Early Old Testament Men & Women

ADAM   God made Adam, the first human being, out of dust from the ground.

You can read about Adam in Genesis 2:4 — 3:24 (page 3).

EVE   God made Eve from one of Adam's ribs. She lived with Adam in the Garden of Eden.

You can read about Eve in Genesis 2:18 — 3:24 (page 4).

NOAH   Because Noah loved God when no one else did, God saved him and his family from the flood.

You can read about Noah in Genesis 6:9 — 9:17 (page 8).

ABRAHAM   Abraham obeyed God and moved away from his familiar homeland into a faraway and unfamiliar country.

You can read about Abraham in Genesis 12—23 (page 14).

SARAH   Sarah was married to Abraham, but they had no children until they were quite old. Then God gave them a son, Isaac.

You can read about Sarah in Genesis 12—23 (page 14).

ISAAC   Isaac, Abraham's son, was forty years old when he married Rebekah. Isaac and Rebekah had twin sons, Jacob and Esau.
You can read about Isaac in Genesis 24—27 (page 27).

REBEKAH   Rebekah left her family and traveled to Canaan with a servant to marry Isaac, a man she had never met.

You can read about Rebekah in Genesis 24—27 (page 27).

JACOB   When Jacob cheated his twin brother Esau out of his inheritance rights, Esau became so angry that Jacob had to leave and live in another country for many years.
You can read about Jacob in Genesis 27—33 and 35 (page 33).

RACHEL   Jacob worked seven years for Rachel's father Laban to gain the right to marry her.

You can read about Rachel in Genesis 29—31 and 35 (page 36).

JOSEPH   Joseph, a favorite son of Jacob, went to Egypt as a slave but became a ruler there. When famine came to Canaan, Joseph was able to get food for his father and brothers.
You can read about Joseph in Genesis 37 and 39—50 (page 48).

continued

this *Adventure* N.I.V. *Bible*

was given to:

Christopher Irwin

on

by

Dad

Early Old Testament Men & Women

MOSES   As a baby, Moses was saved by Pharaoh's daughter from his little basket boat. When he was a man, God chose him to lead Israel out of Egypt to the promised land.
You can read about Moses all through the book of Exodus (page 70).

AARON   Aaron, Moses' brother, served as the first high priest of the Israelites.

You can read about Aaron in Exodus 4:14-17; 28:1—29:46 (page 73).

JOSHUA   Joshua and eleven other men spied out the land of Canaan for Moses. When Moses died God appointed the faithful Joshua to lead Israel into the promised land.
You can read about Joshua in the book of Joshua (page 259).

RAHAB   Rahab lived in Jericho when Joshua conquered it. Because she helped two Israelite spies, she and her family were not killed with the rest of those living in Jericho.
You can read about Rahab in Joshua 2 and 6 (page 259).

DEBORAH   Deborah was one of the judges who ruled Israel. She was known for her wisdom and bravery.

You can read about Deborah in Judges 4 (page 294).

GIDEON   While Gideon was a judge over Israel, he conquered a huge army of Midianites with only three hundred men.

You can read about Gideon in Judges 6—7 (page 297).

SAMSON   Samson, the strongest man who ever lived, was a judge who ruled Israel. However, he was foolish as well as strong and was killed with his enemies, the Philistines.
You can read about Samson in Judges 13—16 (page 308).

NAOMI   Naomi moved to Moab with her husband and sons. After her husband and sons died, she returned to Israel with her daughter-in-law Ruth.
You can read about Naomi in the book of Ruth (page 322).

RUTH   Ruth, who lived in Moab, married Naomi's son. When Ruth's husband and her husband's brother and father died, Ruth went with Naomi to Israel. There she married Boaz.
You can read about Ruth in the book of Ruth (page 322).

SAMUEL   Samuel served God as a prophet, a priest, and a judge in Israel. Samuel anointed Saul and then David to be kings in Israel.
You can read about Samuel in 1 Samuel 1—3, 7—13, and 15—16 (page 328).

Rulers of Israel & Judah

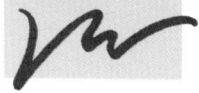

RULERS OF ISRAEL & JUDAH

RULER	DATE	LENGTH OF REIGN	KIND OF REIGN
SAUL	1050 B.C.	40 YEARS	MOSTLY BAD

Saul was the first king to rule Israel and Judah.

DAVID	1010 B.C.	40 YEARS	GOOD

David loved and followed God all his life.

SOLOMON	970 B.C.	40 YEARS	MOSTLY GOOD

Solomon was the wisest man who ever lived.

RULERS OF JUDAH

REHOBOAM	930 B.C.	17 YEARS	BAD

Rehoboam was the first king of Judah after the nation divided.

ABIJAH (Abijam)	913 B.C.	3 YEARS	BAD

Judah and Israel were at war through all of Abijah's reign.

ASA	910 B.C.	41 YEARS	GOOD

Asa loved the Lord and tore down all the idols his father Abijah had made.

JEHOSHAPHAT	872 B.C.	25 YEARS	GOOD

Jehoshaphat built a fleet of ships to sail for gold, but they were wrecked before they ever set sail.

JEHORAM	848 B.C.	8 YEARS	BAD

Jehoram was married to a daughter of wicked King Ahab of Israel.

AHAZIAH	841 B.C.	1 YEAR	BAD

Ahaziah was killed by Jehu just before Jehu took the throne of Israel.

ATHALIAH	841 B.C.	7 YEARS	BAD

Athaliah, Ahaziah's mother, seized the throne for herself when her son was killed.

JOASH	835 B.C.	40 YEARS	GOOD

Joash became king of Judah when he was only seven years old.

AMAZIAH	796 B.C.	29 YEARS	MOSTLY GOOD

During Amaziah's reign, the armies of Israel destroyed part of Jerusalem and stole gold and silver from the temple.

AZARIAH (Uzziah)	792 B.C.	52 YEARS	GOOD

Azariah had the disease of leprosy at the end of his reign.

continued

Rulers of Israel & Judah

RULER	DATE	LENGTH OF REIGN	KIND OF REIGN
JOTHAM	750 B.C.	16 YEARS	GOOD

During the first years of Jotham's reign his father King Azariah was still alive but sick with leprosy.

AHAZ	735 B.C.	16 YEARS	BAD

Ahaz worshiped idols instead of God, even sacrificing his own son.

HEZEKIAH	715 B.C.	29 YEARS	GOOD

Hezekiah built a tunnel to bring water inside the city of Jerusalem.

MANASSEH	697 B.C.	55 YEARS	BAD

Manasseh was only twelve years old when he began to reign.

AMON	642 B.C.	2 YEARS	BAD

Amon was assassinated by some of his own officials.

JOSIAH	640 B.C.	31 YEARS	GOOD

The Book of the Law was discovered in the temple and read to the people during Josiah's reign.

JEHOAHAZ	609 B.C.	3 MONTHS	BAD

After reigning only three months, Jehoahaz was taken captive to Egypt by Pharaoh Neco.

JEHOIAKIM	609 B.C.	11 YEARS	BAD

Eliakim's name was changed to Jehoiakim when Pharaoh Neco of Egypt appointed him king.

JEHOIACHIN	598 B.C.	3 MONTHS	BAD

Nebuchadnezzar took Jehoiachin captive to Babylon.

ZEDEKIAH	597 B.C.	11 YEARS	BAD

During Zedekiah's reign the people of Judah were taken captive into Babylon.

Fall of Jerusalem 586 B.C.

RULERS OF ISRAEL

JEROBOAM	930 B.C.	22 YEARS	BAD

Jeroboam set up two golden calves for the people of Israel to worship, leading them away from God.

NADAB	909 B.C.	2 YEARS	BAD

Baasha killed Nadab and seized the throne for himself.

BAASHA	908 B.C.	24 YEARS	BAD

Baasha killed all of Jeroboam's family in the first years of his reign.

ELAH	886 B.C.	2 YEARS	BAD

One of Elah's officials, Zimri, killed Elah while Elah was drunk.

ZIMRI	885 B.C.	7 DAYS	BAD

Zimri set the palace on fire and died in the blaze.

continued

Rulers of Israel & Judah

RULER	DATE	LENGTH OF REIGN	KIND OF REIGN
TIBNI	885 B.C.	5 YEARS	BAD

Tibni reigned over part of the people of Israel during the first five years of Omri's reign.

OMRI	885 B.C.	12 YEARS	BAD

Omri built the city of Samaria and made it the capital of Israel.

AHAB	874 B.C.	22 YEARS	BAD

Ahab married the wicked Jezebel and refused to listen to God's prophet Elijah.

AHAZIAH	853 B.C.	2 YEARS	BAD

Ahaziah worshiped Baal instead of the Lord.

JORAM (Jehoram)	852 B.C.	12 YEARS	BAD

Joram was killed by Jehu.

JEHU	841 B.C.	28 YEARS	MOSTLY BAD

Jehu killed the priests of Baal but followed the Lord only halfheartedly.

JEHOAHAZ	814 B.C.	17 YEARS	BAD

During most of Jehoahaz's reign, Israel was under the power of Aram.

JEHOASH	798 B.C.	16 YEARS	BAD

Jehoash recovered many Israelite towns that had been under the power of Aram.

JEROBOAM II	793 B.C.	41 YEARS	BAD

During his reign, Jeroboam II recovered the cities of Damascus and Hamath from Judah.

ZECHARIAH	753 B.C.	6 MONTHS	BAD

Shallum attacked and killed Zechariah in front of the people.

SHALLUM	752 B.C.	1 MONTH	BAD

After one month Shallum was assassinated by Menahem.

MENAHEM	752 B.C.	10 YEARS	BAD

The king of Assyria invaded Israel but withdrew when Menahem gave him a large amount of silver.

PEKAHIAH	742 B.C.	2 YEARS	BAD

Pekahiah was killed by Pekah.

PEKAH	752 B.C.	20 YEARS	BAD

Part of Pekah's reign overlapped with Menahem and Pekahiah. He reigned alone beginning in 740 B.C.

HOSHEA	732 B.C.	9 YEARS	MOSTLY BAD

During Hoshea's reign the people of Israel were taken captive to Assyria.

Fall of Samaria 722 B.C.

The Life of Christ

EVENT	PLACE	DATE	PASSAGE
Jesus is born.	Bethlehem	4 B.C.	Luke 2:1-20 *(page 1244)*
When Jesus was born, angels came to announce the news to shepherds.			
Jesus goes to the temple.	Jerusalem	A.D. 9	Luke 2:41-52 *(page 1246)*
When Jesus was twelve years old, he traveled to Jerusalem with his parents to celebrate the Passover.			
Jesus is baptized.	Jordan River	A.D. 26	Matthew 3:13-17 *(page 1171)*
John the Baptist baptized Jesus before Jesus began his ministry.			
Jesus is tempted by Satan.	The Desert	A.D. 26	Luke 4:1-13 *(page 1249)*
While Jesus was in the desert, Satan tried to get Jesus to sin.			
Jesus performs his first miracle.	Cana	A.D. 27	John 2:1-11 *(page 1290)*
Jesus went to a wedding and turned water into wine.			
Jesus chooses his disciples.	Galilee	A.D. 28	Luke 6:12-15 *(page 1252)*
Jesus chose twelve men to be his close companions.			
Jesus feeds 5,000 people.	Bethsaida	A.D. 29	John 6:1-13 *(page 1296)*
Jesus used a young boy's lunch to feed a huge crowd of people.			
Jesus walks on water.	Sea of Galilee	A.D. 29	Mark 6:45-52 *(page 1222)*
The disciples thought that Jesus was a ghost when he came walking on the water toward their boat.			
Jesus raises Lazarus from the dead.	Bethany	A.D. 29	John 11:1-44 *(page 1306)*
Lazarus, Jesus' close friend, had been dead for four days when Jesus raised him.			
Jesus talks to Zacchaeus.	Jericho	A.D. 30	Luke 19:1-10 *(page 1275)*
Zacchaeus was so short he had to climb a tree in order to get a look at Jesus.			

continued

The Life of Christ

Jesus enters Jerusalem. Jesus rode a donkey into Jerusalem on his last visit to that city.	Jerusalem	A.D. 30	Luke 19:28-44 *(page 1276)*
Jesus clears the temple. Jesus was angry when he saw how the people were misusing the temple.	Jerusalem	A.D. 30	Mark 11:15-18 *(page 1230)*
Jesus eats the Last Supper. Jesus ate the Passover meal with his disciples on the night before he died.	Jerusalem	A.D. 30	Matthew 26:17-29 *(page 1205)*
Jesus prays in Gethsemane. Jesus prayed to his Father for strength.	Jerusalem	A.D. 30	Matthew 26:36-46 *(page 1206)*
Jesus is arrested. Judas kissed Jesus to let the crowd know who Jesus was.	Jerusalem	A.D. 30	Luke 22:47-53 *(page 1281)*
Jesus is crucified. Jesus was nailed to a cross to die.	Golgotha	A.D. 30	Matthew 27:27-56 *(page 1209)*
Jesus is buried. A man named Joseph offered his tomb in which Jesus was buried.	Jerusalem	A.D. 30	Matthew 27:57-66 *(page 1210)*
Jesus is raised. On the third day, Jesus came back to life.	Jerusalem	A.D. 30	Mark 16:1-8 *(page 1239)*
Jesus appears to the disciples. Thomas, a disciple, said he wouldn't believe Jesus was alive until he actually saw and touched him.	Jerusalem	A.D. 30	John 20:26-31 *(page 1320)*
Jesus goes to heaven. Forty days after his resurrection, Jesus returned to his Father in heaven.	Mount of Olives	A.D. 30	Acts 1:1-11 *(page 1324)*

The Adventure Bible

NEW INTERNATIONAL VERSION

Features written by:
Lawrence O. Richards
Edited by:
Jean E. Syswerda

The Adventure Bible

NEW INTERNATIONAL VERSION

ZONDERVAN BIBLE PUBLISHERS

GRAND RAPIDS, MICHIGAN

You will be pleased to know that a portion of the purchase price of your new NIV Bible has been provided to the International Bible Society to help spread the Gospel of Jesus Christ around the world!

Illustrated by: Nancy Munger
Designed by: Sharon Wright

CONTENTS

ILLUSTRATIONS

WELCOME!

Welcome to the Adventure Bible!

Welcome to the great adventure of reading, exploring and discovering the Bible for yourself.

Are you looking for adventure? Are you eager to discover God's Word and apply it to your life? Then the Adventure Bible is designed especially for you.

Each feature of the Adventure Bible is designed to introduce you to the wonderful messages and promises in God's Word. Take a few minutes to read these explanations. Then you will know the best way to use your Adventure Bible.

FEATURES YOU SHOULD KNOW ABOUT

WORDS TO REMEMBER Key verses from the Bible appear in large type and are worth memorizing. The best way to live for Jesus is to have his Word in your heart. Memorize the verses from "Words to Remember."

Life in Bible Times Do you ever wonder what it was like to live in the times of Abraham or Ruth or Jesus? What kind of food did they eat? Where did they sleep? What kind of work did they do? "Life in Bible Times" will tell you. One hundred of these entries have pictures with them.

? DID YOU KNOW? This feature points out many of the interesting small facts that are found in the Bible. Learn them all and wow your parents, teachers and friends with your Bible knowledge.

LET'S LIVE IT! It is important to read and memorize God's Word. But what really counts is *living* it, letting the Bible affect how you work, play and live. "Let's Live It!" tells you what the Bible has to say about your life RIGHT NOW!

BOOK INTRODUCTIONS If you need the basic facts about a book of the Bible (who wrote it, where it took place, why it was written), you'll find that information at the beginning of each book. The book introduction will also give you a list of favorite Bible stories and teachings you can find in that Bible book.

INDEX In the back of your Adventure Bible (page 1545) is an index of different subjects and people covered in this Bible. If you need to do a report for school or are wondering about a certain subject or person, look it up in this index and then read about it on the pages listed.

ACTIVITIES If you want to not only *read* your Adventure Bible but also *do* something with what you've learned, turn to the list of Activities at the back of the Bible (page 1558). You'll find there many ideas for things to discuss, to do, and to make.

DICTIONARY-CONCORDANCE When you're reading your Adventure Bible, you may come to a word that you don't understand. Be sure to take a minute to look it up in the Dictionary-Concordance found at the back of your Bible (page 1561). Read the definition so you can better understand God's message.

CHARTS AND WRAPS Scattered throughout your Adventure Bible as well as in the front are some special pages in color that contain important information. Be sure to check out the facts on these pages. You'll be glad you did!

MAPS In the back of this Bible are eight color maps. They will help you better understand where the events in the Bible took place.

WHERE TO START

Don't worry about where to start. Start anywhere. Go through the Bible and see what features interest you. Then begin exploring and reading both the feature and the Bible text. Use your Adventure Bible every day to begin the great adventure of living for Jesus!

P.S. If you have any questions or comments about this Bible, please write and tell us.

The Editors
Zondervan Bible Publishers
1415 Lake Dr.
Grand Rapids, MI 49506

Note to parents and teachers:
The special features of this Adventure Bible can be used as a teaching or devotional tool by parents and teachers, but also may be used to encourage children to explore the Bible on their own and to have their own quiet time with God.

PREFACE
TO THE NEW INTERNATIONAL VERSION

THE NEW INTERNATIONAL VERSION is a completely new translation of the Holy Bible made by over a hundred scholars working directly from the best available Hebrew, Aramaic and Greek texts. It had its beginning in 1965 when, after several years of exploratory study by committees from the Christian Reformed Church and the National Association of Evangelicals, a group of scholars met at Palos Heights, Illinois, and concurred in the need for a new translation of the Bible in contemporary English. This group, though not made up of official church representatives, was transdenominational. Its conclusion was endorsed by a large number of leaders from many denominations who met in Chicago in 1966.

Responsibility for the new version was delegated by the Palos Heights group to a self-governing body of fifteen, the Committee on Bible Translation, composed for the most part of biblical scholars from colleges, universities and seminaries. In 1967 the New York Bible Society (now the International Bible Society) generously undertook the financial sponsorship of the project—a sponsorship that made it possible to enlist the help of many distinguished scholars. The fact that participants from the United States, Great Britain, Canada, Australia and New Zealand worked together gave the project its international scope. That they were from many denominations—including Anglican, Assemblies of God, Baptist, Brethren, Christian Reformed, Church of Christ, Evangelical Free, Lutheran, Mennonite, Methodist, Nazarene, Presbyterian, Wesleyan and other churches—helped to safeguard the translation from sectarian bias.

How it was made helps to give the New International Version its distinctiveness. The translation of each book was assigned to a team of scholars. Next, one of the Intermediate Editorial Committees revised the initial translation, with constant reference to the Hebrew, Aramaic or Greek. Their work then went to one of the General Editorial Committees, which checked it in detail and made another thorough revision. This revision in turn was carefully reviewed by the Committee on Bible Translation, which made further changes and then released the final version for publication. In this way the entire Bible underwent three revisions, during each of which the translation was examined for its faithfulness to the original languages and for its English style.

All this involved many thousands of hours of research and discussion regarding the meaning of the texts and the precise way of putting them into English. It may well be that no other translation has been made by a more thorough process of review and revision from committee to committee than this one.

From the beginning of the project, the Committee on Bible Translation held to certain goals for the New International Version: that it would be an accurate translation and one that would have clarity and literary quality and so prove suitable for public and private reading, teaching, preaching, memorizing and liturgical use. The Committee also sought to preserve some measure of continuity with the long tradition of translating the Scriptures into English.

In working toward these goals, the translators were united in their commitment to the authority and infallibility of the Bible as God's Word in written form. They believe that it contains the divine answer to the deepest needs of humanity, that it sheds unique light on our path in a dark world, and that it sets forth the way to our eternal well-being.

The first concern of the translators has been the accuracy of the translation and its fidelity to the thought of the biblical writers. They have weighed the significance of the lexical and grammatical details of the Hebrew, Aramaic and Greek texts. At the same time, they have striven for more than a word-for-word translation. Because thought patterns and syntax differ from language to language, faithful communication of the meaning of the writers of the Bible demands frequent modifications in sentence structure and constant regard for the contextual meanings of words.

A sensitive feeling for style does not always accompany scholarship. Accordingly the Committee on Bible Translation submitted the developing version to a number of stylistic consultants. Two of them read every book of both Old and New Testaments twice—once before and once after the last major revision—and made invaluable suggestions. Samples of the translation were tested for clarity and ease of reading by various kinds of people—young and old, highly educated and less well educated, ministers and laymen.

Concern for clear and natural English—that the New International Version should be idiomatic but not idiosyncratic, contemporary but not dated—motivated the translators and consultants. At the same time, they tried to reflect the differing styles of the biblical writers. In view of the international use of English, the translators sought to avoid obvious Americanisms on the one hand and obvious Anglicisms on the other. A British edition reflects the comparatively few differences of significant idiom and of spelling.

As for the traditional pronouns "thou," "thee" and "thine" in reference to the Deity, the translators judged that to use these archaisms (along with the old verb forms such as "doest," "wouldest" and "hadst") would violate accuracy in translation. Neither Hebrew, Aramaic nor Greek uses special pronouns for the persons of the Godhead. A present-day translation is not enhanced by forms that in the time of the King James Version were used in everyday speech, whether referring to God or man.

For the Old Testament the standard Hebrew text, the Masoretic Text as published in the latest editions of *Biblia Hebraica,* was used throughout. The Dead Sea Scrolls contain material bearing on an earlier stage of the Hebrew text. They were consulted, as were the Samaritan Pentateuch and the ancient scribal traditions relating to textual changes. Sometimes a variant Hebrew reading in the margin of the Masoretic Text was followed instead of the text itself. Such instances, being variants within the Masoretic tradition, are not specified by footnotes. In rare cases, words in the consonantal text were divided differently from the way they appear in the Masoretic Text. Footnotes indicate this. The translators also consulted the more important early versions—the Septuagint; Aquila, Symmachus and Theodotion; the Vulgate; the Syriac Peshitta; the Targums; and for the Psalms the *Juxta Hebraica* of Jerome. Readings from these versions were occasionally followed where the Masoretic Text seemed doubtful and where accepted principles of textual criticism showed that one or more of these textual witnesses appeared to provide the correct reading. Such instances are footnoted. Sometimes vowel letters and vowel signs did not, in the judgment of the translators, represent the correct vowels for the original consonantal text. Accordingly some words were read with a different set of vowels. These instances are usually not indicated by footnotes.

The Greek text used in translating the New Testament was an eclectic one. No other piece of ancient literature has such an abundance of manuscript witnesses as does the New Testament. Where existing manuscripts differ, the translators made their choice of readings according to accepted principles of New Testament textual criticism. Footnotes call attention to places where there was uncertainty about what the original text was. The best current printed texts of the Greek New Testament were used.

There is a sense in which the work of translation is never wholly finished. This applies to all great literature and uniquely so to the Bible. In 1973 the New Testament in the New International Version was published. Since then, suggestions for corrections and revisions have been received from various sources. The Committee on Bible Translation carefully considered the suggestions and adopted a number of them. These were incorporated in the first printing of the entire Bible in 1978. Additional revisions were made by the Committee on Bible Translation in 1983 and appear in printings after that date.

As in other ancient documents, the precise meaning of the biblical texts is sometimes uncertain. This is more often the case with the Hebrew and Aramaic texts than with the Greek text. Although archaeological and linguistic discoveries in this century aid in understanding difficult passages, some uncertainties remain. The more significant of these have been called to the reader's attention in the footnotes.

In regard to the divine name *YHWH,* commonly referred to as the *Tetragrammaton,* the translators adopted the device used in most English versions of rendering that name as "Lord" in capital letters to distinguish it from *Adonai,* another Hebrew word rendered "Lord," for which small letters are used. Wherever the two names stand together in the Old Testament as a compound name of God, they are rendered "Sovereign Lord."

Because for most readers today the phrases "the Lord of hosts" and "God of hosts" have little meaning, this version renders them "the Lord Almighty" and "God Almighty." These renderings convey the sense of the Hebrew, namely, "he who is sovereign over all the 'hosts' (powers) in heaven and on earth, especially over the 'hosts' (armies) of Israel." For readers unacquainted with Hebrew this does not make clear the distinction between *Sabaoth* ("hosts" or "Almighty") and *Shaddai* (which can also be translated "Almighty"), but the latter occurs infrequently and is always footnoted. When *Adonai* and *YHWH Sabaoth* occur together, they are rendered "the Lord, the Lord Almighty."

As for other proper nouns, the familiar spellings of the King James Version are generally retained. Names traditionally spelled with "ch," except where it is final, are usually spelled in this translation with "k" or "c," since the biblical languages do not have the sound that "ch" frequently indicates in English—for example, in *chant*. For well-known names such as Zechariah, however, the traditional spelling has been retained. Variation in the spelling of names in the original languages has usually not been indicated. Where a person or place has two or more different names in the Hebrew, Aramaic or Greek texts, the more familiar one has generally been used, with footnotes where needed.

To achieve clarity the translators sometimes supplied words not in the original texts but required by the context. If there was uncertainty about such material, it is enclosed in brackets. Also for the sake of clarity or style, nouns, including some proper nouns, are sometimes substituted for pronouns, and vice versa. And though the Hebrew writers often shifted back and forth between first, second and third personal pronouns without change of antecedent, this translation often makes them uniform, in accordance with English style and without the use of footnotes.

Poetical passages are printed as poetry, that is, with indentation of lines and with separate stanzas. These are generally designed to reflect the structure of Hebrew poetry. This poetry is normally characterized by parallelism in balanced lines. Most of the poetry in the Bible is in the Old Testament, and scholars differ regarding the scansion of Hebrew lines. The translators determined the stanza divisions for the most part by analysis of the subject matter. The stanzas therefore serve as poetic paragraphs.

As an aid to the reader, italicized sectional headings are inserted in most of the books. They are not to be regarded as part of the NIV text, are not for oral reading, and are not intended to dictate the interpretation of the sections they head.

The footnotes in this version are of several kinds, most of which need no explanation. Those giving alternative translations begin with "Or" and generally introduce the alternative with the last word preceding it in the text, except when it is a single-word alternative; in poetry quoted in a footnote a slant mark indicates a line division. Footnotes introduced by "Or" do not have uniform significance. In some cases two possible translations were considered to have about equal validity. In other cases, though the translators were convinced that the translation in the text was correct, they judged that another interpretation was possible and of sufficient importance to be represented in a footnote.

In the New Testament, footnotes that refer to uncertainty regarding the original text are introduced by "Some manuscripts" or similar expressions. In the Old Testament, evidence for the reading chosen is given first and evidence for the alternative is added after a semicolon (for example: Septuagint; Hebrew *father*). In such notes the term "Hebrew" refers to the Masoretic Text.

It should be noted that minerals, flora and fauna, architectural details, articles of clothing and jewelry, musical instruments and other articles cannot always be identified with precision. Also measures of capacity in the biblical period are particularly uncertain (see the table of weights and measures following the text).

Like all translations of the Bible, made as they are by imperfect man, this one undoubtedly falls short of its goals. Yet we are grateful to God for the extent to which he has enabled us to realize these goals and for the strength he has given us and our colleagues to complete our task. We offer this version of the Bible to him in whose name and for whose glory it has been made. We pray that it will lead many into a better understanding of the Holy Scriptures and a fuller knowledge of Jesus Christ the incarnate Word, of whom the Scriptures so faithfully testify.

The Committee on Bible Translation

June 1978
(Revised August 1983)

Names of the translators and editors may be secured
from the International Bible Society,
translation sponsors of the New International Version,
P.O. Box 62970, Colorado Springs, Colorado, 80962-2970 U.S.A.

OLD TESTAMENT

GENESIS

WHO WROTE THIS BOOK?

Moses.

WHY WAS THIS BOOK WRITTEN?

Genesis tells how God created the universe and human beings. It also covers the special promises God made to Abraham.

WHAT HAPPENS IN THIS BOOK?

God creates the universe and people. People sin, and God punishes them with a great flood. God speaks to Abraham and gives his family special promises.

WHAT DO WE LEARN ABOUT GOD IN THIS BOOK?

God created all things. God loves people but will punish sin. God promises to save people who trust him.

WHO IS IMPORTANT IN THIS BOOK?

The important people in this book are Adam and Eve, Noah, Abraham, Isaac, Jacob, and Joseph.

WHEN DID THIS HAPPEN?

No one knows when the creation or the flood happened. Abraham was born about 2150 B.C. His great-grandson Joseph died about 1800 B.C.

WHERE DID THIS HAPPEN?

Genesis 1–11 happened in Mesopotamia. Genesis 12–36 takes place in Canaan (Palestine). The rest of Genesis takes place in Egypt.

WHAT ARE SOME OF THE STORIES IN THIS BOOK?

God creates the universe.	Genesis 1
God creates Adam and Eve.	Genesis 2
Adam and Eve sin.	Genesis 3
Noah builds an ark.	Genesis 6
The flood punishes sinners.	Genesis 7–8
God gives Abraham promises.	Genesis 12
Abraham prays for a city.	Genesis 18
Jacob steals Esau's blessing.	Genesis 27
Jacob's name is changed.	Genesis 32
Joseph is sold by his brothers.	Genesis 37
Joseph becomes a ruler.	Genesis 39–41

The Beginning

1 In the beginning God created the heavens and the earth. ²Now the earth was^a formless and empty, darkness was over the surface of the deep, and the Spirit of God was hovering over the waters.

WORDS TO REMEMBER

1:1 In the beginning God created the heavens and the earth.

³And God said, "Let there be light," and there was light. ⁴God saw that the light was good, and he separated the light from the darkness. ⁵God called the light "day," and the darkness he called "night." And there was evening, and there was morning—the first day.

⁶And God said, "Let there be an expanse between the waters to separate water from water." ⁷So God made the expanse and separated the water under the expanse from the water above it. And it was so. ⁸God called the expanse "sky." And there was evening, and there was morning—the second day.

⁹And God said, "Let the water under the sky be gathered to one place, and let dry ground appear." And it was so. ¹⁰God called the dry ground "land," and the gathered waters he called "seas." And God saw that it was good.

¹¹Then God said, "Let the land produce vegetation: seed-bearing plants and trees on the land that bear fruit with seed in it, according to their various kinds." And it was so. ¹²The land produced vegetation: plants bearing seed according to their kinds and trees bearing fruit with seed in it according to their kinds. And God saw that it was good. ¹³And

there was evening, and there was morning—the third day.

?DID YOU KNOW?   1:1

What does create mean?

The Bible word *create* means to make or begin something new. Genesis tells us that God is the creator of all things. You can find many things that God created in Genesis 1.

¹⁴And God said, "Let there be lights in the expanse of the sky to separate the day from the night, and let them serve as signs to mark seasons and days and years, ¹⁵and let them be lights in the expanse of the sky to give light on the earth." And it was so. ¹⁶God made two great lights—the greater light to govern the day and the lesser light to govern the night. He also made the stars. ¹⁷God set them in the expanse of the sky to give light on the earth, ¹⁸to govern the day and the night, and to separate light from darkness. And God saw that it was good. ¹⁹And there was evening, and there was morning—the fourth day.

²⁰And God said, "Let the water teem with living creatures, and let birds fly above the earth across the expanse of the sky." ²¹So God created the great creatures of the sea and every living and moving thing with which the water teems, according to their kinds, and every winged bird according to its kind. And God saw that it was good. ²²God blessed them and said, "Be fruitful and increase in number and fill the water in the seas, and let the birds increase on the earth." ²³And there was evening, and there was morning—the fifth day.

²⁴And God said, "Let the land pro-

duce living creatures according to their kinds: livestock, creatures that move along the ground, and wild animals, each according to its kind." And it was so. ²⁵God made the wild animals according to their kinds, the livestock according to their kinds, and all the creatures that move along the ground according to their kinds. And God saw that it was good.

²⁶Then God said, "Let us make man in our image, in our likeness, and let them rule over the fish of the sea and the birds of the air, over the livestock, over all the earth, ᵃ and over all the creatures that move along the ground."

²⁷So God created man in his own image,
  in the image of God he created him;
  male and female he created them.

²⁸God blessed them and said to them, "Be fruitful and increase in number; fill the earth and subdue it. Rule over the fish of the sea and the birds of the air and over every living creature that moves on the ground."

²⁹Then God said, "I give you every seed-bearing plant on the face of the whole earth and every tree that has fruit with seed in it. They will be yours for food. ³⁰And to all the beasts of the earth and all the birds of the air and all the creatures that move on the ground—everything that has the breath of life in it—I give every green plant for food." And it was so.

³¹God saw all that he had made, and it was very good. And there was evening, and there was morning—the sixth day.

2 Thus the heavens and the earth were completed in all their vast array.

²By the seventh day God had finished the work he had been doing; so on the seventh day he rested ᵇ from all his work. ³And God blessed the seventh day and made it holy, because on it he rested from all the work of creating that he had done.

Adam and Eve

⁴This is the account of the heavens and the earth when they were created.

When the Lᴏʀᴅ God made the earth and the heavens— ⁵and no shrub of the field had yet appeared on the earth ᶜ and no plant of the field had yet sprung up, for the Lᴏʀᴅ God had not sent rain on the earth ᶜ and there was no man to work the ground, ⁶but streams ᵈ came up from the earth and watered the whole surface of the ground— ⁷the Lᴏʀᴅ God formed the

---

ᵃ26 Hebrew; Syriac *all the wild animals*   ᵇ2 Or *ceased*; also in verse 3   ᶜ5 Or *land*; also in verse 6   ᵈ6 Or *mist*

▚ET'S LIVE IT!   Genesis 1:26–27

YOU'RE SPECIAL ➠ Read Genesis 1:26–27. God made us in his own image. We are like God in some ways but different in other ways.

  Look at childhood pictures of your mom or dad. How were they like you? How were they different? Your parents love you very much because you are their child, and you are like them in important ways. Ask your mom or dad to tell you why they think you are special.

  Because God made you in his image, you are special to God, and he loves you. Write a letter to God to thank him for loving you.

man[a] from the dust of the ground and breathed into his nostrils the breath of life, and the man became a living being.

[8]Now the LORD God had planted a garden in the east, in Eden; and there he put the man he had formed. [9]And the LORD God made all kinds of trees grow out of the ground—trees that were pleasing to the eye and good for food. In the middle of the garden were the tree of life and the tree of the knowledge of good and evil.

[10]A river watering the garden flowed from Eden; from there it was separated into four headwaters. [11]The name of the first is the Pishon; it winds through the entire land of Havilah, where there is gold. [12](The gold of that land is good; aromatic resin[b] and onyx are also there.) [13]The name of the second river is the Gihon; it winds through the entire land of Cush.[c] [14]The name of the third river is the Tigris; it runs along the east side of Asshur. And the fourth river is the Euphrates.

[15]The LORD God took the man and put him in the Garden of Eden to work it and take care of it. [16]And the LORD God commanded the man, "You are free to eat from any tree in the garden; [17]but you must not eat from the tree of the knowledge of good and evil, for when you eat of it you will surely die."

[18]The LORD God said, "It is not good for the man to be alone. I will make a helper suitable for him."

[19]Now the LORD God had formed out of the ground all the beasts of the field and all the birds of the air. He brought them to the man to see what he would name them; and whatever the man called each living creature, that was its name. [20]So the man gave names to all the livestock, the birds of the air and all the beasts of the field.

But for Adam[d] no suitable helper was found. [21]So the LORD God caused the man to fall into a deep sleep; and while he was sleeping, he took one of the man's ribs[e] and closed up the place with flesh. [22]Then the LORD God made a woman from the rib[f] he had taken out of the man, and he brought her to the man.

[23]The man said,

"This is now bone of my bones
    and flesh of my flesh;
she shall be called 'woman,[g]'
    for she was taken out of man."

[24]For this reason a man will leave his father and mother and be united to his wife, and they will become one flesh.

[25]The man and his wife were both naked, and they felt no shame.

The Fall of Man

3 Now the serpent was more crafty than any of the wild animals the LORD God had made. He said to the woman, "Did God really say, 'You must not eat from any tree in the garden'?"

[2]The woman said to the serpent, "We may eat fruit from the trees in the garden, [3]but God did say, 'You must not eat fruit from the tree that is in the middle of the garden, and you must not touch it, or you will die.'"

[4]"You will not surely die," the serpent said to the woman. [5]"For God knows that when you eat of it your eyes will be opened, and you will be like God, knowing good and evil."

[6]When the woman saw that the fruit of the tree was good for food and pleasing to the eye, and also desirable for gaining wisdom, she took some and ate it. She also gave some to her husband, who was with her, and he ate it. [7]Then the eyes of both of them were opened, and they realized they were naked; so they sewed

---

[a]7 The Hebrew for *man (adam)* sounds like and may be related to the Hebrew for *ground (adamah)*; it is also the name *Adam* (see Gen. 2:20).   [b]12 Or *good; pearls*   [c]13 Possibly southeast Mesopotamia   [d]20 Or *the man*   [e]21 Or *took part of the man's side*   [f]22 Or *part*   [g]23 The Hebrew for *woman* sounds like the Hebrew for *man*.

fig leaves together and made coverings for themselves.

⁸Then the man and his wife heard the sound of the LORD God as he was walking in the garden in the cool of the day, and they hid from the LORD God among the trees of the garden. ⁹But the LORD God called to the man, "Where are you?"

¹⁰He answered, "I heard you in the garden, and I was afraid because I was naked; so I hid."

¹¹And he said, "Who told you that you were naked? Have you eaten from the tree that I commanded you not to eat from?"

¹²The man said, "The woman you put here with me—she gave me some fruit from the tree, and I ate it."

¹³Then the LORD God said to the woman, "What is this you have done?"

The woman said, "The serpent deceived me, and I ate."

¹⁴So the LORD God said to the serpent, "Because you have done this,

"Cursed are you above all the livestock
  and all the wild animals!
You will crawl on your belly
  and you will eat dust
  all the days of your life.
¹⁵And I will put enmity

ᵃ15 Or *seed*   ᵇ15 Or *strike*

between you and the woman,
  and between your offspringᵃ
  and hers;
he will crushᵇ your head,
  and you will strike his heel."

¹⁶To the woman he said,

"I will greatly increase your pains
  in childbearing;
with pain you will give birth to
  children.
Your desire will be for your
  husband,
  and he will rule over you."

? DID YOU KNOW?   3:6

What kind of fruit did Adam eat?

The Bible does not name the fruit. The important point is that Adam and Eve disobeyed God. Genesis 3 tells what happened because they disobeyed.

---

¹⁷To Adam he said, "Because you listened to your wife and ate from the tree about which I commanded you, 'You must not eat of it,'

"Cursed is the ground because of you;
  through painful toil you will eat of it

LET'S LIVE IT!   Genesis 3:1–13

BAD CHOICES ➡ Adam and Eve made a wrong choice when they disobeyed God. Why did they do it? Read Genesis 3:1–13. Adam and Eve made the wrong choice because:

   3:4: Someone said it was all right to do the wrong thing.
   3:5: It looked like a fun thing to do.
   3:6: A close friend did it first.

After Adam and Eve made that wrong choice, they felt guilty and afraid. But it was too late.

Think about what to say if someone tells you it's all right to do a wrong thing, or if something wrong looks like fun, or if a friend does a wrong thing first and wants you to do it too. If you can't think of a good answer, ask an older friend or your mom or dad for advice.

all the days of your life.
18It will produce thorns and thistles
for you,
and you will eat the plants of
the field.
19By the sweat of your brow
you will eat your food
until you return to the ground,
since from it you were taken;
for dust you are
and to dust you will return."

20Adam*a* named his wife Eve,*b* because she would become the mother
of all the living.

21The LORD God made garments of
skin for Adam and his wife and
clothed them. 22And the LORD God
said, "The man has now become like
one of us, knowing good and evil. He
must not be allowed to reach out his
hand and take also from the tree of
life and eat, and live forever." 23So
the LORD God banished him from the
Garden of Eden to work the ground
from which he had been taken. 24Af-
ter he drove the man out, he placed
on the east side*c* of the Garden of
Eden cherubim and a flaming sword
flashing back and forth to guard the
way to the tree of life.

Cain and Abel

4 Adam*a* lay with his wife Eve,
and she became pregnant and
gave birth to Cain.*d* She said, "With
the help of the LORD I have brought
forth*e* a man." 2Later she gave birth
to his brother Abel.

Now Abel kept flocks, and Cain
worked the soil. 3In the course of time
Cain brought some of the fruits of the
soil as an offering to the LORD. 4But
Abel brought fat portions from some
of the firstborn of his flock. The LORD
looked with favor on Abel and his offering, 5but on Cain and his offering
he did not look with favor. So Cain
was very angry, and his face was
downcast.

6Then the LORD said to Cain, "Why
are you angry? Why is your face
downcast? 7If you do what is right,
will you not be accepted? But if you
do not do what is right, sin is crouching at your door; it desires to have
you, but you must master it."

8Now Cain said to his brother
Abel, "Let's go out to the field."*f* And
while they were in the field, Cain attacked his brother Abel and killed
him.

9Then the LORD said to Cain,
"Where is your brother Abel?"

"I don't know," he replied. "Am I
my brother's keeper?"

10The LORD said, "What have you
done? Listen! Your brother's blood
cries out to me from the ground.
11Now you are under a curse and
driven from the ground, which
opened its mouth to receive your
brother's blood from your hand.
12When you work the ground, it will
no longer yield its crops for you. You
will be a restless wanderer on the
earth."

13Cain said to the LORD, "My punishment is more than I can bear. 14To-
day you are driving me from the land,
and I will be hidden from your presence; I will be a restless wanderer on
the earth, and whoever finds me will
kill me."

15But the LORD said to him, "Not
so*g*; if anyone kills Cain, he will suffer vengeance seven times over."
Then the LORD put a mark on Cain so
that no one who found him would kill
him. 16So Cain went out from the
LORD's presence and lived in the land
of Nod,*h* east of Eden.

17Cain lay with his wife, and she
became pregnant and gave birth to
Enoch. Cain was then building a city,
and he named it after his son Enoch.
18To Enoch was born Irad, and Irad
was the father of Mehujael, and Mehujael was the father of Methushael,

---

*a*20,1 Or *The man*   *b*20 *Eve* probably means *living.*   *c*24 Or *placed in front*   *d*1 *Cain*
sounds like the Hebrew for *brought forth* or *acquired.*   *e*1 Or *have acquired*   *f*8 Samaritan
Pentateuch, Septuagint, Vulgate and Syriac; Masoretic Text does not have *"Let's go out to the field."*
*g*15 Septuagint, Vulgate and Syriac; Hebrew *Very well*   *h*16 *Nod* means *wandering* (see verses
12 and 14).

and Methushael was the father of Lamech.

¹⁹Lamech married two women, one named Adah and the other Zillah. ²⁰Adah gave birth to Jabal; he was the father of those who live in tents and raise livestock. ²¹His brother's name was Jubal; he was the father of all who play the harp and flute. ²²Zillah also had a son, Tubal-Cain, who forged all kinds of tools out of^a bronze and iron. Tubal-Cain's sister was Naamah.

²³Lamech said to his wives,

"Adah and Zillah, listen to me;
    wives of Lamech, hear my
    words.
I have killed^b a man for
    wounding me,
    a young man for injuring me.
²⁴If Cain is avenged seven times,
    then Lamech seventy-seven
    times."

²⁵Adam lay with his wife again, and she gave birth to a son and named him Seth,^c saying, "God has granted me another child in place of Abel, since Cain killed him." ²⁶Seth also had a son, and he named him Enosh.

At that time men began to call on^d the name of the LORD.

From Adam to Noah

5 This is the written account of Adam's line.

When God created man, he made him in the likeness of God. ²He created them male and female and blessed them. And when they were created, he called them "man.^e"

³When Adam had lived 130 years, he had a son in his own likeness, in his own image; and he named him Seth. ⁴After Seth was born, Adam lived 800 years and had other sons and daughters. ⁵Altogether, Adam lived 930 years, and then he died.

⁶When Seth had lived 105 years, he became the father^f of Enosh. ⁷And after he became the father of Enosh, Seth lived 807 years and had other sons and daughters. ⁸Altogether, Seth lived 912 years, and then he died.

⁹When Enosh had lived 90 years, he became the father of Kenan. ¹⁰And after he became the father of Kenan, Enosh lived 815 years and had other sons and daughters. ¹¹Altogether, Enosh lived 905 years, and then he died.

¹²When Kenan had lived 70 years, he became the father of Mahalalel. ¹³And after he became the father of Mahalalel, Kenan lived 840 years and had other sons and daughters. ¹⁴Altogether, Kenan lived 910 years, and then he died.

¹⁵When Mahalalel had lived 65 years, he became the father of Jared. ¹⁶And after he became the father of Jared, Mahalalel lived 830 years and had other sons and daughters. ¹⁷Altogether, Mahalalel lived 895 years, and then he died.

¹⁸When Jared had lived 162 years, he became the father of Enoch. ¹⁹And after he became the father of Enoch, Jared lived 800 years and had other sons and daughters. ²⁰Altogether, Jared lived 962 years, and then he died.

²¹When Enoch had lived 65 years, he became the father of Methuselah. ²²And after he became the father of Methuselah, Enoch walked with God 300 years and had other sons and daughters. ²³Altogether, Enoch lived 365 years. ²⁴Enoch walked with God; then he was no more, because God took him away.

²⁵When Methuselah had lived 187 years, he became the father of Lamech. ²⁶And after he became the father of Lamech, Methuselah lived 782 years and had other sons and daughters. ²⁷Altogether, Methuselah lived 969 years, and then he died.

²⁸When Lamech had lived 182 years, he had a son. ²⁹He named him

---

^a22 Or *who instructed all who work in*   ^b23 Or *I will kill*   ^c25 Seth probably means *granted.*
^d26 Or *to proclaim*   ^e2 Hebrew *adam*   ^f6 *Father* may mean *ancestor*; also in verses 7-26.

Noah[a] and said, "He will comfort us in the labor and painful toil of our hands caused by the ground the LORD has cursed." [30]After Noah was born, Lamech lived 595 years and had other sons and daughters. [31]Altogether, Lamech lived 777 years, and then he died.

[32]After Noah was 500 years old, he became the father of Shem, Ham and Japheth.

The Flood

6 When men began to increase in number on the earth and daughters were born to them, [2]the sons of God saw that the daughters of men were beautiful, and they married any of them they chose. [3]Then the LORD said, "My Spirit will not contend with[b] man forever, for he is mortal[c]; his days will be a hundred and twenty years."

?DID YOU KNOW?   6:3

How long did it take to build the ark?

It took 120 years to build the ark. In order to save faithful Noah and his family, God waited until the ark was ready before he punished the wicked.

---

[4]The Nephilim were on the earth in those days—and also afterward—when the sons of God went to the daughters of men and had children by them. They were the heroes of old, men of renown.

[5]The LORD saw how great man's wickedness on the earth had become, and that every inclination of the thoughts of his heart was only evil all the time. [6]The LORD was grieved that he had made man on the earth, and his heart was filled with pain. [7]So the LORD said, "I will wipe mankind, whom I have created, from the face of the earth—men and animals, and creatures that move along the ground, and birds of the air—for I am grieved that I have made them." [8]But Noah found favor in the eyes of the LORD.

[9]This is the account of Noah.

Noah was a righteous man, blameless among the people of his time, and he walked with God. [10]Noah had three sons: Shem, Ham and Japheth.

[11]Now the earth was corrupt in God's sight and was full of violence. [12]God saw how corrupt the earth had become, for all the people on earth had corrupted their ways. [13]So God said to Noah, "I am going to put an end to all people, for the earth is filled with violence because of them. I am surely going to destroy both them and the earth. [14]So make yourself an ark of cypress[d] wood; make rooms in it and coat it with pitch inside and out. [15]This is how you are to build it: The ark is to be 450 feet long, 75 feet wide and 45 feet high.[e] [16]Make a roof for it and finish[f] the ark to within 18 inches[g] of the top. Put a door in the side of the ark and make lower, middle and upper decks. [17]I am going to bring floodwaters on the earth to destroy all life under the heavens, every creature that has the breath of life in it. Everything on earth will perish. [18]But I will establish my covenant with you, and you will enter the ark—you and your sons and your wife and your sons' wives with you. [19]You are to bring into the ark two of all living creatures, male and female, to keep them alive with you. [20]Two of every kind of bird, of every kind of animal and of every kind of creature that moves along the ground will come to you to be kept alive. [21]You are to take every kind of food that is to be eaten and store it away as food for you and for them."

---

[a]29 *Noah* sounds like the Hebrew for *comfort.*   [b]3 Or *My spirit will not remain in*   [c]3 Or *corrupt*   [d]14 The meaning of the Hebrew for this word is uncertain.   [e]15 Hebrew *300 cubits long, 50 cubits wide and 30 cubits high* (about 140 meters long, 23 meters wide and 13.5 meters high)   [f]16 Or *Make an opening for light by finishing*   [g]16 Hebrew *a cubit* (about 0.5 meter)

²²Noah did everything just as God commanded him.

7 The Lord then said to Noah, "Go into the ark, you and your whole family, because I have found you righteous in this generation. ²Take with you seven*a* of every kind of clean animal, a male and its mate, and two of every kind of unclean animal, a male and its mate, ³and also seven of every kind of bird, male and female, to keep their various kinds alive throughout the earth. ⁴Seven days from now I will send rain on the earth for forty days and forty nights, and I will wipe from the face of the earth every living creature I have made."

⁵And Noah did all that the Lord commanded him.

⁶Noah was six hundred years old when the floodwaters came on the earth. ⁷And Noah and his sons and his wife and his sons' wives entered the ark to escape the waters of the flood. ⁸Pairs of clean and unclean animals, of birds and of all creatures that move along the ground, ⁹male and female, came to Noah and entered the ark, as God had commanded Noah. ¹⁰And after the seven days the floodwaters came on the earth.

¹¹In the six hundredth year of Noah's life, on the seventeenth day of the second month—on that day all the springs of the great deep burst forth, and the floodgates of the heavens were opened. ¹²And rain fell on the earth forty days and forty nights.

¹³On that very day Noah and his sons, Shem, Ham and Japheth, together with his wife and the wives of his three sons, entered the ark. ¹⁴They had with them every wild animal according to its kind, all livestock according to their kinds, every creature that moves along the ground according to its kind and every bird according to its kind, everything with wings. ¹⁵Pairs of all creatures that have the breath of life in them came to Noah and entered the ark. ¹⁶The animals going in were male and female of every living thing, as God had commanded Noah. Then the Lord shut him in.

¹⁷For forty days the flood kept coming on the earth, and as the waters increased they lifted the ark high above the earth. ¹⁸The waters rose and increased greatly on the earth, and the ark floated on the surface of the water. ¹⁹They rose greatly on the earth, and all the high mountains under the entire heavens were covered. ²⁰The waters rose and covered the mountains to a depth of more than twenty feet.*b,c* ²¹Every living thing

a2 Or seven pairs; also in verse 3   *b20 Hebrew fifteen cubits (about 6.9 meters)*   *c20 Or rose more than twenty feet, and the mountains were covered*

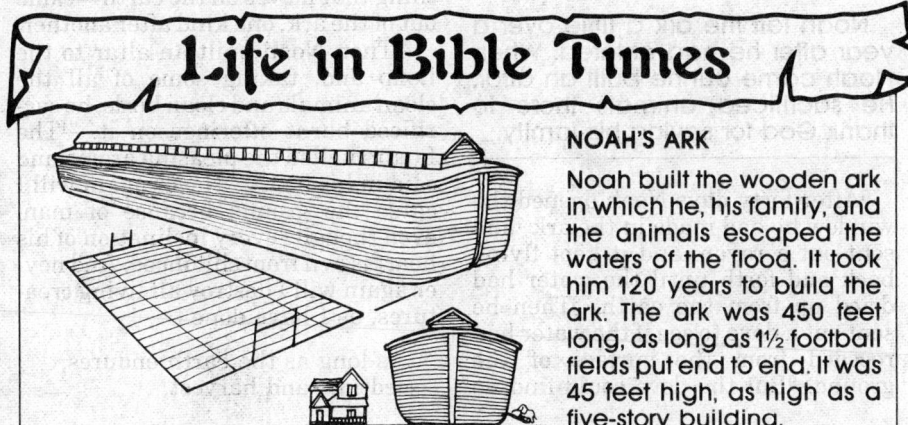

Life in Bible Times

NOAH'S ARK

Noah built the wooden ark in which he, his family, and the animals escaped the waters of the flood. It took him 120 years to build the ark. The ark was 450 feet long, as long as 1½ football fields put end to end. It was 45 feet high, as high as a five-story building.

that moved on the earth perished—birds, livestock, wild animals, all the creatures that swarm over the earth, and all mankind. 22Everything on dry land that had the breath of life in its nostrils died. 23Every living thing on the face of the earth was wiped out; men and animals and the creatures that move along the ground and the birds of the air were wiped from the earth. Only Noah was left, and those with him in the ark.

24The waters flooded the earth for a hundred and fifty days.

8 But God remembered Noah and all the wild animals and the livestock that were with him in the ark, and he sent a wind over the earth, and the waters receded. 2Now the springs of the deep and the floodgates of the heavens had been closed, and the rain had stopped falling from the sky. 3The water receded steadily from the earth. At the end of the hundred and fifty days the water had gone down, 4and on the seventeenth day of the seventh month the ark came to rest on the mountains of Ararat. 5The waters continued to recede until the tenth month, and on the first day of the tenth month the tops of the mountains became visible.

❓ⅅⅼⅅ ㄚoⅠ ㄦⅠoⅣ?   **8:3**

How long was the world covered with water?

Noah left the ark a little over a year after he had entered. When Noah came out he built an altar. He sacrificed animals there to thank God for saving his family.

6After forty days Noah opened the window he had made in the ark 7and sent out a raven, and it kept flying back and forth until the water had dried up from the earth. 8Then he sent out a dove to see if the water had receded from the surface of the ground. 9But the dove could find no place to set its feet because there was water over all the surface of the earth; so it returned to Noah in the ark. He reached out his hand and took the dove and brought it back to himself in the ark. 10He waited seven more days and again sent out the dove from the ark. 11When the dove returned to him in the evening, there in its beak was a freshly plucked olive leaf! Then Noah knew that the water had receded from the earth. 12He waited seven more days and sent the dove out again, but this time it did not return to him.

13By the first day of the first month of Noah's six hundred and first year, the water had dried up from the earth. Noah then removed the covering from the ark and saw that the surface of the ground was dry. 14By the twenty-seventh day of the second month the earth was completely dry.

15Then God said to Noah, 16"Come out of the ark, you and your wife and your sons and their wives. 17Bring out every kind of living creature that is with you—the birds, the animals, and all the creatures that move along the ground—so they can multiply on the earth and be fruitful and increase in number upon it."

18So Noah came out, together with his sons and his wife and his sons' wives. 19All the animals and all the creatures that move along the ground and all the birds—everything that moves on the earth—came out of the ark, one kind after another.

20Then Noah built an altar to the LORD and, taking some of all the clean animals and clean birds, he sacrificed burnt offerings on it. 21The LORD smelled the pleasing aroma and said in his heart: "Never again will I curse the ground because of man, even though[a] every inclination of his heart is evil from childhood. And never again will I destroy all living creatures, as I have done.

22"As long as the earth endures,
  seedtime and harvest,

---

[a]21 Or *man, for*

cold and heat,
summer and winter,
day and night
will never cease."

God's Covenant With Noah

9 Then God blessed Noah and his sons, saying to them, "Be fruitful and increase in number and fill the earth. ²The fear and dread of you will fall upon all the beasts of the earth and all the birds of the air, upon every creature that moves along the ground, and upon all the fish of the sea; they are given into your hands. ³Everything that lives and moves will be food for you. Just as I gave you the green plants, I now give you everything.

⁴"But you must not eat meat that has its lifeblood still in it. ⁵And for your lifeblood I will surely demand an accounting. I will demand an accounting from every animal. And from each man, too, I will demand an accounting for the life of his fellow man.

⁶"Whoever sheds the blood of man,
    by man shall his blood be shed;
for in the image of God
    has God made man.

⁷As for you, be fruitful and increase in number; multiply on the earth and increase upon it."

⁸Then God said to Noah and to his sons with him: ⁹"I now establish my covenant with you and with your descendants after you ¹⁰and with every living creature that was with you—the birds, the livestock and all the wild animals, all those that came out of the ark with you—every living creature on earth. ¹¹I establish my covenant with you: Never again will all life be cut off by the waters of a flood; never again will there be a flood to destroy the earth."

¹²And God said, "This is the sign of the covenant I am making between me and you and every living creature with you, a covenant for all generations to come: ¹³I have set my rainbow in the clouds, and it will be the sign of the covenant between me and the earth. ¹⁴Whenever I bring clouds over the earth and the rainbow appears in the clouds, ¹⁵I will remember my covenant between me and you and all living creatures of every kind. Never again will the waters become a flood to destroy all life. ¹⁶Whenever the rainbow appears in the clouds, I will see it and remember the everlasting covenant between God and all living creatures of every kind on the earth."

¹⁷So God said to Noah, "This is the sign of the covenant I have established between me and all life on the earth."

The Sons of Noah

¹⁸The sons of Noah who came out of the ark were Shem, Ham and Japheth. (Ham was the father of Canaan.) ¹⁹These were the three sons of Noah, and from them came the people who were scattered over the earth.

²⁰Noah, a man of the soil, proceeded[a] to plant a vineyard. ²¹When he drank some of its wine, he became drunk and lay uncovered inside his tent. ²²Ham, the father of Canaan, saw his father's nakedness and told

---

[a]20 Or *soil, was the first*

ＬET'S LIVE IT!   Genesis 8:20–22; 9:12–17

THANK GOD ⟹ Read Genesis 8:20–22; 9:12–17. When Noah and his family left the ark, they built an altar and gave thanks to God. God was pleased. He sent a rainbow as a promise never to send such a flood again. Noah and his family had much for which to be thankful. For fun, make a list of all the things you and your family are thankful for.

his two brothers outside. ²³But Shem and Japheth took a garment and laid it across their shoulders; then they walked in backward and covered their father's nakedness. Their faces were turned the other way so that they would not see their father's nakedness.

²⁴When Noah awoke from his wine and found out what his youngest son had done to him, ²⁵he said,

"Cursed be Canaan!
    The lowest of slaves
    will he be to his brothers."

²⁶He also said,

"Blessed be the Lord, the God of Shem!
    May Canaan be the slave of Shem.ᵃ
²⁷May God extend the territory of Japhethᵇ;
    may Japheth live in the tents of Shem,
    and may Canaan be hisᶜ slave."

²⁸After the flood Noah lived 350 years. ²⁹Altogether, Noah lived 950 years, and then he died.

The Table of Nations

10 This is the account of Shem, Ham and Japheth, Noah's sons, who themselves had sons after the flood.

The Japhethites

²The sonsᵈ of Japheth:
    Gomer, Magog, Madai, Javan, Tubal, Meshech and Tiras.
³The sons of Gomer:
    Ashkenaz, Riphath and Togarmah.
⁴The sons of Javan:
    Elishah, Tarshish, the Kittim and the Rodanim.ᵉ ⁵(From these the maritime peoples spread out into their territories by their clans within their nations, each with its own language.)

The Hamites

⁶The sons of Ham:
    Cush, Mizraim,ᶠ Put and Canaan.
⁷The sons of Cush:
    Seba, Havilah, Sabtah, Raamah and Sabteca.
    The sons of Raamah:
    Sheba and Dedan.

⁸Cush was the fatherᵍ of Nimrod, who grew to be a mighty warrior on the earth. ⁹He was a mighty hunter before the Lord; that is why it is said, "Like Nimrod, a mighty hunter before the Lord." ¹⁰The first centers of his kingdom were Babylon, Erech, Akkad and Calneh, inʰ Shinar.ⁱ ¹¹From that land he went to Assyria, where he built Nineveh, Rehoboth Ir,ʲ Calah ¹²and Resen, which is between Nineveh and Calah; that is the great city.

¹³Mizraim was the father of
    the Ludites, Anamites, Lehabites, Naphtuhites, ¹⁴Pathrusites, Casluhites (from whom the Philistines came) and Caphtorites.
¹⁵Canaan was the father of
    Sidon his firstborn,ᵏ and of the Hittites, ¹⁶Jebusites, Amorites, Girgashites, ¹⁷Hivites, Arkites, Sinites, ¹⁸Arvadites, Zemarites and Hamathites.

Later the Canaanite clans scattered ¹⁹and the borders of Canaan reached from Sidon toward Gerar as far as Gaza, and then toward Sodom, Gomorrah, Admah and Zeboiim, as far as Lasha.

²⁰These are the sons of Ham by

ᵃ26 Or *be his slave*   ᵇ27 *Japheth* sounds like the Hebrew for *extend.*   ᶜ27 Or *their*
ᵈ2 *Sons* may mean *descendants* or *successors* or *nations*; also in verses 3, 4, 6, 7, 20-23, 29 and 31.
ᵉ4 Some manuscripts of the Masoretic Text and Samaritan Pentateuch (see also Septuagint and
1 Chron. 1:7); most manuscripts of the Masoretic Text *Dodanim*   ᶠ6 That is, Egypt; also in verse
13   ᵍ8 *Father* may mean *ancestor* or *predecessor* or *founder*; also in verses 13, 15, 24 and 26.
ʰ10 Or *Erech and Akkad—all of them in*   ⁱ10 That is, Babylonia   ʲ11 Or *Nineveh with its
city squares*   ᵏ15 Or *of the Sidonians, the foremost*

their clans and languages, in their
territories and nations.

The Semites

²¹Sons were also born to Shem,
whose older brother was[a] Japheth;
Shem was the ancestor of all the sons
of Eber.

²²The sons of Shem:

Elam, Asshur, Arphaxad, Lud
and Aram.

²³The sons of Aram:

Uz, Hul, Gether and Me-
shech.[b]

²⁴Arphaxad was the father of[c]
Shelah,

and Shelah the father of Eber.

²⁵Two sons were born to Eber:

One was named Peleg,[d] because in his time the earth was
divided; his brother was
named Joktan.

²⁶Joktan was the father of

Almodad, Sheleph, Hazarmaveth, Jerah, ²⁷Hadoram, Uzal,
Diklah, ²⁸Obal, Abimael, Sheba, ²⁹Ophir, Havilah and Jobab. All these were sons of
Joktan.

³⁰The region where they lived
stretched from Mesha toward Se-
phar, in the eastern hill country.
³¹These are the sons of Shem by
their clans and languages, in their
territories and nations.

³²These are the clans of Noah's
sons, according to their lines of descent, within their nations. From
these the nations spread out over the
earth after the flood.

The Tower of Babel

11 Now the whole world had one
language and a common
speech. ²As men moved eastward,[e]
they found a plain in Shinar[f] and
settled there.
³They said to each other, "Come,
let's make bricks and bake them

thoroughly." They used brick instead
of stone, and tar for mortar. ⁴Then
they said, "Come, let us build ourselves a city, with a tower that
reaches to the heavens, so that we
may make a name for ourselves and
not be scattered over the face of the
whole earth."
⁵But the LORD came down to see the
city and the tower that the men were
building. ⁶The LORD said, "If as one
people speaking the same language
they have begun to do this, then
nothing they plan to do will be impossible for them. ⁷Come, let us go down
and confuse their language so they
will not understand each other."
⁸So the LORD scattered them from
there over all the earth, and they
stopped building the city. ⁹That is
why it was called Babel[g]—because
there the LORD confused the language of the whole world. From there
the LORD scattered them over the face
of the whole earth.

THE TOWER OF BABEL

The tower of Babel was probably a
ziggurat (ZIG-ger-at). A ziggurat
was a tall structure, like a pyramid,
with stairs on the outside. These
towers often had a temple on top,
where people tried to reach
heaven with prayers to false gods.

From Shem to Abram

¹⁰This is the account of Shem.

Two years after the flood, when
Shem was 100 years old, he became
the father[h] of Arphaxad. ¹¹And after

---

[a]21 Or *Shem, the older brother of*   [b]23 See Septuagint and 1 Chron. 1:17; Hebrew *Mash*
[c]24 Hebrew; Septuagint *father of Cainan, and Cainan was the father of*   [d]25 *Peleg* means
division.   [e]2 Or *from the east*; or *in the east*   [f]2 That is, Babylonia   [g]9 That is, Babylon;
Babel sounds like the Hebrew for *confused*.   [h]10 *Father* may mean *ancestor*; also in verses 11-25.

he became the father of Arphaxad, Shem lived 500 years and had other sons and daughters. ¹²When Arphaxad had lived 35 years, he became the father of Shelah. ¹³And after he became the father of Shelah, Arphaxad lived 403 years and had other sons and daughters.ᵃ ¹⁴When Shelah had lived 30 years, he became the father of Eber. ¹⁵And after he became the father of Eber, Shelah lived 403 years and had other sons and daughters.

¹⁶When Eber had lived 34 years, he became the father of Peleg. ¹⁷And after he became the father of Peleg, Eber lived 430 years and had other sons and daughters.

¹⁸When Peleg had lived 30 years, he became the father of Reu. ¹⁹And after he became the father of Reu, Peleg lived 209 years and had other sons and daughters.

²⁰When Reu had lived 32 years, he became the father of Serug. ²¹And after he became the father of Serug, Reu lived 207 years and had other sons and daughters.

²²When Serug had lived 30 years, he became the father of Nahor. ²³And after he became the father of Nahor, Serug lived 200 years and had other sons and daughters.

²⁴When Nahor had lived 29 years, he became the father of Terah. ²⁵And after he became the father of Terah, Nahor lived 119 years and had other sons and daughters.

²⁶After Terah had lived 70 years, he became the father of Abram, Nahor and Haran.

²⁷This is the account of Terah.

Terah became the father of Abram, Nahor and Haran. And Haran became the father of Lot. ²⁸While his father Terah was still alive, Haran died in Ur of the Chaldeans, in the land of his birth. ²⁹Abram and Nahor both married. The name of Abram's wife was Sarai, and the name of Nahor's wife was Milcah; she was the daughter of Haran, the father of both Milcah and Iscah. ³⁰Now Sarai was barren; she had no children.

³¹Terah took his son Abram, his grandson Lot son of Haran, and his daughter-in-law Sarai, the wife of his son Abram, and together they set out from Ur of the Chaldeans to go to Canaan. But when they came to Haran, they settled there. ³²Terah lived 205 years, and he died in Haran.

❓DID YOU KNOW?   12:2

Why is Abram important?

Abram, later known as Abraham, is the ancestor of God's people. The first eleven chapters of the Bible are about the whole human race. The rest of the Old Testament is only about Abraham's descendants, the Hebrew people. Jesus, who came to save all people, is a descendant of Abraham too.

The Call of Abram

12 The LORD had said to Abram, "Leave your country, your people and your father's household and go to the land I will show you.

²"I will make you into a great nation
and I will bless you;
I will make your name great,
and you will be a blessing.
³I will bless those who bless you,
and whoever curses you I will curse;
and all peoples on earth
will be blessed through you."

⁴So Abram left, as the LORD had told him; and Lot went with him.

ᵃ12,13 Hebrew; Septuagint (see also Luke 3:35, 36 and note at Gen. 10:24) *35 years, he became the father of Cainan.* ¹³*And after he became the father of Cainan, Arphaxad lived 430 years and had other sons and daughters, and then he died. When Cainan had lived 130 years, he became the father of Shelah. And after he became the father of Shelah, Cainan lived 330 years and had other sons and daughters*

Abram was seventy-five years old when he set out from Haran. [5]He took his wife Sarai, his nephew Lot, all the possessions they had accumulated and the people they had acquired in Haran, and they set out for the land of Canaan, and they arrived there.

[6]Abram traveled through the land as far as the site of the great tree of Moreh at Shechem. At that time the Canaanites were in the land. [7]The LORD appeared to Abram and said, "To your offspring[a] I will give this land." So he built an altar there to the LORD, who had appeared to him.

[8]From there he went on toward the hills east of Bethel and pitched his tent, with Bethel on the west and Ai on the east. There he built an altar to the LORD and called on the name of the LORD. [9]Then Abram set out and continued toward the Negev.

Abram in Egypt

[10]Now there was a famine in the land, and Abram went down to Egypt to live there for a while because the famine was severe. [11]As he was about to enter Egypt, he said to his wife Sarai, "I know what a beautiful woman you are. [12]When the Egyptians see you, they will say, 'This is his wife.' Then they will kill me but will let you live. [13]Say you are my sister, so that I will be treated well for your sake and my life will be spared because of you."

[14]When Abram came to Egypt, the Egyptians saw that she was a very beautiful woman. [15]And when Pharaoh's officials saw her, they praised her to Pharaoh, and she was taken into his palace. [16]He treated Abram well for her sake, and Abram acquired sheep and cattle, male and female donkeys, menservants and maidservants, and camels.

[17]But the LORD inflicted serious diseases on Pharaoh and his household because of Abram's wife Sarai. [18]So Pharaoh summoned Abram. "What have you done to me?" he said. "Why didn't you tell me she was your wife? [19]Why did you say, 'She is my sister,' so that I took her to be my wife? Now then, here is your wife. Take her and go!" [20]Then Pharaoh gave orders about Abram to his men, and they sent him on his way, with his wife and everything he had.

Abram and Lot Separate

13 So Abram went up from Egypt to the Negev, with his wife and everything he had, and Lot went with him. [2]Abram had become very wealthy in livestock and in silver and gold.

[3]From the Negev he went from place to place until he came to Bethel, to the place between Bethel and Ai where his tent had been earlier [4]and where he had first built an altar. There Abram called on the name of the LORD.

[5]Now Lot, who was moving about with Abram, also had flocks and herds and tents. [6]But the land could not support them while they stayed together, for their possessions were so great that they were not able to stay together. [7]And quarreling arose between Abram's herdsmen and the herdsmen of Lot. The Canaanites and Perizzites were also living in the land at that time.

[8]So Abram said to Lot, "Let's not have any quarreling between you and me, or between your herdsmen and mine, for we are brothers. [9]Is not the whole land before you? Let's part company. If you go to the left, I'll go to the right; if you go to the right, I'll go to the left."

[10]Lot looked up and saw that the whole plain of the Jordan was well watered, like the garden of the LORD, like the land of Egypt, toward Zoar. (This was before the LORD destroyed Sodom and Gomorrah.) [11]So Lot chose for himself the whole plain of the Jordan and set out toward the east. The two men parted company: [12]Abram lived in the land of Canaan, while Lot lived among the cities of the plain and pitched his tents near

---

a7 Or seed

Sodom. ¹³Now the men of Sodom were wicked and were sinning greatly against the LORD.

¹⁴The LORD said to Abram after Lot had parted from him, "Lift up your eyes from where you are and look north and south, east and west. ¹⁵All the land that you see I will give to you and your offspring*a* forever. ¹⁶I will make your offspring like the dust of the earth, so that if anyone could count the dust, then your offspring could be counted. ¹⁷Go, walk through the length and breadth of the land, for I am giving it to you."

¹⁸So Abram moved his tents and went to live near the great trees of Mamre at Hebron, where he built an altar to the LORD.

Abram Rescues Lot

14 At this time Amraphel king of Shinar,*b* Arioch king of Ellasar, Kedorlaomer king of Elam and Tidal king of Goiim ²went to war against Bera king of Sodom, Birsha king of Gomorrah, Shinab king of Admah, Shemeber king of Zeboiim, and the king of Bela (that is, Zoar). ³All these latter kings joined forces in the Valley of Siddim (the Salt Sea*c*). ⁴For twelve years they had been subject to Kedorlaomer, but in the thirteenth year they rebelled.

⁵In the fourteenth year, Kedorlaomer and the kings allied with him went out and defeated the Rephaites in Ashteroth Karnaim, the Zuzites in Ham, the Emites in Shaveh Kiriathaim ⁶and the Horites in the hill country of Seir, as far as El Paran near the desert. ⁷Then they turned back and went to En Mishpat (that is, Kadesh), and they conquered the whole territory of the Amalekites, as well as the Amorites who were living in Hazazon Tamar.

⁸Then the king of Sodom, the king of Gomorrah, the king of Admah, the king of Zeboiim and the king of Bela (that is, Zoar) marched out and drew up their battle lines in the Valley of Siddim ⁹against Kedorlaomer king of Elam, Tidal king of Goiim, Amraphel king of Shinar and Arioch king of Ellasar—four kings against five. ¹⁰Now the Valley of Siddim was full of tar pits, and when the kings of Sodom and Gomorrah fled, some of the men fell into them and the rest fled to the hills. ¹¹The four kings seized all the goods of Sodom and Gomorrah and all their food; then they went away. ¹²They also carried off Abram's nephew Lot and his possessions, since he was living in Sodom.

¹³One who had escaped came and reported this to Abram the Hebrew.

---

a15 Or *seed*; also in verse 16   *b1* That is, Babylonia; also in verse 9   *c3* That is, the Dead Sea

---

ＬET'S LIVE IT!   Genesis 13:1–18

HOW TO STOP FAMILY QUARRELS ➡ The herdsmen of Abram and Lot quarreled about using the land and where to graze and water their flocks. There just wasn't enough room for both groups to live. Abram decided to stop the quarrel. Read Genesis 13:1–18 to find out how he did it.

Most brothers and sisters quarrel at times. Here's how you can stop the quarreling: 1. From the story of Abram, make up rules, such as: Give the other person first choice. Be satisfied with what is left. 2. Make a badge with Abram's name on it. When you have a family quarrel, choose a person to wear the "Abram" badge. Let Abram use the rules you have made to stop the quarrel.

You can take turns being Abram. Then you each can learn how to please God as Abram did.

Now Abram was living near the great trees of Mamre the Amorite, a brother[a] of Eshcol and Aner, all of whom were allied with Abram. [14]When Abram heard that his relative had been taken captive, he called out the 318 trained men born in his household and went in pursuit as far as Dan. [15]During the night Abram divided his men to attack them and he routed them, pursuing them as far as Hobah, north of Damascus. [16]He recovered all the goods and brought back his relative Lot and his possessions, together with the women and the other people.

[17]After Abram returned from defeating Kedorlaomer and the kings allied with him, the king of Sodom came out to meet him in the Valley of Shaveh (that is, the King's Valley).

[18]Then Melchizedek king of Salem[b] brought out bread and wine. He was priest of God Most High, [19]and he blessed Abram, saying,

"Blessed be Abram by God Most
     High,
  Creator[c] of heaven and earth.
[20]And blessed be[d] God Most High,
  who delivered your enemies into
     your hand."

Then Abram gave him a tenth of everything.

[21]The king of Sodom said to Abram, "Give me the people and keep the goods for yourself."

[22]But Abram said to the king of Sodom, "I have raised my hand to the LORD, God Most High, Creator of heaven and earth, and have taken an oath [23]that I will accept nothing belonging to you, not even a thread or the thong of a sandal, so that you will never be able to say, 'I made Abram rich.' [24]I will accept nothing but what my men have eaten and the share that belongs to the men who went with me—to Aner, Eshcol and Mamre. Let them have their share."

God's Covenant With Abram

15 After this, the word of the LORD came to Abram in a vision:

"Do not be afraid, Abram.
  I am your shield,[e]
  your very great reward.[f]"

[2]But Abram said, "O Sovereign LORD, what can you give me since I remain childless and the one who will inherit[g] my estate is Eliezer of Damascus?" [3]And Abram said, "You have given me no children; so a servant in my household will be my heir."

WORDS TO REMEMBER

15:6 Abraham believed the LORD, and he credited it to him as righteousness.

---

[4]Then the word of the LORD came to him: "This man will not be your heir, but a son coming from your own body will be your heir." [5]He took him outside and said, "Look up at the heavens and count the stars—if indeed you can count them." Then he said to him, "So shall your offspring be."

[6]Abram believed the LORD, and he credited it to him as righteousness.

[7]He also said to him, "I am the LORD, who brought you out of Ur of the Chaldeans to give you this land to take possession of it."

[8]But Abram said, "O Sovereign LORD, how can I know that I will gain possession of it?"

[9]So the LORD said to him, "Bring me a heifer, a goat and a ram, each three years old, along with a dove and a young pigeon."

[10]Abram brought all these to him, cut them in two and arranged the halves opposite each other; the birds, however, he did not cut in half. [11]Then birds of prey came down on

---

a13 Or *a relative*; or *an ally*   *b18* That is, Jerusalem   *c19* Or *Possessor*; also in verse 22
d20 Or *And praise be to*   *e1* Or *sovereign*   *f1* Or *shield, / your reward will be very great*
g2 The meaning of the Hebrew for this phrase is uncertain.

the carcasses, but Abram drove them away.

¹²As the sun was setting, Abram fell into a deep sleep, and a thick and dreadful darkness came over him. ¹³Then the LORD said to him, "Know for certain that your descendants will be strangers in a country not their own, and they will be enslaved and mistreated four hundred years. ¹⁴But I will punish the nation they serve as slaves, and afterward they will come out with great possessions. ¹⁵You, however, will go to your fathers in peace and be buried at a good old age. ¹⁶In the fourth generation your descendants will come back here, for the sin of the Amorites has not yet reached its full measure."

¹⁷When the sun had set and darkness had fallen, a smoking firepot with a blazing torch appeared and passed between the pieces. ¹⁸On that day the LORD made a covenant with Abram and said, "To your descendants I give this land, from the river*a* of Egypt to the great river, the Euphrates— ¹⁹the land of the Kenites, Kenizzites, Kadmonites, ²⁰Hittites, Perizzites, Rephaites, ²¹Amorites, Canaanites, Girgashites and Jebusites."

Hagar and Ishmael

16 Now Sarai, Abram's wife, had borne him no children. But

a18 Or Wadi

she had an Egyptian maidservant named Hagar; ²so she said to Abram, "The LORD has kept me from having children. Go, sleep with my maidservant; perhaps I can build a family through her."

Abram agreed to what Sarai said. ³So after Abram had been living in Canaan ten years, Sarai his wife took her Egyptian maidservant Hagar and gave her to her husband to be his wife. ⁴He slept with Hagar, and she conceived.

When she knew she was pregnant, she began to despise her mistress. ⁵Then Sarai said to Abram, "You are responsible for the wrong I am suffering. I put my servant in your arms, and now that she knows she is pregnant, she despises me. May the LORD judge between you and me."

⁶"Your servant is in your hands,"

Abram said. "Do with her whatever you think best." Then Sarai mistreated Hagar; so she fled from her.

？DID YOU KNOW?   16:1

Who was Hagar?

Hagar was Sarah's slave. Because Sarah was childless, she gave her slave Hagar to Abraham to be his wife also. This was quite common practice in Bible times. However, if the slave had a child (which Hagar did), the child belonged to the family of the mistress, not the slave.

---

⁷The angel of the LORD found Hagar near a spring in the desert; it was the spring that is beside the road to Shur. ⁸And he said, "Hagar, servant of Sarai, where have you come from, and where are you going?"

"I'm running away from my mistress Sarai," she answered.

⁹Then the angel of the LORD told her, "Go back to your mistress and submit to her." ¹⁰The angel added, "I will so increase your descendants that they will be too numerous to count."

¹¹The angel of the LORD also said to her:

"You are now with child
  and you will have a son.
You shall name him Ishmael,ᵃ
  for the LORD has heard of your
    misery.
¹²He will be a wild donkey of a
    man;
  his hand will be against
    everyone
  and everyone's hand against
    him,
and he will live in hostility
  towardᵇ all his brothers."

¹³She gave this name to the LORD who spoke to her: "You are the God who sees me," for she said, "I have now seenᶜ the One who sees me." ¹⁴That is why the well was called Beer Lahai Roiᵈ; it is still there, between Kadesh and Bered.

¹⁵So Hagar bore Abram a son, and Abram gave the name Ishmael to the son she had borne. ¹⁶Abram was eighty-six years old when Hagar bore him Ishmael.

The Covenant of Circumcision

17 When Abram was ninety-nine years old, the LORD appeared to him and said, "I am God Almightyᵉ; walk before me and be blameless. ²I will confirm my covenant between me and you and will greatly increase your numbers."

³Abram fell facedown, and God said to him, ⁴"As for me, this is my covenant with you: You will be the father of many nations. ⁵No longer will you be called Abramᶠ; your name will be Abraham,ᵍ for I have made you a father of many nations. ⁶I will make you very fruitful; I will make nations of you, and kings will come from you. ⁷I will establish my covenant as an everlasting covenant between me and you and your descendants after you for the generations to come, to be your God and the God of your descendants after you. ⁸The whole land of Canaan, where you are now an alien, I will give as an everlasting possession to you and your descendants after you; and I will be their God."

？DID YOU KNOW?   17:5

What does the name Abraham mean?

Abram means father. Abraham means father of many. Because Abraham believed God, this childless old man became the ancestor of millions of people.

ᵃ11 *Ishmael* means *God hears.*   ᵇ12 Or *live to the east / of*   ᶜ13 Or *seen the back of*
ᵈ14 *Beer Lahai Roi* means *well of the Living One who sees me.*   ᵉ1 Hebrew *El-Shaddai*
ᶠ5 *Abram* means *exalted father.*   ᵍ5 *Abraham* means *father of many.*

⁹Then God said to Abraham, "As for you, you must keep my covenant, you and your descendants after you for the generations to come. ¹⁰This is my covenant with you and your descendants after you, the covenant you are to keep: Every male among you shall be circumcised. ¹¹You are to undergo circumcision, and it will be the sign of the covenant between me and you. ¹²For the generations to come every male among you who is eight days old must be circumcised, including those born in your household or bought with money from a foreigner—those who are not your offspring. ¹³Whether born in your household or bought with your money, they must be circumcised. My covenant in your flesh is to be an everlasting covenant. ¹⁴Any uncircumcised male, who has not been circumcised in the flesh, will be cut off from his people; he has broken my covenant."

¹⁵God also said to Abraham, "As for Sarai your wife, you are no longer to call her Sarai; her name will be Sarah. ¹⁶I will bless her and will surely give you a son by her. I will bless her so that she will be the mother of nations; kings of peoples will come from her."

¹⁷Abraham fell facedown; he laughed and said to himself, "Will a son be born to a man a hundred years old? Will Sarah bear a child at the age of ninety?" ¹⁸And Abraham said to God, "If only Ishmael might live under your blessing!"

¹⁹Then God said, "Yes, but your wife Sarah will bear you a son, and you will call him Isaac.ᵃ I will establish my covenant with him as an everlasting covenant for his descendants after him. ²⁰And as for Ishmael, I have heard you: I will surely bless him; I will make him fruitful and will greatly increase his numbers. He will be the father of twelve rulers, and I will make him into a great nation. ²¹But my covenant I will establish with Isaac, whom Sarah will bear to you by this time next year." ²²When he had finished speaking with Abraham, God went up from him.

²³On that very day Abraham took his son Ishmael and all those born in his household or bought with his money, every male in his household, and circumcised them, as God told him. ²⁴Abraham was ninety-nine years old when he was circumcised, ²⁵and his son Ishmael was thirteen; ²⁶Abraham and his son Ishmael were both circumcised on that same day. ²⁷And every male in Abraham's household, including those born in his household or bought from a foreigner, was circumcised with him.

The Three Visitors

18 The LORD appeared to Abraham near the great trees of Mamre while he was sitting at the entrance to his tent in the heat of the day. ²Abraham looked up and saw three men standing nearby. When he saw them, he hurried from the entrance of his tent to meet them and bowed low to the ground.

³He said, "If I have found favor in your eyes, my lord,ᵇ do not pass your servant by. ⁴Let a little water be brought, and then you may all wash your feet and rest under this tree. ⁵Let me get you something to eat, so you can be refreshed and then go on your way—now that you have come to your servant."

"Very well," they answered, "do as you say."

⁶So Abraham hurried into the tent to Sarah. "Quick," he said, "get three seahsᶜ of fine flour and knead it and bake some bread."

⁷Then he ran to the herd and selected a choice, tender calf and gave it to a servant, who hurried to prepare it. ⁸He then brought some curds and milk and the calf that had been prepared, and set these before them.

ᵃ19 *Isaac* means *he laughs.*   ᵇ3 Or *O Lord*   ᶜ6 That is, probably about 20 quarts (about 22 liters)

While they ate, he stood near them under a tree.

⁹"Where is your wife Sarah?" they asked him.

"There, in the tent," he said.

¹⁰Then the LORD*ᵃ* said, "I will surely return to you about this time next year, and Sarah your wife will have a son."

Now Sarah was listening at the entrance to the tent, which was behind him. ¹¹Abraham and Sarah were already old and well advanced in years, and Sarah was past the age of childbearing. ¹²So Sarah laughed to herself as she thought, "After I am worn out and my master*ᵇ* is old, will I now have this pleasure?"

¹³Then the LORD said to Abraham, "Why did Sarah laugh and say, 'Will I really have a child, now that I am old?' ¹⁴Is anything too hard for the LORD? I will return to you at the appointed time next year and Sarah will have a son."

¹⁵Sarah was afraid, so she lied and said, "I did not laugh."

But he said, "Yes, you did laugh."

Abraham Pleads for Sodom

¹⁶When the men got up to leave, they looked down toward Sodom, and Abraham walked along with them to see them on their way. ¹⁷Then the LORD said, "Shall I hide from Abraham what I am about to do? ¹⁸Abraham will surely become a great and powerful nation, and all nations on earth will be blessed through him. ¹⁹For I have chosen him, so that he will direct his children and his household after him to keep the way of the LORD by doing what is right and just, so that the LORD will bring about for Abraham what he has promised him."

²⁰Then the LORD said, "The outcry against Sodom and Gomorrah is so great and their sin so grievous ²¹that I will go down and see if what they have done is as bad as the outcry that

has reached me. If not, I will know."

²²The men turned away and went toward Sodom, but Abraham remained standing before the LORD.*ᶜ* ²³Then Abraham approached him and said: "Will you sweep away the righteous with the wicked? ²⁴What if there are fifty righteous people in the city? Will you really sweep it away and not spare*ᵈ* the place for the sake of the fifty righteous people in it? ²⁵Far be it from you to do such a thing—to kill the righteous with the wicked, treating the righteous and the wicked alike. Far be it from you! Will not the Judge*ᵉ* of all the earth do right?"

²⁶The LORD said, "If I find fifty righteous people in the city of Sodom, I will spare the whole place for their sake."

²⁷Then Abraham spoke up again: "Now that I have been so bold as to speak to the Lord, though I am nothing but dust and ashes, ²⁸what if the number of the righteous is five less than fifty? Will you destroy the whole city because of five people?"

"If I find forty-five there," he said, "I will not destroy it."

²⁹Once again he spoke to him, "What if only forty are found there?"

He said, "For the sake of forty, I will not do it."

³⁰Then he said, "May the Lord not be angry, but let me speak. What if only thirty can be found there?"

He answered, "I will not do it if I find thirty there."

³¹Abraham said, "Now that I have been so bold as to speak to the Lord, what if only twenty can be found there?"

He said, "For the sake of twenty, I will not destroy it."

³²Then he said, "May the Lord not be angry, but let me speak just once more. What if only ten can be found there?"

He answered, "For the sake of ten, I will not destroy it."

ᵃ10 Hebrew Then he   ᵇ12 Or husband   ᶜ22 Masoretic Text; an ancient Hebrew scribal tradition but the LORD remained standing before Abraham   ᵈ24 Or forgive, also in verse 26   ᵉ25 Or Ruler

³³When the LORD had finished speaking with Abraham, he left, and Abraham returned home.

Sodom and Gomorrah Destroyed

19 The two angels arrived at Sodom in the evening, and Lot was sitting in the gateway of the city. When he saw them, he got up to meet them and bowed down with his face to the ground. ²"My lords," he said, "please turn aside to your servant's house. You can wash your feet and spend the night and then go on your way early in the morning."

"No," they answered, "we will spend the night in the square."

³But he insisted so strongly that they did go with him and entered his house. He prepared a meal for them, baking bread without yeast, and they ate. ⁴Before they had gone to bed, all the men from every part of the city of Sodom—both young and old—surrounded the house. ⁵They called to Lot, "Where are the men who came to you tonight? Bring them out to us so that we can have sex with them."

⁶Lot went outside to meet them and shut the door behind him ⁷and said, "No, my friends. Don't do this wicked thing. ⁸Look, I have two daughters who have never slept with a man. Let me bring them out to you, and you can do what you like with them. But don't do anything to these men, for they have come under the protection of my roof."

⁹"Get out of our way," they replied. And they said, "This fellow came here as an alien, and now he wants to play the judge! We'll treat you worse than them." They kept bringing pressure on Lot and moved forward to break down the door.

¹⁰But the men inside reached out and pulled Lot back into the house and shut the door. ¹¹Then they struck the men who were at the door of the house, young and old, with blindness so that they could not find the door.

¹²The two men said to Lot, "Do you have anyone else here—sons-in-law, sons or daughters, or anyone else in the city who belongs to you? Get them out of here, ¹³because we are going to destroy this place. The outcry to the LORD against its people is so great that he has sent us to destroy it."

¹⁴So Lot went out and spoke to his sons-in-law, who were pledged to marry*ᵃ* his daughters. He said, "Hurry and get out of this place, because the LORD is about to destroy the city!" But his sons-in-law thought he was joking.

¹⁵With the coming of dawn, the angels urged Lot, saying, "Hurry! Take your wife and your two daughters who are here, or you will be swept away when the city is punished."

¹⁶When he hesitated, the men

a14 Or were married to

▰ET'S LIVE IT!   Genesis 18:16–33

PRAYING FOR OTHERS ➡ Read Genesis 18:16–33 in your Bible. Then try to answer these three questions. If you need help, talk the questions over with a friend or one of your parents.

1. How do I know that God cares about the people I pray for?
2. Whom else should I pray for besides the people I know and like?
3. How does this story show that God will answer my prayers for other people?

Make a list of people to pray for and things to ask God to do for them. Use the list when you pray each day.

grasped his hand and the hands of his wife and of his two daughters and led them safely out of the city, for the LORD was merciful to them. [17]As soon as they had brought them out, one of them said, "Flee for your lives! Don't look back, and don't stop anywhere in the plain! Flee to the mountains or you will be swept away!"

[18]But Lot said to them, "No, my lords,[a] please! [19]Your[b] servant has found favor in your[b] eyes, and you[b] have shown great kindness to me in sparing my life. But I can't flee to the mountains; this disaster will overtake me, and I'll die. [20]Look, here is a town near enough to run to, and it is small. Let me flee to it—it is very small, isn't it? Then my life will be spared."

[21]He said to him, "Very well, I will grant this request too; I will not overthrow the town you speak of. [22]But flee there quickly, because I cannot do anything until you reach it." (That is why the town was called Zoar.[c])

[23]By the time Lot reached Zoar, the sun had risen over the land. [24]Then the LORD rained down burning sulfur on Sodom and Gomorrah—from the LORD out of the heavens. [25]Thus he overthrew those cities and the entire plain, including all those living in the cities—and also the vegetation in the land. [26]But Lot's wife looked back, and she became a pillar of salt.

[27]Early the next morning Abraham got up and returned to the place where he had stood before the LORD. [28]He looked down toward Sodom and Gomorrah, toward all the land of the plain, and he saw dense smoke rising from the land, like smoke from a furnace.

[29]So when God destroyed the cities of the plain, he remembered Abraham, and he brought Lot out of the catastrophe that overthrew the cities where Lot had lived.

Lot and His Daughters

[30]Lot and his two daughters left Zoar and settled in the mountains, for he was afraid to stay in Zoar. He and his two daughters lived in a cave. [31]One day the older daughter said to the younger, "Our father is old, and there is no man around here to lie with us, as is the custom all over the earth. [32]Let's get our father to drink wine and then lie with him and preserve our family line through our father."

?DID YOU KNOW? 19:28

Where are Sodom and Gomorrah?

The ruins of these cities most likely lie under shallow water at the south end of the Dead Sea. God probably destroyed the cities with a large explosion of gases and an earthquake. Today the nation of Israel has oil wells near where Sodom and Gomorrah once stood.

---

[33]That night they got their father to drink wine, and the older daughter went in and lay with him. He was not aware of it when she lay down or when she got up.

[34]The next day the older daughter said to the younger, "Last night I lay with my father. Let's get him to drink wine again tonight, and you go in and lie with him so we can preserve our family line through our father." [35]So they got their father to drink wine that night also, and the younger daughter went and lay with him. Again he was not aware of it when she lay down or when she got up.

[36]So both of Lot's daughters became pregnant by their father. [37]The older daughter had a son, and she named him Moab[d]; he is the father of the Moabites of today. [38]The younger daughter also had a son, and she named him Ben-Ammi[e]; he is the father of the Ammonites of today.

---

[a]18 Or *No, Lord*; or *No, my lord*   [b]19 The Hebrew is singular.   [c]22 *Zoar* means *small*.
[d]37 *Moab* sounds like the Hebrew for *from father*.   [e]38 *Ben-Ammi* means *son of my people*.

Abraham and Abimelech

20 Now Abraham moved on from there into the region of the Negev and lived between Kadesh and Shur. For a while he stayed in Gerar, ²and there Abraham said of his wife Sarah, "She is my sister." Then Abimelech king of Gerar sent for Sarah and took her.

³But God came to Abimelech in a dream one night and said to him, "You are as good as dead because of the woman you have taken; she is a married woman."

⁴Now Abimelech had not gone near her, so he said, "Lord, will you destroy an innocent nation? ⁵Did he not say to me, 'She is my sister,' and didn't she also say, 'He is my brother'? I have done this with a clear conscience and clean hands."

⁶Then God said to him in the dream, "Yes, I know you did this with a clear conscience, and so I have kept you from sinning against me. That is why I did not let you touch her. ⁷Now return the man's wife, for he is a prophet, and he will pray for you and you will live. But if you do not return her, you may be sure that you and all yours will die."

⁸Early the next morning Abimelech summoned all his officials, and when he told them all that had happened, they were very much afraid. ⁹Then Abimelech called Abraham in and said, "What have you done to us? How have I wronged you that you have brought such great guilt upon me and my kingdom? You have done things to me that should not be done." ¹⁰And Abimelech asked Abraham, "What was your reason for doing this?"

¹¹Abraham replied, "I said to myself, 'There is surely no fear of God in this place, and they will kill me because of my wife.' ¹²Besides, she really is my sister, the daughter of my father though not of my mother; and she became my wife. ¹³And when God had me wander from my father's

household, I said to her, 'This is how you can show your love to me: Everywhere we go, say of me, "He is my brother."'"

¹⁴Then Abimelech brought sheep and cattle and male and female slaves and gave them to Abraham, and he returned Sarah his wife to him. ¹⁵And Abimelech said, "My land is before you; live wherever you like."

¹⁶To Sarah he said, "I am giving your brother a thousand shekels[a] of silver. This is to cover the offense against you before all who are with you; you are completely vindicated."

¹⁷Then Abraham prayed to God, and God healed Abimelech, his wife and his slave girls so they could have children again, ¹⁸for the LORD had closed up every womb in Abimelech's household because of Abraham's wife Sarah.

The Birth of Isaac

21 Now the LORD was gracious to Sarah as he had said, and the LORD did for Sarah what he had promised. ²Sarah became pregnant and bore a son to Abraham in his old age, at the very time God had promised him. ³Abraham gave the name Isaac[b] to the son Sarah bore him. ⁴When his son Isaac was eight days old, Abraham circumcised him, as God commanded him. ⁵Abraham was a hundred years old when his son Isaac was born to him.

⁶Sarah said, "God has brought me laughter, and everyone who hears about this will laugh with me." ⁷And she added, "Who would have said to Abraham that Sarah would nurse children? Yet I have borne him a son in his old age."

Hagar and Ishmael Sent Away

⁸The child grew and was weaned, and on the day Isaac was weaned Abraham held a great feast. ⁹But Sarah saw that the son whom Hagar the Egyptian had borne to Abraham was mocking, ¹⁰and she said to Abraham, "Get rid of that slave woman

---

a16 That is, about 25 pounds (about 11.5 kilograms)   *b3 Isaac* means *he laughs.*

and her son, for that slave woman's son will never share in the inheritance with my son Isaac."

¹¹The matter distressed Abraham greatly because it concerned his son. ¹²But God said to him, "Do not be so distressed about the boy and your maidservant. Listen to whatever Sarah tells you, because it is through Isaac that your offspring[a] will be reckoned. ¹³I will make the son of the maidservant into a nation also, because he is your offspring."

¹⁴Early the next morning Abraham took some food and a skin of water and gave them to Hagar. He set them on her shoulders and then sent her off with the boy. She went on her way and wandered in the desert of Beersheba.

¹⁵When the water in the skin was gone, she put the boy under one of the bushes. ¹⁶Then she went off and sat down nearby, about a bowshot away, for she thought, "I cannot watch the boy die." And as she sat there nearby, she[b] began to sob.

¹⁷God heard the boy crying, and the angel of God called to Hagar from heaven and said to her, "What is the matter, Hagar? Do not be afraid; God has heard the boy crying as he lies there. ¹⁸Lift the boy up and take him by the hand, for I will make him into a great nation."

¹⁹Then God opened her eyes and she saw a well of water. So she went and filled the skin with water and gave the boy a drink.

²⁰God was with the boy as he grew up. He lived in the desert and became an archer. ²¹While he was living in the Desert of Paran, his mother got a wife for him from Egypt.

The Treaty at Beersheba

²²At that time Abimelech and Phicol the commander of his forces said to Abraham, "God is with you in everything you do. ²³Now swear to me here before God that you will not deal falsely with me or my children or my descendants. Show to me and the country where you are living as an alien the same kindness I have shown to you."

²⁴Abraham said, "I swear it."

²⁵Then Abraham complained to Abimelech about a well of water that Abimelech's servants had seized. ²⁶But Abimelech said, "I don't know who has done this. You did not tell me, and I heard about it only today."

²⁷So Abraham brought sheep and cattle and gave them to Abimelech, and the two men made a treaty. ²⁸Abraham set apart seven ewe lambs from the flock, ²⁹and Abimelech asked Abraham, "What is the meaning of these seven ewe lambs you have set apart by themselves?"

³⁰He replied, "Accept these seven lambs from my hand as a witness that I dug this well."

³¹So that place was called Beersheba,[c] because the two men swore an oath there.

³²After the treaty had been made at Beersheba, Abimelech and Phicol the commander of his forces returned to the land of the Philistines. ³³Abraham planted a tamarisk tree in Beersheba, and there he called upon the name of the LORD, the Eternal God. ³⁴And Abraham stayed in the land of the Philistines for a long time.

Abraham Tested

22 Some time later God tested Abraham. He said to him, "Abraham!"

"Here I am," he replied.

²Then God said, "Take your son, your only son, Isaac, whom you love, and go to the region of Moriah. Sacrifice him there as a burnt offering on one of the mountains I will tell you about."

³Early the next morning Abraham got up and saddled his donkey. He took with him two of his servants and his son Isaac. When he had cut enough wood for the burnt offering, he set out for the place God had told

---

a12 Or seed   b16 Hebrew; Septuagint the child of the oath.   c31 Beersheba can mean well of seven or well

him about. ⁴On the third day Abraham looked up and saw the place in the distance. ⁵He said to his servants, "Stay here with the donkey while I and the boy go over there. We will worship and then we will come back to you."

⁶Abraham took the wood for the burnt offering and placed it on his son Isaac, and he himself carried the fire and the knife. As the two of them went on together, ⁷Isaac spoke up and said to his father Abraham, "Father?"

"Yes, my son?" Abraham replied.

"The fire and wood are here," Isaac said, "but where is the lamb for the burnt offering?"

⁸Abraham answered, "God himself will provide the lamb for the burnt offering, my son." And the two of them went on together.

⁹When they reached the place God had told him about, Abraham built an altar there and arranged the wood on it. He bound his son Isaac and laid him on the altar, on top of the wood. ¹⁰Then he reached out his hand and took the knife to slay his son. ¹¹But the angel of the LORD called out to him from heaven, "Abraham! Abraham!"

"Here I am," he replied.

¹²"Do not lay a hand on the boy," he said. "Do not do anything to him. Now I know that you fear God, because you have not withheld from me your son, your only son."

¹³Abraham looked up and there in a thicket he saw a ramᵃ caught by its horns. He went over and took the ram and sacrificed it as a burnt offering instead of his son. ¹⁴So Abraham called that place The LORD Will Provide. And to this day it is said, "On the mountain of the LORD it will be provided."

¹⁵The angel of the LORD called to Abraham from heaven a second time ¹⁶and said, "I swear by myself, declares the LORD, that because you

have done this and have not withheld your son, your only son, ¹⁷I will surely bless you and make your descendants as numerous as the stars in the sky and as the sand on the seashore. Your descendants will take possession of the cities of their enemies, ¹⁸and through your offspringᵇ all nations on earth will be blessed, because you have obeyed me."

¹⁹Then Abraham returned to his servants, and they set off together for Beersheba. And Abraham stayed in Beersheba.

Nahor's Sons

²⁰Some time later Abraham was told, "Milcah is also a mother; she has borne sons to your brother Nahor: ²¹Uz the firstborn, Buz his brother, Kemuel (the father of Aram), ²²Kesed, Hazo, Pildash, Jidlaph and Bethuel." ²³Bethuel became the father of Rebekah. Milcah bore these eight sons to Abraham's brother Nahor. ²⁴His concubine, whose name was Reumah, also had sons: Tebah, Gaham, Tahash and Maacah.

The Death of Sarah

23 Sarah lived to be a hundred and twenty-seven years old. ²She died at Kiriath Arba (that is, Hebron) in the land of Canaan, and Abraham went to mourn for Sarah and to weep over her.

³Then Abraham rose from beside his dead wife and spoke to the Hittites.ᶜ He said, ⁴"I am an alien and a stranger among you. Sell me some property for a burial site here so I can bury my dead."

⁵The Hittites replied to Abraham, ⁶"Sir, listen to us. You are a mighty prince among us. Bury your dead in the choicest of our tombs. None of us will refuse you his tomb for burying your dead."

⁷Then Abraham rose and bowed down before the people of the land, the Hittites. ⁸He said to them, "If you

---

ᵃ13 Many manuscripts of the Masoretic Text, Samaritan Pentateuch, Septuagint and Syriac; most manuscripts of the Masoretic Text *a ram behind him;*   ᵇ18 Or *seed*   ᶜ3 Or *the sons of Heth;* also in verses 5, 7, 10, 16, 18 and 20

are willing to let me bury my dead, then listen to me and intercede with Ephron son of Zohar on my behalf ⁹so he will sell me the cave of Machpelah, which belongs to him and is at the end of his field. Ask him to sell it to me for the full price as a burial site among you."

¹⁰Ephron the Hittite was sitting among his people and he replied to Abraham in the hearing of all the Hittites who had come to the gate of his city. ¹¹"No, my lord," he said. "Listen to me; I give*a* you the field, and I give*a* you the cave that is in it. I give*a* it to you in the presence of my people. Bury your dead."

¹²Again Abraham bowed down before the people of the land ¹³and he said to Ephron in their hearing, "Listen to me, if you will. I will pay the price of the field. Accept it from me so I can bury my dead there."

¹⁴Ephron answered Abraham, ¹⁵"Listen to me, my lord; the land is worth four hundred shekels*b* of silver, but what is that between me and you? Bury your dead."

¹⁶Abraham agreed to Ephron's terms and weighed out for him the price he had named in the hearing of the Hittites: four hundred shekels of silver, according to the weight current among the merchants.

¹⁷So Ephron's field in Machpelah near Mamre—both the field and the cave in it, and all the trees within the borders of the field—was deeded ¹⁸to Abraham as his property in the presence of all the Hittites who had come to the gate of the city. ¹⁹Afterward Abraham buried his wife Sarah in the cave in the field of Machpelah near Mamre (which is at Hebron) in the land of Canaan. ²⁰So the field and the cave in it were deeded to Abraham by the Hittites as a burial site.

Isaac and Rebekah

24 Abraham was now old and well advanced in years, and the LORD had blessed him in every way. ²He said to the chief*c* servant in his household, the one in charge of all that he had, "Put your hand under my thigh. ³I want you to swear by the LORD, the God of heaven and the God of earth, that you will not get a wife for my son from the daughters of the Canaanites, among whom I am living, ⁴but will go to my country and my own relatives and get a wife for my son Isaac."

⁵The servant asked him, "What if the woman is unwilling to come back with me to this land? Shall I then take your son back to the country you came from?"

⁶"Make sure that you do not take my son back there," Abraham said. ⁷"The LORD, the God of heaven, who brought me out of my father's household and my native land and who spoke to me and promised me on oath, saying, 'To your offspring*d* I will give this land'—he will send his angel before you so that you can get a wife for my son from there. ⁸If the woman is unwilling to come back with you, then you will be released from this oath of mine. Only do not take my son back there." ⁹So the servant put his hand under the thigh of his master Abraham and swore an oath to him concerning this matter.

¹⁰Then the servant took ten of his master's camels and left, taking with him all kinds of good things from his master. He set out for Aram Naharaim*e* and made his way to the town of Nahor. ¹¹He had the camels kneel down near the well outside the town; it was toward evening, the time the women go out to draw water.

¹²Then he prayed, "O LORD, God of my master Abraham, give me success today, and show kindness to my master Abraham. ¹³See, I am standing beside this spring, and the daughters of the townspeople are coming out to draw water. ¹⁴May it be that when I say to a girl, 'Please let down your jar that I may have a drink,' and she says, 'Drink, and I'll water your cam-

---

*a*11 Or *sell*   *b*15 That is, about 10 pounds (about 4.5 kilograms)   *c*2 Or *oldest*   *d*7 Or *seed*
*e*10 That is, Northwest Mesopotamia

els too'—let her be the one you have chosen for your servant Isaac. By this I will know that you have shown kindness to my master."

¹⁵Before he had finished praying, Rebekah came out with her jar on her shoulder. She was the daughter of Bethuel son of Milcah, who was the wife of Abraham's brother Nahor. ¹⁶The girl was very beautiful, a virgin; no man had ever lain with her. She went down to the spring, filled her jar and came up again.

¹⁷The servant hurried to meet her and said, "Please give me a little water from your jar."

¹⁸"Drink, my lord," she said, and quickly lowered the jar to her hands and gave him a drink.

¹⁹After she had given him a drink, she said, "I'll draw water for your camels too, until they have finished drinking." ²⁰So she quickly emptied her jar into the trough, ran back to the well to draw more water, and drew enough for all his camels. ²¹Without saying a word, the man watched her closely to learn whether or not the LORD had made his journey successful.

²²When the camels had finished drinking, the man took out a gold nose ring weighing a beka*ᵃ* and two gold bracelets weighing ten shekels.*ᵇ* ²³Then he asked, "Whose daughter are you? Please tell me, is there room in your father's house for us to spend the night?"

²⁴She answered him, "I am the daughter of Bethuel, the son that Milcah bore to Nahor." ²⁵And she added, "We have plenty of straw and fodder, as well as room for you to spend the night."

²⁶Then the man bowed down and worshiped the LORD, ²⁷saying, "Praise be to the LORD, the God of my master Abraham, who has not abandoned his kindness and faithfulness to my master. As for me, the LORD has led me on the journey to the house of my master's relatives."

²⁸The girl ran and told her mother's household about these things. ²⁹Now Rebekah had a brother named Laban, and he hurried out to the man at the spring. ³⁰As soon as he had seen the nose ring, and the bracelets on his sister's arms, and had heard Rebekah tell what the man said to her, he went out to the man and found him standing by the camels near the spring. ³¹"Come, you who are blessed by the LORD," he said. "Why are you standing out here? I have prepared the house and a place for the camels."

³²So the man went to the house, and the camels were unloaded. Straw and fodder were brought for the camels, and water for him and his men to wash their feet. ³³Then food was set before him, but he said, "I will not eat until I have told you what I have to say."

"Then tell us," Laban said.

³⁴So he said, "I am Abraham's ser-

ᵃ22 That is, about 1/5 ounce (about 5.5 grams)   *ᵇ22* That is, about 4 ounces (about 110 grams)

▙ET'S LIVE IT!   Genesis 24:1–21

PRAYING IN YOUR HEART ⮕ Praying in your heart means praying to God without saying anything out loud. In Genesis 24:1–21 read what happened when Abraham's servant prayed in his heart.

Here are some places you might want to pray in your heart. 1. In school, you might pray in your heart when you are about to take a test. 2. You might pray in your heart when you are about to cross a dangerous street. 3. You might pray in your heart on the school bus if bigger kids tease you.

Draw pictures of three other places where you might want to pray in your heart.

vant. ³⁵The Lord has blessed my master abundantly, and he has become wealthy. He has given him sheep and cattle, silver and gold, menservants and maidservants, and camels and donkeys. ³⁶My master's wife Sarah has borne him a son in her^a old age, and he has given him everything he owns. ³⁷And my master made me swear an oath, and said, 'You must not get a wife for my son from the daughters of the Canaanites, in whose land I live, ³⁸but go to my father's family and to my own clan, and get a wife for my son.'

³⁹"Then I asked my master, 'What if the woman will not come back with me?'

⁴⁰"He replied, 'The Lord, before whom I have walked, will send his angel with you and make your journey a success, so that you can get a wife for my son from my own clan and from my father's family. ⁴¹Then, when you go to my clan, you will be released from my oath even if they refuse to give her to you—you will be released from my oath.'

⁴²"When I came to the spring today, I said, 'O Lord, God of my master Abraham, if you will, please grant success to the journey on which I have come. ⁴³See, I am standing beside this spring; if a maiden comes out to draw water and I say to her, "Please let me drink a little water from your jar," ⁴⁴and if she says to me, "Drink, and I'll draw water for your camels too," let her be the one the Lord has chosen for my master's son.'

⁴⁵"Before I finished praying in my heart, Rebekah came out, with her jar on her shoulder. She went down to the spring and drew water, and I said to her, 'Please give me a drink.'

⁴⁶"She quickly lowered her jar from her shoulder and said, 'Drink, and I'll water your camels too.' So I drank, and she watered the camels also.

⁴⁷"I asked her, 'Whose daughter are you?'

"She said, 'The daughter of Bethuel son of Nahor, whom Milcah bore to him.'

"Then I put the ring in her nose and the bracelets on her arms, ⁴⁸and I bowed down and worshiped the Lord. I praised the Lord, the God of my master Abraham, who had led me on the right road to get the granddaughter of my master's brother for his son. ⁴⁹Now if you will show kindness and faithfulness to my master, tell me; and if not, tell me, so I may know which way to turn."

⁵⁰Laban and Bethuel answered, "This is from the Lord; we can say nothing to you one way or the other. ⁵¹Here is Rebekah; take her and go, and let her become the wife of your master's son, as the Lord has directed."

⁵²When Abraham's servant heard what they said, he bowed down to the ground before the Lord. ⁵³Then the servant brought out gold and silver jewelry and articles of clothing and gave them to Rebekah; he also gave costly gifts to her brother and to her mother. ⁵⁴Then he and the men who were with him ate and drank and spent the night there.

When they got up the next morning, he said, "Send me on my way to my master."

⁵⁵But her brother and her mother replied, "Let the girl remain with us ten days or so; then you^b may go."

⁵⁶But he said to them, "Do not detain me, now that the Lord has granted success to my journey. Send me on my way so I may go to my master."

⁵⁷Then they said, "Let's call the girl and ask her about it." ⁵⁸So they called Rebekah and asked her, "Will you go with this man?"

"I will go," she said.

⁵⁹So they sent their sister Rebekah on her way, along with her nurse and Abraham's servant and his men. ⁶⁰And they blessed Rebekah and said to her,

"Our sister, may you increase

---

^a36 Or *his*   ^b55 Or *she*

to thousands upon thousands;
may your offspring possess
the gates of their enemies."

⁶¹Then Rebekah and her maids got ready and mounted their camels and went back with the man. So the servant took Rebekah and left.

⁶²Now Isaac had come from Beer Lahai Roi, for he was living in the Negev. ⁶³He went out to the field one evening to meditate,ᵃ and as he looked up, he saw camels approaching. ⁶⁴Rebekah also looked up and saw Isaac. She got down from her camel ⁶⁵and asked the servant, "Who is that man in the field coming to meet us?"

"He is my master," the servant answered. So she took her veil and covered herself.

⁶⁶Then the servant told Isaac all he had done. ⁶⁷Isaac brought her into the tent of his mother Sarah, and he married Rebekah. So she became his wife, and he loved her; and Isaac was comforted after his mother's death.

The Death of Abraham

25 Abraham tookᵇ another wife, whose name was Keturah. ²She bore him Zimran, Jokshan, Medan, Midian, Ishbak and Shuah. ³Jokshan was the father of Sheba and Dedan; the descendants of Dedan were the Asshurites, the Letushites and the Leummites. ⁴The sons of Midian were Ephah, Epher, Hanoch, Abida and Eldaah. All these were descendants of Keturah.

⁵Abraham left everything he owned to Isaac. ⁶But while he was still living, he gave gifts to the sons of his concubines and sent them away from his son Isaac to the land of the east.

⁷Altogether, Abraham lived a hundred and seventy-five years. ⁸Then Abraham breathed his last and died at a good old age, an old man and full of years; and he was gathered to his people. ⁹His sons Isaac and Ishmael

buried him in the cave of Machpelah near Mamre, in the field of Ephron son of Zohar the Hittite, ¹⁰the field Abraham had bought from the Hittites.ᶜ There Abraham was buried with his wife Sarah. ¹¹After Abraham's death, God blessed his son Isaac, who then lived near Beer Lahai Roi.

Ishmael's Sons

¹²This is the account of Abraham's son Ishmael, whom Sarah's maidservant, Hagar the Egyptian, bore to Abraham.

¹³These are the names of the sons of Ishmael, listed in the order of their birth: Nebaioth the firstborn of Ishmael, Kedar, Adbeel, Mibsam, ¹⁴Mishma, Dumah, Massa, ¹⁵Hadad, Tema, Jetur, Naphish and Kedemah. ¹⁶These were the sons of Ishmael, and these are the names of the twelve tribal rulers according to their settlements and camps. ¹⁷Altogether, Ishmael lived a hundred and thirty-seven years. He breathed his last and died, and he was gathered to his people. ¹⁸His descendants settled in the area from Havilah to Shur, near the border of Egypt, as you go toward Asshur. And they lived in hostility towardᵈ all their brothers.

Jacob and Esau

¹⁹This is the account of Abraham's son Isaac.

Abraham became the father of Isaac, ²⁰and Isaac was forty years old when he married Rebekah daughter of Bethuel the Aramean from Paddan Aramᵉ and sister of Laban the Aramean. ²¹Isaac prayed to the LORD on behalf of his wife, because she was barren. The LORD answered his prayer, and his wife Rebekah became pregnant. ²²The babies jostled each other within her, and she said, "Why is this happening to me?" So she went to inquire of the LORD.

ᵃ63 The meaning of the Hebrew for this word is uncertain.   ᵇ1 Or had taken   ᶜ10 Or the sons of Heth   ᵈ18 Or lived to the east of   ᵉ20 That is, Northwest Mesopotamia

²³The LORD said to her,

"Two nations are in your womb,
　and two peoples from within
　　you will be separated;
one people will be stronger than
　　the other,
　and the older will serve the
　　younger."

²⁴When the time came for her to give birth, there were twin boys in her womb. ²⁵The first to come out was red, and his whole body was like a hairy garment; so they named him Esau.ᵃ ²⁶After this, his brother came out, with his hand grasping Esau's heel; so he was named Jacob.ᵇ Isaac was sixty years old when Rebekah gave birth to them.

²⁷The boys grew up, and Esau became a skillful hunter, a man of the open country, while Jacob was a quiet man, staying among the tents. ²⁸Isaac, who had a taste for wild game, loved Esau, but Rebekah loved Jacob.

²⁹Once when Jacob was cooking some stew, Esau came in from the open country, famished. ³⁰He said to Jacob, "Quick, let me have some of that red stew! I'm famished!" (That is why he was also called Edom.ᶜ)

³¹Jacob replied, "First sell me your birthright."

³²"Look, I am about to die," Esau said. "What good is the birthright to me?"

³³But Jacob said, "Swear to me first." So he swore an oath to him, selling his birthright to Jacob.

³⁴Then Jacob gave Esau some bread and some lentil stew. He ate and drank, and then got up and left.

So Esau despised his birthright.

Isaac and Abimelech

26 Now there was a famine in the land—besides the earlier famine of Abraham's time—and Isaac went to Abimelech king of the Philistines in Gerar. ²The LORD appeared to Isaac and said, "Do not go down to Egypt; live in the land where I tell you to live. ³Stay in this land for a while, and I will be with you and will bless you. For to you and your descendants I will give all these lands and will confirm the oath I swore to your father Abraham. ⁴I will make your descendants as numerous

---

ᵃ25 *Esau* may mean *hairy*; he was also called Edom, which means *red*.　ᵇ26 *Jacob* means *he grasps the heel* (figuratively, *he deceives*).　ᶜ30 *Edom* means *red*.

ET'S LIVE IT!　　　　　　　　　　　Genesis 25:27–34

GOD IS IMPORTANT ⟹ Esau's "birthright" was his right as the oldest son to inherit promises God made to his grandfather Abraham. Read Genesis 25:27–34. How did Esau show that God was not important to him?

The way we act shows if God is important to us. Make up an ending to each of these short stories to show how the person will act if God is important to him or her. Tell your endings to a friend or to one of your parents.

1. The guys were throwing stones at passing cars. "Come on, Tim," they said. "It's fun. Here, take this stone."
2. "Sarah, I won't come to your party if Cindy is there," Judy said. "Cindy wears old clothes and looks funny."
3. "Hey, Justin," his best friend said in a loud whisper. "What's the answer to question five?"

Can you tell a true story of something you did that shows God is important to you?

as the stars in the sky and will give them all these lands, and through your offspring*a* all nations on earth will be blessed, 5because Abraham obeyed me and kept my requirements, my commands, my decrees and my laws." 6So Isaac stayed in Gerar.

7When the men of that place asked him about his wife, he said, "She is my sister," because he was afraid to say, "She is my wife." He thought, "The men of this place might kill me on account of Rebekah, because she is beautiful."

8When Isaac had been there a long time, Abimelech king of the Philistines looked down from a window and saw Isaac caressing his wife Rebekah. 9So Abimelech summoned Isaac and said, "She is really your wife! Why did you say, 'She is my sister'?"

Isaac answered him, "Because I thought I might lose my life on account of her."

10Then Abimelech said, "What is this you have done to us? One of the men might well have slept with your wife, and you would have brought guilt upon us."

11So Abimelech gave orders to all the people: "Anyone who molests this man or his wife shall surely be put to death."

12Isaac planted crops in that land and the same year reaped a hundredfold, because the LORD blessed him. 13The man became rich, and his wealth continued to grow until he became very wealthy. 14He had so many flocks and herds and servants that the Philistines envied him. 15So all the wells that his father's servants had dug in the time of his father Abraham, the Philistines stopped up, filling them with earth.

16Then Abimelech said to Isaac, "Move away from us; you have become too powerful for us."

17So Isaac moved away from there and encamped in the Valley of Gerar and settled there. 18Isaac reopened the wells that had been dug in the time of his father Abraham, which the Philistines had stopped up after Abraham died, and he gave them the same names his father had given them.

19Isaac's servants dug in the valley and discovered a well of fresh water there. 20But the herdsmen of Gerar quarreled with Isaac's herdsmen and said, "The water is ours!" So he named the well Esek,*b* because they disputed with him. 21Then they dug another well, but they quarreled over that one also; so he named it Sitnah.*c* 22He moved on from there and dug another well, and no one quarreled over it. He named it Rehoboth,*d* saying, "Now the LORD has given us room and we will flourish in the land."

23From there he went up to Beersheba. 24That night the LORD appeared to him and said, "I am the God of your father Abraham. Do not be afraid, for I am with you; I will bless you and will increase the number of your descendants for the sake of my servant Abraham."

25Isaac built an altar there and called on the name of the LORD. There he pitched his tent, and there his servants dug a well.

26Meanwhile, Abimelech had come to him from Gerar, with Ahuzzath his personal adviser and Phicol the commander of his forces. 27Isaac asked them, "Why have you come to me, since you were hostile to me and sent me away?"

28They answered, "We saw clearly that the LORD was with you; so we said, 'There ought to be a sworn agreement between us'—between us and you. Let us make a treaty with you 29that you will do us no harm, just as we did not molest you but always treated you well and sent you away in peace. And now you are blessed by the LORD."

30Isaac then made a feast for them, and they ate and drank. 31Early the

---

*a*4 Or *seed*   *b*20 *Esek* means *dispute.*   *c*21 *Sitnah* means *opposition.*   *d*22 *Rehoboth* means *room.*

next morning the men swore an oath to each other. Then Isaac sent them on their way, and they left him in peace.

³²That day Isaac's servants came and told him about the well they had dug. They said, "We've found water!" ³³He called it Shibah,ᵃ and to this day the name of the town has been Beersheba.ᵇ

³⁴When Esau was forty years old, he married Judith daughter of Beeri the Hittite, and also Basemath daughter of Elon the Hittite. ³⁵They were a source of grief to Isaac and Rebekah.

Jacob Gets Isaac's Blessing

27 When Isaac was old and his eyes were so weak that he could no longer see, he called for Esau his older son and said to him, "My son."

"Here I am," he answered.

²Isaac said, "I am now an old man and don't know the day of my death. ³Now then, get your weapons—your quiver and bow—and go out to the open country to hunt some wild game for me. ⁴Prepare me the kind of tasty food I like and bring it to me to eat, so that I may give you my blessing before I die."

⁵Now Rebekah was listening as Isaac spoke to his son Esau. When Esau left for the open country to hunt game and bring it back, ⁶Rebekah

said to her son Jacob, "Look, I overheard your father say to your brother Esau, ⁷'Bring me some game and prepare me some tasty food to eat, so that I may give you my blessing in the presence of the LORD before I die.' ⁸Now, my son, listen carefully and do what I tell you: ⁹Go out to the flock and bring me two choice young goats, so I can prepare some tasty food for your father, just the way he likes it. ¹⁰Then take it to your father to eat, so that he may give you his blessing before he dies."

❓DID YOU KNOW?   **27:4**

Why was Isaac's blessing so important to Jacob and Esau?

A father's blessing was like a powerful prayer. People believed the blessing guaranteed success and prosperity. So both Jacob and Esau wanted their father Isaac's blessing.

¹¹Jacob said to Rebekah his mother, "But my brother Esau is a hairy man, and I'm a man with smooth skin. ¹²What if my father touches me? I would appear to be tricking him and would bring down a curse on myself rather than a blessing."

¹³His mother said to him, "My son,

ᵃ33 *Shibah* can mean *oath* or *seven.*   ᵇ33 *Beersheba* can mean *well of the oath* or *well of seven.*

▨ET'S LIVE IT!   **Genesis 26:17–33**

RUNNING AWAY ➡ Whenever Isaac dug a well, other people wanted to take it from him. Every time, Isaac just let them take his well. How do you think Isaac felt? Do you think running away was a good thing to do? Why, or why not?

Read Genesis 26:17–33 to find out what helped Isaac to stop running. Hint: The answer is in Genesis 26:24.

After God told Isaac not to be afraid, he stood up to his enemy. In the end, they made an agreement.

If anyone treats you the way Isaac was treated, talk to an adult friend about it. Tell how you feel. Pray and ask God to help you not to be afraid. Ask for ideas on how to make an agreement to solve the problem.

let the curse fall on me. Just do what I say; go and get them for me."

¹⁴So he went and got them and brought them to his mother, and she prepared some tasty food, just the way his father liked it. ¹⁵Then Rebekah took the best clothes of Esau her older son, which she had in the house, and put them on her younger son Jacob. ¹⁶She also covered his hands and the smooth part of his neck with the goatskins. ¹⁷Then she handed to her son Jacob the tasty food and the bread she had made.

¹⁸He went to his father and said, "My father."

"Yes, my son," he answered. "Who is it?"

¹⁹Jacob said to his father, "I am Esau your firstborn. I have done as you told me. Please sit up and eat some of my game so that you may give me your blessing."

²⁰Isaac asked his son, "How did you find it so quickly, my son?"

"The LORD your God gave me success," he replied.

²¹Then Isaac said to Jacob, "Come near so I can touch you, my son, to know whether you really are my son Esau or not."

²²Jacob went close to his father Isaac, who touched him and said, "The voice is the voice of Jacob, but the hands are the hands of Esau." ²³He did not recognize him, for his hands were hairy like those of his brother Esau; so he blessed him. ²⁴"Are you really my son Esau?" he asked.

"I am," he replied.

²⁵Then he said, "My son, bring me some of your game to eat, so that I may give you my blessing."

Jacob brought it to him and he ate; and he brought some wine and he drank. ²⁶Then his father Isaac said to him, "Come here, my son, and kiss me."

²⁷So he went to him and kissed him. When Isaac caught the smell of his clothes, he blessed him and said,

"Ah, the smell of my son
    is like the smell of a field
    that the LORD has blessed.
²⁸May God give you of heaven's
        dew
    and of earth's richness—
    an abundance of grain and new
        wine.
²⁹May nations serve you
    and peoples bow down to you.
Be lord over your brothers,
    and may the sons of your
        mother bow down to you.
May those who curse you be
        cursed
    and those who bless you be
        blessed."

³⁰After Isaac finished blessing him and Jacob had scarcely left his father's presence, his brother Esau came in from hunting. ³¹He too prepared some tasty food and brought it to his father. Then he said to him, "My father, sit up and eat some of my game, so that you may give me your blessing."

³²His father Isaac asked him, "Who are you?"

"I am your son," he answered, "your firstborn, Esau."

³³Isaac trembled violently and said, "Who was it, then, that hunted game and brought it to me? I ate it just before you came and I blessed him—and indeed he will be blessed!"

³⁴When Esau heard his father's words, he burst out with a loud and bitter cry and said to his father, "Bless me—me too, my father!"

³⁵But he said, "Your brother came deceitfully and took your blessing."

³⁶Esau said, "Isn't he rightly named Jacob*? He has deceived me these two times: He took my birthright, and now he's taken my blessing!" Then he asked, "Haven't you reserved any blessing for me?"

³⁷Isaac answered Esau, "I have made him lord over you and have made all his relatives his servants, and I have sustained him with grain

---

*36 *Jacob* means *he grasps the heel* (figuratively, *he deceives*).

and new wine. So what can I possibly do for you, my son?"

³⁸Esau said to his father, "Do you have only one blessing, my father? Bless me too, my father!" Then Esau wept aloud.

³⁹His father Isaac answered him,

"Your dwelling will be
away from the earth's richness,
away from the dew of heaven
above.
⁴⁰You will live by the sword
and you will serve your brother.
But when you grow restless,
you will throw his yoke
from off your neck."

Jacob Flees to Laban

⁴¹Esau held a grudge against Jacob because of the blessing his father had given him. He said to himself, "The days of mourning for my father are near; then I will kill my brother Jacob."

⁴²When Rebekah was told what her older son Esau had said, she sent for her younger son Jacob and said to him, "Your brother Esau is consoling himself with the thought of killing you. ⁴³Now then, my son, do what I say: Flee at once to my brother Laban in Haran. ⁴⁴Stay with him for a while until your brother's fury subsides. ⁴⁵When your brother is no longer angry with you and forgets what you did to him, I'll send word for you to come back from there. Why should I lose both of you in one day?"

⁴⁶Then Rebekah said to Isaac, "I'm disgusted with living because of these Hittite women. If Jacob takes a wife from among the women of this land, from Hittite women like these, my life will not be worth living."

28 So Isaac called for Jacob and blessed*ᵃ* him and commanded him: "Do not marry a Canaanite woman. ²Go at once to Paddan Aram,*ᵇ* to the house of your mother's father Bethuel. Take a wife for your-

self there, from among the daughters of Laban, your mother's brother. ³May God Almighty*ᶜ* bless you and make you fruitful and increase your numbers until you become a community of peoples. ⁴May he give you and your descendants the blessing given to Abraham, so that you may take possession of the land where you now live as an alien, the land God gave to Abraham." ⁵Then Isaac sent Jacob on his way, and he went to Paddan Aram, to Laban son of Bethuel the Aramean, the brother of Rebekah, who was the mother of Jacob and Esau.

⁶Now Esau learned that Isaac had blessed Jacob and had sent him to Paddan Aram to take a wife from there, and that when he blessed him he commanded him, "Do not marry a Canaanite woman," ⁷and that Jacob had obeyed his father and mother and had gone to Paddan Aram. ⁸Esau then realized how displeasing the Canaanite women were to his father Isaac; ⁹so he went to Ishmael and married Mahalath, the sister of Nebaioth and daughter of Ishmael son of Abraham, in addition to the wives he already had.

Jacob's Dream at Bethel

¹⁰Jacob left Beersheba and set out for Haran. ¹¹When he reached a certain place, he stopped for the night because the sun had set. Taking one of the stones there, he put it under his head and lay down to sleep. ¹²He had a dream in which he saw a stairway*ᵈ* resting on the earth, with its top reaching to heaven, and the angels of God were ascending and descending on it. ¹³There above it*ᵉ* stood the LORD, and he said: "I am the LORD, the God of your father Abraham and the God of Isaac. I will give you and your descendants the land on which you are lying. ¹⁴Your descendants will be like the dust of the earth, and you will spread out to the west and to the east, to the north and to the

---

ᵃ1 Or greeted   *ᵇ2 That is, Northwest Mesopotamia; also in verses 5, 6 and 7*   *ᶜ3 Hebrew El-Shaddai*   *ᵈ12 Or ladder*   *ᵉ13 Or There beside him*

south. All peoples on earth will be blessed through you and your offspring. ¹⁵I am with you and will watch over you wherever you go, and I will bring you back to this land. I will not leave you until I have done what I have promised you."

¹⁶When Jacob awoke from his sleep, he thought, "Surely the LORD is in this place, and I was not aware of it." ¹⁷He was afraid and said, "How awesome is this place! This is none other than the house of God; this is the gate of heaven."

¹⁸Early the next morning Jacob took the stone he had placed under his head and set it up as a pillar and poured oil on top of it. ¹⁹He called that place Bethel,ᵃ though the city used to be called Luz.

²⁰Then Jacob made a vow, saying, "If God will be with me and will watch over me on this journey I am taking and will give me food to eat and clothes to wear ²¹so that I return safely to my father's house, then the LORDᵇ will be my God ²²andᶜ this stone that I have set up as a pillar will be God's house, and of all that you give me I will give you a tenth."

WORDS TO REMEMBER

28:15 I am with you and will watch over you wherever you go.

Jacob Arrives in Paddan Aram

29 Then Jacob continued on his journey and came to the land of the eastern peoples. ²There he saw a well in the field, with three flocks of sheep lying near it because the flocks were watered from that well. The stone over the mouth of the well was large. ³When all the flocks were gathered there, the shepherds would roll the stone away from the well's mouth and water the sheep. Then they would return the stone to its place over the mouth of the well.

⁴Jacob asked the shepherds, "My brothers, where are you from?"

"We're from Haran," they replied.

⁵He said to them, "Do you know Laban, Nahor's grandson?"

"Yes, we know him," they answered.

⁶Then Jacob asked them, "Is he well?"

"Yes, he is," they said, "and here comes his daughter Rachel with the sheep."

⁷"Look," he said, "the sun is still high; it is not time for the flocks to be gathered. Water the sheep and take them back to pasture."

⁸"We can't," they replied, "until all the flocks are gathered and the stone has been rolled away from the mouth of the well. Then we will water the sheep."

⁹While he was still talking with them, Rachel came with her father's sheep, for she was a shepherdess.

ᵃ19 *Bethel* means *house of God.*   ᵇ20,21 Or *Since God ... father's house, the* LORD   ᶜ21,22 Or *house, and the* LORD *will be my God,* ²²*then*

LET'S LIVE IT!   Genesis 28:10–22

WHAT IS IMPORTANT ➠ Make a list of the most important things you can ask God for. Then read Genesis 28:10–22.

Jacob wanted three things from God. You can find them in Genesis 28:20–21. Jacob wanted God to be with him and watch over him on his journey, to give him food to eat and clothes to wear, to return him safely to his father's house.

God gave Jacob the important things he wanted and needed. What are the really important things God has given you? Thank him for these things when you pray.

¹⁰When Jacob saw Rachel daughter of Laban, his mother's brother, and Laban's sheep, he went over and rolled the stone away from the mouth of the well and watered his uncle's sheep. ¹¹Then Jacob kissed Rachel and began to weep aloud. ¹²He had told Rachel that he was a relative of her father and a son of Rebekah. So she ran and told her father.

¹³As soon as Laban heard the news about Jacob, his sister's son, he hurried to meet him. He embraced him and kissed him and brought him to his home, and there Jacob told him all these things. ¹⁴Then Laban said to him, "You are my own flesh and blood."

Jacob Marries Leah and Rachel

After Jacob had stayed with him for a whole month, ¹⁵Laban said to him, "Just because you are a relative of mine, should you work for me for nothing? Tell me what your wages should be."

¹⁶Now Laban had two daughters; the name of the older was Leah, and the name of the younger was Rachel. ¹⁷Leah had weak*a* eyes, but Rachel was lovely in form, and beautiful. ¹⁸Jacob was in love with Rachel and said, "I'll work for you seven years in return for your younger daughter Rachel."

❓DID YOU KNOW?   29:18

Why did Jacob have to work for Laban?

In those times men gave a gift to the father of the woman they married. Jacob had no money, but he loved Rachel so much he was willing to work seven years for her.

---

¹⁹Laban said, "It's better that I give her to you than to some other man. Stay here with me." ²⁰So Jacob served seven years to get Rachel, but they seemed like only a few days to him because of his love for her.

²¹Then Jacob said to Laban, "Give me my wife. My time is completed, and I want to lie with her."

²²So Laban brought together all the people of the place and gave a feast. ²³But when evening came, he took his daughter Leah and gave her to Jacob, and Jacob lay with her. ²⁴And Laban gave his servant girl Zilpah to his daughter as her maidservant.

²⁵When morning came, there was Leah! So Jacob said to Laban, "What is this you have done to me? I served you for Rachel, didn't I? Why have you deceived me?"

²⁶Laban replied, "It is not our custom here to give the younger daughter in marriage before the older one. ²⁷Finish this daughter's bridal week; then we will give you the younger one also, in return for another seven years of work."

²⁸And Jacob did so. He finished the week with Leah, and then Laban gave him his daughter Rachel to be his wife. ²⁹Laban gave his servant girl Bilhah to his daughter Rachel as her maidservant. ³⁰Jacob lay with Rachel also, and he loved Rachel more than Leah. And he worked for Laban another seven years.

Jacob's Children

³¹When the LORD saw that Leah was not loved, he opened her womb, but Rachel was barren. ³²Leah became pregnant and gave birth to a son. She named him Reuben,*b* for she said, "It is because the LORD has seen my misery. Surely my husband will love me now."

³³She conceived again, and when she gave birth to a son she said, "Because the LORD heard that I am not loved, he gave me this one too." So she named him Simeon.*c*

³⁴Again she conceived, and when she gave birth to a son she said, "Now at last my husband will become at-

---

a17 Or *delicate*   *b32 Reuben* sounds like the Hebrew for *he has seen my misery*; the name means *see, a son.*   *c33 Simeon* probably means *one who hears.*

tached to me, because I have borne him three sons." So he was named Levi.[a]

35She conceived again, and when she gave birth to a son she said, "This time I will praise the LORD." So she named him Judah.[b] Then she stopped having children.

30 When Rachel saw that she was not bearing Jacob any children, she became jealous of her sister. So she said to Jacob, "Give me children, or I'll die!"

2Jacob became angry with her and said, "Am I in the place of God, who has kept you from having children?"

3Then she said, "Here is Bilhah, my maidservant. Sleep with her so that she can bear children for me and that through her I too can build a family."

4So she gave him her servant Bilhah as a wife. Jacob slept with her, 5and she became pregnant and bore him a son. 6Then Rachel said, "God has vindicated me; he has listened to my plea and given me a son." Because of this she named him Dan.[c]

7Rachel's servant Bilhah conceived again and bore Jacob a second son. 8Then Rachel said, "I have had a great struggle with my sister, and I have won." So she named him Naphtali.[d]

9When Leah saw that she had stopped having children, she took her maidservant Zilpah and gave her to Jacob as a wife. 10Leah's servant Zilpah bore Jacob a son. 11Then Leah said, "What good fortune!"[e] So she named him Gad.[f]

12Leah's servant Zilpah bore Jacob a second son. 13Then Leah said, "How happy I am! The women will call me happy." So she named him Asher.[g]

14During wheat harvest, Reuben went out into the fields and found some mandrake plants, which he brought to his mother Leah. Rachel said to Leah, "Please give me some of your son's mandrakes."

15But she said to her, "Wasn't it enough that you took away my husband? Will you take my son's mandrakes too?"

"Very well," Rachel said, "he can sleep with you tonight in return for your son's mandrakes."

16So when Jacob came in from the fields that evening, Leah went out to meet him. "You must sleep with me," she said. "I have hired you with my son's mandrakes." So he slept with her that night.

17God listened to Leah, and she became pregnant and bore Jacob a fifth son. 18Then Leah said, "God has rewarded me for giving my maidservant to my husband." So she named him Issachar.[h]

19Leah conceived again and bore Jacob a sixth son. 20Then Leah said, "God has presented me with a precious gift. This time my husband will treat me with honor, because I have borne him six sons." So she named him Zebulun.[i]

21Some time later she gave birth to a daughter and named her Dinah.

22Then God remembered Rachel; he listened to her and opened her womb. 23She became pregnant and gave birth to a son and said, "God has taken away my disgrace." 24She named him Joseph,[j] and said, "May the LORD add to me another son."

Jacob's Flocks Increase

25After Rachel gave birth to Joseph, Jacob said to Laban, "Send me on my way so I can go back to my own homeland. 26Give me my wives and children, for whom I have served you, and I will be on my way. You know how much work I've done for you."

27But Laban said to him, "If I have found favor in your eyes, please stay. I have learned by divination that[k]

---

[a]34 *Levi* sounds like and may be derived from the Hebrew for *attached.*   [b]35 *Judah* sounds like and may be derived from the Hebrew for *praise.*   [c]6 *Dan* here means *he has vindicated.*   [d]8 *Naphtali* means *my struggle.*   [e]11 Or *"A troop is coming!"*   [f]11 *Gad* can mean *good fortune* or *a troop.*   [g]13 *Asher* means *happy.*   [h]18 *Issachar* sounds like the Hebrew for *reward.*   [i]20 *Zebulun* probably means *honor.*   [j]24 *Joseph* means *may he add.*   [k]27 Or possibly *have become rich and*

the LORD has blessed me because of you." ²⁸He added, "Name your wages, and I will pay them."

²⁹Jacob said to him, "You know how I have worked for you and how your livestock has fared under my care. ³⁰The little you had before I came has increased greatly, and the LORD has blessed you wherever I have been. But now, when may I do something for my own household?"

³¹"What shall I give you?" he asked.

"Don't give me anything," Jacob replied. "But if you will do this one thing for me, I will go on tending your flocks and watching over them: ³²Let me go through all your flocks today and remove from them every speckled or spotted sheep, every dark-colored lamb and every spotted or speckled goat. They will be my wages. ³³And my honesty will testify for me in the future, whenever you check on the wages you have paid me. Any goat in my possession that is not speckled or spotted, or any lamb that is not dark-colored, will be considered stolen."

³⁴"Agreed," said Laban. "Let it be as you have said." ³⁵That same day he removed all the male goats that were streaked or spotted, and all the speckled or spotted female goats (all that had white on them) and all the dark-colored lambs, and he placed them in the care of his sons. ³⁶Then he put a three-day journey between himself and Jacob, while Jacob continued to tend the rest of Laban's flocks.

³⁷Jacob, however, took fresh-cut branches from poplar, almond and plane trees and made white stripes on them by peeling the bark and exposing the white inner wood of the branches. ³⁸Then he placed the peeled branches in all the watering troughs, so that they would be directly in front of the flocks when they came to drink. When the flocks were in heat and came to drink, ³⁹they mated in front of the branches. And they bore young that were streaked or speckled or spotted. ⁴⁰Jacob set apart the young of the flock by themselves, but made the rest face the streaked and dark-colored animals that belonged to Laban. Thus he made separate flocks for himself and did not put them with Laban's animals. ⁴¹Whenever the stronger females were in heat, Jacob would place the branches in the troughs in front of the animals so they would mate near the branches, ⁴²but if the animals were weak, he would not place them there. So the weak animals went to Laban and the strong ones to Jacob. ⁴³In this way the man grew exceedingly prosperous and came to own large flocks, and maidservants and menservants, and camels and donkeys.

Jacob Flees From Laban

31 Jacob heard that Laban's sons were saying, "Jacob has taken everything our father owned and has gained all this wealth from what belonged to our father." ²And Jacob noticed that Laban's attitude toward him was not what it had been.

³Then the LORD said to Jacob, "Go back to the land of your fathers and to your relatives, and I will be with you."

⁴So Jacob sent word to Rachel and Leah to come out to the fields where his flocks were. ⁵He said to them, "I see that your father's attitude toward me is not what it was before, but the God of my father has been with me. ⁶You know that I've worked for your father with all my strength, ⁷yet your father has cheated me by changing my wages ten times. However, God has not allowed him to harm me. ⁸If he said, 'The speckled ones will be your wages,' then all the flocks gave birth to speckled young; and if he said, 'The streaked ones will be your wages,' then all the flocks bore streaked young. ⁹So God has taken away your father's livestock and has given them to me.

¹⁰"In breeding season I once had a dream in which I looked up and saw that the male goats mating with the flock were streaked, speckled or spot-

ted. [11]The angel of God said to me in the dream, 'Jacob.' I answered, 'Here I am.' [12]And he said, 'Look up and see that all the male goats mating with the flock are streaked, speckled or spotted, for I have seen all that Laban has been doing to you. [13]I am the God of Bethel, where you anointed a pillar and where you made a vow to me. Now leave this land at once and go back to your native land.'"

[14]Then Rachel and Leah replied, "Do we still have any share in the inheritance of our father's estate? [15]Does he not regard us as foreigners? Not only has he sold us, but he has used up what was paid for us. [16]Surely all the wealth that God took away from our father belongs to us and our children. So do whatever God has told you."

[17]Then Jacob put his children and his wives on camels, [18]and he drove all his livestock ahead of him, along with all the goods he had accumulated in Paddan Aram,[a] to go to his father Isaac in the land of Canaan.

[19]When Laban had gone to shear his sheep, Rachel stole her father's household gods. [20]Moreover, Jacob deceived Laban the Aramean by not telling him he was running away. [21]So he fled with all he had, and crossing the River,[b] he headed for the hill country of Gilead.

Laban Pursues Jacob

[22]On the third day Laban was told that Jacob had fled. [23]Taking his relatives with him, he pursued Jacob for seven days and caught up with him in the hill country of Gilead. [24]Then God came to Laban the Aramean in a dream at night and said to him, "Be careful not to say anything to Jacob, either good or bad."

[25]Jacob had pitched his tent in the hill country of Gilead when Laban overtook him, and Laban and his relatives camped there too. [26]Then Laban said to Jacob, "What have you done? You've deceived me, and you've carried off my daughters like captives in war. [27]Why did you run off secretly and deceive me? Why didn't you tell me, so I could send you away with joy and singing to the music of tambourines and harps? [28]You didn't even let me kiss my grandchildren and my daughters good-by. You have done a foolish thing. [29]I have the power to harm you; but last night the God of your father said to me, 'Be careful not to say anything to Jacob, either good or bad.' [30]Now you have gone off because you longed to return to your father's house. But why did you steal my gods?"

[31]Jacob answered Laban, "I was afraid, because I thought you would take your daughters away from me by force. [32]But if you find anyone who has your gods, he shall not live. In the presence of our relatives, see for yourself whether there is anything of yours here with me; and if so, take it." Now Jacob did not know that Rachel had stolen the gods.

[33]So Laban went into Jacob's tent and into Leah's tent and into the tent of the two maidservants, but he found nothing. After he came out of Leah's tent, he entered Rachel's tent. [34]Now Rachel had taken the household gods and put them inside her camel's saddle and was sitting on them. Laban searched through everything in the tent but found nothing.

[35]Rachel said to her father, "Don't be angry, my lord, that I cannot stand up in your presence; I'm having my period." So he searched but could not find the household gods.

[36]Jacob was angry and took Laban to task. "What is my crime?" he asked Laban. "What sin have I committed that you hunt me down? [37]Now that you have searched through all my goods, what have you found that belongs to your household? Put it here in front of your relatives and mine, and let them judge between the two of us.

[38]"I have been with you for twenty years now. Your sheep and goats have not miscarried, nor have I eaten

---

[a]18 That is, Northwest Mesopotamia   [b]21 That is, the Euphrates

rams from your flocks. ³⁹I did not bring you animals torn by wild beasts; I bore the loss myself. And you demanded payment from me for whatever was stolen by day or night. ⁴⁰This was my situation: The heat consumed me in the daytime and the cold at night, and sleep fled from my eyes. ⁴¹It was like this for the twenty years I was in your household. I worked for you fourteen years for your two daughters and six years for your flocks, and you changed my wages ten times. ⁴²If the God of my father, the God of Abraham and the Fear of Isaac, had not been with me, you would surely have sent me away empty-handed. But God has seen my hardship and the toil of my hands, and last night he rebuked you."

⁴³Laban answered Jacob, "The women are my daughters, the children are my children, and the flocks are my flocks. All you see is mine. Yet what can I do today about these daughters of mine, or about the children they have borne? ⁴⁴Come now, let's make a covenant, you and I, and let it serve as a witness between us."

⁴⁵So Jacob took a stone and set it up as a pillar. ⁴⁶He said to his relatives, "Gather some stones." So they took stones and piled them in a heap, and they ate there by the heap. ⁴⁷Laban called it Jegar Sahadutha,ᵃ and Jacob called it Galeed.ᵇ

⁴⁸Laban said, "This heap is a witness between you and me today." That is why it was called Galeed. ⁴⁹It was also called Mizpah,ᶜ because he said, "May the LORD keep watch between you and me when we are away from each other. ⁵⁰If you mistreat my daughters or if you take any wives besides my daughters, even though no one is with us, remember that God is a witness between you and me."

⁵¹Laban also said to Jacob, "Here is this heap, and here is this pillar I have set up between you and me. ⁵²This heap is a witness, and this pillar is a witness, that I will not go past this heap to your side to harm you and that you will not go past this heap and pillar to my side to harm me. ⁵³May the God of Abraham and the God of Nahor, the God of their father, judge between us."

So Jacob took an oath in the name of the Fear of his father Isaac. ⁵⁴He offered a sacrifice there in the hill country and invited his relatives to a meal. After they had eaten, they spent the night there.

⁵⁵Early the next morning Laban kissed his grandchildren and his daughters and blessed them. Then he left and returned home.

ᵃ47 The Aramaic *Jegar Sahadutha* means *witness heap.*   ᵇ47 The Hebrew *Galeed* means *witness heap.*   ᶜ49 *Mizpah* means *watchtower.*

Life in Bible Times

JACOB'S TENTS

The tents Jacob (as well as Isaac and Abraham) lived in were made of dark cloth or animal skins. These men lived in tents because they traveled back and forth across Palestine. The tents were easy to take down and put up.

Jacob Prepares to Meet Esau

32 Jacob also went on his way, and the angels of God met him. ²When Jacob saw them, he said, "This is the camp of God!" So he named that place Mahanaim.ᵃ

³Jacob sent messengers ahead of him to his brother Esau in the land of Seir, the country of Edom. ⁴He instructed them: "This is what you are to say to my master Esau: 'Your servant Jacob says, I have been staying with Laban and have remained there till now. ⁵I have cattle and donkeys, sheep and goats, menservants and maidservants. Now I am sending this message to my lord, that I may find favor in your eyes.' "

⁶When the messengers returned to Jacob, they said, "We went to your brother Esau, and now he is coming to meet you, and four hundred men are with him."

⁷In great fear and distress Jacob divided the people who were with him into two groups,ᵇ and the flocks and herds and camels as well. ⁸He thought, "If Esau comes and attacks one group,ᶜ the groupᶜ that is left may escape."

⁹Then Jacob prayed, "O God of my father Abraham, God of my father Isaac, O Lᴏʀᴅ, who said to me, 'Go back to your country and your relatives, and I will make you prosper,' ¹⁰I am unworthy of all the kindness and faithfulness you have shown your servant. I had only my staff when I crossed this Jordan, but now I have become two groups. ¹¹Save me, I pray, from the hand of my brother Esau, for I am afraid he will come and attack me, and also the mothers with their children. ¹²But you have said, 'I will surely make you prosper and will make your descendants like the sand of the sea, which cannot be counted.' "

¹³He spent the night there, and from what he had with him he selected a gift for his brother Esau: ¹⁴two hundred female goats and twenty male goats, two hundred ewes and twenty rams, ¹⁵thirty female camels with their young, forty cows and ten bulls, and twenty female donkeys and ten male donkeys. ¹⁶He put them in the care of his servants, each herd by itself, and said to his servants, "Go ahead of me, and keep some space between the herds."

¹⁷He instructed the one in the lead: "When my brother Esau meets you and asks, 'To whom do you belong, and where are you going, and who owns all these animals in front of you?' ¹⁸then you are to say, 'They belong to your servant Jacob. They are a gift sent to my lord Esau, and he is coming behind us.' "

¹⁹He also instructed the second, the third and all the others who followed the herds: "You are to say the same thing to Esau when you meet him. ²⁰And be sure to say, 'Your servant Jacob is coming behind us.' " For he thought, "I will pacify him with these gifts I am sending on ahead; later, when I see him, perhaps he will receive me." ²¹So Jacob's gifts went on ahead of him, but he himself spent the night in the camp.

Jacob Wrestles With God

²²That night Jacob got up and took his two wives, his two maidservants and his eleven sons and crossed the ford of the Jabbok. ²³After he had sent them across the stream, he sent over all his possessions. ²⁴So Jacob was left alone, and a man wrestled with him till daybreak. ²⁵When the man saw that he could not overpower him, he touched the socket of Jacob's hip so that his hip was wrenched as he wrestled with the man. ²⁶Then the man said, "Let me go, for it is daybreak."

But Jacob replied, "I will not let you go unless you bless me."

²⁷The man asked him, "What is your name?"

"Jacob," he answered.

²⁸Then the man said, "Your name

ᵃ2 *Mahanaim* means *two camps.*   ᵇ7 Or *camps*; also in verse 10   ᶜ8 Or *camp*

will no longer be Jacob, but Israel,[a] because you have struggled with God and with men and have overcome."

29Jacob said, "Please tell me your name."

But he replied, "Why do you ask my name?" Then he blessed him there.

30So Jacob called the place Peniel,[b] saying, "It is because I saw God face to face, and yet my life was spared."

31The sun rose above him as he passed Peniel,[c] and he was limping because of his hip. 32Therefore to this day the Israelites do not eat the tendon attached to the socket of the hip, because the socket of Jacob's hip was touched near the tendon.

Jacob Meets Esau

33 Jacob looked up and there was Esau, coming with his four hundred men; so he divided the children among Leah, Rachel and the two maidservants. 2He put the maidservants and their children in front, Leah and her children next, and Rachel and Joseph in the rear. 3He himself went on ahead and bowed down to the ground seven times as he approached his brother.

4But Esau ran to meet Jacob and embraced him; he threw his arms around his neck and kissed him. And they wept. 5Then Esau looked up and saw the women and children. "Who are these with you?" he asked.

Jacob answered, "They are the children God has graciously given your servant."

6Then the maidservants and their children approached and bowed down. 7Next, Leah and her children came and bowed down. Last of all came Joseph and Rachel, and they too bowed down.

8Esau asked, "What do you mean by all these droves I met?"

"To find favor in your eyes, my lord," he said.

9But Esau said, "I already have plenty, my brother. Keep what you have for yourself."

10"No, please!" said Jacob. "If I have found favor in your eyes, accept this gift from me. For to see your face is like seeing the face of God, now that you have received me favorably.

a28 Israel means he struggles with God.   b30 Peniel means face of God.   c31 Hebrew Penuel, a variant of Peniel

---

LET'S LIVE IT!   Genesis 32:22–30

A NEW NAME ➡ This Bible story tells how Jacob got the name Israel, which means, "He struggles with God."

Many Bible people have names that tell something about them. Abraham means "father of many." The Jewish people as well as the Arabs are descended from Abraham. Abraham was indeed the father of many.

Suppose God let you pick a name to tell what you are like. Here is a list of possible names:

Obedient	Contented	Peacemaker
Smiling	Prayerful	Thoughtful
Neat	Helpful	Truthful
Patient	Cheerful	Thankful
Hard Working	Trustworthy	Loving

Pick the one you want to describe you. Just for fun, ask your family to use the new name for a day or two, to remind you of the kind of person you want to be.

11Please accept the present that was brought to you, for God has been gracious to me and I have all I need." And because Jacob insisted, Esau accepted it.

12Then Esau said, "Let us be on our way; I'll accompany you."

13But Jacob said to him, "My lord knows that the children are tender and that I must care for the ewes and cows that are nursing their young. If they are driven hard just one day, all the animals will die. 14So let my lord go on ahead of his servant, while I move along slowly at the pace of the droves before me and that of the children, until I come to my lord in Seir."

15Esau said, "Then let me leave some of my men with you."

"But why do that?" Jacob asked. "Just let me find favor in the eyes of my lord."

16So that day Esau started on his way back to Seir. 17Jacob, however, went to Succoth, where he built a place for himself and made shelters for his livestock. That is why the place is called Succoth.a

18After Jacob came from Paddan Aram,b he arrived safely at thec city of Shechem in Canaan and camped within sight of the city. 19For a hundred pieces of silver,d he bought from the sons of Hamor, the father of Shechem, the plot of ground where he pitched his tent. 20There he set up an altar and called it El Elohe Israel.e

Dinah and the Shechemites

34 Now Dinah, the daughter Leah had borne to Jacob, went out to visit the women of the land. 2When Shechem son of Hamor the Hivite, the ruler of that area, saw her, he took her and violated her. 3His heart was drawn to Dinah daughter of Jacob, and he loved the girl and spoke tenderly to her. 4And Shechem said to his father Hamor, "Get me this girl as my wife."

5When Jacob heard that his daughter Dinah had been defiled, his sons were in the fields with his livestock; so he kept quiet about it until they came home.

6Then Shechem's father Hamor went out to talk with Jacob. 7Now Jacob's sons had come in from the fields as soon as they heard what had happened. They were filled with grief and fury, because Shechem had done a disgraceful thing inf Israel by lying with Jacob's daughter—a thing that should not be done.

8But Hamor said to them, "My son Shechem has his heart set on your daughter. Please give her to him as his wife. 9Intermarry with us; give us your daughters and take our daughters for yourselves. 10You can settle among us; the land is open to you. Live in it, tradeg in it, and acquire property in it."

11Then Shechem said to Dinah's father and brothers, "Let me find favor in your eyes, and I will give you whatever you ask. 12Make the price for the bride and the gift I am to bring as great as you like, and I'll pay whatever you ask me. Only give me the girl as my wife."

13Because their sister Dinah had been defiled, Jacob's sons replied deceitfully as they spoke to Shechem and his father Hamor. 14They said to them, "We can't do such a thing; we can't give our sister to a man who is not circumcised. That would be a disgrace to us. 15We will give our consent to you on one condition only: that you become like us by circumcising all your males. 16Then we will give you our daughters and take your daughters for ourselves. We'll settle among you and become one people with you. 17But if you will not agree to be circumcised, we'll take our sisterh and go."

18Their proposal seemed good to Hamor and his son Shechem. 19The

---

a17 Succoth means shelters.   b18 That is, Northwest Mesopotamia   c18 Or arrived at Shalem, a   d19 Hebrew hundred kesitahs; a kesitah was a unit of money of unknown weight and value.   e20 El Elohe Israel can mean God, the God of Israel or mighty is the God of Israel.   f7 Or against   g10 Or move about freely; also in verse 21   h17 Hebrew daughter

young man, who was the most honored of all his father's household, lost no time in doing what they said, because he was delighted with Jacob's daughter. 20So Hamor and his son Shechem went to the gate of their city to speak to their fellow townsmen. 21"These men are friendly toward us," they said. "Let them live in our land and trade in it; the land has plenty of room for them. We can marry their daughters and they can marry ours. 22But the men will consent to live with us as one people only on the condition that our males be circumcised, as they themselves are. 23Won't their livestock, their property and all their other animals become ours? So let us give our consent to them, and they will settle among us."

24All the men who went out of the city gate agreed with Hamor and his son Shechem, and every male in the city was circumcised.

25Three days later, while all of them were still in pain, two of Jacob's sons, Simeon and Levi, Dinah's brothers, took their swords and attacked the unsuspecting city, killing every male. 26They put Hamor and his son Shechem to the sword and took Dinah from Shechem's house and left. 27The sons of Jacob came upon the dead bodies and looted the city where*a* their sister had been defiled. 28They seized their flocks and herds and donkeys and everything else of theirs in the city and out in the fields. 29They carried off all their wealth and all their women and children, taking as plunder everything in the houses.

30Then Jacob said to Simeon and Levi, "You have brought trouble on me by making me a stench to the Canaanites and Perizzites, the people living in this land. We are few in number, and if they join forces against me and attack me, I and my household will be destroyed."

31But they replied, "Should he have treated our sister like a prostitute?"

Jacob Returns to Bethel

35 Then God said to Jacob, "Go up to Bethel and settle there, and build an altar there to God, who appeared to you when you were fleeing from your brother Esau."

? DID YOU KNOW?   35:1

What does Bethel mean?

Bethel means "house of God." Jacob gave it that name because God spoke to him there. This chapter tells some of the wonderful things that God told Jacob. Later Bethel became an important city and a place where the Israelites worshiped God.

2So Jacob said to his household and to all who were with him, "Get rid of the foreign gods you have with you, and purify yourselves and change your clothes. 3Then come, let us go up to Bethel, where I will build an altar to God, who answered me in the day of my distress and who has been with me wherever I have gone." 4So they gave Jacob all the foreign gods they had and the rings in their ears, and Jacob buried them under the oak at Shechem. 5Then they set out, and the terror of God fell upon the towns all around them so that no one pursued them.

6Jacob and all the people with him came to Luz (that is, Bethel) in the land of Canaan. 7There he built an altar, and he called the place El Bethel,*b* because it was there that God revealed himself to him when he was fleeing from his brother.

8Now Deborah, Rebekah's nurse, died and was buried under the oak below Bethel. So it was named Allon Bacuth.*c*

9After Jacob returned from Paddan Aram,*d* God appeared to him again and blessed him. 10God said to him,

---

*a*27 Or *because*   *b*7 *El Bethel* means *God of Bethel.*   *c*8 *Allon Bacuth* means *oak of weeping.*
*d*9 That is, Northwest Mesopotamia; also in verse 26

"Your name is Jacob,[a] but you will no longer be called Jacob; your name will be Israel.[b]" So he named him Israel.

[11] And God said to him, "I am God Almighty[c]; be fruitful and increase in number. A nation and a community of nations will come from you, and kings will come from your body. [12] The land I gave to Abraham and Isaac I also give to you, and I will give this land to your descendants after you." [13] Then God went up from him at the place where he had talked with him.

[14] Jacob set up a stone pillar at the place where God had talked with him, and he poured out a drink offering on it; he also poured oil on it. [15] Jacob called the place where God had talked with him Bethel.[d]

The Deaths of Rachel and Isaac

[16] Then they moved on from Bethel. While they were still some distance from Ephrath, Rachel began to give birth and had great difficulty. [17] And as she was having great difficulty in childbirth, the midwife said to her, "Don't be afraid, for you have another son." [18] As she breathed her last—for she was dying—she named her son Ben-Oni.[e] But his father named him Benjamin.[f]

[19] So Rachel died and was buried on the way to Ephrath (that is, Bethlehem). [20] Over her tomb Jacob set up a pillar, and to this day that pillar marks Rachel's tomb.

[21] Israel moved on again and pitched his tent beyond Migdal Eder. [22] While Israel was living in that region, Reuben went in and slept with his father's concubine Bilhah, and Israel heard of it.

Jacob had twelve sons:

[23] The sons of Leah:

Reuben the firstborn of Jacob, Simeon, Levi, Judah, Issachar and Zebulun.

[24] The sons of Rachel:

Joseph and Benjamin.

[25] The sons of Rachel's maidservant Bilhah:

Dan and Naphtali.

[26] The sons of Leah's maidservant Zilpah:

Gad and Asher.

These were the sons of Jacob, who were born to him in Paddan Aram.

[27] Jacob came home to his father Isaac in Mamre, near Kiriath Arba (that is, Hebron), where Abraham and Isaac had stayed. [28] Isaac lived a hundred and eighty years. [29] Then he breathed his last and died and was gathered to his people, old and full of years. And his sons Esau and Jacob buried him.

Esau's Descendants

36 This is the account of Esau (that is, Edom).

[2] Esau took his wives from the women of Canaan: Adah daughter of Elon the Hittite, and Oholibamah daughter of Anah and granddaughter of Zibeon the Hivite— [3] also Basemath daughter of Ishmael and sister of Nebaioth.

[4] Adah bore Eliphaz to Esau, Basemath bore Reuel, [5] and Oholibamah bore Jeush, Jalam and Korah. These were the sons of Esau, who were born to him in Canaan.

[6] Esau took his wives and sons and daughters and all the members of his household, as well as his livestock and all his other animals and all the goods he had acquired in Canaan, and moved to a land some distance from his brother Jacob. [7] Their possessions were too great for them to remain together; the land where they were staying could not support them both because of their livestock. [8] So Esau (that is,

---

a10 Jacob means he grasps the heel (figuratively, *he deceives*).   *b10 Israel means he struggles with God.*   *c11 Hebrew El-Shaddai*   *d15 Bethel means house of God.*   *e18 Ben-Oni means son of my trouble.*   *f18 Benjamin means son of my right hand.*

Edom) settled in the hill country of Seir.

⁹This is the account of Esau the father of the Edomites in the hill country of Seir.

¹⁰These are the names of Esau's sons:
    Eliphaz, the son of Esau's wife Adah, and Reuel, the son of Esau's wife Basemath.
¹¹The sons of Eliphaz:
    Teman, Omar, Zepho, Gatam and Kenaz.
¹²Esau's son Eliphaz also had a concubine named Timna, who bore him Amalek. These were grandsons of Esau's wife Adah.
¹³The sons of Reuel:
    Nahath, Zerah, Shammah and Mizzah. These were grandsons of Esau's wife Basemath.
¹⁴The sons of Esau's wife Oholibamah daughter of Anah and granddaughter of Zibeon, whom she bore to Esau:
    Jeush, Jalam and Korah.

¹⁵These were the chiefs among Esau's descendants:
The sons of Eliphaz the firstborn of Esau:
    Chiefs Teman, Omar, Zepho, Kenaz, ¹⁶Korah,ᵃ Gatam and Amalek. These were the chiefs descended from Eliphaz in Edom; they were grandsons of Adah.
¹⁷The sons of Esau's son Reuel:
    Chiefs Nahath, Zerah, Shammah and Mizzah. These were the chiefs descended from Reuel in Edom; they were grandsons of Esau's wife Basemath.
¹⁸The sons of Esau's wife Oholibamah:
    Chiefs Jeush, Jalam and Korah. These were the chiefs descended from Esau's wife

Oholibamah daughter of Anah.
¹⁹These were the sons of Esau (that is, Edom), and these were their chiefs.

²⁰These were the sons of Seir the Horite, who were living in the region:
    Lotan, Shobal, Zibeon, Anah, ²¹Dishon, Ezer and Dishan. These sons of Seir in Edom were Horite chiefs.
²²The sons of Lotan:
    Hori and Homam.ᵇ Timna was Lotan's sister.
²³The sons of Shobal:
    Alvan, Manahath, Ebal, Shepho and Onam.
²⁴The sons of Zibeon:
    Aiah and Anah. This is the Anah who discovered the hot springsᶜ in the desert while he was grazing the donkeys of his father Zibeon.
²⁵The children of Anah:
    Dishon and Oholibamah daughter of Anah.
²⁶The sons of Dishonᵈ:
    Hemdan, Eshban, Ithran and Keran.
²⁷The sons of Ezer:
    Bilhan, Zaavan and Akan.
²⁸The sons of Dishan:
    Uz and Aran.
²⁹These were the Horite chiefs:
    Lotan, Shobal, Zibeon, Anah, ³⁰Dishon, Ezer and Dishan. These were the Horite chiefs, according to their divisions, in the land of Seir.

The Rulers of Edom

³¹These were the kings who reigned in Edom before any Israelite king reignedᵉ:
    ³²Bela son of Beor became king of Edom. His city was named Dinhabah.
³³When Bela died, Jobab son of Zerah from Bozrah succeeded him as king.

ᵃ16 Masoretic Text; Samaritan Pentateuch (see also Gen. 36:11 and 1 Chron. 1:36) does not have *Korah.*   ᵇ22 Hebrew *Hemam,* a variant of *Homam* (see 1 Chron. 1:39)   ᶜ24 Vulgate; Syriac *discovered water;* the meaning of the Hebrew for this word is uncertain.   ᵈ26 Hebrew *Dishan,* a variant of *Dishon*   ᵉ31 Or *before an Israelite king reigned over them*

³⁴When Jobab died, Husham from the land of the Temanites succeeded him as king.

³⁵When Husham died, Hadad son of Bedad, who defeated Midian in the country of Moab, succeeded him as king. His city was named Avith.

³⁶When Hadad died, Samlah from Masrekah succeeded him as king.

³⁷When Samlah died, Shaul from Rehoboth on the river[a] succeeded him as king.

³⁸When Shaul died, Baal-Hanan son of Acbor succeeded him as king.

³⁹When Baal-Hanan son of Acbor died, Hadad[b] succeeded him as king. His city was named Pau, and his wife's name was Mehetabel daughter of Matred, the daughter of Me-Zahab.

⁴⁰These were the chiefs descended from Esau, by name, according to their clans and regions:

Timna, Alvah, Jetheth, ⁴¹Oholibamah, Elah, Pinon, ⁴²Kenaz, Teman, Mibzar, ⁴³Magdiel and Iram. These were the chiefs of Edom, according to their settlements in the land they occupied.

This was Esau the father of the Edomites.

Joseph's Dreams

37 Jacob lived in the land where his father had stayed, the land of Canaan.

²This is the account of Jacob.

Joseph, a young man of seventeen, was tending the flocks with his brothers, the sons of Bilhah and the sons of Zilpah, his father's wives, and he brought their father a bad report about them.

³Now Israel loved Joseph more than any of his other sons, because he had been born to him in his old age; and he made a richly ornamented[c] robe for him. ⁴When his brothers saw that their father loved him more than any of them, they hated him and could not speak a kind word to him.

⁵Joseph had a dream, and when he told it to his brothers, they hated him all the more. ⁶He said to them, "Listen to this dream I had: ⁷We were binding sheaves of grain out in the field when suddenly my sheaf rose and stood upright, while your sheaves gathered around mine and bowed down to it."

⁸His brothers said to him, "Do you intend to reign over us? Will you actually rule us?" And they hated him all the more because of his dream and what he had said.

⁹Then he had another dream, and he told it to his brothers. "Listen," he said, "I had another dream, and this

---

a37 Possibly the Euphrates　　*b39* Many manuscripts of the Masoretic Text, Samaritan Pentateuch and Syriac (see also 1 Chron. 1:50); most manuscripts of the Masoretic Text *Hadar*　*c3* The meaning of the Hebrew for *richly ornamented* is uncertain; also in verses 23 and 32.

◤ ET'S LIVE IT!　　Genesis 37:1–11

FAMILY FAVORITISM ▶ Read Genesis 37:1–11. Jacob showed he loved Joseph best by giving him a beautiful coat. The story says Joseph's brothers "hated him." Joseph didn't help the situation by being proud over his dream.

Do you ever feel as if your parents love a brother or sister more than you? Ask your parents if they ever felt that way when they were young.

Read this Bible story aloud one mealtime and have your family talk about how Joseph and his father could have helped the family feel closer and happier.

time the sun and moon and eleven stars were bowing down to me."

¹⁰When he told his father as well as his brothers, his father rebuked him and said, "What is this dream you had? Will your mother and I and your brothers actually come and bow down to the ground before you?" ¹¹His brothers were jealous of him, but his father kept the matter in mind.

Joseph Sold by His Brothers

¹²Now his brothers had gone to graze their father's flocks near Shechem, ¹³and Israel said to Joseph, "As you know, your brothers are grazing the flocks near Shechem. Come, I am going to send you to them."

"Very well," he replied.

¹⁴So he said to him, "Go and see if all is well with your brothers and with the flocks, and bring word back to me." Then he sent him off from the Valley of Hebron.

When Joseph arrived at Shechem, ¹⁵a man found him wandering around in the fields and asked him, "What are you looking for?"

¹⁶He replied, "I'm looking for my brothers. Can you tell me where they are grazing their flocks?"

¹⁷"They have moved on from here," the man answered. "I heard them say, 'Let's go to Dothan.'"

So Joseph went after his brothers and found them near Dothan. ¹⁸But they saw him in the distance, and before he reached them, they plotted to kill him.

¹⁹"Here comes that dreamer!" they said to each other. ²⁰"Come now, let's kill him and throw him into one of these cisterns and say that a ferocious animal devoured him. Then we'll see what comes of his dreams."

²¹When Reuben heard this, he tried to rescue him from their hands. "Let's not take his life," he said. ²²"Don't shed any blood. Throw him into this cistern here in the desert, but don't lay a hand on him." Reuben said this to rescue him from them and take him back to his father.

²³So when Joseph came to his brothers, they stripped him of his robe—the richly ornamented robe he was wearing— ²⁴and they took him and threw him into the cistern. Now the cistern was empty; there was no water in it.

²⁵As they sat down to eat their meal, they looked up and saw a caravan of Ishmaelites coming from Gilead. Their camels were loaded with spices, balm and myrrh, and they were on their way to take them down to Egypt.

²⁶Judah said to his brothers, "What will we gain if we kill our brother and cover up his blood? ²⁷Come, let's sell him to the Ishmaelites and not lay our hands on him; after all, he is our brother, our own flesh and blood." His brothers agreed.

²⁸So when the Midianite merchants came by, his brothers pulled Joseph up out of the cistern and sold him for twenty shekels*ᵃ* of silver to the Ishmaelites, who took him to Egypt.

²⁹When Reuben returned to the cistern and saw that Joseph was not there, he tore his clothes. ³⁰He went back to his brothers and said, "The boy isn't there! Where can I turn now?"

³¹Then they got Joseph's robe, slaughtered a goat and dipped the robe in the blood. ³²They took the ornamented robe back to their father and said, "We found this. Examine it to see whether it is your son's robe."

³³He recognized it and said, "It is my son's robe! Some ferocious animal has devoured him. Joseph has surely been torn to pieces."

³⁴Then Jacob tore his clothes, put on sackcloth and mourned for his son many days. ³⁵All his sons and daughters came to comfort him, but he refused to be comforted. "No," he said, "in mourning will I go down to the grave*ᵇ* to my son." So his father wept for him.

ᵃ28 That is, about 8 ounces (about 0.2 kilogram)   *ᵇ35* Hebrew *Sheol*

³⁶Meanwhile, the Midianites*ᵃ* sold Joseph in Egypt to Potiphar, one of Pharaoh's officials, the captain of the guard.

❓DID YOU KNOW?   37:36

Why is Joseph important?

Joseph is important because this young son of Jacob saved his family from a famine and brought the Israelites to Egypt to live. Joseph was not treated fairly by his brothers or others, but God helped him become the second most powerful person in Egypt, which at that time was a great country.

Judah and Tamar

38 At that time, Judah left his brothers and went down to stay with a man of Adullam named Hirah. ²There Judah met the daughter of a Canaanite man named Shua. He married her and lay with her; ³she became pregnant and gave birth to a son, who was named Er. ⁴She conceived again and gave birth to a son and named him Onan. ⁵She gave birth to still another son and named him Shelah. It was at Kezib that she gave birth to him.

⁶Judah got a wife for Er, his firstborn, and her name was Tamar. ⁷But Er, Judah's firstborn, was wicked in the LORD's sight; so the LORD put him to death.

⁸Then Judah said to Onan, "Lie with your brother's wife and fulfill your duty to her as a brother-in-law to produce offspring for your brother." ⁹But Onan knew that the offspring would not be his; so whenever he lay with his brother's wife, he spilled his semen on the ground to keep from producing offspring for his brother. ¹⁰What he did was wicked in the LORD's sight; so he put him to death also.

¹¹Judah then said to his daughter-in-law Tamar, "Live as a widow in your father's house until my son Shelah grows up." For he thought, "He may die too, just like his brothers." So Tamar went to live in her father's house.

¹²After a long time Judah's wife, the daughter of Shua, died. When Judah had recovered from his grief, he went up to Timnah, to the men who were shearing his sheep, and his

---

ᵃ36 Samaritan Pentateuch, Septuagint, Vulgate and Syriac (see also verse 28); Masoretic Text *Medanites*

Life in Bible Times

JOSEPH'S ROBE

People in Bible times liked beautiful clothes. They made their clothing out of black or white cloth, as well as from cloth of more vivid colors like purple, red, blue and yellow. Joseph's robe was embroidered by working colored threads into patterns in the cloth. The cloth could be woven with patterns too. The robe was not only a beautiful gift that Jacob gave Joseph. It probably showed position in the family as well, placing Joseph ahead of his older brothers. This picture shows ornamented clothes worn by Egyptians in Joseph's time. Probably Joseph's robe looked something like this.

friend Hirah the Adullamite went with him.

¹³When Tamar was told, "Your father-in-law is on his way to Timnah to shear his sheep," ¹⁴she took off her widow's clothes, covered herself with a veil to disguise herself, and then sat down at the entrance to Enaim, which is on the road to Timnah. For she saw that, though Shelah had now grown up, she had not been given to him as his wife.

¹⁵When Judah saw her, he thought she was a prostitute, for she had covered her face. ¹⁶Not realizing that she was his daughter-in-law, he went over to her by the roadside and said, "Come now, let me sleep with you."

"And what will you give me to sleep with you?" she asked.

¹⁷"I'll send you a young goat from my flock," he said.

"Will you give me something as a pledge until you send it?" she asked.

¹⁸He said, "What pledge should I give you?"

"Your seal and its cord, and the staff in your hand," she answered. So he gave them to her and slept with her, and she became pregnant by him. ¹⁹After she left, she took off her veil and put on her widow's clothes again.

²⁰Meanwhile Judah sent the young goat by his friend the Adullamite in order to get his pledge back from the woman, but he did not find her. ²¹He asked the men who lived there, "Where is the shrine prostitute who was beside the road at Enaim?"

"There hasn't been any shrine prostitute here," they said.

²²So he went back to Judah and said, "I didn't find her. Besides, the men who lived there said, 'There hasn't been any shrine prostitute here.'"

²³Then Judah said, "Let her keep what she has, or we will become a laughingstock. After all, I did send her this young goat, but you didn't find her."

²⁴About three months later Judah was told, "Your daughter-in-law Tamar is guilty of prostitution, and as a result she is now pregnant."

Judah said, "Bring her out and have her burned to death!"

²⁵As she was being brought out, she sent a message to her father-in-law. "I am pregnant by the man who owns these," she said. And she added, "See if you recognize whose seal and cord and staff these are."

²⁶Judah recognized them and said, "She is more righteous than I, since I wouldn't give her to my son Shelah." And he did not sleep with her again.

²⁷When the time came for her to give birth, there were twin boys in her womb. ²⁸As she was giving birth, one of them put out his hand; so the midwife took a scarlet thread and tied it on his wrist and said, "This one came out first." ²⁹But when he drew back his hand, his brother came out, and she said, "So this is how you have broken out!" And he was named Perez.ᵃ ³⁰Then his brother, who had the scarlet thread on his wrist, came out and he was given the name Zerah.ᵇ

Joseph and Potiphar's Wife

39 Now Joseph had been taken down to Egypt. Potiphar, an Egyptian who was one of Pharaoh's officials, the captain of the guard, bought him from the Ishmaelites who had taken him there.

²The LORD was with Joseph and he prospered, and he lived in the house of his Egyptian master. ³When his master saw that the LORD was with him and that the LORD gave him success in everything he did, ⁴Joseph found favor in his eyes and became his attendant. Potiphar put him in charge of his household, and he entrusted to his care everything he owned. ⁵From the time he put him in charge of his household and of all that he owned, the LORD blessed the household of the Egyptian because of Joseph. The blessing of the LORD was on everything Potiphar had, both in the house and in the field. ⁶So he left

ᵃ29 *Perez* means *breaking out.*   ᵇ30 *Zerah* can mean *scarlet* or *brightness.*

in Joseph's care everything he had; with Joseph in charge, he did not concern himself with anything except the food he ate.

Now Joseph was well-built and handsome, 7and after a while his master's wife took notice of Joseph and said, "Come to bed with me!"

8But he refused. "With me in charge," he told her, "my master does not concern himself with anything in the house; everything he owns he has entrusted to my care. 9No one is greater in this house than I am. My master has withheld nothing from me except you, because you are his wife. How then could I do such a wicked thing and sin against God?" 10And though she spoke to Joseph day after day, he refused to go to bed with her or even be with her.

11One day he went into the house to attend to his duties, and none of the household servants was inside. 12She caught him by his cloak and said, "Come to bed with me!" But he left his cloak in her hand and ran out of the house.

13When she saw that he had left his cloak in her hand and had run out of the house, 14she called her household servants. "Look," she said to them, "this Hebrew has been brought to us to make sport of us! He came in here to sleep with me, but I screamed. 15When he heard me scream for help, he left his cloak beside me and ran out of the house."

16She kept his cloak beside her until his master came home. 17Then she told him this story: "That Hebrew slave you brought us came to me to make sport of me. 18But as soon as I screamed for help, he left his cloak beside me and ran out of the house."

19When his master heard the story his wife told him, saying, "This is how your slave treated me," he burned with anger. 20Joseph's master took him and put him in prison, the place where the king's prisoners were confined.

But while Joseph was there in the prison, 21the LORD was with him; he showed him kindness and granted him favor in the eyes of the prison warden. 22So the warden put Joseph in charge of all those held in the prison, and he was made responsible for all that was done there. 23The warden paid no attention to anything under Joseph's care, because the LORD was with Joseph and gave him success in whatever he did.

The Cupbearer and the Baker

40 Some time later, the cupbearer and the baker of the king of Egypt offended their master, the king of Egypt. 2Pharaoh was angry with his two officials, the chief cupbearer and the chief baker, 3and put them in custody in the house of the captain of the guard, in the same prison where Joseph was confined. 4The captain of the guard assigned them to Joseph, and he attended them.

After they had been in custody for some time, 5each of the two men—the

---

LET'S LIVE IT!

Genesis 39:1–23

WHEN LIFE ISN'T FAIR ➡ Draw a cartoon strip story, telling about a time when life wasn't fair to you. Have two of the pictures show what you did after you were treated unfairly.

Life wasn't fair to Joseph after his brothers sold him to be a slave. Read Genesis 39:1–23. What happened to Joseph that wasn't fair? What did Joseph do when life wasn't fair to him? Sulk and stop trying? Or keep on working hard?

Look back at your cartoon strip story. Did you act like Joseph when you were treated unfairly? If not, redraw the last two pictures to show what Joseph would have done.

cupbearer and the baker of the king of Egypt, who were being held in prison—had a dream the same night, and each dream had a meaning of its own. 6When Joseph came to them the next morning, he saw that they were dejected. 7So he asked Pharaoh's officials who were in custody with him in his master's house, "Why are your faces so sad today?"

8"We both had dreams," they answered, "but there is no one to interpret them."

Then Joseph said to them, "Do not interpretations belong to God? Tell me your dreams."

❓DID YOU KNOW?   40:8

Are dreams messages from God?

Most dreams are not messages from God; but God has spoken to people in dreams. God gave dreams to three people in Genesis 40–41, so Joseph could explain what the dreams meant. When Joseph's interpretation turned out to be right, the Egyptians knew God had given Joseph great wisdom.

9So the chief cupbearer told Joseph his dream. He said to him, "In my dream I saw a vine in front of me, 10and on the vine were three branches. As soon as it budded, it blossomed, and its clusters ripened into grapes. 11Pharaoh's cup was in my hand, and I took the grapes, squeezed them into Pharaoh's cup and put the cup in his hand."

12"This is what it means," Joseph said to him. "The three branches are three days. 13Within three days Pharaoh will lift up your head and restore you to your position, and you will put Pharaoh's cup in his hand, just as you used to do when you were his cupbearer. 14But when all goes well with you, remember me and show me kindness; mention me to

Pharaoh and get me out of this prison. 15For I was forcibly carried off from the land of the Hebrews, and even here I have done nothing to deserve being put in a dungeon."

16When the chief baker saw that Joseph had given a favorable interpretation, he said to Joseph, "I too had a dream: On my head were three baskets of bread.a 17In the top basket were all kinds of baked goods for Pharaoh, but the birds were eating them out of the basket on my head."

18"This is what it means," Joseph said. "The three baskets are three days. 19Within three days Pharaoh will lift off your head and hang you on a tree.b And the birds will eat away your flesh."

20Now the third day was Pharaoh's birthday, and he gave a feast for all his officials. He lifted up the heads of the chief cupbearer and the chief baker in the presence of his officials: 21He restored the chief cupbearer to his position, so that he once again put the cup into Pharaoh's hand, 22but he hangedc the chief baker, just as Joseph had said to them in his interpretation.

23The chief cupbearer, however, did not remember Joseph; he forgot him.

Pharaoh's Dreams

41 When two full years had passed, Pharaoh had a dream: He was standing by the Nile, 2when out of the river there came up seven cows, sleek and fat, and they grazed among the reeds. 3After them, seven other cows, ugly and gaunt, came up out of the Nile and stood beside those on the riverbank. 4And the cows that were ugly and gaunt ate up the seven sleek, fat cows. Then Pharaoh woke up.

5He fell asleep again and had a second dream: Seven heads of grain, healthy and good, were growing on a single stalk. 6After them, seven other heads of grain sprouted—thin and

---

a16 Or *three wicker baskets*   b19 Or *and impale you on a pole*   c22 Or *impaled*

scorched by the east wind. 7The thin heads of grain swallowed up the seven healthy, full heads. Then Pharaoh woke up; it had been a dream.

8In the morning his mind was troubled, so he sent for all the magicians and wise men of Egypt. Pharaoh told them his dreams, but no one could interpret them for him.

9Then the chief cupbearer said to Pharaoh, "Today I am reminded of my shortcomings. 10Pharaoh was once angry with his servants, and he imprisoned me and the chief baker in the house of the captain of the guard. 11Each of us had a dream the same night, and each dream had a meaning of its own. 12Now a young Hebrew was there with us, a servant of the captain of the guard. We told him our dreams, and he interpreted them for us, giving each man the interpretation of his dream. 13And things turned out exactly as he interpreted them to us: I was restored to my position, and the other man was hanged.ᵃ"

14So Pharaoh sent for Joseph, and he was quickly brought from the dungeon. When he had shaved and changed his clothes, he came before Pharaoh.

15Pharaoh said to Joseph, "I had a dream, and no one can interpret it. But I have heard it said of you that when you hear a dream you can interpret it."

16"I cannot do it," Joseph replied to Pharaoh, "but God will give Pharaoh the answer he desires."

17Then Pharaoh said to Joseph, "In my dream I was standing on the bank of the Nile, 18when out of the river there came up seven cows, fat and sleek, and they grazed among the reeds. 19After them, seven other cows came up—scrawny and very ugly and lean. I had never seen such ugly cows in all the land of Egypt. 20The lean, ugly cows ate up the seven fat cows that came up first. 21But even after they ate them, no one could tell that they had done so; they looked just as ugly as before. Then I woke up.

22"In my dreams I also saw seven heads of grain, full and good, growing on a single stalk. 23After them, seven other heads sprouted—withered and thin and scorched by the east wind. 24The thin heads of grain swallowed up the seven good heads. I told this to the magicians, but none could explain it to me."

25Then Joseph said to Pharaoh, "The dreams of Pharaoh are one and the same. God has revealed to Pharaoh what he is about to do. 26The seven good cows are seven years, and the seven good heads of grain are seven years; it is one and the same dream. 27The seven lean, ugly cows that came up afterward are seven years, and so are the seven worthless heads of grain scorched by the east wind: They are seven years of famine.

28"It is just as I said to Pharaoh: God has shown Pharaoh what he is about to do. 29Seven years of great abundance are coming throughout the land of Egypt, 30but seven years of famine will follow them. Then all the abundance in Egypt will be forgotten, and the famine will ravage the land. 31The abundance in the land will not be remembered, because the famine that follows it will be so severe. 32The reason the dream was given to Pharaoh in two forms is that the matter has been firmly decided by God, and God will do it soon.

33"And now let Pharaoh look for a discerning and wise man and put him in charge of the land of Egypt. 34Let Pharaoh appoint commissioners over the land to take a fifth of the harvest of Egypt during the seven years of abundance. 35They should collect all the food of these good years that are coming and store up the grain under the authority of Pharaoh, to be kept in the cities for food. 36This food should be held in reserve for the country, to be used during the seven years of famine that will come upon

ᵃ13 Or impaled

Egypt, so that the country may not be ruined by the famine."

37The plan seemed good to Pharaoh and to all his officials. 38So Pharaoh asked them, "Can we find anyone like this man, one in whom is the spirit of God*a*?"

39Then Pharaoh said to Joseph, "Since God has made all this known to you, there is no one so discerning and wise as you. 40You shall be in charge of my palace, and all my people are to submit to your orders. Only with respect to the throne will I be greater than you."

Joseph in Charge of Egypt

41So Pharaoh said to Joseph, "I hereby put you in charge of the whole land of Egypt." 42Then Pharaoh took his signet ring from his finger and put it on Joseph's finger. He dressed him in robes of fine linen and put a gold chain around his neck. 43He had him ride in a chariot as his second-in-command,*b* and men shouted before him, "Make way*c*!" Thus he put him in charge of the whole land of Egypt.

44Then Pharaoh said to Joseph, "I am Pharaoh, but without your word no one will lift hand or foot in all Egypt." 45Pharaoh gave Joseph the name Zaphenath-Paneah and gave him Asenath daughter of Potiphera, priest of On,*d* to be his wife. And Joseph went throughout the land of Egypt.

46Joseph was thirty years old when he entered the service of Pharaoh king of Egypt. And Joseph went out from Pharaoh's presence and traveled throughout Egypt. 47During the seven years of abundance the land produced plentifully. 48Joseph collected all the food produced in those seven years of abundance in Egypt and stored it in the cities. In each city he put the food grown in the fields surrounding it. 49Joseph stored up huge quantities of grain, like the sand of the sea; it was so much that he stopped keeping records because it was beyond measure.

50Before the years of famine came, two sons were born to Joseph by Asenath daughter of Potiphera, priest of On. 51Joseph named his firstborn Manasseh*e* and said, "It is because God has made me forget all my trouble and all my father's household." 52The second son he named Ephraim*f* and said, "It is because God has made me fruitful in the land of my suffering."

53The seven years of abundance in Egypt came to an end, 54and the seven years of famine began, just as Joseph had said. There was famine in all the other lands, but in the whole land of Egypt there was food. 55When all Egypt began to feel the famine, the people cried to Pharaoh for food. Then Pharaoh told all the Egyptians, "Go to Joseph and do what he tells you."

56When the famine had spread over the whole country, Joseph opened the storehouses and sold grain to the Egyptians, for the famine was severe throughout Egypt. 57And all the countries came to Egypt to buy grain from Joseph, because the famine was severe in all the world.

Joseph's Brothers Go to Egypt

42 When Jacob learned that there was grain in Egypt, he said to his sons, "Why do you just keep looking at each other?" 2He continued, "I have heard that there is grain in Egypt. Go down there and buy some for us, so that we may live and not die."

3Then ten of Joseph's brothers went down to buy grain from Egypt. 4But Jacob did not send Benjamin, Joseph's brother, with the others, because he was afraid that harm might come to him. 5So Israel's sons were among those who went to buy grain,

---

*a*38 Or *of the gods*   *b*43 Or *in the chariot of his second-in-command*; or *in his second chariot*
*c*43 Or *Bow down*   *d*45 That is, Heliopolis; also in verse 50   *e*51 *Manasseh* sounds like and
may be derived from the Hebrew for *forget*.   *f*52 *Ephraim* sounds like the Hebrew for *twice fruitful*.

for the famine was in the land of Canaan also.

⁶Now Joseph was the governor of the land, the one who sold grain to all its people. So when Joseph's brothers arrived, they bowed down to him with their faces to the ground. ⁷As soon as Joseph saw his brothers, he recognized them, but he pretended to be a stranger and spoke harshly to them. "Where do you come from?" he asked.

"From the land of Canaan," they replied, "to buy food."

❓DID YOU KNOW?   42:8

Why did Joseph pretend to be a stranger to his brothers?

Joseph wanted to find out if his brothers realized what they did to him was wrong. Joseph kept on testing them, until at last they showed they really cared for their father and each other too.

---

⁸Although Joseph recognized his brothers, they did not recognize him. ⁹Then he remembered his dreams about them and said to them, "You are spies! You have come to see where our land is unprotected."

¹⁰"No, my lord," they answered. "Your servants have come to buy food. ¹¹We are all the sons of one man. Your servants are honest men, not spies."

¹²"No!" he said to them. "You have come to see where our land is unprotected."

¹³But they replied, "Your servants were twelve brothers, the sons of one man, who lives in the land of Canaan. The youngest is now with our father, and one is no more."

¹⁴Joseph said to them, "It is just as I told you: You are spies! ¹⁵And this is how you will be tested: As surely as Pharaoh lives, you will not leave this place unless your youngest brother comes here. ¹⁶Send one of your number to get your brother; the rest of you will be kept in prison, so that your words may be tested to see if you are telling the truth. If you are not, then as surely as Pharaoh lives, you are spies!" ¹⁷And he put them all in custody for three days.

¹⁸On the third day, Joseph said to them, "Do this and you will live, for I fear God: ¹⁹If you are honest men, let one of your brothers stay here in prison, while the rest of you go and take grain back for your starving households. ²⁰But you must bring your youngest brother to me, so that your words may be verified and that

Life in Bible Times

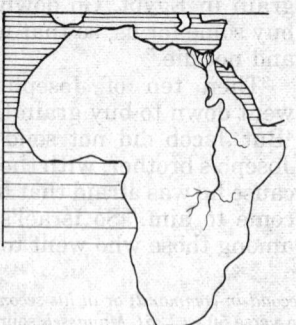

THE NILE

The Nile is one of the longest rivers in the world. The people of Egypt lived along the top, or northern, part of the river on the map. Every year the river overflowed, leaving rich new soil where crops could grow. When lands that depended on rainfall had famines, there was often still food in Egypt.

you may not die." This they proceeded to do.

²¹They said to one another, "Surely we are being punished because of our brother. We saw how distressed he was when he pleaded with us for his life, but we would not listen; that's why this distress has come upon us."

²²Reuben replied, "Didn't I tell you not to sin against the boy? But you wouldn't listen! Now we must give an accounting for his blood." ²³They did not realize that Joseph could understand them, since he was using an interpreter.

²⁴He turned away from them and began to weep, but then turned back and spoke to them again. He had Simeon taken from them and bound before their eyes.

²⁵Joseph gave orders to fill their bags with grain, to put each man's silver back in his sack, and to give them provisions for their journey. After this was done for them, ²⁶they loaded their grain on their donkeys and left.

²⁷At the place where they stopped for the night one of them opened his sack to get feed for his donkey, and he saw his silver in the mouth of his sack. ²⁸"My silver has been returned," he said to his brothers. "Here it is in my sack."

Their hearts sank and they turned to each other trembling and said, "What is this that God has done to us?"

²⁹When they came to their father Jacob in the land of Canaan, they told him all that had happened to them. They said, ³⁰"The man who is lord over the land spoke harshly to us and treated us as though we were spying on the land. ³¹But we said to him, 'We are honest men; we are not spies. ³²We were twelve brothers, sons of one father. One is no more, and the youngest is now with our father in Canaan.'

³³"Then the man who is lord over the land said to us, 'This is how I will know whether you are honest men:

Leave one of your brothers here with me, and take food for your starving households and go. ³⁴But bring your youngest brother to me so I will know that you are not spies but honest men. Then I will give your brother back to you, and you can trade^a in the land.'"

³⁵As they were emptying their sacks, there in each man's sack was his pouch of silver! When they and their father saw the money pouches, they were frightened. ³⁶Their father Jacob said to them, "You have deprived me of my children. Joseph is no more and Simeon is no more, and now you want to take Benjamin. Everything is against me!"

³⁷Then Reuben said to his father, "You may put both of my sons to death if I do not bring him back to you. Entrust him to my care, and I will bring him back."

³⁸But Jacob said, "My son will not go down there with you; his brother is dead and he is the only one left. If harm comes to him on the journey you are taking, you will bring my gray head down to the grave^b in sorrow."

The Second Journey to Egypt

43 Now the famine was still severe in the land. ²So when they had eaten all the grain they had brought from Egypt, their father said to them, "Go back and buy us a little more food."

³But Judah said to him, "The man warned us solemnly, 'You will not see my face again unless your brother is with you.' ⁴If you will send our brother along with us, we will go down and buy food for you. ⁵But if you will not send him, we will not go down, because the man said to us, 'You will not see my face again unless your brother is with you.'"

⁶Israel asked, "Why did you bring this trouble on me by telling the man you had another brother?"

⁷They replied, "The man questioned us closely about ourselves and

---

^{a}34 Or *move about freely* ^{b}38 Hebrew *Sheol*

our family. 'Is your father still living?' he asked us. 'Do you have another brother?' We simply answered his questions. How were we to know he would say, 'Bring your brother down here'?"

⁸Then Judah said to Israel his father, "Send the boy along with me and we will go at once, so that we and you and our children may live and not die. ⁹I myself will guarantee his safety; you can hold me personally responsible for him. If I do not bring him back to you and set him here before you, I will bear the blame before you all my life. ¹⁰As it is, if we had not delayed, we could have gone and returned twice."

¹¹Then their father Israel said to them, "If it must be, then do this: Put some of the best products of the land in your bags and take them down to the man as a gift—a little balm and a little honey, some spices and myrrh, some pistachio nuts and almonds. ¹²Take double the amount of silver with you, for you must return the silver that was put back into the mouths of your sacks. Perhaps it was a mistake. ¹³Take your brother also and go back to the man at once. ¹⁴And may God Almighty[a] grant you mercy before the man so that he will let your other brother and Benjamin come back with you. As for me, if I am bereaved, I am bereaved."

¹⁵So the men took the gifts and double the amount of silver, and Benjamin also. They hurried down to Egypt and presented themselves to Joseph. ¹⁶When Joseph saw Benjamin with them, he said to the steward of his house, "Take these men to my house, slaughter an animal and prepare dinner; they are to eat with me at noon."

¹⁷The man did as Joseph told him and took the men to Joseph's house. ¹⁸Now the men were frightened when they were taken to his house. They thought, "We were brought here because of the silver that was put back into our sacks the first time. He

wants to attack us and overpower us and seize us as slaves and take our donkeys."

¹⁹So they went up to Joseph's steward and spoke to him at the entrance to the house. ²⁰"Please, sir," they said, "we came down here the first time to buy food. ²¹But at the place where we stopped for the night we opened our sacks and each of us found his silver—the exact weight—in the mouth of his sack. So we have brought it back with us. ²²We have also brought additional silver with us to buy food. We don't know who put our silver in our sacks."

²³"It's all right," he said. "Don't be afraid. Your God, the God of your father, has given you treasure in your sacks; I received your silver." Then he brought Simeon out to them.

²⁴The steward took the men into Joseph's house, gave them water to wash their feet and provided fodder for their donkeys. ²⁵They prepared their gifts for Joseph's arrival at noon, because they had heard that they were to eat there.

²⁶When Joseph came home, they presented to him the gifts they had brought into the house, and they bowed down before him to the ground. ²⁷He asked them how they were, and then he said, "How is your aged father you told me about? Is he still living?"

²⁸They replied, "Your servant our father is still alive and well." And they bowed low to pay him honor.

²⁹As he looked about and saw his brother Benjamin, his own mother's son, he asked, "Is this your youngest brother, the one you told me about?" And he said, "God be gracious to you, my son." ³⁰Deeply moved at the sight of his brother, Joseph hurried out and looked for a place to weep. He went into his private room and wept there.

³¹After he had washed his face, he came out and, controlling himself, said, "Serve the food."

³²They served him by himself, the brothers by themselves, and the

^a14 Hebrew *El-Shaddai*

Egyptians who ate with him by themselves, because Egyptians could not eat with Hebrews, for that is detestable to Egyptians. ³³The men had been seated before him in the order of their ages, from the firstborn to the youngest; and they looked at each other in astonishment. ³⁴When portions were served to them from Joseph's table, Benjamin's portion was five times as much as anyone else's. So they feasted and drank freely with him.

A Silver Cup in a Sack

44 Now Joseph gave these instructions to the steward of his house: "Fill the men's sacks with as much food as they can carry, and put each man's silver in the mouth of his sack. ²Then put my cup, the silver one, in the mouth of the youngest one's sack, along with the silver for his grain." And he did as Joseph said.

³As morning dawned, the men were sent on their way with their donkeys. ⁴They had not gone far from the city when Joseph said to his steward, "Go after those men at once, and when you catch up with them, say to them, 'Why have you repaid good with evil? ⁵Isn't this the cup my master drinks from and also uses for divination? This is a wicked thing you have done.'"

⁶When he caught up with them, he repeated these words to them. ⁷But they said to him, "Why does my lord say such things? Far be it from your servants to do anything like that! ⁸We even brought back to you from the land of Canaan the silver we found inside the mouths of our sacks. So why would we steal silver or gold from your master's house? ⁹If any of your servants is found to have it, he will die; and the rest of us will become my lord's slaves."

¹⁰"Very well, then," he said, "let it be as you say. Whoever is found to have it will become my slave; the rest of you will be free from blame."

¹¹Each of them quickly lowered his sack to the ground and opened it. ¹²Then the steward proceeded to search, beginning with the oldest and ending with the youngest. And the cup was found in Benjamin's sack. ¹³At this, they tore their clothes. Then they all loaded their donkeys and returned to the city.

¹⁴Joseph was still in the house when Judah and his brothers came in, and they threw themselves to the ground before him. ¹⁵Joseph said to them, "What is this you have done? Don't you know that a man like me can find things out by divination?"

¹⁶"What can we say to my lord?" Judah replied. "What can we say? How can we prove our innocence? God has uncovered your servants' guilt. We are now my lord's slaves —we ourselves and the one who was found to have the cup."

¹⁷But Joseph said, "Far be it from me to do such a thing! Only the man who was found to have the cup will become my slave. The rest of you, go back to your father in peace."

¹⁸Then Judah went up to him and said: "Please, my lord, let your servant speak a word to my lord. Do not be angry with your servant, though you are equal to Pharaoh himself. ¹⁹My lord asked his servants, 'Do you have a father or a brother?' ²⁰And we answered, 'We have an aged father, and there is a young son born to him in his old age. His brother is dead, and he is the only one of his mother's sons left, and his father loves him.'

²¹"Then you said to your servants, 'Bring him down to me so I can see him for myself.' ²²And we said to my lord, 'The boy cannot leave his father; if he leaves him, his father will die.' ²³But you told your servants, 'Unless your youngest brother comes down with you, you will not see my face again.' ²⁴When we went back to your servant my father, we told him what my lord had said.

²⁵"Then our father said, 'Go back and buy a little more food.' ²⁶But we said, 'We cannot go down. Only if our youngest brother is with us will we go. We cannot see the man's face unless our youngest brother is with us.' ²⁷"Your servant my father said to

us, 'You know that my wife bore me two sons. 28One of them went away from me, and I said, "He has surely been torn to pieces." And I have not seen him since. 29If you take this one from me too and harm comes to him, you will bring my gray head down to the grave^a in misery.'

30"So now, if the boy is not with us when I go back to your servant my father and if my father, whose life is closely bound up with the boy's life, 31sees that the boy isn't there, he will die. Your servants will bring the gray head of our father down to the grave in sorrow. 32Your servant guaranteed the boy's safety to my father. I said, 'If I do not bring him back to you, I will bear the blame before you, my father, all my life!'

33"Now then, please let your servant remain here as my lord's slave in place of the boy, and let the boy return with his brothers. 34How can I go back to my father if the boy is not with me? No! Do not let me see the misery that would come upon my father."

Joseph Makes Himself Known

45 Then Joseph could no longer control himself before all his attendants, and he cried out, "Have everyone leave my presence!" So there was no one with Joseph when he made himself known to his brothers. 2And he wept so loudly that the Egyptians heard him, and Pharaoh's household heard about it.

3Joseph said to his brothers, "I am Joseph! Is my father still living?" But his brothers were not able to answer him, because they were terrified at his presence.

4Then Joseph said to his brothers, "Come close to me." When they had done so, he said, "I am your brother Joseph, the one you sold into Egypt! 5And now, do not be distressed and do not be angry with yourselves for selling me here, because it was to save lives that God sent me ahead of you.

6For two years now there has been famine in the land, and for the next five years there will not be plowing and reaping. 7But God sent me ahead of you to preserve for you a remnant on earth and to save your lives by a great deliverance.^b

8"So then, it was not you who sent me here, but God. He made me father to Pharaoh, lord of his entire household and ruler of all Egypt. 9Now hurry back to my father and say to him, 'This is what your son Joseph says: God has made me lord of all Egypt. Come down to me; don't delay. 10You shall live in the region of Goshen and be near me—you, your children and grandchildren, your flocks and herds, and all you have. 11I will provide for you there, because five years of famine are still to come. Otherwise you and your household and all who belong to you will become destitute.'

12"You can see for yourselves, and so can my brother Benjamin, that it is really I who am speaking to you. 13Tell my father about all the honor accorded me in Egypt and about everything you have seen. And bring my father down here quickly."

14Then he threw his arms around his brother Benjamin and wept, and Benjamin embraced him, weeping. 15And he kissed all his brothers and wept over them. Afterward his brothers talked with him.

16When the news reached Pharaoh's palace that Joseph's brothers had come, Pharaoh and all his officials were pleased. 17Pharaoh said to Joseph, "Tell your brothers, 'Do this: Load your animals and return to the land of Canaan, 18and bring your father and your families back to me. I will give you the best of the land of Egypt and you can enjoy the fat of the land.'

19"You are also directed to tell them, 'Do this: Take some carts from Egypt for your children and your wives, and get your father and come. 20Never mind about your belongings,

---

^a29 Hebrew Sheol; also in verse 31   ^b7 Or save you as a great band of survivors

because the best of all Egypt will be yours.' "

²¹So the sons of Israel did this. Joseph gave them carts, as Pharaoh had commanded, and he also gave them provisions for their journey. ²²To each of them he gave new clothing, but to Benjamin he gave three hundred shekels *a* of silver and five sets of clothes. ²³And this is what he sent to his father: ten donkeys loaded with the best things of Egypt, and ten female donkeys loaded with grain and bread and other provisions for his journey. ²⁴Then he sent his brothers away, and as they were leaving he said to them, "Don't quarrel on the way!"

²⁵So they went up out of Egypt and came to their father Jacob in the land of Canaan. ²⁶They told him, "Joseph is still alive! In fact, he is ruler of all Egypt." Jacob was stunned; he did not believe them. ²⁷But when they told him everything Joseph had said to them, and when he saw the carts Joseph had sent to carry him back, the spirit of their father Jacob revived. ²⁸And Israel said, "I'm convinced! My son Joseph is still alive. I will go and see him before I die."

Jacob Goes to Egypt

46 So Israel set out with all that was his, and when he reached Beersheba, he offered sacrifices to the God of his father Isaac.

²And God spoke to Israel in a vision at night and said, "Jacob! Jacob!"

"Here I am," he replied.

³"I am God, the God of your father," he said. "Do not be afraid to go down to Egypt, for I will make you into a great nation there. ⁴I will go down to Egypt with you, and I will surely bring you back again. And Joseph's own hand will close your eyes."

⁵Then Jacob left Beersheba, and Israel's sons took their father Jacob

and their children and their wives in the carts that Pharaoh had sent to transport him. ⁶They also took with them their livestock and the possessions they had acquired in Canaan, and Jacob and all his offspring went to Egypt. ⁷He took with him to Egypt his sons and grandsons and his daughters and granddaughters—all his offspring.

⁸These are the names of the sons of Israel (Jacob and his descendants) who went to Egypt:

Reuben the firstborn of Jacob.
⁹The sons of Reuben:
　Hanoch, Pallu, Hezron and Carmi.
¹⁰The sons of Simeon:
　Jemuel, Jamin, Ohad, Jakin, Zohar and Shaul the son of a Canaanite woman.
¹¹The sons of Levi:
　Gershon, Kohath and Merari.
¹²The sons of Judah:
　Er, Onan, Shelah, Perez and Zerah (but Er and Onan had died in the land of Canaan).
　The sons of Perez:
　　Hezron and Hamul.
¹³The sons of Issachar:
　Tola, Puah, *b* Jashub *c* and Shimron.
¹⁴The sons of Zebulun:
　Sered, Elon and Jahleel.
¹⁵These were the sons Leah bore to Jacob in Paddan Aram, *d* besides his daughter Dinah. These sons and daughters of his were thirty-three in all.

¹⁶The sons of Gad:
　Zephon, *e* Haggi, Shuni, Ezbon, Eri, Arodi and Areli.
¹⁷The sons of Asher:
　Imnah, Ishvah, Ishvi and Beriah.
　Their sister was Serah.
　The sons of Beriah:
　　Heber and Malkiel.

---

a22 That is, about 7 1/2 pounds (about 3.5 kilograms) (see also 1 Chron. 7:1); Masoretic Text *Puvah* manuscripts (see also Num. 26:24 and 1 Chron. 7:1); Masoretic Text *Iob* Mesopotamia *e16* Samaritan Pentateuch and Septuagint (see also Num. 26:15); Masoretic Text *Ziphion*
b13 Samaritan Pentateuch and Syriac *c13* Samaritan Pentateuch and some Septuagint *d15* That is, Northwest

18These were the children born to Jacob by Zilpah, whom Laban had given to his daughter Leah—sixteen in all.

19The sons of Jacob's wife Rachel: Joseph and Benjamin. 20In Egypt, Manasseh and Ephraim were born to Joseph by Asenath daughter of Potiphera, priest of On.ᵃ

21The sons of Benjamin: Bela, Beker, Ashbel, Gera, Naaman, Ehi, Rosh, Muppim, Huppim and Ard.

22These were the sons of Rachel who were born to Jacob—fourteen in all.

23The son of Dan: Hushim.

24The sons of Naphtali: Jahziel, Guni, Jezer and Shillem.

25These were the sons born to Jacob by Bilhah, whom Laban had given to his daughter Rachel—seven in all.

26All those who went to Egypt with Jacob—those who were his direct descendants, not counting his sons' wives—numbered sixty-six persons. 27With the two sonsᵇ who had been born to Joseph in Egypt, the members of Jacob's family, which went to Egypt, were seventyᶜ in all.

?DID YOU KNOW?   46:26

Why did God send Jacob's family to Egypt?

God sent Jacob to Egypt so his family could multiply in safety. There were many wars as well as famine in Canaan. But in Egypt the seventy people in Jacob's family multiplied to become millions in the next four hundred years.

28Now Jacob sent Judah ahead of him to Joseph to get directions to Go-shen. When they arrived in the region of Goshen, 29Joseph had his chariot made ready and went to Goshen to meet his father Israel. As soon as Joseph appeared before him, he threw his arms around his fatherᵈ and wept for a long time.

30Israel said to Joseph, "Now I am ready to die, since I have seen for myself that you are still alive."

31Then Joseph said to his brothers and to his father's household, "I will go up and speak to Pharaoh and will say to him, 'My brothers and my father's household, who were living in the land of Canaan, have come to me. 32The men are shepherds; they tend livestock, and they have brought along their flocks and herds and everything they own.' 33When Pharaoh calls you in and asks, 'What is your occupation?' 34you should answer, 'Your servants have tended livestock from our boyhood on, just as our fathers did.' Then you will be allowed to settle in the region of Goshen, for all shepherds are detestable to the Egyptians."

47 Joseph went and told Pharaoh, "My father and brothers, with their flocks and herds and everything they own, have come from the land of Canaan and are now in Goshen." 2He chose five of his brothers and presented them before Pharaoh.

3Pharaoh asked the brothers, "What is your occupation?"

"Your servants are shepherds," they replied to Pharaoh, "just as our fathers were." 4They also said to him, "We have come to live here awhile, because the famine is severe in Canaan and your servants' flocks have no pasture. So now, please let your servants settle in Goshen."

5Pharaoh said to Joseph, "Your father and your brothers have come to you, 6and the land of Egypt is before you; settle your father and your brothers in the best part of the land. Let them live in Goshen. And if you

---

ᵃ20 That is, Heliopolis   ᵇ27 Hebrew; Septuagint *the nine children*   ᶜ27 Hebrew (see also Exodus 1:5 and footnote); Septuagint (see also Acts 7:14) *seventy-five*   ᵈ29 Hebrew *around him*

know of any among them with special ability, put them in charge of my own livestock."

7Then Joseph brought his father Jacob in and presented him before Pharaoh. After Jacob blessed*a* Pharaoh, 8Pharaoh asked him, "How old are you?"

9And Jacob said to Pharaoh, "The years of my pilgrimage are a hundred and thirty. My years have been few and difficult, and they do not equal the years of the pilgrimage of my fathers." 10Then Jacob blessed*b* Pharaoh and went out from his presence.

11So Joseph settled his father and his brothers in Egypt and gave them property in the best part of the land, the district of Rameses, as Pharaoh directed. 12Joseph also provided his father and his brothers and all his father's household with food, according to the number of their children.

Joseph and the Famine

13There was no food, however, in the whole region because the famine was severe; both Egypt and Canaan wasted away because of the famine. 14Joseph collected all the money that was to be found in Egypt and Canaan in payment for the grain they were buying, and he brought it to Pharaoh's palace. 15When the money of the people of Egypt and Canaan was gone, all Egypt came to Joseph and said, "Give us food. Why should we die before your eyes? Our money is used up."

16"Then bring your livestock," said Joseph. "I will sell you food in exchange for your livestock, since your money is gone." 17So they brought their livestock to Joseph, and he gave them food in exchange for their horses, their sheep and goats, their cattle and donkeys. And he brought them through that year with food in exchange for all their livestock.

18When that year was over, they came to him the following year and said, "We cannot hide from our lord the fact that since our money is gone and our livestock belongs to you, there is nothing left for our lord except our bodies and our land. 19Why should we perish before your eyes —we and our land as well? Buy us and our land in exchange for food, and we with our land will be in bondage to Pharaoh. Give us seed so that we may live and not die, and that the land may not become desolate."

20So Joseph bought all the land in Egypt for Pharaoh. The Egyptians, one and all, sold their fields, because the famine was too severe for them. The land became Pharaoh's, 21and Joseph reduced the people to servitude,*c* from one end of Egypt to the other. 22However, he did not buy the land of the priests, because they received a regular allotment from Pharaoh and had food enough from the allotment Pharaoh gave them. That is why they did not sell their land.

23Joseph said to the people, "Now that I have bought you and your land today for Pharaoh, here is seed for you so you can plant the ground. 24But when the crop comes in, give a fifth of it to Pharaoh. The other four-fifths you may keep as seed for the fields and as food for yourselves and your households and your children."

25"You have saved our lives," they said. "May we find favor in the eyes of our lord; we will be in bondage to Pharaoh."

26So Joseph established it as a law concerning land in Egypt—still in force today—that a fifth of the produce belongs to Pharaoh. It was only the land of the priests that did not become Pharaoh's.

27Now the Israelites settled in Egypt in the region of Goshen. They acquired property there and were fruitful and increased greatly in number.

28Jacob lived in Egypt seventeen years, and the years of his life were a

---

*a*7 Or *greeted*   *b*10 Or *said farewell to*   *c*21 Samaritan Pentateuch and Septuagint (see also Vulgate); Masoretic Text *and he moved the people into the cities*

hundred and forty-seven. ²⁹When the time drew near for Israel to die, he called for his son Joseph and said to him, "If I have found favor in your eyes, put your hand under my thigh and promise that you will show me kindness and faithfulness. Do not bury me in Egypt, ³⁰but when I rest with my fathers, carry me out of Egypt and bury me where they are buried."

"I will do as you say," he said.

³¹"Swear to me," he said. Then Joseph swore to him, and Israel worshiped as he leaned on the top of his staff.^a

Manasseh and Ephraim

48 Some time later Joseph was told, "Your father is ill." So he took his two sons Manasseh and Ephraim along with him. ²When Jacob was told, "Your son Joseph has come to you," Israel rallied his strength and sat up on the bed.

³Jacob said to Joseph, "God Almighty^b appeared to me at Luz in the land of Canaan, and there he blessed me ⁴and said to me, 'I am going to make you fruitful and will increase your numbers. I will make you a community of peoples, and I will give this land as an everlasting possession to your descendants after you.'

⁵"Now then, your two sons born to you in Egypt before I came to you here will be reckoned as mine; Ephraim and Manasseh will be mine, just as Reuben and Simeon are mine. ⁶Any children born to you after them will be yours; in the territory they inherit they will be reckoned under the names of their brothers. ⁷As I was returning from Paddan,^c to my sorrow Rachel died in the land of Canaan while we were still on the way, a little distance from Ephrath. So I buried her there beside the road to Ephrath" (that is, Bethlehem).

⁸When Israel saw the sons of Joseph, he asked, "Who are these?"

⁹"They are the sons God has given

me here," Joseph said to his father.

Then Israel said, "Bring them to me so I may bless them."

¹⁰Now Israel's eyes were failing because of old age, and he could hardly see. So Joseph brought his sons close to him, and his father kissed them and embraced them.

¹¹Israel said to Joseph, "I never expected to see your face again, and now God has allowed me to see your children too."

¹²Then Joseph removed them from Israel's knees and bowed down with his face to the ground. ¹³And Joseph took both of them, Ephraim on his right toward Israel's left hand and Manasseh on his left toward Israel's right hand, and brought them close to him. ¹⁴But Israel reached out his right hand and put it on Ephraim's head, though he was the younger, and crossing his arms, he put his left hand on Manasseh's head, even though Manasseh was the firstborn.

¹⁵Then he blessed Joseph and said,

"May the God before whom my
  fathers
  Abraham and Isaac walked,
the God who has been my
  shepherd
  all my life to this day,
¹⁶the Angel who has delivered me
  from all harm
  —may he bless these boys.
May they be called by my name
  and the names of my fathers
  Abraham and Isaac,
and may they increase greatly
  upon the earth."

¹⁷When Joseph saw his father placing his right hand on Ephraim's head he was displeased; so he took hold of his father's hand to move it from Ephraim's head to Manasseh's head. ¹⁸Joseph said to him, "No, my father, this one is the firstborn; put your right hand on his head."

¹⁹But his father refused and said, "I know, my son, I know. He too will become a people, and he too will be-

^a31 Or *Israel bowed down at the head of his bed*   ^b3 Hebrew *El-Shaddai*   ^c7 That is,
Northwest Mesopotamia

come great. Nevertheless, his younger brother will be greater than he, and his descendants will become a group of nations." [20]He blessed them that day and said,

"In your[a] name will Israel
　　pronounce this blessing:
'May God make you like
　　Ephraim and Manasseh.' "

So he put Ephraim ahead of Manasseh.

[21]Then Israel said to Joseph, "I am about to die, but God will be with you[b] and take you[b] back to the land of your[b] fathers. [22]And to you, as one who is over your brothers, I give the ridge of land[c] I took from the Amorites with my sword and my bow."

❓DID YOU KNOW?   49:1

How is Jacob's blessing of his sons special?

Jacob's blessing is a prophecy as well as a prayer. It tells what will happen to each family and what will be special about each family many years later. The prophecy about Judah is most important. King David and Jesus came from this family group. Jesus is the one who will rule all nations (Genesis 49:10).

Jacob Blesses His Sons

49 Then Jacob called for his sons and said: "Gather around so I can tell you what will happen to you in days to come.

[2]"Assemble and listen, sons of
　　Jacob;
　　listen to your father Israel.

[3]"Reuben, you are my firstborn,
　　my might, the first sign of my
　　strength,

excelling in honor, excelling in
　　power.
[4]Turbulent as the waters, you will
　　no longer excel,
　　for you went up onto your
　　　　father's bed,
　　onto my couch and defiled it.

[5]"Simeon and Levi are brothers—
　　their swords[d] are weapons of
　　violence.
[6]Let me not enter their council,
　　let me not join their assembly,
　　for they have killed men in their
　　　　anger
　　and hamstrung oxen as they
　　　　pleased.
[7]Cursed be their anger, so fierce,
　　and their fury, so cruel!
I will scatter them in Jacob
　　and disperse them in Israel.

[8]"Judah,[e] your brothers will praise
　　you;
　　your hand will be on the neck
　　　　of your enemies;
　　your father's sons will bow
　　　　down to you.
[9]You are a lion's cub, O Judah;
　　you return from the prey, my
　　　　son.
Like a lion he crouches and lies
　　down,
　　like a lioness—who dares to
　　　　rouse him?
[10]The scepter will not depart from
　　Judah,
　　nor the ruler's staff from
　　　　between his feet,
until he comes to whom it
　　belongs[f]
　　and the obedience of the nations
　　　　is his.
[11]He will tether his donkey to a
　　vine,
　　his colt to the choicest branch;
he will wash his garments in
　　wine,
　　his robes in the blood of grapes.
[12]His eyes will be darker than
　　wine,

---

a20 The Hebrew is singular.   b21 The Hebrew is plural.   c22 Or And to you I give one portion more than to your brothers—the portion   d5 The meaning of the Hebrew for this word is uncertain.   e8 Judah sounds like and may be derived from the Hebrew for praise.   f10 Or until Shiloh comes; or until he comes to whom tribute belongs

his teeth whiter than milk. *a*

13"Zebulun will live by the seashore
  and become a haven for ships;
  his border will extend toward
    Sidon.

14"Issachar is a rawboned *b* donkey
  lying down between two
    saddlebags. *c*
15When he sees how good is his
    resting place
  and how pleasant is his land,
  he will bend his shoulder to the
    burden
  and submit to forced labor.

16"Dan *d* will provide justice for his
    people
  as one of the tribes of Israel.
17Dan will be a serpent by the
    roadside,
  a viper along the path,
  that bites the horse's heels
  so that its rider tumbles
    backward.

18"I look for your deliverance,
  O LORD.

19"Gad *e* will be attacked by a band
    of raiders,
  but he will attack them at their
    heels.

20"Asher's food will be rich;
  he will provide delicacies fit for
    a king.

21"Naphtali is a doe set free
  that bears beautiful fawns. *f*

22"Joseph is a fruitful vine,
  a fruitful vine near a spring,
  whose branches climb over a
    wall. *g*
23With bitterness archers attacked
    him;
  they shot at him with hostility.
24But his bow remained steady,
  his strong arms stayed *h* limber,

because of the hand of the Mighty
    One of Jacob,
  because of the Shepherd, the
    Rock of Israel,
25because of your father's God, who
    helps you,
  because of the Almighty, *i* who
    blesses you
with blessings of the heavens
    above,
  blessings of the deep that lies
    below,
  blessings of the breast and
    womb.
26Your father's blessings are
    greater
  than the blessings of the
    ancient mountains,
  than *j* the bounty of the age-old
    hills.
Let all these rest on the head of
    Joseph,
  on the brow of the prince
    among *k* his brothers.

27"Benjamin is a ravenous wolf;
  in the morning he devours the
    prey,
  in the evening he divides the
    plunder."

28All these are the twelve tribes of
Israel, and this is what their father
said to them when he blessed them,
giving each the blessing appropriate
to him.

❓DID YOU KNOW?   49:28

**Why isn't Joseph the name of
one of the twelve tribes of
Israel?**

Jacob adopted Joseph's two
sons Ephraim and Manasseh as his
own. Their names are found on later lists of the twelve tribes, or family
groups, of Israel.

---

*a*12 Or *will be dull from wine, / his teeth white from milk*   *b*14 Or *strong*   *c*14 Or *campfires*
*d*16 *Dan* here means *he provides justice.*   *e*19 *Gad* can mean *attack* and *band of raiders.*
*f*21 Or *free; / he utters beautiful words*   *g*22 Or *Joseph is a wild colt, / a wild colt near a spring, /
a wild donkey on a terraced hill*   *h*23,24 Or *archers will attack . . . will shoot . . . will remain . . .
will stay*   *i*25 Hebrew *Shaddai*   *j*26 Or *of my progenitors, / as great as*   *k*26 Or *the one
separated from*

The Death of Jacob

29Then he gave them these instructions: "I am about to be gathered to my people. Bury me with my fathers in the cave in the field of Ephron the Hittite, 30the cave in the field of Machpelah, near Mamre in Canaan, which Abraham bought as a burial place from Ephron the Hittite, along with the field. 31There Abraham and his wife Sarah were buried, there Isaac and his wife Rebekah were buried, and there I buried Leah. 32The field and the cave in it were bought from the Hittites.*a*"

33When Jacob had finished giving instructions to his sons, he drew his feet up into the bed, breathed his last and was gathered to his people.

50 Joseph threw himself upon his father and wept over him and kissed him. 2Then Joseph directed the physicians in his service to embalm his father Israel. So the physicians embalmed him, 3taking a full forty days, for that was the time required for embalming. And the Egyptians mourned for him seventy days.

4When the days of mourning had passed, Joseph said to Pharaoh's court, "If I have found favor in your eyes, speak to Pharaoh for me. Tell him, 5'My father made me swear an oath and said, "I am about to die; bury me in the tomb I dug for myself in the land of Canaan." Now let me go up and bury my father; then I will return.'"

6Pharaoh said, "Go up and bury your father, as he made you swear to do."

7So Joseph went up to bury his father. All Pharaoh's officials accompanied him—the dignitaries of his court and all the dignitaries of Egypt— 8besides all the members of Joseph's household and his brothers and those belonging to his father's household. Only their children and their flocks and herds were left in Go-

shen. 9Chariots and horsemen*b* also went up with him. It was a very large company.

10When they reached the threshing floor of Atad, near the Jordan, they lamented loudly and bitterly; and there Joseph observed a seven-day period of mourning for his father. 11When the Canaanites who lived there saw the mourning at the threshing floor of Atad, they said, "The Egyptians are holding a solemn ceremony of mourning." That is why that place near the Jordan is called Abel Mizraim.*c*

12So Jacob's sons did as he had commanded them: 13They carried him to the land of Canaan and buried him in the cave in the field of Machpelah, near Mamre, which Abraham had bought as a burial place from Ephron the Hittite, along with the field. 14After burying his father, Joseph returned to Egypt, together with his brothers and all the others who had gone with him to bury his father.

Joseph Reassures His Brothers

15When Joseph's brothers saw that their father was dead, they said, "What if Joseph holds a grudge against us and pays us back for all the wrongs we did to him?" 16So they sent word to Joseph, saying, "Your father left these instructions before he died: 17'This is what you are to say to Joseph: I ask you to forgive your brothers the sins and the wrongs they committed in treating you so badly.' Now please forgive the sins of the servants of the God of your father." When their message came to him, Joseph wept.

18His brothers then came and threw themselves down before him. "We are your slaves," they said.

19But Joseph said to them, "Don't be afraid. Am I in the place of God? 20You intended to harm me, but God intended it for good to accomplish what is now being done, the saving of many lives. 21So then, don't be afraid.

---

*a*32 Or *the sons of Heth*   *b*9 Or *charioteers*   *c*11 *Abel Mizraim* means *mourning of the Egyptians.*

I will provide for you and your children." And he reassured them and spoke kindly to them.

The Death of Joseph

22Joseph stayed in Egypt, along with all his father's family. He lived a hundred and ten years 23and saw the third generation of Ephraim's children. Also the children of Makir son of Manasseh were placed at birth on Joseph's knees.ᵃ

24Then Joseph said to his brothers,

ᵃ23 That is, were counted as his

"I am about to die. But God will surely come to your aid and take you up out of this land to the land he promised on oath to Abraham, Isaac and Jacob." 25And Joseph made the sons of Israel swear an oath and said, "God will surely come to your aid, and then you must carry my bones up from this place."

26So Joseph died at the age of a hundred and ten. And after they embalmed him, he was placed in a coffin in Egypt.

ET'S LIVE IT!   Genesis 50:15–21

ASKING FORGIVENESS ➠ Can you think of a time when you have done something wrong to someone? Have you ever said something unkind or done something mean to a friend or brother or sister?

Read Genesis 50:15–21. If you have wronged someone, use Joseph's brothers' plan. First write a letter asking that person to forgive you. Then go see him or her in person and ask forgiveness.

Joseph's brothers felt much better when they knew Joseph forgave them. You will feel better when you are forgiven too.

EXODUS

Moses.

WHO WROTE THIS BOOK?

Moses.

WHY WAS THIS BOOK WRITTEN?

Exodus shows how God used his power to rescue the Israelites from slavery.

WHAT HAPPENS IN THIS BOOK?

God brings ten terrible plagues on Egypt. He forces Pharaoh to let God's people go. God gives the Israelites the Ten Commandments and other laws by which to live.

WHAT DO WE LEARN ABOUT GOD IN THIS BOOK?

God uses his power to rescue helpless people. God expects his people to live moral and righteous lives.

WHO IS IMPORTANT IN THIS BOOK?

The important people in this book are Moses and Aaron.

WHEN DID THIS HAPPEN?

The Israelites left Egypt about 1446 B.C. The Law was given at Sinai a year later.

WHERE DID THIS HAPPEN?

Exodus 1–12 took place in Egypt. Most other events took place at Mount Sinai.

WHAT ARE SOME OF THE STORIES IN THIS BOOK?

Baby Moses.	Exodus 2
A burning bush.	Exodus 3
The ten plagues.	Exodus 7–11
The Passover.	Exodus 12
Crossing the Red Sea.	Exodus 14
The Ten Commandments.	Exodus 20
Building the tabernacle.	Exodus 25–27
The golden calf.	Exodus 32

The Israelites Oppressed

1 These are the names of the sons of Israel who went to Egypt with Jacob, each with his family: ²Reuben, Simeon, Levi and Judah; ³Issachar, Zebulun and Benjamin; ⁴Dan and Naphtali; Gad and Asher. ⁵The descendants of Jacob numbered seventy[a] in all; Joseph was already in Egypt.

⁶Now Joseph and all his brothers and all that generation died, ⁷but the Israelites were fruitful and multiplied greatly and became exceedingly numerous, so that the land was filled with them.

⁸Then a new king, who did not know about Joseph, came to power in Egypt. ⁹"Look," he said to his people, "the Israelites have become much too numerous for us. ¹⁰Come, we must deal shrewdly with them or they will become even more numerous and, if war breaks out, will join our enemies, fight against us and leave the country."

¹¹So they put slave masters over them to oppress them with forced labor, and they built Pithom and Rameses as store cities for Pharaoh. ¹²But the more they were oppressed, the more they multiplied and spread; so the Egyptians came to dread the Israelites ¹³and worked them ruthlessly. ¹⁴They made their lives bitter with hard labor in brick and mortar and with all kinds of work in the fields; in all their hard labor the Egyptians used them ruthlessly.

¹⁵The king of Egypt said to the Hebrew midwives, whose names were Shiphrah and Puah, ¹⁶"When you help the Hebrew women in childbirth and observe them on the delivery stool, if it is a boy, kill him; but if it is a girl, let her live." ¹⁷The midwives, however, feared God and did not do what the king of Egypt had told them to do; they let the boys live. ¹⁸Then the king of Egypt summoned the midwives and asked them, "Why have you done this? Why have you let the boys live?"

¹⁹The midwives answered Pharaoh, "Hebrew women are not like Egyptian women; they are vigorous and give birth before the midwives arrive."

²⁰So God was kind to the midwives and the people increased and became even more numerous. ²¹And because the midwives feared God, he gave them families of their own.

²²Then Pharaoh gave this order to all his people: "Every boy that is born[b] you must throw into the Nile, but let every girl live."

Life in Bible Times

MOSES' BASKET BOAT

The Egyptians built boats by tying together bundles of dried papyrus (pu-PIE-rus) reeds. The papyrus reed basket boat that Moses' mother made probably looked like one of those boats.

The Birth of Moses

2 Now a man of the house of Levi married a Levite woman, ²and she became pregnant and gave birth to a son. When she saw that he was a fine child, she hid him for three months. ³But when she could hide him no longer, she got a papyrus basket for him and coated it with tar and pitch. Then she placed the child in it and put it among the reeds along the bank of the Nile. ⁴His sister stood at a distance to see what would happen to him.

⁵Then Pharaoh's daughter went down to the Nile to bathe, and her attendants were walking along the river bank. She saw the basket among the reeds and sent her slave girl to get it. ⁶She opened it and saw the baby. He was crying, and she felt sorry for him. "This is one of the Hebrew babies," she said.

⁷Then his sister asked Pharaoh's daughter, "Shall I go and get one of the Hebrew women to nurse the baby for you?"

⁸"Yes, go," she answered. And the girl went and got the baby's mother. ⁹Pharaoh's daughter said to her, "Take this baby and nurse him for me, and I will pay you." So the woman took the baby and nursed him. ¹⁰When the child grew older, she took him to Pharaoh's daughter and he became her son. She named him Moses,ᵃ saying, "I drew him out of the water."

Moses Flees to Midian

¹¹One day, after Moses had grown up, he went out to where his own people were and watched them at their hard labor. He saw an Egyptian beating a Hebrew, one of his own people. ¹²Glancing this way and that and seeing no one, he killed the Egyptian and hid him in the sand. ¹³The next day he went out and saw two Hebrews fighting. He asked the one in the wrong, "Why are you hitting your fellow Hebrew?"

¹⁴The man said, "Who made you ruler and judge over us? Are you thinking of killing me as you killed the Egyptian?" Then Moses was afraid and thought, "What I did must have become known."

¹⁵When Pharaoh heard of this, he tried to kill Moses, but Moses fled from Pharaoh and went to live in Midian, where he sat down by a well. ¹⁶Now a priest of Midian had seven daughters, and they came to draw water and fill the troughs to water their father's flock. ¹⁷Some shepherds came along and drove them away, but Moses got up and came to their rescue and watered their flock.

¹⁸When the girls returned to Reuel their father, he asked them, "Why have you returned so early today?"

¹⁹They answered, "An Egyptian rescued us from the shepherds. He even drew water for us and watered the flock."

²⁰"And where is he?" he asked his daughters. "Why did you leave him? Invite him to have something to eat."

²¹Moses agreed to stay with the man, who gave his daughter Zipporah to Moses in marriage. ²²Zipporah gave birth to a son, and Moses named him Gershom,ᵇ saying, "I have become an alien in a foreign land."

²³During that long period, the king of Egypt died. The Israelites groaned in their slavery and cried out, and their cry for help because of their slavery went up to God. ²⁴God heard their groaning and he remembered his covenant with Abraham, with Isaac and with Jacob. ²⁵So God looked on the Israelites and was concerned about them.

Moses and the Burning Bush

3 Now Moses was tending the flock of Jethro his father-in-law, the priest of Midian, and he led the flock to the far side of the desert and came to Horeb, the mountain of God. ²There the angel of the LORD ap-

---

ᵃ10 Moses sounds like the Hebrew for *draw out*.   ᵇ22 Gershom sounds like the Hebrew for *an*
alien there.

peared to him in flames of fire from within a bush. Moses saw that though the bush was on fire it did not burn up. [3]So Moses thought, "I will go over and see this strange sight—why the bush does not burn up."

[4]When the LORD saw that he had gone over to look, God called to him from within the bush, "Moses! Moses!"

And Moses said, "Here I am."

[5]"Do not come any closer," God said. "Take off your sandals, for the place where you are standing is holy ground." [6]Then he said, "I am the God of your father, the God of Abraham, the God of Isaac and the God of Jacob." At this, Moses hid his face, because he was afraid to look at God.

[7]The LORD said, "I have indeed seen the misery of my people in Egypt. I have heard them crying out because of their slave drivers, and I am concerned about their suffering. [8]So I have come down to rescue them from the hand of the Egyptians and to bring them up out of that land into a good and spacious land, a land flowing with milk and honey—the home of the Canaanites, Hittites, Amorites, Perizzites, Hivites and Jebusites. [9]And now the cry of the Israelites has reached me, and I have seen the way the Egyptians are oppressing them. [10]So now, go. I am sending you to Pharaoh to bring my people the Israelites out of Egypt."

[11]But Moses said to God, "Who am I, that I should go to Pharaoh and bring the Israelites out of Egypt?"

[12]And God said, "I will be with you. And this will be the sign to you that it is I who have sent you: When you have brought the people out of Egypt, you[a] will worship God on this mountain."

[13]Moses said to God, "Suppose I go to the Israelites and say to them, 'The God of your fathers has sent me to you,' and they ask me, 'What is his name?' Then what shall I tell them?"

[14]God said to Moses, "I AM WHO I AM.[b] This is what you are to say to the Israelites: 'I AM has sent me to you.'"

[15]God also said to Moses, "Say to the Israelites, 'The LORD,[c] the God of your fathers—the God of Abraham, the God of Isaac and the God of Jacob—has sent me to you.' This is my name forever, the name by which I am to be remembered from generation to generation.

[16]"Go, assemble the elders of Israel and say to them, 'The LORD, the God of your fathers—the God of Abraham, Isaac and Jacob— appeared to me and said: I have watched over you and have seen what has been done to you in Egypt. [17]And I have promised to bring you up out of your misery in

---

[a]12 The Hebrew is plural.   [b]14 Or *I WILL BE WHAT I WILL BE*   [c]15 The Hebrew for LORD sounds like and may be derived from the Hebrew for *I AM* in verse 14.

LET'S LIVE IT!   Exodus 3:1–12

DON'T GIVE UP ➠ Sarah was seven. All her friends rode bicycles. But when Sarah got on a two-wheeler, she was afraid. Instead of pushing the pedals hard, she stopped trying. And the bike fell over. "I'm just no good," Sarah thought. "I can't do it."

Read Exodus 3:1–12. In Exodus 3:11 Moses' words, "Who am I," mean the same thing as Sarah's "I'm just no good." Read Exodus 3:12, and find a five-word promise that God gave Moses. How would remembering this promise help Moses not give up? How might it help Sarah, or help you at times when you feel like giving up?

Make a poster for your room. Draw a scene from this Bible story, and print the five-word promise on your poster.

Egypt into the land of the Canaanites, Hittites, Amorites, Perizzites, Hivites and Jebusites—a land flowing with milk and honey.'

18"The elders of Israel will listen to you. Then you and the elders are to go to the king of Egypt and say to him, 'The LORD, the God of the Hebrews, has met with us. Let us take a three-day journey into the desert to offer sacrifices to the LORD our God.' 19But I know that the king of Egypt will not let you go unless a mighty hand compels him. 20So I will stretch out my hand and strike the Egyptians with all the wonders that I will perform among them. After that, he will let you go.

21"And I will make the Egyptians favorably disposed toward this people, so that when you leave you will not go empty-handed. 22Every woman is to ask her neighbor and any woman living in her house for articles of silver and gold and for clothing, which you will put on your sons and daughters. And so you will plunder the Egyptians."

Signs for Moses

4 Moses answered, "What if they do not believe me or listen to me and say, 'The LORD did not appear to you'?"

2Then the LORD said to him, "What is that in your hand?"

"A staff," he replied.

3The LORD said, "Throw it on the ground."

Moses threw it on the ground and it became a snake, and he ran from it. 4Then the LORD said to him, "Reach out your hand and take it by the tail." So Moses reached out and took hold of the snake and it turned back into a staff in his hand. 5"This," said the LORD, "is so that they may believe that the LORD, the God of their fathers—the God of Abraham, the God of Isaac and the God of Jacob—has appeared to you."

6Then the LORD said, "Put your hand inside your cloak." So Moses put his hand into his cloak, and when he took it out, it was leprous,[a] like snow.

7"Now put it back into your cloak," he said. So Moses put his hand back into his cloak, and when he took it out, it was restored, like the rest of his flesh.

8Then the LORD said, "If they do not believe you or pay attention to the first miraculous sign, they may believe the second. 9But if they do not believe these two signs or listen to you, take some water from the Nile and pour it on the dry ground. The water you take from the river will become blood on the ground."

10Moses said to the LORD, "O Lord, I have never been eloquent, neither in the past nor since you have spoken to your servant. I am slow of speech and tongue."

11The LORD said to him, "Who gave man his mouth? Who makes him deaf or mute? Who gives him sight or makes him blind? Is it not I, the LORD? 12Now go; I will help you speak and will teach you what to say."

WORDS TO REMEMBER

4:12 I will help you speak and will teach you what to say.

13But Moses said, "O Lord, please send someone else to do it."

14Then the LORD's anger burned against Moses and he said, "What about your brother, Aaron the Levite? I know he can speak well. He is already on his way to meet you, and his heart will be glad when he sees you. 15You shall speak to him and put words in his mouth; I will help both of you speak and will teach you what to do. 16He will speak to the people for you, and it will be as if he were your mouth and as if you were God to him. 17But take this staff in your hand so you can perform miraculous signs with it."

---

a6 The Hebrew word was used for various diseases affecting the skin—not necessarily leprosy.

Moses Returns to Egypt

[18]Then Moses went back to Jethro his father-in-law and said to him, "Let me go back to my own people in Egypt to see if any of them are still alive."

Jethro said, "Go, and I wish you well."

[19]Now the LORD had said to Moses in Midian, "Go back to Egypt, for all the men who wanted to kill you are dead." [20]So Moses took his wife and sons, put them on a donkey and started back to Egypt. And he took the staff of God in his hand.

[21]The LORD said to Moses, "When you return to Egypt, see that you perform before Pharaoh all the wonders I have given you the power to do. But I will harden his heart so that he will not let the people go. [22]Then say to Pharaoh, 'This is what the LORD says: Israel is my firstborn son, [23]and I told you, "Let my son go, so he may worship me." But you refused to let him go; so I will kill your firstborn son.'"

[24]At a lodging place on the way, the LORD met Moses,[a] and was about to kill him. [25]But Zipporah took a flint knife, cut off her son's foreskin and touched Moses' feet with it.[b] "Surely you are a bridegroom of blood to me," she said. [26]So the LORD let him alone. (At that time she said "bridegroom of blood," referring to circumcision.)

[27]The LORD said to Aaron, "Go into the desert to meet Moses." So he met Moses at the mountain of God and kissed him. [28]Then Moses told Aaron everything the LORD had sent him to say, and also about all the miraculous signs he had commanded him to perform.

[29]Moses and Aaron brought together all the elders of the Israelites, [30]and Aaron told them everything the LORD had said to Moses. He also performed the signs before the people, [31]and they believed. And when they heard that the LORD was concerned about them and had seen their misery, they bowed down and worshiped.

Life In Bible Times

MAKING BRICKS

People made brick by mixing mud with straw and pressing it into molds. An acid in the straw made the bricks stronger. A person could make only about sixty-five bricks a day.

Bricks Without Straw

5 Afterward Moses and Aaron went to Pharaoh and said, "This is what the LORD, the God of Israel, says: 'Let my people go, so that they may hold a festival to me in the desert.'"

[2]Pharaoh said, "Who is the LORD, that I should obey him and let Israel go? I do not know the LORD and I will not let Israel go."

[3]Then they said, "The God of the Hebrews has met with us. Now let us take a three-day journey into the desert to offer sacrifices to the LORD our God, or he may strike us with plagues or with the sword."

[4]But the king of Egypt said, "Moses and Aaron, why are you taking the people away from their labor? Get back to your work!" [5]Then Pharaoh said, "Look, the people of the land are now numerous, and you are stopping them from working."

[6]That same day Pharaoh gave this order to the slave drivers and foremen in charge of the people: [7]"You are no longer to supply the people with straw for making bricks; let them go and gather their own straw. [8]But require them to make the same number of bricks as before; don't re-

duce the quota. They are lazy; that is why they are crying out, 'Let us go and sacrifice to our God.' ⁹Make the work harder for the men so that they keep working and pay no attention to lies."

¹⁰Then the slave drivers and the foremen went out and said to the people, "This is what Pharaoh says: 'I will not give you any more straw. ¹¹Go and get your own straw wherever you can find it, but your work will not be reduced at all.' " ¹²So the people scattered all over Egypt to gather stubble to use for straw. ¹³The slave drivers kept pressing them, saying, "Complete the work required of you for each day, just as when you had straw." ¹⁴The Israelite foremen appointed by Pharaoh's slave drivers were beaten and were asked, "Why didn't you meet your quota of bricks yesterday or today, as before?"

¹⁵Then the Israelite foremen went and appealed to Pharaoh: "Why have you treated your servants this way? ¹⁶Your servants are given no straw, yet we are told, 'Make bricks!' Your servants are being beaten, but the fault is with your own people."

¹⁷Pharaoh said, "Lazy, that's what you are—lazy! That is why you keep saying, 'Let us go and sacrifice to the LORD.' ¹⁸Now get to work. You will

not be given any straw, yet you must produce your full quota of bricks."

¹⁹The Israelite foremen realized they were in trouble when they were told, "You are not to reduce the number of bricks required of you for each day." ²⁰When they left Pharaoh, they found Moses and Aaron waiting to meet them, ²¹and they said, "May the LORD look upon you and judge you! You have made us a stench to Pharaoh and his officials and have put a sword in their hand to kill us."

God Promises Deliverance

²²Moses returned to the LORD and said, "O Lord, why have you brought trouble upon this people? Is this why you sent me? ²³Ever since I went to Pharaoh to speak in your name, he has brought trouble upon this people, and you have not rescued your people at all."

6 Then the LORD said to Moses, "Now you will see what I will do to Pharaoh: Because of my mighty hand he will let them go; because of my mighty hand he will drive them out of his country."

²God also said to Moses, "I am the LORD. ³I appeared to Abraham, to Isaac and to Jacob as God Almighty,ᵃ but by my name the LORDᵇ I did not

---

a3 Hebrew *El-Shaddai*   *b3* See note at Exodus 3:15.

▌ET'S LIVE IT!   Exodus 5:1–21

WHEN THINGS GO WRONG ➡ Read Exodus 5:1–21, and answer these questions.

1. When Moses did what God said, did something good happen right away?
2. Whom did the Israelites blame when they were told to work harder?
3. How did Moses feel when he obeyed God and the troubles of the Israelite slaves were made worse?

Sometimes things get worse before they get better. In the end, Moses led the Israelites to freedom. Remember some things that have happened to you. Draw an up and down line to show ups (happy times) and downs (unhappy times) in your life. If you keep on doing what God says, as Moses did, where do you think your line will go in the end?

make myself known to them.*a* 4I also established my covenant with them to give them the land of Canaan, where they lived as aliens. 5Moreover, I have heard the groaning of the Israelites, whom the Egyptians are enslaving, and I have remembered my covenant.

6"Therefore, say to the Israelites: 'I am the LORD, and I will bring you out from under the yoke of the Egyptians. I will free you from being slaves to them, and I will redeem you with an outstretched arm and with mighty acts of judgment. 7I will take you as my own people, and I will be your God. Then you will know that I am the LORD your God, who brought you out from under the yoke of the Egyptians. 8And I will bring you to the land I swore with uplifted hand to give to Abraham, to Isaac and to Jacob. I will give it to you as a possession. I am the LORD.'"

9Moses reported this to the Israelites, but they did not listen to him because of their discouragement and cruel bondage.

10Then the LORD said to Moses, 11"Go, tell Pharaoh king of Egypt to let the Israelites go out of his country."

12But Moses said to the LORD, "If the Israelites will not listen to me, why would Pharaoh listen to me, since I speak with faltering lips*b*?"

Family Record of Moses and Aaron

13Now the LORD spoke to Moses and Aaron about the Israelites and Pharaoh king of Egypt, and he commanded them to bring the Israelites out of Egypt.

14These were the heads of their families*c*:

The sons of Reuben the firstborn son of Israel were Hanoch and Pallu, Hezron and Carmi. These were the clans of Reuben.

15The sons of Simeon were Jemuel, Jamin, Ohad, Jakin, Zohar and Shaul the son of a Canaanite woman. These were the clans of Simeon.

16These were the names of the sons of Levi according to their records: Gershon, Kohath and Merari. Levi lived 137 years.

17The sons of Gershon, by clans, were Libni and Shimei.

18The sons of Kohath were Amram, Izhar, Hebron and Uzziel. Kohath lived 133 years.

19The sons of Merari were Mahli and Mushi.

These were the clans of Levi according to their records.

20Amram married his father's sister Jochebed, who bore him Aaron and Moses. Amram lived 137 years.

21The sons of Izhar were Korah, Nepheg and Zicri.

22The sons of Uzziel were Mishael, Elzaphan and Sithri.

23Aaron married Elisheba, daughter of Amminadab and sister of Nahshon, and she bore him Nadab and Abihu, Eleazar and Ithamar.

24The sons of Korah were Assir, Elkanah and Abiasaph. These were the Korahite clans.

25Eleazar son of Aaron married one of the daughters of Putiel, and she bore him Phinehas.

These were the heads of the Levite families, clan by clan.

26It was this same Aaron and Moses to whom the LORD said, "Bring the Israelites out of Egypt by their divisions." 27They were the ones who spoke to Pharaoh king of Egypt about bringing the Israelites out of Egypt. It was the same Moses and Aaron.

Aaron to Speak for Moses

28Now when the LORD spoke to Moses in Egypt, 29he said to him, "I am

---

a3 Or *Almighty, and by my name the LORD did I not let myself be known to them?*   *b12* Hebrew *I am uncircumcised of lips*; also in verse 30   *c14* The Hebrew for *families* here and in verse 25 refers to units larger than clans.

the LORD. Tell Pharaoh king of Egypt everything I tell you."

³⁰But Moses said to the LORD, "Since I speak with faltering lips, why would Pharaoh listen to me?"

7 Then the LORD said to Moses, "See, I have made you like God to Pharaoh, and your brother Aaron will be your prophet. ²You are to say everything I command you, and your brother Aaron is to tell Pharaoh to let the Israelites go out of his country. ³But I will harden Pharaoh's heart, and though I multiply my miraculous signs and wonders in Egypt, ⁴he will not listen to you. Then I will lay my hand on Egypt and with mighty acts of judgment I will bring out my divisions, my people the Israelites. ⁵And the Egyptians will know that I am the LORD when I stretch out my hand against Egypt and bring the Israelites out of it."

❓DID YOU KNOW? 7:4

What are God's "mighty acts"?

The ten terrible plagues God brought on Egypt are his "mighty acts." They are also called "miraculous signs and wonders." Each plague was worse than any in Egypt's history. Each one came and went at Moses' command. Each one showed God's power to Pharaoh.

⁶Moses and Aaron did just as the LORD commanded them. ⁷Moses was eighty years old and Aaron eighty-three when they spoke to Pharaoh.

Aaron's Staff Becomes a Snake

⁸The LORD said to Moses and Aaron, ⁹"When Pharaoh says to you, 'Perform a miracle,' then say to Aaron, 'Take your staff and throw it down before Pharaoh,' and it will become a snake."

¹⁰So Moses and Aaron went to Pharaoh and did just as the LORD commanded. Aaron threw his staff down in front of Pharaoh and his offi-

cials, and it became a snake. ¹¹Pharaoh then summoned wise men and sorcerers, and the Egyptian magicians also did the same things by their secret arts: ¹²Each one threw down his staff and it became a snake. But Aaron's staff swallowed up their staffs. ¹³Yet Pharaoh's heart became hard and he would not listen to them, just as the LORD had said.

The Plague of Blood

¹⁴Then the LORD said to Moses, "Pharaoh's heart is unyielding; he refuses to let the people go. ¹⁵Go to Pharaoh in the morning as he goes out to the water. Wait on the bank of the Nile to meet him, and take in your hand the staff that was changed into a snake. ¹⁶Then say to him, 'The LORD, the God of the Hebrews, has sent me to say to you: Let my people go, so that they may worship me in the desert. But until now you have not listened. ¹⁷This is what the LORD says: By this you will know that I am the LORD: With the staff that is in my hand I will strike the water of the Nile, and it will be changed into blood. ¹⁸The fish in the Nile will die, and the river will stink; the Egyptians will not be able to drink its water.'"

¹⁹The LORD said to Moses, "Tell Aaron, 'Take your staff and stretch out your hand over the waters of Egypt—over the streams and canals, over the ponds and all the reservoirs'—and they will turn to blood. Blood will be everywhere in Egypt, even in the wooden buckets and stone jars."

²⁰Moses and Aaron did just as the LORD had commanded. He raised his staff in the presence of Pharaoh and his officials and struck the water of the Nile, and all the water was changed into blood. ²¹The fish in the Nile died, and the river smelled so bad that the Egyptians could not drink its water. Blood was everywhere in Egypt.

²²But the Egyptian magicians did the same things by their secret arts, and Pharaoh's heart became hard; he

would not listen to Moses and Aaron, just as the LORD had said. ²³Instead, he turned and went into his palace, and did not take even this to heart. ²⁴And all the Egyptians dug along the Nile to get drinking water, because they could not drink the water of the river.

The Plague of Frogs

²⁵Seven days passed after the LORD struck the Nile. ¹Then the LORD **8** said to Moses, "Go to Pharaoh and say to him, 'This is what the LORD says: Let my people go, so that they may worship me. ²If you refuse to let them go, I will plague your whole country with frogs. ³The Nile will teem with frogs. They will come up into your palace and your bedroom and onto your bed, into the houses of your officials and on your people, and into your ovens and kneading troughs. ⁴The frogs will go up on you and your people and all your officials.' "

⁵Then the LORD said to Moses, "Tell Aaron, 'Stretch out your hand with your staff over the streams and canals and ponds, and make frogs come up on the land of Egypt.' "

⁶So Aaron stretched out his hand over the waters of Egypt, and the frogs came up and covered the land. ⁷But the magicians did the same things by their secret arts; they also made frogs come up on the land of Egypt.

⁸Pharaoh summoned Moses and Aaron and said, "Pray to the LORD to take the frogs away from me and my people, and I will let your people go to offer sacrifices to the LORD."

⁹Moses said to Pharaoh, "I leave to you the honor of setting the time for me to pray for you and your officials and your people that you and your houses may be rid of the frogs, except for those that remain in the Nile."

¹⁰"Tomorrow," Pharaoh said.

Moses replied, "It will be as you say, so that you may know there is no one like the LORD our God. ¹¹The frogs will leave you and your houses, your officials and your people; they will remain only in the Nile."

¹²After Moses and Aaron left Pharaoh, Moses cried out to the LORD about the frogs he had brought on Pharaoh. ¹³And the LORD did what Moses asked. The frogs died in the houses, in the courtyards and in the fields. ¹⁴They were piled into heaps, and the land reeked of them. ¹⁵But when Pharaoh saw that there was relief, he hardened his heart and would not listen to Moses and Aaron, just as the LORD had said.

The Plague of Gnats

¹⁶Then the LORD said to Moses, "Tell Aaron, 'Stretch out your staff and strike the dust of the ground,' and throughout the land of Egypt the dust will become gnats." ¹⁷They did this, and when Aaron stretched out his hand with the staff and struck the dust of the ground, gnats came upon

---

▚ET'S LIVE IT!   Exodus 7:14–24

HARD HEART, SOFT HEART ➡ A person with a "hard heart" is someone who will not do what God says. Read this story. What do you think made Pharaoh's heart hard?

On a warm, sunny day take two small plastic bowls. In one bowl, put a marshmallow. In the other bowl, put an ice cube. Put both bowls in the sun for one hour. What happened to the ice cube? What happened to the marshmallow? In this experiment, the hot sun is like God's Word. The ice cube is like the heart of people who trust God. The marshmallow is like the heart of Pharaoh.

Let the melted ice and the hardened marshmallow remind you to keep your heart soft and obey God when you hear his Word.

men and animals. All the dust throughout the land of Egypt became gnats. [18]But when the magicians tried to produce gnats by their secret arts, they could not. And the gnats were on men and animals.

[19]The magicians said to Pharaoh, "This is the finger of God." But Pharaoh's heart was hard and he would not listen, just as the LORD had said.

The Plague of Flies

[20]Then the LORD said to Moses, "Get up early in the morning and confront Pharaoh as he goes to the water and say to him, 'This is what the LORD says: Let my people go, so that they may worship me. [21]If you do not let my people go, I will send swarms of flies on you and your officials, on your people and into your houses. The houses of the Egyptians will be full of flies, and even the ground where they are.

[22]" 'But on that day I will deal differently with the land of Goshen, where my people live; no swarms of flies will be there, so that you will know that I, the LORD, am in this land. [23]I will make a distinction[a] between my people and your people. This miraculous sign will occur tomorrow.' "

[24]And the LORD did this. Dense swarms of flies poured into Pharaoh's palace and into the houses of his officials, and throughout Egypt the land was ruined by the flies.

[25]Then Pharaoh summoned Moses and Aaron and said, "Go, sacrifice to your God here in the land."

[26]But Moses said, "That would not be right. The sacrifices we offer the LORD our God would be detestable to the Egyptians. And if we offer sacrifices that are detestable in their eyes, will they not stone us? [27]We must take a three-day journey into the desert to offer sacrifices to the LORD our God, as he commands us."

[28]Pharaoh said, "I will let you go to offer sacrifices to the LORD your God in the desert, but you must not go very far. Now pray for me."

[29]Moses answered, "As soon as I leave you, I will pray to the LORD, and tomorrow the flies will leave Pharaoh and his officials and his people. Only be sure that Pharaoh does not act deceitfully again by not letting the people go to offer sacrifices to the LORD."

[30]Then Moses left Pharaoh and prayed to the LORD, [31]and the LORD did what Moses asked: The flies left Pharaoh and his officials and his people; not a fly remained. [32]But this time also Pharaoh hardened his heart and would not let the people go.

The Plague on Livestock

9 Then the LORD said to Moses, "Go to Pharaoh and say to him,

[a]23 Septuagint and Vulgate; Hebrew *will put a deliverance*

Life in Bible Times

PHARAOH ON HIS THRONE

When Pharaoh summoned Moses he probably sat on an impressive throne, holding the symbols of his power. Even though Pharaoh was the ruler of all Egypt, he could do nothing against the power of God.

'This is what the LORD, the God of the Hebrews, says: "Let my people go, so that they may worship me." ²If you refuse to let them go and continue to hold them back, ³the hand of the LORD will bring a terrible plague on your livestock in the field—on your horses and donkeys and camels and on your cattle and sheep and goats. ⁴But the LORD will make a distinction between the livestock of Israel and that of Egypt, so that no animal belonging to the Israelites will die.' "

⁵The LORD set a time and said, "Tomorrow the LORD will do this in the land." ⁶And the next day the LORD did it: All the livestock of the Egyptians died, but not one animal belonging to the Israelites died. ⁷Pharaoh sent men to investigate and found that not even one of the animals of the Israelites had died. Yet his heart was unyielding and he would not let the people go.

The Plague of Boils

⁸Then the LORD said to Moses and Aaron, "Take handfuls of soot from a furnace and have Moses toss it into the air in the presence of Pharaoh. ⁹It will become fine dust over the whole land of Egypt, and festering boils will break out on men and animals throughout the land."

¹⁰So they took soot from a furnace and stood before Pharaoh. Moses tossed it into the air, and festering boils broke out on men and animals. ¹¹The magicians could not stand before Moses because of the boils that were on them and on all the Egyptians. ¹²But the LORD hardened Pharaoh's heart and he would not listen to Moses and Aaron, just as the LORD had said to Moses.

The Plague of Hail

¹³Then the LORD said to Moses, "Get up early in the morning, confront Pharaoh and say to him, 'This is what the LORD, the God of the Hebrews, says: Let my people go, so that they may worship me, ¹⁴or this time I will send the full force of my plagues against you and against your officials and your people, so you may know that there is no one like me in all the earth. ¹⁵For by now I could have stretched out my hand and struck you and your people with a plague that would have wiped you off the earth. ¹⁶But I have raised you up ᵃ for this very purpose, that I might show you my power and that my name might be proclaimed in all the earth. ¹⁷You still set yourself against my people and will not let them go. ¹⁸Therefore, at this time tomorrow I will send the worst hailstorm that has ever fallen on Egypt, from the day it was founded till now. ¹⁹Give an order now to bring your livestock and everything you have in the field to a place of shelter, because the hail will fall on every man and animal that has not been brought in and is still out in the field, and they will die.' "

²⁰Those officials of Pharaoh who feared the word of the LORD hurried to bring their slaves and their livestock inside. ²¹But those who ignored the word of the LORD left their slaves and livestock in the field.

²²Then the LORD said to Moses, "Stretch out your hand toward the sky so that hail will fall all over Egypt—on men and animals and on everything growing in the fields of Egypt." ²³When Moses stretched out his staff toward the sky, the LORD sent thunder and hail, and lightning flashed down to the ground. So the LORD rained hail on the land of Egypt; ²⁴hail fell and lightning flashed back and forth. It was the worst storm in all the land of Egypt since it had become a nation. ²⁵Throughout Egypt hail struck everything in the fields—both men and animals; it beat down everything growing in the fields and stripped every tree. ²⁶The only place it did not hail was the land of Goshen, where the Israelites were.

²⁷Then Pharaoh summoned Moses and Aaron. "This time I have

ᵃ16 Or have spared you

sinned," he said to them. "The LORD is in the right, and I and my people are in the wrong. 28Pray to the LORD, for we have had enough thunder and hail. I will let you go; you don't have to stay any longer."

29Moses replied, "When I have gone out of the city, I will spread out my hands in prayer to the LORD. The thunder will stop and there will be no more hail, so you may know that the earth is the LORD's. 30But I know that you and your officials still do not fear the LORD God."

31(The flax and barley were destroyed, since the barley had headed and the flax was in bloom. 32The wheat and spelt, however, were not destroyed, because they ripen later.)

33Then Moses left Pharaoh and went out of the city. He spread out his hands toward the LORD; the thunder and hail stopped, and the rain no longer poured down on the land. 34When Pharaoh saw that the rain and hail and thunder had stopped, he sinned again: He and his officials hardened their hearts. 35So Pharaoh's heart was hard and he would not let the Israelites go, just as the LORD had said through Moses.

The Plague of Locusts

10 Then the LORD said to Moses, "Go to Pharaoh, for I have hardened his heart and the hearts of his officials so that I may perform these miraculous signs of mine among them 2that you may tell your children and grandchildren how I dealt harshly with the Egyptians and how I performed my signs among them, and that you may know that I am the LORD."

3So Moses and Aaron went to Pharaoh and said to him, "This is what the LORD, the God of the Hebrews, says: 'How long will you refuse to humble yourself before me? Let my people go, so that they may worship me. 4If you refuse to let them go, I will bring locusts into your country tomorrow. 5They will cover the face of the

ground so that it cannot be seen. They will devour what little you have left after the hail, including every tree that is growing in your fields. 6They will fill your houses and those of all your officials and all the Egyptians—something neither your fathers nor your forefathers have ever seen from the day they settled in this land till now.'" Then Moses turned and left Pharaoh.

7Pharaoh's officials said to him, "How long will this man be a snare to us? Let the people go, so that they may worship the LORD their God. Do you not yet realize that Egypt is ruined?"

8Then Moses and Aaron were brought back to Pharaoh. "Go, worship the LORD your God," he said. "But just who will be going?"

9Moses answered, "We will go with our young and old, with our sons and daughters, and with our flocks and herds, because we are to celebrate a festival to the LORD."

10Pharaoh said, "The LORD be with you—if I let you go, along with your women and children! Clearly you are bent on evil.a 11No! Have only the men go; and worship the LORD, since that's what you have been asking for." Then Moses and Aaron were driven out of Pharaoh's presence.

12And the LORD said to Moses, "Stretch out your hand over Egypt so that locusts will swarm over the land and devour everything growing in the fields, everything left by the hail."

13So Moses stretched out his staff over Egypt, and the LORD made an east wind blow across the land all that day and all that night. By morning the wind had brought the locusts; 14they invaded all Egypt and settled down in every area of the country in great numbers. Never before had there been such a plague of locusts, nor will there ever be again. 15They covered all the ground until it was black. They devoured all that was left after the hail—everything growing in the fields and the fruit on the trees. Nothing green remained on tree or plant in all the land of Egypt.

[16]Pharaoh quickly summoned Moses and Aaron and said, "I have sinned against the LORD your God and against you. [17]Now forgive my sin once more and pray to the LORD your God to take this deadly plague away from me."

[18]Moses then left Pharaoh and prayed to the LORD. [19]And the LORD changed the wind to a very strong west wind, which caught up the locusts and carried them into the Red Sea.[a] Not a locust was left anywhere in Egypt. [20]But the LORD hardened Pharaoh's heart, and he would not let the Israelites go.

The Plague of Darkness

[21]Then the LORD said to Moses, "Stretch out your hand toward the sky so that darkness will spread over Egypt—darkness that can be felt." [22]So Moses stretched out his hand toward the sky, and total darkness covered all Egypt for three days. [23]No one could see anyone else or leave his place for three days. Yet all the Israelites had light in the places where they lived.

[24]Then Pharaoh summoned Moses and said, "Go, worship the LORD. Even your women and children may go with you; only leave your flocks and herds behind."

[25]But Moses said, "You must allow us to have sacrifices and burnt offerings to present to the LORD our God. [26]Our livestock too must go with us; not a hoof is to be left behind. We have to use some of them in worshiping the LORD our God, and until we get there we will not know what we are to use to worship the LORD."

[27]But the LORD hardened Pharaoh's heart, and he was not willing to let them go. [28]Pharaoh said to Moses, "Get out of my sight! Make sure you do not appear before me again! The day you see my face you will die."

[29]"Just as you say," Moses replied,

"I will never appear before you again."

The Plague on the Firstborn

11 Now the LORD had said to Moses, "I will bring one more plague on Pharaoh and on Egypt. After that, he will let you go from here, and when he does, he will drive you out completely. [2]Tell the people that men and women alike are to ask their neighbors for articles of silver and gold." [3](The LORD made the Egyptians favorably disposed toward the people, and Moses himself was highly regarded in Egypt by Pharaoh's officials and by the people.)

[4]So Moses said, "This is what the LORD says: 'About midnight I will go throughout Egypt. [5]Every firstborn son in Egypt will die, from the firstborn son of Pharaoh, who sits on the throne, to the firstborn son of the slave girl, who is at her hand mill, and all the firstborn of the cattle as well. [6]There will be loud wailing throughout Egypt—worse than there has ever been or ever will be again. [7]But among the Israelites not a dog will bark at any man or animal.' Then you will know that the LORD makes a distinction between Egypt and Israel. [8]All these officials of yours will come to me, bowing down before me and saying, 'Go, you and all the people who follow you!' After that I will leave." Then Moses, hot with anger, left Pharaoh.

[9]The LORD had said to Moses, "Pharaoh will refuse to listen to you—so that my wonders may be multiplied in Egypt." [10]Moses and Aaron performed all these wonders before Pharaoh, but the LORD hardened Pharaoh's heart, and he would not let the Israelites go out of his country.

The Passover

12 The LORD said to Moses and Aaron in Egypt, [2]"This month is to be for you the first month, the first month of your year. [3]Tell the

a19 Hebrew *Yam Suph*; that is, Sea of Reeds

whole community of Israel that on the tenth day of this month each man is to take a lamb[a] for his family, one for each household. [4]If any household is too small for a whole lamb, they must share one with their nearest neighbor, having taken into account the number of people there are. You are to determine the amount of lamb needed in accordance with what each person will eat. [5]The animals you choose must be year-old males without defect, and you may take them from the sheep or the goats. [6]Take care of them until the fourteenth day of the month, when all the people of the community of Israel must slaughter them at twilight. [7]Then they are to take some of the blood and put it on the sides and tops of the doorframes of the houses where they eat the lambs. [8]That same night they are to eat the meat roasted over the fire, along with bitter herbs, and bread made without yeast. [9]Do not eat the meat raw or cooked in water, but roast it over the fire—head, legs and inner parts. [10]Do not leave any of it till morning; if some is left till morning, you must burn it. [11]This is how you are to eat it: with your cloak tucked into your belt, your sandals on your feet and your staff in your hand. Eat it in haste; it is the LORD's Passover.

❓DID YOU KNOW?   12:11

What is the Passover?

Passover is the name given to the night that God killed the firstborn sons of the Egyptians but "passed over" Israelite families. God told the Israelites to hold a special meal each year on that date. This Passover meal helps Jewish families remember that God saved their ancestors when they were slaves in Egypt.

---

[12]"On that same night I will pass through Egypt and strike down every firstborn—both men and animals— and I will bring judgment on all the gods of Egypt. I am the LORD. [13]The blood will be a sign for you on the houses where you are; and when I see the blood, I will pass over you. No destructive plague will touch you when I strike Egypt.

[14]"This is a day you are to commemorate; for the generations to come you shall celebrate it as a festival to the LORD—a lasting ordinance. [15]For seven days you are to eat bread made without yeast. On the first day remove the yeast from your houses, for whoever eats anything with yeast in it from the first day through the seventh must be cut off from Israel. [16]On the first day hold a sacred assembly, and another one on the seventh day. Do no work at all on these days, except to prepare food for everyone to eat—that is all you may do.

[17]"Celebrate the Feast of Unleavened Bread, because it was on this very day that I brought your divisions out of Egypt. Celebrate this day as a lasting ordinance for the generations to come. [18]In the first month you are to eat bread made without yeast, from the evening of the fourteenth day until the evening of the twenty-first day. [19]For seven days no yeast is to be found in your houses. And whoever eats anything with yeast in it must be cut off from the community of Israel, whether he is an alien or native-born. [20]Eat nothing made with yeast. Wherever you live, you must eat unleavened bread."

[21]Then Moses summoned all the elders of Israel and said to them, "Go at once and select the animals for your families and slaughter the Passover lamb. [22]Take a bunch of hyssop, dip it into the blood in the basin and put some of the blood on the top and on both sides of the doorframe. Not one of you shall go out the door of his house until morning. [23]When the LORD goes through the land to strike down the Egyptians, he will see the

---

[a]3 The Hebrew word can mean *lamb* or *kid*; also in verse 4.

blood on the top and sides of the doorframe and will pass over that doorway, and he will not permit the destroyer to enter your houses and strike you down.

24"Obey these instructions as a lasting ordinance for you and your descendants. 25When you enter the land that the LORD will give you as he promised, observe this ceremony. 26And when your children ask you, 'What does this ceremony mean to you?' 27then tell them, 'It is the Passover sacrifice to the LORD, who passed over the houses of the Israelites in Egypt and spared our homes when he struck down the Egyptians.'" Then the people bowed down and worshiped. 28The Israelites did just what the LORD commanded Moses and Aaron.

29At midnight the LORD struck down all the firstborn in Egypt, from the firstborn of Pharaoh, who sat on the throne, to the firstborn of the prisoner, who was in the dungeon, and the firstborn of all the livestock as well. 30Pharaoh and all his officials and all the Egyptians got up during the night, and there was loud wailing in Egypt, for there was not a house without someone dead.

The Exodus

31During the night Pharaoh summoned Moses and Aaron and said, "Up! Leave my people, you and the Israelites! Go, worship the LORD as you have requested. 32Take your flocks and herds, as you have said, and go. And also bless me."

33The Egyptians urged the people to hurry and leave the country. "For otherwise," they said, "we will all die!" 34So the people took their dough before the yeast was added, and carried it on their shoulders in kneading troughs wrapped in clothing. 35The Israelites did as Moses instructed and asked the Egyptians for articles of silver and gold and for clothing. 36The LORD had made the Egyptians favorably disposed toward the people, and they gave them what they asked for; so they plundered the Egyptians.

37The Israelites journeyed from Rameses to Succoth. There were about six hundred thousand men on foot, besides women and children. 38Many other people went up with them, as well as large droves of livestock, both flocks and herds. 39With the dough they had brought from Egypt, they baked cakes of unleavened bread. The dough was without yeast because they had been driven out of Egypt and did not have time to prepare food for themselves.

40Now the length of time the Israelite people lived in Egypt*a* was 430 years. 41At the end of the 430 years, to the very day, all the LORD's divisions left Egypt. 42Because the LORD kept vigil that night to bring them out of Egypt, on this night all the Israelites are to keep vigil to honor the LORD for the generations to come.

Passover Restrictions

43The LORD said to Moses and Aaron, "These are the regulations for the Passover:

"No foreigner is to eat of it. 44Any slave you have bought may eat of it after you have circumcised him, 45but a temporary resident and a hired worker may not eat of it.

46"It must be eaten inside one house; take none of the meat outside the house. Do not break any of the bones. 47The whole community of Israel must celebrate it.

48"An alien living among you who wants to celebrate the LORD's Passover must have all the males in his household circumcised; then he may take part like one born in the land. No uncircumcised male may eat of it. 49The same law applies to the native-born and to the alien living among you."

50All the Israelites did just what the LORD had commanded Moses and Aaron. 51And on that very day the

---

a40 Masoretic Text; Samaritan Pentateuch and Septuagint *Egypt and Canaan*

LORD brought the Israelites out of Egypt by their divisions.

Consecration of the Firstborn

13 The LORD said to Moses, ²"Consecrate to me every firstborn male. The first offspring of every womb among the Israelites belongs to me, whether man or animal."

³Then Moses said to the people, "Commemorate this day, the day you came out of Egypt, out of the land of slavery, because the LORD brought you out of it with a mighty hand. Eat nothing containing yeast. ⁴Today, in the month of Abib, you are leaving. ⁵When the LORD brings you into the land of the Canaanites, Hittites, Amorites, Hivites and Jebusites—the land he swore to your forefathers to give you, a land flowing with milk and honey—you are to observe this ceremony in this month: ⁶For seven days eat bread made without yeast and on the seventh day hold a festival to the LORD. ⁷Eat unleavened bread during those seven days; nothing with yeast in it is to be seen among you, nor shall any yeast be seen anywhere within your borders. ⁸On that day tell your son, 'I do this because of what the LORD did for me when I came out of Egypt.' ⁹This observance will be for you like a sign on your hand and a reminder on your forehead that the law of the LORD is to be on your lips. For the LORD brought you out of Egypt with his mighty hand. ¹⁰You must keep this ordinance at the appointed time year after year.

¹¹"After the LORD brings you into the land of the Canaanites and gives it to you, as he promised on oath to you and your forefathers, ¹²you are to give over to the LORD the first offspring of every womb. All the firstborn males of your livestock belong to the LORD. ¹³Redeem with a lamb every firstborn donkey, but if you do not redeem it, break its neck. Redeem every firstborn among your sons.

¹⁴"In days to come, when your son asks you, 'What does this mean?' say to him, 'With a mighty hand the LORD brought us out of Egypt, out of the land of slavery. ¹⁵When Pharaoh stubbornly refused to let us go, the LORD killed every firstborn in Egypt, both man and animal. This is why I sacrifice to the LORD the first male offspring of every womb and redeem each of my firstborn sons.' ¹⁶And it will be like a sign on your hand and a symbol on your forehead that the LORD brought us out of Egypt with his mighty hand."

Crossing the Sea

¹⁷When Pharaoh let the people go, God did not lead them on the road through the Philistine country, though that was shorter. For God said, "If they face war, they might change their minds and return to Egypt." ¹⁸So God led the people around by the desert road toward the Red Sea.ᵃ The Israelites went up out of Egypt armed for battle.

¹⁹Moses took the bones of Joseph with him because Joseph had made the sons of Israel swear an oath. He had said, "God will surely come to your aid, and then you must carry my bones up with you from this place."ᵇ ²⁰After leaving Succoth they camped at Etham on the edge of the desert. ²¹By day the LORD went ahead of them in a pillar of cloud to guide them on their way and by night in a pillar of fire to give them light, so that they could travel by day or night. ²²Neither the pillar of cloud by day nor the pillar of fire by night left its place in front of the people.

14 Then the LORD said to Moses, ²"Tell the Israelites to turn back and encamp near Pi Hahiroth, between Migdol and the sea. They are to encamp by the sea, directly opposite Baal Zephon. ³Pharaoh will think, 'The Israelites are wandering around the land in confusion, hemmed in by the desert.' ⁴And I will harden Pharaoh's heart, and he will pursue them. But I will gain glory for

---

ᵃ18 Hebrew *Yam Suph*; that is, Sea of Reeds   ᵇ19 See Gen. 50:25.

myself through Pharaoh and all his army, and the Egyptians will know that I am the LORD." So the Israelites did this.

⁵When the king of Egypt was told that the people had fled, Pharaoh and his officials changed their minds about them and said, "What have we done? We have let the Israelites go and have lost their services!" ⁶So he had his chariot made ready and took his army with him. ⁷He took six hundred of the best chariots, along with all the other chariots of Egypt, with officers over all of them. ⁸The LORD hardened the heart of Pharaoh king of Egypt, so that he pursued the Israelites, who were marching out boldly. ⁹The Eyptians—all Pharaoh's horses and chariots, horsemen*a* and troops—pursued the Israelites and overtook them as they camped by the sea near Pi Hahiroth, opposite Baal Zephon.

¹⁰As Pharaoh approached, the Israelites looked up, and there were the Egyptians, marching after them. They were terrified and cried out to the LORD. ¹¹They said to Moses, "Was it because there were no graves in Egypt that you brought us to the desert to die? What have you done to us by bringing us out of Egypt? ¹²Didn't we say to you in Egypt, 'Leave us alone; let us serve the Egyptians'? It would have been better for us to serve the Egyptians than to die in the desert!"

¹³Moses answered the people, "Do not be afraid. Stand firm and you will see the deliverance the LORD will bring you today. The Egyptians you see today you will never see again. ¹⁴The LORD will fight for you; you need only to be still."

¹⁵Then the LORD said to Moses, "Why are you crying out to me? Tell the Israelites to move on. ¹⁶Raise your staff and stretch out your hand over the sea to divide the water so that the Israelites can go through the sea on dry ground. ¹⁷I will harden the hearts of the Egyptians so that they will go in after them. And I will gain glory through Pharaoh and all his army, through his chariots and his horsemen. ¹⁸The Egyptians will know that I am the LORD when I gain glory through Pharaoh, his chariots and his horsemen."

a9 Or charioteers; also in verses 17, 18, 23, 26 and 28

LET'S LIVE IT!   Exodus 14:1–31

SAND, SEA, AND SORRY ➡ Here's a fun game you can play at a birthday party or any other time. Mark off part of your yard to be "sand," but make most of it "sea." Divide into two teams. One team is Israelite, the other team is Egyptian. The Egyptians try to recapture their Israelite slaves before the whistle blows and the sea covers them up.

Follow these rules: 1. Everyone must walk. No one can run. 2. The Israelites get a three-second head start walking into the "sea." 3. Egyptians must tag the Israelites in the "sea" to capture them and then walk them slowly back to the "sand." A captured Israelite brought back to the sand is out of the game. 4. At the beginning decide how many seconds each "play" will last. Blow a whistle when that play is over. 5. An Egyptian caught in the "sea" when the whistle blows has "drowned" and is out of the game. Israelites cannot be hurt by the water when the whistle blows. 6. The team that has all its members either captured or drowned loses.

After you play the game, talk about the story in Exodus 14:1–31. In that Bible story how many Israelites were captured? How many Egyptian soldiers escaped drowning? God really does take care of his own.

[19]Then the angel of God, who had been traveling in front of Israel's army, withdrew and went behind them. The pillar of cloud also moved from in front and stood behind them, [20]coming between the armies of Egypt and Israel. Throughout the night the cloud brought darkness to the one side and light to the other side; so neither went near the other all night long.

[21]Then Moses stretched out his hand over the sea, and all that night the LORD drove the sea back with a strong east wind and turned it into dry land. The waters were divided, [22]and the Israelites went through the sea on dry ground, with a wall of water on their right and on their left.

[23]The Egyptians pursued them, and all Pharaoh's horses and chariots and horsemen followed them into the sea. [24]During the last watch of the night the LORD looked down from the pillar of fire and cloud at the Egyptian army and threw it into confusion. [25]He made the wheels of their chariots come off[a] so that they had difficulty driving. And the Egyptians said, "Let's get away from the Israelites! The LORD is fighting for them against Egypt."

[26]Then the LORD said to Moses, "Stretch out your hand over the sea so that the waters may flow back over the Egyptians and their chariots and horsemen." [27]Moses stretched out his hand over the sea, and at daybreak the sea went back to its place. The Egyptians were fleeing toward[b] it, and the LORD swept them into the sea. [28]The water flowed back and covered the chariots and horsemen—the entire army of Pharaoh that had followed the Israelites into the sea. Not one of them survived.

[29]But the Israelites went through the sea on dry ground, with a wall of water on their right and on their left. [30]That day the LORD saved Israel from the hands of the Egyptians, and Israel saw the Egyptians lying dead on the shore. [31]And when the Israelites saw the great power the LORD displayed against the Egyptians, the people feared the LORD and put their trust in him and in Moses his servant.

The Song of Moses and Miriam

15 Then Moses and the Israelites sang this song to the LORD:

"I will sing to the LORD,
  for he is highly exalted.
The horse and its rider
  he has hurled into the sea.
[2]The LORD is my strength and my song;
  he has become my salvation.
He is my God, and I will praise him,
  my father's God, and I will exalt him.
[3]The LORD is a warrior;
  the LORD is his name.
[4]Pharaoh's chariots and his army
  he has hurled into the sea.
The best of Pharaoh's officers
  are drowned in the Red Sea.[c]
[5]The deep waters have covered them;
  they sank to the depths like a stone.

[6]"Your right hand, O LORD,
  was majestic in power.
Your right hand, O LORD,
  shattered the enemy.
[7]In the greatness of your majesty
  you threw down those who opposed you.
You unleashed your burning anger;
  it consumed them like stubble.
[8]By the blast of your nostrils
  the waters piled up.
The surging waters stood firm like a wall;
  the deep waters congealed in the heart of the sea.

[9]"The enemy boasted,

[a]25 Or *He jammed the wheels of their chariots* (see Samaritan Pentateuch, Septuagint and Syriac) [b]27 Or *from*   [c]4 Hebrew *Yam Suph*; that is, Sea of Reeds; also in verse 22

'I will pursue, I will overtake
them.
I will divide the spoils;
I will gorge myself on them.
I will draw my sword
and my hand will destroy them.'
10But you blew with your breath,
and the sea covered them.
They sank like lead
in the mighty waters.

11"Who among the gods is like you,
O LORD?
Who is like you—
majestic in holiness,
awesome in glory,
working wonders?
12You stretched out your right
hand
and the earth swallowed them.

13"In your unfailing love you will
lead
the people you have redeemed.
In your strength you will guide
them
to your holy dwelling.
14The nations will hear and
tremble;
anguish will grip the people of
Philistia.
15The chiefs of Edom will be
terrified,
the leaders of Moab will be
seized with trembling,
the people*a* of Canaan will melt
away;
16 terror and dread will fall upon
them.
By the power of your arm
they will be as still as a stone—
until your people pass by, O LORD,
until the people you bought*b*
pass by.
17You will bring them in and plant
them
on the mountain of your
inheritance—
the place, O LORD, you made for
your dwelling,
the sanctuary, O Lord, your
hands established.
18The LORD will reign
for ever and ever."

19When Pharaoh's horses, chariots
and horsemen*c* went into the sea, the
LORD brought the waters of the sea
back over them, but the Israelites
walked through the sea on dry
ground. 20Then Miriam the prophetess, Aaron's sister, took a tambourine
in her hand, and all the women followed her, with tambourines and
dancing. 21Miriam sang to them:

"Sing to the LORD,
for he is highly exalted.
The horse and its rider
he has hurled into the sea."

The Waters of Marah and Elim

22Then Moses led Israel from the
Red Sea and they went into the
Desert of Shur. For three days they
traveled in the desert without finding water. 23When they came to Marah, they could not drink its water
because it was bitter. (That is why
the place is called Marah.*d*) 24So the
people grumbled against Moses, saying, "What are we to drink?"
25Then Moses cried out to the LORD,
and the LORD showed him a piece of
wood. He threw it into the water, and
the water became sweet.
There the LORD made a decree and
a law for them, and there he tested
them. 26He said, "If you listen carefully to the voice of the LORD your
God and do what is right in his eyes,
if you pay attention to his commands
and keep all his decrees, I will not
bring on you any of the diseases I
brought on the Egyptians, for I am
the LORD, who heals you."
27Then they came to Elim, where
there were twelve springs and seventy palm trees, and they camped there
near the water.

Manna and Quail

16 The whole Israelite community set out from Elim and
came to the Desert of Sin, which is
between Elim and Sinai, on the fifteenth day of the second month after
they had come out of Egypt. 2In the

---

*a*15 Or *rulers*   *b*16 Or *created*   *c*19 Or *charioteers*   *d*23 *Marah* means *bitter.*

desert the whole community grumbled against Moses and Aaron. ³The Israelites said to them, "If only we had died by the LORD's hand in Egypt! There we sat around pots of meat and ate all the food we wanted, but you have brought us out into this desert to starve this entire assembly to death."

⁴Then the LORD said to Moses, "I will rain down bread from heaven for you. The people are to go out each day and gather enough for that day. In this way I will test them and see whether they will follow my instructions. ⁵On the sixth day they are to prepare what they bring in, and that is to be twice as much as they gather on the other days."

⁶So Moses and Aaron said to all the Israelites, "In the evening you will know that it was the LORD who brought you out of Egypt, ⁷and in the morning you will see the glory of the LORD, because he has heard your grumbling against him. Who are we, that you should grumble against us?" ⁸Moses also said, "You will know that it was the LORD when he gives you meat to eat in the evening and all the bread you want in the morning, because he has heard your grumbling against him. Who are we? You are not grumbling against us, but against the LORD."

⁹Then Moses told Aaron, "Say to the entire Israelite community, 'Come before the LORD, for he has heard your grumbling.'"

¹⁰While Aaron was speaking to the whole Israelite community, they looked toward the desert, and there was the glory of the LORD appearing in the cloud.

¹¹The LORD said to Moses, ¹²"I have heard the grumbling of the Israelites. Tell them, 'At twilight you will eat meat, and in the morning you will be filled with bread. Then you will know that I am the LORD your God.'"

¹³That evening quail came and covered the camp, and in the morning there was a layer of dew around the camp. ¹⁴When the dew was gone, thin flakes like frost on the ground appeared on the desert floor. ¹⁵When the Israelites saw it, they said to each other, "What is it?" For they did not know what it was.

MANNA

Manna was a special food that God gave the Israelites the entire time they were in the desert. The people collected the manna from the ground every day except the Sabbath. The Hebrew meaning for the word *manna* was probably "What is it?" The Israelites didn't know exactly what manna was when they first saw it, but they soon realized it was a delicious and nourishing food given to them by God.

Moses said to them, "It is the bread the LORD has given you to eat. ¹⁶This is what the LORD has commanded: 'Each one is to gather as much as he needs. Take an omer ᵃ for each person you have in your tent.'"

¹⁷The Israelites did as they were told; some gathered much, some little. ¹⁸And when they measured it by the omer, he who gathered much did not have too much, and he who gathered little did not have too little. Each one gathered as much as he needed.

¹⁹Then Moses said to them, "No one is to keep any of it until morning."

²⁰However, some of them paid no attention to Moses; they kept part of it until morning, but it was full of maggots and began to smell. So Moses was angry with them.

ᵃ16 That is, probably about 2 quarts (about 2 liters); also in verses 18, 32, 33 and 36

21Each morning everyone gathered as much as he needed, and when the sun grew hot, it melted away. 22On the sixth day, they gathered twice as much—two omers[a] for each person —and the leaders of the community came and reported this to Moses. 23He said to them, "This is what the LORD commanded: 'Tomorrow is to be a day of rest, a holy Sabbath to the LORD. So bake what you want to bake and boil what you want to boil. Save whatever is left and keep it until morning.'"

24So they saved it until morning, as Moses commanded, and it did not stink or get maggots in it. 25"Eat it today," Moses said, "because today is a Sabbath to the LORD. You will not find any of it on the ground today. 26Six days you are to gather it, but on the seventh day, the Sabbath, there will not be any."

27Nevertheless, some of the people went out on the seventh day to gather it, but they found none. 28Then the LORD said to Moses, "How long will you[b] refuse to keep my commands and my instructions? 29Bear in mind that the LORD has given you the Sabbath; that is why on the sixth day he gives you bread for two days. Everyone is to stay where he is on the seventh day; no one is to go out." 30So the people rested on the seventh day.

31The people of Israel called the bread manna.[c] It was white like coriander seed and tasted like wafers made with honey. 32Moses said, "This is what the LORD has commanded: 'Take an omer of manna and keep it for the generations to come, so they can see the bread I gave you to eat in the desert when I brought you out of Egypt.'"

33So Moses said to Aaron, "Take a jar and put an omer of manna in it. Then place it before the LORD to be kept for the generations to come."

34As the LORD commanded Moses, Aaron put the manna in front of the Testimony, that it might be kept. 35The Israelites ate manna forty years, until they came to a land that was settled; they ate manna until they reached the border of Canaan. 36(An omer is one tenth of an ephah.)

Water From the Rock

17 The whole Israelite community set out from the Desert of Sin, traveling from place to place as the LORD commanded. They camped at Rephidim, but there was no water for the people to drink. 2So they quarreled with Moses and said, "Give us water to drink."

Moses replied, "Why do you quarrel with me? Why do you put the LORD to the test?"

3But the people were thirsty for wa-

a22 That is, probably about 4 quarts (about 4.5 liters)   b28 The Hebrew is plural.
c31 Manna means What is it? (see verse 15).

▉ET'S LIVE IT!   Exodus 16:13–30

DAILY BREAD ➡ Moses probably led some two million Israelites in the desert. God provided them with a special kind of food, called *manna*. Read Exodus 16:13–30, and answer these questions. 1. What happened when people took more manna than they could eat in one day? 2. What happened when they took extra on the sixth day?

God could have given the Israelites enough manna on one day for the whole week. But God wanted his people to trust him every day and to be satisfied with each day's food.

Do you think you would like to eat only manna every day? Try for one whole day to eat only bread. No peanut butter or jelly ... just the bread for each meal. Now picture the Israelites and their manna again.

ter there, and they grumbled against Moses. They said, "Why did you bring us up out of Egypt to make us and our children and livestock die of thirst?"

⁴Then Moses cried out to the LORD, "What am I to do with these people? They are almost ready to stone me."

⁵The LORD answered Moses, "Walk on ahead of the people. Take with you some of the elders of Israel and take in your hand the staff with which you struck the Nile, and go. ⁶I will stand there before you by the rock at Horeb. Strike the rock, and water will come out of it for the people to drink." So Moses did this in the sight of the elders of Israel. ⁷And he called the place Massah ᵃ and Meribah ᵇ because the Israelites quarreled and because they tested the LORD saying, "Is the LORD among us or not?"

The Amalekites Defeated

⁸The Amalekites came and attacked the Israelites at Rephidim. ⁹Moses said to Joshua, "Choose some of our men and go out to fight the Amalekites. Tomorrow I will stand on top of the hill with the staff of God in my hands."

¹⁰So Joshua fought the Amalekites as Moses had ordered, and Moses, Aaron and Hur went to the top of the hill. ¹¹As long as Moses held up his hands, the Israelites were winning, but whenever he lowered his hands, the Amalekites were winning. ¹²When Moses' hands grew tired, they took a stone and put it under him and he sat on it. Aaron and Hur held his hands up—one on one side, one on the other—so that his hands remained steady till sunset. ¹³So Joshua overcame the Amalekite army with the sword.

¹⁴Then the LORD said to Moses, "Write this on a scroll as something to be remembered and make sure that Joshua hears it, because I will completely blot out the memory of Amalek from under heaven."

¹⁵Moses built an altar and called it The LORD is my Banner. ¹⁶He said, "For hands were lifted up to the throne of the LORD. The ᶜ LORD will be at war against the Amalekites from generation to generation."

❓DID YOU KNOW?   17:11

Why did Moses hold up his staff when the Israelites were at war?

When Moses held up his staff, the Israelites won. When Moses did not hold up his staff, the Israelites were defeated. This showed the Israelites that God gave them victory. They could not win in their own strength.

Jethro Visits Moses

18 Now Jethro, the priest of Midian and father-in-law of Moses, heard of everything God had done for Moses and for his people Israel, and how the LORD had brought Israel out of Egypt.

²After Moses had sent away his wife Zipporah, his father-in-law Jethro received her ³and her two sons. One son was named Gershom, ᵈ for Moses said, "I have become an alien in a foreign land"; ⁴and the other was named Eliezer, ᵉ for he said, "My father's God was my helper; he saved me from the sword of Pharaoh."

⁵Jethro, Moses' father-in-law, together with Moses' sons and wife, came to him in the desert, where he was camped near the mountain of God. ⁶Jethro had sent word to him, "I, your father-in-law Jethro, am coming to you with your wife and her two sons."

⁷So Moses went out to meet his father-in-law and bowed down and kissed him. They greeted each other and then went into the tent. ⁸Moses told his father-in-law about every-

---

ᵃ7 Massah means testing.   ᵇ7 Meribah means quarreling.   ᶜ16 Or "Because a hand was against the throne of the LORD, the   ᵈ3 Gershom sounds like the Hebrew for an alien there. ᵉ4 Eliezer means my God is helper.

thing the LORD had done to Pharaoh and the Egyptians for Israel's sake and about all the hardships they had met along the way and how the LORD had saved them.

9Jethro was delighted to hear about all the good things the LORD had done for Israel in rescuing them from the hand of the Egyptians. 10He said, "Praise be to the LORD, who rescued you from the hand of the Egyptians and of Pharaoh, and who rescued the people from the hand of the Egyptians. 11Now I know that the LORD is greater than all other gods, for he did this to those who had treated Israel arrogantly." 12Then Jethro, Moses' father-in-law, brought a burnt offering and other sacrifices to God, and Aaron came with all the elders of Israel to eat bread with Moses' father-in-law in the presence of God.

13The next day Moses took his seat to serve as judge for the people, and they stood around him from morning till evening. 14When his father-in-law saw all that Moses was doing for the people, he said, "What is this you are doing for the people? Why do you alone sit as judge, while all these people stand around you from morning till evening?"

15Moses answered him, "Because the people come to me to seek God's will. 16Whenever they have a dispute, it is brought to me, and I decide between the parties and inform them of God's decrees and laws."

17Moses' father-in-law replied, "What you are doing is not good. 18You and these people who come to you will only wear yourselves out. The work is too heavy for you; you cannot handle it alone. 19Listen now to me and I will give you some advice, and may God be with you. You must be the people's representative before God and bring their disputes to him. 20Teach them the decrees and laws, and show them the way to live and the duties they are to perform. 21But select capable men from all the people—men who fear God, trustworthy men who hate dishonest gain—and appoint them as officials over thousands, hundreds, fifties and tens. 22Have them serve as judges for the people at all times, but have them bring every difficult case to you; the simple cases they can decide themselves. That will make your load lighter, because they will share it with you. 23If you do this and God so commands, you will be able to stand the strain, and all these people will go home satisfied."

24Moses listened to his father-in-law and did everything he said. 25He chose capable men from all Israel and made them leaders of the people, officials over thousands, hundreds, fifties and tens. 26They served as judges for the people at all times. The difficult cases they brought to Moses, but the simple ones they decided themselves.

27Then Moses sent his father-in-law on his way, and Jethro returned to his own country.

At Mount Sinai

19 In the third month after the Israelites left Egypt—on the very day—they came to the Desert of Sinai. 2After they set out from Rephidim, they entered the Desert of Sinai, and Israel camped there in the desert in front of the mountain.

3Then Moses went up to God, and the LORD called to him from the mountain and said, "This is what you are to say to the house of Jacob and what you are to tell the people of Israel: 4'You yourselves have seen what I did to Egypt, and how I carried you on eagles' wings and brought you to myself. 5Now if you obey me fully and keep my covenant, then out of all nations you will be my treasured possession. Although the whole earth is mine, 6you*a* will be for me a kingdom of priests and a holy nation.' These are the words you are to speak to the Israelites."

7So Moses went back and summoned the elders of the people and

a5,6 Or possession, for the whole earth is mine. 6You

set before them all the words the LORD had commanded him to speak. [8]The people all responded together, "We will do everything the LORD has said." So Moses brought their answer back to the LORD.

[9]The LORD said to Moses, "I am going to come to you in a dense cloud, so that the people will hear me speaking with you and will always put their trust in you." Then Moses told the LORD what the people had said.

[10]And the LORD said to Moses, "Go to the people and consecrate them today and tomorrow. Have them wash their clothes [11]and be ready by the third day, because on that day the LORD will come down on Mount Sinai in the sight of all the people. [12]Put limits for the people around the mountain and tell them, 'Be careful that you do not go up the mountain or touch the foot of it. Whoever touches the mountain shall surely be put to death. [13]He shall surely be stoned or shot with arrows; not a hand is to be laid on him. Whether man or animal, he shall not be permitted to live.' Only when the ram's horn sounds a long blast may they go up to the mountain."

[14]After Moses had gone down the mountain to the people, he consecrated them, and they washed their clothes. [15]Then he said to the people, "Prepare yourselves for the third day. Abstain from sexual relations."

[16]On the morning of the third day there was thunder and lightning, with a thick cloud over the mountain, and a very loud trumpet blast. Everyone in the camp trembled. [17]Then Moses led the people out of the camp to meet with God, and they stood at the foot of the mountain. [18]Mount Sinai was covered with smoke, because the LORD descended on it in fire. The smoke billowed up from it like smoke from a furnace, the whole mountain[a] trembled violently, [19]and the sound of the trumpet grew louder and louder. Then Moses spoke and the voice of God answered him.[b]

[20]The LORD descended to the top of Mount Sinai and called Moses to the top of the mountain. So Moses went up [21]and the LORD said to him, "Go down and warn the people so they do not force their way through to see the LORD and many of them perish. [22]Even the priests, who approach the LORD, must consecrate themselves, or the LORD will break out against them."

❓DID YOU KNOW?　　19:20

Why is Mount Sinai important?

Mount Sinai is the place where two important things happened. God spoke to Moses from the burning bush (Exodus 3:12). And God gave the Israelites his law there (Exodus 19).

---

[23]Moses said to the LORD, "The people cannot come up Mount Sinai, because you yourself warned us, 'Put limits around the mountain and set it apart as holy.'"

[24]The LORD replied, "Go down and bring Aaron up with you. But the priests and the people must not force their way through to come up to the LORD, or he will break out against them."

[25]So Moses went down to the people and told them.

The Ten Commandments

20 And God spoke all these words:

[2]"I am the LORD your God, who brought you out of Egypt, out of the land of slavery.

[3]"You shall have no other gods before[c] me.

[4]"You shall not make for yourself an idol in the form of any-

---

[a]18 Most Hebrew manuscripts; a few Hebrew manuscripts and Septuagint *all the people* [b]19 Or *and God answered him with thunder* [c]3 Or *besides*

thing in heaven above or on the earth beneath or in the waters below. ⁵You shall not bow down to them or worship them; for I, the LORD your God, am a jealous God, punishing the children for the sin of the fathers to the third and fourth generation of those who hate me, ⁶but showing love to a thousand generations, of those who love me and keep my commandments.

⁷"You shall not misuse the name of the LORD your God, for the LORD will not hold anyone guiltless who misuses his name.

⁸"Remember the Sabbath day by keeping it holy. ⁹Six days you shall labor and do all your work, ¹⁰but the seventh day is a Sabbath to the LORD your God. On it you shall not do any work, neither you, nor your son or daughter, nor your manservant or maidservant, nor your animals, nor the alien within your gates. ¹¹For in six days the LORD made the heavens and the earth, the sea, and all that is in them, but he rested

---

▚ET'S LIVE IT!

Exodus 20:1–17

TEN COMMANDMENTS ➡ God's Ten Commandments show us how to love God and how to love people. Here is a list of the commandments, with an explanation of what each one means and how you can obey these commandments each day.

The Commandment	Meaning	I Obey It by:
How to show love to God.		
1. Have no gods before me.	Trust God only.	Praying about my needs.
2. Have no idols.	Worship God only.	Thanking and praising God.
3. Don't misuse God's name.	Use God's name respectfully.	Not swearing with God's name.
4. Keep the Sabbath holy.	Rest and think about God.	Going to Church school. Talking about God at home.
How to show love to people.		
5. Honor father and mother.	Respect parents.	Obeying my mom and dad.
6. Do not murder.	Protect human life.	Helping others not get hurt.
7. Do not commit adultery.	Be true to husband or wife.	Keeping promises I make to others.
8. Do not steal.	Don't take what belongs to others.	Not taking things that belong to others.
9. Do not give false testimony.	Don't lie about others.	Being truthful and not gossiping.
10. Do not covet.	Don't want what others have.	Being satisfied with what I have.

on the seventh day. Therefore the LORD blessed the Sabbath day and made it holy.

12"Honor your father and your mother, so that you may live long in the land the LORD your God is giving you.

13"You shall not murder.

14"You shall not commit adultery.

15"You shall not steal.

16"You shall not give false testimony against your neighbor.

17"You shall not covet your neighbor's house. You shall not covet your neighbor's wife, or his manservant or maidservant, his ox or donkey, or anything that belongs to your neighbor."

18When the people saw the thunder and lightning and heard the trumpet and saw the mountain in smoke, they trembled with fear. They stayed at a distance 19and said to Moses, "Speak to us yourself and we will listen. But do not have God speak to us or we will die."

20Moses said to the people, "Do not be afraid. God has come to test you, so that the fear of God will be with you to keep you from sinning."

21The people remained at a distance, while Moses approached the thick darkness where God was.

Idols and Altars

22Then the LORD said to Moses, "Tell the Israelites this: 'You have seen for yourselves that I have spoken to you from heaven: 23Do not make any gods to be alongside me; do not make for yourselves gods of silver or gods of gold.

24" 'Make an altar of earth for me and sacrifice on it your burnt offerings and fellowship offerings,ᵃ your sheep and goats and your cattle. Wherever I cause my name to be honored, I will come to you and bless you. 25If you make an altar of stones for me, do not build it with dressed stones, for you will defile it if you use a tool on it. 26And do not go up to my altar on steps, lest your nakedness be exposed on it.'

21 "These are the laws you are to set before them:

Hebrew Servants

2"If you buy a Hebrew servant, he is to serve you for six years. But in the seventh year, he shall go free, without paying anything. 3If he comes alone, he is to go free alone; but if he has a wife when he comes, she is to go with him. 4If his master gives him a wife and she bears him sons or daughters, the woman and her children shall belong to her master, and only the man shall go free.

5"But if the servant declares, 'I love my master and my wife and children and do not want to go free,' 6then his master must take him before the judges.ᵇ He shall take him to the door or the doorpost and pierce his ear with an awl. Then he will be his servant for life.

7"If a man sells his daughter as a servant, she is not to go free as menservants do. 8If she does not please the master who has selected her for himself,ᶜ he must let her be redeemed. He has no right to sell her to foreigners, because he has broken faith with her. 9If he selects her for his son, he must grant her the rights of a daughter. 10If he marries another woman, he must not deprive the first one of her food, clothing and marital rights. 11If he does not provide her with these three things, she is to go free, without any payment of money.

Personal Injuries

12"Anyone who strikes a man and kills him shall surely be put to death. 13However, if he does not do it intentionally, but God lets it happen, he is to flee to a place I will designate. 14But if a man schemes and kills an-

a24 Traditionally *peace offerings*   b6 Or *before God*   c8 Or *master so that he does not choose her*

other man deliberately, take him away from my altar and put him to death.

15"Anyone who attacks*a* his father or his mother must be put to death.

16"Anyone who kidnaps another and either sells him or still has him when he is caught must be put to death.

17"Anyone who curses his father or mother must be put to death.

18"If men quarrel and one hits the other with a stone or with his fist*b* and he does not die but is confined to bed, 19the one who struck the blow will not be held responsible if the other gets up and walks around outside with his staff; however, he must pay the injured man for the loss of his time and see that he is completely healed.

20"If a man beats his male or female slave with a rod and the slave dies as a direct result, he must be punished, 21but he is not to be punished if the slave gets up after a day or two, since the slave is his property.

22"If men who are fighting hit a pregnant woman and she gives birth prematurely*c* but there is no serious injury, the offender must be fined whatever the woman's husband demands and the court allows. 23But if there is serious injury, you are to take life for life, 24eye for eye, tooth for tooth, hand for hand, foot for foot, 25burn for burn, wound for wound, bruise for bruise.

26"If a man hits a manservant or maidservant in the eye and destroys it, he must let the servant go free to compensate for the eye. 27And if he knocks out the tooth of a manservant or maidservant, he must let the servant go free to compensate for the tooth.

28"If a bull gores a man or a woman to death, the bull must be stoned to death, and its meat must not be eaten. But the owner of the bull will not be held responsible. 29If, however, the bull has had the habit of goring and the owner has been warned but has not kept it penned up and it kills a man or woman, the bull must be stoned and the owner also must be put to death. 30However, if payment is demanded of him, he may redeem his life by paying whatever is demanded. 31This law also applies if the bull gores a son or daughter. 32If the bull gores a male or female slave, the owner must pay thirty shekels*d* of silver to the master of the slave, and the bull must be stoned.

33"If a man uncovers a pit or digs one and fails to cover it and an ox or a donkey falls into it, 34the owner of the pit must pay for the loss; he must pay its owner, and the dead animal will be his.

35"If a man's bull injures the bull of another and it dies, they are to sell the live one and divide both the money and the dead animal equally. 36However, if it was known that the bull had the habit of goring, yet the owner did not keep it penned up, the owner must pay, animal for animal, and the dead animal will be his.

Protection of Property

22 "If a man steals an ox or a sheep and slaughters it or sells it, he must pay back five head of cattle for the ox and four sheep for the sheep.

2"If a thief is caught breaking in and is struck so that he dies, the defender is not guilty of bloodshed; 3but if it happens*e* after sunrise, he is guilty of bloodshed.

"A thief must certainly make restitution, but if he has nothing, he must be sold to pay for his theft.

4"If the stolen animal is found alive in his possession—whether ox or donkey or sheep—he must pay back double.

5"If a man grazes his livestock in a field or vineyard and lets them stray and they graze in another man's field, he must make restitution from the best of his own field or vineyard.

---

*a*15 Or *kills*　　*b*18 Or *with a tool*　　*c*22 Or *she has a miscarriage*　　*d*32 That is, about 12 ounces (about 0.3 kilogram)　　*e*3 Or *if he strikes him*

⁶"If a fire breaks out and spreads into thornbushes so that it burns shocks of grain or standing grain or the whole field, the one who started the fire must make restitution.

❓DID YOU KNOW?　　22:1

How did God's law punish thieves?

People who stole or cheated others did not go to jail. Instead they had to pay back the person they stole from—two or even five times as much as they took! This way of punishing is called "making restitution."

---

⁷"If a man gives his neighbor silver or goods for safekeeping and they are stolen from the neighbor's house, the thief, if he is caught, must pay back double. ⁸But if the thief is not found, the owner of the house must appear before the judges*a* to determine whether he has laid his hands on the other man's property. ⁹In all cases of illegal possession of an ox, a donkey, a sheep, a garment, or any other lost property about which somebody says, 'This is mine,' both parties are to bring their cases before the judges.

The one whom the judges declare*b* guilty must pay back double to his neighbor.

¹⁰"If a man gives a donkey, an ox, a sheep or any other animal to his neighbor for safekeeping and it dies or is injured or is taken away while no one is looking, ¹¹the issue between them will be settled by the taking of an oath before the LORD that the neighbor did not lay hands on the other person's property. The owner is to accept this, and no restitution is required. ¹²But if the animal was stolen from the neighbor, he must make restitution to the owner. ¹³If it was torn to pieces by a wild animal, he shall bring in the remains as evidence and he will not be required to pay for the torn animal.

¹⁴"If a man borrows an animal from his neighbor and it is injured or dies while the owner is not present, he must make restitution. ¹⁵But if the owner is with the animal, the borrower will not have to pay. If the animal was hired, the money paid for the hire covers the loss.

Social Responsibility

¹⁶"If a man seduces a virgin who is not pledged to be married and sleeps with her, he must pay the bride-price, and she shall be his wife. ¹⁷If her fa-

a8 Or before God; also in verse 9　　*b9 Or whom God declares*

ＬET'S LIVE IT!　　　Exodus 21:28–36

PROTECT OTHERS ➠ Read Exodus 21:28–36. The laws given here show that God's people are to be careful to protect the lives and property of other people.

Perform a "safety check" on your home. Are any toys that someone might trip over put away? Are tools put away? Are there any fire hazards in your home, like frayed electrical cords or paint cans and rags piled in a corner? If your dog bites, is he safely tied? Are things that are poisonous kept out of the reach of children?

Give yourself ten points for each thing you do to make your house and yard safer for your family and other people:

10 points . . . doing good!
30 points . . . super!
50 points . . . you are great!

ther absolutely refuses to give her to him, he must still pay the bride-price for virgins.

18"Do not allow a sorceress to live.

19"Anyone who has sexual relations with an animal must be put to death.

20"Whoever sacrifices to any god other than the LORD must be destroyed.ᵃ

21"Do not mistreat an alien or oppress him, for you were aliens in Egypt.

22"Do not take advantage of a widow or an orphan. 23If you do and they cry out to me, I will certainly hear their cry. 24My anger will be aroused, and I will kill you with the sword; your wives will become widows and your children fatherless.

25"If you lend money to one of my people among you who is needy, do not be like a moneylender; charge him no interest.ᵇ 26If you take your neighbor's cloak as a pledge, return it to him by sunset, 27because his cloak is the only covering he has for his body. What else will he sleep in? When he cries out to me, I will hear, for I am compassionate.

28"Do not blaspheme Godᶜ or curse the ruler of your people.

29"Do not hold back offerings from your granaries or your vats.ᵈ

"You must give me the firstborn of your sons. 30Do the same with your cattle and your sheep. Let them stay with their mothers for seven days, but give them to me on the eighth day.

31"You are to be my holy people. So do not eat the meat of an animal torn by wild beasts; throw it to the dogs.

Laws of Justice and Mercy

23 "Do not spread false reports. Do not help a wicked man by being a malicious witness.

2"Do not follow the crowd in doing wrong. When you give testimony in a lawsuit, do not pervert justice by siding with the crowd, 3and do not show favoritism to a poor man in his lawsuit.

4"If you come across your enemy's ox or donkey wandering off, be sure to take it back to him. 5If you see the donkey of someone who hates you fallen down under its load, do not leave it there; be sure you help him with it.

6"Do not deny justice to your poor people in their lawsuits. 7Have nothing to do with a false charge and do not put an innocent or honest person to death, for I will not acquit the guilty.

❓DID YOU KNOW?   23:2

What does justice mean?

Justice means doing the right thing for other people. The first nine verses of Exodus 23 list twelve ways that God's people can do the right thing for people they know.

8"Do not accept a bribe, for a bribe blinds those who see and twists the words of the righteous.

9"Do not oppress an alien; you yourselves know how it feels to be aliens, because you were aliens in Egypt.

Sabbath Laws

10"For six years you are to sow your fields and harvest the crops, 11but during the seventh year let the land lie unplowed and unused. Then the poor among your people may get food from it, and the wild animals may eat what they leave. Do the same with your vineyard and your olive grove.

12"Six days do your work, but on the seventh day do not work, so that your ox and your donkey may rest and the slave born in your household,

---

ᵃ20 The Hebrew term refers to the irrevocable giving over of things or persons to the LORD, often by totally destroying them.   ᵇ25 Or *excessive interest*   ᶜ28 Or *Do not revile the judges*
ᵈ29 The meaning of the Hebrew for this phrase is uncertain.

and the alien as well, may be refreshed.

¹³"Be careful to do everything I have said to you. Do not invoke the names of other gods; do not let them be heard on your lips.

The Three Annual Festivals

¹⁴"Three times a year you are to celebrate a festival to me.

¹⁵"Celebrate the Feast of Unleavened Bread; for seven days eat bread made without yeast, as I commanded you. Do this at the appointed time in the month of Abib, for in that month you came out of Egypt.

"No one is to appear before me empty-handed.

¹⁶"Celebrate the Feast of Harvest with the firstfruits of the crops you sow in your field.

"Celebrate the Feast of Ingathering at the end of the year, when you gather in your crops from the field.

¹⁷"Three times a year all the men are to appear before the Sovereign LORD.

¹⁸"Do not offer the blood of a sacrifice to me along with anything containing yeast.

"The fat of my festival offerings must not be kept until morning.

¹⁹"Bring the best of the firstfruits of your soil to the house of the LORD your God.

"Do not cook a young goat in its mother's milk.

God's Angel to Prepare the Way

²⁰"See, I am sending an angel ahead of you to guard you along the way and to bring you to the place I have prepared. ²¹Pay attention to him and listen to what he says. Do not rebel against him; he will not forgive your rebellion, since my Name is in him. ²²If you listen carefully to what he says and do all that I say, I will be an enemy to your enemies and will oppose those who oppose you. ²³My angel will go ahead of you and bring you into the land of the Amorites, Hittites, Perizzites, Canaanites, Hivites and Jebusites, and I will wipe them out. ²⁴Do not bow down before their gods or worship them or follow their practices. You must demolish them and break their sacred stones to pieces. ²⁵Worship the LORD your God, and his blessing will be on your food and water. I will take away sickness from among you, ²⁶and none will miscarry or be barren in your land. I will give you a full life span.

²⁷"I will send my terror ahead of you and throw into confusion every nation you encounter. I will make all your enemies turn their backs and run. ²⁸I will send the hornet ahead of you to drive the Hivites, Canaanites and Hittites out of your way. ²⁹But I will not drive them out in a single year, because the land would become desolate and the wild animals too numerous for you. ³⁰Little by little I will drive them out before you, until you have increased enough to take possession of the land.

³¹"I will establish your borders from the Red Sea*ᵃ* to the Sea of the Philistines,*ᵇ* and from the desert to the River.*ᶜ* I will hand over to you the people who live in the land and you will drive them out before you. ³²Do not make a covenant with them or with their gods. ³³Do not let them live in your land, or they will cause you to sin against me, because the worship of their gods will certainly be a snare to you."

The Covenant Confirmed

24 Then he said to Moses, "Come up to the LORD, you and Aaron, Nadab and Abihu, and seventy of the elders of Israel. You are to worship at a distance, ²but Moses alone is to approach the LORD; the others must not come near. And the people may not come up with him."

³When Moses went and told the people all the LORD's words and laws, they responded with one voice, "Everything the LORD has said we will

---

ᵃ31 Hebrew *Yam Suph*; that is, Sea of Reeds   *ᵇ31* That is, the Mediterranean   *ᶜ31* That is, the Euphrates

do." ⁴Moses then wrote down everything the LORD had said.

He got up early the next morning and built an altar at the foot of the mountain and set up twelve stone pillars representing the twelve tribes of Israel. ⁵Then he sent young Israelite men, and they offered burnt offerings and sacrificed young bulls as fellowship offeringsᵃ to the LORD. ⁶Moses took half of the blood and put it in bowls, and the other half he sprinkled on the altar. ⁷Then he took the Book of the Covenant and read it to the people. They responded, "We will do everything the LORD has said; we will obey."

Words to Remember

24:7 We will do everything the LORD has said; we will obey.

---

⁸Moses then took the blood, sprinkled it on the people and said, "This is the blood of the covenant that the LORD has made with you in accordance with all these words."

⁹Moses and Aaron, Nadab and Abihu, and the seventy elders of Israel went up ¹⁰and saw the God of Israel. Under his feet was something like a pavement made of sapphire,ᵇ clear as the sky itself. ¹¹But God did not raise his hand against these leaders of the Israelites; they saw God, and they ate and drank.

¹²The LORD said to Moses, "Come up to me on the mountain and stay here, and I will give you the tablets of stone, with the law and commands I have written for their instruction."

¹³Then Moses set out with Joshua his aide, and Moses went up on the mountain of God. ¹⁴He said to the elders, "Wait here for us until we come back to you. Aaron and Hur are with you, and anyone involved in a dispute can go to them."

¹⁵When Moses went up on the mountain, the cloud covered it, ¹⁶and the glory of the LORD settled on Mount Sinai. For six days the cloud covered the mountain, and on the seventh day the LORD called to Moses from within the cloud. ¹⁷To the Israelites the glory of the LORD looked like a consuming fire on top of the mountain. ¹⁸Then Moses entered the cloud as he went on up the mountain. And he stayed on the mountain forty days and forty nights.

Offerings for the Tabernacle

25 The LORD said to Moses, ²"Tell the Israelites to bring me an offering. You are to receive the offering for me from each man whose heart prompts him to give. ³These are the offerings you are to receive from them: gold, silver and bronze; ⁴blue, purple and scarlet yarn and fine linen; goat hair; ⁵ram skins dyed red and hides of sea cowsᶜ; acacia wood; ⁶olive oil for the light; spices for the anointing oil and for the fragrant incense; ⁷and onyx stones and other gems to be mounted on the ephod and breastpiece.

⁸"Then have them make a sanctuary for me, and I will dwell among them. ⁹Make this tabernacle and all its furnishings exactly like the pattern I will show you.

The Ark

¹⁰"Have them make a chest of acacia wood—two and a half cubits long, a cubit and a half wide, and a cubit and a half high.ᵈ ¹¹Overlay it with pure gold, both inside and out, and make a gold molding around it. ¹²Cast four gold rings for it and fasten them to its four feet, with two rings on one side and two rings on the other. ¹³Then make poles of acacia wood and overlay them with gold. ¹⁴Insert the poles into the rings on the sides of the chest to carry it. ¹⁵The poles are to remain in the rings of this ark;

ᵃ5 Traditionally *peace offerings*   ᵇ10 Or *lapis lazuli*   ᶜ5 That is, dugongs   ᵈ10 That is, about 3 3/4 feet (about 1.1 meters) long and 2 1/4 feet (about 0.7 meter) wide and high

they are not to be removed. ¹⁶Then put in the ark the Testimony, which I will give you.

¹⁷"Make an atonement cover*ᵃ* of pure gold—two and a half cubits long and a cubit and a half wide.*ᵇ* ¹⁸And make two cherubim out of hammered gold at the ends of the cover. ¹⁹Make one cherub on one end and the second cherub on the other; make the cherubim of one piece with the cover, at the two ends. ²⁰The cherubim are to have their wings spread upward, overshadowing the cover with them. The cherubim are to face each other, looking toward the cover. ²¹Place the cover on top of the ark and put in the ark the Testimony, which I will give you. ²²There, above the cover between the two cherubim that are over the ark of the Testimony, I will meet with you and give you all my commands for the Israelites.

THE ARK OF THE COVENANT

The ark of the covenant was the most important object in the tabernacle. It was placed in the Most Holy Place and only once a year, on the Day of Atonement, did a priest go in and pour the blood of a sacrifice on the cover. The "atonement cover" of the ark was made of pure gold and had two cherubim on it, facing each other with their wings spread upward. According to Hebrews 9:4 the ark held the two tablets of the law that God gave to Moses, a jar of manna and Aaron's rod that had budded.

The Table

²³"Make a table of acacia wood— two cubits long, a cubit wide and a cubit and a half high.*ᶜ* ²⁴Overlay it with pure gold and make a gold molding around it. ²⁵Also make around it a rim a handbreadth*ᵈ* wide and put a gold molding on the rim. ²⁶Make four gold rings for the table and fasten them to the four corners, where the four legs are. ²⁷The rings are to be close to the rim to hold the poles used in carrying the table. ²⁸Make the poles of acacia wood, overlay them with gold and carry the table with them. ²⁹And make its plates and dishes of pure gold, as well as its pitchers and bowls for the pouring out of offerings. ³⁰Put the bread of the Presence on this table to be before me at all times.

The Lampstand

³¹"Make a lampstand of pure gold and hammer it out, base and shaft; its flowerlike cups, buds and blossoms shall be of one piece with it. ³²Six branches are to extend from the sides of the lampstand—three on one side and three on the other. ³³Three cups shaped like almond flowers with buds and blossoms are to be on one branch, three on the next branch, and the same for all six branches extending from the lampstand. ³⁴And on the lampstand there are to be four cups shaped like almond flowers with buds and blossoms. ³⁵One bud shall be under the first pair of branches extending from the lampstand, a second bud under the second pair, and a third bud under the third pair—six branches in all. ³⁶The buds and branches shall all be of one piece with the lampstand, hammered out of pure gold.

³⁷"Then make its seven lamps and set them up on it so that they light the space in front of it. ³⁸Its wick trimmers and trays are to be of pure

---

ᵃ17 Traditionally *a mercy seat*   *ᵇ17* That is, about 3 3/4 feet (about 1.1 meters) long and 2 1/4 feet (about 0.7 meter) wide   *ᶜ23* That is, about 3 feet (about 0.9 meter) long and 1 1/2 feet (about 0.5 meter) wide and 2 1/4 feet (about 0.7 meter) high   *ᵈ25* That is, about 3 inches (about 8 centimeters)

gold. ³⁹A talent*a* of pure gold is to be used for the lampstand and all these accessories. ⁴⁰See that you make them according to the pattern shown you on the mountain.

The Tabernacle

26 ¹"Make the tabernacle with ten curtains of finely twisted linen and blue, purple and scarlet yarn, with cherubim worked into them by a skilled craftsman. ²All the curtains are to be the same size—twenty-eight cubits long and four cubits wide.*b* ³Join five of the curtains together, and do the same with the other five. ⁴Make loops of blue material along the edge of the end curtain in one set, and do the same with the end curtain in the other set. ⁵Make fifty loops on one curtain and fifty loops on the end curtain of the other set, with the loops opposite each other. ⁶Then make fifty gold clasps and use them to fasten the curtains together so that the tabernacle is a unit.

⁷"Make curtains of goat hair for the tent over the tabernacle—eleven altogether. ⁸All eleven curtains are to be the same size—thirty cubits long and four cubits wide.*c* ⁹Join five of the curtains together into one set and the other six into another set. Fold the sixth curtain double at the front of the tent. ¹⁰Make fifty loops along the edge of the end curtain in one set and also along the edge of the end curtain in the other set. ¹¹Then make fifty bronze clasps and put them in the loops to fasten the tent together as a unit. ¹²As for the additional length of the tent curtains, the half curtain that is left over is to hang down at the rear of the tabernacle. ¹³The tent curtains will be a cubit*d* longer on both sides; what is left will hang over the sides of the tabernacle so as to cover it. ¹⁴Make for the tent a covering of ram skins dyed red, and

over that a covering of hides of sea cows.*e*

¹⁵"Make upright frames of acacia wood for the tabernacle. ¹⁶Each frame is to be ten cubits long and a cubit and a half wide,*f* ¹⁷with two projections set parallel to each other. Make all the frames of the tabernacle in this way. ¹⁸Make twenty frames for the south side of the tabernacle ¹⁹and make forty silver bases to go under them—two bases for each frame, one under each projection. ²⁰For the other side, the north side of the tabernacle, make twenty frames ²¹and forty silver bases—two under each frame. ²²Make six frames for the far end, that is, the west end of the tabernacle, ²³and make two frames for the corners at the far end. ²⁴At these two corners they must be double from the bottom all the way to the top, and fitted into a single ring; both shall be like that. ²⁵So there will be eight frames and sixteen silver bases—two under each frame.

²⁶"Also make crossbars of acacia wood: five for the frames on one side of the tabernacle, ²⁷five for those on the other side, and five for the frames on the west, at the far end of the tabernacle. ²⁸The center crossbar is to extend from end to end at the middle of the frames. ²⁹Overlay the frames with gold and make gold rings to hold the crossbars. Also overlay the crossbars with gold.

³⁰"Set up the tabernacle according to the plan shown you on the mountain.

³¹"Make a curtain of blue, purple and scarlet yarn and finely twisted linen, with cherubim worked into it by a skilled craftsman. ³²Hang it with gold hooks on four posts of acacia wood overlaid with gold and standing on four silver bases. ³³Hang the curtain from the clasps and place the ark of the Testimony behind the curtain. The curtain will separate

---

a39 That is, about 75 pounds (about 34 kilograms)   *b2* That is, about 42 feet (about 12.5 meters) long and 6 feet (about 1.8 meters) wide   *c8* That is, about 45 feet (about 13.5 meters) long and 6 feet (about 1.8 meters) wide   *d13* That is, about 1 1/2 feet (about 0.5 meter)   *e14* That is, dugongs   *f16* That is, about 15 feet (about 4.5 meters) long and 2 1/4 feet (about 0.7 meter) wide

the Holy Place from the Most Holy Place. ³⁴Put the atonement cover on the ark of the Testimony in the Most Holy Place. ³⁵Place the table outside the curtain on the north side of the tabernacle and put the lampstand opposite it on the south side.

³⁶"For the entrance to the tent make a curtain of blue, purple and scarlet yarn and finely twisted linen—the work of an embroiderer. ³⁷Make gold hooks for this curtain and five posts of acacia wood overlaid with gold. And cast five bronze bases for them.

The Altar of Burnt Offering

27 "Build an altar of acacia wood, three cubits*a* high; it is to be square, five cubits long and five cubits wide.*b* ²Make a horn at each of the four corners, so that the horns and the altar are of one piece, and overlay the altar with bronze. ³Make all its utensils of bronze—its pots to remove the ashes, and its shovels, sprinkling bowls, meat forks and firepans. ⁴Make a grating for it, a bronze network, and make a bronze ring at each of the four corners of the network. ⁵Put it under the ledge of the altar so that it is halfway up the altar. ⁶Make poles of acacia wood for the altar and overlay them with bronze. ⁷The poles are to be inserted into the rings so they will be on two sides of the altar when it is carried. ⁸Make the altar hollow, out of boards. It is to be made just as you were shown on the mountain.

The Courtyard

⁹"Make a courtyard for the tabernacle. The south side shall be a hundred cubits*c* long and is to have curtains of finely twisted linen, ¹⁰with twenty posts and twenty bronze bases and with silver hooks and bands on the posts. ¹¹The north side shall also

be a hundred cubits long and is to have curtains, with twenty posts and twenty bronze bases and with silver hooks and bands on the posts.

¹²"The west end of the courtyard shall be fifty cubits*d* wide and have curtains, with ten posts and ten bases. ¹³On the east end, toward the sunrise, the courtyard shall also be fifty cubits wide. ¹⁴Curtains fifteen cubits*e* long are to be on one side of the entrance, with three posts and three bases, ¹⁵and curtains fifteen cubits long are to be on the other side, with three posts and three bases.

¹⁶"For the entrance to the courtyard, provide a curtain twenty cubits*f* long, of blue, purple and scarlet yarn and finely twisted linen—the work of an embroiderer—with four posts and four bases. ¹⁷All the posts around the courtyard are to have silver bands and hooks, and bronze bases. ¹⁸The courtyard shall be a hundred cubits long and fifty cubits wide,*g* with curtains of finely twisted linen five cubits*h* high, and with bronze bases. ¹⁹All the other articles used in the service of the tabernacle, whatever their function, including all the tent pegs for it and those for the courtyard, are to be of bronze.

Oil for the Lampstand

²⁰"Command the Israelites to bring you clear oil of pressed olives for the light so that the lamps may be kept burning. ²¹In the Tent of Meeting, outside the curtain that is in front of the Testimony, Aaron and his sons are to keep the lamps burning before the LORD from evening till morning. This is to be a lasting ordinance among the Israelites for the generations to come.

The Priestly Garments

28 "Have Aaron your brother brought to you from among

---

*a*1 That is, about 4 1/2 feet (about 1.3 meters)   *b*1 That is, about 7 1/2 feet (about 2.3 meters) long and wide   *c*9 That is, about 150 feet (about 46 meters); also in verse 11   *d*12 That is, about 75 feet (about 23 meters); also in verse 13   *e*14 That is, about 22 1/2 feet (about 6.9 meters); also in verse 15   *f*16 That is, about 30 feet (about 9 meters)   *g*18 That is, about 150 feet (about 46 meters) long and 75 feet (about 23 meters) wide   *h*18 That is, about 7 1/2 feet (about 2.3 meters)

the Israelites, along with his sons Nadab and Abihu, Eleazar and Ithamar, so they may serve me as priests. ²Make sacred garments for your brother Aaron, to give him dignity and honor. ³Tell all the skilled men to whom I have given wisdom in such matters that they are to make garments for Aaron, for his consecration, so he may serve me as priest. ⁴These are the garments they are to make: a breastpiece, an ephod, a robe, a woven tunic, a turban and a sash. They are to make these sacred garments for your brother Aaron and his sons, so they may serve me as priests. ⁵Have them use gold, and blue, purple and scarlet yarn, and fine linen.

The Ephod

⁶"Make the ephod of gold, and of blue, purple and scarlet yarn, and of finely twisted linen—the work of a skilled craftsman. ⁷It is to have two shoulder pieces attached to two of its corners, so it can be fastened. ⁸Its skillfully woven waistband is to be like it—of one piece with the ephod and made with gold, and with blue, purple and scarlet yarn, and with finely twisted linen.

⁹"Take two onyx stones and engrave on them the names of the sons of Israel ¹⁰in the order of their birth—six names on one stone and the remaining six on the other. ¹¹Engrave the names of the sons of Israel on the two stones the way a gem cutter engraves a seal. Then mount the stones in gold filigree settings ¹²and fasten them on the shoulder pieces of the ephod as memorial stones for the sons of Israel. Aaron is to bear the names on his shoulders as a memorial before the LORD. ¹³Make gold filigree settings ¹⁴and two braided chains of pure gold, like a rope, and attach the chains to the settings.

The Breastpiece

¹⁵"Fashion a breastpiece for making decisions—the work of a skilled craftsman. Make it like the ephod: of gold, and of blue, purple and scarlet yarn, and of finely twisted linen. ¹⁶It is to be square—a span*a* long and a span wide—and folded double. ¹⁷Then mount four rows of precious stones on it. In the first row there shall be a ruby, a topaz and a beryl; ¹⁸in the second row a turquoise, a sapphire*b* and an emerald; ¹⁹in the third row a jacinth, an agate and an amethyst; ²⁰in the fourth row a chrysolite, an onyx and a jasper.*c* Mount them in gold filigree settings. ²¹There are to be twelve stones, one for each of the names of the sons of Israel, each engraved like a seal with the name of one of the twelve tribes.

²²"For the breastpiece make braided chains of pure gold, like a rope. ²³Make two gold rings for it and fasten them to two corners of the breastpiece. ²⁴Fasten the two gold chains to the rings at the corners of the breastpiece, ²⁵and the other ends of the chains to the two settings, attaching them to the shoulder pieces of the ephod at the front. ²⁶Make two gold rings and attach them to the other two corners of the breastpiece on the inside edge next to the ephod. ²⁷Make two more gold rings and attach them to the bottom of the shoulder pieces on the front of the ephod, close to the seam just above the waistband of the ephod. ²⁸The rings of the breastpiece are to be tied to the rings of the ephod with blue cord, connecting it to the waistband, so that the breastpiece will not swing out from the ephod.

²⁹"Whenever Aaron enters the Holy Place, he will bear the names of the sons of Israel over his heart on the breastpiece of decision as a continuing memorial before the LORD. ³⁰Also put the Urim and the Thummim in the breastpiece, so they may be over Aaron's heart whenever he enters the presence of the LORD. Thus Aaron will always bear the means of making decisions for the Israelites over his heart before the LORD.

---

a16 That is, about 9 inches (about 22 centimeters)   *b18* Or *lapis lazuli*   *c20* The precise identification of some of these precious stones is uncertain.

Other Priestly Garments

³¹"Make the robe of the ephod entirely of blue cloth, ³²with an opening for the head in its center. There shall be a woven edge like a collar*ᵃ* around this opening, so that it will not tear. ³³Make pomegranates of blue, purple and scarlet yarn around the hem of the robe, with gold bells between them. ³⁴The gold bells and the pomegranates are to alternate around the hem of the robe. ³⁵Aaron must wear it when he ministers. The sound of the bells will be heard when he enters the Holy Place before the LORD and when he comes out, so that he will not die.

³⁶"Make a plate of pure gold and engrave on it as on a seal: HOLY TO THE LORD. ³⁷Fasten a blue cord to it to attach it to the turban; it is to be on the front of the turban. ³⁸It will be on Aaron's forehead, and he will bear the guilt involved in the sacred gifts the Israelites consecrate, whatever their gifts may be. It will be on Aar-

on's forehead continually so that they will be acceptable to the LORD.

³⁹"Weave the tunic of fine linen and make the turban of fine linen. The sash is to be the work of an embroiderer. ⁴⁰Make tunics, sashes and headbands for Aaron's sons, to give them dignity and honor. ⁴¹After you put these clothes on your brother Aaron and his sons, anoint and ordain them. Consecrate them so they may serve me as priests.

⁴²"Make linen undergarments as a covering for the body, reaching from the waist to the thigh. ⁴³Aaron and his sons must wear them whenever they enter the Tent of Meeting or approach the altar to minister in the Holy Place, so that they will not incur guilt and die.

"This is to be a lasting ordinance for Aaron and his descendants.

Consecration of the Priests

29 "This is what you are to do to consecrate them, so they may serve me as priests: Take a young

---

ᵃ32 The meaning of the Hebrew for this word is uncertain.

Life in Bible Times

ISRAEL'S HIGH PRIEST

Aaron, Moses' brother, was the first high priest. The high priest was head over all the other priests. He was in charge of the sacrifices in the tabernacle, either doing them himself or making sure they were properly done. He was the only priest allowed to enter the Most Holy Place in the tabernacle, and that was allowed only once each year on the Day of Atonement. The high priest was the one who found God's will with the use of Urim and Thummim.

bull and two rams without defect.
²And from fine wheat flour, without
yeast, make bread, and cakes mixed
with oil, and wafers spread with oil.
³Put them in a basket and present
them in it—along with the bull and
the two rams. ⁴Then bring Aaron and
his sons to the entrance to the Tent of
Meeting and wash them with water.
⁵Take the garments and dress Aaron
with the tunic, the robe of the ephod,
the ephod itself and the breastpiece.
Fasten the ephod on him by its skillfully woven waistband. ⁶Put the turban on his head and attach the sacred
diadem to the turban. ⁷Take the
anointing oil and anoint him by pouring it on his head. ⁸Bring his sons and
dress them in tunics ⁹and put headbands on them. Then tie sashes on
Aaron and his sons.ᵃ The priesthood
is theirs by a lasting ordinance. In
this way you shall ordain Aaron and
his sons.

❓DID YOU KNOW?　　29:1

What does consecrate mean?

To consecrate means to set
something apart for God's special
use. All the things in the tabernacle were to be used in the worship
of God. The priests were consecrated because they were to lead Israel in worship.

---

¹⁰"Bring the bull to the front of the
Tent of Meeting, and Aaron and his
sons shall lay their hands on its head.
¹¹Slaughter it in the LORD's presence
at the entrance to the Tent of Meeting. ¹²Take some of the bull's blood
and put it on the horns of the altar
with your finger, and pour out the
rest of it at the base of the altar.
¹³Then take all the fat around the inner parts, the covering of the liver,
and both kidneys with the fat on
them, and burn them on the altar.
¹⁴But burn the bull's flesh and its

hide and its offal outside the camp. It
is a sin offering.

¹⁵"Take one of the rams, and Aaron
and his sons shall lay their hands on
its head. ¹⁶Slaughter it and take the
blood and sprinkle it against the altar on all sides. ¹⁷Cut the ram into
pieces and wash the inner parts and
the legs, putting them with the head
and the other pieces. ¹⁸Then burn the
entire ram on the altar. It is a burnt
offering to the LORD, a pleasing aroma, an offering made to the LORD by
fire.

¹⁹"Take the other ram, and Aaron
and his sons shall lay their hands on
its head. ²⁰Slaughter it, take some of
its blood and put it on the lobes of the
right ears of Aaron and his sons, on
the thumbs of their right hands, and
on the big toes of their right feet.
Then sprinkle blood against the altar
on all sides. ²¹And take some of the
blood on the altar and some of the
anointing oil and sprinkle it on Aaron and his garments and on his sons
and their garments. Then he and his
sons and their garments will be consecrated.

²²"Take from this ram the fat, the
fat tail, the fat around the inner
parts, the covering of the liver, both
kidneys with the fat on them, and the
right thigh. (This is the ram for the
ordination.) ²³From the basket of
bread made without yeast, which is
before the LORD, take a loaf, and a
cake made with oil, and a wafer.
²⁴Put all these in the hands of Aaron
and his sons and wave them before
the LORD as a wave offering. ²⁵Then
take them from their hands and burn
them on the altar along with the
burnt offering for a pleasing aroma to
the LORD, an offering made to the
LORD by fire. ²⁶After you take the
breast of the ram for Aaron's ordination, wave it before the LORD as a
wave offering, and it will be your
share.

²⁷"Consecrate those parts of the ordination ram that belong to Aaron
and his sons: the breast that was

ᵃ9 Hebrew; Septuagint *on them*

waved and the thigh that was presented. 28This is always to be the regular share from the Israelites for Aaron and his sons. It is the contribution the Israelites are to make to the LORD from their fellowship offerings.*a*

29"Aaron's sacred garments will belong to his descendants so that they can be anointed and ordained in them. 30The son who succeeds him as priest and comes to the Tent of Meeting to minister in the Holy Place is to wear them seven days.

31"Take the ram for the ordination and cook the meat in a sacred place. 32At the entrance to the Tent of Meeting, Aaron and his sons are to eat the meat of the ram and the bread that is in the basket. 33They are to eat these offerings by which atonement was made for their ordination and consecration. But no one else may eat them, because they are sacred. 34And if any of the meat of the ordination ram or any bread is left over till morning, burn it up. It must not be eaten, because it is sacred.

35"Do for Aaron and his sons everything I have commanded you, taking seven days to ordain them. 36Sacrifice a bull each day as a sin offering to make atonement. Purify the altar by making atonement for it, and anoint it to consecrate it. 37For seven days make atonement for the altar and consecrate it. Then the altar will be most holy, and whatever touches it will be holy.

38"This is what you are to offer on the altar regularly each day: two lambs a year old. 39Offer one in the morning and the other at twilight. 40With the first lamb offer a tenth of an ephah*b* of fine flour mixed with a quarter of a hin*c* of oil from pressed olives, and a quarter of a hin of wine as a drink offering. 41Sacrifice the other lamb at twilight with the same grain offering and its drink offering as in the morning—a pleasing aro-

ma, an offering made to the LORD by fire.

42"For the generations to come this burnt offering is to be made regularly at the entrance to the Tent of Meeting before the LORD. There I will meet you and speak to you; 43there also I will meet with the Israelites, and the place will be consecrated by my glory.

44"So I will consecrate the Tent of Meeting and the altar and will consecrate Aaron and his sons to serve me as priests. 45Then I will dwell among the Israelites and be their God. 46They will know that I am the LORD their God, who brought them out of Egypt so that I might dwell among them. I am the LORD their God.

The Altar of Incense

30 "Make an altar of acacia wood for burning incense. 2It is to be square, a cubit long and a cubit wide, and two cubits high*d*—its horns of one piece with it. 3Overlay the top and all the sides and the horns with pure gold, and make a gold molding around it. 4Make two gold rings for the altar below the molding—two on opposite sides—to hold the poles used to carry it. 5Make the poles of acacia wood and overlay them with gold. 6Put the altar in front of the curtain that is before the ark of the Testimony—before the atonement cover that is over the Testimony—where I will meet with you.

7"Aaron must burn fragrant incense on the altar every morning when he tends the lamps. 8He must burn incense again when he lights the lamps at twilight so incense will burn regularly before the LORD for the generations to come. 9Do not offer on this altar any other incense or any burnt offering or grain offering, and do not pour a drink offering on it. 10Once a year Aaron shall make atonement on its horns. This annual atonement must be made with the blood of the atoning sin offering for

---

a28 Traditionally *peace offerings*   *b40* That is, probably about 2 quarts (about 2 liters)
c40 That is, probably about 1 quart (about 1 liter)   *d2* That is, about 1 1/2 feet (about 0.5 meter)
long and wide and about 3 feet (about 0.9 meter) high

the generations to come. It is most holy to the LORD."

Atonement Money

[11]Then the LORD said to Moses, [12]"When you take a census of the Israelites to count them, each one must pay the LORD a ransom for his life at the time he is counted. Then no plague will come on them when you number them. [13]Each one who crosses over to those already counted is to give a half shekel, [a] according to the sanctuary shekel, which weighs twenty gerahs. This half shekel is an offering to the LORD. [14]All who cross over, those twenty years old or more, are to give an offering to the LORD. [15]The rich are not to give more than a half shekel and the poor are not to give less when you make the offering to the LORD to atone for your lives. [16]Receive the atonement money from the Israelites and use it for the service of the Tent of Meeting. It will be a memorial for the Israelites before the LORD, making atonement for your lives."

Basin for Washing

[17]Then the LORD said to Moses, [18]"Make a bronze basin, with its bronze stand, for washing. Place it between the Tent of Meeting and the altar, and put water in it. [19]Aaron and his sons are to wash their hands and feet with water from it. [20]Whenever they enter the Tent of Meeting, they shall wash with water so that they will not die. Also, when they approach the altar to minister by presenting an offering made to the LORD

by fire, [21]they shall wash their hands and feet so that they will not die. This is to be a lasting ordinance for Aaron and his descendants for the generations to come."

Anointing Oil

[22]Then the LORD said to Moses, [23]"Take the following fine spices: 500 shekels [b] of liquid myrrh, half as much (that is, 250 shekels) of fragrant cinnamon, 250 shekels of fragrant cane, [24]500 shekels of cassia —all according to the sanctuary shekel—and a hin [c] of olive oil. [25]Make these into a sacred anointing oil, a fragrant blend, the work of a perfumer. It will be the sacred anointing oil. [26]Then use it to anoint the Tent of Meeting, the ark of the Testimony, [27]the table and all its articles, the lampstand and its accessories, the altar of incense, [28]the altar of burnt offering and all its utensils, and the basin with its stand. [29]You shall consecrate them so they will be most holy, and whatever touches them will be holy.

[30]"Anoint Aaron and his sons and consecrate them so they may serve me as priests. [31]Say to the Israelites, 'This is to be my sacred anointing oil for the generations to come. [32]Do not pour it on men's bodies and do not make any oil with the same formula. It is sacred, and you are to consider it sacred. [33]Whoever makes perfume like it and whoever puts it on anyone other than a priest must be cut off from his people.' "

Incense

[34]Then the LORD said to Moses, "Take fragrant spices—gum resin, onycha and galbanum—and pure frankincense, all in equal amounts, [35]and make a fragrant blend of incense, the work of a perfumer. It is to be salted and pure and sacred. [36]Grind some of it to powder and place it in front of the Testimony in the Tent of Meeting, where I will

---

[a]13 That is, about 1/5 ounce (about 6 grams); also in verse 15   [b]23 That is, about 12 1/2 pounds (about 6 kilograms)   [c]24 That is, probably about 4 quarts (about 4 liters)

meet with you. It shall be most holy to you. ³⁷Do not make any incense with this formula for yourselves; consider it holy to the LORD. ³⁸Whoever makes any like it to enjoy its fragrance must be cut off from his people."

Bezalel and Oholiab

31 Then the LORD said to Moses, ²"See, I have chosen Bezalel son of Uri, the son of Hur, of the tribe of Judah, ³and I have filled him with the Spirit of God, with skill, ability and knowledge in all kinds of crafts— ⁴to make artistic designs for work in gold, silver and bronze, ⁵to cut and set stones, to work in wood, and to engage in all kinds of craftsmanship. ⁶Moreover, I have appointed Oholiab son of Ahisamach, of the tribe of Dan, to help him. Also I have given skill to all the craftsmen to make everything I have commanded you: ⁷the Tent of Meeting, the ark of the Testimony with the atonement cover on it, and all the other furnishings of the tent— ⁸the table and its articles, the pure gold lampstand and all its accessories, the altar of incense, ⁹the altar of burnt offering and all its utensils, the basin with its stand— ¹⁰and also the woven garments, both the sacred garments for Aaron the priest and the garments for his sons when they serve as priests, ¹¹and the anointing oil and fragrant incense for the Holy Place. They are to make them just as I commanded you."

The Sabbath

¹²Then the LORD said to Moses, ¹³"Say to the Israelites, 'You must observe my Sabbaths. This will be a sign between me and you for the generations to come, so you may know that I am the LORD, who makes you holy.ᵃ

¹⁴"'Observe the Sabbath, because it is holy to you. Anyone who desecrates it must be put to death; whoev-

er does any work on that day must be cut off from his people. ¹⁵For six days, work is to be done, but the seventh day is a Sabbath of rest, holy to the LORD. Whoever does any work on the Sabbath day must be put to death. ¹⁶The Israelites are to observe the Sabbath, celebrating it for the generations to come as a lasting covenant. ¹⁷It will be a sign between me and the Israelites forever, for in six days the LORD made the heavens and the earth, and on the seventh day he abstained from work and rested.'"

¹⁸When the LORD finished speaking to Moses on Mount Sinai, he gave him the two tablets of the Testimony, the tablets of stone inscribed by the finger of God.

The Golden Calf

32 When the people saw that Moses was so long in coming down from the mountain, they gathered around Aaron and said, "Come, make us godsᵇ who will go before us. As for this fellow Moses who brought us up out of Egypt, we don't know what has happened to him."

²Aaron answered them, "Take off the gold earrings that your wives, your sons and your daughters are wearing, and bring them to me." ³So all the people took off their earrings and brought them to Aaron. ⁴He took what they handed him and made it into an idol cast in the shape of a calf, fashioning it with a tool. Then they said, "These are your gods,ᶜ O Israel, who brought you up out of Egypt."

⁵When Aaron saw this, he built an altar in front of the calf and announced, "Tomorrow there will be a festival to the LORD." ⁶So the next day the people rose early and sacrificed burnt offerings and presented fellowship offerings.ᵈ Afterward they sat down to eat and drink and got up to indulge in revelry.

⁷Then the LORD said to Moses, "Go down, because your people, whom you brought up out of Egypt, have be-

---

ᵃ13 Or *who sanctifies you*; or *who sets you apart as holy*   ᵇ1 Or *a god*; also in verses 23 and 31
ᶜ4 Or *This is your god*; also in verse 8   ᵈ6 Traditionally *peace offerings*

come corrupt. ⁸They have been quick to turn away from what I commanded them and have made themselves an idol cast in the shape of a calf. They have bowed down to it and sacrificed to it and have said, 'These are your gods, O Israel, who brought you up out of Egypt.'

⁹"I have seen these people," the LORD said to Moses, "and they are a stiff-necked people. ¹⁰Now leave me alone so that my anger may burn against them and that I may destroy them. Then I will make you into a great nation."

¹¹But Moses sought the favor of the LORD his God. "O LORD," he said, "why should your anger burn against your people, whom you brought out of Egypt with great power and a mighty hand? ¹²Why should the Egyptians say, 'It was with evil intent that he brought them out, to kill them in the mountains and to wipe them off the face of the earth'? Turn from your fierce anger; relent and do not bring disaster on your people. ¹³Remember your servants Abraham, Isaac and Israel, to whom you swore by your own self: 'I will make your descendants as numerous as the stars in the sky and I will give your descendants all this land I promised them, and it will be their inheritance forever.'" ¹⁴Then the LORD relented and did not bring on his people the disaster he had threatened.

¹⁵Moses turned and went down the mountain with the two tablets of the Testimony in his hands. They were inscribed on both sides, front and back. ¹⁶The tablets were the work of God; the writing was the writing of God, engraved on the tablets.

¹⁷When Joshua heard the noise of the people shouting, he said to Moses, "There is the sound of war in the camp."

¹⁸Moses replied:

"It is not the sound of victory,
　it is not the sound of defeat;
　　it is the sound of singing that I
　　　hear."

¹⁹When Moses approached the camp and saw the calf and the dancing, his anger burned and he threw the tablets out of his hands, breaking them to pieces at the foot of the mountain. ²⁰And he took the calf they had made and burned it in the fire; then he ground it to powder, scattered it on the water and made the Israelites drink it.

²¹He said to Aaron, "What did these people do to you, that you led them into such great sin?"

²²"Do not be angry, my lord," Aaron answered. "You know how prone these people are to evil. ²³They said to me, 'Make us gods who will go before us. As for this fellow Moses who brought us up out of Egypt, we don't know what has happened to him.' ²⁴So I told them, 'Whoever has any gold jewelry, take it off.' Then they

Life in Bible Times

THE GOLDEN CALF

Moses had been up on the mountain for so long that the people said, "We don't know what has happened to him." They asked Aaron to make them a god. So Aaron made a golden calf at Mount Sinai. He took the gold jewelry that the people gave him and made it into an idol for the people to worship. The idols people worshiped at that time were often in the form of a calf or a bull.

gave me the gold, and I threw it into the fire, and out came this calf!"

25Moses saw that the people were running wild and that Aaron had let them get out of control and so become a laughingstock to their enemies. 26So he stood at the entrance to the camp and said, "Whoever is for the LORD, come to me." And all the Levites rallied to him.

27Then he said to them, "This is what the LORD, the God of Israel, says: 'Each man strap a sword to his side. Go back and forth through the camp from one end to the other, each killing his brother and friend and neighbor.'" 28The Levites did as Moses commanded, and that day about three thousand of the people died. 29Then Moses said, "You have been set apart to the LORD today, for you were against your own sons and brothers, and he has blessed you this day."

30The next day Moses said to the people, "You have committed a great sin. But now I will go up to the LORD; perhaps I can make atonement for your sin."

31So Moses went back to the LORD and said, "Oh, what a great sin these people have committed! They have made themselves gods of gold. 32But now, please forgive their sin—but if not, then blot me out of the book you have written."

33The LORD replied to Moses, "Whoever has sinned against me I will blot out of my book. 34Now go, lead the people to the place I spoke of, and my angel will go before you. However, when the time comes for me to punish, I will punish them for their sin."

35And the LORD struck the people with a plague because of what they did with the calf Aaron had made.

33 Then the LORD said to Moses, "Leave this place, you and the people you brought up out of Egypt, and go up to the land I promised on oath to Abraham, Isaac and Jacob, saying, 'I will give it to your descendants.' 2I will send an angel before you and drive out the Canaanites, Amorites, Hittites, Perizzites, Hi-

vites and Jebusites. 3Go up to the land flowing with milk and honey. But I will not go with you, because you are a stiff-necked people and I might destroy you on the way."

4When the people heard these distressing words, they began to mourn and no one put on any ornaments. 5For the LORD had said to Moses, "Tell the Israelites, 'You are a stiff-necked people. If I were to go with you even for a moment, I might destroy you. Now take off your ornaments and I will decide what to do with you.'" 6So the Israelites stripped off their ornaments at Mount Horeb.

The Tent of Meeting

7Now Moses used to take a tent and pitch it outside the camp some distance away, calling it the "tent of meeting." Anyone inquiring of the LORD would go to the tent of meeting outside the camp. 8And whenever Moses went out to the tent, all the people rose and stood at the entrances to their tents, watching Moses until he entered the tent. 9As Moses went into the tent, the pillar of cloud would come down and stay at the entrance, while the LORD spoke with Moses. 10Whenever the people saw the pillar of cloud standing at the entrance to the tent, they all stood and worshiped, each at the entrance to his tent. 11The LORD would speak to Moses face to face, as a man speaks with his friend. Then Moses would return to the camp, but his young aide Joshua son of Nun did not leave the tent.

Moses and the Glory of the LORD

12Moses said to the LORD, "You have been telling me, 'Lead these people,' but you have not let me know whom you will send with me. You have said, 'I know you by name and you have found favor with me.' 13If you are pleased with me, teach me your ways so I may know you and continue to find favor with you. Remember that this nation is your people."

14The Lord replied, "My Presence will go with you, and I will give you rest."

WORDS TO REMEMBER

33:14 My Presence will go with you, and I will give you rest.

15Then Moses said to him, "If your Presence does not go with us, do not send us up from here. 16How will anyone know that you are pleased with me and with your people unless you go with us? What else will distinguish me and your people from all the other people on the face of the earth?"

17And the Lord said to Moses, "I will do the very thing you have asked, because I am pleased with you and I know you by name."

18Then Moses said, "Now show me your glory."

19And the Lord said, "I will cause all my goodness to pass in front of you, and I will proclaim my name, the Lord, in your presence. I will have mercy on whom I will have mercy, and I will have compassion on whom I will have compassion. 20But," he said, "you cannot see my face, for no one may see me and live."

21Then the Lord said, "There is a place near me where you may stand on a rock. 22When my glory passes by, I will put you in a cleft in the rock and cover you with my hand until I have passed by. 23Then I will remove my hand and you will see my back; but my face must not be seen."

The New Stone Tablets

34 The Lord said to Moses, "Chisel out two stone tablets like the first ones, and I will write on them the words that were on the first tablets, which you broke. 2Be ready in the morning, and then come up on Mount Sinai. Present yourself to me

there on top of the mountain. 3No one is to come with you or be seen anywhere on the mountain; not even the flocks and herds may graze in front of the mountain."

4So Moses chiseled out two stone tablets like the first ones and went up Mount Sinai early in the morning, as the Lord had commanded him; and he carried the two stone tablets in his hands. 5Then the Lord came down in the cloud and stood there with him and proclaimed his name, the Lord. 6And he passed in front of Moses, proclaiming, "The Lord, the Lord, the compassionate and gracious God, slow to anger, abounding in love and faithfulness, 7maintaining love to thousands, and forgiving wickedness, rebellion and sin. Yet he does not leave the guilty unpunished; he punishes the children and their children for the sin of the fathers to the third and fourth generation."

8Moses bowed to the ground at once and worshiped. 9"O Lord, if I have found favor in your eyes," he said, "then let the Lord go with us. Although this is a stiff-necked people, forgive our wickedness and our sin, and take us as your inheritance."

10Then the Lord said: "I am making a covenant with you. Before all your people I will do wonders never before done in any nation in all the world. The people you live among will see how awesome is the work that I, the Lord, will do for you. 11Obey what I command you today. I will drive out before you the Amorites, Canaanites, Hittites, Perizzites, Hivites and Jebusites. 12Be careful not to make a treaty with those who live in the land where you are going, or they will be a snare among you. 13Break down their altars, smash their sacred stones and cut down their Asherah poles.a 14Do not worship any other god, for the Lord, whose name is Jealous, is a jealous God. 15"Be careful not to make a treaty with those who live in the land; for

a13 That is, symbols of the goddess Asherah

when they prostitute themselves to their gods and sacrifice to them, they will invite you and you will eat their sacrifices. [16]And when you choose some of their daughters as wives for your sons and those daughters prostitute themselves to their gods, they will lead your sons to do the same.

[17]"Do not make cast idols.

[18]"Celebrate the Feast of Unleavened Bread. For seven days eat bread made without yeast, as I commanded you. Do this at the appointed time in the month of Abib, for in that month you came out of Egypt.

[19]"The first offspring of every womb belongs to me, including all the firstborn males of your livestock, whether from herd or flock. [20]Redeem the firstborn donkey with a lamb, but if you do not redeem it, break its neck. Redeem all your firstborn sons.

"No one is to appear before me empty-handed.

[21]"Six days you shall labor, but on the seventh day you shall rest; even during the plowing season and harvest you must rest.

[22]"Celebrate the Feast of Weeks with the firstfruits of the wheat harvest, and the Feast of Ingathering at the turn of the year.[a] [23]Three times a year all your men are to appear before the Sovereign LORD, the God of Israel. [24]I will drive out nations before you and enlarge your territory, and no one will covet your land when you go up three times each year to appear before the LORD your God.

[25]"Do not offer the blood of a sacrifice to me along with anything containing yeast, and do not let any of the sacrifice from the Passover Feast remain until morning.

[26]"Bring the best of the firstfruits of your soil to the house of the LORD your God.

"Do not cook a young goat in its mother's milk."

[27]Then the LORD said to Moses, "Write down these words, for in accordance with these words I have made a covenant with you and with

Israel." [28]Moses was there with the LORD forty days and forty nights without eating bread or drinking water. And he wrote on the tablets the words of the covenant—the Ten Commandments.

The Radiant Face of Moses

[29]When Moses came down from Mount Sinai with the two tablets of the Testimony in his hands, he was not aware that his face was radiant because he had spoken with the LORD. [30]When Aaron and all the Israelites saw Moses, his face was radiant, and they were afraid to come near him. [31]But Moses called to them; so Aaron and all the leaders of the community came back to him, and he spoke to them. [32]Afterward all the Israelites came near him, and he gave them all the commands the LORD had given him on Mount Sinai.

[33]When Moses finished speaking to them, he put a veil over his face. [34]But whenever he entered the LORD's presence to speak with him, he removed the veil until he came out. And when he came out and told the Israelites what he had been commanded, [35]they saw that his face was radiant. Then Moses would put the veil back over his face until he went in to speak with the LORD.

Sabbath Regulations

35 Moses assembled the whole Israelite community and said to them, "These are the things the LORD has commanded you to do: [2]For six days, work is to be done, but the seventh day shall be your holy day, a Sabbath of rest to the LORD. Whoever does any work on it must be put to death. [3]Do not light a fire in any of your dwellings on the Sabbath day."

Materials for the Tabernacle

[4]Moses said to the whole Israelite community, "This is what the LORD has commanded: [5]From what you have, take an offering for the LORD.

[a]22 That is, in the fall

Everyone who is willing is to bring to the LORD an offering of gold, silver and bronze; 6blue, purple and scarlet yarn and fine linen; goat hair; 7ram skins *a* dyed red and hides of sea cows*a*; acacia wood; 8olive oil for the light; spices for the anointing oil and for the fragrant incense; 9and onyx stones and other gems to be mounted on the ephod and breastpiece.

?DID YOU KNOW?   35:2

What day is the Sabbath?

Saturday, the seventh day of the week, is the Old Testament Sabbath. On this holy day the Israelites were not supposed to work but were to rest and think about the Lord. Many Christians keep Sunday as a special day, because Jesus was raised from the dead on a Sunday morning.

10"All who are skilled among you are to come and make everything the LORD has commanded: 11the tabernacle with its tent and its covering, clasps, frames, crossbars, posts and bases; 12the ark with its poles and the atonement cover and the curtain that shields it; 13the table with its poles and all its articles and the bread of the Presence; 14the lampstand that is for light with its accessories, lamps and oil for the light; 15the altar of incense with its poles, the anointing oil and the fragrant incense; the curtain for the doorway at the entrance to the tabernacle; 16the altar of burnt offering with its bronze grating, its poles and all its utensils; the bronze basin with its stand; 17the curtains of the courtyard with its posts and bases, and the curtain for the entrance to the courtyard; 18the tent pegs for the tabernacle and for the courtyard, and their ropes; 19the woven garments worn for ministering in the sanctuary—both the sacred garments for Aaron the priest and the garments for his sons when they serve as priests."

20Then the whole Israelite community withdrew from Moses' presence, 21and everyone who was willing and whose heart moved him came and brought an offering to the LORD for the work on the Tent of Meeting, for all its service, and for the sacred garments. 22All who were willing, men and women alike, came and brought gold jewelry of all kinds: brooches, earrings, rings and ornaments. They all presented their gold as a wave offering to the LORD. 23Everyone who had blue, purple or scarlet yarn or fine linen, or goat hair, ram skins dyed red or hides of sea cows brought them. 24Those presenting an offering of silver or bronze brought it as an offering to the LORD, and everyone who had acacia wood for any part of the work brought it. 25Every skilled woman spun with her hands and brought what she had spun—blue, purple or scarlet yarn or fine linen. 26And all the women who were willing and had the skill spun the goat hair. 27The leaders brought onyx stones and other gems to be mounted on the ephod and breastpiece. 28They also brought spices and olive oil for the light and for the anointing oil and for the fragrant incense. 29All the Israelite men and women who were willing brought to the LORD freewill offerings for all the work the LORD through Moses had commanded them to do.

?DID YOU KNOW?   35:11

What was the tabernacle?

The tabernacle was a tent church where the Israelites worshiped God. When it was time to build the tabernacle, everyone who was willing and who had skill was allowed to help.

---

*a*7 That is, dugongs; also in verse 23

Bezalel and Oholiab

[30]Then Moses said to the Israelites, "See, the LORD has chosen Bezalel son of Uri, the son of Hur, of the tribe of Judah, [31]and he has filled him with the Spirit of God, with skill, ability and knowledge in all kinds of crafts— [32]to make artistic designs for work in gold, silver and bronze, [33]to cut and set stones, to work in wood and to engage in all kinds of artistic craftsmanship. [34]And he has given both him and Oholiab son of Ahisamach, of the tribe of Dan, the ability to teach others. [35]He has filled them with skill to do all kinds of work as craftsmen, designers, embroiderers in blue, purple and scarlet yarn and fine linen, and weavers—all of them master craftsmen and designers.

36 [1]So Bezalel, Oholiab and every skilled person to whom the LORD has given skill and ability to know how to carry out all the work of constructing the sanctuary are to do the work just as the Lord has commanded."

[2]Then Moses summoned Bezalel and Oholiab and every skilled person to whom the LORD had given ability and who was willing to come and do the work. [3]They received from Moses all the offerings the Israelites had brought to carry out the work of constructing the sanctuary. And the people continued to bring freewill offerings morning after morning. [4]So all the skilled craftsmen who were doing all the work on the sanctuary left their work [5]and said to Moses, "The people are bringing more than enough for doing the work the LORD commanded to be done."

[6]Then Moses gave an order and they sent this word throughout the camp: "No man or woman is to make anything else as an offering for the sanctuary." And so the people were restrained from bringing more, [7]because what they already had was more than enough to do all the work.

The Tabernacle

[8]All the skilled men among the workmen made the tabernacle with ten curtains of finely twisted linen and blue, purple and scarlet yarn, with cherubim worked into them by a skilled craftsman. [9]All the curtains were the same size—twenty-eight cubits long and four cubits wide.[a] [10]They joined five of the curtains together and did the same with the other five. [11]Then they made loops of blue material along the edge of the end curtain in one set, and the same was done with the end curtain in the other set. [12]They also made fifty loops on one curtain and fifty loops on the end curtain of the other set, with the loops opposite each other. [13]Then they made fifty gold clasps and used them to fasten the two sets of curtains together so that the tabernacle was a unit.

[14]They made curtains of goat hair for the tent over the tabernacle—eleven altogether. [15]All eleven curtains were the same size—thirty cubits long and four cubits wide.[b] [16]They joined five of the curtains into one set and the other six into another set. [17]Then they made fifty loops along the edge of the end curtain in one set and also along the edge of the end curtain in the other set. [18]They made fifty bronze clasps to fasten the tent together as a unit. [19]Then they made for the tent a covering of ram skins dyed red, and over that a covering of hides of sea cows.[c]

[20]They made upright frames of acacia wood for the tabernacle. [21]Each frame was ten cubits long and a cubit and a half wide,[d] [22]with two projections set parallel to each other. They made all the frames of the tabernacle in this way. [23]They made twenty frames for the south side of the tabernacle [24]and made forty silver bases to go under them—two bases for each frame, one under each projection. [25]For the other side, the north side of

---

[a]9 That is, about 42 feet (about 12.5 meters) long and 6 feet (about 1.8 meters) wide   [b]15 That is, about 45 feet (about 13.5 meters) long and 6 feet (about 1.8 meters) wide   [c]19 That is, dugongs   [d]21 That is, about 15 feet (about 4.5 meters) long and 2 1/4 feet (about 0.7 meter) wide

the tabernacle, they made twenty frames [26]and forty silver bases—two under each frame. [27]They made six frames for the far end, that is, the west end of the tabernacle, [28]and two frames were made for the corners of the tabernacle at the far end. [29]At these two corners the frames were double from the bottom all the way to the top and fitted into a single ring; both were made alike. [30]So there were eight frames and sixteen silver bases—two under each frame.

[31]They also made crossbars of acacia wood: five for the frames on one side of the tabernacle, [32]five for those on the other side, and five for the frames on the west, at the far end of the tabernacle. [33]They made the center crossbar so that it extended from end to end at the middle of the frames. [34]They overlaid the frames with gold and made gold rings to hold the crossbars. They also overlaid the crossbars with gold.

[35]They made the curtain of blue, purple and scarlet yarn and finely twisted linen, with cherubim worked into it by a skilled craftsman. [36]They made four posts of acacia wood for it and overlaid them with gold. They made gold hooks for them and cast their four silver bases. [37]For the entrance to the tent they made a curtain of blue, purple and scarlet yarn and finely twisted linen—the work of an embroiderer; [38]and they made five posts with hooks for them. They overlaid the tops of the posts and their bands with gold and made their five bases of bronze.

The Ark

37 Bezalel made the ark of acacia wood—two and a half cubits long, a cubit and a half wide, and a cubit and a half high. [a] [2]He overlaid it with pure gold, both inside and out, and made a gold molding around it. [3]He cast four gold rings for it and fastened them to its four feet, with two rings on one side and two rings on the other. [4]Then he made poles of acacia wood and overlaid them with gold. [5]And he inserted the poles into the rings on the sides of the ark to carry it.

[6]He made the atonement cover of pure gold—two and a half cubits long and a cubit and a half wide. [b] [7]Then he made two cherubim out of hammered gold at the ends of the cover. [8]He made one cherub on one end and the second cherub on the other; at the two ends he made them of one piece with the cover. [9]The cherubim had their wings spread upward, overshadowing the cover with them. The

[a]1 That is, about 3 3/4 feet (about 1.1 meters) long and 2 1/4 feet (about 0.7 meter) wide and high
[b]6 That is, about 3 3/4 feet (about 1.1 meters) long and 2 1/4 feet (about 0.7 meter) wide

---

LET'S LIVE IT!   Exodus 37:1–9

MAKE A MODEL ARK ➠ The ark was a wooden box covered with gold. Figures of two angels sat on the lid of the ark. Long poles were used to carry it.

In Israel the ark was the symbol, or sign, of God's presence. The ark belonged in the tabernacle, where Israel worshiped. Read about it in Exodus 37:1–9.

Make a model ark to remind you of how powerful our God is and that he is with you. Get a small box and cover it with gold paper. Cut out cardboard angels, and color them gold or cover them with gold paper too. Then glue them to the top of the box. You can buy small sticks, called dowels, at a hardware or hobby store. Glue them to the side of your box.

Put the model ark in your room as a reminder of God's presence.

cherubim faced each other, looking toward the cover.

The Table

¹⁰They*a* made the table of acacia wood—two cubits long, a cubit wide, and a cubit and a half high.*b* ¹¹Then they overlaid it with pure gold and made a gold molding around it. ¹²They also made around it a rim a handbreadth*c* wide and put a gold molding on the rim. ¹³They cast four gold rings for the table and fastened them to the four corners, where the four legs were. ¹⁴The rings were put close to the rim to hold the poles used in carrying the table. ¹⁵The poles for carrying the table were made of acacia wood and were overlaid with gold. ¹⁶And they made from pure gold the articles for the table—its plates and dishes and bowls and its pitchers for the pouring out of drink offerings.

The Lampstand

¹⁷They made the lampstand of pure gold and hammered it out, base and shaft; its flowerlike cups, buds and blossoms were of one piece with it. ¹⁸Six branches extended from the sides of the lampstand—three on one side and three on the other. ¹⁹Three cups shaped like almond flowers with buds and blossoms were on one branch, three on the next branch and the same for all six branches extending from the lampstand. ²⁰And on the lampstand were four cups shaped like almond flowers with buds and blossoms. ²¹One bud was under the first pair of branches extending from the lampstand, a second bud under the second pair, and a third bud under the third pair—six branches in all. ²²The buds and the branches were all of one piece with the lampstand, hammered out of pure gold. ²³They made its seven lamps, as well as its wick trimmers and trays,

of pure gold. ²⁴They made the lampstand and all its accessories from one talent*d* of pure gold.

The Altar of Incense

²⁵They made the altar of incense out of acacia wood. It was square, a cubit long and a cubit wide, and two cubits high*e*—its horns of one piece with it. ²⁶They overlaid the top and all the sides and the horns with pure gold, and made a gold molding around it. ²⁷They made two gold rings below the molding—two on opposite sides—to hold the poles used to carry it. ²⁸They made the poles of acacia wood and overlaid them with gold. ²⁹They also made the sacred anointing oil and the pure, fragrant incense—the work of a perfumer.

The Altar of Burnt Offering

38 They*f* built the altar of burnt offering of acacia wood, three cubits*g* high; it was square, five cubits long and five cubits wide.*h* ²They made a horn at each of the four corners, so that the horns and the altar were of one piece, and they overlaid the altar with bronze. ³They made all its utensils of bronze—its pots, shovels, sprinkling bowls, meat forks and firepans. ⁴They made a grating for the altar, a bronze network, to be under its ledge, halfway up the altar. ⁵They cast bronze rings to hold the poles for the four corners of the bronze grating. ⁶They made the poles of acacia wood and overlaid them with bronze. ⁷They inserted the poles into the rings so they would be on the sides of the altar for carrying it. They made it hollow, out of boards.

Basin for Washing

⁸They made the bronze basin and its bronze stand from the mirrors of

a10 Or *He*; also in verses 11-29   *b10* That is, about 3 feet (about 0.9 meter) long, 1 1/2 feet (about 0.5 meter) wide, and 2 1/4 feet (about 0.7 meter) high   *c12* That is, about 3 inches (about 8 centimeters)   *d24* That is, about 75 pounds (about 34 kilograms)   *e25* That is, about 1 1/2 feet (about 0.5 meter) long and wide, and about 3 feet (about 0.9 meter) high   *f1* Or *He*; also in verses 2-9   *g1* That is, about 4 1/2 feet (about 1.3 meters)   *h1* That is, about 7 1/2 feet (about 2.3 meters) long and wide

the women who served at the entrance to the Tent of Meeting.

The Courtyard

⁹Next they made the courtyard. The south side was a hundred cubits[a] long and had curtains of finely twisted linen, ¹⁰with twenty posts and twenty bronze bases, and with silver hooks and bands on the posts. ¹¹The north side was also a hundred cubits long and had twenty posts and twenty bronze bases, with silver hooks and bands on the posts.

¹²The west end was fifty cubits[b] wide and had curtains, with ten posts and ten bases, with silver hooks and bands on the posts. ¹³The east end, toward the sunrise, was also fifty cubits wide. ¹⁴Curtains fifteen cubits[c] long were on one side of the entrance, with three posts and three bases,

¹⁵and curtains fifteen cubits long were on the other side of the entrance to the courtyard, with three posts and three bases. ¹⁶All the curtains around the courtyard were of finely twisted linen. ¹⁷The bases for the posts were bronze. The hooks and bands on the posts were silver, and their tops were overlaid with silver; so all the posts of the courtyard had silver bands.

¹⁸The curtain for the entrance to the courtyard was of blue, purple and scarlet yarn and finely twisted linen—the work of an embroiderer. It was twenty cubits[d] long and, like the curtains of the courtyard, five cubits[e] high, ¹⁹with four posts and four bronze bases. Their hooks and bands were silver, and their tops were overlaid with silver. ²⁰All the tent pegs of the tabernacle and of the surrounding courtyard were bronze.

---

a9 That is, about 150 feet (about 46 meters)
c14 That is, about 22 1/2 feet (about 6.9 meters)
e18 That is, about 7 1/2 feet (about 2.3 meters)

b12 That is, about 75 feet (about 23 meters)
d18 That is, about 30 feet (about 9 meters)

Life in Bible Times

THE TABERNACLE

The tabernacle was where Israel worshiped God. It was called the "Tent of Meeting," where God met his chosen people. The tabernacle had many parts, but all were built so they could be easily moved as

Israel wandered in the desert. The courtyard had only one door to remind the people that there is only one way to come to God. The tabernacle had two rooms. They were called the Holy Place and the Most Holy Place. Read Exodus 40:34–38 to see how God showed his presence in the tabernacle.

The Materials Used

21These are the amounts of the materials used for the tabernacle, the tabernacle of the Testimony, which were recorded at Moses' command by the Levites under the direction of Ithamar son of Aaron, the priest. 22(Bezalel son of Uri, the son of Hur, of the tribe of Judah, made everything the LORD commanded Moses; 23with him was Oholiab son of Ahisamach, of the tribe of Dan—a craftsman and designer, and an embroiderer in blue, purple and scarlet yarn and fine linen.) 24The total amount of the gold from the wave offering used for all the work on the sanctuary was 29 talents and 730 shekels,*a* according to the sanctuary shekel.

25The silver obtained from those of the community who were counted in the census was 100 talents and 1,775 shekels,*b* according to the sanctuary shekel— 26one beka per person, that is, half a shekel,*c* according to the sanctuary shekel, from everyone who had crossed over to those counted, twenty years old or more, a total of 603,550 men. 27The 100 talents*d* of silver were used to cast the bases for the sanctuary and for the curtain— 100 bases from the 100 talents, one talent for each base. 28They used the 1,775 shekels*e* to make the hooks for the posts, to overlay the tops of the posts, and to make their bands.

29The bronze from the wave offering was 70 talents and 2,400 shekels.*f* 30They used it to make the bases for the entrance to the Tent of Meeting, the bronze altar with its bronze grating and all its utensils, 31the bases for the surrounding courtyard and those for its entrance and all the tent pegs for the tabernacle and those for the surrounding courtyard.

The Priestly Garments

39 From the blue, purple and scarlet yarn they made woven garments for ministering in the sanctuary. They also made sacred garments for Aaron, as the LORD commanded Moses.

The Ephod

2They*g* made the ephod of gold, and of blue, purple and scarlet yarn, and of finely twisted linen. 3They hammered out thin sheets of gold and cut strands to be worked into the blue, purple and scarlet yarn and fine linen—the work of a skilled craftsman. 4They made shoulder pieces for the ephod, which were attached to two of its corners, so it could be fastened. 5Its skillfully woven waistband was like it—of one piece with the ephod and made with gold, and with blue, purple and scarlet yarn, and with finely twisted linen, as the LORD commanded Moses.

6They mounted the onyx stones in gold filigree settings and engraved them like a seal with the names of the sons of Israel. 7Then they fastened them on the shoulder pieces of the ephod as memorial stones for the sons of Israel, as the LORD commanded Moses.

The Breastpiece

8They fashioned the breastpiece— the work of a skilled craftsman. They made it like the ephod: of gold, and of blue, purple and scarlet yarn, and of finely twisted linen. 9It was square —a span*h* long and a span wide— and folded double. 10Then they mounted four rows of precious stones on it. In the first row there was a ruby, a topaz and a beryl; 11in the second row a turquoise, a sapphire*i* and an emerald; 12in the third row a jacinth, an agate and an amethyst; 13in

---

a24 The weight of the gold was a little over one ton (about 1 metric ton).　　*b25* The weight of the silver was a little over 3 3/4 tons (about 3.4 metric tons).　　*c26* That is, about 1/5 ounce (about 5.5 grams)　　*d27* That is, about 3 3/4 tons (about 3.4 metric tons)　　*e28* That is, about 45 pounds (about 20 kilograms)　　*f29* The weight of the bronze was about 2 1/2 tons (about 2.4 metric tons).　　*g2* Or *He*; also in verses 7, 8 and 22　　*h9* That is, about 9 inches (about 22 centimeters)　　*i11* Or *lapis lazuli*

the fourth row a chrysolite, an onyx and a jasper.[a] They were mounted in gold filigree settings. [14]There were twelve stones, one for each of the names of the sons of Israel, each engraved like a seal with the name of one of the twelve tribes.

[15]For the breastpiece they made braided chains of pure gold, like a rope. [16]They made two gold filigree settings and two gold rings, and fastened the rings to two of the corners of the breastpiece. [17]They fastened the two gold chains to the rings at the corners of the breastpiece, [18]and the other ends of the chains to the two settings, attaching them to the shoulder pieces of the ephod at the front. [19]They made two gold rings and attached them to the other two corners of the breastpiece on the inside edge next to the ephod. [20]Then they made two more gold rings and attached them to the bottom of the shoulder pieces on the front of the ephod, close to the seam just above the waistband of the ephod. [21]They tied the rings of the breastpiece to the rings of the ephod with blue cord, connecting it to the waistband so that the breastpiece would not swing out from the ephod—as the LORD commanded Moses.

Other Priestly Garments

[22]They made the robe of the ephod entirely of blue cloth—the work of a weaver— [23]with an opening in the center of the robe like the opening of a collar,[b] and a band around this opening, so that it would not tear. [24]They made pomegranates of blue, purple and scarlet yarn and finely twisted linen around the hem of the robe. [25]And they made bells of pure gold and attached them around the hem between the pomegranates. [26]The bells and pomegranates alternated around the hem of the robe to be worn for ministering, as the LORD commanded Moses.

[27]For Aaron and his sons, they made tunics of fine linen—the work of a weaver— [28]and the turban of fine linen, the linen headbands and the undergarments of finely twisted linen. [29]The sash was of finely twisted linen and blue, purple and scarlet yarn—the work of an embroiderer —as the LORD commanded Moses.

[30]They made the plate, the sacred diadem, out of pure gold and engraved on it, like an inscription on a seal: HOLY TO THE LORD. [31]Then they fastened a blue cord to it to attach it to the turban, as the LORD commanded Moses.

Moses Inspects the Tabernacle

[32]So all the work on the tabernacle, the Tent of Meeting, was completed. The Israelites did everything just as the LORD commanded Moses. [33]Then they brought the tabernacle to Moses: the tent and all its furnishings, its clasps, frames, crossbars, posts and bases; [34]the covering of ram skins dyed red, the covering of hides of sea cows[c] and the shielding curtain; [35]the ark of the Testimony with its poles and the atonement cover; [36]the table with all its articles and the bread of the Presence; [37]the pure gold lampstand with its row of lamps and all its accessories, and the oil for the light; [38]the gold altar, the anointing oil, the fragrant incense, and the curtain for the entrance to the tent; [39]the bronze altar with its bronze grating, its poles and all its utensils; the basin with its stand; [40]the curtains of the courtyard with its posts and bases, and the curtain for the entrance to the courtyard; the ropes and tent pegs for the courtyard; all the furnishings for the tabernacle, the Tent of Meeting; [41]and the woven garments worn for ministering in the sanctuary, both the sacred garments for Aaron the priest and the garments for his sons when serving as priests.

[42]The Israelites had done all the work just as the LORD had command-

---

[a]13 The precise identification of some of these precious stones is uncertain.   [b]23 The meaning of the Hebrew for this word is uncertain.   [c]34 That is, dugongs

ed Moses. ⁴³Moses inspected the work and saw that they had done it just as the LORD had commanded. So Moses blessed them.

Setting Up the Tabernacle

40 Then the LORD said to Moses: ²"Set up the tabernacle, the Tent of Meeting, on the first day of the first month. ³Place the ark of the Testimony in it and shield the ark with the curtain. ⁴Bring in the table and set out what belongs on it. Then bring in the lampstand and set up its lamps. ⁵Place the gold altar of incense in front of the ark of the Testimony and put the curtain at the entrance to the tabernacle.

⁶"Place the altar of burnt offering in front of the entrance to the tabernacle, the Tent of Meeting; ⁷place the basin between the Tent of Meeting and the altar and put water in it. ⁸Set up the courtyard around it and put the curtain at the entrance to the courtyard.

⁹"Take the anointing oil and anoint the tabernacle and everything in it; consecrate it and all its furnishings, and it will be holy. ¹⁰Then anoint the altar of burnt offering and all its utensils; consecrate the altar, and it will be most holy. ¹¹Anoint the basin and its stand and consecrate them.

¹²"Bring Aaron and his sons to the entrance to the Tent of Meeting and wash them with water. ¹³Then dress Aaron in the sacred garments, anoint him and consecrate him so he may serve me as priest. ¹⁴Bring his sons and dress them in tunics. ¹⁵Anoint them just as you anointed their father, so they may serve me as priests. Their anointing will be to a priesthood that will continue for all generations to come." ¹⁶Moses did everything just as the LORD commanded him.

¹⁷So the tabernacle was set up on the first day of the first month in the second year. ¹⁸When Moses set up the tabernacle, he put the bases in place, erected the frames, inserted the crossbars and set up the posts. ¹⁹Then he spread the tent over the taberna-cle and put the covering over the tent, as the LORD commanded him.

²⁰He took the Testimony and placed it in the ark, attached the poles to the ark and put the atonement cover over it. ²¹Then he brought the ark into the tabernacle and hung the shielding curtain and shielded the ark of the Testimony, as the LORD commanded him.

²²Moses placed the table in the Tent of Meeting on the north side of the tabernacle outside the curtain ²³and set out the bread on it before the LORD, as the LORD commanded him.

²⁴He placed the lampstand in the Tent of Meeting opposite the table on the south side of the tabernacle ²⁵and set up the lamps before the LORD, as the LORD commanded him.

²⁶Moses placed the gold altar in the Tent of Meeting in front of the curtain ²⁷and burned fragrant incense on it, as the LORD commanded him. ²⁸Then he put up the curtain at the entrance to the tabernacle.

²⁹He set the altar of burnt offering near the entrance to the tabernacle, the Tent of Meeting, and offered on it burnt offerings and grain offerings, as the LORD commanded him.

³⁰He placed the basin between the Tent of Meeting and the altar and put water in it for washing, ³¹and Moses and Aaron and his sons used it to wash their hands and feet. ³²They washed whenever they entered the Tent of Meeting or approached the altar, as the LORD commanded Moses.

³³Then Moses set up the courtyard around the tabernacle and altar and put up the curtain at the entrance to the courtyard. And so Moses finished the work.

The Glory of the LORD

³⁴Then the cloud covered the Tent of Meeting, and the glory of the LORD filled the tabernacle. ³⁵Moses could not enter the Tent of Meeting because the cloud had settled upon it, and the glory of the LORD filled the tabernacle.

³⁶In all the travels of the Israelites, whenever the cloud lifted from above the tabernacle, they would set out; ³⁷but if the cloud did not lift, they did not set out—until the day it lifted.

³⁸So the cloud of the LORD was over the tabernacle by day, and fire was in the cloud by night, in the sight of all the house of Israel during all their travels.

LEVITICUS

The Burnt Offering

1 The LORD called to Moses and spoke to him from the Tent of Meeting. He said, [2]"Speak to the Israelites and say to them: 'When any of you brings an offering to the LORD, bring as your offering an animal from either the herd or the flock.

[3]" 'If the offering is a burnt offering from the herd, he is to offer a male without defect. He must present it at the entrance to the Tent of Meeting so that it[a] will be acceptable to the LORD. [4]He is to lay his hand on the head of the burnt offering, and it will be accepted on his behalf to make atonement for him. [5]He is to slaughter the young bull before the LORD, and then Aaron's sons the priests shall bring the blood and sprinkle it against the altar on all sides at the entrance to the Tent of Meeting. [6]He is to skin the burnt offering and cut it into pieces. [7]The sons of Aaron the priest are to put fire on the altar and arrange wood on the fire. [8]Then Aaron's sons the priests shall arrange the pieces, including the head and the fat, on the burning wood that is on the altar. [9]He is to wash the inner parts and the legs with water, and the priest is to burn all of it on the altar. It is a burnt offering, an offering made by fire, an aroma pleasing to the LORD.

❓DID YOU KNOW?   1:9

What is a burnt offering?

When the Israelites made a sacrifice or offering to God, they burned an animal on a special altar. Special laws told the priests and people just how to make burnt offerings.

---

[10]" 'If the offering is a burnt offering from the flock, from either the sheep or the goats, he is to offer a male without defect. [11]He is to slaughter it at the north side of the altar before the LORD, and Aaron's sons the priests shall sprinkle its blood against the altar on all sides. [12]He is to cut it into pieces, and the priest shall arrange them, including the head and the fat, on the burning wood that is on the altar. [13]He is to wash the inner parts and the legs with water, and the priest is to bring all of it and burn it on the altar. It is a burnt offering, an offering made by fire, an aroma pleasing to the LORD.

[14]" 'If the offering to the LORD is a burnt offering of birds, he is to offer a dove or a young pigeon. [15]The priest shall bring it to the altar, wring off the head and burn it on the altar; its blood shall be drained out on the side of the altar. [16]He is to remove the crop with its contents[b] and throw it to the east side of the altar, where the ashes are. [17]He shall tear it open by the wings, not severing it completely, and then the priest shall burn it on the wood that is on the fire on the altar. It is a burnt offering, an offering made by fire, an aroma pleasing to the LORD.

The Grain Offering

2 " 'When someone brings a grain offering to the LORD, his offering is to be of fine flour. He is to pour oil on it, put incense on it [2]and take it to Aaron's sons the priests. The priest shall take a handful of the fine flour and oil, together with all the incense, and burn this as a memorial portion on the altar, an offering made by fire, an aroma pleasing to the LORD. [3]The rest of the grain offering belongs to Aaron and his sons; it is a most holy part of the offerings made to the LORD by fire.

[4]" 'If you bring a grain offering baked in an oven, it is to consist of fine flour: cakes made without yeast and mixed with oil, or[c] wafers made without yeast and spread with oil. [5]If your grain offering is prepared on a griddle, it is to be made of fine flour

---

[a]3 Or he   [b]16 Or crop and the feathers; the meaning of the Hebrew for this word is uncertain.
[c]4 Or and

mixed with oil, and without yeast.
⁶Crumble it and pour oil on it; it is a
grain offering. ⁷If your grain offering
is cooked in a pan, it is to be made of
fine flour and oil. ⁸Bring the grain
offering made of these things to the
LORD; present it to the priest, who
shall take it to the altar. ⁹He shall
take out the memorial portion from
the grain offering and burn it on the
altar as an offering made by fire, an
aroma pleasing to the LORD. ¹⁰The
rest of the grain offering belongs to
Aaron and his sons; it is a most holy
part of the offerings made to the LORD
by fire.

¹¹" 'Every grain offering you bring
to the LORD must be made without
yeast, for you are not to burn any
yeast or honey in an offering made to
the LORD by fire. ¹²You may bring
them to the LORD as an offering of the
firstfruits, but they are not to be offered on the altar as a pleasing aroma. ¹³Season all your grain offerings
with salt. Do not leave the salt of the
covenant of your God out of your
grain offerings; add salt to all your
offerings.

¹⁴" 'If you bring a grain offering of
firstfruits to the LORD, offer crushed
heads of new grain roasted in the fire.
¹⁵Put oil and incense on it; it is a
grain offering. ¹⁶The priest shall
burn the memorial portion of the
crushed grain and the oil, together
with all the incense, as an offering
made to the LORD by fire.

The Fellowship Offering

3 " 'If someone's offering is a fellowship offering,ᵃ and he offers
an animal from the herd, whether
male or female, he is to present before the LORD an animal without defect. ²He is to lay his hand on the
head of his offering and slaughter it
at the entrance to the Tent of Meeting. Then Aaron's sons the priests
shall sprinkle the blood against the
altar on all sides. ³From the fellowship offering he is to bring a sacrifice
made to the LORD by fire: all the fat

that covers the inner parts or is connected to them, ⁴both kidneys with
the fat on them near the loins, and
the covering of the liver, which he
will remove with the kidneys. ⁵Then
Aaron's sons are to burn it on the altar on top of the burnt offering that is
on the burning wood, as an offering
made by fire, an aroma pleasing to
the LORD.

⁶" 'If he offers an animal from the
flock as a fellowship offering to the
LORD, he is to offer a male or female
without defect. ⁷If he offers a lamb,
he is to present it before the LORD.
⁸He is to lay his hand on the head of
his offering and slaughter it in front
of the Tent of Meeting. Then Aaron's
sons shall sprinkle its blood against
the altar on all sides. ⁹From the fellowship offering he is to bring a sacrifice made to the LORD by fire: its fat,
the entire fat tail cut off close to the
backbone, all the fat that covers the
inner parts or is connected to them,
¹⁰both kidneys with the fat on them
near the loins, and the covering of the
liver, which he will remove with the
kidneys. ¹¹The priest shall burn them
on the altar as food, an offering made
to the LORD by fire.

? DID YOU KNOW?   3:6

**What happened to the meat of
a fellowship offering?**

The family of the person who offered the sacrifice ate most of the
meat of a fellowship offering. The
Israelites thought of this as eating a
friendship meal with God himself.

---

¹²" 'If his offering is a goat, he is to
present it before the LORD. ¹³He is to
lay his hand on its head and slaughter it in front of the Tent of Meeting.
Then Aaron's sons shall sprinkle its
blood against the altar on all sides.
¹⁴From what he offers he is to make
this offering to the LORD by fire: all
the fat that covers the inner parts or

ᵃ1 Traditionally *peace offering*; also in verses 3, 6 and 9

is connected to them, [15]both kidneys with the fat on them near the loins, and the covering of the liver, which he will remove with the kidneys. [16]The priest shall burn them on the altar as food, an offering made by fire, a pleasing aroma. All the fat is the LORD's.

[17]" 'This is a lasting ordinance for the generations to come, wherever you live: You must not eat any fat or any blood.' "

The Sin Offering

4 The LORD said to Moses, [2]"Say to the Israelites: 'When anyone sins unintentionally and does what is forbidden in any of the LORD's commands—

[3]" 'If the anointed priest sins, bringing guilt on the people, he must bring to the LORD a young bull without defect as a sin offering for the sin he has committed. [4]He is to present the bull at the entrance to the Tent of Meeting before the LORD. He is to lay his hand on its head and slaughter it before the LORD. [5]Then the anointed priest shall take some of the bull's blood and carry it into the Tent of Meeting. [6]He is to dip his finger into the blood and sprinkle some of it seven times before the LORD, in front of the curtain of the sanctuary. [7]The priest shall then put some of the blood on the horns of the altar of fragrant incense that is before the LORD in the Tent of Meeting. The rest of the bull's blood he shall pour out at the base of the altar of burnt offering at the entrance to the Tent of Meeting. [8]He shall remove all the fat from the bull of the sin offering—the fat that covers the inner parts or is connected to them, [9]both kidneys with the fat on them near the loins, and the covering of the liver, which he will remove with the kidneys— [10]just as the fat is removed from the ox[a] sacrificed as a fellowship offering.[b] Then the priest shall burn them on the altar of burnt

offering. [11]But the hide of the bull and all its flesh, as well as the head and legs, the inner parts and offal— [12]that is, all the rest of the bull—he must take outside the camp to a place ceremonially clean, where the ashes are thrown, and burn it in a wood fire on the ash heap.

[13]" 'If the whole Israelite community sins unintentionally and does what is forbidden in any of the LORD's commands, even though the community is unaware of the matter, they are guilty. [14]When they become aware of the sin they committed, the assembly must bring a young bull as a sin offering and present it before the Tent of Meeting. [15]The elders of the community are to lay their hands on the bull's head before the LORD, and the bull shall be slaughtered before the LORD. [16]Then the anointed priest is to take some of the bull's blood into the Tent of Meeting. [17]He shall dip his finger into the blood and sprinkle it before the LORD seven times in front of the curtain. [18]He is to put some of the blood on the horns of the altar that is before the LORD in the Tent of Meeting. The rest of the blood he shall pour out at the base of the altar of burnt offering at the entrance to the Tent of Meeting. [19]He shall remove all the fat from it and burn it on the altar, [20]and do with this bull just as he did with the bull for the sin offering. In this way the priest will make atonement for them, and they will be forgiven. [21]Then he shall take the bull outside the camp and burn it as he burned the first bull. This is the sin offering for the community.

[22]" 'When a leader sins unintentionally and does what is forbidden in any of the commands of the LORD his God, he is guilty. [23]When he is made aware of the sin he committed, he must bring as his offering a male goat without defect. [24]He is to lay his hand on the goat's head and slaugh-

---

[a]10 The Hebrew word can include both male and female, also in verses 26, 31 and 35   [b]10 Traditionally *peace offering*; also

ter it at the place where the burnt offering is slaughtered before the LORD. It is a sin offering. 25Then the priest shall take some of the blood of the sin offering with his finger and put it on the horns of the altar of burnt offering and pour out the rest of the blood at the base of the altar. 26He shall burn all the fat on the altar as he burned the fat of the fellowship offering. In this way the priest will make atonement for the man's sin, and he will be forgiven.

27" 'If a member of the community sins unintentionally and does what is forbidden in any of the LORD's commands, he is guilty. 28When he is made aware of the sin he committed, he must bring as his offering for the sin he committed a female goat without defect. 29He is to lay his hand on the head of the sin offering and slaughter it at the place of the burnt offering. 30Then the priest is to take some of the blood with his finger and put it on the horns of the altar of burnt offering and pour out the rest of the blood at the base of the altar. 31He shall remove all the fat, just as the fat is removed from the fellowship offering, and the priest shall burn it on the altar as an aroma pleasing to the LORD. In this way the priest will make atonement for him, and he will be forgiven.

32" 'If he brings a lamb as his sin offering, he is to bring a female without defect. 33He is to lay his hand on its head and slaughter it for a sin of-

fering at the place where the burnt offering is slaughtered. 34Then the priest shall take some of the blood of the sin offering with his finger and put it on the horns of the altar of burnt offering and pour out the rest of the blood at the base of the altar. 35He shall remove all the fat, just as the fat is removed from the lamb of the fellowship offering, and the priest shall burn it on the altar on top of the offerings made to the LORD by fire. In this way the priest will make atonement for him for the sin he has committed, and he will be forgiven.

5 " 'If a person sins because he does not speak up when he hears a public charge to testify regarding something he has seen or learned about, he will be held responsible.

2" 'Or if a person touches anything ceremonially unclean—whether the carcasses of unclean wild animals or of unclean livestock or of unclean creatures that move along the ground—even though he is unaware of it, he has become unclean and is guilty.

3" 'Or if he touches human uncleanness—anything that would make him unclean—even though he is unaware of it, when he learns of it he will be guilty.

4" 'Or if a person thoughtlessly takes an oath to do anything, whether good or evil—in any matter one might carelessly swear about—even

---

LET'S LIVE IT! Leviticus 4:22–31

I FORGOT! ➡ "Kenny, did you take my hammer?"

Kenny nodded. "Yes, Dad. I had to fix a board in the dog house."

Dad looked angry. "Did you leave the hammer outside when you were done? Didn't I tell you when you used my tools to put them back again?"

"Oh, no," Kenny thought. Then he told his dad, "I'm sorry. I forgot."

Kenny didn't do wrong on purpose. But he did do wrong. You be the judge. Is Kenny guilty? Should Kenny be punished? Read Leviticus 4:22–31. What does it say about unintentional sins? (Unintentional means not done on purpose.)

though he is unaware of it, in any case when he learns of it he will be guilty.

5" 'When anyone is guilty in any of these ways, he must confess in what way he has sinned 6and, as a penalty for the sin he has committed, he must bring to the LORD a female lamb or goat from the flock as a sin offering; and the priest shall make atonement for him for his sin.

7" 'If he cannot afford a lamb, he is to bring two doves or two young pigeons to the LORD as a penalty for his sin—one for a sin offering and the other for a burnt offering. 8He is to bring them to the priest, who shall first offer the one for the sin offering. He is to wring its head from its neck, not severing it completely, 9and is to sprinkle some of the blood of the sin offering against the side of the altar; the rest of the blood must be drained out at the base of the altar. It is a sin offering. 10The priest shall then offer the other as a burnt offering in the prescribed way and make atonement for him for the sin he has committed, and he will be forgiven.

11" 'If, however, he cannot afford two doves or two young pigeons, he is to bring as an offering for his sin a tenth of an ephah*a* of fine flour for a sin offering. He must not put oil or incense on it, because it is a sin offering. 12He is to bring it to the priest, who shall take a handful of it as a memorial portion and burn it on the altar on top of the offerings made to the LORD by fire. It is a sin offering. 13In this way the priest will make atonement for him for any of these sins he has committed, and he will be forgiven. The rest of the offering will belong to the priest, as in the case of the grain offering.' "

The Guilt Offering

14The LORD said to Moses: 15"When a person commits a violation and sins unintentionally in regard to any of the LORD's holy things, he is to bring to the LORD as a penalty a ram from the flock, one without defect and of the proper value in silver, according to the sanctuary shekel.*b* It is a guilt offering. 16He must make restitution for what he has failed to do in regard to the holy things, add a fifth of the value to that and give it all to the priest, who will make atonement for him with the ram as a guilt offering, and he will be forgiven.

17"If a person sins and does what is forbidden in any of the LORD's commands, even though he does not know it, he is guilty and will be held responsible. 18He is to bring to the priest as a guilt offering a ram from the flock, one without defect and of the proper value. In this way the priest will make atonement for him for the wrong he has committed unintentionally, and he will be forgiven. 19It is a guilt offering; he has been guilty of*c* wrongdoing against the LORD."

6 The LORD said to Moses: 2"If anyone sins and is unfaithful to the LORD by deceiving his neighbor about something entrusted to him or left in his care or stolen, or if he cheats him, 3or if he finds lost property and lies about it, or if he swears falsely, or if he commits any such sin that people may do— 4when he thus sins and becomes guilty, he must return what he has stolen or taken by extortion, or what was entrusted to him, or the lost property he found, 5or whatever it was he swore falsely about. He must make restitution in full, add a fifth of the value to it and give it all to the owner on the day he presents his guilt offering. 6And as a penalty he must bring to the priest, that is, to the LORD, his guilt offering, a ram from the flock, one without defect and of the proper value. 7In this way the priest will make atonement for him before the LORD, and he will be forgiven for any of these things he did that made him guilty."

---

a11 That is, probably about 2 quarts (about 2 liters) grams)   *c19* Or *has made full expiation for his*

b15 That is, about 2/5 ounce (about 11.5

The Burnt Offering

[8]The LORD said to Moses: [9]"Give Aaron and his sons this command: 'These are the regulations for the burnt offering: The burnt offering is to remain on the altar hearth throughout the night, till morning, and the fire must be kept burning on the altar. [10]The priest shall then put on his linen clothes, with linen undergarments next to his body, and shall remove the ashes of the burnt offering that the fire has consumed on the altar and place them beside the altar. [11]Then he is to take off these clothes and put on others, and carry the ashes outside the camp to a place that is ceremonially clean. [12]The fire on the altar must be kept burning; it must not go out. Every morning the priest is to add firewood and arrange the burnt offering on the fire and burn the fat of the fellowship offerings[a] on it. [13]The fire must be kept burning on the altar continuously; it must not go out.

The Grain Offering

[14]" 'These are the regulations for the grain offering: Aaron's sons are to bring it before the LORD, in front of the altar. [15]The priest is to take a handful of fine flour and oil, together with all the incense on the grain offering, and burn the memorial portion on the altar as an aroma pleasing to the LORD. [16]Aaron and his sons shall eat the rest of it, but it is to be eaten without yeast in a holy place; they are to eat it in the courtyard of the Tent of Meeting. [17]It must not be baked with yeast; I have given it as their share of the offerings made to me by fire. Like the sin offering and the guilt offering, it is most holy. [18]Any male descendant of Aaron may eat it. It is his regular share of the offerings made to the LORD by fire for the generations to come. Whatever touches them will become holy.[b] '"

[19]The LORD also said to Moses, [20]"This is the offering Aaron and his sons are to bring to the LORD on the day he[c] is anointed: a tenth of an ephah[d] of fine flour as a regular grain offering, half of it in the morning and half in the evening. [21]Prepare it with oil on a griddle; bring it well-mixed and present the grain offering broken[e] in pieces as an aroma pleasing to the LORD. [22]The son who is to succeed him as anointed priest shall prepare it. It is the LORD's regular share and is to be burned completely. [23]Every grain offering of a

---

*a12 Traditionally *peace offerings*   *b18 Or *Whoever touches them must be holy*; similarly in verse 27   *c20 Or *each*   *d20 That is, probably about 2 quarts (about 2 liters)   *e21 The meaning of the Hebrew for this word is uncertain.

▟ET'S LIVE IT!   Leviticus 6:1–7

FINDERS KEEPERS? ➠ Have you ever heard the saying, "finders keepers, losers weepers"? It means that if I find something you lost... too bad. I get to keep it, and you just get to cry because you lost it.

Now read Leviticus 6:1–7. What do you think you should do in each of the following situations?

    1. You find a five-dollar bill in the hall at school.
    2. You borrow your friend's good ink pen and forget to return it.
    3. You discover that the jacket you brought home from the game isn't yours.

What do you suppose God thinks about "finders keepers, losers weepers"?

priest shall be burned completely; it must not be eaten."

The Sin Offering

24The LORD said to Moses, 25"Say to Aaron and his sons: 'These are the regulations for the sin offering: The sin offering is to be slaughtered before the LORD in the place the burnt offering is slaughtered; it is most holy. 26The priest who offers it shall eat it; it is to be eaten in a holy place, in the courtyard of the Tent of Meeting. 27Whatever touches any of the flesh will become holy, and if any of the blood is spattered on a garment, you must wash it in a holy place. 28The clay pot the meat is cooked in must be broken; but if it is cooked in a bronze pot, the pot is to be scoured and rinsed with water. 29Any male in a priest's family may eat it; it is most holy. 30But any sin offering whose blood is brought into the Tent of Meeting to make atonement in the Holy Place must not be eaten; it must be burned.

The Guilt Offering

7 " 'These are the regulations for the guilt offering, which is most holy: 2The guilt offering is to be slaughtered in the place where the burnt offering is slaughtered, and its blood is to be sprinkled against the altar on all sides. 3All its fat shall be offered: the fat tail and the fat that covers the inner parts, 4both kidneys with the fat on them near the loins, and the covering of the liver, which is to be removed with the kidneys. 5The priest shall burn them on the altar as an offering made to the LORD by fire. It is a guilt offering. 6Any male in a priest's family may eat it, but it must be eaten in a holy place; it is most holy.

7" 'The same law applies to both the sin offering and the guilt offering: They belong to the priest who makes atonement with them. 8The priest who offers a burnt offering for anyone may keep its hide for himself. 9Every grain offering baked in an oven or cooked in a pan or on a griddle belongs to the priest who offers it, 10and every grain offering, whether mixed with oil or dry, belongs equally to all the sons of Aaron.

❓DID YOU KNOW?   7:6

What happened to the meat of guilt and sin offerings?

Much of these offerings was burned. The part that was not burned belonged to the priests. The Israelites were commanded to make these offerings whenever they had accidentally broken one of God's laws.

The Fellowship Offering

11" 'These are the regulations for the fellowship offeringa a person may present to the LORD:

12" 'If he offers it as an expression of thankfulness, then along with this thank offering he is to offer cakes of bread made without yeast and mixed with oil, wafers made without yeast and spread with oil, and cakes of fine flour well-kneaded and mixed with oil. 13Along with his fellowship offering of thanksgiving he is to present an offering with cakes of bread made with yeast. 14He is to bring one of each kind as an offering, a contribution to the LORD; it belongs to the priest who sprinkles the blood of the fellowship offerings. 15The meat of his fellowship offering of thanksgiving must be eaten on the day it is offered; he must leave none of it till morning.

16" 'If, however, his offering is the result of a vow or is a freewill offering, the sacrifice shall be eaten on the day he offers it, but anything left over may be eaten on the next day. 17Any meat of the sacrifice left over till the third day must be burned up. 18If any meat of the fellowship offer-

---

a11 Traditionally *peace offering*; also in verses 13-37

ing is eaten on the third day, it will not be accepted. It will not be credited to the one who offered it, for it is impure; the person who eats any of it will be held responsible.

19"'Meat that touches anything ceremonially unclean must not be eaten; it must be burned up. As for other meat, anyone ceremonially clean may eat it. 20But if anyone who is unclean eats any meat of the fellowship offering belonging to the LORD, that person must be cut off from his people. 21If anyone touches something unclean—whether human uncleanness or an unclean animal or any unclean, detestable thing—and then eats any of the meat of the fellowship offering belonging to the LORD, that person must be cut off from his people.' "

Eating Fat and Blood Forbidden

22The LORD said to Moses, 23"Say to the Israelites: 'Do not eat any of the fat of cattle, sheep or goats. 24The fat of an animal found dead or torn by wild animals may be used for any other purpose, but you must not eat it. 25Anyone who eats the fat of an animal from which an offering by fire may be*a* made to the LORD must be cut off from his people. 26And wherever you live, you must not eat the blood of any bird or animal. 27If anyone eats blood, that person must be cut off from his people.' "

The Priests' Share

28The LORD said to Moses, 29"Say to the Israelites: 'Anyone who brings a fellowship offering to the LORD is to bring part of it as his sacrifice to the LORD. 30With his own hands he is to bring the offering made to the LORD by fire; he is to bring the fat, together with the breast, and wave the breast before the LORD as a wave offering. 31The priest shall burn the fat on the altar, but the breast belongs to Aaron and his sons. 32You are to give the right thigh of your fellowship offerings to the priest as a contribution.

33The son of Aaron who offers the blood and the fat of the fellowship offering shall have the right thigh as his share. 34From the fellowship offerings of the Israelites, I have taken the breast that is waved and the thigh that is presented and have given them to Aaron the priest and his sons as their regular share from the Israelites.' "

35This is the portion of the offerings made to the LORD by fire that were allotted to Aaron and his sons on the day they were presented to serve the LORD as priests. 36On the day they were anointed, the LORD commanded that the Israelites give this to them as their regular share for the generations to come.

37These, then, are the regulations for the burnt offering, the grain offering, the sin offering, the guilt offering, the ordination offering and the fellowship offering, 38which the LORD gave Moses on Mount Sinai on the day he commanded the Israelites to bring their offerings to the LORD, in the Desert of Sinai.

The Ordination of Aaron and His Sons

8 The LORD said to Moses, 2"Bring Aaron and his sons, their garments, the anointing oil, the bull for the sin offering, the two rams and the basket containing bread made without yeast, 3and gather the entire assembly at the entrance to the Tent of Meeting." 4Moses did as the LORD commanded him, and the assembly gathered at the entrance to the Tent of Meeting.

5Moses said to the assembly, "This is what the LORD has commanded to be done." 6Then Moses brought Aaron and his sons forward and washed them with water. 7He put the tunic on Aaron, tied the sash around him, clothed him with the robe and put the ephod on him. He also tied the ephod to him by its skillfully woven waistband; so it was fastened on him. 8He

a25 Or fire is

placed the breastpiece on him and put the Urim and Thummim in the breastpiece. ⁹Then he placed the turban on Aaron's head and set the gold plate, the sacred diadem, on the front of it, as the LORD commanded Moses.

❓DID YOU KNOW?   8:2

What was the job of the priest in Israel?

The priests made the sacrifices that God commanded. The priests took care of the tabernacle and were also to teach the Israelites God's rules for holy living.

¹⁰Then Moses took the anointing oil and anointed the tabernacle and everything in it, and so consecrated them. ¹¹He sprinkled some of the oil on the altar seven times, anointing the altar and all its utensils and the basin with its stand, to consecrate them. ¹²He poured some of the anointing oil on Aaron's head and anointed him to consecrate him. ¹³Then he brought Aaron's sons forward, put tunics on them, tied sashes around them and put headbands on them, as the LORD commanded Moses.

¹⁴He then presented the bull for the sin offering, and Aaron and his sons laid their hands on its head. ¹⁵Moses slaughtered the bull and took some of the blood, and with his finger he put it on all the horns of the altar to purify the altar. He poured out the rest of the blood at the base of the altar. So he consecrated it to make atonement for it. ¹⁶Moses also took all the fat around the inner parts, the covering of the liver, and both kidneys and their fat, and burned it on the altar. ¹⁷But the bull with its hide and its flesh and its offal he burned up outside the camp, as the LORD commanded Moses.

¹⁸He then presented the ram for the burnt offering, and Aaron and his sons laid their hands on its head. ¹⁹Then Moses slaughtered the ram

and sprinkled the blood against the altar on all sides. ²⁰He cut the ram into pieces and burned the head, the pieces and the fat. ²¹He washed the inner parts and the legs with water and burned the whole ram on the altar as a burnt offering, a pleasing aroma, an offering made to the LORD by fire, as the LORD commanded Moses.

²²He then presented the other ram, the ram for the ordination, and Aaron and his sons laid their hands on its head. ²³Moses slaughtered the ram and took some of its blood and put it on the lobe of Aaron's right ear, on the thumb of his right hand and on the big toe of his right foot. ²⁴Moses also brought Aaron's sons forward and put some of the blood on the lobes of their right ears, on the thumbs of their right hands and on the big toes of their right feet. Then he sprinkled blood against the altar on all sides. ²⁵He took the fat, the fat tail, all the fat around the inner parts, the covering of the liver, both kidneys and their fat and the right thigh. ²⁶Then from the basket of bread made without yeast, which was before the LORD, he took a cake of bread, and one made with oil, and a wafer; he put these on the fat portions and on the right thigh. ²⁷He put all these in the hands of Aaron and his sons and waved them before the LORD as a wave offering. ²⁸Then Moses took them from their hands and burned them on the altar on top of the burnt offering as an ordination offering, a pleasing aroma, an offering made to the LORD by fire. ²⁹He also took the breast— Moses' share of the ordination ram —and waved it before the LORD as a wave offering, as the LORD commanded Moses.

³⁰Then Moses took some of the anointing oil and some of the blood from the altar and sprinkled them on Aaron and his garments and on his sons and their garments. So he consecrated Aaron and his garments and his sons and their garments.

³¹Moses then said to Aaron and his sons, "Cook the meat at the entrance

to the Tent of Meeting and eat it
there with the bread from the basket
of ordination offerings, as I commanded, saying,[a] 'Aaron and his
sons are to eat it.' ³²Then burn up the
rest of the meat and the bread. ³³Do
not leave the entrance to the Tent of
Meeting for seven days, until the
days of your ordination are completed, for your ordination will last seven
days. ³⁴What has been done today
was commanded by the LORD to make
atonement for you. ³⁵You must stay
at the entrance to the Tent of Meeting day and night for seven days and
do what the LORD requires, so you
will not die; for that is what I have
been commanded." ³⁶So Aaron and
his sons did everything the LORD
commanded through Moses.

The Priests Begin Their Ministry

9 On the eighth day Moses summoned Aaron and his sons and
the elders of Israel. ²He said to Aaron, "Take a bull calf for your sin offering and a ram for your burnt offering,
both without defect, and present
them before the LORD. ³Then say to
the Israelites: 'Take a male goat for a
sin offering, a calf and a lamb—both
a year old and without defect—for a
burnt offering, ⁴and an ox[b] and a ram
for a fellowship offering[c] to sacrifice
before the LORD, together with
a grain offering mixed with oil. For
today the LORD will appear to
you.' "

⁵They took the things Moses commanded to the front of the Tent of
Meeting, and the entire assembly
came near and stood before the LORD.
⁶Then Moses said, "This is what the
LORD has commanded you to do, so
that the glory of the LORD may appear to you."

⁷Moses said to Aaron, "Come to the
altar and sacrifice your sin offering
and your burnt offering and make
atonement for yourself and the people; sacrifice the offering that is for

the people and make atonement for
them, as the LORD has commanded."
⁸So Aaron came to the altar and
slaughtered the calf as a sin offering
for himself. ⁹His sons brought the
blood to him, and he dipped his finger
into the blood and put it on the horns
of the altar; the rest of the blood he
poured out at the base of the altar.
¹⁰On the altar he burned the fat, the
kidneys and the covering of the liver
from the sin offering, as the LORD
commanded Moses; ¹¹the flesh and
the hide he burned up outside the
camp.

¹²Then he slaughtered the burnt offering. His sons handed him the
blood, and he sprinkled it against the
altar on all sides. ¹³They handed him
the burnt offering piece by piece, including the head, and he burned
them on the altar. ¹⁴He washed the
inner parts and the legs and burned
them on top of the burnt offering on
the altar.

¹⁵Aaron then brought the offering
that was for the people. He took the
goat for the people's sin offering and
slaughtered it and offered it for a sin
offering as he did with the first one.

¹⁶He brought the burnt offering
and offered it in the prescribed way.
¹⁷He also brought the grain offering,
took a handful of it and burned it on
the altar in addition to the morning's
burnt offering.

¹⁸He slaughtered the ox and the
ram as the fellowship offering for the
people. His sons handed him the
blood, and he sprinkled it against the
altar on all sides. ¹⁹But the fat portions of the ox and the ram—the fat
tail, the layer of fat, the kidneys and
the covering of the liver— ²⁰these
they laid on the breasts, and then
Aaron burned the fat on the altar.
²¹Aaron waved the breasts and the
right thigh before the LORD as a wave
offering, as Moses commanded.

²²Then Aaron lifted his hands toward the people and blessed them.
And having sacrificed the sin offer-

---

a31 Or I was commanded: *b4 The Hebrew word can include both male and female; also in
verses 18 and 19.*   *c4 Traditionally peace offering; also in verses 18 and 22*

ing, the burnt offering and the fellowship offering, he stepped down. 23Moses and Aaron then went into the Tent of Meeting. When they came out, they blessed the people; and the glory of the LORD appeared to all the people. 24Fire came out from the presence of the LORD and consumed the burnt offering and the fat portions on the altar. And when all the people saw it, they shouted for joy and fell facedown.

The Death of Nadab and Abihu

10 Aaron's sons Nadab and Abihu took their censers, put fire in them and added incense; and they offered unauthorized fire before the LORD, contrary to his command. 2So fire came out from the presence of the LORD and consumed them, and they died before the LORD. 3Moses then said to Aaron, "This is what the LORD spoke of when he said:

" 'Among those who approach me
    I will show myself holy;
in the sight of all the people
    I will be honored.' "

Aaron remained silent.

❓DID YOU KNOW?   10:1

Why was the sin of Nadab and Abihu so terrible?

Nadab and Abihu were priests. Priests were supposed to teach others God's law. Instead, these priests disobeyed a law about how they were to worship God.

4Moses summoned Mishael and Elzaphan, sons of Aaron's uncle Uzziel, and said to them, "Come here; carry your cousins outside the camp, away from the front of the sanctuary." 5So they came and carried them, still in their tunics, outside the camp, as Moses ordered.

6Then Moses said to Aaron and his sons Eleazar and Ithamar, "Do not let your hair become unkempt,a and do not tear your clothes, or you will die and the LORD will be angry with the whole community. But your relatives, all the house of Israel, may mourn for those the LORD has destroyed by fire. 7Do not leave the entrance to the Tent of Meeting or you will die, because the LORD's anointing oil is on you." So they did as Moses said.

8Then the LORD said to Aaron, 9"You and your sons are not to drink wine or other fermented drink whenever you go into the Tent of Meeting, or you will die. This is a lasting ordinance for the generations to come. 10You must distinguish between the holy and the common, between the unclean and the clean, 11and you must teach the Israelites all the decrees the LORD has given them through Moses."

12Moses said to Aaron and his remaining sons, Eleazar and Ithamar, "Take the grain offering left over from the offerings made to the LORD by fire and eat it prepared without yeast beside the altar, for it is most holy. 13Eat it in a holy place, because it is your share and your sons' share of the offerings made to the LORD by fire; for so I have been commanded. 14But you and your sons and your daughters may eat the breast that was waved and the thigh that was presented. Eat them in a ceremonially clean place; they have been given to you and your children as your share of the Israelites' fellowship offerings.b 15The thigh that was presented and the breast that was waved must be brought with the fat portions of the offerings made by fire, to be waved before the LORD as a wave offering. This will be the regular share for you and your children, as the LORD has commanded."

16When Moses inquired about the goat of the sin offering and found that it had been burned up, he was angry with Eleazar and Ithamar, Aaron's

---

a6 Or Do not uncover your heads   b14 Traditionally peace offerings

remaining sons, and asked, [17]"Why didn't you eat the sin offering in the sanctuary area? It is most holy; it was given to you to take away the guilt of the community by making atonement for them before the LORD. [18]Since its blood was not taken into the Holy Place, you should have eaten the goat in the sanctuary area, as I commanded."

[19]Aaron replied to Moses, "Today they sacrificed their sin offering and their burnt offering before the LORD, but such things as this have happened to me. Would the LORD have been pleased if I had eaten the sin offering today?" [20]When Moses heard this, he was satisfied.

Clean and Unclean Food

11 The LORD said to Moses and Aaron, [2]"Say to the Israelites: 'Of all the animals that live on land, these are the ones you may eat: [3]You may eat any animal that has a split hoof completely divided and that chews the cud.

[4]"'There are some that only chew the cud or only have a split hoof, but you must not eat them. The camel, though it chews the cud, does not have a split hoof; it is ceremonially

a5 That is, the hyrax or rock badger

unclean for you. [5]The coney,[a] though it chews the cud, does not have a split hoof; it is unclean for you. [6]The rabbit, though it chews the cud, does not have a split hoof; it is unclean for you. [7]And the pig, though it has a split hoof completely divided, does not chew the cud; it is unclean for you. [8]You must not eat their meat or touch their carcasses; they are unclean for you.

[9]"'Of all the creatures living in the water of the seas and the streams, you may eat any that have fins and scales. [10]But all creatures in the seas or streams that do not have fins and scales—whether among all the swarming things or among all the other living creatures in the water—you are to detest. [11]And since you are to detest them, you must not eat their meat and you must detest their carcasses. [12]Anything living in the water that does not have fins and scales is to be detestable to you.

[13]"'These are the birds you are to detest and not eat because they are detestable: the eagle, the vulture, the black vulture, [14]the red kite, any kind of black kite, [15]any kind of raven, [16]the horned owl, the screech

Life in Bible Times

EATING IN BIBLE TIMES

In Bible times it was important to show hospitality. Old Testament people did this by serving visitors a meal. They probably sat down at a round reed mat or leather "table," laid flat on the floor. Food was served in large dishes. Each person dipped into these dishes with his or her fingers or with a piece of bread.

owl, the gull, any kind of hawk, ¹⁷the little owl, the cormorant, the great owl, ¹⁸the white owl, the desert owl, the osprey, ¹⁹the stork, any kind of heron, the hoopoe and the bat.ᵃ

²⁰" 'All flying insects that walk on all fours are to be detestable to you. ²¹There are, however, some winged creatures that walk on all fours that you may eat: those that have jointed legs for hopping on the ground. ²²Of these you may eat any kind of locust, katydid, cricket or grasshopper. ²³But all other winged creatures that have four legs you are to detest.

²⁴" 'You will make yourselves unclean by these; whoever touches their carcasses will be unclean till evening. ²⁵Whoever picks up one of their carcasses must wash his clothes, and he will be unclean till evening.

²⁶" 'Every animal that has a split hoof not completely divided or that does not chew the cud is unclean for you; whoever touches the carcass of any of them will be unclean. ²⁷Of all the animals that walk on all fours, those that walk on their paws are unclean for you; whoever touches their carcasses will be unclean till evening. ²⁸Anyone who picks up their carcasses must wash his clothes, and he will be unclean till evening. They are unclean for you.

²⁹" 'Of the animals that move about on the ground, these are unclean for you: the weasel, the rat, any kind of great lizard, ³⁰the gecko, the monitor lizard, the wall lizard, the skink and the chameleon. ³¹Of all those that move along the ground, these are unclean for you. Whoever touches them when they are dead will be unclean till evening. ³²When one of them dies and falls on something, that article, whatever its use, will be unclean, whether it is made of wood, cloth, hide or sackcloth. Put it in water; it will be unclean till evening, and then it will be clean. ³³If one of them falls into a clay pot, everything in it will be unclean, and you must break the pot. ³⁴Any food that could be eaten but has water on it from such a pot is unclean, and any liquid that could be drunk from it is unclean. ³⁵Anything that one of their carcasses falls on becomes unclean; an oven or cooking pot must be broken up. They are unclean, and you are to regard them as unclean. ³⁶A spring, however, or a cistern for collecting water remains clean, but anyone who touches one of these carcasses is unclean. ³⁷If a carcass falls on any seeds that are to be planted, they remain clean. ³⁸But if water has been put on the seed and a carcass falls on it, it is unclean for you.

³⁹" 'If an animal that you are allowed to eat dies, anyone who touches the carcass will be unclean till evening. ⁴⁰Anyone who eats some of the carcass must wash his clothes, and he will be unclean till evening. Anyone who picks up the carcass must wash his clothes, and he will be unclean till evening.

⁴¹" 'Every creature that moves about on the ground is detestable; it is not to be eaten. ⁴²You are not to eat any creature that moves about on the ground, whether it moves on its belly or walks on all fours or on many feet; it is detestable. ⁴³Do not defile yourselves by any of these creatures. Do not make yourselves unclean by means of them or be made unclean by them. ⁴⁴I am the LORD your God; consecrate yourselves and be holy, because I am holy. Do not make yourselves unclean by any creature that moves about on the ground. ⁴⁵I am the LORD who brought you up out of Egypt to be your God; therefore be holy, because I am holy.

⁴⁶" 'These are the regulations concerning animals, birds, every living thing that moves in the water and every creature that moves about on the ground. ⁴⁷You must distinguish between the unclean and the clean, between living creatures that may be eaten and those that may not be eaten.' "

ᵃ19 The precise identification of some of the birds, insects and animals in this chapter is uncertain.

Purification After Childbirth

12 The LORD said to Moses, [2]"Say to the Israelites: 'A woman who becomes pregnant and gives birth to a son will be ceremonially unclean for seven days, just as she is unclean during her monthly period. [3]On the eighth day the boy is to be circumcised. [4]Then the woman must wait thirty-three days to be purified from her bleeding. She must not touch anything sacred or go to the sanctuary until the days of her purification are over. [5]If she gives birth to a daughter, for two weeks the woman will be unclean, as during her period. Then she must wait sixty-six days to be purified from her bleeding.

[6]" 'When the days of her purification for a son or daughter are over, she is to bring to the priest at the entrance to the Tent of Meeting a year-old lamb for a burnt offering and a young pigeon or a dove for a sin offering. [7]He shall offer them before the LORD to make atonement for her, and then she will be ceremonially clean from her flow of blood.

" 'These are the regulations for the woman who gives birth to a boy or a girl. [8]If she cannot afford a lamb, she is to bring two doves or two young pigeons, one for a burnt offering and the other for a sin offering. In this way the priest will make atonement for her, and she will be clean.' "

Regulations About Infectious Skin Diseases

13 The LORD said to Moses and Aaron, [2]"When anyone has a swelling or a rash or a bright spot on his skin that may become an infectious skin disease,[a] he must be brought to Aaron the priest or to one of his sons[b] who is a priest. [3]The priest is to examine the sore on his skin, and if the hair in the sore has turned white and the sore appears to be more than skin deep,[c] it is an infectious skin disease. When the priest examines him, he shall pronounce him ceremonially unclean. [4]If the spot on his skin is white but does not appear to be more than skin deep and the hair in it has not turned white, the priest is to put the infected person in isolation for seven days. [5]On the seventh day the priest is to examine him, and if he sees that the

---

[a]2 Traditionally *leprosy*; the Hebrew word was used for various diseases affecting the skin—not necessarily leprosy; also elsewhere in this chapter.   [b]2 Or *descendants*   [c]3 Or *be lower than the rest of the skin*; also elsewhere in this chapter

Life in Bible Times

CLEAN AND UNCLEAN ANIMALS

God set certain rules for what animals the Israelites could and could not eat or sacrifice. Animals that were acceptable as sacrifices or for eating were called clean animals. The Israelites were not allowed to eat or sacrifice unclean animals. Look at the picture to see some clean and some unclean animals.

sore is unchanged and has not spread in the skin, he is to keep him in isolation another seven days. [6]On the seventh day the priest is to examine him again, and if the sore has faded and has not spread in the skin, the priest shall pronounce him clean; it is only a rash. The man must wash his clothes, and he will be clean. [7]But if the rash does spread in his skin after he has shown himself to the priest to be pronounced clean, he must appear before the priest again. [8]The priest is to examine him, and if the rash has spread in the skin, he shall pronounce him unclean; it is an infectious disease.

[9]"When anyone has an infectious skin disease, he must be brought to the priest. [10]The priest is to examine him, and if there is a white swelling in the skin that has turned the hair white and if there is raw flesh in the swelling, [11]it is a chronic skin disease and the priest shall pronounce him unclean. He is not to put him in isolation, because he is already unclean.

[12]"If the disease breaks out all over his skin and, so far as the priest can see, it covers all the skin of the infected person from head to foot, [13]the priest is to examine him, and if the disease has covered his whole body, he shall pronounce that person clean. Since it has all turned white, he is clean. [14]But whenever raw flesh appears on him, he will be unclean. [15]When the priest sees the raw flesh, he shall pronounce him unclean. The raw flesh is unclean; he has an infectious disease. [16]Should the raw flesh change and turn white, he must go to the priest. [17]The priest is to examine him, and if the sores have turned white, the priest shall pronounce the infected person clean; then he will be clean.

[18]"When someone has a boil on his skin and it heals, [19]and in the place where the boil was, a white swelling or reddish-white spot appears, he must present himself to the priest. [20]The priest is to examine it, and if it appears to be more than skin deep and the hair in it has turned white,

the priest shall pronounce him unclean. It is an infectious skin disease that has broken out where the boil was. [21]But if, when the priest examines it, there is no white hair in it and it is not more than skin deep and has faded, then the priest is to put him in isolation for seven days. [22]If it is spreading in the skin, the priest shall pronounce him unclean; it is infectious. [23]But if the spot is unchanged and has not spread, it is only a scar from the boil, and the priest shall pronounce him clean.

?DID YOU KNOW?   13:9

What is the worst infectious skin disease?

The worst of the diseases described here is leprosy. A person with leprosy could lose fingers, toes, nose or ears. The Old Testament tells people with infectious skin diseases to live apart from others, so others will not catch their illness.

---

[24]"When someone has a burn on his skin and a reddish-white or white spot appears in the raw flesh of the burn, [25]the priest is to examine the spot, and if the hair in it has turned white, and it appears to be more than skin deep, it is an infectious disease that has broken out in the burn. The priest shall pronounce him unclean; it is an infectious skin disease. [26]But if the priest examines it and there is no white hair in the spot and if it is not more than skin deep and has faded, then the priest is to put him in isolation for seven days. [27]On the seventh day the priest is to examine him, and if it is spreading in the skin, the priest shall pronounce him unclean; it is an infectious skin disease. [28]If, however, the spot is unchanged and has not spread in the skin but has faded, it is a swelling from the burn, and the priest shall pronounce him clean; it is only a scar from the burn.

²⁹"If a man or woman has a sore on the head or on the chin, ³⁰the priest is to examine the sore, and if it appears to be more than skin deep and the hair in it is yellow and thin, the priest shall pronounce that person unclean; it is an itch, an infectious disease of the head or chin. ³¹But if, when the priest examines this kind of sore, it does not seem to be more than skin deep and there is no black hair in it, then the priest is to put the infected person in isolation for seven days. ³²On the seventh day the priest is to examine the sore, and if the itch has not spread and there is no yellow hair in it and it does not appear to be more than skin deep, ³³he must be shaved except for the diseased area, and the priest is to keep him in isolation another seven days. ³⁴On the seventh day the priest is to examine the itch, and if it has not spread in the skin and appears to be no more than skin deep, the priest shall pronounce him clean. He must wash his clothes, and he will be clean. ³⁵But if the itch does spread in the skin after he is pronounced clean, ³⁶the priest is to examine him, and if the itch has spread in the skin, the priest does not need to look for yellow hair; the person is unclean. ³⁷If, however, in his judgment it is unchanged and black hair has grown in it, the itch is healed. He is clean, and the priest shall pronounce him clean.

³⁸"When a man or woman has white spots on the skin, ³⁹the priest is to examine them, and if the spots are dull white, it is a harmless rash that has broken out on the skin; that person is clean.

⁴⁰"When a man has lost his hair and is bald, he is clean. ⁴¹If he has lost his hair from the front of his scalp and has a bald forehead, he is clean. ⁴²But if he has a reddish-white sore on his bald head or forehead, it is an infectious disease breaking out on his head or forehead. ⁴³The priest is to examine him, and if the swollen sore on his head or forehead is reddish-white like an infectious skin disease, ⁴⁴the man is diseased and is unclean. The priest shall pronounce him unclean because of the sore on his head.

⁴⁵"The person with such an infectious disease must wear torn clothes, let his hair be unkempt,ᵃ cover the lower part of his face and cry out, 'Unclean! Unclean!' ⁴⁶As long as he has the infection he remains unclean. He must live alone; he must live outside the camp.

Regulations About Mildew

⁴⁷"If any clothing is contaminated with mildew—any woolen or linen clothing, ⁴⁸any woven or knitted material of linen or wool, any leather or anything made of leather— ⁴⁹and if the contamination in the clothing, or leather, or woven or knitted material, or any leather article, is greenish or reddish, it is a spreading mildew and must be shown to the priest. ⁵⁰The priest is to examine the mildew and isolate the affected article for seven days. ⁵¹On the seventh day he is to examine it, and if the mildew has spread in the clothing, or the woven or knitted material, or the leather, whatever its use, it is a destructive mildew; the article is unclean. ⁵²He must burn up the clothing, or the woven or knitted material of wool or linen, or any leather article that has the contamination in it, because the mildew is destructive; the article must be burned up.

⁵³"But if, when the priest examines it, the mildew has not spread in the clothing, or the woven or knitted material, or the leather article, ⁵⁴he shall order that the contaminated article be washed. Then he is to isolate it for another seven days. ⁵⁵After the affected article has been washed, the priest is to examine it, and if the mildew has not changed its appearance, even though it has not spread, it is unclean. Burn it with fire, whether the mildew has affected one side or the other. ⁵⁶If, when the priest examines it, the mildew has faded after the

ᵃ45 Or *clothes, uncover his head*

article has been washed, he is to tear the contaminated part out of the clothing, or the leather, or the woven or knitted material. ⁵⁷But if it reappears in the clothing, or in the woven or knitted material, or in the leather article, it is spreading, and whatever has the mildew must be burned with fire. ⁵⁸The clothing, or the woven or knitted material, or any leather article that has been washed and is rid of the mildew, must be washed again, and it will be clean."

⁵⁹These are the regulations concerning contamination by mildew in woolen or linen clothing, woven or knitted material, or any leather article, for pronouncing them clean or unclean.

Cleansing From Infectious Skin Diseases

14 The LORD said to Moses, ²"These are the regulations for the diseased person at the time of his ceremonial cleansing, when he is brought to the priest: ³The priest is to go outside the camp and examine him. If the person has been healed of his infectious skin disease,ᵃ ⁴the priest shall order that two live clean birds and some cedar wood, scarlet yarn and hyssop be brought for the one to be cleansed. ⁵Then the priest shall order that one of the birds be killed over fresh water in a clay pot. ⁶He is then to take the live bird and dip it, together with the cedar wood, the scarlet yarn and the hyssop, into the blood of the bird that was killed over the fresh water. ⁷Seven times he shall sprinkle the one to be cleansed of the infectious disease and pronounce him clean. Then he is to release the live bird in the open fields.

⁸"The person to be cleansed must wash his clothes, shave off all his hair and bathe with water; then he will be ceremonially clean. After this he may come into the camp, but he must stay outside his tent for seven

days. ⁹On the seventh day he must shave off all his hair; he must shave his head, his beard, his eyebrows and the rest of his hair. He must wash his clothes and bathe himself with water, and he will be clean.

❓DID YOU KNOW?   14:2

What does cleansing mean?

Cleansing here is not making a thing clean, like washing our hands. Here cleansing means the ceremony that permitted Israelites who were healed of things like infectious skin diseases to live and worship with others again.

---

¹⁰"On the eighth day he must bring two male lambs and one ewe lamb a year old, each without defect, along with three-tenths of an ephahᵇ of fine flour mixed with oil for a grain offering, and one logᶜ of oil. ¹¹The priest who pronounces him clean shall present both the one to be cleansed and his offerings before the LORD at the entrance to the Tent of Meeting.

¹²"Then the priest is to take one of the male lambs and offer it as a guilt offering, along with the log of oil; he shall wave them before the LORD as a wave offering. ¹³He is to slaughter the lamb in the holy place where the sin offering and the burnt offering are slaughtered. Like the sin offering, the guilt offering belongs to the priest; it is most holy. ¹⁴The priest is to take some of the blood of the guilt offering and put it on the lobe of the right ear of the one to be cleansed, on the thumb of his right hand and on the big toe of his right foot. ¹⁵The priest shall then take some of the log of oil, pour it in the palm of his own left hand, ¹⁶dip his right forefinger into the oil in his palm, and with his finger sprinkle some of it before the

---

ᵃ3 Traditionally *leprosy*; the Hebrew word was used for various diseases affecting the skin—not necessarily leprosy; also elsewhere in this chapter.   ᵇ10 That is, probably about 6 quarts (about 6.5 liters)   ᶜ10 That is, probably about 2/3 pint (about 0.3 liter); also in verses 12, 15, 21 and 24

LORD seven times. [17]The priest is to put some of the oil remaining in his palm on the lobe of the right ear of the one to be cleansed, on the thumb of his right hand and on the big toe of his right foot, on top of the blood of the guilt offering. [18]The rest of the oil in his palm the priest shall put on the head of the one to be cleansed and make atonement for him before the LORD.

[19]"Then the priest is to sacrifice the sin offering and make atonement for the one to be cleansed from his uncleanness. After that, the priest shall slaughter the burnt offering [20]and offer it on the altar, together with the grain offering, and make atonement for him, and he will be clean.

[21]"If, however, he is poor and cannot afford these, he must take one male lamb as a guilt offering to be waved to make atonement for him, together with a tenth of an ephah[a] of fine flour mixed with oil for a grain offering, a log of oil, [22]and two doves or two young pigeons, which he can afford, one for a sin offering and the other for a burnt offering.

[23]"On the eighth day he must bring them for his cleansing to the priest at the entrance to the Tent of Meeting, before the LORD. [24]The priest is to take the lamb for the guilt offering, together with the log of oil, and wave them before the LORD as a wave offering. [25]He shall slaughter the lamb for the guilt offering and take some of its blood and put it on the lobe of the right ear of the one to be cleansed, on the thumb of his right hand and on the big toe of his right foot. [26]The priest is to pour some of the oil into the palm of his own left hand, [27]and with his right forefinger sprinkle some of the oil from his palm seven times before the LORD. [28]Some of the oil in his palm he is to put on the same places he put the blood of the guilt offering—on the lobe of the right ear of the one to be cleansed, on the thumb of his right hand and on

the big toe of his right foot. [29]The rest of the oil in his palm the priest shall put on the head of the one to be cleansed, to make atonement for him before the LORD. [30]Then he shall sacrifice the doves or the young pigeons, which the person can afford, [31]one[b] as a sin offering and the other as a burnt offering, together with the grain offering. In this way the priest will make atonement before the LORD on behalf of the one to be cleansed."

[32]These are the regulations for anyone who has an infectious skin disease and who cannot afford the regular offerings for his cleansing.

Cleansing From Mildew

[33]The LORD said to Moses and Aaron, [34]"When you enter the land of Canaan, which I am giving you as your possession, and I put a spreading mildew in a house in that land, [35]the owner of the house must go and tell the priest, 'I have seen something that looks like mildew in my house.' [36]The priest is to order the house to be emptied before he goes in to examine the mildew, so that nothing in the house will be pronounced unclean. After this the priest is to go in and inspect the house. [37]He is to examine the mildew on the walls, and if it has greenish or reddish depressions that appear to be deeper than the surface of the wall, [38]the priest shall go out the doorway of the house and close it up for seven days. [39]On the seventh day the priest shall return to inspect the house. If the mildew has spread on the walls, [40]he is to order that the contaminated stones be torn out and thrown into an unclean place outside the town. [41]He must have all the inside walls of the house scraped and the material that is scraped off dumped into an unclean place outside the town. [42]Then they are to take other stones to replace these and take new clay and plaster the house.

[43]"If the mildew reappears in the house after the stones have been torn

---

out and the house scraped and plastered, ⁴⁴the priest is to go and examine it and, if the mildew has spread in the house, it is a destructive mildew; the house is unclean. ⁴⁵It must be torn down—its stones, timbers and all the plaster—and taken out of the town to an unclean place.

⁴⁶"Anyone who goes into the house while it is closed up will be unclean till evening. ⁴⁷Anyone who sleeps or eats in the house must wash his clothes.

⁴⁸"But if the priest comes to examine it and the mildew has not spread after the house has been plastered, he shall pronounce the house clean, because the mildew is gone. ⁴⁹To purify the house he is to take two birds and some cedar wood, scarlet yarn and hyssop. ⁵⁰He shall kill one of the birds over fresh water in a clay pot. ⁵¹Then he is to take the cedar wood, the hyssop, the scarlet yarn and the live bird, dip them into the blood of the dead bird and the fresh water, and sprinkle the house seven times. ⁵²He shall purify the house with the bird's blood, the fresh water, the live bird, the cedar wood, the hyssop and the scarlet yarn. ⁵³Then he is to release the live bird in the open fields outside the town. In this way he will make atonement for the house, and it will be clean."

⁵⁴These are the regulations for any infectious skin disease, for an itch, ⁵⁵for mildew in clothing or in a house, ⁵⁶and for a swelling, a rash or a bright spot, ⁵⁷to determine when something is clean or unclean.

These are the regulations for infectious skin diseases and mildew.

Discharges Causing Uncleanness

15 The LORD said to Moses and Aaron, ²"Speak to the Israelites and say to them: 'When any man has a bodily discharge, the discharge is unclean. ³Whether it continues flowing from his body or is blocked, it will make him unclean. This is how his discharge will bring about uncleanness:

⁴"'Any bed the man with a discharge lies on will be unclean, and anything he sits on will be unclean. ⁵Anyone who touches his bed must wash his clothes and bathe with water, and he will be unclean till evening. ⁶Whoever sits on anything that the man with a discharge sat on must wash his clothes and bathe with water, and he will be unclean till evening.

⁷"'Whoever touches the man who has a discharge must wash his clothes and bathe with water, and he will be unclean till evening.

⁸"'If the man with the discharge spits on someone who is clean, that person must wash his clothes and bathe with water, and he will be unclean till evening.

⁹"'Everything the man sits on when riding will be unclean, ¹⁰and whoever touches any of the things that were under him will be unclean till evening; whoever picks up those things must wash his clothes and bathe with water, and he will be unclean till evening.

¹¹"'Anyone the man with a discharge touches without rinsing his hands with water must wash his clothes and bathe with water, and he will be unclean till evening.

¹²"'A clay pot that the man touches must be broken, and any wooden article is to be rinsed with water.

¹³"'When a man is cleansed from his discharge, he is to count off seven days for his ceremonial cleansing; he must wash his clothes and bathe himself with fresh water, and he will be clean. ¹⁴On the eighth day he must take two doves or two young pigeons and come before the LORD to the entrance to the Tent of Meeting and give them to the priest. ¹⁵The priest is to sacrifice them, the one for a sin offering and the other for a burnt offering. In this way he will make atonement before the LORD for the man because of his discharge.

¹⁶"'When a man has an emission of semen, he must bathe his whole body with water, and he will be unclean till evening. ¹⁷Any clothing or leath-

er that has semen on it must be washed with water, and it will be unclean till evening. ¹⁸When a man lies with a woman and there is an emission of semen, both must bathe with water, and they will be unclean till evening.

¹⁹" 'When a woman has her regular flow of blood, the impurity of her monthly period will last seven days, and anyone who touches her will be unclean till evening.

²⁰" 'Anything she lies on during her period will be unclean, and anything she sits on will be unclean. ²¹Whoever touches her bed must wash his clothes and bathe with water, and he will be unclean till evening. ²²Whoever touches anything she sits on must wash his clothes and bathe with water, and he will be unclean till evening. ²³Whether it is the bed or anything she was sitting on, when anyone touches it, he will be unclean till evening.

²⁴" 'If a man lies with her and her monthly flow touches him, he will be unclean for seven days; any bed he lies on will be unclean.

²⁵" 'When a woman has a discharge of blood for many days at a time other than her monthly period or has a discharge that continues beyond her period, she will be unclean as long as she has the discharge, just as in the days of her period. ²⁶Any bed she lies on while her discharge continues will be unclean, as is her bed during her monthly period, and anything she sits on will be unclean, as during her period. ²⁷Whoever touches them will be unclean; he must wash his clothes and bathe with water, and he will be unclean till evening.

²⁸" 'When she is cleansed from her discharge, she must count off seven days, and after that she will be ceremonially clean. ²⁹On the eighth day she must take two doves or two young pigeons and bring them to the priest at the entrance to the Tent of Meeting. ³⁰The priest is to sacrifice one for a sin offering and the other for a burnt offering. In this way he will make atonement for her before the LORD for the uncleanness of her discharge.

³¹" 'You must keep the Israelites separate from things that make them unclean, so they will not die in their uncleanness for defiling my dwelling place,ᵃ which is among them.' "

³²These are the regulations for a man with a discharge, for anyone made unclean by an emission of semen, ³³for a woman in her monthly period, for a man or a woman with a discharge, and for a man who lies with a woman who is ceremonially unclean.

The Day of Atonement

16 The LORD spoke to Moses after the death of the two sons of Aaron who died when they approached the LORD. ²The LORD said to Moses: "Tell your brother Aaron not to come whenever he chooses into the Most Holy Place behind the curtain in front of the atonement cover on the ark, or else he will die, because I appear in the cloud over the atonement cover.

³"This is how Aaron is to enter the sanctuary area: with a young bull for a sin offering and a ram for a burnt offering. ⁴He is to put on the sacred linen tunic, with linen undergarments next to his body; he is to tie the linen sash around him and put on the linen turban. These are sacred garments; so he must bathe himself with water before he puts them on. ⁵From the Israelite community he is to take two male goats for a sin offering and a ram for a burnt offering.

⁶"Aaron is to offer the bull for his own sin offering to make atonement for himself and his household. ⁷Then he is to take the two goats and present them before the LORD at the entrance to the Tent of Meeting. ⁸He is to cast lots for the two goats—one lot for the LORD and the other for the scapegoat.ᵇ ⁹Aaron shall bring the goat whose lot falls to the LORD and

---

ᵃ31 Or *my tabernacle*   ᵇ8 That is, the goat of removal; Hebrew *azazel*; also in verses 10 and 26

sacrifice it for a sin offering. [10]But the goat chosen by lot as the scapegoat shall be presented alive before the LORD to be used for making atonement by sending it into the desert as a scapegoat.

[11]"Aaron shall bring the bull for his own sin offering to make atonement for himself and his household, and he is to slaughter the bull for his own sin offering. [12]He is to take a censer full of burning coals from the altar before the LORD and two handfuls of finely ground fragrant incense and take them behind the curtain. [13]He is to put the incense on the fire before the LORD, and the smoke of the incense will conceal the atonement cover above the Testimony, so that he will not die. [14]He is to take some of the bull's blood and with his finger sprinkle it on the front of the atonement cover; then he shall sprinkle some of it with his finger seven times before the atonement cover.

? DID YOU KNOW?   16:16

What was the Day of Atonement?

Every year, on the Day of Atonement the high priest offered a special sacrifice. He took the blood of that sacrifice into the Most Holy Place of the tabernacle and sprinkled it on the cover of God's ark. This sacrifice was special because it made atonement for all the sins of the Israelites, even sins that were committed on purpose.

[15]"He shall then slaughter the goat for the sin offering for the people and take its blood behind the curtain and do with it as he did with the bull's blood: He shall sprinkle it on the atonement cover and in front of it. [16]In this way he will make atonement for the Most Holy Place because of the uncleanness and rebellion of the Israelites, whatever their sins have been. He is to do the same for the Tent of Meeting, which is among

them in the midst of their uncleanness. [17]No one is to be in the Tent of Meeting from the time Aaron goes in to make atonement in the Most Holy Place until he comes out, having made atonement for himself, his household and the whole community of Israel.

[18]"Then he shall come out to the altar that is before the LORD and make atonement for it. He shall take some of the bull's blood and some of the goat's blood and put it on all the horns of the altar. [19]He shall sprinkle some of the blood on it with his finger seven times to cleanse it and to consecrate it from the uncleanness of the Israelites.

[20]"When Aaron has finished making atonement for the Most Holy Place, the Tent of Meeting and the altar, he shall bring forward the live goat. [21]He is to lay both hands on the head of the live goat and confess over it all the wickedness and rebellion of the Israelites—all their sins—and put them on the goat's head. He shall send the goat away into the desert in the care of a man appointed for the task. [22]The goat will carry on itself all their sins to a solitary place; and the man shall release it in the desert.

[23]"Then Aaron is to go into the Tent of Meeting and take off the linen garments he put on before he entered the Most Holy Place, and he is to leave them there. [24]He shall bathe himself with water in a holy place and put on his regular garments. Then he shall come out and sacrifice the burnt offering for himself and the burnt offering for the people, to make atonement for himself and for the people. [25]He shall also burn the fat of the sin offering on the altar.

[26]"The man who releases the goat as a scapegoat must wash his clothes and bathe himself with water; afterward he may come into the camp. [27]The bull and the goat for the sin offerings, whose blood was brought into the Most Holy Place to make atonement, must be taken outside the camp; their hides, flesh and offal are to be burned up. [28]The man who

burns them must wash his clothes and bathe himself with water; afterward he may come into the camp.

29"This is to be a lasting ordinance for you: On the tenth day of the seventh month you must deny yourselves[a] and not do any work—whether native-born or an alien living among you— 30because on this day atonement will be made for you, to cleanse you. Then, before the LORD, you will be clean from all your sins. 31It is a sabbath of rest, and you must deny yourselves; it is a lasting ordinance. 32The priest who is anointed and ordained to succeed his father as high priest is to make atonement. He is to put on the sacred linen garments 33and make atonement for the Most Holy Place, for the Tent of Meeting and the altar, and for the priests and all the people of the community.

34"This is to be a lasting ordinance for you: Atonement is to be made once a year for all the sins of the Israelites."

And it was done, as the LORD commanded Moses.

Eating Blood Forbidden

17 The LORD said to Moses, 2"Speak to Aaron and his sons and to all the Israelites and say to them: 'This is what the LORD has commanded: 3Any Israelite who sacrifices an ox,[b] a lamb or a goat in the camp or outside of it 4instead of bringing it to the entrance to the Tent of Meeting to present it as an offering to the LORD in front of the tabernacle of the LORD—that man shall be considered guilty of bloodshed; he has shed blood and must be cut off from his people. 5This is so the Israelites will bring to the LORD the sacrifices they are now making in the open fields. They must bring them to the priest, that is, to the LORD, at the entrance to the Tent of Meeting and sacrifice them as fellowship offerings.[c] 6The priest is to sprinkle the blood against the altar of the LORD at the entrance to the Tent of Meeting and burn the fat as an aroma pleasing to the LORD. 7They must no longer offer any of their sacrifices to the goat idols[d] to whom they prostitute themselves. This is to be a lasting ordinance for them and for the generations to come.'

8"Say to them: 'Any Israelite or any alien living among them who offers a burnt offering or sacrifice 9and does not bring it to the entrance to the Tent of Meeting to sacrifice it to the LORD—that man must be cut off from his people.

10"'Any Israelite or any alien living among them who eats any blood—I will set my face against that person who eats blood and will cut him off from his people. 11For the life of a creature is in the blood, and I have given it to you to make atonement for yourselves on the altar; it is the blood that makes atonement for one's life. 12Therefore I say to the Israelites, "None of you may eat blood, nor may an alien living among you eat blood."

? DID YOU KNOW?　17:10

Why were the Israelites told not to eat blood?

Israelites could not eat blood because blood represented the life of an animal. The blood of the animals that were sacrificed on altars cleansed the Israelites' sins. This was so special that the blood could only be used for this holy purpose.

13"'Any Israelite or any alien living among you who hunts any animal or bird that may be eaten must drain out the blood and cover it with earth, 14because the life of every creature is its blood. That is why I have said to the Israelites, "You must not eat the blood of any creature, because the life

---

a29 Or *must fast*; also in verse 31　b3 The Hebrew word can include both male and female.
c5 Traditionally *peace offerings*　d7 Or *demons*

of every creature is its blood; anyone who eats it must be cut off.' "

15" 'Anyone, whether native-born or alien, who eats anything found dead or torn by wild animals must wash his clothes and bathe with water, and he will be ceremonially unclean till evening; then he will be clean. 16But if he does not wash his clothes and bathe himself, he will be held responsible.' "

Unlawful Sexual Relations

18 The LORD said to Moses, 2"Speak to the Israelites and say to them: 'I am the LORD your God. 3You must not do as they do in Egypt, where you used to live, and you must not do as they do in the land of Canaan, where I am bringing you. Do not follow their practices. 4You must obey my laws and be careful to follow my decrees. I am the LORD your God. 5Keep my decrees and laws, for the man who obeys them will live by them. I am the LORD.

6" 'No one is to approach any close relative to have sexual relations. I am the LORD.

7" 'Do not dishonor your father by having sexual relations with your mother. She is your mother; do not have relations with her.

8" 'Do not have sexual relations with your father's wife; that would dishonor your father.

9" 'Do not have sexual relations with your sister, either your father's daughter or your mother's daughter, whether she was born in the same home or elsewhere.

10" 'Do not have sexual relations with your son's daughter or your daughter's daughter; that would dishonor you.

11" 'Do not have sexual relations with the daughter of your father's wife, born to your father; she is your sister.

12" 'Do not have sexual relations with your father's sister; she is your father's close relative.

13" 'Do not have sexual relations with your mother's sister, because she is your mother's close relative.

14" 'Do not dishonor your father's brother by approaching his wife to have sexual relations; she is your aunt.

15" 'Do not have sexual relations with your daughter-in-law. She is your son's wife; do not have relations with her.

16" 'Do not have sexual relations with your brother's wife; that would dishonor your brother.

17" 'Do not have sexual relations with both a woman and her daughter. Do not have sexual relations with either her son's daughter or her daughter's daughter; they are her close relatives. That is wickedness.

18" 'Do not take your wife's sister as a rival wife and have sexual relations with her while your wife is living.

19" 'Do not approach a woman to have sexual relations during the uncleanness of her monthly period.

20" 'Do not have sexual relations with your neighbor's wife and defile yourself with her.

21" 'Do not give any of your children to be sacrificed[a] to Molech, for you must not profane the name of your God. I am the LORD.

22" 'Do not lie with a man as one lies with a woman; that is detestable.

23" 'Do not have sexual relations with an animal and defile yourself with it. A woman must not present herself to an animal to have sexual relations with it; that is a perversion.

24" 'Do not defile yourselves in any of these ways, because this is how the nations that I am going to drive out before you became defiled. 25Even the land was defiled; so I punished it for its sin, and the land vomited out its inhabitants. 26But you must keep my decrees and my laws. The native-born and the aliens living among you must not do any of these detestable things, 27for all these things were done by the people who lived in the land before you, and the land became defiled. 28And if you defile the land, it

a21 Or to be passed through the fire

will vomit you out as it vomited out the nations that were before you.

²⁹" 'Everyone who does any of these detestable things—such persons must be cut off from their people. ³⁰Keep my requirements and do not follow any of the detestable customs that were practiced before you came and do not defile yourselves with them. I am the LORD your God.' "

Various Laws

19 The LORD said to Moses, ²"Speak to the entire assembly of Israel and say to them: 'Be holy because I, the LORD your God, am holy.

³" 'Each of you must respect his mother and father, and you must observe my Sabbaths. I am the LORD your God.

⁴" 'Do not turn to idols or make gods of cast metal for yourselves. I am the LORD your God.

⁵" 'When you sacrifice a fellowship offering^a to the LORD, sacrifice it in such a way that it will be accepted on your behalf. ⁶It shall be eaten on the day you sacrifice it or on the next day; anything left over until the third day must be burned up. ⁷If any of it is eaten on the third day, it is impure and will not be accepted. ⁸Whoever eats it will be held responsible because he has desecrated what is holy to the LORD; that person must be cut off from his people.

⁹" 'When you reap the harvest of your land, do not reap to the very edges of your field or gather the gleanings of your harvest. ¹⁰Do not go over your vineyard a second time or pick up the grapes that have fallen. Leave them for the poor and the alien. I am the LORD your God.

¹¹" 'Do not steal.

" 'Do not lie.

" 'Do not deceive one another.

¹²" 'Do not swear falsely by my name and so profane the name of your God. I am the LORD.

¹³" 'Do not defraud your neighbor or rob him.

" 'Do not hold back the wages of a hired man overnight.

Life In Bible Times

FOOD FOR THE POOR

God's law told farmers to leave for the poor any grain that fell on the ground and any grapes that were not ripe. Many laws in the Old Testament show that God cares very much for poor people.

---

¹⁴" 'Do not curse the deaf or put a stumbling block in front of the blind, but fear your God. I am the LORD.

¹⁵" 'Do not pervert justice; do not show partiality to the poor or favoritism to the great, but judge your neighbor fairly.

¹⁶" 'Do not go about spreading slander among your people.

" 'Do not do anything that endangers your neighbor's life. I am the LORD.

¹⁷" 'Do not hate your brother in your heart. Rebuke your neighbor frankly so you will not share in his guilt.

¹⁸" 'Do not seek revenge or bear a grudge against one of your people, but love your neighbor as yourself. I am the LORD.

¹⁹" 'Keep my decrees.

" 'Do not mate different kinds of animals.

" 'Do not plant your field with two kinds of seed.

" 'Do not wear clothing woven of two kinds of material.

²⁰" 'If a man sleeps with a woman who is a slave girl promised to another man but who has not been ransomed or given her freedom, there must be due punishment. Yet they

^a5 Traditionally *peace offering*

are not to be put to death, because she had not been freed. 21The man, however, must bring a ram to the entrance to the Tent of Meeting for a guilt offering to the LORD. 22With the ram of the guilt offering the priest is to make atonement for him before the LORD for the sin he has committed, and his sin will be forgiven.

23" 'When you enter the land and plant any kind of fruit tree, regard its fruit as forbidden.ᵃ For three years you are to consider it forbiddenᵃ; it must not be eaten. 24In the fourth year all its fruit will be holy, an offering of praise to the LORD. 25But in the fifth year you may eat its fruit. In this way your harvest will be increased. I am the LORD your God.

26" 'Do not eat any meat with the blood still in it.

" 'Do not practice divination or sorcery.

27" 'Do not cut the hair at the sides of your head or clip off the edges of your beard.

28" 'Do not cut your bodies for the dead or put tattoo marks on yourselves. I am the LORD.

29" 'Do not degrade your daughter by making her a prostitute, or the land will turn to prostitution and be filled with wickedness.

30" 'Observe my Sabbaths and have reverence for my sanctuary. I am the LORD.

31" 'Do not turn to mediums or seek out spiritists, for you will be defiled by them. I am the LORD your God.

32" 'Rise in the presence of the aged, show respect for the elderly and revere your God. I am the LORD.

33" 'When an alien lives with you in your land, do not mistreat him. 34The alien living with you must be treated as one of your native-born. Love him as yourself, for you were aliens in Egypt. I am the LORD your God.

35" 'Do not use dishonest standards when measuring length, weight or quantity. 36Use honest scales and honest weights, an honest ephahᵇ and an honest hin.ᶜ I am the LORD your God, who brought you out of Egypt.

37" 'Keep all my decrees and all my laws and follow them. I am the LORD.' "

Punishments for Sin

20 The LORD said to Moses, 2"Say to the Israelites: 'Any Israelite or any alien living in Israel who givesᵈ any of his children to Molech must be put to death. The people of the community are to stone him. 3I will set my face against that man and I will cut him off from his people; for by giving his children to Molech, he has defiled my sanctuary and profaned my holy name. 4If the people of the community close their eyes when that man gives one of his children to Molech and they fail to put him to death, 5I will set my face against that man and his family and will cut off from their people both him and all who follow him in prostituting themselves to Molech.

6" 'I will set my face against the person who turns to mediums and spiritists to prostitute himself by following them, and I will cut him off from his people.

7" 'Consecrate yourselves and be holy, because I am the LORD your God. 8Keep my decrees and follow them. I am the LORD, who makes you holy.ᵉ

9" 'If anyone curses his father or mother, he must be put to death. He has cursed his father or his mother, and his blood will be on his own head.

10" 'If a man commits adultery with another man's wife—with the wife of his neighbor—both the adulterer and the adulteress must be put to death.

11" 'If a man sleeps with his father's wife, he has dishonored his father. Both the man and the woman must

---

ᵃ23 Hebrew *uncircumcised*   ᵇ36 An ephah was a dry measure.   ᶜ36 A hin was a liquid measure.   ᵈ2 Or *sacrifices*; also in verses 3 and 4   ᵉ8 Or *who sanctifies you*; or *who sets you apart as holy*

be put to death; their blood will be on their own heads.

¹²" 'If a man sleeps with his daughter-in-law, both of them must be put to death. What they have done is a perversion; their blood will be on their own heads.

¹³" 'If a man lies with a man as one lies with a woman, both of them have done what is detestable. They must be put to death; their blood will be on their own heads.

¹⁴" 'If a man marries both a woman and her mother, it is wicked. Both he and they must be burned in the fire, so that no wickedness will be among you.

¹⁵" 'If a man has sexual relations with an animal, he must be put to death, and you must kill the animal.

¹⁶" 'If a woman approaches an animal to have sexual relations with it, kill both the woman and the animal. They must be put to death; their blood will be on their own heads.

¹⁷" 'If a man marries his sister, the daughter of either his father or his mother, and they have sexual relations, it is a disgrace. They must be cut off before the eyes of their people. He has dishonored his sister and will be held responsible.

¹⁸" 'If a man lies with a woman during her monthly period and has sexual relations with her, he has exposed the source of her flow, and she has also uncovered it. Both of them must be cut off from their people.

¹⁹" 'Do not have sexual relations with the sister of either your mother or your father, for that would dishonor a close relative; both of you would be held responsible.

²⁰" 'If a man sleeps with his aunt, he has dishonored his uncle. They will be held responsible; they will die childless.

²¹" 'If a man marries his brother's wife, it is an act of impurity; he has dishonored his brother. They will be childless.

²²" 'Keep all my decrees and laws and follow them, so that the land

where I am bringing you to live may not vomit you out. ²³You must not live according to the customs of the nations I am going to drive out before you. Because they did all these things, I abhorred them. ²⁴But I said to you, "You will possess their land; I will give it to you as an inheritance, a land flowing with milk and honey." I am the LORD your God, who has set you apart from the nations.

²⁵" 'You must therefore make a distinction between clean and unclean animals and between unclean and clean birds. Do not defile yourselves by any animal or bird or anything that moves along the ground—those which I have set apart as unclean for you. ²⁶You are to be holy to me *a* because I, the LORD, am holy, and I have set you apart from the nations to be my own.

²⁷" 'A man or woman who is a medium or spiritist among you must be put to death. You are to stone them; their blood will be on their own heads.' "

Rules for Priests

21 The LORD said to Moses, "Speak to the priests, the sons of Aaron, and say to them: 'A priest must not make himself ceremonially unclean for any of his people who die, ²except for a close relative, such as his mother or father, his son or daughter, his brother, ³or an unmarried sister who is dependent on him since she has no husband—for her he may make himself unclean. ⁴He must not make himself unclean for people related to him by marriage, *b* and so defile himself.

⁵" 'Priests must not shave their heads or shave off the edges of their beards or cut their bodies. ⁶They must be holy to their God and must not profane the name of their God. Because they present the offerings made to the LORD by fire, the food of their God, they are to be holy.

⁷" 'They must not marry women defiled by prostitution or divorced from

---

*a26 Or *be my holy ones*   *b4 Or *unclean as a leader among his people*

their husbands, because priests are holy to their God. [8]Regard them as holy, because they offer up the food of your God. Consider them holy, because I the LORD am holy—I who make you holy.[a]

[9] 'If a priest's daughter defiles herself by becoming a prostitute, she disgraces her father; she must be burned in the fire.

[10] 'The high priest, the one among his brothers who has had the anointing oil poured on his head and who has been ordained to wear the priestly garments, must not let his hair become unkempt[b] or tear his clothes. [11]He must not enter a place where there is a dead body. He must not make himself unclean, even for his father or mother, [12]nor leave the sanctuary of his God or desecrate it, because he has been dedicated by the anointing oil of his God. I am the LORD.

[13] 'The woman he marries must be a virgin. [14]He must not marry a widow, a divorced woman, or a woman defiled by prostitution, but only a virgin from his own people, [15]so he will not defile his offspring among his people. I am the LORD, who makes him holy.[c] '

[16]The LORD said to Moses, [17]"Say to Aaron: 'For the generations to come none of your descendants who has a defect may come near to offer the food of his God. [18]No man who has any defect may come near: no man who is blind or lame, disfigured or deformed; [19]no man with a crippled foot or hand, [20]or who is hunchbacked or dwarfed, or who has any eye defect, or who has festering or running sores or damaged testicles. [21]No descendant of Aaron the priest who has any defect is to come near to present the offerings made to the LORD by fire. He has a defect; he must not come near to offer the food of his God. [22]He may

eat the most holy food of his God, as well as the holy food; [23]yet because of his defect, he must not go near the curtain or approach the altar, and so desecrate my sanctuary. I am the LORD, who makes them holy.[d] '"

[24]So Moses told this to Aaron and his sons and to all the Israelites.

22 The LORD said to Moses, [2]"Tell Aaron and his sons to treat with respect the sacred offerings the Israelites consecrate to me, so they will not profane my holy name. I am the LORD.

[3]"Say to them: 'For the generations to come, if any of your descendants is ceremonially unclean and yet comes near the sacred offerings the Israelites consecrate to the LORD, that person must be cut off from my presence. I am the LORD.

[4] 'If a descendant of Aaron has an infectious skin disease[e] or a bodily discharge, he may not eat the sacred offerings until he is cleansed. He will also be unclean if he touches something defiled by a corpse or by anyone who has an emission of semen, [5]or if he touches any crawling thing that makes him unclean, or any person who makes him unclean, whatever the uncleanness may be. [6]The one who touches any such thing will be unclean till evening. He must not eat any of the sacred offerings unless he has bathed himself with water. [7]When the sun goes down, he will be clean, and after that he may eat the sacred offerings, for they are his food. [8]He must not eat anything found dead or torn by wild animals, and so become unclean through it. I am the LORD.

[9] 'The priests are to keep my requirements so that they do not become guilty and die for treating them with contempt. I am the LORD, who makes them holy.[f]

[10] 'No one outside a priest's family

---

[a]8 Or who sanctify you; or who set you apart as holy who sanctifies him; or who sets him apart as holy   [b]10 Or not uncover his head   [c]15 Or who sanctifies them; or who sets him apart as holy   [d]23 Or who sanctifies them; or who sets them apart as holy   [e]4 Traditionally leprosy; the Hebrew word was used for various diseases affecting the skin—not necessarily leprosy.   [f]9 Or who sanctifies them; or who sets them apart as holy; also in verse 16

may eat the sacred offering, nor may the guest of a priest or his hired worker eat it. [11]But if a priest buys a slave with money, or if a slave is born in his household, that slave may eat his food. [12]If a priest's daughter marries anyone other than a priest, she may not eat any of the sacred contributions. [13]But if a priest's daughter becomes a widow or is divorced, yet has no children, and she returns to live in her father's house as in her youth, she may eat of her father's food. No unauthorized person, however, may eat any of it.

[14]" 'If anyone eats a sacred offering by mistake, he must make restitution to the priest for the offering and add a fifth of the value to it. [15]The priests must not desecrate the sacred offerings the Israelites present to the LORD [16]by allowing them to eat the sacred offerings and so bring upon them guilt requiring payment. I am the LORD, who makes them holy.' "

Unacceptable Sacrifices

[17]The LORD said to Moses, [18]"Speak to Aaron and his sons and to all the Israelites and say to them: 'If any of you—either an Israelite or an alien living in Israel—presents a gift for a burnt offering to the LORD, either to fulfill a vow or as a freewill offering, [19]you must present a male without defect from the cattle, sheep or goats in order that it may be accepted on your behalf. [20]Do not bring anything with a defect, because it will not be accepted on your behalf. [21]When anyone brings from the herd or flock a fellowship offering[a] to the LORD to fulfill a special vow or as a freewill offering, it must be without defect or blemish to be acceptable. [22]Do not offer to the LORD the blind, the injured or the maimed, or anything with warts or festering or running sores. Do not place any of these on the altar as an offering made to the LORD by fire. [23]You may, however, present as a freewill offering an ox[b] or a sheep

that is deformed or stunted, but it will not be accepted in fulfillment of a vow. [24]You must not offer to the LORD an animal whose testicles are bruised, crushed, torn or cut. You must not do this in your own land, [25]and you must not accept such animals from the hand of a foreigner and offer them as the food of your God. They will not be accepted on your behalf, because they are deformed and have defects.' "

[26]The LORD said to Moses, [27]"When a calf, a lamb or a goat is born, it is to remain with its mother for seven days. From the eighth day on, it will be acceptable as an offering made to the LORD by fire. [28]Do not slaughter a cow or a sheep and its young on the same day.

[29]"When you sacrifice a thank offering to the LORD, sacrifice it in such a way that it will be accepted on your behalf. [30]It must be eaten that same day; leave none of it till morning. I am the LORD.

[31]"Keep my commands and follow them. I am the LORD. [32]Do not profane my holy name. I must be acknowledged as holy by the Israelites. I am the LORD, who makes[c] you holy[d] [33]and who brought you out of Egypt to be your God. I am the LORD."

23 The LORD said to Moses, [2]"Speak to the Israelites and say to them: 'These are my appointed feasts, the appointed feasts of the LORD, which you are to proclaim as sacred assemblies.

The Sabbath

[3]" 'There are six days when you may work, but the seventh day is a Sabbath of rest, a day of sacred assembly. You are not to do any work; wherever you live, it is a Sabbath to the LORD.

The Passover and Unleavened Bread

[4]" 'These are the LORD's appointed

---

[a]21 Traditionally *peace offering*   [b]23 The Hebrew word can include both male and female.
[c]32 Or *made*   [d]32 Or *who sanctifies you*; or *who sets you apart as holy*

feasts, the sacred assemblies you are to proclaim at their appointed times: ⁵The LORD's Passover begins at twilight on the fourteenth day of the first month. ⁶On the fifteenth day of that month the LORD's Feast of Unleavened Bread begins; for seven days you must eat bread made without yeast. ⁷On the first day hold a sacred assembly and do no regular work. ⁸For seven days present an offering made to the LORD by fire. And on the seventh day hold a sacred assembly and do no regular work.'"

Firstfruits

⁹The LORD said to Moses, ¹⁰"Speak to the Israelites and say to them: 'When you enter the land I am going to give you and you reap its harvest, bring to the priest a sheaf of the first grain you harvest. ¹¹He is to wave the sheaf before the LORD so it will be accepted on your behalf; the priest is to wave it on the day after the Sabbath. ¹²On the day you wave the sheaf, you must sacrifice as a burnt offering to the LORD a lamb a year old without defect, ¹³together with its grain offering of two-tenths of an ephah ᵃ of fine flour mixed with oil—an offering made to the LORD by fire, a pleasing aroma—and its drink offering of a quarter of a hin ᵇ of wine. ¹⁴You must not eat any bread, or roasted or new grain, until the very day you bring this offering to your God. This is to be a lasting ordinance for the generations to come, wherever you live.

Feast of Weeks

¹⁵"'From the day after the Sabbath, the day you brought the sheaf of the wave offering, count off seven full weeks. ¹⁶Count off fifty days up to the day after the seventh Sabbath, and then present an offering of new grain to the LORD. ¹⁷From wherever you live, bring two loaves made of two-tenths of an ephah of fine flour, baked with yeast, as a wave offering of firstfruits to the LORD. ¹⁸Present

with this bread seven male lambs, each a year old and without defect, one young bull and two rams. They will be a burnt offering to the LORD, together with their grain offerings and drink offerings—an offering made by fire, an aroma pleasing to the LORD. ¹⁹Then sacrifice one male goat for a sin offering and two lambs, each a year old, for a fellowship offering.ᶜ ²⁰The priest is to wave the two lambs before the LORD as a wave offering, together with the bread of the firstfruits. They are a sacred offering to the LORD for the priest. ²¹On that same day you are to proclaim a sacred assembly and do no regular work. This is to be a lasting ordinance for the generations to come, wherever you live.

²²"'When you reap the harvest of your land, do not reap to the very edges of your field or gather the gleanings of your harvest. Leave them for the poor and the alien. I am the LORD your God.'"

❓DID YOU KNOW?   23:6,34

What does feast mean in the Old Testament?

The word feast is often used to describe the special religious holidays that God told his people to keep. They are called feasts or festivals because they were times of great joy, when Israel worshiped their wonderful and loving God.

Feast of Trumpets

²³The LORD said to Moses, ²⁴"Say to the Israelites: 'On the first day of the seventh month you are to have a day of rest, a sacred assembly commemorated with trumpet blasts. ²⁵Do no regular work, but present an offering made to the LORD by fire.'"

Day of Atonement

²⁶The LORD said to Moses, ²⁷"The

ᵃ13 That is, probably about 4 quarts (about 4.5 liters); also in verse 17   ᵇ13 That is, probably about 1 quart (about 1 liter)   ᶜ19 Traditionally *peace offering*

tenth day of this seventh month is the Day of Atonement. Hold a sacred assembly and deny yourselves,[a] and present an offering made to the LORD by fire. 28Do no work on that day, because it is the Day of Atonement, when atonement is made for you before the LORD your God. 29Anyone who does not deny himself on that day must be cut off from his people. 30I will destroy from among his people anyone who does any work on that day. 31You shall do no work at all. This is to be a lasting ordinance for the generations to come, wherever you live. 32It is a sabbath of rest for you, and you must deny yourselves. From the evening of the ninth day of the month until the following evening you are to observe your sabbath."

Feast of Tabernacles

33The LORD said to Moses, 34"Say to the Israelites: 'On the fifteenth day of the seventh month the LORD's Feast of Tabernacles begins, and it lasts for seven days. 35The first day is a sacred assembly; do no regular work. 36For seven days present offerings made to the LORD by fire, and on the eighth day hold a sacred assembly and present an offering made to the LORD by fire. It is the closing assembly; do no regular work.

37(" 'These are the LORD's appointed feasts, which you are to proclaim as sacred assemblies for bringing offerings made to the LORD by fire—the burnt offerings and grain offerings, sacrifices and drink offerings required for each day. 38These offerings are in addition to those for the LORD's Sabbaths and[b] in addition to your gifts and whatever you have vowed and all the freewill offerings you give to the LORD.)

39" 'So beginning with the fifteenth day of the seventh month, after you have gathered the crops of the land, celebrate the festival to the LORD for seven days; the first day is a day of rest, and the eighth day also is a day of rest. 40On the first day you are to take choice fruit from the trees, and palm fronds, leafy branches and poplars, and rejoice before the LORD your God for seven days. 41Celebrate this as a festival to the LORD for seven days each year. This is to be a lasting ordinance for the generations to come; celebrate it in the seventh month. 42Live in booths for seven days: All native-born Israelites are to live in booths 43so your descendants will know that I had the Israelites live in booths when I brought them out of Egypt. I am the LORD your God.' "

44So Moses announced to the Israelites the appointed feasts of the LORD.

BOOTHS

Each year during the Feast of Tabernacles, Israelite families lived outdoors for a week in shelters made of branches. This reminded them that God kept their ancestors safe in the wilderness when they traveled from Egypt to the promised land.

Oil and Bread Set Before the LORD

24 The LORD said to Moses, 2"Command the Israelites to bring you clear oil of pressed olives for the light so that the lamps may be kept burning continually. 3Outside the curtain of the Testimony in the Tent of Meeting, Aaron is to tend the lamps before the LORD from evening till morning, continually. This is to be a lasting ordinance for the generations to come. [4]The lamps on the pure gold lampstand before the LORD must be tended continually.

[5]"Take fine flour and bake twelve loaves of bread, using two-tenths of an ephah[a] for each loaf. [6]Set them in two rows, six in each row, on the table of pure gold before the LORD. [7]Along each row put some pure incense as a memorial portion to represent the bread and to be an offering made to the LORD by fire. [8]This bread is to be set out before the LORD regularly, Sabbath after Sabbath, on behalf of the Israelites, as a lasting covenant. [9]It belongs to Aaron and his sons, who are to eat it in a holy place, because it is a most holy part of their regular share of the offerings made to the LORD by fire."

A Blasphemer Stoned

[10]Now the son of an Israelite mother and an Egyptian father went out among the Israelites, and a fight broke out in the camp between him and an Israelite. [11]The son of the Israelite woman blasphemed the Name with a curse; so they brought him to Moses. (His mother's name was Shelomith, the daughter of Dibri the Danite.) [12]They put him in custody until the will of the LORD should be made clear to them.

[13]Then the LORD said to Moses: [14]"Take the blasphemer outside the camp. All those who heard him are to lay their hands on his head, and the entire assembly is to stone him. [15]Say to the Israelites: 'If anyone curses his God, he will be held responsible; [16]anyone who blasphemes the name of the LORD must be put to death. The entire assembly must stone him. Whether an alien or native-born, when he blasphemes the Name, he must be put to death.

[17]"'If anyone takes the life of a human being, he must be put to death. [18]Anyone who takes the life of someone's animal must make restitution —life for life. [19]If anyone injures his

neighbor, whatever he has done must be done to him: [20]fracture for fracture, eye for eye, tooth for tooth. As he has injured the other, so he is to be injured. [21]Whoever kills an animal must make restitution, but whoever kills a man must be put to death. [22]You are to have the same law for the alien and the native-born. I am the LORD your God.'"

❓DID YOU KNOW?   24:14

Was a young man really stoned for swearing?

The Bible says he "blasphemed the [Lord's] Name with a curse." This means he tried to use God's name to make magic in order to harm another person. It was for this terrible sin, not for swearing, that the man was put to death.

---

[23]Then Moses spoke to the Israelites, and they took the blasphemer outside the camp and stoned him. The Israelites did as the LORD commanded Moses.

The Sabbath Year

25 The LORD said to Moses on Mount Sinai, [2]"Speak to the Israelites and say to them: 'When you enter the land I am going to give you, the land itself must observe a sabbath to the LORD. [3]For six years sow your fields, and for six years prune your vineyards and gather their crops. [4]But in the seventh year the land is to have a sabbath of rest, a sabbath to the LORD. Do not sow your fields or prune your vineyards. [5]Do not reap what grows of itself or harvest the grapes of your untended vines. The land is to have a year of rest. [6]Whatever the land yields during the sabbath year will be food for you—for yourself, your manservant and maidservant, and the hired worker and temporary resident who live among you, [7]as well as for your

---

[a]5 That is, probably about 4 quarts (about 4.5 liters)

livestock and the wild animals in your land. Whatever the land produces may be eaten.

The Year of Jubilee

8" 'Count off seven sabbaths of years—seven times seven years—so that the seven sabbaths of years amount to a period of forty-nine years. 9Then have the trumpet sounded everywhere on the tenth day of the seventh month; on the Day of Atonement sound the trumpet throughout your land. 10Consecrate the fiftieth year and proclaim liberty throughout the land to all its inhabitants. It shall be a jubilee for you; each one of you is to return to his family property and each to his own clan. 11The fiftieth year shall be a jubilee for you; do not sow and do not reap what grows of itself or harvest the untended vines. 12For it is a jubilee and is to be holy for you; eat only what is taken directly from the fields.

13" 'In this Year of Jubilee everyone is to return to his own property.

14" 'If you sell land to one of your countrymen or buy any from him, do not take advantage of each other. 15You are to buy from your countryman on the basis of the number of years since the Jubilee. And he is to sell to you on the basis of the number of years left for harvesting crops. 16When the years are many, you are to increase the price, and when the years are few, you are to decrease the price, because what he is really selling you is the number of crops. 17Do not take advantage of each other, but fear your God. I am the LORD your God.

18" 'Follow my decrees and be careful to obey my laws, and you will live safely in the land. 19Then the land will yield its fruit, and you will eat your fill and live there in safety. 20You may ask, "What will we eat in the seventh year if we do not plant or harvest our crops?" 21I will send you such a blessing in the sixth year that the land will yield enough for three years. 22While you plant during the eighth year, you will eat from the old crop and will continue to eat from it until the harvest of the ninth year comes in.

23" 'The land must not be sold permanently, because the land is mine and you are but aliens and my tenants. 24Throughout the country that you hold as a possession, you must provide for the redemption of the land.

25" 'If one of your countrymen becomes poor and sells some of his property, his nearest relative is to come and redeem what his countryman has sold. 26If, however, a man has no one to redeem it for him but he himself prospers and acquires sufficient means to redeem it, 27he is to determine the value for the years since he sold it and refund the balance to the man to whom he sold it; he can then go back to his own property. 28But if he does not acquire the means to repay him, what he sold will remain in the possession of the buyer until the Year of Jubilee. It will be returned in the Jubilee, and he can then go back to his property.

29" 'If a man sells a house in a walled city, he retains the right of redemption a full year after its sale. During that time he may redeem it. 30If it is not redeemed before a full year has passed, the house in the walled city shall belong permanently to the buyer and his descendants. It is not to be returned in the Jubilee. 31But houses in villages without walls around them are to be considered as open country. They can be redeemed, and they are to be returned in the Jubilee.

32" 'The Levites always have the right to redeem their houses in the Levitical towns, which they possess. 33So the property of the Levites is redeemable—that is, a house sold in any town they hold—and is to be returned in the Jubilee, because the houses in the towns of the Levites are their property among the Israelites. 34But the pastureland belonging to their towns must not be sold; it is their permanent possession.

35" 'If one of your countrymen becomes poor and is unable to support himself among you, help him as you would an alien or a temporary resident, so he can continue to live among you. ³⁶Do not take interest of any kind^a from him, but fear your God, so that your countryman may continue to live among you. ³⁷You must not lend him money at interest or sell him food at a profit. ³⁸I am the LORD your God, who brought you out of Egypt to give you the land of Canaan and to be your God.

³⁹" 'If one of your countrymen becomes poor among you and sells himself to you, do not make him work as a slave. ⁴⁰He is to be treated as a hired worker or a temporary resident among you; he is to work for you until the Year of Jubilee. ⁴¹Then he and his children are to be released, and he will go back to his own clan and to the property of his forefathers. ⁴²Because the Israelites are my servants, whom I brought out of Egypt, they must not be sold as slaves. ⁴³Do not rule over them ruthlessly, but fear your God.

⁴⁴" 'Your male and female slaves are to come from the nations around you; from them you may buy slaves. ⁴⁵You may also buy some of the temporary residents living among you and members of their clans born in your country, and they will become your property. ⁴⁶You can will them to your children as inherited property and can make them slaves for life, but you must not rule over your fellow Israelites ruthlessly.

⁴⁷" 'If an alien or a temporary resident among you becomes rich and one of your countrymen becomes poor and sells himself to the alien living among you or to a member of the alien's clan, ⁴⁸he retains the right of redemption after he has sold himself. One of his relatives may redeem him: ⁴⁹An uncle or a cousin or any blood relative in his clan may redeem him. Or if he prospers, he may redeem himself. ⁵⁰He and his buyer are to count the time from the year he sold himself up to the Year of Jubilee. The price for his release is to be based on the rate paid to a hired man for that number of years. ⁵¹If many years remain, he must pay for his redemption a larger share of the price paid for him. ⁵²If only a few years remain until the Year of Jubilee, he is to compute that and pay for his redemption accordingly. ⁵³He is to be treated as a man hired from year to year; you must see to it that his owner does not rule over him ruthlessly.

⁵⁴" 'Even if he is not redeemed in any of these ways, he and his children are to be released in the Year of Jubilee, ⁵⁵for the Israelites belong to me as servants. They are my servants, whom I brought out of Egypt. I am the LORD your God.

Reward for Obedience

26 " 'Do not make idols or set up an image or a sacred stone for yourselves, and do not place a carved stone in your land to bow down before it. I am the LORD your God.

²" 'Observe my Sabbaths and have reverence for my sanctuary. I am the LORD.

³" 'If you follow my decrees and are careful to obey my commands, ⁴I will send you rain in its season, and the ground will yield its crops and the trees of the field their fruit. ⁵Your threshing will continue until grape harvest and the grape harvest will continue until planting, and you will eat all the food you want and live in safety in your land.

⁶" 'I will grant peace in the land, and you will lie down and no one will make you afraid. I will remove savage beasts from the land, and the sword will not pass through your country. ⁷You will pursue your enemies, and they will fall by the sword before you. ⁸Five of you will chase a hundred, and a hundred of you will chase ten thousand, and your enemies will fall by the sword before you.

⁹" 'I will look on you with favor and make you fruitful and increase your numbers, and I will keep my cov-

---

^a36 Or *take excessive interest*; similarly in verse 37

enant with you. ¹⁰You will still be eating last year's harvest when you will have to move it out to make room for the new. ¹¹I will put my dwelling place *a* among you, and I will not abhor you. ¹²I will walk among you and be your God, and you will be my people. ¹³I am the LORD your God, who brought you out of Egypt so that you would no longer be slaves to the Egyptians; I broke the bars of your yoke and enabled you to walk with heads held high.

Punishment for Disobedience

¹⁴" 'But if you will not listen to me and carry out all these commands, ¹⁵and if you reject my decrees and abhor my laws and fail to carry out all my commands and so violate my covenant, ¹⁶then I will do this to you: I will bring upon you sudden terror, wasting diseases and fever that will destroy your sight and drain away your life. You will plant seed in vain, because your enemies will eat it. ¹⁷I will set my face against you so that you will be defeated by your enemies; those who hate you will rule over you, and you will flee even when no one is pursuing you.

¹⁸" 'If after all this you will not listen to me, I will punish you for your sins seven times over. ¹⁹I will break down your stubborn pride and make the sky above you like iron and the ground beneath you like bronze.

a11 Or my tabernacle

²⁰Your strength will be spent in vain, because your soil will not yield its crops, nor will the trees of the land yield their fruit.

²¹" 'If you remain hostile toward me and refuse to listen to me, I will multiply your afflictions seven times over, as your sins deserve. ²²I will send wild animals against you, and they will rob you of your children, destroy your cattle and make you so few in number that your roads will be deserted.

²³" 'If in spite of these things you do not accept my correction but continue to be hostile toward me, ²⁴I myself will be hostile toward you and will afflict you for your sins seven times over. ²⁵And I will bring the sword upon you to avenge the breaking of the covenant. When you withdraw into your cities, I will send a plague among you, and you will be given into enemy hands. ²⁶When I cut off your supply of bread, ten women will be able to bake your bread in one oven, and they will dole out the bread by weight. You will eat, but you will not be satisfied.

²⁷" 'If in spite of this you still do not listen to me but continue to be hostile toward me, ²⁸then in my anger I will be hostile toward you, and I myself will punish you for your sins seven times over. ²⁹You will eat the flesh of your sons and the flesh of your daughters. ³⁰I will destroy your high

▚ET'S LIVE IT! Leviticus 26:3–22

REWARDS AND PUNISHMENTS ➡ Read Leviticus 26:3–22 to find out what God told the Israelites about rewards and punishments. God loved the Israelites and he loves you. He wants you to love and obey him. If you do, he will send rewards just as he promised the Israelites. But punishment is just as certain if you disobey.

Make a list of all the rewards and all the punishments you can find in this part of Leviticus. Give yourself ten points for each reward and punishment.

200 points: Good.
250 points: Super!

places, cut down your incense altars and pile your dead bodies on the lifeless forms of your idols, and I will abhor you. 31I will turn your cities into ruins and lay waste your sanctuaries, and I will take no delight in the pleasing aroma of your offerings. 32I will lay waste the land, so that your enemies who live there will be appalled. 33I will scatter you among the nations and will draw out my sword and pursue you. Your land will be laid waste, and your cities will lie in ruins. 34Then the land will enjoy its sabbath years all the time that it lies desolate and you are in the country of your enemies; then the land will rest and enjoy its sabbaths. 35All the time that it lies desolate, the land will have the rest it did not have during the sabbaths you lived in it.

36" 'As for those of you who are left, I will make their hearts so fearful in the lands of their enemies that the sound of a windblown leaf will put them to flight. They will run as though fleeing from the sword, and they will fall, even though no one is pursuing them. 37They will stumble over one another as though fleeing from the sword, even though no one is pursuing them. So you will not be able to stand before your enemies. 38You will perish among the nations; the land of your enemies will devour you. 39Those of you who are left will waste away in the lands of their enemies because of their sins; also because of their fathers' sins they will waste away.

40" 'But if they will confess their sins and the sins of their fathers—their treachery against me and their hostility toward me, 41which made me hostile toward them so that I sent them into the land of their enemies —then when their uncircumcised hearts are humbled and they pay for their sin, 42I will remember my covenant with Jacob and my covenant with Isaac and my covenant with Abraham, and I will remember the land. 43For the land will be deserted by them and will enjoy its sabbaths while it lies desolate without them. They will pay for their sins because they rejected my laws and abhorred my decrees. 44Yet in spite of this, when they are in the land of their enemies, I will not reject them or abhor them so as to destroy them completely, breaking my covenant with them. I am the LORD their God. 45But for their sake I will remember the covenant with their ancestors whom I brought out of Egypt in the sight of the nations to be their God. I am the LORD.' "

46These are the decrees, the laws and the regulations that the LORD established on Mount Sinai between himself and the Israelites through Moses.

Redeeming What Is the LORD's

27 The LORD said to Moses, 2"Speak to the Israelites and say to them: 'If anyone makes a special vow to dedicate persons to the LORD by giving equivalent values, 3set the value of a male between the ages of twenty and sixty at fifty shekels*a* of silver, according to the sanctuary shekel*b*; 4and if it is a female, set her value at thirty shekels.*c* 5If it is a person between the ages of five and twenty, set the value of a male at twenty shekels*d* and of a female at ten shekels.*e* 6If it is a person between one month and five years, set the value of a male at five shekels*f* of silver and that of a female at three shekels*g* of silver. 7If it is a person sixty years old or more, set the value of a male at fifteen shekels*h* and of a female at ten shekels. 8If anyone making the vow is too poor to pay the specified amount, he is to present the

---

a3 That is, about 1 1/4 pounds (about 0.6 kilogram); also in verse 16   *b3* That is, about 2/5 ounce (about 11.5 grams); also in verse 25   *c4* That is, about 12 ounces (about 0.3 kilogram)
d5 That is, about 8 ounces (about 0.2 kilogram)   *e5* That is, about 4 ounces (about 110 grams); also in verse 7   *f6* That is, about 2 ounces (about 55 grams)   *g6* That is, about 1 1/4 ounces (about 35 grams)   *h7* That is, about 6 ounces (about 170 grams)

person to the priest, who will set the value for him according to what the man making the vow can afford.

9" 'If what he vowed is an animal that is acceptable as an offering to the LORD, such an animal given to the LORD becomes holy. 10He must not exchange it or substitute a good one for a bad one, or a bad one for a good one; if he should substitute one animal for another, both it and the substitute become holy. 11If what he vowed is a ceremonially unclean animal—one that is not acceptable as an offering to the LORD—the animal must be presented to the priest, 12who will judge its quality as good or bad. Whatever value the priest then sets, that is what it will be. 13If the owner wishes to redeem the animal, he must add a fifth to its value.

14" 'If a man dedicates his house as something holy to the LORD, the priest will judge its quality as good or bad. Whatever value the priest then sets, so it will remain. 15If the man who dedicates his house redeems it, he must add a fifth to its value, and the house will again become his.

16" 'If a man dedicates to the LORD part of his family land, its value is to be set according to the amount of seed required for it—fifty shekels of silver to a homer a of barley seed. 17If he dedicates his field during the Year of Jubilee, the value that has been set remains. 18But if he dedicates his field after the Jubilee, the priest will determine the value according to the number of years that remain until the next Year of Jubilee, and its set value will be reduced. 19If the man who dedicates the field wishes to redeem it, he must add a fifth to its value, and the field will again become his. 20If, however, he does not redeem the field, or if he has sold it to someone else, it can never be redeemed. 21When the field is released in the Jubilee, it will become holy, like a field devoted to the LORD; it will become the property of the priests. b

22" 'If a man dedicates to the LORD a field he has bought, which is not part of his family land, 23the priest will determine its value up to the Year of Jubilee, and the man must pay its value on that day as something holy to the LORD. 24In the Year of Jubilee the field will revert to the person from whom he bought it, the one whose land it was. 25Every value is to be set according to the sanctuary shekel, twenty gerahs to the shekel.

26" 'No one, however, may dedicate the firstborn of an animal, since the firstborn already belongs to the LORD; whether an ox c or a sheep, it is the LORD's. 27If it is one of the unclean animals, he may buy it back at its set value, adding a fifth of the value to it. If he does not redeem it, it is to be sold at its set value.

28" 'But nothing that a man owns and devotes d to the LORD—whether man or animal or family land—may be sold or redeemed; everything so devoted is most holy to the LORD.

29" 'No person devoted to destruction e may be ransomed; he must be put to death.

30" 'A tithe of everything from the land, whether grain from the soil or fruit from the trees, belongs to the LORD; it is holy to the LORD. 31If a man redeems any of his tithe, he must add a fifth of the value to it. 32The entire tithe of the herd and flock—every tenth animal that passes under the shepherd's rod—will be holy to the LORD. 33He must not pick out the good from the bad or make any substitution. If he does make a substitution, both the animal and its substitute become holy and cannot be redeemed.' "

34These are the commands the LORD gave Moses on Mount Sinai for the Israelites.

---

a16 That is, probably about 6 bushels (about 220 liters)   b21 Or priest   c26 The Hebrew word can include both male and female.   d28 The Hebrew term refers to the irrevocable giving over of things or persons to the LORD.   e29 The Hebrew term refers to the irrevocable giving over of things or persons to the LORD, often by totally destroying them.

NUMBERS

WHO WROTE THIS BOOK?

Moses.

WHY WAS THIS BOOK WRITTEN?

Numbers tells how Israel's disobedience kept the Israelites from entering the promised land.

WHAT HAPPENS IN THIS BOOK?

The Israelites are frightened by the power of the Canaanites. They disobey when God tells them to attack Canaan. The Israelites wander in the desert for forty years, until all the adults who disobeyed God have died.

WHAT DO WE LEARN ABOUT GOD IN THIS BOOK?

God will not bless people who refuse to trust and obey him.

WHO IS IMPORTANT IN THIS BOOK?

The important people in this book are Moses and Aaron.

WHEN DID THIS HAPPEN?

The events in this book happened between 1445 and 1405 B.C.

WHERE DID THIS HAPPEN?

Numbers 1–10 happened at Mount Sinai. Numbers 11–14 happened just outside Canaan. The rest of the book took place in the wilderness and on the way back to Canaan forty years later.

WHAT ARE SOME OF THE STORIES IN THIS BOOK?

The Israelites complain.	Numbers 11
Aaron turns against Moses.	Numbers 12
Spies explore Canaan.	Numbers 13
The Israelites disobey God.	Numbers 14
Korah leads a rebellion.	Numbers 16
Aaron's staff buds.	Numbers 17
Balaam tries to curse Israel.	Numbers 22–24
Israel defeats the Midianites.	Numbers 31

The Census

1 The LORD spoke to Moses in the Tent of Meeting in the Desert of Sinai on the first day of the second month of the second year after the Israelites came out of Egypt. He said: ²"Take a census of the whole Israelite community by their clans and families, listing every man by name, one by one. ³You and Aaron are to number by their divisions all the men in Israel twenty years old or more who are able to serve in the army. ⁴One man from each tribe, each the head of his family, is to help you. ⁵These are the names of the men who are to assist you:

from Reuben, Elizur son of Shedeur;
⁶from Simeon, Shelumiel son of Zurishaddai;
⁷from Judah, Nahshon son of Amminadab;
⁸from Issachar, Nethanel son of Zuar;
⁹from Zebulun, Eliab son of Helon;
¹⁰from the sons of Joseph:
from Ephraim, Elishama son of Ammihud;
from Manasseh, Gamaliel son of Pedahzur;
¹¹from Benjamin, Abidan son of Gideoni;
¹²from Dan, Ahiezer son of Ammishaddai;
¹³from Asher, Pagiel son of Ocran;
¹⁴from Gad, Eliasaph son of Deuel;
¹⁵from Naphtali, Ahira son of Enan."

¹⁶These were the men appointed from the community, the leaders of their ancestral tribes. They were the heads of the clans of Israel.

¹⁷Moses and Aaron took these men whose names had been given, ¹⁸and they called the whole community together on the first day of the second month. The people indicated their ancestry by their clans and families, and the men twenty years old or more were listed by name, one by one, ¹⁹as the LORD commanded Moses. And so he counted them in the Desert of Sinai:

²⁰From the descendants of Reuben the firstborn son of Israel:

All the men twenty years old or more who were able to serve in the army were listed by name, one by one, according to the records of their clans and families. ²¹The number from the tribe of Reuben was 46,500.

²²From the descendants of Simeon:

All the men twenty years old or more who were able to serve in the army were counted and listed by name, one by one, according to the records of their clans and families. ²³The number from the tribe of Simeon was 59,300.

²⁴From the descendants of Gad:

All the men twenty years old or more who were able to serve in the army were listed by name, according to the records of their clans and families. ²⁵The number from the tribe of Gad was 45,650.

²⁶From the descendants of Judah:

All the men twenty years old or more who were able to serve in the army were listed by name, according to the records of their clans and families. ²⁷The number from the tribe of Judah was 74,600.

²⁸From the descendants of Issachar:

All the men twenty years old or more who were able to serve in the army were listed by name, according to the records of their clans and families. ²⁹The number from the tribe of Issachar was 54,400.

³⁰From the descendants of Zebulun:

All the men twenty years old or more who were able to serve in the army were listed by name, according to the records of their clans and families.

³¹The number from the tribe of Zebulun was 57,400.

³²From the sons of Joseph:
From the descendants of Ephraim:
All the men twenty years old or more who were able to serve in the army were listed by name, according to the records of their clans and families. ³³The number from the tribe of Ephraim was 40,500.

³⁴From the descendants of Manasseh:
All the men twenty years old or more who were able to serve in the army were listed by name, according to the records of their clans and families. ³⁵The number from the tribe of Manasseh was 32,200.

³⁶From the descendants of Benjamin:
All the men twenty years old or more who were able to serve in the army were listed by name, according to the records of their clans and families. ³⁷The number from the tribe of Benjamin was 35,400.

³⁸From the descendants of Dan:
All the men twenty years old or more who were able to serve in the army were listed by name, according to the records of their clans and families. ³⁹The number from the tribe of Dan was 62,700.

⁴⁰From the descendants of Asher:
All the men twenty years old or more who were able to serve in the army were listed by name, according to the records of their clans and families. ⁴¹The number from the tribe of Asher was 41,500.

⁴²From the descendants of Naphtali:
All the men twenty years old or more who were able to serve in the army were listed by name, according to the records of their clans and families. ⁴³The number from the tribe of Naphtali was 53,400.

⁴⁴These were the men counted by Moses and Aaron and the twelve leaders of Israel, each one representing his family. ⁴⁵All the Israelites twenty years old or more who were able to serve in Israel's army were counted according to their families. ⁴⁶The total number was 603,550.

❓DID YOU KNOW?   1:46

Do we know how many Israelites came out of Egypt?

This chapter tells the number of men twenty years and older. Most men this age were married, and many had families. If you multiply the total number of men given in Numbers 1:46 by four, you will know about how many Israelites Moses led from slavery in Egypt.

---

⁴⁷The families of the tribe of Levi, however, were not counted along with the others. ⁴⁸The LORD had said to Moses: ⁴⁹"You must not count the tribe of Levi or include them in the census of the other Israelites. ⁵⁰Instead, appoint the Levites to be in charge of the tabernacle of the Testimony—over all its furnishings and everything belonging to it. They are to carry the tabernacle and all its furnishings; they are to take care of it and encamp around it. ⁵¹Whenever the tabernacle is to move, the Levites are to take it down, and whenever the tabernacle is to be set up, the Levites shall do it. Anyone else who goes near it shall be put to death. ⁵²The Israelites are to set up their tents by divisions, each man in his own camp under his own standard. ⁵³The Levites, however, are to set up their tents around the tabernacle of the Testimony so that wrath will not fall on the Israelite community. The Levites are to be responsible for the care of the tabernacle of the Testimony."

⁵⁴The Israelites did all this just as the LORD commanded Moses.

The Arrangement of the Tribal Camps

2 The LORD said to Moses and Aaron: 2"The Israelites are to camp around the Tent of Meeting some distance from it, each man under his standard with the banners of his family."

3On the east, toward the sunrise, the divisions of the camp of Judah are to encamp under their standard. The leader of the people of Judah is Nahshon son of Amminadab. 4His division numbers 74,600.

5The tribe of Issachar will camp next to them. The leader of the people of Issachar is Nethanel son of Zuar. 6His division numbers 54,400.

7The tribe of Zebulun will be next. The leader of the people of Zebulun is Eliab son of Helon. 8His division numbers 57,400.

9All the men assigned to the camp of Judah, according to their divisions, number 186,400. They will set out first.

10On the south will be the divisions of the camp of Reuben under their standard. The leader of the people of Reuben is Elizur son of Shedeur. 11His division numbers 46,500.

12The tribe of Simeon will camp next to them. The leader of the people of Simeon is Shelumiel son of Zurishaddai. 13His division numbers 59,300.

14The tribe of Gad will be next. The leader of the people of Gad is Eliasaph son of Deuel.*a* 15His division numbers 45,650.

16All the men assigned to the camp of Reuben, according to their divisions, number 151,450. They will set out second.

17Then the Tent of Meeting and the camp of the Levites will set out in the middle of the camps. They will set out in the same order as they encamp, each in his own place under his standard.

?DID YOU KNOW?   2:17

What was in the center of the Israelite camp?

The tabernacle was in the center of the camp. Here the tabernacle is called the Tent of Meeting, because this tent church was where God met with his people. Each Israelite tribe had its own area to the north, south, east, or west of the tabernacle.

18On the west will be the divisions of the camp of Ephraim under their standard. The leader of the people of Ephraim is Elishama son of Ammihud. 19His division numbers 40,500.

20The tribe of Manasseh will be next to them. The leader of the people of Manasseh is Gamaliel son of Pedahzur. 21His division numbers 32,200.

22The tribe of Benjamin will be next. The leader of the people of Benjamin is Abidan son of Gideoni. 23His division numbers 35,-400.

24All the men assigned to the camp of Ephraim, according to their divisions, number 108,100. They will set out third.

25On the north will be the divisions of the camp of Dan, under their standard. The leader of the people of Dan is Ahiezer son of Ammishaddai. 26His division numbers 62,700.

27The tribe of Asher will camp next to them. The leader of the people of Asher is Pagiel son of Ocran. 28His division numbers 41,500.

---

a14 Many manuscripts of the Masoretic Text, Samaritan Pentateuch and Vulgate (see also Num. 1:14); most manuscripts of the Masoretic Text *Reuel*

²⁹The tribe of Naphtali will be next. The leader of the people of Naphtali is Ahira son of Enan. ³⁰His division numbers 53,400.

³¹All the men assigned to the camp of Dan number 157,600. They will set out last, under their standards.

³²These are the Israelites, counted according to their families. All those in the camps, by their divisions, number 603,550. ³³The Levites, however, were not counted along with the other Israelites, as the LORD commanded Moses.

³⁴So the Israelites did everything the LORD commanded Moses; that is the way they encamped under their standards, and that is the way they set out, each with his clan and family.

The Levites

3 This is the account of the family of Aaron and Moses at the time the LORD talked with Moses on Mount Sinai.

²The names of the sons of Aaron were Nadab the firstborn and Abihu, Eleazar and Ithamar. ³Those were the names of Aaron's sons, the anointed priests, who were ordained to serve as priests. ⁴Nadab and Abihu, however, fell dead before the LORD when they made an offering with unauthorized fire before him in the Desert of Sinai. They had no sons; so only Eleazar and Ithamar served as priests during the lifetime of their father Aaron.

⁵The LORD said to Moses, ⁶"Bring the tribe of Levi and present them to Aaron the priest to assist him. ⁷They are to perform duties for him and for the whole community at the Tent of Meeting by doing the work of the tabernacle. ⁸They are to take care of all the furnishings of the Tent of Meeting, fulfilling the obligations of the Israelites by doing the work of the

tabernacle. ⁹Give the Levites to Aaron and his sons; they are the Israelites who are to be given wholly to him.ᵃ ¹⁰Appoint Aaron and his sons to serve as priests; anyone else who approaches the sanctuary must be put to death."

❓DID YOU KNOW?   3:6

How were the Levites special?

The tribe of Levi was set apart. Members of this tribe helped the priests take care of and move the tabernacle. Numbers 3–4 tell the different jobs given to Levite families.

---

¹¹The LORD also said to Moses, ¹²"I have taken the Levites from among the Israelites in place of the first male offspring of every Israelite woman. The Levites are mine, ¹³for all the firstborn are mine. When I struck down all the firstborn in Egypt, I set apart for myself every firstborn in Israel, whether man or animal. They are to be mine. I am the LORD."

¹⁴The LORD said to Moses in the Desert of Sinai, ¹⁵"Count the Levites by their families and clans. Count every male a month old or more." ¹⁶So Moses counted them, as he was commanded by the word of the LORD.

¹⁷These were the names of the sons of Levi:

Gershon, Kohath and Merari.
¹⁸These were the names of the Gershonite clans:

Libni and Shimei.
¹⁹The Kohathite clans:

Amram, Izhar, Hebron and Uzziel.
²⁰The Merarite clans:

Mahli and Mushi.
These were the Levite clans, according to their families.

²¹To Gershon belonged the clans of

ᵃ9 Most manuscripts of the Masoretic Text; some manuscripts of the Masoretic Text, Samaritan Pentateuch and Septuagint (see also Num. 8:16) *to me* the Libnites and Shimeites; these were the Gershonite clans. ²²The number of all the males a month old or more who were counted was 7,500. ²³The Gershonite clans were to camp on the west, behind the tabernacle. ²⁴The leader of the families of the Gershonites was Eliasaph son of Lael. ²⁵At the Tent of Meeting the Gershonites were responsible for the care of the tabernacle and tent, its coverings, the curtain at the entrance to the Tent of Meeting, ²⁶the curtains of the courtyard, the curtain at the entrance to the courtyard surrounding the tabernacle and altar, and the ropes—and everything related to their use.

²⁷To Kohath belonged the clans of the Amramites, Izharites, Hebronites and Uzzielites; these were the Kohathite clans. ²⁸The number of all the males a month old or more was 8,600.ᵃ The Kohathites were responsible for the care of the sanctuary. ²⁹The Kohathite clans were to camp on the south side of the tabernacle. ³⁰The leader of the families of the Kohathite clans was Elizaphan son of Uzziel. ³¹They were responsible for the care of the ark, the table, the lampstand, the altars, the articles of the sanctuary used in ministering, the curtain, and everything related to their use. ³²The chief leader of the Levites was Eleazar son of Aaron, the priest. He was appointed over those who were responsible for the care of the sanctuary.

³³To Merari belonged the clans of the Mahlites and the Mushites; these were the Merarite clans. ³⁴The number of all the males a month old or more who were counted was 6,200. ³⁵The leader of the families of the Merarite clans was Zuriel son of Abihail; they were to camp on the north side of the tabernacle. ³⁶The Merarites were appointed to take care of the frames of the tabernacle, its crossbars, posts, bases, all its equipment, and everything related to their use, ³⁷as well as the posts of the surrounding courtyard with their bases, tent pegs and ropes.

³⁸Moses and Aaron and his sons were to camp to the east of the tabernacle, toward the sunrise, in front of the Tent of Meeting. They were responsible for the care of the sanctuary on behalf of the Israelites. Anyone else who approached the sanctuary was to be put to death.

³⁹The total number of Levites counted at the LORD's command by Moses and Aaron according to their clans, including every male a month old or more, was 22,000.

⁴⁰The LORD said to Moses, "Count all the firstborn Israelite males who are a month old or more and make a list of their names. ⁴¹Take the Levites for me in place of all the firstborn of the Israelites, and the livestock of the Levites in place of all the firstborn of the livestock of the Israelites. I am the LORD."

⁴²So Moses counted all the firstborn of the Israelites, as the LORD commanded him. ⁴³The total number of firstborn males a month old or more, listed by name, was 22,273.

⁴⁴The LORD also said to Moses, ⁴⁵"Take the Levites in place of all the firstborn of Israel, and the livestock of the Levites in place of their livestock. The Levites are to be mine. I am the LORD. ⁴⁶To redeem the 273 firstborn Israelites who exceed the number of the Levites, ⁴⁷collect five shekelsᵇ for each one, according to the sanctuary shekel, which weighs twenty gerahs. ⁴⁸Give the money for the redemption of the additional Israelites to Aaron and his sons."

⁴⁹So Moses collected the redemption money from those who exceeded the number redeemed by the Levites. ⁵⁰From the firstborn of the Israelites he collected silver weighing 1,365

ᵃ28 Hebrew; some Septuagint manuscripts 8,300   ᵇ47 That is, about 2 ounces (about 55 grams) shekels,[a] according to the sanctuary shekel. [51]Moses gave the redemption money to Aaron and his sons, as he was commanded by the word of the LORD.

The Kohathites

4 The LORD said to Moses and Aaron: [2]"Take a census of the Kohathite branch of the Levites by their clans and families. [3]Count all the men from thirty to fifty years of age who come to serve in the work in the Tent of Meeting.

[4]"This is the work of the Kohathites in the Tent of Meeting: the care of the most holy things. [5]When the camp is to move, Aaron and his sons are to go in and take down the shielding curtain and cover the ark of the Testimony with it. [6]Then they are to cover this with hides of sea cows,[b] spread a cloth of solid blue over that and put the poles in place.

[7]"Over the table of the Presence they are to spread a blue cloth and put on it the plates, dishes and bowls, and the jars for drink offerings; the bread that is continually there is to remain on it. [8]Over these they are to spread a scarlet cloth, cover that with hides of sea cows and put its poles in place.

[9]"They are to take a blue cloth and cover the lampstand that is for light, together with its lamps, its wick trimmers and trays, and all its jars for the oil used to supply it. [10]Then they are to wrap it and all its accessories in a covering of hides of sea cows and put it on a carrying frame.

[11]"Over the gold altar they are to spread a blue cloth and cover that with hides of sea cows and put its poles in place. [12]"They are to take all the articles used for ministering in the sanctuary, wrap them in a blue cloth, cover that with hides of sea cows and put them on a carrying frame. [13]"They are to remove the ashes from the bronze altar and spread a

purple cloth over it. [14]Then they are to place on it all the utensils used for ministering at the altar, including the firepans, meat forks, shovels and sprinkling bowls. Over it they are to spread a covering of hides of sea cows and put its poles in place.

THE LAMPSTAND

The lampstand, called the *menorah* (men-OH-rah), had to be packed very carefully by the Levites who took care of the tabernacle and later of God's temple. According to Exodus 37:17–24 the lampstand was made of seventy-five pounds of pure gold!

---

[15]"After Aaron and his sons have finished covering the holy furnishings and all the holy articles, and when the camp is ready to move, the Kohathites are to come to do the carrying. But they must not touch the holy things or they will die. The Kohathites are to carry those things that are in the Tent of Meeting.

[16]"Eleazar son of Aaron, the priest, is to have charge of the oil for the light, the fragrant incense, the regular grain offering and the anointing oil. He is to be in charge of the entire tabernacle and everything in it, including its holy furnishings and articles."

[17]The LORD said to Moses and Aaron, [18]"See that the Kohathite tribal clans are not cut off from the Levites. [19]So that they may live and not die when they come near the most holy things, do this for them: Aaron and his sons are to go into the sanctuary

---

[a]50 That is, about 35 pounds (about 15.5 kilograms)
11, 12, 14 and 25   [b]6 That is, dugongs; also in verses 8, 10,

and assign to each man his work and
what he is to carry. ²⁰But the Kohathites must not go in to look at the holy
things, even for a moment, or they
will die."

The Gershonites

²¹The LORD said to Moses, ²²"Take
a census also of the Gershonites by
their families and clans. ²³Count all
the men from thirty to fifty years of
age who come to serve in the work at
the Tent of Meeting.

²⁴"This is the service of the Gershonite clans as they work and carry
burdens: ²⁵They are to carry the curtains of the tabernacle, the Tent of
Meeting, its covering and the outer
covering of hides of sea cows, the curtains for the entrance to the Tent of
Meeting, ²⁶the curtains of the courtyard surrounding the tabernacle and
altar, the curtain for the entrance,
the ropes and all the equipment used
in its service. The Gershonites are to
do all that needs to be done with
these things. ²⁷All their service,
whether carrying or doing other
work, is to be done under the direction of Aaron and his sons. You shall
assign to them as their responsibility
all they are to carry. ²⁸This is the service of the Gershonite clans at the
Tent of Meeting. Their duties are to
be under the direction of Ithamar son
of Aaron, the priest.

The Merarites

²⁹"Count the Merarites by their
clans and families. ³⁰Count all the
men from thirty to fifty years of age
who come to serve in the work at the
Tent of Meeting. ³¹This is their duty
as they perform service at the Tent of
Meeting: to carry the frames of the
tabernacle, its crossbars, posts and
bases, ³²as well as the posts of the
surrounding courtyard with their
bases, tent pegs, ropes, all their
equipment and everything related to
their use. Assign to each man the
specific things he is to carry. ³³This is
the service of the Merarite clans as
they work at the Tent of Meeting un-

der the direction of Ithamar son of
Aaron, the priest."

The Numbering of the Levite Clans

³⁴Moses, Aaron and the leaders of
the community counted the Kohathites by their clans and families. ³⁵All
the men from thirty to fifty years of
age who came to serve in the work in
the Tent of Meeting, ³⁶counted by
clans, were 2,750. ³⁷This was the total of all those in the Kohathite clans
who served in the Tent of Meeting.
Moses and Aaron counted them according to the LORD's command
through Moses.

³⁸The Gershonites were counted by
their clans and families. ³⁹All the
men from thirty to fifty years of age
who came to serve in the work at the
Tent of Meeting, ⁴⁰counted by their
clans and families, were 2,630.
⁴¹This was the total of those in the
Gershonite clans who served at the
Tent of Meeting. Moses and Aaron
counted them according to the LORD's
command.

⁴²The Merarites were counted by
their clans and families. ⁴³All the
men from thirty to fifty years of age
who came to serve in the work at the
Tent of Meeting, ⁴⁴counted by their
clans, were 3,200. ⁴⁵This was the total of those in the Merarite clans. Moses and Aaron counted them according to the LORD's command through
Moses.

⁴⁶So Moses, Aaron and the leaders
of Israel counted all the Levites by
their clans and families. ⁴⁷All the
men from thirty to fifty years of age
who came to do the work of serving
and carrying the Tent of Meeting
⁴⁸numbered 8,580. ⁴⁹At the LORD's
command through Moses, each was
assigned his work and told what to
carry.

Thus they were counted, as the
LORD commanded Moses.

The Purity of the Camp

5 The LORD said to Moses, ²"Command the Israelites to send away
from the camp anyone who has an in-

fectious skin disease*a* or a discharge of any kind, or who is ceremonially unclean because of a dead body. ³Send away male and female alike; send them outside the camp so they will not defile their camp, where I dwell among them." ⁴The Israelites did this; they sent them outside the camp. They did just as the LORD had instructed Moses.

Restitution for Wrongs

⁵The LORD said to Moses, ⁶"Say to the Israelites: 'When a man or woman wrongs another in any way*b* and so is unfaithful to the LORD, that person is guilty ⁷and must confess the sin he has committed. He must make full restitution for his wrong, add one fifth to it and give it all to the person he has wronged. ⁸But if that person has no close relative to whom restitution can be made for the wrong, the restitution belongs to the LORD and must be given to the priest, along with the ram with which atonement is made for him. ⁹All the sacred contributions the Israelites bring to a priest will belong to him. ¹⁰Each man's sacred gifts are his own, but what he gives to the priest will belong to the priest.' "

The Test for an Unfaithful Wife

¹¹Then the LORD said to Moses, ¹²"Speak to the Israelites and say to them: 'If a man's wife goes astray and is unfaithful to him ¹³by sleeping with another man, and this is hidden from her husband and her impurity is undetected (since there is no witness against her and she has not been caught in the act), ¹⁴and if feelings of jealousy come over her husband and he suspects his wife and she is impure—or if he is jealous and suspects her even though she is not impure— ¹⁵then he is to take his wife to the priest. He must also take an offering of a tenth of an ephah*c* of barley flour

on her behalf. He must not pour oil on it or put incense on it, because it is a grain offering for jealousy, a reminder offering to draw attention to guilt.

¹⁶" 'The priest shall bring her and have her stand before the LORD. ¹⁷Then he shall take some holy water in a clay jar and put some dust from the tabernacle floor into the water. ¹⁸After the priest has had the woman stand before the LORD, he shall loosen her hair and place in her hands the reminder offering, the grain offering for jealousy, while he himself holds the bitter water that brings a curse. ¹⁹Then the priest shall put the woman under oath and say to her, "If no other man has slept with you and you have not gone astray and become impure while married to your husband, may this bitter water that brings a curse not harm you. ²⁰But if you have gone astray while married to your husband and you have defiled yourself by sleeping with a man other than your husband"— ²¹here the priest is to put the woman under this curse of the oath—"may the LORD cause your people to curse and denounce you when he causes your thigh to waste away and your abdomen to swell.*d* ²²May this water that brings a curse enter your body so that your abdomen swells and your thigh wastes away.*e* "

" 'Then the woman is to say, "Amen. So be it."

²³" 'The priest is to write these curses on a scroll and then wash them off into the bitter water. ²⁴He shall have the woman drink the bitter water that brings a curse, and this water will enter her and cause bitter suffering. ²⁵The priest is to take from her hands the grain offering for jealousy, wave it before the LORD and bring it to the altar. ²⁶The priest is then to take a handful of the grain offering as a memorial offering and burn it on the altar; after that, he

---

a2 Traditionally *leprosy*; the Hebrew word was used for various diseases affecting the skin—not necessarily leprosy.   *b6* Or *woman commits any wrong common to mankind*   *c15* That is, probably about 2 quarts (about 2 liters)   *d21* Or *causes you to have a miscarrying womb and barrenness*   *e22* Or *body and cause you to be barren and have a miscarrying womb*

is to have the woman drink the water. ²⁷If she has defiled herself and been unfaithful to her husband, then when she is made to drink the water that brings a curse, it will go into her and cause bitter suffering; her abdomen will swell and her thigh waste away,ᵃ and she will become accursed among her people. ²⁸If, however, the woman has not defiled herself and is free from impurity, she will be cleared of guilt and will be able to have children.

²⁹" 'This, then, is the law of jealousy when a woman goes astray and defiles herself while married to her husband, ³⁰or when feelings of jealousy come over a man because he suspects his wife. The priest is to have her stand before the LORD and is to apply this entire law to her. ³¹The husband will be innocent of any wrongdoing, but the woman will bear the consequences of her sin.' "

The Nazirite

6 The LORD said to Moses, ²"Speak to the Israelites and say to them: 'If a man or woman wants to make a special vow, a vow of separation to the LORD as a Nazirite, ³he must abstain from wine and other fermented drink and must not drink vinegar made from wine or from other fermented drink. He must not drink grape juice or eat grapes or raisins. ⁴As long as he is a Nazirite, he must not eat anything that comes from the grapevine, not even the seeds or skins.

⁵" 'During the entire period of his vow of separation no razor may be used on his head. He must be holy until the period of his separation to the LORD is over; he must let the hair of his head grow long. ⁶Throughout the period of his separation to the LORD he must not go near a dead body. ⁷Even if his own father or mother or brother or sister dies, he must not make himself ceremonially unclean on account of them, because the symbol of his separation to God is

on his head. ⁸Throughout the period of his separation he is consecrated to the LORD.

MEN'S HAIRSTYLES

Most men in Israel did not have long hair. But a man who made a special "Nazirite" vow to God had to let his hair grow. The most famous Nazirite in the Bible was Samson. He lost his amazing strength when his hair was cut off. You can read about Samson in Judges 16.

---

⁹" 'If someone dies suddenly in his presence, thus defiling the hair he has dedicated, he must shave his head on the day of his cleansing—the seventh day. ¹⁰Then on the eighth day he must bring two doves or two young pigeons to the priest at the entrance to the Tent of Meeting. ¹¹The priest is to offer one as a sin offering and the other as a burnt offering to make atonement for him because he sinned by being in the presence of the dead body. That same day he is to consecrate his head. ¹²He must dedicate himself to the LORD for the period of his separation and must bring a year-old male lamb as a guilt offering. The previous days do not count, because he became defiled during his separation.

¹³" 'Now this is the law for the Nazirite when the period of his separation is over. He is to be brought to the entrance to the Tent of Meeting. ¹⁴There he is to present his offerings to the LORD: a year-old male lamb without defect for a burnt offering, a year-old ewe lamb without defect for

ᵃ27 Or suffering; she will have barrenness and a miscarrying womb a sin offering, a ram without defect for a fellowship offering,a 15together with their grain offerings and drink offerings, and a basket of bread made without yeast—cakes made of fine flour mixed with oil, and wafers spread with oil.

16" 'The priest is to present them before the LORD and make the sin offering and the burnt offering. 17He is to present the basket of unleavened bread and is to sacrifice the ram as a fellowship offering to the LORD, together with its grain offering and drink offering.

18" 'Then at the entrance to the Tent of Meeting, the Nazirite must shave off the hair that he dedicated. He is to take the hair and put it in the fire that is under the sacrifice of the fellowship offering.

19" 'After the Nazirite has shaved off the hair of his dedication, the priest is to place in his hands a boiled shoulder of the ram, and a cake and a wafer from the basket, both made without yeast. 20The priest shall then wave them before the LORD as a wave offering; they are holy and belong to the priest, together with the breast that was waved and the thigh that was presented. After that, the Nazirite may drink wine.

21" 'This is the law of the Nazirite who vows his offering to the LORD in accordance with his separation, in addition to whatever else he can afford. He must fulfill the vow he has made, according to the law of the Nazirite.' "

The Priestly Blessing

22The LORD said to Moses, 23"Tell Aaron and his sons, 'This is how you are to bless the Israelites. Say to them:

24" ' "The LORD bless you
    and keep you;
25the LORD make his face shine
    upon you
    and be gracious to you;
26the LORD turn his face toward you

and give you peace." '

27"So they will put my name on the Israelites, and I will bless them."

Offerings at the Dedication of the Tabernacle

7 When Moses finished setting up the tabernacle, he anointed it and consecrated it and all its furnishings. He also anointed and consecrated the altar and all its utensils. 2Then the leaders of Israel, the heads of families who were the tribal leaders in charge of those who were counted, made offerings. 3They brought as their gifts before the LORD six covered carts and twelve oxen—an ox from each leader and a cart from every two. These they presented before the tabernacle.

4The LORD said to Moses, 5"Accept these from them, that they may be used in the work at the Tent of Meeting. Give them to the Levites as each man's work requires."

6So Moses took the carts and oxen and gave them to the Levites. 7He gave two carts and four oxen to the Gershonites, as their work required, 8and he gave four carts and eight oxen to the Merarites, as their work required. They were all under the direction of Ithamar son of Aaron, the priest. 9But Moses did not give any to the Kohathites, because they were to carry on their shoulders the holy things, for which they were responsible.

---

a14 Traditionally peace offering; also in verses 17 and 18

¹⁰When the altar was anointed, the leaders brought their offerings for its dedication and presented them before the altar. ¹¹For the LORD had said to Moses, "Each day one leader is to bring his offering for the dedication of the altar."

¹²The one who brought his offering on the first day was Nahshon son of Amminadab of the tribe of Judah.

¹³His offering was one silver plate weighing a hundred and thirty shekels,ᵃ and one silver sprinkling bowl weighing seventy shekels,ᵇ both according to the sanctuary shekel, each filled with fine flour mixed with oil as a grain offering; ¹⁴one gold dish weighing ten shekels,ᶜ filled with incense; ¹⁵one young bull, one ram and one male lamb a year old, for a burnt offering; ¹⁶one male goat for a sin offering; ¹⁷and two oxen, five rams, five male goats and five male lambs a year old, to be sacrificed as a fellowship offering.ᵈ This was the offering of Nahshon son of Amminadab.

¹⁸On the second day Nethanel son of Zuar, the leader of Issachar, brought his offering.

¹⁹The offering he brought was one silver plate weighing a hundred and thirty shekels, and one silver sprinkling bowl weighing seventy shekels, both according to the sanctuary shekel, each filled with fine flour mixed with oil as a grain offering; ²⁰one gold dish weighing ten shekels, filled with incense; ²¹one young bull, one ram and one male lamb a year old, for a burnt offering; ²²one male goat for a sin offering; ²³and two oxen, five rams, five male goats and five male lambs a year old, to be sacrificed as a fellowship offering. This was the offering of Nethanel son of Zuar.

²⁴On the third day, Eliab son of Helon, the leader of the people of Zebulun, brought his offering.

²⁵His offering was one silver plate weighing a hundred and thirty shekels, and one silver sprinkling bowl weighing seventy shekels, both according to the sanctuary shekel, each filled with fine flour mixed with oil as a grain offering; ²⁶one gold dish weighing ten shekels, filled with incense; ²⁷one young bull, one ram and one male lamb a year old, for a burnt offering; ²⁸one male goat for a sin offering; ²⁹and two oxen, five rams, five male goats and five male lambs a year old, to be sacrificed as a fellowship offering. This was the offering of Eliab son of Helon.

³⁰On the fourth day Elizur son of Shedeur, the leader of the people of Reuben, brought his offering.

³¹His offering was one silver plate weighing a hundred and thirty shekels, and one silver sprinkling bowl weighing seventy shekels, both according to the sanctuary shekel, each filled with fine flour mixed with oil as a grain offering; ³²one gold dish weighing ten shekels, filled with incense; ³³one young bull, one ram and one male lamb a year old, for a burnt offering; ³⁴one male goat for a sin offering; ³⁵and two oxen, five rams, five male goats and five male lambs a year old, to be sacrificed as a fellowship offering. This was the offering of Elizur son of Shedeur.

³⁶On the fifth day Shelumiel son of Zurishaddai, the leader of the people of Simeon, brought his offering.

³⁷His offering was one silver plate weighing a hundred and thirty shekels, and one silver

---

ᵃ13 That is, about 3 1/4 pounds (about 1.5 kilograms); also elsewhere in this chapter   ᵇ13 That is, about 1 3/4 pounds (about 0.8 kilogram); also elsewhere in this chapter   ᶜ14 That is, about 4 ounces (about 110 grams); also elsewhere in this chapter   ᵈ17 Traditionally *peace offering*; also elsewhere in this chapter

sprinkling bowl weighing seventy shekels, both according to the sanctuary shekel, each filled with fine flour mixed with oil as a grain offering; [38]one gold dish weighing ten shekels, filled with incense; [39]one young bull, one ram and one male lamb a year old, for a burnt offering; [40]one male goat for a sin offering; [41]and two oxen, five rams, five male goats and five male lambs a year old, to be sacrificed as a fellowship offering. This was the offering of Shelumiel son of Zurishaddai.

[42]On the sixth day Eliasaph son of Deuel, the leader of the people of Gad, brought his offering.

[43]His offering was one silver plate weighing a hundred and thirty shekels, and one silver sprinkling bowl weighing seventy shekels, both according to the sanctuary shekel, each filled with fine flour mixed with oil as a grain offering; [44]one gold dish weighing ten shekels, filled with incense; [45]one young bull, one ram and one male lamb a year old, for a burnt offering; [46]one male goat for a sin offering; [47]and two oxen, five rams, five male goats and five male lambs a year old, to be sacrificed as a fellowship offering. This was the offering of Eliasaph son of Deuel.

[48]On the seventh day Elishama son of Ammihud, the leader of the people of Ephraim, brought his offering.

[49]His offering was one silver plate weighing a hundred and thirty shekels, and one silver sprinkling bowl weighing seventy shekels, both according to the sanctuary shekel, each filled with fine flour mixed with oil as a grain offering; [50]one gold dish weighing ten shekels, filled with incense; [51]one young bull, one ram and one male lamb a year old, for a burnt offering; [52]one male goat for a sin offering; [53]and two oxen, five rams, five

male goats and five male lambs a year old, to be sacrificed as a fellowship offering. This was the offering of Elishama son of Ammihud.

[54]On the eighth day Gamaliel son of Pedahzur, the leader of the people of Manasseh, brought his offering.

[55]His offering was one silver plate weighing a hundred and thirty shekels, and one silver sprinkling bowl weighing seventy shekels, both according to the sanctuary shekel, each filled with fine flour mixed with oil as a grain offering; [56]one gold dish weighing ten shekels, filled with incense; [57]one young bull, one ram and one male lamb a year old, for a burnt offering; [58]one male goat for a sin offering; [59]and two oxen, five rams, five male goats and five male lambs a year old, to be sacrificed as a fellowship offering. This was the offering of Gamaliel son of Pedahzur.

[60]On the ninth day Abidan son of Gideoni, the leader of the people of Benjamin, brought his offering.

[61]His offering was one silver plate weighing a hundred and thirty shekels, and one silver sprinkling bowl weighing seventy shekels, both according to the sanctuary shekel, each filled with fine flour mixed with oil as a grain offering; [62]one gold dish weighing ten shekels, filled with incense; [63]one young bull, one ram and one male lamb a year old, for a burnt offering; [64]one male goat for a sin offering; [65]and two oxen, five rams, five male goats and five male lambs a year old, to be sacrificed as a fellowship offering. This was the offering of Abidan son of Gideoni.

[66]On the tenth day Ahiezer son of Ammishaddai, the leader of the people of Dan, brought his offering. [67]His offering was one silver

plate weighing a hundred and thirty shekels, and one silver sprinkling bowl weighing seventy shekels, both according to the sanctuary shekel, each filled with fine flour mixed with oil as a grain offering; [68]one gold dish weighing ten shekels, filled with incense; [69]one young bull, one ram and one male lamb a year old, for a burnt offering; [70]one male goat for a sin offering; [71]and two oxen, five rams, five male goats and five male lambs a year old, to be sacrificed as a fellowship offering. This was the offering of Ahiezer son of Ammishaddai.

[72]On the eleventh day Pagiel son of Ocran, the leader of the people of Asher, brought his offering.

[73]His offering was one silver plate weighing a hundred and thirty shekels, and one silver sprinkling bowl weighing seventy shekels, both according to the sanctuary shekel, each filled with fine flour mixed with oil as a grain offering; [74]one gold dish weighing ten shekels, filled with incense; [75]one young bull, one ram and one male lamb a year old, for a burnt offering; [76]one male goat for a sin offering; [77]and two oxen, five rams, five male goats and five male lambs a year old, to be sacrificed as a fellowship offering. This was the offering of Pagiel son of Ocran.

[78]On the twelfth day Ahira son of Enan, the leader of the people of Naphtali, brought his offering.

[79]His offering was one silver plate weighing a hundred and thirty shekels, and one silver sprinkling bowl weighing seventy shekels, both according to the sanctuary shekel, each filled with fine flour mixed with oil as a grain offering; [80]one gold dish weighing ten shekels, filled with

incense; [81]one young bull, one ram and one male lamb a year old, for a burnt offering; [82]one male goat for a sin offering; [83]and two oxen, five rams, five male goats and five male lambs a year old, to be sacrificed as a fellowship offering. This was the offering of Ahira son of Enan.

[84]These were the offerings of the Israelite leaders for the dedication of the altar when it was anointed: twelve silver plates, twelve silver sprinkling bowls and twelve gold dishes. [85]Each silver plate weighed a hundred and thirty shekels, and each sprinkling bowl seventy shekels. Altogether, the silver dishes weighed two thousand four hundred shekels,[a] according to the sanctuary shekel. [86]The twelve gold dishes filled with incense weighed ten shekels each, according to the sanctuary shekel. Altogether, the gold dishes weighed a hundred and twenty shekels.[b] [87]The total number of animals for the burnt offering came to twelve young bulls, twelve rams and twelve male lambs a year old, together with their grain offering. Twelve male goats were used for the sin offering. [88]The total number of animals for the sacrifice of the fellowship offering came to twenty-four oxen, sixty rams, sixty male goats and sixty male lambs a year old. These were the offerings for the dedication of the altar after it was anointed.

[89]When Moses entered the Tent of Meeting to speak with the LORD, he heard the voice speaking to him from between the two cherubim above the atonement cover on the ark of the Testimony. And he spoke with him.

Setting Up the Lamps

8 The LORD said to Moses, [2]"Speak to Aaron and say to him, 'When you set up the seven lamps, they are to light the area in front of the lampstand.'"

[a]85 That is, about 60 pounds (about 28 kilograms)

[b]86 That is, about 3 pounds (about 1.4 kilograms)

³Aaron did so; he set up the lamps so that they faced forward on the lampstand, just as the LORD commanded Moses. ⁴This is how the lampstand was made: It was made of hammered gold—from its base to its blossoms. The lampstand was made exactly like the pattern the LORD had shown Moses.

The Setting Apart of the Levites

⁵The LORD said to Moses: ⁶"Take the Levites from among the other Israelites and make them ceremonially clean. ⁷To purify them, do this: Sprinkle the water of cleansing on them; then have them shave their whole bodies and wash their clothes, and so purify themselves. ⁸Have them take a young bull with its grain offering of fine flour mixed with oil; then you are to take a second young bull for a sin offering. ⁹Bring the Levites to the front of the Tent of Meeting and assemble the whole Israelite community. ¹⁰You are to bring the Levites before the LORD, and the Israelites are to lay their hands on them. ¹¹Aaron is to present the Levites before the LORD as a wave offering from the Israelites, so that they may be ready to do the work of the LORD.

¹²"After the Levites lay their hands on the heads of the bulls, use the one for a sin offering to the LORD and the other for a burnt offering, to make atonement for the Levites. ¹³Have the Levites stand in front of Aaron and his sons and then present them as a wave offering to the LORD. ¹⁴In this way you are to set the Levites apart from the other Israelites, and the Levites will be mine.

¹⁵"After you have purified the Levites and presented them as a wave offering, they are to come to do their work at the Tent of Meeting. ¹⁶They are the Israelites who are to be given wholly to me. I have taken them as my own in place of the firstborn, the first male offspring from every Israelite woman. ¹⁷Every firstborn male in Israel, whether man or animal, is mine. When I struck down all the firstborn in Egypt, I set them apart for myself. ¹⁸And I have taken the Levites in place of all the firstborn sons in Israel. ¹⁹Of all the Israelites, I have given the Levites as gifts to Aaron and his sons to do the work at the Tent of Meeting on behalf of the Israelites and to make atonement for them so that no plague will strike the Israelites when they go near the sanctuary."

²⁰Moses, Aaron and the whole Israelite community did with the Levites just as the LORD commanded Moses. ²¹The Levites purified themselves and washed their clothes. Then Aaron presented them as a wave offering before the LORD and made atonement for them to purify them. ²²After that, the Levites came to do their work at the Tent of Meeting under the supervision of Aaron and his sons. They did with the Levites just as the LORD commanded Moses.

²³The LORD said to Moses, ²⁴"This applies to the Levites: Men twenty-five years old or more shall come to take part in the work at the Tent of Meeting, ²⁵but at the age of fifty, they must retire from their regular service and work no longer. ²⁶They may assist their brothers in performing their duties at the Tent of Meeting, but they themselves must not do the work. This, then, is how you are to assign the responsibilities of the Levites."

The Passover

9 The LORD spoke to Moses in the Desert of Sinai in the first month of the second year after they came out of Egypt. He said, ²"Have the Israelites celebrate the Passover at the appointed time. ³Celebrate it at the appointed time, at twilight on the fourteenth day of this month, in accordance with all its rules and regulations."

⁴So Moses told the Israelites to celebrate the Passover, ⁵and they did so in the Desert of Sinai at twilight on the fourteenth day of the first month. The Israelites did everything just as the LORD commanded Moses.

⁶But some of them could not cele-

brate the Passover on that day because they were ceremonially unclean on account of a dead body. So they came to Moses and Aaron that same day [7]and said to Moses, "We have become unclean because of a dead body, but why should we be kept from presenting the LORD's offering with the other Israelites at the appointed time?"

[8]Moses answered them, "Wait until I find out what the LORD commands concerning you."

[9]Then the LORD said to Moses, [10]"Tell the Israelites: 'When any of you or your descendants are unclean because of a dead body or are away on a journey, they may still celebrate the LORD's Passover. [11]They are to celebrate it on the fourteenth day of the second month at twilight. They are to eat the lamb, together with unleavened bread and bitter herbs. [12]They must not leave any of it till morning or break any of its bones. When they celebrate the Passover, they must follow all the regulations. [13]But if a man who is ceremonially clean and not on a journey fails to celebrate the Passover, that person must be cut off from his people because he did not present the LORD's offering at the appointed time. That man will bear the consequences of his sin.

[14]" 'An alien living among you who wants to celebrate the LORD's Passover must do so in accordance with its rules and regulations. You must have the same regulations for the alien and the native-born.' "

The Cloud Above the Tabernacle

[15]On the day the tabernacle, the Tent of the Testimony, was set up, the cloud covered it. From evening till morning the cloud above the tabernacle looked like fire. [16]That is how it continued to be; the cloud covered it, and at night it looked like fire. [17]Whenever the cloud lifted from above the Tent, the Israelites set out; wherever the cloud settled, the Israelites encamped. [18]At the LORD's com-

mand the Israelites set out, and at his command they encamped. As long as the cloud stayed over the tabernacle, they remained in camp. [19]When the cloud remained over the tabernacle a long time, the Israelites obeyed the LORD's order and did not set out. [20]Sometimes the cloud was over the tabernacle only a few days; at the LORD's command they would encamp, and then at his command they would set out. [21]Sometimes the cloud stayed only from evening till morning, and when it lifted in the morning, they set out. Whether by day or by night, whenever the cloud lifted, they set out. [22]Whether the cloud stayed over the tabernacle for two days or a month or a year, the Israelites would remain in camp and not set out; but when it lifted, they would set out. [23]At the LORD's command they encamped, and at the LORD's command they set out. They obeyed the LORD's order, in accordance with his command through Moses.

❓ DID YOU KNOW?   9:22

Why did God place a cloud over the tabernacle?

The cloud reminded the Israelites that God was with them. The cloud also guided the Israelites in the wilderness. The Israelites followed the cloud when it moved, and stopped when the cloud stopped moving.

The Silver Trumpets

10 The LORD said to Moses: [2]"Make two trumpets of hammered silver, and use them for calling the community together and for having the camps set out. [3]When both are sounded, the whole community is to assemble before you at the entrance to the Tent of Meeting. [4]If only one is sounded, the leaders—the heads of the clans of Israel—are to assemble before you. [5]When a trumpet blast is sounded, the tribes camping on the east are to set out. ⁶At the sounding of a second blast, the camps on the south are to set out. The blast will be the signal for setting out. ⁷To gather the assembly, blow the trumpets, but not with the same signal.

⁸"The sons of Aaron, the priests, are to blow the trumpets. This is to be a lasting ordinance for you and the generations to come. ⁹When you go into battle in your own land against an enemy who is oppressing you, sound a blast on the trumpets. Then you will be remembered by the LORD your God and rescued from your enemies. ¹⁰Also at your times of rejoicing—your appointed feasts and New Moon festivals—you are to sound the trumpets over your burnt offerings and fellowship offerings,ᵃ and they will be a memorial for you before your God. I am the LORD your God."

The Israelites Leave Sinai

¹¹On the twentieth day of the second month of the second year, the cloud lifted from above the tabernacle of the Testimony. ¹²Then the Israelites set out from the Desert of Sinai and traveled from place to place until the cloud came to rest in the Desert of Paran. ¹³They set out, this first time, at the LORD's command through Moses.

¹⁴The divisions of the camp of Judah went first, under their standard. Nahshon son of Amminadab was in command. ¹⁵Nethanel son of Zuar was over the division of the tribe of Issachar, ¹⁶and Eliab son of Helon was over the division of the tribe of Zebulun. ¹⁷Then the tabernacle was taken down, and the Gershonites and Merarites, who carried it, set out.

¹⁸The divisions of the camp of Reuben went next, under their standard. Elizur son of Shedeur was in command. ¹⁹Shelumiel son of Zurishaddai was over the division of the tribe of Simeon, ²⁰and Eliasaph son of Deuel was over the division of the tribe of Gad. ²¹Then the Kohathites set out, carrying the holy things. The taber-

nacle was to be set up before they arrived.

²²The divisions of the camp of Ephraim went next, under their standard. Elishama son of Ammihud was in command. ²³Gamaliel son of Pedahzur was over the division of the tribe of Manasseh, ²⁴and Abidan son of Gideoni was over the division of the tribe of Benjamin.

²⁵Finally, as the rear guard for all the units, the divisions of the camp of Dan set out, under their standard. Ahiezer son of Ammishaddai was in command. ²⁶Pagiel son of Ocran was over the division of the tribe of Asher, ²⁷and Ahira son of Enan was over the division of the tribe of Naphtali. ²⁸This was the order of march for the Israelite divisions as they set out.

²⁹Now Moses said to Hobab son of Reuel the Midianite, Moses' father-in-law, "We are setting out for the place about which the LORD said, 'I will give it to you.' Come with us and we will treat you well, for the LORD has promised good things to Israel."

³⁰He answered, "No, I will not go; I am going back to my own land and my own people."

³¹But Moses said, "Please do not leave us. You know where we should camp in the desert, and you can be our eyes. ³²If you come with us, we will share with you whatever good things the LORD gives us."

³³So they set out from the mountain of the LORD and traveled for three days. The ark of the covenant of the LORD went before them during those three days to find them a place to rest. ³⁴The cloud of the LORD was over them by day when they set out from the camp.

³⁵Whenever the ark set out, Moses said,

"Rise up, O LORD!
May your enemies be scattered;
may your foes flee before you."

³⁶Whenever it came to rest, he said,

"Return, O LORD,

ᵃ10 Traditionally *peace offerings*

to the countless thousands of Israel."

Fire From the LORD

11 Now the people complained about their hardships in the hearing of the LORD, and when he heard them his anger was aroused. Then fire from the LORD burned among them and consumed some of the outskirts of the camp. ²When the people cried out to Moses, he prayed to the LORD and the fire died down. ³So that place was called Taberah,ᵃ because fire from the LORD had burned among them.

Quail From the LORD

⁴The rabble with them began to crave other food, and again the Israelites started wailing and said, "If only we had meat to eat! ⁵We remember the fish we ate in Egypt at no cost—also the cucumbers, melons, leeks, onions and garlic. ⁶But now we have lost our appetite; we never see anything but this manna!"

⁷The manna was like coriander seed and looked like resin. ⁸The people went around gathering it, and then ground it in a handmill or crushed it in a mortar. They cooked it in a pot or made it into cakes. And it tasted like something made with olive oil. ⁹When the dew settled on the camp at night, the manna also came down.

¹⁰Moses heard the people of every family wailing, each at the entrance to his tent. The LORD became exceedingly angry, and Moses was troubled. ¹¹He asked the LORD, "Why have you brought this trouble on your servant? What have I done to displease you that you put the burden of all these people on me? ¹²Did I conceive all these people? Did I give them birth? Why do you tell me to carry them in my arms, as a nurse carries an infant, to the land you promised on oath to their forefathers? ¹³Where can I get meat for all these people? They keep wailing to me, 'Give us meat to eat!' ¹⁴I cannot carry all these people by myself; the burden is too heavy for me. ¹⁵If this is how you are going to treat me, put me to death right now—if I have found favor in your eyes—and do not let me face my own ruin."

¹⁶The LORD said to Moses: "Bring me seventy of Israel's elders who are known to you as leaders and officials among the people. Have them come to the Tent of Meeting, that they may stand there with you. ¹⁷I will come

ᵃ3 *Taberah* means *burning.*

▚ET'S LIVE IT!   Numbers 11:1–9,31–34

BE SATISFIED ▧➡ Before you read the Bible story check on what God has given you. Count (or guess) how many you have of each thing on this list.

___ shirts or blouses	___ toys
___ pants or jeans	___ books
___ pairs of socks	___ markers or crayons
___ pairs of shoes	___ meals & snacks a day
___ sweaters	___ TV's, radios, video games

Thank God for all that you have. If your list shows there is something you really need, then you can pray for it.

Read Numbers 11:1–9,31–34. The Israelites had everything they needed, but they still complained and wanted more. Do you have everything you need? Do you ever still grumble or complain?

down and speak with you there, and I will take of the Spirit that is on you and put the Spirit on them. They will help you carry the burden of the people so that you will not have to carry it alone.

18"Tell the people: 'Consecrate yourselves in preparation for tomorrow, when you will eat meat. The LORD heard you when you wailed, "If only we had meat to eat! We were better off in Egypt!" Now the LORD will give you meat, and you will eat it. 19You will not eat it for just one day, or two days, or five, ten or twenty days, 20but for a whole month—until it comes out of your nostrils and you loathe it—because you have rejected the LORD, who is among you, and have wailed before him, saying, "Why did we ever leave Egypt?"'"

21But Moses said, "Here I am among six hundred thousand men on foot, and you say, 'I will give them meat to eat for a whole month!' 22Would they have enough if flocks and herds were slaughtered for them? Would they have enough if all the fish in the sea were caught for them?"

23The LORD answered Moses, "Is the LORD's arm too short? You will now see whether or not what I say will come true for you."

24So Moses went out and told the people what the LORD had said. He brought together seventy of their elders and had them stand around the Tent. 25Then the LORD came down in the cloud and spoke with him, and he took of the Spirit that was on him and put the Spirit on the seventy elders. When the Spirit rested on them, they prophesied, but they did not do so again.ᵃ

26However, two men, whose names were Eldad and Medad, had remained in the camp. They were listed among the elders, but did not go out to the Tent. Yet the Spirit also rested on them, and they prophesied in the

camp. 27A young man ran and told Moses, "Eldad and Medad are prophesying in the camp."

28Joshua son of Nun, who had been Moses' aide since youth, spoke up and said, "Moses, my lord, stop them!"

29But Moses replied, "Are you jealous for my sake? I wish that all the LORD's people were prophets and that the LORD would put his Spirit on them!" 30Then Moses and the elders of Israel returned to the camp.

31Now a wind went out from the LORD and drove quail ᵇ down in from the sea. It brought them ᵇ down all around the camp to about three feetᶜ above the ground, as far as a day's walk in any direction. 32All that day and night and all the next day the people went out and gathered quail. No one gathered less than ten homers.ᵈ Then they spread them out all around the camp. 33But while the meat was still between their teeth and before it could be consumed, the anger of the LORD burned against the people, and he struck them with a severe plague. 34Therefore the place was named Kibroth Hattaavah,ᵉ because there they buried the people who had craved other food.

35From Kibroth Hattaavah the people traveled to Hazeroth and stayed there.

Miriam and Aaron Oppose Moses

12 Miriam and Aaron began to talk against Moses because of his Cushite wife, for he had married a Cushite. 2"Has the LORD spoken only through Moses?" they asked. "Hasn't he also spoken through us?" And the LORD heard this.

3(Now Moses was a very humble man, more humble than anyone else on the face of the earth.)

4At once the LORD said to Moses, Aaron and Miriam, "Come out to the Tent of Meeting, all three of you." So the three of them came out. 5Then the

---

ᵃ25 Or prophesied and continued to do so   ᵇ31 Or They flew   ᶜ31 Hebrew two cubits (about 1 meter)   ᵈ32 That is, probably about 60 bushels (about 2.2 kiloliters)   ᵉ34 Kibroth Hattaavah means graves of craving.

LORD came down in a pillar of cloud; he stood at the entrance to the Tent and summoned Aaron and Miriam. When both of them stepped forward, ⁶he said, "Listen to my words:

"When a prophet of the LORD is
   among you,
I reveal myself to him in
   visions,
I speak to him in dreams.
⁷But this is not true of my servant
   Moses;
he is faithful in all my house.
⁸With him I speak face to face,
   clearly and not in riddles;
he sees the form of the LORD.
Why then were you not afraid
   to speak against my servant
   Moses?"

⁹The anger of the LORD burned against them, and he left them.

¹⁰When the cloud lifted from above the Tent, there stood Miriam—leprous,ᵃ like snow. Aaron turned toward her and saw that she had leprosy; ¹¹and he said to Moses, "Please, my lord, do not hold against us the sin we have so foolishly committed. ¹²Do not let her be like a stillborn infant coming from its mother's womb with its flesh half eaten away."

¹³So Moses cried out to the LORD, "O God, please heal her!"

¹⁴The LORD replied to Moses, "If her father had spit in her face, would she not have been in disgrace for seven days? Confine her outside the camp for seven days; after that she can be brought back." ¹⁵So Miriam was confined outside the camp for seven days, and the people did not move on till she was brought back.

¹⁶After that, the people left Hazeroth and encamped in the Desert of Paran.

Exploring Canaan

13 The LORD said to Moses, ²"Send some men to explore the land of Canaan, which I am giving to the Israelites. From each an-cestral tribe send one of its leaders."

³So at the LORD's command Moses sent them out from the Desert of Paran. All of them were leaders of the Israelites. ⁴These are their names:

from the tribe of Reuben, Shammua son of Zaccur;
⁵from the tribe of Simeon, Shaphat son of Hori;
⁶from the tribe of Judah, Caleb son of Jephunneh;
⁷from the tribe of Issachar, Igal son of Joseph;
⁸from the tribe of Ephraim, Hoshea son of Nun;
⁹from the tribe of Benjamin, Palti son of Raphu;
¹⁰from the tribe of Zebulun, Gaddiel son of Sodi;
¹¹from the tribe of Manasseh (a tribe of Joseph), Gaddi son of Susi;
¹²from the tribe of Dan, Ammiel son of Gemalli;
¹³from the tribe of Asher, Sethur son of Michael;
¹⁴from the tribe of Naphtali, Nahbi son of Vophsi;
¹⁵from the tribe of Gad, Geuel son of Maki.

¹⁶These are the names of the men Moses sent to explore the land. (Moses gave Hoshea son of Nun the name Joshua.)

¹⁷When Moses sent them to explore Canaan, he said, "Go up through the Negev and on into the hill country. ¹⁸See what the land is like and whether the people who live there are strong or weak, few or many. ¹⁹What kind of land do they live in? Is it good or bad? What kind of towns do they live in? Are they unwalled or fortified? ²⁰How is the soil? Is it fertile or poor? Are there trees on it or not? Do your best to bring back some of the fruit of the land." (It was the season for the first ripe grapes.)

²¹So they went up and explored the land from the Desert of Zin as far as Rehob, toward Leboᵇ Hamath.

ᵃ10 The Hebrew word was used for various diseases affecting the skin—not necessarily leprosy.
ᵇ21 Or *toward the entrance to*

22They went up through the Negev and came to Hebron, where Ahiman, Sheshai and Talmai, the descendants of Anak, lived. (Hebron had been built seven years before Zoan in Egypt.) 23When they reached the Valley of Eshcol,*a* they cut off a branch bearing a single cluster of grapes. Two of them carried it on a pole between them, along with some pomegranates and figs. 24That place was called the Valley of Eshcol because of the cluster of grapes the Israelites cut off there. 25At the end of forty days they returned from exploring the land.

Report on the Exploration

26They came back to Moses and Aaron and the whole Israelite community at Kadesh in the Desert of Paran. There they reported to them and to the whole assembly and showed them the fruit of the land. 27They gave Moses this account: "We went into the land to which you sent us, and it does flow with milk and honey! Here is its fruit. 28But the people who live there are powerful, and the cities are fortified and very large. We even saw descendants of Anak there. 29The Amalekites live in the Negev; the Hittites, Jebusites and Amorites live in the hill country; and the Canaanites live near the sea and along the Jordan."

30Then Caleb silenced the people before Moses and said, "We should go up and take possession of the land, for we can certainly do it."

31But the men who had gone up with him said, "We can't attack those people; they are stronger than we are." 32And they spread among the Israelites a bad report about the land they had explored. They said, "The land we explored devours those living in it. All the people we saw there are of great size. 33We saw the Nephilim there (the descendants of Anak come from the Nephilim). We seemed like grasshoppers in our own eyes, and we looked the same to them."

The People Rebel

14 That night all the people of the community raised their voices and wept aloud. 2All the Israelites grumbled against Moses and Aaron, and the whole assembly said to them, "If only we had died in Egypt! Or in this desert! 3Why is the LORD bringing us to this land only to let us fall by the sword? Our wives and children will be taken as plunder. Wouldn't it be better for us to go back to Egypt?" 4And they said to each other, "We should choose a leader and go back to Egypt."

5Then Moses and Aaron fell facedown in front of the whole Israelite assembly gathered there. 6Joshua son of Nun and Caleb son of Jephunneh, who were among those who had explored the land, tore their clothes 7and said to the entire Israelite assembly, "The land we passed through and explored is exceedingly good. 8If the LORD is pleased with us, he will lead us into that land, a land flowing with milk and honey, and will give it to us. 9Only do not rebel against the LORD. And do not be afraid of the people of the land, because we will swallow them up. Their protection is gone, but the LORD is with us. Do not be afraid of them."

10But the whole assembly talked about stoning them. Then the glory of the LORD appeared at the Tent of Meeting to all the Israelites. 11The LORD said to Moses, "How long will these people treat me with contempt? How long will they refuse to believe in me, in spite of all the miraculous signs I have performed among them? 12I will strike them down with a plague and destroy them, but I will make you into a nation greater and stronger than they."

13Moses said to the LORD, "Then the Egyptians will hear about it! By your power you brought these people up from among them. 14And they will tell the inhabitants of this land about it. They have already heard that you,

a23 Eshcol means cluster; also in verse 24.

O LORD, are with these people and that you, O LORD, have been seen face to face, that your cloud stays over them, and that you go before them in a pillar of cloud by day and a pillar of fire by night. 15If you put these people to death all at one time, the nations who have heard this report about you will say, 16'The LORD was not able to bring these people into the land he promised them on oath; so he slaughtered them in the desert.'

17"Now may the Lord's strength be displayed, just as you have declared: 18'The LORD is slow to anger, abounding in love and forgiving sin and rebellion. Yet he does not leave the guilty unpunished; he punishes the children for the sin of the fathers to the third and fourth generation.' 19In accordance with your great love, forgive the sin of these people, just as you have pardoned them from the time they left Egypt until now."

20The LORD replied, "I have forgiven them, as you asked. 21Nevertheless, as surely as I live and as surely as the glory of the LORD fills the whole earth, 22not one of the men who saw my glory and the miraculous signs I performed in Egypt and in the desert but who disobeyed me and tested me ten times— 23not one of them will ever see the land I promised on oath to their forefathers. No one who has treated me with contempt will ever see it. 24But because my servant Caleb has a different spirit and follows me wholeheartedly, I will bring him into the land he went to, and his descendants will inherit it. 25Since the Amalekites and Canaanites are living in the valleys, turn back tomorrow and set out toward the desert along the route to the Red Sea.a"

26The LORD said to Moses and Aaron: 27"How long will this wicked community grumble against me? I have heard the complaints of these grumbling Israelites. 28So tell them, 'As surely as I live, declares the LORD, I will do to you the very things I heard you say: 29In this desert your bodies will fall—every one of you twenty years old or more who was counted in the census and who has grumbled against me. 30Not one of you will enter the land I swore with uplifted hand to make your home, except Ca-

a25 Hebrew *Yam Suph*; that is, Sea of Reeds

LET'S LIVE IT!   Numbers 14:1–24

CONSEQUENCES ⟹ Read Numbers 14:1–24. God forgave his people when they did not obey. But those people had to live in the wilderness for forty years, until all the adults who would not obey had died.

Being forgiven means someone is not angry with us anymore. But we may still have to take the consequences for what we did. Read this story and decide what you think this dad should do.

Dad told Andy, "Don't bounce your ball off the side of the house." But later Andy felt bored. He tossed his ball toward the side of the house—and hit a window! Crash! The ball went through the window. "Andy!" Dad called. "Come in here!"

What do you think Andy's dad should do? Spank him? Forgive him and then spank him? Make Andy pay for the window? Forgive Andy and make him pay for the window? Just tell Andy, "I forgive you"? Tell your parents the story of Andy and then explain to them what you think Andy's dad should do, and why.

leb son of Jephunneh and Joshua son of Nun. 31As for your children that you said would be taken as plunder, I will bring them in to enjoy the land you have rejected. 32But you—your bodies will fall in this desert. 33Your children will be shepherds here for forty years, suffering for your unfaithfulness, until the last of your bodies lies in the desert. 34For forty years—one year for each of the forty days you explored the land—you will suffer for your sins and know what it is like to have me against you.' 35I, the LORD, have spoken, and I will surely do these things to this whole wicked community, which has banded together against me. They will meet their end in this desert; here they will die."

36So the men Moses had sent to explore the land, who returned and made the whole community grumble against him by spreading a bad report about it— 37these men responsible for spreading the bad report about the land were struck down and died of a plague before the LORD. 38Of the men who went to explore the land, only Joshua son of Nun and Caleb son of Jephunneh survived.

39When Moses reported this to all the Israelites, they mourned bitterly. 40Early the next morning they went up toward the high hill country. "We have sinned," they said. "We will go up to the place the LORD promised."

41But Moses said, "Why are you disobeying the LORD's command? This will not succeed! 42Do not go up, because the LORD is not with you. You will be defeated by your enemies, 43for the Amalekites and Canaanites will face you there. Because you have turned away from the LORD, he will not be with you and you will fall by the sword."

44Nevertheless, in their presumption they went up toward the high hill country, though neither Moses nor the ark of the LORD's covenant moved from the camp. 45Then the Amalekites and Canaanites who lived in that hill country came down and attacked them and beat them down all the way to Hormah.

Supplementary Offerings

15 The LORD said to Moses, 2"Speak to the Israelites and say to them: 'After you enter the land I am giving you as a home 3and you present to the LORD offerings made by fire, from the herd or the flock, as an aroma pleasing to the LORD—whether burnt offerings or sacrifices, for special vows or freewill offerings or festival offerings— 4then the one who brings his offering shall present to the LORD a grain offering of a tenth of an ephah^a of fine flour mixed with a quarter of a hin^b of oil. 5With each lamb for the burnt offering or the sacrifice, prepare a quarter of a hin of wine as a drink offering.

6" 'With a ram prepare a grain offering of two-tenths of an ephah^c of fine flour mixed with a third of a hin^d of oil, 7and a third of a hin of wine as a drink offering. Offer it as an aroma pleasing to the LORD.

8" 'When you prepare a young bull as a burnt offering or sacrifice, for a special vow or a fellowship offering^e to the LORD, 9bring with the bull a grain offering of three-tenths of an ephah^f of fine flour mixed with half a hin^g of oil. 10Also bring half a hin of wine as a drink offering. It will be an offering made by fire, an aroma pleasing to the LORD. 11Each bull or ram, each lamb or young goat, is to be prepared in this manner. 12Do this for each one, for as many as you prepare.

13" 'Everyone who is native-born must do these things in this way when he brings an offering made by fire as an aroma pleasing to the LORD.

---

^{a}4 That is, probably about 2 quarts (about 2 liters) 1 liter); also in verse 5　^{c}6 That is, probably about 4 quarts (about 4.5 liters)　^{b}4 That is, probably about 1 quart (about ^{d}6 That is, probably about 1 1/4 quarts (about 1.2 liters); also in verse 7　^{e}8 Traditionally *peace offering* ^{f}9 That is, probably about 6 quarts (about 6.5 liters)　^{g}9 That is, probably about 2 quarts (about 2 liters); also in verse 10

14For the generations to come, whenever an alien or anyone else living among you presents an offering made by fire as an aroma pleasing to the LORD, he must do exactly as you do. 15The community is to have the same rules for you and for the alien living among you; this is a lasting ordinance for the generations to come. You and the alien shall be the same before the LORD: 16The same laws and regulations will apply both to you and to the alien living among you.' "

17The LORD said to Moses, 18"Speak to the Israelites and say to them: 'When you enter the land to which I am taking you 19and you eat the food of the land, present a portion as an offering to the LORD. 20Present a cake from the first of your ground meal and present it as an offering from the threshing floor. 21Throughout the generations to come you are to give this offering to the LORD from the first of your ground meal.

Offerings for Unintentional Sins

22" 'Now if you unintentionally fail to keep any of these commands the LORD gave Moses— 23any of the LORD's commands to you through him, from the day the LORD gave them and continuing through the generations to come— 24and if this is done unintentionally without the community being aware of it, then the whole community is to offer a young bull for a burnt offering as an aroma pleasing to the LORD, along with its prescribed grain offering and drink offering, and a male goat for a sin offering. 25The priest is to make atonement for the whole Israelite community, and they will be forgiven, for it was not intentional and they have brought to the LORD for their wrong an offering made by fire and a sin offering. 26The whole Israelite community and the aliens living among them will be forgiven, because all the people were involved in the unintentional wrong.

27" 'But if just one person sins unintentionally, he must bring a year-old female goat for a sin offering. 28The priest is to make atonement before the LORD for the one who erred by sinning unintentionally, and when atonement has been made for him, he will be forgiven. 29One and the same law applies to everyone who sins unintentionally, whether he is a native-born Israelite or an alien.

30" 'But anyone who sins defiantly, whether native-born or alien, blasphemes the LORD, and that person must be cut off from his people. 31Because he has despised the LORD's word and broken his commands, that person must surely be cut off; his guilt remains on him.' "

The Sabbath-Breaker Put to Death

32While the Israelites were in the desert, a man was found gathering wood on the Sabbath day. 33Those who found him gathering wood brought him to Moses and Aaron and the whole assembly, 34and they kept him in custody, because it was not clear what should be done to him. 35Then the LORD said to Moses, "The man must die. The whole assembly must stone him outside the camp." 36So the assembly took him outside the camp and stoned him to death, as the LORD commanded Moses.

Tassels on Garments

37The LORD said to Moses, 38"Speak to the Israelites and say to them: 'Throughout the generations to come you are to make tassels on the corners of your garments, with a blue cord on each tassel. 39You will have these tassels to look at and so you will remember all the commands of the LORD, that you may obey them and not prostitute yourselves by going after the lusts of your own hearts and eyes. 40Then you will remember to obey all my commands and will be consecrated to your God. 41I am the LORD your God, who brought you out of Egypt to be your God. I am the LORD your God.' "

Korah, Dathan and Abiram

16 Korah son of Izhar, the son of Kohath, the son of Levi, and certain Reubenites—Dathan and Abiram, sons of Eliab, and On son of Peleth—became insolent[a] [2]and rose up against Moses. With them were 250 Israelite men, well-known community leaders who had been appointed members of the council. [3]They came as a group to oppose Moses and Aaron and said to them, "You have gone too far! The whole community is holy, every one of them, and the LORD is with them. Why then do you set yourselves above the LORD's assembly?"

TASSELS ON CLOTHING

Blue cords, or long fringes containing a blue thread, were sewed as tassels on the corner of Hebrew clothing. The blue tassels were to help the Israelites remember God, so they would obey his commandments.

[4]When Moses heard this, he fell facedown. [5]Then he said to Korah and all his followers: "In the morning the LORD will show who belongs to him and who is holy, and he will have that person come near him. The man he chooses he will cause to come near him. [6]You, Korah, and all your followers are to do this: Take censers [7]and tomorrow put fire and incense in them before the LORD. The man the LORD chooses will be the one who is holy. You Levites have gone too far!"

[8]Moses also said to Korah, "Now listen, you Levites! [9]Isn't it enough for you that the God of Israel has sep-

arated you from the rest of the Israelite community and brought you near himself to do the work at the LORD's tabernacle and to stand before the community and minister to them? [10]He has brought you and all your fellow Levites near himself, but now you are trying to get the priesthood too. [11]It is against the LORD that you and all your followers have banded together. Who is Aaron that you should grumble against him?"

[12]Then Moses summoned Dathan and Abiram, the sons of Eliab. But they said, "We will not come! [13]Isn't it enough that you have brought us up out of a land flowing with milk and honey to kill us in the desert? And now you also want to lord it over us? [14]Moreover, you haven't brought us into a land flowing with milk and honey or given us an inheritance of fields and vineyards. Will you gouge out the eyes of[b] these men? No, we will not come!"

[15]Then Moses became very angry and said to the LORD, "Do not accept their offering. I have not taken so much as a donkey from them, nor have I wronged any of them."

[16]Moses said to Korah, "You and all your followers are to appear before the LORD tomorrow—you and they and Aaron. [17]Each man is to take his censer and put incense in it—250 censers in all—and present it before the LORD. You and Aaron are to present your censers also." [18]So each man took his censer, put fire and incense in it, and stood with Moses and Aaron at the entrance to the Tent of Meeting. [19]When Korah had gathered all his followers in opposition to them at the entrance to the Tent of Meeting, the glory of the LORD appeared to the entire assembly. [20]The LORD said to Moses and Aaron, [21]"Separate yourselves from this assembly so I can put an end to them at once."

[22]But Moses and Aaron fell facedown and cried out, "O God, God of the spirits of all mankind, will you be

a1 Or Peleth—took men,   *b14 Or you make slaves of; or you deceive* angry with the entire assembly when only one man sins?"

CENSERS

Israel's priests burned sweet-smelling incense in censers that looked like small shovels or scoops. Incense was burned with fire from the altar of sacrifice.

23Then the LORD said to Moses, 24"Say to the assembly, 'Move away from the tents of Korah, Dathan and Abiram.' "

25Moses got up and went to Dathan and Abiram, and the elders of Israel followed him. 26He warned the assembly, "Move back from the tents of these wicked men! Do not touch anything belonging to them, or you will be swept away because of all their sins." 27So they moved away from the tents of Korah, Dathan and Abiram. Dathan and Abiram had come out and were standing with their wives, children and little ones at the entrances to their tents.

28Then Moses said, "This is how you will know that the LORD has sent me to do all these things and that it was not my idea: 29If these men die a natural death and experience only what usually happens to men, then the LORD has not sent me. 30But if the LORD brings about something totally new, and the earth opens its mouth and swallows them, with everything that belongs to them, and they go down alive into the grave,*a* then you will know that these men have treated the LORD with contempt."

31As soon as he finished saying all this, the ground under them split

apart 32and the earth opened its mouth and swallowed them, with their households and all Korah's men and all their possessions. 33They went down alive into the grave, with everything they owned; the earth closed over them, and they perished and were gone from the community. 34At their cries, all the Israelites around them fled, shouting, "The earth is going to swallow us too!"

35And fire came out from the LORD and consumed the 250 men who were offering the incense.

36The LORD said to Moses, 37"Tell Eleazar son of Aaron, the priest, to take the censers out of the smoldering remains and scatter the coals some distance away, for the censers are holy— 38the censers of the men who sinned at the cost of their lives. Hammer the censers into sheets to overlay the altar, for they were presented before the LORD and have become holy. Let them be a sign to the Israelites."

39So Eleazar the priest collected the bronze censers brought by those who had been burned up, and he had them hammered out to overlay the altar, 40as the LORD directed him through Moses. This was to remind the Israelites that no one except a descendant of Aaron should come to burn incense before the LORD, or he would become like Korah and his followers.

41The next day the whole Israelite community grumbled against Moses and Aaron. "You have killed the LORD's people," they said.

42But when the assembly gathered in opposition to Moses and Aaron and turned toward the Tent of Meeting, suddenly the cloud covered it and the glory of the LORD appeared. 43Then Moses and Aaron went to the front of the Tent of Meeting, 44and the LORD said to Moses, 45"Get away from this assembly so I can put an end to them at once." And they fell facedown.

46Then Moses said to Aaron, "Take your censer and put incense in it,

a30 Hebrew Sheol; also in verse 33

along with fire from the altar, and hurry to the assembly to make atonement for them. Wrath has come out from the LORD; the plague has started." ⁴⁷So Aaron did as Moses said, and ran into the midst of the assembly. The plague had already started among the people, but Aaron offered the incense and made atonement for them. ⁴⁸He stood between the living and the dead, and the plague stopped. ⁴⁹But 14,700 people died from the plague, in addition to those who had died because of Korah. ⁵⁰Then Aaron returned to Moses at the entrance to the Tent of Meeting, for the plague had stopped.

The Budding of Aaron's Staff

17 The LORD said to Moses, ²"Speak to the Israelites and get twelve staffs from them, one from the leader of each of their ancestral tribes. Write the name of each man on his staff. ³On the staff of Levi write Aaron's name, for there must be one staff for the head of each ancestral tribe. ⁴Place them in the Tent of Meeting in front of the Testimony, where I meet with you. ⁵The staff belonging to the man I choose will sprout, and I will rid myself of this constant grumbling against you by the Israelites."

⁶So Moses spoke to the Israelites, and their leaders gave him twelve staffs, one for the leader of each of their ancestral tribes, and Aaron's staff was among them. ⁷Moses placed the staffs before the LORD in the Tent of the Testimony.

⁸The next day Moses entered the Tent of the Testimony and saw that Aaron's staff, which represented the house of Levi, had not only sprouted but had budded, blossomed and produced almonds. ⁹Then Moses brought out all the staffs from the LORD's presence to all the Israelites. They looked at them, and each man took his own staff.

¹⁰The LORD said to Moses, "Put back Aaron's staff in front of the Testimony, to be kept as a sign to the rebellious. This will put an end to

their grumbling against me, so that they will not die." ¹¹Moses did just as the LORD commanded him.

¹²The Israelites said to Moses, "We will die! We are lost, we are all lost! ¹³Anyone who even comes near the tabernacle of the LORD will die. Are we all going to die?"

Duties of Priests and Levites

18 The LORD said to Aaron, "You, your sons and your father's family are to bear the responsibility for offenses against the sanctuary, and you and your sons alone are to bear the responsibility for offenses against the priesthood. ²Bring your fellow Levites from your ancestral tribe to join you and assist you when you and your sons minister before the Tent of the Testimony. ³They are to be responsible to you and are to perform all the duties of the Tent, but they must not go near the furnishings of the sanctuary or the altar, or both they and you will die. ⁴They are to join you and be responsible for the care of the Tent of Meeting—all the work at the Tent—and no one else may come near where you are.

⁵"You are to be responsible for the care of the sanctuary and the altar, so that wrath will not fall on the Israelites again. ⁶I myself have selected your fellow Levites from among the Israelites as a gift to you, dedicated to the LORD to do the work at the Tent of Meeting. ⁷But only you and your sons may serve as priests in connection with everything at the altar and inside the curtain. I am giving you the service of the priesthood as a gift. Anyone else who comes near the sanctuary must be put to death."

Offerings for Priests and Levites

⁸Then the LORD said to Aaron, "I myself have put you in charge of the offerings presented to me; all the holy offerings the Israelites give me I give to you and your sons as your portion and regular share. ⁹You are to have the part of the most holy offerings that is kept from the fire. From all the gifts they bring me as most holy

offerings, whether grain or sin or guilt offerings, that part belongs to you and your sons. ¹⁰Eat it as something most holy; every male shall eat it. You must regard it as holy.

¹¹"This also is yours: whatever is set aside from the gifts of all the wave offerings of the Israelites. I give this to you and your sons and daughters as your regular share. Everyone in your household who is ceremonially clean may eat it.

¹²"I give you all the finest olive oil and all the finest new wine and grain they give the LORD as the firstfruits of their harvest. ¹³All the land's firstfruits that they bring to the LORD will be yours. Everyone in your household who is ceremonially clean may eat it.

¹⁴"Everything in Israel that is devoted*ᵃ* to the LORD is yours. ¹⁵The first offspring of every womb, both man and animal, that is offered to the LORD is yours. But you must redeem every firstborn son and every firstborn male of unclean animals. ¹⁶When they are a month old, you must redeem them at the redemption price set at five shekels*ᵇ* of silver, according to the sanctuary shekel, which weighs twenty gerahs.

¹⁷"But you must not redeem the firstborn of an ox, a sheep or a goat; they are holy. Sprinkle their blood on the altar and burn their fat as an of-fering made by fire, an aroma pleasing to the LORD. ¹⁸Their meat is to be yours, just as the breast of the wave offering and the right thigh are yours. ¹⁹Whatever is set aside from the holy offerings the Israelites present to the LORD I give to you and your sons and daughters as your regular share. It is an everlasting covenant of salt before the LORD for both you and your offspring."

²⁰The LORD said to Aaron, "You will have no inheritance in their land, nor will you have any share among them; I am your share and your inheritance among the Israelites.

²¹"I give to the Levites all the tithes in Israel as their inheritance in return for the work they do while serving at the Tent of Meeting. ²²From now on the Israelites must not go near the Tent of Meeting, or they will bear the consequences of their sin and will die. ²³It is the Levites who are to do the work at the Tent of Meeting and bear the responsibility for offenses against it. This is a lasting ordinance for the generations to come. They will receive no inheritance among the Israelites. ²⁴Instead, I give to the Levites as their inheritance the tithes that the Israelites present as an offering to the LORD. That is why I said concern-

ᵃ14 The Hebrew term refers to the irrevocable giving over of things or persons to the LORD.
ᵇ16 That is, about 2 ounces (about 55 grams)

▓ET'S LIVE IT!   Numbers 18:1–7

BEING RESPONSIBLE ➡ The family of Aaron was responsible for taking care of the tent church where the Israelites worshiped. But there was too much work for so few people to do. Read Numbers 18:1–7. Whom did God give Aaron's family to "join you and be responsible for the care of the Tent of Meeting"? (If you want to find out just what the Levites did, read Numbers 3:21–4:49.)

God makes parents responsible for the family. And God gives them children to help them. Ask your mom or dad to make a list of the things they are responsible for around your house. You can write the list down for them. After you have worked on the list together, ask your mom or dad to pick some things you can be responsible for, as a helper given to them by God.

ing them: 'They will have no inheritance among the Israelites.' "

²⁵The LORD said to Moses, ²⁶"Speak to the Levites and say to them: 'When you receive from the Israelites the tithe I give you as your inheritance, you must present a tenth of that tithe as the LORD's offering. ²⁷Your offering will be reckoned to you as grain from the threshing floor or juice from the winepress. ²⁸In this way you also will present an offering to the LORD from all the tithes you receive from the Israelites. From these tithes you must give the LORD's portion to Aaron the priest. ²⁹You must present as the LORD's portion the best and holiest part of everything given to you.'

³⁰"Say to the Levites: 'When you present the best part, it will be reckoned to you as the product of the threshing floor or the winepress. ³¹You and your households may eat the rest of it anywhere, for it is your wages for your work at the Tent of Meeting. ³²By presenting the best part of it you will not be guilty in this matter; then you will not defile the holy offerings of the Israelites, and you will not die.' "

The Water of Cleansing

19 The LORD said to Moses and Aaron: ²"This is a requirement of the law that the LORD has commanded: Tell the Israelites to bring you a red heifer without defect or blemish and that has never been under a yoke. ³Give it to Eleazar the priest; it is to be taken outside the camp and slaughtered in his presence. ⁴Then Eleazar the priest is to take some of its blood on his finger and sprinkle it seven times toward the front of the Tent of Meeting. ⁵While he watches, the heifer is to be burned—its hide, flesh, blood and offal. ⁶The priest is to take some cedar wood, hyssop and scarlet wool and throw them onto the burning heifer. ⁷After that, the priest must wash his clothes and bathe himself with water. He may then come into the camp, but he will be ceremonially unclean till evening. ⁸The man who burns it

must also wash his clothes and bathe with water, and he too will be unclean till evening.

⁹"A man who is clean shall gather up the ashes of the heifer and put them in a ceremonially clean place outside the camp. They shall be kept by the Israelite community for use in the water of cleansing; it is for purification from sin. ¹⁰The man who gathers up the ashes of the heifer must also wash his clothes, and he too will be unclean till evening. This will be a lasting ordinance both for the Israelites and for the aliens living among them.

¹¹"Whoever touches the dead body of anyone will be unclean for seven days. ¹²He must purify himself with the water on the third day and on the seventh day; then he will be clean. But if he does not purify himself on the third and seventh days, he will not be clean. ¹³Whoever touches the dead body of anyone and fails to purify himself defiles the LORD's tabernacle. That person must be cut off from Israel. Because the water of cleansing has not been sprinkled on him, he is unclean; his uncleanness remains on him.

¹⁴"This is the law that applies when a person dies in a tent: Anyone who enters the tent and anyone who is in it will be unclean for seven days, ¹⁵and every open container without a lid fastened on it will be unclean.

¹⁶"Anyone out in the open who touches someone who has been killed with a sword or someone who has died a natural death, or anyone who touches a human bone or a grave, will be unclean for seven days.

¹⁷"For the unclean person, put some ashes from the burned purification offering into a jar and pour fresh water over them. ¹⁸Then a man who is ceremonially clean is to take some hyssop, dip it in the water and sprinkle the tent and all the furnishings and the people who were there. He must also sprinkle anyone who has touched a human bone or a grave or someone who has been killed or someone who has died a natural

death. ¹⁹The man who is clean is to sprinkle the unclean person on the third and seventh days, and on the seventh day he is to purify him. The person being cleansed must wash his clothes and bathe with water, and that evening he will be clean. ²⁰But if a person who is unclean does not purify himself, he must be cut off from the community, because he has defiled the sanctuary of the LORD. The water of cleansing has not been sprinkled on him, and he is unclean. ²¹This is a lasting ordinance for them.

"The man who sprinkles the water of cleansing must also wash his clothes, and anyone who touches the water of cleansing will be unclean till evening. ²²Anything that an unclean person touches becomes unclean, and anyone who touches it becomes unclean till evening."

Water From the Rock

20 In the first month the whole Israelite community arrived at the Desert of Zin, and they stayed at Kadesh. There Miriam died and was buried.

²Now there was no water for the community, and the people gathered in opposition to Moses and Aaron. ³They quarreled with Moses and said, "If only we had died when our brothers fell dead before the LORD! ⁴Why did you bring the LORD's community into this desert, that we and our livestock should die here? ⁵Why did you bring us up out of Egypt to this terrible place? It has no grain or figs, grapevines or pomegranates. And there is no water to drink!"

⁶Moses and Aaron went from the assembly to the entrance to the Tent of Meeting and fell facedown, and the glory of the LORD appeared to them. ⁷The LORD said to Moses, ⁸"Take the staff, and you and your brother Aaron gather the assembly together. Speak to that rock before their eyes and it will pour out its water. You will bring water out of the rock for

the community so they and their livestock can drink."

⁹So Moses took the staff from the LORD's presence, just as he commanded him. ¹⁰He and Aaron gathered the assembly together in front of the rock and Moses said to them, "Listen, you rebels, must we bring you water out of this rock?" ¹¹Then Moses raised his arm and struck the rock twice with his staff. Water gushed out, and the community and their livestock drank.

¹²But the LORD said to Moses and Aaron, "Because you did not trust in me enough to honor me as holy in the sight of the Israelites, you will not bring this community into the land I give them."

? DID YOU KNOW? 20:12

Why didn't God let Moses enter the promised land?

God was punishing Moses for disobedience. God had told Moses to speak to a rock, and it would give the Israelites water. Instead, Moses took his staff and hit the rock two times. It is important to do what God wants us to do, and to do it his way. We show respect for God by obeying him in all things.

¹³These were the waters of Meribah,ᵃ where the Israelites quarreled with the LORD and where he showed himself holy among them.

Edom Denies Israel Passage

¹⁴Moses sent messengers from Kadesh to the king of Edom, saying:

"This is what your brother Israel says: You know about all the hardships that have come upon us. ¹⁵Our forefathers went down into Egypt, and we lived there many years. The Egyptians mistreated us and our fathers, ¹⁶but when we cried out to the LORD,

ᵃ13 Meribah means quarreling.

he heard our cry and sent an angel and brought us out of Egypt.

"Now we are here at Kadesh, a town on the edge of your territory. ¹⁷Please let us pass through your country. We will not go through any field or vineyard, or drink water from any well. We will travel along the king's highway and not turn to the right or to the left until we have passed through your territory."

¹⁸But Edom answered:

"You may not pass through here; if you try, we will march out and attack you with the sword."

¹⁹The Israelites replied:

"We will go along the main road, and if we or our livestock drink any of your water, we will pay for it. We only want to pass through on foot—nothing else."

²⁰Again they answered:

"You may not pass through."

Then Edom came out against them with a large and powerful army. ²¹Since Edom refused to let them go through their territory, Israel turned away from them.

The Death of Aaron

²²The whole Israelite community set out from Kadesh and came to Mount Hor. ²³At Mount Hor, near the border of Edom, the LORD said to Moses and Aaron, ²⁴"Aaron will be gathered to his people. He will not enter the land I give the Israelites, because both of you rebelled against my command at the waters of Meribah. ²⁵Get Aaron and his son Eleazar and take them up Mount Hor. ²⁶Remove Aaron's garments and put them on his son Eleazar, for Aaron will be gathered to his people; he will die there."

²⁷Moses did as the LORD command-

ed: They went up Mount Hor in the sight of the whole community. ²⁸Moses removed Aaron's garments and put them on his son Eleazar. And Aaron died there on top of the mountain. Then Moses and Eleazar came down from the mountain, ²⁹and when the whole community learned that Aaron had died, the entire house of Israel mourned for him thirty days.

Arad Destroyed

21 When the Canaanite king of Arad, who lived in the Negev, heard that Israel was coming along the road to Atharim, he attacked the Israelites and captured some of them. ²Then Israel made this vow to the LORD: "If you will deliver these people into our hands, we will totally destroy*ᵃ* their cities." ³The LORD listened to Israel's plea and gave the Canaanites over to them. They completely destroyed them and their towns; so the place was named Hormah.*ᵇ*

The Bronze Snake

⁴They traveled from Mount Hor along the route to the Red Sea,*ᶜ* to go around Edom. But the people grew impatient on the way; ⁵they spoke against God and against Moses, and said, "Why have you brought us up out of Egypt to die in the desert? There is no bread! There is no water! And we detest this miserable food!"

⁶Then the LORD sent venomous snakes among them; they bit the people and many Israelites died. ⁷The people came to Moses and said, "We sinned when we spoke against the LORD and against you. Pray that the LORD will take the snakes away from us." So Moses prayed for the people.

⁸The LORD said to Moses, "Make a snake and put it up on a pole; anyone who is bitten can look at it and live." ⁹So Moses made a bronze snake and put it up on a pole. Then when any-

---

*ᵃ2 The Hebrew term refers to the irrevocable giving over of things or persons to the LORD, often by totally destroying them; also in verse 3.   *ᵇ3 Hormah* means *destruction.   *ᶜ4 Hebrew *Yam Suph*; that is, Sea of Reeds

one was bitten by a snake and looked at the bronze snake, he lived.

❓DID YOU KNOW?   21:9

What did Jesus say about the bronze snake?

Jesus said that he would be lifted up on a pole (John 3:14) like the bronze snake Moses made. Jesus was talking about being crucified. People in Moses' time who believed God enough to look at the bronze snake were saved from the poisonous snakes. People today who believe God enough to look to Jesus for forgiveness are saved from their sins.

The Journey to Moab

[10]The Israelites moved on and camped at Oboth. [11]Then they set out from Oboth and camped in Iye Abarim, in the desert that faces Moab toward the sunrise. [12]From there they moved on and camped in the Zered Valley. [13]They set out from there and camped alongside the Arnon, which is in the desert extending into Amorite territory. The Arnon is the border of Moab, between Moab and the Amorites. [14]That is why the Book of the Wars of the LORD says:

". . . Waheb in Suphah[a] and the ravines,
    the Arnon [15]and[b] the slopes of the ravines
that lead to the site of Ar
    and lie along the border of Moab."

[16]From there they continued on to Beer, the well where the LORD said to Moses, "Gather the people together and I will give them water."

[17]Then Israel sang this song:

"Spring up, O well!
    Sing about it,

[18]about the well that the princes dug,
    that the nobles of the people sank—
    the nobles with scepters and staffs."

Then they went from the desert to Mattanah, [19]from Mattanah to Nahaliel, from Nahaliel to Bamoth, [20]and from Bamoth to the valley in Moab where the top of Pisgah overlooks the wasteland.

Defeat of Sihon and Og

[21]Israel sent messengers to say to Sihon king of the Amorites:

[22]"Let us pass through your country. We will not turn aside into any field or vineyard, or drink water from any well. We will travel along the king's highway until we have passed through your territory."

[23]But Sihon would not let Israel pass through his territory. He mustered his entire army and marched out into the desert against Israel. When he reached Jahaz, he fought with Israel. [24]Israel, however, put him to the sword and took over his land from the Arnon to the Jabbok, but only as far as the Ammonites, because their border was fortified. [25]Israel captured all the cities of the Amorites and occupied them, including Heshbon and all its surrounding settlements. [26]Heshbon was the city of Sihon king of the Amorites, who had fought against the former king of Moab and had taken from him all his land as far as the Arnon.

[27]That is why the poets say:

"Come to Heshbon and let it be rebuilt;
    let Sihon's city be restored.

[28]"Fire went out from Heshbon,
    a blaze from the city of Sihon.
It consumed Ar of Moab,
    the citizens of Arnon's heights.

---

[a]14 The meaning of the Hebrew for this phrase is uncertain. Suphah and the ravines / of the Arnon [15]to   [b]14,15 Or "I have been given from

²⁹Woe to you, O Moab!
　　You are destroyed, O people of
　　　Chemosh!
He has given up his sons as
　　fugitives
and his daughters as captives
　to Sihon king of the Amorites.

³⁰"But we have overthrown them;
　　Heshbon is destroyed all the
　　　way to Dibon.
We have demolished them as far
　　as Nophah,
which extends to Medeba."

³¹So Israel settled in the land of the Amorites.

³²After Moses had sent spies to Jazer, the Israelites captured its surrounding settlements and drove out the Amorites who were there. ³³Then they turned and went up along the road toward Bashan, and Og king of Bashan and his whole army marched out to meet them in battle at Edrei.

³⁴The LORD said to Moses, "Do not be afraid of him, for I have handed him over to you, with his whole army and his land. Do to him what you did to Sihon king of the Amorites, who reigned in Heshbon."

³⁵So they struck him down, together with his sons and his whole army, leaving them no survivors. And they took possession of his land.

Balak Summons Balaam

22 Then the Israelites traveled to the plains of Moab and camped along the Jordan across from Jericho.ᵃ

²Now Balak son of Zippor saw all that Israel had done to the Amorites, ³and Moab was terrified because there were so many people. Indeed, Moab was filled with dread because of the Israelites.

⁴The Moabites said to the elders of Midian, "This horde is going to lick up everything around us, as an ox licks up the grass of the field."

So Balak son of Zippor, who was king of Moab at that time, ⁵sent messengers to summon Balaam son of Beor, who was at Pethor, near the River,ᵇ in his native land. Balak said:

"A people has come out of Egypt; they cover the face of the land and have settled next to me. ⁶Now come and put a curse on these people, because they are too powerful for me. Perhaps then I will be able to defeat them and drive them out of the country. For I know that those you bless are blessed, and those you curse are cursed."

⁷The elders of Moab and Midian left, taking with them the fee for divination. When they came to Balaam, they told him what Balak had said.

⁸"Spend the night here," Balaam said to them, "and I will bring you back the answer the LORD gives me." So the Moabite princes stayed with him.

⁹God came to Balaam and asked, "Who are these men with you?"

¹⁰Balaam said to God, "Balak son of Zippor, king of Moab, sent me this message: ¹¹'A people that has come out of Egypt covers the face of the land. Now come and put a curse on them for me. Perhaps then I will be able to fight them and drive them away.'"

¹²But God said to Balaam, "Do not go with them. You must not put a curse on those people, because they are blessed."

¹³The next morning Balaam got up and said to Balak's princes, "Go back to your own country, for the LORD has refused to let me go with you."

¹⁴So the Moabite princes returned to Balak and said, "Balaam refused to come with us."

¹⁵Then Balak sent other princes, more numerous and more distinguished than the first. ¹⁶They came to Balaam and said:

ᵃ1 Hebrew *Jordan of Jericho*; possibly an ancient name for the Jordan River   ᵇ5 That is, the Euphrates

"This is what Balak son of Zippor says: Do not let anything keep you from coming to me, [17]because I will reward you handsomely and do whatever you say. Come and put a curse on these people for me."

[18]But Balaam answered them, "Even if Balak gave me his palace filled with silver and gold, I could not do anything great or small to go beyond the command of the LORD my God. [19]Now stay here tonight as the others did, and I will find out what else the LORD will tell me."

[20]That night God came to Balaam and said, "Since these men have come to summon you, go with them, but do only what I tell you."

Balaam's Donkey

[21]Balaam got up in the morning, saddled his donkey and went with the princes of Moab. [22]But God was very angry when he went, and the angel of the LORD stood in the road to oppose him. Balaam was riding on his donkey, and his two servants were with him. [23]When the donkey saw the angel of the LORD standing in the road with a drawn sword in his hand, she turned off the road into a field. Balaam beat her to get her back on the road.

[24]Then the angel of the LORD stood in a narrow path between two vineyards, with walls on both sides. [25]When the donkey saw the angel of the LORD, she pressed close to the wall, crushing Balaam's foot against it. So he beat her again.

[26]Then the angel of the LORD moved on ahead and stood in a narrow place where there was no room to turn, either to the right or to the left. [27]When the donkey saw the angel of the LORD, she lay down under Balaam, and he was angry and beat her with his staff. [28]Then the LORD opened the donkey's mouth, and she said to Balaam, "What have I done to you to make you beat me these three times?"

[29]Balaam answered the donkey, "You have made a fool of me! If I had a sword in my hand, I would kill you right now."

[30]The donkey said to Balaam, "Am I not your own donkey, which you have always ridden, to this day? Have I been in the habit of doing this to you?"

"No," he said.

[31]Then the LORD opened Balaam's eyes, and he saw the angel of the LORD standing in the road with his sword drawn. So he bowed low and fell facedown.

[32]The angel of the LORD asked him, "Why have you beaten your donkey these three times? I have come here to oppose you because your path is a reckless one before me.[a] [33]The donkey saw me and turned away from me these three times. If she had not turned away, I would certainly have killed you by now, but I would have spared her."

[34]Balaam said to the angel of the LORD, "I have sinned. I did not realize

---

[a]32 The meaning of the Hebrew for this clause is uncertain.

LET'S LIVE IT!   Numbers 22:1–20; 24:10–14

WHO IS IN CONTROL? ➤ Read this story about Balaam. Balak, king of Moab, wanted Balaam to curse the Israelites so that bad things would happen to them. Then the Israelites would not be able to conquer Moab.

But Balaam couldn't curse the Israelites. He could only say what God told him to say, good things about the Israelites and their God.

Does God control what you say? At your next mealtime listen to what is said by each family member. Was it a good thing to say or not? Is God in control of what your family talks about?

you were standing in the road to oppose me. Now if you are displeased, I will go back."

³⁵The angel of the LORD said to Balaam, "Go with the men, but speak only what I tell you." So Balaam went with the princes of Balak.

³⁶When Balak heard that Balaam was coming, he went out to meet him at the Moabite town on the Arnon border, at the edge of his territory. ³⁷Balak said to Balaam, "Did I not send you an urgent summons? Why didn't you come to me? Am I really not able to reward you?"

³⁸"Well, I have come to you now," Balaam replied. "But can I say just anything? I must speak only what God puts in my mouth."

³⁹Then Balaam went with Balak to Kiriath Huzoth. ⁴⁰Balak sacrificed cattle and sheep, and gave some to Balaam and the princes who were with him. ⁴¹The next morning Balak took Balaam up to Bamoth Baal, and from there he saw part of the people.

Balaam's First Oracle

23 Balaam said, "Build me seven altars here, and prepare seven bulls and seven rams for me." ²Balak did as Balaam said, and the two of them offered a bull and a ram on each altar.

³Then Balaam said to Balak, "Stay here beside your offering while I go aside. Perhaps the LORD will come to meet with me. Whatever he reveals to me I will tell you." Then he went off to a barren height.

⁴God met with him, and Balaam said, "I have prepared seven altars, and on each altar I have offered a bull and a ram."

⁵The LORD put a message in Balaam's mouth and said, "Go back to Balak and give him this message."

⁶So he went back to him and found him standing beside his offering, with all the princes of Moab. ⁷Then Balaam uttered his oracle:

"Balak brought me from Aram,
    the king of Moab from the
        eastern mountains.
'Come,' he said, 'curse Jacob for
        me;
    come, denounce Israel.'
⁸How can I curse
    those whom God has not
        cursed?
How can I denounce
    those whom the LORD has not
        denounced?
⁹From the rocky peaks I see them,
    from the heights I view them.
I see a people who live apart
    and do not consider themselves
        one of the nations.
¹⁰Who can count the dust of Jacob
    or number the fourth part of
        Israel?

Life in Bible Times

DONKEYS

In Bible times even important people rode on small donkeys. When a king rode a donkey into a nation or city, it meant he was coming in peace. A king who was going to war rode a horse. The most important person to ever ride a donkey was Jesus. He rode a donkey into Jerusalem to show he came in peace. Matthew 21 tells us that the people who were in Jerusalem that day praised God and threw branches and their coats on the road in front of Jesus.

Let me die the death of the
righteous,
and may my end be like theirs!"

?DID YOU KNOW?   23:7

What is an oracle?

An oracle is a message from
God. Often an oracle is a message
of judgment. Even though Balaam
wanted to harm Israel, the only
message God gave Balaam was
a message of blessing.

---

¹¹Balak said to Balaam, "What
have you done to me? I brought you
to curse my enemies, but you have
done nothing but bless them!"
¹²He answered, "Must I not speak
what the LORD puts in my mouth?"

Balaam's Second Oracle

¹³Then Balak said to him, "Come
with me to another place where you
can see them; you will see only a part
but not all of them. And from there,
curse them for me." ¹⁴So he took him
to the field of Zophim on the top of
Pisgah, and there he built seven altars and offered a bull and a ram on
each altar.
¹⁵Balaam said to Balak, "Stay here
beside your offering while I meet
with him over there."
¹⁶The LORD met with Balaam and
put a message in his mouth and said,
"Go back to Balak and give him this
message."
¹⁷So he went to him and found him
standing beside his offering, with the
princes of Moab. Balak asked him,
"What did the LORD say?"
¹⁸Then he uttered his oracle:

"Arise, Balak, and listen;
hear me, son of Zippor.
¹⁹God is not a man, that he should
lie,
nor a son of man, that he
should change his mind.
Does he speak and then not act?
Does he promise and not fulfill?
²⁰I have received a command to
bless;
he has blessed, and I cannot
change it.

²¹"No misfortune is seen in Jacob,
no misery observed in Israel.ᵃ
The LORD their God is with them;
the shout of the King is among
them.
²²God brought them out of Egypt;
they have the strength of a wild
ox.
²³There is no sorcery against Jacob,
no divination against Israel.
It will now be said of Jacob
and of Israel, 'See what God has
done!'
²⁴The people rise like a lioness;
they rouse themselves like a
lion
that does not rest till he devours
his prey
and drinks the blood of his
victims."

²⁵Then Balak said to Balaam, "Neither curse them at all nor bless them
at all!"
²⁶Balaam answered, "Did I not tell
you I must do whatever the LORD
says?"

Balaam's Third Oracle

²⁷Then Balak said to Balaam,
"Come, let me take you to another
place. Perhaps it will please God to
let you curse them for me from
there." ²⁸And Balak took Balaam to
the top of Peor, overlooking the
wasteland.
²⁹Balaam said, "Build me seven altars here, and prepare seven bulls
and seven rams for me." ³⁰Balak did
as Balaam had said, and offered a
bull and a ram on each altar.

24 Now when Balaam saw that
it pleased the LORD to bless Israel, he did not resort to sorcery as at
other times, but turned his face toward the desert. ²When Balaam
looked out and saw Israel encamped
tribe by tribe, the Spirit of God came

ᵃ21 Or *He has not looked on Jacob's offenses / or on the wrongs found in Israel.*

upon him ³and he uttered his oracle:

"The oracle of Balaam son of
      Beor,
   the oracle of one whose eye sees
      clearly,
⁴the oracle of one who hears the
      words of God,
   who sees a vision from the
      Almighty,ᵃ
   who falls prostrate, and whose
      eyes are opened:

⁵"How beautiful are your tents,
      O Jacob,
   your dwelling places, O Israel!

⁶"Like valleys they spread out,
   like gardens beside a river,
like aloes planted by the LORD,
   like cedars beside the waters.
⁷Water will flow from their
      buckets;
   their seed will have abundant
      water.

"Their king will be greater than
      Agag;
   their kingdom will be exalted.

⁸"God brought them out of Egypt;
   they have the strength of a wild
      ox.
They devour hostile nations
   and break their bones in pieces;
   with their arrows they pierce
      them.
⁹Like a lion they crouch and lie
      down,
   like a lioness—who dares to
      rouse them?

"May those who bless you be
      blessed
   and those who curse you be
      cursed!"

¹⁰Then Balak's anger burned
against Balaam. He struck his hands
together and said to him, "I summoned you to curse my enemies, but
you have blessed them these three
times. ¹¹Now leave at once and go
home! I said I would reward you

handsomely, but the LORD has kept
you from being rewarded."

¹²Balaam answered Balak, "Did I
not tell the messengers you sent me,
¹³'Even if Balak gave me his palace
filled with silver and gold, I could not
do anything of my own accord, good
or bad, to go beyond the command of
the LORD—and I must say only what
the LORD says'? ¹⁴Now I am going
back to my people, but come, let me
warn you of what this people will do
to your people in days to come."

Balaam's Fourth Oracle

¹⁵Then he uttered his oracle:

"The oracle of Balaam son of
      Beor,
   the oracle of one whose eye sees
      clearly,
¹⁶the oracle of one who hears the
      words of God,
   who has knowledge from the
      Most High,
who sees a vision from the
      Almighty,
   who falls prostrate, and whose
      eyes are opened:

¹⁷"I see him, but not now;
   I behold him, but not near.
A star will come out of Jacob;
   a scepter will rise out of Israel.
He will crush the foreheads of
      Moab,
   the skullsᵇ ofᶜ all the sons of
      Sheth.ᵈ
¹⁸Edom will be conquered;
   Seir, his enemy, will be
      conquered,
   but Israel will grow strong.
¹⁹A ruler will come out of Jacob
   and destroy the survivors of the
      city."

Balaam's Final Oracles

²⁰Then Balaam saw Amalek and
uttered his oracle:

"Amalek was first among the
      nations,

ᵃ4 Hebrew *Shaddai;* also in verse 16   ᵇ17 Samaritan Pentateuch (see also Jer. 48:45); the
meaning of the word in the Masoretic Text is uncertain.   ᶜ17 Or possibly *Moab,* / *batter*
ᵈ17 Or *all the noisy boasters*

but he will come to ruin at
last."

21Then he saw the Kenites and uttered his oracle:

"Your dwelling place is secure,
    your nest is set in a rock;
22yet you Kenites will be destroyed
    when Asshur takes you
        captive."

23Then he uttered his oracle:

"Ah, who can live when God does
    this?ᵃ
24 Ships will come from the shores
        of Kittim;
they will subdue Asshur and
        Eber,
    but they too will come to ruin."

25Then Balaam got up and returned home and Balak went his own
way.

Moab Seduces Israel

25 While Israel was staying in
Shittim, the men began to indulge in sexual immorality with Moabite women, 2who invited them to
the sacrifices to their gods. The people ate and bowed down before these
gods. 3So Israel joined in worshiping
the Baal of Peor. And the LORD's anger burned against them.

4The LORD said to Moses, "Take all
the leaders of these people, kill them
and expose them in broad daylight
before the LORD, so that the LORD's
fierce anger may turn away from Israel."

5So Moses said to Israel's judges,
"Each of you must put to death those
of your men who have joined in worshiping the Baal of Peor."

6Then an Israelite man brought to
his family a Midianite woman right
before the eyes of Moses and the
whole assembly of Israel while they
were weeping at the entrance to the
Tent of Meeting. 7When Phinehas
son of Eleazar, the son of Aaron, the

priest, saw this, he left the assembly,
took a spear in his hand 8and followed the Israelite into the tent. He
drove the spear through both of
them—through the Israelite and into
the woman's body. Then the plague
against the Israelites was stopped;
9but those who died in the plague
numbered 24,000.

10The LORD said to Moses, 11"Phinehas son of Eleazar, the son of Aaron,
the priest, has turned my anger away
from the Israelites; for he was as zealous as I am for my honor among
them, so that in my zeal I did not put
an end to them. 12Therefore tell him
I am making my covenant of peace
with him. 13He and his descendants
will have a covenant of a lasting
priesthood, because he was zealous
for the honor of his God and made
atonement for the Israelites."

14The name of the Israelite who
was killed with the Midianite woman
was Zimri son of Salu, the leader of a
Simeonite family. 15And the name of
the Midianite woman who was put to
death was Cozbi daughter of Zur, a
tribal chief of a Midianite family.

16The LORD said to Moses, 17"Treat
the Midianites as enemies and kill
them, 18because they treated you as
enemies when they deceived you in
the affair of Peor and their sister
Cozbi, the daughter of a Midianite
leader, the woman who was killed
when the plague came as a result of
Peor."

The Second Census

26 After the plague the LORD
said to Moses and Eleazar son
of Aaron, the priest, 2"Take a census
of the whole Israelite community by
families—all those twenty years old
or more who are able to serve in the
army of Israel." 3So on the plains of
Moab by the Jordan across from Jericho,ᵇ Moses and Eleazar the priest
spoke with them and said, 4"Take a
census of the men twenty years old or

ᵃ23 Masoretic Text; with a different word division of the Hebrew A people will gather from the
north.   ᵇ3 Hebrew Jordan of Jericho; possibly an ancient name for the Jordan River; also in
verse 63

more, as the LORD commanded Moses."

These were the Israelites who came out of Egypt:

5The descendants of Reuben, the firstborn son of Israel, were:

through Hanoch, the Hanochite clan;

through Pallu, the Palluite clan;

6through Hezron, the Hezronite clan;

through Carmi, the Carmite clan.

7These were the clans of Reuben; those numbered were 43,730.

8The son of Pallu was Eliab, 9and the sons of Eliab were Nemuel, Dathan and Abiram. The same Dathan and Abiram were the community officials who rebelled against Moses and Aaron and were among Korah's followers when they rebelled against the LORD. 10The earth opened its mouth and swallowed them along with Korah, whose followers died when the fire devoured the 250 men. And they served as a warning sign. 11The line of Korah, however, did not die out.

12The descendants of Simeon by their clans were:

through Nemuel, the Nemuelite clan;

through Jamin, the Jaminite clan;

through Jakin, the Jakinite clan;

13through Zerah, the Zerahite clan;

through Shaul, the Shaulite clan.

14These were the clans of Simeon; there were 22,200 men.

15The descendants of Gad by their clans were:

through Zephon, the Zephonite clan;

through Haggi, the Haggite clan;

through Shuni, the Shunite clan;

16through Ozni, the Oznite clan;

through Eri, the Erite clan;

17through Arodi,[a] the Arodite clan;

through Areli, the Arelite clan.

18These were the clans of Gad; those numbered were 40,500.

19Er and Onan were sons of Judah, but they died in Canaan.

20The descendants of Judah by their clans were:

through Shelah, the Shelanite clan;

through Perez, the Perezite clan;

through Zerah, the Zerahite clan.

21The descendants of Perez were:

through Hezron, the Hezronite clan;

through Hamul, the Hamulite clan.

22These were the clans of Judah; those numbered were 76,500.

23The descendants of Issachar by their clans were:

through Tola, the Tolaite clan;

through Puah, the Puite[b] clan;

24through Jashub, the Jashubite clan;

through Shimron, the Shimronite clan.

25These were the clans of Issachar; those numbered were 64,300.

26The descendants of Zebulun by their clans were:

through Sered, the Seredite clan;

through Elon, the Elonite clan;

through Jahleel, the Jahleelite clan.

27These were the clans of Zebulun; those numbered were 60,500.

28The descendants of Joseph by their clans through Manasseh and Ephraim were:

29The descendants of Manasseh:

through Makir, the Makirite

---

[a]17 Samaritan Pentateuch and Syriac (see also Gen. 46:16); Masoretic Text *Arod*
[b]23 Samaritan Pentateuch, Septuagint, Vulgate and Syriac (see also 1 Chron. 7:1); Masoretic Text *through Puvah, the Punite*

clan (Makir was the father of Gilead);

through Gilead, the Gileadite clan.

³⁰These were the descendants of Gilead:

through Iezer, the Iezerite clan;

through Helek, the Helekite clan;

³¹through Asriel, the Asrielite clan;

through Shechem, the Shechemite clan;

³²through Shemida, the Shemidaite clan;

through Hepher, the Hepherite clan.

³³(Zelophehad son of Hepher had no sons; he had only daughters, whose names were Mahlah, Noah, Hoglah, Milcah and Tirzah.)

³⁴These were the clans of Manasseh; those numbered were 52,700.

³⁵These were the descendants of Ephraim by their clans:

through Shuthelah, the Shuthelahite clan;

through Beker, the Bekerite clan;

through Tahan, the Tahanite clan.

³⁶These were the descendants of Shuthelah:

through Eran, the Eranite clan.

³⁷These were the clans of Ephraim; those numbered were 32,500.

These were the descendants of Joseph by their clans.

³⁸The descendants of Benjamin by their clans were:

through Bela, the Belaite clan;

through Ashbel, the Ashbelite clan;

through Ahiram, the Ahiramite clan;

³⁹through Shupham,^{*a*} the Shuphamite clan;

through Hupham, the Huphamite clan.

⁴⁰The descendants of Bela through Ard and Naaman were:

through Ard,^{*b*} the Ardite clan;

through Naaman, the Naamite clan.

⁴¹These were the clans of Benjamin; those numbered were 45,600.

⁴²These were the descendants of Dan by their clans:

through Shuham, the Shuhamite clan.

These were the clans of Dan: ⁴³All of them were Shuhamite clans; and those numbered were 64,400.

⁴⁴The descendants of Asher by their clans were:

through Imnah, the Imnite clan;

through Ishvi, the Ishvite clan;

through Beriah, the Beriite clan;

⁴⁵and through the descendants of Beriah:

through Heber, the Heberite clan;

through Malkiel, the Malkielite clan.

⁴⁶(Asher had a daughter named Serah.)

⁴⁷These were the clans of Asher; those numbered were 53,400.

⁴⁸The descendants of Naphtali by their clans were:

through Jahzeel, the Jahzeelite clan;

through Guni, the Gunite clan;

⁴⁹through Jezer, the Jezerite clan;

through Shillem, the Shillemite clan.

⁵⁰These were the clans of Naphtali; those numbered were 45,400.

⁵¹The total number of the men of Israel was 601,730.

⁵²The LORD said to Moses, ⁵³"The land is to be allotted to them as an

---

^{*a*}39 A few manuscripts of the Masoretic Text, Samaritan Pentateuch, Vulgate and Syriac (see also Septuagint); most manuscripts of the Masoretic Text *Shephupham*   ^{*b*}40 Samaritan Pentateuch and Vulgate (see also Septuagint); Masoretic Text does not have *through Ard.*

inheritance based on the number of names. ⁵⁴To a larger group give a larger inheritance, and to a smaller group a smaller one; each is to receive its inheritance according to the number of those listed. ⁵⁵Be sure that the land is distributed by lot. What each group inherits will be according to the names for its ancestral tribe. ⁵⁶Each inheritance is to be distributed by lot among the larger and smaller groups."

⁵⁷These were the Levites who were counted by their clans:

through Gershon, the Gershonite clan;

through Kohath, the Kohathite clan;

through Merari, the Merarite clan.

⁵⁸These also were Levite clans:

the Libnite clan,

the Hebronite clan,

the Mahlite clan,

the Mushite clan,

the Korahite clan.

(Kohath was the forefather of Amram; ⁵⁹the name of Amram's wife was Jochebed, a descendant of Levi, who was born to the Levites*a* in Egypt. To Amram she bore Aaron, Moses and their sister Miriam. ⁶⁰Aaron was the father of Nadab and Abihu, Eleazar and Ithamar. ⁶¹But Nadab and Abihu died when they made an offering before the LORD with unauthorized fire.)

⁶²All the male Levites a month old or more numbered 23,000. They were not counted along with the other Israelites because they received no inheritance among them.

⁶³These are the ones counted by Moses and Eleazar the priest when they counted the Israelites on the plains of Moab by the Jordan across from Jericho. ⁶⁴Not one of them was among those counted by Moses and Aaron the priest when they counted the Israelites in the Desert of Sinai.

⁶⁵For the LORD had told those Israelites they would surely die in the desert, and not one of them was left except Caleb son of Jephunneh and Joshua son of Nun.

Zelophehad's Daughters

27 The daughters of Zelophehad son of Hepher, the son of Gilead, the son of Makir, the son of Manasseh, belonged to the clans of Manasseh son of Joseph. The names of the daughters were Mahlah, Noah, Hoglah, Milcah and Tirzah. They approached ²the entrance to the Tent of Meeting and stood before Moses, Eleazar the priest, the leaders and the whole assembly, and said, ³"Our father died in the desert. He was not among Korah's followers, who banded together against the LORD, but he died for his own sin and left no sons. ⁴Why should our father's name disappear from his clan because he had no son? Give us property among our father's relatives."

❓DID YOU KNOW?   27:7

Why are the daughters of Zelophehad important?

In Israel, sons inherited family property. However, the daughters of Zelophehad said they should get property because they had no brother. The Lord told Moses the women were right. Women as well as men could inherit property.

---

⁵So Moses brought their case before the LORD ⁶and the LORD said to him, ⁷"What Zelophehad's daughters are saying is right. You must certainly give them property as an inheritance among their father's relatives and turn their father's inheritance over to them.

⁸"Say to the Israelites, 'If a man dies and leaves no son, turn his inheritance over to his daughter. ⁹If he has no daughter, give his inheritance

---

a59 Or Jochebed, a daughter of Levi, who was born to Levi

to his brothers. ¹⁰If he has no brothers, give his inheritance to his fa-
ther's brothers. ¹¹If his father had no
brothers, give his inheritance to the
nearest relative in his clan, that he
may possess it. This is to be a legal
requirement for the Israelites, as the
LORD commanded Moses.' "

Joshua to Succeed Moses

¹²Then the LORD said to Moses, "Go
up this mountain in the Abarim
range and see the land I have given
the Israelites. ¹³After you have seen
it, you too will be gathered to your
people, as your brother Aaron was,
¹⁴for when the community rebelled at
the waters in the Desert of Zin, both
of you disobeyed my command to hon-
or me as holy before their eyes."
(These were the waters of Meribah
Kadesh, in the Desert of Zin.)

¹⁵Moses said to the LORD, ¹⁶"May
the LORD, the God of the spirits of all
mankind, appoint a man over this
community ¹⁷to go out and come in
before them, one who will lead them
out and bring them in, so the LORD's
people will not be like sheep without
a shepherd."

¹⁸So the LORD said to Moses, "Take
Joshua son of Nun, a man in whom is
the spirit,^a and lay your hand on
him. ¹⁹Have him stand before Eleazar the priest and the entire assembly and commission him in their
presence. ²⁰Give him some of your authority so the whole Israelite community will obey him. ²¹He is to stand
before Eleazar the priest, who will
obtain decisions for him by inquiring
of the Urim before the LORD. At his
command he and the entire community of the Israelites will go out,
and at his command they will come
in."

²²Moses did as the LORD command-
ed him. He took Joshua and had him
stand before Eleazar the priest and
the whole assembly. ²³Then he laid
his hands on him and commissioned

him, as the LORD instructed through
Moses.

Daily Offerings

28 The LORD said to Moses,
²"Give this command to the
Israelites and say to them: 'See that
you present to me at the appointed
time the food for my offerings made
by fire, as an aroma pleasing to me.'
³Say to them: 'This is the offering
made by fire that you are to present
to the LORD: two lambs a year old
without defect, as a regular burnt offering each day. ⁴Prepare one lamb in
the morning and the other at twi-
light, ⁵together with a grain offering
of a tenth of an ephah^b of fine flour
mixed with a quarter of a hin^c of oil
from pressed olives. ⁶This is the regular burnt offering instituted at
Mount Sinai as a pleasing aroma, an
offering made to the LORD by fire.
⁷The accompanying drink offering is
to be a quarter of a hin of fermented
drink with each lamb. Pour out the
drink offering to the LORD at the
sanctuary. ⁸Prepare the second lamb
at twilight, along with the same kind
of grain offering and drink offering
that you prepare in the morning.
This is an offering made by fire, an
aroma pleasing to the LORD.

Sabbath Offerings

⁹" 'On the Sabbath day, make an of-
fering of two lambs a year old without defect, together with its drink offering and a grain offering of two-
tenths of an ephah^d of fine flour
mixed with oil. ¹⁰This is the burnt offering for every Sabbath, in addition
to the regular burnt offering and its
drink offering.

Monthly Offerings

¹¹" 'On the first of every month,
present to the LORD a burnt offering
of two young bulls, one ram and sev-
en male lambs a year old, all without
defect. ¹²With each bull there is to be

---

^a18 Or *Spirit*   ^b5 That is, probably about 2 quarts (about 2 liters); also in verses 13, 21 and 29
^c5 That is, probably about 1 quart (about 1 liter); also in verses 7 and 14   ^d9 That is, probably
about 4 quarts (about 4.5 liters); also in verses 12, 20 and 28

a grain offering of three-tenths of an ephah[a] of fine flour mixed with oil; with the ram, a grain offering of two-tenths of an ephah of fine flour mixed with oil; [13]and with each lamb, a grain offering of a tenth of an ephah of fine flour mixed with oil. This is for a burnt offering, a pleasing aroma, an offering made to the LORD by fire. [14]With each bull there is to be a drink offering of half a hin[b] of wine; with the ram, a third of a hin[c]; and with each lamb, a quarter of a hin. This is the monthly burnt offering to be made at each new moon during the year. [15]Besides the regular burnt offering with its drink offering, one male goat is to be presented to the LORD as a sin offering.

The Passover

[16]" 'On the fourteenth day of the first month the LORD's Passover is to be held. [17]On the fifteenth day of this month there is to be a festival; for seven days eat bread made without yeast. [18]On the first day hold a sacred assembly and do no regular work. [19]Present to the LORD an offering made by fire, a burnt offering of two young bulls, one ram and seven male lambs a year old, all without defect. [20]With each bull prepare a grain offering of three-tenths of an ephah of fine flour mixed with oil; with the ram, two-tenths; [21]and with each of the seven lambs, one-tenth. [22]Include one male goat as a sin offering to make atonement for you. [23]Prepare these in addition to the regular morning burnt offering. [24]In this way prepare the food for the offering made by fire every day for seven days as an aroma pleasing to the LORD; it is to be prepared in addition to the regular burnt offering and its drink offering. [25]On the seventh day hold a sacred assembly and do no regular work.

Feast of Weeks

[26]" 'On the day of firstfruits, when you present to the LORD an offering of new grain during the Feast of Weeks, hold a sacred assembly and do no regular work. [27]Present a burnt offering of two young bulls, one ram and seven male lambs a year old as an aroma pleasing to the LORD. [28]With each bull there is to be a grain offering of three-tenths of an ephah of fine flour mixed with oil; with the ram, two-tenths; [29]and with each of the seven lambs, one-tenth. [30]Include one male goat to make atonement for you. [31]Prepare these together with their drink offerings, in addition to the regular burnt offering and its grain offering. Be sure the animals are without defect.

Feast of Trumpets

29 " 'On the first day of the seventh month hold a sacred assembly and do no regular work. It is a day for you to sound the trumpets. [2]As an aroma pleasing to the LORD, prepare a burnt offering of one young bull, one ram and seven male lambs a year old, all without defect. [3]With the bull prepare a grain offering of three-tenths of an ephah[d] of fine flour mixed with oil; with the ram, two-tenths[e]; [4]and with each of the seven lambs, one-tenth.[f] [5]Include one male goat as a sin offering to make atonement for you. [6]These are in addition to the monthly and daily burnt offerings with their grain offerings and drink offerings as specified. They are offerings made to the LORD by fire—a pleasing aroma.

Day of Atonement

[7]" 'On the tenth day of this seventh month hold a sacred assembly. You must deny yourselves[g] and do no work. [8]Present as an aroma pleasing to the LORD a burnt offering of one

---

[a]12 That is, probably about 6 quarts (about 6.5 liters); also in verses 20 and 28   [b]14 That is, probably about 2 quarts (about 2 liters)   [c]14 That is, probably about 1 1/4 quarts (about 1.2 liters)   [d]3 That is, probably about 6 quarts (about 6.5 liters); also in verses 9 and 14   [e]3 That is, probably about 4 quarts (about 4.5 liters); also in verses 9 and 14   [f]4 That is, probably about 2 quarts (about 2 liters); also in verses 10 and 15   [g]7 Or *must fast*

young bull, one ram and seven male lambs a year old, all without defect. [9]With the bull prepare a grain offering of three-tenths of an ephah of fine flour mixed with oil; with the ram, two-tenths; [10]and with each of the seven lambs, one-tenth. [11]Include one male goat as a sin offering, in addition to the sin offering for atonement and the regular burnt offering with its grain offering, and their drink offerings.

Feast of Tabernacles

[12]" 'On the fifteenth day of the seventh month, hold a sacred assembly and do no regular work. Celebrate a festival to the LORD for seven days. [13]Present an offering made by fire as an aroma pleasing to the LORD, a burnt offering of thirteen young bulls, two rams and fourteen male lambs a year old, all without defect. [14]With each of the thirteen bulls prepare a grain offering of three-tenths of an ephah of fine flour mixed with oil; with each of the two rams, two-tenths; [15]and with each of the fourteen lambs, one-tenth. [16]Include one male goat as a sin offering, in addition to the regular burnt offering with its grain offering and drink offering.

[17]" 'On the second day prepare twelve young bulls, two rams and fourteen male lambs a year old, all without defect. [18]With the bulls, rams and lambs, prepare their grain offerings and drink offerings according to the number specified. [19]Include one male goat as a sin offering, in addition to the regular burnt offering with its grain offering, and their drink offerings.

[20]" 'On the third day prepare eleven bulls, two rams and fourteen male lambs a year old, all without defect. [21]With the bulls, rams and lambs, prepare their grain offerings and drink offerings according to the number specified. [22]Include one male goat as a sin offering, in addition to the regular burnt offering with its grain offering and drink offering.

[23]" 'On the fourth day prepare ten bulls, two rams and fourteen male lambs a year old, all without defect. [24]With the bulls, rams and lambs, prepare their grain offerings and drink offerings according to the number specified. [25]Include one male goat as a sin offering, in addition to the regular burnt offering with its grain offering and drink offering.

[26]" 'On the fifth day prepare nine bulls, two rams and fourteen male lambs a year old, all without defect. [27]With the bulls, rams and lambs, prepare their grain offerings and drink offerings according to the number specified. [28]Include one male goat as a sin offering, in addition to the regular burnt offering with its grain offering and drink offering.

[29]" 'On the sixth day prepare eight bulls, two rams and fourteen male lambs a year old, all without defect. [30]With the bulls, rams and lambs, prepare their grain offerings and drink offerings according to the number specified. [31]Include one male goat as a sin offering, in addition to the regular burnt offering with its grain offering and drink offering.

[32]" 'On the seventh day prepare seven bulls, two rams and fourteen male lambs a year old, all without defect. [33]With the bulls, rams and lambs, prepare their grain offerings and drink offerings according to the number specified. [34]Include one male goat as a sin offering, in addition to the regular burnt offering with its grain offering and drink offering.

[35]" 'On the eighth day hold an assembly and do no regular work. [36]Present an offering made by fire as an aroma pleasing to the LORD, a burnt offering of one bull, one ram and seven male lambs a year old, all without defect. [37]With the bull, the ram and the lambs, prepare their grain offerings and drink offerings according to the number specified. [38]Include one male goat as a sin offering, in addition to the regular burnt offering with its grain offering and drink offering.

[39]" 'In addition to what you vow and your freewill offerings, prepare

these for the LORD at your appointed feasts: your burnt offerings, grain offerings, drink offerings and fellowship offerings.ᵃ' "

⁴⁰Moses told the Israelites all that the LORD commanded him.

Vows

30 Moses said to the heads of the tribes of Israel: "This is what the LORD commands: ²When a man makes a vow to the LORD or takes an oath to obligate himself by a pledge, he must not break his word but must do everything he said.

³"When a young woman still living in her father's house makes a vow to the LORD or obligates herself by a pledge ⁴and her father hears about her vow or pledge but says nothing to her, then all her vows and every pledge by which she obligated herself will stand. ⁵But if her father forbids her when he hears about it, none of her vows or the pledges by which she obligated herself will stand; the LORD will release her because her father has forbidden her.

⁶"If she marries after she makes a vow or after her lips utter a rash promise by which she obligates herself ⁷and her husband hears about it but says nothing to her, then her vows or the pledges by which she obligated herself will stand. ⁸But if her husband forbids her when he hears about it, he nullifies the vow that obligates her or the rash promise by which she obligates herself, and the LORD will release her.

⁹"Any vow or obligation taken by a widow or divorced woman will be binding on her.

¹⁰"If a woman living with her husband makes a vow or obligates herself by a pledge under oath ¹¹and her husband hears about it but says nothing to her and does not forbid her, then all her vows or the pledges by which she obligated herself will stand. ¹²But if her husband nullifies them when he hears about them, then none of the vows or pledges that came from her lips will stand. Her husband has nullified them, and the LORD will release her. ¹³Her husband

ᵃ39 Traditionally peace offerings

❚ET'S LIVE IT!   Numbers 30:1–5

WHY CAN'T I DO WHAT I WANT? ▤➡ "Dad, I told Allison I'd come over to her house," Judy said when she came home from school.

"Is your homework done?" her dad asked.

Judy shook her head. "I'll do it later," she offered.

"No," he said. "Call Allison and tell her you can't come over."

Do you think it's fair for her dad to say no after Judy promised to go to Allison's house? Read Numbers 30:1–5. In Israel a man was responsible for his whole family. Husbands could even say no to promises (vows) their wives or children made to God! Today parents are still responsible for children, so children can't do just anything they want to do. Because moms and dads are responsible, they have to say no at times.

Here are some rules for saying no. Talk them over with your parents. Do you think the rules are fair?

Have a good reason for saying no.
Tell the reasons for saying no.
Don't argue after the reason is explained.
Don't keep on asking after being told no.
Listen to the child before saying no.

may confirm or nullify any vow she makes or any sworn pledge to deny herself. ¹⁴But if her husband says nothing to her about it from day to day, then he confirms all her vows or the pledges binding on her. He confirms them by saying nothing to her when he hears about them. ¹⁵If, however, he nullifies them some time after he hears about them, then he is responsible for her guilt.'"

¹⁶These are the regulations the LORD gave Moses concerning relationships between a man and his wife, and between a father and his young daughter still living in his house.

Vengeance on the Midianites

31 The LORD said to Moses, ²"Take vengeance on the Midianites for the Israelites. After that, you will be gathered to your people."

³So Moses said to the people, "Arm some of your men to go to war against the Midianites and to carry out the LORD's vengeance on them. ⁴Send into battle a thousand men from each of the tribes of Israel." ⁵So twelve thousand men armed for battle, a thousand from each tribe, were supplied from the clans of Israel. ⁶Moses sent them into battle, a thousand from each tribe, along with Phinehas son of Eleazar, the priest, who took with him articles from the sanctuary and the trumpets for signaling.

⁷They fought against Midian, as the LORD commanded Moses, and killed every man. ⁸Among their victims were Evi, Rekem, Zur, Hur and Reba—the five kings of Midian. They also killed Balaam son of Beor with the sword. ⁹The Israelites captured the Midianite women and children and took all the Midianite herds, flocks and goods as plunder. ¹⁰They burned all the towns where the Midianites had settled, as well as all their camps. ¹¹They took all the plunder and spoils, including the people and animals, ¹²and brought the captives,

spoils and plunder to Moses and Eleazar the priest and the Israelite assembly at their camp on the plains of Moab, by the Jordan across from Jericho.ᵃ

¹³Moses, Eleazar the priest and all the leaders of the community went to meet them outside the camp. ¹⁴Moses was angry with the officers of the army—the commanders of thousands and commanders of hundreds —who returned from the battle.

¹⁵"Have you allowed all the women to live?" he asked them. ¹⁶"They were the ones who followed Balaam's advice and were the means of turning the Israelites away from the LORD in what happened at Peor, so that a plague struck the LORD's people. ¹⁷Now kill all the boys. And kill every woman who has slept with a man, ¹⁸but save for yourselves every girl who has never slept with a man.

¹⁹"All of you who have killed anyone or touched anyone who was killed must stay outside the camp seven days. On the third and seventh days you must purify yourselves and your captives. ²⁰Purify every garment as well as everything made of leather, goat hair or wood.'"

²¹Then Eleazar the priest said to the soldiers who had gone into battle, "This is the requirement of the law that the LORD gave Moses: ²²Gold, silver, bronze, iron, tin, lead ²³and anything else that can withstand fire must be put through the fire, and then it will be clean. But it must also be purified with the water of cleansing. And whatever cannot withstand fire must be put through that water. ²⁴On the seventh day wash your clothes and you will be clean. Then you may come into the camp."

Dividing the Spoils

²⁵The LORD said to Moses, ²⁶"You and Eleazar the priest and the family heads of the community are to count all the people and animals that were captured. ²⁷Divide the spoils between the soldiers who took part in the bat-

---

ᵃ12 Hebrew *Jordan of Jericho*; possibly an ancient name for the Jordan River

tle and the rest of the community.
²⁸From the soldiers who fought in the
battle, set apart as tribute for the
LORD one out of every five hundred,
whether persons, cattle, donkeys,
sheep or goats. ²⁹Take this tribute
from their half share and give it to
Eleazar the priest as the LORD's part.
³⁰From the Israelites' half, select one
out of every fifty, whether persons,
cattle, donkeys, sheep, goats or other
animals. Give them to the Levites,
who are responsible for the care of
the LORD's tabernacle." ³¹So Moses
and Eleazar the priest did as the
LORD commanded Moses.

³²The plunder remaining from the
spoils that the soldiers took was 675,-
000 sheep, ³³72,000 cattle, ³⁴61,000
donkeys ³⁵and 32,000 women who
had never slept with a man.

³⁶The half share of those who
fought in the battle was:

337,500 sheep, ³⁷of which the
    tribute for the LORD was 675;
³⁸36,000 cattle, of which the trib-
    ute for the LORD was 72;
³⁹30,500 donkeys, of which the
    tribute for the LORD was 61;
⁴⁰16,000 people, of which the trib-
    ute for the LORD was 32.

⁴¹Moses gave the tribute to Eleazar
the priest as the LORD's part, as the
LORD commanded Moses.

⁴²The half belonging to the Israelites, which Moses set apart from that
of the fighting men— ⁴³the community's half—was 337,500 sheep,
⁴⁴36,000 cattle, ⁴⁵30,500 donkeys
⁴⁶and 16,000 people. ⁴⁷From the Israelites' half, Moses selected one out of
every fifty persons and animals, as
the LORD commanded him, and gave
them to the Levites, who were responsible for the care of the LORD's
tabernacle.

⁴⁸Then the officers who were over
the units of the army—the commanders of thousands and commanders of hundreds—went to Moses
⁴⁹and said to him, "Your servants
have counted the soldiers under our

command, and not one is missing.
⁵⁰So we have brought as an offering
to the LORD the gold articles each of
us acquired—armlets, bracelets, signet rings, earrings and necklaces—
to make atonement for ourselves before the LORD."

⁵¹Moses and Eleazar the priest accepted from them the gold—all the
crafted articles. ⁵²All the gold from
the commanders of thousands and
commanders of hundreds that Moses
and Eleazar presented as a gift to the
LORD weighed 16,750 shekels.ᵃ
⁵³Each soldier had taken plunder for
himself. ⁵⁴Moses and Eleazar the
priest accepted the gold from the
commanders of thousands and commanders of hundreds and brought it
into the Tent of Meeting as a memorial for the Israelites before the LORD.

The Transjordan Tribes

32 The Reubenites and Gadites,
who had very large herds and
flocks, saw that the lands of Jazer
and Gilead were suitable for livestock. ²So they came to Moses and Eleazar the priest and to the leaders of
the community, and said, ³"Ataroth,
Dibon, Jazer, Nimrah, Heshbon, Elealeh, Sebam, Nebo and Beon— ⁴the
land the LORD subdued before the
people of Israel—are suitable for
livestock, and your servants have
livestock. ⁵If we have found favor in
your eyes," they said, "let this land be
given to your servants as our possession. Do not make us cross the Jordan."

⁶Moses said to the Gadites and
Reubenites, "Shall your countrymen
go to war while you sit here? ⁷Why do
you discourage the Israelites from going over into the land the LORD has
given them? ⁸This is what your fathers did when I sent them from Kadesh Barnea to look over the land.
⁹After they went up to the Valley of
Eshcol and viewed the land, they discouraged the Israelites from entering
the land the LORD had given them.
¹⁰The LORD's anger was aroused that

ᵃ52 That is, about 420 pounds (about 190 kilograms)

day and he swore this oath: [11]"Because they have not followed me wholeheartedly, not one of the men twenty years old or more who came up out of Egypt will see the land I promised on oath to Abraham, Isaac and Jacob— [12]not one except Caleb son of Jephunneh the Kenizzite and Joshua son of Nun, for they followed the LORD wholeheartedly.' [13]The LORD's anger burned against Israel and he made them wander in the desert forty years, until the whole generation of those who had done evil in his sight was gone.

❓ DID YOU KNOW?   32:1

What are the Transjordan tribes?

The tribes of Reuben, Gad, and Manasseh are the Transjordan tribes. The men in these tribes built farms and homes on the east side of the Jordan river. The other Israelite tribes settled on the west side. The name *Transjordan* means "across the Jordan" from the other Israelites.

---

[14]"And here you are, a brood of sinners, standing in the place of your fathers and making the LORD even more angry with Israel. [15]If you turn away from following him, he will again leave all this people in the desert, and you will be the cause of their destruction."

[16]Then they came up to him and said, "We would like to build pens here for our livestock and cities for our women and children. [17]But we are ready to arm ourselves and go ahead of the Israelites until we have brought them to their place. Meanwhile our women and children will live in fortified cities, for protection from the inhabitants of the land. [18]We will not return to our homes until every Israelite has received his inheritance. [19]We will not receive any inheritance with them on the other side of the Jordan, because our inher-itance has come to us on the east side of the Jordan."

[20]Then Moses said to them, "If you will do this—if you will arm yourselves before the LORD for battle, [21]and if all of you will go armed over the Jordan before the LORD until he has driven his enemies out before him— [22]then when the land is subdued before the LORD, you may return and be free from your obligation to the LORD and to Israel. And this land will be your possession before the LORD.

[23]"But if you fail to do this, you will be sinning against the LORD; and you may be sure that your sin will find you out. [24]Build cities for your women and children, and pens for your flocks, but do what you have promised."

[25]The Gadites and Reubenites said to Moses, "We your servants will do as our lord commands. [26]Our children and wives, our flocks and herds will remain here in the cities of Gilead. [27]But your servants, every man armed for battle, will cross over to fight before the LORD, just as our lord says."

[28]Then Moses gave orders about them to Eleazar the priest and Joshua son of Nun and to the family heads of the Israelite tribes. [29]He said to them, "If the Gadites and Reubenites, every man armed for battle, cross over the Jordan with you before the LORD, then when the land is subdued before you, give them the land of Gilead as their possession. [30]But if they do not cross over with you armed, they must accept their possession with you in Canaan."

[31]The Gadites and Reubenites answered, "Your servants will do what the LORD has said. [32]We will cross over before the LORD into Canaan armed, but the property we inherit will be on this side of the Jordan."

[33]Then Moses gave to the Gadites, the Reubenites and the half-tribe of Manasseh son of Joseph the kingdom of Sihon king of the Amorites and the kingdom of Og king of Bashan—the

whole land with its cities and the territory around them.

[34]The Gadites built up Dibon, Ataroth, Aroer, [35]Atroth Shophan, Jazer, Jogbehah, [36]Beth Nimrah and Beth Haran as fortified cities, and built pens for their flocks. [37]And the Reubenites rebuilt Heshbon, Elealeh and Kiriathaim, [38]as well as Nebo and Baal Meon (these names were changed) and Sibmah. They gave names to the cities they rebuilt.

[39]The descendants of Makir son of Manasseh went to Gilead, captured it and drove out the Amorites who were there. [40]So Moses gave Gilead to the Makirites, the descendants of Manasseh, and they settled there. [41]Jair, a descendant of Manasseh, captured their settlements and called them Havvoth Jair.[a] [42]And Nobah captured Kenath and its surrounding settlements and called it Nobah after himself.

Stages in Israel's Journey

33 Here are the stages in the journey of the Israelites when they came out of Egypt by divisions under the leadership of Moses and Aaron. [2]At the LORD's command Moses recorded the stages in their journey. This is their journey by stages:

[3]The Israelites set out from Rameses on the fifteenth day of the first month, the day after the Passover. They marched out boldly in full view of all the Egyptians, [4]who were burying all their firstborn, whom the LORD had struck down among them; for the LORD had brought judgment on their gods.

[5]The Israelites left Rameses and camped at Succoth.

[6]They left Succoth and camped at Etham, on the edge of the desert.

[7]They left Etham, turned back to Pi Hahiroth, to the east of Baal Zephon, and camped near Migdol.

[8]They left Pi Hahiroth[b] and passed through the sea into the desert, and when they had traveled for three days in the Desert of Etham, they camped at Marah.

[9]They left Marah and went to Elim, where there were twelve springs and seventy palm trees, and they camped there.

[10]They left Elim and camped by the Red Sea.[c]

[11]They left the Red Sea and camped in the Desert of Sin.

[12]They left the Desert of Sin and camped at Dophkah.

[13]They left Dophkah and camped at Alush.

[14]They left Alush and camped at Rephidim, where there was no water for the people to drink.

[15]They left Rephidim and camped in the Desert of Sinai.

[16]They left the Desert of Sinai and camped at Kibroth Hattaavah.

[17]They left Kibroth Hattaavah and camped at Hazeroth.

[18]They left Hazeroth and camped at Rithmah.

[19]They left Rithmah and camped at Rimmon Perez.

[20]They left Rimmon Perez and camped at Libnah.

[21]They left Libnah and camped at Rissah.

[22]They left Rissah and camped at Kehelathah.

[23]They left Kehelathah and camped at Mount Shepher.

[24]They left Mount Shepher and camped at Haradah.

[25]They left Haradah and camped at Makheloth.

[26]They left Makheloth and camped at Tahath.

[27]They left Tahath and camped at Terah.

---

[a]41 Or *them the settlements of Jair*   [b]8 Many manuscripts of the Masoretic Text, Samaritan Pentateuch and Vulgate; most manuscripts of the Masoretic Text *left from before Hahiroth*   [c]10 Hebrew *Yam Suph*; that is, Sea of Reeds; also in verse 11

28They left Terah and camped at Mithcah. 29They left Mithcah and camped at Hashmonah. 30They left Hashmonah and camped at Moseroth. 31They left Moseroth and camped at Bene Jaakan. 32They left Bene Jaakan and camped at Hor Haggidgad. 33They left Hor Haggidgad and camped at Jotbathah. 34They left Jotbathah and camped at Abronah. 35They left Abronah and camped at Ezion Geber. 36They left Ezion Geber and camped at Kadesh, in the Desert of Zin. 37They left Kadesh and camped at Mount Hor, on the border of Edom. 38At the LORD's command Aaron the priest went up Mount Hor, where he died on the first day of the fifth month of the fortieth year after the Israelites came out of Egypt. 39Aaron was a hundred and twenty-three years old when he died on Mount Hor.

40The Canaanite king of Arad, who lived in the Negev of Canaan, heard that the Israelites were coming.

41They left Mount Hor and camped at Zalmonah. 42They left Zalmonah and camped at Punon. 43They left Punon and camped at Oboth. 44They left Oboth and camped at Iye Abarim, on the border of Moab. 45They left Iyim*a* and camped at Dibon Gad. 46They left Dibon Gad and camped at Almon Diblathaim. 47They left Almon Diblathaim and camped in the mountains of Abarim, near Nebo. 48They left the mountains of Abarim and camped on the plains of Moab by the Jordan across from Jericho.*b* 49There on the plains of Moab they camped along the Jordan from Beth Jeshimoth to Abel Shittim.

50On the plains of Moab by the Jordan across from Jericho the LORD said to Moses, 51"Speak to the Israelites and say to them: 'When you cross the Jordan into Canaan, 52drive out all the inhabitants of the land before you. Destroy all their carved images and their cast idols, and demolish all their high places. 53Take possession of the land and settle in it, for I have given you the land to possess. 54Distribute the land by lot, according to your clans. To a larger group give a larger inheritance, and to a smaller group a smaller one. Whatever falls to them by lot will be theirs. Distribute it according to your ancestral tribes.

55" 'But if you do not drive out the inhabitants of the land, those you allow to remain will become barbs in your eyes and thorns in your sides. They will give you trouble in the land where you will live. 56And then I will do to you what I plan to do to them.' "

Boundaries of Canaan

34 The LORD said to Moses, 2"Command the Israelites and say to them: 'When you enter Canaan, the land that will be allotted to you as an inheritance will have these boundaries:

3" 'Your southern side will include some of the Desert of Zin along the border of Edom. On the east, your southern boundary will start from the end of the Salt Sea,*c* 4cross south of Scorpion*d* Pass, continue on to Zin and go south of Kadesh Barnea. Then it will go to Hazar Addar and over to Azmon, 5where it will turn, join the Wadi of Egypt and end at the Sea.*e* 6" 'Your western boundary will be

---

a45 That is, Iye Abarim   *b48* Hebrew *Jordan of Jericho;* possibly an ancient name for the Jordan River; also in verse 50   *c3* That is, the Dead Sea; also in verse 12   *d4* Hebrew *Akrabbim*   *e5* That is, the Mediterranean; also in verses 6 and 7

the coast of the Great Sea. This will be your boundary on the west.

7"'For your northern boundary, run a line from the Great Sea to Mount Hor 8and from Mount Hor to Lebo*a* Hamath. Then the boundary will go to Zedad, 9continue to Ziphron and end at Hazar Enan. This will be your boundary on the north.

10"'For your eastern boundary, run a line from Hazar Enan to Shepham. 11The boundary will go down from Shepham to Riblah on the east side of Ain and continue along the slopes east of the Sea of Kinnereth.*b* 12Then the boundary will go down along the Jordan and end at the Salt Sea.

"'This will be your land, with its boundaries on every side.'"

13Moses commanded the Israelites: "Assign this land by lot as an inheritance. The LORD has ordered that it be given to the nine and a half tribes, 14because the families of the tribe of Reuben, the tribe of Gad and the half-tribe of Manasseh have received their inheritance. 15These two and a half tribes have received their inheritance on the east side of the Jordan of Jericho,*c* toward the sunrise."

16The LORD said to Moses, 17"'These are the names of the men who are to assign the land for you as an inheritance: Eleazar the priest and Joshua son of Nun. 18And appoint one leader from each tribe to help assign the land. 19These are their names:

Caleb son of Jephunneh,
    from the tribe of Judah;
20Shemuel son of Ammihud,
    from the tribe of Simeon;
21Elidad son of Kislon,
    from the tribe of Benjamin;
22Bukki son of Jogli,
    the leader from the tribe of Dan;
23Hanniel son of Ephod,
    the leader from the tribe of Manasseh son of Joseph;
24Kemuel son of Shiphtan,
    the leader from the tribe of Ephraim son of Joseph;
25Elizaphan son of Parnach,
    the leader from the tribe of Zebulun;
26Paltiel son of Azzan,
    the leader from the tribe of Issachar;
27Ahihud son of Shelomi,
    the leader from the tribe of Asher;
28Pedahel son of Ammihud,
    the leader from the tribe of Naphtali."

29These are the men the LORD commanded to assign the inheritance to the Israelites in the land of Canaan.

Towns for the Levites

35 On the plains of Moab by the Jordan across from Jericho,*d* the LORD said to Moses, 2"Command the Israelites to give the Levites towns to live in from the inheritance the Israelites will possess. And give them pasturelands around the towns. 3Then they will have towns to live in and pasturelands for their cattle, flocks and all their other livestock.

4"The pasturelands around the towns that you give the Levites will extend out fifteen hundred feet*e* from the town wall. 5Outside the town, measure three thousand feet*f* on the east side, three thousand on the south side, three thousand on the west and three thousand on the north, with the town in the center. They will have this area as pastureland for the towns.

Cities of Refuge

6"Six of the towns you give the Levites will be cities of refuge, to which a person who has killed someone may flee. In addition, give them forty-two other towns. 7In all you must give the Levites forty-eight towns, together with their pasturelands. 8The towns you give the Levites from the land

*a*8 Or *to the entrance to* *b*11 That is, Galilee *c*15 *Jordan of Jericho* was possibly an ancient name for the Jordan River. *d*1 Hebrew *Jordan of Jericho*; possibly an ancient name for the Jordan River *e*4 Hebrew *a thousand cubits* (about 450 meters) *f*5 Hebrew *two thousand cubits* (about 900 meters)

the Israelites possess are to be given in proportion to the inheritance of each tribe: Take many towns from a tribe that has many, but few from one that has few."

⁹Then the LORD said to Moses: ¹⁰"Speak to the Israelites and say to them: 'When you cross the Jordan into Canaan, ¹¹select some towns to be your cities of refuge, to which a person who has killed someone accidentally may flee. ¹²They will be places of refuge from the avenger, so that a person accused of murder may not die before he stands trial before the assembly. ¹³These six towns you give will be your cities of refuge. ¹⁴Give three on this side of the Jordan and three in Canaan as cities of refuge. ¹⁵These six towns will be a place of refuge for Israelites, aliens and any other people living among them, so that anyone who has killed another accidentally can flee there.

Life In Bible Times

CITIES OF REFUGE

God said that people who murder others must die (Numbers 35:16–21). But someone who kills another accidentally should not die (Numbers 35:22–25). In Israel when a person killed someone by accident he or she could hurry to one of these six cities of refuge and be safe. No one in Israel lived more than one day's journey from a city of refuge.

---

¹⁶"'If a man strikes someone with an iron object so that he dies, he is a murderer; the murderer shall be put to death. ¹⁷Or if anyone has a stone in his hand that could kill, and he strikes someone so that he dies, he is a murderer; the murderer shall be

put to death. ¹⁸Or if anyone has a wooden object in his hand that could kill, and he hits someone so that he dies, he is a murderer; the murderer shall be put to death. ¹⁹The avenger of blood shall put the murderer to death; when he meets him, he shall put him to death. ²⁰If anyone with malice aforethought shoves another or throws something at him intentionally so that he dies ²¹or if in hostility he hits him with his fist so that he dies, that person shall be put to death; he is a murderer. The avenger of blood shall put the murderer to death when he meets him.

²²"'But if without hostility someone suddenly shoves another or throws something at him unintentionally ²³or, without seeing him, drops a stone on him that could kill him, and he dies, then since he was not his enemy and he did not intend to harm him, ²⁴the assembly must judge between him and the avenger of blood according to these regulations. ²⁵The assembly must protect the one accused of murder from the avenger of blood and send him back to the city of refuge to which he fled. He must stay there until the death of the high priest, who was anointed with the holy oil.

²⁶"'But if the accused ever goes outside the limits of the city of refuge to which he has fled ²⁷and the avenger of blood finds him outside the city, the avenger of blood may kill the accused without being guilty of murder. ²⁸The accused must stay in his city of refuge until the death of the high priest; only after the death of the high priest may he return to his own property.

²⁹"'These are to be legal requirements for you throughout the generations to come, wherever you live.

³⁰"'Anyone who kills a person is to be put to death as a murderer only on the testimony of witnesses. But no one is to be put to death on the testimony of only one witness.

³¹"'Do not accept a ransom for the life of a murderer, who deserves to die. He must surely be put to death.

[32]" 'Do not accept a ransom for anyone who has fled to a city of refuge and so allow him to go back and live on his own land before the death of the high priest.

[33]" 'Do not pollute the land where you are. Bloodshed pollutes the land, and atonement cannot be made for the land on which blood has been shed, except by the blood of the one who shed it. [34]Do not defile the land where you live and where I dwell, for I, the LORD, dwell among the Israelites.' "

Inheritance of Zelophehad's Daughters

36 The family heads of the clan of Gilead son of Makir, the son of Manasseh, who were from the clans of the descendants of Joseph, came and spoke before Moses and the leaders, the heads of the Israelite families. [2]They said, "When the LORD commanded my lord to give the land as an inheritance to the Israelites by lot, he ordered you to give the inheritance of our brother Zelophehad to his daughters. [3]Now suppose they marry men from other Israelite tribes; then their inheritance will be taken from our ancestral inheritance and added to that of the tribe they marry into. And so part of the inheritance allotted to us will be taken away. [4]When the Year of Jubilee for the Israelites comes, their inheritance will be added to that of the tribe

into which they marry, and their property will be taken from the tribal inheritance of our forefathers."

[5]Then at the LORD's command Moses gave this order to the Israelites: "What the tribe of the descendants of Joseph is saying is right. [6]This is what the LORD commands for Zelophehad's daughters: They may marry anyone they please as long as they marry within the tribal clan of their father. [7]No inheritance in Israel is to pass from tribe to tribe, for every Israelite shall keep the tribal land inherited from his forefathers. [8]Every daughter who inherits land in any Israelite tribe must marry someone in her father's tribal clan, so that every Israelite will possess the inheritance of his fathers. [9]No inheritance may pass from tribe to tribe, for each Israelite tribe is to keep the land it inherits."

[10]So Zelophehad's daughters did as the LORD commanded Moses. [11]Zelophehad's daughters—Mahlah, Tirzah, Hoglah, Milcah and Noah—married their cousins on their father's side. [12]They married within the clans of the descendants of Manasseh son of Joseph, and their inheritance remained in their father's clan and tribe.

[13]These are the commands and regulations the LORD gave through Moses to the Israelites on the plains of Moab by the Jordan across from Jericho. [a]

---

[a]13 Hebrew *Jordan of Jericho*; possibly an ancient name for the Jordan River

DEUTERONOMY

The Command to Leave Horeb

1 These are the words Moses spoke to all Israel in the desert east of the Jordan—that is, in the Arabah —opposite Suph, between Paran and Tophel, Laban, Hazeroth and Dizahab. ²(It takes eleven days to go from Horeb to Kadesh Barnea by the Mount Seir road.)

³In the fortieth year, on the first day of the eleventh month, Moses proclaimed to the Israelites all that the LORD had commanded him concerning them. ⁴This was after he had defeated Sihon king of the Amorites, who reigned in Heshbon, and at Edrei had defeated Og king of Bashan, who reigned in Ashtaroth.

⁵East of the Jordan in the territory of Moab, Moses began to expound this law, saying:

⁶The LORD our God said to us at Horeb, "You have stayed long enough at this mountain. ⁷Break camp and advance into the hill country of the Amorites; go to all the neighboring peoples in the Arabah, in the mountains, in the western foothills, in the Negev and along the coast, to the land of the Canaanites and to Lebanon, as far as the great river, the Euphrates. ⁸See, I have given you this land. Go in and take possession of the land that the LORD swore he would give to your fathers—to Abraham, Isaac and Jacob—and to their descendants after them."

The Appointment of Leaders

⁹At that time I said to you, "You are too heavy a burden for me to carry alone. ¹⁰The LORD your God has increased your numbers so that today you are as many as the stars in the sky. ¹¹May the LORD, the God of your fathers, increase you a thousand times and bless you as he has promised! ¹²But how can I bear your problems and your burdens and your disputes all by myself? ¹³Choose some wise, understanding and respected men from each of your tribes, and I will set them over you."

¹⁴You answered me, "What you propose to do is good."

¹⁵So I took the leading men of your tribes, wise and respected men, and appointed them to have authority over you—as commanders of thousands, of hundreds, of fifties and of tens and as tribal officials. ¹⁶And I charged your judges at that time: Hear the disputes between your brothers and judge fairly, whether the case is between brother Israelites or between one of them and an alien. ¹⁷Do not show partiality in judging; hear both small and great alike. Do not be afraid of any man, for judgment belongs to God. Bring me any case too hard for you, and I will hear it. ¹⁸And at that time I told you everything you were to do.

Spies Sent Out

¹⁹Then, as the LORD our God commanded us, we set out from Horeb and went toward the hill country of the Amorites through all that vast and dreadful desert that you have seen, and so we reached Kadesh Barnea. ²⁰Then I said to you, "You have reached the hill country of the Amorites, which the LORD our God is giving us. ²¹See, the LORD your God has given you the land. Go up and take possession of it as the LORD, the God of your fathers, told you. Do not be afraid; do not be discouraged."

²²Then all of you came to me and said, "Let us send men ahead to spy out the land for us and bring back a report about the route we are to take and the towns we will come to."

²³The idea seemed good to me; so I selected twelve of you, one man from each tribe. ²⁴They left and went up into the hill country, and came to the Valley of Eshcol and explored it. ²⁵Taking with them some of the fruit of the land, they brought it down to us and reported, "It is a good land that the LORD our God is giving us."

Rebellion Against the LORD

²⁶But you were unwilling to go up; you rebelled against the command of the LORD your God. ²⁷You grumbled

in your tents and said, "The LORD hates us; so he brought us out of Egypt to deliver us into the hands of the Amorites to destroy us. 28Where can we go? Our brothers have made us lose heart. They say, 'The people are stronger and taller than we are; the cities are large, with walls up to the sky. We even saw the Anakites there.' "

29Then I said to you, "Do not be terrified; do not be afraid of them. 30The LORD your God, who is going before you, will fight for you, as he did for you in Egypt, before your very eyes, 31and in the desert. There you saw how the LORD your God carried you, as a father carries his son, all the way you went until you reached this place."

32In spite of this, you did not trust in the LORD your God, 33who went ahead of you on your journey, in fire by night and in a cloud by day, to search out places for you to camp and to show you the way you should go.

34When the LORD heard what you said, he was angry and solemnly swore: 35"Not a man of this evil generation shall see the good land I swore to give your forefathers, 36except Caleb son of Jephunneh. He will see it, and I will give him and his descendants the land he set his feet on, because he followed the LORD wholeheartedly."

37Because of you the LORD became angry with me also and said, "You shall not enter it, either. 38But your assistant, Joshua son of Nun, will enter it. Encourage him, because he will lead Israel to inherit it. 39And the little ones that you said would be taken captive, your children who do not yet know good from bad—they will enter the land. I will give it to them and they will take possession of it. 40But as for you, turn around and set out toward the desert along the route to the Red Sea.a"

41Then you replied, "We have sinned against the LORD. We will go up and fight, as the LORD our God commanded us." So every one of you put on his weapons, thinking it easy to go up into the hill country.

42But the LORD said to me, "Tell them, 'Do not go up and fight, because I will not be with you. You will be defeated by your enemies.' "

43So I told you, but you would not listen. You rebelled against the LORD's command and in your arrogance you marched up into the hill country. 44The Amorites who lived in those hills came out against you; they chased you like a swarm of bees and beat you down from Seir all the way to Hormah. 45You came back and wept before the LORD, but he paid no attention to your weeping and turned a deaf ear to you. 46And so you stayed in Kadesh many days—all the time you spent there.

Wanderings in the Desert

2 Then we turned back and set out toward the desert along the route to the Red Sea,a as the LORD had directed me. For a long time we made our way around the hill country of Seir.

2Then the LORD said to me, 3"You have made your way around this hill country long enough; now turn north. 4Give the people these orders: 'You are about to pass through the territory of your brothers the descendants of Esau, who live in Seir. They will be afraid of you, but be very careful. 5Do not provoke them to war, for I will not give you any of their land, not even enough to put your foot on. I have given Esau the hill country of Seir as his own. 6You are to pay them in silver for the food you eat and the water you drink.' "

7The LORD your God has blessed you in all the work of your hands. He has watched over your journey through this vast desert. These forty years the LORD your God has been with you, and you have not lacked anything.

8So we went on past our brothers the descendants of Esau, who live in

---

a40,1 Hebrew *Yam Suph*; that is, Sea of Reeds

Seir. We turned from the Arabah road, which comes up from Elath and Ezion Geber, and traveled along the desert road of Moab.

⁹Then the LORD said to me, "Do not harass the Moabites or provoke them to war, for I will not give you any part of their land. I have given Ar to the descendants of Lot as a possession."

¹⁰(The Emites used to live there—a people strong and numerous, and as tall as the Anakites. ¹¹Like the Anakites, they too were considered Rephaites, but the Moabites called them Emites. ¹²Horites used to live in Seir, but the descendants of Esau drove them out. They destroyed the Horites from before them and settled in their place, just as Israel did in the land the LORD gave them as their possession.)

¹³And the LORD said, "Now get up and cross the Zered Valley." So we crossed the valley.

¹⁴Thirty-eight years passed from the time we left Kadesh Barnea until we crossed the Zered Valley. By then, that entire generation of fighting men had perished from the camp, as the LORD had sworn to them. ¹⁵The LORD's hand was against them until he had completely eliminated them from the camp.

¹⁶Now when the last of these fighting men among the people had died, ¹⁷the LORD said to me, ¹⁸"Today you are to pass by the region of Moab at Ar. ¹⁹When you come to the Ammonites, do not harass them or provoke them to war, for I will not give you possession of any land belonging to the Ammonites. I have given it as a possession to the descendants of Lot."

²⁰(That too was considered a land of the Rephaites, who used to live there; but the Ammonites called them Zamzummites. ²¹They were a people strong and numerous, and as tall as the Anakites. The LORD destroyed them from before the Ammonites, who drove them out and settled in their place. ²²The LORD had done the same for the descendants of Esau, who lived in Seir, when he destroyed the Horites from before them. They drove them out and have lived in their place to this day. ²³And as for the Avvites who lived in villages as far as Gaza, the Caphtorites coming out from Caphtor[a] destroyed them and settled in their place.)

Defeat of Sihon King of Heshbon

²⁴"Set out now and cross the Arnon Gorge. See, I have given into your hand Sihon the Amorite, king of Heshbon, and his country. Begin to take possession of it and engage him in battle. ²⁵This very day I will begin to put the terror and fear of you on all the nations under heaven. They will hear reports of you and will tremble and be in anguish because of you."

²⁶From the desert of Kedemoth I sent messengers to Sihon king of Heshbon offering peace and saying, ²⁷"Let us pass through your country. We will stay on the main road; we will not turn aside to the right or to the left. ²⁸Sell us food to eat and water to drink for their price in silver. Only let us pass through on foot— ²⁹as the descendants of Esau, who live in Seir, and the Moabites, who live in Ar, did for us—until we cross the Jordan into the land the LORD our God is giving us." ³⁰But Sihon king of Heshbon refused to let us pass through. For the LORD your God had made his spirit stubborn and his heart obstinate in order to give him into your hands, as he has now done.

³¹The LORD said to me, "See, I have begun to deliver Sihon and his country over to you. Now begin to conquer and possess his land."

³²When Sihon and all his army came out to meet us in battle at Jahaz, ³³the LORD our God delivered him over to us and we struck him down, together with his sons and his whole army. ³⁴At that time we took all his towns and completely de-

stroyed*a* them—men, women and children. We left no survivors. ³⁵But the livestock and the plunder from the towns we had captured we carried off for ourselves. ³⁶From Aroer on the rim of the Arnon Gorge, and from the town in the gorge, even as far as Gilead, not one town was too strong for us. The LORD our God gave us all of them. ³⁷But in accordance with the command of the LORD our God, you did not encroach on any of the land of the Ammonites, neither the land along the course of the Jabbok nor that around the towns in the hills.

Defeat of Og King of Bashan

3 Next we turned and went up along the road toward Bashan, and Og king of Bashan with his whole army marched out to meet us in battle at Edrei. ²The LORD said to me, "Do not be afraid of him, for I have handed him over to you with his whole army and his land. Do to him what you did to Sihon king of the Amorites, who reigned in Heshbon."

³So the LORD our God also gave into our hands Og king of Bashan and all his army. We struck them down, leaving no survivors. ⁴At that time we took all his cities. There was not one of the sixty cities that we did not take from them—the whole region of Argob, Og's kingdom in Bashan. ⁵All these cities were fortified with high walls and with gates and bars, and there were also a great many unwalled villages. ⁶We completely destroyed*a* them, as we had done with Sihon king of Heshbon, destroying*a* every city—men, women and children. ⁷But all the livestock and the plunder from their cities we carried off for ourselves.

⁸So at that time we took from these two kings of the Amorites the territory east of the Jordan, from the Arnon Gorge as far as Mount Hermon. ⁹(Hermon is called Sirion by the Sido-

nians; the Amorites call it Senir.) ¹⁰We took all the towns on the plateau, and all Gilead, and all Bashan as far as Salecah and Edrei, towns of Og's kingdom in Bashan. ¹¹(Only Og king of Bashan was left of the remnant of the Rephaites. His bed*b* was made of iron and was more than thirteen feet long and six feet wide.*c* It is still in Rabbah of the Ammonites.)

Division of the Land

¹²Of the land that we took over at that time, I gave the Reubenites and the Gadites the territory north of Aroer by the Arnon Gorge, including half the hill country of Gilead, together with its towns. ¹³The rest of Gilead and also all of Bashan, the kingdom of Og, I gave to the half tribe of Manasseh. (The whole region of Argob in Bashan used to be known as a land of the Rephaites. ¹⁴Jair, a descendant of Manasseh, took the whole region of Argob as far as the border of the Geshurites and the Maacathites; it was named after him, so that to this day Bashan is called Havvoth Jair.*d*) ¹⁵And I gave Gilead to Makir. ¹⁶But to the Reubenites and the Gadites I gave the territory extending from Gilead down to the Arnon Gorge (the middle of the gorge being the border) and out to the Jabbok River, which is the border of the Ammonites. ¹⁷Its western border was the Jordan in the Arabah, from Kinnereth to the Sea of the Arabah (the Salt Sea*e*), below the slopes of Pisgah.

¹⁸I commanded you at that time: "The LORD your God has given you this land to take possession of it. But all your able-bodied men, armed for battle, must cross over ahead of your brother Israelites. ¹⁹However, your wives, your children and your livestock (I know you have much livestock) may stay in the towns I have given you, ²⁰until the LORD gives rest

---

a34,6 The Hebrew term refers to the irrevocable giving over of things or persons to the LORD, often by totally destroying them.   *b11* Or *sarcophagus*   *c11* Hebrew *nine cubits long and four cubits wide* (about 4 meters long and 1.8 meters wide)   *d14* Or *called the settlements of Jair* *e17* That is, the Dead Sea

to your brothers as he has to you, and they too have taken over the land that the LORD your God is giving them, across the Jordan. After that, each of you may go back to the possession I have given you."

Moses Forbidden to Cross the Jordan

21At that time I commanded Joshua: "You have seen with your own eyes all that the LORD your God has done to these two kings. The LORD will do the same to all the kingdoms over there where you are going. 22Do not be afraid of them; the LORD your God himself will fight for you."

23At that time I pleaded with the LORD: 24"O Sovereign LORD, you have begun to show to your servant your greatness and your strong hand. For what god is there in heaven or on earth who can do the deeds and mighty works you do? 25Let me go over and see the good land beyond the Jordan—that fine hill country and Lebanon."

26But because of you the LORD was angry with me and would not listen to me. "That is enough," the LORD said. "Do not speak to me anymore about this matter. 27Go up to the top of Pisgah and look west and north and south and east. Look at the land with your own eyes, since you are not going to cross this Jordan. 28But commission Joshua, and encourage and strengthen him, for he will lead this people across and will cause them to inherit the land that you will see." 29So we stayed in the valley near Beth Peor.

Obedience Commanded

4 Hear now, O Israel, the decrees and laws I am about to teach you. Follow them so that you may live and may go in and take possession of the land that the LORD, the God of your fathers, is giving you. 2Do not add to what I command you and do not subtract from it, but keep the commands of the LORD your God that I give you.

3You saw with your own eyes what the LORD did at Baal Peor. The LORD

your God destroyed from among you everyone who followed the Baal of Peor, 4but all of you who held fast to the LORD your God are still alive today.

5See, I have taught you decrees and laws as the LORD my God commanded me, so that you may follow them in the land you are entering to take possession of it. 6Observe them carefully, for this will show your wisdom and understanding to the nations, who will hear about all these decrees and say, "Surely this great nation is a wise and understanding people." 7What other nation is so great as to have their gods near them the way the LORD our God is near us whenever we pray to him? 8And what other nation is so great as to have such righteous decrees and laws as this body of laws I am setting before you today?

9Only be careful, and watch yourselves closely so that you do not forget the things your eyes have seen or let them slip from your heart as long as you live. Teach them to your children and to their children after them. 10Remember the day you stood before the LORD your God at Horeb, when he said to me, "Assemble the people before me to hear my words so that they may learn to revere me as long as they live in the land and may teach them to their children." 11You came near and stood at the foot of the mountain while it blazed with fire to the very heavens, with black clouds and deep darkness. 12Then the LORD spoke to you out of the fire. You heard the sound of words but saw no form; there was only a voice. 13He declared to you his covenant, the Ten Commandments, which he commanded you to follow and then wrote them on two stone tablets. 14And the LORD directed me at that time to teach you the decrees and laws you are to follow in the land that you are crossing the Jordan to possess.

Idolatry Forbidden

15You saw no form of any kind the day the LORD spoke to you at Horeb out of the fire. Therefore watch your-selves very carefully, [16]so that you do not become corrupt and make for yourselves an idol, an image of any shape, whether formed like a man or a woman, [17]or like any animal on earth or any bird that flies in the air, [18]or like any creature that moves along the ground or any fish in the waters below. [19]And when you look up to the sky and see the sun, the moon and the stars—all the heaven-ly array—do not be enticed into bow-ing down to them and worshiping things the LORD your God has appor-tioned to all the nations under heav-en. [20]But as for you, the LORD took you and brought you out of the iron-smelting furnace, out of Egypt, to be the people of his inheritance, as you now are.

PAGAN IDOLS

The idols that pagan people worshiped as gods in Moses' time were made of wood or metal. These idols obviously could not hear or see or speak. God promised the Israelites that if they loved and followed him, he would protect and care for them, something no idol could ever do.

[21]The LORD was angry with me be-cause of you, and he solemnly swore that I would not cross the Jordan and enter the good land the LORD your God is giving you as your inheri-tance. [22]I will die in this land; I will not cross the Jordan; but you are about to cross over and take posses-sion of that good land. [23]Be careful not to forget the covenant of the LORD

your God that he made with you; do not make for yourselves an idol in the form of anything the LORD your God has forbidden. [24]For the LORD your God is a consuming fire, a jealous God.

[25]After you have had children and grandchildren and have lived in the land a long time—if you then become corrupt and make any kind of idol, doing evil in the eyes of the LORD your God and provoking him to an-ger, [26]I call heaven and earth as wit-nesses against you this day that you will quickly perish from the land that you are crossing the Jordan to pos-sess. You will not live there long but will certainly be destroyed. [27]The LORD will scatter you among the peo-ples, and only a few of you will sur-vive among the nations to which the LORD will drive you. [28]There you will worship man-made gods of wood and stone, which cannot see or hear or eat or smell. [29]But if from there you seek the LORD your God, you will find him if you look for him with all your heart and with all your soul. [30]When you are in distress and all these things have happened to you, then in later days you will return to the LORD your God and obey him. [31]For the LORD your God is a merciful God; he will not abandon or destroy you or forget the covenant with your forefathers, which he confirmed to them by oath.

The LORD Is God

[32]Ask now about the former days, long before your time, from the day God created man on the earth; ask from one end of the heavens to the other. Has anything so great as this ever happened, or has anything like it ever been heard of? [33]Has any other people heard the voice of God[a] speak-ing out of fire, as you have, and lived? [34]Has any god ever tried to take for himself one nation out of another na-tion, by testings, by miraculous signs and wonders, by war, by a mighty hand and an outstretched arm, or by great and awesome deeds, like all the

[a]33 Or *of a god*

things the LORD your God did for you in Egypt before your very eyes? ³⁵You were shown these things so that you might know that the LORD is God; besides him there is no other. ³⁶From heaven he made you hear his voice to discipline you. On earth he showed you his great fire, and you heard his words from out of the fire. ³⁷Because he loved your forefathers and chose their descendants after them, he brought you out of Egypt by his Presence and his great strength, ³⁸to drive out before you nations greater and stronger than you and to bring you into their land to give it to you for your inheritance, as it is today.

WORDS TO REMEMBER

4:35 The LORD is God; besides him there is no other.

---

³⁹Acknowledge and take to heart this day that the LORD is God in heaven above and on the earth below. There is no other. ⁴⁰Keep his decrees and commands, which I am giving you today, so that it may go well with you and your children after you and that you may live long in the land the LORD your God gives you for all time.

Cities of Refuge

⁴¹Then Moses set aside three cities east of the Jordan, ⁴²to which anyone who had killed a person could flee if he had unintentionally killed his neighbor without malice aforethought. He could flee into one of these cities and save his life. ⁴³The cities were these: Bezer in the desert plateau, for the Reubenites; Ramoth in Gilead, for the Gadites; and Golan in Bashan, for the Manassites.

Introduction to the Law

⁴⁴This is the law Moses set before the Israelites. ⁴⁵These are the stipulations, decrees and laws Moses gave

them when they came out of Egypt ⁴⁶and were in the valley near Beth Peor east of the Jordan, in the land of Sihon king of the Amorites, who reigned in Heshbon and was defeated by Moses and the Israelites as they came out of Egypt. ⁴⁷They took possession of his land and the land of Og king of Bashan, the two Amorite kings east of the Jordan. ⁴⁸This land extended from Aroer on the rim of the Arnon Gorge to Mount Siyon^a (that is, Hermon), ⁴⁹and included all the Arabah east of the Jordan, as far as the Sea of the Arabah,^{b} below the slopes of Pisgah.

The Ten Commandments

5 Moses summoned all Israel and said:

Hear, O Israel, the decrees and laws I declare in your hearing today. Learn them and be sure to follow them. ²The LORD our God made a covenant with us at Horeb. ³It was not with our fathers that the LORD made this covenant, but with us, with all of us who are alive here today. ⁴The LORD spoke to you face to face out of the fire on the mountain. ⁵(At that time I stood between the LORD and you to declare to you the word of the LORD, because you were afraid of the fire and did not go up the mountain.) And he said:

6"I am the LORD your God, who brought you out of Egypt, out of the land of slavery.

7"You shall have no other gods before^c me.

8"You shall not make for yourself an idol in the form of anything in heaven above or on the earth beneath or in the waters below. ⁹You shall not bow down to them or worship them; for I, the LORD your God, am a jealous God, punishing the children for the sin of the fathers to the third and fourth generation of

---

^{a}48 Hebrew; Syriac (see also Deut. 3:9) *Sirion* ^{b}49 That is, the Dead Sea ^{c}7 Or *besides*

those who hate me, ¹⁰but showing love to a thousand generations of those who love me and keep my commandments.

¹¹"You shall not misuse the name of the LORD your God, for the LORD will not hold anyone guiltless who misuses his name.

¹²"Observe the Sabbath day by keeping it holy, as the LORD your God has commanded you. ¹³Six days you shall labor and do all your work, ¹⁴but the seventh day is a Sabbath to the LORD your God. On it you shall not do any work, neither you, nor your son or daughter, nor your manservant or maidservant, nor your ox, your donkey or any of your animals, nor the alien within your gates, so that your manservant and maidservant may rest, as you do. ¹⁵Remember that you were slaves in Egypt and that the LORD your God brought you out of there with a mighty hand and an outstretched arm. Therefore the LORD your God has commanded you to observe the Sabbath day.

¹⁶"Honor your father and your mother, as the LORD your God has commanded you, so that you may live long and that it may go well with you in the land the LORD your God is giving you.

¹⁷"You shall not murder.

¹⁸"You shall not commit adultery.

¹⁹"You shall not steal.

²⁰"You shall not give false testimony against your neighbor.

²¹"You shall not covet your neighbor's wife. You shall not set your desire on your neighbor's house or land, his manservant or maidservant, his ox or donkey, or anything that belongs to your neighbor."

²²These are the commandments the LORD proclaimed in a loud voice to your whole assembly there on the mountain from out of the fire, the cloud and the deep darkness; and he added nothing more. Then he wrote them on two stone tablets and gave them to me.

❓DID YOU KNOW?　5:22

What are the Ten Commandments?

The Ten Commandments are special rules God gave the Israelites and us. Following these rules will help people to show love to God and to one another.

---

²³When you heard the voice out of the darkness, while the mountain was ablaze with fire, all the leading men of your tribes and your elders came to me. ²⁴And you said, "The LORD our God has shown us his glory and his majesty, and we have heard his voice from the fire. Today we have seen that a man can live even if God speaks with him. ²⁵But now, why should we die? This great fire will consume us, and we will die if we hear the voice of the LORD our God any longer. ²⁶For what mortal man has ever heard the voice of the living God speaking out of fire, as we have, and survived? ²⁷Go near and listen to all that the LORD our God says. Then tell us whatever the LORD our God tells you. We will listen and obey."

²⁸The LORD heard you when you spoke to me and the LORD said to me, "I have heard what this people said to you. Everything they said was good. ²⁹Oh, that their hearts would be inclined to fear me and keep all my commands always, so that it might go well with them and their children forever!

³⁰"Go, tell them to return to their tents. ³¹But you stay here with me so

that I may give you all the commands, decrees and laws you are to teach them to follow in the land I am giving them to possess."

³²So be careful to do what the LORD your God has commanded you; do not turn aside to the right or to the left. ³³Walk in all the way that the LORD your God has commanded you, so that you may live and prosper and prolong your days in the land that you will possess.

Love the LORD Your God

6 These are the commands, decrees and laws the LORD your God directed me to teach you to observe in the land that you are crossing the Jordan to possess, ²so that you, your children and their children after them may fear the LORD your God as long as you live by keeping all his decrees and commands that I give you, and so that you may enjoy long life. ³Hear, O Israel, and be careful to obey so that it may go well with you and that you may increase greatly in a land flowing with milk and honey, just as the LORD, the God of your fathers, promised you.

⁴Hear, O Israel: The LORD our God, the LORD is one.ᵃ ⁵Love the LORD your God with all your heart and with all your soul and with all your strength. ⁶These commandments that I give you today are to be upon your hearts. ⁷Impress them on your children. Talk about them when you sit at home and when you walk along the road, when you lie down and when you get up. ⁸Tie them as symbols on your hands and bind them on your foreheads. ⁹Write them on the doorframes of your houses and on your gates.

¹⁰When the LORD your God brings you into the land he swore to your fathers, to Abraham, Isaac and Jacob, to give you—a land with large, flourishing cities you did not build, ¹¹houses filled with all kinds of good things you did not provide, wells you did not dig, and vineyards and olive groves you did not plant—then when you eat and are satisfied, ¹²be careful that you do not forget the LORD, who brought you out of Egypt, out of the land of slavery.

¹³Fear the LORD your God, serve him only and take your oaths in his name. ¹⁴Do not follow other gods, the gods of the peoples around you; ¹⁵for the LORD your God, who is among you, is a jealous God and his anger will burn against you, and he will destroy you from the face of the land. ¹⁶Do not test the LORD your God as you did at Massah. ¹⁷Be sure to keep the commands of the LORD your God and the stipulations and decrees he has given you. ¹⁸Do what is right and good in the LORD's sight, so that it may go well with you and you may go in and take over the good land that the LORD promised on oath to your forefathers, ¹⁹thrusting out all your enemies before you, as the LORD said.

²⁰In the future, when your son asks you, "What is the meaning of the stipulations, decrees and laws the LORD our God has commanded you?" ²¹tell him: "We were slaves of Pharaoh in Egypt, but the LORD brought us out of Egypt with a mighty hand.

ᵃ4 Or *The LORD our God is one LORD*; or *The LORD is our God, the LORD is one*; or *The LORD is our God, the LORD alone*

▖ET'S LIVE IT!   Deuteronomy 6:1–9

LEARNING FROM YOUR MOM AND DAD ▪▶ Read Deuteronomy 6:1–9. What should moms and dads teach their children about God?

It would make your mom or dad happy if you wrote them a letter. Tell them what you have learned about God from them. Tell them thanks for teaching you about the Lord.

²²Before our eyes the LORD sent miraculous signs and wonders—great and terrible—upon Egypt and Pharaoh and his whole household. ²³But he brought us out from there to bring us in and give us the land that he promised on oath to our forefathers. ²⁴The LORD commanded us to obey all these decrees and to fear the LORD our God, so that we might always prosper and be kept alive, as is the case today. ²⁵And if we are careful to obey all this law before the LORD our God, as he has commanded us, that will be our righteousness."

Driving Out the Nations

7 When the LORD your God brings you into the land you are entering to possess and drives out before you many nations—the Hittites, Girgashites, Amorites, Canaanites, Perizzites, Hivites and Jebusites, seven nations larger and stronger than you— ²and when the LORD your God has delivered them over to you and you have defeated them, then you must destroy them totally.ᵃ Make no treaty with them, and show them no mercy. ³Do not intermarry with them. Do not give your daughters to their sons or take their daughters for your sons, ⁴for they will turn your sons away from following me to serve other gods, and the LORD's anger will burn against you and will quickly destroy you. ⁵This is what you are to do to them: Break down their altars, smash their sacred stones, cut down their Asherah polesᵇ and burn their idols in the fire. ⁶For you are a people holy to the LORD your God. The LORD your God has chosen you out of all the peoples on the face of the earth to be his people, his treasured possession. ⁷The LORD did not set his affection on you and choose you because you were more numerous than other peoples, for you were the fewest of all peoples. ⁸But it was because the LORD loved you and kept the oath he swore to your forefathers that he brought you out with a mighty hand and redeemed you from the land of slavery, from the power of Pharaoh king of Egypt. ⁹Know therefore that the LORD your God is God; he is the faithful God, keeping his covenant of love to a thousand generations of those who love him and keep his commands. ¹⁰But

those who hate him he will repay
  to their face by destruction;
he will not be slow to repay to
  their face those who hate
  him.

❓DID YOU KNOW?   7:6

Why did God tell his people to kill all the Canaanites?

The Canaanites had a very evil pagan religion. They practiced witchcraft, and some even burned their own children as sacrifices to their gods. God intended to destroy the Canaanites, both to punish them for their sins and to keep the Canaanites from leading Israel away from the Lord.

¹¹Therefore, take care to follow the commands, decrees and laws I give you today. ¹²If you pay attention to these laws and are careful to follow them, then the LORD your God will keep his covenant of love with you, as he swore to your forefathers. ¹³He will love you and bless you and increase your numbers. He will bless the fruit of your womb, the crops of your land—your grain, new wine and oil—the calves of your herds and the lambs of your flocks in the land that he swore to your forefathers to give you. ¹⁴You will be blessed more than any other people; none of your men or women will be childless, nor any of your livestock without young. ¹⁵The LORD will

---

ᵃ2 The Hebrew term refers to the irrevocable giving over of things or persons to the LORD, often by totally destroying them; also in verse 26.   ᵇ5 That is, symbols of the goddess Asherah; here and elsewhere in Deuteronomy

keep you free from every disease. He will not inflict on you the horrible diseases you knew in Egypt, but he will inflict them on all who hate you. 16You must destroy all the peoples the LORD your God gives over to you. Do not look on them with pity and do not serve their gods, for that will be a snare to you.

17You may say to yourselves, "These nations are stronger than we are. How can we drive them out?" 18But do not be afraid of them; remember well what the LORD your God did to Pharaoh and to all Egypt. 19You saw with your own eyes the great trials, the miraculous signs and wonders, the mighty hand and outstretched arm, with which the LORD your God brought you out. The LORD your God will do the same to all the peoples you now fear. 20Moreover, the LORD your God will send the hornet among them until even the survivors who hide from you have perished. 21Do not be terrified by them, for the LORD your God, who is among you, is a great and awesome God. 22The LORD your God will drive out those nations before you, little by little. You will not be allowed to eliminate them all at once, or the wild animals will multiply around you. 23But the LORD your God will deliver them over to you, throwing them into great confusion until they are destroyed. 24He will give their kings into your hand, and you will wipe out their names from under heaven. No one will be able to stand up against you; you will destroy them. 25The images of their gods you are to burn in the fire. Do not covet the silver and gold on them, and do not take it for yourselves, or you will be ensnared by it, for it is detestable to the LORD your God. 26Do not bring a detestable thing into your house or you, like it, will be set apart for destruction. Utterly abhor and detest it, for it is set apart for destruction.

Do Not Forget the LORD

8 Be careful to follow every command I am giving you today, so that you may live and increase and may enter and possess the land that the LORD promised on oath to your forefathers. 2Remember how the LORD your God led you all the way in the desert these forty years, to humble you and to test you in order to know what was in your heart, whether or not you would keep his commands. 3He humbled you, causing you to hunger and then feeding you with manna, which neither you nor your fathers had known, to teach you that man does not live on bread alone but on every word that comes from the mouth of the LORD. 4Your clothes did not wear out and your feet did not swell during these forty years. 5Know then in your heart that as a man disciplines his son, so the LORD your God disciplines you.

❓DID YOU KNOW?   8:1

Why did God give us laws and rules to live by?

God gives us rules to live by because he loves us. When we do what is right, God can bless us. When we do what is wrong, God must punish us. People who obey God are the happiest, and God wants only the best for his people.

6Observe the commands of the LORD your God, walking in his ways and revering him. 7For the LORD your God is bringing you into a good land—a land with streams and pools of water, with springs flowing in the valleys and hills; 8a land with wheat and barley, vines and fig trees, pomegranates, olive oil and honey; 9a land where bread will not be scarce and you will lack nothing; a land where the rocks are iron and you can dig copper out of the hills.

10When you have eaten and are satisfied, praise the LORD your God for the good land he has given you. 11Be careful that you do not forget the LORD your God, failing to observe his commands, his laws and his decrees that I am giving you this day. [12]Otherwise, when you eat and are satisfied, when you build fine houses and settle down, [13]and when your herds and flocks grow large and your silver and gold increase and all you have is multiplied, [14]then your heart will become proud and you will forget the LORD your God, who brought you out of Egypt, out of the land of slavery. [15]He led you through the vast and dreadful desert, that thirsty and waterless land, with its venomous snakes and scorpions. He brought you water out of hard rock. [16]He gave you manna to eat in the desert, something your fathers had never known, to humble and to test you so that in the end it might go well with you. [17]You may say to yourself, "My power and the strength of my hands have produced this wealth for me." [18]But remember the LORD your God, for it is he who gives you the ability to produce wealth, and so confirms his covenant, which he swore to your forefathers, as it is today.

[19]If you ever forget the LORD your God and follow other gods and worship and bow down to them, I testify against you today that you will surely be destroyed. [20]Like the nations the LORD destroyed before you, so you will be destroyed for not obeying the LORD your God.

Not Because of Israel's Righteousness

9 Hear, O Israel. You are now about to cross the Jordan to go in and dispossess nations greater and stronger than you, with large cities that have walls up to the sky. [2]The people are strong and tall—Anakites! You know about them and have heard it said: "Who can stand up against the Anakites?" [3]But be assured today that the LORD your God is the one who goes across ahead of you like a devouring fire. He will destroy them; he will subdue them before you. And you will drive them out and annihilate them quickly, as the LORD has promised you.

[4]After the LORD your God has driven them out before you, do not say to yourself, "The LORD has brought me here to take possession of this land because of my righteousness." No, it is on account of the wickedness of these nations that the LORD is going to drive them out before you. [5]It is not because of your righteousness or your integrity that you are going in to take possession of their land; but on account of the wickedness of these nations, the LORD your God will drive them out before you, to accomplish what he swore to your fathers, to Abraham, Isaac and Jacob. [6]Understand, then, that it is not because of your righteousness that the LORD your God is giving you this good land to possess, for you are a stiff-necked people.

The Golden Calf

[7]Remember this and never forget how you provoked the LORD your God to anger in the desert. From the day you left Egypt until you arrived here, you have been rebellious against the LORD. [8]At Horeb you aroused the LORD's wrath so that he was angry enough to destroy you. [9]When I went up on the mountain to receive the tablets of stone, the tablets of the covenant that the LORD had made with you, I stayed on the mountain forty days and forty nights; I ate no bread and drank no water. [10]The LORD gave me two stone tablets inscribed by the finger of God. On them were all the commandments the LORD proclaimed to you on the mountain out of the fire, on the day of the assembly.

[11]At the end of the forty days and forty nights, the LORD gave me the two stone tablets, the tablets of the covenant. [12]Then the LORD told me, "Go down from here at once, because your people whom you brought out of Egypt have become corrupt. They have turned away quickly from what I commanded them and have made a cast idol for themselves."

[13]And the LORD said to me, "I have seen this people, and they are a stiff-necked people indeed! [14]Let me alone, so that I may destroy them and

blot out their name from under heaven. And I will make you into a nation stronger and more numerous than they."

15So I turned and went down from the mountain while it was ablaze with fire. And the two tablets of the covenant were in my hands. *a* 16When I looked, I saw that you had sinned against the LORD your God; you had made for yourselves an idol cast in the shape of a calf. You had turned aside quickly from the way that the LORD had commanded you. 17So I took the two tablets and threw them out of my hands, breaking them to pieces before your eyes.

18Then once again I fell prostrate before the LORD for forty days and forty nights; I ate no bread and drank no water, because of all the sin you had committed, doing what was evil in the LORD's sight and so provoking him to anger. 19I feared the anger and wrath of the LORD, for he was angry enough with you to destroy you. But again the LORD listened to me. 20And the LORD was angry enough with Aaron to destroy him, but at that time I prayed for Aaron too. 21Also I took that sinful thing of yours, the calf you had made, and burned it in the fire. Then I crushed it and ground it to powder as fine as dust and threw the dust into a stream that flowed down the mountain.

22You also made the LORD angry at Taberah, at Massah and at Kibroth Hattaavah.

23And when the LORD sent you out from Kadesh Barnea, he said, "Go up and take possession of the land I have given you." But you rebelled against the command of the LORD your God. You did not trust him or obey him. 24You have been rebellious against the LORD ever since I have known you.

25I lay prostrate before the LORD those forty days and forty nights because the LORD had said he would destroy you. 26I prayed to the LORD and said, "O Sovereign LORD, do not destroy your people, your own inheritance that you redeemed by your great power and brought out of Egypt with a mighty hand. 27Remember your servants Abraham, Isaac and Jacob. Overlook the stubbornness of this people, their wickedness and their sin. 28Otherwise, the country from which you brought us will say, 'Because the LORD was not able to take them into the land he had promised them, and because he hated them, he brought them out to put them to death in the desert.' 29But they are your people, your inheritance that you brought out by your great power and your outstretched arm."

a15 Or And I had the two tablets of the covenant with me, one in each hand

---

▚ET'S LIVE IT!   Deuteronomy 9:7–21

OUT OF SIGHT, OUT OF MIND? ➡ Moses climbed Mount Sinai to speak with God. He was gone for 40 days. In Exodus 32 we can read about the golden calf the Israelites built and worshiped while Moses was gone. Now read Deuteronomy 9:7–21. Do you think God and Moses were angry?

Some boys and girls do things when adults aren't watching that they would never do if adults were around. Do you know any children who act that way?

Talk about this Bible story with your mom or dad. Ask how they would feel if you did something bad when they weren't there. Ask them the most important thing they want you to remember when they aren't with you.

Tablets Like the First Ones

10 At that time the LORD said to me, "Chisel out two stone tablets like the first ones and come up to me on the mountain. Also make a wooden chest.*a* ²I will write on the tablets the words that were on the first tablets, which you broke. Then you are to put them in the chest."

³So I made the ark out of acacia wood and chiseled out two stone tablets like the first ones, and I went up on the mountain with the two tablets in my hands. ⁴The LORD wrote on these tablets what he had written before, the Ten Commandments he had proclaimed to you on the mountain, out of the fire, on the day of the assembly. And the LORD gave them to me. ⁵Then I came back down the mountain and put the tablets in the ark I had made, as the LORD commanded me, and they are there now.

⁶(The Israelites traveled from the wells of the Jaakanites to Moserah. There Aaron died and was buried, and Eleazar his son succeeded him as priest. ⁷From there they traveled to Gudgodah and on to Jotbathah, a land with streams of water. ⁸At that time the LORD set apart the tribe of Levi to carry the ark of the covenant of the LORD, to stand before the LORD to minister and to pronounce blessings in his name, as they still do today. ⁹That is why the Levites have no share or inheritance among their brothers; the LORD is their inheritance, as the LORD your God told them.)

¹⁰Now I had stayed on the mountain forty days and nights, as I did the first time, and the LORD listened to me at this time also. It was not his will to destroy you. ¹¹"Go," the LORD said to me, "and lead the people on their way, so that they may enter and possess the land that I swore to their fathers to give them."

Fear the LORD

¹²And now, O Israel, what does the LORD your God ask of you but to fear the LORD your God, to walk in all his ways, to love him, to serve the LORD your God with all your heart and with all your soul, ¹³and to observe the LORD's commands and decrees that I am giving you today for your own good?

¹⁴To the LORD your God belong the heavens, even the highest heavens, the earth and everything in it. ¹⁵Yet the LORD set his affection on your forefathers and loved them, and he chose you, their descendants, above all the nations, as it is today. ¹⁶Cir-

a1 That is, an ark

Life in Bible Times

STONE TABLETS

Moses chiseled two tablets out of stone, and God wrote the Ten Commandments on them. We don't know for sure what these tablets looked like. The letters on the tablets pictured here are Hebrew. Moses put both tablets in the ark of the covenant that he had made.

cumcise your hearts, therefore, and do not be stiff-necked any longer. ¹⁷For the Lord your God is God of gods and Lord of lords, the great God, mighty and awesome, who shows no partiality and accepts no bribes. ¹⁸He defends the cause of the fatherless and the widow, and loves the alien, giving him food and clothing. ¹⁹And you are to love those who are aliens, for you yourselves were aliens in Egypt. ²⁰Fear the Lord your God and serve him. Hold fast to him and take your oaths in his name. ²¹He is your praise; he is your God, who performed for you those great and awesome wonders you saw with your own eyes. ²²Your forefathers who went down into Egypt were seventy in all, and now the Lord your God has made you as numerous as the stars in the sky.

WORDS TO REMEMBER

10:12 What does the Lord your God ask of you but to fear the Lord your God, to walk in all his ways, to love him, to serve the Lord your God with all your heart and with all your soul.

Love and Obey the Lord

11 Love the Lord your God and keep his requirements, his decrees, his laws and his commands always. ²Remember today that your children were not the ones who saw and experienced the discipline of the Lord your God: his majesty, his mighty hand, his outstretched arm; ³the signs he performed and the things he did in the heart of Egypt, both to Pharaoh king of Egypt and to his whole country; ⁴what he did to the Egyptian army, to its horses and chariots, how he overwhelmed them with the waters of the Red Sea*a* as they were pursuing you, and how the Lord brought lasting ruin on them. ⁵It was not your children who saw what he did for you in the desert until

you arrived at this place, ⁶and what he did to Dathan and Abiram, sons of Eliab the Reubenite, when the earth opened its mouth right in the middle of all Israel and swallowed them up with their households, their tents and every living thing that belonged to them. ⁷But it was your own eyes that saw all these great things the Lord has done.

⁸Observe therefore all the commands I am giving you today, so that you may have the strength to go in and take over the land that you are crossing the Jordan to possess, ⁹and so that you may live long in the land that the Lord swore to your forefathers to give to them and their descendants, a land flowing with milk and honey. ¹⁰The land you are entering to take over is not like the land of Egypt, from which you have come, where you planted your seed and irrigated it by foot as in a vegetable garden. ¹¹But the land you are crossing the Jordan to take possession of is a land of mountains and valleys that drinks rain from heaven. ¹²It is a land the Lord your God cares for; the eyes of the Lord your God are continually on it from the beginning of the year to its end.

¹³So if you faithfully obey the commands I am giving you today—to love the Lord your God and to serve him with all your heart and with all your soul— ¹⁴then I will send rain on your land in its season, both autumn and spring rains, so that you may gather in your grain, new wine and oil. ¹⁵I will provide grass in the fields for your cattle, and you will eat and be satisfied.

¹⁶Be careful, or you will be enticed to turn away and worship other gods and bow down to them. ¹⁷Then the Lord's anger will burn against you, and he will shut the heavens so that it will not rain and the ground will yield no produce, and you will soon perish from the good land the Lord is giving you. ¹⁸Fix these words of mine in your hearts and minds; tie them as

*a4 Hebrew *Yam Suph*; that is, Sea of Reeds

symbols on your hands and bind them on your foreheads. ¹⁹Teach them to your children, talking about them when you sit at home and when you walk along the road, when you lie down and when you get up. ²⁰Write them on the doorframes of your houses and on your gates, ²¹so that your days and the days of your children may be many in the land that the LORD swore to give your forefathers, as many as the days that the heavens are above the earth.

²²If you carefully observe all these commands I am giving you to follow—to love the LORD your God, to walk in all his ways and to hold fast to him— ²³then the LORD will drive out all these nations before you, and you will dispossess nations larger and stronger than you. ²⁴Every place where you set your foot will be yours: Your territory will extend from the desert to Lebanon, and from the Euphrates River to the western sea.ᵃ ²⁵No man will be able to stand against you. The LORD your God, as he promised you, will put the terror and fear of you on the whole land, wherever you go.

²⁶See, I am setting before you today a blessing and a curse— ²⁷the blessing if you obey the commands of the LORD your God that I am giving you today; ²⁸the curse if you disobey the commands of the LORD your God and turn from the way that I command you today by following other gods, which you have not known. ²⁹When the LORD your God has brought you into the land you are entering to possess, you are to proclaim on Mount Gerizim the blessings, and on Mount Ebal the curses. ³⁰As you know, these mountains are across the Jordan, west of the road,ᵇ toward the setting sun, near the great trees of Moreh, in the territory of those Canaanites living in the Arabah in the vicinity of Gilgal. ³¹You are about to cross the Jordan to enter and take possession of the land the LORD your God is giving you. When you have taken it over and are living there, ³²be sure that you obey all the decrees and laws I am setting before you today.

The One Place of Worship

12 These are the decrees and laws you must be careful to follow in the land that the LORD, the God of your fathers, has given you to

---

ᵃ24 That is, the Mediterranean   ᵇ30 Or *Jordan, westward*

Life in Bible Times

THE MEZUZAH

Deuteronomy 11:20 told the Hebrew people to write God's word on the door frames of their houses. Many copied verses of the Bible on bits of paper and put them in little boxes hung by the door. Jewish children were taught to touch this *mezuzah* (meh-ZOO-zuh) whenever they went in or out of the house, to remind them to obey the Lord.

possess—as long as you live in the land. ²Destroy completely all the places on the high mountains and on the hills and under every spreading tree where the nations you are dispossessing worship their gods. ³Break down their altars, smash their sacred stones and burn their Asherah poles in the fire; cut down the idols of their gods and wipe out their names from those places.

⁴You must not worship the LORD your God in their way. ⁵But you are to seek the place the LORD your God will choose from among all your tribes to put his Name there for his dwelling. To that place you must go; ⁶there bring your burnt offerings and sacrifices, your tithes and special gifts, what you have vowed to give and your freewill offerings, and the firstborn of your herds and flocks. ⁷There, in the presence of the LORD your God, you and your families shall eat and shall rejoice in everything you have put your hand to, because the LORD your God has blessed you.

⁸You are not to do as we do here today, everyone as he sees fit, ⁹since you have not yet reached the resting place and the inheritance the LORD your God is giving you. ¹⁰But you will cross the Jordan and settle in the land the LORD your God is giving you as an inheritance, and he will give you rest from all your enemies around you so that you will live in safety. ¹¹Then to the place the LORD your God will choose as a dwelling for his Name—there you are to bring everything I command you: your burnt offerings and sacrifices, your tithes and special gifts, and all the choice possessions you have vowed to the LORD. ¹²And there rejoice before the LORD your God, you, your sons and daughters, your menservants and maidservants, and the Levites from your towns, who have no allotment or inheritance of their own. ¹³Be careful not to sacrifice your burnt offerings anywhere you please. ¹⁴Offer them only at the place the LORD will choose in one of your tribes, and there observe everything I command you.

¹⁵Nevertheless, you may slaughter your animals in any of your towns and eat as much of the meat as you want, as if it were gazelle or deer, according to the blessing the LORD your God gives you. Both the ceremonially unclean and the clean may eat it. ¹⁶But you must not eat the blood; pour it out on the ground like water. ¹⁷You must not eat in your own towns the tithe of your grain and new wine and oil, or the firstborn of your herds and flocks, or whatever you have vowed to give, or your freewill offerings or special gifts. ¹⁸Instead, you are to eat them in the presence of the LORD your God at the place the LORD your God will choose—you, your sons and daughters, your menservants and maidservants, and the Levites from your towns—and you are to rejoice before the LORD your God in everything you put your hand to. ¹⁹Be careful not to neglect the Levites as long as you live in your land.

²⁰When the LORD your God has enlarged your territory as he promised you, and you crave meat and say, "I would like some meat," then you may eat as much of it as you want. ²¹If the place where the LORD your God chooses to put his Name is too far away from you, you may slaughter animals from the herds and flocks the LORD has given you, as I have commanded you, and in your own towns you may eat as much of them as you want. ²²Eat them as you would gazelle or deer. Both the ceremonially unclean and the clean may eat. ²³But be sure you do not eat the blood, because the blood is the life, and you must not eat the life with the meat. ²⁴You must not eat the blood; pour it out on the ground like water. ²⁵Do not eat it, so that it may go well with you and your children after you, because you will be doing what is right in the eyes of the LORD.

²⁶But take your consecrated things and whatever you have vowed to give, and go to the place the LORD will choose. ²⁷Present your burnt offerings on the altar of the LORD your God, both the meat and the blood.

The blood of your sacrifices must be poured beside the altar of the LORD your God, but you may eat the meat. 28Be careful to obey all these regulations I am giving you, so that it may always go well with you and your children after you, because you will be doing what is good and right in the eyes of the LORD your God.

29The LORD your God will cut off before you the nations you are about to invade and dispossess. But when you have driven them out and settled in their land, 30and after they have been destroyed before you, be careful not to be ensnared by inquiring about their gods, saying, "How do these nations serve their gods? We will do the same." 31You must not worship the LORD your God in their way, because in worshiping their gods, they do all kinds of detestable things the LORD hates. They even burn their sons and daughters in the fire as sacrifices to their gods.

32See that you do all I command you; do not add to it or take away from it.

Worshiping Other Gods

13 If a prophet, or one who foretells by dreams, appears among you and announces to you a miraculous sign or wonder, 2and if the sign or wonder of which he has spoken takes place, and he says, "Let us follow other gods" (gods you have not known) "and let us worship them," 3you must not listen to the words of that prophet or dreamer. The LORD your God is testing you to find out whether you love him with all your heart and with all your soul. 4It is the LORD your God you must follow, and him you must revere. Keep his commands and obey him; serve him and hold fast to him. 5That prophet or dreamer must be put to death, because he preached rebellion against the LORD your God, who brought you out of Egypt and redeemed you from the land of slavery;

he has tried to turn you from the way the LORD your God commanded you to follow. You must purge the evil from among you.

WORDS TO REMEMBER

13:4 It is the LORD your God you must follow, and him you must revere.

6If your very own brother, or your son or daughter, or the wife you love, or your closest friend secretly entices you, saying, "Let us go and worship other gods" (gods that neither you nor your fathers have known, 7gods of the peoples around you, whether near or far, from one end of the land to the other), 8do not yield to him or listen to him. Show him no pity. Do not spare him or shield him. 9You must certainly put him to death. Your hand must be the first in putting him to death, and then the hands of all the people. 10Stone him to death, because he tried to turn you away from the LORD your God, who brought you out of Egypt, out of the land of slavery. 11Then all Israel will hear and be afraid, and no one among you will do such an evil thing again.

12If you hear it said about one of the towns the LORD your God is giving you to live in 13that wicked men have arisen among you and have led the people of their town astray, saying, "Let us go and worship other gods" (gods you have not known), 14then you must inquire, probe and investigate it thoroughly. And if it is true and it has been proved that this detestable thing has been done among you, 15you must certainly put to the sword all who live in that town. Destroy it completely,ᵃ both its people and its livestock. 16Gather all the plunder of the town into the middle of the public square and completely burn the town and all its plunder as

---

ᵃ15,17 The Hebrew term refers to the irrevocable giving over of things or persons to the LORD, often by totally destroying them.

a whole burnt offering to the LORD your God. It is to remain a ruin forever, never to be rebuilt. [17]None of those condemned things[a] shall be found in your hands, so that the LORD will turn from his fierce anger; he will show you mercy, have compassion on you, and increase your numbers, as he promised on oath to your forefathers, [18]because you obey the LORD your God, keeping all his commands that I am giving you today and doing what is right in his eyes.

Clean and Unclean Food

14 You are the children of the LORD your God. Do not cut yourselves or shave the front of your heads for the dead, [2]for you are a people holy to the LORD your God. Out of all the peoples on the face of the earth, the LORD has chosen you to be his treasured possession.

[3]Do not eat any detestable thing. [4]These are the animals you may eat: the ox, the sheep, the goat, [5]the deer, the gazelle, the roe deer, the wild goat, the ibex, the antelope and the mountain sheep.[b] [6]You may eat any animal that has a split hoof divided in two and that chews the cud. [7]However, of those that chew the cud or that have a split hoof completely divided you may not eat the camel, the rabbit or the coney.[c] Although they chew the cud, they do not have a split hoof; they are ceremonially unclean for you. [8]The pig is also unclean; although it has a split hoof, it does not chew the cud. You are not to eat their meat or touch their carcasses.

[9]Of all the creatures living in the water, you may eat any that has fins and scales. [10]But anything that does not have fins and scales you may not eat; for you it is unclean.

[11]You may eat any clean bird. [12]But these you may not eat: the eagle, the vulture, the black vulture, [13]the red kite, the black kite, any kind of falcon, [14]any kind of raven, [15]the horned owl, the screech owl, the gull, any kind of hawk, [16]the little owl, the great owl, the white owl, [17]the desert owl, the osprey, the cormorant, [18]the stork, any kind of heron, the hoopoe and the bat.

[19]All flying insects that swarm are unclean to you; do not eat them. [20]But any winged creature that is clean you may eat.

[21]Do not eat anything you find already dead. You may give it to an alien living in any of your towns, and he may eat it, or you may sell it to a foreigner. But you are a people holy to the LORD your God.

Do not cook a young goat in its mother's milk.

Tithes

[22]Be sure to set aside a tenth of all that your fields produce each year. [23]Eat the tithe of your grain, new wine and oil, and the firstborn of your herds and flocks in the presence of the LORD your God at the place he will choose as a dwelling for his Name, so that you may learn to revere the LORD your God always. [24]But if that place is too distant and you have been blessed by the LORD your God and cannot carry your tithe (because the place where the LORD will choose to put his Name is so far away), [25]then exchange your tithe for silver, and take the silver with you and go to the place the LORD your God will choose. [26]Use the silver to buy whatever you like: cattle, sheep, wine or other fermented drink, or anything you wish. Then you and your household shall eat there in the presence of the LORD your God and rejoice. [27]And do not neglect the Levites living in your towns, for they have no allotment or inheritance of their own.

[28]At the end of every three years, bring all the tithes of that year's produce and store it in your towns, [29]so that the Levites (who have no allot-

---

[a]15,17 The Hebrew term refers to the irrevocable giving over of things or persons to the LORD, often by totally destroying them.   [b]5 The precise identification of some of the birds and animals in this chapter is uncertain.   [c]7 That is, the hyrax or rock badger

ment or inheritance of their own) and the aliens, the fatherless and the widows who live in your towns may come and eat and be satisfied, and so that the LORD your God may bless you in all the work of your hands.

The Year for Canceling Debts

15 At the end of every seven years you must cancel debts. ²This is how it is to be done: Every creditor shall cancel the loan he has made to his fellow Israelite. He shall not require payment from his fellow Israelite or brother, because the LORD's time for canceling debts has been proclaimed. ³You may require payment from a foreigner, but you must cancel any debt your brother owes you. ⁴However, there should be no poor among you, for in the land the LORD your God is giving you to possess as your inheritance, he will richly bless you, ⁵if only you fully obey the LORD your God and are careful to follow all these commands I am giving you today. ⁶For the LORD your God will bless you as he has promised, and you will lend to many nations but will borrow from none. You will rule over many nations but none will rule over you.

⁷If there is a poor man among your brothers in any of the towns of the land that the LORD your God is giving you, do not be hardhearted or tightfisted toward your poor brother. ⁸Rather be openhanded and freely lend him whatever he needs. ⁹Be careful not to harbor this wicked thought: "The seventh year, the year for canceling debts, is near," so that you do not show ill will toward your needy brother and give him nothing. He may then appeal to the LORD against you, and you will be found guilty of sin. ¹⁰Give generously to him and do so without a grudging heart; then because of this the LORD your God will bless you in all your work and in everything you put your hand to. ¹¹There will always be poor people in the land. Therefore I command you to be openhanded toward your brothers and toward the poor and needy in your land.

Freeing Servants

¹²If a fellow Hebrew, a man or a woman, sells himself to you and serves you six years, in the seventh year you must let him go free. ¹³And when you release him, do not send him away empty-handed. ¹⁴Supply him liberally from your flock, your threshing floor and your winepress. Give to him as the LORD your God has blessed you. ¹⁵Remember that you were slaves in Egypt and the LORD your God redeemed you. That is why I give you this command today.

¹⁶But if your servant says to you, "I do not want to leave you," because he loves you and your family and is well off with you, ¹⁷then take an awl and push it through his ear lobe into the door, and he will become your servant for life. Do the same for your maidservant.

¹⁸Do not consider it a hardship to set your servant free, because his service to you these six years has been

LET'S LIVE IT!   Deuteronomy 14:22–29

GIVING TO GOD ➡ Read Deuteronomy 14:22–29. How much did God tell the Israelites to give to the Lord? How was the money used?

Even children can give to God. Find two boxes or jars for money. Label one "giving." Label the other "spending." When you earn money or get your allowance, put some in the giving jar. How much of what you get do you think you should put in the giving jar?

Ask a leader in your church how your gifts to the Lord could be used. Draw a picture showing one of the ways the money you give can be used. Tape it to your giving jar.

worth twice as much as that of a hired hand. And the LORD your God will bless you in everything you do.

❓DID YOU KNOW?   15:12

How does God's law show that he cares about the poor?

God's law told the Israelites to lend money to the needy without charging interest. Sometimes the only way an Israelite could get out of debt was to be sold as a servant. But he or she only had to serve seven years. After that the Israelite was set free and given enough money for a new start in life. These and other laws show that God cares for the poor. If we are able, he wants us to help others.

The Firstborn Animals

19Set apart for the LORD your God every firstborn male of your herds and flocks. Do not put the firstborn of your oxen to work, and do not shear the firstborn of your sheep. 20Each year you and your family are to eat them in the presence of the LORD your God at the place he will choose. 21If an animal has a defect, is lame or blind, or has any serious flaw, you must not sacrifice it to the LORD your God. 22You are to eat it in your own towns. Both the ceremonially unclean and the clean may eat it, as if it were gazelle or deer. 23But you must not eat the blood; pour it out on the ground like water.

Passover

16 Observe the month of Abib and celebrate the Passover of the LORD your God, because in the month of Abib he brought you out of Egypt by night. 2Sacrifice as the Passover to the LORD your God an animal from your flock or herd at the place the LORD will choose as a dwelling for his Name. 3Do not eat it with bread made with yeast, but for seven days eat unleavened bread, the bread of affliction, because you left Egypt in haste—so that all the days of your life you may remember the time of your departure from Egypt. 4Let no yeast be found in your possession in all your land for seven days. Do not let any of the meat you sacrifice on the evening of the first day remain until morning.

5You must not sacrifice the Passover in any town the LORD your God gives you 6except in the place he will choose as a dwelling for his Name. There you must sacrifice the Passover in the evening, when the sun goes down, on the anniversary*a* of your departure from Egypt. 7Roast it and eat it at the place the LORD your God will choose. Then in the morning return to your tents. 8For six days eat unleavened bread and on the seventh day hold an assembly to the LORD your God and do no work.

Feast of Weeks

9Count off seven weeks from the time you begin to put the sickle to the standing grain. 10Then celebrate the Feast of Weeks to the LORD your God by giving a freewill offering in proportion to the blessings the LORD your God has given you. 11And rejoice before the LORD your God at the place he will choose as a dwelling for his Name—you, your sons and daughters, your menservants and maidservants, the Levites in your towns, and the aliens, the fatherless and the widows living among you. 12Remember that you were slaves in Egypt, and follow carefully these decrees.

Feast of Tabernacles

13Celebrate the Feast of Tabernacles for seven days after you have gathered the produce of your threshing floor and your winepress. 14Be joyful at your Feast—you, your sons and daughters, your menservants and maidservants, and the Levites, the aliens, the fatherless and the wid-

---

a6 Or down, at the time of day

ows who live in your towns. [15]For seven days celebrate the Feast to the LORD your God at the place the LORD will choose. For the LORD your God will bless you in all your harvest and in all the work of your hands, and your joy will be complete.

[16]Three times a year all your men must appear before the LORD your God at the place he will choose: at the Feast of Unleavened Bread, the Feast of Weeks and the Feast of Tabernacles. No man should appear before the LORD empty-handed: [17]Each of you must bring a gift in proportion to the way the LORD your God has blessed you.

❓DID YOU KNOW?   16:16

What three feasts were all Israelites to celebrate together?

All Israelites were to gather in one place to celebrate the feasts of Passover, Weeks, and Tabernacles. Deuteronomy 16 says these religious holidays were to be celebrated in a place God would choose later. The place God chose was Jerusalem, which King David made Israel's capital about four hundred years after Moses died.

Judges

[18]Appoint judges and officials for each of your tribes in every town the LORD your God is giving you, and they shall judge the people fairly. [19]Do not pervert justice or show partiality. Do not accept a bribe, for a bribe blinds the eyes of the wise and twists the words of the righteous. [20]Follow justice and justice alone, so that you may live and possess the land the LORD your God is giving you.

Worshiping Other Gods

[21]Do not set up any wooden Asherah pole[a] beside the altar you build

to the LORD your God, [22]and do not erect a sacred stone, for these the LORD your God hates.

17 Do not sacrifice to the LORD your God an ox or a sheep that has any defect or flaw in it, for that would be detestable to him.

[2]If a man or woman living among you in one of the towns the LORD gives you is found doing evil in the eyes of the LORD your God in violation of his covenant, [3]and contrary to my command has worshiped other gods, bowing down to them or to the sun or the moon or the stars of the sky, [4]and this has been brought to your attention, then you must investigate it thoroughly. If it is true and it has been proved that this detestable thing has been done in Israel, [5]take the man or woman who has done this evil deed to your city gate and stone that person to death. [6]On the testimony of two or three witnesses a man shall be put to death, but no one shall be put to death on the testimony of only one witness. [7]The hands of the witnesses must be the first in putting him to death, and then the hands of all the people. You must purge the evil from among you.

Law Courts

[8]If cases come before your courts that are too difficult for you to judge—whether bloodshed, lawsuits or assaults—take them to the place the LORD your God will choose. [9]Go to the priests, who are Levites, and to the judge who is in office at that time. Inquire of them and they will give you the verdict. [10]You must act according to the decisions they give you at the place the LORD will choose. Be careful to do everything they direct you to do. [11]Act according to the law they teach you and the decisions they give you. Do not turn aside from what they tell you, to the right or to the left. [12]The man who shows contempt for the judge or for the priest who stands ministering there to the LORD your God must be put to death. You

---

a21 Or Do not plant any tree dedicated to Asherah

must purge the evil from Israel. [13]All the people will hear and be afraid, and will not be contemptuous again.

The King

[14]When you enter the land the LORD your God is giving you and have taken possession of it and settled in it, and you say, "Let us set a king over us like all the nations around us," [15]be sure to appoint over you the king the LORD your God chooses. He must be from among your own brothers. Do not place a foreigner over you, one who is not a brother Israelite. [16]The king, moreover, must not acquire great numbers of horses for himself or make the people return to Egypt to get more of them, for the LORD has told you, "You are not to go back that way again." [17]He must not take many wives, or his heart will be led astray. He must not accumulate large amounts of silver and gold.

[18]When he takes the throne of his kingdom, he is to write for himself on a scroll a copy of this law, taken from that of the priests, who are Levites. [19]It is to be with him, and he is to read it all the days of his life so that he may learn to revere the LORD his God and follow carefully all the words of this law and these decrees [20]and not consider himself better than his brothers and turn from the law to the right or to the left. Then he and his descendants will reign a long time over his kingdom in Israel.

Offerings for Priests and Levites

18 The priests, who are Levites —indeed the whole tribe of Levi—are to have no allotment or inheritance with Israel. They shall live on the offerings made to the LORD by fire, for that is their inheritance. [2]They shall have no inheritance among their brothers; the LORD is their inheritance, as he promised them.

[3]This is the share due the priests from the people who sacrifice a bull or a sheep: the shoulder, the jowls and the inner parts. [4]You are to give them the firstfruits of your grain, new wine and oil, and the first wool from the shearing of your sheep, [5]for the LORD your God has chosen them and their descendants out of all your tribes to stand and minister in the LORD's name always.

[6]If a Levite moves from one of your towns anywhere in Israel where he is living, and comes in all earnestness to the place the LORD will choose, [7]he may minister in the name of the LORD his God like all his fellow Levites who serve there in the presence of the LORD. [8]He is to share equally in their benefits, even though he has received money from the sale of family possessions.

Detestable Practices

[9]When you enter the land the LORD your God is giving you, do not learn to imitate the detestable ways of the nations there. [10]Let no one be found among you who sacrifices his son or daughter in*a* the fire, who practices divination or sorcery, interprets omens, engages in witchcraft, [11]or casts spells, or who is a medium or spiritist or who consults the dead. [12]Anyone who does these things is detestable to the LORD, and because of these detestable practices the LORD your God will drive out those nations before you. [13]You must be blameless before the LORD your God.

The Prophet

[14]The nations you will dispossess listen to those who practice sorcery or divination. But as for you, the LORD your God has not permitted you to do so. [15]The LORD your God will raise up for you a prophet like me from among your own brothers. You must listen to him. [16]For this is what you asked of the LORD your God at Horeb on the day of the assembly when you said, "Let us not hear the voice of the LORD our God nor see this great fire anymore, or we will die."

[17]The LORD said to me: "What they

---

a10 Or *who makes his son or daughter pass through*

say is good. [18]I will raise up for them a prophet like you from among their brothers; I will put my words in his mouth, and he will tell them everything I command him. [19]If anyone does not listen to my words that the prophet speaks in my name, I myself will call him to account. [20]But a prophet who presumes to speak in my name anything I have not commanded him to say, or a prophet who speaks in the name of other gods, must be put to death."

[21]You may say to yourselves, "How can we know when a message has not been spoken by the LORD?" [22]If what a prophet proclaims in the name of the LORD does not take place or come true, that is a message the LORD has not spoken. That prophet has spoken presumptuously. Do not be afraid of him.

Cities of Refuge

19 When the LORD your God has destroyed the nations whose land he is giving you, and when you have driven them out and settled in their towns and houses, [2]then set aside for yourselves three cities centrally located in the land the LORD your God is giving you to possess. [3]Build roads to them and divide into three parts the land the LORD your God is giving you as an inheritance, so that anyone who kills a man may flee there.

[4]This is the rule concerning the man who kills another and flees there to save his life—one who kills his neighbor unintentionally, without malice aforethought. [5]For instance, a man may go into the forest with his neighbor to cut wood, and as he swings his ax to fell a tree, the head may fly off and hit his neighbor and kill him. That man may flee to one of these cities and save his life. [6]Otherwise, the avenger of blood might pursue him in a rage, overtake him if the distance is too great, and kill him even though he is not deserving of death, since he did it to his neighbor without malice aforethought. [7]This is why I command you to set aside for yourselves three cities.

[8]If the LORD your God enlarges your territory, as he promised on oath to your forefathers, and gives you the whole land he promised them, [9]because you carefully follow all these laws I command you today —to love the LORD your God and to walk always in his ways—then you are to set aside three more cities. [10]Do this so that innocent blood will not be shed in your land, which the LORD your God is giving you as your inheritance, and so that you will not be guilty of bloodshed.

[11]But if a man hates his neighbor and lies in wait for him, assaults and kills him, and then flees to one of these cities, [12]the elders of his town shall send for him, bring him back from the city, and hand him over to the avenger of blood to die. [13]Show him no pity. You must purge from Israel the guilt of shedding innocent

---

LET'S LIVE IT!

Deuteronomy 18:9–13

GOOD MOVIES? ⇒ Some people like horror movies about people possessed by demons or about witches who can hurt someone by sticking pins in a doll.

In Moses' time, in the land of Canaan, there were real witches! Read Deuteronomy 18:9–13 to see what God said about them.

Now talk over these questions, first with a friend, then with an adult: Is it good to watch horror movies with pretend supernatural things in them? Would it be all right to watch them on TV or the VCR? Would God want us to watch things he says are evil, even if we don't plan to do such things ourselves? Why, or why not?

blood, so that it may go well with you.

¹⁴Do not move your neighbor's boundary stone set up by your predecessors in the inheritance you receive in the land the LORD your God is giving you to possess.

Witnesses

¹⁵One witness is not enough to convict a man accused of any crime or offense he may have committed. A matter must be established by the testimony of two or three witnesses.

¹⁶If a malicious witness takes the stand to accuse a man of a crime, ¹⁷the two men involved in the dispute must stand in the presence of the LORD before the priests and the judges who are in office at the time. ¹⁸The judges must make a thorough investigation, and if the witness proves to be a liar, giving false testimony against his brother, ¹⁹then do to him as he intended to do to his brother. You must purge the evil from among you. ²⁰The rest of the people will hear of this and be afraid, and never again will such an evil thing be done among you. ²¹Show no pity: life for life, eye for eye, tooth for tooth, hand for hand, foot for foot.

Going to War

20 When you go to war against your enemies and see horses and chariots and an army greater than yours, do not be afraid of them, because the LORD your God, who brought you up out of Egypt, will be with you. ²When you are about to go into battle, the priest shall come forward and address the army. ³He shall say: "Hear, O Israel, today you are going into battle against your enemies. Do not be fainthearted or afraid; do not be terrified or give way to panic before them. ⁴For the LORD your God is the one who goes with you to fight for you against your enemies to give you victory."

⁵The officers shall say to the army: "Has anyone built a new house and not dedicated it? Let him go home, or

he may die in battle and someone else may dedicate it. ⁶Has anyone planted a vineyard and not begun to enjoy it? Let him go home, or he may die in battle and someone else enjoy it. ⁷Has anyone become pledged to a woman and not married her? Let him go home, or he may die in battle and someone else marry her." ⁸Then the officers shall add, "Is any man afraid or fainthearted? Let him go home so that his brothers will not become disheartened too." ⁹When the officers have finished speaking to the army, they shall appoint commanders over it.

❓DID YOU KNOW?   20:5–8

Who did not have to fight if Israel went to war?

When Israel went to war, men who had just married or built a new house were sent home. Men who were afraid were also told to go home. Men with new vineyards were not required to go to war either.

¹⁰When you march up to attack a city, make its people an offer of peace. ¹¹If they accept and open their gates, all the people in it shall be subject to forced labor and shall work for you. ¹²If they refuse to make peace and they engage you in battle, lay siege to that city. ¹³When the LORD your God delivers it into your hand, put to the sword all the men in it. ¹⁴As for the women, the children, the livestock and everything else in the city, you may take these as plunder for yourselves. And you may use the plunder the LORD your God gives you from your enemies. ¹⁵This is how you are to treat all the cities that are at a distance from you and do not belong to the nations nearby.

¹⁶However, in the cities of the nations the LORD your God is giving you as an inheritance, do not leave alive anything that breathes. ¹⁷Complete-

ly destroy*a* them—the Hittites, Amorites, Canaanites, Perizzites, Hivites and Jebusites—as the Lord your God has commanded you. 18Otherwise, they will teach you to follow all the detestable things they do in worshiping their gods, and you will sin against the Lord your God.

19When you lay siege to a city for a long time, fighting against it to capture it, do not destroy its trees by putting an ax to them, because you can eat their fruit. Do not cut them down. Are the trees of the field people, that you should besiege them?*b* 20However, you may cut down trees that you know are not fruit trees and use them to build siege works until the city at war with you falls.

Atonement for an Unsolved Murder

21 If a man is found slain, lying in a field in the land the Lord your God is giving you to possess, and it is not known who killed him, 2your elders and judges shall go out and measure the distance from the body to the neighboring towns. 3Then the elders of the town nearest the body shall take a heifer that has never been worked and has never worn a yoke 4and lead her down to a valley that has not been plowed or planted and where there is a flowing stream. There in the valley they are to break the heifer's neck. 5The priests, the sons of Levi, shall step forward, for the Lord your God has chosen them to minister and to pronounce blessings in the name of the Lord and to decide all cases of dispute and assault. 6Then all the elders of the town nearest the body shall wash their hands over the heifer whose neck was broken in the valley, 7and they shall declare: "Our hands did not shed this blood, nor did our eyes see it done. 8Accept this atonement for your people Israel, whom you have redeemed, O Lord, and do not hold your people

guilty of the blood of an innocent man." And the bloodshed will be atoned for. 9So you will purge from yourselves the guilt of shedding innocent blood, since you have done what is right in the eyes of the Lord.

Marrying a Captive Woman

10When you go to war against your enemies and the Lord your God delivers them into your hands and you take captives, 11if you notice among the captives a beautiful woman and are attracted to her, you may take her as your wife. 12Bring her into your home and have her shave her head, trim her nails 13and put aside the clothes she was wearing when captured. After she has lived in your house and mourned her father and mother for a full month, then you may go to her and be her husband and she shall be your wife. 14If you are not pleased with her, let her go wherever she wishes. You must not sell her or treat her as a slave, since you have dishonored her.

The Right of the Firstborn

15If a man has two wives, and he loves one but not the other, and both bear him sons but the firstborn is the son of the wife he does not love, 16when he wills his property to his sons, he must not give the rights of the firstborn to the son of the wife he loves in preference to his actual firstborn, the son of the wife he does not love. 17He must acknowledge the son of his unloved wife as the firstborn by giving him a double share of all he has. That son is the first sign of his father's strength. The right of the firstborn belongs to him.

A Rebellious Son

18If a man has a stubborn and rebellious son who does not obey his father and mother and will not listen to them when they discipline him, 19his father and mother shall take hold of

---

a17 The Hebrew term refers to the irrevocable giving over of things or persons to the Lord, often by totally destroying them.   *b19* Or *down to use in the siege, for the fruit trees are for the benefit of man.*

him and bring him to the elders at the gate of his town. ²⁰They shall say to the elders, "This son of ours is stubborn and rebellious. He will not obey us. He is a profligate and a drunkard." ²¹Then all the men of his town shall stone him to death. You must purge the evil from among you. All Israel will hear of it and be afraid.

Various Laws

²²If a man guilty of a capital offense is put to death and his body is hung on a tree, ²³you must not leave his body on the tree overnight. Be sure to bury him that same day, because anyone who is hung on a tree is under God's curse. You must not desecrate the land the LORD your God is giving you as an inheritance.

22 If you see your brother's ox or sheep straying, do not ignore it but be sure to take it back to him. ²If the brother does not live near you or if you do not know who he is, take it home with you and keep it until he comes looking for it. Then give it back to him. ³Do the same if you find your brother's donkey or his cloak or anything he loses. Do not ignore it.

⁴If you see your brother's donkey or his ox fallen on the road, do not ignore it. Help him get it to its feet.

⁵A woman must not wear men's clothing, nor a man wear women's clothing, for the LORD your God detests anyone who does this.

⁶If you come across a bird's nest beside the road, either in a tree or on the ground, and the mother is sitting on the young or on the eggs, do not take the mother with the young. ⁷You may take the young, but be sure to let the mother go, so that it may go well with you and you may have a long life.

⁸When you build a new house, make a parapet around your roof so that you may not bring the guilt of bloodshed on your house if someone falls from the roof.

⁹Do not plant two kinds of seed in your vineyard; if you do, not only the crops you plant but also the fruit of the vineyard will be defiled.ᵃ

¹⁰Do not plow with an ox and a donkey yoked together.

¹¹Do not wear clothes of wool and linen woven together.

¹²Make tassels on the four corners of the cloak you wear.

Marriage Violations

¹³If a man takes a wife and, after lying with her, dislikes her ¹⁴and slanders her and gives her a bad name, saying, "I married this woman, but when I approached her, I did not find proof of her virginity," ¹⁵then the girl's father and mother shall bring proof that she was a virgin to the town elders at the gate. ¹⁶The girl's father will say to the elders, "I gave my daughter in marriage to this man, but he dislikes her. ¹⁷Now he has slandered her and said, 'I did not find your daughter to be a virgin.' But here is the proof of my daughter's virginity." Then her parents shall display the cloth before the elders of the town, ¹⁸and the elders shall take the man and punish him. ¹⁹They shall fine him a hundred shekels of silverᵇ and give them to the girl's father, because this man has given an Israelite virgin a bad name. She shall continue to be his wife; he must not divorce her as long as he lives.

²⁰If, however, the charge is true and no proof of the girl's virginity can be found, ²¹she shall be brought to the door of her father's house and there the men of her town shall stone her to death. She has done a disgraceful thing in Israel by being promiscuous while still in her father's house. You must purge the evil from among you.

²²If a man is found sleeping with another man's wife, both the man who slept with her and the woman must die. You must purge the evil from Israel.

²³If a man happens to meet in a town a virgin pledged to be married and he sleeps with her, ²⁴you shall take both of them to the gate of that

---

ᵃ9 Or *be forfeited to the sanctuary*   ᵇ19 That is, about 2 1/2 pounds (about 1 kilogram)

ABOUT THE

Bible

QUESTION: What is the Bible?
ANSWER: The Bible is a book that tells us about God.

It shows us what he is like,
    what he has done and
        what he wants us to do.
It tells us about ourselves — about how God made us and about how sin came into the world.
It tells us about Jesus, who came to show us how much God loves us and wants to forgive our sins.

QUESTION: How was the Bible written?
ANSWER: The simplest answer is: God wrote the Bible.

But he used humans to write down what he wanted us to know.
    We can trust God that he worked in the writers
        so that they wrote down what is really God's Word,
            even though God let each writer use
                his own personality and style.

QUESTION: Who are these people who wrote the Bible?
ANSWER: The people who wrote the Bible lived a long time ago.

Some, like Moses, lived as long ago as 3,500 years.
    Others, like John, lived about 1,900 years ago.
In lots of ways they were people just like we are...
    people who had doubts,
        people who did some bad things and some good things.
God used them to write down words that tell us about him and his love for us.

QUESTION: Why is the Bible important for me?
ANSWER: The Bible is one of the most important ways that God uses to talk to you and let you know that he is real.

The Bible is more than just a bunch of old stories about some people who lived a long time ago.
    It is God's love letter to you,
        assuring you that he is interested in you
            and will take care of you every day.

About the Old Testament Books

THE PENTATEUCH

The first five books of the Old Testament are called the Pentateuch, meaning "five books." These books cover the creation of the world and the beginning of the nation of Israel.

GENESIS
EXODUS
LEVITICUS
NUMBERS
DEUTERONOMY

HISTORY

Many years of Jewish history are covered in these history books of the Bible. Some of the best stories ever written can be found in these books.

JOSHUA
JUDGES
RUTH
1, 2 SAMUEL
1, 2 KINGS
1, 2 CHRONICLES
EZRA
NEHEMIAH
ESTHER

POETRY

Hebrew poetry was not written exactly like English poetry but is still very beautiful. These writers used poetry to express many feelings, from sadness to happiness, from fear to praise to God for his protection and love.

JOB
PSALMS
PROVERBS
ECCLESIASTES
SONG OF SONGS
LAMENTATIONS

PROPHECY

God spoke to Israel through men called prophets. Their stories, and the messages they gave Israel from God, are found in these books.

ISAIAH
JEREMIAH
EZEKIEL
DANIEL
HOSEA
JOEL
AMOS
OBADIAH
JONAH
MICAH
NAHUM
HABAKKUK
ZEPHANIAH
HAGGAI
ZECHARIAH
MALACHI

town and stone them to death—the girl because she was in a town and did not scream for help, and the man because he violated another man's wife. You must purge the evil from among you.

25But if out in the country a man happens to meet a girl pledged to be married and rapes her, only the man who has done this shall die. 26Do nothing to the girl; she has committed no sin deserving death. This case is like that of someone who attacks and murders his neighbor, 27for the man found the girl out in the country, and though the betrothed girl screamed, there was no one to rescue her.

28If a man happens to meet a virgin who is not pledged to be married and rapes her and they are discovered, 29he shall pay the girl's father fifty shekels of silver.*a* He must marry the girl, for he has violated her. He can never divorce her as long as he lives.

30A man is not to marry his father's wife; he must not dishonor his father's bed.

Exclusion From the Assembly

23 No one who has been emasculated by crushing or cutting may enter the assembly of the LORD.

2No one born of a forbidden marriage*b* nor any of his descendants may enter the assembly of the LORD, even down to the tenth generation.

3No Ammonite or Moabite or any of his descendants may enter the assembly of the LORD, even down to the tenth generation. 4For they did not come to meet you with bread and water on your way when you came out of Egypt, and they hired Balaam son of Beor from Pethor in Aram Naharaim*c* to pronounce a curse on you. 5However, the LORD your God would not listen to Balaam but turned the curse into a blessing for you, because the LORD your God loves you. 6Do not

seek a treaty of friendship with them as long as you live.

7Do not abhor an Edomite, for he is your brother. Do not abhor an Egyptian, because you lived as an alien in his country. 8The third generation of children born to them may enter the assembly of the LORD.

Uncleanness in the Camp

9When you are encamped against your enemies, keep away from everything impure. 10If one of your men is unclean because of a nocturnal emission, he is to go outside the camp and stay there. 11But as evening approaches he is to wash himself, and at sunset he may return to the camp.

12Designate a place outside the camp where you can go to relieve yourself. 13As part of your equipment have something to dig with, and when you relieve yourself, dig a hole and cover up your excrement. 14For the LORD your God moves about in your camp to protect you and to deliver your enemies to you. Your camp must be holy, so that he will not see among you anything indecent and turn away from you.

Miscellaneous Laws

15If a slave has taken refuge with you, do not hand him over to his master. 16Let him live among you wherever he likes and in whatever town he chooses. Do not oppress him.

17No Israelite man or woman is to become a shrine prostitute. 18You must not bring the earnings of a female prostitute or of a male prostitute*d* into the house of the LORD your God to pay any vow, because the LORD your God detests them both.

19Do not charge your brother interest, whether on money or food or anything else that may earn interest. 20You may charge a foreigner interest, but not a brother Israelite, so that the LORD your God may bless you in everything you put your hand

---

a29 That is, about 1 1/4 pounds (about 0.6 kilogram) is, Northwest Mesopotamia   *b2* Or *one of illegitimate birth*   *c4* That   *d18* Hebrew *of a dog*

to in the land you are entering to possess.

21If you make a vow to the LORD your God, do not be slow to pay it, for the LORD your God will certainly demand it of you and you will be guilty of sin. 22But if you refrain from making a vow, you will not be guilty. 23Whatever your lips utter you must be sure to do, because you made your vow freely to the LORD your God with your own mouth.

24If you enter your neighbor's vineyard, you may eat all the grapes you want, but do not put any in your basket. 25If you enter your neighbor's grainfield, you may pick kernels with your hands, but you must not put a sickle to his standing grain.

24 If a man marries a woman who becomes displeasing to him because he finds something indecent about her, and he writes her a certificate of divorce, gives it to her and sends her from his house, 2and if after she leaves his house she becomes the wife of another man, 3and her second husband dislikes her and writes her a certificate of divorce, gives it to her and sends her from his house, or if he dies, 4then her first husband, who divorced her, is not allowed to marry her again after she has been defiled. That would be detestable in the eyes of the LORD. Do not bring sin upon the land the LORD your God is giving you as an inheritance.

5If a man has recently married, he must not be sent to war or have any other duty laid on him. For one year he is to be free to stay at home and bring happiness to the wife he has married.

6Do not take a pair of millstones —not even the upper one—as security for a debt, because that would be taking a man's livelihood as security.

7If a man is caught kidnapping one of his brother Israelites and treats him as a slave or sells him, the kidnapper must die. You must purge the evil from among you.

8In cases of leprous*a* diseases be very careful to do exactly as the priests, who are Levites, instruct you. You must follow carefully what I have commanded them. 9Remember what the LORD your God did to Miriam along the way after you came out of Egypt.

10When you make a loan of any kind to your neighbor, do not go into his house to get what he is offering as a pledge. 11Stay outside and let the man to whom you are making the loan bring the pledge out to you. 12If the man is poor, do not go to sleep with his pledge in your possession. 13Return his cloak to him by sunset so that he may sleep in it. Then he will thank you, and it will be regarded as a righteous act in the sight of the LORD your God.

14Do not take advantage of a hired man who is poor and needy, whether he is a brother Israelite or an alien living in one of your towns. 15Pay him his wages each day before sunset, because he is poor and is counting on it. Otherwise he may cry to the LORD against you, and you will be guilty of sin.

16Fathers shall not be put to death for their children, nor children put to death for their fathers; each is to die for his own sin.

17Do not deprive the alien or the fatherless of justice, or take the cloak of the widow as a pledge. 18Remember that you were slaves in Egypt and the LORD your God redeemed you from there. That is why I command you to do this.

19When you are harvesting in your field and you overlook a sheaf, do not go back to get it. Leave it for the alien, the fatherless and the widow, so that the LORD your God may bless you in all the work of your hands. 20When you beat the olives from your trees, do not go over the branches a second time. Leave what remains for the alien, the fatherless and the widow. 21When you harvest the grapes in your vineyard, do not go over the

---

*a8 The Hebrew word was used for various diseases affecting the skin—not necessarily leprosy.

vines again. Leave what remains for the alien, the fatherless and the widow. [22]Remember that you were slaves in Egypt. That is why I command you to do this.

25 When men have a dispute, they are to take it to court and the judges will decide the case, acquitting the innocent and condemning the guilty. [2]If the guilty man deserves to be beaten, the judge shall make him lie down and have him flogged in his presence with the number of lashes his crime deserves, [3]but he must not give him more than forty lashes. If he is flogged more than that, your brother will be degraded in your eyes.

[4]Do not muzzle an ox while it is treading out the grain.

[5]If brothers are living together and one of them dies without a son, his widow must not marry outside the family. Her husband's brother shall take her and marry her and fulfill the duty of a brother-in-law to her. [6]The first son she bears shall carry on the name of the dead brother so that his name will not be blotted out from Israel.

[7]However, if a man does not want to marry his brother's wife, she shall go to the elders at the town gate and say, "My husband's brother refuses to carry on his brother's name in Israel. He will not fulfill the duty of a brother-in-law to me." [8]Then the elders of his town shall summon him and talk to him. If he persists in saying, "I do not want to marry her," [9]his brother's widow shall go up to him in the presence of the elders, take off one of his sandals, spit in his face and say, "This is what is done to the man who will not build up his brother's family line." [10]That man's line shall be known in Israel as The Family of the Unsandaled.

[11]If two men are fighting and the wife of one of them comes to rescue her husband from his assailant, and she reaches out and seizes him by his private parts, [12]you shall cut off her hand. Show her no pity.

[13]Do not have two differing weights in your bag—one heavy, one light. [14]Do not have two differing measures in your house—one large, one small. [15]You must have accurate and honest weights and measures, so that you may live long in the land the LORD your God is giving you. [16]For the LORD your God detests anyone who does these things, anyone who deals dishonestly.

[17]Remember what the Amalekites did to you along the way when you came out of Egypt. [18]When you were weary and worn out, they met you on your journey and cut off all who were lagging behind; they had no fear of God. [19]When the LORD your God gives you rest from all the enemies around you in the land he is giving you to possess as an inheritance, you shall blot out the memory of Amalek from under heaven. Do not forget!

Firstfruits and Tithes

26 When you have entered the land the LORD your God is giving you as an inheritance and have taken possession of it and settled in it, [2]take some of the firstfruits of all that you produce from the soil of the land the LORD your God is giving you and put them in a basket. Then go to the place the LORD your God will choose as a dwelling for his Name [3]and say to the priest in office at the time, "I declare today to the LORD your God that I have come to the land the LORD swore to our forefathers to give us." [4]The priest shall take the basket from your hands and set it down in front of the altar of the LORD your God. [5]Then you shall declare before the LORD your God: "My father was a wandering Aramean, and he went down into Egypt with a few people and lived there and became a great nation, powerful and numerous. [6]But the Egyptians mistreated us and made us suffer, putting us to hard labor. [7]Then we cried out to the LORD, the God of our fathers, and the LORD heard our voice and saw our misery, toil and oppression. [8]So the LORD brought us out of Egypt with a mighty hand and an outstretched arm, with great terror and with miraculous signs and wonders. [9]He brought us to this place and gave us this land, a land flowing with milk and honey; [10]and now I bring the firstfruits of the soil that you, O LORD, have given me." Place the basket before the LORD your God and bow down before him. [11]And you and the Levites and the aliens among you shall rejoice in all the good things the LORD your God has given to you and your household.

❓DID YOU KNOW?   26:12

What were tithes, and what were they used for?

The tithe for an Israelite was 10% of their crops or income. For two years, the tithe was to be taken to the tabernacle or temple. It was used to support the Levites and priests who served God. The third year, the tithe was stored in each town and used to feed the poor.

---

[12]When you have finished setting aside a tenth of all your produce in the third year, the year of the tithe, you shall give it to the Levite, the alien, the fatherless and the widow, so that they may eat in your towns and be satisfied. [13]Then say to the LORD your God: "I have removed from my house the sacred portion and have given it to the Levite, the alien, the fatherless and the widow, according to all you commanded. I have not turned aside from your commands nor have I forgotten any of them. [14]I have not eaten any of the sacred portion while I was in mourning, nor have I removed any of it while I was unclean, nor have I offered any of it to the dead. I have obeyed the LORD my God; I have done everything you commanded me. [15]Look down from heaven, your holy dwelling place, and bless your people Israel and the

land you have given us as you promised on oath to our forefathers, a land flowing with milk and honey."

Follow the LORD's Commands

[16]The LORD your God commands you this day to follow these decrees and laws; carefully observe them with all your heart and with all your soul. [17]You have declared this day that the LORD is your God and that you will walk in his ways, that you will keep his decrees, commands and laws, and that you will obey him. [18]And the LORD has declared this day that you are his people, his treasured possession as he promised, and that you are to keep all his commands. [19]He has declared that he will set you in praise, fame and honor high above all the nations he has made and that you will be a people holy to the LORD your God, as he promised.

The Altar on Mount Ebal

27 Moses and the elders of Israel commanded the people: "Keep all these commands that I give you today. [2]When you have crossed the Jordan into the land the LORD your God is giving you, set up some large stones and coat them with plaster. [3]Write on them all the words of this law when you have crossed over to enter the land the LORD your God is giving you, a land flowing with milk and honey, just as the LORD, the God of your fathers, promised you. [4]And when you have crossed the Jordan, set up these stones on Mount Ebal, as I command you today, and coat them with plaster. [5]Build there an altar to the LORD your God, an altar of stones. Do not use any iron tool upon them. [6]Build the altar of the LORD your God with fieldstones and offer burnt offerings on it to the LORD your God. [7]Sacrifice fellowship offerings[a] there, eating them and rejoicing in the presence of the LORD your God. [8]And you shall write very clearly all the words of this law on these stones you have set up."

---

[a]7 Traditionally *peace offerings*

Curses From Mount Ebal

⁹Then Moses and the priests, who are Levites, said to all Israel, "Be silent, O Israel, and listen! You have now become the people of the LORD your God. ¹⁰Obey the LORD your God and follow his commands and decrees that I give you today."

¹¹On the same day Moses commanded the people:

¹²When you have crossed the Jordan, these tribes shall stand on Mount Gerizim to bless the people: Simeon, Levi, Judah, Issachar, Joseph and Benjamin. ¹³And these tribes shall stand on Mount Ebal to pronounce curses: Reuben, Gad, Asher, Zebulun, Dan and Naphtali.

¹⁴The Levites shall recite to all the people of Israel in a loud voice:

¹⁵"Cursed is the man who carves an image or casts an idol—a thing detestable to the LORD, the work of the craftsman's hands—and sets it up in secret."

Then all the people shall say,
"Amen!"

¹⁶"Cursed is the man who dishonors his father or his mother."

Then all the people shall say,
"Amen!"

¹⁷"Cursed is the man who moves his neighbor's boundary stone."

Then all the people shall say,
"Amen!"

¹⁸"Cursed is the man who leads the blind astray on the road."

Then all the people shall say,
"Amen!"

¹⁹"Cursed is the man who withholds justice from the alien, the fatherless or the widow."

Then all the people shall say,
"Amen!"

²⁰"Cursed is the man who sleeps with his father's wife, for he dishonors his father's bed."

Then all the people shall say,
"Amen!"

²¹"Cursed is the man who has sexual relations with any animal."

Then all the people shall say,
"Amen!"

²²"Cursed is the man who sleeps with his sister, the daughter of his father or the daughter of his mother."

Then all the people shall say,
"Amen!"

²³"Cursed is the man who sleeps with his mother-in-law."

Then all the people shall say,
"Amen!"

²⁴"Cursed is the man who kills his neighbor secretly."

Then all the people shall say,
"Amen!"

²⁵"Cursed is the man who accepts a bribe to kill an innocent person."

Then all the people shall say,
"Amen!"

²⁶"Cursed is the man who does not uphold the words of this law by carrying them out."

Then all the people shall say,
"Amen!"

Blessings for Obedience

28 If you fully obey the LORD your God and carefully follow all his commands I give you today, the LORD your God will set you high above all the nations on earth. ²All these blessings will come upon you and accompany you if you obey the LORD your God:

³You will be blessed in the city and blessed in the country.

⁴The fruit of your womb will be blessed, and the crops of your land and the young of your livestock—the calves of your herds and the lambs of your flocks.

⁵Your basket and your kneading trough will be blessed.

⁶You will be blessed when you come in and blessed when you go out.

⁷The LORD will grant that the enemies who rise up against you will be

defeated before you. They will come at you from one direction but flee from you in seven.

8The LORD will send a blessing on your barns and on everything you put your hand to. The LORD your God will bless you in the land he is giving you.

9The LORD will establish you as his holy people, as he promised you on oath, if you keep the commands of the LORD your God and walk in his ways. 10Then all the peoples on earth will see that you are called by the name of the LORD, and they will fear you. 11The LORD will grant you abundant prosperity—in the fruit of your womb, the young of your livestock and the crops of your ground—in the land he swore to your forefathers to give you.

12The LORD will open the heavens, the storehouse of his bounty, to send rain on your land in season and to bless all the work of your hands. You will lend to many nations but will borrow from none. 13The LORD will make you the head, not the tail. If you pay attention to the commands of the LORD your God that I give you this day and carefully follow them, you will always be at the top, never at the bottom. 14Do not turn aside from any of the commands I give you today, to the right or to the left, following other gods and serving them.

Curses for Disobedience

15However, if you do not obey the LORD your God and do not carefully follow all his commands and decrees I am giving you today, all these curses will come upon you and over-take you:

16You will be cursed in the city and cursed in the country.

17Your basket and your kneading trough will be cursed.

18The fruit of your womb will be cursed, and the crops of your land, and the calves of your herds and the lambs of your flocks.

19You will be cursed when you come in and cursed when you go out.

? DID YOU KNOW?   28:1,15

What difference did it make if the Israelites obeyed God or disobeyed him?

Deuteronomy 28 tells how God would bless the Israelites if they obeyed him. It also tells how God would punish Israel if they dis-obeyed. It really did make a differ-ence if they obeyed God.

20The LORD will send on you curses, confusion and rebuke in everything you put your hand to, until you are destroyed and come to sudden ruin because of the evil you have done in forsaking him.a 21The LORD will plague you with diseases until he has destroyed you from the land you are entering to possess. 22The LORD will strike you with wasting disease, with fever and inflammation, with scorch-ing heat and drought, with blight and mildew, which will plague you until you perish. 23The sky over your head will be bronze, the ground beneath you iron. 24The LORD will turn the rain of your country into dust and powder; it will come down from the skies until you are destroyed.

25The LORD will cause you to be de-feated before your enemies. You will come at them from one direction but flee from them in seven, and you will become a thing of horror to all the kingdoms on earth. 26Your carcasses will be food for all the birds of the air and the beasts of the earth, and there will be no one to frighten them away. 27The LORD will afflict you with the boils of Egypt and with tumors, fes-tering sores and the itch, from which

a20 Hebrew me

you cannot be cured. 28The LORD will afflict you with madness, blindness and confusion of mind. 29At midday you will grope about like a blind man in the dark. You will be unsuccessful in everything you do; day after day you will be oppressed and robbed, with no one to rescue you.

30You will be pledged to be married to a woman, but another will take her and ravish her. You will build a house, but you will not live in it. You will plant a vineyard, but you will not even begin to enjoy its fruit. 31Your ox will be slaughtered before your eyes, but you will eat none of it. Your donkey will be forcibly taken from you and will not be returned. Your sheep will be given to your enemies, and no one will rescue them. 32Your sons and daughters will be given to another nation, and you will wear out your eyes watching for them day after day, powerless to lift a hand. 33A people that you do not know will eat what your land and labor produce, and you will have nothing but cruel oppression all your days. 34The sights you see will drive you mad. 35The LORD will afflict your knees and legs with painful boils that cannot be cured, spreading from the soles of your feet to the top of your head.

36The LORD will drive you and the king you set over you to a nation unknown to you or your fathers. There you will worship other gods, gods of wood and stone. 37You will become a thing of horror and an object of scorn and ridicule to all the nations where the LORD will drive you.

38You will sow much seed in the field but you will harvest little, because locusts will devour it. 39You will plant vineyards and cultivate them but you will not drink the wine or gather the grapes, because worms will eat them. 40You will have olive trees throughout your country but you will not use the oil, because the olives will drop off. 41You will have sons and daughters but you will not keep them, because they will go into captivity. 42Swarms of locusts will take over all your trees and the crops of your land.

43The alien who lives among you will rise above you higher and higher, but you will sink lower and lower. 44He will lend to you, but you will not lend to him. He will be the head, but you will be the tail.

45All these curses will come upon you. They will pursue you and overtake you until you are destroyed, because you did not obey the LORD your God and observe the commands and decrees he gave you. 46They will be a sign and a wonder to you and your descendants forever. 47Because you did not serve the LORD your God joyfully and gladly in the time of prosperity, 48therefore in hunger and thirst, in nakedness and dire poverty, you will serve the enemies the LORD sends against you. He will put an iron yoke on your neck until he has destroyed you.

49The LORD will bring a nation against you from far away, from the ends of the earth, like an eagle swooping down, a nation whose language you will not understand, 50a fierce-looking nation without respect for the old or pity for the young. 51They will devour the young of your livestock and the crops of your land until you are destroyed. They will leave you no grain, new wine or oil, nor any calves of your herds or lambs of your flocks until you are ruined. 52They will lay siege to all the cities throughout your land until the high fortified walls in which you trust fall down. They will besiege all the cities throughout the land the LORD your God is giving you.

53Because of the suffering that your enemy will inflict on you during the siege, you will eat the fruit of the womb, the flesh of the sons and daughters the LORD your God has given you. 54Even the most gentle and sensitive man among you will have no compassion on his own brother or the wife he loves or his surviving children, 55and he will not give to one of them any of the flesh of his children that he is eating. It will be all he has left because of the suffering your enemy will inflict on you during the siege of all your cities. ⁵⁶The most gentle and sensitive woman among you—so sensitive and gentle that she would not venture to touch the ground with the sole of her foot—will begrudge the husband she loves and her own son or daughter ⁵⁷the after-birth from her womb and the children she bears. For she intends to eat them secretly during the siege and in the distress that your enemy will inflict on you in your cities.

⁵⁸If you do not carefully follow all the words of this law, which are written in this book, and do not revere this glorious and awesome name— the LORD your God— ⁵⁹the LORD will send fearful plagues on you and your descendants, harsh and prolonged disasters, and severe and lingering illnesses. ⁶⁰He will bring upon you all the diseases of Egypt that you dreaded, and they will cling to you. ⁶¹The LORD will also bring on you every kind of sickness and disaster not recorded in this Book of the Law, until you are destroyed. ⁶²You who were as numerous as the stars in the sky will be left but few in number, because you did not obey the LORD your God. ⁶³Just as it pleased the LORD to make you prosper and increase in number, so it will please him to ruin and destroy you. You will be uprooted from the land you are entering to possess.

⁶⁴Then the LORD will scatter you among all nations, from one end of the earth to the other. There you will worship other gods—gods of wood and stone, which neither you nor your fathers have known. ⁶⁵Among those nations you will find no repose, no resting place for the sole of your foot. There the LORD will give you an anxious mind, eyes weary with longing, and a despairing heart. ⁶⁶You will live in constant suspense, filled with dread both night and day, never sure of your life. ⁶⁷In the morning you will say, "If only it were evening!"

and in the evening, "If only it were morning!"—because of the terror that will fill your hearts and the sights that your eyes will see. ⁶⁸The LORD will send you back in ships to Egypt on a journey I said you should never make again. There you will offer yourselves for sale to your enemies as male and female slaves, but no one will buy you.

Renewal of the Covenant

29 These are the terms of the covenant the LORD commanded Moses to make with the Israelites in Moab, in addition to the covenant he had made with them at Horeb.

²Moses summoned all the Israelites and said to them:

Your eyes have seen all that the LORD did in Egypt to Pharaoh, to all his officials and to all his land. ³With your own eyes you saw those great trials, those miraculous signs and great wonders. ⁴But to this day the LORD has not given you a mind that understands or eyes that see or ears that hear. ⁵During the forty years that I led you through the desert, your clothes did not wear out, nor did the sandals on your feet. ⁶You ate no bread and drank no wine or other fermented drink. I did this so that you might know that I am the LORD your God.

⁷When you reached this place, Sihon king of Heshbon and Og king of Bashan came out to fight against us, but we defeated them. ⁸We took their land and gave it as an inheritance to the Reubenites, the Gadites and the half-tribe of Manasseh.

⁹Carefully follow the terms of this covenant, so that you may prosper in everything you do. ¹⁰All of you are standing today in the presence of the LORD your God—your leaders and chief men, your elders and officials, and all the other men of Israel, ¹¹together with your children and your wives, and the aliens living in your camps who chop your wood and carry your water. ¹²You are standing here

in order to enter into a covenant with the LORD your God, a covenant the LORD is making with you this day and sealing with an oath, [13]to confirm you this day as his people, that he may be your God as he promised you and as he swore to your fathers, Abraham, Isaac and Jacob. [14]I am making this covenant, with its oath, not only with you [15]who are standing here with us today in the presence of the LORD our God but also with those who are not here today.

[16]You yourselves know how we lived in Egypt and how we passed through the countries on the way here. [17]You saw among them their detestable images and idols of wood and stone, of silver and gold. [18]Make sure there is no man or woman, clan or tribe among you today whose heart turns away from the LORD our God to go and worship the gods of those nations; make sure there is no root among you that produces such bitter poison.

[19]When such a person hears the words of this oath, he invokes a blessing on himself and therefore thinks, "I will be safe, even though I persist in going my own way." This will bring disaster on the watered land as well as the dry.[a] [20]The LORD will never be willing to forgive him; his wrath and zeal will burn against that man. All the curses written in this book will fall upon him, and the LORD will blot out his name from under heaven. [21]The LORD will single him out from all the tribes of Israel for disaster, according to all the curses of the covenant written in this Book of the Law.

[22]Your children who follow you in later generations and foreigners who come from distant lands will see the calamities that have fallen on the land and the diseases with which the LORD has afflicted it. [23]The whole land will be a burning waste of salt and sulfur—nothing planted, nothing sprouting, no vegetation growing on it. It will be like the destruction of Sodom and Gomorrah, Admah and Zeboiim, which the LORD overthrew in fierce anger. [24]All the nations will ask: "Why has the LORD done this to this land? Why this fierce, burning anger?"

[25]And the answer will be: "It is because this people abandoned the covenant of the LORD, the God of their fathers, the covenant he made with them when he brought them out of Egypt. [26]They went off and worshiped other gods and bowed down to them, gods they did not know, gods he had not given them. [27]Therefore the LORD's anger burned against this land, so that he brought on it all the curses written in this book. [28]In furious anger and in great wrath the LORD uprooted them from their land and thrust them into another land, as it is now."

[29]The secret things belong to the LORD our God, but the things revealed belong to us and to our children forever, that we may follow all the words of this law.

Prosperity After Turning to the LORD

30 When all these blessings and curses I have set before you come upon you and you take them to heart wherever the LORD your God disperses you among the nations, [2]and when you and your children return to the LORD your God and obey him with all your heart and with all your soul according to everything I command you today, [3]then the LORD your God will restore your fortunes[b] and have compassion on you and gather you again from all the nations where he scattered you. [4]Even if you have been banished to the most distant land under the heavens, from there the LORD your God will gather you and bring you back. [5]He will bring you to the land that belonged to your fathers, and you will take possession of it. He will make you more prosperous and numerous than your fathers. [6]The LORD your God will cir-

---

[a]19 Or *way, in order to add drunkenness to thirst."*   [b]3 Or *will bring you back from captivity*

cumcise your hearts and the hearts of your descendants, so that you may love him with all your heart and with all your soul, and live. 7The LORD your God will put all these curses on your enemies who hate and persecute you. 8You will again obey the LORD and follow all his commands I am giving you today. 9Then the LORD your God will make you most prosperous in all the work of your hands and in the fruit of your womb, the young of your livestock and the crops of your land. The LORD will again delight in you and make you prosperous, just as he delighted in your fathers, 10if you obey the LORD your God and keep his commands and decrees that are written in this Book of the Law and turn to the LORD your God with all your heart and with all your soul.

WORDS TO REMEMBER

30:2-3 When you and your children return to the LORD your God and obey him with all your heart and with all your soul according to everything I command you today, then the LORD your God will restore your fortunes and have compassion on you.

The Offer of Life or Death

11Now what I am commanding you today is not too difficult for you or beyond your reach. 12It is not up in heaven, so that you have to ask, "Who will ascend into heaven to get it and proclaim it to us so we may obey it?" 13Nor is it beyond the sea, so that you have to ask, "Who will cross the sea to get it and proclaim it to us so we may obey it?" 14No, the word is very near you; it is in your mouth and in your heart so you may obey it.

15See, I set before you today life and prosperity, death and destruction. 16For I command you today to love the LORD your God, to walk in his ways, and to keep his commands, decrees and laws; then you will live and increase, and the LORD your God will

bless you in the land you are entering to possess.

17But if your heart turns away and you are not obedient, and if you are drawn away to bow down to other gods and worship them, 18I declare to you this day that you will certainly be destroyed. You will not live long in the land you are crossing the Jordan to enter and possess.

19This day I call heaven and earth as witnesses against you that I have set before you life and death, blessings and curses. Now choose life, so that you and your children may live 20and that you may love the LORD your God, listen to his voice, and hold fast to him. For the LORD is your life, and he will give you many years in the land he swore to give to your fathers, Abraham, Isaac and Jacob.

WORDS TO REMEMBER

30:19-20 Choose life, so that you and your children may live and that you may love the LORD your God, listen to his voice, and hold fast to him.

Joshua to Succeed Moses

31 Then Moses went out and spoke these words to all Israel: 2"I am now a hundred and twenty years old and I am no longer able to lead you. The LORD has said to me, 'You shall not cross the Jordan.' 3The LORD your God himself will cross over ahead of you. He will destroy these nations before you, and you will take possession of their land. Joshua also will cross over ahead of you, as the LORD said. 4And the LORD will do to them what he did to Sihon and Og, the kings of the Amorites, whom he destroyed along with their land. 5The LORD will deliver them to you, and you must do to them all that I have commanded you. 6Be strong and courageous. Do not be afraid or terrified because of them, for the LORD your God goes with you; he will never leave you nor forsake you."

7Then Moses summoned Joshua and said to him in the presence of all Israel, "Be strong and courageous, for you must go with this people into the land that the Lord swore to their forefathers to give them, and you must divide it among them as their inheritance. 8The Lord himself goes before you and will be with you; he will never leave you nor forsake you. Do not be afraid; do not be discouraged."

The Reading of the Law

9So Moses wrote down this law and gave it to the priests, the sons of Levi, who carried the ark of the covenant of the Lord, and to all the elders of Israel. 10Then Moses commanded them: "At the end of every seven years, in the year for canceling debts, during the Feast of Tabernacles, 11when all Israel comes to appear before the Lord your God at the place he will choose, you shall read this law before them in their hearing. 12Assemble the people—men, women and children, and the aliens living in your towns—so they can listen and learn to fear the Lord your God and follow carefully all the words of this law. 13Their children, who do not know this law, must hear it and learn to fear the Lord your God as long as you live in the land you are crossing the Jordan to possess."

Israel's Rebellion Predicted

14The Lord said to Moses, "Now the day of your death is near. Call Joshua and present yourselves at the Tent of Meeting, where I will commission him." So Moses and Joshua came and presented themselves at the Tent of Meeting.
15Then the Lord appeared at the Tent in a pillar of cloud, and the cloud stood over the entrance to the Tent. 16And the Lord said to Moses: "You are going to rest with your fathers, and these people will soon prostitute themselves to the foreign gods of the land they are entering. They will forsake me and break the covenant I made with them. 17On that day I will

become angry with them and forsake them; I will hide my face from them, and they will be destroyed. Many disasters and difficulties will come upon them, and on that day they will ask, 'Have not these disasters come upon us because our God is not with us?' 18And I will certainly hide my face on that day because of all their wickedness in turning to other gods.

? DID YOU KNOW?   31:14

Who became the leader of all Israel when Moses died?

Joshua, who had led Israel's soldiers from the time they left Egypt, became leader of all Israel. He was one of the spies Moses sent into Canaan. Only Joshua and another spy, Caleb, wanted to obey God when they were told to attack Canaan. God rewarded Joshua and Caleb. Every other adult who left Egypt died before Israel finally entered Canaan. Joshua is one of the greatest Old Testament heroes.

19"Now write down for yourselves this song and teach it to the Israelites and have them sing it, so that it may be a witness for me against them. 20When I have brought them into the land flowing with milk and honey, the land I promised on oath to their forefathers, and when they eat their fill and thrive, they will turn to other gods and worship them, rejecting me and breaking my covenant. 21And when many disasters and difficulties come upon them, this song will testify against them, because it will not be forgotten by their descendants. I know what they are disposed to do, even before I bring them into the land I promised them on oath." 22So Moses wrote down this song that day and taught it to the Israelites.
23The Lord gave this command to Joshua son of Nun: "Be strong and courageous, for you will bring the Israelites into the land I promised

them on oath, and I myself will be with you."

24After Moses finished writing in a book the words of this law from beginning to end, 25he gave this command to the Levites who carried the ark of the covenant of the LORD: 26"Take this Book of the Law and place it beside the ark of the covenant of the LORD your God. There it will remain as a witness against you. 27For I know how rebellious and stiff-necked you are. If you have been rebellious against the LORD while I am still alive and with you, how much more will you rebel after I die! 28Assemble before me all the elders of your tribes and all your officials, so that I can speak these words in their hearing and call heaven and earth to testify against them. 29For I know that after my death you are sure to become utterly corrupt and to turn from the way I have commanded you. In days to come, disaster will fall upon you because you will do evil in the sight of the LORD and provoke him to anger by what your hands have made."

The Song of Moses

30And Moses recited the words of this song from beginning to end in the hearing of the whole assembly of Israel:

32 Listen, O heavens, and I will speak;
hear, O earth, the words of my mouth.
2Let my teaching fall like rain
and my words descend like dew,
like showers on new grass,
like abundant rain on tender plants.
3I will proclaim the name of the LORD.
Oh, praise the greatness of our God!
4He is the Rock, his works are perfect,

and all his ways are just.
A faithful God who does no wrong,
upright and just is he.
5They have acted corruptly toward him;
to their shame they are no longer his children,
but a warped and crooked generation. a
6Is this the way you repay the LORD,
O foolish and unwise people?
Is he not your Father, your Creator, b
who made you and formed you?
7Remember the days of old;
consider the generations long past.
Ask your father and he will tell you,
your elders, and they will explain to you.
8When the Most High gave the nations their inheritance,
when he divided all mankind,
he set up boundaries for the peoples
according to the number of the sons of Israel. c
9For the LORD's portion is his people,
Jacob his allotted inheritance.
10In a desert land he found him,
in a barren and howling waste.
He shielded him and cared for him;
he guarded him as the apple of his eye,
11like an eagle that stirs up its nest
and hovers over its young,
that spreads its wings to catch them
and carries them on its pinions.
12The LORD alone led him;
no foreign god was with him.
13He made him ride on the heights of the land
and fed him with the fruit of the fields.

---

a5 Or Corrupt are they and not his children, / a generation warped and twisted to their shame
b6 Or Father, who bought you   c8 Masoretic Text; Dead Sea Scrolls (see also Septuagint) sons of God

He nourished him with honey
        from the rock,
    and with oil from the flinty
        crag,
14with curds and milk from herd
        and flock
    and with fattened lambs and
        goats,
    with choice rams of Bashan
        and the finest kernels of wheat.
    You drank the foaming blood of
        the grape.

? DID YOU KNOW?   31:30

Why did Moses teach Israel this song?

Moses taught Israel this song because he knew that it is easy to remember songs. Moses wanted the Israelites to learn this song and to think about its words.

15Jeshuruna grew fat and kicked;
    filled with food, he became
        heavy and sleek.
    He abandoned the God who made
        him
    and rejected the Rock his
        Savior.
16They made him jealous with their
        foreign gods
    and angered him with their
        detestable idols.
17They sacrificed to demons, which
        are not God—
    gods they had not known,
    gods that recently appeared,
    gods your fathers did not fear.
18You deserted the Rock, who
        fathered you;
    you forgot the God who gave
        you birth.

19The LORD saw this and rejected
        them
    because he was angered by his
        sons and daughters.

20"I will hide my face from them,"
        he said,
    "and see what their end will be;
    for they are a perverse
        generation,
    children who are unfaithful.
21They made me jealous by what is
        no god
    and angered me with their
        worthless idols.
    I will make them envious by
        those who are not a people;
    I will make them angry by a
        nation that has no
        understanding.
22For a fire has been kindled by my
        wrath,
    one that burns to the realm of
        deathb below.
    It will devour the earth and its
        harvests
    and set afire the foundations of
        the mountains.

23"I will heap calamities upon them
    and spend my arrows against
        them.
24I will send wasting famine
        against them,
    consuming pestilence and
        deadly plague;
    I will send against them the fangs
        of wild beasts,
    the venom of vipers that glide
        in the dust.
25In the street the sword will make
        them childless;
    in their homes terror will reign.
    Young men and young women
        will perish,
    infants and gray-haired men.
26I said I would scatter them
    and blot out their memory from
        mankind,
27but I dreaded the taunt of the
        enemy,
    lest the adversary
        misunderstand
    and say, 'Our hand has
        triumphed;
    the LORD has not done all
        this.'"

28They are a nation without sense,

---

a15 Jeshurun means the upright one, that is, Israel.   b22 Hebrew to Sheol

there is no discernment in
them.
²⁹If only they were wise and would
understand this
and discern what their end will
be!
³⁰How could one man chase a
thousand,
or two put ten thousand to
flight,
unless their Rock had sold them,
unless the LORD had given them
up?
³¹For their rock is not like our
Rock,
as even our enemies concede.
³²Their vine comes from the vine of
Sodom
and from the fields of
Gomorrah.
Their grapes are filled with
poison,
and their clusters with
bitterness.
³³Their wine is the venom of
serpents,
the deadly poison of cobras.

³⁴"Have I not kept this in reserve
and sealed it in my vaults?
³⁵It is mine to avenge; I will repay.
In due time their foot will slip;
their day of disaster is near
and their doom rushes upon
them."

³⁶The LORD will judge his people
and have compassion on his
servants
when he sees their strength is
gone
and no one is left, slave or free.
³⁷He will say: "Now where are
their gods,
the rock they took refuge in,
³⁸the gods who ate the fat of their
sacrifices
and drank the wine of their
drink offerings?
Let them rise up to help you!
Let them give you shelter!
³⁹"See now that I myself am He!

There is no god besides me.
I put to death and I bring to life,
I have wounded and I will heal,
and no one can deliver out of
my hand.
⁴⁰I lift my hand to heaven and
declare:
As surely as I live forever,
⁴¹when I sharpen my flashing
sword
and my hand grasps it in
judgment,
I will take vengeance on my
adversaries
and repay those who hate me.
⁴²I will make my arrows drunk
with blood,
while my sword devours flesh:
the blood of the slain and the
captives,
the heads of the enemy
leaders."

⁴³Rejoice, O nations, with his
people,ᵃ,ᵇ
for he will avenge the blood of
his servants;
he will take vengeance on his
enemies
and make atonement for his
land and people.

⁴⁴Moses came with Joshuaᶜ son of
Nun and spoke all the words of this
song in the hearing of the people.
⁴⁵When Moses finished reciting all
these words to all Israel, ⁴⁶he said to
them, "Take to heart all the words I
have solemnly declared to you this
day, so that you may command your
children to obey carefully all the
words of this law. ⁴⁷They are not just
idle words for you—they are your
life. By them you will live long in the
land you are crossing the Jordan to
possess."

Moses to Die on Mount Nebo

⁴⁸On that same day the LORD told
Moses, ⁴⁹"Go up into the Abarim
Range to Mount Nebo in Moab,

ᵃ43 Or *Make his people rejoice, O nations*   ᵇ43 Masoretic Text; Dead Sea Scrolls (see also
Septuagint) *people, / and let all the angels worship him /*   ᶜ44 Hebrew *Hoshea,* a variant of
Joshua

across from Jericho, and view Canaan, the land I am giving the Israelites as their own possession. ⁵⁰There on the mountain that you have climbed you will die and be gathered to your people, just as your brother Aaron died on Mount Hor and was gathered to his people. ⁵¹This is because both of you broke faith with me in the presence of the Israelites at the waters of Meribah Kadesh in the Desert of Zin and because you did not uphold my holiness among the Israelites. ⁵²Therefore, you will see the land only from a distance; you will not enter the land I am giving to the people of Israel."

Moses Blesses the Tribes

33 This is the blessing that Moses the man of God pronounced on the Israelites before his death. ²He said:

"The LORD came from Sinai
    and dawned over them from
       Seir;
he shone forth from Mount
       Paran.
He came withᵃ myriads of holy
       ones
    from the south, from his
       mountain slopes.ᵇ
³Surely it is you who love the
       people;
    all the holy ones are in your
       hand.
At your feet they all bow down,
    and from you receive
       instruction,
⁴the law that Moses gave us,
    the possession of the assembly
       of Jacob.
⁵He was king over Jeshurunᶜ
    when the leaders of the people
       assembled,
    along with the tribes of Israel.

⁶"Let Reuben live and not die,
    norᵈ his men be few."

⁷And this he said about Judah:

"Hear, O LORD, the cry of Judah;

bring him to his people.
With his own hands he defends
    his cause.
Oh, be his help against his
       foes!"

⁸About Levi he said:

"Your Thummim and Urim
       belong
    to the man you favored.
You tested him at Massah;
    you contended with him at the
       waters of Meribah.
⁹He said of his father and mother,
    'I have no regard for them.'
He did not recognize his brothers
    or acknowledge his own
       children,
but he watched over your word
    and guarded your covenant.
¹⁰He teaches your precepts to Jacob
    and your law to Israel.
He offers incense before you
    and whole burnt offerings on
       your altar.
¹¹Bless all his skills, O LORD,
    and be pleased with the work of
       his hands.
Smite the loins of those who rise
       up against him;
    strike his foes till they rise no
       more."

¹²About Benjamin he said:

"Let the beloved of the LORD rest
       secure in him,
    for he shields him all day long,
    and the one the LORD loves
       rests between his
       shoulders."

¹³About Joseph he said:

"May the LORD bless his land
    with the precious dew from
       heaven above
    and with the deep waters that
       lie below;
¹⁴with the best the sun brings forth
    and the finest the moon can
       yield;
¹⁵with the choicest gifts of the
       ancient mountains

---

*a*2 Or *from*   *b*2 The meaning of the Hebrew for this phrase is uncertain.   *c*5 *Jeshurun* means *the upright one,* that is, Israel; also in verse 26.   *d*6 Or *but let*

and the fruitfulness of the
everlasting hills;
¹⁶with the best gifts of the earth
and its fullness
and the favor of him who dwelt
in the burning bush.
Let all these rest on the head of
Joseph,
on the brow of the prince
among*ᵃ* his brothers.
¹⁷In majesty he is like a firstborn
bull;
his horns are the horns of a
wild ox.
With them he will gore the
nations,
even those at the ends of the
earth.
Such are the ten thousands of
Ephraim;
such are the thousands of
Manasseh."

¹⁸About Zebulun he said:

"Rejoice, Zebulun, in your going
out,
and you, Issachar, in your tents.
¹⁹They will summon peoples to the
mountain
and there offer sacrifices of
righteousness;
they will feast on the abundance
of the seas,
on the treasures hidden in the
sand."

²⁰About Gad he said:

"Blessed is he who enlarges Gad's
domain!
Gad lives there like a lion,
tearing at arm or head.
²¹He chose the best land for
himself;
the leader's portion was kept for
him.
When the heads of the people
assembled,
he carried out the Lord's
righteous will,
and his judgments concerning
Israel."

²²About Dan he said:

"Dan is a lion's cub,
springing out of Bashan."

²³About Naphtali he said:

"Naphtali is abounding with the
favor of the Lord
and is full of his blessing;
he will inherit southward to the
lake."

²⁴About Asher he said:

"Most blessed of sons is Asher;
let him be favored by his
brothers,
and let him bathe his feet in
oil.
²⁵The bolts of your gates will be
iron and bronze,
and your strength will equal
your days.

²⁶"There is no one like the God of
Jeshurun,
who rides on the heavens to
help you
and on the clouds in his
majesty.
²⁷The eternal God is your refuge,
and underneath are the
everlasting arms.
He will drive out your enemy
before you,
saying, 'Destroy him!'
²⁸So Israel will live in safety alone;
Jacob's spring is secure
in a land of grain and new wine,
where the heavens drop dew.
²⁹Blessed are you, O Israel!
Who is like you,
a people saved by the Lord?
He is your shield and helper
and your glorious sword.
Your enemies will cower before
you,
and you will trample down their
high places.*ᵇ*"

The Death of Moses

34 Then Moses climbed Mount
Nebo from the plains of Moab
to the top of Pisgah, across from Jericho. There the Lord showed him the
whole land—from Gilead to Dan, ²all

ᵃ16 Or *of the one separated from*   *ᵇ29* Or *will tread upon their bodies*

of Naphtali, the territory of Ephraim and Manasseh, all the land of Judah as far as the western sea,ᵃ ³the Negev and the whole region from the Valley of Jericho, the City of Palms, as far as Zoar. ⁴Then the LORD said to him, "This is the land I promised on oath to Abraham, Isaac and Jacob when I said, 'I will give it to your descendants.' I have let you see it with your eyes, but you will not cross over into it."

⁵And Moses the servant of the LORD died there in Moab, as the LORD had said. ⁶He buried himᵇ in Moab, in the valley opposite Beth Peor, but to this day no one knows where his grave is. ⁷Moses was a hundred and twenty years old when he died, yet his eyes were not weak nor his strength gone.

⁸The Israelites grieved for Moses in the plains of Moab thirty days, until the time of weeping and mourning was over.

⁹Now Joshua son of Nun was filled with the spiritᶜ of wisdom because Moses had laid his hands on him. So the Israelites listened to him and did what the LORD had commanded Moses.

¹⁰Since then, no prophet has risen in Israel like Moses, whom the LORD knew face to face, ¹¹who did all those miraculous signs and wonders the LORD sent him to do in Egypt—to Pharaoh and to all his officials and to his whole land. ¹²For no one has ever shown the mighty power or performed the awesome deeds that Moses did in the sight of all Israel.

ᵃ2 That is, the Mediterranean   ᵇ6 Or *He was buried*   ᶜ9 Or *Spirit*

LET'S LIVE IT!   Deuteronomy 34:1–8

WHEN A LOVED ONE DIES ➠ Ten-year-old Paul sat very still. It was quiet in the funeral home. Dad was standing by Grandma's casket. Paul sat very still through the funeral too. But that night, when Dad talked about how he cried when they buried Grandma, Paul cried too. Grandma had been so special. And now she was dead.

Dad said it was all right to cry. One day they would see Grandma in heaven. But now it was all right to feel sad. Grandma was special, and the whole family would miss her.

Deuteronomy 34:1–8 tells us what happened when Moses died. If someone you have loved has died, read this Bible passage with one of your parents and talk about these things:

How did the Israelites feel when Moses died?

What were some of the things that made Moses special to the Israelites?

What do you think the people of Israel remembered best about Moses?

How did you feel when the person you loved died?

What were some of the things that made that person special to you?

What is your favorite memory of that person?

JOSHUA

WHO WROTE THIS BOOK?

The author of Joshua is not named, but probably was someone who witnessed the events described.

WHY WAS THIS BOOK WRITTEN?

Joshua tells how God helped the Israelites defeat the Canaanites.

WHAT HAPPENS IN THIS BOOK?

Joshua becomes Israel's leader. Joshua leads Israel's armies to victory. Joshua assigns land to Israel's twelve tribes.

WHAT DO WE LEARN ABOUT GOD IN THIS BOOK?

God will give victory to his people when they obey him.

WHO IS IMPORTANT IN THIS BOOK?

The important person in this book is Joshua.

WHEN DID THIS HAPPEN?

The Israelite conquest of Canaan probably happened between 1405 and 1390 B.C.

WHERE DID THIS HAPPEN?

The events in this book happened in the land of Canaan. Today we call that land Israel or Palestine.

WHAT ARE SOME OF THE STORIES IN THIS BOOK?

The Lord Commands Joshua

1 After the death of Moses the servant of the Lord, the Lord said to Joshua son of Nun, Moses' aide: ²"Moses my servant is dead. Now then, you and all these people, get ready to cross the Jordan River into the land I am about to give to them —to the Israelites. ³I will give you every place where you set your foot, as I promised Moses. ⁴Your territory will extend from the desert to Lebanon, and from the great river, the Euphrates—all the Hittite country—to the Great Sea*a* on the west. ⁵No one will be able to stand up against you all the days of your life. As I was with Moses, so I will be with you; I will never leave you nor forsake you.

⁶"Be strong and courageous, because you will lead these people to inherit the land I swore to their forefathers to give them. ⁷Be strong and very courageous. Be careful to obey all the law my servant Moses gave you; do not turn from it to the right or to the left, that you may be successful wherever you go. ⁸Do not let this Book of the Law depart from your mouth; meditate on it day and night, so that you may be careful to do everything written in it. Then you will be prosperous and successful. ⁹Have I not commanded you? Be strong and courageous. Do not be terrified; do not be discouraged, for the Lord your God will be with you wherever you go."

¹⁰So Joshua ordered the officers of the people: ¹¹"Go through the camp and tell the people, 'Get your supplies ready. Three days from now you will cross the Jordan here to go in and take possession of the land the Lord your God is giving you for your own.'"

¹²But to the Reubenites, the Gadites and the half-tribe of Manasseh, Joshua said, ¹³"Remember the command that Moses the servant of the Lord gave you: 'The Lord your God is giving you rest and has granted you

this land.' ¹⁴Your wives, your children and your livestock may stay in the land that Moses gave you east of the Jordan, but all your fighting men, fully armed, must cross over ahead of your brothers. You are to help your brothers ¹⁵until the Lord gives them rest, as he has done for you, and until they too have taken possession of the land that the Lord your God is giving them. After that, you may go back and occupy your own land, which Moses the servant of the Lord gave you east of the Jordan toward the sunrise."

¹⁶Then they answered Joshua, "Whatever you have commanded us we will do, and wherever you send us we will go. ¹⁷Just as we fully obeyed Moses, so we will obey you. Only may the Lord your God be with you as he was with Moses. ¹⁸Whoever rebels against your word and does not obey your words, whatever you may command them, will be put to death. Only be strong and courageous!"

DRYING FLAX

The houses of Canaan had flat roofs, and the rooftops were used for many things. Flax plants were piled on rooftops to dry. Stringy fibers taken from dried flax plants were woven to make linen cloth. In Jericho the Israelite spies hid under piles of drying flax plants.

Rahab and the Spies

2 Then Joshua son of Nun secretly sent two spies from Shittim. "Go, look over the land," he said, "especially Jericho." So they went and en-

a4 That is, the Mediterranean

tered the house of a prostitute[a] named Rahab and stayed there.

2The king of Jericho was told, "Look! Some of the Israelites have come here tonight to spy out the land." 3So the king of Jericho sent this message to Rahab: "Bring out the men who came to you and entered your house, because they have come to spy out the whole land."

4But the woman had taken the two men and hidden them. She said, "Yes, the men came to me, but I did not know where they had come from. 5At dusk, when it was time to close the city gate, the men left. I don't know which way they went. Go after them quickly. You may catch up with them." 6(But she had taken them up to the roof and hidden them under the stalks of flax she had laid out on the roof.) 7So the men set out in pursuit of the spies on the road that leads to the fords of the Jordan, and as soon as the pursuers had gone out, the gate was shut.

8Before the spies lay down for the night, she went up on the roof 9and said to them, "I know that the LORD has given this land to you and that a great fear of you has fallen on us, so that all who live in this country are melting in fear because of you. 10We have heard how the LORD dried up the water of the Red Sea[b] for you when you came out of Egypt, and what you did to Sihon and Og, the two kings of the Amorites east of the Jordan, whom you completely destroyed.[c] 11When we heard of it, our hearts melted and everyone's courage failed because of you, for the LORD your God is God in heaven above and on the earth below. 12Now then, please swear to me by the LORD that you will show kindness to my family, because I have shown kindness to you. Give me a sure sign 13that you will spare the lives of my father and mother, my brothers and sisters, and all who belong to them, and that you will save us from death."

14"Our lives for your lives!" the men assured her. "If you don't tell what we are doing, we will treat you kindly and faithfully when the LORD gives us the land."

15So she let them down by a rope through the window, for the house she lived in was part of the city wall. 16Now she had said to them, "Go to the hills so the pursuers will not find you. Hide yourselves there three days until they return, and then go on your way."

17The men said to her, "This oath you made us swear will not be binding on us 18unless, when we enter the land, you have tied this scarlet cord in the window through which you let us down, and unless you have

---

a1 Or possibly *an innkeeper*   b10 Hebrew *Yam Suph*; that is, Sea of Reeds   c10 The Hebrew term refers to the irrevocable giving over of things or persons to the LORD, often by totally destroying them.

LET'S LIVE IT!   Joshua 2:1–21

FAITH LIKE RAHAB'S ➡ Rahab was a woman who believed in the God of Israel even though she lived in Jericho. Read Joshua 2:1–21. Joshua 2:18 tells of the red cord Rahab put in her window in order to save her own life and her family. You can make a "Rahab cord." Take nine pieces of red yarn, each about eighteen inches long. Tie a knot at one end and divide the yarn into three groups with three strands of yarn in each group. Braid the strands together and tie the end or secure it with a rubber band. Hang the cord inside your window. Every time you look at it let it remind you to be like Rahab. Rahab trusted God and was willing to help others. You can too.

brought your father and mother, your brothers and all your family into your house. ¹⁹If anyone goes outside your house into the street, his blood will be on his own head; we will not be responsible. As for anyone who is in the house with you, his blood will be on our head if a hand is laid on him. ²⁰But if you tell what we are doing, we will be released from the oath you made us swear."

²¹"Agreed," she replied. "Let it be as you say." So she sent them away and they departed. And she tied the scarlet cord in the window.

²²When they left, they went into the hills and stayed there three days, until the pursuers had searched all along the road and returned without finding them. ²³Then the two men started back. They went down out of the hills, forded the river and came to Joshua son of Nun and told him everything that had happened to them. ²⁴They said to Joshua, "The LORD has surely given the whole land into our hands; all the people are melting in fear because of us."

Crossing the Jordan

3 Early in the morning Joshua and all the Israelites set out from Shittim and went to the Jordan, where they camped before crossing over. ²After three days the officers went throughout the camp, ³giving orders to the people: "When you see the ark of the covenant of the LORD your God, and the priests, who are Levites, carrying it, you are to move out from your positions and follow it. ⁴Then you will know which way to go, since you have never been this way before. But keep a distance of about a thousand yards*ᵃ* between you and the ark; do not go near it."

⁵Joshua told the people, "Consecrate yourselves, for tomorrow the LORD will do amazing things among you."

⁶Joshua said to the priests, "Take up the ark of the covenant and pass on ahead of the people." So they took it up and went ahead of them.

⁷And the LORD said to Joshua, "Today I will begin to exalt you in the eyes of all Israel, so they may know that I am with you as I was with Moses. ⁸Tell the priests who carry the ark of the covenant: 'When you reach the edge of the Jordan's waters, go and stand in the river.'"

⁹Joshua said to the Israelites, "Come here and listen to the words of the LORD your God. ¹⁰This is how you will know that the living God is among you and that he will certainly drive out before you the Canaanites, Hittites, Hivites, Perizzites, Girgashites, Amorites and Jebusites. ¹¹See, the ark of the covenant of the Lord of all the earth will go into the Jordan ahead of you. ¹²Now then, choose twelve men from the tribes of Israel, one from each tribe. ¹³And as soon as the priests who carry the ark of the LORD—the Lord of all the earth—set foot in the Jordan, its waters flowing downstream will be cut off and stand up in a heap."

¹⁴So when the people broke camp to cross the Jordan, the priests carrying the ark of the covenant went ahead of them. ¹⁵Now the Jordan is at flood stage all during harvest. Yet as soon as the priests who carried the ark reached the Jordan and their feet touched the water's edge, ¹⁶the water from upstream stopped flowing. It piled up in a heap a great distance away, at a town called Adam in the vicinity of Zarethan, while the water flowing down to the Sea of the Arabah (the Salt Sea ᵇ) was completely cut off. So the people crossed over opposite Jericho. ¹⁷The priests who carried the ark of the covenant of the LORD stood firm on dry ground in the middle of the Jordan, while all Israel passed by until the whole nation had completed the crossing on dry ground.

4 When the whole nation had finished crossing the Jordan, the LORD said to Joshua, ²"Choose twelve

---

a4 Hebrew *about two thousand cubits* (about 900 meters)   *b16* That is, the Dead Sea

men from among the people, one from each tribe, ³and tell them to take up twelve stones from the middle of the Jordan from right where the priests stood and to carry them over with you and put them down at the place where you stay tonight."

⁴So Joshua called together the twelve men he had appointed from the Israelites, one from each tribe, ⁵and said to them, "Go over before the ark of the LORD your God into the middle of the Jordan. Each of you is to take up a stone on his shoulder, according to the number of the tribes of the Israelites, ⁶to serve as a sign among you. In the future, when your children ask you, 'What do these stones mean?' ⁷tell them that the flow of the Jordan was cut off before the ark of the covenant of the LORD. When it crossed the Jordan, the waters of the Jordan were cut off. These stones are to be a memorial to the people of Israel forever."

⁸So the Israelites did as Joshua commanded them. They took twelve stones from the middle of the Jordan, according to the number of the tribes of the Israelites, as the LORD had told Joshua; and they carried them over with them to their camp, where they put them down. ⁹Joshua set up the twelve stones that had been*a* in the middle of the Jordan at the spot where the priests who carried the ark

of the covenant had stood. And they are there to this day.

¹⁰Now the priests who carried the ark remained standing in the middle of the Jordan until everything the LORD had commanded Joshua was done by the people, just as Moses had directed Joshua. The people hurried over, ¹¹and as soon as all of them had crossed, the ark of the LORD and the priests came to the other side while the people watched. ¹²The men of Reuben, Gad and the half-tribe of Manasseh crossed over, armed, in front of the Israelites, as Moses had directed them. ¹³About forty thousand armed for battle crossed over before the LORD to the plains of Jericho for war.

¹⁴That day the LORD exalted Joshua in the sight of all Israel; and they revered him all the days of his life, just as they had revered Moses.

¹⁵Then the LORD said to Joshua, ¹⁶"Command the priests carrying the ark of the Testimony to come up out of the Jordan."

¹⁷So Joshua commanded the priests, "Come up out of the Jordan."

¹⁸And the priests came up out of the river carrying the ark of the covenant of the LORD. No sooner had they set their feet on the dry ground than the waters of the Jordan returned to their place and ran at flood stage as before.

---

a9 Or *Joshua also set up twelve stones*

Life in Bible Times

MEMORIALS

Joshua piled twelve stones from the Jordan river on its bank for a "memorial," or special reminder. One man from each of the twelve tribes carried a stone. The stones reminded God's people how God parted the waters and let the Israelites cross the river on dry ground.

19On the tenth day of the first month the people went up from the Jordan and camped at Gilgal on the eastern border of Jericho. 20And Joshua set up at Gilgal the twelve stones they had taken out of the Jordan. 21He said to the Israelites, "In the future when your descendants ask their fathers, 'What do these stones mean?' 22tell them, 'Israel crossed the Jordan on dry ground.' 23For the LORD your God dried up the Jordan before you until you had crossed over. The LORD your God did to the Jordan just what he had done to the Red Sea*a* when he dried it up before us until we had crossed over. 24He did this so that all the peoples of the earth might know that the hand of the LORD is powerful and so that you might always fear the LORD your God."

Circumcision at Gilgal

5 Now when all the Amorite kings west of the Jordan and all the Canaanite kings along the coast heard how the LORD had dried up the Jordan before the Israelites until we had crossed over, their hearts melted and they no longer had the courage to face the Israelites.

2At that time the LORD said to Joshua, "Make flint knives and circumcise the Israelites again." 3So Joshua made flint knives and circumcised the Israelites at Gibeath Haaraloth.*b*

4Now this is why he did so: All those who came out of Egypt—all the men of military age—died in the desert on the way after leaving Egypt. 5All the people that came out had been circumcised, but all the people born in the desert during the journey from Egypt had not. 6The Israelites had moved about in the desert forty years until all the men who were of military age when they left Egypt had died, since they had not obeyed the LORD. For the LORD had sworn to them that they would not

see the land that he had solemnly promised their fathers to give us, a land flowing with milk and honey. 7So he raised up their sons in their place, and these were the ones Joshua circumcised. They were still uncircumcised because they had not been circumcised on the way. 8And after the whole nation had been circumcised, they remained where they were in camp until they were healed.

9Then the LORD said to Joshua, "Today I have rolled away the reproach of Egypt from you." So the place has been called Gilgal*c* to this day.

10On the evening of the fourteenth day of the month, while camped at Gilgal on the plains of Jericho, the Israelites celebrated the Passover. 11The day after the Passover, that very day, they ate some of the produce of the land: unleavened bread and roasted grain. 12The manna stopped the day after*d* they ate this food from the land; there was no longer any manna for the Israelites, but that year they ate of the produce of Canaan.

The Fall of Jericho

13Now when Joshua was near Jericho, he looked up and saw a man standing in front of him with a drawn sword in his hand. Joshua went up to him and asked, "Are you for us or for our enemies?"

14"Neither," he replied, "but as commander of the army of the LORD I have now come." Then Joshua fell facedown to the ground in reverence, and asked him, "What message does my Lord*e* have for his servant?"

15The commander of the LORD's army replied, "Take off your sandals, for the place where you are standing is holy." And Joshua did so.

6 Now Jericho was tightly shut up because of the Israelites. No one went out and no one came in.

2Then the LORD said to Joshua, "See, I have delivered Jericho into your hands, along with its king and

---

a23 Hebrew *Yam Suph*; that is, Sea of Reeds   *b3* Gibeath Haaraloth means *hill of foreskins.*
c9 Gilgal sounds like the Hebrew for *roll.*   *d12* Or *the day*   *e14* Or *lord*

its fighting men. ³March around the city once with all the armed men. Do this for six days. ⁴Have seven priests carry trumpets of rams' horns in front of the ark. On the seventh day, march around the city seven times, with the priests blowing the trumpets. ⁵When you hear them sound a long blast on the trumpets, have all the people give a loud shout; then the wall of the city will collapse and the people will go up, every man straight in."

⁶So Joshua son of Nun called the priests and said to them, "Take up the ark of the covenant of the LORD and have seven priests carry trumpets in front of it." ⁷And he ordered the people, "Advance! March around the city, with the armed guard going ahead of the ark of the LORD."

⁸When Joshua had spoken to the people, the seven priests carrying the seven trumpets before the LORD went forward, blowing their trumpets, and the ark of the LORD's covenant followed them. ⁹The armed guard marched ahead of the priests who blew the trumpets, and the rear guard followed the ark. All this time the trumpets were sounding. ¹⁰But

Joshua had commanded the people, "Do not give a war cry, do not raise your voices, do not say a word until the day I tell you to shout. Then shout!" ¹¹So he had the ark of the LORD carried around the city, circling it once. Then the people returned to camp and spent the night there.

¹²Joshua got up early the next morning and the priests took up the ark of the LORD. ¹³The seven priests carrying the seven trumpets went forward, marching before the ark of the LORD and blowing the trumpets. The armed men went ahead of them and the rear guard followed the ark of the LORD, while the trumpets kept sounding. ¹⁴So on the second day they marched around the city once and returned to the camp. They did this for six days.

¹⁵On the seventh day, they got up at daybreak and marched around the city seven times in the same manner, except that on that day they circled the city seven times. ¹⁶The seventh time around, when the priests sounded the trumpet blast, Joshua commanded the people, "Shout! For the LORD has given you the city! ¹⁷The

Life in Bible Times

JERICHO'S WALL

Jericho was not a huge city, but it sat high up on a mound. Its walls were high and thick—so thick people built their houses in them (see Joshua 2:15)! The Israelite soldiers probably looked at Jericho and wondered how they would ever be able to scramble up that hill and then go over such huge walls. But God had an answer for the high walls of Jericho. You can read about it in Joshua 6.

city and all that is in it are to be devoted[a] to the LORD. Only Rahab the prostitute[b] and all who are with her in her house shall be spared, because she hid the spies we sent. [18]But keep away from the devoted things, so that you will not bring about your own destruction by taking any of them. Otherwise you will make the camp of Israel liable to destruction and bring trouble on it. [19]All the silver and gold and the articles of bronze and iron are sacred to the LORD and must go into his treasury."

[20]When the trumpets sounded, the people shouted, and at the sound of the trumpet, when the people gave a loud shout, the wall collapsed; so every man charged straight in, and they took the city. [21]They devoted the city to the LORD and destroyed with the sword every living thing in it— men and women, young and old, cattle, sheep and donkeys.

[22]Joshua said to the two men who had spied out the land, "Go into the prostitute's house and bring her out and all who belong to her, in accordance with your oath to her." [23]So the young men who had done the spying went in and brought out Rahab, her father and mother and brothers and all who belonged to her. They brought out her entire family and put them in a place outside the camp of Israel.

[24]Then they burned the whole city and everything in it, but they put the silver and gold and the articles of bronze and iron into the treasury of the LORD's house. [25]But Joshua spared Rahab the prostitute, with her family and all who belonged to her, because she hid the men Joshua had sent as spies to Jericho—and she lives among the Israelites to this day.

[26]At that time Joshua pronounced this solemn oath: "Cursed before the LORD is the man who undertakes to rebuild this city, Jericho:

"At the cost of his firstborn son
 will he lay its foundations;
at the cost of his youngest
 will he set up its gates."

[27]So the LORD was with Joshua, and his fame spread throughout the land.

Achan's Sin

7 But the Israelites acted unfaithfully in regard to the devoted things[c]; Achan son of Carmi, the son of Zimri,[d] the son of Zerah, of the tribe of Judah, took some of them. So the LORD's anger burned against Israel.

[2]Now Joshua sent men from Jericho to Ai, which is near Beth Aven to

---

a17 The Hebrew term refers to the irrevocable giving over of things or persons to the LORD, often by totally destroying them; also in verses 18 and 21.   *b17* Or possibly *innkeeper*; also in verses 22 and 25   *c1* The Hebrew term refers to the irrevocable giving over of things or persons to the LORD, often by totally destroying them; also in verses 11, 12, 13 and 15.   *d1* See Septuagint and 1 Chron. 2:6; Hebrew *Zabdi*; also in verses 17 and 18.

 LET'S LIVE IT!   Joshua 6:1–21

A DUMB THING TO DO? ➡ When armies attacked walled cities, they piled dirt against the walls until they could climb over them. Read Joshua 6:1–15. What do you suppose the people in Jericho thought when the Israelites just walked around their walls? Make up three things the people of Jericho might have yelled at the Israelites to tease or try to scare them.

Now read Joshua 6:16–21. The Israelites did not know why they were told to march around the city. But they obeyed God and won!

There are many things that grown-ups understand better than children. It is not dumb to obey your mom and dad, even if you don't always understand why they want you to do what they ask.

the east of Bethel, and told them, "Go up and spy out the region." So the men went up and spied out Ai.

³When they returned to Joshua, they said, "Not all the people will have to go up against Ai. Send two or three thousand men to take it and do not weary all the people, for only a few men are there." ⁴So about three thousand men went up; but they were routed by the men of Ai, ⁵who killed about thirty-six of them. They chased the Israelites from the city gate as far as the stone quarries*a* and struck them down on the slopes. At this the hearts of the people melted and became like water.

⁶Then Joshua tore his clothes and fell facedown to the ground before the ark of the LORD, remaining there till evening. The elders of Israel did the same, and sprinkled dust on their heads. ⁷And Joshua said, "Ah, Sovereign LORD, why did you ever bring this people across the Jordan to deliver us into the hands of the Amorites to destroy us? If only we had been content to stay on the other side of the Jordan! ⁸O Lord, what can I say, now that Israel has been routed by its enemies? ⁹The Canaanites and the other people of the country will hear about this and they will surround us and wipe out our name from the earth. What then will you do for your own great name?"

¹⁰The LORD said to Joshua, "Stand up! What are you doing down on your face? ¹¹Israel has sinned; they have violated my covenant, which I commanded them to keep. They have taken some of the devoted things; they have stolen, they have lied, they have put them with their own possessions. ¹²That is why the Israelites cannot stand against their enemies; they turn their backs and run because they have been made liable to destruction. I will not be with you anymore unless you destroy whatever among you is devoted to destruction.

¹³"Go, consecrate the people. Tell them, 'Consecrate yourselves in preparation for tomorrow; for this is what the LORD, the God of Israel, says: That which is devoted is among you, O Israel. You cannot stand against your enemies until you remove it.

¹⁴" 'In the morning, present yourselves tribe by tribe. The tribe that the LORD takes shall come forward clan by clan; the clan that the LORD takes shall come forward family by family; and the family that the LORD takes shall come forward man by man. ¹⁵He who is caught with the devoted things shall be destroyed by fire, along with all that belongs to him. He has violated the covenant of the LORD and has done a disgraceful thing in Israel!' "

¹⁶Early the next morning Joshua had Israel come forward by tribes, and Judah was taken. ¹⁷The clans of Judah came forward, and he took the Zerahites. He had the clan of the Zerahites come forward by families, and Zimri was taken. ¹⁸Joshua had his family come forward man by man, and Achan son of Carmi, the son of Zimri, the son of Zerah, of the tribe of Judah, was taken.

¹⁹Then Joshua said to Achan, "My son, give glory to the LORD,*b* the God of Israel, and give him the praise.*c* Tell me what you have done; do not hide it from me."

²⁰Achan replied, "It is true! I have sinned against the LORD, the God of Israel. This is what I have done: ²¹When I saw in the plunder a beautiful robe from Babylonia,*d* two hundred shekels*e* of silver and a wedge of gold weighing fifty shekels,*f* I coveted them and took them. They are hidden in the ground inside my tent, with the silver underneath."

²²So Joshua sent messengers, and they ran to the tent, and there it was, hidden in his tent, with the silver underneath. ²³They took the things

---

a5 Or *as far as Shebarim*   *b19* A solemn charge to tell the truth   *c19* Or *and confess to him*
d21 Hebrew *Shinar*   *e21* That is, about 5 pounds (about 2.3 kilograms)   *f21* That is, about 1 1/4 pounds (about 0.6 kilogram)

from the tent, brought them to Joshua and all the Israelites and spread them out before the LORD.

❓DID YOU KNOW?   7:11

Why was Achan's sin so terrible?

God would help Israel fight their enemies only if his people obeyed him completely. Achan had disobeyed. Because God would not help after Achan sinned, thirty-six Israelite soldiers were killed at Ai. Only after Achan confessed and was punished did God again go with the Israelite soldiers into battle.

24Then Joshua, together with all Israel, took Achan son of Zerah, the silver, the robe, the gold wedge, his sons and daughters, his cattle, donkeys and sheep, his tent and all that he had, to the Valley of Achor. 25Joshua said, "Why have you brought this trouble on us? The LORD will bring trouble on you today."

Then all Israel stoned him, and after they had stoned the rest, they burned them. 26Over Achan they heaped up a large pile of rocks, which remains to this day. Then the LORD turned from his fierce anger. Therefore that place has been called the Valley of Achor*a* ever since.

Ai Destroyed

8 Then the LORD said to Joshua, "Do not be afraid; do not be discouraged. Take the whole army with you, and go up and attack Ai. For I have delivered into your hands the king of Ai, his people, his city and his land. 2You shall do to Ai and its king as you did to Jericho and its king, except that you may carry off their plunder and livestock for yourselves. Set an ambush behind the city."

3So Joshua and the whole army moved out to attack Ai. He chose thirty thousand of his best fighting men and sent them out at night 4with these orders: "Listen carefully. You are to set an ambush behind the city. Don't go very far from it. All of you be on the alert. 5I and all those with me will advance on the city, and when the men come out against us, as they did before, we will flee from them. 6They will pursue us until we have lured them away from the city, for they will say, 'They are running away from us as they did before.' So when we flee from them, 7you are to rise up from ambush and take the city. The LORD your God will give it into your hand. 8When you have taken the city, set it on fire. Do what the LORD has commanded. See to it; you have my orders."

9Then Joshua sent them off, and they went to the place of ambush and lay in wait between Bethel and Ai, to the west of Ai—but Joshua spent that night with the people.

10Early the next morning Joshua mustered his men, and he and the leaders of Israel marched before them to Ai. 11The entire force that was with him marched up and approached the city and arrived in front of it. They set up camp north of Ai, with the valley between them and the city. 12Joshua had taken about five thousand men and set them in ambush between Bethel and Ai, to the west of the city. 13They had the soldiers take up their positions—all those in the camp to the north of the city and the ambush to the west of it. That night Joshua went into the valley.

14When the king of Ai saw this, he and all the men of the city hurried out early in the morning to meet Israel in battle at a certain place overlooking the Arabah. But he did not know that an ambush had been set against him behind the city. 15Joshua and all Israel let themselves be driven back before them, and they fled toward the desert. 16All the men of Ai were called to pursue them, and they

---

a26 Achor means *trouble.*

pursued Joshua and were lured away from the city. [17]Not a man remained in Ai or Bethel who did not go after Israel. They left the city open and went in pursuit of Israel.

[18]Then the LORD said to Joshua, "Hold out toward Ai the javelin that is in your hand, for into your hand I will deliver the city." So Joshua held out his javelin toward Ai. [19]As soon as he did this, the men in the ambush rose quickly from their position and rushed forward. They entered the city and captured it and quickly set it on fire.

[20]The men of Ai looked back and saw the smoke of the city rising against the sky, but they had no chance to escape in any direction, for the Israelites who had been fleeing toward the desert had turned back against their pursuers. [21]For when Joshua and all Israel saw that the ambush had taken the city and that smoke was going up from the city, they turned around and attacked the men of Ai. [22]The men of the ambush also came out of the city against them, so that they were caught in the middle, with Israelites on both sides. Israel cut them down, leaving them neither survivors nor fugitives. [23]But they took the king of Ai alive and brought him to Joshua.

[24]When Israel had finished killing all the men of Ai in the fields and in the desert where they had chased them, and when every one of them had been put to the sword, all the Israelites returned to Ai and killed those who were in it. [25]Twelve thousand men and women fell that day —all the people of Ai. [26]For Joshua did not draw back the hand that held out his javelin until he had destroyed[a] all who lived in Ai. [27]But Israel did carry off for themselves the livestock and plunder of this city, as the LORD had instructed Joshua.

[28]So Joshua burned Ai and made it a permanent heap of ruins, a desolate place to this day. [29]He hung the king of Ai on a tree and left him there until evening. At sunset, Joshua ordered them to take his body from the tree and throw it down at the entrance of the city gate. And they raised a large pile of rocks over it, which remains to this day.

The Covenant Renewed at Mount Ebal

[30]Then Joshua built on Mount Ebal an altar to the LORD, the God of Israel, [31]as Moses the servant of the LORD had commanded the Israelites. He built it according to what is written in the Book of the Law of Moses—an altar of uncut stones, on which no iron tool had been used. On it they offered to the LORD burnt offerings and sacrificed fellowship offerings.[b] [32]There, in the presence of the Israelites, Joshua copied on stones the law of Moses, which he had written. [33]All Israel, aliens and citizens alike, with their elders, officials and judges, were standing on both sides of the ark of the covenant of the LORD, facing those who carried it—the priests, who were Levites. Half of the people stood in front of Mount Gerizim and half of them in front of Mount Ebal, as Moses the servant of the LORD had formerly commanded when he gave instructions to bless the people of Israel.

[34]Afterward, Joshua read all the words of the law—the blessings and the curses—just as it is written in the Book of the Law. [35]There was not a word of all that Moses had commanded that Joshua did not read to the whole assembly of Israel, including the women and children, and the aliens who lived among them.

The Gibeonite Deception

9 Now when all the kings west of the Jordan heard about these things—those in the hill country, in the western foothills, and along the entire coast of the Great Sea[c] as far

---

[a]26 The Hebrew term refers to the irrevocable giving over of things or persons to the LORD, often by totally destroying them.   [b]31 Traditionally *peace offerings*   [c]1 That is, the Mediterranean

as Lebanon (the kings of the Hittites, Amorites, Canaanites, Perizzites, Hivites and Jebusites)— ²they came together to make war against Joshua and Israel.

³However, when the people of Gibeon heard what Joshua had done to Jericho and Ai, ⁴they resorted to a ruse: They went as a delegation whose donkeys were loaded*a* with worn-out sacks and old wineskins, cracked and mended. ⁵The men put worn and patched sandals on their feet and wore old clothes. All the bread of their food supply was dry and moldy. ⁶Then they went to Joshua in the camp at Gilgal and said to him and the men of Israel, "We have come from a distant country; make a treaty with us."

⁷The men of Israel said to the Hivites, "But perhaps you live near us. How then can we make a treaty with you?"

⁸"We are your servants," they said to Joshua.

But Joshua asked, "Who are you and where do you come from?"

⁹They answered: "Your servants have come from a very distant country because of the fame of the LORD your God. For we have heard reports of him: all that he did in Egypt, ¹⁰and all that he did to the two kings of the Amorites east of the Jordan—Sihon king of Heshbon, and Og king of Bashan, who reigned in Ashtaroth. ¹¹And our elders and all those living in our country said to us, 'Take provisions for your journey; go and meet them and say to them, "We are your servants; make a treaty with us."'

¹²This bread of ours was warm when we packed it at home on the day we left to come to you. But now see how dry and moldy it is. ¹³And these wineskins that we filled were new, but see how cracked they are. And our clothes and sandals are worn out by the very long journey."

¹⁴The men of Israel sampled their provisions but did not inquire of the LORD. ¹⁵Then Joshua made a treaty of peace with them to let them live, and the leaders of the assembly ratified it by oath.

¹⁶Three days after they made the treaty with the Gibeonites, the Israelites heard that they were neighbors, living near them. ¹⁷So the Israelites set out and on the third day came to their cities: Gibeon, Kephirah, Beeroth and Kiriath Jearim. ¹⁸But the Israelites did not attack them, because the leaders of the as-

---

a4 Most Hebrew manuscripts; some Hebrew manuscripts, Vulgate and Syriac (see also Septuagint) *They prepared provisions and loaded their donkeys*

ET'S LIVE IT!   Joshua 9:1–18

ASK FIRST ➠ God had told Joshua to drive all the different peoples out of the land of Canaan. But one people, the Gibeonites, tricked Joshua and the Israelites. Read Joshua 9:1–18 to find out how.

The Bible says the people of Israel "did not inquire of the Lord (Joshua 9:14)." This means they didn't ask before they acted. When a person isn't sure about something, he or she should ask first.

Here are some questions that maybe should be asked before you act: Can I use the hammer if I put it back when I'm done? Is it all right if I cut across your yard? What should I do with the money I found in the street? Can I read my library book if I get my math done early?

Think up other questions you should ask before you go ahead and do something. Give yourself three points for each question you think of. See how many points you can earn in ten minutes. Or play the game at the supper table, with your whole family helping you think of things to ask about before acting.

sembly had sworn an oath to them by the LORD, the God of Israel.

The whole assembly grumbled against the leaders, [19]but all the leaders answered, "We have given them our oath by the LORD, the God of Israel, and we cannot touch them now. [20]This is what we will do to them: We will let them live, so that wrath will not fall on us for breaking the oath we swore to them." [21]They continued, "Let them live, but let them be woodcutters and water carriers for the entire community." So the leaders' promise to them was kept.

[22]Then Joshua summoned the Gibeonites and said, "Why did you deceive us by saying, 'We live a long way from you,' while actually you live near us? [23]You are now under a curse: You will never cease to serve as woodcutters and water carriers for the house of my God."

[24]They answered Joshua, "Your servants were clearly told how the LORD your God had commanded his servant Moses to give you the whole land and to wipe out all its inhabitants from before you. So we feared for our lives because of you, and that is why we did this. [25]We are now in your hands. Do to us whatever seems good and right to you."

[26]So Joshua saved them from the Israelites, and they did not kill them. [27]That day he made the Gibeonites woodcutters and water carriers for the community and for the altar of the LORD at the place the LORD would choose. And that is what they are to this day.

The Sun Stands Still

10 Now Adoni-Zedek king of Jerusalem heard that Joshua had taken Ai and totally destroyed[a] it, doing to Ai and its king as he had done to Jericho and its king, and that the people of Gibeon had made a treaty of peace with Israel and were living near them. [2]He and his people were very much alarmed at this, because Gibeon was an important city, like one of the royal cities; it was larger than Ai, and all its men were good fighters. [3]So Adoni-Zedek king of Jerusalem appealed to Hoham king of Hebron, Piram king of Jarmuth, Japhia king of Lachish and Debir king of Eglon. [4]"Come up and help me attack Gibeon," he said, "because it has made peace with Joshua and the Israelites."

[5]Then the five kings of the Amorites—the kings of Jerusalem, Hebron, Jarmuth, Lachish and Eglon —joined forces. They moved up with all their troops and took up positions against Gibeon and attacked it.

[6]The Gibeonites then sent word to Joshua in the camp at Gilgal: "Do not abandon your servants. Come up to us quickly and save us! Help us, because all the Amorite kings from the hill country have joined forces against us."

[7]So Joshua marched up from Gilgal with his entire army, including all the best fighting men. [8]The LORD said to Joshua, "Do not be afraid of them; I have given them into your hand. Not one of them will be able to withstand you."

[9]After an all-night march from Gilgal, Joshua took them by surprise. [10]The LORD threw them into confusion before Israel, who defeated them in a great victory at Gibeon. Israel pursued them along the road going up to Beth Horon and cut them down all the way to Azekah and Makkedah. [11]As they fled before Israel on the road down from Beth Horon to Azekah, the LORD hurled large hailstones down on them from the sky, and more of them died from the hailstones than were killed by the swords of the Israelites.

[12]On the day the LORD gave the Amorites over to Israel, Joshua said to the LORD in the presence of Israel:

"O sun, stand still over Gibeon,

---

[a]1 The Hebrew term refers to the irrevocable giving over of things or persons to the LORD, often by totally destroying them; also in verses 28, 35, 37, 39 and 40.

O moon, over the Valley of
   Aijalon."
¹³So the sun stood still,
  and the moon stopped,
   till the nation avenged itself
    on*ᵃ* its enemies,

as it is written in the Book of Jashar.

The sun stopped in the middle of
the sky and delayed going down
about a full day. ¹⁴There has never
been a day like it before or since, a
day when the LORD listened to a man.
Surely the LORD was fighting for Israel!

¹⁵Then Joshua returned with all Israel to the camp at Gilgal.

Five Amorite Kings Killed

¹⁶Now the five kings had fled and
hidden in the cave at Makkedah.
¹⁷When Joshua was told that the five
kings had been found hiding in the
cave at Makkedah, ¹⁸he said, "Roll
large rocks up to the mouth of the
cave, and post some men there to
guard it. ¹⁹But don't stop! Pursue
your enemies, attack them from the
rear and don't let them reach their
cities, for the LORD your God has given them into your hand."

²⁰So Joshua and the Israelites destroyed them completely—almost to
a man—but the few who were left
reached their fortified cities. ²¹The
whole army then returned safely to
Joshua in the camp at Makkedah,
and no one uttered a word against the
Israelites.

²²Joshua said, "Open the mouth of
the cave and bring those five kings
out to me." ²³So they brought the five
kings out of the cave—the kings of
Jerusalem, Hebron, Jarmuth, Lachish and Eglon. ²⁴When they had
brought these kings to Joshua, he
summoned all the men of Israel and
said to the army commanders who
had come with him, "Come here and
put your feet on the necks of these
kings." So they came forward and
placed their feet on their necks.

²⁵Joshua said to them, "Do not be

afraid; do not be discouraged. Be
strong and courageous. This is what
the LORD will do to all the enemies
you are going to fight." ²⁶Then Joshua struck and killed the kings and
hung them on five trees, and they
were left hanging on the trees until
evening.

DEFEATED KINGS

Joshua had his army commanders
put their feet on the necks of
enemy kings. This was a sign of
how helpless their enemies were.
The sign reminded the Israelites of
God's promise to go with them into
battles and to give them victory
over their enemies.

---

²⁷At sunset Joshua gave the order
and they took them down from the
trees and threw them into the cave
where they had been hiding. At
the mouth of the cave they placed
large rocks, which are there to this
day.

²⁸That day Joshua took Makkedah.
He put the city and its king to the
sword and totally destroyed everyone
in it. He left no survivors. And he did
to the king of Makkedah as he had
done to the king of Jericho.

Southern Cities Conquered

²⁹Then Joshua and all Israel with
him moved on from Makkedah to Libnah and attacked it. ³⁰The LORD also
gave that city and its king into Israel's hand. The city and everyone in it
Joshua put to the sword. He left no
survivors there. And he did to its
king as he had done to the king of
Jericho.

ᵃ13 Or nation triumphed over

³¹Then Joshua and all Israel with him moved on from Libnah to Lachish; he took up positions against it and attacked it. ³²The LORD handed Lachish over to Israel, and Joshua took it on the second day. The city and everyone in it he put to the sword, just as he had done to Libnah. ³³Meanwhile, Horam king of Gezer had come up to help Lachish, but Joshua defeated him and his army —until no survivors were left.

³⁴Then Joshua and all Israel with him moved on from Lachish to Eglon; they took up positions against it and attacked it. ³⁵They captured it that same day and put it to the sword and totally destroyed everyone in it, just as they had done to Lachish.

³⁶Then Joshua and all Israel with him went up from Eglon to Hebron and attacked it. ³⁷They took the city and put it to the sword, together with its king, its villages and everyone in it. They left no survivors. Just as at Eglon, they totally destroyed it and everyone in it.

³⁸Then Joshua and all Israel with him turned around and attacked Debir. ³⁹They took the city, its king and its villages, and put them to the sword. Everyone in it they totally destroyed. They left no survivors. They did to Debir and its king as they had done to Libnah and its king and to Hebron.

⁴⁰So Joshua subdued the whole region, including the hill country, the Negev, the western foothills and the mountain slopes, together with all their kings. He left no survivors. He totally destroyed all who breathed, just as the LORD, the God of Israel, had commanded. ⁴¹Joshua subdued them from Kadesh Barnea to Gaza and from the whole region of Goshen to Gibeon. ⁴²All these kings and their lands Joshua conquered in one campaign, because the LORD, the God of Israel, fought for Israel.

⁴³Then Joshua returned with all Israel to the camp at Gilgal.

a2 Or in the heights of Dor

Northern Kings Defeated

11 When Jabin king of Hazor heard of this, he sent word to Jobab king of Madon, to the kings of Shimron and Acshaph, ²and to the northern kings who were in the mountains, in the Arabah south of Kinnereth, in the western foothills and in Naphoth Dor*ᵃ* on the west; ³to the Canaanites in the east and west; to the Amorites, Hittites, Perizzites and Jebusites in the hill country; and to the Hivites below Hermon in the region of Mizpah. ⁴They came out with all their troops and a large number of horses and chariots—a huge army, as numerous as the sand on the seashore. ⁵All these kings joined forces and made camp together at the Waters of Merom, to fight against Israel.

❓DID YOU KNOW?   10:40

How did Joshua conquer Canaan?

Joshua's army drove into the center of Canaan and divided it. Joshua first defeated the kings of the south cities. Then he turned and defeated the kings of the north. Officers in modern war colleges still study the strategy Joshua used.

---

⁶The LORD said to Joshua, "Do not be afraid of them, because by this time tomorrow I will hand all of them over to Israel, slain. You are to hamstring their horses and burn their chariots."

⁷So Joshua and his whole army came against them suddenly at the Waters of Merom and attacked them, ⁸and the LORD gave them into the hand of Israel. They defeated them and pursued them all the way to Greater Sidon, to Misrephoth Maim, and to the Valley of Mizpah on the east, until no survivors were left. ⁹Joshua did to them as the LORD had

directed: He hamstrung their horses and burned their chariots.

¹⁰At that time Joshua turned back and captured Hazor and put its king to the sword. (Hazor had been the head of all these kingdoms.) ¹¹Everyone in it they put to the sword. They totally destroyed*a* them, not sparing anything that breathed, and he burned up Hazor itself.

¹²Joshua took all these royal cities and their kings and put them to the sword. He totally destroyed them, as Moses the servant of the LORD had commanded. ¹³Yet Israel did not burn any of the cities built on their mounds—except Hazor, which Joshua burned. ¹⁴The Israelites carried off for themselves all the plunder and livestock of these cities, but all the people they put to the sword until they completely destroyed them, not sparing anyone that breathed. ¹⁵As the LORD commanded his servant Moses, so Moses commanded Joshua, and Joshua did it; he left nothing undone of all that the LORD commanded Moses.

¹⁶So Joshua took this entire land: the hill country, all the Negev, the whole region of Goshen, the western foothills, the Arabah and the mountains of Israel with their foothills, ¹⁷from Mount Halak, which rises toward Seir, to Baal Gad in the Valley of Lebanon below Mount Hermon. He captured all their kings and struck them down, putting them to death. ¹⁸Joshua waged war against all these kings for a long time. ¹⁹Except for the Hivites living in Gibeon, not one city made a treaty of peace with the Israelites, who took them all in battle. ²⁰For it was the LORD himself who hardened their hearts to wage war against Israel, so that he might destroy them totally, exterminating them without mercy, as the LORD had commanded Moses.

²¹At that time Joshua went and destroyed the Anakites from the hill country: from Hebron, Debir and Anab, from all the hill country of Judah, and from all the hill country of Israel. Joshua totally destroyed them and their towns. ²²No Anakites were left in Israelite territory; only in Gaza, Gath and Ashdod did any survive. ²³So Joshua took the entire land, just as the LORD had directed Moses, and he gave it as an inheritance to Israel according to their tribal divisions.

Then the land had rest from war.

List of Defeated Kings

12 These are the kings of the land whom the Israelites had defeated and whose territory they took over east of the Jordan, from the Arnon Gorge to Mount Hermon, including all the eastern side of the Arabah:

²Sihon king of the Amorites,
   who reigned in Heshbon. He ruled from Aroer on the rim of the Arnon Gorge—from the middle of the gorge—to the Jabbok River, which is the border of the Ammonites. This included half of Gilead. ³He also ruled over the eastern Arabah from the Sea of Kinnereth*b* to the Sea of the Arabah (the Salt Sea*c*), to Beth Jeshimoth, and then southward below the slopes of Pisgah.

⁴And the territory of Og king of Bashan,
   one of the last of the Rephaites, who reigned in Ashtaroth and Edrei. ⁵He ruled over Mount Hermon, Salecah, all of Bashan to the border of the people of Geshur and Maacah, and half of Gilead to the border of Sihon king of Heshbon.

⁶Moses, the servant of the LORD, and the Israelites conquered them. And Moses the servant of the LORD

---

a11 The Hebrew term refers to the irrevocable giving over of things or persons to the LORD, often by totally destroying them; also in verses 12, 20 and 21.   *b3* That is, Galilee   *c3* That is, the Dead Sea

gave their land to the Reubenites, the Gadites and the half-tribe of Manasseh to be their possession.

⁷These are the kings of the land that Joshua and the Israelites conquered on the west side of the Jordan, from Baal Gad in the Valley of Lebanon to Mount Halak, which rises toward Seir (their lands Joshua gave as an inheritance to the tribes of Israel according to their tribal divisions— ⁸the hill country, the western foothills, the Arabah, the mountain slopes, the desert and the Negev— the lands of the Hittites, Amorites, Canaanites, Perizzites, Hivites and Jebusites):

⁹the king of Jericho	one
the king of Ai	
(near Bethel)	one
¹⁰the king of Jerusalem	one
the king of Hebron	one
¹¹the king of Jarmuth	one
the king of Lachish	one
¹²the king of Eglon	one
the king of Gezer	one
¹³the king of Debir	one
the king of Geder	one
¹⁴the king of Hormah	one
the king of Arad	one
¹⁵the king of Libnah	one
the king of Adullam	one
¹⁶the king of Makkedah	one
the king of Bethel	one
¹⁷the king of Tappuah	one
the king of Hepher	one
¹⁸the king of Aphek	one
the king of Lasharon	one
¹⁹the king of Madon	one
the king of Hazor	one
²⁰the king of Shimron	
Meron	one
the king of Acshaph	one
²¹the king of Taanach	one
the king of Megiddo	one
²²the king of Kedesh	one
the king of Jokneam in	
Carmel	one
²³the king of Dor (in	
Naphoth Dor ᵃ)	one
the king of Goyim in	
Gilgal	one

²⁴the king of Tirzah   one
thirty-one kings in all.

Land Still to Be Taken

13 When Joshua was old and well advanced in years, the LORD said to him, "You are very old, and there are still very large areas of land to be taken over.

²"This is the land that remains: all the regions of the Philistines and Geshurites: ³from the Shihor River on the east of Egypt to the territory of Ekron on the north, all of it counted as Canaanite (the territory of the five Philistine rulers in Gaza, Ashdod, Ashkelon, Gath and Ekron —that of the Avvites); ⁴from the south, all the land of the Canaanites, from Arah of the Sidonians as far as Aphek, the region of the Amorites, ⁵the area of the Gebalites ᵇ; and all Lebanon to the east, from Baal Gad below Mount Hermon to Lebo ᶜ Hamath.

❓DID YOU KNOW?   13:1

Were all the Canaanites killed by Joshua?

No. The Canaanite armies were defeated, but many Canaanites still lived in the land. Each Israelite tribe was supposed to fight the Canaanites that remained in the land assigned to them.

---

⁶"As for all the inhabitants of the mountain regions from Lebanon to Misrephoth Maim, that is, all the Sidonians, I myself will drive them out before the Israelites. Be sure to allocate this land to Israel for an inheritance, as I have instructed you, ⁷and divide it as an inheritance among the nine tribes and half of the tribe of Manasseh."

Division of the Land East of the Jordan

[8]The other half of Manasseh,[a] the Reubenites and the Gadites had received the inheritance that Moses had given them east of the Jordan, as he, the servant of the LORD, had assigned it to them.

[9]It extended from Aroer on the rim of the Arnon Gorge, and from the town in the middle of the gorge, and included the whole plateau of Medeba as far as Dibon, [10]and all the towns of Sihon king of the Amorites, who ruled in Heshbon, out to the border of the Ammonites. [11]It also included Gilead, the territory of the people of Geshur and Maacah, all of Mount Hermon and all Bashan as far as Salecah— [12]that is, the whole kingdom of Og in Bashan, who had reigned in Ashtaroth and Edrei and had survived as one of the last of the Rephaites. Moses had defeated them and taken over their land. [13]But the Israelites did not drive out the people of Geshur and Maacah, so they continue to live among the Israelites to this day.

[14]But to the tribe of Levi he gave no inheritance, since the offerings made by fire to the LORD, the God of Israel, are their inheritance, as he promised them.

[15]This is what Moses had given to the tribe of Reuben, clan by clan:

[16]The territory from Aroer on the rim of the Arnon Gorge, and from the town in the middle of the gorge, and the whole plateau past Medeba [17]to Heshbon and all its towns on the plateau, including Dibon, Bamoth Baal, Beth Baal Meon, [18]Jahaz, Kedemoth, Mephaath, [19]Kiriathaim, Sibmah, Zereth Shahar on the hill in the valley, [20]Beth Peor, the slopes of Pisgah, and Beth Jeshimoth [21]—all the towns on the plateau and the entire realm of Sihon king of the Amorites, who ruled at Heshbon. Moses had defeated him and the Midianite chiefs, Evi, Rekem, Zur, Hur and Reba—princes allied with Sihon—who lived in that country. [22]In addition to those slain in battle, the Israelites had put to the sword Balaam son of Beor, who practiced divination. [23]The boundary of the Reubenites was the bank of the Jordan. These towns and their villages were the inheritance of the Reubenites, clan by clan.

[24]This is what Moses had given to the tribe of Gad, clan by clan:

[25]The territory of Jazer, all the towns of Gilead and half the Ammonite country as far as Aroer, near Rabbah; [26]and from Heshbon to Ramath Mizpah and Betonim, and from Mahanaim to the territory of Debir; [27]and in the valley, Beth Haram, Beth Nimrah, Succoth and Zaphon with the rest of the realm of Sihon king of Heshbon (the east side of the Jordan, the territory up to the end of the Sea of Kinnereth[b]). [28]These towns and their villages were the inheritance of the Gadites, clan by clan.

[29]This is what Moses had given to the half-tribe of Manasseh, that is, to half the family of the descendants of Manasseh, clan by clan:

[30]The territory extending from Mahanaim and including all of Bashan, the entire realm of Og king of Bashan—all the settlements of Jair in Bashan, sixty towns, [31]half of Gilead, and Ashtaroth and Edrei (the royal cities of Og in Bashan). This was for the descendants of Makir son of Manasseh—for half of the sons of Makir, clan by clan.

---

a8 Hebrew *With it* (that is, with the other half of Manasseh)   b27 That is, Galilee

³²This is the inheritance Moses had given when he was in the plains of Moab across the Jordan east of Jericho. ³³But to the tribe of Levi, Moses had given no inheritance; the LORD, the God of Israel, is their inheritance, as he promised them.

Division of the Land West of the Jordan

14 Now these are the areas the Israelites received as an inheritance in the land of Canaan, which Eleazar the priest, Joshua son of Nun and the heads of the tribal clans of Israel allotted to them. ²Their inheritances were assigned by lot to the nine-and-a-half tribes, as the LORD had commanded through Moses. ³Moses had granted the two-and-a-half tribes their inheritance east of the Jordan but had not granted the Levites an inheritance among the rest, ⁴for the sons of Joseph had become two tribes—Manasseh and Ephraim. The Levites received no share of the land but only towns to live in, with pasturelands for their flocks and herds. ⁵So the Israelites divided the land, just as the LORD had commanded Moses.

Hebron Given to Caleb

⁶Now the men of Judah approached Joshua at Gilgal, and Caleb son of Jephunneh the Kenizzite said to him, "You know what the LORD said to Moses the man of God at Kadesh Barnea about you and me. ⁷I was forty years old when Moses the servant of the LORD sent me from Kadesh Barnea to explore the land. And I brought him back a report according to my convictions, ⁸but my brothers who went up with me made the hearts of the people melt with fear. I, however, followed the LORD my God wholeheartedly. ⁹So on that day Moses swore to me, 'The land on which your feet have walked will be your inheritance and that of your children forever, because you have followed the LORD my God wholeheartedly.'ᵃ

¹⁰"Now then, just as the LORD promised, he has kept me alive for forty-five years since the time he said this to Moses, while Israel moved about in the desert. So here I am today, eighty-five years old! ¹¹I am still as strong today as the day Moses sent me out; I'm just as vigorous to go out to battle now as I was then. ¹²Now give me this hill country that the LORD promised me that day. You yourself heard then that the Anakites were there and their cities were large and fortified, but, the LORD helping me, I will drive them out just as he said."

❓DID YOU KNOW?   14:6

Who was Caleb?

Caleb was one of the spies Moses sent to scout Canaan when the Israelites first came out of Egypt. Only Caleb and Joshua wanted to obey God and attack Canaan at that time. As a reward, God let Caleb live when the other Israelite adults died in the wilderness.

¹³Then Joshua blessed Caleb son of Jephunneh and gave him Hebron as his inheritance. ¹⁴So Hebron has belonged to Caleb son of Jephunneh the Kenizzite ever since, because he followed the LORD, the God of Israel, wholeheartedly. ¹⁵(Hebron used to be called Kiriath Arba after Arba, who was the greatest man among the Anakites.)

Then the land had rest from war.

Allotment for Judah

15 The allotment for the tribe of Judah, clan by clan, extended down to the territory of Edom, to the Desert of Zin in the extreme south.

²Their southern boundary started from the bay at the southern end of the Salt Sea,ᵇ ³crossed south of Scorpionᶜ Pass, continued on to Zin and went

---

ᵃ9 Deut. 1:36   ᵇ2 That is, the Dead Sea; also in verse 5   ᶜ3 Hebrew *Akrabbim* over to the south of Kadesh Barnea. Then it ran past Hezron up to Addar and curved around to Karka. ⁴It then passed along to Azmon and joined the Wadi of Egypt, ending at the sea. This is their*a* southern boundary.

⁵The eastern boundary is the Salt Sea as far as the mouth of the Jordan.

The northern boundary started from the bay of the sea at the mouth of the Jordan, ⁶went up to Beth Hoglah and continued north of Beth Arabah to the Stone of Bohan son of Reuben. ⁷The boundary then went up to Debir from the Valley of Achor and turned north to Gilgal, which faces the Pass of Adummim south of the gorge. It continued along to the waters of En Shemesh and came out at En Rogel. ⁸Then it ran up the Valley of Ben Hinnom along the southern slope of the Jebusite city (that is, Jerusalem). From there it climbed to the top of the hill west of the Hinnom Valley at the northern end of the Valley of Rephaim. ⁹From the hilltop the boundary headed toward the spring of the waters of Nephtoah, came out at the towns of Mount Ephron and went down toward Baalah (that is, Kiriath Jearim). ¹⁰Then it curved westward from Baalah to Mount Seir, ran along the northern slope of Mount Jearim (that is, Kesalon), continued down to Beth Shemesh and crossed to Timnah. ¹¹It went to the northern slope of Ekron, turned toward Shikkeron, passed along to Mount Baalah and reached Jabneel. The boundary ended at the sea.

¹²The western boundary is the coastline of the Great Sea.*b* These are the boundaries around the people of Judah by their clans.

¹³In accordance with the Lord's command to him, Joshua gave to Caleb son of Jephunneh a portion in Judah—Kiriath Arba, that is, Hebron. (Arba was the forefather of Anak.) ¹⁴From Hebron Caleb drove out the three Anakites—Sheshai, Ahiman and Talmai—descendants of Anak. ¹⁵From there he marched against the people living in Debir (formerly called Kiriath Sepher). ¹⁶And Caleb said, "I will give my daughter Acsah in marriage to the man who attacks and captures Kiriath Sepher." ¹⁷Othniel son of Kenaz, Caleb's brother, took it; so Caleb gave his daughter Acsah to him in marriage.

¹⁸One day when she came to Othniel, she urged him*c* to ask her father for a field. When she got off her donkey, Caleb asked her, "What can I do for you?"

¹⁹She replied, "Do me a special favor. Since you have given me land in the Negev, give me also springs of water." So Caleb gave her the upper and lower springs.

²⁰This is the inheritance of the tribe of Judah, clan by clan:

²¹The southernmost towns of the tribe of Judah in the Negev toward the boundary of Edom were:

Kabzeel, Eder, Jagur, ²²Kinah, Dimonah, Adadah, ²³Kedesh, Hazor, Ithnan, ²⁴Ziph, Telem, Bealoth, ²⁵Hazor Hadattah, Kerioth Hezron (that is, Hazor), ²⁶Amam, Shema, Moladah, ²⁷Hazar Gaddah, Heshmon, Beth Pelet, ²⁸Hazar Shual, Beersheba, Biziothiah, ²⁹Baalah, Iim, Ezem, ³⁰Eltolad, Kesil, Hormah, ³¹Ziklag, Madmannah, Sansannah, ³²Lebaoth, Shilhim, Ain and Rimmon—a total of twenty-nine towns and their villages.

³³In the western foothills:

Eshtaol, Zorah, Ashnah, ³⁴Zanoah, En Gannim, Tappuah,

---

a4 Hebrew *your*　　*b12* That is, the Mediterranean; also in verse 47　　*c18* Hebrew and some Septuagint manuscripts; other Septuagint manuscripts (see also note at Judges 1:14) *Othniel, he urged her*

Enam, 35Jarmuth, Adullam, Socoh, Azekah, 36Shaaraim, Adi-
thaim and Gederah (or Gederothaim)*—fourteen towns and
their villages.

37Zenan, Hadashah, Migdal
Gad, 38Dilean, Mizpah, Joktheel,
39Lachish, Bozkath, Eglon,
40Cabbon, Lahmas, Kitlish,
41Gederoth, Beth Dagon, Naamah and Makkedah—sixteen
towns and their villages.

42Libnah, Ether, Ashan, 43Iph-
tah, Ashnah, Nezib, 44Keilah,
Aczib and Mareshah—nine
towns and their villages.

45Ekron, with its surrounding
settlements and villages; 46west
of Ekron, all that were in the vicinity of Ashdod, together with
their villages; 47Ashdod, its surrounding settlements and villages; and Gaza, its settlements
and villages, as far as the Wadi
of Egypt and the coastline of the
Great Sea.

48In the hill country:
Shamir, Jattir, Socoh, 49Dan-
nah, Kiriath Sannah (that is,
Debir), 50Anab, Eshtemoh,
Anim, 51Goshen, Holon and Giloh—eleven towns and their villages.

52Arab, Dumah, Eshan, 53Ja-
nim, Beth Tappuah, Aphekah,
54Humtah, Kiriath Arba (that is,
Hebron) and Zior—nine towns
and their villages.

55Maon, Carmel, Ziph, Juttah,
56Jezreel, Jokdeam, Zanoah,
57Kain, Gibeah and Timnah—
ten towns and their villages.

58Halhul, Beth Zur, Gedor,
59Maarath, Beth Anoth and Elte-
kon—six towns and their villages.

60Kiriath Baal (that is, Kiriath Jearim) and Rabbah—two
towns and their villages.

61In the desert:
Beth Arabah, Middin, Seca-

cah, 62Nibshan, the City of Salt
and En Gedi—six towns and
their villages.

63Judah could not dislodge the Jebusites, who were living in Jerusalem;
to this day the Jebusites live there
with the people of Judah.

Allotment for Ephraim and Manasseh

16 The allotment for Joseph
began at the Jordan of
Jericho,*b* east of the waters of
Jericho, and went up from there
through the desert into the hill
country of Bethel. 2It went on
from Bethel (that is, Luz),*c*
crossed over to the territory of
the Arkites in Ataroth, 3de-
scended westward to the territory of the Japhletites as far as the
region of Lower Beth Horon and
on to Gezer, ending at the sea.
4So Manasseh and Ephraim, the
descendants of Joseph, received their
inheritance.

5This was the territory of Ephraim,
clan by clan:
The boundary of their inheritance went from Ataroth Addar
in the east to Upper Beth Horon
6and continued to the sea. From
Micmethath on the north it
curved eastward to Taanath Shiloh, passing by it to Janoah on
the east. 7Then it went down
from Janoah to Ataroth and Naarah, touched Jericho and came
out at the Jordan. 8From Tappuah the border went west to the
Kanah Ravine and ended at the
sea. This was the inheritance of
the tribe of the Ephraimites,
clan by clan. 9It also included all
the towns and their villages that
were set aside for the Ephraimites within the inheritance of the
Manassites.

10They did not dislodge the Canaanites living in Gezer; to this day the
Canaanites live among the people of

---

*a36 Or Gederah and Gederothaim   b1 Jordan of Jericho was possibly an ancient name for the
Jordan River.   c2 Septuagint; Hebrew Bethel to Luz*

Ephraim but are required to do forced labor.

17 This was the allotment for the tribe of Manasseh as Joseph's firstborn, that is, for Makir, Manasseh's firstborn. Makir was the ancestor of the Gileadites, who had received Gilead and Bashan because the Makirites were great soldiers. ²So this allotment was for the rest of the people of Manasseh—the clans of Abiezer, Helek, Asriel, Shechem, Hepher and Shemida. These are the other male descendants of Manasseh son of Joseph by their clans.

³Now Zelophehad son of Hepher, the son of Gilead, the son of Makir, the son of Manasseh, had no sons but only daughters, whose names were Mahlah, Noah, Hoglah, Milcah and Tirzah. ⁴They went to Eleazar the priest, Joshua son of Nun, and the leaders and said, "The LORD commanded Moses to give us an inheritance among our brothers." So Joshua gave them an inheritance along with the brothers of their father, according to the LORD's command. ⁵Manasseh's share consisted of ten tracts of land besides Gilead and Bashan east of the Jordan, ⁶because the daughters of the tribe of Manasseh received an inheritance among the sons. The land of Gilead belonged to the rest of the descendants of Manasseh.

⁷The territory of Manasseh extended from Asher to Micmethath east of Shechem. The boundary ran southward from there to include the people living at En Tappuah. ⁸(Manasseh had the land of Tappuah, but Tappuah itself, on the boundary of Manasseh, belonged to the Ephraimites.) ⁹Then the boundary continued south to the Kanah Ravine. There were towns belonging to Ephraim lying among the towns of Manasseh, but the boundary of Manasseh was the northern side of the ravine and ended at the sea. ¹⁰On the south

the land belonged to Ephraim, on the north to Manasseh. The territory of Manasseh reached the sea and bordered Asher on the north and Issachar on the east.

¹¹Within Issachar and Asher, Manasseh also had Beth Shan, Ibleam and the people of Dor, Endor, Taanach and Megiddo, together with their surrounding settlements (the third in the list is Naphoth*a*).

¹²Yet the Manassites were not able to occupy these towns, for the Canaanites were determined to live in that region. ¹³However, when the Israelites grew stronger, they subjected the Canaanites to forced labor but did not drive them out completely.

¹⁴The people of Joseph said to Joshua, "Why have you given us only one allotment and one portion for an inheritance? We are a numerous people and the LORD has blessed us abundantly."

¹⁵"If you are so numerous," Joshua answered, "and if the hill country of Ephraim is too small for you, go up into the forest and clear land for yourselves there in the land of the Perizzites and Rephaites."

¹⁶The people of Joseph replied, "The hill country is not enough for us, and all the Canaanites who live in the plain have iron chariots, both those in Beth Shan and its settlements and those in the Valley of Jezreel."

¹⁷But Joshua said to the house of Joseph—to Ephraim and Manasseh —"You are numerous and very powerful. You will have not only one allotment ¹⁸but the forested hill country as well. Clear it, and its farthest limits will be yours; though the Canaanites have iron chariots and though they are strong, you can drive them out."

Division of the Rest of the Land

18 The whole assembly of the Israelites gathered at Shiloh

*a11 That is, Naphoth Dor

and set up the Tent of Meeting there. The country was brought under their control, 2but there were still seven Israelite tribes who had not yet received their inheritance.

3So Joshua said to the Israelites: "How long will you wait before you begin to take possession of the land that the LORD, the God of your fathers, has given you? 4Appoint three men from each tribe. I will send them out to make a survey of the land and to write a description of it, according to the inheritance of each. Then they will return to me. 5You are to divide the land into seven parts. Judah is to remain in its territory on the south and the house of Joseph in its territory on the north. 6After you have written descriptions of the seven parts of the land, bring them here to me and I will cast lots for you in the presence of the LORD our God. 7The Levites, however, do not get a portion among you, because the priestly service of the LORD is their inheritance. And Gad, Reuben and the half-tribe of Manasseh have already received their inheritance on the east side of the Jordan. Moses the servant of the LORD gave it to them."

8As the men started on their way to map out the land, Joshua instructed them, "Go and make a survey of the land and write a description of it. Then return to me, and I will cast lots for you here at Shiloh in the presence of the LORD." 9So the men left and went through the land. They wrote its description on a scroll, town by town, in seven parts, and returned to Joshua in the camp at Shiloh. 10Joshua then cast lots for them in Shiloh in the presence of the LORD, and there he distributed the land to the Israelites according to their tribal divisions.

Allotment for Benjamin

11The lot came up for the tribe of Benjamin, clan by clan. Their allotted territory lay between the tribes of Judah and Joseph:

12On the north side their boundary began at the Jordan,

passed the northern slope of Jericho and headed west into the hill country, coming out at the desert of Beth Aven. 13From there it crossed to the south slope of Luz (that is, Bethel) and went down to Ataroth Addar on the hill south of Lower Beth Horon.

Life In Bible Times

THE LAND DIVIDED

When the Israelites entered the promised land, Joshua divided the land up. He gave each tribe an area in which to live. The only tribe not assigned an area was the tribe of Levi. They were assigned forty-eight towns and the land that was around them. These towns were inside the areas given to the other tribes and were located so that some Levites lived with each tribe of Israel.

14From the hill facing Beth Horon on the south the boundary turned south along the western side and came out at Kiriath Baal (that is, Kiriath Jearim), a town of the people of Judah. This was the western side.

15The southern side began at the outskirts of Kiriath Jearim on the west, and the boundary came out at the spring of the waters of Nephtoah. 16The boundary went down to the foot of the hill facing the Valley of Ben Hinnom, north of the Valley of Rephaim. It continued down the Hinnom Valley along the southern slope of the Jebusite city and so to En Rogel. 17It then curved north, went to En Shemesh, continued to Geliloth, which faces the Pass of Adummim, and ran down to the Stone of Bohan son of Reuben. ¹⁸It continued to the northern slope of Beth Arabah^a and on down into the Arabah. ¹⁹It then went to the northern slope of Beth Hoglah and came out at the northern bay of the Salt Sea,^b at the mouth of the Jordan in the south. This was the southern boundary.

²⁰The Jordan formed the boundary on the eastern side.

These were the boundaries that marked out the inheritance of the clans of Benjamin on all sides.

²¹The tribe of Benjamin, clan by clan, had the following cities:

Jericho, Beth Hoglah, Emek Keziz, ²²Beth Arabah, Zemaraim, Bethel, ²³Avvim, Parah, Ophrah, ²⁴Kephar Ammoni, Ophni and Geba—twelve towns and their villages.

²⁵Gibeon, Ramah, Beeroth, ²⁶Mizpah, Kephirah, Mozah, ²⁷Rekem, Irpeel, Taralah, ²⁸Zelah, Haeleph, the Jebusite city (that is, Jerusalem), Gibeah and Kiriath—fourteen towns and their villages.

This was the inheritance of Benjamin for its clans.

Allotment for Simeon

19 The second lot came out for the tribe of Simeon, clan by clan. Their inheritance lay within the territory of Judah. ²It included:

Beersheba (or Sheba),^c Moladah, ³Hazar Shual, Balah, Ezem, ⁴Eltolad, Bethul, Hormah, ⁵Ziklag, Beth Marcaboth, Hazar Susah, ⁶Beth Lebaoth and Sharuhen—thirteen towns and their villages;

⁷Ain, Rimmon, Ether and Ashan—four towns and their villages— ⁸and all the villages around these towns as far as Baalath Beer (Ramah in the Negev).

This was the inheritance of the tribe of the Simeonites, clan by clan. ⁹The inheritance of the Simeonites was taken from the share of Judah, because Judah's portion was more than they needed. So the Simeonites received their inheritance within the territory of Judah.

Allotment for Zebulun

¹⁰The third lot came up for Zebulun, clan by clan:

The boundary of their inheritance went as far as Sarid. ¹¹Going west it ran to Maralah, touched Dabbesheth, and extended to the ravine near Jokneam. ¹²It turned east from Sarid toward the sunrise to the territory of Kisloth Tabor and went on to Daberath and up to Japhia. ¹³Then it continued eastward to Gath Hepher and Eth Kazin; it came out at Rimmon and turned toward Neah. ¹⁴There the boundary went around on the north to Hannathon and ended at the Valley of Iphtah El. ¹⁵Included were Kattath, Nahalal, Shimron, Idalah and Bethlehem. There were twelve towns and their villages.

¹⁶These towns and their villages were the inheritance of Zebulun, clan by clan.

Allotment for Issachar

¹⁷The fourth lot came out for Issachar, clan by clan. ¹⁸Their territory included:

Jezreel, Kesulloth, Shunem, ¹⁹Hapharaim, Shion, Anaharath, ²⁰Rabbith, Kishion, Ebez, ²¹Remeth, En Gannim, En Haddah and Beth Pazzez. ²²The boundary touched Tabor, Shahazumah and Beth Shemesh, and ended at the Jordan. There were sixteen towns and their villages.

²³These towns and their villages were the inheritance of the tribe of Issachar, clan by clan.

---

^a18 Septuagint; Hebrew *slope facing the Arabah*   ^b19 That is, the Dead Sea   ^c2 Or *Beersheba, Sheba*; 1 Chron. 4:28 does not have *Sheba*.

Allotment for Asher

²⁴The fifth lot came out for the tribe of Asher, clan by clan. ²⁵Their territory included:

Helkath, Hali, Beten, Acshaph, ²⁶Allammelech, Amad and Mishal. On the west the boundary touched Carmel and Shihor Libnath. ²⁷It then turned east toward Beth Dagon, touched Zebulun and the Valley of Iphtah El, and went north to Beth Emek and Neiel, passing Cabul on the left. ²⁸It went to Abdon,ᵃ Rehob, Hammon and Kanah, as far as Greater Sidon. ²⁹The boundary then turned back toward Ramah and went to the fortified city of Tyre, turned toward Hosah and came out at the sea in the region of Aczib, ³⁰Ummah, Aphek and Rehob. There were twenty-two towns and their villages.

³¹These towns and their villages were the inheritance of the tribe of Asher, clan by clan.

Allotment for Naphtali

³²The sixth lot came out for Naphtali, clan by clan:

³³Their boundary went from Heleph and the large tree in Zaanannim, passing Adami Nekeb and Jabneel to Lakkum and ending at the Jordan. ³⁴The boundary ran west through Aznoth Tabor and came out at Hukkok. It touched Zebulun on the south, Asher on the west and the Jordanᵇ on the east. ³⁵The fortified cities were Ziddim, Zer, Hammath, Rakkath, Kinnereth, ³⁶Adamah, Ramah, Hazor, ³⁷Kedesh, Edrei, En Hazor, ³⁸Iron, Migdal El, Horem, Beth Anath and Beth Shemesh. There were nineteen towns and their villages.

³⁹These towns and their villages were the inheritance of the tribe of Naphtali, clan by clan.

Allotment for Dan

⁴⁰The seventh lot came out for the tribe of Dan, clan by clan. ⁴¹The territory of their inheritance included:

Zorah, Eshtaol, Ir Shemesh, ⁴²Shaalabbin, Aijalon, Ithlah, ⁴³Elon, Timnah, Ekron, ⁴⁴Eltekeh, Gibbethon, Baalath, ⁴⁵Jehud, Bene Berak, Gath Rimmon, ⁴⁶Me Jarkon and Rakkon, with the area facing Joppa.

⁴⁷(But the Danites had difficulty taking possession of their territory, so they went up and attacked Leshem, took it, put it to the sword and occupied it. They settled in Leshem and named it Dan after their forefather.)

⁴⁸These towns and their villages were the inheritance of the tribe of Dan, clan by clan.

Allotment for Joshua

⁴⁹When they had finished dividing the land into its allotted portions, the Israelites gave Joshua son of Nun an inheritance among them, ⁵⁰as the LORD had commanded. They gave him the town he asked for—Timnath Serahᶜ in the hill country of Ephraim. And he built up the town and settled there.

⁵¹These are the territories that Eleazar the priest, Joshua son of Nun and the heads of the tribal clans of Israel assigned by lot at Shiloh in the presence of the LORD at the entrance to the Tent of Meeting. And so they finished dividing the land.

Cities of Refuge

20 Then the LORD said to Joshua: ²"Tell the Israelites to designate the cities of refuge, as I instructed you through Moses, ³so that anyone who kills a person accidentally and unintentionally may flee there

---

ᵃ28 Some Hebrew manuscripts (see also Joshua 21:30); most Hebrew manuscripts *Ebron*   ᵇ34 Septuagint; Hebrew *west, and Judah, the Jordan,*   ᶜ50 Also known as *Timnath Heres* (see Judges 2:9)

and find protection from the avenger of blood.

4"When he flees to one of these cities, he is to stand in the entrance of the city gate and state his case before the elders of that city. Then they are to admit him into their city and give him a place to live with them. 5If the avenger of blood pursues him, they must not surrender the one accused, because he killed his neighbor unintentionally and without malice aforethought. 6He is to stay in that city until he has stood trial before the assembly and until the death of the high priest who is serving at that time. Then he may go back to his own home in the town from which he fled."

7So they set apart Kedesh in Galilee in the hill country of Naphtali, Shechem in the hill country of Ephraim, and Kiriath Arba (that is, Hebron) in the hill country of Judah. 8On the east side of the Jordan of Jericho[a] they designated Bezer in the desert on the plateau in the tribe of Reuben, Ramoth in Gilead in the tribe of Gad, and Golan in Bashan in the tribe of Manasseh. 9Any of the Israelites or any alien living among them who killed someone accidentally could flee to these designated cities and not be killed by the avenger of blood prior to standing trial before the assembly.

Towns for the Levites

21 Now the family heads of the Levites approached Eleazar the priest, Joshua son of Nun, and the heads of the other tribal families of Israel 2at Shiloh in Canaan and said to them, "The LORD commanded through Moses that you give us towns to live in, with pasturelands for our livestock." 3So, as the LORD had commanded, the Israelites gave the Levites the following towns and pasturelands out of their own inheritance:

4The first lot came out for the Kohathites, clan by clan. The Levites who were descendants of Aaron the priest were allotted thirteen towns from the tribes of Judah, Simeon and Benjamin. 5The rest of Kohath's descendants were allotted ten towns from the clans of the tribes of Ephraim, Dan and half of Manasseh.

6The descendants of Gershon were allotted thirteen towns from the clans of the tribes of Issachar, Asher, Naphtali and the half-tribe of Manasseh in Bashan.

7The descendants of Merari, clan by clan, received twelve towns from the tribes of Reuben, Gad and Zebulun.

8So the Israelites allotted to the Levites these towns and their pasturelands, as the LORD had commanded through Moses.

9From the tribes of Judah and Simeon they allotted the following towns by name 10(these towns were assigned to the descendants of Aaron who were from the Kohathite clans of the Levites, because the first lot fell to them):

11They gave them Kiriath Arba (that is, Hebron), with its surrounding pastureland, in the hill country of Judah. (Arba was the forefather of Anak.) 12But the fields and villages around the city they had given to Caleb son of Jephunneh as his possession.

13So to the descendants of Aaron the priest they gave Hebron (a city of refuge for one accused of murder), Libnah, 14Jattir, Eshtemoa, 15Holon, Debir, 16Ain, Juttah and Beth Shemesh, together with their pasturelands—nine towns from these two tribes.

17And from the tribe of Benjamin they gave them Gibeon, Geba, 18Anathoth and Almon, together with their pasturelands —four towns.

19All the towns for the priests, the descendants of Aaron, were thirteen, together with their pasturelands.

a8 Jordan of Jericho was possibly an ancient name for the Jordan River.

²⁰The rest of the Kohathite clans of the Levites were allotted towns from the tribe of Ephraim:

²¹In the hill country of Ephraim they were given Shechem (a city of refuge for one accused of murder) and Gezer, ²²Kibzaim and Beth Horon, together with their pasturelands—four towns.

²³Also from the tribe of Dan they received Eltekeh, Gibbethon, ²⁴Aijalon and Gath Rimmon, together with their pasturelands—four towns.

²⁵From half the tribe of Manasseh they received Taanach and Gath Rimmon, together with their pasturelands—two towns.

²⁶All these ten towns and their pasturelands were given to the rest of the Kohathite clans.

²⁷The Levite clans of the Gershonites were given:
from the half-tribe of Manasseh,
Golan in Bashan (a city of refuge for one accused of murder) and Be Eshtarah, together with their pasturelands—two towns;
²⁸from the tribe of Issachar,
Kishion, Daberath, ²⁹Jarmuth and En Gannim, together with their pasturelands—four towns;
³⁰from the tribe of Asher,
Mishal, Abdon, ³¹Helkath and Rehob, together with their pasturelands—four towns;
³²from the tribe of Naphtali,
Kedesh in Galilee (a city of refuge for one accused of murder), Hammoth Dor and Kartan, together with their pasturelands—three towns.

³³All the towns of the Gershonite clans were thirteen, together with their pasturelands.

³⁴The Merarite clans (the rest of the Levites) were given:
from the tribe of Zebulun,
Jokneam, Kartah, ³⁵Dimnah and Nahalal, together with their pasturelands—four towns;
³⁶from the tribe of Reuben,
Bezer, Jahaz, ³⁷Kedemoth and Mephaath, together with their pasturelands—four towns;
³⁸from the tribe of Gad,
Ramoth in Gilead (a city of refuge for one accused of murder), Mahanaim, ³⁹Heshbon and Jazer, together with their pasturelands—four towns in all.

⁴⁰All the towns allotted to the Merarite clans, who were the rest of the Levites, were twelve.

⁴¹The towns of the Levites in the territory held by the Israelites were forty-eight in all, together with their pasturelands. ⁴²Each of these towns had pasturelands surrounding it; this was true for all these towns.

⁴³So the LORD gave Israel all the land he had sworn to give their forefathers, and they took possession of it and settled there. ⁴⁴The LORD gave them rest on every side, just as he had sworn to their forefathers. Not one of their enemies withstood them; the LORD handed all their enemies over to them. ⁴⁵Not one of all the LORD's good promises to the house of Israel failed; every one was fulfilled.

Eastern Tribes Return Home

22 Then Joshua summoned the Reubenites, the Gadites and the half-tribe of Manasseh ²and said to them, "You have done all that Moses the servant of the LORD commanded, and you have obeyed me in everything I commanded. ³For a long time now—to this very day—you have not deserted your brothers but have carried out the mission the LORD your God gave you. ⁴Now that the LORD your God has given your brothers rest as he promised, return to your homes in the land that Moses the servant of the LORD gave you on the other side of the Jordan. ⁵But be very careful to keep the commandment and the law that Moses the servant of the LORD gave you: to love the LORD your God, to walk in all his ways, to obey his commands, to hold fast to him and to serve him with all your heart and all your soul."

⁶Then Joshua blessed them and

sent them away, and they went to their homes. ⁷(To the half-tribe of Manasseh Moses had given land in Bashan, and to the other half of the tribe Joshua gave land on the west side of the Jordan with their brothers.) When Joshua sent them home, he blessed them, ⁸saying, "Return to your homes with your great wealth —with large herds of livestock, with silver, gold, bronze and iron, and a great quantity of clothing—and divide with your brothers the plunder from your enemies."

⁹So the Reubenites, the Gadites and the half-tribe of Manasseh left the Israelites at Shiloh in Canaan to return to Gilead, their own land, which they had acquired in accordance with the command of the LORD through Moses.

¹⁰When they came to Geliloth near the Jordan in the land of Canaan, the Reubenites, the Gadites and the half-tribe of Manasseh built an imposing altar there by the Jordan. ¹¹And when the Israelites heard that they had built the altar on the border of Canaan at Geliloth near the Jordan on the Israelite side, ¹²the whole assembly of Israel gathered at Shiloh to go to war against them.

¹³So the Israelites sent Phinehas son of Eleazar, the priest, to the land of Gilead—to Reuben, Gad and the half-tribe of Manasseh. ¹⁴With him they sent ten of the chief men, one for each of the tribes of Israel, each the head of a family division among the Israelite clans.

¹⁵When they went to Gilead—to Reuben, Gad and the half-tribe of Manasseh—they said to them: ¹⁶"The whole assembly of the LORD says: 'How could you break faith with the God of Israel like this? How could you turn away from the LORD and build yourselves an altar in rebellion against him now? ¹⁷Was not the sin of Peor enough for us? Up to this very day we have not cleansed ourselves from that sin, even though a plague

fell on the community of the LORD! ¹⁸And are you now turning away from the LORD?

" 'If you rebel against the LORD today, tomorrow he will be angry with the whole community of Israel. ¹⁹If the land you possess is defiled, come over to the LORD's land, where the LORD's tabernacle stands, and share the land with us. But do not rebel against the LORD or against us by building an altar for yourselves, other than the altar of the LORD our God. ²⁰When Achan son of Zerah acted unfaithfully regarding the devoted things,ᵃ did not wrath come upon the whole community of Israel? He was not the only one who died for his sin.' "

²¹Then Reuben, Gad and the half-tribe of Manasseh replied to the heads of the clans of Israel: ²²"The Mighty One, God, the LORD! The Mighty One, God, the LORD! He knows! And let Israel know! If this has been in rebellion or disobedience to the LORD, do not spare us this day. ²³If we have built our own altar to turn away from the LORD and to offer burnt offerings and grain offerings, or to sacrifice fellowship offeringsᵇ on it, may the LORD himself call us to account.

²⁴"No! We did it for fear that some day your descendants might say to ours, 'What do you have to do with the LORD, the God of Israel? ²⁵The LORD has made the Jordan a boundary between us and you—you Reubenites and Gadites! You have no share in the LORD.' So your descendants might cause ours to stop fearing the LORD.

²⁶"That is why we said, 'Let us get ready and build an altar—but not for burnt offerings or sacrifices.' ²⁷On the contrary, it is to be a witness between us and you and the generations that follow, that we will worship the LORD at his sanctuary with our burnt offerings, sacrifices and fellowship offerings. Then in the future

---

ᵃ20 The Hebrew term refers to the irrevocable giving over of things or persons to the LORD, often by totally destroying them.   ᵇ23 Traditionally *peace offerings*; also in verse 27

your descendants will not be able to say to ours, 'You have no share in the LORD.'

28"And we said, 'If they ever say this to us, or to our descendants, we will answer: Look at the replica of the LORD's altar, which our fathers built, not for burnt offerings and sacrifices, but as a witness between us and you.'

29"Far be it from us to rebel against the LORD and turn away from him today by building an altar for burnt offerings, grain offerings and sacrifices, other than the altar of the LORD our God that stands before his tabernacle."

30When Phinehas the priest and the leaders of the community—the heads of the clans of the Israelites —heard what Reuben, Gad and Manasseh had to say, they were pleased. 31And Phinehas son of Eleazar, the priest, said to Reuben, Gad and Manasseh, "Today we know that the LORD is with us, because you have not acted unfaithfully toward the LORD in this matter. Now you have rescued the Israelites from the LORD's hand."

32Then Phinehas son of Eleazar, the priest, and the leaders returned to Canaan from their meeting with the Reubenites and Gadites in Gilead and reported to the Israelites. 33They were glad to hear the report and praised God. And they talked no more about going to war against them to devastate the country where the Reubenites and the Gadites lived.

34And the Reubenites and the Gadites gave the altar this name: A Witness Between Us that the LORD is God.

Joshua's Farewell to the Leaders

23 After a long time had passed and the LORD had given Israel rest from all their enemies around them, Joshua, by then old and well advanced in years, 2summoned all Israel—their elders, leaders, judges and officials—and said to them: "I am old and well advanced in years.

3You yourselves have seen everything the LORD your God has done to all these nations for your sake; it was the LORD your God who fought for you. 4Remember how I have allotted as an inheritance for your tribes all the land of the nations that remain —the nations I conquered—between the Jordan and the Great Sea*a* in the west. 5The LORD your God himself will drive them out of your way. He will push them out before you, and you will take possession of their land, as the LORD your God promised you.

6"Be very strong; be careful to obey all that is written in the Book of the Law of Moses, without turning aside to the right or to the left. 7Do not associate with these nations that remain among you; do not invoke the names of their gods or swear by them. You must not serve them or bow down to them. 8But you are to hold fast to the LORD your God, as you have until now.

9"The LORD has driven out before you great and powerful nations; to this day no one has been able to withstand you. 10One of you routs a thousand, because the LORD your God fights for you, just as he promised. 11So be very careful to love the LORD your God.

12"But if you turn away and ally yourselves with the survivors of these nations that remain among you and if you intermarry with them and associate with them, 13then you may be sure that the LORD your God will no longer drive out these nations before you. Instead, they will become snares and traps for you, whips on your backs and thorns in your eyes, until you perish from this good land, which the LORD your God has given you.

14"Now I am about to go the way of all the earth. You know with all your heart and soul that not one of all the good promises the LORD your God gave you has failed. Every promise has been fulfilled; not one has failed. 15But just as every good promise of

a4 That is, the Mediterranean

the LORD your God has come true, so the LORD will bring on you all the evil he has threatened, until he has destroyed you from this good land he has given you. 16If you violate the covenant of the LORD your God, which he commanded you, and go and serve other gods and bow down to them, the LORD's anger will burn against you, and you will quickly perish from the good land he has given you."

The Covenant Renewed at Shechem

24 Then Joshua assembled all the tribes of Israel at Shechem. He summoned the elders, leaders, judges and officials of Israel, and they presented themselves before God.

2Joshua said to all the people, "This is what the LORD, the God of Israel, says: 'Long ago your forefathers, including Terah the father of Abraham and Nahor, lived beyond the River*a* and worshiped other gods. 3But I took your father Abraham from the land beyond the River and led him throughout Canaan and gave him many descendants. I gave him Isaac, 4and to Isaac I gave Jacob and Esau. I assigned the hill country of Seir to Esau, but Jacob and his sons went down to Egypt.

5"'Then I sent Moses and Aaron, and I afflicted the Egyptians by what I did there, and I brought you out. 6When I brought your fathers out of Egypt, you came to the sea, and the Egyptians pursued them with chariots and horsemen*b* as far as the Red Sea.*c* 7But they cried to the LORD for help, and he put darkness between you and the Egyptians; he brought the sea over them and covered them. You saw with your own eyes what I did to the Egyptians. Then you lived in the desert for a long time.

8"'I brought you to the land of the Amorites who lived east of the Jordan. They fought against you, but I gave them into your hands. I destroyed them from before you, and you took possession of their land. 9When Balak son of Zippor, the king of Moab, prepared to fight against Israel, he sent for Balaam son of Beor to put a curse on you. 10But I would not listen to Balaam, so he blessed you again and again, and I delivered you out of his hand.

11"'Then you crossed the Jordan and came to Jericho. The citizens of Jericho fought against you, as did also the Amorites, Perizzites, Canaanites, Hittites, Girgashites, Hivites and Jebusites, but I gave them into your hands. 12I sent the hornet ahead of you, which drove them out before you—also the two Amorite kings. You did not do it with your own sword and bow. 13So I gave you a land on which you did not toil and cities you did not build; and you live in them and eat from vineyards and olive groves that you did not plant.'

14"Now fear the LORD and serve him with all faithfulness. Throw away the gods your forefathers worshiped beyond the River and in Egypt, and serve the LORD. 15But if serving the LORD seems undesirable to you, then choose for yourselves this day whom you will serve, whether the gods your forefathers served beyond the River, or the gods of the Amorites, in whose land you are living. But as for me and my household, we will serve the LORD."

WORDS TO REMEMBER

24:15 As for me and my household, we will serve the LORD.

16Then the people answered, "Far be it from us to forsake the LORD to serve other gods! 17It was the LORD our God himself who brought us and our fathers up out of Egypt, from that land of slavery, and performed those great signs before our eyes. He pro-

---

*a*2 That is, the Euphrates; also in verses 3, 14 and 15 Suph; that is, Sea of Reeds   *b*6 Or charioteers   *c*6 Hebrew Yam

tected us on our entire journey and among all the nations through which we traveled. ¹⁸And the LORD drove out before us all the nations, including the Amorites, who lived in the land. We too will serve the LORD, because he is our God."

¹⁹Joshua said to the people, "You are not able to serve the LORD. He is a holy God; he is a jealous God. He will not forgive your rebellion and your sins. ²⁰If you forsake the LORD and serve foreign gods, he will turn and bring disaster on you and make an end of you, after he has been good to you."

²¹But the people said to Joshua, "No! We will serve the LORD."

²²Then Joshua said, "You are witnesses against yourselves that you have chosen to serve the LORD."

"Yes, we are witnesses," they replied.

²³"Now then," said Joshua, "throw away the foreign gods that are among you and yield your hearts to the LORD, the God of Israel."

²⁴And the people said to Joshua, "We will serve the LORD our God and obey him."

²⁵On that day Joshua made a covenant for the people, and there at Shechem he drew up for them decrees and laws. ²⁶And Joshua recorded these things in the Book of the Law of God. Then he took a large stone

and set it up there under the oak near the holy place of the LORD.

²⁷"See!" he said to all the people. "This stone will be a witness against us. It has heard all the words the LORD has said to us. It will be a witness against you if you are untrue to your God."

Buried in the Promised Land

²⁸Then Joshua sent the people away, each to his own inheritance.

²⁹After these things, Joshua son of Nun, the servant of the LORD, died at the age of a hundred and ten. ³⁰And they buried him in the land of his inheritance, at Timnath Serah ᵃ in the hill country of Ephraim, north of Mount Gaash.

³¹Israel served the LORD throughout the lifetime of Joshua and of the elders who outlived him and who had experienced everything the LORD had done for Israel.

³²And Joseph's bones, which the Israelites had brought up from Egypt, were buried at Shechem in the tract of land that Jacob bought for a hundred pieces of silver ᵇ from the sons of Hamor, the father of Shechem. This became the inheritance of Joseph's descendants.

³³And Eleazar son of Aaron died and was buried at Gibeah, which had been allotted to his son Phinehas in the hill country of Ephraim.

ᵃ30 Also known as *Timnath Heres* (see Judges 2:9)   ᵇ32 Hebrew *hundred kesitahs*; a kesitah was
a unit of money of unknown weight and value.

▍ET'S LIVE IT!   Joshua 24:14–27

CHOOSING TO SERVE GOD ➠ When Joshua was old, he called all the Israelites together. What did he ask them to do?

Joshua said, "As for me and my household, we will serve the LORD." This special verse is Joshua 24:15. Ask your mom or dad, "When did you choose to serve the Lord? Why did you decide to serve him?" After your mom or dad answers, here's another question to ask, "Why do you want me to choose to serve God?"

JUDGES

WHO WROTE THIS BOOK?

No one knows for sure. Many people think Samuel is the author.

WHY WAS THIS BOOK WRITTEN?

Judges shows what happened when the Israelites abandoned God to worship idols.

WHAT HAPPENS IN THIS BOOK?

God's people sin again and again. God lets Israel's enemies win. When the Israelites suffer, they turn to God. Then God sends a "judge" to defeat the enemy and lead Israel.

WHAT DO WE LEARN ABOUT GOD IN THIS BOOK?

God is eager to forgive and help people who have sinned if only they will turn to him.

WHO IS IMPORTANT IN THIS BOOK?

The most important people in this book are Deborah, Gideon, Jephthah and Samson.

WHEN DID THIS HAPPEN?

The events in this book happened between 1390 and 1050 B.C.

WHERE DID THIS HAPPEN?

The events of this book happened in different parts of Palestine, then called Canaan.

WHAT ARE SOME OF THE STORIES IN THIS BOOK?

Israel Fights the Remaining Canaanites

1 After the death of Joshua, the Israelites asked the LORD, "Who will be the first to go up and fight for us against the Canaanites?"

2The LORD answered, "Judah is to go; I have given the land into their hands."

3Then the men of Judah said to the Simeonites their brothers, "Come up with us into the territory allotted to us, to fight against the Canaanites. We in turn will go with you into yours." So the Simeonites went with them.

4When Judah attacked, the LORD gave the Canaanites and Perizzites into their hands and they struck down ten thousand men at Bezek. 5It was there that they found Adoni-Bezek and fought against him, putting to rout the Canaanites and Perizzites. 6Adoni-Bezek fled, but they chased him and caught him, and cut off his thumbs and big toes.

7Then Adoni-Bezek said, "Seventy kings with their thumbs and big toes cut off have picked up scraps under my table. Now God has paid me back for what I did to them." They brought him to Jerusalem, and he died there.

8The men of Judah attacked Jerusalem also and took it. They put the city to the sword and set it on fire.

9After that, the men of Judah went down to fight against the Canaanites living in the hill country, the Negev and the western foothills. 10They advanced against the Canaanites living in Hebron (formerly called Kiriath Arba) and defeated Sheshai, Ahiman and Talmai.

11From there they advanced against the people living in Debir (formerly called Kiriath Sepher). 12And Caleb said, "I will give my daughter Acsah in marriage to the man who attacks and captures Kiriath Sepher." 13Othniel son of Kenaz,

Caleb's younger brother, took it; so Caleb gave his daughter Acsah to him in marriage.

14One day when she came to Othniel, she urged him*a* to ask her father for a field. When she got off her donkey, Caleb asked her, "What can I do for you?"

15She replied, "Do me a special favor. Since you have given me land in the Negev, give me also springs of water." Then Caleb gave her the upper and lower springs.

16The descendants of Moses' father-in-law, the Kenite, went up from the City of Palms*b* with the men of Judah to live among the people of the Desert of Judah in the Negev near Arad.

17Then the men of Judah went with the Simeonites their brothers and attacked the Canaanites living in Zephath, and they totally destroyed*c* the city. Therefore it was called Hormah.*d* 18The men of Judah also took*e* Gaza, Ashkelon and Ekron—each city with its territory.

19The LORD was with the men of Judah. They took possession of the hill country, but they were unable to drive the people from the plains, because they had iron chariots. 20As Moses had promised, Hebron was given to Caleb, who drove from it the three sons of Anak. 21The Benjamites, however, failed to dislodge the Jebusites, who were living in Jerusalem; to this day the Jebusites live there with the Benjamites.

22Now the house of Joseph attacked Bethel, and the LORD was with them. 23When they sent men to spy out Bethel (formerly called Luz), 24the spies saw a man coming out of the city and they said to him, "Show us how to get into the city and we will see that you are treated well." 25So he showed them, and they put the city to the sword but spared the man and his whole family. 26He then went to the

---

a14 Hebrew; Septuagint and Vulgate *Othniel, he urged her*   *b16* That is, Jericho   *c17* The Hebrew term refers to the irrevocable giving over of things or persons to the LORD, often by totally destroying them.   *d17 Hormah* means *destruction.*   *e18* Hebrew; Septuagint *Judah did not take*

land of the Hittites, where he built a city and called it Luz, which is its name to this day.

27But Manasseh did not drive out the people of Beth Shan or Taanach or Dor or Ibleam or Megiddo and their surrounding settlements, for the Canaanites were determined to live in that land. 28When Israel became strong, they pressed the Canaanites into forced labor but never drove them out completely. 29Nor did Ephraim drive out the Canaanites living in Gezer, but the Canaanites continued to live there among them. 30Neither did Zebulun drive out the Canaanites living in Kitron or Nahalol, who remained among them; but they did subject them to forced labor. 31Nor did Asher drive out those living in Acco or Sidon or Ahlab or Aczib or Helbah or Aphek or Rehob, 32and because of this the people of Asher lived among the Canaanite inhabitants of the land. 33Neither did Naphtali drive out those living in Beth Shemesh or Beth Anath; but the Naphtalites too lived among the Canaanite inhabitants of the land, and those living in Beth Shemesh and Beth Anath became forced laborers for them. 34The Amorites confined the Danites to the hill country, not allowing them to come down into the plain. 35And the Amorites were determined also to

hold out in Mount Heres, Aijalon and Shaalbim, but when the power of the house of Joseph increased, they too were pressed into forced labor. 36The boundary of the Amorites was from Scorpion*a* Pass to Sela and beyond.

The Angel of the LORD at Bokim

2 The angel of the LORD went up from Gilgal to Bokim and said, "I brought you up out of Egypt and led you into the land that I swore to give to your forefathers. I said, 'I will never break my covenant with you, 2and you shall not make a covenant with the people of this land, but you shall break down their altars.' Yet you have disobeyed me. Why have you done this? 3Now therefore I tell you that I will not drive them out before you; they will be thorns in your sides and their gods will be a snare to you."

4When the angel of the LORD had spoken these things to all the Israelites, the people wept aloud, 5and they called that place Bokim.*b* There they offered sacrifices to the LORD.

Disobedience and Defeat

6After Joshua had dismissed the Israelites, they went to take possession of the land, each to his own inheritance. 7The people served the LORD throughout the lifetime of Joshua

*a36 Hebrew Akrabbim   *b5 Bokim means weepers.

Life in Bible Times

CANAANITE WAR CHARIOTS

The Canaanites fought from heavy chariots covered with iron. These chariots were the tanks of ancient armies. War chariots could only be used on flat ground, not on rocky hillsides. The Israelites had no iron chariots.

and of the elders who outlived him and who had seen all the great things the LORD had done for Israel.

8Joshua son of Nun, the servant of the LORD, died at the age of a hundred and ten. 9And they buried him in the land of his inheritance, at Timnath Heres*a* in the hill country of Ephraim, north of Mount Gaash.

10After that whole generation had been gathered to their fathers, another generation grew up, who knew neither the LORD nor what he had done for Israel. 11Then the Israelites did evil in the eyes of the LORD and served the Baals. 12They forsook the LORD, the God of their fathers, who had brought them out of Egypt. They followed and worshiped various gods of the peoples around them. They provoked the LORD to anger 13because they forsook him and served Baal and the Ashtoreths. 14In his anger against Israel the LORD handed them over to raiders who plundered them. He sold them to their enemies all around, whom they were no longer able to resist. 15Whenever Israel went out to fight, the hand of the LORD was against them to defeat them, just as he had sworn to them. They were in great distress.

16Then the LORD raised up judges,*b* who saved them out of the hands of these raiders. 17Yet they would not listen to their judges but prostituted themselves to other gods and wor-

shiped them. Unlike their fathers, they quickly turned from the way in which their fathers had walked, the way of obedience to the LORD's commands. 18Whenever the LORD raised up a judge for them, he was with the judge and saved them out of the hands of their enemies as long as the judge lived; for the LORD had compassion on them as they groaned under those who oppressed and afflicted them. 19But when the judge died, the people returned to ways even more corrupt than those of their fathers, following other gods and serving and worshiping them. They refused to give up their evil practices and stubborn ways.

❓DID YOU KNOW?   2:18

What were judges?

The judges of the Bible were rulers. They led the Israelites in war and governed them in peacetime.

20Therefore the LORD was very angry with Israel and said, "Because this nation has violated the covenant that I laid down for their forefathers and has not listened to me, 21I will no longer drive out before them any of the nations Joshua left when he died. 22I will use them to test Israel and see

a9 Also known as *Timnath Serah* (see Joshua 19:50 and 24:30)   *b16* Or *leaders*; similarly in verses 17-19

▌ET'S LIVE IT!   Judges 2:6–7

A FAMILY HISTORY ➠ If your parents, grandparents, uncles and aunts are Christians, make a history book to help you remember what God means to your family. Ask your parents to get you a picture album. Then get pictures of your mom and dad, your grandparents, aunts and uncles, and other relatives. Ask each relative to write you a letter about his or her life and what God has meant to him or her. Put the pictures and letters in the album. Then you will never forget what God has done for your own family.

It really is important to remember God. Read Judges 2:10–23 and see what happened when the young Israelites did not remember God.

whether they will keep the way of the LORD and walk in it as their forefathers did." 23The LORD had allowed those nations to remain; he did not drive them out at once by giving them into the hands of Joshua.

3 These are the nations the LORD left to test all those Israelites who had not experienced any of the wars in Canaan 2(he did this only to teach warfare to the descendants of the Israelites who had not had previous battle experience): 3the five rulers of the Philistines, all the Canaanites, the Sidonians, and the Hivites living in the Lebanon mountains from Mount Baal Hermon to Lebo*a* Hamath. 4They were left to test the Israelites to see whether they would obey the LORD's commands, which he had given their forefathers through Moses.

5The Israelites lived among the Canaanites, Hittites, Amorites, Perizzites, Hivites and Jebusites. 6They took their daughters in marriage and gave their own daughters to their sons, and served their gods.

Othniel

7The Israelites did evil in the eyes of the LORD; they forgot the LORD their God and served the Baals and the Asherahs. 8The anger of the LORD burned against Israel so that he sold them into the hands of Cushan-Rishathaim king of Aram Naharaim,*b* to whom the Israelites were subject for eight years. 9But when they cried out to the LORD, he raised up for them a deliverer, Othniel son of Kenaz, Caleb's younger brother, who saved them. 10The Spirit of the LORD came upon him, so that he became Israel's judge*c* and went to war. The LORD gave Cushan-Rishathaim king of Aram into the hands of Othniel, who overpowered him. 11So the land had peace for forty years, until Othniel son of Kenaz died.

Ehud

12Once again the Israelites did evil in the eyes of the LORD, and because they did this evil the LORD gave Eglon king of Moab power over Israel. 13Getting the Ammonites and Amalekites to join him, Eglon came and attacked Israel, and they took possession of the City of Palms.*d* 14The Israelites were subject to Eglon king of Moab for eighteen years.

15Again the Israelites cried out to the LORD, and he gave them a deliverer—Ehud, a left-handed man, the son of Gera the Benjamite. The Israelites sent him with tribute to Eglon king of Moab. 16Now Ehud had made a double-edged sword about a foot and a half*e* long, which he strapped to his right thigh under his clothing. 17He presented the tribute to Eglon king of Moab, who was a very fat man. 18After Ehud had presented the tribute, he sent on their way the men who had carried it. 19At the idols*f* near Gilgal he himself turned back and said, "I have a secret message for you, O king."

The king said, "Quiet!" And all his attendants left him.

20Ehud then approached him while he was sitting alone in the upper room of his summer palace*g* and said, "I have a message from God for you." As the king rose from his seat, 21Ehud reached with his left hand, drew the sword from his right thigh and plunged it into the king's belly. 22Even the handle sank in after the blade, which came out his back. Ehud did not pull the sword out, and the fat closed in over it. 23Then Ehud went out to the porch*h*; he shut the doors of the upper room behind him and locked them.

24After he had gone, the servants came and found the doors of the upper room locked. They said, "He must be relieving himself in the inner room of the house." 25They waited to

---

a3 Or *to the entrance to*   *b8* That is, Northwest Mesopotamia   *c10* Or *leader*   *d13* That is, Jericho   *e16* Hebrew *a cubit* (about 0.5 meter)   *f19* Or *the stone quarries*; also in verse 26   *g20* The meaning of the Hebrew for this phrase is uncertain.   *h23* The meaning of the Hebrew for this word is uncertain.

the point of embarrassment, but when he did not open the doors of the room, they took a key and unlocked them. There they saw their lord fallen to the floor, dead.

²⁶While they waited, Ehud got away. He passed by the idols and escaped to Seirah. ²⁷When he arrived there, he blew a trumpet in the hill country of Ephraim, and the Israelites went down with him from the hills, with him leading them.

²⁸"Follow me," he ordered, "for the LORD has given Moab, your enemy, into your hands." So they followed him down and, taking possession of the fords of the Jordan that led to Moab, they allowed no one to cross over. ²⁹At that time they struck down about ten thousand Moabites, all vigorous and strong; not a man escaped. ³⁰That day Moab was made subject to Israel, and the land had peace for eighty years.

Shamgar

³¹After Ehud came Shamgar son of Anath, who struck down six hundred Philistines with an oxgoad. He too saved Israel.

Deborah

4 After Ehud died, the Israelites once again did evil in the eyes of the LORD. ²So the LORD sold them into the hands of Jabin, a king of Canaan, who reigned in Hazor. The command-er of his army was Sisera, who lived in Harosheth Haggoyim. ³Because he had nine hundred iron chariots and had cruelly oppressed the Israelites for twenty years, they cried to the LORD for help.

⁴Deborah, a prophetess, the wife of Lappidoth, was leading *a* Israel at that time. ⁵She held court under the Palm of Deborah between Ramah and Bethel in the hill country of Ephraim, and the Israelites came to her to have their disputes decided. ⁶She sent for Barak son of Abinoam from Kedesh in Naphtali and said to him, "The LORD, the God of Israel, commands you: 'Go, take with you ten thousand men of Naphtali and Zebulun and lead the way to Mount Tabor. ⁷I will lure Sisera, the commander of Jabin's army, with his chariots and his troops to the Kishon River and give him into your hands.'"

⁸Barak said to her, "If you go with me, I will go; but if you don't go with me, I won't go."

⁹"Very well," Deborah said, "I will go with you. But because of the way you are going about this, *b* the honor will not be yours, for the LORD will hand Sisera over to a woman." So Deborah went with Barak to Kedesh, ¹⁰where he summoned Zebulun and Naphtali. Ten thousand men followed him, and Deborah also went with him.

---

a4 Traditionally *judging*   *b9* Or *But on the expedition you are undertaking*

▌ET'S LIVE IT!   Judges 4:1–10

JUST FOR GIRLS ➠ The word *judge* in this Bible book means leader or ruler. Deborah was a prophetess who spoke the Word of God. Deborah was a judge, too, and ruled the Israelites. The people counted on Deborah so much that General Barak, the head of the army, said he would not fight the enemy unless Deborah went with him! Read Judges 4:1–10 to learn more about this important Bible woman.

Women are important in the church today too. Talk to a woman leader in your church. Ask what she does to serve God. Ask how other women can serve God. Ask how you will be able to serve God when you grow up. Then write her a letter and tell her how you want to serve God when you grow up.

¹¹Now Heber the Kenite had left the other Kenites, the descendants of Hobab, Moses' brother-in-law,ᵃ and pitched his tent by the great tree in Zaanannim near Kedesh.

¹²When they told Sisera that Barak son of Abinoam had gone up to Mount Tabor, ¹³Sisera gathered together his nine hundred iron chariots and all the men with him, from Harosheth Haggoyim to the Kishon River. ¹⁴Then Deborah said to Barak, "Go! This is the day the LORD has given Sisera into your hands. Has not the LORD gone ahead of you?" So Barak went down Mount Tabor, followed by ten thousand men. ¹⁵At Barak's advance, the LORD routed Sisera and all his chariots and army by the sword, and Sisera abandoned his chariot and fled on foot. ¹⁶But Barak pursued the chariots and army as far as Harosheth Haggoyim. All the troops of Sisera fell by the sword; not a man was left.

¹⁷Sisera, however, fled on foot to the tent of Jael, the wife of Heber the Kenite, because there were friendly relations between Jabin king of Hazor and the clan of Heber the Kenite. ¹⁸Jael went out to meet Sisera and said to him, "Come, my lord, come right in. Don't be afraid." So he entered her tent, and she put a covering over him.

¹⁹"I'm thirsty," he said. "Please give me some water." She opened a skin of milk, gave him a drink, and covered him up.

²⁰"Stand in the doorway of the tent," he told her. "If someone comes by and asks you, 'Is anyone here?' say 'No.'"

²¹But Jael, Heber's wife, picked up a tent peg and a hammer and went quietly to him while he lay fast asleep, exhausted. She drove the peg through his temple into the ground, and he died.

²²Barak came by in pursuit of Sisera, and Jael went out to meet him. "Come," she said, "I will show you the man you're looking for." So he went in with her, and there lay Sisera with the tent peg through his temple— dead.

SKIN BOTTLES

In Bible times liquids were often kept in containers made of goat skin. The skin was sewed up with the hair on the outside. Milk was put into these skin bottles to make yogurt. Water and wine were put into skin bottles to be carried from place to place.

---

²³On that day God subdued Jabin, the Canaanite king, before the Israelites. ²⁴And the hand of the Israelites grew stronger and stronger against Jabin, the Canaanite king, until they destroyed him.

The Song of Deborah

5 On that day Deborah and Barak son of Abinoam sang this song:

²"When the princes in Israel take
 the lead,
 when the people willingly offer
  themselves—
 praise the LORD!

³"Hear this, you kings! Listen, you
 rulers!
 I will sing toᵇ the LORD, I will
  sing;
 I will make music toᶜ the LORD,
  the God of Israel.

⁴"O LORD, when you went out from
 Seir,
 when you marched from the
  land of Edom,

ᵃ11 Or *father-in-law* ᵇ3 Or *of* ᶜ3 Or *I with song I will praise*

the earth shook, the heavens
poured,
the clouds poured down water.

WORDS TO REMEMBER

5:3 I will sing to the LORD, I will
sing;
I will make music to the
LORD, the God of Israel.

---

⁵The mountains quaked before the
LORD, the One of Sinai,
before the LORD, the God of
Israel.

⁶"In the days of Shamgar son of
Anath,
in the days of Jael, the roads
were abandoned;
travelers took to winding paths.
⁷Village life*a* in Israel ceased,
ceased until I,*b* Deborah, arose,
arose a mother in Israel.
⁸When they chose new gods,
war came to the city gates,
and not a shield or spear was
seen
among forty thousand in Israel.
⁹My heart is with Israel's princes,
with the willing volunteers
among the people.
Praise the LORD!

¹⁰"You who ride on white donkeys,
sitting on your saddle blankets,
and you who walk along the
road,
consider ¹¹the voice of the
singers*c* at the watering
places.
They recite the righteous acts of
the LORD,
the righteous acts of his
warriors*d* in Israel.

"Then the people of the LORD
went down to the city gates.
¹²'Wake up, wake up, Deborah!
Wake up, wake up, break out in
song!
Arise, O Barak!

Take captive your captives,
O son of Abinoam.'

¹³"Then the men who were left
came down to the nobles;
the people of the LORD
came to me with the mighty.
¹⁴Some came from Ephraim, whose
roots were in Amalek;
Benjamin was with the people
who followed you.
From Makir captains came down,
from Zebulun those who bear a
commander's staff.
¹⁵The princes of Issachar were with
Deborah;
yes, Issachar was with Barak,
rushing after him into the
valley.
In the districts of Reuben
there was much searching of
heart.
¹⁶Why did you stay among the
campfires*e*
to hear the whistling for the
flocks?
In the districts of Reuben
there was much searching of
heart.
¹⁷Gilead stayed beyond the Jordan.
And Dan, why did he linger by
the ships?
Asher remained on the coast
and stayed in his coves.
¹⁸The people of Zebulun risked
their very lives;
so did Naphtali on the heights
of the field.

¹⁹"Kings came, they fought;
the kings of Canaan fought
at Taanach by the waters of
Megiddo,
but they carried off no silver, no
plunder.
²⁰From the heavens the stars
fought,
from their courses they fought
against Sisera.
²¹The river Kishon swept them
away,
the age-old river, the river
Kishon.

---

a7 Or *Warriors*   *b7* Or *you*   *c11* Or *archers*; the meaning of the Hebrew for this word is
uncertain.   *d11* Or *villagers*   *e16* Or *saddlebags*

March on, my soul; be strong!
²²Then thundered the horses'
        hoofs—
    galloping, galloping go his
        mighty steeds.
²³'Curse Meroz,' said the angel of
        the LORD.
    'Curse its people bitterly,
    because they did not come to help
        the LORD,
    to help the LORD against the
        mighty.'

²⁴"Most blessed of women be Jael,
    the wife of Heber the Kenite,
    most blessed of tent-dwelling
        women.
²⁵He asked for water, and she gave
        him milk;
    in a bowl fit for nobles she
        brought him curdled milk.
²⁶Her hand reached for the tent
        peg,
    her right hand for the
        workman's hammer.
    She struck Sisera, she crushed his
        head,
    she shattered and pierced his
        temple.
²⁷At her feet he sank,
    he fell; there he lay.
    At her feet he sank, he fell;
    where he sank, there he
        fell—dead.

²⁸"Through the window peered
        Sisera's mother;
    behind the lattice she cried out,
    'Why is his chariot so long in
        coming?
    Why is the clatter of his
        chariots delayed?'
²⁹The wisest of her ladies answer
        her;
    indeed, she keeps saying to
        herself,
³⁰'Are they not finding and dividing
        the spoils:
    a girl or two for each man,
    colorful garments as plunder for
        Sisera,
    colorful garments embroidered,
    highly embroidered garments
        for my neck—
    all this as plunder?'

³¹"So may all your enemies perish,
        O LORD!
    But may they who love you be
        like the sun
    when it rises in its strength."

Then the land had peace forty years.

Gideon

6 Again the Israelites did evil in the eyes of the LORD, and for seven years he gave them into the hands of the Midianites. ²Because the power of Midian was so oppressive, the Israelites prepared shelters for themselves in mountain clefts, caves and strongholds. ³Whenever the Israelites planted their crops, the Midianites, Amalekites and other eastern peoples invaded the country. ⁴They camped on the land and ruined the crops all the way to Gaza and did not spare a living thing for Israel, neither sheep nor cattle nor donkeys. ⁵They came up with their livestock and their tents like swarms of locusts. It was impossible to count the men and their camels; they invaded the land to ravage it. ⁶Midian so impoverished the Israelites that they cried out to the LORD for help.

⁷When the Israelites cried to the LORD because of Midian, ⁸he sent them a prophet, who said, "This is what the LORD, the God of Israel, says: I brought you up out of Egypt, out of the land of slavery. ⁹I snatched you from the power of Egypt and from the hand of all your oppressors. I drove them from before you and gave you their land. ¹⁰I said to you, 'I am the LORD your God; do not worship the gods of the Amorites, in whose land you live.' But you have not listened to me."

¹¹The angel of the LORD came and sat down under the oak in Ophrah that belonged to Joash the Abiezrite, where his son Gideon was threshing wheat in a winepress to keep it from the Midianites. ¹²When the angel of the LORD appeared to Gideon, he said, "The LORD is with you, mighty warrior."

¹³"But sir," Gideon replied, "if the LORD is with us, why has all this happened to us? Where are all his wonders that our fathers told us about when they said, 'Did not the LORD bring us up out of Egypt?' But now the LORD has abandoned us and put us into the hand of Midian."

? DID YOU KNOW?   6:12

Who was Gideon?

Gideon was a young man whom God used to save the Israelites from an enemy called the Midianites. He was one of the most important judges. Although Gideon was often afraid, he was determined to obey God.

¹⁴The LORD turned to him and said, "Go in the strength you have and save Israel out of Midian's hand. Am I not sending you?"

¹⁵"But Lord,ᵃ" Gideon asked, "how can I save Israel? My clan is the weakest in Manasseh, and I am the least in my family."

¹⁶The LORD answered, "I will be with you, and you will strike down all the Midianites together."

¹⁷Gideon replied, "If now I have found favor in your eyes, give me a sign that it is really you talking to me. ¹⁸Please do not go away until I come back and bring my offering and set it before you."

And the LORD said, "I will wait until you return."

¹⁹Gideon went in, prepared a young goat, and from an ephahᵇ of flour he made bread without yeast. Putting the meat in a basket and its broth in a pot, he brought them out and offered them to him under the oak.

²⁰The angel of God said to him, "Take the meat and the unleavened bread, place them on this rock, and pour out the broth." And Gideon did so. ²¹With the tip of the staff that was in his hand, the angel of the LORD touched the meat and the unleavened bread. Fire flared from the rock, consuming the meat and the bread. And the angel of the LORD disappeared. ²²When Gideon realized that it was the angel of the LORD, he exclaimed, "Ah, Sovereign LORD! I have seen the angel of the LORD face to face!"

²³But the LORD said to him, "Peace! Do not be afraid. You are not going to die."

²⁴So Gideon built an altar to the LORD there and called it The LORD is Peace. To this day it stands in Ophrah of the Abiezrites.

²⁵That same night the LORD said to him, "Take the second bull from your father's herd, the one seven years old.ᶜ Tear down your father's altar to Baal and cut down the Asherah poleᵈ beside it. ²⁶Then build a proper kind ofᵉ altar to the LORD your God on the top of this height. Using the wood of the Asherah pole that you cut down, offer the secondᶠ bull as a burnt offering."

Life In Bible Times

BAAL AND ASHERAH

Baal was the chief Canaanite god in Old Testament times. Asherah was the chief goddess. Her symbol was a tall wooden pole. Gideon destroyed the altar of Baal and cut down the Asherah pole. Then he built a "proper kind of altar" (Judges 6:26) to use in worshiping the Lord.

ᵃ15 Or sir   ᵇ19 That is, probably about 3/5 bushel (about 22 liters)   ᶜ25 Or Take a full-grown, mature bull from your father's herd here and elsewhere in Judges   ᵈ25 That is, a symbol of the goddess Asherah; in verse 28   ᵉ26 Or build with layers of stone an   ᶠ26 Or full-grown; also

²⁷So Gideon took ten of his servants and did as the LORD told him. But because he was afraid of his family and the men of the town, he did it at night rather than in the daytime.

²⁸In the morning when the men of the town got up, there was Baal's altar, demolished, with the Asherah pole beside it cut down and the second bull sacrificed on the newly built altar!

²⁹They asked each other, "Who did this?"

When they carefully investigated, they were told, "Gideon son of Joash did it."

³⁰The men of the town demanded of Joash, "Bring out your son. He must die, because he has broken down Baal's altar and cut down the Asherah pole beside it."

³¹But Joash replied to the hostile crowd around him, "Are you going to plead Baal's cause? Are you trying to save him? Whoever fights for him shall be put to death by morning! If Baal really is a god, he can defend himself when someone breaks down his altar." ³²So that day they called Gideon "Jerub-Baal,ᵃ" saying, "Let Baal contend with him," because he broke down Baal's altar.

³³Now all the Midianites, Amalekites and other eastern peoples joined forces and crossed over the Jordan and camped in the Valley of Jezreel. ³⁴Then the Spirit of the LORD came upon Gideon, and he blew a trumpet, summoning the Abiezrites to follow him. ³⁵He sent messengers throughout Manasseh, calling them to arms, and also into Asher, Zebulun and Naphtali, so that they too went up to meet them.

³⁶Gideon said to God, "If you will save Israel by my hand as you have promised— ³⁷look, I will place a wool fleece on the threshing floor. If there is dew only on the fleece and all the ground is dry, then I will know that you will save Israel by my hand, as you said." ³⁸And that is what happened. Gideon rose early the next day; he squeezed the fleece and wrung out the dew—a bowlful of water.

³⁹Then Gideon said to God, "Do not be angry with me. Let me make just one more request. Allow me one more test with the fleece. This time make the fleece dry and the ground covered with dew." ⁴⁰That night God did so. Only the fleece was dry; all the ground was covered with dew.

Gideon Defeats the Midianites

7 Early in the morning, Jerub-Baal (that is, Gideon) and all his men camped at the spring of Harod. The camp of Midian was north of them in the valley near the hill of Moreh. ²The LORD said to Gideon, "You have too many men for me to deliver Midian into their hands. In order that Israel may not boast against me that her own strength has saved her, ³announce now to the people, 'Anyone who trembles with fear may turn back and leave Mount Gilead.'" So twenty-two thousand men left, while ten thousand remained.

⁴But the LORD said to Gideon, "There are still too many men. Take them down to the water, and I will sift them for you there. If I say, 'This one shall go with you,' he shall go; but if I say, 'This one shall not go with you,' he shall not go."

⁵So Gideon took the men down to the water. There the LORD told him, "Separate those who lap the water with their tongues like a dog from those who kneel down to drink." ⁶Three hundred men lapped with their hands to their mouths. All the rest got down on their knees to drink.

⁷The LORD said to Gideon, "With the three hundred men that lapped I will save you and give the Midianites into your hands. Let all the other men go, each to his own place." ⁸So Gideon sent the rest of the Israelites to their tents but kept the three hundred, who took over the provisions and trumpets of the others.

Now the camp of Midian lay below

ᵃ32 *Jerub-Baal* means *let Baal contend.*

him in the valley. ⁹During that night the LORD said to Gideon, "Get up, go down against the camp, because I am going to give it into your hands. ¹⁰If you are afraid to attack, go down to the camp with your servant Purah ¹¹and listen to what they are saying. Afterward, you will be encouraged to attack the camp." So he and Purah his servant went down to the outposts of the camp. ¹²The Midianites, the Amalekites and all the other eastern peoples had settled in the valley, thick as locusts. Their camels could no more be counted than the sand on the seashore.

¹³Gideon arrived just as a man was telling a friend his dream. "I had a dream," he was saying. "A round loaf of barley bread came tumbling into the Midianite camp. It struck the tent with such force that the tent overturned and collapsed."

¹⁴His friend responded, "This can be nothing other than the sword of Gideon son of Joash, the Israelite. God has given the Midianites and the whole camp into his hands."

¹⁵When Gideon heard the dream and its interpretation, he worshiped God. He returned to the camp of Israel and called out, "Get up! The LORD has given the Midianite camp into your hands." ¹⁶Dividing the three hundred men into three companies, he placed trumpets and empty jars in the hands of all of them, with torches inside.

¹⁷"Watch me," he told them. "Follow my lead. When I get to the edge of the camp, do exactly as I do. ¹⁸When I and all who are with me blow our trumpets, then from all around the camp blow yours and shout, 'For the LORD and for Gideon.'"

¹⁹Gideon and the hundred men with him reached the edge of the camp at the beginning of the middle watch, just after they had changed the guard. They blew their trumpets and broke the jars that were in their hands. ²⁰The three companies blew the trumpets and smashed the jars. Grasping the torches in their left hands and holding in their right hands the trumpets they were to blow, they shouted, "A sword for the LORD and for Gideon!" ²¹While each man held his position around the camp, all the Midianites ran, crying out as they fled.

²²When the three hundred trumpets sounded, the LORD caused the men throughout the camp to turn on each other with their swords. The army fled to Beth Shittah toward Zererah as far as the border of Abel Meholah near Tabbath. ²³Israelites from Naphtali, Asher and all Manasseh were called out, and they pursued the Midianites. ²⁴Gideon sent mes-

---

▌ET'S LIVE IT!   Judges 7:1–21

SCARED, BUT WILLING ➠ Even though Gideon was afraid, he trusted God. Read Judges 7:1–21. Gideon's three hundred men must have been frightened too. But Gideon said "Follow my lead.... Do exactly as I do" (Judges 7:17). Is there someone who is a good example to you? Write that person a thank you letter. Here's a good way to start your letter:

> "Dear_____,
> I just read the story of Gideon in Judges 7. He was a good example to his men. He helped them trust God and showed them what to do to please God. This Bible story made me think of you. You are a good example to me. Here are some of the ways I want to be like you as I grow up ...."

When you finish writing your letter, be sure to mail it!

sengers throughout the hill country of Ephraim, saying, "Come down against the Midianites and seize the waters of the Jordan ahead of them as far as Beth Barah."

So all the men of Ephraim were called out and they took the waters of the Jordan as far as Beth Barah. 25They also captured two of the Midianite leaders, Oreb and Zeeb. They killed Oreb at the rock of Oreb, and Zeeb at the winepress of Zeeb. They pursued the Midianites and brought the heads of Oreb and Zeeb to Gideon, who was by the Jordan.

Zebah and Zalmunna

8 Now the Ephraimites asked Gideon, "Why have you treated us like this? Why didn't you call us when you went to fight Midian?" And they criticized him sharply.

2But he answered them, "What have I accomplished compared to you? Aren't the gleanings of Ephraim's grapes better than the full grape harvest of Abiezer? 3God gave Oreb and Zeeb, the Midianite leaders, into your hands. What was I able to do compared to you?" At this, their resentment against him subsided.

4Gideon and his three hundred men, exhausted yet keeping up the pursuit, came to the Jordan and crossed it. 5He said to the men of Succoth, "Give my troops some bread; they are worn out, and I am still pursuing Zebah and Zalmunna, the kings of Midian."

6But the officials of Succoth said, "Do you already have the hands of Zebah and Zalmunna in your possession? Why should we give bread to your troops?"

7Then Gideon replied, "Just for that, when the LORD has given Zebah and Zalmunna into my hand, I will tear your flesh with desert thorns and briers."

8From there he went up to Peniel^a and made the same request of them, but they answered as the men of Succoth had. 9So he said to the men of Peniel, "When I return in triumph, I will tear down this tower."

10Now Zebah and Zalmunna were in Karkor with a force of about fifteen thousand men, all that were left of the armies of the eastern peoples; a hundred and twenty thousand swordsmen had fallen. 11Gideon went up by the route of the nomads east of Nobah and Jogbehah and fell upon the unsuspecting army. 12Zebah and Zalmunna, the two kings of Midian, fled, but he pursued them and captured them, routing their entire army.

13Gideon son of Joash then returned from the battle by the Pass of Heres. 14He caught a young man of Succoth and questioned him, and the young man wrote down for him the names of the seventy-seven officials of Succoth, the elders of the town. 15Then Gideon came and said to the men of Succoth, "Here are Zebah and Zalmunna, about whom you taunted me by saying, 'Do you already have the hands of Zebah and Zalmunna in your possession? Why should we give bread to your exhausted men?' " 16He took the elders of the town and taught the men of Succoth a lesson by punishing them with desert thorns and briers. 17He also pulled down the tower of Peniel and killed the men of the town.

18Then he asked Zebah and Zalmunna, "What kind of men did you kill at Tabor?"

"Men like you," they answered, "each one with the bearing of a prince."

19Gideon replied, "Those were my brothers, the sons of my own mother. As surely as the LORD lives, if you had spared their lives, I would not kill you." 20Turning to Jether, his oldest son, he said, "Kill them!" But Jether did not draw his sword, because he was only a boy and was afraid.

21Zebah and Zalmunna said, "Come, do it yourself. 'As is the man, so is his strength.' " So Gideon stepped forward and killed them, and

---

a8 Hebrew Penuel, a variant of Peniel; also in verses 9 and 17 took the ornaments off their camels' necks.

Gideon's Ephod

²²The Israelites said to Gideon, "Rule over us—you, your son and your grandson—because you have saved us out of the hand of Midian." ²³But Gideon told them, "I will not rule over you, nor will my son rule over you. The LORD will rule over you." ²⁴And he said, "I do have one request, that each of you give me an earring from your share of the plunder." (It was the custom of the Ishmaelites to wear gold earrings.) ²⁵They answered, "We'll be glad to give them." So they spread out a garment, and each man threw a ring from his plunder onto it. ²⁶The weight of the gold rings he asked for came to seventeen hundred shekels,ᵃ not counting the ornaments, the pendants and the purple garments worn by the kings of Midian or the chains that were on their camels' necks. ²⁷Gideon made the gold into an ephod, which he placed in Ophrah, his town. All Israel prostituted themselves by worshiping it there, and it became a snare to Gideon and his family.

❓DID YOU KNOW?   8:27

What was an ephod?

An ephod was a vest-type garment that priests wore when they led worship. The ephod Gideon made was not used by priests. Later some Israelites began to worship Gideon's ephod.

Gideon's Death

²⁸Thus Midian was subdued before the Israelites and did not raise its head again. During Gideon's lifetime, the land enjoyed peace forty years.

²⁹Jerub-Baal son of Joash went back home to live. ³⁰He had seventy sons of his own, for he had many wives. ³¹His concubine, who lived in Shechem, also bore him a son, whom he named Abimelech. ³²Gideon son of Joash died at a good old age and was buried in the tomb of his father Joash in Ophrah of the Abiezrites.

³³No sooner had Gideon died than the Israelites again prostituted themselves to the Baals. They set up Baal-Berith as their god and ³⁴did not remember the LORD their God, who had rescued them from the hands of all their enemies on every side. ³⁵They also failed to show kindness to the family of Jerub-Baal (that is, Gideon) for all the good things he had done for them.

Abimelech

9 Abimelech son of Jerub-Baal went to his mother's brothers in Shechem and said to them and to all his mother's clan, ²"Ask all the citizens of Shechem, 'Which is better for you: to have all seventy of Jerub-Baal's sons rule over you, or just one man?' Remember, I am your flesh and blood."

³When the brothers repeated all this to the citizens of Shechem, they were inclined to follow Abimelech, for they said, "He is our brother." ⁴They gave him seventy shekelsᵇ of silver from the temple of Baal-Berith, and Abimelech used it to hire reckless adventurers, who became his followers. ⁵He went to his father's home in Ophrah and on one stone murdered his seventy brothers, the sons of Jerub-Baal. But Jotham, the youngest son of Jerub-Baal, escaped by hiding. ⁶Then all the citizens of Shechem and Beth Millo gathered beside the great tree at the pillar in Shechem to crown Abimelech king.

⁷When Jotham was told about this, he climbed up on the top of Mount Gerizim and shouted to them, "Listen to me, citizens of Shechem, so that God may listen to you. ⁸One day the

---

ᵃ26 That is, about 43 pounds (about 19.5 kilograms)   ᵇ4 That is, about 1 3/4 pounds (about 0.8 kilogram)

trees went out to anoint a king for themselves. They said to the olive tree, 'Be our king.'

9"But the olive tree answered, 'Should I give up my oil, by which both gods and men are honored, to hold sway over the trees?'

10"Next, the trees said to the fig tree, 'Come and be our king.'

11"But the fig tree replied, 'Should I give up my fruit, so good and sweet, to hold sway over the trees?'

12"Then the trees said to the vine, 'Come and be our king.'

13"But the vine answered, 'Should I give up my wine, which cheers both gods and men, to hold sway over the trees?'

14"Finally all the trees said to the thornbush, 'Come and be our king.'

15"The thornbush said to the trees, 'If you really want to anoint me king over you, come and take refuge in my shade; but if not, then let fire come out of the thornbush and consume the cedars of Lebanon!'

16"Now if you have acted honorably and in good faith when you made Abimelech king, and if you have been fair to Jerub-Baal and his family, and if you have treated him as he deserves— 17and to think that my father fought for you, risked his life to rescue you from the hand of Midian 18(but today you have revolted against my father's family, murdered his seventy sons on a single stone, and made Abimelech, the son of his slave girl, king over the citizens of Shechem because he is your brother)— 19if then you have acted honorably and in good faith toward Jerub-Baal and his family today, may Abimelech be your joy, and may you be his, too! 20But if you have not, let fire come out from Abimelech and consume you, citizens of Shechem and Beth Millo, and let fire come out from you, citizens of Shechem and Beth Millo, and consume Abimelech!"

21Then Jotham fled, escaping to Beer, and he lived there because he was afraid of his brother Abimelech.

22After Abimelech had governed Israel three years, 23God sent an evil spirit between Abimelech and the citizens of Shechem, who acted treacherously against Abimelech. 24God did this in order that the crime against Jerub-Baal's seventy sons, the shedding of their blood, might be avenged on their brother Abimelech and on the citizens of Shechem, who had helped him murder his brothers. 25In opposition to him these citizens of Shechem set men on the hilltops to ambush and rob everyone who passed by, and this was reported to Abimelech.

❓DID YOU KNOW?   9:22

Was Abimelech a judge?

No. Abimelech was a son of Gideon who tried to make himself king. He killed his brothers, and later he himself was killed in battle. The story of Abimelech shows how God will punish people who do wicked things.

26Now Gaal son of Ebed moved with his brothers into Shechem, and its citizens put their confidence in him. 27After they had gone out into the fields and gathered the grapes and trodden them, they held a festival in the temple of their god. While they were eating and drinking, they cursed Abimelech. 28Then Gaal son of Ebed said, "Who is Abimelech, and who is Shechem, that we should be subject to him? Isn't he Jerub-Baal's son, and isn't Zebul his deputy? Serve the men of Hamor, Shechem's father! Why should we serve Abimelech? 29If only this people were under my command! Then I would get rid of him. I would say to Abimelech, 'Call out your whole army!'"a

30When Zebul the governor of the city heard what Gaal son of Ebed

---

a29 Septuagint; Hebrew him." Then he said to Abimelech, "Call out your whole army!"

said, he was very angry. [31]Under cover he sent messengers to Abimelech, saying, "Gaal son of Ebed and his brothers have come to Shechem and are stirring up the city against you. [32]Now then, during the night you and your men should come and lie in wait in the fields. [33]In the morning at sunrise, advance against the city. When Gaal and his men come out against you, do whatever your hand finds to do."

[34]So Abimelech and all his troops set out by night and took up concealed positions near Shechem in four companies. [35]Now Gaal son of Ebed had gone out and was standing at the entrance to the city gate just as Abimelech and his soldiers came out from their hiding place.

[36]When Gaal saw them, he said to Zebul, "Look, people are coming down from the tops of the mountains!"

Zebul replied, "You mistake the shadows of the mountains for men."

[37]But Gaal spoke up again: "Look, people are coming down from the center of the land, and a company is coming from the direction of the soothsayers' tree."

[38]Then Zebul said to him, "Where is your big talk now, you who said, 'Who is Abimelech that we should be subject to him?' Aren't these the men you ridiculed? Go out and fight them!"

[39]So Gaal led out[a] the citizens of Shechem and fought Abimelech. [40]Abimelech chased him, and many fell wounded in the flight—all the way to the entrance to the gate. [41]Abimelech stayed in Arumah, and Zebul drove Gaal and his brothers out of Shechem.

[42]The next day the people of Shechem went out to the fields, and this was reported to Abimelech. [43]So he took his men, divided them into three companies and set an ambush in the fields. When he saw the people coming out of the city, he rose to attack them. [44]Abimelech and the companies with him rushed forward to a position at the entrance to the city gate. Then two companies rushed upon those in the fields and struck them down. [45]All that day Abimelech pressed his attack against the city until he had captured it and killed its people. Then he destroyed the city and scattered salt over it.

[46]On hearing this, the citizens in the tower of Shechem went into the stronghold of the temple of El-Berith. [47]When Abimelech heard that they had assembled there, [48]he and all his men went up Mount Zalmon. He took an ax and cut off some branches, which he lifted to his shoulders. He ordered the men with him, "Quick! Do what you have seen me do!" [49]So all the men cut branches and followed Abimelech. They piled them against the stronghold and set it on fire over the people inside. So all the people in the tower of Shechem, about a thousand men and women, also died.

[50]Next Abimelech went to Thebez and besieged it and captured it. [51]Inside the city, however, was a strong tower, to which all the men and women—all the people of the city—fled. They locked themselves in and climbed up on the tower roof. [52]Abimelech went to the tower and stormed it. But as he approached the entrance to the tower to set it on fire, [53]a woman dropped an upper millstone on his head and cracked his skull.

[54]Hurriedly he called to his armor-bearer, "Draw your sword and kill me, so that they can't say, 'A woman killed him.'" So his servant ran him through, and he died. [55]When the Israelites saw that Abimelech was dead, they went home.

[56]Thus God repaid the wickedness that Abimelech had done to his father by murdering his seventy brothers. [57]God also made the men of Shechem pay for all their wickedness. The curse of Jotham son of Jerub-Baal came on them.

---

[a]39 Or *Gaal went out in the sight of*

Tola

10 After the time of Abimelech a man of Issachar, Tola son of Puah, the son of Dodo, rose to save Israel. He lived in Shamir, in the hill country of Ephraim. ²He led*ᵃ* Israel twenty-three years; then he died, and was buried in Shamir.

Jair

³He was followed by Jair of Gilead, who led Israel twenty-two years. ⁴He had thirty sons, who rode thirty donkeys. They controlled thirty towns in Gilead, which to this day are called Havvoth Jair.*ᵇ* ⁵When Jair died, he was buried in Kamon.

Jephthah

⁶Again the Israelites did evil in the eyes of the LORD. They served the Baals and the Ashtoreths, and the gods of Aram, the gods of Sidon, the gods of Moab, the gods of the Ammonites and the gods of the Philistines. And because the Israelites forsook the LORD and no longer served him, ⁷he became angry with them. He sold them into the hands of the Philistines and the Ammonites, ⁸who that year shattered and crushed them. For eighteen years they oppressed all the Israelites on the east side of the Jordan in Gilead, the land of the Amorites. ⁹The Ammonites also crossed the Jordan to fight against Judah, Benjamin and the house of Ephraim; and Israel was in great distress. ¹⁰Then the Israelites cried out to the LORD, "We have sinned against you, forsaking our God and serving the Baals."

¹¹The LORD replied, "When the Egyptians, the Amorites, the Ammonites, the Philistines, ¹²the Sidonians, the Amalekites and the Maonites*ᶜ* oppressed you and you cried to me for help, did I not save you from their hands? ¹³But you have forsaken me and served other gods, so I will no longer save you. ¹⁴Go and cry out to the gods you have chosen. Let them save you when you are in trouble!"

¹⁵But the Israelites said to the LORD, "We have sinned. Do with us whatever you think best, but please rescue us now." ¹⁶Then they got rid of the foreign gods among them and served the LORD. And he could bear Israel's misery no longer.

¹⁷When the Ammonites were called to arms and camped in Gilead, the Israelites assembled and camped at Mizpah. ¹⁸The leaders of the people of Gilead said to each other, "Whoever will launch the attack against the Ammonites will be the head of all those living in Gilead."

11 Jephthah the Gileadite was a mighty warrior. His father was Gilead; his mother was a prostitute. ²Gilead's wife also bore him sons, and when they were grown up, they drove Jephthah away. "You are not going to get any inheritance in our family," they said, "because you are the son of another woman." ³So Jephthah fled from his brothers and settled in the land of Tob, where a group of adventurers gathered around him and followed him.

❓DID YOU KNOW?   **11:1**

Who was Jephthah?

Jephthah was a person who was hated and rejected by his family. But he was able to overcome all of that, and he became a judge and the leader of his tribe.

---

⁴Some time later, when the Ammonites made war on Israel, ⁵the elders of Gilead went to get Jephthah from the land of Tob. ⁶"Come," they said, "be our commander, so we can fight the Ammonites."

⁷Jephthah said to them, "Didn't you hate me and drive me from my father's house? Why do you come to me now, when you're in trouble?"

---

*ᵃ*2 Traditionally *judged*; also in verse 3 some Septuagint manuscripts *Midianites*   *ᵇ*4 Or *called the settlements of Jair*   *ᶜ*12 Hebrew;

[8]The elders of Gilead said to him, "Nevertheless, we are turning to you now; come with us to fight the Ammonites, and you will be our head over all who live in Gilead."

[9]Jephthah answered, "Suppose you take me back to fight the Ammonites and the LORD gives them to me—will I really be your head?"

[10]The elders of Gilead replied, "The LORD is our witness; we will certainly do as you say." [11]So Jephthah went with the elders of Gilead, and the people made him head and commander over them. And he repeated all his words before the LORD in Mizpah.

[12]Then Jephthah sent messengers to the Ammonite king with the question: "What do you have against us that you have attacked our country?"

[13]The king of the Ammonites answered Jephthah's messengers, "When Israel came up out of Egypt, they took away my land from the Arnon to the Jabbok, all the way to the Jordan. Now give it back peaceably."

[14]Jephthah sent back messengers to the Ammonite king, [15]saying:

"This is what Jephthah says: Israel did not take the land of Moab or the land of the Ammonites. [16]But when they came up out of Egypt, Israel went through the desert to the Red Sea[a] and on to Kadesh. [17]Then Israel sent messengers to the king of Edom, saying, 'Give us permission to go through your country,' but the king of Edom would not listen. They sent also to the king of Moab, and he refused. So Israel stayed at Kadesh.

[18]"Next they traveled through the desert, skirted the lands of Edom and Moab, passed along the eastern side of the country of Moab, and camped on the other side of the Arnon. They did not enter the territory of Moab, for the Arnon was its border.

[19]"Then Israel sent messengers to Sihon king of the Amorites, who ruled in Heshbon, and said to him, 'Let us pass through your country to our own place.' [20]Sihon, however, did not trust Israel[b] to pass through his territory. He mustered all his men and encamped at Jahaz and fought with Israel.

[21]"Then the LORD, the God of Israel, gave Sihon and all his men into Israel's hands, and they defeated them. Israel took over all the land of the Amorites who lived in that country, [22]capturing all of it from the Arnon to the Jabbok and from the desert to the Jordan.

[23]"Now since the LORD, the God of Israel, has driven the Amorites out before his people Israel, what right have you to take it over? [24]Will you not take what your god Chemosh gives you? Likewise, whatever the LORD our God has given us, we will possess. [25]Are you better than Balak son of Zippor, king of Moab? Did he ever quarrel with Israel or fight with them? [26]For three hundred years Israel occupied Heshbon, Aroer, the surrounding settlements and all the towns along the Arnon. Why didn't you retake them during that time? [27]I have not wronged you, but you are doing me wrong by waging war against me. Let the LORD, the Judge,[c] decide the dispute this day between the Israelites and the Ammonites."

[28]The king of Ammon, however, paid no attention to the message Jephthah sent him.

[29]Then the Spirit of the LORD came upon Jephthah. He crossed Gilead and Manasseh, passed through Mizpah of Gilead, and from there he advanced against the Ammonites. [30]And Jephthah made a vow to the

---

[a]16 Hebrew *Yam Suph*; that is, Sea of Reeds [b]20 Or *however, would not make an agreement for Israel* [c]27 Or *Ruler*

LORD: "If you give the Ammonites into my hands, ³¹whatever comes out of the door of my house to meet me when I return in triumph from the Ammonites will be the LORD's, and I will sacrifice it as a burnt offering."

³²Then Jephthah went over to fight the Ammonites, and the LORD gave them into his hands. ³³He devastated twenty towns from Aroer to the vicinity of Minnith, as far as Abel Keramim. Thus Israel subdued Ammon.

³⁴When Jephthah returned to his home in Mizpah, who should come out to meet him but his daughter, dancing to the sound of tambourines! She was an only child. Except for her he had neither son nor daughter. ³⁵When he saw her, he tore his clothes and cried, "Oh! My daughter! You have made me miserable and wretched, because I have made a vow to the LORD that I cannot break."

³⁶"My father," she replied, "you have given your word to the LORD. Do to me just as you promised, now that the LORD has avenged you of your enemies, the Ammonites. ³⁷But grant me this one request," she said. "Give me two months to roam the hills and weep with my friends, because I will never marry."

³⁸"You may go," he said. And he let her go for two months. She and the girls went into the hills and wept because she would never marry. ³⁹After the two months, she returned to her father and he did to her as he had vowed. And she was a virgin.

From this comes the Israelite custom ⁴⁰that each year the young women of Israel go out for four days to commemorate the daughter of Jephthah the Gileadite.

Jephthah and Ephraim

12 The men of Ephraim called out their forces, crossed over to Zaphon and said to Jephthah, "Why did you go to fight the Ammonites without calling us to go with you? We're going to burn down your house over your head."

²Jephthah answered, "I and my people were engaged in a great struggle with the Ammonites, and although I called, you didn't save me out of their hands. ³When I saw that you wouldn't help, I took my life in my hands and crossed over to fight the Ammonites, and the LORD gave me the victory over them. Now why have you come up today to fight me?"

⁴Jephthah then called together the men of Gilead and fought against Ephraim. The Gileadites struck them down because the Ephraimites had said, "You Gileadites are renegades from Ephraim and Manasseh." ⁵The Gileadites captured the fords of

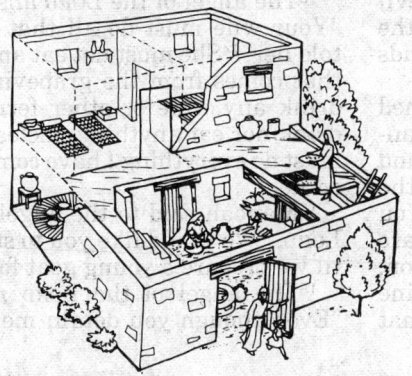

Life in Bible Times

OLD TESTAMENT HOUSES

Houses in the time of the judges were usually made of stone, with straw or brush roofs. Most had only four or five small rooms. Usually six to eight people lived in a house. The ceilings of these houses were less than six feet high inside. Of course, the people of those times were much shorter than people are today.

the Jordan leading to Ephraim, and whenever a survivor of Ephraim said, "Let me cross over," the men of Gilead asked him, "Are you an Ephraimite?" If he replied, "No," 6they said, "All right, say 'Shibboleth.'" If he said, "Sibboleth," because he could not pronounce the word correctly, they seized him and killed him at the fords of the Jordan. Forty-two thousand Ephraimites were killed at that time.

7Jephthah led*a* Israel six years. Then Jephthah the Gileadite died, and was buried in a town in Gilead.

Ibzan, Elon and Abdon

8After him, Ibzan of Bethlehem led Israel. 9He had thirty sons and thirty daughters. He gave his daughters away in marriage to those outside his clan, and for his sons he brought in thirty young women as wives from outside his clan. Ibzan led Israel seven years. 10Then Ibzan died, and was buried in Bethlehem.

11After him, Elon the Zebulunite led Israel ten years. 12Then Elon died, and was buried in Aijalon in the land of Zebulun.

13After him, Abdon son of Hillel, from Pirathon, led Israel. 14He had forty sons and thirty grandsons, who rode on seventy donkeys. He led Israel eight years. 15Then Abdon son of Hillel died, and was buried at Pirathon in Ephraim, in the hill country of the Amalekites.

The Birth of Samson

13 Again the Israelites did evil in the eyes of the LORD, so the LORD delivered them into the hands of the Philistines for forty years.

2A certain man of Zorah, named Manoah, from the clan of the Danites, had a wife who was sterile and remained childless. 3The angel of the LORD appeared to her and said, "You are sterile and childless, but you are going to conceive and have a son. 4Now see to it that you drink no wine or other fermented drink and that

you do not eat anything unclean, 5because you will conceive and give birth to a son. No razor may be used on his head, because the boy is to be a Nazirite, set apart to God from birth, and he will begin the deliverance of Israel from the hands of the Philistines."

6Then the woman went to her husband and told him, "A man of God came to me. He looked like an angel of God, very awesome. I didn't ask him where he came from, and he didn't tell me his name. 7But he said to me, 'You will conceive and give birth to a son. Now then, drink no wine or other fermented drink and do not eat anything unclean, because the boy will be a Nazirite of God from birth until the day of his death.'"

8Then Manoah prayed to the LORD: "O Lord, I beg you, let the man of God you sent to us come again to teach us how to bring up the boy who is to be born."

9God heard Manoah, and the angel of God came again to the woman while she was out in the field; but her husband Manoah was not with her. 10The woman hurried to tell her husband, "He's here! The man who appeared to me the other day!"

11Manoah got up and followed his wife. When he came to the man, he said, "Are you the one who talked to my wife?"

"I am," he said.

12So Manoah asked him, "When your words are fulfilled, what is to be the rule for the boy's life and work?"

13The angel of the LORD answered, "Your wife must do all that I have told her. 14She must not eat anything that comes from the grapevine, nor drink any wine or other fermented drink nor eat anything unclean. She must do everything I have commanded her."

15Manoah said to the angel of the LORD, "We would like you to stay until we prepare a young goat for you."

16The angel of the LORD replied, "Even though you detain me, I will

---

a7 Traditionally *judged*; also in verses 8-14

not eat any of your food. But if you prepare a burnt offering, offer it to the LORD." (Manoah did not realize that it was the angel of the LORD.)

¹⁷Then Manoah inquired of the angel of the LORD, "What is your name, so that we may honor you when your word comes true?"

¹⁸He replied, "Why do you ask my name? It is beyond understanding.ᵃ"

¹⁹Then Manoah took a young goat, together with the grain offering, and sacrificed it on a rock to the LORD. And the LORD did an amazing thing while Manoah and his wife watched: ²⁰As the flame blazed up from the altar toward heaven, the angel of the LORD ascended in the flame. Seeing this, Manoah and his wife fell with their faces to the ground. ²¹When the angel of the LORD did not show himself again to Manoah and his wife, Manoah realized that it was the angel of the LORD.

²²"We are doomed to die!" he said to his wife. "We have seen God!"

²³But his wife answered, "If the LORD had meant to kill us, he would not have accepted a burnt offering and grain offering from our hands, nor shown us all these things or now told us this."

²⁴The woman gave birth to a boy and named him Samson. He grew and the LORD blessed him, ²⁵and the Spirit of the LORD began to stir him

ᵃ18 Or *is wonderful*

while he was in Mahaneh Dan, between Zorah and Eshtaol.

Samson's Marriage

14 Samson went down to Timnah and saw there a young Philistine woman. ²When he returned, he said to his father and mother, "I have seen a Philistine woman in Timnah; now get her for me as my wife."

³His father and mother replied, "Isn't there an acceptable woman among your relatives or among all our people? Must you go to the uncircumcised Philistines to get a wife?"

But Samson said to his father, "Get her for me. She's the right one for me." ⁴(His parents did not know that this was from the LORD, who was seeking an occasion to confront the Philistines; for at that time they were ruling over Israel.) ⁵Samson went down to Timnah together with his father and mother. As they approached the vineyards of Timnah, suddenly a young lion came roaring toward him. ⁶The Spirit of the LORD came upon him in power so that he tore the lion apart with his bare hands as he might have torn a young goat. But he told neither his father nor his mother what he had done. ⁷Then he went down and talked with the woman, and he liked her.

⁸Some time later, when he went back to marry her, he turned aside to

ᴸET'S LIVE IT!   Judges 13:1–14

DEDICATING CHILDREN TO THE LORD ➡ A "Nazirite" was a person dedicated to God by a special promise or "vow." Read Judges 13:1–14 to find out what special things Samson's mother and father were to do to dedicate their son.

Christians often dedicate their children to the Lord too. Many parents dedicate or baptize children when they are babies. Ask your parents if you were dedicated or baptized as a baby. Ask them why they did this and what promises they made then.

A dedication or baptism service may be printed in your church hymnal. If so, read for yourself the special service your mom and dad may have had at church for you when you were a baby.

look at the lion's carcass. In it was a swarm of bees and some honey, [9]which he scooped out with his hands and ate as he went along. When he rejoined his parents, he gave them some, and they too ate it. But he did not tell them that he had taken the honey from the lion's carcass.

[10]Now his father went down to see the woman. And Samson made a feast there, as was customary for bridegrooms. [11]When he appeared, he was given thirty companions.

[12]"Let me tell you a riddle," Samson said to them. "If you can give me the answer within the seven days of the feast, I will give you thirty linen garments and thirty sets of clothes. [13]If you can't tell me the answer, you must give me thirty linen garments and thirty sets of clothes."

"Tell us your riddle," they said. "Let's hear it."

[14]He replied,

"Out of the eater, something to eat;
    out of the strong, something sweet."

For three days they could not give the answer.

[15]On the fourth[a] day, they said to Samson's wife, "Coax your husband into explaining the riddle for us, or we will burn you and your father's household to death. Did you invite us here to rob us?"

[16]Then Samson's wife threw herself on him, sobbing, "You hate me! You don't really love me. You've given my people a riddle, but you haven't told me the answer."

"I haven't even explained it to my father or mother," he replied, "so why should I explain it to you?" [17]She cried the whole seven days of the feast. So on the seventh day he finally told her, because she continued to press him. She in turn explained the riddle to her people.

[18]Before sunset on the seventh day the men of the town said to him,

"What is sweeter than honey?
    What is stronger than a lion?"

Samson said to them,

"If you had not plowed with my heifer,
    you would not have solved my riddle."

[19]Then the Spirit of the LORD came upon him in power. He went down to Ashkelon, struck down thirty of their men, stripped them of their belongings and gave their clothes to those who had explained the riddle. Burning with anger, he went up to his father's house. [20]And Samson's wife was given to the friend who had attended him at his wedding.

Samson's Vengeance on the Philistines

15 Later on, at the time of wheat harvest, Samson took a young goat and went to visit his wife. He said, "I'm going to my wife's room." But her father would not let him go in.

[2]"I was so sure you thoroughly hated her," he said, "that I gave her to your friend. Isn't her younger sister more attractive? Take her instead."

[3]Samson said to them, "This time I have a right to get even with the Philistines; I will really harm them." [4]So he went out and caught three hundred foxes and tied them tail to tail in pairs. He then fastened a torch to every pair of tails, [5]lit the torches and let the foxes loose in the standing grain of the Philistines. He burned up the shocks and standing grain, together with the vineyards and olive groves.

[6]When the Philistines asked, "Who did this?" they were told, "Samson, the Timnite's son-in-law, because his wife was given to his friend."

So the Philistines went up and burned her and her father to death. [7]Samson said to them, "Since you've acted like this, I won't stop until I get my revenge on you." [8]He attacked

---

[a]15 Some Septuagint manuscripts and Syriac; Hebrew *seventh*

them viciously and slaughtered many of them. Then he went down and stayed in a cave in the rock of Etam.

⁹The Philistines went up and camped in Judah, spreading out near Lehi. ¹⁰The men of Judah asked, "Why have you come to fight us?"

"We have come to take Samson prisoner," they answered, "to do to him as he did to us."

¹¹Then three thousand men from Judah went down to the cave in the rock of Etam and said to Samson, "Don't you realize that the Philistines are rulers over us? What have you done to us?"

He answered, "I merely did to them what they did to me."

¹²They said to him, "We've come to tie you up and hand you over to the Philistines."

Samson said, "Swear to me that you won't kill me yourselves."

¹³"Agreed," they answered. "We will only tie you up and hand you over to them. We will not kill you." So they bound him with two new ropes and led him up from the rock. ¹⁴As he approached Lehi, the Philistines came toward him shouting. The Spirit of the LORD came upon him in power. The ropes on his arms became like charred flax, and the bindings

dropped from his hands. ¹⁵Finding a fresh jawbone of a donkey, he grabbed it and struck down a thousand men.

¹⁶Then Samson said,

"With a donkey's jawbone
    I have made donkeys of them.ᵃ
With a donkey's jawbone
    I have killed a thousand men."

¹⁷When he finished speaking, he threw away the jawbone; and the place was called Ramath Lehi.ᵇ

¹⁸Because he was very thirsty, he cried out to the LORD, "You have given your servant this great victory. Must I now die of thirst and fall into the hands of the uncircumcised?" ¹⁹Then God opened up the hollow place in Lehi, and water came out of it. When Samson drank, his strength returned and he revived. So the spring was called En Hakkore,ᶜ and it is still there in Lehi.

²⁰Samson ledᵈ Israel for twenty years in the days of the Philistines.

Samson and Delilah

16 One day Samson went to Gaza, where he saw a prostitute. He went in to spend the night with her. ²The people of Gaza were told, "Samson is here!" So they sur-

---

ᵃ16 Or *made a heap or two*; the Hebrew for *donkey* sounds like the Hebrew for *heap.*
ᵇ17 *Ramath Lehi* means *jawbone hill.*   ᶜ19 *En Hakkore* means *caller's spring.*
ᵈ20 Traditionally *judged*

LET'S LIVE IT! Judges 15:1–17

REVENGE ➡ Samson was strong, but he was not always good or wise. Once when the Philistines had tricked Samson, he became very angry and decided to get even, to get revenge.

Read Judges 15:1–17. Did Samson's revenge help anyone? The Philistines? The Israelites? Samson?

Look at the three situations below where you might be tempted to get even. What should you do?

1. Your sister borrows your bike and brings it home with a flat tire.
2. While on the playground at school a classmate runs by and accidentally knocks you over.
3. Your parents punish you for something that isn't your fault.

rounded the place and lay in wait for him all night at the city gate. They made no move during the night, saying, "At dawn we'll kill him."

³But Samson lay there only until the middle of the night. Then he got up and took hold of the doors of the city gate, together with the two posts, and tore them loose, bar and all. He lifted them to his shoulders and carried them to the top of the hill that faces Hebron.

⁴Some time later, he fell in love with a woman in the Valley of Sorek whose name was Delilah. ⁵The rulers of the Philistines went to her and said, "See if you can lure him into showing you the secret of his great strength and how we can overpower him so we may tie him up and subdue him. Each one of us will give you eleven hundred shekels ᵃ of silver."

⁶So Delilah said to Samson, "Tell me the secret of your great strength and how you can be tied up and subdued."

⁷Samson answered her, "If anyone ties me with seven fresh thongs ᵇ that have not been dried, I'll become as weak as any other man."

⁸Then the rulers of the Philistines brought her seven fresh thongs that had not been dried, and she tied him with them. ⁹With men hidden in the room, she called to him, "Samson, the Philistines are upon you!" But he snapped the thongs as easily as a piece of string snaps when it comes close to a flame. So the secret of his strength was not discovered.

¹⁰Then Delilah said to Samson, "You have made a fool of me; you lied to me. Come now, tell me how you can be tied."

¹¹He said, "If anyone ties me securely with new ropes that have never been used, I'll become as weak as any other man."

¹²So Delilah took new ropes and tied him with them. Then, with men hidden in the room, she called to him, "Samson, the Philistines are upon you!" But he snapped the ropes off his arms as if they were threads.

¹³Delilah then said to Samson, "Until now, you have been making a fool of me and lying to me. Tell me how you can be tied."

He replied, "If you weave the seven braids of my head into the fabric on the loom, and tighten it with the pin, I'll become as weak as any other man." So while he was sleeping, Delilah took the seven braids of his head,

ᵃ5 That is, about 28 pounds (about 13 kilograms)

ᵇ7 Or *bowstrings*; also in verses 8 and 9

LET'S LIVE IT!　　　Judges 16:1–3

THE STRONGEST MAN IN THE WORLD? ➡ Read Judges 16:1–3. In Bible times city gates were made of stone or metal or thick wood held together with strips of iron. The distance from Gaza to the top of the hill that faces Hebron is thirty miles!

But was Samson really strong? This chapter tells us that Samson was tempted to stay with a woman he was not married to. He knew this was wrong, but Samson gave in to his temptation. Inside, Samson was weak, not strong! If you are tempted to do something you know is wrong, and you do what is right instead, you are stronger than Samson!

Ask your dad or mom to draw seven small pictures of an arm with muscles. Make each picture about the size of a stamp. Under the row of pictures write "Stronger than Samson!"

When you are tempted to do something wrong, and do what is right instead, tell your mom or dad what happened. They will tape a "Stronger than Samson" stamp to that date on their calendar. See how soon you can earn all your "Stronger than Samson" awards.

wove them into the fabric [14]and[a] tightened it with the pin.

Again she called to him, "Samson, the Philistines are upon you!" He awoke from his sleep and pulled up the pin and the loom, with the fabric.

[15]Then she said to him, "How can you say, 'I love you,' when you won't confide in me? This is the third time you have made a fool of me and haven't told me the secret of your great strength." [16]With such nagging she prodded him day after day until he was tired to death.

[17]So he told her everything. "No razor has ever been used on my head," he said, "because I have been a Nazirite set apart to God since birth. If my head were shaved, my strength would leave me, and I would become as weak as any other man."

[18]When Delilah saw that he had told her everything, she sent word to the rulers of the Philistines, "Come back once more; he has told me everything." So the rulers of the Philistines returned with the silver in their hands. [19]Having put him to sleep on her lap, she called a man to shave off the seven braids of his hair, and so began to subdue him.[b] And his strength left him.

[20]Then she called, "Samson, the Philistines are upon you!"

He awoke from his sleep and thought, "I'll go out as before and shake myself free." But he did not know that the LORD had left him. [21]Then the Philistines seized him, gouged out his eyes and took him down to Gaza. Binding him with bronze shackles, they set him to grinding in the prison. [22]But the hair on his head began to grow again after it had been shaved.

The Death of Samson

[23]Now the rulers of the Philistines assembled to offer a great sacrifice to Dagon their god and to celebrate,

saying, "Our god has delivered Samson, our enemy, into our hands."

[24]When the people saw him, they praised their god, saying,

"Our god has delivered our enemy
    into our hands,
the one who laid waste our land
    and multiplied our slain."

[25]While they were in high spirits, they shouted, "Bring out Samson to entertain us." So they called Samson out of the prison, and he performed for them.

When they stood him among the pillars, [26]Samson said to the servant who held his hand, "Put me where I can feel the pillars that support the temple, so that I may lean against them." [27]Now the temple was crowded with men and women; all the rulers of the Philistines were there, and on the roof were about three thousand men and women watching Samson perform. [28]Then Samson prayed to the LORD, "O Sovereign LORD, remember me. O God, please strengthen me just once more, and let me with one blow get revenge on the Philistines for my two eyes." [29]Then Samson reached toward the two central pillars on which the temple stood. Bracing himself against them, his right hand on the one and his left hand on the other, [30]Samson said, "Let me die with the Philistines!" Then he pushed with all his might, and down came the temple on the rulers and all the people in it. Thus he killed many more when he died than while he lived.

[31]Then his brothers and his father's whole family went down to get him. They brought him back and buried him between Zorah and Eshtaol in the tomb of Manoah his father. He had led[c] Israel twenty years.

Micah's Idols

17 Now a man named Micah from the hill country of

---

[a]13,14 Some Septuagint manuscripts; Hebrew "*I can, if you weave the seven braids of my head into the fabric on the loom,.*" [14]*So she*   [b]19 Hebrew; some Septuagint manuscripts *and he began to weaken*   [c]31 Traditionally *judged*

Ephraim [2]said to his mother, "The eleven hundred shekels[a] of silver that were taken from you and about which I heard you utter a curse—I have that silver with me; I took it."

❓DID YOU KNOW?   16:30

How did Samson die?

Samson was killed when he pulled down a Philistine temple. Samson was strong, but he was not always wise. He killed many Philistines, the enemies of Israel. But because he did not always obey God, he was unable to free Israel from the Philistines.

Then his mother said, "The LORD bless you, my son!"

[3]When he returned the eleven hundred shekels of silver to his mother, she said, "I solemnly consecrate my silver to the LORD for my son to make a carved image and a cast idol. I will give it back to you."

[4]So he returned the silver to his mother, and she took two hundred shekels[b] of silver and gave them to a silversmith, who made them into the image and the idol. And they were put in Micah's house.

[5]Now this man Micah had a shrine, and he made an ephod and some idols and installed one of his sons as his priest. [6]In those days Israel had no king; everyone did as he saw fit.

[7]A young Levite from Bethlehem in Judah, who had been living within the clan of Judah, [8]left that town in search of some other place to stay. On his way[c] he came to Micah's house in the hill country of Ephraim.

[9]Micah asked him, "Where are you from?"

"I'm a Levite from Bethlehem in Judah," he said, "and I'm looking for a place to stay."

[10]Then Micah said to him, "Live with me and be my father and priest, and I'll give you ten shekels[d] of silver a year, your clothes and your food." [11]So the Levite agreed to live with him, and the young man was to him like one of his sons. [12]Then Micah installed the Levite, and the young man became his priest and lived in his house. [13]And Micah said, "Now I know that the LORD will be good to me, since this Levite has become my priest."

Danites Settle in Laish

18 In those days Israel had no king.

And in those days the tribe of the Danites was seeking a place of their own where they might settle, because they had not yet come into an inheritance among the tribes of Israel. [2]So the Danites sent five warriors from Zorah and Eshtaol to spy out the land and explore it. These men represented all their clans. They told them, "Go, explore the land."

The men entered the hill country of Ephraim and came to the house of Micah, where they spent the night. [3]When they were near Micah's house, they recognized the voice of the young Levite; so they turned in there and asked him, "Who brought you here? What are you doing in this place? Why are you here?"

[4]He told them what Micah had done for him, and said, "He has hired me and I am his priest."

[5]Then they said to him, "Please inquire of God to learn whether our journey will be successful."

[6]The priest answered them, "Go in peace. Your journey has the LORD's approval."

[7]So the five men left and came to Laish, where they saw that the people were living in safety, like the Sidonians, unsuspecting and secure. And since their land lacked nothing, they were prosperous.[e] Also, they lived a long way from the Sidonians

---

[a]2 That is, about 28 pounds (about 13 kilograms)
2.3 kilograms)   [c]8 Or *To carry on his profession*
110 grams)   [e]7 The meaning of the Hebrew for this clause is uncertain.

[b]4 That is, about 5 pounds (about
[d]10 That is, about 4 ounces (about

and had no relationship with anyone else.*

⁸When they returned to Zorah and Eshtaol, their brothers asked them, "How did you find things?"

⁹They answered, "Come on, let's attack them! We have seen that the land is very good. Aren't you going to do something? Don't hesitate to go there and take it over. ¹⁰When you get there, you will find an unsuspecting people and a spacious land that God has put into your hands, a land that lacks nothing whatever."

¹¹Then six hundred men from the clan of the Danites, armed for battle, set out from Zorah and Eshtaol. ¹²On their way they set up camp near Kiriath Jearim in Judah. This is why the place west of Kiriath Jearim is called Mahaneh Dan*b* to this day. ¹³From there they went on to the hill country of Ephraim and came to Micah's house.

¹⁴Then the five men who had spied out the land of Laish said to their brothers, "Do you know that one of these houses has an ephod, other household gods, a carved image and a cast idol? Now you know what to do." ¹⁵So they turned in there and went to the house of the young Levite at Micah's place and greeted him. ¹⁶The six hundred Danites, armed for battle, stood at the entrance to the gate. ¹⁷The five men who had spied out the land went inside and took the carved image, the ephod, the other household gods and the cast idol while the priest and the six hundred armed men stood at the entrance to the gate.

¹⁸When these men went into Micah's house and took the carved image, the ephod, the other household gods and the cast idol, the priest said to them, "What are you doing?"

¹⁹They answered him, "Be quiet! Don't say a word. Come with us, and be our father and priest. Isn't it better that you serve a tribe and clan in Israel as priest rather than just one

man's household?" ²⁰Then the priest was glad. He took the ephod, the other household gods and the carved image and went along with the people. ²¹Putting their little children, their livestock and their possessions in front of them, they turned away and left.

²²When they had gone some distance from Micah's house, the men who lived near Micah were called together and overtook the Danites. ²³As they shouted after them, the Danites turned and said to Micah, "What's the matter with you that you called out your men to fight?"

²⁴He replied, "You took the gods I made, and my priest, and went away. What else do I have? How can you ask, 'What's the matter with you?'"

²⁵The Danites answered, "Don't argue with us, or some hot-tempered men will attack you, and you and your family will lose your lives." ²⁶So the Danites went their way, and Micah, seeing that they were too strong for him, turned around and went back home.

²⁷Then they took what Micah had made, and his priest, and went on to Laish, against a peaceful and unsuspecting people. They attacked them with the sword and burned down their city. ²⁸There was no one to rescue them because they lived a long way from Sidon and had no relationship with anyone else. The city was in a valley near Beth Rehob.

The Danites rebuilt the city and settled there. ²⁹They named it Dan after their forefather Dan, who was born to Israel—though the city used to be called Laish. ³⁰There the Danites set up for themselves the idols, and Jonathan son of Gershom, the son of Moses,*c* and his sons were priests for the tribe of Dan until the time of the captivity of the land. ³¹They continued to use the idols Micah had made, all the time the house of God was in Shiloh.

---

a7 Hebrew; some Septuagint manuscripts *with the Arameans*　　*b12 Mahaneh Dan* means *Dan's camp.*　　*c30* An ancient Hebrew scribal tradition, some Septuagint manuscripts and Vulgate; Masoretic Text *Manasseh*

A Levite and His Concubine

19 In those days Israel had no king.

Now a Levite who lived in a remote area in the hill country of Ephraim took a concubine from Bethlehem in Judah. ²But she was unfaithful to him. She left him and went back to her father's house in Bethlehem, Judah. After she had been there four months, ³her husband went to her to persuade her to return. He had with him his servant and two donkeys. She took him into her father's house, and when her father saw him, he gladly welcomed him. ⁴His father-in-law, the girl's father, prevailed upon him to stay; so he remained with him three days, eating and drinking, and sleeping there.

❓DID YOU KNOW?　　　19:1

What was a concubine?

In Old Testament times some men had more than one wife at the same time. The first wife had special rights. Other wives were often called concubines.

---

⁵On the fourth day they got up early and he prepared to leave, but the girl's father said to his son-in-law, "Refresh yourself with something to eat; then you can go." ⁶So the two of them sat down to eat and drink together. Afterward the girl's father said, "Please stay tonight and enjoy yourself." ⁷And when the man got up to go, his father-in-law persuaded him, so he stayed there that night. ⁸On the morning of the fifth day, when he rose to go, the girl's father said, "Refresh yourself. Wait till afternoon!" So the two of them ate together.

⁹Then when the man, with his concubine and his servant, got up to leave, his father-in-law, the girl's father, said, "Now look, it's almost evening. Spend the night here; the day is nearly over. Stay and enjoy yourself.

Early tomorrow morning you can get up and be on your way home." ¹⁰But, unwilling to stay another night, the man left and went toward Jebus (that is, Jerusalem), with his two saddled donkeys and his concubine.

¹¹When they were near Jebus and the day was almost gone, the servant said to his master, "Come, let's stop at this city of the Jebusites and spend the night."

¹²His master replied, "No. We won't go into an alien city, whose people are not Israelites. We will go on to Gibeah." ¹³He added, "Come, let's try to reach Gibeah or Ramah and spend the night in one of those places." ¹⁴So they went on, and the sun set as they neared Gibeah in Benjamin. ¹⁵There they stopped to spend the night. They went and sat in the city square, but no one took them into his home for the night.

¹⁶That evening an old man from the hill country of Ephraim, who was living in Gibeah (the men of the place were Benjamites), came in from his work in the fields. ¹⁷When he looked and saw the traveler in the city square, the old man asked, "Where are you going? Where did you come from?"

¹⁸He answered, "We are on our way from Bethlehem in Judah to a remote area in the hill country of Ephraim where I live. I have been to Bethlehem in Judah and now I am going to the house of the LORD. No one has taken me into his house. ¹⁹We have both straw and fodder for our donkeys and bread and wine for ourselves your servants—me, your maidservant, and the young man with us. We don't need anything."

²⁰"You are welcome at my house," the old man said. "Let me supply whatever you need. Only don't spend the night in the square." ²¹So he took him into his house and fed his donkeys. After they had washed their feet, they had something to eat and drink.

²²While they were enjoying themselves, some of the wicked men of the city surrounded the house. Pounding

on the door, they shouted to the old man who owned the house, "Bring out the man who came to your house so we can have sex with him."

²³The owner of the house went outside and said to them, "No, my friends, don't be so vile. Since this man is my guest, don't do this disgraceful thing. ²⁴Look, here is my virgin daughter, and his concubine. I will bring them out to you now, and you can use them and do to them whatever you wish. But to this man, don't do such a disgraceful thing."

²⁵But the men would not listen to him. So the man took his concubine and sent her outside to them, and they raped her and abused her throughout the night, and at dawn they let her go. ²⁶At daybreak the woman went back to the house where her master was staying, fell down at the door and lay there until daylight.

²⁷When her master got up in the morning and opened the door of the house and stepped out to continue on his way, there lay his concubine, fallen in the doorway of the house, with her hands on the threshold. ²⁸He said to her, "Get up; let's go." But there was no answer. Then the man put her on his donkey and set out for home.

²⁹When he reached home, he took a knife and cut up his concubine, limb by limb, into twelve parts and sent them into all the areas of Israel. ³⁰Everyone who saw it said, "Such a thing has never been seen or done, not since the day the Israelites came up out of Egypt. Think about it! Consider it! Tell us what to do!"

Israelites Fight the Benjamites

20 Then all the Israelites from Dan to Beersheba and from the land of Gilead came out as one man and assembled before the LORD in Mizpah. ²The leaders of all the people of the tribes of Israel took their places in the assembly of the people of God, four hundred thousand soldiers armed with swords. ³(The Benjamites heard that the Israelites had gone up to Mizpah.) Then the Israelites said, "Tell us how this awful thing happened."

? DID YOU KNOW?   20:3

Who were the Benjamites?

The Benjamites were one of the Israelite tribes. Each Israelite tribe or family was called by the name of one of the sons of Jacob. You can find the names of all twelve sons of Jacob in Genesis 35:23–26.

---

⁴So the Levite, the husband of the murdered woman, said, "I and my concubine came to Gibeah in Benjamin to spend the night. ⁵During the night the men of Gibeah came after me and surrounded the house, intending to kill me. They raped my concubine, and she died. ⁶I took my concubine, cut her into pieces and sent one piece to each region of Israel's inheritance, because they committed this lewd and disgraceful act in Israel. ⁷Now, all you Israelites, speak up and give your verdict."

⁸All the people rose as one man, saying, "None of us will go home. No, not one of us will return to his house. ⁹But now this is what we'll do to Gibeah: We'll go up against it as the lot directs. ¹⁰We'll take ten men out of every hundred from all the tribes of Israel, and a hundred from a thousand, and a thousand from ten thousand, to get provisions for the army. Then, when the army arrives at Gibeah*ᵃ* in Benjamin, it can give them what they deserve for all this vileness done in Israel." ¹¹So all the men of Israel got together and united as one man against the city.

¹²The tribes of Israel sent men throughout the tribe of Benjamin, saying, "What about this awful crime that was committed among you? ¹³Now surrender those wicked men of Gibeah so that we may put them to

---

ᵃ10 One Hebrew manuscript; most Hebrew manuscripts Geba, a variant of Gibeah

death and purge the evil from Israel."

But the Benjamites would not listen to their fellow Israelites. ¹⁴From their towns they came together at Gibeah to fight against the Israelites. ¹⁵At once the Benjamites mobilized twenty-six thousand swordsmen from their towns, in addition to seven hundred chosen men from those living in Gibeah. ¹⁶Among all these soldiers there were seven hundred chosen men who were left-handed, each of whom could sling a stone at a hair and not miss.

THE SLING

A sling had two cords tied to a small pad. A smooth stone was put into the pad and swung around and around. When one string was released, the stone flew very fast toward its target. Shepherds used slings to protect their flocks. Many armies had units of men whose main weapon was the sling. David was the world's most famous user of a sling. You can read about him in 1 Samuel 17.

¹⁷Israel, apart from Benjamin, mustered four hundred thousand swordsmen, all of them fighting men.

¹⁸The Israelites went up to Bethel*a* and inquired of God. They said, "Who of us shall go first to fight against the Benjamites?"

The LORD replied, "Judah shall go first."

¹⁹The next morning the Israelites got up and pitched camp near Gibeah. ²⁰The men of Israel went out to fight the Benjamites and took up bat-

tle positions against them at Gibeah. ²¹The Benjamites came out of Gibeah and cut down twenty-two thousand Israelites on the battlefield that day. ²²But the men of Israel encouraged one another and again took up their positions where they had stationed themselves the first day. ²³The Israelites went up and wept before the LORD until evening, and they inquired of the LORD. They said, "Shall we go up again to battle against the Benjamites, our brothers?"

The LORD answered, "Go up against them."

²⁴Then the Israelites drew near to Benjamin the second day. ²⁵This time, when the Benjamites came out from Gibeah to oppose them, they cut down another eighteen thousand Israelites, all of them armed with swords.

²⁶Then the Israelites, all the people, went up to Bethel, and there they sat weeping before the LORD. They fasted that day until evening and presented burnt offerings and fellowship offerings*b* to the LORD. ²⁷And the Israelites inquired of the LORD. (In those days the ark of the covenant of God was there, ²⁸with Phinehas son of Eleazar, the son of Aaron, ministering before it.) They asked, "Shall we go up again to battle with Benjamin our brother, or not?"

The LORD responded, "Go, for tomorrow I will give them into your hands."

²⁹Then Israel set an ambush around Gibeah. ³⁰They went up against the Benjamites on the third day and took up positions against Gibeah as they had done before. ³¹The Benjamites came out to meet them and were drawn away from the city. They began to inflict casualties on the Israelites as before, so that about thirty men fell in the open field and on the roads—the one leading to Bethel and the other to Gibeah. ³²While the Benjamites were saying, "We are defeating them as before," the Israelites were saying,

a18 Or to the house of God; also in verse 26   b26 Traditionally peace offerings

"Let's retreat and draw them away from the city to the roads."

³³All the men of Israel moved from their places and took up positions at Baal Tamar, and the Israelite ambush charged out of its place on the west[a] of Gibeah.[b] ³⁴Then ten thousand of Israel's finest men made a frontal attack on Gibeah. The fighting was so heavy that the Benjamites did not realize how near disaster was. ³⁵The LORD defeated Benjamin before Israel, and on that day the Israelites struck down 25,100 Benjamites, all armed with swords. ³⁶Then the Benjamites saw that they were beaten.

Now the men of Israel had given way before Benjamin, because they relied on the ambush they had set near Gibeah. ³⁷The men who had been in ambush made a sudden dash into Gibeah, spread out and put the whole city to the sword. ³⁸The men of Israel had arranged with the ambush that they should send up a great cloud of smoke from the city, ³⁹and then the men of Israel would turn in the battle.

The Benjamites had begun to inflict casualties on the men of Israel (about thirty), and they said, "We are defeating them as in the first battle." ⁴⁰But when the column of smoke began to rise from the city, the Benjamites turned and saw the smoke of the whole city going up into the sky. ⁴¹Then the men of Israel turned on them, and the men of Benjamin were terrified, because they realized that disaster had come upon them. ⁴²So they fled before the Israelites in the direction of the desert, but they could not escape the battle. And the men of Israel who came out of the towns cut them down there. ⁴³They surrounded the Benjamites, chased them and easily[c] overran them in the vicinity of Gibeah on the east. ⁴⁴Eighteen thousand Benjamites fell, all of them valiant fighters. ⁴⁵As they turned and fled toward the desert to the rock

of Rimmon, the Israelites cut down five thousand men along the roads. They kept pressing after the Benjamites as far as Gidom and struck down two thousand more. ⁴⁶On that day twenty-five thousand Benjamite swordsmen fell, all of them valiant fighters. ⁴⁷But six hundred men turned and fled into the desert to the rock of Rimmon, where they stayed four months. ⁴⁸The men of Israel went back to Benjamin and put all the towns to the sword, including the animals and everything else they found. All the towns they came across they set on fire.

Wives for the Benjamites

21 The men of Israel had taken an oath at Mizpah: "Not one of us will give his daughter in marriage to a Benjamite." ²The people went to Bethel,[d] where they sat before God until evening, raising their voices and weeping bitterly. ³"O LORD, the God of Israel," they cried, "why has this happened to Israel? Why should one tribe be missing from Israel today?"

⁴Early the next day the people built an altar and presented burnt offerings and fellowship offerings.[e] ⁵Then the Israelites asked, "Who from all the tribes of Israel has failed to assemble before the LORD?" For they had taken a solemn oath that anyone who failed to assemble before the LORD at Mizpah should certainly be put to death. ⁶Now the Israelites grieved for their brothers, the Benjamites. "Today one tribe is cut off from Israel," they said. ⁷"How can we provide wives for those who are left, since we have taken an oath by the LORD not to give them any of our daughters in marriage?" ⁸Then they asked, "Which one of the tribes of Israel failed to assemble before the LORD at Mizpah?" They discovered that no one from Jabesh Gilead had come to

---

^a33 Some Septuagint manuscripts and Vulgate; the meaning of the Hebrew for this word is uncertain.   ^b33 Hebrew *Geba*, a variant of *Gibeah*   ^c43 The meaning of the Hebrew for this word is uncertain.   ^d2 Or *to the house of God*   ^e4 Traditionally *peace offerings*

the camp for the assembly. [9]For when they counted the people, they found that none of the people of Jabesh Gilead were there.

[10]So the assembly sent twelve thousand fighting men with instructions to go to Jabesh Gilead and put to the sword those living there, including the women and children. [11]"This is what you are to do," they said. "Kill every male and every woman who is not a virgin." [12]They found among the people living in Jabesh Gilead four hundred young women who had never slept with a man, and they took them to the camp at Shiloh in Canaan.

[13]Then the whole assembly sent an offer of peace to the Benjamites at the rock of Rimmon. [14]So the Benjamites returned at that time and were given the women of Jabesh Gilead who had been spared. But there were not enough for all of them.

[15]The people grieved for Benjamin, because the LORD had made a gap in the tribes of Israel. [16]And the elders of the assembly said, "With the women of Benjamin destroyed, how shall we provide wives for the men who are left? [17]The Benjamite survivors must have heirs," they said, "so that a tribe of Israel will not be wiped out. [18]We can't give them our daughters as wives, since we Israelites have taken this oath: 'Cursed be anyone who gives a wife to a Benjamite.' [19]But look, there is the annual festival of the LORD in Shiloh, to the north of Bethel, and east of the road that goes from Bethel to Shechem, and to the south of Lebonah."

[20]So they instructed the Benjamites, saying, "Go and hide in the vineyards [21]and watch. When the girls of Shiloh come out to join in the dancing, then rush from the vineyards and each of you seize a wife from the girls of Shiloh and go to the land of Benjamin. [22]When their fathers or brothers complain to us, we will say to them, 'Do us a kindness by helping them, because we did not get wives for them during the war, and you are innocent, since you did not give your daughters to them.' "

[23]So that is what the Benjamites did. While the girls were dancing, each man caught one and carried her off to be his wife. Then they returned to their inheritance and rebuilt the towns and settled in them.

[24]At that time the Israelites left that place and went home to their tribes and clans, each to his own inheritance.

[25]In those days Israel had no king; everyone did as he saw fit.

RUTH

WHO WROTE THIS BOOK?	The author of Ruth is unknown.
WHY WAS THIS BOOK WRITTEN?	Ruth shows that some people trusted God even in the time of the judges.
WHAT HAPPENS IN THIS BOOK?	Ruth, a young Moabite widow, travels to Israel with her Jewish mother-in-law and marries a good man there.
WHAT DO WE LEARN ABOUT GOD IN THIS BOOK?	God loves people of every nation who put their trust in him.
WHO IS IMPORTANT IN THIS BOOK?	The important people in this book are Naomi, Ruth and Boaz.
WHEN DID THIS HAPPEN?	The story of Ruth took place in the days of the judges, probably about 1100 B.C.
WHERE DID THIS HAPPEN?	Ruth and Naomi lived in Bethlehem, the city where David and Jesus were born.
WHAT ARE SOME OF THE STORIES IN THIS BOOK?	Ruth goes with Naomi. Ruth 1 Ruth meets Boaz. Ruth 2 Boaz marries Ruth. Ruth 4

Naomi and Ruth

1 In the days when the judges ruled,*a* there was a famine in the land, and a man from Bethlehem in Judah, together with his wife and two sons, went to live for a while in the country of Moab. ²The man's name was Elimelech, his wife's name Naomi, and the names of his two sons were Mahlon and Kilion. They were Ephrathites from Bethlehem, Judah. And they went to Moab and lived there.

³Now Elimelech, Naomi's husband, died, and she was left with her two sons. ⁴They married Moabite women, one named Orpah and the other Ruth. After they had lived there about ten years, ⁵both Mahlon and Kilion also died, and Naomi was left without her two sons and her husband.

⁶When she heard in Moab that the LORD had come to the aid of his people by providing food for them, Naomi and her daughters-in-law prepared to return home from there. ⁷With her two daughters-in-law she left the place where she had been living and set out on the road that would take them back to the land of Judah.

⁸Then Naomi said to her two daughters-in-law, "Go back, each of you, to your mother's home. May the LORD show kindness to you, as you have shown to your dead and to me. ⁹May the LORD grant that each of you will find rest in the home of another husband."

Then she kissed them and they wept aloud ¹⁰and said to her, "We will go back with you to your people."

¹¹But Naomi said, "Return home, my daughters. Why would you come with me? Am I going to have any more sons, who could become your husbands? ¹²Return home, my daughters; I am too old to have another husband. Even if I thought there was still hope for me—even if I had a husband tonight and then gave birth to sons— ¹³would you wait until they grew up? Would you remain unmarried for them? No, my daughters. It is more bitter for me than for you, because the LORD's hand has gone out against me!"

¹⁴At this they wept again. Then Orpah kissed her mother-in-law goodby, but Ruth clung to her.

¹⁵"Look," said Naomi, "your sister-in-law is going back to her people and her gods. Go back with her."

¹⁶But Ruth replied, "Don't urge me to leave you or to turn back from you. Where you go I will go, and where you stay I will stay. Your people will be my people and your God my God. ¹⁷Where you die I will die, and there I will be buried. May the LORD deal with me, be it ever so severely, if anything but death separates you and me." ¹⁸When Naomi realized that Ruth was determined to go with her, she stopped urging her.

¹⁹So the two women went on until they came to Bethlehem. When they arrived in Bethlehem, the whole town was stirred because of them, and the women exclaimed, "Can this be Naomi?"

²⁰"Don't call me Naomi,*b*" she told them. "Call me Mara,*c* because the Almighty*d* has made my life very bitter. ²¹I went away full, but the LORD has brought me back empty. Why call me Naomi? The LORD has afflicted*e* me; the Almighty has brought misfortune upon me."

²²So Naomi returned from Moab accompanied by Ruth the Moabitess, her daughter-in-law, arriving in Bethlehem as the barley harvest was beginning.

Ruth Meets Boaz

2 Now Naomi had a relative on her husband's side, from the clan of Elimelech, a man of standing, whose name was Boaz.

²And Ruth the Moabitess said to Naomi, "Let me go to the fields and pick up the leftover grain behind

---

a1 Traditionally *judged*   *b20 Naomi* means *pleasant*; also in verse 21.   *c20 Mara* means *bitter*.   *d20* Hebrew *Shaddai*; also in verse 21   *e21* Or *has testified against*

anyone in whose eyes I find favor."

Naomi said to her, "Go ahead, my daughter." ³So she went out and began to glean in the fields behind the harvesters. As it turned out, she found herself working in a field belonging to Boaz, who was from the clan of Elimelech.

⁴Just then Boaz arrived from Bethlehem and greeted the harvesters, "The LORD be with you!"

"The LORD bless you!" they called back.

⁵Boaz asked the foreman of his harvesters, "Whose young woman is that?"

⁶The foreman replied, "She is the Moabitess who came back from Moab with Naomi. ⁷She said, 'Please let me glean and gather among the sheaves behind the harvesters.' She went into the field and has worked steadily from morning till now, except for a short rest in the shelter."

⁸So Boaz said to Ruth, "My daughter, listen to me. Don't go and glean in another field and don't go away from here. Stay here with my servant girls. ⁹Watch the field where the men are harvesting, and follow along after the girls. I have told the men not to touch you. And whenever you are thirsty, go and get a drink from the water jars the men have filled."

¹⁰At this, she bowed down with her face to the ground. She exclaimed, "Why have I found such favor in your eyes that you notice me—a foreigner?"

¹¹Boaz replied, "I've been told all about what you have done for your mother-in-law since the death of your husband—how you left your father and mother and your homeland and came to live with a people you did not know before. ¹²May the LORD repay you for what you have done. May you be richly rewarded by the LORD, the God of Israel, under whose wings you have come to take refuge."

¹³"May I continue to find favor in your eyes, my lord," she said. "You have given me comfort and have spoken kindly to your servant—though I do not have the standing of one of your servant girls."

¹⁴At mealtime Boaz said to her, "Come over here. Have some bread and dip it in the wine vinegar."

When she sat down with the harvesters, he offered her some roasted grain. She ate all she wanted and had some left over. ¹⁵As she got up to glean, Boaz gave orders to his men, "Even if she gathers among the sheaves, don't embarrass her. ¹⁶Rather, pull out some stalks for her from the bundles and leave them for her to pick up, and don't rebuke her."

¹⁷So Ruth gleaned in the field until evening. Then she threshed the barley she had gathered, and it amounted to about an ephah.ᵃ ¹⁸She carried it back to town, and her mother-in-law saw how much she had gathered. Ruth also brought out and gave her what she had left over after she had eaten enough.

ᵃ17 That is, probably about 3/5 bushel (about 22 liters)

 ET'S LIVE IT!   Ruth 1:11—2:3

CHOOSE FRIENDS WISELY ➡ Write down the names of two or three of your close friends. Under their names list the things that a good friend does or does not do. For instance, a good friend takes turns, isn't bossy, helps you out, and won't leave you when you're in trouble. How many more things can you add to this list? Read Ruth 1:11—2:3. How did Ruth show she was a good friend to Naomi? Did Ruth do any of the things on your friendship list? Sometimes boys and girls don't choose their friends wisely. Keep the friendship list you made as a reminder of the kind of person you want to choose for a friend.

¹⁹Her mother-in-law asked her, "Where did you glean today? Where did you work? Blessed be the man who took notice of you!"

Then Ruth told her mother-in-law about the one at whose place she had been working. "The name of the man I worked with today is Boaz," she said.

²⁰"The LORD bless him!" Naomi said to her daughter-in-law. "He has not stopped showing his kindness to the living and the dead." She added, "That man is our close relative; he is one of our kinsman-redeemers."

²¹Then Ruth the Moabitess said, "He even said to me, 'Stay with my workers until they finish harvesting all my grain.'"

²²Naomi said to Ruth her daughter-in-law, "It will be good for you, my daughter, to go with his girls, because in someone else's field you might be harmed."

²³So Ruth stayed close to the servant girls of Boaz to glean until the barley and wheat harvests were finished. And she lived with her mother-in-law.

Ruth and Boaz at the Threshing Floor

3 One day Naomi her mother-in-law said to her, "My daughter, should I not try to find a home^a for you, where you will be well provided for? ²Is not Boaz, with whose servant girls you have been, a kinsman of ours? Tonight he will be winnowing barley on the threshing floor. ³Wash and perfume yourself, and put on your best clothes. Then go down to the threshing floor, but don't let him know you are there until he has finished eating and drinking. ⁴When he lies down, note the place where he is lying. Then go and uncover his feet and lie down. He will tell you what to do."

⁵"I will do whatever you say," Ruth answered. ⁶So she went down to the threshing floor and did everything her mother-in-law told her to do.

⁷When Boaz had finished eating and drinking and was in good spirits, he went over to lie down at the far end of the grain pile. Ruth approached quietly, uncovered his feet and lay down. ⁸In the middle of the night something startled the man, and he turned and discovered a woman lying at his feet.

⁹"Who are you?" he asked.

"I am your servant Ruth," she said. "Spread the corner of your garment over me, since you are a kinsman-redeemer."

¹⁰"The LORD bless you, my daughter," he replied. "This kindness is greater than that which you showed earlier: You have not run after the younger men, whether rich or poor. ¹¹And now, my daughter, don't be afraid. I will do for you all you ask. All my fellow townsmen know that you are a woman of noble character. ¹²Although it is true that I am near of kin, there is a kinsman-redeemer nearer than I. ¹³Stay here for the night, and in the morning if he wants to redeem, good; let him redeem. But if he is not willing, as surely as the LORD lives I will do it. Lie here until morning."

¹⁴So she lay at his feet until morning, but got up before anyone could be recognized; and he said, "Don't let it be known that a woman came to the threshing floor."

¹⁵He also said, "Bring me the shawl you are wearing and hold it out." When she did so, he poured into it six measures of barley and put it on her. Then he^b went back to town.

¹⁶When Ruth came to her mother-in-law, Naomi asked, "How did it go, my daughter?"

Then she told her everything Boaz had done for her ¹⁷and added, "He gave me these six measures of barley, saying, 'Don't go back to your mother-in-law empty-handed.'"

¹⁸Then Naomi said, "Wait, my

---

^a1 Hebrew *find rest* (see Ruth 1:9)   ^b15 Most Hebrew manuscripts; many Hebrew manuscripts, Vulgate and Syriac *she*

daughter, until you find out what happens. For the man will not rest until the matter is settled today."

Boaz Marries Ruth

4 Meanwhile Boaz went up to the town gate and sat there. When the kinsman-redeemer he had mentioned came along, Boaz said, "Come over here, my friend, and sit down." So he went over and sat down.

²Boaz took ten of the elders of the town and said, "Sit here," and they did so. ³Then he said to the kinsman-redeemer, "Naomi, who has come back from Moab, is selling the piece of land that belonged to our brother Elimelech. ⁴I thought I should bring the matter to your attention and suggest that you buy it in the presence of these seated here and in the presence of the elders of my people. If you will redeem it, do so. But if you ᵃ will not, tell me, so I will know. For no one has the right to do it except you, and I am next in line."

"I will redeem it," he said.

⁵Then Boaz said, "On the day you buy the land from Naomi and from Ruth the Moabitess, you acquire ᵇ the dead man's widow, in order to maintain the name of the dead with his property."

⁶At this, the kinsman-redeemer said, "Then I cannot redeem it because I might endanger my own estate. You redeem it yourself. I cannot do it."

⁷(Now in earlier times in Israel, for the redemption and transfer of property to become final, one party took off his sandal and gave it to the other. This was the method of legalizing transactions in Israel.)

⁸So the kinsman-redeemer said to Boaz, "Buy it yourself." And he removed his sandal.

⁹Then Boaz announced to the elders and all the people, "Today you are witnesses that I have bought from Naomi all the property of Elimelech, Kilion and Mahlon. ¹⁰I have

also acquired Ruth the Moabitess, Mahlon's widow, as my wife, in order to maintain the name of the dead with his property, so that his name will not disappear from among his family or from the town records. Today you are witnesses!"

Life In Bible Times

TAKING OFF A SANDAL

Today people sign papers to show they have made an agreement. In the days of the judges a person showed that an agreement had been made by taking off a sandal (shoe) and handing it over. People who saw the sandal handed over could be witnesses in court if the agreement was broken.

---

¹¹Then the elders and all those at the gate said, "We are witnesses. May the LORD make the woman who is coming into your home like Rachel and Leah, who together built up the house of Israel. May you have standing in Ephrathah and be famous in Bethlehem. ¹²Through the offspring the LORD gives you by this young woman, may your family be like that of Perez, whom Tamar bore to Judah."

The Genealogy of David

¹³So Boaz took Ruth and she became his wife. Then he went to her, and the LORD enabled her to conceive, and she gave birth to a son. ¹⁴The women said to Naomi: "Praise be to the LORD, who this day has not left you without a kinsman-redeemer. May he become famous throughout Israel! ¹⁵He will renew your life and sustain you in your old age. For your

---

ᵃ4 Many Hebrew manuscripts, Septuagint, Vulgate and Syriac; most Hebrew manuscripts *he*
ᵇ5 Hebrew; Vulgate and Syriac *Naomi, you acquire Ruth the Moabitess,*

daughter-in-law, who loves you and who is better to you than seven sons, has given him birth."

¹⁶Then Naomi took the child, laid him in her lap and cared for him. ¹⁷The women living there said, "Naomi has a son." And they named him Obed. He was the father of Jesse, the father of David.

¹⁸This, then, is the family line of Perez:

Perez was the father of Hezron,
¹⁹Hezron the father of Ram,
Ram the father of Amminadab,
²⁰Amminadab the father of Nahshon,
Nahshon the father of Salmon,ᵃ
²¹Salmon the father of Boaz,
Boaz the father of Obed,
²²Obed the father of Jesse,
and Jesse the father of David.

---

a20 A few Hebrew manuscripts, some Septuagint manuscripts and Vulgate (see also verse 21 and Septuagint of 1 Chron. 2:11); most Hebrew manuscripts *Salma*

LET'S LIVE IT!   Ruth 4:1–22

RICH REWARDS ➠ When Ruth decided to be Naomi's friend and to help her, Ruth did not expect any rewards. But everyone in Bethlehem noticed what a good friend and nice person Ruth was. Even the rich Boaz said, "I've been told all about what you have done for your mother-in-law. . . . May you be richly rewarded by the LORD" (Ruth 2:11–12).

Read Ruth 4:1–22 to find out what Ruth's reward was.

Ruth didn't choose to be Naomi's friend to get a reward. Your close friends didn't choose you in order to get a reward either. But sometimes it's nice to surprise people who are nice to us. Ask your mom if you can have a Friendship Party for one or two or maybe three good friends. Have cake and ice cream at the party. Using some pretty wrapping paper, make a special card for your friends to tell them why you're glad they are your friends.

1 SAMUEL

The Birth of Samuel

1 There was a certain man from Ramathaim, a Zuphite[a] from the hill country of Ephraim, whose name was Elkanah son of Jeroham, the son of Elihu, the son of Tohu, the son of Zuph, an Ephraimite. ²He had two wives; one was called Hannah and the other Peninnah. Peninnah had children, but Hannah had none.

³Year after year this man went up from his town to worship and sacrifice to the LORD Almighty at Shiloh, where Hophni and Phinehas, the two sons of Eli, were priests of the LORD. ⁴Whenever the day came for Elkanah to sacrifice, he would give portions of the meat to his wife Peninnah and to all her sons and daughters. ⁵But to Hannah he gave a double portion because he loved her, and the LORD had closed her womb. ⁶And because the LORD had closed her womb, her rival kept provoking her in order to irritate her. ⁷This went on year after year. Whenever Hannah went up to the house of the LORD, her rival provoked her till she wept and would not eat. ⁸Elkanah her husband would say to her, "Hannah, why are you weeping? Why don't you eat? Why are you downhearted? Don't I mean more to you than ten sons?"

⁹Once when they had finished eating and drinking in Shiloh, Hannah stood up. Now Eli the priest was sitting on a chair by the doorpost of the LORD's temple.[b] ¹⁰In bitterness of soul Hannah wept much and prayed to the LORD. ¹¹And she made a vow, saying, "O LORD Almighty, if you will only look upon your servant's misery and remember me, and not forget your servant but give her a son, then I will give him to the LORD for all the days of his life, and no razor will ever be used on his head."

¹²As she kept on praying to the LORD, Eli observed her mouth. ¹³Hannah was praying in her heart, and her lips were moving but her voice was not heard. Eli thought she was drunk ¹⁴and said to her, "How long will you keep on getting drunk? Get rid of your wine."

¹⁵"Not so, my lord," Hannah replied, "I am a woman who is deeply troubled. I have not been drinking wine or beer; I was pouring out my soul to the LORD. ¹⁶Do not take your servant for a wicked woman; I have been praying here out of my great anguish and grief."

¹⁷Eli answered, "Go in peace, and may the God of Israel grant you what you have asked of him."

¹⁸She said, "May your servant find favor in your eyes." Then she went her way and ate something, and her face was no longer downcast.

¹⁹Early the next morning they arose and worshiped before the LORD and then went back to their home at Ramah. Elkanah lay with Hannah his wife, and the LORD remembered her. ²⁰So in the course of time Hannah conceived and gave birth to a son. She named him Samuel,[c] saying, "Because I asked the LORD for him."

a1 Or from Ramathaim Zuphim   b9 That is, tabernacle   c20 Samuel sounds like the Hebrew for heard of God.

LET'S LIVE IT!

1 Samuel 1:1–20

A GIFT TO AND FROM GOD ➥ Did you know that many mothers pray for their children before the children are born? Ask your mom if she prayed for you before you were born. Ask her what she said when she prayed for you. Ask if she prays for you now.

Then read 1 Samuel 1:1–20. What did Hannah say when she prayed to God for her child? Was anything in Hannah's prayer like your mother's prayers for you?

Hannah Dedicates Samuel

²¹When the man Elkanah went up with all his family to offer the annual sacrifice to the LORD and to fulfill his vow, ²²Hannah did not go. She said to her husband, "After the boy is weaned, I will take him and present him before the LORD, and he will live there always."

²³"Do what seems best to you," Elkanah her husband told her. "Stay here until you have weaned him; only may the LORD make good his*ᵃ* word." So the woman stayed at home and nursed her son until she had weaned him.

²⁴After he was weaned, she took the boy with her, young as he was, along with a three-year-old bull,*ᵇ* an ephah*ᶜ* of flour and a skin of wine, and brought him to the house of the LORD at Shiloh. ²⁵When they had slaughtered the bull, they brought the boy to Eli, ²⁶and she said to him, "As surely as you live, my lord, I am the woman who stood here beside you praying to the LORD. ²⁷I prayed for this child, and the LORD has granted me what I asked of him. ²⁸So now I give him to the LORD. For his whole life he will be given over to the LORD." And he worshiped the LORD there.

Hannah's Prayer

2 Then Hannah prayed and said:

"My heart rejoices in the LORD;
    in the LORD my horn*ᵈ* is lifted
        high.
My mouth boasts over my
        enemies,
    for I delight in your
        deliverance.

²"There is no one holy*ᵉ* like the
        LORD;
    there is no one besides you;
    there is no Rock like our God.

³"Do not keep talking so proudly

or let your mouth speak such
        arrogance,
for the LORD is a God who knows,
    and by him deeds are weighed.

⁴"The bows of the warriors are
        broken,
    but those who stumbled are
        armed with strength.
⁵Those who were full hire
        themselves out for food,
    but those who were hungry
        hunger no more.
She who was barren has borne
        seven children,
    but she who has had many sons
        pines away.

⁶"The LORD brings death and
        makes alive;
    he brings down to the grave*ᶠ*
        and raises up.
⁷The LORD sends poverty and
        wealth;
    he humbles and he exalts.
⁸He raises the poor from the dust
    and lifts the needy from the ash
        heap;
he seats them with princes
    and has them inherit a throne
        of honor.

"For the foundations of the earth
        are the LORD's;
    upon them he has set the world.
⁹He will guard the feet of his
        saints,
    but the wicked will be silenced
        in darkness.

"It is not by strength that one
        prevails;
10   those who oppose the LORD will
        be shattered.
He will thunder against them
        from heaven;
    the LORD will judge the ends of
        the earth.

"He will give strength to his king
    and exalt the horn of his
        anointed."

ᵃ23 Masoretic Text; Dead Sea Scrolls, Septuagint and Syriac *your*   *ᵇ24* Dead Sea Scrolls, Septuagint and Syriac; Masoretic Text *with three bulls*   *ᶜ24* That is, probably about 3/5 bushel (about 22 liters)   *ᵈ1 Horn* here symbolizes strength; also in verse 10.   *ᵉ2* Or *no Holy One*   *ᶠ6* Hebrew *Sheol*

¹¹Then Elkanah went home to Ramah, but the boy ministered before the Lord under Eli the priest.

Eli's Wicked Sons

¹²Eli's sons were wicked men; they had no regard for the Lord. ¹³Now it was the practice of the priests with the people that whenever anyone offered a sacrifice and while the meat was being boiled, the servant of the priest would come with a three-pronged fork in his hand. ¹⁴He would plunge it into the pan or kettle or caldron or pot, and the priest would take for himself whatever the fork brought up. This is how they treated all the Israelites who came to Shiloh. ¹⁵But even before the fat was burned, the servant of the priest would come and say to the man who was sacrificing, "Give the priest some meat to roast; he won't accept boiled meat from you, but only raw."

❓DID YOU KNOW?　　　2:12

What was Eli's sin?

Eli was high priest. He let his sons, who were also priests, keep on disobeying God and doing wicked things. This chapter tells what happened to Eli for letting his sons sin. It also tells what will happen to Eli's sons.

¹⁶If the man said to him, "Let the fat be burned up first, and then take whatever you want," the servant would then answer, "No, hand it over now; if you don't, I'll take it by force."

¹⁷This sin of the young men was very great in the Lord's sight, for they^a were treating the Lord's offering with contempt.

¹⁸But Samuel was ministering before the Lord—a boy wearing a linen ephod. ¹⁹Each year his mother made him a little robe and took it to him when she went up with her husband to offer the annual sacrifice. ²⁰Eli would bless Elkanah and his wife, saying, "May the Lord give you children by this woman to take the place of the one she prayed for and gave to the Lord." Then they would go home. ²¹And the Lord was gracious to Hannah; she conceived and gave birth to three sons and two daughters. Meanwhile, the boy Samuel grew up in the presence of the Lord.

²²Now Eli, who was very old, heard about everything his sons were doing to all Israel and how they slept with the women who served at the entrance to the Tent of Meeting. ²³So he said to them, "Why do you do such things? I hear from all the people about these wicked deeds of yours. ²⁴No, my sons; it is not a good report that I hear spreading among the Lord's people. ²⁵If a man sins against another man, God^b may mediate for him; but if a man sins against the Lord, who will intercede for him?" His sons, however, did not listen to their father's rebuke, for it was the Lord's will to put them to death.

²⁶And the boy Samuel continued to grow in stature and in favor with the Lord and with men.

Prophecy Against the House of Eli

²⁷Now a man of God came to Eli and said to him, "This is what the Lord says: 'Did I not clearly reveal myself to your father's house when they were in Egypt under Pharaoh? ²⁸I chose your father out of all the tribes of Israel to be my priest, to go up to my altar, to burn incense, and to wear an ephod in my presence. I also gave your father's house all the offerings made with fire by the Israelites. ²⁹Why do you^c scorn my sacrifice and offering that I prescribed for my dwelling? Why do you honor your sons more than me by fattening yourselves on the choice parts of every offering made by my people Israel?'

³⁰"Therefore the Lord, the God of Israel, declares: 'I promised that your house and your father's house would

---

^a17 Or men　　^b25 Or the judges　　^c29 The Hebrew is plural.

minister before me forever.' But now the LORD declares: 'Far be it from me! Those who honor me I will honor, but those who despise me will be disdained. ³¹The time is coming when I will cut short your strength and the strength of your father's house, so that there will not be an old man in your family line ³²and you will see distress in my dwelling. Although good will be done to Israel, in your family line there will never be an old man. ³³Every one of you that I do not cut off from my altar will be spared only to blind your eyes with tears and to grieve your heart, and all your descendants will die in the prime of life.

³⁴" 'And what happens to your two sons, Hophni and Phinehas, will be a sign to you—they will both die on the same day. ³⁵I will raise up for myself a faithful priest, who will do according to what is in my heart and mind. I will firmly establish his house, and he will minister before my anointed one always. ³⁶Then everyone left in your family line will come and bow down before him for a piece of silver and a crust of bread and plead, "Appoint me to some priestly office so I can have food to eat." ' "

? DID YOU KNOW?   3:1

How old was Samuel when God called him in the night?

The Hebrew word for *boy* means that Samuel was probably about twelve when God spoke to him. A person does not have to be grown-up to listen to God or to obey him.

The LORD Calls Samuel

3 The boy Samuel ministered before the LORD under Eli. In those days the word of the LORD was rare; there were not many visions.

²One night Eli, whose eyes were becoming so weak that he could barely see, was lying down in his usual place. ³The lamp of God had not yet gone out, and Samuel was lying down in the temple^a of the LORD, where the ark of God was. ⁴Then the LORD called Samuel.

Samuel answered, "Here I am." ⁵And he ran to Eli and said, "Here I am; you called me."

But Eli said, "I did not call; go back and lie down." So he went and lay down.

⁶Again the LORD called, "Samuel!" And Samuel got up and went to Eli and said, "Here I am; you called me."

"My son," Eli said, "I did not call; go back and lie down."

⁷Now Samuel did not yet know the LORD: The word of the LORD had not yet been revealed to him.

⁸The LORD called Samuel a third time, and Samuel got up and went to Eli and said, "Here I am; you called me."

Then Eli realized that the LORD was calling the boy. ⁹So Eli told Samuel, "Go and lie down, and if he calls you, say, 'Speak, LORD, for your servant is listening.' " So Samuel went and lay down in his place.

¹⁰The LORD came and stood there, calling as at the other times, "Samuel! Samuel!"

Then Samuel said, "Speak, for your servant is listening."

¹¹And the LORD said to Samuel: "See, I am about to do something in Israel that will make the ears of everyone who hears of it tingle. ¹²At that time I will carry out against Eli everything I spoke against his family—from beginning to end. ¹³For I told him that I would judge his family forever because of the sin he knew about; his sons made themselves contemptible,^b and he failed to restrain them. ¹⁴Therefore, I swore to the house of Eli, 'The guilt of Eli's house will never be atoned for by sacrifice or offering.' "

¹⁵Samuel lay down until morning

^a3 That is, tabernacle   ^b13 Masoretic Text; an ancient Hebrew scribal tradition and Septuagint *sons blasphemed God*

and then opened the doors of the house of the LORD. He was afraid to tell Eli the vision, [16]but Eli called him and said, "Samuel, my son."

Samuel answered, "Here I am."

[17]"What was it he said to you?" Eli asked. "Do not hide it from me. May God deal with you, be it ever so severely, if you hide from me anything he told you." [18]So Samuel told him everything, hiding nothing from him. Then Eli said, "He is the LORD; let him do what is good in his eyes."

[19]The LORD was with Samuel as he grew up, and he let none of his words fall to the ground. [20]And all Israel from Dan to Beersheba recognized that Samuel was attested as a prophet of the LORD. [21]The LORD continued to appear at Shiloh, and there he revealed himself to Samuel through his word.

4 And Samuel's word came to all Israel.

The Philistines Capture the Ark

Now the Israelites went out to fight against the Philistines. The Israelites camped at Ebenezer, and the Philistines at Aphek. [2]The Philistines deployed their forces to meet Israel, and as the battle spread, Israel was defeated by the Philistines, who killed about four thousand of them on the battlefield. [3]When the soldiers returned to camp, the elders of Israel asked, "Why did the LORD bring defeat upon us today before the Philistines? Let us bring the ark of the LORD's covenant from Shiloh, so that it[a] may go with us and save us from the hand of our enemies."

[4]So the people sent men to Shiloh, and they brought back the ark of the covenant of the LORD Almighty, who is enthroned between the cherubim. And Eli's two sons, Hophni and Phinehas, were there with the ark of the covenant of God.

[5]When the ark of the LORD's covenant came into the camp, all Israel raised such a great shout that the

ground shook. [6]Hearing the uproar, the Philistines asked, "What's all this shouting in the Hebrew camp?"

When they learned that the ark of the LORD had come into the camp, [7]the Philistines were afraid. "A god has come into the camp," they said. "We're in trouble! Nothing like this has happened before. [8]Woe to us! Who will deliver us from the hand of these mighty gods? They are the gods who struck the Egyptians with all kinds of plagues in the desert. [9]Be strong, Philistines! Be men, or you will be subject to the Hebrews, as they have been to you. Be men, and fight!"

[10]So the Philistines fought, and the Israelites were defeated and every man fled to his tent. The slaughter was very great; Israel lost thirty thousand foot soldiers. [11]The ark of God was captured, and Eli's two sons, Hophni and Phinehas, died.

Death of Eli

[12]That same day a Benjamite ran from the battle line and went to Shiloh, his clothes torn and dust on his head. [13]When he arrived, there was Eli sitting on his chair by the side of the road, watching, because his heart feared for the ark of God. When the man entered the town and told what had happened, the whole town sent up a cry.

[14]Eli heard the outcry and asked, "What is the meaning of this uproar?"

The man hurried over to Eli, [15]who was ninety-eight years old and whose eyes were set so that he could not see. [16]He told Eli, "I have just come from the battle line; I fled from it this very day."

Eli asked, "What happened, my son?"

[17]The man who brought the news replied, "Israel fled before the Philistines, and the army has suffered heavy losses. Also your two sons, Hophni and Phinehas, are dead, and the ark of God has been captured."

¹⁸When he mentioned the ark of God, Eli fell backward off his chair by the side of the gate. His neck was broken and he died, for he was an old man and heavy. He had led*ᵃ* Israel forty years.

¹⁹His daughter-in-law, the wife of Phinehas, was pregnant and near the time of delivery. When she heard the news that the ark of God had been captured and that her father-in-law and her husband were dead, she went into labor and gave birth, but was overcome by her labor pains. ²⁰As she was dying, the women attending her said, "Don't despair; you have given birth to a son." But she did not respond or pay any attention.

²¹She named the boy Ichabod,*ᵇ* saying, "The glory has departed from Israel"—because of the capture of the ark of God and the deaths of her father-in-law and her husband. ²²She said, "The glory has departed from Israel, for the ark of God has been captured."

The Ark in Ashdod and Ekron

5 After the Philistines had captured the ark of God, they took it from Ebenezer to Ashdod. ²Then they carried the ark into Dagon's temple and set it beside Dagon. ³When the people of Ashdod rose early the next day, there was Dagon, fallen on his face on the ground before the ark of the LORD! They took Dagon and put him back in his place. ⁴But the following morning when they rose, there was Dagon, fallen on his face on the ground before the ark of the LORD! His head and hands had been broken off and were lying on the threshold; only his body remained. ⁵That is why to this day neither the priests of Dagon nor any others who enter Dagon's temple at Ashdod step on the threshold.

⁶The LORD's hand was heavy upon the people of Ashdod and its vicinity; he brought devastation upon them and afflicted them with tumors.*ᶜ* ⁷When the men of Ashdod saw what was happening, they said, "The ark of the god of Israel must not stay here with us, because his hand is heavy upon us and upon Dagon our god." ⁸So they called together all the rulers of the Philistines and asked them, "What shall we do with the ark of the god of Israel?"

Life In Bible Times

THE BROKEN IDOL

The Philistines worshiped an idol made of clay and called it their god, Dagon. The god had many human features like a head and hands. Dagon fell and broke apart before the ark of God. This showed that the Lord is the true God.

They answered, "Have the ark of the god of Israel moved to Gath." So they moved the ark of the God of Israel.

⁹But after they had moved it, the LORD's hand was against that city, throwing it into a great panic. He afflicted the people of the city, both young and old, with an outbreak of tumors.*ᵈ* ¹⁰So they sent the ark of God to Ekron.

As the ark of God was entering Ekron, the people of Ekron cried out, "They have brought the ark of the god of Israel around to us to kill us and our people." ¹¹So they called together all the rulers of the Philistines and said, "Send the ark of the god of Israel away; let it go back to its own place, or it*ᵉ* will kill us and our people." For death had filled the city with panic; God's hand was very

---

a18 Traditionally *judged*   *b21 Ichabod* means *no glory.*   *c6* Hebrew; Septuagint and Vulgate *tumors. And rats appeared in their land, and death and destruction were throughout the city*   *d9* Or *with tumors in the groin* (see Septuagint)   *e11* Or *he*

heavy upon it. [12]Those who did not die were afflicted with tumors, and the outcry of the city went up to heaven.

❓DID YOU KNOW?   5:6,10

What were Ashdod and Ekron?

Ashdod and Ekron were Philistine cities. The Philistines had five large cities. These were two of the important centers of Philistine power.

The Ark Returned to Israel

6 When the ark of the LORD had been in Philistine territory seven months, [2]the Philistines called for the priests and the diviners and said, "What shall we do with the ark of the LORD? Tell us how we should send it back to its place."

[3]They answered, "If you return the ark of the god of Israel, do not send it away empty, but by all means send a guilt offering to him. Then you will be healed, and you will know why his hand has not been lifted from you."

[4]The Philistines asked, "What guilt offering should we send to him?"

They replied, "Five gold tumors and five gold rats, according to the number of the Philistine rulers, because the same plague has struck both you and your rulers. [5]Make models of the tumors and of the rats that are destroying the country, and pay honor to Israel's god. Perhaps he will lift his hand from you and your gods and your land. [6]Why do you harden your hearts as the Egyptians and Pharaoh did? When he[a] treated them harshly, did they not send the Israelites out so they could go on their way?

[7]"Now then, get a new cart ready, with two cows that have calved and have never been yoked. Hitch the cows to the cart, but take their calves away and pen them up. [8]Take the ark of the LORD and put it on the cart, and in a chest beside it put the gold objects you are sending back to him as a guilt offering. Send it on its way, [9]but keep watching it. If it goes up to its own territory, toward Beth Shemesh, then the LORD has brought this great disaster on us. But if it does not, then we will know that it was not his hand that struck us and that it happened to us by chance."

[10]So they did this. They took two such cows and hitched them to the cart and penned up their calves. [11]They placed the ark of the LORD on the cart and along with it the chest containing the gold rats and the models of the tumors. [12]Then the cows went straight up toward Beth Shemesh, keeping on the road and lowing all the way; they did not turn to the right or to the left. The rulers of the Philistines followed them as far as the border of Beth Shemesh.

[13]Now the people of Beth Shemesh were harvesting their wheat in the valley, and when they looked up and saw the ark, they rejoiced at the sight. [14]The cart came to the field of Joshua of Beth Shemesh, and there it stopped beside a large rock. The people chopped up the wood of the cart and sacrificed the cows as a burnt offering to the LORD. [15]The Levites took down the ark of the LORD, together with the chest containing the gold objects, and placed them on the large rock. On that day the people of Beth Shemesh offered burnt offerings and made sacrifices to the LORD. [16]The five rulers of the Philistines saw all this and then returned that same day to Ekron.

[17]These are the gold tumors the Philistines sent as a guilt offering to the LORD—one each for Ashdod, Gaza, Ashkelon, Gath and Ekron. [18]And the number of the gold rats was according to the number of Philistine towns belonging to the five rulers—the fortified towns with their country villages. The large rock, on

---

a6 That is, God

which*a* they set the ark of the LORD, is a witness to this day in the field of Joshua of Beth Shemesh.

¹⁹But God struck down some of the men of Beth Shemesh, putting seventy*b* of them to death because they had looked into the ark of the LORD. The people mourned because of the heavy blow the LORD had dealt them, ²⁰and the men of Beth Shemesh asked, "Who can stand in the presence of the LORD, this holy God? To whom will the ark go up from here?"

²¹Then they sent messengers to the people of Kiriath Jearim, saying, "The Philistines have returned the ark of the LORD. Come down and take it up to your place." ¹So the men of Kiriath Jearim came and took up the ark of the LORD. They took it to Abinadab's house on the hill and consecrated Eleazar his son to guard the ark of the LORD.

Samuel Subdues the Philistines at Mizpah

²It was a long time, twenty years in all, that the ark remained at Kiriath Jearim, and all the people of Israel mourned and sought after the LORD. ³And Samuel said to the whole house of Israel, "If you are returning to the LORD with all your hearts, then rid yourselves of the foreign gods and the Ashtoreths and commit yourselves to the LORD and serve him only, and he will deliver you out of the hand of the Philistines." ⁴So the Israelites put away their Baals and Ashtoreths, and served the LORD only.

⁵Then Samuel said, "Assemble all Israel at Mizpah and I will intercede with the LORD for you." ⁶When they had assembled at Mizpah, they drew water and poured it out before the LORD. On that day they fasted and there they confessed, "We have sinned against the LORD." And Samuel was leader*c* of Israel at Mizpah.

⁷When the Philistines heard that Israel had assembled at Mizpah, the rulers of the Philistines came up to attack them. And when the Israelites heard of it, they were afraid because of the Philistines. ⁸They said to Samuel, "Do not stop crying out to the LORD our God for us, that he may rescue us from the hand of the Philistines." ⁹Then Samuel took a suckling lamb and offered it up as a whole burnt offering to the LORD. He cried out to the LORD on Israel's behalf, and the LORD answered him.

¹⁰While Samuel was sacrificing the burnt offering, the Philistines drew near to engage Israel in battle. But that day the LORD thundered with loud thunder against the Philistines and threw them into such a panic that they were routed before the Israelites. ¹¹The men of Israel rushed out of Mizpah and pursued the Philistines, slaughtering them along the way to a point below Beth Car.

¹²Then Samuel took a stone and set it up between Mizpah and Shen. He named it Ebenezer,*d* saying, "Thus far has the LORD helped us." ¹³So the Philistines were subdued and did not invade Israelite territory again.

Throughout Samuel's lifetime, the hand of the LORD was against the Philistines. ¹⁴The towns from Ekron to Gath that the Philistines had captured from Israel were restored to her, and Israel delivered the neighboring territory from the power of the Philistines. And there was peace between Israel and the Amorites.

¹⁵Samuel continued as judge over Israel all the days of his life. ¹⁶From year to year he went on a circuit from Bethel to Gilgal to Mizpah, judging Israel in all those places. ¹⁷But he always went back to Ramah, where his home was, and there he also judged Israel. And he built an altar there to the LORD.

Israel Asks for a King

8 When Samuel grew old, he appointed his sons as judges for Is-

a18 A few Hebrew manuscripts (see also Septuagint); most Hebrew manuscripts *villages as far as Greater Abel, where*   *b19* A few Hebrew manuscripts; most Hebrew manuscripts and Septuagint *50,070*   *c6* Traditionally *judge*   *d12* Ebenezer means *stone of help.*

rael. ²The name of his firstborn was Joel and the name of his second was Abijah, and they served at Beersheba. ³But his sons did not walk in his ways. They turned aside after dishonest gain and accepted bribes and perverted justice.

❓DID YOU KNOW?　　　7:14

How did the Israelites defeat the Philistines?

Samuel persuaded the Israelites to give up worshiping pagan gods. When the Israelites worshiped only God, he gave them victory at Mizpah. As long as Samuel lived, and as long as Israel worshiped God, the people were safe from the Philistines.

⁴So all the elders of Israel gathered together and came to Samuel at Ramah. ⁵They said to him, "You are old, and your sons do not walk in your ways; now appoint a king to lead^a us, such as all the other nations have." ⁶But when they said, "Give us a king to lead us," this displeased Samuel; so he prayed to the LORD. ⁷And the LORD told him: "Listen to all that the people are saying to you; it is not you they have rejected, but they have rejected me as their king. ⁸As they have done from the day I brought them up out of Egypt until this day, forsaking me and serving other gods, so they are doing to you. ⁹Now listen to them; but warn them solemnly and let them know what the king who will reign over them will do."

¹⁰Samuel told all the words of the LORD to the people who were asking him for a king. ¹¹He said, "This is what the king who will reign over you will do: He will take your sons and make them serve with his chariots and horses, and they will run in front of his chariots. ¹²Some he will assign to be commanders of thousands and commanders of fifties, and

others to plow his ground and reap his harvest, and still others to make weapons of war and equipment for his chariots. ¹³He will take your daughters to be perfumers and cooks and bakers. ¹⁴He will take the best of your fields and vineyards and olive groves and give them to his attendants. ¹⁵He will take a tenth of your grain and of your vintage and give it to his officials and attendants. ¹⁶Your menservants and maidservants and the best of your cattle^b and donkeys he will take for his own use. ¹⁷He will take a tenth of your flocks, and you yourselves will become his slaves. ¹⁸When that day comes, you will cry out for relief from the king you have chosen, and the LORD will not answer you in that day."

❓DID YOU KNOW?　　　8:5

Why did the Israelites want a king?

The Israelites wanted to be like other nations, but Israel was not like other nations. Israel had God as its king and leader. It was not wrong to have a king, but Israel wanted a king for the wrong reason.

¹⁹But the people refused to listen to Samuel. "No!" they said. "We want a king over us. ²⁰Then we will be like all the other nations, with a king to lead us and to go out before us and fight our battles."

²¹When Samuel heard all that the people said, he repeated it before the LORD. ²²The LORD answered, "Listen to them and give them a king."

Then Samuel said to the men of Israel, "Everyone go back to his town."

Samuel Anoints Saul

9 There was a Benjamite, a man of standing, whose name was Kish son of Abiel, the son of Zeror, the son of Becorath, the son of Aphiah of Ben-

---

^a5 Traditionally *judge*; also in verses 6 and 20　　　^b16 Septuagint; Hebrew *young men*

jamin. ²He had a son named Saul, an impressive young man without equal among the Israelites—a head taller than any of the others.

³Now the donkeys belonging to Saul's father Kish were lost, and Kish said to his son Saul, "Take one of the servants with you and go and look for the donkeys." ⁴So he passed through the hill country of Ephraim and through the area around Shalisha, but they did not find them. They went on into the district of Shaalim, but the donkeys were not there. Then he passed through the territory of Benjamin, but they did not find them.

⁵When they reached the district of Zuph, Saul said to the servant who was with him, "Come, let's go back, or my father will stop thinking about the donkeys and start worrying about us."

⁶But the servant replied, "Look, in this town there is a man of God; he is highly respected, and everything he says comes true. Let's go there now. Perhaps he will tell us what way to take."

⁷Saul said to his servant, "If we go, what can we give the man? The food in our sacks is gone. We have no gift to take to the man of God. What do we have?"

⁸The servant answered him again. "Look," he said, "I have a quarter of a shekel*ᵃ* of silver. I will give it to the man of God so that he will tell us what way to take." ⁹(Formerly in Israel, if a man went to inquire of God, he would say, "Come, let us go to the seer," because the prophet of today used to be called a seer.)

¹⁰"Good," Saul said to his servant. "Come, let's go." So they set out for the town where the man of God was.

¹¹As they were going up the hill to the town, they met some girls coming out to draw water, and they asked them, "Is the seer here?"

¹²"He is," they answered. "He's ahead of you. Hurry now; he has just come to our town today, for the people have a sacrifice at the high place.

¹³As soon as you enter the town, you will find him before he goes up to the high place to eat. The people will not begin eating until he comes, because he must bless the sacrifice; afterward, those who are invited will eat. Go up now; you should find him about this time."

¹⁴They went up to the town, and as they were entering it, there was Samuel, coming toward them on his way up to the high place.

¹⁵Now the day before Saul came, the LORD had revealed this to Samuel: ¹⁶"About this time tomorrow I will send you a man from the land of Benjamin. Anoint him leader over my people Israel; he will deliver my people from the hand of the Philistines. I have looked upon my people, for their cry has reached me."

¹⁷When Samuel caught sight of Saul, the LORD said to him, "This is the man I spoke to you about; he will govern my people."

❓DID YOU KNOW? 9:17

Who was Israel's first king?

Saul was Israel's first king. People were impressed with Saul because he was so tall. At first Saul was a good king. He trusted God and showed good judgment. But later he began to forget God.

---

¹⁸Saul approached Samuel in the gateway and asked, "Would you please tell me where the seer's house is?"

¹⁹"I am the seer," Samuel replied. "Go up ahead of me to the high place, for today you are to eat with me, and in the morning I will let you go and will tell you all that is in your heart. ²⁰As for the donkeys you lost three days ago, do not worry about them; they have been found. And to whom is all the desire of Israel turned, if not to you and all your father's family?"

²¹Saul answered, "But am I not a

ᵃ8 That is, about 1/10 ounce (about 3 grams)

Benjamite, from the smallest tribe of Israel, and is not my clan the least of all the clans of the tribe of Benjamin? Why do you say such a thing to me?"

²²Then Samuel brought Saul and his servant into the hall and seated them at the head of those who were invited—about thirty in number. ²³Samuel said to the cook, "Bring the piece of meat I gave you, the one I told you to lay aside."

²⁴So the cook took up the leg with what was on it and set it in front of Saul. Samuel said, "Here is what has been kept for you. Eat, because it was set aside for you for this occasion, from the time I said, 'I have invited guests.'" And Saul dined with Samuel that day.

²⁵After they came down from the high place to the town, Samuel talked with Saul on the roof of his house. ²⁶They rose about daybreak and Samuel called to Saul on the roof, "Get ready, and I will send you on your way." When Saul got ready, he and Samuel went outside together. ²⁷As they were going down to the edge of the town, Samuel said to Saul, "Tell the servant to go on ahead of us"—and the servant did so—"but you stay here awhile, so that I may give you a message from God."

10 Then Samuel took a flask of oil and poured it on Saul's head and kissed him, saying, "Has not the LORD anointed you leader over his inheritance?ᵃ ²When you leave me today, you will meet two men near Rachel's tomb, at Zelzah on the border of Benjamin. They will say to you, 'The donkeys you set out to look for have been found. And now your father has stopped thinking about them and is worried about you. He is asking, "What shall I do about my son?"'

³"Then you will go on from there until you reach the great tree of Tabor. Three men going up to God at Bethel will meet you there. One will be carrying three young goats, another three loaves of bread, and another a skin of wine. ⁴They will greet you and offer you two loaves of bread, which you will accept from them.

⁵"After that you will go to Gibeah of God, where there is a Philistine outpost. As you approach the town, you will meet a procession of prophets coming down from the high place with lyres, tambourines, flutes and harps being played before them, and

ᵃ1 Hebrew; Septuagint and Vulgate *over his people Israel? You will reign over the LORD's people and save them from the power of their enemies round about. And this will be a sign to you that the LORD has anointed you leader over his inheritance:*

Life in Bible Times

ANOINTING WITH OIL

Pouring oil on a person's head was a special act in Old Testament times. It was done when God gave a person an important job, like being king or being high priest. Our greatest high priest and king of kings is Jesus Christ. The name "Christ" means "anointed one."

they will be prophesying. 6The Spirit of the LORD will come upon you in power, and you will prophesy with them; and you will be changed into a different person. 7Once these signs are fulfilled, do whatever your hand finds to do, for God is with you.

8"Go down ahead of me to Gilgal. I will surely come down to you to sacrifice burnt offerings and fellowship offerings,*a* but you must wait seven days until I come to you and tell you what you are to do."

Saul Made King

9As Saul turned to leave Samuel, God changed Saul's heart, and all these signs were fulfilled that day. 10When they arrived at Gibeah, a procession of prophets met him; the Spirit of God came upon him in power, and he joined in their prophesying. 11When all those who had formerly known him saw him prophesying with the prophets, they asked each other, "What is this that has happened to the son of Kish? Is Saul also among the prophets?"

12A man who lived there answered, "And who is their father?" So it became a saying: "Is Saul also among the prophets?" 13After Saul stopped prophesying, he went to the high place.

14Now Saul's uncle asked him and his servant, "Where have you been?"

"Looking for the donkeys," he said. "But when we saw they were not to be found, we went to Samuel."

15Saul's uncle said, "Tell me what Samuel said to you."

16Saul replied, "He assured us that the donkeys had been found." But he did not tell his uncle what Samuel had said about the kingship.

17Samuel summoned the people of Israel to the LORD at Mizpah 18and said to them, "This is what the LORD, the God of Israel, says: 'I brought Israel up out of Egypt, and I delivered you from the power of Egypt and all the kingdoms that oppressed you.' 19But you have now rejected your God, who saves you out of all your calamities and distresses. And you have said, 'No, set a king over us.' So now present yourselves before the LORD by your tribes and clans."

20When Samuel brought all the tribes of Israel near, the tribe of Benjamin was chosen. 21Then he brought forward the tribe of Benjamin, clan by clan, and Matri's clan was chosen. Finally Saul son of Kish was chosen. But when they looked for him, he was not to be found. 22So they inquired further of the LORD, "Has the man come here yet?"

And the LORD said, "Yes, he has hidden himself among the baggage."

23They ran and brought him out, and as he stood among the people he was a head taller than any of the others. 24Samuel said to all the people, "Do you see the man the LORD has chosen? There is no one like him among all the people."

Then the people shouted, "Long live the king!"

25Samuel explained to the people the regulations of the kingship. He wrote them down on a scroll and deposited it before the LORD. Then Samuel dismissed the people, each to his own home.

26Saul also went to his home in Gibeah, accompanied by valiant men whose hearts God had touched. 27But some troublemakers said, "How can this fellow save us?" They despised him and brought him no gifts. But Saul kept silent.

Saul Rescues the City of Jabesh

11 Nahash the Ammonite went up and besieged Jabesh Gilead. And all the men of Jabesh said to him, "Make a treaty with us, and we will be subject to you."

2But Nahash the Ammonite replied, "I will make a treaty with you only on the condition that I gouge out the right eye of every one of you and so bring disgrace on all Israel."

3The elders of Jabesh said to him, "Give us seven days so we can send

a8 Traditionally peace offerings

messengers throughout Israel; if no one comes to rescue us, we will surrender to you."

4When the messengers came to Gibeah of Saul and reported these terms to the people, they all wept aloud. 5Just then Saul was returning from the fields, behind his oxen, and he asked, "What is wrong with the people? Why are they weeping?" Then they repeated to him what the men of Jabesh had said.

6When Saul heard their words, the Spirit of God came upon him in power, and he burned with anger. 7He took a pair of oxen, cut them into pieces, and sent the pieces by messengers throughout Israel, proclaiming, "This is what will be done to the oxen of anyone who does not follow Saul and Samuel." Then the terror of the LORD fell on the people, and they turned out as one man. 8When Saul mustered them at Bezek, the men of Israel numbered three hundred thousand and the men of Judah thirty thousand.

9They told the messengers who had come, "Say to the men of Jabesh Gilead, 'By the time the sun is hot tomorrow, you will be delivered.'" When the messengers went and reported this to the men of Jabesh, they were elated. 10They said to the Ammonites, "Tomorrow we will surrender to you, and you can do to us whatever seems good to you."

11The next day Saul separated his men into three divisions; during the last watch of the night they broke into the camp of the Ammonites and slaughtered them until the heat of the day. Those who survived were scattered, so that no two of them were left together.

Saul Confirmed as King

12The people then said to Samuel, "Who was it that asked, 'Shall Saul reign over us?' Bring these men to us and we will put them to death."

13But Saul said, "No one shall be put to death today, for this day the LORD has rescued Israel."

14Then Samuel said to the people, "Come, let us go to Gilgal and there reaffirm the kingship." 15So all the people went to Gilgal and confirmed Saul as king in the presence of the LORD. There they sacrificed fellowship offerings[a] before the LORD, and Saul and all the Israelites held a great celebration.

Samuel's Farewell Speech

12 Samuel said to all Israel, "I have listened to everything you said to me and have set a king over you. 2Now you have a king as your leader. As for me, I am old and gray, and my sons are here with you. I have been your leader from my youth until this day. 3Here I stand. Testify against me in the presence of the LORD and his anointed. Whose ox have I taken? Whose donkey have I taken? Whom have I cheated? Whom have I oppressed? From whose hand have I accepted a bribe to make me shut my eyes? If I have done any of these, I will make it right."

4"You have not cheated or oppressed us," they replied. "You have not taken anything from anyone's hand."

5Samuel said to them, "The LORD is witness against you, and also his anointed is witness this day, that you have not found anything in my hand."

"He is witness," they said.

6Then Samuel said to the people, "It is the LORD who appointed Moses and Aaron and brought your forefathers up out of Egypt. 7Now then, stand here, because I am going to confront you with evidence before the LORD as to all the righteous acts performed by the LORD for you and your fathers.

8"After Jacob entered Egypt, they cried to the LORD for help, and the LORD sent Moses and Aaron, who brought your forefathers out of Egypt and settled them in this place.

⁹"But they forgot the LORD their God; so he sold them into the hand of Sisera, the commander of the army of Hazor, and into the hands of the Philistines and the king of Moab, who fought against them. ¹⁰They cried out to the LORD and said, 'We have sinned; we have forsaken the LORD and served the Baals and the Ashtoreths. But now deliver us from the hands of our enemies, and we will serve you.' ¹¹Then the LORD sent Jerub-Baal,ᵃ Barak,ᵇ Jephthah and Samuel,ᶜ and he delivered you from the hands of your enemies on every side, so that you lived securely.

¹²"But when you saw that Nahash king of the Ammonites was moving against you, you said to me, 'No, we want a king to rule over us'—even though the LORD your God was your king. ¹³Now here is the king you have chosen, the one you asked for; see, the LORD has set a king over you. ¹⁴If you fear the LORD and serve and obey him and do not rebel against his commands, and if both you and the king who reigns over you follow the LORD your God—good! ¹⁵But if you do not obey the LORD, and if you rebel against his commands, his hand will be against you, as it was against your fathers.

¹⁶"Now then, stand still and see this great thing the LORD is about to do before your eyes! ¹⁷Is it not wheat harvest now? I will call upon the LORD to send thunder and rain. And you will realize what an evil thing you did in the eyes of the LORD when you asked for a king."

¹⁸Then Samuel called upon the LORD, and that same day the LORD sent thunder and rain. So all the people stood in awe of the LORD and of Samuel.

¹⁹The people all said to Samuel, "Pray to the LORD your God for your servants so that we will not die, for we have added to all our other sins the evil of asking for a king."

²⁰"Do not be afraid," Samuel replied. "You have done all this evil; yet do not turn away from the LORD, but serve the LORD with all your heart. ²¹Do not turn away after useless idols. They can do you no good, nor can they rescue you, because they are useless. ²²For the sake of his great name the LORD will not reject his people, because the LORD was pleased to make you his own. ²³As for me, far be it from me that I should sin against the LORD by failing to pray for you. And I will teach you the way that is good and right. ²⁴But be sure to fear the LORD and serve him faithfully with all your heart; consider what great things he has done for you. ²⁵Yet if you persist in doing evil, both you and your king will be swept away."

❓DID YOU KNOW?   12:17

Why couldn't a king help the Israelites?

The only thing that really helped the Israelites was to worship and obey God. When God's people served him, God took care of them. A king would not be a better leader than God.

Samuel Rebukes Saul

13 Saul was ⌜thirty⌝ᵈ years old when he became king, and he reigned over Israel ⌜forty-⌝ᵉ two years.

²Saulᶠ chose three thousand men from Israel; two thousand were with him at Micmash and in the hill country of Bethel, and a thousand were with Jonathan at Gibeah in Benjamin. The rest of the men he sent back to their homes.

³Jonathan attacked the Philistine

ᵃ11 Also called *Gideon*   ᵇ11 Some Septuagint manuscripts and Syriac; Hebrew *Bedan*   ᶜ11 Hebrew; some Septuagint manuscripts and Syriac *Samson*   ᵈ1 A few late manuscripts of the Septuagint; Hebrew does not have *thirty.*   ᵉ1 See the round number in Acts 13:21; Hebrew does not have *forty-.*   ᶠ1,2 Or *and when he had reigned over Israel two years,* ²he

outpost at Geba, and the Philistines heard about it. Then Saul had the trumpet blown throughout the land and said, "Let the Hebrews hear!" [4]So all Israel heard the news: "Saul has attacked the Philistine outpost, and now Israel has become a stench to the Philistines." And the people were summoned to join Saul at Gilgal.

[5]The Philistines assembled to fight Israel, with three thousand[a] chariots, six thousand charioteers, and soldiers as numerous as the sand on the seashore. They went up and camped at Micmash, east of Beth Aven. [6]When the men of Israel saw that their situation was critical and that their army was hard pressed, they hid in caves and thickets, among the rocks, and in pits and cisterns. [7]Some Hebrews even crossed the Jordan to the land of Gad and Gilead.

Saul remained at Gilgal, and all the troops with him were quaking with fear. [8]He waited seven days, the time set by Samuel; but Samuel did not come to Gilgal, and Saul's men began to scatter. [9]So he said, "Bring me the burnt offering and the fellowship offerings.[b]" And Saul offered up the burnt offering. [10]Just as he finished making the offering, Samuel

arrived, and Saul went out to greet him.

[11]"What have you done?" asked Samuel.

Saul replied, "When I saw that the men were scattering, and that you did not come at the set time, and that the Philistines were assembling at Micmash, [12]I thought, 'Now the Philistines will come down against me at Gilgal, and I have not sought the LORD's favor.' So I felt compelled to offer the burnt offering."

[13]"You acted foolishly," Samuel said. "You have not kept the command the LORD your God gave you; if you had, he would have established your kingdom over Israel for all time. [14]But now your kingdom will not endure; the LORD has sought out a man after his own heart and appointed him leader of his people, because you have not kept the LORD's command."

[15]Then Samuel left Gilgal[c] and went up to Gibeah in Benjamin, and Saul counted the men who were with him. They numbered about six hundred.

Israel Without Weapons

[16]Saul and his son Jonathan and the men with them were staying in Gibeah[d] in Benjamin, while the Phil-

a5 Some Septuagint manuscripts and Syriac; Hebrew *thirty thousand*   b9 Traditionally *peace offerings*   c15 Hebrew; Septuagint *Gilgal and went his way; the rest of the people went after Saul to meet the army, and they went out of Gilgal*   d16 Two Hebrew manuscripts; most Hebrew manuscripts *Geba,* a variant of *Gibeah*

▌ET'S LIVE IT!   1 Samuel 13:5–14

ACTING FOOLISHLY ➤ Eric's dad was supposed to come home in the afternoon to take him fishing. By the middle of the afternoon Eric was tired of waiting. He took his pole, dug a few worms, hopped on his bike, and went to the river to fish by himself.

Half an hour later Eric's dad found him. "Eric, why didn't you wait? We were supposed to go fishing with Mr. Carson in his bass boat until late tonight. It was a special surprise for you. But Mr. Carson has already left. Now it's too late. You should have waited."

Read 1 Samuel 13:5–14. Saul didn't wait either. Eric missed out on a fishing trip because he didn't wait. What Saul missed is recorded in 1 Samuel 13:14.

Eric and Saul both were impatient. More than that, they both disobeyed. Can you see from these stories how important it is to obey?

istines camped at Micmash. [17]Raiding parties went out from the Philistine camp in three detachments. One turned toward Ophrah in the vicinity of Shual, [18]another toward Beth Horon, and the third toward the borderland overlooking the Valley of Zeboim facing the desert.

[19]Not a blacksmith could be found in the whole land of Israel, because the Philistines had said, "Otherwise the Hebrews will make swords or spears!" [20]So all Israel went down to the Philistines to have their plowshares, mattocks, axes and sickles[a] sharpened. [21]The price was two thirds of a shekel[b] for sharpening plowshares and mattocks, and a third of a shekel[c] for sharpening forks and axes and for repointing goads.

❓DID YOU KNOW?   13:19

Why didn't the Israelites have any weapons?

The Philistines knew how to make and sharpen iron. The Israelites did not. So for many years the Israelites could not make iron swords or even sharpen the tools they used in farming.

[22]So on the day of the battle not a soldier with Saul and Jonathan had a sword or spear in his hand; only Saul and his son Jonathan had them.

Jonathan Attacks the Philistines

[23]Now a detachment of Philistines had gone out to the pass at Micmash.

14 [1]One day Jonathan son of Saul said to the young man bearing his armor, "Come, let's go over to the Philistine outpost on the other side." But he did not tell his father.

[2]Saul was staying on the outskirts of Gibeah under a pomegranate tree in Migron. With him were about six hundred men, [3]among whom was Ahijah, who was wearing an ephod. He was a son of Ichabod's brother Ahitub son of Phinehas, the son of Eli, the LORD's priest in Shiloh. No one was aware that Jonathan had left.

❓DID YOU KNOW?   14:1

Who was Jonathan?

Jonathan was King Saul's son. He was a brave fighter who trusted God. Later he became David's very best friend.

[4]On each side of the pass that Jonathan intended to cross to reach the Philistine outpost was a cliff; one was called Bozez, and the other Seneh. [5]One cliff stood to the north toward Micmash, the other to the south toward Geba.

[6]Jonathan said to his young armor-bearer, "Come, let's go over to the outpost of those uncircumcised fellows. Perhaps the LORD will act in our behalf. Nothing can hinder the LORD from saving, whether by many or by few."

[7]"Do all that you have in mind," his armor-bearer said. "Go ahead; I am with you heart and soul."

[8]Jonathan said, "Come, then; we will cross over toward the men and let them see us. [9]If they say to us, 'Wait there until we come to you,' we will stay where we are and not go up to them. [10]But if they say, 'Come up to us,' we will climb up, because that will be our sign that the LORD has given them into our hands."

[11]So both of them showed themselves to the Philistine outpost. "Look!" said the Philistines. "The Hebrews are crawling out of the holes they were hiding in." [12]The men of the outpost shouted to Jonathan and his armor-bearer, "Come up to us and we'll teach you a lesson."

So Jonathan said to his armor-

---

[a]20 Septuagint; Hebrew *plowshares*   [b]21 Hebrew *pim*; that is, about 1/4 ounce (about 8 grams)
[c]21 That is, about 1/8 ounce (about 4 grams)

bearer, "Climb up after me; the LORD has given them into the hand of Israel."

¹³Jonathan climbed up, using his hands and feet, with his armor-bearer right behind him. The Philistines fell before Jonathan, and his armor-bearer followed and killed behind him. ¹⁴In that first attack Jonathan and his armor-bearer killed some twenty men in an area of about half an acre.ᵃ

Israel Routs the Philistines

¹⁵Then panic struck the whole army—those in the camp and field, and those in the outposts and raiding parties—and the ground shook. It was a panic sent by God.ᵇ

¹⁶Saul's lookouts at Gibeah in Benjamin saw the army melting away in all directions. ¹⁷Then Saul said to the men who were with him, "Muster the forces and see who has left us." When they did, it was Jonathan and his armor-bearer who were not there.

¹⁸Saul said to Ahijah, "Bring the ark of God." (At that time it was with the Israelites.)ᶜ ¹⁹While Saul was talking to the priest, the tumult in the Philistine camp increased more and more. So Saul said to the priest, "Withdraw your hand."

²⁰Then Saul and all his men assembled and went to the battle. They found the Philistines in total confusion, striking each other with their swords. ²¹Those Hebrews who had previously been with the Philistines and had gone up with them to their camp went over to the Israelites who were with Saul and Jonathan. ²²When all the Israelites who had hidden in the hill country of Ephraim heard that the Philistines were on the run, they joined the battle in hot pursuit. ²³So the LORD rescued Israel that day, and the battle moved on beyond Beth Aven.

Jonathan Eats Honey

²⁴Now the men of Israel were in distress that day, because Saul had bound the people under an oath, saying, "Cursed be any man who eats food before evening comes, before I have avenged myself on my enemies!" So none of the troops tasted food.

²⁵The entire armyᵈ entered the woods, and there was honey on the ground. ²⁶When they went into the woods, they saw the honey oozing out, yet no one put his hand to his mouth, because they feared the oath. ²⁷But Jonathan had not heard that his father had bound the people with the oath, so he reached out the end of the staff that was in his hand and dipped it into the honeycomb. He raised his hand to his mouth, and his eyes brightened.ᵉ ²⁸Then one of the soldiers told him, "Your father bound the army under a strict oath, saying, 'Cursed be any man who eats food today!' That is why the men are faint."

²⁹Jonathan said, "My father has made trouble for the country. See how my eyes brightenedᶠ when I tasted a little of this honey. ³⁰How much better it would have been if the men had eaten today some of the plunder they took from their enemies. Would not the slaughter of the Philistines have been even greater?"

³¹That day, after the Israelites had struck down the Philistines from Micmash to Aijalon, they were exhausted. ³²They pounced on the plunder and, taking sheep, cattle and calves, they butchered them on the ground and ate them, together with the blood. ³³Then someone said to Saul, "Look, the men are sinning against the LORD by eating meat that has blood in it."

"You have broken faith," he said. "Roll a large stone over here at once." ³⁴Then he said, "Go out among the men and tell them, 'Each of you bring

---

ᵃ14 Hebrew *half a yoke*; a "yoke" was the land plowed by a yoke of oxen in one day.　　ᵇ15 Or *a terrible panic*　　ᶜ18 Hebrew; Septuagint *"Bring the ephod." (At that time he wore the ephod before the Israelites.)*　　ᵈ25 Or *Now all the people of the land*　　ᵉ27 Or *his strength was renewed*　　ᶠ29 Or *my strength was renewed*

me your cattle and sheep, and slaughter them here and eat them. Do not sin against the LORD by eating meat with blood still in it.' "

So everyone brought his ox that night and slaughtered it there. 35Then Saul built an altar to the LORD; it was the first time he had done this.

36Saul said, "Let us go down after the Philistines by night and plunder them till dawn, and let us not leave one of them alive."

"Do whatever seems best to you," they replied.

But the priest said, "Let us inquire of God here."

37So Saul asked God, "Shall I go down after the Philistines? Will you give them into Israel's hand?" But God did not answer him that day.

38Saul therefore said, "Come here, all you who are leaders of the army, and let us find out what sin has been committed today. 39As surely as the LORD who rescues Israel lives, even if it lies with my son Jonathan, he must die." But not one of the men said a word.

40Saul then said to all the Israelites, "You stand over there; I and Jonathan my son will stand over here."

"Do what seems best to you," the men replied.

? DID YOU KNOW?　　14:39

Why was Jonathan condemned to die for eating honey?

Jonathan's father made the army promise to eat nothing all day. Jonathan didn't know this and ate some honey. Saul was ready to put Jonathan to death, but the men did not let that happen.

41Then Saul prayed to the LORD, the God of Israel, "Give me the right answer."[a] And Jonathan and Saul were taken by lot, and the men were cleared. 42Saul said, "Cast the lot between me and Jonathan my son." And Jonathan was taken.

43Then Saul said to Jonathan, "Tell me what you have done."

So Jonathan told him, "I merely tasted a little honey with the end of my staff. And now must I die?"

44Saul said, "May God deal with me, be it ever so severely, if you do not die, Jonathan."

45But the men said to Saul, "Should Jonathan die—he who has brought about this great deliverance in Israel? Never! As surely as the LORD lives, not a hair of his head will fall to the ground, for he did this today with God's help." So the men rescued Jonathan, and he was not put to death.

46Then Saul stopped pursuing the Philistines, and they withdrew to their own land.

47After Saul had assumed rule over Israel, he fought against their enemies on every side: Moab, the Ammonites, Edom, the kings[b] of Zobah, and the Philistines. Wherever he turned, he inflicted punishment on them.[c] 48He fought valiantly and defeated the Amalekites, delivering Israel from the hands of those who had plundered them.

Saul's Family

49Saul's sons were Jonathan, Ishvi and Malki-Shua. The name of his older daughter was Merab, and that of the younger was Michal. 50His wife's name was Ahinoam daughter of Ahimaaz. The name of the commander of Saul's army was Abner son of Ner, and Ner was Saul's uncle. 51Saul's father Kish and Abner's father Ner were sons of Abiel.

52All the days of Saul there was bit-

---

a41 Hebrew; Septuagint "Why have you not answered your servant today? If the fault is in me or my son Jonathan, respond with Urim, but if the men of Israel are at fault, respond with Thummim."　b47 Masoretic Text; Dead Sea Scrolls and Septuagint king　c47 Hebrew; Septuagint he was victorious

ter war with the Philistines, and whenever Saul saw a mighty or brave man, he took him into his service.

The LORD Rejects Saul as King

15 Samuel said to Saul, "I am the one the LORD sent to anoint you king over his people Israel; so listen now to the message from the LORD. ²This is what the LORD Almighty says: 'I will punish the Amalekites for what they did to Israel when they waylaid them as they came up from Egypt. ³Now go, attack the Amalekites and totally destroy*a* everything that belongs to them. Do not spare them; put to death men and women, children and infants, cattle and sheep, camels and donkeys.'"

⁴So Saul summoned the men and mustered them at Telaim—two hundred thousand foot soldiers and ten thousand men from Judah. ⁵Saul went to the city of Amalek and set an ambush in the ravine. ⁶Then he said to the Kenites, "Go away, leave the Amalekites so that I do not destroy you along with them; for you showed kindness to all the Israelites when they came up out of Egypt." So the Kenites moved away from the Amalekites.

⁷Then Saul attacked the Amalekites all the way from Havilah to Shur, to the east of Egypt. ⁸He took Agag king of the Amalekites alive, and all his people he totally destroyed with the sword. ⁹But Saul and the army spared Agag and the best of the sheep and cattle, the fat calves*b* and lambs—everything that was good. These they were unwilling to destroy completely, but everything that was despised and weak they totally destroyed.

¹⁰Then the word of the LORD came to Samuel: ¹¹"I am grieved that I have made Saul king, because he has turned away from me and has not carried out my instructions." Samuel was troubled, and he cried out to the LORD all that night.

?DID YOU KNOW?   15:11

Why did God reject Saul as king?

Saul was rejected because he did not obey God. Anyone who leads God's people must be sure to obey God always.

¹²Early in the morning Samuel got up and went to meet Saul, but he was told, "Saul has gone to Carmel. There he has set up a monument in his own honor and has turned and gone on down to Gilgal."

¹³When Samuel reached him, Saul said, "The LORD bless you! I have carried out the LORD's instructions."

¹⁴But Samuel said, "What then is this bleating of sheep in my ears? What is this lowing of cattle that I hear?"

¹⁵Saul answered, "The soldiers brought them from the Amalekites; they spared the best of the sheep and cattle to sacrifice to the LORD your God, but we totally destroyed the rest."

¹⁶"Stop!" Samuel said to Saul. "Let me tell you what the LORD said to me last night."

"Tell me," Saul replied.

¹⁷Samuel said, "Although you were once small in your own eyes, did you not become the head of the tribes of Israel? The LORD anointed you king over Israel. ¹⁸And he sent you on a mission, saying, 'Go and completely destroy those wicked people, the Amalekites; make war on them until you have wiped them out.' ¹⁹Why did you not obey the LORD? Why did you pounce on the plunder and do evil in the eyes of the LORD?"

²⁰"But I did obey the LORD," Saul said. "I went on the mission the LORD

---

a3 The Hebrew term refers to the irrevocable giving over of things or persons to the LORD, often by totally destroying them; also in verses 8, 9, 15, 18, 20 and 21.   *b9* Or *the grown bulls*; the meaning of the Hebrew for this phrase is uncertain.

assigned me. I completely destroyed the Amalekites and brought back Agag their king. [21]The soldiers took sheep and cattle from the plunder, the best of what was devoted to God, in order to sacrifice them to the LORD your God at Gilgal."

[22]But Samuel replied:

"Does the LORD delight in burnt
　　offerings and sacrifices
as much as in obeying the voice
　　of the LORD?
To obey is better than sacrifice,
　　and to heed is better than the
　　fat of rams.
[23]For rebellion is like the sin of
　　divination,
　　and arrogance like the evil of
　　idolatry.
Because you have rejected the
　　word of the LORD,
　　he has rejected you as king."

WORDS TO REMEMBER

15:22 To obey is better than sacrifice.

[24]Then Saul said to Samuel, "I have sinned. I violated the LORD's command and your instructions. I was afraid of the people and so I gave in to them. [25]Now I beg you, forgive my sin and come back with me, so that I may worship the LORD."

[26]But Samuel said to him, "I will not go back with you. You have rejected the word of the LORD, and the LORD has rejected you as king over Israel!"

[27]As Samuel turned to leave, Saul caught hold of the hem of his robe, and it tore. [28]Samuel said to him, "The LORD has torn the kingdom of Israel from you today and has given it to one of your neighbors—to one better than you. [29]He who is the Glory of Israel does not lie or change his mind; for he is not a man, that he should change his mind."

[30]Saul replied, "I have sinned. But

please honor me before the elders of my people and before Israel; come back with me, so that I may worship the LORD your God." [31]So Samuel went back with Saul, and Saul worshiped the LORD.

[32]Then Samuel said, "Bring me Agag king of the Amalekites."

Agag came to him confidently,[a] thinking, "Surely the bitterness of death is past."

[33]But Samuel said,

"As your sword has made women
　　childless,
so will your mother be childless
　　among women."

And Samuel put Agag to death before the LORD at Gilgal.

[34]Then Samuel left for Ramah, but Saul went up to his home in Gibeah of Saul. [35]Until the day Samuel died, he did not go to see Saul again, though Samuel mourned for him. And the LORD was grieved that he had made Saul king over Israel.

Samuel Anoints David

16 The LORD said to Samuel, "How long will you mourn for Saul, since I have rejected him as king over Israel? Fill your horn with oil and be on your way; I am sending you to Jesse of Bethlehem. I have chosen one of his sons to be king."

[2]But Samuel said, "How can I go? Saul will hear about it and kill me."

The LORD said, "Take a heifer with you and say, 'I have come to sacrifice to the LORD.' [3]Invite Jesse to the sacrifice, and I will show you what to do. You are to anoint for me the one I indicate."

[4]Samuel did what the LORD said. When he arrived at Bethlehem, the elders of the town trembled when they met him. They asked, "Do you come in peace?"

[5]Samuel replied, "Yes, in peace; I have come to sacrifice to the LORD. Consecrate yourselves and come to the sacrifice with me." Then he con-

[a]32 Or *him trembling, yet*

secrated Jesse and his sons and invited them to the sacrifice.

WORDS TO REMEMBER

16:7 Man looks at the outward appearance, but the LORD looks at the heart.

⁶When they arrived, Samuel saw Eliab and thought, "Surely the LORD's anointed stands here before the LORD."

⁷But the LORD said to Samuel, "Do not consider his appearance or his height, for I have rejected him. The LORD does not look at the things man looks at. Man looks at the outward appearance, but the LORD looks at the heart."

⁸Then Jesse called Abinadab and had him pass in front of Samuel. But Samuel said, "The LORD has not chosen this one either." ⁹Jesse then had Shammah pass by, but Samuel said, "Nor has the LORD chosen this one." ¹⁰Jesse had seven of his sons pass before Samuel, but Samuel said to him, "The LORD has not chosen these." ¹¹So he asked Jesse, "Are these all the sons you have?"

"There is still the youngest," Jesse answered, "but he is tending the sheep."

Samuel said, "Send for him; we will not sit down*a* until he arrives."

¹²So he sent and had him brought in. He was ruddy, with a fine appearance and handsome features.

Then the LORD said, "Rise and anoint him; he is the one."

¹³So Samuel took the horn of oil and anointed him in the presence of his brothers, and from that day on the Spirit of the LORD came upon David in power. Samuel then went to Ramah.

David in Saul's Service

¹⁴Now the Spirit of the LORD had departed from Saul, and an evil*b* spirit from the LORD tormented him. ¹⁵Saul's attendants said to him, "See, an evil spirit from God is tormenting you. ¹⁶Let our lord command his servants here to search for someone who can play the harp. He will play when the evil spirit from God comes upon you, and you will feel better."

¹⁷So Saul said to his attendants, "Find someone who plays well and bring him to me."

¹⁸One of the servants answered, "I have seen a son of Jesse of Bethlehem who knows how to play the harp. He is a brave man and a warrior. He speaks well and is a fine-looking man. And the LORD is with him."

¹⁹Then Saul sent messengers to Jesse and said, "Send me your son David, who is with the sheep." ²⁰So Jesse took a donkey loaded with

a11 Some Septuagint manuscripts; Hebrew *not gather around*   *b14* Or *injurious*; also in verses 15, 16 and 23

LET'S LIVE IT!   1 Samuel 16:1–13

WHAT IS IMPORTANT ABOUT YOU? ➡ Read 1 Samuel 16:1–13. When Samuel saw the first of Jesse's sons, he thought he knew who Israel's next king would be. But he was looking at the wrong thing, the outside. What part of a person is important to God?

Cut a heart from red construction paper. Make it large enough to cover your face if you tape the heart to a mirror. On the heart write something that God thinks is important in a person who loves him, like "most helpful," "most caring," "most honest," or "most friendly."

Put up the heart where you will see it, to help you remember that what is really important about you is the kind of person you are inside.

bread, a skin of wine and a young goat and sent them with his son David to Saul.

21David came to Saul and entered his service. Saul liked him very much, and David became one of his armor-bearers. 22Then Saul sent word to Jesse, saying, "Allow David to remain in my service, for I am pleased with him."

23Whenever the spirit from God came upon Saul, David would take his harp and play. Then relief would come to Saul; he would feel better, and the evil spirit would leave him.

David and Goliath

17 Now the Philistines gathered their forces for war and assembled at Socoh in Judah. They pitched camp at Ephes Dammim, between Socoh and Azekah. 2Saul and the Israelites assembled and camped in the Valley of Elah and drew up their battle line to meet the Philistines. 3The Philistines occupied one hill and the Israelites another, with the valley between them.

4A champion named Goliath, who was from Gath, came out of the Philistine camp. He was over nine feet*a* tall. 5He had a bronze helmet on his head and wore a coat of scale armor of bronze weighing five thousand shekels*b*; 6on his legs he wore bronze greaves, and a bronze javelin was slung on his back. 7His spear shaft was like a weaver's rod, and its iron point weighed six hundred shekels.*c* His shield bearer went ahead of him.

8Goliath stood and shouted to the ranks of Israel, "Why do you come out and line up for battle? Am I not a Philistine, and are you not the servants of Saul? Choose a man and have him come down to me. 9If he is able to fight and kill me, we will become your subjects; but if I overcome him and kill him, you will become our subjects and serve us." 10Then the Philistine said, "This day I defy the

ranks of Israel! Give me a man and let us fight each other." 11On hearing the Philistine's words, Saul and all the Israelites were dismayed and terrified.

12Now David was the son of an Ephrathite named Jesse, who was from Bethlehem in Judah. Jesse had eight sons, and in Saul's time he was old and well advanced in years. 13Jesse's three oldest sons had followed Saul to the war: The firstborn was Eliab; the second, Abinadab; and the third, Shammah. 14David was the youngest. The three oldest followed Saul, 15but David went back and forth from Saul to tend his father's sheep at Bethlehem.

16For forty days the Philistine came forward every morning and evening and took his stand.

17Now Jesse said to his son David, "Take this ephah*d* of roasted grain and these ten loaves of bread for your brothers and hurry to their camp. 18Take along these ten cheeses to the commander of their unit.*e* See how your brothers are and bring back some assurance*f* from them. 19They are with Saul and all the men of Israel in the Valley of Elah, fighting against the Philistines."

20Early in the morning David left the flock with a shepherd, loaded up and set out, as Jesse had directed. He reached the camp as the army was going out to its battle positions, shouting the war cry. 21Israel and the Philistines were drawing up their lines facing each other. 22David left his things with the keeper of supplies, ran to the battle lines and greeted his brothers. 23As he was talking with them, Goliath, the Philistine champion from Gath, stepped out from his lines and shouted his usual defiance, and David heard it. 24When the Israelites saw the man, they all ran from him in great fear.

25Now the Israelites had been saying, "Do you see how this man keeps

---

a4 Hebrew *was six cubits and a span* (about 3 meters)   *b5* That is, about 125 pounds (about 57 kilograms)   *c7* That is, about 15 pounds (about 7 kilograms)   *d17* That is, probably about 3/5 bushel (about 22 liters)   *e18* Hebrew *thousand*   *f18* Or *some token*; or *some pledge of spoils*

coming out? He comes out to defy Israel. The king will give great wealth to the man who kills him. He will also give him his daughter in marriage and will exempt his father's family from taxes in Israel."

26David asked the men standing near him, "What will be done for the man who kills this Philistine and removes this disgrace from Israel? Who is this uncircumcised Philistine that he should defy the armies of the living God?"

27They repeated to him what they had been saying and told him, "This is what will be done for the man who kills him."

28When Eliab, David's oldest brother, heard him speaking with the men, he burned with anger at him and asked, "Why have you come down here? And with whom did you leave those few sheep in the desert? I know how conceited you are and how wicked your heart is; you came down only to watch the battle."

29"Now what have I done?" said David. "Can't I even speak?" 30He then turned away to someone else and brought up the same matter, and the men answered him as before. 31What David said was overheard and reported to Saul, and Saul sent for him.

32David said to Saul, "Let no one lose heart on account of this Philistine; your servant will go and fight him."

33Saul replied, "You are not able to go out against this Philistine and fight him; you are only a boy, and he has been a fighting man from his youth."

34But David said to Saul, "Your servant has been keeping his father's sheep. When a lion or a bear came and carried off a sheep from the flock, 35I went after it, struck it and rescued the sheep from its mouth. When it turned on me, I seized it by its hair, struck it and killed it. 36Your servant has killed both the lion and the bear; this uncircumcised Philistine will be like one of them, because he has defied the armies of the living God. 37The LORD who delivered me from the paw of the lion and the paw of the bear will deliver me from the hand of this Philistine."

Saul said to David, "Go, and the LORD be with you."

38Then Saul dressed David in his own tunic. He put a coat of armor on him and a bronze helmet on his head. 39David fastened on his sword over the tunic and tried walking around, because he was not used to them.

"I cannot go in these," he said to Saul, "because I am not used to them." So he took them off. 40Then he took his staff in his hand, chose five smooth stones from the stream, put them in the pouch of his shepherd's bag and, with his sling in his hand, approached the Philistine.

41Meanwhile, the Philistine, with his shield bearer in front of him, kept

Life in Bible Times

GOLIATH THE GIANT

David was just a boy, but he fought the giant Goliath. Even the big men in Saul's army wouldn't fight Goliath.

This picture shows a six-foot-tall basketball player, and Goliath, who was over nine feet tall! How did David dare to fight such a giant? See 1 Samuel 17:45–47.

coming closer to David. [42]He looked David over and saw that he was only a boy, ruddy and handsome, and he despised him. [43]He said to David, "Am I a dog, that you come at me with sticks?" And the Philistine cursed David by his gods. [44]"Come here," he said, "and I'll give your flesh to the birds of the air and the beasts of the field!"

[45]David said to the Philistine, "You come against me with sword and spear and javelin, but I come against you in the name of the LORD Almighty, the God of the armies of Israel, whom you have defied. [46]This day the LORD will hand you over to me, and I'll strike you down and cut off your head. Today I will give the carcasses of the Philistine army to the birds of the air and the beasts of the earth, and the whole world will know that there is a God in Israel. [47]All those gathered here will know that it is not by sword or spear that the LORD saves; for the battle is the LORD's, and he will give all of you into our hands."

[48]As the Philistine moved closer to attack him, David ran quickly toward the battle line to meet him. [49]Reaching into his bag and taking out a stone, he slung it and struck the Philistine on the forehead. The stone sank into his forehead, and he fell facedown on the ground.

[50]So David triumphed over the Philistine with a sling and a stone; without a sword in his hand he struck down the Philistine and killed him. [51]David ran and stood over him. He took hold of the Philistine's sword

and drew it from the scabbard. After he killed him, he cut off his head with the sword.

When the Philistines saw that their hero was dead, they turned and ran. [52]Then the men of Israel and Judah surged forward with a shout and pursued the Philistines to the entrance of Gath[a] and to the gates of Ekron. Their dead were strewn along the Shaaraim road to Gath and Ekron. [53]When the Israelites returned from chasing the Philistines, they plundered their camp. [54]David took the Philistine's head and brought it to Jerusalem, and he put the Philistine's weapons in his own tent.

[55]As Saul watched David going out to meet the Philistine, he said to Abner, commander of the army, "Abner, whose son is that young man?"

Abner replied, "As surely as you live, O king, I don't know."

[56]The king said, "Find out whose son this young man is."

[57]As soon as David returned from killing the Philistine, Abner took him and brought him before Saul, with David still holding the Philistine's head.

[58]"Whose son are you, young man?" Saul asked him.

David said, "I am the son of your servant Jesse of Bethlehem."

Saul's Jealousy of David

18 After David had finished talking with Saul, Jonathan became one in spirit with David, and he loved him as himself. [2]From that day Saul kept David with him and

[a]52 Some Septuagint manuscripts; Hebrew *a valley*

ET'S LIVE IT!

THE BIBLE STORY EVERYBODY KNOWS ➡ Do you think that everyone knows the story of David and the giant Goliath? Just for fun, ask five of your neighborhood or school friends if they know the story. Read 1 Samuel 17 to make sure that you remember every part of this famous Bible story. It is a long chapter, but it is exciting reading.

David was able to face the giant because he trusted God. David was not afraid. He knew that God could help him defeat Israel's enemy.

did not let him return to his father's house. ³And Jonathan made a covenant with David because he loved him as himself. ⁴Jonathan took off the robe he was wearing and gave it to David, along with his tunic, and even his sword, his bow and his belt.

⁵Whatever Saul sent him to do, David did it so successfully*a* that Saul gave him a high rank in the army. This pleased all the people, and Saul's officers as well.

⁶When the men were returning home after David had killed the Philistine, the women came out from all the towns of Israel to meet King Saul with singing and dancing, with joyful songs and with tambourines and lutes. ⁷As they danced, they sang:

"Saul has slain his thousands,
　and David his tens of
　　thousands."

⁸Saul was very angry; this refrain galled him. "They have credited David with tens of thousands," he thought, "but me with only thousands. What more can he get but the kingdom?" ⁹And from that time on Saul kept a jealous eye on David.

❓DID YOU KNOW?　　18:8

Why was Saul jealous of David?

David was so successful as an army leader that people praised him more than they praised Saul. That made Saul jealous. Saul was afraid of David too. Saul had disobeyed God and knew that God had rejected him as king of Israel. He also knew that David obeyed God and that David was victorious because God was with him.

---

¹⁰The next day an evil*b* spirit from God came forcefully upon Saul. He was prophesying in his house, while David was playing the harp, as he usually did. Saul had a spear in his hand ¹¹and he hurled it, saying to himself, "I'll pin David to the wall." But David eluded him twice.

¹²Saul was afraid of David, because the Lord was with David but had left Saul. ¹³So he sent David away from him and gave him command over a thousand men, and David led the troops in their campaigns. ¹⁴In everything he did he had great success,*c* because the Lord was with him. ¹⁵When Saul saw how successful*d* he was, he was afraid of him. ¹⁶But all Israel and Judah loved David, because he led them in their campaigns.

¹⁷Saul said to David, "Here is my older daughter Merab. I will give her to you in marriage; only serve me bravely and fight the battles of the Lord." For Saul said to himself, "I will not raise a hand against him. Let the Philistines do that!"

¹⁸But David said to Saul, "Who am I, and what is my family or my father's clan in Israel, that I should become the king's son-in-law?" ¹⁹So*e* when the time came for Merab, Saul's daughter, to be given to David, she was given in marriage to Adriel of Meholah.

²⁰Now Saul's daughter Michal was in love with David, and when they told Saul about it, he was pleased. ²¹"I will give her to him," he thought, "so that she may be a snare to him and so that the hand of the Philistines may be against him." So Saul said to David, "Now you have a second opportunity to become my son-in-law."

²²Then Saul ordered his attendants: "Speak to David privately and say, 'Look, the king is pleased with you, and his attendants all like you; now become his son-in-law.'"

²³They repeated these words to David. But David said, "Do you think it is a small matter to become the king's son-in-law? I'm only a poor man and little known."

²⁴When Saul's servants told him what David had said, ²⁵Saul replied,

---

a5 Or *wisely*　　*b10* Or *injurious*　　*c14* Or *he was very wise*　　*d15* Or *wise*　　*e19* Or *However,*

"Say to David, 'The king wants no other price for the bride than a hundred Philistine foreskins, to take revenge on his enemies.' " Saul's plan was to have David fall by the hands of the Philistines.

26When the attendants told David these things, he was pleased to become the king's son-in-law. So before the allotted time elapsed, 27David and his men went out and killed two hundred Philistines. He brought their foreskins and presented the full number to the king so that he might become the king's son-in-law. Then Saul gave him his daughter Michal in marriage.

28When Saul realized that the LORD was with David and that his daughter Michal loved David, 29Saul became still more afraid of him, and he remained his enemy the rest of his days.

30The Philistine commanders continued to go out to battle, and as often as they did, David met with more success*a* than the rest of Saul's officers, and his name became well known.

Saul Tries to Kill David

19 Saul told his son Jonathan and all the attendants to kill David. But Jonathan was very fond of David 2and warned him, "My father Saul is looking for a chance to kill you. Be on your guard tomorrow morning; go into hiding and stay there. 3I will go out and stand with my father in the field where you are. I'll speak to him about you and will tell you what I find out."

4Jonathan spoke well of David to Saul his father and said to him, "Let not the king do wrong to his servant David; he has not wronged you, and what he has done has benefited you greatly. 5He took his life in his hands when he killed the Philistine. The LORD won a great victory for all Israel, and you saw it and were glad. Why then would you do wrong to an innocent man like David by killing him for no reason?"

6Saul listened to Jonathan and took this oath: "As surely as the LORD lives, David will not be put to death."

7So Jonathan called David and told him the whole conversation. He brought him to Saul, and David was with Saul as before.

8Once more war broke out, and David went out and fought the Philistines. He struck them with such force that they fled before him.

9But an evil*b* spirit from the LORD came upon Saul as he was sitting in his house with his spear in his hand. While David was playing the harp, 10Saul tried to pin him to the wall with his spear, but David eluded him as Saul drove the spear into the wall. That night David made good his escape.

? DID YOU KNOW?　　19:9

What is an "evil spirit from the LORD"?

The Lord has control over everything, even evil spirits. Because Saul disobeyed God, he was punished by the presence of this evil spirit, which made him jealous, angry, and even violent.

11Saul sent men to David's house to watch it and to kill him in the morning. But Michal, David's wife, warned him, "If you don't run for your life tonight, tomorrow you'll be killed." 12So Michal let David down through a window, and he fled and escaped. 13Then Michal took an idol*c* and laid it on the bed, covering it with a garment and putting some goats' hair at the head.

14When Saul sent the men to capture David, Michal said, "He is ill."

15Then Saul sent the men back to see David and told them, "Bring him up to me in his bed so that I may kill him." 16But when the men entered, there was the idol in the bed, and at the head was some goats' hair.

---

*a*30 Or *David acted more wisely*　　*b*9 Or *injurious*　　*c*13 Hebrew *teraphim*; also in verse 16

17Saul said to Michal, "Why did you deceive me like this and send my enemy away so that he escaped?"

Michal told him, "He said to me, 'Let me get away. Why should I kill you?' "

18When David had fled and made his escape, he went to Samuel at Ramah and told him all that Saul had done to him. Then he and Samuel went to Naioth and stayed there. 19Word came to Saul: "David is in Naioth at Ramah"; 20so he sent men to capture him. But when they saw a group of prophets prophesying, with Samuel standing there as their leader, the Spirit of God came upon Saul's men and they also prophesied. 21Saul was told about it, and he sent more men, and they prophesied too. Saul sent men a third time, and they also prophesied. 22Finally, he himself left for Ramah and went to the great cistern at Secu. And he asked, "Where are Samuel and David?"

"Over in Naioth at Ramah," they said.

23So Saul went to Naioth at Ramah. But the Spirit of God came even upon him, and he walked along prophesying until he came to Naioth. 24He stripped off his robes and also prophesied in Samuel's presence. He lay that way all that day and night. This is why people say, "Is Saul also among the prophets?"

David and Jonathan

20 Then David fled from Naioth at Ramah and went to Jonathan and asked, "What have I done? What is my crime? How have I wronged your father, that he is trying to take my life?"

2"Never!" Jonathan replied. "You are not going to die! Look, my father doesn't do anything, great or small, without confiding in me. Why would he hide this from me? It's not so!"

3But David took an oath and said, "Your father knows very well that I have found favor in your eyes, and he has said to himself, 'Jonathan must not know this or he will be grieved.' Yet as surely as the LORD lives and as

you live, there is only a step between me and death."

4Jonathan said to David, "Whatever you want me to do, I'll do for you."

5So David said, "Look, tomorrow is the New Moon festival, and I am supposed to dine with the king; but let me go and hide in the field until the evening of the day after tomorrow. 6If your father misses me at all, tell him, 'David earnestly asked my permission to hurry to Bethlehem, his hometown, because an annual sacrifice is being made there for his whole clan.' 7If he says, 'Very well,' then your servant is safe. But if he loses his temper, you can be sure that he is determined to harm me. 8As for you, show kindness to your servant, for you have brought him into a covenant with you before the LORD. If I am guilty, then kill me yourself! Why hand me over to your father?"

9"Never!" Jonathan said. "If I had the least inkling that my father was determined to harm you, wouldn't I tell you?"

10David asked, "Who will tell me if your father answers you harshly?"

11"Come," Jonathan said, "let's go out into the field." So they went there together.

12Then Jonathan said to David: "By the LORD, the God of Israel, I will surely sound out my father by this time the day after tomorrow! If he is favorably disposed toward you, will I not send you word and let you know? 13But if my father is inclined to harm you, may the LORD deal with me, be it ever so severely, if I do not let you know and send you away safely. May the LORD be with you as he has been with my father. 14But show me unfailing kindness like that of the LORD as long as I live, so that I may not be killed, 15and do not ever cut off your kindness from my family—not even when the LORD has cut off every one of David's enemies from the face of the earth."

16So Jonathan made a covenant with the house of David, saying, "May the LORD call David's enemies to account." 17And Jonathan had David reaffirm his oath out of love for him, because he loved him as he loved himself.

18Then Jonathan said to David: "Tomorrow is the New Moon festival. You will be missed, because your seat will be empty. 19The day after tomorrow, toward evening, go to the place where you hid when this trouble began, and wait by the stone Ezel. 20I will shoot three arrows to the side of it, as though I were shooting at a target. 21Then I will send a boy and say, 'Go, find the arrows.' If I say to him, 'Look, the arrows are on this side of you; bring them here,' then come, because, as surely as the LORD lives, you are safe; there is no danger. 22But if I say to the boy, 'Look, the arrows are beyond you,' then you must go, because the LORD has sent you away. 23And about the matter you and I discussed—remember, the LORD is witness between you and me forever."

24So David hid in the field, and when the New Moon festival came, the king sat down to eat. 25He sat in his customary place by the wall, opposite Jonathan,ᵃ and Abner sat next to Saul, but David's place was empty. 26Saul said nothing that day, for he thought, "Something must have happened to David to make him ceremonially unclean—surely he is unclean." 27But the next day, the second day of the month, David's place was empty again. Then Saul said to his son Jonathan, "Why hasn't the son of Jesse come to the meal, either yesterday or today?"

28Jonathan answered, "David earnestly asked me for permission to go to Bethlehem. 29He said, 'Let me go, because our family is observing a sacrifice in the town and my brother has ordered me to be there. If I have found favor in your eyes, let me get away to see my brothers.' That is why he has not come to the king's table."

30Saul's anger flared up at Jonathan and he said to him, "You son of a perverse and rebellious woman! Don't I know that you have sided with the son of Jesse to your own shame and to the shame of the mother who bore you? 31As long as the son of Jesse lives on this earth, neither you nor your kingdom will be established. Now send and bring him to me, for he must die!"

32"Why should he be put to death? What has he done?" Jonathan asked his father. 33But Saul hurled his spear at him to kill him. Then Jonathan knew that his father intended to kill David.

34Jonathan got up from the table in fierce anger; on that second day of the month he did not eat, because he was grieved at his father's shameful treatment of David.

35In the morning Jonathan went out to the field for his meeting with David. He had a small boy with him, 36and he said to the boy, "Run and find the arrows I shoot." As the boy ran, he shot an arrow beyond him. 37When the boy came to the place where Jonathan's arrow had fallen, Jonathan called out after him, "Isn't

ᵃ25 Septuagint; Hebrew wall. Jonathan arose

⬛LET'S LIVE IT!
1 Samuel 20:1–42

SHOWING FRIENDSHIP ⬛➡ Read about the friendship of David and Jonathan in 1 Samuel 20:1–42. After reading the story, name three ways that Jonathan showed his friendship with David. Name three ways you can be a friend to someone.

Make posters showing each of the three important things friends do. A good Bible verse to put on your posters is, "A friend loves at all times" (Proverbs 17:17). Ask if you can put the posters up where everyone in your family will see them.

the arrow beyond you?" ³⁸Then he shouted, "Hurry! Go quickly! Don't stop!" The boy picked up the arrow and returned to his master. ³⁹(The boy knew nothing of all this; only Jonathan and David knew.) ⁴⁰Then Jonathan gave his weapons to the boy and said, "Go, carry them back to town."

⁴¹After the boy had gone, David got up from the south side of the stone, and bowed down before Jonathan three times, with his face to the ground. Then they kissed each other and wept together—but David wept the most.

⁴²Jonathan said to David, "Go in peace, for we have sworn friendship with each other in the name of the LORD, saying, 'The LORD is witness between you and me, and between your descendants and my descendants forever.'" Then David left, and Jonathan went back to the town.

David at Nob

21 David went to Nob, to Ahimelech the priest. Ahimelech trembled when he met him, and asked, "Why are you alone? Why is no one with you?"

²David answered Ahimelech the priest, "The king charged me with a certain matter and said to me, 'No one is to know anything about your mission and your instructions.' As for my men, I have told them to meet me at a certain place. ³Now then, what do you have on hand? Give me five loaves of bread, or whatever you can find."

⁴But the priest answered David, "I don't have any ordinary bread on hand; however, there is some consecrated bread here—provided the men have kept themselves from women."

⁵David replied, "Indeed women have been kept from us, as usual whenever*ᵃ* I set out. The men's things*ᵇ* are holy even on missions that are not holy. How much more so today!" ⁶So the priest gave him the consecrated bread, since there was no bread there except the bread of the Presence that had been removed from before the LORD and replaced by hot bread on the day it was taken away.

⁷Now one of Saul's servants was there that day, detained before the LORD; he was Doeg the Edomite, Saul's head shepherd.

⁸David asked Ahimelech, "Don't you have a spear or a sword here? I haven't brought my sword or any other weapon, because the king's business was urgent."

⁹The priest replied, "The sword of Goliath the Philistine, whom you killed in the Valley of Elah, is here; it is wrapped in a cloth behind the ephod. If you want it, take it; there is no sword here but that one."

David said, "There is none like it; give it to me."

David at Gath

¹⁰That day David fled from Saul and went to Achish king of Gath. ¹¹But the servants of Achish said to him, "Isn't this David, the king of the land? Isn't he the one they sing about in their dances:

"'Saul has slain his thousands,
   and David his tens of
     thousands'?"

¹²David took these words to heart and was very much afraid of Achish king of Gath. ¹³So he pretended to be insane in their presence; and while he was in their hands he acted like a madman, making marks on the doors of the gate and letting saliva run down his beard.

¹⁴Achish said to his servants, "Look at the man! He is insane! Why bring him to me? ¹⁵Am I so short of madmen that you have to bring this fellow here to carry on like this in front of me? Must this man come into my house?"

David at Adullam and Mizpah

22 David left Gath and escaped to the cave of Adullam. When

---

*ᵃ*5 Or *from us in the past few days since*   *ᵇ*5 Or *bodies*

his brothers and his father's household heard about it, they went down to him there. ²All those who were in distress or in debt or discontented gathered around him, and he became their leader. About four hundred men were with him.

³From there David went to Mizpah in Moab and said to the king of Moab, "Would you let my father and mother come and stay with you until I learn what God will do for me?" ⁴So he left them with the king of Moab, and they stayed with him as long as David was in the stronghold.

⁵But the prophet Gad said to David, "Do not stay in the stronghold. Go into the land of Judah." So David left and went to the forest of Hereth.

Saul Kills the Priests of Nob

⁶Now Saul heard that David and his men had been discovered. And Saul, spear in hand, was seated under the tamarisk tree on the hill at Gibeah, with all his officials standing around him. ⁷Saul said to them, "Listen, men of Benjamin! Will the son of Jesse give all of you fields and vineyards? Will he make all of you commanders of thousands and commanders of hundreds? ⁸Is that why you have all conspired against me? No one tells me when my son makes a covenant with the son of Jesse. None of you is concerned about me or tells me that my son has incited my servant to lie in wait for me, as he does today."

⁹But Doeg the Edomite, who was standing with Saul's officials, said, "I saw the son of Jesse come to Ahimelech son of Ahitub at Nob. ¹⁰Ahimelech inquired of the LORD for him; he also gave him provisions and the sword of Goliath the Philistine."

¹¹Then the king sent for the priest Ahimelech son of Ahitub and his father's whole family, who were the priests at Nob, and they all came to the king. ¹²Saul said, "Listen now, son of Ahitub."

"Yes, my lord," he answered.

¹³Saul said to him, "Why have you conspired against me, you and the

son of Jesse, giving him bread and a sword and inquiring of God for him, so that he has rebelled against me and lies in wait for me, as he does today?"

¹⁴Ahimelech answered the king, "Who of all your servants is as loyal as David, the king's son-in-law, captain of your bodyguard and highly respected in your household? ¹⁵Was that day the first time I inquired of God for him? Of course not! Let not the king accuse your servant or any of his father's family, for your servant knows nothing at all about this whole affair."

¹⁶But the king said, "You will surely die, Ahimelech, you and your father's whole family."

¹⁷Then the king ordered the guards at his side: "Turn and kill the priests of the LORD, because they too have sided with David. They knew he was fleeing, yet they did not tell me."

But the king's officials were not willing to raise a hand to strike the priests of the LORD.

¹⁸The king then ordered Doeg, "You turn and strike down the priests." So Doeg the Edomite turned and struck them down. That day he killed eighty-five men who wore the linen ephod. ¹⁹He also put to the sword Nob, the town of the priests, with its men and women, its children and infants, and its cattle, donkeys and sheep.

²⁰But Abiathar, a son of Ahimelech son of Ahitub, escaped and fled to join David. ²¹He told David that Saul had killed the priests of the LORD. ²²Then David said to Abiathar: "That day, when Doeg the Edomite was there, I knew he would be sure to tell Saul. I am responsible for the death of your father's whole family. ²³Stay with me; don't be afraid; the man who is seeking your life is seeking mine also. You will be safe with me."

David Saves Keilah

23 When David was told, "Look, the Philistines are fighting against Keilah and are looting the threshing floors," ²he inquired of the

LORD, saying, "Shall I go and attack these Philistines?"

The LORD answered him, "Go, attack the Philistines and save Keilah."

3But David's men said to him, "Here in Judah we are afraid. How much more, then, if we go to Keilah against the Philistine forces!"

4Once again David inquired of the LORD, and the LORD answered him, "Go down to Keilah, for I am going to give the Philistines into your hand." 5So David and his men went to Keilah, fought the Philistines and carried off their livestock. He inflicted heavy losses on the Philistines and saved the people of Keilah. 6(Now Abiathar son of Ahimelech had brought the ephod down with him when he fled to David at Keilah.)

Saul Pursues David

7Saul was told that David had gone to Keilah, and he said, "God has handed him over to me, for David has imprisoned himself by entering a town with gates and bars." 8And Saul called up all his forces for battle, to go down to Keilah to besiege David and his men.

9When David learned that Saul was plotting against him, he said to Abiathar the priest, "Bring the ephod." 10David said, "O LORD, God of Israel, your servant has heard definitely that Saul plans to come to Keilah and destroy the town on account of me. 11Will the citizens of Keilah surrender me to him? Will Saul come down, as your servant has heard? O LORD, God of Israel, tell your servant."

And the LORD said, "He will."

12Again David asked, "Will the citizens of Keilah surrender me and my men to Saul?"

And the LORD said, "They will."

13So David and his men, about six hundred in number, left Keilah and kept moving from place to place. When Saul was told that David had

escaped from Keilah, he did not go there.

14David stayed in the desert strongholds and in the hills of the Desert of Ziph. Day after day Saul searched for him, but God did not give David into his hands.

15While David was at Horesh in the Desert of Ziph, he learned that Saul had come out to take his life. 16And Saul's son Jonathan went to David at Horesh and helped him find strength in God. 17"Don't be afraid," he said. "My father Saul will not lay a hand on you. You will be king over Israel, and I will be second to you. Even my father Saul knows this." 18The two of them made a covenant before the LORD. Then Jonathan went home, but David remained at Horesh.

19The Ziphites went up to Saul at Gibeah and said, "Is not David hiding among us in the strongholds at Horesh, on the hill of Hakilah, south of Jeshimon? 20Now, O king, come down whenever it pleases you to do so, and we will be responsible for handing him over to the king."

21Saul replied, "The LORD bless you for your concern for me. 22Go and make further preparation. Find out where David usually goes and who has seen him there. They tell me he is very crafty. 23Find out about all the hiding places he uses and come back to me with definite information.a Then I will go with you; if he is in the area, I will track him down among all the clans of Judah."

24So they set out and went to Ziph ahead of Saul. Now David and his men were in the Desert of Maon, in the Arabah south of Jeshimon. 25Saul and his men began the search, and when David was told about it, he went down to the rock and stayed in the Desert of Maon. When Saul heard this, he went into the Desert of Maon in pursuit of David.

26Saul was going along one side of the mountain, and David and his men were on the other side, hurrying to get away from Saul. As Saul and

a23 Or me at Nacon

his forces were closing in on David and his men to capture them, ²⁷a messenger came to Saul, saying, "Come quickly! The Philistines are raiding the land." ²⁸Then Saul broke off his pursuit of David and went to meet the Philistines. That is why they call this place Sela Hammahlekoth.ᵃ ²⁹And David went up from there and lived in the strongholds of En Gedi.

David Spares Saul's Life

24 After Saul returned from pursuing the Philistines, he was told, "David is in the Desert of En Gedi." ²So Saul took three thousand chosen men from all Israel and set out to look for David and his men near the Crags of the Wild Goats.

³He came to the sheep pens along the way; a cave was there, and Saul went in to relieve himself. David and his men were far back in the cave. ⁴The men said, "This is the day the LORD spoke of when he saidᵇ to you, 'I will give your enemy into your hands for you to deal with as you wish.'" Then David crept up unnoticed and cut off a corner of Saul's robe.

⁵Afterward, David was conscience-stricken for having cut off a corner of his robe. ⁶He said to his men, "The LORD forbid that I should do such a thing to my master, the LORD's anointed, or lift my hand against him; for he is the anointed of the LORD." ⁷With these words David rebuked his men and did not allow them to attack Saul. And Saul left the cave and went his way.

⁸Then David went out of the cave and called out to Saul, "My lord the king!" When Saul looked behind him, David bowed down and prostrated himself with his face to the ground. ⁹He said to Saul, "Why do you listen when men say, 'David is bent on harming you'? ¹⁰This day you have seen with your own eyes how the LORD delivered you into my hands in the cave. Some urged me to kill you, but I spared you; I said, 'I will not lift

my hand against my master, because he is the LORD's anointed.' ¹¹See, my father, look at this piece of your robe in my hand! I cut off the corner of your robe but did not kill you. Now understand and recognize that I am not guilty of wrongdoing or rebellion. I have not wronged you, but you are hunting me down to take my life. ¹²May the LORD judge between you and me. And may the LORD avenge the wrongs you have done to me, but my hand will not touch you. ¹³As the old saying goes, 'From evildoers come evil deeds,' so my hand will not touch you.

?DID YOU KNOW?   **24:5**

Why was David "conscience-stricken" for cutting off the hem of Saul's robe?

David did not hurt the king. But in those days the hem of a person's clothes had special markings. These markings showed what the person did. David had so much respect for God, who had made Saul king, that he felt sorry when he cut Saul's hem, a symbol of his royal power.

---

¹⁴"Against whom has the king of Israel come out? Whom are you pursuing? A dead dog? A flea? ¹⁵May the LORD be our judge and decide between us. May he consider my cause and uphold it; may he vindicate me by delivering me from your hand."

¹⁶When David finished saying this, Saul asked, "Is that your voice, David my son?" And he wept aloud. ¹⁷"You are more righteous than I," he said. "You have treated me well, but I have treated you badly. ¹⁸You have just now told me of the good you did to me; the LORD delivered me into your hands, but you did not kill me. ¹⁹When a man finds his enemy, does he let him get away unharmed? May the LORD reward you well for the way

---

ᵃ28 *Sela Hammahlekoth* means *rock of parting.*   ᵇ4 Or *"Today the* LORD *is saying*

you treated me today. ²⁰I know that you will surely be king and that the kingdom of Israel will be established in your hands. ²¹Now swear to me by the LORD that you will not cut off my descendants or wipe out my name from my father's family."

²²So David gave his oath to Saul. Then Saul returned home, but David and his men went up to the stronghold.

David, Nabal and Abigail

25 Now Samuel died, and all Israel assembled and mourned for him; and they buried him at his home in Ramah.

Then David moved down into the Desert of Maon.ᵃ ²A certain man in Maon, who had property there at Carmel, was very wealthy. He had a thousand goats and three thousand sheep, which he was shearing in Carmel. ³His name was Nabal and his wife's name was Abigail. She was an intelligent and beautiful woman, but her husband, a Calebite, was surly and mean in his dealings.

⁴While David was in the desert, he heard that Nabal was shearing sheep. ⁵So he sent ten young men and said to them, "Go up to Nabal at Carmel and greet him in my name. ⁶Say to him: 'Long life to you! Good health to you and your household! And good health to all that is yours!

⁷" 'Now I hear that it is sheep-shearing time. When your shepherds were with us, we did not mistreat

them, and the whole time they were at Carmel nothing of theirs was missing. ⁸Ask your own servants and they will tell you. Therefore be favorable toward my young men, since we come at a festive time. Please give your servants and your son David whatever you can find for them.' "

⁹When David's men arrived, they gave Nabal this message in David's name. Then they waited.

¹⁰Nabal answered David's servants, "Who is this David? Who is this son of Jesse? Many servants are breaking away from their masters these days. ¹¹Why should I take my bread and water, and the meat I have slaughtered for my shearers, and give it to men coming from who knows where?"

¹²David's men turned around and went back. When they arrived, they reported every word. ¹³David said to his men, "Put on your swords!" So they put on their swords, and David put on his. About four hundred men went up with David, while two hundred stayed with the supplies.

¹⁴One of the servants told Nabal's wife Abigail: "David sent messengers from the desert to give our master his greetings, but he hurled insults at them. ¹⁵Yet these men were very good to us. They did not mistreat us, and the whole time we were out in the fields near them nothing was missing. ¹⁶Night and day they were a wall around us all the time we were herding our sheep near them. ¹⁷Now

ᵃ1 Some Septuagint manuscripts; Hebrew *Paran*

▌ET'S LIVE IT!   1 Samuel 25:1–19,35–42

SPECIAL WOMEN DESERVE PRAISE ➡ Abigail is a famous Bible woman. How can you tell from this Bible story that she was both brave and wise?

When David saw how special Abigail was, he did two things. He praised (thanked) God for her (1 Samuel 25:32). And he praised Abigail for her good judgment (1 Samuel 25:33).

You can praise the women you know just as David praised Abigail. Think about what makes each one special. Tell God thank you for them. Now choose one of the women and write her a letter. In your letter, tell her why you think she is special.

think it over and see what you can do, because disaster is hanging over our master and his whole household. He is such a wicked man that no one can talk to him."

¹⁸Abigail lost no time. She took two hundred loaves of bread, two skins of wine, five dressed sheep, five seahs^a of roasted grain, a hundred cakes of raisins and two hundred cakes of pressed figs, and loaded them on donkeys. ¹⁹Then she told her servants, "Go on ahead; I'll follow you." But she did not tell her husband Nabal.

²⁰As she came riding her donkey into a mountain ravine, there were David and his men descending toward her, and she met them. ²¹David had just said, "It's been useless—all my watching over this fellow's property in the desert so that nothing of his was missing. He has paid me back evil for good. ²²May God deal with David,^b be it ever so severely, if by morning I leave alive one male of all who belong to him!"

²³When Abigail saw David, she quickly got off her donkey and bowed down before David with her face to the ground. ²⁴She fell at his feet and said: "My lord, let the blame be on me alone. Please let your servant speak to you; hear what your servant has to say. ²⁵May my lord pay no attention to that wicked man Nabal. He is just like his name—his name is Fool, and folly goes with him. But as for me, your servant, I did not see the men my master sent.

²⁶"Now since the LORD has kept you, my master, from bloodshed and from avenging yourself with your own hands, as surely as the LORD lives and as you live, may your enemies and all who intend to harm my master be like Nabal. ²⁷And let this gift, which your servant has brought to my master, be given to the men who follow you. ²⁸Please forgive your servant's offense, for the LORD will certainly make a lasting dynasty for my master, because he fights the LORD's battles. Let no wrongdoing be found in you as long as you live. ²⁹Even though someone is pursuing you to take your life, the life of my master will be bound securely in the bundle of the living by the LORD your God. But the lives of your enemies he will hurl away as from the pocket of a sling. ³⁰When the LORD has done for my master every good thing he promised concerning him and has appointed him leader over Israel, ³¹my master will not have on his conscience the staggering burden of needless bloodshed or of having avenged himself. And when the LORD has brought my master success, remember your servant."

³²David said to Abigail, "Praise be to the LORD, the God of Israel, who has sent you today to meet me. ³³May you be blessed for your good judgment and for keeping me from bloodshed this day and from avenging myself with my own hands. ³⁴Otherwise, as surely as the LORD, the God of Israel, lives, who has kept me from harming you, if you had not come quickly to meet me, not one male belonging to Nabal would have been left alive by daybreak."

³⁵Then David accepted from her hand what she had brought him and said, "Go home in peace. I have heard your words and granted your request."

³⁶When Abigail went to Nabal, he was in the house holding a banquet like that of a king. He was in high spirits and very drunk. So she told him nothing until daybreak. ³⁷Then in the morning, when Nabal was sober, his wife told him all these things, and his heart failed him and he became like a stone. ³⁸About ten days later, the LORD struck Nabal and he died.

³⁹When David heard that Nabal was dead, he said, "Praise be to the LORD, who has upheld my cause against Nabal for treating me with contempt. He has kept his servant

^a18 That is, probably about a bushel (about 37 liters)   ^b22 Some Septuagint manuscripts;
Hebrew *with David's enemies*

from doing wrong and has brought Nabal's wrongdoing down on his own head."

Then David sent word to Abigail, asking her to become his wife. 40His servants went to Carmel and said to Abigail, "David has sent us to you to take you to become his wife."

41She bowed down with her face to the ground and said, "Here is your maidservant, ready to serve you and wash the feet of my master's servants." 42Abigail quickly got on a donkey and, attended by her five maids, went with David's messengers and became his wife. 43David had also married Ahinoam of Jezreel, and they both were his wives. 44But Saul had given his daughter Michal, David's wife, to Paltiel*a* son of Laish, who was from Gallim.

David Again Spares Saul's Life

26 The Ziphites went to Saul at Gibeah and said, "Is not David hiding on the hill of Hakilah, which faces Jeshimon?"

2So Saul went down to the Desert of Ziph, with his three thousand chosen men of Israel, to search there for David. 3Saul made his camp beside the road on the hill of Hakilah facing Jeshimon, but David stayed in the desert. When he saw that Saul had followed him there, 4he sent out scouts and learned that Saul had definitely arrived.*b*

5Then David set out and went to the place where Saul had camped. He saw where Saul and Abner son of Ner, the commander of the army, had lain down. Saul was lying inside the camp, with the army encamped around him.

6David then asked Ahimelech the Hittite and Abishai son of Zeruiah, Joab's brother, "Who will go down into the camp with me to Saul?"

"I'll go with you," said Abishai.

7So David and Abishai went to the army by night, and there was Saul, lying asleep inside the camp with his spear stuck in the ground near his head. Abner and the soldiers were lying around him.

8Abishai said to David, "Today God has delivered your enemy into your hands. Now let me pin him to the ground with one thrust of my spear; I won't strike him twice."

9But David said to Abishai, "Don't destroy him! Who can lay a hand on the LORD's anointed and be guiltless? 10As surely as the LORD lives," he said, "the LORD himself will strike him; either his time will come and he

a44 Hebrew Palti, a variant of *Paltiel*   *b4 Or had come to Nacon* will die, or he will go into battle and perish. [11]But the LORD forbid that I should lay a hand on the LORD's anointed. Now get the spear and water jug that are near his head, and let's go."

[12]So David took the spear and water jug near Saul's head, and they left. No one saw or knew about it, nor did anyone wake up. They were all sleeping, because the LORD had put them into a deep sleep.

[13]Then David crossed over to the other side and stood on top of the hill some distance away; there was a wide space between them. [14]He called out to the army and to Abner son of Ner, "Aren't you going to answer me, Abner?"

Abner replied, "Who are you who calls to the king?"

[15]David said, "You're a man, aren't you? And who is like you in Israel? Why didn't you guard your lord the king? Someone came to destroy your lord the king. [16]What you have done is not good. As surely as the LORD lives, you and your men deserve to die, because you did not guard your master, the LORD's anointed. Look around you. Where are the king's spear and water jug that were near his head?"

[17]Saul recognized David's voice and said, "Is that your voice, David my son?"

David replied, "Yes it is, my lord the king." [18]And he added, "Why is my lord pursuing his servant? What have I done, and what wrong am I guilty of? [19]Now let my lord the king listen to his servant's words. If the LORD has incited you against me, then may he accept an offering. If, however, men have done it, may they be cursed before the LORD! They have now driven me from my share in the LORD's inheritance and have said, 'Go, serve other gods.' [20]Now do not let my blood fall to the ground far from the presence of the LORD. The king of Israel has come out to look for a flea—as one hunts a partridge in the mountains."

[21]Then Saul said, "I have sinned. Come back, David my son. Because you considered my life precious today, I will not try to harm you again. Surely I have acted like a fool and have erred greatly."

❓DID YOU KNOW?   26:21

How many chances did David have to kill King Saul?

David had at least two chances (see 1 Samuel 24 and 26) to kill Saul. But David knew God had made Saul king. David would not harm the man God had made king, even though Saul had tried to kill David.

---

[22]"Here is the king's spear," David answered. "Let one of your young men come over and get it. [23]The LORD rewards every man for his righteousness and faithfulness. The LORD delivered you into my hands today, but I would not lay a hand on the LORD's anointed. [24]As surely as I valued your life today, so may the LORD value my life and deliver me from all trouble."

[25]Then Saul said to David, "May you be blessed, my son David; you will do great things and surely triumph."

So David went on his way, and Saul returned home.

David Among the Philistines

27 But David thought to himself, "One of these days I will be destroyed by the hand of Saul. The best thing I can do is to escape to the land of the Philistines. Then Saul will give up searching for me anywhere in Israel, and I will slip out of his hand."

[2]So David and the six hundred men with him left and went over to Achish son of Maoch king of Gath. [3]David and his men settled in Gath with Achish. Each man had his family with him, and David had his two wives: Ahinoam of Jezreel and Abigail of Carmel, the widow of Nabal.

⁴When Saul was told that David had fled to Gath, he no longer searched for him.

⁵Then David said to Achish, "If I have found favor in your eyes, let a place be assigned to me in one of the country towns, that I may live there. Why should your servant live in the royal city with you?"

⁶So on that day Achish gave him Ziklag, and it has belonged to the kings of Judah ever since. ⁷David lived in Philistine territory a year and four months.

⁸Now David and his men went up and raided the Geshurites, the Girzites and the Amalekites. (From ancient times these peoples had lived in the land extending to Shur and Egypt.) ⁹Whenever David attacked an area, he did not leave a man or woman alive, but took sheep and cattle, donkeys and camels, and clothes. Then he returned to Achish.

¹⁰When Achish asked, "Where did you go raiding today?" David would say, "Against the Negev of Judah" or "Against the Negev of Jerahmeel" or "Against the Negev of the Kenites." ¹¹He did not leave a man or woman alive to be brought to Gath, for he thought, "They might inform on us and say, 'This is what David did.'" And such was his practice as long as he lived in Philistine territory. ¹²Achish trusted David and said to himself, "He has become so odious to his people, the Israelites, that he will be my servant forever."

Saul and the Witch of Endor

28 In those days the Philistines gathered their forces to fight against Israel. Achish said to David, "You must understand that you and your men will accompany me in the army."

²David said, "Then you will see for yourself what your servant can do."

Achish replied, "Very well, I will make you my bodyguard for life."

³Now Samuel was dead, and all Israel had mourned for him and buried him in his own town of Ramah. Saul had expelled the mediums and spiritists from the land.

⁴The Philistines assembled and came and set up camp at Shunem, while Saul gathered all the Israelites and set up camp at Gilboa. ⁵When Saul saw the Philistine army, he was afraid; terror filled his heart. ⁶He inquired of the LORD, but the LORD did not answer him by dreams or Urim or prophets. ⁷Saul then said to his attendants, "Find me a woman who is a medium, so I may go and inquire of her."

❓ DID YOU KNOW?　　28:3

Why was it wrong for Saul to consult a medium?

A medium is someone who claims to talk with the dead or with spirits. God told his people not to go to witches or astrologers or anyone like them. Saul knew this law, so what he did was very wrong.

"There is one in Endor," they said.

⁸So Saul disguised himself, putting on other clothes, and at night he and two men went to the woman. "Consult a spirit for me," he said, "and bring up for me the one I name."

⁹But the woman said to him, "Surely you know what Saul has done. He has cut off the mediums and spiritists from the land. Why have you set a trap for my life to bring about my death?"

¹⁰Saul swore to her by the LORD, "As surely as the LORD lives, you will not be punished for this."

¹¹Then the woman asked, "Whom shall I bring up for you?"

"Bring up Samuel," he said.

¹²When the woman saw Samuel, she cried out at the top of her voice and said to Saul, "Why have you deceived me? You are Saul!"

¹³The king said to her, "Don't be afraid. What do you see?"

The woman said, "I see a spirit[a] coming up out of the ground."

[14]"What does he look like?" he asked.

"An old man wearing a robe is coming up," she said.

Then Saul knew it was Samuel, and he bowed down and prostrated himself with his face to the ground.

[15]Samuel said to Saul, "Why have you disturbed me by bringing me up?"

"I am in great distress," Saul said. "The Philistines are fighting against me, and God has turned away from me. He no longer answers me, either by prophets or by dreams. So I have called on you to tell me what to do."

[16]Samuel said, "Why do you consult me, now that the LORD has turned away from you and become your enemy? [17]The LORD has done what he predicted through me. The LORD has torn the kingdom out of your hands and given it to one of your neighbors—to David. [18]Because you did not obey the LORD or carry out his fierce wrath against the Amalekites, the LORD has done this to you today. [19]The LORD will hand over both Israel and you to the Philistines, and tomorrow you and your sons will be with me. The LORD will also hand over the army of Israel to the Philistines."

[20]Immediately Saul fell full length on the ground, filled with fear because of Samuel's words. His strength was gone, for he had eaten nothing all that day and night.

[21]When the woman came to Saul and saw that he was greatly shaken, she said, "Look, your maidservant has obeyed you. I took my life in my hands and did what you told me to do. [22]Now please listen to your servant and let me give you some food so you may eat and have the strength to go on your way."

[23]He refused and said, "I will not eat."

But his men joined the woman in urging him, and he listened to them.

He got up from the ground and sat on the couch.

[24]The woman had a fattened calf at the house, which she butchered at once. She took some flour, kneaded it and baked bread without yeast. [25]Then she set it before Saul and his men, and they ate. That same night they got up and left.

Achish Sends David Back to Ziklag

29 The Philistines gathered all their forces at Aphek, and Israel camped by the spring in Jezreel. [2]As the Philistine rulers marched with their units of hundreds and thousands, David and his men were marching at the rear with Achish. [3]The commanders of the Philistines asked, "What about these Hebrews?"

Achish replied, "Is this not David, who was an officer of Saul king of Israel? He has already been with me for over a year, and from the day he left Saul until now, I have found no fault in him."

[4]But the Philistine commanders were angry with him and said, "Send the man back, that he may return to the place you assigned him. He must not go with us into battle, or he will turn against us during the fighting. How better could he regain his master's favor than by taking the heads of our own men? [5]Isn't this the David they sang about in their dances:

" 'Saul has slain his thousands,
    and David his tens of
        thousands'?"

[6]So Achish called David and said to him, "As surely as the LORD lives, you have been reliable, and I would be pleased to have you serve with me in the army. From the day you came to me until now, I have found no fault in you, but the rulers don't approve of you. [7]Turn back and go in peace; do nothing to displease the Philistine rulers."

[8]"But what have I done?" asked David. "What have you found against

---

[a]13 Or see spirits; or see gods

your servant from the day I came to you until now? Why can't I go and fight against the enemies of my lord the king?"

❓DID YOU KNOW?   29:4

Why didn't the Philistine rulers want David in their army?

The Philistines were going to fight the Israelites. They were afraid that when the battle started David would fight against them, not with them. So the Philistines sent David home, and he did not have to fight against his own people.

9Achish answered, "I know that you have been as pleasing in my eyes as an angel of God; nevertheless, the Philistine commanders have said, 'He must not go up with us into battle.' 10Now get up early, along with your master's servants who have come with you, and leave in the morning as soon as it is light."

11So David and his men got up early in the morning to go back to the land of the Philistines, and the Philistines went up to Jezreel.

David Destroys the Amalekites

30 David and his men reached Ziklag on the third day. Now the Amalekites had raided the Negev and Ziklag. They had attacked Ziklag and burned it, 2and had taken captive the women and all who were in it, both young and old. They killed none of them, but carried them off as they went on their way.

3When David and his men came to Ziklag, they found it destroyed by fire and their wives and sons and daughters taken captive. 4So David and his men wept aloud until they had no strength left to weep. 5David's two wives had been captured—Ahinoam of Jezreel and Abigail, the widow of Nabal of Carmel. 6David was greatly distressed because the men were talking of stoning him; each one was bitter in spirit because of his sons and

daughters. But David found strength in the LORD his God.

7Then David said to Abiathar the priest, the son of Ahimelech, "Bring me the ephod." Abiathar brought it to him, 8and David inquired of the LORD, "Shall I pursue this raiding party? Will I overtake them?"

"Pursue them," he answered. "You will certainly overtake them and succeed in the rescue."

9David and the six hundred men with him came to the Besor Ravine, where some stayed behind, 10for two hundred men were too exhausted to cross the ravine. But David and four hundred men continued the pursuit.

11They found an Egyptian in a field and brought him to David. They gave him water to drink and food to eat— 12part of a cake of pressed figs and two cakes of raisins. He ate and was revived, for he had not eaten any food or drunk any water for three days and three nights.

13David asked him, "To whom do you belong, and where do you come from?"

He said, "I am an Egyptian, the slave of an Amalekite. My master abandoned me when I became ill three days ago. 14We raided the Negev of the Kerethites and the territory belonging to Judah and the Negev of Caleb. And we burned Ziklag."

15David asked him, "Can you lead me down to this raiding party?"

He answered, "Swear to me before God that you will not kill me or hand me over to my master, and I will take you down to them."

16He led David down, and there they were, scattered over the countryside, eating, drinking and reveling because of the great amount of plunder they had taken from the land of the Philistines and from Judah. 17David fought them from dusk until the evening of the next day, and none of them got away, except four hundred young men who rode off on camels and fled. 18David recovered everything the Amalekites had taken, including his two wives. 19Nothing was missing: young or old, boy or girl, plunder or anything else they had taken. David brought everything back. ²⁰He took all the flocks and herds, and his men drove them ahead of the other livestock, saying, "This is David's plunder."

²¹Then David came to the two hundred men who had been too exhausted to follow him and who were left behind at the Besor Ravine. They came out to meet David and the people with him. As David and his men approached, he greeted them. ²²But all the evil men and troublemakers among David's followers said, "Because they did not go out with us, we will not share with them the plunder we recovered. However, each man may take his wife and children and go."

²³David replied, "No, my brothers, you must not do that with what the LORD has given us. He has protected us and handed over to us the forces that came against us. ²⁴Who will listen to what you say? The share of the man who stayed with the supplies is to be the same as that of him who went down to the battle. All will share alike." ²⁵David made this a statute and ordinance for Israel from that day to this.

²⁶When David arrived in Ziklag, he sent some of the plunder to the elders of Judah, who were his friends, saying, "Here is a present for you from the plunder of the LORD's enemies."

²⁷He sent it to those who were in Bethel, Ramoth Negev and Jattir; ²⁸to those in Aroer, Siphmoth, Eshtemoa ²⁹and Racal; to those in the towns of the Jerahmeelites and the Kenites; ³⁰to those in Hormah, Bor Ashan, Athach ³¹and Hebron; and to those in all the other places where David and his men had roamed.

Saul Takes His Life

31 Now the Philistines fought against Israel; the Israelites fled before them, and many fell slain on Mount Gilboa. ²The Philistines pressed hard after Saul and his sons, and they killed his sons Jonathan, Abinadab and Malki-Shua. ³The fighting grew fierce around Saul, and when the archers overtook him, they wounded him critically.

❓ DID YOU KNOW? 31:3

Who killed King Saul?

Saul was badly wounded by a Philistine arrow. He did not want to be taken alive, so he fell on his own sword. But this still did not kill him. Later he asked a passing Amalekite to finish killing him so the Philistines would not capture him. Part of this story is told in 1 Samuel 31 and part in 2 Samuel 1.

⁴Saul said to his armor-bearer, "Draw your sword and run me through, or these uncircumcised fellows will come and run me through and abuse me."

But his armor-bearer was terrified and would not do it; so Saul took his own sword and fell on it. ⁵When the armor-bearer saw that Saul was dead, he too fell on his sword and died with him. ⁶So Saul and his three sons and his armor-bearer and all his men died together that same day.

⁷When the Israelites along the valley and those across the Jordan saw that the Israelite army had fled and that Saul and his sons had died, they

Life In Bible Times

SAUL'S ARMOR

In Old Testament times coats of armor were usually made by fastening metal scales together. Heavy metal helmets protected the head. Saul was a big man with heavy, strong armor. You can read about a boy who put on Saul's armor in 1 Samuel 17.

abandoned their towns and fled. And the Philistines came and occupied them.

8The next day, when the Philistines came to strip the dead, they found Saul and his three sons fallen on Mount Gilboa. 9They cut off his head and stripped off his armor, and they sent messengers throughout the land of the Philistines to proclaim the news in the temple of their idols and among their people. 10They put his armor in the temple of the Ashto-

reths and fastened his body to the wall of Beth Shan.

11When the people of Jabesh Gilead heard of what the Philistines had done to Saul, 12all their valiant men journeyed through the night to Beth Shan. They took down the bodies of Saul and his sons from the wall of Beth Shan and went to Jabesh, where they burned them. 13Then they took their bones and buried them under a tamarisk tree at Jabesh, and they fasted seven days.

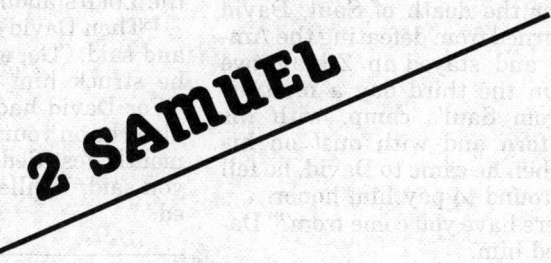

2 SAMUEL

David Hears of Saul's Death

1 After the death of Saul, David returned from defeating the Amalekites and stayed in Ziklag two days. [2]On the third day a man arrived from Saul's camp, with his clothes torn and with dust on his head. When he came to David, he fell to the ground to pay him honor.

[3]"Where have you come from?" David asked him.

He answered, "I have escaped from the Israelite camp."

[4]"What happened?" David asked. "Tell me."

He said, "The men fled from the battle. Many of them fell and died. And Saul and his son Jonathan are dead."

[5]Then David said to the young man who brought him the report, "How do you know that Saul and his son Jonathan are dead?"

[6]"I happened to be on Mount Gilboa," the young man said, "and there was Saul, leaning on his spear, with the chariots and riders almost upon him. [7]When he turned around and saw me, he called out to me, and I said, 'What can I do?'

[8]"He asked me, 'Who are you?'

" 'An Amalekite,' I answered.

[9]"Then he said to me, 'Stand over me and kill me! I am in the throes of death, but I'm still alive.'

[10]"So I stood over him and killed him, because I knew that after he had fallen he could not survive. And I took the crown that was on his head and the band on his arm and have brought them here to my lord."

[11]Then David and all the men with him took hold of their clothes and tore them. [12]They mourned and wept and fasted till evening for Saul and his son Jonathan, and for the army of the LORD and the house of Israel, because they had fallen by the sword.

[13]David said to the young man who brought him the report, "Where are you from?"

"I am the son of an alien, an Amalekite," he answered.

[14]David asked him, "Why were you not afraid to lift your hand to destroy the LORD's anointed?"

[15]Then David called one of his men and said, "Go, strike him down!" So he struck him down, and he died. [16]For David had said to him, "Your blood be on your own head. Your own mouth testified against you when you said, 'I killed the LORD's anointed.' "

? DID YOU KNOW? 1:16

Did David reward the young man who killed Saul?

No. The young man thought that David would reward him for killing Saul. But David had him killed! There could only be punishment, not reward, for killing Israel's anointed king, even if that king was as bad as Saul.

David's Lament for Saul and Jonathan

[17]David took up this lament concerning Saul and his son Jonathan, [18]and ordered that the men of Judah be taught this lament of the bow (it is written in the Book of Jashar):

[19]"Your glory, O Israel, lies slain
 on your heights.
 How the mighty have fallen!

[20]"Tell it not in Gath,
 proclaim it not in the streets of
  Ashkelon,
 lest the daughters of the
  Philistines be glad,
 lest the daughters of the
  uncircumcised rejoice.

[21]"O mountains of Gilboa,
 may you have neither dew nor
  rain,
 nor fields that yield offerings of
  grain.
 For there the shield of the mighty
  was defiled,
 the shield of Saul—no longer
  rubbed with oil.

[22]From the blood of the slain,
 from the flesh of the mighty,

the bow of Jonathan did not turn
  back,
the sword of Saul did not return
  unsatisfied.

23"Saul and Jonathan—
  in life they were loved and
    gracious,
  and in death they were not
    parted.
They were swifter than eagles,
  they were stronger than lions.

24"O daughters of Israel,
  weep for Saul,
who clothed you in scarlet and
    finery,
who adorned your garments
  with ornaments of gold.

25"How the mighty have fallen in
    battle!
  Jonathan lies slain on your
    heights.
26I grieve for you, Jonathan my
    brother;
  you were very dear to me.
Your love for me was wonderful,
  more wonderful than that of
    women.

27"How the mighty have fallen!
  The weapons of war have
    perished!"

❓DID YOU KNOW?   1:17

What is a lament?

A lament is a sad song. The tune
of a lament is very sad, and the
words tell why the person singing it
feels bad. David wrote this lament
to help Israel remember the good
things about Saul and Jonathan.

David Anointed King Over Judah

2 In the course of time, David inquired of the LORD. "Shall I go up
to one of the towns of Judah?" he
asked.
  The LORD said, "Go up."

David asked, "Where shall I go?"
  "To Hebron," the LORD answered.
²So David went up there with his
two wives, Ahinoam of Jezreel and
Abigail, the widow of Nabal of Carmel. ³David also took the men who
were with him, each with his family,
and they settled in Hebron and its
towns. ⁴Then the men of Judah came
to Hebron and there they anointed
David king over the house of Judah.
  When David was told that it was
the men of Jabesh Gilead who had
buried Saul, ⁵he sent messengers to
the men of Jabesh Gilead to say to
them, "The LORD bless you for showing this kindness to Saul your master
by burying him. ⁶May the LORD now
show you kindness and faithfulness,
and I too will show you the same favor because you have done this. ⁷Now
then, be strong and brave, for Saul
your master is dead, and the house of
Judah has anointed me king over
them."

War Between the Houses of David and Saul

⁸Meanwhile, Abner son of Ner, the
commander of Saul's army, had tak-
en Ish-Bosheth son of Saul and
brought him over to Mahanaim. ⁹He
made him king over Gilead, Ashuri*a*
and Jezreel, and also over Ephraim,
Benjamin and all Israel.
  ¹⁰Ish-Bosheth son of Saul was forty
years old when he became king over
Israel, and he reigned two years. The
house of Judah, however, followed
David. ¹¹The length of time David
was king in Hebron over the house of
Judah was seven years and six
months.
  ¹²Abner son of Ner, together with
the men of Ish-Bosheth son of Saul,
left Mahanaim and went to Gibeon.
¹³Joab son of Zeruiah and David's
men went out and met them at the
pool of Gibeon. One group sat down
on one side of the pool and one group
on the other side.
  ¹⁴Then Abner said to Joab, "Let's
have some of the young men get up

---

a9 Or Asher

and fight hand to hand in front of us."

"All right, let them do it," Joab said.

¹⁵So they stood up and were counted off—twelve men for Benjamin and Ish-Bosheth son of Saul, and twelve for David. ¹⁶Then each man grabbed his opponent by the head and thrust his dagger into his opponent's side, and they fell down together. So that place in Gibeon was called Helkath Hazzurim.ᵃ

¹⁷The battle that day was very fierce, and Abner and the men of Israel were defeated by David's men.

¹⁸The three sons of Zeruiah were there: Joab, Abishai and Asahel. Now Asahel was as fleet-footed as a wild gazelle. ¹⁹He chased Abner, turning neither to the right nor to the left as he pursued him. ²⁰Abner looked behind him and asked, "Is that you, Asahel?"

"It is," he answered.

²¹Then Abner said to him, "Turn aside to the right or to the left; take on one of the young men and strip him of his weapons." But Asahel would not stop chasing him.

²²Again Abner warned Asahel, "Stop chasing me! Why should I strike you down? How could I look your brother Joab in the face?"

²³But Asahel refused to give up the pursuit; so Abner thrust the butt of his spear into Asahel's stomach, and the spear came out through his back. He fell there and died on the spot. And every man stopped when he came to the place where Asahel had fallen and died.

²⁴But Joab and Abishai pursued Abner, and as the sun was setting, they came to the hill of Ammah, near Giah on the way to the wasteland of Gibeon. ²⁵Then the men of Benjamin rallied behind Abner. They formed themselves into a group and took their stand on top of a hill.

²⁶Abner called out to Joab, "Must the sword devour forever? Don't you realize that this will end in bitterness? How long before you order your men to stop pursuing their brothers?"

²⁷Joab answered, "As surely as God lives, if you had not spoken, the men would have continued the pursuit of their brothers until morning.ᵇ"

ᵃ16 *Helkath Hazzurim* means *field of daggers* or *field of hostilities.*   ᵇ27 Or *spoken this morning, the men would not have taken up the pursuit of their brothers*; or *spoken, the men would have given up the pursuit of their brothers by morning*

▌ET'S LIVE IT! 2 Samuel 2:8–28

AVOID BITTERNESS ➠ The Israelites were all descendants of Abraham, Isaac, and Jacob. So they were really family. Read 2 Samuel 2:8–28 and find out what happened when members of the Israelite family went to war with each other.

Most brothers and sisters fight now and then. Here are some rules you can follow to stop family fights before they end in bitterness.

Rule #1. When you realize you are having a fight, try to stop and walk away.

Rule #2. If the other person keeps after you, ask that person to please stop. Tell him or her you don't want anyone to become bitter.

Rule #3. After the fight ends, it's good to get away from the other for a while, so everyone can calm down.

Tell your family about these rules and the Bible story. If your family agrees to follow these rules when arguments start, make copies of the rules and post them in places where you are likely to fight. Try following the rules for one month. Then have the family talk about whether the rules helped avoid bitterness.

²⁸So Joab blew the trumpet, and all the men came to a halt; they no longer pursued Israel, nor did they fight anymore.

²⁹All that night Abner and his men marched through the Arabah. They crossed the Jordan, continued through the whole Bithron[a] and came to Mahanaim.

³⁰Then Joab returned from pursuing Abner and assembled all his men. Besides Asahel, nineteen of David's men were found missing. ³¹But David's men had killed three hundred and sixty Benjamites who were with Abner. ³²They took Asahel and buried him in his father's tomb at Bethlehem. Then Joab and his men marched all night and arrived at Hebron by daybreak.

3 The war between the house of Saul and the house of David lasted a long time. David grew stronger and stronger, while the house of Saul grew weaker and weaker.

²Sons were born to David in Hebron:

His firstborn was Amnon the son of Ahinoam of Jezreel;

³his second, Kileab the son of Abigail the widow of Nabal of Carmel;

the third, Absalom the son of Maacah daughter of Talmai king of Geshur;

⁴the fourth, Adonijah the son of Haggith;

the fifth, Shephatiah the son of Abital;

⁵and the sixth, Ithream the son of David's wife Eglah.

These were born to David in Hebron.

Abner Goes Over to David

⁶During the war between the house of Saul and the house of David, Abner had been strengthening his own position in the house of Saul. ⁷Now Saul had had a concubine named Rizpah daughter of Aiah. And Ish-Bosheth said to Abner, "Why did you sleep with my father's concubine?"

⁸Abner was very angry because of what Ish-Bosheth said and he answered, "Am I a dog's head—on Judah's side? This very day I am loyal to the house of your father Saul and to his family and friends. I haven't handed you over to David. Yet now you accuse me of an offense involving this woman! ⁹May God deal with Abner, be it ever so severely, if I do not do for David what the LORD promised him on oath ¹⁰and transfer the kingdom from the house of Saul and establish David's throne over Israel and Judah from Dan to Beersheba." ¹¹Ish-Bosheth did not dare to say another word to Abner, because he was afraid of him.

¹²Then Abner sent messengers on his behalf to say to David, "Whose land is it? Make an agreement with me, and I will help you bring all Israel over to you."

¹³"Good," said David. "I will make an agreement with you. But I demand one thing of you: Do not come into my presence unless you bring Michal daughter of Saul when you come to see me." ¹⁴Then David sent messengers to Ish-Bosheth son of Saul, demanding, "Give me my wife Michal, whom I betrothed to myself for the price of a hundred Philistine foreskins."

¹⁵So Ish-Bosheth gave orders and had her taken away from her husband Paltiel son of Laish. ¹⁶Her husband, however, went with her, weeping behind her all the way to Bahurim. Then Abner said to him, "Go back home!" So he went back.

¹⁷Abner conferred with the elders of Israel and said, "For some time you have wanted to make David your king. ¹⁸Now do it! For the LORD promised David, 'By my servant David I will rescue my people Israel from the hand of the Philistines and from the hand of all their enemies.'"

¹⁹Abner also spoke to the Benjamites in person. Then he went to Hebron to tell David everything that Israel and the whole house of Benjamin

---

a29 Or *morning*; or *ravine*; the meaning of the Hebrew for this word is uncertain.

wanted to do. [20]When Abner, who had twenty men with him, came to David at Hebron, David prepared a feast for him and his men. [21]Then Abner said to David, "Let me go at once and assemble all Israel for my lord the king, so that they may make a compact with you, and that you may rule over all that your heart desires." So David sent Abner away, and he went in peace.

❓DID YOU KNOW?   3:17

Who was Abner?

Abner was Saul's general. He helped Saul's son Ish-Bosheth become king of ten of Israel's twelve tribes. He helped Ish-Bosheth fight against David, who was king of the other two tribes. When Abner became angry at Ish-Bosheth, he decided to help David be king of all twelve tribes.

Joab Murders Abner

[22]Just then David's men and Joab returned from a raid and brought with them a great deal of plunder. But Abner was no longer with David in Hebron, because David had sent him away, and he had gone in peace. [23]When Joab and all the soldiers with him arrived, he was told that Abner son of Ner had come to the king and that the king had sent him away and that he had gone in peace.

[24]So Joab went to the king and said, "What have you done? Look, Abner came to you. Why did you let him go? Now he is gone! [25]You know Abner son of Ner; he came to deceive you and observe your movements and find out everything you are doing."

[26]Joab then left David and sent messengers after Abner, and they brought him back from the well of Sirah. But David did not know it. [27]Now when Abner returned to Hebron, Joab took him aside into the gateway, as though to speak with him privately. And there, to avenge the blood of his brother Asahel, Joab stabbed him in the stomach, and he died.

[28]Later, when David heard about this, he said, "I and my kingdom are forever innocent before the LORD concerning the blood of Abner son of Ner. [29]May his blood fall upon the head of Joab and upon all his father's house! May Joab's house never be without someone who has a running sore or leprosy[a] or who leans on a crutch or who falls by the sword or who lacks food."

[30](Joab and his brother Abishai murdered Abner because he had killed their brother Asahel in the battle at Gibeon.)

❓DID YOU KNOW?   3:30

Who was Joab?

Joab was David's general. When Abner, Saul's old general, came over to David's side, Joab murdered him. Joab did this because Abner had killed Joab's brother in a battle, and also because he was jealous and afraid Abner might become David's general.

[31]Then David said to Joab and all the people with him, "Tear your clothes and put on sackcloth and walk in mourning in front of Abner." King David himself walked behind the bier. [32]They buried Abner in Hebron, and the king wept aloud at Abner's tomb. All the people wept also.

[33]The king sang this lament for Abner:

"Should Abner have died as the
    lawless die?
[34] Your hands were not bound,
    your feet were not fettered.
You fell as one falls before wicked
    men."

[a]29 The Hebrew word was used for various diseases affecting the skin—not necessarily leprosy.

And all the people wept over him again.

35Then they all came and urged David to eat something while it was still day; but David took an oath, saying, "May God deal with me, be it ever so severely, if I taste bread or anything else before the sun sets!"

36All the people took note and were pleased; indeed, everything the king did pleased them. 37So on that day all the people and all Israel knew that the king had no part in the murder of Abner son of Ner.

38Then the king said to his men, "Do you not realize that a prince and a great man has fallen in Israel this day? 39And today, though I am the anointed king, I am weak, and these sons of Zeruiah are too strong for me. May the LORD repay the evildoer according to his evil deeds!"

Ish-Bosheth Murdered

4 When Ish-Bosheth son of Saul heard that Abner had died in Hebron, he lost courage, and all Israel became alarmed. 2Now Saul's son had two men who were leaders of raiding bands. One was named Baanah and the other Recab; they were sons of Rimmon the Beerothite from the tribe of Benjamin—Beeroth is considered part of Benjamin, 3because the people of Beeroth fled to Gittaim and have lived there as aliens to this day.

4(Jonathan son of Saul had a son who was lame in both feet. He was five years old when the news about Saul and Jonathan came from Jezreel. His nurse picked him up and fled, but as she hurried to leave, he fell and became crippled. His name was Mephibosheth.)

5Now Recab and Baanah, the sons of Rimmon the Beerothite, set out for the house of Ish-Bosheth, and they arrived there in the heat of the day while he was taking his noonday rest. 6They went into the inner part of the house as if to get some wheat, and they stabbed him in the stomach. Then Recab and his brother Baanah slipped away.

7They had gone into the house while he was lying on the bed in his bedroom. After they stabbed and killed him, they cut off his head. Taking it with them, they traveled all night by way of the Arabah. 8They brought the head of Ish-Bosheth to David at Hebron and said to the king, "Here is the head of Ish-Bosheth son of Saul, your enemy, who tried to take your life. This day the LORD has avenged my lord the king against Saul and his offspring."

9David answered Recab and his brother Baanah, the sons of Rimmon the Beerothite, "As surely as the LORD lives, who has delivered me out of all trouble, 10when a man told me, 'Saul is dead,' and thought he was bringing good news, I seized him and put him to death in Ziklag. That was the reward I gave him for his news! 11How much more—when wicked men have killed an innocent man in his own house and on his own bed —should I not now demand his blood from your hand and rid the earth of you!"

❓DID YOU KNOW?   4:11

How did David reward the men who killed Saul's son Ish-Bosheth?

David didn't reward them. He had them killed. The death of Ish-Bosheth meant David would become king of all Israel. But it was wicked for the men to murder Ish-Bosheth. David never rewarded anyone for doing wicked things.

12So David gave an order to his men, and they killed them. They cut off their hands and feet and hung the bodies by the pool in Hebron. But they took the head of Ish-Bosheth and buried it in Abner's tomb at Hebron.

David Becomes King Over Israel

5 All the tribes of Israel came to David at Hebron and said, "We

are your own flesh and blood. ²In the past, while Saul was king over us, you were the one who led Israel on their military campaigns. And the LORD said to you, 'You will shepherd my people Israel, and you will become their ruler.'"

³When all the elders of Israel had come to King David at Hebron, the king made a compact with them at Hebron before the LORD, and they anointed David king over Israel. ⁴David was thirty years old when he became king, and he reigned forty years. ⁵In Hebron he reigned over Judah seven years and six months, and in Jerusalem he reigned over all Israel and Judah thirty-three years.

David Conquers Jerusalem

⁶The king and his men marched to Jerusalem to attack the Jebusites, who lived there. The Jebusites said to David, "You will not get in here; even the blind and the lame can ward you off." They thought, "David cannot get in here." ⁷Nevertheless, David captured the fortress of Zion, the City of David.

⁸On that day, David said, "Anyone who conquers the Jebusites will have to use the water shaft *a* to reach those 'lame and blind' who are David's enemies. *b* " That is why they say, "The 'blind and lame' will not enter the palace."

⁹David then took up residence in the fortress and called it the City of David. He built up the area around it, from the supporting terraces *c* inward. ¹⁰And he became more and more powerful, because the LORD God Almighty was with him.

¹¹Now Hiram king of Tyre sent messengers to David, along with cedar logs and carpenters and stonemasons, and they built a palace for David. ¹²And David knew that the LORD had established him as king over Israel and had exalted his kingdom for the sake of his people Israel.

¹³After he left Hebron, David took more concubines and wives in Jerusalem, and more sons and daughters were born to him. ¹⁴These are the names of the children born to him there: Shammua, Shobab, Nathan, Solomon, ¹⁵Ibhar, Elishua, Nepheg, Japhia, ¹⁶Elishama, Eliada and Eliphelet.

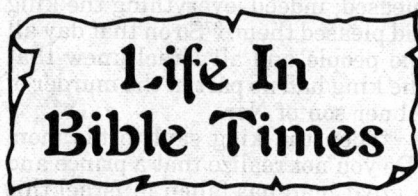

THE CITY OF DAVID

David captured the city of Jerusalem from the Jebusites and made it his capital. Only about 3500 people lived there when he captured it. In the Bible, Jerusalem is often referred to as Zion and as the City of David.

David Defeats the Philistines

¹⁷When the Philistines heard that David had been anointed king over Israel, they went up in full force to search for him, but David heard about it and went down to the stronghold. ¹⁸Now the Philistines had come and spread out in the Valley of Rephaim; ¹⁹so David inquired of the LORD, "Shall I go and attack the Philistines? Will you hand them over to me?"

The LORD answered him, "Go, for I will surely hand the Philistines over to you."

²⁰So David went to Baal Perazim, and there he defeated them. He said, "As waters break out, the LORD has broken out against my enemies before me." So that place was called Baal Perazim. *d* ²¹The Philistines abandoned their idols there, and David and his men carried them off.

²²Once more the Philistines came

---

a8 Or use scaling hooks   *b8 Or are hated by David*   *c9 Or the Millo*   *d20 Baal Perazim* means *the lord who breaks out.*

up and spread out in the Valley of Rephaim; [23]so David inquired of the LORD, and he answered, "Do not go straight up, but circle around behind them and attack them in front of the balsam trees. [24]As soon as you hear the sound of marching in the tops of the balsam trees, move quickly, because that will mean the LORD has gone out in front of you to strike the Philistine army." [25]So David did as the LORD commanded him, and he struck down the Philistines all the way from Gibeon[a] to Gezer.

The Ark Brought to Jerusalem

6 David again brought together out of Israel chosen men, thirty thousand in all. [2]He and all his men set out from Baalah of Judah[b] to bring up from there the ark of God, which is called by the Name,[c] the name of the LORD Almighty, who is enthroned between the cherubim that are on the ark. [3]They set the ark of God on a new cart and brought it from the house of Abinadab, which was on the hill. Uzzah and Ahio, sons of Abinadab, were guiding the new cart [4]with the ark of God on it,[d] and Ahio was walking in front of it. [5]David and the whole house of Israel were celebrating with all their might

before the LORD, with songs[e] and with harps, lyres, tambourines, sistrums and cymbals.

[6]When they came to the threshing floor of Nacon, Uzzah reached out and took hold of the ark of God, because the oxen stumbled. [7]The LORD's anger burned against Uzzah because of his irreverent act; therefore God struck him down and he died there beside the ark of God.

[8]Then David was angry because the LORD's wrath had broken out against Uzzah, and to this day that place is called Perez Uzzah.[f]

[9]David was afraid of the LORD that day and said, "How can the ark of the LORD ever come to me?" [10]He was not willing to take the ark of the LORD to be with him in the City of David. Instead, he took it aside to the house of Obed-Edom the Gittite. [11]The ark of the LORD remained in the house of Obed-Edom the Gittite for three months, and the LORD blessed him and his entire household.

[12]Now King David was told, "The LORD has blessed the household of Obed-Edom and everything he has, because of the ark of God." So David went down and brought up the ark of God from the house of Obed-Edom to the City of David with rejoicing.

---

[a]25 Septuagint (see also 1 Chron. 14:16); Hebrew *Geba*   [b]2 That is, Kiriath Jearim; Hebrew *Baale Judah*, a variant of *Baalah of Judah*   [c]2 Hebrew; Septuagint and Vulgate do not have *the Name.*   [d]3,4 Dead Sea Scrolls and some Septuagint manuscripts; Masoretic Text *cart* [4]*and they brought it with the ark of God from the house of Abinadab, which was on the hill*   [e]5 See Dead Sea Scrolls, Septuagint and 1 Chronicles 13:8; Masoretic Text *celebrating before the LORD with all kinds of instruments made of pine.*   [f]8 *Perez Uzzah* means *outbreak against Uzzah.*

▟ET'S LIVE IT!   2 Samuel 6:1–11

SHOW RESPECT FOR GOD ➠ David wanted to bring the ark of God to Jerusalem. This special box was the most holy object in Israel. This story tells something that happened that made David afraid and angry. Read 2 Samuel 6:1–11.

Why was Uzzah (UH-zuh) killed? God's law said the ark was to be carried very carefully on poles and that no one could touch it. People had to show respect for God by doing exactly what God said, not by doing what they thought would be all right. Later David had men carry the ark to Jerusalem exactly the way God asked. The story of Uzzah reminds us to show respect for God, because God is very great. We show respect for God as David finally did, by carefully obeying him.

¹³When those who were carrying the ark of the LORD had taken six steps, he sacrificed a bull and a fattened calf. ¹⁴David, wearing a linen ephod, danced before the LORD with all his might, ¹⁵while he and the entire house of Israel brought up the ark of the LORD with shouts and the sound of trumpets.

¹⁶As the ark of the LORD was entering the City of David, Michal daughter of Saul watched from a window. And when she saw King David leaping and dancing before the LORD, she despised him in her heart.

¹⁷They brought the ark of the LORD and set it in its place inside the tent that David had pitched for it, and David sacrificed burnt offerings and fellowship offerings*a* before the LORD. ¹⁸After he had finished sacrificing the burnt offerings and fellowship offerings, he blessed the people in the name of the LORD Almighty. ¹⁹Then he gave a loaf of bread, a cake of dates and a cake of raisins to each person in the whole crowd of Israelites, both men and women. And all the people went to their homes.

²⁰When David returned home to bless his household, Michal daughter of Saul came out to meet him and said, "How the king of Israel has distinguished himself today, disrobing in the sight of the slave girls of his servants as any vulgar fellow would!"

²¹David said to Michal, "It was before the LORD, who chose me rather than your father or anyone from his house when he appointed me ruler over the LORD's people Israel—I will celebrate before the LORD. ²²I will become even more undignified than this, and I will be humiliated in my own eyes. But by these slave girls you spoke of, I will be held in honor."

²³And Michal daughter of Saul had no children to the day of her death.

God's Promise to David

7 After the king was settled in his palace and the LORD had given him rest from all his enemies around

him, ²he said to Nathan the prophet, "Here I am, living in a palace of cedar, while the ark of God remains in a tent."

³Nathan replied to the king, "Whatever you have in mind, go ahead and do it, for the LORD is with you."

⁴That night the word of the LORD came to Nathan, saying:

⁵"Go and tell my servant David, 'This is what the LORD says: Are you the one to build me a house to dwell in? ⁶I have not dwelt in a house from the day I brought the Israelites up out of Egypt to this day. I have been moving from place to place with a tent as my dwelling. ⁷Wherever I have moved with all the Israelites, did I ever say to any of their rulers whom I commanded to shepherd my people Israel, "Why have you not built me a house of cedar?"'

⁸"Now then, tell my servant David, 'This is what the LORD Almighty says: I took you from the pasture and from following the flock to be ruler over my people Israel. ⁹I have been with you wherever you have gone, and I have cut off all your enemies from before you. Now I will make your name great, like the names of the greatest men of the earth. ¹⁰And I will provide a place for my people Israel and will plant them so that they can have a home of their own and no longer be disturbed. Wicked people will not oppress them anymore, as they did at the beginning ¹¹and have done ever since the time I appointed leaders*b* over my people Israel. I will also give you rest from all your enemies.

"'The LORD declares to you that the LORD himself will establish a house for you: ¹²When your days are over and you rest with your fathers, I will raise up your

---

offspring to succeed you, who will come from your own body, and I will establish his kingdom. [13]He is the one who will build a house for my Name, and I will establish the throne of his kingdom forever. [14]I will be his father, and he will be my son. When he does wrong, I will punish him with the rod of men, with floggings inflicted by men. [15]But my love will never be taken away from him, as I took it away from Saul, whom I removed from before you. [16]Your house and your kingdom will endure forever before me[a]; your throne will be established forever.' "

[17]Nathan reported to David all the words of this entire revelation.

David's Prayer

[18]Then King David went in and sat before the LORD, and he said:

"Who am I, O Sovereign LORD, and what is my family, that you have brought me this far? [19]And as if this were not enough in your sight, O Sovereign LORD, you have also spoken about the future of the house of your servant. Is this your usual way of dealing with man, O Sovereign LORD?

[20]"What more can David say to you? For you know your servant, O Sovereign LORD. [21]For the sake of your word and according to your will, you have done this great thing and made it known to your servant.

[22]"How great you are, O Sovereign LORD! There is no one like you, and there is no God but you, as we have heard with our own ears. [23]And who is like your people Israel—the one nation on earth that God went out to redeem as a people for himself, and to make a name for himself, and to perform great and awesome wonders by driving out nations and their gods from before your people, whom you redeemed from Egypt?[b] [24]You have established your people Israel as your very own forever, and you, O LORD, have become their God.

[25]"And now, LORD God, keep forever the promise you have made concerning your servant and his house. Do as you promised, [26]so that your name will be great forever. Then men will say, 'The LORD Almighty is God over Israel!' And the house of your servant David will be established before you.

[27]"O LORD Almighty, God of Israel, you have revealed this to

---

[a]16 Some Hebrew manuscripts and Septuagint; most Hebrew manuscripts *you*   [b]23 See Septuagint and 1 Chron. 17:21; Hebrew *wonders for your land and before your people, whom you redeemed from Egypt, from the nations and their gods.*

╲ET'S LIVE IT!   2 Samuel 7:1–16

LOVED FOREVER ➡ Read 2 Samuel 7:1–16. Then memorize this part of 2 Samuel 7:15: "My love will never be taken away from him."

God loves us just the same way. To remind you of God's kind of love, cut a strip of paper about one half inch wide and eleven inches long. Twist the paper strip one time, and tape the two ends together. Then take a pen. Start drawing a line on the inside of the strip. Keep turning the strip, but do not lift the pen from the paper. You'll find you've made a line on both sides of the strip, without ever taking the pen off the paper!

Keep this "magic" strip to remind you that God will never take his love away from you. You are marked as someone God loves, and that love continues forever.

your servant, saying, 'I will build a house for you.' So your servant has found courage to offer you this prayer. 28O Sovereign LORD, you are God! Your words are trustworthy, and you have promised these good things to your servant. 29Now be pleased to bless the house of your servant, that it may continue forever in your sight; for you, O Sovereign LORD, have spoken, and with your blessing the house of your servant will be blessed forever."

David's Victories

8 In the course of time, David defeated the Philistines and subdued them, and he took Metheg Ammah from the control of the Philistines.

2David also defeated the Moabites. He made them lie down on the ground and measured them off with a length of cord. Every two lengths of them were put to death, and the third length was allowed to live. So the Moabites became subject to David and brought tribute.

3Moreover, David fought Hadadezer son of Rehob, king of Zobah, when he went to restore his control along the Euphrates River. 4David captured a thousand of his chariots, seven thousand charioteers[a] and twenty thousand foot soldiers. He hamstrung all but a hundred of the chariot horses.

5When the Arameans of Damascus came to help Hadadezer king of Zobah, David struck down twenty-two thousand of them. 6He put garrisons in the Aramean kingdom of Damascus, and the Arameans became subject to him and brought tribute. The LORD gave David victory wherever he went.

7David took the gold shields that belonged to the officers of Hadadezer and brought them to Jerusalem. 8From Tebah[b] and Berothai, towns that belonged to Hadadezer, King David took a great quantity of bronze.

? DID YOU KNOW?   8:4

Why did David hamstring captured horses?

To hamstring means to cut a tendon in the leg, so a horse could no longer run or pull a war chariot. God's law told Israel's kings not to have chariot armies (see Deuteronomy 17:16). God gave Israel this law because he wanted them to rely on the LORD, not on military strength.

9When Tou[c] king of Hamath heard that David had defeated the entire army of Hadadezer, 10he sent his son Joram[d] to King David to greet him and congratulate him on his victory in battle over Hadadezer, who had been at war with Tou. Joram brought with him articles of silver and gold and bronze.

11King David dedicated these articles to the LORD, as he had done with the silver and gold from all the nations he had subdued: 12Edom[e] and Moab, the Ammonites and the Philistines, and Amalek. He also dedicated the plunder taken from Hadadezer son of Rehob, king of Zobah.

13And David became famous after he returned from striking down eighteen thousand Edomites[f] in the Valley of Salt.

14He put garrisons throughout Edom, and all the Edomites became subject to David. The LORD gave David victory wherever he went.

---

a4 Septuagint (see also Dead Sea Scrolls and 1 Chron. 18:4); Masoretic Text *captured seventeen hundred of his charioteers*   b8 See some Septuagint manuscripts (see also 1 Chron. 18:8); Hebrew *Betah*.   c9 Hebrew *Toi*, a variant of *Tou*; also in verse 10   d10 A variant of *Hadoram*   e12 Some Hebrew manuscripts, Septuagint and Syriac (see also 1 Chron. 18:11); most Hebrew manuscripts *Aram*   f13 A few Hebrew manuscripts, Septuagint and Syriac (see also 1 Chron. 18:12); most Hebrew manuscripts *Aram* (that is, Arameans)

David's Officials

15David reigned over all Israel, doing what was just and right for all his people. 16Joab son of Zeruiah was over the army; Jehoshaphat son of Ahilud was recorder; 17Zadok son of Ahitub and Ahimelech son of Abiathar were priests; Seraiah was secretary; 18Benaiah son of Jehoiada was over the Kerethites and Pelethites; and David's sons were royal advisers.[a]

David and Mephibosheth

9 David asked, "Is there anyone still left of the house of Saul to whom I can show kindness for Jonathan's sake?"

2Now there was a servant of Saul's household named Ziba. They called him to appear before David, and the king said to him, "Are you Ziba?"

"Your servant," he replied.

3The king asked, "Is there no one still left of the house of Saul to whom I can show God's kindness?"

Ziba answered the king, "There is still a son of Jonathan; he is crippled in both feet."

4"Where is he?" the king asked.

Ziba answered, "He is at the house of Makir son of Ammiel in Lo Debar."

5So King David had him brought from Lo Debar, from the house of Makir son of Ammiel.

6When Mephibosheth son of Jonathan, the son of Saul, came to David, he bowed down to pay him honor.

David said, "Mephibosheth!"

"Your servant," he replied.

7"Don't be afraid," David said to him, "for I will surely show you kindness for the sake of your father Jonathan. I will restore to you all the land that belonged to your grandfather Saul, and you will always eat at my table."

8Mephibosheth bowed down and said, "What is your servant, that you should notice a dead dog like me?"

9Then the king summoned Ziba, Saul's servant, and said to him, "I have given your master's grandson everything that belonged to Saul and his family. 10You and your sons and your servants are to farm the land for him and bring in the crops, so that your master's grandson may be provided for. And Mephibosheth, grandson of your master, will always eat at my table." (Now Ziba had fifteen sons and twenty servants.)

11Then Ziba said to the king, "Your servant will do whatever my lord the king commands his servant to do." So Mephibosheth ate at David's[b] table like one of the king's sons.

12Mephibosheth had a young son named Mica, and all the members of Ziba's household were servants of Mephibosheth. 13And Mephibosheth lived in Jerusalem, because he al-

---

a18 Or *were priests*   b11 Septuagint; Hebrew *my*

▚ET'S LIVE IT!   2 Samuel 9:1–13

SHOWING KINDNESS ⟹ Read 2 Samuel 9:12–13. Mephibosheth (Meh-FIB-o-sheth) was crippled in both feet. Why did David show him kindness? How did David show him kindness?

Children who are crippled or sick or who look different from other boys and girls have a special need for kindness. They need friends who will play with them and talk to them. If you know any children who have a special need, like Mephibosheth, you can be like David and show kindness. How? Here are some ideas. Send him a card. Take a game to her house and play it together. Talk to him when others go off to play. Call her regularly on the phone. Get your other friends to visit him with you. Take her to Sunday school. Help him with missed school work. Pray for him or her every day.

ways ate at the king's table, and he was crippled in both feet.

David Defeats the Ammonites

10 In the course of time, the king of the Ammonites died, and his son Hanun succeeded him as king. ²David thought, "I will show kindness to Hanun son of Nahash, just as his father showed kindness to me." So David sent a delegation to express his sympathy to Hanun concerning his father.

When David's men came to the land of the Ammonites, ³the Ammonite nobles said to Hanun their lord, "Do you think David is honoring your father by sending men to you to express sympathy? Hasn't David sent them to you to explore the city and spy it out and overthrow it?" ⁴So Hanun seized David's men, shaved off half of each man's beard, cut off their garments in the middle at the buttocks, and sent them away.

⁵When David was told about this, he sent messengers to meet the men, for they were greatly humiliated. The king said, "Stay at Jericho till your beards have grown, and then come back."

⁶When the Ammonites realized that they had become a stench in David's nostrils, they hired twenty thousand Aramean foot soldiers from Beth Rehob and Zobah, as well as the king of Maacah with a thousand men, and also twelve thousand men from Tob.

⁷On hearing this, David sent Joab out with the entire army of fighting men. ⁸The Ammonites came out and drew up in battle formation at the entrance to their city gate, while the Arameans of Zobah and Rehob and the men of Tob and Maacah were by themselves in the open country.

⁹Joab saw that there were battle lines in front of him and behind him; so he selected some of the best troops in Israel and deployed them against the Arameans. ¹⁰He put the rest of the men under the command of Abishai his brother and deployed them against the Ammonites. ¹¹Joab said, "If the Arameans are too strong for me, then you are to come to my rescue; but if the Ammonites are too strong for you, then I will come to rescue you. ¹²Be strong and let us fight bravely for our people and the cities of our God. The LORD will do what is good in his sight."

WORDS TO REMEMBER

10:12 The LORD will do what is good in his sight.

¹³Then Joab and the troops with him advanced to fight the Arameans, and they fled before him. ¹⁴When the Ammonites saw that the Arameans were fleeing, they fled before Abishai and went inside the city. So Joab returned from fighting the Ammonites and came to Jerusalem.

¹⁵After the Arameans saw that they had been routed by Israel, they regrouped. ¹⁶Hadadezer had Arameans brought from beyond the River*a*; they went to Helam, with Shobach the commander of Hadadezer's army leading them.

¹⁷When David was told of this, he gathered all Israel, crossed the Jordan and went to Helam. The Arameans formed their battle lines to meet David and fought against him. ¹⁸But they fled before Israel, and David killed seven hundred of their charioteers and forty thousand of their foot soldiers.*b* He also struck down Shobach the commander of their army, and he died there. ¹⁹When all the kings who were vassals of Hadadezer saw that they had been defeated by Israel, they made peace with the Israelites and became subject to them.

So the Arameans were afraid to help the Ammonites anymore.

---

a16 That is, the Euphrates   *b18* Some Septuagint manuscripts (see also 1 Chron. 19:18); Hebrew *horsemen*

David and Bathsheba

11 In the spring, at the time when kings go off to war, David sent Joab out with the king's men and the whole Israelite army. They destroyed the Ammonites and besieged Rabbah. But David remained in Jerusalem.

2One evening David got up from his bed and walked around on the roof of the palace. From the roof he saw a woman bathing. The woman was very beautiful, 3and David sent someone to find out about her. The man said, "Isn't this Bathsheba, the daughter of Eliam and the wife of Uriah the Hittite?" 4Then David sent messengers to get her. She came to him, and he slept with her. (She had purified herself from her uncleanness.) Then*a* she went back home. 5The woman conceived and sent word to David, saying, "I am pregnant."

6So David sent this word to Joab: "Send me Uriah the Hittite." And Joab sent him to David. 7When Uriah came to him, David asked him how Joab was, how the soldiers were and how the war was going. 8Then David said to Uriah, "Go down to your house and wash your feet." So Uriah left the palace, and a gift from the king was sent after him. 9But Uriah slept at the entrance to the palace with all his master's servants and did not go down to his house.

10When David was told, "Uriah did not go home," he asked him, "Haven't you just come from a distance? Why didn't you go home?"

11Uriah said to David, "The ark and Israel and Judah are staying in tents, and my master Joab and my lord's men are camped in the open fields. How could I go to my house to eat and drink and lie with my wife? As surely as you live, I will not do such a thing!"

12Then David said to him, "Stay here one more day, and tomorrow I will send you back." So Uriah remained in Jerusalem that day and the next. 13At David's invitation, he ate and drank with him, and David made him drunk. But in the evening Uriah went out to sleep on his mat among his master's servants; he did not go home.

14In the morning David wrote a letter to Joab and sent it with Uriah. 15In it he wrote, "Put Uriah in the front line where the fighting is fiercest. Then withdraw from him so he will be struck down and die."

16So while Joab had the city under siege, he put Uriah at a place where he knew the strongest defenders were. 17When the men of the city came out and fought against Joab, some of the men in David's army fell; moreover, Uriah the Hittite died.

18Joab sent David a full account of the battle. 19He instructed the messenger: "When you have finished giving the king this account of the battle, 20the king's anger may flare up, and he may ask you, 'Why did you get so close to the city to fight? Didn't you know they would shoot arrows from the wall? 21Who killed Abimelech son of Jerub-Besheth*b*? Didn't a woman throw an upper millstone on him from the wall, so that he died in Thebez? Why did you get so close to the wall?' If he asks you this, then say to him, 'Also, your servant Uriah the Hittite is dead.'"

22The messenger set out, and when he arrived he told David everything Joab had sent him to say. 23The messenger said to David, "The men overpowered us and came out against us in the open, but we drove them back to the entrance to the city gate. 24Then the archers shot arrows at your servants from the wall, and some of the king's men died. Moreover, your servant Uriah the Hittite is dead."

25David told the messenger, "Say this to Joab: 'Don't let this upset you; the sword devours one as well as another. Press the attack against the

---

*a*4 Or *with her. When she purified herself from her uncleanness,* (that is, Gideon)   *b*21 Also known as *Jerub-Baal*

city and destroy it.' Say this to encourage Joab."

26When Uriah's wife heard that her husband was dead, she mourned for him. 27After the time of mourning was over, David had her brought to his house, and she became his wife and bore him a son. But the thing David had done displeased the LORD.

❓DID YOU KNOW?   11:27

Did David ever sin?

Yes. 2 Samuel 11 tells about a terrible sin of David. But David confessed his sin, and God forgave him. You can read about David's confession in 2 Samuel 12 and Psalm 51.

Nathan Rebukes David

12 The LORD sent Nathan to David. When he came to him, he said, "There were two men in a certain town, one rich and the other poor. 2The rich man had a very large number of sheep and cattle, 3but the poor man had nothing except one little ewe lamb he had bought. He raised it, and it grew up with him and his children. It shared his food, drank from his cup and even slept in his arms. It was like a daughter to him.

4"Now a traveler came to the rich man, but the rich man refrained from taking one of his own sheep or cattle

to prepare a meal for the traveler who had come to him. Instead, he took the ewe lamb that belonged to the poor man and prepared it for the one who had come to him."

5David burned with anger against the man and said to Nathan, "As surely as the LORD lives, the man who did this deserves to die! 6He must pay for that lamb four times over, because he did such a thing and had no pity."

7Then Nathan said to David, "You are the man! This is what the LORD, the God of Israel, says: 'I anointed you king over Israel, and I delivered you from the hand of Saul. 8I gave your master's house to you, and your master's wives into your arms. I gave you the house of Israel and Judah. And if all this had been too little, I would have given you even more. 9Why did you despise the word of the LORD by doing what is evil in his eyes? You struck down Uriah the Hittite with the sword and took his wife to be your own. You killed him with the sword of the Ammonites. 10Now, therefore, the sword will never depart from your house, because you despised me and took the wife of Uriah the Hittite to be your own.'

11"This is what the LORD says: 'Out of your own household I am going to bring calamity upon you. Before your very eyes I will take your wives and give them to one who is close to you, and he will lie with your wives in broad daylight. 12You did it in secret,

---

▓ LET'S LIVE IT!   2 Samuel 12:1–14

FORGIVENESS FROM SIN ➡ Even people who love God, as King David did, sin sometimes. God forgives our sin. But sin still has consequences. Read 2 Samuel 12:1–14. Find: 1. Where David confesses his sin. 2. Where David is forgiven. 3. What happened because David sinned.

David sinned but was forgiven. God will forgive the sin of anyone who is sorry and asks to be forgiven.

Ask your parents or your pastor to help you find the name and address of someone who is in your local jail or prison for doing something wrong. Write a letter to that person. First tell him or her something about yourself. Then explain how God loves and forgives those who are sorry and ask for forgiveness. Show the letter to your mom or dad before you mail it.

but I will do this thing in broad daylight before all Israel.' "

[13]Then David said to Nathan, "I have sinned against the LORD."

Nathan replied, "The LORD has taken away your sin. You are not going to die. [14]But because by doing this you have made the enemies of the LORD show utter contempt,[a] the son born to you will die."

[15]After Nathan had gone home, the LORD struck the child that Uriah's wife had borne to David, and he became ill. [16]David pleaded with God for the child. He fasted and went into his house and spent the nights lying on the ground. [17]The elders of his household stood beside him to get him up from the ground, but he refused, and he would not eat any food with them.

[18]On the seventh day the child died. David's servants were afraid to tell him that the child was dead, for they thought, "While the child was still living, we spoke to David but he would not listen to us. How can we tell him the child is dead? He may do something desperate."

[19]David noticed that his servants were whispering among themselves and he realized the child was dead. "Is the child dead?" he asked.

"Yes," they replied, "he is dead."

[20]Then David got up from the ground. After he had washed, put on lotions and changed his clothes, he went into the house of the LORD and worshiped. Then he went to his own house, and at his request they served him food, and he ate.

[21]His servants asked him, "Why are you acting this way? While the child was alive, you fasted and wept, but now that the child is dead, you get up and eat!"

[22]He answered, "While the child was still alive, I fasted and wept. I thought, 'Who knows? The LORD may be gracious to me and let the child live.' [23]But now that he is dead, why should I fast? Can I bring him back again? I will go to him, but he will not return to me."

FASTING AND PRAYER

Old Testament people sometimes wore old, rough clothes when they prayed and would not eat food. This was to show they were very sorry for sins or that they desperately wanted God's help. David fasted, which means going without food, while he prayed for his sick son.

[24]Then David comforted his wife Bathsheba, and he went to her and lay with her. She gave birth to a son, and they named him Solomon. The LORD loved him; [25]and because the LORD loved him, he sent word through Nathan the prophet to name him Jedidiah.[b]

[26]Meanwhile Joab fought against Rabbah of the Ammonites and captured the royal citadel. [27]Joab then sent messengers to David, saying, "I have fought against Rabbah and taken its water supply. [28]Now muster the rest of the troops and besiege the city and capture it. Otherwise I will take the city, and it will be named after me."

[29]So David mustered the entire army and went to Rabbah, and attacked and captured it. [30]He took the crown from the head of their king[c] —its weight was a talent[d] of gold, and it was set with precious stones —and it was placed on David's head. He took a great quantity of plunder from the city [31]and brought out the

---

[a]14 Masoretic Text; an ancient Hebrew scribal tradition *this you have shown utter contempt for the* LORD   [b]25 *Jedidiah* means *loved by the* LORD.   [c]30 Or *of Milcom* (that is, Molech)
[d]30 That is, about 75 pounds (about 34 kilograms)

people who were there, consigning them to labor with saws and with iron picks and axes, and he made them work at brickmaking.*a* He did this to all the Ammonite towns. Then David and his entire army returned to Jerusalem.

Amnon and Tamar

13 In the course of time, Amnon son of David fell in love with Tamar, the beautiful sister of Absalom son of David.

²Amnon became frustrated to the point of illness on account of his sister Tamar, for she was a virgin, and it seemed impossible for him to do anything to her.

³Now Amnon had a friend named Jonadab son of Shimeah, David's brother. Jonadab was a very shrewd man. ⁴He asked Amnon, "Why do you, the king's son, look so haggard morning after morning? Won't you tell me?"

Amnon said to him, "I'm in love with Tamar, my brother Absalom's sister."

⁵"Go to bed and pretend to be ill," Jonadab said. "When your father comes to see you, say to him, 'I would like my sister Tamar to come and give me something to eat. Let her prepare the food in my sight so I may watch her and then eat it from her hand.'"

⁶So Amnon lay down and pretended to be ill. When the king came to see him, Amnon said to him, "I would like my sister Tamar to come and make some special bread in my sight, so I may eat from her hand."

⁷David sent word to Tamar at the palace: "Go to the house of your brother Amnon and prepare some food for him." ⁸So Tamar went to the house of her brother Amnon, who was lying down. She took some dough, kneaded it, made the bread in his sight and baked it. ⁹Then she took the pan and served him the bread, but he refused to eat.

"Send everyone out of here," Amnon said. So everyone left him. ¹⁰Then Amnon said to Tamar, "Bring the food here into my bedroom so I may eat from your hand." And Tamar took the bread she had prepared and brought it to her brother Amnon in his bedroom. ¹¹But when she took it to him to eat, he grabbed her and said, "Come to bed with me, my sister."

¹²"Don't, my brother!" she said to him. "Don't force me. Such a thing should not be done in Israel! Don't do this wicked thing. ¹³What about me? Where could I get rid of my disgrace? And what about you? You would be like one of the wicked fools in Israel. Please speak to the king; he will not keep me from being married to you." ¹⁴But he refused to listen to her, and since he was stronger than she, he raped her.

¹⁵Then Amnon hated her with intense hatred. In fact, he hated her more than he had loved her. Amnon said to her, "Get up and get out!"

¹⁶"No!" she said to him. "Sending me away would be a greater wrong than what you have already done to me."

But he refused to listen to her. ¹⁷He called his personal servant and said, "Get this woman out of here and bolt the door after her." ¹⁸So his servant put her out and bolted the door after her. She was wearing a richly ornamented*b* robe, for this was the kind of garment the virgin daughters of the king wore. ¹⁹Tamar put ashes on her head and tore the ornamented*c* robe she was wearing. She put her hand on her head and went away, weeping aloud as she went.

²⁰Her brother Absalom said to her, "Has that Amnon, your brother, been with you? Be quiet now, my sister; he is your brother. Don't take this thing to heart." And Tamar lived in her brother Absalom's house, a desolate woman.

²¹When King David heard all this,

---

a31 The meaning of the Hebrew for this clause is uncertain.   *b18* The meaning of the Hebrew for this phrase is uncertain.   *c19* The meaning of the Hebrew for this word is uncertain.

he was furious. ²²Absalom never said a word to Amnon, either good or bad; he hated Amnon because he had disgraced his sister Tamar.

❓ DID YOU KNOW? 13:21

Was David a good father?

David was a great soldier and a great king, but he was not a good father. He did not discipline his children when they did wrong. 2 Samuel 13 shows what can happen when a father does not discipline his children.

Absalom Kills Amnon

²³Two years later, when Absalom's sheepshearers were at Baal Hazor near the border of Ephraim, he invited all the king's sons to come there. ²⁴Absalom went to the king and said, "Your servant has had shearers come. Will the king and his officials please join me?"

²⁵"No, my son," the king replied. "All of us should not go; we would only be a burden to you." Although Absalom urged him, he still refused to go, but gave him his blessing.

²⁶Then Absalom said, "If not, please let my brother Amnon come with us."

The king asked him, "Why should he go with you?" ²⁷But Absalom urged him, so he sent with him Amnon and the rest of the king's sons.

²⁸Absalom ordered his men, "Listen! When Amnon is in high spirits from drinking wine and I say to you, 'Strike Amnon down,' then kill him. Don't be afraid. Have not I given you this order? Be strong and brave." ²⁹So Absalom's men did to Amnon what Absalom had ordered. Then all the king's sons got up, mounted their mules and fled.

³⁰While they were on their way, the report came to David: "Absalom has struck down all the king's sons; not one of them is left." ³¹The king stood up, tore his clothes and lay down on the ground; and all his servants stood by with their clothes torn.

³²But Jonadab son of Shimeah, David's brother, said, "My lord should not think that they killed all the princes; only Amnon is dead. This has been Absalom's expressed intention ever since the day Amnon raped his sister Tamar. ³³My lord the king should not be concerned about the report that all the king's sons are dead. Only Amnon is dead."

³⁴Meanwhile, Absalom had fled.

Now the man standing watch looked up and saw many people on the road west of him, coming down the side of the hill. The watchman went and told the king, "I see men in the direction of Horonaim, on the side of the hill."ᵃ

³⁵Jonadab said to the king, "See, the king's sons are here; it has happened just as your servant said."

³⁶As he finished speaking, the king's sons came in, wailing loudly. The king, too, and all his servants wept very bitterly.

³⁷Absalom fled and went to Talmai son of Ammihud, the king of Geshur. But King David mourned for his son every day.

³⁸After Absalom fled and went to Geshur, he stayed there three years. ³⁹And the spirit of the kingᵇ longed to go to Absalom, for he was consoled concerning Amnon's death.

❓ DID YOU KNOW? 13:38

Who was Absalom?

Absalom was a handsome son of David. But Absalom killed one of his brothers and ran away. David would not punish Absalom or forgive him. Later Absalom led a rebellion against his father, and many people were killed.

ᵃ34 Septuagint; Hebrew does not have this sentence.   ᵇ39 Dead Sea Scrolls and some Septuagint manuscripts; Masoretic Text *But the spirit of David the king*

Absalom Returns to Jerusalem

14 Joab son of Zeruiah knew that the king's heart longed for Absalom. [2]So Joab sent someone to Tekoa and had a wise woman brought from there. He said to her, "Pretend you are in mourning. Dress in mourning clothes, and don't use any cosmetic lotions. Act like a woman who has spent many days grieving for the dead. [3]Then go to the king and speak these words to him." And Joab put the words in her mouth.

[4]When the woman from Tekoa went[a] to the king, she fell with her face to the ground to pay him honor, and she said, "Help me, O king!"

[5]The king asked her, "What is troubling you?"

She said, "I am indeed a widow; my husband is dead. [6]I your servant had two sons. They got into a fight with each other in the field, and no one was there to separate them. One struck the other and killed him. [7]Now the whole clan has risen up against your servant; they say, 'Hand over the one who struck his brother down, so that we may put him to death for the life of his brother whom he killed; then we will get rid of the heir as well.' They would put out the only burning coal I have left, leaving my husband neither name nor descendant on the face of the earth."

[8]The king said to the woman, "Go home, and I will issue an order in your behalf."

[9]But the woman from Tekoa said to him, "My lord the king, let the blame rest on me and on my father's family, and let the king and his throne be without guilt."

[10]The king replied, "If anyone says anything to you, bring him to me, and he will not bother you again."

[11]She said, "Then let the king invoke the LORD his God to prevent the avenger of blood from adding to the destruction, so that my son will not be destroyed."

"As surely as the LORD lives," he said, "not one hair of your son's head will fall to the ground."

[12]Then the woman said, "Let your servant speak a word to my lord the king."

"Speak," he replied.

[13]The woman said, "Why then have you devised a thing like this against the people of God? When the king says this, does he not convict himself, for the king has not brought back his banished son? [14]Like water spilled on the ground, which cannot be recovered, so we must die. But God does not take away life; instead, he devises ways so that a banished person may not remain estranged from him.

[15]"And now I have come to say this to my lord the king because the people have made me afraid. Your servant thought, 'I will speak to the king; perhaps he will do what his servant asks. [16]Perhaps the king will agree to deliver his servant from the hand of the man who is trying to cut off both me and my son from the inheritance God gave us.'

[17]"And now your servant says, 'May the word of my lord the king bring me rest, for my lord the king is like an angel of God in discerning good and evil. May the LORD your God be with you.'"

[18]Then the king said to the woman, "Do not keep from me the answer to what I am going to ask you."

"Let my lord the king speak," the woman said.

[19]The king asked, "Isn't the hand of Joab with you in all this?"

The woman answered, "As surely as you live, my lord the king, no one can turn to the right or to the left from anything my lord the king says. Yes, it was your servant Joab who instructed me to do this and who put all these words into the mouth of your servant. [20]Your servant Joab did this to change the present situation. My lord has wisdom like that of an angel of God—he knows everything that happens in the land."

[21]The king said to Joab, "Very well,

---

a4 Many Hebrew manuscripts, Septuagint, Vulgate and Syriac; most Hebrew manuscripts *spoke*

I will do it. Go, bring back the young man Absalom."

²²Joab fell with his face to the ground to pay him honor, and he blessed the king. Joab said, "Today your servant knows that he has found favor in your eyes, my lord the king, because the king has granted his servant's request."

²³Then Joab went to Geshur and brought Absalom back to Jerusalem. ²⁴But the king said, "He must go to his own house; he must not see my face." So Absalom went to his own house and did not see the face of the king.

²⁵In all Israel there was not a man so highly praised for his handsome appearance as Absalom. From the top of his head to the sole of his foot there was no blemish in him. ²⁶Whenever he cut the hair of his head—he used to cut his hair from time to time when it became too heavy for him—he would weigh it, and its weight was two hundred shekels*a* by the royal standard. ²⁷Three sons and a daughter were born to Absalom. The daughter's name was Tamar, and she became a beautiful woman.

²⁸Absalom lived two years in Jerusalem without seeing the king's face. ²⁹Then Absalom sent for Joab in order to send him to the king, but Joab refused to come to him. So he sent a second time, but he refused to come. ³⁰Then he said to his servants, "Look, Joab's field is next to mine, and he has barley there. Go and set it on fire." So Absalom's servants set the field on fire.

³¹Then Joab did go to Absalom's house and he said to him, "Why have your servants set my field on fire?"

³²Absalom said to Joab, "Look, I sent word to you and said, 'Come here so I can send you to the king to ask, "Why have I come from Geshur? It would be better for me if I were still there!"' Now then, I want to see the king's face, and if I am guilty of anything, let him put me to death."

³³So Joab went to the king and told him this. Then the king summoned Absalom, and he came in and bowed down with his face to the ground before the king. And the king kissed Absalom.

Absalom's Conspiracy

15 In the course of time, Absalom provided himself with a chariot and horses and with fifty men to run ahead of him. ²He would get up early and stand by the side of the road leading to the city gate. Whenever anyone came with a complaint to be placed before the king for a decision, Absalom would call out to him, "What town are you from?" He would answer, "Your servant is from one of the tribes of Israel." ³Then Absalom would say to him, "Look, your claims are valid and proper, but there is no representative of the king to hear you." ⁴And Absalom would add, "If only I were appointed judge in the land! Then everyone who has a complaint or case could come to me and I would see that he gets justice."

⁵Also, whenever anyone approached him to bow down before him, Absalom would reach out his hand, take hold of him and kiss him. ⁶Absalom behaved in this way toward all the Israelites who came to the king asking for justice, and so he stole the hearts of the men of Israel.

⁷At the end of four*b* years, Absalom said to the king, "Let me go to Hebron and fulfill a vow I made to the LORD. ⁸While your servant was living at Geshur in Aram, I made this vow: 'If the LORD takes me back to Jerusalem, I will worship the LORD in Hebron.*c*'"

⁹The king said to him, "Go in peace." So he went to Hebron.

¹⁰Then Absalom sent secret messengers throughout the tribes of Israel to say, "As soon as you hear the sound of the trumpets, then say, 'Ab-

*a*26 That is, about 5 pounds (about 2.3 kilograms)
Josephus; Hebrew *forty*   *c*8 Some Septuagint manuscripts; Hebrew does not have *in Hebron.*
*b*7 Some Septuagint manuscripts, Syriac and

salom is king in Hebron.'" [11]Two hundred men from Jerusalem had accompanied Absalom. They had been invited as guests and went quite innocently, knowing nothing about the matter. [12]While Absalom was offering sacrifices, he also sent for Ahithophel the Gilonite, David's counselor, to come from Giloh, his hometown. And so the conspiracy gained strength, and Absalom's following kept on increasing.

David Flees

[13]A messenger came and told David, "The hearts of the men of Israel are with Absalom."

[14]Then David said to all his officials who were with him in Jerusalem, "Come! We must flee, or none of us will escape from Absalom. We must leave immediately, or he will move quickly to overtake us and bring ruin upon us and put the city to the sword."

[15]The king's officials answered him, "Your servants are ready to do whatever our lord the king chooses."

[16]The king set out, with his entire household following him; but he left ten concubines to take care of the palace. [17]So the king set out, with all the people following him, and they halted at a place some distance away. [18]All his men marched past him, along with all the Kerethites and Pelethites; and all the six hundred Gittites who had accompanied him from Gath marched before the king.

[19]The king said to Ittai the Gittite, "Why should you come along with us? Go back and stay with King Absalom. You are a foreigner, an exile from your homeland. [20]You came only yesterday. And today shall I make you wander about with us, when I do not know where I am going? Go back, and take your countrymen. May kindness and faithfulness be with you."

[21]But Ittai replied to the king, "As surely as the LORD lives, and as my lord the king lives, wherever my lord

the king may be, whether it means life or death, there will your servant be."

[22]David said to Ittai, "Go ahead, march on." So Ittai the Gittite marched on with all his men and the families that were with him.

[23]The whole countryside wept aloud as all the people passed by. The king also crossed the Kidron Valley, and all the people moved on toward the desert.

[24]Zadok was there, too, and all the Levites who were with him were carrying the ark of the covenant of God. They set down the ark of God, and Abiathar offered sacrifices[a] until all the people had finished leaving the city.

[25]Then the king said to Zadok, "Take the ark of God back into the city. If I find favor in the LORD's eyes, he will bring me back and let me see it and his dwelling place again. [26]But if he says, 'I am not pleased with you,' then I am ready; let him do to me whatever seems good to him."

[27]The king also said to Zadok the priest, "Aren't you a seer? Go back to the city in peace, with your son Ahimaaz and Jonathan son of Abiathar. You and Abiathar take your two sons with you. [28]I will wait at the fords in the desert until word comes from you to inform me." [29]So Zadok and Abiathar took the ark of God back to Jerusalem and stayed there.

[30]But David continued up the Mount of Olives, weeping as he went; his head was covered and he was barefoot. All the people with him covered their heads too and were weeping as they went up. [31]Now David had been told, "Ahithophel is among the conspirators with Absalom." So David prayed, "O LORD, turn Ahithophel's counsel into foolishness."

[32]When David arrived at the summit, where people used to worship God, Hushai the Arkite was there to meet him, his robe torn and dust on his head. [33]David said to him, "If you go with me, you will be a burden to

---

a24 Or Abiathar went up

me. ³⁴But if you return to the city and say to Absalom, 'I will be your servant, O king; I was your father's servant in the past, but now I will be your servant,' then you can help me by frustrating Ahithophel's advice. ³⁵Won't the priests Zadok and Abiathar be there with you? Tell them anything you hear in the king's palace. ³⁶Their two sons, Ahimaaz son of Zadok and Jonathan son of Abiathar, are there with them. Send them to me with anything you hear."

³⁷So David's friend Hushai arrived at Jerusalem as Absalom was entering the city.

David and Ziba

16 When David had gone a short distance beyond the summit, there was Ziba, the steward of Mephibosheth, waiting to meet him. He had a string of donkeys saddled and loaded with two hundred loaves of bread, a hundred cakes of raisins, a hundred cakes of figs and a skin of wine.

²The king asked Ziba, "Why have you brought these?"

Ziba answered, "The donkeys are for the king's household to ride on, the bread and fruit are for the men to eat, and the wine is to refresh those who become exhausted in the desert."

³The king then asked, "Where is your master's grandson?"

Ziba said to him, "He is staying in Jerusalem, because he thinks, 'Today the house of Israel will give me back my grandfather's kingdom.'"

⁴Then the king said to Ziba, "All that belonged to Mephibosheth is now yours."

"I humbly bow," Ziba said. "May I find favor in your eyes, my lord the king."

Shimei Curses David

⁵As King David approached Bahurim, a man from the same clan as Saul's family came out from there. His name was Shimei son of Gera, and he cursed as he came out. ⁶He pelted David and all the king's officials with stones, though all the troops and the special guard were on David's right and left. ⁷As he cursed, Shimei said, "Get out, get out, you man of blood, you scoundrel! ⁸The LORD has repaid you for all the blood you shed in the household of Saul, in whose place you have reigned. The LORD has handed the kingdom over to your son Absalom. You have come to ruin because you are a man of blood!"

⁹Then Abishai son of Zeruiah said to the king, "Why should this dead dog curse my lord the king? Let me go over and cut off his head."

¹⁰But the king said, "What do you and I have in common, you sons of Zeruiah? If he is cursing because the LORD said to him, 'Curse David,' who can ask, 'Why do you do this?'"

¹¹David then said to Abishai and all his officials, "My son, who is of my own flesh, is trying to take my life. How much more, then, this Benjamite! Leave him alone; let him curse, for the LORD has told him to. ¹²It may be that the LORD will see my distress and repay me with good for the cursing I am receiving today."

¹³So David and his men continued along the road while Shimei was going along the hillside opposite him, cursing as he went and throwing stones at him and showering him with dirt. ¹⁴The king and all the people with him arrived at their destination exhausted. And there he refreshed himself.

The Advice of Hushai and Ahithophel

¹⁵Meanwhile, Absalom and all the men of Israel came to Jerusalem, and Ahithophel was with him. ¹⁶Then Hushai the Arkite, David's friend, went to Absalom and said to him, "Long live the king! Long live the king!"

¹⁷Absalom asked Hushai, "Is this the love you show your friend? Why didn't you go with your friend?"

¹⁸Hushai said to Absalom, "No, the one chosen by the LORD, by these people, and by all the men of Israel—his I will be, and I will remain with him. ¹⁹Furthermore, whom should I serve?

Should I not serve the son? Just as I served your father, so I will serve you."

²⁰Absalom said to Ahithophel, "Give us your advice. What should we do?"

²¹Ahithophel answered, "Lie with your father's concubines whom he left to take care of the palace. Then all Israel will hear that you have made yourself a stench in your father's nostrils, and the hands of everyone with you will be strengthened." ²²So they pitched a tent for Absalom on the roof, and he lay with his father's concubines in the sight of all Israel.

²³Now in those days the advice Ahithophel gave was like that of one who inquires of God. That was how both David and Absalom regarded all of Ahithophel's advice.

17 Ahithophel said to Absalom, "I would*ᵃ* choose twelve thousand men and set out tonight in pursuit of David. ²I would*ᵇ* attack him while he is weary and weak. I would*ᵇ* strike him with terror, and then all the people with him will flee. I would*ᵇ* strike down only the king ³and bring all the people back to you.

The death of the man you seek will mean the return of all; all the people will be unharmed." ⁴This plan seemed good to Absalom and to all the elders of Israel.

⁵But Absalom said, "Summon also Hushai the Arkite, so we can hear what he has to say." ⁶When Hushai came to him, Absalom said, "Ahithophel has given this advice. Should we do what he says? If not, give us your opinion."

⁷Hushai replied to Absalom, "The advice Ahithophel has given is not good this time. ⁸You know your father and his men; they are fighters, and as fierce as a wild bear robbed of her cubs. Besides, your father is an experienced fighter; he will not spend the night with the troops. ⁹Even now, he is hidden in a cave or some other place. If he should attack your troops first,*ᶜ* whoever hears about it will say, 'There has been a slaughter among the troops who follow Absalom.' ¹⁰Then even the bravest soldier, whose heart is like the heart of a lion, will melt with fear, for all Israel knows that your father is a fighter and that those with him are brave.

¹¹"So I advise you: Let all Israel,

ᵃ1 Or *Let me*　　*ᵇ2* Or *will*　　*ᶜ9* Or *When some of the men fall at the first attack*

◣ET'S LIVE IT! 　　　2 Samuel 16:5–14

WHEN OTHERS CALL YOU NAMES ⮕ Have you ever recited this little poem?

　　Sticks and stones
　　Will break my bones,
　　But names will never hurt me.

But being called names *does* hurt, doesn't it? What do you do when someone calls you names?

In this Bible story a man named Shimei (SHIM-ee-eye) called King David bad names and even threw stones at him. Read 2 Samuel 16:5–14 and answer these true/false questions:

　1. David told his soldiers to kill Shimei.
　2. David told his friends to pay no attention to Shimei.
　3. David said God would hear and repay good for all the bad things Shimei said.
　4. David called Shimei names and chased him away.

Now decide what you will do next time someone calls you names.

from Dan to Beersheba—as numerous as the sand on the seashore—be gathered to you, with you yourself leading them into battle. [12]Then we will attack him wherever he may be found, and we will fall on him as dew settles on the ground. Neither he nor any of his men will be left alive. [13]If he withdraws into a city, then all Israel will bring ropes to that city, and we will drag it down to the valley until not even a piece of it can be found."

[14]Absalom and all the men of Israel said, "The advice of Hushai the Arkite is better than that of Ahithophel." For the LORD had determined to frustrate the good advice of Ahithophel in order to bring disaster on Absalom.

[15]Hushai told Zadok and Abiathar, the priests, "Ahithophel has advised Absalom and the elders of Israel to do such and such, but I have advised them to do so and so. [16]Now send a message immediately and tell David, 'Do not spend the night at the fords in the desert; cross over without fail, or the king and all the people with him will be swallowed up.'"

[17]Jonathan and Ahimaaz were staying at En Rogel. A servant girl was to go and inform them, and they were to go and tell King David, for they could not risk being seen entering the city. [18]But a young man saw them and told Absalom. So the two of them left quickly and went to the house of a man in Bahurim. He had a well in his courtyard, and they climbed down into it. [19]His wife took a covering and spread it out over the opening of the well and scattered grain over it. No one knew anything about it.

[20]When Absalom's men came to the woman at the house, they asked, "Where are Ahimaaz and Jonathan?"

The woman answered them, "They crossed over the brook."[a] The men searched but found no one, so they returned to Jerusalem.

[21]After the men had gone, the two climbed out of the well and went to inform King David. They said to him, "Set out and cross the river at once; Ahithophel has advised such and such against you." [22]So David and all the people with him set out and crossed the Jordan. By daybreak, no one was left who had not crossed the Jordan.

[23]When Ahithophel saw that his advice had not been followed, he saddled his donkey and set out for his house in his hometown. He put his house in order and then hanged himself. So he died and was buried in his father's tomb.

[24]David went to Mahanaim, and Absalom crossed the Jordan with all the men of Israel. [25]Absalom had appointed Amasa over the army in place of Joab. Amasa was the son of a man named Jether,[b] an Israelite[c] who had married Abigail,[d] the daughter of Nahash and sister of Zeruiah the mother of Joab. [26]The Israelites and Absalom camped in the land of Gilead.

[27]When David came to Mahanaim, Shobi son of Nahash from Rabbah of the Ammonites, and Makir son of Ammiel from Lo Debar, and Barzillai the Gileadite from Rogelim [28]brought bedding and bowls and articles of pottery. They also brought wheat and barley, flour and roasted grain, beans and lentils,[e] [29]honey and curds, sheep, and cheese from cows' milk for David and his people to eat. For they said, "The people have become hungry and tired and thirsty in the desert."

Absalom's Death

18 David mustered the men who were with him and appointed over them commanders of thousands and commanders of hundreds. [2]David

---

[a]20 Or "They passed by the sheep pen toward the water."   [b]25 Hebrew *Ithra*, a variant of *Jether*
[c]25 Hebrew and some Septuagint manuscripts; other Septuagint manuscripts (see also 1 Chron. 2:17) *Ishmaelite* or *Jezreelite*   [d]25 Hebrew *Abigal*, a variant of *Abigail*   [e]28 Most Septuagint manuscripts and Syriac; Hebrew *lentils, and roasted grain*

sent the troops out—a third under the command of Joab, a third under Joab's brother Abishai son of Zeruiah, and a third under Ittai the Gittite. The king told the troops, "I myself will surely march out with you."

3But the men said, "You must not go out; if we are forced to flee, they won't care about us. Even if half of us die, they won't care; but you are worth ten thousand of us.ᵃ It would be better now for you to give us support from the city."

4The king answered, "I will do whatever seems best to you."

So the king stood beside the gate while all the men marched out in units of hundreds and of thousands. 5The king commanded Joab, Abishai and Ittai, "Be gentle with the young man Absalom for my sake." And all the troops heard the king giving orders concerning Absalom to each of the commanders.

Life In Bible Times

THE CITY GATE

Doors, or gates, in the walls of a city were very heavy. Some were made of stone several inches thick and were as much as ten feet tall. Others were made of thick wood strengthened with strips of iron. In Judges 16 you can read about a strong man who carried a city gate thirty miles!

6The army marched into the field to fight Israel, and the battle took place in the forest of Ephraim. 7There the army of Israel was defeated by Da-vid's men, and the casualties that day were great—twenty thousand men. 8The battle spread out over the whole countryside, and the forest claimed more lives that day than the sword.

9Now Absalom happened to meet David's men. He was riding his mule, and as the mule went under the thick branches of a large oak, Absalom's head got caught in the tree. He was left hanging in midair, while the mule he was riding kept on going.

10When one of the men saw this, he told Joab, "I just saw Absalom hanging in an oak tree."

11Joab said to the man who had told him this, "What! You saw him? Why didn't you strike him to the ground right there? Then I would have had to give you ten shekelsᵇ of silver and a warrior's belt."

12But the man replied, "Even if a thousand shekelsᶜ were weighed out into my hands, I would not lift my hand against the king's son. In our hearing the king commanded you and Abishai and Ittai, 'Protect the young man Absalom for my sake.ᵈ' 13And if I had put my life in jeopardyᵉ—and nothing is hidden from the king—you would have kept your distance from me."

14Joab said, "I'm not going to wait like this for you." So he took three javelins in his hand and plunged them into Absalom's heart while Absalom was still alive in the oak tree. 15And ten of Joab's armor-bearers surrounded Absalom, struck him and killed him.

16Then Joab sounded the trumpet, and the troops stopped pursuing Israel, for Joab halted them. 17They took Absalom, threw him into a big pit in the forest and piled up a large heap of rocks over him. Meanwhile, all the Israelites fled to their homes.

18During his lifetime Absalom had taken a pillar and erected it in the

ᵃ3 Two Hebrew manuscripts, some Septuagint manuscripts and Vulgate; most Hebrew manuscripts care; for now there are ten thousand like us   ᵇ11 That is, about 4 ounces (about 115 grams)   ᶜ12 That is, about 25 pounds (about 11 kilograms)   ᵈ12 A few Hebrew manuscripts, Septuagint, Vulgate and Syriac; most Hebrew manuscripts may be translated Absalom, whoever you may be. ᵉ13 Or Otherwise, if I had acted treacherously toward him

King's Valley as a monument to himself, for he thought, "I have no son to carry on the memory of my name." He named the pillar after himself, and it is called Absalom's Monument to this day.

David Mourns

¹⁹Now Ahimaaz son of Zadok said, "Let me run and take the news to the king that the LORD has delivered him from the hand of his enemies."

²⁰"You are not the one to take the news today," Joab told him. "You may take the news another time, but you must not do so today, because the king's son is dead."

²¹Then Joab said to a Cushite, "Go, tell the king what you have seen." The Cushite bowed down before Joab and ran off.

²²Ahimaaz son of Zadok again said to Joab, "Come what may, please let me run behind the Cushite."

But Joab replied, "My son, why do you want to go? You don't have any news that will bring you a reward."

²³He said, "Come what may, I want to run."

So Joab said, "Run!" Then Ahimaaz ran by way of the plain^a and outran the Cushite.

²⁴While David was sitting between the inner and outer gates, the watchman went up to the roof of the gateway by the wall. As he looked out, he saw a man running alone. ²⁵The watchman called out to the king and reported it.

The king said, "If he is alone, he must have good news." And the man came closer and closer.

²⁶Then the watchman saw another man running, and he called down to the gatekeeper, "Look, another man running alone!"

The king said, "He must be bringing good news, too."

²⁷The watchman said, "It seems to me that the first one runs like Ahimaaz son of Zadok."

"He's a good man," the king said. "He comes with good news."

²⁸Then Ahimaaz called out to the king, "All is well!" He bowed down before the king with his face to the ground and said, "Praise be to the LORD your God! He has delivered up the men who lifted their hands against my lord the king."

²⁹The king asked, "Is the young man Absalom safe?"

Ahimaaz answered, "I saw great confusion just as Joab was about to send the king's servant and me, your servant, but I don't know what it was."

³⁰The king said, "Stand aside and wait here." So he stepped aside and stood there.

³¹Then the Cushite arrived and said, "My lord the king, hear the good news! The LORD has delivered you today from all who rose up against you."

³²The king asked the Cushite, "Is the young man Absalom safe?"

The Cushite replied, "May the enemies of my lord the king and all who rise up to harm you be like that young man."

³³The king was shaken. He went up to the room over the gateway and wept. As he went, he said: "O my son Absalom! My son, my son Absalom! If only I had died instead of you—O Absalom, my son, my son!"

19 Joab was told, "The king is weeping and mourning for Absalom." ²And for the whole army the victory that day was turned into mourning, because on that day the troops heard it said, "The king is grieving for his son." ³The men stole into the city that day as men steal in who are ashamed when they flee from battle. ⁴The king covered his face and cried aloud, "O my son Absalom! O Absalom, my son, my son!"

⁵Then Joab went into the house to the king and said, "Today you have humiliated all your men, who have just saved your life and the lives of your sons and daughters and the lives of your wives and concubines. ⁶You love those who hate you and

^a23 That is, the plain of the Jordan

hate those who love you. You have made it clear today that the commanders and their men mean nothing to you. I see that you would be pleased if Absalom were alive today and all of us were dead. 7Now go out and encourage your men. I swear by the LORD that if you don't go out, not a man will be left with you by nightfall. This will be worse for you than all the calamities that have come upon you from your youth till now."

8So the king got up and took his seat in the gateway. When the men were told, "The king is sitting in the gateway," they all came before him.

David Returns to Jerusalem

Meanwhile, the Israelites had fled to their homes. 9Throughout the tribes of Israel, the people were all arguing with each other, saying, "The king delivered us from the hand of our enemies; he is the one who rescued us from the hand of the Philistines. But now he has fled the country because of Absalom; 10and Absalom, whom we anointed to rule over us, has died in battle. So why do you say nothing about bringing the king back?"

11King David sent this message to Zadok and Abiathar, the priests: "Ask the elders of Judah, 'Why should you be the last to bring the king back to his palace, since what is being said throughout Israel has reached the king at his quarters? 12You are my brothers, my own flesh and blood. So why should you be the last to bring back the king?' 13And say to Amasa, 'Are you not my own flesh and blood? May God deal with me, be it ever so severely, if from now on you are not the commander of my army in place of Joab.' "

14He won over the hearts of all the men of Judah as though they were one man. They sent word to the king, "Return, you and all your men." 15Then the king returned and went as far as the Jordan.

Now the men of Judah had come to Gilgal to go out and meet the king and bring him across the Jordan.

16Shimei son of Gera, the Benjamite from Bahurim, hurried down with the men of Judah to meet King David. 17With him were a thousand Benjamites, along with Ziba, the steward of Saul's household, and his fifteen sons and twenty servants. They rushed to the Jordan, where the king was. 18They crossed at the ford to take the king's household over and to do whatever he wished.

When Shimei son of Gera crossed the Jordan, he fell prostrate before the king 19and said to him, "May my lord not hold me guilty. Do not remember how your servant did wrong on the day my lord the king left Jerusalem. May the king put it out of his mind. 20For I your servant know that I have sinned, but today I have come here as the first of the whole house of Joseph to come down and meet my lord the king."

21Then Abishai son of Zeruiah said, "Shouldn't Shimei be put to death for this? He cursed the LORD's anointed."

22David replied, "What do you and I have in common, you sons of Zeruiah? This day you have become my adversaries! Should anyone be put to death in Israel today? Do I not know that today I am king over Israel?" 23So the king said to Shimei, "You shall not die." And the king promised him on oath.

24Mephibosheth, Saul's grandson, also went down to meet the king. He had not taken care of his feet or trimmed his mustache or washed his clothes from the day the king left until the day he returned safely. 25When he came from Jerusalem to meet the king, the king asked him, "Why didn't you go with me, Mephibosheth?"

26He said, "My lord the king, since I your servant am lame, I said, 'I will have my donkey saddled and will ride on it, so I can go with the king.' But Ziba my servant betrayed me. 27And he has slandered your servant to my lord the king. My lord the king is like an angel of God; so do whatever pleases you. 28All my grandfather's descendants deserved nothing but death from my lord the king, but you gave your servant a place among those who sat at your table. So what right do I have to make any more appeals to the king?"

²⁹The king said to him, "Why say more? I order you and Ziba to divide the fields."

³⁰Mephibosheth said to the king, "Let him take everything, now that my lord the king has arrived home safely."

³¹Barzillai the Gileadite also came down from Rogelim to cross the Jordan with the king and to send him on his way from there. ³²Now Barzillai was a very old man, eighty years of age. He had provided for the king during his stay in Mahanaim, for he was a very wealthy man. ³³The king said to Barzillai, "Cross over with me and stay with me in Jerusalem, and I will provide for you."

³⁴But Barzillai answered the king, "How many more years will I live, that I should go up to Jerusalem with the king? ³⁵I am now eighty years old. Can I tell the difference between what is good and what is not? Can your servant taste what he eats and drinks? Can I still hear the voices of men and women singers? Why should your servant be an added burden to my lord the king? ³⁶Your servant will cross over the Jordan with the king for a short distance, but why should the king reward me in this way? ³⁷Let your servant return, that I may die in my own town near the tomb of my father and mother. But here is your servant Kimham. Let him cross over with my lord the king. Do for him whatever pleases you."

³⁸The king said, "Kimham shall cross over with me, and I will do for him whatever pleases you. And anything you desire from me I will do for you."

³⁹So all the people crossed the Jordan, and then the king crossed over. The king kissed Barzillai and gave him his blessing, and Barzillai returned to his home.

⁴⁰When the king crossed over to Gilgal, Kimham crossed with him. All the troops of Judah and half the troops of Israel had taken the king over.

⁴¹Soon all the men of Israel were coming to the king and saying to him, "Why did our brothers, the men of Judah, steal the king away and bring him and his household across the Jordan, together with all his men?"

⁴²All the men of Judah answered the men of Israel, "We did this because the king is closely related to us. Why are you angry about it? Have we eaten any of the king's provisions? Have we taken anything for ourselves?"

⁴³Then the men of Israel answered the men of Judah, "We have ten shares in the king; and besides, we have a greater claim on David than you have. So why do you treat us with contempt? Were we not the first to speak of bringing back our king?"

But the men of Judah responded even more harshly than the men of Israel.

Sheba Rebels Against David

20 Now a troublemaker named Sheba son of Bicri, a Benjamite, happened to be there. He sounded the trumpet and shouted,

"We have no share in David,
　no part in Jesse's son!
Every man to his tent, O Israel!"

²So all the men of Israel deserted David to follow Sheba son of Bicri. But the men of Judah stayed by their king all the way from the Jordan to Jerusalem.

³When David returned to his palace in Jerusalem, he took the ten concubines he had left to take care of the palace and put them in a house under guard. He provided for them, but did not lie with them. They were kept in confinement till the day of their death, living as widows.

⁴Then the king said to Amasa, "Summon the men of Judah to come to me within three days, and be here yourself." ⁵But when Amasa went to summon Judah, he took longer than the time the king had set for him.

⁶David said to Abishai, "Now Sheba son of Bicri will do us more harm than Absalom did. Take your master's men and pursue him, or he will find fortified cities and escape from us." ⁷So Joab's men and the Kerethites and Pelethites and all the mighty warriors went out under the command of Abishai. They marched out from Jerusalem to pursue Sheba son of Bicri.

⁸While they were at the great rock in Gibeon, Amasa came to meet them. Joab was wearing his military tunic, and strapped over it at his waist was a belt with a dagger in its sheath. As he stepped forward, it dropped out of its sheath.

⁹Joab said to Amasa, "How are you, my brother?" Then Joab took Amasa by the beard with his right hand to kiss him. ¹⁰Amasa was not on his guard against the dagger in Joab's hand, and Joab plunged it into his belly, and his intestines spilled out on the ground. Without being stabbed again, Amasa died. Then Joab and his brother Abishai pursued Sheba son of Bicri.

¹¹One of Joab's men stood beside Amasa and said, "Whoever favors Joab, and whoever is for David, let him follow Joab!" ¹²Amasa lay wallowing in his blood in the middle of the road, and the man saw that all the troops came to a halt there. When he realized that everyone who came up to Amasa stopped, he dragged him from the road into a field and threw a garment over him. ¹³After Amasa had been removed from the road, all the men went on with Joab to pursue Sheba son of Bicri.

¹⁴Sheba passed through all the tribes of Israel to Abel Beth Maacah*a* and through the entire region of the Berites, who gathered together and followed him. ¹⁵All the troops with Joab came and besieged Sheba in Abel Beth Maacah. They built a siege ramp up to the city, and it stood against the outer fortifications. While they were battering the wall to

bring it down, ¹⁶a wise woman called from the city, "Listen! Listen! Tell Joab to come here so I can speak to him." ¹⁷He went toward her, and she asked, "Are you Joab?"

Life In Bible Times

ATTACKING A WALLED CITY

When attacking a walled city, ancient armies built siege ramps by piling dirt and stones up against one wall. Soldiers climbed up this ramp and used heavy logs to knock the upper walls apart. The walls of ancient cities were thinner and weaker at the top.

"I am," he answered.

She said, "Listen to what your servant has to say."

"I'm listening," he said.

¹⁸She continued, "Long ago they used to say, 'Get your answer at Abel,' and that settled it. ¹⁹We are the peaceful and faithful in Israel. You are trying to destroy a city that is a mother in Israel. Why do you want to swallow up the LORD's inheritance?"

²⁰"Far be it from me!" Joab replied, "Far be it from me to swallow up or destroy! ²¹That is not the case. A man named Sheba son of Bicri, from the hill country of Ephraim, has lifted up his hand against the king, against David. Hand over this one man, and I'll withdraw from the city."

The woman said to Joab, "His head will be thrown to you from the wall."

²²Then the woman went to all the people with her wise advice, and they cut off the head of Sheba son of Bicri and threw it to Joab. So he sounded

a14 Or Abel, even Beth Maacah; also in verse 15

the trumpet, and his men dispersed from the city, each returning to his home. And Joab went back to the king in Jerusalem.

[23]Joab was over Israel's entire army; Benaiah son of Jehoiada was over the Kerethites and Pelethites; [24]Adoniram[a] was in charge of forced labor; Jehoshaphat son of Ahilud was recorder; [25]Sheva was secretary; Zadok and Abiathar were priests; [26]and Ira the Jairite was David's priest.

The Gibeonites Avenged

21 During the reign of David, there was a famine for three successive years; so David sought the face of the LORD. The LORD said, "It is on account of Saul and his bloodstained house; it is because he put the Gibeonites to death."

[2]The king summoned the Gibeonites and spoke to them. (Now the Gibeonites were not a part of Israel but were survivors of the Amorites; the Israelites had sworn to spare them, but Saul in his zeal for Israel and Judah had tried to annihilate them.) [3]David asked the Gibeonites, "What shall I do for you? How shall I make amends so that you will bless the LORD's inheritance?"

? DID YOU KNOW?   21:1

Who were the Gibeonites?

The Gibeonites were Canaanites who had tricked Joshua into making a treaty of peace (see Joshua 9). King Saul broke that treaty and tried to wipe out the Gibeonites. 2 Samuel 21 tells what David had to do to make up for Saul's sin against the Gibeonites.

[4]The Gibeonites answered him, "We have no right to demand silver or gold from Saul or his family, nor do we have the right to put anyone in Israel to death."

"What do you want me to do for you?" David asked.

[5]They answered the king, "As for the man who destroyed us and plotted against us so that we have been decimated and have no place anywhere in Israel, [6]let seven of his male descendants be given to us to be killed and exposed before the LORD at Gibeah of Saul—the LORD's chosen one."

So the king said, "I will give them to you."

[7]The king spared Mephibosheth son of Jonathan, the son of Saul, because of the oath before the LORD between David and Jonathan son of Saul. [8]But the king took Armoni and Mephibosheth, the two sons of Aiah's daughter Rizpah, whom she had borne to Saul, together with the five sons of Saul's daughter Merab,[b] whom she had borne to Adriel son of Barzillai the Meholathite. [9]He handed them over to the Gibeonites, who killed and exposed them on a hill before the LORD. All seven of them fell together; they were put to death during the first days of the harvest, just as the barley harvest was beginning.

[10]Rizpah daughter of Aiah took sackcloth and spread it out for herself on a rock. From the beginning of the harvest till the rain poured down from the heavens on the bodies, she did not let the birds of the air touch them by day or the wild animals by night. [11]When David was told what Aiah's daughter Rizpah, Saul's concubine, had done, [12]he went and took the bones of Saul and his son Jonathan from the citizens of Jabesh Gilead. (They had taken them secretly from the public square at Beth Shan, where the Philistines had hung them after they struck Saul down on Gilboa.) [13]David brought the bones of Saul and his son Jonathan from

---

[a]24 Some Septuagint manuscripts (see also 1 Kings 4:6 and 5:14); Hebrew *Adoram*   [b]8 Two Hebrew manuscripts, some Septuagint manuscripts and Syriac (see also 1 Samuel 18:19); most Hebrew and Septuagint manuscripts *Michal*

there, and the bones of those who had been killed and exposed were gathered up.

¹⁴They buried the bones of Saul and his son Jonathan in the tomb of Saul's father Kish, at Zela in Benjamin, and did everything the king commanded. After that, God answered prayer in behalf of the land.

Wars Against the Philistines

¹⁵Once again there was a battle between the Philistines and Israel. David went down with his men to fight against the Philistines, and he became exhausted. ¹⁶And Ishbi-Benob, one of the descendants of Rapha, whose bronze spearhead weighed three hundred shekels *a* and who was armed with a new ˌswordˌ, said he would kill David. ¹⁷But Abishai son of Zeruiah came to David's rescue; he struck the Philistine down and killed him. Then David's men swore to him, saying, "Never again will you go out with us to battle, so that the lamp of Israel will not be extinguished."

¹⁸In the course of time, there was another battle with the Philistines, at Gob. At that time Sibbecai the Hushathite killed Saph, one of the descendants of Rapha.

¹⁹In another battle with the Philistines at Gob, Elhanan son of Jaare-Oregim *b* the Bethlehemite killed Goliath *c* the Gittite, who had a spear with a shaft like a weaver's rod.

²⁰In still another battle, which took place at Gath, there was a huge man with six fingers on each hand and six toes on each foot—twenty-four in all. He also was descended from Rapha. ²¹When he taunted Israel, Jonathan son of Shimeah, David's brother, killed him.

²²These four were descendants of Rapha in Gath, and they fell at the hands of David and his men.

David's Song of Praise

22 David sang to the LORD the words of this song when the LORD delivered him from the hand of all his enemies and from the hand of Saul. ²He said:

"The LORD is my rock, my fortress
   and my deliverer;
³ my God is my rock, in whom I
      take refuge,
   my shield and the horn *d* of my
      salvation.
He is my stronghold, my refuge
      and my savior—
   from violent men you save me.
⁴I call to the LORD, who is worthy
      of praise,
   and I am saved from my
      enemies.

⁵"The waves of death swirled about
      me;
   the torrents of destruction
      overwhelmed me.
⁶The cords of the grave *e* coiled
      around me;
   the snares of death confronted
      me.
⁷In my distress I called to the
      LORD;
   I called out to my God.
From his temple he heard my
      voice;
   my cry came to his ears.

⁸"The earth trembled and quaked,
   the foundations of the heavens *f*
      shook;
   they trembled because he was
      angry.
⁹Smoke rose from his nostrils;
   consuming fire came from his
      mouth,
   burning coals blazed out of it.
¹⁰He parted the heavens and came
      down;
   dark clouds were under his
      feet.
¹¹He mounted the cherubim and
      flew;

---

a16 That is, about 7 1/2 pounds (about 3.5 kilograms)   *b19* Or *son of Jair the weaver*
c19 Hebrew and Septuagint; 1 Chron. 20:5 *son of Jair killed Lahmi the brother of Goliath*
d3 Horn here symbolizes strength.   *e6* Hebrew *Sheol*   *f8* Hebrew; Vulgate and Syriac (see also Psalm 18:7) *mountains*

he soared[a] on the wings of the
    wind.
12He made darkness his canopy
    around him—
  the dark[b] rain clouds of the
    sky.
13Out of the brightness of his
    presence
  bolts of lightning blazed forth.
14The LORD thundered from
    heaven;
  the voice of the Most High
    resounded.
15He shot arrows and scattered the
    enemies,
  bolts of lightning and routed
    them.
16The valleys of the sea were
    exposed
  and the foundations of the earth
    laid bare
at the rebuke of the LORD,
  at the blast of breath from his
    nostrils.

17"He reached down from on high
    and took hold of me;
  he drew me out of deep waters.
18He rescued me from my powerful
    enemy,
  from my foes, who were too
    strong for me.
19They confronted me in the day of
    my disaster,
  but the LORD was my support.
20He brought me out into a
    spacious place;
  he rescued me because he
    delighted in me.

21"The LORD has dealt with me
    according to my
    righteousness;
  according to the cleanness of my
    hands he has rewarded me.
22For I have kept the ways of the
    LORD;
  I have not done evil by turning
    from my God.
23All his laws are before me;

I have not turned away from
    his decrees.
24I have been blameless before him
  and have kept myself from sin.
25The LORD has rewarded me
    according to my
    righteousness,
  according to my cleanness[c] in
    his sight.

❓DID YOU KNOW?   22:1

What is another name for a song of praise?

A song of praise can also be
called a psalm. David wrote many
of the psalms in our Bible. His most
famous psalm is Psalm 23, where
he says "The LORD is my shepherd."

26"To the faithful you show yourself
    faithful,
  to the blameless you show
    yourself blameless,
27to the pure you show yourself
    pure,
  but to the crooked you show
    yourself shrewd.
28You save the humble,
  but your eyes are on the
    haughty to bring them low.
29You are my lamp, O LORD;
  the LORD turns my darkness
    into light.
30With your help I can advance
    against a troop[d];
  with my God I can scale a wall.

31"As for God, his way is perfect;
  the word of the LORD is
    flawless.
He is a shield
  for all who take refuge in him.
32For who is God besides the LORD?
  And who is the Rock except our
    God?
33It is God who arms me with
    strength[e]

---

a11 Many Hebrew manuscripts (see also Psalm 18:10); most Hebrew manuscripts *appeared*
b12 Septuagint and Vulgate (see also Psalm 18:11); Hebrew *massed*   c25 Hebrew; Septuagint
and Vulgate (see also Psalm 18:24) *to the cleanness of my hands*   d30 Or *can run through a*
barricade   e33 Dead Sea Scrolls, some Septuagint manuscripts, Vulgate and Syriac (see also
Psalm 18:32); Masoretic Text *who is my strong refuge*

and makes my way perfect.
³⁴He makes my feet like the feet of
a deer;
he enables me to stand on the
heights.
³⁵He trains my hands for battle;
my arms can bend a bow of
bronze.
³⁶You give me your shield of
victory;
you stoop down to make me
great.
³⁷You broaden the path beneath
me,
so that my ankles do not turn.

³⁸"I pursued my enemies and
crushed them;
I did not turn back till they
were destroyed.
³⁹I crushed them completely, and
they could not rise;
they fell beneath my feet.
⁴⁰You armed me with strength for
battle;
you made my adversaries bow
at my feet.
⁴¹You made my enemies turn their
backs in flight,
and I destroyed my foes.
⁴²They cried for help, but there was
no one to save them—
to the LORD, but he did not
answer.
⁴³I beat them as fine as the dust of
the earth;
I pounded and trampled them
like mud in the streets.

⁴⁴"You have delivered me from the
attacks of my people;
you have preserved me as the
head of nations.
People I did not know are subject
to me,
⁴⁵ and foreigners come cringing to
me;
as soon as they hear me, they
obey me.
⁴⁶They all lose heart;
they come trembling*ᵃ* from
their strongholds.

⁴⁷"The LORD lives! Praise be to my
Rock!
Exalted be God, the Rock, my
Savior!
⁴⁸He is the God who avenges me,
who puts the nations under me,
⁴⁹ who sets me free from my
enemies.
You exalted me above my foes;
from violent men you rescued
me.
⁵⁰Therefore I will praise you,
O LORD, among the nations;
I will sing praises to your
name.
⁵¹He gives his king great victories;
he shows unfailing kindness to
his anointed,
to David and his descendants
forever."

The Last Words of David

23 These are the last words of
David:

ᵃ46 Some Septuagint manuscripts and Vulgate (see also Psalm 18:45); Masoretic Text *they arm themselves.*

▌ET'S LIVE IT!   2 Samuel 22:47–51

PRAISE GOD WITH POEMS ➠ David wrote many psalms, or poems, to praise God. 2 Samuel 22 is one of his praise poems. In his poem, David listed many of the good things God had done for him. He praised and thanked God for the good things God had brought into his life.
You can write a praise poem, too. Use 2 Samuel 22:47–51 as an example. Your praise poem could have 5 verses instead of 50.
Have verse 1 of your poem praise God.
Have verses 2 and 3 tell something God does for you.
Have verse 4 tell how you will praise God.
Have verse 5 tell something else God does for you.

"The oracle of David son of Jesse,
　the oracle of the man exalted by
　　the Most High,
the man anointed by the God of
　　Jacob,
　Israel's singer of songs[a]:

[2]"The Spirit of the LORD spoke
　　through me;
　his word was on my tongue.
[3]The God of Israel spoke,
　the Rock of Israel said to me:
'When one rules over men in
　　righteousness,
　when he rules in the fear of
　　God,
[4]he is like the light of morning at
　　sunrise
on a cloudless morning,
like the brightness after rain
　that brings the grass from the
　　earth.'

[5]"Is not my house right with God?
Has he not made with me an
　　everlasting covenant,
　arranged and secured in every
　　part?
Will he not bring to fruition my
　　salvation
　and grant me my every desire?
[6]But evil men are all to be cast
　　aside like thorns,
　which are not gathered with the
　　hand.
[7]Whoever touches thorns
　uses a tool of iron or the shaft
　　of a spear;
　they are burned up where they
　　lie."

David's Mighty Men

[8]These are the names of David's
mighty men:

Josheb-Basshebeth,[b] a Tahkemo-
nite,[c] was chief of the Three; he
raised his spear against eight hundred men, whom he killed[d] in one encounter.
[9]Next to him was Eleazar son of
Dodai the Ahohite. As one of the
three mighty men, he was with David
when they taunted the Philistines
gathered ₍at Pas Dammim₎[e] for battle. Then the men of Israel retreated,
[10]but he stood his ground and struck
down the Philistines till his hand
grew tired and froze to the sword. The
LORD brought about a great victory
that day. The troops returned to Eleazar, but only to strip the dead.

[11]Next to him was Shammah son of
Agee the Hararite. When the Philistines banded together at a place
where there was a field full of lentils,
Israel's troops fled from them. [12]But
Shammah took his stand in the middle of the field. He defended it and
struck the Philistines down, and the
LORD brought about a great victory.

[13]During harvest time, three of the
thirty chief men came down to David
at the cave of Adullam, while a band
of Philistines was encamped in the
Valley of Rephaim. [14]At that time
David was in the stronghold, and the
Philistine garrison was at Bethlehem. [15]David longed for water and
said, "Oh, that someone would get me
a drink of water from the well near
the gate of Bethlehem!" [16]So the
three mighty men broke through the
Philistine lines, drew water from the
well near the gate of Bethlehem and
carried it back to David. But he refused to drink it; instead, he poured it
out before the LORD. [17]"Far be it from
me, O LORD, to do this!" he said. "Is it
not the blood of men who went at the
risk of their lives?" And David would
not drink it.

Such were the exploits of the three
mighty men.

[18]Abishai the brother of Joab son of
Zeruiah was chief of the Three.[f] He
raised his spear against three hundred men, whom he killed, and so he
became as famous as the Three.
[19]Was he not held in greater honor

---

[a]1 Or *Israel's beloved singer*　　[b]8 Hebrew; some Septuagint manuscripts suggest *Ish-Bosheth*, that
is, *Esh-Baal* (see also 1 Chron. 11:11 *Jashobeam*).　　[c]8 Probably a variant of *Hacmonite* (see
1 Chron. 11:11)　　[d]8 Some Septuagint manuscripts (see also 1 Chron. 11:11); Hebrew and other
Septuagint manuscripts *Three; it was Adino the Eznite who killed eight hundred men*　　[e]9 See
1 Chron. 11:13; Hebrew *gathered there.*　　[f]18 Most Hebrew manuscripts (see also 1 Chron. 11:20);
two Hebrew manuscripts and Syriac *Thirty*

than the Three? He became their commander, even though he was not included among them.

? DID YOU KNOW?　　23:8

What were David's mighty men?

David's mighty men were war heroes. Each of the mighty men was a famous fighter who had won some great victory over Israel's enemies. Some of these heroes and their acts are highlighted in 2 Samuel 23.

---

[20]Benaiah son of Jehoiada was a valiant fighter from Kabzeel, who performed great exploits. He struck down two of Moab's best men. He also went down into a pit on a snowy day and killed a lion. [21]And he struck down a huge Egyptian. Although the Egyptian had a spear in his hand, Benaiah went against him with a club. He snatched the spear from the Egyptian's hand and killed him with his own spear. [22]Such were the exploits of Benaiah son of Jehoiada; he too was as famous as the three mighty men. [23]He was held in greater honor than any of the Thirty, but he was not included among the Three. And David put him in charge of his bodyguard.

[24]Among the Thirty were:
Asahel the brother of Joab,
Elhanan son of Dodo from Bethlehem,
[25]Shammah the Harodite,
Elika the Harodite,
[26]Helez the Paltite,
Ira son of Ikkesh from Tekoa,
[27]Abiezer from Anathoth,
Mebunnai[a] the Hushathite,
[28]Zalmon the Ahohite,
Maharai the Netophathite,
[29]Heled[b] son of Baanah the Netophathite,
Ithai son of Ribai from Gibeah in Benjamin,
[30]Benaiah the Pirathonite,
Hiddai[c] from the ravines of Gaash,
[31]Abi-Albon the Arbathite,
Azmaveth the Barhumite,
[32]Eliahba the Shaalbonite,
the sons of Jashen,
Jonathan [33]son of[d] Shammah the Hararite,
Ahiam son of Sharar[e] the Hararite,
[34]Eliphelet son of Ahasbai the Maacathite,
Eliam son of Ahithophel the Gilonite,
[35]Hezro the Carmelite,
Paarai the Arbite,
[36]Igal son of Nathan from Zobah,
the son of Hagri,[f]
[37]Zelek the Ammonite,
Naharai the Beerothite, the armor-bearer of Joab son of Zeruiah,
[38]Ira the Ithrite,
Gareb the Ithrite
[39]and Uriah the Hittite.
There were thirty-seven in all.

David Counts the Fighting Men

24 Again the anger of the LORD burned against Israel, and he incited David against them, saying, "Go and take a census of Israel and Judah."

[2]So the king said to Joab and the army commanders[g] with him, "Go throughout the tribes of Israel from Dan to Beersheba and enroll the fighting men, so that I may know how many there are."

[3]But Joab replied to the king, "May the LORD your God multiply the troops a hundred times over, and may

---

[a]27 Hebrew; some Septuagint manuscripts (see also 1 Chron. 11:29) *Sibbecai*　　[b]29 Some Hebrew manuscripts and Vulgate (see also 1 Chron. 11:30); most Hebrew manuscripts *Heleb*　　[c]30 Hebrew; some Septuagint manuscripts (see also 1 Chron. 11:32) *Hurai*　　[d]33 Some Septuagint manuscripts (see also 1 Chron. 11:34); Hebrew does not have *son of*.　　[e]33 Hebrew; some Septuagint manuscripts (see also 1 Chron. 11:35) *Sacar*　　[f]36 Some Septuagint manuscripts (see also 1 Chron. 11:38); Hebrew *Haggadi*　　[g]2 Septuagint (see also verse 4 and 1 Chron. 21:2); Hebrew *Joab the army commander*

the eyes of my lord the king see it. But why does my lord the king want to do such a thing?"

⁴The king's word, however, overruled Joab and the army commanders; so they left the presence of the king to enroll the fighting men of Israel.

⁵After crossing the Jordan, they camped near Aroer, south of the town in the gorge, and then went through Gad and on to Jazer. ⁶They went to Gilead and the region of Tahtim Hodshi, and on to Dan Jaan and around toward Sidon. ⁷Then they went toward the fortress of Tyre and all the towns of the Hivites and Canaanites. Finally, they went on to Beersheba in the Negev of Judah.

⁸After they had gone through the entire land, they came back to Jerusalem at the end of nine months and twenty days.

⁹Joab reported the number of the fighting men to the king: In Israel there were eight hundred thousand able-bodied men who could handle a sword, and in Judah five hundred thousand.

❓DID YOU KNOW?   24:3

Why was it wrong for David to count his army?

The Bible does not say why. Many think that this was a sign of pride in how large David's army had grown. Others think David began to rely on military might instead of on the Lord. But even Joab knew it was wrong and tried to keep David from ordering the census.

¹⁰David was conscience-stricken after he had counted the fighting men, and he said to the LORD, "I have sinned greatly in what I have done. Now, O LORD, I beg you, take away the guilt of your servant. I have done a very foolish thing."

¹¹Before David got up the next morning, the word of the LORD had come to Gad the prophet, David's seer: ¹²"Go and tell David, 'This is what the LORD says: I am giving you three options. Choose one of them for me to carry out against you.'"

¹³So Gad went to David and said to him, "Shall there come upon you threeᵃ years of famine in your land? Or three months of fleeing from your enemies while they pursue you? Or three days of plague in your land? Now then, think it over and decide how I should answer the one who sent me."

¹⁴David said to Gad, "I am in deep distress. Let us fall into the hands of the LORD, for his mercy is great; but do not let me fall into the hands of men."

¹⁵So the LORD sent a plague on Israel from that morning until the end of the time designated, and seventy thousand of the people from Dan to Beersheba died. ¹⁶When the angel stretched out his hand to destroy Jerusalem, the LORD was grieved because of the calamity and said to the angel who was afflicting the people, "Enough! Withdraw your hand." The angel of the LORD was then at the threshing floor of Araunah the Jebusite.

¹⁷When David saw the angel who was striking down the people, he said to the LORD, "I am the one who has sinned and done wrong. These are but sheep. What have they done? Let your hand fall upon me and my family."

David Builds an Altar

¹⁸On that day Gad went to David and said to him, "Go up and build an altar to the LORD on the threshing floor of Araunah the Jebusite." ¹⁹So David went up, as the LORD had commanded through Gad. ²⁰When Araunah looked and saw the king and his men coming toward him, he went out

ᵃ13 Septuagint (see also 1 Chron. 21:12); Hebrew *seven*

and bowed down before the king with his face to the ground. ²¹Araunah said, "Why has my lord the king come to his servant?"

"To buy your threshing floor," David answered, "so I can build an altar to the LORD, that the plague on the people may be stopped."

²²Araunah said to David, "Let my lord the king take whatever pleases him and offer it up. Here are oxen for the burnt offering, and here are threshing sledges and ox yokes for the wood. ²³O king, Araunah gives all this to the king." Araunah also said

to him, "May the LORD your God accept you."

²⁴But the king replied to Araunah, "No, I insist on paying you for it. I will not sacrifice to the LORD my God burnt offerings that cost me nothing."

So David bought the threshing floor and the oxen and paid fifty shekels*a* of silver for them. ²⁵David built an altar to the LORD there and sacrificed burnt offerings and fellowship offerings.*b* Then the LORD answered prayer in behalf of the land, and the plague on Israel was stopped.

a24 That is, about 1 1/4 pounds (about 0.6 kilogram)   *b25* Traditionally *peace offerings*

ET'S LIVE IT!   2 Samuel 24:18–25

USING YOUR OWN MONEY ➡ David wanted some land where he could build an altar and offer sacrifices to God. Read 2 Samuel 24:18–25 and find out why David insisted on paying for the land and animals himself.

What do you think would please God most? 1. To use your mom's or dad's money in your Sunday school offering. 2. To use allowance money in your offering. 3. To use money you earn yourself in your offering.

Talk to your mom or dad about your choice, and decide with them what to do.

1 KINGS

WHO WROTE THIS BOOK?

The author of this book is unknown.

WHY WAS THIS BOOK WRITTEN?

The book of 1 Kings shows how the kings of Israel and Judah obeyed or disobeyed God.

WHAT HAPPENS IN THIS BOOK?

Solomon rules for forty years. When he dies his kingdom is divided. The northern ten tribes are called Israel. The southern two tribes are called Judah.

WHAT DO WE LEARN ABOUT GOD IN THIS BOOK?

God sends prophets to turn disobedient people back to him.

WHO IS IMPORTANT IN THIS BOOK?

The important people in this book are Solomon, Elijah, and evil King Ahab of Israel.

WHEN DID THIS HAPPEN?

The stories in this book took place between 970 and 853 B.C.

WHERE DID THIS HAPPEN?

The events happened in Israel and Judah.

WHAT ARE SOME OF THE STORIES IN THIS BOOK?

Solomon asks for wisdom.	1 Kings 3
Solomon builds the temple.	1 Kings 6
Solomon dedicates the temple.	1 Kings 8
A queen visits Solomon.	1 Kings 10
A prophet warns Jeroboam.	1 Kings 13
Elijah is fed by ravens.	1 Kings 17
Elijah on Mount Carmel.	1 Kings 18
Elijah runs away.	1 Kings 19
Ahab steals a vineyard.	1 Kings 21
Ahab dies in battle.	1 Kings 22

Adonijah Sets Himself Up as King

1 When King David was old and well advanced in years, he could not keep warm even when they put covers over him. ²So his servants said to him, "Let us look for a young virgin to attend the king and take care of him. She can lie beside him so that our lord the king may keep warm."

³Then they searched throughout Israel for a beautiful girl and found Abishag, a Shunammite, and brought her to the king. ⁴The girl was very beautiful; she took care of the king and waited on him, but the king had no intimate relations with her.

⁵Now Adonijah, whose mother was Haggith, put himself forward and said, "I will be king." So he got chariots and horses*a* ready, with fifty men to run ahead of him. ⁶(His father had never interfered with him by asking, "Why do you behave as you do?" He was also very handsome and was born next after Absalom.)

? DID YOU KNOW?   1:5

Who was Adonijah?

Adonijah was a son of David. He tried to have himself crowned king. However, David decided to make his son Solomon king instead.

---

⁷Adonijah conferred with Joab son of Zeruiah and with Abiathar the priest, and they gave him their support. ⁸But Zadok the priest, Benaiah son of Jehoiada, Nathan the prophet, Shimei and Rei*b* and David's special guard did not join Adonijah.

⁹Adonijah then sacrificed sheep, cattle and fattened calves at the Stone of Zoheleth near En Rogel. He invited all his brothers, the king's sons, and all the men of Judah who were royal officials, ¹⁰but he did not invite Nathan the prophet or Bena-

iah or the special guard or his brother Solomon.

¹¹Then Nathan asked Bathsheba, Solomon's mother, "Have you not heard that Adonijah, the son of Haggith, has become king without our lord David's knowing it? ¹²Now then, let me advise you how you can save your own life and the life of your son Solomon. ¹³Go in to King David and say to him, 'My lord the king, did you not swear to me your servant: "Surely Solomon your son shall be king after me, and he will sit on my throne"? Why then has Adonijah become king?' ¹⁴While you are still there talking to the king, I will come in and confirm what you have said."

¹⁵So Bathsheba went to see the aged king in his room, where Abishag the Shunammite was attending him. ¹⁶Bathsheba bowed low and knelt before the king.

"What is it you want?" the king asked.

¹⁷She said to him, "My lord, you yourself swore to me your servant by the LORD your God: 'Solomon your son shall be king after me, and he will sit on my throne.' ¹⁸But now Adonijah has become king, and you, my lord the king, do not know about it. ¹⁹He has sacrificed great numbers of cattle, fattened calves, and sheep, and has invited all the king's sons, Abiathar the priest and Joab the commander of the army, but he has not invited Solomon your servant. ²⁰My lord the king, the eyes of all Israel are on you, to learn from you who will sit on the throne of my lord the king after him. ²¹Otherwise, as soon as my lord the king is laid to rest with his fathers, I and my son Solomon will be treated as criminals."

²²While she was still speaking with the king, Nathan the prophet arrived. ²³And they told the king, "Nathan the prophet is here." So he went before the king and bowed with his face to the ground.

²⁴Nathan said, "Have you, my lord the king, declared that Adonijah

---

a5 Or *charioteers*   *b8* Or *and his friends*

shall be king after you, and that he will sit on your throne? ²⁵Today he has gone down and sacrificed great numbers of cattle, fattened calves, and sheep. He has invited all the king's sons, the commanders of the army and Abiathar the priest. Right now they are eating and drinking with him and saying, 'Long live King Adonijah!' ²⁶But me your servant, and Zadok the priest, and Benaiah son of Jehoiada, and your servant Solomon he did not invite. ²⁷Is this something my lord the king has done without letting his servants know who should sit on the throne of my lord the king after him?"

David Makes Solomon King

²⁸Then King David said, "Call in Bathsheba." So she came into the king's presence and stood before him. ²⁹The king then took an oath: "As surely as the LORD lives, who has delivered me out of every trouble, ³⁰I will surely carry out today what I swore to you by the LORD, the God of Israel: Solomon your son shall be king after me, and he will sit on my throne in my place."

³¹Then Bathsheba bowed low with her face to the ground and, kneeling before the king, said, "May my lord King David live forever!"

³²King David said, "Call in Zadok the priest, Nathan the prophet and Benaiah son of Jehoiada." When they came before the king, ³³he said to them: "Take your lord's servants with you and set Solomon my son on my own mule and take him down to Gihon. ³⁴There have Zadok the priest and Nathan the prophet anoint him king over Israel. Blow the trumpet and shout, 'Long live King Solomon!' ³⁵Then you are to go up with him, and he is to come and sit on my throne and reign in my place. I have appointed him ruler over Israel and Judah."

³⁶Benaiah son of Jehoiada answered the king, "Amen! May the LORD, the God of my lord the king, so declare it. ³⁷As the LORD was with my lord the king, so may he be with Solo-

mon to make his throne even greater than the throne of my lord King David!"

³⁸So Zadok the priest, Nathan the prophet, Benaiah son of Jehoiada, the Kerethites and the Pelethites went down and put Solomon on King David's mule and escorted him to Gihon. ³⁹Zadok the priest took the horn of oil from the sacred tent and anointed Solomon. Then they sounded the trumpet and all the people shouted, "Long live King Solomon!" ⁴⁰And all the people went up after him, playing flutes and rejoicing greatly, so that the ground shook with the sound.

⁴¹Adonijah and all the guests who were with him heard it as they were finishing their feast. On hearing the sound of the trumpet, Joab asked, "What's the meaning of all the noise in the city?"

⁴²Even as he was speaking, Jonathan son of Abiathar the priest arrived. Adonijah said, "Come in. A worthy man like you must be bringing good news."

⁴³"Not at all!" Jonathan answered. "Our lord King David has made Solomon king. ⁴⁴The king has sent with him Zadok the priest, Nathan the prophet, Benaiah son of Jehoiada, the Kerethites and the Pelethites, and they have put him on the king's mule, ⁴⁵and Zadok the priest and Nathan the prophet have anointed him king at Gihon. From there they have gone up cheering, and the city resounds with it. That's the noise you hear. ⁴⁶Moreover, Solomon has taken his seat on the royal throne. ⁴⁷Also, the royal officials have come to congratulate our lord King David, saying, 'May your God make Solomon's name more famous than yours and his throne greater than yours!' And the king bowed in worship on his bed ⁴⁸and said, 'Praise be to the LORD, the God of Israel, who has allowed my eyes to see a successor on my throne today.'"

⁴⁹At this, all Adonijah's guests rose in alarm and dispersed. ⁵⁰But Adonijah, in fear of Solomon, went and took hold of the horns of the altar. ⁵¹Then

Solomon was told, "Adonijah is afraid of King Solomon and is clinging to the horns of the altar. He says, 'Let King Solomon swear to me today that he will not put his servant to death with the sword.'"

⁵²Solomon replied, "If he shows himself to be a worthy man, not a hair of his head will fall to the ground; but if evil is found in him, he will die." ⁵³Then King Solomon sent men, and they brought him down from the altar. And Adonijah came and bowed down to King Solomon, and Solomon said, "Go to your home."

David's Charge to Solomon

2 When the time drew near for David to die, he gave a charge to Solomon his son.

²"I am about to go the way of all the earth," he said. "So be strong, show yourself a man, ³and observe what the LORD your God requires: Walk in his ways, and keep his decrees and commands, his laws and requirements, as written in the Law of Moses, so that you may prosper in all you do and wherever you go, ⁴and that the LORD may keep his promise to me: 'If your descendants watch how they live, and if they walk faithfully before me with all their heart and soul, you will never fail to have a man on the throne of Israel.'

⁵"Now you yourself know what Joab son of Zeruiah did to me—what he did to the two commanders of Israel's armies, Abner son of Ner and Amasa son of Jether. He killed them, shedding their blood in peacetime as

a6 Hebrew *Sheol*; also in verse 9

if in battle, and with that blood stained the belt around his waist and the sandals on his feet. ⁶Deal with him according to your wisdom, but do not let his gray head go down to the grave*ᵃ* in peace.

⁷"But show kindness to the sons of Barzillai of Gilead and let them be among those who eat at your table. They stood by me when I fled from your brother Absalom.

⁸"And remember, you have with you Shimei son of Gera, the Benjamite from Bahurim, who called down bitter curses on me the day I went to Mahanaim. When he came down to meet me at the Jordan, I swore to him by the LORD: 'I will not put you to death by the sword.' ⁹But now, do not consider him innocent. You are a man of wisdom; you will know what to do to him. Bring his gray head down to the grave in blood."

¹⁰Then David rested with his fathers and was buried in the City of David. ¹¹He had reigned forty years over Israel—seven years in Hebron and thirty-three in Jerusalem. ¹²So Solomon sat on the throne of his father David, and his rule was firmly established.

Solomon's Throne Established

¹³Now Adonijah, the son of Haggith, went to Bathsheba, Solomon's mother. Bathsheba asked him, "Do you come peacefully?"

He answered, "Yes, peacefully." ¹⁴Then he added, "I have something to say to you."

"You may say it," she replied.

LET'S LIVE IT! 1 Kings 2:1–4

WHAT A FATHER WANTS HIS CHILD TO REMEMBER ➡ When David grew old he gave his son Solomon a charge. "Charge" means advice. David told Solomon the really important things he wanted him to remember. Read 1 Kings 2:1–4 and write down things David wanted Solomon to remember.

Ask your mom or dad to give you a "charge," like David gave Solomon, so you will know what they want you to remember all your life.

15"As you know," he said, "the kingdom was mine. All Israel looked to me as their king. But things changed, and the kingdom has gone to my brother; for it has come to him from the LORD. 16Now I have one request to make of you. Do not refuse me."

"You may make it," she said.

17So he continued, "Please ask King Solomon—he will not refuse you—to give me Abishag the Shunammite as my wife."

18"Very well," Bathsheba replied, "I will speak to the king for you."

19When Bathsheba went to King Solomon to speak to him for Adonijah, the king stood up to meet her, bowed down to her and sat down on his throne. He had a throne brought for the king's mother, and she sat down at his right hand.

20"I have one small request to make of you," she said. "Do not refuse me."

The king replied, "Make it, my mother; I will not refuse you."

21So she said, "Let Abishag the Shunammite be given in marriage to your brother Adonijah."

22King Solomon answered his mother, "Why do you request Abishag the Shunammite for Adonijah? You might as well request the kingdom for him—after all, he is my older brother—yes, for him and for Abiathar the priest and Joab son of Zeruiah!"

?DID YOU KNOW?   2:17

What did Adonijah's request to marry Abishag mean?

Abishag was a girl who had taken care of King David. The man who married her would have a claim to the throne of Israel. Adonijah's request showed that he would try to steal the throne that God had given to Solomon.

23Then King Solomon swore by the LORD: "May God deal with me, be it ever so severely, if Adonijah does not pay with his life for this request! 24And now, as surely as the LORD lives—he who has established me securely on the throne of my father David and has founded a dynasty for me as he promised—Adonijah shall be put to death today!" 25So King Solomon gave orders to Benaiah son of Jehoiada, and he struck down Adonijah and he died.

26To Abiathar the priest the king said, "Go back to your fields in Anathoth. You deserve to die, but I will not put you to death now, because you carried the ark of the Sovereign LORD before my father David and shared all my father's hardships." 27So Solomon removed Abiathar from the priesthood of the LORD, fulfilling the word the LORD had spoken at Shiloh about the house of Eli.

28When the news reached Joab, who had conspired with Adonijah though not with Absalom, he fled to the tent of the LORD and took hold of the horns of the altar. 29King Solomon was told that Joab had fled to the tent of the LORD and was beside the altar. Then Solomon ordered Benaiah son of Jehoiada, "Go, strike him down!"

30So Benaiah entered the tent of the LORD and said to Joab, "The king says, 'Come out!'"

But he answered, "No, I will die here."

Benaiah reported to the king, "This is how Joab answered me."

31Then the king commanded Benaiah, "Do as he says. Strike him down and bury him, and so clear me and my father's house of the guilt of the innocent blood that Joab shed. 32The LORD will repay him for the blood he shed, because without the knowledge of my father David he attacked two men and killed them with the sword. Both of them—Abner son of Ner, commander of Israel's army, and Amasa son of Jether, commander of Judah's army—were better men and more upright than he. 33May the guilt of their blood rest on the head of Joab and his descendants forever. But on David and his descendants, his house and his throne, may there be the LORD's peace forever."

³⁴So Benaiah son of Jehoiada went up and struck down Joab and killed him, and he was buried on his own land*ᵃ* in the desert. ³⁵The king put Benaiah son of Jehoiada over the army in Joab's position and replaced Abiathar with Zadok the priest.

³⁶Then the king sent for Shimei and said to him, "Build yourself a house in Jerusalem and live there, but do not go anywhere else. ³⁷The day you leave and cross the Kidron Valley, you can be sure you will die; your blood will be on your own head."

³⁸Shimei answered the king, "What you say is good. Your servant will do as my lord the king has said." And Shimei stayed in Jerusalem for a long time.

³⁹But three years later, two of Shimei's slaves ran off to Achish son of Maacah, king of Gath, and Shimei was told, "Your slaves are in Gath." ⁴⁰At this, he saddled his donkey and went to Achish at Gath in search of his slaves. So Shimei went away and brought the slaves back from Gath.

⁴¹When Solomon was told that Shimei had gone from Jerusalem to Gath and had returned, ⁴²the king summoned Shimei and said to him, "Did I not make you swear by the LORD and warn you, 'On the day you leave to go anywhere else, you can be sure you will die'? At that time you said to me, 'What you say is good. I will obey.' ⁴³Why then did you not keep your oath to the LORD and obey the command I gave you?"

⁴⁴The king also said to Shimei, "You know in your heart all the wrong you did to my father David. Now the LORD will repay you for your wrongdoing. ⁴⁵But King Solomon will be blessed, and David's throne will remain secure before the LORD forever."

⁴⁶Then the king gave the order to Benaiah son of Jehoiada, and he went out and struck Shimei down and killed him.

ᵃ34 Or buried in his tomb

The kingdom was now firmly established in Solomon's hands.

❓DID YOU KNOW?   2:36

Who was Shimei?

Shimei was a man who had cursed David as he ran from Jerusalem when Absalom rebelled. David had not punished Shimei, but Solomon did. Solomon ordered Shimei to stay in Jerusalem. 1 Kings 2 tells what happened when Shimei disobeyed King Solomon.

Solomon Asks for Wisdom

3 Solomon made an alliance with Pharaoh king of Egypt and married his daughter. He brought her to the City of David until he finished building his palace and the temple of the LORD, and the wall around Jerusalem. ²The people, however, were still sacrificing at the high places, because a temple had not yet been built for the Name of the LORD. ³Solomon showed his love for the LORD by walking according to the statutes of his father David, except that he offered sacrifices and burned incense on the high places.

⁴The king went to Gibeon to offer sacrifices, for that was the most important high place, and Solomon offered a thousand burnt offerings on that altar. ⁵At Gibeon the LORD appeared to Solomon during the night in a dream, and God said, "Ask for whatever you want me to give you."

⁶Solomon answered, "You have shown great kindness to your servant, my father David, because he was faithful to you and righteous and upright in heart. You have continued this great kindness to him and have given him a son to sit on his throne this very day.

⁷"Now, O LORD my God, you have made your servant king in place of

my father David. But I am only a little child and do not know how to carry out my duties. ⁸Your servant is here among the people you have chosen, a great people, too numerous to count or number. ⁹So give your servant a discerning heart to govern your people and to distinguish between right and wrong. For who is able to govern this great people of yours?"

¹⁰The Lord was pleased that Solomon had asked for this. ¹¹So God said to him, "Since you have asked for this and not for long life or wealth for yourself, nor have asked for the death of your enemies but for discernment in administering justice, ¹²I will do what you have asked. I will give you a wise and discerning heart, so that there will never have been anyone like you, nor will there ever be. ¹³Moreover, I will give you what you have not asked for—both riches and honor—so that in your lifetime you will have no equal among kings. ¹⁴And if you walk in my ways and obey my statutes and commands as David your father did, I will give you a long life." ¹⁵Then Solomon awoke —and he realized it had been a dream.

ᵃ15 Traditionally *peace offerings*

He returned to Jerusalem, stood before the ark of the Lord's covenant and sacrificed burnt offerings and fellowship offerings.ᵃ Then he gave a feast for all his court.

A Wise Ruling

¹⁶Now two prostitutes came to the king and stood before him. ¹⁷One of them said, "My lord, this woman and I live in the same house. I had a baby while she was there with me. ¹⁸The third day after my child was born, this woman also had a baby. We were alone; there was no one in the house but the two of us.

¹⁹"During the night this woman's son died because she lay on him. ²⁰So she got up in the middle of the night and took my son from my side while I your servant was asleep. She put him by her breast and put her dead son by my breast. ²¹The next morning, I got up to nurse my son—and he was dead! But when I looked at him closely in the morning light, I saw that it wasn't the son I had borne."

²²The other woman said, "No! The living one is my son; the dead one is yours."

But the first one insisted, "No! The dead one is yours; the living one is

---

╲ET'S LIVE IT!   1 Kings 3:4–15

FOUR PRAYERS GOD WILL ANSWER ➡ God hears all our prayers. But God doesn't always answer yes. Read 1 Kings 3:4–15. Find out what Solomon prayed for.

Here are four prayers you can pray that are like Solomon's. Find the words below that best complete each prayer.

1. God, at school help me to _____ to be a good student.
2. God, as a son or daughter help me to _____ my parents.
3. God, as a brother or sister help me to be _____ to my brothers and sisters.
4. God, as a friend help me to _____ when I play with my friends.

a. obey   b. kind   c. study hard   d. take turns.

Write each prayer on a small piece of paper. Each day choose one and make that request part of your prayers for that day.

mine." And so they argued before the king.

²³The king said, "This one says, 'My son is alive and your son is dead,' while that one says, 'No! Your son is dead and mine is alive.'"

²⁴Then the king said, "Bring me a sword." So they brought a sword for the king. ²⁵He then gave an order: "Cut the living child in two and give half to one and half to the other."

²⁶The woman whose son was alive was filled with compassion for her son and said to the king, "Please, my lord, give her the living baby! Don't kill him!"

But the other said, "Neither I nor you shall have him. Cut him in two!"

²⁷Then the king gave his ruling: "Give the living baby to the first woman. Do not kill him; she is his mother."

²⁸When all Israel heard the verdict the king had given, they held the king in awe, because they saw that he had wisdom from God to administer justice.

Solomon's Officials and Governors

4 So King Solomon ruled over all Israel. ²And these were his chief officials:

Azariah son of Zadok—the priest;
³Elihoreph and Ahijah, sons of Shisha—secretaries;
Jehoshaphat son of Ahilud—recorder;
⁴Benaiah son of Jehoiada—commander in chief;
Zadok and Abiathar—priests;
⁵Azariah son of Nathan—in charge of the district officers;
Zabud son of Nathan—a priest and personal adviser to the king;
⁶Ahishar—in charge of the palace;
Adoniram son of Abda—in charge of forced labor.

⁷Solomon also had twelve district governors over all Israel, who supplied provisions for the king and the royal household. Each one had to provide supplies for one month in the year. ⁸These are their names:

Ben-Hur—in the hill country of Ephraim;
⁹Ben-Deker—in Makaz, Shaalbim, Beth Shemesh and Elon Bethhanan;
¹⁰Ben-Hesed—in Arubboth (Socoh and all the land of Hepher were his);
¹¹Ben-Abinadab—in Naphoth Dor ᵃ (he was married to Taphath daughter of Solomon);
¹²Baana son of Ahilud—in Taanach and Megiddo, and in all of Beth Shan next to Zarethan below Jezreel, from Beth Shan to Abel Meholah across to Jokmeam;
¹³Ben-Geber—in Ramoth Gilead (the settlements of Jair son of Manasseh in Gilead were his, as well as the district of Argob in Bashan and its sixty large walled cities with bronze gate bars);
¹⁴Ahinadab son of Iddo—in Mahanaim;
¹⁵Ahimaaz—in Naphtali (he had married Basemath daughter of Solomon);
¹⁶Baana son of Hushai—in Asher and in Aloth;
¹⁷Jehoshaphat son of Paruah—in Issachar;
¹⁸Shimei son of Ela—in Benjamin;
¹⁹Geber son of Uri—in Gilead (the country of Sihon king of the Amorites and the country of Og king of Bashan). He was the only governor over the district.

Solomon's Daily Provisions

²⁰The people of Judah and Israel were as numerous as the sand on the seashore; they ate, they drank and they were happy. ²¹And Solomon

ᵃ11 Or *in the heights of Dor*

ruled over all the kingdoms from the River[a] to the land of the Philistines, as far as the border of Egypt. These countries brought tribute and were Solomon's subjects all his life.

[22]Solomon's daily provisions were thirty cors[b] of fine flour and sixty cors[c] of meal, [23]ten head of stall-fed cattle, twenty of pasture-fed cattle and a hundred sheep and goats, as well as deer, gazelles, roebucks and choice fowl. [24]For he ruled over all the kingdoms west of the River, from Tiphsah to Gaza, and had peace on all sides. [25]During Solomon's lifetime Judah and Israel, from Dan to Beersheba, lived in safety, each man under his own vine and fig tree.

[26]Solomon had four[d] thousand stalls for chariot horses, and twelve thousand horses.[e]

[27]The district officers, each in his month, supplied provisions for King Solomon and all who came to the king's table. They saw to it that nothing was lacking. [28]They also brought to the proper place their quotas of barley and straw for the chariot horses and the other horses.

Solomon's Wisdom

[29]God gave Solomon wisdom and very great insight, and a breadth of understanding as measureless as the sand on the seashore. [30]Solomon's wisdom was greater than the wisdom of all the men of the East, and greater than all the wisdom of Egypt. [31]He was wiser than any other man, including Ethan the Ezrahite—wiser than Heman, Calcol and Darda, the sons of Mahol. And his fame spread to all the surrounding nations. [32]He spoke three thousand proverbs and his songs numbered a thousand and five. [33]He described plant life, from the cedar of Lebanon to the hyssop that grows out of walls. He also taught about animals and birds, reptiles and fish. [34]Men of all nations came to listen to Solomon's wisdom,

sent by all the kings of the world, who had heard of his wisdom.

❓DID YOU KNOW?   4:34

How wise was Solomon?

Solomon was very wise. He wrote many of the sayings found in the book of Proverbs. He studied plants and animals, built great buildings, and kept Israel at peace all forty years of his rule. Solomon also wrote the book of Ecclesiastes. That book tells us that wisdom isn't as important as remembering God and trying to please him.

Preparations for Building the Temple

5 When Hiram king of Tyre heard that Solomon had been anointed king to succeed his father David, he sent his envoys to Solomon, because he had always been on friendly terms with David. [2]Solomon sent back this message to Hiram:

[3]"You know that because of the wars waged against my father David from all sides, he could not build a temple for the Name of the LORD his God until the LORD put his enemies under his feet. [4]But now the LORD my God has given me rest on every side, and there is no adversary or disaster. [5]I intend, therefore, to build a temple for the Name of the LORD my God, as the LORD told my father David, when he said, 'Your son whom I will put on the throne in your place will build the temple for my Name.'

[6]"So give orders that cedars of Lebanon be cut for me. My men will work with yours, and I will pay you for your men whatever wages you set. You know that we

---

[a]21 That is, the Euphrates; also in verse 24   [b]22 That is, probably about 185 bushels (about 6.6 kiloliters)   [c]22 That is, probably about 375 bushels (about 13.2 kiloliters)   [d]26 Some Septuagint manuscripts (see also 2 Chron. 9:25); Hebrew *forty*   [e]26 Or *charioteers*

have no one so skilled in felling timber as the Sidonians."

7When Hiram heard Solomon's message, he was greatly pleased and said, "Praise be to the LORD today, for he has given David a wise son to rule over this great nation."

8So Hiram sent word to Solomon:

"I have received the message you sent me and will do all you want in providing the cedar and pine logs. 9My men will haul them down from Lebanon to the sea, and I will float them in rafts by sea to the place you specify. There I will separate them and you can take them away. And you are to grant my wish by providing food for my royal household."

10In this way Hiram kept Solomon supplied with all the cedar and pine logs he wanted, 11and Solomon gave Hiram twenty thousand cors*a* of wheat as food for his household, in addition to twenty thousand baths*b,c* of pressed olive oil. Solomon continued to do this for Hiram year after year. 12The LORD gave Solomon wisdom, just as he had promised him. There were peaceful relations between Hiram and Solomon, and the two of them made a treaty.

13King Solomon conscripted laborers from all Israel—thirty thousand men. 14He sent them off to Lebanon in shifts of ten thousand a month, so that they spent one month in Lebanon and two months at home. Adoniram was in charge of the forced labor. 15Solomon had seventy thousand carriers and eighty thousand stonecutters in the hills, 16as well as thirty-three hundred*d* foremen who supervised the project and directed the

workmen. 17At the king's command they removed from the quarry large blocks of quality stone to provide a foundation of dressed stone for the temple. 18The craftsmen of Solomon and Hiram and the men of Gebal*e* cut and prepared the timber and stone for the building of the temple.

Solomon Builds the Temple

6 In the four hundred and eightieth*f* year after the Israelites had come out of Egypt, in the fourth year of Solomon's reign over Israel, in the month of Ziv, the second month, he began to build the temple of the LORD.

2The temple that King Solomon built for the LORD was sixty cubits long, twenty wide and thirty high.*g* 3The portico at the front of the main hall of the temple extended the width of the temple, that is twenty cubits,*h* and projected ten cubits*i* from the front of the temple. 4He made narrow clerestory windows in the temple. 5Against the walls of the main hall and inner sanctuary he built a structure around the building, in which there were side rooms. 6The lowest floor was five cubits*j* wide, the middle floor six cubits*k* and the third floor seven.*l* He made offset ledges around the outside of the temple so that nothing would be inserted into the temple walls.

7In building the temple, only blocks dressed at the quarry were used, and no hammer, chisel or any other iron tool was heard at the temple site while it was being built.

8The entrance to the lowest*m* floor was on the south side of the temple; a stairway led up to the middle level and from there to the third. 9So he built the temple and completed it,

a11 That is, probably about 125,000 bushels (about 4,400 kiloliters)   *b11* Septuagint (see also 2 Chron. 2:10); Hebrew *twenty cors*   *c11* That is, about 115,000 gallons (about 440 kiloliters)
d16 Hebrew; some Septuagint manuscripts (see also 2 Chron. 2:2, 18) *thirty-six hundred*
e18 That is, Byblos   *f1* Hebrew; Septuagint *four hundred and fortieth*   *g2* That is, about 90 feet (about 27 meters) long and 30 feet (about 9 meters) wide and 45 feet (about 13.5 meters) high
h3 That is, about 30 feet (about 9 meters)   *i3* That is, about 15 feet (about 4.5 meters)
j6 That is, about 7 1/2 feet (about 2.3 meters); also in verses 10 and 24   *k6* That is, about 9 feet (about 2.7 meters)   *l6* That is, about 10 1/2 feet (about 3.1 meters)   *m8* Septuagint; Hebrew *middle*

roofing it with beams and cedar planks. ¹⁰And he built the side rooms all along the temple. The height of each was five cubits, and they were attached to the temple by beams of cedar.

¹¹The word of the LORD came to Solomon: ¹²"As for this temple you are building, if you follow my decrees, carry out my regulations and keep all my commands and obey them, I will fulfill through you the promise I gave to David your father. ¹³And I will live among the Israelites and will not abandon my people Israel."

¹⁴So Solomon built the temple and completed it. ¹⁵He lined its interior walls with cedar boards, paneling them from the floor of the temple to the ceiling, and covered the floor of the temple with planks of pine. ¹⁶He partitioned off twenty cubits*a* at the rear of the temple with cedar boards from floor to ceiling to form within the temple an inner sanctuary, the Most Holy Place. ¹⁷The main hall in front of this room was forty cubits*b* long. ¹⁸The inside of the temple was cedar, carved with gourds and open flowers. Everything was cedar; no stone was to be seen.

¹⁹He prepared the inner sanctuary within the temple to set the ark of the covenant of the LORD there. ²⁰The inner sanctuary was twenty cubits long, twenty wide and twenty high.*c* He overlaid the inside with pure gold, and he also overlaid the altar of cedar. ²¹Solomon covered the inside of the temple with pure gold, and he extended gold chains across the front of the inner sanctuary, which was overlaid with gold. ²²So he overlaid the whole interior with gold. He also overlaid with gold the altar that belonged to the inner sanctuary.

²³In the inner sanctuary he made a pair of cherubim of olive wood, each ten cubits*d* high. ²⁴One wing of the first cherub was five cubits long, and the other wing five cubits—ten cu-

bits from wing tip to wing tip. ²⁵The second cherub also measured ten cubits, for the two cherubim were identical in size and shape. ²⁶The height of each cherub was ten cubits. ²⁷He placed the cherubim inside the innermost room of the temple, with their wings spread out. The wing of one cherub touched one wall, while the wing of the other touched the other wall, and their wings touched each other in the middle of the room. ²⁸He overlaid the cherubim with gold.

²⁹On the walls all around the temple, in both the inner and outer rooms, he carved cherubim, palm trees and open flowers. ³⁰He also covered the floors of both the inner and outer rooms of the temple with gold.

³¹For the entrance of the inner sanctuary he made doors of olive wood with five-sided jambs. ³²And on the two olive wood doors he carved cherubim, palm trees and open flowers, and overlaid the cherubim and palm trees with beaten gold. ³³In the same way he made four-sided jambs of olive wood for the entrance to the main hall. ³⁴He also made two pine doors, each having two leaves that turned in sockets. ³⁵He carved cherubim, palm trees and open flowers on them and overlaid them with gold hammered evenly over the carvings.

³⁶And he built the inner courtyard of three courses of dressed stone and one course of trimmed cedar beams.

³⁷The foundation of the temple of the LORD was laid in the fourth year, in the month of Ziv. ³⁸In the eleventh year in the month of Bul, the eighth month, the temple was finished in all its details according to its specifications. He had spent seven years building it.

Solomon Builds His Palace

7 It took Solomon thirteen years, however, to complete the construction of his palace. ²He built the

a16 That is, about 30 feet (about 9 meters)   *b17* That is, about 60 feet (about 18 meters)
c20 That is, about 30 feet (about 9 meters) long, wide and high   *d23* That is, about 15 feet (about 4.5 meters)

Palace of the Forest of Lebanon a hundred cubits long, fifty wide and thirty high, *a* with four rows of cedar columns supporting trimmed cedar beams. ³It was roofed with cedar above the beams that rested on the columns—forty-five beams, fifteen to a row. ⁴Its windows were placed high in sets of three, facing each other. ⁵All the doorways had rectangular frames; they were in the front part in sets of three, facing each other. *b*

⁶He made a colonnade fifty cubits long and thirty wide. *c* In front of it was a portico, and in front of that were pillars and an overhanging roof.

⁷He built the throne hall, the Hall of Justice, where he was to judge, and he covered it with cedar from floor to ceiling. *d* ⁸And the palace in which he was to live, set farther back, was similar in design. Solomon also made a palace like this hall for Pharaoh's daughter, whom he had married.

⁹All these structures, from the outside to the great courtyard and from foundation to eaves, were made of blocks of high-grade stone cut to size and trimmed with a saw on their inner and outer faces. ¹⁰The foundations were laid with large stones of good quality, some measuring ten cubits *e* and some eight. *f* ¹¹Above were high-grade stones, cut to size, and cedar beams. ¹²The great courtyard was surrounded by a wall of three courses of dressed stone and one course of trimmed cedar beams, as was the inner courtyard of the temple of the LORD with its portico.

The Temple's Furnishings

¹³King Solomon sent to Tyre and brought Huram, *g* ¹⁴whose mother was a widow from the tribe of Naphtali and whose father was a man of Tyre and a craftsman in bronze. Huram was highly skilled and experienced in all kinds of bronze work. He came to King Solomon and did all the work assigned to him.

¹⁵He cast two bronze pillars, each eighteen cubits high and twelve cu-

---

*a*2 That is, about 150 feet (about 46 meters) long, 75 feet (about 23 meters) wide and 45 feet (about 13.5 meters) high   *b*5 The meaning of the Hebrew for this verse is uncertain.   *c*6 That is, about 75 feet (about 23 meters) long and 45 feet (about 13.5 meters) wide   *d*7 Vulgate and Syriac; Hebrew *floor*   *e*10 That is, about 15 feet (about 4.5 meters)   *f*10 That is, about 12 feet (about 3.6 meters)   *g*13 Hebrew *Hiram,* a variant of *Huram*; also in verses 40 and 45

Life in Bible Times

SOLOMON'S TEMPLE

Solomon built the temple in Jerusalem and it was a beautiful structure. He used stone, carved wood, and a lot of gold. Because it was the house of God, all hammering and chiseling were done away from the temple site. No noisy iron tools were used there (see 1 Kings 6:7). God promised to live among the Israelites if Solomon would obey and build the temple as God told him to.

bits around,[a] by line. [16]He also made two capitals of cast bronze to set on the tops of the pillars; each capital was five cubits[b] high. [17]A network of interwoven chains festooned the capitals on top of the pillars, seven for each capital. [18]He made pomegranates in two rows[c] encircling each network to decorate the capitals on top of the pillars.[d] He did the same for each capital. [19]The capitals on top of the pillars in the portico were in the shape of lilies, four cubits[e] high. [20]On the capitals of both pillars, above the bowl-shaped part next to the network, were the two hundred pomegranates in rows all around. [21]He erected the pillars at the portico of the temple. The pillar to the south he named Jakin[f] and the one to the north Boaz.[g] [22]The capitals on top were in the shape of lilies. And so the work on the pillars was completed.

[23]He made the Sea of cast metal, circular in shape, measuring ten cubits[h] from rim to rim and five cubits high. It took a line of thirty cubits[i] to measure around it. [24]Below the rim, gourds encircled it—ten to a cubit. The gourds were cast in two rows in one piece with the Sea.

[25]The Sea stood on twelve bulls, three facing north, three facing west, three facing south and three facing east. The Sea rested on top of them, and their hindquarters were toward the center. [26]It was a handbreadth[j] in thickness, and its rim was like the rim of a cup, like a lily blossom. It held two thousand baths.[k]

[27]He also made ten movable stands of bronze; each was four cubits long, four wide and three high.[l] [28]This is how the stands were made: They had side panels attached to uprights. [29]On the panels between the uprights were lions, bulls and cherubim—and on the uprights as well. Above and below the lions and bulls were wreaths of hammered work. [30]Each stand had four bronze wheels with bronze axles, and each had a basin resting on four supports, cast with wreaths on each side. [31]On the inside of the stand there was an opening that had a circular frame one cubit[m] deep. This opening was round, and with its basework it measured a cubit and a half.[n] Around its opening there was engraving. The panels of the stands were square, not round. [32]The four wheels were under the panels, and the axles of the wheels were attached to the stand. The diameter of each wheel was a cubit and a half. [33]The wheels were made like chariot wheels; the axles, rims, spokes and hubs were all of cast metal.

[34]Each stand had four handles, one on each corner, projecting from the stand. [35]At the top of the stand there was a circular band half a cubit[o] deep. The supports and panels were attached to the top of the stand. [36]He engraved cherubim, lions and palm trees on the surfaces of the supports and on the panels, in every available space, with wreaths all around. [37]This is the way he made the ten stands. They were all cast in the same molds and were identical in size and shape.

[38]He then made ten bronze basins, each holding forty baths[p] and measuring four cubits across, one basin to go on each of the ten stands. [39]He placed five of the stands on the south side of the temple and five on the

---

[a]15 That is, about 27 feet (about 8.1 meters) high and 18 feet (about 5.4 meters) around
[b]16 That is, about 7 1/2 feet (about 2.3 meters); also in verse 23   [c]18 Two Hebrew manuscripts and Septuagint; most Hebrew manuscripts *made the pillars, and there were two rows*   [d]18 Many Hebrew manuscripts and Syriac; most Hebrew manuscripts *pomegranates*   [e]19 That is, about 6 feet (about 1.8 meters); also in verse 38   [f]21 *Jakin* probably means *he establishes.*   [g]21 *Boaz* probably means *in him is strength.*   [h]23 That is, about 15 feet (about 4.5 meters)   [i]23 That is, about 45 feet (about 13.5 meters)   [j]26 That is, about 3 inches (about 8 centimeters)   [k]26 That is, probably about 11,500 gallons (about 44 kiloliters); the Septuagint does not have this sentence.   [l]27 That is, about 6 cubit (about 1.8 meters) long and wide and about 4 1/2 feet (about 1.3 meters) high   [m]31 That is, about 1 1/2 feet (about 0.5 meter)   [n]31 That is, about 2 1/4 feet (about 0.7 meter); also in verse 32   [o]35 That is, about 3/4 foot (about 0.2 meter)
[p]38 That is, about 230 gallons (about 880 liters)

north. He placed the Sea on the south side, at the southeast corner of the temple. ⁴⁰He also made the basins and shovels and sprinkling bowls.

So Huram finished all the work he had undertaken for King Solomon in the temple of the LORD:

⁴¹the two pillars;

  the two bowl-shaped capitals on top of the pillars;

  the two sets of network decorating the two bowl-shaped capitals on top of the pillars;

⁴²the four hundred pomegranates for the two sets of network (two rows of pomegranates for each network, decorating the bowl-shaped capitals on top of the pillars);

⁴³the ten stands with their ten basins;

⁴⁴the Sea and the twelve bulls under it;

⁴⁵the pots, shovels and sprinkling bowls.

All these objects that Huram made for King Solomon for the temple of the LORD were of burnished bronze. ⁴⁶The king had them cast in clay molds in the plain of the Jordan between Succoth and Zarethan. ⁴⁷Solomon left all these things unweighed, because there were so many; the weight of the bronze was not determined.

⁴⁸Solomon also made all the furnishings that were in the LORD's temple:

  the golden altar;

  the golden table on which was the bread of the Presence;

⁴⁹the lampstands of pure gold (five on the right and five on the left, in front of the inner sanctuary);

  the gold floral work and lamps and tongs;

⁵⁰the pure gold basins, wick trimmers, sprinkling bowls, dishes and censers;

  and the gold sockets for the doors of the innermost room, the Most Holy Place, and also for the doors of the main hall of the temple.

⁵¹When all the work King Solomon had done for the temple of the LORD was finished, he brought in the things his father David had dedicated—the silver and gold and the furnishings—and he placed them in the treasuries of the LORD's temple.

The Ark Brought to the Temple

8 Then King Solomon summoned into his presence at Jerusalem the elders of Israel, all the heads of the tribes and the chiefs of the Israelite families, to bring up the ark of the LORD's covenant from Zion, the City of David. ²All the men of Israel came together to King Solomon at the time of the festival in the month of Ethanim, the seventh month.

³When all the elders of Israel had arrived, the priests took up the ark, ⁴and they brought up the ark of the LORD and the Tent of Meeting and all the sacred furnishings in it. The priests and Levites carried them up, ⁵and King Solomon and the entire assembly of Israel that had gathered about him were before the ark, sacrificing so many sheep and cattle that they could not be recorded or counted.

⁶The priests then brought the ark of the LORD's covenant to its place in the inner sanctuary of the temple, the Most Holy Place, and put it beneath the wings of the cherubim. ⁷The cherubim spread their wings over the place of the ark and overshadowed the ark and its carrying poles. ⁸These poles were so long that their ends could be seen from the Holy Place in front of the inner sanctuary, but not from outside the Holy Place; and they are still there today. ⁹There was nothing in the ark except the two stone tablets that Moses had placed in it at Horeb, where the LORD made a covenant with the Israelites after they came out of Egypt.

¹⁰When the priests withdrew from the Holy Place, the cloud filled the temple of the LORD. ¹¹And the priests could not perform their service be-

cause of the cloud, for the glory of the LORD filled his temple.

¹²Then Solomon said, "The LORD has said that he would dwell in a dark cloud; ¹³I have indeed built a magnificent temple for you, a place for you to dwell forever."

¹⁴While the whole assembly of Israel was standing there, the king turned around and blessed them. ¹⁵Then he said:

"Praise be to the LORD, the God of Israel, who with his own hand has fulfilled what he promised with his own mouth to my father David. For he said, ¹⁶'Since the day I brought my people Israel out of Egypt, I have not chosen a city in any tribe of Israel to have a temple built for my Name to be there, but I have chosen David to rule my people Israel.'

¹⁷"My father David had it in his heart to build a temple for the Name of the LORD, the God of Israel. ¹⁸But the LORD said to my father David, 'Because it was in your heart to build a temple for my Name, you did well to have this in your heart. ¹⁹Nevertheless, you are not the one to build the temple, but your son, who is your own flesh and blood—he is the one who will build the temple for my Name.'

²⁰"The LORD has kept the promise he made: I have succeeded David my father and now I sit on the throne of Israel, just as the LORD promised, and I have built the temple for the Name of the LORD, the God of Israel. ²¹I have provided a place there for the ark, in which is the covenant of the LORD that he made with our fathers when he brought them out of Egypt."

Solomon's Prayer of Dedication

²²Then Solomon stood before the altar of the LORD in front of the whole assembly of Israel, spread out his hands toward heaven ²³and said:

"O LORD, God of Israel, there is no God like you in heaven above or on earth below—you who keep your covenant of love with your servants who continue wholeheartedly in your way. ²⁴You have kept your promise to your servant David my father; with your mouth you have promised and with your hand you have fulfilled it—as it is today.

²⁵"Now LORD, God of Israel, keep for your servant David my father the promises you made to him when you said, 'You shall never fail to have a man to sit before me on the throne of Israel, if only your sons are careful in all they do to walk before me as you have done.' ²⁶And now, O God of Israel, let your word that you promised your servant David my father come true.

²⁷"But will God really dwell on earth? The heavens, even the highest heaven, cannot contain you. How much less this temple I have built! ²⁸Yet give attention to your servant's prayer and his plea for mercy, O LORD my God. Hear the cry and the prayer that your servant is praying in your presence this day. ²⁹May your eyes be open toward this temple night and day, this place of which you said, 'My Name shall be there,' so that you will hear the prayer your servant prays toward this place. ³⁰Hear the supplication of your servant and of your people Israel when they pray toward this place. Hear from heaven, your dwelling place, and when you hear, forgive.

³¹"When a man wrongs his neighbor and is required to take an oath and he comes and swears the oath before your altar in this

---

𝕎ORDS TO REMEMBER

8:20 The LORD has kept the promise he made.

temple, [32]then hear from heaven and act. Judge between your servants, condemning the guilty and bringing down on his own head what he has done. Declare the innocent not guilty, and so establish his innocence.

[33]"When your people Israel have been defeated by an enemy because they have sinned against you, and when they turn back to you and confess your name, praying and making supplication to you in this temple, [34]then hear from heaven and forgive the sin of your people Israel and bring them back to the land you gave to their fathers.

[35]"When the heavens are shut up and there is no rain because your people have sinned against you, and when they pray toward this place and confess your name and turn from their sin because you have afflicted them, [36]then hear from heaven and forgive the sin of your servants, your people Israel. Teach them the right way to live, and send rain on the land you gave your people for an inheritance.

[37]"When famine or plague comes to the land, or blight or mildew, locusts or grasshoppers, or when an enemy besieges them in any of their cities, whatever disaster or disease may come,

[38]and when a prayer or plea is made by any of your people Israel—each one aware of the afflictions of his own heart, and spreading out his hands toward this temple— [39]then hear from heaven, your dwelling place. Forgive and act; deal with each man according to all he does, since you know his heart (for you alone know the hearts of all men), [40]so that they will fear you all the time they live in the land you gave our fathers.

[41]"As for the foreigner who does not belong to your people Israel but has come from a distant land because of your name— [42]for men will hear of your great name and your mighty hand and your outstretched arm—when he comes and prays toward this temple, [43]then hear from heaven, your dwelling place, and do whatever the foreigner asks of you, so that all the peoples of the earth may know your name and fear you, as do your own people Israel, and may know that this house I have built bears your Name.

[44]"When your people go to war against their enemies, wherever you send them, and when they pray to the LORD toward the city you have chosen and the temple I have built for your Name, [45]then hear from heaven their

---

▌ ET'S LIVE IT!   1 Kings 8:41–43

REMEMBERING ANSWERED PRAYERS ➠ King Solomon prayed when he dedicated the great temple to God in Jerusalem. Read 1 Kings 8:41–43. Why did Solomon want God to answer the prayers of foreigners?

Answered prayer is still a good way to help people learn that God is real. Pray about a friend's problem. Or tell your friend to pray about the problem. When God answers the prayer, it will help your friend know God is real.

In a small notebook list the people or problems that you are praying for. When God answers your prayer, put the date and the answer next to the prayer in your notebook. It will help you remember to praise God for answering your prayers, and it will make you more and more sure that God is real.

prayer and their plea, and uphold their cause.

⁴⁶"When they sin against you —for there is no one who does not sin—and you become angry with them and give them over to the enemy, who takes them captive to his own land, far away or near; ⁴⁷and if they have a change of heart in the land where they are held captive, and repent and plead with you in the land of their conquerors and say, 'We have sinned, we have done wrong, we have acted wickedly'; ⁴⁸and if they turn back to you with all their heart and soul in the land of their enemies who took them captive, and pray to you toward the land you gave their fathers, toward the city you have chosen and the temple I have built for your Name; ⁴⁹then from heaven, your dwelling place, hear their prayer and their plea, and uphold their cause. ⁵⁰And forgive your people, who have sinned against you; forgive all the offenses they have committed against you, and cause their conquerors to show them mercy; ⁵¹for they are your people and your inheritance, whom you brought out of Egypt, out of that iron-smelting furnace.

⁵²"May your eyes be open to your servant's plea and to the plea of your people Israel, and may you listen to them whenever they cry out to you. ⁵³For you singled them out from all the nations of the world to be your own inheritance, just as you declared through your servant Moses when you, O Sovereign LORD, brought our fathers out of Egypt."

⁵⁴When Solomon had finished all these prayers and supplications to the LORD, he rose from before the altar of the LORD, where he had been kneeling with his hands spread out toward heaven. ⁵⁵He stood and blessed the whole assembly of Israel in a loud voice, saying:

⁵⁶"Praise be to the LORD, who has given rest to his people Israel just as he promised. Not one word has failed of all the good promises he gave through his servant Moses. ⁵⁷May the LORD our God be with us as he was with our fathers; may he never leave us nor forsake us. ⁵⁸May he turn our hearts to him, to walk in all his ways and to keep the commands, decrees and regulations he gave our fathers. ⁵⁹And may these words of mine, which I have prayed before the LORD, be near to the LORD our God day and night, that he may uphold the cause of his servant and the cause of his people Israel according to each day's need, ⁶⁰so that all the peoples of the earth may know that the LORD is God and that there is no other. ⁶¹But your hearts must be fully committed to the LORD our God, to live by his decrees and obey his commands, as at this time."

The Dedication of the Temple

⁶²Then the king and all Israel with him offered sacrifices before the LORD. ⁶³Solomon offered a sacrifice of fellowship offerings[a] to the LORD: twenty-two thousand cattle and a hundred and twenty thousand sheep and goats. So the king and all the Israelites dedicated the temple of the LORD.

⁶⁴On that same day the king consecrated the middle part of the courtyard in front of the temple of the LORD, and there he offered burnt offerings, grain offerings and the fat of the fellowship offerings, because the bronze altar before the LORD was too small to hold the burnt offerings, the grain offerings and the fat of the fellowship offerings.

a63 Traditionally *peace offerings*; also in verse 64

⁶⁵So Solomon observed the festival at that time, and all Israel with him—a vast assembly, people from Lebo*ᵃ* Hamath to the Wadi of Egypt. They celebrated it before the LORD our God for seven days and seven days more, fourteen days in all. ⁶⁶On the following day he sent the people away. They blessed the king and then went home, joyful and glad in heart for all the good things the LORD had done for his servant David and his people Israel.

The LORD Appears to Solomon

9 When Solomon had finished building the temple of the LORD and the royal palace, and had achieved all he had desired to do, ²the LORD appeared to him a second time, as he had appeared to him at Gibeon. ³The LORD said to him:

"I have heard the prayer and plea you have made before me; I have consecrated this temple, which you have built, by putting my Name there forever. My eyes and my heart will always be there.

⁴"As for you, if you walk before me in integrity of heart and uprightness, as David your father did, and do all I command and observe my decrees and laws, ⁵I will establish your royal throne over Israel forever, as I promised David your father when I said, 'You shall never fail to have a man on the throne of Israel.'

⁶"But if you*ᵇ* or your sons turn away from me and do not observe the commands and decrees I have given you*ᵇ* and go off to serve other gods and worship them, ⁷then I will cut off Israel from the land I have given them and will reject this temple I have consecrated for my Name. Israel will then become a byword and an object of ridicule among all

peoples. ⁸And though this temple is now imposing, all who pass by will be appalled and will scoff and say, 'Why has the LORD done such a thing to this land and to this temple?' ⁹People will answer, 'Because they have forsaken the LORD their God, who brought their fathers out of Egypt, and have embraced other gods, worshiping and serving them—that is why the LORD brought all this disaster on them.'"

Solomon's Other Activities

¹⁰At the end of twenty years, during which Solomon built these two buildings—the temple of the LORD and the royal palace— ¹¹King Solomon gave twenty towns in Galilee to Hiram king of Tyre, because Hiram had supplied him with all the cedar and pine and gold he wanted. ¹²But when Hiram went from Tyre to see the towns that Solomon had given him, he was not pleased with them. ¹³"What kind of towns are these you have given me, my brother?" he asked. And he called them the Land of Cabul,*ᶜ* a name they have to this day. ¹⁴Now Hiram had sent to the king 120 talents*ᵈ* of gold.

¹⁵Here is the account of the forced labor King Solomon conscripted to build the LORD's temple, his own palace, the supporting terraces,*ᵉ* the wall of Jerusalem, and Hazor, Megiddo and Gezer. ¹⁶(Pharaoh king of Egypt had attacked and captured Gezer. He had set it on fire. He killed its Canaanite inhabitants and then gave it as a wedding gift to his daughter, Solomon's wife. ¹⁷And Solomon rebuilt Gezer.) He built up Lower Beth Horon, ¹⁸Baalath, and Tadmor*ᶠ* in the desert, within his land, ¹⁹as well as all his store cities and the towns for his chariots and for his horses*ᵍ*—whatever he desired to build in Jerusalem, in Lebanon and

---

ᵃ65 Or from the entrance to   *ᵇ6 The Hebrew is plural.*   *ᶜ13 Cabul sounds like the Hebrew for good-for-nothing.*   *ᵈ14 That is, about 4 1/2 tons (about 4 metric tons)*   *ᵉ15 Or the Millo; also in verse 24*   *ᶠ18 The Hebrew may also be read Tamar.*   *ᵍ19 Or charioteers*

throughout all the territory he ruled.

20All the people left from the Amorites, Hittites, Perizzites, Hivites and Jebusites (these peoples were not Israelites), 21that is, their descendants remaining in the land, whom the Israelites could not exterminate*a*— these Solomon conscripted for his slave labor force, as it is to this day. 22But Solomon did not make slaves of any of the Israelites; they were his fighting men, his government officials, his officers, his captains, and the commanders of his chariots and charioteers. 23They were also the chief officials in charge of Solomon's projects—550 officials supervising the men who did the work.

24After Pharaoh's daughter had come up from the City of David to the palace Solomon had built for her, he constructed the supporting terraces.

25Three times a year Solomon sacrificed burnt offerings and fellowship offerings*b* on the altar he had built for the Lord, burning incense before the Lord along with them, and so fulfilled the temple obligations.

26King Solomon also built ships at Ezion Geber, which is near Elath in Edom, on the shore of the Red Sea.*c* 27And Hiram sent his men—sailors who knew the sea—to serve in the fleet with Solomon's men. 28They sailed to Ophir and brought back 420 talents*d* of gold, which they delivered to King Solomon.

The Queen of Sheba Visits Solomon

10 When the queen of Sheba heard about the fame of Solomon and his relation to the name of the Lord, she came to test him with hard questions. 2Arriving at Jerusalem with a very great caravan—with

a21 The Hebrew term refers to the irrevocable giving over of things or persons to the Lord, often by totally destroying them.   *b25* Traditionally *peace offerings*   *c26* Hebrew *Yam Suph*; that is, Sea of Reeds   *d28* That is, about 16 tons (about 14.5 metric tons)

Life in Bible Times

CAMELS

Camels were the trucks of Bible times. A camel could carry four hundred pounds and travel up to ten miles an hour. Camels carried spices and other goods along trade routes thousands of years before Christ was born. Because camels could hold five gallons of water in each of their three stomachs, they could go without drinking for three days. Fat, not water, is stored in the hump. Camel milk was used to make cheese, and camel hair was woven into tent cloth and used to make rope.

camels carrying spices, large quantities of gold, and precious stones—she came to Solomon and talked with him about all that she had on her mind. ³Solomon answered all her questions; nothing was too hard for the king to explain to her. ⁴When the queen of Sheba saw all the wisdom of Solomon and the palace he had built, ⁵the food on his table, the seating of his officials, the attending servants in their robes, his cupbearers, and the burnt offerings he made at*a* the temple of the Lord, she was overwhelmed.

⁶She said to the king, "The report I heard in my own country about your achievements and your wisdom is true. ⁷But I did not believe these things until I came and saw with my own eyes. Indeed, not even half was told me; in wisdom and wealth you have far exceeded the report I heard. ⁸How happy your men must be! How happy your officials, who continually stand before you and hear your wisdom! ⁹Praise be to the Lord your God, who has delighted in you and placed you on the throne of Israel. Because of the Lord's eternal love for Israel, he has made you king, to maintain justice and righteousness."

¹⁰And she gave the king 120 talents*b* of gold, large quantities of spices, and precious stones. Never again were so many spices brought in as those the queen of Sheba gave to King Solomon.

¹¹(Hiram's ships brought gold from Ophir; and from there they brought great cargoes of almugwood*c* and precious stones. ¹²The king used the almugwood to make supports for the temple of the Lord and for the royal palace, and to make harps and lyres for the musicians. So much almugwood has never been imported or seen since that day.)

¹³King Solomon gave the queen of Sheba all she desired and asked for, besides what he had given her out of his royal bounty. Then she left and returned with her retinue to her own country.

Solomon's Splendor

¹⁴The weight of the gold that Solomon received yearly was 666 talents,*d* ¹⁵not including the revenues from merchants and traders and from all the Arabian kings and the governors of the land.

¹⁶King Solomon made two hundred large shields of hammered gold; six hundred bekas*e* of gold went into each shield. ¹⁷He also made three hundred small shields of hammered gold, with three minas*f* of gold in each shield. The king put them in the Palace of the Forest of Lebanon.

¹⁸Then the king made a great throne inlaid with ivory and overlaid with fine gold. ¹⁹The throne had six steps, and its back had a rounded top. On both sides of the seat were armrests, with a lion standing beside each of them. ²⁰Twelve lions stood on the six steps, one at either end of each step. Nothing like it had ever been made for any other kingdom. ²¹All King Solomon's goblets were gold, and all the household articles in the Palace of the Forest of Lebanon were pure gold. Nothing was made of silver, because silver was considered of little value in Solomon's days. ²²The king had a fleet of trading ships*g* at sea along with the ships of Hiram. Once every three years it returned, carrying gold, silver and ivory, and apes and baboons.

²³King Solomon was greater in riches and wisdom than all the other kings of the earth. ²⁴The whole world sought audience with Solomon to hear the wisdom God had put in his heart. ²⁵Year after year, everyone who came brought a gift—articles of silver and gold, robes, weapons and spices, and horses and mules.

²⁶Solomon accumulated chariots

---

a5 Or *the ascent by which he went up to*　　*b10* That is, about 4 1/2 tons (about 4 metric tons)
c11 Probably a variant of *algumwood*; also in verse 12　　*d14* That is, about 25 tons (about 23 metric tons)　　*e16* That is, about 7 1/2 pounds (about 3.5 kilograms)　　*f17* That is, about 3 3/4 pounds (about 1.7 kilograms)　　*g22* Hebrew *of ships of Tarshish*

and horses; he had fourteen hundred chariots and twelve thousand horses,*a* which he kept in the chariot cities and also with him in Jerusalem. 27The king made silver as common in Jerusalem as stones, and cedar as plentiful as sycamore-fig trees in the foothills. 28Solomon's horses were imported from Egypt*b* and from Kue*c*—the royal merchants purchased them from Kue. 29They imported a chariot from Egypt for six hundred shekels*d* of silver, and a horse for a hundred and fifty.*e* They also exported them to all the kings of the Hittites and of the Arameans.

SOLOMON'S SHIPS

King Solomon had a fleet of trading ships that brought many interesting and valuable items back to Israel. Each voyage lasted three years! According to Ezekiel 27 these ships of Tyre were beautifully made, with embroidered sails and inlaid ivory decks and awnings of blue and purple.

Solomon's Wives

11 King Solomon, however, loved many foreign women besides Pharaoh's daughter—Moabites, Ammonites, Edomites, Sidonians and Hittites. 2They were from nations about which the LORD had told the Israelites, "You must not intermarry with them, because they will surely turn your hearts after their gods." Nevertheless, Solomon held fast to them in love. 3He had seven

hundred wives of royal birth and three hundred concubines, and his wives led him astray. 4As Solomon grew old, his wives turned his heart after other gods, and his heart was not fully devoted to the LORD his God, as the heart of David his father had been. 5He followed Ashtoreth the goddess of the Sidonians, and Molech*f* the detestable god of the Ammonites. 6So Solomon did evil in the eyes of the LORD; he did not follow the LORD completely, as David his father had done.

? DID YOU KNOW?   11:1

Why did Solomon marry so many women?

Treaties with other nations were often sealed by marrying one ruler's daughter to the other country's king. Many of Solomon's wives came from such treaty marriages. But God had told the Israelites not to marry foreign women.

7On a hill east of Jerusalem, Solomon built a high place for Chemosh the detestable god of Moab, and for Molech the detestable god of the Ammonites. 8He did the same for all his foreign wives, who burned incense and offered sacrifices to their gods.

9The LORD became angry with Solomon because his heart had turned away from the LORD, the God of Israel, who had appeared to him twice. 10Although he had forbidden Solomon to follow other gods, Solomon did not keep the LORD's command. 11So the LORD said to Solomon, "Since this is your attitude and you have not kept my covenant and my decrees, which I commanded you, I will most certainly tear the kingdom away from you and give it to one of your subordinates. 12Nevertheless, for the sake of David your father, I will not

---

a26 Or *charioteers*   *b28* Or possibly *Muzur*, a region in Cilicia; also in verse 29
c28 Probably *Cilicia*   *d29* That is, about 15 pounds (about 7 kilograms)   *e29* That is, about
3 3/4 pounds about (1.7 kilograms)   *f5* Hebrew *Milcom*; also in verse 33

do it during your lifetime. I will tear it out of the hand of your son. ¹³Yet I will not tear the whole kingdom from him, but will give him one tribe for the sake of David my servant and for the sake of Jerusalem, which I have chosen."

Solomon's Adversaries

¹⁴Then the LORD raised up against Solomon an adversary, Hadad the Edomite, from the royal line of Edom. ¹⁵Earlier when David was fighting with Edom, Joab the commander of the army, who had gone up to bury the dead, had struck down all the men in Edom. ¹⁶Joab and all the Israelites stayed there for six months, until they had destroyed all the men in Edom. ¹⁷But Hadad, still only a boy, fled to Egypt with some Edomite officials who had served his father. ¹⁸They set out from Midian and went to Paran. Then taking men from Paran with them, they went to Egypt, to Pharaoh king of Egypt, who gave Hadad a house and land and provided him with food.

¹⁹Pharaoh was so pleased with Hadad that he gave him a sister of his own wife, Queen Tahpenes, in marriage. ²⁰The sister of Tahpenes bore him a son named Genubath, whom Tahpenes brought up in the royal palace. There Genubath lived with Pharaoh's own children.

²¹While he was in Egypt, Hadad heard that David rested with his fathers and that Joab the commander of the army was also dead. Then Hadad said to Pharaoh, "Let me go, that I may return to my own country."

²²"What have you lacked here that you want to go back to your own country?" Pharaoh asked.

"Nothing," Hadad replied, "but do let me go!"

²³And God raised up against Solomon another adversary, Rezon son of Eliada, who had fled from his master, Hadadezer king of Zobah. ²⁴He gathered men around him and became the leader of a band of rebels when David

destroyed the forces*a* of Zobah; the rebels went to Damascus, where they settled and took control. ²⁵Rezon was Israel's adversary as long as Solomon lived, adding to the trouble caused by Hadad. So Rezon ruled in Aram and was hostile toward Israel.

❓DID YOU KNOW?   11:26

Who was Jeroboam?

Jeroboam was one of Solomon's officials. A prophet told Jeroboam that he would become king of ten of Israel's tribes. When Solomon heard this he tried to kill Jeroboam. The prophet's words came true after Solomon had died.

Jeroboam Rebels Against Solomon

²⁶Also, Jeroboam son of Nebat rebelled against the king. He was one of Solomon's officials, an Ephraimite from Zeredah, and his mother was a widow named Zeruah.

²⁷Here is the account of how he rebelled against the king: Solomon had built the supporting terraces*b* and had filled in the gap in the wall of the city of David his father. ²⁸Now Jeroboam was a man of standing, and when Solomon saw how well the young man did his work, he put him in charge of the whole labor force of the house of Joseph.

²⁹About that time Jeroboam was going out of Jerusalem, and Ahijah the prophet of Shiloh met him on the way, wearing a new cloak. The two of them were alone out in the country, ³⁰and Ahijah took hold of the new cloak he was wearing and tore it into twelve pieces. ³¹Then he said to Jeroboam, "Take ten pieces for yourself, for this is what the LORD, the God of Israel, says: 'See, I am going to tear the kingdom out of Solomon's hand and give you ten tribes. ³²But for the sake of my servant David and the city

---

a24 Hebrew destroyed them   *b27 Or the Millo*

of Jerusalem, which I have chosen out of all the tribes of Israel, he will have one tribe. [33]I will do this because they have[a] forsaken me and worshiped Ashtoreth the goddess of the Sidonians, Chemosh the god of the Moabites, and Molech the god of the Ammonites, and have not walked in my ways, nor done what is right in my eyes, nor kept my statutes and laws as David, Solomon's father, did.

[34]" 'But I will not take the whole kingdom out of Solomon's hand; I have made him ruler all the days of his life for the sake of David my servant, whom I chose and who observed my commands and statutes. [35]I will take the kingdom from his son's hands and give you ten tribes. [36]I will give one tribe to his son so that David my servant may always have a lamp before me in Jerusalem, the city where I chose to put my Name. [37]However, as for you, I will take you, and you will rule over all that your heart desires; you will be king over Israel. [38]If you do whatever I command you and walk in my ways and do what is right in my eyes by keeping my statutes and commands, as David my servant did, I will be with you. I will build you a dynasty as enduring as the one I built for David and will give Israel to you. [39]I will humble David's descendants because of this, but not forever.' "

[40]Solomon tried to kill Jeroboam, but Jeroboam fled to Egypt, to Shishak the king, and stayed there until Solomon's death.

Solomon's Death

[41]As for the other events of Solomon's reign—all he did and the wisdom he displayed—are they not written in the book of the annals of Solomon? [42]Solomon reigned in Jerusalem over all Israel forty years. [43]Then he rested with his fathers and was buried in the city of David his father. And Rehoboam his son succeeded him as king.

Israel Rebels Against Rehoboam

12 Rehoboam went to Shechem, for all the Israelites had gone there to make him king. [2]When Jeroboam son of Nebat heard this (he was still in Egypt, where he had fled from King Solomon), he returned from[b] Egypt. [3]So they sent for Jeroboam, and he and the whole assembly of Israel went to Rehoboam and said to him: [4]"Your father put a heavy yoke on us, but now lighten the harsh labor and the heavy yoke he put on us, and we will serve you."

[5]Rehoboam answered, "Go away for three days and then come back to me." So the people went away.

[6]Then King Rehoboam consulted the elders who had served his father Solomon during his lifetime. "How would you advise me to answer these people?" he asked.

[7]They replied, "If today you will be a servant to these people and serve them and give them a favorable answer, they will always be your servants."

[8]But Rehoboam rejected the advice the elders gave him and consulted the young men who had grown up with him and were serving him. [9]He asked them, "What is your advice? How should we answer these people who say to me, 'Lighten the yoke your father put on us'?"

[10]The young men who had grown up with him replied, "Tell these people who have said to you, 'Your father put a heavy yoke on us, but make our yoke lighter'—tell them, 'My little finger is thicker than my father's waist. [11]My father laid on you a heavy yoke; I will make it even heavier. My father scourged you with whips; I will scourge you with scorpions.' "

[12]Three days later Jeroboam and all the people returned to Rehoboam, as the king had said, "Come back to me in three days." [13]The king answered the people harshly. Rejecting the advice given him by the elders,

a33 Hebrew; Septuagint, Vulgate and Syriac *because he has*　　　b2 Or *he remained in*

¹⁴he followed the advice of the young men and said, "My father made your yoke heavy; I will make it even heavier. My father scourged you with whips; I will scourge you with scorpions." ¹⁵So the king did not listen to the people, for this turn of events was from the LORD, to fulfill the word the LORD had spoken to Jeroboam son of Nebat through Ahijah the Shilonite.

¹⁶When all Israel saw that the king refused to listen to them, they answered the king:

"What share do we have in David,
    what part in Jesse's son?
To your tents, O Israel!
    Look after your own house,
        O David!"

So the Israelites went home. ¹⁷But as for the Israelites who were living in the towns of Judah, Rehoboam still ruled over them.

¹⁸King Rehoboam sent out Adoniram,ᵃ who was in charge of forced labor, but all Israel stoned him to death. King Rehoboam, however, managed to get into his chariot and escape to Jerusalem. ¹⁹So Israel has been in rebellion against the house of David to this day.

²⁰When all the Israelites heard that Jeroboam had returned, they sent and called him to the assembly and made him king over all Israel. Only the tribe of Judah remained loyal to the house of David.

²¹When Rehoboam arrived in Jerusalem, he mustered the whole house of Judah and the tribe of Benjamin —a hundred and eighty thousand fighting men—to make war against the house of Israel and to regain the kingdom for Rehoboam son of Solomon.

²²But this word of God came to Shemaiah the man of God: ²³"Say to Rehoboam son of Solomon king of Judah, to the whole house of Judah and Benjamin, and to the rest of the people, ²⁴'This is what the LORD says: Do not go up to fight against your broth-

ers, the Israelites. Go home, every one of you, for this is my doing.' " So they obeyed the word of the LORD and went home again, as the LORD had ordered.

Golden Calves at Bethel and Dan

²⁵Then Jeroboam fortified Shechem in the hill country of Ephraim and lived there. From there he went out and built up Peniel.ᵇ

²⁶Jeroboam thought to himself, "The kingdom will now likely revert to the house of David. ²⁷If these people go up to offer sacrifices at the temple of the LORD in Jerusalem, they will again give their allegiance to their lord, Rehoboam king of Judah. They will kill me and return to King Rehoboam."

²⁸After seeking advice, the king made two golden calves. He said to the people, "It is too much for you to go up to Jerusalem. Here are your gods, O Israel, who brought you up out of Egypt." ²⁹One he set up in Bethel, and the other in Dan. ³⁰And this thing became a sin; the people went even as far as Dan to worship the one there.

³¹Jeroboam built shrines on high places and appointed priests from all sorts of people, even though they were not Levites. ³²He instituted a festival on the fifteenth day of the eighth month, like the festival held in Judah, and offered sacrifices on the altar. This he did in Bethel, sacrificing to the calves he had made. And at Bethel he also installed priests at the high places he had made. ³³On the fifteenth day of the eighth month, a month of his own choosing, he offered sacrifices on the altar he had built at Bethel. So he instituted the festival for the Israelites and went up to the altar to make offerings.

The Man of God From Judah

13 By the word of the LORD a man of God came from Judah

ᵃ18 Some Septuagint manuscripts and Syriac (see also 1 Kings 4:6 and 5:14); Hebrew *Adoram*
ᵇ25 Hebrew *Penuel,* a variant of *Peniel*

to Bethel, as Jeroboam was standing by the altar to make an offering. ²He cried out against the altar by the word of the LORD: "O altar, altar! This is what the LORD says: 'A son named Josiah will be born to the house of David. On you he will sacrifice the priests of the high places who now make offerings here, and human bones will be burned on you.'" ³That same day the man of God gave a sign: "This is the sign the LORD has declared: The altar will be split apart and the ashes on it will be poured out."

❓DID YOU KNOW?   12:33

What evil thing did King Jeroboam do?

Jeroboam set up a false religion for his kingdom. He put up golden calves for Israel to worship. He established new religious holidays in place of the ones God's law had established. For the next two hundred years, every king of the ten tribes of Israel led people to worship God in this false and evil way.

---

⁴When King Jeroboam heard what the man of God cried out against the altar at Bethel, he stretched out his hand from the altar and said, "Seize him!" But the hand he stretched out toward the man shriveled up, so that he could not pull it back. ⁵Also, the altar was split apart and its ashes poured out according to the sign given by the man of God by the word of the LORD.

⁶Then the king said to the man of God, "Intercede with the LORD your God and pray for me that my hand may be restored." So the man of God interceded with the LORD, and the king's hand was restored and became as it was before.

⁷The king said to the man of God, "Come home with me and have something to eat, and I will give you a gift."

⁸But the man of God answered the king, "Even if you were to give me half your possessions, I would not go with you, nor would I eat bread or drink water here. ⁹For I was commanded by the word of the LORD: 'You must not eat bread or drink water or return by the way you came.'" ¹⁰So he took another road and did not return by the way he had come to Bethel.

¹¹Now there was a certain old prophet living in Bethel, whose sons came and told him all that the man of God had done there that day. They also told their father what he had said to the king. ¹²Their father asked them, "Which way did he go?" And his sons showed him which road the man of God from Judah had taken. ¹³So he said to his sons, "Saddle the donkey for me." And when they had saddled the donkey for him, he mounted it ¹⁴and rode after the man of God. He found him sitting under an oak tree and asked, "Are you the man of God who came from Judah?"

"I am," he replied.

¹⁵So the prophet said to him, "Come home with me and eat."

¹⁶The man of God said, "I cannot turn back and go with you, nor can I eat bread or drink water with you in this place. ¹⁷I have been told by the word of the LORD: 'You must not eat bread or drink water there or return by the way you came.'"

¹⁸The old prophet answered, "I too am a prophet, as you are. And an angel said to me by the word of the LORD: 'Bring him back with you to your house so that he may eat bread and drink water.'" (But he was lying to him.) ¹⁹So the man of God returned with him and ate and drank in his house.

²⁰While they were sitting at the table, the word of the LORD came to the old prophet who had brought him back. ²¹He cried out to the man of God who had come from Judah, "This is what the LORD says: 'You have defied the word of the LORD and have not kept the command the LORD your God gave you. ²²You came back and ate bread and drank water in the place

where he told you not to eat or drink. Therefore your body will not be buried in the tomb of your fathers.' "

23When the man of God had finished eating and drinking, the prophet who had brought him back saddled his donkey for him. 24As he went on his way, a lion met him on the road and killed him, and his body was thrown down on the road, with both the donkey and the lion standing beside it. 25Some people who passed by saw the body thrown down there, with the lion standing beside the body, and they went and reported it in the city where the old prophet lived.

26When the prophet who had brought him back from his journey heard of it, he said, "It is the man of God who defied the word of the LORD. The LORD has given him over to the lion, which has mauled him and killed him, as the word of the LORD had warned him."

27The prophet said to his sons, "Saddle the donkey for me," and they did so. 28Then he went out and found the body thrown down on the road, with the donkey and the lion standing beside it. The lion had neither eaten the body nor mauled the donkey. 29So the prophet picked up the body of the man of God, laid it on the donkey, and brought it back to his own city to mourn for him and bury him. 30Then he laid the body in his own tomb, and they mourned over him and said, "Oh, my brother!"

31After burying him, he said to his sons, "When I die, bury me in the grave where the man of God is buried; lay my bones beside his bones. 32For the message he declared by the word of the LORD against the altar in Bethel and against all the shrines on the high places in the towns of Samaria will certainly come true."

33Even after this, Jeroboam did not change his evil ways, but once more appointed priests for the high places from all sorts of people. Anyone who wanted to become a priest he consecrated for the high places. 34This was the sin of the house of Jeroboam that led to its downfall and to its destruction from the face of the earth.

? DID YOU KNOW?   13:34

Was Jeroboam ever punished for the evil he did?

Yes, God punished Jeroboam. God also punished the people of Israel, who let Jeroboam lead them away from the Lord.

Ahijah's Prophecy Against Jeroboam

14 At that time Abijah son of Jeroboam became ill, 2and Jeroboam said to his wife, "Go, disguise yourself, so you won't be recognized as the wife of Jeroboam. Then go to Shiloh. Ahijah the prophet is there—the one who told me I would be king over this people. 3Take ten loaves of bread with you, some cakes and a jar of honey, and go to him. He will tell you what will happen to the boy." 4So Jeroboam's wife did what he said and went to Ahijah's house in Shiloh.

Now Ahijah could not see; his sight was gone because of his age. 5But the LORD had told Ahijah, "Jeroboam's wife is coming to ask you about her son, for he is ill, and you are to give her such and such an answer. When she arrives, she will pretend to be someone else."

6So when Ahijah heard the sound of her footsteps at the door, he said, "Come in, wife of Jeroboam. Why this pretense? I have been sent to you with bad news. 7Go, tell Jeroboam that this is what the LORD, the God of Israel, says: 'I raised you up from among the people and made you a leader over my people Israel. 8I tore the kingdom away from the house of David and gave it to you, but you have not been like my servant David, who kept my commands and followed me with all his heart, doing only what was right in my eyes. 9You have done more evil than all who lived before you. You have made for yourself other gods, idols made of metal; you have provoked me to anger and thrust me behind your back.

10" 'Because of this, I am going to bring disaster on the house of Jeroboam. I will cut off from Jeroboam every last male in Israel—slave or free. I will burn up the house of Jeroboam as one burns dung, until it is all gone. 11Dogs will eat those belonging to Jeroboam who die in the city, and the birds of the air will feed on those who die in the country. The LORD has spoken!'

12"As for you, go back home. When you set foot in your city, the boy will die. 13All Israel will mourn for him and bury him. He is the only one belonging to Jeroboam who will be buried, because he is the only one in the house of Jeroboam in whom the LORD, the God of Israel, has found anything good.

14"The LORD will raise up for himself a king over Israel who will cut off the family of Jeroboam. This is the day! What? Yes, even now.ᵃ 15And the LORD will strike Israel, so that it will be like a reed swaying in the water. He will uproot Israel from this good land that he gave to their forefathers and scatter them beyond the River,ᵇ because they provoked the LORD to anger by making Asherah poles.ᶜ 16And he will give Israel up because of the sins Jeroboam has committed and has caused Israel to commit."

17Then Jeroboam's wife got up and left and went to Tirzah. As soon as she stepped over the threshold of the house, the boy died. 18They buried him, and all Israel mourned for him, as the LORD had said through his servant the prophet Ahijah.

19The other events of Jeroboam's reign, his wars and how he ruled, are written in the book of the annals of the kings of Israel. 20He reigned for twenty-two years and then rested with his fathers. And Nadab his son succeeded him as king.

Rehoboam King of Judah

21Rehoboam son of Solomon was king in Judah. He was forty-one years old when he became king, and he reigned seventeen years in Jerusalem, the city the LORD had chosen out of all the tribes of Israel in which to put his Name. His mother's name was Naamah; she was an Ammonite.

22Judah did evil in the eyes of the LORD. By the sins they committed they stirred up his jealous anger more than their fathers had done. 23They also set up for themselves high places, sacred stones and Asherah poles on every high hill and under every spreading tree. 24There were even male shrine prostitutes in the land; the people engaged in all the detestable practices of the nations the LORD had driven out before the Israelites.

25In the fifth year of King Rehoboam, Shishak king of Egypt attacked Jerusalem. 26He carried off the treasures of the temple of the LORD and the treasures of the royal palace. He took everything, including all the gold shields Solomon had made. 27So King Rehoboam made bronze shields to replace them and assigned these to the commanders of the guard on duty at the entrance to the royal palace. 28Whenever the king went to the LORD's temple, the guards bore the shields, and afterward they returned them to the guardroom.

29As for the other events of Rehoboam's reign, and all he did, are they not written in the book of the annals of the kings of Judah? 30There was continual warfare between Rehoboam and Jeroboam. 31And Rehoboam rested with his fathers and was buried with them in the City of David. His mother's name was Naamah; she was an Ammonite. And Abijahᵈ his son succeeded him as king.

ᵃ14 The meaning of the Hebrew for this sentence is uncertain.   ᵇ15 That is, the Euphrates
ᶜ15 That is, symbols of the goddess Asherah; here and elsewhere in 1 Kings   ᵈ31 Some Hebrew
manuscripts and Septuagint (see also 2 Chron. 12:16); most Hebrew manuscripts Abijam

Abijah King of Judah

15 In the eighteenth year of the reign of Jeroboam son of Nebat, Abijah[a] became king of Judah, [2]and he reigned in Jerusalem three years. His mother's name was Maacah daughter of Abishalom.[b]

❓DID YOU KNOW?   15:1,25

What were Israel and Judah?

When Solomon died his kingdom was divided. The southern part of the kingdom became a separate nation called Judah. The northern part of the kingdom became a separate nation and was called Israel. The first king of Judah was Rehoboam. The first king of Israel was Jeroboam. In the rest of 1 Kings and in 2 Kings, Israel and Judah are the names of these two separate nations.

---

[3]He committed all the sins his father had done before him; his heart was not fully devoted to the LORD his God, as the heart of David his forefather had been. [4]Nevertheless, for David's sake the LORD his God gave him a lamp in Jerusalem by raising up a son to succeed him and by making Jerusalem strong. [5]For David had done what was right in the eyes of the LORD and had not failed to keep any of the LORD's commands all the days of his life—except in the case of Uriah the Hittite.

[6]There was war between Rehoboam[c] and Jeroboam throughout Abijah's lifetime. [7]As for the other events of Abijah's reign, and all he did, are they not written in the book of the annals of the kings of Judah? There was war between Abijah and Jeroboam. [8]And Abijah rested with his fathers and was buried in the City of David. And Asa his son succeeded him as king.

Asa King of Judah

[9]In the twentieth year of Jeroboam king of Israel, Asa became king of Judah, [10]and he reigned in Jerusalem forty-one years. His grandmother's name was Maacah daughter of Abishalom.

[11]Asa did what was right in the eyes of the LORD, as his father David had done. [12]He expelled the male shrine prostitutes from the land and got rid of all the idols his fathers had made. [13]He even deposed his grandmother Maacah from her position as queen mother, because she had made a repulsive Asherah pole. Asa cut the pole down and burned it in the Kidron Valley. [14]Although he did not remove the high places, Asa's heart was fully committed to the LORD all his life. [15]He brought into the temple of the LORD the silver and gold and the articles that he and his father had dedicated.

[16]There was war between Asa and Baasha king of Israel throughout their reigns. [17]Baasha king of Israel went up against Judah and fortified Ramah to prevent anyone from leaving or entering the territory of Asa king of Judah.

[18]Asa then took all the silver and gold that was left in the treasuries of the LORD's temple and of his own palace. He entrusted it to his officials and sent them to Ben-Hadad son of Tabrimmon, the son of Hezion, the king of Aram, who was ruling in Damascus. [19]"Let there be a treaty between me and you," he said, "as there was between my father and your father. See, I am sending you a gift of silver and gold. Now break your treaty with Baasha king of Israel so he will withdraw from me."

[20]Ben-Hadad agreed with King Asa and sent the commanders of his forces against the towns of Israel. He conquered Ijon, Dan, Abel Beth Maacah and all Kinnereth in addition to Naphtali. [21]When Baasha heard this,

---

[a]1 Some Hebrew manuscripts and Septuagint (see also 2 Chron. 12:16); most Hebrew manuscripts *Abijam*; also in verses 7 and 8   [b]2 A variant of *Absalom*; also in verse 10   [c]6 Most Hebrew manuscripts; some Hebrew manuscripts and Syriac *Abijam* (that is, Abijah)

he stopped building Ramah and withdrew to Tirzah. 22Then King Asa issued an order to all Judah—no one was exempt—and they carried away from Ramah the stones and timber Baasha had been using there. With them King Asa built up Geba in Benjamin, and also Mizpah.

23As for all the other events of Asa's reign, all his achievements, all he did and the cities he built, are they not written in the book of the annals of the kings of Judah? In his old age, however, his feet became diseased. 24Then Asa rested with his fathers and was buried with them in the city of his father David. And Jehoshaphat his son succeeded him as king.

Nadab King of Israel

25Nadab son of Jeroboam became king of Israel in the second year of Asa king of Judah, and he reigned over Israel two years. 26He did evil in the eyes of the LORD, walking in the ways of his father and in his sin, which he had caused Israel to commit.

27Baasha son of Ahijah of the house of Issachar plotted against him, and he struck him down at Gibbethon, a Philistine town, while Nadab and all Israel were besieging it. 28Baasha killed Nadab in the third year of Asa king of Judah and succeeded him as king.

29As soon as he began to reign, he killed Jeroboam's whole family. He did not leave Jeroboam anyone that breathed, but destroyed them all, according to the word of the LORD given through his servant Ahijah the Shilonite— 30because of the sins Jeroboam had committed and had caused Israel to commit, and because he provoked the LORD, the God of Israel, to anger.

31As for the other events of Nadab's reign, and all he did, are they not written in the book of the annals of the kings of Israel? 32There was war between Asa and Baasha king of Israel throughout their reigns.

Baasha King of Israel

33In the third year of Asa king of Judah, Baasha son of Ahijah became king of all Israel in Tirzah, and he reigned twenty-four years. 34He did evil in the eyes of the LORD, walking in the ways of Jeroboam and in his sin, which he had caused Israel to commit.

16 Then the word of the LORD came to Jehu son of Hanani against Baasha: 2"I lifted you up from the dust and made you leader of my people Israel, but you walked in the ways of Jeroboam and caused my people Israel to sin and to provoke me to anger by their sins. 3So I am about to consume Baasha and his house, and I will make your house like that of Jeroboam son of Nebat. 4Dogs will eat those belonging to Baasha who die in the city, and the birds of the air will feed on those who die in the country."

5As for the other events of Baasha's reign, what he did and his achievements, are they not written in the book of the annals of the kings of Israel? 6Baasha rested with his fathers and was buried in Tirzah. And Elah his son succeeded him as king.

7Moreover, the word of the LORD came through the prophet Jehu son of Hanani to Baasha and his house, because of all the evil he had done in the eyes of the LORD, provoking him to anger by the things he did, and becoming like the house of Jeroboam —and also because he destroyed it.

Elah King of Israel

8In the twenty-sixth year of Asa king of Judah, Elah son of Baasha became king of Israel, and he reigned in Tirzah two years.

9Zimri, one of his officials, who had command of half his chariots, plotted against him. Elah was in Tirzah at the time, getting drunk in the home of Arza, the man in charge of the palace at Tirzah. 10Zimri came in, struck him down and killed him in the twenty-seventh year of Asa king of Judah. Then he succeeded him as king.

11As soon as he began to reign and was seated on the throne, he killed off Baasha's whole family. He did not spare a single male, whether relative or friend. [12]So Zimri destroyed the whole family of Baasha, in accordance with the word of the LORD spoken against Baasha through the prophet Jehu— [13]because of all the sins Baasha and his son Elah had committed and had caused Israel to commit, so that they provoked the LORD, the God of Israel, to anger by their worthless idols.

[14]As for the other events of Elah's reign, and all he did, are they not written in the book of the annals of the kings of Israel?

Zimri King of Israel

[15]In the twenty-seventh year of Asa king of Judah, Zimri reigned in Tirzah seven days. The army was encamped near Gibbethon, a Philistine town. [16]When the Israelites in the camp heard that Zimri had plotted against the king and murdered him, they proclaimed Omri, the commander of the army, king over Israel that very day there in the camp. [17]Then Omri and all the Israelites with him withdrew from Gibbethon and laid siege to Tirzah. [18]When Zimri saw that the city was taken, he went into the citadel of the royal palace and set the palace on fire around him. So he died, [19]because of the sins he had committed, doing evil in the eyes of the LORD and walking in the ways of Jeroboam and in the sin he had committed and had caused Israel to commit.

[20]As for the other events of Zimri's reign, and the rebellion he carried out, are they not written in the book of the annals of the kings of Israel?

Omri King of Israel

[21]Then the people of Israel were split into two factions; half supported Tibni son of Ginath for king, and the other half supported Omri. [22]But Omri's followers proved stronger than those of Tibni son of Ginath. So Tibni died and Omri became king.

[23]In the thirty-first year of Asa king of Judah, Omri became king of Israel, and he reigned twelve years, six of them in Tirzah. [24]He bought the hill of Samaria from Shemer for two talents[a] of silver and built a city on the hill, calling it Samaria, after Shemer, the name of the former owner of the hill.

[25]But Omri did evil in the eyes of the LORD and sinned more than all those before him. [26]He walked in all the ways of Jeroboam son of Nebat and in his sin, which he had caused Israel to commit, so that they provoked the LORD, the God of Israel, to anger by their worthless idols.

[27]As for the other events of Omri's reign, what he did and the things he achieved, are they not written in the book of the annals of the kings of Israel? [28]Omri rested with his fathers and was buried in Samaria. And Ahab his son succeeded him as king.

?DID YOU KNOW?   16:25

How many good kings did Israel have?

Not one king of Israel worshiped God. They all did "evil in the eyes of the LORD." Many evil kings of Israel are listed in 1 Kings 15–16. The worst king of all was Ahab, who was the enemy of Elijah the prophet.

Ahab Becomes King of Israel

[29]In the thirty-eighth year of Asa king of Judah, Ahab son of Omri became king of Israel, and he reigned in Samaria over Israel twenty-two years. [30]Ahab son of Omri did more evil in the eyes of the LORD than any of those before him. [31]He not only considered it trivial to commit the sins of Jeroboam son of Nebat, but he also married Jezebel daughter of Ethbaal king of the Sidonians, and began to serve Baal and worship him. [32]He set up an altar for Baal in the

---

[a]24 That is, about 150 pounds (about 70 kilograms)

temple of Baal that he built in Samaria. ³³Ahab also made an Asherah pole and did more to provoke the Lord, the God of Israel, to anger than did all the kings of Israel before him.

³⁴In Ahab's time, Hiel of Bethel rebuilt Jericho. He laid its foundations at the cost of his firstborn son Abiram, and he set up its gates at the cost of his youngest son Segub, in accordance with the word of the Lord spoken by Joshua son of Nun.

Elijah Fed by Ravens

17 Now Elijah the Tishbite, from Tishbe*ᵃ* in Gilead, said to Ahab, "As the Lord, the God of Israel, lives, whom I serve, there will be neither dew nor rain in the next few years except at my word."

²Then the word of the Lord came to Elijah: ³"Leave here, turn eastward and hide in the Kerith Ravine, east of the Jordan. ⁴You will drink from the brook, and I have ordered the ravens to feed you there."

⁵So he did what the Lord had told him. He went to the Kerith Ravine, east of the Jordan, and stayed there. ⁶The ravens brought him bread and meat in the morning and bread and meat in the evening, and he drank from the brook.

The Widow at Zarephath

⁷Some time later the brook dried up

ᵃ1 Or Tishbite, of the settlers

because there had been no rain in the land. ⁸Then the word of the Lord came to him: ⁹"Go at once to Zarephath of Sidon and stay there. I have commanded a widow in that place to supply you with food." ¹⁰So he went to Zarephath. When he came to the town gate, a widow was there gathering sticks. He called to her and asked, "Would you bring me a little water in a jar so I may have a drink?" ¹¹As she was going to get it, he called, "And bring me, please, a piece of bread."

¹²"As surely as the Lord your God lives," she replied, "I don't have any bread—only a handful of flour in a jar and a little oil in a jug. I am gathering a few sticks to take home and make a meal for myself and my son, that we may eat it—and die."

¹³Elijah said to her, "Don't be afraid. Go home and do as you have said. But first make a small cake of bread for me from what you have and bring it to me, and then make something for yourself and your son. ¹⁴For this is what the Lord, the God of Israel, says: 'The jar of flour will not be used up and the jug of oil will not run dry until the day the Lord gives rain on the land.'"

¹⁵She went away and did as Elijah had told her. So there was food every day for Elijah and for the woman and her family. ¹⁶For the jar of flour was not used up and the jug of oil did not

---

▌ET'S LIVE IT!   1 Kings 17:1–6

GOD'S CARE ➠ Somtimes God uses unusual ways to take care of those he loves. Read 1 Kings 17:1–6. How did God take care of Elijah?

Usually God takes care of children through their parents. He gives their mom or dad a job so there is money for what the family needs. But not always.

Sometimes God has the government help out a poor family. Sometimes one family can help out another family. There are many ways you could be used by God to help someone. If you have Christian magazines in your home, look in them for advertisements asking readers to help poor children. Perhaps your town has a food pantry to which you could donate some canned goods. Maybe you know a family in your church or town who could use the clothes you have outgrown.

run dry, in keeping with the word of the LORD spoken by Elijah.

¹⁷Some time later the son of the woman who owned the house became ill. He grew worse and worse, and finally stopped breathing. ¹⁸She said to Elijah, "What do you have against me, man of God? Did you come to remind me of my sin and kill my son?"

¹⁹"Give me your son," Elijah replied. He took him from her arms, carried him to the upper room where he was staying, and laid him on his bed. ²⁰Then he cried out to the LORD, "O LORD my God, have you brought tragedy also upon this widow I am staying with, by causing her son to die?" ²¹Then he stretched himself out on the boy three times and cried to the LORD, "O LORD my God, let this boy's life return to him!"

²²The LORD heard Elijah's cry, and the boy's life returned to him, and he lived. ²³Elijah picked up the child and carried him down from the room into the house. He gave him to his mother and said, "Look, your son is alive!"

²⁴Then the woman said to Elijah, "Now I know that you are a man of God and that the word of the LORD from your mouth is the truth."

❓ DID YOU KNOW?   17:1

Who was Elijah?

Elijah was a very famous prophet. He lived when King Ahab and his evil wife Jezebel tried to get everyone in Israel to worship Baal instead of the Lord. God gave Elijah the power to do miracles to fight against Baal worship.

Elijah and Obadiah

18 After a long time, in the third year, the word of the LORD came to Elijah: "Go and present yourself to Ahab, and I will send rain on the land." ²So Elijah went to present himself to Ahab.

Now the famine was severe in Samaria, ³and Ahab had summoned Obadiah, who was in charge of his palace. (Obadiah was a devout believer in the LORD. ⁴While Jezebel was killing off the LORD's prophets, Obadiah had taken a hundred prophets and hidden them in two caves, fifty in each, and had supplied them with food and water.) ⁵Ahab had said to Obadiah, "Go through the land to all the springs and valleys. Maybe we can find some grass to keep the horses and mules alive so we will not have to kill any of our animals." ⁶So they divided the land they were to cover, Ahab going in one direction and Obadiah in another.

⁷As Obadiah was walking along, Elijah met him. Obadiah recognized him, bowed down to the ground, and said, "Is it really you, my lord Elijah?"

⁸"Yes," he replied. "Go tell your master, 'Elijah is here.' "

⁹"What have I done wrong," asked Obadiah, "that you are handing your servant over to Ahab to be put to death? ¹⁰As surely as the LORD your God lives, there is not a nation or kingdom where my master has not sent someone to look for you. And whenever a nation or kingdom claimed you were not there, he made them swear they could not find you. ¹¹But now you tell me to go to my master and say, 'Elijah is here.' ¹²I don't know where the Spirit of the LORD may carry you when I leave you. If I go and tell Ahab and he doesn't find you, he will kill me. Yet I your servant have worshiped the LORD since my youth. ¹³Haven't you heard, my lord, what I did while Jezebel was killing the prophets of the LORD? I hid a hundred of the LORD's prophets in two caves, fifty in each, and supplied them with food and water. ¹⁴And now you tell me to go to my master and say, 'Elijah is here.' He will kill me!"

¹⁵Elijah said, "As the LORD Almighty lives, whom I serve, I will surely present myself to Ahab today."

Elijah on Mount Carmel

[16]So Obadiah went to meet Ahab and told him, and Ahab went to meet Elijah. [17]When he saw Elijah, he said to him, "Is that you, you troubler of Israel?"

[18]"I have not made trouble for Israel," Elijah replied. "But you and your father's family have. You have abandoned the LORD's commands and have followed the Baals. [19]Now summon the people from all over Israel to meet me on Mount Carmel. And bring the four hundred and fifty prophets of Baal and the four hundred prophets of Asherah, who eat at Jezebel's table."

[20]So Ahab sent word throughout all Israel and assembled the prophets on Mount Carmel. [21]Elijah went before the people and said, "How long will you waver between two opinions? If the LORD is God, follow him; but if Baal is God, follow him."

But the people said nothing.

[22]Then Elijah said to them, "I am the only one of the LORD's prophets left, but Baal has four hundred and fifty prophets. [23]Get two bulls for us. Let them choose one for themselves, and let them cut it into pieces and put it on the wood but not set fire to it. I will prepare the other bull and put it on the wood but not set fire to it. [24]Then you call on the name of your god, and I will call on the name of the LORD. The god who answers by fire —he is God."

Then all the people said, "What you say is good."

[25]Elijah said to the prophets of Baal, "Choose one of the bulls and prepare it first, since there are so many of you. Call on the name of your god, but do not light the fire." [26]So they took the bull given them and prepared it.

Then they called on the name of Baal from morning till noon. "O Baal, answer us!" they shouted. But there was no response; no one answered.

And they danced around the altar they had made.

[27]At noon Elijah began to taunt them. "Shout louder!" he said. "Surely he is a god! Perhaps he is deep in thought, or busy, or traveling. Maybe he is sleeping and must be awakened." [28]So they shouted louder and slashed themselves with swords and spears, as was their custom, until their blood flowed. [29]Midday passed, and they continued their frantic prophesying until the time for the evening sacrifice. But there was no response, no one answered, no one paid attention.

Life In Bible Times

CUTTING THEMSELVES

Some people in Bible times cut themselves with knives to show grief. But the prophets of the pagan god Baal cut themselves for a different reason. They thought Baal liked the smell of blood. The prophets of Baal cut themselves hoping to get their god's attention.

[30]Then Elijah said to all the people, "Come here to me." They came to him, and he repaired the altar of the LORD, which was in ruins. [31]Elijah took twelve stones, one for each of the tribes descended from Jacob, to whom the word of the LORD had come, saying, "Your name shall be Israel." [32]With the stones he built an altar in the name of the LORD, and he dug a trench around it large enough to hold two seahs[a] of seed. [33]He arranged the wood, cut the bull into pieces and laid it on the wood. Then he said to them,

---

[a]32 That is, probably about 13 quarts (about 15 liters)

"Fill four large jars with water and pour it on the offering and on the wood."

34"Do it again," he said, and they did it again.

"Do it a third time," he ordered, and they did it the third time. 35The water ran down around the altar and even filled the trench.

36At the time of sacrifice, the prophet Elijah stepped forward and prayed: "O Lord, God of Abraham, Isaac and Israel, let it be known today that you are God in Israel and that I am your servant and have done all these things at your command. 37Answer me, O Lord, answer me, so these people will know that you, O Lord, are God, and that you are turning their hearts back again."

38Then the fire of the Lord fell and burned up the sacrifice, the wood, the stones and the soil, and also licked up the water in the trench.

39When all the people saw this, they fell prostrate and cried, "The Lord—he is God! The Lord—he is God!"

40Then Elijah commanded them, "Seize the prophets of Baal. Don't let anyone get away!" They seized them, and Elijah had them brought down to the Kishon Valley and slaughtered there.

41And Elijah said to Ahab, "Go, eat and drink, for there is the sound of a heavy rain." 42So Ahab went off to eat and drink, but Elijah climbed to the top of Carmel, bent down to the ground and put his face between his knees.

43"Go and look toward the sea," he told his servant. And he went up and looked.

"There is nothing there," he said.

Seven times Elijah said, "Go back."

44The seventh time the servant reported, "A cloud as small as a man's hand is rising from the sea."

So Elijah said, "Go and tell Ahab, 'Hitch up your chariot and go down before the rain stops you.'"

45Meanwhile, the sky grew black with clouds, the wind rose, a heavy rain came on and Ahab rode off to Jezreel. 46The power of the Lord came upon Elijah and, tucking his cloak into his belt, he ran ahead of Ahab all the way to Jezreel.

Elijah Flees to Horeb

19 Now Ahab told Jezebel everything Elijah had done and how he had killed all the prophets with the sword. 2So Jezebel sent a messenger to Elijah to say, "May the gods deal with me, be it ever so severely, if by this time tomorrow I do not make your life like that of one of them."

3Elijah was afraid*a* and ran for his life. When he came to Beersheba in Judah, he left his servant there, 4while he himself went a day's journey into the desert. He came to a broom tree, sat down under it and prayed that he might die. "I have had enough, Lord," he said. "Take my life; I am no better than my ancestors." 5Then he lay down under the tree and fell asleep.

All at once an angel touched him and said, "Get up and eat." 6He looked around, and there by his head was a cake of bread baked over hot coals, and a jar of water. He ate and drank and then lay down again.

7The angel of the Lord came back a second time and touched him and said, "Get up and eat, for the journey is too much for you." 8So he got up and ate and drank. Strengthened by that food, he traveled forty days and forty nights until he reached Horeb,

---

❓DID YOU KNOW?   19:8

What is Horeb?

Horeb is another name for Mount Sinai, where God gave his people the Ten Commandments.

---

*a*3 Or *Elijah saw*

the mountain of God. ⁹There he went into a cave and spent the night.

The LORD Appears to Elijah

And the word of the LORD came to him: "What are you doing here, Elijah?"

¹⁰He replied, "I have been very zealous for the LORD God Almighty. The Israelites have rejected your covenant, broken down your altars, and put your prophets to death with the sword. I am the only one left, and now they are trying to kill me too."

¹¹The LORD said, "Go out and stand on the mountain in the presence of the LORD, for the LORD is about to pass by."

Then a great and powerful wind tore the mountains apart and shattered the rocks before the LORD, but the LORD was not in the wind. After the wind there was an earthquake, but the LORD was not in the earthquake. ¹²After the earthquake came a fire, but the LORD was not in the fire. And after the fire came a gentle whisper. ¹³When Elijah heard it, he pulled his cloak over his face and went out and stood at the mouth of the cave.

Then a voice said to him, "What are you doing here, Elijah?"

¹⁴He replied, "I have been very zealous for the LORD God Almighty. The Israelites have rejected your covenant, broken down your altars, and put your prophets to death with the sword. I am the only one left, and now they are trying to kill me too."

¹⁵The LORD said to him, "Go back the way you came, and go to the Desert of Damascus. When you get there, anoint Hazael king over Aram. ¹⁶Also, anoint Jehu son of Nimshi king over Israel, and anoint Elisha son of Shaphat from Abel Meholah to succeed you as prophet. ¹⁷Jehu will put to death any who escape the sword of Hazael, and Elisha will put to death any who escape the sword of Jehu. ¹⁸Yet I reserve seven thousand in Israel—all whose knees have not bowed down to Baal and all whose mouths have not kissed him."

The Call of Elisha

¹⁹So Elijah went from there and found Elisha son of Shaphat. He was plowing with twelve yoke of oxen, and he himself was driving the twelfth pair. Elijah went up to him and threw his cloak around him. ²⁰Elisha then left his oxen and ran after Elijah. "Let me kiss my father and mother good-by," he said, "and then I will come with you."

"Go back," Elijah replied. "What have I done to you?"

²¹So Elisha left him and went back. He took his yoke of oxen and slaughtered them. He burned the plowing equipment to cook the meat and gave it to the people, and they ate. Then he set out to follow Elijah and became his attendant.

Ben-Hadad Attacks Samaria

20 Now Ben-Hadad king of Aram mustered his entire army. Accompanied by thirty-two kings with their horses and chariots, he went up and besieged Samaria and attacked it. ²He sent messengers into the city to Ahab king of Israel, saying, "This is what Ben-Hadad says: ³'Your silver and gold are mine, and the best of your wives and children are mine.'"

⁴The king of Israel answered, "Just as you say, my lord the king. I and all I have are yours."

⁵The messengers came again and said, "This is what Ben-Hadad says: 'I sent to demand your silver and gold, your wives and your children. ⁶But about this time tomorrow I am going to send my officials to search your palace and the houses of your officials. They will seize everything you value and carry it away.'"

⁷The king of Israel summoned all the elders of the land and said to them, "See how this man is looking for trouble! When he sent for my wives and my children, my silver and my gold, I did not refuse him."

⁸The elders and the people all answered, "Don't listen to him or agree to his demands."

⁹So he replied to Ben-Hadad's messengers, "Tell my lord the king, 'Your servant will do all you demanded the first time, but this demand I cannot meet.' " They left and took the answer back to Ben-Hadad.

¹⁰Then Ben-Hadad sent another message to Ahab: "May the gods deal with me, be it ever so severely, if enough dust remains in Samaria to give each of my men a handful."

¹¹The king of Israel answered, "Tell him: 'One who puts on his armor should not boast like one who takes it off.' "

¹²Ben-Hadad heard this message while he and the kings were drinking in their tents,ᵃ and he ordered his men: "Prepare to attack." So they prepared to attack the city.

Ahab Defeats Ben-Hadad

¹³Meanwhile a prophet came to Ahab king of Israel and announced, "This is what the LORD says: 'Do you see this vast army? I will give it into your hand today, and then you will know that I am the LORD.' "

¹⁴"But who will do this?" asked Ahab.

The prophet replied, "This is what the LORD says: 'The young officers of the provincial commanders will do it.' "

"And who will start the battle?" he asked.

The prophet answered, "You will."

¹⁵So Ahab summoned the young officers of the provincial commanders, 232 men. Then he assembled the rest of the Israelites, 7,000 in all. ¹⁶They set out at noon while Ben-Hadad and the 32 kings allied with him were in their tents getting drunk. ¹⁷The young officers of the provincial commanders went out first.

Now Ben-Hadad had dispatched scouts, who reported, "Men are advancing from Samaria."

¹⁸He said, "If they have come out for peace, take them alive; if they have come out for war, take them alive."

¹⁹The young officers of the provincial commanders marched out of the city with the army behind them ²⁰and each one struck down his opponent. At that, the Arameans fled, with the Israelites in pursuit. But Ben-Hadad king of Aram escaped on horseback with some of his horsemen. ²¹The king of Israel advanced and overpowered the horses and chariots and inflicted heavy losses on the Arameans.

²²Afterward, the prophet came to the king of Israel and said, "Strengthen your position and see what must be done, because next spring the king of Aram will attack you again."

²³Meanwhile, the officials of the king of Aram advised him, "Their gods are gods of the hills. That is why they were too strong for us. But if we fight them on the plains, surely we will be stronger than they. ²⁴Do this: Remove all the kings from their commands and replace them with other officers. ²⁵You must also raise an army like the one you lost—horse for horse and chariot for chariot—so we can fight Israel on the plains. Then surely we will be stronger than they." He agreed with them and acted accordingly.

²⁶The next spring Ben-Hadad mustered the Arameans and went up to Aphek to fight against Israel. ²⁷When the Israelites were also mustered and given provisions, they marched out to meet them. The Israelites camped opposite them like two small flocks of goats, while the Arameans covered the countryside.

²⁸The man of God came up and told the king of Israel, "This is what the LORD says: 'Because the Arameans think the LORD is a god of the hills and not a god of the valleys, I will deliver this vast army into your hands, and you will know that I am the LORD.' "

²⁹For seven days they camped opposite each other, and on the seventh day the battle was joined. The Israelites inflicted a hundred thousand ca-

ᵃ12 Or in Succoth; also in verse 16

sualties on the Aramean foot soldiers in one day. [30]The rest of them escaped to the city of Aphek, where the wall collapsed on twenty-seven thousand of them. And Ben-Hadad fled to the city and hid in an inner room.

[31]His officials said to him, "Look, we have heard that the kings of the house of Israel are merciful. Let us go to the king of Israel with sackcloth around our waists and ropes around our heads. Perhaps he will spare your life."

[32]Wearing sackcloth around their waists and ropes around their heads, they went to the king of Israel and said, "Your servant Ben-Hadad says: 'Please let me live.'"

The king answered, "Is he still alive? He is my brother."

[33]The men took this as a good sign and were quick to pick up his word. "Yes, your brother Ben-Hadad!" they said.

"Go and get him," the king said. When Ben-Hadad came out, Ahab had him come up into his chariot.

[34]"I will return the cities my father took from your father," Ben-Hadad offered. "You may set up your own market areas in Damascus, as my father did in Samaria."

Ahab said, "On the basis of a treaty I will set you free." So he made a treaty with him, and let him go.

A Prophet Condemns Ahab

[35]By the word of the LORD one of the sons of the prophets said to his companion, "Strike me with your weapon," but the man refused.

[36]So the prophet said, "Because you have not obeyed the LORD, as soon as you leave me a lion will kill you." And after the man went away, a lion found him and killed him.

[37]The prophet found another man and said, "Strike me, please." So the man struck him and wounded him. [38]Then the prophet went and stood by the road waiting for the king. He disguised himself with his headband

down over his eyes. [39]As the king passed by, the prophet called out to him, "Your servant went into the thick of the battle, and someone came to me with a captive and said, 'Guard this man. If he is missing, it will be your life for his life, or you must pay a talent[a] of silver.' [40]While your servant was busy here and there, the man disappeared."

"That is your sentence," the king of Israel said. "You have pronounced it yourself."

[41]Then the prophet quickly removed the headband from his eyes, and the king of Israel recognized him as one of the prophets. [42]He said to the king, "This is what the LORD says: 'You have set free a man I had determined should die.[b] Therefore it is your life for his life, your people for his people.'" [43]Sullen and angry, the king of Israel went to his palace in Samaria.

Naboth's Vineyard

21 Some time later there was an incident involving a vineyard belonging to Naboth the Jezreelite. The vineyard was in Jezreel, close to the palace of Ahab king of Samaria. [2]Ahab said to Naboth, "Let me have your vineyard to use for a vegetable garden, since it is close to my palace. In exchange I will give you a better vineyard or, if you prefer, I will pay you whatever it is worth."

[3]But Naboth replied, "The LORD forbid that I should give you the inheritance of my fathers."

[4]So Ahab went home, sullen and angry because Naboth the Jezreelite had said, "I will not give you the inheritance of my fathers." He lay on his bed sulking and refused to eat.

[5]His wife Jezebel came in and asked him, "Why are you so sullen? Why won't you eat?"

[6]He answered her, "Because I said to Naboth the Jezreelite, 'Sell me your vineyard; or if you prefer, I will give you another vineyard in its

---

[a]39 That is, about 75 pounds (about 34 kilograms)   [b]42 The Hebrew term refers to the irrevocable giving over of things or persons to the LORD, often by totally destroying them.

place.' But he said, 'I will not give you my vineyard.' "

7Jezebel his wife said, "Is this how you act as king over Israel? Get up and eat! Cheer up. I'll get you the vineyard of Naboth the Jezreelite." 8So she wrote letters in Ahab's name, placed his seal on them, and sent them to the elders and nobles who lived in Naboth's city with him. 9In those letters she wrote:

"Proclaim a day of fasting and seat Naboth in a prominent place among the people. 10But seat two scoundrels opposite him and have them testify that he has cursed both God and the king. Then take him out and stone him to death."

11So the elders and nobles who lived in Naboth's city did as Jezebel directed in the letters she had written to them. 12They proclaimed a fast and seated Naboth in a prominent place among the people. 13Then two scoundrels came and sat opposite him and brought charges against Naboth before the people, saying, "Naboth has cursed both God and the king." So they took him outside the city and stoned him to death. 14Then they sent word to Jezebel: "Naboth has been stoned and is dead." 15As soon as Jezebel heard that Naboth had been stoned to death, she said to Ahab, "Get up and take pos-

session of the vineyard of Naboth the Jezreelite that he refused to sell you. He is no longer alive, but dead." 16When Ahab heard that Naboth was dead, he got up and went down to take possession of Naboth's vineyard.

17Then the word of the LORD came to Elijah the Tishbite: 18"Go down to meet Ahab king of Israel, who rules in Samaria. He is now in Naboth's vineyard, where he has gone to take possession of it. 19Say to him, 'This is what the LORD says: Have you not murdered a man and seized his property?' Then say to him, 'This is what the LORD says: In the place where dogs licked up Naboth's blood, dogs will lick up your blood—yes, yours!' "

20Ahab said to Elijah, "So you have found me, my enemy!"

"I have found you," he answered, "because you have sold yourself to do evil in the eyes of the LORD. 21I am going to bring disaster on you. I will consume your descendants and cut off from Ahab every last male in Israel—slave or free. 22I will make your house like that of Jeroboam son of Nebat and that of Baasha son of Ahijah, because you have provoked me to anger and have caused Israel to sin.'

23"And also concerning Jezebel the LORD says: 'Dogs will devour Jezebel by the wall of[a] Jezreel.'

24"Dogs will eat those belonging to Ahab who die in the city, and the

___

a23 Most Hebrew manuscripts; a few Hebrew manuscripts, Vulgate and Syriac (see also 2 Kings 9:26) *the plot of ground at*

Life in Bible Times

GRAPEVINES

Ahab thought Naboth's vineyard was worth stealing. Grapes were one of the most important crops of Palestine. They were squeezed for their juice or dried to make raisins.

birds of the air will feed on those who die in the country."

25(There was never a man like Ahab, who sold himself to do evil in the eyes of the LORD, urged on by Jezebel his wife. 26He behaved in the vilest manner by going after idols, like the Amorites the LORD drove out before Israel.)

27When Ahab heard these words, he tore his clothes, put on sackcloth and fasted. He lay in sackcloth and went around meekly.

28Then the word of the LORD came to Elijah the Tishbite: 29"Have you noticed how Ahab has humbled himself before me? Because he has humbled himself, I will not bring this disaster in his day, but I will bring it on his house in the days of his son."

Micaiah Prophesies Against Ahab

22 For three years there was no war between Aram and Israel. 2But in the third year Jehoshaphat king of Judah went down to see the king of Israel. 3The king of Israel had said to his officials, "Don't you know that Ramoth Gilead belongs to us and yet we are doing nothing to retake it from the king of Aram?"

4So he asked Jehoshaphat, "Will you go with me to fight against Ramoth Gilead?"

Jehoshaphat replied to the king of Israel, "I am as you are, my people as your people, my horses as your horses." 5But Jehoshaphat also said to the king of Israel, "First seek the counsel of the LORD."

6So the king of Israel brought together the prophets—about four hundred men—and asked them, "Shall I go to war against Ramoth Gilead, or shall I refrain?"

"Go," they answered, "for the Lord will give it into the king's hand."

7But Jehoshaphat asked, "Is there not a prophet of the LORD here whom we can inquire of?"

8The king of Israel answered Jehoshaphat, "There is still one man through whom we can inquire of the LORD, but I hate him because he never prophesies anything good about me, but always bad. He is Micaiah son of Imlah."

"The king should not say that," Jehoshaphat replied.

9So the king of Israel called one of his officials and said, "Bring Micaiah son of Imlah at once."

10Dressed in their royal robes, the king of Israel and Jehoshaphat king of Judah were sitting on their thrones at the threshing floor by the entrance of the gate of Samaria, with all the prophets prophesying before them. 11Now Zedekiah son of Kenaanah had made iron horns and he declared, "This is what the LORD says: 'With these you will gore the Arameans until they are destroyed.'"

▌ET'S LIVE IT!　　1 Kings 21:1–29

WANTING SOMETHING TOO MUCH ➠ One of the Ten Commandments is "Do not covet." This means to not want something that belongs to another person. In this Bible story, King Ahab coveted a field of grape vines that belonged to Naboth.

Read 1 Kings 21:1–29 and answer these questions about coveting. 1. How did coveting something make Ahab feel (1 Kings 21:4)? 2. What did Ahab's wife do to get him the field he coveted (1 Kings 21:7–16)? 3. What did God tell Ahab would happen, and why (1 Kings 21:17–22)?

Here are some things you can do to stop coveting. List all the good things you have. Choose a favorite thing to play with. Invite a friend to play with you, and share your favorite toy or game with your friend. Thank God for all the good things you do have, and the thing you wanted won't seem so important.

¹²All the other prophets were prophesying the same thing. "Attack Ramoth Gilead and be victorious," they said, "for the LORD will give it into the king's hand."

¹³The messenger who had gone to summon Micaiah said to him, "Look, as one man the other prophets are predicting success for the king. Let your word agree with theirs, and speak favorably."

¹⁴But Micaiah said, "As surely as the LORD lives, I can tell him only what the LORD tells me."

¹⁵When he arrived, the king asked him, "Micaiah, shall we go to war against Ramoth Gilead, or shall I refrain?"

"Attack and be victorious," he answered, "for the LORD will give it into the king's hand."

¹⁶The king said to him, "How many times must I make you swear to tell me nothing but the truth in the name of the LORD?"

¹⁷Then Micaiah answered, "I saw all Israel scattered on the hills like sheep without a shepherd, and the LORD said, 'These people have no master. Let each one go home in peace.' "

¹⁸The king of Israel said to Jehoshaphat, "Didn't I tell you that he never prophesies anything good about me, but only bad?"

¹⁹Micaiah continued, "Therefore hear the word of the LORD: I saw the LORD sitting on his throne with all the host of heaven standing around him on his right and on his left. ²⁰And the LORD said, 'Who will entice Ahab into attacking Ramoth Gilead and going to his death there?'

"One suggested this, and another that. ²¹Finally, a spirit came forward, stood before the LORD and said, 'I will entice him.'

²²" 'By what means?' the LORD asked.

" 'I will go out and be a lying spirit in the mouths of all his prophets,' he said.

" 'You will succeed in enticing him,' said the LORD. 'Go and do it.'

²³"So now the LORD has put a lying spirit in the mouths of all these prophets of yours. The LORD has decreed disaster for you."

²⁴Then Zedekiah son of Kenaanah went up and slapped Micaiah in the face. "Which way did the spirit from ᵃ the LORD go when he went from me to speak to you?" he asked.

²⁵Micaiah replied, "You will find out on the day you go to hide in an inner room."

²⁶The king of Israel then ordered, "Take Micaiah and send him back to Amon the ruler of the city and to Joash the king's son ²⁷and say, 'This is what the king says: Put this fellow in prison and give him nothing but bread and water until I return safely.' "

²⁸Micaiah declared, "If you ever return safely, the LORD has not spoken through me." Then he added, "Mark my words, all you people!"

Ahab Killed at Ramoth Gilead

²⁹So the king of Israel and Jehoshaphat king of Judah went up to Ramoth Gilead. ³⁰The king of Israel said to Jehoshaphat, "I will enter the battle in disguise, but you wear your royal robes." So the king of Israel disguised himself and went into battle.

³¹Now the king of Aram had ordered his thirty-two chariot commanders, "Do not fight with anyone, small or great, except the king of Israel." ³²When the chariot commanders saw Jehoshaphat, they thought, "Surely this is the king of Israel." So they turned to attack him, but when Jehoshaphat cried out, ³³the chariot commanders saw that he was not the king of Israel and stopped pursuing him.

³⁴But someone drew his bow at random and hit the king of Israel between the sections of his armor. The king told his chariot driver, "Wheel around and get me out of the fighting. I've been wounded." ³⁵All day long the battle raged, and the king

ᵃ24 Or *Spirit of*

was propped up in his chariot facing the Arameans. The blood from his wound ran onto the floor of the chariot, and that evening he died. ³⁶As the sun was setting, a cry spread through the army: "Every man to his town; everyone to his land!"

³⁷So the king died and was brought to Samaria, and they buried him there. ³⁸They washed the chariot at a pool in Samaria (where the prostitutes bathed),ᵃ and the dogs licked up his blood, as the word of the LORD had declared.

³⁹As for the other events of Ahab's reign, including all he did, the palace he built and inlaid with ivory, and the cities he fortified, are they not written in the book of the annals of the kings of Israel? ⁴⁰Ahab rested with his fathers. And Ahaziah his son succeeded him as king.

Jehoshaphat King of Judah

⁴¹Jehoshaphat son of Asa became king of Judah in the fourth year of Ahab king of Israel. ⁴²Jehoshaphat was thirty-five years old when he became king, and he reigned in Jerusalem twenty-five years. His mother's name was Azubah daughter of Shilhi. ⁴³In everything he walked in the ways of his father Asa and did not stray from them; he did what was right in the eyes of the LORD. The high places, however, were not removed, and the people continued to offer sacrifices and burn incense there. ⁴⁴Jehoshaphat was also at peace with the king of Israel.

⁴⁵As for the other events of Jehoshaphat's reign, the things he achieved and his military exploits, are they not written in the book of the annals of the kings of Judah? ⁴⁶He rid the land of the rest of the male shrine prostitutes who remained there even after the reign of his father Asa. ⁴⁷There was then no king in Edom; a deputy ruled.

⁴⁸Now Jehoshaphat built a fleet of trading shipsᵇ to go to Ophir for gold, but they never set sail—they were wrecked at Ezion Geber. ⁴⁹At that time Ahaziah son of Ahab said to Jehoshaphat, "Let my men sail with your men," but Jehoshaphat refused.

⁵⁰Then Jehoshaphat rested with his fathers and was buried with them in the city of David his father. And Jehoram his son succeeded him.

Ahaziah King of Israel

⁵¹Ahaziah son of Ahab became king of Israel in Samaria in the seventeenth year of Jehoshaphat king of Judah, and he reigned over Israel two years. ⁵²He did evil in the eyes of the LORD, because he walked in the ways of his father and mother and in the ways of Jeroboam son of Nebat, who caused Israel to sin. ⁵³He served and worshiped Baal and provoked the LORD, the God of Israel, to anger, just as his father had done.

ᵃ38 Or *Samaria and cleaned the weapons*   ᵇ48 Hebrew *of ships of Tarshish*

2 KINGS

WHO WROTE THIS BOOK?

The author of this book is unknown.

WHY WAS THIS BOOK WRITTEN?

The book of 2 Kings shows why God finally exiled Israel and Judah from the promised land.

WHAT HAPPENS IN THIS BOOK?

The stories of many kings of Judah and Israel are told in this book.

WHAT DO WE LEARN ABOUT GOD IN THIS BOOK?

God is very patient. But God will punish his people if they keep on disobeying him.

WHO IS IMPORTANT IN THIS BOOK?

The most important people in this book are Elisha, Joash, Hezekiah, and Josiah.

WHEN DID THIS HAPPEN?

The events in this book happened between 853 and 586 B.C.

WHERE DID THIS HAPPEN?

These stories happened in Israel and Judah.

WHAT ARE SOME OF THE STORIES IN THIS BOOK?

The LORD's Judgment on Ahaziah

1 After Ahab's death, Moab rebelled against Israel. ²Now Ahaziah had fallen through the lattice of his upper room in Samaria and injured himself. So he sent messengers, saying to them, "Go and consult Baal-Zebub, the god of Ekron, to see if I will recover from this injury."

³But the angel of the LORD said to Elijah the Tishbite, "Go up and meet the messengers of the king of Samaria and ask them, 'Is it because there is no God in Israel that you are going off to consult Baal-Zebub, the god of Ekron?' ⁴Therefore this is what the LORD says: 'You will not leave the bed you are lying on. You will certainly die!' " So Elijah went.

⁵When the messengers returned to the king, he asked them, "Why have you come back?"

⁶"A man came to meet us," they replied. "And he said to us, 'Go back to the king who sent you and tell him, "This is what the LORD says: Is it because there is no God in Israel that you are sending men to consult Baal-Zebub, the god of Ekron? Therefore you will not leave the bed you are lying on. You will certainly die!" ' "

⁷The king asked them, "What kind of man was it who came to meet you and told you this?"

⁸They replied, "He was a man with a garment of hair and with a leather belt around his waist."

The king said, "That was Elijah the Tishbite."

⁹Then he sent to Elijah a captain with his company of fifty men. The captain went up to Elijah, who was sitting on the top of a hill, and said to him, "Man of God, the king says, 'Come down!' "

¹⁰Elijah answered the captain, "If I am a man of God, may fire come down from heaven and consume you and your fifty men!" Then fire fell from heaven and consumed the captain and his men.

¹¹At this the king sent to Elijah another captain with his fifty men. The captain said to him, "Man of God, this is what the king says, 'Come down at once!' "

¹²"If I am a man of God," Elijah replied, "may fire come down from heaven and consume you and your fifty men!" Then the fire of God fell from heaven and consumed him and his fifty men.

¹³So the king sent a third captain with his fifty men. This third captain went up and fell on his knees before Elijah. "Man of God," he begged, "please have respect for my life and the lives of these fifty men, your servants! ¹⁴See, fire has fallen from heaven and consumed the first two captains and all their men. But now have respect for my life!"

¹⁵The angel of the LORD said to Elijah, "Go down with him; do not be afraid of him." So Elijah got up and went down with him to the king.

¹⁶He told the king, "This is what the LORD says: Is it because there is no God in Israel for you to consult that you have sent messengers to consult Baal-Zebub, the god of Ekron? Because you have done this, you will never leave the bed you are lying on. You will certainly die!" ¹⁷So he died, according to the word of the LORD that Elijah had spoken.

Because Ahaziah had no son, Joram*a* succeeded him as king in the second year of Jehoram son of Jehoshaphat king of Judah. ¹⁸As for all the other events of Ahaziah's reign, and what he did, are they not written in the book of the annals of the kings of Israel?

Elijah Taken Up to Heaven

2 When the LORD was about to take Elijah up to heaven in a whirlwind, Elijah and Elisha were on their way from Gilgal. ²Elijah said to Elisha, "Stay here; the LORD has sent me to Bethel."

But Elisha said, "As surely as the LORD lives and as you live, I will not

---

a17 Hebrew *Jehoram,* a variant of *Joram*

leave you." So they went down to
Bethel.

❓DID YOU KNOW?   2:2

How many people have gone directly to heaven without dying first?

The Bible mentions two people who went to heaven without dying: Enoch (Genesis 5:24) and Elijah (2 Kings 2).

---

³The company of the prophets at Bethel came out to Elisha and asked, "Do you know that the LORD is going to take your master from you today?"

"Yes, I know," Elisha replied, "but do not speak of it."

⁴Then Elijah said to him, "Stay here, Elisha; the LORD has sent me to Jericho."

And he replied, "As surely as the LORD lives and as you live, I will not leave you." So they went to Jericho.

⁵The company of the prophets at Jericho went up to Elisha and asked him, "Do you know that the LORD is going to take your master from you today?"

"Yes, I know," he replied, "but do not speak of it."

⁶Then Elijah said to him, "Stay here; the LORD has sent me to the Jordan."

And he replied, "As surely as the LORD lives and as you live, I will not leave you." So the two of them walked on.

⁷Fifty men of the company of the prophets went and stood at a distance, facing the place where Elijah and Elisha had stopped at the Jordan. ⁸Elijah took his cloak, rolled it up and struck the water with it. The water divided to the right and to the left, and the two of them crossed over on dry ground.

⁹When they had crossed, Elijah said to Elisha, "Tell me, what can I do for you before I am taken from you?"

"Let me inherit a double portion of your spirit," Elisha replied.

¹⁰"You have asked a difficult thing," Elijah said, "yet if you see me when I am taken from you, it will be yours—otherwise not."

❓DID YOU KNOW?   2:9

What does "a double portion of your spirit" mean?

When a father died, his oldest son inherited two times as much as any other son. Elisha wanted to be Elijah's heir. He wanted to inherit all of Elijah's abilities as a prophet, times two! God gave Elisha what he wanted. Elisha performed twice as many miracles (14) as Elijah did (7)! You can read about Elisha's miracles in 2 Kings 1–7.

---

¹¹As they were walking along and talking together, suddenly a chariot of fire and horses of fire appeared and separated the two of them, and Elijah went up to heaven in a whirlwind. ¹²Elisha saw this and cried out, "My father! My father! The chariots and horsemen of Israel!" And Elisha saw him no more. Then he took hold of his own clothes and tore them apart.

¹³He picked up the cloak that had fallen from Elijah and went back and stood on the bank of the Jordan. ¹⁴Then he took the cloak that had fallen from him and struck the water with it. "Where now is the LORD, the God of Elijah?" he asked. When he struck the water, it divided to the right and to the left, and he crossed over.

¹⁵The company of the prophets from Jericho, who were watching, said, "The spirit of Elijah is resting on Elisha." And they went to meet him and bowed to the ground before him. ¹⁶"Look," they said, "we your servants have fifty able men. Let them go and look for your master. Perhaps the Spirit of the LORD has picked him up and set him down on some mountain or in some valley."

"No," Elisha replied, "do not send them."

[17]But they persisted until he was too ashamed to refuse. So he said, "Send them." And they sent fifty men, who searched for three days but did not find him. [18]When they returned to Elisha, who was staying in Jericho, he said to them, "Didn't I tell you not to go?"

Healing of the Water

[19]The men of the city said to Elisha, "Look, our lord, this town is well situated, as you can see, but the water is bad and the land is unproductive."

[20]"Bring me a new bowl," he said, "and put salt in it." So they brought it to him.

[21]Then he went out to the spring and threw the salt into it, saying, "This is what the LORD says: 'I have healed this water. Never again will it cause death or make the land unproductive.'" [22]And the water has remained wholesome to this day, according to the word Elisha had spoken.

Elisha Is Jeered

[23]From there Elisha went up to Bethel. As he was walking along the road, some youths came out of the town and jeered at him. "Go on up, you baldhead!" they said. "Go on up, you baldhead!" [24]He turned around, looked at them and called down a curse on them in the name of the LORD. Then two bears came out of the woods and mauled forty-two of the youths. [25]And he went on to Mount Carmel and from there returned to Samaria.

Moab Revolts

3 Joram[a] son of Ahab became king of Israel in Samaria in the eighteenth year of Jehoshaphat king of Judah, and he reigned twelve years. [2]He did evil in the eyes of the LORD, but not as his father and mother had done. He got rid of the sacred stone of Baal that his father had made. [3]Nevertheless he clung to the sins of Jeroboam son of Nebat, which he had caused Israel to commit; he did not turn away from them.

[4]Now Mesha king of Moab raised sheep, and he had to supply the king of Israel with a hundred thousand lambs and with the wool of a hundred thousand rams. [5]But after Ahab died, the king of Moab rebelled against the king of Israel. [6]So at that time King Joram set out from Samaria and mobilized all Israel. [7]He also sent this message to Jehoshaphat king of Judah: "The king of Moab has rebelled against me. Will you go with me to fight against Moab?"

"I will go with you," he replied. "I am as you are, my people as your people, my horses as your horses."

[8]"By what route shall we attack?" he asked.

"Through the Desert of Edom," he answered.

[9]So the king of Israel set out with the king of Judah and the king of Edom. After a roundabout march of seven days, the army had no more water for themselves or for the animals with them.

[10]"What!" exclaimed the king of Israel. "Has the LORD called us three kings together only to hand us over to Moab?"

[11]But Jehoshaphat asked, "Is there no prophet of the LORD here, that we may inquire of the LORD through him?"

An officer of the king of Israel answered, "Elisha son of Shaphat is here. He used to pour water on the hands of Elijah.[b]"

[12]Jehoshaphat said, "The word of the LORD is with him." So the king of Israel and Jehoshaphat and the king of Edom went down to him.

[13]Elisha said to the king of Israel, "What do we have to do with each other? Go to the prophets of your father and the prophets of your mother."

"No," the king of Israel answered, "because it was the LORD who called

---

[a]1 Hebrew *Jehoram*, a variant of *Joram*; also in verse 6   [b]11 That is, he was Elijah's personal servant.

us three kings together to hand us over to Moab."

¹⁴Elisha said, "As surely as the LORD Almighty lives, whom I serve, if I did not have respect for the presence of Jehoshaphat king of Judah, I would not look at you or even notice you. ¹⁵But now bring me a harpist."

While the harpist was playing, the hand of the LORD came upon Elisha ¹⁶and he said, "This is what the LORD says: Make this valley full of ditches. ¹⁷For this is what the LORD says: You will see neither wind nor rain, yet this valley will be filled with water, and you, your cattle and your other animals will drink. ¹⁸This is an easy thing in the eyes of the LORD; he will also hand Moab over to you. ¹⁹You will overthrow every fortified city and every major town. You will cut down every good tree, stop up all the springs, and ruin every good field with stones."

²⁰The next morning, about the time for offering the sacrifice, there it was—water flowing from the direction of Edom! And the land was filled with water.

²¹Now all the Moabites had heard that the kings had come to fight against them; so every man, young and old, who could bear arms was called up and stationed on the border. ²²When they got up early in the morning, the sun was shining on the water. To the Moabites across the way, the water looked red—like blood. ²³"That's blood!" they said. "Those kings must have fought and slaughtered each other. Now to the plunder, Moab!"

²⁴But when the Moabites came to the camp of Israel, the Israelites rose up and fought them until they fled. And the Israelites invaded the land and slaughtered the Moabites. ²⁵They destroyed the towns, and each man threw a stone on every good field until it was covered. They stopped up all the springs and cut down every good tree. Only Kir Hareseth was left with its stones in place, but men armed with slings surrounded it and attacked it as well.

²⁶When the king of Moab saw that the battle had gone against him, he took with him seven hundred swordsmen to break through to the king of Edom, but they failed. ²⁷Then he took his firstborn son, who was to succeed him as king, and offered him as a sacrifice on the city wall. The fury against Israel was great; they withdrew and returned to their own land.

The Widow's Oil

4 The wife of a man from the company of the prophets cried out to Elisha, "Your servant my husband is dead, and you know that he revered the LORD. But now his creditor is coming to take my two boys as his slaves."

²Elisha replied to her, "How can I help you? Tell me, what do you have in your house?"

"Your servant has nothing there at all," she said, "except a little oil."

³Elisha said, "Go around and ask all your neighbors for empty jars. Don't ask for just a few. ⁴Then go inside and shut the door behind you and your sons. Pour oil into all the jars, and as each is filled, put it to one side."

⁵She left him and afterward shut the door behind her and her sons. They brought the jars to her and she kept pouring. ⁶When all the jars were full, she said to her son, "Bring me another one."

But he replied, "There is not a jar left." Then the oil stopped flowing.

⁷She went and told the man of God, and he said, "Go, sell the oil and pay your debts. You and your sons can live on what is left."

The Shunammite's Son Restored to Life

⁸One day Elisha went to Shunem. And a well-to-do woman was there, who urged him to stay for a meal. So whenever he came by, he stopped there to eat. ⁹She said to her husband, "I know that this man who often comes our way is a holy man of God. ¹⁰Let's make a small room on the roof and put in it a bed and a ta-

ble, a chair and a lamp for him. Then he can stay there whenever he comes to us."

¹¹One day when Elisha came, he went up to his room and lay down there. ¹²He said to his servant Gehazi, "Call the Shunammite." So he called her, and she stood before him. ¹³Elisha said to him, "Tell her, 'You have gone to all this trouble for us. Now what can be done for you? Can we speak on your behalf to the king or the commander of the army?' "

She replied, "I have a home among my own people."

¹⁴"What can be done for her?" Elisha asked.

Gehazi said, "Well, she has no son and her husband is old."

¹⁵Then Elisha said, "Call her." So he called her, and she stood in the doorway. ¹⁶"About this time next year," Elisha said, "you will hold a son in your arms."

"No, my lord," she objected. "Don't mislead your servant, O man of God!"

¹⁷But the woman became pregnant, and the next year about that same time she gave birth to a son, just as Elisha had told her.

¹⁸The child grew, and one day he went out to his father, who was with the reapers. ¹⁹"My head! My head!" he said to his father.

His father told a servant, "Carry him to his mother." ²⁰After the servant had lifted him up and carried him to his mother, the boy sat on her lap until noon, and then he died. ²¹She went up and laid him on the bed of the man of God, then shut the door and went out.

²²She called her husband and said, "Please send me one of the servants and a donkey so I can go to the man of God quickly and return."

²³"Why go to him today?" he asked. "It's not the New Moon or the Sabbath."

"It's all right," she said.

²⁴She saddled the donkey and said to her servant, "Lead on; don't slow down for me unless I tell you." ²⁵So she set out and came to the man of God at Mount Carmel.

When he saw her in the distance, the man of God said to his servant Gehazi, "Look! There's the Shunammite! ²⁶Run to meet her and ask her,

Life in Bible Times

POTS AND JARS

Pottery jars made of hardened clay were used everywhere during Bible times. Pottery making is one of the oldest crafts in Bible lands. By looking at the shape of pottery jars archaeologists, who study the past, can tell when and where they were made! Clay pots and jars were used for every type of storage as well as for eating and cooking. Some pots were very plain while others were beautifully decorated.

'Are you all right? Is your husband all right? Is your child all right?' "

"Everything is all right," she said.

²⁷When she reached the man of God at the mountain, she took hold of his feet. Gehazi came over to push her away, but the man of God said, "Leave her alone! She is in bitter distress, but the LORD has hidden it from me and has not told me why."

²⁸"Did I ask you for a son, my lord?" she said. "Didn't I tell you, 'Don't raise my hopes'?"

²⁹Elisha said to Gehazi, "Tuck your cloak into your belt, take my staff in your hand and run. If you meet anyone, do not greet him, and if anyone greets you, do not answer. Lay my staff on the boy's face."

³⁰But the child's mother said, "As surely as the LORD lives and as you live, I will not leave you." So he got up and followed her.

³¹Gehazi went on ahead and laid the staff on the boy's face, but there was no sound or response. So Gehazi went back to meet Elisha and told him, "The boy has not awakened."

³²When Elisha reached the house, there was the boy lying dead on his couch. ³³He went in, shut the door on the two of them and prayed to the LORD. ³⁴Then he got on the bed and lay upon the boy, mouth to mouth, eyes to eyes, hands to hands. As he stretched himself out upon him, the boy's body grew warm. ³⁵Elisha turned away and walked back and forth in the room and then got on the bed and stretched out upon him once more. The boy sneezed seven times and opened his eyes.

³⁶Elisha summoned Gehazi and said, "Call the Shunammite." And he did. When she came, he said, "Take your son." ³⁷She came in, fell at his feet and bowed to the ground. Then she took her son and went out.

Death in the Pot

³⁸Elisha returned to Gilgal and there was a famine in that region.

While the company of the prophets was meeting with him, he said to his servant, "Put on the large pot and cook some stew for these men."

³⁹One of them went out into the fields to gather herbs and found a wild vine. He gathered some of its gourds and filled the fold of his cloak. When he returned, he cut them up into the pot of stew, though no one knew what they were. ⁴⁰The stew was poured out for the men, but as they began to eat it, they cried out, "O man of God, there is death in the pot!" And they could not eat it.

⁴¹Elisha said, "Get some flour." He put it into the pot and said, "Serve it to the people to eat." And there was nothing harmful in the pot.

Feeding of a Hundred

⁴²A man came from Baal Shalishah, bringing the man of God twenty loaves of barley bread baked from the first ripe grain, along with some heads of new grain. "Give it to the people to eat," Elisha said.

⁴³"How can I set this before a hundred men?" his servant asked.

But Elisha answered, "Give it to the people to eat. For this is what the LORD says: 'They will eat and have some left over.'" ⁴⁴Then he set it before them, and they ate and had some left over, according to the word of the LORD.

Naaman Healed of Leprosy

5 Now Naaman was commander of the army of the king of Aram. He was a great man in the sight of his master and highly regarded, because through him the LORD had given victory to Aram. He was a valiant soldier, but he had leprosy.^a

²Now bands from Aram had gone out and had taken captive a young girl from Israel, and she served Naaman's wife. ³She said to her mistress, "If only my master would see the prophet who is in Samaria! He would cure him of his leprosy."

---

^a1 The Hebrew word was used for various diseases affecting the skin—not necessarily leprosy; also in verses 3, 6, 7, 11 and 27.

⁴Naaman went to his master and told him what the girl from Israel had said. ⁵"By all means, go," the king of Aram replied. "I will send a letter to the king of Israel." So Naaman left, taking with him ten talentsª of silver, six thousand shekelsᵇ of gold and ten sets of clothing. ⁶The letter that he took to the king of Israel read: "With this letter I am sending my servant Naaman to you so that you may cure him of his leprosy."

⁷As soon as the king of Israel read the letter, he tore his robes and said, "Am I God? Can I kill and bring back to life? Why does this fellow send someone to me to be cured of his leprosy? See how he is trying to pick a quarrel with me!"

⁸When Elisha the man of God heard that the king of Israel had torn his robes, he sent him this message: "Why have you torn your robes? Have the man come to me and he will know that there is a prophet in Israel." ⁹So Naaman went with his horses and chariots and stopped at the door of Elisha's house. ¹⁰Elisha sent a messenger to say to him, "Go, wash yourself seven times in the Jordan, and your flesh will be restored and you will be cleansed."

¹¹But Naaman went away angry and said, "I thought that he would surely come out to me and stand and call on the name of the Lord his God, wave his hand over the spot and cure me of my leprosy. ¹²Are not Abana and Pharpar, the rivers of Damascus,

better than any of the waters of Israel? Couldn't I wash in them and be cleansed?" So he turned and went off in a rage.

¹³Naaman's servants went to him and said, "My father, if the prophet had told you to do some great thing, would you not have done it? How much more, then, when he tells you, 'Wash and be cleansed'!" ¹⁴So he went down and dipped himself in the Jordan seven times, as the man of God had told him, and his flesh was restored and became clean like that of a young boy.

¹⁵Then Naaman and all his attendants went back to the man of God. He stood before him and said, "Now I know that there is no God in all the world except in Israel. Please accept now a gift from your servant."

¹⁶The prophet answered, "As surely as the Lord lives, whom I serve, I will not accept a thing." And even though Naaman urged him, he refused.

¹⁷"If you will not," said Naaman, "please let me, your servant, be given as much earth as a pair of mules can carry, for your servant will never again make burnt offerings and sacrifices to any other god but the Lord. ¹⁸But may the Lord forgive your servant for this one thing: When my master enters the temple of Rimmon to bow down and he is leaning on my arm and I bow there also—when I bow down in the temple of Rimmon, may the Lord forgive your servant for this."

ª5 That is, about 750 pounds (about 340 kilograms)
ᵇ5 That is, about 150 pounds (about 70 kilograms)

⬛LET'S LIVE IT!
2 Kings 5:1–14

TELLING THE GOOD NEWS ➡ Read in 2 Kings 5:1–14 about a girl who was probably about your age. She was a slave for the wife of Naaman, the army commander. The girl in the Bible story helped just by telling what she knew about God. Write down five important things you know about God. Show the list to your Sunday school teacher or your mom or dad, and ask if you have left out anything important. Then tell a friend what you know about God and Jesus.

¹⁹"Go in peace," Elisha said.

After Naaman had traveled some distance, ²⁰Gehazi, the servant of Elisha the man of God, said to himself, "My master was too easy on Naaman, this Aramean, by not accepting from him what he brought. As surely as the LORD lives, I will run after him and get something from him."

²¹So Gehazi hurried after Naaman. When Naaman saw him running toward him, he got down from the chariot to meet him. "Is everything all right?" he asked.

²²"Everything is all right," Gehazi answered. "My master sent me to say, 'Two young men from the company of the prophets have just come to me from the hill country of Ephraim. Please give them a talent*a* of silver and two sets of clothing.' "

²³"By all means, take two talents," said Naaman. He urged Gehazi to accept them, and then tied up the two talents of silver in two bags, with two sets of clothing. He gave them to two of his servants, and they carried them ahead of Gehazi. ²⁴When Gehazi came to the hill, he took the things from the servants and put them away in the house. He sent the men away and they left. ²⁵Then he went in and stood before his master Elisha.

"Where have you been, Gehazi?" Elisha asked.

"Your servant didn't go anywhere," Gehazi answered.

²⁶But Elisha said to him, "Was not my spirit with you when the man got down from his chariot to meet you? Is this the time to take money, or to accept clothes, olive groves, vineyards, flocks, herds, or menservants and maidservants? ²⁷Naaman's leprosy will cling to you and to your descendants forever." Then Gehazi went from Elisha's presence and he was leprous, as white as snow.

An Axhead Floats

6 The company of the prophets said to Elisha, "Look, the place where we meet with you is too small for us. ²Let us go to the Jordan, where each of us can get a pole; and let us build a place there for us to live."

And he said, "Go."

³Then one of them said, "Won't you please come with your servants?"

"I will," Elisha replied. ⁴And he went with them.

They went to the Jordan and began to cut down trees. ⁵As one of them was cutting down a tree, the iron axhead fell into the water. "Oh, my lord," he cried out, "it was borrowed!"

⁶The man of God asked, "Where did it fall?" When he showed him the place, Elisha cut a stick and threw it there, and made the iron float. ⁷"Lift it out," he said. Then the man reached out his hand and took it.

Elisha Traps Blinded Arameans

⁸Now the king of Aram was at war with Israel. After conferring with his officers, he said, "I will set up my camp in such and such a place."

⁹The man of God sent word to the king of Israel: "Beware of passing that place, because the Arameans are going down there." ¹⁰So the king of Israel checked on the place indicated by the man of God. Time and again Elisha warned the king, so that he was on his guard in such places.

¹¹This enraged the king of Aram. He summoned his officers and demanded of them, "Will you not tell me which of us is on the side of the king of Israel?"

¹²"None of us, my lord the king," said one of his officers, "but Elisha, the prophet who is in Israel, tells the king of Israel the very words you speak in your bedroom."

¹³"Go, find out where he is," the king ordered, "so I can send men and capture him." The report came back: "He is in Dothan." ¹⁴Then he sent horses and chariots and a strong force there. They went by night and surrounded the city.

¹⁵When the servant of the man of

---

a22 That is, about 75 pounds (about 34 kilograms)

God got up and went out early the next morning, an army with horses and chariots had surrounded the city. "Oh, my lord, what shall we do?" the servant asked.

16"Don't be afraid," the prophet answered. "Those who are with us are more than those who are with them."

17And Elisha prayed, "O LORD, open his eyes so he may see." Then the LORD opened the servant's eyes, and he looked and saw the hills full of horses and chariots of fire all around Elisha.

18As the enemy came down toward him, Elisha prayed to the LORD, "Strike these people with blindness." So he struck them with blindness, as Elisha had asked.

19Elisha told them, "This is not the road and this is not the city. Follow me, and I will lead you to the man you are looking for." And he led them to Samaria.

20After they entered the city, Elisha said, "LORD, open the eyes of these men so they can see." Then the LORD opened their eyes and they looked, and there they were, inside Samaria.

21When the king of Israel saw them, he asked Elisha, "Shall I kill them, my father? Shall I kill them?"

22"Do not kill them," he answered. "Would you kill men you have captured with your own sword or bow? Set food and water before them so that they may eat and drink and then go back to their master." 23So he prepared a great feast for them, and after they had finished eating and drinking, he sent them away, and they returned to their master. So the bands from Aram stopped raiding Israel's territory.

Famine in Besieged Samaria

24Some time later, Ben-Hadad king of Aram mobilized his entire army and marched up and laid siege to Samaria. 25There was a great famine in the city; the siege lasted so long that a donkey's head sold for eighty shekels*a* of silver, and a quarter of a cab*b* of seed pods*c* for five shekels. *d*

26As the king of Israel was passing by on the wall, a woman cried to him, "Help me, my lord the king!"

27The king replied, "If the LORD does not help you, where can I get help for you? From the threshing floor? From the winepress?" 28Then he asked her, "What's the matter?"

She answered, "This woman said to me, 'Give up your son so we may eat him today, and tomorrow we'll eat my son.' 29So we cooked my son and ate him. The next day I said to her, 'Give up your son so we may eat him,' but she had hidden him."

30When the king heard the woman's words, he tore his robes. As he went along the wall, the people looked, and there, underneath, he had sackcloth on his body. 31He said, "May God deal with me, be it ever so severely, if the head of Elisha son of Shaphat remains on his shoulders today!"

32Now Elisha was sitting in his house, and the elders were sitting with him. The king sent a messenger ahead, but before he arrived, Elisha said to the elders, "Don't you see how this murderer is sending someone to cut off my head? Look, when the messenger comes, shut the door and hold it shut against him. Is not the sound of his master's footsteps behind him?"

33While he was still talking to them, the messenger came down to him. And ‚the king‚ said, "This disaster is from the LORD. Why should I wait for the LORD any longer?"

7 Elisha said, "Hear the word of the LORD. This is what the LORD says: About this time tomorrow, a seah*e* of flour will sell for a shekel*f*

---

a25 That is, about 2 pounds (about 1 kilogram)   *b25* That is, probably about 1/2 pint (about 0.3 liter)   *c25* Or *of dove's dung*   *d25* That is, about 2 ounces (about 55 grams)   *e1* That is, probably about 7 quarts (about 7.3 liters); also in verses 16 and 18   *f1* That is, about 2/5 ounce (about 11 grams); also in verses 16 and 18

and two seahs*a* of barley for a shekel at the gate of Samaria."

²The officer on whose arm the king was leaning said to the man of God, "Look, even if the LORD should open the floodgates of the heavens, could this happen?"

"You will see it with your own eyes," answered Elisha, "but you will not eat any of it!"

The Siege Lifted

³Now there were four men with leprosy*b* at the entrance of the city gate. They said to each other, "Why stay here until we die? ⁴If we say, 'We'll go into the city'—the famine is there, and we will die. And if we stay here, we will die. So let's go over to the camp of the Arameans and surrender. If they spare us, we live; if they kill us, then we die."

⁵At dusk they got up and went to the camp of the Arameans. When they reached the edge of the camp, not a man was there, ⁶for the Lord had caused the Arameans to hear the sound of chariots and horses and a great army, so that they said to one another, "Look, the king of Israel has hired the Hittite and Egyptian kings to attack us!" ⁷So they got up and fled in the dusk and abandoned their tents and their horses and donkeys. They left the camp as it was and ran for their lives.

⁸The men who had leprosy reached the edge of the camp and entered one of the tents. They ate and drank, and carried away silver, gold and clothes, and went off and hid them. They returned and entered another tent and took some things from it and hid them also.

⁹Then they said to each other, "We're not doing right. This is a day of good news and we are keeping it to ourselves. If we wait until daylight, punishment will overtake us. Let's go at once and report this to the royal palace."

¹⁰So they went and called out to the city gatekeepers and told them, "We went into the Aramean camp and not a man was there—not a sound of anyone—only tethered horses and donkeys, and the tents left just as they were." ¹¹The gatekeepers shouted the news, and it was reported within the palace.

¹²The king got up in the night and said to his officers, "I will tell you what the Arameans have done to us. They know we are starving; so they have left the camp to hide in the countryside, thinking, 'They will surely come out, and then we will take them alive and get into the city.'"

¹³One of his officers answered, "Have some men take five of the horses that are left in the city. Their plight will be like that of all the Israelites left here—yes, they will only be like all these Israelites who are

---

a1 That is, probably about 13 quarts (about 15 liters); also in verses 16 and 18   *b3* The Hebrew word is used for various diseases affecting the skin—not necessarily leprosy; also in verse 8

▌ET'S LIVE IT!   2 Kings 7:3–11

KEEP IT TO YOURSELF? ➟ The Arameans were camped all around the city of Samaria. They were not letting anyone or anything go in or out of the city, so the people inside were starving. Read 2 Kings 7:3–11 to find out what four men with leprosy did.

Now read 2 Kings 7:9 again. Do you think Christians today sometimes do the same thing? Our Good News is that Jesus died to save us from sin so we can go to heaven. People who don't believe in Jesus will not go to heaven. If you don't tell people about the Good News, they may never hear it. Do you think God wants you to tell them?

doomed. So let us send them to find
out what happened."

¹⁴So they selected two chariots
with their horses, and the king sent
them after the Aramean army. He
commanded the drivers, "Go and find
out what has happened." ¹⁵They followed them as far as the Jordan, and
they found the whole road strewn
with the clothing and equipment the
Arameans had thrown away in their
headlong flight. So the messengers
returned and reported to the king.
¹⁶Then the people went out and plundered the camp of the Arameans. So
a seah of flour sold for a shekel, and
two seahs of barley sold for a shekel,
as the Lord had said.

¹⁷Now the king had put the officer
on whose arm he leaned in charge of
the gate, and the people trampled
him in the gateway, and he died, just
as the man of God had foretold when
the king came down to his house. ¹⁸It
happened as the man of God had said
to the king: "About this time tomorrow, a seah of flour will sell for a
shekel and two seahs of barley for a
shekel at the gate of Samaria."

¹⁹The officer had said to the man of
God, "Look, even if the Lord should
open the floodgates of the heavens,
could this happen?" The man of God
had replied, "You will see it with
your own eyes, but you will not eat
any of it!" ²⁰And that is exactly what
happened to him, for the people trampled him in the gateway, and he
died.

The Shunammite's Land Restored

8 Now Elisha had said to the woman whose son he had restored to
life, "Go away with your family and
stay for a while wherever you can,
because the Lord has decreed a famine in the land that will last seven
years." ²The woman proceeded to do
as the man of God said. She and her
family went away and stayed in the
land of the Philistines seven years.

³At the end of the seven years she
came back from the land of the Philistines and went to the king to beg for

her house and land. ⁴The king was
talking to Gehazi, the servant of the
man of God, and had said, "Tell me
about all the great things Elisha has
done." ⁵Just as Gehazi was telling the
king how Elisha had restored the
dead to life, the woman whose son
Elisha had brought back to life came
to beg the king for her house and
land.

Gehazi said, "This is the woman,
my lord the king, and this is her son
whom Elisha restored to life." ⁶The
king asked the woman about it, and
she told him.

Then he assigned an official to her
case and said to him, "Give back everything that belonged to her, including all the income from her land from
the day she left the country until
now."

Hazael Murders Ben-Hadad

⁷Elisha went to Damascus, and
Ben-Hadad king of Aram was ill.
When the king was told, "The man of
God has come all the way up here,"
⁸he said to Hazael, "Take a gift with
you and go to meet the man of God.
Consult the Lord through him; ask
him, 'Will I recover from this illness?' "

?DID YOU KNOW?   **8:9**

Who was Hazael?

Hazael was a soldier who became king of Aram (Syria). He became a powerful enemy of Israel
and killed many Israelites.

---

⁹Hazael went to meet Elisha, taking with him as a gift forty camel-
loads of all the finest wares of Damascus. He went in and stood before
him, and said, "Your son Ben-Hadad
king of Aram has sent me to ask,
'Will I recover from this illness?' "

¹⁰Elisha answered, "Go and say to
him, 'You will certainly recover';

but*ª* the LORD has revealed to me that he will in fact die." ¹¹He stared at him with a fixed gaze until Hazael felt ashamed. Then the man of God began to weep.

¹²"Why is my lord weeping?" asked Hazael.

"Because I know the harm you will do to the Israelites," he answered. "You will set fire to their fortified places, kill their young men with the sword, dash their little children to the ground, and rip open their pregnant women."

¹³Hazael said, "How could your servant, a mere dog, accomplish such a feat?"

"The LORD has shown me that you will become king of Aram," answered Elisha.

¹⁴Then Hazael left Elisha and returned to his master. When Ben-Hadad asked, "What did Elisha say to you?" Hazael replied, "He told me that you would certainly recover." ¹⁵But the next day he took a thick cloth, soaked it in water and spread it over the king's face, so that he died. Then Hazael succeeded him as king.

Jehoram King of Judah

¹⁶In the fifth year of Joram son of Ahab king of Israel, when Jehoshaphat was king of Judah, Jehoram son of Jehoshaphat began his reign as king of Judah. ¹⁷He was thirty-two years old when he became king, and he reigned in Jerusalem eight years. ¹⁸He walked in the ways of the kings of Israel, as the house of Ahab had done, for he married a daughter of Ahab. He did evil in the eyes of the LORD. ¹⁹Nevertheless, for the sake of his servant David, the LORD was not willing to destroy Judah. He had promised to maintain a lamp for David and his descendants forever.

²⁰In the time of Jehoram, Edom rebelled against Judah and set up its own king. ²¹So Jehoram*ᵇ* went to Zair with all his chariots. The Edomites surrounded him and his chariot

commanders, but he rose up and broke through by night; his army, however, fled back home. ²²To this day Edom has been in rebellion against Judah. Libnah revolted at the same time.

²³As for the other events of Jehoram's reign, and all he did, are they not written in the book of the annals of the kings of Judah? ²⁴Jehoram rested with his fathers and was buried with them in the City of David. And Ahaziah his son succeeded him as king.

Ahaziah King of Judah

²⁵In the twelfth year of Joram son of Ahab king of Israel, Ahaziah son of Jehoram king of Judah began to reign. ²⁶Ahaziah was twenty-two years old when he became king, and he reigned in Jerusalem one year. His mother's name was Athaliah, a granddaughter of Omri king of Israel. ²⁷He walked in the ways of the house of Ahab and did evil in the eyes of the LORD, as the house of Ahab had done, for he was related by marriage to Ahab's family.

²⁸Ahaziah went with Joram son of Ahab to war against Hazael king of Aram at Ramoth Gilead. The Arameans wounded Joram; ²⁹so King Joram returned to Jezreel to recover from the wounds the Arameans had inflicted on him at Ramoth*ᶜ* in his battle with Hazael king of Aram.

Then Ahaziah son of Jehoram king of Judah went down to Jezreel to see Joram son of Ahab, because he had been wounded.

Jehu Anointed King of Israel

9 The prophet Elisha summoned a man from the company of the prophets and said to him, "Tuck your cloak into your belt, take this flask of oil with you and go to Ramoth Gilead. ²When you get there, look for Jehu son of Jehoshaphat, the son of Nimshi. Go to him, get him away from his companions and take him into an in-

---

ª10 The Hebrew may also be read *Go and say, 'You will certainly not recover,' for.*   *ᵇ21* Hebrew *Joram*, a variant of *Jehoram*; also in verses 23 and 24   *ᶜ29* Hebrew *Ramah*, a variant of *Ramoth*

ner room. ³Then take the flask and pour the oil on his head and declare, 'This is what the LORD says: I anoint you king over Israel.' Then open the door and run; don't delay!"

?ᴅɪᴅ ʏᴏᴜ ᴋɴᴏᴡ?   9:2

Who was Jehu?

Jehu was a general who became king of Israel. He killed the family of evil King Ahab and all the priests of Baal. But he still did not follow God with all his heart, and so continued Israel's line of wicked kings.

---

⁴So the young man, the prophet, went to Ramoth Gilead. ⁵When he arrived, he found the army officers sitting together. "I have a message for you, commander," he said.

"For which of us?" asked Jehu.

"For you, commander," he replied.

⁶Jehu got up and went into the house. Then the prophet poured the oil on Jehu's head and declared, "This is what the LORD, the God of Israel, says: 'I anoint you king over the LORD's people Israel. ⁷You are to destroy the house of Ahab your master, and I will avenge the blood of my servants the prophets and the blood of all the LORD's servants shed by Jezebel. ⁸The whole house of Ahab will perish. I will cut off from Ahab every last male in Israel—slave or free. ⁹I will make the house of Ahab like the house of Jeroboam son of Nebat and like the house of Baasha son of Ahijah. ¹⁰As for Jezebel, dogs will devour her on the plot of ground at Jezreel, and no one will bury her.' " Then he opened the door and ran.

¹¹When Jehu went out to his fellow officers, one of them asked him, "Is everything all right? Why did this madman come to you?"

"You know the man and the sort of things he says," Jehu replied.

¹²"That's not true!" they said. "Tell us."

Jehu said, "Here is what he told me: 'This is what the LORD says: I anoint you king over Israel.' "

¹³They hurried and took their cloaks and spread them under him on the bare steps. Then they blew the trumpet and shouted, "Jehu is king!"

Jehu Kills Joram and Ahaziah

¹⁴So Jehu son of Jehoshaphat, the son of Nimshi, conspired against Joram. (Now Joram and all Israel had been defending Ramoth Gilead against Hazael king of Aram, ¹⁵but King Joramᵃ had returned to Jezreel to recover from the wounds the Arameans had inflicted on him in the battle with Hazael king of Aram.) Jehu said, "If this is the way you feel, don't let anyone slip out of the city to go and tell the news in Jezreel." ¹⁶Then he got into his chariot and rode to Jezreel, because Joram was resting there and Ahaziah king of Judah had gone down to see him.

¹⁷When the lookout standing on the tower in Jezreel saw Jehu's troops approaching, he called out, "I see some troops coming."

"Get a horseman," Joram ordered. "Send him to meet them and ask, 'Do you come in peace?' "

¹⁸The horseman rode off to meet Jehu and said, "This is what the king says: 'Do you come in peace?' "

"What do you have to do with peace?" Jehu replied. "Fall in behind me."

The lookout reported, "The messenger has reached them, but he isn't coming back."

¹⁹So the king sent out a second horseman. When he came to them he said, "This is what the king says: 'Do you come in peace?' "

Jehu replied, "What do you have to do with peace? Fall in behind me."

²⁰The lookout reported, "He has reached them, but he isn't coming

---

ᵃ15 Hebrew *Jehoram*, a variant of *Joram*; also in verses 17 and 21-24 back either. The driving is like that of Jehu son of Nimshi—he drives like a madman."

21"Hitch up my chariot," Joram ordered. And when it was hitched up, Joram king of Israel and Ahaziah king of Judah rode out, each in his own chariot, to meet Jehu. They met him at the plot of ground that had belonged to Naboth the Jezreelite. 22When Joram saw Jehu he asked, "Have you come in peace, Jehu?"

"How can there be peace," Jehu replied, "as long as all the idolatry and witchcraft of your mother Jezebel abound?"

23Joram turned about and fled, calling out to Ahaziah, "Treachery, Ahaziah!"

24Then Jehu drew his bow and shot Joram between the shoulders. The arrow pierced his heart and he slumped down in his chariot. 25Jehu said to Bidkar, his chariot officer, "Pick him up and throw him on the field that belonged to Naboth the Jezreelite. Remember how you and I were riding together in chariots behind Ahab his father when the LORD made this prophecy about him: 26'Yesterday I saw the blood of Naboth and the blood of his sons, declares the LORD, and I will surely make you pay for it on this plot of ground, declares the LORD.'a Now then, pick him up and throw him on that plot, in accordance with the word of the LORD."

27When Ahaziah king of Judah saw what had happened, he fled up the road to Beth Haggan.b Jehu chased him, shouting, "Kill him too!" They wounded him in his chariot on the way up to Gur near Ibleam, but he escaped to Megiddo and died there. 28His servants took him by chariot to Jerusalem and buried him with his fathers in his tomb in the City of David. 29(In the eleventh year of Joram son of Ahab, Ahaziah had become king of Judah.)

Jezebel Killed

30Then Jehu went to Jezreel. When Jezebel heard about it, she painted her eyes, arranged her hair and looked out of a window. 31As Jehu entered the gate, she asked, "Have you come in peace, Zimri, you murderer of your master?"c

32He looked up at the window and called out, "Who is on my side? Who?" Two or three eunuchs looked down at him. 33"Throw her down!" Jehu said. So they threw her down, and some of her blood spattered the wall and the horses as they trampled her underfoot.

34Jehu went in and ate and drank. "Take care of that cursed woman," he said, "and bury her, for she was a king's daughter." 35But when they went out to bury her, they found nothing except her skull, her feet and her hands. 36They went back and told Jehu, who said, "This is the word of the LORD that he spoke through his servant Elijah the Tishbite: On the plot of ground at Jezreel dogs will devour Jezebel's flesh.d 37Jezebel's body will be like refuse on the ground in the plot at Jezreel, so that no one will be able to say, 'This is Jezebel.' "

Ahab's Family Killed

10 Now there were in Samaria seventy sons of the house of Ahab. So Jehu wrote letters and sent them to Samaria: to the officials of Jezreel,e to the elders and to the guardians of Ahab's children. He said, 2"As soon as this letter reaches you, since your master's sons are with you and you have chariots and horses, a fortified city and weapons, 3choose the best and most worthy of your master's sons and set him on his father's throne. Then fight for your master's house."

4But they were terrified and said, "If two kings could not resist him, how can we?"

5So the palace administrator, the

city governor, the elders and the guardians sent this message to Jehu: "We are your servants and we will do anything you say. We will not appoint anyone as king; you do whatever you think best."

⁶Then Jehu wrote them a second letter, saying, "If you are on my side and will obey me, take the heads of your master's sons and come to me in Jezreel by this time tomorrow."

Now the royal princes, seventy of them, were with the leading men of the city, who were rearing them. ⁷When the letter arrived, these men took the princes and slaughtered all seventy of them. They put their heads in baskets and sent them to Jehu in Jezreel. ⁸When the messenger arrived, he told Jehu, "They have brought the heads of the princes."

Then Jehu ordered, "Put them in two piles at the entrance of the city gate until morning."

⁹The next morning Jehu went out. He stood before all the people and said, "You are innocent. It was I who conspired against my master and killed him, but who killed all these? ¹⁰Know then, that not a word the LORD has spoken against the house of Ahab will fail. The LORD has done what he promised through his servant Elijah." ¹¹So Jehu killed everyone in Jezreel who remained of the house of Ahab, as well as all his chief men, his close friends and his priests, leaving him no survivor.

¹²Jehu then set out and went toward Samaria. At Beth Eked of the Shepherds, ¹³he met some relatives of Ahaziah king of Judah and asked, "Who are you?"

They said, "We are relatives of Ahaziah, and we have come down to greet the families of the king and of the queen mother."

¹⁴"Take them alive!" he ordered. So they took them alive and slaughtered them by the well of Beth Eked—forty-two men. He left no survivor.

¹⁵After he left there, he came upon Jehonadab son of Recab, who was on his way to meet him. Jehu greeted him and said, "Are you in accord with me, as I am with you?"

"I am," Jehonadab answered.

"If so," said Jehu, "give me your hand." So he did, and Jehu helped him up into the chariot. ¹⁶Jehu said, "Come with me and see my zeal for the LORD." Then he had him ride along in his chariot.

¹⁷When Jehu came to Samaria, he killed all who were left there of Ahab's family; he destroyed them, according to the word of the LORD spoken to Elijah.

Ministers of Baal Killed

¹⁸Then Jehu brought all the people together and said to them, "Ahab served Baal a little; Jehu will serve him much. ¹⁹Now summon all the prophets of Baal, all his ministers and all his priests. See that no one is missing, because I am going to hold a great sacrifice for Baal. Anyone who fails to come will no longer live." But Jehu was acting deceptively in order to destroy the ministers of Baal.

²⁰Jehu said, "Call an assembly in honor of Baal." So they proclaimed it. ²¹Then he sent word throughout Israel, and all the ministers of Baal came; not one stayed away. They crowded into the temple of Baal until it was full from one end to the other. ²²And Jehu said to the keeper of the wardrobe, "Bring robes for all the ministers of Baal." So he brought out robes for them.

²³Then Jehu and Jehonadab son of Recab went into the temple of Baal. Jehu said to the ministers of Baal, "Look around and see that no servants of the LORD are here with you—only ministers of Baal." ²⁴So they went in to make sacrifices and burnt offerings. Now Jehu had posted eighty men outside with this warning: "If one of you lets any of the men I am placing in your hands escape, it will be your life for his life."

²⁵As soon as Jehu had finished making the burnt offering, he ordered the guards and officers: "Go in and kill them; let no one escape." So they cut them down with the sword.

The guards and officers threw the bodies out and then entered the inner shrine of the temple of Baal. [26]They brought the sacred stone out of the temple of Baal and burned it. [27]They demolished the sacred stone of Baal and tore down the temple of Baal, and people have used it for a latrine to this day.

[28]So Jehu destroyed Baal worship in Israel. [29]However, he did not turn away from the sins of Jeroboam son of Nebat, which he had caused Israel to commit—the worship of the golden calves at Bethel and Dan.

[30]The LORD said to Jehu, "Because you have done well in accomplishing what is right in my eyes and have done to the house of Ahab all I had in mind to do, your descendants will sit on the throne of Israel to the fourth generation." [31]Yet Jehu was not careful to keep the law of the LORD, the God of Israel, with all his heart. He did not turn away from the sins of Jeroboam, which he had caused Israel to commit.

[32]In those days the LORD began to reduce the size of Israel. Hazael overpowered the Israelites throughout their territory [33]east of the Jordan in all the land of Gilead (the region of Gad, Reuben and Manasseh), from Aroer by the Arnon Gorge through Gilead to Bashan.

[34]As for the other events of Jehu's reign, all he did, and all his achievements, are they not written in the book of the annals of the kings of Israel?

[35]Jehu rested with his fathers and was buried in Samaria. And Jehoahaz his son succeeded him as king. [36]The time that Jehu reigned over Israel in Samaria was twenty-eight years.

Athaliah and Joash

11 When Athaliah the mother of Ahaziah saw that her son was dead, she proceeded to destroy the whole royal family. [2]But Jehosheba, the daughter of King Jehoram[a] and sister of Ahaziah, took Joash son of Ahaziah and stole him away from among the royal princes, who were about to be murdered. She put him and his nurse in a bedroom to hide him from Athaliah; so he was not killed. [3]He remained hidden with his nurse at the temple of the LORD for six years while Athaliah ruled the land.

[4]In the seventh year Jehoiada sent for the commanders of units of a hundred, the Carites and the guards and had them brought to him at the temple of the LORD. He made a covenant with them and put them under oath at the temple of the LORD. Then he showed them the king's son. [5]He commanded them, saying, "This is what you are to do: You who are in the three companies that are going on duty on the Sabbath—a third of you guarding the royal palace, [6]a third at the Sur Gate, and a third at the gate behind the guard, who take turns guarding the temple— [7]and you who are in the other two companies that normally go off Sabbath duty are all to guard the temple for the king. [8]Station yourselves around the king, each man with his weapon in his hand. Anyone who approaches your ranks[b] must be put to death. Stay close to the king wherever he goes."

[9]The commanders of units of a hundred did just as Jehoiada the priest ordered. Each one took his men—those who were going on duty on the Sabbath and those who were going off duty—and came to Jehoiada the priest. [10]Then he gave the commanders the spears and shields that had belonged to King David and that were in the temple of the LORD. [11]The guards, each with his weapon in his hand, stationed themselves around the king—near the altar and the temple, from the south side to the north side of the temple.

[12]Jehoiada brought out the king's son and put the crown on him; he presented him with a copy of the covenant and proclaimed him king.

---

a2 Hebrew Joram, a variant of *Jehoram*   *b8 Or approaches the precincts*

They anointed him, and the people clapped their hands and shouted, "Long live the king!"

13When Athaliah heard the noise made by the guards and the people, she went to the people at the temple of the LORD. 14She looked and there was the king, standing by the pillar, as the custom was. The officers and the trumpeters were beside the king, and all the people of the land were rejoicing and blowing trumpets. Then Athaliah tore her robes and called out, "Treason! Treason!"

15Jehoiada the priest ordered the commanders of units of a hundred, who were in charge of the troops: "Bring her out between the ranksa and put to the sword anyone who follows her." For the priest had said, "She must not be put to death in the temple of the LORD." 16So they seized her as she reached the place where the horses enter the palace grounds, and there she was put to death.

17Jehoiada then made a covenant between the LORD and the king and people that they would be the LORD's people. He also made a covenant between the king and the people. 18All the people of the land went to the temple of Baal and tore it down. They smashed the altars and idols to pieces and killed Mattan the priest of Baal in front of the altars.

Then Jehoiada the priest posted guards at the temple of the LORD. 19He took with him the commanders of hundreds, the Carites, the guards and all the people of the land, and together they brought the king down from the temple of the LORD and went into the palace, entering by way of the gate of the guards. The king then took his place on the royal throne, 20and all the people of the land rejoiced. And the city was quiet, because Athaliah had been slain with the sword at the palace.

21Joashb was seven years old when he began to reign.

Joash Repairs the Temple

12 In the seventh year of Jehu, Joashc became king, and he reigned in Jerusalem forty years. His mother's name was Zibiah; she was from Beersheba. 2Joash did what was right in the eyes of the LORD all the years Jehoiada the priest instructed him. 3The high places, however, were not removed; the people continued to offer sacrifices and burn incense there.

4Joash said to the priests, "Collect all the money that is brought as sacred offerings to the temple of the LORD—the money collected in the census, the money received from personal vows and the money brought

a15 Or out from the precincts   b21 Hebrew Jehoash, a variant of Joash   c1 Hebrew Jehoash, a variant of Joash; also in verses 2, 4, 6, 7 and 18

Life in Bible Times

JOASH'S CROWN
The kings of many ancient empires had heavy crowns made of silver and gold and sometimes covered with jewels. However, the kings of Israel had a different kind of crown. Their crown was a flat, thin plate of gold that was fastened to the king's soft cloth headdress.

voluntarily to the temple. ⁵Let every priest receive the money from one of the treasurers, and let it be used to repair whatever damage is found in the temple."

⁶But by the twenty-third year of King Joash the priests still had not repaired the temple. ⁷Therefore King Joash summoned Jehoiada the priest and the other priests and asked them, "Why aren't you repairing the damage done to the temple? Take no more money from your treasurers, but hand it over for repairing the temple." ⁸The priests agreed that they would not collect any more money from the people and that they would not repair the temple themselves.

⁹Jehoiada the priest took a chest and bored a hole in its lid. He placed it beside the altar, on the right side as one enters the temple of the LORD. The priests who guarded the entrance put into the chest all the money that was brought to the temple of the LORD. ¹⁰Whenever they saw that there was a large amount of money in the chest, the royal secretary and the high priest came, counted the money that had been brought into the temple of the LORD and put it into bags. ¹¹When the amount had been determined, they gave the money to the men appointed to supervise the work on the temple. With it they paid those who worked on the temple of the LORD—the carpenters and builders, ¹²the masons and stonecutters. They purchased timber and dressed stone

for the repair of the temple of the LORD, and met all the other expenses of restoring the temple.

¹³The money brought into the temple was not spent for making silver basins, wick trimmers, sprinkling bowls, trumpets or any other articles of gold or silver for the temple of the LORD; ¹⁴it was paid to the workmen, who used it to repair the temple. ¹⁵They did not require an accounting from those to whom they gave the money to pay the workers, because they acted with complete honesty. ¹⁶The money from the guilt offerings and sin offerings was not brought into the temple of the LORD; it belonged to the priests.

¹⁷About this time Hazael king of Aram went up and attacked Gath and captured it. Then he turned to attack Jerusalem. ¹⁸But Joash king of Judah took all the sacred objects dedicated by his fathers—Jehoshaphat, Jehoram and Ahaziah, the kings of Judah—and the gifts he himself had dedicated and all the gold found in the treasuries of the temple of the LORD and of the royal palace, and he sent them to Hazael king of Aram, who then withdrew from Jerusalem.

¹⁹As for the other events of the reign of Joash, and all he did, are they not written in the book of the annals of the kings of Judah? ²⁰His officials conspired against him and assassinated him at Beth Millo, on the road down to Silla. ²¹The officials

---

▌ET'S LIVE IT!   2 Kings 12:1–12

A CHURCH BUILDING PROGRAM ▶ Joash became king when he was only seven years old. Read 2 Kings 12:1–12 and find out what Joash did to show he loved God. How did others who loved God help him?

Sometimes churches need to be repaired. Many churches have building programs to build more rooms for Church school or a bigger room for worship services. Here are some ways you can earn money to give, just as the people gave to help Joash repair God's temple.

1. Collect newspapers. 2. Collect returnable soda pop bottles. 3. Wash cars. 4. Mow lawns, rake leaves or sweep a garage. 5. Collect things for a garage sale. 6. Bake and sell cookies and cakes.

What will you do to earn money for your church?

who murdered him were Jozabad son of Shimeath and Jehozabad son of Shomer. He died and was buried with his fathers in the City of David. And Amaziah his son succeeded him as king.

Jehoahaz King of Israel

13 In the twenty-third year of Joash son of Ahaziah king of Judah, Jehoahaz son of Jehu became king of Israel in Samaria, and he reigned seventeen years. ²He did evil in the eyes of the LORD by following the sins of Jeroboam son of Nebat, which he had caused Israel to commit, and he did not turn away from them. ³So the LORD's anger burned against Israel, and for a long time he kept them under the power of Hazael king of Aram and Ben-Hadad his son.

⁴Then Jehoahaz sought the LORD's favor, and the LORD listened to him, for he saw how severely the king of Aram was oppressing Israel. ⁵The LORD provided a deliverer for Israel, and they escaped from the power of Aram. So the Israelites lived in their own homes as they had before. ⁶But they did not turn away from the sins of the house of Jeroboam, which he had caused Israel to commit; they continued in them. Also, the Asherah pole*a* remained standing in Samaria.

⁷Nothing had been left of the army of Jehoahaz except fifty horsemen, ten chariots and ten thousand foot soldiers, for the king of Aram had destroyed the rest and made them like the dust at threshing time.

⁸As for the other events of the reign of Jehoahaz, all he did and his achievements, are they not written in the book of the annals of the kings of Israel? ⁹Jehoahaz rested with his fathers and was buried in Samaria. And Jehoash*b* his son succeeded him as king.

Jehoash King of Israel

¹⁰In the thirty-seventh year of Joash king of Judah, Jehoash son of Je-hoahaz became king of Israel in Samaria, and he reigned sixteen years. ¹¹He did evil in the eyes of the LORD and did not turn away from any of the sins of Jeroboam son of Nebat, which he had caused Israel to commit; he continued in them.

¹²As for the other events of the reign of Jehoash, all he did and his achievements, including his war against Amaziah king of Judah, are they not written in the book of the annals of the kings of Israel? ¹³Jeho-ash rested with his fathers, and Jeroboam succeeded him on the throne. Jehoash was buried in Samaria with the kings of Israel.

¹⁴Now Elisha was suffering from the illness from which he died. Jeho-ash king of Israel went down to see him and wept over him. "My father! My father!" he cried. "The chariots and horsemen of Israel!"

¹⁵Elisha said, "Get a bow and some arrows," and he did so. ¹⁶"Take the bow in your hands," he said to the king of Israel. When he had taken it, Elisha put his hands on the king's hands.

¹⁷"Open the east window," he said, and he opened it. "Shoot!" Elisha said, and he shot. "The LORD's arrow of victory, the arrow of victory over Aram!" Elisha declared. "You will completely destroy the Arameans at Aphek."

¹⁸Then he said, "Take the arrows," and the king took them. Elisha told him, "Strike the ground." He struck it three times and stopped. ¹⁹The man of God was angry with him and said, "You should have struck the ground five or six times; then you would have defeated Aram and completely destroyed it. But now you will defeat it only three times."

²⁰Elisha died and was buried.

Now Moabite raiders used to enter the country every spring. ²¹Once while some Israelites were burying a man, suddenly they saw a band of raiders; so they threw the man's body

---

a6 That is, a symbol of the goddess Asherah; here and elsewhere in 2 Kings   *b9* Hebrew *Joash,* a variant of *Jehoash*; also in verses 12-14 and 25

into Elisha's tomb. When the body touched Elisha's bones, the man came to life and stood up on his feet.

²²Hazael king of Aram oppressed Israel throughout the reign of Jehoahaz. ²³But the LORD was gracious to them and had compassion and showed concern for them because of his covenant with Abraham, Isaac and Jacob. To this day he has been unwilling to destroy them or banish them from his presence.

²⁴Hazael king of Aram died, and Ben-Hadad his son succeeded him as king. ²⁵Then Jehoash son of Jehoahaz recaptured from Ben-Hadad son of Hazael the towns he had taken in battle from his father Jehoahaz. Three times Jehoash defeated him, and so he recovered the Israelite towns.

Amaziah King of Judah

14 In the second year of Jehoash[a] son of Jehoahaz king of Israel, Amaziah son of Joash king of Judah began to reign. ²He was twenty-five years old when he became king, and he reigned in Jerusalem twenty-nine years. His mother's name was Jehoaddin; she was from Jerusalem. ³He did what was right in the eyes of the LORD, but not as his father David had done. In everything he followed the example of his father Joash. ⁴The high places, however, were not removed; the people continued to offer sacrifices and burn incense there.

⁵After the kingdom was firmly in his grasp, he executed the officials who had murdered his father the king. ⁶Yet he did not put the sons of the assassins to death, in accordance with what is written in the Book of the Law of Moses where the LORD commanded: "Fathers shall not be put to death for their children, nor children put to death for their fathers; each is to die for his own sins."[b]

⁷He was the one who defeated ten thousand Edomites in the Valley of Salt and captured Sela in battle, calling it Joktheel, the name it has to this day.

⁸Then Amaziah sent messengers to Jehoash son of Jehoahaz, the son of Jehu, king of Israel, with the challenge: "Come, meet me face to face."

⁹But Jehoash king of Israel replied to Amaziah king of Judah: "A thistle in Lebanon sent a message to a cedar in Lebanon, 'Give your daughter to my son in marriage.' Then a wild beast in Lebanon came along and trampled the thistle underfoot. ¹⁰You have indeed defeated Edom and now you are arrogant. Glory in your victory, but stay at home! Why ask for trouble and cause your own downfall and that of Judah also?"

¹¹Amaziah, however, would not listen, so Jehoash king of Israel attacked. He and Amaziah king of Judah faced each other at Beth Shemesh in Judah. ¹²Judah was routed by Israel, and every man fled to his home. ¹³Jehoash king of Israel captured Amaziah king of Judah, the son of Joash, the son of Ahaziah, at Beth Shemesh. Then Jehoash went to Jerusalem and broke down the wall of Jerusalem from the Ephraim Gate to the Corner Gate—a section about six hundred feet long.[c] ¹⁴He took all the gold and silver and all the articles found in the temple of the LORD and in the treasuries of the royal palace. He also took hostages and returned to Samaria.

¹⁵As for the other events of the reign of Jehoash, what he did and his achievements, including his war against Amaziah king of Judah, are they not written in the book of the annals of the kings of Israel? ¹⁶Jehoash rested with his fathers and was buried in Samaria with the kings of Israel. And Jeroboam his son succeeded him as king.

¹⁷Amaziah son of Joash king of Judah lived for fifteen years after the death of Jehoash son of Jehoahaz

---

a1 Hebrew *Joash*, a variant of *Jehoash*; also in verses 13, 23 and 27   b6 Deut. 24:16
c13 Hebrew *four hundred cubits* (about 180 meters)

king of Israel. ¹⁸As for the other events of Amaziah's reign, are they not written in the book of the annals of the kings of Judah?

¹⁹They conspired against him in Jerusalem, and he fled to Lachish, but they sent men after him to Lachish and killed him there. ²⁰He was brought back by horse and was buried in Jerusalem with his fathers, in the City of David.

²¹Then all the people of Judah took Azariah,ᵃ who was sixteen years old, and made him king in place of his father Amaziah. ²²He was the one who rebuilt Elath and restored it to Judah after Amaziah rested with his fathers.

Jeroboam II King of Israel

²³In the fifteenth year of Amaziah son of Joash king of Judah, Jeroboam son of Jehoash king of Israel became king in Samaria, and he reigned forty-one years. ²⁴He did evil in the eyes of the LORD and did not turn away from any of the sins of Jeroboam son of Nebat, which he had caused Israel to commit. ²⁵He was the one who restored the boundaries of Israel from Leboᵇ Hamath to the Sea of the Arabah,ᶜ in accordance with the word of the LORD, the God of Israel, spoken through his servant Jonah son of Amittai, the prophet from Gath Hepher.

❓DID YOU KNOW?　　14:23

Who was Jeroboam II?

Jeroboam II was an important king of Israel. In his time Israel became very powerful and rich. The Bible books of Jonah and Amos were written while Jeroboam II was king of Israel.

---

²⁶The LORD had seen how bitterly everyone in Israel, whether slave or free, was suffering; there was no one to help them. ²⁷And since the LORD had not said he would blot out the name of Israel from under heaven, he saved them by the hand of Jeroboam son of Jehoash.

²⁸As for the other events of Jeroboam's reign, all he did, and his military achievements, including how he recovered for Israel both Damascus and Hamath, which had belonged to Yaudi,ᵈ are they not written in the book of the annals of the kings of Israel? ²⁹Jeroboam rested with his fathers, the kings of Israel. And Zechariah his son succeeded him as king.

Azariah King of Judah

15 In the twenty-seventh year of Jeroboam king of Israel, Azariah son of Amaziah king of Judah began to reign. ²He was sixteen years old when he became king, and he reigned in Jerusalem fifty-two years. His mother's name was Jecoliah; she was from Jerusalem. ³He did what was right in the eyes of the LORD, just as his father Amaziah had done. ⁴The high places, however, were not removed; the people continued to offer sacrifices and burn incense there.

⁵The LORD afflicted the king with leprosyᵉ until the day he died, and he lived in a separate house.ᶠ Jotham the king's son had charge of the palace and governed the people of the land.

⁶As for the other events of Azariah's reign, and all he did, are they not written in the book of the annals of the kings of Judah? ⁷Azariah rested with his fathers and was buried near them in the City of David. And Jotham his son succeeded him as king.

Zechariah King of Israel

⁸In the thirty-eighth year of Azariah king of Judah, Zechariah son of Jeroboam became king of Israel in Samaria, and he reigned six months. ⁹He did evil in the eyes of the LORD,

---

ᵃ21 Also called *Uzziah*　　ᵇ25 Or *from the entrance to*　　ᶜ25 That is, the Dead Sea　　ᵈ28 Or *Judah*　　ᵉ5 The Hebrew word was used for various diseases affecting the skin—not necessarily leprosy.　　ᶠ5 Or *in a house where he was relieved of responsibility*

as his fathers had done. He did not turn away from the sins of Jeroboam son of Nebat, which he had caused Israel to commit.

[10]Shallum son of Jabesh conspired against Zechariah. He attacked him in front of the people,[a] assassinated him and succeeded him as king. [11]The other events of Zechariah's reign are written in the book of the annals of the kings of Israel. [12]So the word of the LORD spoken to Jehu was fulfilled: "Your descendants will sit on the throne of Israel to the fourth generation."[b]

Shallum King of Israel

[13]Shallum son of Jabesh became king in the thirty-ninth year of Uzziah king of Judah, and he reigned in Samaria one month. [14]Then Menahem son of Gadi went from Tirzah up to Samaria. He attacked Shallum son of Jabesh in Samaria, assassinated him and succeeded him as king.

[15]The other events of Shallum's reign, and the conspiracy he led, are written in the book of the annals of the kings of Israel.

[16]At that time Menahem, starting out from Tirzah, attacked Tiphsah and everyone in the city and its vicinity, because they refused to open their gates. He sacked Tiphsah and ripped open all the pregnant women.

Menahem King of Israel

[17]In the thirty-ninth year of Azariah king of Judah, Menahem son of Gadi became king of Israel, and he reigned in Samaria ten years. [18]He did evil in the eyes of the LORD. During his entire reign he did not turn away from the sins of Jeroboam son of Nebat, which he had caused Israel to commit.

[19]Then Pul[c] king of Assyria invaded the land, and Menahem gave him a thousand talents[d] of silver to gain his support and strengthen his own hold on the kingdom. [20]Menahem exacted this money from Israel. Every wealthy man had to contribute fifty shekels[e] of silver to be given to the king of Assyria. So the king of Assyria withdrew and stayed in the land no longer.

[21]As for the other events of Menahem's reign, and all he did, are they not written in the book of the annals of the kings of Israel? [22]Menahem rested with his fathers. And Pekahiah his son succeeded him as king.

Pekahiah King of Israel

[23]In the fiftieth year of Azariah king of Judah, Pekahiah son of Menahem became king of Israel in Samaria, and he reigned two years. [24]Pekahiah did evil in the eyes of the LORD. He did not turn away from the sins of Jeroboam son of Nebat, which he had caused Israel to commit. [25]One of his chief officers, Pekah son of Remaliah, conspired against him. Taking fifty men of Gilead with him, he assassinated Pekahiah, along with Argob and Arieh, in the citadel of the royal palace at Samaria. So Pekah killed Pekahiah and succeeded him as king.

[26]The other events of Pekahiah's reign, and all he did, are written in the book of the annals of the kings of Israel.

Pekah King of Israel

[27]In the fifty-second year of Azariah king of Judah, Pekah son of Remaliah became king of Israel in Samaria, and he reigned twenty years. [28]He did evil in the eyes of the LORD. He did not turn away from the sins of Jeroboam son of Nebat, which he had caused Israel to commit.

[29]In the time of Pekah king of Israel, Tiglath-Pileser king of Assyria came and took Ijon, Abel Beth Maacah, Janoah, Kedesh and Hazor. He took Gilead and Galilee, including all the land of Naphtali, and deported the people to Assyria. [30]Then Hoshea

---

[a]10 Hebrew; some Septuagint manuscripts in Ibleam   [b]12 2 Kings 10:30   [c]19 Also called Tiglath-Pileser   [d]19 That is, about 37 tons (about 34 metric tons)   [e]20 That is, about 1 1/4 pounds (about 0.6 kilogram)

son of Elah conspired against Pekah son of Remaliah. He attacked and assassinated him, and then succeeded him as king in the twentieth year of Jotham son of Uzziah.

31As for the other events of Pekah's reign, and all he did, are they not written in the book of the annals of the kings of Israel?

Jotham King of Judah

32In the second year of Pekah son of Remaliah king of Israel, Jotham son of Uzziah king of Judah began to reign. 33He was twenty-five years old when he became king, and he reigned in Jerusalem sixteen years. His mother's name was Jerusha daughter of Zadok. 34He did what was right in the eyes of the LORD, just as his father Uzziah had done. 35The high places, however, were not removed; the people continued to offer sacrifices and burn incense there. Jotham rebuilt the Upper Gate of the temple of the LORD.

36As for the other events of Jotham's reign, and what he did, are they not written in the book of the annals of the kings of Judah? 37(In those days the LORD began to send Rezin king of Aram and Pekah son of Remaliah against Judah.) 38Jotham rested with his fathers and was buried with them in the City of David, the city of his father. And Ahaz his son succeeded him as king.

Ahaz King of Judah

16 In the seventeenth year of Pekah son of Remaliah, Ahaz son of Jotham king of Judah began to reign. 2Ahaz was twenty years old when he became king, and he reigned in Jerusalem sixteen years. Unlike David his father, he did not do what was right in the eyes of the LORD his God. 3He walked in the ways of the kings of Israel and even sacrificed his son in*a* the fire, following the detestable ways of the nations the LORD had driven out before the Israelites. 4He offered sacrifices and burned incense

at the high places, on the hilltops and under every spreading tree.

5Then Rezin king of Aram and Pekah son of Remaliah king of Israel marched up to fight against Jerusalem and besieged Ahaz, but they could not overpower him. 6At that time, Rezin king of Aram recovered Elath for Aram by driving out the men of Judah. Edomites then moved into Elath and have lived there to this day.

7Ahaz sent messengers to say to Tiglath-Pileser king of Assyria, "I am your servant and vassal. Come up and save me out of the hand of the king of Aram and of the king of Israel, who are attacking me." 8And Ahaz took the silver and gold found in the temple of the LORD and in the treasuries of the royal palace and sent it as a gift to the king of Assyria. 9The king of Assyria complied by attacking Damascus and capturing it. He deported its inhabitants to Kir and put Rezin to death.

10Then King Ahaz went to Damascus to meet Tiglath-Pileser king of Assyria. He saw an altar in Damascus and sent to Uriah the priest a sketch of the altar, with detailed plans for its construction. 11So Uriah the priest built an altar in accordance with all the plans that King Ahaz had sent from Damascus and finished it before King Ahaz returned. 12When the king came back from Damascus and saw the altar, he approached it and presented offerings*b* on it. 13He offered up his burnt offering and grain offering, poured out his drink offering, and sprinkled the blood of his fellowship offerings*c* on the altar. 14The bronze altar that stood before the LORD he brought from the front of the temple—from between the new altar and the temple of the LORD—and put it on the north side of the new altar.

15King Ahaz then gave these orders to Uriah the priest: "On the large new altar, offer the morning burnt offering and the evening grain

---

a3 Or even made his son pass through   *b12 Or and went up*   *c13 Traditionally peace offerings* offering, the king's burnt offering and his grain offering, and the burnt offering of all the people of the land, and their grain offering and their drink offering. Sprinkle on the altar all the blood of the burnt offerings and sacrifices. But I will use the bronze altar for seeking guidance." ¹⁶And Uriah the priest did just as King Ahaz had ordered.

¹⁷King Ahaz took away the side panels and removed the basins from the movable stands. He removed the Sea from the bronze bulls that supported it and set it on a stone base. ¹⁸He took away the Sabbath canopy[a] that had been built at the temple and removed the royal entryway outside the temple of the LORD, in deference to the king of Assyria.

¹⁹As for the other events of the reign of Ahaz, and what he did, are they not written in the book of the annals of the kings of Judah? ²⁰Ahaz rested with his fathers and was buried with them in the City of David. And Hezekiah his son succeeded him as king.

Hoshea Last King of Israel

17 In the twelfth year of Ahaz king of Judah, Hoshea son of Elah became king of Israel in Samaria, and he reigned nine years. ²He did evil in the eyes of the LORD, but not like the kings of Israel who preceded him.

³Shalmaneser king of Assyria came up to attack Hoshea, who had been Shalmaneser's vassal and had paid him tribute. ⁴But the king of Assyria discovered that Hoshea was a traitor, for he had sent envoys to So[b] king of Egypt, and he no longer paid tribute to the king of Assyria, as he had done year by year. Therefore Shalmaneser seized him and put him in prison. ⁵The king of Assyria invaded the entire land, marched against Samaria and laid siege to it for three years. ⁶In the ninth year of Hoshea, the king of Assyria captured Samaria

and deported the Israelites to Assyria. He settled them in Halah, in Gozan on the Habor River and in the towns of the Medes.

Israel Exiled Because of Sin

⁷All this took place because the Israelites had sinned against the LORD their God, who had brought them up out of Egypt from under the power of Pharaoh king of Egypt. They worshiped other gods ⁸and followed the practices of the nations the LORD had driven out before them, as well as the practices that the kings of Israel had introduced. ⁹The Israelites secretly did things against the LORD their God that were not right. From watchtower to fortified city they built themselves high places in all their towns. ¹⁰They set up sacred stones and Asherah poles on every high hill and under every spreading tree. ¹¹At every high place they burned incense, as the nations whom the LORD had driven out before them had done. They did wicked things that provoked the LORD to anger. ¹²They worshiped idols, though the LORD had said, "You shall not do this."[c] ¹³The LORD warned Israel and Judah through all his prophets and seers: "Turn from your evil ways. Observe my commands and decrees, in accordance with the entire Law that I commanded your fathers to obey and that I delivered to you through my servants the prophets."

¹⁴But they would not listen and were as stiff-necked as their fathers, who did not trust in the LORD their God. ¹⁵They rejected his decrees and the covenant he had made with their fathers and the warnings he had given them. They followed worthless idols and themselves became worthless. They imitated the nations around them although the LORD had ordered them, "Do not do as they do," and they did the things the LORD had forbidden them to do.

¹⁶They forsook all the commands of

---

a18 Or the dais of his throne (see Septuagint) abbreviation for Osorkon.   c12 Exodus 20:4, 5   b4 Or to Sais, to the; So is possibly an

the LORD their God and made for themselves two idols cast in the shape of calves, and an Asherah pole. They bowed down to all the starry hosts, and they worshiped Baal. [17]They sacrificed their sons and daughters in[a] the fire. They practiced divination and sorcery and sold themselves to do evil in the eyes of the LORD, provoking him to anger.

[18]So the LORD was very angry with Israel and removed them from his presence. Only the tribe of Judah was left, [19]and even Judah did not keep the commands of the LORD their God. They followed the practices Israel had introduced. [20]Therefore the LORD rejected all the people of Israel; he afflicted them and gave them into the hands of plunderers, until he thrust them from his presence.

[21]When he tore Israel away from the house of David, they made Jeroboam son of Nebat their king. Jeroboam enticed Israel away from following the LORD and caused them to commit a great sin. [22]The Israelites persisted in all the sins of Jeroboam and did not turn away from them [23]until the LORD removed them from his presence, as he had warned through all his servants the prophets. So the people of Israel were taken from their homeland into exile in Assyria, and they are still there.

Samaria Resettled

[24]The king of Assyria brought people from Babylon, Cuthah, Avva, Hamath and Sepharvaim and settled them in the towns of Samaria to replace the Israelites. They took over Samaria and lived in its towns. [25]When they first lived there, they did not worship the LORD; so he sent lions among them and they killed some of the people. [26]It was reported to the king of Assyria: "The people you deported and resettled in the towns of Samaria do not know what the god of that country requires. He has sent lions among them, which are killing them off, because the people do not know what he requires."

[27]Then the king of Assyria gave this order: "Have one of the priests you took captive from Samaria go back to live there and teach the people what the god of the land requires." [28]So one of the priests who had been exiled from Samaria came to live in Bethel and taught them how to worship the LORD.

[29]Nevertheless, each national group made its own gods in the several towns where they settled, and set them up in the shrines the people of Samaria had made at the high places. [30]The men from Babylon made Succoth Benoth, the men from Cuthah made Nergal, and the men from Ha-

[a]17 Or *They made their sons and daughters pass through*

▌ET'S LIVE IT!   2 Kings 17:1–23

PUNISHMENT ⟹ Read 2 Kings 17:1–23. How did God punish the Israelites? What did they do to deserve punishment? Before God punished Israel:

   1. God told them what they must not do, so they would know right from wrong (2 Kings 17:12).
   2. God warned them to stop doing wrong (2 Kings 17:13).
   3. Only then did God punish them (2 Kings 17:18).

Show your mom and dad this story. Ask about when they were punished as children. Did their parents follow God's example of telling, warning, and then punishing? Talk about times you have been punished. Can you see how your mom and dad have followed God's example when they punished you?

math made Ashima; ³¹the Avvites made Nibhaz and Tartak, and the Sepharvites burned their children in the fire as sacrifices to Adrammelech and Anammelech, the gods of Sepharvaim. ³²They worshiped the LORD, but they also appointed all sorts of their own people to officiate for them as priests in the shrines at the high places. ³³They worshiped the LORD, but they also served their own gods in accordance with the customs of the nations from which they had been brought.

³⁴To this day they persist in their former practices. They neither worship the LORD nor adhere to the decrees and ordinances, the laws and commands that the LORD gave the descendants of Jacob, whom he named Israel. ³⁵When the LORD made a covenant with the Israelites, he commanded them: "Do not worship any other gods or bow down to them, serve them or sacrifice to them. ³⁶But the LORD, who brought you up out of Egypt with mighty power and outstretched arm, is the one you must worship. To him you shall bow down and to him offer sacrifices. ³⁷You must always be careful to keep the decrees and ordinances, the laws and commands he wrote for you. Do not worship other gods. ³⁸Do not forget the covenant I have made with you, and do not worship other gods. ³⁹Rather, worship the LORD your God; it is he who will deliver you from the hand of all your enemies."

⁴⁰They would not listen, however, but persisted in their former practices. ⁴¹Even while these people were worshiping the LORD, they were serving their idols. To this day their children and grandchildren continue to do as their fathers did.

Hezekiah King of Judah

18 In the third year of Hoshea son of Elah king of Israel, Hezekiah son of Ahaz king of Judah began to reign. ²He was twenty-five

years old when he became king, and he reigned in Jerusalem twenty-nine years. His mother's name was Abijah[a] daughter of Zechariah. ³He did what was right in the eyes of the LORD, just as his father David had done. ⁴He removed the high places, smashed the sacred stones and cut down the Asherah poles. He broke into pieces the bronze snake Moses had made, for up to that time the Israelites had been burning incense to it. (It was called[b] Nehushtan.[c])

❓DID YOU KNOW?　　18:1

Who was Hezekiah?

Hezekiah was one of Judah's most godly kings. He ruled Judah when the Assyrians destroyed the kingdom of Israel. The Assyrians tried to invade Judah too, but were unsuccessful because Judah depended on God for deliverance.

---

⁵Hezekiah trusted in the LORD, the God of Israel. There was no one like him among all the kings of Judah, either before him or after him. ⁶He held fast to the LORD and did not cease to follow him; he kept the commands the LORD had given Moses. ⁷And the LORD was with him; he was successful in whatever he undertook. He rebelled against the king of Assyria and did not serve him. ⁸From watchtower to fortified city, he defeated the Philistines, as far as Gaza and its territory.

⁹In King Hezekiah's fourth year, which was the seventh year of Hoshea son of Elah king of Israel, Shalmaneser king of Assyria marched against Samaria and laid siege to it. ¹⁰At the end of three years the Assyrians took it. So Samaria was captured in Hezekiah's sixth year, which was the ninth year of Hoshea king of Israel. ¹¹The king of Assyria deported Israel to Assyria and settled them in

---

a2 Hebrew *Abi*, a variant of *Abijah*　　*b4* Or *He called it*　　*c4 Nehushtan* sounds like the Hebrew for *bronze* and *snake* and *unclean thing.*

Halah, in Gozan on the Habor River and in towns of the Medes. ¹²This happened because they had not obeyed the LORD their God, but had violated his covenant—all that Moses the servant of the LORD commanded. They neither listened to the commands nor carried them out.

¹³In the fourteenth year of King Hezekiah's reign, Sennacherib king of Assyria attacked all the fortified cities of Judah and captured them. ¹⁴So Hezekiah king of Judah sent this message to the king of Assyria at Lachish: "I have done wrong. Withdraw from me, and I will pay whatever you demand of me." The king of Assyria exacted from Hezekiah king of Judah three hundred talents*a* of silver and thirty talents*b* of gold. ¹⁵So Hezekiah gave him all the silver that was found in the temple of the LORD and in the treasuries of the royal palace.

¹⁶At this time Hezekiah king of Judah stripped off the gold with which he had covered the doors and doorposts of the temple of the LORD, and gave it to the king of Assyria.

Sennacherib Threatens Jerusalem

¹⁷The king of Assyria sent his supreme commander, his chief officer and his field commander with a large army, from Lachish to King Hezekiah at Jerusalem. They came up to Jerusalem and stopped at the aqueduct of the Upper Pool, on the road to the Washerman's Field. ¹⁸They called for the king; and Eliakim son of Hilkiah the palace administrator, Shebna the secretary, and Joah son of Asaph the recorder went out to them.

¹⁹The field commander said to them, "Tell Hezekiah:

" 'This is what the great king, the king of Assyria, says: On what are you basing this confidence of yours? ²⁰You say you have strategy and military strength—but you speak only empty words. On whom are you depending, that you rebel against me? ²¹Look now, you are depending on Egypt, that splintered reed of a staff, which pierces a man's hand and wounds him if he leans on it! Such is Pharaoh king of Egypt to all who depend on him. ²²And if you say to me, "We are depending on the LORD our God"—isn't he the one whose high places and altars Hezekiah removed, saying to Judah and Jerusalem, "You must worship before this altar in Jerusalem"?

²³" 'Come now, make a bargain with my master, the king of Assyria: I will give you two thousand horses—if you can put riders on them! ²⁴How can you repulse one officer of the least of my master's officials, even though you are depending on Egypt for chariots and horsemen*c*? ²⁵Furthermore, have I come to attack and destroy this place without word from the LORD? The LORD himself told me to march against this country and destroy it.' "

²⁶Then Eliakim son of Hilkiah, and Shebna and Joah said to the field commander, "Please speak to your servants in Aramaic, since we understand it. Don't speak to us in Hebrew in the hearing of the people on the wall."

²⁷But the commander replied, "Was it only to your master and you that my master sent me to say these things, and not to the men sitting on the wall—who, like you, will have to eat their own filth and drink their own urine?"

²⁸Then the commander stood and called out in Hebrew: "Hear the word of the great king, the king of Assyria! ²⁹This is what the king says: Do not let Hezekiah deceive you. He cannot deliver you from my hand. ³⁰Do not let Hezekiah persuade you to trust in

---

a14 That is, about 11 tons (about 10 metric tons)   *b14* That is, about 1 ton (about 1 metric ton)
c24 Or *charioteers*

the LORD when he says, 'The LORD will surely deliver us; this city will not be given into the hand of the king of Assyria.'

³¹"Do not listen to Hezekiah. This is what the king of Assyria says: Make peace with me and come out to me. Then every one of you will eat from his own vine and fig tree and drink water from his own cistern, ³²until I come and take you to a land like your own, a land of grain and new wine, a land of bread and vineyards, a land of olive trees and honey. Choose life and not death!

"Do not listen to Hezekiah, for he is misleading you when he says, 'The LORD will deliver us.' ³³Has the god of any nation ever delivered his land from the hand of the king of Assyria? ³⁴Where are the gods of Hamath and Arpad? Where are the gods of Sepharvaim, Hena and Ivvah? Have they rescued Samaria from my hand? ³⁵Who of all the gods of these countries has been able to save his land from me? How then can the LORD deliver Jerusalem from my hand?"

³⁶But the people remained silent and said nothing in reply, because the king had commanded, "Do not answer him."

³⁷Then Eliakim son of Hilkiah the palace administrator, Shebna the secretary and Joah son of Asaph the recorder went to Hezekiah, with their clothes torn, and told him what the field commander had said.

Jerusalem's Deliverance Foretold

19 When King Hezekiah heard this, he tore his clothes and put on sackcloth and went into the temple of the LORD. ²He sent Eliakim the palace administrator, Shebna the secretary and the leading priests, all wearing sackcloth, to the prophet Isaiah son of Amoz. ³They told him, "This is what Hezekiah says: This day is a day of distress and rebuke and disgrace, as when children come to the point of birth and there is no

strength to deliver them. ⁴It may be that the LORD your God will hear all the words of the field commander, whom his master, the king of Assyria, has sent to ridicule the living God, and that he will rebuke him for the words the LORD your God has heard. Therefore pray for the remnant that still survives."

⁵When King Hezekiah's officials came to Isaiah, ⁶Isaiah said to them, "Tell your master, 'This is what the LORD says: Do not be afraid of what you have heard—those words with which the underlings of the king of Assyria have blasphemed me. ⁷Listen! I am going to put such a spirit in him that when he hears a certain report, he will return to his own country, and there I will have him cut down with the sword.' "

⁸When the field commander heard that the king of Assyria had left Lachish, he withdrew and found the king fighting against Libnah.

⁹Now Sennacherib received a report that Tirhakah, the Cushite*ᵃ* king ¸of Egypt¸, was marching out to fight against him. So he again sent messengers to Hezekiah with this word: ¹⁰"Say to Hezekiah king of Judah: Do not let the god you depend on deceive you when he says, 'Jerusalem will not be handed over to the king of Assyria.' ¹¹Surely you have heard what the kings of Assyria have done to all the countries, destroying them completely. And will you be delivered? ¹²Did the gods of the nations that were destroyed by my forefathers deliver them: the gods of Gozan, Haran, Rezeph and the people of Eden who were in Tel Assar? ¹³Where is the king of Hamath, the king of Arpad, the king of the city of Sepharvaim, or of Hena or Ivvah?"

Hezekiah's Prayer

¹⁴Hezekiah received the letter from the messengers and read it. Then he went up to the temple of the LORD and spread it out before the LORD. ¹⁵And

ᵃ9 That is, from the upper Nile region

Hezekiah prayed to the LORD: "O LORD, God of Israel, enthroned between the cherubim, you alone are God over all the kingdoms of the earth. You have made heaven and earth. ¹⁶Give ear, O LORD, and hear; open your eyes, O LORD, and see; listen to the words Sennacherib has sent to insult the living God.

¹⁷"It is true, O LORD, that the Assyrian kings have laid waste these nations and their lands. ¹⁸They have thrown their gods into the fire and destroyed them, for they were not gods but only wood and stone, fashioned by men's hands. ¹⁹Now, O LORD our God, deliver us from his hand, so that all kingdoms on earth may know that you alone, O LORD, are God."

Isaiah Prophesies Sennacherib's Fall

²⁰Then Isaiah son of Amoz sent a message to Hezekiah: "This is what the LORD, the God of Israel, says: I have heard your prayer concerning Sennacherib king of Assyria. ²¹This is the word that the LORD has spoken against him:

" 'The Virgin Daughter of Zion
    despises you and mocks you.
The Daughter of Jerusalem
    tosses her head as you flee.
²²Who is it you have insulted and
    blasphemed?

Against whom have you raised
    your voice
and lifted your eyes in pride?
    Against the Holy One of Israel!
²³By your messengers
    you have heaped insults on the
        Lord.
And you have said,
    "With my many chariots
I have ascended the heights of the
        mountains,
    the utmost heights of Lebanon.
I have cut down its tallest cedars,
    the choicest of its pines.
I have reached its remotest parts,
    the finest of its forests.
²⁴I have dug wells in foreign lands
    and drunk the water there.
With the soles of my feet
    I have dried up all the streams
        of Egypt."

²⁵" 'Have you not heard?
    Long ago I ordained it.
In days of old I planned it;
    now I have brought it to pass,
that you have turned fortified
        cities
    into piles of stone.
²⁶Their people, drained of power,
    are dismayed and put to shame.
They are like plants in the field,
    like tender green shoots,
like grass sprouting on the roof,
    scorched before it grows up.

²⁷" 'But I know where you stay

▌ET'S LIVE IT!   2 Kings 18:13–16; 19:1–19,35–37

PRAY WHEN AFRAID ➡ Read how the terrible Assyrian army marched on Jerusalem in 2 Kings 18:13–16. Think how the people in Jerusalem must have felt as the enemy came nearer.

Before you read any more of the story, think about other kids your age. Make a list of things they and you are afraid of today.

Now read 2 Kings 19:1–19. What did King Hezekiah do when he was afraid? To find out what happened next, read 2 Kings 19:35–37.

Pick out something on your list of what boys and girls are afraid of today. Write a prayer, as Hezekiah did, asking the Lord to protect you from the thing you fear.

and when you come and go
and how you rage against me.
28Because you rage against me
    and your insolence has reached
        my ears,
I will put my hook in your nose
    and my bit in your mouth,
and I will make you return
    by the way you came.'

29"This will be the sign for you,
O Hezekiah:

"This year you will eat what
    grows by itself,
    and the second year what
        springs from that.
But in the third year sow and
    reap,
    plant vineyards and eat their
        fruit.
30Once more a remnant of the
    house of Judah
    will take root below and bear
        fruit above.
31For out of Jerusalem will come a
    remnant,
    and out of Mount Zion a band of
        survivors.

The zeal of the LORD Almighty will
accomplish this.

32"Therefore this is what the LORD
says concerning the king of Assyria:

"He will not enter this city
    or shoot an arrow here.
He will not come before it with
    shield
    or build a siege ramp against it.
33By the way that he came he will
    return;
    he will not enter this city,
        declares the LORD.
34I will defend this city and save it,
    for my sake and for the sake of
        David my servant."

35That night the angel of the LORD
went out and put to death a hundred
and eighty-five thousand men in the
Assyrian camp. When the people got
up the next morning—there were all
the dead bodies! 36So Sennacherib
king of Assyria broke camp and withdrew. He returned to Nineveh and
stayed there.

37One day, while he was worshiping in the temple of his god Nisroch,
his sons Adrammelech and Sharezer
cut him down with the sword, and
they escaped to the land of Ararat.
And Esarhaddon his son succeeded
him as king.

Hezekiah's Illness

20 In those days Hezekiah became ill and was at the point
of death. The prophet Isaiah son of
Amoz went to him and said, "This is
what the LORD says: Put your house
in order, because you are going to die;
you will not recover."

2Hezekiah turned his face to the
wall and prayed to the LORD, 3"Remember, O LORD, how I have walked
before you faithfully and with wholehearted devotion and have done what
is good in your eyes." And Hezekiah
wept bitterly.

4Before Isaiah had left the middle
court, the word of the LORD came to
him: 5"Go back and tell Hezekiah, the
leader of my people, 'This is what the
LORD, the God of your father David,
says: I have heard your prayer and
seen your tears; I will heal you. On
the third day from now you will go up
to the temple of the LORD. 6I will add
fifteen years to your life. And I will
deliver you and this city from the
hand of the king of Assyria. I will defend this city for my sake and for the
sake of my servant David.' "

7Then Isaiah said, "Prepare a poultice of figs." They did so and applied
it to the boil, and he recovered.

8Hezekiah had asked Isaiah,
"What will be the sign that the LORD
will heal me and that I will go up to
the temple of the LORD on the third
day from now?"

9Isaiah answered, "This is the
LORD's sign to you that the LORD will
do what he has promised: Shall the
shadow go forward ten steps, or shall
it go back ten steps?"

10"It is a simple matter for the
shadow to go forward ten steps," said
Hezekiah. "Rather, have it go back
ten steps."

11Then the prophet Isaiah called

upon the LORD, and the LORD made the shadow go back the ten steps it had gone down on the stairway of Ahaz.

Envoys From Babylon

¹²At that time Merodach-Baladan son of Baladan king of Babylon sent Hezekiah letters and a gift, because he had heard of Hezekiah's illness. ¹³Hezekiah received the messengers and showed them all that was in his storehouses—the silver, the gold, the spices and the fine oil—his armory and everything found among his treasures. There was nothing in his palace or in all his kingdom that Hezekiah did not show them.

¹⁴Then Isaiah the prophet went to King Hezekiah and asked, "What did those men say, and where did they come from?"

"From a distant land," Hezekiah replied. "They came from Babylon."

¹⁵The prophet asked, "What did they see in your palace?"

"They saw everything in my palace," Hezekiah said. "There is nothing among my treasures that I did not show them."

¹⁶Then Isaiah said to Hezekiah, "Hear the word of the LORD: ¹⁷The time will surely come when everything in your palace, and all that your fathers have stored up until this day, will be carried off to Babylon. Nothing will be left, says the LORD. ¹⁸And some of your descendants, your own flesh and blood, that will be born

a6 Or He made his own son pass through

to you, will be taken away, and they will become eunuchs in the palace of the king of Babylon."

¹⁹"The word of the LORD you have spoken is good," Hezekiah replied. For he thought, "Will there not be peace and security in my lifetime?"

²⁰As for the other events of Hezekiah's reign, all his achievements and how he made the pool and the tunnel by which he brought water into the city, are they not written in the book of the annals of the kings of Judah? ²¹Hezekiah rested with his fathers. And Manasseh his son succeeded him as king.

Manasseh King of Judah

21 Manasseh was twelve years old when he became king, and he reigned in Jerusalem fifty-five years. His mother's name was Hephzibah. ²He did evil in the eyes of the LORD, following the detestable practices of the nations the LORD had driven out before the Israelites. ³He rebuilt the high places his father Hezekiah had destroyed; he also erected altars to Baal and made an Asherah pole, as Ahab king of Israel had done. He bowed down to all the starry hosts and worshiped them. ⁴He built altars in the temple of the LORD, of which the LORD had said, "In Jerusalem I will put my Name." ⁵In both courts of the temple of the LORD, he built altars to all the starry hosts. ⁶He sacrificed his own son in*ᵃ* the fire, practiced sorcery and divina-

---

 ET'S LIVE IT!					2 Kings 20:1–11

PRAY WHEN SICK ➠ Hezekiah had prayed when Jerusalem was to be attacked by Assyria (see 2 Kings 18–19). God answered his prayer and saved the city. So when Hezekiah became sick and was about to die, he prayed. Read 2 Kings 20:1–11. Then draw a picture of Hezekiah. Draw a large boil (red, raised sore) somewhere on him. Now get a Band-Aid and put it over the boil. Write Psalm 30:2 on your picture.

Put your picture and Bible verse inside the door of your family medicine cabinet to remind you to pray when you or a family member gets sick.

tion, and consulted mediums and spiritists. He did much evil in the eyes of the LORD, provoking him to anger.

7He took the carved Asherah pole he had made and put it in the temple, of which the LORD had said to David and to his son Solomon, "In this temple and in Jerusalem, which I have chosen out of all the tribes of Israel, I will put my Name forever. 8I will not again make the feet of the Israelites wander from the land I gave their forefathers, if only they will be careful to do everything I commanded them and will keep the whole Law that my servant Moses gave them." 9But the people did not listen. Manasseh led them astray, so that they did more evil than the nations the LORD had destroyed before the Israelites.

10The LORD said through his servants the prophets: 11"Manasseh king of Judah has committed these detestable sins. He has done more evil than the Amorites who preceded him and has led Judah into sin with his idols. 12Therefore this is what the LORD, the God of Israel, says: I am going to bring such disaster on Jerusalem and Judah that the ears of everyone who hears of it will tingle. 13I will stretch out over Jerusalem the measuring line used against Samaria and the plumb line used against the house of Ahab. I will wipe out Jerusalem as one wipes a dish, wiping it and turning it upside down. 14I will forsake the remnant of my inheritance and hand them over to their enemies. They will be looted and plundered by all their foes, 15because they have done evil in my eyes and have provoked me to anger from the day their forefathers came out of Egypt until this day."

16Moreover, Manasseh also shed so much innocent blood that he filled Jerusalem from end to end—besides the sin that he had caused Judah to commit, so that they did evil in the eyes of the LORD.

17As for the other events of Manasseh's reign, and all he did, including the sin he committed, are they not written in the book of the annals of the kings of Judah? 18Manasseh rested with his fathers and was buried in his palace garden, the garden of Uzza. And Amon his son succeeded him as king.

Amon King of Judah

19Amon was twenty-two years old when he became king, and he reigned in Jerusalem two years. His mother's name was Meshullemeth daughter of Haruz; she was from Jotbah. 20He did evil in the eyes of the LORD, as his father Manasseh had done. 21He walked in all the ways of his father; he worshiped the idols his father had worshiped, and bowed down to them. 22He forsook the LORD, the God of his fathers, and did not walk in the way of the LORD.

23Amon's officials conspired against him and assassinated the king in his palace. 24Then the people of the land killed all who had plotted against King Amon, and they made Josiah his son king in his place.

25As for the other events of Amon's reign, and what he did, are they not written in the book of the annals of the kings of Judah? 26He was buried in his grave in the garden of Uzza. And Josiah his son succeeded him as king.

The Book of the Law Found

22 Josiah was eight years old when he became king, and he reigned in Jerusalem thirty-one years. His mother's name was Jedidah daughter of Adaiah; she was from Bozkath. 2He did what was right in the eyes of the LORD and walked in all the ways of his father David, not turning aside to the right or to the left.

3In the eighteenth year of his reign, King Josiah sent the secretary, Shaphan son of Azaliah, the son of Meshullam, to the temple of the LORD. He said: 4"Go up to Hilkiah the high priest and have him get ready the money that has been brought into the temple of the LORD, which the doorkeepers have collected from the people. ⁵Have them entrust it to the men appointed to supervise the work on the temple. And have these men pay the workers who repair the temple of the LORD— ⁶the carpenters, the builders and the masons. Also have them purchase timber and dressed stone to repair the temple. ⁷But they need not account for the money entrusted to them, because they are acting faithfully."

⁸Hilkiah the high priest said to Shaphan the secretary, "I have found the Book of the Law in the temple of the LORD." He gave it to Shaphan, who read it. ⁹Then Shaphan the secretary went to the king and reported to him: "Your officials have paid out the money that was in the temple of the LORD and have entrusted it to the workers and supervisors at the temple." ¹⁰Then Shaphan the secretary informed the king, "Hilkiah the priest has given me a book." And Shaphan read from it in the presence of the king.

¹¹When the king heard the words of the Book of the Law, he tore his robes. ¹²He gave these orders to Hilkiah the priest, Ahikam son of Shaphan, Acbor son of Micaiah, Shaphan the secretary and Asaiah the king's attendant: ¹³"Go and inquire of the LORD for me and for the people and for all Judah about what is written in this book that has been found. Great is the LORD's anger that burns against us because our fathers have not obeyed the words of this book;

they have not acted in accordance with all that is written there concerning us."

¹⁴Hilkiah the priest, Ahikam, Acbor, Shaphan and Asaiah went to speak to the prophetess Huldah, who was the wife of Shallum son of Tikvah, the son of Harhas, keeper of the wardrobe. She lived in Jerusalem, in the Second District.

¹⁵She said to them, "This is what the LORD, the God of Israel, says: Tell the man who sent you to me, ¹⁶'This is what the LORD says: I am going to bring disaster on this place and its people, according to everything written in the book the king of Judah has read. ¹⁷Because they have forsaken me and burned incense to other gods and provoked me to anger by all the idols their hands have made,ᵃ my anger will burn against this place and will not be quenched.' ¹⁸Tell the king of Judah, who sent you to inquire of the LORD, 'This is what the LORD, the God of Israel, says concerning the words you heard: ¹⁹Because your heart was responsive and you humbled yourself before the LORD when you heard what I have spoken against this place and its people, that they would become accursed and laid waste, and because you tore your robes and wept in my presence, I have heard you, declares the LORD. ²⁰Therefore I will gather you to your fathers, and you will be buried in peace. Your eyes will not see all the disaster I am going to bring on this place.' "

ᵃ17 Or by everything they have done

▉ET'S LIVE IT!   2 Kings 22:1–20

EVEN A CHILD ➠ Proverbs 20:11 says, "Even a child is known by his actions." Josiah was only eight years old when he became king over Judah. Read about him in 2 Kings 22:1–20. How old are you? Can you imagine being a king at your age?
   Now read 2 Kings 22:2. What does this verse tell you about Josiah? As you go through your day today, whatever you do, think about young Josiah. You may not be a king, but no matter how young you are, you can do what God wants.

So they took her answer back to the king.

Josiah Renews the Covenant

23 Then the king called together all the elders of Judah and Jerusalem. [2]He went up to the temple of the LORD with the men of Judah, the people of Jerusalem, the priests and the prophets—all the people from the least to the greatest. He read in their hearing all the words of the Book of the Covenant, which had been found in the temple of the LORD. [3]The king stood by the pillar and renewed the covenant in the presence of the LORD—to follow the LORD and keep his commands, regulations and decrees with all his heart and all his soul, thus confirming the words of the covenant written in this book. Then all the people pledged themselves to the covenant.

❓ DID YOU KNOW?   23:2

What was the Book of the Covenant?

The Book of the Covenant was probably the Bible book of Deuteronomy. *Covenant* means "agreement." Josiah and his people promised to do what God had commanded. The Lord then could bless Judah.

---

[4]The king ordered Hilkiah the high priest, the priests next in rank and the doorkeepers to remove from the temple of the LORD all the articles made for Baal and Asherah and all the starry hosts. He burned them outside Jerusalem in the fields of the Kidron Valley and took the ashes to Bethel. [5]He did away with the pagan priests appointed by the kings of Judah to burn incense on the high places of the towns of Judah and on those around Jerusalem—those who burned incense to Baal, to the sun and moon, to the constellations and to all the starry hosts. [6]He took the Asherah pole from the temple of the LORD to the Kidron Valley outside Jerusalem and burned it there. He ground it to powder and scattered the dust over the graves of the common people. [7]He also tore down the quarters of the male shrine prostitutes, which were in the temple of the LORD and where women did weaving for Asherah.

[8]Josiah brought all the priests from the towns of Judah and desecrated the high places, from Geba to Beersheba, where the priests had burned incense. He broke down the shrines*a* at the gates—at the entrance to the Gate of Joshua, the city governor, which is on the left of the city gate. [9]Although the priests of the high places did not serve at the altar of the LORD in Jerusalem, they ate unleavened bread with their fellow priests.

[10]He desecrated Topheth, which was in the Valley of Ben Hinnom, so no one could use it to sacrifice his son or daughter in*b* the fire to Molech. [11]He removed from the entrance to the temple of the LORD the horses that the kings of Judah had dedicated to the sun. They were in the court near the room of an official named Nathan-Melech. Josiah then burned the chariots dedicated to the sun.

[12]He pulled down the altars the kings of Judah had erected on the roof near the upper room of Ahaz, and the altars Manasseh had built in the two courts of the temple of the LORD. He removed them from there, smashed them to pieces and threw the rubble into the Kidron Valley. [13]The king also desecrated the high places that were east of Jerusalem on the south of the Hill of Corruption—the ones Solomon king of Israel had built for Ashtoreth the vile goddess of the Sidonians, for Chemosh the vile god of Moab, and for Molech*c* the detestable god of the people of Ammon. [14]Josiah smashed the sacred stones and cut down the Asherah

---

a8 Or *high places*   *b10* Or *to make his son or daughter pass through*   *c13* Hebrew *Milcom*

poles and covered the sites with human bones.

¹⁵Even the altar at Bethel, the high place made by Jeroboam son of Nebat, who had caused Israel to sin— even that altar and high place he demolished. He burned the high place and ground it to powder, and burned the Asherah pole also. ¹⁶Then Josiah looked around, and when he saw the tombs that were there on the hillside, he had the bones removed from them and burned on the altar to defile it, in accordance with the word of the LORD proclaimed by the man of God who foretold these things.

¹⁷The king asked, "What is that tombstone I see?"

The men of the city said, "It marks the tomb of the man of God who came from Judah and pronounced against the altar of Bethel the very things you have done to it."

¹⁸"Leave it alone," he said. "Don't let anyone disturb his bones." So they spared his bones and those of the prophet who had come from Samaria.

¹⁹Just as he had done at Bethel, Josiah removed and defiled all the shrines at the high places that the kings of Israel had built in the towns of Samaria that had provoked the LORD to anger. ²⁰Josiah slaughtered all the priests of those high places on the altars and burned human bones on them. Then he went back to Jerusalem.

²¹The king gave this order to all the people: "Celebrate the Passover to the LORD your God, as it is written in this Book of the Covenant." ²²Not since the days of the judges who led Israel, nor throughout the days of the kings of Israel and the kings of Judah, had any such Passover been observed. ²³But in the eighteenth year of King Josiah, this Passover was celebrated to the LORD in Jerusalem.

²⁴Furthermore, Josiah got rid of the mediums and spiritists, the household gods, the idols and all the other detestable things seen in Judah and Jerusalem. This he did to fulfill the requirements of the law written in the book that Hilkiah the priest had discovered in the temple of the LORD. ²⁵Neither before nor after Josiah was there a king like him who turned to the LORD as he did—with all his heart and with all his soul and with all his strength, in accordance with all the Law of Moses.

²⁶Nevertheless, the LORD did not turn away from the heat of his fierce anger, which burned against Judah because of all that Manasseh had done to provoke him to anger. ²⁷So the LORD said, "I will remove Judah also from my presence as I removed Israel, and I will reject Jerusalem, the city I chose, and this temple, about which I said, 'There shall my Name be.'ᵃ"

²⁸As for the other events of Josiah's reign, and all he did, are they not written in the book of the annals of the kings of Judah?

²⁹While Josiah was king, Pharaoh Neco king of Egypt went up to the Euphrates River to help the king of Assyria. King Josiah marched out to meet him in battle, but Neco faced him and killed him at Megiddo. ³⁰Josiah's servants brought his body in a chariot from Megiddo to Jerusalem and buried him in his own tomb. And the people of the land took Jehoahaz son of Josiah and anointed him and made him king in place of his father.

Jehoahaz King of Judah

³¹Jehoahaz was twenty-three years old when he became king, and he reigned in Jerusalem three months. His mother's name was Hamutal daughter of Jeremiah; she was from Libnah. ³²He did evil in the eyes of the LORD, just as his fathers had done. ³³Pharaoh Neco put him in chains at Riblah in the land of Hamathᵇ so that he might not reign in Jerusalem, and he imposed on Judah a levy of a hundred talentsᶜ of silver

---

ᵃ27 1 Kings 8:29   ᵇ33 Hebrew; Septuagint (see also 2 Chron. 36:3) Neco at Riblah in Hamath removed him   ᶜ33 That is, about 3 3/4 tons (about 3.4 metric tons)

and a talent^a of gold. ³⁴Pharaoh Neco made Eliakim son of Josiah king in place of his father Josiah and changed Eliakim's name to Jehoiakim. But he took Jehoahaz and carried him off to Egypt, and there he died. ³⁵Jehoiakim paid Pharaoh Neco the silver and gold he demanded. In order to do so, he taxed the land and exacted the silver and gold from the people of the land according to their assessments.

Jehoiakim King of Judah

³⁶Jehoiakim was twenty-five years old when he became king, and he reigned in Jerusalem eleven years. His mother's name was Zebidah daughter of Pedaiah; she was from Rumah. ³⁷And he did evil in the eyes of the LORD, just as his fathers had done.

24 During Jehoiakim's reign, Nebuchadnezzar king of Babylon invaded the land, and Jehoiakim became his vassal for three years. But then he changed his mind and rebelled against Nebuchadnezzar. ²The LORD sent Babylonian,^b Aramean, Moabite and Ammonite raiders against him. He sent them to destroy Judah, in accordance with the word of the LORD proclaimed by his servants the prophets. ³Surely these things happened to Judah according to the LORD's command, in order to remove them from his presence because of the sins of Manasseh and all he had done, ⁴including the shedding of innocent blood. For he had filled Jerusalem with innocent blood, and the LORD was not willing to forgive.

⁵As for the other events of Jehoiakim's reign, and all he did, are they not written in the book of the annals of the kings of Judah? ⁶Jehoiakim rested with his fathers. And Jehoiachin his son succeeded him as king.

⁷The king of Egypt did not march out from his own country again, because the king of Babylon had taken all his territory, from the Wadi of Egypt to the Euphrates River.

Jehoiachin King of Judah

⁸Jehoiachin was eighteen years old when he became king, and he reigned in Jerusalem three months. His mother's name was Nehushta daughter of Elnathan; she was from Jerusalem. ⁹He did evil in the eyes of the LORD, just as his father had done.

¹⁰At that time the officers of Nebuchadnezzar king of Babylon advanced on Jerusalem and laid siege to it, ¹¹and Nebuchadnezzar himself came up to the city while his officers were besieging it. ¹²Jehoiachin king of Judah, his mother, his attendants, his nobles and his officials all surrendered to him.

In the eighth year of the reign of the king of Babylon, he took Jehoiachin prisoner. ¹³As the LORD had declared, Nebuchadnezzar removed all the treasures from the temple of the LORD and from the royal palace, and took away all the gold articles that Solomon king of Israel had made for the temple of the LORD. ¹⁴He carried into exile all Jerusalem: all the officers and fighting men, and all the craftsmen and artisans—a total of ten thousand. Only the poorest people of the land were left.

¹⁵Nebuchadnezzar took Jehoiachin captive to Babylon. He also took from Jerusalem to Babylon the king's mother, his wives, his officials and the leading men of the land. ¹⁶The king of Babylon also deported to Babylon the entire force of seven thousand fighting men, strong and fit for war, and a thousand craftsmen and artisans. ¹⁷He made Mattaniah, Jehoiachin's uncle, king in his place and changed his name to Zedekiah.

Zedekiah King of Judah

¹⁸Zedekiah was twenty-one years old when he became king, and he reigned in Jerusalem eleven years. His mother's name was Hamutal daughter of Jeremiah; she was from Libnah. ¹⁹He did evil in the eyes of the LORD, just as Jehoiakim had

---

^a33 That is, about 75 pounds (about 34 kilograms)   ^b2 Or *Chaldean*

done. ²⁰It was because of the LORD's anger that all this happened to Jerusalem and Judah, and in the end he thrust them from his presence.

? DID YOU KNOW?   24:20

What happened to the nation of Judah?

Judah's last kings were evil and led the people away from God. To punish these sins God let the Babylonians attack and destroy Jerusalem. The people of Judah were either taken captive to Babylon or fled into Egypt.

The Fall of Jerusalem

Now Zedekiah rebelled against the king of Babylon.

25 So in the ninth year of Zedekiah's reign, on the tenth day of the tenth month, Nebuchadnezzar king of Babylon marched against Jerusalem with his whole army. He encamped outside the city and built siege works all around it. ²The city was kept under siege until the eleventh year of King Zedekiah. ³By the ninth day of the ,fourth,^a month the famine in the city had become so severe that there was no food for the people to eat. ⁴Then the city wall was broken through, and the whole army fled at night through the gate between the two walls near the king's garden, though the Babylonians^b were surrounding the city. They fled toward the Arabah,^c ⁵but the Babylonian^d army pursued the king and overtook him in the plains of Jericho. All his soldiers were separated from him and scattered, ⁶and he was captured. He was taken to the king of Babylon at Riblah, where sentence was pronounced on him. ⁷They killed the sons of Zedekiah before his eyes. Then they put out his eyes, bound

him with bronze shackles and took him to Babylon.

⁸On the seventh day of the fifth month, in the nineteenth year of Nebuchadnezzar king of Babylon, Nebuzaradan commander of the imperial guard, an official of the king of Babylon, came to Jerusalem. ⁹He set fire to the temple of the LORD, the royal palace and all the houses of Jerusalem. Every important building he burned down. ¹⁰The whole Babylonian army, under the commander of the imperial guard, broke down the walls around Jerusalem. ¹¹Nebuzaradan the commander of the guard carried into exile the people who remained in the city, along with the rest of the populace and those who had gone over to the king of Babylon. ¹²But the commander left behind some of the poorest people of the land to work the vineyards and fields.

¹³The Babylonians broke up the bronze pillars, the movable stands and the bronze Sea that were at the temple of the LORD and they carried the bronze to Babylon. ¹⁴They also took away the pots, shovels, wick trimmers, dishes and all the bronze articles used in the temple service. ¹⁵The commander of the imperial guard took away the censers and sprinkling bowls—all that were made of pure gold or silver.

¹⁶The bronze from the two pillars, the Sea and the movable stands, which Solomon had made for the temple of the LORD, was more than could be weighed. ¹⁷Each pillar was twenty-seven feet^e high. The bronze capital on top of one pillar was four and a half feet^f high and was decorated with a network and pomegranates of bronze all around. The other pillar, with its network, was similar.

¹⁸The commander of the guard took as prisoners Seraiah the chief priest, Zephaniah the priest next in rank and the three doorkeepers. ¹⁹Of those still in the city, he took the officer in

---

^a3 See Jer. 52:6.   ^b4 Or *Chaldeans*; also in verses 13, 25 and 26   ^c4 Or *the Jordan Valley*
^d5 Or *Chaldean*; also in verses 10 and 24   ^e17 Hebrew *eighteen cubits* (about 8.1 meters)
^f17 Hebrew *three cubits* (about 1.3 meters)

charge of the fighting men and five royal advisers. He also took the secretary who was chief officer in charge of conscripting the people of the land and sixty of his men who were found in the city. ²⁰Nebuzaradan the commander took them all and brought them to the king of Babylon at Riblah. ²¹There at Riblah, in the land of Hamath, the king had them executed.

So Judah went into captivity, away from her land.

²²Nebuchadnezzar king of Babylon appointed Gedaliah son of Ahikam, the son of Shaphan, to be over the people he had left behind in Judah. ²³When all the army officers and their men heard that the king of Babylon had appointed Gedaliah as governor, they came to Gedaliah at Mizpah—Ishmael son of Nethaniah, Johanan son of Kareah, Seraiah son of Tanhumeth the Netophathite, Jaazaniah the son of the Maacathite, and their men. ²⁴Gedaliah took an oath to reassure them and their men. "Do not be afraid of the Babylonian officials," he said. "Settle down in the land and serve the king of Babylon, and it will go well with you."

²⁵In the seventh month, however, Ishmael son of Nethaniah, the son of Elishama, who was of royal blood, came with ten men and assassinated Gedaliah and also the men of Judah and the Babylonians who were with him at Mizpah. ²⁶At this, all the people from the least to the greatest, together with the army officers, fled to Egypt for fear of the Babylonians.

Jehoiachin Released

²⁷In the thirty-seventh year of the exile of Jehoiachin king of Judah, in the year Evil-Merodach^a became king of Babylon, he released Jehoiachin from prison on the twenty-seventh day of the twelfth month. ²⁸He spoke kindly to him and gave him a seat of honor higher than those of the other kings who were with him in Babylon. ²⁹So Jehoiachin put aside his prison clothes and for the rest of his life ate regularly at the king's table. ³⁰Day by day the king gave Jehoiachin a regular allowance as long as he lived.

^a27 Also called *Amel-Marduk*

1 CHRONICLES

WHO WROTE THIS BOOK?

The author is unknown. Many think the book was written by Ezra.

WHY WAS THIS BOOK WRITTEN?

The book of 1 Chronicles gives God's evaluation of David's rule.

WHAT HAPPENS IN THIS BOOK?

David becomes king of Israel. He defeats Israel's enemies and works to make Israel a mighty nation.

WHAT DO WE LEARN ABOUT GOD IN THIS BOOK?

God gives people who serve him many different abilities.

WHO IS IMPORTANT IN THIS BOOK?

The important person in this book is David.

WHEN DID THIS HAPPEN?

The events in this book happened between 1010 and 970 B.C.

WHERE DID THIS HAPPEN?

These events took place in the land of Israel, united by David into a powerful nation.

WHAT ARE SOME OF THE STORIES IN THIS BOOK?

The ark comes to Jerusalem. 1 Chronicles 15
God's promise to David. 1 Chronicles 17
David counts his army. 1 Chronicles 21
David's plan for the temple. 1 Chronicles 28

Historical Records From Adam to Abraham

To Noah's Sons

1 Adam, Seth, Enosh, [2]Kenan, Mahalalel, Jared, [3]Enoch, Methuselah, Lamech, Noah.

[4]The sons of Noah:[a]
Shem, Ham and Japheth.

The Japhethites

[5]The sons[b] of Japheth:
Gomer, Magog, Madai, Javan, Tubal, Meshech and Tiras.
[6]The sons of Gomer:
Ashkenaz, Riphath[c] and Togarmah.
[7]The sons of Javan:
Elishah, Tarshish, the Kittim and the Rodanim.

The Hamites

[8]The sons of Ham:
Cush, Mizraim,[d] Put and Canaan.
[9]The sons of Cush:
Seba, Havilah, Sabta, Raamah and Sabteca.
The sons of Raamah:
Sheba and Dedan.
[10]Cush was the father[e] of
Nimrod, who grew to be a mighty warrior on earth.
[11]Mizraim was the father of
the Ludites, Anamites, Lehabites, Naphtuhites, [12]Pathrusites, Casluhites (from whom the Philistines came) and Caphtorites.
[13]Canaan was the father of
Sidon his firstborn,[f] and of the Hittites, [14]Jebusites, Amorites, Girgashites, [15]Hivites, Arkites, Sinites, [16]Arvadites, Zemarites and Hamathites.

The Semites

[17]The sons of Shem:
Elam, Asshur, Arphaxad, Lud and Aram.
The sons of Aram[g]:
Uz, Hul, Gether and Meshech.
[18]Arphaxad was the father of Shelah,
and Shelah the father of Eber.
[19]Two sons were born to Eber:
One was named Peleg,[h] because in his time the earth was divided; his brother was named Joktan.
[20]Joktan was the father of
Almodad, Sheleph, Hazarmaveth, Jerah, [21]Hadoram, Uzal, Diklah, [22]Obal,[i] Abimael, Sheba, [23]Ophir, Havilah and Jobab. All these were sons of Joktan.

[24]Shem, Arphaxad,[j] Shelah,
[25]Eber, Peleg, Reu,
[26]Serug, Nahor, Terah
[27]and Abram (that is, Abraham).

The Family of Abraham

[28]The sons of Abraham:
Isaac and Ishmael.

Descendants of Hagar

[29]These were their descendants:
Nebaioth the firstborn of Ishmael, Kedar, Adbeel, Mibsam, [30]Mishma, Dumah, Massa, Hadad, Tema, [31]Jetur, Naphish and Kedemah. These were the sons of Ishmael.

Descendants of Keturah

[32]The sons born to Keturah, Abraham's concubine:
Zimran, Jokshan, Medan, Midian, Ishbak and Shuah.

---

a4 Septuagint; Hebrew does not have *The sons of Noah: successors* or *nations*; also in verses 6-10, 17 and 20.　　*b5 Sons* may mean *descendants* or *c6* Many Hebrew manuscripts and Vulgate (see also Septuagint and Gen. 10:3); most Hebrew manuscripts *Diphath*　　*d8* That is, Egypt; also in verse 11　　*e10 Father* may mean *ancestor* or *predecessor* or *founder*; also in verses 11, 13, 18 and 20.　　*f13* Or *of the Sidonians, the foremost*　　*g17* One Hebrew manuscript and some Septuagint manuscripts (see also Gen. 10:23); most Hebrew manuscripts do not have this line.　　*h19 Peleg* means *division.*　　*i22* Some Hebrew manuscripts and Syriac (see also Gen. 10:28); most Hebrew manuscripts *Ebal*　　*j24* Hebrew; some Septuagint manuscripts *Arphaxad, Cainan* (see also note at Gen. 11:10)

The sons of Jokshan:
Sheba and Dedan.
33The sons of Midian:
Ephah, Epher, Hanoch, Abida
and Eldaah.
All these were descendants of
Keturah.

Descendants of Sarah

34Abraham was the father of Isaac.
The sons of Isaac:
Esau and Israel.

Esau's Sons

35The sons of Esau:
Eliphaz, Reuel, Jeush, Jalam
and Korah.
36The sons of Eliphaz:
Teman, Omar, Zepho,ᵃ Gatam
and Kenaz;
by Timna: Amalek.ᵇ
37The sons of Reuel:
Nahath, Zerah, Shammah and
Mizzah.

The People of Seir in Edom

38The sons of Seir:
Lotan, Shobal, Zibeon, Anah,
Dishon, Ezer and Dishan.
39The sons of Lotan:
Hori and Homam. Timna was
Lotan's sister.
40The sons of Shobal:
Alvan,ᶜ Manahath, Ebal,
Shepho and Onam.
The sons of Zibeon:
Aiah and Anah.
41The son of Anah:
Dishon.
The sons of Dishon:
Hemdan,ᵈ Eshban, Ithran
and Keran.
42The sons of Ezer:
Bilhan, Zaavan and Akan.ᵉ

The sons of Dishanᶠ:
Uz and Aran.

The Rulers of Edom

43These were the kings who
reigned in Edom before any Israelite king reignedᵍ:
Bela son of Beor, whose city
was named Dinhabah.
44When Bela died, Jobab son of Zerah from Bozrah succeeded
him as king.
45When Jobab died, Husham from
the land of the Temanites succeeded him as king.
46When Husham died, Hadad son
of Bedad, who defeated Midian
in the country of Moab, succeeded him as king. His city
was named Avith.
47When Hadad died, Samlah from
Masrekah succeeded him as
king.
48When Samlah died, Shaul from
Rehoboth on the riverʰ succeeded him as king.
49When Shaul died, Baal-Hanan
son of Acbor succeeded him as
king.
50When Baal-Hanan died, Hadad
succeeded him as king. His
city was named Pau,ⁱ and his
wife's name was Mehetabel
daughter of Matred, the
daughter of Me-Zahab. 51Ha-
dad also died.

The chiefs of Edom were:
Timna, Alvah, Jetheth,
52Oholibamah, Elah, Pinon,
53Kenaz, Teman, Mibzar,
54Magdiel and Iram. These
were the chiefs of Edom.

Israel's Sons

2 These were the sons of Israel:
Reuben, Simeon, Levi, Judah,

ᵃ36 Many Hebrew manuscripts, some Septuagint manuscripts and Syriac (see also Gen. 36:11); most
Hebrew manuscripts Zephi   ᵇ36 Some Septuagint manuscripts (see also Gen. 36:12); Hebrew
Gatam, Kenaz, Timna and Amalek   ᶜ40 Many Hebrew manuscripts and some Septuagint
manuscripts (see also Gen. 36:23); most Hebrew manuscripts Alian   ᵈ41 Many Hebrew
manuscripts and some Septuagint manuscripts (see also Gen. 36:26); most Hebrew manuscripts
Hamran   ᵉ42 Many Hebrew and Septuagint manuscripts (see also Gen. 36:27); most Hebrew
manuscripts Zaavan, Jaakan   ᶠ42 Hebrew Dishon, a variant of Dishan   ᵍ43 Or before an
Israelite king reigned over them   ʰ48 Possibly the Euphrates   ⁱ50 Many Hebrew manuscripts,
some Septuagint manuscripts, Vulgate and Syriac (see also Gen. 36:39); most Hebrew manuscripts
Pai

Issachar, Zebulun, [2]Dan, Joseph, Benjamin, Naphtali, Gad and Asher.

Judah

To Hezron's Sons

[3]The sons of Judah:
Er, Onan and Shelah. These three were born to him by a Canaanite woman, the daughter of Shua. Er, Judah's firstborn, was wicked in the LORD's sight; so the LORD put him to death. [4]Tamar, Judah's daughter-in-law, bore him Perez and Zerah. Judah had five sons in all.

[5]The sons of Perez:
Hezron and Hamul.
[6]The sons of Zerah:
Zimri, Ethan, Heman, Calcol and Darda[a]—five in all.
[7]The son of Carmi:
Achar,[b] who brought trouble on Israel by violating the ban on taking devoted things.[c]
[8]The son of Ethan:
Azariah.
[9]The sons born to Hezron were:
Jerahmeel, Ram and Caleb.[d]

From Ram Son of Hezron

[10]Ram was the father of Amminadab, and Amminadab the father of Nahshon, the leader of the people of Judah. [11]Nahshon was the father of Salmon,[e] Salmon the father of Boaz, [12]Boaz the father of Obed and Obed the father of Jesse.
[13]Jesse was the father of Eliab his firstborn; the second son was Abinadab, the third Shimea, [14]the fourth Nethanel, the fifth Raddai, [15]the sixth Ozem and the seventh David.

[16]Their sisters were Zeruiah and Abigail. Zeruiah's three sons were Abishai, Joab and Asahel. [17]Abigail was the mother of Amasa, whose father was Jether the Ishmaelite.

Caleb Son of Hezron

[18]Caleb son of Hezron had children by his wife Azubah (and by Jerioth). These were her sons: Jesher, Shobab and Ardon. [19]When Azubah died, Caleb married Ephrath, who bore him Hur. [20]Hur was the father of Uri, and Uri the father of Bezalel.
[21]Later, Hezron lay with the daughter of Makir the father of Gilead (he had married her when he was sixty years old), and she bore him Segub. [22]Segub was the father of Jair, who controlled twenty-three towns in Gilead. [23](But Geshur and Aram captured Havvoth Jair,[f] as well as Kenath with its surrounding settlements —sixty towns.) All these were descendants of Makir the father of Gilead.

[24]After Hezron died in Caleb Ephrathah, Abijah the wife of Hezron bore him Ashhur the father[g] of Tekoa.

Jerahmeel Son of Hezron

[25]The sons of Jerahmeel the firstborn of Hezron:
Ram his firstborn, Bunah, Oren, Ozem and[h] Ahijah. [26]Jerahmeel had another wife, whose name was Atarah; she was the mother of Onam.
[27]The sons of Ram the firstborn of Jerahmeel:

---

[a]6 Many Hebrew manuscripts, some Septuagint manuscripts and Syriac (see also 1 Kings 4:31); most Hebrew manuscripts *Dara*   [b]7 *Achar* means *trouble*; *Achar* is called *Achan* in Joshua.   [c]7 The Hebrew term refers to the irrevocable giving over of things or persons to the LORD, often by totally destroying them.   [d]9 Hebrew *Kelubai*, a variant of *Caleb*   [e]11 Septuagint (see also Ruth 4:21); Hebrew *Salma*   [f]23 Or *captured the settlements of Jair*   [g]24 *Father* may mean *civic leader* or *military leader*; also in verses 42, 45, 49-52 and possibly elsewhere.   [h]25 Or *Oren and Ozem, by*

Maaz, Jamin and Eker.
²⁸The sons of Onam:
Shammai and Jada.
The sons of Shammai:
Nadab and Abishur.
²⁹Abishur's wife was named Abihail, who bore him Ahban and
Molid.
³⁰The sons of Nadab:
Seled and Appaim. Seled died
without children.
³¹The son of Appaim:
Ishi, who was the father of
Sheshan.
Sheshan was the father of Ahlai.
³²The sons of Jada, Shammai's
brother:
Jether and Jonathan. Jether
died without children.
³³The sons of Jonathan:
Peleth and Zaza.
These were the descendants of
Jerahmeel.
³⁴Sheshan had no sons—only
daughters.
He had an Egyptian servant
named Jarha. ³⁵Sheshan gave
his daughter in marriage to
his servant Jarha, and she
bore him Attai.
³⁶Attai was the father of Nathan,
Nathan the father of Zabad,
³⁷Zabad the father of Ephlal,
Ephlal the father of Obed,
³⁸Obed the father of Jehu,
Jehu the father of Azariah,
³⁹Azariah the father of Helez,
Helez the father of Eleasah,
⁴⁰Eleasah the father of Sismai,
Sismai the father of Shallum,
⁴¹Shallum the father of Jekamiah,
and Jekamiah the father of
Elishama.

The Clans of Caleb

⁴²The sons of Caleb the brother of
Jerahmeel:
Mesha his firstborn, who was
the father of Ziph, and his son

Mareshah,ᵃ who was the father of Hebron.
⁴³The sons of Hebron:
Korah, Tappuah, Rekem and
Shema. ⁴⁴Shema was the father of Raham, and Raham the
father of Jorkeam. Rekem was
the father of Shammai. ⁴⁵The
son of Shammai was Maon,
and Maon was the father of
Beth Zur.
⁴⁶Caleb's concubine Ephah was
the mother of Haran, Moza
and Gazez. Haran was the father of Gazez.
⁴⁷The sons of Jahdai:
Regem, Jotham, Geshan, Pelet, Ephah and Shaaph.
⁴⁸Caleb's concubine Maacah was
the mother of Sheber and Tir-
hanah. ⁴⁹She also gave birth to
Shaaph the father of Madmannah and to Sheva the father of
Macbenah and Gibea. Caleb's
daughter was Acsah. ⁵⁰These
were the descendants of Caleb.

The sons of Hur the firstborn of
Ephrathah:
Shobal the father of Kiriath
Jearim, ⁵¹Salma the father of
Bethlehem, and Hareph the
father of Beth Gader.
⁵²The descendants of Shobal the
father of Kiriath Jearim were:
Haroeh, half the Manahathites, ⁵³and the clans of Kiriath
Jearim: the Ithrites, Puthites,
Shumathites and Mishraites.
From these descended the Zo-
rathites and Eshtaolites.
⁵⁴The descendants of Salma:
Bethlehem, the Netopha-
thites, Atroth Beth Joab, half
the Manahathites, the Zorites,
⁵⁵and the clans of scribesᵇ who
lived at Jabez: the Tirathites,
Shimeathites and Sucathites.
These are the Kenites who
came from Hammath, the father of the house of Recab.ᶜ

ᵃ42 The meaning of the Hebrew for this phrase is uncertain.　　ᵇ55 Or of the Sopherites
ᶜ55 Or father of Beth Recab

The Sons of David

3 These were the sons of David born to him in Hebron:
The firstborn was Amnon the son of Ahinoam of Jezreel;
the second, Daniel the son of Abigail of Carmel;
²the third, Absalom the son of Maacah daughter of Talmai king of Geshur;
the fourth, Adonijah the son of Haggith;
³the fifth, Shephatiah the son of Abital;
and the sixth, Ithream, by his wife Eglah.
⁴These six were born to David in Hebron, where he reigned seven years and six months.

David reigned in Jerusalem thirty-three years, ⁵and these were the children born to him there:
Shammua,ᵃ Shobab, Nathan and Solomon. These four were by Bathshebaᵇ daughter of Ammiel. ⁶There were also Ibhar, Elishua,ᶜ Eliphelet, ⁷Nogah, Nepheg, Japhia, ⁸Elishama, Eliada and Eliphelet— nine in all. ⁹All these were the sons of David, besides his sons by his concubines. And Tamar was their sister.

The Kings of Judah

¹⁰Solomon's son was Rehoboam,
Abijah his son,
Asa his son,
Jehoshaphat his son,
¹¹Jehoramᵈ his son,
Ahaziah his son,
Joash his son,
¹²Amaziah his son,
Azariah his son,
Jotham his son,
¹³Ahaz his son,
Hezekiah his son,
Manasseh his son,
¹⁴Amon his son,
Josiah his son.
¹⁵The sons of Josiah:
Johanan the firstborn,
Jehoiakim the second son,
Zedekiah the third,
Shallum the fourth.
¹⁶The successors of Jehoiakim:
Jehoiachinᵉ his son,
and Zedekiah.

The Royal Line After the Exile

¹⁷The descendants of Jehoiachin the captive:
Shealtiel his son, ¹⁸Malkiram,

ᵃ5 Hebrew *Shimea*, a variant of *Shammua*   ᵇ5 One Hebrew manuscript and Vulgate (see also Septuagint and 2 Samuel 11:3); most Hebrew manuscripts *Bathshua*   ᶜ6 Two Hebrew manuscripts (see also 2 Samuel 5:15 and 1 Chron. 14:5); most Hebrew manuscripts *Elishama*
ᵈ11 Hebrew *Joram*, a variant of *Jehoram*   ᵉ16 Hebrew *Jeconiah*, a variant of *Jehoiachin*; also in verse 17

▌ET'S LIVE IT!   1 Chronicles 3:1–16

YOUR BRANCH OF THE FAMILY TREE ➠ Lists of names in the Bible seem very boring. But the Hebrew people were very proud of their ancestors. They kept careful records, called "genealogies," showing their grandparents and great-grandparents and great-great-grandparents and so on.

Today we call genealogical records "family trees." On a long strip of paper tablecloth, draw your family tree. Ask your mom or dad to help you get pictures of each person. Tape the pictures to your family tree. Beside each person write one interesting thing about him or her.

Then decide with your parents on a title for your family tree. Maybe your title will be "hard workers," or "Michigan farmers," or "people helpers" or "praying Christians." Choose any title that tells something about your family that you are proud of.

Pedaiah, Shenazzar, Jekami-
ah, Hoshama and Nedabiah.
¹⁹The sons of Pedaiah:
Zerubbabel and Shimei.
The sons of Zerubbabel:
Meshullam and Hananiah.
Shelomith was their sister.
²⁰There were also five others:
Hashubah, Ohel, Berekiah,
Hasadiah and Jushab-Hesed.
²¹The descendants of Hananiah:
Pelatiah and Jeshaiah, and
the sons of Rephaiah, of Ar-
nan, of Obadiah and of Sheca-
niah.
²²The descendants of Shecaniah:
Shemaiah and his sons:
Hattush, Igal, Bariah, Neari-
ah and Shaphat—six in all.
²³The sons of Neariah:
Elioenai, Hizkiah and Azri-
kam—three in all.
²⁴The sons of Elioenai:
Hodaviah, Eliashib, Pelaiah,
Akkub, Johanan, Delaiah and
Anani—seven in all.

Other Clans of Judah

4 The descendants of Judah:
Perez, Hezron, Carmi, Hur
and Shobal.
²Reaiah son of Shobal was the fa-
ther of Jahath, and Jahath the
father of Ahumai and Lahad.
These were the clans of the Zo-
rathites.
³These were the sons^a of Etam:
Jezreel, Ishma and Idbash.
Their sister was named Hazze-
lelponi. ⁴Penuel was the father of Gedor, and Ezer the father of Hushah.
These were the descendants of
Hur, the firstborn of Ephrathah and father^b of Bethlehem.
⁵Ashhur the father of Tekoa had
two wives, Helah and Naarah.
⁶Naarah bore him Ahuzzam, He-
pher, Temeni and Haahashta-
ri. These were the descendants
of Naarah.
⁷The sons of Helah:
Zereth, Zohar, Ethnan, ⁸and
Koz, who was the father of
Anub and Hazzobebah and of
the clans of Aharhel son of Ha-
rum.

⁹Jabez was more honorable than
his brothers. His mother had named
him Jabez,^c saying, "I gave birth to
him in pain." ¹⁰Jabez cried out to the
God of Israel, "Oh, that you would
bless me and enlarge my territory!
Let your hand be with me, and keep
me from harm so that I will be free
from pain." And God granted his request.

¹¹Kelub, Shuhah's brother, was
the father of Mehir, who was
the father of Eshton. ¹²Eshton
was the father of Beth Rapha,
Paseah and Tehinnah the father of Ir Nahash.^d These
were the men of Recah.

¹³The sons of Kenaz:
Othniel and Seraiah.
The sons of Othniel:
Hathath and Meonothai.^e
¹⁴Meonothai was the father of
Ophrah.
Seraiah was the father of Joab,
the father of Ge Harashim.^f It
was called this because its peo-
ple were craftsmen.
¹⁵The sons of Caleb son of Jephun-
neh:
Iru, Elah and Naam.
The son of Elah:
Kenaz.
¹⁶The sons of Jehallelel:
Ziph, Ziphah, Tiria and Asa-
rel.
¹⁷The sons of Ezrah:
Jether, Mered, Epher and Ja-
lon. One of Mered's wives gave
birth to Miriam, Shammai
and Ishbah the father of Eshtemoa. ¹⁸(His Judean wife

---

^a3 Some Septuagint manuscripts (see also Vulgate); Hebrew *father*   ^b4 *Father* may mean *civic leader* or *military leader*; also in verses 12, 14, 17, 18 and possibly elsewhere.   ^c9 *Jabez* sounds like the Hebrew for *pain*.   ^d12 Or *of the city of Nahash*   ^e13 Some Septuagint manuscripts and Vulgate; Hebrew does not have *and Meonothai*.   ^f14 *Ge Harashim* means *valley of craftsmen*.

gave birth to Jered the father of Gedor, Heber the father of Soco, and Jekuthiel the father of Zanoah.) These were the children of Pharaoh's daughter Bithiah, whom Mered had married.

19The sons of Hodiah's wife, the sister of Naham:
the father of Keilah the Garmite, and Eshtemoa the Maacathite.

20The sons of Shimon:
Amnon, Rinnah, Ben-Hanan and Tilon.

The descendants of Ishi:
Zoheth and Ben-Zoheth.

21The sons of Shelah son of Judah:
Er the father of Lecah, Laadah the father of Mareshah and the clans of the linen workers at Beth Ashbea, 22Jokim, the men of Cozeba, and Joash and Saraph, who ruled in Moab and Jashubi Lehem. (These records are from ancient times.) 23They were the potters who lived at Netaim and Gederah; they stayed there and worked for the king.

Simeon

24The descendants of Simeon:
Nemuel, Jamin, Jarib, Zerah and Shaul;

25Shallum was Shaul's son, Mibsam his son and Mishma his son.

26The descendants of Mishma:
Hammuel his son, Zaccur his son and Shimei his son.

27Shimei had sixteen sons and six daughters, but his brothers did not have many children; so their entire clan did not become as numerous as the people of Judah. 28They lived in Beersheba, Moladah, Hazar Shual, 29Bilhah, Ezem, Tolad, 30Bethuel, Hormah, Ziklag, 31Beth Marcaboth, Hazar Susim, Beth Biri and Shaaraim. These were their towns until the reign of David. 32Their surrounding villages were Etam, Ain, Rimmon, Token and Ashan—five towns— 33and all the villages around these towns as far as Baalath.a These were their settlements. And they kept a genealogical record.

34Meshobab, Jamlech, Joshah son of Amaziah, 35Joel, Jehu son of Joshibiah, the son of Seraiah, the son of Asiel, 36also Elioenai, Jaakobah, Jeshohaiah, Asaiah, Adiel, Jesimiel, Benaiah, 37and Ziza son of Shiphi, the son of Allon, the son of Jedaiah, the son of Shimri, the son of Shemaiah.

38The men listed above by name were leaders of their clans. Their families increased greatly, 39and they went to the outskirts of Gedor to the east of the valley in search of pasture for their flocks. 40They found rich, good pasture, and the land was spacious, peaceful and quiet. Some Hamites had lived there formerly.

41The men whose names were listed came in the days of Hezekiah king of Judah. They attacked the Hamites in their dwellings and also the Meunites who were there and completely destroyedb them, as is evident to this day. Then they settled in their place, because there was pasture for their flocks. 42And five hundred of these Simeonites, led by Pelatiah, Neariah, Rephaiah and Uzziel, the sons of Ishi, invaded the hill country of Seir. 43They killed the remaining Amalekites who had escaped, and they have lived there to this day.

Reuben

5 The sons of Reuben the firstborn of Israel (he was the firstborn, but when he defiled his father's marriage bed, his rights as firstborn were given to the sons of Joseph son of Israel; so he could not be listed in the genealogical record in accordance with his birthright, 2and though Ju-

---

a33 Some Septuagint manuscripts (see also Joshua 19:8); Hebrew Baal   b41 The Hebrew term refers to the irrevocable giving over of things or persons to the LORD, often by totally destroying them.

dah was the strongest of his brothers and a ruler came from him, the rights of the firstborn belonged to Joseph)—
³the sons of Reuben the firstborn of Israel:

Hanoch, Pallu, Hezron and Carmi.
⁴The descendants of Joel:
Shemaiah his son, Gog his son, Shimei his son, ⁵Micah his son,
Reaiah his son, Baal his son, ⁶and Beerah his son, whom Tiglath-Pileser[a] king of Assyria took into exile. Beerah was a leader of the Reubenites.
⁷Their relatives by clans, listed according to their genealogical records:
Jeiel the chief, Zechariah, ⁸and Bela son of Azaz, the son of Shema, the son of Joel. They settled in the area from Aroer to Nebo and Baal Meon. ⁹To the east they occupied the land up to the edge of the desert that extends to the Euphrates River, because their livestock had increased in Gilead.
¹⁰During Saul's reign they waged war against the Hagrites, who were defeated at their hands; they occupied the dwellings of the Hagrites throughout the entire region east of Gilead.

Gad

¹¹The Gadites lived next to them in Bashan, as far as Salecah:
¹²Joel was the chief, Shapham the second, then Janai and Shaphat, in Bashan.
¹³Their relatives, by families, were:
Michael, Meshullam, Sheba, Jorai, Jacan, Zia and Eber—seven in all.
¹⁴These were the sons of Abihail son of Huri, the son of Jaroah, the son of Gilead, the son of Michael, the son of Jeshishai, the son of Jahdo, the son of Buz.

¹⁵Ahi son of Abdiel, the son of Guni, was head of their family.

Life In Bible Times

THE CAPTIVITY

Babylonian records show Jewish captives being led away from Jerusalem. Hundreds of years earlier Moses urged the Israelites to obey God and warned that if they would not obey, "You will be uprooted from the land you are entering to possess" (Deuteronomy 28:63). God's people did not obey him. Captivity in Babylon was their punishment.

---

¹⁶The Gadites lived in Gilead, in Bashan and its outlying villages, and on all the pasturelands of Sharon as far as they extended.
¹⁷All these were entered in the genealogical records during the reigns of Jotham king of Judah and Jeroboam king of Israel.

¹⁸The Reubenites, the Gadites and the half-tribe of Manasseh had 44,-760 men ready for military service—able-bodied men who could handle shield and sword, who could use a bow, and who were trained for battle. ¹⁹They waged war against the Hagrites, Jetur, Naphish and Nodab. ²⁰They were helped in fighting them, and God handed the Hagrites and all their allies over to them, because they cried out to him during the battle. He answered their prayers, because they trusted in him. ²¹They seized the livestock of the Hagrites—fifty thousand camels, two hundred fifty thousand sheep and two

---

ᵃ6 Hebrew *Tilgath-Pilneser*, a variant of *Tiglath-Pileser*; also in verse 26

thousand donkeys. They also took one hundred thousand people captive, 22and many others fell slain, because the battle was God's. And they occupied the land until the exile.

The Half-Tribe of Manasseh

23The people of the half-tribe of Manasseh were numerous; they settled in the land from Bashan to Baal Hermon, that is, to Senir (Mount Hermon).

24These were the heads of their families: Epher, Ishi, Eliel, Azriel, Jeremiah, Hodaviah and Jahdiel. They were brave warriors, famous men, and heads of their families. 25But they were unfaithful to the God of their fathers and prostituted themselves to the gods of the peoples of the land, whom God had destroyed before them. 26So the God of Israel stirred up the spirit of Pul king of Assyria (that is, Tiglath-Pileser king of Assyria), who took the Reubenites, the Gadites and the half-tribe of Manasseh into exile. He took them to Halah, Habor, Hara and the river of Gozan, where they are to this day.

Levi

6 The sons of Levi:
Gershon, Kohath and Merari.
2The sons of Kohath:
Amram, Izhar, Hebron and Uzziel.
3The children of Amram:
Aaron, Moses and Miriam.
The sons of Aaron:
Nadab, Abihu, Eleazar and Ithamar.
4Eleazar was the father of Phinehas,
Phinehas the father of Abishua,
5Abishua the father of Bukki,
Bukki the father of Uzzi,
6Uzzi the father of Zerahiah,
Zerahiah the father of Meraioth,
7Meraioth the father of Amariah,
Amariah the father of Ahitub,

8Ahitub the father of Zadok,
Zadok the father of Ahimaaz,
9Ahimaaz the father of Azariah,
Azariah the father of Johanan,
10Johanan the father of Azariah (it was he who served as priest in the temple Solomon built in Jerusalem),
11Azariah the father of Amariah,
Amariah the father of Ahitub,
12Ahitub the father of Zadok,
Zadok the father of Shallum,
13Shallum the father of Hilkiah,
Hilkiah the father of Azariah,
14Azariah the father of Seraiah,
and Seraiah the father of Jehozadak.

15Jehozadak was deported when the LORD sent Judah and Jerusalem into exile by the hand of Nebuchadnezzar.

16The sons of Levi:
Gershon,*a* Kohath and Merari.
17These are the names of the sons of Gershon:
Libni and Shimei.
18The sons of Kohath:
Amram, Izhar, Hebron and Uzziel.
19The sons of Merari:
Mahli and Mushi.
These are the clans of the Levites listed according to their fathers:
20Of Gershon:
Libni his son, Jehath his son, Zimmah his son, 21Joah his son,
Iddo his son, Zerah his son and Jeatherai his son.
22The descendants of Kohath:
Amminadab his son, Korah his son,
Assir his son, 23Elkanah his son,
Ebiasaph his son, Assir his son,
24Tahath his son, Uriel his son,

---

a16 Hebrew *Gershom*, a variant of *Gershon*; also in verses 17, 20, 43, 62 and 71

10 Commandments

FOR KIDS

1 You may not love anyone or anything more than you love God.

2 You may not worship, or put more importance on, any person or thing, other than God. You must worship only the Lord, not your parents, not a friend, not a movie star or sports hero, not a car or boat or skateboard. Nothing.

3 You may not swear. Use God's holy name only in a loving way, never to express anger or frustration.

4 One day of your week should be set aside for rest and the worship of God. Work six days of the week only. You need a special day set aside to relax and meet with other Christians.

5 Be respectful to your parents. Love them, and the Lord will reward you with a long life.

6 You may not hate other people; don't ever think of hurting someone else in any way.

7 Keep your thoughts and actions pure. Sex is a gift of God to married couples.

8 You may not take and keep anything that doesn't belong to you.

9 You may not tell lies, especially when that lie will hurt someone else.

10 You may not be jealous of what others have. You may not be jealous of your friend's new toy or clothes or the big house your neighbor lives in. Be satisfied with what you have.

THE BOOKS OF THE Bible

Genesis tells how God created us.
Next come Exodus and Leviticus.
    Numbers and Deuteronomy tell
    Great stories of wandering Israel.
Joshua has stories of war and victory.
Judges tells of problems in Jewish history.
    Next comes Ruth — you'll find in this book
    The story of Boaz and the wife he took.
Samuel contains books one and two.
Kings and Chronicles also do.
    In Ezra and Nehemiah the Jews come home.
    Esther is the story of a rise to the throne.
Job is a story of hope and sadness.
The Psalms are poems of praise and gladness.
    Proverbs gives us wise things to do;
    Ecclesiastes contains much good advice too.
Song of Songs — a poem of love and devotion —
Is expressed in words of strong emotion.
    Isaiah and Jeremiah are books of prophecy.
    Lamentations laments a sad time in history.
Ezekiel and Daniel take place in captivity.
Hosea, Joel and Amos are the next three.
    Obadiah is a short little book.
    Jonah is a great story — take a look.
Micah, Nahum, and Habakkuk prophesy,
Then come Zephaniah and Haggai.
    Zechariah and Malachi are at the end;
    Then a long time of silence God did send.

Matthew and Mark with Luke and John
Tell of the teachings of God's Son.
    Acts reports on the apostles' work
    With the people of the early church.
Take a look at Romans — you'll find within
How faith in Jesus can cover sin.
    Next come First and Second Corinthians
    Followed by Galatians, Ephesians, and Philippians.
Colossians explains what faith can do.
Thessalonians and Timothy have books one and two.
    Titus tells us to carry on.
    The next in line is Philemon.
Hebrews follows — a well-known book —
Chapter eleven at the subject of faith takes a look.
    James tells what a Christian should do.
    Followed by Peter — books one and two.
Then come John's letters — one, two and three.
Jude is next, and as brief as can be.
    The Revelation of John comes at the end
    And tells of a Savior who's coming again.

Uzziah his son and Shaul his son.

25The descendants of Elkanah:
Amasai, Ahimoth,
26Elkanah his son,[a] Zophai his son,
Nahath his son, 27Eliab his son,
Jeroham his son, Elkanah his son
and Samuel his son.[b]

28The sons of Samuel:
Joel[c] the firstborn
and Abijah the second son.

29The descendants of Merari:
Mahli, Libni his son,
Shimei his son, Uzzah his son,
30Shimea his son, Haggiah his son
and Asaiah his son.

The Temple Musicians

31These are the men David put in charge of the music in the house of the LORD after the ark came to rest there. 32They ministered with music before the tabernacle, the Tent of Meeting, until Solomon built the temple of the LORD in Jerusalem. They performed their duties according to the regulations laid down for them.

33Here are the men who served, together with their sons:

From the Kohathites:
Heman, the musician,
the son of Joel, the son of Samuel,
34the son of Elkanah, the son of Jeroham,
the son of Eliel, the son of Toah,
35the son of Zuph, the son of Elkanah,
the son of Mahath, the son of Amasai,
36the son of Elkanah, the son of Joel,
the son of Azariah, the son of Zephaniah,
37the son of Tahath, the son of Assir,
the son of Ebiasaph, the son of Korah,
38the son of Izhar, the son of Kohath,
the son of Levi, the son of Israel;
39and Heman's associate Asaph, who served at his right hand:
Asaph son of Berekiah, the son of Shimea,
40the son of Michael, the son of Baaseiah,[d]

---

[a]26 Some Hebrew manuscripts, Septuagint and Syriac; most Hebrew manuscripts *Ahimoth* 26and *Elkanah. The sons of Elkanah:* [b]27 Some Septuagint manuscripts (see also 1 Samuel 1:19,20 and 1 Chron. 6:33,34); Hebrew does not have *and Samuel his son.* [c]28 Some Septuagint manuscripts and Syriac (see also 1 Samuel 8:2 and 1 Chron. 6:33); Hebrew does not have *Joel.* [d]40 Most Hebrew manuscripts; some Hebrew manuscripts, one Septuagint manuscript and Syriac *Maaseiah*

Life in Bible Times

TEMPLE MUSICIANS

In King David's time the temple musicians used instruments like the lyre, the flute, cymbals, tambourines, and trumpets. All of these were played with shouts of joy to worship the Lord (Psalm 33:1–3).

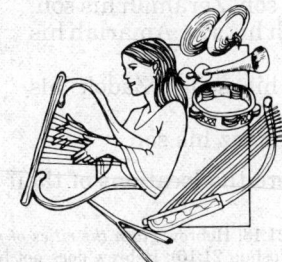

the son of Malkijah, ⁴¹the son
of Ethni,
the son of Zerah, the son of
Adaiah,
⁴²the son of Ethan, the son of
Zimmah,
the son of Shimei, ⁴³the son of
Jahath,
the son of Gershon, the son of
Levi;
⁴⁴and from their associates, the
Merarites, at his left hand:
Ethan son of Kishi, the son of
Abdi,
the son of Malluch, ⁴⁵the son of
Hashabiah,
the son of Amaziah, the son of
Hilkiah,
⁴⁶the son of Amzi, the son of
Bani,
the son of Shemer, ⁴⁷the son of
Mahli,
the son of Mushi, the son of
Merari,
the son of Levi.

⁴⁸Their fellow Levites were assigned to all the other duties of the
tabernacle, the house of God. ⁴⁹But
Aaron and his descendants were the
ones who presented offerings on the
altar of burnt offering and on the altar of incense in connection with all
that was done in the Most Holy Place,
making atonement for Israel, in accordance with all that Moses the servant of God had commanded.

⁵⁰These were the descendants of
Aaron:
Eleazar his son, Phinehas his
son,
Abishua his son, ⁵¹Bukki his
son,
Uzzi his son, Zerahiah his son,
⁵²Meraioth his son, Amariah his
son,
Ahitub his son, ⁵³Zadok his
son
and Ahimaaz his son.

⁵⁴These were the locations of their
settlements allotted as their territory (they were assigned to the descendants of Aaron who were from the
Kohathite clan, because the first lot
was for them):
⁵⁵They were given Hebron in
Judah with its surrounding pasturelands. ⁵⁶But the fields and
villages around the city were
given to Caleb son of Jephunneh.
⁵⁷So the descendants of Aaron
were given Hebron (a city of refuge), and Libnah,ᵃ Jattir, Eshtemoa, ⁵⁸Hilen, Debir, ⁵⁹Ashan,
Juttahᵇ and Beth Shemesh, together with their pasturelands.
⁶⁰And from the tribe of Benjamin
they were given Gibeon,ᶜ Geba,
Alemeth and Anathoth, together
with their pasturelands.
These towns, which were distributed among the Kohathite
clans, were thirteen in all.
⁶¹The rest of Kohath's descendants
were allotted ten towns from the
clans of half the tribe of Manasseh.
⁶²The descendants of Gershon, clan
by clan, were allotted thirteen towns
from the tribes of Issachar, Asher and
Naphtali, and from the part of the
tribe of Manasseh that is in Bashan.
⁶³The descendants of Merari, clan
by clan, were allotted twelve towns
from the tribes of Reuben, Gad and
Zebulun.
⁶⁴So the Israelites gave the Levites
these towns and their pasturelands.
⁶⁵From the tribes of Judah, Simeon
and Benjamin they allotted the previously named towns.
⁶⁶Some of the Kohathite clans were
given as their territory towns from
the tribe of Ephraim.
⁶⁷In the hill country of Ephraim they were given Shechem (a
city of refuge), and Gezer,ᵈ
⁶⁸Jokmeam, Beth Horon, ⁶⁹Aija-
lon and Gath Rimmon, together
with their pasturelands.
⁷⁰And from half the tribe of
Manasseh the Israelites gave

ᵃ57 See Joshua 21:13; Hebrew *given the cities of refuge: Hebron, Libnah.*   ᵇ59 Syriac (see also
Septuagint and Joshua 21:16); Hebrew does not have *Juttah.*   ᶜ60 See Joshua 21:17; Hebrew
does not have *Gibeon.*   ᵈ67 See Joshua 21:21; Hebrew *given the cities of refuge: Shechem, Gezer.*

Aner and Bileam, together with their pasturelands, to the rest of the Kohathite clans.

⁷¹The Gershonites received the following:

From the clan of the half-tribe of Manasseh

they received Golan in Bashan and also Ashtaroth, together with their pasturelands;

⁷²from the tribe of Issachar

they received Kedesh, Daberath, ⁷³Ramoth and Anem, together with their pasturelands;

⁷⁴from the tribe of Asher

they received Mashal, Abdon, ⁷⁵Hukok and Rehob, together with their pasturelands;

⁷⁶and from the tribe of Naphtali

they received Kedesh in Galilee, Hammon and Kiriathaim, together with their pasturelands.

⁷⁷The Merarites (the rest of the Levites) received the following:

From the tribe of Zebulun

they received Jokneam, Kartah,ᵃ Rimmono and Tabor, together with their pasturelands;

⁷⁸from the tribe of Reuben across the Jordan east of Jericho

they received Bezer in the desert, Jahzah, ⁷⁹Kedemoth and Mephaath, together with their pasturelands;

⁸⁰and from the tribe of Gad

they received Ramoth in Gilead, Mahanaim, ⁸¹Heshbon and Jazer, together with their pasturelands.

Issachar

7 The sons of Issachar:
Tola, Puah, Jashub and Shimron—four in all.
²The sons of Tola:
Uzzi, Rephaiah, Jeriel, Jahmai, Ibsam and Samuel—heads of their families. During the reign of David, the descen-

dants of Tola listed as fighting men in their genealogy numbered 22,600.
³The son of Uzzi:
Izrahiah.
The sons of Izrahiah:
Michael, Obadiah, Joel and Isshiah. All five of them were chiefs. ⁴According to their family genealogy, they had 36,000 men ready for battle, for they had many wives and children.
⁵The relatives who were fighting men belonging to all the clans of Issachar, as listed in their genealogy, were 87,000 in all.

Benjamin

⁶Three sons of Benjamin:
Bela, Beker and Jediael.
⁷The sons of Bela:
Ezbon, Uzzi, Uzziel, Jerimoth and Iri, heads of families—five in all. Their genealogical record listed 22,034 fighting men.
⁸The sons of Beker:
Zemirah, Joash, Eliezer, Elioenai, Omri, Jeremoth, Abijah, Anathoth and Alemeth. All these were the sons of Beker. ⁹Their genealogical record listed the heads of families and 20,200 fighting men.
¹⁰The son of Jediael:
Bilhan.
The sons of Bilhan:
Jeush, Benjamin, Ehud, Kenaanah, Zethan, Tarshish and Ahishahar. ¹¹All these sons of Jediael were heads of families. There were 17,200 fighting men ready to go out to war. ¹²The Shuppites and Huppites were the descendants of Ir, and the Hushites the descendants of Aher.

Naphtali

¹³The sons of Naphtali:
Jahziel, Guni, Jezer and Shil-

ᵃ77 See Septuagint and Joshua 21:34; Hebrew does not have *Jokneam, Kartah.*

lem*ᵃ*—the descendants of Bilhah.

Manasseh

¹⁴The descendants of Manasseh:
Asriel was his descendant through his Aramean concubine. She gave birth to Makir the father of Gilead. ¹⁵Makir took a wife from among the Huppites and Shuppites. His sister's name was Maacah.

Another descendant was named Zelophehad, who had only daughters.

¹⁶Makir's wife Maacah gave birth to a son and named him Peresh. His brother was named Sheresh, and his sons were Ulam and Rakem.

¹⁷The son of Ulam:
Bedan.

These were the sons of Gilead son of Makir, the son of Manasseh. ¹⁸His sister Hammoleketh gave birth to Ishhod, Abiezer and Mahlah.

¹⁹The sons of Shemida were:
Ahian, Shechem, Likhi and Aniam.

Ephraim

²⁰The descendants of Ephraim:
Shuthelah, Bered his son,
Tahath his son, Eleadah his son,
Tahath his son, ²¹Zabad his son
and Shuthelah his son.

Ezer and Elead were killed by the native-born men of Gath, when they went down to seize their livestock. ²²Their father Ephraim mourned for them many days, and his relatives came to comfort him. ²³Then he lay with his wife again, and she became pregnant and gave birth to a son. He named him Beriah,*ᵇ* because there had been misfortune in his family. ²⁴His daughter was Sheerah, who built Lower and Upper Beth Horon as well as Uzzen Sheerah.

²⁵Rephah was his son, Resheph his son,*ᶜ*
Telah his son, Tahan his son,
²⁶Ladan his son, Ammihud his son,
Elishama his son, ²⁷Nun his son
and Joshua his son.

²⁸Their lands and settlements included Bethel and its surrounding villages, Naaran to the east, Gezer and its villages to the west, and Shechem and its villages all the way to Ayyah and its villages. ²⁹Along the borders of Manasseh were Beth Shan, Taanach, Megiddo and Dor, together with their villages. The descendants of Joseph son of Israel lived in these towns.

Asher

³⁰The sons of Asher:
Imnah, Ishvah, Ishvi and Beriah. Their sister was Serah.

³¹The sons of Beriah:
Heber and Malkiel, who was the father of Birzaith.

³²Heber was the father of Japhlet, Shomer and Hotham and of their sister Shua.

³³The sons of Japhlet:
Pasach, Bimhal and Ashvath.
These were Japhlet's sons.

³⁴The sons of Shomer:
Ahi, Rohgah,*ᵈ* Hubbah and Aram.

³⁵The sons of his brother Helem:
Zophah, Imna, Shelesh and Amal.

³⁶The sons of Zophah:
Suah, Harnepher, Shual, Beri, Imrah, ³⁷Bezer, Hod, Shamma, Shilshah, Ithran*ᵉ* and Beera.

³⁸The sons of Jether:
Jephunneh, Pispah and Ara.

ᵃ13 Some Hebrew and Septuagint manuscripts (see also Gen. 46:24 and Num. 26:49); most Hebrew manuscripts *Shallum*   *ᵇ23 Beriah* sounds like the Hebrew for *misfortune.*   *ᶜ25* Some Septuagint manuscripts; Hebrew does not have *his son.*   *ᵈ34* Or *of his brother Shomer: Rohgah*   *ᵉ37* Possibly a variant of *Jether*

³⁹The sons of Ulla:

Arah, Hanniel and Rizia.

⁴⁰All these were descendants of Asher—heads of families, choice men, brave warriors and outstanding leaders. The number of men ready for battle, as listed in their genealogy, was 26,000.

?DID YOU KNOW?   7:40

Why are there so many lists of names in this book?

It was important to the Jewish people to know who their ancestors were. They kept careful records of their families. These records, called "genealogies," are found in 1 Chronicles 1–10.

The Genealogy of Saul the Benjamite

8 Benjamin was the father of Bela his firstborn,

Ashbel the second son, Aharah the third,

²Nohah the fourth and Rapha the fifth.

³The sons of Bela were:

Addar, Gera, Abihud,ᵃ ⁴Abishua, Naaman, Ahoah, ⁵Gera, Shephuphan and Huram.

⁶These were the descendants of Ehud, who were heads of families of those living in Geba and were deported to Manahath:

⁷Naaman, Ahijah, and Gera, who deported them and who was the father of Uzza and Ahihud.

⁸Sons were born to Shaharaim in Moab after he had divorced his wives Hushim and Baara. ⁹By his wife Hodesh he had Jobab, Zibia, Mesha, Malcam, ¹⁰Jeuz, Sakia and Mirmah. These were his sons, heads of families. ¹¹By Hushim he had Abitub and Elpaal.

¹²The sons of Elpaal:

Eber, Misham, Shemed (who built Ono and Lod with its surrounding villages), ¹³and Beriah and Shema, who were heads of families of those living in Aijalon and who drove out the inhabitants of Gath.

¹⁴Ahio, Shashak, Jeremoth, ¹⁵Zebadiah, Arad, Eder, ¹⁶Michael, Ishpah and Joha were the sons of Beriah.

¹⁷Zebadiah, Meshullam, Hizki, Heber, ¹⁸Ishmerai, Izliah and Jobab were the sons of Elpaal.

¹⁹Jakim, Zicri, Zabdi, ²⁰Elienai, Zillethai, Eliel, ²¹Adaiah, Beraiah and Shimrath were the sons of Shimei.

²²Ishpan, Eber, Eliel, ²³Abdon, Zicri, Hanan, ²⁴Hananiah, Elam, Anthothijah, ²⁵Iphdeiah and Penuel were the sons of Shashak.

²⁶Shamsherai, Shehariah, Athaliah, ²⁷Jaareshiah, Elijah and Zicri were the sons of Jeroham.

²⁸All these were heads of families, chiefs as listed in their genealogy, and they lived in Jerusalem.

²⁹Jeielᵇ the fatherᶜ of Gibeon lived in Gibeon.

His wife's name was Maacah, ³⁰and his firstborn son was Abdon, followed by Zur, Kish, Baal, Ner,ᵈ Nadab, ³¹Gedor, Ahio, Zeker ³²and Mikloth, who was the father of Shimeah. They too lived near their relatives in Jerusalem.

³³Ner was the father of Kish, Kish the father of Saul, and Saul the father of Jonathan, Malki-Shua, Abinadab and Esh-Baal.ᵉ

³⁴The son of Jonathan:

ᵃ3 Or *Gera the father of Ehud* ᵇ29 Some Septuagint manuscripts (see also 1 Chron. 9:35); Hebrew does not have *Jeiel*. ᶜ29 *Father* may mean *civic leader* or *military leader*. ᵈ30 Some Septuagint manuscripts (see also 1 Chron. 9:36); Hebrew does not have *Ner*. ᵉ33 Also known as *Ish-Bosheth*

Merib-Baal,ᵃ who was the father of Micah.

³⁵The sons of Micah:

Pithon, Melech, Tarea and Ahaz.

³⁶Ahaz was the father of Jehoaddah, Jehoaddah was the father of Alemeth, Azmaveth and Zimri, and Zimri was the father of Moza. ³⁷Moza was the father of Binea; Raphah was his son, Eleasah his son and Azel his son.

³⁸Azel had six sons, and these were their names:

Azrikam, Bokeru, Ishmael, Sheariah, Obadiah and Hanan. All these were the sons of Azel.

³⁹The sons of his brother Eshek:

Ulam his firstborn, Jeush the second son and Eliphelet the third. ⁴⁰The sons of Ulam were brave warriors who could handle the bow. They had many sons and grandsons—150 in all.

All these were the descendants of Benjamin.

9 All Israel was listed in the genealogies recorded in the book of the kings of Israel.

The People in Jerusalem

The people of Judah were taken captive to Babylon because of their unfaithfulness. ²Now the first to resettle on their own property in their own towns were some Israelites, priests, Levites and temple servants.

³Those from Judah, from Benjamin, and from Ephraim and Manasseh who lived in Jerusalem were:

⁴Uthai son of Ammihud, the son of Omri, the son of Imri, the son of Bani, a descendant of Perez son of Judah.

⁵Of the Shilonites:

Asaiah the firstborn and his sons.

⁶Of the Zerahites:

Jeuel.

The people from Judah numbered 690.

⁷Of the Benjamites:

Sallu son of Meshullam, the son of Hodaviah, the son of Hassenuah;

⁸Ibneiah son of Jeroham; Elah son of Uzzi, the son of Micri; and Meshullam son of Shephatiah, the son of Reuel, the son of Ibnijah.

⁹The people from Benjamin, as listed in their genealogy, numbered 956. All these men were heads of their families.

¹⁰Of the priests:

Jedaiah; Jehoiarib; Jakin;

¹¹Azariah son of Hilkiah, the son of Meshullam, the son of Zadok, the son of Meraioth, the son of Ahitub, the official in charge of the house of God;

¹²Adaiah son of Jeroham, the son of Pashhur, the son of Malkijah; and Maasai son of Adiel, the son of Jahzerah, the son of Meshullam, the son of Meshillemith, the son of Immer.

¹³The priests, who were heads of families, numbered 1,760. They were able men, responsible for ministering in the house of God.

¹⁴Of the Levites:

Shemaiah son of Hasshub, the son of Azrikam, the son of Hashabiah, a Merarite; ¹⁵Bakbakkar, Heresh, Galal and Mattaniah son of Mica, the son of Zicri, the son of Asaph; ¹⁶Obadiah son of Shemaiah, the son of Galal, the son of Jeduthun; and Berekiah son of Asa, the son of Elkanah, who lived in the villages of the Netophathites.

¹⁷The gatekeepers:

Shallum, Akkub, Talmon, Ahiman and their brothers, Shallum their chief ¹⁸being stationed at the King's Gate on the east, up to the present time. These were the gate-

---

ᵃ34 Also known as *Mephibosheth*

keepers belonging to the camp of the Levites. ¹⁹Shallum son of Kore, the son of Ebiasaph, the son of Korah, and his fellow gatekeepers from his family (the Korahites) were responsible for guarding the thresholds of the Tent ª just as their fathers had been responsible for guarding the entrance to the dwelling of the LORD. ²⁰In earlier times Phinehas son of Eleazar was in charge of the gatekeepers, and the LORD was with him. ²¹Zechariah son of Meshelemiah was the gatekeeper at the entrance to the Tent of Meeting.

²²Altogether, those chosen to be gatekeepers at the thresholds numbered 212. They were registered by genealogy in their villages. The gatekeepers had been assigned to their positions of trust by David and Samuel the seer. ²³They and their descendants were in charge of guarding the gates of the house of the LORD—the house called the Tent. ²⁴The gatekeepers were on the four sides: east, west, north and south. ²⁵Their brothers in their villages had to come from time to time and share their duties for seven-day periods. ²⁶But the four principal gatekeepers, who were Levites, were entrusted with the responsibility for the rooms and treasuries in the house of God. ²⁷They would spend the night stationed around the house of God, because they had to guard it; and they had charge of the key for opening it each morning.

²⁸Some of them were in charge of the articles used in the temple service; they counted them when they were brought in and when they were taken out. ²⁹Others were assigned to take care of the furnishings and all the other articles of the sanctuary, as well as the flour and wine, and the oil, incense and spices. ³⁰But some of the priests took care of mixing the spices. ³¹A Levite named Mattithiah, the firstborn son of Shallum the Korahite, was entrusted with the responsibility for baking the offering bread. ³²Some of their Kohathite brothers were in charge of preparing for every Sabbath the bread set out on the table.

³³Those who were musicians, heads of Levite families, stayed in the rooms of the temple and were exempt from other duties because they were responsible for the work day and night.

³⁴All these were heads of Levite families, chiefs as listed in their genealogy, and they lived in Jerusalem.

The Genealogy of Saul

³⁵Jeiel the father ᵇ of Gibeon lived in Gibeon.

His wife's name was Maacah, ³⁶and his firstborn son was Abdon, followed by Zur, Kish, Baal, Ner, Nadab, ³⁷Gedor, Ahio, Zechariah and Mikloth. ³⁸Mikloth was the father of Shimeam. They too lived near their relatives in Jerusalem.

³⁹Ner was the father of Kish, Kish the father of Saul, and Saul the father of Jonathan, Malki-Shua, Abinadab and Esh-Baal. ᶜ

⁴⁰The son of Jonathan:

Merib-Baal, ᵈ who was the father of Micah.

⁴¹The sons of Micah:

Pithon, Melech, Tahrea and Ahaz. ᵉ

⁴²Ahaz was the father of Jadah, Jadah ᶠ was the father of Alemeth, Azmaveth and Zimri, and Zimri was the father of Moza. ⁴³Moza was the father of

---

ª19 That is, the temple; also in verses 21 and 23
leader.   ᶜ39 Also known as Ish-Bosheth   ᵈ40 Also known as Mephibosheth   ᵉ41 Vulgate and Syriac (see also Septuagint and 1 Chron. 8:35); Hebrew does not have and Ahaz.   ᶠ42 Some Hebrew manuscripts and Septuagint (see also 1 Chron. 8:36); most Hebrew manuscripts Jarah, Jarah
ᵇ35 Father may mean civic leader or military

Binea; Rephaiah was his son, Eleasah his son and Azel his son.

⁴⁴Azel had six sons, and these were their names:

Azrikam, Bokeru, Ishmael, Sheariah, Obadiah and Hanan. These were the sons of Azel.

Saul Takes His Life

10 Now the Philistines fought against Israel; the Israelites fled before them, and many fell slain on Mount Gilboa. ²The Philistines pressed hard after Saul and his sons, and they killed his sons Jonathan, Abinadab and Malki-Shua. ³The fighting grew fierce around Saul, and when the archers overtook him, they wounded him.

⁴Saul said to his armor-bearer, "Draw your sword and run me through, or these uncircumcised fellows will come and abuse me."

But his armor-bearer was terrified and would not do it; so Saul took his own sword and fell on it. ⁵When the armor-bearer saw that Saul was dead, he too fell on his sword and died. ⁶So Saul and his three sons died, and all his house died together.

⁷When all the Israelites in the valley saw that the army had fled and that Saul and his sons had died, they abandoned their towns and fled. And the Philistines came and occupied them.

⁸The next day, when the Philistines came to strip the dead, they found Saul and his sons fallen on Mount Gilboa. ⁹They stripped him and took his head and his armor, and sent messengers throughout the land of the Philistines to proclaim the news among their idols and their people. ¹⁰They put his armor in the temple of their gods and hung up his head in the temple of Dagon.

¹¹When all the inhabitants of Jabesh Gilead heard of everything the Philistines had done to Saul, ¹²all their valiant men went and took the bodies of Saul and his sons and brought them to Jabesh. Then they

buried their bones under the great tree in Jabesh, and they fasted seven days.

¹³Saul died because he was unfaithful to the LORD; he did not keep the word of the LORD and even consulted a medium for guidance, ¹⁴and did not inquire of the LORD. So the LORD put him to death and turned the kingdom over to David son of Jesse.

David Becomes King Over Israel

11 All Israel came together to David at Hebron and said, "We are your own flesh and blood. ²In the past, even while Saul was king, you were the one who led Israel on their military campaigns. And the LORD your God said to you, 'You will shepherd my people Israel, and you will become their ruler.'"

³When all the elders of Israel had come to King David at Hebron, he made a compact with them at Hebron before the LORD, and they anointed David king over Israel, as the LORD had promised through Samuel.

David Conquers Jerusalem

⁴David and all the Israelites marched to Jerusalem (that is, Jebus). The Jebusites who lived there ⁵said to David, "You will not get in here." Nevertheless, David captured the fortress of Zion, the City of David.

⁶David had said, "Whoever leads the attack on the Jebusites will become commander-in-chief." Joab son of Zeruiah went up first, and so he received the command.

❓DID YOU KNOW?   11:7

What was the City of David?

Jerusalem was called the City of David because David captured the city and made it the capital of his kingdom.

⁷David then took up residence in the fortress, and so it was called the City of David. ⁸He built up the city around it, from the supporting ter-

races[a] to the surrounding wall, while Joab restored the rest of the city. [9]And David became more and more powerful, because the LORD Almighty was with him.

David's Mighty Men

[10]These were the chiefs of David's mighty men—they, together with all Israel, gave his kingship strong support to extend it over the whole land, as the LORD had promised— [11]this is the list of David's mighty men:

Jashobeam,[b] a Hacmonite, was chief of the officers[c]; he raised his spear against three hundred men, whom he killed in one encounter.

[12]Next to him was Eleazar son of Dodai the Ahohite, one of the three mighty men. [13]He was with David at Pas Dammim when the Philistines gathered there for battle. At a place where there was a field full of barley, the troops fled from the Philistines. [14]But they took their stand in the middle of the field. They defended it and struck the Philistines down, and the LORD brought about a great victory.

[15]Three of the thirty chiefs came down to David to the rock at the cave of Adullam, while a band of Philis-tines was encamped in the Valley of Rephaim. [16]At that time David was in the stronghold, and the Philistine garrison was at Bethlehem. [17]David longed for water and said, "Oh, that someone would get me a drink of water from the well near the gate of Bethlehem!" [18]So the Three broke through the Philistine lines, drew water from the well near the gate of Bethlehem and carried it back to David. But he refused to drink it; instead, he poured it out before the LORD. [19]"God forbid that I should do this!" he said. "Should I drink the blood of these men who went at the risk of their lives?" Because they risked their lives to bring it back, David would not drink it.

Such were the exploits of the three mighty men.

[20]Abishai the brother of Joab was chief of the Three. He raised his spear against three hundred men, whom he killed, and so he became as famous as the Three. [21]He was doubly honored above the Three and became their commander, even though he was not included among them.

[22]Benaiah son of Jehoiada was a valiant fighter from Kabzeel, who performed great exploits. He struck

---

a8 Or *the Millo*   *b11* Possibly a variant of *Jashob-Baal*   *c11* Or *Thirty*; some Septuagint manuscripts *Three* (see also 2 Samuel 23:8)

▨ET'S LIVE IT!   1 Chronicles 11:10–25

DOING IT ALONE ➠ King David was brave and strong. As a boy, he fought off a lion and a bear that tried to kill his sheep. As a teen-ager David killed the giant Goliath. But as king, David needed an army to help him. Read 1 Chronicles 11:10–25 to find out who helped David.

Here are three things to try doing alone.

1. Carry ten pennies, one at a time, from one side of a room to the other. 2. Play a game, like Candyland or Monopoly or Chinese checkers. 3. Pick up a long board and carry it across your yard.

Now do the same three things with another person. When you have finished, decide which is easier when you have a helper? Which is more fun when you have a helper? Which is quicker to do when you have a helper?

Think about this. Which chores that you and your brothers or sisters do might be easier or more fun or done more quickly if you helped each other?

down two of Moab's best men. He also
went down into a pit on a snowy day
and killed a lion. ²³And he struck
down an Egyptian who was seven
and a half feet*a* tall. Although the
Egyptian had a spear like a weaver's
rod in his hand, Benaiah went
against him with a club. He snatched
the spear from the Egyptian's hand
and killed him with his own spear.
²⁴Such were the exploits of Benaiah
son of Jehoiada; he too was as famous
as the three mighty men. ²⁵He was
held in greater honor than any of the
Thirty, but he was not included
among the Three. And David put him
in charge of his bodyguard.

²⁶The mighty men were:
 Asahel the brother of Joab,
 Elhanan son of Dodo from
   Bethlehem,
²⁷Shammoth the Harorite,
 Helez the Pelonite,
²⁸Ira son of Ikkesh from Tekoa,
 Abiezer from Anathoth,
²⁹Sibbecai the Hushathite,
 Ilai the Ahohite,
³⁰Maharai the Netophathite,
 Heled son of Baanah the Netophathite,
³¹Ithai son of Ribai from Gibeah
   in Benjamin,
 Benaiah the Pirathonite,
³²Hurai from the ravines of Gaash,
 Abiel the Arbathite,
³³Azmaveth the Baharumite,
 Eliahba the Shaalbonite,
³⁴the sons of Hashem the Gizo-
   nite,
 Jonathan son of Shagee the
   Hararite,
³⁵Ahiam son of Sacar the Hararite,
 Eliphal son of Ur,
³⁶Hepher the Mekerathite,
 Ahijah the Pelonite,
³⁷Hezro the Carmelite,
 Naarai son of Ezbai,
³⁸Joel the brother of Nathan,
 Mibhar son of Hagri,
³⁹Zelek the Ammonite,

Naharai the Berothite, the armor-bearer of Joab son of Zeruiah,
⁴⁰Ira the Ithrite,
 Gareb the Ithrite,
⁴¹Uriah the Hittite,
 Zabad son of Ahlai,
⁴²Adina son of Shiza the Reubenite, who was chief of the
   Reubenites, and the thirty
   with him,
⁴³Hanan son of Maacah,
 Joshaphat the Mithnite,
⁴⁴Uzzia the Ashterathite,
 Shama and Jeiel the sons of
   Hotham the Aroerite,
⁴⁵Jediael son of Shimri,
 his brother Joha the Tizite,
⁴⁶Eliel the Mahavite,
 Jeribai and Joshaviah the
   sons of Elnaam,
 Ithmah the Moabite,
⁴⁷Eliel, Obed and Jaasiel the
   Mezobaite.

Warriors Join David

12 These were the men who
   came to David at Ziklag,
while he was banished from the presence of Saul son of Kish (they were
among the warriors who helped him
in battle; ²they were armed with
bows and were able to shoot arrows or
to sling stones right-handed or left-
handed; they were kinsmen of Saul
from the tribe of Benjamin):

³Ahiezer their chief and Joash
the sons of Shemaah the Gibe-
athite; Jeziel and Pelet the sons
of Azmaveth; Beracah, Jehu the
Anathothite, ⁴and Ishmaiah the
Gibeonite, a mighty man among
the Thirty, who was a leader of
the Thirty; Jeremiah, Jahaziel,
Johanan, Jozabad the Gedera-
thite, ⁵Eluzai, Jerimoth, Beali-
ah, Shemariah and Shephatiah
the Haruphite; ⁶Elkanah, Isshiah, Azarel, Joezer and Jashobeam the Korahites; ⁷and Joelah
and Zebadiah the sons of Jeroham from Gedor.

⁸Some Gadites defected to David at his stronghold in the desert. They were brave warriors, ready for battle and able to handle the shield and spear. Their faces were the faces of lions, and they were as swift as gazelles in the mountains.

⁹Ezer was the chief,
Obadiah the second in command,
Eliab the third,
¹⁰Mishmannah the fourth, Jeremiah the fifth,
¹¹Attai the sixth, Eliel the seventh,
¹²Johanan the eighth, Elzabad the ninth,
¹³Jeremiah the tenth and Macbannai the eleventh.

¹⁴These Gadites were army commanders; the least was a match for a hundred, and the greatest for a thousand. ¹⁵It was they who crossed the Jordan in the first month when it was overflowing all its banks, and they put to flight everyone living in the valleys, to the east and to the west.

¹⁶Other Benjamites and some men from Judah also came to David in his stronghold. ¹⁷David went out to meet them and said to them, "If you have come to me in peace, to help me, I am ready to have you unite with me. But if you have come to betray me to my enemies when my hands are free from violence, may the God of our fathers see it and judge you."

¹⁸Then the Spirit came upon Amasai, chief of the Thirty, and he said:

"We are yours, O David!
We are with you, O son of
Jesse!
Success, success to you,
and success to those who help
you,
for your God will help you."

So David received them and made them leaders of his raiding bands.

¹⁹Some of the men of Manasseh defected to David when he went with the Philistines to fight against Saul. (He and his men did not help the Philistines because, after consultation, their rulers sent him away. They said, "It will cost us our heads if he deserts to his master Saul.") ²⁰When David went to Ziklag, these were the men of Manasseh who defected to him: Adnah, Jozabad, Jediael, Michael, Jozabad, Elihu and Zillethai, leaders of units of a thousand in Manasseh. ²¹They helped David against raiding bands, for all of them were brave warriors, and they were commanders in his army. ²²Day after day men came to help David, until he had a great army, like the army of God.ᵃ

Others Join David at Hebron

²³These are the numbers of the men armed for battle who came to David at Hebron to turn Saul's kingdom over to him, as the LORD had said:

²⁴men of Judah, carrying shield and spear— 6,800 armed for battle;
²⁵men of Simeon, warriors ready for battle— 7,100;
²⁶men of Levi— 4,600, ²⁷including Jehoiada, leader of the family of Aaron, with 3,700 men, ²⁸and Zadok, a brave young warrior, with 22 officers from his family;
²⁹men of Benjamin, Saul's kinsmen— 3,000, most of whom had remained loyal to Saul's house until then;
³⁰men of Ephraim, brave warriors, famous in their own clans— 20,800;
³¹men of half the tribe of Manasseh, designated by name to come and make David king—18,000;
³²men of Issachar, who understood the times and knew what Israel should do—200 chiefs, with all their relatives under their command;
³³men of Zebulun, experienced soldiers prepared for battle with every type of weapon, to help David with undivided loyalty—50,000;

ᵃ22 Or a great and mighty army

³⁴men of Naphtali— 1,000 officers, together with 37,000 men carrying shields and spears;
³⁵men of Dan, ready for battle— 28,600;
³⁶men of Asher, experienced soldiers prepared for battle— 40,000;
³⁷and from east of the Jordan, men of Reuben, Gad and the half-tribe of Manasseh, armed with every type of weapon— 120,000.

³⁸All these were fighting men who volunteered to serve in the ranks. They came to Hebron fully determined to make David king over all Israel. All the rest of the Israelites were also of one mind to make David king. ³⁹The men spent three days there with David, eating and drinking, for their families had supplied provisions for them. ⁴⁰Also, their neighbors from as far away as Issachar, Zebulun and Naphtali came bringing food on donkeys, camels, mules and oxen. There were plentiful supplies of flour, fig cakes, raisin cakes, wine, oil, cattle and sheep, for there was joy in Israel.

Bringing Back the Ark

13 David conferred with each of his officers, the commanders of thousands and commanders of hundreds. ²He then said to the whole assembly of Israel, "If it seems good to you and if it is the will of the LORD our God, let us send word far and wide to the rest of our brothers throughout the territories of Israel, and also to the priests and Levites who are with them in their towns and pasturelands, to come and join us. ³Let us bring the ark of our God back to us, for we did not inquire of ᵃ it ᵇ during the reign of Saul." ⁴The whole assembly agreed to do this, because it seemed right to all the people.

⁵So David assembled all the Israelites, from the Shihor River in Egypt to Lebo ᶜ Hamath, to bring the ark of God from Kiriath Jearim. ⁶David and all the Israelites with him went to Baalah of Judah (Kiriath Jearim) to bring up from there the ark of God the LORD, who is enthroned between the cherubim—the ark that is called by the Name.

⁷They moved the ark of God from Abinadab's house on a new cart, with Uzzah and Ahio guiding it. ⁸David and all the Israelites were celebrating with all their might before God, with songs and with harps, lyres, tambourines, cymbals and trumpets.

⁹When they came to the threshing floor of Kidon, Uzzah reached out his hand to steady the ark, because the oxen stumbled. ¹⁰The LORD's anger burned against Uzzah, and he struck him down because he had put his hand on the ark. So he died there before God.

❓DID YOU KNOW?   13:10

Why did God kill Uzzah?

Some people think it was unfair of God to kill Uzzah, who was only trying to keep the ark from falling off a cart. But the ark was holy, and no one was allowed to touch it. The ark should have been carried by means of poles put through the rings on each side of the ark. It should not have been placed on a cart. Uzzah's death reminded everyone that God is holy and must be obeyed.

---

¹¹Then David was angry because the LORD's wrath had broken out against Uzzah, and to this day that place is called Perez Uzzah. ᵈ
¹²David was afraid of God that day and asked, "How can I ever bring the ark of God to me?" ¹³He did not take the ark to be with him in the City of David. Instead, he took it aside to the house of Obed-Edom the Gittite.

ᵃ3 Or we neglected   ᵇ3 Or him   ᶜ5 Or to the entrance to   ᵈ11 Perez Uzzah means outbreak against Uzzah.

[14]The ark of God remained with the family of Obed-Edom in his house for three months, and the LORD blessed his household and everything he had.

David's House and Family

14 Now Hiram king of Tyre sent messengers to David, along with cedar logs, stonemasons and carpenters to build a palace for him. [2]And David knew that the LORD had established him as king over Israel and that his kingdom had been highly exalted for the sake of his people Israel.

[3]In Jerusalem David took more wives and became the father of more sons and daughters. [4]These are the names of the children born to him there: Shammua, Shobab, Nathan, Solomon, [5]Ibhar, Elishua, Elpelet, [6]Nogah, Nepheg, Japhia, [7]Elishama, Beeliada[a] and Eliphelet.

David Defeats the Philistines

[8]When the Philistines heard that David had been anointed king over all Israel, they went up in full force to search for him, but David heard about it and went out to meet them. [9]Now the Philistines had come and raided the Valley of Rephaim; [10]so David inquired of God: "Shall I go and attack the Philistines? Will you hand them over to me?"

The LORD answered him, "Go, I will hand them over to you."

[11]So David and his men went up to Baal Perazim, and there he defeated them. He said, "As waters break out, God has broken out against my enemies by my hand." So that place was called Baal Perazim.[b] [12]The Philistines had abandoned their gods there, and David gave orders to burn them in the fire.

[13]Once more the Philistines raided the valley; [14]so David inquired of God again, and God answered him, "Do not go straight up, but circle around them and attack them in front of the balsam trees. [15]As soon as you hear the sound of marching in the tops of the balsam trees, move out to battle, because that will mean God has gone out in front of you to strike the Philistine army." [16]So David did as God commanded him, and they struck down the Philistine army, all the way from Gibeon to Gezer.

[17]So David's fame spread throughout every land, and the LORD made all the nations fear him.

The Ark Brought to Jerusalem

15 After David had constructed buildings for himself in the City of David, he prepared a place for the ark of God and pitched a tent for it. [2]Then David said, "No one but the Levites may carry the ark of God, because the LORD chose them to carry the ark of the LORD and to minister before him forever."

[3]David assembled all Israel in Jerusalem to bring up the ark of the LORD to the place he had prepared for it. [4]He called together the descendants of Aaron and the Levites:

[5]From the descendants of Kohath,
  Uriel the leader and 120 relatives;
[6]from the descendants of Merari,
  Asaiah the leader and 220 relatives;
[7]from the descendants of Gershon,[c]
  Joel the leader and 130 relatives;
[8]from the descendants of Elizaphan,
  Shemaiah the leader and 200 relatives;
[9]from the descendants of Hebron,
  Eliel the leader and 80 relatives;
[10]from the descendants of Uzziel,
  Amminadab the leader and 112 relatives.

[11]Then David summoned Zadok and Abiathar the priests, and Uriel, Asaiah, Joel, Shemaiah, Eliel and Amminadab the Levites. [12]He said to

---

a7 A variant of Eliada   *b11 Baal Perazim means the lord who breaks out.*   *c7 Hebrew Gershom, a variant of Gershon*

them, "You are the heads of the Levitical families; you and your fellow Levites are to consecrate yourselves and bring up the ark of the LORD, the God of Israel, to the place I have prepared for it. ¹³It was because you, the Levites, did not bring it up the first time that the LORD our God broke out in anger against us. We did not inquire of him about how to do it in the prescribed way." ¹⁴So the priests and Levites consecrated themselves in order to bring up the ark of the LORD, the God of Israel. ¹⁵And the Levites carried the ark of God with the poles on their shoulders, as Moses had commanded in accordance with the word of the LORD.

¹⁶David told the leaders of the Levites to appoint their brothers as singers to sing joyful songs, accompanied by musical instruments: lyres, harps and cymbals.

¹⁷So the Levites appointed Heman son of Joel; from his brothers, Asaph son of Berekiah; and from their brothers the Merarites, Ethan son of Kushaiah; ¹⁸and with them their brothers next in rank: Zechariah,ᵃ Jaaziel, Shemiramoth, Jehiel, Unni, Eliab, Benaiah, Maaseiah, Mattithiah, Eliphelehu, Mikneiah, Obed-Edom and Jeiel,ᵇ the gatekeepers.

¹⁹The musicians Heman, Asaph and Ethan were to sound the bronze cymbals; ²⁰Zechariah, Aziel, Shemiramoth, Jehiel, Unni, Eliab, Maaseiah and Benaiah were to play the lyres according to *alamoth*,ᶜ ²¹and Mattithiah, Eliphelehu, Mikneiah, Obed-Edom, Jeiel and Azaziah were to play the harps, directing according to *sheminith*.ᶜ ²²Kenaniah the head Levite was in charge of the singing; that was his responsibility because he was skillful at it.

²³Berekiah and Elkanah were to be doorkeepers for the ark. ²⁴Shebaniah, Joshaphat, Nethanel, Amasai, Zechariah, Benaiah and Eliezer the priests were to blow trumpets before the ark of God. Obed-Edom and Jehiah were also to be doorkeepers for the ark.

²⁵So David and the elders of Israel and the commanders of units of a thousand went to bring up the ark of the covenant of the LORD from the house of Obed-Edom, with rejoicing. ²⁶Because God had helped the Levites who were carrying the ark of the covenant of the LORD, seven bulls and seven rams were sacrificed. ²⁷Now David was clothed in a robe of fine linen, as were all the Levites who were carrying the ark, and as were the singers, and Kenaniah, who was in charge of the singing of the choirs. David also wore a linen ephod. ²⁸So all Israel brought up the ark of the covenant of the LORD with shouts, with the sounding of rams' horns and trumpets, and of cymbals, and the playing of lyres and harps.

²⁹As the ark of the covenant of the LORD was entering the City of David,

---

ᵃ18 Three Hebrew manuscripts and most Septuagint manuscripts (see also verse 20 and 1 Chron. 16:5); most Hebrew manuscripts *Zechariah son and* or *Zechariah, Ben and*   ᵇ18 Hebrew; Septuagint (see also verse 21) *Jeiel and Azaziah*   ᶜ20,21 Probably a musical term

---

▚ET'S LIVE IT!   1 Chronicles 15:16–22

SING JOYFUL SONGS ➡ Read 1 Chronicles 15:16–22. What did David do to improve worship in Jerusalem?

Here's something your family can do to make worship better and more fun. Find a hymnal. Pick out songs you sing at church or Sunday school. Pick some that are new to you, as well as those that are your favorites. Then at suppertime or bedtime, sing one or two of the songs together. Soon you will know the songs better and be able to worship God more joyfully.

Michal daughter of Saul watched from a window. And when she saw King David dancing and celebrating, she despised him in her heart.

16 They brought the ark of God and set it inside the tent that David had pitched for it, and they presented burnt offerings and fellowship offerings[a] before God. ²After David had finished sacrificing the burnt offerings and fellowship offerings, he blessed the people in the name of the LORD. ³Then he gave a loaf of bread, a cake of dates and a cake of raisins to each Israelite man and woman.

⁴He appointed some of the Levites to minister before the ark of the LORD, to make petition, to give thanks, and to praise the LORD, the God of Israel: ⁵Asaph was the chief, Zechariah second, then Jeiel, Shemiramoth, Jehiel, Mattithiah, Eliab, Benaiah, Obed-Edom and Jeiel. They were to play the lyres and harps, Asaph was to sound the cymbals, ⁶and Benaiah and Jahaziel the priests were to blow the trumpets regularly before the ark of the covenant of God.

David's Psalm of Thanks

⁷That day David first committed to Asaph and his associates this psalm of thanks to the LORD:

⁸Give thanks to the LORD, call on his name;
　make known among the nations what he has done.
⁹Sing to him, sing praise to him;
　tell of all his wonderful acts.
¹⁰Glory in his holy name;
　let the hearts of those who seek the LORD rejoice.
¹¹Look to the LORD and his strength;
　seek his face always.
¹²Remember the wonders he has done,

　his miracles, and the judgments he pronounced,
¹³O descendants of Israel his servant,
　O sons of Jacob, his chosen ones.

¹⁴He is the LORD our God;
　his judgments are in all the earth.
¹⁵He remembers[b] his covenant forever,
　the word he commanded, for a thousand generations,
¹⁶the covenant he made with Abraham,
　the oath he swore to Isaac.
¹⁷He confirmed it to Jacob as a decree,
　to Israel as an everlasting covenant:
¹⁸"To you I will give the land of Canaan
　as the portion you will inherit."

¹⁹When they were but few in number,
　few indeed, and strangers in it,
²⁰they[c] wandered from nation to nation,
　from one kingdom to another.
²¹He allowed no man to oppress them;
　for their sake he rebuked kings:
²²"Do not touch my anointed ones;
　do my prophets no harm."

²³Sing to the LORD, all the earth;
　proclaim his salvation day after day.
²⁴Declare his glory among the nations,
　his marvelous deeds among all peoples.
²⁵For great is the LORD and most worthy of praise;
　he is to be feared above all gods.
²⁶For all the gods of the nations are idols,
　but the LORD made the heavens.

---

a1 Traditionally *peace offerings*; also in verse 2 *b15* Some Septuagint manuscripts (see also Psalm 105:8); Hebrew *Remember* *c18-20* One Hebrew manuscript, Septuagint and Vulgate (see also Psalm 105:12); most Hebrew manuscripts *inherit, / ¹⁹though you are but few in number, / few indeed, and strangers in it." / ²⁰They*

²⁷Splendor and majesty are before
him;
strength and joy in his dwelling
place.
²⁸Ascribe to the LORD, O families of
nations,
ascribe to the LORD glory and
strength,
²⁹ ascribe to the LORD the glory
due his name.
Bring an offering and come before
him;
worship the LORD in the
splendor of his*a* holiness.

WORDS TO REMEMBER

**16:29   Ascribe to the LORD the
glory due his name.
Bring an offering and
come before him.**

---

³⁰Tremble before him, all the earth!
The world is firmly established;
it cannot be moved.
³¹Let the heavens rejoice, let the
earth be glad;
let them say among the nations,
"The LORD reigns!"
³²Let the sea resound, and all that
is in it;
let the fields be jubilant, and
everything in them!
³³Then the trees of the forest will
sing,
they will sing for joy before the
LORD,
for he comes to judge the earth.
³⁴Give thanks to the LORD, for he is
good;
his love endures forever.
³⁵Cry out, "Save us, O God our
Savior;
gather us and deliver us from
the nations,
that we may give thanks to your
holy name,
that we may glory in your
praise."
³⁶Praise be to the LORD, the God of
Israel,

from everlasting to everlasting.
Then all the people said "Amen" and
"Praise the LORD."

³⁷David left Asaph and his associates before the ark of the covenant of the LORD to minister there regularly, according to each day's requirements. ³⁸He also left Obed-Edom and his sixty-eight associates to minister with them. Obed-Edom son of Jeduthun, and also Hosah, were gatekeepers. ³⁹David left Zadok the priest and his fellow priests before the tabernacle of the LORD at the high place in Gibeon ⁴⁰to present burnt offerings to the LORD on the altar of burnt offering regularly, morning and evening, in accordance with everything written in the Law of the LORD, which he had given Israel. ⁴¹With them were Heman and Jeduthun and the rest of those chosen and designated by name to give thanks to the LORD, "for his love endures forever." ⁴²Heman and Jeduthun were responsible for the sounding of the trumpets and cymbals and for the playing of the other instruments for sacred song. The sons of Jeduthun were stationed at the gate.

⁴³Then all the people left, each for his own home, and David returned home to bless his family.

God's Promise to David

17 After David was settled in his palace, he said to Nathan the prophet, "Here I am, living in a palace of cedar, while the ark of the covenant of the LORD is under a tent."

²Nathan replied to David, "Whatever you have in mind, do it, for God is with you."

³That night the word of God came to Nathan, saying:

⁴"Go and tell my servant David, 'This is what the LORD says: You are not the one to build me a house to dwell in. ⁵I have not

---

a29 Or LORD *with the splendor of*

dwelt in a house from the day I brought Israel up out of Egypt to this day. I have moved from one tent site to another, from one dwelling place to another. [6]Wherever I have moved with all the Israelites, did I ever say to any of their leaders[a] whom I commanded to shepherd my people, "Why have you not built me a house of cedar?" '

[7]"Now then, tell my servant David, 'This is what the LORD Almighty says: I took you from the pasture and from following the flock, to be ruler over my people Israel. [8]I have been with you wherever you have gone, and I have cut off all your enemies from before you. Now I will make your name like the names of the greatest men of the earth. [9]And I will provide a place for my people Israel and will plant them so that they can have a home of their own and no longer be disturbed. Wicked people will not oppress them anymore, as they did at the beginning [10]and have done ever since the time I appointed leaders over my people Israel. I will also subdue all your enemies.

" 'I declare to you that the LORD will build a house for you: [11]When your days are over and you go to be with your fathers, I will raise up your offspring to succeed you, one of your own sons, and I will establish his kingdom. [12]He is the one who will build a house for me, and I will establish his throne forever. [13]I will be his father, and he will be my son. I will never take my love away from him, as I took it away from your predecessor. [14]I will set him over my house and my kingdom forever; his throne will be established forever.' "

[15]Nathan reported to David all the words of this entire revelation.

David's Prayer

[16]Then King David went in and sat before the LORD, and he said:

? DID YOU KNOW?   **17:11**

What did God promise David?

God promised that one of David's descendants would always sit on the throne. God kept this promise. Today Jesus, who is David's descendant, is alive in heaven. One day Jesus will come again to rule the whole earth and the universe.

"Who am I, O LORD God, and what is my family, that you have brought me this far? [17]And as if this were not enough in your sight, O God, you have spoken about the future of the house of your servant. You have looked on me as though I were the most exalted of men, O LORD God.

[18]"What more can David say to you for honoring your servant? For you know your servant, [19]O LORD. For the sake of your servant and according to your will, you have done this great thing and made known all these great promises.

[20]"There is no one like you, O LORD, and there is no God but you, as we have heard with our own ears. [21]And who is like your people Israel—the one nation on earth whose God went out to redeem a people for himself, and to make a name for yourself, and to perform great and awesome wonders by driving out nations from before your people, whom you redeemed from Egypt? [22]You made your people Israel your very own forever, and you, O LORD, have become their God.

[23]"And now, LORD, let the promise you have made concern-

---

[a]6 Traditionally *judges*; also in verse 10

ing your servant and his house be established forever. Do as you promised, 24so that it will be established and that your name will be great forever. Then men will say, 'The LORD Almighty, the God over Israel, is Israel's God!' And the house of your servant David will be established before you.

25"You, my God, have revealed to your servant that you will build a house for him. So your servant has found courage to pray to you. 26O LORD, you are God! You have promised these good things to your servant. 27Now you have been pleased to bless the house of your servant, that it may continue forever in your sight; for you, O LORD, have blessed it, and it will be blessed forever."

WORDS TO REMEMBER

17:26 O LORD, you are God! You have promised these good things to your servant.

David's Victories

18 In the course of time, David defeated the Philistines and subdued them, and he took Gath and its surrounding villages from the control of the Philistines.

2David also defeated the Moabites, and they became subject to him and brought tribute.

3Moreover, David fought Hadadezer king of Zobah, as far as Hamath, when he went to establish his control along the Euphrates River. 4David captured a thousand of his chariots, seven thousand charioteers and twenty thousand foot soldiers. He hamstrung all but a hundred of the chariot horses.

5When the Arameans of Damascus came to help Hadadezer king of Zobah, David struck down twenty-two thousand of them. 6He put garrisons in the Aramean kingdom of Damascus, and the Arameans became subject to him and brought tribute. The LORD gave David victory everywhere he went.

7David took the gold shields carried by the officers of Hadadezer and brought them to Jerusalem. 8From Tebah[a] and Cun, towns that belonged to Hadadezer, David took a great quantity of bronze, which Solomon used to make the bronze Sea, the pillars and various bronze articles.

9When Tou king of Hamath heard that David had defeated the entire army of Hadadezer king of Zobah, 10he sent his son Hadoram to King David to greet him and congratulate him on his victory in battle over Hadadezer, who had been at war with Tou. Hadoram brought all kinds of articles of gold and silver and bronze.

11King David dedicated these articles to the LORD, as he had done with the silver and gold he had taken from all these nations: Edom and Moab, the Ammonites and the Philistines, and Amalek.

12Abishai son of Zeruiah struck down eighteen thousand Edomites in the Valley of Salt. 13He put garrisons in Edom, and all the Edomites became subject to David. The LORD gave David victory everywhere he went.

David's Officials

14David reigned over all Israel, doing what was just and right for all his people. 15Joab son of Zeruiah was over the army; Jehoshaphat son of Ahilud was recorder; 16Zadok son of Ahitub and Ahimelech[b] son of Abiathar were priests; Shavsha was secretary; 17Benaiah son of Jehoiada was over the Kerethites and Pelethites; and David's sons were chief officials at the king's side.

---

a8 Hebrew *Tibhath,* a variant of *Tebah*   *b16* Some Hebrew manuscripts, Vulgate and Syriac (see also 2 Samuel 8:17); most Hebrew manuscripts *Abimelech*

The Battle Against the Ammonites

19 In the course of time, Nahash king of the Ammonites died, and his son succeeded him as king. ²David thought, "I will show kindness to Hanun son of Nahash, because his father showed kindness to me." So David sent a delegation to express his sympathy to Hanun concerning his father.

When David's men came to Hanun in the land of the Ammonites to express sympathy to him, ³the Ammonite nobles said to Hanun, "Do you think David is honoring your father by sending men to you to express sympathy? Haven't his men come to you to explore and spy out the country and overthrow it?" ⁴So Hanun seized David's men, shaved them, cut off their garments in the middle at the buttocks, and sent them away.

⁵When someone came and told David about the men, he sent messengers to meet them, for they were greatly humiliated. The king said, "Stay at Jericho till your beards have grown, and then come back."

⁶When the Ammonites realized that they had become a stench in David's nostrils, Hanun and the Ammonites sent a thousand talents*a* of silver to hire chariots and charioteers from Aram Naharaim,*b* Aram Maacah and Zobah. ⁷They hired thirty-two thousand chariots and charioteers, as well as the king of Maacah with his troops, who came and camped near Medeba, while the Ammonites were mustered from their towns and moved out for battle.

⁸On hearing this, David sent Joab out with the entire army of fighting men. ⁹The Ammonites came out and drew up in battle formation at the entrance to their city, while the kings who had come were by themselves in the open country.

¹⁰Joab saw that there were battle lines in front of him and behind him; so he selected some of the best troops in Israel and deployed them against the Arameans. ¹¹He put the rest of the men under the command of Abishai his brother, and they were deployed against the Ammonites. ¹²Joab said, "If the Arameans are too strong for me, then you are to rescue me; but if the Ammonites are too strong for you, then I will rescue you. ¹³Be strong and let us fight bravely for our people and the cities of our God. The LORD will do what is good in his sight."

¹⁴Then Joab and the troops with him advanced to fight the Arameans, and they fled before him. ¹⁵When the Ammonites saw that the Arameans were fleeing, they too fled before his brother Abishai and went inside the city. So Joab went back to Jerusalem.

¹⁶After the Arameans saw that they had been routed by Israel, they sent messengers and had Arameans brought from beyond the River,*c* with Shophach the commander of Hadadezer's army leading them.

¹⁷When David was told of this, he gathered all Israel and crossed the Jordan; he advanced against them and formed his battle lines opposite them. David formed his lines to meet the Arameans in battle, and they fought against him. ¹⁸But they fled before Israel, and David killed seven thousand of their charioteers and forty thousand of their foot soldiers. He also killed Shophach the commander of their army.

¹⁹When the vassals of Hadadezer saw that they had been defeated by Israel, they made peace with David and became subject to him.

So the Arameans were not willing to help the Ammonites anymore.

The Capture of Rabbah

20 In the spring, at the time when kings go off to war, Joab led out the armed forces. He laid waste the land of the Ammonites and went to Rabbah and besieged it, but

---

a6 That is, about 37 tons (about 34 metric tons)   *b6* That is, Northwest Mesopotamia
c16 That is, the Euphrates

David remained in Jerusalem. Joab attacked Rabbah and left it in ruins. ²David took the crown from the head of their king*a*—its weight was found to be a talent*b* of gold, and it was set with precious stones—and it was placed on David's head. He took a great quantity of plunder from the city ³and brought out the people who were there, consigning them to labor with saws and with iron picks and axes. David did this to all the Ammonite towns. Then David and his entire army returned to Jerusalem.

?DID YOU KNOW?   20:1

How successful were David's wars?

David had so much military success that his kingdom had ten times as much land when he died as it had before he became ruler!

War With the Philistines

⁴In the course of time, war broke out with the Philistines, at Gezer. At that time Sibbecai the Hushathite killed Sippai, one of the descendants of the Rephaites, and the Philistines were subjugated.

⁵In another battle with the Philistines, Elhanan son of Jair killed Lahmi the brother of Goliath the Gittite, who had a spear with a shaft like a weaver's rod.

⁶In still another battle, which took place at Gath, there was a huge man with six fingers on each hand and six toes on each foot—twenty-four in all. He also was descended from Rapha. ⁷When he taunted Israel, Jonathan son of Shimea, David's brother, killed him.

⁸These were descendants of Rapha in Gath, and they fell at the hands of David and his men.

David Numbers the Fighting Men

21 Satan rose up against Israel and incited David to take a census of Israel. ²So David said to Joab and the commanders of the troops, "Go and count the Israelites from Beersheba to Dan. Then report back to me so that I may know how many there are."

³But Joab replied, "May the LORD multiply his troops a hundred times over. My lord the king, are they not all my lord's subjects? Why does my lord want to do this? Why should he bring guilt on Israel?"

⁴The king's word, however, overruled Joab; so Joab left and went throughout Israel and then came back to Jerusalem. ⁵Joab reported the number of the fighting men to David: In all Israel there were one million one hundred thousand men who could handle a sword, including four hundred and seventy thousand in Judah.

⁶But Joab did not include Levi and Benjamin in the numbering, because the king's command was repulsive to him. ⁷This command was also evil in the sight of God; so he punished Israel.

⁸Then David said to God, "I have sinned greatly by doing this. Now, I beg you, take away the guilt of your servant. I have done a very foolish thing."

⁹The LORD said to Gad, David's seer, ¹⁰"Go and tell David, 'This is what the LORD says: I am giving you three options. Choose one of them for me to carry out against you.'"

¹¹So Gad went to David and said to him, "This is what the LORD says: 'Take your choice: ¹²three years of famine, three months of being swept away*c* before your enemies, with their swords overtaking you, or three days of the sword of the LORD—days of plague in the land, with the angel of the LORD ravaging every part of

---

a2 Or *of Milcom*, that is, Molech   *b2* That is, about 75 pounds (about 34 kilograms)
c12 Hebrew; Septuagint and Vulgate (see also 2 Samuel 24:13) *of fleeing*

Israel.' Now then, decide how I should answer the one who sent me."

¹³David said to Gad, "I am in deep distress. Let me fall into the hands of the LORD, for his mercy is very great; but do not let me fall into the hands of men."

¹⁴So the LORD sent a plague on Israel, and seventy thousand men of Israel fell dead. ¹⁵And God sent an angel to destroy Jerusalem. But as the angel was doing so, the LORD saw it and was grieved because of the calamity and said to the angel who was destroying the people, "Enough! Withdraw your hand." The angel of the LORD was then standing at the threshing floor of Araunah[a] the Jebusite.

¹⁶David looked up and saw the angel of the LORD standing between heaven and earth, with a drawn sword in his hand extended over Jerusalem. Then David and the elders, clothed in sackcloth, fell facedown.

¹⁷David said to God, "Was it not I who ordered the fighting men to be counted? I am the one who has sinned and done wrong. These are but sheep. What have they done? O LORD my God, let your hand fall upon me and my family, but do not let this plague remain on your people."

¹⁸Then the angel of the LORD ordered Gad to tell David to go up and build an altar to the LORD on the threshing floor of Araunah the Jebusite. ¹⁹So David went up in obedience to the word that Gad had spoken in the name of the LORD.

²⁰While Araunah was threshing wheat, he turned and saw the angel; his four sons who were with him hid themselves. ²¹Then David approached, and when Araunah looked and saw him, he left the threshing floor and bowed down before David with his face to the ground.

²²David said to him, "Let me have the site of your threshing floor so I can build an altar to the LORD, that the plague on the people may be stopped. Sell it to me at the full price."

²³Araunah said to David, "Take it! Let my lord the king do whatever pleases him. Look, I will give the oxen for the burnt offerings, the threshing sledges for the wood, and the wheat for the grain offering. I will give all this."

²⁴But King David replied to Araunah, "No, I insist on paying the full price. I will not take for the LORD what is yours, or sacrifice a burnt offering that costs me nothing."

²⁵So David paid Araunah six hundred shekels[b] of gold for the site. ²⁶David built an altar to the LORD there and sacrificed burnt offerings and fellowship offerings.[c] He called on the LORD, and the LORD answered him with fire from heaven on the altar of burnt offering.

²⁷Then the LORD spoke to the angel, and he put his sword back into its sheath. ²⁸At that time, when David saw that the LORD had answered him on the threshing floor of Araunah the Jebusite, he offered sacrifices there. ²⁹The tabernacle of the LORD, which Moses had made in the desert, and the altar of burnt offering were at that time on the high place at Gibeon. ³⁰But David could not go before it to inquire of God, because he was afraid of the sword of the angel of the LORD.

22 Then David said, "The house of the LORD God is to be here, and also the altar of burnt offering for Israel."

Preparations for the Temple

²So David gave orders to assemble the aliens living in Israel, and from among them he appointed stonecutters to prepare dressed stone for building the house of God. ³He provided a large amount of iron to make nails for the doors of the gateways and for the fittings, and more bronze than could be weighed. ⁴He also provided more cedar logs than could be

---

*a*15 Hebrew *Ornan*, a variant of *Araunah*; also in verses 18-28 (about 7 kilograms)   *c*26 Traditionally *peace offerings*   *b*25 That is, about 15 pounds

counted, for the Sidonians and Tyrians had brought large numbers of them to David.

⁵David said, "My son Solomon is young and inexperienced, and the house to be built for the LORD should be of great magnificence and fame and splendor in the sight of all the nations. Therefore I will make preparations for it." So David made extensive preparations before his death.

⁶Then he called for his son Solomon and charged him to build a house for the LORD, the God of Israel. ⁷David said to Solomon: "My son, I had it in my heart to build a house for the Name of the LORD my God. ⁸But this word of the LORD came to me: 'You have shed much blood and have fought many wars. You are not to build a house for my Name, because you have shed much blood on the earth in my sight. ⁹But you will have a son who will be a man of peace and rest, and I will give him rest from all his enemies on every side. His name will be Solomon,ᵃ and I will grant Israel peace and quiet during his reign. ¹⁰He is the one who will build a house for my Name. He will be my son, and I will be his father. And I will establish the throne of his kingdom over Israel forever.'

¹¹"Now, my son, the LORD be with you, and may you have success and build the house of the LORD your God, as he said you would. ¹²May the LORD give you discretion and understanding when he puts you in command over Israel, so that you may keep the law of the LORD your God. ¹³Then you will have success if you are careful to observe the decrees and laws that the LORD gave Moses for Israel. Be strong and courageous. Do not be afraid or discouraged.

¹⁴"I have taken great pains to provide for the temple of the LORD a hundred thousand talentsᵇ of gold, a million talentsᶜ of silver, quantities of bronze and iron too great to be weighed, and wood and stone. And you may add to them. ¹⁵You have many workmen: stonecutters, masons and carpenters, as well as men skilled in every kind of work ¹⁶in gold and silver, bronze and iron—craftsmen beyond number. Now begin the work, and the LORD be with you."

¹⁷Then David ordered all the leaders of Israel to help his son Solomon. ¹⁸He said to them, "Is not the LORD your God with you? And has he not granted you rest on every side? For he has handed the inhabitants of the land over to me, and the land is sub-

---

ᵃ9 *Solomon* sounds like and may be derived from the Hebrew for *peace.*   ᵇ14 That is, about 3,750 tons (about 3,450 metric tons)   ᶜ14 That is, about 37,500 tons (about 34,500 metric tons)

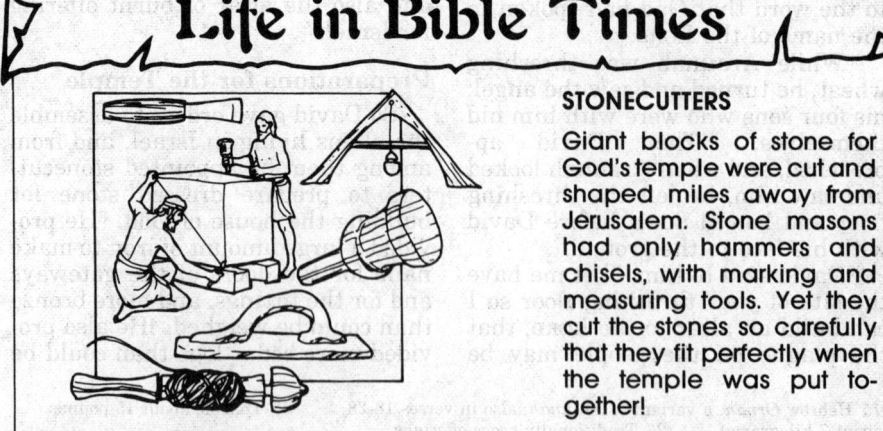

Life in Bible Times

STONECUTTERS

Giant blocks of stone for God's temple were cut and shaped miles away from Jerusalem. Stone masons had only hammers and chisels, with marking and measuring tools. Yet they cut the stones so carefully that they fit perfectly when the temple was put together!

ject to the LORD and to his people. ¹⁹Now devote your heart and soul to seeking the LORD your God. Begin to build the sanctuary of the LORD God, so that you may bring the ark of the covenant of the LORD and the sacred articles belonging to God into the temple that will be built for the Name of the LORD."

WORDS TO REMEMBER

22:19 Now devote your heart and soul to seeking the LORD your God.

The Levites

23 When David was old and full of years, he made his son Solomon king over Israel. ²He also gathered together all the leaders of Israel, as well as the priests and Levites. ³The Levites thirty years old or more were counted, and the total number of men was thirty-eight thousand. ⁴David said, "Of these, twenty-four thousand are to supervise the work of the temple of the LORD and six thousand are to be officials and judges. ⁵Four thousand are to be gatekeepers and four thousand are to praise the LORD with the musical instruments I have provided for that purpose."

? DID YOU KNOW?   23:2

Who were the Levites?

The Levites were a tribe, or family group, of Israelites. They were set apart to serve the Lord. David organized the Levites to serve God at the temple Solomon would build.

---

⁶David divided the Levites into groups corresponding to the sons of Levi: Gershon, Kohath and Merari.

Gershonites

⁷Belonging to the Gershonites:
Ladan and Shimei.
⁸The sons of Ladan:
Jehiel the first, Zetham and Joel—three in all.
⁹The sons of Shimei:
Shelomoth, Haziel and Haran—three in all.
These were the heads of the families of Ladan.
¹⁰And the sons of Shimei:
Jahath, Ziza,ᵃ Jeush and Beriah.
These were the sons of Shimei—four in all.
¹¹Jahath was the first and Ziza the second, but Jeush and Beriah did not have many sons; so they were counted as one family with one assignment.

Kohathites

¹²The sons of Kohath:
Amram, Izhar, Hebron and Uzziel—four in all.
¹³The sons of Amram:
Aaron and Moses.
Aaron was set apart, he and his descendants forever, to consecrate the most holy things, to offer sacrifices before the LORD, to minister before him and to pronounce blessings in his name forever.
¹⁴The sons of Moses the man of God were counted as part of the tribe of Levi.
¹⁵The sons of Moses:
Gershom and Eliezer.
¹⁶The descendants of Gershom:
Shubael was the first.
¹⁷The descendants of Eliezer:
Rehabiah was the first.
Eliezer had no other sons, but the sons of Rehabiah were very numerous.
¹⁸The sons of Izhar:
Shelomith was the first.
¹⁹The sons of Hebron:
Jeriah the first, Amariah the

ᵃ10 One Hebrew manuscript, Septuagint and Vulgate (see also verse 11); most Hebrew manuscripts *Zina*

second, Jahaziel the third and Jekameam the fourth.
20The sons of Uzziel:
Micah the first and Isshiah the second.

Merarites

21The sons of Merari:
Mahli and Mushi.
The sons of Mahli:
Eleazar and Kish.
22Eleazar died without having sons: he had only daughters. Their cousins, the sons of Kish, married them.
23The sons of Mushi:
Mahli, Eder and Jerimoth—three in all.

24These were the descendants of Levi by their families—the heads of families as they were registered under their names and counted individually, that is, the workers twenty years old or more who served in the temple of the LORD. 25For David had said, "Since the LORD, the God of Israel, has granted rest to his people and has come to dwell in Jerusalem forever, 26the Levites no longer need to carry the tabernacle or any of the articles used in its service." 27According to the last instructions of David, the Levites were counted from those twenty years old or more.

28The duty of the Levites was to help Aaron's descendants in the service of the temple of the LORD: to be in charge of the courtyards, the side rooms, the purification of all sacred things and the performance of other duties at the house of God. 29They were in charge of the bread set out on the table, the flour for the grain offerings, the unleavened wafers, the baking and the mixing, and all measurements of quantity and size. 30They were also to stand every morning to thank and praise the LORD. They were to do the same in the evening 31and whenever burnt offerings were presented to the LORD on Sabbaths and at New Moon festivals and at appointed feasts. They were to serve before the LORD regularly in the proper

number and in the way prescribed for them.

32And so the Levites carried out their responsibilities for the Tent of Meeting, for the Holy Place and, under their brothers the descendants of Aaron, for the service of the temple of the LORD.

The Divisions of Priests

24 These were the divisions of the sons of Aaron:

The sons of Aaron were Nadab, Abihu, Eleazar and Ithamar. 2But Nadab and Abihu died before their father did, and they had no sons; so Eleazar and Ithamar served as the priests. 3With the help of Zadok a descendant of Eleazar and Ahimelech a descendant of Ithamar, David separated them into divisions for their appointed order of ministering. 4A larger number of leaders were found among Eleazar's descendants than among Ithamar's, and they were divided accordingly: sixteen heads of families from Eleazar's descendants and eight heads of families from Ithamar's descendants. 5They divided them impartially by drawing lots, for there were officials of the sanctuary and officials of God among the descendants of both Eleazar and Ithamar.

6The scribe Shemaiah son of Nethanel, a Levite, recorded their names in the presence of the king and of the officials: Zadok the priest, Ahimelech son of Abiathar and the heads of families of the priests and of the Levites—one family being taken from Eleazar and then one from Ithamar.

7The first lot fell to Jehoiarib,
the second to Jedaiah,
8the third to Harim,
the fourth to Seorim,
9the fifth to Malkijah,
the sixth to Mijamin,
10the seventh to Hakkoz,
the eighth to Abijah,
11the ninth to Jeshua,
the tenth to Shecaniah,
12the eleventh to Eliashib,

the twelfth to Jakim,
¹³the thirteenth to Huppah,
the fourteenth to Jeshebeab,
¹⁴the fifteenth to Bilgah,
the sixteenth to Immer,
¹⁵the seventeenth to Hezir,
the eighteenth to Happizzez,
¹⁶the nineteenth to Pethahiah,
the twentieth to Jehezkel,
¹⁷the twenty-first to Jakin,
the twenty-second to Gamul,
¹⁸the twenty-third to Delaiah
and the twenty-fourth to Maaziah.

¹⁹This was their appointed order of ministering when they entered the temple of the LORD, according to the regulations prescribed for them by their forefather Aaron, as the LORD, the God of Israel, had commanded him.

The Rest of the Levites

²⁰As for the rest of the descendants of Levi:
from the sons of Amram: Shubael;
from the sons of Shubael: Jehdeiah.
²¹As for Rehabiah, from his sons:
Isshiah was the first.
²²From the Izharites: Shelomoth;
from the sons of Shelomoth: Jahath.
²³The sons of Hebron: Jeriah the first,ᵃ Amariah the second, Jahaziel the third and Jekameam the fourth.
²⁴The son of Uzziel: Micah;
from the sons of Micah: Shamir.
²⁵The brother of Micah: Isshiah;
from the sons of Isshiah: Zechariah.
²⁶The sons of Merari: Mahli and Mushi.
The son of Jaaziah: Beno.
²⁷The sons of Merari:

from Jaaziah: Beno, Shoham, Zaccur and Ibri.
²⁸From Mahli: Eleazar, who had no sons.
²⁹From Kish: the son of Kish: Jerahmeel.
³⁰And the sons of Mushi: Mahli, Eder and Jerimoth.

These were the Levites, according to their families. ³¹They also cast lots, just as their brothers the descendants of Aaron did, in the presence of King David and of Zadok, Ahimelech, and the heads of families of the priests and of the Levites. The families of the oldest brother were treated the same as those of the youngest.

The Singers

25 David, together with the commanders of the army, set apart some of the sons of Asaph, Heman and Jeduthun for the ministry of prophesying, accompanied by harps, lyres and cymbals. Here is the list of the men who performed this service:

²From the sons of Asaph:
Zaccur, Joseph, Nethaniah and Asarelah. The sons of Asaph were under the supervision of Asaph, who prophesied under the king's supervision.
³As for Jeduthun, from his sons:
Gedaliah, Zeri, Jeshaiah, Shimei,ᵇ Hashabiah and Mattithiah, six in all, under the supervision of their father Jeduthun, who prophesied, using the harp in thanking and praising the LORD.
⁴As for Heman, from his sons:
Bukkiah, Mattaniah, Uzziel, Shubael and Jerimoth; Hananiah, Hanani, Eliathah, Giddalti and Romamti-Ezer; Joshbekashah, Mallothi, Hothir and Mahazioth. ⁵All these were sons of Heman the king's seer. They were given him through the promises of God to exalt him.ᶜ

ᵃ23 Two Hebrew manuscripts and some Septuagint manuscripts (see also 1 Chron. 23:19); most Hebrew manuscripts *The sons of Jeriah:*   ᵇ3 One Hebrew manuscript and some Septuagint manuscripts (see also verse 17); most Hebrew manuscripts do not have *Shimei.*   ᶜ5 Hebrew *exalt the horn*

God gave Heman fourteen sons and three daughters.

6All these men were under the supervision of their fathers for the music of the temple of the LORD, with cymbals, lyres and harps, for the ministry at the house of God. Asaph, Jeduthun and Heman were under the supervision of the king. 7Along with their relatives—all of them trained and skilled in music for the LORD—they numbered 288. 8Young and old alike, teacher as well as student, cast lots for their duties.

9The first lot, which was for Asaph, fell to Joseph,
   his sons and relatives,a   12b
the second to Gedaliah,
   he and his relatives and
   sons,   12
10the third to Zaccur,
   his sons and relatives,   12
11the fourth to Izri,c
   his sons and relatives,   12
12the fifth to Nethaniah,
   his sons and relatives,   12
13the sixth to Bukkiah,
   his sons and relatives,   12
14the seventh to Jesarelah,d
   his sons and relatives,   12
15the eighth to Jeshaiah,
   his sons and relatives,   12
16the ninth to Mattaniah,
   his sons and relatives,   12
17the tenth to Shimei,
   his sons and relatives,   12
18the eleventh to Azarel,e
   his sons and relatives,   12
19the twelfth to Hashabiah,
   his sons and relatives,   12
20the thirteenth to Shubael,
   his sons and relatives,   12
21the fourteenth to Mattithiah,
   his sons and relatives,   12
22the fifteenth to Jerimoth,
   his sons and relatives,   12
23the sixteenth to Hananiah,
   his sons and relatives,   12
24the seventeenth to
   Joshbekashah,

   his sons and relatives,   12
25the eighteenth to Hanani,
   his sons and relatives,   12
26the nineteenth to Mallothi,
   his sons and relatives,   12
27the twentieth to Eliathah,
   his sons and relatives,   12
28the twenty-first to Hothir,
   his sons and relatives,   12
29the twenty-second to Giddalti,
   his sons and relatives,   12
30the twenty-third to Mahazioth,
   his sons and relatives,   12
31the twenty-fourth to
   Romamti-Ezer,
   his sons and relatives,   12

The Gatekeepers

26 The divisions of the gatekeepers:

From the Korahites: Meshelemiah son of Kore, one of the sons of Asaph.
2Meshelemiah had sons:
   Zechariah the firstborn,
   Jediael the second,
   Zebadiah the third,
   Jathniel the fourth,
   3Elam the fifth,
   Jehohanan the sixth
   and Eliehoenai the seventh.
4Obed-Edom also had sons:
   Shemaiah the firstborn,
   Jehozabad the second,
   Joah the third,
   Sacar the fourth,
   Nethanel the fifth,
   5Ammiel the sixth,
   Issachar the seventh
   and Peullethai the eighth.
   (For God had blessed Obed-Edom.)

6His son Shemaiah also had sons, who were leaders in their father's family because they were very capable men. 7The sons of Shemaiah: Othni, Rephael, Obed and Elzabad; his relatives Elihu and Semakiah were also able men. 8All these

---

a9 See Septuagint; Hebrew does not have *his sons and relatives*.   b9 See the total in verse 7; Hebrew does not have *twelve*.   c11 A variant of *Zeri*   d14 A variant of *Asarelah*   e18 A variant of *Uzziel*

were descendants of Obed-Edom; they and their sons and their relatives were capable men with the strength to do the work—descendants of Obed-Edom, 62 in all.

⁹Meshelemiah had sons and relatives, who were able men—18 in all.

¹⁰Hosah the Merarite had sons: Shimri the first (although he was not the firstborn, his father had appointed him the first), ¹¹Hilkiah the second, Tabaliah the third and Zechariah the fourth. The sons and relatives of Hosah were 13 in all.

¹²These divisions of the gatekeepers, through their chief men, had duties for ministering in the temple of the LORD, just as their relatives had. ¹³Lots were cast for each gate, according to their families, young and old alike.

¹⁴The lot for the East Gate fell to Shelemiah.ᵃ Then lots were cast for his son Zechariah, a wise counselor, and the lot for the North Gate fell to him. ¹⁵The lot for the South Gate fell to Obed-Edom, and the lot for the storehouse fell to his sons. ¹⁶The lots for the West Gate and the Shalleketh Gate on the upper road fell to Shuppim and Hosah.

Guard was alongside of guard: ¹⁷There were six Levites a day on the east, four a day on the north, four a day on the south and two at a time at the storehouse. ¹⁸As for the court to the west, there were four at the road and two at the court itself.

¹⁹These were the divisions of the gatekeepers who were descendants of Korah and Merari.

The Treasurers and Other Officials

²⁰Their fellow Levites wereᵇ in charge of the treasuries of the house of God and the treasuries for the dedicated things.

²¹The descendants of Ladan, who were Gershonites through Ladan and who were heads of families belonging to Ladan the Gershonite, were Jehieli, ²²the sons of Jehieli, Zetham and his brother Joel. They were in charge of the treasuries of the temple of the LORD.

²³From the Amramites, the Izharites, the Hebronites and the Uzzielites:

²⁴Shubael, a descendant of Gershom son of Moses, was the officer in charge of the treasuries. ²⁵His relatives through Eliezer: Rehabiah his son, Jeshaiah his son, Joram his son, Zicri his son and Shelomith his son. ²⁶Shelomith and his relatives were in charge of all the treasuries for the things dedicated by King David, by the heads of families who were the commanders of thousands and commanders of hundreds, and by the other army commanders. ²⁷Some of the plunder taken in battle they dedicated for the repair of the temple of the LORD. ²⁸And everything dedicated by Samuel the seer and by Saul son of Kish, Abner son of Ner and Joab son of Zeruiah, and all the other dedicated things were in the care of Shelomith and his relatives.

²⁹From the Izharites: Kenaniah and his sons were assigned duties away from the temple, as officials and judges over Israel.

³⁰From the Hebronites: Hashabiah and his relatives—seventeen hundred able men—were responsible in Israel west of the Jordan for all the work of the LORD and for the king's service. ³¹As for the Hebronites, Jeriah was their chief according to the genealogical records of their families. In the

fortieth year of David's reign a search was made in the records, and capable men among the Hebronites were found at Jazer in Gilead. ³²Jeriah had twenty-seven hundred relatives, who were able men and heads of families, and King David put them in charge of the Reubenites, the Gadites and the half-tribe of Manasseh for every matter pertaining to God and for the affairs of the king.

Army Divisions

27 This is the list of the Israelites—heads of families, commanders of thousands and commanders of hundreds, and their officers, who served the king in all that concerned the army divisions that were on duty month by month throughout the year. Each division consisted of 24,000 men.

²In charge of the first division, for the first month, was Jashobeam son of Zabdiel. There were 24,000 men in his division. ³He was a descendant of Perez and chief of all the army officers for the first month.

⁴In charge of the division for the second month was Dodai the Ahohite; Mikloth was the leader of his division. There were 24,000 men in his division.

⁵The third army commander, for the third month, was Benaiah son of Jehoiada the priest. He was chief and there were 24,000 men in his division. ⁶This was the Benaiah who was a mighty man among the Thirty and was over the Thirty. His son Ammizabad was in charge of his division.

⁷The fourth, for the fourth month, was Asahel the brother of Joab; his son Zebadiah was his successor. There were 24,000 men in his division.

⁸The fifth, for the fifth month, was the commander Shamhuth the Izrahite. There were 24,000 men in his division.

⁹The sixth, for the sixth month, was Ira the son of Ikkesh the Tekoite. There were 24,000 men in his division.

¹⁰The seventh, for the seventh month, was Helez the Pelonite, an Ephraimite. There were 24,000 men in his division.

¹¹The eighth, for the eighth month, was Sibbecai the Hushathite, a Zerahite. There were 24,000 men in his division.

¹²The ninth, for the ninth month, was Abiezer the Anathothite, a Benjamite. There were 24,000 men in his division.

¹³The tenth, for the tenth month, was Maharai the Netophathite, a Zerahite. There were 24,000 men in his division.

¹⁴The eleventh, for the eleventh month, was Benaiah the Pirathonite, an Ephraimite. There were 24,000 men in his division.

¹⁵The twelfth, for the twelfth month, was Heldai the Netophathite, from the family of Othniel. There were 24,000 men in his division.

Officers of the Tribes

¹⁶The officers over the tribes of Israel:

over the Reubenites: Eliezer son of Zicri;

over the Simeonites: Shephatiah son of Maacah;

¹⁷over Levi: Hashabiah son of Kemuel;

over Aaron: Zadok;

¹⁸over Judah: Elihu, a brother of David;

over Issachar: Omri son of Michael;

¹⁹over Zebulun: Ishmaiah son of Obadiah;

over Naphtali: Jerimoth son of Azriel;

²⁰over the Ephraimites: Hoshea son of Azaziah;

over half the tribe of Manasseh: Joel son of Pedaiah;

²¹over the half-tribe of Manasseh

in Gilead: Iddo son of Zechariah;

over Benjamin: Jaasiel son of Abner;

²²over Dan: Azarel son of Jeroham.

These were the officers over the tribes of Israel.

²³David did not take the number of the men twenty years old or less, because the LORD had promised to make Israel as numerous as the stars in the sky. ²⁴Joab son of Zeruiah began to count the men but did not finish. Wrath came on Israel on account of this numbering, and the number was not entered in the book*ᵃ* of the annals of King David.

The King's Overseers

²⁵Azmaveth son of Adiel was in charge of the royal storehouses.

Jonathan son of Uzziah was in charge of the storehouses in the outlying districts, in the towns, the villages and the watchtowers.

²⁶Ezri son of Kelub was in charge of the field workers who farmed the land.

²⁷Shimei the Ramathite was in charge of the vineyards.

Zabdi the Shiphmite was in charge of the produce of the vineyards for the wine vats.

²⁸Baal-Hanan the Gederite was in charge of the olive and sycamore-fig trees in the western foothills.

Joash was in charge of the supplies of olive oil.

²⁹Shitrai the Sharonite was in charge of the herds grazing in Sharon.

Shaphat son of Adlai was in charge of the herds in the valleys.

³⁰Obil the Ishmaelite was in charge of the camels.

Jehdeiah the Meronothite was in charge of the donkeys.

³¹Jaziz the Hagrite was in charge of the flocks.

All these were the officials in charge of King David's property.

³²Jonathan, David's uncle, was a counselor, a man of insight and a scribe. Jehiel son of Hacmoni took care of the king's sons.

³³Ahithophel was the king's counselor.

Hushai the Arkite was the king's friend. ³⁴Ahithophel was succeeded by Jehoiada son of Benaiah and by Abiathar.

Joab was the commander of the royal army.

David's Plans for the Temple

28 David summoned all the officials of Israel to assemble at Jerusalem: the officers over the tribes, the commanders of the divisions in the service of the king, the commanders of thousands and commanders of hundreds, and the offi-

---

ᵃ24 Septuagint; Hebrew *number*

LET'S LIVE IT!   1 Chronicles 27:25–34

TRY A JOB CHART ➡ 1 Chronicles 27:25–34 is a list of jobs David gave the men who helped him rule Israel. The list is a job chart: It names David's helpers and tells the job each one had. Which job would you have wanted? I would have liked Hushai's job (1 Chronicles 27:33)!

Make a family job chart by writing down the different jobs that have to be done: bag the garbage, put away dishes, sweep the porch, fold clothes, and so on. Then make a chart listing the names of each family member. Beside each name write the jobs that person will do. Once every two weeks, switch jobs. The job chart will tell how every member of the family helps, just as this Bible passage tells the jobs of David's helpers.

cials in charge of all the property and livestock belonging to the king and his sons, together with the palace officials, the mighty men and all the brave warriors.

²King David rose to his feet and said: "Listen to me, my brothers and my people. I had it in my heart to build a house as a place of rest for the ark of the covenant of the LORD, for the footstool of our God, and I made plans to build it. ³But God said to me, 'You are not to build a house for my Name, because you are a warrior and have shed blood.'

⁴"Yet the LORD, the God of Israel, chose me from my whole family to be king over Israel forever. He chose Judah as leader, and from the house of Judah he chose my family, and from my father's sons he was pleased to make me king over all Israel. ⁵Of all my sons—and the LORD has given me many—he has chosen my son Solomon to sit on the throne of the kingdom of the LORD over Israel. ⁶He said to me: 'Solomon your son is the one who will build my house and my courts, for I have chosen him to be my son, and I will be his father. ⁷I will establish his kingdom forever if he is unswerving in carrying out my commands and laws, as is being done at this time.'

⁸"So now I charge you in the sight of all Israel and of the assembly of the LORD, and in the hearing of our God: Be careful to follow all the commands of the LORD your God, that you may possess this good land and pass it on as an inheritance to your descendants forever.

⁹"And you, my son Solomon, acknowledge the God of your father, and serve him with wholehearted devotion and with a willing mind, for the LORD searches every heart and understands every motive behind the thoughts. If you seek him, he will be found by you; but if you forsake him, he will reject you forever. ¹⁰Consider now, for the LORD has chosen you to build a temple as a sanctuary. Be strong and do the work."

¹¹Then David gave his son Solomon the plans for the portico of the temple, its buildings, its storerooms, its upper parts, its inner rooms and the place of atonement. ¹²He gave him the plans of all that the Spirit had put in his mind for the courts of the temple of the LORD and all the surrounding rooms, for the treasuries of the temple of God and for the treasuries for the dedicated things. ¹³He gave him instructions for the divisions of the priests and Levites, and for all the work of serving in the temple of the LORD, as well as for all the articles to be used in its service. ¹⁴He designated the weight of gold for all the gold articles to be used in various kinds of service, and the weight of silver for all the silver articles to be used in various kinds of service: ¹⁵the weight of gold for the gold lampstands and their lamps, with the weight for each lampstand and its lamps; and the weight of silver for each silver lampstand and its lamps, according to the use of each lampstand; ¹⁶the weight of gold for each table for consecrated bread; the weight of silver for the silver tables; ¹⁷the weight of pure gold for the forks, sprinkling bowls and pitchers; the weight of gold for each gold dish; the weight of silver for each silver dish; ¹⁸and the weight of the refined gold for the altar of incense. He also gave him the plan for the chariot, that is, the cherubim of gold that spread their wings and shelter the ark of the covenant of the LORD.

¹⁹"All this," David said, "I have in writing from the hand of the LORD upon me, and he gave me understanding in all the details of the plan."

²⁰David also said to Solomon his son, "Be strong and courageous, and do the work. Do not be afraid or discouraged, for the LORD God, my God, is with you. He will not fail you or forsake you until all the work for the service of the temple of the LORD is finished. ²¹The divisions of the priests and Levites are ready for all the work on the temple of God, and every willing man skilled in any craft

will help you in all the work. The officials and all the people will obey your every command."

Gifts for Building the Temple

29 Then King David said to the whole assembly: "My son Solomon, the one whom God has chosen, is young and inexperienced. The task is great, because this palatial structure is not for man but for the LORD God. ²With all my resources I have provided for the temple of my God —gold for the gold work, silver for the silver, bronze for the bronze, iron for the iron and wood for the wood, as well as onyx for the settings, turquoise,ᵃ stones of various colors, and all kinds of fine stone and marble —all of these in large quantities. ³Besides, in my devotion to the temple of my God I now give my personal treasures of gold and silver for the temple of my God, over and above everything I have provided for this holy temple: ⁴three thousand talentsᵇ of gold (gold of Ophir) and seven thousand talentsᶜ of refined silver, for the overlaying of the walls of the buildings, ⁵for the gold work and the silver work, and for all the work to be done by the craftsmen. Now, who is willing to consecrate himself today to the LORD?"

⁶Then the leaders of families, the officers of the tribes of Israel, the commanders of thousands and commanders of hundreds, and the officials in charge of the king's work gave willingly. ⁷They gave toward the work on the temple of God five thousand talentsᵈ and ten thousand daricsᵉ of gold, ten thousand talentsᶠ of silver, eighteen thousand talentsᵍ of bronze and a hundred thousand talentsʰ of iron. ⁸Any who had precious stones gave them to the treasury of the temple of the LORD in the custody of Jehiel the Gershonite. ⁹The people rejoiced at the willing response of their leaders, for they had given freely and wholeheartedly to the LORD. David the king also rejoiced greatly.

David's Prayer

¹⁰David praised the LORD in the presence of the whole assembly, saying,

"Praise be to you, O LORD,
 God of our father Israel,
 from everlasting to everlasting.
¹¹Yours, O LORD, is the greatness
 and the power
 and the glory and the majesty
 and the splendor,
 for everything in heaven and
 earth is yours.
 Yours, O LORD, is the kingdom;

ᵃ2 The meaning of the Hebrew for this word is uncertain.   ᵇ4 That is, about 110 tons (about 100 metric tons)   ᶜ4 That is, about 260 tons (about 240 metric tons)   ᵈ7 That is, about 190 tons (about 170 metric tons)   ᵉ7 That is, about 185 pounds (about 84 kilograms)   ᶠ7 That is, about 375 tons (about 345 metric tons)   ᵍ7 That is, about 675 tons (about 610 metric tons)   ʰ7 That is, about 3,750 tons (about 3,450 metric tons)

▌ET'S LIVE IT! 1 Chronicles 28:11–19

ORGANIZE YOUR WORK ➡ Read 1 Chronicles 28:11–19. What plans did David make for building God's temple?

It is always wise to plan work. Try planning ahead how you will pick up your room. Use this work list to help you.

1. Pick up clothes. 2. Put away books, crayons and pencils. 3. Put away toys. 4. Put old papers in the waste basket. 5. Clean up closet. 6. Put away things on tables and dressers. 7. Dust furniture.

Any job is easier when you are organized. Think about the other jobs you have. Try to organize them so you can do them one step at a time. If you need help, ask your mom or dad to help you organize.

you are exalted as head over
all.
[12]Wealth and honor come from
you;
you are the ruler of all things.
In your hands are strength and
power
to exalt and give strength to
all.
[13]Now, our God, we give you
thanks,
and praise your glorious
name.

[14]"But who am I, and who are my
people, that we should be able to give
as generously as this? Everything
comes from you, and we have given
you only what comes from your hand.
[15]We are aliens and strangers in your
sight, as were all our forefathers. Our
days on earth are like a shadow,
without hope. [16]O LORD our God, as
for all this abundance that we have
provided for building you a temple for
your Holy Name, it comes from your
hand, and all of it belongs to you. [17]I
know, my God, that you test the
heart and are pleased with integrity.
All these things have I given willingly and with honest intent. And now I
have seen with joy how willingly
your people who are here have given
to you. [18]O LORD, God of our fathers
Abraham, Isaac and Israel, keep this
desire in the hearts of your people
forever, and keep their hearts loyal to
you. [19]And give my son Solomon the
wholehearted devotion to keep your
commands, requirements and decrees and to do everything to build
the palatial structure for which I
have provided."

[20]Then David said to the whole assembly, "Praise the LORD your God."
So they all praised the LORD, the God
of their fathers; they bowed low and
fell prostrate before the LORD and the
king.

Solomon Acknowledged as King

[21]The next day they made sacrifices to the LORD and presented burnt
offerings to him: a thousand bulls, a
thousand rams and a thousand male
lambs, together with their drink offerings, and other sacrifices in abundance for all Israel. [22]They ate and
drank with great joy in the presence
of the LORD that day.

Then they acknowledged Solomon
son of David as king a second time,
anointing him before the LORD to be
ruler and Zadok to be priest. [23]So Solomon sat on the throne of the LORD as
king in place of his father David. He
prospered and all Israel obeyed him.
[24]All the officers and mighty men, as
well as all of King David's sons,
pledged their submission to King Solomon.

[25]The LORD highly exalted Solomon
in the sight of all Israel and bestowed
on him royal splendor such as no king
over Israel ever had before.

The Death of David

[26]David son of Jesse was king over
all Israel. [27]He ruled over Israel forty
years—seven in Hebron and thirty-
three in Jerusalem. [28]He died at a
good old age, having enjoyed long
life, wealth and honor. His son Solomon succeeded him as king.

[29]As for the events of King David's
reign, from beginning to end, they
are written in the records of Samuel
the seer, the records of Nathan the
prophet and the records of Gad the
seer, [30]together with the details of his
reign and power, and the circumstances that surrounded him and Israel and the kingdoms of all the other
lands.

2 CHRONICLES

WHO WROTE THIS BOOK?

The author of this book is unknown. Some think he was Ezra.

WHY WAS THIS BOOK WRITTEN?

The book of 2 Chronicles tells what God thought of the kings of Israel and Judah.

WHAT HAPPENS IN THIS BOOK?

Solomon is king for forty years. When he dies, his kingdom is divided into two nations. The people of both Hebrew nations sin, and God punishes them by sending them into exile.

WHAT DO WE LEARN ABOUT GOD IN THIS BOOK?

God rescues godly leaders who depend on him for help.

WHO IS IMPORTANT IN THIS BOOK?

The most important people in this book are Solomon, Ahab, Jehoshaphat, Joash, Hezekiah, and Josiah.

WHEN DID THIS HAPPEN?

The events in this book happened between 970 and 586 B.C.

WHERE DID THIS HAPPEN?

These things happened in the two kingdoms of Israel and Judah, in Palestine.

WHAT ARE SOME OF THE STORIES IN THIS BOOK?

Solomon builds the temple.   2 Chronicles 3
Solomon dedicates the temple.   2 Chronicles 7
Egypt attacks Judah.   2 Chronicles 12
Asa worships God.   2 Chronicles 15
Ahab is killed.   2 Chronicles 18
Jehoshaphat defeats Moab.   2 Chronicles 20
Joash repairs the temple.   2 Chronicles 24
Hezekiah trusts God.   2 Chronicles 29–32
Josiah reforms Judah.   2 Chronicles 34–35

Solomon Asks for Wisdom

1 Solomon son of David established himself firmly over his kingdom, for the LORD his God was with him and made him exceedingly great.

2Then Solomon spoke to all Israel —to the commanders of thousands and commanders of hundreds, to the judges and to all the leaders in Israel, the heads of families— 3and Solomon and the whole assembly went to the high place at Gibeon, for God's Tent of Meeting was there, which Moses the LORD's servant had made in the desert. 4Now David had brought up the ark of God from Kiriath Jearim to the place he had prepared for it, because he had pitched a tent for it in Jerusalem. 5But the bronze altar that Bezalel son of Uri, the son of Hur, had made was in Gibeon in front of the tabernacle of the LORD; so Solomon and the assembly inquired of him there. 6Solomon went up to the bronze altar before the LORD in the Tent of Meeting and offered a thousand burnt offerings on it.

❓DID YOU KNOW?   1:10

Why did Solomon ask God for wisdom?

Solomon wanted to be a good ruler of God's people. He could have asked God to make him rich or famous, but he asked for wisdom instead. This request pleased God so much that he promised Solomon riches and honor as well.

7That night God appeared to Solomon and said to him, "Ask for whatever you want me to give you."

8Solomon answered God, "You have shown great kindness to David my father and have made me king in his place. 9Now, LORD God, let your promise to my father David be confirmed, for you have made me king over a people who are as numerous as the dust of the earth. 10Give me wisdom and knowledge, that I may lead this people, for who is able to govern this great people of yours?"

ⓌORDS TO REMEMBER

1:10 Give me wisdom and knowledge, that I may lead this people.

11God said to Solomon, "Since this is your heart's desire and you have not asked for wealth, riches or honor, nor for the death of your enemies, and since you have not asked for a long life but for wisdom and knowledge to govern my people over whom I have made you king, 12therefore wisdom and knowledge will be given you. And I will also give you wealth, riches and honor, such as no king who was before you ever had and none after you will have."

13Then Solomon went to Jerusalem from the high place at Gibeon, from before the Tent of Meeting. And he reigned over Israel.

14Solomon accumulated chariots and horses; he had fourteen hundred chariots and twelve thousand horses,a which he kept in the chariot cities and also with him in Jerusalem. 15The king made silver and gold as common in Jerusalem as stones, and cedar as plentiful as sycamore-fig trees in the foothills. 16Solomon's horses were imported from Egyptb and from Kuec—the royal merchants purchased them from Kue. 17They imported a chariot from Egypt for six hundred shekelsd of silver, and a horse for a hundred and fifty.e They also exported them to all the kings of the Hittites and of the Arameans.

---

a14 Or charioteers   b16 Or possibly Muzur, a region in Cilicia; also in verse 17
c16 Probably Cilicia   d17 That is, about 15 pounds (about 7 kilograms)   e17 That is, about
3 3/4 pounds (about 1.7 kilograms)

Preparations for Building the Temple

2 Solomon gave orders to build a temple for the Name of the LORD and a royal palace for himself. ²He conscripted seventy thousand men as carriers and eighty thousand as stonecutters in the hills and thirty-six hundred as foremen over them.

³Solomon sent this message to Hiram*a* king of Tyre:

"Send me cedar logs as you did for my father David when you sent him cedar to build a palace to live in. ⁴Now I am about to build a temple for the Name of the LORD my God and to dedicate it to him for burning fragrant incense before him, for setting out the consecrated bread regularly, and for making burnt offerings every morning and evening and on Sabbaths and New Moons and at the appointed feasts of the LORD our God. This is a lasting ordinance for Israel.

⁵"The temple I am going to build will be great, because our God is greater than all other gods. ⁶But who is able to build a temple for him, since the heavens, even the highest heavens, cannot contain him? Who then am I to build a temple for him, except as a place to burn sacrifices before him?

⁷"Send me, therefore, a man skilled to work in gold and silver, bronze and iron, and in purple, crimson and blue yarn, and experienced in the art of engraving, to work in Judah and Jerusalem with my skilled craftsmen, whom my father David provided.

⁸"Send me also cedar, pine and algum*b* logs from Lebanon, for I know that your men are skilled in cutting timber there. My men will work with yours ⁹to provide me with plenty of lumber, be-cause the temple I build must be large and magnificent. ¹⁰I will give your servants, the woodsmen who cut the timber, twenty thousand cors*c* of ground wheat, twenty thousand cors of barley, twenty thousand baths*d* of wine and twenty thousand baths of olive oil."

¹¹Hiram king of Tyre replied by letter to Solomon:

"Because the LORD loves his people, he has made you their king."

¹²And Hiram added:

"Praise be to the LORD, the God of Israel, who made heaven and earth! He has given King David a wise son, endowed with intelligence and discernment, who will build a temple for the LORD and a palace for himself.

¹³"I am sending you Huram-Abi, a man of great skill, ¹⁴whose mother was from Dan and whose father was from Tyre. He is trained to work in gold and silver, bronze and iron, stone and wood, and with purple and blue and crimson yarn and fine linen. He is experienced in all kinds of engraving and can execute any design given to him. He will work with your craftsmen and with those of my lord, David your father.

¹⁵"Now let my lord send his servants the wheat and barley and the olive oil and wine he promised, ¹⁶and we will cut all the logs from Lebanon that you need and will float them in rafts by sea down to Joppa. You can then take them up to Jerusalem."

¹⁷Solomon took a census of all the aliens who were in Israel, after the census his father David had taken;

---

*a*3 Hebrew *Huram*, a variant of *Hiram*; also in verses 11 and 12   *b*8 Probably a variant of *almug*; possibly juniper   *c*10 That is, probably about 125,000 bushels (about 4,400 kiloliters)   *d*10 That is, probably about 115,000 gallons (about 440 kiloliters)

and they were found to be 153,600. [18]He assigned 70,000 of them to be carriers and 80,000 to be stonecutters in the hills, with 3,600 foremen over them to keep the people working.

Solomon Builds the Temple

3 Then Solomon began to build the temple of the LORD in Jerusalem on Mount Moriah, where the LORD had appeared to his father David. It was on the threshing floor of Araunah[a] the Jebusite, the place provided by David. [2]He began building on the second day of the second month in the fourth year of his reign.

[3]The foundation Solomon laid for building the temple of God was sixty cubits long and twenty cubits wide[b] (using the cubit of the old standard). [4]The portico at the front of the temple was twenty cubits[c] long across the width of the building and twenty cubits[d] high.

He overlaid the inside with pure gold. [5]He paneled the main hall with pine and covered it with fine gold and decorated it with palm tree and chain designs. [6]He adorned the temple with precious stones. And the gold he used was gold of Parvaim. [7]He overlaid the ceiling beams, doorframes, walls and doors of the temple with gold, and he carved cherubim on the walls.

[8]He built the Most Holy Place, its length corresponding to the width of the temple—twenty cubits long and twenty cubits wide. He overlaid the inside with six hundred talents[e] of fine gold. [9]The gold nails weighed fifty shekels.[f] He also overlaid the upper parts with gold.

[10]In the Most Holy Place he made a pair of sculptured cherubim and overlaid them with gold. [11]The total wingspan of the cherubim was twenty cubits. One wing of the first cherub was five cubits[g] long and touched the temple wall, while its other wing, also five cubits long, touched the wing of the other cherub. [12]Similarly one wing of the second cherub was five cubits long and touched the other temple wall, and its other wing, also five cubits long, touched the wing of the first cherub. [13]The wings of these cherubim extended twenty cubits. They stood on their feet, facing the main hall.[h]

[14]He made the curtain of blue, purple and crimson yarn and fine linen, with cherubim worked into it.

[15]In the front of the temple he made two pillars, which together were thirty-five cubits[i] long, each with a capital on top measuring five cubits. [16]He made interwoven chains[j] and put them on top of the pillars. He also made a hundred pomegranates and attached them to the chains. [17]He erected the pillars in the front of temple, one to the south and one to the north. The one to the south he named Jakin[k] and the one to the north Boaz.[l]

The Temple's Furnishings

4 He made a bronze altar twenty cubits long, twenty cubits wide and ten cubits high.[m] [2]He made the Sea of cast metal, circular in shape, measuring ten cubits from rim to rim and five cubits[n] high. It took a line of thirty cubits[o] to measure around it. [3]Below the rim, figures of bulls encircled it—ten to a cubit.[p] The bulls were cast in two rows in one piece with the Sea.

[4]The Sea stood on twelve bulls, three facing north, three facing west,

---

[a]1 Hebrew *Ornan*, a variant of *Araunah*   [b]3 That is, about 90 feet (about 27 meters) long and 30 feet (about 9 meters) wide   [c]4 That is, about 30 feet (about 9 meters); also in verses 8, 11 and 13   [d]4 Some Septuagint and Syriac manuscripts; Hebrew *and a hundred and twenty*   [e]8 That is, about 23 tons (about 21 metric tons)   [f]9 That is, about 1 1/4 pounds (about 0.6 kilogram)   [g]11 That is, about 7 1/2 feet (about 2.3 meters); also in verse 15   [h]13 Or *facing inward*   [i]15 That is, about 52 feet (about 16 meters)   [j]16 Or possibly *made chains in the inner sanctuary*; the meaning of the Hebrew for this phrase is uncertain.   [k]17 *Jakin* probably means *he establishes*.   [l]17 *Boaz* probably means *in him is strength*.   [m]1 That is, about 30 feet (about 9 meters) long and wide, and about 15 feet (about 4.5 meters) high   [n]2 That is, about 7 1/2 feet (about 2.3 meters)   [o]2 That is, about 45 feet (about 13.5 meters)   [p]3 That is, about 1 1/2 feet (about 0.5 meter)

three facing south and three facing east. The Sea rested on top of them, and their hindquarters were toward the center. ⁵It was a handbreadth*a* in thickness, and its rim was like the rim of a cup, like a lily blossom. It held three thousand baths.*b*

THE SEA OF METAL

This giant Sea held over 17,500 gallons of water. It was like a large round pool, resting on the backs of twelve metal bulls, three facing in each direction. It was used to fill the smaller basins the priests washed in before approaching God's temple.

⁶He then made ten basins for washing and placed five on the south side and five on the north. In them the things to be used for the burnt offerings were rinsed, but the Sea was to be used by the priests for washing. ⁷He made ten gold lampstands according to the specifications for them and placed them in the temple, five on the south side and five on the north. ⁸He made ten tables and placed them in the temple, five on the south side and five on the north. He also made a hundred gold sprinkling bowls. ⁹He made the courtyard of the priests, and the large court and the doors for the court, and overlaid the doors with bronze. ¹⁰He placed the Sea on the south side, at the southeast corner. ¹¹He also made the pots and shovels and sprinkling bowls.

So Huram finished the work he had undertaken for King Solomon in the temple of God:

¹²the two pillars;
the two bowl-shaped capitals on top of the pillars;
the two sets of network decorating the two bowl-shaped capitals on top of the pillars;
¹³the four hundred pomegranates for the two sets of network (two rows of pomegranates for each network, decorating the bowl-shaped capitals on top of the pillars);
¹⁴the stands with their basins;
¹⁵the Sea and the twelve bulls under it;
¹⁶the pots, shovels, meat forks and all related articles.

All the objects that Huram-Abi made for King Solomon for the temple of the Lᴏʀᴅ were of polished bronze. ¹⁷The king had them cast in clay molds in the plain of the Jordan between Succoth and Zarethan.*c* ¹⁸All these things that Solomon made amounted to so much that the weight of the bronze was not determined.

¹⁹Solomon also made all the furnishings that were in God's temple:

the golden altar;
the tables on which was the bread of the Presence;
²⁰the lampstands of pure gold with their lamps, to burn in front of the inner sanctuary as prescribed;
²¹the gold floral work and lamps and tongs (they were solid gold);
²²the pure gold wick trimmers, sprinkling bowls, dishes and censers; and the gold doors of the temple: the inner doors to the Most Holy Place and the doors of the main hall.

5 When all the work Solomon had done for the temple of the Lᴏʀᴅ was finished, he brought in the things his father David had dedicat-

---

a5 That is, about 3 inches (about 8 centimeters)   *b5* That is, about 17,500 gallons (about 66 kiloliters)   *c17* Hebrew *Zeredatha*, a variant of *Zarethan*

ed—the silver and gold and all the furnishings—and he placed them in the treasuries of God's temple.

The Ark Brought to the Temple

2Then Solomon summoned to Jerusalem the elders of Israel, all the heads of the tribes and the chiefs of the Israelite families, to bring up the ark of the LORD's covenant from Zion, the City of David. 3And all the men of Israel came together to the king at the time of the festival in the seventh month.

4When all the elders of Israel had arrived, the Levites took up the ark, 5and they brought up the ark and the Tent of Meeting and all the sacred furnishings in it. The priests, who were Levites, carried them up; 6and King Solomon and the entire assembly of Israel that had gathered about him were before the ark, sacrificing so many sheep and cattle that they could not be recorded or counted.

7The priests then brought the ark of the LORD's covenant to its place in the inner sanctuary of the temple, the Most Holy Place, and put it beneath the wings of the cherubim. 8The cherubim spread their wings over the place of the ark and covered the ark and its carrying poles. 9These poles were so long that their ends, extending from the ark, could be seen from in front of the inner sanctuary, but not from outside the Holy Place; and they are still there today. 10There was nothing in the ark ex-

cept the two tablets that Moses had placed in it at Horeb, where the LORD made a covenant with the Israelites after they came out of Egypt.

11The priests then withdrew from the Holy Place. All the priests who were there had consecrated themselves, regardless of their divisions. 12All the Levites who were musicians—Asaph, Heman, Jeduthun and their sons and relatives—stood on the east side of the altar, dressed in fine linen and playing cymbals, harps and lyres. They were accompanied by 120 priests sounding trumpets. 13The trumpeters and singers joined in unison, as with one voice, to give praise and thanks to the LORD. Accompanied by trumpets, cymbals and other instruments, they raised their voices in praise to the LORD and sang:

"He is good;
    his love endures forever."

Then the temple of the LORD was filled with a cloud, 14and the priests could not perform their service because of the cloud, for the glory of the LORD filled the temple of God.

6 Then Solomon said, "The LORD has said that he would dwell in a dark cloud; 2I have built a magnificent temple for you, a place for you to dwell forever."

3While the whole assembly of Israel was standing there, the king turned around and blessed them. 4Then he said:

LET'S LIVE IT!   2 Chronicles 5:2–14

WRITE A COMMERCIAL ➡ Watch several TV programs with your mom or dad. Make a list of the different commercials you see. Then discuss them. Why do people put commercials on TV? How do commercials get people to buy what they advertise? How is the music in the commercials important?

Read 2 Chronicles 5:2–14. King David had the Levites, who led in music, write songs and lead the people in praising God. One song they wrote was something like a TV commercial for God (2 Chronicles 5:13)!

Write a family commercial for God. Think what to say about him that would make other people want to know and worship God too. Make up music to go with your commercial for God.

"Praise be to the LORD, the God of Israel, who with his hands has fulfilled what he promised with his mouth to my father David. For he said, ⁵'Since the day I brought my people out of Egypt, I have not chosen a city in any tribe of Israel to have a temple built for my Name to be there, nor have I chosen anyone to be the leader over my people Israel. ⁶But now I have chosen Jerusalem for my Name to be there, and I have chosen David to rule my people Israel.'

⁷"My father David had it in his heart to build a temple for the Name of the LORD, the God of Israel. ⁸But the LORD said to my father David, 'Because it was in your heart to build a temple for my Name, you did well to have this in your heart. ⁹Nevertheless, you are not the one to build the temple, but your son, who is your own flesh and blood—he is the one who will build the temple for my Name.'

¹⁰"The LORD has kept the promise he made. I have succeeded David my father and now I sit on the throne of Israel, just as the LORD promised, and I have built the temple for the Name of the LORD, the God of Israel. ¹¹There I have placed the ark, in which is the covenant of the LORD that he made with the people of Israel."

Solomon's Prayer of Dedication

¹²Then Solomon stood before the altar of the LORD in front of the whole assembly of Israel and spread out his hands. ¹³Now he had made a bronze platform, five cubits*ᵃ* long, five cubits wide and three cubits*ᵇ* high, and had placed it in the center of the outer court. He stood on the platform and then knelt down before the whole assembly of Israel and spread out his hands toward heaven. ¹⁴He said:

"O LORD, God of Israel, there is no God like you in heaven or on earth—you who keep your covenant of love with your servants who continue wholeheartedly in your way. ¹⁵You have kept your promise to your servant David my father; with your mouth you have promised and with your hand you have fulfilled it—as it is today.

¹⁶"Now LORD, God of Israel, keep for your servant David my father the promises you made to him when you said, 'You shall never fail to have a man to sit before me on the throne of Israel, if only your sons are careful in all they do to walk before me according to my law, as you have done.' ¹⁷And now, O LORD, God of Israel, let your word that you promised your servant David come true.

¹⁸"But will God really dwell on earth with men? The heavens, even the highest heavens, cannot contain you. How much less this temple I have built! ¹⁹Yet give attention to your servant's prayer and his plea for mercy, O LORD my God. Hear the cry and the prayer that your servant is praying in your presence. ²⁰May your eyes be open toward this temple day and night, this place of which you said you would put your Name there. May you hear the prayer your servant prays toward this place. ²¹Hear the supplications of your servant and of your people Israel when they pray toward this place. Hear from heaven, your dwelling place; and when you hear, forgive.

²²"When a man wrongs his neighbor and is required to take an oath and he comes and swears the oath before your altar in this temple, ²³then hear from heaven and act. Judge between your servants, repaying the guilty by

ᵃ13 That is, about 7 1/2 feet (about 2.3 meters)   *ᵇ13* That is, about 4 1/2 feet (about 1.3 meters)

bringing down on his own head what he has done. Declare the innocent not guilty and so establish his innocence.

24"When your people Israel have been defeated by an enemy because they have sinned against you and when they turn back and confess your name, praying and making supplication before you in this temple, 25then hear from heaven and forgive the sin of your people Israel and bring them back to the land you gave to them and their fathers.

WORDS TO REMEMBER

6:25 Hear from heaven and forgive the sin of your people.

26"When the heavens are shut up and there is no rain because your people have sinned against you, and when they pray toward this place and confess your name and turn from their sin because you have afflicted them, 27then hear from heaven and forgive the sin of your servants, your people Israel. Teach them the right way to live, and send rain on the land you gave your people for an inheritance.

28"When famine or plague comes to the land, or blight or mildew, locusts or grasshoppers, or when enemies besiege them in any of their cities, whatever disaster or disease may come, 29and when a prayer or plea is made by any of your people Israel—each one aware of his afflictions and pains, and spreading out his hands toward this temple— 30then hear from heaven, your dwelling place. Forgive, and deal with each man according to all he does, since you know his heart (for you alone know the hearts of men), 31so that they will fear you and walk in your

ways all the time they live in the land you gave our fathers.

32"As for the foreigner who does not belong to your people Israel but has come from a distant land because of your great name and your mighty hand and your outstretched arm—when he comes and prays toward this temple, 33then hear from heaven, your dwelling place, and do whatever the foreigner asks of you, so that all the peoples of the earth may know your name and fear you, as do your own people Israel, and may know that this house I have built bears your Name.

34"When your people go to war against their enemies, wherever you send them, and when they pray to you toward this city you have chosen and the temple I have built for your Name, 35then hear from heaven their prayer and their plea, and uphold their cause.

36"When they sin against you —for there is no one who does not sin—and you become angry with them and give them over to the enemy, who takes them captive to a land far away or near; 37and if they have a change of heart in the land where they are held captive, and repent and plead with you in the land of their captivity and say, 'We have sinned, we have done wrong and acted wickedly'; 38and if they turn back to you with all their heart and soul in the land of their captivity where they were taken, and pray toward the land you gave their fathers, toward the city you have chosen and toward the temple I have built for your Name; 39then from heaven, your dwelling place, hear their prayer and their pleas, and uphold their cause. And forgive your people, who have sinned against you.

40"Now, my God, may your eyes be open and your ears attentive to the prayers offered in this place.

41"Now arise, O LORD God, and
  come to your resting
    place,
  you and the ark of your
    might.
May your priests, O LORD
  God, be clothed with
    salvation,
  may your saints rejoice in
    your goodness.
42O LORD God, do not reject
  your anointed one.
  Remember the great love
    promised to David your
    servant."

The Dedication of the Temple

7 When Solomon finished praying, fire came down from heaven and consumed the burnt offering and the sacrifices, and the glory of the LORD filled the temple. 2The priests could not enter the temple of the LORD because the glory of the LORD filled it. 3When all the Israelites saw the fire coming down and the glory of the LORD above the temple, they knelt on the pavement with their faces to the ground, and they worshiped and gave thanks to the LORD, saying,

"He is good;
  his love endures forever."

4Then the king and all the people offered sacrifices before the LORD. 5And King Solomon offered a sacrifice of twenty-two thousand head of cattle and a hundred and twenty thousand sheep and goats. So the king and all the people dedicated the temple of God. 6The priests took their positions, as did the Levites with the LORD's musical instruments, which King David had made for praising the LORD and which were used when he gave thanks, saying, "His love endures forever." Opposite the Levites, the priests blew their trumpets, and all the Israelites were standing.

WORDS TO REMEMBER

7:6 His love endures forever.

7Solomon consecrated the middle part of the courtyard in front of the temple of the LORD, and there he offered burnt offerings and the fat of the fellowship offerings,a because the bronze altar he had made could not hold the burnt offerings, the grain offerings and the fat portions.

8So Solomon observed the festival at that time for seven days, and all Israel with him—a vast assembly, people from Lebob Hamath to the Wadi of Egypt. 9On the eighth day they held an assembly, for they had celebrated the dedication of the altar for seven days and the festival for seven days more. 10On the twenty-third day of the seventh month he sent the people to their homes, joyful and glad in heart for the good things

a7 Traditionally peace offerings   b8 Or from the entrance to

LET'S LIVE IT!   2 Chronicles 7:1–3

THE TEMPLE IN JERUSALEM ➡ Read 2 Chronicles 7:1–3 to find out how God showed he was present in Solomon's temple. The beautiful temple was God's house in the country of Israel.

Draw a picture of the house or apartment where you live. Make it look as much like your home as you can. Under the picture of your house, write Hebrews 13:5: "Never will I leave you; never will I forsake you."

Hang the picture up in your room to remind you that God is with you now, even though you cannot see him.

the Lord had done for David and Solomon and for his people Israel.

The Lord Appears to Solomon

[11]When Solomon had finished the temple of the Lord and the royal palace, and had succeeded in carrying out all he had in mind to do in the temple of the Lord and in his own palace, [12]the Lord appeared to him at night and said:

"I have heard your prayer and have chosen this place for myself as a temple for sacrifices.

[13]"When I shut up the heavens so that there is no rain, or command locusts to devour the land or send a plague among my people, [14]if my people, who are called by my name, will humble themselves and pray and seek my face and turn from their wicked ways, then will I hear from heaven and will forgive their sin and will heal their land. [15]Now my eyes will be open and my ears attentive to the prayers offered in this place. [16]I have chosen and consecrated this temple so that my Name may be there forever. My eyes and my heart will always be there.

[17]"As for you, if you walk before me as David your father did, and do all I command, and observe my decrees and laws, [18]I will establish your royal throne, as I covenanted with David your father when I said, 'You shall never fail to have a man to rule over Israel.'

[19]"But if you[a] turn away and forsake the decrees and commands I have given you[a] and go off to serve other gods and worship them, [20]then I will uproot Israel from my land, which I have given them, and will reject this temple I have consecrated for my Name. I will make it a byword and an object of ridicule among all peoples. [21]And though this temple is now so imposing, all who pass by will be appalled and say, 'Why has the Lord done such a thing to this land and to this temple?' [22]People will answer, 'Because they have forsaken the Lord, the God of their fathers, who brought them out of Egypt, and have embraced other gods, worshiping and serving them—that is why he brought all this disaster on them.'"

❓DID YOU KNOW?　　　　7:16

Why was the temple so important?

God promised that he would accept sacrifices and hear prayers offered at the temple. So in Old Testament times, God was in the Jerusalem temple in a special way.

Solomon's Other Activities

8 At the end of twenty years, during which Solomon built the temple of the Lord and his own palace, [2]Solomon rebuilt the villages that Hiram[b] had given him, and settled Israelites in them. [3]Solomon then went to Hamath Zobah and captured it. [4]He also built up Tadmor in the desert and all the store cities he had built in Hamath. [5]He rebuilt Upper Beth Horon and Lower Beth Horon as fortified cities, with walls and with gates and bars, [6]as well as Baalath and all his store cities, and all the cities for his chariots and for his horses[c]—whatever he desired to build in Jerusalem, in Lebanon and throughout all the territory he ruled. [7]All the people left from the Hittites, Amorites, Perizzites, Hivites and Jebusites (these peoples were not Israelites), [8]that is, their descendants remaining in the land, whom

---

a19 The Hebrew is plural.　　*b2* Hebrew *Huram*, a variant of *Hiram*; also in verse 18　　*c6* Or *charioteers*

the Israelites had not destroyed—
these Solomon conscripted for his
slave labor force, as it is to this day.
⁹But Solomon did not make slaves of
the Israelites for his work; they were
his fighting men, commanders of his
captains, and commanders of his
chariots and charioteers. ¹⁰They were
also King Solomon's chief officials
—two hundred and fifty officials supervising the men.

¹¹Solomon brought Pharaoh's
daughter up from the City of David to
the palace he had built for her, for he
said, "My wife must not live in the
palace of David king of Israel, because the places the ark of the LORD
has entered are holy."

¹²On the altar of the LORD that he
had built in front of the portico, Solomon sacrificed burnt offerings to the
LORD, ¹³according to the daily requirement for offerings commanded
by Moses for Sabbaths, New Moons
and the three annual feasts—the
Feast of Unleavened Bread, the
Feast of Weeks and the Feast of Tabernacles. ¹⁴In keeping with the ordinance of his father David, he appointed the divisions of the priests for
their duties, and the Levites to lead
the praise and to assist the priests
according to each day's requirement.
He also appointed the gatekeepers by
divisions for the various gates, because this was what David the man of
God had ordered. ¹⁵They did not devi-
ate from the king's commands to the
priests or to the Levites in any matter, including that of the treasuries.

¹⁶All Solomon's work was carried
out, from the day the foundation of
the temple of the LORD was laid until
its completion. So the temple of the
LORD was finished.

¹⁷Then Solomon went to Ezion Geber and Elath on the coast of Edom.
¹⁸And Hiram sent him ships commanded by his own officers, men who
knew the sea. These, with Solomon's
men, sailed to Ophir and brought
back four hundred and fifty talentsᵃ

of gold, which they delivered to King
Solomon.

The Queen of Sheba Visits Solomon

9 When the queen of Sheba heard
of Solomon's fame, she came to
Jerusalem to test him with hard
questions. Arriving with a very great
caravan—with camels carrying
spices, large quantities of gold, and
precious stones—she came to Solomon and talked with him about all
she had on her mind. ²Solomon answered all her questions; nothing
was too hard for him to explain to
her. ³When the queen of Sheba saw
the wisdom of Solomon, as well as the
palace he had built, ⁴the food on his
table, the seating of his officials, the
attending servants in their robes, the
cupbearers in their robes and the
burnt offerings he made atᵇ the temple of the LORD, she was overwhelmed.

⁵She said to the king, "The report I
heard in my own country about your
achievements and your wisdom is
true. ⁶But I did not believe what they
said until I came and saw with my
own eyes. Indeed, not even half the
greatness of your wisdom was told
me; you have far exceeded the report
I heard. ⁷How happy your men must
be! How happy your officials, who
continually stand before you and
hear your wisdom! ⁸Praise be to the
LORD your God, who has delighted in
you and placed you on his throne as
king to rule for the LORD your God.
Because of the love of your God for
Israel and his desire to uphold them
forever, he has made you king over
them, to maintain justice and righteousness."

⁹Then she gave the king 120 talentsᶜ of gold, large quantities of
spices, and precious stones. There
had never been such spices as those
the queen of Sheba gave to King Solomon.

¹⁰(The men of Hiram and the men

ᵃ18 That is, about 17 tons (about 16 metric tons)
ᶜ9 That is, about 4 1/2 tons (about 4 metric tons)
ᵇ4 Or the ascent by which he went up to

of Solomon brought gold from Ophir; they also brought algumwood[a] and precious stones. [11]The king used the algumwood to make steps for the temple of the LORD and for the royal palace, and to make harps and lyres for the musicians. Nothing like them had ever been seen in Judah.)

[12]King Solomon gave the queen of Sheba all she desired and asked for; he gave her more than she had brought to him. Then she left and returned with her retinue to her own country.

Solomon's Splendor

[13]The weight of the gold that Solomon received yearly was 666 talents,[b] [14]not including the revenues brought in by merchants and traders. Also all the kings of Arabia and the governors of the land brought gold and silver to Solomon.

[15]King Solomon made two hundred large shields of hammered gold; six hundred bekas[c] of hammered gold went into each shield. [16]He also made three hundred small shields of hammered gold, with three hundred bekas[d] of gold in each shield. The king put them in the Palace of the Forest of Lebanon.

[17]Then the king made a great throne inlaid with ivory and overlaid with pure gold. [18]The throne had six steps, and a footstool of gold was attached to it. On both sides of the seat were armrests, with a lion standing beside each of them. [19]Twelve lions stood on the six steps, one at either end of each step. Nothing like it had ever been made for any other kingdom. [20]All King Solomon's goblets were gold, and all the household articles in the Palace of the Forest of Lebanon were pure gold. Nothing was made of silver, because silver was considered of little value in Solomon's day. [21]The king had a fleet of trading ships[e] manned by Hiram's[f] men. Once every three years it returned, carrying gold, silver and ivory, and apes and baboons.

[22]King Solomon was greater in riches and wisdom than all the other kings of the earth. [23]All the kings of the earth sought audience with Solomon to hear the wisdom God had put in his heart. [24]Year after year, everyone who came brought a gift—articles of silver and gold, and robes, weapons and spices, and horses and mules.

[25]Solomon had four thousand stalls for horses and chariots, and twelve thousand horses,[g] which he kept in the chariot cities and also with him in Jerusalem. [26]He ruled over all the kings from the River[h] to the land of the Philistines, as far as the border of Egypt. [27]The king made silver as common in Jerusalem as stones, and cedar as plentiful as sycamore-fig trees in the foothills. [28]Solomon's horses were imported from Egypt[i] and from all other countries.

---

[a]10 Probably a variant of *almugwood*   [b]13 That is, about 25 tons (about 23 metric tons) [c]15 That is, about 7 1/2 pounds (about 3.5 kilograms)   [d]16 That is, about 3 3/4 pounds (about 1.7 kilograms)   [e]21 Hebrew *of ships that could go to Tarshish*   [f]21 Hebrew *Huram*, a variant of *Hiram*   [g]25 Or *charioteers*   [h]26 That is, the Euphrates   [i]28 Or possibly *Muzur*, a region in Cilicia

---

▌ET'S LIVE IT!   2 Chronicles 9:1–9

INTERVIEWING SOLOMON ⇒ Solomon was famous for his wisdom. Read 2 Chronicles 9:1–9 to find out what happened when a queen came to Solomon to "test him with hard questions."

Think of a wise person you know, someone who could answer questions about God and the Bible. Make a list of things that puzzle you or that you worry about sometimes. Then see if the wise person you thought of will talk with you about your questions.

Solomon's Death

29As for the other events of Solomon's reign, from beginning to end, are they not written in the records of Nathan the prophet, in the prophecy of Ahijah the Shilonite and in the visions of Iddo the seer concerning Jeroboam son of Nebat? 30Solomon reigned in Jerusalem over all Israel forty years. 31Then he rested with his fathers and was buried in the city of David his father. And Rehoboam his son succeeded him as king.

Israel Rebels Against Rehoboam

10 Rehoboam went to Shechem, for all the Israelites had gone there to make him king. 2When Jeroboam son of Nebat heard this (he was in Egypt, where he had fled from King Solomon), he returned from Egypt. 3So they sent for Jeroboam, and he and all Israel went to Rehoboam and said to him: 4"Your father put a heavy yoke on us, but now lighten the harsh labor and the heavy yoke he put on us, and we will serve you."

5Rehoboam answered, "Come back to me in three days." So the people went away.

6Then King Rehoboam consulted the elders who had served his father Solomon during his lifetime. "How would you advise me to answer these people?" he asked.

7They replied, "If you will be kind to these people and please them and give them a favorable answer, they will always be your servants."

8But Rehoboam rejected the advice the elders gave him and consulted the young men who had grown up with him and were serving him. 9He asked them, "What is your advice? How should we answer these people who say to me, 'Lighten the yoke your father put on us'?"

10The young men who had grown up with him replied, "Tell the people who have said to you, 'Your father put a heavy yoke on us, but make our yoke lighter'—tell them, 'My little finger is thicker than my father's waist. 11My father laid on you a heavy yoke; I will make it even heavier. My father scourged you with whips; I will scourge you with scorpions.'"

12Three days later Jeroboam and all the people returned to Rehoboam, as the king had said, "Come back to me in three days." 13The king answered them harshly. Rejecting the advice of the elders, 14he followed the advice of the young men and said, "My father made your yoke heavy; I will make it even heavier. My father scourged you with whips; I will scourge you with scorpions." 15So the king did not listen to the people, for this turn of events was from God, to fulfill the word the Lord had spoken to Jeroboam son of Nebat through Ahijah the Shilonite.

16When all Israel saw that the king refused to listen to them, they answered the king:

"What share do we have in David,
    what part in Jesse's son?
To your tents, O Israel!
    Look after your own house,
        O David!"

So all the Israelites went home. 17But as for the Israelites who were living in the towns of Judah, Rehoboam still ruled over them.

18King Rehoboam sent out Adoniram,a who was in charge of forced labor, but the Israelites stoned him to death. King Rehoboam, however, managed to get into his chariot and escape to Jerusalem. 19So Israel has been in rebellion against the house of David to this day.

11 When Rehoboam arrived in Jerusalem, he mustered the house of Judah and Benjamin—a hundred and eighty thousand fighting men—to make war against Israel and to regain the kingdom for Rehoboam.

2But this word of the Lord came to Shemaiah the man of God: 3"Say to Rehoboam son of Solomon king of Ju-

---

a18 Hebrew *Hadoram*, a variant of *Adoniram*

dah and to all the Israelites in Judah and Benjamin, [4]'This is what the LORD says: Do not go up to fight against your brothers. Go home, every one of you, for this is my doing.' " So they obeyed the words of the LORD and turned back from marching against Jeroboam.

? DID YOU KNOW?   10:19

What happened when Solomon died?

Solomon's kingdom was divided into two separate nations. The north was called Israel. The south was called Judah.

Rehoboam Fortifies Judah

[5]Rehoboam lived in Jerusalem and built up towns for defense in Judah: [6]Bethlehem, Etam, Tekoa, [7]Beth Zur, Soco, Adullam, [8]Gath, Mareshah, Ziph, [9]Adoraim, Lachish, Azekah, [10]Zorah, Aijalon and Hebron. These were fortified cities in Judah and Benjamin. [11]He strengthened their defenses and put commanders in them, with supplies of food, olive oil and wine. [12]He put shields and spears in all the cities, and made them very strong. So Judah and Benjamin were his.

[13]The priests and Levites from all their districts throughout Israel sided with him. [14]The Levites even abandoned their pasturelands and property, and came to Judah and Jerusalem because Jeroboam and his sons had rejected them as priests of the LORD. [15]And he appointed his own priests for the high places and for the goat and calf idols he had made. [16]Those from every tribe of Israel who set their hearts on seeking the LORD, the God of Israel, followed the Levites to Jerusalem to offer sacrifices to the LORD, the God of their fathers. [17]They strengthened the kingdom of Judah and supported Rehoboam son of Solo-

mon three years, walking in the ways of David and Solomon during this time.

Rehoboam's Family

[18]Rehoboam married Mahalath, who was the daughter of David's son Jerimoth and of Abihail, the daughter of Jesse's son Eliab. [19]She bore him sons: Jeush, Shemariah and Zaham. [20]Then he married Maacah daughter of Absalom, who bore him Abijah, Attai, Ziza and Shelomith. [21]Rehoboam loved Maacah daughter of Absalom more than any of his other wives and concubines. In all, he had eighteen wives and sixty concubines, twenty-eight sons and sixty daughters.

[22]Rehoboam appointed Abijah son of Maacah to be the chief prince among his brothers, in order to make him king. [23]He acted wisely, dispersing some of his sons throughout the districts of Judah and Benjamin, and to all the fortified cities. He gave them abundant provisions and took many wives for them.

Shishak Attacks Jerusalem

12 After Rehoboam's position as king was established and he had become strong, he and all Israel[a] with him abandoned the law of the LORD. [2]Because they had been unfaithful to the LORD, Shishak king of Egypt attacked Jerusalem in the fifth year of King Rehoboam. [3]With twelve hundred chariots and sixty thousand horsemen and the innumerable troops of Libyans, Sukkites and Cushites[b] that came with him from Egypt, [4]he captured the fortified cities of Judah and came as far as Jerusalem.

[5]Then the prophet Shemaiah came to Rehoboam and to the leaders of Judah who had assembled in Jerusalem for fear of Shishak, and he said to them, "This is what the LORD says, 'You have abandoned me; therefore, I now abandon you to Shishak.' "

[6]The leaders of Israel and the king

---

[a]1 That is, Judah, as frequently in 2 Chronicles   [b]3 That is, people from the upper Nile region

humbled themselves and said, "The LORD is just."

⁷When the LORD saw that they humbled themselves, this word of the LORD came to Shemaiah: "Since they have humbled themselves, I will not destroy them but will soon give them deliverance. My wrath will not be poured out on Jerusalem through Shishak. ⁸They will, however, become subject to him, so that they may learn the difference between serving me and serving the kings of other lands."

⁹When Shishak king of Egypt attacked Jerusalem, he carried off the treasures of the temple of the LORD and the treasures of the royal palace. He took everything, including the gold shields Solomon had made. ¹⁰So King Rehoboam made bronze shields to replace them and assigned these to the commanders of the guard on duty at the entrance to the royal palace. ¹¹Whenever the king went to the LORD's temple, the guards went with him, bearing the shields, and afterward they returned them to the guardroom.

❓DID YOU KNOW?   12:9

What happened to all the gold Solomon put in the Jerusalem temple?

The Egyptians invaded Judah and took all the gold away. The war with the Egyptian king Shishak (SHIE-shack) happened when Rehoboam was king of Judah.

---

¹²Because Rehoboam humbled himself, the LORD's anger turned from him, and he was not totally destroyed. Indeed, there was some good in Judah.

¹³King Rehoboam established himself firmly in Jerusalem and continued as king. He was forty-one years old when he became king, and he

reigned seventeen years in Jerusalem, the city the LORD had chosen out of all the tribes of Israel in which to put his Name. His mother's name was Naamah; she was an Ammonite. ¹⁴He did evil because he had not set his heart on seeking the LORD.

¹⁵As for the events of Rehoboam's reign, from beginning to end, are they not written in the records of Shemaiah the prophet and of Iddo the seer that deal with genealogies? There was continual warfare between Rehoboam and Jeroboam. ¹⁶Rehoboam rested with his fathers and was buried in the City of David. And Abijah his son succeeded him as king.

Abijah King of Judah

13 In the eighteenth year of the reign of Jeroboam, Abijah became king of Judah, ²and he reigned in Jerusalem three years. His mother's name was Maacah,ᵃ a daughterᵇ of Uriel of Gibeah.

There was war between Abijah and Jeroboam. ³Abijah went into battle with a force of four hundred thousand able fighting men, and Jeroboam drew up a battle line against him with eight hundred thousand able troops.

⁴Abijah stood on Mount Zemaraim, in the hill country of Ephraim, and said, "Jeroboam and all Israel, listen to me! ⁵Don't you know that the LORD, the God of Israel, has given the kingship of Israel to David and his descendants forever by a covenant of salt? ⁶Yet Jeroboam son of Nebat, an official of Solomon son of David, rebelled against his master. ⁷Some worthless scoundrels gathered around him and opposed Rehoboam son of Solomon when he was young and indecisive and not strong enough to resist them.

⁸"And now you plan to resist the kingdom of the LORD, which is in the hands of David's descendants. You are indeed a vast army and have with

---

ᵃ2 Most Septuagint manuscripts and Syriac (see also 2 Chron. 11:20 and 1 Kings 15:2); Hebrew *Micaiah*   ᵇ2 Or *granddaughter*

you the golden calves that Jeroboam made to be your gods. ⁹But didn't you drive out the priests of the LORD, the sons of Aaron, and the Levites, and make priests of your own as the peoples of other lands do? Whoever comes to consecrate himself with a young bull and seven rams may become a priest of what are not gods.

¹⁰"As for us, the LORD is our God, and we have not forsaken him. The priests who serve the LORD are sons of Aaron, and the Levites assist them. ¹¹Every morning and evening they present burnt offerings and fragrant incense to the LORD. They set out the bread on the ceremonially clean table and light the lamps on the gold lampstand every evening. We are observing the requirements of the LORD our God. But you have forsaken him. ¹²God is with us; he is our leader. His priests with their trumpets will sound the battle cry against you. Men of Israel, do not fight against the LORD, the God of your fathers, for you will not succeed."

WORDS TO REMEMBER

13:10 The LORD is our God, and we have not forsaken him.

¹³Now Jeroboam had sent troops around to the rear, so that while he was in front of Judah the ambush was behind them. ¹⁴Judah turned and saw that they were being attacked at both front and rear. Then they cried out to the LORD. The priests blew their trumpets ¹⁵and the men of Judah raised the battle cry. At the sound of their battle cry, God routed Jeroboam and all Israel before Abijah and Judah. ¹⁶The Israelites fled before Judah, and God delivered them into their hands. ¹⁷Abijah and his men inflicted heavy losses on them, so that there were five hundred thousand casualties among Israel's able men. ¹⁸The men of Israel were subdued on that occasion, and the men of Judah were victorious because they relied on the LORD, the God of their fathers.

¹⁹Abijah pursued Jeroboam and took from him the towns of Bethel, Jeshanah and Ephron, with their surrounding villages. ²⁰Jeroboam did not regain power during the time of Abijah. And the LORD struck him down and he died.

²¹But Abijah grew in strength. He married fourteen wives and had twenty-two sons and sixteen daughters.

²²The other events of Abijah's reign, what he did and what he said, are written in the annotations of the prophet Iddo.

14 And Abijah rested with his fathers and was buried in the City of David. Asa his son succeeded him as king, and in his days the country was at peace for ten years.

Asa King of Judah

²Asa did what was good and right in the eyes of the LORD his God. ³He removed the foreign altars and the high places, smashed the sacred stones and cut down the Asherah poles.ᵃ ⁴He commanded Judah to seek the LORD, the God of their fathers, and to obey his laws and commands. ⁵He removed the high places and incense altars in every town in Judah, and the kingdom was at peace under him. ⁶He built up the fortified cities of Judah, since the land was at peace. No one was at war with him during those years, for the LORD gave him rest.

⁷"Let us build up these towns," he said to Judah, "and put walls around them, with towers, gates and bars. The land is still ours, because we have sought the LORD our God; we sought him and he has given us rest on every side." So they built and prospered.

⁸Asa had an army of three hundred thousand men from Judah, equipped with large shields and with spears,

ᵃ3 That is, symbols of the goddess Asherah; here and elsewhere in 2 Chronicles

and two hundred and eighty thousand from Benjamin, armed with small shields and with bows. All these were brave fighting men.

⁹Zerah the Cushite marched out against them with a vast army*a* and three hundred chariots, and came as far as Mareshah. ¹⁰Asa went out to meet him, and they took up battle positions in the Valley of Zephathah near Mareshah.

¹¹Then Asa called to the LORD his God and said, "LORD, there is no one like you to help the powerless against the mighty. Help us, O LORD our God, for we rely on you, and in your name we have come against this vast army. O LORD, you are our God; do not let man prevail against you."

¹²The LORD struck down the Cushites before Asa and Judah. The Cushites fled, ¹³and Asa and his army pursued them as far as Gerar. Such a great number of Cushites fell that they could not recover; they were crushed before the LORD and his forces. The men of Judah carried off a large amount of plunder. ¹⁴They destroyed all the villages around Gerar, for the terror of the LORD had fallen upon them. They plundered all these villages, since there was much booty there. ¹⁵They also attacked the camps of the herdsmen and carried off droves of sheep and goats and camels. Then they returned to Jerusalem.

Asa's Reform

15 The Spirit of God came upon Azariah son of Oded. ²He went out to meet Asa and said to him, "Listen to me, Asa and all Judah and Benjamin. The LORD is with you when you are with him. If you seek him, he will be found by you, but if you forsake him, he will forsake you. ³For a long time Israel was without the true God, without a priest to teach and without the law. ⁴But in their distress they turned to the LORD, the God of Israel, and sought him, and he was found by them. ⁵In those days it was not safe to travel about, for all the inhabitants of the lands were in great turmoil. ⁶One nation was being crushed by another and one city by another, because God was troubling them with every kind of distress. ⁷But as for you, be strong and do not give up, for your work will be rewarded."

⁸When Asa heard these words and the prophecy of Azariah son of*b* Oded the prophet, he took courage. He removed the detestable idols from the whole land of Judah and Benjamin and from the towns he had captured in the hills of Ephraim. He repaired the altar of the LORD that was in front of the portico of the LORD's temple.

⁹Then he assembled all Judah and Benjamin and the people from Ephraim, Manasseh and Simeon who had settled among them, for large

---

*a*9 Hebrew *with an army of a thousand thousands* or *with an army of thousands upon thousands*
*b*8 Vulgate and Syriac (see also Septuagint and verse 1); Hebrew does not have *Azariah son of*.

▌ET'S LIVE IT!   2 Chronicles 14:2–15

THE REST OF THE STORY ➡ Have you ever read a story and thought, "I know what's going to happen next," before you reach the end? Read 2 Chronicles 14, but *stop reading* at 2 Chronicles 14:11. Then write down your own ending for the story. Tell your mom or dad you are trying to guess what happened in a Bible story. Read what you wrote out loud. Then read 2 Chronicles 14:12–15 in the Bible. Ask your mom or dad about a time when they prayed to God for help. Why did they pray? What happened when they prayed? If there is anything that you are worried about or afraid of right now, ask your mom or dad to pray with you about it.

numbers had come over to him from Israel when they saw that the LORD his God was with him.

¹⁰They assembled at Jerusalem in the third month of the fifteenth year of Asa's reign. ¹¹At that time they sacrificed to the LORD seven hundred head of cattle and seven thousand sheep and goats from the plunder they had brought back. ¹²They entered into a covenant to seek the LORD, the God of their fathers, with all their heart and soul. ¹³All who would not seek the LORD, the God of Israel, were to be put to death, whether small or great, man or woman. ¹⁴They took an oath to the LORD with loud acclamation, with shouting and with trumpets and horns. ¹⁵All Judah rejoiced about the oath because they had sworn it wholeheartedly. They sought God eagerly, and he was found by them. So the LORD gave them rest on every side.

¹⁶King Asa also deposed his grandmother Maacah from her position as queen mother, because she had made a repulsive Asherah pole. Asa cut the pole down, broke it up and burned it in the Kidron Valley. ¹⁷Although he did not remove the high places from Israel, Asa's heart was fully committed to the LORD all his life. ¹⁸He brought into the temple of God the silver and gold and the articles that he and his father had dedicated.

¹⁹There was no more war until the thirty-fifth year of Asa's reign.

Asa's Last Years

16 In the thirty-sixth year of Asa's reign Baasha king of Israel went up against Judah and fortified Ramah to prevent anyone from leaving or entering the territory of Asa king of Judah.

²Asa then took the silver and gold out of the treasuries of the LORD's temple and of his own palace and sent it to Ben-Hadad king of Aram, who was ruling in Damascus. ³"Let there be a treaty between me and you," he said, "as there was between my father and your father. See, I am sending you silver and gold. Now break your treaty with Baasha king of Israel so he will withdraw from me."

⁴Ben-Hadad agreed with King Asa and sent the commanders of his forces against the towns of Israel. They conquered Ijon, Dan, Abel Maim*ᵃ* and all the store cities of Naphtali. ⁵When Baasha heard this, he stopped building Ramah and abandoned his work. ⁶Then King Asa brought all the men of Judah, and they carried away from Ramah the stones and timber Baasha had been using. With them he built up Geba and Mizpah.

⁷At that time Hanani the seer came to Asa king of Judah and said to him: "Because you relied on the king of Aram and not on the LORD your God, the army of the king of Aram has escaped from your hand. ⁸Were not the Cushites*ᵇ* and Libyans a mighty army with great numbers of chariots and horsemen*ᶜ*? Yet when you relied on the LORD, he delivered them into your hand. ⁹For the eyes of the LORD range throughout the earth to strengthen those whose hearts are fully committed to him. You have done a foolish thing, and from now on you will be at war."

¹⁰Asa was angry with the seer because of this; he was so enraged that he put him in prison. At the same time Asa brutally oppressed some of the people.

¹¹The events of Asa's reign, from beginning to end, are written in the book of the kings of Judah and Israel. ¹²In the thirty-ninth year of his reign Asa was afflicted with a disease in his feet. Though his disease was severe, even in his illness he did not seek help from the LORD, but only from the physicians. ¹³Then in the forty-first year of his reign Asa died and rested with his fathers. ¹⁴They buried him in the tomb that he had

---

ᵃ4 Also known as *Abel Beth Maacah*   *ᵇ8* That is, people from the upper Nile region   *ᶜ8* Or *charioteers*

cut out for himself in the City of David. They laid him on a bier covered with spices and various blended perfumes, and they made a huge fire in his honor.

Jehoshaphat King of Judah

17 Jehoshaphat his son succeeded him as king and strengthened himself against Israel. ²He stationed troops in all the fortified cities of Judah and put garrisons in Judah and in the towns of Ephraim that his father Asa had captured.

³The LORD was with Jehoshaphat because in his early years he walked in the ways his father David had followed. He did not consult the Baals ⁴but sought the God of his father and followed his commands rather than the practices of Israel. ⁵The LORD established the kingdom under his control; and all Judah brought gifts to Jehoshaphat, so that he had great wealth and honor. ⁶His heart was devoted to the ways of the LORD; furthermore, he removed the high places and the Asherah poles from Judah.

⁷In the third year of his reign he sent his officials Ben-Hail, Obadiah, Zechariah, Nethanel and Micaiah to teach in the towns of Judah. ⁸With them were certain Levites—Shemaiah, Nethaniah, Zebadiah, Asahel, Shemiramoth, Jehonathan, Adonijah, Tobijah and Tob-Adonijah—and the priests Elishama and Jehoram. ⁹They taught throughout Judah, taking with them the Book of the Law of the LORD; they went around to all the towns of Judah and taught the people.

¹⁰The fear of the LORD fell on all the kingdoms of the lands surrounding Judah, so that they did not make war with Jehoshaphat. ¹¹Some Philistines brought Jehoshaphat gifts and silver as tribute, and the Arabs brought him flocks: seven thousand seven hundred rams and seven thousand seven hundred goats.

¹²Jehoshaphat became more and more powerful; he built forts and store cities in Judah ¹³and had large supplies in the towns of Judah. He also kept experienced fighting men in Jerusalem. ¹⁴Their enrollment by families was as follows:

From Judah, commanders of units of 1,000:
  Adnah the commander, with 300,000 fighting men;
  ¹⁵next, Jehohanan the commander, with 280,000;
  ¹⁶next, Amasiah son of Zicri, who volunteered himself for the service of the LORD, with 200,000.
¹⁷From Benjamin:
  Eliada, a valiant soldier, with 200,000 men armed with bows and shields;

Life in Bible Times

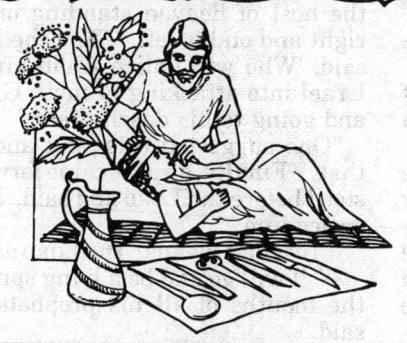

DOCTORS AND MEDICINES

In Bible times medicines were made from herbs and parts of different plants. Olive oil and wine were also used as medicine. The Bible says little about doctors, though by the time of the New Testament, surgeons used tools like scalpels, tweezers and clamps.

18next, Jehozabad, with 180,000 men armed for battle.

19These were the men who served the king, besides those he stationed in the fortified cities throughout Judah.

Micaiah Prophesies Against Ahab

18 Now Jehoshaphat had great wealth and honor, and he allied himself with Ahab by marriage. 2Some years later he went down to visit Ahab in Samaria. Ahab slaughtered many sheep and cattle for him and the people with him and urged him to attack Ramoth Gilead. 3Ahab king of Israel asked Jehoshaphat king of Judah, "Will you go with me against Ramoth Gilead?"

Jehoshaphat replied, "I am as you are, and my people as your people; we will join you in the war." 4But Jehoshaphat also said to the king of Israel, "First seek the counsel of the LORD."

5So the king of Israel brought together the prophets—four hundred men—and asked them, "Shall we go to war against Ramoth Gilead, or shall I refrain?"

"Go," they answered, "for God will give it into the king's hand."

6But Jehoshaphat asked, "Is there not a prophet of the LORD here whom we can inquire of?"

7The king of Israel answered Jehoshaphat, "There is still one man through whom we can inquire of the LORD, but I hate him because he never prophesies anything good about me, but always bad. He is Micaiah son of Imlah."

"The king should not say that," Jehoshaphat replied.

8So the king of Israel called one of his officials and said, "Bring Micaiah son of Imlah at once."

9Dressed in their royal robes, the king of Israel and Jehoshaphat king of Judah were sitting on their thrones at the threshing floor by the entrance to the gate of Samaria, with all the prophets prophesying before them. 10Now Zedekiah son of Kenaa-nah had made iron horns, and he declared, "This is what the LORD says: 'With these you will gore the Arameans until they are destroyed.'"

11All the other prophets were prophesying the same thing. "Attack Ramoth Gilead and be victorious," they said, "for the LORD will give it into the king's hand."

12The messenger who had gone to summon Micaiah said to him, "Look, as one man the other prophets are predicting success for the king. Let your word agree with theirs, and speak favorably."

13But Micaiah said, "As surely as the LORD lives, I can tell him only what my God says."

14When he arrived, the king asked him, "Micaiah, shall we go to war against Ramoth Gilead, or shall I refrain?"

"Attack and be victorious," he answered, "for they will be given into your hand."

15The king said to him, "How many times must I make you swear to tell me nothing but the truth in the name of the LORD?"

16Then Micaiah answered, "I saw all Israel scattered on the hills like sheep without a shepherd, and the LORD said, 'These people have no master. Let each one go home in peace.'"

17The king of Israel said to Jehoshaphat, "Didn't I tell you that he never prophesies anything good about me, but only bad?"

18Micaiah continued, "Therefore hear the word of the LORD: I saw the LORD sitting on his throne with all the host of heaven standing on his right and on his left. 19And the LORD said, 'Who will entice Ahab king of Israel into attacking Ramoth Gilead and going to his death there?'

"One suggested this, and another that. 20Finally, a spirit came forward, stood before the LORD and said, 'I will entice him.'

"'By what means?' the LORD asked.

21"'I will go and be a lying spirit in the mouths of all his prophets,' he said.

" 'You will succeed in enticing him,' said the LORD. 'Go and do it.'
²²"So now the LORD has put a lying spirit in the mouths of these prophets of yours. The LORD has decreed disaster for you."

²³Then Zedekiah son of Kenaanah went up and slapped Micaiah in the face. "Which way did the spirit from ᵃ the LORD go when he went from me to speak to you?" he asked.

²⁴Micaiah replied, "You will find out on the day you go to hide in an inner room."

²⁵The king of Israel then ordered, "Take Micaiah and send him back to Amon the ruler of the city and to Joash the king's son, ²⁶and say, 'This is what the king says: Put this fellow in prison and give him nothing but bread and water until I return safely.' "

²⁷Micaiah declared, "If you ever return safely, the LORD has not spoken through me." Then he added, "Mark my words, all you people!"

Ahab Killed at Ramoth Gilead

²⁸So the king of Israel and Jehoshaphat king of Judah went up to Ramoth Gilead. ²⁹The king of Israel said to Jehoshaphat, "I will enter the battle in disguise, but you wear your royal robes." So the king of Israel disguised himself and went into battle.

³⁰Now the king of Aram had ordered his chariot commanders, "Do not fight with anyone, small or great, except the king of Israel." ³¹When the chariot commanders saw Jehoshaphat, they thought, "This is the king of Israel." So they turned to attack him, but Jehoshaphat cried out, and the LORD helped him. God drew them away from him, ³²for when the chariot commanders saw that he was not the king of Israel, they stopped pursuing him.

³³But someone drew his bow at random and hit the king of Israel between the sections of his armor. The king told the chariot driver, "Wheel around and get me out of the fight-ing. I've been wounded." ³⁴All day long the battle raged, and the king of Israel propped himself up in his chariot facing the Arameans until evening. Then at sunset he died.

19 When Jehoshaphat king of Judah returned safely to his palace in Jerusalem, ²Jehu the seer, the son of Hanani, went out to meet him and said to the king, "Should you help the wicked and love ᵇ those who hate the LORD? Because of this, the wrath of the LORD is upon you. ³There is, however, some good in you, for you have rid the land of the Asherah poles and have set your heart on seeking God."

Jehoshaphat Appoints Judges

⁴Jehoshaphat lived in Jerusalem, and he went out again among the people from Beersheba to the hill country of Ephraim and turned them back to the LORD, the God of their fathers. ⁵He appointed judges in the land, in each of the fortified cities of Judah. ⁶He told them, "Consider carefully what you do, because you are not judging for man but for the LORD, who is with you whenever you give a verdict. ⁷Now let the fear of the LORD be upon you. Judge carefully, for with the LORD our God there is no injustice or partiality or bribery."

⁸In Jerusalem also, Jehoshaphat appointed some of the Levites, priests and heads of Israelite families to administer the law of the LORD and to settle disputes. And they lived in Jerusalem. ⁹He gave them these orders: "You must serve faithfully and wholeheartedly in the fear of the LORD. ¹⁰In every case that comes before you from your fellow countrymen who live in the cities—whether bloodshed or other concerns of the law, commands, decrees or ordinances—you are to warn them not to sin against the LORD; otherwise his wrath will come on you and your brothers. Do this, and you will not sin.

¹¹"Amariah the chief priest will be

ᵃ23 Or *Spirit of*   ᵇ2 Or *and make alliances with*

over you in any matter concerning the LORD, and Zebadiah son of Ishmael, the leader of the tribe of Judah, will be over you in any matter concerning the king, and the Levites will serve as officials before you. Act with courage, and may the LORD be with those who do well."

Jehoshaphat Defeats Moab and Ammon

20 After this, the Moabites and Ammonites with some of the Meunites*a* came to make war on Jehoshaphat.

²Some men came and told Jehoshaphat, "A vast army is coming against you from Edom,*b* from the other side of the Sea.*c* It is already in Hazazon Tamar" (that is, En Gedi). ³Alarmed, Jehoshaphat resolved to inquire of the LORD, and he proclaimed a fast for all Judah. ⁴The people of Judah came together to seek help from the LORD; indeed, they came from every town in Judah to seek him.

⁵Then Jehoshaphat stood up in the assembly of Judah and Jerusalem at the temple of the LORD in the front of the new courtyard ⁶and said:

"O LORD, God of our fathers, are you not the God who is in heaven? You rule over all the kingdoms of the nations. Power and might are in your hand, and no one can withstand you. ⁷O our God, did you not drive out the inhabitants of this land before

your people Israel and give it forever to the descendants of Abraham your friend? ⁸They have lived in it and have built in it a sanctuary for your Name, saying, ⁹'If calamity comes upon us, whether the sword of judgment, or plague or famine, we will stand in your presence before this temple that bears your Name and will cry out to you in our distress, and you will hear us and save us.'

❓DID YOU KNOW?   20:3

Why did Jehoshaphat tell Judah to fast?

To fast means to go without food. In Old Testament times when people felt helpless, they would often go without food to show how sincere their prayers were. Jehoshaphat knew that his armies could only defeat Moab and Ammon if they had God's help.

---

¹⁰"But now here are men from Ammon, Moab and Mount Seir, whose territory you would not allow Israel to invade when they came from Egypt; so they turned away from them and did not destroy them. ¹¹See how they are repaying us by coming to drive us out of the possession you gave

---

a1 Some Septuagint manuscripts; Hebrew *Ammonites*   *b2* One Hebrew manuscript; most Hebrew manuscripts, Septuagint and Vulgate *Aram*   *c2* That is, the Dead Sea

---

◣ET'S LIVE IT!   2 Chronicles 19:4–10

YOU BE THE JUDGE. ➡ In 2 Chronicles 19:4–10 you can read about the judges that King Jehoshaphat appointed. He told them things like: Be fair. Be careful. Use the rules in God's Word. Judge to please God.

Family members argue too. If you were judge in your family and had to settle arguments, how good a judge would you be? Have each family member decide how to settle these real life cases.

Case #1. Tom complains that Kristi takes the biggest piece of cake.
Case #2. Kristi says Tom took a toy out of her room.
Case #3. Tom and Kristi each complain their chores are hardest.

us as an inheritance. ¹²O our God, will you not judge them? For we have no power to face this vast army that is attacking us. We do not know what to do, but our eyes are upon you."

WORDS TO REMEMBER

20:12 We do not know what to do, but our eyes are upon you.

¹³All the men of Judah, with their wives and children and little ones, stood there before the LORD.

¹⁴Then the Spirit of the LORD came upon Jahaziel son of Zechariah, the son of Benaiah, the son of Jeiel, the son of Mattaniah, a Levite and descendant of Asaph, as he stood in the assembly.

¹⁵He said: "Listen, King Jehoshaphat and all who live in Judah and Jerusalem! This is what the LORD says to you: 'Do not be afraid or discouraged because of this vast army. For the battle is not yours, but God's. ¹⁶Tomorrow march down against them. They will be climbing up by the Pass of Ziz, and you will find them at the end of the gorge in the Desert of Jeruel. ¹⁷You will not have to fight this battle. Take up your positions; stand firm and see the deliverance the LORD will give you, O Judah and Jerusalem. Do not be afraid; do not be discouraged. Go out to face them tomorrow, and the LORD will be with you.'"

¹⁸Jehoshaphat bowed with his face to the ground, and all the people of Judah and Jerusalem fell down in worship before the LORD. ¹⁹Then some Levites from the Kohathites and Korahites stood up and praised the LORD, the God of Israel, with very loud voice.

²⁰Early in the morning they left for the Desert of Tekoa. As they set out, Jehoshaphat stood and said, "Listen to me, Judah and people of Jerusalem! Have faith in the LORD your God and you will be upheld; have faith in his prophets and you will be successful." ²¹After consulting the people, Jehoshaphat appointed men to sing to the LORD and to praise him for the splendor of his*a* holiness as they went out at the head of the army, saying:

"Give thanks to the LORD,
    for his love endures forever."

²²As they began to sing and praise, the LORD set ambushes against the men of Ammon and Moab and Mount Seir who were invading Judah, and they were defeated. ²³The men of Ammon and Moab rose up against the men from Mount Seir to destroy and annihilate them. After they finished slaughtering the men from Seir, they helped to destroy one another.

²⁴When the men of Judah came to the place that overlooks the desert and looked toward the vast army, they saw only dead bodies lying on the ground; no one had escaped. ²⁵So Jehoshaphat and his men went to carry off their plunder, and they found among them a great amount of equipment and clothing*b* and also articles of value—more than they could take away. There was so much plunder that it took three days to collect it. ²⁶On the fourth day they assembled in the Valley of Beracah, where they praised the LORD. This is why it is called the Valley of Beracah*c* to this day.

²⁷Then, led by Jehoshaphat, all the men of Judah and Jerusalem returned joyfully to Jerusalem, for the LORD had given them cause to rejoice over their enemies. ²⁸They entered Jerusalem and went to the temple of the LORD with harps and lutes and trumpets.

²⁹The fear of God came upon all the kingdoms of the countries when they heard how the LORD had fought against the enemies of Israel. ³⁰And

---

*a*21 Or *him with the splendor of* *b*25 Some Hebrew manuscripts and Vulgate; most Hebrew manuscripts *corpses*   *c*26 *Beracah* means *praise*.

the kingdom of Jehoshaphat was at peace, for his God had given him rest on every side.

The End of Jehoshaphat's Reign

³¹So Jehoshaphat reigned over Judah. He was thirty-five years old when he became king of Judah, and he reigned in Jerusalem twenty-five years. His mother's name was Azubah daughter of Shilhi. ³²He walked in the ways of his father Asa and did not stray from them; he did what was right in the eyes of the LORD. ³³The high places, however, were not removed, and the people still had not set their hearts on the God of their fathers.

³⁴The other events of Jehoshaphat's reign, from beginning to end, are written in the annals of Jehu son of Hanani, which are recorded in the book of the kings of Israel.

³⁵Later, Jehoshaphat king of Judah made an alliance with Ahaziah king of Israel, who was guilty of wickedness. ³⁶He agreed with him to construct a fleet of trading ships.ᵃ After these were built at Ezion Geber, ³⁷Eliezer son of Dodavahu of Mareshah prophesied against Jehoshaphat, saying, "Because you have made an alliance with Ahaziah, the LORD will destroy what you have made." The ships were wrecked and were not able to set sail to trade.ᵇ

21 Then Jehoshaphat rested with his fathers and was buried with them in the City of David. And Jehoram his son succeeded him as king. ²Jehoram's brothers, the sons of Jehoshaphat, were Azariah, Jehiel, Zechariah, Azariahu, Michael and Shephatiah. All these were sons of Jehoshaphat king of Israel.ᶜ ³Their father had given them many gifts of silver and gold and articles of value, as well as fortified cities in Judah, but he had given the kingdom to Jehoram because he was his firstborn son.

Jehoram King of Judah

⁴When Jehoram established himself firmly over his father's kingdom, he put all his brothers to the sword along with some of the princes of Israel. ⁵Jehoram was thirty-two years old when he became king, and he reigned in Jerusalem eight years. ⁶He walked in the ways of the kings of Israel, as the house of Ahab had done, for he married a daughter of Ahab. He did evil in the eyes of the LORD. ⁷Nevertheless, because of the covenant the LORD had made with David, the LORD was not willing to destroy the house of David. He had promised to maintain a lamp for him and his descendants forever.

⁸In the time of Jehoram, Edom rebelled against Judah and set up its own king. ⁹So Jehoram went there with his officers and all his chariots. The Edomites surrounded him and his chariot commanders, but he rose up and broke through by night. ¹⁰To this day Edom has been in rebellion against Judah.

Libnah revolted at the same time, because Jehoram had forsaken the LORD, the God of his fathers. ¹¹He had also built high places on the hills of Judah and had caused the people of Jerusalem to prostitute themselves and had led Judah astray.

¹²Jehoram received a letter from Elijah the prophet, which said:

"This is what the LORD, the God of your father David, says: 'You have not walked in the ways of your father Jehoshaphat or of Asa king of Judah. ¹³But you have walked in the ways of the kings of Israel, and you have led Judah and the people of Jerusalem to prostitute themselves, just as the house of Ahab did. You have also murdered your own brothers, members of your father's house, men who were better than you. ¹⁴So now the LORD is about to strike your peo-

---

ᵃ36 Hebrew *of ships that could go to Tarshish* Judah, as frequently in 2 Chronicles   ᵇ37 Hebrew *sail for Tarshish*   ᶜ2 That is,

ple, your sons, your wives and everything that is yours, with a heavy blow. ¹⁵You yourself will be very ill with a lingering disease of the bowels, until the disease causes your bowels to come out.'"

¹⁶The LORD aroused against Jehoram the hostility of the Philistines and of the Arabs who lived near the Cushites. ¹⁷They attacked Judah, invaded it and carried off all the goods found in the king's palace, together with his sons and wives. Not a son was left to him except Ahaziah,ᵃ the youngest.

¹⁸After all this, the LORD afflicted Jehoram with an incurable disease of the bowels. ¹⁹In the course of time, at the end of the second year, his bowels came out because of the disease, and he died in great pain. His people made no fire in his honor, as they had for his fathers.

²⁰Jehoram was thirty-two years old when he became king, and he reigned in Jerusalem eight years. He passed away, to no one's regret, and was buried in the City of David, but not in the tombs of the kings.

Ahaziah King of Judah

22 The people of Jerusalem made Ahaziah, Jehoram's youngest son, king in his place, since the raiders, who came with the Arabs into the camp, had killed all the older sons. So Ahaziah son of Jehoram king of Judah began to reign.

²Ahaziah was twenty-twoᵇ years old when he became king, and he reigned in Jerusalem one year. His mother's name was Athaliah, a granddaughter of Omri.

³He too walked in the ways of the house of Ahab, for his mother encouraged him in doing wrong. ⁴He did evil in the eyes of the LORD, as the house of Ahab had done, for after his fa-

ther's death they became his advisers, to his undoing. ⁵He also followed their counsel when he went with Joramᶜ son of Ahab king of Israel to war against Hazael king of Aram at Ramoth Gilead. The Arameans wounded Joram; ⁶so he returned to Jezreel to recover from the wounds they had inflicted on him at Ramothᵈ in his battle with Hazael king of Aram.

Then Ahaziahᵉ son of Jehoram king of Judah went down to Jezreel to see Joram son of Ahab because he had been wounded.

⁷Through Ahaziah's visit to Joram, God brought about Ahaziah's downfall. When Ahaziah arrived, he went out with Joram to meet Jehu son of Nimshi, whom the LORD had anointed to destroy the house of Ahab. ⁸While Jehu was executing judgment on the house of Ahab, he found the princes of Judah and the sons of Ahaziah's relatives, who had been attending Ahaziah, and he killed them. ⁹He then went in search of Ahaziah, and his men captured him while he was hiding in Samaria. He was brought to Jehu and put to death. They buried him, for they said, "He was a son of Jehoshaphat, who sought the LORD with all his heart." So there was no one in the house of Ahaziah powerful enough to retain the kingdom.

Athaliah and Joash

¹⁰When Athaliah the mother of Ahaziah saw that her son was dead, she proceeded to destroy the whole royal family of the house of Judah. ¹¹But Jehosheba,ᶠ the daughter of King Jehoram, took Joash son of Ahaziah and stole him away from among the royal princes who were about to be murdered and put him and his nurse in a bedroom. Because Jehosheba,ᶠ the daughter of King Je-

---

ᵃ17 Hebrew *Jehoahaz*, a variant of *Ahaziah* (see also 2 Kings 8:26); Hebrew *forty-two*   ᵇ2 Some Septuagint manuscripts and Syriac (see   ᶜ5 Hebrew *Jehoram*, a variant of *Joram*; also in verses 6 and 7   ᵈ6 Hebrew *Ramah*, a variant of *Ramoth* (see also 2 Kings 8:29); most Hebrew manuscripts *Azariah*   ᵉ6 Some Hebrew manuscripts, Septuagint, Vulgate and Syriac (see also 2 Kings 8:29); most Hebrew manuscripts *Azariah*   ᶠ11 Hebrew *Jehoshabeath*, a variant of *Jehosheba*

horam and wife of the priest Jehoiada, was Ahaziah's sister, she hid the child from Athaliah so she could not kill him. ¹²He remained hidden with them at the temple of God for six years while Athaliah ruled the land.

? DID YOU KNOW?   22:10

Who was Athaliah?

Athaliah was the daugher of evil King Ahab and Queen Jezebel of Israel. She was so evil that she killed her own grandchildren to become queen of Judah. Only one child, Joash, escaped.

---

23 In the seventh year Jehoiada showed his strength. He made a covenant with the commanders of units of a hundred: Azariah son of Jeroham, Ishmael son of Jehohanan, Azariah son of Obed, Maaseiah son of Adaiah, and Elishaphat son of Zicri. ²They went throughout Judah and gathered the Levites and the heads of Israelite families from all the towns. When they came to Jerusalem, ³the whole assembly made a covenant with the king at the temple of God.

Jehoiada said to them, "The king's son shall reign, as the LORD promised concerning the descendants of David. ⁴Now this is what you are to do: A third of you priests and Levites who are going on duty on the Sabbath are to keep watch at the doors, ⁵a third of you at the royal palace and a third at the Foundation Gate, and all the other men are to be in the courtyards of the temple of the LORD. ⁶No one is to enter the temple of the LORD except the priests and Levites on duty; they may enter because they are consecrated, but all the other men are to guard what the LORD has assigned to them.ᵃ ⁷The Levites are to station themselves around the king, each man with his weapons in his hand.

Anyone who enters the temple must be put to death. Stay close to the king wherever he goes."

⁸The Levites and all the men of Judah did just as Jehoiada the priest ordered. Each one took his men—those who were going on duty on the Sabbath and those who were going off duty—for Jehoiada the priest had not released any of the divisions. ⁹Then he gave the commanders of units of a hundred the spears and the large and small shields that had belonged to King David and that were in the temple of God. ¹⁰He stationed all the men, each with his weapon in his hand, around the king—near the altar and the temple, from the south side to the north side of the temple.

¹¹Jehoiada and his sons brought out the king's son and put the crown on him; they presented him with a copy of the covenant and proclaimed him king. They anointed him and shouted, "Long live the king!"

¹²When Athaliah heard the noise of the people running and cheering the king, she went to them at the temple of the LORD. ¹³She looked, and there was the king, standing by his pillar at the entrance. The officers and the trumpeters were beside the king, and all the people of the land were rejoicing and blowing trumpets, and singers with musical instruments were leading the praises. Then Athaliah tore her robes and shouted, "Treason! Treason!"

¹⁴Jehoiada the priest sent out the commanders of units of a hundred, who were in charge of the troops, and said to them: "Bring her out between the ranksᵇ and put to the sword anyone who follows her." For the priest had said, "Do not put her to death at the temple of the LORD." ¹⁵So they seized her as she reached the entrance of the Horse Gate on the palace grounds, and there they put her to death.

¹⁶Jehoiada then made a covenant that he and the people and the kingᶜ

ᵃ6 Or *to observe the LORD's command not to enter,*   ᵇ14 Or *out from the precincts*   ᶜ16 Or *covenant between the LORD, and the people and the king that they* (see 2 Kings 11:17)

would be the LORD's people. ¹⁷All the people went to the temple of Baal and tore it down. They smashed the altars and idols and killed Mattan the priest of Baal in front of the altars.

¹⁸Then Jehoiada placed the oversight of the temple of the LORD in the hands of the priests, who were Levites, to whom David had made assignments in the temple, to present the burnt offerings of the LORD as written in the Law of Moses, with rejoicing and singing, as David had ordered. ¹⁹He also stationed doorkeepers at the gates of the LORD's temple so that no one who was in any way unclean might enter.

²⁰He took with him the commanders of hundreds, the nobles, the rulers of the people and all the people of the land and brought the king down from the temple of the LORD. They went into the palace through the Upper Gate and seated the king on the royal throne, ²¹and all the people of the land rejoiced. And the city was quiet, because Athaliah had been slain with the sword.

Joash Repairs the Temple

24 Joash was seven years old when he became king, and he reigned in Jerusalem forty years. His mother's name was Zibiah; she was from Beersheba. ²Joash did what was right in the eyes of the LORD all the years of Jehoiada the priest. ³Jehoiada chose two wives for him, and he had sons and daughters.

⁴Some time later Joash decided to restore the temple of the LORD. ⁵He called together the priests and Levites and said to them, "Go to the towns of Judah and collect the money due annually from all Israel, to repair the temple of your God. Do it now." But the Levites did not act at once.

⁶Therefore the king summoned Jehoiada the chief priest and said to him, "Why haven't you required the Levites to bring in from Judah and Jerusalem the tax imposed by Moses the servant of the LORD and by the assembly of Israel for the Tent of the Testimony?'"

⁷Now the sons of that wicked woman Athaliah had broken into the temple of God and had used even its sacred objects for the Baals.

⁸At the king's command, a chest was made and placed outside, at the gate of the temple of the LORD. ⁹A proclamation was then issued in Judah and Jerusalem that they should bring to the LORD the tax that Moses the servant of God had required of Israel in the desert. ¹⁰All the officials and all the people brought their contributions gladly, dropping them into the chest until it was full. ¹¹Whenever the chest was brought in by the Levites to the king's officials and they saw that there was a large amount of money, the royal secretary and the officer of the chief priest would come and empty the chest and carry it back to its place. They did this regularly and collected a great amount of money. ¹²The king and Jehoiada gave it to the men who carried out the work required for the temple of the LORD. They hired masons and carpenters to restore the LORD's temple, and also workers in iron and bronze to repair the temple.

¹³The men in charge of the work were diligent, and the repairs progressed under them. They rebuilt the temple of God according to its original design and reinforced it. ¹⁴When they had finished, they brought the rest of the money to the king and Jehoiada, and with it were made articles for the LORD's temple: articles for the service and for the burnt offerings, and also dishes and other objects of gold and silver. As long as Jehoiada lived, burnt offerings were presented continually in the temple of the LORD.

¹⁵Now Jehoiada was old and full of years, and he died at the age of a hundred and thirty. ¹⁶He was buried with the kings in the City of David, because of the good he had done in Israel for God and his temple.

The Wickedness of Joash

17After the death of Jehoiada, the officials of Judah came and paid homage to the king, and he listened to them. 18They abandoned the temple of the LORD, the God of their fathers, and worshiped Asherah poles and idols. Because of their guilt, God's anger came upon Judah and Jerusalem. 19Although the LORD sent prophets to the people to bring them back to him, and though they testified against them, they would not listen.

20Then the Spirit of God came upon Zechariah son of Jehoiada the priest. He stood before the people and said, "This is what God says: 'Why do you disobey the LORD's commands? You will not prosper. Because you have forsaken the LORD, he has forsaken you.'"

21But they plotted against him, and by order of the king they stoned him to death in the courtyard of the LORD's temple. 22King Joash did not remember the kindness Zechariah's father Jehoiada had shown him but killed his son, who said as he lay dying, "May the LORD see this and call you to account."

23At the turn of the year,a the army of Aram marched against Joash; it invaded Judah and Jerusalem and killed all the leaders of the people. They sent all the plunder to their king in Damascus. 24Although the Aramean army had come with only a few men, the LORD delivered into their hands a much larger army. Because Judah had forsaken the LORD, the God of their fathers, judgment was executed on Joash. 25When the Arameans withdrew, they left Joash severely wounded. His officials conspired against him for murdering the son of Jehoiada the priest, and they killed him in his bed. So he died and was buried in the City of David, but not in the tombs of the kings. 26Those who conspired against him were Zabad,b son of Shimeath an Ammonite woman, and Jehozabad, son of Shimrithc a Moabite woman. 27The account of his sons, the many prophecies about him, and the record of the restoration of the temple of God are written in the annotations on the book of the kings. And Amaziah his son succeeded him as king.

?DID YOU KNOW?   24:24

What kind of king was Joash?

Joash was weak. As long as the priest Jehoiada lived, Joash did well. When the priest died, Joash listened to others and became very wicked.

Amaziah King of Judah

25 Amaziah was twenty-five years old when he became king, and he reigned in Jerusalem twenty-nine years. His mother's name was Jehoaddind; she was from Jerusalem. 2He did what was right in the eyes of the LORD, but not wholeheartedly. 3After the kingdom was firmly in his control, he executed the officials who had murdered his father the king. 4Yet he did not put their sons to death, but acted in accordance with what is written in the Law, in the Book of Moses, where the LORD commanded: "Fathers shall not be put to death for their children, nor children put to death for their fathers; each is to die for his own sins."e

5Amaziah called the people of Judah together and assigned them according to their families to commanders of thousands and commanders of hundreds for all Judah and Benjamin. He then mustered those twenty years old or more and found that there were three hundred thousand men ready for military service, able to handle the spear and shield. 6He also hired a hundred thousand fight-

a23 Probably in the spring   b26 A variant of Jozabad   c26 A variant of Shomer
d1 Hebrew Jehoaddan, a variant of Jehoaddin   e4 Deut. 24:16

ing men from Israel for a hundred talents[a] of silver.

[7]But a man of God came to him and said, "O king, these troops from Israel must not march with you, for the LORD is not with Israel—not with any of the people of Ephraim. [8]Even if you go and fight courageously in battle, God will overthrow you before the enemy, for God has the power to help or to overthrow."

[9]Amaziah asked the man of God, "But what about the hundred talents I paid for these Israelite troops?"

The man of God replied, "The LORD can give you much more than that."

[10]So Amaziah dismissed the troops who had come to him from Ephraim and sent them home. They were furious with Judah and left for home in a great rage.

[11]Amaziah then marshaled his strength and led his army to the Valley of Salt, where he killed ten thousand men of Seir. [12]The army of Judah also captured ten thousand men alive, took them to the top of a cliff and threw them down so that all were dashed to pieces.

[13]Meanwhile the troops that Amaziah had sent back and had not allowed to take part in the war raided Judean towns from Samaria to Beth Horon. They killed three thousand people and carried off great quantities of plunder.

[14]When Amaziah returned from slaughtering the Edomites, he brought back the gods of the people of Seir. He set them up as his own gods, bowed down to them and burned sacrifices to them. [15]The anger of the LORD burned against Amaziah, and he sent a prophet to him, who said, "Why do you consult this people's gods, which could not save their own people from your hand?"

[16]While he was still speaking, the king said to him, "Have we appointed you an adviser to the king? Stop! Why be struck down?"

So the prophet stopped but said, "I know that God has determined to destroy you, because you have done this and have not listened to my counsel."

[17]After Amaziah king of Judah consulted his advisers, he sent this challenge to Jehoash[b] son of Jehoahaz, the son of Jehu, king of Israel: "Come, meet me face to face."

[18]But Jehoash king of Israel replied to Amaziah king of Judah: "A thistle in Lebanon sent a message to a cedar in Lebanon, 'Give your daughter to my son in marriage.' Then a wild beast in Lebanon came along and trampled the thistle underfoot. [19]You say to yourself that you have defeated Edom, and now you are arrogant and proud. But stay at home! Why ask for trouble and cause your own downfall and that of Judah also?"

[20]Amaziah, however, would not listen, for God so worked that he might hand them over to ⌊Jehoash⌋, because they sought the gods of Edom. [21]So Jehoash king of Israel attacked. He and Amaziah king of Judah faced each other at Beth Shemesh in Judah. [22]Judah was routed by Israel, and every man fled to his home. [23]Jehoash king of Israel captured Amaziah king of Judah, the son of Joash, the son of Ahaziah,[c] at Beth Shemesh. Then Jehoash brought him to Jerusalem and broke down the wall of Jerusalem from the Ephraim Gate to the Corner Gate—a section about six hundred feet[d] long. [24]He took all the gold and silver and all the articles found in the temple of God that had been in the care of Obed-Edom, together with the palace treasures and the hostages, and returned to Samaria.

[25]Amaziah son of Joash king of Judah lived for fifteen years after the death of Jehoash son of Jehoahaz king of Israel. [26]As for the other events of Amaziah's reign, from beginning to end, are they not written

---

[a]6 That is, about 3 3/4 tons (about 3.4 metric tons); also in verse 9   [b]17 Hebrew *Joash*, a variant of *Jehoash*; also in verses 18, 21, 23 and 25   [c]23 Hebrew *Jehoahaz*, a variant of *Ahaziah*   [d]23 Hebrew *four hundred cubits* (about 180 meters)

in the book of the kings of Judah and Israel? [27]From the time that Amaziah turned away from following the LORD, they conspired against him in Jerusalem and he fled to Lachish, but they sent men after him to Lachish and killed him there. [28]He was brought back by horse and was buried with his fathers in the City of Judah.

Uzziah King of Judah

26 Then all the people of Judah took Uzziah,[a] who was sixteen years old, and made him king in place of his father Amaziah. [2]He was the one who rebuilt Elath and restored it to Judah after Amaziah rested with his fathers.

[3]Uzziah was sixteen years old when he became king, and he reigned in Jerusalem fifty-two years. His mother's name was Jecoliah; she was from Jerusalem. [4]He did what was right in the eyes of the LORD, just as his father Amaziah had done. [5]He sought God during the days of Zechariah, who instructed him in the fear[b] of God. As long as he sought the LORD, God gave him success.

[6]He went to war against the Philistines and broke down the walls of Gath, Jabneh and Ashdod. He then rebuilt towns near Ashdod and elsewhere among the Philistines. [7]God helped him against the Philistines and against the Arabs who lived in Gur Baal and against the Meunites. [8]The Ammonites brought tribute to Uzziah, and his fame spread as far as the border of Egypt, because he had become very powerful.

[9]Uzziah built towers in Jerusalem at the Corner Gate, at the Valley Gate and at the angle of the wall, and he fortified them. [10]He also built towers in the desert and dug many cisterns, because he had much livestock in the foothills and in the plain. He had people working his fields and vineyards in the hills and in the fertile lands, for he loved the soil.

[11]Uzziah had a well-trained army, ready to go out by divisions according to their numbers as mustered by Jeiel the secretary and Maaseiah the officer under the direction of Hananiah, one of the royal officials. [12]The total number of family leaders over the fighting men was 2,600. [13]Under their command was an army of 307,500 men trained for war, a powerful force to support the king against his enemies. [14]Uzziah provided shields, spears, helmets, coats of armor, bows and slingstones for the entire army. [15]In Jerusalem he made machines designed by skillful men for use on the towers and on the corner defenses to shoot arrows and hurl large stones. His fame spread far and wide, for he was greatly helped until he became powerful.

[16]But after Uzziah became powerful, his pride led to his downfall. He was unfaithful to the LORD his God, and entered the temple of the LORD to burn incense on the altar of incense. [17]Azariah the priest with eighty other courageous priests of the LORD followed him in. [18]They confronted him and said, "It is not right for you, Uzziah, to burn incense to the LORD. That is for the priests, the descendants of Aaron, who have been consecrated to burn incense. Leave the sanctuary, for you have been unfaithful; and you will not be honored by the LORD God." [19]Uzziah, who had a censer in his hand ready to burn incense, became angry. While he was raging at the priests in their presence before the incense altar in the LORD's temple, leprosy[c] broke out on his forehead. [20]When Azariah the chief priest and all the other priests looked at him, they saw that he had leprosy on his forehead, so they hurried him out. Indeed, he himself was eager to leave, because the LORD had afflicted him. [21]King Uzziah had leprosy until

---

[a]1 Also called *Azariah*   [b]5 Many Hebrew manuscripts, Septuagint and Syriac; other Hebrew manuscripts *vision*   [c]19 The Hebrew word was used for various diseases affecting the skin—not necessarily leprosy; also in verses 20, 21 and 23.

the day he died. He lived in a separate house[a] —leprous, and excluded from the temple of the LORD. Jotham his son had charge of the palace and governed the people of the land.

²²The other events of Uzziah's reign, from beginning to end, are recorded by the prophet Isaiah son of Amoz. ²³Uzziah rested with his fathers and was buried near them in a field for burial that belonged to the kings, for people said, "He had leprosy." And Jotham his son succeeded him as king.

? **ᗡIᗡ YOU KᑎOW?**   26:16

What was the great sin of Uzziah?

Uzziah's sin was pride. He was a powerful king as long as he trusted God. But when Uzziah became famous and powerful, he stopped trusting God. God then made him sick with the awful disease of leprosy.

Jotham King of Judah

27 Jotham was twenty-five years old when he became king, and he reigned in Jerusalem sixteen years. His mother's name was Jerusha daughter of Zadok. ²He did what was right in the eyes of the LORD, just as his father Uzziah had done, but unlike him he did not enter the temple of the LORD. The people, however, continued their corrupt practices. ³Jotham rebuilt the Upper Gate of the temple of the LORD and did extensive work on the wall at the hill of Ophel. ⁴He built towns in the Judean hills and forts and towers in the wooded areas.

⁵Jotham made war on the king of the Ammonites and conquered them. That year the Ammonites paid him a hundred talents[b] of silver, ten thousand cors[c] of wheat and ten thousand

cors of barley. The Ammonites brought him the same amount also in the second and third years.

⁶Jotham grew powerful because he walked steadfastly before the LORD his God.

ᗯ **ORᗡS TO REMEMBER**

27:6 Jotham grew powerful because he walked steadfastly before the LORD his God.

---

⁷The other events in Jotham's reign, including all his wars and the other things he did, are written in the book of the kings of Israel and Judah. ⁸He was twenty-five years old when he became king, and he reigned in Jerusalem sixteen years. ⁹Jotham rested with his fathers and was buried in the City of David. And Ahaz his son succeeded him as king.

Ahaz King of Judah

28 Ahaz was twenty years old when he became king, and he reigned in Jerusalem sixteen years. Unlike David his father, he did not do what was right in the eyes of the LORD. ²He walked in the ways of the kings of Israel and also made cast idols for worshiping the Baals. ³He burned sacrifices in the Valley of Ben Hinnom and sacrificed his sons in the fire, following the detestable ways of the nations the LORD had driven out before the Israelites. ⁴He offered sacrifices and burned incense at the high places, on the hilltops and under every spreading tree.

⁵Therefore the LORD his God handed him over to the king of Aram. The Arameans defeated him and took many of his people as prisoners and brought them to Damascus.

He was also given into the hands of the king of Israel, who inflicted heavy casualties on him. ⁶In one day

---

a21 Or in a house where he was relieved of responsibilities   *b5 That is, about 3 3/4 tons (about 3.4 metric tons)*   *c5 That is, probably about 62,000 bushels (about 2,200 kiloliters)*

Pekah son of Remaliah killed a hundred and twenty thousand soldiers in Judah—because Judah had forsaken the LORD, the God of their fathers. [7]Zicri, an Ephraimite warrior, killed Maaseiah the king's son, Azrikam the officer in charge of the palace, and Elkanah, second to the king. [8]The Israelites took captive from their kinsmen two hundred thousand wives, sons and daughters. They also took a great deal of plunder, which they carried back to Samaria.

[9]But a prophet of the LORD named Oded was there, and he went out to meet the army when it returned to Samaria. He said to them, "Because the LORD, the God of your fathers, was angry with Judah, he gave them into your hand. But you have slaughtered them in a rage that reaches to heaven. [10]And now you intend to make the men and women of Judah and Jerusalem your slaves. But aren't you also guilty of sins against the LORD your God? [11]Now listen to me! Send back your fellow countrymen you have taken as prisoners, for the LORD's fierce anger rests on you."

[12]Then some of the leaders in Ephraim—Azariah son of Jehohanan, Berekiah son of Meshillemoth, Jehizkiah son of Shallum, and Amasa son of Hadlai—confronted those who were arriving from the war. [13]"You must not bring those prisoners here," they said, "or we will be guilty before the LORD. Do you intend to add to our sin and guilt? For our guilt is already great, and his fierce anger rests on Israel."

[14]So the soldiers gave up the prisoners and plunder in the presence of the officials and all the assembly. [15]The men designated by name took the prisoners, and from the plunder they clothed all who were naked. They provided them with clothes and sandals, food and drink, and healing balm. All those who were weak they put on donkeys. So they took them back to their fellow countrymen at Jericho, the City of Palms, and returned to Samaria.

[16]At that time King Ahaz sent to the king[a] of Assyria for help. [17]The Edomites had again come and attacked Judah and carried away prisoners, [18]while the Philistines had raided towns in the foothills and in the Negev of Judah. They captured and occupied Beth Shemesh, Aijalon and Gederoth, as well as Soco, Timnah and Gimzo, with their surrounding villages. [19]The LORD had humbled Judah because of Ahaz king of Israel,[b] for he had promoted wickedness in Judah and had been most unfaithful to the LORD. [20]Tiglath-Pileser[c] king of Assyria came to him, but he gave him trouble instead of help. [21]Ahaz took some of the things from the temple of the LORD and from the royal palace and from the princes and presented them to the king of Assyria, but that did not help him.

[22]In his time of trouble King Ahaz became even more unfaithful to the LORD. [23]He offered sacrifices to the gods of Damascus, who had defeated him; for he thought, "Since the gods of the kings of Aram have helped them, I will sacrifice to them so they will help me." But they were his downfall and the downfall of all Israel.

[24]Ahaz gathered together the furnishings from the temple of God and took them away.[d] He shut the doors of the LORD's temple and set up altars at every street corner in Jerusalem. [25]In every town in Judah he built high places to burn sacrifices to other gods and provoked the LORD, the God of his fathers, to anger.

[26]The other events of his reign and all his ways, from beginning to end, are written in the book of the kings of Judah and Israel. [27]Ahaz rested with his fathers and was buried in the city of Jerusalem, but he was not placed in the tombs of the kings of Israel.

---

a16 One Hebrew manuscript, Septuagint and Vulgate (see also 2 Kings 16:7); most Hebrew manuscripts *kings*　　b19 That is, Judah, as frequently in 2 Chronicles　　c20 Hebrew *Tilgath-Pilneser*, a variant of *Tiglath-Pileser*　　d24 Or *and cut them up*

And Hezekiah his son succeeded him as king.

Hezekiah Purifies the Temple

29 Hezekiah was twenty-five years old when he became king, and he reigned in Jerusalem twenty-nine years. His mother's name was Abijah daughter of Zechariah. ²He did what was right in the eyes of the LORD, just as his father David had done.

³In the first month of the first year of his reign, he opened the doors of the temple of the LORD and repaired them. ⁴He brought in the priests and the Levites, assembled them in the square on the east side ⁵and said: "Listen to me, Levites! Consecrate yourselves now and consecrate the temple of the LORD, the God of your fathers. Remove all defilement from the sanctuary. ⁶Our fathers were unfaithful; they did evil in the eyes of the LORD our God and forsook him. They turned their faces away from the LORD's dwelling place and turned their backs on him. ⁷They also shut the doors of the portico and put out the lamps. They did not burn incense or present any burnt offerings at the sanctuary to the God of Israel. ⁸Therefore, the anger of the LORD has fallen on Judah and Jerusalem; he has made them an object of dread and horror and scorn, as you can see with your own eyes. ⁹This is why our fathers have fallen by the sword and why our sons and daughters and our wives are in captivity. ¹⁰Now I intend to make a covenant with the LORD, the God of Israel, so that his fierce anger will turn away from us. ¹¹My sons, do not be negligent now, for the LORD has chosen you to stand before him and serve him, to minister before him and to burn incense."

¹²Then these Levites set to work:
from the Kohathites,
    Mahath son of Amasai and
    Joel son of Azariah;
from the Merarites,
    Kish son of Abdi and Azariah
    son of Jehallelel;
from the Gershonites,

Joah son of Zimmah and Eden
    son of Joah;
¹³from the descendants of Elizaphan,
    Shimri and Jeiel;
from the descendants of Asaph,
    Zechariah and Mattaniah;
¹⁴from the descendants of Heman,
    Jehiel and Shimei;
from the descendants of Jeduthun,
    Shemaiah and Uzziel.

¹⁵When they had assembled their brothers and consecrated themselves, they went in to purify the temple of the LORD, as the king had ordered, following the word of the LORD. ¹⁶The priests went into the sanctuary of the LORD to purify it. They brought out to the courtyard of the LORD's temple everything unclean that they found in the temple of the LORD. The Levites took it and carried it out to the Kidron Valley. ¹⁷They began the consecration on the first day of the first month, and by the eighth day of the month they reached the portico of the LORD. For eight more days they consecrated the temple of the LORD itself, finishing on the sixteenth day of the first month.

¹⁸Then they went in to King Hezekiah and reported: "We have purified the entire temple of the LORD, the altar of burnt offering with all its utensils, and the table for setting out the consecrated bread, with all its articles. ¹⁹We have prepared and consecrated all the articles that King Ahaz removed in his unfaithfulness while he was king. They are now in front of the LORD's altar."

²⁰Early the next morning King Hezekiah gathered the city officials together and went up to the temple of the LORD. ²¹They brought seven bulls, seven rams, seven male lambs and seven male goats as a sin offering for the kingdom, for the sanctuary and for Judah. The king commanded the priests, the descendants of Aaron, to offer these on the altar of the LORD. ²²So they slaughtered the bulls, and the priests took the blood and sprinkled it on the altar; next they slaugh-

tered the rams and sprinkled their blood on the altar; then they slaughtered the lambs and sprinkled their blood on the altar. ²³The goats for the sin offering were brought before the king and the assembly, and they laid their hands on them. ²⁴The priests then slaughtered the goats and presented their blood on the altar for a sin offering to atone for all Israel, because the king had ordered the burnt offering and the sin offering for all Israel.

²⁵He stationed the Levites in the temple of the Lᴏʀᴅ with cymbals, harps and lyres in the way prescribed by David and Gad the king's seer and Nathan the prophet; this was commanded by the Lᴏʀᴅ through his prophets. ²⁶So the Levites stood ready with David's instruments, and the priests with their trumpets.

²⁷Hezekiah gave the order to sacrifice the burnt offering on the altar. As the offering began, singing to the Lᴏʀᴅ began also, accompanied by trumpets and the instruments of David king of Israel. ²⁸The whole assembly bowed in worship, while the singers sang and the trumpeters played. All this continued until the sacrifice of the burnt offering was completed.

²⁹When the offerings were finished, the king and everyone present with him knelt down and worshiped. ³⁰King Hezekiah and his officials ordered the Levites to praise the Lᴏʀᴅ with the words of David and of Asaph the seer. So they sang praises with gladness and bowed their heads and worshiped.

³¹Then Hezekiah said, "You have now dedicated yourselves to the Lᴏʀᴅ. Come and bring sacrifices and thank offerings to the temple of the Lᴏʀᴅ." So the assembly brought sacrifices and thank offerings, and all whose hearts were willing brought burnt offerings.

³²The number of burnt offerings the assembly brought was seventy bulls, a hundred rams and two hun-

dred male lambs—all of them for burnt offerings to the Lᴏʀᴅ. ³³The animals consecrated as sacrifices amounted to six hundred bulls and three thousand sheep and goats. ³⁴The priests, however, were too few to skin all the burnt offerings; so their kinsmen the Levites helped them until the task was finished and until other priests had been consecrated, for the Levites had been more conscientious in consecrating themselves than the priests had been. ³⁵There were burnt offerings in abundance, together with the fat of the fellowship offerings*a* and the drink offerings that accompanied the burnt offerings.

So the service of the temple of the Lᴏʀᴅ was reestablished. ³⁶Hezekiah and all the people rejoiced at what God had brought about for his people, because it was done so quickly.

❓DID YOU KNOW?   29:36

What shows that Hezekiah was a godly king?

Hezekiah showed his faithfulness to God in many ways: He reopened God's temple, and he promised to obey God. He celebrated the Passover. He smashed the places where people worshiped pagan gods. In 2 Chronicles 29–31, you can read all about the good things Hezekiah did.

Hezekiah Celebrates the Passover

30 Hezekiah sent word to all Israel and Judah and also wrote letters to Ephraim and Manasseh, inviting them to come to the temple of the Lᴏʀᴅ in Jerusalem and celebrate the Passover to the Lᴏʀᴅ, the God of Israel. ²The king and his officials and the whole assembly in Jerusalem decided to celebrate the

---

a35 Traditionally *peace offerings*

Passover in the second month. [3]They had not been able to celebrate it at the regular time because not enough priests had consecrated themselves and the people had not assembled in Jerusalem. [4]The plan seemed right both to the king and to the whole assembly. [5]They decided to send a proclamation throughout Israel, from Beersheba to Dan, calling the people to come to Jerusalem and celebrate the Passover to the LORD, the God of Israel. It had not been celebrated in large numbers according to what was written.

[6]At the king's command, couriers went throughout Israel and Judah with letters from the king and from his officials, which read:

"People of Israel, return to the LORD, the God of Abraham, Isaac and Israel, that he may return to you who are left, who have escaped from the hand of the kings of Assyria. [7]Do not be like your fathers and brothers, who were unfaithful to the LORD, the God of their fathers, so that he made them an object of horror, as you see. [8]Do not be stiff-necked, as your fathers were; submit to the LORD. Come to the sanctuary, which he has consecrated forever. Serve the LORD your God, so that his fierce anger will turn away from you. [9]If you return to the LORD, then your brothers and your children will be shown compassion by their captors and will come back to this land, for the LORD your God is gracious and compassionate. He will not turn his face from you if you return to him."

[10]The couriers went from town to town in Ephraim and Manasseh, as far as Zebulun, but the people scorned and ridiculed them. [11]Nevertheless, some men of Asher, Manasseh and Zebulun humbled themselves and went to Jerusalem. [12]Also in Judah the hand of God was on the people to give them unity of mind to carry out what the king and his officials had ordered, following the word of the LORD.

[13]A very large crowd of people assembled in Jerusalem to celebrate the Feast of Unleavened Bread in the second month. [14]They removed the altars in Jerusalem and cleared away the incense altars and threw them into the Kidron Valley.

[15]They slaughtered the Passover lamb on the fourteenth day of the second month. The priests and the Levites were ashamed and consecrated themselves and brought burnt offerings to the temple of the LORD. [16]Then they took up their regular positions as prescribed in the Law of Moses the man of God. The priests sprinkled the blood handed to them by the Levites. [17]Since many in the crowd had not consecrated themselves, the Levites had to kill the Passover lambs for all those who were not ceremonially clean and could not consecrate their lambs to the LORD. [18]Although most of the many people who came from Ephraim, Manasseh, Issachar and Zebulun had not purified themselves, yet they ate the Passover, contrary to what was written. But Hezekiah prayed for them, saying, "May the LORD, who is good, pardon everyone [19]who sets his heart on seeking God —the LORD, the God of his fathers —even if he is not clean according to the rules of the sanctuary." [20]And the LORD heard Hezekiah and healed the people.

[21]The Israelites who were present in Jerusalem celebrated the Feast of Unleavened Bread for seven days with great rejoicing, while the Levites and priests sang to the LORD every day, accompanied by the LORD's instruments of praise. [a]

[22]Hezekiah spoke encouragingly to all the Levites, who showed good understanding of the service of the LORD. For the seven days they ate their assigned portion and offered fel-

---

[a]21 Or *priests praised the LORD every day with resounding instruments belonging to the LORD*

lowship offerings[a] and praised the LORD, the God of their fathers.

23The whole assembly then agreed to celebrate the festival seven more days; so for another seven days they celebrated joyfully. 24Hezekiah king of Judah provided a thousand bulls and seven thousand sheep and goats for the assembly, and the officials provided them with a thousand bulls and ten thousand sheep and goats. A great number of priests consecrated themselves. 25The entire assembly of Judah rejoiced, along with the priests and Levites and all who had assembled from Israel, including the aliens who had come from Israel and those who lived in Judah. 26There was great joy in Jerusalem, for since the days of Solomon son of David king of Israel there had been nothing like this in Jerusalem. 27The priests and the Levites stood to bless the people, and God heard them, for their prayer reached heaven, his holy dwelling place.

31 When all this had ended, the Israelites who were there went out to the towns of Judah, smashed the sacred stones and cut down the Asherah poles. They destroyed the high places and the altars throughout Judah and Benjamin and in Ephraim and Manasseh. After they had destroyed all of them, the Israelites returned to their own towns and to their own property.

Contributions for Worship

2Hezekiah assigned the priests and Levites to divisions—each of them according to their duties as priests or Levites—to offer burnt offerings and fellowship offerings,[a] to minister, to give thanks and to sing praises at the gates of the LORD's dwelling. 3The king contributed from his own possessions for the morning and evening burnt offerings and for the burnt offerings on the Sabbaths, New Moons and appointed feasts as written in the Law of the LORD. 4He ordered the people living in Jerusalem to give the

portion due the priests and Levites so they could devote themselves to the Law of the LORD. 5As soon as the order went out, the Israelites generously gave the firstfruits of their grain, new wine, oil and honey and all that the fields produced. They brought a great amount, a tithe of everything. 6The men of Israel and Judah who lived in the towns of Judah also brought a tithe of their herds and flocks and a tithe of the holy things dedicated to the LORD their God, and they piled them in heaps. 7They began doing this in the third month and finished in the seventh month. 8When Hezekiah and his officials came and saw the heaps, they praised the LORD and blessed his people Israel.

9Hezekiah asked the priests and Levites about the heaps; 10and Azariah the chief priest, from the family of Zadok, answered, "Since the people began to bring their contributions to the temple of the LORD, we have had enough to eat and plenty to spare, because the LORD has blessed his people, and this great amount is left over."

11Hezekiah gave orders to prepare storerooms in the temple of the LORD, and this was done. 12Then they faithfully brought in the contributions, tithes and dedicated gifts. Conaniah, a Levite, was in charge of these things, and his brother Shimei was next in rank. 13Jehiel, Azaziah, Nahath, Asahel, Jerimoth, Jozabad, Eliel, Ismakiah, Mahath and Benaiah were supervisors under Conaniah and Shimei his brother, by appointment of King Hezekiah and Azariah the official in charge of the temple of God.

14Kore son of Imnah the Levite, keeper of the East Gate, was in charge of the freewill offerings given to God, distributing the contributions made to the LORD and also the consecrated gifts. 15Eden, Miniamin, Jeshua, Shemaiah, Amariah and Shecaniah assisted him faithfully in the towns of the priests, distributing to their fellow priests according to their divisions, old and young alike.

¹⁶In addition, they distributed to the males three years old or more whose names were in the genealogical records—all who would enter the temple of the LORD to perform the daily duties of their various tasks, according to their responsibilities and their divisions. ¹⁷And they distributed to the priests enrolled by their families in the genealogical records and likewise to the Levites twenty years old or more, according to their responsibilities and their divisions. ¹⁸They included all the little ones, the wives, and the sons and daughters of the whole community listed in these genealogical records. For they were faithful in consecrating themselves.

¹⁹As for the priests, the descendants of Aaron, who lived on the farm lands around their towns or in any other towns, men were designated by name to distribute portions to every male among them and to all who were recorded in the genealogies of the Levites.

²⁰This is what Hezekiah did throughout Judah, doing what was good and right and faithful before the LORD his God. ²¹In everything that he undertook in the service of God's temple and in obedience to the law and the commands, he sought his God and worked wholeheartedly. And so he prospered.

Sennacherib Threatens Jerusalem

32 After all that Hezekiah had so faithfully done, Sennacherib king of Assyria came and invaded Judah. He laid siege to the fortified cities, thinking to conquer them for himself. ²When Hezekiah saw that Sennacherib had come and that he intended to make war on Jerusalem, ³he consulted with his officials and military staff about blocking off the water from the springs outside the city, and they helped him. ⁴A large force of men assembled, and they blocked all the springs and the stream that flowed through the land. "Why should the kings*a* of Assyria come and find plenty of water?" they said. ⁵Then he worked hard repairing all the broken sections of the wall and building towers on it. He built another wall outside that one and reinforced the supporting terraces*b* of the City of David. He also made large numbers of weapons and shields.

⁶He appointed military officers over the people and assembled them before him in the square at the city gate and encouraged them with these words: ⁷"Be strong and courageous. Do not be afraid or discouraged because of the king of Assyria and the vast army with him, for there is a greater power with us than with him. ⁸With him is only the arm of flesh, but with us is the LORD our God to help us and to fight our battles." And the people gained confidence from what Hezekiah the king of Judah said.

⁹Later, when Sennacherib king of Assyria and all his forces were laying siege to Lachish, he sent his officers to Jerusalem with this message for Hezekiah king of Judah and for all the people of Judah who were there:

¹⁰"This is what Sennacherib king of Assyria says: On what are you basing your confidence, that you remain in Jerusalem under siege? ¹¹When Hezekiah says, 'The LORD our God will save us from the hand of the king of Assyria,' he is misleading you, to let you die of hunger and thirst. ¹²Did not Hezekiah himself remove this god's high places and altars, saying to Judah and Jerusalem, 'You must worship before one altar and burn sacrifices on it'?

¹³"Do you not know what I and my fathers have done to all the peoples of the other lands? Were

a4 Hebrew; Septuagint and Syriac *king*   *b5* Or *the Millo*

the gods of those nations ever able to deliver their land from my hand? ¹⁴Who of all the gods of these nations that my fathers destroyed has been able to save his people from me? How then can your god deliver you from my hand? ¹⁵Now do not let Hezekiah deceive you and mislead you like this. Do not believe him, for no god of any nation or kingdom has been able to deliver his people from my hand or the hand of my fathers. How much less will your god deliver you from my hand!"

¹⁶Sennacherib's officers spoke further against the LORD God and against his servant Hezekiah. ¹⁷The king also wrote letters insulting the LORD, the God of Israel, and saying this against him: "Just as the gods of the peoples of the other lands did not rescue their people from my hand, so the god of Hezekiah will not rescue his people from my hand." ¹⁸Then they called out in Hebrew to the people of Jerusalem who were on the wall, to terrify them and make them afraid in order to capture the city. ¹⁹They spoke about the God of Jerusalem as they did about the gods of the other peoples of the world—the work of men's hands.

²⁰King Hezekiah and the prophet

Isaiah son of Amoz cried out in prayer to heaven about this. ²¹And the LORD sent an angel, who annihilated all the fighting men and the leaders and officers in the camp of the Assyrian king. So he withdrew to his own land in disgrace. And when he went into the temple of his god, some of his sons cut him down with the sword.

²²So the LORD saved Hezekiah and the people of Jerusalem from the hand of Sennacherib king of Assyria and from the hand of all others. He took care of them*a* on every side. ²³Many brought offerings to Jerusalem for the LORD and valuable gifts for Hezekiah king of Judah. From then on he was highly regarded by all the nations.

Hezekiah's Pride, Success and Death

²⁴In those days Hezekiah became ill and was at the point of death. He prayed to the LORD, who answered him and gave him a miraculous sign. ²⁵But Hezekiah's heart was proud and he did not respond to the kindness shown him; therefore the LORD's wrath was on him and on Judah and Jerusalem. ²⁶Then Hezekiah repented of the pride of his heart, as did the people of Jerusalem; therefore the

a22 Hebrew; Septuagint and Vulgate He gave them rest

LET'S LIVE IT!   2 Chronicles 32:1–23

WHEN OTHERS DON'T BELIEVE ➠ Not everyone believes in God and Jesus. Some don't believe God created the world and people. Some don't believe in the Bible's rules of right and wrong. Some people think there isn't any God. They say people who believe in God are foolish.

Read this story about an Assyrian army general who laughed at the idea that God could save the Jews from the Assyrian army. It was hard for Hezekiah and the Jews to be laughed at. But who turned out to be right?

If anyone makes fun of you because you believe in God, ask a grown-up these questions. Why do people laugh at us for believing in God? Have you ever been laughed at for something you believe? How did you feel? What is the best thing to do when someone laughs at our faith in God? When will the people who make fun of God stop laughing?

LORD's wrath did not come upon them during the days of Hezekiah.

27Hezekiah had very great riches and honor, and he made treasuries for his silver and gold and for his precious stones, spices, shields and all kinds of valuables. 28He also made buildings to store the harvest of grain, new wine and oil; and he made stalls for various kinds of cattle, and pens for the flocks. 29He built villages and acquired great numbers of flocks and herds, for God had given him very great riches.

30It was Hezekiah who blocked the upper outlet of the Gihon spring and channeled the water down to the west side of the City of David. He succeeded in everything he undertook. 31But when envoys were sent by the rulers of Babylon to ask him about the miraculous sign that had occurred in the land, God left him to test him and to know everything that was in his heart.

32The other events of Hezekiah's reign and his acts of devotion are written in the vision of the prophet Isaiah son of Amoz in the book of the kings of Judah and Israel. 33Hezekiah rested with his fathers and was buried on the hill where the tombs of David's descendants are. All Judah and the people of Jerusalem honored him when he died. And Manasseh his son succeeded him as king.

Manasseh King of Judah

33 Manasseh was twelve years old when he became king, and he reigned in Jerusalem fifty-five years. 2He did evil in the eyes of the LORD, following the detestable practices of the nations the LORD had driven out before the Israelites. 3He rebuilt the high places his father Hezekiah had demolished; he also erected altars to the Baals and made Asherah poles. He bowed down to all the starry hosts and worshiped them. 4He built altars in the temple of the LORD, of which the LORD had said, "My Name will remain in Jerusalem

forever." 5In both courts of the temple of the LORD, he built altars to all the starry hosts. 6He sacrificed his sons in*a* the fire in the Valley of Ben Hinnom, practiced sorcery, divination and witchcraft, and consulted mediums and spiritists. He did much evil in the eyes of the LORD, provoking him to anger.

7He took the carved image he had made and put it in God's temple, of which God had said to David and to his son Solomon, "In this temple and in Jerusalem, which I have chosen out of all the tribes of Israel, I will put my Name forever. 8I will not again make the feet of the Israelites leave the land I assigned to your forefathers, if only they will be careful to do everything I commanded them concerning all the laws, decrees and ordinances given through Moses." 9But Manasseh led Judah and the people of Jerusalem astray, so that they did more evil than the nations the LORD had destroyed before the Israelites.

10The LORD spoke to Manasseh and his people, but they paid no attention. 11So the LORD brought against them the army commanders of the king of Assyria, who took Manasseh prisoner, put a hook in his nose, bound him with bronze shackles and took him to Babylon. 12In his distress he sought the favor of the LORD his God and humbled himself greatly before the God of his fathers. 13And when he prayed to him, the LORD was moved by his entreaty and listened to his plea; so he brought him back to Jerusalem and to his kingdom. Then Manasseh knew that the LORD is God.

14Afterward he rebuilt the outer wall of the City of David, west of the Gihon spring in the valley, as far as the entrance of the Fish Gate and encircling the hill of Ophel; he also made it much higher. He stationed military commanders in all the fortified cities in Judah.

15He got rid of the foreign gods and removed the image from the temple of the LORD, as well as all the altars

a6 Or He made his sons pass through

he had built on the temple hill and in Jerusalem; and he threw them out of the city. ¹⁶Then he restored the altar of the LORD and sacrificed fellowship offerings*a* and thank offerings on it, and told Judah to serve the LORD, the God of Israel. ¹⁷The people, however, continued to sacrifice at the high places, but only to the LORD their God.

❓DID YOU KNOW?   33:12

Could an evil king change?

King Manasseh was very evil, but when he was captured and taken to Babylon, he admitted he had done wrong and started praying to God. God heard him and gave him a chance to do right. You can read about it in 2 Chronicles 33:10–20.

---

¹⁸The other events of Manasseh's reign, including his prayer to his God and the words the seers spoke to him in the name of the LORD, the God of Israel, are written in the annals of the kings of Israel.*b* ¹⁹His prayer and how God was moved by his entreaty, as well as all his sins and unfaithfulness, and the sites where he built high places and set up Asherah poles and idols before he humbled himself—all are written in the records of the seers.*c* ²⁰Manasseh rested with his fathers and was buried in his palace. And Amon his son succeeded him as king.

Amon King of Judah

²¹Amon was twenty-two years old when he became king, and he reigned in Jerusalem two years. ²²He did evil in the eyes of the LORD, as his father Manasseh had done. Amon worshiped and offered sacrifices to all the idols Manasseh had made. ²³But unlike his father Manasseh, he did not

humble himself before the LORD; Amon increased his guilt.

²⁴Amon's officials conspired against him and assassinated him in his palace. ²⁵Then the people of the land killed all who had plotted against King Amon, and they made Josiah his son king in his place.

Josiah's Reforms

34 Josiah was eight years old when he became king, and he reigned in Jerusalem thirty-one years. ²He did what was right in the eyes of the LORD and walked in the ways of his father David, not turning aside to the right or to the left.

³In the eighth year of his reign, while he was still young, he began to seek the God of his father David. In his twelfth year he began to purge Judah and Jerusalem of high places, Asherah poles, carved idols and cast images. ⁴Under his direction the altars of the Baals were torn down; he cut to pieces the incense altars that were above them, and smashed the Asherah poles, the idols and the images. These he broke to pieces and scattered over the graves of those who had sacrificed to them. ⁵He burned the bones of the priests on their altars, and so he purged Judah and Jerusalem. ⁶In the towns of Manasseh, Ephraim and Simeon, as far as Naphtali, and in the ruins around them, ⁷he tore down the altars and the Asherah poles and crushed the idols to powder and cut to pieces all the incense altars throughout Israel. Then he went back to Jerusalem.

❓DID YOU KNOW?   34:1

Who was Josiah?

Josiah was one of the most godly kings of Judah. He was only eight years old when he became king.

---

a16 Traditionally *peace offerings*   *b18* That is, Judah, as frequently in 2 Chronicles   *c19* One Hebrew manuscript and Septuagint; most Hebrew manuscripts *of Hozai*

⁸In the eighteenth year of Josiah's reign, to purify the land and the temple, he sent Shaphan son of Azaliah and Maaseiah the ruler of the city, with Joah son of Joahaz, the recorder, to repair the temple of the LORD his God.

⁹They went to Hilkiah the high priest and gave him the money that had been brought into the temple of God, which the Levites who were the doorkeepers had collected from the people of Manasseh, Ephraim and the entire remnant of Israel and from all the people of Judah and Benjamin and the inhabitants of Jerusalem. ¹⁰Then they entrusted it to the men appointed to supervise the work on the LORD's temple. These men paid the workers who repaired and restored the temple. ¹¹They also gave money to the carpenters and builders to purchase dressed stone, and timber for joists and beams for the buildings that the kings of Judah had allowed to fall into ruin.

¹²The men did the work faithfully. Over them to direct them were Jahath and Obadiah, Levites descended from Merari, and Zechariah and Meshullam, descended from Kohath. The Levites—all who were skilled in playing musical instruments— ¹³had charge of the laborers and supervised all the workers from job to job. Some of the Levites were secretaries, scribes and doorkeepers.

The Book of the Law Found

¹⁴While they were bringing out the money that had been taken into the temple of the LORD, Hilkiah the priest found the Book of the Law of the LORD that had been given through Moses. ¹⁵Hilkiah said to Shaphan the secretary, "I have found the Book of the Law in the temple of the LORD." He gave it to Shaphan.

¹⁶Then Shaphan took the book to the king and reported to him: "Your officials are doing everything that has been committed to them. ¹⁷They have paid out the money that was in the temple of the LORD and have entrusted it to the supervisors and workers." ¹⁸Then Shaphan the secretary informed the king, "Hilkiah the priest has given me a book." And Shaphan read from it in the presence of the king.

¹⁹When the king heard the words of the Law, he tore his robes. ²⁰He gave these orders to Hilkiah, Ahikam son of Shaphan, Abdon son of Micah,ᵃ Shaphan the secretary and Asaiah the king's attendant: ²¹"Go and inquire of the LORD for me and for the remnant in Israel and Judah about what is written in this book that has been found. Great is the LORD's anger that is poured out on us because our fathers have not kept the word of the LORD; they have not acted in accordance with all that is written in this book."

²²Hilkiah and those the king had sent with himᵇ went to speak to the prophetess Huldah, who was the wife of Shallum son of Tokhath,ᶜ the son of Hasrah,ᵈ keeper of the wardrobe. She lived in Jerusalem, in the Second District.

²³She said to them, "This is what the LORD, the God of Israel, says: Tell the man who sent you to me, ²⁴'This is what the LORD says: I am going to bring disaster on this place and its people—all the curses written in the book that has been read in the presence of the king of Judah. ²⁵Because they have forsaken me and burned incense to other gods and provoked me to anger by all that their hands have made,ᵉ my anger will be poured out on this place and will not be quenched.' ²⁶Tell the king of Judah, who sent you to inquire of the LORD, 'This is what the LORD, the God of Israel, says concerning the words you heard: ²⁷Because your heart was responsive and you humbled yourself before God when you heard what he

ᵃ20 Also called Acbor son of Micaiah   ᵇ22 One Hebrew manuscript, Vulgate and Syriac; most Hebrew manuscripts do not have had sent with him.   ᶜ22 Also called Tikvah   ᵈ22 Also called Harhas   ᵉ25 Or by everything they have done

spoke against this place and its people, and because you humbled yourself before me and tore your robes and wept in my presence, I have heard you, declares the LORD. 28Now I will gather you to your fathers, and you will be buried in peace. Your eyes will not see all the disaster I am going to bring on this place and on those who live here.'"

So they took her answer back to the king.

29Then the king called together all the elders of Judah and Jerusalem. 30He went up to the temple of the LORD with the men of Judah, the people of Jerusalem, the priests and the Levites—all the people from the least to the greatest. He read in their hearing all the words of the Book of the Covenant, which had been found in the temple of the LORD. 31The king stood by his pillar and renewed the covenant in the presence of the LORD—to follow the LORD and keep his commands, regulations and decrees with all his heart and all his soul, and to obey the words of the covenant written in this book.

32Then he had everyone in Jerusalem and Benjamin pledge themselves to it; the people of Jerusalem did this in accordance with the covenant of God, the God of their fathers.

33Josiah removed all the detestable idols from all the territory belonging to the Israelites, and he had all who were present in Israel serve the LORD their God. As long as he lived, they did not fail to follow the LORD, the God of their fathers.

Josiah Celebrates the Passover

35 Josiah celebrated the Passover to the LORD in Jerusalem, and the Passover lamb was slaughtered on the fourteenth day of the first month. 2He appointed the priests to their duties and encouraged them in the service of the LORD's temple. 3He said to the Levites, who instructed all Israel and who had been consecrated to the LORD: "Put the sacred ark in the temple that Solomon son of David king of Israel

built. It is not to be carried about on your shoulders. Now serve the LORD your God and his people Israel. 4Prepare yourselves by families in your divisions, according to the directions written by David king of Israel and by his son Solomon.

5"Stand in the holy place with a group of Levites for each subdivision of the families of your fellow countrymen, the lay people. 6Slaughter the Passover lambs, consecrate yourselves and prepare ͺthe lambsͺ for your fellow countrymen, doing what the LORD commanded through Moses."

7Josiah provided for all the lay people who were there a total of thirty thousand sheep and goats for the Passover offerings, and also three thousand cattle—all from the king's own possessions.

8His officials also contributed voluntarily to the people and the priests and Levites. Hilkiah, Zechariah and Jehiel, the administrators of God's temple, gave the priests twenty-six hundred Passover offerings and three hundred cattle. 9Also Conaniah along with Shemaiah and Nethanel, his brothers, and Hashabiah, Jeiel and Jozabad, the leaders of the Levites, provided five thousand Passover offerings and five hundred head of cattle for the Levites.

10The service was arranged and the priests stood in their places with the Levites in their divisions as the king had ordered. 11The Passover lambs were slaughtered, and the priests sprinkled the blood handed to them, while the Levites skinned the animals. 12They set aside the burnt offerings to give them to the subdivisions of the families of the people to offer to the LORD, as is written in the Book of Moses. They did the same with the cattle. 13They roasted the Passover animals over the fire as prescribed, and boiled the holy offerings in pots, caldrons and pans and served them quickly to all the people. 14After this, they made preparations for themselves and for the priests, because the priests, the descendants of

Aaron, were sacrificing the burnt offerings and the fat portions until nightfall. So the Levites made preparations for themselves and for the Aaronic priests.

15The musicians, the descendants of Asaph, were in the places prescribed by David, Asaph, Heman and Jeduthun the king's seer. The gatekeepers at each gate did not need to leave their posts, because their fellow Levites made the preparations for them.

16So at that time the entire service of the LORD was carried out for the celebration of the Passover and the offering of burnt offerings on the altar of the LORD, as King Josiah had ordered. 17The Israelites who were present celebrated the Passover at that time and observed the Feast of Unleavened Bread for seven days. 18The Passover had not been observed like this in Israel since the days of the prophet Samuel; and none of the kings of Israel had ever celebrated such a Passover as did Josiah, with the priests, the Levites and all Judah and Israel who were there with the people of Jerusalem. 19This Passover was celebrated in the eighteenth year of Josiah's reign.

The Death of Josiah

20After all this, when Josiah had set the temple in order, Neco king of Egypt went up to fight at Carchemish on the Euphrates, and Josiah marched out to meet him in battle. 21But Neco sent messengers to him, saying, "What quarrel is there between you and me, O king of Judah? It is not you I am attacking at this time, but the house with which I am at war. God has told me to hurry; so stop opposing God, who is with me, or he will destroy you."

22Josiah, however, would not turn away from him, but disguised himself to engage him in battle. He would not listen to what Neco had

said at God's command but went to fight him on the plain of Megiddo.

23Archers shot King Josiah, and he told his officers, "Take me away; I am badly wounded." 24So they took him out of his chariot, put him in the other chariot he had and brought him to Jerusalem, where he died. He was buried in the tombs of his fathers, and all Judah and Jerusalem mourned for him.

25Jeremiah composed laments for Josiah, and to this day all the men and women singers commemorate Josiah in the laments. These became a tradition in Israel and are written in the Laments.

26The other events of Josiah's reign and his acts of devotion, according to what is written in the Law of the LORD— 27all the events, from beginning to end, are written in the book of the kings of Israel and Judah.

36 1And the people of the land took Jehoahaz son of Josiah and made him king in Jerusalem in place of his father.

Jehoahaz King of Judah

2Jehoahaz*a* was twenty-three years old when he became king, and he reigned in Jerusalem three months. 3The king of Egypt dethroned him in Jerusalem and imposed on Judah a levy of a hundred talents*b* of silver and a talent*c* of gold. 4The king of Egypt made Eliakim, a brother of Jehoahaz, king over Judah and Jerusalem and changed Eliakim's name to Jehoiakim. But Neco took Eliakim's brother Jehoahaz and carried him off to Egypt.

Jehoiakim King of Judah

5Jehoiakim was twenty-five years old when he became king, and he reigned in Jerusalem eleven years. He did evil in the eyes of the LORD his God. 6Nebuchadnezzar king of Babylon attacked him and bound him with bronze shackles to take him to Babylon. 7Nebuchadnezzar also took

---

a2 Hebrew *Joahaz*, a variant of *Jehoahaz*; also in verse 4   b3 That is, about 3 3/4 tons (about 3.4 metric tons)   c3 That is, about 75 pounds (about 34 kilograms)

to Babylon articles from the temple of the LORD and put them in his temple[a] there.

8The other events of Jehoiakim's reign, the detestable things he did and all that was found against him, are written in the book of the kings of Israel and Judah. And Jehoiachin his son succeeded him as king.

Jehoiachin King of Judah

9Jehoiachin was eighteen[b] years old when he became king, and he reigned in Jerusalem three months and ten days. He did evil in the eyes of the LORD. 10In the spring, King Nebuchadnezzar sent for him and brought him to Babylon, together with articles of value from the temple of the LORD, and he made Jehoiachin's uncle,[c] Zedekiah, king over Judah and Jerusalem.

Zedekiah King of Judah

11Zedekiah was twenty-one years old when he became king, and he reigned in Jerusalem eleven years. 12He did evil in the eyes of the LORD his God and did not humble himself before Jeremiah the prophet, who spoke the word of the LORD. 13He also rebelled against King Nebuchadnezzar, who had made him take an oath in God's name. He became stiff-necked and hardened his heart and would not turn to the LORD, the God of Israel. 14Furthermore, all the leaders of the priests and the people became more and more unfaithful, following all the detestable practices of the nations and defiling the temple of the LORD, which he had consecrated in Jerusalem.

The Fall of Jerusalem

15The LORD, the God of their fathers, sent word to them through his messengers again and again, because he had pity on his people and on his dwelling place. 16But they mocked God's messengers, despised his words and scoffed at his prophets until the wrath of the LORD was aroused against his people and there was no remedy. 17He brought up against them the king of the Babylonians,[d] who killed their young men with the sword in the sanctuary, and spared neither young man nor young woman, old man or aged. God handed all of them over to Nebuchadnezzar. 18He carried to Babylon all the articles from the temple of God, both large and small, and the treasures of the LORD's temple and the treasures of the king and his officials. 19They set fire to God's temple and broke down the wall of Jerusalem; they burned all the palaces and destroyed everything of value there.

20He carried into exile to Babylon the remnant, who escaped from the sword, and they became servants to him and his sons until the kingdom of Persia came to power. 21The land enjoyed its sabbath rests; all the time of its desolation it rested, until the seventy years were completed in fulfillment of the word of the LORD spoken by Jeremiah.

22In the first year of Cyrus king of Persia, in order to fulfill the word of the LORD spoken by Jeremiah, the LORD moved the heart of Cyrus king of Persia to make a proclamation throughout his realm and to put it in writing:

23"This is what Cyrus king of Persia says:

" 'The LORD, the God of heaven, has given me all the kingdoms of the earth and he has appointed me to build a temple for him at Jerusalem in Judah. Anyone of his people among you—may the LORD his God be with him, and let him go up.' "

---

a7 Or palace   b9 One Hebrew manuscript, some Septuagint manuscripts and Syriac (see also 2 Kings 24:8); most Hebrew manuscripts eight   c10 Hebrew brother, that is, relative (see 2 Kings 24:17)   d17 Or Chaldeans

EZRA

WHO WROTE THIS BOOK?	The author is unknown. Many people think Ezra wrote much of this book.
WHY WAS THIS BOOK WRITTEN?	Ezra shows how God kept his promise and brought the Jews back to their homeland.
WHAT HAPPENS IN THIS BOOK?	The Persian ruler Cyrus lets captive people return home. Some of the Jews in Babylon go back to Judah. They rebuild God's temple. Later Ezra comes from Babylon to teach God's law.
WHAT DO WE LEARN ABOUT GOD IN THIS BOOK?	God is faithful and keeps his promises.
WHO IS IMPORTANT IN THIS BOOK?	The important people in this book are King Cyrus and Ezra.
WHEN DID THIS HAPPEN?	The first Jews returned to Judah in 538 B.C. Ezra returned in 458 B.C.
WHERE DID THIS HAPPEN?	The events of this book happened in the little land of Judah and the city of Jerusalem.
WHAT ARE SOME OF THE STORIES IN THIS BOOK?	Exiled Jews return home. Ezra 1–2 Rebuilding the temple. Ezra 3–6 Ezra returns to Jerusalem. Ezra 7 Ezra confesses Judah's sins. Ezra 9 The people of Judah confess. Ezra 10

Cyrus Helps the Exiles to Return

1 In the first year of Cyrus king of Persia, in order to fulfill the word of the LORD spoken by Jeremiah, the LORD moved the heart of Cyrus king of Persia to make a proclamation throughout his realm and to put it in writing:

2"This is what Cyrus king of Persia says:

" 'The LORD, the God of heaven, has given me all the kingdoms of the earth and he has appointed me to build a temple for him at Jerusalem in Judah. 3Anyone of his people among you—may his God be with him, and let him go up to Jerusalem in Judah and build the temple of the LORD, the God of Israel, the God who is in Jerusalem. 4And the people of any place where survivors may now be living are to provide him with silver and gold, with goods and livestock, and with freewill offerings for the temple of God in Jerusalem.' "

5Then the family heads of Judah and Benjamin, and the priests and Levites—everyone whose heart God had moved—prepared to go up and build the house of the LORD in Jerusalem. 6All their neighbors assisted them with articles of silver and gold, with goods and livestock, and with valuable gifts, in addition to all the freewill offerings. 7Moreover, King Cyrus brought out the articles belonging to the temple of the LORD, which Nebuchadnezzar had carried away from Jerusalem and had placed in the temple of his god.*a* 8Cyrus king of Persia had them brought by Mithredath the treasurer, who counted them out to Sheshbazzar the prince of Judah.

9This was the inventory:

gold dishes	30
silver dishes	1,000
silver pans*b*	29
10gold bowls	30
matching silver bowls	410
other articles	1,000

11In all, there were 5,400 articles of gold and of silver. Sheshbazzar brought all these along when the exiles came up from Babylon to Jerusalem.

*a*7 Or *gods*   *b*9 The meaning of the Hebrew for this word is uncertain.

⬛ ET'S LIVE IT!   Ezra 1:1–11

LEAVING HOME ⮕ The Jews had been in Babylon for seventy years. Most had never seen the land their fathers and grandfathers came from. They had homes in Babylon. So most of the Jews decided to stay in Babylon and not move to Judah. Read Ezra 1:1–11. Why did some want to go back to Judah?

Pretend that you are in one of the Jewish families in Babylon. Your father asks, "Do you want to move to Judah?" What will you tell him? Write down reasons not to move. Write down reasons you should move.

If your family does move, here are some things to do to make it easier. Find out about the new area before you leave. What is special about the new area? Draw pictures of how you would like to decorate your new room. Get together for a moving party with your friends before you leave. Get addresses so you can write. Take a vacation on your drive to your new home. Look at maps to see what would be fun to do along the way. And, begin praying that you will find a special new friend when you get to your new home.

The List of the Exiles Who Returned

2 Now these are the people of the province who came up from the captivity of the exiles, whom Nebuchadnezzar king of Babylon had taken captive to Babylon (they returned to Jerusalem and Judah, each to his own town, [2]in company with Zerubbabel, Jeshua, Nehemiah, Seraiah, Reelaiah, Mordecai, Bilshan, Mispar, Bigvai, Rehum and Baanah):

The list of the men of the people of Israel:

[3]the descendants of Parosh	2,172
[4]of Shephatiah	372
[5]of Arah	775
[6]of Pahath-Moab (through the line of Jeshua and Joab)	2,812
[7]of Elam	1,254
[8]of Zattu	945
[9]of Zaccai	760
[10]of Bani	642
[11]of Bebai	623
[12]of Azgad	1,222
[13]of Adonikam	666
[14]of Bigvai	2,056
[15]of Adin	454
[16]of Ater (through Hezekiah)	98
[17]of Bezai	323
[18]of Jorah	112
[19]of Hashum	223
[20]of Gibbar	95
[21]the men of Bethlehem	123
[22]of Netophah	56
[23]of Anathoth	128
[24]of Azmaveth	42
[25]of Kiriath Jearim,[a] Kephirah and Beeroth	743
[26]of Ramah and Geba	621
[27]of Micmash	122
[28]of Bethel and Ai	223
[29]of Nebo	52
[30]of Magbish	156
[31]of the other Elam	1,254
[32]of Harim	320
[33]of Lod, Hadid and Ono	725
[34]of Jericho	345
[35]of Senaah	3,630

[36]The priests:

the descendants of Jedaiah (through the family of Jeshua)	973
[37]of Immer	1,052
[38]of Pashhur	1,247
[39]of Harim	1,017

[40]The Levites:

the descendants of Jeshua and Kadmiel (through the line of Hodaviah)	74

[41]The singers:

the descendants of Asaph	128

[42]The gatekeepers of the temple:

the descendants of Shallum, Ater, Talmon, Akkub, Hatita and Shobai	139

[43]The temple servants:

the descendants of
Ziha, Hasupha, Tabbaoth,
[44]Keros, Siaha, Padon,
[45]Lebanah, Hagabah, Akkub,
[46]Hagab, Shalmai, Hanan,
[47]Giddel, Gahar, Reaiah,
[48]Rezin, Nekoda, Gazzam,
[49]Uzza, Paseah, Besai,
[50]Asnah, Meunim, Nephussim,
[51]Bakbuk, Hakupha, Harhur,
[52]Bazluth, Mehida, Harsha,
[53]Barkos, Sisera, Temah,
[54]Neziah and Hatipha

[55]The descendants of the servants of Solomon:

the descendants of
Sotai, Hassophereth, Peruda,
[56]Jaala, Darkon, Giddel,
[57]Shephatiah, Hattil,
Pokereth-Hazzebaim and
Ami

[58]The temple servants and the descendants of the servants of Solomon	392

[59]The following came up from the towns of Tel Melah, Tel Har-

[a]25 See Septuagint (see also Neh. 7:29); Hebrew *Kiriath Arim.*

sha, Kerub, Addon and Immer, but they could not show that their families were descended from Israel:

⁶⁰The descendants of
Delaiah, Tobiah and
Nekoda   652

⁶¹And from among the priests:

The descendants of
Hobaiah, Hakkoz and
Barzillai (a man who had
married a daughter of
Barzillai the Gileadite and
was called by that name).
⁶²These searched for their family records, but they could not find them and so were excluded from the priesthood as unclean. ⁶³The governor ordered them not to eat any of the most sacred food until there was a priest ministering with the Urim and Thummim.

⁶⁴The whole company numbered 42,360, ⁶⁵besides their 7,337 menservants and maidservants; and they also had 200 men and women singers. ⁶⁶They had 736 horses, 245 mules, ⁶⁷435 camels and 6,720 donkeys.

⁶⁸When they arrived at the house of the LORD in Jerusalem, some of the heads of the families gave freewill offerings toward the rebuilding of the house of God on its site. ⁶⁹According to their ability they gave to the treasury for this work 61,000 drachmas*a* of gold, 5,000 minas*b* of silver and 100 priestly garments.

⁷⁰The priests, the Levites, the singers, the gatekeepers and the temple servants settled in their own towns, along with some of the other people, and the rest of the Israelites settled in their towns.

Rebuilding the Altar

3 When the seventh month came and the Israelites had settled in

their towns, the people assembled as one man in Jerusalem. ²Then Jeshua son of Jozadak and his fellow priests and Zerubbabel son of Shealtiel and his associates began to build the altar of the God of Israel to sacrifice burnt offerings on it, in accordance with what is written in the Law of Moses the man of God. ³Despite their fear of the peoples around them, they built the altar on its foundation and sacrificed burnt offerings on it to the LORD, both the morning and evening sacrifices. ⁴Then in accordance with what is written, they celebrated the Feast of Tabernacles with the required number of burnt offerings prescribed for each day. ⁵After that, they presented the regular burnt offerings, the New Moon sacrifices and the sacrifices for all the appointed sacred feasts of the LORD, as well as those brought as freewill offerings to the LORD. ⁶On the first day of the seventh month they began to offer burnt offerings to the LORD, though the foundation of the LORD's temple had not yet been laid.

Rebuilding the Temple

⁷Then they gave money to the masons and carpenters, and gave food and drink and oil to the people of Sidon and Tyre, so that they would bring cedar logs by sea from Lebanon to Joppa, as authorized by Cyrus king of Persia.

⁸In the second month of the second year after their arrival at the house of God in Jerusalem, Zerubbabel son of Shealtiel, Jeshua son of Jozadak and the rest of their brothers (the priests and the Levites and all who had returned from the captivity to Jerusalem) began the work, appointing Levites twenty years of age and older to supervise the building of the house of the LORD. ⁹Jeshua and his sons and brothers and Kadmiel and his sons (descendants of Hodaviah*c*) and the sons of Henadad and their sons and brothers—all Levites—joined to-

---

a69 That is, about 1,100 pounds (about 500 kilograms)   *b69 That is, about 3 tons (about 2.9 metric tons)*   *c9 Hebrew Yehudah, probably a variant of Hodaviah*

gether in supervising those working on the house of God.

¹⁰When the builders laid the foundation of the temple of the Lord, the priests in their vestments and with trumpets, and the Levites (the sons of Asaph) with cymbals, took their places to praise the Lord, as prescribed by David king of Israel. ¹¹With praise and thanksgiving they sang to the Lord:

> "He is good;
> his love to Israel endures forever."

And all the people gave a great shout of praise to the Lord, because the foundation of the house of the Lord was laid. ¹²But many of the older priests and Levites and family heads, who had seen the former temple, wept aloud when they saw the foundation of this temple being laid, while many others shouted for joy. ¹³No one could distinguish the sound of the shouts of joy from the sound of weeping, because the people made so much noise. And the sound was heard far away.

Opposition to the Rebuilding

4 When the enemies of Judah and Benjamin heard that the exiles were building a temple for the Lord, the God of Israel, ²they came to Zerubbabel and to the heads of the families and said, "Let us help you build because, like you, we seek your God and have been sacrificing to him since the time of Esarhaddon king of Assyria, who brought us here."

❓DID YOU KNOW?   4:1

Who were the enemies of the Jews?

When the king of Assyria took the people of Israel captive, he settled other people in their land. Those people were pagans. Because they thought the Lord owned the land of Israel, they started to worship the Lord along with their old pagan idols. Now they offered to help the Jews rebuild their temple. The Jewish people would not let the pagan settlers help. This made the settlers angry, and they tried to stop the Jews.

---

³But Zerubbabel, Jeshua and the rest of the heads of the families of Israel answered, "You have no part with us in building a temple to our God. We alone will build it for the Lord, the God of Israel, as King Cyrus, the king of Persia, commanded us."

⁴Then the peoples around them set out to discourage the people of Judah and make them afraid to go on build-

---

▟ET'S LIVE IT!   Ezra 3:1–6

CELEBRATION ➠ Read Ezra 3:1–6. "Tabernacles" was a holiday for the Israelites. The word means "tents" or "outdoor shelters." The Israelites who had returned all came to Jerusalem to celebrate the Feast of Tabernacles.

Leviticus 23:33–44 tells us that the Israelites lived in these tents for seven days each year to help them remember how they lived when God brought them out of Egypt. Also, the verses in Leviticus tell them that this was a holiday to *celebrate*. What do you think of when you think of a celebration?

Your family could have a one-day Feast of Tabernacles. Put up a tent in your yard and live in it for one day. Think of how God has taken care of your family and given you a home to live in. It will be like a small vacation... so celebrate!

ing.*a* *5*They hired counselors to work against them and frustrate their plans during the entire reign of Cyrus king of Persia and down to the reign of Darius king of Persia.

Later Opposition Under Xerxes and Artaxerxes

*6*At the beginning of the reign of Xerxes,*b* they lodged an accusation against the people of Judah and Jerusalem.

*7*And in the days of Artaxerxes king of Persia, Bishlam, Mithredath, Tabeel and the rest of his associates wrote a letter to Artaxerxes. The letter was written in Aramaic script and in the Aramaic language.*c, d*

*8*Rehum the commanding officer and Shimshai the secretary wrote a letter against Jerusalem to Artaxerxes the king as follows:

*9*Rehum the commanding officer and Shimshai the secretary, together with the rest of their associates—the judges and officials over the men from Tripolis, Per-

sia,*e* Erech and Babylon, the Elamites of Susa, *10*and the other people whom the great and honorable Ashurbanipal*f* deported and settled in the city of Samaria and elsewhere in Trans-Euphrates.

11(This is a copy of the letter they sent him.)

To King Artaxerxes,

From your servants, the men of Trans-Euphrates:

*12*The king should know that the Jews who came up to us from you have gone to Jerusalem and are rebuilding that rebellious and wicked city. They are restoring the walls and repairing the foundations.

*13*Furthermore, the king should know that if this city is built and its walls are restored, no more taxes, tribute or duty will be paid, and the royal revenues will suffer. *14*Now since we

---

a4 Or *and troubled them as they built*   *b6* Hebrew *Ahasuerus,* a variant of Xerxes' Persian name   *c7* Or *written in Aramaic and translated*   *d7* The text of Ezra 4:8—6:18 is in Aramaic.   *e9* Or *officials, magistrates and governors over the men from Ashurbanipal*   *f10* Aramaic *Osnappar,* a variant of

---

Life in Bible Times

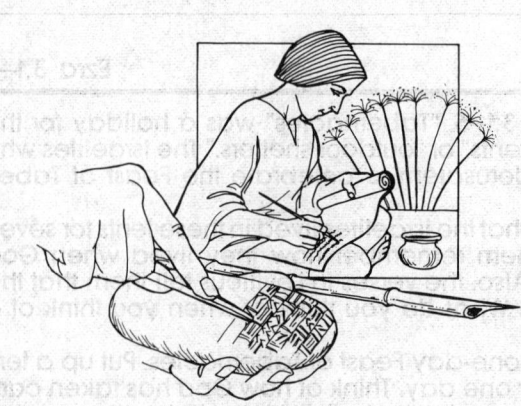

LETTERS

In Old Testament times, letters were often written on clay tablets. Marks were pressed into soft clay, which was then hardened and placed in clay envelopes. Later, letters were written on animal skin or on a kind of paper. The paper was made by gluing together flat layers of the stem of the papyrus reed. Our word *paper* has its beginnings in the word *papyrus.*

are under obligation to the palace and it is not proper for us to see the king dishonored, we are sending this message to inform the king, 15so that a search may be made in the archives of your predecessors. In these records you will find that this city is a rebellious city, troublesome to kings and provinces, a place of rebellion from ancient times. That is why this city was destroyed. 16We inform the king that if this city is built and its walls are restored, you will be left with nothing in Trans-Euphrates.

17The king sent this reply:

To Rehum the commanding officer, Shimshai the secretary and the rest of their associates living in Samaria and elsewhere in Trans-Euphrates:

Greetings.

18The letter you sent us has been read and translated in my presence. 19I issued an order and a search was made, and it was found that this city has a long history of revolt against kings and has been a place of rebellion and sedition. 20Jerusalem has had powerful kings ruling over the whole of Trans-Euphrates, and taxes, tribute and duty were paid to them. 21Now issue an order to these men to stop work, so that this city will not be rebuilt until I so order. 22Be careful not to neglect this matter. Why let this threat grow, to the detriment of the royal interests?

23As soon as the copy of the letter of King Artaxerxes was read to Rehum and Shimshai the secretary and their associates, they went immediately to the Jews in Jerusalem and compelled them by force to stop.

24Thus the work on the house of

God in Jerusalem came to a standstill until the second year of the reign of Darius king of Persia.

Tattenai's Letter to Darius

5 Now Haggai the prophet and Zechariah the prophet, a descendant of Iddo, prophesied to the Jews in Judah and Jerusalem in the name of the God of Israel, who was over them. 2Then Zerubbabel son of Shealtiel and Jeshua son of Jozadak set to work to rebuild the house of God in Jerusalem. And the prophets of God were with them, helping them.

3At that time Tattenai, governor of Trans-Euphrates, and Shethar-Bozenai and their associates went to them and asked, "Who authorized you to rebuild this temple and restore this structure?" 4They also asked, "What are the names of the men constructing this building?"ᵃ 5But the eye of their God was watching over the elders of the Jews, and they were not stopped until a report could go to Darius and his written reply be received.

6This is a copy of the letter that Tattenai, governor of Trans-Euphrates, and Shethar-Bozenai and their associates, the officials of Trans-Euphrates, sent to King Darius. 7The report they sent him read as follows:

To King Darius:

Cordial greetings.

8The king should know that we went to the district of Judah, to the temple of the great God. The people are building it with large stones and placing the timbers in the walls. The work is being carried on with diligence and is making rapid progress under their direction.

9We questioned the elders and asked them, "Who authorized you to rebuild this temple and restore this structure?" 10We also asked them their names, so that we could write down the names

---

ᵃ4 See Septuagint; Aramaic 4We told them the names of the men constructing this building.

of their leaders for your information.

¹¹This is the answer they gave us:

"We are the servants of the God of heaven and earth, and we are rebuilding the temple that was built many years ago, one that a great king of Israel built and finished. ¹²But because our fathers angered the God of heaven, he handed them over to Nebuchadnezzar the Chaldean, king of Babylon, who destroyed this temple and deported the people to Babylon.

¹³"However, in the first year of Cyrus king of Babylon, King Cyrus issued a decree to rebuild this house of God. ¹⁴He even removed from the temple*a* of Babylon the gold and silver articles of the house of God, which Nebuchadnezzar had taken from the temple in Jerusalem and brought to the temple*a* in Babylon.

"Then King Cyrus gave them to a man named Sheshbazzar, whom he had appointed governor, ¹⁵and he told him, 'Take these articles and go and deposit them in the temple in Jerusalem. And rebuild the house of God on its site.' ¹⁶So this Sheshbazzar came and laid the foundations of the house of God in Jerusalem. From that day to the present it has been under construction but is not yet finished."

¹⁷Now if it pleases the king, let a search be made in the royal archives of Babylon to see if King Cyrus did in fact issue a decree to rebuild this house of God in Jerusalem. Then let the king send us his decision in this matter.

The Decree of Darius

6 King Darius then issued an order, and they searched in the archives stored in the treasury at Bab-

ylon. ²A scroll was found in the citadel of Ecbatana in the province of Media, and this was written on it:

Memorandum:

³In the first year of King Cyrus, the king issued a decree concerning the temple of God in Jerusalem:

Let the temple be rebuilt as a place to present sacrifices, and let its foundations be laid. It is to be ninety feet*b* high and ninety feet wide, ⁴with three courses of large stones and one of timbers. The costs are to be paid by the royal treasury. ⁵Also, the gold and silver articles of the house of God, which Nebuchadnezzar took from the temple in Jerusalem and brought to Babylon, are to be returned to their places in the temple in Jerusalem; they are to be deposited in the house of God.

⁶Now then, Tattenai, governor of Trans-Euphrates, and Shethar-Bozenai and you, their fellow officials of that province, stay away from there. ⁷Do not interfere with the work on this temple of God. Let the governor of the Jews and the Jewish elders rebuild this house of God on its site.

⁸Moreover, I hereby decree what you are to do for these elders of the Jews in the construction of this house of God:

The expenses of these men are to be fully paid out of the royal treasury, from the revenues of Trans-Euphrates, so that the work will not stop. ⁹Whatever is needed—young bulls, rams, male lambs for burnt offerings to the God of heaven, and wheat, salt, wine and oil, as requested by the priests in Jerusalem—must be given them daily without fail, ¹⁰so that they may offer

---

a14 Or *palace*   *b3* Aramaic *sixty cubits* (about 27 meters)

sacrifices pleasing to the God of heaven and pray for the well-being of the king and his sons.

11Furthermore, I decree that if anyone changes this edict, a beam is to be pulled from his house and he is to be lifted up and impaled on it. And for this crime his house is to be made a pile of rubble. 12May God, who has caused his Name to dwell there, overthrow any king or people who lifts a hand to change this decree or to destroy this temple in Jerusalem.

I Darius have decreed it. Let it be carried out with diligence.

Completion and Dedication of the Temple

13Then, because of the decree King Darius had sent, Tattenai, governor of Trans-Euphrates, and Shethar-Bozenai and their associates carried it out with diligence. 14So the elders of the Jews continued to build and prosper under the preaching of Haggai the prophet and Zechariah, a descendant of Iddo. They finished building the temple according to the command of the God of Israel and the decrees of Cyrus, Darius and Artaxerxes, kings of Persia. 15The temple was completed on the third day of the month Adar, in the sixth year of the reign of King Darius.

16Then the people of Israel—the priests, the Levites and the rest of the exiles—celebrated the dedication of the house of God with joy. 17For the dedication of this house of God they offered a hundred bulls, two hundred rams, four hundred male lambs and, as a sin offering for all Israel, twelve male goats, one for each of the tribes of Israel. 18And they installed the priests in their divisions and the Levites in their groups for the service of God at Jerusalem, according to what is written in the Book of Moses.

The Passover

19On the fourteenth day of the first month, the exiles celebrated the Passover. 20The priests and Levites had purified themselves and were all ceremonially clean. The Levites slaughtered the Passover lamb for all the exiles, for their brothers the priests and for themselves. 21So the Israelites who had returned from the exile ate it, together with all who had separated themselves from the unclean practices of their Gentile neighbors in order to seek the LORD, the God of Israel. 22For seven days they celebrated with joy the Feast of Unleavened Bread, because the LORD had filled them with joy by changing the attitude of the king of Assyria, so that he assisted them in the work on the house of God, the God of Israel.

ᴸET'S LIVE IT!　　　Ezra 6:13–18

DEDICATED TO GOD ➡ "Dedicate" here means promise to use the temple to worship God and serve him there. Read about the dedication service in Ezra 6:13–18.

Here are some ways you can learn more about dedicating things to God:

1. If people dedicate babies at your church, listen carefully. What do the mom and dad promise? What does the minister say in his prayer?

2. Listen carefully to the prayer of dedication when the church offering is brought forward on Sunday.

3. Think about the things you have. Is there anything you would like to dedicate to God? For instance, you might dedicate your school books to God. Pray and tell God you will study hard, so you can be ready to serve him when you grow up.

Ezra Comes to Jerusalem

7 After these things, during the reign of Artaxerxes king of Persia, Ezra son of Seraiah, the son of Azariah, the son of Hilkiah, ²the son of Shallum, the son of Zadok, the son of Ahitub, ³the son of Amariah, the son of Azariah, the son of Meraioth, ⁴the son of Zerahiah, the son of Uzzi, the son of Bukki, ⁵the son of Abishua, the son of Phinehas, the son of Eleazar, the son of Aaron the chief priest— ⁶this Ezra came up from Babylon. He was a teacher well versed in the Law of Moses, which the LORD, the God of Israel, had given. The king had granted him everything he asked, for the hand of the LORD his God was on him. ⁷Some of the Israelites, including priests, Levites, singers, gatekeepers and temple servants, also came up to Jerusalem in the seventh year of King Artaxerxes.

⁸Ezra arrived in Jerusalem in the fifth month of the seventh year of the king. ⁹He had begun his journey from Babylon on the first day of the first month, and he arrived in Jerusalem on the first day of the fifth month, for the gracious hand of his God was on him. ¹⁰For Ezra had devoted himself to the study and observance of the Law of the LORD, and to teaching its decrees and laws in Israel.

𝖂ORDS TO REMEMBER

7:10 Ezra had devoted himself to the study and observance of the Law of the LORD.

King Artaxerxes' Letter to Ezra

¹¹This is a copy of the letter King Artaxerxes had given to Ezra the priest and teacher, a man learned in matters concerning the commands and decrees of the LORD for Israel:

¹²ᵃArtaxerxes, king of kings,

To Ezra the priest, a teacher of the Law of the God of heaven:

Greetings.

¹³Now I decree that any of the Israelites in my kingdom, including priests and Levites, who wish to go to Jerusalem with you, may go. ¹⁴You are sent by the king and his seven advisers to inquire about Judah and Jerusalem with regard to the Law of your God, which is in your hand. ¹⁵Moreover, you are to take with you the silver and gold that the king and his advisers have freely given to the God of Israel, whose dwelling is in Jerusalem, ¹⁶together with all the silver and gold you may obtain from the province of Babylon, as well as the freewill offerings of the people and priests for the temple of their God in Jerusalem. ¹⁷With this money be sure to buy bulls, rams and male lambs, together with their grain offerings and drink offerings, and sacrifice them on the altar of the temple of your God in Jerusalem.

¹⁸You and your brother Jews may then do whatever seems best with the rest of the silver and gold, in accordance with the will of your God. ¹⁹Deliver to the God of Jerusalem all the articles entrusted to you for worship in the temple of your God. ²⁰And anything else needed for the temple of your God that you may have occasion to supply, you may provide from the royal treasury.

²¹Now I, King Artaxerxes, order all the treasurers of Trans-Euphrates to provide with diligence whatever Ezra the priest, a teacher of the Law of the God of heaven, may ask of you— ²²up to a hundred talentsᵇ of silver, a hundred corsᶜ of wheat, a hun-

---

ᵃ12 The text of Ezra 7:12-26 is in Aramaic.　　ᵇ22 That is, about 3 3/4 tons (about 3.4 metric tons)
ᶜ22 That is, probably about 600 bushels (about 22 kiloliters)

dred baths[a] of wine, a hundred baths[a] of olive oil, and salt without limit. 23Whatever the God of heaven has prescribed, let it be done with diligence for the temple of the God of heaven. Why should there be wrath against the realm of the king and of his sons? 24You are also to know that you have no authority to impose taxes, tribute or duty on any of the priests, Levites, singers, gatekeepers, temple servants or other workers at this house of God.

25And you, Ezra, in accordance with the wisdom of your God, which you possess, appoint magistrates and judges to administer justice to all the people of Trans-Euphrates—all who know the laws of your God. And you are to teach any who do not know them. 26Whoever does not obey the law of your God and the law of the king must surely be punished by death, banishment, confiscation of property, or imprisonment.

27Praise be to the LORD, the God of our fathers, who has put it into the king's heart to bring honor to the house of the LORD in Jerusalem in this way 28and who has extended his good favor to me before the king and his advisers and all the king's powerful officials. Because the hand of the LORD my God was on me, I took courage and gathered leading men from Israel to go up with me.

List of the Family Heads Returning With Ezra

8 These are the family heads and those registered with them who came up with me from Babylon during the reign of King Artaxerxes:

2of the descendants of Phinehas, Gershom;

of the descendants of Ithamar, Daniel;
of the descendants of David, Hattush 3of the descendants of Shecaniah;

? DID YOU KNOW?   8:1

When did Ezra come to Jerusalem?

Ezra came to Jerusalem in 458 B.C. The first six chapters of the book of Ezra are about things that happened eighty years earlier, when the first Jews came back to Judah from Babylon in 538 B.C. The last four chapters tell what happened when Ezra returned.

---

of the descendants of Parosh, Zechariah, and with him were registered 150 men;
4of the descendants of Pahath-Moab, Eliehoenai son of Zerahiah, and with him 200 men;
5of the descendants of Zattu,[b] Shecaniah son of Jahaziel, and with him 300 men;
6of the descendants of Adin, Ebed son of Jonathan, and with him 50 men;
7of the descendants of Elam, Jeshaiah son of Athaliah, and with him 70 men;
8of the descendants of Shephatiah, Zebadiah son of Michael, and with him 80 men;
9of the descendants of Joab, Obadiah son of Jehiel, and with him 218 men;
10of the descendants of Bani,[c] Shelomith son of Josiphiah, and with him 160 men;
11of the descendants of Bebai, Zechariah son of Bebai, and with him 28 men;
12of the descendants of Azgad, Johanan son of Hakkatan, and with him 110 men;

---

a22 That is, probably about 600 gallons (about 2.2 kiloliters) (also 1 Esdras 8:32); Hebrew does not have Zattu. 1 Esdras 8:36); Hebrew does not have Bani.　　b5 Some Septuagint manuscripts c10 Some Septuagint manuscripts (also

¹³of the descendants of Adonikam, the last ones, whose names were Eliphelet, Jeuel and Shemaiah, and with them 60 men; ¹⁴of the descendants of Bigvai, Uthai and Zaccur, and with them 70 men.

The Return to Jerusalem

¹⁵I assembled them at the canal that flows toward Ahava, and we camped there three days. When I checked among the people and the priests, I found no Levites there. ¹⁶So I summoned Eliezer, Ariel, Shemaiah, Elnathan, Jarib, Elnathan, Nathan, Zechariah and Meshullam, who were leaders, and Joiarib and Elnathan, who were men of learning, ¹⁷and I sent them to Iddo, the leader in Casiphia. I told them what to say to Iddo and his kinsmen, the temple servants in Casiphia, so that they might bring attendants to us for the house of our God. ¹⁸Because the gracious hand of our God was on us, they brought us Sherebiah, a capable man, from the descendants of Mahli son of Levi, the son of Israel, and Sherebiah's sons and brothers, 18 men; ¹⁹and Hashabiah, together with Jeshaiah from the descendants of Merari, and his brothers and nephews, 20 men. ²⁰They also brought 220 of the temple servants—a body that David and the officials had established to assist the Levites. All were registered by name.

²¹There, by the Ahava Canal, I proclaimed a fast, so that we might humble ourselves before our God and ask him for a safe journey for us and our children, with all our possessions. ²²I was ashamed to ask the king for soldiers and horsemen to protect us from enemies on the road, because we had told the king, "The gracious hand of our God is on everyone who looks to him, but his great anger is against all who forsake him." ²³So we fasted and petitioned our God about this, and he answered our prayer.

²⁴Then I set apart twelve of the leading priests, together with Sherebiah, Hashabiah and ten of their brothers, ²⁵and I weighed out to them the offering of silver and gold and the articles that the king, his advisers, his officials and all Israel present there had donated for the house of our God. ²⁶I weighed out to them 650 talents^a of silver, silver articles weighing 100 talents,^b 100 talents^b of gold, ²⁷20 bowls of gold valued at 1,000 darics,^c and two fine articles of polished bronze, as precious as gold.

²⁸I said to them, "You as well as these articles are consecrated to the LORD. The silver and gold are a freewill offering to the LORD, the God of your fathers. ²⁹Guard them carefully until you weigh them out in the chambers of the house of the LORD in Jerusalem before the leading priests and the Levites and the family heads of Israel." ³⁰Then the priests and Levites received the silver and gold and sacred articles that had been weighed out to be taken to the house of our God in Jerusalem.

³¹On the twelfth day of the first month we set out from the Ahava Canal to go to Jerusalem. The hand of our God was on us, and he protected us from enemies and bandits along the way. ³²So we arrived in Jerusalem, where we rested three days.

³³On the fourth day, in the house of our God, we weighed out the silver and gold and the sacred articles into the hands of Meremoth son of Uriah, the priest. Eleazar son of Phinehas was with him, and so were the Levites Jozabad son of Jeshua and Noadiah son of Binnui. ³⁴Everything was accounted for by number and weight, and the entire weight was recorded at that time.

³⁵Then the exiles who had returned from captivity sacrificed burnt offerings to the God of Israel: twelve bulls for all Israel, ninety-six rams, seventy-seven male lambs and, as a sin of-

---

^a26 That is, about 25 tons (about 22 metric tons)   ^b26 That is, about 3 3/4 tons (about 3.4 metric tons)   ^c27 That is, about 19 pounds (about 8.5 kilograms)

fering, twelve male goats. All this was a burnt offering to the LORD. [36]They also delivered the king's orders to the royal satraps and to the governors of Trans-Euphrates, who then gave assistance to the people and to the house of God.

Ezra's Prayer About Intermarriage

9 After these things had been done, the leaders came to me and said, "The people of Israel, including the priests and the Levites, have not kept themselves separate from the neighboring peoples with their detestable practices, like those of the Canaanites, Hittites, Perizzites, Jebusites, Ammonites, Moabites, Egyptians and Amorites. [2]They have taken some of their daughters as wives for themselves and their sons, and have mingled the holy race with the peoples around them. And the leaders and officials have led the way in this unfaithfulness."

[3]When I heard this, I tore my tunic and cloak, pulled hair from my head and beard and sat down appalled. [4]Then everyone who trembled at the words of the God of Israel gathered around me because of this unfaithfulness of the exiles. And I sat there appalled until the evening sacrifice.

[5]Then, at the evening sacrifice, I rose from my self-abasement, with my tunic and cloak torn, and fell on my knees with my hands spread out to the LORD my God [6]and prayed:

"O my God, I am too ashamed and disgraced to lift up my face to you, my God, because our sins are higher than our heads and our guilt has reached to the heavens. [7]From the days of our forefathers until now, our guilt has been great. Because of our sins, we and our kings and our priests have been subjected to the sword and captivity, to pillage and humiliation at the hand of foreign kings, as it is today.

[8]"But now, for a brief moment, the LORD our God has been gracious in leaving us a remnant and giving us a firm place in his sanctuary, and so our God gives light to our eyes and a little relief in our bondage. [9]Though we are slaves, our God has not deserted us in our bondage. He has shown us kindness in the sight of the kings of Persia: He has granted us new life to rebuild the house of our God and repair its ruins, and he has given us a wall

Life in Bible Times

WEDDING CELEBRATIONS

Weddings were happy times in Israel. For a week the bride and groom were treated like a queen and king. There was music, dancing, and feasting. But Israelites were forbidden to marry pagans, who did not worship the Lord. When Ezra heard about such weddings, he did not rejoice. He wept for shame and confessed the sin to God.

of protection in Judah and Jerusalem.

¹⁰"But now, O our God, what can we say after this? For we have disregarded the commands ¹¹you gave through your servants the prophets when you said: 'The land you are entering to possess is a land polluted by the corruption of its peoples. By their detestable practices they have filled it with their impurity from one end to the other. ¹²Therefore, do not give your daughters in marriage to their sons or take their daughters for your sons. Do not seek a treaty of friendship with them at any time, that you may be strong and eat the good things of the land and leave it to your children as an everlasting inheritance.'

¹³"What has happened to us is a result of our evil deeds and our great guilt, and yet, our God, you have punished us less than our sins have deserved and have given us a remnant like this. ¹⁴Shall we again break your commands and intermarry with the peoples who commit such detestable practices? Would you not be angry enough with us to destroy us, leaving us no remnant or survivor? ¹⁵O LORD, God of Israel, you are righteous! We are left this day as a remnant. Here we are before you in our guilt, though because of it not one of us can stand in your presence."

The People's Confession of Sin

10 While Ezra was praying and confessing, weeping and throwing himself down before the house of God, a large crowd of Israelites—men, women and children—gathered around him. They too wept bitterly. ²Then Shecaniah son of Jehiel, one of the descendants of Elam, said to Ezra, "We have been unfaithful to our God by marrying foreign women from the peoples around us. But in spite of this, there is still hope for Israel. ³Now let us make a cov-

enant before our God to send away all these women and their children, in accordance with the counsel of my lord and of those who fear the commands of our God. Let it be done according to the Law. ⁴Rise up; this matter is in your hands. We will support you, so take courage and do it."

❓DID YOU KNOW?   9:15
What is said in a prayer of confession?

In a prayer of confession, people tell God about their sins and ask God for forgiveness. Ezra 9:6–15 records Ezra's prayer confessing that his people had done wrong. Because Ezra was so upset, the people realized they had sinned and they confessed. Ezra 10 tells how the people of Judah showed they were truly sorry for their sin.

⁵So Ezra rose up and put the leading priests and Levites and all Israel under oath to do what had been suggested. And they took the oath. ⁶Then Ezra withdrew from before the house of God and went to the room of Jehohanan son of Eliashib. While he was there, he ate no food and drank no water, because he continued to mourn over the unfaithfulness of the exiles.

⁷A proclamation was then issued throughout Judah and Jerusalem for all the exiles to assemble in Jerusalem. ⁸Anyone who failed to appear within three days would forfeit all his property, in accordance with the decision of the officials and elders, and would himself be expelled from the assembly of the exiles.

⁹Within the three days, all the men of Judah and Benjamin had gathered in Jerusalem. And on the twentieth day of the ninth month, all the people were sitting in the square before the house of God, greatly distressed by the occasion and because of the rain.

¹⁰Then Ezra the priest stood up and said to them, "You have been unfaithful; you have married foreign women, adding to Israel's guilt. ¹¹Now make confession to the LORD, the God of your fathers, and do his will. Separate yourselves from the peoples around you and from your foreign wives."

¹²The whole assembly responded with a loud voice: "You are right! We must do as you say. ¹³But there are many people here and it is the rainy season; so we cannot stand outside. Besides, this matter cannot be taken care of in a day or two, because we have sinned greatly in this thing. ¹⁴Let our officials act for the whole assembly. Then let everyone in our towns who has married a foreign woman come at a set time, along with the elders and judges of each town, until the fierce anger of our God in this matter is turned away from us." ¹⁵Only Jonathan son of Asahel and Jahzeiah son of Tikvah, supported by Meshullam and Shabbethai the Levite, opposed this.

¹⁶So the exiles did as was proposed. Ezra the priest selected men who were family heads, one from each family division, and all of them designated by name. On the first day of the tenth month they sat down to investigate the cases, ¹⁷and by the first day of the first month they finished dealing with all the men who had married foreign women.

Those Guilty of Intermarriage

¹⁸Among the descendants of the priests, the following had married foreign women:

From the descendants of Jeshua son of Jozadak, and his brothers: Maaseiah, Eliezer, Jarib and Gedaliah. ¹⁹(They all gave their hands in pledge to put away their wives, and for their guilt they each presented a ram from the flock as a guilt offering.)

²⁰From the descendants of Immer: Hanani and Zebadiah.

²¹From the descendants of Harim: Maaseiah, Elijah, Shemaiah, Jehiel and Uzziah.

²²From the descendants of Pashhur: Elioenai, Maaseiah, Ishmael, Nethanel, Jozabad and Elasah.

²³Among the Levites:

Jozabad, Shimei, Kelaiah (that is, Kelita), Pethahiah, Judah and Eliezer.

²⁴From the singers:
Eliashib.

From the gatekeepers:
Shallum, Telem and Uri.

²⁵And among the other Israelites:

From the descendants of Parosh: Ramiah, Izziah, Malkijah, Mijamin, Eleazar, Malkijah and Benaiah.

²⁶From the descendants of Elam: Mattaniah, Zechariah, Jehiel, Abdi, Jeremoth and Elijah.

²⁷From the descendants of Zattu: Elioenai, Eliashib, Mattaniah, Jeremoth, Zabad and Aziza.

²⁸From the descendants of Bebai: Jehohanan, Hananiah, Zabbai and Athlai.

²⁹From the descendants of Bani: Meshullam, Malluch, Adaiah, Jashub, Sheal and Jeremoth.

³⁰From the descendants of Pahath-Moab: Adna, Kelal, Benaiah, Maaseiah, Mattaniah, Bezalel, Binnui and Manasseh.

³¹From the descendants of Harim: Eliezer, Ishijah, Malkijah, Shemaiah, Shimeon, ³²Benjamin, Malluch and Shemariah.

³³From the descendants of Hashum: Mattenai, Mattattah, Zabad, Eliphelet, Jeremai, Manasseh and Shimei.

³⁴From the descendants of Bani: Maadai, Amram, Uel, ³⁵Benaiah, Bedeiah, Keluhi, ³⁶Vaniah, Meremoth, Eliashib,

37Mattaniah, Mattenai and Jaasu.
38From the descendants of Binnui:*a*
Shimei, 39Shelemiah, Nathan, Adaiah, 40Macnadebai, Shashai, Sharai, 41Azarel, Shelemiah, Shemariah, 42Shallum, Amariah and Joseph.
43From the descendants of Nebo: Jeiel, Mattithiah, Zabad, Zebina, Jaddai, Joel and Benaiah.

44All these had married foreign women, and some of them had children by these wives.*b*

---

a37,38 See Septuagint (also 1 Esdras 9:34); Hebrew *Jaasu 38and Bani and Binnui,* *b44* Or *and they sent them away with their children*

NEHEMIAH

NEH
EST
JOB

WHO WROTE THIS BOOK?
The author of Nehemiah is unknown. Many people think the book was written by Ezra.

WHY WAS THIS BOOK WRITTEN?
The book of Nehemiah tells how God used Nehemiah to rebuild the walls of Jerusalem.

WHAT HAPPENS IN THIS BOOK?
Nehemiah is made governor of Judah. He has the Jews rebuild the city walls. Nehemiah also makes the people of Judah stop sinning.

WHAT DO WE LEARN ABOUT GOD IN THIS BOOK?
God wants his people to be courageous and keep on doing his work.

WHO IS IMPORTANT IN THIS BOOK?
The important person in this book is Nehemiah.

WHEN DID THIS HAPPEN?
The events of this book happened between 444 and 430 B.C.

WHERE DID THIS HAPPEN?
These things took place in the little land of Judah and the city of Jerusalem.

WHAT ARE SOME OF THE STORIES IN THIS BOOK?

The walls are rebuilt.	Nehemiah 3
Nehemiah helps the poor.	Nehemiah 5
Opposition to the rebuilding.	Nehemiah 6
Ezra reads God's law.	Nehemiah 8
The Israelites confess their sins.	Nehemiah 9
Nehemiah asks to be remembered.	Nehemiah 13

Nehemiah's Prayer

1 The words of Nehemiah son of Hacaliah:

In the month of Kislev in the twentieth year, while I was in the citadel of Susa, [2]Hanani, one of my brothers, came from Judah with some other men, and I questioned them about the Jewish remnant that survived the exile, and also about Jerusalem. [3]They said to me, "Those who survived the exile and are back in the province are in great trouble and disgrace. The wall of Jerusalem is broken down, and its gates have been burned with fire."

[4]When I heard these things, I sat down and wept. For some days I mourned and fasted and prayed before the God of heaven. [5]Then I said:

"O LORD, God of heaven, the great and awesome God, who keeps his covenant of love with those who love him and obey his commands, [6]let your ear be attentive and your eyes open to hear the prayer your servant is praying before you day and night for your servants, the people of Israel. I confess the sins we Israelites, including myself and my father's house, have committed against you. [7]We have acted very wickedly toward you. We have not obeyed the commands, decrees and laws you gave your servant Moses.

[8]"Remember the instruction you gave your servant Moses, saying, 'If you are unfaithful, I will scatter you among the nations, [9]but if you return to me and obey my commands, then even if your exiled people are at the farthest horizon, I will gather them from there and bring them to the place I have chosen as a dwelling for my Name.'

[10]"They are your servants and your people, whom you redeemed by your great strength and your mighty hand. [11]O Lord, let your ear be attentive to the prayer of this your servant and to the prayer of your servants who delight in revering your name. Give your servant success today by granting him favor in the presence of this man."

I was cupbearer to the king.

CUPBEARER

The cupbearer was a very high government official in Bible times. It was an honor to fill the king's cup when he ate. Ordinary people drank out of shallow clay cups but kings drank out of golden cups.

Artaxerxes Sends Nehemiah to Jerusalem

2 In the month of Nisan in the twentieth year of King Artaxerxes, when wine was brought for him, I took the wine and gave it to the king. I had not been sad in his presence before; [2]so the king asked me, "Why does your face look so sad when you are not ill? This can be nothing but sadness of heart."

I was very much afraid, [3]but I said to the king, "May the king live forever! Why should my face not look sad when the city where my fathers are buried lies in ruins, and its gates have been destroyed by fire?"

[4]The king said to me, "What is it you want?"

Then I prayed to the God of heaven, [5]and I answered the king, "If it pleases the king and if your servant has found favor in his sight, let him send me to the city in Judah where my fathers are buried so that I can rebuild it."

[6]Then the king, with the queen sitting beside him, asked me, "How long will your journey take, and when will

you get back?" It pleased the king to send me; so I set a time.

7I also said to him, "If it pleases the king, may I have letters to the governors of Trans-Euphrates, so that they will provide me safe-conduct until I arrive in Judah? 8And may I have a letter to Asaph, keeper of the king's forest, so he will give me timber to make beams for the gates of the citadel by the temple and for the city wall and for the residence I will occupy?" And because the gracious hand of my God was upon me, the king granted my requests. 9So I went to the governors of Trans-Euphrates and gave them the king's letters. The king had also sent army officers and cavalry with me.

10When Sanballat the Horonite and Tobiah the Ammonite official heard about this, they were very much disturbed that someone had come to promote the welfare of the Israelites.

Nehemiah Inspects Jerusalem's Walls

11I went to Jerusalem, and after staying there three days 12I set out during the night with a few men. I had not told anyone what my God had put in my heart to do for Jerusalem. There were no mounts with me except the one I was riding on. 13By night I went out through the

Valley Gate toward the Jackal*a* Well and the Dung Gate, examining the walls of Jerusalem, which had been broken down, and its gates, which had been destroyed by fire. 14Then I moved on toward the Fountain Gate and the King's Pool, but there was not enough room for my mount to get through; 15so I went up the valley by night, examining the wall. Finally, I turned back and reentered through the Valley Gate. 16The officials did not know where I had gone or what I was doing, because as yet I had said nothing to the Jews or the priests or nobles or officials or any others who would be doing the work.

17Then I said to them, "You see the trouble we are in: Jerusalem lies in ruins, and its gates have been burned with fire. Come, let us rebuild the wall of Jerusalem, and we will no longer be in disgrace." 18I also told them about the gracious hand of my God upon me and what the king had said to me.

They replied, "Let us start rebuilding." So they began this good work.

19But when Sanballat the Horonite, Tobiah the Ammonite official and Geshem the Arab heard about it, they mocked and ridiculed us. "What is this you are doing?" they asked. "Are you rebelling against the king?"

20I answered them by saying, "The

a13 Or Serpent or Fig

LET'S LIVE IT!　　　　Nehemiah 2:1–5

FAST, SILENT PRAYER ➡ In Bible times, some kings would kill anyone who made them feel upset. Read Nehemiah 2:1–5. Why was Nehemiah afraid? What did Nehemiah do when the king asked why he looked sad?

We don't know what Nehemiah prayed. But it must have been a fast, silent prayer, because Nehemiah answered the king's question right away.

Can you think of times boys and girls might want to say fast, silent prayers? You might pray: "God, help me remember what I studied" just before you take a test. Think of at least five situations and write down a fast prayer for each. It is good to know that God listens to fast, silent prayers, as well as to long ones.

God of heaven will give us success. We his servants will start rebuilding, but as for you, you have no share in Jerusalem or any claim or historic right to it."

Builders of the Wall

3 Eliashib the high priest and his fellow priests went to work and rebuilt the Sheep Gate. They dedicated it and set its doors in place, building as far as the Tower of the Hundred, which they dedicated, and as far as the Tower of Hananel. ²The men of Jericho built the adjoining section, and Zaccur son of Imri built next to them.

³The Fish Gate was rebuilt by the sons of Hassenaah. They laid its beams and put its doors and bolts and bars in place. ⁴Meremoth son of Uriah, the son of Hakkoz, repaired the next section. Next to him Meshullam son of Berekiah, the son of Meshezabel, made repairs, and next to him Zadok son of Baana also made repairs. ⁵The next section was repaired by the men of Tekoa, but their nobles would not put their shoulders to the work under their supervisors.ᵃ

⁶The Jeshanahᵇ Gate was repaired by Joiada son of Paseah and Meshullam son of Besodeiah. They laid its beams and put its doors and bolts and bars in place. ⁷Next to them, repairs were made by men from Gibeon and Mizpah—Melatiah of Gibeon and Jadon of Meronoth—places under the authority of the governor of Trans-Euphrates. ⁸Uzziel son of Harhaiah, one of the goldsmiths, repaired the next section; and Hananiah, one of the perfume-makers, made repairs next to that. They restoredᶜ Jerusalem as far as the Broad Wall. ⁹Rephaiah son of Hur, ruler of a half-district of Jerusalem, repaired the next section. ¹⁰Adjoining this, Jedaiah son of

Harumaph made repairs opposite his house, and Hattush son of Hashabneiah made repairs next to him. ¹¹Malkijah son of Harim and Hasshub son of Pahath-Moab repaired another section and the Tower of the Ovens. ¹²Shallum son of Hallohesh, ruler of a half-district of Jerusalem, repaired the next section with the help of his daughters.

¹³The Valley Gate was repaired by Hanun and the residents of Zanoah. They rebuilt it and put its doors and bolts and bars in place. They also repaired five hundred yardsᵈ of the wall as far as the Dung Gate.

¹⁴The Dung Gate was repaired by Malkijah son of Recab, ruler of the district of Beth Hakkerem. He rebuilt it and put its doors and bolts and bars in place.

¹⁵The Fountain Gate was repaired by Shallun son of Col-Hozeh, ruler of the district of Mizpah. He rebuilt it, roofing it over and putting its doors and bolts and bars in place. He also repaired the wall of the Pool of Siloam,ᵉ by the King's Garden, as far as the steps going down from the City of David. ¹⁶Beyond him, Nehemiah son of Azbuk, ruler of a half-district of Beth Zur, made repairs up to a point opposite the tombsᶠ of David, as far as the artificial pool and the House of the Heroes.

¹⁷Next to him, the repairs were made by the Levites under Rehum son of Bani. Beside him, Hashabiah, ruler of half the district of Keilah, carried out repairs for his district. ¹⁸Next to him, the repairs were made by their countrymen under Binnuiᵍ son of Henadad, ruler of the other half-district of Keilah. ¹⁹Next to him, Ezer son of Jeshua, ruler of Mizpah, repaired another section, from a point facing the ascent to the armory as far as the angle. ²⁰Next to him, Baruch son of Zabbai zealously re-

---

ᵃ5 Or *their Lord* or *the governor*   ᵇ6 Or *Old*   ᶜ8 Or *They left out part of*   ᵈ13 Hebrew *a thousand cubits* (about 450 meters)   ᵉ15 Hebrew *Shelah*, a variant of *Shiloah*, that is, Siloam   ᶠ16 Hebrew; Septuagint, some Vulgate manuscripts and Syriac *tomb*   ᵍ18 Two Hebrew manuscripts and Syriac (see also Septuagint and verse 24); most Hebrew manuscripts *Bavvai*

paired another section, from the angle to the entrance of the house of Eliashib the high priest. 21Next to him, Meremoth son of Uriah, the son of Hakkoz, repaired another section, from the entrance of Eliashib's house to the end of it.

22The repairs next to him were made by the priests from the surrounding region. 23Beyond them, Benjamin and Hasshub made repairs in front of their house; and next to them, Azariah son of Maaseiah, the son of Ananiah, made repairs beside his house. 24Next to him, Binnui son of Henadad repaired another section, from Azariah's house to the angle and the corner, 25and Palal son of Uzai worked opposite the angle and the tower projecting from the upper palace near the court of the guard. Next to him, Pedaiah son of Parosh 26and the temple servants living on the hill of Ophel made repairs up to a point opposite the Water Gate toward the east and the projecting tower. 27Next to them, the men of Tekoa repaired another section, from the great projecting tower to the wall of Ophel.

28Above the Horse Gate, the priests made repairs, each in front of his own house. 29Next to them, Zadok son of Immer made repairs opposite his house. Next to him, Shemaiah son of Shecaniah, the guard at the East Gate, made repairs. 30Next to him, Hananiah son of Shelemiah, and Hanun, the sixth son of Zalaph, repaired another section. Next to them, Meshullam son of Berekiah made repairs opposite his living quarters. 31Next to him, Malkijah, one of the goldsmiths, made repairs as far as the house of the temple servants and the merchants, opposite the Inspection Gate, and as far as the room above the corner; 32and between the room above the corner and the Sheep Gate the goldsmiths and merchants made repairs.

Opposition to the Rebuilding

4 When Sanballat heard that we were rebuilding the wall, he became angry and was greatly incensed. He ridiculed the Jews, 2and in the presence of his associates and the army of Samaria, he said, "What are those feeble Jews doing? Will they restore their wall? Will they offer sacrifices? Will they finish in a day? Can they bring the stones back to life from those heaps of rubble—burned as they are?"

3Tobiah the Ammonite, who was at his side, said, "What they are building—if even a fox climbed up on it, he would break down their wall of stones!"

4Hear us, O our God, for we are despised. Turn their insults back on their own heads. Give them over as plunder in a land of captivity. 5Do not cover up their guilt or blot out their sins from your sight, for they have thrown insults in the face of[a] the builders.

6So we rebuilt the wall till all of it reached half its height, for the people worked with all their heart.

7But when Sanballat, Tobiah, the Arabs, the Ammonites and the men of Ashdod heard that the repairs to Jerusalem's walls had gone ahead and that the gaps were being closed, they were very angry. 8They all plotted together to come and fight against Jerusalem and stir up trouble against it. 9But we prayed to our God and posted a guard day and night to meet this threat.

10Meanwhile, the people in Judah said, "The strength of the laborers is giving out, and there is so much rubble that we cannot rebuild the wall."

11Also our enemies said, "Before they know it or see us, we will be right there among them and will kill them and put an end to the work."

12Then the Jews who lived near them came and told us ten times

---

a5 Or *have provoked you to anger before*

over, "Wherever you turn, they will attack us."

[13] Therefore I stationed some of the people behind the lowest points of the wall at the exposed places, posting them by families, with their swords, spears and bows. [14] After I looked things over, I stood up and said to the nobles, the officials and the rest of the people, "Don't be afraid of them. Remember the Lord, who is great and awesome, and fight for your brothers, your sons and your daughters, your wives and your homes."

[15] When our enemies heard that we were aware of their plot and that God had frustrated it, we all returned to the wall, each to his own work.

[16] From that day on, half of my men did the work, while the other half were equipped with spears, shields, bows and armor. The officers posted themselves behind all the people of Judah [17] who were building the wall. Those who carried materials did their work with one hand and held a weapon in the other, [18] and each of the builders wore his sword at his side as he worked. But the man who sounded the trumpet stayed with me.

[19] Then I said to the nobles, the officials and the rest of the people, "The work is extensive and spread out, and we are widely separated from each other along the wall. [20] Wherever you hear the sound of the trumpet, join us there. Our God will fight for us!"

[21] So we continued the work with half the men holding spears, from the first light of dawn till the stars came out. [22] At that time I also said to the people, "Have every man and his helper stay inside Jerusalem at night, so they can serve us as guards by night and workmen by day." [23] Neither I nor my brothers nor my men nor the guards with me took off our clothes; each had his weapon, even when he went for water.[a]

Nehemiah Helps the Poor

5 Now the men and their wives raised a great outcry against their Jewish brothers. [2] Some were saying, "We and our sons and daughters are numerous; in order for us to

---

[a]23 The meaning of the Hebrew for this clause is uncertain.

LET'S LIVE IT!   Nehemiah 4:1–23

READY TO FIGHT ➡ Read this story about Tim and Bruce:

"I'm going to get you after school," Tim threatened. Tim was bigger than Bruce, and Bruce didn't want to fight. That afternoon Bruce walked home from school a different way. The next day when Tim saw Bruce he said, "You can't hide from me again."

That afternoon Bruce went out in front of the school. He asked a friend to hold his books. When Tim came out, Bruce was waiting. Bruce just stared at Tim, and waited. Tim looked at Bruce. Bruce didn't look afraid. So Tim. . . . "

Finish the story of Bruce and Tim. Now read Nehemiah 4. How do you think Nehemiah would finish the story of Bruce and Tim?

Christians don't agree on whether or not it is right to fight back. Some think Christians should never fight. Others think Christians should not start fights, but should fight back. This is the kind of question you should talk about with your parents or your pastor. So tell a grown-up the story of Bruce and Tim, and ask him or her to finish the story. Read Nehemiah 4 together and talk about if it is ever right for Christians to fight back.

eat and stay alive, we must get grain."

³Others were saying, "We are mortgaging our fields, our vineyards and our homes to get grain during the famine."

⁴Still others were saying, "We have had to borrow money to pay the king's tax on our fields and vineyards. ⁵Although we are of the same flesh and blood as our countrymen and though our sons are as good as theirs, yet we have to subject our sons and daughters to slavery. Some of our daughters have already been enslaved, but we are powerless, because our fields and our vineyards belong to others."

⁶When I heard their outcry and these charges, I was very angry. ⁷I pondered them in my mind and then accused the nobles and officials. I told them, "You are exacting usury from your own countrymen!" So I called together a large meeting to deal with them ⁸and said: "As far as possible, we have bought back our Jewish brothers who were sold to the Gentiles. Now you are selling your brothers, only for them to be sold back to us!" They kept quiet, because they could find nothing to say.

⁹So I continued, "What you are doing is not right. Shouldn't you walk in the fear of our God to avoid the reproach of our Gentile enemies? ¹⁰I and my brothers and my men are also lending the people money and grain. But let the exacting of usury stop! ¹¹Give back to them immediately their fields, vineyards, olive groves and houses, and also the usury you are charging them—the hundredth part of the money, grain, new wine and oil."

¹²"We will give it back," they said. "And we will not demand anything more from them. We will do as you say."

Then I summoned the priests and made the nobles and officials take an oath to do what they had promised. ¹³I also shook out the folds of my robe and said, "In this way may God shake out of his house and possessions every man who does not keep this promise. So may such a man be shaken out and emptied!"

At this the whole assembly said, "Amen," and praised the LORD. And the people did as they had promised.

¹⁴Moreover, from the twentieth year of King Artaxerxes, when I was appointed to be their governor in the land of Judah, until his thirty-second year—twelve years—neither I nor my brothers ate the food allotted to the governor. ¹⁵But the earlier governors—those preceding me—placed a heavy burden on the people and took

---

▌ET'S LIVE IT!   Nehemiah 5:1–12

TAKING ADVANTAGE ➡ What do you think?

Matt was laughing. He had just sold an old GI Joe toy to Jeff. Jeff paid Matt $5. Matt was laughing because he got that toy at a garage sale for $2.

Was Matt just being a good businessman? Was Matt fair to Jeff? What if Jeff finds out how much the toy cost Matt? What if Jeff never finds out?

Read Nehemiah 5:1–12. How were some people in Judah unfair to poor people? What did Nehemiah say about this? What did he tell the rich to do?

Jesus said, "Do to others what you would have them do to you" (Matthew 7:12). If Matt used this rule, what would he do for Jeff? Can you think of times when you can use Jesus' rule and not take advantage of others?

forty shekels[a] of silver from them in addition to food and wine. Their assistants also lorded it over the people. But out of reverence for God I did not act like that. [16]Instead, I devoted myself to the work on this wall. All my men were assembled there for the work; we[b] did not acquire any land.

[17]Furthermore, a hundred and fifty Jews and officials ate at my table, as well as those who came to us from the surrounding nations. [18]Each day one ox, six choice sheep and some poultry were prepared for me, and every ten days an abundant supply of wine of all kinds. In spite of all this, I never demanded the food allotted to the governor, because the demands were heavy on these people.

[19]Remember me with favor, O my God, for all I have done for these people.

Further Opposition to the Rebuilding

6 When word came to Sanballat, Tobiah, Geshem the Arab and the rest of our enemies that I had rebuilt the wall and not a gap was left in it—though up to that time I had not set the doors in the gates— [2]Sanballat and Geshem sent me this message: "Come, let us meet together in one of the villages[c] on the plain of Ono."

But they were scheming to harm me; [3]so I sent messengers to them with this reply: "I am carrying on a great project and cannot go down. Why should the work stop while I leave it and go down to you?" [4]Four times they sent me the same message, and each time I gave them the same answer.

[5]Then, the fifth time, Sanballat sent his aide to me with the same message, and in his hand was an unsealed letter [6]in which was written:

"It is reported among the nations—and Geshem[d] says it is true—that you and the Jews are plotting to revolt, and therefore you are building the wall. Moreover, according to these reports you are about to become their king [7]and have even appointed prophets to make this proclamation about you in Jerusalem: 'There is a king in Judah!' Now this report will get back to the king; so come, let us confer together."

[8]I sent him this reply: "Nothing like what you are saying is happening; you are just making it up out of your head."

[9]They were all trying to frighten us, thinking, "Their hands will get too weak for the work, and it will not be completed."

But I prayed, "Now strengthen my hands."

[10]One day I went to the house of Shemaiah son of Delaiah, the son of Mehetabel, who was shut in at his home. He said, "Let us meet in the house of God, inside the temple, and let us close the temple doors, because men are coming to kill you—by night they are coming to kill you."

[11]But I said, "Should a man like me run away? Or should one like me go into the temple to save his life? I will not go!" [12]I realized that God had not sent him, but that he had prophesied against me because Tobiah and Sanballat had hired him. [13]He had been hired to intimidate me so that I would commit a sin by doing this, and then they would give me a bad name to discredit me.

[14]Remember Tobiah and Sanballat, O my God, because of what they have done; remember also the prophetess Noadiah and the rest of the prophets who have been trying to intimidate me.

The Completion of the Wall

[15]So the wall was completed on the

---

a15 That is, about 1 pound (about 0.5 kilogram)   b16 Most Hebrew manuscripts; some Hebrew
manuscripts, Septuagint, Vulgate and Syriac I   c2 Or in Kephirim   d6 Hebrew Gashmu, a
variant of Geshem

twenty-fifth of Elul, in fifty-two days. [16]When all our enemies heard about this, all the surrounding nations were afraid and lost their self-confidence, because they realized that this work had been done with the help of our God.

WORDS TO REMEMBER

6:16 This work had been done with the help of our God.

---

[17]Also, in those days the nobles of Judah were sending many letters to Tobiah, and replies from Tobiah kept coming to them. [18]For many in Judah were under oath to him, since he was son-in-law to Shecaniah son of Arah, and his son Jehohanan had married the daughter of Meshullam son of Berekiah. [19]Moreover, they kept reporting to me his good deeds and then telling him what I said. And Tobiah sent letters to intimidate me.

7 After the wall had been rebuilt and I had set the doors in place, the gatekeepers and the singers and the Levites were appointed. [2]I put in charge of Jerusalem my brother Hanani, along with[a] Hananiah the commander of the citadel, because he was a man of integrity and feared God more than most men do. [3]I said to them, "The gates of Jerusalem are not to be opened until the sun is hot. While the gatekeepers are still on duty, have them shut the doors and bar them. Also appoint residents of Jerusalem as guards, some at their posts and some near their own houses."

The List of the Exiles Who Returned

[4]Now the city was large and spacious, but there were few people in it, and the houses had not yet been rebuilt. [5]So my God put it into my heart to assemble the nobles, the officials and the common people for registra-

tion by families. I found the genealogical record of those who had been the first to return. This is what I found written there:

[6]These are the people of the province who came up from the captivity of the exiles whom Nebuchadnezzar king of Babylon had taken captive (they returned to Jerusalem and Judah, each to his own town, [7]in company with Zerubbabel, Jeshua, Nehemiah, Azariah, Raamiah, Nahamani, Mordecai, Bilshan, Mispereth, Bigvai, Nehum and Baanah):

The list of the men of Israel:

[8]the descendants of Parosh 2,172

[9]of Shephatiah	372
[10]of Arah	652
[11]of Pahath-Moab (through the line of Jeshua and Joab)	2,818
[12]of Elam	1,254
[13]of Zattu	845
[14]of Zaccai	760
[15]of Binnui	648
[16]of Bebai	628
[17]of Azgad	2,322
[18]of Adonikam	667
[19]of Bigvai	2,067
[20]of Adin	655
[21]of Ater (through Hezekiah)	98
[22]of Hashum	328
[23]of Bezai	324
[24]of Hariph	112
[25]of Gibeon	95
[26]the men of Bethlehem and Netophah	188
[27]of Anathoth	128
[28]of Beth Azmaveth	42
[29]of Kiriath Jearim, Kephirah and Beeroth	743
[30]of Ramah and Geba	621
[31]of Micmash	122
[32]of Bethel and Ai	123
[33]of the other Nebo	52
[34]of the other Elam	1,254
[35]of Harim	320

³⁶of Jericho　345
³⁷of Lod, Hadid and Ono　721
³⁸of Senaah　3,930

³⁹The priests:

the descendants of Jedaiah
(through the family of
Jeshua)　973
⁴⁰of Immer　1,052
⁴¹of Pashhur　1,247
⁴²of Harim　1,017

⁴³The Levites:

the descendants of Jeshua
(through Kadmiel through
the line of Hodaviah)　74

⁴⁴The singers:

the descendants of Asaph　148

⁴⁵The gatekeepers:

the descendants of
Shallum, Ater, Talmon,
Akkub, Hatita and
Shobai　138

⁴⁶The temple servants:

the descendants of
Ziha, Hasupha, Tabbaoth,
⁴⁷Keros, Sia, Padon,
⁴⁸Lebana, Hagaba, Shalmai,
⁴⁹Hanan, Giddel, Gahar,
⁵⁰Reaiah, Rezin, Nekoda,
⁵¹Gazzam, Uzza, Paseah,
⁵²Besai, Meunim, Nephussim,
⁵³Bakbuk, Hakupha, Harhur,
⁵⁴Bazluth, Mehida, Harsha,
⁵⁵Barkos, Sisera, Temah,
⁵⁶Neziah and Hatipha

⁵⁷The descendants of the servants
of Solomon:

the descendants of
Sotai, Sophereth, Perida,
⁵⁸Jaala, Darkon, Giddel,
⁵⁹Shephatiah, Hattil,
Pokereth-Hazzebaim and
Amon

⁶⁰The temple servants and the
descendants of the servants

of Solomon　392

⁶¹The following came up from
the towns of Tel Melah, Tel Harsha, Kerub, Addon and Immer,
but they could not show that
their families were descended
from Israel:

⁶²the descendants of
Delaiah, Tobiah and
Nekoda　642

⁶³And from among the priests:

the descendants of
Hobaiah, Hakkoz and
Barzillai (a man who had
married a daughter of
Barzillai the Gileadite and
was called by that name).

⁶⁴These searched for their family records, but they could not
find them and so were excluded
from the priesthood as unclean.
⁶⁵The governor, therefore, ordered them not to eat any of the
most sacred food until there
should be a priest ministering
with the Urim and Thummim.

⁶⁶The whole company numbered 42,360, ⁶⁷besides their
7,337 menservants and maidservants; and they also had 245 men
and women singers. ⁶⁸There
were 736 horses, 245 mules,ᵃ
⁶⁹435 camels and 6,720 donkeys.

⁷⁰Some of the heads of the families contributed to the work.
The governor gave to the treasury 1,000 drachmasᵇ of gold, 50
bowls and 530 garments for
priests. ⁷¹Some of the heads of
the families gave to the treasury
for the work 20,000 drachmasᶜ
of gold and 2,200 minasᵈ of silver. ⁷²The total given by the rest
of the people was 20,000 drachmas of gold, 2,000 minasᵉ of silver and 67 garments for priests.

ᵃ68 Some Hebrew manuscripts (see also Ezra 2:66); most Hebrew manuscripts do not have this
verse.　ᵇ70 That is, about 19 pounds (about 8.5 kilograms)　ᶜ71 That is, about 375 pounds
(about 170 kilograms); also in verse 72　ᵈ71 That is, about 1 1/3 tons (about 1.2 metric tons)
ᵉ72 That is, about 1 1/4 tons (about 1.1 metric tons)

73The priests, the Levites, the gatekeepers, the singers and the temple servants, along with certain of the people and the rest of the Israelites, settled in their own towns.

Ezra Reads the Law

8 When the seventh month came and the Israelites had settled in their towns, 1all the people assembled as one man in the square before the Water Gate. They told Ezra the scribe to bring out the Book of the Law of Moses, which the LORD had commanded for Israel.

2So on the first day of the seventh month Ezra the priest brought the Law before the assembly, which was made up of men and women and all who were able to understand. 3He read it aloud from daybreak till noon as he faced the square before the Water Gate in the presence of the men, women and others who could understand. And all the people listened attentively to the Book of the Law.

4Ezra the scribe stood on a high wooden platform built for the occasion. Beside him on his right stood

---

a8 Or God, translating it

Mattithiah, Shema, Anaiah, Uriah, Hilkiah and Maaseiah; and on his left were Pedaiah, Mishael, Malkijah, Hashum, Hashbaddanah, Zechariah and Meshullam.

5Ezra opened the book. All the people could see him because he was standing above them; and as he opened it, the people all stood up. 6Ezra praised the LORD, the great God; and all the people lifted their hands and responded, "Amen! Amen!" Then they bowed down and worshiped the LORD with their faces to the ground.

7The Levites—Jeshua, Bani, Sherebiah, Jamin, Akkub, Shabbethai, Hodiah, Maaseiah, Kelita, Azariah, Jozabad, Hanan and Pelaiah—instructed the people in the Law while the people were standing there. 8They read from the Book of the Law of God, making it clear*a* and giving the meaning so that the people could understand what was being read.

9Then Nehemiah the governor, Ezra the priest and scribe, and the Levites who were instructing the people said to them all, "This day is sacred to the LORD your God. Do not mourn or weep." For all the people

---

Life in Bible Times

BOOKS

In Old Testament times a book was a scroll. A strip of parchment (animal skin) or papyrus (paper) was rolled up on two sticks. One copy of Isaiah, made two hundred years before Christ, is ten inches high and twenty-four feet long! It was about a hundred years after Christ that sheets of papyrus began to be stacked together into something like our books.

had been weeping as they listened to the words of the Law.

¹⁰Nehemiah said, "Go and enjoy choice food and sweet drinks, and send some to those who have nothing prepared. This day is sacred to our Lord. Do not grieve, for the joy of the LORD is your strength."

? DID YOU KNOW?   8:8

Why did Ezra have to give the meaning when he read God's Word to the people?

The Old Testament was written in Hebrew. But by this time, the Jewish people spoke a language called Aramaic. Ezra had to give the meaning of many Hebrew words that the people could not understand.

---

¹¹The Levites calmed all the people, saying, "Be still, for this is a sacred day. Do not grieve."

¹²Then all the people went away to eat and drink, to send portions of food and to celebrate with great joy, because they now understood the words that had been made known to them.

¹³On the second day of the month, the heads of all the families, along with the priests and the Levites, gathered around Ezra the scribe to give attention to the words of the Law. ¹⁴They found written in the Law, which the LORD had commanded through Moses, that the Israelites were to live in booths during the feast of the seventh month ¹⁵and that they should proclaim this word and spread it throughout their towns and in Jerusalem: "Go out into the hill country and bring back branches from olive and wild olive trees, and from myrtles, palms and shade trees, to make booths"—as it is written.ᵃ

¹⁶So the people went out and brought back branches and built themselves booths on their own roofs,

in their courtyards, in the courts of the house of God and in the square by the Water Gate and the one by the Gate of Ephraim. ¹⁷The whole company that had returned from exile built booths and lived in them. From the days of Joshua son of Nun until that day, the Israelites had not celebrated it like this. And their joy was very great.

¹⁸Day after day, from the first day to the last, Ezra read from the Book of the Law of God. They celebrated the feast for seven days, and on the eighth day, in accordance with the regulation, there was an assembly.

The Israelites Confess Their Sins

9 On the twenty-fourth day of the same month, the Israelites gathered together, fasting and wearing sackcloth and having dust on their heads. ²Those of Israelite descent had separated themselves from all foreigners. They stood in their places and confessed their sins and the wickedness of their fathers. ³They stood where they were and read from the Book of the Law of the LORD their God for a quarter of the day, and spent another quarter in confession and in worshiping the LORD their God. ⁴Standing on the stairs were the Levites—Jeshua, Bani, Kadmiel, Shebaniah, Bunni, Sherebiah, Bani and Kenani—who called with loud voices to the LORD their God. ⁵And the Levites—Jeshua, Kadmiel, Bani, Hashabneiah, Sherebiah, Hodiah, Shebaniah and Pethahiah—said: "Stand up and praise the LORD your God, who is from everlasting to everlasting.ᵇ"

"Blessed be your glorious name, and may it be exalted above all blessing and praise. ⁶You alone are the LORD. You made the heavens, even the highest heavens, and all their starry host, the earth and all that is on it, the seas and all that is in them. You give life to every-

---

ᵃ15 See Lev. 23:37-40.   ᵇ5 Or God for ever and ever

thing, and the multitudes of heaven worship you.

7"You are the LORD God, who chose Abram and brought him out of Ur of the Chaldeans and named him Abraham. 8You found his heart faithful to you, and you made a covenant with him to give to his descendants the land of the Canaanites, Hittites, Amorites, Perizzites, Jebusites and Girgashites. You have kept your promise because you are righteous.

9"You saw the suffering of our forefathers in Egypt; you heard their cry at the Red Sea.*a* 10You sent miraculous signs and wonders against Pharaoh, against all his officials and all the people of his land, for you knew how arrogantly the Egyptians treated them. You made a name for yourself, which remains to this day. 11You divided the sea before them, so that they passed through it on dry ground, but you hurled their pursuers into the depths, like a stone into mighty waters. 12By day you led them with a pillar of cloud, and by night with a pillar of fire to give them light on the way they were to take.

13"You came down on Mount Sinai; you spoke to them from heaven. You gave them regulations and laws that are just and right, and decrees and commands that are good. 14You made known to them your holy Sabbath and gave them commands, decrees and laws through your servant Moses. 15In their hunger you gave them bread from heaven and in their thirst you brought them water from the rock; you told them to go in and take possession of the land you had sworn with uplifted hand to give them.

16"But they, our forefathers, became arrogant and stiff-necked, and did not obey your commands. 17They refused to listen and failed to remember the miracles you performed among them. They became stiff-necked and in their rebellion appointed a leader in order to return to their slavery. But you are a forgiving God, gracious and compassionate, slow to anger and abounding in love. Therefore you did not desert them, 18even when they cast for themselves an image of a calf and said, 'This is your god, who brought you up out of Egypt,' or when they committed awful blasphemies.

19"Because of your great compassion you did not abandon them in the desert. By day the pillar of cloud did not cease to guide them on their path, nor the pillar of fire by night to shine on the way they were to take. 20You gave your good Spirit to instruct them. You did not withhold your manna from their mouths, and you gave them water for their thirst. 21For forty years you sustained them in the desert; they lacked nothing, their clothes did not wear out nor did their feet become swollen.

22"You gave them kingdoms and nations, allotting to them even the remotest frontiers. They took over the country of Sihon*b* king of Heshbon and the country of Og king of Bashan. 23You made their sons as numerous as the stars in the sky, and you brought them into the land that you told their fathers to enter and possess. 24Their sons went in and took possession of the land. You subdued before them the Canaanites, who lived in the land; you handed the Canaanites over to them, along with their kings and the peoples of the land, to deal with them as

---

a9 Hebrew *Yam Suph*; that is, Sea of Reeds   *b22* One Hebrew manuscript and Septuagint; most
Hebrew manuscripts *Sihon, that is, the country of the*

they pleased. 25They captured fortified cities and fertile land; they took possession of houses filled with all kinds of good things, wells already dug, vineyards, olive groves and fruit trees in abundance. They ate to the full and were well-nourished; they reveled in your great goodness.

26"But they were disobedient and rebelled against you; they put your law behind their backs. They killed your prophets, who had admonished them in order to turn them back to you; they committed awful blasphemies. 27So you handed them over to their enemies, who oppressed them. But when they were oppressed they cried out to you. From heaven you heard them, and in your great compassion you gave them deliverers, who rescued them from the hand of their enemies.

28"But as soon as they were at rest, they again did what was evil in your sight. Then you abandoned them to the hand of their enemies so that they ruled over them. And when they cried out to you again, you heard from heaven, and in your compassion you delivered them time after time.

29"You warned them to return to your law, but they became arrogant and disobeyed your commands. They sinned against your ordinances, by which a man will live if he obeys them. Stubbornly they turned their backs on you, became stiff-necked and refused to listen. 30For many years you were patient with them. By your Spirit you admonished them through your prophets. Yet they paid no attention, so you handed them over to the neighboring peoples. 31But in your great mercy you did not put an end to them or abandon them, for you are a gracious and merciful God.

32"Now therefore, O our God, the great, mighty and awesome God, who keeps his covenant of love, do not let all this hardship seem trifling in your eyes—the hardship that has come upon us, upon our kings and leaders, upon our priests and prophets, upon our fathers and all your people, from the days of the kings of Assyria until today. 33In all that has happened to us, you have been just; you have acted faithfully, while we did wrong. 34Our kings, our leaders, our priests and our fathers did not follow your law; they did not pay attention to your commands or the warnings you gave them. 35Even while they were in their kingdom, enjoying your great goodness to them in the spacious and fertile land you gave them, they did not serve you or turn from their evil ways.

36"But see, we are slaves today, slaves in the land you gave our forefathers so they could eat its fruit and the other good things it produces. 37Because of our sins, its abundant harvest goes to the kings you have placed over us. They rule over our bodies and our cattle as they please. We are in great distress.

The Agreement of the People

38"In view of all this, we are making a binding agreement, putting it in writing, and our leaders, our Levites and our priests are affixing their seals to it."

10 Those who sealed it were:

Nehemiah the governor, the son of Hacaliah.

Zedekiah, 2Seraiah, Azariah, Jeremiah,
3Pashhur, Amariah, Malkijah,
4Hattush, Shebaniah, Malluch,
5Harim, Meremoth, Obadiah,
6Daniel, Ginnethon, Baruch,
7Meshullam, Abijah, Mijamin,
8Maaziah, Bilgai and Shemaiah. These were the priests.

⁹The Levites:

> Jeshua son of Azaniah, Binnui of the sons of Henadad, Kadmiel,
> ¹⁰and their associates: Shebaniah, Hodiah, Kelita, Pelaiah, Hanan,
> ¹¹Mica, Rehob, Hashabiah,
> ¹²Zaccur, Sherebiah, Shebaniah,
> ¹³Hodiah, Bani and Beninu.

¹⁴The leaders of the people:

> Parosh, Pahath-Moab, Elam, Zattu, Bani,
> ¹⁵Bunni, Azgad, Bebai,
> ¹⁶Adonijah, Bigvai, Adin,
> ¹⁷Ater, Hezekiah, Azzur,
> ¹⁸Hodiah, Hashum, Bezai,
> ¹⁹Hariph, Anathoth, Nebai,
> ²⁰Magpiash, Meshullam, Hezir,
> ²¹Meshezabel, Zadok, Jaddua,
> ²²Pelatiah, Hanan, Anaiah,
> ²³Hoshea, Hananiah, Hasshub,
> ²⁴Hallohesh, Pilha, Shobek,
> ²⁵Rehum, Hashabnah, Maaseiah,
> ²⁶Ahiah, Hanan, Anan,
> ²⁷Malluch, Harim and Baanah.

²⁸"The rest of the people—priests, Levites, gatekeepers, singers, temple servants and all who separated themselves from the neighboring peoples for the sake of the Law of God, together with their wives and all their sons and daughters who are able to understand— ²⁹all these now join their brothers the nobles, and bind themselves with a curse and an oath to follow the Law of God given through Moses the servant of God and to obey carefully all the commands, regulations and decrees of the Lord our Lord.

³⁰"We promise not to give our daughters in marriage to the peoples around us or take their daughters for our sons.

³¹"When the neighboring peoples bring merchandise or grain to sell on the Sabbath, we will not buy from them on the Sabbath or on any holy day. Every seventh year we will forgo working the land and will cancel all debts.

³²"We assume the responsibility for carrying out the commands to give a third of a shekel[a] each year for the service of the house of our God: ³³for the bread set out on the table; for the regular grain offerings and burnt offerings; for the offerings on the Sabbaths, New Moon festivals and appointed feasts; for the holy offerings; for sin offerings to make atonement for Israel; and for all the duties of the house of our God.

³⁴"We—the priests, the Levites and the people—have cast lots to determine when each of our families is to bring to the house of our God at set times each year a contribution of wood to burn on the altar of the Lord our God, as it is written in the Law.

³⁵"We also assume responsibility for bringing to the house of the Lord each year the firstfruits of our crops and of every fruit tree.

³⁶"As it is also written in the Law, we will bring the firstborn of our sons and of our cattle, of our herds and of our flocks to the house of our God, to the priests ministering there.

³⁷"Moreover, we will bring to the storerooms of the house of our God, to the priests, the first of our ground meal, of our grain offerings, of the fruit of all our trees and of our new wine and oil. And we will bring a tithe of our crops to the Levites, for it is the Levites who collect the tithes in all the towns where we work. ³⁸A priest descended from Aaron is to accompany the Levites when they receive the tithes, and the Levites are to bring a tenth of the tithes up to the house of

---

a32 That is, about 1/8 ounce (about 4 grams)

our God, to the storerooms of the treasury. ³⁹The people of Israel, including the Levites, are to bring their contributions of grain, new wine and oil to the storerooms where the articles for the sanctuary are kept and where the ministering priests, the gatekeepers and the singers stay.

"We will not neglect the house of our God."

WORDS TO REMEMBER

10:39 We will not neglect the house of our God.

The New Residents of Jerusalem

11 Now the leaders of the people settled in Jerusalem, and the rest of the people cast lots to bring one out of every ten to live in Jerusalem, the holy city, while the remaining nine were to stay in their own towns. ²The people commended all the men who volunteered to live in Jerusalem.

³These are the provincial leaders who settled in Jerusalem (now some Israelites, priests, Levites, temple servants and descendants of Solomon's servants lived in the towns of Judah, each on his own property in the various towns, ⁴while other peo-

ple from both Judah and Benjamin lived in Jerusalem):

From the descendants of Judah:

Athaiah son of Uzziah, the son of Zechariah, the son of Amariah, the son of Shephatiah, the son of Mahalalel, a descendant of Perez; ⁵and Maaseiah son of Baruch, the son of Col-Hozeh, the son of Hazaiah, the son of Adaiah, the son of Joiarib, the son of Zechariah, a descendant of Shelah. ⁶The descendants of Perez who lived in Jerusalem totaled 468 able men.

⁷From the descendants of Benjamin:

Sallu son of Meshullam, the son of Joed, the son of Pedaiah, the son of Kolaiah, the son of Maaseiah, the son of Ithiel, the son of Jeshaiah, ⁸and his followers, Gabbai and Sallai—928 men. ⁹Joel son of Zicri was their chief officer, and Judah son of Hassenuah was over the Second District of the city.

¹⁰From the priests:

Jedaiah; the son of Joiarib; Jakin; ¹¹Seraiah son of Hilkiah, the son of Meshullam, the son of Zadok, the son of Meraioth, the son of Ahitub, supervisor in the house of God, ¹²and their associates, who carried on work for the temple—822 men; Adaiah son of Jeroham, the son of Pelaliah, the

LET'S LIVE IT!   Nehemiah 10:28–39

A "DO GOOD" PLAN ➡ The people of Judah had confessed their sins (Nehemiah 9). Then they did something else. They promised God they would do better and even put their promises in writing (Nehemiah 9:38). To find out what the people of Judah promised God they would do, read Nehemiah 10:28–39.

When we sin it is important to tell God we are sorry. It is also important to plan how to do good in the future.

You can plan ahead to please God. Get a sheet of notebook paper. Write down one thing you will do to please God this week. Write your "do good" plan as a letter to God. Begin as the people in Nehemiah's time did, by writing, "I promise."

son of Amzi, the son of Zechariah, the son of Pashhur, the son of Malkijah, ¹³and his associates, who were heads of families—242 men; Amashsai son of Azarel, the son of Ahzai, the son of Meshillemoth, the son of Immer, ¹⁴and his*a* associates, who were able men—128. Their chief officer was Zabdiel son of Haggedolim.

¹⁵From the Levites:

Shemaiah son of Hasshub, the son of Azrikam, the son of Hashabiah, the son of Bunni; ¹⁶Shabbethai and Jozabad, two of the heads of the Levites, who had charge of the outside work of the house of God; ¹⁷Mattaniah son of Mica, the son of Zabdi, the son of Asaph, the director who led in thanksgiving and prayer; Bakbukiah, second among his associates; and Abda son of Shammua, the son of Galal, the son of Jeduthun. ¹⁸The Levites in the holy city totaled 284.

¹⁹The gatekeepers:

Akkub, Talmon and their associates, who kept watch at the gates—172 men.

²⁰The rest of the Israelites, with the priests and Levites, were in all the towns of Judah, each on his ancestral property.

²¹The temple servants lived on the hill of Ophel, and Ziha and Gishpa were in charge of them.

²²The chief officer of the Levites in Jerusalem was Uzzi son of Bani, the son of Hashabiah, the son of Mattaniah, the son of Mica. Uzzi was one of Asaph's descendants, who were the singers responsible for the service of the house of God. ²³The singers were under the king's orders, which regulated their daily activity.

²⁴Pethahiah son of Meshezabel, one of the descendants of Zerah son of Judah, was the king's agent in all affairs relating to the people.

²⁵As for the villages with their fields, some of the people of Judah lived in Kiriath Arba and its surrounding settlements, in Dibon and its settlements, in Jekabzeel and its villages, ²⁶in Jeshua, in Moladah, in Beth Pelet, ²⁷in Hazar Shual, in Beersheba and its settlements, ²⁸in Ziklag, in Meconah and its settlements, ²⁹in En Rimmon, in Zorah, in Jarmuth, ³⁰Zanoah, Adullam and their villages, in Lachish and its fields, and in Azekah and its settlements. So they were living all the way from Beersheba to the Valley of Hinnom.

³¹The descendants of the Benjamites from Geba lived in Micmash, Aija, Bethel and its settlements, ³²in Anathoth, Nob and Ananiah, ³³in Hazor, Ramah and Gittaim, ³⁴in Hadid, Zeboim and Neballat, ³⁵in Lod and Ono, and in the Valley of the Craftsmen.

³⁶Some of the divisions of the Levites of Judah settled in Benjamin.

Priests and Levites

12 These were the priests and Levites who returned with Zerubbabel son of Shealtiel and with Jeshua:

Seraiah, Jeremiah, Ezra, ²Amariah, Malluch, Hattush, ³Shecaniah, Rehum, Meremoth, ⁴Iddo, Ginnethon,*b* Abijah, ⁵Mijamin,*c* Moadiah, Bilgah, ⁶Shemaiah, Joiarib, Jedaiah, ⁷Sallu, Amok, Hilkiah and Jedaiah.

These were the leaders of the priests and their associates in the days of Jeshua.

⁸The Levites were Jeshua, Binnui, Kadmiel, Sherebiah, Judah, and also Mattaniah, who, together with his associates, was in charge of the songs of thanksgiving. ⁹Bakbukiah and Unni, their associates, stood opposite them in the services.

¹⁰Jeshua was the father of Joiakim,

---

a14 Most Septuagint manuscripts; Hebrew their (also Neh. 12:16); most Hebrew manuscripts Ginnethoi
b4 Many Hebrew manuscripts and Vulgate (see
c5 A variant of Miniamin

Joiakim the father of Eliashib, Eliashib the father of Joiada, [11]Joiada the father of Jonathan, and Jonathan the father of Jaddua.

[12]In the days of Joiakim, these were the heads of the priestly families:

of Seraiah's family, Meraiah;
of Jeremiah's, Hananiah;
[13]of Ezra's, Meshullam;
of Amariah's, Jehohanan;
[14]of Malluch's, Jonathan;
of Shecaniah's,[a] Joseph;
[15]of Harim's, Adna;
of Meremoth's,[b] Helkai;
[16]of Iddo's, Zechariah;
of Ginnethon's, Meshullam;
[17]of Abijah's, Zicri;
of Miniamin's and of Moadiah's, Piltai;
[18]of Bilgah's, Shammua;
of Shemaiah's, Jehonathan;
[19]of Joiarib's, Mattenai;
of Jedaiah's, Uzzi;
[20]of Sallu's, Kallai;
of Amok's, Eber;
[21]of Hilkiah's, Hashabiah;
of Jedaiah's, Nethanel.

[22]The family heads of the Levites in the days of Eliashib, Joiada, Johanan and Jaddua, as well as those of the priests, were recorded in the reign of Darius the Persian. [23]The family heads among the descendants of Levi up to the time of Johanan son of Eliashib were recorded in the book of the annals. [24]And the leaders of the Levites were Hashabiah, Sherebiah, Jeshua son of Kadmiel, and their associates, who stood opposite them to give praise and thanksgiving, one section responding to the other, as prescribed by David the man of God.

[25]Mattaniah, Bakbukiah, Obadiah, Meshullam, Talmon and Akkub were gatekeepers who guarded the storerooms at the gates. [26]They served in the days of Joiakim son of Jeshua, the son of Jozadak, and in the days of Nehemiah the governor and of Ezra the priest and scribe.

Dedication of the Wall of Jerusalem

[27]At the dedication of the wall of Jerusalem, the Levites were sought out from where they lived and were brought to Jerusalem to celebrate joyfully the dedication with songs of thanksgiving and with the music of cymbals, harps and lyres. [28]The singers also were brought together from the region around Jerusalem—from the villages of the Netophathites, [29]from Beth Gilgal, and from the area of Geba and Azmaveth, for the singers had built villages for themselves around Jerusalem. [30]When the priests and Levites had purified themselves ceremonially, they purified the people, the gates and the wall.

[31]I had the leaders of Judah go up on top[c] of the wall. I also assigned two large choirs to give thanks. One was to proceed on top[d] of the wall to the right, toward the Dung Gate. [32]Hoshaiah and half the leaders of Judah followed them, [33]along with Azariah, Ezra, Meshullam, [34]Judah, Benjamin, Shemaiah, Jeremiah, [35]as well as some priests with trumpets, and also Zechariah son of Jonathan, the son of Shemaiah, the son of Mattaniah, the son of Micaiah, the son of Zaccur, the son of Asaph, [36]and his associates—Shemaiah, Azarel, Milalai, Gilalai, Maai, Nethanel, Judah and Hanani—with musical instruments prescribed by David the man of God. Ezra the scribe led the procession. [37]At the Fountain Gate they continued directly up the steps of the City of David on the ascent to the wall and passed above the house of David to the Water Gate on the east.

[38]The second choir proceeded in the opposite direction. I followed them on top[e] of the wall, together with half

---

[a]14 Very many Hebrew manuscripts, some Septuagint manuscripts and Syriac (see also Neh. 12:3); most Hebrew manuscripts *Shebaniah's*   [b]15 Some Septuagint manuscripts (see also Neh. 12:3); Hebrew *Meraioth's*   [c]31 Or *go alongside*   [d]31 Or *proceed alongside*   [e]38 Or *them alongside*

the people—past the Tower of the Ovens to the Broad Wall, 39over the Gate of Ephraim, the Jeshanah*a* Gate, the Fish Gate, the Tower of Hananel and the Tower of the Hundred, as far as the Sheep Gate. At the Gate of the Guard they stopped.

40The two choirs that gave thanks then took their places in the house of God; so did I, together with half the officials, 41as well as the priests— Eliakim, Maaseiah, Miniamin, Micaiah, Elioenai, Zechariah and Hananiah with their trumpets— 42and also Maaseiah, Shemaiah, Eleazar, Uzzi, Jehohanan, Malkijah, Elam and Ezer. The choirs sang under the direction of Jezrahiah. 43And on that day they offered great sacrifices, rejoicing because God had given them great joy. The women and children also rejoiced. The sound of rejoicing in Jerusalem could be heard far away.

44At that time men were appointed to be in charge of the storerooms for the contributions, firstfruits and tithes. From the fields around the towns they were to bring into the storerooms the portions required by the Law for the priests and the Le-

vites, for Judah was pleased with the ministering priests and Levites. 45They performed the service of their God and the service of purification, as did also the singers and gatekeepers, according to the commands of David and his son Solomon. 46For long ago, in the days of David and Asaph, there had been directors for the singers and for the songs of praise and thanksgiving to God. 47So in the days of Zerubbabel and of Nehemiah, all Israel contributed the daily portions for the singers and gatekeepers. They also set aside the portion for the other Levites, and the Levites set aside the portion for the descendants of Aaron.

Nehemiah's Final Reforms

13 On that day the Book of Moses was read aloud in the hearing of the people and there it was found written that no Ammonite or Moabite should ever be admitted into the assembly of God, 2because they had not met the Israelites with food and water but had hired Balaam to call a curse down on them. (Our God, however, turned the curse into a blessing.) 3When the people heard

a39 Or Old

Life in Bible Times

AN OUTDOOR MARKET

Markets in Bible lands were noisy, exciting places. All sorts of food, lamps, blankets, garments and other things were sold outdoors. The sellers shouted. Buyers argued loudly to get a lower price. In chapter 13 Nehemiah reminded the Israelites that it was wrong to hold a market on the Sabbath. God had set that day aside for the Israelites to rest and to worship him.

this law, they excluded from Israel all who were of foreign descent.

⁴Before this, Eliashib the priest had been put in charge of the storerooms of the house of our God. He was closely associated with Tobiah, ⁵and he had provided him with a large room formerly used to store the grain offerings and incense and temple articles, and also the tithes of grain, new wine and oil prescribed for the Levites, singers and gatekeepers, as well as the contributions for the priests.

⁶But while all this was going on, I was not in Jerusalem, for in the thirty-second year of Artaxerxes king of Babylon I had returned to the king. Some time later I asked his permission ⁷and came back to Jerusalem. Here I learned about the evil thing Eliashib had done in providing Tobiah a room in the courts of the house of God. ⁸I was greatly displeased and threw all Tobiah's household goods out of the room. ⁹I gave orders to purify the rooms, and then I put back into them the equipment of the house of God, with the grain offerings and the incense.

¹⁰I also learned that the portions assigned to the Levites had not been given to them, and that all the Levites and singers responsible for the service had gone back to their own fields. ¹¹So I rebuked the officials and asked them, "Why is the house of God neglected?" Then I called them together and stationed them at their posts.

¹²All Judah brought the tithes of grain, new wine and oil into the storerooms. ¹³I put Shelemiah the priest, Zadok the scribe, and a Levite named Pedaiah in charge of the storerooms and made Hanan son of Zaccur, the son of Mattaniah, their assistant, because these men were considered trustworthy. They were made responsible for distributing the supplies to their brothers.

¹⁴Remember me for this, O my God, and do not blot out what I have so faithfully done for the house of my God and its services.

¹⁵In those days I saw men in Judah treading winepresses on the Sabbath and bringing in grain and loading it on donkeys, together with wine, grapes, figs and all other kinds of loads. And they were bringing all this into Jerusalem on the Sabbath. Therefore I warned them against selling food on that day. ¹⁶Men from Tyre who lived in Jerusalem were bringing in fish and all kinds of merchandise and selling them in Jerusalem on the Sabbath to the people of Judah. ¹⁷I rebuked the nobles of Judah and said to them, "What is this wicked thing you are doing—desecrating the Sabbath day? ¹⁸Didn't your forefathers do the same things, so that our God brought all this calamity upon us and upon this city? Now you are stirring up more wrath against Israel by desecrating the Sabbath."

¹⁹When evening shadows fell on the gates of Jerusalem before the Sabbath, I ordered the doors to be

▌ET'S LIVE IT! — Nehemiah 13:10–22

REMEMBER ME, GOD ➡ In Nehemiah 13:10–22, Nehemiah writes down some of the good things that he has done. He asks God to remember him for his good work because he was trying to please God and help his people.

God was pleased when he saw Nehemiah doing good. And he's pleased when he sees you do good things too. Write down on a piece of paper some of the good things that you've done. Show your list to your parents. Ask if there is anything they think you should add to your list.

shut and not opened until the Sabbath was over. I stationed some of my own men at the gates so that no load could be brought in on the Sabbath day. ²⁰Once or twice the merchants and sellers of all kinds of goods spent the night outside Jerusalem. ²¹But I warned them and said, "Why do you spend the night by the wall? If you do this again, I will lay hands on you." From that time on they no longer came on the Sabbath. ²²Then I commanded the Levites to purify themselves and go and guard the gates in order to keep the Sabbath day holy.

Remember me for this also, O my God, and show mercy to me according to your great love.

²³Moreover, in those days I saw men of Judah who had married women from Ashdod, Ammon and Moab. ²⁴Half of their children spoke the language of Ashdod or the language of one of the other peoples, and did not know how to speak the language of Judah. ²⁵I rebuked them and called curses down on them. I beat some of the men and pulled out their hair. I made them take an oath in God's name and said: "You are not to give your daughters in marriage to their sons, nor are you to take their daughters in marriage for your sons or for yourselves. ²⁶Was it not because of marriages like these that Solomon king of Israel sinned? Among the many nations there was no king like him. He was loved by his God, and God made him king over all Israel, but even he was led into sin by foreign women. ²⁷Must we hear now that you too are doing all this terrible wickedness and are being unfaithful to our God by marrying foreign women?"

²⁸One of the sons of Joiada son of Eliashib the high priest was son-in-law to Sanballat the Horonite. And I drove him away from me.

²⁹Remember them, O my God, because they defiled the priestly office and the covenant of the priesthood and of the Levites.

³⁰So I purified the priests and the Levites of everything foreign, and assigned them duties, each to his own task. ³¹I also made provision for contributions of wood at designated times, and for the firstfruits.

Remember me with favor, O my God.

ESTHER

Queen Vashti Deposed

1 This is what happened during the time of Xerxes,[a] the Xerxes who ruled over 127 provinces stretching from India to Cush[b]: ²At that time King Xerxes reigned from his royal throne in the citadel of Susa, ³and in the third year of his reign he gave a banquet for all his nobles and officials. The military leaders of Persia and Media, the princes, and the nobles of the provinces were present.

⁴For a full 180 days he displayed the vast wealth of his kingdom and the splendor and glory of his majesty. ⁵When these days were over, the king gave a banquet, lasting seven days, in the enclosed garden of the king's palace, for all the people from the least to the greatest, who were in the citadel of Susa. ⁶The garden had hangings of white and blue linen, fastened with cords of white linen and purple material to silver rings on marble pillars. There were couches of gold and silver on a mosaic pavement of porphyry, marble, mother-of-pearl and other costly stones. ⁷Wine was served in goblets of gold, each one different from the other, and the royal wine was abundant, in keeping with the king's liberality. ⁸By the king's command each guest was allowed to drink in his own way, for the king instructed all the wine stewards to serve each man what he wished.

⁹Queen Vashti also gave a banquet for the women in the royal palace of King Xerxes.

¹⁰On the seventh day, when King Xerxes was in high spirits from wine, he commanded the seven eunuchs who served him—Mehuman, Biztha, Harbona, Bigtha, Abagtha, Zethar and Carcas— ¹¹to bring before him Queen Vashti, wearing her royal crown, in order to display her beauty to the people and nobles, for she was lovely to look at. ¹²But when the attendants delivered the king's command, Queen Vashti refused to come.

Then the king became furious and burned with anger.

¹³Since it was customary for the king to consult experts in matters of law and justice, he spoke with the wise men who understood the times ¹⁴and were closest to the king—Carshena, Shethar, Admatha, Tarshish, Meres, Marsena and Memucan, the seven nobles of Persia and Media who had special access to the king and were highest in the kingdom.

¹⁵"According to law, what must be done to Queen Vashti?" he asked. "She has not obeyed the command of King Xerxes that the eunuchs have taken to her."

¹⁶Then Memucan replied in the presence of the king and the nobles, "Queen Vashti has done wrong, not only against the king but also against all the nobles and the peoples of all the provinces of King Xerxes. ¹⁷For the queen's conduct will become known to all the women, and so they will despise their husbands and say, 'King Xerxes commanded Queen Vashti to be brought before him, but she would not come.' ¹⁸This very day the Persian and Median women of the nobility who have heard about the queen's conduct will respond to all the king's nobles in the same way. There will be no end of disrespect and discord.

¹⁹"Therefore, if it pleases the king, let him issue a royal decree and let it be written in the laws of Persia and Media, which cannot be repealed, that Vashti is never again to enter the presence of King Xerxes. Also let the king give her royal position to someone else who is better than she. ²⁰Then when the king's edict is proclaimed throughout all his vast realm, all the women will respect their husbands, from the least to the greatest."

²¹The king and his nobles were pleased with this advice, so the king did as Memucan proposed. ²²He sent dispatches to all parts of the king-

---

[a]1 Hebrew *Ahasuerus*, a variant of Xerxes' Persian name; here and throughout Esther   [b]1 That is, the upper Nile region

dom, to each province in its own script and to each people in its own language, proclaiming in each people's tongue that every man should be ruler over his own household.

Esther Made Queen

2 Later when the anger of King Xerxes had subsided, he remembered Vashti and what she had done and what he had decreed about her. ²Then the king's personal attendants proposed, "Let a search be made for beautiful young virgins for the king. ³Let the king appoint commissioners in every province of his realm to bring all these beautiful girls into the harem at the citadel of Susa. Let them be placed under the care of Hegai, the king's eunuch, who is in charge of the women; and let beauty treatments be given to them. ⁴Then let the girl who pleases the king be queen instead of Vashti." This advice appealed to the king, and he followed it.

⁵Now there was in the citadel of Susa a Jew of the tribe of Benjamin, named Mordecai son of Jair, the son of Shimei, the son of Kish, ⁶who had been carried into exile from Jerusalem by Nebuchadnezzar king of Babylon, among those taken captive with Jehoiachin*ᵃ* king of Judah. ⁷Mordecai had a cousin named Hadassah, whom he had brought up because she had neither father nor mother. This

girl, who was also known as Esther, was lovely in form and features, and Mordecai had taken her as his own daughter when her father and mother died.

⁸When the king's order and edict had been proclaimed, many girls were brought to the citadel of Susa and put under the care of Hegai. Esther also was taken to the king's palace and entrusted to Hegai, who had charge of the harem. ⁹The girl pleased him and won his favor. Immediately he provided her with her beauty treatments and special food. He assigned to her seven maids selected from the king's palace and moved her and her maids into the best place in the harem.

¹⁰Esther had not revealed her nationality and family background, because Mordecai had forbidden her to do so. ¹¹Every day he walked back and forth near the courtyard of the harem to find out how Esther was and what was happening to her.

¹²Before a girl's turn came to go in to King Xerxes, she had to complete twelve months of beauty treatments prescribed for the women, six months with oil of myrrh and six with perfumes and cosmetics. ¹³And this is how she would go to the king: Anything she wanted was given her to take with her from the harem to the king's palace. ¹⁴In the evening she would go there and in the morning

ᵃ6 Hebrew Jeconiah, *a variant of* Jehoiachin

▚ET'S LIVE IT!   Esther 2:1–18

NOBODY SPECIAL ➡ Esther's mother and father died, so Esther was brought up by her cousin. No one would have thought Esther was special when she was growing up. But when she did grow up, something happened that made her very special. Read Esther 2:1–8 and find out what happened that made Esther special. Sometimes you may not feel very special. Others may be smarter. Or faster runners. Or have nicer clothes. But you are special to God. Just as he had a plan for Esther, he has a plan for your life. Read about it in Jeremiah 29:11. Draw a picture of yourself doing something special when you grow up. Show the picture to a friend and tell him or her what you would like to be when you are older.

return to another part of the harem to the care of Shaashgaz, the king's eunuch who was in charge of the concubines. She would not return to the king unless he was pleased with her and summoned her by name.

15When the turn came for Esther (the girl Mordecai had adopted, the daughter of his uncle Abihail) to go to the king, she asked for nothing other than what Hegai, the king's eunuch who was in charge of the harem, suggested. And Esther won the favor of everyone who saw her. 16She was taken to King Xerxes in the royal residence in the tenth month, the month of Tebeth, in the seventh year of his reign.

17Now the king was attracted to Esther more than to any of the other women, and she won his favor and approval more than any of the other virgins. So he set a royal crown on her head and made her queen instead of Vashti. 18And the king gave a great banquet, Esther's banquet, for all his nobles and officials. He proclaimed a holiday throughout the provinces and distributed gifts with royal liberality.

Mordecai Uncovers a Conspiracy

19When the virgins were assembled a second time, Mordecai was sitting at the king's gate. 20But Esther had kept secret her family background and nationality just as Mordecai had told her to do, for she continued to follow Mordecai's instructions as she had done when he was bringing her up.

21During the time Mordecai was sitting at the king's gate, Bigthana*a* and Teresh, two of the king's officers who guarded the doorway, became angry and conspired to assassinate King Xerxes. 22But Mordecai found out about the plot and told Queen Esther, who in turn reported it to the king, giving credit to Mordecai. 23And when the report was investi-gated and found to be true, the two officials were hanged on a gallows.*b* All this was recorded in the book of the annals in the presence of the king.

Haman's Plot to Destroy the Jews

3 After these events, King Xerxes honored Haman son of Hammedatha, the Agagite, elevating him and giving him a seat of honor higher than that of all the other nobles. 2All the royal officials at the king's gate knelt down and paid honor to Haman, for the king had commanded this concerning him. But Mordecai would not kneel down or pay him honor.

3Then the royal officials at the king's gate asked Mordecai, "Why do you disobey the king's command?" 4Day after day they spoke to him but he refused to comply. Therefore they told Haman about it to see whether Mordecai's behavior would be tolerated, for he had told them he was a Jew.

5When Haman saw that Mordecai would not kneel down or pay him honor, he was enraged. 6Yet having learned who Mordecai's people were, he scorned the idea of killing only Mordecai. Instead Haman looked for a way to destroy all Mordecai's people, the Jews, throughout the whole kingdom of Xerxes.

7In the twelfth year of King Xerxes, in the first month, the month of Nisan, they cast the *pur* (that is, the lot) in the presence of Haman to select a day and month. And the lot fell on*c* the twelfth month, the month of Adar.

8Then Haman said to King Xerxes, "There is a certain people dispersed and scattered among the peoples in all the provinces of your kingdom whose customs are different from those of all other people and who do not obey the king's laws; it is not in the king's best interest to tolerate

---

*a*21 Hebrew *Bigthan,* a variant of *Bigthana* elsewhere in Esther　　*b*23 Or *were hung* (or *impaled*) *on poles*; similarly *c*7 Septuagint; Hebrew does not have *And the lot fell on.*

them. [9]If it pleases the king, let a decree be issued to destroy them, and I will put ten thousand talents[a] of silver into the royal treasury for the men who carry out this business."

Life In Bible Times

CASTING LOTS

People in Babylon and Persia cast lots for "divining." Divining is trying to learn what will happen in the future. We're not sure today exactly what methods or articles were used to "cast lots." Whatever the method, Haman cast lots to find a good day to ask the king of Persia to let him destroy the Jewish people.

---

[10]So the king took his signet ring from his finger and gave it to Haman son of Hammedatha, the Agagite, the enemy of the Jews. [11]"Keep the money," the king said to Haman, "and do with the people as you please."

[12]Then on the thirteenth day of the first month the royal secretaries were summoned. They wrote out in the script of each province and in the language of each people all Haman's orders to the king's satraps, the governors of the various provinces and the nobles of the various peoples. These were written in the name of King Xerxes himself and sealed with his own ring. [13]Dispatches were sent by couriers to all the king's provinces with the order to destroy, kill and annihilate all the Jews—young and old, women and little children—on a single day, the thirteenth day of the twelfth month, the month of Adar, and to plunder their goods. [14]A copy of the text of the edict was to be is-

sued as law in every province and made known to the people of every nationality so they would be ready for that day.

[15]Spurred on by the king's command, the couriers went out, and the edict was issued in the citadel of Susa. The king and Haman sat down to drink, but the city of Susa was bewildered.

Mordecai Persuades Esther to Help

4 When Mordecai learned of all that had been done, he tore his clothes, put on sackcloth and ashes, and went out into the city, wailing loudly and bitterly. [2]But he went only as far as the king's gate, because no one clothed in sackcloth was allowed to enter it. [3]In every province to which the edict and order of the king came, there was great mourning among the Jews, with fasting, weeping and wailing. Many lay in sackcloth and ashes.

[4]When Esther's maids and eunuchs came and told her about Mordecai, she was in great distress. She sent clothes for him to put on instead of his sackcloth, but he would not accept them. [5]Then Esther summoned Hathach, one of the king's eunuchs assigned to attend her, and ordered him to find out what was troubling Mordecai and why.

[6]So Hathach went out to Mordecai in the open square of the city in front of the king's gate. [7]Mordecai told him everything that had happened to him, including the exact amount of money Haman had promised to pay into the royal treasury for the destruction of the Jews. [8]He also gave him a copy of the text of the edict for their annihilation, which had been published in Susa, to show to Esther and explain it to her, and he told him to urge her to go into the king's presence to beg for mercy and plead with him for her people.

[9]Hathach went back and reported to Esther what Mordecai had said.

[a]9 That is, about 375 tons (about 345 metric tons)

[10]Then she instructed him to say to Mordecai, [11]"All the king's officials and the people of the royal provinces know that for any man or woman who approaches the king in the inner court without being summoned the king has but one law: that he be put to death. The only exception to this is for the king to extend the gold scepter to him and spare his life. But thirty days have passed since I was called to go to the king."

[12]When Esther's words were reported to Mordecai, [13]he sent back this answer: "Do not think that because you are in the king's house you alone of all the Jews will escape. [14]For if you remain silent at this time, relief and deliverance for the Jews will arise from another place, but you and your father's family will perish. And who knows but that you have come to royal position for such a time as this?"

[15]Then Esther sent this reply to Mordecai: [16]"Go, gather together all the Jews who are in Susa, and fast for me. Do not eat or drink for three days, night or day. I and my maids will fast as you do. When this is done, I will go to the king, even though it is against the law. And if I perish, I perish."

[17]So Mordecai went away and carried out all of Esther's instructions.

Esther's Request to the King

5 On the third day Esther put on her royal robes and stood in the inner court of the palace, in front of the king's hall. The king was sitting on his royal throne in the hall, facing the entrance. [2]When he saw Queen Esther standing in the court, he was pleased with her and held out to her the gold scepter that was in his hand. So Esther approached and touched the tip of the scepter.

[3]Then the king asked, "What is it, Queen Esther? What is your request? Even up to half the kingdom, it will be given you."

[4]"If it pleases the king," replied Esther, "let the king, together with Haman, come today to a banquet I have prepared for him."

[5]"Bring Haman at once," the king said, "so that we may do what Esther asks."

So the king and Haman went to the banquet Esther had prepared. [6]As they were drinking wine, the king again asked Esther, "Now what is your petition? It will be given you. And what is your request? Even up to half the kingdom, it will be granted."

[7]Esther replied, "My petition and my request is this: [8]If the king regards me with favor and if it pleases the king to grant my petition and fulfill my request, let the king and Haman come tomorrow to the banquet I will prepare for them. Then I will answer the king's question."

Haman's Rage Against Mordecai

[9]Haman went out that day happy and in high spirits. But when he saw Mordecai at the king's gate and observed that he neither rose nor showed fear in his presence, he was filled with rage against Mordecai. [10]Nevertheless, Haman restrained himself and went home.

Calling together his friends and Zeresh, his wife, [11]Haman boasted to them about his vast wealth, his many sons, and all the ways the king had honored him and how he had elevated him above the other nobles and officials. [12]"And that's not all," Haman added. "I'm the only person Queen Esther invited to accompany the king to the banquet she gave. And she has invited me along with the king tomorrow. [13]But all this gives me no satisfaction as long as I see that Jew Mordecai sitting at the king's gate."

[14]His wife Zeresh and all his friends said to him, "Have a gallows built, seventy-five feet[a] high, and ask the king in the morning to have Mordecai hanged on it. Then go with the king to the dinner and be happy."

---

[a]14 Hebrew *fifty cubits* (about 23 meters)

This suggestion delighted Haman, and he had the gallows built.

Mordecai Honored

6 That night the king could not sleep; so he ordered the book of the chronicles, the record of his reign, to be brought in and read to him. ²It was found recorded there that Mordecai had exposed Bigthana and Teresh, two of the king's officers who guarded the doorway, who had conspired to assassinate King Xerxes.

³"What honor and recognition has Mordecai received for this?" the king asked.

"Nothing has been done for him," his attendants answered.

⁴The king said, "Who is in the court?" Now Haman had just entered the outer court of the palace to speak to the king about hanging Mordecai on the gallows he had erected for him.

⁵His attendants answered, "Haman is standing in the court."

"Bring him in," the king ordered.

⁶When Haman entered, the king asked him, "What should be done for the man the king delights to honor?" Now Haman thought to himself, "Who is there that the king would rather honor than me?" ⁷So he answered the king, "For the man the king delights to honor, ⁸have them bring a royal robe the king has worn and a horse the king has ridden, one with a royal crest placed on its head. ⁹Then let the robe and horse be entrusted to one of the king's most noble princes. Let them robe the man the king delights to honor, and lead him on the horse through the city streets, proclaiming before him, 'This is what is done for the man the king delights to honor!' "

¹⁰"Go at once," the king commanded Haman. "Get the robe and the horse and do just as you have suggested for Mordecai the Jew, who sits at the king's gate. Do not neglect anything you have recommended."

¹¹So Haman got the robe and the horse. He robed Mordecai, and led him on horseback through the city streets, proclaiming before him, "This is what is done for the man the king delights to honor!"

¹²Afterward Mordecai returned to the king's gate. But Haman rushed home, with his head covered in grief, ¹³and told Zeresh his wife and all his friends everything that had happened to him.

His advisers and his wife Zeresh said to him, "Since Mordecai, before whom your downfall has started, is of Jewish origin, you cannot stand against him—you will surely come to ruin!" ¹⁴While they were still talking with him, the king's eunuchs arrived and hurried Haman away to the banquet Esther had prepared.

❓DID YOU KNOW?   6:1

What is Providence?

Providence is a word used to talk about God's control of everything that happens. God does not need to use miracles to help his people. God can control events that seem very natural and normal. God had control of all the events of Esther 6—even an event so ordinary as Xerxes' sleeplessness. And he used all the events to help his people.

Haman Hanged

7 So the king and Haman went to dine with Queen Esther, ²and as they were drinking wine on that second day, the king again asked, "Queen Esther, what is your petition? It will be given you. What is your request? Even up to half the kingdom, it will be granted."

³Then Queen Esther answered, "If I have found favor with you, O king, and if it pleases your majesty, grant me my life—this is my petition. And spare my people—this is my request. ⁴For I and my people have been sold for destruction and slaughter and annihilation. If we had merely been sold as male and female slaves, I would

have kept quiet, because no such distress would justify disturbing the king.[a]"

[5]King Xerxes asked Queen Esther, "Who is he? Where is the man who has dared to do such a thing?"

[6]Esther said, "The adversary and enemy is this vile Haman."

Then Haman was terrified before the king and queen. [7]The king got up in a rage, left his wine and went out into the palace garden. But Haman, realizing that the king had already decided his fate, stayed behind to beg Queen Esther for his life.

[8]Just as the king returned from the palace garden to the banquet hall, Haman was falling on the couch where Esther was reclining.

The king exclaimed, "Will he even molest the queen while she is with me in the house?"

As soon as the word left the king's mouth, they covered Haman's face. [9]Then Harbona, one of the eunuchs attending the king, said, "A gallows seventy-five feet[b] high stands by Haman's house. He had it made for Mordecai, who spoke up to help the king."

The king said, "Hang him on it!" [10]So they hanged Haman on the gallows he had prepared for Mordecai. Then the king's fury subsided.

The King's Edict in Behalf of the Jews

8 That same day King Xerxes gave Queen Esther the estate of Haman, the enemy of the Jews. And Mordecai came into the presence of the king, for Esther had told how he was related to her. [2]The king took off his signet ring, which he had reclaimed from Haman, and presented it to Mordecai. And Esther appointed him over Haman's estate.

[3]Esther again pleaded with the king, falling at his feet and weeping. She begged him to put an end to the evil plan of Haman the Agagite, which he had devised against the Jews. [4]Then the king extended the gold scepter to Esther and she arose and stood before him.

Life In Bible Times

THE KING'S SIGNET RING

People in Bible times did not sign important papers. Instead they pressed their signet ring into a bit of clay that was pressed on to papers that had been tied together. When the king gave Mordecai his signet ring, it meant Mordecai could write any orders he wanted in the king's name.

---

[5]"If it pleases the king," she said, "and if he regards me with favor and thinks it the right thing to do, and if he is pleased with me, let an order be written overruling the dispatches that Haman son of Hammedatha, the Agagite, devised and wrote to destroy the Jews in all the king's provinces. [6]For how can I bear to see disaster fall on my people? How can I bear to see the destruction of my family?"

[7]King Xerxes replied to Queen Esther and to Mordecai the Jew, "Because Haman attacked the Jews, I have given his estate to Esther, and they have hanged him on the gallows. [8]Now write another decree in the king's name in behalf of the Jews as seems best to you, and seal it with the king's signet ring—for no document written in the king's name and sealed with his ring can be revoked."

[9]At once the royal secretaries were summoned—on the twenty-third day of the third month, the month of Sivan. They wrote out all Mordecai's orders to the Jews, and to the satraps, governors and nobles of the 127 provinces stretching from India to Cush.[c]

---

[a]4 Or *quiet, but the compensation our adversary offers cannot be compared with the loss the king would suffer*   [b]9 Hebrew *fifty cubits* (about 23 meters)   [c]9 That is, the upper Nile region

These orders were written in the script of each province and the language of each people and also to the Jews in their own script and language. [10]Mordecai wrote in the name of King Xerxes, sealed the dispatches with the king's signet ring, and sent them by mounted couriers, who rode fast horses especially bred for the king.

[11]The king's edict granted the Jews in every city the right to assemble and protect themselves; to destroy, kill and annihilate any armed force of any nationality or province that might attack them and their women and children; and to plunder the property of their enemies. [12]The day appointed for the Jews to do this in all the provinces of King Xerxes was the thirteenth day of the twelfth month, the month of Adar. [13]A copy of the text of the edict was to be issued as law in every province and made known to the people of every nationality so that the Jews would be ready on that day to avenge themselves on their enemies.

[14]The couriers, riding the royal horses, raced out, spurred on by the king's command. And the edict was also issued in the citadel of Susa.

[15]Mordecai left the king's presence wearing royal garments of blue and white, a large crown of gold and a purple robe of fine linen. And the city of Susa held a joyous celebration. [16]For the Jews it was a time of happiness and joy, gladness and honor. [17]In every province and in every city, wherever the edict of the king went, there was joy and gladness among the Jews, with feasting and celebrating. And many people of other nationalities became Jews because fear of the Jews had seized them.

Triumph of the Jews

9 On the thirteenth day of the twelfth month, the month of Adar, the edict commanded by the king was to be carried out. On this day the enemies of the Jews had hoped to overpower them, but now the tables were turned and the Jews

got the upper hand over those who hated them. [2]The Jews assembled in their cities in all the provinces of King Xerxes to attack those seeking their destruction. No one could stand against them, because the people of all the other nationalities were afraid of them. [3]And all the nobles of the provinces, the satraps, the governors and the king's administrators helped the Jews, because fear of Mordecai had seized them. [4]Mordecai was prominent in the palace; his reputation spread throughout the provinces, and he became more and more powerful.

[5]The Jews struck down all their enemies with the sword, killing and destroying them, and they did what they pleased to those who hated them. [6]In the citadel of Susa, the Jews killed and destroyed five hundred men. [7]They also killed Parshandatha, Dalphon, Aspatha, [8]Poratha, Adalia, Aridatha, [9]Parmashta, Arisai, Aridai and Vaizatha, [10]the ten sons of Haman son of Hammedatha, the enemy of the Jews. But they did not lay their hands on the plunder.

[11]The number of those slain in the citadel of Susa was reported to the king that same day. [12]The king said to Queen Esther, "The Jews have killed and destroyed five hundred men and the ten sons of Haman in the citadel of Susa. What have they done in the rest of the king's provinces? Now what is your petition? It will be given you. What is your request? It will also be granted."

[13]"If it pleases the king," Esther answered, "give the Jews in Susa permission to carry out this day's edict tomorrow also, and let Haman's ten sons be hanged on gallows."

[14]So the king commanded that this be done. An edict was issued in Susa, and they hanged the ten sons of Haman. [15]The Jews in Susa came together on the fourteenth day of the month of Adar, and they put to death in Susa three hundred men, but they did not lay their hands on the plunder.

[16]Meanwhile, the remainder of the

Jews who were in the king's provinces also assembled to protect themselves and get relief from their enemies. They killed seventy-five thousand of them but did not lay their
hands on the plunder. [17]This happened on the thirteenth day of the
month of Adar, and on the fourteenth
they rested and made it a day of feasting and joy.

Purim Celebrated

[18]The Jews in Susa, however, had
assembled on the thirteenth and
fourteenth, and then on the fifteenth
they rested and made it a day of feasting and joy.
[19]That is why rural Jews—those
living in villages—observe the fourteenth of the month of Adar as a day
of joy and feasting, a day for giving
presents to each other.
[20]Mordecai recorded these events,
and he sent letters to all the Jews
throughout the provinces of King
Xerxes, near and far, [21]to have them
celebrate annually the fourteenth
and fifteenth days of the month of
Adar [22]as the time when the Jews got
relief from their enemies, and as the
month when their sorrow was turned
into joy and their mourning into a
day of celebration. He wrote them to
observe the days as days of feasting
and joy and giving presents of food to
one another and gifts to the poor.
[23]So the Jews agreed to continue
the celebration they had begun, doing what Mordecai had written to
them. [24]For Haman son of Hammedatha, the Agagite, the enemy of all the
Jews, had plotted against the Jews to
destroy them and had cast the *pur*
(that is, the lot) for their ruin and destruction. [25]But when the plot came
to the king's attention,[a] he issued
written orders that the evil scheme
Haman had devised against the Jews
should come back onto his own head,
and that he and his sons should be
hanged on the gallows. [26](Therefore
these days were called Purim, from
the word *pur*.) Because of everything
written in this letter and because of
what they had seen and what had
happened to them, [27]the Jews took it
upon themselves to establish the custom that they and their descendants
and all who join them should without
fail observe these two days every
year, in the way prescribed and at the
time appointed. [28]These days should
be remembered and observed in every generation by every family, and
in every province and in every city.
And these days of Purim should never cease to be celebrated by the Jews,
nor should the memory of them die
out among their descendants.

❓DID YOU KNOW?   **9:28**

**Why is the holiday that cele-
brates the Jews' deliverance
called Purim?**

The word *pur* means "lot." The
holiday is named Purim to remind
everyone how Haman cast lots to
pick a day to try to kill all the Jews.
God made the lot fall on a day far
enough away so everything could
be arranged to save his people.
The name of the celebration is a
reminder of God's providence and
his love.

---

[29]So Queen Esther, daughter of Abihail, along with Mordecai the Jew,
wrote with full authority to confirm
this second letter concerning Purim.
[30]And Mordecai sent letters to all the
Jews in the 127 provinces of the kingdom of Xerxes—words of goodwill
and assurance— [31]to establish these
days of Purim at their designated
times, as Mordecai the Jew and
Queen Esther had decreed for them,
and as they had established for themselves and their descendants in regard to their times of fasting and
lamentation. [32]Esther's decree confirmed these regulations about Purim, and it was written down in the
records.

---

a25 Or when Esther came before the king

The Greatness of Mordecai

10 King Xerxes imposed tribute throughout the empire, to its distant shores. ²And all his acts of power and might, together with a full account of the greatness of Mordecai to which the king had raised him, are they not written in the book of the annals of the kings of Media and Persia? ³Mordecai the Jew was second in rank to King Xerxes, preeminent among the Jews, and held in high esteem by his many fellow Jews, because he worked for the good of his people and spoke up for the welfare of all the Jews.

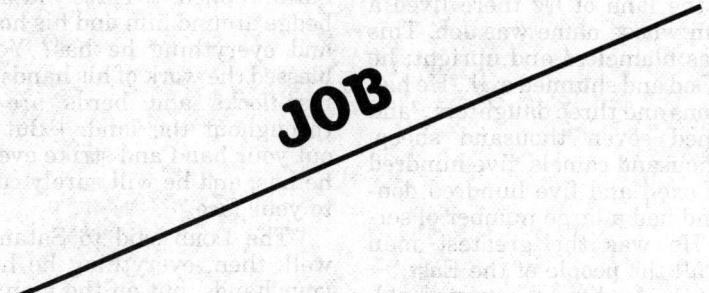
JOB

WHO WROTE THIS BOOK?

The writer of Job is unknown.

WHY WAS THIS BOOK WRITTEN?

Job was written to help people learn that suffering is not always punishment from God.

WHAT HAPPENS IN THIS BOOK?

Terrible things happen to Job. Job and his three friends discuss why God has let these things happen. God tells Job and his friends to just trust him. God then heals Job and makes him wealthy again.

WHAT DO WE LEARN ABOUT GOD IN THIS BOOK?

God does let bad things happen to good people. When bad things happen, it does not mean that God is punishing them for some sin.

WHO IS IMPORTANT IN THIS BOOK?

Job is the important person in this book.

WHEN DID THIS HAPPEN?

We do not know when this happened. It may have happened as early as the time of Abraham, about 2100 B.C.

WHERE DID THIS HAPPEN?

The story of Job took place in a land called Uz, probably in Syria or Palestine.

WHAT ARE SOME OF THE STORIES IN THIS BOOK?

Satan destroys Job's wealth and
family.   Job 1
Satan makes Job very ill.   Job 2
Job says God isn't fair.   Job 9,12
God shows his greatness to Job.   Job 40–41
God makes Job well and wealthy.   Job 42

Prologue

1 In the land of Uz there lived a man whose name was Job. This man was blameless and upright; he feared God and shunned evil. ²He had seven sons and three daughters, ³and he owned seven thousand sheep, three thousand camels, five hundred yoke of oxen and five hundred donkeys, and had a large number of servants. He was the greatest man among all the people of the East.

⁴His sons used to take turns holding feasts in their homes, and they would invite their three sisters to eat and drink with them. ⁵When a period of feasting had run its course, Job would send and have them purified. Early in the morning he would sacrifice a burnt offering for each of them, thinking, "Perhaps my children have sinned and cursed God in their hearts." This was Job's regular custom.

Job's First Test

⁶One day the angels*a* came to present themselves before the LORD, and Satan*b* also came with them. ⁷The LORD said to Satan, "Where have you come from?"

Satan answered the LORD, "From roaming through the earth and going back and forth in it."

⁸Then the LORD said to Satan, "Have you considered my servant Job? There is no one on earth like him; he is blameless and upright, a man who fears God and shuns evil."

⁹"Does Job fear God for nothing?" Satan replied. ¹⁰"Have you not put a hedge around him and his household and everything he has? You have blessed the work of his hands, so that his flocks and herds are spread throughout the land. ¹¹But stretch out your hand and strike everything he has, and he will surely curse you to your face."

¹²The LORD said to Satan, "Very well, then, everything he has is in your hands, but on the man himself do not lay a finger."

Then Satan went out from the presence of the LORD.

¹³One day when Job's sons and daughters were feasting and drinking wine at the oldest brother's house, ¹⁴a messenger came to Job and said, "The oxen were plowing and the donkeys were grazing nearby, ¹⁵and the Sabeans attacked and carried them off. They put the servants to the sword, and I am the only one who has escaped to tell you!"

¹⁶While he was still speaking, another messenger came and said, "The fire of God fell from the sky and burned up the sheep and the servants, and I am the only one who has escaped to tell you!"

¹⁷While he was still speaking, another messenger came and said, "The Chaldeans formed three raiding parties and swept down on your camels and carried them off. They put the servants to the sword, and I am the only one who has escaped to tell you!"

a6 Hebrew the sons of God   *b6 Satan means accuser.*

⬛ET'S LIVE IT!   Job 1:1–22

BAD THINGS HAPPEN TO GOOD PEOPLE ⮕ Read Job 1. Can you find a verse that tells you Job was a good person? Find three terrible things that happened to Job.

Sometimes bad things do happen to good people. If something bad happens to you, you may feel as if you are being punished. But even if terrible things happen, they do not mean God is punishing you.

What do you think happened to Job in the end? Read Job 42:12–17. What do you think will happen to you in the end if you love God as Job did?

18While he was still speaking, yet another messenger came and said, "Your sons and daughters were feasting and drinking wine at the oldest brother's house, 19when suddenly a mighty wind swept in from the desert and struck the four corners of the house. It collapsed on them and they are dead, and I am the only one who has escaped to tell you!"

20At this, Job got up and tore his robe and shaved his head. Then he fell to the ground in worship 21and said:

> "Naked I came from my mother's
>   womb,
>   and naked I will depart.*a*
> The LORD gave and the LORD has
>   taken away;
>   may the name of the LORD be
>   praised."

22In all this, Job did not sin by charging God with wrongdoing.

Job's Second Test

2 On another day the angels*b* came to present themselves before the LORD, and Satan also came with them to present himself before him. 2And the LORD said to Satan, "Where have you come from?"

Satan answered the LORD, "From roaming through the earth and going back and forth in it."

3Then the LORD said to Satan, "Have you considered my servant Job? There is no one on earth like him; he is blameless and upright, a man who fears God and shuns evil. And he still maintains his integrity, though you incited me against him to ruin him without any reason."

4"Skin for skin!" Satan replied. "A man will give all he has for his own life. 5But stretch out your hand and strike his flesh and bones, and he will surely curse you to your face."

6The LORD said to Satan, "Very well, then, he is in your hands; but you must spare his life."

7So Satan went out from the presence of the LORD and afflicted Job with painful sores from the soles of his feet to the top of his head. 8Then Job took a piece of broken pottery and scraped himself with it as he sat among the ashes.

9His wife said to him, "Are you still holding on to your integrity? Curse God and die!"

10He replied, "You are talking like a foolish*c* woman. Shall we accept good from God, and not trouble?"

In all this, Job did not sin in what he said.

WORDS TO REMEMBER

2:10 Shall we accept good from God, and not trouble?

Job's Three Friends

11When Job's three friends, Eliphaz the Temanite, Bildad the Shuhite and Zophar the Naamathite, heard about all the troubles that had come upon him, they set out from their homes and met together by agreement to go and sympathize with him and comfort him. 12When they saw him from a distance, they could hardly recognize him; they began to weep aloud, and they tore their robes and sprinkled dust on their heads. 13Then they sat on the ground with him for seven days and seven nights. No one said a word to him, because they saw how great his suffering was.

Job Speaks

3 After this, Job opened his mouth and cursed the day of his birth. 2He said:

> 3"May the day of my birth perish,
>   and the night it was said, 'A
>   boy is born!'
> 4That day—may it turn to
>   darkness;
>   may God above not care about
>   it;

---

may no light shine upon it.

⁵May darkness and deep shadow*ᵃ*
    claim it once more;
    may a cloud settle over it;
    may blackness overwhelm its
      light.

Life In Bible Times

SHOWING GRIEF

In Bible times people expressed their grief in very open and vivid ways. When something sad happened to them or someone they loved, they would often cry loudly, tear their clothing, sit on the bare ground, and sprinkle dust or ashes on their heads. Job's friends were very upset because of all that had happened to him. For seven days and nights they showed their grief in all these ways.

---

⁶That night—may thick darkness
    seize it;
    may it not be included among
      the days of the year
    nor be entered in any of the
      months.
⁷May that night be barren;
    may no shout of joy be heard in
      it.
⁸May those who curse days*ᵇ* curse
    that day,
    those who are ready to rouse
      Leviathan.
⁹May its morning stars become
    dark;
    may it wait for daylight in vain
    and not see the first rays of
      dawn,
¹⁰for it did not shut the doors of the
    womb on me
    to hide trouble from my eyes.

¹¹"Why did I not perish at birth,
    and die as I came from the
      womb?
¹²Why were there knees to receive
    me
    and breasts that I might be
      nursed?
¹³For now I would be lying down in
    peace;
    I would be asleep and at rest
¹⁴with kings and counselors of the
    earth,
    who built for themselves places
      now lying in ruins,
¹⁵with rulers who had gold,
    who filled their houses with
      silver.
¹⁶Or why was I not hidden in the
    ground like a stillborn
      child,
    like an infant who never saw
      the light of day?
¹⁷There the wicked cease from
    turmoil,
    and there the weary are at rest.
¹⁸Captives also enjoy their ease;
    they no longer hear the slave
      driver's shout.
¹⁹The small and the great are
    there,
    and the slave is freed from his
      master.

²⁰"Why is light given to those in
    misery,
    and life to the bitter of soul,
²¹to those who long for death that
    does not come,
    who search for it more than for
      hidden treasure,
²²who are filled with gladness
    and rejoice when they reach the
      grave?
²³Why is life given to a man
    whose way is hidden,
    whom God has hedged in?
²⁴For sighing comes to me instead
    of food;
    my groans pour out like water.
²⁵What I feared has come upon me;
    what I dreaded has happened to
      me.
²⁶I have no peace, no quietness;

ᵃ5 Or and the shadow of death   ᵇ8 Or the sea

I have no rest, but only
turmoil."

❓DID YOU KNOW?   3:1

How bad did Job feel?

So much had happened to Job
and he was so sad that he said he
wished he had never been born.

Eliphaz

4 Then Eliphaz the Temanite replied:

2"If someone ventures a word with
you, will you be impatient?
But who can keep from
speaking?
3Think how you have instructed
many,
how you have strengthened
feeble hands.
4Your words have supported those
who stumbled;
you have strengthened faltering
knees.
5But now trouble comes to you,
and you are discouraged;
it strikes you, and you are
dismayed.
6Should not your piety be your
confidence
and your blameless ways your
hope?

7"Consider now: Who, being
innocent, has ever perished?
Where were the upright ever
destroyed?
8As I have observed, those who
plow evil
and those who sow trouble reap
it.
9At the breath of God they are
destroyed;
at the blast of his anger they
perish.
10The lions may roar and growl,
yet the teeth of the great lions
are broken.
11The lion perishes for lack of prey,

and the cubs of the lioness are
scattered.
12"A word was secretly brought to
me,
my ears caught a whisper of it.
13Amid disquieting dreams in the
night,
when deep sleep falls on men,
14fear and trembling seized me
and made all my bones shake.
15A spirit glided past my face,
and the hair on my body stood
on end.
16It stopped,
but I could not tell what it was.
A form stood before my eyes,
and I heard a hushed voice:
17'Can a mortal be more righteous
than God?
Can a man be more pure than
his Maker?
18If God places no trust in his
servants,
if he charges his angels with
error,
19how much more those who live in
houses of clay,
whose foundations are in the
dust,
who are crushed more readily
than a moth!
20Between dawn and dusk they are
broken to pieces;
unnoticed, they perish forever.
21Are not the cords of their tent
pulled up,
so that they die without
wisdom?'ᵃ

5 "Call if you will, but who will
answer you?
To which of the holy ones will
you turn?
2Resentment kills a fool,
and envy slays the simple.
3I myself have seen a fool taking
root,
but suddenly his house was
cursed.
4His children are far from safety,
crushed in court without a
defender.
5The hungry consume his harvest,

ᵃ21 Some interpreters end the quotation after verse 17.

taking it even from among
thorns,
and the thirsty pant after his
wealth.
⁶For hardship does not spring from
the soil,
nor does trouble sprout from the
ground.
⁷Yet man is born to trouble
as surely as sparks fly upward.

⁸"But if it were I, I would appeal
to God;
I would lay my cause before
him.
⁹He performs wonders that cannot
be fathomed,
miracles that cannot be
counted.
¹⁰He bestows rain on the earth;
he sends water upon the
countryside.
¹¹The lowly he sets on high,
and those who mourn are lifted
to safety.
¹²He thwarts the plans of the
crafty,
so that their hands achieve no
success.
¹³He catches the wise in their
craftiness,
and the schemes of the wily are
swept away.
¹⁴Darkness comes upon them in the
daytime;
at noon they grope as in the
night.
¹⁵He saves the needy from the
sword in their mouth;
he saves them from the clutches
of the powerful.
¹⁶So the poor have hope,
and injustice shuts its mouth.

¹⁷"Blessed is the man whom God
corrects;
so do not despise the discipline
of the Almighty.ᵃ
¹⁸For he wounds, but he also binds
up;
he injures, but his hands also
heal.
¹⁹From six calamities he will
rescue you;

in seven no harm will befall
you.
²⁰In famine he will ransom you
from death,
and in battle from the stroke of
the sword.
²¹You will be protected from the
lash of the tongue,
and need not fear when
destruction comes.
²²You will laugh at destruction and
famine,
and need not fear the beasts of
the earth.
²³For you will have a covenant
with the stones of the field,
and the wild animals will be at
peace with you.
²⁴You will know that your tent is
secure;
you will take stock of your
property and find nothing
missing.
²⁵You will know that your children
will be many,
and your descendants like the
grass of the earth.
²⁶You will come to the grave in full
vigor,
like sheaves gathered in season.

²⁷"We have examined this, and it is
true.
So hear it and apply it to
yourself."

Job

6 Then Job replied:

²"If only my anguish could be
weighed
and all my misery be placed on
the scales!
³It would surely outweigh the sand
of the seas—
no wonder my words have been
impetuous.
⁴The arrows of the Almighty are
in me,
my spirit drinks in their poison;
God's terrors are marshaled
against me.
⁵Does a wild donkey bray when it
has grass,

ᵃ17 Hebrew *Shaddai*; here and throughout Job

or an ox bellow when it has
  fodder?
6Is tasteless food eaten without
    salt,
  or is there flavor in the white of
    an egg*a*?
7I refuse to touch it;
  such food makes me ill.

8"Oh, that I might have my
    request,
  that God would grant what I
    hope for,
9that God would be willing to
    crush me,
  to let loose his hand and cut me
    off!
10Then I would still have this
    consolation—
  my joy in unrelenting pain—
  that I had not denied the words
    of the Holy One.

11"What strength do I have, that I
    should still hope?
  What prospects, that I should be
    patient?
12Do I have the strength of stone?
  Is my flesh bronze?
13Do I have any power to help
    myself,
  now that success has been
    driven from me?

14"A despairing man should have
    the devotion of his friends,
  even though he forsakes the
    fear of the Almighty.
15But my brothers are as
    undependable as
    intermittent streams,
  as the streams that overflow
16when darkened by thawing ice
  and swollen with melting snow,
17but that cease to flow in the dry
    season,
  and in the heat vanish from
    their channels.
18Caravans turn aside from their
    routes;
  they go up into the wasteland
    and perish.

19The caravans of Tema look for
    water,
  the traveling merchants of
    Sheba look in hope.
20They are distressed, because they
    had been confident;
  they arrive there, only to be
    disappointed.
21Now you too have proved to be of
    no help;
  you see something dreadful and
    are afraid.
22Have I ever said, 'Give something
    on my behalf,
  pay a ransom for me from your
    wealth,
23deliver me from the hand of the
    enemy,
  ransom me from the clutches of
    the ruthless'?

24"Teach me, and I will be quiet;
  show me where I have been
    wrong.
25How painful are honest words!
  But what do your arguments
    prove?
26Do you mean to correct what I
    say,
  and treat the words of a
    despairing man as wind?
27You would even cast lots for the
    fatherless
  and barter away your friend.

28"But now be so kind as to look at
    me.
  Would I lie to your face?
29Relent, do not be unjust;
  reconsider, for my integrity is
    at stake.*b*
30Is there any wickedness on my
    lips?
  Can my mouth not discern
    malice?

7 "Does not man have hard
    service on earth?
  Are not his days like those of a
    hired man?
2Like a slave longing for the
    evening shadows,

---

*a*6 The meaning of the Hebrew for this phrase is uncertain.   *b*29 Or *my righteousness still
stands*

or a hired man waiting eagerly
for his wages,
³so I have been allotted months of
futility,
and nights of misery have been
assigned to me.
⁴When I lie down I think, 'How
long before I get up?'
The night drags on, and I toss
till dawn.
⁵My body is clothed with worms
and scabs,
my skin is broken and festering.

⁶"My days are swifter than a
weaver's shuttle,
and they come to an end
without hope.

Life In Bible Times

WEAVING

Weaving in Bible times was done
mostly by women. Cloth was
made by weaving threads together and then was used to make
clothing and household articles
and even tents. Fabrics were woven from thread made from goat
hair or sheep wool or plants. Some
cloth was coarse and rough, but
some was fine and soft and beautifully colored.

⁷Remember, O God, that my life is
but a breath;
my eyes will never see
happiness again.
⁸The eye that now sees me will see
me no longer;
you will look for me, but I will
be no more.
⁹As a cloud vanishes and is gone,
so he who goes down to the
grave*a* does not return.

¹⁰He will never come to his house
again;
his place will know him no
more.

¹¹"Therefore I will not keep silent;
I will speak out in the anguish
of my spirit,
I will complain in the bitterness
of my soul.
¹²Am I the sea, or the monster of
the deep,
that you put me under guard?
¹³When I think my bed will comfort
me
and my couch will ease my
complaint,
¹⁴even then you frighten me with
dreams
and terrify me with visions,
¹⁵so that I prefer strangling and
death,
rather than this body of mine.
¹⁶I despise my life; I would not live
forever.
Let me alone; my days have no
meaning.

¹⁷"What is man that you make so
much of him,
that you give him so much
attention,
¹⁸that you examine him every
morning
and test him every moment?
¹⁹Will you never look away from
me,
or let me alone even for an
instant?
²⁰If I have sinned, what have I
done to you,
O watcher of men?
Why have you made me your
target?
Have I become a burden to
you?*b*
²¹Why do you not pardon my
offenses
and forgive my sins?
For I will soon lie down in the
dust;
you will search for me, but I
will be no more."

---

a9 Hebrew *Sheol*　　*b20* A few manuscripts of the Masoretic Text, an ancient Hebrew scribal
tradition and Septuagint; most manuscripts of the Masoretic Text *I have become a burden to myself.*

Bildad

8 Then Bildad the Shuhite replied:

2"How long will you say such
things?
Your words are a blustering
wind.
3Does God pervert justice?
Does the Almighty pervert what
is right?
4When your children sinned
against him,
he gave them over to the
penalty of their sin.
5But if you will look to God
and plead with the Almighty,
6if you are pure and upright,
even now he will rouse himself
on your behalf
and restore you to your rightful
place.
7Your beginnings will seem
humble,
so prosperous will your future
be.

8"Ask the former generations
and find out what their fathers
learned,
9for we were born only yesterday
and know nothing,
and our days on earth are but a
shadow.
10Will they not instruct you and
tell you?
Will they not bring forth words
from their understanding?
11Can papyrus grow tall where
there is no marsh?
Can reeds thrive without
water?
12While still growing and uncut,
they wither more quickly than
grass.
13Such is the destiny of all who
forget God;
so perishes the hope of the
godless.
14What he trusts in is fragile*a*;
what he relies on is a spider's
web.
15He leans on his web, but it gives
way;

he clings to it, but it does not
hold.
16He is like a well-watered plant in
the sunshine,
spreading its shoots over the
garden;
17it entwines its roots around a pile
of rocks
and looks for a place among the
stones.
18But when it is torn from its spot,
that place disowns it and says,
'I never saw you.'
19Surely its life withers away,
and*b* from the soil other plants
grow.

20"Surely God does not reject a
blameless man
or strengthen the hands of
evildoers.
21He will yet fill your mouth with
laughter
and your lips with shouts of joy.
22Your enemies will be clothed in
shame,
and the tents of the wicked will
be no more."

Job

9 Then Job replied:

2"Indeed, I know that this is
true.
But how can a mortal be
righteous before God?
3Though one wished to dispute
with him,
he could not answer him one
time out of a thousand.
4His wisdom is profound, his power
is vast.
Who has resisted him and come
out unscathed?
5He moves mountains without
their knowing it
and overturns them in his
anger.
6He shakes the earth from its
place
and makes its pillars tremble.
7He speaks to the sun and it does
not shine;

---

a14 The meaning of the Hebrew for this word is uncertain.
that

b19 Or *Surely all the joy it has / is*

he seals off the light of the
stars.
⁸He alone stretches out the
heavens
and treads on the waves of the
sea.
⁹He is the Maker of the Bear and
Orion,
the Pleiades and the
constellations of the south.
¹⁰He performs wonders that cannot
be fathomed,
miracles that cannot be
counted.
¹¹When he passes me, I cannot see
him;
when he goes by, I cannot
perceive him.
¹²If he snatches away, who can stop
him?
Who can say to him, 'What are
you doing?'
¹³God does not restrain his anger;
even the cohorts of Rahab
cowered at his feet.

¹⁴"How then can I dispute with
him?
How can I find words to argue
with him?
¹⁵Though I were innocent, I could
not answer him;
I could only plead with my
Judge for mercy.
¹⁶Even if I summoned him and he
responded,
I do not believe he would give
me a hearing.
¹⁷He would crush me with a storm
and multiply my wounds for no
reason.
¹⁸He would not let me regain my
breath
but would overwhelm me with
misery.
¹⁹If it is a matter of strength, he is
mighty!
And if it is a matter of justice,
who will summon him*a*?
²⁰Even if I were innocent, my
mouth would condemn me;
if I were blameless, it would
pronounce me guilty.

²¹"Although I am blameless,
I have no concern for myself;
I despise my own life.
²²It is all the same; that is why I
say,
'He destroys both the blameless
and the wicked.'
²³When a scourge brings sudden
death,
he mocks the despair of the
innocent.
²⁴When a land falls into the hands
of the wicked,
he blindfolds its judges.
If it is not he, then who is it?

²⁵"My days are swifter than a
runner;
they fly away without a glimpse
of joy.
²⁶They skim past like boats of
papyrus,
like eagles swooping down on
their prey.
²⁷If I say, 'I will forget my
complaint,
I will change my expression,
and smile,'
²⁸I still dread all my sufferings,
for I know you will not hold me
innocent.
²⁹Since I am already found guilty,
why should I struggle in vain?
³⁰Even if I washed myself with
soap*b*
and my hands with washing
soda,
³¹you would plunge me into a slime
pit
so that even my clothes would
detest me.

³²"He is not a man like me that I
might answer him,
that we might confront each
other in court.
³³If only there were someone to
arbitrate between us,
to lay his hand upon us both,
³⁴someone to remove God's rod from
me,
so that his terror would frighten
me no more.

---

a19 See Septuagint; Hebrew *me.*   *b30* Or *snow*

35Then I would speak up without
fear of him,
but as it now stands with me, I
cannot.

10 "I loathe my very life;
therefore I will give free
rein to my complaint
and speak out in the bitterness
of my soul.
2I will say to God: Do not condemn
me,
but tell me what charges you
have against me.
3Does it please you to oppress me,
to spurn the work of your
hands,
while you smile on the schemes
of the wicked?
4Do you have eyes of flesh?
Do you see as a mortal sees?
5Are your days like those of a
mortal
or your years like those of a
man,
6that you must search out my
faults
and probe after my sin—
7though you know that I am not
guilty
and that no one can rescue me
from your hand?

8"Your hands shaped me and made
me.
Will you now turn and destroy
me?
9Remember that you molded me
like clay.
Will you now turn me to dust
again?
10Did you not pour me out like
milk
and curdle me like cheese,
11clothe me with skin and flesh
and knit me together with
bones and sinews?
12You gave me life and showed me
kindness,
and in your providence watched
over my spirit.

13"But this is what you concealed
in your heart,
and I know that this was in
your mind:
14If I sinned, you would be
watching me
and would not let my offense go
unpunished.
15If I am guilty—woe to me!
Even if I am innocent, I cannot
lift my head,
for I am full of shame
and drowned in*a* my affliction.
16If I hold my head high, you stalk
me like a lion
and again display your
awesome power against me.
17You bring new witnesses against
me
and increase your anger toward
me;
your forces come against me
wave upon wave.

18"Why then did you bring me out
of the womb?
I wish I had died before any eye
saw me.
19If only I had never come into
being,
or had been carried straight
from the womb to the
grave!
20Are not my few days almost over?
Turn away from me so I can
have a moment's joy
21before I go to the place of no
return,
to the land of gloom and deep
shadow,*b*
22to the land of deepest night,
of deep shadow and disorder,
where even the light is like
darkness."

Zophar

11 Then Zophar the Naamathite
replied:

2"Are all these words to go
unanswered?
Is this talker to be vindicated?
3Will your idle talk reduce men to
silence?
Will no one rebuke you when
you mock?

---

*a*15 Or *and aware of*   *b*21 Or *and the shadow of death;* also in verse 22

⁴You say to God, 'My beliefs are
flawless

❓ DID YOU KNOW?   10:20

Did Job's friends help him?

Three of Job's friends—Eliphaz,
Bildad and Zophar—came to
comfort Job. But they kept saying
that Job's wickedness was the reason why God had sent so much
trouble to Job. They said God was
punishing Job for his sins. But Job
knew in his heart he had not
sinned. Job 1:8 tells what God
thought of Job.

---

and I am pure in your sight.'
⁵Oh, how I wish that God would
speak,
that he would open his lips
against you
⁶and disclose to you the secrets of
wisdom,
for true wisdom has two sides.
Know this: God has even
forgotten some of your sin.

⁷"Can you fathom the mysteries of
God?
Can you probe the limits of the
Almighty?
⁸They are higher than the
heavens—what can you do?
They are deeper than the
depths of the grave*ᵃ*—what
can you know?
⁹Their measure is longer than the
earth
and wider than the sea.

¹⁰"If he comes along and confines
you in prison
and convenes a court, who can
oppose him?
¹¹Surely he recognizes deceitful
men;
and when he sees evil, does he
not take note?
¹²But a witless man can no more
become wise

than a wild donkey's colt can be
born a man.*ᵇ*

¹³"Yet if you devote your heart to
him
and stretch out your hands to
him,
¹⁴if you put away the sin that is in
your hand
and allow no evil to dwell in
your tent,
¹⁵then you will lift up your face
without shame;
you will stand firm and without
fear.
¹⁶You will surely forget your
trouble,
recalling it only as waters gone
by.
¹⁷Life will be brighter than
noonday,
and darkness will become like
morning.
¹⁸You will be secure, because there
is hope;
you will look about you and
take your rest in safety.
¹⁹You will lie down, with no one to
make you afraid,
and many will court your favor.
²⁰But the eyes of the wicked will
fail,
and escape will elude them;
their hope will become a dying
gasp."

Job

12 Then Job replied:

²"Doubtless you are the
people,
and wisdom will die with you!
³But I have a mind as well as
you;
I am not inferior to you.
Who does not know all these
things?

⁴"I have become a laughingstock to
my friends,
though I called upon God and
he answered—
a mere laughingstock, though
righteous and blameless!

ᵃ8 Hebrew *than Sheol*   *ᵇ12* Or *wild donkey can be born tame*

⁵Men at ease have contempt for misfortune
as the fate of those whose feet are slipping.
⁶The tents of marauders are undisturbed,
and those who provoke God are secure—
those who carry their god in their hands.ᵃ

⁷"But ask the animals, and they will teach you,
or the birds of the air, and they will tell you;
⁸or speak to the earth, and it will teach you,
or let the fish of the sea inform you.
⁹Which of all these does not know that the hand of the LORD has done this?
¹⁰In his hand is the life of every creature
and the breath of all mankind.
¹¹Does not the ear test words as the tongue tastes food?
¹²Is not wisdom found among the aged?
Does not long life bring understanding?

¹³"To God belong wisdom and power;
counsel and understanding are his.
¹⁴What he tears down cannot be rebuilt;
the man he imprisons cannot be released.
¹⁵If he holds back the waters, there is drought;
if he lets them loose, they devastate the land.
¹⁶To him belong strength and victory;
both deceived and deceiver are his.
¹⁷He leads counselors away stripped and makes fools of judges.
¹⁸He takes off the shackles put on by kings
and ties a loinclothᵇ around their waist.

¹⁹He leads priests away stripped and overthrows men long established.
²⁰He silences the lips of trusted advisers
and takes away the discernment of elders.
²¹He pours contempt on nobles and disarms the mighty.
²²He reveals the deep things of darkness
and brings deep shadows into the light.
²³He makes nations great, and destroys them;
he enlarges nations, and disperses them.
²⁴He deprives the leaders of the earth of their reason;
he sends them wandering through a trackless waste.
²⁵They grope in darkness with no light;
he makes them stagger like drunkards.

13 "My eyes have seen all this, my ears have heard and understood it.
²What you know, I also know; I am not inferior to you.
³But I desire to speak to the Almighty
and to argue my case with God.
⁴You, however, smear me with lies;
you are worthless physicians, all of you!
⁵If only you would be altogether silent!
For you, that would be wisdom.
⁶Hear now my argument;
listen to the plea of my lips.
⁷Will you speak wickedly on God's behalf?
Will you speak deceitfully for him?
⁸Will you show him partiality?
Will you argue the case for God?
⁹Would it turn out well if he examined you?

ᵃ6 Or secure / in what God's hand brings them   ᵇ18 Or shackles of kings / and ties a belt

Could you deceive him as you
might deceive men?
¹⁰He would surely rebuke you
if you secretly showed
partiality.
¹¹Would not his splendor terrify
you?
Would not the dread of him fall
on you?
¹²Your maxims are proverbs of
ashes;
your defenses are defenses of
clay.

¹³"Keep silent and let me speak;
then let come to me what may.
¹⁴Why do I put myself in jeopardy
and take my life in my hands?
¹⁵Though he slay me, yet will I
hope in him;
I will surely*a* defend my ways
to his face.
¹⁶Indeed, this will turn out for my
deliverance,
for no godless man would dare
come before him!
¹⁷Listen carefully to my words;
let your ears take in what I say.
¹⁸Now that I have prepared my
case,
I know I will be vindicated.
¹⁹Can anyone bring charges against
me?
If so, I will be silent and die.

²⁰"Only grant me these two things,
O God,
and then I will not hide from
you:
²¹Withdraw your hand far from me,
and stop frightening me with
your terrors.
²²Then summon me and I will
answer,
or let me speak, and you reply.
²³How many wrongs and sins have
I committed?
Show me my offense and my
sin.
²⁴Why do you hide your face
and consider me your enemy?
²⁵Will you torment a windblown
leaf?

Will you chase after dry chaff?
²⁶For you write down bitter things
against me
and make me inherit the sins of
my youth.
²⁷You fasten my feet in shackles;
you keep close watch on all my
paths
by putting marks on the soles of
my feet.

²⁸"So man wastes away like
something rotten,
like a garment eaten by moths.

14 "Man born of woman
is of few days and full of
trouble.
²He springs up like a flower and
withers away;
like a fleeting shadow, he does
not endure.
³Do you fix your eye on such a
one?
Will you bring him*b* before you
for judgment?
⁴Who can bring what is pure from
the impure?
No one!
⁵Man's days are determined;
you have decreed the number of
his months
and have set limits he cannot
exceed.
⁶So look away from him and let
him alone,
till he has put in his time like a
hired man.

⁷"At least there is hope for a tree:
If it is cut down, it will sprout
again,
and its new shoots will not fail.
⁸Its roots may grow old in the
ground
and its stump die in the soil,
⁹yet at the scent of water it will
bud
and put forth shoots like a
plant.
¹⁰But man dies and is laid low;
he breathes his last and is no
more.

---

a15 Or *He will surely slay me; I have no hope — / yet I will*
Hebrew *me*　　　　*b3* Septuagint, Vulgate and Syriac;

¹¹As water disappears from the sea
or a riverbed becomes parched
and dry,
¹²so man lies down and does not
rise;
till the heavens are no more,
men will not awake
or be roused from their sleep.

¹³"If only you would hide me in the
grave^a
and conceal me till your anger
has passed!
If only you would set me a time
and then remember me!
¹⁴If a man dies, will he live again?
All the days of my hard service
I will wait for my renewal^b to
come.
¹⁵You will call and I will answer
you;
you will long for the creature
your hands have made.
¹⁶Surely then you will count my
steps
but not keep track of my sin.
¹⁷My offenses will be sealed up in a
bag;
you will cover over my sin.

¹⁸"But as a mountain erodes and
crumbles
and as a rock is moved from its
place,
¹⁹as water wears away stones
and torrents wash away the
soil,
so you destroy man's hope.
²⁰You overpower him once for all,
and he is gone;
you change his countenance and
send him away.
²¹If his sons are honored, he does
not know it;
if they are brought low, he does
not see it.
²²He feels but the pain of his own
body
and mourns only for himself."

Eliphaz

15 Then Eliphaz the Temanite
replied:

²"Would a wise man answer with
empty notions
or fill his belly with the hot
east wind?
³Would he argue with useless
words,
with speeches that have no
value?
⁴But you even undermine piety
and hinder devotion to God.
⁵Your sin prompts your mouth;
you adopt the tongue of the
crafty.
⁶Your own mouth condemns you,
not mine;
your own lips testify against
you.

⁷"Are you the first man ever born?
Were you brought forth before
the hills?
⁸Do you listen in on God's council?
Do you limit wisdom to
yourself?
⁹What do you know that we do not
know?
What insights do you have that
we do not have?
¹⁰The gray-haired and the aged are
on our side,
men even older than your
father.
¹¹Are God's consolations not enough
for you,
words spoken gently to you?
¹²Why has your heart carried you
away,
and why do your eyes flash,
¹³so that you vent your rage
against God
and pour out such words from
your mouth?

¹⁴"What is man, that he could be
pure,
or one born of woman, that he
could be righteous?
¹⁵If God places no trust in his holy
ones,
if even the heavens are not
pure in his eyes,
¹⁶how much less man, who is vile
and corrupt,
who drinks up evil like water!

^a13 Hebrew *Sheol*   ^b14 Or *release*

¹⁷"Listen to me and I will explain
  to you;
  let me tell you what I have
    seen,
¹⁸what wise men have declared,
  hiding nothing received from
    their fathers
¹⁹(to whom alone the land was
    given
  when no alien passed among
    them):
²⁰All his days the wicked man
    suffers torment,
  the ruthless through all the
    years stored up for him.
²¹Terrifying sounds fill his ears;
  when all seems well, marauders
    attack him.
²²He despairs of escaping the
    darkness;
  he is marked for the sword.
²³He wanders about—food for
    vultures^a;
  he knows the day of darkness is
    at hand.
²⁴Distress and anguish fill him
    with terror;
  they overwhelm him, like a
    king poised to attack,
²⁵because he shakes his fist at God
  and vaunts himself against the
    Almighty,
²⁶defiantly charging against him
  with a thick, strong shield.

²⁷"Though his face is covered with
    fat
  and his waist bulges with flesh,
²⁸he will inhabit ruined towns
  and houses where no one lives,
  houses crumbling to rubble.
²⁹He will no longer be rich and his
    wealth will not endure,
  nor will his possessions spread
    over the land.
³⁰He will not escape the darkness;
  a flame will wither his shoots,
  and the breath of God's mouth
    will carry him away.
³¹Let him not deceive himself by
    trusting what is worthless,
  for he will get nothing in
    return.

³²Before his time he will be paid in
    full,
  and his branches will not
    flourish.
³³He will be like a vine stripped of
    its unripe grapes,
  like an olive tree shedding its
    blossoms.
³⁴For the company of the godless
    will be barren,
  and fire will consume the tents
    of those who love bribes.
³⁵They conceive trouble and give
    birth to evil;
  their womb fashions deceit."

Job

16 Then Job replied:

²"I have heard many things
    like these;
  miserable comforters are you
    all!
³Will your long-winded speeches
    never end?
  What ails you that you keep on
    arguing?
⁴I also could speak like you,
  if you were in my place;
  I could make fine speeches
    against you
  and shake my head at you.
⁵But my mouth would encourage
    you;
  comfort from my lips would
    bring you relief.

⁶"Yet if I speak, my pain is not
    relieved;
  and if I refrain, it does not go
    away.
⁷Surely, O God, you have worn me
    out;
  you have devastated my entire
    household.
⁸You have bound me—and it has
    become a witness;
  my gauntness rises up and
    testifies against me.
⁹God assails me and tears me in
    his anger
  and gnashes his teeth at me;
  my opponent fastens on me his
    piercing eyes.

^a23 Or about, looking for food

¹⁰Men open their mouths to jeer at
   me;
   they strike my cheek in scorn
   and unite together against me.
¹¹God has turned me over to evil
   men
   and thrown me into the clutches
   of the wicked.
¹²All was well with me, but he
   shattered me;
   he seized me by the neck and
   crushed me.
He has made me his target;
¹³   his archers surround me.
Without pity, he pierces my
   kidneys
   and spills my gall on the
   ground.
¹⁴Again and again he bursts upon
   me;
   he rushes at me like a warrior.

¹⁵"I have sewed sackcloth over my
   skin
   and buried my brow in the
   dust.
¹⁶My face is red with weeping,
   deep shadows ring my eyes;
¹⁷yet my hands have been free of
   violence
   and my prayer is pure.

¹⁸"O earth, do not cover my blood;
   may my cry never be laid to
   rest!
¹⁹Even now my witness is in
   heaven;
   my advocate is on high.
²⁰My intercessor is my friend*ᵃ*
   as my eyes pour out tears to
   God;
²¹on behalf of a man he pleads with
   God
   as a man pleads for his friend.

²²"Only a few years will pass
   before I go on the journey of no
   return.

17 ¹My spirit is broken,
   my days are cut short,
   the grave awaits me.
²Surely mockers surround me;
   my eyes must dwell on their
   hostility.

³"Give me, O God, the pledge you
   demand.

❓DID YOU KNOW?   16:17

**How did Job answer his friends
when they said all his troubles
were because he had sinned?**

Job said that everyone knows
wicked people whom God has
not punished and good people
who have hard times. What his
friends had said was not true.

Who else will put up security
   for me?
⁴You have closed their minds to
   understanding;
   therefore you will not let them
   triumph.
⁵If a man denounces his friends for
   reward,
   the eyes of his children will fail.

⁶"God has made me a byword to
   everyone,
   a man in whose face people spit.
⁷My eyes have grown dim with
   grief;
   my whole frame is but a
   shadow.
⁸Upright men are appalled at this;
   the innocent are aroused
   against the ungodly.
⁹Nevertheless, the righteous will
   hold to their ways,
   and those with clean hands will
   grow stronger.

¹⁰"But come on, all of you, try
   again!
   I will not find a wise man
   among you.
¹¹My days have passed, my plans
   are shattered,
   and so are the desires of my
   heart.
¹²These men turn night into day;
   in the face of darkness they say,
   'Light is near.'
¹³If the only home I hope for is the
   grave,*ᵇ*

ᵃ20 Or *My friends treat me with scorn*   *ᵇ13* Hebrew *Sheol*

if I spread out my bed in
darkness,
¹⁴if I say to corruption, 'You are my
father,'
and to the worm, 'My mother'
or 'My sister,'
¹⁵where then is my hope?
Who can see any hope for
me?
¹⁶Will it go down to the gates of
death*a*?
Will we descend together into
the dust?"

Bildad

18 Then Bildad the Shuhite replied:

²"When will you end these
speeches?
Be sensible, and then we can
talk.
³Why are we regarded as cattle
and considered stupid in your
sight?
⁴You who tear yourself to pieces in
your anger,
is the earth to be abandoned for
your sake?
Or must the rocks be moved
from their place?

⁵"The lamp of the wicked is
snuffed out;
the flame of his fire stops
burning.
⁶The light in his tent becomes
dark;
the lamp beside him goes
out.
⁷The vigor of his step is weakened;
his own schemes throw him
down.
⁸His feet thrust him into a net
and he wanders into its
mesh.
⁹A trap seizes him by the heel;
a snare holds him fast.
¹⁰A noose is hidden for him on the
ground;
a trap lies in his path.
¹¹Terrors startle him on every side
and dog his every step.
¹²Calamity is hungry for him;

disaster is ready for him when
he falls.
¹³It eats away parts of his skin;
death's firstborn devours his
limbs.

SLEEPING LAMPS

During Bible times people kept an
olive oil lamp burning all night. A
dark house or tent meant no one
was there. Job says that the lamp
of the wicked will be put out (Job
18:5–8). This means the wicked will
die, and their houses will be
empty.

---

¹⁴He is torn from the security of his
tent
and marched off to the king of
terrors.
¹⁵Fire resides*b* in his tent;
burning sulfur is scattered over
his dwelling.
¹⁶His roots dry up below
and his branches wither above.
¹⁷The memory of him perishes from
the earth;
he has no name in the land.
¹⁸He is driven from light into
darkness
and is banished from the world.
¹⁹He has no offspring or
descendants among his
people,
no survivor where once he lived.
²⁰Men of the west are appalled at
his fate;
men of the east are seized with
horror.
²¹Surely such is the dwelling of an
evil man;
such is the place of one who
knows not God."

---

*a*16 Hebrew *Sheol*   *b*15 Or *Nothing he had remains*

Job

19

Then Job replied:

²"How long will you
torment me
and crush me with words?
³Ten times now you have
reproached me;
shamelessly you attack me.
⁴If it is true that I have gone
astray,
my error remains my concern
alone.
⁵If indeed you would exalt
yourselves above me
and use my humiliation against
me,
⁶then know that God has wronged
me
and drawn his net around me.

⁷"Though I cry, 'I've been
wronged!' I get no response;
though I call for help, there is
no justice.
⁸He has blocked my way so I
cannot pass;
he has shrouded my paths in
darkness.
⁹He has stripped me of my honor
and removed the crown from my
head.
¹⁰He tears me down on every side
till I am gone;
he uproots my hope like a tree.
¹¹His anger burns against me;
he counts me among his
enemies.
¹²His troops advance in force;
they build a siege ramp against
me
and encamp around my tent.

¹³"He has alienated my brothers
from me;
my acquaintances are
completely estranged from
me.
¹⁴My kinsmen have gone away;
my friends have forgotten me.
¹⁵My guests and my maidservants
count me a stranger;

they look upon me as an alien.
¹⁶I summon my servant, but he
does not answer,
though I beg him with my own
mouth.
¹⁷My breath is offensive to my wife;
I am loathsome to my own
brothers.
¹⁸Even the little boys scorn me;
when I appear, they ridicule
me.
¹⁹All my intimate friends detest
me;
those I love have turned against
me.
²⁰I am nothing but skin and bones;
I have escaped with only the
skin of my teeth.ᵃ

²¹"Have pity on me, my friends,
have pity,
for the hand of God has struck
me.
²²Why do you pursue me as God
does?
Will you never get enough of
my flesh?

²³"Oh, that my words were
recorded,
that they were written on a
scroll,
²⁴that they were inscribed with an
iron tool onᵇ lead,
or engraved in rock forever!
²⁵I know that my Redeemerᶜ lives,
and that in the end he will
stand upon the earth.ᵈ
²⁶And after my skin has been
destroyed,
yetᵉ inᶠ my flesh I will see
God;
²⁷I myself will see him
with my own eyes—I, and not
another.
How my heart yearns within
me!

²⁸"If you say, 'How we will hound
him,
since the root of the trouble lies
in him,ᵍ'

ᵃ20 Or only my gums   ᵇ24 Or and   ᶜ25 Or defender   ᵈ25 Or upon my grave   ᵉ26 Or
And after I awake, / though this body has been destroyed, / then   ᶠ26 Or / apart from
ᵍ28 Many Hebrew manuscripts, Septuagint and Vulgate; most Hebrew manuscripts me

²⁹you should fear the sword
　　yourselves;

𝕎ORDS TO REMEMBER

19:25-27 I know that my
　　　Redeemer lives,
　　　and that in the end he
　　　will stand upon the
　　　earth....
　　　in my flesh I will see
　　　God;
　　　I myself will see him
　　　with my own eyes—
　　　I, and not another.

---

for wrath will bring punishment
　　by the sword,
　　and then you will know that
　　there is judgment.ᵃ"

Zophar

20 Then Zophar the Naamathite
　　replied:

²"My troubled thoughts prompt me
　　to answer
　　because I am greatly disturbed.
³I hear a rebuke that dishonors
　　me,
　　and my understanding inspires
　　me to reply.

⁴"Surely you know how it has been
　　from of old,
　　ever since manᵇ was placed on
　　the earth,
⁵that the mirth of the wicked is
　　brief,
　　the joy of the godless lasts but a
　　moment.
⁶Though his pride reaches to the
　　heavens
　　and his head touches the clouds,
⁷he will perish forever, like his
　　own dung;
　　those who have seen him will
　　say, 'Where is he?'
⁸Like a dream he flies away, no
　　more to be found,
　　banished like a vision of the
　　night.

⁹The eye that saw him will not see
　　him again;
　　his place will look on him no
　　more.
¹⁰His children must make amends
　　to the poor;
　　his own hands must give back
　　his wealth.
¹¹The youthful vigor that fills his
　　bones
　　will lie with him in the dust.

¹²"Though evil is sweet in his
　　mouth
　　and he hides it under his
　　tongue,
¹³though he cannot bear to let it
　　go
　　and keeps it in his mouth,
¹⁴yet his food will turn sour in his
　　stomach;
　　it will become the venom of
　　serpents within him.
¹⁵He will spit out the riches he
　　swallowed;
　　God will make his stomach
　　vomit them up.
¹⁶He will suck the poison of
　　serpents;
　　the fangs of an adder will kill
　　him.
¹⁷He will not enjoy the streams,
　　the rivers flowing with honey
　　and cream.
¹⁸What he toiled for he must give
　　back uneaten;
　　he will not enjoy the profit from
　　his trading.
¹⁹For he has oppressed the poor and
　　left them destitute;
　　he has seized houses he did not
　　build.

²⁰"Surely he will have no respite
　　from his craving;
　　he cannot save himself by his
　　treasure.
²¹Nothing is left for him to devour;
　　his prosperity will not endure.
²²In the midst of his plenty,
　　distress will overtake him;
　　the full force of misery will
　　come upon him.
²³When he has filled his belly,

ᵃ29 Or / that you may come to know the Almighty　　ᵇ4 Or Adam

God will vent his burning anger
　against him
and rain down his blows upon
　him.
24Though he flees from an iron
　weapon,
　a bronze-tipped arrow pierces
　him.
25He pulls it out of his back,
　the gleaming point out of his
　liver.
　Terrors will come over him;
26　total darkness lies in wait for
　his treasures.
　A fire unfanned will consume
　him
　and devour what is left in his
　tent.
27The heavens will expose his guilt;
　the earth will rise up against
　him.
28A flood will carry off his house,
　rushing waters*a* on the day of
　God's wrath.
29Such is the fate God allots the
　wicked,
　the heritage appointed for them
　by God."

Job
21
Then Job replied:
2"Listen carefully to my
　words;
　let this be the consolation you
　give me.
3Bear with me while I speak,
　and after I have spoken, mock
　on.

4"Is my complaint directed to
　man?
　Why should I not be impatient?
5Look at me and be astonished;
　clap your hand over your
　mouth.
6When I think about this, I am
　terrified;
　trembling seizes my body.
7Why do the wicked live on,
　growing old and increasing in
　power?

8They see their children
　established around them,
　their offspring before their eyes.
9Their homes are safe and free
　from fear;
　the rod of God is not upon
　them.
10Their bulls never fail to breed;
　their cows calve and do not
　miscarry.
11They send forth their children as
　a flock;
　their little ones dance about.
12They sing to the music of
　tambourine and harp;
　they make merry to the sound
　of the flute.
13They spend their years in
　prosperity
　and go down to the grave*b* in
　peace.*c*
14Yet they say to God, 'Leave us
　alone!
　We have no desire to know your
　ways.
15Who is the Almighty, that we
　should serve him?
　What would we gain by praying
　to him?'
16But their prosperity is not in
　their own hands,
　so I stand aloof from the
　counsel of the wicked.

17"Yet how often is the lamp of the
　wicked snuffed out?
　How often does calamity come
　upon them,
　the fate God allots in his
　anger?
18How often are they like straw
　before the wind,
　like chaff swept away by a
　gale?
19⸤It is said,⸥ 'God stores up a man's
　punishment for his sons.'
　Let him repay the man himself,
　so that he will know it!
20Let his own eyes see his
　destruction;
　let him drink of the wrath of
　the Almighty.*d*

---

*a*28 Or *The possessions in his house will be carried off, / washed away*　　*b*13 Hebrew *Sheol*
*c*13 Or *in an instant*　　*d*17-20 Verses 17 and 18 may be taken as exclamations and 19 and 20 as
declarations.

²¹For what does he care about the
family he leaves behind
when his allotted months come
to an end?

²²"Can anyone teach knowledge to
God,
since he judges even the
highest?
²³One man dies in full vigor,
completely secure and at ease,
²⁴his body*ᵃ* well nourished,
his bones rich with marrow.
²⁵Another man dies in bitterness of
soul,
never having enjoyed anything
good.
²⁶Side by side they lie in the dust,
and worms cover them both.

²⁷"I know full well what you are
thinking,
the schemes by which you
would wrong me.
²⁸You say, 'Where now is the great
man's house,
the tents where wicked men
lived?'
²⁹Have you never questioned those
who travel?
Have you paid no regard to
their accounts—
³⁰that the evil man is spared from
the day of calamity,
that he is delivered fromᵇ the
day of wrath?
³¹Who denounces his conduct to his
face?
Who repays him for what he
has done?
³²He is carried to the grave,
and watch is kept over his
tomb.
³³The soil in the valley is sweet to
him;
all men follow after him,
and a countless throng goesᶜ
before him.

³⁴"So how can you console me with
your nonsense?
Nothing is left of your answers
but falsehood!"

Eliphaz

22 Then Eliphaz the Temanite
replied:

²"Can a man be of benefit to God?
Can even a wise man benefit
him?
³What pleasure would it give the
Almighty if you were
righteous?
What would he gain if your
ways were blameless?

⁴"Is it for your piety that he
rebukes you
and brings charges against you?
⁵Is not your wickedness great?
Are not your sins endless?
⁶You demanded security from your
brothers for no reason;
you stripped men of their
clothing, leaving them
naked.
⁷You gave no water to the weary
and you withheld food from the
hungry,
⁸though you were a powerful man,
owning land—
an honored man, living on it.
⁹And you sent widows away
empty-handed
and broke the strength of the
fatherless.
¹⁰That is why snares are all around
you,
why sudden peril terrifies you,
¹¹why it is so dark you cannot see,
and why a flood of water covers
you.

¹²"Is not God in the heights of
heaven?
And see how lofty are the
highest stars!
¹³Yet you say, 'What does God
know?
Does he judge through such
darkness?
¹⁴Thick clouds veil him, so he does
not see us
as he goes about in the vaulted
heavens.'
¹⁵Will you keep to the old path

*ᵃ24 The meaning of the Hebrew for this word is uncertain.   ᵇ30 Or man is reserved for the day
of calamity, / that he is brought forth to   ᶜ33 Or / as a countless throng went*

that evil men have trod?
16They were carried off before their
time,
their foundations washed away
by a flood.
17They said to God, 'Leave us alone!
What can the Almighty do to
us?'
18Yet it was he who filled their
houses with good things,
so I stand aloof from the
counsel of the wicked.

19"The righteous see their ruin and
rejoice;
the innocent mock them,
saying,
20'Surely our foes are destroyed,
and fire devours their wealth.'

21"Submit to God and be at peace
with him;
in this way prosperity will come
to you.
22Accept instruction from his
mouth
and lay up his words in your
heart.
23If you return to the Almighty,
you will be restored:
If you remove wickedness far
from your tent
24and assign your nuggets to the
dust,
your gold of Ophir to the rocks
in the ravines,
25then the Almighty will be your
gold,
the choicest silver for you.
26Surely then you will find delight
in the Almighty
and will lift up your face to
God.
27You will pray to him, and he will
hear you,
and you will fulfill your vows.
28What you decide on will be done,
and light will shine on your
ways.
29When men are brought low and
you say, 'Lift them up!'
then he will save the downcast.
30He will deliver even one who is
not innocent,

who will be delivered through
the cleanness of your
hands."

Job

23 Then Job replied:
2"Even today my complaint
is bitter;
his hand[a] is heavy in spite of[b]
my groaning.
3If only I knew where to find him;
if only I could go to his
dwelling!
4I would state my case before him
and fill my mouth with
arguments.
5I would find out what he would
answer me,
and consider what he would say.
6Would he oppose me with great
power?
No, he would not press charges
against me.
7There an upright man could
present his case before him,
and I would be delivered forever
from my judge.

8"But if I go to the east, he is not
there;
if I go to the west, I do not find
him.
9When he is at work in the north,
I do not see him;
when he turns to the south, I
catch no glimpse of him.
10But he knows the way that I
take;
when he has tested me, I will
come forth as gold.
11My feet have closely followed his
steps;
I have kept to his way without
turning aside.
12I have not departed from the
commands of his lips;
I have treasured the words of
his mouth more than my
daily bread.

13"But he stands alone, and who
can oppose him?
He does whatever he pleases.

---

a2 Septuagint and Syriac; Hebrew / *the hand on me*   b2 Or *heavy on me in*

¹⁴He carries out his decree against
    me,
  and many such plans he still
    has in store.
¹⁵That is why I am terrified before
    him;
  when I think of all this, I fear
    him.
¹⁶God has made my heart faint;
  the Almighty has terrified me.
¹⁷Yet I am not silenced by the
    darkness,
  by the thick darkness that
    covers my face.

24   "Why does the Almighty not
    set times for judgment?
  Why must those who know him
    look in vain for such days?
²Men move boundary stones;
  they pasture flocks they have
    stolen.
³They drive away the orphan's
    donkey
  and take the widow's ox in
    pledge.
⁴They thrust the needy from the
    path
  and force all the poor of the
    land into hiding.
⁵Like wild donkeys in the desert,
  the poor go about their labor of
    foraging food;
  the wasteland provides food for
    their children.
⁶They gather fodder in the fields
  and glean in the vineyards of
    the wicked.

⁷Lacking clothes, they spend the
    night naked;
  they have nothing to cover
    themselves in the cold.
⁸They are drenched by mountain
    rains
  and hug the rocks for lack of
    shelter.
⁹The fatherless child is snatched
    from the breast;
  the infant of the poor is seized
    for a debt.
¹⁰Lacking clothes, they go about
    naked;
  they carry the sheaves, but still
    go hungry.
¹¹They crush olives among the
    terraces*a*;
  they tread the winepresses, yet
    suffer thirst.
¹²The groans of the dying rise from
    the city,
  and the souls of the wounded
    cry out for help.
  But God charges no one with
    wrongdoing.

¹³"There are those who rebel
    against the light,
  who do not know its ways
    or stay in its paths.
¹⁴When daylight is gone, the
    murderer rises up
  and kills the poor and needy;
  in the night he steals forth like
    a thief.
¹⁵The eye of the adulterer watches
    for dusk;

---

a11 Or *olives between the millstones*; the meaning of the Hebrew for this word is uncertain.

Life in Bible Times

CRUSHING OLIVES

Olives were crushed with heavy stones to get oil (Job 24:11). Olive oil was used in lamps and in cooking. People also used olive oil in medicines.

he thinks, 'No eye will see me,'
and he keeps his face concealed.
16In the dark, men break into
houses,
but by day they shut
themselves in;
they want nothing to do with
the light.
17For all of them, deep darkness is
their morning[a];
they make friends with the
terrors of darkness. [b]

18"Yet they are foam on the surface
of the water;
their portion of the land is
cursed,
so that no one goes to the
vineyards.
19As heat and drought snatch away
the melted snow,
so the grave[c] snatches away
those who have sinned.
20The womb forgets them,
the worm feasts on them;
evil men are no longer
remembered
but are broken like a tree.
21They prey on the barren and
childless woman,
and to the widow show no
kindness.
22But God drags away the mighty
by his power;
though they become established,
they have no assurance of
life.
23He may let them rest in a feeling
of security,
but his eyes are on their ways.
24For a little while they are
exalted, and then they are
gone;
they are brought low and
gathered up like all others;
they are cut off like heads of
grain.

25"If this is not so, who can prove
me false
and reduce my words to
nothing?"

Bildad

25 Then Bildad the Shuhite replied:

2"Dominion and awe belong to
God;
he establishes order in the
heights of heaven.
3Can his forces be numbered?
Upon whom does his light not
rise?
4How then can a man be righteous
before God?
How can one born of woman be
pure?
5If even the moon is not bright
and the stars are not pure in
his eyes,
6how much less man, who is but a
maggot—
a son of man, who is only a
worm!"

Job

26 Then Job replied:

2"How you have helped the
powerless!
How you have saved the arm
that is feeble!
3What advice you have offered to
one without wisdom!
And what great insight you
have displayed!
4Who has helped you utter these
words?
And whose spirit spoke from
your mouth?

5"The dead are in deep anguish,
those beneath the waters and
all that live in them.
6Death[c] is naked before God;
Destruction[d] lies uncovered.
7He spreads out the northern
ͺskiesͺ over empty space;
he suspends the earth over
nothing.
8He wraps up the waters in his
clouds,
yet the clouds do not burst
under their weight.

---

[a]17 Or *them, their morning is like the shadow of death*   [b]17 Or *of the shadow of death*
[c]19,6 Hebrew *Sheol*   [d]6 Hebrew *Abaddon*

⁹He covers the face of the full
     moon,
  spreading his clouds over it.
¹⁰He marks out the horizon on the
     face of the waters
  for a boundary between light
     and darkness.
¹¹The pillars of the heavens quake,
  aghast at his rebuke.
¹²By his power he churned up the
     sea;
  by his wisdom he cut Rahab to
     pieces.
¹³By his breath the skies became
     fair;
  his hand pierced the gliding
     serpent.
¹⁴And these are but the outer
     fringe of his works;
  how faint the whisper we hear
     of him!
  Who then can understand the
     thunder of his power?"

27 And Job continued his dis-
     course:

²"As surely as God lives, who has
     denied me justice,
  the Almighty, who has made
     me taste bitterness of soul,
³as long as I have life within
     me,
  the breath of God in my
     nostrils,
⁴my lips will not speak
     wickedness,
  and my tongue will utter no
     deceit.
⁵I will never admit you are in the
     right;
  till I die, I will not deny my
     integrity.
⁶I will maintain my righteousness
     and never let go of it;
  my conscience will not reproach
     me as long as I live.

⁷"May my enemies be like the
     wicked,
  my adversaries like the unjust!
⁸For what hope has the godless
     when he is cut off,
  when God takes away his life?
⁹Does God listen to his cry
  when distress comes upon him?

¹⁰Will he find delight in the
     Almighty?
  Will he call upon God at all
     times?

¹¹"I will teach you about the power
     of God;
  the ways of the Almighty I will
     not conceal.
¹²You have all seen this yourselves.
  Why then this meaningless
     talk?

¹³"Here is the fate God allots to the
     wicked,
  the heritage a ruthless man
     receives from the Almighty:
¹⁴However many his children, their
     fate is the sword;
  his offspring will never have
     enough to eat.
¹⁵The plague will bury those who
     survive him,
  and their widows will not weep
     for them.
¹⁶Though he heaps up silver like
     dust
  and clothes like piles of clay,
¹⁷what he lays up the righteous
     will wear,
  and the innocent will divide his
     silver.
¹⁸The house he builds is like a
     moth's cocoon,
  like a hut made by a
     watchman.
¹⁹He lies down wealthy, but will do
     so no more;
  when he opens his eyes, all is
     gone.
²⁰Terrors overtake him like a flood;
  a tempest snatches him away in
     the night.
²¹The east wind carries him off,
     and he is gone;
  it sweeps him out of his place.
²²It hurls itself against him
     without mercy
  as he flees headlong from its
     power.
²³It claps its hands in derision
  and hisses him out of his place.

28 "There is a mine for silver
     and a place where gold is
     refined.

²Iron is taken from the earth,
   and copper is smelted from
      ore.
³Man puts an end to the darkness;
   he searches the farthest
      recesses
   for ore in the blackest darkness.
⁴Far from where people dwell he
      cuts a shaft,
   in places forgotten by the foot of
      man;
   far from men he dangles and
      sways.
⁵The earth, from which food comes,
   is transformed below as by fire;
⁶sapphires*ᵃ* come from its rocks,
   and its dust contains nuggets of
      gold.
⁷No bird of prey knows that
      hidden path,
   no falcon's eye has seen it.
⁸Proud beasts do not set foot on it,
   and no lion prowls there.
⁹Man's hand assaults the flinty
      rock
   and lays bare the roots of the
      mountains.
¹⁰He tunnels through the rock;
   his eyes see all its treasures.
¹¹He searchesᵇ the sources of the
      rivers
   and brings hidden things to
      light.
¹²"But where can wisdom be found?
   Where does understanding
      dwell?
¹³Man does not comprehend its
      worth;
   it cannot be found in the land of
      the living.
¹⁴The deep says, 'It is not in me';
   the sea says, 'It is not with me.'
¹⁵It cannot be bought with the
      finest gold,
   nor can its price be weighed in
      silver.
¹⁶It cannot be bought with the gold
      of Ophir,
   with precious onyx or sapphires.
¹⁷Neither gold nor crystal can
      compare with it,

nor can it be had for jewels of
      gold.
¹⁸Coral and jasper are not worthy
      of mention;
   the price of wisdom is beyond
      rubies.
¹⁹The topaz of Cush cannot
      compare with it;
   it cannot be bought with pure
      gold.
²⁰"Where then does wisdom come
      from?
   Where does understanding
      dwell?
²¹It is hidden from the eyes of
      every living thing,
   concealed even from the birds of
      the air.
²²Destructionᶜ and Death say,
   'Only a rumor of it has reached
      our ears.'
²³God understands the way to it
   and he alone knows where it
      dwells,
²⁴for he views the ends of the
      earth
   and sees everything under the
      heavens.
²⁵When he established the force of
      the wind
   and measured out the waters,
²⁶when he made a decree for the
      rain
   and a path for the
      thunderstorm,
²⁷then he looked at wisdom and
      appraised it;
   he confirmed it and tested it.
²⁸And he said to man,
   'The fear of the Lord—that is
      wisdom,
   and to shun evil is
      understanding.' "

29

Job continued his discourse:
²"How I long for the months
      gone by,
   for the days when God watched
      over me,
³when his lamp shone upon my
      head

---

a6 Or *lapis lazuli*; also in verse 16   *b11* Septuagint, Aquila and Vulgate; Hebrew *He dams up*
c22 Hebrew *Abaddon*

and by his light I walked
through darkness!
⁴Oh, for the days when I was in
my prime,
when God's intimate friendship
blessed my house,
⁵when the Almighty was still with
me
and my children were around
me,
⁶when my path was drenched with
cream
and the rock poured out for me
streams of olive oil.

⁷"When I went to the gate of the
city
and took my seat in the public
square,
⁸the young men saw me and
stepped aside
and the old men rose to their
feet;
⁹the chief men refrained from
speaking
and covered their mouths with
their hands;
¹⁰the voices of the nobles were
hushed,
and their tongues stuck to the
roof of their mouths.
¹¹Whoever heard me spoke well of
me,
and those who saw me
commended me,
¹²because I rescued the poor who
cried for help,
and the fatherless who had
none to assist him.
¹³The man who was dying blessed
me;
I made the widow's heart
sing.
¹⁴I put on righteousness as my
clothing;
justice was my robe and my
turban.
¹⁵I was eyes to the blind
and feet to the lame.
¹⁶I was a father to the needy;
I took up the case of the
stranger.
¹⁷I broke the fangs of the wicked

and snatched the victims from
their teeth.

¹⁸"I thought, 'I will die in my own
house,
my days as numerous as the
grains of sand.
¹⁹My roots will reach to the water,
and the dew will lie all night on
my branches.
²⁰My glory will remain fresh in
me,
the bow ever new in my hand.'

²¹"Men listened to me expectantly,
waiting in silence for my
counsel.
²²After I had spoken, they spoke no
more;
my words fell gently on their
ears.
²³They waited for me as for
showers
and drank in my words as the
spring rain.
²⁴When I smiled at them, they
scarcely believed it;
the light of my face was
precious to them.ᵃ
²⁵I chose the way for them and sat
as their chief;
I dwelt as a king among his
troops;
I was like one who comforts
mourners.

30 "But now they mock me,
men younger than I,
whose fathers I would have
disdained
to put with my sheep dogs.
²Of what use was the strength of
their hands to me,
since their vigor had gone from
them?
³Haggard from want and hunger,
they roamedᵇ the parched land
in desolate wastelands at night.
⁴In the brush they gathered salt
herbs,
and their foodᶜ was the root of
the broom tree.
⁵They were banished from their
fellow men,

---

shouted at as if they were
thieves.
⁶They were forced to live in the
dry stream beds,
among the rocks and in holes in
the ground.
⁷They brayed among the bushes
and huddled in the
undergrowth.
⁸A base and nameless brood,
they were driven out of the
land.

⁹"And now their sons mock me in
song;
I have become a byword among
them.
¹⁰They detest me and keep their
distance;
they do not hesitate to spit in
my face.
¹¹Now that God has unstrung my
bow and afflicted me,
they throw off restraint in my
presence.
¹²On my right the tribe*ᵃ* attacks;
they lay snares for my feet,
they build their siege ramps
against me.
¹³They break up my road;
they succeed in destroying me—
without anyone's helping
them.*ᵇ*
¹⁴They advance as through a
gaping breach;
amid the ruins they come
rolling in.
¹⁵Terrors overwhelm me;
my dignity is driven away as by
the wind,
my safety vanishes like a cloud.

¹⁶"And now my life ebbs away;
days of suffering grip me.
¹⁷Night pierces my bones;
my gnawing pains never rest.
¹⁸In his great power ‚God‚ becomes
like clothing to me*ᶜ*;
he binds me like the neck of my
garment.
¹⁹He throws me into the mud,
and I am reduced to dust and
ashes.

²⁰"I cry out to you, O God, but you
do not answer;
I stand up, but you merely look
at me.
²¹You turn on me ruthlessly;
with the might of your hand
you attack me.
²²You snatch me up and drive me
before the wind;
you toss me about in the storm.
²³I know you will bring me down to
death,
to the place appointed for all
the living.

²⁴"Surely no one lays a hand on a
broken man
when he cries for help in his
distress.
²⁵Have I not wept for those in
trouble?
Has not my soul grieved for the
poor?
²⁶Yet when I hoped for good, evil
came;
when I looked for light, then
came darkness.
²⁷The churning inside me never
stops;
days of suffering confront me.
²⁸I go about blackened, but not by
the sun;
I stand up in the assembly and
cry for help.
²⁹I have become a brother of
jackals,
a companion of owls.
³⁰My skin grows black and peels;
my body burns with fever.
³¹My harp is tuned to mourning,
and my flute to the sound of
wailing.

31 "I made a covenant with my
eyes
not to look lustfully at a girl.
²For what is man's lot from God
above,
his heritage from the Almighty
on high?
³Is it not ruin for the wicked,
disaster for those who do
wrong?

---

*ᵃ12 The meaning of the Hebrew for this word is uncertain.   *ᵇ13 Or me. / 'No one can help him,'
they say‚.   *ᶜ18 Hebrew; Septuagint ‚God‚ grasps my clothing

⁴Does he not see my ways
  and count my every step?

⁵"If I have walked in falsehood
  or my foot has hurried after
    deceit—
⁶let God weigh me in honest scales
  and he will know that I am
    blameless—
⁷if my steps have turned from the
    path,
  if my heart has been led by my
    eyes,
  or if my hands have been
    defiled,
⁸then may others eat what I have
    sown,
  and may my crops be uprooted.

⁹"If my heart has been enticed by
    a woman,
  or if I have lurked at my
    neighbor's door,
¹⁰then may my wife grind another
    man's grain,
  and may other men sleep with
    her.
¹¹For that would have been
    shameful,
  a sin to be judged.
¹²It is a fire that burns to
    Destruction*a*;
  it would have uprooted my
    harvest.

¹³"If I have denied justice to my
    menservants and
    maidservants

a12 Hebrew Abaddon

when they had a grievance
    against me,
¹⁴what will I do when God
    confronts me?
  What will I answer when called
    to account?
¹⁵Did not he who made me in the
    womb make them?
  Did not the same one form us
    both within our mothers?

¹⁶"If I have denied the desires of
    the poor
  or let the eyes of the widow
    grow weary,
¹⁷if I have kept my bread to myself,
  not sharing it with the
    fatherless—
¹⁸but from my youth I reared him
    as would a father,
  and from my birth I guided the
    widow—
¹⁹if I have seen anyone perishing
    for lack of clothing,
  or a needy man without a
    garment,
²⁰and his heart did not bless me
  for warming him with the fleece
    from my sheep,
²¹if I have raised my hand against
    the fatherless,
  knowing that I had influence in
    court,
²²then let my arm fall from the
    shoulder,
  let it be broken off at the
    joint.

Life in Bible Times

GRINDING GRAIN

Each day women ground
grain between two heavy
stones to make coarse
flour. They mixed the flour
with water, salt and yeast
to bake bread for their family.

23For I dreaded destruction from
      God,
   and for fear of his splendor I
      could not do such things.

24"If I have put my trust in gold
      or said to pure gold, 'You are
      my security,'
25if I have rejoiced over my great
      wealth,
   the fortune my hands had
      gained,
26if I have regarded the sun in its
      radiance
   or the moon moving in splendor,
27so that my heart was secretly
      enticed
   and my hand offered them a
      kiss of homage,
28then these also would be sins to
      be judged,
   for I would have been unfaithful
      to God on high.

29"If I have rejoiced at my enemy's
      misfortune
   or gloated over the trouble that
      came to him—
30I have not allowed my mouth to
      sin
   by invoking a curse against his
      life—
31if the men of my household have
      never said,
   'Who has not had his fill of
      Job's meat?'—
32but no stranger had to spend the
      night in the street,
   for my door was always open to
      the traveler—

a33 Or as Adam did

33if I have concealed my sin as men
      do,a
   by hiding my guilt in my heart
34because I so feared the crowd
      and so dreaded the contempt of
      the clans
   that I kept silent and would not
      go outside

35("Oh, that I had someone to hear
      me!
   I sign now my defense—let the
      Almighty answer me;
   let my accuser put his
      indictment in writing.
36Surely I would wear it on my
      shoulder,
   I would put it on like a crown.
37I would give him an account of
      my every step;
   like a prince I would approach
      him.)—

38"if my land cries out against me
      and all its furrows are wet with
      tears,
39if I have devoured its yield
      without payment
   or broken the spirit of its
      tenants,
40then let briers come up instead of
      wheat
   and weeds instead of barley."

   The words of Job are ended.

Elihu

32 So these three men stopped
answering Job, because he
was righteous in his own eyes. 2But

┃ET'S LIVE IT!   Job 31:16–23

HELP FOR THE NEEDY ➡ One thing that made Job such a good man was
that he cared about other people. Read Job 31:16–23. What did Job do
to show he cared about people who were poor and needy?

   Name several ways that Christians today can help others in need.
You can help too. Ask your mom or dad if you can go through your
clothes and toys. Neatly put into bags some clothes and toys you no
longer use. Ask someone in your church or community if there is a needy
family with a boy or girl who could wear what you've outgrown. Bring
the bags of clothes and toys to the family.

Elihu son of Barakel the Buzite, of the family of Ram, became very angry with Job for justifying himself rather than God. ³He was also angry with the three friends, because they had found no way to refute Job, and yet had condemned him.ᵃ ⁴Now Elihu had waited before speaking to Job because they were older than he. ⁵But when he saw that the three men had nothing more to say, his anger was aroused.

⁶So Elihu son of Barakel the Buzite said:

"I am young in years,
    and you are old;
that is why I was fearful,
    not daring to tell you what I
        know.
⁷I thought, 'Age should speak;
    advanced years should teach
        wisdom.'
⁸But it is the spiritᵇ in a man,
    the breath of the Almighty, that
        gives him understanding.
⁹It is not only the oldᶜ who are
        wise,
    not only the aged who
        understand what is right.

¹⁰"Therefore I say: Listen to me;
    I too will tell you what I know.
¹¹I waited while you spoke,
    I listened to your reasoning;
while you were searching for
        words,
¹²   I gave you my full attention.
But not one of you has proved Job
        wrong;
    none of you has answered his
        arguments.
¹³Do not say, 'We have found
        wisdom;
    let God refute him, not man.'
¹⁴But Job has not marshaled his
        words against me,
    and I will not answer him with
        your arguments.

¹⁵"They are dismayed and have no
        more to say;
    words have failed them.

¹⁶Must I wait, now that they are
        silent,
    now that they stand there with
        no reply?
¹⁷I too will have my say;
    I too will tell what I know.
¹⁸For I am full of words,
    and the spirit within me
        compels me;
¹⁹inside I am like bottled-up wine,
    like new wineskins ready to
        burst.
²⁰I must speak and find relief;
    I must open my lips and reply.
²¹I will show partiality to no one,
    nor will I flatter any man;
²²for if I were skilled in flattery,
    my Maker would soon take me
        away.

33 "But now, Job, listen to my
        words;
    pay attention to everything I
        say.
²I am about to open my mouth;
    my words are on the tip of my
        tongue.
³My words come from an upright
        heart;
    my lips sincerely speak what I
        know.
⁴The Spirit of God has made me;
    the breath of the Almighty
        gives me life.
⁵Answer me then, if you can;
    prepare yourself and confront
        me.
⁶I am just like you before God;
    I too have been taken from clay.
⁷No fear of me should alarm you,
    nor should my hand be heavy
        upon you.

⁸"But you have said in my
        hearing—
    I heard the very words—
⁹'I am pure and without sin;
    I am clean and free from guilt.
¹⁰Yet God has found fault with me;
    he considers me his enemy.
¹¹He fastens my feet in shackles;
    he keeps close watch on all my
        paths.'

ᵃ3 Masoretic Text; an ancient Hebrew scribal tradition *Job, and so had condemned God*   ᵇ8 Or
Spirit; also in verse 18   ᶜ9 Or *many*; or *great*

12"But I tell you, in this you are
      not right,
    for God is greater than man.
13Why do you complain to him
    that he answers none of man's
      words^a?
14For God does speak—now one
      way, now another—
    though man may not perceive
      it.
15In a dream, in a vision of the
      night,
    when deep sleep falls on men
    as they slumber in their beds,
16he may speak in their ears
    and terrify them with warnings,
17to turn man from wrongdoing
    and keep him from pride,
18to preserve his soul from the pit,^b
    his life from perishing by the
      sword.^c
19Or a man may be chastened on a
      bed of pain
    with constant distress in his
      bones,
20so that his very being finds food
      repulsive
    and his soul loathes the choicest
      meal.
21His flesh wastes away to nothing,
    and his bones, once hidden, now
      stick out.
22His soul draws near to the pit,^d
    and his life to the messengers of
      death.^e

23"Yet if there is an angel on his
      side
    as a mediator, one out of a
      thousand,
    to tell a man what is right for
      him,
24to be gracious to him and say,
    'Spare him from going down to
      the pit^f;
    I have found a ransom for
      him'—
25then his flesh is renewed like a
      child's;
    it is restored as in the days of
      his youth.

26He prays to God and finds favor
      with him,
    he sees God's face and shouts
      for joy;
    he is restored by God to his
      righteous state.
27Then he comes to men and says,
    'I sinned, and perverted what
      was right,
    but I did not get what I
      deserved.
28He redeemed my soul from going
      down to the pit,^g
    and I will live to enjoy the
      light.'

29"God does all these things to a
      man—
    twice, even three times—
30to turn back his soul from the
      pit,^h
    that the light of life may shine
      on him.

31"Pay attention, Job, and listen to
      me;
    be silent, and I will speak.
32If you have anything to say,
      answer me;
    speak up, for I want you to be
      cleared.
33But if not, then listen to me;
    be silent, and I will teach you
      wisdom."

34 Then Elihu said:
2"Hear my words, you wise
      men;
    listen to me, you men of
      learning.
3For the ear tests words
    as the tongue tastes food.
4Let us discern for ourselves what
      is right;
    let us learn together what is
      good.

5"Job says, 'I am innocent,
    but God denies me justice.
6Although I am right,
    I am considered a liar;

---

^a13 Or *that he does not answer for any of his actions*   ^b18 Or *preserve him from the grave*
^c18 Or *from crossing the River*   ^d22 Or *He draws near to the grave*   ^e22 Or *to the dead*
^f24 Or *grave*   ^g28 Or *redeemed me from going down to the grave*   ^h30 Or *turn him back from the grave*

although I am guiltless,
his arrow inflicts an incurable
wound.'
7What man is like Job,
who drinks scorn like water?
8He keeps company with evildoers;
he associates with wicked men.
9For he says, 'It profits a man
nothing
when he tries to please God.'

10"So listen to me, you men of
understanding.
Far be it from God to do evil,
from the Almighty to do wrong.
11He repays a man for what he has
done;
he brings upon him what his
conduct deserves.
12It is unthinkable that God would
do wrong,
that the Almighty would
pervert justice.
13Who appointed him over the
earth?
Who put him in charge of the
whole world?
14If it were his intention
and he withdrew his spirit*a* and
breath,
15all mankind would perish
together
and man would return to the
dust.

16"If you have understanding, hear
this;
listen to what I say.
17Can he who hates justice govern?
Will you condemn the just and
mighty One?
18Is he not the One who says to
kings, 'You are worthless,'
and to nobles, 'You are wicked,'
19who shows no partiality to
princes
and does not favor the rich over
the poor,
for they are all the work of his
hands?
20They die in an instant, in the
middle of the night;
the people are shaken and they
pass away;

the mighty are removed without
human hand.
21"His eyes are on the ways of
men;
he sees their every step.
22There is no dark place, no deep
shadow,
where evildoers can hide.
23God has no need to examine men
further,
that they should come before
him for judgment.
24Without inquiry he shatters the
mighty
and sets up others in their
place.
25Because he takes note of their
deeds,
he overthrows them in the
night and they are crushed.
26He punishes them for their
wickedness
where everyone can see them,
27because they turned from
following him
and had no regard for any of his
ways.
28They caused the cry of the poor to
come before him,
so that he heard the cry of the
needy.
29But if he remains silent, who can
condemn him?
If he hides his face, who can see
him?
Yet he is over man and nation
alike,
30 to keep a godless man from
ruling,
from laying snares for the
people.

31"Suppose a man says to God,
'I am guilty but will offend no
more.
32Teach me what I cannot see;
if I have done wrong, I will not
do so again.'
33Should God then reward you on
your terms,
when you refuse to repent?
You must decide, not I;
so tell me what you know.

a14 Or *Spirit*

34"Men of understanding declare,
    wise men who hear me say to
    me,
35'Job speaks without knowledge;
    his words lack insight.'
36Oh, that Job might be tested to
    the utmost
    for answering like a wicked
    man!
37To his sin he adds rebellion;
    scornfully he claps his hands
    among us
    and multiplies his words
    against God."

35

Then Elihu said:

2"Do you think this is just?
You say, 'I will be cleared by
    God.ᵃ'
3Yet you ask him, 'What profit is
    it to me,ᵇ
    and what do I gain by not
    sinning?'

4"I would like to reply to you
    and to your friends with you.
5Look up at the heavens and see;
    gaze at the clouds so high above
    you.
6If you sin, how does that affect
    him?
    If your sins are many, what
    does that do to him?
7If you are righteous, what do you
    give to him,
    or what does he receive from
    your hand?
8Your wickedness affects only a
    man like yourself,
    and your righteousness only the
    sons of men.

9"Men cry out under a load of
    oppression;
    they plead for relief from the
    arm of the powerful.
10But no one says, 'Where is God
    my Maker,
    who gives songs in the night,
11who teaches more to us than toᶜ
    the beasts of the earth

and makes us wiser thanᵈ the
    birds of the air?'
12He does not answer when men
    cry out
    because of the arrogance of the
    wicked.
13Indeed, God does not listen to
    their empty plea;
    the Almighty pays no attention
    to it.
14How much less, then, will he
    listen
    when you say that you do not
    see him,
    that your case is before him
    and you must wait for him,
15and further, that his anger never
    punishes
    and he does not take the least
    notice of wickedness.ᵉ
16So Job opens his mouth with
    empty talk;
    without knowledge he
    multiplies words."

36

Elihu continued:

2"Bear with me a little
    longer and I will show you
    that there is more to be said in
    God's behalf.
3I get my knowledge from afar;
    I will ascribe justice to my
    Maker.
4Be assured that my words are not
    false;
    one perfect in knowledge is with
    you.

5"God is mighty, but does not
    despise men;
    he is mighty, and firm in his
    purpose.
6He does not keep the wicked alive
    but gives the afflicted their
    rights.
7He does not take his eyes off the
    righteous;
    he enthrones them with kings
    and exalts them forever.
8But if men are bound in chains,
    held fast by cords of affliction,

ᵃ2 Or *My righteousness is more than God's*   ᵇ3 Or *you*   ᶜ11 Or *teaches us by*   ᵈ11 Or *us
wise by*   ᵉ15 Symmachus, Theodotion and Vulgate; the meaning of the Hebrew for this word is
uncertain.

⁹he tells them what they have
    done—
  that they have sinned
    arrogantly.
¹⁰He makes them listen to
    correction
  and commands them to repent
    of their evil.
¹¹If they obey and serve him,
  they will spend the rest of their
    days in prosperity
  and their years in contentment.
¹²But if they do not listen,
  they will perish by the sword*a*
  and die without knowledge.

¹³"The godless in heart harbor
    resentment;
  even when he fetters them, they
    do not cry for help.
¹⁴They die in their youth,
  among male prostitutes of the
    shrines.
¹⁵But those who suffer he delivers
    in their suffering;
  he speaks to them in their
    affliction.

¹⁶"He is wooing you from the jaws
    of distress
  to a spacious place free from
    restriction,
  to the comfort of your table
    laden with choice food.
¹⁷But now you are laden with the
    judgment due the wicked;
  judgment and justice have
    taken hold of you.
¹⁸Be careful that no one entices you
    by riches;
  do not let a large bribe turn you
    aside.
¹⁹Would your wealth
  or even all your mighty efforts
  sustain you so you would not be
    in distress?
²⁰Do not long for the night,
  to drag people away from their
    homes.*b*
²¹Beware of turning to evil,
  which you seem to prefer to
    affliction.

²²"God is exalted in his power.
  Who is a teacher like him?
²³Who has prescribed his ways for
    him,
  or said to him, 'You have done
    wrong'?
²⁴Remember to extol his work,
  which men have praised in
    song.
²⁵All mankind has seen it;
  men gaze on it from afar.
²⁶How great is God—beyond our
    understanding!
  The number of his years is past
    finding out.

²⁷"He draws up the drops of water,
  which distill as rain to the
    streams*c*;
²⁸the clouds pour down their
    moisture
  and abundant showers fall on
    mankind.
²⁹Who can understand how he
    spreads out the clouds,
  how he thunders from his
    pavilion?
³⁰See how he scatters his lightning
    about him,
  bathing the depths of the
    sea.
³¹This is the way he governs*d* the
    nations
  and provides food in abundance.
³²He fills his hands with lightning
  and commands it to strike its
    mark.
³³His thunder announces the
    coming storm;
  even the cattle make known its
    approach.*e*

37 "At this my heart pounds
    and leaps from its place.
²Listen! Listen to the roar of his
    voice,
  to the rumbling that comes
    from his mouth.
³He unleashes his lightning
    beneath the whole heaven
  and sends it to the ends of the
    earth.

---

a12 Or *will cross the River*   *b20* The meaning of the Hebrew for verses 18-20 is uncertain.
c27 Or *distill from the mist as rain*   *d31* Or *nourishes*   *e33* Or *announces his coming— l the*
One zealous against evil

⁹he tells them what they have
done—
that they have sinned
arrogantly.
¹⁰He makes them listen to
correction
and commands them to repent
of their evil.
¹¹If they obey and serve him,
they will spend the rest of their
days in prosperity
and their years in contentment.
¹²But if they do not listen,
they will perish by the sword^a
and die without knowledge.

¹³"The godless in heart harbor
resentment;
even when he fetters them, they
do not cry for help.
¹⁴They die in their youth,
among male prostitutes of the
shrines.
¹⁵But those who suffer he delivers
in their suffering;
he speaks to them in their
affliction.

¹⁶"He is wooing you from the jaws
of distress
to a spacious place free from
restriction,
to the comfort of your table
laden with choice food.
¹⁷But now you are laden with the
judgment due the wicked;
judgment and justice have
taken hold of you.
¹⁸Be careful that no one entices you
by riches;
do not let a large bribe turn you
aside.
¹⁹Would your wealth
or even all your mighty efforts
sustain you so you would not be
in distress?
²⁰Do not long for the night,
to drag people away from their
homes.^b
²¹Beware of turning to evil,
which you seem to prefer to
affliction.

²²"God is exalted in his power.
Who is a teacher like him?
²³Who has prescribed his ways for
him,
or said to him, 'You have done
wrong'?
²⁴Remember to extol his work,
which men have praised in
song.
²⁵All mankind has seen it;
men gaze on it from afar.
²⁶How great is God—beyond our
understanding!
The number of his years is past
finding out.

²⁷"He draws up the drops of water,
which distill as rain to the
streams^c;
²⁸the clouds pour down their
moisture
and abundant showers fall on
mankind.
²⁹Who can understand how he
spreads out the clouds,
how he thunders from his
pavilion?
³⁰See how he scatters his lightning
about him,
bathing the depths of the
sea.
³¹This is the way he governs^d the
nations
and provides food in abundance.
³²He fills his hands with lightning
and commands it to strike its
mark.
³³His thunder announces the
coming storm;
even the cattle make known its
approach.^e

37 "At this my heart pounds
and leaps from its place.
²Listen! Listen to the roar of his
voice,
to the rumbling that comes
from his mouth.
³He unleashes his lightning
beneath the whole heaven
and sends it to the ends of the
earth.

---

^a12 Or *will cross the River*　　^b20 The meaning of the Hebrew for verses 18-20 is uncertain.
^c27 Or *distill from the mist as rain*　　^d31 Or *nourishes*　　^e33 Or *announces his coming— l the
One zealous against evil*

34"Men of understanding declare,
  wise men who hear me say to
  me,
35'Job speaks without knowledge;
  his words lack insight.'
36Oh, that Job might be tested to
  the utmost
  for answering like a wicked
  man!
37To his sin he adds rebellion;
  scornfully he claps his hands
  among us
  and multiplies his words
  against God."

35

Then Elihu said:

2"Do you think this is just?
You say, 'I will be cleared by
  God.'*a*
3Yet you ask him, 'What profit is
  it to me,*b*
  and what do I gain by not
  sinning?'

4"I would like to reply to you
  and to your friends with you.
5Look up at the heavens and see;
  gaze at the clouds so high above
  you.
6If you sin, how does that affect
  him?
  If your sins are many, what
  does that do to him?
7If you are righteous, what do you
  give to him,
  or what does he receive from
  your hand?
8Your wickedness affects only a
  man like yourself,
  and your righteousness only the
  sons of men.

9"Men cry out under a load of
  oppression;
  they plead for relief from the
  arm of the powerful.
10But no one says, 'Where is God
  my Maker,
  who gives songs in the night,
11who teaches more to us than to*c*
  the beasts of the earth

and makes us wiser than*d* the
  birds of the air?'
12He does not answer when men
  cry out
  because of the arrogance of the
  wicked.
13Indeed, God does not listen to
  their empty plea;
  the Almighty pays no attention
  to it.
14How much less, then, will he
  listen
  when you say that you do not
  see him,
  that your case is before him
  and you must wait for him,
15and further, that his anger never
  punishes
  and he does not take the least
  notice of wickedness.*e*
16So Job opens his mouth with
  empty talk;
  without knowledge he
  multiplies words."

36

Elihu continued:

2"Bear with me a little
  longer and I will show you
  that there is more to be said in
  God's behalf.
3I get my knowledge from afar;
  I will ascribe justice to my
  Maker.
4Be assured that my words are not
  false;
  one perfect in knowledge is with
  you.

5"God is mighty, but does not
  despise men;
  he is mighty, and firm in his
  purpose.
6He does not keep the wicked alive
  but gives the afflicted their
  rights.
7He does not take his eyes off the
  righteous;
  he enthrones them with kings
  and exalts them forever.
8But if men are bound in chains,
  held fast by cords of affliction,

---

a2 Or My righteousness is more than God's   *b3 Or you*   *c11 Or teaches us by*   *d11 Or us
wise by*   *e15 Symmachus, Theodotion and Vulgate; the meaning of the Hebrew for this word is
uncertain.*

⁴After that comes the sound of his
    roar;
  he thunders with his majestic
    voice.
  When his voice resounds,
    he holds nothing back.
⁵God's voice thunders in marvelous
    ways;
  he does great things beyond our
    understanding.
⁶He says to the snow, 'Fall on the
    earth,'
  and to the rain shower, 'Be a
    mighty downpour.'
⁷So that all men he has made may
    know his work,
  he stops every man from his
    labor.ᵃ
⁸The animals take cover;
  they remain in their dens.
⁹The tempest comes out from its
    chamber,
  the cold from the driving winds.
¹⁰The breath of God produces ice,
  and the broad waters become
    frozen.
¹¹He loads the clouds with
    moisture;
  he scatters his lightning
    through them.
¹²At his direction they swirl around
    over the face of the whole earth
  to do whatever he commands
    them.
¹³He brings the clouds to punish
    men,
  or to water his earthᵇ and show
    his love.

¹⁴"Listen to this, Job;
  stop and consider God's
    wonders.
¹⁵Do you know how God controls
    the clouds
  and makes his lightning flash?
¹⁶Do you know how the clouds hang
    poised,
  those wonders of him who is
    perfect in knowledge?
¹⁷You who swelter in your clothes
  when the land lies hushed
    under the south wind,

¹⁸can you join him in spreading out
    the skies,
  hard as a mirror of cast bronze?

¹⁹"Tell us what we should say to
    him;
  we cannot draw up our case
    because of our darkness.
²⁰Should he be told that I want to
    speak?
  Would any man ask to be
    swallowed up?
²¹Now no one can look at the sun,
    bright as it is in the skies
  after the wind has swept them
    clean.
²²Out of the north he comes in
    golden splendor;
  God comes in awesome majesty.
²³The Almighty is beyond our reach
    and exalted in power;
  in his justice and great
    righteousness, he does not
    oppress.
²⁴Therefore, men revere him,
  for does he not have regard for
    all the wise in heart?ᶜ"

The LORD Speaks

38 Then the LORD answered Job
    out of the storm. He said:

²"Who is this that darkens my
    counsel
  with words without knowledge?
³Brace yourself like a man;
  I will question you,
    and you shall answer me.

⁴"Where were you when I laid the
    earth's foundation?
  Tell me, if you understand.
⁵Who marked off its dimensions?
    Surely you know!
  Who stretched a measuring line
    across it?
⁶On what were its footings set,
    or who laid its cornerstone—
⁷while the morning stars sang
    together
  and all the angelsᵈ shouted for
    joy?

ᵃ7 Or / he fills all men with fear by his power   ᵇ13 Or to favor them   ᶜ24 Or for he does not
have regard for any who think they are wise   ᵈ7 Hebrew the sons of God

⁸"Who shut up the sea behind
    doors
  when it burst forth from the
    womb,
⁹when I made the clouds its
    garment
  and wrapped it in thick
    darkness,
¹⁰when I fixed limits for it
  and set its doors and bars in
    place,
¹¹when I said, 'This far you may
    come and no farther;
  here is where your proud waves
    halt'?

¹²"Have you ever given orders to
    the morning,
  or shown the dawn its place,
¹³that it might take the earth by
    the edges
  and shake the wicked out of it?
¹⁴The earth takes shape like clay
    under a seal;
  its features stand out like those
    of a garment.
¹⁵The wicked are denied their light,
  and their upraised arm is
    broken.

¹⁶"Have you journeyed to the
    springs of the sea
  or walked in the recesses of the
    deep?
¹⁷Have the gates of death been
    shown to you?
  Have you seen the gates of the
    shadow of death ᵃ?
¹⁸Have you comprehended the vast
    expanses of the earth?
  Tell me, if you know all this.

¹⁹"What is the way to the abode of
    light?
  And where does darkness
    reside?
²⁰Can you take them to their
    places?
  Do you know the paths to their
    dwellings?
²¹Surely you know, for you were
    already born!
  You have lived so many years!

²²"Have you entered the
    storehouses of the snow
  or seen the storehouses of the
    hail,
²³which I reserve for times of
    trouble,
  for days of war and battle?
²⁴What is the way to the place
    where the lightning is
    dispersed,
  or the place where the east
    winds are scattered over the
    earth?
²⁵Who cuts a channel for the
    torrents of rain,
  and a path for the
    thunderstorm,
²⁶to water a land where no man
    lives,
  a desert with no one in it,
²⁷to satisfy a desolate wasteland
  and make it sprout with grass?
²⁸Does the rain have a father?
  Who fathers the drops of dew?
²⁹From whose womb comes the
    ice?
  Who gives birth to the frost
    from the heavens
³⁰when the waters become hard as
    stone,
  when the surface of the deep is
    frozen?

³¹"Can you bind the beautiful ᵇ
    Pleiades?
  Can you loose the cords of
    Orion?
³²Can you bring forth the
    constellations in their
    seasons ᶜ
  or lead out the Bear ᵈ with its
    cubs?
³³Do you know the laws of the
    heavens?
  Can you set up ⌊God's ᵉ⌋
    dominion over the earth?

³⁴"Can you raise your voice to the
    clouds
  and cover yourself with a flood
    of water?
³⁵Do you send the lightning bolts
    on their way?

ᵃ17 Or *gates of deep shadows*   ᵇ31 Or *the twinkling;* or *the chains of the*   ᶜ32 Or *the morning star in its season*   ᵈ32 Or *out Leo*   ᵉ33 Or *his;* or *their*

Do they report to you, 'Here we
are'?
36Who endowed the heart[a] with
wisdom
or gave understanding to the
mind[a]?
37Who has the wisdom to count the
clouds?
Who can tip over the water jars
of the heavens
38when the dust becomes hard
and the clods of earth stick
together?

39"Do you hunt the prey for the
lioness
and satisfy the hunger of the
lions
40when they crouch in their dens
or lie in wait in a thicket?
41Who provides food for the raven
when its young cry out to
God
and wander about for lack of
food?

39 "Do you know when the
mountain goats give birth?
Do you watch when the doe
bears her fawn?
2Do you count the months till they
bear?
Do you know the time they give
birth?
3They crouch down and bring forth
their young;
their labor pains are ended.
4Their young thrive and grow
strong in the wilds;
they leave and do not return.

5"Who let the wild donkey go free?
Who untied his ropes?
6I gave him the wasteland as his
home,
the salt flats as his habitat.
7He laughs at the commotion in
the town;
he does not hear a driver's
shout.
8He ranges the hills for his
pasture
and searches for any green
thing.

9"Will the wild ox consent to serve
you?
Will he stay by your manger at
night?
10Can you hold him to the furrow
with a harness?
Will he till the valleys behind
you?
11Will you rely on him for his great
strength?
Will you leave your heavy work
to him?
12Can you trust him to bring in
your grain
and gather it to your threshing
floor?

13"The wings of the ostrich flap
joyfully,
but they cannot compare with
the pinions and feathers of
the stork.
14She lays her eggs on the ground
and lets them warm in the
sand,
15unmindful that a foot may crush
them,
that some wild animal may
trample them.
16She treats her young harshly, as
if they were not hers;
she cares not that her labor was
in vain,
17for God did not endow her with
wisdom
or give her a share of good
sense.
18Yet when she spreads her
feathers to run,
she laughs at horse and rider.

19"Do you give the horse his
strength
or clothe his neck with a
flowing mane?
20Do you make him leap like a
locust,
striking terror with his proud
snorting?
21He paws fiercely, rejoicing in his
strength,
and charges into the fray.
22He laughs at fear, afraid of
nothing;

a36 The meaning of the Hebrew for this word is uncertain.

he does not shy away from the
    sword.
23The quiver rattles against his
    side,
along with the flashing spear
    and lance.
24In frenzied excitement he eats up
    the ground;
he cannot stand still when the
    trumpet sounds.
25At the blast of the trumpet he
    snorts, 'Aha!'
He catches the scent of battle
    from afar,
the shout of commanders and
    the battle cry.

26"Does the hawk take flight by
    your wisdom
and spread his wings toward
    the south?
27Does the eagle soar at your
    command
and build his nest on high?
28He dwells on a cliff and stays
    there at night;
a rocky crag is his stronghold.
29From there he seeks out his food;
    his eyes detect it from afar.
30His young ones feast on blood,
    and where the slain are, there
    is he."

40 The LORD said to Job:
    2"Will the one who contends
    with the Almighty correct
    him?
Let him who accuses God
    answer him!"

3Then Job answered the LORD:

4"I am unworthy—how can I reply
    to you?
I put my hand over my mouth.
5I spoke once, but I have no
    answer—
twice, but I will say no more."

6Then the LORD spoke to Job out of
the storm:

7"Brace yourself like a man;
I will question you,
    and you shall answer me.

8"Would you discredit my justice?
Would you condemn me to
    justify yourself?
9Do you have an arm like God's,
    and can your voice thunder like
    his?
10Then adorn yourself with glory
    and splendor,
and clothe yourself in honor and
    majesty.
11Unleash the fury of your wrath,
    look at every proud man and
    bring him low,
12look at every proud man and
    humble him,
crush the wicked where they
    stand.
13Bury them all in the dust
    together;
shroud their faces in the grave.
14Then I myself will admit to you
    that your own right hand can
    save you.

15"Look at the behemoth,ª
    which I made along with you
    and which feeds on grass like
    an ox.
16What strength he has in his loins,

ª15 Possibly the hippopotamus or the elephant

ET'S LIVE IT!   Job 39:1–30

DISPLAY GOD'S GREATNESS ⇒ In Job 39 God reminds Job of some of
the wonders he created. Make a list of the birds and animals God speaks
about.
    See if you can find pictures of some of these birds and animals in
magazines. Cut them out, and paste them on a large sheet of cardboard. Ask your mom or dad where to put your poster, to remind your
whole family that God is the great creator.

what power in the muscles of
his belly!

?DID YOU KNOW?　　40:9

What did God say to Job?

God told Job to consider how
great the Lord is. Job cannot even
understand the things God does in
nature. How can Job expect to understand what God is doing in his
life?

17His tail*a* sways like a cedar;
　the sinews of his thighs are
　　close-knit.
18His bones are tubes of bronze,
　his limbs like rods of iron.
19He ranks first among the works
　　of God,
　yet his Maker can approach him
　　with his sword.
20The hills bring him their produce,
　and all the wild animals play
　　nearby.
21Under the lotus plants he lies,
　hidden among the reeds in the
　　marsh.
22The lotuses conceal him in their
　　shadow;
　the poplars by the stream
　　surround him.
23When the river rages, he is not
　　alarmed;
　he is secure, though the Jordan
　　should surge against his
　　mouth.
24Can anyone capture him by the
　　eyes,*b*
　or trap him and pierce his nose?

41 "Can you pull in the
　　leviathan*c* with a fishhook
　or tie down his tongue with a
　　rope?
2Can you put a cord through his
　　nose
　or pierce his jaw with a hook?
3Will he keep begging you for
　　mercy?

Will he speak to you with
　gentle words?
4Will he make an agreement with
　　you
　for you to take him as your
　　slave for life?
5Can you make a pet of him like a
　　bird
　or put him on a leash for your
　　girls?
6Will traders barter for him?
　Will they divide him up among
　　the merchants?
7Can you fill his hide with
　　harpoons
　or his head with fishing spears?
8If you lay a hand on him,
　you will remember the struggle
　　and never do it again!
9Any hope of subduing him is
　　false;
　the mere sight of him is
　　overpowering.
10No one is fierce enough to rouse
　　him.
　Who then is able to stand
　　against me?
11Who has a claim against me that
　　I must pay?
　Everything under heaven
　　belongs to me.

12"I will not fail to speak of his
　　limbs,
　his strength and his graceful
　　form.
13Who can strip off his outer
　　coat?
　Who would approach him with
　　a bridle?
14Who dares open the doors of his
　　mouth,
　ringed about with his fearsome
　　teeth?
15His back has*d* rows of shields
　tightly sealed together;
16each is so close to the next
　that no air can pass between.
17They are joined fast to one
　　another;
　they cling together and cannot
　　be parted.

---

*a*17 Possibly trunk　　*b*24 Or *by a water hole*　　*c*1 Possibly the crocodile　　*d*15 Or *His pride*
is his

18His snorting throws out flashes of
light;
his eyes are like the rays of
dawn.
19Firebrands stream from his
mouth;
sparks of fire shoot out.
20Smoke pours from his nostrils
as from a boiling pot over a fire
of reeds.
21His breath sets coals ablaze,
and flames dart from his mouth.
22Strength resides in his neck;
dismay goes before him.
23The folds of his flesh are tightly
joined;
they are firm and immovable.
24His chest is hard as rock,
hard as a lower millstone.
25When he rises up, the mighty are
terrified;
they retreat before his
thrashing.
26The sword that reaches him has
no effect,
nor does the spear or the dart
or the javelin.
27Iron he treats like straw
and bronze like rotten wood.
28Arrows do not make him flee;
slingstones are like chaff to him.
29A club seems to him but a piece
of straw;

he laughs at the rattling of the
lance.
30His undersides are jagged
potsherds,
leaving a trail in the mud like
a threshing sledge.
31He makes the depths churn like a
boiling caldron
and stirs up the sea like a pot
of ointment.
32Behind him he leaves a glistening
wake;
one would think the deep had
white hair.
33Nothing on earth is his equal—
a creature without fear.
34He looks down on all that are
haughty;
he is king over all that are
proud."

Job

42

Then Job replied to the LORD:

2"I know that you can do all
things;
no plan of yours can be
thwarted.
3You asked, 'Who is this that
obscures my counsel
without knowledge?'
Surely I spoke of things I did
not understand,

Life in Bible Times

LEVIATHAN

Leviathan probably means
crocodile. In any case, it
must have been a fierce,
dangerous animal. Job 41
describes his "fearsome
teeth," his breath that "sets
coals ablaze," and his
strength that makes iron
"like straw." To see if you
would ever want to get
near this "leviathan" or
crocodile, read what Job
41:8 says!

things too wonderful for me to know.

⁴"You said, 'Listen now, and I will
  speak;
  I will question you,
  and you shall answer me.'
⁵My ears had heard of you
  but now my eyes have seen you.
⁶Therefore I despise myself
  and repent in dust and ashes."

Epilogue

⁷After the LORD had said these things to Job, he said to Eliphaz the Temanite, "I am angry with you and your two friends, because you have not spoken of me what is right, as my servant Job has. ⁸So now take seven bulls and seven rams and go to my servant Job and sacrifice a burnt offering for yourselves. My servant Job will pray for you, and I will accept his prayer and not deal with you according to your folly. You have not spoken of me what is right, as my servant Job has." ⁹So Eliphaz the Temanite, Bildad the Shuhite and Zophar the Naamathite did what the LORD told them; and the LORD accepted Job's prayer.

¹⁰After Job had prayed for his friends, the LORD made him prosperous again and gave him twice as much as he had before. ¹¹All his brothers and sisters and everyone who had known him before came and ate with him in his house. They comforted and consoled him over all the trouble the LORD had brought upon him, and each one gave him a piece of silver*ᵃ* and a gold ring.

❓DID YOU KNOW?   42:12

What happened to Job?

God healed Job and gave Job much wealth and a new family. Job had tried hard to understand God and be honest, and God was pleased with Job.

---

¹²The LORD blessed the latter part of Job's life more than the first. He had fourteen thousand sheep, six thousand camels, a thousand yoke of oxen and a thousand donkeys. ¹³And he also had seven sons and three daughters. ¹⁴The first daughter he named Jemimah, the second Keziah and the third Keren-Happuch. ¹⁵Nowhere in all the land were there found women as beautiful as Job's daughters, and their father granted them an inheritance along with their brothers.

¹⁶After this, Job lived a hundred and forty years; he saw his children and their children to the fourth generation. ¹⁷And so he died, old and full of years.

ᵃ11 Hebrew *him a kesitah*; a kesitah was a unit of money of unknown weight and value.

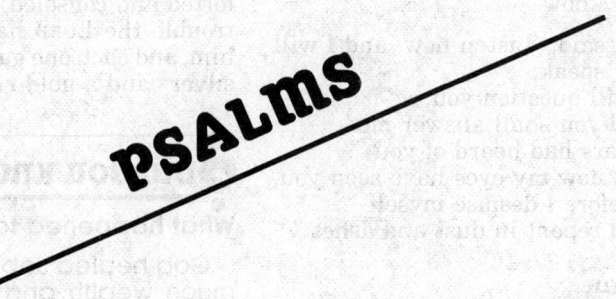

PSALMS

WHO WROTE THIS BOOK?

WHY WAS THIS BOOK WRITTEN?

WHAT KINDS OF PSALMS ARE THERE?

David wrote 73 of the 150 psalms. Several people wrote the others.

The psalms show God's people how to talk to him and to worship him.

There are seven kinds of psalms:

1. Praise psalms like Psalms 33 and 103 show us how to thank God for who he is.
2. History psalms like Psalms 68 and 106 tell what God has done for his people.
3. Friendship psalms like Psalms 8 and 23 remind us that God loves us and tell us how we can show our love to him.
4. Anger psalms like Psalms 35 and 137 ask God to punish evil people.
5. Confession psalms like Psalms 32 and 51 show how to talk to God about our sins.
6. Messiah psalms like Psalms 22 and 89 tell us about Jesus.
7. Worship psalms like Psalms 30 and 120 were used on special religious holidays to worship God with other people.

WHAT KIND OF POETRY IS USED IN THIS BOOK?

WHEN WERE THE PSALMS WRITTEN?

WHAT ARE SOME FAVORITE PSALMS?

The psalms do not rhyme. Hebrew poetry repeats ideas instead of repeating sounds.

The psalms were probably written between about 1400 and 500 B.C.

God's creation and Word.	Psalm 19
God is our shepherd.	Psalm 23
Confessing sin to God.	Psalm 32
Trusting God.	Psalm 37
Don't be jealous.	Psalm 74
God's great love.	Psalm 89
How great God is.	Psalm 104
Loving God's Word.	Psalm 119

BOOK I

Psalms 1–41

Psalm 1

¹Blessed is the man
　who does not walk in the
　　counsel of the wicked
or stand in the way of sinners
　or sit in the seat of mockers.
²But his delight is in the law of
　　the LORD,
　and on his law he meditates
　　day and night.
³He is like a tree planted by
　　streams of water,
　which yields its fruit in season
and whose leaf does not wither.
　Whatever he does prospers.

⁴Not so the wicked!
　They are like chaff
　that the wind blows away.
⁵Therefore the wicked will not
　　stand in the judgment,
　nor sinners in the assembly of
　　the righteous.

⁶For the LORD watches over the
　　way of the righteous,
　but the way of the wicked will
　　perish.

Psalm 2

¹Why do the nations conspire*ᵃ*
　and the peoples plot in vain?
²The kings of the earth take their
　　stand
　and the rulers gather together
against the LORD
　and against his Anointed One.*ᵇ*
³"Let us break their chains," they
　　say,
　"and throw off their fetters."

⁴The One enthroned in heaven
　　laughs;
　the Lord scoffs at them.
⁵Then he rebukes them in his
　　anger

and terrifies them in his wrath,
　saying,
⁶"I have installed my King*ᶜ*
　on Zion, my holy hill."

WHAT GOD IS LIKE

Psalm 2:4 says God is like a king on heaven's throne. In Bible times a king sat on his throne to give orders and make decisions. To say God is a king on heaven's throne means that what he commands will happen.

⁷I will proclaim the decree of the
LORD:

He said to me, "You are my Son*ᵈ*;
　today I have become your
　　Father.*ᵉ*
⁸Ask of me,
　and I will make the nations
　　your inheritance,
　the ends of the earth your
　　possession.
⁹You will rule them with an iron
　　scepter*ᶠ*;
　you will dash them to pieces
　　like pottery."

¹⁰Therefore, you kings, be wise;
　be warned, you rulers of the
　　earth.
¹¹Serve the LORD with fear
　and rejoice with trembling.
¹²Kiss the Son, lest he be angry
　and you be destroyed in your
　　way,
　for his wrath can flare up in a
　　moment.
　Blessed are all who take refuge
　　in him.

ᵃ1 Hebrew; Septuagint *rage*　　*ᵇ2* Or *anointed one*　　*ᶜ6* Or *king*　　*ᵈ7* Or *son; also in verse 12*
ᵉ7 Or *have begotten you*　　*ᶠ9* Or *will break them with a rod of iron*

Psalm 3

A psalm of David. When he fled from
his son Absalom.

[1]O LORD, how many are my foes!
How many rise up against me!
[2]Many are saying of me,
"God will not deliver
him."   *Selah*[a]

[3]But you are a shield around me,
O LORD;
you bestow glory on me and
lift[b] up my head.
[4]To the LORD I cry aloud,
and he answers me from his
holy hill.   *Selah*

[5]I lie down and sleep;
I wake again, because the LORD
sustains me.
[6]I will not fear the tens of
thousands
drawn up against me on every
side.

[7]Arise, O LORD!
Deliver me, O my God!
Strike all my enemies on the
jaw;
break the teeth of the wicked.

[8]From the LORD comes deliverance.
May your blessing be on your
people.   *Selah*

Psalm 4

For the director of music. With
stringed instruments. A psalm
of David.

[1]Answer me when I call to you,
O my righteous God.
Give me relief from my distress;
be merciful to me and hear my
prayer.

[2]How long, O men, will you turn
my glory into shame[c]?
How long will you love
delusions and seek false
gods[d]?   *Selah*
[3]Know that the LORD has set apart
the godly for himself;
the LORD will hear when I call
to him.

[4]In your anger do not sin;
when you are on your beds,
search your hearts and be
silent.   *Selah*
[5]Offer right sacrifices
and trust in the LORD.

[6]Many are asking, "Who can show
us any good?"
Let the light of your face shine
upon us, O LORD.
[7]You have filled my heart with
greater joy
than when their grain and new
wine abound.
[8]I will lie down and sleep in peace,

[a]2 A word of uncertain meaning, occurring frequently in the Psalms; possibly a musical term
[b]3 Or LORD, / my Glorious One, who lifts   [c]2 Or you dishonor my Glorious One   [d]2 Or seek
lies

█LET'S LIVE IT!   Psalm 3:1–8

SAFE AT NIGHT ➠ David was running from an enemy army when he
wrote this psalm. You can read the story in 2 Samuel 15:10–14. Now read
Psalm 3. Verses 1 and 2 tell how David felt. Verses 3 and 4 tell what
David remembered about God. Verses 5 and 6 tell how David was able
to sleep, even when he was in danger. Verses 7 and 8 tell what David
prayed.

Here's something to help you if you are afraid at night. Cut a shield
from a piece of cardboard. Cover it with blue construction paper. Tape
on two strips of aluminum foil in the shape of a cross. Put the shield under
your pillow at night to remind you that God will guard you, just as he
guarded King David.

for you alone, O LORD,
make me dwell in safety.

Psalm 5

For the director of music. For flutes.
A psalm of David.

¹Give ear to my words, O LORD,
consider my sighing.
²Listen to my cry for help,
my King and my God,
for to you I pray.
³In the morning, O LORD, you hear
my voice;
in the morning I lay my
requests before you
and wait in expectation.

⁴You are not a God who takes
pleasure in evil;
with you the wicked cannot
dwell.
⁵The arrogant cannot stand in
your presence;
you hate all who do wrong.
⁶You destroy those who tell lies;
bloodthirsty and deceitful men
the LORD abhors.

⁷But I, by your great mercy,
will come into your house;
in reverence will I bow down
toward your holy temple.
⁸Lead me, O LORD, in your
righteousness
because of my enemies—
make straight your way before
me.

⁹Not a word from their mouth can
be trusted;
their heart is filled with
destruction.
Their throat is an open grave;
with their tongue they speak
deceit.
¹⁰Declare them guilty, O God!
Let their intrigues be their
downfall.
Banish them for their many sins,
for they have rebelled against
you.

¹¹But let all who take refuge in you
be glad;
let them ever sing for joy.
Spread your protection over them,
that those who love your name
may rejoice in you.
¹²For surely, O LORD, you bless the
righteous;
you surround them with your
favor as with a shield.

Psalm 6

For the director of music. With
stringed instruments. According to
*sheminith.*ᵃ A psalm of David.

¹O LORD, do not rebuke me in your
anger
or discipline me in your wrath.
²Be merciful to me, LORD, for I am
faint;
O LORD, heal me, for my bones
are in agony.
³My soul is in anguish.
How long, O LORD, how long?

⁴Turn, O LORD, and deliver me;
save me because of your
unfailing love.
⁵No one remembers you when he
is dead.
Who praises you from the
graveᵇ?

⁶I am worn out from groaning;
all night long I flood my bed
with weeping
and drench my couch with
tears.
⁷My eyes grow weak with sorrow;
they fail because of all my foes.

⁸Away from me, all you who do
evil,
for the LORD has heard my
weeping.
⁹The LORD has heard my cry for
mercy;
the LORD accepts my prayer.
¹⁰All my enemies will be ashamed
and dismayed;
they will turn back in sudden
disgrace.

ᵃTitle: Probably a musical term   ᵇ5 Hebrew *Sheol*

Psalm 7

*A shiggaion^a of David, which he sang
to the LORD concerning Cush,
a Benjamite.*

¹O LORD my God, I take refuge in
    you;
  save and deliver me from all
    who pursue me,
²or they will tear me like a lion
  and rip me to pieces with no
    one to rescue me.

³O LORD my God, if I have done
    this
  and there is guilt on my
    hands—
⁴if I have done evil to him who is
    at peace with me
  or without cause have robbed
    my foe—
⁵then let my enemy pursue and
    overtake me;
  let him trample my life to the
    ground
  and make me sleep in the dust.
                   Selah

⁶Arise, O LORD, in your anger;
  rise up against the rage of my
    enemies.
  Awake, my God; decree justice.
⁷Let the assembled peoples gather
    around you.
  Rule over them from on high;
⁸ let the LORD judge the peoples.
Judge me, O LORD, according to
    my righteousness,
  according to my integrity,
    O Most High.
⁹O righteous God,
  who searches minds and hearts,
  bring to an end the violence of
    the wicked
  and make the righteous secure.

¹⁰My shield^b is God Most High,
  who saves the upright in heart.
¹¹God is a righteous judge,
  a God who expresses his wrath
    every day.
¹²If he does not relent,
  he^c will sharpen his sword;

he will bend and string his
    bow.
¹³He has prepared his deadly
    weapons;
  he makes ready his flaming
    arrows.

WHAT GOD IS LIKE

Psalm 7:10 says God is like a
shield. A shield protected a soldier
from the spears and arrows of his
enemies. To call God a shield
means God will protect the person
who trusts him.

¹⁴He who is pregnant with evil
  and conceives trouble gives
    birth to disillusionment.
¹⁵He who digs a hole and scoops it
    out
  falls into the pit he has made.
¹⁶The trouble he causes recoils on
    himself;
  his violence comes down on his
    own head.

¹⁷I will give thanks to the LORD
    because of his righteousness
  and will sing praise to the
    name of the LORD Most
    High.

Psalm 8

*For the director of music. According to
gittith.^d A psalm of David.*

¹O LORD, our Lord,
  how majestic is your name in
    all the earth!

You have set your glory

---

^aTitle: Probably a literary or musical term   ^b10 Or *sovereign*   ^c12 Or *If a man does not
repent, / God*   ^dTitle: Probably a musical term

above the heavens.
²From the lips of children and
infants
you have ordained praise*a*
because of your enemies,
to silence the foe and the
avenger.

³When I consider your heavens,
the work of your fingers,
the moon and the stars,
which you have set in
place,
⁴what is man that you are mindful
of him,
the son of man that you care for
him?
⁵You made him a little lower than
the heavenly beings*b*
and crowned him with glory
and honor.

⁶You made him ruler over the
works of your hands;
you put everything under his
feet:
⁷all flocks and herds,
and the beasts of the field,
⁸the birds of the air,
and the fish of the sea,
all that swim the paths of the
seas.

⁹O LORD, our Lord,
how majestic is your name in
all the earth!

Psalm 9*c*

For the director of music. To the tune
of "The Death of the Son." A psalm
of David.

¹I will praise you, O LORD, with all
my heart;
I will tell of all your wonders.
²I will be glad and rejoice in you;
I will sing praise to your name,
O Most High.

³My enemies turn back;
they stumble and perish before
you.
⁴For you have upheld my right
and my cause;
you have sat on your throne,
judging righteously.
⁵You have rebuked the nations
and destroyed the wicked;
you have blotted out their name
for ever and ever.
⁶Endless ruin has overtaken the
enemy,
you have uprooted their cities;
even the memory of them has
perished.

⁷The LORD reigns forever;
he has established his throne
for judgment.
⁸He will judge the world in
righteousness;
he will govern the peoples with
justice.

*a*2 Or *strength*   *b*5 Or *than God*   *c*Psalms 9 and 10 may have been originally a single
acrostic poem, the stanzas of which begin with the successive letters of the Hebrew alphabet. In the
Septuagint they constitute one psalm.

▚ET'S LIVE IT!   Psalm 8:1–5

LOOK AT THE HEAVENS ➡ David often slept outside at night when he
cared for his father's sheep. He watched the moon and the stars and
thought about God. Read Psalm 8 and see what David thought when
he looked up.

Some summer night go outside and look at the stars. Without a telescope you can see just over one thousand stars. If you looked through
the first telescope, made many years ago by Galileo, you could see
over three thousand. With today's big telescopes you can see millions
of stars in the sky! It's good to lie on your back, look at the stars, and
think how great God is.

⁹The LORD is a refuge for the
oppressed,
a stronghold in times of
trouble.
¹⁰Those who know your name will
trust in you,
for you, LORD, have never
forsaken those who seek
you.

¹¹Sing praises to the LORD,
enthroned in Zion;
proclaim among the nations
what he has done.
¹²For he who avenges blood
remembers;
he does not ignore the cry of the
afflicted.

¹³O LORD, see how my enemies
persecute me!
Have mercy and lift me up from
the gates of death,
¹⁴that I may declare your praises
in the gates of the Daughter of
Zion
and there rejoice in your
salvation.
¹⁵The nations have fallen into the
pit they have dug;
their feet are caught in the net
they have hidden.
¹⁶The LORD is known by his justice;
the wicked are ensnared by the
work of their hands.
Higgaion.ᵃ Selah
¹⁷The wicked return to the grave,ᵇ
all the nations that forget
God.
¹⁸But the needy will not always be
forgotten,
nor the hope of the afflicted
ever perish.

¹⁹Arise, O LORD, let not man
triumph;
let the nations be judged in
your presence.
²⁰Strike them with terror, O LORD;
let the nations know they are
but men. *Selah*

Psalm 10ᶜ

¹Why, O LORD, do you stand far
off?
Why do you hide yourself in
times of trouble?

²In his arrogance the wicked man
hunts down the weak,
who are caught in the schemes
he devises.
³He boasts of the cravings of his
heart;
he blesses the greedy and
reviles the LORD.
⁴In his pride the wicked does not
seek him;
in all his thoughts there is no
room for God.
⁵His ways are always prosperous;
he is haughty and your laws
are far from him;
he sneers at all his enemies.
⁶He says to himself, "Nothing will
shake me;
I'll always be happy and never
have trouble."
⁷His mouth is full of curses and
lies and threats;
trouble and evil are under his
tongue.
⁸He lies in wait near the villages;
from ambush he murders the
innocent,
watching in secret for his
victims.
⁹He lies in wait like a lion in
cover;
he lies in wait to catch the
helpless;
he catches the helpless and
drags them off in his net.
¹⁰His victims are crushed, they
collapse;
they fall under his strength.
¹¹He says to himself, "God has
forgotten;
he covers his face and never
sees."

¹²Arise, LORD! Lift up your hand,
O God.

ᵃ16 Or *Meditation*; possibly a musical notation   ᵇ17 Hebrew *Sheol*   ᶜPsalms 9 and 10 may
have been originally a single acrostic poem, the stanzas of which begin with the successive letters of
the Hebrew alphabet. In the Septuagint they constitute one psalm.

Do not forget the helpless.

13Why does the wicked man revile
God?

Why does he say to himself,
"He won't call me to account"?

14But you, O God, do see trouble
and grief;

you consider it to take it in
hand.

The victim commits himself to
you;

you are the helper of the
fatherless.

15Break the arm of the wicked and
evil man;

call him to account for his
wickedness

that would not be found out.

16The LORD is King for ever and
ever;

the nations will perish from his
land.

17You hear, O LORD, the desire of
the afflicted;

you encourage them, and you
listen to their cry,

18defending the fatherless and the
oppressed,

in order that man, who is of the
earth, may terrify no more.

Psalm 11

For the director of music. Of David.

1In the LORD I take refuge.
How then can you say to me:
"Flee like a bird to your
mountain.

2For look, the wicked bend their
bows;

they set their arrows against
the strings

to shoot from the shadows
at the upright in heart.

3When the foundations are being
destroyed,

what can the righteous do*a*?"

4The LORD is in his holy temple;
the LORD is on his heavenly
throne.

He observes the sons of men;
his eyes examine them.

5The LORD examines the righteous,
but the wicked *b* and those who
love violence

his soul hates.

6On the wicked he will rain
fiery coals and burning sulfur;
a scorching wind will be their
lot.

7For the LORD is righteous,
he loves justice;
upright men will see his face.

Psalm 12

For the director of music. According to
sheminith. *c* A psalm of David.

1Help, LORD, for the godly are no
more;

the faithful have vanished from
among men.

2Everyone lies to his neighbor;
their flattering lips speak with
deception.

3May the LORD cut off all
flattering lips

and every boastful tongue

4that says, "We will triumph with
our tongues;

we own our lips*d*—who is our
master?"

5"Because of the oppression of the
weak

and the groaning of the needy,
I will now arise," says the LORD.
"I will protect them from those
who malign them."

6And the words of the LORD are
flawless,

like silver refined in a furnace
of clay,

purified seven times.

7O LORD, you will keep us safe
and protect us from such people
forever.

8The wicked freely strut about
when what is vile is honored
among men.

---

a3 Or *what is the Righteous One doing
wicked, |*   *c*Title: Probably a musical term   *b5* Or *The LORD, the Righteous One, examines the*   *d4* Or */ our lips are our plowshares*

Psalm 13

For the director of music. A psalm
of David.

[1]How long, O Lord? Will you
    forget me forever?
How long will you hide your
    face from me?
[2]How long must I wrestle with my
    thoughts
and every day have sorrow in
    my heart?
How long will my enemy
    triumph over me?

[3]Look on me and answer, O Lord
    my God.
Give light to my eyes, or I will
    sleep in death;
[4]my enemy will say, "I have
    overcome him,"
and my foes will rejoice when I
    fall.

[5]But I trust in your unfailing love;
    my heart rejoices in your
    salvation.
[6]I will sing to the Lord,
    for he has been good to me.

WORDS TO REMEMBER

**13:6   I will sing to the Lord,
    for he has been good to
    me.**

Psalm 14

For the director of music. Of David.

[1]The fool[a] says in his heart,
    "There is no God."
They are corrupt, their deeds are
    vile;
there is no one who does good.

[2]The Lord looks down from heaven
    on the sons of men
to see if there are any who
    understand,
any who seek God.
[3]All have turned aside,

they have together become
    corrupt;
there is no one who does good,
    not even one.

[4]Will evildoers never learn—
    those who devour my people as
    men eat bread
and who do not call on the
    Lord?
[5]There they are, overwhelmed with
    dread,
for God is present in the
    company of the righteous.
[6]You evildoers frustrate the plans
    of the poor,
but the Lord is their refuge.

[7]Oh, that salvation for Israel
    would come out of Zion!
When the Lord restores the
    fortunes of his people,
let Jacob rejoice and Israel be
    glad!

Psalm 15

A psalm of David.

[1]Lord, who may dwell in your
    sanctuary?
Who may live on your holy hill?

[2]He whose walk is blameless
    and who does what is righteous,
who speaks the truth from his
    heart
[3] and has no slander on his
    tongue,
who does his neighbor no wrong
    and casts no slur on his
    fellowman,
[4]who despises a vile man
    but honors those who fear the
    Lord,
who keeps his oath
    even when it hurts,
[5]who lends his money without
    usury
and does not accept a bribe
    against the innocent.

He who does these things
    will never be shaken.

---

a1 The Hebrew words rendered *fool* in Psalms denote one who is morally deficient.

Psalm 16

A miktam[a] of David.

¹Keep me safe, O God,
   for in you I take refuge.

²I said to the LORD, "You are my
      Lord;
   apart from you I have no good
      thing."
³As for the saints who are in the
      land,
   they are the glorious ones in
      whom is all my delight.[b]
⁴The sorrows of those will increase
   who run after other gods.
I will not pour out their libations
      of blood
   or take up their names on my
      lips.

⁵LORD, you have assigned me my
      portion and my cup;
   you have made my lot secure.
⁶The boundary lines have fallen
      for me in pleasant places;
   surely I have a delightful
      inheritance.

⁷I will praise the LORD, who
      counsels me;
   even at night my heart
      instructs me.
⁸I have set the LORD always before
      me.
   Because he is at my right hand,
   I will not be shaken.

⁹Therefore my heart is glad and
      my tongue rejoices;
   my body also will rest secure,
¹⁰because you will not abandon me
      to the grave,[c]
   nor will you let your Holy One[d]
      see decay.
¹¹You have made[e] known to me
      the path of life;
   you will fill me with joy in your
      presence,
   with eternal pleasures at your
      right hand.

Psalm 17

A prayer of David.

¹Hear, O LORD, my righteous plea;
   listen to my cry.
Give ear to my prayer—
   it does not rise from deceitful
      lips.
²May my vindication come from
      you;
   may your eyes see what is
      right.

³Though you probe my heart and
      examine me at night,
   though you test me, you will
      find nothing;
   I have resolved that my mouth
      will not sin.
⁴As for the deeds of men—
   by the word of your lips
I have kept myself
   from the ways of the violent.
⁵My steps have held to your paths;
   my feet have not slipped.

⁶I call on you, O God, for you will
      answer me;
   give ear to me and hear my
      prayer.
⁷Show the wonder of your great
      love,
   you who save by your right
      hand
   those who take refuge in you
      from their foes.
⁸Keep me as the apple of your eye;
   hide me in the shadow of your
      wings
⁹from the wicked who assail me,
   from my mortal enemies who
      surround me.

¹⁰They close up their callous
      hearts,
   and their mouths speak with
      arrogance.
¹¹They have tracked me down, they
      now surround me,
   with eyes alert, to throw me to
      the ground.

---

a Title: Probably a literary or musical term   *b 3 Or As for the pagan priests who are in the land /*
and the nobles in whom all delight, I said: *c 10 Hebrew Sheol   d 10 Or your faithful one*
e 11 Or You will make

12They are like a lion hungry for
    prey,
  like a great lion crouching in
    cover.

WHAT GOD IS LIKE

Psalm 17:13 says God is like a
warrior who comes to our rescue.
When others threaten us and we
feel helpless, it is good to
remember that God is on our side.

13Rise up, O LORD, confront them,
    bring them down;
  rescue me from the wicked by
    your sword.
14O LORD, by your hand save me
    from such men,
  from men of this world whose
    reward is in this life.

You still the hunger of those you
    cherish;
  their sons have plenty,
  and they store up wealth for
    their children.
15And I—in righteousness I will see
    your face;
  when I awake, I will be
    satisfied with seeing your
    likeness.

Psalm 18

For the director of music. Of David the
servant of the LORD. He sang to the
LORD the words of this song when the
LORD delivered him from the hand of
all his enemies and from the hand of
Saul. He said:

1I love you, O LORD, my
    strength.

2The LORD is my rock, my fortress
    and my deliverer;
  my God is my rock, in whom I
    take refuge.
  He is my shield and the horn a
    of my salvation, my
    stronghold.
3I call to the LORD, who is worthy
    of praise,
  and I am saved from my
    enemies.

4The cords of death entangled me;
  the torrents of destruction
    overwhelmed me.
5The cords of the grave b coiled
    around me;
  the snares of death confronted
    me.
6In my distress I called to the
    LORD;
  I cried to my God for help.
From his temple he heard my
    voice;
  my cry came before him, into
    his ears.

7The earth trembled and quaked,
  and the foundations of the
    mountains shook;
  they trembled because he was
    angry.
8Smoke rose from his nostrils;
  consuming fire came from his
    mouth,
  burning coals blazed out
    of it.
9He parted the heavens and came
    down;
  dark clouds were under his feet.
10He mounted the cherubim and
    flew;
  he soared on the wings of the
    wind.
11He made darkness his covering,
    his canopy around him—
  the dark rain clouds of the
    sky.
12Out of the brightness of his
    presence clouds advanced,
  with hailstones and bolts of
    lightning.
13The LORD thundered from heaven;

---

a2 Horn here symbolizes strength.   b5 Hebrew Sheol

the voice of the Most High
resounded. ^a

¹⁴He shot his arrows and scattered
the enemies,
great bolts of lightning and
routed them.

¹⁵The valleys of the sea were
exposed
and the foundations of the earth
laid bare
at your rebuke, O LORD,
at the blast of breath from your
nostrils.

¹⁶He reached down from on high
and took hold of me;
he drew me out of deep waters.

¹⁷He rescued me from my powerful
enemy,
from my foes, who were too
strong for me.

¹⁸They confronted me in the day of
my disaster,
but the LORD was my support.

¹⁹He brought me out into a
spacious place;
he rescued me because he
delighted in me.

²⁰The LORD has dealt with me
according to my
righteousness;
according to the cleanness of my
hands he has rewarded me.

²¹For I have kept the ways of the
LORD;
I have not done evil by turning
from my God.

²²All his laws are before me;
I have not turned away from
his decrees.

²³I have been blameless before him
and have kept myself from sin.

²⁴The LORD has rewarded me
according to my
righteousness,
according to the cleanness of my
hands in his sight.

²⁵To the faithful you show yourself
faithful,
to the blameless you show
yourself blameless,

²⁶to the pure you show yourself
pure,
but to the crooked you show
yourself shrewd.

²⁷You save the humble
but bring low those whose eyes
are haughty.

²⁸You, O LORD, keep my lamp
burning;
my God turns my darkness into
light.

²⁹With your help I can advance
against a troop ^b;
with my God I can scale a
wall.

³⁰As for God, his way is perfect;
the word of the LORD is
flawless.
He is a shield
for all who take refuge in him.

³¹For who is God besides the LORD?
And who is the Rock except our
God?

³²It is God who arms me with
strength
and makes my way perfect.

³³He makes my feet like the feet of
a deer;
he enables me to stand on the
heights.

³⁴He trains my hands for battle;
my arms can bend a bow of
bronze.

³⁵You give me your shield of
victory,
and your right hand sustains
me;
you stoop down to make me
great.

³⁶You broaden the path beneath
me,
so that my ankles do not turn.

³⁷I pursued my enemies and
overtook them;
I did not turn back till they
were destroyed.

³⁸I crushed them so that they could
not rise;
they fell beneath my feet.

³⁹You armed me with strength for
battle;

---

a13 Some Hebrew manuscripts and Septuagint (see also 2 Samuel 22:14); most Hebrew manuscripts
resounded, / amid hailstones and bolts of lightning   *b29* Or *can run through a barricade*

you made my adversaries bow
    at my feet.
⁴⁰You made my enemies turn their
    backs in flight,
and I destroyed my foes.
⁴¹They cried for help, but there was
    no one to save them—
to the LORD, but he did not
    answer.
⁴²I beat them as fine as dust borne
    on the wind;
I poured them out like mud in
    the streets.

⁴³You have delivered me from the
    attacks of the people;
you have made me the head of
    nations;
people I did not know are
    subject to me.
⁴⁴As soon as they hear me, they
    obey me;
foreigners cringe before me.
⁴⁵They all lose heart;
    they come trembling from their
    strongholds.

⁴⁶The LORD lives! Praise be to my
    Rock!
Exalted be God my Savior!
⁴⁷He is the God who avenges me,
    who subdues nations under me,
⁴⁸ who saves me from my enemies.
You exalted me above my foes;
    from violent men you rescued
    me.
⁴⁹Therefore I will praise you among
    the nations, O LORD;
I will sing praises to your
    name.
⁵⁰He gives his king great victories;
    he shows unfailing kindness to
    his anointed,
to David and his descendants
    forever.

Psalm 19

For the director of music. A psalm
of David.

¹The heavens declare the glory of
    God;

the skies proclaim the work of
    his hands.
²Day after day they pour forth
    speech;
night after night they display
    knowledge.
³There is no speech or language
    where their voice is not heard.ᵃ
⁴Their voiceᵇ goes out into all the
    earth,
their words to the ends of the
    world.

In the heavens he has pitched a
    tent for the sun,
⁵ which is like a bridegroom
    coming forth from his
    pavilion,
like a champion rejoicing to run
    his course.
⁶It rises at one end of the heavens
    and makes its circuit to the
    other;
nothing is hidden from its heat.

⁷The law of the LORD is perfect,
    reviving the soul.
The statutes of the LORD are
    trustworthy,
making wise the simple.
⁸The precepts of the LORD are
    right,
giving joy to the heart.
The commands of the LORD are
    radiant,
giving light to the eyes.
⁹The fear of the LORD is pure,
    enduring forever.
The ordinances of the LORD are
    sure
and altogether righteous.
¹⁰They are more precious than gold,
    than much pure gold;
they are sweeter than honey,
    than honey from the comb.
¹¹By them is your servant warned;
    in keeping them there is great
    reward.

¹²Who can discern his errors?
    Forgive my hidden faults.
¹³Keep your servant also from
    willful sins;

ᵃ3 Or *They have no speech, there are no words; / no sound is heard from them*   ᵇ4 Septuagint,
Jerome and Syriac; Hebrew *line*

may they not rule over me.
Then will I be blameless,
 innocent of great transgression.

¹⁴May the words of my mouth and
  the meditation of my heart
be pleasing in your sight,
 O LORD, my Rock and my
  Redeemer.

Psalm 20

For the director of music. A psalm
of David.

¹May the LORD answer you when
  you are in distress;
may the name of the God of
 Jacob protect you.
²May he send you help from the
  sanctuary
and grant you support from
 Zion.
³May he remember all your
  sacrifices
and accept your burnt offerings.
                         Selah
⁴May he give you the desire of
  your heart
and make all your plans
 succeed.
⁵We will shout for joy when you
  are victorious
and will lift up our banners in
 the name of our God.
May the LORD grant all your
 requests.

a9 Or save! / O King, answer

⁶Now I know that the LORD saves
 his anointed;
he answers him from his holy
 heaven
with the saving power of his
 right hand.
⁷Some trust in chariots and some
  in horses,
but we trust in the name of the
 LORD our God.
⁸They are brought to their knees
  and fall,
but we rise up and stand firm.

⁹O LORD, save the king!
 Answer*ᵃ* us when we call!

Psalm 21

For the director of music. A psalm
of David.

¹O LORD, the king rejoices in your
  strength.
How great is his joy in the
 victories you give!
²You have granted him the desire
  of his heart
and have not withheld the
 request of his lips.   *Selah*
³You welcomed him with rich
  blessings
and placed a crown of pure gold
 on his head.
⁴He asked you for life, and you
  gave it to him—
length of days, for ever and
 ever.

LET'S LIVE IT!   Psalm 19:1–6

IN CONTROL ➠ Read Psalm 19:1–6. God placed the earth just far enough
from the sun to give us light and warmth. He made the earth rotate so
the warmth would be spread everywhere. He makes sure the sun rises
and sets every day, just as it should. If you watch the sun do its work
each day, it will show you that God is in control.
   Cut a round circle in the center of a piece of blue construction paper.
Over the hole tape a piece of red or brown cellophane or plastic wrap
(the darker plastic that bread is wrapped in will work). Hang the paper
in your bedroom window. Every day when the sun shines through the
hole, let it remind you that God is in control and cares not only about
the sun, but about you.

⁵Through the victories you gave,
   his glory is great;
  you have bestowed on him
   splendor and majesty.
⁶Surely you have granted him
   eternal blessings
  and made him glad with the joy
   of your presence.
⁷For the king trusts in the LORD;
  through the unfailing love of
   the Most High
  he will not be shaken.

⁸Your hand will lay hold on all
   your enemies;
  your right hand will seize your
   foes.
⁹At the time of your appearing
  you will make them like a fiery
   furnace.
In his wrath the LORD will
   swallow them up,
  and his fire will consume them.
¹⁰You will destroy their
   descendants from the earth,
  their posterity from mankind.
¹¹Though they plot evil against you
  and devise wicked schemes,
   they cannot succeed;
¹²for you will make them turn their
   backs
  when you aim at them with
   drawn bow.

¹³Be exalted, O LORD, in your
   strength;
  we will sing and praise your
   might.

Psalm 22

For the director of music. To the tune
of "The Doe of the Morning." A psalm
     of David.

¹My God, my God, why have you
   forsaken me?
  Why are you so far from saving
   me,
  so far from the words of my
   groaning?
²O my God, I cry out by day, but
   you do not answer,
  by night, and am not silent.

³Yet you are enthroned as the
   Holy One;
  you are the praise of Israel.ᵃ
⁴In you our fathers put their trust;
  they trusted and you delivered
   them.
⁵They cried to you and were
   saved;
  in you they trusted and were
   not disappointed.

⁶But I am a worm and not a man,
  scorned by men and despised by
   the people.
⁷All who see me mock me;
  they hurl insults, shaking their
   heads:
⁸"He trusts in the LORD;
  let the LORD rescue him.
Let him deliver him,
  since he delights in him."

⁹Yet you brought me out of the
   womb;
  you made me trust in you
   even at my mother's breast.
¹⁰From birth I was cast upon you;
  from my mother's womb you
   have been my God.
¹¹Do not be far from me,
  for trouble is near
  and there is no one to help.

¹²Many bulls surround me;
  strong bulls of Bashan encircle
   me.
¹³Roaring lions tearing their prey
  open their mouths wide against
   me.
¹⁴I am poured out like water,
  and all my bones are out of
   joint.
My heart has turned to wax;
  it has melted away within
   me.
¹⁵My strength is dried up like a
   potsherd,
  and my tongue sticks to the roof
   of my mouth;
  you lay meᵇ in the dust of
   death.
¹⁶Dogs have surrounded me;
  a band of evil men has encircled
   me,

ᵃ3 Or Yet you are holy, / enthroned on the praises of Israel   ᵇ15 Or / I am laid

they have pierced^a my hands
and my feet.
¹⁷I can count all my bones;
people stare and gloat over
me.
¹⁸They divide my garments among
them
and cast lots for my clothing.

¹⁹But you, O LORD, be not far off;
O my Strength, come quickly to
help me.
²⁰Deliver my life from the sword,
my precious life from the power
of the dogs.
²¹Rescue me from the mouth of the
lions;
save^b me from the horns of the
wild oxen.

²²I will declare your name to my
brothers;
in the congregation I will praise
you.
²³You who fear the LORD, praise
him!
All you descendants of Jacob,
honor him!
Revere him, all you descendants
of Israel!
²⁴For he has not despised or
disdained
the suffering of the afflicted
one;
he has not hidden his face from
him
but has listened to his cry for
help.

²⁵From you comes the theme of my
praise in the great
assembly;
before those who fear you^c will
I fulfill my vows.
²⁶The poor will eat and be satisfied;
they who seek the LORD will
praise him—
may your hearts live forever!
²⁷All the ends of the earth
will remember and turn to the
LORD,
and all the families of the nations
will bow down before him,
²⁸for dominion belongs to the LORD
and he rules over the nations.

²⁹All the rich of the earth will feast
and worship;
all who go down to the dust will
kneel before him—
those who cannot keep
themselves alive.
³⁰Posterity will serve him;
future generations will be told
about the Lord.
³¹They will proclaim his
righteousness
to a people yet unborn—
for he has done it.

Psalm 23

A psalm of David.

¹The LORD is my shepherd, I shall
not be in want.

a16 Some Hebrew manuscripts, Septuagint and Syriac; most Hebrew manuscripts / *like the lion,*
b21 Or / *you have heard*   *c25* Hebrew *him*

Life in Bible Times

WHAT GOD IS LIKE

Psalm 23 says God is like
a shepherd. A shepherd
loves and cares for his
sheep. To say God is our
shepherd means that he
watches over us and will
show us what is best for us.

2 He makes me lie down in green
    pastures,
he leads me beside quiet waters,
3 he restores my soul.
He guides me in paths of
    righteousness
    for his name's sake.
4Even though I walk
    through the valley of the
    shadow of death,ᵃ
I will fear no evil,
    for you are with me;
your rod and your staff,
    they comfort me.

5You prepare a table before
    me
    in the presence of my enemies.
You anoint my head with
    oil;
    my cup overflows.
6Surely goodness and love will
    follow me
    all the days of my life,
and I will dwell in the house of
    the LORD
    forever.

Psalm 24

Of David. A psalm.

1The earth is the LORD's, and
    everything in it,
    the world, and all who live in
    it;
2for he founded it upon the seas

and established it upon the
    waters.
3Who may ascend the hill of the
    LORD?
Who may stand in his holy
    place?
4He who has clean hands and a
    pure heart,
who does not lift up his soul to
    an idol
    or swear by what is false.ᵇ
5He will receive blessing from the
    LORD
    and vindication from God his
    Savior.
6Such is the generation of those
    who seek him,
who seek your face, O God of
    Jacob.ᶜ   *Selah*

7Lift up your heads, O you
    gates;
be lifted up, you ancient
    doors,
    that the King of glory may
    come in.
8Who is this King of glory?
The LORD strong and mighty,
    the LORD mighty in battle.
9Lift up your heads, O you gates;
lift them up, you ancient doors,
    that the King of glory may
    come in.
10Who is he, this King of glory?
The LORD Almighty—
    he is the King of glory.   *Selah*

ᵃ4 Or *through the darkest valley*   ᵇ4 Or *swear falsely*   ᶜ6 Two Hebrew manuscripts and
Syriac (see also Septuagint); most Hebrew manuscripts *face, Jacob*

▐ ET'S LIVE IT!   Psalm 23:1–6

GOD IS MY SHEPHERD ➡ Read Psalm 23. God loves you, just as a shepherd loves the sheep. God wants to take care of you and protect you, just as a shepherd cares for and protects the sheep.

On a large piece of poster board make a Psalm 23 mural. Use strips of green paper for grass, tin foil for the quiet water, and cotton balls for the sheep. Draw in a shepherd and put a twig in his hand for a shepherd's staff.

You could even make the mural together as a family project. When you are finished, ask a parent where to hang it so the whole family is reminded of God's care.

Psalm 25[a]

Of David.

[1]To you, O LORD, I lift up my
    soul;
[2] in you I trust, O my God.
Do not let me be put to shame,
    nor let my enemies triumph
        over me.
[3]No one whose hope is in you
    will ever be put to shame,
but they will be put to shame
    who are treacherous without
        excuse.

[4]Show me your ways, O LORD,
    teach me your paths;
[5]guide me in your truth and teach
        me,
    for you are God my Savior,
    and my hope is in you all day
        long.
[6]Remember, O LORD, your great
        mercy and love,
    for they are from of old.
[7]Remember not the sins of my
        youth
    and my rebellious ways;
according to your love remember
        me,
    for you are good, O LORD.

[8]Good and upright is the LORD;
    therefore he instructs sinners in
        his ways.
[9]He guides the humble in what is
        right
    and teaches them his way.
[10]All the ways of the LORD are
        loving and faithful
    for those who keep the demands
        of his covenant.
[11]For the sake of your name,
        O LORD,
    forgive my iniquity, though it is
        great.
[12]Who, then, is the man that fears
        the LORD?
    He will instruct him in the way
        chosen for him.
[13]He will spend his days in
        prosperity,

and his descendants will inherit
    the land.
[14]The LORD confides in those who
        fear him;
    he makes his covenant known
        to them.
[15]My eyes are ever on the LORD,
    for only he will release my feet
        from the snare.

[16]Turn to me and be gracious to
        me,
    for I am lonely and afflicted.
[17]The troubles of my heart have
        multiplied;
    free me from my anguish.
[18]Look upon my affliction and my
        distress
    and take away all my sins.
[19]See how my enemies have
        increased
    and how fiercely they hate
        me!
[20]Guard my life and rescue me;
    let me not be put to shame,
    for I take refuge in you.
[21]May integrity and uprightness
        protect me,
    because my hope is in you.

[22]Redeem Israel, O God,
    from all their troubles!

Psalm 26

Of David.

[1]Vindicate me, O LORD,
    for I have led a blameless life;
I have trusted in the LORD
    without wavering.
[2]Test me, O LORD, and try me,
    examine my heart and my
        mind;
[3]for your love is ever before me,
    and I walk continually in your
        truth.
[4]I do not sit with deceitful men,
    nor do I consort with hypocrites;
[5]I abhor the assembly of evildoers
    and refuse to sit with the
        wicked.
[6]I wash my hands in innocence,

---

[a]This psalm is an acrostic poem, the verses of which begin with the successive letters of the Hebrew
alphabet.

and go about your altar,
  O Lord,
7proclaiming aloud your praise
  and telling of all your
    wonderful deeds.
8I love the house where you live,
  O Lord,
  the place where your glory
    dwells.

9Do not take away my soul along
  with sinners,
  my life with bloodthirsty men,
10in whose hands are wicked
  schemes,
  whose right hands are full of
    bribes.
11But I lead a blameless life;
  redeem me and be merciful to
    me.

12My feet stand on level ground;
  in the great assembly I will
    praise the Lord.

Psalm 27

Of David.

1The Lord is my light and my
  salvation—
  whom shall I fear?
The Lord is the stronghold of my
  life—
  of whom shall I be afraid?
2When evil men advance against
  me
  to devour my flesh,a
when my enemies and my foes
  attack me,
  they will stumble and fall.
3Though an army besiege me,
  my heart will not fear;
though war break out against me,
  even then will I be confident.

4One thing I ask of the Lord,
  this is what I seek:
that I may dwell in the house of
  the Lord
  all the days of my life,
to gaze upon the beauty of the
  Lord
  and to seek him in his temple.

5For in the day of trouble
  he will keep me safe in his
    dwelling;
he will hide me in the shelter of
  his tabernacle
  and set me high upon a rock.
6Then my head will be exalted
  above the enemies who
    surround me;
at his tabernacle will I sacrifice
  with shouts of joy;
  I will sing and make music to
    the Lord.

7Hear my voice when I call,
  O Lord;
  be merciful to me and answer
    me.
8My heart says of you, "Seek hisb
  face!"
  Your face, Lord, I will seek.
9Do not hide your face from me,
  do not turn your servant away
    in anger;
  you have been my helper.
Do not reject me or forsake me,
  O God my Savior.
10Though my father and mother
  forsake me,
  the Lord will receive me.
11Teach me your way, O Lord;
  lead me in a straight path
  because of my oppressors.
12Do not turn me over to the desire
  of my foes,
for false witnesses rise up
  against me,
  breathing out violence.

13I am still confident of this:
  I will see the goodness of the
    Lord
  in the land of the living.
14Wait for the Lord;
  be strong and take heart
  and wait for the Lord.

Psalm 28

Of David.

1To you I call, O Lord my Rock;
  do not turn a deaf ear to me.
For if you remain silent,

---

a2 Or *to slander me*   b8 Or *To you, O my heart, he has said, "Seek my*

I will be like those who have
  gone down to the pit.
[2]Hear my cry for mercy
  as I call to you for help,
  as I lift up my hands
  toward your Most Holy Place.

[3]Do not drag me away with the
    wicked,
  with those who do evil,
who speak cordially with their
    neighbors
  but harbor malice in their
    hearts.
[4]Repay them for their deeds
  and for their evil work;
repay them for what their hands
    have done
  and bring back upon them what
    they deserve.
[5]Since they show no regard for the
    works of the LORD
  and what his hands have done,
he will tear them down
  and never build them up again.

[6]Praise be to the LORD,
  for he has heard my cry for
    mercy.
[7]The LORD is my strength and my
    shield;
  my heart trusts in him, and I
    am helped.
My heart leaps for joy
  and I will give thanks to him in
    song.

[8]The LORD is the strength of his
    people,
  a fortress of salvation for his
    anointed one.
[9]Save your people and bless your
    inheritance;
  be their shepherd and carry
    them forever.

Psalm 29

A psalm of David.

[1]Ascribe to the LORD, O mighty
    ones,
  ascribe to the LORD glory and
    strength.

[2]Ascribe to the LORD the glory due
    his name;
  worship the LORD in the
    splendor of his[a] holiness.
[3]The voice of the LORD is over the
    waters;
  the God of glory thunders,
  the LORD thunders over the
    mighty waters.
[4]The voice of the LORD is powerful;
  the voice of the LORD is
    majestic.
[5]The voice of the LORD breaks the
    cedars;
  the LORD breaks in pieces the
    cedars of Lebanon.
[6]He makes Lebanon skip like a
    calf,
  Sirion[b] like a young wild ox.
[7]The voice of the LORD strikes
  with flashes of lightning.
[8]The voice of the LORD shakes the
    desert;
  the LORD shakes the Desert of
    Kadesh.
[9]The voice of the LORD twists the
    oaks[c]
  and strips the forests bare.
And in his temple all cry,
    "Glory!"

[10]The LORD sits[d] enthroned over
    the flood;
  the LORD is enthroned as King
    forever.
[11]The LORD gives strength to his
    people;
  the LORD blesses his people with
    peace.

Psalm 30

*A psalm. A song. For the dedication of
the temple.[e] Of David.*

[1]I will exalt you, O LORD,
  for you lifted me out of the
    depths
  and did not let my enemies
    gloat over me.
[2]O LORD my God, I called to you
    for help

---

[a]2 Or LORD *with the splendor of*   [b]6 *That is, Mount Hermon*   [c]9 Or LORD *makes the deer give
birth*   [d]10 Or *sat*   [e]Title: Or *palace*

and you healed me.
³O LORD, you brought me up from
the grave[a];
you spared me from going down
into the pit.

⁴Sing to the LORD, you saints of
his;
praise his holy name.
⁵For his anger lasts only a
moment,
but his favor lasts a lifetime;
weeping may remain for a night,
but rejoicing comes in the
morning.

⁶When I felt secure, I said,
"I will never be shaken."
⁷O LORD, when you favored me,
you made my mountain[b] stand
firm;
but when you hid your face,
I was dismayed.

⁸To you, O LORD, I called;
to the Lord I cried for mercy:
⁹"What gain is there in my
destruction,[c]
in my going down into the pit?
Will the dust praise you?
Will it proclaim your
faithfulness?
¹⁰Hear, O LORD, and be merciful to
me;
O LORD, be my help."

¹¹You turned my wailing into
dancing;
you removed my sackcloth and
clothed me with joy,
¹²that my heart may sing to you
and not be silent.

O LORD my God, I will give you
thanks forever.

Psalm 31

For the director of music. A psalm
of David.

¹In you, O LORD, I have taken
refuge;
let me never be put to shame;
deliver me in your
righteousness.
²Turn your ear to me,
come quickly to my rescue;
be my rock of refuge,
a strong fortress to save me.
³Since you are my rock and my
fortress,
for the sake of your name lead
and guide me.
⁴Free me from the trap that is set
for me,
for you are my refuge.
⁵Into your hands I commit my
spirit;
redeem me, O LORD, the God of
truth.

⁶I hate those who cling to
worthless idols;
I trust in the LORD.
⁷I will be glad and rejoice in your
love,
for you saw my affliction
and knew the anguish of my
soul.
⁸You have not handed me over to
the enemy
but have set my feet in a
spacious place.

---

a3 Hebrew Sheol   *b7 Or hill country*   *c9 Or there if I am silenced*

LET'S LIVE IT!   Psalm 30:4–5

GOOD THINGS AHEAD ➠ Ask your mom or dad about a time when one
of them felt very sad. Why was he or she sad? How long before the
sadness went away? Ask too about times your mom or dad felt very
happy.
Then read Psalm 30:4–5. Sadness is like the night, when everything
seems dark. But God says joy will come in the morning. There are good
things ahead for all God's people.

⁹Be merciful to me, O Lord, for I
    am in distress;
my eyes grow weak with
    sorrow,
my soul and my body with
    grief.
¹⁰My life is consumed by anguish
    and my years by groaning;
my strength fails because of my
    affliction,ᵃ
and my bones grow weak.
¹¹Because of all my enemies,
    I am the utter contempt of my
    neighbors;
I am a dread to my friends—
    those who see me on the street
    flee from me.
¹²I am forgotten by them as though
    I were dead;
I have become like broken
    pottery.
¹³For I hear the slander of many;
    there is terror on every side;
they conspire against me
    and plot to take my life.

¹⁴But I trust in you, O Lord;
    I say, "You are my God."
¹⁵My times are in your hands;
    deliver me from my enemies
    and from those who pursue me.
¹⁶Let your face shine on your
    servant;
save me in your unfailing love.
¹⁷Let me not be put to shame,
    O Lord,
for I have cried out to you;
but let the wicked be put to
    shame
and lie silent in the grave.ᵇ
¹⁸Let their lying lips be silenced,
    for with pride and contempt
    they speak arrogantly against
    the righteous.

¹⁹How great is your goodness,
    which you have stored up for
    those who fear you,
which you bestow in the sight of
    men
on those who take refuge in
    you.
²⁰In the shelter of your presence
    you hide them

from the intrigues of men;
in your dwelling you keep them
    safe
from accusing tongues.

²¹Praise be to the Lord,
    for he showed his wonderful
    love to me
when I was in a besieged city.
²²In my alarm I said,
    "I am cut off from your sight!"
Yet you heard my cry for mercy
    when I called to you for help.

²³Love the Lord, all his saints!
    The Lord preserves the faithful,
but the proud he pays back in
    full.
²⁴Be strong and take heart,
    all you who hope in the Lord.

Psalm 32

Of David. A *maskil.*ᶜ

¹Blessed is he
    whose transgressions are
    forgiven,
    whose sins are covered.
²Blessed is the man
    whose sin the Lord does not
    count against him
and in whose spirit is no deceit.

³When I kept silent,
    my bones wasted away
    through my groaning all day
    long.
⁴For day and night
    your hand was heavy upon me;
my strength was sapped
    as in the heat of summer. *Selah*
⁵Then I acknowledged my sin to
    you
    and did not cover up my
    iniquity.
I said, "I will confess
    my transgressions to the
    Lord"—
and you forgave
    the guilt of my sin.   *Selah*

⁶Therefore let everyone who is
    godly pray to you
    while you may be found;

ᵃ10 Or *guilt*   ᵇ17 Hebrew *Sheol*   ᶜTitle: Probably a literary or musical term

surely when the mighty waters
rise,
they will not reach him.
⁷You are my hiding place;
you will protect me from trouble
and surround me with songs of
deliverance.   *Selah*

⁸I will instruct you and teach you
in the way you should go;
I will counsel you and watch
over you.
⁹Do not be like the horse or the
mule,
which have no understanding
but must be controlled by bit and
bridle
or they will not come to you.
¹⁰Many are the woes of the wicked,
but the LORD's unfailing love
surrounds the man who trusts
in him.

¹¹Rejoice in the LORD and be glad,
you righteous;
sing, all you who are upright in
heart!

Psalm 33

¹Sing joyfully to the LORD, you
righteous;
it is fitting for the upright to
praise him.
²Praise the LORD with the harp;
make music to him on the
ten-stringed lyre.

ᵃ7 Or sea as into a heap

³Sing to him a new song;
play skillfully, and shout for
joy.

⁴For the word of the LORD is right
and true;
he is faithful in all he does.
⁵The LORD loves righteousness and
justice;
the earth is full of his unfailing
love.

⁶By the word of the LORD were the
heavens made,
their starry host by the breath
of his mouth.
⁷He gathers the waters of the sea
into jarsᵃ;
he puts the deep into
storehouses.
⁸Let all the earth fear the LORD;
let all the people of the world
revere him.
⁹For he spoke, and it came to be;
he commanded, and it stood
firm.
¹⁰The LORD foils the plans of the
nations;
he thwarts the purposes of the
peoples.
¹¹But the plans of the LORD stand
firm forever,
the purposes of his heart
through all generations.

¹²Blessed is the nation whose God
is the LORD,

▌ET'S LIVE IT!   Psalm 32:3–5

ADMIT SINS AND FEEL BETTER ➠ Even Bible heroes like David sinned. This
psalm tells how David felt when he did wrong.

Read Psalm 32:3–4. Can you think of three times when you did something wrong and felt very bad, as David did?

Psalm 32:5 tells what David did to feel better. He admitted (confessed)
his sin to God. Then God forgave David, and he felt better.

Ask your mom for some nail polish, and paint one side of a quarter
red. The red represents sin and the unhappiness we feel when we do
something wrong. The shiny other side represents admitting sins to God
and being forgiven. Flip the coin. Any time it comes up red you can
turn it over, to remind you that any time you sin you can confess to God
and be forgiven.

the people he chose for his
inheritance.
¹³From heaven the LORD looks
down
and sees all mankind;
¹⁴from his dwelling place he
watches
all who live on earth—
¹⁵he who forms the hearts of all,
who considers everything they
do.
¹⁶No king is saved by the size of
his army;
no warrior escapes by his great
strength.
¹⁷A horse is a vain hope for
deliverance;
despite all its great strength it
cannot save.
¹⁸But the eyes of the LORD are on
those who fear him,
on those whose hope is in his
unfailing love,
¹⁹to deliver them from death
and keep them alive in famine.

²⁰We wait in hope for the LORD;
he is our help and our shield.
²¹In him our hearts rejoice,
for we trust in his holy name.
²²May your unfailing love rest upon
us, O LORD,
even as we put our hope in you.

Psalm 34 ᵃ

Of David. When he pretended to be
insane before Abimelech, who drove
him away, and he left.

¹I will extol the LORD at all times;
his praise will always be on my
lips.
²My soul will boast in the LORD;
let the afflicted hear and
rejoice.
³Glorify the LORD with me;
let us exalt his name together.

⁴I sought the LORD, and he
answered me;
he delivered me from all my
fears.

⁵Those who look to him are
radiant;
their faces are never covered
with shame.
⁶This poor man called, and the
LORD heard him;
he saved him out of all his
troubles.
⁷The angel of the LORD encamps
around those who fear him,
and he delivers them.

⁸Taste and see that the LORD is
good;
blessed is the man who takes
refuge in him.
⁹Fear the LORD, you his saints,
for those who fear him lack
nothing.
¹⁰The lions may grow weak and
hungry,
but those who seek the LORD
lack no good thing.

¹¹Come, my children, listen to me;
I will teach you the fear of the
LORD.
¹²Whoever of you loves life
and desires to see many good
days,
¹³keep your tongue from evil
and your lips from speaking
lies.
¹⁴Turn from evil and do good;
seek peace and pursue it.

¹⁵The eyes of the LORD are on the
righteous
and his ears are attentive to
their cry;
¹⁶the face of the LORD is against
those who do evil,
to cut off the memory of them
from the earth.

¹⁷The righteous cry out, and the
LORD hears them;
he delivers them from all their
troubles.
¹⁸The LORD is close to the
brokenhearted
and saves those who are
crushed in spirit.

ᵃThis psalm is an acrostic poem, the verses of which begin with the successive letters of the Hebrew
alphabet.

¹⁹A righteous man may have many
    troubles,
  but the LORD delivers him from
    them all;
²⁰he protects all his bones,
  not one of them will be broken.

²¹Evil will slay the wicked;
  the foes of the righteous will be
    condemned.
²²The LORD redeems his servants;
  no one will be condemned who
    takes refuge in him.

Psalm 35

Of David.

¹Contend, O LORD, with those who
    contend with me;
  fight against those who fight
    against me.
²Take up shield and buckler;
  arise and come to my aid.
³Brandish spear and javelin*a*
  against those who pursue me.
Say to my soul,
  "I am your salvation."

⁴May those who seek my life
  be disgraced and put to shame;
  may those who plot my ruin
  be turned back in dismay.
⁵May they be like chaff before the
    wind,
  with the angel of the LORD
    driving them away;
⁶may their path be dark and
    slippery,
  with the angel of the LORD
    pursuing them.
⁷Since they hid their net for me
    without cause
  and without cause dug a pit for
    me,
⁸may ruin overtake them by
    surprise—
  may the net they hid entangle
    them,
  may they fall into the pit, to
    their ruin.
⁹Then my soul will rejoice in the
    LORD
  and delight in his salvation.

¹⁰My whole being will exclaim,
  "Who is like you, O LORD?
You rescue the poor from those
    too strong for them,
  the poor and needy from those
    who rob them."

¹¹Ruthless witnesses come forward;
  they question me on things I
    know nothing about.
¹²They repay me evil for good
  and leave my soul forlorn.
¹³Yet when they were ill, I put on
    sackcloth
  and humbled myself with
    fasting.
When my prayers returned to me
    unanswered,
¹⁴ I went about mourning
  as though for my friend or
    brother.
I bowed my head in grief
  as though weeping for my
    mother.
¹⁵But when I stumbled, they
    gathered in glee;
  attackers gathered against me
    when I was unaware.
They slandered me without
    ceasing.
¹⁶Like the ungodly they maliciously
    mocked*b*;
  they gnashed their teeth at me.
¹⁷O Lord, how long will you look
    on?
  Rescue my life from their
    ravages,
  my precious life from these
    lions.
¹⁸I will give you thanks in the
    great assembly;
  among throngs of people I will
    praise you.

¹⁹Let not those gloat over me
  who are my enemies without
    cause;
  let not those who hate me without
    reason
  maliciously wink the eye.
²⁰They do not speak peaceably,
  but devise false accusations
  against those who live quietly
    in the land.

---

a3 Or *and block the way*   *b16* Septuagint; Hebrew may mean *ungodly circle of mockers.*

²¹They gape at me and say, "Aha!
  Aha!
  With our own eyes we have
  seen it."

²²O LORD, you have seen this; be
  not silent.
  Do not be far from me, O Lord.
²³Awake, and rise to my defense!
  Contend for me, my God and
  Lord.
²⁴Vindicate me in your
  righteousness, O LORD my
  God;
  do not let them gloat over me.
²⁵Do not let them think, "Aha, just
  what we wanted!"
  or say, "We have swallowed him
  up."

²⁶May all who gloat over my
  distress
  be put to shame and confusion;
  may all who exalt themselves
  over me
  be clothed with shame and
  disgrace.
²⁷May those who delight in my
  vindication
  shout for joy and gladness;
  may they always say, "The LORD
  be exalted,
  who delights in the well-being
  of his servant."
²⁸My tongue will speak of your
  righteousness
  and of your praises all day long.

Psalm 36

For the director of music. Of David the
servant of the LORD.

¹An oracle is within my heart
  concerning the sinfulness of the
  wicked:ᵃ
  There is no fear of God
  before his eyes.
²For in his own eyes he flatters
  himself
  too much to detect or hate his
  sin.

³The words of his mouth are
  wicked and deceitful;
  he has ceased to be wise and to
  do good.
⁴Even on his bed he plots evil;
  he commits himself to a sinful
  course
  and does not reject what is
  wrong.

⁵Your love, O LORD, reaches to the
  heavens,
  your faithfulness to the
  skies.
⁶Your righteousness is like the
  mighty mountains,
  your justice like the great deep.
  O LORD, you preserve both man
  and beast.
⁷ How priceless is your unfailing
  love!
  Both high and low among men
  findᵇ refuge in the shadow of
  your wings.
⁸They feast on the abundance of
  your house;
  you give them drink from your
  river of delights.
⁹For with you is the fountain of
  life;
  in your light we see light.

¹⁰Continue your love to those who
  know you,
  your righteousness to the
  upright in heart.
¹¹May the foot of the proud not
  come against me,
  nor the hand of the wicked
  drive me away.
¹²See how the evildoers lie fallen—
  thrown down, not able to rise!

Psalm 37ᶜ

Of David.

¹Do not fret because of evil men
  or be envious of those who do
  wrong;
²for like the grass they will soon
  wither,

ᵃ1 Or heart: / Sin proceeds from the wicked.   ᵇ7 Or love, O God! / Men find; or love! / Both
heavenly beings and men / find   ᶜThis psalm is an acrostic poem, the stanzas of which begin with
the successive letters of the Hebrew alphabet.

like green plants they will soon
die away.

³Trust in the LORD and do good;
dwell in the land and enjoy safe
pasture.
⁴Delight yourself in the LORD
and he will give you the desires
of your heart.

WORDS TO REMEMBER

37:3-4 Trust in the LORD and do
good;
dwell in the land and
enjoy safe pasture.
Delight yourself in the
LORD
and he will give you
the desires of your
heart.

---

⁵Commit your way to the LORD;
trust in him and he will do this:
⁶He will make your righteousness
shine like the dawn,
the justice of your cause like
the noonday sun.

⁷Be still before the LORD and wait
patiently for him;
do not fret when men succeed in
their ways,
when they carry out their
wicked schemes.

⁸Refrain from anger and turn from
wrath;
do not fret—it leads only to
evil.
⁹For evil men will be cut off,
but those who hope in the LORD
will inherit the land.

¹⁰A little while, and the wicked
will be no more;
though you look for them, they
will not be found.
¹¹But the meek will inherit the
land
and enjoy great peace.

¹²The wicked plot against the
righteous
and gnash their teeth at them;

¹³but the Lord laughs at the
wicked,
for he knows their day is
coming.

¹⁴The wicked draw the sword
and bend the bow
to bring down the poor and needy,
to slay those whose ways are
upright.
¹⁵But their swords will pierce their
own hearts,
and their bows will be broken.

¹⁶Better the little that the
righteous have
than the wealth of many
wicked;
¹⁷for the power of the wicked will
be broken,
but the LORD upholds the
righteous.

¹⁸The days of the blameless are
known to the LORD,
and their inheritance will
endure forever.
¹⁹In times of disaster they will not
wither;
in days of famine they will
enjoy plenty.

²⁰But the wicked will perish:
The LORD's enemies will be like
the beauty of the fields,
they will vanish—vanish like
smoke.

²¹The wicked borrow and do not
repay,
but the righteous give
generously;
²²those the LORD blesses will
inherit the land,
but those he curses will be cut
off.

²³If the LORD delights in a man's
way,
he makes his steps firm;
²⁴though he stumble, he will not
fall,
for the LORD upholds him with
his hand.

²⁵I was young and now I am old,
yet I have never seen the
righteous forsaken

or their children begging bread.
26They are always generous and
lend freely;
their children will be blessed.

27Turn from evil and do good;
then you will dwell in the land
forever.
28For the LORD loves the just
and will not forsake his faithful
ones.

They will be protected forever,
but the offspring of the wicked
will be cut off;
29the righteous will inherit the
land
and dwell in it forever.

30The mouth of the righteous man
utters wisdom,
and his tongue speaks what is
just.
31The law of his God is in his
heart;
his feet do not slip.

32The wicked lie in wait for the
righteous,
seeking their very lives;
33but the LORD will not leave them
in their power
or let them be condemned when
brought to trial.

34Wait for the LORD
and keep his way.
He will exalt you to inherit the
land;
when the wicked are cut off,
you will see it.

35I have seen a wicked and ruthless
man
flourishing like a green tree in
its native soil,
36but he soon passed away and was
no more;
though I looked for him, he
could not be found.

37Consider the blameless, observe
the upright;
there is a future a for the man
of peace.
38But all sinners will be destroyed;

the future b of the wicked will
be cut off.

39The salvation of the righteous
comes from the LORD;
he is their stronghold in time of
trouble.
40The LORD helps them and delivers
them;
he delivers them from the
wicked and saves them,
because they take refuge in
him.

Psalm 38

A psalm of David. A petition.

1O LORD, do not rebuke me in your
anger
or discipline me in your wrath.
2For your arrows have pierced me,
and your hand has come down
upon me.
3Because of your wrath there is no
health in my body;
my bones have no soundness
because of my sin.
4My guilt has overwhelmed me
like a burden too heavy to bear.

5My wounds fester and are
loathsome
because of my sinful folly.
6I am bowed down and brought
very low;
all day long I go about
mourning.
7My back is filled with searing
pain;
there is no health in my body.
8I am feeble and utterly crushed;
I groan in anguish of heart.

9All my longings lie open before
you, O Lord;
my sighing is not hidden from
you.
10My heart pounds, my strength
fails me;
even the light has gone from
my eyes.
11My friends and companions avoid
me because of my wounds;

a37 Or *there will be posterity*   b38 Or *posterity*

my neighbors stay far away.
¹²Those who seek my life set their
traps,
those who would harm me talk
of my ruin;
all day long they plot
deception.

¹³I am like a deaf man, who cannot
hear,
like a mute, who cannot open
his mouth;
¹⁴I have become like a man who
does not hear,
whose mouth can offer no
reply.
¹⁵I wait for you, O Lord;
you will answer, O Lord my
God.
¹⁶For I said, "Do not let them gloat
or exalt themselves over me
when my foot slips."

¹⁷For I am about to fall,
and my pain is ever with me.
¹⁸I confess my iniquity;
I am troubled by my sin.
¹⁹Many are those who are my
vigorous enemies;
those who hate me without
reason are numerous.
²⁰Those who repay my good with
evil
slander me when I pursue what
is good.

²¹O Lord, do not forsake me;
be not far from me, O my God.
²²Come quickly to help me,
O Lord my Savior.

Psalm 39

For the director of music. For
Jeduthun. A psalm of David.

¹I said, "I will watch my ways
and keep my tongue from sin;
I will put a muzzle on my mouth
as long as the wicked are in my
presence."
²But when I was silent and still,
not even saying anything good,
my anguish increased.
³My heart grew hot within me,
and as I meditated, the fire
burned;
then I spoke with my tongue:

⁴"Show me, O Lord, my life's end
and the number of my days;
let me know how fleeting is my
life.
⁵You have made my days a mere
handbreadth;
the span of my years is as
nothing before you.
Each man's life is but a breath.
Selah
⁶Man is a mere phantom as he
goes to and fro:
He bustles about, but only in
vain;
he heaps up wealth, not
knowing who will get it.

⁷"But now, Lord, what do I look
for?
My hope is in you.
⁸Save me from all my
transgressions;

Life in Bible Times

WHAT GOD IS LIKE

Psalm 38 pictures God as
an archer. His arrows
wound a person who does
wrong. But God hurts only to
help us. When we feel bad
about doing wrong, we
confess our sins. Then God
will forgive and heal us.

do not make me the scorn of
fools.

WORDS TO REMEMBER

39:7 My hope is in you.

9I was silent; I would not open my
mouth,
for you are the one who has
done this.
10Remove your scourge from me;
I am overcome by the blow of
your hand.
11You rebuke and discipline men
for their sin;
you consume their wealth like a
moth—
each man is but a breath. *Selah*

12"Hear my prayer, O LORD,
listen to my cry for help;
be not deaf to my weeping.
For I dwell with you as an alien,
a stranger, as all my fathers
were.
13Look away from me, that I may
rejoice again
before I depart and am no
more."

Psalm 40

*For the director of music. Of David.
A psalm.*

1I waited patiently for the LORD;
he turned to me and heard my
cry.
2He lifted me out of the slimy pit,
out of the mud and mire;
he set my feet on a rock
and gave me a firm place to
stand.
3He put a new song in my mouth,
a hymn of praise to our God.
Many will see and fear
and put their trust in the LORD.

4Blessed is the man
who makes the LORD his trust,
who does not look to the proud,

to those who turn aside to false
gods.*a*
5Many, O LORD my God,
are the wonders you have done.
The things you planned for us
no one can recount to you;
were I to speak and tell of them,
they would be too many to
declare.

6Sacrifice and offering you did not
desire,
but my ears you have
pierced*b, c*;
burnt offerings and sin offerings
you did not require.
7Then I said, "Here I am, I have
come—
it is written about me in the
scroll.*d*
8I desire to do your will, O my
God;
your law is within my heart."

9I proclaim righteousness in the
great assembly;
I do not seal my lips,
as you know, O LORD.
10I do not hide your righteousness
in my heart;
I speak of your faithfulness and
salvation.
I do not conceal your love and
your truth
from the great assembly.

11Do not withhold your mercy from
me, O LORD;
may your love and your truth
always protect me.
12For troubles without number
surround me;
my sins have overtaken me, and
I cannot see.
They are more than the hairs of
my head,
and my heart fails within me.

13Be pleased, O LORD, to save me;
O LORD, come quickly to help
me.
14May all who seek to take my life
be put to shame and confusion;
may all who desire my ruin

---

*a*4 Or *to falsehood*   *b*6 Hebrew; Septuagint *but a body you have prepared for me* (see also
Symmachus and Theodotion)   *c*6 Or *opened*   *d*7 Or *come / with the scroll written for me*

be turned back in disgrace.
¹⁵May those who say to me, "Aha!
Aha!"
be appalled at their own shame.
¹⁶But may all who seek you
rejoice and be glad in you;
may those who love your
salvation always say,
"The LORD be exalted!"

¹⁷Yet I am poor and needy;
may the Lord think of me.
You are my help and my
deliverer;
O my God, do not delay.

Psalm 41

For the director of music. A psalm
of David.

¹Blessed is he who has regard for
the weak;
the LORD delivers him in times
of trouble.
²The LORD will protect him and
preserve his life;
he will bless him in the land
and not surrender him to the
desire of his foes.
³The LORD will sustain him on his
sickbed
and restore him from his bed of
illness.

⁴I said, "O LORD, have mercy on
me;
heal me, for I have sinned
against you."
⁵My enemies say of me in malice,
"When will he die and his name
perish?"
⁶Whenever one comes to see me,
he speaks falsely, while his
heart gathers slander;
then he goes out and spreads it
abroad.

⁷All my enemies whisper together
against me;
they imagine the worst for me,
saying,
⁸"A vile disease has beset him;

he will never get up from the
place where he lies."
⁹Even my close friend, whom I
trusted,
he who shared my bread,
has lifted up his heel against
me.

¹⁰But you, O LORD, have mercy on
me;
raise me up, that I may repay
them.
¹¹I know that you are pleased with
me,
for my enemy does not triumph
over me.
¹²In my integrity you uphold me
and set me in your presence
forever.

¹³Praise be to the LORD, the God of
Israel,
from everlasting to everlasting.
Amen and Amen.

BOOK II

Psalms 42–72

Psalm 42^a

For the director of music. A *maskil*^b of
the Sons of Korah.

¹As the deer pants for streams of
water,
so my soul pants for you,
O God.
²My soul thirsts for God, for the
living God.
When can I go and meet with
God?
³My tears have been my food
day and night,
while men say to me all day long,
"Where is your God?"
⁴These things I remember
as I pour out my soul:
how I used to go with the
multitude,
leading the procession to the
house of God,

---

^aIn many Hebrew manuscripts Psalms 42 and 43 constitute one psalm.   ^bTitle: Probably a
literary or musical term

with shouts of joy and
   thanksgiving
among the festive throng.

⁵Why are you downcast, O my
   soul?
  Why so disturbed within me?
Put your hope in God,
  for I will yet praise him,
  my Savior and ⁶my God.

My*a* soul is downcast within me;
  therefore I will remember you
from the land of the Jordan,
  the heights of Hermon—from
   Mount Mizar.
⁷Deep calls to deep
  in the roar of your waterfalls;
all your waves and breakers
  have swept over me.

⁸By day the LORD directs his love,
  at night his song is with me—
  a prayer to the God of my life.

⁹I say to God my Rock,
  "Why have you forgotten me?
Why must I go about mourning,
  oppressed by the enemy?"
¹⁰My bones suffer mortal agony
  as my foes taunt me,
saying to me all day long,
  "Where is your God?"

¹¹Why are you downcast, O my
   soul?
  Why so disturbed within me?
Put your hope in God,
  for I will yet praise him,
  my Savior and my God.

Psalm 43*b*

¹Vindicate me, O God,
  and plead my cause against an
   ungodly nation;
rescue me from deceitful and
   wicked men.
²You are God my stronghold.
  Why have you rejected me?
Why must I go about mourning,
  oppressed by the enemy?
³Send forth your light and your
   truth,

let them guide me;

let them bring me to your holy
   mountain,
  to the place where you dwell.
⁴Then will I go to the altar of God,
  to God, my joy and my delight.
I will praise you with the harp,
  O God, my God.

Life In Bible Times

WHAT GOD IS LIKE

Psalm 43:2 says God is like a stronghold. A stronghold was a walled city or fort where people went when an enemy army invaded the land. To say God is a stronghold means he will keep us safe in times of danger.

---

⁵Why are you downcast, O my
   soul?
  Why so disturbed within me?
Put your hope in God,
  for I will yet praise him,
  my Savior and my God.

Psalm 44

For the director of music. Of the Sons
of Korah. A *maskil.c*

¹We have heard with our ears,
   O God;
our fathers have told us
what you did in their days,
  in days long ago.
²With your hand you drove out the
   nations
  and planted our fathers;
you crushed the peoples
  and made our fathers flourish.
³It was not by their sword that
  they won the land,

---

a5,6 A few Hebrew manuscripts, Septuagint and Syriac; most Hebrew manuscripts *praise him for his saving help.* / *6O my God, my*   *b*In many Hebrew manuscripts Psalms 42 and 43 constitute one psalm.   *c*Title: Probably a literary or musical term

nor did their arm bring them
victory;
it was your right hand, your arm,
and the light of your face, for
you loved them.

⁴You are my King and my God,
who decrees^a victories for
Jacob.
⁵Through you we push back our
enemies;
through your name we trample
our foes.
⁶I do not trust in my bow,
my sword does not bring me
victory;
⁷but you give us victory over our
enemies,
you put our adversaries to
shame.
⁸In God we make our boast all day
long,
and we will praise your name
forever.   *Selah*

⁹But now you have rejected and
humbled us;
you no longer go out with our
armies.
¹⁰You made us retreat before the
enemy,
and our adversaries have
plundered us.
¹¹You gave us up to be devoured
like sheep
and have scattered us among
the nations.
¹²You sold your people for a
pittance,
gaining nothing from their sale.

¹³You have made us a reproach to
our neighbors,
the scorn and derision of those
around us.
¹⁴You have made us a byword
among the nations;
the peoples shake their heads at
us.
¹⁵My disgrace is before me all day
long,
and my face is covered with
shame

¹⁶at the taunts of those who
reproach and revile me,
because of the enemy, who is
bent on revenge.

¹⁷All this happened to us,
though we had not forgotten
you
or been false to your covenant.
¹⁸Our hearts had not turned back;
our feet had not strayed from
your path.
¹⁹But you crushed us and made us
a haunt for jackals
and covered us over with deep
darkness.

²⁰If we had forgotten the name of
our God
or spread out our hands to a
foreign god,
²¹would not God have discovered it,
since he knows the secrets of
the heart?
²²Yet for your sake we face death
all day long;
we are considered as sheep to
be slaughtered.

²³Awake, O Lord! Why do you
sleep?
Rouse yourself! Do not reject us
forever.
²⁴Why do you hide your face
and forget our misery and
oppression?

²⁵We are brought down to the dust;
our bodies cling to the ground.
²⁶Rise up and help us;
redeem us because of your
unfailing love.

Psalm 45

For the director of music. To the tune
of "Lilies." Of the Sons of Korah. A
maskil.^b A wedding song.

¹My heart is stirred by a noble
theme
as I recite my verses for the
king;

---

^a4 Septuagint, Aquila and Syriac; Hebrew *King, O God; / command*
or musical term   ^bTitle: Probably a literary

my tongue is the pen of a
skillful writer.

2You are the most excellent of men
and your lips have been
anointed with grace,
since God has blessed you
forever.
3Gird your sword upon your side,
O mighty one;
clothe yourself with splendor
and majesty.
4In your majesty ride forth
victoriously
in behalf of truth, humility and
righteousness;
let your right hand display
awesome deeds.
5Let your sharp arrows pierce the
hearts of the king's
enemies;
let the nations fall beneath your
feet.
6Your throne, O God, will last for
ever and ever;
a scepter of justice will be the
scepter of your kingdom.
7You love righteousness and hate
wickedness;
therefore God, your God, has set
you above your companions
by anointing you with the oil of
joy.
8All your robes are fragrant with
myrrh and aloes and cassia;
from palaces adorned with ivory
the music of the strings makes
you glad.
9Daughters of kings are among
your honored women;
at your right hand is the royal
bride in gold of Ophir.

10Listen, O daughter, consider and
give ear:
Forget your people and your
father's house.
11The king is enthralled by your
beauty;
honor him, for he is your lord.
12The Daughter of Tyre will come
with a gift,a
men of wealth will seek your
favor.

13All glorious is the princess within
her chamber;
her gown is interwoven with
gold.
14In embroidered garments she is
led to the king;
her virgin companions follow
her
and are brought to you.
15They are led in with joy and
gladness;
they enter the palace of the
king.
16Your sons will take the place of
your fathers;
you will make them princes
throughout the land.
17I will perpetuate your memory
through all generations;
therefore the nations will praise
you for ever and ever.

Psalm 46

For the director of music. Of the Sons
of Korah. According to *alamoth.b*
A song.

1God is our refuge and strength,
an ever-present help in trouble.
2Therefore we will not fear, though
the earth give way
and the mountains fall into the
heart of the sea,
3though its waters roar and foam
and the mountains quake with
their surging. *Selah*

4There is a river whose streams
make glad the city of God,
the holy place where the Most
High dwells.
5God is within her, she will not
fall;
God will help her at break of
day.
6Nations are in uproar, kingdoms
fall;
he lifts his voice, the earth
melts.

7The LORD Almighty is with us;
the God of Jacob is our fortress.
Selah

---

a12 Or *A Tyrian robe is among the gifts*   bTitle: Probably a musical term

8Come and see the works of the
    Lord,
  the desolations he has brought
    on the earth.
9He makes wars cease to the ends
    of the earth;
  he breaks the bow and shatters
    the spear,
  he burns the shields*a* with fire.
10"Be still, and know that I am
    God;
  I will be exalted among the
    nations,
  I will be exalted in the earth."

11The Lord Almighty is with us;
  the God of Jacob is our fortress.
                              Selah

Psalm 47

For the director of music. Of the Sons
of Korah. A psalm.

1Clap your hands, all you nations;
  shout to God with cries of joy.
2How awesome is the Lord Most
    High,
  the great King over all the
    earth!
3He subdued nations under us,
  peoples under our feet.
4He chose our inheritance for us,
  the pride of Jacob, whom he
    loved.   *Selah*

5God has ascended amid shouts of
    joy,
  the Lord amid the sounding of
    trumpets.
6Sing praises to God, sing praises;
  sing praises to our King, sing
    praises.

7For God is the King of all the
    earth;
  sing to him a psalm*b* of praise.
8God reigns over the nations;
  God is seated on his holy
    throne.
9The nobles of the nations
    assemble

as the people of the God of
    Abraham,
  for the kings*c* of the earth belong
    to God;

WORDS TO REMEMBER

47:7 God is the King of all the
    earth;
  sing to him a psalm of
    praise.

---

he is greatly exalted.

Psalm 48

A song. A psalm of the Sons of Korah.

1Great is the Lord, and most
    worthy of praise,
  in the city of our God, his holy
    mountain.
2It is beautiful in its loftiness,
  the joy of the whole earth.
  Like the utmost heights of
    Zaphon*d* is Mount Zion,
  the*e* city of the Great King.
3God is in her citadels;
  he has shown himself to be her
    fortress.

4When the kings joined forces,
  when they advanced together,
5they saw ˌherˎ and were
    astounded;
  they fled in terror.
6Trembling seized them there,
  pain like that of a woman in
    labor.
7You destroyed them like ships of
    Tarshish
  shattered by an east wind.

8As we have heard,
  so have we seen
  in the city of the Lord Almighty,
  in the city of our God:
  God makes her secure forever.
                              Selah

9Within your temple, O God,

---

*a*9 Or *chariots*   *b*7 Or *a maskil* (probably a literary or musical term)   *c*9 Or *shields*
*d*2 *Zaphon* can refer to a sacred mountain or the direction north.   *e*2 Or *earth,* / *Mount Zion, on
the northern side* / *of the*

we meditate on your unfailing
love.
¹⁰Like your name, O God,
  your praise reaches to the ends
    of the earth;
  your right hand is filled with
    righteousness.
¹¹Mount Zion rejoices,
  the villages of Judah are glad
    because of your judgments.

¹²Walk about Zion, go around her,
    count her towers,
¹³consider well her ramparts,
    view her citadels,
  that you may tell of them to the
    next generation.
¹⁴For this God is our God for ever
    and ever;
  he will be our guide even to the
    end.

Psalm 49

For the director of music. Of the Sons
of Korah. A psalm.

¹Hear this, all you peoples;
  listen, all who live in this
    world,
²both low and high,
  rich and poor alike:
³My mouth will speak words of
    wisdom;
  the utterance from my heart
    will give understanding.
⁴I will turn my ear to a proverb;
  with the harp I will expound
    my riddle:

⁵Why should I fear when evil days
    come,
  when wicked deceivers surround
    me—
⁶those who trust in their wealth
  and boast of their great
    riches?
⁷No man can redeem the life of
    another
  or give to God a ransom for
    him—
⁸the ransom for a life is costly,

no payment is ever enough—
⁹that he should live on forever
  and not see decay.

¹⁰For all can see that wise men
    die;
  the foolish and the senseless
    alike perish
  and leave their wealth to
    others.
¹¹Their tombs will remain their
    houses[a] forever,
  their dwellings for endless
    generations,
  though they had[b] named lands
    after themselves.

¹²But man, despite his riches, does
    not endure;
  he is[c] like the beasts that
    perish.

¹³This is the fate of those who trust
    in themselves,
  and of their followers, who
    approve their sayings. *Selah*
¹⁴Like sheep they are destined for
    the grave,[d]
  and death will feed on them.
  The upright will rule over them
    in the morning;
  their forms will decay in the
    grave,[d]
  far from their princely
    mansions.
¹⁵But God will redeem my life[e]
    from the grave;
  he will surely take me to
    himself.   *Selah*

¹⁶Do not be overawed when a man
    grows rich,
  when the splendor of his house
    increases;
¹⁷for he will take nothing with him
    when he dies,
  his splendor will not descend
    with him.
¹⁸Though while he lived he counted
    himself blessed—
  and men praise you when you
    prosper—

---

a11 Septuagint and Syriac; Hebrew *In their thoughts their houses will remain*   *b11* Or *I for they*
have   *c12* Hebrew; Septuagint and Syriac read verse 12 the same as verse 20.   *d14* Hebrew
Sheol; also in verse 15   *e15* Or *soul*

¹⁹he will join the generation of his
    fathers,
    who will never see the light ˌof
    lifeˌ.
²⁰A man who has riches without
    understanding
    is like the beasts that perish.

Psalm 50

A psalm of Asaph.

¹The Mighty One, God, the Lord,
    speaks and summons the earth
    from the rising of the sun to the
    place where it sets.
²From Zion, perfect in beauty,
    God shines forth.
³Our God comes and will not be
    silent;
    a fire devours before him,
    and around him a tempest
    rages.
⁴He summons the heavens above,
    and the earth, that he may
    judge his people:
⁵"Gather to me my consecrated
    ones,
    who made a covenant with me
    by sacrifice."
⁶And the heavens proclaim his
    righteousness,
    for God himself is judge.   *Selah*

⁷"Hear, O my people, and I will
    speak,
    O Israel, and I will testify
    against you:
    I am God, your God.
⁸I do not rebuke you for your
    sacrifices
    or your burnt offerings, which
    are ever before me.
⁹I have no need of a bull from your
    stall
    or of goats from your pens,
¹⁰for every animal of the forest is
    mine,
    and the cattle on a thousand
    hills.
¹¹I know every bird in the
    mountains,

    and the creatures of the field
    are mine.
¹²If I were hungry I would not tell
    you,
    for the world is mine, and all
    that is in it.
¹³Do I eat the flesh of bulls
    or drink the blood of goats?
¹⁴Sacrifice thank offerings to God,
    fulfill your vows to the Most
    High,
¹⁵and call upon me in the day of
    trouble;
    I will deliver you, and you will
    honor me."

¹⁶But to the wicked, God says:

    "What right have you to recite
    my laws
    or take my covenant on your
    lips?
¹⁷You hate my instruction
    and cast my words behind
    you.
¹⁸When you see a thief, you join
    with him;
    you throw in your lot with
    adulterers.
¹⁹You use your mouth for evil
    and harness your tongue to
    deceit.
²⁰You speak continually against
    your brother
    and slander your own mother's
    son.
²¹These things you have done and I
    kept silent;
    you thought I was altogether^a
    like you.
  But I will rebuke you
    and accuse you to your face.

²²"Consider this, you who forget
    God,
    or I will tear you to pieces, with
    none to rescue:
²³He who sacrifices thank offerings
    honors me,
    and he prepares the way
    so that I may show him^b the
    salvation of God."

---

^a21 Or *thought the 'I am' was*   ^b23 Or *and to him who considers his way / I will show*

Psalm 51

For the director of music. A psalm of
David. When the prophet Nathan
came to him after David had
committed adultery with Bathsheba.

¹Have mercy on me, O God,
    according to your unfailing love;
according to your great
        compassion
    blot out my transgressions.
²Wash away all my iniquity
    and cleanse me from my sin.

WORDS TO REMEMBER

**51:2   Wash away all my iniquity
        and cleanse me from my
        sin.**

---

³For I know my transgressions,
    and my sin is always before me.
⁴Against you, you only, have I
        sinned
    and done what is evil in your
        sight,
    so that you are proved right when
        you speak
    and justified when you judge.
⁵Surely I was sinful at birth,
    sinful from the time my mother
        conceived me.
⁶Surely you desire truth in the
        inner parts*a*;
    you teach*b* me wisdom in the
        inmost place.

⁷Cleanse me with hyssop, and I
        will be clean;
    wash me, and I will be whiter
        than snow.
⁸Let me hear joy and gladness;
    let the bones you have crushed
        rejoice.
⁹Hide your face from my sins
    and blot out all my iniquity.

¹⁰Create in me a pure heart,
        O God,
    and renew a steadfast spirit
        within me.

¹¹Do not cast me from your
        presence
    or take your Holy Spirit from
        me.
¹²Restore to me the joy of your
        salvation
    and grant me a willing spirit, to
        sustain me.

¹³Then I will teach transgressors
        your ways,
    and sinners will turn back to
        you.
¹⁴Save me from bloodguilt, O God,
    the God who saves me,
    and my tongue will sing of your
        righteousness.
¹⁵O Lord, open my lips,
    and my mouth will declare your
        praise.
¹⁶You do not delight in sacrifice, or
        I would bring it;
    you do not take pleasure in
        burnt offerings.
¹⁷The sacrifices of God are*c* a
        broken spirit;
    a broken and contrite heart,
    O God, you will not despise.

¹⁸In your good pleasure make Zion
        prosper;
    build up the walls of Jerusalem.
¹⁹Then there will be righteous
        sacrifices,
    whole burnt offerings to delight
        you;
    then bulls will be offered on
        your altar.

Psalm 52

For the director of music. A *maskil*d
of David. When Doeg the Edomite had
gone to Saul and told him: "David has
gone to the house of Ahimelech."

¹Why do you boast of evil, you
        mighty man?
    Why do you boast all day long,
    you who are a disgrace in the
        eyes of God?
²Your tongue plots destruction;
    it is like a sharpened razor,
    you who practice deceit.

---

a6 The meaning of the Hebrew for this phrase is uncertain.   *b6* Or *you desired . . . ; / you taught*
c17 Or *My sacrifice, O God, is*   *d*Title: Probably a literary or musical term

³You love evil rather than good,
　falsehood rather than speaking
　　the truth.　　*Selah*
⁴You love every harmful word,
　O you deceitful tongue!

⁵Surely God will bring you down
　to everlasting ruin:
He will snatch you up and tear
　you from your tent;
he will uproot you from the
　land of the living.　*Selah*
⁶The righteous will see and fear;
　they will laugh at him, saying,
⁷"Here now is the man
　who did not make God his
　　stronghold
but trusted in his great wealth
and grew strong by destroying
　others!"

⁸But I am like an olive tree
　flourishing in the house of God;
I trust in God's unfailing love
　for ever and ever.

WORDS TO REMEMBER

**52:8 I trust in God's unfailing
love
for ever and ever.**

---

⁹I will praise you forever for what
　you have done;
in your name I will hope, for
　your name is good.
I will praise you in the presence
　of your saints.

Psalm 53

For the director of music. According to
mahalath.ᵃ A *maskilᵇ* of David.

¹The fool says in his heart,
　"There is no God."
They are corrupt, and their ways
　are vile;
there is no one who does good.

²God looks down from heaven
　on the sons of men

to see if there are any who
　understand,
　any who seek God.
³Everyone has turned away,
　they have together become
　　corrupt;
there is no one who does good,
　not even one.

⁴Will the evildoers never learn—
　those who devour my people as
　　men eat bread
and who do not call on God?
⁵There they were, overwhelmed
　with dread,
　where there was nothing to
　　dread.
God scattered the bones of those
　who attacked you;
　you put them to shame, for God
　　despised them.

⁶Oh, that salvation for Israel
　　would come out of Zion!
When God restores the fortunes
　of his people,
　let Jacob rejoice and Israel be
　　glad!

Psalm 54

For the director of music. With
stringed instruments. A *maskilᵇ* of
David. When the Ziphites had gone to
Saul and said, "Is not David hiding
among us?"

¹Save me, O God, by your name;
　vindicate me by your might.
²Hear my prayer, O God;
　listen to the words of my
　　mouth.

³Strangers are attacking me;
　ruthless men seek my life—
　men without regard for God.
　　　　　　　　　　　Selah

⁴Surely God is my help;
　the Lord is the one who
　　sustains me.

⁵Let evil recoil on those who
　slander me;
　in your faithfulness destroy
　　them.

ᵃTitle: Probably a musical term　　　ᵇTitle: Probably a literary or musical term

⁶I will sacrifice a freewill offering
    to you;
I will praise your name,
    O LORD,
for it is good.
⁷For he has delivered me from all
    my troubles,
and my eyes have looked in
    triumph on my foes.

Psalm 55

For the director of music. With
stringed instruments. A *maskil*ᵃ
    of David.

¹Listen to my prayer, O God,
    do not ignore my plea;
² hear me and answer me.
My thoughts trouble me and I am
    distraught
³ at the voice of the enemy,
    at the stares of the wicked;
for they bring down suffering
    upon me
    and revile me in their anger.

⁴My heart is in anguish within
    me;
    the terrors of death assail me.
⁵Fear and trembling have beset
    me;
    horror has overwhelmed me.
⁶I said, "Oh, that I had the wings
    of a dove!
I would fly away and be at
    rest—
⁷I would flee far away
    and stay in the desert;   *Selah*
⁸I would hurry to my place of
    shelter,
    far from the tempest and
        storm."

⁹Confuse the wicked, O Lord,
    confound their speech,
for I see violence and strife in
    the city.
¹⁰Day and night they prowl about
    on its walls;
    malice and abuse are within
        it.
¹¹Destructive forces are at work in
    the city;

threats and lies never leave its
    streets.

¹²If an enemy were insulting me,
    I could endure it;
if a foe were raising himself
    against me,
    I could hide from him.
¹³But it is you, a man like myself,
    my companion, my close friend,
¹⁴with whom I once enjoyed sweet
    fellowship
as we walked with the throng
    at the house of God.

¹⁵Let death take my enemies by
    surprise;
let them go down alive to the
    grave,ᵇ
    for evil finds lodging among
        them.

¹⁶But I call to God,
    and the LORD saves me.

WORDS TO REMEMBER

55:16 I call to God,
    and the LORD saves me.

---

¹⁷Evening, morning and noon
    I cry out in distress,
    and he hears my voice.
¹⁸He ransoms me unharmed
    from the battle waged against
        me,
    even though many oppose me.
¹⁹God, who is enthroned forever,
    will hear them and afflict
        them—   *Selah*
men who never change their ways
    and have no fear of God.

²⁰My companion attacks his friends;
    he violates his covenant.
²¹His speech is smooth as butter,
    yet war is in his heart;
his words are more soothing than
    oil,
    yet they are drawn swords.

²²Cast your cares on the LORD
    and he will sustain you;

ᵃTitle: Probably a literary or musical term   ᵇ15 Hebrew *Sheol*

he will never let the righteous
fall.
²³But you, O God, will bring down
the wicked
into the pit of corruption;
bloodthirsty and deceitful men
will not live out half their days.

But as for me, I trust in you.

Psalm 56

For the director of music. To the tune
of "A Dove on Distant Oaks." Of
David. A *miktam.*ᵃ When the
Philistines had seized him in Gath.

¹Be merciful to me, O God, for
men hotly pursue me;
all day long they press their
attack.
²My slanderers pursue me all day
long;
many are attacking me in their
pride.

³When I am afraid,
I will trust in you.
⁴In God, whose word I praise,
in God I trust; I will not be
afraid.
What can mortal man do to me?

⁵All day long they twist my words;
they are always plotting to
harm me.
⁶They conspire, they lurk,
they watch my steps,
eager to take my life.

⁷On no account let them escape;
in your anger, O God, bring
down the nations.
⁸Record my lament;
list my tears on your scrollᵇ—
are they not in your record?

⁹Then my enemies will turn back
when I call for help.
By this I will know that God is
for me.
¹⁰In God, whose word I praise,
in the LORD, whose word I
praise—

¹¹in God I trust; I will not be
afraid.
What can man do to me?

¹²I am under vows to you, O God;
I will present my thank
offerings to you.
¹³For you have delivered meᶜ from
death
and my feet from stumbling,
that I may walk before God
in the light of life. ᵈ

Psalm 57

For the director of music. To the tune
of "Do Not Destroy." Of David. A
*miktam.*ᵃ When he had fled from Saul
into the cave.

¹Have mercy on me, O God, have
mercy on me,
for in you my soul takes refuge.
I will take refuge in the shadow
of your wings
until the disaster has passed.

²I cry out to God Most High,
to God, who fulfills his purpose
for me.
³He sends from heaven and saves
me,
rebuking those who hotly
pursue me;   *Selah*
God sends his love and his
faithfulness.

⁴I am in the midst of lions;
I lie among ravenous beasts—
men whose teeth are spears and
arrows,
whose tongues are sharp
swords.

⁵Be exalted, O God, above the
heavens;
let your glory be over all the
earth.

⁶They spread a net for my feet—
I was bowed down in distress.
They dug a pit in my path—
but they have fallen into it
themselves.   *Selah*

⁷My heart is steadfast, O God,

ᵃTitle: Probably a literary or musical term   ᵇ8 Or / *put my tears in your wineskin*   ᶜ13 Or
my soul   ᵈ13 Or *the land of the living*

my heart is steadfast;
I will sing and make music.
⁸Awake, my soul!
Awake, harp and lyre!
I will awaken the dawn.

⁹I will praise you, O Lord, among
the nations;
I will sing of you among the
peoples.
¹⁰For great is your love, reaching to
the heavens;
your faithfulness reaches to the
skies.

¹¹Be exalted, O God, above the
heavens;
let your glory be over all the
earth.

Psalm 58

For the director of music. To the tune
of "Do Not Destroy." Of David.
A *miktam.*ᵃ

¹Do you rulers indeed speak justly?
Do you judge uprightly among
men?
²No, in your heart you devise
injustice,
and your hands mete out
violence on the earth.
³Even from birth the wicked go
astray;
from the womb they are
wayward and speak lies.
⁴Their venom is like the venom of
a snake,
like that of a cobra that has
stopped its ears,
⁵that will not heed the tune of the
charmer,
however skillful the enchanter
may be.

⁶Break the teeth in their mouths,
O God;
tear out, O Lord, the fangs of
the lions!
⁷Let them vanish like water that
flows away;
when they draw the bow, let
their arrows be blunted.

⁸Like a slug melting away as it
moves along,
like a stillborn child, may they
not see the sun.

⁹Before your pots can feel the heat
of the thorns—
whether they be green or
dry—the wicked will be
swept away.ᵇ

¹⁰The righteous will be glad when
they are avenged,
when they bathe their feet in
the blood of the wicked.
¹¹Then men will say,
"Surely the righteous still are
rewarded;
surely there is a God who
judges the earth."

Psalm 59

For the director of music. To the tune
of "Do Not Destroy." Of David. A
*miktam.*ᵃ When Saul had sent men to
watch David's house in order
to kill him.

¹Deliver me from my enemies,
O God;
protect me from those who rise
up against me.
²Deliver me from evildoers
and save me from bloodthirsty
men.

³See how they lie in wait for me!
Fierce men conspire against
me
for no offense or sin of mine,
O Lord.
⁴I have done no wrong, yet they
are ready to attack me.
Arise to help me; look on my
plight!
⁵O Lord God Almighty, the God of
Israel,
rouse yourself to punish all the
nations;
show no mercy to wicked
traitors.   *Selah*

⁶They return at evening,

ᵃTitle: Probably a literary or musical term
uncertain.   ᵇ9 The meaning of the Hebrew for this verse is

snarling like dogs,
and prowl about the city.
⁷See what they spew from their
mouths—
they spew out swords from their
lips,
and they say, "Who can hear
us?"
⁸But you, O Lord, laugh at them;
you scoff at all those nations.

⁹O my Strength, I watch for you;
you, O God, are my fortress,
¹⁰my loving God.

God will go before me
and will let me gloat over those
who slander me.
¹¹But do not kill them, O Lord our
shield,ᵃ
or my people will forget.
In your might make them wander
about,
and bring them down.
¹²For the sins of their mouths,
for the words of their lips,
let them be caught in their
pride.
For the curses and lies they
utter,
¹³ consume them in wrath,
consume them till they are no
more.
Then it will be known to the ends
of the earth
that God rules over Jacob.
Selah

¹⁴They return at evening,
snarling like dogs,
and prowl about the city.
¹⁵They wander about for food
and howl if not satisfied.
¹⁶But I will sing of your strength,
in the morning I will sing of
your love;
for you are my fortress,
my refuge in times of trouble.

¹⁷O my Strength, I sing praise to
you;
you, O God, are my fortress, my
loving God.

Psalm 60

For the director of music. To the tune
of, "The Lily of the Covenant." A
*miktam*ᵇ of David. For teaching.
When he fought Aram Naharaimᶜ
and Aram Zobah,ᵈ and when Joab
returned and struck down twelve
thousand Edomites in the
Valley of Salt.

¹You have rejected us, O God, and
burst forth upon us;
you have been angry—now
restore us!
²You have shaken the land and
torn it open;
mend its fractures, for it is
quaking.
³You have shown your people
desperate times;
you have given us wine that
makes us stagger.

⁴But for those who fear you, you
have raised a banner
to be unfurled against the bow.
Selah

⁵Save us and help us with your
right hand,
that those you love may be
delivered.
⁶God has spoken from his
sanctuary:
"In triumph I will parcel out
Shechem
and measure off the Valley of
Succoth.
⁷Gilead is mine, and Manasseh is
mine;
Ephraim is my helmet,
Judah my scepter.
⁸Moab is my washbasin,
upon Edom I toss my sandal;
over Philistia I shout in
triumph."

⁹Who will bring me to the fortified
city?
Who will lead me to Edom?
¹⁰Is it not you, O God, you who
have rejected us
and no longer go out with our
armies?

ᵃ11 Or *sovereign*   ᵇTitle: Probably a literary or musical term   ᶜTitle: That is, Arameans of
Northwest Mesopotamia   ᵈTitle: That is, Arameans of central Syria

¹¹Give us aid against the enemy,
  for the help of man is worthless.
¹²With God we will gain the
    victory,
  and he will trample down our
    enemies.

Psalm 61

For the director of music. With
stringed instruments. Of David.

¹Hear my cry, O God;
  listen to my prayer.

²From the ends of the earth I call
    to you,
  I call as my heart grows faint;
  lead me to the rock that is
    higher than I.
³For you have been my refuge,
  a strong tower against the foe.

Life In Bible Times

WHAT GOD IS LIKE

Psalm 61:3 says God is like a strong
tower. Strong towers were built
inside walled cities. Even if the
walls were broken down, the
people of the city would be safe
inside the tower.

⁴I long to dwell in your tent
    forever
  and take refuge in the shelter
    of your wings. *Selah*
⁵For you have heard my vows,
    O God;
  you have given me the heritage
    of those who fear your
    name.

⁶Increase the days of the king's
    life,
  his years for many generations.

⁷May he be enthroned in God's
    presence forever;
  appoint your love and
    faithfulness to protect him.

⁸Then will I ever sing praise to
    your name
  and fulfill my vows day after
    day.

Psalm 62

For the director of music. For
Jeduthun. A psalm of David.

¹My soul finds rest in God alone;
  my salvation comes from him.
²He alone is my rock and my
    salvation;
  he is my fortress, I will never
    be shaken.

³How long will you assault a man?
  Would all of you throw him
    down—
  this leaning wall, this tottering
    fence?
⁴They fully intend to topple him
  from his lofty place;
  they take delight in lies.
With their mouths they bless,
  but in their hearts they curse.
                Selah

⁵Find rest, O my soul, in God
    alone;
  my hope comes from him.
⁶He alone is my rock and my
    salvation;
  he is my fortress, I will not be
    shaken.
⁷My salvation and my honor
    depend on God^a;
  he is my mighty rock, my
    refuge.
⁸Trust in him at all times,
    O people;
  pour out your hearts to him,
  for God is our refuge.   *Selah*

⁹Lowborn men are but a breath,
  the highborn are but a lie;
  if weighed on a balance, they are
    nothing;
  together they are only a breath.

a7 Or / God Most High is my salvation and my honor

¹⁰Do not trust in extortion
    or take pride in stolen goods;
though your riches increase,
    do not set your heart on them.

¹¹One thing God has spoken,
    two things have I heard:
that you, O God, are strong,
¹²   and that you, O Lord, are
      loving.
Surely you will reward each
    person
    according to what he has done.

Psalm 63

A psalm of David. When he was in the
Desert of Judah.

¹O God, you are my God,
    earnestly I seek you;
my soul thirsts for you,
    my body longs for you,
in a dry and weary land
    where there is no water.

²I have seen you in the sanctuary
    and beheld your power and your
      glory.
³Because your love is better than
    life,
    my lips will glorify you.
⁴I will praise you as long as I live,
    and in your name I will lift up
      my hands.
⁵My soul will be satisfied as with
    the richest of foods;
    with singing lips my mouth will
      praise you.

⁶On my bed I remember you;
    I think of you through the
      watches of the night.

⁷Because you are my help,
    I sing in the shadow of your
      wings.
⁸My soul clings to you;
    your right hand upholds me.

⁹They who seek my life will be
    destroyed;
    they will go down to the depths
      of the earth.
¹⁰They will be given over to the
    sword
    and become food for jackals.

¹¹But the king will rejoice in God;
    all who swear by God's name
      will praise him,
    while the mouths of liars will
      be silenced.

Psalm 64

For the director of music. A psalm
of David.

¹Hear me, O God, as I voice my
    complaint;
    protect my life from the threat
      of the enemy.
²Hide me from the conspiracy of
    the wicked,
    from that noisy crowd of
      evildoers.

³They sharpen their tongues like
    swords
    and aim their words like deadly
      arrows.
⁴They shoot from ambush at the
    innocent man;
    they shoot at him suddenly,
      without fear.

◣ET'S LIVE IT!
Psalm 63:6–8

LYING AWAKE AT NIGHT ➧ Do you have a hard time going to sleep
sometimes? This psalm tells what David did when he couldn't get to
sleep. Read Psalm 63:6–8 and see if you can find these things to do
when lying awake:

1. Remember Bible stories and things God does for people.
2. Quietly sing the songs about God that you can remember.
3. Snuggle down in your blankets, close your eyes, and as you feel
   the warmth remember that God is close to you.

5They encourage each other in evil
  plans,
  they talk about hiding their
    snares;
  they say, "Who will see
    them*a*?"
6They plot injustice and say,
  "We have devised a perfect
    plan!"
  Surely the mind and heart of
    man are cunning.

7But God will shoot them with
    arrows;
  suddenly they will be struck
    down.
8He will turn their own tongues
    against them
  and bring them to ruin;
  all who see them will shake
    their heads in scorn.

9All mankind will fear;
  they will proclaim the works of
    God
  and ponder what he has done.
10Let the righteous rejoice in the
    LORD
  and take refuge in him;
  let all the upright in heart
    praise him!

Psalm 65

For the director of music. A psalm
of David. A song.

1Praise awaits*b* you, O God, in
    Zion;
  to you our vows will be
    fulfilled.
2O you who hear prayer,
  to you all men will come.
3When we were overwhelmed by
    sins,
  you forgave*c* our
    transgressions.
4Blessed are those you choose
  and bring near to live in your
    courts!
  We are filled with the good things
    of your house,
  of your holy temple.

5You answer us with awesome
    deeds of righteousness,
  O God our Savior,
  the hope of all the ends of the
    earth
  and of the farthest seas,
6who formed the mountains by
    your power,
  having armed yourself with
    strength,
7who stilled the roaring of the
    seas,
  the roaring of their waves,
  and the turmoil of the nations.
8Those living far away fear your
    wonders;
  where morning dawns and
    evening fades
  you call forth songs of joy.

9You care for the land and water
    it;
  you enrich it abundantly.
  The streams of God are filled with
    water
  to provide the people with
    grain,
  for so you have ordained it.*d*
10You drench its furrows
  and level its ridges;
  you soften it with showers
  and bless its crops.
11You crown the year with your
    bounty,
  and your carts overflow with
    abundance.
12The grasslands of the desert
    overflow;
  the hills are clothed with
    gladness.
13The meadows are covered with
    flocks
  and the valleys are mantled
    with grain;
  they shout for joy and sing.

Psalm 66

For the director of music. A song.
A psalm.

1Shout with joy to God, all the
    earth!

---

a5 Or *us*   *b1* Or *befits*; the meaning of the Hebrew for this word is uncertain.   *c3* Or *made*
atonement for   *d9* Or *for that is how you prepare the land*

2 Sing the glory of his name;
   make his praise glorious!
³Say to God, "How awesome are
   your deeds!
   So great is your power
   that your enemies cringe before
   you.
⁴All the earth bows down to you;
   they sing praise to you,
   they sing praise to your name."
                              Selah

⁵Come and see what God has
   done,
   how awesome his works in
   man's behalf!
⁶He turned the sea into dry land,
   they passed through the waters
   on foot—
   come, let us rejoice in him.
⁷He rules forever by his power,
   his eyes watch the nations—
   let not the rebellious rise up
   against him. *Selah*

⁸Praise our God, O peoples,
   let the sound of his praise be
   heard;
⁹he has preserved our lives
   and kept our feet from slipping.
¹⁰For you, O God, tested us;
   you refined us like silver.
¹¹You brought us into prison
   and laid burdens on our backs.
¹²You let men ride over our heads;
   we went through fire and water,
   but you brought us to a place of
   abundance.

¹³I will come to your temple with
   burnt offerings
   and fulfill my vows to you—
¹⁴vows my lips promised and my
   mouth spoke
   when I was in trouble.
¹⁵I will sacrifice fat animals to
   you
   and an offering of rams;
   I will offer bulls and goats.
                              Selah

¹⁶Come and listen, all you who fear
   God;
   let me tell you what he has
   done for me.

¹⁷I cried out to him with my mouth;
   his praise was on my tongue.
¹⁸If I had cherished sin in my
   heart,
   the Lord would not have
   listened;
¹⁹but God has surely listened
   and heard my voice in prayer.
²⁰Praise be to God,
   who has not rejected my prayer
   or withheld his love from me!

Psalm 67

For the director of music. With
stringed instruments. A psalm.
A song.

¹May God be gracious to us and
   bless us
   and make his face shine upon
   us, *Selah*
²that your ways may be known on
   earth,
   your salvation among all
   nations.

WORDS TO REMEMBER

67:1 **May God be gracious to
   us and bless us
   and make his face shine
   upon us.**

---

³May the peoples praise you,
   O God;
   may all the peoples praise
   you.
⁴May the nations be glad and sing
   for joy,
   for you rule the peoples justly
   and guide the nations of the
   earth. *Selah*
⁵May the peoples praise you,
   O God;
   may all the peoples praise you.

⁶Then the land will yield its
   harvest,
   and God, our God, will bless us.
⁷God will bless us,
   and all the ends of the earth
   will fear him.

Psalm 68

For the director of music. Of David.
A psalm. A song.

1May God arise, may his enemies
    be scattered;
  may his foes flee before him.
2As smoke is blown away by the
    wind,
  may you blow them away;
as wax melts before the fire,
  may the wicked perish before
    God.
3But may the righteous be glad
  and rejoice before God;
  may they be happy and joyful.

4Sing to God, sing praise to his
    name,
  extol him who rides on the
    clouds[a]—
his name is the LORD—
  and rejoice before him.
5A father to the fatherless, a
    defender of widows,
  is God in his holy dwelling.
6God sets the lonely in families,[b]
  he leads forth the prisoners
    with singing;
but the rebellious live in a
    sun-scorched land.

7When you went out before your
    people, O God,
  when you marched through the
    wasteland,   *Selah*
8the earth shook,
  the heavens poured down rain,
before God, the One of Sinai,
  before God, the God of Israel.
9You gave abundant showers,
    O God;
  you refreshed your weary
    inheritance.
10Your people settled in it,
  and from your bounty, O God,
    you provided for the poor.

11The Lord announced the word,
  and great was the company of
    those who proclaimed it:
12"Kings and armies flee in haste;

in the camps men divide the
    plunder.
13Even while you sleep among the
    campfires,[c]
the wings of my dove are
    sheathed with silver,
  its feathers with shining gold."
14When the Almighty[d] scattered
    the kings in the land,
  it was like snow fallen on
    Zalmon.

15The mountains of Bashan are
    majestic mountains;
  rugged are the mountains of
    Bashan.
16Why gaze in envy, O rugged
    mountains,
  at the mountain where God
    chooses to reign,
  where the LORD himself will
    dwell forever?
17The chariots of God are tens of
    thousands
  and thousands of thousands;
  the Lord has come from Sinai
    into his sanctuary.
18When you ascended on high,
  you led captives in your train;
  you received gifts from men,
even from[e] the rebellious—
  that you,[f] O LORD God, might
    dwell there.

19Praise be to the Lord, to God our
    Savior,
  who daily bears our burdens.
                  Selah
20Our God is a God who saves;
  from the Sovereign LORD comes
    escape from death.

21Surely God will crush the heads
    of his enemies,
  the hairy crowns of those who
    go on in their sins.
22The Lord says, "I will bring them
    from Bashan;
  I will bring them from the
    depths of the sea,
23that you may plunge your feet in
    the blood of your foes,

---

a4 Or / *prepare the way for him who rides through the deserts*   b6 Or *the desolate in a homeland*
c13 Or *saddlebags*   d14 Hebrew *Shaddai*   e18 Or *gifts for men, / even*   f18 Or *they*

while the tongues of your dogs
  have their share.''

24Your procession has come into
    view, O God,
  the procession of my God and
    King into the sanctuary.
25In front are the singers, after
    them the musicians;
  with them are the maidens
    playing tambourines.
26Praise God in the great
    congregation;
  praise the LORD in the assembly
    of Israel.
27There is the little tribe of
    Benjamin, leading them,
  there the great throng of
    Judah's princes,
  and there the princes of
    Zebulun and of Naphtali.

28Summon your power, O Goda;
  show us your strength, O God,
    as you have done before.
29Because of your temple at
    Jerusalem
  kings will bring you gifts.
30Rebuke the beast among the
    reeds,
  the herd of bulls among the
    calves of the nations.
  Humbled, may it bring bars of
    silver.
  Scatter the nations who delight
    in war.
31Envoys will come from Egypt;
  Cushb will submit herself to
    God.

32Sing to God, O kingdoms of the
    earth,
  sing praise to the Lord,
                              Selah
33to him who rides the ancient
    skies above,
  who thunders with mighty
    voice.
34Proclaim the power of God,
  whose majesty is over Israel,
  whose power is in the skies.
35You are awesome, O God, in your
    sanctuary;

the God of Israel gives power
  and strength to his people.

Praise be to God!

Psalm 69

For the director of music. To the tune
of "Lilies." Of David.

1Save me, O God,
  for the waters have come up to
    my neck.
2I sink in the miry depths,
  where there is no foothold.
  I have come into the deep waters;
    the floods engulf me.
3I am worn out calling for help;
  my throat is parched.
  My eyes fail,
    looking for my God.
4Those who hate me without
    reason
  outnumber the hairs of my
    head;
  many are my enemies without
    cause,
    those who seek to destroy me.
  I am forced to restore
    what I did not steal.

5You know my folly, O God;
  my guilt is not hidden from
    you.

6May those who hope in you
  not be disgraced because of me,
  O Lord, the LORD Almighty;
  may those who seek you
  not be put to shame because of
    me,
  O God of Israel.
7For I endure scorn for your sake,
  and shame covers my face.
8I am a stranger to my brothers,
  an alien to my own mother's
    sons;
9for zeal for your house consumes
    me,
  and the insults of those who
    insult you fall on me.
10When I weep and fast,
  I must endure scorn;
11when I put on sackcloth,

a28 Many Hebrew manuscripts, Septuagint and Syriac; most Hebrew manuscripts Your God has
summoned power for you   b31 That is, the upper Nile region

people make sport of me.
¹²Those who sit at the gate mock
     me,
  and I am the song of the
     drunkards.

¹³But I pray to you, O Lord,
  in the time of your favor;
  in your great love, O God,
     answer me with your sure
     salvation.
¹⁴Rescue me from the mire,
  do not let me sink;
  deliver me from those who hate
     me,
  from the deep waters.
¹⁵Do not let the floodwaters engulf
     me
  or the depths swallow me up
  or the pit close its mouth over
     me.
¹⁶Answer me, O Lord, out of the
     goodness of your love;
  in your great mercy turn to me.
¹⁷Do not hide your face from your
     servant;
  answer me quickly, for I am in
     trouble.
¹⁸Come near and rescue me;
  redeem me because of my foes.

¹⁹You know how I am scorned,
     disgraced and shamed;
  all my enemies are before you.
²⁰Scorn has broken my heart
  and has left me helpless;
  I looked for sympathy, but there
     was none,
  for comforters, but I found none.
²¹They put gall in my food
  and gave me vinegar for my
     thirst.

²²May the table set before them
     become a snare;
  may it become retribution and*a*
     a trap.
²³May their eyes be darkened so
     they cannot see,
  and their backs be bent forever.
²⁴Pour out your wrath on them;
  let your fierce anger overtake
     them.
²⁵May their place be deserted;

let there be no one to dwell in
     their tents.
²⁶For they persecute those you
     wound
  and talk about the pain of those
     you hurt.
²⁷Charge them with crime upon
     crime;
  do not let them share in your
     salvation.
²⁸May they be blotted out of the
     book of life
  and not be listed with the
     righteous.

²⁹I am in pain and distress;
  may your salvation, O God,
     protect me.

³⁰I will praise God's name in song
  and glorify him with
     thanksgiving.
³¹This will please the Lord more
     than an ox,
  more than a bull with its horns
     and hoofs.
³²The poor will see and be glad—
  you who seek God, may your
     hearts live!
³³The Lord hears the needy
  and does not despise his captive
     people.

³⁴Let heaven and earth praise him,
  the seas and all that move in
     them,
³⁵for God will save Zion
  and rebuild the cities of Judah.
  Then people will settle there and
     possess it;
36   the children of his servants will
     inherit it,
  and those who love his name
     will dwell there.

Psalm 70

For the director of music. Of David.
A petition.

¹Hasten, O God, to save me;
  O Lord, come quickly to help
     me.
²May those who seek my life
  be put to shame and confusion;

---

*a*22 Or *snare / and their fellowship become*

may all who desire my ruin
  be turned back in disgrace.
3May those who say to me, "Aha!
    Aha!"
  turn back because of their
    shame.
4But may all who seek you
  rejoice and be glad in you;
may those who love your
    salvation always say,
  "Let God be exalted!"

5Yet I am poor and needy;
  come quickly to me, O God.
You are my help and my
    deliverer;
  O LORD, do not delay.

Psalm 71

1In you, O LORD, I have taken
    refuge;
  let me never be put to shame.
2Rescue me and deliver me in your
    righteousness;
  turn your ear to me and save
    me.
3Be my rock of refuge,
  to which I can always go;
give the command to save me,
  for you are my rock and my
    fortress.
4Deliver me, O my God, from the
    hand of the wicked,
  from the grasp of evil and cruel
    men.

5For you have been my hope,
  O Sovereign LORD,
  my confidence since my youth.
6From birth I have relied on you;

you brought me forth from my
    mother's womb.
  I will ever praise you.
7I have become like a portent to
    many,
  but you are my strong refuge.
8My mouth is filled with your
    praise,
  declaring your splendor all day
    long.

9Do not cast me away when I am
    old;
  do not forsake me when my
    strength is gone.
10For my enemies speak against
    me;
  those who wait to kill me
    conspire together.
11They say, "God has forsaken him;
  pursue him and seize him,
  for no one will rescue him."
12Be not far from me, O God;
  come quickly, O my God, to
    help me.
13May my accusers perish in
    shame;
  may those who want to harm
    me
  be covered with scorn and
    disgrace.

14But as for me, I will always have
    hope;
  I will praise you more and
    more.
15My mouth will tell of your
    righteousness,
  of your salvation all day long,
  though I know not its measure.
16I will come and proclaim your

Life in Bible Times

WHAT GOD IS LIKE

Psalm 71:3 says God is a rock of refuge. Some cities and forts were built on high rocky mountain cliffs. To call God a rock of refuge means we are safest when we trust in him.

mighty acts, O Sovereign
LORD;
I will proclaim your
righteousness, yours alone.
17Since my youth, O God, you have
taught me,
and to this day I declare your
marvelous deeds.
18Even when I am old and gray,
do not forsake me, O God,
till I declare your power to the
next generation,
your might to all who are to
come.

19Your righteousness reaches to the
skies, O God,
you who have done great
things.
Who, O God, is like you?
20Though you have made me see
troubles, many and bitter,
you will restore my life again;
from the depths of the earth
you will again bring me up.
21You will increase my honor
and comfort me once again.

22I will praise you with the harp
for your faithfulness, O my God;
I will sing praise to you with the
lyre,
O Holy One of Israel.
23My lips will shout for joy
when I sing praise to you—
I, whom you have redeemed.
24My tongue will tell of your
righteous acts
all day long,
for those who wanted to harm me
have been put to shame and
confusion.

Psalm 72

Of Solomon.

1Endow the king with your justice,
O God,
the royal son with your
righteousness.
2He willᵃ judge your people in
righteousness,

your afflicted ones with justice.
3The mountains will bring
prosperity to the people,
the hills the fruit of
righteousness.
4He will defend the afflicted
among the people
and save the children of the
needy;
he will crush the oppressor.

5He will endureᵇ as long as the
sun,
as long as the moon, through
all generations.
6He will be like rain falling on a
mown field,
like showers watering the
earth.
7In his days the righteous will
flourish;
prosperity will abound till the
moon is no more.

8He will rule from sea to sea
and from the Riverᶜ to the ends
of the earth.ᵈ
9The desert tribes will bow before
him
and his enemies will lick the
dust.
10The kings of Tarshish and of
distant shores
will bring tribute to him;
the kings of Sheba and Seba
will present him gifts.
11All kings will bow down to him
and all nations will serve him.

12For he will deliver the needy who
cry out,
the afflicted who have no one to
help.
13He will take pity on the weak
and the needy
and save the needy from death.
14He will rescue them from
oppression and violence,
for precious is their blood in his
sight.

15Long may he live!
May gold from Sheba be given
him.

ᵃ2 Or *May he*; similarly in verses 3-11 and 17   ᵇ5 Septuagint; Hebrew *You will be feared*
ᶜ8 That is, the Euphrates   ᵈ8 Or *the end of the land*

May people ever pray for him
and bless him all day long.
16Let grain abound throughout the
land;
on the tops of the hills may it
sway.
Let its fruit flourish like Lebanon;
let it thrive like the grass of the
field.
17May his name endure forever;
may it continue as long as the
sun.

All nations will be blessed
through him,
and they will call him blessed.

18Praise be to the Lord God, the
God of Israel,
who alone does marvelous
deeds.
19Praise be to his glorious name
forever;
may the whole earth be filled
with his glory.
Amen and Amen.

20This concludes the prayers of
David son of Jesse.

BOOK III

Psalms 73–89

Psalm 73

A psalm of Asaph.

1Surely God is good to Israel,
to those who are pure in heart.

2But as for me, my feet had almost
slipped;
I had nearly lost my foothold.
3For I envied the arrogant
when I saw the prosperity of
the wicked.

4They have no struggles;
their bodies are healthy and
strong.*a*

5They are free from the burdens
common to man;
they are not plagued by human
ills.
6Therefore pride is their necklace;
they clothe themselves with
violence.
7From their callous hearts comes
iniquity *b*;
the evil conceits of their minds
know no limits.
8They scoff, and speak with malice;
in their arrogance they threaten
oppression.
9Their mouths lay claim to heaven,
and their tongues take
possession of the earth.
10Therefore their people turn to
them
and drink up waters in
abundance.*c*
11They say, "How can God know?
Does the Most High have
knowledge?"

12This is what the wicked are
like—
always carefree, they increase
in wealth.

13Surely in vain have I kept my
heart pure;
in vain have I washed my
hands in innocence.
14All day long I have been plagued;
I have been punished every
morning.

15If I had said, "I will speak thus,"
I would have betrayed your
children.
16When I tried to understand all
this,
it was oppressive to me
17till I entered the sanctuary of
God;
then I understood their final
destiny.

18Surely you place them on slippery
ground;
you cast them down to ruin.
19How suddenly are they destroyed,

---

*a4 With a different word division of the Hebrew; Masoretic Text struggles at their death; / their
bodies are healthy   b7 Syriac (see also Septuagint); Hebrew Their eyes bulge with fat
c10 The meaning of the Hebrew for this verse is uncertain.*

completely swept away by
terrors!
20As a dream when one awakes,
so when you arise, O Lord,
you will despise them as
fantasies.

21When my heart was grieved
and my spirit embittered,
22I was senseless and ignorant;
I was a brute beast before you.

23Yet I am always with you;
you hold me by my right hand.
24You guide me with your counsel,
and afterward you will take me
into glory.

WORDS TO REMEMBER

73:24 You guide me with your
counsel,
and afterward you will
take me into glory.

25Whom have I in heaven but you?
And earth has nothing I desire
besides you.
26My flesh and my heart may fail,
but God is the strength of my
heart
and my portion forever.

27Those who are far from you will
perish;
you destroy all who are
unfaithful to you.
28But as for me, it is good to be
near God.
I have made the Sovereign LORD
my refuge;
I will tell of all your deeds.

Psalm 74

A maskil[a] of Asaph.

1Why have you rejected us forever,
O God?
Why does your anger smolder
against the sheep of your
pasture?

2Remember the people you
purchased of old,
the tribe of your inheritance,
whom you redeemed—
Mount Zion, where you dwelt.
3Turn your steps toward these
everlasting ruins,
all this destruction the enemy
has brought on the
sanctuary.

4Your foes roared in the place
where you met with us;
they set up their standards as
signs.
5They behaved like men wielding
axes
to cut through a thicket of
trees.
6They smashed all the carved
paneling
with their axes and hatchets.
7They burned your sanctuary to
the ground;
they defiled the dwelling place
of your Name.
8They said in their hearts, "We
will crush them
completely!"
They burned every place where
God was worshiped in the
land.
9We are given no miraculous signs;
no prophets are left,
and none of us knows how long
this will be.

10How long will the enemy mock
you, O God?
Will the foe revile your name
forever?
11Why do you hold back your hand,
your right hand?
Take it from the folds of your
garment and destroy them!

12But you, O God, are my king
from of old;
you bring salvation upon the
earth.
13It was you who split open the sea
by your power;
you broke the heads of the
monster in the waters.

aTitle: Probably a literary or musical term

¹⁴It was you who crushed the heads
of Leviathan
and gave him as food to the
creatures of the desert.
¹⁵It was you who opened up springs
and streams;
you dried up the ever flowing
rivers.
¹⁶The day is yours, and yours also
the night;
you established the sun and
moon.
¹⁷It was you who set all the
boundaries of the earth;
you made both summer and
winter.

¹⁸Remember how the enemy has
mocked you, O LORD,
how foolish people have reviled
your name.
¹⁹Do not hand over the life of your
dove to wild beasts;
do not forget the lives of your
afflicted people forever.
²⁰Have regard for your covenant,
because haunts of violence fill
the dark places of the land.
²¹Do not let the oppressed retreat
in disgrace;
may the poor and needy praise
your name.

²²Rise up, O God, and defend your
cause;
remember how fools mock you
all day long.
²³Do not ignore the clamor of your
adversaries,
the uproar of your enemies,
which rises continually.

Psalm 75

For the director of music. To the tune
of "Do Not Destroy." A psalm of
Asaph. A song.

¹We give thanks to you, O God,
we give thanks, for your Name
is near;
men tell of your wonderful
deeds.

²You say, "I choose the appointed
time;
it is I who judge uprightly.

³When the earth and all its people
quake,
it is I who hold its pillars firm.
Selah
⁴To the arrogant I say, 'Boast no
more,'
and to the wicked, 'Do not lift
up your horns.
⁵Do not lift your horns against
heaven;
do not speak with outstretched
neck.'"

⁶No one from the east or the west
or from the desert can exalt a
man.
⁷But it is God who judges:
He brings one down, he exalts
another.
⁸In the hand of the LORD is a cup
full of foaming wine mixed with
spices;
he pours it out, and all the
wicked of the earth
drink it down to its very dregs.

⁹As for me, I will declare this
forever;
I will sing praise to the God of
Jacob.
¹⁰I will cut off the horns of all the
wicked,
but the horns of the righteous
will be lifted up.

Psalm 76

For the director of music. With
stringed instruments. A psalm of
Asaph. A song.

¹In Judah God is known;
his name is great in Israel.
²His tent is in Salem,
his dwelling place in Zion.
³There he broke the flashing
arrows,
the shields and the swords, the
weapons of war. *Selah*

⁴You are resplendent with light,
more majestic than mountains
rich with game.
⁵Valiant men lie plundered,
they sleep their last sleep;
not one of the warriors
can lift his hands.

⁶At your rebuke, O God of Jacob,
  both horse and chariot lie still.
⁷You alone are to be feared.
  Who can stand before you when
    you are angry?
⁸From heaven you pronounced
    judgment,
  and the land feared and was
    quiet—
⁹when you, O God, rose up to
    judge,
  to save all the afflicted of the
    land.   *Selah*
¹⁰Surely your wrath against men
    brings you praise,
  and the survivors of your wrath
    are restrained.ᵃ

¹¹Make vows to the LORD your God
    and fulfill them;
  let all the neighboring lands
    bring gifts to the One to be
    feared.
¹²He breaks the spirit of rulers;
  he is feared by the kings of the
    earth.

Psalm 77

For the director of music. For
Jeduthun. Of Asaph. A psalm.

¹I cried out to God for help;
  I cried out to God to hear me.
²When I was in distress, I sought
    the Lord;
  at night I stretched out untiring
    hands
  and my soul refused to be
    comforted.

³I remembered you, O God, and I
    groaned;
  I mused, and my spirit grew
    faint.   *Selah*
⁴You kept my eyes from closing;
  I was too troubled to speak.
⁵I thought about the former days,
  the years of long ago;
⁶I remembered my songs in the
    night.
  My heart mused and my spirit
    inquired:

⁷"Will the Lord reject forever?
  Will he never show his favor
    again?
⁸Has his unfailing love vanished
    forever?
  Has his promise failed for all
    time?
⁹Has God forgotten to be merciful?
  Has he in anger withheld his
    compassion?"   *Selah*

¹⁰Then I thought, "To this I will
    appeal:
  the years of the right hand of
    the Most High."
¹¹I will remember the deeds of the
    LORD;
  yes, I will remember your
    miracles of long ago.
¹²I will meditate on all your works
  and consider all your mighty
    deeds.

WORDS TO REMEMBER

**77:12 I will meditate on all your
works
and consider all your
mighty deeds.**

¹³Your ways, O God, are holy.
  What god is so great as our
    God?
¹⁴You are the God who performs
    miracles;
  you display your power among
    the peoples.
¹⁵With your mighty arm you
    redeemed your people,
  the descendants of Jacob and
    Joseph.   *Selah*

¹⁶The waters saw you, O God,
  the waters saw you and
    writhed;
  the very depths were convulsed.
¹⁷The clouds poured down water,
  the skies resounded with
    thunder;
  your arrows flashed back and
    forth.

ᵃ10 Or *Surely the wrath of men brings you praise, / and with the remainder of wrath you arm*
yourself

18Your thunder was heard in the
whirlwind,
your lightning lit up the world;
the earth trembled and quaked.
19Your path led through the sea,
your way through the mighty
waters,
though your footprints were not
seen.

20You led your people like a flock
by the hand of Moses and
Aaron.

Psalm 78

A *maskil*[a] of Asaph.

1O my people, hear my teaching;
listen to the words of my
mouth.
2I will open my mouth in parables,
I will utter hidden things,
things from of old—
3what we have heard and known,
what our fathers have told us.
4We will not hide them from their
children;
we will tell the next generation
the praiseworthy deeds of the
Lord,
his power, and the wonders he
has done.
5He decreed statutes for Jacob
and established the law in
Israel,
which he commanded our
forefathers
to teach their children,
6so the next generation would
know them,
even the children yet to be
born,
and they in turn would tell
their children.
7Then they would put their trust
in God
and would not forget his deeds
but would keep his commands.
8They would not be like their
forefathers—
a stubborn and rebellious
generation,

whose hearts were not loyal to
God,
whose spirits were not faithful
to him.

9The men of Ephraim, though
armed with bows,
turned back on the day of
battle;
10they did not keep God's covenant
and refused to live by his law.
11They forgot what he had done,
the wonders he had shown
them.
12He did miracles in the sight of
their fathers
in the land of Egypt, in the
region of Zoan.
13He divided the sea and led them
through;
he made the water stand firm
like a wall.
14He guided them with the cloud by
day
and with light from the fire all
night.
15He split the rocks in the desert
and gave them water as
abundant as the seas;
16he brought streams out of a rocky
crag
and made water flow down like
rivers.

17But they continued to sin against
him,
rebelling in the desert against
the Most High.
18They willfully put God to the
test
by demanding the food they
craved.
19They spoke against God, saying,
"Can God spread a table in the
desert?
20When he struck the rock, water
gushed out,
and streams flowed abundantly.
But can he also give us food?
Can he supply meat for his
people?"
21When the Lord heard them, he
was very angry;
his fire broke out against Jacob,

---

aTitle: Probably a literary or musical term

and his wrath rose against
Israel,
²²for they did not believe in God
or trust in his deliverance.
²³Yet he gave a command to the
skies above
and opened the doors of the
heavens;
²⁴he rained down manna for the
people to eat,
he gave them the grain of
heaven.
²⁵Men ate the bread of angels;
he sent them all the food they
could eat.
²⁶He let loose the east wind from
the heavens
and led forth the south wind by
his power.
²⁷He rained meat down on them
like dust,
flying birds like sand on the
seashore.
²⁸He made them come down inside
their camp,
all around their tents.
²⁹They ate till they had more than
enough,
for he had given them what
they craved.
³⁰But before they turned from the
food they craved,
even while it was still in their
mouths,
³¹God's anger rose against them;
he put to death the sturdiest
among them,
cutting down the young men of
Israel.

³²In spite of all this, they kept on
sinning;
in spite of his wonders, they did
not believe.
³³So he ended their days in futility
and their years in terror.
³⁴Whenever God slew them, they
would seek him;
they eagerly turned to him
again.
³⁵They remembered that God was
their Rock,
that God Most High was their
Redeemer.

³⁶But then they would flatter him
with their mouths,
lying to him with their tongues;
³⁷their hearts were not loyal to
him,
they were not faithful to his
covenant.
³⁸Yet he was merciful;
he forgave their iniquities
and did not destroy them.
Time after time he restrained his
anger
and did not stir up his full
wrath.
³⁹He remembered that they were
but flesh,
a passing breeze that does not
return.

⁴⁰How often they rebelled against
him in the desert
and grieved him in the
wasteland!
⁴¹Again and again they put God to
the test;
they vexed the Holy One of
Israel.
⁴²They did not remember his
power—
the day he redeemed them from
the oppressor,
⁴³the day he displayed his
miraculous signs in Egypt,
his wonders in the region of
Zoan.
⁴⁴He turned their rivers to blood;
they could not drink from their
streams.
⁴⁵He sent swarms of flies that
devoured them,
and frogs that devastated them.
⁴⁶He gave their crops to the
grasshopper,
their produce to the locust.
⁴⁷He destroyed their vines with
hail
and their sycamore-figs with
sleet.
⁴⁸He gave over their cattle to the
hail,
their livestock to bolts of
lightning.
⁴⁹He unleashed against them his
hot anger,

his wrath, indignation and
hostility—
a band of destroying angels.
⁵⁰He prepared a path for his
anger;
he did not spare them from
death
but gave them over to the
plague.
⁵¹He struck down all the firstborn
of Egypt,
the firstfruits of manhood in the
tents of Ham.
⁵²But he brought his people out
like a flock;
he led them like sheep through
the desert.
⁵³He guided them safely, so they
were unafraid;
but the sea engulfed their
enemies.
⁵⁴Thus he brought them to the
border of his holy land,
to the hill country his right
hand had taken.
⁵⁵He drove out nations before
them
and allotted their lands to them
as an inheritance;
he settled the tribes of Israel in
their homes.
⁵⁶But they put God to the test
and rebelled against the Most
High;
they did not keep his statutes.
⁵⁷Like their fathers they were
disloyal and faithless,
as unreliable as a faulty bow.
⁵⁸They angered him with their high
places;
they aroused his jealousy with
their idols.
⁵⁹When God heard them, he was
very angry;
he rejected Israel completely.
⁶⁰He abandoned the tabernacle of
Shiloh,
the tent he had set up among
men.
⁶¹He sent the ark of his might into
captivity,
his splendor into the hands of
the enemy.

⁶²He gave his people over to the
sword;
he was very angry with his
inheritance.
⁶³Fire consumed their young men,
and their maidens had no
wedding songs;
⁶⁴their priests were put to the
sword,
and their widows could not
weep.

⁶⁵Then the Lord awoke as from
sleep,
as a man wakes from the stupor
of wine.
⁶⁶He beat back his enemies;
he put them to everlasting
shame.
⁶⁷Then he rejected the tents of
Joseph,
he did not choose the tribe of
Ephraim;
⁶⁸but he chose the tribe of Judah,
Mount Zion, which he loved.
⁶⁹He built his sanctuary like the
heights,
like the earth that he
established forever.
⁷⁰He chose David his servant
and took him from the sheep
pens;
⁷¹from tending the sheep he
brought him
to be the shepherd of his people
Jacob,
of Israel his inheritance.
⁷²And David shepherded them with
integrity of heart;
with skillful hands he led them.

Psalm 79

A psalm of Asaph.

¹O God, the nations have invaded
your inheritance;
they have defiled your holy
temple,
they have reduced Jerusalem to
rubble.
²They have given the dead bodies
of your servants
as food to the birds of the air,

the flesh of your saints to the
beasts of the earth.
³They have poured out blood like
water
all around Jerusalem,
and there is no one to bury the
dead.
⁴We are objects of reproach to our
neighbors,
of scorn and derision to those
around us.

⁵How long, O LORD? Will you be
angry forever?
How long will your jealousy
burn like fire?
⁶Pour out your wrath on the
nations
that do not acknowledge
you,
on the kingdoms
that do not call on your name;
⁷for they have devoured Jacob
and destroyed his homeland.
⁸Do not hold against us the sins of
the fathers;
may your mercy come quickly
to meet us,
for we are in desperate need.

⁹Help us, O God our Savior,
for the glory of your name;
deliver us and forgive our sins
for your name's sake.
¹⁰Why should the nations say,
"Where is their God?"
Before our eyes, make known
among the nations
that you avenge the outpoured
blood of your servants.
¹¹May the groans of the prisoners
come before you;
by the strength of your arm
preserve those condemned to
die.

¹²Pay back into the laps of our
neighbors seven times
the reproach they have hurled
at you, O Lord.
¹³Then we your people, the sheep of
your pasture,
will praise you forever;
from generation to generation
we will recount your praise.

Psalm 80

For the director of music. To ⌊the tune
of⌋ "The Lilies of the Covenant."
Of Asaph. A psalm.

¹Hear us, O Shepherd of Israel,
you who lead Joseph like a
flock;

Words to Remember

**79:13 We your people, the sheep
of your pasture,
will praise you forever.**

---

you who sit enthroned between
the cherubim, shine forth
2 before Ephraim, Benjamin and
Manasseh.
Awaken your might;
come and save us.

³Restore us, O God;
make your face shine upon us,
that we may be saved.

⁴O LORD God Almighty,
how long will your anger
smolder
against the prayers of your
people?
⁵You have fed them with the bread
of tears;
you have made them drink
tears by the bowlful.
⁶You have made us a source of
contention to our neighbors,
and our enemies mock us.

⁷Restore us, O God Almighty;
make your face shine upon us,
that we may be saved.

⁸You brought a vine out of Egypt;
you drove out the nations and
planted it.
⁹You cleared the ground for it,
and it took root and filled the
land.
¹⁰The mountains were covered with
its shade,
the mighty cedars with its
branches.

¹¹It sent out its boughs to the Sea,ᵃ
  its shoots as far as the River.ᵇ

¹²Why have you broken down its
    walls
  so that all who pass by pick its
    grapes?
¹³Boars from the forest ravage it
  and the creatures of the field
    feed on it.
¹⁴Return to us, O God Almighty!
  Look down from heaven and
    see!
  Watch over this vine,
¹⁵ the root your right hand has
    planted,
  the sonᶜ you have raised up for
    yourself.

¹⁶Your vine is cut down, it is
    burned with fire;
  at your rebuke your people
    perish.
¹⁷Let your hand rest on the man at
    your right hand,
  the son of man you have raised
    up for yourself.
¹⁸Then we will not turn away from
    you;
  revive us, and we will call on
    your name.

¹⁹Restore us, O LORD God
    Almighty;
  make your face shine upon us,
  that we may be saved.

Psalm 81

For the director of music. According to
  *gittith.*ᵈ Of Asaph.

¹Sing for joy to God our strength;
  shout aloud to the God of Jacob!
²Begin the music, strike the
    tambourine,
  play the melodious harp and
    lyre.

³Sound the ram's horn at the New
    Moon,
  and when the moon is full, on
    the day of our Feast;

⁴this is a decree for Israel,
  an ordinance of the God of
    Jacob.
⁵He established it as a statute for
    Joseph
  when he went out against
    Egypt,
  where we heard a language we
    did not understand.ᵉ

⁶He says, "I removed the burden
    from their shoulders;
  their hands were set free from
    the basket.
⁷In your distress you called and I
    rescued you,
  I answered you out of a
    thundercloud;
  I tested you at the waters of
    Meribah.   *Selah*

⁸"Hear, O my people, and I will
    warn you—
  if you would but listen to me,
    O Israel!
⁹You shall have no foreign god
    among you;
  you shall not bow down to an
    alien god.
¹⁰I am the LORD your God,
  who brought you up out of
    Egypt.
  Open wide your mouth and I
    will fill it.

¹¹"But my people would not listen
    to me;
  Israel would not submit to me.
¹²So I gave them over to their
    stubborn hearts
  to follow their own devices.

¹³"If my people would but listen to
    me,
  if Israel would follow my ways,
¹⁴how quickly would I subdue their
    enemies
  and turn my hand against their
    foes!
¹⁵Those who hate the LORD would
    cringe before him,
  and their punishment would
    last forever.

ᵃ11 Probably the Mediterranean   ᵇ11 That is, the Euphrates   ᶜ15 Or *branch*   ᵈTitle:
Probably a musical term   ᵉ5 Or / *and we heard a voice we had not known*

[16]But you would be fed with the
finest of wheat;
with honey from the rock I
would satisfy you."

Psalm 82

A psalm of Asaph.

[1]God presides in the great
assembly;
he gives judgment among the
"gods":

[2]"How long will you[a] defend the
unjust
and show partiality to the
wicked?   *Selah*
[3]Defend the cause of the weak and
fatherless;
maintain the rights of the poor
and oppressed.
[4]Rescue the weak and needy;
deliver them from the hand of
the wicked.

[5]"They know nothing, they
understand nothing.
They walk about in darkness;
all the foundations of the earth
are shaken.

[6]"I said, 'You are "gods";
you are all sons of the Most
High.'
[7]But you will die like mere men;
you will fall like every other
ruler."

[8]Rise up, O God, judge the earth,
for all the nations are your
inheritance.

Psalm 83

A song. A psalm of Asaph.

[1]O God, do not keep silent;
be not quiet, O God, be not
still.
[2]See how your enemies are astir,
how your foes rear their
heads.

[3]With cunning they conspire
against your people;
they plot against those you
cherish.
[4]"Come," they say, "let us destroy
them as a nation,
that the name of Israel be
remembered no more."

[5]With one mind they plot together;
they form an alliance against
you—
[6]the tents of Edom and the
Ishmaelites,
of Moab and the Hagrites,
[7]Gebal,[b] Ammon and Amalek,
Philistia, with the people of
Tyre.
[8]Even Assyria has joined them
to lend strength to the
descendants of Lot.   *Selah*

[9]Do to them as you did to Midian,
as you did to Sisera and Jabin
at the river Kishon,
[10]who perished at Endor
and became like refuse on the
ground.
[11]Make their nobles like Oreb and
Zeeb,
all their princes like Zebah and
Zalmunna,
[12]who said, "Let us take possession
of the pasturelands of God."

[13]Make them like tumbleweed,
O my God,
like chaff before the wind.
[14]As fire consumes the forest
or a flame sets the mountains
ablaze,
[15]so pursue them with your tempest
and terrify them with your
storm.
[16]Cover their faces with shame
so that men will seek your
name, O LORD.

[17]May they ever be ashamed and
dismayed;
may they perish in disgrace.
[18]Let them know that you, whose
name is the LORD—
that you alone are the Most
High over all the earth.

*a*2 The Hebrew is plural.   *b*7 That is, Byblos

Psalm 84

For the director of music. According to *gittith.ᵃ* Of the Sons of Korah. A psalm.

¹How lovely is your dwelling place,
O Lord Almighty!
²My soul yearns, even faints,
for the courts of the Lord;
my heart and my flesh cry out
for the living God.

³Even the sparrow has found a
home,
and the swallow a nest for
herself,
where she may have her
young—
a place near your altar,
O Lord Almighty, my King and
my God.
⁴Blessed are those who dwell in
your house;
they are ever praising you.
Selah

⁵Blessed are those whose strength
is in you,
who have set their hearts on
pilgrimage.
⁶As they pass through the Valley
of Baca,
they make it a place of springs;
the autumn rains also cover it
with pools.ᵇ
⁷They go from strength to
strength,
till each appears before God in
Zion.

⁸Hear my prayer, O Lord God
Almighty;
listen to me, O God of Jacob.
Selah
⁹Look upon our shield,ᶜ O God;
look with favor on your
anointed one.

¹⁰Better is one day in your courts
than a thousand elsewhere;
I would rather be a doorkeeper in
the house of my God
than dwell in the tents of the
wicked.

¹¹For the Lord God is a sun and
shield;
the Lord bestows favor and
honor;
no good thing does he withhold
from those whose walk is
blameless.

¹²O Lord Almighty,
blessed is the man who trusts
in you.

Psalm 85

For the director of music. Of the Sons of Korah. A psalm.

¹You showed favor to your land,
O Lord;
you restored the fortunes of
Jacob.
²You forgave the iniquity of your
people
and covered all their sins. *Selah*
³You set aside all your wrath
and turned from your fierce
anger.

⁴Restore us again, O God our
Savior,
and put away your displeasure
toward us.
⁵Will you be angry with us
forever?
Will you prolong your anger
through all generations?
⁶Will you not revive us again,
that your people may rejoice in
you?
⁷Show us your unfailing love,
O Lord,
and grant us your salvation.

⁸I will listen to what God the Lord
will say;
he promises peace to his people,
his saints—
but let them not return to folly.
⁹Surely his salvation is near those
who fear him,
that his glory may dwell in our
land.

¹⁰Love and faithfulness meet
together;

ᵃTitle: Probably a musical term   ᵇ6 Or *blessings*   ᶜ9 Or *sovereign*

righteousness and peace kiss
each other.
[11]Faithfulness springs forth from
the earth,
and righteousness looks down
from heaven.
[12]The LORD will indeed give what is
good,
and our land will yield its
harvest.
[13]Righteousness goes before him
and prepares the way for his
steps.

Psalm 86

A prayer of David.

[1]Hear, O LORD, and answer me,
for I am poor and needy.
[2]Guard my life, for I am devoted to
you.
You are my God; save your
servant
who trusts in you.
[3]Have mercy on me, O Lord,
for I call to you all day long.
[4]Bring joy to your servant,
for to you, O Lord,
I lift up my soul.

[5]You are forgiving and good,
O Lord,
abounding in love to all who
call to you.
[6]Hear my prayer, O LORD;
listen to my cry for mercy.
[7]In the day of my trouble I will
call to you,
for you will answer me.

[8]Among the gods there is none like
you, O Lord;
no deeds can compare with
yours.
[9]All the nations you have made
will come and worship before
you, O Lord;
they will bring glory to your
name.
[10]For you are great and do
marvelous deeds;
you alone are God.

[11]Teach me your way, O LORD,
and I will walk in your truth;
give me an undivided heart,
that I may fear your name.

WORDS TO REMEMBER

**86:11 Teach me your way,
O LORD,
and I will walk in your
truth;
give me an undivided
heart,
that I may fear your
name.**

---

[12]I will praise you, O Lord my God,
with all my heart;
I will glorify your name forever.
[13]For great is your love toward me;
you have delivered me from the
depths of the grave.[a]

[14]The arrogant are attacking me,
O God;
a band of ruthless men seeks
my life—
men without regard for you.
[15]But you, O Lord, are a
compassionate and gracious
God,
slow to anger, abounding in
love and faithfulness.
[16]Turn to me and have mercy on
me;
grant your strength to your
servant
and save the son of your
maidservant.[b]
[17]Give me a sign of your goodness,
that my enemies may see it and
be put to shame,
for you, O LORD, have helped
me and comforted me.

Psalm 87

*Of the Sons of Korah. A psalm.
A song.*

[1]He has set his foundation on the
holy mountain;

---

[a]13 Hebrew *Sheol*   [b]16 Or *save your faithful son*

2 the LORD loves the gates of
Zion
more than all the dwellings of
Jacob.
3Glorious things are said of you,
O city of God: *Selah*
4"I will record Rahab*a* and
Babylon
among those who acknowledge
me—
Philistia too, and Tyre, along with
Cush*b*—
and will say, 'This*c* one was
born in Zion.'"

5Indeed, of Zion it will be said,
"This one and that one were
born in her,
and the Most High himself will
establish her."
6The LORD will write in the
register of the peoples:
"This one was born in Zion."
          Selah
7As they make music they will
sing,
"All my fountains are in you."

Psalm 88

A song. A psalm of the Sons of Korah.
For the director of music. According to
mahalath leannoth.^d A *maskil*^e of
Heman the Ezrahite.

1O LORD, the God who saves me,
day and night I cry out before
you.
2May my prayer come before
you;
turn your ear to my cry.

3For my soul is full of trouble
and my life draws near the
grave.*f*
4I am counted among those who go
down to the pit;
I am like a man without
strength.
5I am set apart with the dead,
like the slain who lie in the
grave,
whom you remember no more,
who are cut off from your care.
6You have put me in the lowest
pit,
in the darkest depths.
7Your wrath lies heavily upon me;
you have overwhelmed me with
all your waves.   *Selah*
8You have taken from me my
closest friends
and have made me repulsive to
them.
I am confined and cannot escape;
9 my eyes are dim with grief.

I call to you, O LORD, every day;
I spread out my hands to you.
10Do you show your wonders to the
dead?
Do those who are dead rise up
and praise you?   *Selah*
11Is your love declared in the grave,
your faithfulness in
Destruction*g*?
12Are your wonders known in the
place of darkness,
or your righteous deeds in the
land of oblivion?

13But I cry to you for help, O LORD;
in the morning my prayer
comes before you.
14Why, O LORD, do you reject me
and hide your face from me?

15From my youth I have been
afflicted and close to death;
I have suffered your terrors and
am in despair.
16Your wrath has swept over me;
your terrors have destroyed me.
17All day long they surround me
like a flood;
they have completely engulfed
me.
18You have taken my companions
and loved ones from me;
the darkness is my closest
friend.

---

*a4 A poetic name for Egypt   b4 That is, the upper Nile region   c4 Or "O Rahab and
Babylon, / Philistia, Tyre and Cush, / I will record concerning those who acknowledge me: / 'This
d Title: Possibly a tune, "The Suffering of Affliction"   e Title: Probably a literary or musical term
f3 Hebrew Sheol   g11 Hebrew Abaddon*

Psalm 89

A *maskil*[a] of Ethan the Ezrahite.

[1]I will sing of the LORD's great love
forever;
with my mouth I will make
your faithfulness known
through all generations.
[2]I will declare that your love
stands firm forever,
that you established your
faithfulness in heaven
itself.

[3]You said, "I have made a
covenant with my chosen
one,
I have sworn to David my
servant,
[4]'I will establish your line forever
and make your throne firm
through all generations.' "
Selah

[5]The heavens praise your wonders,
O LORD,
your faithfulness too, in the
assembly of the holy ones.
[6]For who in the skies above can
compare with the LORD?
Who is like the LORD among the
heavenly beings?
[7]In the council of the holy ones
God is greatly feared;
he is more awesome than all
who surround him.
[8]O LORD God Almighty, who is like
you?
You are mighty, O LORD, and
your faithfulness surrounds
you.

[9]You rule over the surging sea;
when its waves mount up, you
still them.
[10]You crushed Rahab like one of
the slain;
with your strong arm you
scattered your enemies.
[11]The heavens are yours, and yours
also the earth;
you founded the world and all
that is in it.

[12]You created the north and the
south;
Tabor and Hermon sing for joy
at your name.
[13]Your arm is endued with power;
your hand is strong, your right
hand exalted.

WHAT GOD IS LIKE

**Psalm 89 says God is "LORD God
Almighty." He is the one who
created the whole universe. Such
a powerful God is surely able to
take care of us.**

[14]Righteousness and justice are the
foundation of your throne;
love and faithfulness go before
you.
[15]Blessed are those who have
learned to acclaim you,
who walk in the light of your
presence, O LORD.
[16]They rejoice in your name all day
long;
they exult in your
righteousness.
[17]For you are their glory and
strength,
and by your favor you exalt our
horn.[b]
[18]Indeed, our shield[c] belongs to the
LORD,
our king to the Holy One of
Israel.

[19]Once you spoke in a vision,
to your faithful people you said:
"I have bestowed strength on a
warrior;
I have exalted a young man
from among the people.
[20]I have found David my servant;

---

[a]Title: Probably a literary or musical term
sovereign   [b]17 *Horn* here symbolizes strong one.   [c]18 Or

with my sacred oil I have
  anointed him.
²¹My hand will sustain him;
  surely my arm will strengthen
    him.
²²No enemy will subject him to
    tribute;
  no wicked man will oppress
    him.
²³I will crush his foes before him
  and strike down his adversaries.
²⁴My faithful love will be with him,
  and through my name his
    horn^a will be exalted.
²⁵I will set his hand over the sea,
  his right hand over the rivers.
²⁶He will call out to me, 'You are
    my Father,
  my God, the Rock my Savior.'
²⁷I will also appoint him my
    firstborn,
  the most exalted of the kings of
    the earth.
²⁸I will maintain my love to him
    forever,
  and my covenant with him will
    never fail.
²⁹I will establish his line forever,
  his throne as long as the
    heavens endure.

³⁰"If his sons forsake my law
  and do not follow my statutes,
³¹if they violate my decrees
  and fail to keep my commands,
³²I will punish their sin with the
    rod,
  their iniquity with flogging;
³³but I will not take my love from
    him,
  nor will I ever betray my
    faithfulness.
³⁴I will not violate my covenant
  or alter what my lips have
    uttered.
³⁵Once for all, I have sworn by my
    holiness—
  and I will not lie to David—
³⁶that his line will continue forever
  and his throne endure before
    me like the sun;
³⁷it will be established forever like
    the moon,

the faithful witness in the sky."
                    Selah
³⁸But you have rejected, you have
    spurned,
  you have been very angry with
    your anointed one.
³⁹You have renounced the covenant
    with your servant
  and have defiled his crown in
    the dust.
⁴⁰You have broken through all his
    walls
  and reduced his strongholds to
    ruins.
⁴¹All who pass by have plundered
    him;
  he has become the scorn of his
    neighbors.
⁴²You have exalted the right hand
    of his foes;
  you have made all his enemies
    rejoice.
⁴³You have turned back the edge of
    his sword
  and have not supported him in
    battle.
⁴⁴You have put an end to his
    splendor
  and cast his throne to the
    ground.
⁴⁵You have cut short the days of
    his youth;
  you have covered him with a
    mantle of shame.   *Selah*

⁴⁶How long, O LORD? Will you hide
    yourself forever?
  How long will your wrath burn
    like fire?
⁴⁷Remember how fleeting is my
    life.
  For what futility you have
    created all men!
⁴⁸What man can live and not see
    death,
  or save himself from the power
    of the grave^b?   *Selah*
⁴⁹O Lord, where is your former
    great love,
  which in your faithfulness you
    swore to David?
⁵⁰Remember, Lord, how your
    servant has^c been mocked,

---

^a24 *Horn* here symbolizes strength.   ^b48 Hebrew *Sheol*   ^c50 Or *your servants have*

how I bear in my heart the
    taunts of all the nations,
⁵¹the taunts with which your
    enemies have mocked,
    O Lᴏʀᴅ,
    with which they have mocked
    every step of your anointed
    one.

⁵²Praise be to the Lᴏʀᴅ forever!
    Amen and Amen.

BOOK IV

Psalms 90–106

Psalm 90

A prayer of Moses the man of God.

¹Lord, you have been our dwelling
    place
    throughout all generations.
²Before the mountains were born
    or you brought forth the earth
    and the world,
    from everlasting to everlasting
    you are God.

³You turn men back to dust,
    saying, "Return to dust, O sons
    of men."
⁴For a thousand years in your
    sight
    are like a day that has just
    gone by,
    or like a watch in the night.
⁵You sweep men away in the sleep
    of death;
    they are like the new grass of
    the morning—
⁶though in the morning it springs
    up new,
    by evening it is dry and
    withered.

⁷We are consumed by your anger
    and terrified by your
    indignation.
⁸You have set our iniquities before
    you,
    our secret sins in the light of
    your presence.

⁹All our days pass away under
    your wrath;
    we finish our years with a
    moan.
¹⁰The length of our days is seventy
    years—
    or eighty, if we have the
    strength;
    yet their span[a] is but trouble and
    sorrow,
    for they quickly pass, and we
    fly away.

¹¹Who knows the power of your
    anger?
    For your wrath is as great as
    the fear that is due you.
¹²Teach us to number our days
    aright,
    that we may gain a heart of
    wisdom.

¹³Relent, O Lᴏʀᴅ! How long will it
    be?
    Have compassion on your
    servants.
¹⁴Satisfy us in the morning with
    your unfailing love,
    that we may sing for joy and be
    glad all our days.
¹⁵Make us glad for as many days as
    you have afflicted us,
    for as many years as we have
    seen trouble.
¹⁶May your deeds be shown to your
    servants,
    your splendor to their children.

¹⁷May the favor[b] of the Lord our
    God rest upon us;
    establish the work of our hands
    for us—
    yes, establish the work of our
    hands.

Psalm 91

¹He who dwells in the shelter of
    the Most High
    will rest in the shadow of the
    Almighty.[c]
²I will say[d] of the Lᴏʀᴅ, "He is my
    refuge and my fortress,
    my God, in whom I trust."

---

a10 Or *yet the best of them*   *b17* Or *beauty*   *c1* Hebrew *Shaddai*   *d2* Or *He says*

³Surely he will save you from the
   fowler's snare
and from the deadly pestilence.
⁴He will cover you with his
   feathers,
   and under his wings you will
      find refuge;
   his faithfulness will be your
      shield and rampart.
⁵You will not fear the terror of
   night,
   nor the arrow that flies by
      day,
⁶nor the pestilence that stalks in
   the darkness,
   nor the plague that destroys at
      midday.
⁷A thousand may fall at your side,
   ten thousand at your right
      hand,
   but it will not come near you.
⁸You will only observe with your
   eyes
   and see the punishment of the
      wicked.

⁹If you make the Most High your
   dwelling—
   even the LORD, who is my
      refuge—
¹⁰then no harm will befall you,
   no disaster will come near your
      tent.
¹¹For he will command his angels
   concerning you
   to guard you in all your ways;
¹²they will lift you up in their
   hands,
   so that you will not strike your
      foot against a stone.
¹³You will tread upon the lion and
   the cobra;
   you will trample the great lion
      and the serpent.

¹⁴"Because he loves me," says the
   LORD, "I will rescue him;
   I will protect him, for he
      acknowledges my name.
¹⁵He will call upon me, and I will
   answer him;
   I will be with him in trouble,
   I will deliver him and honor
      him.

¹⁶With long life will I satisfy him
   and show him my salvation."

Psalm 92

A psalm. A song. For the Sabbath day.

¹It is good to praise the LORD
   and make music to your name,
      O Most High,
²to proclaim your love in the
   morning
   and your faithfulness at night,
³to the music of the ten-stringed
   lyre
   and the melody of the harp.

⁴For you make me glad by your
   deeds, O LORD;
   I sing for joy at the works of
      your hands.
⁵How great are your works,
   O LORD,
   how profound your thoughts!
⁶The senseless man does not know,
   fools do not understand,
⁷that though the wicked spring up
   like grass
   and all evildoers flourish,
   they will be forever destroyed.

⁸But you, O LORD, are exalted
   forever.

⁹For surely your enemies, O LORD,
   surely your enemies will perish;
   all evildoers will be scattered.
¹⁰You have exalted my horn ᵃ like
   that of a wild ox;
   fine oils have been poured upon
      me.
¹¹My eyes have seen the defeat of
   my adversaries;
   my ears have heard the rout of
      my wicked foes.

¹²The righteous will flourish like a
   palm tree,
   they will grow like a cedar of
      Lebanon;
¹³planted in the house of the LORD,
   they will flourish in the courts
      of our God.
¹⁴They will still bear fruit in old
   age,
   they will stay fresh and green,

ᵃ10 Horn here symbolizes strength.

¹⁵proclaiming, "The LORD is
upright;
he is my Rock, and there is no
wickedness in him."

Psalm 93

¹The LORD reigns, he is robed in
majesty;
the LORD is robed in majesty
and is armed with strength.
The world is firmly established;
it cannot be moved.
²Your throne was established long
ago;
you are from all eternity.

³The seas have lifted up, O LORD,
the seas have lifted up their
voice;
the seas have lifted up their
pounding waves.
⁴Mightier than the thunder of the
great waters,
mightier than the breakers of
the sea—
the LORD on high is mighty.

⁵Your statutes stand firm;
holiness adorns your house
for endless days, O LORD.

Psalm 94

¹O LORD, the God who avenges,
O God who avenges, shine forth.
²Rise up, O Judge of the earth;
pay back to the proud what
they deserve.
³How long will the wicked,
O LORD,
how long will the wicked be
jubilant?

⁴They pour out arrogant words;
all the evildoers are full of
boasting.
⁵They crush your people, O LORD;
they oppress your inheritance.
⁶They slay the widow and the
alien;
they murder the fatherless.
⁷They say, "The LORD does not see;
the God of Jacob pays no heed."

⁸Take heed, you senseless ones
among the people;
you fools, when will you become
wise?
⁹Does he who implanted the ear
not hear?
Does he who formed the eye not
see?
¹⁰Does he who disciplines nations
not punish?
Does he who teaches man lack
knowledge?
¹¹The LORD knows the thoughts of
man;
he knows that they are futile.

¹²Blessed is the man you discipline,
O LORD,
the man you teach from your
law;
¹³you grant him relief from days of
trouble,
till a pit is dug for the wicked.
¹⁴For the LORD will not reject his
people;
he will never forsake his
inheritance.
¹⁵Judgment will again be founded
on righteousness,
and all the upright in heart will
follow it.

¹⁶Who will rise up for me against
the wicked?
Who will take a stand for me
against evildoers?
¹⁷Unless the LORD had given me
help,
I would soon have dwelt in the
silence of death.
¹⁸When I said, "My foot is
slipping,"
your love, O LORD, supported
me.
¹⁹When anxiety was great within
me,
your consolation brought joy to
my soul.

²⁰Can a corrupt throne be allied
with you—
one that brings on misery by its
decrees?
²¹They band together against the
righteous
and condemn the innocent to
death.

²²But the Lord has become my
    fortress,
  and my God the rock in whom I
    take refuge.
²³He will repay them for their sins
  and destroy them for their
    wickedness;
  the Lord our God will destroy
    them.

Psalm 95

¹Come, let us sing for joy to the
    Lord;
  let us shout aloud to the Rock
    of our salvation.
²Let us come before him with
    thanksgiving
  and extol him with music and
    song.

³For the Lord is the great God,
  the great King above all
    gods.
⁴In his hand are the depths of the
    earth,
  and the mountain peaks belong
    to him.
⁵The sea is his, for he made it,
  and his hands formed the dry
    land.

⁶Come, let us bow down in
    worship,
  let us kneel before the Lord our
    Maker;
⁷for he is our God
  and we are the people of his
    pasture,
  the flock under his care.

Today, if you hear his voice,

Words to Remember

95:7 He is our God
        and we are the people
        of his pasture,
        the flock under his care.

---

  ⁸ do not harden your hearts as
      you did at Meribah,ᵃ

  as you did that day at Massahᵇ
    in the desert,
⁹where your fathers tested and
    tried me,
  though they had seen what I
    did.
¹⁰For forty years I was angry with
    that generation;
  I said, "They are a people whose
    hearts go astray,
  and they have not known my
    ways."
¹¹So I declared on oath in my
    anger,
  "They shall never enter my
    rest."

Psalm 96

¹Sing to the Lord a new song;
  sing to the Lord, all the earth.
²Sing to the Lord, praise his
    name;
  proclaim his salvation day after
    day.
³Declare his glory among the
    nations,
  his marvelous deeds among all
    peoples.

⁴For great is the Lord and most
    worthy of praise;
  he is to be feared above all
    gods.
⁵For all the gods of the nations are
    idols,
  but the Lord made the heavens.
⁶Splendor and majesty are before
    him;
  strength and glory are in his
    sanctuary.

⁷Ascribe to the Lord, O families of
    nations,
  ascribe to the Lord glory and
    strength.
⁸Ascribe to the Lord the glory due
    his name;
  bring an offering and come into
    his courts.
⁹Worship the Lord in the splendor
    of hisᶜ holiness;
  tremble before him, all the
    earth.

ᵃ8 Meribah means quarreling.   ᵇ8 Massah means testing.   ᶜ9 Or Lord with the splendor of

¹⁰Say among the nations, "The
   LORD reigns."
The world is firmly established,
   it cannot be moved;
   he will judge the peoples with
      equity.
¹¹Let the heavens rejoice, let the
      earth be glad;
   let the sea resound, and all that
      is in it;
¹² let the fields be jubilant, and
      everything in them.
Then all the trees of the forest
   will sing for joy;
¹³ they will sing before the LORD,
      for he comes,
   he comes to judge the earth.
He will judge the world in
   righteousness
   and the peoples in his truth.

Psalm 97

¹The LORD reigns, let the earth be
   glad;
   let the distant shores rejoice.

²Clouds and thick darkness
      surround him;
   righteousness and justice are
      the foundation of his
      throne.
³Fire goes before him
   and consumes his foes on every
      side.
⁴His lightning lights up the world;
   the earth sees and trembles.
⁵The mountains melt like wax
      before the LORD,
   before the Lord of all the earth.
⁶The heavens proclaim his
      righteousness,
   and all the peoples see his
      glory.

⁷All who worship images are put
      to shame,
   those who boast in idols—
   worship him, all you gods!

⁸Zion hears and rejoices
   and the villages of Judah are
      glad
   because of your judgments,
   O LORD.

⁹For you, O LORD, are the Most
      High over all the earth;
   you are exalted far above all
      gods.

¹⁰Let those who love the LORD hate
      evil,
   for he guards the lives of his
      faithful ones
   and delivers them from the
      hand of the wicked.
¹¹Light is shed upon the righteous
   and joy on the upright in heart.
¹²Rejoice in the LORD, you who are
      righteous,
   and praise his holy name.

Psalm 98

A psalm.

¹Sing to the LORD a new song,
   for he has done marvelous
      things;
   his right hand and his holy arm
   have worked salvation for him.
²The LORD has made his salvation
      known
   and revealed his righteousness
      to the nations.
³He has remembered his love
   and his faithfulness to the
      house of Israel;
   all the ends of the earth have
      seen
   the salvation of our God.

⁴Shout for joy to the LORD, all the
      earth,
   burst into jubilant song with
      music;
⁵make music to the LORD with the
      harp,
   with the harp and the sound of
      singing,
⁶with trumpets and the blast of
      the ram's horn—
   shout for joy before the LORD,
      the King.

⁷Let the sea resound, and
      everything in it,
   the world, and all who live in
      it.

8Let the rivers clap their hands,
  let the mountains sing together
    for joy;
9let them sing before the LORD,
  for he comes to judge the
    earth.
He will judge the world in
  righteousness
and the peoples with equity.

Psalm 99

1The LORD reigns,
  let the nations tremble;
he sits enthroned between the
  cherubim,
  let the earth shake.
2Great is the LORD in Zion;
  he is exalted over all the
    nations.
3Let them praise your great and
  awesome name—
  he is holy.

4The King is mighty, he loves
  justice—
  you have established equity;
in Jacob you have done
  what is just and right.
5Exalt the LORD our God
  and worship at his footstool;
  he is holy.

6Moses and Aaron were among his
  priests,
  Samuel was among those who
    called on his name;
they called on the LORD
  and he answered them.
7He spoke to them from the pillar
  of cloud;
  they kept his statutes and the
    decrees he gave them.

8O LORD our God,
  you answered them;
you were to Israel*a* a forgiving
  God,
  though you punished their
    misdeeds.*b*
9Exalt the LORD our God
  and worship at his holy
    mountain,
for the LORD our God is holy.

Psalm 100

A psalm. For giving thanks.

1Shout for joy to the LORD, all the
  earth.
2 Worship the LORD with
  gladness;
  come before him with joyful
    songs.
3Know that the LORD is God.
  It is he who made us, and we
    are his*c*;
  we are his people, the sheep of
    his pasture.

4Enter his gates with thanksgiving
  and his courts with praise;
  give thanks to him and praise
    his name.
5For the LORD is good and his love
  endures forever;
  his faithfulness continues
    through all generations.

Psalm 101

Of David. A psalm.

1I will sing of your love and
  justice;
  to you, O LORD, I will sing
    praise.
2I will be careful to lead a
  blameless life—
  when will you come to me?

I will walk in my house
  with blameless heart.
3I will set before my eyes
  no vile thing.

The deeds of faithless men I hate;
  they will not cling to me.
4Men of perverse heart shall be far
  from me;
  I will have nothing to do with
    evil.

5Whoever slanders his neighbor in
  secret,
  him will I put to silence;
whoever has haughty eyes and a
  proud heart,
  him will I not endure.

---

*a*8 Hebrew *them*   *b*8 Or / *an avenger of the wrongs done to them*   *c*3 Or *and not we ourselves*

⁶My eyes will be on the faithful in
      the land,
    that they may dwell with me;
  he whose walk is blameless
      will minister to me.

⁷No one who practices deceit
    will dwell in my house;
  no one who speaks falsely
    will stand in my presence.

⁸Every morning I will put to
      silence
    all the wicked in the land;
  I will cut off every evildoer
    from the city of the LORD.

Psalm 102

*A prayer of an afflicted man. When he
is faint and pours out his lament
before the LORD.*

¹Hear my prayer, O LORD;
    let my cry for help come to you.
²Do not hide your face from me
    when I am in distress.
  Turn your ear to me;
    when I call, answer me quickly.

³For my days vanish like smoke;
    my bones burn like glowing
      embers.
⁴My heart is blighted and withered
      like grass;
    I forget to eat my food.
⁵Because of my loud groaning
    I am reduced to skin and bones.
⁶I am like a desert owl,
    like an owl among the ruins.
⁷I lie awake; I have become
    like a bird alone on a roof.
⁸All day long my enemies taunt
      me;

those who rail against me use
    my name as a curse.
⁹For I eat ashes as my food
    and mingle my drink with
      tears
¹⁰because of your great wrath,
    for you have taken me up and
      thrown me aside.
¹¹My days are like the evening
      shadow;
    I wither away like grass.

¹²But you, O LORD, sit enthroned
      forever;
    your renown endures through
      all generations.
¹³You will arise and have
      compassion on Zion,
    for it is time to show favor to
      her;
    the appointed time has come.
¹⁴For her stones are dear to your
      servants;
    her very dust moves them to
      pity.
¹⁵The nations will fear the name of
      the LORD,
    all the kings of the earth will
      revere your glory.
¹⁶For the LORD will rebuild Zion
    and appear in his glory.
¹⁷He will respond to the prayer of
      the destitute;
    he will not despise their plea.

¹⁸Let this be written for a future
      generation,
    that a people not yet created
      may praise the LORD:
¹⁹"The LORD looked down from his
      sanctuary on high,
    from heaven he viewed the
      earth,

▩ET'S LIVE IT!   Psalm 102:1-11

TELL GOD YOUR FEELINGS ➡ No one likes to feel upset. Or afraid. Or
angry. But sometimes we all have feelings like these. Read the first eleven
verses of Psalm 102. What words tell you how the psalmist feels?

The person who wrote this psalm knew God would listen to his feelings
and that telling God would help. Next time you're feeling bad, write
your feelings down for God to see. Maybe by the time you're done
writing you'll feel better, just like the person who wrote this psalm (see
Psalm 102:16-17).

²⁰to hear the groans of the
prisoners
and release those condemned to
death."
²¹So the name of the LORD will be
declared in Zion
and his praise in Jerusalem
²²when the peoples and the
kingdoms
assemble to worship the LORD.

²³In the course of my life^a he broke
my strength;
he cut short my days.
²⁴So I said:
"Do not take me away, O my
God, in the midst of my
days;
your years go on through all
generations.
²⁵In the beginning you laid the
foundations of the earth,
and the heavens are the work of
your hands.
²⁶They will perish, but you remain;
they will all wear out like a
garment.
Like clothing you will change
them
and they will be discarded.
²⁷But you remain the same,
and your years will never end.
²⁸The children of your servants will
live in your presence;
their descendants will be
established before you."

Psalm 103

Of David.

¹Praise the LORD, O my soul;
all my inmost being, praise his
holy name.
²Praise the LORD, O my soul,
and forget not all his
benefits—
³who forgives all your sins
and heals all your diseases,
⁴who redeems your life from the
pit
and crowns you with love and
compassion,

⁵who satisfies your desires with
good things
so that your youth is renewed
like the eagle's.

⁶The LORD works righteousness
and justice for all the oppressed.

⁷He made known his ways to
Moses,
his deeds to the people of Israel:
⁸The LORD is compassionate and
gracious,
slow to anger, abounding in
love.
⁹He will not always accuse,
nor will he harbor his anger
forever;
¹⁰he does not treat us as our sins
deserve
or repay us according to our
iniquities.
¹¹For as high as the heavens are
above the earth,
so great is his love for those
who fear him;
¹²as far as the east is from the
west,
so far has he removed our
transgressions from us.
¹³As a father has compassion on his
children,
so the LORD has compassion on
those who fear him;
¹⁴for he knows how we are formed,
he remembers that we are dust.
¹⁵As for man, his days are like
grass,
he flourishes like a flower of
the field;
¹⁶the wind blows over it and it is
gone,
and its place remembers it no
more.
¹⁷But from everlasting to
everlasting
the LORD's love is with those
who fear him,
and his righteousness with their
children's children—
¹⁸with those who keep his covenant
and remember to obey his
precepts.

^a23 Or By his power

¹⁹The LORD has established his
throne in heaven,
and his kingdom rules over all.

²⁰Praise the LORD, you his angels,
you mighty ones who do his
bidding,
who obey his word.
²¹Praise the LORD, all his heavenly
hosts,
you his servants who do his
will.
²²Praise the LORD, all his works
everywhere in his dominion.

Praise the LORD, O my soul.

Psalm 104

¹Praise the LORD, O my soul.

O LORD my God, you are very
great;
you are clothed with splendor
and majesty.
²He wraps himself in light as with
a garment;
he stretches out the heavens
like a tent
³ and lays the beams of his upper
chambers on their waters.
He makes the clouds his chariot
and rides on the wings of the
wind.
⁴He makes winds his messengers,ᵃ
flames of fire his servants.

⁵He set the earth on its
foundations;

ᵃ4 Or angels

it can never be moved.
⁶You covered it with the deep as
with a garment;
the waters stood above the
mountains.
⁷But at your rebuke the waters
fled,
at the sound of your thunder
they took to flight;
⁸they flowed over the mountains,
they went down into the
valleys,
to the place you assigned for
them.
⁹You set a boundary they cannot
cross;
never again will they cover the
earth.

¹⁰He makes springs pour water into
the ravines;
it flows between the mountains.
¹¹They give water to all the beasts
of the field;
the wild donkeys quench their
thirst.
¹²The birds of the air nest by the
waters;
they sing among the branches.
¹³He waters the mountains from
his upper chambers;
the earth is satisfied by the
fruit of his work.
¹⁴He makes grass grow for the
cattle,
and plants for man to
cultivate—
bringing forth food from the
earth:

Life in Bible Times

WHAT GOD IS LIKE

Psalm 103:13 says God is
like a compassionate fa-
ther. This means God loves
us very much. He will not
stay angry when we sin, but
he will forgive us.

¹⁵wine that gladdens the heart of
man,
oil to make his face shine,
and bread that sustains his
heart.
¹⁶The trees of the LORD are well
watered,
the cedars of Lebanon that he
planted.
¹⁷There the birds make their nests;
the stork has its home in the
pine trees.
¹⁸The high mountains belong to the
wild goats;
the crags are a refuge for the
coneys.ᵃ

¹⁹The moon marks off the seasons,
and the sun knows when to go
down.
²⁰You bring darkness, it becomes
night,
and all the beasts of the forest
prowl.
²¹The lions roar for their prey
and seek their food from God.
²²The sun rises, and they steal
away;
they return and lie down in
their dens.
²³Then man goes out to his work,
to his labor until evening.

²⁴How many are your works,
O LORD!
In wisdom you made them all;
the earth is full of your
creatures.
²⁵There is the sea, vast and
spacious,
teeming with creatures beyond
number—
living things both large and
small.
²⁶There the ships go to and fro,
and the leviathan, which you
formed to frolic there.

²⁷These all look to you
to give them their food at the
proper time.
²⁸When you give it to them,
they gather it up;

when you open your hand,
they are satisfied with good
things.
²⁹When you hide your face,
they are terrified;
when you take away their breath,
they die and return to the dust.
³⁰When you send your Spirit,
they are created,
and you renew the face of the
earth.

³¹May the glory of the LORD endure
forever;
may the LORD rejoice in his
works—
³²he who looks at the earth, and it
trembles,
who touches the mountains, and
they smoke.

³³I will sing to the LORD all my life;
I will sing praise to my God as
long as I live.
³⁴May my meditation be pleasing to
him,
as I rejoice in the LORD.
³⁵But may sinners vanish from the
earth
and the wicked be no more.

Praise the LORD, O my soul.

Praise the LORD.ᵇ

Psalm 105

¹Give thanks to the LORD, call on
his name;
make known among the nations
what he has done.
²Sing to him, sing praise to him;
tell of all his wonderful acts.
³Glory in his holy name;
let the hearts of those who seek
the LORD rejoice.
⁴Look to the LORD and his
strength;
seek his face always.

⁵Remember the wonders he has
done,
his miracles, and the judgments
he pronounced,

ᵃ18 That is, the hyrax or rock badger   ᵇ35 Hebrew *Hallelu Yah*; in the Septuagint this line
stands at the beginning of Psalm 105.

⁶O descendants of Abraham his
   servant,
   O sons of Jacob, his chosen
     ones.
⁷He is the LORD our God;
   his judgments are in all the
     earth.

⁸He remembers his covenant
   forever,
   the word he commanded, for a
     thousand generations,
⁹the covenant he made with
   Abraham,
   the oath he swore to Isaac.
¹⁰He confirmed it to Jacob as a
   decree,
   to Israel as an everlasting
     covenant:
¹¹"To you I will give the land of
   Canaan
   as the portion you will inherit."

¹²When they were but few in
   number,
   few indeed, and strangers in it,
¹³they wandered from nation to
   nation,
   from one kingdom to another.
¹⁴He allowed no one to oppress
   them;
   for their sake he rebuked kings:
¹⁵"Do not touch my anointed ones;
   do my prophets no harm."

¹⁶He called down famine on the
   land
   and destroyed all their supplies
     of food;
¹⁷and he sent a man before them—
   Joseph, sold as a slave.
¹⁸They bruised his feet with
   shackles,
   his neck was put in irons,
¹⁹till what he foretold came to pass,
   till the word of the LORD proved
     him true.
²⁰The king sent and released him,
   the ruler of peoples set him
     free.
²¹He made him master of his
   household,
   ruler over all he possessed,
²²to instruct his princes as he
   pleased
   and teach his elders wisdom.

²³Then Israel entered Egypt;
   Jacob lived as an alien in the
     land of Ham.
²⁴The LORD made his people very
   fruitful;
   he made them too numerous for
     their foes,
²⁵whose hearts he turned to hate
   his people,
   to conspire against his servants.
²⁶He sent Moses his servant,
   and Aaron, whom he had
     chosen.
²⁷They performed his miraculous
   signs among them,
   his wonders in the land of Ham.
²⁸He sent darkness and made the
   land dark—
   for had they not rebelled
     against his words?
²⁹He turned their waters into blood,
   causing their fish to die.
³⁰Their land teemed with frogs,
   which went up into the
     bedrooms of their rulers.
³¹He spoke, and there came swarms
   of flies,
   and gnats throughout their
     country.
³²He turned their rain into hail,
   with lightning throughout their
     land;
³³he struck down their vines and
   fig trees
   and shattered the trees of their
     country.
³⁴He spoke, and the locusts came,
   grasshoppers without number;
³⁵they ate up every green thing in
   their land,
   ate up the produce of their soil.
³⁶Then he struck down all the
   firstborn in their land,
   the firstfruits of all their
     manhood.
³⁷He brought out Israel, laden with
   silver and gold,
   and from among their tribes no
     one faltered.
³⁸Egypt was glad when they left,
   because dread of Israel had
     fallen on them.
³⁹He spread out a cloud as a
   covering,

and a fire to give light at night.
40They asked, and he brought them
    quail
and satisfied them with the
    bread of heaven.
41He opened the rock, and water
    gushed out;
like a river it flowed in the
    desert.

42For he remembered his holy
    promise
given to his servant Abraham.
43He brought out his people with
    rejoicing,
his chosen ones with shouts of
    joy;
44he gave them the lands of the
    nations,
and they fell heir to what
    others had toiled for—
45that they might keep his precepts
and observe his laws.

Praise the LORD.*a*

Psalm 106

1Praise the LORD.*b*

Give thanks to the LORD, for he is
    good;
his love endures forever.

WORDS TO REMEMBER

106:1 Give thanks to the LORD, for
    he is good;
        his love endures forever.

2Who can proclaim the mighty acts
    of the LORD
or fully declare his praise?
3Blessed are they who maintain
    justice,
who constantly do what is right.
4Remember me, O LORD, when you
    show favor to your people,
come to my aid when you save
    them,
5that I may enjoy the prosperity of
    your chosen ones,

that I may share in the joy of
    your nation
and join your inheritance in
    giving praise.

6We have sinned, even as our
    fathers did;
we have done wrong and acted
    wickedly.
7When our fathers were in Egypt,
    they gave no thought to your
    miracles;
they did not remember your many
    kindnesses,
and they rebelled by the sea,
    the Red Sea.*c*
8Yet he saved them for his name's
    sake,
to make his mighty power
    known.
9He rebuked the Red Sea, and it
    dried up;
he led them through the depths
    as through a desert.
10He saved them from the hand of
    the foe;
from the hand of the enemy he
    redeemed them.
11The waters covered their
    adversaries;
not one of them survived.
12Then they believed his promises
and sang his praise.
13But they soon forgot what he had
    done
and did not wait for his
    counsel.
14In the desert they gave in to their
    craving;
in the wasteland they put God
    to the test.
15So he gave them what they asked
    for,
but sent a wasting disease upon
    them.
16In the camp they grew envious of
    Moses
and of Aaron, who was
    consecrated to the LORD.
17The earth opened up and
    swallowed Dathan;

---

*a*45 Hebrew *Hallelu Yah*   *b*1 Hebrew *Hallelu Yah*; also in verse 48   *c*7 Hebrew *Yam Suph*;
that is, Sea of Reeds; also in verses 9 and 22

it buried the company of
      Abiram.
¹⁸Fire blazed among their followers;
      a flame consumed the wicked.

¹⁹At Horeb they made a calf
      and worshiped an idol cast from
      metal.
²⁰They exchanged their Glory
      for an image of a bull, which
      eats grass.
²¹They forgot the God who saved
      them,
      who had done great things in
      Egypt,
²²miracles in the land of Ham
      and awesome deeds by the Red
      Sea.
²³So he said he would destroy
      them—
      had not Moses, his chosen one,
   stood in the breach before him
   to keep his wrath from
      destroying them.

²⁴Then they despised the pleasant
      land;
      they did not believe his
      promise.
²⁵They grumbled in their tents
      and did not obey the LORD.
²⁶So he swore to them with uplifted
      hand
      that he would make them fall
      in the desert,
²⁷make their descendants fall
      among the nations
      and scatter them throughout
      the lands.

²⁸They yoked themselves to the
      Baal of Peor
      and ate sacrifices offered to
      lifeless gods;
²⁹they provoked the LORD to anger
      by their wicked deeds,
      and a plague broke out among
      them.
³⁰But Phinehas stood up and
      intervened,
      and the plague was checked.
³¹This was credited to him as
      righteousness
      for endless generations to come.

³²By the waters of Meribah they
      angered the LORD,
      and trouble came to Moses
      because of them;
³³for they rebelled against the
      Spirit of God,
      and rash words came from
      Moses' lips. *a*

³⁴They did not destroy the peoples
      as the LORD had commanded
      them,
³⁵but they mingled with the
      nations
      and adopted their customs.
³⁶They worshiped their idols,
      which became a snare to them.
³⁷They sacrificed their sons
      and their daughters to demons.
³⁸They shed innocent blood,
      the blood of their sons and
      daughters,
   whom they sacrificed to the idols
      of Canaan,
      and the land was desecrated by
      their blood.
³⁹They defiled themselves by what
      they did;
      by their deeds they prostituted
      themselves.

⁴⁰Therefore the LORD was angry
      with his people
      and abhorred his inheritance.
⁴¹He handed them over to the
      nations,
      and their foes ruled over them.
⁴²Their enemies oppressed them
      and subjected them to their
      power.
⁴³Many times he delivered them,
      but they were bent on rebellion
      and they wasted away in their
      sin.

⁴⁴But he took note of their distress
      when he heard their cry;
⁴⁵for their sake he remembered his
      covenant
      and out of his great love he
      relented.
⁴⁶He caused them to be pitied
      by all who held them captive.

⁴⁷Save us, O LORD our God,

a33 Or against his spirit, / and rash words came from his lips

and gather us from the nations,
that we may give thanks to your
   holy name
and glory in your praise.

⁴⁸Praise be to the LORD, the God of
   Israel,
from everlasting to everlasting.
Let all the people say, "Amen!"

Praise the LORD.

BOOK V

Psalms 107–150

Psalm 107

¹Give thanks to the LORD, for he is
   good;
   his love endures forever.
²Let the redeemed of the LORD say
   this—
   those he redeemed from the
   hand of the foe,
³those he gathered from the lands,
   from east and west, from north
   and south. ᵃ

⁴Some wandered in desert
   wastelands,
   finding no way to a city where
   they could settle.
⁵They were hungry and thirsty,
   and their lives ebbed away.
⁶Then they cried out to the LORD
   in their trouble,
   and he delivered them from
   their distress.
⁷He led them by a straight way
   to a city where they could
   settle.
⁸Let them give thanks to the LORD
   for his unfailing love
   and his wonderful deeds for
   men,
⁹for he satisfies the thirsty
   and fills the hungry with good
   things.

¹⁰Some sat in darkness and the
   deepest gloom,
   prisoners suffering in iron
   chains,

¹¹for they had rebelled against the
   words of God
   and despised the counsel of the
   Most High.
¹²So he subjected them to bitter
   labor;
   they stumbled, and there was
   no one to help.
¹³Then they cried to the LORD in
   their trouble,
   and he saved them from their
   distress.
¹⁴He brought them out of darkness
   and the deepest gloom
   and broke away their chains.
¹⁵Let them give thanks to the LORD
   for his unfailing love
   and his wonderful deeds for
   men,

WORDS TO REMEMBER

**107:15   Give thanks to the LORD
            for his unfailing love.**

¹⁶for he breaks down gates of
   bronze
   and cuts through bars of iron.

¹⁷Some became fools through their
   rebellious ways
   and suffered affliction because
   of their iniquities.
¹⁸They loathed all food
   and drew near the gates of
   death.
¹⁹Then they cried to the LORD in
   their trouble,
   and he saved them from their
   distress.
²⁰He sent forth his word and healed
   them;
   he rescued them from the grave.
²¹Let them give thanks to the LORD
   for his unfailing love
   and his wonderful deeds for
   men.
²²Let them sacrifice thank offerings
   and tell of his works with songs
   of joy.

ᵃ3 Hebrew *north and the sea*

²³Others went out on the sea in
  ships;
  they were merchants on the
  mighty waters.
²⁴They saw the works of the Lord,
  his wonderful deeds in the
  deep.
²⁵For he spoke and stirred up a
  tempest
  that lifted high the waves.
²⁶They mounted up to the heavens
  and went down to the
  depths;
  in their peril their courage
  melted away.
²⁷They reeled and staggered like
  drunken men;
  they were at their wits' end.
²⁸Then they cried out to the Lord
  in their trouble,
  and he brought them out of
  their distress.
²⁹He stilled the storm to a whisper;
  the waves of the sea were
  hushed.
³⁰They were glad when it grew
  calm,
  and he guided them to their
  desired haven.
³¹Let them give thanks to the Lord
  for his unfailing love
  and his wonderful deeds for
  men.
³²Let them exalt him in the
  assembly of the people
  and praise him in the council of
  the elders.

³³He turned rivers into a desert,
  flowing springs into thirsty
  ground,
³⁴and fruitful land into a salt
  waste,
  because of the wickedness of
  those who lived there.
³⁵He turned the desert into pools of
  water
  and the parched ground into
  flowing springs;
³⁶there he brought the hungry to
  live,
  and they founded a city where
  they could settle.
³⁷They sowed fields and planted
  vineyards

that yielded a fruitful harvest;
³⁸he blessed them, and their
  numbers greatly increased,
  and he did not let their herds
  diminish.

³⁹Then their numbers decreased,
  and they were humbled
  by oppression, calamity and
  sorrow;
⁴⁰he who pours contempt on nobles
  made them wander in a
  trackless waste.
⁴¹But he lifted the needy out of
  their affliction
  and increased their families like
  flocks.
⁴²The upright see and rejoice,
  but all the wicked shut their
  mouths.

⁴³Whoever is wise, let him heed
  these things
  and consider the great love of
  the Lord.

Psalm 108

A song. A psalm of David.

¹My heart is steadfast, O God;
  I will sing and make music
  with all my soul.
²Awake, harp and lyre!
  I will awaken the dawn.
³I will praise you, O Lord, among
  the nations;
  I will sing of you among the
  peoples.
⁴For great is your love, higher
  than the heavens;
  your faithfulness reaches to the
  skies.
⁵Be exalted, O God, above the
  heavens,
  and let your glory be over all
  the earth.

⁶Save us and help us with your
  right hand,
  that those you love may be
  delivered.
⁷God has spoken from his
  sanctuary:
  "In triumph I will parcel out
  Shechem

and measure off the Valley of
Succoth.
8Gilead is mine, Manasseh is mine;
Ephraim is my helmet,
Judah my scepter.
9Moab is my washbasin,
upon Edom I toss my sandal;
over Philistia I shout in
triumph."

10Who will bring me to the fortified
city?
Who will lead me to Edom?
11Is it not you, O God, you who
have rejected us
and no longer go out with our
armies?
12Give us aid against the enemy,
for the help of man is worthless.
13With God we will gain the
victory,
and he will trample down our
enemies.

Psalm 109

For the director of music. Of David.
A psalm.

1O God, whom I praise,
do not remain silent,
2for wicked and deceitful men
have opened their mouths
against me;
they have spoken against me
with lying tongues.
3With words of hatred they
surround me;
they attack me without cause.
4In return for my friendship they
accuse me,
but I am a man of prayer.
5They repay me evil for good,
and hatred for my friendship.

6Appoint*a* an evil man*b* to oppose
him;
let an accuser*c* stand at his
right hand.
7When he is tried, let him be
found guilty,
and may his prayers condemn
him.

8May his days be few;
may another take his place of
leadership.
9May his children be fatherless
and his wife a widow.
10May his children be wandering
beggars;
may they be driven*d* from their
ruined homes.
11May a creditor seize all he has;
may strangers plunder the
fruits of his labor.
12May no one extend kindness to
him
or take pity on his fatherless
children.
13May his descendants be cut off,
their names blotted out from
the next generation.
14May the iniquity of his fathers be
remembered before the
LORD;
may the sin of his mother never
be blotted out.
15May their sins always remain
before the LORD,
that he may cut off the memory
of them from the earth.

16For he never thought of doing a
kindness,
but hounded to death the poor
and the needy and the
brokenhearted.
17He loved to pronounce a curse—
may it*e* come on him;
he found no pleasure in
blessing—
may it be*f* far from him.
18He wore cursing as his garment;
it entered into his body like
water,
into his bones like oil.
19May it be like a cloak wrapped
about him,
like a belt tied forever around
him.
20May this be the LORD's payment
to my accusers,
to those who speak evil of me.

21But you, O Sovereign LORD,

---

*a*6 Or ,They say:, "Appoint (with quotation marks at the end of verse 19)   *b*6 Or the Evil One
*c*6 Or let Satan   *d*10 Septuagint; Hebrew sought   *e*17 Or curse, / and it has   *f*17 Or
blessing, / and it is

deal well with me for your
name's sake;
out of the goodness of your love,
deliver me.
²²For I am poor and needy,
and my heart is wounded
within me.
²³I fade away like an evening
shadow;
I am shaken off like a locust.
²⁴My knees give way from fasting;
my body is thin and gaunt.
²⁵I am an object of scorn to my
accusers;
when they see me, they shake
their heads.

²⁶Help me, O LORD my God;
save me in accordance with
your love.
²⁷Let them know that it is your
hand,
that you, O LORD, have done it.
²⁸They may curse, but you will
bless;
when they attack they will be
put to shame,
but your servant will rejoice.
²⁹My accusers will be clothed with
disgrace
and wrapped in shame as in a
cloak.

³⁰With my mouth I will greatly
extol the LORD;
in the great throng I will praise
him.
³¹For he stands at the right hand of
the needy one,
to save his life from those who
condemn him.

Psalm 110

Of David. A psalm.

¹The LORD says to my Lord:
"Sit at my right hand
until I make your enemies
a footstool for your feet."

²The LORD will extend your mighty
scepter from Zion;

you will rule in the midst of
your enemies.
³Your troops will be willing
on your day of battle.
Arrayed in holy majesty,
from the womb of the dawn
you will receive the dew of your
youth.ᵃ

⁴The LORD has sworn
and will not change his mind:
"You are a priest forever,
in the order of Melchizedek."

⁵The Lord is at your right hand;
he will crush kings on the day
of his wrath.
⁶He will judge the nations,
heaping up the dead
and crushing the rulers of the
whole earth.
⁷He will drink from a brook beside
the wayᵇ;
therefore he will lift up his
head.

Psalm 111ᶜ

¹Praise the LORD.ᵈ

I will extol the LORD with all my
heart
in the council of the upright
and in the assembly.

²Great are the works of the LORD;
they are pondered by all who
delight in them.
³Glorious and majestic are his
deeds,
and his righteousness endures
forever.
⁴He has caused his wonders to be
remembered;
the LORD is gracious and
compassionate.
⁵He provides food for those who
fear him;
he remembers his covenant
forever.
⁶He has shown his people the
power of his works,

ᵃ3 Or / your young men will come to you like the dew   ᵇ7 Or / The One who grants succession
will set him in authority   ᶜThis psalm is an acrostic poem, the lines of which begin with the
successive letters of the Hebrew alphabet.   ᵈ1 Hebrew Hallelu Yah

giving them the lands of other
nations.
⁷The works of his hands are
faithful and just;
all his precepts are trustworthy.
⁸They are steadfast for ever and
ever,
done in faithfulness and
uprightness.
⁹He provided redemption for his
people;
he ordained his covenant
forever—
holy and awesome is his name.

¹⁰The fear of the LORD is the
beginning of wisdom;
all who follow his precepts have
good understanding.
To him belongs eternal praise.

Psalm 112ᵃ

¹Praise the LORD.ᵇ

Blessed is the man who fears the
LORD,
who finds great delight in his
commands.

²His children will be mighty in the
land;
the generation of the upright
will be blessed.
³Wealth and riches are in his
house,
and his righteousness endures
forever.
⁴Even in darkness light dawns for
the upright,
for the gracious and
compassionate and
righteous man.ᶜ
⁵Good will come to him who is
generous and lends freely,
who conducts his affairs with
justice.
⁶Surely he will never be shaken;
a righteous man will be
remembered forever.
⁷He will have no fear of bad
news;

his heart is steadfast, trusting
in the LORD.
⁸His heart is secure, he will have
no fear;
in the end he will look in
triumph on his foes.
⁹He has scattered abroad his gifts
to the poor,
his righteousness endures
forever;
his hornᵈ will be lifted high in
honor.

¹⁰The wicked man will see and be
vexed,
he will gnash his teeth and
waste away;
the longings of the wicked will
come to nothing.

Psalm 113

¹Praise the LORD.ᵉ

Praise, O servants of the LORD,
praise the name of the LORD.
²Let the name of the LORD be
praised,
both now and forevermore.
³From the rising of the sun to the
place where it sets,
the name of the LORD is to be
praised.

⁴The LORD is exalted over all the
nations,
his glory above the heavens.
⁵Who is like the LORD our God,
the One who sits enthroned on
high,
⁶who stoops down to look
on the heavens and the earth?

⁷He raises the poor from the dust
and lifts the needy from the ash
heap;
⁸he seats them with princes,
with the princes of their people.
⁹He settles the barren woman in
her home
as a happy mother of children.

Praise the LORD.

ᵃThis psalm is an acrostic poem, the lines of which begin with the successive letters of the
Hebrew alphabet.   ᵇ1 Hebrew *Hallelu Yah*   ᶜ4 Or / *for the LORD, is gracious and
compassionate and righteous*   ᵈ9 *Horn* here symbolizes dignity.   ᵉ1 Hebrew *Hallelu Yah*;
also in verse 9

Psalm 114

¹When Israel came out of Egypt,
　　the house of Jacob from a
　　people of foreign tongue,
²Judah became God's sanctuary,
　　Israel his dominion.

³The sea looked and fled,
　　the Jordan turned back;
⁴the mountains skipped like rams,
　　the hills like lambs.

⁵Why was it, O sea, that you fled,
　　O Jordan, that you turned back,
⁶you mountains, that you skipped
　　like rams,
　　you hills, like lambs?

⁷Tremble, O earth, at the presence
　　of the Lord,
　　at the presence of the God of
　　Jacob,
⁸who turned the rock into a pool,
　　the hard rock into springs of
　　water.

Psalm 115

¹Not to us, O Lord, not to us
　　but to your name be the glory,
　　because of your love and
　　faithfulness.

²Why do the nations say,
　　"Where is their God?"
³Our God is in heaven;
　　he does whatever pleases him.
⁴But their idols are silver and
　　gold,
　　made by the hands of men.
⁵They have mouths, but cannot
　　speak,
　　eyes, but they cannot see;

⁶they have ears, but cannot hear,
　　noses, but they cannot smell;
⁷they have hands, but cannot feel,
　　feet, but they cannot walk;
　　nor can they utter a sound with
　　their throats.
⁸Those who make them will be
　　like them,
　　and so will all who trust in
　　them.

⁹O house of Israel, trust in the
　　Lord—
　　he is their help and shield.
¹⁰O house of Aaron, trust in the
　　Lord—
　　he is their help and shield.
¹¹You who fear him, trust in the
　　Lord—
　　he is their help and shield.

¹²The Lord remembers us and will
　　bless us:
　　He will bless the house of
　　Israel,
　　he will bless the house of
　　Aaron,
¹³he will bless those who fear the
　　Lord—
　　small and great alike.

¹⁴May the Lord make you increase,
　　both you and your children.
¹⁵May you be blessed by the Lord,
　　the Maker of heaven and earth.

¹⁶The highest heavens belong to
　　the Lord,
　　but the earth he has given to
　　man.
¹⁷It is not the dead who praise the
　　Lord,
　　those who go down to silence;
¹⁸it is we who extol the Lord,

LET'S LIVE IT!　　　　　　Psalm 113:1–9

PRAISE GOD ➠ Praise is telling God how great he is. Sometimes we praise God by talking to him. Sometimes we praise God by talking to others about him. Read Psalm 113.

　　You can praise God too. One way would be to write down two lines telling God what you like about him. Another way would be to write down two lines that tell others why God is so special. When it's your turn to pray before a meal or during your bedtime prayers, start with one of the praise verses you wrote.

both now and forevermore.

Praise the LORD.ᵃ

Psalm 116

¹I love the LORD, for he heard my
    voice;
  he heard my cry for mercy.
²Because he turned his ear to me,
  I will call on him as long as I
    live.

³The cords of death entangled me,
  the anguish of the graveᵇ came
    upon me;
  I was overcome by trouble and
    sorrow.
⁴Then I called on the name of the
    LORD:
  "O LORD, save me!"

⁵The LORD is gracious and
    righteous;
  our God is full of compassion.
⁶The LORD protects the
    simplehearted;
  when I was in great need, he
    saved me.

⁷Be at rest once more, O my soul,
  for the LORD has been good to
    you.

⁸For you, O LORD, have delivered
    my soul from death,
  my eyes from tears,
  my feet from stumbling,
⁹that I may walk before the LORD
  in the land of the living.
¹⁰I believed; thereforeᶜ I said,
  "I am greatly afflicted."
¹¹And in my dismay I said,
  "All men are liars."

¹²How can I repay the LORD
  for all his goodness to me?
¹³I will lift up the cup of salvation
  and call on the name of the
    LORD.
¹⁴I will fulfill my vows to the LORD
  in the presence of all his people.

¹⁵Precious in the sight of the LORD
  is the death of his saints.

¹⁶O LORD, truly I am your servant;
  I am your servant, the son of
    your maidservantᵈ;
  you have freed me from my
    chains.

¹⁷I will sacrifice a thank offering to
    you
  and call on the name of the
    LORD.
¹⁸I will fulfill my vows to the LORD
  in the presence of all his people,
¹⁹in the courts of the house of the
    LORD—
  in your midst, O Jerusalem.

Praise the LORD.ᵃ

Psalm 117

¹Praise the LORD, all you nations;
  extol him, all you peoples.
²For great is his love toward us,
  and the faithfulness of the LORD
    endures forever.

Praise the LORD.ᵃ

Psalm 118

¹Give thanks to the LORD, for he is
    good;
  his love endures forever.

²Let Israel say:
  "His love endures forever."
³Let the house of Aaron say:
  "His love endures forever."
⁴Let those who fear the LORD say:
  "His love endures forever."

⁵In my anguish I cried to the
    LORD,
  and he answered by setting me
    free.
⁶The LORD is with me; I will not be
    afraid.
  What can man do to me?
⁷The LORD is with me; he is my
    helper.
  I will look in triumph on my
    enemies.

⁸It is better to take refuge in the
    LORD

ᵃ18,19,2 Hebrew *Hallelu Yah*   ᵇ3 Hebrew *Sheol*   ᶜ10 Or *believed even when*   ᵈ16 Or
servant, your faithful son

than to trust in man.
⁹It is better to take refuge in the
    LORD
    than to trust in princes.

¹⁰All the nations surrounded me,
    but in the name of the LORD I
    cut them off.
¹¹They surrounded me on every
    side,
    but in the name of the LORD I
    cut them off.
¹²They swarmed around me like
    bees,
    but they died out as quickly as
    burning thorns;
    in the name of the LORD I cut
    them off.

¹³I was pushed back and about to
    fall,
    but the LORD helped me.
¹⁴The LORD is my strength and my
    song;
    he has become my salvation.

¹⁵Shouts of joy and victory
    resound in the tents of the
    righteous:
    "The LORD's right hand has done
    mighty things!
¹⁶ The LORD's right hand is lifted
    high;
    the LORD's right hand has done
    mighty things!"

¹⁷I will not die but live,
    and will proclaim what the
    LORD has done.
¹⁸The LORD has chastened me
    severely,
    but he has not given me over to
    death.

¹⁹Open for me the gates of
    righteousness;
    I will enter and give thanks to
    the LORD.
²⁰This is the gate of the LORD
    through which the righteous
    may enter.
²¹I will give you thanks, for you
    answered me;

you have become my salvation.

²²The stone the builders rejected
    has become the capstone;
²³the LORD has done this,
    and it is marvelous in our eyes.
²⁴This is the day the LORD has
    made;
    let us rejoice and be glad in it.

²⁵O LORD, save us;
    O LORD, grant us success.
²⁶Blessed is he who comes in the
    name of the LORD.
    From the house of the LORD we
    bless you.ᵃ
²⁷The LORD is God,
    and he has made his light shine
    upon us.
    With boughs in hand, join in the
    festal procession
    upᵇ to the horns of the altar.

²⁸You are my God, and I will give
    you thanks;
    you are my God, and I will
    exalt you.

²⁹Give thanks to the LORD, for he is
    good;
    his love endures forever.

Psalm 119ᶜ

א Aleph

¹Blessed are they whose ways are
    blameless,
    who walk according to the law
    of the LORD.
²Blessed are they who keep his
    statutes
    and seek him with all their
    heart.
³They do nothing wrong;
    they walk in his ways.
⁴You have laid down precepts
    that are to be fully obeyed.
⁵Oh, that my ways were steadfast
    in obeying your decrees!
⁶Then I would not be put to shame
    when I consider all your
    commands.

ᵃ26 The Hebrew is plural.   ᵇ27 Or *Bind the festal sacrifice with ropes / and take it*   ᶜThis
psalm is an acrostic poem; the verses of each stanza begin with the same letter of the Hebrew
alphabet.

⁷I will praise you with an upright
    heart
  as I learn your righteous laws.
⁸I will obey your decrees;
  do not utterly forsake me.

ב Beth

⁹How can a young man keep his
    way pure?
  By living according to your
    word.
¹⁰I seek you with all my heart;
  do not let me stray from your
    commands.
¹¹I have hidden your word in my
    heart
  that I might not sin against
    you.
¹²Praise be to you, O LORD;
  teach me your decrees.
¹³With my lips I recount
  all the laws that come from
    your mouth.
¹⁴I rejoice in following your
    statutes
  as one rejoices in great riches.
¹⁵I meditate on your precepts
  and consider your ways.
¹⁶I delight in your decrees;
  I will not neglect your word.

ג Gimel

¹⁷Do good to your servant, and I
    will live;
  I will obey your word.
¹⁸Open my eyes that I may see
  wonderful things in your
    law.

¹⁹I am a stranger on earth;
  do not hide your commands
    from me.
²⁰My soul is consumed with longing
  for your laws at all times.
²¹You rebuke the arrogant, who are
    cursed
  and who stray from your
    commands.
²²Remove from me scorn and
    contempt,
  for I keep your statutes.
²³Though rulers sit together and
    slander me,
  your servant will meditate on
    your decrees.
²⁴Your statutes are my delight;
  they are my counselors.

ד Daleth

²⁵I am laid low in the dust;
  preserve my life according to
    your word.
²⁶I recounted my ways and you
    answered me;
  teach me your decrees.
²⁷Let me understand the teaching
  of your precepts;
  then I will meditate on your
    wonders.
²⁸My soul is weary with sorrow;
  strengthen me according to your
    word.
²⁹Keep me from deceitful ways;
  be gracious to me through your
    law.
³⁰I have chosen the way of truth;
  I have set my heart on your
    laws.

╲ET'S LIVE IT!   Psalm 119:9–16

MEMORIZE SCRIPTURE ➠ Read Psalm 119:9–16. To hide God's word in your heart (Psalm 119:11) means to memorize a verse and then to do what it says. Here are fun ways to memorize Bible verses with a friend.

1. Read the verse aloud, but leave out one word. Have your friend fill in the word you left out. Take turns reading the verse, and each time leave out a different word.

2. Each time you read the verse aloud leave out one *more* word. The first time, one word; the second time, two words; and so on. You or your friend fill in the words left out.

3. Write the Bible verse on a card. Cut out each word, and scramble them. See who can put the words in the right order in the shortest time.

Famous Children in the Bible

Children are an important part of many of the stories in the Bible. "Famous Children in the Bible" gives you information about some of the children mentioned in God's Word. Turn to the page listed to read more about that story or to discover the name of the child (or did you know it already?).

This boy was left to die in the desert.	Genesis 21:8-21 *(page 24)*
This boy's life was saved by a ram.	Genesis 22:1-19 *(page 25)*
This young woman went with a servant to marry a man she had never seen.	Genesis 24:34-67 *(page 28)*
This boy was born holding on to his twin brother's heel.	Genesis 25:19-28 *(page 30)*
This boy had a colorful coat that made his brothers jealous.	Genesis 37:3-4 *(page 48)*
This boy grew up in the palace of Pharaoh.	Exodus 2:1-10 *(page 71)*
This young girl watched her brother be rescued by a princess.	Exodus 2:1-10 *(page 71)*
This boy liked to tell riddles.	Judges 13 *(page 308)*
This boy heard God's voice calling him.	1 Samuel 3 *(page 331)*
This boy killed a giant.	1 Samuel 17 *(page 349)*
This boy picked up the arrows that Jonathan shot.	1 Samuel 20:35-42 *(page 355)*
This baby boy's life was saved by King Solomon.	1 Kings 3:16-28 *(page 413)*
This boy was brought back to life by the prayers of Elijah.	1 Kings 17:17-24 *(page 438)*
These young men mocked a bald-headed man.	2 Kings 2:23-25 *(page 451)*
These boys were saved from slavery by some oil.	2 Kings 4:1-7 *(page 452)*
This young boy sneezed seven times when he was brought back to life.	2 Kings 4:8-37 *(page 452)*
This slave girl helped her master find healing from leprosy.	2 Kings 5:1-18 *(page 454)*

continued

Famous Children in the Bible

This boy was only seven when he became king.	2 Kings 11:12-21 *(page 464)*
This boy, who was eight when he became king, read to the people from a book of the law.	2 Kings 22:1-13 *(page 480)*
This young Jewish girl became queen of Persia.	Esther 2:1-18 *(page 612)*
This young child will befriend wild animals.	Isaiah 11:6 *(page 847)*
This young man said "I am only a child" when he was asked to speak for God.	Jeremiah 1:4-10 *(page 916)*
This young man knew the meaning of a king's dreams.	Daniel 2:24-49 *(page 1064)*
These young men were thrown into a fire.	Daniel 3 *(page 1065)*
These children were given meaningful names by their father.	Hosea 1:4-9; 2:23 *(page 1083)*
This boy grew up to be the Savior of the world.	Matthew 1:18-25 *(page 1168)*
This boy ate locusts and honey.	Matthew 3:1-12 *(page 1170)*
This little girl was brought back to life by Jesus.	Mark 5:35-43 *(page 1220)*
This girl danced for King Herod.	Mark 6:21-29 *(page 1221)*
These children were hugged by Jesus.	Mark 10:13-16 *(page 1228)*
This girl was told by an angel that she would have a baby boy.	Luke 1:26-38 *(page 1242)*
This boy knew more than his teachers.	Luke 2:41-52 *(page 1246)*
This boy was healed of seizures by Jesus.	Luke 9:37-43 *(page 1260)*
This servant girl asked Peter if he knew Jesus.	Luke 22:54-62 *(page 1282)*
This boy was healed by Jesus even though Jesus never went to see him.	John 4:46-54 *(page 1294)*
This boy gave Jesus his lunch to feed a huge crowd of people.	John 6:1-15 *(page 1296)*
This young man fell asleep during a long sermon.	Acts 20:7-12 *(page 1354)*
This young man saved Paul's life.	Acts 23:12-22 *(page 1359)*
This young man was encouraged by Paul to be a leader.	1 Timothy 4:12 *(page 1460)*

³¹I hold fast to your statutes,
  O Lord;
  do not let me be put to shame.
³²I run in the path of your
    commands,
  for you have set my heart free.

ה He

³³Teach me, O Lord, to follow your
    decrees;
  then I will keep them to the
    end.
³⁴Give me understanding, and I
    will keep your law
  and obey it with all my heart.
³⁵Direct me in the path of your
    commands,
  for there I find delight.
³⁶Turn my heart toward your
    statutes
  and not toward selfish gain.
³⁷Turn my eyes away from
    worthless things;
  preserve my life according to
    your word.ᵃ
³⁸Fulfill your promise to your
    servant,
  so that you may be feared.
³⁹Take away the disgrace I dread,
  for your laws are good.
⁴⁰How I long for your precepts!
  Preserve my life in your
    righteousness.

ו Waw

⁴¹May your unfailing love come to
    me, O Lord,
  your salvation according to your
    promise;
⁴²then I will answer the one who
    taunts me,
  for I trust in your word.
⁴³Do not snatch the word of truth
    from my mouth,
  for I have put my hope in your
    laws.
⁴⁴I will always obey your law,
  for ever and ever.
⁴⁵I will walk about in freedom,
  for I have sought out your
    precepts.

⁴⁶I will speak of your statutes
    before kings
  and will not be put to shame,
⁴⁷for I delight in your commands
  because I love them.
⁴⁸I lift up my hands toᵇ your
    commands, which I love,
  and I meditate on your decrees.

ז Zayin

⁴⁹Remember your word to your
    servant,
  for you have given me hope.
⁵⁰My comfort in my suffering is
    this:
  Your promise preserves my life.
⁵¹The arrogant mock me without
    restraint,
  but I do not turn from your
    law.
⁵²I remember your ancient laws,
    O Lord,
  and I find comfort in them.
⁵³Indignation grips me because of
    the wicked,
  who have forsaken your law.
⁵⁴Your decrees are the theme of my
    song
  wherever I lodge.
⁵⁵In the night I remember your
    name, O Lord,
  and I will keep your law.
⁵⁶This has been my practice:
  I obey your precepts.

ח Heth

⁵⁷You are my portion, O Lord;
  I have promised to obey your
    words.
⁵⁸I have sought your face with all
    my heart;
  be gracious to me according to
    your promise.
⁵⁹I have considered my ways
  and have turned my steps to
    your statutes.
⁶⁰I will hasten and not delay
  to obey your commands.
⁶¹Though the wicked bind me with
    ropes,
  I will not forget your law.

ᵃ37 Two manuscripts of the Masoretic Text and Dead Sea Scrolls; most manuscripts of the Masoretic
Text *life in your way*   ᵇ48 Or *for*

62At midnight I rise to give you
thanks
for your righteous laws.
63I am a friend to all who fear you,
to all who follow your precepts.
64The earth is filled with your love,
O LORD;
teach me your decrees.

ט　Teth

65Do good to your servant
according to your word, O LORD.
66Teach me knowledge and good
judgment,
for I believe in your commands.
67Before I was afflicted I went
astray,
but now I obey your word.
68You are good, and what you do is
good;
teach me your decrees.

Ⓦ ORDS TO REMEMBER

119:68　　You are good, and what
you do is good.

69Though the arrogant have
smeared me with lies,
I keep your precepts with all
my heart.
70Their hearts are callous and
unfeeling,
but I delight in your law.
71It was good for me to be afflicted
so that I might learn your
decrees.
72The law from your mouth is more
precious to me
than thousands of pieces of
silver and gold.

י　Yodh

73Your hands made me and formed
me;
give me understanding to learn
your commands.
74May those who fear you rejoice
when they see me,
for I have put my hope in your
word.

75I know, O LORD, that your laws
are righteous,
and in faithfulness you have
afflicted me.
76May your unfailing love be my
comfort,
according to your promise to
your servant.
77Let your compassion come to me
that I may live,
for your law is my delight.
78May the arrogant be put to
shame for wronging me
without cause;
but I will meditate on your
precepts.
79May those who fear you turn to
me,
those who understand your
statutes.
80May my heart be blameless
toward your decrees,
that I may not be put to shame.

כ　Kaph

81My soul faints with longing for
your salvation,
but I have put my hope in your
word.
82My eyes fail, looking for your
promise;
I say, "When will you comfort
me?"
83Though I am like a wineskin in
the smoke,
I do not forget your decrees.
84How long must your servant
wait?
When will you punish my
persecutors?
85The arrogant dig pitfalls for me,
contrary to your law.
86All your commands are
trustworthy;
help me, for men persecute me
without cause.
87They almost wiped me from the
earth,
but I have not forsaken your
precepts.
88Preserve my life according to
your love,
and I will obey the statutes of
your mouth.

ל Lamedh

89Your word, O Lord, is eternal;
  it stands firm in the heavens.
90Your faithfulness continues
      through all generations;
  you established the earth, and
      it endures.
91Your laws endure to this day,
  for all things serve you.
92If your law had not been my
      delight,
  I would have perished in my
      affliction.
93I will never forget your precepts,
  for by them you have preserved
      my life.
94Save me, for I am yours;
  I have sought out your precepts.
95The wicked are waiting to destroy
      me,
  but I will ponder your statutes.
96To all perfection I see a limit;
  but your commands are
      boundless.

מ Mem

97Oh, how I love your law!
  I meditate on it all day long.

Life In Bible Times

WHAT GOD IS LIKE

Psalm 119:97 says God is the
lawgiver. He gives us rules to live
by, to keep us from doing wrong.
God is good, and he shows us how
to do good.

98Your commands make me wiser
      than my enemies,
  for they are ever with me.
99I have more insight than all my
      teachers,
  for I meditate on your statutes.
100I have more understanding than
      the elders,

for I obey your precepts.
101I have kept my feet from every
      evil path
  so that I might obey your word.
102I have not departed from your
      laws,
  for you yourself have taught
      me.
103How sweet are your words to my
      taste,
  sweeter than honey to my
      mouth!
104I gain understanding from your
      precepts;
  therefore I hate every wrong
      path.

נ Nun

105Your word is a lamp to my feet
  and a light for my path.
106I have taken an oath and
      confirmed it,
  that I will follow your righteous
      laws.
107I have suffered much;
  preserve my life, O Lord,
  according to your word.
108Accept, O Lord, the willing
      praise of my mouth,
  and teach me your laws.
109Though I constantly take my life
      in my hands,
  I will not forget your law.
110The wicked have set a snare for
      me,
  but I have not strayed from
      your precepts.
111Your statutes are my heritage
      forever;
  they are the joy of my heart.
112My heart is set on keeping your
      decrees
  to the very end.

ס Samekh

113I hate double-minded men,
  but I love your law.
114You are my refuge and my
      shield;
  I have put my hope in your
      word.
115Away from me, you evildoers,
  that I may keep the commands
      of my God!

116Sustain me according to your
  promise, and I will live;
 do not let my hopes be dashed.
117Uphold me, and I will be
  delivered;
 I will always have regard for
  your decrees.
118You reject all who stray from
  your decrees,
 for their deceitfulness is in
  vain.
119All the wicked of the earth you
  discard like dross;
 therefore I love your statutes.
120My flesh trembles in fear of you;
 I stand in awe of your laws.

ע Ayin

121I have done what is righteous
  and just;
 do not leave me to my
  oppressors.
122Ensure your servant's well-being;
 let not the arrogant oppress me.
123My eyes fail, looking for your
  salvation,
 looking for your righteous
  promise.
124Deal with your servant according
  to your love
 and teach me your decrees.
125I am your servant; give me
  discernment
 that I may understand your
  statutes.
126It is time for you to act, O LORD;
 your law is being broken.
127Because I love your commands
  more than gold, more than pure
  gold,
128and because I consider all your
  precepts right,
 I hate every wrong path.

פ Pe

129Your statutes are wonderful;
 therefore I obey them.
130The unfolding of your words
  gives light;
 it gives understanding to the
  simple.
131I open my mouth and pant,
 longing for your commands.

132Turn to me and have mercy on
  me,
 as you always do to those who
  love your name.
133Direct my footsteps according to
  your word;
 let no sin rule over me.
134Redeem me from the oppression
  of men,
 that I may obey your precepts.
135Make your face shine upon your
  servant
 and teach me your decrees.
136Streams of tears flow from my
  eyes,
 for your law is not obeyed.

צ Tsadhe

137Righteous are you, O LORD,
 and your laws are right.
138The statutes you have laid down
  are righteous;
 they are fully trustworthy.
139My zeal wears me out,
 for my enemies ignore your
  words.
140Your promises have been
  thoroughly tested,
 and your servant loves them.
141Though I am lowly and despised,
 I do not forget your precepts.
142Your righteousness is everlasting
 and your law is true.
143Trouble and distress have come
  upon me,
 but your commands are my
  delight.
144Your statutes are forever right;
 give me understanding that I
  may live.

ק Qoph

145I call with all my heart; answer
  me, O LORD,
 and I will obey your decrees.
146I call out to you; save me
 and I will keep your statutes.
147I rise before dawn and cry for
  help;
 I have put my hope in your
  word.
148My eyes stay open through the
  watches of the night,

that I may meditate on your
promises.
149Hear my voice in accordance
with your love;
preserve my life, O Lord,
according to your laws.
150Those who devise wicked
schemes are near,
but they are far from your
law.
151Yet you are near, O Lord,
and all your commands are
true.
152Long ago I learned from your
statutes
that you established them to
last forever.

ר   Resh

153Look upon my suffering and
deliver me,
for I have not forgotten your
law.
154Defend my cause and redeem
me;
preserve my life according to
your promise.
155Salvation is far from the wicked,
for they do not seek out your
decrees.
156Your compassion is great,
O Lord;
preserve my life according to
your laws.
157Many are the foes who persecute
me,
but I have not turned from your
statutes.

Ⓦ ORDS TO REMEMBER

119:160 All your words are true.

158I look on the faithless with
loathing,
for they do not obey your word.
159See how I love your precepts;
preserve my life, O Lord,
according to your love.
160All your words are true;
all your righteous laws are
eternal.

שׁ   Sin and Shin

161Rulers persecute me without
cause,
but my heart trembles at your
word.
162I rejoice in your promise
like one who finds great spoil.
163I hate and abhor falsehood
but I love your law.
164Seven times a day I praise you
for your righteous laws.
165Great peace have they who love
your law,
and nothing can make them
stumble.
166I wait for your salvation,
O Lord,
and I follow your commands.
167I obey your statutes,
for I love them greatly.
168I obey your precepts and your
statutes,
for all my ways are known to
you.

ת   Taw

169May my cry come before you,
O Lord;
give me understanding
according to your word.
170May my supplication come before
you;
deliver me according to your
promise.
171May my lips overflow with
praise,
for you teach me your decrees.
172May my tongue sing of your
word,
for all your commands are
righteous.
173May your hand be ready to help
me,
for I have chosen your precepts.
174I long for your salvation,
O Lord,
and your law is my delight.
175Let me live that I may praise
you,
and may your laws sustain me.
176I have strayed like a lost sheep.
Seek your servant,
for I have not forgotten your
commands.

Psalm 120

A song of ascents.

¹I call on the LORD in my distress,
and he answers me.
²Save me, O LORD, from lying lips
and from deceitful tongues.

³What will he do to you,
and what more besides,
O deceitful tongue?
⁴He will punish you with a
warrior's sharp arrows,
with burning coals of the broom
tree.

⁵Woe to me that I dwell in
Meshech,
that I live among the tents of
Kedar!
⁶Too long have I lived
among those who hate peace.
⁷I am a man of peace;
but when I speak, they are for
war.

Psalm 121

A song of ascents.

¹I lift up my eyes to the hills—
where does my help come
from?
²My help comes from the LORD,
the Maker of heaven and
earth.

³He will not let your foot slip—
he who watches over you will
not slumber;
⁴indeed, he who watches over
Israel
will neither slumber nor sleep.

⁵The LORD watches over you—
the LORD is your shade at your
right hand;
⁶the sun will not harm you by
day,
nor the moon by night.

⁷The LORD will keep you from all
harm—
he will watch over your life;
⁸the LORD will watch over your
coming and going
both now and forevermore.

Psalm 122

A song of ascents. Of David.

¹I rejoiced with those who said to
me,
"Let us go to the house of the
LORD."
²Our feet are standing
in your gates, O Jerusalem.

³Jerusalem is built like a city
that is closely compacted
together.
⁴That is where the tribes go up,
the tribes of the LORD,
to praise the name of the LORD
according to the statute given to
Israel.
⁵There the thrones for judgment
stand,
the thrones of the house of
David.

⁶Pray for the peace of Jerusalem:
"May those who love you be
secure.
⁷May there be peace within your
walls
and security within your
citadels."
⁸For the sake of my brothers and
friends,
I will say, "Peace be within
you."
⁹For the sake of the house of the
LORD our God,
I will seek your prosperity.

Psalm 123

A song of ascents.

¹I lift up my eyes to you,
to you whose throne is in
heaven.
²As the eyes of slaves look to the
hand of their master,
as the eyes of a maid look to
the hand of her mistress,
so our eyes look to the LORD our
God,
till he shows us his mercy.

³Have mercy on us, O LORD, have
mercy on us,

for we have endured much
contempt.
4We have endured much ridicule
from the proud,
much contempt from the
arrogant.

Psalm 124

A song of ascents. Of David.

1If the LORD had not been on our
side—
let Israel say—
2if the LORD had not been on our
side
when men attacked us,
3when their anger flared against
us,
they would have swallowed us
alive;
4the flood would have engulfed us,
the torrent would have swept
over us,
5the raging waters
would have swept us away.

6Praise be to the LORD,
who has not let us be torn by
their teeth.
7We have escaped like a bird
out of the fowler's snare;
the snare has been broken,
and we have escaped.
8Our help is in the name of the
LORD,
the Maker of heaven and earth.

Psalm 125

A song of ascents.

1Those who trust in the LORD are
like Mount Zion,
which cannot be shaken but
endures forever.
2As the mountains surround
Jerusalem,
so the LORD surrounds his
people
both now and forevermore.

3The scepter of the wicked will not
remain

over the land allotted to the
righteous,
for then the righteous might use
their hands to do evil.

4Do good, O LORD, to those who are
good,
to those who are upright in
heart.
5But those who turn to crooked
ways
the LORD will banish with the
evildoers.

Peace be upon Israel.

Psalm 126

A song of ascents.

1When the LORD brought back the
captives toª Zion,
we were like men who
dreamed.ᵇ
2Our mouths were filled with
laughter,
our tongues with songs of joy.
Then it was said among the
nations,
"The LORD has done great
things for them."
3The LORD has done great things
for us,
and we are filled with joy.

4Restore our fortunes,ᶜ O LORD,
like streams in the Negev.
5Those who sow in tears
will reap with songs of joy.
6He who goes out weeping,
carrying seed to sow,
will return with songs of joy,
carrying sheaves with him.

Psalm 127

A song of ascents. Of Solomon.

1Unless the LORD builds the house,
its builders labor in vain.
Unless the LORD watches over the
city,
the watchmen stand guard in
vain.

ª1 Or LORD *restored the fortunes of*
captives   ᵇ1 Or *men restored to health*   ᶜ4 Or *Bring back our*

2In vain you rise early
and stay up late,
toiling for food to eat—
for he grants sleep to*a* those he
loves.

3Sons are a heritage from the
Lord,
children a reward from him.
4Like arrows in the hands of a
warrior
are sons born in one's youth.
5Blessed is the man
whose quiver is full of them.
They will not be put to shame
when they contend with their
enemies in the gate.

Psalm 128

A song of ascents.

1Blessed are all who fear the Lord,
who walk in his ways.

WORDS TO REMEMBER

**128:1 Blessed are all who fear
the Lord,
who walk in his ways.**

2You will eat the fruit of your
labor;
blessings and prosperity will be
yours.
3Your wife will be like a fruitful
vine
within your house;
your sons will be like olive shoots
around your table.
4Thus is the man blessed
who fears the Lord.

5May the Lord bless you from Zion
all the days of your life;
may you see the prosperity of
Jerusalem,
6 and may you live to see your
children's children.

Peace be upon Israel.

Psalm 129

A song of ascents.

1They have greatly oppressed me
from my youth—
let Israel say—
2they have greatly oppressed me
from my youth,
but they have not gained the
victory over me.
3Plowmen have plowed my back
and made their furrows long.
4But the Lord is righteous;
he has cut me free from the
cords of the wicked.

5May all who hate Zion
be turned back in shame.
6May they be like grass on the
roof,
which withers before it can
grow;
7with it the reaper cannot fill his
hands,
nor the one who gathers fill his
arms.
8May those who pass by not say,
"The blessing of the Lord be
upon you;
we bless you in the name of the
Lord."

Psalm 130

A song of ascents.

1Out of the depths I cry to you,
O Lord;
2 O Lord, hear my voice.
Let your ears be attentive
to my cry for mercy.

3If you, O Lord, kept a record of
sins,
O Lord, who could stand?
4But with you there is forgiveness;
therefore you are feared.

5I wait for the Lord, my soul
waits,
and in his word I put my hope.
6My soul waits for the Lord
more than watchmen wait for
the morning,

---

a2 Or eat— / for while they sleep he provides for

more than watchmen wait for
  the morning.
⁷O Israel, put your hope in the
  LORD,
    for with the LORD is unfailing
      love
    and with him is full
      redemption.
⁸He himself will redeem Israel
  from all their sins.

Psalm 131

A song of ascents. Of David.

¹My heart is not proud, O LORD,
  my eyes are not haughty;
I do not concern myself with great
    matters
  or things too wonderful for me.
²But I have stilled and quieted my
    soul;
  like a weaned child with its
    mother,
  like a weaned child is my soul
    within me.

³O Israel, put your hope in the
  LORD
  both now and forevermore.

Psalm 132

A song of ascents.

¹O LORD, remember David
  and all the hardships he
    endured.
²He swore an oath to the LORD
  and made a vow to the Mighty
    One of Jacob:
³"I will not enter my house
  or go to my bed—
⁴I will allow no sleep to my eyes,
  no slumber to my eyelids,
⁵till I find a place for the LORD,
  a dwelling for the Mighty One
    of Jacob."

⁶We heard it in Ephrathah,
  we came upon it in the fields of
    Jaar[a]:[b]
⁷"Let us go to his dwelling place;

  let us worship at his footstool—
⁸arise, O LORD, and come to your
    resting place,
  you and the ark of your might.
⁹May your priests be clothed with
    righteousness;
  may your saints sing for joy."

¹⁰For the sake of David your
    servant,
  do not reject your anointed one.
¹¹The LORD swore an oath to David,
  a sure oath that he will not
    revoke:
"One of your own descendants
  I will place on your throne—
¹²if your sons keep my covenant
  and the statutes I teach them,
then their sons will sit
  on your throne for ever and
    ever."

¹³For the LORD has chosen Zion,
  he has desired it for his
    dwelling:
¹⁴"This is my resting place for ever
    and ever;
  here I will sit enthroned, for I
    have desired it—
¹⁵I will bless her with abundant
    provisions;
  her poor will I satisfy with food.
¹⁶I will clothe her priests with
    salvation,
  and her saints will ever sing for
    joy.

¹⁷"Here I will make a horn[c] grow
    for David
  and set up a lamp for my
    anointed one.
¹⁸I will clothe his enemies with
    shame,
  but the crown on his head will
    be resplendent."

Psalm 133

A song of ascents. Of David.

¹How good and pleasant it is
  when brothers live together in
    unity!

---

[a]6 That is, Kiriath Jearim   [b]6 Or *heard of it in Ephrathah, / we found it in the fields of Jaar.*
(And no quotes around verses 7-9)   [c]17 *Horn* here symbolizes strong one, that is, king.

²It is like precious oil poured on
the head,
running down on the beard,
running down on Aaron's beard,
down upon the collar of his
robes.
³It is as if the dew of Hermon
were falling on Mount Zion.
For there the LORD bestows his
blessing,
even life forevermore.

Psalm 134

A song of ascents.

¹Praise the LORD, all you servants
of the LORD
who minister by night in the
house of the LORD.
²Lift up your hands in the
sanctuary
and praise the LORD.

³May the LORD, the Maker of
heaven and earth,
bless you from Zion.

Psalm 135

¹Praise the LORD.^a

Praise the name of the LORD;
praise him, you servants of the
LORD,
²you who minister in the house of
the LORD,
in the courts of the house of our
God.

³Praise the LORD, for the LORD is
good;
sing praise to his name, for that
is pleasant.
⁴For the LORD has chosen Jacob to
be his own,
Israel to be his treasured
possession.

⁵I know that the LORD is great,
that our Lord is greater than
all gods.
⁶The LORD does whatever pleases
him,

in the heavens and on the
earth,
in the seas and all their depths.
⁷He makes clouds rise from the
ends of the earth;
he sends lightning with the rain
and brings out the wind from
his storehouses.

⁸He struck down the firstborn of
Egypt,
the firstborn of men and
animals.
⁹He sent his signs and wonders
into your midst, O Egypt,
against Pharaoh and all his
servants.
¹⁰He struck down many nations
and killed mighty kings—
¹¹Sihon king of the Amorites,
Og king of Bashan
and all the kings of Canaan—
¹²and he gave their land as an
inheritance,
an inheritance to his people
Israel.

¹³Your name, O LORD, endures
forever,
your renown, O LORD, through
all generations.
¹⁴For the LORD will vindicate his
people
and have compassion on his
servants.

¹⁵The idols of the nations are silver
and gold,
made by the hands of men.
¹⁶They have mouths, but cannot
speak,
eyes, but they cannot see;
¹⁷they have ears, but cannot hear,
nor is there breath in their
mouths.
¹⁸Those who make them will be
like them,
and so will all who trust in
them.

¹⁹O house of Israel, praise the
LORD;
O house of Aaron, praise the
LORD;
²⁰O house of Levi, praise the LORD;

^a1 Hebrew *Hallelu Yah*; also in verses 3 and 21

you who fear him, praise the
LORD.
²¹Praise be to the LORD from Zion,
to him who dwells in
Jerusalem.

Praise the LORD.

Psalm 136

¹Give thanks to the LORD, for he is
good.
His love endures forever.
²Give thanks to the God of gods.
His love endures forever.
³Give thanks to the Lord of lords:
His love endures forever.

⁴to him who alone does great
wonders,
His love endures forever.
⁵who by his understanding made
the heavens,
His love endures forever.
⁶who spread out the earth upon
the waters,
His love endures forever.
⁷who made the great lights—
His love endures forever.
⁸the sun to govern the day,
His love endures forever.
⁹the moon and stars to govern the
night;
His love endures forever.

¹⁰to him who struck down the
firstborn of Egypt
His love endures forever.
¹¹and brought Israel out from
among them
His love endures forever.

¹²with a mighty hand and
outstretched arm;
His love endures forever.

¹³to him who divided the Red Seaᵃ
asunder
His love endures forever.
¹⁴and brought Israel through the
midst of it,
His love endures forever.
¹⁵but swept Pharaoh and his army
into the Red Sea;
His love endures forever.

¹⁶to him who led his people through
the desert,
His love endures forever.
¹⁷who struck down great kings,
His love endures forever.
¹⁸and killed mighty kings—
His love endures forever.
¹⁹Sihon king of the Amorites
His love endures forever.
²⁰and Og king of Bashan—
His love endures forever.
²¹and gave their land as an
inheritance,
His love endures forever.
²²an inheritance to his servant
Israel;
His love endures forever.

²³to the One who remembered us in
our low estate
His love endures forever.
²⁴and freed us from our enemies,
His love endures forever.
²⁵and who gives food to every
creature.
His love endures forever.

²⁶Give thanks to the God of heaven.
His love endures forever.

ᵃ13 Hebrew *Yam Suph*; that is, Sea of Reeds; also in verse 15

LET'S LIVE IT!   Psalm 135:1–21

FAMILY PRAISE FUN ➡ Read Psalm 135. It praises God for the many great things he did for the Israelites.

For family fun at the table, take turns telling something great that God has done. Each person must tell something God has done that no one else has said. A person who can't think of something in five seconds loses a turn. Count and see how many great things your family can tell about God.

Psalm 137

¹By the rivers of Babylon we sat
  and wept
  when we remembered Zion.
²There on the poplars
  we hung our harps,
³for there our captors asked us for
    songs,
  our tormentors demanded songs
    of joy;
  they said, "Sing us one of the
    songs of Zion!"

⁴How can we sing the songs of the
    Lord
  while in a foreign land?
⁵If I forget you, O Jerusalem,
  may my right hand forget ₍its
    skill₎.
⁶May my tongue cling to the roof
    of my mouth
  if I do not remember you,
  if I do not consider Jerusalem
  my highest joy.

⁷Remember, O Lord, what the
    Edomites did
  on the day Jerusalem fell.
"Tear it down," they cried,
  "tear it down to its
    foundations!"

⁸O Daughter of Babylon, doomed
    to destruction,
  happy is he who repays you
  for what you have done to us—
⁹he who seizes your infants
  and dashes them against the
    rocks.

Psalm 138

Of David.

¹I will praise you, O Lord, with all
    my heart;
  before the "gods" I will sing
    your praise.
²I will bow down toward your holy
    temple
  and will praise your name
  for your love and your
    faithfulness,
for you have exalted above all
    things
  your name and your word.

³When I called, you answered me;
  you made me bold and
    stouthearted.

⁴May all the kings of the earth
    praise you, O Lord,
  when they hear the words of
    your mouth.
⁵May they sing of the ways of the
    Lord,
  for the glory of the Lord is
    great.

⁶Though the Lord is on high, he
    looks upon the lowly,
  but the proud he knows from
    afar.
⁷Though I walk in the midst of
    trouble,
  you preserve my life;
you stretch out your hand against
    the anger of my foes,
  with your right hand you save
    me.
⁸The Lord will fulfill ₍his purpose₎
    for me;
  your love, O Lord, endures
    forever—
  do not abandon the works of
    your hands.

Psalm 139

*For the director of music. Of David.
A psalm.*

¹O Lord, you have searched me
  and you know me.
²You know when I sit and when I
    rise;
  you perceive my thoughts from
    afar.
³You discern my going out and my
    lying down;
  you are familiar with all my
    ways.
⁴Before a word is on my tongue
  you know it completely, O Lord.

⁵You hem me in—behind and
    before;
  you have laid your hand upon
    me.
⁶Such knowledge is too wonderful
    for me,
  too lofty for me to attain.

⁷Where can I go from your Spirit?
  Where can I flee from your
    presence?
⁸If I go up to the heavens, you are
    there;
  if I make my bed in the
    depths,ᵃ you are there.
⁹If I rise on the wings of the dawn,
  if I settle on the far side of the
    sea,
¹⁰even there your hand will guide
    me,
  your right hand will hold me
    fast.

¹¹If I say, "Surely the darkness will
    hide me
  and the light become night
    around me,"
¹²even the darkness will not be
    dark to you;
  the night will shine like the
    day,
  for darkness is as light to you.

¹³For you created my inmost being;
  you knit me together in my
    mother's womb.
¹⁴I praise you because I am
    fearfully and wonderfully
    made;
  your works are wonderful,
  I know that full well.
¹⁵My frame was not hidden from
    you
  when I was made in the secret
    place.
  When I was woven together in
    the depths of the earth,

¹⁶ your eyes saw my unformed
      body.
  All the days ordained for me
    were written in your book
    before one of them came to be.

¹⁷How precious toᵇ me are your
    thoughts, O God!
  How vast is the sum of them!
¹⁸Were I to count them,
  they would outnumber the
    grains of sand.
  When I awake,
  I am still with you.

¹⁹If only you would slay the wicked,
    O God!
  Away from me, you bloodthirsty
    men!
²⁰They speak of you with evil
    intent;
  your adversaries misuse your
    name.
²¹Do I not hate those who hate you,
    O LORD,
  and abhor those who rise up
    against you?
²²I have nothing but hatred for
    them;
  I count them my enemies.

²³Search me, O God, and know my
    heart;
  test me and know my anxious
    thoughts.
²⁴See if there is any offensive way
    in me,
  and lead me in the way
    everlasting.

ᵃ8 Hebrew *Sheol*   ᵇ17 Or *concerning*

Life in Bible Times

WHAT GOD IS LIKE

Psalm 139:13 says that God knew David even before he was born. God knew you and watched over you before you were born too. You are special to God because he made you.

Psalm 140

*For the director of music. A psalm
of David.*

¹Rescue me, O LORD, from evil
    men;
  protect me from men of
    violence,
²who devise evil plans in their
    hearts
  and stir up war every day.
³They make their tongues as sharp
    as a serpent's;
  the poison of vipers is on their
    lips.   *Selah*

⁴Keep me, O LORD, from the hands
    of the wicked;
  protect me from men of violence
  who plan to trip my feet.
⁵Proud men have hidden a snare
    for me;
  they have spread out the cords
    of their net
  and have set traps for me along
    my path.   *Selah*

⁶O LORD, I say to you, "You are my
    God."
  Hear, O LORD, my cry for
    mercy.
⁷O Sovereign LORD, my strong
    deliverer,
  who shields my head in the day
    of battle—
⁸do not grant the wicked their
    desires, O LORD;
  do not let their plans succeed,
  or they will become proud.
                                Selah

⁹Let the heads of those who
    surround me
  be covered with the trouble
    their lips have caused.
¹⁰Let burning coals fall upon them;
  may they be thrown into the
    fire,
  into miry pits, never to rise.
¹¹Let slanderers not be established
    in the land;
  may disaster hunt down men of
    violence.

¹²I know that the LORD secures
    justice for the poor
  and upholds the cause of the
    needy.
¹³Surely the righteous will praise
    your name
  and the upright will live before
    you.

Psalm 141

A psalm of David.

¹O LORD, I call to you; come
    quickly to me.
  Hear my voice when I call to
    you.
²May my prayer be set before you
    like incense;
  may the lifting up of my hands
    be like the evening
    sacrifice.

³Set a guard over my mouth,
    O LORD;
  keep watch over the door of my
    lips.
⁴Let not my heart be drawn to
    what is evil,
  to take part in wicked deeds
  with men who are evildoers;
  let me not eat of their
    delicacies.

⁵Let a righteous man*ᵃ* strike
    me—it is a kindness;
  let him rebuke me—it is oil on
    my head.
  My head will not refuse it.

  Yet my prayer is ever against the
    deeds of evildoers;
⁶ their rulers will be thrown
    down from the cliffs,
  and the wicked will learn that
    my words were well spoken.
⁷They will say, "As one plows and
    breaks up the earth,
  so our bones have been
    scattered at the mouth of
    the grave.*ᵇ*"

⁸But my eyes are fixed on you,
    O Sovereign LORD;

ᵃ5 Or Let the Righteous One   *ᵇ7 Hebrew Sheol*

in you I take refuge—do not
    give me over to death.
⁹Keep me from the snares they
    have laid for me,
  from the traps set by evildoers.
¹⁰Let the wicked fall into their own
    nets,
  while I pass by in safety.

Psalm 142

A *maskil*ᵃ of David. When he was in
    the cave. A prayer.

¹I cry aloud to the LORD;
  I lift up my voice to the LORD
    for mercy.
²I pour out my complaint before
    him;
  before him I tell my trouble.

³When my spirit grows faint
    within me,
  it is you who know my way.
In the path where I walk
  men have hidden a snare for
    me.
⁴Look to my right and see;
  no one is concerned for me.
I have no refuge;
  no one cares for my life.

⁵I cry to you, O LORD;
  I say, "You are my refuge,
  my portion in the land of the
    living."
⁶Listen to my cry,
  for I am in desperate need;
rescue me from those who pursue
    me,
  for they are too strong for me.
⁷Set me free from my prison,
  that I may praise your name.

Then the righteous will gather
    about me
  because of your goodness to me.

Psalm 143

A psalm of David.

¹O LORD, hear my prayer,
  listen to my cry for mercy;

in your faithfulness and
    righteousness
  come to my relief.
²Do not bring your servant into
    judgment,
  for no one living is righteous
    before you.

³The enemy pursues me,
  he crushes me to the ground;
he makes me dwell in darkness
  like those long dead.
⁴So my spirit grows faint within
    me;
  my heart within me is
    dismayed.

⁵I remember the days of long ago;
  I meditate on all your works
  and consider what your hands
    have done.
⁶I spread out my hands to you;
  my soul thirsts for you like a
    parched land.   *Selah*

⁷Answer me quickly, O LORD;
  my spirit fails.
Do not hide your face from me
  or I will be like those who go
    down to the pit.
⁸Let the morning bring me word of
    your unfailing love,
  for I have put my trust in you.
Show me the way I should go,
  for to you I lift up my soul.

Words to Remember

**143:8 I have put my trust in you.
    Show me the way I
    should go.**

---

⁹Rescue me from my enemies,
    O LORD,
  for I hide myself in you.
¹⁰Teach me to do your will,
  for you are my God;
may your good Spirit
  lead me on level ground.

¹¹For your name's sake, O LORD,
  preserve my life;

ᵃTitle: Probably a literary or musical term

in your righteousness, bring me
out of trouble.
¹²In your unfailing love, silence my
enemies;
destroy all my foes,
for I am your servant.

Psalm 144

Of David.

¹Praise be to the LORD my Rock,
who trains my hands for war,
my fingers for battle.
²He is my loving God and my
fortress,
my stronghold and my
deliverer,
my shield, in whom I take refuge,
who subdues peoples*ᵃ* under
me.

³O LORD, what is man that you
care for him,
the son of man that you think
of him?
⁴Man is like a breath;
his days are like a fleeting
shadow.

⁵Part your heavens, O LORD, and
come down;
touch the mountains, so that
they smoke.
⁶Send forth lightning and scatter
the enemies;
shoot your arrows and rout
them.
⁷Reach down your hand from on
high;
deliver me and rescue me
from the mighty waters,
from the hands of foreigners
⁸whose mouths are full of lies,
whose right hands are deceitful.

⁹I will sing a new song to you,
O God;
on the ten-stringed lyre I will
make music to you,
¹⁰to the One who gives victory to
kings,

who delivers his servant David
from the deadly sword.

¹¹Deliver me and rescue me
from the hands of foreigners
whose mouths are full of lies,
whose right hands are deceitful.

¹²Then our sons in their youth
will be like well-nurtured
plants,
and our daughters will be like
pillars
carved to adorn a palace.
¹³Our barns will be filled
with every kind of provision.
Our sheep will increase by
thousands,
by tens of thousands in our
fields;
14   our oxen will draw heavy
loads.*ᵇ*
There will be no breaching of
walls,
no going into captivity,
no cry of distress in our streets.

¹⁵Blessed are the people of whom
this is true;
blessed are the people whose
God is the LORD.

Psalm 145*ᶜ*

A psalm of praise. Of David.

¹I will exalt you, my God the
King;
I will praise your name for ever
and ever.
²Every day I will praise you
and extol your name for ever
and ever.

³Great is the LORD and most
worthy of praise;
his greatness no one can
fathom.
⁴One generation will commend
your works to another;
they will tell of your mighty
acts.

---

*ᵃ2 Many manuscripts of the Masoretic Text, Dead Sea Scrolls, Aquila, Jerome and Syriac; most
manuscripts of the Masoretic Text *subdues my people*   *ᵇ14 Or *our chieftains will be firmly
established*   *ᶜThis psalm is an acrostic poem, the verses of which (including verse 13b) begin
with the successive letters of the Hebrew alphabet.

⁵They will speak of the glorious
  splendor of your majesty,
  and I will meditate on your
    wonderful works.ᵃ
⁶They will tell of the power of your
    awesome works,
  and I will proclaim your great
    deeds.
⁷They will celebrate your
    abundant goodness
  and joyfully sing of your
    righteousness.

⁸The LORD is gracious and
    compassionate,
  slow to anger and rich in love.
⁹The LORD is good to all;
  he has compassion on all he has
    made.

WORDS TO REMEMBER

145:9 The LORD is good to all.

---

¹⁰All you have made will praise
    you, O LORD;
  your saints will extol you.
¹¹They will tell of the glory of your
    kingdom
  and speak of your might,
¹²so that all men may know of your
    mighty acts
  and the glorious splendor of
    your kingdom.
¹³Your kingdom is an everlasting
    kingdom,
  and your dominion endures
    through all generations.

  The LORD is faithful to all his
    promises
  and loving toward all he has
    made.ᵇ
¹⁴The LORD upholds all those who
    fall
  and lifts up all who are bowed
    down.
¹⁵The eyes of all look to you,

and you give them their food at
  the proper time.
¹⁶You open your hand
  and satisfy the desires of every
    living thing.

¹⁷The LORD is righteous in all his
    ways
  and loving toward all he has
    made.
¹⁸The LORD is near to all who call
    on him,
  to all who call on him in truth.
¹⁹He fulfills the desires of those
    who fear him;
  he hears their cry and saves
    them.
²⁰The LORD watches over all who
    love him,
  but all the wicked he will
    destroy.

²¹My mouth will speak in praise of
    the LORD.
  Let every creature praise his
    holy name
  for ever and ever.

Psalm 146

¹Praise the LORD.ᶜ

  Praise the LORD, O my soul.
² I will praise the LORD all my
    life;
  I will sing praise to my God as
    long as I live.

³Do not put your trust in princes,
  in mortal men, who cannot
    save.
⁴When their spirit departs, they
    return to the ground;
  on that very day their plans
    come to nothing.

⁵Blessed is he whose help is the
    God of Jacob,
  whose hope is in the LORD his
    God,
⁶the Maker of heaven and earth,

ᵃ5 Dead Sea Scrolls and Syriac (see also Septuagint); Masoretic Text *On the glorious splendor of
your majesty / and on your wonderful works I will meditate*   ᵇ13 One manuscript of the
Masoretic Text, Dead Sea Scrolls and Syriac (see also Septuagint); most manuscripts of the
Masoretic Text do not have the last two lines of verse 13.   ᶜ1 Hebrew *Hallelu Yah*; also in
verse 10

the sea, and everything in
  them—
the LORD, who remains faithful
  forever.
⁷He upholds the cause of the
  oppressed
and gives food to the hungry.
The LORD sets prisoners free,
⁸ the LORD gives sight to the
  blind,
the LORD lifts up those who are
  bowed down,
the LORD loves the righteous.
⁹The LORD watches over the alien
and sustains the fatherless and
  the widow,
but he frustrates the ways of
  the wicked.

¹⁰The LORD reigns forever,
  your God, O Zion, for all
  generations.

Praise the LORD.

Psalm 147

¹Praise the LORD.ᵃ

How good it is to sing praises to
  our God,
how pleasant and fitting to
  praise him!

²The LORD builds up Jerusalem;
he gathers the exiles of Israel.
³He heals the brokenhearted
and binds up their wounds.
⁴He determines the number of the
  stars
and calls them each by name.
⁵Great is our Lord and mighty in
  power;
his understanding has no limit.
⁶The LORD sustains the humble
but casts the wicked to the
  ground.

⁷Sing to the LORD with
  thanksgiving;
make music to our God on the
  harp.
⁸He covers the sky with clouds;

he supplies the earth with rain
and makes grass grow on the
  hills.
⁹He provides food for the cattle
and for the young ravens when
  they call.

¹⁰His pleasure is not in the
  strength of the horse,
nor his delight in the legs of a
  man;
¹¹the LORD delights in those who
  fear him,
who put their hope in his
  unfailing love.

¹²Extol the LORD, O Jerusalem;
praise your God, O Zion,
¹³for he strengthens the bars of
  your gates
and blesses your people within
  you.
¹⁴He grants peace to your borders
and satisfies you with the finest
  of wheat.

¹⁵He sends his command to the
  earth;
his word runs swiftly.
¹⁶He spreads the snow like wool
and scatters the frost like ashes.
¹⁷He hurls down his hail like
  pebbles.
Who can withstand his icy
  blast?
¹⁸He sends his word and melts
  them;
he stirs up his breezes, and the
  waters flow.

¹⁹He has revealed his word to
  Jacob,
his laws and decrees to Israel.
²⁰He has done this for no other
  nation;
they do not know his laws.

Praise the LORD.

Psalm 148

¹Praise the LORD.ᵇ

Praise the LORD from the heavens,

ᵃ1 Hebrew *Hallelu Yah*; also in verse 20   ᵇ1 Hebrew *Hallelu Yah*; also in verse 14

praise him in the heights above.
²Praise him, all his angels,
　praise him, all his heavenly
　　hosts.
³Praise him, sun and moon,
　praise him, all you shining
　　stars.
⁴Praise him, you highest heavens
　and you waters above the skies.
⁵Let them praise the name of the
　　LORD,
　for he commanded and they
　　were created.
⁶He set them in place for ever and
　　ever;
　he gave a decree that will never
　　pass away.

⁷Praise the LORD from the earth,
　you great sea creatures and all
　　ocean depths,
⁸lightning and hail, snow and
　　clouds,
　stormy winds that do his
　　bidding,
⁹you mountains and all hills,
　fruit trees and all cedars,
¹⁰wild animals and all cattle,
　small creatures and flying
　　birds,
¹¹kings of the earth and all
　　nations,

you princes and all rulers on
　earth,
¹²young men and maidens,
　old men and children.

¹³Let them praise the name of the
　　LORD,
　for his name alone is exalted;
　his splendor is above the earth
　　and the heavens.
¹⁴He has raised up for his people a
　　horn,ᵃ
　the praise of all his saints,
　of Israel, the people close to his
　　heart.

Praise the LORD.

Psalm 149

¹Praise the LORD.ᵇ
Sing to the LORD a new song,
　his praise in the assembly of
　　the saints.
²Let Israel rejoice in their Maker;
　let the people of Zion be glad in
　　their King.
³Let them praise his name with
　　dancing
　and make music to him with
　　tambourine and harp.

ᵃ14 *Horn* here symbolizes strong one, that is, king.　ᵇ1 Hebrew *Hallelu Yah*; also in verse 9

Life in Bible Times

DANCING

In Bible times a man and a woman did not dance together. Usually a group of men danced, or a group of women danced. People danced at weddings to show happiness. They danced at great feasts held to worship the Lord. David danced and leaped for joy when God's ark entered Jerusalem (1 Chronicles 15:29).

4For the LORD takes delight in his
   people;
   he crowns the humble with
      salvation.
5Let the saints rejoice in this
   honor
   and sing for joy on their
      beds.

6May the praise of God be in their
   mouths
   and a double-edged sword in
      their hands,
7to inflict vengeance on the
   nations
   and punishment on the
      peoples,
8to bind their kings with fetters,
   their nobles with shackles of
      iron,
9to carry out the sentence written
   against them.
   This is the glory of all his
      saints.

Praise the LORD.

Psalm 150

1Praise the LORD.[a]

Praise God in his sanctuary;
   praise him in his mighty
      heavens.
2Praise him for his acts of power;
   praise him for his surpassing
      greatness.
3Praise him with the sounding of
   the trumpet,
   praise him with the harp and
      lyre,
4praise him with tambourine and
   dancing,
   praise him with the strings and
      flute,
   praise him with resounding
      cymbals.
5praise him with the clash of
   cymbals,

6Let everything that has breath
   praise the LORD.

Praise the LORD.

PROVERBS

WHO WROTE THIS BOOK?
Solomon wrote many of the proverbs. Wise men added others.

WHY WAS THIS BOOK WRITTEN?
This book was written to help people make wise choices.

FOR WHOM WAS THIS BOOK WRITTEN?
This book was written for everyone. Even people who do not believe in God can use its good advice.

WHAT KIND OF ADVICE IS FOUND IN PROVERBS?
This book gives advice on making friends, on living in the family, on money, on doing right, on caring about poor people, and on many other important things.

WHEN WAS THIS BOOK WRITTEN?
The proverbs in this book were probably written between 970 and 686 B.C.

WHAT ARE SOME PROVERBS FOR CHILDREN IN THIS BOOK?

Advice about trusting God.	Proverbs 3:5–6
Advice on working hard.	Proverbs 6:6–11
Advice about insults.	Proverbs 12:16
Advice about gossip.	Proverbs 17:9
Advice about revenge.	Proverbs 20:22
Advice on discipline.	Proverbs 22:15

Prologue: Purpose and Theme

1 The proverbs of Solomon son of David, king of Israel:

²for attaining wisdom and discipline;
for understanding words of insight;
³for acquiring a disciplined and prudent life,
doing what is right and just and fair;
⁴for giving prudence to the simple,
knowledge and discretion to the young—
⁵let the wise listen and add to their learning,
and let the discerning get guidance—
⁶for understanding proverbs and parables,
the sayings and riddles of the wise.

⁷The fear of the LORD is the beginning of knowledge,
but fools*ᵃ* despise wisdom and discipline.

Exhortations to Embrace Wisdom

Warning Against Enticement

⁸Listen, my son, to your father's instruction
and do not forsake your mother's teaching.
⁹They will be a garland to grace your head
and a chain to adorn your neck.

¹⁰My son, if sinners entice you,
do not give in to them.
¹¹If they say, "Come along with us;
let's lie in wait for someone's blood,
let's waylay some harmless soul;
¹²let's swallow them alive, like the grave,*ᵇ*
and whole, like those who go down to the pit;
¹³we will get all sorts of valuable things
and fill our houses with plunder;
¹⁴throw in your lot with us,
and we will share a common purse"—
¹⁵my son, do not go along with them,
do not set foot on their paths;
¹⁶for their feet rush into sin,
they are swift to shed blood.
¹⁷How useless to spread a net
in full view of all the birds!
¹⁸These men lie in wait for their own blood;
they waylay only themselves!
¹⁹Such is the end of all who go after ill-gotten gain;
it takes away the lives of those who get it.

Warning Against Rejecting Wisdom

²⁰Wisdom calls aloud in the street,
she raises her voice in the public squares;
²¹at the head of the noisy streets*ᶜ* she cries out,
in the gateways of the city she makes her speech:

²²"How long will you simple ones*ᵈ* love your simple ways?
How long will mockers delight in mockery
and fools hate knowledge?
²³If you had responded to my rebuke,
I would have poured out my heart to you
and made my thoughts known to you.
²⁴But since you rejected me when I called
and no one gave heed when I stretched out my hand,
²⁵since you ignored all my advice

ᵃ7 The Hebrew words rendered *fool* in Proverbs, and often elsewhere in the Old Testament, denote one who is morally deficient.   *ᵇ12* Hebrew *Sheol*   *ᶜ21* Hebrew; Septuagint / *on the tops of the walls*   *ᵈ22* The Hebrew word rendered *simple* in Proverbs generally denotes one without moral direction and inclined to evil.

and would not accept my
rebuke,
26I in turn will laugh at your
disaster;
I will mock when calamity
overtakes you—
27when calamity overtakes you like
a storm,
when disaster sweeps over you
like a whirlwind,
when distress and trouble
overwhelm you.

28"Then they will call to me but I
will not answer;
they will look for me but will
not find me.
29Since they hated knowledge
and did not choose to fear the
Lord,
30since they would not accept my
advice
and spurned my rebuke,
31they will eat the fruit of their
ways
and be filled with the fruit of
their schemes.
32For the waywardness of the
simple will kill them,
and the complacency of fools
will destroy them;
33but whoever listens to me will
live in safety
and be at ease, without fear of
harm."

Moral Benefits of Wisdom

2 My son, if you accept my words
and store up my commands
within you,
2turning your ear to wisdom
and applying your heart to
understanding,
3and if you call out for insight
and cry aloud for
understanding,
4and if you look for it as for silver
and search for it as for hidden
treasure,
5then you will understand the fear
of the Lord
and find the knowledge of God.
6For the Lord gives wisdom,

and from his mouth come
knowledge and
understanding.
7He holds victory in store for the
upright,
he is a shield to those whose
walk is blameless,
8for he guards the course of the
just
and protects the way of his
faithful ones.

9Then you will understand what is
right and just
and fair—every good path.
10For wisdom will enter your heart,
and knowledge will be pleasant
to your soul.
11Discretion will protect you,
and understanding will guard
you.

12Wisdom will save you from the
ways of wicked men,
from men whose words are
perverse,
13who leave the straight paths
to walk in dark ways,
14who delight in doing wrong
and rejoice in the perverseness
of evil,
15whose paths are crooked
and who are devious in their
ways.

16It will save you also from the
adulteress,
from the wayward wife with her
seductive words,
17who has left the partner of her
youth
and ignored the covenant she
made before God. a
18For her house leads down to
death
and her paths to the spirits of
the dead.
19None who go to her return
or attain the paths of life.

20Thus you will walk in the ways of
good men
and keep to the paths of the
righteous.

a17 Or covenant of her God

21For the upright will live in the
land,
and the blameless will remain
in it;
22but the wicked will be cut off
from the land,
and the unfaithful will be torn
from it.

Further Benefits of Wisdom

3 My son, do not forget my
teaching,
but keep my commands in your
heart,
2for they will prolong your life
many years
and bring you prosperity.

3Let love and faithfulness never
leave you;
bind them around your neck,
write them on the tablet of your
heart.
4Then you will win favor and a
good name
in the sight of God and man.

5Trust in the LORD with all your
heart
and lean not on your own
understanding;
6in all your ways acknowledge
him,

a6 Or *will direct your paths*

and he will make your paths
straight.a

WORDS TO REMEMBER

3:5-6 Trust in the LORD with all
your heart
and lean not on your
own understanding;
in all your ways
acknowledge him,
and he will make your
paths straight.

7Do not be wise in your own eyes;
fear the LORD and shun evil.
8This will bring health to your
body
and nourishment to your bones.

9Honor the LORD with your wealth,
with the firstfruits of all your
crops;
10then your barns will be filled to
overflowing,
and your vats will brim over
with new wine.

11My son, do not despise the LORD's
discipline
and do not resent his rebuke,

LET'S LIVE IT!
Proverbs 2:6–15

THINK BEFORE YOU ACT ➡ "Come on, gang! Let's go get him!" Greg
started running, and everyone ran after him. Everyone but Kevin.
    Kevin had read Proverbs 2:6–15, and he knew "wisdom will save you
from the ways of wicked men" (Proverbs 2:12). Here's what Kevin did—
and what you can do to help you think before you act. Kevin counted
to five by asking himself these questions:

1. Is it right?
2. Is it good?
3. Is it helpful?
4. Would my parents approve?
5. Would God approve?

    If the answer to any of the questions is no, stop counting. And go the
other way!

¹²because the LORD disciplines those
    he loves,
  as a father^a the son he delights
    in.

¹³Blessed is the man who finds
    wisdom,
  the man who gains
    understanding,
¹⁴for she is more profitable than
    silver
  and yields better returns than
    gold.
¹⁵She is more precious than rubies;
  nothing you desire can compare
    with her.
¹⁶Long life is in her right hand;
  in her left hand are riches and
    honor.
¹⁷Her ways are pleasant ways,
  and all her paths are peace.
¹⁸She is a tree of life to those who
    embrace her;
  those who lay hold of her will
    be blessed.

¹⁹By wisdom the LORD laid the
    earth's foundations,
  by understanding he set the
    heavens in place;
²⁰by his knowledge the deeps were
    divided,
  and the clouds let drop the
    dew.

²¹My son, preserve sound judgment
    and discernment,
  do not let them out of your
    sight;
²²they will be life for you,
  an ornament to grace your
    neck.
²³Then you will go on your way in
    safety,
  and your foot will not stumble;
²⁴when you lie down, you will not
    be afraid;
  when you lie down, your sleep
    will be sweet.
²⁵Have no fear of sudden disaster
  or of the ruin that overtakes
    the wicked,
²⁶for the LORD will be your
    confidence

and will keep your foot from
    being snared.

²⁷Do not withhold good from those
    who deserve it,
  when it is in your power to act.
²⁸Do not say to your neighbor,
  "Come back later; I'll give it
    tomorrow"—
  when you now have it with you.

²⁹Do not plot harm against your
    neighbor,
  who lives trustfully near you.
³⁰Do not accuse a man for no
    reason—
  when he has done you no harm.

³¹Do not envy a violent man
  or choose any of his ways,
³²for the LORD detests a perverse
    man
  but takes the upright into his
    confidence.

³³The LORD's curse is on the house
    of the wicked,
  but he blesses the home of the
    righteous.
³⁴He mocks proud mockers
  but gives grace to the humble.
³⁵The wise inherit honor,
  but fools he holds up to shame.

Wisdom Is Supreme

4 Listen, my sons, to a father's
    instruction;
  pay attention and gain
    understanding.
²I give you sound learning,
  so do not forsake my teaching.
³When I was a boy in my father's
    house,
  still tender, and an only child of
    my mother,
⁴he taught me and said,
  "Lay hold of my words with all
    your heart;
  keep my commands and you
    will live.
⁵Get wisdom, get understanding;
  do not forget my words or
    swerve from them.

^a12 Hebrew; Septuagint / *and he punishes*

⁶Do not forsake wisdom, and she
will protect you;
love her, and she will watch
over you.
⁷Wisdom is supreme; therefore get
wisdom.
Though it cost all you have,ᵃ
get understanding.
⁸Esteem her, and she will exalt
you;
embrace her, and she will honor
you.
⁹She will set a garland of grace on
your head
and present you with a crown of
splendor."

¹⁰Listen, my son, accept what I say,
and the years of your life will
be many.
¹¹I guide you in the way of wisdom
and lead you along straight
paths.
¹²When you walk, your steps will
not be hampered;
when you run, you will not
stumble.
¹³Hold on to instruction, do not let
it go;
guard it well, for it is your life.
¹⁴Do not set foot on the path of the
wicked
or walk in the way of evil men.
¹⁵Avoid it, do not travel on it;
turn from it and go on your
way.
¹⁶For they cannot sleep till they do
evil;
they are robbed of slumber till
they make someone fall.
¹⁷They eat the bread of wickedness
and drink the wine of violence.

¹⁸The path of the righteous is like
the first gleam of dawn,
shining ever brighter till the
full light of day.
¹⁹But the way of the wicked is like
deep darkness;
they do not know what makes
them stumble.

²⁰My son, pay attention to what I
say;

listen closely to my words.
²¹Do not let them out of your sight,
keep them within your heart;
²²for they are life to those who find
them
and health to a man's whole
body.
²³Above all else, guard your heart,
for it is the wellspring of life.
²⁴Put away perversity from your
mouth;
keep corrupt talk far from your
lips.
²⁵Let your eyes look straight
ahead,
fix your gaze directly before
you.
²⁶Make levelᵇ paths for your feet
and take only ways that are
firm.
²⁷Do not swerve to the right or the
left;
keep your foot from evil.

Warning Against Adultery

5 My son, pay attention to my
wisdom,
listen well to my words of
insight,
²that you may maintain discretion
and your lips may preserve
knowledge.
³For the lips of an adulteress drip
honey,
and her speech is smoother than
oil;
⁴but in the end she is bitter as
gall,
sharp as a double-edged sword.
⁵Her feet go down to death;
her steps lead straight to the
grave.ᶜ
⁶She gives no thought to the way
of life;
her paths are crooked, but she
knows it not.

⁷Now then, my sons, listen to me;
do not turn aside from what I
say.
⁸Keep to a path far from her,
do not go near the door of her
house,

ᵃ7 Or *Whatever else you get*   ᵇ26 Or *Consider the*   ᶜ5 Hebrew *Sheol*

⁹lest you give your best strength to others
and your years to one who is cruel,
¹⁰lest strangers feast on your wealth
and your toil enrich another man's house.
¹¹At the end of your life you will groan,
when your flesh and body are spent.
¹²You will say, "How I hated discipline!
How my heart spurned correction!
¹³I would not obey my teachers
or listen to my instructors.
¹⁴I have come to the brink of utter ruin
in the midst of the whole assembly."

¹⁵Drink water from your own cistern,
running water from your own well.
¹⁶Should your springs overflow in the streets,
your streams of water in the public squares?
¹⁷Let them be yours alone,
never to be shared with strangers.
¹⁸May your fountain be blessed,
and may you rejoice in the wife of your youth.
¹⁹A loving doe, a graceful deer—
may her breasts satisfy you always,
may you ever be captivated by her love.
²⁰Why be captivated, my son, by an adulteress?
Why embrace the bosom of another man's wife?

²¹For a man's ways are in full view of the LORD,
and he examines all his paths.
²²The evil deeds of a wicked man ensnare him;
the cords of his sin hold him fast.

²³He will die for lack of discipline,
led astray by his own great folly.

Warnings Against Folly

6 My son, if you have put up security for your neighbor,
if you have struck hands in pledge for another,
²if you have been trapped by what you said,
ensnared by the words of your mouth,
³then do this, my son, to free yourself,
since you have fallen into your neighbor's hands:
Go and humble yourself;
press your plea with your neighbor!
⁴Allow no sleep to your eyes,
no slumber to your eyelids.
⁵Free yourself, like a gazelle from the hand of the hunter,
like a bird from the snare of the fowler.

⁶Go to the ant, you sluggard;
consider its ways and be wise!
⁷It has no commander,
no overseer or ruler,
⁸yet it stores its provisions in summer
and gathers its food at harvest.

⁹How long will you lie there, you sluggard?
When will you get up from your sleep?
¹⁰A little sleep, a little slumber,
a little folding of the hands to rest—
¹¹and poverty will come on you like a bandit
and scarcity like an armed man.ᵃ

¹²A scoundrel and villain,
who goes about with a corrupt mouth,
¹³ who winks with his eye,
signals with his feet
and motions with his fingers,

ᵃ11 Or *like a vagrant / and scarcity like a beggar*

14 who plots evil with deceit in his
     heart—
  he always stirs up dissension.
15Therefore disaster will overtake
     him in an instant;
  he will suddenly be
     destroyed—without remedy.

16There are six things the LORD
     hates,
  seven that are detestable to
     him:
17   haughty eyes,
  a lying tongue,
  hands that shed innocent
     blood,
18   a heart that devises wicked
     schemes,
  feet that are quick to rush
     into evil,
19   a false witness who pours out
     lies
  and a man who stirs up
     dissension among brothers.

Warning Against Adultery

20My son, keep your father's
     commands
  and do not forsake your
     mother's teaching.
21Bind them upon your heart
     forever;
  fasten them around your
     neck.
22When you walk, they will guide
     you;
  when you sleep, they will watch
     over you;
  when you awake, they will
     speak to you.
23For these commands are a lamp,
  this teaching is a light,
  and the corrections of discipline

  are the way to life,
24keeping you from the immoral
     woman,
  from the smooth tongue of the
     wayward wife.
25Do not lust in your heart after
     her beauty
  or let her captivate you with
     her eyes,
26for the prostitute reduces you to a
     loaf of bread,
  and the adulteress preys upon
     your very life.
27Can a man scoop fire into his lap
  without his clothes being
     burned?
28Can a man walk on hot coals
  without his feet being scorched?
29So is he who sleeps with another
     man's wife;
  no one who touches her will go
     unpunished.

30Men do not despise a thief if he
     steals
  to satisfy his hunger when he is
     starving.
31Yet if he is caught, he must pay
     sevenfold,
  though it costs him all the
     wealth of his house.
32But a man who commits adultery
     lacks judgment;
  whoever does so destroys
     himself.
33Blows and disgrace are his lot,
  and his shame will never be
     wiped away;
34for jealousy arouses a husband's
     fury,
  and he will show no mercy
     when he takes revenge.
35He will not accept any
     compensation;

LET'S LIVE IT!   Proverbs 6:6–11

WORK HARD ➥ Read Proverbs 6:6–11. Then look outside for an anthill.
Watch the ants going in and out. See the loads they carry. The writer of
Proverbs urges people to follow the example of ants and to work hard.
   An easy way to draw an ant is to use just three circles and stick legs.
If you need a reminder to work hard on your school work, on your chores,
or on some other project, draw a picture of an ant and tape it where it
can remind you.

he will refuse the bribe,
  however great it is.

Warning Against the Adulteress

7 My son, keep my words
  and store up my commands
    within you.
²Keep my commands and you will
    live;
  guard my teachings as the
    apple of your eye.
³Bind them on your fingers;
  write them on the tablet of your
    heart.
⁴Say to wisdom, "You are my
    sister,"
  and call understanding your
    kinsman;
⁵they will keep you from the
    adulteress,
  from the wayward wife with her
    seductive words.

⁶At the window of my house
  I looked out through the lattice.
⁷I saw among the simple,
  I noticed among the young men,
  a youth who lacked judgment.
⁸He was going down the street
    near her corner,
  walking along in the direction
    of her house
⁹at twilight, as the day was fading,
  as the dark of night set in.

¹⁰Then out came a woman to meet
    him,
  dressed like a prostitute and
    with crafty intent.
¹¹(She is loud and defiant,
  her feet never stay at home;
¹²now in the street, now in the
    squares,
  at every corner she lurks.)
¹³She took hold of him and kissed
    him
  and with a brazen face she said:

¹⁴"I have fellowship offerings[a] at
    home;
  today I fulfilled my vows.
¹⁵So I came out to meet you;

I looked for you and have found
    you!
¹⁶I have covered my bed
  with colored linens from Egypt.
¹⁷I have perfumed my bed
  with myrrh, aloes and
    cinnamon.
¹⁸Come, let's drink deep of love till
    morning;
  let's enjoy ourselves with love!
¹⁹My husband is not at home;
  he has gone on a long journey.
²⁰He took his purse filled with
    money
  and will not be home till full
    moon."

²¹With persuasive words she led
    him astray;
  she seduced him with her
    smooth talk.
²²All at once he followed her
  like an ox going to the
    slaughter,
  like a deer[b] stepping into a
    noose[c]
²³ till an arrow pierces his liver,
  like a bird darting into a snare,
  little knowing it will cost him
    his life.

²⁴Now then, my sons, listen to me;
  pay attention to what I say.
²⁵Do not let your heart turn to her
    ways
  or stray into her paths.
²⁶Many are the victims she has
    brought down;
  her slain are a mighty throng.
²⁷Her house is a highway to the
    grave,[d]
  leading down to the chambers of
    death.

Wisdom's Call

8 Does not wisdom call out?
  Does not understanding raise
    her voice?
²On the heights along the way,
  where the paths meet, she takes
    her stand;
³beside the gates leading into the
    city,

---

a14 Traditionally *peace offerings*   b22 Syriac (see also Septuagint); Hebrew *fool*   c22 The
meaning of the Hebrew for this line is uncertain.   d27 Hebrew *Sheol*

at the entrances, she cries
aloud:
⁴"To you, O men, I call out;
I raise my voice to all mankind.
⁵You who are simple, gain
prudence;
you who are foolish, gain
understanding.
⁶Listen, for I have worthy things
to say;
I open my lips to speak what is
right.
⁷My mouth speaks what is true,
for my lips detest wickedness.
⁸All the words of my mouth are
just;
none of them is crooked or
perverse.
⁹To the discerning all of them are
right;
they are faultless to those who
have knowledge.
¹⁰Choose my instruction instead of
silver,
knowledge rather than choice
gold,
¹¹for wisdom is more precious than
rubies,
and nothing you desire can
compare with her.

¹²"I, wisdom, dwell together with
prudence;
I possess knowledge and
discretion.
¹³To fear the LORD is to hate evil;
I hate pride and arrogance,
evil behavior and perverse
speech.
¹⁴Counsel and sound judgment are
mine;
I have understanding and
power.
¹⁵By me kings reign
and rulers make laws that are
just;
¹⁶by me princes govern,
and all nobles who rule on
earth.ᵃ
¹⁷I love those who love me,
and those who seek me find me.

¹⁸With me are riches and honor,
enduring wealth and prosperity.
¹⁹My fruit is better than fine gold;
what I yield surpasses choice
silver.
²⁰I walk in the way of
righteousness,
along the paths of justice,
²¹bestowing wealth on those who
love me
and making their treasuries
full.

²²"The LORD brought me forth as
the first of his works,ᵇ, ᶜ
before his deeds of old;
²³I was appointedᵈ from eternity,
from the beginning, before the
world began.
²⁴When there were no oceans, I was
given birth,
when there were no springs
abounding with water;
²⁵before the mountains were settled
in place,
before the hills, I was given
birth,
²⁶before he made the earth or its
fields
or any of the dust of the world.
²⁷I was there when he set the
heavens in place,
when he marked out the
horizon on the face of the
deep,
²⁸when he established the clouds
above
and fixed securely the fountains
of the deep,
²⁹when he gave the sea its
boundary
so the waters would not
overstep his command,
and when he marked out the
foundations of the earth.
³⁰ Then I was the craftsman at his
side.
I was filled with delight day after
day,
rejoicing always in his presence,
³¹rejoicing in his whole world

ᵃ16 Many Hebrew manuscripts and Septuagint; most Hebrew manuscripts *and nobles—all righteous
rulers*   ᵇ22 Or *way;* or *dominion*   ᶜ22 Or *The LORD possessed me at the beginning of his work;*
or *The LORD brought me forth at the beginning of his work*   ᵈ23 Or *fashioned*

and delighting in mankind.

³²"Now then, my sons, listen to me;
blessed are those who keep my
ways.
³³Listen to my instruction and be
wise;
do not ignore it.
³⁴Blessed is the man who listens to
me,
watching daily at my doors,
waiting at my doorway.
³⁵For whoever finds me finds life
and receives favor from the
LORD.
³⁶But whoever fails to find me
harms himself;
all who hate me love death."

Invitations of Wisdom and of Folly

9 Wisdom has built her house;
she has hewn out its seven
pillars.
²She has prepared her meat and
mixed her wine;
she has also set her table.
³She has sent out her maids, and
she calls
from the highest point of the
city.
⁴"Let all who are simple come in
here!"
she says to those who lack
judgment.
⁵"Come, eat my food
and drink the wine I have
mixed.
⁶Leave your simple ways and you
will live;
walk in the way of
understanding.

⁷"Whoever corrects a mocker
invites insult;
whoever rebukes a wicked man
incurs abuse.
⁸Do not rebuke a mocker or he will
hate you;
rebuke a wise man and he will
love you.
⁹Instruct a wise man and he will
be wiser still;

teach a righteous man and he
will add to his learning.
¹⁰"The fear of the LORD is the
beginning of wisdom,
and knowledge of the Holy One
is understanding.
¹¹For through me your days will be
many,
and years will be added to your
life.
¹²If you are wise, your wisdom will
reward you;
if you are a mocker, you alone
will suffer."

¹³The woman Folly is loud;
she is undisciplined and without
knowledge.
¹⁴She sits at the door of her house,
on a seat at the highest point of
the city,
¹⁵calling out to those who pass by,
who go straight on their way.
¹⁶"Let all who are simple come in
here!"
she says to those who lack
judgment.
¹⁷"Stolen water is sweet;
food eaten in secret is
delicious!"
¹⁸But little do they know that the
dead are there,
that her guests are in the
depths of the grave.ᵃ

Proverbs of Solomon

10 The proverbs of Solomon:

A wise son brings joy to his
father,
but a foolish son grief to his
mother.

²Ill-gotten treasures are of no
value,
but righteousness delivers from
death.

³The LORD does not let the
righteous go hungry
but he thwarts the craving of
the wicked.

⁴Lazy hands make a man poor,

ᵃ18 Hebrew *Sheol*

but diligent hands bring wealth.

⁵He who gathers crops in summer
　is a wise son,
but he who sleeps during
　harvest is a disgraceful son.

⁶Blessings crown the head of the
　righteous,
but violence overwhelms the
　mouth of the wicked. *ᵃ*

⁷The memory of the righteous will
　be a blessing,
but the name of the wicked will
　rot.

⁸The wise in heart accept
　commands,
but a chattering fool comes to
　ruin.

⁹The man of integrity walks
　securely,
but he who takes crooked paths
　will be found out.

¹⁰He who winks maliciously causes
　grief,
and a chattering fool comes to
　ruin.

¹¹The mouth of the righteous is a
　fountain of life,
but violence overwhelms the
　mouth of the wicked.

¹²Hatred stirs up dissension,
but love covers over all wrongs.

¹³Wisdom is found on the lips of the
　discerning,
but a rod is for the back of him
　who lacks judgment.

¹⁴Wise men store up knowledge,
but the mouth of a fool invites
　ruin.

¹⁵The wealth of the rich is their
　fortified city,
but poverty is the ruin of the
　poor.

¹⁶The wages of the righteous bring
　them life,
but the income of the wicked
　brings them punishment.

¹⁷He who heeds discipline shows
　the way to life,
but whoever ignores correction
　leads others astray.

¹⁸He who conceals his hatred has
　lying lips,
and whoever spreads slander is
　a fool.

¹⁹When words are many, sin is not
　absent,
but he who holds his tongue is
　wise.

²⁰The tongue of the righteous is
　choice silver,
but the heart of the wicked is of
　little value.

²¹The lips of the righteous nourish
　many,
but fools die for lack of
　judgment.

²²The blessing of the Lord brings
　wealth,
and he adds no trouble to it.

²³A fool finds pleasure in evil
　conduct,
but a man of understanding
　delights in wisdom.

²⁴What the wicked dreads will
　overtake him;
what the righteous desire will
　be granted.

²⁵When the storm has swept by, the
　wicked are gone,
but the righteous stand firm
　forever.

²⁶As vinegar to the teeth and
　smoke to the eyes,
so is a sluggard to those who
　send him.

²⁷The fear of the Lord adds length
　to life,
but the years of the wicked are
　cut short.

²⁸The prospect of the righteous is
　joy,
but the hopes of the wicked
　come to nothing.

ᵃ6 Or but the mouth of the wicked conceals violence; *also in verse 11*

²⁹The way of the LORD is a refuge
for the righteous,
but it is the ruin of those who
do evil.

³⁰The righteous will never be
uprooted,
but the wicked will not remain
in the land.

³¹The mouth of the righteous
brings forth wisdom,
but a perverse tongue will be
cut out.

³²The lips of the righteous know
what is fitting,
but the mouth of the wicked
only what is perverse.

11 The LORD abhors dishonest
scales,
but accurate weights are his
delight.

²When pride comes, then comes
disgrace,
but with humility comes
wisdom.

³The integrity of the upright
guides them,
but the unfaithful are destroyed
by their duplicity.

⁴Wealth is worthless in the day of
wrath,
but righteousness delivers from
death.

⁵The righteousness of the
blameless makes a straight
way for them,
but the wicked are brought
down by their own
wickedness.

⁶The righteousness of the upright
delivers them,
but the unfaithful are trapped
by evil desires.

⁷When a wicked man dies, his
hope perishes;
all he expected from his power
comes to nothing.

⁸The righteous man is rescued
from trouble,
and it comes on the wicked
instead.

⁹With his mouth the godless
destroys his neighbor,
but through knowledge the
righteous escape.

¹⁰When the righteous prosper, the
city rejoices;
when the wicked perish, there
are shouts of joy.

¹¹Through the blessing of the
upright a city is exalted,
but by the mouth of the wicked
it is destroyed.

¹²A man who lacks judgment
derides his neighbor,
but a man of understanding
holds his tongue.

¹³A gossip betrays a confidence,
but a trustworthy man keeps a
secret.

¹⁴For lack of guidance a nation
falls,
but many advisers make victory
sure.

¹⁵He who puts up security for
another will surely suffer,
but whoever refuses to strike
hands in pledge is safe.

¹⁶A kindhearted woman gains
respect,
but ruthless men gain only
wealth.

¹⁷A kind man benefits himself,
but a cruel man brings trouble
on himself.

¹⁸The wicked man earns deceptive
wages,
but he who sows righteousness
reaps a sure reward.

¹⁹The truly righteous man attains
life,
but he who pursues evil goes to
his death.

²⁰The LORD detests men of perverse
heart
but he delights in those whose
ways are blameless.

²¹Be sure of this: The wicked will
not go unpunished,
but those who are righteous will
go free.

²²Like a gold ring in a pig's snout
is a beautiful woman who shows
no discretion.

²³The desire of the righteous ends
only in good,
but the hope of the wicked only
in wrath.

²⁴One man gives freely, yet gains
even more;
another withholds unduly, but
comes to poverty.

²⁵A generous man will prosper;
he who refreshes others will
himself be refreshed.

²⁶People curse the man who hoards
grain,
but blessing crowns him who is
willing to sell.

²⁷He who seeks good finds goodwill,
but evil comes to him who
searches for it.

²⁸Whoever trusts in his riches will
fall,
but the righteous will thrive
like a green leaf.

²⁹He who brings trouble on his
family will inherit only
wind,
and the fool will be servant to
the wise.

³⁰The fruit of the righteous is a
tree of life,
and he who wins souls is wise.

³¹If the righteous receive their due
on earth,
how much more the ungodly
and the sinner!

12 Whoever loves discipline
loves knowledge,
but he who hates correction is
stupid.

²A good man obtains favor from
the LORD,
but the LORD condemns a crafty
man.

³A man cannot be established
through wickedness,
but the righteous cannot be
uprooted.

⁴A wife of noble character is her
husband's crown,
but a disgraceful wife is like
decay in his bones.

⁵The plans of the righteous are
just,
but the advice of the wicked is
deceitful.

⁶The words of the wicked lie in
wait for blood,
but the speech of the upright
rescues them.

⁷Wicked men are overthrown and
are no more,
but the house of the righteous
stands firm.

⁸A man is praised according to his
wisdom,
but men with warped minds are
despised.

⁹Better to be a nobody and yet
have a servant
than pretend to be somebody
and have no food.

¹⁰A righteous man cares for the
needs of his animal,
but the kindest acts of the
wicked are cruel.

¹¹He who works his land will have
abundant food,
but he who chases fantasies
lacks judgment.

¹²The wicked desire the plunder of
evil men,
but the root of the righteous
flourishes.

¹³An evil man is trapped by his
sinful talk,
but a righteous man escapes
trouble.

¹⁴From the fruit of his lips a man
is filled with good things
as surely as the work of his
hands rewards him.

15The way of a fool seems right to
  him,
    but a wise man listens to
    advice.

16A fool shows his annoyance at
  once,
    but a prudent man overlooks an
    insult.

17A truthful witness gives honest
  testimony,
    but a false witness tells lies.

18Reckless words pierce like a
  sword,
    but the tongue of the wise
    brings healing.

19Truthful lips endure forever,
    but a lying tongue lasts only a
    moment.

20There is deceit in the hearts of
  those who plot evil,
    but joy for those who promote
    peace.

21No harm befalls the righteous,
    but the wicked have their fill of
    trouble.

22The LORD detests lying lips,
    but he delights in men who are
    truthful.

23A prudent man keeps his
  knowledge to himself,
    but the heart of fools blurts out
    folly.

24Diligent hands will rule,
    but laziness ends in slave labor.

25An anxious heart weighs a man
  down,
    but a kind word cheers him up.

26A righteous man is cautious in
  friendship,a
    but the way of the wicked leads
    them astray.

27The lazy man does not roastb his
  game,
    but the diligent man prizes his
    possessions.

28In the way of righteousness there
  is life;
    along that path is immortality.

13 A wise son heeds his
    father's instruction,
    but a mocker does not listen to
    rebuke.

2From the fruit of his lips a man
  enjoys good things,
    but the unfaithful have a
    craving for violence.

3He who guards his lips guards his
  life,
    but he who speaks rashly will
    come to ruin.

4The sluggard craves and gets
  nothing,
    but the desires of the diligent
    are fully satisfied.

5The righteous hate what is false,
    but the wicked bring shame and
    disgrace.

6Righteousness guards the man of
  integrity,
    but wickedness overthrows the
    sinner.

7One man pretends to be rich, yet
  has nothing;
    another pretends to be poor, yet
    has great wealth.

8A man's riches may ransom his
  life,
    but a poor man hears no threat.

9The light of the righteous shines
  brightly,
    but the lamp of the wicked is
    snuffed out.

10Pride only breeds quarrels,
    but wisdom is found in those
    who take advice.

11Dishonest money dwindles away,
    but he who gathers money little
    by little makes it grow.

12Hope deferred makes the heart
  sick,

a26 Or man is a guide to his neighbor   b27 The meaning of the Hebrew for this word is
uncertain.

but a longing fulfilled is a tree
of life.

¹³He who scorns instruction will
pay for it,
but he who respects a command
is rewarded.

¹⁴The teaching of the wise is a
fountain of life,
turning a man from the snares
of death.

¹⁵Good understanding wins favor,
but the way of the unfaithful is
hard.ᵃ

¹⁶Every prudent man acts out of
knowledge,
but a fool exposes his folly.

¹⁷A wicked messenger falls into
trouble,
but a trustworthy envoy brings
healing.

¹⁸He who ignores discipline comes
to poverty and shame,
but whoever heeds correction is
honored.

¹⁹A longing fulfilled is sweet to the
soul,
but fools detest turning from
evil.

²⁰He who walks with the wise
grows wise,
but a companion of fools suffers
harm.

²¹Misfortune pursues the sinner,
but prosperity is the reward of
the righteous.

²²A good man leaves an inheritance
for his children's children,
but a sinner's wealth is stored
up for the righteous.

²³A poor man's field may produce
abundant food,
but injustice sweeps it away.

²⁴He who spares the rod hates his
son,
but he who loves him is careful
to discipline him.

²⁵The righteous eat to their hearts'
content,
but the stomach of the wicked
goes hungry.

14 The wise woman builds her
house,
but with her own hands the
foolish one tears hers down.

²He whose walk is upright fears
the LORD,
but he whose ways are devious
despises him.

³A fool's talk brings a rod to his
back,
but the lips of the wise protect
them.

⁴Where there are no oxen, the
manger is empty,
but from the strength of an ox
comes an abundant harvest.

⁵A truthful witness does not
deceive,
but a false witness pours out
lies.

⁶The mocker seeks wisdom and
finds none,
but knowledge comes easily to
the discerning.

⁷Stay away from a foolish man,
for you will not find knowledge
on his lips.

⁸The wisdom of the prudent is to
give thought to their ways,
but the folly of fools is
deception.

⁹Fools mock at making amends for
sin,
but goodwill is found among the
upright.

¹⁰Each heart knows its own
bitterness,
and no one else can share its
joy.

¹¹The house of the wicked will be
destroyed,
but the tent of the upright will
flourish.

ᵃ15 Or *unfaithful does not endure*

¹²There is a way that seems right
to a man,
but in the end it leads to death.

¹³Even in laughter the heart may
ache,
and joy may end in grief.

¹⁴The faithless will be fully repaid
for their ways,
and the good man rewarded for
his.

¹⁵A simple man believes anything,
but a prudent man gives
thought to his steps.

¹⁶A wise man fears the LORD and
shuns evil,
but a fool is hotheaded and
reckless.

¹⁷A quick-tempered man does
foolish things,
and a crafty man is hated.

¹⁸The simple inherit folly,
but the prudent are crowned
with knowledge.

¹⁹Evil men will bow down in the
presence of the good,
and the wicked at the gates of
the righteous.

²⁰The poor are shunned even by
their neighbors,
but the rich have many friends.

²¹He who despises his neighbor
sins,

but blessed is he who is kind to
the needy.

²²Do not those who plot evil go
astray?
But those who plan what is
good find*a* love and
faithfulness.

²³All hard work brings a profit,
but mere talk leads only to
poverty.

²⁴The wealth of the wise is their
crown,
but the folly of fools yields folly.

²⁵A truthful witness saves lives,
but a false witness is deceitful.

²⁶He who fears the LORD has a
secure fortress,
and for his children it will be a
refuge.

²⁷The fear of the LORD is a fountain
of life,
turning a man from the snares
of death.

²⁸A large population is a king's
glory,
but without subjects a prince is
ruined.

²⁹A patient man has great
understanding,
but a quick-tempered man
displays folly.

³⁰A heart at peace gives life to the
body,

a22 Or *show*

Life in Bible Times

WHAT MAKES LIFE GOOD

Work makes life good
(Proverbs 14:23). Most people in Palestine were farmers. Farming wasn't easy,
but people who worked
hard had food and cloth-
ing for their families.

but envy rots the bones.

³¹He who oppresses the poor shows
   contempt for their Maker,
but whoever is kind to the
   needy honors God.

³²When calamity comes, the wicked
   are brought down,
but even in death the righteous
   have a refuge.

³³Wisdom reposes in the heart of
   the discerning
and even among fools she lets
   herself be known.ᵃ

³⁴Righteousness exalts a nation,
but sin is a disgrace to any
   people.

³⁵A king delights in a wise servant,
but a shameful servant incurs
   his wrath.

15 A gentle answer turns away
   wrath,
but a harsh word stirs up
   anger.

²The tongue of the wise commends
   knowledge,
but the mouth of the fool
   gushes folly.

³The eyes of the LORD are
   everywhere,
keeping watch on the wicked
   and the good.

⁴The tongue that brings healing is
   a tree of life,
but a deceitful tongue crushes
   the spirit.

⁵A fool spurns his father's
   discipline,
but whoever heeds correction
   shows prudence.

⁶The house of the righteous
   contains great treasure,
but the income of the wicked
   brings them trouble.

⁷The lips of the wise spread
   knowledge;
not so the hearts of fools.

⁸The LORD detests the sacrifice of
   the wicked,
but the prayer of the upright
   pleases him.

⁹The LORD detests the way of the
   wicked
but he loves those who pursue
   righteousness.

¹⁰Stern discipline awaits him who
   leaves the path;
he who hates correction will die.

¹¹Death and Destructionᵇ lie open
   before the LORD—
how much more the hearts of
   men!

¹²A mocker resents correction;
he will not consult the wise.

¹³A happy heart makes the face
   cheerful,
but heartache crushes the
   spirit.

¹⁴The discerning heart seeks
   knowledge,
but the mouth of a fool feeds on
   folly.

¹⁵All the days of the oppressed are
   wretched,
but the cheerful heart has a
   continual feast.

¹⁶Better a little with the fear of the
   LORD
than great wealth with turmoil.

¹⁷Better a meal of vegetables where
   there is love
than a fattened calf with
   hatred.

¹⁸A hot-tempered man stirs up
   dissension,
but a patient man calms a
   quarrel.

¹⁹The way of the sluggard is
   blocked with thorns,
but the path of the upright is a
   highway.

²⁰A wise son brings joy to his
   father,

ᵃ33 Hebrew; Septuagint and Syriac / *but in the heart of fools she is not known*   ᵇ11 Hebrew
Sheol and Abaddon

but a foolish man despises his
mother.

²¹Folly delights a man who lacks
judgment,
but a man of understanding
keeps a straight course.

²²Plans fail for lack of counsel,
but with many advisers they
succeed.

²³A man finds joy in giving an apt
reply—
and how good is a timely word!

²⁴The path of life leads upward for
the wise
to keep him from going down to
the grave.ᵃ

²⁵The LORD tears down the proud
man's house
but he keeps the widow's
boundaries intact.

²⁶The LORD detests the thoughts of
the wicked,
but those of the pure are
pleasing to him.

²⁷A greedy man brings trouble to
his family,
but he who hates bribes will
live.

²⁸The heart of the righteous weighs
its answers,
but the mouth of the wicked
gushes evil.

²⁹The LORD is far from the wicked
but he hears the prayer of the
righteous.

³⁰A cheerful look brings joy to the
heart,
and good news gives health to
the bones.

³¹He who listens to a life-giving
rebuke
will be at home among the
wise.

³²He who ignores discipline
despises himself,
but whoever heeds correction
gains understanding.

³³The fear of the LORD teaches a
man wisdom,ᵇ
and humility comes before
honor.

16 To man belong the plans of
the heart,
but from the LORD comes the
reply of the tongue.

²All a man's ways seem innocent
to him,
but motives are weighed by the
LORD.

³Commit to the LORD whatever you
do,
and your plans will succeed.

⁴The LORD works out everything
for his own ends—
even the wicked for a day of
disaster.

⁵The LORD detests all the proud of
heart.
Be sure of this: They will not go
unpunished.

⁶Through love and faithfulness sin
is atoned for;
through the fear of the LORD a
man avoids evil.

⁷When a man's ways are pleasing
to the LORD,
he makes even his enemies live
at peace with him.

⁸Better a little with righteousness
than much gain with injustice.

⁹In his heart a man plans his
course,
but the LORD determines his
steps.

¹⁰The lips of a king speak as an
oracle,
and his mouth should not
betray justice.

¹¹Honest scales and balances are
from the LORD;
all the weights in the bag are of
his making.

¹²Kings detest wrongdoing,

ᵃ24 Hebrew *Sheol*   ᵇ33 Or *Wisdom teaches the fear of the LORD*

for a throne is established
through righteousness.

¹³Kings take pleasure in honest
lips;
they value a man who speaks
the truth.

¹⁴A king's wrath is a messenger of
death,
but a wise man will appease it.

¹⁵When a king's face brightens, it
means life;
his favor is like a rain cloud in
spring.

¹⁶How much better to get wisdom
than gold,
to choose understanding rather
than silver!

¹⁷The highway of the upright
avoids evil;
he who guards his way guards
his life.

¹⁸Pride goes before destruction,
a haughty spirit before a fall.

¹⁹Better to be lowly in spirit and
among the oppressed
than to share plunder with the
proud.

²⁰Whoever gives heed to instruction
prospers,
and blessed is he who trusts in
the LORD.

²¹The wise in heart are called
discerning,
and pleasant words promote
instruction.ᵃ

²²Understanding is a fountain of
life to those who have it,
but folly brings punishment to
fools.

²³A wise man's heart guides his
mouth,
and his lips promote
instruction.ᵇ

²⁴Pleasant words are a honeycomb,
sweet to the soul and healing to
the bones.

²⁵There is a way that seems right
to a man,
but in the end it leads to death.

²⁶The laborer's appetite works for
him;
his hunger drives him on.

²⁷A scoundrel plots evil,
and his speech is like a
scorching fire.

²⁸A perverse man stirs up
dissension,
and a gossip separates close
friends.

²⁹A violent man entices his
neighbor
and leads him down a path that
is not good.

³⁰He who winks with his eye is
plotting perversity;
he who purses his lips is bent
on evil.

³¹Gray hair is a crown of splendor;
it is attained by a righteous
life.

³²Better a patient man than a
warrior,
a man who controls his temper
than one who takes a city.

³³The lot is cast into the lap,
but its every decision is from
the LORD.

17 Better a dry crust with
peace and quiet
than a house full of feasting,ᶜ
with strife.

²A wise servant will rule over a
disgraceful son,
and will share the inheritance
as one of the brothers.

³The crucible for silver and the
furnace for gold,
but the LORD tests the heart.

⁴A wicked man listens to evil lips;
a liar pays attention to a
malicious tongue.

ᵃ21 Or *words make a man persuasive*   ᵇ23 Or *mouth / and makes his lips persuasive*
ᶜ1 Hebrew *sacrifices*

⁵He who mocks the poor shows
contempt for their Maker;
whoever gloats over disaster
will not go unpunished.

⁶Children's children are a crown to
the aged,
and parents are the pride of
their children.

⁷Arrogant*a* lips are unsuited to a
fool—
how much worse lying lips to a
ruler!

⁸A bribe is a charm to the one who
gives it;
wherever he turns, he succeeds.

⁹He who covers over an offense
promotes love,
but whoever repeats the matter
separates close friends.

¹⁰A rebuke impresses a man of
discernment
more than a hundred lashes a
fool.

¹¹An evil man is bent only on
rebellion;
a merciless official will be sent
against him.

¹²Better to meet a bear robbed of
her cubs
than a fool in his folly.

¹³If a man pays back evil for good,
evil will never leave his house.

a7 Or Eloquent

¹⁴Starting a quarrel is like
breaching a dam;
so drop the matter before a
dispute breaks out.

¹⁵Acquitting the guilty and
condemning the innocent—
the LORD detests them both.

¹⁶Of what use is money in the hand
of a fool,
since he has no desire to get
wisdom?

¹⁷A friend loves at all times,
and a brother is born for
adversity.

¹⁸A man lacking in judgment
strikes hands in pledge
and puts up security for his
neighbor.

¹⁹He who loves a quarrel loves sin;
he who builds a high gate
invites destruction.

²⁰A man of perverse heart does not
prosper;
he whose tongue is deceitful
falls into trouble.

²¹To have a fool for a son brings
grief;
there is no joy for the father of
a fool.

²²A cheerful heart is good medicine,
but a crushed spirit dries up the
bones.

Life in Bible Times

WHAT MAKES LIFE GOOD

One of the good things of
life that God has given is
the family. Parents and
children, aunts and uncles,
and even friends are God's
way of making us feel that
we have a special place
in the world, somewhere
that we belong.

23A wicked man accepts a bribe in
secret
to pervert the course of justice.

24A discerning man keeps wisdom
in view,
but a fool's eyes wander to the
ends of the earth.

25A foolish son brings grief to his
father
and bitterness to the one who
bore him.

26It is not good to punish an
innocent man,
or to flog officials for their
integrity.

27A man of knowledge uses words
with restraint,
and a man of understanding is
even-tempered.

28Even a fool is thought wise if he
keeps silent,
and discerning if he holds his
tongue.

18 An unfriendly man pursues
selfish ends;
he defies all sound judgment.

2A fool finds no pleasure in
understanding
but delights in airing his own
opinions.

3When wickedness comes, so does
contempt,
and with shame comes disgrace.

4The words of a man's mouth are
deep waters,

but the fountain of wisdom is a
bubbling brook.

5It is not good to be partial to the
wicked
or to deprive the innocent of
justice.

6A fool's lips bring him strife,
and his mouth invites a
beating.

7A fool's mouth is his undoing,
and his lips are a snare to his
soul.

8The words of a gossip are like
choice morsels;
they go down to a man's inmost
parts.

9One who is slack in his work
is brother to one who destroys.

10The name of the LORD is a strong
tower;
the righteous run to it and are
safe.

11The wealth of the rich is their
fortified city;
they imagine it an unscalable
wall.

12Before his downfall a man's heart
is proud,
but humility comes before
honor.

13He who answers before
listening—
that is his folly and his shame.

14A man's spirit sustains him in
sickness,

▟ET'S LIVE IT!

TURN GOSSIP AROUND ➠ Gossip is saying something bad or embar-
rassing about another person. Read what the Bible says about gossip
in Proverbs 16:28; 26:20, and 2 Corinthians 12:20.

Proverbs 17:9 tells you how to turn gossip around and help people
stay friends. Read the verse. Then the next time you hear gossip, turn the
gossip around. How? When you hear someone say something bad
about a person, you say something good about that person!

If you practice turning gossip around, you'll keep your friends and be
someone others can trust and like.

but a crushed spirit who can
bear?

15The heart of the discerning
acquires knowledge;
the ears of the wise seek it out.

16A gift opens the way for the giver
and ushers him into the
presence of the great.

17The first to present his case
seems right,
till another comes forward and
questions him.

18Casting the lot settles disputes
and keeps strong opponents
apart.

19An offended brother is more
unyielding than a fortified
city,
and disputes are like the barred
gates of a citadel.

20From the fruit of his mouth a
man's stomach is filled;
with the harvest from his lips
he is satisfied.

21The tongue has the power of life
and death,
and those who love it will eat
its fruit.

22He who finds a wife finds what is
good
and receives favor from the
LORD.

23A poor man pleads for mercy,
but a rich man answers
harshly.

24A man of many companions may
come to ruin,
but there is a friend who sticks
closer than a brother.

19 Better a poor man whose
walk is blameless
than a fool whose lips are
perverse.

2It is not good to have zeal without
knowledge,
nor to be hasty and miss the
way.

3A man's own folly ruins his life,
yet his heart rages against the
LORD.

4Wealth brings many friends,
but a poor man's friend deserts
him.

5A false witness will not go
unpunished,
and he who pours out lies will
not go free.

6Many curry favor with a ruler,
and everyone is the friend of a
man who gives gifts.

7A poor man is shunned by all his
relatives—
how much more do his friends
avoid him!
Though he pursues them with
pleading,
they are nowhere to be found.ᵃ

8He who gets wisdom loves his
own soul;
he who cherishes understanding
prospers.

9A false witness will not go
unpunished,
and he who pours out lies will
perish.

10It is not fitting for a fool to live
in luxury—
how much worse for a slave to
rule over princes!

11A man's wisdom gives him
patience;
it is to his glory to overlook an
offense.

12A king's rage is like the roar of a
lion,
but his favor is like dew on the
grass.

13A foolish son is his father's ruin,
and a quarrelsome wife is like a
constant dripping.

14Houses and wealth are inherited
from parents,
but a prudent wife is from the
LORD.

ᵃ7 The meaning of the Hebrew for this sentence is uncertain.

¹⁵Laziness brings on deep sleep,
   and the shiftless man goes
     hungry.

¹⁶He who obeys instructions guards
   his life,
   but he who is contemptuous of
     his ways will die.

¹⁷He who is kind to the poor lends
   to the Lord,
   and he will reward him for
     what he has done.

¹⁸Discipline your son, for in that
   there is hope;
   do not be a willing party to his
     death.

¹⁹A hot-tempered man must pay
   the penalty;
   if you rescue him, you will have
     to do it again.

²⁰Listen to advice and accept
   instruction,
   and in the end you will be wise.

²¹Many are the plans in a man's
   heart,
   but it is the Lord's purpose that
     prevails.

²²What a man desires is unfailing
   love[a];
   better to be poor than a liar.

²³The fear of the Lord leads to life:
   Then one rests content,
     untouched by trouble.

²⁴The sluggard buries his hand in
   the dish;
   he will not even bring it back to
     his mouth!

²⁵Flog a mocker, and the simple
   will learn prudence;
   rebuke a discerning man, and
     he will gain knowledge.

²⁶He who robs his father and drives
   out his mother
   is a son who brings shame and
     disgrace.

²⁷Stop listening to instruction, my
   son,

and you will stray from the
   words of knowledge.

²⁸A corrupt witness mocks at
   justice,
   and the mouth of the wicked
     gulps down evil.

²⁹Penalties are prepared for
   mockers,
   and beatings for the backs of
     fools.

20 Wine is a mocker and beer
   a brawler;
   whoever is led astray by them
     is not wise.

²A king's wrath is like the roar of
   a lion;
   he who angers him forfeits his
     life.

³It is to a man's honor to avoid
   strife,
   but every fool is quick to
     quarrel.

⁴A sluggard does not plow in
   season;
   so at harvest time he looks but
     finds nothing.

⁵The purposes of a man's heart are
   deep waters,
   but a man of understanding
     draws them out.

⁶Many a man claims to have
   unfailing love,
   but a faithful man who can
     find?

⁷The righteous man leads a
   blameless life;
   blessed are his children after
     him.

⁸When a king sits on his throne to
   judge,
   he winnows out all evil with his
     eyes.

⁹Who can say, "I have kept my
   heart pure;
   I am clean and without sin"?

¹⁰Differing weights and differing
   measures—

---

[a]22 Or *A man's greed is his shame*

the LORD detests them both.

11Even a child is known by his
actions,
by whether his conduct is pure
and right.

12Ears that hear and eyes that
see—
the LORD has made them both.

13Do not love sleep or you will grow
poor;
stay awake and you will have
food to spare.

14"It's no good, it's no good!" says
the buyer;
then off he goes and boasts
about his purchase.

15Gold there is, and rubies in
abundance,
but lips that speak knowledge
are a rare jewel.

16Take the garment of one who
puts up security for a
stranger;
hold it in pledge if he does it for
a wayward woman.

17Food gained by fraud tastes sweet
to a man,
but he ends up with a mouth
full of gravel.

18Make plans by seeking advice;
if you wage war, obtain
guidance.

WORDS TO REMEMBER

20:18 Make plans by seeking
advice.

19A gossip betrays a confidence;
so avoid a man who talks too
much.

20If a man curses his father or
mother,
his lamp will be snuffed out in
pitch darkness.

21An inheritance quickly gained at
the beginning
will not be blessed at the end.

22Do not say, "I'll pay you back for
this wrong!"
Wait for the LORD, and he will
deliver you.

23The LORD detests differing
weights,
and dishonest scales do not
please him.

24A man's steps are directed by the
LORD.
How then can anyone
understand his own way?

25It is a trap for a man to dedicate
something rashly
and only later to consider his
vows.

26A wise king winnows out the
wicked;
he drives the threshing wheel
over them.

27The lamp of the LORD searches
the spirit of a man[a];
it searches out his inmost being.

28Love and faithfulness keep a king
safe;
through love his throne is made
secure.

29The glory of young men is their
strength,
gray hair the splendor of the
old.

30Blows and wounds cleanse away
evil,
and beatings purge the inmost
being.

21 The king's heart is in the
hand of the LORD;
he directs it like a watercourse
wherever he pleases.

2All a man's ways seem right to
him,
but the LORD weighs the heart.

3To do what is right and just

---

a27 Or The spirit of man is the LORD's lamp

is more acceptable to the LORD
than sacrifice.

4Haughty eyes and a proud heart,
the lamp of the wicked, are sin!

5The plans of the diligent lead to
profit
as surely as haste leads to
poverty.

6A fortune made by a lying tongue
is a fleeting vapor and a deadly
snare.[a]

7The violence of the wicked will
drag them away,
for they refuse to do what is
right.

8The way of the guilty is devious,
but the conduct of the innocent
is upright.

9Better to live on a corner of the
roof
than share a house with a
quarrelsome wife.

10The wicked man craves evil;
his neighbor gets no mercy from
him.

11When a mocker is punished, the
simple gain wisdom;
when a wise man is instructed,
he gets knowledge.

12The Righteous One[b] takes note of
the house of the wicked
and brings the wicked to ruin.

13If a man shuts his ears to the cry
of the poor,
he too will cry out and not be
answered.

14A gift given in secret soothes
anger,
and a bribe concealed in the
cloak pacifies great wrath.

15When justice is done, it brings joy
to the righteous
but terror to evildoers.

16A man who strays from the path
of understanding

comes to rest in the company of
the dead.

17He who loves pleasure will
become poor;
whoever loves wine and oil will
never be rich.

18The wicked become a ransom for
the righteous,
and the unfaithful for the
upright.

19Better to live in a desert
than with a quarrelsome and
ill-tempered wife.

20In the house of the wise are
stores of choice food and oil,
but a foolish man devours all he
has.

21He who pursues righteousness
and love
finds life, prosperity[c] and
honor.

22A wise man attacks the city of
the mighty
and pulls down the stronghold
in which they trust.

23He who guards his mouth and his
tongue
keeps himself from calamity.

24The proud and arrogant
man—"Mocker" is his
name;
he behaves with overweening
pride.

25The sluggard's craving will be the
death of him,
because his hands refuse to
work.

26All day long he craves for more,
but the righteous give without
sparing.

27The sacrifice of the wicked is
detestable—
how much more so when
brought with evil intent!

28A false witness will perish,

---

[a]6 Some Hebrew manuscripts, Septuagint and Vulgate; most Hebrew manuscripts *vapor for those
who seek death*   [b]12 Or *The righteous man*   [c]21 Or *righteousness*

and whoever listens to him will
  be destroyed forever.[a]

²⁹A wicked man puts up a bold
  front,
  but an upright man gives
  thought to his ways.

³⁰There is no wisdom, no insight,
  no plan
  that can succeed against the
  LORD.

³¹The horse is made ready for the
  day of battle,
  but victory rests with the LORD.

22 A good name is more
  desirable than great riches;
  to be esteemed is better than
  silver or gold.

²Rich and poor have this in
  common:
  The LORD is the Maker of them
  all.

³A prudent man sees danger and
  takes refuge,
  but the simple keep going and
  suffer for it.

⁴Humility and the fear of the LORD
  bring wealth and honor and life.

⁵In the paths of the wicked lie
  thorns and snares,
  but he who guards his soul
  stays far from them.

⁶Train[b] a child in the way he
  should go,
  and when he is old he will not
  turn from it.

⁷The rich rule over the poor,
  and the borrower is servant to
  the lender.

⁸He who sows wickedness reaps
  trouble,
  and the rod of his fury will be
  destroyed.

⁹A generous man will himself be
  blessed,
  for he shares his food with the
  poor.

¹⁰Drive out the mocker, and out
  goes strife;
  quarrels and insults are ended.

¹¹He who loves a pure heart and
  whose speech is gracious
  will have the king for his
  friend.

¹²The eyes of the LORD keep watch
  over knowledge,
  but he frustrates the words of
  the unfaithful.

¹³The sluggard says, "There is a
  lion outside!"
  or, "I will be murdered in the
  streets!"

¹⁴The mouth of an adulteress is a
  deep pit;
  he who is under the LORD's
  wrath will fall into it.

¹⁵Folly is bound up in the heart of
  a child,
  but the rod of discipline will
  drive it far from him.

WHAT MAKES LIFE GOOD

No one likes to get a spanking. But
Proverbs 22:15 says that spankings
can help us. They keep us from
doing wrong and foolish things,
and that makes life good.

¹⁶He who oppresses the poor to
  increase his wealth
  and he who gives gifts to the
  rich—both come to poverty.

Sayings of the Wise

¹⁷Pay attention and listen to the
  sayings of the wise;

---

[a]28 Or / but the words of an obedient man will live on   [b]6 Or Start

apply your heart to what I
  teach,
¹⁸for it is pleasing when you keep
  them in your heart
and have all of them ready on
  your lips.
¹⁹So that your trust may be in the
  LORD,
I teach you today, even you.
²⁰Have I not written thirty[a]
  sayings for you,
sayings of counsel and
  knowledge,
²¹teaching you true and reliable
  words,
so that you can give sound
  answers
to him who sent you?

²²Do not exploit the poor because
  they are poor
and do not crush the needy in
  court,
²³for the LORD will take up their
  case
and will plunder those who
  plunder them.

²⁴Do not make friends with a
  hot-tempered man,
do not associate with one easily
  angered,
²⁵or you may learn his ways
and get yourself ensnared.

²⁶Do not be a man who strikes
  hands in pledge
or puts up security for debts;
²⁷if you lack the means to pay,
your very bed will be snatched
  from under you.

²⁸Do not move an ancient boundary
  stone
set up by your forefathers.

²⁹Do you see a man skilled in his
  work?
He will serve before kings;
he will not serve before obscure
  men.

23 When you sit to dine with a
  ruler,
note well what[b] is before you,

²and put a knife to your throat
if you are given to gluttony.
³Do not crave his delicacies,
for that food is deceptive.

⁴Do not wear yourself out to get
  rich;
have the wisdom to show
  restraint.
⁵Cast but a glance at riches, and
  they are gone,
for they will surely sprout
  wings
and fly off to the sky like an
  eagle.

⁶Do not eat the food of a stingy
  man,
do not crave his delicacies;
⁷for he is the kind of man
who is always thinking about
  the cost.[c]
"Eat and drink," he says to you,
but his heart is not with you.
⁸You will vomit up the little you
  have eaten
and will have wasted your
  compliments.

⁹Do not speak to a fool,
for he will scorn the wisdom of
  your words.

¹⁰Do not move an ancient boundary
  stone
or encroach on the fields of the
  fatherless,
¹¹for their Defender is strong;
he will take up their case
against you.

¹²Apply your heart to instruction
and your ears to words of
  knowledge.

¹³Do not withhold discipline from a
  child;
if you punish him with the rod,
he will not die.
¹⁴Punish him with the rod
and save his soul from death.[d]

¹⁵My son, if your heart is wise,
then my heart will be glad;
¹⁶my inmost being will rejoice

---

a20 Or *not formerly written*; or *not written excellent*   b1 Or *who*   c7 Or *for as he thinks*
within himself, | so he is; or *for as he puts on a feast, | so he is*   d14 Hebrew *Sheol*

when your lips speak what is
right.

¹⁷Do not let your heart envy
sinners,
but always be zealous for the
fear of the LORD.
¹⁸There is surely a future hope for
you,
and your hope will not be cut
off.

¹⁹Listen, my son, and be wise,
and keep your heart on the
right path.
²⁰Do not join those who drink too
much wine
or gorge themselves on meat,
²¹for drunkards and gluttons
become poor,
and drowsiness clothes them in
rags.

²²Listen to your father, who gave
you life,
and do not despise your mother
when she is old.
²³Buy the truth and do not sell it;
get wisdom, discipline and
understanding.
²⁴The father of a righteous man has
great joy;
he who has a wise son delights
in him.
²⁵May your father and mother be
glad;
may she who gave you birth
rejoice!

²⁶My son, give me your heart
and let your eyes keep to my
ways,
²⁷for a prostitute is a deep pit
and a wayward wife is a narrow
well.
²⁸Like a bandit she lies in wait,
and multiplies the unfaithful
among men.

²⁹Who has woe? Who has sorrow?
Who has strife? Who has
complaints?
Who has needless bruises? Who
has bloodshot eyes?
³⁰Those who linger over wine,
who go to sample bowls of
mixed wine.

³¹Do not gaze at wine when it is
red,
when it sparkles in the cup,
when it goes down smoothly!
³²In the end it bites like a snake
and poisons like a viper.
³³Your eyes will see strange sights
and your mind imagine
confusing things.
³⁴You will be like one sleeping on
the high seas,
lying on top of the rigging.
³⁵"They hit me," you will say, "but
I'm not hurt!
They beat me, but I don't feel
it!
When will I wake up
so I can find another drink?"

24 Do not envy wicked men,
do not desire their company;
²for their hearts plot violence,
and their lips talk about
making trouble.

³By wisdom a house is built,
and through understanding it is
established;
⁴through knowledge its rooms are
filled
with rare and beautiful
treasures.

⁵A wise man has great power,
and a man of knowledge
increases strength;
⁶for waging war you need
guidance,
and for victory many advisers.

⁷Wisdom is too high for a fool;
in the assembly at the gate he
has nothing to say.

⁸He who plots evil
will be known as a schemer.
⁹The schemes of folly are sin,
and men detest a mocker.

¹⁰If you falter in times of trouble,
how small is your strength!

¹¹Rescue those being led away to
death;
hold back those staggering
toward slaughter.
¹²If you say, "But we knew nothing
about this,"

does not he who weighs the
heart perceive it?
Does not he who guards your life
know it?
Will he not repay each person
according to what he has
done?

13Eat honey, my son, for it is good;
honey from the comb is sweet to
your taste.
14Know also that wisdom is sweet
to your soul;
if you find it, there is a future
hope for you,
and your hope will not be cut
off.

15Do not lie in wait like an outlaw
against a righteous man's
house,
do not raid his dwelling place;
16for though a righteous man falls
seven times, he rises again,
but the wicked are brought
down by calamity.

17Do not gloat when your enemy
falls;
when he stumbles, do not let
your heart rejoice,
18or the LORD will see and
disapprove
and turn his wrath away from
him.

19Do not fret because of evil
men
or be envious of the wicked,
20for the evil man has no future
hope,
and the lamp of the wicked will
be snuffed out.

21Fear the LORD and the king, my
son,
and do not join with the
rebellious,
22for those two will send sudden
destruction upon them,
and who knows what calamities
they can bring?

Further Sayings of the Wise

23These also are sayings of the
wise:

To show partiality in judging is
not good:
24Whoever says to the guilty, "You
are innocent"—
peoples will curse him and
nations denounce him.
25But it will go well with those who
convict the guilty,
and rich blessing will come
upon them.

26An honest answer
is like a kiss on the lips.

27Finish your outdoor work
and get your fields ready;
after that, build your house.

28Do not testify against your
neighbor without cause,
or use your lips to deceive.
29Do not say, "I'll do to him as he
has done to me;
I'll pay that man back for what
he did."

30I went past the field of the
sluggard,
past the vineyard of the man
who lacks judgment;

LET'S LIVE IT!   Proverbs 24:17–18

LAUGHING AT OTHERS ⇒ Think about a time when you made a mistake
or goofed up somehow and someone laughed at you. Perhaps you
answered a question wrong or tripped on the steps of the school bus
or had a tear in your shirt. How did the laughter make you feel?
     Now think about a time when you laughed at someone else. What
did he or she do to make you laugh? How do you think that person felt?
     Read Proverbs 24:17–18. The wise person who wrote Proverbs says
something about what happens when we laugh ("gloat") at someone.
What will you do next time you see someone make a mistake?

³¹thorns had come up everywhere,
  the ground was covered with
    weeds,
  and the stone wall was in ruins.
³²I applied my heart to what I
    observed
  and learned a lesson from what
    I saw:
³³A little sleep, a little slumber,
  a little folding of the hands to
    rest—
³⁴and poverty will come on you like
    a bandit
  and scarcity like an armed
    man.ᵃ

More Proverbs of Solomon

25 These are more proverbs of
  Solomon, copied by the men of
Hezekiah king of Judah:

²It is the glory of God to conceal a
    matter;
  to search out a matter is the
    glory of kings.

³As the heavens are high and the
    earth is deep,
  so the hearts of kings are
    unsearchable.

⁴Remove the dross from the silver,
  and out comes material forᵇ the
    silversmith;
⁵remove the wicked from the
    king's presence,
  and his throne will be
    established through
    righteousness.

⁶Do not exalt yourself in the king's
    presence,
  and do not claim a place among
    great men;
⁷it is better for him to say to you,
    "Come up here,"
  than for him to humiliate you
    before a nobleman.

  What you have seen with your
    eyes
⁸ do not bringᶜ hastily to court,
  for what will you do in the end

if your neighbor puts you to
    shame?

⁹If you argue your case with a
    neighbor,
  do not betray another man's
    confidence,
¹⁰or he who hears it may shame
    you
  and you will never lose your
    bad reputation.

¹¹A word aptly spoken
  is like apples of gold in settings
    of silver.

¹²Like an earring of gold or an
    ornament of fine gold
  is a wise man's rebuke to a
    listening ear.

¹³Like the coolness of snow at
    harvest time
  is a trustworthy messenger to
    those who send him;
  he refreshes the spirit of his
    masters.

¹⁴Like clouds and wind without
    rain
  is a man who boasts of gifts he
    does not give.

¹⁵Through patience a ruler can be
    persuaded,
  and a gentle tongue can break a
    bone.

¹⁶If you find honey, eat just
    enough—
  too much of it, and you will
    vomit.
¹⁷Seldom set foot in your neighbor's
    house—
  too much of you, and he will
    hate you.

¹⁸Like a club or a sword or a sharp
    arrow
  is the man who gives false
    testimony against his
    neighbor.

¹⁹Like a bad tooth or a lame foot
  is reliance on the unfaithful in
    times of trouble.

ᵃ34 Or *like a vagrant / and scarcity like a beggar*   ᵇ4 Or *comes a vessel from*   ᶜ7,8 Or
nobleman / on whom you had set your eyes. / ⁸*Do not go*

²⁰Like one who takes away a
    garment on a cold day,
  or like vinegar poured on soda,
  is one who sings songs to a
    heavy heart.

²¹If your enemy is hungry, give
    him food to eat;
  if he is thirsty, give him water
    to drink.
²²In doing this, you will heap
    burning coals on his head,
  and the LORD will reward you.

WORDS TO REMEMBER

25:21-22 If your enemy is hungry,
    give him food to eat;
    if he is thirsty, give him
    water to drink.
    In doing this, you will
      heap burning coals
      on his head,
    and the LORD will
    reward you.

---

²³As a north wind brings rain,
  so a sly tongue brings angry
    looks.

²⁴Better to live on a corner of the
    roof
  than share a house with a
    quarrelsome wife.

²⁵Like cold water to a weary soul
  is good news from a distant
    land.

²⁶Like a muddied spring or a
    polluted well
  is a righteous man who gives
    way to the wicked.

²⁷It is not good to eat too much
    honey,
  nor is it honorable to seek one's
    own honor.

²⁸Like a city whose walls are
    broken down
  is a man who lacks self-control.

26 Like snow in summer or
    rain in harvest,
  honor is not fitting for a fool.

²Like a fluttering sparrow or a
    darting swallow,
  an undeserved curse does not
    come to rest.

³A whip for the horse, a halter for
    the donkey,
  and a rod for the backs of fools!

⁴Do not answer a fool according to
    his folly,
  or you will be like him yourself.

⁵Answer a fool according to his
    folly,
  or he will be wise in his own
    eyes.

⁶Like cutting off one's feet or
    drinking violence
  is the sending of a message by
    the hand of a fool.

⁷Like a lame man's legs that hang
    limp
  is a proverb in the mouth of a
    fool.

⁸Like tying a stone in a sling
  is the giving of honor to a fool.

⁹Like a thornbush in a drunkard's
    hand
  is a proverb in the mouth of a
    fool.

¹⁰Like an archer who wounds at
    random
  is he who hires a fool or any
    passer-by.

¹¹As a dog returns to its vomit,
  so a fool repeats his folly.

¹²Do you see a man wise in his own
    eyes?
  There is more hope for a fool
    than for him.

¹³The sluggard says, "There is a
    lion in the road,
  a fierce lion roaming the
    streets!"

¹⁴As a door turns on its hinges,
  so a sluggard turns on his bed.

¹⁵The sluggard buries his hand in
    the dish;
  he is too lazy to bring it back to
    his mouth.

¹⁶The sluggard is wiser in his own
eyes
than seven men who answer
discreetly.

¹⁷Like one who seizes a dog by the
ears
is a passer-by who meddles in a
quarrel not his own.

¹⁸Like a madman shooting
firebrands or deadly arrows
¹⁹is a man who deceives his
neighbor
and says, "I was only joking!"

²⁰Without wood a fire goes out;
without gossip a quarrel dies
down.

²¹As charcoal to embers and as
wood to fire,
so is a quarrelsome man for
kindling strife.

²²The words of a gossip are like
choice morsels;
they go down to a man's inmost
parts.

²³Like a coating of glaze^a over
earthenware
are fervent lips with an evil
heart.

²⁴A malicious man disguises
himself with his lips,
but in his heart he harbors
deceit.
²⁵Though his speech is charming,
do not believe him,
for seven abominations fill his
heart.
²⁶His malice may be concealed by
deception,
but his wickedness will be
exposed in the assembly.

²⁷If a man digs a pit, he will fall
into it;
if a man rolls a stone, it will
roll back on him.

²⁸A lying tongue hates those it
hurts,
and a flattering mouth works
ruin.

27 Do not boast about
tomorrow,
for you do not know what a day
may bring forth.

²Let another praise you, and not
your own mouth;
someone else, and not your own
lips.

³Stone is heavy and sand a
burden,
but provocation by a fool is
heavier than both.

⁴Anger is cruel and fury
overwhelming,
but who can stand before
jealousy?

⁵Better is open rebuke
than hidden love.

⁶Wounds from a friend can be
trusted,
but an enemy multiplies kisses.

⁷He who is full loathes honey,
but to the hungry even what is
bitter tastes sweet.

⁸Like a bird that strays from its
nest
is a man who strays from his
home.

⁹Perfume and incense bring joy to
the heart,
and the pleasantness of one's
friend springs from his
earnest counsel.

¹⁰Do not forsake your friend and
the friend of your father,
and do not go to your brother's
house when disaster strikes
you—
better a neighbor nearby than a
brother far away.

¹¹Be wise, my son, and bring joy to
my heart;
then I can answer anyone who
treats me with contempt.

¹²The prudent see danger and take
refuge,

---

a23 With a different word division of the Hebrew; Masoretic Text *of silver dross*

but the simple keep going and
suffer for it.

13Take the garment of one who
puts up security for a
stranger;
hold it in pledge if he does it for
a wayward woman.

14If a man loudly blesses his
neighbor early in the
morning,
it will be taken as a curse.

15A quarrelsome wife is like
a constant dripping on a rainy
day;
16restraining her is like restraining
the wind
or grasping oil with the hand.

17As iron sharpens iron,
so one man sharpens another.

18He who tends a fig tree will eat
its fruit,
and he who looks after his
master will be honored.

19As water reflects a face,
so a man's heart reflects the
man.

20Death and Destruction*a* are never
satisfied,
and neither are the eyes of
man.

21The crucible for silver and the
furnace for gold,
but man is tested by the praise
he receives.

22Though you grind a fool in a
mortar,
grinding him like grain with a
pestle,
you will not remove his folly
from him.

23Be sure you know the condition of
your flocks,
give careful attention to your
herds;
24for riches do not endure forever,
and a crown is not secure for all
generations.

25When the hay is removed and
new growth appears
and the grass from the hills is
gathered in,
26the lambs will provide you with
clothing,
and the goats with the price of
a field.
27You will have plenty of goats'
milk
to feed you and your family
and to nourish your servant
girls.

28 The wicked man flees
though no one pursues,
but the righteous are as bold as
a lion.

2When a country is rebellious, it
has many rulers,
but a man of understanding and
knowledge maintains order.

3A ruler*b* who oppresses the poor
is like a driving rain that
leaves no crops.

4Those who forsake the law praise
the wicked,
but those who keep the law
resist them.

5Evil men do not understand
justice,
but those who seek the LORD
understand it fully.

6Better a poor man whose walk is
blameless
than a rich man whose ways
are perverse.

7He who keeps the law is a
discerning son,
but a companion of gluttons
disgraces his father.

8He who increases his wealth by
exorbitant interest
amasses it for another, who will
be kind to the poor.

9If anyone turns a deaf ear to the
law,
even his prayers are detestable.

---

a20 Hebrew *Sheol and Abaddon*   *b3* Or *A poor man*

10He who leads the upright along
    an evil path
will fall into his own trap,
but the blameless will receive a
    good inheritance.

11A rich man may be wise in his
    own eyes,
    but a poor man who has
    discernment sees through
    him.

12When the righteous triumph,
    there is great elation;
but when the wicked rise to
    power, men go into hiding.

13He who conceals his sins does not
    prosper,
    but whoever confesses and
    renounces them finds
    mercy.

14Blessed is the man who always
    fears the LORD,
    but he who hardens his heart
    falls into trouble.

WORDS TO REMEMBER

28:14 Blessed is the man who
        always fears the LORD.

15Like a roaring lion or a charging
    bear
    is a wicked man ruling over a
    helpless people.

16A tyrannical ruler lacks
    judgment,
    but he who hates ill-gotten gain
    will enjoy a long life.

17A man tormented by the guilt of
    murder
    will be a fugitive till death;
    let no one support him.

18He whose walk is blameless is
    kept safe,
    but he whose ways are perverse
    will suddenly fall.

19He who works his land will have
    abundant food,
    but the one who chases

fantasies will have his fill
    of poverty.

20A faithful man will be richly
    blessed,
    but one eager to get rich will
    not go unpunished.

21To show partiality is not good—
    yet a man will do wrong for a
    piece of bread.

22A stingy man is eager to get rich
    and is unaware that poverty
    awaits him.

23He who rebukes a man will in the
    end gain more favor
than he who has a flattering
    tongue.

24He who robs his father or mother
    and says, "It's not wrong"—
he is partner to him who
    destroys.

25A greedy man stirs up dissension,
    but he who trusts in the LORD
    will prosper.

26He who trusts in himself is a fool,
    but he who walks in wisdom is
    kept safe.

27He who gives to the poor will lack
    nothing,
    but he who closes his eyes to
    them receives many curses.

28When the wicked rise to power,
    people go into hiding;
    but when the wicked perish, the
    righteous thrive.

29 A man who remains
    stiff-necked after many
    rebukes
will suddenly be
    destroyed—without remedy.

2When the righteous thrive, the
    people rejoice;
    when the wicked rule, the
    people groan.

3A man who loves wisdom brings
    joy to his father,
    but a companion of prostitutes
    squanders his wealth.

⁴By justice a king gives a country
   stability,
   but one who is greedy for bribes
      tears it down.

⁵Whoever flatters his neighbor
   is spreading a net for his feet.

⁶An evil man is snared by his own
      sin,
   but a righteous one can sing
      and be glad.

⁷The righteous care about justice
      for the poor,
   but the wicked have no such
      concern.

⁸Mockers stir up a city,
   but wise men turn away anger.

⁹If a wise man goes to court with a
      fool,
   the fool rages and scoffs, and
      there is no peace.

¹⁰Bloodthirsty men hate a man of
      integrity
   and seek to kill the upright.

¹¹A fool gives full vent to his anger,
   but a wise man keeps himself
      under control.

¹²If a ruler listens to lies,
   all his officials become wicked.

¹³The poor man and the oppressor
      have this in common:
   The LORD gives sight to the
      eyes of both.

¹⁴If a king judges the poor with
      fairness,
   his throne will always be
      secure.

¹⁵The rod of correction imparts
      wisdom,
   but a child left to himself
      disgraces his mother.

¹⁶When the wicked thrive, so does
      sin,
   but the righteous will see their
      downfall.

¹⁷Discipline your son, and he will
      give you peace;

he will bring delight to your
   soul.

¹⁸Where there is no revelation, the
      people cast off restraint;
   but blessed is he who keeps the
      law.

¹⁹A servant cannot be corrected by
      mere words;
   though he understands, he will
      not respond.

²⁰Do you see a man who speaks in
      haste?
   There is more hope for a fool
      than for him.

²¹If a man pampers his servant
      from youth,
   he will bring grief*a* in the end.

²²An angry man stirs up
      dissension,
   and a hot-tempered one
      commits many sins.

²³A man's pride brings him low,
   but a man of lowly spirit gains
      honor.

²⁴The accomplice of a thief is his
      own enemy;
   he is put under oath and dare
      not testify.

²⁵Fear of man will prove to be a
      snare,
   but whoever trusts in the LORD
      is kept safe.

²⁶Many seek an audience with a
      ruler,
   but it is from the LORD that
      man gets justice.

²⁷The righteous detest the
      dishonest;
   the wicked detest the upright.

Sayings of Agur

30 The sayings of Agur son of Ja-
      keh—an oracle*b*:

This man declared to Ithiel,

---

a21 The meaning of the Hebrew for this word is uncertain.   *b1* Or *Jakeh of Massa*

to Ithiel and to Ucal:ᵃ

²"I am the most ignorant of men;
  I do not have a man's
    understanding.
³I have not learned wisdom,
  nor have I knowledge of the
    Holy One.
⁴Who has gone up to heaven and
    come down?
  Who has gathered up the wind
    in the hollow of his hands?
  Who has wrapped up the waters
    in his cloak?
  Who has established all the
    ends of the earth?
  What is his name, and the name
    of his son?
  Tell me if you know!

⁵"Every word of God is flawless;
  he is a shield to those who take
    refuge in him.
⁶Do not add to his words,
  or he will rebuke you and prove
    you a liar.

⁷"Two things I ask of you, O Lord;
  do not refuse me before I die:
⁸Keep falsehood and lies far from
    me;
  give me neither poverty nor
    riches,
  but give me only my daily
    bread.
⁹Otherwise, I may have too much
  and disown you
  and say, 'Who is the Lord?'
  Or I may become poor and steal,
  and so dishonor the name of my
    God.

¹⁰"Do not slander a servant to his
    master,
  or he will curse you, and you
    will pay for it.

¹¹"There are those who curse their
    fathers
  and do not bless their mothers;
¹²those who are pure in their own
    eyes
  and yet are not cleansed of
    their filth;

¹³those whose eyes are ever so
    haughty,
  whose glances are so disdainful;
¹⁴those whose teeth are swords
  and whose jaws are set with
    knives
  to devour the poor from the earth,
  the needy from among
    mankind.

¹⁵"The leech has two daughters.
  'Give! Give!' they cry.

"There are three things that are
    never satisfied,
  four that never say, 'Enough!':
¹⁶the grave,ᵇ the barren womb,
  land, which is never satisfied
    with water,
  and fire, which never says,
    'Enough!'

¹⁷"The eye that mocks a father,
  that scorns obedience to a
    mother,
  will be pecked out by the ravens
    of the valley,
  will be eaten by the vultures.

¹⁸"There are three things that are
    too amazing for me,
  four that I do not understand:
¹⁹the way of an eagle in the sky,
  the way of a snake on a rock,
  the way of a ship on the high
    seas,
  and the way of a man with a
    maiden.

²⁰"This is the way of an adulteress:
  She eats and wipes her mouth
  and says, 'I've done nothing
    wrong.'

²¹"Under three things the earth
    trembles,
  under four it cannot bear up:
²²a servant who becomes king,
  a fool who is full of food,
²³an unloved woman who is
    married,
  and a maidservant who
    displaces her mistress.

²⁴"Four things on earth are small,

ᵃ1 Masoretic Text; with a different word division of the Hebrew *declared, "I am weary, O God; / I
am weary, O God, and faint.*   ᵇ16 Hebrew *Sheol*

yet they are extremely wise:
²⁵Ants are creatures of little
strength,
   yet they store up their food in
the summer;
²⁶coneys^a are creatures of little
power,
   yet they make their home in
the crags;
²⁷locusts have no king,
   yet they advance together in
ranks;
²⁸a lizard can be caught with the
hand,
   yet it is found in kings' palaces.

²⁹"There are three things that are
stately in their stride,
   four that move with stately
bearing:
³⁰a lion, mighty among beasts,
   who retreats before nothing;
³¹a strutting rooster, a he-goat,
   and a king with his army
around him.^b

³²"If you have played the fool and
exalted yourself,
   or if you have planned evil,
clap your hand over your
mouth!
³³For as churning the milk
produces butter,
   and as twisting the nose
produces blood,
so stirring up anger produces
strife."

Sayings of King Lemuel

31 The sayings of King Lemuel
—an oracle^c his mother
taught him:

²"O my son, O son of my womb,
   O son of my vows,^d
³do not spend your strength on
women,
   your vigor on those who ruin
kings.

⁴"It is not for kings, O Lemuel—

not for kings to drink wine,
   not for rulers to crave beer,
⁵lest they drink and forget what
the law decrees,
   and deprive all the oppressed of
their rights.
⁶Give beer to those who are
perishing,
   wine to those who are in
anguish;
⁷let them drink and forget their
poverty
   and remember their misery no
more.

⁸"Speak up for those who cannot
speak for themselves,
   for the rights of all who are
destitute.
⁹Speak up and judge fairly;
   defend the rights of the poor
and needy."

Epilogue: The Wife of Noble Character

^{10e}A wife of noble character who
can find?
   She is worth far more than
rubies.
¹¹Her husband has full confidence
in her
   and lacks nothing of value.
¹²She brings him good, not harm,
   all the days of her life.
¹³She selects wool and flax
   and works with eager hands.
¹⁴She is like the merchant ships,
   bringing her food from afar.
¹⁵She gets up while it is still dark;
   she provides food for her
family
   and portions for her servant
girls.
¹⁶She considers a field and buys it;
   out of her earnings she plants a
vineyard.
¹⁷She sets about her work
vigorously;
   her arms are strong for her
tasks.

---

^a26 That is, the hyrax or rock badger   ^b31 Or king secure against revolt   ^c1 Or of Lemuel
king of Massa, which   ^d2 Or / the answer to my prayers   ^e10 Verses 10-31 are an acrostic,
each verse beginning with a successive letter of the Hebrew alphabet.

¹⁸She sees that her trading is
profitable,
and her lamp does not go out at
night.
¹⁹In her hand she holds the distaff
and grasps the spindle with her
fingers.

WHAT MAKES LIFE GOOD

In Bible times women did
important work for their families.
They made thread on a spindle,
wove cloth and made clothing.
Life is good when men and
women both do important things.

²⁰She opens her arms to the poor
and extends her hands to the
needy.
²¹When it snows, she has no fear
for her household;
for all of them are clothed in
scarlet.
²²She makes coverings for her bed;

she is clothed in fine linen and
purple.
²³Her husband is respected at the
city gate,
where he takes his seat among
the elders of the land.
²⁴She makes linen garments and
sells them,
and supplies the merchants
with sashes.
²⁵She is clothed with strength and
dignity;
she can laugh at the days to
come.
²⁶She speaks with wisdom,
and faithful instruction is on
her tongue.
²⁷She watches over the affairs of
her household
and does not eat the bread of
idleness.
²⁸Her children arise and call her
blessed;
her husband also, and he
praises her:
²⁹"Many women do noble things,
but you surpass them all."
³⁰Charm is deceptive, and beauty is
fleeting;
but a woman who fears the
LORD is to be praised.
³¹Give her the reward she has
earned,
and let her works bring her
praise at the city gate.

ECCLESIASTES

WHO WROTE THIS BOOK?	This book was probably written by Solomon.
WHY WAS THIS BOOK WRITTEN?	Ecclesiastes shows that no one can have a happy life without God.
FOR WHOM WAS THIS BOOK WRITTEN?	Ecclesiastes was written for anyone who thinks that God is not important.
WHAT DO WE LEARN ABOUT GOD IN THIS BOOK?	God is more important than money, pleasure, work or anything else in life.
WHEN WAS THIS BOOK WRITTEN?	If Solomon wrote Ecclesiastes, it was written sometime during the tenth century B.C. If it was written by someone else, the date is unknown.
WHAT ARE SOME IMPORTANT PASSAGES IN THIS BOOK?	Pleasure can't make people happy. Ecclesiastes 2:1–11 Success can't make people happy. Ecclesiastes 2:17–26 Riches can't make people happy. Ecclesiastes 5:8–6:2

Everything Is Meaningless

1 The words of the Teacher,[a] son of David, king in Jerusalem:

2"Meaningless! Meaningless!"
   says the Teacher.
"Utterly meaningless!
   Everything is meaningless."

3What does man gain from all his labor
   at which he toils under the sun?
4Generations come and generations go,
   but the earth remains forever.
5The sun rises and the sun sets,
   and hurries back to where it rises.
6The wind blows to the south
   and turns to the north;
round and round it goes,
   ever returning on its course.
7All streams flow into the sea,
   yet the sea is never full.
To the place the streams come from,
   there they return again.
8All things are wearisome,
   more than one can say.
The eye never has enough of seeing,
   nor the ear its fill of hearing.
9What has been will be again,
   what has been done will be done again;
   there is nothing new under the sun.
10Is there anything of which one can say,
   "Look! This is something new"?
It was here already, long ago;
   it was here before our time.
11There is no remembrance of men of old,
   and even those who are yet to come
will not be remembered
   by those who follow.

Wisdom Is Meaningless

12I, the Teacher, was king over Israel in Jerusalem. 13I devoted myself to study and to explore by wisdom all that is done under heaven. What a heavy burden God has laid on men! 14I have seen all the things that are done under the sun; all of them are meaningless, a chasing after the wind.

15What is twisted cannot be straightened;
   what is lacking cannot be counted.

16I thought to myself, "Look, I have grown and increased in wisdom more than anyone who has ruled over Jerusalem before me; I have experienced much of wisdom and knowledge." 17Then I applied myself to the understanding of wisdom, and also of madness and folly, but I learned that this, too, is a chasing after the wind.

18For with much wisdom comes much sorrow;
   the more knowledge, the more grief.

Pleasures Are Meaningless

2 I thought in my heart, "Come now, I will test you with pleasure to find out what is good." But that also proved to be meaningless. 2"Laughter," I said, "is foolish. And what does pleasure accomplish?" 3I tried cheering myself with wine, and embracing folly—my mind still guiding me with wisdom. I wanted to see what was worthwhile for men to do under heaven during the few days of their lives.

4I undertook great projects: I built houses for myself and planted vineyards. 5I made gardens and parks and planted all kinds of fruit trees in them. 6I made reservoirs to water groves of flourishing trees. 7I bought male and female slaves and had other slaves who were born in my house. I also owned more herds and flocks than anyone in Jerusalem before me. 8I amassed silver and gold for myself, and the treasure of kings and provinces. I acquired men and women

---

a1 Or *leader of the assembly*; also in verses 2 and 12

singers, and a harem*a* as well—the delights of the heart of man. ⁹I became greater by far than anyone in Jerusalem before me. In all this my wisdom stayed with me.

¹⁰I denied myself nothing my eyes
      desired;
   I refused my heart no pleasure.
My heart took delight in all my
      work,
   and this was the reward for all
      my labor.
¹¹Yet when I surveyed all that my
      hands had done
   and what I had toiled to
      achieve,
everything was meaningless, a
      chasing after the wind;
   nothing was gained under the
      sun.

Wisdom and Folly Are Meaningless

¹²Then I turned my thoughts to
      consider wisdom,
   and also madness and folly.
What more can the king's
      successor do
   than what has already been
      done?
¹³I saw that wisdom is better than
      folly,
   just as light is better than
      darkness.
¹⁴The wise man has eyes in his
      head,

while the fool walks in the
      darkness;
but I came to realize
   that the same fate overtakes
      them both.

¹⁵Then I thought in my heart,

"The fate of the fool will overtake
      me also.
   What then do I gain by being
      wise?"
I said in my heart,
   "This too is meaningless."
¹⁶For the wise man, like the fool,
      will not be long
      remembered;
   in days to come both will be
      forgotten.
Like the fool, the wise man too
      must die!

Toil Is Meaningless

¹⁷So I hated life, because the work that is done under the sun was grievous to me. All of it is meaningless, a chasing after the wind. ¹⁸I hated all the things I had toiled for under the sun, because I must leave them to the one who comes after me. ¹⁹And who knows whether he will be a wise man or a fool? Yet he will have control over all the work into which I have poured my effort and skill under the sun. This too is meaningless. ²⁰So my heart began to despair over all my toilsome labor under the sun. ²¹For a man may do his work with wisdom,

a8 The meaning of the Hebrew for this phrase is uncertain.

Life in Bible Times

GARDENS

Wealthy people planted vegetables, spices and fruit trees in walled gardens. They liked to relax in their gardens. In summertime many slept outdoors in their gardens. You can read about gardens in Ecclesiastes 2:5–6.

knowledge and skill, and then he must leave all he owns to someone who has not worked for it. This too is meaningless and a great misfortune. ²²What does a man get for all the toil and anxious striving with which he labors under the sun? ²³All his days his work is pain and grief; even at night his mind does not rest. This too is meaningless.

²⁴A man can do nothing better than to eat and drink and find satisfaction in his work. This too, I see, is from the hand of God, ²⁵for without him, who can eat or find enjoyment? ²⁶To the man who pleases him, God gives wisdom, knowledge and happiness, but to the sinner he gives the task of gathering and storing up wealth to hand it over to the one who pleases God. This too is meaningless, a chasing after the wind.

WORDS TO REMEMBER

3:1 There is a time for everything,
and a season for every
activity under heaven.

A Time for Everything

3 There is a time for everything,
and a season for every activity
under heaven:

2 a time to be born and a time to
die,
a time to plant and a time to
uproot,
3 a time to kill and a time to
heal,
a time to tear down and a time
to build,
4 a time to weep and a time to
laugh,
a time to mourn and a time to
dance,
5 a time to scatter stones and a
time to gather them,
a time to embrace and a time to
refrain,

6 a time to search and a time to
give up,
a time to keep and a time to
throw away,
7 a time to tear and a time to
mend,
a time to be silent and a time to
speak,
8 a time to love and a time to
hate,
a time for war and a time for
peace.

⁹What does the worker gain from his toil? ¹⁰I have seen the burden God has laid on men. ¹¹He has made everything beautiful in its time. He has also set eternity in the hearts of men; yet they cannot fathom what God has done from beginning to end. ¹²I know that there is nothing better for men than to be happy and do good while they live. ¹³That everyone may eat and drink, and find satisfaction in all his toil—this is the gift of God. ¹⁴I know that everything God does will endure forever; nothing can be added to it and nothing taken from it. God does it so that men will revere him.

¹⁵Whatever is has already been,
and what will be has been
before;
and God will call the past to
account.ᵃ

¹⁶And I saw something else under the sun:

In the place of
judgment—wickedness was
there,
in the place of
justice—wickedness was
there.

¹⁷I thought in my heart,

"God will bring to judgment
both the righteous and the
wicked,
for there will be a time for every
activity,
a time for every deed."

¹⁸I also thought, "As for men, God

ᵃ15 Or God calls back the past

tests them so that they may see that they are like the animals. ¹⁹Man's fate is like that of the animals; the same fate awaits them both: As one dies, so dies the other. All have the same breath*a*; man has no advantage over the animal. Everything is meaningless. ²⁰All go to the same place; all come from dust, and to dust all return. ²¹Who knows if the spirit of man rises upward and if the spirit of the animal*b* goes down into the earth?"

²²So I saw that there is nothing better for a man than to enjoy his work, because that is his lot. For who can bring him to see what will happen after him?

Oppression, Toil, Friendlessness

4 Again I looked and saw all the oppression that was taking place under the sun:

I saw the tears of the oppressed—
and they have no comforter;
power was on the side of their
oppressors—
and they have no comforter.
²And I declared that the dead,
who had already died,
are happier than the living,
who are still alive.
³But better than both
is he who has not yet been,
who has not seen the evil
that is done under the sun.

⁴And I saw that all labor and all achievement spring from man's envy of his neighbor. This too is meaningless, a chasing after the wind.

⁵The fool folds his hands
and ruins himself.
⁶Better one handful with
tranquillity
than two handfuls with toil
and chasing after the wind.

⁷Again I saw something meaningless under the sun:

⁸There was a man all alone;

he had neither son nor brother.
There was no end to his toil,
yet his eyes were not content
with his wealth.
"For whom am I toiling," he
asked,
"and why am I depriving myself
of enjoyment?"
This too is meaningless—
a miserable business!

⁹Two are better than one,
because they have a good return
for their work:
¹⁰If one falls down,
his friend can help him up.
But pity the man who falls
and has no one to help him up!
¹¹Also, if two lie down together,
they will keep warm.
But how can one keep warm
alone?
¹²Though one may be overpowered,
two can defend themselves.
A cord of three strands is not
quickly broken.

Advancement Is Meaningless

¹³Better a poor but wise youth than an old but foolish king who no longer knows how to take warning. ¹⁴The youth may have come from prison to the kingship, or he may have been born in poverty within his kingdom. ¹⁵I saw that all who lived and walked under the sun followed the youth, the king's successor. ¹⁶There was no end to all the people who were before them. But those who came later were not pleased with the successor. This too is meaningless, a chasing after the wind.

Stand in Awe of God

5 Guard your steps when you go to the house of God. Go near to listen rather than to offer the sacrifice of fools, who do not know that they do wrong.

²Do not be quick with your mouth,
do not be hasty in your heart
to utter anything before God.

---

a19 Or *spirit*   *b21* Or *Who knows the spirit of man, which rises upward, or the spirit of the animal, which*

God is in heaven
and you are on earth,
so let your words be few.
3As a dream comes when there are
many cares,
so the speech of a fool when
there are many words.

4When you make a vow to God, do
not delay in fulfilling it. He has no
pleasure in fools; fulfill your vow. 5It
is better not to vow than to make a
vow and not fulfill it. 6Do not let your
mouth lead you into sin. And do not
protest to the temple messenger,
"My vow was a mistake." Why should
God be angry at what you say and
destroy the work of your hands?
7Much dreaming and many words are
meaningless. Therefore stand in awe
of God.

Riches Are Meaningless

8If you see the poor oppressed in a
district, and justice and rights denied, do not be surprised at such
things; for one official is eyed by a
higher one, and over them both are
others higher still. 9The increase
from the land is taken by all; the king
himself profits from the fields.

10Whoever loves money never has
money enough;
whoever loves wealth is never
satisfied with his income.
This too is meaningless.

11As goods increase,
so do those who consume them.
And what benefit are they to the
owner
except to feast his eyes on
them?

12The sleep of a laborer is sweet,
whether he eats little or much,
but the abundance of a rich man
permits him no sleep.

13I have seen a grievous evil under
the sun:

wealth hoarded to the harm of its
owner,
14   or wealth lost through some
misfortune,
so that when he has a son

there is nothing left for him.
15Naked a man comes from his
mother's womb,
and as he comes, so he departs.
He takes nothing from his labor
that he can carry in his hand.

16This too is a grievous evil:

As a man comes, so he departs,
and what does he gain,
since he toils for the wind?
17All his days he eats in darkness,
with great frustration, affliction
and anger.

18Then I realized that it is good and
proper for a man to eat and drink,
and to find satisfaction in his toilsome labor under the sun during the
few days of life God has given him
—for this is his lot. 19Moreover, when
God gives any man wealth and possessions, and enables him to enjoy
them, to accept his lot and be happy
in his work—this is a gift of God.
20He seldom reflects on the days of his
life, because God keeps him occupied
with gladness of heart.

6 I have seen another evil under
the sun, and it weighs heavily on
men: 2God gives a man wealth, possessions and honor, so that he lacks
nothing his heart desires, but God
does not enable him to enjoy them,
and a stranger enjoys them instead.
This is meaningless, a grievous evil.

3A man may have a hundred children and live many years; yet no
matter how long he lives, if he cannot
enjoy his prosperity and does not receive proper burial, I say that a stillborn child is better off than he. 4It
comes without meaning, it departs in
darkness, and in darkness its name is
shrouded. 5Though it never saw the
sun or knew anything, it has more
rest than does that man— 6even if he
lives a thousand years twice over but
fails to enjoy his prosperity. Do not
all go to the same place?

7All man's efforts are for his
mouth,
yet his appetite is never
satisfied.
8What advantage has a wise man

over a fool?
What does a poor man gain
    by knowing how to conduct
      himself before others?
⁹Better what the eye sees
    than the roving of the appetite.
This too is meaningless,
    a chasing after the wind.

¹⁰Whatever exists has already been
      named,
    and what man is has been
      known;
no man can contend
    with one who is stronger than
      he.
¹¹The more the words,
    the less the meaning,
    and how does that profit
      anyone?

¹²For who knows what is good for a
man in life, during the few and meaningless days he passes through like a
shadow? Who can tell him what will
happen under the sun after he is
gone?

Wisdom

7 A good name is better than
      fine perfume,
    and the day of death better
      than the day of birth.
²It is better to go to a house of
      mourning
    than to go to a house of
      feasting,
for death is the destiny of every
      man;
    the living should take this to
      heart.
³Sorrow is better than laughter,
    because a sad face is good for
      the heart.
⁴The heart of the wise is in the
      house of mourning,
    but the heart of fools is in the
      house of pleasure.
⁵It is better to heed a wise man's
      rebuke
    than to listen to the song of
      fools.
⁶Like the crackling of thorns under
      the pot,
    so is the laughter of fools.

This too is meaningless.

⁷Extortion turns a wise man into a
      fool,
    and a bribe corrupts the heart.

⁸The end of a matter is better than
      its beginning,
    and patience is better than
      pride.
⁹Do not be quickly provoked in
      your spirit,
    for anger resides in the lap of
      fools.

¹⁰Do not say, "Why were the old
      days better than these?"
    For it is not wise to ask such
      questions.

¹¹Wisdom, like an inheritance, is a
      good thing
    and benefits those who see the
      sun.
¹²Wisdom is a shelter
    as money is a shelter,
but the advantage of knowledge is
      this:
    that wisdom preserves the life
      of its possessor.

¹³Consider what God has done:

Who can straighten
    what he has made crooked?
¹⁴When times are good, be happy;
    but when times are bad,
      consider:
God has made the one
    as well as the other.
Therefore, a man cannot discover
    anything about his future.

¹⁵In this meaningless life of mine I
have seen both of these:

a righteous man perishing in his
      righteousness,
    and a wicked man living long
      in his wickedness.
¹⁶Do not be overrighteous,
    neither be overwise—
    why destroy yourself?
¹⁷Do not be overwicked,
    and do not be a fool—
    why die before your time?
¹⁸It is good to grasp the one
    and not let go of the other.

The man who fears God will
avoid all ⌐extremes⌐.*a*

¹⁹Wisdom makes one wise man
more powerful
than ten rulers in a city.

²⁰There is not a righteous man on
earth
who does what is right and
never sins.

²¹Do not pay attention to every
word people say,
or you may hear your servant
cursing you—
²²for you know in your heart
that many times you yourself
have cursed others.

²³All this I tested by wisdom and I
said,

"I am determined to be wise"—
but this was beyond me.
²⁴Whatever wisdom may be,
it is far off and most profound—
who can discover it?
²⁵So I turned my mind to
understand,
to investigate and to search out
wisdom and the scheme of
things
and to understand the stupidity of
wickedness
and the madness of folly.

²⁶I find more bitter than death
the woman who is a snare,
whose heart is a trap
and whose hands are chains.
The man who pleases God will
escape her,
but the sinner she will ensnare.

²⁷"Look," says the Teacher,*b* "this
is what I have discovered:

"Adding one thing to another to
discover the scheme of
things—
²⁸ while I was still searching
but not finding—
I found one ⌐upright⌐ man among a
thousand,

but not one ⌐upright⌐ woman
among them all.
²⁹This only have I found:
God made mankind upright,
but men have gone in search of
many schemes."

8 Who is like the wise man?
Who knows the explanation of
things?
Wisdom brightens a man's face
and changes its hard
appearance.

Obey the King

²Obey the king's command, I say,
because you took an oath before God.
³Do not be in a hurry to leave the
king's presence. Do not stand up for a
bad cause, for he will do whatever he
pleases. ⁴Since a king's word is supreme, who can say to him, "What
are you doing?"

⁵Whoever obeys his command will
come to no harm,
and the wise heart will know
the proper time and
procedure.
⁶For there is a proper time and
procedure for every matter,
though a man's misery weighs
heavily upon him.

⁷Since no man knows the future,
who can tell him what is to
come?
⁸No man has power over the wind
to contain it*c*;
so no one has power over the
day of his death.
As no one is discharged in time of
war,
so wickedness will not release
those who practice it.

⁹All this I saw, as I applied my
mind to everything done under the
sun. There is a time when a man
lords it over others to his own*d* hurt.
¹⁰Then too, I saw the wicked buried
—those who used to come and go
from the holy place and receive

praise*a* in the city where they did this. This too is meaningless.

¹¹When the sentence for a crime is not quickly carried out, the hearts of the people are filled with schemes to do wrong. ¹²Although a wicked man commits a hundred crimes and still lives a long time, I know that it will go better with God-fearing men, who are reverent before God. ¹³Yet because the wicked do not fear God, it will not go well with them, and their days will not lengthen like a shadow.

¹⁴There is something else meaningless that occurs on earth: righteous men who get what the wicked deserve, and wicked men who get what the righteous deserve. This too, I say, is meaningless. ¹⁵So I commend the enjoyment of life, because nothing is better for a man under the sun than to eat and drink and be glad. Then joy will accompany him in his work all the days of the life God has given him under the sun.

¹⁶When I applied my mind to know wisdom and to observe man's labor on earth—his eyes not seeing sleep day or night— ¹⁷then I saw all that God has done. No one can comprehend what goes on under the sun. Despite all his efforts to search it out, man cannot discover its meaning. Even if a wise man claims he knows, he cannot really comprehend it.

A Common Destiny for All

9 So I reflected on all this and concluded that the righteous and the wise and what they do are in God's hands, but no man knows whether love or hate awaits him. ²All share a common destiny—the righteous and the wicked, the good and the bad,*b* the clean and the unclean, those who offer sacrifices and those who do not.

As it is with the good man,
 so with the sinner;
as it is with those who take oaths,

so with those who are afraid to
 take them.

³This is the evil in everything that happens under the sun: The same destiny overtakes all. The hearts of men, moreover, are full of evil and there is madness in their hearts while they live, and afterward they join the dead. ⁴Anyone who is among the living has hope*c*—even a live dog is better off than a dead lion!

⁵For the living know that they will
 die,
 but the dead know nothing;
they have no further reward,
 and even the memory of them is
 forgotten.
⁶Their love, their hate
 and their jealousy have long
 since vanished;
never again will they have a part
 in anything that happens under
 the sun.

⁷Go, eat your food with gladness, and drink your wine with a joyful heart, for it is now that God favors what you do. ⁸Always be clothed in white, and always anoint your head with oil. ⁹Enjoy life with your wife, whom you love, all the days of this meaningless life that God has given you under the sun— all your meaningless days. For this is your lot in life and in your toilsome labor under the sun. ¹⁰Whatever your hand finds to do, do it with all your might, for in the grave,*d* where you are going, there is neither working nor planning nor knowledge nor wisdom.

¹¹I have seen something else under the sun:

The race is not to the swift
 or the battle to the strong,
nor does food come to the wise
 or wealth to the brilliant
 or favor to the learned;
but time and chance happen to
 them all.

---

a10 Some Hebrew manuscripts and Septuagint (Aquila); most Hebrew manuscripts *and are forgotten*
b2 Septuagint (Aquila), Vulgate and Syriac; Hebrew does not have *and the bad.*   *c4* Or *What then is to be chosen? With all who live, there is hope*   *d10* Hebrew *Sheol*

¹²Moreover, no man knows when his hour will come:

As fish are caught in a cruel net,
or birds are taken in a snare,
so men are trapped by evil times
that fall unexpectedly upon
them.

Life In Bible Times

HUNTING

Sometimes men in Bible times hunted animals with bows and arrows. But usually they tried to catch birds and small animals with traps. The first hunter mentioned in the Bible is Nimrod, way back in Genesis 10:9.

Wisdom Better Than Folly

¹³I also saw under the sun this example of wisdom that greatly impressed me: ¹⁴There was once a small city with only a few people in it. And a powerful king came against it, surrounded it and built huge siegeworks against it. ¹⁵Now there lived in that city a man poor but wise, and he saved the city by his wisdom. But nobody remembered that poor man. ¹⁶So I said, "Wisdom is better than strength." But the poor man's wisdom is despised, and his words are no longer heeded.

¹⁷The quiet words of the wise are
more to be heeded
than the shouts of a ruler of
fools.
¹⁸Wisdom is better than weapons of
war,
but one sinner destroys much
good.

10 As dead flies give perfume a
bad smell,
so a little folly outweighs
wisdom and honor.

²The heart of the wise inclines to
the right,
but the heart of the fool to the
left.
³Even as he walks along the road,
the fool lacks sense
and shows everyone how stupid
he is.
⁴If a ruler's anger rises against
you,
do not leave your post;
calmness can lay great errors to
rest.

⁵There is an evil I have seen under
the sun,
the sort of error that arises
from a ruler:
⁶Fools are put in many high
positions,
while the rich occupy the low
ones.
⁷I have seen slaves on horseback,
while princes go on foot like
slaves.

⁸Whoever digs a pit may fall into
it;
whoever breaks through a wall
may be bitten by a snake.
⁹Whoever quarries stones may be
injured by them;
whoever splits logs may be
endangered by them.

¹⁰If the ax is dull
and its edge unsharpened,
more strength is needed
but skill will bring success.

¹¹If a snake bites before it is
charmed,
there is no profit for the
charmer.

¹²Words from a wise man's mouth
are gracious,
but a fool is consumed by his
own lips.
¹³At the beginning his words are
folly;
at the end they are wicked
madness—
¹⁴ and the fool multiplies words.

No one knows what is coming—
who can tell him what will
happen after him?

15A fool's work wearies him;
    he does not know the way to
        town.

16Woe to you, O land whose king
        was a servant[a]
    and whose princes feast in the
        morning.
17Blessed are you, O land whose
        king is of noble birth
    and whose princes eat at a
        proper time—
    for strength and not for
        drunkenness.

18If a man is lazy, the rafters sag;
    if his hands are idle, the house
        leaks.

19A feast is made for laughter,
    and wine makes life merry,
    but money is the answer for
        everything.

20Do not revile the king even in
        your thoughts,
    or curse the rich in your
        bedroom,
    because a bird of the air may
        carry your words,
    and a bird on the wing may
        report what you say.

Bread Upon the Waters

11 Cast your bread upon the
    waters,
    for after many days you will
        find it again.
2Give portions to seven, yes to
        eight,
    for you do not know what
        disaster may come upon the
        land.

3If clouds are full of water,
    they pour rain upon the earth.
Whether a tree falls to the south
        or to the north,
    in the place where it falls, there
        will it lie.
4Whoever watches the wind will
        not plant;
    whoever looks at the clouds will
        not reap.

5As you do not know the path of
        the wind,
    or how the body is formed[b] in a
        mother's womb,
    so you cannot understand the
        work of God,
    the Maker of all things.

6Sow your seed in the morning,
    and at evening let not your
        hands be idle,
    for you do not know which will
        succeed,
    whether this or that,
    or whether both will do equally
        well.

Remember Your Creator While Young

7Light is sweet,
    and it pleases the eyes to see
        the sun.
8However many years a man may
        live,
    let him enjoy them all.
But let him remember the days of
        darkness,
    for they will be many.
    Everything to come is
        meaningless.

9Be happy, young man, while you
        are young,
    and let your heart give you joy
        in the days of your youth.
Follow the ways of your heart
    and whatever your eyes see,
but know that for all these things
    God will bring you to judgment.
10So then, banish anxiety from your
        heart
    and cast off the troubles of your
        body,
    for youth and vigor are
        meaningless.

12 Remember your Creator
    in the days of your youth,
before the days of trouble come
    and the years approach when
        you will say,
    "I find no pleasure in them"—
2before the sun and the light

---

a16 Or *king is a child*   b5 Or *know how life (or the spirit) / enters the body being formed*

and the moon and the stars
grow dark,
and the clouds return after the
rain;

12:1   Remember your Creator
in the days of your youth.

³when the keepers of the house
tremble,
and the strong men stoop,
when the grinders cease because
they are few,
and those looking through the
windows grow dim;
⁴when the doors to the street are
closed
and the sound of grinding fades;
when men rise up at the sound of
birds,
but all their songs grow faint;
⁵when men are afraid of heights
and of dangers in the streets;
when the almond tree blossoms
and the grasshopper drags
himself along
and desire no longer is stirred.
Then man goes to his eternal
home
and mourners go about the
streets.

⁶Remember him—before the silver
cord is severed,
or the golden bowl is broken;

before the pitcher is shattered at
the spring,
or the wheel broken at the well,
⁷and the dust returns to the
ground it came from,
and the spirit returns to God
who gave it.

⁸"Meaningless! Meaningless!" says
the Teacher.ᵃ
"Everything is meaningless!"

The Conclusion of the Matter

⁹Not only was the Teacher wise,
but also he imparted knowledge to
the people. He pondered and
searched out and set in order many
proverbs. ¹⁰The Teacher searched to
find just the right words, and what he
wrote was upright and true.

¹¹The words of the wise are like
goads, their collected sayings like
firmly embedded nails—given by one
Shepherd. ¹²Be warned, my son, of
anything in addition to them.

Of making many books there is no
end, and much study wearies the
body.

¹³Now all has been heard;
here is the conclusion of the
matter:
Fear God and keep his
commandments,
for this is the whole ⌊duty⌋ of
man.
¹⁴For God will bring every deed
into judgment,
including every hidden thing,
whether it is good or evil.

ᵃ8 Or *the leader of the assembly*; also in verses 9 and 10

SONG OF SONGS

WHO WROTE THIS BOOK? This book was probably written by Solomon.

WHAT IS THIS BOOK ABOUT? This book is a collection of poems about grown-up love between a man and a woman.

FOR WHOM WAS THIS BOOK WRITTEN? The book was written for grown-ups to help them understand love and marriage.

WHEN WAS THIS BOOK WRITTEN? If Solomon wrote Song of Songs, it was written sometime during the tenth century B.C. If it was written by someone else, the date is unknown.

1

Solomon's Song of Songs.

Beloved[a]

²Let him kiss me with the kisses
of his mouth—
for your love is more delightful
than wine.
³Pleasing is the fragrance of your
perfumes;
your name is like perfume
poured out.
No wonder the maidens love
you!
⁴Take me away with you—let us
hurry!
Let the king bring me into his
chambers.

Friends

We rejoice and delight in you[b];
we will praise your love more
than wine.

Beloved

How right they are to adore you!

⁵Dark am I, yet lovely,
O daughters of Jerusalem,
dark like the tents of Kedar,
like the tent curtains of
Solomon.[c]
⁶Do not stare at me because I am
dark,
because I am darkened by the
sun.
My mother's sons were angry
with me
and made me take care of the
vineyards;
my own vineyard I have
neglected.
⁷Tell me, you whom I love, where
you graze your flock
and where you rest your sheep
at midday.
Why should I be like a veiled
woman
beside the flocks of your
friends?

Friends

⁸If you do not know, most
beautiful of women,
follow the tracks of the
sheep
and graze your young goats
by the tents of the shepherds.

Lover

⁹I liken you, my darling, to a mare
harnessed to one of the chariots
of Pharaoh.
¹⁰Your cheeks are beautiful with
earrings,
your neck with strings of
jewels.
¹¹We will make you earrings of
gold,
studded with silver.

Beloved

¹²While the king was at his table,
my perfume spread its
fragrance.
¹³My lover is to me a sachet of
myrrh
resting between my breasts.
¹⁴My lover is to me a cluster of
henna blossoms
from the vineyards of En Gedi.

Life In Bible Times

PERFUME

Women and sometimes men used
sweet-smelling perfume. Perfume
was made from spices like cinnamon and from crushed flower petals. These were mixed in oil and
kept in delicate stone or glass bottles.

---

[a]Primarily on the basis of the gender of the Hebrew pronouns used, male and female speakers are
indicated in the margins by the captions *Lover* and *Beloved* respectively. The words of others are
marked *Friends*. In some instances the divisions and their captions are debatable.   [b]4 The
Hebrew is masculine singular.   [c]5 Or *Salma*

Lover

15How beautiful you are, my
     darling!
  Oh, how beautiful!
  Your eyes are doves.

Beloved

16How handsome you are, my lover!
  Oh, how charming!
  And our bed is verdant.

Lover

17The beams of our house are
     cedars;
  our rafters are firs.

Beloved[a]

2 I am a rose[b] of Sharon,
  a lily of the valleys.

Lover

2Like a lily among thorns
  is my darling among the
     maidens.

Beloved

3Like an apple tree among the
     trees of the forest
  is my lover among the young
     men.
  I delight to sit in his shade,
     and his fruit is sweet to my
        taste.
4He has taken me to the banquet
     hall,
  and his banner over me is love.
5Strengthen me with raisins,
  refresh me with apples,
  for I am faint with love.
6His left arm is under my head,
  and his right arm embraces me.
7Daughters of Jerusalem, I charge
     you
  by the gazelles and by the does
     of the field:
  Do not arouse or awaken love
     until it so desires.

8Listen! My lover!
  Look! Here he comes,
  leaping across the mountains,
     bounding over the hills.

9My lover is like a gazelle or a
     young stag.
  Look! There he stands behind
     our wall,
  gazing through the windows,
     peering through the lattice.
10My lover spoke and said to me,
  "Arise, my darling,
  my beautiful one, and come
     with me.
11See! The winter is past;
  the rains are over and gone.
12Flowers appear on the earth;
  the season of singing has come,
  the cooing of doves
  is heard in our land.
13The fig tree forms its early fruit;
  the blossoming vines spread
     their fragrance.
  Arise, come, my darling;
  my beautiful one, come with
     me."

Lover

14My dove in the clefts of the rock,
  in the hiding places on the
     mountainside,
  show me your face,
  let me hear your voice;
  for your voice is sweet,
  and your face is lovely.
15Catch for us the foxes,
  the little foxes
  that ruin the vineyards,
  our vineyards that are in bloom.

Beloved

16My lover is mine and I am his;
  he browses among the lilies.
17Until the day breaks
  and the shadows flee,
  turn, my lover,
  and be like a gazelle
  or like a young stag
  on the rugged hills.[c]

3 All night long on my bed
  I looked for the one my heart
     loves;
  I looked for him but did not find
     him.
2I will get up now and go about
     the city,

---

a1 Or *Lover*   b1 Possibly a member of the crocus family   c17 Or *the hills of Bether*

through its streets and squares;
  I will search for the one my heart
      loves.
    So I looked for him but did not
      find him.
³The watchmen found me
  as they made their rounds in
      the city.
    "Have you seen the one my
      heart loves?"
⁴Scarcely had I passed them
  when I found the one my heart
      loves.
  I held him and would not let him
      go
    till I had brought him to my
      mother's house,
    to the room of the one who
      conceived me.
⁵Daughters of Jerusalem, I charge
      you
  by the gazelles and by the does
      of the field:
  Do not arouse or awaken love
    until it so desires.

⁶Who is this coming up from the
      desert
  like a column of smoke,
  perfumed with myrrh and incense
    made from all the spices of the
      merchant?
⁷Look! It is Solomon's carriage,
  escorted by sixty warriors,
  the noblest of Israel,
⁸all of them wearing the sword,

all experienced in battle,
  each with his sword at his side,
  prepared for the terrors of the
      night.
⁹King Solomon made for himself
    the carriage;
  he made it of wood from
      Lebanon.
¹⁰Its posts he made of silver,
    its base of gold.
  Its seat was upholstered with
      purple,
    its interior lovingly inlaid
    by*ᵃ* the daughters of Jerusalem.
¹¹Come out, you daughters of Zion,
    and look at King Solomon
      wearing the crown,
  the crown with which his
      mother crowned him
  on the day of his wedding,
    the day his heart rejoiced.

Lover

4 How beautiful you are, my
      darling!
    Oh, how beautiful!
  Your eyes behind your veil are
      doves.
  Your hair is like a flock of goats
    descending from Mount Gilead.
²Your teeth are like a flock of
    sheep just shorn,
  coming up from the washing.
  Each has its twin;
    not one of them is alone.

ᵃ10 Or its inlaid interior a gift of love / from

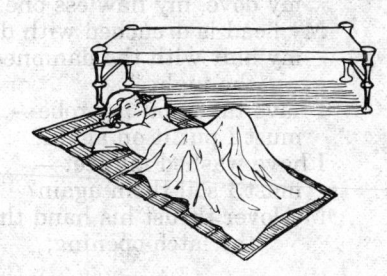

Life in Bible Times

BEDS

Most people in Israel slept
on woven mats or animal
skins that were thrown on
the floor. Some wealthy
people slept on real beds.
Beds were made of wood
or metal and sometimes
even had linen sheets and
pillows.

³Your lips are like a scarlet
  ribbon;
  your mouth is lovely.
Your temples behind your veil
  are like the halves of a
  pomegranate.
⁴Your neck is like the tower of
  David,
  built with elegance*a*;
on it hang a thousand shields,
  all of them shields of warriors.
⁵Your two breasts are like two
  fawns,
  like twin fawns of a gazelle
  that browse among the lilies.
⁶Until the day breaks
  and the shadows flee,
I will go to the mountain of
  myrrh
  and to the hill of incense.
⁷All beautiful you are, my darling;
  there is no flaw in you.

⁸Come with me from Lebanon, my
  bride,
  come with me from Lebanon.
Descend from the crest of Amana,
  from the top of Senir, the
  summit of Hermon,
from the lions' dens
  and the mountain haunts of the
  leopards.
⁹You have stolen my heart, my
  sister, my bride;
  you have stolen my heart
with one glance of your eyes,
  with one jewel of your necklace.
¹⁰How delightful is your love, my
  sister, my bride!
  How much more pleasing is
  your love than wine,
  and the fragrance of your
  perfume than any spice!
¹¹Your lips drop sweetness as the
  honeycomb, my bride;
  milk and honey are under your
  tongue.
  The fragrance of your garments
  is like that of Lebanon.
¹²You are a garden locked up, my
  sister, my bride;
  you are a spring enclosed, a
  sealed fountain.

¹³Your plants are an orchard of
  pomegranates
  with choice fruits,
  with henna and nard,
¹⁴ nard and saffron,
  calamus and cinnamon,
  with every kind of incense tree,
  with myrrh and aloes
  and all the finest spices.
¹⁵You are*b* a garden fountain,
  a well of flowing water
  streaming down from Lebanon.

Beloved

¹⁶Awake, north wind,
  and come, south wind!
Blow on my garden,
  that its fragrance may spread
  abroad.
Let my lover come into his garden
  and taste its choice fruits.

Lover

5 I have come into my garden,
  my sister, my bride;
  I have gathered my myrrh with
  my spice.
I have eaten my honeycomb and
  my honey;
  I have drunk my wine and my
  milk.

Friends

  Eat, O friends, and drink;
  drink your fill, O lovers.

Beloved

²I slept but my heart was awake.
  Listen! My lover is knocking:
"Open to me, my sister, my
  darling,
  my dove, my flawless one.
My head is drenched with dew,
  my hair with the dampness of
  the night."
³I have taken off my robe—
  must I put it on again?
I have washed my feet—
  must I soil them again?
⁴My lover thrust his hand through
  the latch-opening;

---

a4 The meaning of the Hebrew for this word is uncertain.   *b15* Or *I am* (spoken by the *Beloved*)

my heart began to pound for
him.
⁵I arose to open for my lover,
and my hands dripped with
myrrh,
my fingers with flowing myrrh,
on the handles of the lock.
⁶I opened for my lover,
but my lover had left; he was
gone.
My heart sank at his
departure.ᵃ
I looked for him but did not find
him.
I called him but he did not
answer.
⁷The watchmen found me
as they made their rounds in
the city.
They beat me, they bruised me;
they took away my cloak,
those watchmen of the walls!
⁸O daughters of Jerusalem, I
charge you—
if you find my lover,
what will you tell him?
Tell him I am faint with
love.

Friends

⁹How is your beloved better than
others,
most beautiful of women?

How is your beloved better than
others,
that you charge us so?

Beloved

¹⁰My lover is radiant and ruddy,
outstanding among ten
thousand.
¹¹His head is purest gold;
his hair is wavy
and black as a raven.
¹²His eyes are like doves
by the water streams,
washed in milk,
mounted like jewels.
¹³His cheeks are like beds of
spice
yielding perfume.
His lips are like lilies
dripping with myrrh.
¹⁴His arms are rods of gold
set with chrysolite.
His body is like polished ivory
decorated with sapphires.ᵇ
¹⁵His legs are pillars of marble
set on bases of pure gold.
His appearance is like Lebanon,
choice as its cedars.
¹⁶His mouth is sweetness itself;
he is altogether lovely.
This is my lover, this my
friend,
O daughters of Jerusalem.

ᵃ6 Or *heart had gone out to him when he spoke*   ᵇ14 Or *lapis lazuli*

Life in Bible Times

SPICES

Spices are herbs that have a pleasant odor, like cinnamon or myrrh. In Bible times some spices were brought to Arabia by boat, and then on to Israel by camel caravan. Spices were used in the sweet-smelling incense burned when people worshiped the Lord.

Friends

6 Where has your lover gone,
　　most beautiful of women?
Which way did your lover turn,
　　that we may look for him with
　　you?

Beloved

2My lover has gone down to his
　　garden,
　　to the beds of spices,
to browse in the gardens
　　and to gather lilies.
3I am my lover's and my lover is
　　mine;
　　he browses among the lilies.

Lover

4You are beautiful, my darling, as
　　Tirzah,
　　lovely as Jerusalem,
　　majestic as troops with banners.
5Turn your eyes from me;
　　they overwhelm me.
Your hair is like a flock of goats
　　descending from Gilead.
6Your teeth are like a flock of
　　sheep
　　coming up from the washing.
Each has its twin,
　　not one of them is alone.
7Your temples behind your veil
　　are like the halves of a
　　pomegranate.
8Sixty queens there may be,
　　and eighty concubines,
　　and virgins beyond number;
9but my dove, my perfect one, is
　　unique,
　　the only daughter of her
　　mother,
　　the favorite of the one who bore
　　her.
The maidens saw her and called
　　her blessed;
　　the queens and concubines
　　praised her.

Friends

10Who is this that appears like the
　　dawn,

fair as the moon, bright as the
　　sun,
majestic as the stars in
　　procession?

Lover

11I went down to the grove of nut
　　trees
　　to look at the new growth in
　　the valley,
to see if the vines had budded
　　or the pomegranates were in
　　bloom.
12Before I realized it,
　　my desire set me among the
　　royal chariots of my
　　people.[a]

Friends

13Come back, come back,
　　O Shulammite;
come back, come back, that we
　　may gaze on you!

Lover

Why would you gaze on the
　　Shulammite
as on the dance of Mahanaim?

7 How beautiful your sandaled
　　feet,
　　O prince's daughter!
Your graceful legs are like jewels,
　　the work of a craftsman's
　　hands.
2Your navel is a rounded goblet
　　that never lacks blended wine.
Your waist is a mound of wheat
　　encircled by lilies.
3Your breasts are like two fawns,
　　twins of a gazelle.
4Your neck is like an ivory tower.
Your eyes are the pools of
　　Heshbon
　　by the gate of Bath Rabbim.
Your nose is like the tower of
　　Lebanon
　　looking toward Damascus.
5Your head crowns you like Mount
　　Carmel.
Your hair is like royal tapestry;

---

a12 Or *among the chariots of Amminadab*; or *among the chariots of the people of the prince*

the king is held captive by its
   tresses.
6How beautiful you are and how
   pleasing,
  O love, with your delights!
7Your stature is like that of the
   palm,
  and your breasts like clusters of
   fruit.
8I said, "I will climb the palm
   tree;
  I will take hold of its fruit."
May your breasts be like the
   clusters of the vine,
  the fragrance of your breath
   like apples,
9   and your mouth like the best
   wine.

Beloved

May the wine go straight to my
   lover,
  flowing gently over lips and
   teeth.*a*
10I belong to my lover,
  and his desire is for me.
11Come, my lover, let us go to the
   countryside,
  let us spend the night in the
   villages.*b*
12Let us go early to the vineyards
  to see if the vines have budded,
  if their blossoms have opened,
  and if the pomegranates are in
   bloom—
  there I will give you my love.
13The mandrakes send out their
   fragrance,
  and at our door is every
   delicacy,
both new and old,
  that I have stored up for you,
   my lover.

8 If only you were to me like a
   brother,
  who was nursed at my mother's
   breasts!
Then, if I found you outside,
  I would kiss you,
  and no one would despise me.
2I would lead you

and bring you to my mother's
   house—
  she who has taught me.
I would give you spiced wine to
   drink,
  the nectar of my pomegranates.
3His left arm is under my head
  and his right arm embraces me.
4Daughters of Jerusalem, I charge
   you:
  Do not arouse or awaken love
  until it so desires.

Friends

5Who is this coming up from the
   desert
  leaning on her lover?

Beloved

Under the apple tree I roused
   you;
  there your mother conceived
   you,
  there she who was in labor gave
   you birth.
6Place me like a seal over your
   heart,
  like a seal on your arm;
for love is as strong as death,
  its jealousy*c* unyielding as the
   grave.*d*
It burns like blazing fire,
  like a mighty flame.*e*
7Many waters cannot quench love;
  rivers cannot wash it away.
If one were to give
  all the wealth of his house for
   love,
  it*f* would be utterly scorned.

Friends

8We have a young sister,
  and her breasts are not yet
   grown.
What shall we do for our sister
  for the day she is spoken for?
9If she is a wall,
  we will build towers of silver on
   her.
If she is a door,

---

a9 Septuagint, Aquila, Vulgate and Syriac; Hebrew *lips of sleepers*   *b11* Or *henna bushes*
c6 Or *ardor*   *d6* Hebrew *Sheol*   *e6* Or / *like the very flame of the* LORD   *f7* Or *he*

we will enclose her with panels
of cedar.

Beloved

[10]I am a wall,
and my breasts are like towers.
Thus I have become in his eyes
like one bringing contentment.
[11]Solomon had a vineyard in Baal
Hamon;
he let out his vineyard to
tenants.
Each was to bring for its fruit
a thousand shekels[a] of silver.
[12]But my own vineyard is mine to
give;

the thousand shekels are for
you, O Solomon,
and two hundred[b] are for those
who tend its fruit.

Lover

[13]You who dwell in the gardens
with friends in attendance,
let me hear your voice!

Beloved

[14]Come away, my lover,
and be like a gazelle
or like a young stag
on the spice-laden mountains.

---

[a]11 That is, about 25 pounds (about 11.5 kilograms); also in verse 12   [b]12 That is, about 5
pounds (about 2.3 kilograms)

ISAIAH

WHO WROTE THIS BOOK?	The prophet Isaiah.
WHY WAS THIS BOOK WRITTEN?	Isaiah warns the people of Judah that God will punish them just as he is punishing Israel, if they keep on doing wicked things. Isaiah also promises that God will comfort his people after punishing them and make their nation strong again.
WHAT DO WE LEARN ABOUT GOD IN THIS BOOK?	Isaiah uses many special names for God. These names show that God is holy, God is judge, and God is our salvation.
WHAT IS SPECIAL ABOUT THIS BOOK?	Isaiah gives many wonderful prophecies about Jesus, the coming Savior.
WHEN WAS THIS BOOK WRITTEN?	Isaiah was written between 739 and 680 B.C. During this time the Assyrian armies that took Israel captive were driven out of Judah by God.
WHAT ARE SOME IMPORTANT CHAPTERS IN THIS BOOK?	The wickedness of Judah. Isaiah 1 God's holiness. Isaiah 6 Who Jesus is. Isaiah 9:1–7 What Jesus will do. Isaiah 11 God is better than idols. Isaiah 44 Jesus' death on the cross. Isaiah 53 A new heaven and earth. Isaiah 65

1 The vision concerning Judah and Jerusalem that Isaiah son of Amoz saw during the reigns of Uzziah, Jotham, Ahaz and Hezekiah, kings of Judah.

A Rebellious Nation

²Hear, O heavens! Listen, O earth!
  For the LORD has spoken:
"I reared children and brought
    them up,
  but they have rebelled against
    me.
³The ox knows his master,
  the donkey his owner's manger,
but Israel does not know,
  my people do not understand."

⁴Ah, sinful nation,
  a people loaded with guilt,
a brood of evildoers,
  children given to corruption!
They have forsaken the LORD;
  they have spurned the Holy
    One of Israel
  and turned their backs on him.

⁵Why should you be beaten
    anymore?
  Why do you persist in rebellion?
Your whole head is injured,
  your whole heart afflicted.
⁶From the sole of your foot to the
    top of your head
  there is no soundness—
only wounds and welts
  and open sores,
not cleansed or bandaged
  or soothed with oil.

⁷Your country is desolate,
  your cities burned with fire;
your fields are being stripped by
    foreigners
  right before you,
  laid waste as when overthrown
    by strangers.
⁸The Daughter of Zion is left
  like a shelter in a vineyard,
like a hut in a field of melons,
  like a city under siege.
⁹Unless the LORD Almighty
  had left us some survivors,

we would have become like
    Sodom,
  we would have been like
    Gomorrah.

¹⁰Hear the word of the LORD,
  you rulers of Sodom;
listen to the law of our God,
  you people of Gomorrah!
¹¹"The multitude of your
    sacrifices—
  what are they to me?" says the
    LORD.
"I have more than enough of
    burnt offerings,
  of rams and the fat of fattened
    animals;
I have no pleasure
  in the blood of bulls and lambs
    and goats.
¹²When you come to appear before
    me,
  who has asked this of you,
  this trampling of my courts?
¹³Stop bringing meaningless
    offerings!
  Your incense is detestable to
    me.
New Moons, Sabbaths and
    convocations—
  I cannot bear your evil
    assemblies.
¹⁴Your New Moon festivals and
    your appointed feasts
  my soul hates.
They have become a burden to
    me;
  I am weary of bearing them.
¹⁵When you spread out your hands
    in prayer,
  I will hide my eyes from you;
even if you offer many prayers,
  I will not listen.
Your hands are full of blood;
¹⁶ wash and make yourselves
    clean.
Take your evil deeds
  out of my sight!
Stop doing wrong,
¹⁷ learn to do right!
Seek justice,
  encourage the oppressed.^a
Defend the cause of the fatherless,

---

^a17 Or / rebuke the oppressor

plead the case of the widow.

18"Come now, let us reason
    together,"
  says the LORD.
  "Though your sins are like
    scarlet,
    they shall be as white as
      snow;
  though they are red as crimson,
    they shall be like wool.
19If you are willing and obedient,
    you will eat the best from the
      land;
20but if you resist and rebel,
    you will be devoured by the
      sword."
      For the mouth of the LORD
        has spoken.

21See how the faithful city
    has become a harlot!
  She once was full of justice;
    righteousness used to dwell in
      her—
    but now murderers!
22Your silver has become dross,
    your choice wine is diluted with
      water.
23Your rulers are rebels,
    companions of thieves;
  they all love bribes
    and chase after gifts.
  They do not defend the cause of
    the fatherless;
    the widow's case does not come
      before them.
24Therefore the Lord, the LORD
    Almighty,
  the Mighty One of Israel,
    declares:
  "Ah, I will get relief from my foes
    and avenge myself on my
      enemies.
25I will turn my hand against you;
    I will thoroughly purge away
      your dross
    and remove all your impurities.
26I will restore your judges as in
    days of old,
    your counselors as at the
      beginning.
  Afterward you will be called
    the City of Righteousness,
    the Faithful City."

27Zion will be redeemed with
    justice,
  her penitent ones with
    righteousness.
28But rebels and sinners will both
    be broken,
  and those who forsake the LORD
    will perish.

29"You will be ashamed because of
    the sacred oaks
  in which you have delighted;
  you will be disgraced because of
    the gardens
    that you have chosen.
30You will be like an oak with
    fading leaves,
  like a garden without water.
31The mighty man will become
    tinder
    and his work a spark;
  both will burn together,
    with no one to quench the fire."

The Mountain of the LORD

2 This is what Isaiah son of Amoz
  saw concerning Judah and Jerusalem:

2In the last days

the mountain of the LORD's temple
    will be established
  as chief among the mountains;
  it will be raised above the hills,
    and all nations will stream to
      it.

3Many peoples will come and say,

"Come, let us go up to the
    mountain of the LORD,
  to the house of the God of
    Jacob.
  He will teach us his ways,
    so that we may walk in his
      paths."
  The law will go out from Zion,
    the word of the LORD from
      Jerusalem.
4He will judge between the nations
    and will settle disputes for
      many peoples.
  They will beat their swords into
    plowshares
    and their spears into pruning
      hooks.

Nation will not take up sword
    against nation,
nor will they train for war
    anymore.

⁵Come, O house of Jacob,
    let us walk in the light of the
    LORD.

The Day of the LORD

⁶You have abandoned your people,
    the house of Jacob.
They are full of superstitions from
    the East;
    they practice divination like the
      Philistines
and clasp hands with pagans.
⁷Their land is full of silver and
    gold;
    there is no end to their
      treasures.
Their land is full of horses;
    there is no end to their chariots.
⁸Their land is full of idols;
    they bow down to the work of
      their hands,
to what their fingers have
    made.
⁹So man will be brought low
    and mankind humbled—
    do not forgive them. ᵃ

¹⁰Go into the rocks,
    hide in the ground

from dread of the LORD
    and the splendor of his majesty!
¹¹The eyes of the arrogant man will
    be humbled
and the pride of men brought
    low;
the LORD alone will be exalted in
    that day.

¹²The LORD Almighty has a day in
    store
for all the proud and lofty,
for all that is exalted
    (and they will be humbled),
¹³for all the cedars of Lebanon, tall
    and lofty,
and all the oaks of Bashan,
¹⁴for all the towering mountains
    and all the high hills,
¹⁵for every lofty tower
    and every fortified wall,
¹⁶for every trading ship ᵇ
    and every stately vessel.
¹⁷The arrogance of man will be
    brought low
and the pride of men humbled;
the LORD alone will be exalted in
    that day,
¹⁸ and the idols will totally
    disappear.

¹⁹Men will flee to caves in the
    rocks
and to holes in the ground
from dread of the LORD

ᵃ9 Or *not raise them up*   ᵇ16 Hebrew *every ship of Tarshish*

Life in Bible Times

PLOWING

Oxen pulled plows that were made of heavy, forked tree branches. The part of the plow that turned over the earth was called the plowshare. Metal blades on plowshares made plowing easier. In wartime metal plowshares were hammered into swords.

and the splendor of his majesty,
when he rises to shake the
earth.
20In that day men will throw away
to the rodents and bats
their idols of silver and idols of
gold,
which they made to worship.
21They will flee to caverns in the
rocks
and to the overhanging crags
from dread of the LORD
and the splendor of his majesty,
when he rises to shake the
earth.

22Stop trusting in man,
who has but a breath in his
nostrils.
Of what account is he?

Judgment on Jerusalem and Judah

3 See now, the Lord,
the LORD Almighty,
is about to take from Jerusalem
and Judah
both supply and support:
all supplies of food and all
supplies of water,
2 the hero and warrior,
the judge and prophet,
the soothsayer and elder,
3the captain of fifty and man of
rank,
the counselor, skilled craftsman
and clever enchanter.

4I will make boys their officials;
mere children will govern them.
5People will oppress each other—
man against man, neighbor
against neighbor.
The young will rise up against
the old,
the base against the honorable.

6A man will seize one of his
brothers
at his father's home, and say,
"You have a cloak, you be our
leader;
take charge of this heap of
ruins!"
7But in that day he will cry out,
"I have no remedy.

I have no food or clothing in my
house;
do not make me the leader of
the people."

8Jerusalem staggers,
Judah is falling;
their words and deeds are against
the LORD,
defying his glorious presence.
9The look on their faces testifies
against them;
they parade their sin like
Sodom;
they do not hide it.
Woe to them!
They have brought disaster
upon themselves.

10Tell the righteous it will be well
with them,
for they will enjoy the fruit of
their deeds.
11Woe to the wicked! Disaster is
upon them!
They will be paid back for what
their hands have done.

12Youths oppress my people,
women rule over them.
O my people, your guides lead
you astray;
they turn you from the path.

13The LORD takes his place in court;
he rises to judge the people.
14The LORD enters into judgment
against the elders and leaders
of his people:
"It is you who have ruined my
vineyard;
the plunder from the poor is in
your houses.
15What do you mean by crushing
my people
and grinding the faces of the
poor?"
declares the Lord, the LORD
Almighty.

16The LORD says,
"The women of Zion are
haughty,
walking along with outstretched
necks,
flirting with their eyes,
tripping along with mincing steps,

with ornaments jingling on
their ankles.
¹⁷Therefore the Lord will bring
    sores on the heads of the
    women of Zion;
    the LORD will make their scalps
      bald."

¹⁸In that day the Lord will snatch
away their finery: the bangles and
headbands and crescent necklaces,
¹⁹the earrings and bracelets and
veils, ²⁰the headdresses and ankle
chains and sashes, the perfume bottles and charms, ²¹the signet rings
and nose rings, ²²the fine robes and
the capes and cloaks, the purses
²³and mirrors, and the linen gar-
ments and tiaras and shawls.

²⁴Instead of fragrance there will be
    a stench;
    instead of a sash, a rope;
  instead of well-dressed hair,
      baldness;
    instead of fine clothing,
      sackcloth;
    instead of beauty, branding.
²⁵Your men will fall by the sword,
    your warriors in battle.
²⁶The gates of Zion will lament and
      mourn;
    destitute, she will sit on the
      ground.

4 In that day seven women
    will take hold of one man
and say, "We will eat our own
    food
  and provide our own clothes;
only let us be called by your
    name.
    Take away our disgrace!"

The Branch of the LORD

²In that day the Branch of the LORD
will be beautiful and glorious, and
the fruit of the land will be the pride
and glory of the survivors in Israel.
³Those who are left in Zion, who re-
main in Jerusalem, will be called
holy, all who are recorded among the
living in Jerusalem. ⁴The Lord will
wash away the filth of the women of

Zion; he will cleanse the bloodstains
from Jerusalem by a spirit^a of judgment and a spirit^a of fire. ⁵Then the
LORD will create over all of Mount
Zion and over those who assemble
there a cloud of smoke by day and a
glow of flaming fire by night; over all
the glory will be a canopy. ⁶It will be
a shelter and shade from the heat of
the day, and a refuge and hiding
place from the storm and rain.

The Song of the Vineyard

5 I will sing for the one I love
    a song about his vineyard:
My loved one had a vineyard
    on a fertile hillside.
²He dug it up and cleared it of
      stones
    and planted it with the choicest
      vines.
He built a watchtower in it
    and cut out a winepress as
      well.
Then he looked for a crop of good
      grapes,
    but it yielded only bad fruit.

³"Now you dwellers in Jerusalem
    and men of Judah,
    judge between me and my
      vineyard.
⁴What more could have been done
    for my vineyard
    than I have done for it?
When I looked for good grapes,
    why did it yield only bad?
⁵Now I will tell you
    what I am going to do to my
      vineyard:
I will take away its hedge,
    and it will be destroyed;
I will break down its wall,
    and it will be trampled.
⁶I will make it a wasteland,
    neither pruned nor cultivated,
    and briers and thorns will grow
      there.
I will command the clouds
    not to rain on it."

⁷The vineyard of the LORD
    Almighty

is the house of Israel,
and the men of Judah
   are the garden of his delight.
And he looked for justice, but saw
   bloodshed;
   for righteousness, but heard
   cries of distress.

Woes and Judgments

⁸Woe to you who add house to
   house
   and join field to field
till no space is left
   and you live alone in the land.

⁹The LORD Almighty has declared
in my hearing:

"Surely the great houses will
   become desolate,
   the fine mansions left without
   occupants.
¹⁰A ten-acre*a* vineyard will
   produce
   only a bath*b* of wine,
a homer*c* of seed only an
   ephah*d* of grain."

¹¹Woe to those who rise early in
   the morning
   to run after their drinks,
who stay up late at night
   till they are inflamed with
   wine.

¹²They have harps and lyres at
   their banquets,
   tambourines and flutes and
   wine,
but they have no regard for the
   deeds of the LORD,
   no respect for the work of his
   hands.
¹³Therefore my people will go into
   exile
   for lack of understanding;
their men of rank will die of
   hunger
   and their masses will be
   parched with thirst.
¹⁴Therefore the grave*e* enlarges its
   appetite
   and opens its mouth without
   limit;
into it will descend their nobles
   and masses
   with all their brawlers and
   revelers.
¹⁵So man will be brought low
   and mankind humbled,
   the eyes of the arrogant
   humbled.
¹⁶But the LORD Almighty will be
   exalted by his justice,
   and the holy God will show
   himself holy by his
   righteousness.
¹⁷Then sheep will graze as in their
   own pasture;

a10 Hebrew *ten-yoke,* that is, the land plowed by 10 yoke of oxen in one day   *b10* That is,
probably about 6 gallons (about 22 liters)   *c10* That is, probably about 6 bushels (about 220
liters)   *d10* That is, probably about 3/5 bushel (about 22 liters)   *e14* Hebrew *Sheol*

Life in Bible Times

WINEPRESSES

Ripe grapes were put into
a large stone vat, called a
winepress. Men stamped
on the grapes to get juice.
The juice flowed out a hole
near the bottom of the vat.
The men held on to ropes
so they would not fall on
the slippery grape skins.

lambs will feed*a* among the
ruins of the rich.

¹⁸Woe to those who draw sin along
with cords of deceit,
and wickedness as with cart
ropes,
¹⁹to those who say, "Let God hurry,
let him hasten his work
so we may see it.
Let it approach,
let the plan of the Holy One of
Israel come,
so we may know it."

²⁰Woe to those who call evil good
and good evil,
who put darkness for light
and light for darkness,
who put bitter for sweet
and sweet for bitter.

²¹Woe to those who are wise in
their own eyes
and clever in their own
sight.

²²Woe to those who are heroes at
drinking wine
and champions at mixing
drinks,
²³who acquit the guilty for a bribe,
but deny justice to the innocent.
²⁴Therefore, as tongues of fire lick
up straw
and as dry grass sinks down in
the flames,
so their roots will decay
and their flowers blow away
like dust;
for they have rejected the law of
the LORD Almighty
and spurned the word of the
Holy One of Israel.
²⁵Therefore the LORD's anger burns
against his people;
his hand is raised and he
strikes them down.
The mountains shake,
and the dead bodies are like
refuse in the streets.

Yet for all this, his anger is not
turned away,
his hand is still upraised.

²⁶He lifts up a banner for the
distant nations,
he whistles for those at the
ends of the earth.
Here they come,
swiftly and speedily!
²⁷Not one of them grows tired or
stumbles,
not one slumbers or sleeps;
not a belt is loosened at the waist,
not a sandal thong is broken.
²⁸Their arrows are sharp,
all their bows are strung;
their horses' hoofs seem like flint,
their chariot wheels like a
whirlwind.
²⁹Their roar is like that of the lion,
they roar like young lions;
they growl as they seize their
prey
and carry it off with no one to
rescue.
³⁰In that day they will roar over it
like the roaring of the sea.
And if one looks at the land,
he will see darkness and
distress;
even the light will be darkened
by the clouds.

Isaiah's Commission

6 In the year that King Uzziah
died, I saw the Lord seated on a
throne, high and exalted, and the
train of his robe filled the temple.
²Above him were seraphs, each with
six wings: With two wings they covered their faces, with two they covered their feet, and with two they
were flying. ³And they were calling
to one another:

"Holy, holy, holy is the LORD
Almighty;
the whole earth is full of his
glory."

⁴At the sound of their voices the door-
posts and thresholds shook and the
temple was filled with smoke.

⁵"Woe to me!" I cried. "I am ruined!
For I am a man of unclean lips, and
I live among a people of unclean lips,

---

*a*17 Septuagint; Hebrew / *strangers will eat*

and my eyes have seen the King, the
LORD Almighty.'"

[6]Then one of the seraphs flew to me
with a live coal in his hand, which he
had taken with tongs from the altar.
[7]With it he touched my mouth and
said, "See, this has touched your lips;
your guilt is taken away and your sin
atoned for."

[8]Then I heard the voice of the Lord
saying, "Whom shall I send? And who
will go for us?"

And I said, "Here am I. Send me!"
[9]He said, "Go and tell this people:

" 'Be ever hearing, but never
    understanding;
  be ever seeing, but never
    perceiving.'
[10]Make the heart of this people
    calloused;
  make their ears dull
  and close their eyes.[a]
Otherwise they might see with
    their eyes,
  hear with their ears,
  understand with their hearts,
and turn and be healed."

[11]Then I said, "For how long,
O Lord?"

And he answered:

"Until the cities lie ruined
  and without inhabitant,

until the houses are left deserted
  and the fields ruined and
    ravaged,
[12]until the LORD has sent everyone
    far away
  and the land is utterly forsaken.
[13]And though a tenth remains in
    the land,
  it will again be laid waste.
But as the terebinth and oak
  leave stumps when they are cut
    down,
  so the holy seed will be the
    stump in the land."

The Sign of Immanuel

7 When Ahaz son of Jotham, the
  son of Uzziah, was king of Judah,
King Rezin of Aram and Pekah son of
Remaliah king of Israel marched up
to fight against Jerusalem, but they
could not overpower it.

[2]Now the house of David was told,
"Aram has allied itself with[b] Ephraim"; so the hearts of Ahaz and his
people were shaken, as the trees of
the forest are shaken by the wind.

[3]Then the LORD said to Isaiah, "Go
out, you and your son Shear-Jashub,[c] to meet Ahaz at the end of the
aqueduct of the Upper Pool, on the
road to the Washerman's Field. [4]Say
to him, 'Be careful, keep calm and

---

[a]9,10 Hebrew; Septuagint 'You will be ever hearing, but never understanding; / you will be ever
seeing, but never perceiving.' / [10]This people's heart has become calloused; / they hardly hear with
their ears, / and they have closed their eyes   [b]2 Or has set up camp in   [c]3 Shear-Jashub
means a remnant will return.

▚ET'S LIVE IT!   Isaiah 6:1–8

MEET A HOLY GOD ➡ Read Isaiah 6:1–8. This is the story of Isaiah's "commission," when God told Isaiah he wanted him to be a prophet.

What do you think Isaiah wanted to be when he was young? Maybe
a shepherd? Or a farmer? Or a carpenter? What do children today often
want to be when they grow up? For Isaiah, and for children today, the
most important thing is to grow up to be what God wants. Read Isaiah
6:8, where Isaiah answers God.

What do you want to be when you grow up? A teacher? A farmer? A
computer expert? Whatever you want to be, write it down on a piece
of paper and put it in this Bible. Put today's date on the piece of paper.
Look at the paper every once in a while. Do you still want to be what
you wrote? Do you still want to be what God wants?

don't be afraid. Do not lose heart because of these two smoldering stubs of firewood—because of the fierce anger of Rezin and Aram and of the son of Remaliah. ⁵Aram, Ephraim and Remaliah's son have plotted your ruin, saying, ⁶"Let us invade Judah; let us tear it apart and divide it among ourselves, and make the son of Tabeel king over it." ⁷Yet this is what the Sovereign LORD says:

" 'It will not take place,
    it will not happen,
⁸for the head of Aram is
        Damascus,
    and the head of Damascus is
        only Rezin.
Within sixty-five years
    Ephraim will be too shattered
        to be a people.
⁹The head of Ephraim is Samaria,
    and the head of Samaria is only
        Remaliah's son.
If you do not stand firm in your
        faith,
    you will not stand at all.' "

¹⁰Again the LORD spoke to Ahaz, ¹¹"Ask the LORD your God for a sign, whether in the deepest depths or in the highest heights."

¹²But Ahaz said, "I will not ask; I will not put the LORD to the test."

¹³Then Isaiah said, "Hear now, you house of David! Is it not enough to try the patience of men? Will you try the patience of my God also? ¹⁴Therefore the Lord himself will give youᵃ a sign: The virgin will be with child and will give birth to a son, andᵇ will call him Immanuel.ᶜ ¹⁵He will eat curds and honey when he knows enough to reject the wrong and choose the right. ¹⁶But before the boy knows enough to reject the wrong and choose the right, the land of the two kings you dread will be laid waste. ¹⁷The LORD will bring on you and on your people and on the house of your father a time unlike any since

Ephraim broke away from Judah— he will bring the king of Assyria."

¹⁸In that day the LORD will whistle for flies from the distant streams of Egypt and for bees from the land of Assyria. ¹⁹They will all come and settle in the steep ravines and in the crevices in the rocks, on all the thornbushes and at all the water holes. ²⁰In that day the Lord will use a razor hired from beyond the Riverᵈ—the king of Assyria—to shave your head and the hair of your legs, and to take off your beards also. ²¹In that day, a man will keep alive a young cow and two goats. ²²And because of the abundance of the milk they give, he will have curds to eat. All who remain in the land will eat curds and honey. ²³In that day, in every place where there were a thousand vines worth a thousand silver shekels,ᵉ there will be only briers and thorns. ²⁴Men will go there with bow and arrow, for the land will be covered with briers and thorns. ²⁵As for all the hills once cultivated by the hoe, you will no longer go there for fear of the briers and thorns; they will become places where cattle are turned loose and where sheep run.

Assyria, the LORD's Instrument

8 The LORD said to me, "Take a large scroll and write on it with an ordinary pen: Maher-Shalal-Hash-Baz.ᶠ ²And I will call in Uriah the priest and Zechariah son of Jeberekiah as reliable witnesses for me."

³Then I went to the prophetess, and she conceived and gave birth to a son. And the LORD said to me, "Name him Maher-Shalal-Hash-Baz. ⁴Before the boy knows how to say 'My father' or 'My mother,' the wealth of Damascus and the plunder of Samaria will be carried off by the king of Assyria."

⁵The LORD spoke to me again:

⁶"Because this people has rejected

ᵃ14 The Hebrew is plural.   ᵇ14 Masoretic Text; Dead Sea Scrolls *and he* or *and they*   ᶜ14 *Immanuel* means *God with us.*   ᵈ20 That is, the Euphrates   ᵉ23 That is, about 25 pounds (about 11.5 kilograms)   ᶠ1 *Maher-Shalal-Hash-Baz* means *quick to the plunder, swift to the spoil*; also in verse 3.

the gently flowing waters of
　　Shiloah
and rejoices over Rezin
　　and the son of Remaliah,
⁷therefore the Lord is about to
　　bring against them
　　the mighty floodwaters of the
　　　River ᵃ—
　　the king of Assyria with all his
　　　pomp.
It will overflow all its channels,
　　run over all its banks
⁸and sweep on into Judah, swirling
　　over it,
　　passing through it and reaching
　　　up to the neck.
Its outspread wings will cover the
　　breadth of your land,
　　O Immanuel ᵇ!”

⁹Raise the war cry,ᶜ you nations,
　　and be shattered!
　　Listen, all you distant lands.
　　Prepare for battle, and be
　　　shattered!
　　Prepare for battle, and be
　　　shattered!
¹⁰Devise your strategy, but it will
　　be thwarted;
　　propose your plan, but it will
　　　not stand,
　　for God is with us.ᵈ

Fear God

¹¹The LORD spoke to me with his
strong hand upon me, warning me
not to follow the way of this people.
He said:

¹²“Do not call conspiracy
　　everything that these people
　　　call conspiracyᵉ;
　　do not fear what they fear,
　　and do not dread it.
¹³The LORD Almighty is the one
　　you are to regard as holy,
　　he is the one you are to fear,
　　he is the one you are to dread,
¹⁴and he will be a sanctuary;
　　but for both houses of Israel he
　　　will be
　　a stone that causes men to
　　　stumble

and a rock that makes them
　　fall.
And for the people of Jerusalem
　　he will be
　　a trap and a snare.
¹⁵Many of them will stumble;
　　they will fall and be broken,
　　they will be snared and
　　　captured.”

¹⁶Bind up the testimony
　　and seal up the law among my
　　　disciples.
¹⁷I will wait for the LORD,
　　who is hiding his face from the
　　　house of Jacob.
　　I will put my trust in him.

¹⁸Here am I, and the children the
LORD has given me. We are signs and
symbols in Israel from the LORD
Almighty, who dwells on Mount
Zion.

¹⁹When men tell you to consult mediums and spiritists, who whisper
and mutter, should not a people inquire of their God? Why consult the
dead on behalf of the living? ²⁰To the
law and to the testimony! If they do
not speak according to this word,
they have no light of dawn. ²¹Dis-
tressed and hungry, they will roam
through the land; when they are famished, they will become enraged and,
looking upward, will curse their king
and their God. ²²Then they will look
toward the earth and see only distress and darkness and fearful gloom,
and they will be thrust into utter
darkness.

To Us a Child Is Born

9 Nevertheless, there will be no
　　more gloom for those who were
in distress. In the past he humbled
the land of Zebulun and the land of
Naphtali, but in the future he will
honor Galilee of the Gentiles, by the
way of the sea, along the Jordan—

²The people walking in darkness
　　have seen a great light;

ᵃ7 That is, the Euphrates　　　ᵇ8 *Immanuel* means *God with us.*　　　ᶜ9 Or *Do your worst*
ᵈ10 Hebrew *Immanuel*　　　ᵉ12 Or *Do not call for a treaty / every time these people call for a treaty*

on those living in the land of the
  shadow of death^a
a light has dawned.
³You have enlarged the nation
  and increased their joy;
they rejoice before you
  as people rejoice at the
    harvest,
as men rejoice
  when dividing the plunder.
⁴For as in the day of Midian's
    defeat,
  you have shattered
the yoke that burdens them,
  the bar across their shoulders,
  the rod of their oppressor.
⁵Every warrior's boot used in
    battle
  and every garment rolled in
    blood
will be destined for burning,
  will be fuel for the fire.
⁶For to us a child is born,
  to us a son is given,
  and the government will be on
    his shoulders.
And he will be called
  Wonderful Counselor,^b Mighty
    God,
  Everlasting Father, Prince of
    Peace.
⁷Of the increase of his government
    and peace
  there will be no end.
He will reign on David's throne
  and over his kingdom,
establishing and upholding it
  with justice and righteousness
  from that time on and forever.
The zeal of the LORD Almighty
  will accomplish this.

The LORD's Anger Against Israel

⁸The Lord has sent a message
    against Jacob;
  it will fall on Israel.
⁹All the people will know it—
  Ephraim and the inhabitants of
    Samaria—
who say with pride
  and arrogance of heart,
¹⁰"The bricks have fallen down,

but we will rebuild with dressed
    stone;
the fig trees have been felled,
  but we will replace them with
    cedars."

? DID YOU KNOW?   9:6

**Does the Old Testament speak
about Jesus?**

  There are many prophecies
about Jesus in the Old Testament.
A prophecy tells ahead of time
something that will happen in the
future. Both Isaiah 9:1–7 and 11:1–9
are prophecies about Jesus.

---

¹¹But the LORD has strengthened
    Rezin's foes against them
  and has spurred their enemies
    on.
¹²Arameans from the east and
    Philistines from the west
  have devoured Israel with open
    mouth.

Yet for all this, his anger is not
    turned away,
  his hand is still upraised.

¹³But the people have not returned
    to him who struck them,
  nor have they sought the LORD
    Almighty.
¹⁴So the LORD will cut off from
    Israel both head and tail,
  both palm branch and reed in a
    single day;
¹⁵the elders and prominent men are
    the head,
  the prophets who teach lies are
    the tail.
¹⁶Those who guide this people
    mislead them,
  and those who are guided are
    led astray.
¹⁷Therefore the Lord will take no
    pleasure in the young men,
  nor will he pity the fatherless
    and widows,
for everyone is ungodly and
    wicked,

---

^a2 Or *land of darkness*   ^b6 Or *Wonderful, Counselor*

every mouth speaks vileness.

Yet for all this, his anger is not
turned away,
his hand is still upraised.

18Surely wickedness burns like a
fire;
it consumes briers and thorns,
it sets the forest thickets ablaze,
so that it rolls upward in a
column of smoke.
19By the wrath of the LORD
Almighty
the land will be scorched
and the people will be fuel for the
fire;
no one will spare his brother.
20On the right they will devour,
but still be hungry;
on the left they will eat,
but not be satisfied.
Each will feed on the flesh of his
own offspring*a*:
21 Manasseh will feed on
Ephraim, and Ephraim on
Manasseh;
together they will turn against
Judah.

Yet for all this, his anger is not
turned away,
his hand is still upraised.

10 Woe to those who make
unjust laws,
to those who issue oppressive
decrees,
2to deprive the poor of their
rights
and withhold justice from the
oppressed of my people,
making widows their prey
and robbing the fatherless.
3What will you do on the day of
reckoning,
when disaster comes from
afar?
To whom will you run for help?
Where will you leave your
riches?
4Nothing will remain but to cringe
among the captives
or fall among the slain.

Yet for all this, his anger is not
turned away,
his hand is still upraised.

God's Judgment on Assyria

5"Woe to the Assyrian, the rod of
my anger,
in whose hand is the club of my
wrath!
6I send him against a godless
nation,
I dispatch him against a people
who anger me,
to seize loot and snatch plunder,
and to trample them down like
mud in the streets.
7But this is not what he intends,
this is not what he has in mind;
his purpose is to destroy,
to put an end to many nations.
8'Are not my commanders all
kings?' he says.
9 'Has not Calno fared like
Carchemish?
Is not Hamath like Arpad,
and Samaria like Damascus?
10As my hand seized the kingdoms
of the idols,
kingdoms whose images
excelled those of Jerusalem
and Samaria—
11shall I not deal with Jerusalem
and her images
as I dealt with Samaria and her
idols?' "

12When the Lord has finished all
his work against Mount Zion and Jerusalem, he will say, "I will punish
the king of Assyria for the willful
pride of his heart and the haughty
look in his eyes. 13For he says:

" 'By the strength of my hand I
have done this,
and by my wisdom, because I
have understanding.
I removed the boundaries of
nations,
I plundered their treasures;
like a mighty one I subdued*b*
their kings.
14As one reaches into a nest,

a20 Or arm   *b13 Or / I subdued the mighty,*

so my hand reached for the
  wealth of the nations;
as men gather abandoned eggs,
  so I gathered all the countries;
not one flapped a wing,
  or opened its mouth to chirp.' "

¹⁵Does the ax raise itself above him
    who swings it,
  or the saw boast against him
    who uses it?
As if a rod were to wield him who
    lifts it up,
  or a club brandish him who is
    not wood!
¹⁶Therefore, the Lord, the LORD
    Almighty,
  will send a wasting disease
    upon his sturdy warriors;
under his pomp a fire will be
    kindled
  like a blazing flame.
¹⁷The Light of Israel will become a
    fire,
  their Holy One a flame;
in a single day it will burn and
    consume
  his thorns and his briers.
¹⁸The splendor of his forests and
    fertile fields
  it will completely destroy,
    as when a sick man wastes
    away.
¹⁹And the remaining trees of his
    forests will be so few
  that a child could write them
    down.

The Remnant of Israel

²⁰In that day the remnant of Israel,
  the survivors of the house of
    Jacob,
will no longer rely on him
  who struck them down
but will truly rely on the LORD,
  the Holy One of Israel.
²¹A remnant will return,ᵃ a
    remnant of Jacob
  will return to the Mighty God.
²²Though your people, O Israel, be
    like the sand by the sea,
  only a remnant will return.

Destruction has been decreed,
  overwhelming and righteous.
²³The Lord, the LORD Almighty,
  will carry out
the destruction decreed upon
  the whole land.

²⁴Therefore, this is what the Lord,
the LORD Almighty, says:

"O my people who live in Zion,
  do not be afraid of the
    Assyrians,
who beat you with a rod
  and lift up a club against you,
    as Egypt did.
²⁵Very soon my anger against you
    will end
  and my wrath will be directed
    to their destruction."

²⁶The LORD Almighty will lash
    them with a whip,
  as when he struck down Midian
    at the rock of Oreb;
and he will raise his staff over
    the waters,
  as he did in Egypt.
²⁷In that day their burden will be
    lifted from your shoulders,
  their yoke from your neck;
the yoke will be broken
  because you have grown so fat.ᵇ

²⁸They enter Aiath;
  they pass through Migron;
  they store supplies at Micmash.
²⁹They go over the pass, and say,
  "We will camp overnight at
    Geba."
Ramah trembles;
  Gibeah of Saul flees.
³⁰Cry out, O Daughter of Gallim!
  Listen, O Laishah!
  Poor Anathoth!
³¹Madmenah is in flight;
  the people of Gebim take cover.
³²This day they will halt at Nob;
  they will shake their fist
at the mount of the Daughter of
    Zion,
  at the hill of Jerusalem.

³³See, the Lord, the LORD Almighty,

ᵃ21 Hebrew *shear-jashub*; also in verse 22
shoulders   ᵇ27 Hebrew; Septuagint *broken / from your*

will lop off the boughs with
　　great power.
The lofty trees will be felled,
　　the tall ones will be brought
　　low.
34He will cut down the forest
　　thickets with an ax;
　　Lebanon will fall before the
　　Mighty One.

The Branch From Jesse

11 A shoot will come up from
　　the stump of Jesse;
　　from his roots a Branch will
　　bear fruit.
2The Spirit of the LORD will rest on
　　him—
　　the Spirit of wisdom and of
　　understanding,
　　the Spirit of counsel and of
　　power,
　　the Spirit of knowledge and of
　　the fear of the LORD—
3and he will delight in the fear of
　　the LORD.

He will not judge by what he sees
　　with his eyes,
　　or decide by what he hears with
　　his ears;
4but with righteousness he will
　　judge the needy,
　　with justice he will give
　　decisions for the poor of the
　　earth.
He will strike the earth with the
　　rod of his mouth;

with the breath of his lips he
　　will slay the wicked.
5Righteousness will be his belt
　　and faithfulness the sash
　　around his waist.

6The wolf will live with the lamb,
　　the leopard will lie down with
　　the goat,
　　the calf and the lion and the
　　yearling[a] together;
　　and a little child will lead
　　them.
7The cow will feed with the bear,
　　their young will lie down
　　together,
　　and the lion will eat straw like
　　the ox.
8The infant will play near the hole
　　of the cobra,
　　and the young child put his
　　hand into the viper's nest.
9They will neither harm nor
　　destroy
　　on all my holy mountain,
　　for the earth will be full of the
　　knowledge of the LORD
　　as the waters cover the sea.

10In that day the Root of Jesse will
stand as a banner for the peoples; the
nations will rally to him, and his
place of rest will be glorious. 11In that
day the Lord will reach out his hand
a second time to reclaim the remnant
that is left of his people from Assyria,
from Lower Egypt, from Upper

a6 Hebrew; Septuagint *lion will feed*

LET'S LIVE IT!　　　　　　　Isaiah 11:6–9

A PERFECT WORLD ➠ Have you ever seen a cat catch a mouse? Or a
cat and a dog in a fight? Animals in today's world often fight and hurt
each other.
　　Read Isaiah 11:6–9. This is a picture of what the perfect world will be
like when Jesus returns. Can you picture all these animals in the new
world?
　　It would be fun to get as many animals together as you can with your
friends for an animal parade. You could have pet dogs and cats, ham-
sters, rabbits, and toads. Most will have to be on a leash or in a cage
or box. Form a parade through your neighborhood with your friends and
the animals. If anyone asks why you are doing this, tell that person what
you read about in Isaiah 11.

Egypt,[a] from Cush,[b] from Elam,
from Babylonia,[c] from Hamath and
from the islands of the sea.

12He will raise a banner for the
    nations
  and gather the exiles of Israel;
he will assemble the scattered
    people of Judah
  from the four quarters of the
    earth.
13Ephraim's jealousy will vanish,
  and Judah's enemies[d] will be
    cut off;
Ephraim will not be jealous of
    Judah,
  nor Judah hostile toward
    Ephraim.
14They will swoop down on the
    slopes of Philistia to the
    west;
  together they will plunder the
    people to the east.
They will lay hands on Edom and
    Moab,
  and the Ammonites will be
    subject to them.
15The Lord will dry up
  the gulf of the Egyptian sea;
with a scorching wind he will
    sweep his hand
  over the Euphrates River.[e]
He will break it up into seven
    streams
  so that men can cross over in
    sandals.
16There will be a highway for the
    remnant of his people
  that is left from Assyria,
as there was for Israel
  when they came up from Egypt.

Songs of Praise

12 In that day you will say:
    "I will praise you, O Lord.
  Although you were angry with
    me,
  your anger has turned away
    and you have comforted me.
2Surely God is my salvation;
  I will trust and not be afraid.

The Lord, the Lord, is my
    strength and my song;
  he has become my salvation."
3With joy you will draw water
  from the wells of salvation.

4In that day you will say:

"Give thanks to the Lord, call on
    his name;
  make known among the nations
    what he has done,
  and proclaim that his name is
    exalted.
5Sing to the Lord, for he has done
    glorious things;
  let this be known to all the
    world.
6Shout aloud and sing for joy,
    people of Zion,
  for great is the Holy One of
    Israel among you."

A Prophecy Against Babylon

13 An oracle concerning Bab-
    ylon that Isaiah son of Amoz
saw:

2Raise a banner on a bare hilltop,
    shout to them;
  beckon to them
    to enter the gates of the nobles.
3I have commanded my holy ones;
  I have summoned my warriors
    to carry out my wrath—
  those who rejoice in my
    triumph.

4Listen, a noise on the mountains,
  like that of a great multitude!
Listen, an uproar among the
    kingdoms,
  like nations massing together!
The Lord Almighty is mustering
  an army for war.
5They come from faraway lands,
  from the ends of the heavens—
the Lord and the weapons of his
    wrath—
  to destroy the whole country.

6Wail, for the day of the Lord is
    near;

---

it will come like destruction
from the Almighty.[a]
7Because of this, all hands will go
limp,
every man's heart will melt.
8Terror will seize them,
pain and anguish will grip
them;
they will writhe like a woman
in labor.
They will look aghast at each
other,
their faces aflame.

9See, the day of the LORD is
coming
—a cruel day, with wrath and
fierce anger—
to make the land desolate
and destroy the sinners within
it.
10The stars of heaven and their
constellations
will not show their light.
The rising sun will be darkened
and the moon will not give its
light.
11I will punish the world for its
evil,
the wicked for their sins.
I will put an end to the arrogance
of the haughty
and will humble the pride of
the ruthless.
12I will make man scarcer than
pure gold,
more rare than the gold of
Ophir.
13Therefore I will make the
heavens tremble;
and the earth will shake from
its place
at the wrath of the LORD
Almighty,
in the day of his burning anger.

14Like a hunted gazelle,
like sheep without a shepherd,
each will return to his own
people,
each will flee to his native land.
15Whoever is captured will be
thrust through;

all who are caught will fall by
the sword.
16Their infants will be dashed to
pieces before their eyes;
their houses will be looted and
their wives ravished.

17See, I will stir up against them
the Medes,
who do not care for silver
and have no delight in gold.
18Their bows will strike down the
young men;
they will have no mercy on
infants
nor will they look with
compassion on children.
19Babylon, the jewel of kingdoms,
the glory of the Babylonians'[b]
pride,
will be overthrown by God
like Sodom and Gomorrah.
20She will never be inhabited
or lived in through all
generations;
no Arab will pitch his tent there,
no shepherd will rest his flocks
there.
21But desert creatures will lie
there,
jackals will fill her houses;
there the owls will dwell,
and there the wild goats will
leap about.
22Hyenas will howl in her
strongholds,
jackals in her luxurious palaces.
Her time is at hand,
and her days will not be
prolonged.

14 The LORD will have
compassion on Jacob;
once again he will choose Israel
and will settle them in their
own land.
Aliens will join them
and unite with the house of
Jacob.
2Nations will take them
and bring them to their own
place.

a6 Hebrew Shaddai   b19 Or Chaldeans'

And the house of Israel will
   possess the nations
as menservants and
   maidservants in the LORD's
   land.
They will make captives of their
   captors
and rule over their oppressors.

³On the day the LORD gives you relief from suffering and turmoil and
cruel bondage, ⁴you will take up this
taunt against the king of Babylon:

How the oppressor has come to an
   end!
   How his fury*a* has ended!
⁵The LORD has broken the rod of
   the wicked,
   the scepter of the rulers,
⁶which in anger struck down
   peoples
   with unceasing blows,
and in fury subdued nations
   with relentless aggression.
⁷All the lands are at rest and at
   peace;
   they break into singing.
⁸Even the pine trees and the
   cedars of Lebanon
exult over you and say,
"Now that you have been laid
   low,
   no woodsman comes to cut us
   down."

⁹The grave*b* below is all astir
   to meet you at your coming;
it rouses the spirits of the
   departed to greet you—
   all those who were leaders in
   the world;
it makes them rise from their
   thrones—
   all those who were kings over
   the nations.
¹⁰They will all respond,
   they will say to you,
"You also have become weak, as
   we are;
   you have become like us."
¹¹All your pomp has been brought
   down to the grave,

along with the noise of your
   harps;
maggots are spread out beneath
   you
   and worms cover you.

¹²How you have fallen from
   heaven,
   O morning star, son of the
   dawn!
You have been cast down to the
   earth,
   you who once laid low the
   nations!
¹³You said in your heart,
   "I will ascend to heaven;
I will raise my throne
   above the stars of God;
I will sit enthroned on the mount
   of assembly,
   on the utmost heights of the
   sacred mountain.*c*
¹⁴I will ascend above the tops of the
   clouds;
   I will make myself like the
   Most High."
¹⁵But you are brought down to the
   grave,
   to the depths of the pit.

¹⁶Those who see you stare at you,
   they ponder your fate:
"Is this the man who shook the
   earth
   and made kingdoms tremble,
¹⁷the man who made the world a
   desert,
   who overthrew its cities
   and would not let his captives
   go home?"

¹⁸All the kings of the nations lie in
   state,
   each in his own tomb.
¹⁹But you are cast out of your tomb
   like a rejected branch;
you are covered with the slain,
   with those pierced by the sword,
   those who descend to the stones
   of the pit.
Like a corpse trampled underfoot,
20   you will not join them in burial,
for you have destroyed your land

---

a4 Dead Sea Scrolls, Septuagint and Syriac; the meaning of the word in the Masoretic Text is
uncertain.   *b9* Hebrew *Sheol*; also in verses 11 and 15   *c13* Or *the north*; Hebrew *Zaphon*

and killed your people.

The offspring of the wicked
will never be mentioned again.
²¹Prepare a place to slaughter his
sons
for the sins of their forefathers;
they are not to rise to inherit the
land
and cover the earth with their
cities.

²²"I will rise up against them,"
declares the LORD Almighty.
"I will cut off from Babylon her
name and survivors,
her offspring and descendants,"
declares the LORD.
²³"I will turn her into a place for
owls
and into swampland;
I will sweep her with the broom
of destruction,"
declares the LORD Almighty.

A Prophecy Against Assyria

²⁴The LORD Almighty has sworn,

"Surely, as I have planned, so it
will be,
and as I have purposed, so it
will stand.
²⁵I will crush the Assyrian in my
land;
on my mountains I will trample
him down.
His yoke will be taken from my
people,
and his burden removed from
their shoulders."

²⁶This is the plan determined for
the whole world;
this is the hand stretched out
over all nations.
²⁷For the LORD Almighty has
purposed, and who can
thwart him?
His hand is stretched out, and
who can turn it back?

A Prophecy Against the Philistines

²⁸This oracle came in the year King
Ahaz died:

²⁹Do not rejoice, all you Philistines,

that the rod that struck you is
broken;
from the root of that snake will
spring up a viper,
its fruit will be a darting,
venomous serpent.
³⁰The poorest of the poor will find
pasture,
and the needy will lie down in
safety.
But your root I will destroy by
famine;
it will slay your survivors.

³¹Wail, O gate! Howl, O city!
Melt away, all you Philistines!
A cloud of smoke comes from the
north,
and there is not a straggler in
its ranks.
³²What answer shall be given
to the envoys of that nation?
"The LORD has established Zion,
and in her his afflicted people
will find refuge."

A Prophecy Against Moab

15 An oracle concerning Moab:

Ar in Moab is ruined,
destroyed in a night!
Kir in Moab is ruined,
destroyed in a night!
²Dibon goes up to its temple,
to its high places to weep;
Moab wails over Nebo and
Medeba.
Every head is shaved
and every beard cut off.
³In the streets they wear
sackcloth;
on the roofs and in the public
squares
they all wail,
prostrate with weeping.
⁴Heshbon and Elealeh cry out,
their voices are heard all the
way to Jahaz.
Therefore the armed men of Moab
cry out,
and their hearts are faint.

⁵My heart cries out over Moab;
her fugitives flee as far as Zoar,
as far as Eglath Shelishiyah.
They go up the way to Luhith,

weeping as they go;
on the road to Horonaim
they lament their destruction.
⁶The waters of Nimrim are dried
up
and the grass is withered;
the vegetation is gone
and nothing green is left.
⁷So the wealth they have acquired
and stored up
they carry away over the
Ravine of the Poplars.
⁸Their outcry echoes along the
border of Moab;
their wailing reaches as far as
Eglaim,
their lamentation as far as Beer
Elim.
⁹Dimon's*a* waters are full of blood,
but I will bring still more upon
Dimon*a*—
a lion upon the fugitives of Moab
and upon those who remain in
the land.

16
Send lambs as tribute
to the ruler of the land,
from Sela, across the desert,
to the mount of the Daughter of
Zion.
²Like fluttering birds
pushed from the nest,
so are the women of Moab
at the fords of the Arnon.

³"Give us counsel,
render a decision.
Make your shadow like night—
at high noon.
Hide the fugitives,
do not betray the refugees.
⁴Let the Moabite fugitives stay
with you;
be their shelter from the
destroyer."

The oppressor will come to an
end,
and destruction will cease;
the aggressor will vanish from
the land.
⁵In love a throne will be
established;

in faithfulness a man will sit on
it—
one from the house*b* of David—
one who in judging seeks justice
and speeds the cause of
righteousness.

⁶We have heard of Moab's pride—
her overweening pride and
conceit,
her pride and her insolence—
but her boasts are empty.
⁷Therefore the Moabites wail,
they wail together for Moab.
Lament and grieve
for the men*c* of Kir Hareseth.
⁸The fields of Heshbon wither,
the vines of Sibmah also.
The rulers of the nations
have trampled down the
choicest vines,
which once reached Jazer
and spread toward the desert.
Their shoots spread out
and went as far as the sea.
⁹So I weep, as Jazer weeps,
for the vines of Sibmah.
O Heshbon, O Elealeh,
I drench you with tears!
The shouts of joy over your
ripened fruit
and over your harvests have
been stilled.
¹⁰Joy and gladness are taken away
from the orchards;
no one sings or shouts in the
vineyards;
no one treads out wine at the
presses,
for I have put an end to the
shouting.
¹¹My heart laments for Moab like a
harp,
my inmost being for Kir
Hareseth.
¹²When Moab appears at her high
place,
she only wears herself out;
when she goes to her shrine to
pray,
it is to no avail.

¹³This is the word the LORD has al-

---

ready spoken concerning Moab. ¹⁴But now the LORD says: "Within three years, as a servant bound by contract would count them, Moab's splendor and all her many people will be despised, and her survivors will be very few and feeble."

An Oracle Against Damascus

17 An oracle concerning Damascus:

"See, Damascus will no longer be
      a city
   but will become a heap of ruins.
²The cities of Aroer will be
      deserted
   and left to flocks, which will lie
      down,
   with no one to make them
      afraid.
³The fortified city will disappear
      from Ephraim,
   and royal power from
      Damascus;
   the remnant of Aram will be
   like the glory of the Israelites,"
      declares the LORD Almighty.

⁴"In that day the glory of Jacob
      will fade;
   the fat of his body will waste
      away.
⁵It will be as when a reaper
      gathers the standing grain
   and harvests the grain with his
      arm—
as when a man gleans heads of
      grain
   in the Valley of Rephaim.
⁶Yet some gleanings will remain,
   as when an olive tree is beaten,
   leaving two or three olives on the
      topmost branches,
   four or five on the fruitful
      boughs,"
         declares the LORD, the God
            of Israel.

⁷In that day men will look to their
      Maker
   and turn their eyes to the Holy
      One of Israel.

⁸They will not look to the altars,
   the work of their hands,
and they will have no regard for
      the Asherah poles^a
   and the incense altars their
      fingers have made.

⁹In that day their strong cities,
which they left because of the Israelites, will be like places abandoned to thickets and undergrowth. And all will be desolation.

¹⁰You have forgotten God your
      Savior;
   you have not remembered the
      Rock, your fortress.
Therefore, though you set out the
      finest plants
   and plant imported vines,
¹¹though on the day you set them
      out, you make them grow,
   and on the morning when you
      plant them, you bring them
         to bud,
   yet the harvest will be as nothing
   in the day of disease and
      incurable pain.

¹²Oh, the raging of many nations—
   they rage like the raging sea!
Oh, the uproar of the peoples—
   they roar like the roaring of
      great waters!
¹³Although the peoples roar like
      the roar of surging waters,
   when he rebukes them they flee
      far away,
driven before the wind like chaff
      on the hills,
   like tumbleweed before a gale.
¹⁴In the evening, sudden terror!
Before the morning, they are
      gone!
This is the portion of those who
      loot us,
   the lot of those who plunder us.

A Prophecy Against Cush

18 Woe to the land of whirring
   wings^b
   along the rivers of Cush,^c

---

^a8 That is, symbols of the goddess Asherah region   ^b1 Or of locusts   ^c1 That is, the upper Nile

²which sends envoys by sea
   in papyrus boats over the water.

Go, swift messengers,
to a people tall and
   smooth-skinned,
to a people feared far and wide,
an aggressive nation of strange
   speech,
   whose land is divided by rivers.

³All you people of the world,
   you who live on the earth,
when a banner is raised on the
   mountains,
   you will see it,
and when a trumpet sounds,
   you will hear it.
⁴This is what the LORD says to me:
   "I will remain quiet and will
     look on from my dwelling
     place,
like shimmering heat in the
   sunshine,
like a cloud of dew in the heat
   of harvest."
⁵For, before the harvest, when the
   blossom is gone
and the flower becomes a
   ripening grape,
he will cut off the shoots with
   pruning knives,
and cut down and take away
   the spreading branches.
⁶They will all be left to the
   mountain birds of prey
and to the wild animals;
the birds will feed on them all
   summer,
   the wild animals all winter.

⁷At that time gifts will be brought
to the LORD Almighty

from a people tall and
   smooth-skinned,
from a people feared far and
   wide,
an aggressive nation of strange
   speech,
   whose land is divided by
     rivers—

the gifts will be brought to Mount
Zion, the place of the Name of the
LORD Almighty.

A Prophecy About Egypt

19 An oracle concerning Egypt:
   See, the LORD rides on a
     swift cloud
   and is coming to Egypt.
The idols of Egypt tremble before
   him,
and the hearts of the Egyptians
   melt within them.

²"I will stir up Egyptian against
   Egyptian—
brother will fight against
   brother,
neighbor against neighbor,
city against city,
kingdom against kingdom.
³The Egyptians will lose heart,
   and I will bring their plans to
     nothing;
they will consult the idols and the
   spirits of the dead,
the mediums and the spiritists.
⁴I will hand the Egyptians over
   to the power of a cruel master,
and a fierce king will rule over
   them,"
   declares the Lord, the LORD
     Almighty.

⁵The waters of the river will dry
   up,
and the riverbed will be
   parched and dry.
⁶The canals will stink;
   the streams of Egypt will
     dwindle and dry up.
The reeds and rushes will wither,
⁷ also the plants along the Nile,
   at the mouth of the river.
Every sown field along the Nile
   will become parched, will blow
     away and be no more.
⁸The fishermen will groan and
   lament,
all who cast hooks into the
   Nile;
those who throw nets on the
   water
   will pine away.
⁹Those who work with combed flax
   will despair,
the weavers of fine linen will
   lose hope.

¹⁰The workers in cloth will be
  dejected,
    and all the wage earners will be
      sick at heart.

¹¹The officials of Zoan are nothing
  but fools;
    the wise counselors of Pharaoh
      give senseless advice.
How can you say to Pharaoh,
  "I am one of the wise men,
    a disciple of the ancient kings"?

¹²Where are your wise men now?
  Let them show you and make
    known
what the LORD Almighty
  has planned against Egypt.
¹³The officials of Zoan have become
  fools,
    the leaders of Memphis*ᵃ* are
      deceived;
the cornerstones of her peoples
  have led Egypt astray.
¹⁴The LORD has poured into them
  a spirit of dizziness;
    they make Egypt stagger in all
      that she does,
as a drunkard staggers around
  in his vomit.
¹⁵There is nothing Egypt can do—
  head or tail, palm branch or
    reed.

¹⁶In that day the Egyptians will be
like women. They will shudder with
fear at the uplifted hand that the
LORD Almighty raises against them.
¹⁷And the land of Judah will bring
terror to the Egyptians; everyone to
whom Judah is mentioned will be terrified, because of what the LORD Almighty is planning against them.
¹⁸In that day five cities in Egypt
will speak the language of Canaan
and swear allegiance to the LORD Almighty. One of them will be called
the City of Destruction.*ᵇ*
¹⁹In that day there will be an altar
to the LORD in the heart of Egypt, and
a monument to the LORD at its border. ²⁰It will be a sign and witness to

the LORD Almighty in the land of
Egypt. When they cry out to the LORD
because of their oppressors, he will
send them a savior and defender, and
he will rescue them. ²¹So the LORD
will make himself known to the
Egyptians, and in that day they will
acknowledge the LORD. They will
worship with sacrifices and grain offerings; they will make vows to the
LORD and keep them. ²²The LORD will
strike Egypt with a plague; he will
strike them and heal them. They will
turn to the LORD, and he will respond
to their pleas and heal them.
²³In that day there will be a highway from Egypt to Assyria. The Assyrians will go to Egypt and the
Egyptians to Assyria. The Egyptians
and Assyrians will worship together.
²⁴In that day Israel will be the third,
along with Egypt and Assyria, a
blessing on the earth. ²⁵The LORD Almighty will bless them, saying,
"Blessed be Egypt my people, Assyria
my handiwork, and Israel my inheritance."

A Prophecy Against Egypt and Cush

20 In the year that the supreme
commander, sent by Sargon
king of Assyria, came to Ashdod and
attacked and captured it— ²at that
time the LORD spoke through Isaiah
son of Amoz. He said to him, "Take off
the sackcloth from your body and the
sandals from your feet." And he did
so, going around stripped and barefoot.
³Then the LORD said, "Just as my
servant Isaiah has gone stripped and
barefoot for three years, as a sign and
portent against Egypt and Cush,*ᶜ* ⁴so
the king of Assyria will lead away
stripped and barefoot the Egyptian
captives and Cushite exiles, young
and old, with buttocks bared—to
Egypt's shame. ⁵Those who trusted in
Cush and boasted in Egypt will be
afraid and put to shame. ⁶In that day

ᵃ13 Hebrew *Noph*   *ᵇ18* Most manuscripts of the Masoretic Text; some manuscripts of the
Masoretic Text, Dead Sea Scrolls and Vulgate *City of the Sun* (that is, Heliopolis)   *ᶜ3* That is,
the upper Nile region; also in verse 5

the people who live on this coast will say, 'See what has happened to those we relied on, those we fled to for help and deliverance from the king of Assyria! How then can we escape?' "

A Prophecy Against Babylon

21 An oracle concerning the Desert by the Sea:

Like whirlwinds sweeping
    through the southland,
an invader comes from the
    desert,
from a land of terror.

2A dire vision has been shown to
    me:
The traitor betrays, the looter
    takes loot.
Elam, attack! Media, lay siege!
I will bring to an end all the
    groaning she caused.

3At this my body is racked with
    pain,
pangs seize me, like those of a
    woman in labor;
I am staggered by what I hear,
I am bewildered by what I see.
4My heart falters,
    fear makes me tremble;
the twilight I longed for
    has become a horror to me.

5They set the tables,
    they spread the rugs,
    they eat, they drink!
Get up, you officers,
    oil the shields!

6This is what the Lord says to me:

"Go, post a lookout
    and have him report what he
        sees.
7When he sees chariots
    with teams of horses,
riders on donkeys
    or riders on camels,
let him be alert,
    fully alert."

8And the lookout*a* shouted,

"Day after day, my lord, I stand
    on the watchtower;
every night I stay at my post.
9Look, here comes a man in a
    chariot
with a team of horses.
And he gives back the answer:
    'Babylon has fallen, has fallen!
All the images of its gods
    lie shattered on the ground!' "

10O my people, crushed on the
    threshing floor,
I tell you what I have heard
from the LORD Almighty,
    from the God of Israel.

A Prophecy Against Edom

11An oracle concerning Dumah*b*:

Someone calls to me from Seir,
    "Watchman, what is left of the
        night?
Watchman, what is left of the
    night?"
12The watchman replies,
    "Morning is coming, but also
        the night.
If you would ask, then ask;
    and come back yet again."

A Prophecy Against Arabia

13An oracle concerning Arabia:

You caravans of Dedanites,
    who camp in the thickets of
        Arabia,
14 bring water for the thirsty;
you who live in Tema,
    bring food for the fugitives.
15They flee from the sword,
    from the drawn sword,
from the bent bow
    and from the heat of battle.

16This is what the Lord says to me:
"Within one year, as a servant bound by contract would count it, all the pomp of Kedar will come to an end. 17The survivors of the bowmen, the warriors of Kedar, will be few." The LORD, the God of Israel, has spoken.

a8 Dead Sea Scrolls and Syriac; Masoretic Text A lion wordplay on Edom.   *b11 Dumah means silence or stillness, a*

A Prophecy About Jerusalem

22 An oracle concerning the Valley of Vision:

What troubles you now,
    that you have all gone up on
        the roofs,
²O town full of commotion,
    O city of tumult and revelry?
Your slain were not killed by the
        sword,
    nor did they die in battle.
³All your leaders have fled
        together;
    they have been captured
        without using the bow.
All you who were caught were
        taken prisoner together,
    having fled while the enemy
        was still far away.
⁴Therefore I said, "Turn away from
        me;
    let me weep bitterly.
Do not try to console me
    over the destruction of my
        people."

⁵The Lord, the LORD Almighty, has
        a day
    of tumult and trampling and
        terror
    in the Valley of Vision,
a day of battering down walls
    and of crying out to the
        mountains.
⁶Elam takes up the quiver,
    with her charioteers and horses;
Kir uncovers the shield.
⁷Your choicest valleys are full of
        chariots,
    and horsemen are posted at the
        city gates;
⁸   the defenses of Judah are
        stripped away.

And you looked in that day
    to the weapons in the Palace of
        the Forest;
⁹you saw that the City of David
    had many breaches in its
        defenses;
you stored up water
    in the Lower Pool.
¹⁰You counted the buildings in
        Jerusalem

and tore down houses to
    strengthen the wall.
¹¹You built a reservoir between the
        two walls
    for the water of the Old Pool,
but you did not look to the One
        who made it,
    or have regard for the One who
        planned it long ago.

¹²The Lord, the LORD Almighty,
        called you on that day
    to weep and to wail,
    to tear out your hair and put on
        sackcloth.
¹³But see, there is joy and revelry,
    slaughtering of cattle and
        killing of sheep,
    eating of meat and drinking of
        wine!
"Let us eat and drink," you say,
    "for tomorrow we die!"

¹⁴The LORD Almighty has revealed
this in my hearing: "Till your dying
day this sin will not be atoned for,"
says the Lord, the LORD Almighty.

¹⁵This is what the Lord, the LORD
Almighty, says:

"Go, say to this steward,
    to Shebna, who is in charge of
        the palace:
¹⁶What are you doing here and who
        gave you permission
    to cut out a grave for yourself
        here,
hewing your grave on the height
    and chiseling your resting place
        in the rock?

¹⁷"Beware, the LORD is about to
        take firm hold of you
    and hurl you away, O you
        mighty man.
¹⁸He will roll you up tightly like a
        ball
    and throw you into a large
        country.
There you will die
    and there your splendid chariots
        will remain—
    you disgrace to your master's
        house!
¹⁹I will depose you from your office,

and you will be ousted from
　　your position.

20"In that day I will summon my
servant, Eliakim son of Hilkiah. 21I
will clothe him with your robe and
fasten your sash around him and
hand your authority over to him. He
will be a father to those who live in
Jerusalem and to the house of Judah.
22I will place on his shoulder the key
to the house of David; what he opens
no one can shut, and what he shuts no
one can open. 23I will drive him like
a peg into a firm place; he will be a
seat[a] of honor for the house of his father. 24All the glory of his family will
hang on him: its offspring and off-
shoots—all its lesser vessels, from
the bowls to all the jars.

25"In that day," declares the LORD
Almighty, "the peg driven into the
firm place will give way; it will be
sheared off and will fall, and the load
hanging on it will be cut down." The
LORD has spoken.

A Prophecy About Tyre

23 An oracle concerning Tyre:

Wail, O ships of Tarshish!
For Tyre is destroyed
and left without house or
　　harbor.
From the land of Cyprus[b]
word has come to them.

2Be silent, you people of the island
　　and you merchants of Sidon,
　　whom the seafarers have
　　　enriched.
3On the great waters
　　came the grain of the Shihor;
the harvest of the Nile[c] was the
　　revenue of Tyre,
　　and she became the
　　　marketplace of the nations.

4Be ashamed, O Sidon, and you,
　　O fortress of the sea,
for the sea has spoken:

"I have neither been in labor nor
　　given birth;
I have neither reared sons nor
　　brought up daughters."
5When word comes to Egypt,
　　they will be in anguish at the
　　report from Tyre.

6Cross over to Tarshish;
　　wail, you people of the island.
7Is this your city of revelry,
　　the old, old city,
whose feet have taken her
　　to settle in far-off lands?
8Who planned this against Tyre,
　　the bestower of crowns,
whose merchants are princes,
　　whose traders are renowned in
　　the earth?
9The LORD Almighty planned it,
　　to bring low the pride of all
　　glory
　　and to humble all who are
　　renowned on the earth.

10Till[d] your land as along the Nile,
　　O Daughter of Tarshish,
　　for you no longer have a harbor.
11The LORD has stretched out his
　　hand over the sea
　　and made its kingdoms tremble.
He has given an order concerning
　　Phoenicia[e]
　　that her fortresses be destroyed.
12He said, "No more of your
　　reveling,
　　O Virgin Daughter of Sidon,
　　now crushed!

"Up, cross over to Cyprus[b];
　　even there you will find no
　　rest."
13Look at the land of the
　　Babylonians,[f]
　　this people that is now of no
　　account!
The Assyrians have made it
　　a place for desert creatures;
they raised up their siege towers,
　　they stripped its fortresses bare
　　and turned it into a ruin.

a23 Or throne　　b1,12 Hebrew Kittim　　c2,3 Masoretic Text; one Dead Sea Scroll Sidon, / who
cross over the sea; / your envoys 3are on the great waters. / The grain of the Shihor, / the harvest of
the Nile,　　d10 Dead Sea Scrolls and some Septuagint manuscripts; Masoretic Text Go through
e11 Hebrew Canaan　　f13 Or Chaldeans

¹⁴Wail, you ships of Tarshish;
  your fortress is destroyed!

¹⁵At that time Tyre will be forgotten for seventy years, the span of a king's life. But at the end of these seventy years, it will happen to Tyre as in the song of the prostitute:

¹⁶"Take up a harp, walk through
    the city,
  O prostitute forgotten;
  play the harp well, sing many a
    song,
    so that you will be
    remembered."

¹⁷At the end of seventy years, the LORD will deal with Tyre. She will return to her hire as a prostitute and will ply her trade with all the kingdoms on the face of the earth. ¹⁸Yet her profit and her earnings will be set apart for the LORD; they will not be stored up or hoarded. Her profits will go to those who live before the LORD, for abundant food and fine clothes.

The LORD's Devastation of the Earth

24 See, the LORD is going to lay
    waste the earth
  and devastate it;
  he will ruin its face
  and scatter its inhabitants—
²it will be the same
  for priest as for people,
  for master as for servant,
  for mistress as for maid,
  for seller as for buyer,
  for borrower as for lender,
  for debtor as for creditor.
³The earth will be completely laid
    waste
  and totally plundered.
              The LORD has spoken
                  this word.

⁴The earth dries up and withers,
  the world languishes and
    withers,
  the exalted of the earth
    languish.
⁵The earth is defiled by its people;
  they have disobeyed the laws,
  violated the statutes

and broken the everlasting
    covenant.
⁶Therefore a curse consumes the
    earth;
  its people must bear their guilt.
  Therefore earth's inhabitants are
    burned up,
  and very few are left.
⁷The new wine dries up and the
    vine withers;
  all the merrymakers groan.
⁸The gaiety of the tambourines is
    stilled,
  the noise of the revelers has
    stopped,
  the joyful harp is silent.
⁹No longer do they drink wine
    with a song;
  the beer is bitter to its drinkers.
¹⁰The ruined city lies desolate;
  the entrance to every house is
    barred.
¹¹In the streets they cry out for
    wine;
  all joy turns to gloom,
  all gaiety is banished from the
    earth.
¹²The city is left in ruins,
  its gate is battered to pieces.
¹³So will it be on the earth
  and among the nations,
  as when an olive tree is beaten,
  or as when gleanings are left
    after the grape harvest.

¹⁴They raise their voices, they
    shout for joy;
  from the west they acclaim the
    LORD's majesty.
¹⁵Therefore in the east give glory to
    the LORD;
  exalt the name of the LORD, the
    God of Israel,
  in the islands of the sea.
¹⁶From the ends of the earth we
    hear singing:
  "Glory to the Righteous One."

But I said, "I waste away, I waste
    away!
  Woe to me!
  The treacherous betray!
  With treachery the treacherous
    betray!"
¹⁷Terror and pit and snare await
    you,

O people of the earth.
18Whoever flees at the sound of
      terror
   will fall into a pit;
whoever climbs out of the pit
   will be caught in a snare.

The floodgates of the heavens are
      opened,
   the foundations of the earth
      shake.
19The earth is broken up,
   the earth is split asunder,
   the earth is thoroughly shaken.
20The earth reels like a drunkard,
   it sways like a hut in the wind;
so heavy upon it is the guilt of its
      rebellion
   that it falls—never to rise
      again.

21In that day the LORD will punish
   the powers in the heavens
      above
   and the kings on the earth
      below.
22They will be herded together
   like prisoners bound in a
      dungeon;
they will be shut up in prison
   and be punished^a after many
      days.
23The moon will be abashed, the
      sun ashamed;
   for the LORD Almighty will
      reign
on Mount Zion and in Jerusalem,
   and before its elders, gloriously.

Praise to the LORD

25 O LORD, you are my God;
   I will exalt you and praise
      your name,
for in perfect faithfulness
   you have done marvelous
      things,
   things planned long ago.
2You have made the city a heap of
      rubble,
   the fortified town a ruin,
   the foreigners' stronghold a city
      no more;
   it will never be rebuilt.

3Therefore strong peoples will
      honor you;
   cities of ruthless nations will
      revere you.
4You have been a refuge for the
      poor,
   a refuge for the needy in his
      distress,
a shelter from the storm
   and a shade from the heat.
For the breath of the ruthless
   is like a storm driving against a
      wall
5 and like the heat of the desert.
You silence the uproar of
      foreigners;
   as heat is reduced by the
      shadow of a cloud,
   so the song of the ruthless is
      stilled.

6On this mountain the LORD
      Almighty will prepare
   a feast of rich food for all
      peoples,
   a banquet of aged wine—
   the best of meats and the finest
      of wines.
7On this mountain he will destroy
   the shroud that enfolds all
      peoples,
   the sheet that covers all nations;
8 he will swallow up death
      forever.
The Sovereign LORD will wipe
      away the tears
   from all faces;
he will remove the disgrace of his
      people
   from all the earth.
                  The LORD has spoken.

9In that day they will say,

"Surely this is our God;
   we trusted in him, and he saved
      us.
This is the LORD, we trusted in
      him;
   let us rejoice and be glad in his
      salvation."

10The hand of the LORD will rest on
      this mountain;

^a22 Or released

but Moab will be trampled
　　under him
as straw is trampled down in
　　the manure.

WORDS TO REMEMBER

25:9 Surely this is our God;
　　we trusted in him, and he
　　saved us.

---

¹¹They will spread out their hands
　　in it,
　　as a swimmer spreads out his
　　　hands to swim.
God will bring down their pride
　　despite the cleverness*ᵃ* of their
　　　hands.
¹²He will bring down your high
　　fortified walls
　　and lay them low;
he will bring them down to the
　　ground,
　　to the very dust.

A Song of Praise

26 In that day this song will be
sung in the land of Judah:

We have a strong city;
　　God makes salvation
　　its walls and ramparts.
²Open the gates
　　that the righteous nation may
　　　enter,
　　the nation that keeps faith.
³You will keep in perfect peace
　　him whose mind is steadfast,
　　because he trusts in you.
⁴Trust in the LORD forever,
　　for the LORD, the LORD, is the
　　　Rock eternal.
⁵He humbles those who dwell on
　　high,
　　he lays the lofty city low;
he levels it to the ground
　　and casts it down to the dust.
⁶Feet trample it down—
　　the feet of the oppressed,
　　the footsteps of the poor.

⁷The path of the righteous is level;

O upright One, you make the
　　way of the righteous
　　smooth.
⁸Yes, LORD, walking in the way of
　　your laws,*ᵇ*
　　we wait for you;
your name and renown
　　are the desire of our hearts.
⁹My soul yearns for you in the
　　night;
　　in the morning my spirit longs
　　　for you.
When your judgments come upon
　　the earth,
　　the people of the world learn
　　　righteousness.
¹⁰Though grace is shown to the
　　wicked,
　　they do not learn righteousness;
even in a land of uprightness they
　　go on doing evil
　　and regard not the majesty of
　　　the LORD.
¹¹O LORD, your hand is lifted high,
　　but they do not see it.
Let them see your zeal for your
　　people and be put to shame;
　　let the fire reserved for your
　　　enemies consume them.

¹²LORD, you establish peace for us;
　　all that we have accomplished
　　　you have done for us.
¹³O LORD, our God, other lords
　　besides you have ruled over
　　　us,
　　but your name alone do we
　　　honor.
¹⁴They are now dead, they live no
　　more;
　　those departed spirits do not
　　　rise.
You punished them and brought
　　them to ruin;
　　you wiped out all memory of
　　　them.
¹⁵You have enlarged the nation,
　　O LORD;
　　you have enlarged the nation.
You have gained glory for
　　yourself;
　　you have extended all the
　　　borders of the land.

ᵃ11 The meaning of the Hebrew for this word is uncertain.　　*ᵇ8* Or *judgments*

¹⁶Lord, they came to you in their
   distress;
  when you disciplined them,
  they could barely whisper a
    prayer.ᵃ
¹⁷As a woman with child and about
   to give birth
  writhes and cries out in her
   pain,
  so were we in your presence,
   O Lord.
¹⁸We were with child, we writhed
   in pain,
  but we gave birth to wind.
We have not brought salvation to
   the earth;
  we have not given birth to
   people of the world.

¹⁹But your dead will live;
   their bodies will rise.
You who dwell in the dust,
  wake up and shout for joy.
Your dew is like the dew of the
   morning;
  the earth will give birth to her
   dead.

²⁰Go, my people, enter your rooms
  and shut the doors behind
   you;
  hide yourselves for a little while
   until his wrath has passed by.
²¹See, the Lord is coming out of his
   dwelling
  to punish the people of the
   earth for their sins.
The earth will disclose the blood
   shed upon her;

ᵃ16 The meaning of the Hebrew for this clause is uncertain.

she will conceal her slain no
   longer.

Deliverance of Israel

27 In that day,

  the Lord will punish with
   his sword,
  his fierce, great and powerful
   sword,
Leviathan the gliding serpent,
  Leviathan the coiling serpent;
he will slay the monster of the
   sea.

²In that day—

"Sing about a fruitful vineyard:
³ I, the Lord, watch over it;
  I water it continually.
I guard it day and night
  so that no one may harm it.
⁴ I am not angry.
If only there were briers and
   thorns confronting me!
  I would march against them in
   battle;
  I would set them all on fire.
⁵Or else let them come to me for
   refuge;
  let them make peace with me,
  yes, let them make peace with
   me."

⁶In days to come Jacob will take
   root,
  Israel will bud and blossom
  and fill all the world with fruit.

LET'S LIVE IT!   Isaiah 26:19

JOY AFTER SORROW ⟫ People are often sad at funerals. The body of
someone they love is buried in the ground. It's all right to cry when a
person we love dies and is buried. But Isaiah 26:19 is about joy. Read
it to find out why, even when Christians feel sorrow, we know joy will
come.
   Make a picture reminder that your loved one will rise from the dead.
Fold a sheet of paper in two. Draw a grave on the outside of the fold.
Inside the fold glue a photo or draw a picture of your friend or relative.
When the paper is folded, you see only the grave. When the paper is
unfolded, you see your loved one alive again, and happy.

7Has ˌthe LORDˌ struck her
  as he struck down those who
    struck her?
Has she been killed
  as those were killed who killed
    her?
8By warfare*a* and exile you
    contend with her—
  with his fierce blast he drives
    her out,
  as on a day the east wind
    blows.
9By this, then, will Jacob's guilt be
    atoned for,
  and this will be the full fruitage
    of the removal of his sin:
When he makes all the altar
    stones
  to be like chalk stones crushed
    to pieces,
  no Asherah poles*b* or incense
    altars
  will be left standing.
10The fortified city stands
    desolate,
  an abandoned settlement,
    forsaken like the desert;
  there the calves graze,
    there they lie down;
    they strip its branches bare.
11When its twigs are dry, they are
    broken off
  and women come and make
    fires with them.
For this is a people without
    understanding;
  so their Maker has no
    compassion on them,
  and their Creator shows them
    no favor.

12In that day the LORD will thresh
from the flowing Euphrates*c* to the
Wadi of Egypt, and you, O Israelites,
will be gathered up one by one. 13And
in that day a great trumpet will
sound. Those who were perishing in
Assyria and those who were exiled in
Egypt will come and worship the
LORD on the holy mountain in Jerusalem.

Woe to Ephraim

28 Woe to that wreath, the
    pride of Ephraim's
    drunkards,
  to the fading flower, his
    glorious beauty,
set on the head of a fertile
    valley—
  to that city, the pride of those
    laid low by wine!
2See, the Lord has one who is
    powerful and strong.
Like a hailstorm and a
    destructive wind,
  like a driving rain and a flooding
    downpour,
  he will throw it forcefully to the
    ground.
3That wreath, the pride of
    Ephraim's drunkards,
  will be trampled underfoot.
4That fading flower, his glorious
    beauty,
  set on the head of a fertile
    valley,
will be like a fig ripe before
    harvest—
  as soon as someone sees it and
    takes it in his hand,
  he swallows it.

5In that day the LORD Almighty
  will be a glorious crown,
a beautiful wreath
  for the remnant of his people.
6He will be a spirit of justice
  to him who sits in judgment,
a source of strength
  to those who turn back the
    battle at the gate.

7And these also stagger from wine
    and reel from beer:
Priests and prophets stagger from
    beer
  and are befuddled with wine;
they reel from beer,
  they stagger when seeing
    visions,
  they stumble when rendering
    decisions.

a8 See Septuagint; the meaning of the Hebrew for this word is uncertain.　*b9* That is, symbols of the goddess Asherah　*c12* Hebrew *River*

8All the tables are covered with
vomit
and there is not a spot without
filth.

9"Who is it he is trying to teach?
To whom is he explaining his
message?
To children weaned from their
milk,
to those just taken from the
breast?
10For it is:
Do and do, do and do,
rule on rule, rule on rule*a*;
a little here, a little there."

11Very well then, with foreign lips
and strange tongues
God will speak to this people,
12to whom he said,
"This is the resting place, let
the weary rest";
and, "This is the place of
repose"—
but they would not listen.
13So then, the word of the LORD to
them will become:
Do and do, do and do,
rule on rule, rule on rule;
a little here, a little there—
so that they will go and fall
backward,
be injured and snared and
captured.

14Therefore hear the word of the
LORD, you scoffers
who rule this people in
Jerusalem.
15You boast, "We have entered into
a covenant with death,
with the grave*b* we have made
an agreement.
When an overwhelming scourge
sweeps by,
it cannot touch us,
for we have made a lie our refuge
and falsehood*c* our hiding
place."

16So this is what the Sovereign
LORD says:

"See, I lay a stone in Zion,
a tested stone,
a precious cornerstone for a sure
foundation;
the one who trusts will never be
dismayed.
17I will make justice the measuring
line
and righteousness the plumb
line;
hail will sweep away your refuge,
the lie,
and water will overflow your
hiding place.
18Your covenant with death will be
annulled;
your agreement with the grave
will not stand.
When the overwhelming scourge
sweeps by,
you will be beaten down by it.
19As often as it comes it will carry
you away;
morning after morning, by day
and by night,
it will sweep through."

The understanding of this
message
will bring sheer terror.
20The bed is too short to stretch out
on,
the blanket too narrow to wrap
around you.
21The LORD will rise up as he did at
Mount Perazim,
he will rouse himself as in the
Valley of Gibeon—
to do his work, his strange work,
and perform his task, his alien
task.
22Now stop your mocking,
or your chains will become
heavier;
the Lord, the LORD Almighty, has
told me
of the destruction decreed
against the whole land.

23Listen and hear my voice;
pay attention and hear what I
say.

---

a10 Hebrew / *sav lasav sav lasav* / *kav lakav kav lakav* (possibly meaningless sounds; perhaps a
mimicking of the prophet's words); also in verse 13   *b15* Hebrew *Sheol*; also in verse 18
c15 Or *false gods*

24When a farmer plows for
   planting, does he plow
   continually?
Does he keep on breaking up
   and harrowing the soil?
25When he has leveled the surface,
   does he not sow caraway and
   scatter cummin?
Does he not plant wheat in its
   place,*a*
   barley in its plot,*a*
   and spelt in its field?
26His God instructs him
   and teaches him the right
   way.

27Caraway is not threshed with a
   sledge,
   nor is a cartwheel rolled over
   cummin;
caraway is beaten out with a rod,
   and cummin with a stick.
28Grain must be ground to make
   bread;
   so one does not go on threshing
   it forever.
Though he drives the wheels of
   his threshing cart over it,
his horses do not grind it.
29All this also comes from the LORD
   Almighty,
   wonderful in counsel and
   magnificent in wisdom.

Woe to David's City

29 Woe to you, Ariel, Ariel,
   the city where David
   settled!
Add year to year
   and let your cycle of festivals go
   on.
2Yet I will besiege Ariel;
   she will mourn and lament,
   she will be to me like an altar
   hearth.*b*
3I will encamp against you all
   around;
   I will encircle you with towers
   and set up my siege works
   against you.
4Brought low, you will speak from
   the ground;

your speech will mumble out of
   the dust.
Your voice will come ghostlike
   from the earth;
   out of the dust your speech will
   whisper.

5But your many enemies will
   become like fine dust,
   the ruthless hordes like blown
   chaff.
Suddenly, in an instant,
6   the LORD Almighty will come
with thunder and earthquake and
   great noise,
   with windstorm and tempest
   and flames of a devouring
   fire.
7Then the hordes of all the nations
   that fight against Ariel,
   that attack her and her fortress
   and besiege her,
will be as it is with a dream,
   with a vision in the night—
8as when a hungry man dreams
   that he is eating,
   but he awakens, and his hunger
   remains;
as when a thirsty man dreams
   that he is drinking,
   but he awakens faint, with his
   thirst unquenched.
So will it be with the hordes of all
   the nations
   that fight against Mount Zion.

9Be stunned and amazed,
   blind yourselves and be
   sightless;
be drunk, but not from wine,
   stagger, but not from beer.
10The LORD has brought over you a
   deep sleep:
   He has sealed your eyes (the
   prophets);
   he has covered your heads (the
   seers).

11For you this whole vision is nothing but words sealed in a scroll. And
if you give the scroll to someone who
can read, and say to him, "Read this,
please," he will answer, "I can't; it is

---

*a*25 The meaning of the Hebrew for this word is uncertain.   *b*2 The Hebrew for *altar hearth*
sounds like the Hebrew for *Ariel*.

sealed." ¹²Or if you give the scroll to someone who cannot read, and say, "Read this, please," he will answer, "I don't know how to read."

¹³The Lord says:

"These people come near to me
with their mouth
and honor me with their lips,
but their hearts are far from
me.
Their worship of me
is made up only of rules taught
by men.ᵃ
¹⁴Therefore once more I will
astound these people
with wonder upon wonder;
the wisdom of the wise will
perish,
the intelligence of the
intelligent will vanish."
¹⁵Woe to those who go to great
depths
to hide their plans from the
Lord,
who do their work in darkness
and think,
"Who sees us? Who will know?"
¹⁶You turn things upside down,
as if the potter were thought to
be like the clay!
Shall what is formed say to him
who formed it,
"He did not make me"?
Can the pot say of the potter,
"He knows nothing"?

¹⁷In a very short time, will not
Lebanon be turned into a
fertile field
and the fertile field seem like a
forest?
¹⁸In that day the deaf will hear the
words of the scroll,
and out of gloom and darkness
the eyes of the blind will see.
¹⁹Once more the humble will
rejoice in the Lord;
the needy will rejoice in the
Holy One of Israel.
²⁰The ruthless will vanish,
the mockers will disappear,
and all who have an eye for evil
will be cut down—
²¹those who with a word make a
man out to be guilty,
who ensnare the defender in
court
and with false testimony
deprive the innocent of
justice.

²²Therefore this is what the Lord,
who redeemed Abraham, says to the
house of Jacob:

"No longer will Jacob be
ashamed;
no longer will their faces grow
pale.
²³When they see among them their
children,
the work of my hands,
they will keep my name holy;
they will acknowledge the
holiness of the Holy One of
Jacob,
and will stand in awe of the
God of Israel.
²⁴Those who are wayward in spirit
will gain understanding;
those who complain will accept
instruction."

Woe to the Obstinate Nation

30 "Woe to the obstinate
children,"
declares the Lord,
"to those who carry out plans that
are not mine,
forming an alliance, but not by
my Spirit,
heaping sin upon sin;
²who go down to Egypt
without consulting me;
who look for help to Pharaoh's
protection,
to Egypt's shade for refuge.
³But Pharaoh's protection will be
to your shame,
Egypt's shade will bring you
disgrace.
⁴Though they have officials in
Zoan

ᵃ13 Hebrew; Septuagint *They worship me in vain; / their teachings are but rules taught by men*

and their envoys have arrived
in Hanes,
⁵everyone will be put to shame
because of a people useless to
them,
who bring neither help nor
advantage,
but only shame and disgrace."

⁶An oracle concerning the animals
of the Negev:

Through a land of hardship and
distress,
of lions and lionesses,
of adders and darting snakes,
the envoys carry their riches on
donkeys' backs,
their treasures on the humps of
camels,
to that unprofitable nation,
⁷ to Egypt, whose help is utterly
useless.
Therefore I call her
Rahab the Do-Nothing.

⁸Go now, write it on a tablet for
them,
inscribe it on a scroll,
that for the days to come
it may be an everlasting
witness.
⁹These are rebellious people,
deceitful children,
children unwilling to listen to
the LORD's instruction.
¹⁰They say to the seers,
"See no more visions!"
and to the prophets,
"Give us no more visions of
what is right!
Tell us pleasant things,
prophesy illusions.
¹¹Leave this way,
get off this path,
and stop confronting us
with the Holy One of Israel!"

¹²Therefore, this is what the Holy
One of Israel says:

"Because you have rejected this
message,
relied on oppression
and depended on deceit,
¹³this sin will become for you

like a high wall, cracked and
bulging,
that collapses suddenly, in an
instant.
¹⁴It will break in pieces like
pottery,
shattered so mercilessly
that among its pieces not a
fragment will be found
for taking coals from a hearth
or scooping water out of a
cistern."

¹⁵This is what the Sovereign LORD,
the Holy One of Israel, says:

"In repentance and rest is your
salvation,
in quietness and trust is your
strength,
but you would have none of it.
¹⁶You said, 'No, we will flee on
horses.'
Therefore you will flee!
You said, 'We will ride off on
swift horses.'
Therefore your pursuers will be
swift!
¹⁷A thousand will flee
at the threat of one;
at the threat of five
you will all flee away,
till you are left
like a flagstaff on a
mountaintop,
like a banner on a hill."

¹⁸Yet the LORD longs to be gracious
to you;
he rises to show you
compassion.
For the LORD is a God of justice.
Blessed are all who wait for
him!

¹⁹O people of Zion, who live in Jerusalem, you will weep no more. How gracious he will be when you cry for help! As soon as he hears, he will answer you. ²⁰Although the Lord gives you the bread of adversity and the water of affliction, your teachers will be hidden no more; with your own eyes you will see them. ²¹Whether you turn to the right or to the left, your ears will hear a voice behind you, saying, "This is the way; walk in

it." 22Then you will defile your idols overlaid with silver and your images covered with gold; you will throw them away like a menstrual cloth and say to them, "Away with you!"

23He will also send you rain for the seed you sow in the ground, and the food that comes from the land will be rich and plentiful. In that day your cattle will graze in broad meadows. 24The oxen and donkeys that work the soil will eat fodder and mash, spread out with fork and shovel. 25In the day of great slaughter, when the towers fall, streams of water will flow on every high mountain and every lofty hill. 26The moon will shine like the sun, and the sunlight will be seven times brighter, like the light of seven full days, when the LORD binds up the bruises of his people and heals the wounds he inflicted.

27See, the Name of the LORD comes
　　from afar,
　with burning anger and dense
　　clouds of smoke;
his lips are full of wrath,
　and his tongue is a consuming
　　fire.
28His breath is like a rushing
　　torrent,
　rising up to the neck.
He shakes the nations in the
　　sieve of destruction;
　he places in the jaws of the
　　peoples
　a bit that leads them
　　astray.
29And you will sing
　as on the night you celebrate a
　　holy festival;
your hearts will rejoice
　as when people go up with
　　flutes
to the mountain of the LORD,
　to the Rock of Israel.
30The LORD will cause men to hear
　　his majestic voice
　and will make them see his arm
　　coming down
with raging anger and consuming
　　fire,
　with cloudburst, thunderstorm
　　and hail.

31The voice of the LORD will shatter
　　Assyria;
　with his scepter he will strike
　　them down.
32Every stroke the LORD lays on
　　them
　with his punishing rod
will be to the music of
　　tambourines and harps,
　as he fights them in battle with
　　the blows of his arm.
33Topheth has long been prepared;
　it has been made ready for the
　　king.
Its fire pit has been made deep
　　and wide,
　with an abundance of fire and
　　wood;
the breath of the LORD,
　like a stream of burning sulfur,
　sets it ablaze.

Woe to Those Who Rely on Egypt

31 Woe to those who go down
　　to Egypt for help,
who rely on horses,
who trust in the multitude of
　　their chariots
　and in the great strength of
　　their horsemen,
but do not look to the Holy One of
　　Israel,
　or seek help from the LORD.
2Yet he too is wise and can bring
　　disaster;
　he does not take back his
　　words.
He will rise up against the house
　　of the wicked,
　against those who help
　　evildoers.
3But the Egyptians are men and
　　not God;
　their horses are flesh and not
　　spirit.
When the LORD stretches out his
　　hand,
　he who helps will stumble,
　he who is helped will fall;
　both will perish together.

4This is what the LORD says to me:

"As a lion growls,

a great lion over his prey—
and though a whole band of
    shepherds
is called together against him,
he is not frightened by their
    shouts
or disturbed by their clamor—
so the LORD Almighty will come
    down
    to do battle on Mount Zion and
    on its heights.
⁵Like birds hovering overhead,
    the LORD Almighty will shield
    Jerusalem;
he will shield it and deliver it,
    he will 'pass over' it and will
    rescue it."

⁶Return to him you have so greatly
revolted against, O Israelites. ⁷For in
that day every one of you will reject
the idols of silver and gold your sinful
hands have made.

⁸"Assyria will fall by a sword that
    is not of man;
    a sword, not of mortals, will
    devour them.
They will flee before the sword
    and their young men will be
    put to forced labor.
⁹Their stronghold will fall because
    of terror;
    at sight of the battle standard
    their commanders will
    panic,"
declares the LORD,
    whose fire is in Zion,
    whose furnace is in Jerusalem.

The Kingdom of Righteousness

32 See, a king will reign in
    righteousness
    and rulers will rule with justice.
²Each man will be like a shelter
    from the wind
    and a refuge from the storm,
like streams of water in the
    desert
    and the shadow of a great rock
    in a thirsty land.

³Then the eyes of those who see
    will no longer be closed,
    and the ears of those who hear
    will listen.

⁴The mind of the rash will know
    and understand,
    and the stammering tongue will
    be fluent and clear.
⁵No longer will the fool be called
    noble
    nor the scoundrel be highly
    respected.
⁶For the fool speaks folly,
    his mind is busy with evil:
He practices ungodliness
    and spreads error concerning
    the LORD;
the hungry he leaves empty
    and from the thirsty he
    withholds water.
⁷The scoundrel's methods are
    wicked,
    he makes up evil schemes
to destroy the poor with lies,
    even when the plea of the needy
    is just.
⁸But the noble man makes noble
    plans,
    and by noble deeds he stands.

The Women of Jerusalem

⁹You women who are so
    complacent,
    rise up and listen to me;
you daughters who feel secure,
    hear what I have to say!
¹⁰In little more than a year
    you who feel secure will
    tremble;
the grape harvest will fail,
    and the harvest of fruit will not
    come.
¹¹Tremble, you complacent women;
    shudder, you daughters who feel
    secure!
Strip off your clothes,
    put sackcloth around your
    waists.
¹²Beat your breasts for the pleasant
    fields,
    for the fruitful vines
¹³and for the land of my people,
    a land overgrown with thorns
    and briers—
yes, mourn for all houses of
    merriment
    and for this city of revelry.
¹⁴The fortress will be abandoned,

the noisy city deserted;
citadel and watchtower will
     become a wasteland forever,
   the delight of donkeys, a
     pasture for flocks,
¹⁵till the Spirit is poured upon us
     from on high,
   and the desert becomes a fertile
     field,
   and the fertile field seems like
     a forest.
¹⁶Justice will dwell in the desert
   and righteousness live in the
     fertile field.
¹⁷The fruit of righteousness will be
     peace;
   the effect of righteousness will
     be quietness and confidence
     forever.
¹⁸My people will live in peaceful
     dwelling places,
   in secure homes,
   in undisturbed places of rest.
¹⁹Though hail flattens the forest
   and the city is leveled
     completely,
²⁰how blessed you will be,
   sowing your seed by every
     stream,
   and letting your cattle and
     donkeys range free.

Distress and Help

33 Woe to you, O destroyer,
     you who have not been
     destroyed!
   Woe to you, O traitor,
     you who have not been
     betrayed!
   When you stop destroying,
     you will be destroyed;
   when you stop betraying,
     you will be betrayed.

²O LORD, be gracious to us;
   we long for you.
   Be our strength every morning,
     our salvation in time of distress.
³At the thunder of your voice, the
     peoples flee;
   when you rise up, the nations
     scatter.
⁴Your plunder, O nations, is

harvested as by young
     locusts;
   like a swarm of locusts men
     pounce on it.

⁵The LORD is exalted, for he dwells
     on high;
   he will fill Zion with justice and
     righteousness.
⁶He will be the sure foundation for
     your times,
   a rich store of salvation and
     wisdom and knowledge;
   the fear of the LORD is the key
     to this treasure.ᵃ

⁷Look, their brave men cry aloud
     in the streets;
   the envoys of peace weep
     bitterly.
⁸The highways are deserted,
   no travelers are on the roads.
   The treaty is broken,
     its witnessesᵇ are despised,
   no one is respected.
⁹The land mournsᶜ and wastes
     away,
   Lebanon is ashamed and
     withers;
   Sharon is like the Arabah,
     and Bashan and Carmel drop
     their leaves.

¹⁰"Now will I arise," says the LORD.
   "Now will I be exalted;
   now will I be lifted up.
¹¹You conceive chaff,
   you give birth to straw;
   your breath is a fire that
     consumes you.
¹²The peoples will be burned as if
     to lime;
   like cut thornbushes they will
     be set ablaze."

¹³You who are far away, hear what
     I have done;
   you who are near, acknowledge
     my power!
¹⁴The sinners in Zion are terrified;
   trembling grips the godless:
   "Who of us can dwell with the
     consuming fire?
   Who of us can dwell with
     everlasting burning?"

ᵃ6 Or *is a treasure from him*   ᵇ8 Dead Sea Scrolls; Masoretic Text / *the cities*   ᶜ9 Or *dries up*

¹⁵He who walks righteously
and speaks what is right,
who rejects gain from extortion
and keeps his hand from
accepting bribes,
who stops his ears against plots of
murder
and shuts his eyes against
contemplating evil—
¹⁶this is the man who will dwell on
the heights,
whose refuge will be the
mountain fortress.
His bread will be supplied,
and water will not fail him.

¹⁷Your eyes will see the king in his
beauty
and view a land that stretches
afar.
¹⁸In your thoughts you will ponder
the former terror:
"Where is that chief officer?
Where is the one who took the
revenue?
Where is the officer in charge of
the towers?"
¹⁹You will see those arrogant
people no more,
those people of an obscure
speech,
with their strange,
incomprehensible tongue.

²⁰Look upon Zion, the city of our
festivals;
your eyes will see Jerusalem,
a peaceful abode, a tent that
will not be moved;
its stakes will never be pulled up,
nor any of its ropes broken.
²¹There the LORD will be our
Mighty One.
It will be like a place of broad
rivers and streams.
No galley with oars will ride
them,
no mighty ship will sail
them.
²²For the LORD is our judge,
the LORD is our lawgiver,
the LORD is our king;
it is he who will save us.

²³Your rigging hangs loose:
The mast is not held secure,
the sail is not spread.
Then an abundance of spoils will
be divided
and even the lame will carry off
plunder.
²⁴No one living in Zion will say, "I
am ill";
and the sins of those who dwell
there will be forgiven.

Judgment Against the Nations

34 Come near, you nations,
and listen;
pay attention, you peoples!
Let the earth hear, and all that is
in it,
the world, and all that comes
out of it!
²The LORD is angry with all
nations;
his wrath is upon all their
armies.
He will totally destroyª them,
he will give them over to
slaughter.
³Their slain will be thrown out,
their dead bodies will send up a
stench;
the mountains will be soaked
with their blood.
⁴All the stars of the heavens will
be dissolved
and the sky rolled up like a
scroll;
all the starry host will fall
like withered leaves from the
vine,
like shriveled figs from the fig
tree.

⁵My sword has drunk its fill in the
heavens;
see, it descends in judgment on
Edom,
the people I have totally
destroyed.
⁶The sword of the LORD is bathed
in blood,
it is covered with fat—
the blood of lambs and goats,

fat from the kidneys of rams.
For the LORD has a sacrifice in
    Bozrah
  and a great slaughter in
    Edom.
⁷And the wild oxen will fall with
    them,
  the bull calves and the great
    bulls.
Their land will be drenched with
    blood,
  and the dust will be soaked
    with fat.

⁸For the LORD has a day of
    vengeance,
  a year of retribution, to uphold
    Zion's cause.
⁹Edom's streams will be turned
    into pitch,
  her dust into burning sulfur;
  her land will become blazing
    pitch!
¹⁰It will not be quenched night and
    day;
  its smoke will rise forever.
From generation to generation it
    will lie desolate;
  no one will ever pass through it
    again.
¹¹The desert owlᵃ and screech owlᵃ
    will possess it;
  the great owlᵃ and the raven
    will nest there.
God will stretch out over Edom
    the measuring line of chaos
  and the plumb line of
    desolation.
¹²Her nobles will have nothing
    there to be called a
    kingdom,
  all her princes will vanish
    away.
¹³Thorns will overrun her citadels,
  nettles and brambles her
    strongholds.
She will become a haunt for
    jackals,
  a home for owls.
¹⁴Desert creatures will meet with
    hyenas,
  and wild goats will bleat to
    each other;

there the night creatures will also
    repose
  and find for themselves places
    of rest.
¹⁵The owl will nest there and lay
    eggs,
  she will hatch them, and care
    for her young under the
    shadow of her wings;
there also the falcons will gather,
  each with its mate.

¹⁶Look in the scroll of the LORD and
read:

None of these will be missing,
  not one will lack her mate.
For it is his mouth that has given
    the order,
  and his Spirit will gather them
    together.
¹⁷He allots their portions;
  his hand distributes them by
    measure.
They will possess it forever
  and dwell there from generation
    to generation.

Joy of the Redeemed

35 The desert and the parched
    land will be glad;
  the wilderness will rejoice and
    blossom.
Like the crocus, ²it will burst into
    bloom;
  it will rejoice greatly and shout
    for joy.
The glory of Lebanon will be
    given to it,
  the splendor of Carmel and
    Sharon;
they will see the glory of the
    LORD,
  the splendor of our God.

³Strengthen the feeble hands,
  steady the knees that give way;
⁴say to those with fearful hearts,
  "Be strong, do not fear;
  your God will come,
    he will come with vengeance;
with divine retribution
    he will come to save you."

ᵃ11 The precise identification of these birds is uncertain.

⁵Then will the eyes of the blind be
    opened
and the ears of the deaf
    unstopped.

Words to Remember

35:4 Say to those with fearful
      hearts,
    "Be strong, do not fear;
    your God will come."

---

⁶Then will the lame leap like a
    deer,
    and the mute tongue shout for
      joy.
Water will gush forth in the
    wilderness
    and streams in the desert.
⁷The burning sand will become a
    pool,
    the thirsty ground bubbling
      springs.
In the haunts where jackals once
    lay,
    grass and reeds and papyrus
      will grow.

⁸And a highway will be there;
    it will be called the Way of
      Holiness.
The unclean will not journey on
    it;
    it will be for those who walk in
      that Way;
    wicked fools will not go about
      on it.ᵃ
⁹No lion will be there,
    nor will any ferocious beast get
      up on it;
    they will not be found there.
But only the redeemed will walk
    there,
10 and the ransomed of the LORD
    will return.
They will enter Zion with singing;
    everlasting joy will crown their
      heads.
Gladness and joy will overtake
    them,
    and sorrow and sighing will flee
      away.

ᵃ8 Or / *the simple will not stray from it*

Sennacherib Threatens Jerusalem

36 In the fourteenth year of
King Hezekiah's reign, Sennacherib king of Assyria attacked all
the fortified cities of Judah and captured them. ²Then the king of Assyria sent his field commander with a
large army from Lachish to King
Hezekiah at Jerusalem. When the
commander stopped at the aqueduct
of the Upper Pool, on the road to the
Washerman's Field, ³Eliakim son of
Hilkiah the palace administrator,
Shebna the secretary, and Joah son of
Asaph the recorder went out to him.
⁴The field commander said to them,
"Tell Hezekiah,

" 'This is what the great king,
the king of Assyria, says: On
what are you basing this confidence of yours? ⁵You say you
have strategy and military
strength—but you speak only
empty words. On whom are you
depending, that you rebel
against me? ⁶Look now, you are
depending on Egypt, that splintered reed of a staff, which pierces
a man's hand and wounds him if
he leans on it! Such is Pharaoh
king of Egypt to all who depend
on him. ⁷And if you say to me,
"We are depending on the LORD
our God"—isn't he the one whose
high places and altars Hezekiah
removed, saying to Judah and
Jerusalem, "You must worship
before this altar"?

⁸" 'Come now, make a bargain
with my master, the king of Assyria: I will give you two thousand horses—if you can put riders on them! ⁹How then can you
repulse one officer of the least of
my master's officials, even
though you are depending on
Egypt for chariots and horsemen? ¹⁰Furthermore, have I
come to attack and destroy this
land without the LORD? The
LORD himself told me to march

against this country and destroy it.' "

11Then Eliakim, Shebna and Joah said to the field commander, "Please speak to your servants in Aramaic, since we understand it. Don't speak to us in Hebrew in the hearing of the people on the wall."

12But the commander replied, "Was it only to your master and you that my master sent me to say these things, and not to the men sitting on the wall—who, like you, will have to eat their own filth and drink their own urine?"

13Then the commander stood and called out in Hebrew, "Hear the words of the great king, the king of Assyria! 14This is what the king says: Do not let Hezekiah deceive you. He cannot deliver you! 15Do not let Hezekiah persuade you to trust in the LORD when he says, 'The LORD will surely deliver us; this city will not be given into the hand of the king of Assyria.'

16"Do not listen to Hezekiah. This is what the king of Assyria says: Make peace with me and come out to me. Then every one of you will eat from his own vine and fig tree and drink water from his own cistern, 17until I come and take you to a land like your own—a land of grain and new wine, a land of bread and vineyards.

18"Do not let Hezekiah mislead you when he says, 'The LORD will deliver us.' Has the god of any nation ever delivered his land from the hand of the king of Assyria? 19Where are the gods of Hamath and Arpad? Where are the gods of Sepharvaim? Have they rescued Samaria from my hand? 20Who of all the gods of these countries has been able to save his land from me? How then can the LORD deliver Jerusalem from my hand?"

21But the people remained silent and said nothing in reply, because the king had commanded, "Do not answer him."

22Then Eliakim son of Hilkiah the palace administrator, Shebna the secretary, and Joah son of Asaph the recorder went to Hezekiah, with their clothes torn, and told him what the field commander had said.

Jerusalem's Deliverance Foretold

37 When King Hezekiah heard this, he tore his clothes and put on sackcloth and went into the temple of the LORD. 2He sent Eliakim the palace administrator, Shebna the secretary, and the leading priests, all wearing sackcloth, to the prophet Isaiah son of Amoz. 3They told him, "This is what Hezekiah says: This day is a day of distress and rebuke and disgrace, as when children come to the point of birth and there is no strength to deliver them. 4It may be that the LORD your God will hear the words of the field commander, whom his master, the king of Assyria, has sent to ridicule the living God, and that he will rebuke him for the words the LORD your God has heard. Therefore pray for the remnant that still survives."

5When King Hezekiah's officials came to Isaiah, 6Isaiah said to them, "Tell your master, 'This is what the LORD says: Do not be afraid of what you have heard—those words with which the underlings of the king of Assyria have blasphemed me. 7Listen! I am going to put a spirit in him so that when he hears a certain report, he will return to his own country, and there I will have him cut down with the sword.' "

8When the field commander heard that the king of Assyria had left Lachish, he withdrew and found the king fighting against Libnah.

9Now Sennacherib received a report that Tirhakah, the Cushite[a] king ⸢of Egypt⸣, was marching out to fight against him. When he heard it, he sent messengers to Hezekiah with this word: 10"Say to Hezekiah king of Judah: Do not let the god you depend on deceive you when he says, 'Jerusalem will not be handed over to the king of Assyria.' ¹¹Surely you have heard what the kings of Assyria have done to all the countries, destroying them completely. And will you be delivered? ¹²Did the gods of the nations that were destroyed by my forefathers deliver them—the gods of Gozan, Haran, Rezeph and the people of Eden who were in Tel Assar? ¹³Where is the king of Hamath, the king of Arpad, the king of the city of Sepharvaim, or of Hena or Ivvah?"

Hezekiah's Prayer

¹⁴Hezekiah received the letter from the messengers and read it. Then he went up to the temple of the LORD and spread it out before the LORD. ¹⁵And Hezekiah prayed to the LORD: ¹⁶"O LORD Almighty, God of Israel, enthroned between the cherubim, you alone are God over all the kingdoms of the earth. You have made heaven and earth. ¹⁷Give ear, O LORD, and hear; open your eyes, O LORD, and see; listen to all the words Sennacherib has sent to insult the living God.

¹⁸"It is true, O LORD, that the Assyrian kings have laid waste all these peoples and their lands. ¹⁹They have thrown their gods into the fire and destroyed them, for they were not gods but only wood and stone, fashioned by human hands. ²⁰Now, O LORD our God, deliver us from his hand, so that all kingdoms on earth may know that you alone, O LORD, are God.*a*"

Sennacherib's Fall

²¹Then Isaiah son of Amoz sent a message to Hezekiah: "This is what the LORD, the God of Israel, says: Because you have prayed to me concerning Sennacherib king of Assyria, ²²this is the word the LORD has spoken against him:

"The Virgin Daughter of Zion

despises and mocks you.
The Daughter of Jerusalem
   tosses her head as you flee.
²³Who is it you have insulted and
   blasphemed?
Against whom have you raised
   your voice
and lifted your eyes in pride?
   Against the Holy One of Israel!
²⁴By your messengers
   you have heaped insults on the
     Lord.
And you have said,
   'With my many chariots
I have ascended the heights of the
   mountains,
   the utmost heights of Lebanon.
I have cut down its tallest cedars,
   the choicest of its pines.
I have reached its remotest
   heights,
   the finest of its forests.
²⁵I have dug wells in foreign lands*b*
   and drunk the water there.
With the soles of my feet
   I have dried up all the streams
     of Egypt.'

²⁶"Have you not heard?
   Long ago I ordained it.
In days of old I planned it;
   now I have brought it to pass,
that you have turned fortified
   cities
   into piles of stone.
²⁷Their people, drained of power,
   are dismayed and put to shame.
They are like plants in the field,
   like tender green shoots,
like grass sprouting on the roof,
   scorched*c* before it grows up.

²⁸"But I know where you stay
   and when you come and go
   and how you rage against me.
²⁹Because you rage against me
   and because your insolence has
     reached my ears,
I will put my hook in your nose
   and my bit in your mouth,
and I will make you return

a20 Dead Sea Scrolls (see also 2 Kings 19:19); Masoretic Text *alone are the LORD*   *b25* Dead Sea Scrolls (see also 2 Kings 19:24); Masoretic Text does not have *in foreign lands.*   *c27* Some manuscripts of the Masoretic Text, Dead Sea Scrolls and some Septuagint manuscripts (see also 2 Kings 19:26); most manuscripts of the Masoretic Text *roof / and terraced fields* by the way you came.

30"This will be the sign for you, O Hezekiah:

"This year you will eat what
grows by itself,
and the second year what
springs from that.
But in the third year sow and
reap,
plant vineyards and eat their
fruit.
31Once more a remnant of the
house of Judah
will take root below and bear
fruit above.
32For out of Jerusalem will come a
remnant,
and out of Mount Zion a band of
survivors.
The zeal of the LORD Almighty
will accomplish this.

33"Therefore this is what the LORD says concerning the king of Assyria:

"He will not enter this city
or shoot an arrow here.
He will not come before it with
shield
or build a siege ramp against it.
34By the way that he came he will
return;
he will not enter this city,"
declares the LORD.
35"I will defend this city and save
it,
for my sake and for the sake of
David my servant!"

36Then the angel of the LORD went out and put to death a hundred and eighty-five thousand men in the Assyrian camp. When the people got up the next morning—there were all the dead bodies! 37So Sennacherib king of Assyria broke camp and withdrew. He returned to Nineveh and stayed there.

38One day, while he was worshiping in the temple of his god Nisroch, his sons Adrammelech and Sharezer cut him down with the sword, and they escaped to the land of Ararat. And Esarhaddon his son succeeded him as king.

Hezekiah's Illness

38 In those days Hezekiah became ill and was at the point of death. The prophet Isaiah son of Amoz went to him and said, "This is what the LORD says: Put your house in order, because you are going to die; you will not recover."

2Hezekiah turned his face to the wall and prayed to the LORD, 3"Remember, O LORD, how I have walked before you faithfully and with wholehearted devotion and have done what is good in your eyes." And Hezekiah wept bitterly.

4Then the word of the LORD came to Isaiah: 5"Go and tell Hezekiah, 'This is what the LORD, the God of your father David, says: I have heard your prayer and seen your tears; I will add fifteen years to your life. 6And I will deliver you and this city from the hand of the king of Assyria. I will defend this city.

7" 'This is the LORD's sign to you that the LORD will do what he has promised: 8I will make the shadow cast by the sun go back the ten steps it has gone down on the stairway of Ahaz.' " So the sunlight went back the ten steps it had gone down.

9A writing of Hezekiah king of Judah after his illness and recovery:

10I said, "In the prime of my life
must I go through the gates of
death a
and be robbed of the rest of my
years?"
11I said, "I will not again see the
LORD,
the LORD, in the land of the
living;
no longer will I look on mankind,
or be with those who now dwell
in this world. b
12Like a shepherd's tent my house

a10 Hebrew Sheol   b11 A few Hebrew manuscripts; most Hebrew manuscripts in the place of cessation

has been pulled down and taken
from me.
Like a weaver I have rolled up
my life,
and he has cut me off from the
loom;
day and night you made an end
of me.
13I waited patiently till dawn,
but like a lion he broke all my
bones;
day and night you made an end
of me.
14I cried like a swift or thrush,
I moaned like a mourning
dove.
My eyes grew weak as I looked to
the heavens.
I am troubled; O Lord, come to
my aid!"

15But what can I say?
He has spoken to me, and he
himself has done this.
I will walk humbly all my years
because of this anguish of my
soul.
16Lord, by such things men live;
and my spirit finds life in them
too.
You restored me to health
and let me live.
17Surely it was for my benefit
that I suffered such anguish.

a18 Hebrew *Sheol*

In your love you kept me
from the pit of destruction;
you have put all my sins
behind your back.
18For the grave*a* cannot praise you,
death cannot sing your praise;
those who go down to the pit
cannot hope for your
faithfulness.
19The living, the living—they
praise you,
as I am doing today;
fathers tell their children
about your faithfulness.

20The LORD will save me,
and we will sing with stringed
instruments
all the days of our lives
in the temple of the LORD.

21Isaiah had said, "Prepare a poultice of figs and apply it to the boil, and he will recover."

22Hezekiah had asked, "What will be the sign that I will go up to the temple of the LORD?"

Envoys From Babylon

39 At that time Merodach-Baladan son of Baladan king of Babylon sent Hezekiah letters and a gift, because he had heard of his illness and recovery. 2Hezekiah re-

Life in Bible Times

BABYLONIANS

Pictures carved in rocks tell us how ancient peoples looked. Each area or nation had its own special way of dressing, of cutting hair, of shaving or not shaving their beards. The Babylonians were a large and powerful nation during the time of Isaiah, and they too dressed in their own special way.

ceived the envoys gladly and showed them what was in his storehouses —the silver, the gold, the spices, the fine oil, his entire armory and everything found among his treasures. There was nothing in his palace or in all his kingdom that Hezekiah did not show them.

3Then Isaiah the prophet went to King Hezekiah and asked, "What did those men say, and where did they come from?"

"From a distant land," Hezekiah replied. "They came to me from Babylon."

4The prophet asked, "What did they see in your palace?"

"They saw everything in my palace," Hezekiah said. "There is nothing among my treasures that I did not show them."

5Then Isaiah said to Hezekiah, "Hear the word of the LORD Almighty: 6The time will surely come when everything in your palace, and all that your fathers have stored up until this day, will be carried off to Babylon. Nothing will be left, says the LORD. 7And some of your descendants, your own flesh and blood who will be born to you, will be taken away, and they will become eunuchs in the palace of the king of Babylon."

8"The word of the LORD you have spoken is good," Hezekiah replied. For he thought, "There will be peace and security in my lifetime."

Comfort for God's People

40 Comfort, comfort my people, says your God.
2Speak tenderly to Jerusalem, and proclaim to her that her hard service has been completed, that her sin has been paid for, that she has received from the LORD's hand double for all her sins.

3A voice of one calling:

"In the desert prepare the way for the LORD[a];
make straight in the wilderness a highway for our God.[b]
4Every valley shall be raised up, every mountain and hill made low;
the rough ground shall become level, the rugged places a plain.
5And the glory of the LORD will be revealed, and all mankind together will see it.
For the mouth of the LORD has spoken."

6A voice says, "Cry out." And I said, "What shall I cry?"

"All men are like grass, and all their glory is like the flowers of the field.
7The grass withers and the flowers fall, because the breath of the LORD blows on them.
Surely the people are grass.
8The grass withers and the flowers fall, but the word of our God stands forever."

9You who bring good tidings to Zion, go up on a high mountain.
You who bring good tidings to Jerusalem,[c]
lift up your voice with a shout, lift it up, do not be afraid;
say to the towns of Judah, "Here is your God!"
10See, the Sovereign LORD comes with power, and his arm rules for him.
See, his reward is with him, and his recompense accompanies him.
11He tends his flock like a shepherd:
He gathers the lambs in his arms

---

a3 Or A voice of one calling in the desert: / "Prepare the way for the LORD   b3 Hebrew; Septuagint make straight the paths of our God   c9 Or O Zion, bringer of good tidings, / go up on a high mountain. / O Jerusalem, bringer of good tidings

and carries them close to his
    heart;
  he gently leads those that have
    young.

12Who has measured the waters in
    the hollow of his hand,
  or with the breadth of his hand
    marked off the heavens?
Who has held the dust of the
    earth in a basket,
  or weighed the mountains on
    the scales
  and the hills in a balance?
13Who has understood the mind*a* of
    the LORD,
  or instructed him as his
    counselor?
14Whom did the LORD consult to
    enlighten him,
  and who taught him the right
    way?
Who was it that taught him
    knowledge
  or showed him the path of
    understanding?

15Surely the nations are like a drop
    in a bucket;
  they are regarded as dust on
    the scales;
  he weighs the islands as though
    they were fine dust.
16Lebanon is not sufficient for altar
    fires,
  nor its animals enough for
    burnt offerings.
17Before him all the nations are as
    nothing;
  they are regarded by him as
    worthless
  and less than nothing.

18To whom, then, will you compare
    God?
  What image will you compare
    him to?
19As for an idol, a craftsman casts
    it,
  and a goldsmith overlays it
    with gold
  and fashions silver chains for it.
20A man too poor to present such
    an offering

selects wood that will not rot.
He looks for a skilled craftsman
  to set up an idol that will not
    topple.

21Do you not know?
  Have you not heard?
Has it not been told you from the
    beginning?
  Have you not understood since
    the earth was founded?
22He sits enthroned above the circle
    of the earth,
  and its people are like
    grasshoppers.
He stretches out the heavens like
    a canopy,
  and spreads them out like a
    tent to live in.
23He brings princes to naught
  and reduces the rulers of this
    world to nothing.
24No sooner are they planted,
  no sooner are they sown,
  no sooner do they take root in
    the ground,
than he blows on them and they
    wither,
  and a whirlwind sweeps them
    away like chaff.

25"To whom will you compare me?
  Or who is my equal?" says the
    Holy One.
26Lift your eyes and look to the
    heavens:
  Who created all these?
He who brings out the starry host
    one by one,
  and calls them each by name.
Because of his great power and
    mighty strength,
  not one of them is missing.

27Why do you say, O Jacob,
  and complain, O Israel,
"My way is hidden from the LORD;
  my cause is disregarded by my
    God"?
28Do you not know?
  Have you not heard?
The LORD is the everlasting God,
  the Creator of the ends of the
    earth.

a13 Or Spirit; or spirit

He will not grow tired or weary,
and his understanding no one
can fathom.
²⁹He gives strength to the weary
and increases the power of the
weak.
³⁰Even youths grow tired and
weary,
and young men stumble and
fall;
³¹but those who hope in the LORD
will renew their strength.
They will soar on wings like
eagles;
they will run and not grow
weary,
they will walk and not be faint.

WORDS TO REMEMBER

40:31 Those who hope in the LORD
will renew their strength.
They will soar on wings like
eagles;
they will run and not
grow weary,
they will walk and not be
faint.

The Helper of Israel

41 "Be silent before me, you
islands!
Let the nations renew their
strength!
Let them come forward and
speak;
let us meet together at the
place of judgment.

²"Who has stirred up one from the
east,
calling him in righteousness to
his service^a?
He hands nations over to him
and subdues kings before him.
He turns them to dust with his
sword,
to windblown chaff with his
bow.
³He pursues them and moves on
unscathed,
by a path his feet have not
traveled before.
⁴Who has done this and carried it
through,
calling forth the generations
from the beginning?
I, the LORD—with the first of
them
and with the last—I am he."

⁵The islands have seen it and fear;
the ends of the earth tremble.
They approach and come forward;
⁶ each helps the other
and says to his brother, "Be
strong!"
⁷The craftsman encourages the
goldsmith,
and he who smooths with the
hammer
spurs on him who strikes the
anvil.
He says of the welding, "It is
good."
He nails down the idol so it will
not topple.

⁸"But you, O Israel, my servant,
Jacob, whom I have chosen,
you descendants of Abraham
my friend,
⁹I took you from the ends of the
earth,
from its farthest corners I called
you.
I said, 'You are my servant';
I have chosen you and have not
rejected you.
¹⁰So do not fear, for I am with you;
do not be dismayed, for I am
your God.
I will strengthen you and help
you;
I will uphold you with my
righteous right hand.

¹¹"All who rage against you
will surely be ashamed and
disgraced;
those who oppose you
will be as nothing and perish.
¹²Though you search for your
enemies,
you will not find them.

---

^a2 Or / whom victory meets at every step

Those who wage war against
you
will be as nothing at all.
13For I am the LORD, your God,
who takes hold of your right
hand
and says to you, Do not fear;
I will help you.
14Do not be afraid, O worm Jacob,
O little Israel,
for I myself will help you,"
declares the LORD,
your Redeemer, the Holy One of
Israel.
15"See, I will make you into a
threshing sledge,
new and sharp, with many
teeth.
You will thresh the mountains
and crush them,
and reduce the hills to chaff.
16You will winnow them, the wind
will pick them up,
and a gale will blow them
away.
But you will rejoice in the LORD
and glory in the Holy One of
Israel.

17"The poor and needy search for
water,
but there is none;
their tongues are parched with
thirst.
But I the LORD will answer them;
I, the God of Israel, will not
forsake them.
18I will make rivers flow on barren
heights,
and springs within the valleys.
I will turn the desert into pools of
water,
and the parched ground into
springs.
19I will put in the desert
the cedar and the acacia, the
myrtle and the olive.
I will set pines in the wasteland,
the fir and the cypress together,
20so that people may see and know,
may consider and understand,
that the hand of the LORD has
done this,
that the Holy One of Israel has
created it.

21"Present your case," says the
LORD.
"Set forth your arguments,"
says Jacob's King.
22"Bring in ˻your idols˼ to tell us
what is going to happen.
Tell us what the former things
were,
so that we may consider them
and know their final outcome.
Or declare to us the things to
come,
23   tell us what the future holds,
so we may know that you are
gods.
Do something, whether good or
bad,
so that we will be dismayed and
filled with fear.
24But you are less than nothing
and your works are utterly
worthless;
he who chooses you is
detestable.

25"I have stirred up one from the
north, and he comes—
one from the rising sun who
calls on my name.
He treads on rulers as if they
were mortar,
as if he were a potter treading
the clay.
26Who told of this from the
beginning, so we could
know,
or beforehand, so we could say,
'He was right'?
No one told of this,
no one foretold it,
no one heard any words from
you.
27I was the first to tell Zion, 'Look,
here they are!'
I gave to Jerusalem a
messenger of good tidings.
28I look but there is no one—
no one among them to give
counsel,
no one to give answer when I
ask them.
29See, they are all false!
Their deeds amount to nothing;
their images are but wind and
confusion.

The Servant of the LORD

42 "Here is my servant, whom I uphold,
my chosen one in whom I delight;
I will put my Spirit on him
and he will bring justice to the nations.
²He will not shout or cry out,
or raise his voice in the streets.
³A bruised reed he will not break,
and a smoldering wick he will not snuff out.
In faithfulness he will bring forth justice;
⁴ he will not falter or be discouraged
till he establishes justice on earth.
In his law the islands will put their hope."

⁵This is what God the LORD says—
he who created the heavens and stretched them out,
who spread out the earth and all that comes out of it,
who gives breath to its people,
and life to those who walk on it:
⁶"I, the LORD, have called you in righteousness;
I will take hold of your hand.
I will keep you and will make you
to be a covenant for the people
and a light for the Gentiles,
⁷to open eyes that are blind,

to free captives from prison
and to release from the dungeon
those who sit in darkness.

⁸"I am the LORD; that is my name!
I will not give my glory to another
or my praise to idols.
⁹See, the former things have taken place,
and new things I declare;
before they spring into being
I announce them to you."

Song of Praise to the LORD

¹⁰Sing to the LORD a new song,
his praise from the ends of the earth,
you who go down to the sea, and all that is in it,
you islands, and all who live in them.
¹¹Let the desert and its towns raise their voices;
let the settlements where Kedar lives rejoice.
Let the people of Sela sing for joy;
let them shout from the mountaintops.
¹²Let them give glory to the LORD
and proclaim his praise in the islands.
¹³The LORD will march out like a mighty man,

▌ET'S LIVE IT!

Isaiah 42:1–4

NO UNIMPORTANT PEOPLE ➠ Read Isaiah 42:1–4. In verse 3, the bruised reed and smoldering wick stand for unimportant people. No one will be unimportant when Jesus, God's servant, comes to make everything right.

You can show people are important as Mike did in this true story.

No one liked Ken. He was overweight and not very nice. When the kids on the playground lined up to play kickball, Ken went on one side—and everyone else in the fourth grade went on the other! Mike thought that wasn't very nice. After a minute, he went over to be on Ken's side. Then some of the other kids followed Mike.

When you are nice to people who aren't very attractive or who aren't always nice, you please God and help to make things right.

like a warrior he will stir up
  his zeal;
with a shout he will raise the
    battle cry
and will triumph over his
    enemies.

14"For a long time I have kept
    silent,
  I have been quiet and held
    myself back.
But now, like a woman in
    childbirth,
  I cry out, I gasp and pant.
15I will lay waste the mountains
    and hills
  and dry up all their vegetation;
  I will turn rivers into islands
  and dry up the pools.
16I will lead the blind by ways they
    have not known,
  along unfamiliar paths I will
    guide them;
  I will turn the darkness into light
    before them
  and make the rough places
    smooth.
These are the things I will do;
  I will not forsake them.
17But those who trust in idols,
  who say to images, 'You are our
    gods,'
  will be turned back in utter
    shame.

Israel Blind and Deaf

18"Hear, you deaf;
  look, you blind, and see!
19Who is blind but my servant,
  and deaf like the messenger I
    send?
Who is blind like the one
    committed to me,
  blind like the servant of the
    LORD?
20You have seen many things, but
    have paid no attention;
  your ears are open, but you
    hear nothing."
21It pleased the LORD
  for the sake of his righteousness
  to make his law great and
    glorious.

22But this is a people plundered
    and looted,
  all of them trapped in pits
  or hidden away in prisons.
They have become plunder,
  with no one to rescue them;
they have been made loot,
  with no one to say, "Send them
    back."

23Which of you will listen to this
  or pay close attention in time to
    come?
24Who handed Jacob over to become
    loot,
  and Israel to the plunderers?
Was it not the LORD,
  against whom we have sinned?
For they would not follow his
    ways;
  they did not obey his law.
25So he poured out on them his
    burning anger,
  the violence of war.
It enveloped them in flames, yet
    they did not understand;
  it consumed them, but they did
    not take it to heart.

Israel's Only Savior

43 But now, this is what the
   LORD says—
he who created you, O Jacob,
  he who formed you, O Israel:
"Fear not, for I have redeemed
    you;
  I have summoned you by name;
    you are mine.
2When you pass through the
    waters,
  I will be with you;
and when you pass through the
    rivers,
  they will not sweep over you.
When you walk through the fire,
  you will not be burned;
  the flames will not set you
    ablaze.
3For I am the LORD, your God,
  the Holy One of Israel, your
    Savior;
I give Egypt for your ransom,
  Cush*a* and Seba in your stead.

a3 That is, the upper Nile region

⁴Since you are precious and
   honored in my sight,
and because I love you,
I will give men in exchange for
   you,
   and people in exchange for your
   life.
⁵Do not be afraid, for I am with
   you;
   I will bring your children from
      the east
   and gather you from the
      west.
⁶I will say to the north, 'Give them
   up!'
   and to the south, 'Do not hold
      them back.'
Bring my sons from afar
   and my daughters from the
      ends of the earth—
⁷everyone who is called by my
   name,
   whom I created for my glory,
   whom I formed and made."

⁸Lead out those who have eyes but
   are blind,
who have ears but are deaf.
⁹All the nations gather together
   and the peoples assemble.
Which of them foretold this
   and proclaimed to us the former
      things?
Let them bring in their witnesses
   to prove they were right,
   so that others may hear and
      say, "It is true."
¹⁰"You are my witnesses," declares
   the LORD,
   "and my servant whom I have
      chosen,
   so that you may know and believe
      me
   and understand that I am he.
Before me no god was formed,
   nor will there be one after
      me.
¹¹I, even I, am the LORD,
   and apart from me there is no
      savior.
¹²I have revealed and saved and
      proclaimed—
   I, and not some foreign god
      among you.

You are my witnesses," declares
   the LORD, "that I am God.
¹³ Yes, and from ancient days I
      am he.
No one can deliver out of my
      hand.
When I act, who can reverse
      it?"

God's Mercy and Israel's Unfaithfulness

¹⁴This is what the LORD says—
   your Redeemer, the Holy One of
      Israel:
"For your sake I will send to
      Babylon
   and bring down as fugitives all
      the Babylonians,ᵃ
   in the ships in which they took
      pride.
¹⁵I am the LORD, your Holy One,
   Israel's Creator, your King."

¹⁶This is what the LORD says—
   he who made a way through the
      sea,
   a path through the mighty
      waters,
¹⁷who drew out the chariots and
      horses,
   the army and reinforcements
      together,
   and they lay there, never to rise
      again,
   extinguished, snuffed out like a
      wick:
¹⁸"Forget the former things;
   do not dwell on the past.
¹⁹See, I am doing a new thing!
   Now it springs up; do you not
      perceive it?
I am making a way in the desert
   and streams in the wasteland.
²⁰The wild animals honor me,
   the jackals and the owls,
because I provide water in the
      desert
   and streams in the wasteland,
to give drink to my people, my
      chosen,
²¹ the people I formed for myself
      that they may proclaim my
      praise.

ᵃ14 Or Chaldeans

²²"Yet you have not called upon
me, O Jacob,
you have not wearied
yourselves for me, O Israel.
²³You have not brought me sheep
for burnt offerings,
nor honored me with your
sacrifices.
I have not burdened you with
grain offerings
nor wearied you with demands
for incense.
²⁴You have not bought any
fragrant calamus for me,
or lavished on me the fat of
your sacrifices.
But you have burdened me with
your sins
and wearied me with your
offenses.

²⁵"I, even I, am he who blots out
your transgressions, for my own
sake,
and remembers your sins no
more.
²⁶Review the past for me,
let us argue the matter
together;
state the case for your
innocence.
²⁷Your first father sinned;
your spokesmen rebelled
against me.
²⁸So I will disgrace the dignitaries
of your temple,
and I will consign Jacob to
destruction[a]
and Israel to scorn.

Israel the Chosen

44 "But now listen, O Jacob,
my servant,
Israel, whom I have chosen.
²This is what the LORD says—
he who made you, who formed
you in the womb,
and who will help you:
Do not be afraid, O Jacob, my
servant,
Jeshurun, whom I have
chosen.

³For I will pour water on the
thirsty land,
and streams on the dry ground;
I will pour out my Spirit on your
offspring,
and my blessing on your
descendants.
⁴They will spring up like grass in
a meadow,
like poplar trees by flowing
streams.
⁵One will say, 'I belong to the
LORD';
another will call himself by the
name of Jacob;
still another will write on his
hand, 'The LORD's,'
and will take the name Israel.

The LORD, Not Idols

⁶"This is what the LORD says—
Israel's King and Redeemer, the
LORD Almighty:
I am the first and I am the last;
apart from me there is no God.
⁷Who then is like me? Let him
proclaim it.
Let him declare and lay out
before me
what has happened since I
established my ancient
people,
and what is yet to come—
yes, let him foretell what will
come.
⁸Do not tremble, do not be afraid.
Did I not proclaim this and
foretell it long ago?
You are my witnesses. Is there
any God besides me?
No, there is no other Rock; I
know not one."

⁹All who make idols are nothing,
and the things they treasure
are worthless.
Those who would speak up for
them are blind;
they are ignorant, to their own
shame.
¹⁰Who shapes a god and casts an
idol,

---

*a28 The Hebrew term refers to the irrevocable giving over of things or persons to the LORD, often by
totally destroying them.*

which can profit him nothing?
11He and his kind will be put to
　　shame;
　　craftsmen are nothing but men.
Let them all come together and
　　take their stand;
　　they will be brought down to
　　terror and infamy.

12The blacksmith takes a tool
　　and works with it in the coals;
he shapes an idol with hammers,
　　he forges it with the might of
　　his arm.
He gets hungry and loses his
　　strength;
　　he drinks no water and grows
　　faint.
13The carpenter measures with a
　　line
　　and makes an outline with a
　　marker;
he roughs it out with chisels
　　and marks it with compasses.
He shapes it in the form of man,
　　of man in all his glory,
　　that it may dwell in a shrine.
14He cut down cedars,
　　or perhaps took a cypress or
　　oak.
He let it grow among the trees of
　　the forest,
　　or planted a pine, and the rain
　　made it grow.
15It is man's fuel for burning;
　　some of it he takes and warms
　　himself,
　　he kindles a fire and bakes
　　bread.
But he also fashions a god and
　　worships it;
　　he makes an idol and bows
　　down to it.
16Half of the wood he burns in the
　　fire;
　　over it he prepares his meal,
　　he roasts his meat and eats his
　　fill.
He also warms himself and says,
　　"Ah! I am warm; I see the fire."
17From the rest he makes a god, his
　　idol;
　　he bows down to it and
　　worships.
He prays to it and says,

"Save me; you are my god."
18They know nothing, they
　　understand nothing;
　　their eyes are plastered over so
　　they cannot see,
　　and their minds closed so they
　　cannot understand.
19No one stops to think,
　　no one has the knowledge or
　　understanding to say,
"Half of it I used for fuel;
　　I even baked bread over its
　　coals,
　　I roasted meat and I ate.
Shall I make a detestable thing
　　from what is left?
Shall I bow down to a block of
　　wood?"
20He feeds on ashes, a deluded
　　heart misleads him;
　　he cannot save himself, or say,
"Is not this thing in my right
　　hand a lie?"

?DID YOU KNOW? 44:16–17

What are idols? How did people make idols?

Idols were figures, like dolls, that pagan people worshiped as if they were gods. Idols were made of metal or carved from wood. This chapter of Isaiah told the people how foolish they were to think that idols they had made could help them.

21"Remember these things, O Jacob,
　　for you are my servant,
　　　　O Israel.
I have made you, you are my
　　servant;
　　O Israel, I will not forget you.
22I have swept away your offenses
　　like a cloud,
　　your sins like the morning mist.
Return to me,
　　for I have redeemed you."

23Sing for joy, O heavens, for the
　　LORD has done this;
　　shout aloud, O earth beneath.
Burst into song, you mountains,

you forests and all your trees,
for the LORD has redeemed Jacob,
   he displays his glory in Israel.

Jerusalem to Be Inhabited

24"This is what the LORD says—
   your Redeemer, who formed you
    in the womb:

I am the LORD,
who has made all things,
who alone stretched out the
   heavens,
who spread out the earth by
   myself,
25who foils the signs of false
   prophets
   and makes fools of diviners,
who overthrows the learning of
   the wise
   and turns it into nonsense,
26who carries out the words of his
   servants
   and fulfills the predictions of
   his messengers,

who says of Jerusalem, 'It shall
   be inhabited,'
of the towns of Judah, 'They
   shall be built,'
   and of their ruins, 'I will restore
   them,'
27who says to the watery deep, 'Be
   dry,
   and I will dry up your streams,'
28who says of Cyrus, 'He is my
   shepherd
   and will accomplish all that I
   please;
he will say of Jerusalem, "Let it
   be rebuilt,"
   and of the temple, "Let its
   foundations be laid."'

45 "This is what the LORD says
   to his anointed,
   to Cyrus, whose right hand I
   take hold of
to subdue nations before him
   and to strip kings of their
   armor,
to open doors before him
   so that gates will not be shut:

2I will go before you
   and will level the mountainsᵃ;
I will break down gates of bronze
   and cut through bars of iron.
3I will give you the treasures of
   darkness,
   riches stored in secret places,
so that you may know that I am
   the LORD,
   the God of Israel, who summons
   you by name.
4For the sake of Jacob my servant,
   of Israel my chosen,
I summon you by name
   and bestow on you a title of
   honor,
   though you do not acknowledge
   me.
5I am the LORD, and there is no
   other;
   apart from me there is no God.
I will strengthen you,
   though you have not
   acknowledged me,
6so that from the rising of the sun
   to the place of its setting
men may know there is none
   besides me.
I am the LORD, and there is no
   other.
7I form the light and create
   darkness,
   I bring prosperity and create
   disaster;
I, the LORD, do all these things.

8"You heavens above, rain down
   righteousness;
   let the clouds shower it down.
Let the earth open wide,
   let salvation spring up,
let righteousness grow with it;
   I, the LORD, have created it.

9"Woe to him who quarrels with
   his Maker,
   to him who is but a potsherd
   among the potsherds on the
   ground.
Does the clay say to the potter,
   'What are you making?'
Does your work say,
   'He has no hands'?

ᵃ2 Dead Sea Scrolls and Septuagint; the meaning of the word in the Masoretic Text is uncertain.

¹⁰Woe to him who says to his
    father,
    'What have you begotten?'
or to his mother,
    'What have you brought to
        birth?'

¹¹"This is what the LORD says—
    the Holy One of Israel, and its
        Maker:
Concerning things to come,
    do you question me about my
        children,
    or give me orders about the
        work of my hands?
¹²It is I who made the earth
    and created mankind upon it.
My own hands stretched out the
        heavens;
    I marshaled their starry hosts.
¹³I will raise up Cyrus*a* in my
        righteousness:
    I will make all his ways
        straight.
He will rebuild my city
    and set my exiles free,
but not for a price or reward,
    says the LORD Almighty."

¹⁴This is what the LORD says:

"The products of Egypt and the
        merchandise of Cush, *b*
    and those tall Sabeans—
they will come over to you
    and will be yours;
they will trudge behind you,
    coming over to you in chains.
They will bow down before you
    and plead with you, saying,
'Surely God is with you, and there
        is no other;
    there is no other god.' "

¹⁵Truly you are a God who hides
        himself,
    O God and Savior of Israel.
¹⁶All the makers of idols will be
        put to shame and disgraced;
    they will go off into disgrace
        together.
¹⁷But Israel will be saved by the
        LORD
    with an everlasting salvation;

you will never be put to shame or
        disgraced,
    to ages everlasting.

¹⁸For this is what the LORD says—
    he who created the heavens,
        he is God;
    he who fashioned and made the
        earth,
        he founded it;
    he did not create it to be empty,
        but formed it to be inhabited—
    he says:
    "I am the LORD,
        and there is no other.
¹⁹I have not spoken in secret,
    from somewhere in a land of
        darkness;
    I have not said to Jacob's
        descendants,
    'Seek me in vain.'
I, the LORD, speak the truth;
    I declare what is right.

²⁰"Gather together and come;
    assemble, you fugitives from the
        nations.
Ignorant are those who carry
        about idols of wood,
    who pray to gods that cannot
        save.
²¹Declare what is to be, present
        it—
    let them take counsel together.
Who foretold this long ago,
    who declared it from the distant
        past?
Was it not I, the LORD?
    And there is no God apart from
        me,
    a righteous God and a Savior;
        there is none but me.

²²"Turn to me and be saved,
    all you ends of the earth;
    for I am God, and there is no
        other.
²³By myself I have sworn,
    my mouth has uttered in all
        integrity
    a word that will not be revoked:
Before me every knee will bow;
    by me every tongue will swear.

---

a13 Hebrew *him*   *b14* That is, the upper Nile region

24They will say of me, 'In the LORD
 alone
 are righteousness and
 strength.' "
All who have raged against him
 will come to him and be put to
 shame.
25But in the LORD all the
 descendants of Israel
 will be found righteous and will
 exult.

Gods of Babylon

46 Bel bows down, Nebo stoops
 low;
 their idols are borne by beasts
 of burden.a
The images that are carried about
 are burdensome,
 a burden for the weary.
2They stoop and bow down
 together;
 unable to rescue the burden,
 they themselves go off into
 captivity.

3"Listen to me, O house of Jacob,
 all you who remain of the house
 of Israel,
 you whom I have upheld since
 you were conceived,
 and have carried since your
 birth.
4Even to your old age and gray
 hairs
 I am he, I am he who will
 sustain you.
I have made you and I will carry
 you;
 I will sustain you and I will
 rescue you.

5"To whom will you compare me or
 count me equal?
 To whom will you liken me that
 we may be compared?
6Some pour out gold from their
 bags
 and weigh out silver on the
 scales;
 they hire a goldsmith to make it
 into a god,

and they bow down and worship
 it.
7They lift it to their shoulders and
 carry it;
 they set it up in its place, and
 there it stands.
From that spot it cannot move.
Though one cries out to it, it does
 not answer;
 it cannot save him from his
 troubles.

8"Remember this, fix it in mind,
 take it to heart, you rebels.
9Remember the former things,
 those of long ago;
 I am God, and there is no other;
 I am God, and there is none
 like me.
10I make known the end from the
 beginning,
 from ancient times, what is still
 to come.
I say: My purpose will stand,
 and I will do all that I please.
11From the east I summon a bird of
 prey;
 from a far-off land, a man to
 fulfill my purpose.
What I have said, that will I
 bring about;
 what I have planned, that will I
 do.
12Listen to me, you
 stubborn-hearted,
 you who are far from
 righteousness.
13I am bringing my righteousness
 near,
 it is not far away;
 and my salvation will not be
 delayed.
I will grant salvation to Zion,
 my splendor to Israel.

The Fall of Babylon

47 "Go down, sit in the dust,
 Virgin Daughter of Babylon;
sit on the ground without a
 throne,
 Daughter of the Babylonians.b
No more will you be called
 tender or delicate.

a1 Or are but beasts and cattle   b1 Or Chaldeans; also in verse 5

²Take millstones and grind flour;
  take off your veil.
Lift up your skirts, bare your
    legs,
  and wade through the streams.
³Your nakedness will be exposed
  and your shame uncovered.
I will take vengeance;
  I will spare no one."

⁴Our Redeemer—the LORD
      Almighty is his name—
  is the Holy One of Israel.

⁵"Sit in silence, go into darkness,
    Daughter of the Babylonians;
no more will you be called
  queen of kingdoms.
⁶I was angry with my people
  and desecrated my inheritance;
I gave them into your hand,
  and you showed them no mercy.
Even on the aged
  you laid a very heavy yoke.
⁷You said, 'I will continue
    forever—
  the eternal queen!'
But you did not consider these
    things
  or reflect on what might
    happen.

⁸"Now then, listen, you wanton
    creature,
  lounging in your security
and saying to yourself,

'I am, and there is none besides
    me.
I will never be a widow
  or suffer the loss of children.'
⁹Both of these will overtake you
  in a moment, on a single day:
  loss of children and widowhood.
They will come upon you in full
    measure,
  in spite of your many sorceries
  and all your potent spells.
¹⁰You have trusted in your
    wickedness
  and have said, 'No one sees me.'
Your wisdom and knowledge
    mislead you
  when you say to yourself,
  'I am, and there is none besides
    me.'
¹¹Disaster will come upon you,
  and you will not know how to
    conjure it away.
A calamity will fall upon you
  that you cannot ward off with a
    ransom;
a catastrophe you cannot foresee
  will suddenly come upon you.

¹²"Keep on, then, with your magic
    spells
  and with your many sorceries,
  which you have labored at since
    childhood.
Perhaps you will succeed,
  perhaps you will cause terror.

Life in Bible Times

WORKING MAGIC

Pagan peoples often tried to get what they wanted by casting magic spells. They used magic to harm enemies, to gain riches, or to heal sickness. Some spells used things like the skin of toads or feathers along with magic words. But magic is in the end unsuccessful. God is the one who is in control.

¹³All the counsel you have received
     has only worn you out!
  Let your astrologers come
     forward,
  those stargazers who make
     predictions month by
     month,
  let them save you from what is
     coming upon you.
¹⁴Surely they are like stubble;
  the fire will burn them up.
  They cannot even save themselves
     from the power of the flame.
  Here are no coals to warm
     anyone;
  here is no fire to sit by.
¹⁵That is all they can do for you—
     these you have labored with
  and trafficked with since
     childhood.
  Each of them goes on in his error;
     there is not one that can save
     you.

Stubborn Israel

48 "Listen to this, O house of
        Jacob,
  you who are called by the name
     of Israel
  and come from the line of
     Judah,
  you who take oaths in the name
     of the LORD
  and invoke the God of Israel—
     but not in truth or
     righteousness—
²you who call yourselves citizens of
     the holy city
  and rely on the God of Israel—

  the LORD Almighty is his name:
³I foretold the former things long
     ago,
  my mouth announced them and
     I made them known;
  then suddenly I acted, and they
     came to pass.
⁴For I knew how stubborn you
     were;
  the sinews of your neck were
     iron,
  your forehead was bronze.
⁵Therefore I told you these things
     long ago;
  before they happened I
     announced them to you
  so that you could not say,
  'My idols did them;
  my wooden image and metal
     god ordained them.'
⁶You have heard these things; look
     at them all.
  Will you not admit them?

"From now on I will tell you of
     new things,
  of hidden things unknown to
     you.
⁷They are created now, and not
     long ago;
  you have not heard of them
     before today.
  So you cannot say,
  'Yes, I knew of them.'
⁸You have neither heard nor
     understood;
  from of old your ear has not
     been open.
  Well do I know how treacherous
     you are;

▌ET'S LIVE IT!   Isaiah 47:12–15

DON'T TRUST ASTROLOGERS ➡ People in Babylon wanted supernatural
help. They tried magic spells, and they asked astrologers to tell them
what to do. Astrologers are people who think the stars control our future.
Read Isaiah 47:12–15. Could magic or astrology help the Babylonians
avoid God's judgment? Also read Daniel 2:1–11. Could the astrologers
help King Nebuchadnezzar? Most newspapers have an astrology column to give advice to people. If your paper has an astrology column,
write a letter to the editor and tell him what you think about astrology.
When you need help to make a decision, pray to God for help, and
talk to an adult Christian you can trust.

you were called a rebel from
birth.
⁹For my own name's sake I delay
my wrath;
for the sake of my praise I hold
it back from you,
so as not to cut you off.
¹⁰See, I have refined you, though
not as silver;
I have tested you in the furnace
of affliction.
¹¹For my own sake, for my own
sake, I do this.
How can I let myself be
defamed?
I will not yield my glory to
another.

Israel Freed

¹²"Listen to me, O Jacob,
Israel, whom I have called:
I am he;
I am the first and I am the last.
¹³My own hand laid the
foundations of the earth,
and my right hand spread out
the heavens;
when I summon them,
they all stand up together.

¹⁴"Come together, all of you, and
listen:
Which of ˍthe idolsˍ has foretold
these things?
The LORD's chosen ally
will carry out his purpose
against Babylon;
his arm will be against the
Babylonians.ᵃ
¹⁵I, even I, have spoken;
yes, I have called him.
I will bring him,
and he will succeed in his
mission.

¹⁶"Come near me and listen to this:

"From the first announcement I
have not spoken in secret;
at the time it happens, I am
there."

And now the Sovereign LORD has
sent me,

with his Spirit.
¹⁷This is what the LORD says—
your Redeemer, the Holy One of
Israel:
"I am the LORD your God,
who teaches you what is best
for you,
who directs you in the way you
should go.
¹⁸If only you had paid attention to
my commands,
your peace would have been
like a river,
your righteousness like the
waves of the sea.
¹⁹Your descendants would have
been like the sand,
your children like its
numberless grains;
their name would never be cut off
nor destroyed from before me."

²⁰Leave Babylon,
flee from the Babylonians!
Announce this with shouts of joy
and proclaim it.
Send it out to the ends of the
earth;
say, "The LORD has redeemed
his servant Jacob."
²¹They did not thirst when he led
them through the deserts;
he made water flow for them
from the rock;
he split the rock
and water gushed out.

²²"There is no peace," says the
LORD, "for the wicked."

The Servant of the LORD

49 Listen to me, you islands;
hear this, you distant
nations:
Before I was born the LORD called
me;
from my birth he has made
mention of my name.
²He made my mouth like a
sharpened sword,
in the shadow of his hand he
hid me;
he made me into a polished arrow

ᵃ14 Or *Chaldeans*; also in verse 20

and concealed me in his quiver.
³He said to me, "You are my
servant,
Israel, in whom I will display
my splendor."
⁴But I said, "I have labored to no
purpose;
I have spent my strength in
vain and for nothing.
Yet what is due me is in the
LORD's hand,
and my reward is with my
God."

⁵And now the LORD says—
he who formed me in the womb
to be his servant
to bring Jacob back to him
and gather Israel to himself,
for I am honored in the eyes of
the LORD
and my God has been my
strength—
⁶he says:
"It is too small a thing for you to
be my servant
to restore the tribes of Jacob
and bring back those of Israel I
have kept.
I will also make you a light for
the Gentiles,
that you may bring my
salvation to the ends of the
earth."

⁷This is what the LORD says—
the Redeemer and Holy One of
Israel—
to him who was despised and
abhorred by the nation,
to the servant of rulers:
"Kings will see you and rise up,
princes will see and bow down,
because of the LORD, who is
faithful,
the Holy One of Israel, who has
chosen you."

Restoration of Israel

⁸This is what the LORD says:

"In the time of my favor I will
answer you,
and in the day of salvation I
will help you;
I will keep you and will make you
to be a covenant for the people,
to restore the land
and to reassign its desolate
inheritances,
⁹to say to the captives, 'Come out,'
and to those in darkness, 'Be
free!'

"They will feed beside the roads
and find pasture on every
barren hill.
¹⁰They will neither hunger nor
thirst,
nor will the desert heat or the
sun beat upon them.
He who has compassion on them
will guide them
and lead them beside springs of
water.
¹¹I will turn all my mountains into
roads,
and my highways will be raised
up.
¹²See, they will come from afar—
some from the north, some from
the west,
some from the region of
Aswan.ᵃ"

¹³Shout for joy, O heavens;
rejoice, O earth;
burst into song, O mountains!
For the LORD comforts his people
and will have compassion on his
afflicted ones.

¹⁴But Zion said, "The LORD has
forsaken me,
the Lord has forgotten me."

¹⁵"Can a mother forget the baby at
her breast
and have no compassion on the
child she has borne?
Though she may forget,
I will not forget you!
¹⁶See, I have engraved you on the
palms of my hands;
your walls are ever before me.
¹⁷Your sons hasten back,
and those who laid you waste
depart from you.

ᵃ12 Dead Sea Scrolls; Masoretic Text *Sinim*

¹⁸Lift up your eyes and look
　　around;
　all your sons gather and come
　　to you.
As surely as I live," declares the
　LORD,
　"you will wear them all as
　　ornaments;
　you will put them on, like a
　　bride.

¹⁹"Though you were ruined and
　　made desolate
　and your land laid waste,
　now you will be too small for your
　　people,
　and those who devoured you
　　will be far away.
²⁰The children born during your
　　bereavement
　will yet say in your hearing,
　'This place is too small for us;
　give us more space to live in.'
²¹Then you will say in your heart,
　'Who bore me these?
　I was bereaved and barren;
　　I was exiled and rejected.
　Who brought these up?
　I was left all alone,
　　but these—where have they
　　　come from?' "

²²This is what the Sovereign LORD
says:

　"See, I will beckon to the
　　Gentiles,
　I will lift up my banner to the
　　peoples;
　they will bring your sons in their
　　arms
　　and carry your daughters on
　　　their shoulders.
²³Kings will be your foster fathers,
　　and their queens your nursing
　　　mothers.
　They will bow down before you
　　with their faces to the
　　　ground;
　　they will lick the dust at your
　　　feet.
　Then you will know that I am the
　　LORD;

　those who hope in me will not
　　be disappointed."

²⁴Can plunder be taken from
　　warriors,
　or captives rescued from the
　　fierce[a]?

²⁵But this is what the LORD says:

　"Yes, captives will be taken from
　　warriors,
　and plunder retrieved from the
　　fierce;
　I will contend with those who
　　contend with you,
　and your children I will save.
²⁶I will make your oppressors eat
　　their own flesh;
　they will be drunk on their own
　　blood, as with wine.
　Then all mankind will know
　　that I, the LORD, am your
　　　Savior,
　your Redeemer, the Mighty One
　　of Jacob."

Israel's Sin and the Servant's Obedience

50 This is what the LORD says:

　"Where is your mother's
　　certificate of divorce
　with which I sent her away?
　Or to which of my creditors
　　did I sell you?
　Because of your sins you were
　　sold;
　because of your transgressions
　　your mother was sent away.
²When I came, why was there no
　　one?
　When I called, why was there
　　no one to answer?
　Was my arm too short to ransom
　　you?
　Do I lack the strength to rescue
　　you?
　By a mere rebuke I dry up the
　　sea,
　I turn rivers into a desert;
　their fish rot for lack of water
　　and die of thirst.
³I clothe the sky with darkness

---

a24 Dead Sea Scrolls, Vulgate and Syriac (see also Septuagint and verse 25); Masoretic Text
righteous

and make sackcloth its
　covering."

4The Sovereign LORD has given me
　　an instructed tongue,
　to know the word that sustains
　　the weary.
He wakens me morning by
　　morning,
　wakens my ear to listen like
　　one being taught.
5The Sovereign LORD has opened
　　my ears,
　and I have not been rebellious;
　I have not drawn back.
6I offered my back to those who
　　beat me,
　my cheeks to those who pulled
　　out my beard;
I did not hide my face
　from mocking and spitting.
7Because the Sovereign LORD helps
　　me,
　I will not be disgraced.
Therefore have I set my face like
　　flint,
　and I know I will not be put to
　　shame.
8He who vindicates me is near.
　Who then will bring charges
　　against me?
　Let us face each other!
Who is my accuser?
　Let him confront me!
9It is the Sovereign LORD who
　　helps me.
　Who is he that will condemn
　　me?
They will all wear out like a
　　garment;
　the moths will eat them up.

10Who among you fears the LORD
　　and obeys the word of his
　　servant?
Let him who walks in the dark,
　who has no light,
trust in the name of the LORD
　and rely on his God.
11But now, all you who light fires
　and provide yourselves with
　　flaming torches,
go, walk in the light of your fires
　and of the torches you have set
　　ablaze.

This is what you shall receive
　from my hand:
You will lie down in torment.

Everlasting Salvation for Zion

51 "Listen to me, you who
　　pursue righteousness
　and who seek the LORD:
Look to the rock from which you
　　were cut
　and to the quarry from which
　　you were hewn;
2look to Abraham, your father,
　and to Sarah, who gave you
　　birth.
When I called him he was but
　　one,
　and I blessed him and made
　　him many.
3The LORD will surely comfort Zion
　and will look with compassion
　　on all her ruins;
he will make her deserts like
　　Eden,
　her wastelands like the garden
　　of the LORD.
Joy and gladness will be found in
　　her,
　thanksgiving and the sound of
　　singing.

4"Listen to me, my people;
　hear me, my nation:
The law will go out from me;
　my justice will become a light
　　to the nations.
5My righteousness draws near
　　speedily,
　my salvation is on the way,
　and my arm will bring justice
　　to the nations.
The islands will look to me
　and wait in hope for my arm.
6Lift up your eyes to the heavens,
　look at the earth beneath;
the heavens will vanish like
　　smoke,
　the earth will wear out like a
　　garment
　and its inhabitants die like
　　flies.
But my salvation will last forever,
　my righteousness will never
　　fail.

7"Hear me, you who know what is
    right,
  you people who have my law in
    your hearts:
Do not fear the reproach of men
  or be terrified by their insults.
8For the moth will eat them up
    like a garment;
  the worm will devour them like
    wool.
But my righteousness will last
    forever,
  my salvation through all
    generations."

9Awake, awake! Clothe yourself
    with strength,
  O arm of the LORD;
awake, as in days gone by,
  as in generations of old.
Was it not you who cut Rahab to
    pieces,
  who pierced that monster
    through?
10Was it not you who dried up the
    sea,
  the waters of the great deep,
who made a road in the depths of
    the sea
  so that the redeemed might
    cross over?
11The ransomed of the LORD will
    return.
  They will enter Zion with
    singing;
  everlasting joy will crown their
    heads.
Gladness and joy will overtake
    them,
  and sorrow and sighing will flee
    away.

12"I, even I, am he who comforts
    you.
  Who are you that you fear
    mortal men,
  the sons of men, who are but
    grass,
13that you forget the LORD your
    Maker,
  who stretched out the heavens
  and laid the foundations of the
    earth,

that you live in constant terror
    every day
  because of the wrath of the
    oppressor,
  who is bent on destruction?
For where is the wrath of the
    oppressor?
14 The cowering prisoners will
    soon be set free;
  they will not die in their
    dungeon,
  nor will they lack bread.
15For I am the LORD your God,
  who churns up the sea so that
    its waves roar—
  the LORD Almighty is his name.
16I have put my words in your
    mouth
  and covered you with the
    shadow of my hand—
I who set the heavens in place,
  who laid the foundations of the
    earth,
  and who say to Zion, 'You are
    my people.' "

The Cup of the LORD's Wrath

17Awake, awake!
  Rise up, O Jerusalem,
  you who have drunk from the
    hand of the LORD
  the cup of his wrath,
  you who have drained to its dregs
    the goblet that makes men
    stagger.
18Of all the sons she bore
  there was none to guide her;
  of all the sons she reared
  there was none to take her by
    the hand.
19These double calamities have
    come upon you—
  who can comfort you?—
  ruin and destruction, famine and
    sword—
  who cana console you?
20Your sons have fainted;
  they lie at the head of every
    street,
  like antelope caught in a net.
They are filled with the wrath of
    the LORD

a19 Dead Sea Scrolls, Septuagint, Vulgate and Syriac; Masoretic Text / how can I

and the rebuke of your God.

21Therefore hear this, you afflicted
      one,
   made drunk, but not with wine.
22This is what your Sovereign LORD
      says,
   your God, who defends his
      people:
"See, I have taken out of your
      hand
   the cup that made you stagger;
from that cup, the goblet of my
      wrath,
   you will never drink again.
23I will put it into the hands of
      your tormentors,
   who said to you,
   'Fall prostrate that we may
      walk over you.'
And you made your back like the
      ground,
   like a street to be walked over."

52 Awake, awake, O Zion,
      clothe yourself with
      strength.
Put on your garments of splendor,
   O Jerusalem, the holy city.
The uncircumcised and defiled
   will not enter you again.
2Shake off your dust;
   rise up, sit enthroned,
      O Jerusalem.
Free yourself from the chains on
      your neck,
   O captive Daughter of Zion.

3For this is what the LORD says:

"You were sold for nothing,
   and without money you will be
      redeemed."

4For this is what the Sovereign
LORD says:

"At first my people went down to
      Egypt to live;
   lately, Assyria has oppressed
      them.

5"And now what do I have here?"
declares the LORD.

"For my people have been taken
      away for nothing,
   and those who rule them
      mock, a"
                    declares the LORD.
"And all day long
   my name is constantly
      blasphemed.
6Therefore my people will know
      my name;
   therefore in that day they will
      know
that it is I who foretold it.
   Yes, it is I."

7How beautiful on the mountains
   are the feet of those who bring
      good news,
who proclaim peace,
   who bring good tidings,
   who proclaim salvation,
who say to Zion,
   "Your God reigns!"
8Listen! Your watchmen lift up
      their voices;
   together they shout for joy.
When the LORD returns to Zion,
   they will see it with their own
      eyes.
9Burst into songs of joy together,
   you ruins of Jerusalem,
for the LORD has comforted his
      people,
   he has redeemed Jerusalem.
10The LORD will lay bare his holy
      arm
   in the sight of all the nations,
and all the ends of the earth will
      see
   the salvation of our God.

11Depart, depart, go out from there!
   Touch no unclean thing!
Come out from it and be pure,
   you who carry the vessels of the
      LORD.
12But you will not leave in haste
   or go in flight;
for the LORD will go before you,
   the God of Israel will be your
      rear guard.

a5 Dead Sea Scrolls and Vulgate; Masoretic Text *wail*

The Suffering and Glory of the Servant

¹³See, my servant will act wisely*a*;
   he will be raised and lifted up
   and highly exalted.
¹⁴Just as there were many who
      were appalled at him *b*—
   his appearance was so
     disfigured beyond that of
     any man
   and his form marred beyond
     human likeness—
¹⁵so will he sprinkle many
     nations,*c*
   and kings will shut their
     mouths because of him.
For what they were not told, they
     will see,
   and what they have not heard,
     they will understand.

53 Who has believed our
     message
   and to whom has the arm of the
     LORD been revealed?
²He grew up before him like a
     tender shoot,
   and like a root out of dry
     ground.
He had no beauty or majesty to
     attract us to him,
   nothing in his appearance that
     we should desire him.
³He was despised and rejected by
     men,
   a man of sorrows, and familiar
     with suffering.
Like one from whom men hide
     their faces
   he was despised, and we
     esteemed him not.

⁴Surely he took up our infirmities
   and carried our sorrows,
   yet we considered him stricken by
     God,
   smitten by him, and afflicted.
⁵But he was pierced for our
     transgressions,

he was crushed for our
     iniquities;
the punishment that brought us
     peace was upon him,
   and by his wounds we are
     healed.
⁶We all, like sheep, have gone
     astray,
   each of us has turned to his
     own way;
   and the LORD has laid on him
     the iniquity of us all.

⁷He was oppressed and afflicted,
   yet he did not open his mouth;
   he was led like a lamb to the
     slaughter,
   and as a sheep before her
     shearers is silent,
   so he did not open his mouth.
⁸By oppression*d* and judgment he
     was taken away.
And who can speak of his
     descendants?
For he was cut off from the land
     of the living;
   for the transgression of my
     people he was stricken.*e*
⁹He was assigned a grave with the
     wicked,
   and with the rich in his death,
   though he had done no violence,
     nor was any deceit in his
     mouth.

¹⁰Yet it was the LORD's will to
     crush him and cause him to
     suffer,
   and though the LORD makes*f*
     his life a guilt offering,
   he will see his offspring and
     prolong his days,
   and the will of the LORD will
     prosper in his hand.
¹¹After the suffering of his soul,
   he will see the light of life,*g*
     and be satisfied*h*;
   by his knowledge*i* my righteous
     servant will justify many,

---

a13 Or *will prosper*   *b14* Hebrew *you*   *c15* Hebrew; Septuagint *so will many nations marvel at him*   *d8* Or *From arrest*   *e8* Or *away. / Yet who of his generation considered / that he was cut off from the land of the living / for the transgression of my people, / to whom the blow was due?*   *f10* Hebrew *though you make*   *g11* Dead Sea Scrolls (see also Septuagint); Masoretic Text does not have *the light of life*.   *h11* Or (with Masoretic Text) *11He will see the result of the suffering of his soul / and be satisfied*   *i11* Or *by knowledge of him*

and he will bear their
        iniquities.
¹²Therefore I will give him a
        portion among the great,^a
    and he will divide the spoils
        with the strong,^b
    because he poured out his life
        unto death,
    and was numbered with the
        transgressors.
    For he bore the sin of many,
        and made intercession for the
        transgressors.

❓ DID YOU KNOW?   53:4

What does Isaiah 53 describe?

This chapter is about Jesus. It describes his death and burial and explains that Jesus died for our sins. Isaiah wrote these words about seven hundred years before Jesus was born! Only God could know ahead of time how Jesus would die. Prophecies like this one prove that the Bible really is the Word of God.

The Future Glory of Zion

54 "Sing, O barren woman,
        you who never bore a child;
    burst into song, shout for joy,
        you who were never in labor;
    because more are the children of
        the desolate woman
    than of her who has a
        husband,"
                        says the LORD.
²"Enlarge the place of your tent,
        stretch your tent curtains wide,
        do not hold back;
    lengthen your cords,
        strengthen your stakes.
³For you will spread out to the
        right and to the left;
    your descendants will dispossess
        nations
    and settle in their desolate
        cities.

⁴"Do not be afraid; you will not
        suffer shame.
    Do not fear disgrace; you will
        not be humiliated.
    You will forget the shame of your
        youth
    and remember no more the
        reproach of your
        widowhood.
⁵For your Maker is your
        husband—
    the LORD Almighty is his
        name—
    the Holy One of Israel is your
        Redeemer;
    he is called the God of all the
        earth.
⁶The LORD will call you back
    as if you were a wife deserted
        and distressed in spirit—
    a wife who married young,
        only to be rejected," says your
        God.
⁷"For a brief moment I abandoned
        you,
    but with deep compassion I will
        bring you back.
⁸In a surge of anger
    I hid my face from you for a
        moment,
    but with everlasting kindness
    I will have compassion on you,"
        says the LORD your Redeemer.

⁹"To me this is like the days of
        Noah,
    when I swore that the waters of
        Noah would never again
        cover the earth.
    So now I have sworn not to be
        angry with you,
    never to rebuke you again.
¹⁰Though the mountains be shaken
        and the hills be removed,
    yet my unfailing love for you will
        not be shaken
    nor my covenant of peace be
        removed,"
    says the LORD, who has
        compassion on you.

¹¹"O afflicted city, lashed by storms
        and not comforted,

_a12 Or *many*   _b12 Or *numerous*

I will build you with stones of
turquoise,[a]
your foundations with
sapphires.[b]
¹²I will make your battlements of
rubies,
your gates of sparkling jewels,
and all your walls of precious
stones.
¹³All your sons will be taught by
the LORD,
and great will be your
children's peace.
¹⁴In righteousness you will be
established:
Tyranny will be far from you;
you will have nothing to
fear.
Terror will be far removed;
it will not come near you.
¹⁵If anyone does attack you, it will
not be my doing;
whoever attacks you will
surrender to you.

¹⁶"See, it is I who created the
blacksmith
who fans the coals into flame
and forges a weapon fit for its
work.
And it is I who have created the
destroyer to work havoc;
¹⁷ no weapon forged against you
will prevail,
and you will refute every
tongue that accuses you.
This is the heritage of the
servants of the LORD,

and this is their vindication
from me,"
declares the LORD.

Invitation to the Thirsty

55 "Come, all you who are
thirsty,
come to the waters;
and you who have no money,
come, buy and eat!
Come, buy wine and milk
without money and without
cost.
²Why spend money on what is not
bread,
and your labor on what does not
satisfy?
Listen, listen to me, and eat what
is good,
and your soul will delight in
the richest of fare.
³Give ear and come to me;
hear me, that your soul may
live.
I will make an everlasting
covenant with you,
my faithful love promised to
David.
⁴See, I have made him a witness to
the peoples,
a leader and commander of the
peoples.
⁵Surely you will summon nations
you know not,
and nations that do not know
you will hasten to you,
because of the LORD your God,

---

a11 The meaning of the Hebrew for this word is uncertain.   *b11* Or *lapis lazuli*

Life in Bible Times

BLACKSMITHS

Blacksmiths heated metal
in a fire until it was red hot.
Then they could use ham-
mers to shape it. Black-
smiths made tools for farming and swords for fighting
wars.

the Holy One of Israel,
for he has endowed you with
    splendor."

6Seek the LORD while he may be
    found;
call on him while he is near.
7Let the wicked forsake his way
and the evil man his thoughts.
Let him turn to the LORD, and he
    will have mercy on him,
and to our God, for he will
    freely pardon.

8"For my thoughts are not your
    thoughts,
neither are your ways my
    ways,"
        declares the LORD.
9"As the heavens are higher than
    the earth,
so are my ways higher than
    your ways
and my thoughts than your
    thoughts.
10As the rain and the snow
come down from heaven,
and do not return to it
without watering the earth
and making it bud and flourish,
so that it yields seed for the
    sower and bread for the
    eater,
11so is my word that goes out from
    my mouth:
It will not return to me empty,
but will accomplish what I
    desire
and achieve the purpose for
    which I sent it.
12You will go out in joy
and be led forth in peace;
the mountains and hills
will burst into song before you,
and all the trees of the field
will clap their hands.
13Instead of the thornbush will
    grow the pine tree,
and instead of briers the myrtle
    will grow.
This will be for the LORD's
    renown,
for an everlasting sign,
which will not be destroyed."

Salvation for Others

56 This is what the LORD says:
    "Maintain justice
and do what is right,
for my salvation is close at hand
and my righteousness will soon
    be revealed.
2Blessed is the man who does this,
the man who holds it fast,
who keeps the Sabbath without
    desecrating it,
and keeps his hand from doing
    any evil."

3Let no foreigner who has bound
    himself to the LORD say,
"The LORD will surely exclude
    me from his people."
And let not any eunuch complain,
"I am only a dry tree."

4For this is what the LORD says:

"To the eunuchs who keep my
    Sabbaths,
who choose what pleases me
and hold fast to my covenant—
5to them I will give within my
    temple and its walls
a memorial and a name
better than sons and daughters;
I will give them an everlasting
    name
that will not be cut off.
6And foreigners who bind
    themselves to the LORD
to serve him,
to love the name of the LORD,
and to worship him,
all who keep the Sabbath without
    desecrating it
and who hold fast to my
    covenant—
7these I will bring to my holy
    mountain
and give them joy in my house
    of prayer.
Their burnt offerings and
    sacrifices
will be accepted on my altar;
for my house will be called
a house of prayer for all
    nations."
8The Sovereign LORD declares—

he who gathers the exiles of
Israel:
"I will gather still others to them
besides those already gathered."

God's Accusation Against the Wicked

⁹Come, all you beasts of the field,
come and devour, all you beasts
of the forest!
¹⁰Israel's watchmen are blind,
they all lack knowledge;
they are all mute dogs,
they cannot bark;
they lie around and dream,
they love to sleep.
¹¹They are dogs with mighty
appetites;
they never have enough.
They are shepherds who lack
understanding;
they all turn to their own way,
each seeks his own gain.
¹²"Come," each one cries, "let me
get wine!
Let us drink our fill of beer!
And tomorrow will be like today,
or even far better."

57 The righteous perish,
and no one ponders it in his
heart;
devout men are taken away,
and no one understands
that the righteous are taken away
to be spared from evil.
²Those who walk uprightly
enter into peace;

they find rest as they lie in
death.

³"But you—come here, you sons of
a sorceress,
you offspring of adulterers and
prostitutes!
⁴Whom are you mocking?
At whom do you sneer
and stick out your tongue?
Are you not a brood of rebels,
the offspring of liars?
⁵You burn with lust among the
oaks
and under every spreading tree;
you sacrifice your children in the
ravines
and under the overhanging
crags.
⁶The idols among the smooth
stones of the ravines are
your portion;
they, they are your lot.
Yes, to them you have poured out
drink offerings
and offered grain offerings.
In the light of these things,
should I relent?
⁷You have made your bed on a
high and lofty hill;
there you went up to offer your
sacrifices.
⁸Behind your doors and your
doorposts
you have put your pagan
symbols.
Forsaking me, you uncovered
your bed,
you climbed into it and opened
it wide;

Life in Bible Times

DOGS

In Bible times people did not
keep dogs as pets. Dogs lived in
the streets and ate the garbage
people threw outside. People
thought dogs were lazy, noisy,
and mean. In Isaiah 56:10–11, the
Lord compares the prophets of
Israel ("watchmen") to dogs.

you made a pact with those whose
  beds you love,
and you looked on their
  nakedness.
9You went to Molech[a] with olive
  oil
and increased your perfumes.
You sent your ambassadors[b] far
  away;
  you descended to the grave[c]
  itself!
10You were wearied by all your
  ways,
  but you would not say, 'It is
  hopeless.'
You found renewal of your
  strength,
  and so you did not faint.

11"Whom have you so dreaded and
  feared
  that you have been false to me,
and have neither remembered me
  nor pondered this in your
  hearts?
Is it not because I have long been
  silent
  that you do not fear me?
12I will expose your righteousness
  and your works,
  and they will not benefit you.
13When you cry out for help,
  let your collection of idols save
  you!
The wind will carry all of them
  off,
  a mere breath will blow them
  away.
But the man who makes me his
  refuge
  will inherit the land
  and possess my holy mountain."

Comfort for the Contrite

14And it will be said:

"Build up, build up, prepare the
  road!
  Remove the obstacles out of the
  way of my people."
15For this is what the high and
  lofty One says—
  he who lives forever, whose
  name is holy:

"I live in a high and holy place,
  but also with him who is
  contrite and lowly in spirit,
to revive the spirit of the lowly
  and to revive the heart of the
  contrite.
16I will not accuse forever,
  nor will I always be angry,
for then the spirit of man would
  grow faint before me—
  the breath of man that I have
  created.
17I was enraged by his sinful greed;
  I punished him, and hid my
  face in anger,
  yet he kept on in his willful
  ways.
18I have seen his ways, but I will
  heal him;
  I will guide him and restore
  comfort to him,
19 creating praise on the lips of
  the mourners in Israel.
Peace, peace, to those far and
  near,"
  says the LORD. "And I will heal
  them."
20But the wicked are like the
  tossing sea,
  which cannot rest,
  whose waves cast up mire and
  mud.
21"There is no peace," says my God,
  "for the wicked."

True Fasting

58 "Shout it aloud, do not hold
  back.
Raise your voice like a trumpet.
Declare to my people their
  rebellion
  and to the house of Jacob their
  sins.
2For day after day they seek me
  out;
  they seem eager to know my
  ways,
as if they were a nation that does
  what is right
  and has not forsaken the
  commands of its God.
They ask me for just decisions

---

and seem eager for God to come
near them.
³'Why have we fasted,' they say,
'and you have not seen it?
Why have we humbled ourselves,
and you have not noticed?'

"Yet on the day of your fasting,
you do as you please
and exploit all your workers.
⁴Your fasting ends in quarreling
and strife,
and in striking each other with
wicked fists.
You cannot fast as you do today
and expect your voice to be
heard on high.
⁵Is this the kind of fast I have
chosen,
only a day for a man to humble
himself?
Is it only for bowing one's head
like a reed
and for lying on sackcloth and
ashes?
Is that what you call a fast,
a day acceptable to the LORD?

⁶"Is not this the kind of fasting I
have chosen:
to loose the chains of injustice
and untie the cords of the yoke,
to set the oppressed free
and break every yoke?
⁷Is it not to share your food with
the hungry
and to provide the poor
wanderer with shelter—
when you see the naked, to clothe
him,
and not to turn away from your
own flesh and blood?
⁸Then your light will break forth
like the dawn,
and your healing will quickly
appear;
then your righteousness^a will go
before you,
and the glory of the LORD will
be your rear guard.
⁹Then you will call, and the LORD
will answer;
you will cry for help, and he
will say: Here am I.

"If you do away with the yoke of
oppression,
with the pointing finger and
malicious talk,
¹⁰and if you spend yourselves in
behalf of the hungry
and satisfy the needs of the
oppressed,
then your light will rise in the
darkness,
and your night will become like
the noonday.
¹¹The LORD will guide you always;
he will satisfy your needs in a
sun-scorched land
and will strengthen your frame.
You will be like a well-watered
garden,
like a spring whose waters
never fail.
¹²Your people will rebuild the
ancient ruins
and will raise up the age-old
foundations;
you will be called Repairer of
Broken Walls,
Restorer of Streets with
Dwellings.

¹³"If you keep your feet from
breaking the Sabbath
and from doing as you please on
my holy day,
if you call the Sabbath a delight
and the LORD's holy day
honorable,
and if you honor it by not going
your own way
and not doing as you please or
speaking idle words,
¹⁴then you will find your joy in the
LORD,
and I will cause you to ride on
the heights of the land
and to feast on the inheritance
of your father Jacob."
The mouth of the LORD
has spoken.

Sin, Confession and Redemption

59 Surely the arm of the LORD
is not too short to save,
nor his ear too dull to hear.

---

^a8 Or *your righteous One*

²But your iniquities have
    separated
  you from your God;
  your sins have hidden his face
    from you,
    so that he will not hear.
³For your hands are stained with
    blood,
  your fingers with guilt.
Your lips have spoken lies,
  and your tongue mutters wicked
    things.
⁴No one calls for justice;
  no one pleads his case with
    integrity.
They rely on empty arguments
    and speak lies;
  they conceive trouble and give
    birth to evil.
⁵They hatch the eggs of vipers
  and spin a spider's web.
Whoever eats their eggs will die,
  and when one is broken, an
    adder is hatched.
⁶Their cobwebs are useless for
    clothing;
  they cannot cover themselves
    with what they make.
Their deeds are evil deeds,
  and acts of violence are in their
    hands.
⁷Their feet rush into sin;
  they are swift to shed innocent
    blood.
Their thoughts are evil thoughts;
  ruin and destruction mark their
    ways.
⁸The way of peace they do not
    know;
  there is no justice in their
    paths.
They have turned them into
    crooked roads;
  no one who walks in them will
    know peace.

⁹So justice is far from us,
  and righteousness does not
    reach us.
We look for light, but all is
    darkness;
  for brightness, but we walk in
    deep shadows.
¹⁰Like the blind we grope along the
    wall,

feeling our way like men
    without eyes.
At midday we stumble as if it
    were twilight;
  among the strong, we are like
    the dead.
¹¹We all growl like bears;
  we moan mournfully like doves.
We look for justice, but find none;
  for deliverance, but it is far
    away.

¹²For our offenses are many in your
    sight,
  and our sins testify against us.
Our offenses are ever with us,
  and we acknowledge our
    iniquities:
¹³rebellion and treachery against
    the LORD,
  turning our backs on our God,
  fomenting oppression and revolt,
  uttering lies our hearts have
    conceived.
¹⁴So justice is driven back,
  and righteousness stands at a
    distance;
  truth has stumbled in the streets,
    honesty cannot enter.
¹⁵Truth is nowhere to be found,
  and whoever shuns evil becomes
    a prey.

The LORD looked and was
    displeased
  that there was no justice.
¹⁶He saw that there was no one,
  he was appalled that there was
    no one to intervene;
  so his own arm worked salvation
    for him,
  and his own righteousness
    sustained him.
¹⁷He put on righteousness as his
    breastplate,
  and the helmet of salvation on
    his head;
  he put on the garments of
    vengeance
  and wrapped himself in zeal as
    in a cloak.
¹⁸According to what they have
    done,
  so will he repay
  wrath to his enemies
  and retribution to his foes;

he will repay the islands their
due.
19From the west, men will fear the
name of the LORD,
and from the rising of the sun,
they will revere his glory.
For he will come like a pent-up
flood
that the breath of the LORD
drives along.ᵃ

20"The Redeemer will come to Zion,
to those in Jacob who repent of
their sins,"
declares the LORD.

21"As for me, this is my covenant
with them," says the LORD. "My Spirit, who is on you, and my words that
I have put in your mouth will not depart from your mouth, or from the
mouths of your children, or from the
mouths of their descendants from
this time on and forever," says the
LORD.

The Glory of Zion

60 "Arise, shine, for your light
has come,
and the glory of the LORD rises
upon you.
2See, darkness covers the earth
and thick darkness is over the
peoples,
but the LORD rises upon you
and his glory appears over
you.
3Nations will come to your light,
and kings to the brightness of
your dawn.

4"Lift up your eyes and look about
you:
All assemble and come to
you;
your sons come from afar,
and your daughters are carried
on the arm.
5Then you will look and be
radiant,
your heart will throb and swell
with joy;

the wealth on the seas will be
brought to you,
to you the riches of the nations
will come.
6Herds of camels will cover your
land,
young camels of Midian and
Ephah.
And all from Sheba will come,
bearing gold and incense
and proclaiming the praise of
the LORD.
7All Kedar's flocks will be
gathered to you,
the rams of Nebaioth will serve
you;
they will be accepted as offerings
on my altar,
and I will adorn my glorious
temple.

8"Who are these that fly along like
clouds,
like doves to their nests?
9Surely the islands look to me;
in the lead are the ships of
Tarshish,ᵇ
bringing your sons from afar,
with their silver and gold,
to the honor of the LORD your
God,
the Holy One of Israel,
for he has endowed you with
splendor.

10"Foreigners will rebuild your
walls,
and their kings will serve you.
Though in anger I struck you,
in favor I will show you
compassion.
11Your gates will always stand
open,
they will never be shut, day or
night,
so that men may bring you the
wealth of the nations—
their kings led in triumphal
procession.
12For the nation or kingdom that
will not serve you will
perish;
it will be utterly ruined.

ᵃ19 Or When the enemy comes in like a flood, / the Spirit of the LORD will put him to flight
ᵇ9 Or the trading ships

13"The glory of Lebanon will come
    to you,
  the pine, the fir and the cypress
      together,
  to adorn the place of my
      sanctuary;
  and I will glorify the place of
      my feet.
14The sons of your oppressors will
    come bowing before you;
  all who despise you will bow
      down at your feet
  and will call you the City of the
      LORD,
  Zion of the Holy One of Israel.

15"Although you have been
    forsaken and hated,
  with no one traveling through,
  I will make you the everlasting
      pride
  and the joy of all generations.
16You will drink the milk of
    nations
  and be nursed at royal breasts.
  Then you will know that I, the
      LORD, am your Savior,
  your Redeemer, the Mighty One
      of Jacob.
17Instead of bronze I will bring you
    gold,
  and silver in place of iron.
  Instead of wood I will bring you
      bronze,
  and iron in place of stones.
  I will make peace your governor
  and righteousness your ruler.
18No longer will violence be heard
    in your land,
  nor ruin or destruction within
      your borders,
  but you will call your walls
      Salvation
  and your gates Praise.
19The sun will no more be your
    light by day,
  nor will the brightness of the
      moon shine on you,
  for the LORD will be your
      everlasting light,
  and your God will be your
      glory.
20Your sun will never set again,

and your moon will wane no
    more;
  the LORD will be your everlasting
      light,
  and your days of sorrow will
      end.
21Then will all your people be
    righteous
  and they will possess the land
      forever.
  They are the shoot I have
      planted,
  the work of my hands,
  for the display of my splendor.
22The least of you will become a
    thousand,
  the smallest a mighty nation.
  I am the LORD;
  in its time I will do this
      swiftly."

The Year of the LORD's Favor

61 The Spirit of the Sovereign
      LORD is on me,
  because the LORD has anointed
      me
  to preach good news to the
      poor.
  He has sent me to bind up the
      brokenhearted,
  to proclaim freedom for the
      captives
  and release from darkness for
      the prisoners,*a*
  2to proclaim the year of the LORD's
      favor
  and the day of vengeance of our
      God,
  to comfort all who mourn,
  3 and provide for those who
        grieve in Zion—
  to bestow on them a crown of
      beauty
  instead of ashes,
  the oil of gladness
      instead of mourning,
  and a garment of praise
      instead of a spirit of despair.
  They will be called oaks of
      righteousness,
  a planting of the LORD
  for the display of his splendor.

a1 Hebrew; Septuagint the blind

⁴They will rebuild the ancient
  ruins
  and restore the places long
    devastated;
  they will renew the ruined cities
    that have been devastated for
    generations.
⁵Aliens will shepherd your flocks;
  foreigners will work your fields
    and vineyards.
⁶And you will be called priests of
    the LORD,
  you will be named ministers of
    our God.
You will feed on the wealth of
    nations,
  and in their riches you will
    boast.

⁷Instead of their shame
  my people will receive a double
    portion,
  and instead of disgrace
    they will rejoice in their
    inheritance;
  and so they will inherit a double
    portion in their land,
  and everlasting joy will be
    theirs.

⁸"For I, the LORD, love justice;
  I hate robbery and iniquity.
In my faithfulness I will reward
    them
  and make an everlasting
    covenant with them.
⁹Their descendants will be known
    among the nations
  and their offspring among the
    peoples.
All who see them will
    acknowledge
  that they are a people the LORD
    has blessed."

¹⁰I delight greatly in the LORD;
  my soul rejoices in my God.
For he has clothed me with
    garments of salvation
  and arrayed me in a robe of
    righteousness,
  as a bridegroom adorns his head
    like a priest,

and as a bride adorns herself
    with her jewels.
¹¹For as the soil makes the sprout
    come up
  and a garden causes seeds to
    grow,
  so the Sovereign LORD will make
    righteousness and praise
  spring up before all nations.

Zion's New Name

62 For Zion's sake I will not
    keep silent,
  for Jerusalem's sake I will not
    remain quiet,
  till her righteousness shines out
    like the dawn,
  her salvation like a blazing
    torch.
²The nations will see your
    righteousness,
  and all kings your glory;
  you will be called by a new name
    that the mouth of the LORD will
    bestow.
³You will be a crown of splendor in
    the LORD's hand,
  a royal diadem in the hand of
    your God.
⁴No longer will they call you
    Deserted,
  or name your land Desolate.
But you will be called
    Hephzibah,ᵃ
  and your land Beulahᵇ;
  for the LORD will take delight in
    you,
  and your land will be married.
⁵As a young man marries a
    maiden,
  so will your sonsᶜ marry you;
  as a bridegroom rejoices over his
    bride,
  so will your God rejoice over
    you.

⁶I have posted watchmen on your
    walls, O Jerusalem;
  they will never be silent day or
    night.
You who call on the LORD,
  give yourselves no rest,

ᵃ4 *Hephzibah* means *my delight is in her.*   ᵇ4 *Beulah* means *married.*   ᶜ5 Or *Builder*

7and give him no rest till he
　　establishes Jerusalem
　and makes her the praise of the
　　earth.

8The LORD has sworn by his right
　　hand
　and by his mighty arm:
"Never again will I give your
　　grain
　　as food for your enemies,
and never again will foreigners
　　drink the new wine
　for which you have toiled;
9but those who harvest it will eat
　　it
　and praise the LORD,
and those who gather the grapes
　　will drink it
　in the courts of my sanctuary."

10Pass through, pass through the
　　gates!
　Prepare the way for the people.
Build up, build up the highway!
　Remove the stones.
Raise a banner for the nations.

11The LORD has made proclamation
　　to the ends of the earth:
"Say to the Daughter of Zion,
　'See, your Savior comes!
See, his reward is with him,
　and his recompense
　　accompanies him.'"
12They will be called the Holy
　　People,
　the Redeemed of the LORD;
and you will be called Sought
　　After,
　the City No Longer Deserted.

God's Day of Vengeance and Redemption

63 Who is this coming from
　　Edom,
　from Bozrah, with his garments
　　stained crimson?
Who is this, robed in splendor,
　striding forward in the
　　greatness of his strength?

"It is I, speaking in righteousness,
　mighty to save."

2Why are your garments red,
like those of one treading the
　　winepress?

3"I have trodden the winepress
　　alone;
　from the nations no one was
　　with me.
I trampled them in my anger
　and trod them down in my
　　wrath;
their blood spattered my
　　garments,
　and I stained all my clothing.
4For the day of vengeance was in
　　my heart,
　and the year of my redemption
　　has come.
5I looked, but there was no one to
　　help,
　I was appalled that no one gave
　　support;
so my own arm worked salvation
　　for me,
　and my own wrath sustained
　　me.
6I trampled the nations in my
　　anger;
　in my wrath I made them
　　drunk
　and poured their blood on the
　　ground."

Praise and Prayer

7I will tell of the kindnesses of the
　　LORD,
　the deeds for which he is to be
　　praised,
　according to all the LORD has
　　done for us—
yes, the many good things he has
　　done
　for the house of Israel,
　according to his compassion and
　　many kindnesses.
8He said, "Surely they are my
　　people,
　sons who will not be false to
　　me";
　and so he became their Savior.
9In all their distress he too was
　　distressed,
　and the angel of his presence
　　saved them.
In his love and mercy he
　　redeemed them;

he lifted them up and carried
them
all the days of old.
¹⁰Yet they rebelled
and grieved his Holy Spirit.
So he turned and became their
enemy
and he himself fought against
them.

¹¹Then his people recalled*ᵃ* the
days of old,
the days of Moses and his
people—
where is he who brought them
through the sea,
with the shepherd of his flock?
Where is he who set
his Holy Spirit among them,
¹²who sent his glorious arm of
power
to be at Moses' right hand,
who divided the waters before
them,
to gain for himself everlasting
renown,
¹³who led them through the depths?
Like a horse in open country,
they did not stumble;
¹⁴like cattle that go down to the
plain,
they were given rest by the
Spirit of the LORD.
This is how you guided your
people
to make for yourself a glorious
name.

¹⁵Look down from heaven and see
from your lofty throne, holy and
glorious.
Where are your zeal and your
might?
Your tenderness and
compassion are withheld
from us.
¹⁶But you are our Father,
though Abraham does not know
us
or Israel acknowledge us;
you, O LORD, are our Father,
our Redeemer from of old is
your name.

¹⁷Why, O LORD, do you make us
wander from your ways
and harden our hearts so we do
not revere you?
Return for the sake of your
servants,
the tribes that are your
inheritance.
¹⁸For a little while your people
possessed your holy place,
but now our enemies have
trampled down your
sanctuary.
¹⁹We are yours from of old;
but you have not ruled over
them,
they have not been called by
your name.*ᵇ*

64 Oh, that you would rend the
heavens and come down,
that the mountains would
tremble before you!
²As when fire sets twigs ablaze
and causes water to boil,
come down to make your name
known to your enemies
and cause the nations to quake
before you!
³For when you did awesome things
that we did not expect,
you came down, and the
mountains trembled before
you.
⁴Since ancient times no one has
heard,
no ear has perceived,
no eye has seen any God besides
you,
who acts on behalf of those who
wait for him.
⁵You come to the help of those who
gladly do right,
who remember your ways.
But when we continued to sin
against them,
you were angry.
How then can we be saved?
⁶All of us have become like one
who is unclean,
and all our righteous acts are
like filthy rags;

ᵃ11 Or But may he recall   *ᵇ19 Or We are like those you have never ruled, / like those never called
by your name*

we all shrivel up like a leaf,
  and like the wind our sins
    sweep us away.
7No one calls on your name
  or strives to lay hold of you;
for you have hidden your face
    from us
  and made us waste away
    because of our sins.

8Yet, O LORD, you are our Father.
  We are the clay, you are the
    potter;
  we are all the work of your
    hand.
9Do not be angry beyond measure,
    O LORD;
  do not remember our sins
    forever.
Oh, look upon us, we pray,
  for we are all your people.
10Your sacred cities have become a
    desert;
  even Zion is a desert, Jerusalem
    a desolation.
11Our holy and glorious temple,
  where our fathers praised
    you,
  has been burned with fire,
  and all that we treasured lies in
    ruins.
12After all this, O LORD, will you
    hold yourself back?
  Will you keep silent and punish
    us beyond measure?

Judgment and Salvation

65 "I revealed myself to those
     who did not ask for me;
  I was found by those who did
    not seek me.
To a nation that did not call on
    my name,
  I said, 'Here am I, here am I.'
2All day long I have held out my
    hands
  to an obstinate people,
  who walk in ways not good,
    pursuing their own
      imaginations—
3a people who continually provoke
    me
  to my very face,
  offering sacrifices in gardens
  and burning incense on altars of
    brick;
4who sit among the graves
  and spend their nights keeping
    secret vigil;
who eat the flesh of pigs,
  and whose pots hold broth of
    unclean meat;
5who say, 'Keep away; don't come
    near me,
  for I am too sacred for you!'
Such people are smoke in my
    nostrils,
  a fire that keeps burning all
    day.

6"See, it stands written before me:
  I will not keep silent but will
    pay back in full;
  I will pay it back into their
    laps—
7both your sins and the sins of
    your fathers,"
    says the LORD.
"Because they burned sacrifices
    on the mountains
  and defied me on the hills,
  I will measure into their laps
    the full payment for their
      former deeds."

8This is what the LORD says:

"As when juice is still found in a
    cluster of grapes
  and men say, 'Don't destroy it,
    there is yet some good in it,'
  so will I do in behalf of my
    servants;
  I will not destroy them all.
9I will bring forth descendants
    from Jacob,
  and from Judah those who will
    possess my mountains;
  my chosen people will inherit
    them,
  and there will my servants live.
10Sharon will become a pasture for
    flocks,
  and the Valley of Achor a
    resting place for herds,
  for my people who seek me.

11"But as for you who forsake the
    LORD
  and forget my holy mountain,
  who spread a table for Fortune

and fill bowls of mixed wine for
　　Destiny,
¹²I will destine you for the sword,
　and you will all bend down for
　　the slaughter;
　for I called but you did not
　　answer,
　I spoke but you did not listen.
You did evil in my sight
　and chose what displeases me.”

¹³Therefore this is what the Sovereign LORD says:

“My servants will eat,
　but you will go hungry;
my servants will drink,
　but you will go thirsty;
my servants will rejoice,
　but you will be put to shame.
¹⁴My servants will sing
　out of the joy of their hearts,
but you will cry out
　from anguish of heart
　and wail in brokenness of spirit.
¹⁵You will leave your name
　to my chosen ones as a curse;
the Sovereign LORD will put you
　　to death,
　but to his servants he will give
　　another name.
¹⁶Whoever invokes a blessing in
　　the land
will do so by the God of truth;
he who takes an oath in the land
　will swear by the God of truth.
For the past troubles will be
　　forgotten
　and hidden from my eyes.

New Heavens and a New Earth

¹⁷“Behold, I will create
　new heavens and a new earth.
The former things will not be
　　remembered,
　nor will they come to mind.
¹⁸But be glad and rejoice forever
　in what I will create,
for I will create Jerusalem to be a
　　delight
　and its people a joy.
¹⁹I will rejoice over Jerusalem
　and take delight in my people;

the sound of weeping and of
　　crying
　will be heard in it no more.

²⁰“Never again will there be in it
　an infant who lives but a few
　　days,
　or an old man who does not live
　　out his years;
he who dies at a hundred
　will be thought a mere youth;
he who fails to reach*a* a hundred
　will be considered accursed.
²¹They will build houses and dwell
　　in them;
　they will plant vineyards and
　　eat their fruit.
²²No longer will they build houses
　　and others live in them,
　or plant and others eat.
For as the days of a tree,
　so will be the days of my
　　people;
my chosen ones will long enjoy
　the works of their hands.
²³They will not toil in vain
　or bear children doomed to
　　misfortune;
for they will be a people blessed
　　by the LORD,
　they and their descendants with
　　them.
²⁴Before they call I will answer;
　while they are still speaking I
　　will hear.
²⁵The wolf and the lamb will feed
　　together,
　and the lion will eat straw like
　　the ox,
　but dust will be the serpent’s
　　food.
They will neither harm nor
　　destroy
　on all my holy mountain,”
　　　　　　　　says the LORD.

Judgment and Hope

66 This is what the LORD says:

“Heaven is my throne,
　and the earth is my footstool.
Where is the house you will build
　　for me?
Where will my resting place be?

---

a20 Or / the sinner who reaches

²Has not my hand made all these
things,
and so they came into being?"
declares the LORD.

"This is the one I esteem:
he who is humble and contrite
in spirit,
and trembles at my word.
³But whoever sacrifices a bull
is like one who kills a man,
and whoever offers a lamb,
like one who breaks a dog's
neck;
whoever makes a grain offering
is like one who presents pig's
blood,
and whoever burns memorial
incense,
like one who worships an idol.
They have chosen their own ways,
and their souls delight in their
abominations;
⁴so I also will choose harsh
treatment for them
and will bring upon them what
they dread.
For when I called, no one
answered,
when I spoke, no one listened.
They did evil in my sight
and chose what displeases me."

⁵Hear the word of the LORD,
you who tremble at his word:
"Your brothers who hate you,
and exclude you because of my
name, have said,
'Let the LORD be glorified,
that we may see your joy!'
Yet they will be put to shame.
⁶Hear that uproar from the city,
hear that noise from the temple!
It is the sound of the LORD
repaying his enemies all they
deserve.

⁷"Before she goes into labor,
she gives birth;
before the pains come upon her,
she delivers a son.
⁸Who has ever heard of such a
thing?
Who has ever seen such things?
Can a country be born in a day
or a nation be brought forth in
a moment?
Yet no sooner is Zion in labor
than she gives birth to her
children.
⁹Do I bring to the moment of birth
and not give delivery?" says the
LORD.
"Do I close up the womb
when I bring to delivery?" says
your God.
¹⁰"Rejoice with Jerusalem and be
glad for her,
all you who love her;
rejoice greatly with her,
all you who mourn over her.

Life in Bible Times

OLDER PEOPLE

Old men and women were respected in Bible times. Because they were older and more experienced, they were thought to be wiser than the young. People wanted the advice of older people. Living long enough to grow old was seen as a special blessing from God.

¹¹For you will nurse and be
satisfied
  at her comforting breasts;
you will drink deeply
  and delight in her overflowing
  abundance."

¹²For this is what the LORD says:

"I will extend peace to her like a
river,
  and the wealth of nations like a
  flooding stream;
you will nurse and be carried on
her arm
  and dandled on her knees.
¹³As a mother comforts her child,
  so will I comfort you;
and you will be comforted over
Jerusalem."

¹⁴When you see this, your heart
will rejoice
  and you will flourish like grass;
the hand of the LORD will be
  made known to his
  servants,
  but his fury will be shown to
  his foes.
¹⁵See, the LORD is coming with fire,
  and his chariots are like a
  whirlwind;
he will bring down his anger with
fury,
  and his rebuke with flames of
  fire.
¹⁶For with fire and with his sword
  the LORD will execute judgment
  upon all men,
  and many will be those slain by
  the LORD.

¹⁷"Those who consecrate and purify
themselves to go into the gardens,
following the one in the midst of[a]
those who eat the flesh of pigs and
rats and other abominable things—
they will meet their end together,"
declares the LORD.

¹⁸"And I, because of their actions
and their imaginations, am about to
come[b] and gather all nations and
tongues, and they will come and see
my glory.

¹⁹"I will set a sign among them,
and I will send some of those who survive to the nations—to Tarshish, to
the Libyans[c] and Lydians (famous as
archers), to Tubal and Greece, and to
the distant islands that have not
heard of my fame or seen my glory.
They will proclaim my glory among
the nations. ²⁰And they will bring all
your brothers, from all the nations, to
my holy mountain in Jerusalem as
an offering to the LORD—on horses,
in chariots and wagons, and on mules
and camels," says the LORD. "They
will bring them, as the Israelites
bring their grain offerings, to the
temple of the LORD in ceremonially
clean vessels. ²¹And I will select some
of them also to be priests and Le-
vites," says the LORD.

²²"As the new heavens and the new
earth that I make will endure before
me," declares the LORD, "so will your
name and descendants endure.
²³From one New Moon to another and
from one Sabbath to another, all
mankind will come and bow down be-
fore me," says the LORD. ²⁴"And they
will go out and look upon the dead
bodies of those who rebelled against
me; their worm will not die, nor will
their fire be quenched, and they will
be loathsome to all mankind."

---

^a17 Or *gardens behind one of your temples, and
is uncertain.*   ^c19 Some Septuagint manuscripts *Put* (Libyans); Hebrew *Pul*
                                       ^b18 The meaning of the Hebrew for this clause

JEREMIAH

WHO WROTE THIS BOOK?
The prophet Jeremiah.

WHY WAS THIS BOOK WRITTEN?
God intended to use Babylon to punish Judah's sin. Jeremiah urged the king and people to surrender to Babylon.

WHAT IS SPECIAL ABOUT THIS BOOK?
Jeremiah is faithful to God even though the people of Judah ridicule and hate him. Jeremiah prophesies that one day God will forgive and restore his people.

WHEN WAS THIS BOOK WRITTEN?
Jeremiah was written between 627 B.C. and the destruction of Jerusalem in 586 B.C.

WHAT CHAPTERS TELL ABOUT JEREMIAH'S EXPERIENCES?

God calls Jeremiah.	Jeremiah 1
Jeremiah is beaten.	Jeremiah 20
Jeremiah is threatened.	Jeremiah 26
Jeremiah and a false prophet.	Jeremiah 28
Jeremiah buys a field.	Jeremiah 32
Jeremiah in a cistern.	Jeremiah 38
Jeremiah is set free.	Jeremiah 40

WHAT ARE SOME IMPORTANT CHAPTERS IN THIS BOOK?

The wickedness of Judah.	Jeremiah 5
God and idols.	Jeremiah 10
False prophets.	Jeremiah 23
God's lasting love.	Jeremiah 31
A family that obeyed God.	Jeremiah 35
God's future punishment.	Jeremiah 51

1 The words of Jeremiah son of Hilkiah, one of the priests at Anathoth in the territory of Benjamin. ²The word of the LORD came to him in the thirteenth year of the reign of Josiah son of Amon king of Judah, ³and through the reign of Jehoiakim son of Josiah king of Judah, down to the fifth month of the eleventh year of Zedekiah son of Josiah king of Judah, when the people of Jerusalem went into exile.

The Call of Jeremiah

⁴The word of the LORD came to me, saying,

⁵"Before I formed you in the womb
    I knew*ᵃ* you,
  before you were born I set you
      apart;
  I appointed you as a prophet to
      the nations."

⁶"Ah, Sovereign LORD," I said, "I do not know how to speak; I am only a child."

⁷But the LORD said to me, "Do not say, 'I am only a child.' You must go to everyone I send you to and say whatever I command you. ⁸Do not be afraid of them, for I am with you and will rescue you," declares the LORD.

⁹Then the LORD reached out his hand and touched my mouth and said to me, "Now, I have put my words in your mouth. ¹⁰See, today I appoint you over nations and kingdoms to uproot and tear down, to destroy and overthrow, to build and to plant."

¹¹The word of the LORD came to me: "What do you see, Jeremiah?"

"I see the branch of an almond tree," I replied.

¹²The LORD said to me, "You have seen correctly, for I am watching*ᵇ* to see that my word is fulfilled."

¹³The word of the LORD came to me again: "What do you see?"

"I see a boiling pot, tilting away from the north," I answered.

¹⁴The LORD said to me, "From the north disaster will be poured out on all who live in the land. ¹⁵I am about to summon all the peoples of the northern kingdoms," declares the LORD.

"Their kings will come and set up
    their thrones
  in the entrance of the gates of
      Jerusalem;
they will come against all her
    surrounding walls
  and against all the towns of
      Judah.
¹⁶I will pronounce my judgments on
    my people
  because of their wickedness in
      forsaking me,
in burning incense to other gods
  and in worshiping what their
      hands have made.

¹⁷"Get yourself ready! Stand up and say to them whatever I command you. Do not be terrified by them, or I will terrify you before them. ¹⁸Today I have made you a fortified city, an iron pillar and a bronze wall to stand

---

ᵃ5 Or *chose*   *ᵇ12* The Hebrew for *watching* sounds like the Hebrew for *almond tree.*

▌ET'S LIVE IT!   Jeremiah 1:4–8

GOD HAS A PLAN FOR YOUR LIFE ➡ Find the verses in Jeremiah 1:4–8 that say the following things.

1. God knew Jeremiah before he was born. 2. God had planned work for Jeremiah even then. 3. God would help Jeremiah do the work God had for him. 4. Jeremiah had to trust God and do his work.

Jeremiah was a special person. You are special to God too. Begin to pray even now that God will show you his plan for your life.

Think of three things you would like to be when you grow up. Tell an adult how you think you could serve God in each of the three jobs.

against the whole land—against the kings of Judah, its officials, its priests and the people of the land. [19]They will fight against you but will not overcome you, for I am with you and will rescue you," declares the LORD.

Israel Forsakes God

2 The word of the LORD came to me: [2]"Go and proclaim in the hearing of Jerusalem:

" 'I remember the devotion of your
    youth,
  how as a bride you loved me
and followed me through the
    desert,
  through a land not sown.
[3]Israel was holy to the LORD,
  the firstfruits of his harvest;
all who devoured her were held
    guilty,
  and disaster overtook them,' "
              declares the LORD.

[4]Hear the word of the LORD,
  O house of Jacob,
  all you clans of the house of
    Israel.

[5]This is what the LORD says:

"What fault did your fathers find
    in me,
  that they strayed so far from
    me?
They followed worthless idols
  and became worthless
    themselves.
[6]They did not ask, 'Where is the
    LORD,
who brought us up out of Egypt
and led us through the barren
    wilderness,
  through a land of deserts and
    rifts,
a land of drought and darkness,[a]
  a land where no one travels and
    no one lives?'
[7]I brought you into a fertile land
  to eat its fruit and rich produce.

But you came and defiled my land
and made my inheritance
    detestable.
[8]The priests did not ask,
  'Where is the LORD?'
Those who deal with the law did
    not know me;
  the leaders rebelled against me.
The prophets prophesied by Baal,
  following worthless idols.

[9]"Therefore I bring charges against
    you again,"
              declares the LORD.
"And I will bring charges
  against your children's
    children.
[10]Cross over to the coasts of
    Kittim[b] and look,
  send to Kedar[c] and observe
    closely;
  see if there has ever been
    anything like this:
[11]Has a nation ever changed its
    gods?
  (Yet they are not gods at all.)
But my people have exchanged
    their[d] Glory
  for worthless idols.
[12]Be appalled at this, O heavens,
  and shudder with great horror,"
              declares the LORD.
[13]"My people have committed two
    sins:
They have forsaken me,
  the spring of living water,
and have dug their own cisterns,
  broken cisterns that cannot hold
    water.
[14]Is Israel a servant, a slave by
    birth?
  Why then has he become
    plunder?
[15]Lions have roared;
  they have growled at him.
They have laid waste his land;
  his towns are burned and
    deserted.
[16]Also, the men of Memphis[e] and
    Tahpanhes
  have shaved the crown of your
    head.[f]

---

[a]6 Or *and the shadow of death*   [b]10 That is, Cyprus and western coastlands   [c]10 The home of Bedouin tribes in the Syro-Arabian desert   [d]11 Masoretic Text; an ancient Hebrew scribal tradition *my*   [e]16 Hebrew *Noph*   [f]16 Or *have cracked your skull*

¹⁷Have you not brought this on
    yourselves
  by forsaking the LORD your God
    when he led you in the way?
¹⁸Now why go to Egypt
  to drink water from the
    Shihor^a?
  And why go to Assyria
    to drink water from the River^b?
¹⁹Your wickedness will punish you;
  your backsliding will rebuke
    you.
Consider then and realize
  how evil and bitter it is for you
when you forsake the LORD your
    God
  and have no awe of me,"
      declares the Lord, the LORD
        Almighty.

²⁰"Long ago you broke off your
    yoke
  and tore off your bonds;
  you said, 'I will not serve you!'
Indeed, on every high hill
  and under every spreading tree
  you lay down as a prostitute.
²¹I had planted you like a choice
    vine
  of sound and reliable stock.
How then did you turn against
    me
  into a corrupt, wild vine?
²²Although you wash yourself with
    soda
  and use an abundance of soap,
  the stain of your guilt is still
    before me,"
      declares the Sovereign
        LORD.
²³"How can you say, 'I am not
    defiled;
  I have not run after the
    Baals'?
See how you behaved in the
    valley;
  consider what you have done.
You are a swift she-camel
  running here and there,
²⁴a wild donkey accustomed to the
    desert,
  sniffing the wind in her
    craving—

in her heat who can restrain
    her?
Any males that pursue her need
    not tire themselves;
  at mating time they will find
    her.
²⁵Do not run until your feet are
    bare
  and your throat is dry.
But you said, 'It's no use!
  I love foreign gods,
  and I must go after them.'

²⁶"As a thief is disgraced when he
    is caught,
  so the house of Israel is
    disgraced—
they, their kings and their
    officials,
  their priests and their prophets.
²⁷They say to wood, 'You are my
    father,'
  and to stone, 'You gave me
    birth.'
They have turned their backs to
    me
  and not their faces;
yet when they are in trouble, they
    say,
  'Come and save us!'
²⁸Where then are the gods you
    made for yourselves?
  Let them come if they can save
    you
  when you are in trouble!
For you have as many gods
  as you have towns, O Judah.

²⁹"Why do you bring charges
    against me?
  You have all rebelled against
    me,"
          declares the LORD.
³⁰"In vain I punished your people;
  they did not respond to
    correction.
Your sword has devoured your
    prophets
  like a ravening lion.

³¹"You of this generation, consider
the word of the LORD:

"Have I been a desert to Israel
  or a land of great darkness?

---

^a18 That is, a branch of the Nile   ^b18 That is, the Euphrates

Why do my people say, 'We are
　　free to roam;
　　we will come to you no more'?
[32]Does a maiden forget her jewelry,
　　a bride her wedding ornaments?
Yet my people have forgotten me,
　　days without number.

Life In Bible Times

JEWELRY

Israelite men and women wore
jewelry, like bracelets, chains, and
necklaces. Women also wore earrings. Women in some nations
even wore nose rings! Jewelry was
beautifully made of ivory, bronze,
silver, and gold. Sometimes precious stones like rubies and em-
eralds were added.

---

[33]How skilled you are at pursuing
　　love!
　　Even the worst of women can
　　　learn from your ways.
[34]On your clothes men find
　　the lifeblood of the innocent
　　　poor,
　　though you did not catch them
　　　breaking in.
　Yet in spite of all this
[35]　you say, 'I am innocent;
　　he is not angry with me.'
　But I will pass judgment on you
　　because you say, 'I have not
　　　sinned.'
[36]Why do you go about so much,
　　changing your ways?
　You will be disappointed by Egypt
　　as you were by Assyria.
[37]You will also leave that place
　　with your hands on your head,
　for the Lord has rejected those
　　you trust;
　you will not be helped by them.

3 "If a man divorces his wife
　　and she leaves him and
　　　marries another man,
should he return to her again?
Would not the land be
　　completely defiled?
But you have lived as a prostitute
　　with many lovers—
would you now return to me?"
　　　　declares the Lord.
[2]"Look up to the barren heights
　　and see.
Is there any place where you
　　have not been ravished?
By the roadside you sat waiting
　　for lovers,
　sat like a nomad[a] in the desert.
You have defiled the land
　　with your prostitution and
　　　wickedness.
[3]Therefore the showers have been
　　withheld,
　and no spring rains have fallen.
Yet you have the brazen look of a
　　prostitute;
　you refuse to blush with shame.
[4]Have you not just called to me:
　'My Father, my friend from my
　　　youth,
[5]will you always be angry?
　Will your wrath continue
　　　forever?'
This is how you talk,
　but you do all the evil you can."

Unfaithful Israel

[6]During the reign of King Josiah,
the Lord said to me, "Have you seen
what faithless Israel has done? She
has gone up on every high hill and
under every spreading tree and has
committed adultery there. [7]I thought
that after she had done all this she
would return to me but she did not,
and her unfaithful sister Judah saw
it. [8]I gave faithless Israel her certificate of divorce and sent her away because of all her adulteries. Yet I saw
that her unfaithful sister Judah had
no fear; she also went out and committed adultery. [9]Because Israel's
immorality mattered so little to her,
she defiled the land and committed

[a]2 Or an Arab

adultery with stone and wood. ¹⁰In spite of all this, her unfaithful sister Judah did not return to me with all her heart, but only in pretense," declares the LORD.

¹¹The LORD said to me, "Faithless Israel is more righteous than unfaithful Judah. ¹²Go, proclaim this message toward the north:

" 'Return, faithless Israel,'
    declares the LORD,
'I will frown on you no longer,
for I am merciful,' declares the
    LORD,
'I will not be angry forever.
¹³Only acknowledge your guilt—
    you have rebelled against the
    LORD your God,
you have scattered your favors to
    foreign gods
    under every spreading tree,
    and have not obeyed me,' "
                declares the LORD.

¹⁴"Return, faithless people," declares the LORD, "for I am your husband. I will choose you—one from a town and two from a clan—and bring you to Zion. ¹⁵Then I will give you shepherds after my own heart, who will lead you with knowledge and understanding. ¹⁶In those days, when your numbers have increased greatly in the land," declares the LORD, "men will no longer say, 'The ark of the covenant of the LORD.' It will never enter their minds or be remembered; it will not be missed, nor will another one be made. ¹⁷At that time they will call Jerusalem The Throne of the LORD, and all nations will gather in Jerusalem to honor the name of the LORD. No longer will they follow the stubbornness of their evil hearts. ¹⁸In those days the house of Judah will join the house of Israel, and together they will come from a northern land to the land I gave your forefathers as an inheritance.

¹⁹"I myself said,

" 'How gladly would I treat you
    like sons
    and give you a desirable land,

the most beautiful inheritance
    of any nation.'
I thought you would call me
    'Father'
    and not turn away from
    following me.
²⁰But like a woman unfaithful to
    her husband,
so you have been unfaithful to
    me, O house of Israel,"
                declares the LORD.

²¹A cry is heard on the barren
    heights,
    the weeping and pleading of the
    people of Israel,
because they have perverted their
    ways
    and have forgotten the LORD
    their God.

²²"Return, faithless people;
    I will cure you of backsliding."

"Yes, we will come to you,
    for you are the LORD our God.
²³Surely the ⌊idolatrous⌋ commotion
    on the hills
    and mountains is a deception;
surely in the LORD our God
    is the salvation of Israel.
²⁴From our youth shameful gods
    have consumed
    the fruits of our fathers' labor—
their flocks and herds,
    their sons and daughters.
²⁵Let us lie down in our shame,
    and let our disgrace cover us.
We have sinned against the LORD
    our God,
    both we and our fathers;
from our youth till this day
    we have not obeyed the LORD
    our God."

4 "If you will return, O Israel,
    return to me,"
                declares the LORD.
"If you put your detestable idols
    out of my sight
    and no longer go astray,
²and if in a truthful, just and
    righteous way
    you swear, 'As surely as the
    LORD lives,'

then the nations will be blessed
by him
and in him they will glory."

³This is what the LORD says to the
men of Judah and to Jerusalem:

"Break up your unplowed ground
and do not sow among thorns.
⁴Circumcise yourselves to the
LORD,
circumcise your hearts,
you men of Judah and people of
Jerusalem,
or my wrath will break out and
burn like fire
because of the evil you have
done—
burn with no one to quench it.

Disaster From the North

⁵"Announce in Judah and proclaim
in Jerusalem and say:
'Sound the trumpet throughout
the land!'
Cry aloud and say:
'Gather together!
Let us flee to the fortified
cities!'
⁶Raise the signal to go to Zion!
Flee for safety without delay!
For I am bringing disaster from
the north,
even terrible destruction."

⁷A lion has come out of his lair;
a destroyer of nations has set
out.
He has left his place
to lay waste your land.
Your towns will lie in ruins
without inhabitant.
⁸So put on sackcloth,
lament and wail,
for the fierce anger of the LORD
has not turned away from us.

⁹"In that day," declares the LORD,
"the king and the officials will
lose heart,
the priests will be horrified,
and the prophets will be
appalled."

¹⁰Then I said, "Ah, Sovereign LORD,
how completely you have deceived
this people and Jerusalem by saying,
'You will have peace,' when the
sword is at our throats."

¹¹At that time this people and Jerusalem will be told, "A scorching wind
from the barren heights in the desert
blows toward my people, but not to
winnow or cleanse; ¹²a wind too
strong for that comes from me.ᵃ Now
I pronounce my judgments against
them."

¹³Look! He advances like the
clouds,
his chariots come like a
whirlwind,
his horses are swifter than eagles.
Woe to us! We are ruined!
¹⁴O Jerusalem, wash the evil from
your heart and be saved.
How long will you harbor
wicked thoughts?
¹⁵A voice is announcing from Dan,
proclaiming disaster from the
hills of Ephraim.
¹⁶"Tell this to the nations,
proclaim it to Jerusalem:
'A besieging army is coming from
a distant land,
raising a war cry against the
cities of Judah.
¹⁷They surround her like men
guarding a field,
because she has rebelled
against me,'"
declares the LORD.
¹⁸"Your own conduct and actions
have brought this upon you.
This is your punishment.
How bitter it is!
How it pierces to the heart!"

¹⁹Oh, my anguish, my anguish!
I writhe in pain.
Oh, the agony of my heart!
My heart pounds within me,
I cannot keep silent.
For I have heard the sound of the
trumpet;
I have heard the battle cry.
²⁰Disaster follows disaster;
the whole land lies in ruins.

ᵃ12 Or comes at my command

In an instant my tents are
    destroyed,
  my shelter in a moment.
21How long must I see the battle
    standard
  and hear the sound of the
    trumpet?

22"My people are fools;
  they do not know me.
They are senseless children;
  they have no understanding.
They are skilled in doing evil;
  they know not how to do good."

23I looked at the earth,
    and it was formless and empty;
  and at the heavens,
    and their light was gone.
24I looked at the mountains,
    and they were quaking;
  all the hills were swaying.
25I looked, and there were no
    people;
  every bird in the sky had flown
    away.
26I looked, and the fruitful land
    was a desert;
  all its towns lay in ruins
before the Lord, before his
    fierce anger.

27This is what the Lord says:

"The whole land will be ruined,
  though I will not destroy it
    completely.
28Therefore the earth will mourn
  and the heavens above grow
    dark,
because I have spoken and will
    not relent,
  I have decided and will not turn
    back."

29At the sound of horsemen and
    archers
  every town takes to flight.
Some go into the thickets;
  some climb up among the rocks.
All the towns are deserted;
  no one lives in them.

30What are you doing, O devastated
    one?
  Why dress yourself in scarlet
  and put on jewels of gold?

Why shade your eyes with paint?
  You adorn yourself in vain.
Your lovers despise you;
  they seek your life.

31I hear a cry as of a woman in
    labor,
  a groan as of one bearing her
    first child—
the cry of the Daughter of Zion
    gasping for breath,
  stretching out her hands and
    saying,
"Alas! I am fainting;
  my life is given over to
    murderers."

Not One Is Upright

5 "Go up and down the streets of
    Jerusalem,
  look around and consider,
    search through her squares.
If you can find but one person
  who deals honestly and seeks
    the truth,
  I will forgive this city.
2Although they say, 'As surely as
    the Lord lives,'
  still they are swearing falsely."

3O Lord, do not your eyes look for
    truth?
  You struck them, but they felt
    no pain;
  you crushed them, but they
    refused correction.
They made their faces harder
    than stone
  and refused to repent.
4I thought, "These are only the
    poor;
  they are foolish,
for they do not know the way of
    the Lord,
  the requirements of their God.
5So I will go to the leaders
  and speak to them;
surely they know the way of the
    Lord,
  the requirements of their God."
But with one accord they too had
    broken off the yoke
  and torn off the bonds.
6Therefore a lion from the forest
  will attack them,

a wolf from the desert will
   ravage them,
a leopard will lie in wait near
      their towns
   to tear to pieces any who
      venture out,
   for their rebellion is great
   and their backslidings many.

7"Why should I forgive you?
   Your children have forsaken me
   and sworn by gods that are not
      gods.
I supplied all their needs,
   yet they committed adultery
   and thronged to the houses of
      prostitutes.
8They are well-fed, lusty stallions,
   each neighing for another man's
      wife.
9Should I not punish them for
      this?"
   declares the LORD.
"Should I not avenge myself
   on such a nation as this?

10"Go through her vineyards and
      ravage them,
   but do not destroy them
      completely.
Strip off her branches,
   for these people do not belong to
      the LORD.
11The house of Israel and the house
      of Judah
   have been utterly unfaithful to
      me,"
                  declares the LORD.

12They have lied about the LORD;
   they said, "He will do nothing!
No harm will come to us;
   we will never see sword or
      famine.
13The prophets are but wind
   and the word is not in them;
   so let what they say be done to
      them."

14Therefore this is what the LORD
God Almighty says:

"Because the people have spoken
      these words,
   I will make my words in your
      mouth a fire

and these people the wood it
   consumes.
15O house of Israel," declares the
      LORD,
   "I am bringing a distant nation
      against you—
an ancient and enduring nation,
   a people whose language you do
      not know,
   whose speech you do not
      understand.
16Their quivers are like an open
      grave;
   all of them are mighty warriors.
17They will devour your harvests
      and food,
   devour your sons and
      daughters;
   they will devour your flocks and
      herds,
   devour your vines and fig trees.
With the sword they will destroy
   the fortified cities in which you
      trust.

18"Yet even in those days," declares
the LORD, "I will not destroy you completely. 19And when the people ask,
'Why has the LORD our God done all
this to us?' you will tell them, 'As you
have forsaken me and served foreign
gods in your own land, so now you
will serve foreigners in a land not
your own.'

20"Announce this to the house of
      Jacob
   and proclaim it in Judah:
21Hear this, you foolish and
      senseless people,
   who have eyes but do not see,
   who have ears but do not hear:
22Should you not fear me?" declares
      the LORD.
   "Should you not tremble in my
      presence?
I made the sand a boundary for
      the sea,
   an everlasting barrier it cannot
      cross.
The waves may roll, but they
      cannot prevail;
   they may roar, but they cannot
      cross it.
23But these people have stubborn
   and rebellious hearts;

they have turned aside and
    gone away.
²⁴They do not say to themselves,
    'Let us fear the LORD our God,
who gives autumn and spring
    rains in season,
who assures us of the regular
    weeks of harvest.'
²⁵Your wrongdoings have kept
    these away;
    your sins have deprived you of
    good.

²⁶"Among my people are wicked
    men
who lie in wait like men who
    snare birds
and like those who set traps to
    catch men.
²⁷Like cages full of birds,
    their houses are full of deceit;
they have become rich and
    powerful
²⁸ and have grown fat and sleek.
Their evil deeds have no limit;
    they do not plead the case of
    the fatherless to win it,
    they do not defend the rights of
    the poor.
²⁹Should I not punish them for
    this?"
    declares the LORD.
"Should I not avenge myself
    on such a nation as this?

³⁰"A horrible and shocking thing
    has happened in the land:
³¹The prophets prophesy lies,
    the priests rule by their own
    authority,
and my people love it this way.
    But what will you do in the
    end?

Jerusalem Under Siege

6 "Flee for safety, people of
    Benjamin!
Flee from Jerusalem!
Sound the trumpet in Tekoa!
    Raise the signal over Beth
    Hakkerem!
For disaster looms out of the
    north,

even terrible destruction.
²I will destroy the Daughter of
    Zion,
    so beautiful and delicate.
³Shepherds with their flocks will
    come against her;
    they will pitch their tents
    around her,
each tending his own portion."

⁴"Prepare for battle against her!
    Arise, let us attack at noon!
But, alas, the daylight is fading,
    and the shadows of evening
    grow long.
⁵So arise, let us attack at night
    and destroy her fortresses!"

⁶This is what the LORD Almighty
says:

"Cut down the trees
    and build siege ramps against
    Jerusalem.
This city must be punished;
    it is filled with oppression.
⁷As a well pours out its water,
    so she pours out her
    wickedness.
Violence and destruction resound
    in her;
    her sickness and wounds are
    ever before me.
⁸Take warning, O Jerusalem,
    or I will turn away from you
and make your land desolate
    so no one can live in it."

⁹This is what the LORD Almighty
says:

"Let them glean the remnant of
    Israel
    as thoroughly as a vine;
pass your hand over the branches
    again,
    like one gathering grapes."

¹⁰To whom can I speak and give
    warning?
    Who will listen to me?
Their ears are closed ᵃ
    so they cannot hear.
The word of the LORD is offensive
    to them;
    they find no pleasure in it.

ᵃ10 Hebrew *uncircumcised*

¹¹But I am full of the wrath of the
LORD,
  and I cannot hold it in.

"Pour it out on the children in the
  street
  and on the young men gathered
  together;
both husband and wife will be
  caught in it,
  and the old, those weighed
  down with years.
¹²Their houses will be turned over
  to others,
  together with their fields and
  their wives,
when I stretch out my hand
  against those who live in the
  land,"
                    declares the LORD.
¹³"From the least to the greatest,
  all are greedy for gain;
prophets and priests alike,
  all practice deceit.
¹⁴They dress the wound of my
  people
  as though it were not serious.
'Peace, peace,' they say,
  when there is no peace.
¹⁵Are they ashamed of their
  loathsome conduct?
  No, they have no shame at all;
  they do not even know how to
  blush.
So they will fall among the fallen;
  they will be brought down when
  I punish them,"
                    says the LORD.

¹⁶This is what the LORD says:

"Stand at the crossroads and look;
  ask for the ancient paths,
ask where the good way is, and
  walk in it,
  and you will find rest for your
  souls.
  But you said, 'We will not walk
  in it.'
¹⁷I appointed watchmen over you
  and said,
  'Listen to the sound of the
  trumpet!'
  But you said, 'We will not
  listen.'
¹⁸Therefore hear, O nations;

observe, O witnesses,
  what will happen to them.
¹⁹Hear, O earth:
I am bringing disaster on this
  people,
  the fruit of their schemes,
because they have not listened to
  my words
  and have rejected my law.
²⁰What do I care about incense
  from Sheba
  or sweet calamus from a distant
  land?
Your burnt offerings are not
  acceptable;
  your sacrifices do not please
  me."

²¹Therefore this is what the LORD
says:

"I will put obstacles before this
  people.
  Fathers and sons alike will
  stumble over them;
  neighbors and friends will
  perish."

²²This is what the LORD says:

"Look, an army is coming
  from the land of the north;
a great nation is being stirred up
  from the ends of the earth.
²³They are armed with bow and
  spear;
  they are cruel and show no
  mercy.
They sound like the roaring sea
  as they ride on their horses;
they come like men in battle
  formation
  to attack you, O Daughter of
  Zion."

²⁴We have heard reports about
  them,
  and our hands hang limp.
Anguish has gripped us,
  pain like that of a woman in
  labor.
²⁵Do not go out to the fields
  or walk on the roads,
for the enemy has a sword,
  and there is terror on every
  side.
²⁶O my people, put on sackcloth

and roll in ashes;
mourn with bitter wailing
  as for an only son,
for suddenly the destroyer
  will come upon us.

²⁷"I have made you a tester of
    metals
  and my people the ore,
that you may observe
  and test their ways.
²⁸They are all hardened rebels,
  going about to slander.
They are bronze and iron;
  they all act corruptly.
²⁹The bellows blow fiercely
  to burn away the lead with fire,
but the refining goes on in vain;
  the wicked are not purged out.
³⁰They are called rejected silver,
  because the LORD has rejected
    them."

False Religion Worthless

7 This is the word that came to
Jeremiah from the LORD:
²"Stand at the gate of the LORD's
house and there proclaim this message:

" 'Hear the word of the LORD, all
you people of Judah who come
through these gates to worship the
LORD. ³This is what the LORD Almighty, the God of Israel, says: Reform your ways and your actions, and
I will let you live in this place. ⁴Do
not trust in deceptive words and say,
"This is the temple of the LORD, the
temple of the LORD, the temple of the
LORD!" ⁵If you really change your
ways and your actions and deal with
each other justly, ⁶if you do not oppress the alien, the fatherless or the
widow and do not shed innocent blood
in this place, and if you do not follow
other gods to your own harm, ⁷then I
will let you live in this place, in the
land I gave your forefathers for ever
and ever. ⁸But look, you are trusting
in deceptive words that are worthless.

⁹" 'Will you steal and murder, commit adultery and perjury,^a burn incense to Baal and follow other gods
you have not known, ¹⁰and then come
and stand before me in this house,
which bears my Name, and say, "We
are safe"—safe to do all these detestable things? ¹¹Has this house, which
bears my Name, become a den of robbers to you? But I have been watching! declares the LORD.

¹²" 'Go now to the place in Shiloh
where I first made a dwelling for my
Name, and see what I did to it because of the wickedness of my people
Israel. ¹³While you were doing all
these things, declares the LORD, I
spoke to you again and again, but you
did not listen; I called you, but you
did not answer. ¹⁴Therefore, what I
did to Shiloh I will now do to the
house that bears my Name, the temple you trust in, the place I gave to
you and your fathers. ¹⁵I will thrust
you from my presence, just as I did all
your brothers, the people of Ephraim.'

¹⁶"So do not pray for this people nor
offer any plea or petition for them; do
not plead with me, for I will not listen
to you. ¹⁷Do you not see what they are
doing in the towns of Judah and in
the streets of Jerusalem? ¹⁸The children gather wood, the fathers light
the fire, and the women knead the
dough and make cakes of bread for
the Queen of Heaven. They pour out
drink offerings to other gods to provoke me to anger. ¹⁹But am I the one
they are provoking? declares the
LORD. Are they not rather harming
themselves, to their own shame?

²⁰" 'Therefore this is what the Sovereign LORD says: My anger and my
wrath will be poured out on this
place, on man and beast, on the trees
of the field and on the fruit of the
ground, and it will burn and not be
quenched.

²¹" 'This is what the LORD Almighty, the God of Israel, says: Go
ahead, add your burnt offerings to
your other sacrifices and eat the meat
yourselves! ²²For when I brought
your forefathers out of Egypt and

---

^a9 Or *and swear by false gods*

spoke to them, I did not just give them commands about burnt offerings and sacrifices, 23but I gave them this command: Obey me, and I will be your God and you will be my people. Walk in all the ways I command you, that it may go well with you. 24But they did not listen or pay attention; instead, they followed the stubborn inclinations of their evil hearts. They went backward and not forward. 25From the time your forefathers left Egypt until now, day after day, again and again I sent you my servants the prophets. 26But they did not listen to me or pay attention. They were stiff-necked and did more evil than their forefathers.'

27"When you tell them all this, they will not listen to you; when you call to them, they will not answer. 28Therefore say to them, 'This is the nation that has not obeyed the LORD its God or responded to correction. Truth has perished; it has vanished from their lips. 29Cut off your hair and throw it away; take up a lament on the barren heights, for the LORD has rejected and abandoned this generation that is under his wrath.

The Valley of Slaughter

30" 'The people of Judah have done evil in my eyes, declares the LORD. They have set up their detestable idols in the house that bears my Name and have defiled it. 31They have built the high places of Topheth in the Valley of Ben Hinnom to burn their sons and daughters in the fire —something I did not command, nor did it enter my mind. 32So beware, the days are coming, declares the LORD, when people will no longer call it Topheth or the Valley of Ben Hinnom, but the Valley of Slaughter, for they will bury the dead in Topheth until there is no more room. 33Then the carcasses of this people will become food for the birds of the air and the beasts of the earth, and there will be no one to frighten them away. 34I will bring an end to the sounds of joy and gladness and to the voices of bride and bridegroom in the towns of Judah and the streets of Jerusalem, for the land will become desolate.

8 " 'At that time, declares the LORD, the bones of the kings and officials of Judah, the bones of the priests and prophets, and the bones of the people of Jerusalem will be removed from their graves. 2They will be exposed to the sun and the moon and all the stars of the heavens, which they have loved and served and which they have followed and consulted and worshiped. They will not be gathered up or buried, but will be like refuse lying on the ground. 3Wherever I banish them, all the survivors of this evil nation will prefer death to life, declares the LORD Almighty.'

Sin and Punishment

4"Say to them, 'This is what the LORD says:

" 'When men fall down, do they
    not get up?
  When a man turns away, does
    he not return?
5Why then have these people
    turned away?
  Why does Jerusalem always
    turn away?
They cling to deceit;
  they refuse to return.
6I have listened attentively,
  but they do not say what is
    right.
No one repents of his wickedness,
  saying, "What have I done?"
Each pursues his own course
  like a horse charging into
    battle.
7Even the stork in the sky
  knows her appointed seasons,
and the dove, the swift and the
    thrush
  observe the time of their
    migration.
But my people do not know
  the requirements of the LORD.

8" 'How can you say, "We are wise,
  for we have the law of the
    LORD,"
when actually the lying pen of
  the scribes

has handled it falsely?
⁹The wise will be put to shame;
they will be dismayed and
trapped.
Since they have rejected the word
of the LORD,
what kind of wisdom do they
have?
¹⁰Therefore I will give their wives
to other men
and their fields to new owners.
From the least to the greatest,
all are greedy for gain;
prophets and priests alike,
all practice deceit.
¹¹They dress the wound of my
people
as though it were not serious.
"Peace, peace," they say,
when there is no peace.
¹²Are they ashamed of their
loathsome conduct?
No, they have no shame at all;
they do not even know how to
blush.
So they will fall among the
fallen;
they will be brought down when
they are punished,
says the LORD.

¹³" 'I will take away their harvest,
declares the LORD.
There will be no grapes on the
vine.
There will be no figs on the tree,

and their leaves will wither.
What I have given them
will be taken from them.ᵃ' "

¹⁴"Why are we sitting here?
Gather together!
Let us flee to the fortified cities
and perish there!
For the LORD our God has doomed
us to perish
and given us poisoned water to
drink,
because we have sinned against
him.
¹⁵We hoped for peace
but no good has come,
for a time of healing
but there was only terror.
¹⁶The snorting of the enemy's
horses
is heard from Dan;
at the neighing of their stallions
the whole land trembles.
They have come to devour
the land and everything in it,
the city and all who live there."

¹⁷"See, I will send venomous snakes
among you,
vipers that cannot be charmed,
and they will bite you,"
declares the LORD.

¹⁸O my Comforterᵇ in sorrow,
my heart is faint within me.
¹⁹Listen to the cry of my people

ᵃ13 The meaning of the Hebrew for this sentence is uncertain.   ᵇ18 The meaning of the Hebrew for this word is uncertain.

Life in Bible Times

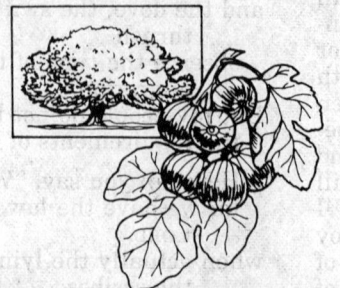

FIGS

Figs grew on trees all over Palestine, so they were handy for everyone to eat. Fig trees have large leaves, and the figs are full of sugar. The Israelites dried and pressed the figs into cakes to eat at home and when traveling.

from a land far away:
"Is the LORD not in Zion?
    Is her King no longer there?"

"Why have they provoked me to
        anger with their images,
    with their worthless foreign
        idols?"

²⁰"The harvest is past,
    the summer has ended,
    and we are not saved."

²¹Since my people are crushed, I
        am crushed;
    I mourn, and horror grips me.
²²Is there no balm in Gilead?
    Is there no physician there?
Why then is there no healing
    for the wound of my people?

9 ¹Oh, that my head were a
        spring of water
    and my eyes a fountain of tears!
I would weep day and night
    for the slain of my people.
²Oh, that I had in the desert
    a lodging place for travelers,
so that I might leave my people
    and go away from them;
for they are all adulterers,
    a crowd of unfaithful people.

³"They make ready their tongue
        like a bow, to shoot lies;
it is not by truth
    that they triumphᵃ in the land.
They go from one sin to another;
    they do not acknowledge me,"
                declares the LORD.
⁴"Beware of your friends;
    do not trust your brothers.
For every brother is a deceiver,ᵇ
    and every friend a slanderer.
⁵Friend deceives friend,
    and no one speaks the truth.
They have taught their tongues to
        lie;
    they weary themselves with
        sinning.
⁶Youᶜ live in the midst of
        deception;
    in their deceit they refuse to
        acknowledge me,"
                declares the LORD.

⁷Therefore this is what the LORD
Almighty says:

"See, I will refine and test them,
    for what else can I do
because of the sin of my people?
⁸Their tongue is a deadly arrow;
    it speaks with deceit.
With his mouth each speaks
        cordially to his neighbor,
    but in his heart he sets a trap
        for him.
⁹Should I not punish them for
        this?"
    declares the LORD.
"Should I not avenge myself
    on such a nation as this?"

¹⁰I will weep and wail for the
        mountains
    and take up a lament
        concerning the desert
        pastures.
They are desolate and untraveled,
    and the lowing of cattle is not
        heard.
The birds of the air have fled
    and the animals are gone.

¹¹"I will make Jerusalem a heap of
        ruins,
    a haunt of jackals;
and I will lay waste the towns of
        Judah
    so no one can live there."

¹²What man is wise enough to understand this? Who has been instructed by the LORD and can explain
it? Why has the land been ruined and
laid waste like a desert that no one
can cross?

¹³The LORD said, "It is because they
have forsaken my law, which I set before them; they have not obeyed me
or followed my law. ¹⁴Instead, they
have followed the stubbornness of
their hearts; they have followed the
Baals, as their fathers taught them."
¹⁵Therefore, this is what the LORD Almighty, the God of Israel, says: "See,
I will make this people eat bitter food
and drink poisoned water. ¹⁶I will
scatter them among nations that nei-

ᵃ3 Or lies; / they are not valiant for truth   ᵇ4 Or a deceiving Jacob   ᶜ6 That is, Jeremiah (the
Hebrew is singular)

ther they nor their fathers have
known, and I will pursue them with
the sword until I have destroyed
them.ˮ

¹⁷This is what the LORD Almighty
says:

"Consider now! Call for the
        wailing women to come;
    send for the most skillful of
        them.
¹⁸Let them come quickly
    and wail over us
till our eyes overflow with tears
    and water streams from our
        eyelids.
¹⁹The sound of wailing is heard
        from Zion:
    'How ruined we are!
    How great is our shame!
We must leave our land
    because our houses are in
        ruins.' "

²⁰Now, O women, hear the word of
        the LORD;
    open your ears to the words of
        his mouth.
Teach your daughters how to
        wail;
    teach one another a lament.
²¹Death has climbed in through our
        windows
    and has entered our fortresses;
it has cut off the children from
        the streets
    and the young men from the
        public squares.

²²Say, "This is what the LORD declares:

" 'The dead bodies of men will lie
    like refuse on the open field,
like cut grain behind the reaper,
    with no one to gather them.' "

²³This is what the LORD says:

"Let not the wise man boast of his
        wisdom
    or the strong man boast of his
        strength
    or the rich man boast of his
        riches,

²⁴but let him who boasts boast
        about this:
    that he understands and knows
        me,
    that I am the LORD, who exercises
        kindness,
    justice and righteousness on
        earth,
    for in these I delight,"
                    declares the LORD.

²⁵"The days are coming," declares
the LORD, "when I will punish all who
are circumcised only in the flesh—
²⁶Egypt, Judah, Edom, Ammon,
Moab and all who live in the desert in
distant places.ᵃ For all these nations
are really uncircumcised, and even
the whole house of Israel is uncircumcised in heart."

God and Idols

10 Hear what the LORD says to
    you, O house of Israel. ²This is
what the LORD says:

"Do not learn the ways of the
        nations
    or be terrified by signs in the
        sky,
    though the nations are terrified
        by them.
³For the customs of the peoples are
        worthless;
    they cut a tree out of the forest,
    and a craftsman shapes it with
        his chisel.
⁴They adorn it with silver and
        gold;
    they fasten it with hammer and
        nails
    so it will not totter.
⁵Like a scarecrow in a melon
        patch,
    their idols cannot speak;
they must be carried
    because they cannot walk.
Do not fear them;
    they can do no harm
    nor can they do any good."

⁶No one is like you, O LORD;
    you are great,

ᵃ26 Or desert and who clip the hair by their foreheads

and your name is mighty in
power.
⁷Who should not revere you,
O King of the nations?
This is your due.
Among all the wise men of the
nations
and in all their kingdoms,
there is no one like you.
⁸They are all senseless and foolish;
they are taught by worthless
wooden idols.
⁹Hammered silver is brought from
Tarshish
and gold from Uphaz.
What the craftsman and
goldsmith have made
is then dressed in blue and
purple—
all made by skilled workers.
¹⁰But the LORD is the true God;
he is the living God, the eternal
King.
When he is angry, the earth
trembles;
the nations cannot endure his
wrath.

¹¹"Tell them this: 'These gods, who
did not make the heavens and the
earth, will perish from the earth and
from under the heavens.' "ᵃ

¹²But God made the earth by his
power;
he founded the world by his
wisdom
and stretched out the heavens
by his understanding.
¹³When he thunders, the waters in
the heavens roar;
he makes clouds rise from the
ends of the earth.
He sends lightning with the
rain
and brings out the wind from
his storehouses.

¹⁴Everyone is senseless and without
knowledge;
every goldsmith is shamed by
his idols.
His images are a fraud;
they have no breath in them.

¹⁵They are worthless, the objects of
mockery;
when their judgment comes,
they will perish.
¹⁶He who is the Portion of Jacob is
not like these,
for he is the Maker of all
things,
including Israel, the tribe of his
inheritance—
the LORD Almighty is his name.

Coming Destruction

¹⁷Gather up your belongings to
leave the land,
you who live under siege.
¹⁸For this is what the LORD says:
"At this time I will hurl out
those who live in this land;
I will bring distress on them
so that they may be captured."

¹⁹Woe to me because of my injury!
My wound is incurable!
Yet I said to myself,
"This is my sickness, and I
must endure it."
²⁰My tent is destroyed;
all its ropes are snapped.
My sons are gone from me and
are no more;
no one is left now to pitch my
tent
or to set up my shelter.
²¹The shepherds are senseless
and do not inquire of the LORD;
so they do not prosper
and all their flock is scattered.
²²Listen! The report is coming—
a great commotion from the
land of the north!
It will make the towns of Judah
desolate,
a haunt of jackals.

Jeremiah's Prayer

²³I know, O LORD, that a man's life
is not his own;
it is not for man to direct his
steps.
²⁴Correct me, LORD, but only with
justice—
not in your anger,

ᵃ11 The text of this verse is in Aramaic.

lest you reduce me to nothing.
²⁵Pour out your wrath on the
      nations
   that do not acknowledge you,
   on the peoples who do not call
      on your name.
For they have devoured Jacob;
   they have devoured him
      completely
   and destroyed his homeland.

The Covenant Is Broken

11 This is the word that came to
Jeremiah from the LORD:
²"Listen to the terms of this covenant
and tell them to the people of Judah
and to those who live in Jerusalem.
³Tell them that this is what the LORD,
the God of Israel, says: 'Cursed is the
man who does not obey the terms of
this covenant— ⁴the terms I commanded your forefathers when I
brought them out of Egypt, out of the
iron-smelting furnace.' I said, 'Obey
me and do everything I command
you, and you will be my people, and
I will be your God. ⁵Then I will fulfill
the oath I swore to your forefathers,
to give them a land flowing with milk
and honey'—the land you possess today."

I answered, "Amen, LORD."

SMELTING METAL

Iron is a strong metal used in Bible
times for many things. The ore was
placed in thick clay pots and
heated in brick furnaces. The
metal in the pots melted and was
poured out by workmen. It could
then be used to make dishes, tools
or weapons.

⁶The LORD said to me, "Proclaim all
these words in the towns of Judah
and in the streets of Jerusalem: 'Listen to the terms of this covenant and
follow them. ⁷From the time I
brought your forefathers up from
Egypt until today, I warned them
again and again, saying, "Obey me."
⁸But they did not listen or pay attention; instead, they followed the stubbornness of their evil hearts. So I
brought on them all the curses of the
covenant I had commanded them to
follow but that they did not keep.' "

⁹Then the LORD said to me, "There
is a conspiracy among the people of
Judah and those who live in Jerusalem. ¹⁰They have returned to the sins
of their forefathers, who refused to
listen to my words. They have followed other gods to serve them. Both
the house of Israel and the house of
Judah have broken the covenant I
made with their forefathers. ¹¹Therefore this is what the LORD says: 'I will
bring on them a disaster they cannot
escape. Although they cry out to me,
I will not listen to them. ¹²The towns
of Judah and the people of Jerusalem
will go and cry out to the gods to
whom they burn incense, but they
will not help them at all when disaster strikes. ¹³You have as many gods
as you have towns, O Judah; and the
altars you have set up to burn incense to that shameful god Baal are
as many as the streets of Jerusalem.'
¹⁴"Do not pray for this people nor
offer any plea or petition for them,
because I will not listen when they
call to me in the time of their distress.

¹⁵"What is my beloved doing in my
      temple
   as she works out her evil
      schemes with many?
   Can consecrated meat avert
      ⌐your punishment⌐?
When you engage in your
      wickedness,
   then you rejoice.ᵃ"

¹⁶The LORD called you a thriving
      olive tree

ᵃ15 Or Could consecrated meat avert your punishment? / Then you would rejoice

with fruit beautiful in form.
But with the roar of a mighty
storm
　he will set it on fire,
　and its branches will be broken.

17The LORD Almighty, who planted you, has decreed disaster for you, because the house of Israel and the house of Judah have done evil and provoked me to anger by burning incense to Baal.

Plot Against Jeremiah

18Because the LORD revealed their plot to me, I knew it, for at that time he showed me what they were doing. 19I had been like a gentle lamb led to the slaughter; I did not realize that they had plotted against me, saying,

"Let us destroy the tree and its
fruit;
　let us cut him off from the land
of the living,
　that his name be remembered
no more."
20But, O LORD Almighty, you who
judge righteously
　and test the heart and mind,
let me see your vengeance upon
them,
　for to you I have committed my
cause.

21"Therefore this is what the LORD says about the men of Anathoth who are seeking your life and saying, 'Do not prophesy in the name of the LORD or you will die by our hands'— 22therefore this is what the LORD Almighty says: 'I will punish them. Their young men will die by the sword, their sons and daughters by famine. 23Not even a remnant will be left to them, because I will bring disaster on the men of Anathoth in the year of their punishment.' "

Jeremiah's Complaint

12 You are always righteous,
O LORD,
　when I bring a case before you.

Yet I would speak with you about
your justice:
　Why does the way of the wicked
prosper?
　Why do all the faithless live at
ease?
2You have planted them, and they
have taken root;
　they grow and bear fruit.
You are always on their lips
　but far from their hearts.
3Yet you know me, O LORD;
　you see me and test my
thoughts about you.
Drag them off like sheep to be
butchered!
　Set them apart for the day of
slaughter!
4How long will the land lie
parched *a*
　and the grass in every field be
withered?
Because those who live in it are
wicked,
　the animals and birds have
perished.
Moreover, the people are saying,
　"He will not see what happens
to us."

God's Answer

5"If you have raced with men on
foot
　and they have worn you out,
　how can you compete with
horses?
If you stumble in safe country, *b*
　how will you manage in the
thickets by *c* the Jordan?
6Your brothers, your own family—
　even they have betrayed you;
　they have raised a loud cry
against you.
Do not trust them,
　though they speak well of you.

7"I will forsake my house,
　abandon my inheritance;
I will give the one I love
　into the hands of her enemies.
8My inheritance has become to me
　like a lion in the forest.
She roars at me;

---

*a*4 Or *land mourn*　　*b*5 Or *If you put your trust in a land of safety*　　*c*5 Or *the flooding of*

therefore I hate her.
⁹Has not my inheritance become to
　me
　like a speckled bird of prey
　that other birds of prey
　　surround and attack?
Go and gather all the wild beasts;
　bring them to devour.
¹⁰Many shepherds will ruin my
　　vineyard
　and trample down my field;
　they will turn my pleasant field
　　into a desolate wasteland.
¹¹It will be made a wasteland,
　parched and desolate before me;
　the whole land will be laid waste
　　because there is no one who
　　cares.
¹²Over all the barren heights in the
　　desert
　destroyers will swarm,
　for the sword of the LORD will
　　devour
　from one end of the land to the
　　other;
　no one will be safe.
¹³They will sow wheat but reap
　　thorns;
　they will wear themselves out
　　but gain nothing.
So bear the shame of your harvest
　because of the LORD's fierce
　　anger."

¹⁴This is what the LORD says: "As
for all my wicked neighbors who seize
the inheritance I gave my people Israel, I will uproot them from their
lands and I will uproot the house of
Judah from among them. ¹⁵But after
I uproot them, I will again have compassion and will bring each of them
back to his own inheritance and his
own country. ¹⁶And if they learn well
the ways of my people and swear by
my name, saying, 'As surely as the
LORD lives'—even as they once
taught my people to swear by Baal
—then they will be established
among my people. ¹⁷But if any nation
does not listen, I will completely uproot and destroy it," declares the
LORD.

A Linen Belt

13 This is what the LORD said to
me: "Go and buy a linen belt
and put it around your waist, but do
not let it touch water." ²So I bought
a belt, as the LORD directed, and put
it around my waist.

³Then the word of the LORD came to
me a second time: ⁴"Take the belt you
bought and are wearing around your
waist, and go now to Perath[a] and
hide it there in a crevice in the
rocks." ⁵So I went and hid it at Perath, as the LORD told me.

⁶Many days later the LORD said to
me, "Go now to Perath and get the
belt I told you to hide there." ⁷So I
went to Perath and dug up the belt
and took it from the place where I had
hidden it, but now it was ruined and
completely useless.

⁸Then the word of the LORD came to
me: ⁹"This is what the LORD says: 'In
the same way I will ruin the pride of
Judah and the great pride of Jerusalem. ¹⁰These wicked people, who refuse to listen to my words, who follow
the stubbornness of their hearts and
go after other gods to serve and worship them, will be like this belt—
completely useless! ¹¹For as a belt is
bound around a man's waist, so I
bound the whole house of Israel and
the whole house of Judah to me,' declares the LORD, 'to be my people for
my renown and praise and honor. But
they have not listened.'

Wineskins

¹²"Say to them: 'This is what the
LORD, the God of Israel, says: Every
wineskin should be filled with wine.'
And if they say to you, 'Don't we
know that every wineskin should be
filled with wine?' ¹³then tell them,
'This is what the LORD says: I am going to fill with drunkenness all who
live in this land, including the kings
who sit on David's throne, the priests,
the prophets and all those living in
Jerusalem. ¹⁴I will smash them one
against the other, fathers and sons

a4 Or possibly the Euphrates; also in verses 5-7

alike, declares the LORD. I will allow no pity or mercy or compassion to keep me from destroying them.' "

Threat of Captivity

15Hear and pay attention,
do not be arrogant,
for the LORD has spoken.
16Give glory to the LORD your God
before he brings the darkness,
before your feet stumble
on the darkening hills.
You hope for light,
but he will turn it to thick
darkness
and change it to deep gloom.
17But if you do not listen,
I will weep in secret
because of your pride;
my eyes will weep bitterly,
overflowing with tears,
because the LORD's flock will be
taken captive.

18Say to the king and to the queen
mother,
"Come down from your thrones,
for your glorious crowns
will fall from your heads."
19The cities in the Negev will be
shut up,
and there will be no one to open
them.
All Judah will be carried into
exile,
carried completely away.

20Lift up your eyes and see
those who are coming from the
north.
Where is the flock that was
entrusted to you,
the sheep of which you boasted?
21What will you say when the
LORD sets over you
those you cultivated as your
special allies?
Will not pain grip you
like that of a woman in labor?
22And if you ask yourself,
"Why has this happened to
me?"—
it is because of your many sins

that your skirts have been torn
off
and your body mistreated.
23Can the Ethiopian[a] change his
skin
or the leopard its spots?
Neither can you do good
who are accustomed to doing
evil.

24"I will scatter you like chaff
driven by the desert wind.
25This is your lot,
the portion I have decreed for
you,"
                    declares the LORD,
"because you have forgotten me
and trusted in false gods.
26I will pull up your skirts over
your face
that your shame may be seen—
27your adulteries and lustful
neighings,
your shameless prostitution!
I have seen your detestable acts
on the hills and in the fields.
Woe to you, O Jerusalem!
How long will you be unclean?"

Drought, Famine, Sword

14 This is the word of the LORD to
Jeremiah concerning the
drought:

2"Judah mourns,
her cities languish;
they wail for the land,
and a cry goes up from
Jerusalem.
3The nobles send their servants for
water;
they go to the cisterns
but find no water.
They return with their jars
unfilled;
dismayed and despairing,
they cover their heads.
4The ground is cracked
because there is no rain in the
land;
the farmers are dismayed
and cover their heads.
5Even the doe in the field
deserts her newborn fawn

---

a23 Hebrew Cushite (probably a person from the upper Nile region)

because there is no grass.
⁶Wild donkeys stand on the barren
    heights
    and pant like jackals;
their eyesight fails
    for lack of pasture."

⁷Although our sins testify against
    us,
    O LORD, do something for the
        sake of your name.
For our backsliding is great;
    we have sinned against you.
⁸O Hope of Israel,
    its Savior in times of distress,
why are you like a stranger in
        the land,
    like a traveler who stays only a
        night?
⁹Why are you like a man taken by
        surprise,
    like a warrior powerless to
        save?
You are among us, O LORD,
    and we bear your name;
    do not forsake us!

¹⁰This is what the LORD says about
this people:

"They greatly love to wander;
    they do not restrain their feet.
So the LORD does not accept them;
    he will now remember their
        wickedness
    and punish them for their sins."

¹¹Then the LORD said to me, "Do not
pray for the well-being of this people.
¹²Although they fast, I will not listen
to their cry; though they offer burnt
offerings and grain offerings, I will
not accept them. Instead, I will destroy them with the sword, famine
and plague."

¹³But I said, "Ah, Sovereign LORD,
the prophets keep telling them, 'You
will not see the sword or suffer famine. Indeed, I will give you lasting
peace in this place.'"

¹⁴Then the LORD said to me, "The
prophets are prophesying lies in my
name. I have not sent them or appointed them or spoken to them.

They are prophesying to you false visions, divinations, idolatries[a] and
the delusions of their own minds.
¹⁵Therefore, this is what the LORD
says about the prophets who are
prophesying in my name: I did not
send them, yet they are saying, 'No
sword or famine will touch this land.'
Those same prophets will perish by
sword and famine. ¹⁶And the people
they are prophesying to will be
thrown out into the streets of Jerusalem because of the famine and sword.
There will be no one to bury them or
their wives, their sons or their
daughters. I will pour out on them
the calamity they deserve.

¹⁷"Speak this word to them:

" 'Let my eyes overflow with tears
    night and day without ceasing;
for my virgin daughter—my
        people—
    has suffered a grievous wound,
    a crushing blow.
¹⁸If I go into the country,
    I see those slain by the sword;
if I go into the city,
    I see the ravages of famine.
Both prophet and priest
    have gone to a land they know
        not.' "

¹⁹Have you rejected Judah
        completely?
    Do you despise Zion?
Why have you afflicted us
    so that we cannot be healed?
We hoped for peace
    but no good has come,
for a time of healing
    but there is only terror.
²⁰O LORD, we acknowledge our
        wickedness
    and the guilt of our fathers;
    we have indeed sinned against
        you.
²¹For the sake of your name do not
        despise us;
    do not dishonor your glorious
        throne.
Remember your covenant with us
    and do not break it.

_____
ᵃ14 Or visions, worthless divinations

22Do any of the worthless idols of
      the nations bring rain?
   Do the skies themselves send
      down showers?
   No, it is you, O LORD our God.
   Therefore our hope is in you,
      for you are the one who does all
      this.

15 Then the LORD said to me:
"Even if Moses and Samuel
were to stand before me, my heart
would not go out to this people. Send
them away from my presence! Let
them go! 2And if they ask you, 'Where
shall we go?' tell them, 'This is what
the LORD says:

   " 'Those destined for death, to
      death;
   those for the sword, to the sword;
   those for starvation, to starvation;
   those for captivity, to captivity.'

   3"I will send four kinds of destroyers against them," declares the LORD,
"the sword to kill and the dogs to drag
away and the birds of the air and the
beasts of the earth to devour and destroy. 4I will make them abhorrent to
all the kingdoms of the earth because
of what Manasseh son of Hezekiah
king of Judah did in Jerusalem.

   5"Who will have pity on you,
      O Jerusalem?
   Who will mourn for you?
   Who will stop to ask how you
      are?
   6You have rejected me," declares
      the LORD.
   "You keep on backsliding.
   So I will lay hands on you and
      destroy you;
      I can no longer show
      compassion.
   7I will winnow them with a
      winnowing fork
      at the city gates of the land.
   I will bring bereavement and
      destruction on my people,
      for they have not changed their
      ways.

   8I will make their widows more
      numerous
      than the sand of the sea.
   At midday I will bring a
      destroyer
      against the mothers of their
      young men;
   suddenly I will bring down on
      them
      anguish and terror.
   9The mother of seven will grow
      faint
      and breathe her last.
   Her sun will set while it is still
      day;
      she will be disgraced and
      humiliated.
   I will put the survivors to the
      sword
      before their enemies,"
                      declares the LORD.

   10Alas, my mother, that you gave
      me birth,
      a man with whom the whole
      land strives and contends!
   I have neither lent nor borrowed,
      yet everyone curses me.

   11The LORD said,

   "Surely I will deliver you for a
      good purpose;
   surely I will make your enemies
      plead with you
      in times of disaster and times of
      distress.

   12"Can a man break iron—
      iron from the north—or bronze?
   13Your wealth and your treasures
      I will give as plunder, without
      charge,
   because of all your sins
      throughout your country.
   14I will enslave you to your
      enemies
      in*a* a land you do not know,
   for my anger will kindle a fire
      that will burn against you."

   15You understand, O LORD;
      remember me and care for me.
   Avenge me on my persecutors.

*a14 Some Hebrew manuscripts, Septuagint and Syriac (see also Jer. 17:4); most Hebrew manuscripts
I will cause your enemies to bring you / into*

You are long-suffering—do not
    take me away;
  think of how I suffer reproach
    for your sake.
16When your words came, I ate
    them;
  they were my joy and my
    heart's delight,
  for I bear your name,
  O Lord God Almighty.
17I never sat in the company of
    revelers,
  never made merry with them;
  I sat alone because your hand was
    on me
  and you had filled me with
    indignation.
18Why is my pain unending
  and my wound grievous and
    incurable?
  Will you be to me like a deceptive
    brook,
  like a spring that fails?

19Therefore this is what the Lord
says:

"If you repent, I will restore you
    that you may serve me;
  if you utter worthy, not worthless,
    words,
  you will be my spokesman.
  Let this people turn to you,
    but you must not turn to them.
20I will make you a wall to this
    people,
  a fortified wall of bronze;
  they will fight against you
    but will not overcome you,
  for I am with you
    to rescue and save you,"
                declares the Lord.
21"I will save you from the hands of
    the wicked
  and redeem you from the grasp
    of the cruel."

Day of Disaster

16 Then the word of the Lord
came to me: 2"You must not
marry and have sons or daughters in
this place." 3For this is what the Lord
says about the sons and daughters
born in this land and about the wom-
en who are their mothers and the
men who are their fathers: 4"They

will die of deadly diseases. They will
not be mourned or buried but will be
like refuse lying on the ground. They
will perish by sword and famine, and
their dead bodies will become food for
the birds of the air and the beasts of
the earth."

5For this is what the Lord says:
"Do not enter a house where there is
a funeral meal; do not go to mourn or
show sympathy, because I have withdrawn my blessing, my love and my
pity from this people," declares the
Lord. 6"Both high and low will die in
this land. They will not be buried or
mourned, and no one will cut himself
or shave his head for them. 7No one
will offer food to comfort those who
mourn for the dead—not even for a
father or a mother—nor will anyone
give them a drink to console them.

8"And do not enter a house where
there is feasting and sit down to eat
and drink. 9For this is what the Lord
Almighty, the God of Israel, says: Before your eyes and in your days I will
bring an end to the sounds of joy and
gladness and to the voices of bride
and bridegroom in this place.

10"When you tell these people all
this and they ask you, 'Why has the
Lord decreed such a great disaster
against us? What wrong have we
done? What sin have we committed
against the Lord our God?' 11then say
to them, 'It is because your fathers
forsook me,' declares the Lord, 'and
followed other gods and served and
worshiped them. They forsook me
and did not keep my law. 12But you
have behaved more wickedly than
your fathers. See how each of you is
following the stubbornness of his evil
heart instead of obeying me. 13So I
will throw you out of this land into a
land neither you nor your fathers
have known, and there you will serve
other gods day and night, for I will
show you no favor.'

14"However, the days are coming,"
declares the Lord, "when men will no
longer say, 'As surely as the Lord
lives, who brought the Israelites up
out of Egypt,' 15but they will say, 'As
surely as the Lord lives, who brought

the Israelites up out of the land of the north and out of all the countries where he had banished them.' For I will restore them to the land I gave their forefathers.

¹⁶"But now I will send for many fishermen," declares the LORD, "and they will catch them. After that I will send for many hunters, and they will hunt them down on every mountain and hill and from the crevices of the rocks. ¹⁷My eyes are on all their ways; they are not hidden from me, nor is their sin concealed from my eyes. ¹⁸I will repay them double for their wickedness and their sin, because they have defiled my land with the lifeless forms of their vile images and have filled my inheritance with their detestable idols."

¹⁹O LORD, my strength and my
    fortress,
  my refuge in time of distress,
to you the nations will come
  from the ends of the earth and
    say,
"Our fathers possessed nothing
    but false gods,
  worthless idols that did them no
    good.
²⁰Do men make their own gods?
  Yes, but they are not gods!"

²¹"Therefore I will teach them—
  this time I will teach them
  my power and might.
Then they will know
  that my name is the LORD.

17 "Judah's sin is engraved
    with an iron tool,
  inscribed with a flint point,
on the tablets of their hearts
  and on the horns of their altars.
²Even their children remember
  their altars and Asherah poles*ᵃ*
beside the spreading trees
  and on the high hills.
³My mountain in the land
  and your*ᵇ* wealth and all your
    treasures
I will give away as plunder,

together with your high places,
  because of sin throughout your
    country.
⁴Through your own fault you will
    lose
  the inheritance I gave you.
I will enslave you to your enemies
  in a land you do not know,
for you have kindled my anger,
  and it will burn forever."

⁵This is what the LORD says:

"Cursed is the one who trusts in
    man,
  who depends on flesh for his
    strength
  and whose heart turns away
    from the LORD.
⁶He will be like a bush in the
    wastelands;
  he will not see prosperity when
    it comes.
He will dwell in the parched
    places of the desert,
  in a salt land where no one
    lives.

⁷"But blessed is the man who
    trusts in the LORD,
  whose confidence is in him.
⁸He will be like a tree planted by
    the water
  that sends out its roots by the
    stream.
It does not fear when heat comes;
  its leaves are always green.
It has no worries in a year of
    drought
  and never fails to bear fruit."

⁹The heart is deceitful above all
    things
  and beyond cure.
  Who can understand it?

¹⁰"I the LORD search the heart
  and examine the mind,
to reward a man according to his
    conduct,
  according to what his deeds
    deserve."

¹¹Like a partridge that hatches
  eggs it did not lay

ᵃ2 That is, symbols of the goddess Asherah   *ᵇ2,3* Or *hills / 3and the mountains of the land. /*
Your

is the man who gains riches by
unjust means.
When his life is half gone, they
will desert him,
and in the end he will prove to
be a fool.

12A glorious throne, exalted from
the beginning,
is the place of our sanctuary.
13O LORD, the hope of Israel,
all who forsake you will be put
to shame.
Those who turn away from you
will be written in the dust
because they have forsaken the
LORD,
the spring of living water.

14Heal me, O LORD, and I will be
healed;
save me and I will be saved,
for you are the one I praise.
15They keep saying to me,
"Where is the word of the LORD?
Let it now be fulfilled!"
16I have not run away from being
your shepherd;
you know I have not desired the
day of despair.
What passes my lips is open
before you.
17Do not be a terror to me;
you are my refuge in the day of
disaster.
18Let my persecutors be put to
shame,
but keep me from shame;
let them be terrified,
but keep me from terror.
Bring on them the day of disaster;
destroy them with double
destruction.

Keeping the Sabbath Holy

19This is what the LORD said to me:
"Go and stand at the gate of the people, through which the kings of Judah go in and out; stand also at all the
other gates of Jerusalem. 20Say to
them, 'Hear the word of the LORD, O
kings of Judah and all people of Judah and everyone living in Jerusalem who come through these gates.
21This is what the LORD says: Be careful not to carry a load on the Sabbath

day or bring it through the gates of
Jerusalem. 22Do not bring a load out
of your houses or do any work on the
Sabbath, but keep the Sabbath day
holy, as I commanded your forefathers. 23Yet they did not listen or pay
attention; they were stiff-necked and
would not listen or respond to discipline. 24But if you are careful to obey
me, declares the LORD, and bring no
load through the gates of this city on
the Sabbath, but keep the Sabbath
day holy by not doing any work on it,
25then kings who sit on David's
throne will come through the gates of
this city with their officials. They and
their officials will come riding in
chariots and on horses, accompanied
by the men of Judah and those living
in Jerusalem, and this city will be inhabited forever. 26People will come
from the towns of Judah and the villages around Jerusalem, from the
territory of Benjamin and the western foothills, from the hill country
and the Negev, bringing burnt offerings and sacrifices, grain offerings,
incense and thank offerings to the
house of the LORD. 27But if you do not
obey me to keep the Sabbath day holy
by not carrying any load as you come
through the gates of Jerusalem on
the Sabbath day, then I will kindle
an unquenchable fire in the gates of
Jerusalem that will consume her fortresses.' "

At the Potter's House

18 This is the word that came to
Jeremiah from the LORD:
2"Go down to the potter's house, and
there I will give you my message."
3So I went down to the potter's house,
and I saw him working at the wheel.
4But the pot he was shaping from the
clay was marred in his hands; so the
potter formed it into another pot,
shaping it as seemed best to him.

5Then the word of the LORD came to
me: 6"O house of Israel, can I not do
with you as this potter does?" declares the LORD. "Like clay in the
hand of the potter, so are you in my
hand, O house of Israel. 7If at any
time I announce that a nation or

kingdom is to be uprooted, torn down and destroyed, ⁸and if that nation I warned repents of its evil, then I will relent and not inflict on it the disaster I had planned. ⁹And if at another time I announce that a nation or kingdom is to be built up and planted, ¹⁰and if it does evil in my sight and does not obey me, then I will reconsider the good I had intended to do for it.

¹¹"Now therefore say to the people of Judah and those living in Jerusalem, 'This is what the LORD says: Look! I am preparing a disaster for you and devising a plan against you. So turn from your evil ways, each one of you, and reform your ways and your actions.' ¹²But they will reply, 'It's no use. We will continue with our own plans; each of us will follow the stubbornness of his evil heart.'"

¹³Therefore this is what the LORD says:

"Inquire among the nations:
  Who has ever heard anything
    like this?
A most horrible thing has been
    done
  by Virgin Israel.
¹⁴Does the snow of Lebanon
  ever vanish from its rocky
    slopes?

a14 The meaning of the Hebrew for this sentence is uncertain.

Do its cool waters from distant
    sources
  ever cease to flow?ᵃ
¹⁵Yet my people have forgotten me;
  they burn incense to worthless
    idols,
which made them stumble in
    their ways
  and in the ancient paths.
They made them walk in bypaths
  and on roads not built up.
¹⁶Their land will be laid waste,
  an object of lasting scorn;
all who pass by will be appalled
  and will shake their heads.
¹⁷Like a wind from the east,
  I will scatter them before their
    enemies;
I will show them my back and not
    my face
  in the day of their disaster."

¹⁸They said, "Come, let's make plans against Jeremiah; for the teaching of the law by the priest will not be lost, nor will counsel from the wise, nor the word from the prophets. So come, let's attack him with our tongues and pay no attention to anything he says."

¹⁹Listen to me, O LORD;
  hear what my accusers are
    saying!
²⁰Should good be repaid with evil?

Life in Bible Times

A POTTER AT WORK

Clay pots were used in Israel for cooking and for holding water, oil and grain. Potters shaped the clay into pots with their hands while the clay was spinning on a flat wheel. Making pots was an important job, because every household needed many clay pots.

Yet they have dug a pit for me.
Remember that I stood before
  you
  and spoke in their behalf
  to turn your wrath away from
  them.
²¹So give their children over to
  famine;
  hand them over to the power of
  the sword.
Let their wives be made childless
  and widows;
  let their men be put to death,
  their young men slain by the
  sword in battle.
²²Let a cry be heard from their
  houses
  when you suddenly bring
  invaders against them,
  for they have dug a pit to capture
  me
  and have hidden snares for my
  feet.
²³But you know, O Lord,
  all their plots to kill me.
Do not forgive their crimes
  or blot out their sins from your
  sight.
Let them be overthrown before
  you;
  deal with them in the time of
  your anger.

19 This is what the Lord says:
"Go and buy a clay jar from a
potter. Take along some of the elders
of the people and of the priests ²and
go out to the Valley of Ben Hinnom,
near the entrance of the Potsherd
Gate. There proclaim the words I tell
you, ³and say, 'Hear the word of the
Lord, O kings of Judah and people of
Jerusalem. This is what the Lord Almighty, the God of Israel, says: Listen! I am going to bring a disaster on
this place that will make the ears of
everyone who hears of it tingle. ⁴For
they have forsaken me and made this
a place of foreign gods; they have
burned sacrifices in it to gods that
neither they nor their fathers nor the
kings of Judah ever knew, and they
have filled this place with the blood

of the innocent. ⁵They have built the
high places of Baal to burn their sons
in the fire as offerings to Baal—
something I did not command or
mention, nor did it enter my mind.
⁶So beware, the days are coming, declares the Lord, when people will no
longer call this place Topheth or the
Valley of Ben Hinnom, but the Valley of Slaughter.

⁷" 'In this place I will ruin*a* the
plans of Judah and Jerusalem. I will
make them fall by the sword before
their enemies, at the hands of those
who seek their lives, and I will give
their carcasses as food to the birds of
the air and the beasts of the earth. ⁸I
will devastate this city and make it
an object of scorn; all who pass by will
be appalled and will scoff because of
all its wounds. ⁹I will make them eat
the flesh of their sons and daughters,
and they will eat one another's flesh
during the stress of the siege imposed
on them by the enemies who seek
their lives.'

¹⁰"Then break the jar while those
who go with you are watching, ¹¹and
say to them, 'This is what the Lord
Almighty says: I will smash this nation and this city just as this potter's
jar is smashed and cannot be repaired. They will bury the dead in Topheth until there is no more room.
¹²This is what I will do to this place
and to those who live here, declares
the Lord. I will make this city like
Topheth. ¹³The houses in Jerusalem
and those of the kings of Judah will
be defiled like this place, Topheth
—all the houses where they burned
incense on the roofs to all the starry
hosts and poured out drink offerings
to other gods.' "

¹⁴Jeremiah then returned from Topheth, where the Lord had sent him
to prophesy, and stood in the court of
the Lord's temple and said to all the
people, ¹⁵"This is what the Lord Almighty, the God of Israel, says: 'Listen! I am going to bring on this city
and the villages around it every disaster I pronounced against them, be-

---

*a7 The Hebrew for *ruin* sounds like the Hebrew for *jar* (see verses 1 and 10).

cause they were stiff-necked and would not listen to my words.' "

Jeremiah and Pashhur

20 When the priest Pashhur son of Immer, the chief officer in the temple of the LORD, heard Jeremiah prophesying these things, ²he had Jeremiah the prophet beaten and put in the stocks at the Upper Gate of Benjamin at the LORD's temple. ³The next day, when Pashhur released him from the stocks, Jeremiah said to him, "The LORD's name for you is not Pashhur, but Magor-Missabib.ᵃ ⁴For this is what the LORD says: 'I will make you a terror to yourself and to all your friends; with your own eyes you will see them fall by the sword of their enemies. I will hand all Judah over to the king of Babylon, who will carry them away to Babylon or put them to the sword. ⁵I will hand over to their enemies all the wealth of this city—all its products, all its valuables and all the treasures of the kings of Judah. They will take it away as plunder and carry it off to Babylon. ⁶And you, Pashhur, and all who live in your house will go into exile to Babylon. There you will die and be buried, you and all your friends to whom you have prophesied lies.' "

Jeremiah's Complaint

⁷O LORD, you deceivedᵇ me, and I
    was deceivedᵇ;
  you overpowered me and
    prevailed.
  I am ridiculed all day long;
    everyone mocks me.
⁸Whenever I speak, I cry out
    proclaiming violence and
    destruction.
  So the word of the LORD has
    brought me
    insult and reproach all day
    long.
⁹But if I say, "I will not mention
    him

or speak any more in his
    name,"
  his word is in my heart like a
    fire,
  a fire shut up in my bones.
  I am weary of holding it in;
    indeed, I cannot.
¹⁰I hear many whispering,
  "Terror on every side!
  Report him! Let's report him!"
  All my friends
    are waiting for me to slip,
    saying,
  "Perhaps he will be deceived;
    then we will prevail over him
    and take our revenge on him."

¹¹But the LORD is with me like a
    mighty warrior;
  so my persecutors will stumble
    and not prevail.
  They will fail and be thoroughly
    disgraced;
    their dishonor will never be
    forgotten.
¹²O LORD Almighty, you who
    examine the righteous
  and probe the heart and mind,
  let me see your vengeance upon
    them,
    for to you I have committed my
    cause.

¹³Sing to the LORD!
  Give praise to the LORD!
  He rescues the life of the needy
    from the hands of the wicked.

¹⁴Cursed be the day I was born!
  May the day my mother bore
    me not be blessed!
¹⁵Cursed be the man who brought
    my father the news,
  who made him very glad,
    saying,
  "A child is born to you—a son!"
¹⁶May that man be like the towns
    the LORD overthrew without
    pity.
  May he hear wailing in the
    morning,
    a battle cry at noon.
¹⁷For he did not kill me in the
    womb,

ᵃ3 *Magor-Missabib* means *terror on every side.*   ᵇ7 Or *persuaded*

with my mother as my grave,
her womb enlarged forever.
¹⁸Why did I ever come out of the
womb
to see trouble and sorrow
and to end my days in shame?

God Rejects Zedekiah's Request

21 The word came to Jeremiah from the LORD when King Zedekiah sent to him Pashhur son of Malkijah and the priest Zephaniah son of Maaseiah. They said: ²"Inquire now of the LORD for us because Nebuchadnezzar*ᵃ* king of Babylon is attacking us. Perhaps the LORD will perform wonders for us as in times past so that he will withdraw from us."

³But Jeremiah answered them, "Tell Zedekiah, ⁴'This is what the LORD, the God of Israel, says: I am about to turn against you the weapons of war that are in your hands, which you are using to fight the king of Babylon and the Babylonians*ᵇ* who are outside the wall besieging you. And I will gather them inside this city. ⁵I myself will fight against you with an outstretched hand and a mighty arm in anger and fury and great wrath. ⁶I will strike down those who live in this city—both men and animals—and they will die of a terrible plague. ⁷After that, declares the LORD, I will hand over Zedekiah king of Judah, his officials and the people in this city who survive the plague, sword and famine, to Nebuchadnezzar king of Babylon and to their enemies who seek their lives. He will put them to the sword; he will show them no mercy or pity or compassion.'

⁸"Furthermore, tell the people, 'This is what the LORD says: See, I am setting before you the way of life and the way of death. ⁹Whoever stays in this city will die by the sword, famine or plague. But whoever goes out and surrenders to the Babylonians who are besieging you will live; he will escape with his life. ¹⁰I have deter-

mined to do this city harm and not good, declares the LORD. It will be given into the hands of the king of Babylon, and he will destroy it with fire.'

¹¹"Moreover, say to the royal house of Judah, 'Hear the word of the LORD; ¹²O house of David, this is what the LORD says:

" 'Administer justice every
morning;
rescue from the hand of his
oppressor
the one who has been robbed,
or my wrath will break out and
burn like fire
because of the evil you have
done—
burn with no one to quench it.
¹³I am against you, ₍Jerusalem₎,
you who live above this valley
on the rocky plateau,
declares the LORD—
you who say, "Who can come
against us?
Who can enter our refuge?"
¹⁴I will punish you as your deeds
deserve,
declares the LORD.
I will kindle a fire in your forests
that will consume everything
around you.' "

Judgment Against Evil Kings

22 This is what the LORD says: "Go down to the palace of the king of Judah and proclaim this message there: ²'Hear the word of the LORD, O king of Judah, you who sit on David's throne—you, your officials and your people who come through these gates. ³This is what the LORD says: Do what is just and right. Rescue from the hand of his oppressor the one who has been robbed. Do no wrong or violence to the alien, the fatherless or the widow, and do not shed innocent blood in this place. ⁴For if you are careful to carry out these commands, then kings who sit on David's throne will come through

---

ᵃ2 Hebrew *Nebuchadrezzar,* of which *Nebuchadnezzar* is a variant; here and often in Jeremiah and Ezekiel   *ᵇ4* Or *Chaldeans*; also in verse 9

the gates of this palace, riding in chariots and on horses, accompanied by their officials and their people. ⁵But if you do not obey these commands, declares the LORD, I swear by myself that this palace will become a ruin.'"

⁶For this is what the LORD says about the palace of the king of Judah:

"Though you are like Gilead to
    me,
  like the summit of Lebanon,
I will surely make you like a
    desert,
  like towns not inhabited.
⁷I will send destroyers against you,
  each man with his weapons,
and they will cut up your fine
    cedar beams
  and throw them into the fire.

⁸"People from many nations will pass by this city and will ask one another, 'Why has the LORD done such a thing to this great city?' ⁹And the answer will be: 'Because they have forsaken the covenant of the LORD their God and have worshiped and served other gods.'"

¹⁰Do not weep for the dead ⌊king⌋ or
    mourn his loss;
  rather, weep bitterly for him
    who is exiled,
because he will never return
  nor see his native land again.

¹¹For this is what the LORD says about Shallum*ᵃ* son of Josiah, who succeeded his father as king of Judah but has gone from this place: "He will never return. ¹²He will die in the place where they have led him captive; he will not see this land again."

¹³"Woe to him who builds his
    palace by unrighteousness,
  his upper rooms by injustice,
making his countrymen work for
    nothing,
  not paying them for their labor.
¹⁴He says, 'I will build myself a
    great palace
  with spacious upper rooms.'

So he makes large windows in it,
  panels it with cedar
  and decorates it in red.

¹⁵"Does it make you a king
  to have more and more cedar?
Did not your father have food and
    drink?
  He did what was right and just,
  so all went well with him.
¹⁶He defended the cause of the poor
    and needy,
  and so all went well.
Is that not what it means to know
    me?"
  declares the LORD.
¹⁷"But your eyes and your heart
  are set only on dishonest gain,
on shedding innocent blood
  and on oppression and
    extortion."

¹⁸Therefore this is what the LORD says about Jehoiakim son of Josiah king of Judah:

"They will not mourn for him:
  'Alas, my brother! Alas, my
    sister!'
They will not mourn for him:
  'Alas, my master! Alas, his
    splendor!'
¹⁹He will have the burial of a
    donkey—
  dragged away and thrown
  outside the gates of Jerusalem."

²⁰"Go up to Lebanon and cry out,
  let your voice be heard in
    Bashan,
cry out from Abarim,
  for all your allies are crushed.
²¹I warned you when you felt
    secure,
  but you said, 'I will not listen!'
This has been your way from your
    youth;
  you have not obeyed me.
²²The wind will drive all your
    shepherds away,
  and your allies will go into
    exile.
Then you will be ashamed and
    disgraced
  because of all your wickedness.

---

*ᵃ11 Also called *Jehoahaz*

²³You who live in 'Lebanon,ᵃ'
　who are nestled in cedar
　　buildings,
how you will groan when pangs
　come upon you,
　　pain like that of a woman in
　　　labor!

²⁴"As surely as I live," declares the
LORD, "even if you, Jehoiachinᵇ son
of Jehoiakim king of Judah, were a
signet ring on my right hand, I would
still pull you off. ²⁵I will hand you
over to those who seek your life, those
you fear—to Nebuchadnezzar king of
Babylon and to the Babylonians.ᶜ ²⁶I
will hurl you and the mother who
gave you birth into another country,
where neither of you was born, and
there you both will die. ²⁷You will
never come back to the land you long
to return to."

²⁸Is this man Jehoiachin a
　　despised, broken pot,
　an object no one wants?
Why will he and his children be
　　hurled out,
　cast into a land they do not
　　know?
²⁹O land, land, land,
　hear the word of the LORD!
³⁰This is what the LORD says:
"Record this man as if childless,
　a man who will not prosper in
　　his lifetime,
for none of his offspring will
　　prosper,
　none will sit on the throne of
　　David
　or rule anymore in Judah."

The Righteous Branch

23 "Woe to the shepherds who
are destroying and scattering
the sheep of my pasture!" declares
the LORD. ²Therefore this is what the
LORD, the God of Israel, says to the
shepherds who tend my people: "Because you have scattered my flock
and driven them away and have not
bestowed care on them, I will bestow

punishment on you for the evil you
have done," declares the LORD. ³"I
myself will gather the remnant of my
flock out of all the countries where I
have driven them and will bring
them back to their pasture, where
they will be fruitful and increase in
number. ⁴I will place shepherds over
them who will tend them, and they
will no longer be afraid or terrified,
nor will any be missing," declares the
LORD.

⁵"The days are coming," declares
　　the LORD,
"when I will raise up to Davidᵈ
　a righteous Branch,
a King who will reign wisely
　and do what is just and right in
　　the land.
⁶In his days Judah will be saved
　and Israel will live in safety.
This is the name by which he will
　　be called:
　The LORD Our Righteousness.

⁷"So then, the days are coming," declares the LORD, "when people will no
longer say, 'As surely as the LORD
lives, who brought the Israelites up
out of Egypt,' ⁸but they will say, 'As
surely as the LORD lives, who brought
the descendants of Israel up out of the
land of the north and out of all the
countries where he had banished
them.' Then they will live in their
own land."

Lying Prophets

⁹Concerning the prophets:

My heart is broken within me;
　all my bones tremble.
I am like a drunken man,
　like a man overcome by wine,
because of the LORD
　and his holy words.
¹⁰The land is full of adulterers;
　because of the curseᵉ the land
　　lies parchedᶠ
　and the pastures in the desert
　　are withered.

ᵃ23 That is, the palace in Jerusalem (see 1 Kings 7:2)
Jehoiachin; also in verse 28　　ᶜ25 Or Chaldeans
because of these things　ᶠ10 Or land mourns
ᵇ24 Hebrew Coniah, a variant of
ᵈ5 Or up from David's line　ᵉ10 Or

The ⌊prophets⌋ follow an evil
  course
and use their power unjustly.
¹¹"Both prophet and priest are
    godless;
  even in my temple I find their
    wickedness,"
            declares the LORD.
¹²"Therefore their path will become
    slippery;
  they will be banished to
    darkness
  and there they will fall.
I will bring disaster on them
  in the year they are punished,"
            declares the LORD.

¹³"Among the prophets of Samaria
  I saw this repulsive thing:
They prophesied by Baal
  and led my people Israel astray.
¹⁴And among the prophets of
    Jerusalem
  I have seen something horrible:
They commit adultery and live
    a lie.
They strengthen the hands of
    evildoers,
  so that no one turns from his
    wickedness.
They are all like Sodom to me;
  the people of Jerusalem are like
    Gomorrah."

¹⁵Therefore, this is what the LORD
Almighty says concerning the prophets:

"I will make them eat bitter food
  and drink poisoned water,
because from the prophets of
    Jerusalem
  ungodliness has spread
    throughout the land."

¹⁶This is what the LORD Almighty
says:

"Do not listen to what the
    prophets are prophesying to
    you;
  they fill you with false hopes.
They speak visions from their
    own minds,
  not from the mouth of the LORD.
¹⁷They keep saying to those who
    despise me,

'The LORD says: You will have
    peace.'
And to all who follow the
    stubbornness of their hearts
  they say, 'No harm will come to
    you.'
¹⁸But which of them has stood in
    the council of the LORD
  to see or to hear his word?
Who has listened and heard his
    word?
¹⁹See, the storm of the LORD
  will burst out in wrath,
a whirlwind swirling down
  on the heads of the wicked.
²⁰The anger of the LORD will not
    turn back
  until he fully accomplishes
    the purposes of his heart.
In days to come
  you will understand it clearly.
²¹I did not send these prophets,
  yet they have run with their
    message;
I did not speak to them,
  yet they have prophesied.
²²But if they had stood in my
    council,
  they would have proclaimed my
    words to my people
and would have turned them from
    their evil ways
  and from their evil deeds.

²³"Am I only a God nearby,"
            declares the LORD,
  "and not a God far away?
²⁴Can anyone hide in secret places
  so that I cannot see him?"
            declares the LORD.
  "Do not I fill heaven and
    earth?"
            declares the LORD.

²⁵"I have heard what the prophets
say who prophesy lies in my name.
They say, 'I had a dream! I had a
dream!' ²⁶How long will this continue
in the hearts of these lying prophets,
who prophesy the delusions of their
own minds? ²⁷They think the dreams
they tell one another will make my
people forget my name, just as their
fathers forgot my name through Baal
worship. ²⁸Let the prophet who has a
dream tell his dream, but let the one

who has my word speak it faithfully. For what has straw to do with grain?" declares the LORD. [29]"Is not my word like fire," declares the LORD, "and like a hammer that breaks a rock in pieces?

[30]"Therefore," declares the LORD, "I am against the prophets who steal from one another words supposedly from me. [31]Yes," declares the LORD, "I am against the prophets who wag their own tongues and yet declare, 'The LORD declares.' [32]Indeed, I am against those who prophesy false dreams," declares the LORD. "They tell them and lead my people astray with their reckless lies, yet I did not send or appoint them. They do not benefit these people in the least," declares the LORD.

False Oracles and False Prophets

[33]"When these people, or a prophet or a priest, ask you, 'What is the oracle[a] of the LORD?' say to them, 'What oracle?[b] I will forsake you, declares the LORD.' [34]If a prophet or a priest or anyone else claims, 'This is the oracle of the LORD,' I will punish that man and his household. [35]This is what each of you keeps on saying to his friend or relative: 'What is the LORD's answer?' or 'What has the LORD spoken?' [36]But you must not mention 'the oracle of the LORD' again, be-

cause every man's own word becomes his oracle and so you distort the words of the living God, the LORD Almighty, our God. [37]This is what you keep saying to a prophet: 'What is the LORD's answer to you?' or 'What has the LORD spoken?' [38]Although you claim, 'This is the oracle of the LORD,' this is what the LORD says: You used the words, 'This is the oracle of the LORD,' even though I told you that you must not claim, 'This is the oracle of the LORD.' [39]Therefore, I will surely forget you and cast you out of my presence along with the city I gave to you and your fathers. [40]I will bring upon you everlasting disgrace —everlasting shame that will not be forgotten.' "

Two Baskets of Figs

24 After Jehoiachin[c] son of Jehoiakim king of Judah and the officials, the craftsmen and the artisans of Judah were carried into exile from Jerusalem to Babylon by Nebuchadnezzar king of Babylon, the LORD showed me two baskets of figs placed in front of the temple of the LORD. [2]One basket had very good figs, like those that ripen early; the other basket had very poor figs, so bad they could not be eaten.

[3]Then the LORD asked me, "What do you see, Jeremiah?"

"Figs," I answered. "The good ones

---

[a]33 Or *burden* (see Septuagint and Vulgate)   [b]33 Hebrew; Septuagint and Vulgate *'You are the burden.* (The Hebrew for *oracle* and *burden* is the same.)   [c]1 Hebrew *Jeconiah,* a variant of *Jehoiachin*

▚ ET'S LIVE IT!   Jeremiah 23:23–24

WHERE IS GOD NOW? ➠ Read Jeremiah 23:23–24. How do these verses tell us that God is everywhere?

If God is everywhere, how many of these statements about him are true?

1. God is with me wherever I go, and he can protect me.
2. God sees all the wrong things people do.
3. No one can run away and hide from God.

Can you think of other things that are true because God is everywhere?

are very good, but the poor ones are so bad they cannot be eaten."

⁴Then the word of the LORD came to me: ⁵"This is what the LORD, the God of Israel, says: 'Like these good figs, I regard as good the exiles from Judah, whom I sent away from this place to the land of the Babylonians.*ᵃ* ⁶My eyes will watch over them for their good, and I will bring them back to this land. I will build them up and not tear them down; I will plant them and not uproot them. ⁷I will give them a heart to know me, that I am the LORD. They will be my people, and I will be their God, for they will return to me with all their heart.

⁸" 'But like the poor figs, which are so bad they cannot be eaten,' says the LORD, 'so will I deal with Zedekiah king of Judah, his officials and the survivors from Jerusalem, whether they remain in this land or live in Egypt. ⁹I will make them abhorrent and an offense to all the kingdoms of the earth, a reproach and a byword, an object of ridicule and cursing, wherever I banish them. ¹⁰I will send the sword, famine and plague against them until they are destroyed from the land I gave to them and their fathers.' "

Seventy Years of Captivity

25 The word came to Jeremiah concerning all the people of Judah in the fourth year of Jehoiakim son of Josiah king of Judah, which was the first year of Nebuchadnezzar king of Babylon. ²So Jeremiah the prophet said to all the people of Judah and to all those living in Jerusalem: ³For twenty-three years —from the thirteenth year of Josiah son of Amon king of Judah until this very day—the word of the LORD has come to me and I have spoken to you again and again, but you have not listened.

⁴And though the LORD has sent all his servants the prophets to you again and again, you have not listened or paid any attention. ⁵They said, "Turn now, each of you, from your evil ways and your evil practices, and you can stay in the land the LORD gave to you and your fathers for ever and ever. ⁶Do not follow other gods to serve and worship them; do not provoke me to anger with what your hands have made. Then I will not harm you."

⁷"But you did not listen to me," declares the LORD, "and you have provoked me with what your hands have made, and you have brought harm to yourselves."

⁸Therefore the LORD Almighty says this: "Because you have not listened to my words, ⁹I will summon all the peoples of the north and my servant Nebuchadnezzar king of Babylon," declares the LORD, "and I will bring them against this land and its inhabitants and against all the surrounding nations. I will completely destroy*ᵇ* them and make them an object of horror and scorn, and an everlasting ruin. ¹⁰I will banish from them the sounds of joy and gladness, the voices of bride and bridegroom, the sound of millstones and the light of the lamp. ¹¹This whole country will become a desolate wasteland, and these nations will serve the king of Babylon seventy years.

¹²"But when the seventy years are fulfilled, I will punish the king of Babylon and his nation, the land of the Babylonians,*ᵃ* for their guilt," declares the LORD, "and will make it desolate forever. ¹³I will bring upon that land all the things I have spoken against it, all that are written in this book and prophesied by Jeremiah against all the nations. ¹⁴They themselves will be enslaved by many nations and great kings; I will repay them according to their deeds and the work of their hands."

The Cup of God's Wrath

¹⁵This is what the LORD, the God of Israel, said to me: "Take from my

---

ᵃ5,12 Or *Chaldeans*   *ᵇ9* The Hebrew term refers to the irrevocable giving over of things or persons to the LORD, often by totally destroying them.

hand this cup filled with the wine of my wrath and make all the nations to whom I send you drink it. ¹⁶When they drink it, they will stagger and go mad because of the sword I will send among them."

¹⁷So I took the cup from the LORD's hand and made all the nations to whom he sent me drink it: ¹⁸Jerusalem and the towns of Judah, its kings and officials, to make them a ruin and an object of horror and scorn and cursing, as they are today; ¹⁹Pharaoh king of Egypt, his attendants, his officials and all his people, ²⁰and all the foreign people there; all the kings of Uz; all the kings of the Philistines (those of Ashkelon, Gaza, Ekron, and the people left at Ashdod); ²¹Edom, Moab and Ammon; ²²all the kings of Tyre and Sidon; the kings of the coastlands across the sea; ²³Dedan, Tema, Buz and all who are in distant places*ᵃ*; ²⁴all the kings of Arabia and all the kings of the foreign people who live in the desert; ²⁵all the kings of Zimri, Elam and Media; ²⁶and all the kings of the north, near and far, one after the other—all the kingdoms on the face of the earth. And after all of them, the king of Sheshach*ᵇ* will drink it too.

²⁷"Then tell them, 'This is what the LORD Almighty, the God of Israel, says: Drink, get drunk and vomit, and fall to rise no more because of the sword I will send among you.' ²⁸But if they refuse to take the cup from your hand and drink, tell them, 'This is what the LORD Almighty says: You must drink it! ²⁹See, I am beginning to bring disaster on the city that bears my Name, and will you indeed go unpunished? You will not go unpunished, for I am calling down a sword upon all who live on the earth, declares the LORD Almighty.'

³⁰"Now prophesy all these words against them and say to them:

" 'The LORD will roar from on
    high;

he will thunder from his holy
    dwelling
and roar mightily against his
    land.
He will shout like those who
    tread the grapes,
shout against all who live on
    the earth.
³¹The tumult will resound to the
    ends of the earth,
for the LORD will bring charges
    against the nations;
he will bring judgment on all
    mankind
and put the wicked to the
    sword,' "
           declares the LORD.

³²This is what the LORD Almighty says:

"Look! Disaster is spreading
    from nation to nation;
a mighty storm is rising
    from the ends of the earth."

³³At that time those slain by the LORD will be everywhere—from one end of the earth to the other. They will not be mourned or gathered up or buried, but will be like refuse lying on the ground.

³⁴Weep and wail, you shepherds;
    roll in the dust, you leaders of
    the flock.
For your time to be slaughtered
    has come;
you will fall and be shattered
    like fine pottery.
³⁵The shepherds will have nowhere
    to flee,
the leaders of the flock no place
    to escape.
³⁶Hear the cry of the shepherds,
    the wailing of the leaders of the
    flock,
for the LORD is destroying their
    pasture.
³⁷The peaceful meadows will be
    laid waste
because of the fierce anger of
    the LORD.
³⁸Like a lion he will leave his lair,

---

*ᵃ*23 Or *who clip the hair by their foreheads*   *ᵇ*26 *Sheshach* is a cryptogram for Babylon.

and their land will become
  desolate
because of the sword*a* of the
  oppressor
and because of the LORD's fierce
  anger.

Jeremiah Threatened With Death

26 Early in the reign of Jehoiakim son of Josiah king of Judah, this word came from the LORD:
²"This is what the LORD says: Stand
in the courtyard of the LORD's house
and speak to all the people of the
towns of Judah who come to worship
in the house of the LORD. Tell them
everything I command you; do not
omit a word. ³Perhaps they will listen
and each will turn from his evil way.
Then I will relent and not bring on
them the disaster I was planning because of the evil they have done. ⁴Say
to them, 'This is what the LORD says:
If you do not listen to me and follow
my law, which I have set before you,
⁵and if you do not listen to the words
of my servants the prophets, whom I
have sent to you again and again
(though you have not listened), ⁶then
I will make this house like Shiloh
and this city an object of cursing
among all the nations of the earth.'"

⁷The priests, the prophets and all
the people heard Jeremiah speak
these words in the house of the LORD.
⁸But as soon as Jeremiah finished
telling all the people everything the
LORD had commanded him to say, the
priests, the prophets and all the people seized him and said, "You must
die! ⁹Why do you prophesy in the
LORD's name that this house will be
like Shiloh and this city will be desolate and deserted?" And all the people crowded around Jeremiah in the
house of the LORD.

¹⁰When the officials of Judah heard
about these things, they went up
from the royal palace to the house of
the LORD and took their places at the
entrance of the New Gate of the
LORD's house. ¹¹Then the priests and
the prophets said to the officials and
all the people, "This man should be
sentenced to death because he has
prophesied against this city. You
have heard it with your own ears!"

¹²Then Jeremiah said to all the officials and all the people: "The LORD
sent me to prophesy against this
house and this city all the things you
have heard. ¹³Now reform your ways
and your actions and obey the LORD
your God. Then the LORD will relent
and not bring the disaster he has pronounced against you. ¹⁴As for me, I
am in your hands; do with me whatever you think is good and right. ¹⁵Be
assured, however, that if you put me
to death, you will bring the guilt of
innocent blood on yourselves and on
this city and on those who live in it,
for in truth the LORD has sent me to
you to speak all these words in your
hearing."

¹⁶Then the officials and all the people said to the priests and the prophets, "This man should not be sentenced to death! He has spoken to us
in the name of the LORD our God."

PROPHETS

God's messengers in Old Testament times were called prophets.
God told each prophet what to
say. Even when God's people did
not want to hear his message, the
prophet had to speak to them.

¹⁷Some of the elders of the land
stepped forward and said to the entire assembly of people, ¹⁸"Micah of
Moresheth prophesied in the days of

---

*a38 Some Hebrew manuscripts and Septuagint (see also Jer. 46:16 and 50:16); most Hebrew
manuscripts *anger*

Hezekiah king of Judah. He told all the people of Judah, 'This is what the LORD Almighty says:

" 'Zion will be plowed like a field,
Jerusalem will become a heap
of rubble,
the temple hill a mound
overgrown with thickets.'ᵃ

¹⁹"Did Hezekiah king of Judah or anyone else in Judah put him to death? Did not Hezekiah fear the LORD and seek his favor? And did not the LORD relent, so that he did not bring the disaster he pronounced against them? We are about to bring a terrible disaster on ourselves!"

²⁰(Now Uriah son of Shemaiah from Kiriath Jearim was another man who prophesied in the name of the LORD; he prophesied the same things against this city and this land as Jeremiah did. ²¹When King Jehoiakim and all his officers and officials heard his words, the king sought to put him to death. But Uriah heard of it and fled in fear to Egypt. ²²King Jehoiakim, however, sent Elnathan son of Acbor to Egypt, along with some other men. ²³They brought Uriah out of Egypt and took him to King Jehoiakim, who had him struck down with a sword and his body thrown into the burial place of the common people.)

²⁴Furthermore, Ahikam son of Shaphan supported Jeremiah, and so he was not handed over to the people to be put to death.

Judah to Serve Nebuchadnezzar

27 Early in the reign of Zedekiahᵇ son of Josiah king of Judah, this word came to Jeremiah from the LORD: ²This is what the LORD said to me: "Make a yoke out of straps and crossbars and put it on your neck. ³Then send word to the kings of Edom, Moab, Ammon, Tyre and Sidon through the envoys who have come to Jerusalem to Zedekiah king of Judah. ⁴Give them a message for their masters and say, 'This is what the LORD Almighty, the God of Israel, says: "Tell this to your masters: ⁵With my great power and outstretched arm I made the earth and its people and the animals that are on it, and I give it to anyone I please. ⁶Now I will hand all your countries over to my servant Nebuchadnezzar king of Babylon; I will make even the wild animals subject to him. ⁷All nations will serve him and his son and his grandson until the time for his land comes; then many nations and great kings will subjugate him.

⁸" ' "If, however, any nation or kingdom will not serve Nebuchadnezzar king of Babylon or bow its neck under his yoke, I will punish that nation with the sword, famine and plague, declares the LORD, until I destroy it by his hand. ⁹So do not listen to your prophets, your diviners, your interpreters of dreams, your mediums or your sorcerers who tell you, 'You will not serve the king of Babylon.' ¹⁰They prophesy lies to you that will only serve to remove you far from your lands; I will banish you and you will perish. ¹¹But if any nation will bow its neck under the yoke of the king of Babylon and serve him, I will let that nation remain in its own land to till it and to live there, declares the LORD." ' "

¹²I gave the same message to Zedekiah king of Judah. I said, "Bow your neck under the yoke of the king of Babylon; serve him and his people, and you will live. ¹³Why will you and your people die by the sword, famine and plague with which the LORD has threatened any nation that will not serve the king of Babylon? ¹⁴Do not listen to the words of the prophets who say to you, 'You will not serve the king of Babylon,' for they are prophesying lies to you. ¹⁵'I have not sent them,' declares the LORD. 'They are prophesying lies in my name. Therefore, I will banish you and you

---

ᵃ18 Micah 3:12   ᵇ1 A few Hebrew manuscripts and Syriac (see also Jer. 27:3, 12 and 28:1); most Hebrew manuscripts *Jehoiakim* (Most Septuagint manuscripts do not have this verse.)

will perish, both you and the prophets who prophesy to you.' "

16Then I said to the priests and all these people, "This is what the LORD says: Do not listen to the prophets who say, 'Very soon now the articles from the LORD's house will be brought back from Babylon.' They are prophesying lies to you. 17Do not listen to them. Serve the king of Babylon, and you will live. Why should this city become a ruin? 18If they are prophets and have the word of the LORD, let them plead with the LORD Almighty that the furnishings remaining in the house of the LORD and in the palace of the king of Judah and in Jerusalem not be taken to Babylon. 19For this is what the LORD Almighty says about the pillars, the Sea, the movable stands and the other furnishings that are left in this city, 20which Nebuchadnezzar king of Babylon did not take away when he carried Jehoiachin[a] son of Jehoiakim king of Judah into exile from Jerusalem to Babylon, along with all the nobles of Judah and Jerusalem— 21yes, this is what the LORD Almighty, the God of Israel, says about the things that are left in the house of the LORD and in the palace of the king of Judah and in Jerusalem: 22'They will be taken to Babylon and there they will remain until the day I come for them,' declares the LORD. 'Then I will bring them back and restore them to this place.' "

The False Prophet Hananiah

28 In the fifth month of that same year, the fourth year, early in the reign of Zedekiah king of Judah, the prophet Hananiah son of Azzur, who was from Gibeon, said to me in the house of the LORD in the presence of the priests and all the people: 2"This is what the LORD Almighty, the God of Israel, says: 'I will break the yoke of the king of Babylon. 3Within two years I will bring back to this place all the articles of the LORD's house that Nebuchadnezzar king of Babylon removed from here and took to Babylon. 4I will also bring back to this place Jehoiachin[a] son of Jehoiakim king of Judah and all the other exiles from Judah who went to Babylon,' declares the LORD, 'for I will break the yoke of the king of Babylon.' "

5Then the prophet Jeremiah replied to the prophet Hananiah before the priests and all the people who were standing in the house of the LORD. 6He said, "Amen! May the LORD do so! May the LORD fulfill the words you have prophesied by bringing the articles of the LORD's house and all the exiles back to this place from Babylon. 7Nevertheless, listen to what I have to say in your hearing and in the hearing of all the people: 8From early times the prophets who preceded you and me have prophesied war, disaster and plague against many countries and great kingdoms. 9But the prophet who prophesies peace will be recognized as one truly sent by the LORD only if his prediction comes true."

10Then the prophet Hananiah took the yoke off the neck of the prophet Jeremiah and broke it, 11and he said before all the people, "This is what the LORD says: 'In the same way will I break the yoke of Nebuchadnezzar king of Babylon off the neck of all the nations within two years.' " At this, the prophet Jeremiah went on his way.

12Shortly after the prophet Hananiah had broken the yoke off the neck of the prophet Jeremiah, the word of the LORD came to Jeremiah: 13"Go and tell Hananiah, 'This is what the LORD says: You have broken a wooden yoke, but in its place you will get a yoke of iron. 14This is what the LORD Almighty, the God of Israel, says: I will put an iron yoke on the necks of all these nations to make them serve Nebuchadnezzar king of Babylon, and they will serve him. I will even give him control over the wild animals.' "

a20,4 Hebrew Jeconiah, a variant of Jehoiachin

¹⁵Then the prophet Jeremiah said to Hananiah the prophet, "Listen, Hananiah! The LORD has not sent you, yet you have persuaded this nation to trust in lies. ¹⁶Therefore, this is what the LORD says: 'I am about to remove you from the face of the earth. This very year you are going to die, because you have preached rebellion against the LORD.'"

¹⁷In the seventh month of that same year, Hananiah the prophet died.

A Letter to the Exiles

29 This is the text of the letter that the prophet Jeremiah sent from Jerusalem to the surviving elders among the exiles and to the priests, the prophets and all the other people Nebuchadnezzar had carried into exile from Jerusalem to Babylon. ²(This was after King Jehoiachin[a] and the queen mother, the court officials and the leaders of Judah and Jerusalem, the craftsmen and the artisans had gone into exile from Jerusalem.) ³He entrusted the letter to Elasah son of Shaphan and to Gemariah son of Hilkiah, whom Zedekiah king of Judah sent to King Nebuchadnezzar in Babylon. It said:

⁴This is what the LORD Almighty, the God of Israel, says to all those I carried into exile from Jerusalem to Babylon: ⁵"Build houses and settle down; plant gardens and eat what they produce. ⁶Marry and have sons and daughters; find wives for your sons and give your daughters in marriage, so that they too may have sons and daughters. Increase in number there; do not decrease. ⁷Also, seek the peace and prosperity of the city to which I have carried you into exile. Pray to the LORD for it, because if it prospers, you too will prosper." ⁸Yes, this is what the LORD Almighty, the God of Israel, says: "Do not let the prophets and diviners among you deceive you. Do not listen to the dreams you encourage them to have. ⁹They are prophesying lies to you in my name. I have not sent them," declares the LORD.

¹⁰This is what the LORD says: "When seventy years are completed for Babylon, I will come to you and fulfill my gracious promise to bring you back to this place. ¹¹For I know the plans I have for you," declares the LORD, "plans to prosper you and not to harm you, plans to give you hope and a future. ¹²Then you will call upon me and come and pray to me, and I will listen to you. ¹³You will seek me and find me when you seek me with all your heart. ¹⁴I will be found by you," declares the LORD, "and will bring you back from captivity.[b] I will gather you from all the nations and places where I have banished you," declares the LORD, "and will bring you back to the place from which I carried you into exile."

¹⁵You may say, "The LORD has raised up prophets for us in Babylon," ¹⁶but this is what the LORD says about the king who sits on David's throne and all the people who remain in this city, your countrymen who did not go with you into exile— ¹⁷yes, this is what the LORD Almighty says: "I will send the sword, famine and plague against them and I will make them like poor figs that are so bad they cannot be eaten. ¹⁸I will pursue them with the sword, famine and plague and will make them abhorrent to all the kingdoms of the earth and an object of cursing and horror, of scorn and reproach, among all the nations where I drive them. ¹⁹For they have not listened to my words," declares the LORD, "words that I sent to them again and again by my servants the

---

prophets. And you exiles have not listened either," declares the LORD.

20Therefore, hear the word of the LORD, all you exiles whom I have sent away from Jerusalem to Babylon. 21This is what the LORD Almighty, the God of Israel, says about Ahab son of Kolaiah and Zedekiah son of Maaseiah, who are prophesying lies to you in my name: "I will hand them over to Nebuchadnezzar king of Babylon, and he will put them to death before your very eyes. 22Because of them, all the exiles from Judah who are in Babylon will use this curse: 'The LORD treat you like Zedekiah and Ahab, whom the king of Babylon burned in the fire.' 23For they have done outrageous things in Israel; they have committed adultery with their neighbors' wives and in my name have spoken lies, which I did not tell them to do. I know it and am a witness to it," declares the LORD.

Message to Shemaiah

24Tell Shemaiah the Nehelamite, 25"This is what the LORD Almighty, the God of Israel, says: You sent letters in your own name to all the people in Jerusalem, to Zephaniah son of Maaseiah the priest, and to all the other priests. You said to Zephaniah, 26'The LORD has appointed you priest in place of Jehoiada to be in charge of the house of the LORD; you should put any madman who acts like a prophet into the stocks and neck-irons. 27So why have you not reprimanded Jeremiah from Anathoth, who poses as a prophet among you? 28He has sent this message to us in Babylon: It will be a long time. Therefore build houses and settle down; plant gardens and eat what they produce.' "

29Zephaniah the priest, however, read the letter to Jeremiah the prophet. 30Then the word of the LORD

came to Jeremiah: 31"Send this message to all the exiles: 'This is what the LORD says about Shemaiah the Nehelamite: Because Shemaiah has prophesied to you, even though I did not send him, and has led you to believe a lie, 32this is what the LORD says: I will surely punish Shemaiah the Nehelamite and his descendants. He will have no one left among this people, nor will he see the good things I will do for my people, declares the LORD, because he has preached rebellion against me.' "

Restoration of Israel

30 This is the word that came to Jeremiah from the LORD: 2"This is what the LORD, the God of Israel, says: 'Write in a book all the words I have spoken to you. 3The days are coming,' declares the LORD, 'when I will bring my people Israel and Judah back from captivity*a* and restore them to the land I gave their forefathers to possess,' says the LORD."

4These are the words the LORD spoke concerning Israel and Judah: 5"This is what the LORD says:

" 'Cries of fear are heard—
    terror, not peace.
6Ask and see:
    Can a man bear children?
Then why do I see every strong
        man
    with his hands on his stomach
        like a woman in labor,
    every face turned deathly pale?
7How awful that day will be!
    None will be like it.
It will be a time of trouble for
        Jacob,
    but he will be saved out of it.

8" ' In that day,' declares the LORD
        Almighty,
    'I will break the yoke off their
        necks
and will tear off their bonds;
    no longer will foreigners
        enslave them.

a3 Or will restore the fortunes of my people Israel and Judah

⁹Instead, they will serve the LORD
    their God
and David their king,
    whom I will raise up for them.

¹⁰" 'So do not fear, O Jacob my
    servant;
do not be dismayed, O Israel,'
        declares the LORD.
'I will surely save you out of a
    distant place,
your descendants from the land
    of their exile.
Jacob will again have peace and
    security,
    and no one will make him
        afraid.
¹¹I am with you and will save you,'
    declares the LORD.
'Though I completely destroy all
    the nations
    among which I scatter you,
I will not completely destroy
    you.
I will discipline you but only with
    justice;
I will not let you go entirely
    unpunished.'

¹²"This is what the LORD says:

" 'Your wound is incurable,
    your injury beyond healing.
¹³There is no one to plead your
    cause,
    no remedy for your sore,
    no healing for you.
¹⁴All your allies have forgotten
    you;
    they care nothing for you.
I have struck you as an enemy
    would
    and punished you as would the
        cruel,
because your guilt is so great
    and your sins so many.
¹⁵Why do you cry out over your
    wound,
    your pain that has no cure?
Because of your great guilt and
    many sins
    I have done these things to you.

¹⁶" 'But all who devour you will be
    devoured;
    all your enemies will go into
        exile.

Those who plunder you will be
    plundered;
    all who make spoil of you I will
        despoil.
¹⁷But I will restore you to health
    and heal your wounds,'
        declares the LORD,
'because you are called an outcast,
    Zion for whom no one cares.'

¹⁸"This is what the LORD says:

" 'I will restore the fortunes of
    Jacob's tents
    and have compassion on his
        dwellings;
the city will be rebuilt on her
    ruins,
    and the palace will stand in its
        proper place.
¹⁹From them will come songs of
    thanksgiving
    and the sound of rejoicing.
I will add to their numbers,
    and they will not be decreased;
I will bring them honor,
    and they will not be disdained.
²⁰Their children will be as in days
    of old,
    and their community will be
        established before me;
I will punish all who oppress
    them.
²¹Their leader will be one of their
    own;
    their ruler will arise from
        among them.
I will bring him near and he will
    come close to me,
    for who is he who will devote
        himself
    to be close to me?'
        declares the LORD.
²²" 'So you will be my people,
    and I will be your God.' "

²³See, the storm of the LORD
    will burst out in wrath,
a driving wind swirling down
    on the heads of the wicked.
²⁴The fierce anger of the LORD will
    not turn back
    until he fully accomplishes
    the purposes of his heart.
In days to come
    you will understand this.

31 "At that time," declares the LORD, "I will be the God of all the clans of Israel, and they will be my people."

²This is what the LORD says:

"The people who survive the sword
will find favor in the desert;
I will come to give rest to Israel."

³The LORD appeared to us in the past,ᵃ saying:

"I have loved you with an everlasting love;
I have drawn you with loving-kindness.

WORDS TO REMEMBER

31:3 I have loved you with an everlasting love.

---

⁴I will build you up again
and you will be rebuilt,
O Virgin Israel.
Again you will take up your tambourines
and go out to dance with the joyful.
⁵Again you will plant vineyards
on the hills of Samaria;
the farmers will plant them
and enjoy their fruit.
⁶There will be a day when watchmen cry out
on the hills of Ephraim,
'Come, let us go up to Zion,
to the LORD our God.' "

⁷This is what the LORD says:

"Sing with joy for Jacob;
shout for the foremost of the nations.
Make your praises heard, and say,
'O LORD, save your people,
the remnant of Israel.'
⁸See, I will bring them from the land of the north
and gather them from the ends of the earth.

Among them will be the blind and the lame,
expectant mothers and women in labor;
a great throng will return.
⁹They will come with weeping;
they will pray as I bring them back.
I will lead them beside streams of water
on a level path where they will not stumble,
because I am Israel's father,
and Ephraim is my firstborn son.

¹⁰"Hear the word of the LORD, O nations;
proclaim it in distant coastlands:
'He who scattered Israel will gather them
and will watch over his flock like a shepherd.'
¹¹For the LORD will ransom Jacob
and redeem them from the hand of those stronger than they.
¹²They will come and shout for joy on the heights of Zion;
they will rejoice in the bounty of the LORD—
the grain, the new wine and the oil,
the young of the flocks and herds.
They will be like a well-watered garden,
and they will sorrow no more.
¹³Then maidens will dance and be glad,
young men and old as well.
I will turn their mourning into gladness;
I will give them comfort and joy instead of sorrow.
¹⁴I will satisfy the priests with abundance,
and my people will be filled with my bounty,"
declares the LORD.

¹⁵This is what the LORD says:

"A voice is heard in Ramah,

ᵃ3 Or LORD *has appeared to us from afar*

mourning and great weeping,
Rachel weeping for her children
and refusing to be comforted,
because her children are no
more."

¹⁶This is what the LORD says:

"Restrain your voice from
weeping
and your eyes from tears,
for your work will be rewarded,"
declares the LORD.
"They will return from the land
of the enemy.
¹⁷So there is hope for your future,"
declares the LORD.
"Your children will return to
their own land.

¹⁸"I have surely heard Ephraim's
moaning:
'You disciplined me like an
unruly calf,
and I have been disciplined.
Restore me, and I will return,
because you are the LORD my
God.
¹⁹After I strayed,
I repented;
after I came to understand,
I beat my breast.
I was ashamed and humiliated
because I bore the disgrace of
my youth.'
²⁰Is not Ephraim my dear son,
the child in whom I delight?
Though I often speak against him,
I still remember him.
Therefore my heart yearns for
him;
I have great compassion for
him,"
declares the LORD.

²¹"Set up road signs;
put up guideposts.
Take note of the highway,
the road that you take.
Return, O Virgin Israel,
return to your towns.
²²How long will you wander,
O unfaithful daughter?

The LORD will create a new thing
on earth—
a woman will surroundᵃ a man."

²³This is what the LORD Almighty,
the God of Israel, says: "When I bring
them back from captivity,ᵇ the people
in the land of Judah and in its
towns will once again use these
words: 'The LORD bless you, O righteous
dwelling, O sacred mountain.'
²⁴People will live together in Judah
and all its towns—farmers and those
who move about with their flocks. ²⁵I
will refresh the weary and satisfy the
faint."

²⁶At this I awoke and looked
around. My sleep had been pleasant
to me.

²⁷"The days are coming," declares
the LORD, "when I will plant the
house of Israel and the house of Judah
with the offspring of men and of
animals. ²⁸Just as I watched over
them to uproot and tear down, and to
overthrow, destroy and bring disaster,
so I will watch over them to build
and to plant," declares the LORD.
²⁹"In those days people will no longer
say,

'The fathers have eaten sour
grapes,
and the children's teeth are set
on edge.'

³⁰Instead, everyone will die for his
own sin; whoever eats sour grapes
—his own teeth will be set on edge.

³¹"The time is coming," declares
the LORD,
"when I will make a new
covenant
with the house of Israel
and with the house of Judah.
³²It will not be like the covenant
I made with their forefathers
when I took them by the hand
to lead them out of Egypt,
because they broke my covenant,
though I was a husband toᶜ
them,ᵈ"
declares the LORD.

ᵃ22 Or *will go about seeking;* or *will protect*
Septuagint and Syriac / *and I turned away from*   ᵇ23 Or *I restore their fortunes*   ᶜ32 Hebrew;
ᵈ32 Or *was their master*

33"This is the covenant I will make
　　with the house of Israel
　　after that time," declares the
　　Lord.
"I will put my law in their
　　minds
　　and write it on their hearts.
I will be their God,
　　and they will be my people.

?DID YOU KNOW?　　31:31

What was the new covenant?

Even though God was about to
punish his people, he still loved
them. Here God promised to make
a new covenant, or agreement,
with his people. Under the new
covenant God would change
people's hearts and forgive their
sins. When Jesus died, the new
covenant Jeremiah talked about
was made.

34No longer will a man teach his
　　neighbor,
　　or a man his brother, saying,
　　'Know the Lord,'
because they will all know me,
　　from the least of them to the
　　greatest,"
　　　　　　　　　declares the Lord.
"For I will forgive their
　　wickedness
　　and will remember their sins no
　　more."

35This is what the Lord says,

he who appoints the sun
　　to shine by day,
who decrees the moon and stars
　　to shine by night,
who stirs up the sea
　　so that its waves roar—
　　the Lord Almighty is his
　　name:
36"Only if these decrees vanish
　　from my sight,"
　　declares the Lord,
"will the descendants of Israel
　　ever cease

to be a nation before me."

37This is what the Lord says:

"Only if the heavens above can be
　　measured
　　and the foundations of the earth
　　below be searched out
will I reject all the descendants of
　　Israel
　　because of all they have done,"
　　　　　　　　declares the Lord.

38"The days are coming," declares
the Lord, "when this city will be rebuilt for me from the Tower of Hananel to the Corner Gate. 39The measuring line will stretch from there
straight to the hill of Gareb and then
turn to Goah. 40The whole valley
where dead bodies and ashes are
thrown, and all the terraces out to
the Kidron Valley on the east as far
as the corner of the Horse Gate, will
be holy to the Lord. The city will never again be uprooted or demolished."

Jeremiah Buys a Field

32 This is the word that came to
Jeremiah from the Lord in
the tenth year of Zedekiah king of Judah, which was the eighteenth year
of Nebuchadnezzar. 2The army of the
king of Babylon was then besieging
Jerusalem, and Jeremiah the prophet was confined in the courtyard of
the guard in the royal palace of Judah.

3Now Zedekiah king of Judah had
imprisoned him there, saying, "Why
do you prophesy as you do? You say,
'This is what the Lord says: I am
about to hand this city over to the
king of Babylon, and he will capture
it. 4Zedekiah king of Judah will not
escape out of the hands of the Babylo-
niansa but will certainly be handed
over to the king of Babylon, and will
speak with him face to face and see
him with his own eyes. 5He will take
Zedekiah to Babylon, where he will
remain until I deal with him, declares the Lord. If you fight against

a4 Or *Chaldeans*; also in verses 5, 24, 25, 28, 29 and 43

the Babylonians, you will not succeed.' "

⁶Jeremiah said, "The word of the LORD came to me: ⁷Hanamel son of Shallum your uncle is going to come to you and say, 'Buy my field at Anathoth, because as nearest relative it is your right and duty to buy it.'

⁸"Then, just as the LORD had said, my cousin Hanamel came to me in the courtyard of the guard and said, 'Buy my field at Anathoth in the territory of Benjamin. Since it is your right to redeem it and possess it, buy it for yourself.'

"I knew that this was the word of the LORD; ⁹so I bought the field at Anathoth from my cousin Hanamel and weighed out for him seventeen shekels*a* of silver. ¹⁰I signed and sealed the deed, had it witnessed, and weighed out the silver on the scales. ¹¹I took the deed of purchase—the sealed copy containing the terms and conditions, as well as the unsealed copy— ¹²and I gave this deed to Baruch son of Neriah, the son of Mahseiah, in the presence of my cousin Hanamel and of the witnesses who had signed the deed and of all the Jews sitting in the courtyard of the guard.

¹³"In their presence I gave Baruch these instructions: ¹⁴'This is what the LORD Almighty, the God of Israel, says: Take these documents, both the sealed and unsealed copies of the deed of purchase, and put them in a clay jar so they will last a long time. ¹⁵For this is what the LORD Almighty, the God of Israel, says: Houses, fields and vineyards will again be bought in this land.'

¹⁶"After I had given the deed of purchase to Baruch son of Neriah, I prayed to the LORD:

¹⁷"Ah, Sovereign LORD, you have made the heavens and the earth by your great power and outstretched arm. Nothing is too hard for you. ¹⁸You show love to thousands but bring the punishment for the fathers' sins into the laps of their children after them. O great and powerful God, whose name is the LORD Almighty, ¹⁹great are your purposes and mighty are your deeds. Your eyes are open to all the ways of men; you reward everyone according to his conduct and as his deeds deserve. ²⁰You performed miraculous signs and wonders in Egypt and have continued them to this day, both in Israel and among all mankind, and have gained the renown that is still yours. ²¹You brought your people Israel out of Egypt with signs and wonders, by a mighty hand and an outstretched arm and with great terror. ²²You gave them this land you had sworn to give their forefathers, a land flowing with milk and honey. ²³They came in and took possession of it, but they did not obey you or follow your law; they did not do what you commanded them to do. So you brought all this disaster upon them.

²⁴"See how the siege ramps are built up to take the city. Because of the sword, famine and plague, the city will be handed over to the Babylonians who are attacking it. What you said has happened, as you now see. ²⁵And though the city will be handed over to the Babylonians, you, O Sovereign LORD, say to me, 'Buy the field with silver and have the transaction witnessed.' "

²⁶Then the word of the LORD came to Jeremiah: ²⁷"I am the LORD, the God of all mankind. Is anything too hard for me? ²⁸Therefore, this is what the LORD says: I am about to hand this city over to the Babylonians and to Nebuchadnezzar king of Babylon, who will capture it. ²⁹The Babylonians who are attacking this city will come in and set it on fire; they will burn it down, along with the houses

---

a9 That is, about 7 ounces (about 200 grams)

where the people provoked me to anger by burning incense on the roofs to Baal and by pouring out drink offerings to other gods.

30"The people of Israel and Judah have done nothing but evil in my sight from their youth; indeed, the people of Israel have done nothing but provoke me with what their hands have made, declares the LORD. 31From the day it was built until now, this city has so aroused my anger and wrath that I must remove it from my sight. 32The people of Israel and Judah have provoked me by all the evil they have done—they, their kings and officials, their priests and prophets, the men of Judah and the people of Jerusalem. 33They turned their backs to me and not their faces; though I taught them again and again, they would not listen or respond to discipline. 34They set up their abominable idols in the house that bears my Name and defiled it. 35They built high places for Baal in the Valley of Ben Hinnom to sacrifice their sons and daughters*a* to Molech, though I never commanded, nor did it enter my mind, that they should do such a detestable thing and so make Judah sin.

36"You are saying about this city, 'By the sword, famine and plague it will be handed over to the king of Babylon'; but this is what the LORD, the God of Israel, says: 37I will surely gather them from all the lands where I banish them in my furious anger and great wrath; I will bring them back to this place and let them live in safety. 38They will be my people, and I will be their God. 39I will give them singleness of heart and action, so that they will always fear me for their own good and the good of their children after them. 40I will make an everlasting covenant with them: I will never stop doing good to them, and I will inspire them to fear me, so that they will never turn away from me. 41I will rejoice in doing them good

and will assuredly plant them in this land with all my heart and soul.

42"This is what the LORD says: As I have brought all this great calamity on this people, so I will give them all the prosperity I have promised them. 43Once more fields will be bought in this land of which you say, 'It is a desolate waste, without men or animals, for it has been handed over to the Babylonians.' 44Fields will be bought for silver, and deeds will be signed, sealed and witnessed in the territory of Benjamin, in the villages around Jerusalem, in the towns of Judah and in the towns of the hill country, of the western foothills and of the Negev, because I will restore their fortunes,*b* declares the LORD."

Promise of Restoration

33 While Jeremiah was still confined in the courtyard of the guard, the word of the LORD came to him a second time: 2"This is what the LORD says, he who made the earth, the LORD who formed it and established it—the LORD is his name: 3'Call to me and I will answer you and tell you great and unsearchable things you do not know.' 4For this is what the LORD, the God of Israel, says about the houses in this city and the royal palaces of Judah that have been torn down to be used against the siege ramps and the sword 5in the fight with the Babylonians*c*: 'They will be filled with the dead bodies of the men I will slay in my anger and wrath. I will hide my face from this city because of all its wickedness.

6"'Nevertheless, I will bring health and healing to it; I will heal my people and will let them enjoy abundant peace and security. 7I will bring Judah and Israel back from captivity*d* and will rebuild them as they were before. 8I will cleanse them from all the sin they have committed against me and will forgive all their sins of rebellion against me. 9Then this city will bring me renown, joy,

---

a35 Or to make their sons and daughters pass through ˌthe fireˌ   *b44 Or will bring them back from captivity*   *c5 Or Chaldeans*   *d7 Or will restore the fortunes of Judah and Israel*

praise and honor before all nations on earth that hear of all the good things I do for it; and they will be in awe and will tremble at the abundant prosperity and peace I provide for it.'

10"This is what the LORD says: 'You say about this place, "It is a desolate waste, without men or animals." Yet in the towns of Judah and the streets of Jerusalem that are deserted, inhabited by neither men nor animals, there will be heard once more 11the sounds of joy and gladness, the voices of bride and bridegroom, and the voices of those who bring thank offerings to the house of the LORD, saying,

"Give thanks to the LORD
    Almighty,
  for the LORD is good;
  his love endures forever."

For I will restore the fortunes of the land as they were before,' says the LORD.

12"This is what the LORD Almighty says: 'In this place, desolate and without men or animals—in all its towns there will again be pastures for shepherds to rest their flocks. 13In the towns of the hill country, of the western foothills and of the Negev, in the territory of Benjamin, in the villages around Jerusalem and in the towns of Judah, flocks will again pass under the hand of the one who counts them,' says the LORD.

14" 'The days are coming,' declares the LORD, 'when I will fulfill the gracious promise I made to the house of Israel and to the house of Judah.

15" 'In those days and at that time
    I will make a righteous Branch
      sprout from David's line;
    he will do what is just and right
      in the land.
16In those days Judah will be saved
    and Jerusalem will live in
      safety.
This is the name by which it*a*
    will be called:
  The LORD Our Righteousness.'

17For this is what the LORD says: 'Da-

vid will never fail to have a man to sit on the throne of the house of Israel, 18nor will the priests, who are Levites, ever fail to have a man to stand before me continually to offer burnt offerings, to burn grain offerings and to present sacrifices.' "

19The word of the LORD came to Jeremiah: 20"This is what the LORD says: 'If you can break my covenant with the day and my covenant with the night, so that day and night no longer come at their appointed time, 21then my covenant with David my servant—and my covenant with the Levites who are priests ministering before me—can be broken and David will no longer have a descendant to reign on his throne. 22I will make the descendants of David my servant and the Levites who minister before me as countless as the stars of the sky and as measureless as the sand on the seashore.' "

23The word of the LORD came to Jeremiah: 24"Have you not noticed that these people are saying, 'The LORD has rejected the two kingdoms*b* he chose'? So they despise my people and no longer regard them as a nation. 25This is what the LORD says: 'If I have not established my covenant with day and night and the fixed laws of heaven and earth, 26then I will reject the descendants of Jacob and David my servant and will not choose one of his sons to rule over the descendants of Abraham, Isaac and Jacob. For I will restore their fortunes*c* and have compassion on them.' "

Warning to Zedekiah

34 While Nebuchadnezzar king of Babylon and all his army and all the kingdoms and peoples in the empire he ruled were fighting against Jerusalem and all its surrounding towns, this word came to Jeremiah from the LORD: 2"This is what the LORD, the God of Israel, says: Go to Zedekiah king of Judah and tell him, 'This is what the LORD

a16 Or he   b24 Or families   c26 Or will bring them back from captivity says: I am about to hand this city over to the king of Babylon, and he will burn it down. [3]You will not escape from his grasp but will surely be captured and handed over to him. You will see the king of Babylon with your own eyes, and he will speak with you face to face. And you will go to Babylon.

[4]" 'Yet hear the promise of the LORD, O Zedekiah king of Judah. This is what the LORD says concerning you: You will not die by the sword; [5]you will die peacefully. As people made a funeral fire in honor of your fathers, the former kings who preceded you, so they will make a fire in your honor and lament, "Alas, O master!" I myself make this promise, declares the LORD.' "

[6]Then Jeremiah the prophet told all this to Zedekiah king of Judah, in Jerusalem, [7]while the army of the king of Babylon was fighting against Jerusalem and the other cities of Judah that were still holding out—Lachish and Azekah. These were the only fortified cities left in Judah.

Freedom for Slaves

[8]The word came to Jeremiah from the LORD after King Zedekiah had made a covenant with all the people in Jerusalem to proclaim freedom for the slaves. [9]Everyone was to free his Hebrew slaves, both male and female; no one was to hold a fellow Jew in bondage. [10]So all the officials and people who entered into this covenant agreed that they would free their male and female slaves and no longer hold them in bondage. They agreed, and set them free. [11]But afterward they changed their minds and took back the slaves they had freed and enslaved them again.

[12]Then the word of the LORD came to Jeremiah: [13]"This is what the LORD, the God of Israel, says: I made a covenant with your forefathers when I brought them out of Egypt, out of the land of slavery. I said, [14]'Every seventh year each of you must free any fellow Hebrew who has sold himself to you. After he has served you six years, you must let him go free.'[a] Your fathers, however, did not listen to me or pay attention to me. [15]Recently you repented and did what is right in my sight: Each of you proclaimed freedom to his countrymen. You even made a covenant before me in the house that bears my Name. [16]But now you have turned around and profaned my name; each of you has taken back the male and

a14 Deut. 15:12

LET'S LIVE IT!   Jeremiah 34:8–16

KEEP ON DOING WHAT IS RIGHT ➡ Sometimes people break promises to God. Read Jeremiah 34:8–16. Jeremiah told the Israelites in this story that it was wrong for them to keep another Israelite as a slave. They agreed together, while worshiping in the temple, to free their slaves. But then they changed their minds and did wrong again. Jeremiah 34:11 tells what they did.

Trace around your foot on blue and on green construction paper. Cut out at least ten footprints of each color. When you do something you know is right, write what you did on one of the blue footprints, and tape it to the wall of your room. Start halfway up the wall and point the blue footprint up. If you do something that is wrong, write what you did on one of the green footprints. Tape it to the wall, but point this footprint down. The footprints will show you which road you are traveling: God's road, doing what is right; or the road toward punishment, doing what is wrong.

female slaves you had set free to go where they wished. You have forced them to become your slaves again.

17"Therefore, this is what the LORD says: You have not obeyed me; you have not proclaimed freedom for your fellow countrymen. So I now proclaim 'freedom' for you, declares the LORD—'freedom' to fall by the sword, plague and famine. I will make you abhorrent to all the kingdoms of the earth. 18The men who have violated my covenant and have not fulfilled the terms of the covenant they made before me, I will treat like the calf they cut in two and then walked between its pieces. 19The leaders of Judah and Jerusalem, the court officials, the priests and all the people of the land who walked between the pieces of the calf, 20I will hand over to their enemies who seek their lives. Their dead bodies will become food for the birds of the air and the beasts of the earth.

21"I will hand Zedekiah king of Judah and his officials over to their enemies who seek their lives, to the army of the king of Babylon, which has withdrawn from you. 22I am going to give the order, declares the LORD, and I will bring them back to this city. They will fight against it, take it and burn it down. And I will lay waste the towns of Judah so no one can live there."

The Recabites

35 This is the word that came to Jeremiah from the LORD during the reign of Jehoiakim son of Josiah king of Judah: 2"Go to the Recabite family and invite them to come to one of the side rooms of the house of the LORD and give them wine to drink."

3So I went to get Jaazaniah son of Jeremiah, the son of Habazziniah, and his brothers and all his sons—the whole family of the Recabites. 4I brought them into the house of the LORD, into the room of the sons of Hanan son of Igdaliah the man of God.

It was next to the room of the officials, which was over that of Maaseiah son of Shallum the doorkeeper. 5Then I set bowls full of wine and some cups before the men of the Recabite family and said to them, "Drink some wine."

6But they replied, "We do not drink wine, because our forefather Jonadab son of Recab gave us this command: 'Neither you nor your descendants must ever drink wine. 7Also you must never build houses, sow seed or plant vineyards; you must never have any of these things, but must always live in tents. Then you will live a long time in the land where you are nomads.' 8We have obeyed everything our forefather Jonadab son of Recab commanded us. Neither we nor our wives nor our sons and daughters have ever drunk wine 9or built houses to live in or had vineyards, fields or crops. 10We have lived in tents and have fully obeyed everything our forefather Jonadab commanded us. 11But when Nebuchadnezzar king of Babylon invaded this land, we said, 'Come, we must go to Jerusalem to escape the Babylonian[a] and Aramean armies.' So we have remained in Jerusalem."

12Then the word of the LORD came to Jeremiah, saying: 13"This is what the LORD Almighty, the God of Israel, says: Go and tell the men of Judah and the people of Jerusalem, 'Will you not learn a lesson and obey my words?' declares the LORD. 14'Jonadab son of Recab ordered his sons not to drink wine and this command has been kept. To this day they do not drink wine, because they obey their forefather's command. But I have spoken to you again and again, yet you have not obeyed me. 15Again and again I sent all my servants the prophets to you. They said, "Each of you must turn from your wicked ways and reform your actions; do not follow other gods to serve them. Then you will live in the land I have given to you and your fathers." But you

a11 Or Chaldean

have not paid attention or listened to me. ¹⁶The descendants of Jonadab son of Recab have carried out the command their forefather gave them, but these people have not obeyed me.'

¹⁷"Therefore, this is what the LORD God Almighty, the God of Israel, says: 'Listen! I am going to bring on Judah and on everyone living in Jerusalem every disaster I pronounced against them. I spoke to them, but they did not listen; I called to them, but they did not answer.'"

¹⁸Then Jeremiah said to the family of the Recabites, "This is what the LORD Almighty, the God of Israel, says: 'You have obeyed the command of your forefather Jonadab and have followed all his instructions and have done everything he ordered.' ¹⁹Therefore, this is what the LORD Almighty, the God of Israel, says: 'Jonadab son of Recab will never fail to have a man to serve me.'"

Jehoiakim Burns Jeremiah's Scroll

36 In the fourth year of Jehoiakim son of Josiah king of Judah, this word came to Jeremiah from the LORD: ²"Take a scroll and write on it all the words I have spoken to you concerning Israel, Judah and all the other nations from the time I began speaking to you in the reign of Josiah till now. ³Perhaps when the people of Judah hear about every disaster I plan to inflict on them, each of them will turn from his wicked way; then I will forgive their wickedness and their sin."

⁴So Jeremiah called Baruch son of Neriah, and while Jeremiah dictated all the words the LORD had spoken to him, Baruch wrote them on the scroll. ⁵Then Jeremiah told Baruch, "I am restricted; I cannot go to the LORD's temple. ⁶So you go to the house of the LORD on a day of fasting and read to the people from the scroll the words of the LORD that you wrote as I dictated. Read them to all the people of Judah who come in from their towns. ⁷Perhaps they will bring their petition before the LORD, and

each will turn from his wicked ways, for the anger and wrath pronounced against this people by the LORD are great."

⁸Baruch son of Neriah did everything Jeremiah the prophet told him to do; at the LORD's temple he read the words of the LORD from the scroll. ⁹In the ninth month of the fifth year of Jehoiakim son of Josiah king of Judah, a time of fasting before the LORD was proclaimed for all the people in Jerusalem and those who had come from the towns of Judah. ¹⁰From the room of Gemariah son of Shaphan the secretary, which was in the upper courtyard at the entrance of the New Gate of the temple, Baruch read to all the people at the LORD's temple the words of Jeremiah from the scroll.

¹¹When Micaiah son of Gemariah, the son of Shaphan, heard all the words of the LORD from the scroll, ¹²he went down to the secretary's room in the royal palace, where all the officials were sitting: Elishama the secretary, Delaiah son of Shemaiah, Elnathan son of Acbor, Gemariah son of Shaphan, Zedekiah son of Hananiah, and all the other officials. ¹³After Micaiah told them everything he had heard Baruch read to the people from the scroll, ¹⁴all the officials sent Jehudi son of Nethaniah, the son of Shelemiah, the son of Cushi, to say to Baruch, "Bring the scroll from which you have read to the people and come." So Baruch son of Neriah went to them with the scroll in his hand. ¹⁵They said to him, "Sit down, please, and read it to us."

So Baruch read it to them. ¹⁶When they heard all these words, they looked at each other in fear and said to Baruch, "We must report all these words to the king." ¹⁷Then they asked Baruch, "Tell us, how did you come to write all this? Did Jeremiah dictate it?"

¹⁸"Yes," Baruch replied, "he dictated all these words to me, and I wrote them in ink on the scroll."

¹⁹Then the officials said to Baruch, "You and Jeremiah, go and hide.

Don't let anyone know where you are."

²⁰After they put the scroll in the room of Elishama the secretary, they went to the king in the courtyard and reported everything to him. ²¹The king sent Jehudi to get the scroll, and Jehudi brought it from the room of Elishama the secretary and read it to the king and all the officials standing beside him. ²²It was the ninth month and the king was sitting in the winter apartment, with a fire burning in the firepot in front of him. ²³Whenever Jehudi had read three or four columns of the scroll, the king cut them off with a scribe's knife and threw them into the firepot, until the entire scroll was burned in the fire. ²⁴The king and all his attendants who heard all these words showed no fear, nor did they tear their clothes. ²⁵Even though Elnathan, Delaiah and Gemariah urged the king not to burn the scroll, he would not listen to them. ²⁶Instead, the king commanded Jerahmeel, a son of the king, Seraiah son of Azriel and Shelemiah son of Abdeel to arrest Baruch the scribe and Jeremiah the prophet. But the LORD had hidden them.

²⁷After the king burned the scroll containing the words that Baruch had written at Jeremiah's dictation, the word of the LORD came to Jeremiah: ²⁸"Take another scroll and write on it all the words that were on the first scroll, which Jehoiakim king of Judah burned up. ²⁹Also tell Jehoiakim king of Judah, 'This is what the LORD says: You burned that scroll and said, "Why did you write on it that the king of Babylon would certainly come and destroy this land and cut off both men and animals from it?" ³⁰Therefore, this is what the LORD says about Jehoiakim king of Judah: He will have no one to sit on the throne of David; his body will be thrown out and exposed to the heat by day and the frost by night. ³¹I will punish him and his children and his attendants for their wickedness; I

will bring on them and those living in Jerusalem and the people of Judah every disaster I pronounced against them, because they have not listened.' "

³²So Jeremiah took another scroll and gave it to the scribe Baruch son of Neriah, and as Jeremiah dictated, Baruch wrote on it all the words of the scroll that Jehoiakim king of Judah had burned in the fire. And many similar words were added to them.

Jeremiah in Prison

37 Zedekiah son of Josiah was made king of Judah by Nebuchadnezzar king of Babylon; he reigned in place of Jehoiachin ᵃ son of Jehoiakim. ²Neither he nor his attendants nor the people of the land paid any attention to the words the LORD had spoken through Jeremiah the prophet.

³King Zedekiah, however, sent Jehucal son of Shelemiah with the priest Zephaniah son of Maaseiah to Jeremiah the prophet with this message: "Please pray to the LORD our God for us."

⁴Now Jeremiah was free to come and go among the people, for he had not yet been put in prison. ⁵Pharaoh's army had marched out of Egypt, and when the Babylonians ᵇ who were besieging Jerusalem heard the report about them, they withdrew from Jerusalem.

⁶Then the word of the LORD came to Jeremiah the prophet: ⁷"This is what the LORD, the God of Israel, says: Tell the king of Judah, who sent you to inquire of me, 'Pharaoh's army, which has marched out to support you, will go back to its own land, to Egypt. ⁸Then the Babylonians will return and attack this city; they will capture it and burn it down.'

⁹"This is what the LORD says: Do not deceive yourselves, thinking, 'The Babylonians will surely leave us.' They will not! ¹⁰Even if you were

---

ᵃ1 Hebrew *Coniah*, a variant of *Jehoiachin*   ᵇ5 Or *Chaldeans*; also in verses 8, 9, 13 and 14

to defeat the entire Babylonian[a] army that is attacking you and only wounded men were left in their tents, they would come out and burn this city down."

[11]After the Babylonian army had withdrawn from Jerusalem because of Pharaoh's army, [12]Jeremiah started to leave the city to go to the territory of Benjamin to get his share of the property among the people there. [13]But when he reached the Benjamin Gate, the captain of the guard, whose name was Irijah son of Shelemiah, the son of Hananiah, arrested him and said, "You are deserting to the Babylonians!"

[14]"That's not true!" Jeremiah said. "I am not deserting to the Babylonians." But Irijah would not listen to him; instead, he arrested Jeremiah and brought him to the officials. [15]They were angry with Jeremiah and had him beaten and imprisoned in the house of Jonathan the secretary, which they had made into a prison.

[16]Jeremiah was put into a vaulted cell in a dungeon, where he remained a long time. [17]Then King Zedekiah sent for him and had him brought to the palace, where he asked him privately, "Is there any word from the LORD?"

"Yes," Jeremiah replied, "you will be handed over to the king of Babylon."

[18]Then Jeremiah said to King Zedekiah, "What crime have I committed against you or your officials or this people, that you have put me in prison? [19]Where are your prophets who prophesied to you, 'The king of Babylon will not attack you or this land'? [20]But now, my lord the king, please listen. Let me bring my petition before you: Do not send me back to the house of Jonathan the secretary, or I will die there."

[21]King Zedekiah then gave orders for Jeremiah to be placed in the courtyard of the guard and given bread from the street of the bakers each day until all the bread in the city was gone. So Jeremiah remained in the courtyard of the guard.

Jeremiah Thrown Into a Cistern

38 Shephatiah son of Mattan, Gedaliah son of Pashhur, Jehucal[b] son of Shelemiah, and Pashhur son of Malkijah heard what Jeremiah was telling all the people when he said, [2]"This is what the LORD says: 'Whoever stays in this city will die by the sword, famine or plague, but whoever goes over to the Babylonians[c] will live. He will escape with his life; he will live.' [3]And this is what the LORD says: 'This city will certainly be handed over to the army of the king of Babylon, who will capture it.' "

[4]Then the officials said to the king, "This man should be put to death. He is discouraging the soldiers who are left in this city, as well as all the people, by the things he is saying to them. This man is not seeking the good of these people but their ruin."

[5]"He is in your hands," King Zedekiah answered. "The king can do nothing to oppose you."

[6]So they took Jeremiah and put him into the cistern of Malkijah, the king's son, which was in the courtyard of the guard. They lowered Jeremiah by ropes into the cistern; it had no water in it, only mud, and Jeremiah sank down into the mud.

[7]But Ebed-Melech, a Cushite,[d] an official[e] in the royal palace, heard that they had put Jeremiah into the cistern. While the king was sitting in the Benjamin Gate, [8]Ebed-Melech went out of the palace and said to him, [9]"My lord the king, these men have acted wickedly in all they have done to Jeremiah the prophet. They have thrown him into a cistern, where he will starve to death when there is no longer any bread in the city."

[10]Then the king commanded Ebed-Melech the Cushite, "Take

---

*a*10 Or *Chaldean;* also in verse 11   *b*1 Hebrew *Jucal,* a variant of *Jehucal*   *c*2 Or *Chaldeans;* also in verses 18, 19 and 23   *d*7 Probably from the upper Nile region   *e*7 Or *a eunuch*

thirty men from here with you and lift Jeremiah the prophet out of the cistern before he dies."

CITY CISTERNS

In Israel, cities often had giant cisterns, like underground water storage tanks. There were thirty-seven cisterns cut in the rock under Jerusalem. One held over two million gallons of water! People needed this water if an enemy army surrounded the city walls and blocked off the streams so no water could get into the city.

---

¹¹So Ebed-Melech took the men with him and went to a room under the treasury in the palace. He took some old rags and worn-out clothes from there and let them down with ropes to Jeremiah in the cistern. ¹²Ebed-Melech the Cushite said to Jeremiah, "Put these old rags and worn-out clothes under your arms to pad the ropes." Jeremiah did so, ¹³and they pulled him up with the ropes and lifted him out of the cistern. And Jeremiah remained in the courtyard of the guard.

Zedekiah Questions Jeremiah Again

¹⁴Then King Zedekiah sent for Jeremiah the prophet and had him brought to the third entrance to the temple of the LORD. "I am going to ask you something," the king said to Jeremiah. "Do not hide anything from me."

¹⁵Jeremiah said to Zedekiah, "If I give you an answer, will you not kill me? Even if I did give you counsel, you would not listen to me."

¹⁶But King Zedekiah swore this oath secretly to Jeremiah: "As surely as the LORD lives, who has given us breath, I will neither kill you nor hand you over to those who are seeking your life."

¹⁷Then Jeremiah said to Zedekiah, "This is what the LORD God Almighty, the God of Israel, says: 'If you surrender to the officers of the king of Babylon, your life will be spared and this city will not be burned down; you and your family will live. ¹⁸But if you will not surrender to the officers of the king of Babylon, this city will be handed over to the Babylonians and they will burn it down; you yourself will not escape from their hands.'"

¹⁹King Zedekiah said to Jeremiah, "I am afraid of the Jews who have gone over to the Babylonians, for the Babylonians may hand me over to them and they will mistreat me."

²⁰"They will not hand you over," Jeremiah replied. "Obey the LORD by doing what I tell you. Then it will go well with you, and your life will be spared. ²¹But if you refuse to surrender, this is what the LORD has revealed to me: ²²All the women left in the palace of the king of Judah will be brought out to the officials of the king of Babylon. Those women will say to you:

" 'They misled you and overcame
        you—
    those trusted friends of yours.
Your feet are sunk in the mud;
    your friends have deserted you.'

²³"All your wives and children will be brought out to the Babylonians. You yourself will not escape from their hands but will be captured by the king of Babylon; and this city willᵃ be burned down."

²⁴Then Zedekiah said to Jeremiah, "Do not let anyone know about this conversation, or you may die. ²⁵If the officials hear that I talked with you, and they come to you and say, 'Tell us

---

ᵃ23 Or and you will cause this city to

what you said to the king and what the king said to you; do not hide it from us or we will kill you,' 26then tell them, 'I was pleading with the king not to send me back to Jonathan's house to die there.'"

27All the officials did come to Jeremiah and question him, and he told them everything the king had ordered him to say. So they said no more to him, for no one had heard his conversation with the king.

28And Jeremiah remained in the courtyard of the guard until the day Jerusalem was captured.

The Fall of Jerusalem

39 This is how Jerusalem was taken: 1In the ninth year of Zedekiah king of Judah, in the tenth month, Nebuchadnezzar king of Babylon marched against Jerusalem with his whole army and laid siege to it. 2And on the ninth day of the fourth month of Zedekiah's eleventh year, the city wall was broken through. 3Then all the officials of the king of Babylon came and took seats in the Middle Gate: Nergal-Sharezer of Samgar, Nebo-Sarsekim*a* a chief officer, Nergal-Sharezer a high official and all the other officials of the king of Babylon. 4When Zedekiah king of Judah and all the soldiers saw them, they fled; they left the city at night by way of the king's garden, through the gate between the two walls, and headed toward the Arabah.*b*

5But the Babylonian*c* army pursued them and overtook Zedekiah in the plains of Jericho. They captured him and took him to Nebuchadnezzar king of Babylon at Riblah in the land of Hamath, where he pronounced sentence on him. 6There at Riblah the king of Babylon slaughtered the sons of Zedekiah before his eyes and also killed all the nobles of Judah. 7Then he put out Zedekiah's eyes and bound him with bronze shackles to take him to Babylon.

8The Babylonians*d* set fire to the royal palace and the houses of the people and broke down the walls of Jerusalem. 9Nebuzaradan commander of the imperial guard carried into exile to Babylon the people who remained in the city, along with those who had gone over to him, and the rest of the people. 10But Nebuzaradan the commander of the guard left behind in the land of Judah some of the poor people, who owned nothing; and at that time he gave them vineyards and fields.

11Now Nebuchadnezzar king of Babylon had given these orders about Jeremiah through Nebuzaradan commander of the imperial guard: 12"Take him and look after him; don't harm him but do for him whatever he asks." 13So Nebuzaradan the commander of the guard, Nebushazban a chief officer, Nergal-Sharezer a high official and all the other officers of the king of Babylon 14sent and had Jeremiah taken out of the courtyard of the guard. They turned him over to Gedaliah son of Ahikam, the son of Shaphan, to take him back to his home. So he remained among his own people.

15While Jeremiah had been confined in the courtyard of the guard, the word of the LORD came to him: 16"Go and tell Ebed-Melech the Cushite, 'This is what the LORD Almighty, the God of Israel, says: I am about to fulfill my words against this city through disaster, not prosperity. At that time they will be fulfilled before your eyes. 17But I will rescue you on that day, declares the LORD; you will not be handed over to those you fear. 18I will save you; you will not fall by the sword but will escape with your life, because you trust in me, declares the LORD.'"

Jeremiah Freed

40 The word came to Jeremiah from the LORD after Nebuzaradan commander of the imperial guard had released him at Ramah.

a3 Or Nergal-Sharezer, Samgar-Nebo, Sarsekim   *b4 Or the Jordan Valley*   *c5 Or Chaldean*
d8 Or Chaldeans

He had found Jeremiah bound in chains among all the captives from Jerusalem and Judah who were being carried into exile to Babylon. ²When the commander of the guard found Jeremiah, he said to him, "The LORD your God decreed this disaster for this place. ³And now the LORD has brought it about; he has done just as he said he would. All this happened because you people sinned against the LORD and did not obey him. ⁴But today I am freeing you from the chains on your wrists. Come with me to Babylon, if you like, and I will look after you; but if you do not want to, then don't come. Look, the whole country lies before you; go wherever you please." ⁵However, before Jeremiah turned to go,ᵃ Nebuzaradan added, "Go back to Gedaliah son of Ahikam, the son of Shaphan, whom the king of Babylon has appointed over the towns of Judah, and live with him among the people, or go anywhere else you please."

Then the commander gave him provisions and a present and let him go. ⁶So Jeremiah went to Gedaliah son of Ahikam at Mizpah and stayed with him among the people who were left behind in the land.

Gedaliah Assassinated

⁷When all the army officers and their men who were still in the open country heard that the king of Babylon had appointed Gedaliah son of Ahikam as governor over the land and had put him in charge of the men, women and children who were the poorest in the land and who had not been carried into exile to Babylon, ⁸they came to Gedaliah at Mizpah—Ishmael son of Nethaniah, Johanan and Jonathan the sons of Kareah, Seraiah son of Tanhumeth, the sons of Ephai the Netophathite, and Jaazaniahᵇ the son of the Maacathite, and their men. ⁹Gedaliah son of Ahikam, the son of Shaphan, took an oath to reassure them and their men.

"Do not be afraid to serve the Babylonians,ᶜ" he said. "Settle down in the land and serve the king of Babylon, and it will go well with you. ¹⁰I myself will stay at Mizpah to represent you before the Babylonians who come to us, but you are to harvest the wine, summer fruit and oil, and put them in your storage jars, and live in the towns you have taken over."

¹¹When all the Jews in Moab, Ammon, Edom and all the other countries heard that the king of Babylon had left a remnant in Judah and had appointed Gedaliah son of Ahikam, the son of Shaphan, as governor over them, ¹²they all came back to the land of Judah, to Gedaliah at Mizpah, from all the countries where they had been scattered. And they harvested an abundance of wine and summer fruit.

¹³Johanan son of Kareah and all the army officers still in the open country came to Gedaliah at Mizpah ¹⁴and said to him, "Don't you know that Baalis king of the Ammonites has sent Ishmael son of Nethaniah to take your life?" But Gedaliah son of Ahikam did not believe them.

¹⁵Then Johanan son of Kareah said privately to Gedaliah in Mizpah, "Let me go and kill Ishmael son of Nethaniah, and no one will know it. Why should he take your life and cause all the Jews who are gathered around you to be scattered and the remnant of Judah to perish?"

¹⁶But Gedaliah son of Ahikam said to Johanan son of Kareah, "Don't do such a thing! What you are saying about Ishmael is not true."

41 In the seventh month Ishmael son of Nethaniah, the son of Elishama, who was of royal blood and had been one of the king's officers, came with ten men to Gedaliah son of Ahikam at Mizpah. While they were eating together there, ²Ishmael son of Nethaniah and the ten men who were with him got up and struck down Gedaliah son of Ahikam, the

---

ᵃ5 Or *Jeremiah answered*   ᵇ8 Hebrew *Jezaniah*, a variant of *Jaazaniah*   ᶜ9 Or *Chaldeans*; also in verse 10

son of Shaphan, with the sword, killing the one whom the king of Babylon had appointed as governor over the land. ³Ishmael also killed all the Jews who were with Gedaliah at Mizpah, as well as the Babylonian*a* soldiers who were there.

⁴The day after Gedaliah's assassination, before anyone knew about it, ⁵eighty men who had shaved off their beards, torn their clothes and cut themselves came from Shechem, Shiloh and Samaria, bringing grain offerings and incense with them to the house of the LORD. ⁶Ishmael son of Nethaniah went out from Mizpah to meet them, weeping as he went. When he met them, he said, "Come to Gedaliah son of Ahikam." ⁷When they went into the city, Ishmael son of Nethaniah and the men who were with him slaughtered them and threw them into a cistern. ⁸But ten of them said to Ishmael, "Don't kill us! We have wheat and barley, oil and honey, hidden in a field." So he let them alone and did not kill them with the others. ⁹Now the cistern where he threw all the bodies of the men he had killed along with Gedaliah was the one King Asa had made as part of his defense against Baasha king of Israel. Ishmael son of Nethaniah filled it with the dead.

¹⁰Ishmael made captives of all the rest of the people who were in Mizpah—the king's daughters along with all the others who were left there, over whom Nebuzaradan commander of the imperial guard had appointed Gedaliah son of Ahikam. Ishmael son of Nethaniah took them captive and set out to cross over to the Ammonites.

¹¹When Johanan son of Kareah and all the army officers who were with him heard about all the crimes Ishmael son of Nethaniah had committed, ¹²they took all their men and went to fight Ishmael son of Nethaniah. They caught up with him near the great pool in Gibeon. ¹³When all the people Ishmael had with him saw Johanan son of Kareah and the army officers who were with him, they were glad. ¹⁴All the people Ishmael had taken captive at Mizpah turned and went over to Johanan son of Kareah. ¹⁵But Ishmael son of Nethaniah and eight of his men escaped from Johanan and fled to the Ammonites.

Flight to Egypt

¹⁶Then Johanan son of Kareah and all the army officers who were with him led away all the survivors from Mizpah whom he had recovered from Ishmael son of Nethaniah after he had assassinated Gedaliah son of Ahikam: the soldiers, women, children and court officials he had brought from Gibeon. ¹⁷And they went on, stopping at Geruth Kimham near Bethlehem on their way to Egypt ¹⁸to escape the Babylonians.*b* They were afraid of them because Ishmael son of Nethaniah had killed Gedaliah son of Ahikam, whom the king of Babylon had appointed as governor over the land.

42 Then all the army officers, including Johanan son of Kareah and Jezaniah*c* son of Hoshaiah, and all the people from the least to the greatest approached ²Jeremiah the prophet and said to him, "Please hear our petition and pray to the LORD your God for this entire remnant. For as you now see, though we were once many, now only a few are left. ³Pray that the LORD your God will tell us where we should go and what we should do."

⁴"I have heard you," replied Jeremiah the prophet. "I will certainly pray to the LORD your God as you have requested; I will tell you everything the LORD says and will keep nothing back from you."

⁵Then they said to Jeremiah, "May the LORD be a true and faithful witness against us if we do not act in accordance with everything the LORD your God sends you to tell us. ⁶Whether it is favorable or unfavorable, we will obey the LORD our God,

---

a3 Or *Chaldean*　　*b18* Or *Chaldeans*　　*c1* Hebrew; Septuagint (see also 43:2) *Azariah*

to whom we are sending you, so that it will go well with us, for we will obey the LORD our God."

⁷Ten days later the word of the LORD came to Jeremiah. ⁸So he called together Johanan son of Kareah and all the army officers who were with him and all the people from the least to the greatest. ⁹He said to them, "This is what the LORD, the God of Israel, to whom you sent me to present your petition, says: ¹⁰'If you stay in this land, I will build you up and not tear you down; I will plant you and not uproot you, for I am grieved over the disaster I have inflicted on you. ¹¹Do not be afraid of the king of Babylon, whom you now fear. Do not be afraid of him, declares the LORD, for I am with you and will save you and deliver you from his hands. ¹²I will show you compassion so that he will have compassion on you and restore you to your land.'

¹³"However, if you say, 'We will not stay in this land,' and so disobey the LORD your God, ¹⁴and if you say, 'No, we will go and live in Egypt, where we will not see war or hear the trumpet or be hungry for bread,' ¹⁵then hear the word of the LORD, O remnant of Judah. This is what the LORD Almighty, the God of Israel, says: 'If you are determined to go to Egypt and you do go to settle there, ¹⁶then the sword you fear will overtake you there, and the famine you dread will follow you into Egypt, and there you will die. ¹⁷Indeed, all who are determined to go to Egypt to settle there will die by the sword, famine and plague; not one of them will survive or escape the disaster I will bring on them.' ¹⁸This is what the LORD Almighty, the God of Israel, says: 'As my anger and wrath have been poured out on those who lived in Jerusalem, so will my wrath be poured out on you when you go to Egypt. You will be an object of cursing and horror, of condemnation and reproach; you will never see this place again.'

¹⁹"O remnant of Judah, the LORD has told you, 'Do not go to Egypt.' Be sure of this: I warn you today ²⁰that you made a fatal mistake*a* when you sent me to the LORD your God and said, 'Pray to the LORD our God for us; tell us everything he says and we will do it.' ²¹I have told you today, but you still have not obeyed the LORD your God in all he sent me to tell you. ²²So now, be sure of this: You will die by the sword, famine and plague in the place where you want to go to settle."

43 When Jeremiah finished telling the people all the words of the LORD their God—everything the LORD had sent him to tell them— ²Azariah son of Hoshaiah and Johanan son of Kareah and all the arrogant men said to Jeremiah, "You are lying! The LORD our God has not sent you to say, 'You must not go to Egypt to settle there.' ³But Baruch son of Neriah is inciting you against us to hand us over to the Babylonians,*b* so they may kill us or carry us into exile to Babylon."

⁴So Johanan son of Kareah and all the army officers and all the people disobeyed the LORD's command to stay in the land of Judah. ⁵Instead, Johanan son of Kareah and all the army officers led away all the remnant of Judah who had come back to live in the land of Judah from all the nations where they had been scattered. ⁶They also led away all the men, women and children and the king's daughters whom Nebuzaradan commander of the imperial guard had left with Gedaliah son of Ahikam, the son of Shaphan, and Jeremiah the prophet and Baruch son of Neriah. ⁷So they entered Egypt in disobedience to the LORD and went as far as Tahpanhes.

⁸In Tahpanhes the word of the LORD came to Jeremiah: ⁹"While the Jews are watching, take some large stones with you and bury them in clay in the brick pavement at the entrance to Pharaoh's palace in Tahpanhes. ¹⁰Then say to them, 'This is what the LORD Almighty, the God of

---

a20 Or *you erred in your hearts*   *b3* Or *Chaldeans*

Israel, says: I will send for my servant Nebuchadnezzar king of Babylon, and I will set his throne over these stones I have buried here; he will spread his royal canopy above them. [11]He will come and attack Egypt, bringing death to those destined for death, captivity to those destined for captivity, and the sword to those destined for the sword. [12]He[a] will set fire to the temples of the gods of Egypt; he will burn their temples and take their gods captive. As a shepherd wraps his garment around him, so will he wrap Egypt around himself and depart from there unscathed. [13]There in the temple of the sun[b] in Egypt he will demolish the sacred pillars and will burn down the temples of the gods of Egypt.' "

Disaster Because of Idolatry

44 This word came to Jeremiah concerning all the Jews living in Lower Egypt—in Migdol, Tahpanhes and Memphis[c]—and in Upper Egypt[d]: [2]"This is what the LORD Almighty, the God of Israel, says: You saw the great disaster I brought on Jerusalem and on all the towns of Judah. Today they lie deserted and in ruins [3]because of the evil they have done. They provoked me to anger by burning incense and by worshiping other gods that neither they nor you nor your fathers ever knew. [4]Again and again I sent my servants the prophets, who said, 'Do not do this detestable thing that I hate!' [5]But they did not listen or pay attention; they did not turn from their wickedness or stop burning incense to other gods. [6]Therefore, my fierce anger was poured out; it raged against the towns of Judah and the streets of Jerusalem and made them the desolate ruins they are today.

[7]"Now this is what the LORD God Almighty, the God of Israel, says: Why bring such great disaster on yourselves by cutting off from Judah the men and women, the children and

infants, and so leave yourselves without a remnant? [8]Why provoke me to anger with what your hands have made, burning incense to other gods in Egypt, where you have come to live? You will destroy yourselves and make yourselves an object of cursing and reproach among all the nations on earth. [9]Have you forgotten the wickedness committed by your fathers and by the kings and queens of Judah and the wickedness committed by you and your wives in the land of Judah and the streets of Jerusalem? [10]To this day they have not humbled themselves or shown reverence, nor have they followed my law and the decrees I set before you and your fathers.

[11]"Therefore, this is what the LORD Almighty, the God of Israel, says: I am determined to bring disaster on you and to destroy all Judah. [12]I will take away the remnant of Judah who were determined to go to Egypt to settle there. They will all perish in Egypt; they will fall by the sword or die from famine. From the least to the greatest, they will die by sword or famine. They will become an object of cursing and horror, of condemnation and reproach. [13]I will punish those who live in Egypt with the sword, famine and plague, as I punished Jerusalem. [14]None of the remnant of Judah who have gone to live in Egypt will escape or survive to return to the land of Judah, to which they long to return and live; none will return except a few fugitives."

[15]Then all the men who knew that their wives were burning incense to other gods, along with all the women who were present—a large assembly—and all the people living in Lower and Upper Egypt,[e] said to Jeremiah, [16]"We will not listen to the message you have spoken to us in the name of the LORD! [17]We will certainly do everything we said we would: We will burn incense to the Queen of Heaven and will pour out drink offer-

---

[a]12 Or *I*   [b]13 Or *in Heliopolis*   [c]1 Hebrew *Noph*   [d]1 Hebrew *in Pathros*   [e]15 Hebrew *in Egypt and Pathros*

ings to her just as we and our fathers, our kings and our officials did in the towns of Judah and in the streets of Jerusalem. At that time we had plenty of food and were well off and suffered no harm. [18]But ever since we stopped burning incense to the Queen of Heaven and pouring out drink offerings to her, we have had nothing and have been perishing by sword and famine."

[19]The women added, "When we burned incense to the Queen of Heaven and poured out drink offerings to her, did not our husbands know that we were making cakes like her image and pouring out drink offerings to her?"

[20]Then Jeremiah said to all the people, both men and women, who were answering him, [21]"Did not the LORD remember and think about the incense burned in the towns of Judah and the streets of Jerusalem by you and your fathers, your kings and your officials and the people of the land? [22]When the LORD could no longer endure your wicked actions and the detestable things you did, your land became an object of cursing and a desolate waste without inhabitants, as it is today. [23]Because you have burned incense and have sinned against the LORD and have not obeyed him or followed his law or his decrees or his stipulations, this disaster has come upon you, as you now see."

[24]Then Jeremiah said to all the people, including the women, "Hear the word of the LORD, all you people of Judah in Egypt. [25]This is what the LORD Almighty, the God of Israel, says: You and your wives have shown by your actions what you promised when you said, 'We will certainly carry out the vows we made to burn incense and pour out drink offerings to the Queen of Heaven.'

"Go ahead then, do what you promised! Keep your vows! [26]But hear the word of the LORD, all Jews living in Egypt: 'I swear by my great name,' says the LORD, 'that no one from Judah living anywhere in Egypt will

ever again invoke my name or swear, "As surely as the Sovereign LORD lives." [27]For I am watching over them for harm, not for good; the Jews in Egypt will perish by sword and famine until they are all destroyed. [28]Those who escape the sword and return to the land of Judah from Egypt will be very few. Then the whole remnant of Judah who came to live in Egypt will know whose word will stand—mine or theirs.

[29]"'This will be the sign to you that I will punish you in this place,' declares the LORD, 'so that you will know that my threats of harm against you will surely stand.' [30]This is what the LORD says: 'I am going to hand Pharaoh Hophra king of Egypt over to his enemies who seek his life, just as I handed Zedekiah king of Judah over to Nebuchadnezzar king of Babylon, the enemy who was seeking his life.'"

A Message to Baruch

45 This is what Jeremiah the prophet told Baruch son of Neriah in the fourth year of Jehoiakim son of Josiah king of Judah, after Baruch had written on a scroll the words Jeremiah was then dictating: [2]"This is what the LORD, the God of Israel, says to you, Baruch: [3]You said, 'Woe to me! The LORD has added sorrow to my pain; I am worn out with groaning and find no rest.'"

[4]The LORD said, "Say this to him: 'This is what the LORD says: I will overthrow what I have built and uproot what I have planted, throughout the land. [5]Should you then seek great things for yourself? Seek them not. For I will bring disaster on all people, declares the LORD, but wherever you go I will let you escape with your life.'"

A Message About Egypt

46 This is the word of the LORD that came to Jeremiah the prophet concerning the nations:

[2]Concerning Egypt:

This is the message against the army of Pharaoh Neco king of Egypt, which was defeated at Carchemish on the Euphrates River by Nebuchadnezzar king of Babylon in the fourth year of Jehoiakim son of Josiah king of Judah:

³"Prepare your shields, both large and small,
　　and march out for battle!
⁴Harness the horses,
　　mount the steeds!
Take your positions
　　with helmets on!
Polish your spears,
　　put on your armor!
⁵What do I see?
　　They are terrified,
　they are retreating,
　　their warriors are defeated.
They flee in haste
　　without looking back,
　　and there is terror on every side,"
　　　　　　　　　declares the LORD.
⁶"The swift cannot flee
　　nor the strong escape.
In the north by the River Euphrates
　　they stumble and fall.

⁷"Who is this that rises like the Nile,
　　like rivers of surging waters?
⁸Egypt rises like the Nile,
　　like rivers of surging waters.
She says, 'I will rise and cover the earth;

a9 That is, the upper Nile region

I will destroy cities and their people.'
⁹Charge, O horses!
　Drive furiously, O charioteers!
March on, O warriors—
　　men of Cush*a* and Put who carry shields,
　　men of Lydia who draw the bow.
¹⁰But that day belongs to the Lord, the LORD Almighty—
　a day of vengeance, for vengeance on his foes.
The sword will devour till it is satisfied,
　　till it has quenched its thirst with blood.
For the Lord, the LORD Almighty, will offer sacrifice
　　in the land of the north by the River Euphrates.

¹¹"Go up to Gilead and get balm, O Virgin Daughter of Egypt.
But you multiply remedies in vain;
　there is no healing for you.
¹²The nations will hear of your shame;
　your cries will fill the earth.
One warrior will stumble over another;
　both will fall down together."

¹³This is the message the LORD spoke to Jeremiah the prophet about the coming of Nebuchadnezzar king of Babylon to attack Egypt:

Life in Bible Times

SCRIBES

Scribes were educated men who earned their living by writing letters or important papers. A scribe named Baruch wrote this Bible book as Jeremiah the prophet dictated it to him.

¹⁴"Announce this in Egypt, and
  proclaim it in Migdol;
  proclaim it also in Memphis^a
    and Tahpanhes:
'Take your positions and get
    ready,
  for the sword devours those
    around you.'
¹⁵Why will your warriors be laid
    low?
  They cannot stand, for the LORD
    will push them down.
¹⁶They will stumble repeatedly;
  they will fall over each other.
They will say, 'Get up, let us go
    back
  to our own people and our
    native lands,
  away from the sword of the
    oppressor.'
¹⁷There they will exclaim,
  'Pharaoh king of Egypt is only
    a loud noise;
  he has missed his opportunity.'

¹⁸"As surely as I live," declares the
    King,
  whose name is the LORD
    Almighty,
  "one will come who is like Tabor
    among the mountains,
  like Carmel by the sea.
¹⁹Pack your belongings for exile,
  you who live in Egypt,
for Memphis will be laid waste
  and lie in ruins without
    inhabitant.

²⁰"Egypt is a beautiful heifer,
  but a gadfly is coming
    against her from the north.
²¹The mercenaries in her ranks
  are like fattened calves.
They too will turn and flee
    together,
  they will not stand their
    ground,
for the day of disaster is coming
    upon them,
  the time for them to be
    punished.
²²Egypt will hiss like a fleeing
    serpent
  as the enemy advances in force;

they will come against her with
    axes,
  like men who cut down trees.
²³They will chop down her forest,"
    declares the LORD,
  "dense though it be.
They are more numerous than
    locusts,
  they cannot be counted.
²⁴The Daughter of Egypt will be
    put to shame,
  handed over to the people of the
    north."

²⁵The LORD Almighty, the God of
Israel, says: "I am about to bring punishment on Amon god of Thebes,^b on
Pharaoh, on Egypt and her gods and
her kings, and on those who rely on
Pharaoh. ²⁶I will hand them over to
those who seek their lives, to Nebuchadnezzar king of Babylon and his
officers. Later, however, Egypt will
be inhabited as in times past," declares the LORD.

²⁷"Do not fear, O Jacob my servant;
  do not be dismayed, O Israel.
I will surely save you out of a
    distant place,
  your descendants from the land
    of their exile.
Jacob will again have peace and
    security,
  and no one will make him
    afraid.
²⁸Do not fear, O Jacob my servant,
  for I am with you," declares the
    LORD.
"Though I completely destroy all
    the nations
  among which I scatter you,
  I will not completely destroy
    you.
I will discipline you but only with
    justice;
  I will not let you go entirely
    unpunished."

A Message About the Philistines

47 This is the word of the LORD
  that came to Jeremiah the
prophet concerning the Philistines
before Pharaoh attacked Gaza:

^a14 Hebrew Noph; also in verse 19   ^b25 Hebrew No

²This is what the LORD says:

"See how the waters are rising in
the north;
they will become an overflowing
torrent.
They will overflow the land and
everything in it,
the towns and those who live in
them.
The people will cry out;
all who dwell in the land will
wail
³at the sound of the hoofs of
galloping steeds,
at the noise of enemy chariots
and the rumble of their wheels.
Fathers will not turn to help their
children;
their hands will hang limp.
⁴For the day has come
to destroy all the Philistines
and to cut off all survivors
who could help Tyre and Sidon.
The LORD is about to destroy the
Philistines,
the remnant from the coasts of
Caphtor.ᵃ
⁵Gaza will shave her head in
mourning;
Ashkelon will be silenced.
O remnant on the plain,
how long will you cut
yourselves?

⁶" 'Ah, sword of the LORD,' ⌊you
cry,⌋
'how long till you rest?
Return to your scabbard;
cease and be still.'
⁷But how can it rest
when the LORD has commanded
it,
when he has ordered it
to attack Ashkelon and the
coast?"

A Message About Moab

48 Concerning Moab:

This is what the LORD Al-
mighty, the God of Israel, says:

"Woe to Nebo, for it will be
ruined.
Kiriathaim will be disgraced
and captured;
the strongholdᵇ will be
disgraced and shattered.
²Moab will be praised no more;
in Heshbonᶜ men will plot her
downfall:
'Come, let us put an end to that
nation.'
You too, O Madmen,ᵈ will be
silenced;
the sword will pursue you.
³Listen to the cries from
Horonaim,
cries of great havoc and
destruction.
⁴Moab will be broken;
her little ones will cry out.ᵉ
⁵They go up the way to Luhith,
weeping bitterly as they
go;
on the road down to Horonaim
anguished cries over the
destruction are heard.
⁶Flee! Run for your lives;
become like a bushᶠ in the
desert.
⁷Since you trust in your deeds and
riches,
you too will be taken
captive,
and Chemosh will go into exile,
together with his priests and
officials.
⁸The destroyer will come against
every town,
and not a town will escape.
The valley will be ruined
and the plateau destroyed,
because the LORD has spoken.
⁹Put salt on Moab,
for she will be laid wasteᵍ;
her towns will become desolate,
with no one to live in them.

¹⁰"A curse on him who is lax in
doing the LORD's work!
A curse on him who keeps his
sword from bloodshed!

ᵃ4 That is, Crete　　ᵇ1 Or / Misgab　　ᶜ2 The Hebrew for Heshbon sounds like the Hebrew for
plot.　　ᵈ2 The name of the Moabite town Madmen sounds like the Hebrew for be silenced.
ᵉ4 Hebrew; Septuagint / proclaim it to Zoar　　ᶠ6 Or like Aroer　　ᵍ9 Or Give wings to Moab, /
for she will fly away

¹¹"Moab has been at rest from
          youth,
     like wine left on its dregs,
not poured from one jar to
          another—
     she has not gone into exile.
So she tastes as she did,
     and her aroma is unchanged.
¹²But days are coming,"
          declares the LORD,
     "when I will send men who pour
          from jars,
     and they will pour her out;
they will empty her jars
     and smash her jugs.
¹³Then Moab will be ashamed of
          Chemosh,
     as the house of Israel was
          ashamed
     when they trusted in Bethel.

¹⁴"How can you say, 'We are
          warriors,
     men valiant in battle'?
¹⁵Moab will be destroyed and her
          towns invaded;
     her finest young men will go
          down in the slaughter,"
          declares the King, whose name
          is the LORD Almighty.
¹⁶"The fall of Moab is at hand;
     her calamity will come quickly.
¹⁷Mourn for her, all who live
          around her,
     all who know her fame;
say, 'How broken is the mighty
          scepter,
     how broken the glorious staff!'

¹⁸"Come down from your glory
     and sit on the parched ground,
     O inhabitants of the Daughter
          of Dibon,
for he who destroys Moab
     will come up against you
     and ruin your fortified cities.
¹⁹Stand by the road and watch,
     you who live in Aroer.
Ask the man fleeing and the
          woman escaping,
     ask them, 'What has happened?'
²⁰Moab is disgraced, for she is
          shattered.
     Wail and cry out!

Announce by the Arnon
     that Moab is destroyed.
²¹Judgment has come to the
          plateau—
     to Holon, Jahzah and
          Mephaath,
²² to Dibon, Nebo and Beth
          Diblathaim,
²³ to Kiriathaim, Beth Gamul and
          Beth Meon,
²⁴ to Kerioth and Bozrah—
     to all the towns of Moab, far
          and near.
²⁵Moab's horn[a] is cut off;
     her arm is broken,"
                    declares the LORD.

²⁶"Make her drunk,
     for she has defied the LORD.
Let Moab wallow in her vomit;
     let her be an object of ridicule.
²⁷Was not Israel the object of your
          ridicule?
Was she caught among thieves,
     that you shake your head in scorn
     whenever you speak of her?
²⁸Abandon your towns and dwell
          among the rocks,
     you who live in Moab.
Be like a dove that makes its nest
     at the mouth of a cave.

²⁹"We have heard of Moab's pride—
     her overweening pride and
          conceit,
     her pride and arrogance
     and the haughtiness of her
          heart.
³⁰I know her insolence but it is
          futile,"
                    declares the LORD,
     "and her boasts accomplish
          nothing.
³¹Therefore I wail over Moab,
     for all Moab I cry out,
     I moan for the men of Kir
          Hareseth.
³²I weep for you, as Jazer weeps,
     O vines of Sibmah.
Your branches spread as far as
          the sea;
     they reached as far as the sea of
          Jazer.
The destroyer has fallen

---

a25 *Horn* here symbolizes strength.

on your ripened fruit and
grapes.
³³Joy and gladness are gone
from the orchards and fields of
Moab.
I have stopped the flow of wine
from the presses;
no one treads them with shouts
of joy.
Although there are shouts,
they are not shouts of joy.

³⁴"The sound of their cry rises
from Heshbon to Elealeh and
Jahaz,
from Zoar as far as Horonaim and
Eglath Shelishiyah,
for even the waters of Nimrim
are dried up.
³⁵In Moab I will put an end
to those who make offerings on
the high places
and burn incense to their gods,"
declares the LORD.
³⁶"So my heart laments for Moab
like a flute;
it laments like a flute for the
men of Kir Hareseth.
The wealth they acquired is
gone.
³⁷Every head is shaved
and every beard cut off;
every hand is slashed
and every waist is covered with
sackcloth.
³⁸On all the roofs in Moab
and in the public squares
there is nothing but mourning,
for I have broken Moab
like a jar that no one wants,"
declares the LORD.
³⁹"How shattered she is! How they
wail!
How Moab turns her back in
shame!
Moab has become an object of
ridicule,
an object of horror to all those
around her."

⁴⁰This is what the LORD says:

"Look! An eagle is swooping
down,

spreading its wings over Moab.
⁴¹Kerioth*a* will be captured
and the strongholds taken.
In that day the hearts of Moab's
warriors
will be like the heart of a
woman in labor.
⁴²Moab will be destroyed as a
nation
because she defied the LORD.
⁴³Terror and pit and snare await
you,
O people of Moab,"
declares the LORD.
⁴⁴"Whoever flees from the terror
will fall into a pit,
whoever climbs out of the pit
will be caught in a snare;
for I will bring upon Moab
the year of her punishment,"
declares the LORD.

⁴⁵"In the shadow of Heshbon
the fugitives stand helpless,
for a fire has gone out from
Heshbon,
a blaze from the midst of Sihon;
it burns the foreheads of Moab,
the skulls of the noisy boasters.
⁴⁶Woe to you, O Moab!
The people of Chemosh are
destroyed;
your sons are taken into exile
and your daughters into
captivity.

⁴⁷"Yet I will restore the fortunes of
Moab
in days to come,"
declares the LORD.

Here ends the judgment on Moab.

A Message About Ammon

49 Concerning the Ammonites:

This is what the LORD says:

"Has Israel no sons?
Has she no heirs?
Why then has Molech*b* taken
possession of Gad?
Why do his people live in its
towns?
²But the days are coming,"

a41 Or The cities   *b1 Or their king; Hebrew malcam; also in verse 3*

declares the LORD,
"when I will sound the battle cry
against Rabbah of the
Ammonites;
it will become a mound of ruins,
and its surrounding villages
will be set on fire.
Then Israel will drive out
those who drove her out,"
                    says the LORD.
3"Wail, O Heshbon, for Ai is
destroyed!
Cry out, O inhabitants of
Rabbah!
Put on sackcloth and mourn;
rush here and there inside the
walls,
for Molech will go into exile,
together with his priests and
officials.
4Why do you boast of your valleys,
boast of your valleys so fruitful?
O unfaithful daughter,
you trust in your riches and
say,
'Who will attack me?'
5I will bring terror on you
from all those around you,"
            declares the Lord, the LORD
                            Almighty.
"Every one of you will be driven
away,
and no one will gather the
fugitives.

6"Yet afterward, I will restore the
fortunes of the Ammonites,"
            declares the LORD.

A Message About Edom

7Concerning Edom:

This is what the LORD Almighty
says:

"Is there no longer wisdom in
Teman?
Has counsel perished from the
prudent?
Has their wisdom decayed?
8Turn and flee, hide in deep caves,
you who live in Dedan,
for I will bring disaster on Esau
at the time I punish him.

9If grape pickers came to you,
would they not leave a few
grapes?
If thieves came during the night,
would they not steal only as
much as they wanted?
10But I will strip Esau bare;
I will uncover his hiding places,
so that he cannot conceal
himself.
His children, relatives and
neighbors will perish,
and he will be no more.
11Leave your orphans; I will protect
their lives.
Your widows too can trust in
me."

12This is what the LORD says: "If
those who do not deserve to drink the
cup must drink it, why should you go
unpunished? You will not go unpunished, but must drink it. 13I swear by
myself," declares the LORD, "that
Bozrah will become a ruin and an object of horror, of reproach and of cursing; and all its towns will be in ruins
forever."

14I have heard a message from the
LORD:
An envoy was sent to the
nations to say,
"Assemble yourselves to attack it!
Rise up for battle!"

15"Now I will make you small
among the nations,
despised among men.
16The terror you inspire
and the pride of your heart
have deceived you,
you who live in the clefts of the
rocks,
who occupy the heights of the
hill.
Though you build your nest as
high as the eagle's,
from there I will bring you
down,"
                    declares the LORD.
17"Edom will become an object of
horror;
all who pass by will be appalled
and will scoff
because of all its wounds.

¹⁸As Sodom and Gomorrah were
overthrown,
along with their neighboring
towns,"
says the LORD,
"so no one will live there;
no man will dwell in it.

¹⁹"Like a lion coming up from
Jordan's thickets
to a rich pastureland,
I will chase Edom from its land in
an instant.
Who is the chosen one I will
appoint for this?
Who is like me and who can
challenge me?
And what shepherd can stand
against me?"
²⁰Therefore, hear what the LORD
has planned against Edom,
what he has purposed against
those who live in Teman:
The young of the flock will be
dragged away;
he will completely destroy their
pasture because of them.
²¹At the sound of their fall the
earth will tremble;
their cry will resound to the
Red Sea.^a
²²Look! An eagle will soar and
swoop down,
spreading its wings over
Bozrah.
In that day the hearts of Edom's
warriors
will be like the heart of a
woman in labor.

A Message About Damascus

²³Concerning Damascus:

"Hamath and Arpad are
dismayed,
for they have heard bad news.
They are disheartened,
troubled like^b the restless sea.
²⁴Damascus has become feeble,
she has turned to flee
and panic has gripped her;
anguish and pain have seized her,

pain like that of a woman in
labor.
²⁵Why has the city of renown not
been abandoned,
the town in which I delight?
²⁶Surely, her young men will fall in
the streets;
all her soldiers will be silenced
in that day,"
declares the LORD Almighty.
²⁷"I will set fire to the walls of
Damascus;
it will consume the fortresses of
Ben-Hadad."

A Message About Kedar and Hazor

²⁸Concerning Kedar and the king-
doms of Hazor, which Nebuchadnezzar king of Babylon attacked:

This is what the LORD says:

"Arise, and attack Kedar
and destroy the people of the
East.
²⁹Their tents and their flocks will
be taken;
their shelters will be carried off
with all their goods and camels.
Men will shout to them,
'Terror on every side!'

³⁰"Flee quickly away!
Stay in deep caves, you who
live in Hazor,"
declares the LORD.
"Nebuchadnezzar king of Babylon
has plotted against you;
he has devised a plan against
you.

³¹"Arise and attack a nation at
ease,
which lives in confidence,"
declares the LORD,
"a nation that has neither gates
nor bars;
its people live alone.
³²Their camels will become plunder,
and their large herds will be
booty.
I will scatter to the winds those
who are in distant places^c

^a21 Hebrew *Yam Suph*; that is, Sea of Reeds
by their foreheads   ^b23 Hebrew *on* or *by*   ^c32 Or *who clip the hair*

and will bring disaster on them
from every side,"
       declares the LORD.
³³"Hazor will become a haunt of
jackals,
a desolate place forever.
No one will live there;
no man will dwell in it."

A Message About Elam

³⁴This is the word of the LORD that
came to Jeremiah the prophet concerning Elam, early in the reign of
Zedekiah king of Judah:

³⁵This is what the LORD Almighty
says:

"See, I will break the bow of
Elam,
the mainstay of their might.
³⁶I will bring against Elam the four
winds
from the four quarters of the
heavens;
I will scatter them to the four
winds,
and there will not be a nation
where Elam's exiles do not go.
³⁷I will shatter Elam before their
foes,
before those who seek their
lives;
I will bring disaster upon them,
even my fierce anger,"
       declares the LORD.
"I will pursue them with the
sword
until I have made an end of
them.
³⁸I will set my throne in Elam
and destroy her king and
officials,"
       declares the LORD.

³⁹"Yet I will restore the fortunes of
Elam
in days to come,"
       declares the LORD.

A Message About Babylon

50 This is the word the LORD
spoke through Jeremiah the
prophet concerning Babylon and the
land of the Babylonians[a]:

²"Announce and proclaim among
the nations,
lift up a banner and proclaim it;
keep nothing back, but say,
'Babylon will be captured;
Bel will be put to shame,
Marduk filled with terror.
Her images will be put to shame
and her idols filled with terror.'
³A nation from the north will
attack her
and lay waste her land.
No one will live in it;
both men and animals will flee
away.

⁴"In those days, at that time,"
       declares the LORD,
"the people of Israel and the
people of Judah together
will go in tears to seek the
LORD their God.
⁵They will ask the way to Zion
and turn their faces toward it.
They will come and bind
themselves to the LORD
in an everlasting covenant
that will not be forgotten.

⁶"My people have been lost sheep;
their shepherds have led them
astray
and caused them to roam on the
mountains.
They wandered over mountain
and hill
and forgot their own resting
place.
⁷Whoever found them devoured
them;
their enemies said, 'We are not
guilty,
for they sinned against the LORD,
their true pasture,
the LORD, the hope of their
fathers.'

⁸"Flee out of Babylon;
leave the land of the
Babylonians,
and be like the goats that lead
the flock.

---

a1 Or *Chaldeans*; also in verses 8, 25, 35 and 45

⁹For I will stir up and bring
    against Babylon
an alliance of great nations
    from the land of the north.
They will take up their positions
    against her,
    and from the north she will be
    captured.
Their arrows will be like skilled
    warriors
    who do not return
    empty-handed.
¹⁰So Babylonia*a* will be plundered;
    all who plunder her will have
    their fill,"
              declares the LORD.

¹¹"Because you rejoice and are glad,
    you who pillage my inheritance,
because you frolic like a heifer
    threshing grain
and neigh like stallions,
¹²your mother will be greatly
    ashamed;
    she who gave you birth will be
    disgraced.
She will be the least of the
    nations—
    a wilderness, a dry land, a
    desert.
¹³Because of the LORD's anger she
    will not be inhabited
    but will be completely
    desolate.
All who pass Babylon will be
    horrified and scoff
    because of all her wounds.
¹⁴"Take up your positions around
    Babylon,
    all you who draw the bow.
Shoot at her! Spare no arrows,
    for she has sinned against the
    LORD.
¹⁵Shout against her on every side!
    She surrenders, her towers fall,
    her walls are torn down.
Since this is the vengeance of the
    LORD,
    take vengeance on her;
    do to her as she has done to
    others.
¹⁶Cut off from Babylon the sower,

and the reaper with his sickle
    at harvest.
Because of the sword of the
    oppressor
    let everyone return to his own
    people,
    let everyone flee to his own
    land.

¹⁷"Israel is a scattered flock
    that lions have chased away.
The first to devour him
    was the king of Assyria;
the last to crush his bones
    was Nebuchadnezzar king of
    Babylon."

¹⁸Therefore this is what the LORD
Almighty, the God of Israel, says:

"I will punish the king of Babylon
    and his land
    as I punished the king of
    Assyria.
¹⁹But I will bring Israel back to his
    own pasture
    and he will graze on Carmel
    and Bashan;
his appetite will be satisfied
    on the hills of Ephraim and
    Gilead.
²⁰In those days, at that time,"
    declares the LORD,
"search will be made for Israel's
    guilt,
    but there will be none,
and for the sins of Judah,
    but none will be found,
for I will forgive the remnant I
    spare.

²¹"Attack the land of Merathaim
    and those who live in Pekod.
Pursue, kill and completely
    destroy*b* them,"
              declares the LORD.
"Do everything I have
    commanded you.
²²The noise of battle is in the land,
    the noise of great destruction!
²³How broken and shattered
    is the hammer of the whole
    earth!
How desolate is Babylon

---

*a*10 Or *Chaldea*   *b*21 The Hebrew term refers to the irrevocable giving over of things or persons
to the LORD, often by totally destroying them; also in verse 26.

among the nations!

²⁴I set a trap for you, O Babylon,
and you were caught before you
knew it;
you were found and captured
because you opposed the LORD.
²⁵The LORD has opened his arsenal
and brought out the weapons of
his wrath,
for the Sovereign LORD Almighty
has work to do
in the land of the Babylonians.
²⁶Come against her from afar.
Break open her granaries;
pile her up like heaps of grain.
Completely destroy her
and leave her no remnant.
²⁷Kill all her young bulls;
let them go down to the
slaughter!
Woe to them! For their day has
come,
the time for them to be
punished.
²⁸Listen to the fugitives and
refugees from Babylon
declaring in Zion
how the LORD our God has taken
vengeance,
vengeance for his temple.

²⁹"Summon archers against
Babylon,
all those who draw the bow.
Encamp all around her;
let no one escape.
Repay her for her deeds;
do to her as she has done.
For she has defied the LORD,
the Holy One of Israel.
³⁰Therefore, her young men will
fall in the streets;
all her soldiers will be silenced
in that day,"
declares the LORD.
³¹"See, I am against you,
O arrogant one,"
declares the Lord, the LORD
Almighty,
"for your day has come,
the time for you to be punished.
³²The arrogant one will stumble
and fall

and no one will help her up;
I will kindle a fire in her towns
that will consume all who are
around her."

³³This is what the LORD Almighty
says:

"The people of Israel are
oppressed,
and the people of Judah as well.
All their captors hold them fast,
refusing to let them go.
³⁴Yet their Redeemer is strong;
the LORD Almighty is his name.
He will vigorously defend their
cause
so that he may bring rest to
their land,
but unrest to those who live in
Babylon.

³⁵"A sword against the
Babylonians!"
declares the LORD—
"against those who live in
Babylon
and against her officials and
wise men!
³⁶A sword against her false
prophets!
They will become fools.
A sword against her warriors!
They will be filled with terror.
³⁷A sword against her horses and
chariots
and all the foreigners in her
ranks!
They will become women.
A sword against her treasures!
They will be plundered.
³⁸A drought on*ᵃ her waters!
They will dry up.
For it is a land of idols,
idols that will go mad with
terror.

³⁹"So desert creatures and hyenas
will live there,
and there the owl will dwell.
It will never again be inhabited
or lived in from generation to
generation.
⁴⁰As God overthrew Sodom and
Gomorrah

ᵃ38 Or *A sword against*

along with their neighboring
   towns,"
            declares the LORD,
"so no one will live there;
   no man will dwell in it.

⁴¹"Look! An army is coming from
      the north;
   a great nation and many kings
   are being stirred up from the
      ends of the earth.
⁴²They are armed with bows and
      spears;
   they are cruel and without
      mercy.
They sound like the roaring sea
   as they ride on their horses;
they come like men in battle
      formation
   to attack you, O Daughter of
      Babylon.
⁴³The king of Babylon has heard
      reports about them,
   and his hands hang limp.
Anguish has gripped him,
   pain like that of a woman in
      labor.
⁴⁴Like a lion coming up from
      Jordan's thickets
   to a rich pastureland,
I will chase Babylon from its land
   in an instant.
Who is the chosen one I will
      appoint for this?
Who is like me and who can
      challenge me?
   And what shepherd can stand
      against me?"
⁴⁵Therefore, hear what the LORD
      has planned against
      Babylon,
   what he has purposed against
      the land of the Babylonians:
The young of the flock will be
      dragged away;
   he will completely destroy their
      pasture because of them.
⁴⁶At the sound of Babylon's capture
      the earth will tremble;
   its cry will resound among the
      nations.

51 This is what the LORD says:

"See, I will stir up the spirit
      of a destroyer
against Babylon and the people
      of Leb Kamai.ᵃ
²I will send foreigners to Babylon
   to winnow her and to devastate
      her land;
they will oppose her on every side
   in the day of her disaster.
³Let not the archer string his bow,
   nor let him put on his armor.
Do not spare her young men;
   completely destroyᵇ her army.
⁴They will fall down slain in
      Babylon,ᶜ
   fatally wounded in her streets.
⁵For Israel and Judah have not
      been forsaken
   by their God, the LORD
      Almighty,
though their landᵈ is full of guilt
   before the Holy One of Israel.

⁶"Flee from Babylon!
   Run for your lives!
   Do not be destroyed because of
      her sins.
It is time for the LORD's
      vengeance;
   he will pay her what she
      deserves.
⁷Babylon was a gold cup in the
      LORD's hand;
   she made the whole earth
      drunk.
The nations drank her wine;
   therefore they have now gone
      mad.
⁸Babylon will suddenly fall and be
      broken.
   Wail over her!
Get balm for her pain;
   perhaps she can be healed.

⁹" 'We would have healed Babylon,
   but she cannot be healed;
let us leave her and each go to his
      own land,
   for her judgment reaches to the
      skies,

ᵃ1 *Leb Kamai* is a cryptogram for Chaldea, that is, Babylonia.   ᵇ3 The Hebrew term refers to
the irrevocable giving over of things or persons to the LORD, often by totally destroying them.
ᶜ4 Or *Chaldea*   ᵈ5 Or / *and the land of the Babylonians*

it rises as high as the clouds.'

¹⁰" 'The LORD has vindicated us;
come, let us tell in Zion
what the LORD our God has
done.'

¹¹"Sharpen the arrows,
take up the shields!
The LORD has stirred up the kings
of the Medes,
because his purpose is to
destroy Babylon.
The LORD will take vengeance,
vengeance for his temple.
¹²Lift up a banner against the
walls of Babylon!
Reinforce the guard,
station the watchmen,
prepare an ambush!
The LORD will carry out his
purpose,
his decree against the people of
Babylon.
¹³You who live by many waters
and are rich in treasures,
your end has come,
the time for you to be cut off.
¹⁴The LORD Almighty has sworn by
himself:
I will surely fill you with men,
as with a swarm of locusts,
and they will shout in triumph
over you.

¹⁵"He made the earth by his power;
he founded the world by his
wisdom
and stretched out the heavens
by his understanding.
¹⁶When he thunders, the waters in
the heavens roar;
he makes clouds rise from the
ends of the earth.
He sends lightning with the rain
and brings out the wind from
his storehouses.

¹⁷"Every man is senseless and
without knowledge;
every goldsmith is shamed by
his idols.
His images are a fraud;
they have no breath in them.

¹⁸They are worthless, the objects of
mockery;
when their judgment comes,
they will perish.
¹⁹He who is the Portion of Jacob is
not like these,
for he is the Maker of all
things,
including the tribe of his
inheritance—
the LORD Almighty is his name.

²⁰"You are my war club,
my weapon for battle—
with you I shatter nations,
with you I destroy kingdoms,
²¹with you I shatter horse and
rider,
with you I shatter chariot and
driver,
²²with you I shatter man and
woman,
with you I shatter old man and
youth,
with you I shatter young man
and maiden,
²³with you I shatter shepherd and
flock,
with you I shatter farmer and
oxen,
with you I shatter governors
and officials.

²⁴"Before your eyes I will repay
Babylon and all who live in Babylo-
niaª for all the wrong they have done
in Zion," declares the LORD.

²⁵"I am against you, O destroying
mountain,
you who destroy the whole
earth,"
declares the LORD.
"I will stretch out my hand
against you,
roll you off the cliffs,
and make you a burned-out
mountain.
²⁶No rock will be taken from you
for a cornerstone,
nor any stone for a foundation,
for you will be desolate forever,"
declares the LORD.

²⁷"Lift up a banner in the land!

ª24 Or *Chaldea*; also in verse 35

Blow the trumpet among the
   nations!
Prepare the nations for battle
   against her;
   summon against her these
    kingdoms:
   Ararat, Minni and Ashkenaz.
Appoint a commander against
   her;
   send up horses like a swarm of
    locusts.
28Prepare the nations for battle
   against her—
   the kings of the Medes,
   their governors and all their
    officials,
   and all the countries they rule.
29The land trembles and writhes,
   for the LORD's purposes against
    Babylon stand—
   to lay waste the land of Babylon
   so that no one will live there.
30Babylon's warriors have stopped
    fighting;
   they remain in their
    strongholds.
Their strength is exhausted;
   they have become like women.
Her dwellings are set on fire;
   the bars of her gates are
    broken.
31One courier follows another
   and messenger follows
    messenger
   to announce to the king of
    Babylon
   that his entire city is captured,
32the river crossings seized,
   the marshes set on fire,
   and the soldiers terrified."

33This is what the LORD Almighty,
the God of Israel, says:

"The Daughter of Babylon is like
   a threshing floor
   at the time it is trampled;
   the time to harvest her will
    soon come."

34"Nebuchadnezzar king of Babylon
   has devoured us,
   he has thrown us into
    confusion,

he has made us an empty jar.
Like a serpent he has swallowed
   us
   and filled his stomach with our
    delicacies,
   and then has spewed us out.
35May the violence done to our
   flesh*a* be upon Babylon,"
   say the inhabitants of Zion.
"May our blood be on those who
   live in Babylonia,"
   says Jerusalem.

36Therefore, this is what the LORD
says:

"See, I will defend your cause
   and avenge you;
I will dry up her sea
   and make her springs dry.
37Babylon will be a heap of ruins,
   a haunt of jackals,
   an object of horror and scorn,
   a place where no one lives.
38Her people all roar like young
    lions,
   they growl like lion cubs.
39But while they are aroused,
   I will set out a feast for them
   and make them drunk,
   so that they shout with
    laughter—
   then sleep forever and not
    awake,"
            declares the LORD.
40"I will bring them down
   like lambs to the slaughter,
   like rams and goats.

41"How Sheshach*b* will be captured,
   the boast of the whole earth
    seized!
What a horror Babylon will be
   among the nations!
42The sea will rise over Babylon;
   its roaring waves will cover
    her.
43Her towns will be desolate,
   a dry and desert land,
   a land where no one lives,
   through which no man travels.
44I will punish Bel in Babylon
   and make him spew out what
    he has swallowed.

---

a35 Or *done to us and to our children*   *b41 Sheshach* is a cryptogram for Babylon.

The nations will no longer stream
to him.
And the wall of Babylon will
fall.

⁴⁵"Come out of her, my people!
Run for your lives!
Run from the fierce anger of the
LORD.
⁴⁶Do not lose heart or be afraid
when rumors are heard in the
land;
one rumor comes this year,
another the next,
rumors of violence in the land
and of ruler against ruler.
⁴⁷For the time will surely come
when I will punish the idols of
Babylon;
her whole land will be disgraced
and her slain will all lie fallen
within her.
⁴⁸Then heaven and earth and all
that is in them
will shout for joy over Babylon,
for out of the north
destroyers will attack her,"
declares the LORD.

⁴⁹"Babylon must fall because of
Israel's slain,
just as the slain in all the
earth
have fallen because of Babylon.
⁵⁰You who have escaped the sword,
leave and do not linger!
Remember the LORD in a distant
land,
and think on Jerusalem."

⁵¹"We are disgraced,
for we have been insulted
and shame covers our faces,
because foreigners have entered
the holy places of the LORD's
house."

⁵²"But days are coming," declares
the LORD,
"when I will punish her idols,
and throughout her land
the wounded will groan.
⁵³Even if Babylon reaches the sky
and fortifies her lofty
stronghold,

I will send destroyers against
her,"
declares the LORD.

⁵⁴"The sound of a cry comes from
Babylon,
the sound of great destruction
from the land of the
Babylonians.ᵃ
⁵⁵The LORD will destroy Babylon;
he will silence her noisy din.
Waves ₗof enemies₎ will rage like
great waters;
the roar of their voices will
resound.
⁵⁶A destroyer will come against
Babylon;
her warriors will be captured,
and their bows will be broken.
For the LORD is a God of
retribution;
he will repay in full.
⁵⁷I will make her officials and wise
men drunk,
her governors, officers and
warriors as well;
they will sleep forever and not
awake,"
declares the King, whose name
is the LORD Almighty.

⁵⁸This is what the LORD Almighty
says:

"Babylon's thick wall will be
leveled
and her high gates set on fire;
the peoples exhaust themselves
for nothing,
the nations' labor is only fuel
for the flames."

⁵⁹This is the message Jeremiah
gave to the staff officer Seraiah son of
Neriah, the son of Mahseiah, when
he went to Babylon with Zedekiah
king of Judah in the fourth year of his
reign. ⁶⁰Jeremiah had written on a
scroll about all the disasters that
would come upon Babylon—all that
had been recorded concerning Babylon. ⁶¹He said to Seraiah, "When
you get to Babylon, see that you read
all these words aloud. ⁶²Then say, 'O
LORD, you have said you will destroy

this place, so that neither man nor animal will live in it; it will be desolate forever.' ⁶³When you finish reading this scroll, tie a stone to it and throw it into the Euphrates. ⁶⁴Then say, 'So will Babylon sink to rise no more because of the disaster I will bring upon her. And her people will fall.'"

The words of Jeremiah end here.

The Fall of Jerusalem

52 Zedekiah was twenty-one years old when he became king, and he reigned in Jerusalem eleven years. His mother's name was Hamutal daughter of Jeremiah; she was from Libnah. ²He did evil in the eyes of the LORD, just as Jehoiakim had done. ³It was because of the LORD's anger that all this happened to Jerusalem and Judah, and in the end he thrust them from his presence.

Now Zedekiah rebelled against the king of Babylon.

⁴So in the ninth year of Zedekiah's reign, on the tenth day of the tenth month, Nebuchadnezzar king of Babylon marched against Jerusalem with his whole army. They camped outside the city and built siege works all around it. ⁵The city was kept under siege until the eleventh year of King Zedekiah.

⁶By the ninth day of the fourth month the famine in the city had become so severe that there was no food for the people to eat. ⁷Then the city wall was broken through, and the whole army fled. They left the city at night through the gate between the two walls near the king's garden, though the Babylonians*ᵃ* were surrounding the city. They fled toward the Arabah,*ᵇ* ⁸but the Babylonian*ᶜ* army pursued King Zedekiah and overtook him in the plains of Jericho. All his soldiers were separated from him and scattered, ⁹and he was captured.

He was taken to the king of Babylon at Riblah in the land of Hamath, where he pronounced sentence on him. ¹⁰There at Riblah the king of Babylon slaughtered the sons of Zedekiah before his eyes; he also killed all the officials of Judah. ¹¹Then he put out Zedekiah's eyes, bound him with bronze shackles and took him to Babylon, where he put him in prison till the day of his death.

¹²On the tenth day of the fifth month, in the nineteenth year of Nebuchadnezzar king of Babylon, Nebuzaradan commander of the imperial guard, who served the king of Babylon, came to Jerusalem. ¹³He set fire to the temple of the LORD, the royal palace and all the houses of Jerusalem. Every important building he burned down. ¹⁴The whole Babylonian army under the commander of the imperial guard broke down all the walls around Jerusalem. ¹⁵Nebuzaradan the commander of the guard carried into exile some of the poorest people and those who remained in the city, along with the rest of the craftsmen*ᵈ* and those who had gone over to the king of Babylon. ¹⁶But Nebuzaradan left behind the rest of the poorest people of the land to work the vineyards and fields.

¹⁷The Babylonians broke up the bronze pillars, the movable stands and the bronze Sea that were at the temple of the LORD and they carried all the bronze to Babylon. ¹⁸They also took away the pots, shovels, wick trimmers, sprinkling bowls, dishes and all the bronze articles used in the temple service. ¹⁹The commander of the imperial guard took away the basins, censers, sprinkling bowls, pots, lampstands, dishes and bowls used for drink offerings—all that were made of pure gold or silver.

²⁰The bronze from the two pillars, the Sea and the twelve bronze bulls under it, and the movable stands, which King Solomon had made for the temple of the LORD, was more

ᵃ7 Or Chaldeans; also in verse 17　*ᵇ7 Or the Jordan Valley*　*ᶜ8 Or Chaldean; also in verse 14*　*ᵈ15 Or populace*

than could be weighed. [21]Each of the pillars was eighteen cubits high and twelve cubits in circumference[a]; each was four fingers thick, and hollow. [22]The bronze capital on top of the one pillar was five cubits[b] high and was decorated with a network and pomegranates of bronze all around. The other pillar, with its pomegranates, was similar. [23]There were ninety-six pomegranates on the sides; the total number of pomegranates above the surrounding network was a hundred.

[24]The commander of the guard took as prisoners Seraiah the chief priest, Zephaniah the priest next in rank and the three doorkeepers. [25]Of those still in the city, he took the officer in charge of the fighting men, and seven royal advisers. He also took the secretary who was chief officer in charge of conscripting the people of the land and sixty of his men who were found in the city. [26]Nebuzaradan the commander took them all and brought them to the king of Babylon at Riblah. [27]There at Riblah, in the land of Hamath, the king had them executed.

So Judah went into captivity, away from her land. [28]This is the number of the people Nebuchadnezzar carried into exile:

in the seventh year, 3,023 Jews;
[29]in Nebuchadnezzar's eighteenth year,
832 people from Jerusalem;
[30]in his twenty-third year,
745 Jews taken into exile by Nebuzaradan the commander of the imperial guard.
There were 4,600 people in all.

Jehoiachin Released

[31]In the thirty-seventh year of the exile of Jehoiachin king of Judah, in the year Evil-Merodach[c] became king of Babylon, he released Jehoiachin king of Judah and freed him from prison on the twenty-fifth day of the twelfth month. [32]He spoke kindly to him and gave him a seat of honor higher than those of the other kings who were with him in Babylon. [33]So Jehoiachin put aside his prison clothes and for the rest of his life ate regularly at the king's table. [34]Day by day the king of Babylon gave Jehoiachin a regular allowance as long as he lived, till the day of his death.

---

[a]21 That is, about 27 feet (about 8.1 meters) high and 18 feet (about 5.4 meters) in circumference
[b]22 That is, about 7 1/2 feet (about 2.3 meters) [c]31 Also called *Amel-Marduk*

LAMENTATIONS

WHO WROTE THIS BOOK?
The writer is unknown for certain, though the prophet Jeremiah may be the author.

WHY WAS THIS BOOK WRITTEN?
Lamentations shows how sad the captives in Babylon were, and shows that they finally realized that they were being punished because of their sin.

WHAT IS SPECIAL ABOUT THIS BOOK?
Lamentations is "dirge poetry." This is very sad poetry, like sadness over a person's death.

WHEN WAS THIS BOOK WRITTEN?
This book was written after Jerusalem was destroyed by the Babylonians in 586 B.C.

LAM
EZE
DAN

1 ^aHow deserted lies the city,
   once so full of people!
How like a widow is she,
   who once was great among the
      nations!
She who was queen among the
      provinces
   has now become a slave.

²Bitterly she weeps at night,
   tears are upon her cheeks.
Among all her lovers
   there is none to comfort her.
All her friends have betrayed her;
   they have become her enemies.

³After affliction and harsh labor,
   Judah has gone into exile.
She dwells among the nations;
   she finds no resting place.
All who pursue her have
      overtaken her
   in the midst of her distress.

⁴The roads to Zion mourn,
   for no one comes to her
      appointed feasts.
All her gateways are desolate,
   her priests groan,
her maidens grieve,
   and she is in bitter anguish.

⁵Her foes have become her
      masters;
   her enemies are at ease.
The LORD has brought her grief
   because of her many sins.
Her children have gone into exile,
   captive before the foe.

⁶All the splendor has departed
   from the Daughter of Zion.
Her princes are like deer
   that find no pasture;
in weakness they have fled
   before the pursuer.

⁷In the days of her affliction and
      wandering
   Jerusalem remembers all the
      treasures
   that were hers in days of old.
When her people fell into enemy
      hands,
   there was no one to help her.

Her enemies looked at her
   and laughed at her destruction.

⁸Jerusalem has sinned greatly
   and so has become unclean.
All who honored her despise her,
   for they have seen her
      nakedness;
she herself groans
   and turns away.

⁹Her filthiness clung to her skirts;
   she did not consider her future.
Her fall was astounding;
   there was none to comfort her.
"Look, O LORD, on my affliction,
   for the enemy has triumphed."

¹⁰The enemy laid hands
   on all her treasures;
she saw pagan nations
   enter her sanctuary—
those you had forbidden
   to enter your assembly.

¹¹All her people groan
   as they search for bread;
they barter their treasures for
      food
   to keep themselves alive.
"Look, O LORD, and consider,
   for I am despised."

¹²"Is it nothing to you, all you who
      pass by?
   Look around and see.
Is any suffering like my suffering
   that was inflicted on me,
that the LORD brought on me
   in the day of his fierce anger?

¹³"From on high he sent fire,
   sent it down into my bones.
He spread a net for my feet
   and turned me back.
He made me desolate,
   faint all the day long.

¹⁴"My sins have been bound into a
      yoke^b;
   by his hands they were woven
      together.
They have come upon my neck
   and the Lord has sapped my
      strength.

---

^aThis chapter is an acrostic poem, the verses of which begin with the successive letters of the
Hebrew alphabet.   ^b14 Most Hebrew manuscripts; Septuagint *He kept watch over my sins*

He has handed me over
  to those I cannot withstand.

15"The Lord has rejected
  all the warriors in my midst;
he has summoned an army
      against me
  to*a* crush my young men.
In his winepress the Lord has
      trampled
  the Virgin Daughter of Judah.

16"This is why I weep
  and my eyes overflow with
      tears.
No one is near to comfort me,
  no one to restore my spirit.
My children are destitute
  because the enemy has
      prevailed."

17Zion stretches out her hands,
  but there is no one to comfort
      her.
The LORD has decreed for Jacob
  that his neighbors become his
      foes;
Jerusalem has become
  an unclean thing among them.

18"The LORD is righteous,
  yet I rebelled against his
      command.
Listen, all you peoples;
  look upon my suffering.
My young men and maidens
  have gone into exile.

19"I called to my allies
  but they betrayed me.
My priests and my elders
  perished in the city
while they searched for food
  to keep themselves alive.

20"See, O LORD, how distressed I
      am!
  I am in torment within,
and in my heart I am disturbed,
  for I have been most rebellious.
Outside, the sword bereaves;
  inside, there is only death.

21"People have heard my groaning,
  but there is no one to comfort
      me.
All my enemies have heard of my
      distress;
  they rejoice at what you have
      done.
May you bring the day you have
      announced
  so they may become like me.

22"Let all their wickedness come
      before you;
  deal with them
as you have dealt with me
  because of all my sins.
My groans are many
  and my heart is faint."

2 *b* How the Lord has covered the
      Daughter of Zion
    with the cloud of his anger*c*!
He has hurled down the splendor
      of Israel
  from heaven to earth;
he has not remembered his
      footstool
  in the day of his anger.

2Without pity the Lord has
      swallowed up
  all the dwellings of Jacob;
in his wrath he has torn down
  the strongholds of the Daughter
      of Judah.
He has brought her kingdom and
      its princes
  down to the ground in dishonor.

3In fierce anger he has cut off
  every horn*d* of Israel.
He has withdrawn his right hand
  at the approach of the enemy.
He has burned in Jacob like a
      flaming fire
  that consumes everything
      around it.

4Like an enemy he has strung his
      bow;
  his right hand is ready.
Like a foe he has slain

---

a15 Or *has set a time for me / when he will*   *b*This chapter is an acrostic poem, the verses of
which begin with the successive letters of the Hebrew alphabet.   *c1* Or *How the Lord in his
anger / has treated the Daughter of Zion with contempt*   *d3* Or / *all the strength*; or *every king*;
horn here symbolizes strength.

all who were pleasing to the
 eye;
he has poured out his wrath like
 fire
on the tent of the Daughter of
 Zion.

⁵The Lord is like an enemy;
 he has swallowed up Israel.
He has swallowed up all her
 palaces
and destroyed her strongholds.
He has multiplied mourning and
 lamentation
for the Daughter of Judah.

⁶He has laid waste his dwelling
 like a garden;
he has destroyed his place of
 meeting.
The LORD has made Zion forget
 her appointed feasts and her
 Sabbaths;
in his fierce anger he has spurned
 both king and priest.

⁷The Lord has rejected his altar
 and abandoned his sanctuary.
He has handed over to the enemy
 the walls of her palaces;
they have raised a shout in the
 house of the LORD
as on the day of an appointed
 feast.

⁸The LORD determined to tear
 down
 the wall around the Daughter of
 Zion.
He stretched out a measuring line
 and did not withhold his hand
 from destroying.
He made ramparts and walls
 lament;
 together they wasted away.

⁹Her gates have sunk into the
 ground;
 their bars he has broken and
 destroyed.
Her king and her princes are
 exiled among the nations,
 the law is no more,
and her prophets no longer find
 visions from the LORD.

¹⁰The elders of the Daughter of
 Zion

sit on the ground in silence;
they have sprinkled dust on their
 heads
 and put on sackcloth.
The young women of Jerusalem
 have bowed their heads to the
 ground.

¹¹My eyes fail from weeping,
 I am in torment within,
my heart is poured out on the
 ground
 because my people are
 destroyed,
because children and infants faint
 in the streets of the city.

¹²They say to their mothers,
 "Where is bread and wine?"
as they faint like wounded men
 in the streets of the city,
as their lives ebb away
 in their mothers' arms.

¹³What can I say for you?
 With what can I compare you,
 O Daughter of Jerusalem?
To what can I liken you,
 that I may comfort you,
 O Virgin Daughter of Zion?
Your wound is as deep as the sea.
 Who can heal you?

¹⁴The visions of your prophets
 were false and worthless;
they did not expose your sin
 to ward off your captivity.
The oracles they gave you
 were false and misleading.

¹⁵All who pass your way
 clap their hands at you;
they scoff and shake their heads
 at the Daughter of Jerusalem:
"Is this the city that was called
 the perfection of beauty,
 the joy of the whole earth?"

¹⁶All your enemies open their
 mouths
 wide against you;
they scoff and gnash their teeth
 and say, "We have swallowed
 her up.
This is the day we have waited
 for;
 we have lived to see it."

¹⁷The Lᴏʀᴅ has done what he
　　planned;
　he has fulfilled his word,
　which he decreed long ago.
He has overthrown you without
　　pity,
　he has let the enemy gloat over
　　you,
　he has exalted the horn*a* of
　　your foes.

¹⁸The hearts of the people
　　cry out to the Lord.
O wall of the Daughter of Zion,
　let your tears flow like a river
　　day and night;
　give yourself no relief,
　your eyes no rest.

¹⁹Arise, cry out in the night,
　as the watches of the night
　　begin;
　pour out your heart like water
　in the presence of the Lord.
Lift up your hands to him
　for the lives of your children,
　who faint from hunger
　at the head of every street.

²⁰"Look, O Lᴏʀᴅ, and consider:
　Whom have you ever treated
　　like this?
　Should women eat their offspring,
　　the children they have cared
　　for?
　Should priest and prophet be
　　killed
　in the sanctuary of the Lord?

²¹"Young and old lie together
　in the dust of the streets;
　my young men and maidens
　have fallen by the sword.
You have slain them in the day of
　　your anger;
　you have slaughtered them
　　without pity.

²²"As you summon to a feast day,
　so you summoned against me
　　terrors on every side.
In the day of the Lᴏʀᴅ's anger
　no one escaped or survived;

those I cared for and reared,
　my enemy has destroyed."

3 *b* I am the man who has seen
　　affliction
　by the rod of his wrath.
²He has driven me away and made
　　me walk
　in darkness rather than
　　light;
³indeed, he has turned his hand
　　against me
　again and again, all day long.

⁴He has made my skin and my
　　flesh grow old
　and has broken my bones.
⁵He has besieged me and
　　surrounded me
　with bitterness and hardship.
⁶He has made me dwell in
　　darkness
　like those long dead.

⁷He has walled me in so I cannot
　　escape;
　he has weighed me down with
　　chains.
⁸Even when I call out or cry for
　　help,
　he shuts out my prayer.
⁹He has barred my way with
　　blocks of stone;
　he has made my paths crooked.

¹⁰Like a bear lying in wait,
　like a lion in hiding,
¹¹he dragged me from the path and
　　mangled me
　and left me without help.
¹²He drew his bow
　and made me the target for his
　　arrows.

¹³He pierced my heart
　with arrows from his quiver.
¹⁴I became the laughingstock of all
　　my people;
　they mock me in song all day
　　long.
¹⁵He has filled me with bitter herbs
　and sated me with gall.

---

a17 Horn here symbolizes strength.　　*b*This chapter is an acrostic poem; the verses of each stanza
begin with the successive letters of the Hebrew alphabet, and the verses within each stanza begin
with the same letter.

16He has broken my teeth with
   gravel;
   he has trampled me in the dust.
17I have been deprived of peace;
   I have forgotten what prosperity
   is.
18So I say, "My splendor is gone
   and all that I had hoped from
   the LORD."

19I remember my affliction and my
   wandering,
   the bitterness and the gall.
20I well remember them,
   and my soul is downcast within
   me.
21Yet this I call to mind
   and therefore I have hope:

22Because of the LORD's great love
   we are not consumed,
   for his compassions never fail.
23They are new every morning;
   great is your faithfulness.
24I say to myself, "The LORD is my
   portion;
   therefore I will wait for him."

25The LORD is good to those whose
   hope is in him,
   to the one who seeks him;
26it is good to wait quietly
   for the salvation of the LORD.

WORDS TO REMEMBER

3:25-26 The LORD is good to
         those whose hope is
         in him,
         to the one who seeks
         him;
         it is good to wait quietly
         for the salvation of the
         LORD.

27It is good for a man to bear the
   yoke
   while he is young.

28Let him sit alone in silence,
   for the LORD has laid it on him.
29Let him bury his face in the
   dust—
   there may yet be hope.

30Let him offer his cheek to one
   who would strike him,
   and let him be filled with
   disgrace.
31For men are not cast off
   by the Lord forever.
32Though he brings grief, he will
   show compassion,
   so great is his unfailing love.
33For he does not willingly bring
   affliction
   or grief to the children of men.

34To crush underfoot
   all prisoners in the land,
35to deny a man his rights
   before the Most High,
36to deprive a man of justice—
   would not the Lord see such
   things?

37Who can speak and have it
   happen
   if the Lord has not decreed it?
38Is it not from the mouth of the
   Most High
   that both calamities and good
   things come?
39Why should any living man
   complain
   when punished for his sins?

40Let us examine our ways and test
   them,
   and let us return to the LORD.
41Let us lift up our hearts and our
   hands
   to God in heaven, and say:
42"We have sinned and rebelled
   and you have not forgiven.

43"You have covered yourself with
   anger and pursued us;
   you have slain without pity.
44You have covered yourself with a
   cloud
   so that no prayer can get
   through.
45You have made us scum and
   refuse
   among the nations.

46"All our enemies have opened
   their mouths
   wide against us.
47We have suffered terror and
   pitfalls,

ruin and destruction."
⁴⁸Streams of tears flow from my
eyes
because my people are
destroyed.

⁴⁹My eyes will flow unceasingly,
without relief,
⁵⁰until the LORD looks down
from heaven and sees.
⁵¹What I see brings grief to my soul
because of all the women of my
city.

⁵²Those who were my enemies
without cause
hunted me like a bird.
⁵³They tried to end my life in a pit
and threw stones at me;
⁵⁴the waters closed over my head,
and I thought I was about to be
cut off.

⁵⁵I called on your name, O LORD,
from the depths of the pit.
⁵⁶You heard my plea: "Do not close
your ears
to my cry for relief."
⁵⁷You came near when I called you,
and you said, "Do not fear."

⁵⁸O Lord, you took up my case;
you redeemed my life.
⁵⁹You have seen, O LORD, the
wrong done to me.
Uphold my cause!
⁶⁰You have seen the depth of their
vengeance,
all their plots against me.

⁶¹O LORD, you have heard their
insults,
all their plots against me—
⁶²what my enemies whisper and
mutter
against me all day long.
⁶³Look at them! Sitting or standing,
they mock me in their songs.

⁶⁴Pay them back what they
deserve, O LORD,
for what their hands have done.
⁶⁵Put a veil over their hearts,
and may your curse be on them!

⁶⁶Pursue them in anger and destroy
them
from under the heavens of the
LORD.

4 ᵃ How the gold has lost its
luster,
the fine gold become dull!
The sacred gems are scattered
at the head of every street.

²How the precious sons of Zion,
once worth their weight in gold,
are now considered as pots of
clay,
the work of a potter's hands!

³Even jackals offer their breasts
to nurse their young,
but my people have become
heartless
like ostriches in the desert.

⁴Because of thirst the infant's
tongue
sticks to the roof of its mouth;
the children beg for bread,
but no one gives it to them.

⁵Those who once ate delicacies
are destitute in the streets.
Those nurtured in purple
now lie on ash heaps.

⁶The punishment of my people
is greater than that of Sodom,
which was overthrown in a
moment
without a hand turned to help
her.

⁷Their princes were brighter than
snow
and whiter than milk,
their bodies more ruddy than
rubies,
their appearance like
sapphires. ᵇ

⁸But now they are blacker than
soot;
they are not recognized in the
streets.
Their skin has shriveled on their
bones;

ᵃThis chapter is an acrostic poem, the verses of which begin with the successive letters of the
Hebrew alphabet.   ᵇ7 Or *lapis lazuli*

it has become as dry as a stick.

⁹Those killed by the sword are
    better off
than those who die of famine;
racked with hunger, they waste
    away
    for lack of food from the field.

¹⁰With their own hands
    compassionate women
    have cooked their own children,
who became their food
    when my people were destroyed.

¹¹The LORD has given full vent to
    his wrath;
    he has poured out his fierce
    anger.
He kindled a fire in Zion
    that consumed her foundations.

¹²The kings of the earth did not
    believe,
    nor did any of the world's
    people,
that enemies and foes could enter
    the gates of Jerusalem.

¹³But it happened because of the
    sins of her prophets
    and the iniquities of her priests,
who shed within her
    the blood of the righteous.

¹⁴Now they grope through the
    streets
    like men who are blind.
They are so defiled with blood
    that no one dares to touch their
    garments.

¹⁵"Go away! You are unclean!" men
    cry to them.
    "Away! Away! Don't touch us!"
When they flee and wander about,
    people among the nations say,
    "They can stay here no longer."

¹⁶The LORD himself has scattered
    them;
    he no longer watches over them.
The priests are shown no honor,
    the elders no favor.

¹⁷Moreover, our eyes failed,
    looking in vain for help;
from our towers we watched
for a nation that could not save
    us.

¹⁸Men stalked us at every step,
    so we could not walk in our
    streets.
Our end was near, our days were
    numbered,
    for our end had come.

¹⁹Our pursuers were swifter
    than eagles in the sky;
they chased us over the
    mountains
    and lay in wait for us in the
    desert.

²⁰The LORD's anointed, our very life
    breath,
    was caught in their traps.
We thought that under his
    shadow
    we would live among the
    nations.

²¹Rejoice and be glad, O Daughter
    of Edom,
    you who live in the land of Uz.
But to you also the cup will be
    passed;
    you will be drunk and stripped
    naked.

²²O Daughter of Zion, your
    punishment will end;
    he will not prolong your exile.
But, O Daughter of Edom, he will
    punish your sin
    and expose your wickedness.

5 Remember, O LORD, what has
    happened to us;
    look, and see our disgrace.
²Our inheritance has been turned
    over to aliens,
    our homes to foreigners.
³We have become orphans and
    fatherless,
    our mothers like widows.
⁴We must buy the water we drink;
    our wood can be had only at a
    price.
⁵Those who pursue us are at our
    heels;
    we are weary and find no rest.
⁶We submitted to Egypt and
    Assyria

to get enough bread.
⁷Our fathers sinned and are no
more,
and we bear their punishment.
⁸Slaves rule over us,
and there is none to free us
from their hands.
⁹We get our bread at the risk of
our lives
because of the sword in the
desert.
¹⁰Our skin is hot as an oven,
feverish from hunger.
¹¹Women have been ravished in
Zion,
and virgins in the towns of
Judah.
¹²Princes have been hung up by
their hands;
elders are shown no respect.
¹³Young men toil at the millstones;
boys stagger under loads of
wood.
¹⁴The elders are gone from the city
gate;
the young men have stopped
their music.

¹⁵Joy is gone from our hearts;
our dancing has turned to
mourning.
¹⁶The crown has fallen from our
head.
Woe to us, for we have sinned!
¹⁷Because of this our hearts are
faint,
because of these things our eyes
grow dim
¹⁸for Mount Zion, which lies
desolate,
with jackals prowling over
it.

¹⁹You, O LORD, reign forever;
your throne endures from
generation to generation.
²⁰Why do you always forget us?
Why do you forsake us so long?
²¹Restore us to yourself, O LORD,
that we may return;
renew our days as of old
²²unless you have utterly rejected
us
and are angry with us beyond
measure.

WHO WROTE THIS BOOK?

The prophet Ezekiel.

WHY WAS THIS BOOK WRITTEN?

The first part of Ezekiel shows why God must punish the wicked people still in Judah. The second part shows that God will bring his people back to their land and that a new temple will be built in Jerusalem.

WHAT DO WE LEARN ABOUT GOD IN THIS BOOK?

God is holy. He will not live among a wicked people.

WHAT IS SPECIAL ABOUT THIS BOOK?

Ezekiel acts out many of his prophecies. Ezekiel also describes a great temple to be built in Jerusalem after the captives return from Babylon.

WHEN WAS THIS BOOK WRITTEN?

Ezekiel was written between 593 and 571 B.C.

WHERE WAS THIS BOOK WRITTEN?

Ezekiel was a captive in Babylon when he wrote this book.

WHAT CHAPTERS TELL ABOUT EZEKIEL'S EXPERIENCES?

Ezekiel's vision.	Ezekiel 1,10
Ezekiel acts out the attack on Jerusalem.	Ezekiel 4
Ezekiel, God's watchman.	Ezekiel 33

The Living Creatures and the Glory of the LORD

1 In the[a] thirtieth year, in the fourth month on the fifth day, while I was among the exiles by the Kebar River, the heavens were opened and I saw visions of God. ²On the fifth of the month—it was the fifth year of the exile of King Jehoiachin— ³the word of the LORD came to Ezekiel the priest, the son of Buzi,[b] by the Kebar River in the land of the Babylonians.[c] There the hand of the LORD was upon him.

⁴I looked, and I saw a windstorm coming out of the north—an immense cloud with flashing lightning and surrounded by brilliant light. The center of the fire looked like glowing metal, ⁵and in the fire was what looked like four living creatures. In appearance their form was that of a man, ⁶but each of them had four faces and four wings. ⁷Their legs were straight; their feet were like those of a calf and gleamed like burnished bronze. ⁸Under their wings on their four sides they had the hands of a man. All four of them had faces and wings, ⁹and their wings touched one another. Each one went straight ahead; they did not turn as they moved.

¹⁰Their faces looked like this: Each of the four had the face of a man, and on the right side each had the face of a lion, and on the left the face of an ox; each also had the face of an eagle. ¹¹Such were their faces. Their wings were spread out upward; each had two wings, one touching the wing of another creature on either side, and two wings covering its body. ¹²Each one went straight ahead. Wherever the spirit would go, they would go, without turning as they went. ¹³The appearance of the living creatures was like burning coals of fire or like torches. Fire moved back and forth among the creatures; it was bright, and lightning flashed out of it. ¹⁴The creatures sped back and forth like flashes of lightning.

¹⁵As I looked at the living creatures, I saw a wheel on the ground beside each creature with its four faces. ¹⁶This was the appearance and structure of the wheels: They sparkled like chrysolite, and all four looked alike. Each appeared to be made like a wheel intersecting a wheel. ¹⁷As they moved, they would go in any one of the four directions the creatures faced; the wheels did not turn about[d] as the creatures went. ¹⁸Their rims were high and awesome, and all four rims were full of eyes all around.

LIFE IN BIBLE TIMES

LIVING CREATURES

Ezekiel describes these "living creatures" in much detail. Read Ezekiel 1:10–14 to find out what their faces were like. The living creatures were special angels, called cherubim. They must have been awesome to see, with their four faces and four wings and the fire and lightning that came with them. Read Ezekiel 10 to find out more about them.

¹⁹When the living creatures moved, the wheels beside them moved; and when the living creatures rose from the ground, the wheels also rose. ²⁰Wherever the spirit would go, they would go, and the wheels would rise along with them, because the spirit of the living creatures was in the wheels. ²¹When the creatures moved, they also moved; when the creatures stood still, they also stood still; and when the creatures rose from the ground, the wheels rose along with them, be-

---

*a*1 Or _my_   *b*3 Or *Ezekiel son of Buzi the priest*   *c*3 Or *Chaldeans*   *d*17 Or *aside* cause the spirit of the living creatures was in the wheels.

²²Spread out above the heads of the living creatures was what looked like an expanse, sparkling like ice, and awesome. ²³Under the expanse their wings were stretched out one toward the other, and each had two wings covering its body. ²⁴When the creatures moved, I heard the sound of their wings, like the roar of rushing waters, like the voice of the Almighty,ᵃ like the tumult of an army. When they stood still, they lowered their wings.

²⁵Then there came a voice from above the expanse over their heads as they stood with lowered wings. ²⁶Above the expanse over their heads was what looked like a throne of sapphire,ᵇ and high above on the throne was a figure like that of a man. ²⁷I saw that from what appeared to be his waist up he looked like glowing metal, as if full of fire, and that from there down he looked like fire; and brilliant light surrounded him. ²⁸Like the appearance of a rainbow in the clouds on a rainy day, so was the radiance around him.

This was the appearance of the likeness of the glory of the LORD. When I saw it, I fell facedown, and I heard the voice of one speaking.

Ezekiel's Call

2 He said to me, "Son of man, stand up on your feet and I will speak to you." ²As he spoke, the Spirit came into me and raised me to my feet, and I heard him speaking to me.

³He said: "Son of man, I am sending you to the Israelites, to a rebellious nation that has rebelled against me; they and their fathers have been in revolt against me to this very day. ⁴The people to whom I am sending you are obstinate and stubborn. Say to them, 'This is what the Sovereign LORD says.' ⁵And whether they listen or fail to listen—for they are a rebellious house—they will know that a prophet has been among them. ⁶And you, son of man, do not be afraid of them or their words. Do not be afraid, though briers and thorns are all around you and you live among scorpions. Do not be afraid of what they say or terrified by them, though they are a rebellious house. ⁷You must speak my words to them, whether they listen or fail to listen, for they are rebellious. ⁸But you, son of man, listen to what I say to you. Do not rebel like that rebellious house; open your mouth and eat what I give you."

⁹Then I looked, and I saw a hand stretched out to me. In it was a scroll, ¹⁰which he unrolled before me. On both sides of it were written words of lament and mourning and woe.

3 And he said to me, "Son of man, eat what is before you, eat this scroll; then go and speak to the house of Israel." ²So I opened my mouth, and he gave me the scroll to eat.

³Then he said to me, "Son of man, eat this scroll I am giving you and fill your stomach with it." So I ate it, and it tasted as sweet as honey in my mouth.

⁴He then said to me: "Son of man, go now to the house of Israel and speak my words to them. ⁵You are not being sent to a people of obscure speech and difficult language, but to the house of Israel— ⁶not to many peoples of obscure speech and difficult language, whose words you cannot understand. Surely if I had sent you to them, they would have listened to you. ⁷But the house of Israel is not willing to listen to you because they are not willing to listen to me, for the whole house of Israel is hardened and obstinate. ⁸But I will make you as unyielding and hardened as they are. ⁹I will make your forehead like the hardest stone, harder than flint. Do not be afraid of them or terrified by them, though they are a rebellious house."

¹⁰And he said to me, "Son of man, listen carefully and take to heart all

ᵃ24 Hebrew *Shaddai*   ᵇ26 Or *lapis lazuli*

the words I speak to you. ¹¹Go now to your countrymen in exile and speak to them. Say to them, 'This is what the Sovereign Lᴏʀᴅ says,' whether they listen or fail to listen."

¹²Then the Spirit lifted me up, and I heard behind me a loud rumbling sound—May the glory of the Lᴏʀᴅ be praised in his dwelling place!— ¹³the sound of the wings of the living creatures brushing against each other and the sound of the wheels beside them, a loud rumbling sound. ¹⁴The Spirit then lifted me up and took me away, and I went in bitterness and in the anger of my spirit, with the strong hand of the Lᴏʀᴅ upon me. ¹⁵I came to the exiles who lived at Tel Abib near the Kebar River. And there, where they were living, I sat among them for seven days—overwhelmed.

Warning to Israel

¹⁶At the end of seven days the word of the Lᴏʀᴅ came to me: ¹⁷"Son of man, I have made you a watchman for the house of Israel; so hear the word I speak and give them warning from me. ¹⁸When I say to a wicked man, 'You will surely die,' and you do not warn him or speak out to dissuade him from his evil ways in order to save his life, that wicked man will die forᵃ his sin, and I will hold you accountable for his blood. ¹⁹But if you do warn the wicked man and he does not turn from his wickedness or from his evil ways, he will die for his sin; but you will have saved yourself.

²⁰"Again, when a righteous man turns from his righteousness and does evil, and I put a stumbling block before him, he will die. Since you did not warn him, he will die for his sin. The righteous things he did will not be remembered, and I will hold you accountable for his blood. ²¹But if you do warn the righteous man not to sin and he does not sin, he will surely live because he took warning, and you will have saved yourself."

²²The hand of the Lᴏʀᴅ was upon me there, and he said to me, "Get up and go out to the plain, and there I will speak to you." ²³So I got up and went out to the plain. And the glory of the Lᴏʀᴅ was standing there, like the glory I had seen by the Kebar River, and I fell facedown.

²⁴Then the Spirit came into me and raised me to my feet. He spoke to me and said: "Go, shut yourself inside your house. ²⁵And you, son of man, they will tie with ropes; you will be bound so that you cannot go out among the people. ²⁶I will make your tongue stick to the roof of your mouth so that you will be silent and unable to rebuke them, though they are a rebellious house. ²⁷But when I speak to you, I will open your mouth and you shall say to them, 'This is what the Sovereign Lᴏʀᴅ says.' Whoever will listen let him listen, and whoever will refuse let him refuse; for they are a rebellious house.

ᵃ18 Or *in*; also in verses 19 and 20

 ᴇᴛ's ʟɪᴠᴇ ɪᴛ!   Ezekiel 3:16–21

THE JOB OF A WATCHMAN ➡ In Bible times watchmen stood on a city wall to warn citizens of danger. Read Ezekiel 3:16–21 to find out what God's watchman does.

Christians today can watch out for others too. You and some of your friends might even start a watchman's club! Pick a club Bible verse, make up club rules, and have a special watchman's salute. Anyone who wants to obey God can join. Club members can promise to help each other do what God says is right.

Siege of Jerusalem Symbolized

4 "Now, son of man, take a clay tablet, put it in front of you and draw the city of Jerusalem on it. ²Then lay siege to it: Erect siege works against it, build a ramp up to it, set up camps against it and put battering rams around it. ³Then take an iron pan, place it as an iron wall between you and the city and turn your face toward it. It will be under siege, and you shall besiege it. This will be a sign to the house of Israel.

⁴"Then lie on your left side and put the sin of the house of Israel upon yourself.ᵃ You are to bear their sin for the number of days you lie on your side. ⁵I have assigned you the same number of days as the years of their sin. So for 390 days you will bear the sin of the house of Israel.

⁶"After you have finished this, lie down again, this time on your right side, and bear the sin of the house of Judah. I have assigned you 40 days, a day for each year. ⁷Turn your face toward the siege of Jerusalem and with bared arm prophesy against her. ⁸I will tie you up with ropes so that you cannot turn from one side to the other until you have finished the days of your siege.

⁹"Take wheat and barley, beans and lentils, millet and spelt; put them in a storage jar and use them to make bread for yourself. You are to eat it during the 390 days you lie on your side. ¹⁰Weigh out twenty shekelsᵇ of food to eat each day and eat it at set times. ¹¹Also measure out a sixth of a hinᶜ of water and drink it at set times. ¹²Eat the food as you would a barley cake; bake it in the sight of the people, using human excrement for fuel." ¹³The LORD said, "In this way the people of Israel will eat defiled food among the nations where I will drive them."

¹⁴Then I said, "Not so, Sovereign LORD! I have never defiled myself. From my youth until now I have nev-

er eaten anything found dead or torn by wild animals. No unclean meat has ever entered my mouth."

¹⁵"Very well," he said, "I will let you bake your bread over cow manure instead of human excrement."

¹⁶He then said to me: "Son of man, I will cut off the supply of food in Jerusalem. The people will eat rationed food in anxiety and drink rationed water in despair, ¹⁷for food and water will be scarce. They will be appalled at the sight of each other and will waste away because ofᵈ their sin.

5 "Now, son of man, take a sharp sword and use it as a barber's razor to shave your head and your beard. Then take a set of scales and divide up the hair. ²When the days of your siege come to an end, burn a third of the hair with fire inside the city. Take a third and strike it with the sword all around the city. And scatter a third to the wind. For I will pursue them with drawn sword. ³But take a few strands of hair and tuck them away in the folds of your garment. ⁴Again, take a few of these and throw them into the fire and burn them up. A fire will spread from there to the whole house of Israel.

⁵"This is what the Sovereign LORD says: This is Jerusalem, which I have set in the center of the nations, with countries all around her. ⁶Yet in her wickedness she has rebelled against my laws and decrees more than the nations and countries around her. She has rejected my laws and has not followed my decrees.

⁷"Therefore this is what the Sovereign LORD says: You have been more unruly than the nations around you and have not followed my decrees or kept my laws. You have not evenᵉ conformed to the standards of the nations around you.

⁸"Therefore this is what the Sovereign LORD says: I myself am against you, Jerusalem, and I will inflict punishment on you in the sight of the na-

---

ᵃ4 Or *your side*   ᵇ10 That is, about 8 ounces (about 0.2 kilogram)   ᶜ11 That is, about 2/3 quart (about 0.6 liter)   ᵈ17 Or *away in*   ᵉ7 Most Hebrew manuscripts; some Hebrew manuscripts and Syriac *You have*

tions. ⁹Because of all your detestable idols, I will do to you what I have never done before and will never do again. ¹⁰Therefore in your midst fathers will eat their children, and children will eat their fathers. I will inflict punishment on you and will scatter all your survivors to the winds. ¹¹Therefore as surely as I live, declares the Sovereign LORD, because you have defiled my sanctuary with all your vile images and detestable practices, I myself will withdraw my favor; I will not look on you with pity or spare you. ¹²A third of your people will die of the plague or perish by famine inside you; a third will fall by the sword outside your walls; and a third I will scatter to the winds and pursue with drawn sword.

¹³"Then my anger will cease and my wrath against them will subside, and I will be avenged. And when I have spent my wrath upon them, they will know that I the LORD have spoken in my zeal.

¹⁴"I will make you a ruin and a reproach among the nations around you, in the sight of all who pass by. ¹⁵You will be a reproach and a taunt, a warning and an object of horror to the nations around you when I inflict punishment on you in anger and in wrath and with stinging rebuke. I the LORD have spoken. ¹⁶When I shoot at you with my deadly and destructive arrows of famine, I will shoot to destroy you. I will bring more and more famine upon you and cut off your supply of food. ¹⁷I will send famine and wild beasts against you, and they will leave you childless. Plague and bloodshed will sweep through you, and I will bring the sword against you. I the LORD have spoken."

A Prophecy Against the Mountains of Israel

6 The word of the LORD came to me: ²"Son of man, set your face against the mountains of Israel; prophesy against them ³and say: 'O mountains of Israel, hear the word of the Sovereign LORD. This is what the Sovereign LORD says to the mountains and hills, to the ravines and valleys: I am about to bring a sword against you, and I will destroy your high places. ⁴Your altars will be demolished and your incense altars will be smashed; and I will slay your people in front of your idols. ⁵I will lay the dead bodies of the Israelites in front of their idols, and I will scatter your bones around your altars. ⁶Wherever you live, the towns will be laid waste and the high places demolished, so that your altars will be laid waste and devastated, your idols smashed and ruined, your incense altars broken down, and what you have made wiped out. ⁷Your people will fall slain among you, and you will know that I am the LORD.

⁸" 'But I will spare some, for some of you will escape the sword when you are scattered among the lands and nations. ⁹Then in the nations where they have been carried captive, those who escape will remember me—how I have been grieved by their adulterous hearts, which have turned away from me, and by their eyes, which have lusted after their idols. They will loathe themselves for the evil they have done and for all their detestable practices. ¹⁰And they will know that I am the LORD; I did not threaten in vain to bring this calamity on them.

¹¹" 'This is what the Sovereign LORD says: Strike your hands together and stamp your feet and cry out "Alas!" because of all the wicked and detestable practices of the house of Israel, for they will fall by the sword, famine and plague. ¹²He that is far away will die of the plague, and he that is near will fall by the sword, and he that survives and is spared will die of famine. So will I spend my wrath upon them. ¹³And they will know that I am the LORD, when their people lie slain among their idols around their altars, on every high hill and on all the mountaintops, under every spreading tree and every leafy oak—places where they offered fragrant incense to all their idols. ¹⁴And I will stretch out my hand

against them and make the land a desolate waste from the desert to Diblah*a*—wherever they live. Then they will know that I am the LORD.' "

The End Has Come

7 The word of the LORD came to me: 2"Son of man, this is what the Sovereign LORD says to the land of Israel: The end! The end has come upon the four corners of the land. 3The end is now upon you and I will unleash my anger against you. I will judge you according to your conduct and repay you for all your detestable practices. 4I will not look on you with pity or spare you; I will surely repay you for your conduct and the detestable practices among you. Then you will know that I am the LORD.

5"This is what the Sovereign LORD says: Disaster! An unheard-of*b* disaster is coming. 6The end has come! The end has come! It has roused itself against you. It has come! 7Doom has come upon you—you who dwell in the land. The time has come, the day is near; there is panic, not joy, upon the mountains. 8I am about to pour out my wrath on you and spend my anger against you; I will judge you according to your conduct and repay you for all your detestable practices. 9I will not look on you with pity or spare you; I will repay you in accordance with your conduct and the detestable practices among you. Then you will know that it is I the LORD who strikes the blow.

10"The day is here! It has come! Doom has burst forth, the rod has budded, arrogance has blossomed! 11Violence has grown into*c* a rod to punish wickedness; none of the people will be left, none of that crowd —no wealth, nothing of value. 12The time has come, the day has arrived. Let not the buyer rejoice nor the seller grieve, for wrath is upon the whole crowd. 13The seller will not recover the land he has sold as long as both of them live, for the vision concerning

the whole crowd will not be reversed. Because of their sins, not one of them will preserve his life. 14Though they blow the trumpet and get everything ready, no one will go into battle, for my wrath is upon the whole crowd.

15"Outside is the sword, inside are plague and famine; those in the country will die by the sword, and those in the city will be devoured by famine and plague. 16All who survive and escape will be in the mountains, moaning like doves of the valleys, each because of his sins. 17Every hand will go limp, and every knee will become as weak as water. 18They will put on sackcloth and be clothed with terror. Their faces will be covered with shame and their heads will be shaved. 19They will throw their silver into the streets, and their gold will be an unclean thing. Their silver and gold will not be able to save them in the day of the LORD's wrath. They will not satisfy their hunger or fill their stomachs with it, for it has made them stumble into sin. 20They were proud of their beautiful jewelry and used it to make their detestable idols and vile images. Therefore I will turn these into an unclean thing for them. 21I will hand it all over as plunder to foreigners and as loot to the wicked of the earth, and they will defile it. 22I will turn my face away from them, and they will desecrate my treasured place; robbers will enter it and desecrate it.

23"Prepare chains, because the land is full of bloodshed and the city is full of violence. 24I will bring the most wicked of the nations to take possession of their houses; I will put an end to the pride of the mighty, and their sanctuaries will be desecrated. 25When terror comes, they will seek peace, but there will be none. 26Calamity upon calamity will come, and rumor upon rumor. They will try to get a vision from the prophet; the teaching of the law by the priest will be lost, as will the counsel of the el-

---

a14 Most Hebrew manuscripts; a few Hebrew manuscripts *Riblah*   *b5* Most Hebrew manuscripts; some Hebrew manuscripts and Syriac *Disaster after*   *c11* Or *The violent one has become*

ders. ²⁷The king will mourn, the prince will be clothed with despair, and the hands of the people of the land will tremble. I will deal with them according to their conduct, and by their own standards I will judge them. Then they will know that I am the LORD."

Idolatry in the Temple

8 In the sixth year, in the sixth month on the fifth day, while I was sitting in my house and the elders of Judah were sitting before me, the hand of the Sovereign LORD came upon me there. ²I looked, and I saw a figure like that of a man.ᵃ From what appeared to be his waist down he was like fire, and from there up his appearance was as bright as glowing metal. ³He stretched out what looked like a hand and took me by the hair of my head. The Spirit lifted me up between earth and heaven and in visions of God he took me to Jerusalem, to the entrance to the north gate of the inner court, where the idol that provokes to jealousy stood. ⁴And there before me was the glory of the God of Israel, as in the vision I had seen in the plain.

⁵Then he said to me, "Son of man, look toward the north." So I looked, and in the entrance north of the gate of the altar I saw this idol of jealousy.

⁶And he said to me, "Son of man, do you see what they are doing—the utterly detestable things the house of Israel is doing here, things that will drive me far from my sanctuary? But you will see things that are even more detestable."

⁷Then he brought me to the entrance to the court. I looked, and I saw a hole in the wall. ⁸He said to me, "Son of man, now dig into the wall." So I dug into the wall and saw a doorway there.

⁹And he said to me, "Go in and see the wicked and detestable things they are doing here." ¹⁰So I went in and looked, and I saw portrayed all over the walls all kinds of crawling things and detestable animals and all the idols of the house of Israel. ¹¹In front of them stood seventy elders of the house of Israel, and Jaazaniah son of Shaphan was standing among them. Each had a censer in his hand, and a fragrant cloud of incense was rising.

¹²He said to me, "Son of man, have you seen what the elders of the house of Israel are doing in the darkness, each at the shrine of his own idol? They say, 'The LORD does not see us; the LORD has forsaken the land.'" ¹³Again, he said, "You will see them doing things that are even more detestable."

¹⁴Then he brought me to the entrance to the north gate of the house of the LORD, and I saw women sitting there, mourning for Tammuz. ¹⁵He said to me, "Do you see this, son of man? You will see things that are even more detestable than this."

¹⁶He then brought me into the inner court of the house of the LORD, and there at the entrance to the temple, between the portico and the altar, were about twenty-five men. With their backs toward the temple of the LORD and their faces toward the east, they were bowing down to the sun in the east.

¹⁷He said to me, "Have you seen this, son of man? Is it a trivial matter for the house of Judah to do the detestable things they are doing here? Must they also fill the land with violence and continually provoke me to anger? Look at them putting the branch to their nose! ¹⁸Therefore I will deal with them in anger; I will not look on them with pity or spare them. Although they shout in my ears, I will not listen to them."

Idolaters Killed

9 Then I heard him call out in a loud voice, "Bring the guards of the city here, each with a weapon in his hand." ²And I saw six men coming from the direction of the upper gate, which faces north, each with a deadly

ᵃ2 Or *saw a fiery figure*

weapon in his hand. With them was a man clothed in linen who had a writing kit at his side. They came in and stood beside the bronze altar.

WORSHIP TOWARD THE TEMPLE

When God's people were away from the promised land, they were supposed to pray with their faces toward the temple (1 Kings 8:42–43). When Daniel prayed while he was in Babylon he faced God's temple (Daniel 6:10). But the people Ezekiel was describing were praying with their backs to the temple. They were facing east, the direction most pagan people faced when praying.

---

³Now the glory of the God of Israel went up from above the cherubim, where it had been, and moved to the threshold of the temple. Then the LORD called to the man clothed in linen who had the writing kit at his side ⁴and said to him, "Go throughout the city of Jerusalem and put a mark on the foreheads of those who grieve and lament over all the detestable things that are done in it."

⁵As I listened, he said to the others, "Follow him through the city and kill, without showing pity or compassion. ⁶Slaughter old men, young men and maidens, women and children, but do not touch anyone who has the mark. Begin at my sanctuary." So they began with the elders who were in front of the temple.

⁷Then he said to them, "Defile the temple and fill the courts with the slain. Go!" So they went out and began killing throughout the city.

⁸While they were killing and I was left alone, I fell facedown, crying out, "Ah, Sovereign LORD! Are you going to destroy the entire remnant of Israel in this outpouring of your wrath on Jerusalem?"

⁹He answered me, "The sin of the house of Israel and Judah is exceedingly great; the land is full of bloodshed and the city is full of injustice. They say, 'The LORD has forsaken the land; the LORD does not see.' ¹⁰So I will not look on them with pity or spare them, but I will bring down on their own heads what they have done."

¹¹Then the man in linen with the writing kit at his side brought back word, saying, "I have done as you commanded."

The Glory Departs From the Temple

10 I looked, and I saw the likeness of a throne of sapphire[a] above the expanse that was over the heads of the cherubim. ²The LORD said to the man clothed in linen, "Go in among the wheels beneath the cherubim. Fill your hands with burning coals from among the cherubim and scatter them over the city." And as I watched, he went in.

³Now the cherubim were standing on the south side of the temple when the man went in, and a cloud filled the inner court. ⁴Then the glory of the LORD rose from above the cherubim and moved to the threshold of the temple. The cloud filled the temple, and the court was full of the radiance of the glory of the LORD. ⁵The sound of the wings of the cherubim could be heard as far away as the outer court, like the voice of God Almighty[b] when he speaks.

⁶When the LORD commanded the man in linen, "Take fire from among the wheels, from among the cherubim," the man went in and stood beside a wheel. ⁷Then one of the cherubim reached out his hand to the fire that was among them. He took up

a1 Or lapis lazuli   b5 Hebrew El-Shaddai

Old Testament Prophets

ISAIAH Isaiah prophesied in Judah during the reigns of Kings Uzziah, Jotham, Ahaz and Hezekiah.
His book (page 834) predicts punishment for wickedness, but it also promises God's comfort.

JEREMIAH Jeremiah prophesied to Judah and was often in danger because his predictions angered the officials.
His book (page 916) gives a good picture of what Judah was like before going into captivity.

EZEKIEL Ezekiel spoke to the Jews who were in exile in Babylon.
His book (page 1001) contains descriptions of several strange visions.

DANIEL Daniel went as a captive to Babylon, where he rose to a position of power because of his God-given wisdom.
His book (page 1062) covers the story of his experiences in Babylon as well as the dreams and visions he had.

HOSEA Hosea prophesied to Israel, probably shortly before the fall of Samaria.
His book (page 1083) uses the story of Hosea's unfaithful wife to describe Israel's unfaithfulness to God.

AMOS Amos was a shepherd from Judah who prophesied God's coming punishment of Israel.
His book (page 1103) calls the people to turn toward God and leave their selfish and often cruel lifestyle.

JONAH Jonah was called to preach to the people of Ninevah, but he ran from God instead.
His book (page 1117) tells the story of his flight and what happened when he finally reached Ninevah.

ZEPHANIAH Zephaniah ministered during the reign of Judah's King Josiah.
His book (page 1140) predicts punishment for Judah as well as the nations around her.

HAGGAI AND ZECHARIAH Haggai and Zechariah prophesied during the time when the temple was being rebuilt.
Their books (pages 1146 and 1149) urge the people to keep a close relationship with God.

The writings of the prophets Joel (page 1097), Obadiah (page 1114), Micah (page 1121), Nahum (page 1130), Habakkuk (page 1133) and Malachi (page 1161) contain important messages from God and are worthwhile reading. However, little else is known about these prophets.

HOW TO *Pray*

QUESTION: How do I start?
ANSWER: Praying is not as hard as you might think.

What is hard is to get into the habit of talking with God every day.
    Sometimes we just get so busy, we forget to talk with God.
Maybe you could start by picking a special time every day.
    Think about things for which you want to say
        "Thank you" or "I'm sorry" or "Please help me."
Then tell God those things.
    You don't have to use fancy words . . . you can talk to God like
    you talk to your dad or mom or a friend.

QUESTION: Can I tell God anything?
ANSWER: You surely can!

There isn't a thing you could say to him that would make him stop
loving you.
    You can tell him when you're sad or grumpy.
You can thank him when everything's going your way.
    You can lean on him when you're having a bad day.
You can talk to him just like you would talk to a friend.
    But you know what?
        Your friends might let you down.
        Your mom and dad might not always listen.
But God will always listen — and he'll understand.

QUESTION: How do I know God hears me?
ANSWER: God promises to listen!

God has promised in the Bible that he will listen to you.
    Look at Psalm 66:17-19 on page 710.
    Now turn to page 1314 and read John 16:23, where
    God promises to listen when you pray in Jesus' name.
Most important of all, the Holy Spirit lives in your heart.
    He helps you know for sure that God listens when you talk
to him.

QUESTION: Must I fold my hands and close my eyes
    when I pray?
ANSWER: That's one way to do it.

Closing your eyes shows you don't want anything to get in the way
of talking with God.
    But it's not the only way to pray.
You can pray while on your knees or standing up.
    You can pray with toys in your hands
        or while you're hugging your mom.
You can talk to God at any time because he's always right there
with you.
    And he wants you to be his friend.

some of it and put it into the hands of the man in linen, who took it and went out. ⁸(Under the wings of the cherubim could be seen what looked like the hands of a man.)

⁹I looked, and I saw beside the cherubim four wheels, one beside each of the cherubim; the wheels sparkled like chrysolite. ¹⁰As for their appearance, the four of them looked alike; each was like a wheel intersecting a wheel. ¹¹As they moved, they would go in any one of the four directions the cherubim faced; the wheels did not turn about*a* as the cherubim went. The cherubim went in whatever direction the head faced, without turning as they went. ¹²Their entire bodies, including their backs, their hands and their wings, were completely full of eyes, as were their four wheels. ¹³I heard the wheels being called "the whirling wheels." ¹⁴Each of the cherubim had four faces: One face was that of a cherub, the second the face of a man, the third the face of a lion, and the fourth the face of an eagle.

¹⁵Then the cherubim rose upward. These were the living creatures I had seen by the Kebar River. ¹⁶When the cherubim moved, the wheels beside them moved; and when the cherubim spread their wings to rise from the ground, the wheels did not leave their side. ¹⁷When the cherubim stood still, they also stood still; and when the cherubim rose, they rose with them, because the spirit of the living creatures was in them.

¹⁸Then the glory of the LORD departed from over the threshold of the temple and stopped above the cherubim. ¹⁹While I watched, the cherubim spread their wings and rose from the ground, and as they went, the wheels went with them. They stopped at the entrance to the east gate of the LORD's house, and the glory of the God of Israel was above them.

²⁰These were the living creatures I had seen beneath the God of Israel by the Kebar River, and I realized that they were cherubim. ²¹Each had four faces and four wings, and under their wings was what looked like the hands of a man. ²²Their faces had the same appearance as those I had seen by the Kebar River. Each one went straight ahead.

Judgment on Israel's Leaders

11 Then the Spirit lifted me up and brought me to the gate of the house of the LORD that faces east. There at the entrance to the gate were twenty-five men, and I saw among them Jaazaniah son of Azzur and Pelatiah son of Benaiah, leaders of the people. ²The LORD said to me, "Son of man, these are the men who are plotting evil and giving wicked advice in this city. ³They say, 'Will it not soon be time to build houses?*b* This city is a cooking pot, and we are the meat.' ⁴Therefore prophesy against them; prophesy, son of man."

⁵Then the Spirit of the LORD came upon me, and he told me to say: "This is what the LORD says: That is what you are saying, O house of Israel, but I know what is going through your mind. ⁶You have killed many people in this city and filled its streets with the dead.

⁷"Therefore this is what the Sovereign LORD says: The bodies you have thrown there are the meat and this city is the pot, but I will drive you out of it. ⁸You fear the sword, and the sword is what I will bring against you, declares the Sovereign LORD. ⁹I will drive you out of the city and hand you over to foreigners and inflict punishment on you. ¹⁰You will fall by the sword, and I will execute judgment on you at the borders of Israel. Then you will know that I am the LORD. ¹¹This city will not be a pot for you, nor will you be the meat in it; I will execute judgment on you at the borders of Israel. ¹²And you will know that I am the LORD, for you have not followed my decrees or kept my laws but have conformed to the standards of the nations around you."

---

a11 Or *aside*　　*b3* Or *This is not the time to build houses.*

¹³Now as I was prophesying, Pelatiah son of Benaiah died. Then I fell facedown and cried out in a loud voice, "Ah, Sovereign LORD! Will you completely destroy the remnant of Israel?"

¹⁴The word of the LORD came to me: ¹⁵"Son of man, your brothers—your brothers who are your blood relatives[a] and the whole house of Israel—are those of whom the people of Jerusalem have said, 'They are[b] far away from the LORD; this land was given to us as our possession.'

Promised Return of Israel

¹⁶"Therefore say: 'This is what the Sovereign LORD says: Although I sent them far away among the nations and scattered them among the countries, yet for a little while I have been a sanctuary for them in the countries where they have gone.'

¹⁷"Therefore say: 'This is what the Sovereign LORD says: I will gather you from the nations and bring you back from the countries where you have been scattered, and I will give you back the land of Israel again.'

¹⁸"They will return to it and remove all its vile images and detestable idols. ¹⁹I will give them an undivided heart and put a new spirit in them; I will remove from them their heart of stone and give them a heart of flesh. ²⁰Then they will follow my decrees and be careful to keep my laws. They will be my people, and I will be their God. ²¹But as for those whose hearts are devoted to their vile images and detestable idols, I will bring down on their own heads what they have done, declares the Sovereign LORD."

²²Then the cherubim, with the wheels beside them, spread their wings, and the glory of the God of Israel was above them. ²³The glory of the LORD went up from within the city and stopped above the mountain east of it. ²⁴The Spirit lifted me up and brought me to the exiles in Babylonia[c] in the vision given by the Spirit of God.

Then the vision I had seen went up from me, ²⁵and I told the exiles everything the LORD had shown me.

The Exile Symbolized

12 The word of the LORD came to me: ²"Son of man, you are living among a rebellious people. They have eyes to see but do not see and ears to hear but do not hear, for they are a rebellious people.

❓DID YOU KNOW?　　12:3

How did Ezekiel prophesy without words?

God had Ezekiel act out things that would happen. Ezekiel 12 tells how Ezekiel acted out what would happen to the people of Jerusalem when that city was captured by the Babylonians.

---

³"Therefore, son of man, pack your belongings for exile and in the daytime, as they watch, set out and go from where you are to another place. Perhaps they will understand, though they are a rebellious house. ⁴During the daytime, while they watch, bring out your belongings packed for exile. Then in the evening, while they are watching, go out like those who go into exile. ⁵While they watch, dig through the wall and take your belongings out through it. ⁶Put them on your shoulder as they are watching and carry them out at dusk. Cover your face so that you cannot see the land, for I have made you a sign to the house of Israel."

⁷So I did as I was commanded. During the day I brought out my things packed for exile. Then in the evening I dug through the wall with my hands. I took my belongings out at dusk, carrying them on my shoulders while they watched.

---

a15 Or are in exile with you (see Septuagint and Syriac)　　*b15 Or those to whom the people of Jerusalem have said, 'Stay*　　*c24 Or Chaldea*

⁸In the morning the word of the LORD came to me: ⁹"Son of man, did not that rebellious house of Israel ask you, 'What are you doing?'

¹⁰"Say to them, 'This is what the Sovereign LORD says: This oracle concerns the prince in Jerusalem and the whole house of Israel who are there.' ¹¹Say to them, 'I am a sign to you.'

"As I have done, so it will be done to them. They will go into exile as captives.

¹²"The prince among them will put his things on his shoulder at dusk and leave, and a hole will be dug in the wall for him to go through. He will cover his face so that he cannot see the land. ¹³I will spread my net for him, and he will be caught in my snare; I will bring him to Babylonia, the land of the Chaldeans, but he will not see it, and there he will die. ¹⁴I will scatter to the winds all those around him—his staff and all his troops—and I will pursue them with drawn sword.

¹⁵"They will know that I am the LORD, when I disperse them among the nations and scatter them through the countries. ¹⁶But I will spare a few of them from the sword, famine and plague, so that in the nations where they go they may acknowledge all their detestable practices. Then they will know that I am the LORD."

¹⁷The word of the LORD came to me: ¹⁸"Son of man, tremble as you eat your food, and shudder in fear as you drink your water. ¹⁹Say to the people of the land: 'This is what the Sovereign LORD says about those living in Jerusalem and in the land of Israel: They will eat their food in anxiety and drink their water in despair, for their land will be stripped of everything in it because of the violence of all who live there. ²⁰The inhabited towns will be laid waste and the land will be desolate. Then you will know that I am the LORD.' "

²¹The word of the LORD came to me: ²²"Son of man, what is this proverb you have in the land of Israel: 'The days go by and every vision comes to nothing'? ²³Say to them, 'This is what the Sovereign LORD says: I am going to put an end to this proverb, and they will no longer quote it in Israel.' Say to them, 'The days are near when every vision will be fulfilled. ²⁴For there will be no more false visions or flattering divinations among the people of Israel. ²⁵But I the LORD will speak what I will, and it shall be fulfilled without delay. For in your days, you rebellious house, I will fulfill whatever I say, declares the Sovereign LORD.' "

²⁶The word of the LORD came to me: ²⁷"Son of man, the house of Israel is saying, 'The vision he sees is for many years from now, and he prophesies about the distant future.'

²⁸"Therefore say to them, 'This is what the Sovereign LORD says: None of my words will be delayed any longer; whatever I say will be fulfilled, declares the Sovereign LORD.' "

False Prophets Condemned

13 The word of the LORD came to me: ²"Son of man, prophesy against the prophets of Israel who are now prophesying. Say to those who prophesy out of their own imagination: 'Hear the word of the LORD! ³This is what the Sovereign LORD says: Woe to the foolishᵃ prophets who follow their own spirit and have seen nothing! ⁴Your prophets, O Israel, are like jackals among ruins. ⁵You have not gone up to the breaks in the wall to repair it for the house of Israel so that it will stand firm in the battle on the day of the LORD. ⁶Their visions are false and their divinations a lie. They say, "The LORD declares," when the LORD has not sent them; yet they expect their words to be fulfilled. ⁷Have you not seen false visions and uttered lying divinations when you say, "The LORD declares," though I have not spoken?

⁸" 'Therefore this is what the Sovereign LORD says: Because of your false words and lying visions, I am

---

ᵃ3 Or *wicked*

against you, declares the Sovereign LORD. 9My hand will be against the prophets who see false visions and utter lying divinations. They will not belong to the council of my people or be listed in the records of the house of Israel, nor will they enter the land of Israel. Then you will know that I am the Sovereign LORD.

10" 'Because they lead my people astray, saying, "Peace," when there is no peace, and because, when a flimsy wall is built, they cover it with whitewash, 11therefore tell those who cover it with whitewash that it is going to fall. Rain will come in torrents, and I will send hailstones hurtling down, and violent winds will burst forth. 12When the wall collapses, will people not ask you, "Where is the whitewash you covered it with?"

Life In Bible Times

PLASTER WALLS

Sometimes the walls of a building would be covered with lime plaster, called "whitewash." This made the wall look smooth and beautiful. But the stones in the wall had to be strong and had to be correctly laid. A wall that was poorly made would collapse no matter how good it looked.

13" 'Therefore this is what the Sovereign LORD says: In my wrath I will unleash a violent wind, and in my anger hailstones and torrents of rain will fall with destructive fury. 14I will tear down the wall you have covered with whitewash and will level it to the ground so that its foundation will be laid bare. When ita falls, you will be destroyed in it; and you will know

that I am the LORD. 15So I will spend my wrath against the wall and against those who covered it with whitewash. I will say to you, "The wall is gone and so are those who whitewashed it, 16those prophets of Israel who prophesied to Jerusalem and saw visions of peace for her when there was no peace, declares the Sovereign LORD." '

17"Now, son of man, set your face against the daughters of your people who prophesy out of their own imagination. Prophesy against them 18and say, 'This is what the Sovereign LORD says: Woe to the women who sew magic charms on all their wrists and make veils of various lengths for their heads in order to ensnare people. Will you ensnare the lives of my people but preserve your own? 19You have profaned me among my people for a few handfuls of barley and scraps of bread. By lying to my people, who listen to lies, you have killed those who should not have died and have spared those who should not live.

20" 'Therefore this is what the Sovereign LORD says: I am against your magic charms with which you ensnare people like birds and I will tear them from your arms; I will set free the people that you ensnare like birds. 21I will tear off your veils and save my people from your hands, and they will no longer fall prey to your power. Then you will know that I am the LORD. 22Because you disheartened the righteous with your lies, when I had brought them no grief, and because you encouraged the wicked not to turn from their evil ways and so save their lives, 23therefore you will no longer see false visions or practice divination. I will save my people from your hands. And then you will know that I am the LORD.' "

Idolaters Condemned

14 Some of the elders of Israel came to me and sat down in

---

a14 Or the city

front of me. ²Then the word of the LORD came to me: ³"Son of man, these men have set up idols in their hearts and put wicked stumbling blocks before their faces. Should I let them inquire of me at all? ⁴Therefore speak to them and tell them, 'This is what the Sovereign LORD says: When any Israelite sets up idols in his heart and puts a wicked stumbling block before his face and then goes to a prophet, I the LORD will answer him myself in keeping with his great idolatry. ⁵I will do this to recapture the hearts of the people of Israel, who have all deserted me for their idols.'

⁶"Therefore say to the house of Israel, 'This is what the Sovereign LORD says: Repent! Turn from your idols and renounce all your detestable practices!

⁷"'When any Israelite or any alien living in Israel separates himself from me and sets up idols in his heart and puts a wicked stumbling block before his face and then goes to a prophet to inquire of me, I the LORD will answer him myself. ⁸I will set my face against that man and make him an example and a byword. I will cut him off from my people. Then you will know that I am the LORD.

⁹"'And if the prophet is enticed to utter a prophecy, I the LORD have enticed that prophet, and I will stretch out my hand against him and destroy him from among my people Israel. ¹⁰They will bear their guilt—the prophet will be as guilty as the one who consults him. ¹¹Then the people of Israel will no longer stray from me, nor will they defile themselves anymore with all their sins. They will be my people, and I will be their God, declares the Sovereign LORD.'"

Judgment Inescapable

¹²The word of the LORD came to me: ¹³"Son of man, if a country sins against me by being unfaithful and I stretch out my hand against it to cut off its food supply and send famine upon it and kill its men and their animals, ¹⁴even if these three men—Noah, Daniel[a] and Job—were in it, they could save only themselves by their righteousness, declares the Sovereign LORD.

¹⁵"Or if I send wild beasts through that country and they leave it childless and it becomes desolate so that no one can pass through it because of the beasts, ¹⁶as surely as I live, declares the Sovereign LORD, even if these three men were in it, they could not save their own sons or daughters. They alone would be saved, but the land would be desolate.

¹⁷"Or if I bring a sword against that country and say, 'Let the sword pass throughout the land,' and I kill its men and their animals, ¹⁸as surely as I live, declares the Sovereign LORD, even if these three men were in it, they could not save their own sons or daughters. They alone would be saved.

¹⁹"Or if I send a plague into that land and pour out my wrath upon it through bloodshed, killing its men and their animals, ²⁰as surely as I live, declares the Sovereign LORD, even if Noah, Daniel and Job were in it, they could save neither son nor daughter. They would save only themselves by their righteousness.

²¹"For this is what the Sovereign LORD says: How much worse will it be when I send against Jerusalem my four dreadful judgments—sword and famine and wild beasts and plague—to kill its men and their animals! ²²Yet there will be some survivors—sons and daughters who will be brought out of it. They will come to you, and when you see their conduct and their actions, you will be consoled regarding the disaster I have brought upon Jerusalem—every disaster I have brought upon it. ²³You will be consoled when you see their conduct and their actions, for you will know that I have done nothing in it

---

a14 Or *Danel*; the Hebrew spelling may suggest a person other than the prophet Daniel; also in verse 20.

without cause, declares the Sovereign LORD."

Jerusalem, A Useless Vine

15 The word of the LORD came to me: [2]"Son of man, how is the wood of a vine better than that of a branch on any of the trees in the forest? [3]Is wood ever taken from it to make anything useful? Do they make pegs from it to hang things on? [4]And after it is thrown on the fire as fuel and the fire burns both ends and chars the middle, is it then useful for anything? [5]If it was not useful for anything when it was whole, how much less can it be made into something useful when the fire has burned it and it is charred?

[6]"Therefore this is what the Sovereign LORD says: As I have given the wood of the vine among the trees of the forest as fuel for the fire, so will I treat the people living in Jerusalem. [7]I will set my face against them. Although they have come out of the fire, the fire will yet consume them. And when I set my face against them, you will know that I am the LORD. [8]I will make the land desolate because they have been unfaithful, declares the Sovereign LORD."

An Allegory of Unfaithful Jerusalem

16 The word of the LORD came to me: [2]"Son of man, confront Jerusalem with her detestable practices [3]and say, 'This is what the Sovereign LORD says to Jerusalem: Your ancestry and birth were in the land of the Canaanites; your father was an Amorite and your mother a Hittite. [4]On the day you were born your cord was not cut, nor were you washed with water to make you clean, nor were you rubbed with salt or wrapped in cloths. [5]No one looked on you with pity or had compassion enough to do any of these things for you. Rather, you were thrown out into the open field, for on the day you were born you were despised.

[6]"'Then I passed by and saw you kicking about in your blood, and as you lay there in your blood I said to you, "Live!"[a] [7]I made you grow like a plant of the field. You grew up and developed and became the most beautiful of jewels.[b] Your breasts were formed and your hair grew, you who were naked and bare.

[8]"'Later I passed by, and when I looked at you and saw that you were old enough for love, I spread the corner of my garment over you and covered your nakedness. I gave you my solemn oath and entered into a covenant with you, declares the Sovereign LORD, and you became mine.

[9]"'I bathed[c] you with water and washed the blood from you and put ointments on you. [10]I clothed you with an embroidered dress and put leather sandals on you. I dressed you in fine linen and covered you with costly garments. [11]I adorned you with jewelry: I put bracelets on your arms and a necklace around your neck, [12]and I put a ring on your nose, earrings on your ears and a beautiful crown on your head. [13]So you were adorned with gold and silver; your clothes were of fine linen and costly fabric and embroidered cloth. Your food was fine flour, honey and olive oil. You became very beautiful and rose to be a queen. [14]And your fame spread among the nations on account of your beauty, because the splendor I had given you made your beauty perfect, declares the Sovereign LORD.

[15]"'But you trusted in your beauty and used your fame to become a prostitute. You lavished your favors on anyone who passed by and your beauty became his.[d] [16]You took some of your garments to make gaudy high places, where you carried on your prostitution. Such things should not

---

[a]6 A few Hebrew manuscripts, Septuagint and Syriac; most Hebrew manuscripts *"Live!" And as you lay there in your blood I said to you, "Live!"*   [b]7 Or *became mature*   [c]9 Or *I had bathed*
[d]15 Most Hebrew manuscripts; one Hebrew manuscript (see some Septuagint manuscripts) *by. Such a thing should not happen*

happen, nor should they ever occur.
¹⁷You also took the fine jewelry I
gave you, the jewelry made of my
gold and silver, and you made for
yourself male idols and engaged in
prostitution with them. ¹⁸And you
took your embroidered clothes to put
on them, and you offered my oil and
incense before them. ¹⁹Also the food I
provided for you—the fine flour, olive oil and honey I gave you to eat
—you offered as fragrant incense before them. That is what happened,
declares the Sovereign LORD.

²⁰" 'And you took your sons and
daughters whom you bore to me and
sacrificed them as food to the idols.
Was your prostitution not enough?
²¹You slaughtered my children and
sacrificed themᵃ to the idols. ²²In all
your detestable practices and your
prostitution you did not remember
the days of your youth, when you
were naked and bare, kicking about
in your blood.

²³" 'Woe! Woe to you, declares the
Sovereign LORD. In addition to all
your other wickedness, ²⁴you built a
mound for yourself and made a lofty
shrine in every public square. ²⁵At
the head of every street you built
your lofty shrines and degraded your
beauty, offering your body with increasing promiscuity to anyone who
passed by. ²⁶You engaged in prostitution with the Egyptians, your lustful
neighbors, and provoked me to anger
with your increasing promiscuity.
²⁷So I stretched out my hand against
you and reduced your territory; I
gave you over to the greed of your
enemies, the daughters of the Philistines, who were shocked by your lewd
conduct. ²⁸You engaged in prostitution with the Assyrians too, because
you were insatiable; and even after
that, you still were not satisfied.
²⁹Then you increased your promiscuity to include Babylonia,ᵇ a land of
merchants, but even with this you
were not satisfied.

³⁰" 'How weak-willed you are, declares the Sovereign LORD, when you

do all these things, acting like a brazen prostitute! ³¹When you built your
mounds at the head of every street
and made your lofty shrines in every
public square, you were unlike a
prostitute, because you scorned payment.

³²" 'You adulterous wife! You prefer strangers to your own husband!
³³Every prostitute receives a fee, but
you give gifts to all your lovers, brib-
ing them to come to you from everywhere for your illicit favors. ³⁴So in
your prostitution you are the opposite of others; no one runs after you
for your favors. You are the very opposite, for you give payment and
none is given to you.

³⁵" 'Therefore, you prostitute, hear
the word of the LORD! ³⁶This is what
the Sovereign LORD says: Because
you poured out your wealthᶜ and exposed your nakedness in your promiscuity with your lovers, and because of all your detestable idols, and
because you gave them your children's blood, ³⁷therefore I am going to
gather all your lovers, with whom
you found pleasure, those you loved
as well as those you hated. I will
gather them against you from all
around and will strip you in front of
them, and they will see all your nakedness. ³⁸I will sentence you to the
punishment of women who commit
adultery and who shed blood; I will
bring upon you the blood vengeance
of my wrath and jealous anger.
³⁹Then I will hand you over to your
lovers, and they will tear down your
mounds and destroy your lofty
shrines. They will strip you of your
clothes and take your fine jewelry
and leave you naked and bare. ⁴⁰They
will bring a mob against you, who
will stone you and hack you to pieces
with their swords. ⁴¹They will burn
down your houses and inflict punishment on you in the sight of many
women. I will put a stop to your prostitution, and you will no longer pay
your lovers. ⁴²Then my wrath against
you will subside and my jealous an-

ger will turn away from you; I will be calm and no longer angry.

43" 'Because you did not remember the days of your youth but enraged me with all these things, I will surely bring down on your head what you have done, declares the Sovereign Lord. Did you not add lewdness to all your other detestable practices?

44" 'Everyone who quotes proverbs will quote this proverb about you: "Like mother, like daughter." 45You are a true daughter of your mother, who despised her husband and her children; and you are a true sister of your sisters, who despised their husbands and their children. Your mother was a Hittite and your father an Amorite. 46Your older sister was Samaria, who lived to the north of you with her daughters; and your younger sister, who lived to the south of you with her daughters, was Sodom. 47You not only walked in their ways and copied their detestable practices, but in all your ways you soon became more depraved than they. 48As surely as I live, declares the Sovereign Lord, your sister Sodom and her daughters never did what you and your daughters have done.

49" 'Now this was the sin of your sister Sodom: She and her daughters were arrogant, overfed and unconcerned; they did not help the poor and needy. 50They were haughty and did detestable things before me. Therefore I did away with them as you have seen. 51Samaria did not commit half the sins you did. You have done more detestable things than they, and have made your sisters seem righteous by all these things you have done. 52Bear your disgrace, for you have furnished some justification for your sisters. Because your sins were more vile than theirs, they appear more righteous than you. So then, be ashamed and bear your disgrace, for you have made your sisters appear righteous.

53" 'However, I will restore the for-

tunes of Sodom and her daughters and of Samaria and her daughters, and your fortunes along with them, 54so that you may bear your disgrace and be ashamed of all you have done in giving them comfort. 55And your sisters, Sodom with her daughters and Samaria with her daughters, will return to what they were before; and you and your daughters will return to what you were before. 56You would not even mention your sister Sodom in the day of your pride, 57before your wickedness was uncovered. Even so, you are now scorned by the daughters of Edom*a* and all her neighbors and the daughters of the Philistines—all those around you who despise you. 58You will bear the consequences of your lewdness and your detestable practices, declares the Lord.

59" 'This is what the Sovereign Lord says: I will deal with you as you deserve, because you have despised my oath by breaking the covenant. 60Yet I will remember the covenant I made with you in the days of your youth, and I will establish an everlasting covenant with you. 61Then you will remember your ways and be ashamed when you receive your sisters, both those who are older than you and those who are younger. I will give them to you as daughters, but not on the basis of my covenant with you. 62So I will establish my covenant with you, and you will know that I am the Lord. 63Then, when I make atonement for you for all you have done, you will remember and be ashamed and never again open your mouth because of your humiliation, declares the Sovereign Lord.' "

Two Eagles and a Vine

17 The word of the Lord came to me: 2"Son of man, set forth an allegory and tell the house of Israel a parable. 3Say to them, 'This is what the Sovereign Lord says: A great eagle with powerful wings, long feath-

---

a57 Many Hebrew manuscripts and Syriac; most Hebrew manuscripts, Septuagint and Vulgate *Aram*

ers and full plumage of varied colors came to Lebanon. Taking hold of the top of a cedar, [4]he broke off its topmost shoot and carried it away to a land of merchants, where he planted it in a city of traders.

[5]" 'He took some of the seed of your land and put it in fertile soil. He planted it like a willow by abundant water, [6]and it sprouted and became a low, spreading vine. Its branches turned toward him, but its roots remained under it. So it became a vine and produced branches and put out leafy boughs.

[7]" 'But there was another great eagle with powerful wings and full plumage. The vine now sent out its roots toward him from the plot where it was planted and stretched out its branches to him for water. [8]It had been planted in good soil by abundant water so that it would produce branches, bear fruit and become a splendid vine.'

[9]"Say to them, 'This is what the Sovereign LORD says: Will it thrive? Will it not be uprooted and stripped of its fruit so that it withers? All its new growth will wither. It will not take a strong arm or many people to pull it up by the roots. [10]Even if it is transplanted, will it thrive? Will it not wither completely when the east wind strikes it—wither away in the plot where it grew?' "

[11]Then the word of the LORD came to me: [12]"Say to this rebellious house, 'Do you not know what these things mean?' Say to them: 'The king of Babylon went to Jerusalem and carried off her king and her nobles, bringing them back with him to Babylon. [13]Then he took a member of the royal family and made a treaty with him, putting him under oath. He also carried away the leading men of the land, [14]so that the kingdom would be brought low, unable to rise again, surviving only by keeping his treaty. [15]But the king rebelled against him by sending his envoys to Egypt to get horses and a large army. Will he succeed? Will he who does such things

escape? Will he break the treaty and yet escape?

[16]" 'As surely as I live, declares the Sovereign LORD, he shall die in Babylon, in the land of the king who put him on the throne, whose oath he despised and whose treaty he broke. [17]Pharaoh with his mighty army and great horde will be of no help to him in war, when ramps are built and siege works erected to destroy many lives. [18]He despised the oath by breaking the covenant. Because he had given his hand in pledge and yet did all these things, he shall not escape.

[19]" 'Therefore this is what the Sovereign LORD says: As surely as I live, I will bring down on his head my oath that he despised and my covenant that he broke. [20]I will spread my net for him, and he will be caught in my snare. I will bring him to Babylon and execute judgment upon him there because he was unfaithful to me. [21]All his fleeing troops will fall by the sword, and the survivors will be scattered to the winds. Then you will know that I the LORD have spoken.

[22]" 'This is what the Sovereign LORD says: I myself will take a shoot from the very top of a cedar and plant it; I will break off a tender sprig from its topmost shoots and plant it on a high and lofty mountain. [23]On the mountain heights of Israel I will plant it; it will produce branches and bear fruit and become a splendid cedar. Birds of every kind will nest in it; they will find shelter in the shade of its branches. [24]All the trees of the field will know that I the LORD bring down the tall tree and make the low tree grow tall. I dry up the green tree and make the dry tree flourish.

" 'I the LORD have spoken, and I will do it.' "

The Soul Who Sins Will Die

18 The word of the LORD came to me: [2]"What do you people mean by quoting this proverb about the land of Israel:

" 'The fathers eat sour grapes,
and the children's teeth are set
on edge'?

3"As surely as I live, declares the
Sovereign LORD, you will no longer
quote this proverb in Israel. 4For every living soul belongs to me, the father as well as the son—both alike
belong to me. The soul who sins is the
one who will die.

5"Suppose there is a righteous man
who does what is just and right.
6He does not eat at the mountain
shrines
or look to the idols of the house
of Israel.
He does not defile his neighbor's
wife
or lie with a woman during her
period.
7He does not oppress anyone,
but returns what he took in
pledge for a loan.

He does not commit robbery
but gives his food to the hungry
and provides clothing for the
naked.
8He does not lend at usury
or take excessive interest.*a*
He withholds his hand from doing
wrong
and judges fairly between man
and man.
9He follows my decrees
and faithfully keeps my laws.
That man is righteous;
he will surely live,
declares the Sovereign
LORD.

10"Suppose he has a violent son,
who sheds blood or does any of these
other things*b* 11(though the father
has done none of them):

"He eats at the mountain shrines.
He defiles his neighbor's wife.
12He oppresses the poor and needy.

a8 Or *take interest*; similarly in verses 13 and 17   *b10* Or *things to a brother*

Life in Bible Times

CLOTHING

In Old Testament times people wore graceful, simple clothing, usually made of wool or linen. Most wore an inner tunic of finer cloth next to the body. Over that they wore a looser outer tunic, held at the waist by a belt made of cloth or leather. For cold weather Old Testament people wore a woolen cloak, which they used as a blanket at night. To protect their heads from the hot sun, both men and women wore a square of fabric draped over the head and held in place with a band. They usually wore leather sandals on their feet.

He commits robbery.
He does not return what he took
in pledge.
He looks to the idols.
He does detestable things.
13He lends at usury and takes
excessive interest.

Will such a man live? He will not!
Because he has done all these detestable things, he will surely be put to
death and his blood will be on his own
head.

14"But suppose this son has a son
who sees all the sins his father commits, and though he sees them, he
does not do such things:

15"He does not eat at the mountain
shrines
or look to the idols of the house
of Israel.
He does not defile his neighbor's
wife.
16He does not oppress anyone
or require a pledge for a loan.
He does not commit robbery
but gives his food to the hungry
and provides clothing for the
naked.
17He withholds his hand from sin[a]
and takes no usury or excessive
interest.
He keeps my laws and follows my
decrees.

He will not die for his father's sin; he
will surely live. 18But his father will
die for his own sin, because he practiced extortion, robbed his brother
and did what was wrong among his
people.

19"Yet you ask, 'Why does the son
not share the guilt of his father?'
Since the son has done what is just
and right and has been careful to
keep all my decrees, he will surely
live. 20The soul who sins is the one
who will die. The son will not share
the guilt of the father, nor will the
father share the guilt of the son. The
righteousness of the righteous man
will be credited to him, and the wick-

edness of the wicked will be charged
against him.

21"But if a wicked man turns away
from all the sins he has committed
and keeps all my decrees and does
what is just and right, he will surely
live; he will not die. 22None of the offenses he has committed will be remembered against him. Because of
the righteous things he has done, he
will live. 23Do I take any pleasure in
the death of the wicked? declares the
Sovereign LORD. Rather, am I not
pleased when they turn from their
ways and live?

24"But if a righteous man turns
from his righteousness and commits
sin and does the same detestable
things the wicked man does, will he
live? None of the righteous things he
has done will be remembered. Because of the unfaithfulness he is
guilty of and because of the sins he
has committed, he will die.

25"Yet you say, 'The way of the
Lord is not just.' Hear, O house of Israel: Is my way unjust? Is it not your
ways that are unjust? 26If a righteous
man turns from his righteousness
and commits sin, he will die for it;
because of the sin he has committed
he will die. 27But if a wicked man
turns away from the wickedness he
has committed and does what is just
and right, he will save his life. 28Be-
cause he considers all the offenses he
has committed and turns away from
them, he will surely live; he will not
die. 29Yet the house of Israel says,
'The way of the Lord is not just.'
Are my ways unjust, O house of Israel? Is it not your ways that are unjust?

30"Therefore, O house of Israel, I
will judge you, each one according to
his ways, declares the Sovereign
LORD. Repent! Turn away from all
your offenses; then sin will not be
your downfall. 31Rid yourselves of all
the offenses you have committed, and
get a new heart and a new spirit.
Why will you die, O house of Israel?
32For I take no pleasure in the death

a17 Septuagint (see also verse 8); Hebrew *from the poor*

of anyone, declares the Sovereign
LORD. Repent and live!

A Lament for Israel's Princes

19 "Take up a lament concerning the princes of Israel ²and say:

" 'What a lioness was your mother
among the lions!
She lay down among the young
lions
and reared her cubs.
³She brought up one of her cubs,
and he became a strong lion.
He learned to tear the prey
and he devoured men.
⁴The nations heard about him,
and he was trapped in their pit.
They led him with hooks
to the land of Egypt.

⁵" 'When she saw her hope
unfulfilled,
her expectation gone,
she took another of her cubs
and made him a strong lion.
⁶He prowled among the lions,
for he was now a strong lion.
He learned to tear the prey
and he devoured men.
⁷He broke down ᵃ their strongholds
and devastated their towns.
The land and all who were in it
were terrified by his roaring.
⁸Then the nations came against
him,
those from regions round about.
They spread their net for him,
and he was trapped in their pit.
⁹With hooks they pulled him into
a cage
and brought him to the king of
Babylon.
They put him in prison,
so his roar was heard no longer
on the mountains of Israel.

¹⁰" 'Your mother was like a vine in
your vineyard ᵇ
planted by the water;
it was fruitful and full of
branches
because of abundant water.
¹¹Its branches were strong,
fit for a ruler's scepter.
It towered high
above the thick foliage,
conspicuous for its height
and for its many branches.
¹²But it was uprooted in fury
and thrown to the ground.
The east wind made it shrivel,
it was stripped of its fruit;
its strong branches withered
and fire consumed them.
¹³Now it is planted in the desert,
in a dry and thirsty land.
¹⁴Fire spread from one of its main ᶜ
branches
and consumed its fruit.
No strong branch is left on it
fit for a ruler's scepter.'

This is a lament and is to be used as
a lament."

Rebellious Israel

20 In the seventh year, in the fifth month on the tenth day, some of the elders of Israel came to inquire of the LORD, and they sat down in front of me.

²Then the word of the LORD came to me: ³"Son of man, speak to the elders of Israel and say to them, 'This is what the Sovereign LORD says: Have you come to inquire of me? As surely as I live, I will not let you inquire of me, declares the Sovereign LORD.'

⁴"Will you judge them? Will you judge them, son of man? Then confront them with the detestable practices of their fathers ⁵and say to them: 'This is what the Sovereign LORD says: On the day I chose Israel, I swore with uplifted hand to the descendants of the house of Jacob and revealed myself to them in Egypt. With uplifted hand I said to them, "I am the LORD your God." ⁶On that day I swore to them that I would bring them out of Egypt into a land I had searched out for them, a land flowing with milk and honey, the most beau-

---

ᵃ7 Targum (see Septuagint); Hebrew *He knew*
manuscripts *your blood*   ᶜ14 Or *from under its*   ᵇ10 Two Hebrew manuscripts; most Hebrew

tiful of all lands. 7And I said to them, "Each of you, get rid of the vile images you have set your eyes on, and do not defile yourselves with the idols of Egypt. I am the LORD your God."

8" 'But they rebelled against me and would not listen to me; they did not get rid of the vile images they had set their eyes on, nor did they forsake the idols of Egypt. So I said I would pour out my wrath on them and spend my anger against them in Egypt. 9But for the sake of my name I did what would keep it from being profaned in the eyes of the nations they lived among and in whose sight I had revealed myself to the Israelites by bringing them out of Egypt. 10Therefore I led them out of Egypt and brought them into the desert. 11I gave them my decrees and made known to them my laws, for the man who obeys them will live by them. 12Also I gave them my Sabbaths as a sign between us, so they would know that I the LORD made them holy.

13" 'Yet the people of Israel rebelled against me in the desert. They did not follow my decrees but rejected my laws—although the man who obeys them will live by them—and they utterly desecrated my Sabbaths. So I said I would pour out my wrath on them and destroy them in the desert. 14But for the sake of my name I did what would keep it from being profaned in the eyes of the nations in whose sight I had brought them out. 15Also with uplifted hand I swore to them in the desert that I would not bring them into the land I had given them—a land flowing with milk and honey, most beautiful of all lands— 16because they rejected my laws and did not follow my decrees and desecrated my Sabbaths. For their hearts were devoted to their idols. 17Yet I looked on them with pity and did not destroy them or put an end to them in the desert. 18I said to their children in the desert, "Do not follow the statutes of your fathers or keep their laws or defile yourselves with their idols. 19I

am the LORD your God; follow my decrees and be careful to keep my laws. 20Keep my Sabbaths holy, that they may be a sign between us. Then you will know that I am the LORD your God."

21" 'But the children rebelled against me: They did not follow my decrees, they were not careful to keep my laws—although the man who obeys them will live by them—and they desecrated my Sabbaths. So I said I would pour out my wrath on them and spend my anger against them in the desert. 22But I withheld my hand, and for the sake of my name I did what would keep it from being profaned in the eyes of the nations in whose sight I had brought them out. 23Also with uplifted hand I swore to them in the desert that I would disperse them among the nations and scatter them through the countries, 24because they had not obeyed my laws but had rejected my decrees and desecrated my Sabbaths, and their eyes ˌlustedˌ after their fathers' idols. 25I also gave them over to statutes that were not good and laws they could not live by; 26I let them become defiled through their gifts —the sacrifice of every firstborn[a] —that I might fill them with horror so they would know that I am the LORD.'

27"Therefore, son of man, speak to the people of Israel and say to them, 'This is what the Sovereign LORD says: In this also your fathers blasphemed me by forsaking me: 28When I brought them into the land I had sworn to give them and they saw any high hill or any leafy tree, there they offered their sacrifices, made offerings that provoked me to anger, presented their fragrant incense and poured out their drink offerings. 29Then I said to them: What is this high place you go to?' " (It is called Bamah[b] to this day.)

Judgment and Restoration

30"Therefore say to the house of Is-

a26 Or *—making every firstborn pass through ˌthe fireˌ*   *b29 Bamah* means *high place.*

rael: 'This is what the Sovereign LORD says: Will you defile yourselves the way your fathers did and lust after their vile images? ³¹When you offer your gifts—the sacrifice of your sons in *a* the fire—you continue to defile yourselves with all your idols to this day. Am I to let you inquire of me, O house of Israel? As surely as I live, declares the Sovereign LORD, I will not let you inquire of me.

³²" 'You say, "We want to be like the nations, like the peoples of the world, who serve wood and stone." But what you have in mind will never happen. ³³As surely as I live, declares the Sovereign LORD, I will rule over you with a mighty hand and an outstretched arm and with outpoured wrath. ³⁴I will bring you from the nations and gather you from the countries where you have been scattered—with a mighty hand and an outstretched arm and with outpoured wrath. ³⁵I will bring you into the desert of the nations and there, face to face, I will execute judgment upon you. ³⁶As I judged your fathers in the desert of the land of Egypt, so I will judge you, declares the Sovereign LORD. ³⁷I will take note of you as you pass under my rod, and I will bring you into the bond of the covenant. ³⁸I will purge you of those who revolt and rebel against me. Although I will bring them out of the land where they are living, yet they will not enter the land of Israel. Then you will know that I am the LORD.

³⁹" 'As for you, O house of Israel, this is what the Sovereign LORD says: Go and serve your idols, every one of you! But afterward you will surely listen to me and no longer profane my holy name with your gifts and idols. ⁴⁰For on my holy mountain, the high mountain of Israel, declares the Sovereign LORD, there in the land the entire house of Israel will serve me, and there I will accept them. There I will require your offerings and your choice gifts, *b* along with all your holy sacrifices. ⁴¹I will accept you as fragrant incense when I bring you out from the nations and gather you from the countries where you have been scattered, and I will show myself holy among you in the sight of the nations. ⁴²Then you will know that I am the LORD, when I bring you into the land of Israel, the land I had sworn with uplifted hand to give to your fathers. ⁴³There you will remember your conduct and all the actions by which you have defiled yourselves, and you will loathe yourselves for all the evil you have done. ⁴⁴You will know that I am the LORD, when I deal with you for my name's sake and not according to your evil ways and your corrupt practices, O house of Israel, declares the Sovereign LORD.' "

Prophecy Against the South

⁴⁵The word of the LORD came to me: ⁴⁶"Son of man, set your face toward the south; preach against the south and prophesy against the forest of the southland. ⁴⁷Say to the southern forest: 'Hear the word of the LORD. This

a31 Or —making your sons pass through   b40 Or and the gifts of your firstfruits

---

▌ET'S LIVE IT!   Ezekiel 20:39–44

GOD CAN CHANGE PEOPLE ➡ In Ezekiel's time God's people worshiped idols. Read Ezekiel 20:39–44. In this passage God tells the Israelites that he is unhappy with what they've been doing, but then he tells them what will happen in the future. The Israelites will return to worshiping God, and they will be very sorry for what they have done wrong.

Do you know any boys and girls who don't act like Christians but do mean and wrong things? You can pray for boys and girls like this. Ask God to change them by helping them know and love Jesus.

is what the Sovereign LORD says: I am about to set fire to you, and it will consume all your trees, both green and dry. The blazing flame will not be quenched, and every face from south to north will be scorched by it. ⁴⁸Everyone will see that I the LORD have kindled it; it will not be quenched.' "

⁴⁹Then I said, "Ah, Sovereign LORD! They are saying of me, 'Isn't he just telling parables?' "

Babylon, God's Sword of Judgment

21 The word of the LORD came to me: ²"Son of man, set your face against Jerusalem and preach against the sanctuary. Prophesy against the land of Israel ³and say to her: 'This is what the LORD says: I am against you. I will draw my sword from its scabbard and cut off from you both the righteous and the wicked. ⁴Because I am going to cut off the righteous and the wicked, my sword will be unsheathed against everyone from south to north. ⁵Then all people will know that I the LORD have drawn my sword from its scabbard; it will not return again.'

⁶"Therefore groan, son of man! Groan before them with broken heart and bitter grief. ⁷And when they ask you, 'Why are you groaning?' you shall say, 'Because of the news that is coming. Every heart will melt and every hand go limp; every spirit will become faint and every knee become as weak as water.' It is coming! It will surely take place, declares the Sovereign LORD."

⁸The word of the LORD came to me: ⁹"Son of man, prophesy and say, 'This is what the Lord says:

" 'A sword, a sword,
    sharpened and polished—
¹⁰sharpened for the slaughter,
    polished to flash like lightning!

" 'Shall we rejoice in the scepter of my son ͺJudah͵? The sword despises every such stick.

¹¹" 'The sword is appointed to be
    polished,
  to be grasped with the hand;
  it is sharpened and polished,
  made ready for the hand of the
    slayer.
¹²Cry out and wail, son of man,
  for it is against my people;
  it is against all the princes of
    Israel.
They are thrown to the sword
  along with my people.
Therefore beat your breast.

¹³" 'Testing will surely come. And what if the scepter ͺof Judah͵, which the sword despises, does not continue? declares the Sovereign LORD.'

¹⁴"So then, son of man, prophesy
  and strike your hands together.
Let the sword strike twice,
  even three times.
It is a sword for slaughter—
  a sword for great slaughter,
  closing in on them from every
    side.
¹⁵So that hearts may melt
  and the fallen be many,
I have stationed the sword for
    slaughter^a
  at all their gates.
Oh! It is made to flash like
    lightning,
  it is grasped for slaughter.
¹⁶O sword, slash to the right,
  then to the left,
  wherever your blade is turned.
¹⁷I too will strike my hands
    together,
  and my wrath will subside.
I the LORD have spoken."

¹⁸The word of the LORD came to me: ¹⁹"Son of man, mark out two roads for the sword of the king of Babylon to take, both starting from the same country. Make a signpost where the road branches off to the city. ²⁰Mark out one road for the sword to come against Rabbah of the Ammonites and another against Judah and fortified Jerusalem. ²¹For the king of Babylon will stop at the fork in the road,

---

^a15 Septuagint; the meaning of the Hebrew for this word is uncertain.

at the junction of the two roads, to seek an omen: He will cast lots with arrows, he will consult his idols, he will examine the liver. ²²Into his right hand will come the lot for Jerusalem, where he is to set up battering rams, to give the command to slaughter, to sound the battle cry, to set battering rams against the gates, to build a ramp and to erect siege works. ²³It will seem like a false omen to those who have sworn allegiance to him, but he will remind them of their guilt and take them captive.

²⁴"Therefore this is what the Sovereign LORD says: 'Because you people have brought to mind your guilt by your open rebellion, revealing your sins in all that you do—because you have done this, you will be taken captive.

²⁵" 'O profane and wicked prince of Israel, whose day has come, whose time of punishment has reached its climax, ²⁶this is what the Sovereign LORD says: Take off the turban, remove the crown. It will not be as it was: The lowly will be exalted and the exalted will be brought low. ²⁷A ruin! A ruin! I will make it a ruin! It will not be restored until he comes to whom it rightfully belongs; to him I will give it.'

²⁸"And you, son of man, prophesy and say, 'This is what the Sovereign LORD says about the Ammonites and their insults:

" 'A sword, a sword,
    drawn for the slaughter,
  polished to consume
    and to flash like lightning!
²⁹Despite false visions concerning
      you
    and lying divinations about you,
  it will be laid on the necks
    of the wicked who are to be
      slain,
  whose day has come,
    whose time of punishment has
      reached its climax.
³⁰Return the sword to its scabbard.
  In the place where you were
    created,

in the land of your ancestry,
  I will judge you.
³¹I will pour out my wrath upon
      you
  and breathe out my fiery anger
    against you;
  I will hand you over to brutal
    men,
  men skilled in destruction.
³²You will be fuel for the fire,
  your blood will be shed in your
    land,
you will be remembered no more;
  for I the LORD have spoken.' "

Jerusalem's Sins

22 The word of the LORD came to me: ²"Son of man, will you judge her? Will you judge this city of bloodshed? Then confront her with all her detestable practices ³and say: 'This is what the Sovereign LORD says: O city that brings on herself doom by shedding blood in her midst and defiles herself by making idols, ⁴you have become guilty because of the blood you have shed and have become defiled by the idols you have made. You have brought your days to a close, and the end of your years has come. Therefore I will make you an object of scorn to the nations and a laughingstock to all the countries. ⁵Those who are near and those who are far away will mock you, O infamous city, full of turmoil.

⁶" 'See how each of the princes of Israel who are in you uses his power to shed blood. ⁷In you they have treated father and mother with contempt; in you they have oppressed the alien and mistreated the fatherless and the widow. ⁸You have despised my holy things and desecrated my Sabbaths. ⁹In you are slanderous men bent on shedding blood; in you are those who eat at the mountain shrines and commit lewd acts. ¹⁰In you are those who dishonor their fathers' bed; in you are those who violate women during their period, when they are ceremonially unclean. ¹¹In you one man commits a detestable offense with his neighbor's wife, another shamefully defiles his

daughter-in-law, and another violates his sister, his own father's daughter. ¹²In you men accept bribes to shed blood; you take usury and excessive interest*ᵃ* and make unjust gain from your neighbors by extortion. And you have forgotten me, declares the Sovereign LORD.

¹³" 'I will surely strike my hands together at the unjust gain you have made and at the blood you have shed in your midst. ¹⁴Will your courage endure or your hands be strong in the day I deal with you? I the LORD have spoken, and I will do it. ¹⁵I will disperse you among the nations and scatter you through the countries; and I will put an end to your uncleanness. ¹⁶When you have been defiled*ᵇ* in the eyes of the nations, you will know that I am the LORD.' "

¹⁷Then the word of the LORD came to me: ¹⁸"Son of man, the house of Israel has become dross to me; all of them are the copper, tin, iron and lead left inside a furnace. They are but the dross of silver. ¹⁹Therefore this is what the Sovereign LORD says: 'Because you have all become dross, I will gather you into Jerusalem. ²⁰As men gather silver, copper, iron, lead and tin into a furnace to melt it with a fiery blast, so will I gather you in my anger and my wrath and put you inside the city and melt you. ²¹I will gather you and I will blow on you with my fiery wrath, and you will be melted inside her. ²²As silver is melted in a furnace, so you will be melted inside her, and you will know that I the LORD have poured out my wrath upon you.' "

²³Again the word of the LORD came to me: ²⁴"Son of man, say to the land, 'You are a land that has had no rain or showers*ᶜ* in the day of wrath.' ²⁵There is a conspiracy of her princes*ᵈ* within her like a roaring lion tearing its prey; they devour people, take treasures and precious things and make many widows within her. ²⁶Her priests do violence to my

law and profane my holy things; they do not distinguish between the holy and the common; they teach that there is no difference between the unclean and the clean; and they shut their eyes to the keeping of my Sabbaths, so that I am profaned among them. ²⁷Her officials within her are like wolves tearing their prey; they shed blood and kill people to make unjust gain. ²⁸Her prophets whitewash these deeds for them by false visions and lying divinations. They say, 'This is what the Sovereign LORD says'—when the LORD has not spoken. ²⁹The people of the land practice extortion and commit robbery; they oppress the poor and needy and mistreat the alien, denying them justice.

³⁰"I looked for a man among them who would build up the wall and stand before me in the gap on behalf of the land so I would not have to destroy it, but I found none. ³¹So I will pour out my wrath on them and consume them with my fiery anger, bringing down on their own heads all they have done, declares the Sovereign LORD."

Two Adulterous Sisters

23 The word of the LORD came to me: ²"Son of man, there were two women, daughters of the same mother. ³They became prostitutes in Egypt, engaging in prostitution from their youth. In that land their breasts were fondled and their virgin bosoms caressed. ⁴The older was named Oholah, and her sister was Oholibah. They were mine and gave birth to sons and daughters. Oholah is Samaria, and Oholibah is Jerusalem.

⁵"Oholah engaged in prostitution while she was still mine; and she lusted after her lovers, the Assyrians—warriors ⁶clothed in blue, governors and commanders, all of them handsome young men, and mounted horsemen. ⁷She gave herself as a prostitute to all the elite of the Assyr-

---

ᵃ12 Or *usury and interest*　　*ᵇ16* Or *When I have allotted you your inheritance*　　*ᶜ24* Septuagint; Hebrew *has not been cleansed or rained on*　　*ᵈ25* Septuagint; Hebrew *prophets*

ians and defiled herself with all the idols of everyone she lusted after. [8]She did not give up the prostitution she began in Egypt, when during her youth men slept with her, caressed her virgin bosom and poured out their lust upon her.

[9]"Therefore I handed her over to her lovers, the Assyrians, for whom she lusted. [10]They stripped her naked, took away her sons and daughters and killed her with the sword. She became a byword among women, and punishment was inflicted on her.

[11]"Her sister Oholibah saw this, yet in her lust and prostitution she was more depraved than her sister. [12]She too lusted after the Assyrians—governors and commanders, warriors in full dress, mounted horsemen, all handsome young men. [13]I saw that she too defiled herself; both of them went the same way.

[14]"But she carried her prostitution still further. She saw men portrayed on a wall, figures of Chaldeans[a] portrayed in red, [15]with belts around their waists and flowing turbans on their heads; all of them looked like Babylonian chariot officers, natives of Chaldea.[b] [16]As soon as she saw them, she lusted after them and sent messengers to them in Chaldea. [17]Then the Babylonians came to her, to the bed of love, and in their lust they defiled her. After she had been defiled by them, she turned away from them in disgust. [18]When she carried on her prostitution openly and exposed her nakedness, I turned away from her in disgust, just as I had turned away from her sister. [19]Yet she became more and more promiscuous as she recalled the days of her youth, when she was a prostitute in Egypt. [20]There she lusted after her lovers, whose genitals were like those of donkeys and whose emission was like that of horses. [21]So you longed for the lewdness of your youth, when in Egypt your bosom was caressed and your young breasts fondled.[c]

[22]"Therefore, Oholibah, this is what the Sovereign LORD says: I will stir up your lovers against you, those you turned away from in disgust, and I will bring them against you from every side— [23]the Babylonians and all the Chaldeans, the men of Pekod and Shoa and Koa, and all the Assyrians with them, handsome young men, all of them governors and commanders, chariot officers and men of high rank, all mounted on horses. [24]They will come against you with weapons,[d] chariots and wagons and with a throng of people; they will take up positions against you on every side with large and small shields and with helmets. I will turn you over to them for punishment, and they will punish you according to their standards. [25]I will direct my jealous anger against you, and they will deal with you in fury. They will cut off your noses and your ears, and those of you who are left will fall by the sword. They will take away your sons and daughters, and those of you who are left will be consumed by fire. [26]They will also strip you of your clothes and take your fine jewelry. [27]So I will put a stop to the lewdness and prostitution you began in Egypt. You will not look on these things with longing or remember Egypt anymore.

[28]"For this is what the Sovereign LORD says: I am about to hand you over to those you hate, to those you turned away from in disgust. [29]They will deal with you in hatred and take away everything you have worked for. They will leave you naked and bare, and the shame of your prostitution will be exposed. Your lewdness and promiscuity [30]have brought this upon you, because you lusted after the nations and defiled yourself with their idols. [31]You have gone the way

---

[a]14 Or Babylonians   [b]15 Or Babylonia; also in verse 16   [c]21 Syriac (see also verse 3);
Hebrew caressed because of your young breasts   [d]24 The meaning of the Hebrew for this word is
uncertain.

of your sister; so I will put her cup into your hand.

³²"This is what the Sovereign LORD says:

"You will drink your sister's cup,
    a cup large and deep;
it will bring scorn and derision,
    for it holds so much.
³³You will be filled with
        drunkenness and sorrow,
    the cup of ruin and desolation,
    the cup of your sister Samaria.
³⁴You will drink it and drain it dry;
    you will dash it to pieces
        and tear your breasts.

I have spoken, declares the Sovereign LORD.

³⁵"Therefore this is what the Sovereign LORD says: Since you have forgotten me and thrust me behind your back, you must bear the consequences of your lewdness and prostitution."

³⁶The LORD said to me: "Son of man, will you judge Oholah and Oholibah? Then confront them with their detestable practices, ³⁷for they have committed adultery and blood is on their hands. They committed adultery with their idols; they even sacrificed their children, whom they bore to me,ᵃ as food for them. ³⁸They have also done this to me: At that same time they defiled my sanctuary and desecrated my Sabbaths. ³⁹On the very day they sacrificed their children to their idols, they entered my sanctuary and desecrated it. That is what they did in my house.

⁴⁰"They even sent messengers for men who came from far away, and when they arrived you bathed yourself for them, painted your eyes and put on your jewelry. ⁴¹You sat on an elegant couch, with a table spread before it on which you had placed the incense and oil that belonged to me.

⁴²"The noise of a carefree crowd was around her; Sabeansᵇ were brought from the desert along with

men from the rabble, and they put bracelets on the arms of the woman and her sister and beautiful crowns on their heads. ⁴³Then I said about the one worn out by adultery, 'Now let them use her as a prostitute, for that is all she is.' ⁴⁴And they slept with her. As men sleep with a prostitute, so they slept with those lewd women, Oholah and Oholibah. ⁴⁵But righteous men will sentence them to the punishment of women who commit adultery and shed blood, because they are adulterous and blood is on their hands.

⁴⁶"This is what the Sovereign LORD says: Bring a mob against them and give them over to terror and plunder. ⁴⁷The mob will stone them and cut them down with their swords; they will kill their sons and daughters and burn down their houses.

⁴⁸"So I will put an end to lewdness in the land, that all women may take warning and not imitate you. ⁴⁹You will suffer the penalty for your lewdness and bear the consequences of your sins of idolatry. Then you will know that I am the Sovereign LORD."

The Cooking Pot

24 In the ninth year, in the tenth month on the tenth day, the word of the LORD came to me: ²"Son of man, record this date, this very date, because the king of Babylon has laid siege to Jerusalem this very day. ³Tell this rebellious house a parable and say to them: 'This is what the Sovereign LORD says:

" 'Put on the cooking pot; put it
        on
    and pour water into it.
⁴Put into it the pieces of meat,
    all the choice pieces—the leg
        and the shoulder.
Fill it with the best of these
        bones;
⁵ take the pick of the flock.
Pile wood beneath it for the
        bones;

ᵃ37 Or *even made the children they bore to me pass through the fire*   ᵇ42 Or *drunkards*

bring it to a boil
and cook the bones in it.

⁶" 'For this is what the Sovereign
LORD says:

" 'Woe to the city of bloodshed,
to the pot now encrusted,
whose deposit will not go
away!
Empty it piece by piece
without casting lots for them.

⁷" 'For the blood she shed is in her
midst:
She poured it on the bare rock;
she did not pour it on the ground,
where the dust would cover it.
⁸To stir up wrath and take
revenge
I put her blood on the bare
rock,
so that it would not be covered.

⁹" 'Therefore this is what the Sover-
eign LORD says:

" 'Woe to the city of bloodshed!
I, too, will pile the wood high.
¹⁰So heap on the wood
and kindle the fire.
Cook the meat well,
mixing in the spices;
and let the bones be charred.
¹¹Then set the empty pot on the
coals
till it becomes hot and its
copper glows
so its impurities may be melted
and its deposit burned away.
¹²It has frustrated all efforts;
its heavy deposit has not been
removed,
not even by fire.

¹³" 'Now your impurity is lewdness.
Because I tried to cleanse you but you
would not be cleansed from your impurity, you will not be clean again
until my wrath against you has subsided.

¹⁴" 'I the LORD have spoken. The
time has come for me to act. I will not
hold back; I will not have pity, nor
will I relent. You will be judged according to your conduct and your actions, declares the Sovereign LORD.' "

Ezekiel's Wife Dies

¹⁵The word of the LORD came to me:
¹⁶"Son of man, with one blow I am
about to take away from you the delight of your eyes. Yet do not lament
or weep or shed any tears. ¹⁷Groan
quietly; do not mourn for the dead.
Keep your turban fastened and your
sandals on your feet; do not cover the
lower part of your face or eat the customary food ˌof mourners˲."

¹⁸So I spoke to the people in the
morning, and in the evening my wife
died. The next morning I did as I had
been commanded.

¹⁹Then the people asked me,
"Won't you tell us what these things
have to do with us?"

²⁰So I said to them, "The word of
the LORD came to me: ²¹Say to the
house of Israel, 'This is what the Sovereign LORD says: I am about to desecrate my sanctuary—the stronghold
in which you take pride, the delight
of your eyes, the object of your affection. The sons and daughters you left
behind will fall by the sword. ²²And
you will do as I have done. You will
not cover the lower part of your face
or eat the customary food ˌof mourn-
ers˲. ²³You will keep your turbans on
your heads and your sandals on your
feet. You will not mourn or weep but
will waste away because of[a] your
sins and groan among yourselves.
²⁴Ezekiel will be a sign to you; you
will do just as he has done. When this
happens, you will know that I am the
Sovereign LORD.'

²⁵"And you, son of man, on the day
I take away their stronghold, their
joy and glory, the delight of their
eyes, their heart's desire, and their
sons and daughters as well— ²⁶on
that day a fugitive will come to tell
you the news. ²⁷At that time your
mouth will be opened; you will speak
with him and will no longer be silent.
So you will be a sign to them, and
they will know that I am the LORD."

^a23 Or away in

A Prophecy Against Ammon

25 The word of the LORD came to me: ²"Son of man, set your face against the Ammonites and prophesy against them. ³Say to them, 'Hear the word of the Sovereign LORD. This is what the Sovereign LORD says: Because you said "Aha!" over my sanctuary when it was desecrated and over the land of Israel when it was laid waste and over the people of Judah when they went into exile, ⁴therefore I am going to give you to the people of the East as a possession. They will set up their camps and pitch their tents among you; they will eat your fruit and drink your milk. ⁵I will turn Rabbah into a pasture for camels and Ammon into a resting place for sheep. Then you will know that I am the LORD. ⁶For this is what the Sovereign LORD says: Because you have clapped your hands and stamped your feet, rejoicing with all the malice of your heart against the land of Israel, ⁷therefore I will stretch out my hand against you and give you as plunder to the nations. I will cut you off from the nations and exterminate you from the countries. I will destroy you, and you will know that I am the LORD.' "

A Prophecy Against Moab

⁸"This is what the Sovereign LORD says: 'Because Moab and Seir said, "Look, the house of Judah has become like all the other nations," ⁹therefore I will expose the flank of Moab, beginning at its frontier towns—Beth Jeshimoth, Baal Meon and Kiriathaim—the glory of that land. ¹⁰I will give Moab along with the Ammonites to the people of the East as a possession, so that the Ammonites will not be remembered among the nations; ¹¹and I will inflict punishment on Moab. Then they will know that I am the LORD.' "

A Prophecy Against Edom

¹²"This is what the Sovereign LORD says: 'Because Edom took revenge on the house of Judah and became very guilty by doing so, ¹³therefore this is what the Sovereign LORD says: I will stretch out my hand against Edom and kill its men and their animals. I will lay it waste, and from Teman to Dedan they will fall by the sword. ¹⁴I will take vengeance on Edom by the hand of my people Israel, and they will deal with Edom in accordance with my anger and my wrath; they will know my vengeance, declares the Sovereign LORD.' "

A Prophecy Against Philistia

¹⁵"This is what the Sovereign LORD says: 'Because the Philistines acted in vengeance and took revenge with malice in their hearts, and with ancient hostility sought to destroy Judah, ¹⁶therefore this is what the Sovereign LORD says: I am about to stretch out my hand against the Philistines, and I will cut off the Kerethites and destroy those remaining along the coast. ¹⁷I will carry out great vengeance on them and punish them in my wrath. Then they will know that I am the LORD, when I take vengeance on them.' "

A Prophecy Against Tyre

26 In the eleventh year, on the first day of the month, the word of the LORD came to me: ²"Son of man, because Tyre has said of Jerusalem, 'Aha! The gate to the nations is broken, and its doors have swung open to me; now that she lies in ruins I will prosper,' ³therefore this is what the Sovereign LORD says: I am against you, O Tyre, and I will bring many nations against you, like the sea casting up its waves. ⁴They will destroy the walls of Tyre and pull down her towers; I will scrape away her rubble and make her a bare rock. ⁵Out in the sea she will become a place to spread fishnets, for I have spoken, declares the Sovereign LORD. She will become plunder for the nations, ⁶and her settlements on the mainland will be ravaged by the sword. Then they will know that I am the LORD.

7"For this is what the Sovereign LORD says: From the north I am going to bring against Tyre Nebuchadnezzar[a] king of Babylon, king of kings, with horses and chariots, with horsemen and a great army. 8He will ravage your settlements on the mainland with the sword; he will set up siege works against you, build a ramp up to your walls and raise his shields against you. 9He will direct the blows of his battering rams against your walls and demolish your towers with his weapons. 10His horses will be so many that they will cover you with dust. Your walls will tremble at the noise of the war horses, wagons and chariots when he enters your gates as men enter a city whose walls have been broken through. 11The hoofs of his horses will trample all your streets; he will kill your people with the sword, and your strong pillars will fall to the ground. 12They will plunder your wealth and loot your merchandise; they will break down your walls and demolish your fine houses and throw your stones, timber and rubble into the sea. 13I will put an end to your noisy songs, and the music of your harps will be heard no more. 14I will make you a bare rock, and you will become a place to spread fishnets. You will never be rebuilt, for I the LORD have spoken, declares the Sovereign LORD.

15"This is what the Sovereign LORD says to Tyre: Will not the coastlands tremble at the sound of your fall, when the wounded groan and the slaughter takes place in you? 16Then all the princes of the coast will step down from their thrones and lay aside their robes and take off their embroidered garments. Clothed with terror, they will sit on the ground, trembling every moment, appalled at you. 17Then they will take up a lament concerning you and say to you:

" 'How you are destroyed, O city
    of renown,
   peopled by men of the sea!
You were a power on the seas,
   you and your citizens;
you put your terror
   on all who lived there.
18Now the coastlands tremble
   on the day of your fall;
the islands in the sea
   are terrified at your collapse.'

19"This is what the Sovereign LORD says: When I make you a desolate city, like cities no longer inhabited, and when I bring the ocean depths over you and its vast waters cover you, 20then I will bring you down with those who go down to the pit, to the people of long ago. I will make you dwell in the earth below, as in ancient ruins, with those who go down to the pit, and you will not return or take your place[b] in the land of the living. 21I will bring you to a horrible end and you will be no more. You will be sought, but you will never again be found, declares the Sovereign LORD."

A Lament for Tyre

27 The word of the LORD came to me: 2"Son of man, take up a lament concerning Tyre. 3Say to Tyre, situated at the gateway to the sea, merchant of peoples on many coasts, 'This is what the Sovereign LORD says:

" 'You say, O Tyre,
   "I am perfect in beauty."
4Your domain was on the high
      seas;
   your builders brought your
      beauty to perfection.
5They made all your timbers
   of pine trees from Senir[c];
they took a cedar from
      Lebanon
   to make a mast for you.
6Of oaks from Bashan
   they made your oars;

a7 Hebrew *Nebuchadrezzar*, of which *Nebuchadnezzar* is a variant; here and often in Ezekiel and Jeremiah   b20 Septuagint; Hebrew *return, and I will give glory*   c5 That is, Hermon

of cypress wood[a] from the coasts
of Cyprus[b]
they made your deck, inlaid
with ivory.
[7]Fine embroidered linen from
Egypt was your sail
and served as your banner;
your awnings were of blue and
purple
from the coasts of Elishah.
[8]Men of Sidon and Arvad were
your oarsmen;
your skilled men, O Tyre, were
aboard as your seamen.
[9]Veteran craftsmen of Gebal[c] were
on board
as shipwrights to caulk your
seams.
All the ships of the sea and their
sailors
came alongside to trade for your
wares.

[10]" 'Men of Persia, Lydia and Put
served as soldiers in your army.
They hung their shields and
helmets on your walls,
bringing you splendor.
[11]Men of Arvad and Helech
manned your walls on every
side;
men of Gammad
were in your towers.
They hung their shields around
your walls;
they brought your beauty to
perfection.

[12]" 'Tarshish did business with you
because of your great wealth of goods;
they exchanged silver, iron, tin and
lead for your merchandise.

[13]" 'Greece, Tubal and Meshech
traded with you; they exchanged
slaves and articles of bronze for your
wares.

[14]" 'Men of Beth Togarmah exchanged work horses, war horses and
mules for your merchandise.

[15]" 'The men of Rhodes[d] traded
with you, and many coastlands were

your customers; they paid you with
ivory tusks and ebony.

[16]" 'Aram[e] did business with you
because of your many products; they
exchanged turquoise, purple fabric,
embroidered work, fine linen, coral
and rubies for your merchandise.

[17]" 'Judah and Israel traded with
you; they exchanged wheat from
Minnith and confections,[f] honey, oil
and balm for your wares.

[18]" 'Damascus, because of your
many products and great wealth of
goods, did business with you in wine
from Helbon and wool from Zahar.

[19]" 'Danites and Greeks from Uzal
bought your merchandise; they exchanged wrought iron, cassia and
calamus for your wares.

[20]" 'Dedan traded in saddle blankets with you.

[21]" 'Arabia and all the princes of
Kedar were your customers; they did
business with you in lambs, rams and
goats.

[22]" 'The merchants of Sheba and
Raamah traded with you; for your
merchandise they exchanged the finest of all kinds of spices and precious
stones, and gold.

[23]" 'Haran, Canneh and Eden and
merchants of Sheba, Asshur and Kil-
mad traded with you. [24]In your marketplace they traded with you beautiful garments, blue fabric, embroidered work and multicolored rugs
with cords twisted and tightly knot-
ted.

[25]" 'The ships of Tarshish serve
as carriers for your wares.
You are filled with heavy cargo
in the heart of the sea.
[26]Your oarsmen take you
out to the high seas.
But the east wind will break you
to pieces
in the heart of the sea.
[27]Your wealth, merchandise and
wares,

---

[a]6 Targum; the Masoretic Text has a different division of the consonants.   [b]6 Hebrew *Kittim*
[c]9 That is, Byblos   [d]15 Septuagint; Hebrew *Dedan*   [e]16 Most Hebrew manuscripts; some
Hebrew manuscripts and Syriac *Edom*   [f]17 The meaning of the Hebrew for this word is
uncertain.

your mariners, seamen and
  shipwrights,
your merchants and all your
  soldiers,
and everyone else on board
will sink into the heart of the
  sea
on the day of your shipwreck.
²⁸The shorelands will quake
  when your seamen cry out.
²⁹All who handle the oars
  will abandon their ships;
the mariners and all the seamen
  will stand on the shore.
³⁰They will raise their voice
  and cry bitterly over you;
they will sprinkle dust on their
  heads
  and roll in ashes.
³¹They will shave their heads
  because of you
  and will put on sackcloth.
They will weep over you with
  anguish of soul
  and with bitter mourning.
³²As they wail and mourn over
  you,
  they will take up a lament
  concerning you:
"Who was ever silenced like
  Tyre,
  surrounded by the sea?"
³³When your merchandise went out
  on the seas,
  you satisfied many nations;
with your great wealth and your
  wares
  you enriched the kings of the
  earth.
³⁴Now you are shattered by the
  sea
  in the depths of the waters;
your wares and all your company
  have gone down with you.
³⁵All who live in the coastlands
  are appalled at you;
their kings shudder with horror
  and their faces are distorted
  with fear.
³⁶The merchants among the nations
  hiss at you;
you have come to a horrible end
  and will be no more.' "

A Prophecy Against the King of Tyre

28 The word of the Lord came to me: ²"Son of man, say to the ruler of Tyre, 'This is what the Sovereign Lord says:

TRADE

Ancient nations have traded goods since very early times. Most goods were carried from place to place by camel caravan, but ships were also used. Solomon was the first Hebrew to organize trade by camel caravan and ship. The countries involved traded a wide variety of exciting as well as ordinary items: spices, gold and silver, bronze and iron, ivory, horses, fabric, turquoise and rubies, wheat, oil, wine, rugs, lambs and goats.

" 'In the pride of your heart
  you say, "I am a god;
I sit on the throne of a god
  in the heart of the seas."
But you are a man and not a god,
  though you think you are as
  wise as a god.
³Are you wiser than Daniel^a?
  Is no secret hidden from you?
⁴By your wisdom and
  understanding
  you have gained wealth for
  yourself
and amassed gold and silver
  in your treasuries.
⁵By your great skill in trading
  you have increased your wealth,
and because of your wealth
  your heart has grown proud.

---

^a3 Or *Danel*; the Hebrew spelling may suggest a person other than the prophet Daniel.

⁶" 'Therefore this is what the Sovereign LORD says:

" 'Because you think you are
    wise,
    as wise as a god,
⁷I am going to bring foreigners
    against you,
    the most ruthless of nations;
they will draw their swords
    against your beauty and
    wisdom
    and pierce your shining
    splendor.
⁸They will bring you down to the
    pit,
    and you will die a violent death
    in the heart of the seas.
⁹Will you then say, "I am a god,"
    in the presence of those who
    kill you?
You will be but a man, not a god,
    in the hands of those who slay
    you.
¹⁰You will die the death of the
    uncircumcised
    at the hands of foreigners.

I have spoken, declares the Sovereign
LORD.' "

¹¹The word of the LORD came to me:
¹²"Son of man, take up a lament concerning the king of Tyre and say to him: 'This is what the Sovereign LORD says:

" 'You were the model of
    perfection,
    full of wisdom and perfect in
    beauty.
¹³You were in Eden,
    the garden of God;
    every precious stone adorned you:
    ruby, topaz and emerald,
    chrysolite, onyx and jasper,
    sapphire,ᵃ turquoise and
    beryl.ᵇ
Your settings and mountingsᶜ
    were made of gold;
    on the day you were created
    they were prepared.
¹⁴You were anointed as a guardian
    cherub,

for so I ordained you.
You were on the holy mount of
    God;
    you walked among the fiery
    stones.
¹⁵You were blameless in your ways
    from the day you were created
    till wickedness was found in
    you.
¹⁶Through your widespread trade
    you were filled with violence,
    and you sinned.
So I drove you in disgrace from
    the mount of God,
    and I expelled you, O guardian
    cherub,
    from among the fiery stones.
¹⁷Your heart became proud
    on account of your beauty,
    and you corrupted your wisdom
    because of your splendor.
So I threw you to the earth;
    I made a spectacle of you before
    kings.
¹⁸By your many sins and dishonest
    trade
    you have desecrated your
    sanctuaries.
So I made a fire come out from
    you,
    and it consumed you,
    and I reduced you to ashes on the
    ground
    in the sight of all who were
    watching.
¹⁹All the nations who knew you
    are appalled at you;
    you have come to a horrible end
    and will be no more.' "

A Prophecy Against Sidon

²⁰The word of the LORD came to me:
²¹"Son of man, set your face against Sidon; prophesy against her ²²and say: 'This is what the Sovereign LORD says:

" 'I am against you, O Sidon,
    and I will gain glory within
    you.
They will know that I am the
    LORD,

ᵃ13 Or *lapis lazuli*   ᵇ13 The precise identification of some of these precious stones is uncertain.
ᶜ13 The meaning of the Hebrew for this phrase is uncertain.

when I inflict punishment on
her
and show myself holy within
her.
23I will send a plague upon her
and make blood flow in her
streets.
The slain will fall within her,
with the sword against her on
every side.
Then they will know that I am
the LORD.

24" 'No longer will the people of Israel have malicious neighbors who are painful briers and sharp thorns. Then they will know that I am the Sovereign LORD.

25" 'This is what the Sovereign LORD says: When I gather the people of Israel from the nations where they have been scattered, I will show myself holy among them in the sight of the nations. Then they will live in their own land, which I gave to my servant Jacob. 26They will live there in safety and will build houses and plant vineyards; they will live in safety when I inflict punishment on all their neighbors who maligned them. Then they will know that I am the LORD their God.' "

A Prophecy Against Egypt

29 In the tenth year, in the tenth month on the twelfth day, the word of the LORD came to me: 2"Son of man, set your face against Pharaoh king of Egypt and prophesy against him and against all Egypt. 3Speak to him and say: 'This is what the Sovereign LORD says:

" 'I am against you, Pharaoh king
of Egypt,
you great monster lying among
your streams.
You say, "The Nile is mine;
I made it for myself."
4But I will put hooks in your jaws
and make the fish of your
streams stick to your scales.

I will pull you out from among
your streams,
with all the fish sticking to
your scales.
5I will leave you in the desert,
you and all the fish of your
streams.
You will fall on the open field
and not be gathered or picked
up.
I will give you as food
to the beasts of the earth and
the birds of the air.

6Then all who live in Egypt will know that I am the LORD.

" 'You have been a staff of reed for the house of Israel. 7When they grasped you with their hands, you splintered and you tore open their shoulders; when they leaned on you, you broke and their backs were wrenched.[a]

8" 'Therefore this is what the Sovereign LORD says: I will bring a sword against you and kill your men and their animals. 9Egypt will become a desolate wasteland. Then they will know that I am the LORD.

" 'Because you said, "The Nile is mine; I made it," 10therefore I am against you and against your streams, and I will make the land of Egypt a ruin and a desolate waste from Migdol to Aswan, as far as the border of Cush.[b] 11No foot of man or animal will pass through it; no one will live there for forty years. 12I will make the land of Egypt desolate among devastated lands, and her cities will lie desolate forty years among ruined cities. And I will disperse the Egyptians among the nations and scatter them through the countries.

13" 'Yet this is what the Sovereign LORD says: At the end of forty years I will gather the Egyptians from the nations where they were scattered. 14I will bring them back from captivity and return them to Upper Egypt,[c] the land of their ancestry. There they will be a lowly kingdom. 15It will be

---

a7 Syriac (see also Septuagint and Vulgate); Hebrew and you caused their backs to stand
b10 That is, the upper Nile region   c14 Hebrew to Pathros

the lowliest of kingdoms and will never again exalt itself above the other nations. I will make it so weak that it will never again rule over the nations. [16]Egypt will no longer be a source of confidence for the people of Israel but will be a reminder of their sin in turning to her for help. Then they will know that I am the Sovereign LORD.' "

[17]In the twenty-seventh year, in the first month on the first day, the word of the LORD came to me: [18]"Son of man, Nebuchadnezzar king of Babylon drove his army in a hard campaign against Tyre; every head was rubbed bare and every shoulder made raw. Yet he and his army got no reward from the campaign he led against Tyre. [19]Therefore this is what the Sovereign LORD says: I am going to give Egypt to Nebuchadnezzar king of Babylon, and he will carry off its wealth. He will loot and plunder the land as pay for his army. [20]I have given him Egypt as a reward for his efforts because he and his army did it for me, declares the Sovereign LORD. [21]"On that day I will make a horn[a] grow for the house of Israel, and I will open your mouth among them. Then they will know that I am the LORD."

A Lament for Egypt

30 The word of the LORD came to me: [2]"Son of man, prophesy and say: 'This is what the Sovereign LORD says:

" 'Wail and say,
  "Alas for that day!"
[3]For the day is near,
  the day of the LORD is near—
a day of clouds,
  a time of doom for the nations.
[4]A sword will come against Egypt,
  and anguish will come upon
    Cush.[b]
When the slain fall in Egypt,
  her wealth will be carried away
  and her foundations torn down.

[5]Cush and Put, Lydia and all Arabia, Libya[c] and the people of the covenant land will fall by the sword along with Egypt.

[6]" 'This is what the LORD says:

" 'The allies of Egypt will fall
  and her proud strength will fail.
From Migdol to Aswan
  they will fall by the sword
    within her,
      declares the Sovereign
        LORD.
[7]" 'They will be desolate
  among desolate lands,
and their cities will lie
  among ruined cities.
[8]Then they will know that I am
    the LORD,
  when I set fire to Egypt
  and all her helpers are crushed.

[9]" 'On that day messengers will go out from me in ships to frighten Cush out of her complacency. Anguish will take hold of them on the day of Egypt's doom, for it is sure to come.

[10]" 'This is what the Sovereign LORD says:

" 'I will put an end to the hordes
    of Egypt
  by the hand of Nebuchadnezzar
    king of Babylon.
[11]He and his army—the most
    ruthless of nations—
  will be brought in to destroy
    the land.
They will draw their swords
    against Egypt
  and fill the land with the slain.
[12]I will dry up the streams of the
    Nile
  and sell the land to evil men;
by the hand of foreigners
  I will lay waste the land and
    everything in it.

I the LORD have spoken.

[13]" 'This is what the Sovereign LORD says:

" 'I will destroy the idols

---

a21 Horn here symbolizes strength. *b4* That is, the upper Nile region; also in verses 5 and 9
c5 Hebrew *Cub*

and put an end to the images in
Memphis. *a*
No longer will there be a prince
in Egypt,
and I will spread fear
throughout the land.
14I will lay waste Upper Egypt, *b*
set fire to Zoan
and inflict punishment on
Thebes. *c*
15I will pour out my wrath on
Pelusium, *d*
the stronghold of Egypt,
and cut off the hordes of
Thebes.
16I will set fire to Egypt;
Pelusium will writhe in agony.
Thebes will be taken by storm;
Memphis will be in constant
distress.
17The young men of Heliopolis*e*
and Bubastis*f*
will fall by the sword,
and the cities themselves will
go into captivity.
18Dark will be the day at
Tahpanhes
when I break the yoke of
Egypt;
there her proud strength will
come to an end.
She will be covered with clouds,
and her villages will go into
captivity.
19So I will inflict punishment on
Egypt,
and they will know that I am
the LORD.' "

20In the eleventh year, in the first
month on the seventh day, the word
of the LORD came to me: 21"Son of
man, I have broken the arm of Pharaoh king of Egypt. It has not been
bound up for healing or put in a splint
so as to become strong enough to hold
a sword. 22Therefore this is what the
Sovereign LORD says: I am against
Pharaoh king of Egypt. I will break
both his arms, the good arm as well
as the broken one, and make the
sword fall from his hand. 23I will dis-

perse the Egyptians among the nations and scatter them through the
countries. 24I will strengthen the
arms of the king of Babylon and put
my sword in his hand, but I will
break the arms of Pharaoh, and he
will groan before him like a mortally
wounded man. 25I will strengthen the
arms of the king of Babylon, but the
arms of Pharaoh will fall limp. Then
they will know that I am the LORD,
when I put my sword into the hand of
the king of Babylon and he bran-
dishes it against Egypt. 26I will disperse the Egyptians among the nations and scatter them through the
countries. Then they will know that
I am the LORD."

A Cedar in Lebanon

31 In the eleventh year, in the
third month on the first day,
the word of the LORD came to me:
2"Son of man, say to Pharaoh king of
Egypt and to his hordes:

" 'Who can be compared with you
in majesty?
3Consider Assyria, once a cedar in
Lebanon,
with beautiful branches
overshadowing the forest;
it towered on high,
its top above the thick foliage.
4The waters nourished it,
deep springs made it grow tall;
their streams flowed
all around its base
and sent their channels
to all the trees of the field.
5So it towered higher
than all the trees of the field;
its boughs increased
and its branches grew long,
spreading because of abundant
waters.
6All the birds of the air
nested in its boughs,
all the beasts of the field
gave birth under its branches;
all the great nations

---

a13 Hebrew *Noph*; also in verse 16   *b14* Hebrew *waste Pathros*   *c14* Hebrew *No*; also in
verses 15 and 16   *d15* Hebrew *Sin*; also in verse 16   *e17* Hebrew *Awen* (or *On*)
f17 Hebrew *Pi Beseth*

lived in its shade.
⁷It was majestic in beauty,
  with its spreading boughs,
for its roots went down
  to abundant waters.
⁸The cedars in the garden of God
  could not rival it,
nor could the pine trees
  equal its boughs,
nor could the plane trees
  compare with its branches—
no tree in the garden of God
  could match its beauty.
⁹I made it beautiful
  with abundant branches,
the envy of all the trees of Eden
  in the garden of God.

¹⁰" 'Therefore this is what the Sovereign LORD says: Because it towered on high, lifting its top above the thick foliage, and because it was proud of its height, ¹¹I handed it over to the ruler of the nations, for him to deal with according to its wickedness. I cast it aside, ¹²and the most ruthless of foreign nations cut it down and left it. Its boughs fell on the mountains and in all the valleys; its branches lay broken in all the ravines of the land. All the nations of the earth came out from under its shade and left it. ¹³All the birds of the air settled on the fallen tree, and all the beasts of the field were among its branches. ¹⁴Therefore no other trees by the waters are ever to tower proudly on high, lifting their tops above the thick foliage. No other trees so well-watered are ever to reach such a height; they are all destined for death, for the earth below, among mortal men, with those who go down to the pit.

¹⁵" 'This is what the Sovereign LORD says: On the day it was brought down to the grave *ᵃ* I covered the deep springs with mourning for it; I held back its streams, and its abundant waters were restrained. Because of it I clothed Lebanon with gloom, and all the trees of the field withered away. ¹⁶I made the nations tremble at the sound of its fall when I brought it down to the grave with those who go down to the pit. Then all the trees of Eden, the choicest and best of Lebanon, all the trees that were well-watered, were consoled in the earth below. ¹⁷Those who lived in its shade, its allies among the nations, had also gone down to the grave with it, joining those killed by the sword.

¹⁸" 'Which of the trees of Eden can be compared with you in splendor and majesty? Yet you, too, will be

ᵃ15 Hebrew *Sheol*; also in verses 16 and 17

Life in Bible Times

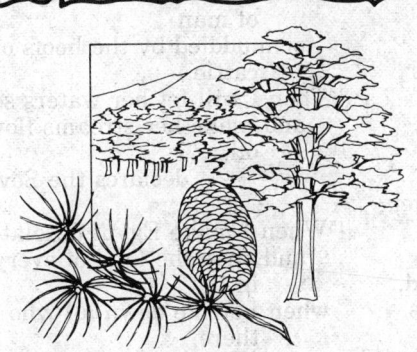

CEDARS OF LEBANON

These tall cedar trees made the best wood in the ancient world. The wood was strong and long-lasting. Insects that attack wood do not like the smell of cedar wood, but people do like it. Masts of ships as well as the walls of God's temple in Jerusalem were made from the cedar wood of Lebanon.

brought down with the trees of Eden to the earth below; you will lie among the uncircumcised, with those killed by the sword.

" 'This is Pharaoh and all his hordes, declares the Sovereign LORD.' "

A Lament for Pharaoh

32 In the twelfth year, in the twelfth month on the first day, the word of the LORD came to me: [2]"Son of man, take up a lament concerning Pharaoh king of Egypt and say to him:

" 'You are like a lion among the
nations;
you are like a monster in the
seas
thrashing about in your streams,
churning the water with your
feet
and muddying the streams.

[3]" 'This is what the Sovereign LORD says:

" 'With a great throng of people
I will cast my net over you,
and they will haul you up in
my net.
[4]I will throw you on the land
and hurl you on the open field.
I will let all the birds of the air
settle on you
and all the beasts of the earth
gorge themselves on you.
[5]I will spread your flesh on the
mountains
and fill the valleys with your
remains.
[6]I will drench the land with your
flowing blood
all the way to the mountains,
and the ravines will be filled
with your flesh.
[7]When I snuff you out, I will cover
the heavens
and darken their stars;
I will cover the sun with a cloud,
and the moon will not give its
light.

[8]All the shining lights in the
heavens
I will darken over you;
I will bring darkness over your
land,
declares the Sovereign
LORD.
[9]I will trouble the hearts of many
peoples
when I bring about your
destruction among the
nations,
among[a] lands you have not
known.
[10]I will cause many peoples to be
appalled at you,
and their kings will shudder
with horror because of you
when I brandish my sword
before them.
On the day of your downfall
each of them will tremble
every moment for his life.

[11]" 'For this is what the Sovereign LORD says:

" 'The sword of the king of
Babylon
will come against you.
[12]I will cause your hordes to fall
by the swords of mighty men—
the most ruthless of all
nations.
They will shatter the pride of
Egypt,
and all her hordes will be
overthrown.
[13]I will destroy all her cattle
from beside abundant waters
no longer to be stirred by the foot
of man
or muddied by the hoofs of
cattle.
[14]Then I will let her waters settle
and make her streams flow like
oil,
declares the Sovereign
LORD.
[15]When I make Egypt desolate
and strip the land of everything
in it,
when I strike down all who live
there,

---

[a]9 Hebrew; Septuagint *bring you into captivity among the nations, / to*

then they will know that I am the LORD.'

16"This is the lament they will chant for her. The daughters of the nations will chant it; for Egypt and all her hordes they will chant it, declares the Sovereign LORD."

17In the twelfth year, on the fifteenth day of the month, the word of the LORD came to me: 18"Son of man, wail for the hordes of Egypt and consign to the earth below both her and the daughters of mighty nations, with those who go down to the pit. 19Say to them, 'Are you more favored than others? Go down and be laid among the uncircumcised.' 20They will fall among those killed by the sword. The sword is drawn; let her be dragged off with all her hordes. 21From within the grave[a] the mighty leaders will say of Egypt and her allies, 'They have come down and they lie with the uncircumcised, with those killed by the sword.'

22"Assyria is there with her whole army; she is surrounded by the graves of all her slain, all who have fallen by the sword. 23Their graves are in the depths of the pit and her army lies around her grave. All who had spread terror in the land of the living are slain, fallen by the sword.

24"Elam is there, with all her hordes around her grave. All of them are slain, fallen by the sword. All who had spread terror in the land of the living went down uncircumcised to the earth below. They bear their shame with those who go down to the pit. 25A bed is made for her among the slain, with all her hordes around her grave. All of them are uncircumcised, killed by the sword. Because their terror had spread in the land of the living, they bear their shame with those who go down to the pit; they are laid among the slain.

26"Meshech and Tubal are there, with all their hordes around their graves. All of them are uncircumcised, killed by the sword because

they spread their terror in the land of the living. 27Do they not lie with the other uncircumcised warriors who have fallen, who went down to the grave with their weapons of war, whose swords were placed under their heads? The punishment for their sins rested on their bones, though the terror of these warriors had stalked through the land of the living.

28"You too, O Pharaoh, will be broken and will lie among the uncircumcised, with those killed by the sword.

29"Edom is there, her kings and all her princes; despite their power, they are laid with those killed by the sword. They lie with the uncircumcised, with those who go down to the pit.

30"All the princes of the north and all the Sidonians are there; they went down with the slain in disgrace despite the terror caused by their power. They lie uncircumcised with those killed by the sword and bear their shame with those who go down to the pit.

31"Pharaoh—he and all his army —will see them and he will be consoled for all his hordes that were killed by the sword, declares the Sovereign LORD. 32Although I had him spread terror in the land of the living, Pharaoh and all his hordes will be laid among the uncircumcised, with those killed by the sword, declares the Sovereign LORD."

Ezekiel a Watchman

33 The word of the LORD came to me: 2"Son of man, speak to your countrymen and say to them: 'When I bring the sword against a land, and the people of the land choose one of their men and make him their watchman, 3and he sees the sword coming against the land and blows the trumpet to warn the people, 4then if anyone hears the trumpet but does not take warning and the sword comes and takes his life,

---

a21 Hebrew *Sheol*; also in verse 27

his blood will be on his own head. ⁵Since he heard the sound of the trumpet but did not take warning, his blood will be on his own head. If he had taken warning, he would have saved himself. ⁶But if the watchman sees the sword coming and does not blow the trumpet to warn the people and the sword comes and takes the life of one of them, that man will be taken away because of his sin, but I will hold the watchman accountable for his blood.'

⁷"Son of man, I have made you a watchman for the house of Israel; so hear the word I speak and give them warning from me. ⁸When I say to the wicked, 'O wicked man, you will surely die,' and you do not speak out to dissuade him from his ways, that wicked man will die for*a* his sin, and I will hold you accountable for his blood. ⁹But if you do warn the wicked man to turn from his ways and he does not do so, he will die for his sin, but you will have saved yourself.

¹⁰"Son of man, say to the house of Israel, 'This is what you are saying: "Our offenses and sins weigh us down, and we are wasting away because of*b* them. How then can we live?"' ¹¹Say to them, 'As surely as I live, declares the Sovereign LORD, I take no pleasure in the death of the wicked, but rather that they turn from their ways and live. Turn! Turn

from your evil ways! Why will you die, O house of Israel?'

¹²"Therefore, son of man, say to your countrymen, 'The righteousness of the righteous man will not save him when he disobeys, and the wickedness of the wicked man will not cause him to fall when he turns from it. The righteous man, if he sins, will not be allowed to live because of his former righteousness.' ¹³If I tell the righteous man that he will surely live, but then he trusts in his righteousness and does evil, none of the righteous things he has done will be remembered; he will die for the evil he has done. ¹⁴And if I say to the wicked man, 'You will surely die,' but he then turns away from his sin and does what is just and right— ¹⁵if he gives back what he took in pledge for a loan, returns what he has stolen, follows the decrees that give life, and does no evil, he will surely live; he will not die. ¹⁶None of the sins he has committed will be remembered against him. He has done what is just and right; he will surely live.

¹⁷"Yet your countrymen say, 'The way of the Lord is not just.' But it is their way that is not just. ¹⁸If a righteous man turns from his righteousness and does evil, he will die for it. ¹⁹And if a wicked man turns away from his wickedness and does what is just and right, he will live by doing

a8 Or *in*; also in verse 9   *b10* Or *away in*

Life in Bible Times

WATCHMEN

Watchmen stood on the high walls of a city to watch for enemies. Their job was to warn the citizens of danger. God wanted Ezekiel to be like a watchman and warn his people of the danger in disobeying the Lord.

so. ²⁰Yet, O house of Israel, you say, 'The way of the Lord is not just.' But I will judge each of you according to his own ways."

Jerusalem's Fall Explained

²¹In the twelfth year of our exile, in the tenth month on the fifth day, a man who had escaped from Jerusalem came to me and said, "The city has fallen!" ²²Now the evening before the man arrived, the hand of the LORD was upon me, and he opened my mouth before the man came to me in the morning. So my mouth was opened and I was no longer silent.

²³Then the word of the LORD came to me: ²⁴"Son of man, the people living in those ruins in the land of Israel are saying, 'Abraham was only one man, yet he possessed the land. But we are many; surely the land has been given to us as our possession.' ²⁵Therefore say to them, 'This is what the Sovereign LORD says: Since you eat meat with the blood still in it and look to your idols and shed blood, should you then possess the land? ²⁶You rely on your sword, you do detestable things, and each of you defiles his neighbor's wife. Should you then possess the land?'

²⁷"Say this to them: 'This is what the Sovereign LORD says: As surely as I live, those who are left in the ruins will fall by the sword, those out in the country I will give to the wild animals to be devoured, and those in strongholds and caves will die of a plague. ²⁸I will make the land a desolate waste, and her proud strength will come to an end, and the mountains of Israel will become desolate so

that no one will cross them. ²⁹Then they will know that I am the LORD, when I have made the land a desolate waste because of all the detestable things they have done.'

³⁰"As for you, son of man, your countrymen are talking together about you by the walls and at the doors of the houses, saying to each other, 'Come and hear the message that has come from the LORD.' ³¹My people come to you, as they usually do, and sit before you to listen to your words, but they do not put them into practice. With their mouths they express devotion, but their hearts are greedy for unjust gain. ³²Indeed, to them you are nothing more than one who sings love songs with a beautiful voice and plays an instrument well, for they hear your words but do not put them into practice.

³³"When all this comes true—and it surely will—then they will know that a prophet has been among them."

Shepherds and Sheep

34 The word of the LORD came to me: ²"Son of man, prophesy against the shepherds of Israel; prophesy and say to them: 'This is what the Sovereign LORD says: Woe to the shepherds of Israel who only take care of themselves! Should not shepherds take care of the flock? ³You eat the curds, clothe yourselves with the wool and slaughter the choice animals, but you do not take care of the flock. ⁴You have not strengthened the weak or healed the sick or bound up the injured. You have not brought back the strays or

---

▚ET'S LIVE IT!   Ezekiel 33:14–16

A PROMISE FOR THE WICKED ➡ Ezekiel brought good news to God's people. Even a wicked person can change, and God will accept him or her. Read the good news Ezekiel brought in Ezekiel 33:14–16.

You can bring good news to others too. Tell them about Jesus. Invite them to Church school where they will learn more about him. You can help them know that God loves and forgives by being loving and forgiving to them.

searched for the lost. You have ruled them harshly and brutally. 5So they were scattered because there was no shepherd, and when they were scattered they became food for all the wild animals. 6My sheep wandered over all the mountains and on every high hill. They were scattered over the whole earth, and no one searched or looked for them.

7"'Therefore, you shepherds, hear the word of the LORD: 8As surely as I live, declares the Sovereign LORD, because my flock lacks a shepherd and so has been plundered and has become food for all the wild animals, and because my shepherds did not search for my flock but cared for themselves rather than for my flock, 9therefore, O shepherds, hear the word of the LORD: 10This is what the Sovereign LORD says: I am against the shepherds and will hold them accountable for my flock. I will remove them from tending the flock so that the shepherds can no longer feed themselves. I will rescue my flock from their mouths, and it will no longer be food for them.

11"'For this is what the Sovereign LORD says: I myself will search for my sheep and look after them. 12As a shepherd looks after his scattered flock when he is with them, so will I look after my sheep. I will rescue them from all the places where they were scattered on a day of clouds and darkness. 13I will bring them out from the nations and gather them from the countries, and I will bring them into their own land. I will pasture them on the mountains of Israel, in the ravines and in all the settlements in the land. 14I will tend them in a good pasture, and the mountain heights of Israel will be their grazing land. There they will lie down in good grazing land, and there they will feed in a rich pasture on the mountains of Israel. 15I myself will tend my sheep and have them lie down, declares the Sovereign LORD. 16I will search for the lost and bring back the strays. I

will bind up the injured and strengthen the weak, but the sleek and the strong I will destroy. I will shepherd the flock with justice.

17"'As for you, my flock, this is what the Sovereign LORD says: I will judge between one sheep and another, and between rams and goats. 18Is it not enough for you to feed on the good pasture? Must you also trample the rest of your pasture with your feet? Is it not enough for you to drink clear water? Must you also muddy the rest with your feet? 19Must my flock feed on what you have trampled and drink what you have muddied with your feet?

20"'Therefore this is what the Sovereign LORD says to them: See, I myself will judge between the fat sheep and the lean sheep. 21Because you shove with flank and shoulder, butting all the weak sheep with your horns until you have driven them away, 22I will save my flock, and they will no longer be plundered. I will judge between one sheep and another. 23I will place over them one shepherd, my servant David, and he will tend them; he will tend them and be their shepherd. 24I the LORD will be their God, and my servant David will be prince among them. I the LORD have spoken.

25"'I will make a covenant of peace with them and rid the land of wild beasts so that they may live in the desert and sleep in the forests in safety. 26I will bless them and the places surrounding my hill.a I will send down showers in season; there will be showers of blessing. 27The trees of the field will yield their fruit and the ground will yield its crops; the people will be secure in their land. They will know that I am the LORD, when I break the bars of their yoke and rescue them from the hands of those who enslaved them. 28They will no longer be plundered by the nations, nor will wild animals devour them. They will live in safety, and no one will make them afraid. 29I will provide for them

a26 Or I will make them and the places surrounding my hill a blessing a land renowned for its crops, and they will no longer be victims of famine in the land or bear the scorn of the nations. ³⁰Then they will know that I, the LORD their God, am with them and that they, the house of Israel, are my people, declares the Sovereign LORD. ³¹You my sheep, the sheep of my pasture, are people, and I am your God, declares the Sovereign LORD.' "

A Prophecy Against Edom

35 The word of the LORD came to me: ²"Son of man, set your face against Mount Seir; prophesy against it ³and say: 'This is what the Sovereign LORD says: I am against you, Mount Seir, and I will stretch out my hand against you and make you a desolate waste. ⁴I will turn your towns into ruins and you will be desolate. Then you will know that I am the LORD.

⁵" 'Because you harbored an ancient hostility and delivered the Israelites over to the sword at the time of their calamity, the time their punishment reached its climax, ⁶therefore as surely as I live, declares the Sovereign LORD, I will give you over to bloodshed and it will pursue you. Since you did not hate bloodshed, bloodshed will pursue you. ⁷I will make Mount Seir a desolate waste and cut off from it all who come and go. ⁸I will fill your mountains with the slain; those killed by the sword will fall on your hills and in your valleys and in all your ravines. ⁹I will make you desolate forever; your towns will not be inhabited. Then you will know that I am the LORD.

¹⁰" 'Because you have said, "These two nations and countries will be ours and we will take possession of them," even though I the LORD was there, ¹¹therefore as surely as I live, declares the Sovereign LORD, I will treat you in accordance with the anger and jealousy you showed in your hatred of them and I will make myself known among them when I judge you. ¹²Then you will know that I the LORD have heard all the contemptible

things you have said against the mountains of Israel. You said, "They have been laid waste and have been given over to us to devour." ¹³You boasted against me and spoke against me without restraint, and I heard it. ¹⁴This is what the Sovereign LORD says: While the whole earth rejoices, I will make you desolate. ¹⁵Because you rejoiced when the inheritance of the house of Israel became desolate, that is how I will treat you. You will be desolate, O Mount Seir, you and all of Edom. Then they will know that I am the LORD.' "

A Prophecy to the Mountains of Israel

36 "Son of man, prophesy to the mountains of Israel and say, 'O mountains of Israel, hear the word of the LORD. ²This is what the Sovereign LORD says: The enemy said of you, "Aha! The ancient heights have become our possession." ' ³Therefore prophesy and say, 'This is what the Sovereign LORD says: Because they ravaged and hounded you from every side so that you became the possession of the rest of the nations and the object of people's malicious talk and slander, ⁴therefore, O mountains of Israel, hear the word of the Sovereign LORD: This is what the Sovereign LORD says to the mountains and hills, to the ravines and valleys, to the desolate ruins and the deserted towns that have been plundered and ridiculed by the rest of the nations around you— ⁵this is what the Sovereign LORD says: In my burning zeal I have spoken against the rest of the nations, and against all Edom, for with glee and with malice in their hearts they made my land their own possession so that they might plunder its pastureland.' ⁶Therefore prophesy concerning the land of Israel and say to the mountains and hills, to the ravines and valleys: 'This is what the Sovereign LORD says: I speak in my jealous wrath because you have suffered the scorn of the nations. ⁷Therefore this is what the Sovereign LORD says: I swear with uplifted hand that the nations around you will also suffer scorn.

8" 'But you, O mountains of Israel, will produce branches and fruit for my people Israel, for they will soon come home. 9I am concerned for you and will look on you with favor; you will be plowed and sown, 10and I will multiply the number of people upon you, even the whole house of Israel. The towns will be inhabited and the ruins rebuilt. 11I will increase the number of men and animals upon you, and they will be fruitful and become numerous. I will settle people on you as in the past and will make you prosper more than before. Then you will know that I am the LORD. 12I will cause people, my people Israel, to walk upon you. They will possess you, and you will be their inheritance; you will never again deprive them of their children.

13" 'This is what the Sovereign LORD says: Because people say to you, "You devour men and deprive your nation of its children," 14therefore you will no longer devour men or make your nation childless, declares the Sovereign LORD. 15No longer will I make you hear the taunts of the nations, and no longer will you suffer the scorn of the peoples or cause your nation to fall, declares the Sovereign LORD.' "

16Again the word of the LORD came to me: 17"Son of man, when the people of Israel were living in their own land, they defiled it by their conduct and their actions. Their conduct was like a woman's monthly uncleanness in my sight. 18So I poured out my wrath on them because they had shed blood in the land and because they had defiled it with their idols. 19I dispersed them among the nations, and they were scattered through the countries; I judged them according to their conduct and their actions. 20And wherever they went among the nations they profaned my holy name, for it was said of them, 'These are the LORD's people, and yet they had to leave his land.' 21I had concern for my holy name, which the house of Israel profaned among the nations where they had gone.

22"Therefore say to the house of Israel, 'This is what the Sovereign LORD says: It is not for your sake, O house of Israel, that I am going to do these things, but for the sake of my holy name, which you have profaned among the nations where you have gone. 23I will show the holiness of my great name, which has been profaned among the nations, the name you have profaned among them. Then the nations will know that I am the LORD, declares the Sovereign LORD, when I show myself holy through you before their eyes.

24" 'For I will take you out of the nations; I will gather you from all the countries and bring you back into your own land. 25I will sprinkle clean water on you, and you will be clean; I will cleanse you from all your impurities and from all your idols. 26I will give you a new heart and put a new spirit in you; I will remove from you your heart of stone and give you a heart of flesh. 27And I will put my Spirit in you and move you to follow my decrees and be careful to keep my laws. 28You will live in the land I gave your forefathers; you will be my people, and I will be your God. 29I will save you from all your uncleanness. I will call for the grain and make it plentiful and will not bring famine upon you. 30I will increase the fruit of the trees and the crops of the field, so that you will no longer suffer disgrace among the nations because of famine. 31Then you will remember your evil ways and wicked deeds, and you will loathe yourselves for your sins and detestable practices. 32I want you to know that I am not doing this for your sake, declares the Sovereign LORD. Be ashamed and disgraced for your conduct, O house of Israel!

33" 'This is what the Sovereign LORD says: On the day I cleanse you from all your sins, I will resettle your towns, and the ruins will be rebuilt. 34The desolate land will be cultivated instead of lying desolate in the sight of all who pass through it. 35They will say, "This land that was laid waste has become like the garden of Eden; the cities that were lying in ruins, desolate and destroyed, are now fortified and inhabited." 36Then the nations around you that remain will know that I the LORD have rebuilt what was destroyed and have replanted what was desolate. I the LORD have spoken, and I will do it.'

37"This is what the Sovereign LORD says: Once again I will yield to the plea of the house of Israel and do this for them: I will make their people as numerous as sheep, 38as numerous as the flocks for offerings at Jerusalem during her appointed feasts. So will the ruined cities be filled with flocks of people. Then they will know that I am the LORD."

The Valley of Dry Bones

37 The hand of the LORD was upon me, and he brought me out by the Spirit of the LORD and set me in the middle of a valley; it was full of bones. 2He led me back and forth among them, and I saw a great many bones on the floor of the valley, bones that were very dry. 3He asked me, "Son of man, can these bones live?"

I said, "O Sovereign LORD, you alone know."

4Then he said to me, "Prophesy to these bones and say to them, 'Dry bones, hear the word of the LORD! 5This is what the Sovereign LORD says to these bones: I will make breath^a enter you, and you will come to life. 6I will attach tendons to you and make flesh come upon you and cover you with skin; I will put breath in you, and you will come to life. Then you will know that I am the LORD.'"

7So I prophesied as I was commanded. And as I was prophesying, there was a noise, a rattling sound, and the bones came together, bone to bone. 8I looked, and tendons and flesh appeared on them and skin covered

them, but there was no breath in them.

9Then he said to me, "Prophesy to the breath; prophesy, son of man, and say to it, 'This is what the Sovereign LORD says: Come from the four winds, O breath, and breathe into these slain, that they may live.'" 10So I prophesied as he commanded me, and breath entered them; they came to life and stood up on their feet—a vast army.

? **DID YOU KNOW?**   37:1

What was the valley of dry bones?

In Ezekiel's vision, this valley represented the whole world. The dry bones represented the Jewish people, who were scattered through the world without any hope of a land of their own. God showed Ezekiel that someday the Jewish people would come back to Israel. Fifty years later King Cyrus permitted the Jewish people to return to Palestine. Recently, again, many people began moving to Israel, and in 1948 they became a nation again.

11Then he said to me: "Son of man, these bones are the whole house of Israel. They say, 'Our bones are dried up and our hope is gone; we are cut off.' 12Therefore prophesy and say to them: 'This is what the Sovereign LORD says: O my people, I am going to open your graves and bring you up from them; I will bring you back to the land of Israel. 13Then you, my people, will know that I am the LORD, when I open your graves and bring you up from them. 14I will put my Spirit in you and you will live, and I will settle you in your own land. Then you will know that I the LORD have spoken, and I have done it, declares the LORD.'"

---

a5 The Hebrew for this word can also mean wind *or* spirit *(see verses 6-14).*

One Nation Under One King

¹⁵The word of the LORD came to me: ¹⁶"Son of man, take a stick of wood and write on it, 'Belonging to Judah and the Israelites associated with him.' Then take another stick of wood, and write on it, 'Ephraim's stick, belonging to Joseph and all the house of Israel associated with him.' ¹⁷Join them together into one stick so that they will become one in your hand.

¹⁸"When your countrymen ask you, 'Won't you tell us what you mean by this?' ¹⁹say to them, 'This is what the Sovereign LORD says: I am going to take the stick of Joseph—which is in Ephraim's hand—and of the Israelite tribes associated with him, and join it to Judah's stick, making them a single stick of wood, and they will become one in my hand.' ²⁰Hold before their eyes the sticks you have written on ²¹and say to them, 'This is what the Sovereign LORD says: I will take the Israelites out of the nations where they have gone. I will gather them from all around and bring them back into their own land. ²²I will make them one nation in the land, on the mountains of Israel. There will be one king over all of them and they will never again be two nations or be divided into two kingdoms. ²³They will no longer defile themselves with their idols and vile images or with any of their offenses, for I will save them from all their sinful backsliding,ᵃ and I will cleanse them. They will be my people, and I will be their God.

²⁴" 'My servant David will be king over them, and they will all have one shepherd. They will follow my laws and be careful to keep my decrees. ²⁵They will live in the land I gave to my servant Jacob, the land where your fathers lived. They and their children and their children's children will live there forever, and David my servant will be their prince forever.

²⁶I will make a covenant of peace with them; it will be an everlasting covenant. I will establish them and increase their numbers, and I will put my sanctuary among them forever. ²⁷My dwelling place will be with them; I will be their God, and they will be my people. ²⁸Then the nations will know that I the LORD make Israel holy, when my sanctuary is among them forever.' "

A Prophecy Against Gog

38 The word of the LORD came to me: ²"Son of man, set your face against Gog, of the land of Magog, the chief prince ofᵇ Meshech and Tubal; prophesy against him ³and say: 'This is what the Sovereign LORD says: I am against you, O Gog, chief prince ofᶜ Meshech and Tubal. ⁴I will turn you around, put hooks in your jaws and bring you out with your whole army—your horses, your horsemen fully armed, and a great horde with large and small shields, all of them brandishing their swords. ⁵Persia, Cushᵈ and Put will be with them, all with shields and helmets, ⁶also Gomer with all its troops, and Beth Togarmah from the far north with all its troops—the many nations with you.

⁷" 'Get ready; be prepared, you and all the hordes gathered about you, and take command of them. ⁸After many days you will be called to arms. In future years you will invade a land that has recovered from war, whose people were gathered from many nations to the mountains of Israel, which had long been desolate. They had been brought out from the nations, and now all of them live in safety. ⁹You and all your troops and the many nations with you will go up, advancing like a storm; you will be like a cloud covering the land.

¹⁰" 'This is what the Sovereign LORD says: On that day thoughts will come into your mind and you will de-

---

ᵃ23 Many Hebrew manuscripts (see also Septuagint); most Hebrew manuscripts *all their dwelling places where they sinned*   ᵇ2 Or *the prince of Rosh,*   ᶜ3 Or *Gog, prince of Rosh,*   ᵈ5 That is, the upper Nile region

vise an evil scheme. [11]You will say, "I will invade a land of unwalled villages; I will attack a peaceful and unsuspecting people—all of them living without walls and without gates and bars. [12]I will plunder and loot and turn my hand against the resettled ruins and the people gathered from the nations, rich in livestock and goods, living at the center of the land." [13]Sheba and Dedan and the merchants of Tarshish and all her villages[a] will say to you, "Have you come to plunder? Have you gathered your hordes to loot, to carry off silver and gold, to take away livestock and goods and to seize much plunder?"'

[14]"Therefore, son of man, prophesy and say to Gog: 'This is what the Sovereign LORD says: In that day, when my people Israel are living in safety, will you not take notice of it? [15]You will come from your place in the far north, you and many nations with you, all of them riding on horses, a great horde, a mighty army. [16]You will advance against my people Israel like a cloud that covers the land. In days to come, O Gog, I will bring you against my land, so that the nations may know me when I show myself holy through you before their eyes.

[17]"'This is what the Sovereign LORD says: Are you not the one I spoke of in former days by my servants the prophets of Israel? At that time they prophesied for years that I would bring you against them. [18]This is what will happen in that day: When Gog attacks the land of Israel, my hot anger will be aroused, declares the Sovereign LORD. [19]In my zeal and fiery wrath I declare that at that time there shall be a great earthquake in the land of Israel. [20]The fish of the sea, the birds of the air, the beasts of the field, every creature that moves along the ground, and all the people on the face of the earth will tremble at my presence. The mountains will be overturned, the cliffs will crumble and every wall will fall to the ground. [21]I will summon a sword against Gog on all my mountains, declares the Sovereign LORD. Every man's sword will be against his brother. [22]I will execute judgment upon him with plague and bloodshed; I will pour down torrents of rain, hailstones and burning sulfur on him and on his troops and on the many nations with him. [23]And so I will show my greatness and my holiness, and I will make myself known in the sight of many nations. Then they will know that I am the LORD.'

39 "Son of man, prophesy against Gog and say: 'This is what the Sovereign LORD says: I am against you, O Gog, chief prince of[b] Meshech and Tubal. [2]I will turn you around and drag you along. I will bring you from the far north and send you against the mountains of Israel. [3]Then I will strike your bow from your left hand and make your arrows drop from your right hand. [4]On the mountains of Israel you will fall, you and all your troops and the nations with you. I will give you as food to all kinds of carrion birds and to the wild animals. [5]You will fall in the open field, for I have spoken, declares the Sovereign LORD. [6]I will send fire on Magog and on those who live in safety in the coastlands, and they will know that I am the LORD.

[7]"'I will make known my holy name among my people Israel. I will no longer let my holy name be profaned, and the nations will know that I the LORD am the Holy One in Israel. [8]It is coming! It will surely take place, declares the Sovereign LORD. This is the day I have spoken of.

[9]"'Then those who live in the towns of Israel will go out and use the weapons for fuel and burn them up —the small and large shields, the bows and arrows, the war clubs and spears. For seven years they will use them for fuel. [10]They will not need to gather wood from the fields or cut it from the forests, because they will use the weapons for fuel. And they will plunder those who plundered

---

[a]13 Or *her strong lions*   [b]1 Or *Gog, prince of Rosh,*

them and loot those who looted them, declares the Sovereign LORD.

11"'On that day I will give Gog a burial place in Israel, in the valley of those who travel east toward[a] the Sea.[b] It will block the way of travelers, because Gog and all his hordes will be buried there. So it will be called the Valley of Hamon Gog.[c]

12"'For seven months the house of Israel will be burying them in order to cleanse the land. 13All the people of the land will bury them, and the day I am glorified will be a memorable day for them, declares the Sovereign LORD.

14"'Men will be regularly employed to cleanse the land. Some will go throughout the land and, in addition to them, others will bury those that remain on the ground. At the end of the seven months they will begin their search. 15As they go through the land and one of them sees a human bone, he will set up a marker beside it until the gravediggers have buried it in the Valley of Hamon Gog. 16(Also a town called Hamonah[d] will be there.) And so they will cleanse the land.'

17"Son of man, this is what the Sovereign LORD says: Call out to every kind of bird and all the wild animals: 'Assemble and come together from all around to the sacrifice I am preparing for you, the great sacrifice on the mountains of Israel. There you will eat flesh and drink blood. 18You will eat the flesh of mighty men and drink the blood of the princes of the earth as if they were rams and lambs, goats and bulls—all of them fattened animals from Bashan. 19At the sacrifice I am preparing for you, you will eat fat till you are glutted and drink blood till you are drunk. 20At my table you will eat your fill of horses and riders, mighty men and soldiers of every kind,' declares the Sovereign LORD.

21"I will display my glory among the nations, and all the nations will see the punishment I inflict and the hand I lay upon them. 22From that day forward the house of Israel will know that I am the LORD their God. 23And the nations will know that the people of Israel went into exile for their sin, because they were unfaithful to me. So I hid my face from them and handed them over to their enemies, and they all fell by the sword. 24I dealt with them according to their uncleanness and their offenses, and I hid my face from them.

25"Therefore this is what the Sovereign LORD says: I will now bring Jacob back from captivity[e] and will have compassion on all the people of Israel, and I will be zealous for my holy name. 26They will forget their shame and all the unfaithfulness they showed toward me when they lived in safety in their land with no one to make them afraid. 27When I have brought them back from the nations and have gathered them from the countries of their enemies, I will show myself holy through them in the sight of many nations. 28Then they will know that I am the LORD their God, for though I sent them into exile among the nations, I will gather them to their own land, not leaving any behind. 29I will no longer hide my face from them, for I will pour out my Spirit on the house of Israel, declares the Sovereign LORD."

The New Temple Area

40 In the twenty-fifth year of our exile, at the beginning of the year, on the tenth of the month, in the fourteenth year after the fall of the city—on that very day the hand of the LORD was upon me and he took me there. 2In visions of God he took me to the land of Israel and set me on a very high mountain, on whose south side were some buildings that looked like a city. 3He took me there, and I saw a man whose appearance was like bronze; he was standing in

---

a11 Or of   b11 That is, the Dead Sea   c11 Hamon Gog means hordes of Gog.
d16 Hamonah means horde.   e25 Or now restore the fortunes of Jacob

the gateway with a linen cord and a measuring rod in his hand. ⁴The man said to me, "Son of man, look with your eyes and hear with your ears and pay attention to everything I am going to show you, for that is why you have been brought here. Tell the house of Israel everything you see."

The East Gate to the Outer Court

⁵I saw a wall completely surrounding the temple area. The length of the measuring rod in the man's hand was six long cubits, each of which was a cubit[a] and a handbreadth.[b] He measured the wall; it was one measuring rod thick and one rod high.

⁶Then he went to the gate facing east. He climbed its steps and measured the threshold of the gate; it was one rod deep.[c] ⁷The alcoves for the guards were one rod long and one rod wide, and the projecting walls between the alcoves were five cubits thick. And the threshold of the gate next to the portico facing the temple was one rod deep.

⁸Then he measured the portico of the gateway; ⁹it[d] was eight cubits deep and its jambs were two cubits thick. The portico of the gateway faced the temple.

¹⁰Inside the east gate were three alcoves on each side; the three had the same measurements, and the faces of the projecting walls on each side had the same measurements. ¹¹Then he measured the width of the entrance to the gateway; it was ten cubits and its length was thirteen cubits. ¹²In front of each alcove was a wall one cubit high, and the alcoves were six cubits square. ¹³Then he measured the gateway from the top of the rear wall of one alcove to the top of the opposite one; the distance was twenty-five cubits from one parapet opening to the opposite one. ¹⁴He measured along the faces of the projecting walls all around the inside of the gateway—sixty cubits. The measurement was up to the portico[e] facing the courtyard.[f] ¹⁵The distance from the entrance of the gateway to the far end of its portico was fifty cubits. ¹⁶The alcoves and the projecting walls inside the gateway were surmounted by narrow parapet openings all around, as was the portico; the openings all around faced inward. The faces of the projecting walls were decorated with palm trees.

The Outer Court

¹⁷Then he brought me into the outer court. There I saw some rooms and a pavement that had been constructed all around the court; there were thirty rooms along the pavement. ¹⁸It abutted the sides of the gateways and was as wide as they were long; this was the lower pavement. ¹⁹Then he measured the distance from the inside of the lower gateway to the outside of the inner court; it was a hundred cubits on the east side as well as on the north.

The North Gate

²⁰Then he measured the length and width of the gate facing north, leading into the outer court. ²¹Its alcoves—three on each side—its projecting walls and its portico had the same measurements as those of the first gateway. It was fifty cubits long and twenty-five cubits wide. ²²Its openings, its portico and its palm tree decorations had the same measurements as those of the gate facing east. Seven steps led up to it, with its portico opposite them. ²³There was a gate to the inner court facing the north gate, just as there was on the east. He measured from one gate to the opposite one; it was a hundred cubits.

---

a5 The common cubit was about 1 1/2 feet (about 0.5 meter).   b5 That is, about 3 inches (about 8 centimeters)   c6 Septuagint; Hebrew deep, the first threshold, one rod deep   d8,9 Many Hebrew manuscripts, Septuagint, Vulgate and Syriac; most Hebrew manuscripts gateway facing the temple; it was one rod deep. 9Then he measured the portico of the gateway; it   e14 Septuagint; Hebrew projecting wall   f14 The meaning of the Hebrew for this verse is uncertain.

The South Gate

24Then he led me to the south side and I saw a gate facing south. He measured its jambs and its portico, and they had the same measurements as the others. 25The gateway and its portico had narrow openings all around, like the openings of the others. It was fifty cubits long and twenty-five cubits wide. 26Seven steps led up to it, with its portico opposite them; it had palm tree decorations on the faces of the projecting walls on each side. 27The inner court also had a gate facing south, and he measured from this gate to the outer gate on the south side; it was a hundred cubits.

Gates to the Inner Court

28Then he brought me into the inner court through the south gate, and he measured the south gate; it had the same measurements as the others. 29Its alcoves, its projecting walls and its portico had the same measurements as the others. The gateway and its portico had openings all around. It was fifty cubits long and twenty-five cubits wide. 30(The porticoes of the gateways around the inner court were twenty-five cubits wide and five cubits deep.) 31Its portico faced the outer court; palm trees decorated its jambs, and eight steps led up to it.

32Then he brought me to the inner court on the east side, and he measured the gateway; it had the same measurements as the others. 33Its alcoves, its projecting walls and its portico had the same measurements as the others. The gateway and its portico had openings all around. It was fifty cubits long and twenty-five cubits wide. 34Its portico faced the outer court; palm trees decorated the jambs on either side, and eight steps led up to it.

35Then he brought me to the north gate and measured it. It had the same measurements as the others, 36as did its alcoves, its projecting walls and its portico, and it had openings all around. It was fifty cubits long and twenty-five cubits wide. 37Its portico*a* faced the outer court; palm trees decorated the jambs on either side, and eight steps led up to it.

The Rooms for Preparing Sacrifices

38A room with a doorway was by the portico in each of the inner gateways, where the burnt offerings were washed. 39In the portico of the gateway were two tables on each side, on which the burnt offerings, sin offerings and guilt offerings were slaughtered. 40By the outside wall of the portico of the gateway, near the steps at the entrance to the north gateway were two tables, and on the other side of the steps were two tables. 41So there were four tables on one side of the gateway and four on the other —eight tables in all—on which the sacrifices were slaughtered. 42There were also four tables of dressed stone for the burnt offerings, each a cubit and a half long, a cubit and a half wide and a cubit high. On them were placed the utensils for slaughtering the burnt offerings and the other sacrifices. 43And double-pronged hooks, each a handbreadth long, were attached to the wall all around. The tables were for the flesh of the offerings.

Rooms for the Priests

44Outside the inner gate, within the inner court, were two rooms, one*b* at the side of the north gate and facing south, and another at the side of the south*c* gate and facing north. 45He said to me, "The room facing south is for the priests who have charge of the temple, 46and the room facing north is for the priests who have charge of the altar. These are the sons of Zadok, who are the only

---

*a*37 Septuagint (see also verses 31 and 34); Hebrew *jambs for singers, which were*   *c*44 Septuagint; Hebrew *east*   *b*44 Septuagint; Hebrew *were rooms*

Levites who may draw near to the LORD to minister before him."

47Then he measured the court: It was square—a hundred cubits long and a hundred cubits wide. And the altar was in front of the temple.

The Temple

48He brought me to the portico of the temple and measured the jambs of the portico; they were five cubits wide on either side. The width of the entrance was fourteen cubits and its projecting walls were[a] three cubits wide on either side. 49The portico was twenty cubits wide, and twelve[b] cubits from front to back. It was reached by a flight of stairs,[c] and there were pillars on each side of the jambs.

41 Then the man brought me to the outer sanctuary and measured the jambs; the width of the jambs was six cubits[d] on each side.[e] 2The entrance was ten cubits wide, and the projecting walls on each side of it were five cubits wide. He also measured the outer sanctuary; it was forty cubits long and twenty cubits wide.

3Then he went into the inner sanctuary and measured the jambs of the entrance; each was two cubits wide. The entrance was six cubits wide, and the projecting walls on each side of it were seven cubits wide. 4And he measured the length of the inner sanctuary; it was twenty cubits, and its width was twenty cubits across the end of the outer sanctuary. He said to me, "This is the Most Holy Place."

5Then he measured the wall of the temple; it was six cubits thick, and each side room around the temple was four cubits wide. 6The side rooms were on three levels, one above another, thirty on each level. There were ledges all around the wall of the temple to serve as supports for the side rooms, so that the supports were

not inserted into the wall of the temple. 7The side rooms all around the temple were wider at each successive level. The structure surrounding the temple was built in ascending stages, so that the rooms widened as one went upward. A stairway went up from the lowest floor to the top floor through the middle floor.

8I saw that the temple had a raised base all around it, forming the foundation of the side rooms. It was the length of the rod, six long cubits. 9The outer wall of the side rooms was five cubits thick. The open area between the side rooms of the temple 10and the ⌊priests'⌋ rooms was twenty cubits wide all around the temple. 11There were entrances to the side rooms from the open area, one on the north and another on the south; and the base adjoining the open area was five cubits wide all around.

12The building facing the temple courtyard on the west side was seventy cubits wide. The wall of the building was five cubits thick all around, and its length was ninety cubits.

13Then he measured the temple; it was a hundred cubits long, and the temple courtyard and the building with its walls were also a hundred cubits long. 14The width of the temple courtyard on the east, including the front of the temple, was a hundred cubits.

15Then he measured the length of the building facing the courtyard at the rear of the temple, including its galleries on each side; it was a hundred cubits.

The outer sanctuary, the inner sanctuary and the portico facing the court, 16as well as the thresholds and the narrow windows and galleries around the three of them—everything beyond and including the threshold was covered with wood. The floor, the wall up to the windows, and the windows were covered. 17In the space above the outside of the en-

---

trance to the inner sanctuary and on the walls at regular intervals all around the inner and outer sanctuary [18]were carved cherubim and palm trees. Palm trees alternated with cherubim. Each cherub had two faces: [19]the face of a man toward the palm tree on one side and the face of a lion toward the palm tree on the other. They were carved all around the whole temple. [20]From the floor to the area above the entrance, cherubim and palm trees were carved on the wall of the outer sanctuary.

[21]The outer sanctuary had a rectangular doorframe, and the one at the front of the Most Holy Place was similar. [22]There was a wooden altar three cubits high and two cubits square[a]; its corners, its base[b] and its sides were of wood. The man said to me, "This is the table that is before the Lord." [23]Both the outer sanctuary and the Most Holy Place had double doors. [24]Each door had two leaves—two hinged leaves for each door. [25]And on the doors of the outer sanctuary were carved cherubim and palm trees like those carved on the walls, and there was a wooden overhang on the front of the portico. [26]On the sidewalls of the portico were narrow windows with palm trees carved on each side. The side rooms of the temple also had overhangs.

Rooms for the Priests

42 Then the man led me northward into the outer court and brought me to the rooms opposite the temple courtyard and opposite the outer wall on the north side. [2]The building whose door faced north was a hundred cubits[c] long and fifty cubits wide. [3]Both in the section twenty cubits from the inner court and in the section opposite the pavement of the outer court, gallery faced gallery at the three levels. [4]In front of the rooms was an inner passageway ten cubits wide and a hundred cubits[d]

long. Their doors were on the north. [5]Now the upper rooms were narrower, for the galleries took more space from them than from the rooms on the lower and middle floors of the building. [6]The rooms on the third floor had no pillars, as the courts had; so they were smaller in floor space than those on the lower and middle floors. [7]There was an outer wall parallel to the rooms and the outer court; it extended in front of the rooms for fifty cubits. [8]While the row of rooms on the side next to the outer court was fifty cubits long, the row on the side nearest the sanctuary was a hundred cubits long. [9]The lower rooms had an entrance on the east side as one enters them from the outer court.

[10]On the south side[e] along the length of the wall of the outer court, adjoining the temple courtyard and opposite the outer wall, were rooms [11]with a passageway in front of them. These were like the rooms on the north; they had the same length and width, with similar exits and dimensions. Similar to the doorways on the north [12]were the doorways of the rooms on the south. There was a doorway at the beginning of the passageway that was parallel to the corresponding wall extending eastward, by which one enters the rooms.

[13]Then he said to me, "The north and south rooms facing the temple courtyard are the priests' rooms, where the priests who approach the Lord will eat the most holy offerings. There they will put the most holy offerings—the grain offerings, the sin offerings and the guilt offerings—for the place is holy. [14]Once the priests enter the holy precincts, they are not to go into the outer court until they leave behind the garments in which they minister, for these are holy. They are to put on other clothes before they go near the places that are for the people."

---

[a]22 Septuagint; Hebrew long   [b]22 Septuagint; Hebrew length   [c]2 The common cubit was about 1 1/2 feet (about 0.5 meter).   [d]4 Septuagint and Syriac; Hebrew and one cubit   [e]10 Septuagint; Hebrew Eastward

[15]When he had finished measuring what was inside the temple area, he led me out by the east gate and measured the area all around: [16]He measured the east side with the measuring rod; it was five hundred cubits.[a] [17]He measured the north side; it was five hundred cubits[b] by the measuring rod. [18]He measured the south side; it was five hundred cubits by the measuring rod. [19]Then he turned to the west side and measured; it was five hundred cubits by the measuring rod. [20]So he measured the area on all four sides. It had a wall around it, five hundred cubits long and five hundred cubits wide, to separate the holy from the common.

The Glory Returns to the Temple

43 Then the man brought me to the gate facing east, [2]and I saw the glory of the God of Israel coming from the east. His voice was like the roar of rushing waters, and the land was radiant with his glory. [3]The vision I saw was like the vision I had seen when he[c] came to destroy the city and like the visions I had seen by the Kebar River, and I fell facedown. [4]The glory of the LORD entered the temple through the gate facing east. [5]Then the Spirit lifted me up and brought me into the inner court, and the glory of the LORD filled the temple.

[6]While the man was standing beside me, I heard someone speaking to me from inside the temple. [7]He said: "Son of man, this is the place of my throne and the place for the soles of my feet. This is where I will live among the Israelites forever. The house of Israel will never again defile my holy name—neither they nor their kings—by their prostitution[d] and the lifeless idols[e] of their kings at their high places. [8]When they placed their threshold next to my threshold and their doorposts beside my doorposts, with only a wall between me and them, they defiled my holy name by their detestable practices. So I destroyed them in my anger. [9]Now let them put away from me their prostitution and the lifeless idols of their kings, and I will live among them forever.

[10]"Son of man, describe the temple to the people of Israel, that they may be ashamed of their sins. Let them consider the plan, [11]and if they are ashamed of all they have done, make known to them the design of the temple—its arrangement, its exits and entrances—its whole design and all its regulations[f] and laws. Write these down before them so that they may be faithful to its design and follow all its regulations.

[12]"This is the law of the temple: All the surrounding area on top of the mountain will be most holy. Such is the law of the temple.

The Altar

[13]"These are the measurements of the altar in long cubits, that cubit being a cubit[g] and a handbreadth[h]: Its gutter is a cubit deep and a cubit wide, with a rim of one span[i] around the edge. And this is the height of the altar: [14]From the gutter on the ground up to the lower ledge it is two cubits high and a cubit wide, and from the smaller ledge up to the larger ledge it is four cubits high and a cubit wide. [15]The altar hearth is four cubits high, and four horns project upward from the hearth. [16]The altar hearth is square, twelve cubits long and twelve cubits wide. [17]The upper ledge also is square, fourteen cubits long and fourteen cubits wide, with a rim of half a cubit and a gutter of a cubit all around. The steps of the altar face east."

---

[a]16 See Septuagint of verse 17; Hebrew *rods*; also in verses 18 and 19.   [b]17 Septuagint; Hebrew *rods*   [c]3 Some Hebrew manuscripts and Vulgate; most Hebrew manuscripts *I*   [d]7 Or *their spiritual adultery*; also in verse 9   [e]7 Or *the corpses*; also in verse 9   [f]11 Some Hebrew manuscripts and Septuagint; most Hebrew manuscripts *regulations and its whole design*   [g]13 The common cubit was about 1 1/2 feet (about 0.5 meter).   [h]13 That is, about 3 inches (about 8 centimeters)   [i]13 That is, about 9 inches (about 22 centimeters)

18Then he said to me, "Son of man, this is what the Sovereign LORD says: These will be the regulations for sacrificing burnt offerings and sprinkling blood upon the altar when it is built: 19You are to give a young bull as a sin offering to the priests, who are Levites, of the family of Zadok, who come near to minister before me, declares the Sovereign LORD. 20You are to take some of its blood and put it on the four horns of the altar and on the four corners of the upper ledge and all around the rim, and so purify the altar and make atonement for it. 21You are to take the bull for the sin offering and burn it in the designated part of the temple area outside the sanctuary.

22"On the second day you are to offer a male goat without defect for a sin offering, and the altar is to be purified as it was purified with the bull. 23When you have finished purifying it, you are to offer a young bull and a ram from the flock, both without defect. 24You are to offer them before the LORD, and the priests are to sprinkle salt on them and sacrifice them as a burnt offering to the LORD.

25"For seven days you are to provide a male goat daily for a sin offering; you are also to provide a young bull and a ram from the flock, both without defect. 26For seven days they are to make atonement for the altar and cleanse it; thus they will dedicate it. 27At the end of these days, from the eighth day on, the priests are to present your burnt offerings and fellowship offerings[a] on the altar. Then I will accept you, declares the Sovereign LORD."

The Prince, the Levites, the Priests

44 Then the man brought me back to the outer gate of the sanctuary, the one facing east, and it was shut. 2The LORD said to me, "This gate is to remain shut. It must not be opened; no one may enter through it. It is to remain shut because the LORD,

the God of Israel, has entered through it. 3The prince himself is the only one who may sit inside the gateway to eat in the presence of the LORD. He is to enter by way of the portico of the gateway and go out the same way."

4Then the man brought me by way of the north gate to the front of the temple. I looked and saw the glory of the LORD filling the temple of the LORD, and I fell facedown.

5The LORD said to me, "Son of man, look carefully, listen closely and give attention to everything I tell you concerning all the regulations regarding the temple of the LORD. Give attention to the entrance of the temple and all the exits of the sanctuary. 6Say to the rebellious house of Israel, 'This is what the Sovereign LORD says: Enough of your detestable practices, O house of Israel! 7In addition to all your other detestable practices, you brought foreigners uncircumcised in heart and flesh into my sanctuary, desecrating my temple while you offered me food, fat and blood, and you broke my covenant. 8Instead of carrying out your duty in regard to my holy things, you put others in charge of my sanctuary. 9This is what the Sovereign LORD says: No foreigner uncircumcised in heart and flesh is to enter my sanctuary, not even the foreigners who live among the Israelites.

10" 'The Levites who went far from me when Israel went astray and who wandered from me after their idols must bear the consequences of their sin. 11They may serve in my sanctuary, having charge of the gates of the temple and serving in it; they may slaughter the burnt offerings and sacrifices for the people and stand before the people and serve them. 12But because they served them in the presence of their idols and made the house of Israel fall into sin, therefore I have sworn with uplifted hand that they must bear the consequences of their sin, declares the Sovereign

LORD. [13]They are not to come near to serve me as priests or come near any of my holy things or my most holy offerings; they must bear the shame of their detestable practices. [14]Yet I will put them in charge of the duties of the temple and all the work that is to be done in it.

[15]" 'But the priests, who are Levites and descendants of Zadok and who faithfully carried out the duties of my sanctuary when the Israelites went astray from me, are to come near to minister before me; they are to stand before me to offer sacrifices of fat and blood, declares the Sovereign LORD. [16]They alone are to enter my sanctuary; they alone are to come near my table to minister before me and perform my service.

[17]" 'When they enter the gates of the inner court, they are to wear linen clothes; they must not wear any woolen garment while ministering at the gates of the inner court or inside the temple. [18]They are to wear linen turbans on their heads and linen undergarments around their waists. They must not wear anything that makes them perspire. [19]When they go out into the outer court where the people are, they are to take off the clothes they have been ministering in and are to leave them in the sacred rooms, and put on other clothes, so that they do not consecrate the people by means of their garments.

[20]" 'They must not shave their heads or let their hair grow long, but they are to keep the hair of their heads trimmed. [21]No priest is to drink wine when he enters the inner court. [22]They must not marry widows or divorced women; they may marry only virgins of Israelite descent or widows of priests. [23]They are to teach my people the difference between the holy and the common and show them how to distinguish between the unclean and the clean.

[24]" 'In any dispute, the priests are to serve as judges and decide it according to my ordinances. They are to keep my laws and my decrees for all my appointed feasts, and they are to keep my Sabbaths holy.

[25]" 'A priest must not defile himself by going near a dead person; however, if the dead person was his father or mother, son or daughter, brother or unmarried sister, then he may defile himself. [26]After he is cleansed, he must wait seven days. [27]On the day he goes into the inner court of the sanctuary to minister in the sanctuary, he is to offer a sin offering for himself, declares the Sovereign LORD.

[28]" 'I am to be the only inheritance the priests have. You are to give them no possession in Israel; I will be their possession. [29]They will eat the grain offerings, the sin offerings and the guilt offerings; and everything in Israel devoted[a] to the LORD will belong to them. [30]The best of all the firstfruits and of all your special gifts will belong to the priests. You are to give them the first portion of your ground meal so that a blessing may rest on your household. [31]The priests must not eat anything, bird or animal, found dead or torn by wild animals.

Division of the Land

45 " 'When you allot the land as an inheritance, you are to present to the LORD a portion of the land as a sacred district, 25,000 cubits long and 20,000[b] cubits wide; the entire area will be holy. [2]Of this, a section 500 cubits square is to be for the sanctuary, with 50 cubits around it for open land. [3]In the sacred district, measure off a section 25,000 cubits[c] long and 10,000 cubits[d] wide. In it will be the sanctuary, the Most Holy Place. [4]It will be the sacred portion of the land for the priests, who minister in the sanctuary and who draw near to minister before the

---

[a]29 The Hebrew term refers to the irrevocable giving over of things or persons to the LORD.   [b]1 Septuagint (see also verses 3 and 5 and 48:9); Hebrew *10,000*   [c]3 That is, about 7 miles (about 12 kilometers)   [d]3 That is, about 3 miles (about 5 kilometers)

LORD. It will be a place for their houses as well as a holy place for the sanctuary. 5An area 25,000 cubits long and 10,000 cubits wide will belong to the Levites, who serve in the temple, as their possession for towns to live in.*a*

6" 'You are to give the city as its property an area 5,000 cubits wide and 25,000 cubits long, adjoining the sacred portion; it will belong to the whole house of Israel.

7" 'The prince will have the land bordering each side of the area formed by the sacred district and the property of the city. It will extend westward from the west side and eastward from the east side, running lengthwise from the western to the eastern border parallel to one of the tribal portions. 8This land will be his possession in Israel. And my princes will no longer oppress my people but will allow the house of Israel to possess the land according to their tribes.

9" 'This is what the Sovereign LORD says: You have gone far enough, O princes of Israel! Give up your violence and oppression and do what is just and right. Stop dispossessing my people, declares the Sovereign LORD. 10You are to use accurate scales, an accurate ephah*b* and an accurate bath.*c* 11The ephah and the bath are to be the same size, the bath containing a tenth of a homer*d* and the ephah a tenth of a homer; the homer is to be the standard measure for both. 12The shekel*e* is to consist of twenty gerahs. Twenty shekels plus twenty-five shekels plus fifteen shekels equal one mina.*f*

Offerings and Holy Days

13" 'This is the special gift you are to offer: a sixth of an ephah from each homer of wheat and a sixth of an ephah from each homer of barley. 14The prescribed portion of oil, mea-

sured by the bath, is a tenth of a bath from each cor (which consists of ten baths or one homer, for ten baths are equivalent to a homer). 15Also one sheep is to be taken from every flock of two hundred from the well-watered pastures of Israel. These will be used for the grain offerings, burnt offerings and fellowship offerings*g* to make atonement for the people, declares the Sovereign LORD. 16All the people of the land will participate in this special gift for the use of the prince in Israel. 17It will be the duty of the prince to provide the burnt offerings, grain offerings and drink offerings at the festivals, the New Moons and the Sabbaths—at all the appointed feasts of the house of Israel. He will provide the sin offerings, grain offerings, burnt offerings and fellowship offerings to make atonement for the house of Israel.

18" 'This is what the Sovereign LORD says: In the first month on the first day you are to take a young bull without defect and purify the sanctuary. 19The priest is to take some of the blood of the sin offering and put it on the doorposts of the temple, on the four corners of the upper ledge of the altar and on the gateposts of the inner court. 20You are to do the same on the seventh day of the month for anyone who sins unintentionally or through ignorance; so you are to make atonement for the temple.

21" 'In the first month on the fourteenth day you are to observe the Passover, a feast lasting seven days, during which you shall eat bread made without yeast. 22On that day the prince is to provide a bull as a sin offering for himself and for all the people of the land. 23Every day during the seven days of the Feast he is to provide seven bulls and seven rams without defect as a burnt offering to the LORD, and a male goat for a sin offering. 24He is to provide as a

---

a5 Septuagint; Hebrew *temple; they will have as their possession 20 rooms*   *b10* An ephah was a dry measure.   *c10* A bath was a liquid measure.   *d11* A homer was a dry measure.
e12 A shekel weighed about 2/5 ounce (about 11.5 grams).   *f12* That is, 60 shekels; the common mina was 50 shekels.   *g15* Traditionally *peace offerings*; also in verse 17

grain offering an ephah for each bull and an ephah for each ram, along with a hin*a* of oil for each ephah.

²⁵" 'During the seven days of the Feast, which begins in the seventh month on the fifteenth day, he is to make the same provision for sin offerings, burnt offerings, grain offerings and oil.

46 " 'This is what the Sovereign LORD says: The gate of the inner court facing east is to be shut on the six working days, but on the Sabbath day and on the day of the New Moon it is to be opened. ²The prince is to enter from the outside through the portico of the gateway and stand by the gatepost. The priests are to sacrifice his burnt offering and his fellowship offerings.*b* He is to worship at the threshold of the gateway and then go out, but the gate will not be shut until evening. ³On the Sabbaths and New Moons the people of the land are to worship in the presence of the LORD at the entrance to that gateway. ⁴The burnt offering the prince brings to the LORD on the Sabbath day is to be six male lambs and a ram, all without defect. ⁵The grain offering given with the ram is to be an ephah,*c* and the grain offering with the lambs is to be as much as he pleases, along with a hin*a* of oil for each ephah. ⁶On the day of the New Moon he is to offer a young bull, six lambs and a ram, all without defect. ⁷He is to provide as a grain offering one ephah with the bull, one ephah with the ram, and with the lambs as much as he wants to give, along with a hin of oil with each ephah. ⁸When the prince enters, he is to go in through the portico of the gateway, and he is to come out the same way.

⁹" 'When the people of the land come before the LORD at the appointed feasts, whoever enters by the north gate to worship is to go out the south gate; and whoever enters by the south gate is to go out the north gate. No one is to return through the gate by which he entered, but each is to go out the opposite gate. ¹⁰The prince is to be among them, going in when they go in and going out when they go out.

¹¹" 'At the festivals and the appointed feasts, the grain offering is to be an ephah with a bull, an ephah with a ram, and with the lambs as much as one pleases, along with a hin of oil for each ephah. ¹²When the prince provides a freewill offering to the LORD—whether a burnt offering or fellowship offerings—the gate facing east is to be opened for him. He shall offer his burnt offering or his fellowship offerings as he does on the Sabbath day. Then he shall go out, and after he has gone out, the gate will be shut.

¹³" 'Every day you are to provide a year-old lamb without defect for a burnt offering to the LORD; morning by morning you shall provide it. ¹⁴You are also to provide with it morning by morning a grain offering, consisting of a sixth of an ephah with a third of a hin of oil to moisten the flour. The presenting of this grain offering to the LORD is a lasting ordinance. ¹⁵So the lamb and the grain offering and the oil shall be provided morning by morning for a regular burnt offering.

¹⁶" 'This is what the Sovereign LORD says: If the prince makes a gift from his inheritance to one of his sons, it will also belong to his descendants; it is to be their property by inheritance. ¹⁷If, however, he makes a gift from his inheritance to one of his servants, the servant may keep it until the year of freedom; then it will revert to the prince. His inheritance belongs to his sons only; it is theirs. ¹⁸The prince must not take any of the inheritance of the people, driving them off their property. He is to give his sons their inheritance out of his own property, so that none of my people will be separated from his property.' "

---

*a*24,5 That is, probably about 4 quarts (about 4 liters)　　*b*2 Traditionally *peace offerings*; also in verse 12　　*c*5 That is, probably about 3/5 bushel (about 22 liters)

¹⁹Then the man brought me through the entrance at the side of the gate to the sacred rooms facing north, which belonged to the priests, and showed me a place at the western end. ²⁰He said to me, "This is the place where the priests will cook the guilt offering and the sin offering and bake the grain offering, to avoid bringing them into the outer court and consecrating the people."

²¹He then brought me to the outer court and led me around to its four corners, and I saw in each corner another court. ²²In the four corners of the outer court were enclosed*a* courts, forty cubits long and thirty cubits wide; each of the courts in the four corners was the same size. ²³Around the inside of each of the four courts was a ledge of stone, with places for fire built all around under the ledge. ²⁴He said to me, "These are the kitchens where those who minister at the temple will cook the sacrifices of the people."

The River From the Temple

47 The man brought me back to the entrance of the temple, and I saw water coming out from under the threshold of the temple toward the east (for the temple faced east). The water was coming down from under the south side of the temple, south of the altar. ²He then brought me out through the north gate and led me around the outside to the outer gate facing east, and the water was flowing from the south side.

³As the man went eastward with a measuring line in his hand, he measured off a thousand cubits*b* and then led me through water that was ankle-deep. ⁴He measured off another thousand cubits and led me through water that was knee-deep. He measured off another thousand and led me through water that was up to the waist. ⁵He measured off another

thousand, but now it was a river that I could not cross, because the water had risen and was deep enough to swim in—a river that no one could cross. ⁶He asked me, "Son of man, do you see this?"

Then he led me back to the bank of the river. ⁷When I arrived there, I saw a great number of trees on each side of the river. ⁸He said to me, "This water flows toward the eastern region and goes down into the Arabah,*c* where it enters the Sea.*d* When it empties into the Sea,*d* the water there becomes fresh. ⁹Swarms of living creatures will live wherever the river flows. There will be large numbers of fish, because this water flows there and makes the salt water fresh; so where the river flows everything will live. ¹⁰Fishermen will stand along the shore; from En Gedi to En Eglaim there will be places for spreading nets. The fish will be of many kinds—like the fish of the Great Sea.*e* ¹¹But the swamps and marshes will not become fresh; they will be left for salt. ¹²Fruit trees of all kinds will grow on both banks of the river. Their leaves will not wither, nor will their fruit fail. Every month they will bear, because the water from the sanctuary flows to them. Their fruit will serve for food and their leaves for healing."

The Boundaries of the Land

¹³This is what the Sovereign LORD says: "These are the boundaries by which you are to divide the land for an inheritance among the twelve tribes of Israel, with two portions for Joseph. ¹⁴You are to divide it equally among them. Because I swore with uplifted hand to give it to your forefathers, this land will become your inheritance.

¹⁵"This is to be the boundary of the land:

"On the north side it will run from

---

a22 The meaning of the Hebrew for this word is uncertain.   *b3* That is, about 1,500 feet (about 450 meters)   *c8* Or *the Jordan Valley*   *d8* That is, the Dead Sea   *e10* That is, the Mediterranean; also in verses 15, 19 and 20

the Great Sea by the Hethlon road past Lebo[a] Hamath to Zedad, [16]Berothah[b] and Sibraim (which lies on the border between Damascus and Hamath), as far as Hazer Hatticon, which is on the border of Hauran. [17]The boundary will extend from the sea to Hazar Enan,[c] along the northern border of Damascus, with the border of Hamath to the north. This will be the north boundary.

[18]"On the east side the boundary will run between Hauran and Damascus, along the Jordan between Gilead and the land of Israel, to the eastern sea and as far as Tamar.[d] This will be the east boundary.

[19]"On the south side it will run from Tamar as far as the waters of Meribah Kadesh, then along the Wadi ⎣of Egypt⎦ to the Great Sea. This will be the south boundary.

[20]"On the west side, the Great Sea will be the boundary to a point opposite Lebo[e] Hamath. This will be the west boundary.

[21]"You are to distribute this land among yourselves according to the tribes of Israel. [22]You are to allot it as an inheritance for yourselves and for the aliens who have settled among you and who have children. You are to consider them as native-born Israelites; along with you they are to be allotted an inheritance among the tribes of Israel. [23]In whatever tribe the alien settles, there you are to give him his inheritance," declares the Sovereign LORD.

The Division of the Land

48 "These are the tribes, listed by name: At the northern frontier, Dan will have one portion; it will follow the Hethlon road to Lebo[f] Hamath; Hazar Enan and the north-

ern border of Damascus next to Hamath will be part of its border from the east side to the west side.

[2]"Asher will have one portion; it will border the territory of Dan from east to west.

[3]"Naphtali will have one portion; it will border the territory of Asher from east to west.

[4]"Manasseh will have one portion; it will border the territory of Naphtali from east to west.

[5]"Ephraim will have one portion; it will border the territory of Manasseh from east to west.

[6]"Reuben will have one portion; it will border the territory of Ephraim from east to west.

[7]"Judah will have one portion; it will border the territory of Reuben from east to west.

[8]"Bordering the territory of Judah from east to west will be the portion you are to present as a special gift. It will be 25,000 cubits[g] wide, and its length from east to west will equal one of the tribal portions; the sanctuary will be in the center of it.

[9]"The special portion you are to offer to the LORD will be 25,000 cubits long and 10,000 cubits[h] wide. [10]This will be the sacred portion for the priests. It will be 25,000 cubits long on the north side, 10,000 cubits wide on the west side, 10,000 cubits wide on the east side and 25,000 cubits long on the south side. In the center of it will be the sanctuary of the LORD. [11]This will be for the consecrated priests, the Zadokites, who were faithful in serving me and did not go astray as the Levites did when the Israelites went astray. [12]It will be a special gift to them from the sacred portion of the land, a most holy portion, bordering the territory of the Levites.

[13]"Alongside the territory of the priests, the Levites will have an al-

---

a15 Or past the entrance to Zedad, 16Hamath, Berothah   *b15,16 See Septuagint and Ezekiel 48:1; Hebrew road to go into*   *c17 Hebrew Enon, a variant of Enan*   *d18 Septuagint and Syriac; Hebrew Israel. You will measure to the eastern sea*   *e20 Or opposite the entrance to*   *f1 Or to the entrance to*   *g8 That is, about 7 miles (about 12 kilometers)*   *h9 That is, about 3 miles (about 5 kilometers)*

lotment 25,000 cubits long and 10,-000 cubits wide. Its total length will be 25,000 cubits and its width 10,000 cubits. ¹⁴They must not sell or exchange any of it. This is the best of the land and must not pass into other hands, because it is holy to the LORD.

¹⁵"The remaining area, 5,000 cubits wide and 25,000 cubits long, will be for the common use of the city, for houses and for pastureland. The city will be in the center of it ¹⁶and will have these measurements: the north side 4,500 cubits, the south side 4,500 cubits, the east side 4,500 cubits, and the west side 4,500 cubits. ¹⁷The pastureland for the city will be 250 cubits on the north, 250 cubits on the south, 250 cubits on the east, and 250 cubits on the west. ¹⁸What remains of the area, bordering on the sacred portion and running the length of it, will be 10,000 cubits on the east side and 10,000 cubits on the west side. Its produce will supply food for the workers of the city. ¹⁹The workers from the city who farm it will come from all the tribes of Israel. ²⁰The entire portion will be a square, 25,000 cubits on each side. As a special gift you will set aside the sacred portion, along with the property of the city.

²¹"What remains on both sides of the area formed by the sacred portion and the city property will belong to the prince. It will extend eastward from the 25,000 cubits of the sacred portion to the eastern border, and westward from the 25,000 cubits to the western border. Both these areas running the length of the tribal portions will belong to the prince, and the sacred portion with the temple sanctuary will be in the center of them. ²²So the property of the Levites and the property of the city will lie in the center of the area that belongs to the prince. The area belonging to the prince will lie between the border of Judah and the border of Benjamin.

²³"As for the rest of the tribes: Ben-jamin will have one portion; it will extend from the east side to the west side.

²⁴"Simeon will have one portion; it will border the territory of Benjamin from east to west.

²⁵"Issachar will have one portion; it will border the territory of Simeon from east to west.

²⁶"Zebulun will have one portion; it will border the territory of Issachar from east to west.

²⁷"Gad will have one portion; it will border the territory of Zebulun from east to west.

²⁸"The southern boundary of Gad will run south from Tamar to the waters of Meribah Kadesh, then along the Wadi ˬof Egyptˏ to the Great Sea.ᵃ

²⁹"This is the land you are to allot as an inheritance to the tribes of Israel, and these will be their portions," declares the Sovereign LORD.

The Gates of the City

³⁰"These will be the exits of the city: Beginning on the north side, which is 4,500 cubits long, ³¹the gates of the city will be named after the tribes of Israel. The three gates on the north side will be the gate of Reuben, the gate of Judah and the gate of Levi.

³²"On the east side, which is 4,500 cubits long, will be three gates: the gate of Joseph, the gate of Benjamin and the gate of Dan.

³³"On the south side, which measures 4,500 cubits, will be three gates: the gate of Simeon, the gate of Issachar and the gate of Zebulun.

³⁴"On the west side, which is 4,500 cubits long, will be three gates: the gate of Gad, the gate of Asher and the gate of Naphtali.

³⁵"The distance all around will be 18,000 cubits.

"And the name of the city from that time on will be:

THE LORD IS THERE."

ᵃ28 That is, the Mediterranean

DANIEL

Daniel's Training in Babylon

1 In the third year of the reign of Jehoiakim king of Judah, Nebuchadnezzar king of Babylon came to Jerusalem and besieged it. ²And the Lord delivered Jehoiakim king of Judah into his hand, along with some of the articles from the temple of God. These he carried off to the temple of his god in Babylonia*a* and put in the treasure house of his god.

³Then the king ordered Ashpenaz, chief of his court officials, to bring in some of the Israelites from the royal family and the nobility— ⁴young men without any physical defect, handsome, showing aptitude for every kind of learning, well informed, quick to understand, and qualified to serve in the king's palace. He was to teach them the language and literature of the Babylonians.*b* ⁵The king assigned them a daily amount of food and wine from the king's table. They were to be trained for three years, and after that they were to enter the king's service.

⁶Among these were some from Judah: Daniel, Hananiah, Mishael and Azariah. ⁷The chief official gave them new names: to Daniel, the name Belteshazzar; to Hananiah, Shadrach; to Mishael, Meshach; and to Azariah, Abednego.

⁸But Daniel resolved not to defile himself with the royal food and wine, and he asked the chief official for permission not to defile himself this way. ⁹Now God had caused the official to show favor and sympathy to Daniel, ¹⁰but the official told Daniel, "I am afraid of my lord the king, who has assigned your*c* food and drink. Why should he see you looking worse than the other young men your age? The king would then have my head because of you."

¹¹Daniel then said to the guard whom the chief official had appointed over Daniel, Hananiah, Mishael and Azariah, ¹²"Please test your servants for ten days: Give us nothing but vegetables to eat and water to drink. ¹³Then compare our appearance with that of the young men who eat the royal food, and treat your servants in accordance with what you see." ¹⁴So he agreed to this and tested them for ten days.

¹⁵At the end of the ten days they looked healthier and better nourished than any of the young men who ate the royal food. ¹⁶So the guard took away their choice food and the wine they were to drink and gave them vegetables instead.

¹⁷To these four young men God gave knowledge and understanding of all kinds of literature and learning. And Daniel could understand visions and dreams of all kinds.

¹⁸At the end of the time set by the king to bring them in, the chief official presented them to Nebuchadnezzar. ¹⁹The king talked with them, and he found none equal to Daniel, Hananiah, Mishael and Azariah; so they entered the king's service. ²⁰In every

a2 Hebrew *Shinar*   *b4* Or *Chaldeans*   *c10* The Hebrew for *your* and *you* in this verse is plural.

▌ET'S LIVE IT!   Daniel 1:8–16

A POLITE WAY ➡ Daniel knew right away that he couldn't eat the food from the king's table and still please God. But he didn't just sit there and refuse to eat. Read Daniel 1:8–16 to find out how Daniel politely spoke to the official and convinced him to let Daniel eat more nourishing food.

Do you ever disagree with your parents over rules they set? At mealtime, ask if you can read this story, then decide how Daniel's way could be your family's way. Decide together to politely discuss your differences and how to handle them.

matter of wisdom and understanding about which the king questioned them, he found them ten times better than all the magicians and enchanters in his whole kingdom. ²¹And Daniel remained there until the first year of King Cyrus.

Nebuchadnezzar's Dream

2 In the second year of his reign, Nebuchadnezzar had dreams; his mind was troubled and he could not sleep. ²So the king summoned the magicians, enchanters, sorcerers and astrologers*a* to tell him what he had dreamed. When they came in and stood before the king, ³he said to them, "I have had a dream that troubles me and I want to know what it means.*b*"

⁴Then the astrologers answered the king in Aramaic,*c* "O king, live forever! Tell your servants the dream, and we will interpret it."

⁵The king replied to the astrologers, "This is what I have firmly decided: If you do not tell me what my dream was and interpret it, I will have you cut into pieces and your houses turned into piles of rubble. ⁶But if you tell me the dream and explain it, you will receive from me gifts and rewards and great honor. So tell me the dream and interpret it for me."

⁷Once more they replied, "Let the king tell his servants the dream, and we will interpret it."

⁸Then the king answered, "I am certain that you are trying to gain time, because you realize that this is what I have firmly decided: ⁹If you do not tell me the dream, there is just one penalty for you. You have conspired to tell me misleading and wicked things, hoping the situation will change. So then, tell me the dream, and I will know that you can interpret it for me."

¹⁰The astrologers answered the king, "There is not a man on earth who can do what the king asks! No king, however great and mighty, has ever asked such a thing of any magician or enchanter or astrologer. ¹¹What the king asks is too difficult. No one can reveal it to the king except the gods, and they do not live among men."

¹²This made the king so angry and furious that he ordered the execution of all the wise men of Babylon. ¹³So the decree was issued to put the wise men to death, and men were sent to look for Daniel and his friends to put them to death.

¹⁴When Arioch, the commander of the king's guard, had gone out to put to death the wise men of Babylon, Daniel spoke to him with wisdom and tact. ¹⁵He asked the king's officer, "Why did the king issue such a harsh decree?" Arioch then explained the matter to Daniel. ¹⁶At this, Daniel went in to the king and asked for time, so that he might interpret the dream for him.

¹⁷Then Daniel returned to his house and explained the matter to his friends Hananiah, Mishael and Azariah. ¹⁸He urged them to plead for mercy from the God of heaven concerning this mystery, so that he and his friends might not be executed with the rest of the wise men of Babylon. ¹⁹During the night the mystery was revealed to Daniel in a vision. Then Daniel praised the God of heaven ²⁰and said:

"Praise be to the name of God for
        ever and ever;
    wisdom and power are his.
²¹He changes times and seasons;
    he sets up kings and deposes
        them.
He gives wisdom to the wise
    and knowledge to the
        discerning.
²²He reveals deep and hidden
        things;
    he knows what lies in
        darkness,
    and light dwells with him.

a2 Or Chaldeans; also in verses 4, 5 and 10 chapter 7 is in Aramaic.   *b3 Or was*   *c4 The text from here through*

²³I thank and praise you, O God of
my fathers:
   You have given me wisdom and
      power,
   you have made known to me what
      we asked of you,
   you have made known to us the
      dream of the king."

Daniel Interprets the Dream

²⁴Then Daniel went to Arioch,
whom the king had appointed to execute the wise men of Babylon, and
said to him, "Do not execute the wise
men of Babylon. Take me to the king,
and I will interpret his dream for
him."

²⁵Arioch took Daniel to the king at
once and said, "I have found a man
among the exiles from Judah who can
tell the king what his dream means."

²⁶The king asked Daniel (also
called Belteshazzar), "Are you able to
tell me what I saw in my dream and
interpret it?"

²⁷Daniel replied, "No wise man, en-
chanter, magician or diviner can explain to the king the mystery he has
asked about, ²⁸but there is a God in
heaven who reveals mysteries. He
has shown King Nebuchadnezzar
what will happen in days to come.
Your dream and the visions that
passed through your mind as you lay
on your bed are these:

²⁹"As you were lying there, O king,
your mind turned to things to come,
and the revealer of mysteries showed
you what is going to happen. ³⁰As for
me, this mystery has been revealed to
me, not because I have greater wisdom than other living men, but so
that you, O king, may know the interpretation and that you may understand what went through your mind.

³¹"You looked, O king, and there
before you stood a large statue—an
enormous, dazzling statue, awesome
in appearance. ³²The head of the statue was made of pure gold, its chest
and arms of silver, its belly and
thighs of bronze, ³³its legs of iron, its
feet partly of iron and partly of baked
clay. ³⁴While you were watching, a
rock was cut out, but not by human

hands. It struck the statue on its feet
of iron and clay and smashed them.
³⁵Then the iron, the clay, the bronze,
the silver and the gold were broken to
pieces at the same time and became
like chaff on a threshing floor in the
summer. The wind swept them away
without leaving a trace. But the rock
that struck the statue became a huge
mountain and filled the whole earth.

³⁶"This was the dream, and now we
will interpret it to the king. ³⁷You, O
king, are the king of kings. The God
of heaven has given you dominion
and power and might and glory; ³⁸in
your hands he has placed mankind
and the beasts of the field and the
birds of the air. Wherever they live,
he has made you ruler over them all.
You are that head of gold.

³⁹"After you, another kingdom will
rise, inferior to yours. Next, a third
kingdom, one of bronze, will rule over
the whole earth. ⁴⁰Finally, there will
be a fourth kingdom, strong as iron
—for iron breaks and smashes everything—and as iron breaks things to
pieces, so it will crush and break all
the others. ⁴¹Just as you saw that the
feet and toes were partly of baked
clay and partly of iron, so this will be
a divided kingdom; yet it will have
some of the strength of iron in it, even
as you saw iron mixed with clay. ⁴²As
the toes were partly iron and partly
clay, so this kingdom will be partly
strong and partly brittle. ⁴³And just
as you saw the iron mixed with baked
clay, so the people will be a mixture
and will not remain united, any more
than iron mixes with clay.

⁴⁴"In the time of those kings, the
God of heaven will set up a kingdom
that will never be destroyed, nor will
it be left to another people. It will
crush all those kingdoms and bring
them to an end, but it will itself endure forever. ⁴⁵This is the meaning of
the vision of the rock cut out of a
mountain, but not by human hands
—a rock that broke the iron, the
bronze, the clay, the silver and the
gold to pieces.

"The great God has shown the king
what will take place in the future.

The dream is true and the interpretation is trustworthy."

46Then King Nebuchadnezzar fell prostrate before Daniel and paid him honor and ordered that an offering and incense be presented to him. 47The king said to Daniel, "Surely your God is the God of gods and the Lord of kings and a revealer of mysteries, for you were able to reveal this mystery."

48Then the king placed Daniel in a high position and lavished many gifts on him. He made him ruler over the entire province of Babylon and placed him in charge of all its wise men. 49Moreover, at Daniel's request the king appointed Shadrach, Meshach and Abednego administrators over the province of Babylon, while Daniel himself remained at the royal court.

The Image of Gold and the Fiery Furnace

3 King Nebuchadnezzar made an image of gold, ninety feet high and nine feet*a* wide, and set it up on the plain of Dura in the province of Babylon. 2He then summoned the satraps, prefects, governors, advisers, treasurers, judges, magistrates and all the other provincial officials to come to the dedication of the image he had set up. 3So the satraps, prefects, governors, advisers, treasurers, judges, magistrates and all the other provincial officials assembled for the dedication of the image that King Nebuchadnezzar had set up, and they stood before it.

4Then the herald loudly proclaimed, "This is what you are commanded to do, O peoples, nations and men of every language: 5As soon as you hear the sound of the horn, flute, zither, lyre, harp, pipes and all kinds of music, you must fall down and worship the image of gold that King Nebuchadnezzar has set up. 6Whoever does not fall down and worship will

immediately be thrown into a blazing furnace."

7Therefore, as soon as they heard the sound of the horn, flute, zither, lyre, harp and all kinds of music, all the peoples, nations and men of every language fell down and worshiped the image of gold that King Nebuchadnezzar had set up.

8At this time some astrologers*b* came forward and denounced the Jews. 9They said to King Nebuchadnezzar, "O king, live forever! 10You have issued a decree, O king, that everyone who hears the sound of the horn, flute, zither, lyre, harp, pipes and all kinds of music must fall down and worship the image of gold, 11and that whoever does not fall down and worship will be thrown into a blazing furnace. 12But there are some Jews whom you have set over the affairs of the province of Babylon—Shadrach, Meshach and Abednego—who pay no attention to you, O king. They neither serve your gods nor worship the image of gold you have set up."

13Furious with rage, Nebuchadnezzar summoned Shadrach, Meshach and Abednego. So these men were brought before the king, 14and Nebuchadnezzar said to them, "Is it true, Shadrach, Meshach and Abednego, that you do not serve my gods or worship the image of gold I have set up? 15Now when you hear the sound of the horn, flute, zither, lyre, harp, pipes and all kinds of music, if you are ready to fall down and worship the image I made, very good. But if you do not worship it, you will be thrown immediately into a blazing furnace. Then what god will be able to rescue you from my hand?"

16Shadrach, Meshach and Abednego replied to the king, "O Nebuchadnezzar, we do not need to defend ourselves before you in this matter. 17If we are thrown into the blazing furnace, the God we serve is able to save us from it, and he will rescue us from

---

*a*1 Aramaic *sixty cubits high and six cubits wide* (about 27 meters high and 2.7 meters wide)
*b*8 Or *Chaldeans*

your hand, O king. [18]But even if he does not, we want you to know, O king, that we will not serve your gods or worship the image of gold you have set up."

[19]Then Nebuchadnezzar was furious with Shadrach, Meshach and Abednego, and his attitude toward them changed. He ordered the furnace heated seven times hotter than usual [20]and commanded some of the strongest soldiers in his army to tie up Shadrach, Meshach and Abednego and throw them into the blazing furnace. [21]So these men, wearing their robes, trousers, turbans and other clothes, were bound and thrown into the blazing furnace. [22]The king's command was so urgent and the furnace so hot that the flames of the fire killed the soldiers who took up Shadrach, Meshach and Abednego, [23]and these three men, firmly tied, fell into the blazing furnace.

[24]Then King Nebuchadnezzar leaped to his feet in amazement and asked his advisers, "Weren't there three men that we tied up and threw into the fire?"

They replied, "Certainly, O king."

[25]He said, "Look! I see four men walking around in the fire, unbound and unharmed, and the fourth looks like a son of the gods."

[26]Nebuchadnezzar then approached the opening of the blazing furnace and shouted, "Shadrach, Meshach and Abednego, servants of the Most High God, come out! Come here!"

So Shadrach, Meshach and Abednego came out of the fire, [27]and the satraps, prefects, governors and royal advisers crowded around them. They saw that the fire had not harmed their bodies, nor was a hair of their heads singed; their robes were not scorched, and there was no smell of fire on them.

[28]Then Nebuchadnezzar said, "Praise be to the God of Shadrach, Meshach and Abednego, who has sent his angel and rescued his servants! They trusted in him and defied the king's command and were willing to give up their lives rather than serve or worship any god except their own God. [29]Therefore I decree that the people of any nation or language who say anything against the God of Shadrach, Meshach and Abednego be cut into pieces and their houses be turned into piles of rubble, for no other god can save in this way."

[30]Then the king promoted Shadrach, Meshach and Abednego in the province of Babylon.

Nebuchadnezzar's Dream of a Tree

4 King Nebuchadnezzar,

To the peoples, nations and men of every language, who live in all the world:

May you prosper greatly!

▌ET'S LIVE IT!   Daniel 3:1–30

TRUSTING GOD WHEN THINGS LOOK BAD ▶ Read Daniel 3. When the three Hebrews were about to be thrown into the fire, they said "the God we serve is able to save us" (Daniel 3:17). Their situation looked so bad, but God was there to help them. Sometimes things can get pretty tough for kids too. Maybe you're having a hard year in school; maybe your parents fight a lot; maybe your friends have turned against you. Try to remember ... no matter how rough things get ... God is there.

Fold a sheet of paper in three sections, so two are like doors. Close the doors and draw flames on the outside. On the inside, paste a picture of you and a picture of Jesus. God is with you when things get difficult even as he was with the three in the fiery furnace.

²It is my pleasure to tell you about the miraculous signs and wonders that the Most High God has performed for me.

³How great are his signs,
  how mighty his wonders!
His kingdom is an eternal
    kingdom;
  his dominion endures from
    generation to
    generation.

⁴I, Nebuchadnezzar, was at home in my palace, contented and prosperous. ⁵I had a dream that made me afraid. As I was lying in my bed, the images and visions that passed through my mind terrified me. ⁶So I commanded that all the wise men of Babylon be brought before me to interpret the dream for me. ⁷When the magicians, enchanters, astrologers*ᵃ* and diviners came, I told them the dream, but they could not interpret it for me. ⁸Finally, Daniel came into my presence and I told him the dream. (He is called Belteshazzar, after the name of my god, and the spirit of the holy gods is in him.)

⁹I said, "Belteshazzar, chief of the magicians, I know that the spirit of the holy gods is in you, and no mystery is too difficult for you. Here is my dream; interpret it for me. ¹⁰These are the visions I saw while lying in my bed: I looked, and there before me stood a tree in the middle of the land. Its height was enormous. ¹¹The tree grew large and strong and its top touched the sky; it was visible to the ends of the earth. ¹²Its leaves were beautiful, its fruit abundant, and on it was food for all. Under it the beasts of the field found shelter, and the birds of the air lived in its branches; from it every creature was fed.

¹³"In the visions I saw while lying in my bed, I looked, and there before me was a messenger,*ᵇ* a holy one, coming down from heaven. ¹⁴He called in a loud voice: 'Cut down the tree and trim off its branches; strip off its leaves and scatter its fruit. Let the animals flee from under it and the birds from its branches. ¹⁵But let the stump and its roots, bound with iron and bronze, remain in the ground, in the grass of the field.

" 'Let him be drenched with the dew of heaven, and let him live with the animals among the plants of the earth. ¹⁶Let his mind be changed from that of a man and let him be given the mind of an animal, till seven times*ᶜ* pass by for him.

¹⁷" 'The decision is announced by messengers, the holy ones declare the verdict, so that the living may know that the Most High is sovereign over the kingdoms of men and gives them to anyone he wishes and sets over them the lowliest of men.'

¹⁸"This is the dream that I, King Nebuchadnezzar, had. Now, Belteshazzar, tell me what it means, for none of the wise men in my kingdom can interpret it for me. But you can, because the spirit of the holy gods is in you."

Daniel Interprets the Dream

¹⁹Then Daniel (also called Belteshazzar) was greatly perplexed for a time, and his thoughts terrified him. So the king said, "Belteshazzar, do not let the dream or its meaning alarm you."

Belteshazzar answered, "My lord, if only the dream applied to your enemies and its meaning to your adversaries! ²⁰The tree you saw, which grew large and strong, with its top touching the

---

ᵃ7 Or *Chaldeans*   *ᵇ13* Or *watchman*; also in verses 17 and 23   *ᶜ16* Or *years*; also in verses 23, 25 and 32

sky, visible to the whole earth, [21]with beautiful leaves and abundant fruit, providing food for all, giving shelter to the beasts of the field, and having nesting places in its branches for the birds of the air— [22]you, O king, are that tree! You have become great and strong; your greatness has grown until it reaches the sky, and your dominion extends to distant parts of the earth.

[23]"You, O king, saw a messenger, a holy one, coming down from heaven and saying, 'Cut down the tree and destroy it, but leave the stump, bound with iron and bronze, in the grass of the field, while its roots remain in the ground. Let him be drenched with the dew of heaven; let him live like the wild animals, until seven times pass by for him.'

[24]"This is the interpretation, O king, and this is the decree the Most High has issued against my lord the king: [25]You will be driven away from people and will live with the wild animals; you will eat grass like cattle and be drenched with the dew of heaven. Seven times will pass by for you until you acknowledge that the Most High is sovereign over the kingdoms of men and gives them to anyone he wishes. [26]The command to leave the stump of the tree with its roots means that your kingdom will be restored to you when you acknowledge that Heaven rules. [27]Therefore, O king, be pleased to accept my advice: Renounce your sins by doing what is right, and your wickedness by being kind to the oppressed. It may be that then your prosperity will continue."

The Dream Is Fulfilled

[28]All this happened to King Nebuchadnezzar. [29]Twelve months later, as the king was walking on the roof of the royal palace of Babylon, [30]he said, "Is not this the great Babylon I have built as the royal residence, by my mighty power and for the glory of my majesty?"

[31]The words were still on his lips when a voice came from heaven, "This is what is decreed for you, King Nebuchadnezzar: Your royal authority has been taken from you. [32]You will be driven away from people and will live with the wild animals; you will eat grass like cattle. Seven times will pass by for you until you acknowledge that the Most High is sovereign over the kingdoms of men and gives them to anyone he wishes."

[33]Immediately what had been said about Nebuchadnezzar was fulfilled. He was driven away from people and ate grass like cattle. His body was drenched with the dew of heaven until his hair grew like the feathers of an eagle and his nails like the claws of a bird.

[34]At the end of that time, I, Nebuchadnezzar, raised my eyes toward heaven, and my sanity was restored. Then I praised the Most High; I honored and glorified him who lives forever.

His dominion is an eternal
      dominion;
   his kingdom endures from
      generation to generation.
[35]All the peoples of the earth
   are regarded as nothing.
He does as he pleases
   with the powers of heaven
   and the peoples of the earth.
No one can hold back his hand
   or say to him: "What have you
      done?"

[36]At the same time that my sanity was restored, my honor and splendor were returned to me for the glory of my kingdom. My advisers and nobles sought me out, and I was restored to my throne and became even greater than before. [37]Now I, Nebuchad-

nezzar, praise and exalt and glorify the King of heaven, because everything he does is right and all his ways are just. And those who walk in pride he is able to humble.

The Writing on the Wall

5 King Belshazzar gave a great banquet for a thousand of his nobles and drank wine with them. ²While Belshazzar was drinking his wine, he gave orders to bring in the gold and silver goblets that Nebuchadnezzar his father*a* had taken from the temple in Jerusalem, so that the king and his nobles, his wives and his concubines might drink from them. ³So they brought in the gold goblets that had been taken from the temple of God in Jerusalem, and the king and his nobles, his wives and his concubines drank from them. ⁴As they drank the wine, they praised the gods of gold and silver, of bronze, iron, wood and stone.

⁵Suddenly the fingers of a human hand appeared and wrote on the plaster of the wall, near the lampstand in the royal palace. The king watched the hand as it wrote. ⁶His face turned pale and he was so frightened that his knees knocked together and his legs gave way.

⁷The king called out for the enchanters, astrologers*b* and diviners to be brought and said to these wise men of Babylon, "Whoever reads this writing and tells me what it means will be clothed in purple and have a gold chain placed around his neck, and he will be made the third highest ruler in the kingdom."

⁸Then all the king's wise men came in, but they could not read the writing or tell the king what it meant. ⁹So King Belshazzar became even more terrified and his face grew more pale. His nobles were baffled.

¹⁰The queen,*c* hearing the voices of the king and his nobles, came into the banquet hall. "O king, live forever!" she said. "Don't be alarmed! Don't look so pale! ¹¹There is a man in your kingdom who has the spirit of the holy gods in him. In the time of your father he was found to have insight and intelligence and wisdom like that of the gods. King Nebuchadnezzar your father—your father the king, I say—appointed him chief of the magicians, enchanters, astrologers and diviners. ¹²This man Daniel, whom the king called Belteshazzar, was found to have a keen mind and knowledge and understanding, and also the ability to interpret dreams, explain riddles and solve difficult problems. Call for Daniel, and he will tell you what the writing means."

BABYLON

By the time Daniel arrived there, the city of Babylon had become the richest and most famous in the world. Its palm trees and hanging gardens and rich architecture made it strikingly beautiful. The huge double wall that surrounded it was constructed not just for defense but for beauty as well with designs and figures worked into its structure. The city had fifty temples dedicated to pagan gods. If Babylon were still in existence today, it would be located in modern Iraq. However, this greatest city of ancient times is now only a bare mound.

¹³So Daniel was brought before the king, and the king said to him, "Are you Daniel, one of the exiles my father the king brought from Judah? ¹⁴I have heard that the spirit of the

---

gods is in you and that you have insight, intelligence and outstanding wisdom. ¹⁵The wise men and enchanters were brought before me to read this writing and tell me what it means, but they could not explain it. ¹⁶Now I have heard that you are able to give interpretations and to solve difficult problems. If you can read this writing and tell me what it means, you will be clothed in purple and have a gold chain placed around your neck, and you will be made the third highest ruler in the kingdom."

¹⁷Then Daniel answered the king, "You may keep your gifts for yourself and give your rewards to someone else. Nevertheless, I will read the writing for the king and tell him what it means.

¹⁸"O king, the Most High God gave your father Nebuchadnezzar sovereignty and greatness and glory and splendor. ¹⁹Because of the high position he gave him, all the peoples and nations and men of every language dreaded and feared him. Those the king wanted to put to death, he put to death; those he wanted to spare, he spared; those he wanted to promote, he promoted; and those he wanted to humble, he humbled. ²⁰But when his heart became arrogant and hardened with pride, he was deposed from his royal throne and stripped of his glory. ²¹He was driven away from people and given the mind of an animal; he lived with the wild donkeys and ate grass like cattle; and his body was drenched with the dew of heaven, until he acknowledged that the Most High God is sovereign over the kingdoms of men and sets over them anyone he wishes.

²²"But you his son,ᵃ O Belshazzar, have not humbled yourself, though you knew all this. ²³Instead, you have set yourself up against the Lord of heaven. You had the goblets from his temple brought to you, and you and

your nobles, your wives and your concubines drank wine from them. You praised the gods of silver and gold, of bronze, iron, wood and stone, which cannot see or hear or understand. But you did not honor the God who holds in his hand your life and all your ways. ²⁴Therefore he sent the hand that wrote the inscription.

²⁵"This is the inscription that was written:

MENE, MENE, TEKEL, PARSINᵇ

²⁶"This is what these words mean:

*Mene*ᶜ: God has numbered the days of your reign and brought it to an end.
²⁷*Tekel*ᵈ: You have been weighed on the scales and found wanting.
²⁸*Peres*ᵉ: Your kingdom is divided and given to the Medes and Persians."

²⁹Then at Belshazzar's command, Daniel was clothed in purple, a gold chain was placed around his neck, and he was proclaimed the third highest ruler in the kingdom.

³⁰That very night Belshazzar, king of the Babylonians,ᶠ was slain, ³¹and Darius the Mede took over the kingdom, at the age of sixty-two.

Daniel in the Den of Lions

6 It pleased Darius to appoint 120 satraps to rule throughout the kingdom, ²with three administrators over them, one of whom was Daniel. The satraps were made accountable to them so that the king might not suffer loss. ³Now Daniel so distinguished himself among the administrators and the satraps by his exceptional qualities that the king planned to set him over the whole kingdom. ⁴At this, the administrators and the satraps tried to find grounds for charges against Daniel in his conduct of government affairs,

---

ᵃ22 Or *descendant*; or *successor*   ᵇ25 Aramaic *UPARSIN* (that is, *AND PARSIN*)   ᶜ26 *Mene* can mean *numbered* or *mina* (a unit of money).   ᵈ27 *Tekel* can mean *weighed* or *shekel*.   ᵉ28 *Peres* (the singular of *Parsin*) can mean *divided* or *Persia* or *a half mina* or *a half shekel*.   ᶠ30 Or *Chaldeans*

but they were unable to do so. They could find no corruption in him, because he was trustworthy and neither corrupt nor negligent. ⁵Finally these men said, "We will never find any basis for charges against this man Daniel unless it has something to do with the law of his God."

⁶So the administrators and the satraps went as a group to the king and said: "O King Darius, live forever! ⁷The royal administrators, prefects, satraps, advisers and governors have all agreed that the king should issue an edict and enforce the decree that anyone who prays to any god or man during the next thirty days, except to you, O king, shall be thrown into the lions' den. ⁸Now, O king, issue the decree and put it in writing so that it cannot be altered—in accordance with the laws of the Medes and Persians, which cannot be repealed." ⁹So King Darius put the decree in writing.

¹⁰Now when Daniel learned that the decree had been published, he went home to his upstairs room where the windows opened toward Jerusalem. Three times a day he got down on his knees and prayed, giving thanks to his God, just as he had done

before. ¹¹Then these men went as a group and found Daniel praying and asking God for help. ¹²So they went to the king and spoke to him about his royal decree: "Did you not publish a decree that during the next thirty days anyone who prays to any god or man except to you, O king, would be thrown into the lions' den?"

The king answered, "The decree stands—in accordance with the laws of the Medes and Persians, which cannot be repealed."

¹³Then they said to the king, "Daniel, who is one of the exiles from Judah, pays no attention to you, O king, or to the decree you put in writing. He still prays three times a day." ¹⁴When the king heard this, he was greatly distressed; he was determined to rescue Daniel and made every effort until sundown to save him.

¹⁵Then the men went as a group to the king and said to him, "Remember, O king, that according to the law of the Medes and Persians no decree or edict that the king issues can be changed."

¹⁶So the king gave the order, and they brought Daniel and threw him into the lions' den. The king said to

Life in Bible Times

PRAYER

People in the Bible prayed in many different places and positions. When Daniel prayed he got down on his knees to show his respect for God (Daniel 6:10). Moses was so upset because of Israel's worship of the golden calf that he fell facedown ("prostrate") before the Lord to pray (Deuteronomy 9:18). Paul urged Timothy to lift up his hands when he prayed (1 Timothy 2:8).

Daniel, "May your God, whom you serve continually, rescue you!"

[17]A stone was brought and placed over the mouth of the den, and the king sealed it with his own signet ring and with the rings of his nobles, so that Daniel's situation might not be changed. [18]Then the king returned to his palace and spent the night without eating and without any entertainment being brought to him. And he could not sleep.

[19]At the first light of dawn, the king got up and hurried to the lions' den. [20]When he came near the den, he called to Daniel in an anguished voice, "Daniel, servant of the living God, has your God, whom you serve continually, been able to rescue you from the lions?"

[21]Daniel answered, "O king, live forever! [22]My God sent his angel, and he shut the mouths of the lions. They have not hurt me, because I was found innocent in his sight. Nor have I ever done any wrong before you, O king."

[23]The king was overjoyed and gave orders to lift Daniel out of the den. And when Daniel was lifted from the den, no wound was found on him, because he had trusted in his God.

[24]At the king's command, the men who had falsely accused Daniel were brought in and thrown into the lions' den, along with their wives and children. And before they reached the floor of the den, the lions overpowered them and crushed all their bones.

[25]Then King Darius wrote to all the peoples, nations and men of every language throughout the land:

"May you prosper greatly!

[26]"I issue a decree that in every part of my kingdom people must fear and reverence the God of Daniel.

"For he is the living God
    and he endures forever;
his kingdom will not be destroyed,
    his dominion will never end.
[27]He rescues and he saves;
    he performs signs and wonders
    in the heavens and on the
        earth.
He has rescued Daniel
    from the power of the lions."

[28]So Daniel prospered during the reign of Darius and the reign of Cyrus[a] the Persian.

Daniel's Dream of Four Beasts

7 In the first year of Belshazzar king of Babylon, Daniel had a dream, and visions passed through his mind as he was lying on his bed. He wrote down the substance of his dream.

[2]Daniel said: "In my vision at night I looked, and there before me were the four winds of heaven churning up the great sea. [3]Four great beasts, each different from the others, came up out of the sea.

[4]"The first was like a lion, and it had the wings of an eagle. I watched until its wings were torn off and it was lifted from the ground so that it

---

[a]28 Or *Darius, that is, the reign of Cyrus*

▉ET'S LIVE IT!   Daniel 6:6–24

DO WHAT GOD SAYS, ALWAYS ➡ Read Daniel 6:6–24. What did Daniel do when the king made a law that no one could pray for thirty days?
    Christians should obey laws. But if a rule is against God's will, we must obey God. Find a picture of a lion. Trace the lion's head on a white strip of cloth about ten inches long and four inches wide. Go over the lion's head with a marker. When you play, tie the cloth on your arm so the lion shows. It will remind you that God protects you when you do right.

stood on two feet like a man, and the heart of a man was given to it.

5"And there before me was a second beast, which looked like a bear. It was raised up on one of its sides, and it had three ribs in its mouth between its teeth. It was told, 'Get up and eat your fill of flesh!'

6"After that, I looked, and there before me was another beast, one that looked like a leopard. And on its back it had four wings like those of a bird. This beast had four heads, and it was given authority to rule.

7"After that, in my vision at night I looked, and there before me was a fourth beast—terrifying and frightening and very powerful. It had large iron teeth; it crushed and devoured its victims and trampled underfoot whatever was left. It was different from all the former beasts, and it had ten horns.

8"While I was thinking about the horns, there before me was another horn, a little one, which came up among them; and three of the first horns were uprooted before it. This horn had eyes like the eyes of a man and a mouth that spoke boastfully.

9"As I looked,

"thrones were set in place,
    and the Ancient of Days took
        his seat.
His clothing was as white as
        snow;
    the hair of his head was white
        like wool.
His throne was flaming with fire,
    and its wheels were all ablaze.
10A river of fire was flowing,
    coming out from before him.
Thousands upon thousands
        attended him;
    ten thousand times ten
        thousand stood before him.
The court was seated,
    and the books were opened.

11"Then I continued to watch because of the boastful words the horn was speaking. I kept looking until the beast was slain and its body destroyed and thrown into the blazing fire. 12(The other beasts had been

stripped of their authority, but were allowed to live for a period of time.)

13"In my vision at night I looked, and there before me was one like a son of man, coming with the clouds of heaven. He approached the Ancient of Days and was led into his presence. 14He was given authority, glory and sovereign power; all peoples, nations and men of every language worshiped him. His dominion is an everlasting dominion that will not pass away, and his kingdom is one that will never be destroyed.

The Interpretation of the Dream

15"I, Daniel, was troubled in spirit, and the visions that passed through my mind disturbed me. 16I approached one of those standing there and asked him the true meaning of all this.

"So he told me and gave me the interpretation of these things: 17'The four great beasts are four kingdoms that will rise from the earth. 18But the saints of the Most High will receive the kingdom and will possess it forever—yes, for ever and ever.'

19"Then I wanted to know the true meaning of the fourth beast, which was different from all the others and most terrifying, with its iron teeth and bronze claws—the beast that crushed and devoured its victims and trampled underfoot whatever was left. 20I also wanted to know about the ten horns on its head and about the other horn that came up, before which three of them fell—the horn that looked more imposing than the others and that had eyes and a mouth that spoke boastfully. 21As I watched, this horn was waging war against the saints and defeating them, 22until the Ancient of Days came and pronounced judgment in favor of the saints of the Most High, and the time came when they possessed the kingdom.

23"He gave me this explanation: 'The fourth beast is a fourth kingdom that will appear on earth. It will be different from all the other kingdoms and will devour the whole earth, trampling it down and crushing it. ²⁴The ten horns are ten kings who will come from this kingdom. After them another king will arise, different from the earlier ones; he will subdue three kings. ²⁵He will speak against the Most High and oppress his saints and try to change the set times and the laws. The saints will be handed over to him for a time, times and half a time.ᵃ

²⁶"'But the court will sit, and his power will be taken away and completely destroyed forever. ²⁷Then the sovereignty, power and greatness of the kingdoms under the whole heaven will be handed over to the saints, the people of the Most High. His kingdom will be an everlasting kingdom, and all rulers will worship and obey him.'

²⁸"This is the end of the matter. I, Daniel, was deeply troubled by my thoughts, and my face turned pale, but I kept the matter to myself."

Daniel's Vision of a Ram and a Goat

8 In the third year of King Belshazzar's reign, I, Daniel, had a vision, after the one that had already appeared to me. ²In my vision I saw myself in the citadel of Susa in the province of Elam; in the vision I was beside the Ulai Canal. ³I looked up, and there before me was a ram with two horns, standing beside the canal, and the horns were long. One of the horns was longer than the other but grew up later. ⁴I watched the ram as he charged toward the west and the north and the south. No animal could stand against him, and none could rescue from his power. He did as he pleased and became great.

⁵As I was thinking about this, suddenly a goat with a prominent horn between his eyes came from the west, crossing the whole earth without touching the ground. ⁶He came toward the two-horned ram I had seen standing beside the canal and charged at him in great rage. ⁷I saw

him attack the ram furiously, striking the ram and shattering his two horns. The ram was powerless to stand against him; the goat knocked him to the ground and trampled on him, and none could rescue the ram from his power. ⁸The goat became very great, but at the height of his power his large horn was broken off, and in its place four prominent horns grew up toward the four winds of heaven.

⁹Out of one of them came another horn, which started small but grew in power to the south and to the east and toward the Beautiful Land. ¹⁰It grew until it reached the host of the heavens, and it threw some of the starry host down to the earth and trampled on them. ¹¹It set itself up to be as great as the Prince of the host; it took away the daily sacrifice from him, and the place of his sanctuary was brought low. ¹²Because of rebellion, the host ₍of the saints₎ᵇ and the daily sacrifice were given over to it. It prospered in everything it did, and truth was thrown to the ground.

¹³Then I heard a holy one speaking, and another holy one said to him, "How long will it take for the vision to be fulfilled—the vision concerning the daily sacrifice, the rebellion that causes desolation, and the surrender of the sanctuary and of the host that will be trampled underfoot?"

¹⁴He said to me, "It will take 2,300 evenings and mornings; then the sanctuary will be reconsecrated."

The Interpretation of the Vision

¹⁵While I, Daniel, was watching the vision and trying to understand it, there before me stood one who looked like a man. ¹⁶And I heard a man's voice from the Ulai calling, "Gabriel, tell this man the meaning of the vision."

¹⁷As he came near the place where I was standing, I was terrified and fell prostrate. "Son of man," he said to me, "understand that the vision concerns the time of the end."

ᵃ25 Or *for a year, two years and half a year*   ᵇ12 Or *rebellion, the armies*

¹⁸While he was speaking to me, I was in a deep sleep, with my face to the ground. Then he touched me and raised me to my feet.

¹⁹He said: "I am going to tell you what will happen later in the time of wrath, because the vision concerns the appointed time of the end. ᵃ ²⁰The two-horned ram that you saw represents the kings of Media and Persia. ²¹The shaggy goat is the king of Greece, and the large horn between his eyes is the first king. ²²The four horns that replaced the one that was broken off represent four kingdoms that will emerge from his nation but will not have the same power.

²³"In the latter part of their reign, when rebels have become completely wicked, a stern-faced king, a master of intrigue, will arise. ²⁴He will become very strong, but not by his own power. He will cause astounding devastation and will succeed in whatever he does. He will destroy the mighty men and the holy people. ²⁵He will cause deceit to prosper, and he will consider himself superior. When they feel secure, he will destroy many and take his stand against the Prince of princes. Yet he will be destroyed, but not by human power.

²⁶"The vision of the evenings and mornings that has been given you is true, but seal up the vision, for it concerns the distant future."

²⁷I, Daniel, was exhausted and lay ill for several days. Then I got up and went about the king's business. I was appalled by the vision; it was beyond understanding.

Daniel's Prayer

9 In the first year of Darius son of Xerxes ᵇ (a Mede by descent), who was made ruler over the Babylonian ᶜ kingdom— ²in the first year of his reign, I, Daniel, understood from the Scriptures, according to the word of the LORD given to Jeremiah the prophet, that the desolation of Jerusalem would last seventy years. ³So I turned to the Lord God and pleaded with him in prayer and petition, in fasting, and in sackcloth and ashes.

❓DID YOU KNOW? 8:19–20

What were Daniel's dream and vision about?

The dream and vision in Daniel 7 and 8 were about the future. Daniel saw what countries would be powerful from his time until when Jesus was born. These dreams about Babylon, Persia, Greece and Rome came true in every way.

⁴I prayed to the LORD my God and confessed:

"O Lord, the great and awesome God, who keeps his covenant of love with all who love him and obey his commands, ⁵we have sinned and done wrong. We have been wicked and have rebelled; we have turned away from your commands and laws. ⁶We have not listened to your servants the prophets, who spoke in your name to our kings, our princes and our fathers, and to all the people of the land.

⁷"Lord, you are righteous, but this day we are covered with shame—the men of Judah and people of Jerusalem and all Israel, both near and far, in all the countries where you have scattered us because of our unfaithfulness to you. ⁸O LORD, we and our kings, our princes and our fathers are covered with shame because we have sinned against you. ⁹The Lord our God is merciful and forgiving, even though we have rebelled against him; ¹⁰we have not obeyed the LORD our God or kept the laws he gave

---

ᵃ19 Or *because the end will be at the appointed time*　　ᵇ1 Hebrew *Ahasuerus*　　ᶜ1 Or *Chaldean*

us through his servants the prophets. [11]All Israel has transgressed your law and turned away, refusing to obey you.

"Therefore the curses and sworn judgments written in the Law of Moses, the servant of God, have been poured out on us, because we have sinned against you. [12]You have fulfilled the words spoken against us and against our rulers by bringing upon us great disaster. Under the whole heaven nothing has ever been done like what has been done to Jerusalem. [13]Just as it is written in the Law of Moses, all this disaster has come upon us, yet we have not sought the favor of the LORD our God by turning from our sins and giving attention to your truth. [14]The LORD did not hesitate to bring the disaster upon us, for the LORD our God is righteous in everything he does; yet we have not obeyed him.

[15]"Now, O Lord our God, who brought your people out of Egypt with a mighty hand and who made for yourself a name that endures to this day, we have sinned, we have done wrong. [16]O Lord, in keeping with all your righteous acts, turn away your anger and your wrath from Jerusalem, your city, your holy hill. Our sins and the iniquities of our fathers have made Jerusalem and your people an object of scorn to all those around us.

[17]"Now, our God, hear the prayers and petitions of your servant. For your sake, O Lord, look with favor on your desolate sanctuary. [18]Give ear, O God, and hear; open your eyes and see the desolation of the city that bears your Name. We do not make requests of you because we are righteous, but because of your great mercy. [19]O Lord, listen! O Lord, forgive! O Lord, hear and act! For your sake, O my God, do not delay, because your city and your people bear your Name."

The Seventy "Sevens"

[20]While I was speaking and praying, confessing my sin and the sin of my people Israel and making my request to the LORD my God for his holy hill— [21]while I was still in prayer, Gabriel, the man I had seen in the earlier vision, came to me in swift flight about the time of the evening sacrifice. [22]He instructed me and said to me, "Daniel, I have now come to give you insight and understanding. [23]As soon as you began to pray, an answer was given, which I have come to tell you, for you are highly esteemed. Therefore, consider the message and understand the vision:

[24]"Seventy 'sevens'[a] are decreed for your people and your holy city to finish[b] transgression, to put an end to sin, to atone for wickedness, to bring in everlasting righteousness, to seal up vision and prophecy and to anoint the most holy.[c]

[25]"Know and understand this: From the issuing of the decree[d] to restore and rebuild Jerusalem until the Anointed One,[e] the ruler, comes, there will be seven 'sevens,' and sixty-two 'sevens.' It will be rebuilt with streets and a trench, but in times of trouble. [26]After the sixty-two 'sevens,' the Anointed One will be cut off and will have nothing.[f] The people of the ruler who will come will destroy the city and the sanctuary. The end will come like a flood: War will continue until the end, and desolations have been decreed. [27]He will confirm a covenant with many for one 'seven.'[g] In the middle of the 'seven'[g] he will put an end to sacrifice and offering. And on a wing of the temple he will set up an abomination that

causes desolation, until the end that is decreed is poured out on him.ᵃ"ᵇ

Daniel's Vision of a Man

10 In the third year of Cyrus king of Persia, a revelation was given to Daniel (who was called Belteshazzar). Its message was true and it concerned a great war.ᶜ The understanding of the message came to him in a vision.

²At that time I, Daniel, mourned for three weeks. ³I ate no choice food; no meat or wine touched my lips; and I used no lotions at all until the three weeks were over.

⁴On the twenty-fourth day of the first month, as I was standing on the bank of the great river, the Tigris, ⁵I looked up and there before me was a man dressed in linen, with a belt of the finest gold around his waist. ⁶His body was like chrysolite, his face like lightning, his eyes like flaming torches, his arms and legs like the gleam of burnished bronze, and his voice like the sound of a multitude.

⁷I, Daniel, was the only one who saw the vision; the men with me did not see it, but such terror overwhelmed them that they fled and hid themselves. ⁸So I was left alone, gazing at this great vision; I had no strength left, my face turned deathly pale and I was helpless. ⁹Then I heard him speaking, and as I listened to him, I fell into a deep sleep, my face to the ground.

¹⁰A hand touched me and set me trembling on my hands and knees. ¹¹He said, "Daniel, you who are highly esteemed, consider carefully the words I am about to speak to you, and stand up, for I have now been sent to you." And when he said this to me, I stood up trembling.

¹²Then he continued, "Do not be afraid, Daniel. Since the first day that you set your mind to gain understanding and to humble yourself before your God, your words were heard, and I have come in response to them. ¹³But the prince of the Persian kingdom resisted me twenty-one days. Then Michael, one of the chief princes, came to help me, because I was detained there with the king of Persia. ¹⁴Now I have come to explain to you what will happen to your people in the future, for the vision concerns a time yet to come."

¹⁵While he was saying this to me, I bowed with my face toward the ground and was speechless. ¹⁶Then one who looked like a manᵈ touched my lips, and I opened my mouth and

---

ᵃ27 Or *it*   ᵇ27 Or *And one who causes desolation will come upon the pinnacle of the abominable temple, until the end that is decreed is poured out on the desolated city*   ᶜ1 Or *true and burdensome*   ᵈ16 Most manuscripts of the Masoretic Text; one manuscript of the Masoretic Text, Dead Sea Scrolls and Septuagint *Then something that looked like a man's hand*

 ET'S LIVE IT!   Daniel 10:2–14

GOD HEARS PRAYERS ➠ Does it seem sometimes as if God doesn't answer your prayer? Ask your mom or dad if this has ever happened to them. Sometimes God answers our prayers very directly; but sometimes we must wait. Sometimes the answer is no. Sometimes God gives us an answer different from the one we were looking for.

Read Daniel 10:2–14. In this story the "man dressed in linen" is a good angel and the "prince of the Persian kingdom" is an evil angel. What did the angel tell Daniel (see Daniel 10:14)?

Draw an ear at the top of a large sheet of paper. Under it write "your words were heard" (Daniel 10:12). If you want, use a *concordance* to look up other verses on prayer to write on this sheet. Let the poster remind you that God hears all your prayers, even if he does not answer them right away.

began to speak. I said to the one standing before me, "I am overcome with anguish because of the vision, my lord, and I am helpless. 17How can I, your servant, talk with you, my lord? My strength is gone and I can hardly breathe."

18Again the one who looked like a man touched me and gave me strength. 19"Do not be afraid, O man highly esteemed," he said. "Peace! Be strong now; be strong."

When he spoke to me, I was strengthened and said, "Speak, my lord, since you have given me strength."

20So he said, "Do you know why I have come to you? Soon I will return to fight against the prince of Persia, and when I go, the prince of Greece will come; 21but first I will tell you what is written in the Book of Truth. (No one supports me against them except Michael, your prince.

11 1And in the first year of Darius the Mede, I took my stand to support and protect him.)

The Kings of the South and the North

2"Now then, I tell you the truth: Three more kings will appear in Per-

sia, and then a fourth, who will be far richer than all the others. When he has gained power by his wealth, he will stir up everyone against the kingdom of Greece. 3Then a mighty king will appear, who will rule with great power and do as he pleases. 4After he has appeared, his empire will be broken up and parceled out toward the four winds of heaven. It will not go to his descendants, nor will it have the power he exercised, because his empire will be uprooted and given to others.

5"The king of the South will become strong, but one of his commanders will become even stronger than he and will rule his own kingdom with great power. 6After some years, they will become allies. The daughter of the king of the South will go to the king of the North to make an alliance, but she will not retain her power, and he and his power *a* will not last. In those days she will be handed over, together with her royal escort and her father *b* and the one who supported her.

7"One from her family line will arise to take her place. He will attack the forces of the king of the North and enter his fortress; he will fight

a6 Or offspring   b6 Or child (see Vulgate and Syriac)

Life in Bible Times

ANGELS

Angels were created by God. Angels are spirit and do not have physical bodies. When angels did appear to people in Old Testament times they looked something like people but they had other things about them that weren't very human. The angel Daniel saw had a "face like lightning" and "eyes like flaming torches."

against them and be victorious. ⁸He will also seize their gods, their metal images and their valuable articles of silver and gold and carry them off to Egypt. For some years he will leave the king of the North alone. ⁹Then the king of the North will invade the realm of the king of the South but will retreat to his own country. ¹⁰His sons will prepare for war and assemble a great army, which will sweep on like an irresistible flood and carry the battle as far as his fortress.

¹¹"Then the king of the South will march out in a rage and fight against the king of the North, who will raise a large army, but it will be defeated. ¹²When the army is carried off, the king of the South will be filled with pride and will slaughter many thousands, yet he will not remain triumphant. ¹³For the king of the North will muster another army, larger than the first; and after several years, he will advance with a huge army fully equipped.

¹⁴"In those times many will rise against the king of the South. The violent men among your own people will rebel in fulfillment of the vision, but without success. ¹⁵Then the king of the North will come and build up siege ramps and will capture a fortified city. The forces of the South will be powerless to resist; even their best troops will not have the strength to stand. ¹⁶The invader will do as he pleases; no one will be able to stand against him. He will establish himself in the Beautiful Land and will have the power to destroy it. ¹⁷He will determine to come with the might of his entire kingdom and will make an alliance with the king of the South. And he will give him a daughter in marriage in order to overthrow the kingdom, but his plans*ᵃ* will not succeed or help him. ¹⁸Then he will turn his attention to the coastlands and will take many of them, but a commander will put an end to his insolence and will turn his insolence back upon him. ¹⁹After this, he will turn back toward the fortresses of his own country but will stumble and fall, to be seen no more.

²⁰"His successor will send out a tax collector to maintain the royal splendor. In a few years, however, he will be destroyed, yet not in anger or in battle.

²¹"He will be succeeded by a contemptible person who has not been given the honor of royalty. He will invade the kingdom when its people feel secure, and he will seize it through intrigue. ²²Then an overwhelming army will be swept away before him; both it and a prince of the covenant will be destroyed. ²³After coming to an agreement with him, he will act deceitfully, and with only a few people he will rise to power. ²⁴When the richest provinces feel secure, he will invade them and will achieve what neither his fathers nor his forefathers did. He will distribute plunder, loot and wealth among his followers. He will plot the overthrow of fortresses—but only for a time.

²⁵"With a large army he will stir up his strength and courage against the king of the South. The king of the South will wage war with a large and very powerful army, but he will not be able to stand because of the plots devised against him. ²⁶Those who eat from the king's provisions will try to destroy him; his army will be swept away, and many will fall in battle. ²⁷The two kings, with their hearts bent on evil, will sit at the same table and lie to each other, but to no avail, because an end will still come at the appointed time. ²⁸The king of the North will return to his own country with great wealth, but his heart will be set against the holy covenant. He will take action against it and then return to his own country.

²⁹"At the appointed time he will invade the South again, but this time the outcome will be different from what it was before. ³⁰Ships of the western coastlands*ᵇ* will oppose him, and he will lose heart. Then he will

---

ᵃ17 Or *but she*   *ᵇ30* Hebrew of *Kittim*

turn back and vent his fury against the holy covenant. He will return and show favor to those who forsake the holy covenant.

[31]"His armed forces will rise up to desecrate the temple fortress and will abolish the daily sacrifice. Then they will set up the abomination that causes desolation. [32]With flattery he will corrupt those who have violated the covenant, but the people who know their God will firmly resist him.

[33]"Those who are wise will instruct many, though for a time they will fall by the sword or be burned or captured or plundered. [34]When they fall, they will receive a little help, and many who are not sincere will join them. [35]Some of the wise will stumble, so that they may be refined, purified and made spotless until the time of the end, for it will still come at the appointed time.

The King Who Exalts Himself

[36]"The king will do as he pleases. He will exalt and magnify himself above every god and will say unheard-of things against the God of gods. He will be successful until the time of wrath is completed, for what has been determined must take place. [37]He will show no regard for the gods of his fathers or for the one desired by women, nor will he regard any god, but will exalt himself above them all. [38]Instead of them, he will honor a god of fortresses; a god unknown to his fathers he will honor with gold and silver, with precious stones and costly gifts. [39]He will attack the mightiest fortresses with the help of a foreign god and will greatly honor those who acknowledge him. He will make them rulers over many people and will distribute the land at a price.[a]

[40]"At the time of the end the king of the South will engage him in battle, and the king of the North will storm out against him with chariots and cavalry and a great fleet of ships.

He will invade many countries and sweep through them like a flood. [41]He will also invade the Beautiful Land. Many countries will fall, but Edom, Moab and the leaders of Ammon will be delivered from his hand. [42]He will extend his power over many countries; Egypt will not escape. [43]He will gain control of the treasures of gold and silver and all the riches of Egypt, with the Libyans and Nubians in submission. [44]But reports from the east and the north will alarm him, and he will set out in a great rage to destroy and annihilate many. [45]He will pitch his royal tents between the seas at[b] the beautiful holy mountain. Yet he will come to his end, and no one will help him.

The End Times

12 "At that time Michael, the great prince who protects your people, will arise. There will be a time of distress such as has not happened from the beginning of nations until then. But at that time your people—everyone whose name is found written in the book—will be delivered. [2]Multitudes who sleep in the dust of the earth will awake: some to everlasting life, others to shame and everlasting contempt. [3]Those who are wise[c] will shine like the brightness of the heavens, and those who lead many to righteousness, like the stars for ever and ever. [4]But you, Daniel, close up and seal the words of the scroll until the time of the end. Many will go here and there to increase knowledge."

[5]Then I, Daniel, looked, and there before me stood two others, one on this bank of the river and one on the opposite bank. [6]One of them said to the man clothed in linen, who was above the waters of the river, "How long will it be before these astonishing things are fulfilled?"

[7]The man clothed in linen, who was above the waters of the river, lifted his right hand and his left hand to-

---

a39 Or land for a reward　　*b45 Or the sea and*　　*c3 Or who impart wisdom* ward heaven, and I heard him swear by him who lives forever, saying, "It will be for a time, times and half a time.[a] When the power of the holy people has been finally broken, all these things will be completed."

?DID YOU KNOW?   12:4

What are the last chapters of Daniel about?

These last chapters of Daniel are about what will happen just before the end of the world. Many things in these chapters are hard to understand. Even Bible scholars disagree about exactly what they mean.

---

[8]I heard, but I did not understand. So I asked, "My lord, what will the outcome of all this be?"

[9]He replied, "Go your way, Daniel, because the words are closed up and sealed until the time of the end. [10]Many will be purified, made spotless and refined, but the wicked will continue to be wicked. None of the wicked will understand, but those who are wise will understand.

[11]"From the time that the daily sacrifice is abolished and the abomination that causes desolation is set up, there will be 1,290 days. [12]Blessed is the one who waits for and reaches the end of the 1,335 days.

[13]"As for you, go your way till the end. You will rest, and then at the end of the days you will rise to receive your allotted inheritance."

---

[a]7 Or *a year, two years and half a year*

HOSEA

WHO WROTE THIS BOOK?

The prophet Hosea.

WHY WAS THIS BOOK WRITTEN?

Hosea warns the people of Israel about their unfaithfulness to God.

WHAT DO WE LEARN ABOUT GOD IN THIS BOOK?

God keeps on loving us even if we are unfaithful. Punishment does not mean God has stopped loving us.

WHAT IS SPECIAL ABOUT THIS BOOK?

Hosea's wife is not faithful to him, but Hosea keeps on loving her. Even though the people of Israel are unfaithful to God, God keeps on loving them.

WHEN WAS THIS BOOK WRITTEN?

The sermons in Hosea were preached between 753 and 723 B.C. This was just before the Assyrians destroyed Israel and took all its people captive.

WHAT ARE SOME IMPORTANT CHAPTERS IN THIS BOOK?

Israel's unfaithfulness.	Hosea 4
God's love for Israel.	Hosea 11

1 The word of the LORD that came to Hosea son of Beeri during the reigns of Uzziah, Jotham, Ahaz and Hezekiah, kings of Judah, and during the reign of Jeroboam son of Jehoash[a] king of Israel:

Hosea's Wife and Children

[2]When the LORD began to speak through Hosea, the LORD said to him, "Go, take to yourself an adulterous wife and children of unfaithfulness, because the land is guilty of the vilest adultery in departing from the LORD." [3]So he married Gomer daughter of Diblaim, and she conceived and bore him a son.

[4]Then the LORD said to Hosea, "Call him Jezreel, because I will soon punish the house of Jehu for the massacre at Jezreel, and I will put an end to the kingdom of Israel. [5]In that day I will break Israel's bow in the Valley of Jezreel."

[6]Gomer conceived again and gave birth to a daughter. Then the LORD said to Hosea, "Call her Lo-Ruhamah,[b] for I will no longer show love to the house of Israel, that I should at all forgive them. [7]Yet I will show love to the house of Judah; and I will save them—not by bow, sword or battle, or by horses and horsemen, but by the LORD their God."

[8]After she had weaned Lo-Ruhamah, Gomer had another son. [9]Then the LORD said, "Call him Lo-Ammi,[c] for you are not my people, and I am not your God.

[10]"Yet the Israelites will be like the sand on the seashore, which cannot be measured or counted. In the place where it was said to them, 'You are not my people,' they will be called 'sons of the living God.' [11]The people of Judah and the people of Israel will be reunited, and they will appoint one leader and will come up out of the land, for great will be the day of Jezreel.

2 "Say of your brothers, 'My people,' and of your sisters, 'My loved one.'

CHILDREN'S NAMES

In Old Testament times the names people gave their children had special meaning. God told Hosea what to name his children in order for those names to be a message to God's people. Find the names and what they mean in Hosea 1.

Israel Punished and Restored

[2]"Rebuke your mother, rebuke her,
  for she is not my wife,
  and I am not her husband.
Let her remove the adulterous
  look from her face
  and the unfaithfulness from
  between her breasts.
[3]Otherwise I will strip her naked
  and make her as bare as on the
  day she was born;
I will make her like a desert,
  turn her into a parched land,
  and slay her with thirst.
[4]I will not show my love to her
  children,
  because they are the children of
  adultery.
[5]Their mother has been unfaithful
  and has conceived them in
  disgrace.
She said, 'I will go after my
  lovers,
  who give me my food and my
  water,
  my wool and my linen, my oil
  and my drink.'

---

a1 Hebrew *Joash,* a variant of *Jehoash*   *b6* Lo-Ruhamah means *not loved.*   *c9* Lo-Ammi
means *not my people.*

⁶Therefore I will block her path
with thornbushes;
I will wall her in so that she
cannot find her way.
⁷She will chase after her lovers
but not catch them;
she will look for them but not
find them.
Then she will say,
'I will go back to my husband
as at first,
for then I was better off than
now.'
⁸She has not acknowledged that I
was the one
who gave her the grain, the
new wine and oil,
who lavished on her the silver
and gold—
which they used for Baal.

⁹"Therefore I will take away my
grain when it ripens,
and my new wine when it is
ready.
I will take back my wool and my
linen,
intended to cover her
nakedness.
¹⁰So now I will expose her lewdness
before the eyes of her lovers;
no one will take her out of my
hands.
¹¹I will stop all her celebrations:
her yearly festivals, her New
Moons,
her Sabbath days—all her
appointed feasts.
¹²I will ruin her vines and her fig
trees,
which she said were her pay
from her lovers;
I will make them a thicket,
and wild animals will devour
them.
¹³I will punish her for the days
she burned incense to the Baals;
she decked herself with rings and
jewelry,
and went after her lovers,
but me she forgot,"
declares the LORD.

¹⁴"Therefore I am now going to
allure her;
I will lead her into the desert
and speak tenderly to her.
¹⁵There I will give her back her
vineyards,
and will make the Valley of
Achorᵃ a door of hope.
There she will singᵇ as in the
days of her youth,
as in the day she came up out
of Egypt.

¹⁶"In that day," declares the LORD,
"you will call me 'my husband';
you will no longer call me 'my
master.ᶜ'
¹⁷I will remove the names of the
Baals from her lips;
no longer will their names be
invoked.
¹⁸In that day I will make a
covenant for them
with the beasts of the field and
the birds of the air
and the creatures that move
along the ground.
Bow and sword and battle
I will abolish from the land,
so that all may lie down in
safety.
¹⁹I will betroth you to me forever;
I will betroth you inᵈ
righteousness and justice,
inᵉ love and compassion.
²⁰I will betroth you in faithfulness,
and you will acknowledge the
LORD.

²¹"In that day I will respond,"
declares the LORD—
"I will respond to the skies,
and they will respond to the
earth;
²²and the earth will respond to the
grain,
the new wine and oil,
and they will respond to
Jezreel.ᶠ
²³I will plant her for myself in the
land;
I will show my love to the one I
called 'Not my loved one.ᵍ'

ᵃ15 *Achor* means *trouble.* ᵇ15 Or *respond* ᶜ16 Hebrew *baal* ᵈ19 Or *with*; also in verse 20 ᵉ19 Or *with* ᶠ22 *Jezreel* means *God plants.* ᵍ23 Hebrew *Lo-Ruhamah*

I will say to those called 'Not my
people,^{a}' 'You are my
people';
and they will say, 'You are my
God.' "

Hosea's Reconciliation With His Wife

3 The LORD said to me, "Go, show
your love to your wife again,
though she is loved by another and is
an adulteress. Love her as the LORD
loves the Israelites, though they turn
to other gods and love the sacred raisin cakes."

^{2}So I bought her for fifteen shek-
els^b of silver and about a homer and
a lethek^c of barley. ^{3}Then I told her,
"You are to live with^d me many days;
you must not be a prostitute or be intimate with any man, and I will live
with^d you."

^{4}For the Israelites will live many
days without king or prince, without
sacrifice or sacred stones, without
ephod or idol. ^{5}Afterward the Israelites will return and seek the LORD
their God and David their king. They
will come trembling to the LORD and
to his blessings in the last days.

The Charge Against Israel

4 Hear the word of the LORD, you
Israelites,
because the LORD has a charge
to bring
against you who live in the
land:

"There is no faithfulness, no love,
no acknowledgment of God in
the land.
^{2}There is only cursing,^{e} lying and
murder,
stealing and adultery;
they break all bounds,
and bloodshed follows
bloodshed.
^{3}Because of this the land mourns,^{f}
and all who live in it waste
away;
the beasts of the field and the
birds of the air
and the fish of the sea are
dying.

^{4}"But let no man bring a charge,
let no man accuse another,
for your people are like those
who bring charges against a
priest.
^{5}You stumble day and night,
and the prophets stumble with
you.
So I will destroy your mother—
^{6} my people are destroyed from
lack of knowledge.

"Because you have rejected
knowledge,
I also reject you as my priests;
because you have ignored the law
of your God,
I also will ignore your
children.
^{7}The more the priests increased,
the more they sinned against
me;

^{a}23 Hebrew *Lo-Ammi* ^{b}2 That is, about 6 ounces (about 170 grams) ^{c}2 That is, probably
about 10 bushels (about 330 liters) ^{d}3 Or *wait for* ^{e}2 That is, to pronounce a curse upon
^{f}3 Or *dries up*

▟ET'S LIVE IT!   Hosea 4:1–3

KNOW RIGHT FROM WRONG ➠ Read Hosea 4:1–3. Divide a sheet of
paper in half with a line down the middle. On one side write WRONG
in large letters. On the other side write RIGHT. On the side headed
WRONG, list all the wrong things these verses say that people do. Add
at least two more things that you know are wrong.

Now on the side headed RIGHT, list the same number of good things
that people do. Show the list to a good friend. Talk about the most
important right things that Christians should do.

they exchanged[a] their[b] Glory
 for something disgraceful.
[8]They feed on the sins of my
 people
and relish their wickedness.
[9]And it will be: Like people, like
 priests.
 I will punish both of them for
 their ways
and repay them for their deeds.

[10]"They will eat but not have
 enough;
 they will engage in prostitution
 but not increase,
because they have deserted the
 LORD
 to give themselves [11]to
 prostitution,
to old wine and new,
 which take away the
 understanding [12]of my
 people.
They consult a wooden idol
 and are answered by a stick of
 wood.
A spirit of prostitution leads them
 astray;
 they are unfaithful to their God.
[13]They sacrifice on the
 mountaintops
 and burn offerings on the hills,
under oak, poplar and terebinth,
 where the shade is pleasant.
Therefore your daughters turn to
 prostitution
 and your daughters-in-law to
 adultery.

[14]"I will not punish your daughters
 when they turn to prostitution,
nor your daughters-in-law
 when they commit adultery,
because the men themselves
 consort with harlots
 and sacrifice with shrine
 prostitutes—
 a people without understanding
 will come to ruin!

[15]"Though you commit adultery,
 O Israel,

let not Judah become guilty.

"Do not go to Gilgal;
 do not go up to Beth Aven.[c]
 And do not swear, 'As surely as
 the LORD lives!'
[16]The Israelites are stubborn,
 like a stubborn heifer.
How then can the LORD pasture
 them
 like lambs in a meadow?
[17]Ephraim is joined to idols;
 leave him alone!
[18]Even when their drinks are gone,
 they continue their prostitution;
 their rulers dearly love
 shameful ways.
[19]A whirlwind will sweep them
 away,
 and their sacrifices will bring
 them shame.

Judgment Against Israel

5 "Hear this, you priests!
 Pay attention, you Israelites!
Listen, O royal house!
 This judgment is against you:
You have been a snare at Mizpah,
 a net spread out on Tabor.
[2]The rebels are deep in slaughter.
 I will discipline all of them.
[3]I know all about Ephraim;
 Israel is not hidden from me.
Ephraim, you have now turned to
 prostitution;
 Israel is corrupt.

[4]"Their deeds do not permit them
 to return to their God.
A spirit of prostitution is in their
 heart;
 they do not acknowledge the
 LORD.
[5]Israel's arrogance testifies against
 them;
 the Israelites, even Ephraim,
 stumble in their sin;
 Judah also stumbles with them.
[6]When they go with their flocks
 and herds
 to seek the LORD,
 they will not find him;

---

[a]7 Syriac and an ancient Hebrew scribal tradition; Masoretic Text *I will exchange*   [b]7 Masoretic Text; an ancient Hebrew scribal tradition *my name for Bethel, which means house of God*).   [c]15 *Beth Aven* means *house of wickedness* (a

he has withdrawn himself from
them.
⁷They are unfaithful to the LORD;
they give birth to illegitimate
children.
Now their New Moon festivals
will devour them and their
fields.

⁸"Sound the trumpet in Gibeah,
the horn in Ramah.
Raise the battle cry in Beth
Aven*a*;
lead on, O Benjamin.
⁹Ephraim will be laid waste
on the day of reckoning.
Among the tribes of Israel
I proclaim what is certain.
¹⁰Judah's leaders are like those
who move boundary stones.
I will pour out my wrath on them
like a flood of water.
¹¹Ephraim is oppressed,
trampled in judgment,
intent on pursuing idols.*b*
¹²I am like a moth to Ephraim,
like rot to the people of Judah.

¹³"When Ephraim saw his sickness,
and Judah his sores,
then Ephraim turned to Assyria,
and sent to the great king for
help.
But he is not able to cure you,
not able to heal your sores.
¹⁴For I will be like a lion to
Ephraim,

like a great lion to Judah.
I will tear them to pieces and go
away;
I will carry them off, with no
one to rescue them.
¹⁵Then I will go back to my place
until they admit their guilt.
And they will seek my face;
in their misery they will
earnestly seek me."

Israel Unrepentant

6 "Come, let us return to the
LORD.
He has torn us to pieces
but he will heal us;
he has injured us
but he will bind up our wounds.
²After two days he will revive us;
on the third day he will restore
us,
that we may live in his
presence.
³Let us acknowledge the LORD;
let us press on to acknowledge
him.
As surely as the sun rises,
he will appear;
he will come to us like the winter
rains,
like the spring rains that water
the earth."

⁴"What can I do with you,
Ephraim?
What can I do with you, Judah?

a8 Beth Aven means *house of wickedness* (a name for Bethel, which means *house of God*).
b11 The meaning of the Hebrew for this word is uncertain.

Life in Bible Times

THE TRUMPET

Trumpets were blown loud-
ly in Bible times, to call
people to prayer, to wor-
ship or to war. There were
two kinds of trumpets. One
was made of metal. The
other was made of a ram's
horn.

Your love is like the morning
mist,
like the early dew that
disappears.
⁵Therefore I cut you in pieces with
my prophets,
I killed you with the words of
my mouth;
my judgments flashed like
lightning upon you.
⁶For I desire mercy, not sacrifice,
and acknowledgment of God
rather than burnt offerings.
⁷Like Adam,ᵃ they have broken
the covenant—
they were unfaithful to me
there.
⁸Gilead is a city of wicked men,
stained with footprints of blood.
⁹As marauders lie in ambush for a
man,
so do bands of priests;
they murder on the road to
Shechem,
committing shameful crimes.
¹⁰I have seen a horrible thing
in the house of Israel.
There Ephraim is given to
prostitution
and Israel is defiled.

¹¹"Also for you, Judah,
a harvest is appointed.

"Whenever I would restore the
fortunes of my people,
7 ¹whenever I would heal Israel,
the sins of Ephraim are
exposed
and the crimes of Samaria
revealed.
They practice deceit,
thieves break into houses,
bandits rob in the streets;
²but they do not realize
that I remember all their evil
deeds.
Their sins engulf them;
they are always before me.

³"They delight the king with their
wickedness,
the princes with their lies.
⁴They are all adulterers,

burning like an oven
whose fire the baker need not stir
from the kneading of the dough
till it rises.
⁵On the day of the festival of our
king
the princes become inflamed
with wine,
and he joins hands with the
mockers.
⁶Their hearts are like an oven;
they approach him with
intrigue.
Their passion smolders all night;
in the morning it blazes like a
flaming fire.
⁷All of them are hot as an oven;
they devour their rulers.
All their kings fall,
and none of them calls on me.

⁸"Ephraim mixes with the nations;
Ephraim is a flat cake not
turned over.
⁹Foreigners sap his strength,
but he does not realize it.
His hair is sprinkled with gray,
but he does not notice.
¹⁰Israel's arrogance testifies against
him,
but despite all this
he does not return to the LORD his
God
or search for him.

¹¹"Ephraim is like a dove,
easily deceived and senseless—
now calling to Egypt,
now turning to Assyria.
¹²When they go, I will throw my
net over them;
I will pull them down like birds
of the air.
When I hear them flocking
together,
I will catch them.
¹³Woe to them,
because they have strayed from
me!
Destruction to them,
because they have rebelled
against me!
I long to redeem them
but they speak lies against me.

ᵃ7 Or As at Adam; or Like men

14They do not cry out to me from
     their hearts
  but wail upon their beds.
They gather together*a* for grain
     and new wine
  but turn away from me.
15I trained them and strengthened
     them,
  but they plot evil against me.
16They do not turn to the Most
     High;
  they are like a faulty bow.
Their leaders will fall by the
     sword
  because of their insolent words.
For this they will be ridiculed
  in the land of Egypt.

Israel to Reap the Whirlwind

8 "Put the trumpet to your lips!
     An eagle is over the house of
     the LORD
  because the people have broken
     my covenant
  and rebelled against my law.
2Israel cries out to me,
  'O our God, we acknowledge
     you!'
3But Israel has rejected what is
     good;
  an enemy will pursue him.
4They set up kings without my
     consent;
  they choose princes without my
     approval.
With their silver and gold
  they make idols for themselves
     to their own destruction.
5Throw out your calf-idol,
     O Samaria!
  My anger burns against them.
How long will they be incapable
     of purity?
6 They are from Israel!
This calf—a craftsman has made
     it;
  it is not God.
It will be broken in pieces,
  that calf of Samaria.

7"They sow the wind
  and reap the whirlwind.
The stalk has no head;

it will produce no flour.
Were it to yield grain,
  foreigners would swallow it up.
8Israel is swallowed up;
  now she is among the nations
  like a worthless thing.
9For they have gone up to Assyria
  like a wild donkey wandering
     alone.
Ephraim has sold herself to
     lovers.
10Although they have sold
     themselves among the
     nations,
  I will now gather them
     together.
They will begin to waste away
  under the oppression of the
     mighty king.

11"Though Ephraim built many
     altars for sin offerings,
  these have become altars for
     sinning.
12I wrote for them the many things
     of my law,
  but they regarded them as
     something alien.
13They offer sacrifices given to me
  and they eat the meat,
  but the LORD is not pleased
     with them.
Now he will remember their
     wickedness
  and punish their sins:
  They will return to Egypt.
14Israel has forgotten his Maker
  and built palaces;
  Judah has fortified many towns.
But I will send fire upon their
     cities
  that will consume their
     fortresses."

Punishment for Israel

9 Do not rejoice, O Israel;
     do not be jubilant like the
     other nations.
For you have been unfaithful to
     your God;
  you love the wages of a
     prostitute
  at every threshing floor.

---

a14 Most Hebrew manuscripts; some Hebrew manuscripts and Septuagint They slash themselves

²Threshing floors and winepresses
 will not feed the people;
the new wine will fail them.
³They will not remain in the
 LORD's land;
 Ephraim will return to
 Egypt
 and eat unclean*a* food in
 Assyria.
⁴They will not pour out wine
 offerings to the LORD,
 nor will their sacrifices please
 him.
Such sacrifices will be to them
 like the bread of mourners;
 all who eat them will be
 unclean.
This food will be for themselves;
 it will not come into the temple
 of the LORD.

⁵What will you do on the day of
 your appointed feasts,
 on the festival days of the
 LORD?
⁶Even if they escape from
 destruction,
 Egypt will gather them,
 and Memphis will bury them.
Their treasures of silver will be
 taken over by briers,
 and thorns will overrun their
 tents.
⁷The days of punishment are
 coming,
 the days of reckoning are at
 hand.
 Let Israel know this.
Because your sins are so many
 and your hostility so great,
the prophet is considered a fool,
 the inspired man a maniac.
⁸The prophet, along with my God,
 is the watchman over
 Ephraim,*b*
yet snares await him on all his
 paths,
 and hostility in the house of his
 God.
⁹They have sunk deep into
 corruption,
 as in the days of Gibeah.

God will remember their
 wickedness
 and punish them for their sins.

¹⁰"When I found Israel,
 it was like finding grapes in the
 desert;
when I saw your fathers,
 it was like seeing the early
 fruit on the fig tree.
But when they came to Baal Peor,
 they consecrated themselves to
 that shameful idol
 and became as vile as the thing
 they loved.
¹¹Ephraim's glory will fly away like
 a bird—
 no birth, no pregnancy, no
 conception.
¹²Even if they rear children,
 I will bereave them of every
 one.
Woe to them
 when I turn away from them!
¹³I have seen Ephraim, like Tyre,
 planted in a pleasant place.
But Ephraim will bring out
 their children to the slayer."

¹⁴Give them, O LORD—
 what will you give them?
Give them wombs that miscarry
 and breasts that are dry.

¹⁵"Because of all their wickedness
 in Gilgal,
 I hated them there.
Because of their sinful deeds,
 I will drive them out of my
 house.
I will no longer love them;
 all their leaders are rebellious.
¹⁶Ephraim is blighted,
 their root is withered,
 they yield no fruit.
Even if they bear children,
 I will slay their cherished
 offspring."

¹⁷My God will reject them
 because they have not obeyed
 him;
 they will be wanderers among
 the nations.

---

a3 That is, ceremonially unclean *b8* Or *The prophet is the watchman over Ephraim, / the people of my God*

10 Israel was a spreading vine;
he brought forth fruit for
himself.
As his fruit increased,
he built more altars;
as his land prospered,
he adorned his sacred stones.
²Their heart is deceitful,
and now they must bear their
guilt.
The LORD will demolish their
altars
and destroy their sacred
stones.

³Then they will say, "We have no
king
because we did not revere the
LORD.
But even if we had a king,
what could he do for us?"
⁴They make many promises,
take false oaths
and make agreements;
therefore lawsuits spring up
like poisonous weeds in a
plowed field.
⁵The people who live in Samaria
fear
for the calf-idol of Beth Aven.ᵃ
Its people will mourn over it,
and so will its idolatrous
priests,
those who had rejoiced over its
splendor,
because it is taken from them
into exile.
⁶It will be carried to Assyria
as tribute for the great king.
Ephraim will be disgraced;
Israel will be ashamed of its
wooden idols.ᵇ
⁷Samaria and its king will float
away
like a twig on the surface of the
waters.
⁸The high places of wickednessᶜ
will be destroyed—
it is the sin of Israel.
Thorns and thistles will grow up
and cover their altars.

Then they will say to the
mountains, "Cover us!"
and to the hills, "Fall on us!"

⁹"Since the days of Gibeah, you
have sinned, O Israel,
and there you have remained.ᵈ
Did not war overtake
the evildoers in Gibeah?
¹⁰When I please, I will punish
them;
nations will be gathered against
them
to put them in bonds for their
double sin.
¹¹Ephraim is a trained heifer
that loves to thresh;
so I will put a yoke
on her fair neck.
I will drive Ephraim,
Judah must plow,
and Jacob must break up the
ground.
¹²Sow for yourselves righteousness,
reap the fruit of unfailing love,
and break up your unplowed
ground;
for it is time to seek the LORD,
until he comes
and showers righteousness on
you.
¹³But you have planted wickedness,
you have reaped evil,
you have eaten the fruit of
deception.
Because you have depended on
your own strength
and on your many warriors,
¹⁴the roar of battle will rise against
your people,
so that all your fortresses will
be devastated—
as Shalman devastated Beth
Arbel on the day of battle,
when mothers were dashed to
the ground with their
children.
¹⁵Thus will it happen to you,
O Bethel,
because your wickedness is
great.

ᵃ5 *Beth Aven* means *house of wickedness* (a name for Bethel, which means *house of God*).   ᵇ6 Or
its counsel   ᶜ8 Hebrew *aven*, a reference to Beth Aven (a derogatory name for Bethel)   ᵈ9 Or
there a stand was taken

When that day dawns,
　the king of Israel will be
　　completely destroyed.

God's Love for Israel

11 "When Israel was a child, I
　　loved him,
　and out of Egypt I called my
　　son.
[2]But the more I[a] called Israel,
　the further they went from
　　me.[b]
They sacrificed to the Baals
　and they burned incense to
　　images.
[3]It was I who taught Ephraim to
　　walk,
　taking them by the arms;
but they did not realize
　it was I who healed them.
[4]I led them with cords of human
　　kindness,
　with ties of love;
I lifted the yoke from their
　　neck
　and bent down to feed them.

[5]"Will they not return to Egypt
　and will not Assyria rule over
　　them
　because they refuse to repent?
[6]Swords will flash in their cities,
　will destroy the bars of their
　　gates

and put an end to their plans.
[7]My people are determined to turn
　　from me.
Even if they call to the Most
　　High,
　he will by no means exalt
　　them.

[8]"How can I give you up,
　　Ephraim?
How can I hand you over,
　　Israel?
How can I treat you like Admah?
How can I make you like
　　Zeboiim?
My heart is changed within me;
　all my compassion is aroused.
[9]I will not carry out my fierce
　　anger,
　nor will I turn and devastate
　　Ephraim.
For I am God, and not man—
　the Holy One among you.
　I will not come in wrath.[c]
[10]They will follow the LORD;
　he will roar like a lion.
When he roars,
　his children will come
　　trembling from the west.
[11]They will come trembling
　like birds from Egypt,
　like doves from Assyria.
I will settle them in their
　　homes,"
　declares the LORD.

---

[a]2 Some Septuagint manuscripts; Hebrew *they
against any city*　　　[b]2 Septuagint; Hebrew *them*　　　[c]9 Or *come*

Life in Bible Times

CHILDREN

The Hebrew people loved children very much. They played with them, cared for them, taught them to walk and taught them about God. To have many children was considered a great blessing from God. Hosea says that God loved Israel as his own child.

Israel's Sin

¹²Ephraim has surrounded me with
    lies,
    the house of Israel with deceit.
And Judah is unruly against God,
    even against the faithful Holy
    One.

12 ¹Ephraim feeds on the wind;
    he pursues the east wind all
    day
and multiplies lies and violence.
He makes a treaty with Assyria
    and sends olive oil to Egypt.
²The LORD has a charge to bring
    against Judah;
    he will punish Jacobᵃ according
    to his ways
and repay him according to his
    deeds.
³In the womb he grasped his
    brother's heel;
    as a man he struggled with
    God.
⁴He struggled with the angel and
    overcame him;
    he wept and begged for his
    favor.
He found him at Bethel
    and talked with him there—
⁵the LORD God Almighty,
    the LORD is his name of renown!
⁶But you must return to your God;
    maintain love and justice,
    and wait for your God always.

⁷The merchant uses dishonest
    scales;
    he loves to defraud.
⁸Ephraim boasts,
    "I am very rich; I have become
    wealthy.
With all my wealth they will not
    find in me
    any iniquity or sin."

⁹"I am the LORD your God,
    ˌwho brought youˌ out ofᵇ Egypt;
I will make you live in tents
    again,
    as in the days of your appointed
    feasts.
¹⁰I spoke to the prophets,

gave them many visions
    and told parables through
    them."

¹¹Is Gilead wicked?
    Its people are worthless!
Do they sacrifice bulls in Gilgal?
    Their altars will be like piles of
    stones
    on a plowed field.
¹²Jacob fled to the country of
    Aramᶜ;
    Israel served to get a wife,
    and to pay for her he tended
    sheep.
¹³The LORD used a prophet to bring
    Israel up from Egypt,
    by a prophet he cared for him.
¹⁴But Ephraim has bitterly
    provoked him to anger;
    his Lord will leave upon him
    the guilt of his bloodshed
and will repay him for his
    contempt.

The LORD's Anger Against Israel

13 When Ephraim spoke, men
    trembled;
    he was exalted in Israel.
But he became guilty of Baal
    worship and died.
²Now they sin more and more;
    they make idols for themselves
    from their silver,
cleverly fashioned images,
    all of them the work of
    craftsmen.
It is said of these people,
    "They offer human sacrifice
    and kissᵈ the calf-idols."
³Therefore they will be like the
    morning mist,
    like the early dew that
    disappears,
    like chaff swirling from a
    threshing floor,
    like smoke escaping through a
    window.

⁴"But I am the LORD your God,
    ˌwho brought youˌ out ofᵇ Egypt.
You shall acknowledge no God
    but me,

ᵃ2 *Jacob* means *he grasps the heel* (figuratively, *he deceives*).   ᵇ9,4 Or *God* / *ever since you were*
in   ᶜ12 That is, Northwest Mesopotamia   ᵈ2 Or *"Men who sacrifice* / *kiss*

no Savior except me.
⁵I cared for you in the desert,
in the land of burning heat.
⁶When I fed them, they were
satisfied;
when they were satisfied, they
became proud;
then they forgot me.
⁷So I will come upon them like a
lion,
like a leopard I will lurk by the
path.
⁸Like a bear robbed of her cubs,
I will attack them and rip them
open.
Like a lion I will devour them;
a wild animal will tear them
apart.

⁹"You are destroyed, O Israel,
because you are against me,
against your helper.
¹⁰Where is your king, that he may
save you?
Where are your rulers in all
your towns,
of whom you said,
'Give me a king and princes'?
¹¹So in my anger I gave you a king,
and in my wrath I took him
away.
¹²The guilt of Ephraim is stored up,
his sins are kept on record.
¹³Pains as of a woman in childbirth
come to him,
but he is a child without
wisdom;
when the time arrives,
he does not come to the opening
of the womb.

¹⁴"I will ransom them from the
power of the grave ᵃ;
I will redeem them from death.
Where, O death, are your
plagues?
Where, O grave, ᵃ is your
destruction?

"I will have no compassion,
15 even though he thrives among
his brothers.
An east wind from the LORD will
come,

blowing in from the desert;
his spring will fail
and his well dry up.
His storehouse will be plundered
of all its treasures.
¹⁶The people of Samaria must bear
their guilt,
because they have rebelled
against their God.
They will fall by the sword;
their little ones will be dashed
to the ground,
their pregnant women ripped
open."

Repentance to Bring Blessing

14 Return, O Israel, to the
LORD your God.
Your sins have been your
downfall!
²Take words with you
and return to the LORD.
Say to him:
"Forgive all our sins
and receive us graciously,
that we may offer the fruit of
our lips. ᵇ
³Assyria cannot save us;
we will not mount war-horses.
We will never again say 'Our
gods'
to what our own hands have
made,
for in you the fatherless find
compassion."

⁴"I will heal their waywardness
and love them freely,
for my anger has turned away
from them.
⁵I will be like the dew to Israel;
he will blossom like a lily.
Like a cedar of Lebanon
he will send down his roots;
6 his young shoots will grow.
His splendor will be like an olive
tree,
his fragrance like a cedar of
Lebanon.
⁷Men will dwell again in his
shade.
He will flourish like the grain.
He will blossom like a vine,

ᵃ14 Hebrew *Sheol*   ᵇ2 Or *offer our lips as sacrifices of bulls*

and his fame will be like the
    wine from Lebanon.
8O Ephraim, what more have I[a] to
    do with idols?
I will answer him and care for
    him.
I am like a green pine tree;
    your fruitfulness comes from
    me."

9Who is wise? He will realize these
    things.
Who is discerning? He will
    understand them.
The ways of the LORD are
    right;
the righteous walk in them,
but the rebellious stumble in
    them.

a8 Or What more has Ephraim

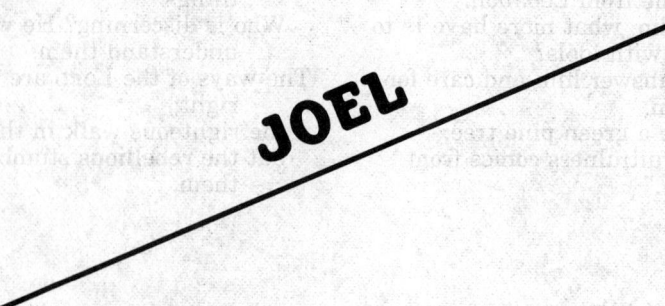

JOEL

WHO WROTE THIS BOOK?

The prophet Joel.

WHY WAS THIS BOOK WRITTEN?

Joel wants the people of Judah to repent and stop sinning.

WHAT DO WE LEARN ABOUT GOD IN THIS BOOK?

God is judge. He will punish people who sin.

WHAT IS SPECIAL ABOUT THIS BOOK?

Joel realizes that the swarm of locusts is like the great enemy army God will use someday to punish his people for their sins. Joel promises that God will save and bless his people after he punishes them.

WHEN WAS THIS BOOK WRITTEN?

Joel was written just after a terrible swarm of locusts destroyed crops in Judah. Exactly when that was is not known.

WHAT ARE SOME IMPORTANT PASSAGES IN THIS BOOK?

How to repent.   Joel 2:12–14
How God will bless.   Joel 2:18–27

1 The word of the Lord that came
to Joel son of Pethuel.

An Invasion of Locusts

²Hear this, you elders;
   listen, all who live in the
      land.
Has anything like this ever
      happened in your days
   or in the days of your
      forefathers?
³Tell it to your children,
   and let your children tell it to
      their children,
   and their children to the next
      generation.
⁴What the locust swarm has left
   the great locusts have eaten;
what the great locusts have left
   the young locusts have eaten;
what the young locusts have left
   other locusts*ᵃ* have eaten.

⁵Wake up, you drunkards, and
      weep!
   Wail, all you drinkers of wine;
wail because of the new wine,
   for it has been snatched from
      your lips.
⁶A nation has invaded my land,
   powerful and without number;
it has the teeth of a lion,
   the fangs of a lioness.
⁷It has laid waste my vines
   and ruined my fig trees.
It has stripped off their bark
   and thrown it away,
   leaving their branches
      white.

⁸Mourn like a virgin*ᵇ* in sackcloth
   grieving for the husband*ᶜ* of
      her youth.
⁹Grain offerings and drink
      offerings
   are cut off from the house of the
      Lord.
The priests are in mourning,
   those who minister before the
      Lord.
¹⁰The fields are ruined,
   the ground is dried up*ᵈ*;
the grain is destroyed,
   the new wine is dried up,
   the oil fails.
¹¹Despair, you farmers,
   wail, you vine growers;
grieve for the wheat and the
      barley,
   because the harvest of the field
      is destroyed.
¹²The vine is dried up
   and the fig tree is withered;
the pomegranate, the palm and
   the apple tree—

ᵃ4 The precise meaning of the four Hebrew words used here for locusts is uncertain.   *ᵇ8 Or
young woman*   *ᶜ8 Or betrothed*   *ᵈ10 Or ground mourns*

Life in Bible Times

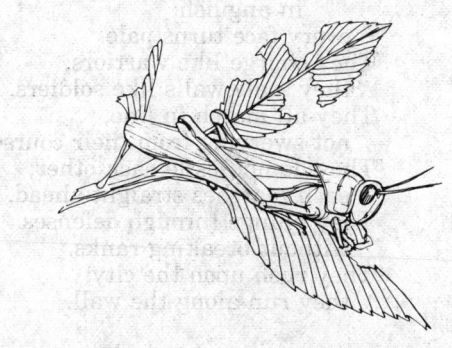

LOCUSTS

In Bible times millions of locusts would sometimes
come and cover the land
and eat every green plant
for miles. The locusts would
lay eggs before moving
on, and the caterpillars
that hatched from these
eggs ate the next year's
crops. When such locust
plagues came, many peo-
ple could starve to death.

all the trees of the field—are
  dried up.
Surely the joy of mankind
  is withered away.

A Call to Repentance

¹³Put on sackcloth, O priests, and
  mourn;
  wail, you who minister before
    the altar.
Come, spend the night in
    sackcloth,
  you who minister before my
    God;
  for the grain offerings and drink
    offerings
  are withheld from the house of
    your God.
¹⁴Declare a holy fast;
  call a sacred assembly.
Summon the elders
  and all who live in the land
to the house of the Lord your
    God,
  and cry out to the Lord.

¹⁵Alas for that day!
  For the day of the Lord is near;
  it will come like destruction
    from the Almighty.^a

¹⁶Has not the food been cut off
  before our very eyes—
joy and gladness
  from the house of our God?
¹⁷The seeds are shriveled
  beneath the clods.^b
The storehouses are in ruins,
  the granaries have been broken
    down,
  for the grain has dried up.
¹⁸How the cattle moan!
  The herds mill about
because they have no pasture;
  even the flocks of sheep are
    suffering.

¹⁹To you, O Lord, I call,
  for fire has devoured the open
    pastures
  and flames have burned up all
    the trees of the field.
²⁰Even the wild animals pant for
    you;

the streams of water have dried
    up
and fire has devoured the open
    pastures.

An Army of Locusts

2 Blow the trumpet in Zion;
  sound the alarm on my holy
    hill.
Let all who live in the land
    tremble,
  for the day of the Lord is
    coming.
It is close at hand—
² a day of darkness and gloom,
  a day of clouds and blackness.
Like dawn spreading across the
    mountains
  a large and mighty army comes,
such as never was of old
  nor ever will be in ages to
    come.

³Before them fire devours,
  behind them a flame blazes.
Before them the land is like the
    garden of Eden,
  behind them, a desert waste—
nothing escapes them.
⁴They have the appearance of
    horses;
  they gallop along like cavalry.
⁵With a noise like that of chariots
  they leap over the
    mountaintops,
like a crackling fire consuming
    stubble,
  like a mighty army drawn up
    for battle.

⁶At the sight of them, nations are
    in anguish;
  every face turns pale.
⁷They charge like warriors;
  they scale walls like soldiers.
They all march in line,
  not swerving from their course.
⁸They do not jostle each other;
  each marches straight ahead.
They plunge through defenses
  without breaking ranks.
⁹They rush upon the city;
  they run along the wall.

^a15 Hebrew *Shaddai*   ^b17 The meaning of the Hebrew for this word is uncertain.

They climb into the houses;
   like thieves they enter through
    the windows.

10Before them the earth shakes,
   the sky trembles,
the sun and moon are darkened,
   and the stars no longer shine.
11The LORD thunders
   at the head of his army;
his forces are beyond number,
   and mighty are those who obey
    his command.
The day of the LORD is great;
   it is dreadful.
   Who can endure it?

Rend Your Heart

12"Even now," declares the LORD,
   "return to me with all your
    heart,
   with fasting and weeping and
    mourning."

13Rend your heart
   and not your garments.
Return to the LORD your God,
   for he is gracious and
    compassionate,
slow to anger and abounding in
    love,
   and he relents from sending
    calamity.

WORDS TO REMEMBER

2:13 Return to the LORD your
      God,
      for he is gracious and
      compassionate,
      slow to anger and
      abounding in love.

14Who knows? He may turn and
   have pity
   and leave behind a blessing—
grain offerings and drink
   offerings
for the LORD your God.

15Blow the trumpet in Zion,
   declare a holy fast,

call a sacred assembly.
16Gather the people,
   consecrate the assembly;
bring together the elders,
   gather the children,
   those nursing at the breast.
Let the bridegroom leave his room
   and the bride her chamber.
17Let the priests, who minister
    before the LORD,
   weep between the temple porch
    and the altar.
Let them say, "Spare your people,
   O LORD.
Do not make your inheritance
   an object of scorn,
a byword among the nations.
Why should they say among the
   peoples,
   'Where is their God?' "

The LORD's Answer

18Then the LORD will be jealous for
    his land
   and take pity on his people.

19The LORD will reply[a] to them:

"I am sending you grain, new
    wine and oil,
   enough to satisfy you fully;
never again will I make you
    an object of scorn to the
    nations.

20"I will drive the northern army
    far from you,
   pushing it into a parched and
    barren land,
with its front columns going into
    the eastern sea[b]
and those in the rear into the
    western sea.[c]
And its stench will go up;
   its smell will rise."

Surely he has done great things.[d]
21 Be not afraid, O land;
   be glad and rejoice.
Surely the LORD has done great
    things.
22 Be not afraid, O wild animals,
   for the open pastures are
    becoming green.

---

[a]18,19 Or LORD was jealous . . . / and took pity . . . / [a]19The LORD replied   [b]20 That is, the Dead
Sea   [c]20 That is, the Mediterranean   [d]20 Or rise. / Surely it has done great things."

The trees are bearing their
    fruit;
    the fig tree and the vine yield
        their riches.
²³Be glad, O people of Zion,
    rejoice in the LORD your God,
for he has given you
    the autumn rains in
        righteousness.^a
He sends you abundant showers,
    both autumn and spring rains,
        as before.
²⁴The threshing floors will be filled
    with grain;
    the vats will overflow with new
        wine and oil.

²⁵"I will repay you for the years the
    locusts have eaten—
    the great locust and the young
        locust,
    the other locusts and the locust
        swarm^b—
my great army that I sent among
    you.
²⁶You will have plenty to eat, until
    you are full,
    and you will praise the name of
        the LORD your God,
    who has worked wonders for
        you;
    never again will my people be
        shamed.
²⁷Then you will know that I am in
    Israel,
    that I am the LORD your God,
    and that there is no other;
never again will my people be
    shamed.

The Day of the LORD

²⁸"And afterward,
    I will pour out my Spirit on all
        people.
Your sons and daughters will
    prophesy,
    your old men will dream
        dreams,
    your young men will see
        visions.
²⁹Even on my servants, both men
    and women,

I will pour out my Spirit in
    those days.
³⁰I will show wonders in the
    heavens
    and on the earth,
    blood and fire and billows of
        smoke.
³¹The sun will be turned to
    darkness
    and the moon to blood
    before the coming of the great
        and dreadful day of the
        LORD.
³²And everyone who calls
    on the name of the LORD will be
        saved;
    for on Mount Zion and in
        Jerusalem
    there will be deliverance,
    as the LORD has said,
among the survivors
    whom the LORD calls.

The Nations Judged

3 "In those days and at that
    time,
    when I restore the fortunes of
        Judah and Jerusalem,
²I will gather all nations
    and bring them down to the
        Valley of Jehoshaphat.^c
There I will enter into judgment
    against them
    concerning my inheritance, my
        people Israel,
for they scattered my people
    among the nations
    and divided up my land.
³They cast lots for my people
    and traded boys for prostitutes;
they sold girls for wine
    that they might drink.

⁴"Now what have you against me,
O Tyre and Sidon and all you regions
of Philistia? Are you repaying me for
something I have done? If you are
paying me back, I will swiftly and
speedily return on your own heads
what you have done. ⁵For you took
my silver and my gold and carried off
my finest treasures to your temples.

---

^a23 Or / the teacher for righteousness: ^b25 The precise meaning of the four Hebrew words used
here for locusts is uncertain.   ^c2 Jehoshaphat means the LORD judges; also in verse 12.

⁶You sold the people of Judah and Jerusalem to the Greeks, that you might send them far from their homeland.

⁷"See, I am going to rouse them out of the places to which you sold them, and I will return on your own heads what you have done. ⁸I will sell your sons and daughters to the people of Judah, and they will sell them to the Sabeans, a nation far away." The LORD has spoken.

⁹Proclaim this among the nations:
Prepare for war!
Rouse the warriors!
Let all the fighting men draw
near and attack.
¹⁰Beat your plowshares into swords
and your pruning hooks into
spears.
Let the weakling say,
"I am strong!"
¹¹Come quickly, all you nations
from every side,
and assemble there.

Bring down your warriors,
O LORD!

¹²"Let the nations be roused;
let them advance into the
Valley of Jehoshaphat,
for there I will sit
to judge all the nations on
every side.
¹³Swing the sickle,
for the harvest is ripe.
Come, trample the grapes,
for the winepress is full
and the vats overflow—
so great is their wickedness!"

¹⁴Multitudes, multitudes
in the valley of decision!
For the day of the LORD is near
in the valley of decision.

¹⁵The sun and moon will be
darkened,
and the stars no longer
shine.
¹⁶The LORD will roar from Zion
and thunder from Jerusalem;
the earth and the sky will
tremble.
But the LORD will be a refuge for
his people,
a stronghold for the people of
Israel.

Blessings for God's People

¹⁷"Then you will know that I, the
LORD your God,
dwell in Zion, my holy hill.
Jerusalem will be holy;
never again will foreigners
invade her.

¹⁸"In that day the mountains will
drip new wine,
and the hills will flow with
milk;
all the ravines of Judah will
run with water.
A fountain will flow out of the
LORD's house
and will water the valley of
acacias.ᵃ
¹⁹But Egypt will be desolate,
Edom a desert waste,
because of violence done to the
people of Judah,
in whose land they shed
innocent blood.
²⁰Judah will be inhabited forever
and Jerusalem through all
generations.
²¹Their bloodguilt, which I have not
pardoned,
I will pardon."

The LORD dwells in Zion!

ᵃ18 Or *Valley of Shittim*

Amos

1 The words of Amos, one of the shepherds of Tekoa—what he saw concerning Israel two years before the earthquake, when Uzziah was king of Judah and Jeroboam son of Jehoash[a] was king of Israel.

2He said:

"The LORD roars from Zion
    and thunders from Jerusalem;
the pastures of the shepherds dry up,[b]
    and the top of Carmel withers."

Judgment on Israel's Neighbors

3This is what the LORD says:

"For three sins of Damascus,
    even for four, I will not turn
        back ⌞my wrath⌟.
Because she threshed Gilead
    with sledges having iron teeth,
4I will send fire upon the house of
        Hazael
    that will consume the fortresses
        of Ben-Hadad.
5I will break down the gate of
        Damascus;
    I will destroy the king who is
        in[c] the Valley of Aven[d]
and the one who holds the scepter
        in Beth Eden.
    The people of Aram will go into
        exile to Kir,"
            says the LORD.

❓DID YOU KNOW? 1:3

What does "for three sins . . . even for four" mean?

It means "for many sins." Amos warns Judah and Israel as well as foreign nations that God will punish them for their many sins.

6This is what the LORD says:

"For three sins of Gaza,
    even for four, I will not turn
        back ⌞my wrath⌟.
Because she took captive whole
        communities
    and sold them to Edom,
7I will send fire upon the walls of
        Gaza
    that will consume her
        fortresses.
8I will destroy the king[e] of Ashdod
    and the one who holds the
        scepter in Ashkelon.
I will turn my hand against
        Ekron,
    till the last of the Philistines is
        dead,"
            says the Sovereign LORD.

9This is what the LORD says:

"For three sins of Tyre,
    even for four, I will not turn
        back ⌞my wrath⌟.
Because she sold whole
        communities of captives to
        Edom,
    disregarding a treaty of
        brotherhood,
10I will send fire upon the walls of
        Tyre
    that will consume her
        fortresses."

11This is what the LORD says:

"For three sins of Edom,
    even for four, I will not turn
        back ⌞my wrath⌟.
Because he pursued his brother
        with a sword,
    stifling all compassion,[f]
because his anger raged
        continually
    and his fury flamed unchecked,
12I will send fire upon Teman
    that will consume the fortresses
        of Bozrah."

13This is what the LORD says:

"For three sins of Ammon,
    even for four, I will not turn
        back ⌞my wrath⌟.
Because he ripped open the
        pregnant women of Gilead
    in order to extend his borders,

---

a1 Hebrew *Joash*, a variant of *Jehoash*   b2 Or *shepherds mourn*   c5 Or *the inhabitants of*
d5 *Aven* means *wickedness.*   e8 Or *inhabitants*   f11 Or *sword / and destroyed his allies*

¹⁴I will set fire to the walls of
    Rabbah
  that will consume her fortresses
amid war cries on the day of
    battle,
  amid violent winds on a stormy
    day.
¹⁵Her king[a] will go into exile,
  he and his officials together,"
                    says the LORD.

2 This is what the LORD says:

  "For three sins of Moab,
    even for four, I will not turn
    back ⸤my wrath⸥.
  Because he burned, as if to lime,
    the bones of Edom's king,
  ²I will send fire upon Moab
    that will consume the fortresses
    of Kerioth.[b]
  Moab will go down in great
    tumult
    amid war cries and the blast of
    the trumpet.
  ³I will destroy her ruler
    and kill all her officials with
    him,"
                    says the LORD.

  ⁴This is what the LORD says:

  "For three sins of Judah,
    even for four, I will not turn
    back ⸤my wrath⸥.
  Because they have rejected the
    law of the LORD
    and have not kept his decrees,
  because they have been led astray
    by false gods,[c]
    the gods[d] their ancestors
    followed,
  ⁵I will send fire upon Judah
    that will consume the fortresses
    of Jerusalem."

Judgment on Israel

  ⁶This is what the LORD says:

  "For three sins of Israel,
    even for four, I will not turn
    back ⸤my wrath⸥.
  They sell the righteous for silver,
    and the needy for a pair of
    sandals.

⁷They trample on the heads of the
    poor
  as upon the dust of the ground
    and deny justice to the
    oppressed.
  Father and son use the same girl
    and so profane my holy name.
⁸They lie down beside every altar
    on garments taken in pledge.
  In the house of their god
    they drink wine taken as fines.

NO BLANKETS

Most people in Israel slept under
the robe they wore during the day.
That is why God's law said no one
who loaned money could keep a
person's robe to make sure that
person paid the money back.

---

⁹"I destroyed the Amorite before
    them,
  though he was tall as the
    cedars
  and strong as the oaks.
  I destroyed his fruit above
    and his roots below.

¹⁰"I brought you up out of Egypt,
    and I led you forty years in the
    desert
  to give you the land of the
    Amorites.
¹¹I also raised up prophets from
    among your sons
  and Nazirites from among your
    young men.
  Is this not true, people of Israel?"
                    declares the LORD.
¹²"But you made the Nazirites
    drink wine
  and commanded the prophets
    not to prophesy.

ᵃ15 Or / Molech; Hebrew malcam   ᵇ2 Or of her cities   ᶜ4 Or by lies   ᵈ4 Or lies

¹³"Now then, I will crush you
    as a cart crushes when loaded
       with grain.
¹⁴The swift will not escape,
    the strong will not muster their
       strength,
    and the warrior will not save
       his life.
¹⁵The archer will not stand his
       ground,
    the fleet-footed soldier will not
       get away,
    and the horseman will not save
       his life.
¹⁶Even the bravest warriors
    will flee naked on that day,"
          declares the LORD.

Witnesses Summoned Against Israel

3 Hear this word the LORD has spoken against you, O people of Israel—against the whole family I
brought up out of Egypt:

²"You only have I chosen
    of all the families of the earth;
    therefore I will punish you
       for all your sins."

³Do two walk together
    unless they have agreed to do
       so?
⁴Does a lion roar in the thicket
    when he has no prey?
Does he growl in his den
    when he has caught nothing?
⁵Does a bird fall into a trap on the
       ground
    where no snare has been set?
Does a trap spring up from the
       earth
    when there is nothing to catch?
⁶When a trumpet sounds in a city,
    do not the people tremble?
When disaster comes to a city,
    has not the LORD caused it?

⁷Surely the Sovereign LORD does
       nothing
    without revealing his plan
    to his servants the prophets.

⁸The lion has roared—
    who will not fear?

The Sovereign LORD has spoken—
    who can but prophesy?

⁹Proclaim to the fortresses of
       Ashdod
    and to the fortresses of Egypt:
"Assemble yourselves on the
       mountains of Samaria;
    see the great unrest within her
    and the oppression among her
       people."

¹⁰"They do not know how to do
       right," declares the LORD,
    "who hoard plunder and loot in
       their fortresses."

¹¹Therefore this is what the Sovereign LORD says:

"An enemy will overrun the land;
    he will pull down your
       strongholds
    and plunder your fortresses."

¹²This is what the LORD says:

"As a shepherd saves from the
       lion's mouth
    only two leg bones or a piece of
       an ear,
    so will the Israelites be saved,
those who sit in Samaria
    on the edge of their beds
    and in Damascus on their
       couches.ᵃ"

¹³"Hear this and testify against the
house of Jacob," declares the Lord,
the LORD God Almighty.

¹⁴"On the day I punish Israel for
       her sins,
    I will destroy the altars of
       Bethel;
    the horns of the altar will be cut
       off
    and fall to the ground.
¹⁵I will tear down the winter house
    along with the summer house;
    the houses adorned with ivory
       will be destroyed
    and the mansions will be
       demolished,"
          declares the LORD.

ᵃ12 The meaning of the Hebrew for this line is uncertain.

Israel Has Not Returned to God

4 Hear this word, you cows of
      Bashan on Mount Samaria,
you women who oppress the
    poor and crush the needy
and say to your husbands,
    "Bring us some drinks!"
²The Sovereign LORD has sworn by
    his holiness:
"The time will surely come
when you will be taken away
    with hooks,
the last of you with fishhooks.
³You will each go straight out
    through breaks in the wall,
and you will be cast out toward
    Harmon,ᵃ"
           declares the LORD.

⁴"Go to Bethel and sin;
    go to Gilgal and sin yet more.
Bring your sacrifices every
    morning,
your tithes every three years.ᵇ
⁵Burn leavened bread as a thank
    offering
and brag about your freewill
    offerings—
boast about them, you Israelites,
    for this is what you love
    to do,"
           declares the Sovereign
              LORD.

⁶"I gave you empty stomachsᶜ in
    every city
and lack of bread in every
    town,
yet you have not returned to
    me,"
           declares the LORD.

⁷"I also withheld rain from you
    when the harvest was still three
    months away.
I sent rain on one town,
    but withheld it from another.
One field had rain;
    another had none and dried up.
⁸People staggered from town to
    town for water
but did not get enough to drink,
    yet you have not returned to
    me,"
           declares the LORD.

⁹"Many times I struck your
    gardens and vineyards,
I struck them with blight and
    mildew.
Locusts devoured your fig and
    olive trees,
yet you have not returned to
    me,"
           declares the LORD.

¹⁰"I sent plagues among you
    as I did to Egypt.
I killed your young men with the
    sword,
along with your captured
    horses.
I filled your nostrils with the
    stench of your camps,
yet you have not returned to
    me,"
           declares the LORD.

ᵃ3 Masoretic Text; with a different word division of the Hebrew (see Septuagint) *out, O mountain of oppression*   ᵇ4 Or *tithes on the third day*   ᶜ6 Hebrew *you cleanness of teeth*

▌ET'S LIVE IT!   Amos 4:7–10

WHY SOME BAD THINGS HAPPEN ➠ The people of Israel had turned away and were not following God. Amos 4:7–10 tells some of the terrible punishments that God brought on Israel. Read these verses to find several things that he did.

The end of each verse shows that Israel did not learn from punishment. But you can learn from punishment if you are sorry and stop doing what is wrong.

Can you think of a time when you learned from being punished? Ask one of your parents what he or she learned from being punished as a child.

¹¹"I overthrew some of you
    as I*ᵃ* overthrew Sodom and
    Gomorrah.
You were like a burning stick
    snatched from the fire,
    yet you have not returned to
    me,"
                    declares the LORD.

¹²"Therefore this is what I will do
    to you, Israel,
    and because I will do this to
    you,
    prepare to meet your God,
    O Israel."

¹³He who forms the mountains,
    creates the wind,
    and reveals his thoughts to
    man,
he who turns dawn to darkness,
    and treads the high places of
    the earth—
    the LORD God Almighty is his
    name.

A Lament and Call to Repentance

5 Hear this word, O house of Israel, this lament I take up concerning you:

²"Fallen is Virgin Israel,
    never to rise again,
deserted in her own land,
    with no one to lift her up."

³This is what the Sovereign LORD
says:

"The city that marches out a
    thousand strong for Israel
will have only a hundred left;
the town that marches out a
    hundred strong
will have only ten left."

⁴This is what the LORD says to the
house of Israel:

"Seek me and live;
⁵   do not seek Bethel,
do not go to Gilgal,
    do not journey to Beersheba.

For Gilgal will surely go into
    exile,
    and Bethel will be reduced to
    nothing.*ᵇ*"
⁶Seek the LORD and live,
    or he will sweep through the
    house of Joseph like a fire;
it will devour,
    and Bethel will have no one to
    quench it.

⁷You who turn justice into
    bitterness
    and cast righteousness to the
    ground
⁸(he who made the Pleiades and
    Orion,
    who turns blackness into dawn
    and darkens day into night,
who calls for the waters of the sea
    and pours them out over the
    face of the land—
    the LORD is his name—
⁹he flashes destruction on the
    stronghold
    and brings the fortified city to
    ruin),
¹⁰you hate the one who reproves in
    court
    and despise him who tells the
    truth.

¹¹You trample on the poor
    and force him to give you grain.
Therefore, though you have built
    stone mansions,
    you will not live in them;
though you have planted lush
    vineyards,
    you will not drink their wine.
¹²For I know how many are your
    offenses
    and how great your sins.

You oppress the righteous and
    take bribes
    and you deprive the poor of
    justice in the courts.
¹³Therefore the prudent man keeps
    quiet in such times,
    for the times are evil.

¹⁴Seek good, not evil,
    that you may live.

ᵃ11 Hebrew *God*   *ᵇ5* Or *grief*; or *wickedness*; Hebrew *aven*, a reference to Beth Aven (a derogatory name for Bethel)

Then the LORD God Almighty will
    be with you,
    just as you say he is.
15Hate evil, love good;
    maintain justice in the courts.
Perhaps the LORD God Almighty
    will have mercy
    on the remnant of Joseph.

16Therefore this is what the Lord,
the LORD God Almighty, says:

"There will be wailing in all the
    streets
    and cries of anguish in every
        public square.
The farmers will be summoned to
        weep
    and the mourners to wail.
17There will be wailing in all the
    vineyards,
    for I will pass through your
        midst,"
                        says the LORD.

The Day of the LORD

18Woe to you who long
    for the day of the LORD!
Why do you long for the day of
    the LORD?
    That day will be darkness, not
        light.
19It will be as though a man fled
    from a lion
    only to meet a bear,
as though he entered his house
    and rested his hand on the wall
    only to have a snake bite him.
20Will not the day of the LORD be
    darkness, not light—
    pitch-dark, without a ray of
        brightness?

21"I hate, I despise your religious
    feasts;
    I cannot stand your assemblies.
22Even though you bring me burnt
        offerings and grain
        offerings,
    I will not accept them.
Though you bring choice
        fellowship offerings,a

I will have no regard for them.
23Away with the noise of your
        songs!

❓DID YOU KNOW?   5:20

What was the "day of the LORD"?

In the Old Testament, the day of
the Lord was any time God did
something that affected history.
Usually a day of the Lord was a
time when God punished his people by bringing on a war or famine
or some other disaster. Amos wanted the sinful people of Israel to realize that when God acted next, it
would be to punish them for their
sins.

I will not listen to the music of
    your harps.
24But let justice roll on like a river,
    righteousness like a
        never-failing stream!

25"Did you bring me sacrifices and
        offerings
    forty years in the desert,
        O house of Israel?
26You have lifted up the shrine of
        your king,
    the pedestal of your idols,
    the star of your godb—
    which you made for yourselves.
27Therefore I will send you into
        exile beyond Damascus,"
    says the LORD, whose name is
        God Almighty.

Woe to the Complacent

6 Woe to you who are
        complacent in Zion,
    and to you who feel secure on
        Mount Samaria,
you notable men of the foremost
        nation,
    to whom the people of Israel
        come!
2Go to Calneh and look at it;

---

a22 Traditionally peace offerings   b26 Or lifted up Sakkuth your king / and Kaiwan your idols, /
your star-gods; Septuagint lifted up the shrine of Molech / and the star of your god Rephan, / their
idols

go from there to great Hamath,
and then go down to Gath in
  Philistia.
Are they better off than your two
  kingdoms?
Is their land larger than yours?
³You put off the evil day
and bring near a reign of terror.
⁴You lie on beds inlaid with ivory
and lounge on your couches.
You dine on choice lambs
and fattened calves.

Life In Bible Times

IVORY COUCHES

The very rich people in Amos's time relaxed on couches and beds decorated with ivory. God was angry, because these people got their wealth by robbing the poor (see Amos 5:7–13).

---

⁵You strum away on your harps
  like David
and improvise on musical
  instruments.
⁶You drink wine by the bowlful
and use the finest lotions,
but you do not grieve over the
  ruin of Joseph.
⁷Therefore you will be among the
  first to go into exile;
your feasting and lounging will
  end.

The LORD Abhors the Pride of Israel

⁸The Sovereign LORD has sworn by himself—the LORD God Almighty declares:

"I abhor the pride of Jacob
and detest his fortresses;
I will deliver up the city

and everything in it."

⁹If ten men are left in one house, they too will die. ¹⁰And if a relative who is to burn the bodies comes to carry them out of the house and asks anyone still hiding there, "Is anyone with you?" and he says, "No," then he will say, "Hush! We must not mention the name of the LORD."

¹¹For the LORD has given the
  command,
and he will smash the great
  house into pieces
and the small house into bits.

¹²Do horses run on the rocky crags?
Does one plow there with oxen?
But you have turned justice into
  poison
and the fruit of righteousness
  into bitterness—
¹³you who rejoice in the conquest of
  Lo Debar ᵃ
and say, "Did we not take
  Karnaim ᵇ by our own
  strength?"

¹⁴For the LORD God Almighty
  declares,
"I will stir up a nation against
  you, O house of Israel,
that will oppress you all the way
  from Lebo ᶜ Hamath to the
  valley of the Arabah."

Locusts, Fire and a Plumb Line

7 This is what the Sovereign LORD showed me: He was preparing swarms of locusts after the king's share had been harvested and just as the second crop was coming up. ²When they had stripped the land clean, I cried out, "Sovereign LORD, forgive! How can Jacob survive? He is so small!"

³So the LORD relented.

"This will not happen," the LORD said.

⁴This is what the Sovereign LORD showed me: The Sovereign LORD was calling for judgment by fire; it dried up the great deep and devoured the

---

ᵃ13 Lo Debar means nothing.   ᵇ13 Karnaim means horns; horn here symbolizes strength.
ᶜ14 Or from the entrance to

land. 5Then I cried out, "Sovereign LORD, I beg you, stop! How can Jacob survive? He is so small!"

6So the LORD relented.

"This will not happen either," the Sovereign LORD said.

7This is what he showed me: The Lord was standing by a wall that had been built true to plumb, with a plumb line in his hand. 8And the LORD asked me, "What do you see, Amos?"

"A plumb line," I replied.

Then the Lord said, "Look, I am setting a plumb line among my people Israel; I will spare them no longer.

9"The high places of Isaac will be
    destroyed
  and the sanctuaries of Israel
    will be ruined;
  with my sword I will rise
    against the house of
    Jeroboam."

Amos and Amaziah

10Then Amaziah the priest of Bethel sent a message to Jeroboam king of Israel: "Amos is raising a conspiracy against you in the very heart of Israel. The land cannot bear all his words. 11For this is what Amos is saying:

" 'Jeroboam will die by the sword,
    and Israel will surely go into
    exile,
  away from their native land.' "

12Then Amaziah said to Amos, "Get out, you seer! Go back to the land of Judah. Earn your bread there and do your prophesying there. 13Don't prophesy anymore at Bethel, because this is the king's sanctuary and the temple of the kingdom."

14Amos answered Amaziah, "I was neither a prophet nor a prophet's son, but I was a shepherd, and I also took care of sycamore-fig trees. 15But the LORD took me from tending the flock and said to me, 'Go, prophesy to my people Israel.' 16Now then, hear the word of the LORD. You say,

" 'Do not prophesy against Israel,
    and stop preaching against the
    house of Isaac.'

17"Therefore this is what the LORD says:

" 'Your wife will become a
    prostitute in the city,
  and your sons and daughters
    will fall by the sword.
Your land will be measured and
    divided up,
  and you yourself will die in a
    pagan*a* country.
And Israel will certainly go into
    exile,
  away from their native land.' "

A Basket of Ripe Fruit

8 This is what the Sovereign LORD showed me: a basket of ripe fruit. 2"What do you see, Amos?" he asked.

"A basket of ripe fruit," I answered.

Then the LORD said to me, "The time is ripe for my people Israel; I will spare them no longer.

3"In that day," declares the Sovereign LORD, "the songs in the temple will turn to wailing.*b* Many, many bodies—flung everywhere! Silence!"

4Hear this, you who trample the
    needy
  and do away with the poor of
    the land,

5saying,

"When will the New Moon be
    over
  that we may sell grain,
and the Sabbath be ended
  that we may market wheat?"—
skimping the measure,
  boosting the price
  and cheating with dishonest
    scales,
6buying the poor with silver
  and the needy for a pair of
    sandals,
  selling even the sweepings with
    the wheat.

---

*a*17 Hebrew *an unclean*   *b*3 Or *"the temple singers will wail*

⁷The Lᴏʀᴅ has sworn by the Pride of Jacob: "I will never forget anything they have done.

⁸"Will not the land tremble for this,
and all who live in it mourn?
The whole land will rise like the Nile;
it will be stirred up and then sink
like the river of Egypt.

⁹"In that day," declares the Sovereign Lᴏʀᴅ,

"I will make the sun go down at noon
and darken the earth in broad daylight.
¹⁰I will turn your religious feasts into mourning
and all your singing into weeping.
I will make all of you wear sackcloth
and shave your heads.
I will make that time like mourning for an only son
and the end of it like a bitter day.

¹¹"The days are coming," declares the Sovereign Lᴏʀᴅ,
"when I will send a famine through the land—
not a famine of food or a thirst for water,

but a famine of hearing the words of the Lᴏʀᴅ.
¹²Men will stagger from sea to sea and wander from north to east,
searching for the word of the Lᴏʀᴅ,
but they will not find it.

¹³"In that day

"the lovely young women and strong young men
will faint because of thirst.
¹⁴They who swear by the shameᵃ of Samaria,
or say, 'As surely as your god lives, O Dan,'
or, 'As surely as the godᵇ of Beersheba lives'—
they will fall,
never to rise again."

Israel to Be Destroyed

9 I saw the Lord standing by the altar, and he said:

"Strike the tops of the pillars
so that the thresholds shake.
Bring them down on the heads of all the people;
those who are left I will kill with the sword.
Not one will get away,
none will escape.
²Though they dig down to the depths of the grave,ᶜ

ᵃ14 Or *by Ashima*; or *by the idol*   ᵇ14 Or *power*   ᶜ2 Hebrew *to Sheol*

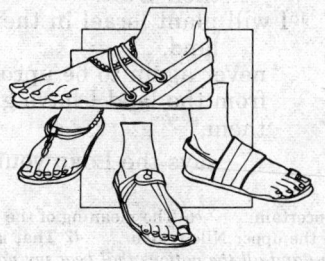

Life in Bible Times

SANDALS

People in Bible times wore sandals on their feet rather than shoes. Some of the rich in Amos's time thought that using their money to buy a pair of fancy sandals was more satisfying than using it to help someone in need.

from there my hand will take
   them.
Though they climb up to the
   heavens,
   from there I will bring them
     down.
³Though they hide themselves on
   the top of Carmel,
   there I will hunt them down
     and seize them.
Though they hide from me at the
   bottom of the sea,
   there I will command the
     serpent to bite them.
⁴Though they are driven into exile
   by their enemies,
   there I will command the sword
     to slay them.
I will fix my eyes upon them
   for evil and not for good."

⁵The Lord, the Lᴏʀᴅ Almighty,
   he who touches the earth and it
     melts,
   and all who live in it mourn—
the whole land rises like the Nile,
   then sinks like the river of
     Egypt—
⁶he who builds his lofty palaceᵃ in
   the heavens
   and sets its foundationᵇ on the
     earth,
who calls for the waters of the sea
   and pours them out over the
     face of the land—
   the Lᴏʀᴅ is his name.

⁷"Are not you Israelites
   the same to me as the
     Cushitesᶜ?"
             declares the Lᴏʀᴅ.
"Did I not bring Israel up from
   Egypt,
   the Philistines from Caphtorᵈ
   and the Arameans from Kir?

⁸"Surely the eyes of the Sovereign
   Lᴏʀᴅ
   are on the sinful kingdom.
I will destroy it
   from the face of the earth—
   yet I will not totally destroy

the house of Jacob,"
             declares the Lᴏʀᴅ.
⁹"For I will give the command,
   and I will shake the house of
     Israel
   among all the nations
as grain is shaken in a sieve,
   and not a pebble will reach the
     ground.
¹⁰All the sinners among my people
   will die by the sword,
all those who say,
   'Disaster will not overtake or
     meet us.'

Israel's Restoration

¹¹"In that day I will restore
   David's fallen tent.
I will repair its broken places,
   restore its ruins,
   and build it as it used to be,
¹²so that they may possess the
     remnant of Edom
   and all the nations that bear
     my name,ᵉ"
       declares the Lᴏʀᴅ, who will
            do these things.
¹³"The days are coming," declares
the Lᴏʀᴅ,

   "when the reaper will be
     overtaken by the plowman
   and the planter by the one
     treading grapes.
New wine will drip from the
     mountains
   and flow from all the hills.
¹⁴I will bring back my exiledᶠ
     people Israel;
   they will rebuild the ruined
     cities and live in them.
They will plant vineyards and
     drink their wine;
   they will make gardens and eat
     their fruit.
¹⁵I will plant Israel in their own
     land,
   never again to be uprooted
   from the land I have given
     them,"
           says the Lᴏʀᴅ your God.

ᵃ6 The meaning of the Hebrew for this phrase is uncertain.   ᵇ6 The meaning of the Hebrew for this word is uncertain.   ᶜ7 That is, people from the upper Nile region   ᵈ7 That is, Crete ᵉ12 Hebrew; Septuagint *so that the remnant of men / and all the nations that bear my name may seek the Lord*,   ᶠ14 Or *will restore the fortunes of my*

OBADIAH

WHO WROTE THIS BOOK?

Obadiah. Nothing more is known about this prophet.

WHY WAS THIS BOOK WRITTEN?

Obadiah speaks of the punishment God will bring on the Edomites, who had invaded Judah and plundered Jerusalem.

WHAT DO WE LEARN ABOUT GOD IN THIS BOOK?

God is faithful. He will keep his promise to Abraham: "Whoever curses you I will curse" (Genesis 12:3).

WHEN WAS THIS BOOK WRITTEN?

No one knows for sure when Obadiah was written.

¹The vision of Obadiah.

This is what the Sovereign LORD says about Edom—

We have heard a message from
    the LORD:
  An envoy was sent to the
    nations to say,
  "Rise, and let us go against her
    for battle"—

²"See, I will make you small
    among the nations;
  you will be utterly despised.
³The pride of your heart has
    deceived you,
  you who live in the clefts of the
    rocks*a*
  and make your home on the
    heights,
you who say to yourself,
  'Who can bring me down to the
    ground?'
⁴Though you soar like the eagle
  and make your nest among the
    stars,
  from there I will bring you
    down,"
            declares the LORD.
⁵"If thieves came to you,
  if robbers in the night—
  Oh, what a disaster awaits you—
  would they not steal only as
    much as they wanted?
  If grape pickers came to you,
  would they not leave a few
    grapes?
⁶But how Esau will be ransacked,
  his hidden treasures pillaged!
⁷All your allies will force you to
    the border;
  your friends will deceive and
    overpower you;
  those who eat your bread will set
    a trap for you,*b*
  but you will not detect it.

⁸"In that day," declares the LORD,
  "will I not destroy the wise men
    of Edom,
  men of understanding in the
    mountains of Esau?

⁹Your warriors, O Teman, will be
    terrified,
  and everyone in Esau's
    mountains
  will be cut down in the
    slaughter.
¹⁰Because of the violence against
    your brother Jacob,
  you will be covered with shame;
  you will be destroyed forever.
¹¹On the day you stood aloof
  while strangers carried off his
    wealth
  and foreigners entered his gates
  and cast lots for Jerusalem,
  you were like one of them.
¹²You should not look down on your
    brother
  in the day of his misfortune,
  nor rejoice over the people of
    Judah
  in the day of their destruction,
  nor boast so much
  in the day of their trouble.
¹³You should not march through
    the gates of my people
  in the day of their disaster,
  nor look down on them in their
    calamity
  in the day of their disaster,
  nor seize their wealth
  in the day of their disaster.
¹⁴You should not wait at the
    crossroads
  to cut down their fugitives,
  nor hand over their survivors
  in the day of their trouble.

¹⁵"The day of the LORD is near
    for all nations.
  As you have done, it will be done
    to you;
  your deeds will return upon
    your own head.
¹⁶Just as you drank on my holy
    hill,
  so all the nations will drink
    continually;
  they will drink and drink
  and be as if they had never
    been.
¹⁷But on Mount Zion will be
    deliverance;

---

*a*3 Or *of Sela*   *b*7 The meaning of the Hebrew for this clause is uncertain.

it will be holy,
and the house of Jacob
will possess its inheritance.
[18]The house of Jacob will be a fire
and the house of Joseph a
flame;
the house of Esau will be stubble,
and they will set it on fire and
consume it.
There will be no survivors
from the house of Esau."
The LORD has spoken.

[19]People from the Negev will
occupy
the mountains of Esau,
and people from the foothills will
possess

the land of the Philistines.
They will occupy the fields of
Ephraim and Samaria,
and Benjamin will possess
Gilead.
[20]This company of Israelite exiles
who are in Canaan
will possess ͺthe landͺ as far as
Zarephath;
the exiles from Jerusalem who
are in Sepharad
will possess the towns of the
Negev.
[21]Deliverers will go up on[a] Mount
Zion
to govern the mountains of
Esau.
And the kingdom will be the
LORD's.

---

a21 Or from

JONAH

WHO WROTE THIS BOOK?

The prophet Jonah.

WHY WAS THIS BOOK WRITTEN?

Jonah shows Israel that God does not punish if people repent and are sorry for their sins.

WHAT DO WE LEARN ABOUT GOD IN THIS BOOK?

God forgives his disobedient prophet and gives Jonah a second chance. God also forgives the people of Nineveh. God does not punish people who repent.

WHAT IS SPECIAL ABOUT THIS BOOK?

God shows love for the foreign people in Nineveh as well as for his own Hebrew people.

WHEN WAS THIS BOOK WRITTEN?

Jonah was written about 760 B.C.

WHAT ARE SOME OF THE STORIES IN THIS BOOK?

Jonah is swallowed by a fish.	Jonah 1
The people of Nineveh repent.	Jonah 3
God teaches Jonah to care about all people.	Jonah 4

Jonah Flees From the LORD

1 The word of the LORD came to Jonah son of Amittai: ²"Go to the great city of Nineveh and preach against it, because its wickedness has come up before me."

³But Jonah ran away from the LORD and headed for Tarshish. He went down to Joppa, where he found a ship bound for that port. After paying the fare, he went aboard and sailed for Tarshish to flee from the LORD.

⁴Then the LORD sent a great wind on the sea, and such a violent storm arose that the ship threatened to break up. ⁵All the sailors were afraid and each cried out to his own god. And they threw the cargo into the sea to lighten the ship.

But Jonah had gone below deck, where he lay down and fell into a deep sleep. ⁶The captain went to him and said, "How can you sleep? Get up and call on your god! Maybe he will take notice of us, and we will not perish."

⁷Then the sailors said to each other, "Come, let us cast lots to find out who is responsible for this calamity." They cast lots and the lot fell on Jonah. ⁸So they asked him, "Tell us, who is responsible for making all this trouble for us? What do you do? Where do you come from? What is your country? From what people are you?"

⁹He answered, "I am a Hebrew and I worship the LORD, the God of heaven, who made the sea and the land."

¹⁰This terrified them and they asked, "What have you done?" (They knew he was running away from the LORD, because he had already told them so.)

¹¹The sea was getting rougher and rougher. So they asked him, "What should we do to you to make the sea calm down for us?"

¹²"Pick me up and throw me into the sea," he replied, "and it will become calm. I know that it is my fault that this great storm has come upon you."

¹³Instead, the men did their best to row back to land. But they could not, for the sea grew even wilder than before. ¹⁴Then they cried to the LORD, "O LORD, please do not let us die for taking this man's life. Do not hold us accountable for killing an innocent man, for you, O LORD, have done as you pleased." ¹⁵Then they took Jonah and threw him overboard, and the raging sea grew calm. ¹⁶At this the men greatly feared the LORD, and they offered a sacrifice to the LORD and made vows to him.

JONAH'S TRIP

Nineveh was far north of Israel, and Tarshish was far to the south. God told Jonah to go to Nineveh, but Jonah got on a ship to Tarshish. This Bible book tells us why, and it tells us what happened to Jonah.

---

¹⁷But the LORD provided a great fish to swallow Jonah, and Jonah was inside the fish three days and three nights.

Jonah's Prayer

2 From inside the fish Jonah prayed to the LORD his God. ²He said:

"In my distress I called to the
    LORD,
    and he answered me.
From the depths of the grave^a I
    called for help,
    and you listened to my cry.
³You hurled me into the deep,
    into the very heart of the seas,

---

^a2 Hebrew *Sheol*

and the currents swirled about
me;
all your waves and breakers
swept over me.
⁴I said, 'I have been banished
from your sight;
yet I will look again
toward your holy temple.'
⁵The engulfing waters threatened
me,ᵃ
the deep surrounded me;
seaweed was wrapped around
my head.
⁶To the roots of the mountains I
sank down;
the earth beneath barred me in
forever.
But you brought my life up from
the pit,
O Lᴏʀᴅ my God.

⁷"When my life was ebbing away,
I remembered you, Lᴏʀᴅ,
and my prayer rose to you,
to your holy temple.

⁸"Those who cling to worthless
idols
forfeit the grace that could be
theirs.
⁹But I, with a song of
thanksgiving,
will sacrifice to you.
What I have vowed I will make
good.
Salvation comes from the
Lᴏʀᴅ."

¹⁰And the Lᴏʀᴅ commanded the
fish, and it vomited Jonah onto dry
land.

Jonah Goes to Nineveh

3 Then the word of the Lᴏʀᴅ came
to Jonah a second time: ²"Go to
the great city of Nineveh and proclaim to it the message I give you."

³Jonah obeyed the word of the Lᴏʀᴅ
and went to Nineveh. Now Nineveh
was a very important city—a visit required three days. ⁴On the first day,
Jonah started into the city. He proclaimed: "Forty more days and Nineveh will be overturned." ⁵The Nine-

vites believed God. They declared a
fast, and all of them, from the greatest to the least, put on sackcloth.

CARGO SHIPS

In ancient times the crew of a
cargo ship (see Jonah 1:3, 5) lived
and slept on the deck of their ship.
When storms came they tried to
find a sheltered harbor, or they
risked being swept overboard.

---

⁶When the news reached the king
of Nineveh, he rose from his throne,
took off his royal robes, covered himself with sackcloth and sat down in
the dust. ⁷Then he issued a proclamation in Nineveh:

"By the decree of the king and his
nobles:

Do not let any man or beast,
herd or flock, taste anything; do
not let them eat or drink. ⁸But
let man and beast be covered
with sackcloth. Let everyone call
urgently on God. Let them give
up their evil ways and their violence. ⁹Who knows? God may yet
relent and with compassion turn
from his fierce anger so that we
will not perish."

¹⁰When God saw what they did and
how they turned from their evil ways,
he had compassion and did not bring
upon them the destruction he had
threatened.

Jonah's Anger at the Lᴏʀᴅ's Compassion

4 But Jonah was greatly displeased and became angry. ²He

ᵃ5 Or *waters were at my throat*

prayed to the LORD, "O LORD, is this not what I said when I was still at home? That is why I was so quick to flee to Tarshish. I knew that you are a gracious and compassionate God, slow to anger and abounding in love, a God who relents from sending calamity. ³Now, O LORD, take away my life, for it is better for me to die than to live."

⁴But the LORD replied, "Have you any right to be angry?"

⁵Jonah went out and sat down at a place east of the city. There he made himself a shelter, sat in its shade and waited to see what would happen to the city. ⁶Then the LORD God provided a vine and made it grow up over Jonah to give shade for his head to ease his discomfort, and Jonah was very happy about the vine. ⁷But at dawn the next day God provided a worm, which chewed the vine so that it withered. ⁸When the sun rose, God provided a scorching east wind, and the sun blazed on Jonah's head so that he grew faint. He wanted to die, and said, "It would be better for me to die than to live."

⁹But God said to Jonah, "Do you have a right to be angry about the vine?"

"I do," he said. "I am angry enough to die."

¹⁰But the LORD said, "You have been concerned about this vine, though you did not tend it or make it grow. It sprang up overnight and died overnight. ¹¹But Nineveh has more than a hundred and twenty thousand people who cannot tell their right hand from their left, and many cattle as well. Should I not be concerned about that great city?"

ET'S LIVE IT!   Jonah 4:1–11

JONAH'S VINE ➠ Jonah told the people of Nineveh that God would destroy the city. The people repented, and God did not destroy Nineveh. Read Jonah 4, and find out how Jonah felt about this. Find out too why God did not destroy Nineveh.

Get a lima bean seed and plant it in dirt in a styrofoam cup. Put it by your window, water it, and watch the plant grow. As you care for your plant, remember how much God loves people. If we remember how much God loves everyone, we won't be jealous when good things happen to others.

MICAH

1 The word of the LORD that came to Micah of Moresheth during the reigns of Jotham, Ahaz and Hezekiah, kings of Judah—the vision he saw concerning Samaria and Jerusalem.

²Hear, O peoples, all of you,
    listen, O earth and all who are
      in it,
that the Sovereign LORD may
    witness against you,
    the Lord from his holy temple.

Judgment Against Samaria and Jerusalem

³Look! The LORD is coming from
    his dwelling place;
he comes down and treads the
    high places of the earth.
⁴The mountains melt beneath
    him
    and the valleys split apart,
like wax before the fire,
    like water rushing down a
      slope.
⁵All this is because of Jacob's
    transgression,
    because of the sins of the house
      of Israel.
What is Jacob's transgression?
    Is it not Samaria?
What is Judah's high place?
    Is it not Jerusalem?

⁶"Therefore I will make Samaria a
    heap of rubble,
    a place for planting vineyards.
I will pour her stones into the
    valley
    and lay bare her foundations.
⁷All her idols will be broken to
    pieces;
    all her temple gifts will be
      burned with fire;
    I will destroy all her images.
Since she gathered her gifts from
    the wages of prostitutes,
    as the wages of prostitutes they
      will again be used."

Weeping and Mourning

⁸Because of this I will weep and
    wail;
    I will go about barefoot and
      naked.
I will howl like a jackal
    and moan like an owl.
⁹For her wound is incurable;
    it has come to Judah.
It^a has reached the very gate of
    my people,
    even to Jerusalem itself.
¹⁰Tell it not in Gath^b;
    weep not at all.^{c}
In Beth Ophrah^d
    roll in the dust.
¹¹Pass on in nakedness and
    shame,
    you who live in Shaphir.^{e}
Those who live in Zaanan^f
    will not come out.
Beth Ezel is in mourning;
    its protection is taken from you.
¹²Those who live in Maroth^g writhe
    in pain,
    waiting for relief,
because disaster has come from
    the LORD,
    even to the gate of Jerusalem.
¹³You who live in Lachish,^{h}
    harness the team to the chariot.
You were the beginning of sin
    to the Daughter of Zion,
for the transgressions of Israel
    were found in you.
¹⁴Therefore you will give parting
    gifts
    to Moresheth Gath.
The town of Aczib^i will prove
    deceptive
    to the kings of Israel.
¹⁵I will bring a conqueror against
    you
    who live in Mareshah.^{j}
He who is the glory of Israel
    will come to Adullam.
¹⁶Shave your heads in mourning
    for the children in whom you
      delight;

---

^{a}9 Or *He* ^{b}10 *Gath* sounds like the Hebrew for *tell.* ^{c}10 Hebrew; Septuagint may suggest *not in Acco.* The Hebrew for *in Acco* sounds like the Hebrew for *weep.* ^{d}10 *Beth Ophrah* means *house of dust.* ^{e}11 *Shaphir* means *pleasant.* ^{f}11 *Zaanan* sounds like the Hebrew for *come out.* ^{g}12 *Maroth* sounds like the Hebrew for *bitter.* ^{h}13 *Lachish* sounds like the Hebrew for *team.* ^{i}14 *Aczib* means *deception.* ^{j}15 *Mareshah* sounds like the Hebrew for *conqueror.*

make yourselves as bald as the
vulture,
for they will go from you into
exile.

Man's Plans and God's

2 Woe to those who plan
iniquity,
to those who plot evil on their
beds!
At morning's light they carry it
out
because it is in their power to
do it.
²They covet fields and seize
them,
and houses, and take
They defraud a man of his
home,
a fellowman of his inheritance.

³Therefore, the LORD says:

"I am planning disaster against
this people,
from which you cannot save
yourselves.
You will no longer walk proudly,
for it will be a time of calamity.
⁴In that day men will ridicule
you;
they will taunt you with this
mournful song:
'We are utterly ruined;
my people's possession is
divided up.
He takes it from me!
He assigns our fields to
traitors.'"

⁵Therefore you will have no one in
the assembly of the LORD
to divide the land by lot.

False Prophets

⁶"Do not prophesy," their prophets
say.
"Do not prophesy about these
things;
disgrace will not overtake us."
⁷Should it be said, O house of
Jacob:
"Is the Spirit of the LORD
angry?
Does he do such things?"

"Do not my words do good
to him whose ways are upright?
⁸Lately my people have risen up
like an enemy.
You strip off the rich robe
from those who pass by without
a care,
like men returning from battle.
⁹You drive the women of my
people
from their pleasant homes.
You take away my blessing
from their children forever.
¹⁰Get up, go away!
For this is not your resting
place,
because it is defiled,
it is ruined, beyond all remedy.
¹¹If a liar and deceiver comes and
says,
'I will prophesy for you plenty
of wine and beer,'
he would be just the prophet for
this people!

Deliverance Promised

¹²"I will surely gather all of you,
O Jacob;
I will surely bring together the
remnant of Israel.

▓ET'S LIVE IT!   Micah 2:1–3

EVIL PEOPLE WILL PAY ➡ Read Micah 2:1–3. What will God do to those
who plan evil?
It's wise for Christians to plan—but we must plan to do good. Get a
pen and paper and write down some plans. Plan something good to
do for your parents. Plan something good to do for two of your friends.
Plan something good to do for a school teacher or Church school teacher. Then carry out your plans!
God, who is watching, will plan something good for you in return!

I will bring them together like
   sheep in a pen,
  like a flock in its pasture;
  the place will throng with
     people.
¹³One who breaks open the way
     will go up before them;
  they will break through the
     gate and go out.
Their king will pass through
     before them,
  the LORD at their head."

Leaders and Prophets Rebuked

3 Then I said,
      "Listen, you leaders of Jacob,
  you rulers of the house of
     Israel.
Should you not know justice,
² you who hate good and love
     evil;
  who tear the skin from my people
  and the flesh from their bones;
³who eat my people's flesh,
  strip off their skin
  and break their bones in pieces;
who chop them up like meat for
     the pan,
  like flesh for the pot?"

⁴Then they will cry out to the
   LORD,
  but he will not answer them.
At that time he will hide his face
     from them
  because of the evil they have
     done.

⁵This is what the LORD says:

"As for the prophets
  who lead my people astray,
if one feeds them,
  they proclaim 'peace';
if he does not,
  they prepare to wage war
     against him.
⁶Therefore night will come over
     you, without visions,
  and darkness, without
     divination.
The sun will set for the prophets,
  and the day will go dark for
     them.
⁷The seers will be ashamed
  and the diviners disgraced.

They will all cover their faces
  because there is no answer from
     God."

⁸But as for me, I am filled with
     power,
  with the Spirit of the LORD,
  and with justice and might,
to declare to Jacob his
     transgression,
  to Israel his sin.
⁹Hear this, you leaders of the
     house of Jacob,
  you rulers of the house of
     Israel,
who despise justice
  and distort all that is right;
¹⁰who build Zion with bloodshed,
  and Jerusalem with wickedness.
¹¹Her leaders judge for a bribe,
  her priests teach for a price,
  and her prophets tell fortunes
     for money.
Yet they lean upon the LORD and
     say,
  "Is not the LORD among us?
  No disaster will come upon us."

Life In Bible Times

BRIBES

In Bible times people often gave
gifts. A person who received a gift
was expected to give a gift in
return. Gifts to judges were bribes,
to get the judge to make a
decision in favor of the one who
gave him the gift. God's Law tells
judges not to accept bribes (see
Exodus 23:8).

¹²Therefore because of you,
  Zion will be plowed like a field,
Jerusalem will become a heap of
     rubble,
  the temple hill a mound
     overgrown with thickets.

The Mountain of the LORD

4 In the last days
the mountain of the LORD's
temple will be established
as chief among the mountains;
it will be raised above the hills,
and peoples will stream to it.

²Many nations will come and
say,

"Come, let us go up to the
mountain of the LORD,
to the house of the God of
Jacob.
He will teach us his ways,
so that we may walk in his
paths."
The law will go out from Zion,
the word of the LORD from
Jerusalem.
³He will judge between many
peoples
and will settle disputes for
strong nations far and
wide.
They will beat their swords into
plowshares
and their spears into pruning
hooks.
Nation will not take up sword
against nation,
nor will they train for war
anymore.
⁴Every man will sit under his own
vine
and under his own fig
tree,
and no one will make them
afraid,
for the LORD Almighty has
spoken.
⁵All the nations may walk
in the name of their gods;
we will walk in the name of the
LORD
our God for ever and ever.

The LORD's Plan

⁶"In that day," declares the LORD,

"I will gather the lame;
I will assemble the exiles

and those I have brought to
grief.
⁷I will make the lame a remnant,
those driven away a strong
nation.
The LORD will rule over them in
Mount Zion
from that day and forever.
⁸As for you, O watchtower of the
flock,
O stronghold*a* of the Daughter
of Zion,
the former dominion will be
restored to you;
kingship will come to the
Daughter of Jerusalem."

⁹Why do you now cry aloud—
have you no king?
Has your counselor perished,
that pain seizes you like that of
a woman in labor?
¹⁰Writhe in agony, O Daughter of
Zion,
like a woman in labor,
for now you must leave the city
to camp in the open field.
You will go to Babylon;
there you will be rescued.
There the LORD will redeem you
out of the hand of your enemies.

¹¹But now many nations
are gathered against you.
They say, "Let her be defiled,
let our eyes gloat over Zion!"
¹²But they do not know
the thoughts of the LORD;
they do not understand his plan,
he who gathers them like
sheaves to the threshing
floor.

¹³"Rise and thresh, O Daughter of
Zion,
for I will give you horns of iron;
I will give you hoofs of bronze
and you will break to pieces
many nations."

You will devote their ill-gotten
gains to the LORD,
their wealth to the Lord of all
the earth.

*a*8 Or *hill*

A Promised Ruler From Bethlehem

5 Marshal your troops, O city of
troops,[a]
for a siege is laid against us.
They will strike Israel's ruler
on the cheek with a rod.

[2]"But you, Bethlehem Ephrathah,
though you are small among
the clans[b] of Judah,
out of you will come for me
one who will be ruler over
Israel,
whose origins[c] are from of old,
from ancient times. [d]"

[3]Therefore Israel will be
abandoned
until the time when she who is
in labor gives birth
and the rest of his brothers return
to join the Israelites.

? DID YOU KNOW?   5:2

**When did Micah predict that
Jesus would be born in
Bethlehem?**

Micah wrote about seven hundred years before Jesus was born!
God knows the future, and through
the Bible he often tells us about the
future.

---

[4]He will stand and shepherd his
flock
in the strength of the LORD,
in the majesty of the name of
the LORD his God.
And they will live securely, for
then his greatness
will reach to the ends of the
earth.
[5] And he will be their peace.

Deliverance and Destruction

When the Assyrian invades our
land

and marches through our
fortresses,
we will raise against him seven
shepherds,
even eight leaders of men.
[6]They will rule[e] the land of
Assyria with the sword,
the land of Nimrod with drawn
sword.[f]
He will deliver us from the
Assyrian
when he invades our land
and marches into our
borders.

[7]The remnant of Jacob will be
in the midst of many peoples
like dew from the LORD,
like showers on the grass,
which do not wait for man
or linger for mankind.
[8]The remnant of Jacob will be
among the nations,
in the midst of many peoples,
like a lion among the beasts of
the forest,
like a young lion among flocks
of sheep,
which mauls and mangles as it
goes,
and no one can rescue.
[9]Your hand will be lifted up in
triumph over your enemies,
and all your foes will be
destroyed.

[10]"In that day," declares the LORD,

"I will destroy your horses from
among you
and demolish your chariots.
[11]I will destroy the cities of your
land
and tear down all your
strongholds.
[12]I will destroy your witchcraft
and you will no longer cast
spells.
[13]I will destroy your carved images
and your sacred stones from
among you;
you will no longer bow down
to the work of your hands.

---

[a]1 Or *Strengthen your walls, O walled city*   [b]2 Or *rulers*   [c]2 Hebrew *goings out*   [d]2 Or
from days of eternity   [e]6 Or *crush*   [f]6 Or *Nimrod in its gates*

14I will uproot from among you
    your Asherah poles[a]
and demolish your cities.
15I will take vengeance in anger
    and wrath
upon the nations that have not
    obeyed me."

The LORD's Case Against Israel

6 Listen to what the LORD says:

"Stand up, plead your case
    before the mountains;
let the hills hear what you have
    to say.
2Hear, O mountains, the LORD's
    accusation;
listen, you everlasting
    foundations of the earth.
For the LORD has a case against
    his people;
he is lodging a charge against
    Israel.

3"My people, what have I done to
    you?
How have I burdened you?
    Answer me.
4I brought you up out of Egypt
    and redeemed you from the land
    of slavery.
I sent Moses to lead you,
    also Aaron and Miriam.
5My people, remember
    what Balak king of Moab
    counseled
and what Balaam son of Beor
    answered.
Remember your journey from
    Shittim to Gilgal,
that you may know the
    righteous acts of the LORD."

6With what shall I come before the
    LORD
and bow down before the
    exalted God?
Shall I come before him with
    burnt offerings,
with calves a year old?
7Will the LORD be pleased with
    thousands of rams,
with ten thousand rivers of oil?

Shall I offer my firstborn for my
    transgression,
the fruit of my body for the sin
    of my soul?

THE OFFERING GOD WANTS

God wanted offerings in Old
Testament times, but he wanted
the people to bring them because
they loved God and were trying to
live good lives. God was not
pleased with offerings of animals
from people who kept doing
wicked things.

8He has showed you, O man, what
    is good.
    And what does the LORD require
    of you?
To act justly and to love mercy
    and to walk humbly with your
    God.

Israel's Guilt and Punishment

9Listen! The LORD is calling to the
    city—
and to fear your name is
    wisdom—
"Heed the rod and the One who
    appointed it.[b]
10Am I still to forget, O wicked
    house,
your ill-gotten treasures
    and the short ephah,[c] which is
    accursed?
11Shall I acquit a man with
    dishonest scales,
with a bag of false weights?
12Her rich men are violent;
    her people are liars
and their tongues speak
    deceitfully.

---

a14 That is, symbols of the goddess Asherah
uncertain.   c10 An ephah was a dry measure.   b9 The meaning of the Hebrew for this line is

¹³Therefore, I have begun to
>destroy you,
>to ruin you because of your
>sins.

¹⁴You will eat but not be satisfied;
>your stomach will still be
>empty.ᵃ
>You will store up but save
>nothing,
>because what you save I will
>give to the sword.

¹⁵You will plant but not harvest;
>you will press olives but not use
>the oil on yourselves,
>you will crush grapes but not
>drink the wine.

¹⁶You have observed the statutes of
>Omri
>and all the practices of Ahab's
>house,
>and you have followed their
>traditions.
>Therefore I will give you over to
>ruin
>and your people to derision;
>you will bear the scorn of the
>nations.ᵇ"

Israel's Misery

7 What misery is mine!
>I am like one who gathers
>summer fruit
>at the gleaning of the vineyard;
>there is no cluster of grapes to
>eat,
>none of the early figs that I
>crave.

²The godly have been swept from
>the land;
>not one upright man
>remains.
>All men lie in wait to shed blood;
>each hunts his brother with a
>net.

³Both hands are skilled in doing
>evil;
>the ruler demands gifts,
>the judge accepts bribes,
>the powerful dictate what they
>desire—
>they all conspire together.

⁴The best of them is like a brier,

the most upright worse than a
>thorn hedge.
>The day of your watchmen has
>come,
>the day God visits you.
>Now is the time of their
>confusion.

⁵Do not trust a neighbor;
>put no confidence in a friend.
>Even with her who lies in your
>embrace
>be careful of your words.

⁶For a son dishonors his father,
>a daughter rises up against her
>mother,
>a daughter-in-law against her
>mother-in-law—
>a man's enemies are the
>members of his own
>household.

⁷But as for me, I watch in hope for
>the Lᴏʀᴅ,
>I wait for God my Savior;
>my God will hear me.

𝗪ORDS TO REMEMBER

7:7 I watch in hope for the
>Lᴏʀᴅ.
>I wait for God my Savior;
>my God will hear me.

Israel Will Rise

⁸Do not gloat over me, my enemy!
>Though I have fallen, I will
>rise.
>Though I sit in darkness,
>the Lᴏʀᴅ will be my light.

⁹Because I have sinned against
>him,
>I will bear the Lᴏʀᴅ's wrath,
>until he pleads my case
>and establishes my right.
>He will bring me out into the
>light;
>I will see his righteousness.

¹⁰Then my enemy will see it
>and will be covered with shame,
>she who said to me,

ᵃ14 The meaning of the Hebrew for this word is uncertain.   ᵇ16 Septuagint; Hebrew *scorn due
my people*

"Where is the LORD your God?"
My eyes will see her downfall;
    even now she will be trampled
      underfoot
    like mire in the streets.

¹¹The day for building your walls
    will come,
    the day for extending your
      boundaries.
¹²In that day people will come to
    you
    from Assyria and the cities of
      Egypt,
even from Egypt to the Euphrates
    and from sea to sea
    and from mountain to
      mountain.
¹³The earth will become desolate
    because of its inhabitants,
    as the result of their deeds.

Prayer and Praise

¹⁴Shepherd your people with your
    staff,
    the flock of your inheritance,
which lives by itself in a forest,
    in fertile pasturelands. ᵃ
Let them feed in Bashan and
    Gilead
    as in days long ago.
¹⁵"As in the days when you came
    out of Egypt,

ᵃ14 Or in the middle of Carmel

I will show them my wonders."

¹⁶Nations will see and be ashamed,
    deprived of all their power.
They will lay their hands on their
    mouths
    and their ears will become
      deaf.
¹⁷They will lick dust like a snake,
    like creatures that crawl on the
      ground.
They will come trembling out of
    their dens;
    they will turn in fear to the
      LORD our God
    and will be afraid of you.
¹⁸Who is a God like you,
    who pardons sin and forgives
      the transgression
    of the remnant of his
      inheritance?
You do not stay angry forever
    but delight to show mercy.
¹⁹You will again have compassion
    on us;
    you will tread our sins
      underfoot
    and hurl all our iniquities into
      the depths of the sea.
²⁰You will be true to Jacob,
    and show mercy to Abraham,
as you pledged on oath to our
    fathers
    in days long ago.

▐ ET'S LIVE IT!   Micah 7:18–20

GOD WILL FORGIVE YOUR SINS ➡ Read Micah 7:18–20. These beautiful verses tell us how God loves us even when we sin and how he wants to forgive us.

If you have done something wrong for which you don't feel forgiven, here's something you can do: Confess the sin by writing it on a piece of paper and telling God you're sorry for what you've done. Tear the paper into tiny pieces, drop them on the floor and step all over them. Now vacuum them up until they are gone!

Now reread Micah 7:19 and thank God that he forgives your sins and treads them underfoot.

NAHUM

The prophet Nahum.

WHY WAS THIS BOOK WRITTEN?

Nahum assures the people of Judah that God will destroy Nineveh, the capital city of their great enemy, Assyria.

WHAT DO WE LEARN ABOUT GOD IN THIS BOOK?

God will punish the enemies of the people he loves.

WHEN WAS THIS BOOK WRITTEN?

Nahum probably preached between 663 and 655 B.C.

NAH HAB ZEP

1 An oracle concerning Nineveh. The book of the vision of Nahum the Elkoshite.

The LORD's Anger Against Nineveh

²The LORD is a jealous and
  avenging God;
  the LORD takes vengeance and
    is filled with wrath.
The LORD takes vengeance on his
    foes
  and maintains his wrath
    against his enemies.
³The LORD is slow to anger and
    great in power;
  the LORD will not leave the
    guilty unpunished.
His way is in the whirlwind and
    the storm,
  and clouds are the dust of his
    feet.
⁴He rebukes the sea and dries it
    up;
  he makes all the rivers run
    dry.
Bashan and Carmel wither
  and the blossoms of Lebanon
    fade.
⁵The mountains quake before him
  and the hills melt away.
The earth trembles at his
    presence,
  the world and all who live
    in it.

𝖂ORDS TO REMEMBER

1:7   The LORD is good,
        a refuge in times of
          trouble.
        He cares for those who trust
          in him.

---

⁶Who can withstand his
    indignation?
  Who can endure his fierce
    anger?
His wrath is poured out like fire;

the rocks are shattered before
  him.
⁷The LORD is good,
  a refuge in times of trouble.
He cares for those who trust in
    him,
⁸ but with an overwhelming
    flood
he will make an end of ⌊Nineveh⌋;
  he will pursue his foes into
    darkness.

⁹Whatever they plot against the
    LORD
  he^a will bring to an end;
  trouble will not come a second
    time.
¹⁰They will be entangled among
    thorns
  and drunk from their wine;
  they will be consumed like dry
    stubble.^b
¹¹From you, ⌊O Nineveh,⌋ has one
    come forth
  who plots evil against the
    LORD
  and counsels wickedness.

¹²This is what the LORD says:

"Although they have allies and
    are numerous,
  they will be cut off and pass
    away.
Although I have afflicted you,
    ⌊O Judah,⌋
  I will afflict you no more.
¹³Now I will break their yoke from
    your neck
  and tear your shackles away."

¹⁴The LORD has given a command
    concerning you, ⌊Nineveh⌋:
  "You will have no descendants
    to bear your name.
I will destroy the carved images
    and cast idols
  that are in the temple of your
    gods.
I will prepare your grave,
  for you are vile."

---

^a9 Or What do you foes plot against the LORD? / He
verse is uncertain.   ^b10 The meaning of the Hebrew for this

¹⁵Look, there on the mountains,
the feet of one who brings good
news,
who proclaims peace!
Celebrate your festivals, O Judah,
and fulfill your vows.
No more will the wicked invade
you;
they will be completely
destroyed.

Nineveh to Fall

2 An attacker advances against
you, ˌNinevehˌ.
Guard the fortress,
watch the road,
brace yourselves,
marshal all your strength!

²The LORD will restore the
splendor of Jacob
like the splendor of Israel,
though destroyers have laid them
waste
and have ruined their vines.

³The shields of his soldiers are red;
the warriors are clad in scarlet.
The metal on the chariots flashes
on the day they are made
ready;
the spears of pine are
brandished.ᵃ
⁴The chariots storm through the
streets,
rushing back and forth through
the squares.
They look like flaming torches;
they dart about like lightning.

⁵He summons his picked troops,
yet they stumble on their way.
They dash to the city wall;
the protective shield is put in
place.
⁶The river gates are thrown open
and the palace collapses.
⁷It is decreedᵇ that ˌthe cityˌ
be exiled and carried away.
Its slave girls moan like doves
and beat upon their breasts.
⁸Nineveh is like a pool,
and its water is draining away.

"Stop! Stop!" they cry,
but no one turns back.
⁹Plunder the silver!
Plunder the gold!
The supply is endless,
the wealth from all its
treasures!
¹⁰She is pillaged, plundered,
stripped!
Hearts melt, knees give way,
bodies tremble, every face grows
pale.

¹¹Where now is the lions' den,
the place where they fed their
young,
where the lion and lioness went,
and the cubs, with nothing to
fear?
¹²The lion killed enough for his
cubs
and strangled the prey for his
mate,
filling his lairs with the kill
and his dens with the prey.

¹³"I am against you,"
declares the LORD Almighty.
"I will burn up your chariots in
smoke,
and the sword will devour your
young lions.
I will leave you no prey on the
earth.
The voices of your messengers
will no longer be heard."

Woe to Nineveh

3 Woe to the city of blood,
full of lies,
full of plunder,
never without victims!
²The crack of whips,
the clatter of wheels,
galloping horses
and jolting chariots!
³Charging cavalry,
flashing swords
and glittering spears!
Many casualties,
piles of dead,
bodies without number,

ᵃ3 Hebrew; Septuagint and Syriac / *the horsemen rush to and fro*   ᵇ7 The meaning of the
Hebrew for this word is uncertain.

people stumbling over the
corpses—
[4]all because of the wanton lust of a
harlot,
alluring, the mistress of
sorceries,
who enslaved nations by her
prostitution
and peoples by her witchcraft.

[5]"I am against you," declares the
LORD Almighty.
"I will lift your skirts over your
face.
I will show the nations your
nakedness
and the kingdoms your shame.
[6]I will pelt you with filth,
I will treat you with contempt
and make you a spectacle.
[7]All who see you will flee from you
and say,
'Nineveh is in ruins—who will
mourn for her?'
Where can I find anyone to
comfort you?"

[8]Are you better than Thebes,[a]
situated on the Nile,
with water around her?
The river was her defense,
the waters her wall.
[9]Cush[b] and Egypt were her
boundless strength;
Put and Libya were among her
allies.
[10]Yet she was taken captive
and went into exile.
Her infants were dashed to pieces
at the head of every street.
Lots were cast for her nobles,
and all her great men were put
in chains.
[11]You too will become drunk;
you will go into hiding
and seek refuge from the
enemy.

[12]All your fortresses are like fig
trees
with their first ripe fruit;

when they are shaken,
the figs fall into the mouth of
the eater.
[13]Look at your troops—
they are all women!
The gates of your land
are wide open to your enemies;
fire has consumed their bars.

[14]Draw water for the siege,
strengthen your defenses!
Work the clay,
tread the mortar,
repair the brickwork!
[15]There the fire will devour you;
the sword will cut you down
and, like grasshoppers, consume
you.
Multiply like grasshoppers,
multiply like locusts!
[16]You have increased the number
of your merchants
till they are more than the
stars of the sky,
but like locusts they strip the
land
and then fly away.
[17]Your guards are like locusts,
your officials like swarms of
locusts
that settle in the walls on a
cold day—
but when the sun appears they fly
away,
and no one knows where.

[18]O king of Assyria, your
shepherds[c] slumber;
your nobles lie down to rest.
Your people are scattered on the
mountains
with no one to gather them.
[19]Nothing can heal your wound;
your injury is fatal.
Everyone who hears the news
about you
claps his hands at your
fall,
for who has not felt
your endless cruelty?

---

a8 Hebrew *No Amon*   *b9* That is, the upper Nile region   *c18* Or *rulers*

HABAKKUK

WHO WROTE THIS BOOK?

The prophet Habakkuk.

WHY WAS THIS BOOK WRITTEN?

Habakkuk shows that people never get away with being wicked but will be punished by God.

WHAT DO WE LEARN ABOUT GOD IN THIS BOOK?

God is too holy to let men get away with sin. He punishes everyone who sins, even people like the Babylonians, who seemed to get rich by being wicked.

WHAT IS SPECIAL ABOUT THIS BOOK?

Habakkuk is afraid when he learns that God will send the Babylonians against Judah. But in the end Habakkuk decides to trust God anyway.

WHEN WAS THIS BOOK WRITTEN?

Habakkuk was written during the reign of good King Josiah, who ruled Judah from 639 to 597 B.C.

1 The oracle that Habakkuk the prophet received.

Habakkuk's Complaint

²How long, O Lord, must I call for help,
    but you do not listen?
Or cry out to you, "Violence!"
    but you do not save?
³Why do you make me look at injustice?
    Why do you tolerate wrong?
Destruction and violence are before me;
    there is strife, and conflict abounds.
⁴Therefore the law is paralyzed,
    and justice never prevails.
The wicked hem in the righteous,
    so that justice is perverted.

❓DID YOU KNOW?   1:2

Why was Habakkuk so unhappy?

Habakkuk saw injustice and sin in Judah. He was unhappy because God let such evil things happen. God told his prophet that he would punish his people by letting the Babylonians invade their country.

The Lord's Answer

⁵"Look at the nations and watch—
    and be utterly amazed.
For I am going to do something in your days
    that you would not believe,
    even if you were told.
⁶I am raising up the Babylonians,^a
    that ruthless and impetuous people,
who sweep across the whole earth
    to seize dwelling places not their own.
⁷They are a feared and dreaded people;
    they are a law to themselves
    and promote their own honor.

⁸Their horses are swifter than leopards,
    fiercer than wolves at dusk.
Their cavalry gallops headlong;
    their horsemen come from afar.
They fly like a vulture swooping to devour;
 ⁹ they all come bent on violence.
Their hordes^b advance like a desert wind
    and gather prisoners like sand.
¹⁰They deride kings
    and scoff at rulers.
They laugh at all fortified cities;
    they build earthen ramps and capture them.
¹¹Then they sweep past like the wind and go on—
    guilty men, whose own strength is their god."

Habakkuk's Second Complaint

¹²O Lord, are you not from everlasting?
    My God, my Holy One, we will not die.
O Lord, you have appointed them to execute judgment;
    O Rock, you have ordained them to punish.
¹³Your eyes are too pure to look on evil;
    you cannot tolerate wrong.
Why then do you tolerate the treacherous?
    Why are you silent while the wicked
swallow up those more righteous than themselves?
¹⁴You have made men like fish in the sea,
    like sea creatures that have no ruler.
¹⁵The wicked foe pulls all of them up with hooks,
    he catches them in his net,
he gathers them up in his dragnet;
    and so he rejoices and is glad.
¹⁶Therefore he sacrifices to his net
    and burns incense to his dragnet,

^a6 Or *Chaldeans*   ^b9 The meaning of the Hebrew for this word is uncertain.

for by his net he lives in luxury
and enjoys the choicest food.
¹⁷Is he to keep on emptying his net,
destroying nations without
mercy?

2 I will stand at my watch
and station myself on the
ramparts;
I will look to see what he will say
to me,
and what answer I am to give
to this complaint. *a*

The LORD's Answer

²Then the LORD replied:

"Write down the revelation
and make it plain on tablets
so that a herald *b* may run with
it.
³For the revelation awaits an
appointed time;
it speaks of the end
and will not prove false.
Though it linger, wait for it;
it*c* will certainly come and will
not delay.

⁴"See, he is puffed up;
his desires are not upright—
but the righteous will live by
his faith*d*—
⁵indeed, wine betrays him;
he is arrogant and never at
rest.

Because he is as greedy as the
grave*e*
and like death is never
satisfied,
he gathers to himself all the
nations
and takes captive all the
peoples.

⁶"Will not all of them taunt him
with ridicule and scorn, saying,

" 'Woe to him who piles up stolen
goods
and makes himself wealthy by
extortion!
How long must this go on?'
⁷Will not your debtors*f* suddenly
arise?
Will they not wake up and
make you tremble?
Then you will become their
victim.
⁸Because you have plundered
many nations,
the peoples who are left will
plunder you.
For you have shed man's blood;
you have destroyed lands and
cities and everyone in them.

⁹"Woe to him who builds his realm
by unjust gain
to set his nest on high,
to escape the clutches of
ruin!

---

a1 Or and what to answer when I am rebuked
he linger, wait for him; / he   *d4 Or faithfulness*
b2 Or so that whoever reads it   *c3 Or Though*
e5 Hebrew Sheol   *f7 Or creditors*

Life in Bible Times

EAGLES' NESTS

Because the eagle built its
nest high up on rocky cliffs,
its nest was a symbol of
safety. Like other Bible writers, Habakkuk uses many
pictures from nature. Ha-
bakkuk is saying here (2:9)
that there is no safety for
those who do wrong.

[10]You have plotted the ruin of
many peoples,
shaming your own house and
forfeiting your life.
[11]The stones of the wall will cry
out,
and the beams of the woodwork
will echo it.

[12]"Woe to him who builds a city
with bloodshed
and establishes a town by
crime!
[13]Has not the LORD Almighty
determined
that the people's labor is only
fuel for the fire,
that the nations exhaust
themselves for nothing?
[14]For the earth will be filled with
the knowledge of the glory
of the LORD,
as the waters cover the
sea.

[15]"Woe to him who gives drink to
his neighbors,
pouring it from the wineskin
till they are drunk,
so that he can gaze on their
naked bodies.
[16]You will be filled with shame
instead of glory.
Now it is your turn! Drink and
be exposed[a]!
The cup from the LORD's right
hand is coming around to
you,
and disgrace will cover your
glory.
[17]The violence you have done to
Lebanon will overwhelm
you,
and your destruction of animals
will terrify you.
For you have shed man's blood;
you have destroyed lands and
cities and everyone in them.

[18]"Of what value is an idol, since a
man has carved it?
Or an image that teaches lies?

For he who makes it trusts in his
own creation;
he makes idols that cannot
speak.
[19]Woe to him who says to wood,
'Come to life!'
Or to lifeless stone, 'Wake up!'
Can it give guidance?
It is covered with gold and
silver;
there is no breath in it.
[20]But the LORD is in his holy
temple;
let all the earth be silent before
him."

Habakkuk's Prayer

3 A prayer of Habakkuk the
prophet. On *shigionoth.*[b]

[2]LORD, I have heard of your fame;
I stand in awe of your deeds,
O LORD.
Renew them in our day,
in our time make them known;
in wrath remember mercy.

[3]God came from Teman,
the Holy One from Mount
Paran.   *Selah*[c]
His glory covered the heavens
and his praise filled the earth.
[4]His splendor was like the sunrise;
rays flashed from his hand,
where his power was hidden.
[5]Plague went before him;
pestilence followed his steps.
[6]He stood, and shook the earth;
he looked, and made the nations
tremble.
The ancient mountains crumbled
and the age-old hills collapsed.
His ways are eternal.
[7]I saw the tents of Cushan in
distress,
the dwellings of Midian in
anguish.

[8]Were you angry with the rivers,
O LORD?
Was your wrath against the
streams?

---

[a]16 Masoretic Text; Dead Sea Scrolls, Aquila, Vulgate and Syriac (see also Septuagint) *and stagger*
[b]1 Probably a literary or musical term   [c]3 A word of uncertain meaning; possibly a musical
term; also in verses 9 and 13

Did you rage against the sea
  when you rode with your horses
  and your victorious chariots?
⁹You uncovered your bow,
  you called for many arrows.
                              Selah
You split the earth with rivers;
10   the mountains saw you and
      writhed.
Torrents of water swept by;
  the deep roared
  and lifted its waves on high.

¹¹Sun and moon stood still in the
      heavens
  at the glint of your flying
      arrows,
  at the lightning of your flashing
      spear.
¹²In wrath you strode through the
      earth
  and in anger you threshed the
      nations.
¹³You came out to deliver your
      people,
  to save your anointed one.
You crushed the leader of the
      land of wickedness,
  you stripped him from head to
      foot.   *Selah*
¹⁴With his own spear you pierced
      his head
  when his warriors stormed out
      to scatter us,
  gloating as though about to
      devour
  the wretched who were in
      hiding.

¹⁵You trampled the sea with your
      horses,
  churning the great waters.

¹⁶I heard and my heart pounded,
  my lips quivered at the sound;
decay crept into my bones,
  and my legs trembled.
Yet I will wait patiently for the
      day of calamity
  to come on the nation invading
      us.
¹⁷Though the fig tree does not bud
  and there are no grapes on the
      vines,
though the olive crop fails
  and the fields produce no food,
though there are no sheep in the
      pen
  and no cattle in the stalls,

? DID YOU KNOW?   3:16

Why was Habakkuk afraid?

  Habakkuk realized that everyone would suffer when God
judged his people. That made him
afraid. But he decided to trust God
to help him through the times to
come.

---

¹⁸yet I will rejoice in the LORD,
  I will be joyful in God my
      Savior.

Life in Bible Times

MOUNTAIN GOATS

High mountain cliffs are dangerous places for people. But
mountain goats, called deer in
Habakkuk 3:19, walk there safely. This picture from nature
teaches that God will keep his
people safe, even in dangerous
places.

19The Sovereign LORD is my
   strength;
he makes my feet like the feet
   of a deer,
he enables me to go on the
   heights.

For the director of music. On my
   stringed instruments.

ZEPHANIAH

WHO WROTE THIS BOOK?	The prophet Zephaniah, a descendant of good King Hezekiah, wrote this book.
WHY WAS THIS BOOK WRITTEN?	Zephaniah prepares Judah for Josiah's revival of 621 B.C. Zephaniah warns Judah that God will judge a sinful people.
WHAT DO WE LEARN ABOUT GOD IN THIS BOOK?	God is a God of judgment. He will punish sin when history comes to an end. But God does not wait. He also punishes sinful nations now.
WHAT IS SPECIAL ABOUT THIS BOOK?	Zephaniah's preaching may have helped to turn people to God during Josiah's revival.
WHEN WAS THIS BOOK WRITTEN?	Zephaniah was written during the reign of Josiah, probably about 620 B.C.

1 The word of the LORD that came to Zephaniah son of Cushi, the son of Gedaliah, the son of Amariah, the son of Hezekiah, during the reign of Josiah son of Amon king of Judah:

Warning of Coming Destruction

2"I will sweep away everything
   from the face of the earth,"
           declares the LORD.
3"I will sweep away both men and
   animals;
  I will sweep away the birds of
   the air
  and the fish of the sea.
The wicked will have only heaps
   of rubble*a*
  when I cut off man from the
   face of the earth,"
          declares the LORD.

Against Judah

4"I will stretch out my hand
   against Judah
  and against all who live in
   Jerusalem.
I will cut off from this place every
   remnant of Baal,
  the names of the pagan and the
   idolatrous priests—
5those who bow down on the roofs
  to worship the starry host,
those who bow down and swear
  by the LORD
and who also swear by Molech,*b*
6those who turn back from
  following the LORD
and neither seek the LORD nor
  inquire of him.
7Be silent before the Sovereign
  LORD,
for the day of the LORD is near.
The LORD has prepared a sacrifice;
  he has consecrated those he has
   invited.
8On the day of the LORD's sacrifice
  I will punish the princes
  and the king's sons
  and all those clad
   in foreign clothes.

9On that day I will punish
  all who avoid stepping on the
   threshold,*c*

Life In Bible Times

FOREIGN CLOTHES

The people of Israel belonged to God. God wanted even their clothes to be different from all other peoples (Zephaniah 1:8). Israelites who wore foreign clothes rejected God.

---

who fill the temple of their gods
  with violence and deceit.

10"On that day," declares the LORD,
  "a cry will go up from the Fish
   Gate,
  wailing from the New Quarter,
  and a loud crash from the
   hills.
11Wail, you who live in the market
  district*d*;
  all your merchants will be
   wiped out,
  all who trade with*e* silver will
   be ruined.
12At that time I will search
  Jerusalem with lamps
  and punish those who are
   complacent,
  who are like wine left on its
   dregs,
  who think, 'The LORD will do
   nothing,
  either good or bad.'
13Their wealth will be plundered,
  their houses demolished.
They will build houses
  but not live in them;
they will plant vineyards
  but not drink the wine.

---

a3 The meaning of the Hebrew for this line is uncertain.   *b5* Hebrew *Malcam,* that is, Milcom
c9 See 1 Samuel 5:5.   *d11* Or *the Mortar*   *e11* Or *in*

The Great Day of the LORD

14"The great day of the LORD is
    near—
    near and coming quickly.
  Listen! The cry on the day of the
    LORD will be bitter,
    the shouting of the warrior
    there.
15That day will be a day of wrath,
    a day of distress and anguish,
    a day of trouble and ruin,
    a day of darkness and gloom,
    a day of clouds and blackness,
16a day of trumpet and battle cry
    against the fortified cities
    and against the corner
    towers.
17I will bring distress on the people
    and they will walk like blind
    men,
    because they have sinned
    against the LORD.
  Their blood will be poured out
    like dust
    and their entrails like filth.
18Neither their silver nor their gold
    will be able to save them
    on the day of the LORD's
    wrath.
  In the fire of his jealousy
    the whole world will be
    consumed,
  for he will make a sudden end
    of all who live in the earth."

2 Gather together, gather
    together,
    O shameful nation,
2before the appointed time arrives
    and that day sweeps on like
    chaff,
  before the fierce anger of the
    LORD comes upon you,
  before the day of the LORD's
    wrath comes upon you.
3Seek the LORD, all you humble of
    the land,
    you who do what he commands.
  Seek righteousness, seek
    humility;
    perhaps you will be sheltered
    on the day of the LORD's anger.

Against Philistia

4Gaza will be abandoned
    and Ashkelon left in ruins.
  At midday Ashdod will be
    emptied
    and Ekron uprooted.
5Woe to you who live by the sea,
    O Kerethite people;
  the word of the LORD is against
    you,
    O Canaan, land of the
    Philistines.
  "I will destroy you,
    and none will be left."

6The land by the sea, where the
    Kerethites*a* dwell,
  will be a place for shepherds
    and sheep pens.
7It will belong to the remnant of
    the house of Judah;
    there they will find pasture.
  In the evening they will lie down
    in the houses of Ashkelon.
  The LORD their God will care for
    them;
    he will restore their fortunes.*b*

Against Moab and Ammon

8"I have heard the insults of Moab
    and the taunts of the
    Ammonites,
  who insulted my people
    and made threats against their
    land.
9Therefore, as surely as I live,"
    declares the LORD Almighty, the
    God of Israel,
  "surely Moab will become like
    Sodom,
    the Ammonites like
    Gomorrah—
  a place of weeds and salt pits,
    a wasteland forever.
  The remnant of my people will
    plunder them;
    the survivors of my nation will
    inherit their land."

10This is what they will get in
    return for their pride,
    for insulting and mocking the

people of the LORD Almighty.

¹¹The LORD will be awesome to them
when he destroys all the gods of the land.
The nations on every shore will worship him,
every one in its own land.

Against Cush

¹²"You too, O Cushites,ᵃ
will be slain by my sword."

Against Assyria

¹³He will stretch out his hand against the north
and destroy Assyria,
leaving Nineveh utterly desolate
and dry as the desert.
¹⁴Flocks and herds will lie down there,
creatures of every kind.
The desert owl and the screech owl
will roost on her columns.
Their calls will echo through the windows,
rubble will be in the doorways,
the beams of cedar will be exposed.
¹⁵This is the carefree city
that lived in safety.
She said to herself,

ᵃ12 That is, people from the upper Nile region

"I am, and there is none besides me."
What a ruin she has become,
a lair for wild beasts!
All who pass by her scoff
and shake their fists.

The Future of Jerusalem

3 Woe to the city of oppressors,
rebellious and defiled!
²She obeys no one,
she accepts no correction.
She does not trust in the LORD,
she does not draw near to her God.
³Her officials are roaring lions,
her rulers are evening wolves,
who leave nothing for the morning.
⁴Her prophets are arrogant;
they are treacherous men.
Her priests profane the sanctuary
and do violence to the law.
⁵The LORD within her is righteous;
he does no wrong.
Morning by morning he dispenses his justice,
and every new day he does not fail,
yet the unrighteous know no shame.

⁶"I have cut off nations;
their strongholds are demolished.

Life in Bible Times

DESERT OWLS

The desert owl of Bible lands chooses to live in lonely places and is very afraid of people. Zephaniah (2:14) uses this picture of the owl to show that Nineveh, the capital of Assyria, will lie in ruins. Desert owls live in Nineveh's ruins even today.

I have left their streets deserted,
    with no one passing through.
Their cities are destroyed;
    no one will be left—no one at
        all.
7I said to the city,
    'Surely you will fear me
    and accept correction!'
Then her dwelling would not be
        cut off,
    nor all my punishments come
        upon her.
But they were still eager
    to act corruptly in all they did.
8Therefore wait for me," declares
        the LORD,
    "for the day I will stand up to
        testify.*a*
I have decided to assemble the
        nations,
    to gather the kingdoms
and to pour out my wrath on
        them—
    all my fierce anger.
The whole world will be consumed
    by the fire of my jealous anger.

9"Then will I purify the lips of the
        peoples,
    that all of them may call on the
        name of the LORD
    and serve him shoulder to
        shoulder.
10From beyond the rivers of Cush*b*
    my worshipers, my scattered
        people,
    will bring me offerings.
11On that day you will not be put
        to shame
    for all the wrongs you have
        done to me,
because I will remove from this
        city
    those who rejoice in their pride.
Never again will you be haughty
    on my holy hill.
12But I will leave within you
    the meek and humble,
    who trust in the name of the
        LORD.
13The remnant of Israel will do no
        wrong;

they will speak no lies,
    nor will deceit be found in their
        mouths.
They will eat and lie down
    and no one will make them
        afraid."

14Sing, O Daughter of Zion;
    shout aloud, O Israel!
Be glad and rejoice with all your
        heart,
    O Daughter of Jerusalem!
15The LORD has taken away your
        punishment,
    he has turned back your enemy.
The LORD, the King of Israel, is
        with you;
    never again will you fear any
        harm.
16On that day they will say to
        Jerusalem,
    "Do not fear, O Zion;
    do not let your hands hang
        limp.
17The LORD your God is with
        you,
    he is mighty to save.
He will take great delight in
        you,
    he will quiet you with his
        love,
    he will rejoice over you with
        singing."

WORDS TO REMEMBER

3:17　The LORD your God is with
        you,
    he is mighty to save.

18"The sorrows for the appointed
        feasts
    I will remove from you;
    they are a burden and a
        reproach to you.*c*
19At that time I will deal
    with all who oppressed you;
I will rescue the lame
    and gather those who have been
        scattered.

a8 Septuagint and Syriac; Hebrew *will rise up to plunder*　　*b10* That is, the upper Nile region
c18 Or *"I will gather you who mourn for the appointed feasts; / your reproach is a burden to you*

I will give them praise and honor
  in every land where they were
    put to shame.
20At that time I will gather you;
  at that time I will bring you
    home.

I will give you honor and praise
  among all the peoples of the
    earth
when I restore your fortunes*a*
  before your very eyes,"
                    says the LORD.

HAGGAI

WHO WROTE THIS BOOK?	The prophet Haggai.
WHY WAS THIS BOOK WRITTEN?	The people stop rebuilding God's temple. Haggai tells them the temple must be rebuilt . . . now.
WHAT DO WE LEARN ABOUT GOD IN THIS BOOK?	God will bless people when they put him first.
WHAT IS SPECIAL ABOUT THIS BOOK?	The people listen to Haggai's preaching. They go to work and finish rebuilding the temple.
WHEN WAS THIS BOOK WRITTEN?	Haggai was written after some of the Jews returned to Judah from captivity in Babylon. Haggai preached in 520 B.C.
WHAT ARE SOME IMPORTANT VERSES IN THIS BOOK?	The people are poor because they have not put God first. Haggai 1:2–11 The people have obeyed and from now on God will bless them. Haggai 2:15–19

A Call to Build the House of the LORD

1 In the second year of King Darius, on the first day of the sixth month, the word of the LORD came through the prophet Haggai to Zerubbabel son of Shealtiel, governor of Judah, and to Joshua*a* son of Jehozadak, the high priest:

²This is what the LORD Almighty says: "These people say, 'The time has not yet come for the LORD's house to be built.' "

³Then the word of the LORD came through the prophet Haggai: ⁴"Is it a time for you yourselves to be living in your paneled houses, while this house remains a ruin?"

⁵Now this is what the LORD Almighty says: "Give careful thought to your ways. ⁶You have planted much, but have harvested little. You eat, but never have enough. You drink, but never have your fill. You put on clothes, but are not warm. You earn wages, only to put them in a purse with holes in it."

⁷This is what the LORD Almighty says: "Give careful thought to your ways. ⁸Go up into the mountains and bring down timber and build the house, so that I may take pleasure in it and be honored," says the LORD. ⁹"You expected much, but see, it turned out to be little. What you brought home, I blew away. Why?" declares the LORD Almighty. "Because of my house, which remains a ruin, while each of you is busy with his own house. ¹⁰Therefore, because of you the heavens have withheld their dew and the earth its crops. ¹¹I called for a drought on the fields and the mountains, on the grain, the new wine, the oil and whatever the ground produces, on men and cattle, and on the labor of your hands."

¹²Then Zerubbabel son of Shealtiel, Joshua son of Jehozadak, the high priest, and the whole remnant of the people obeyed the voice of the LORD their God and the message of the prophet Haggai, because the LORD their God had sent him. And the people feared the LORD.

¹³Then Haggai, the LORD's messenger, gave this message of the LORD to the people: "I am with you," declares the LORD. ¹⁴So the LORD stirred up the spirit of Zerubbabel son of Shealtiel, governor of Judah, and the spirit of Joshua son of Jehozadak, the high priest, and the spirit of the whole remnant of the people. They came and began to work on the house of the LORD Almighty, their God, ¹⁵on the twenty-fourth day of the sixth month in the second year of King Darius.

The Promised Glory of the New House

2 On the twenty-first day of the seventh month, the word of the LORD came through the prophet Haggai: ²"Speak to Zerubbabel son of Shealtiel, governor of Judah, to Joshua son of Jehozadak, the high priest, and to the remnant of the people. Ask them, ³'Who of you is left who saw this house in its former glory? How does it look to you now? Does it not seem to you like nothing? ⁴But now be strong, O Zerubbabel,' declares the LORD. 'Be strong, O Joshua son of Jehozadak, the high priest. Be strong, all you people of the land,' declares the LORD, 'and work. For I am with you,' declares the LORD Almighty. ⁵'This is what I covenanted with you when you came out of Egypt. And my Spirit remains among you. Do not fear.'

⁶"This is what the LORD Almighty says: 'In a little while I will once more shake the heavens and the earth, the sea and the dry land. ⁷I will shake all nations, and the desired of all nations will come, and I will fill this house with glory,' says the LORD Almighty. ⁸'The silver is mine and the gold is mine,' declares the LORD Almighty. ⁹'The glory of this present house will be greater than the glory of the former house,' says the LORD Almighty.

a1 A variant of Jeshua; here and elsewhere in Haggai

'And in this place I will grant peace,' declares the Lord Almighty."

Blessings for a Defiled People

¹⁰On the twenty-fourth day of the ninth month, in the second year of Darius, the word of the Lord came to the prophet Haggai: ¹¹"This is what the Lord Almighty says: 'Ask the priests what the law says: ¹²If a person carries consecrated meat in the fold of his garment, and that fold touches some bread or stew, some wine, oil or other food, does it become consecrated?'"

The priests answered, "No."

¹³Then Haggai said, "If a person defiled by contact with a dead body touches one of these things, does it become defiled?"

"Yes," the priests replied, "it becomes defiled."

¹⁴Then Haggai said, "'So it is with this people and this nation in my sight,' declares the Lord. 'Whatever they do and whatever they offer there is defiled.

¹⁵"'Now give careful thought to this from this day on ᵃ—consider how things were before one stone was laid on another in the Lord's temple. ¹⁶When anyone came to a heap of twenty measures, there were only ten. When anyone went to a wine vat to draw fifty measures, there were only twenty. ¹⁷I struck all the work of your hands with blight, mildew and hail, yet you did not turn to me,' declares the Lord. ¹⁸'From this day on, from this twenty-fourth day of the ninth month, give careful thought to the day when the foundation of the Lord's temple was laid. Give careful thought: ¹⁹Is there yet any seed left in the barn? Until now, the vine and the fig tree, the pomegranate and the olive tree have not borne fruit.

"'From this day on I will bless you.'"

Zerubbabel the Lord's Signet Ring

²⁰The word of the Lord came to Haggai a second time on the twenty-fourth day of the month: ²¹"Tell Zerubbabel governor of Judah that I will shake the heavens and the earth. ²²I will overturn royal thrones and shatter the power of the foreign kingdoms. I will overthrow chariots and their drivers; horses and their riders will fall, each by the sword of his brother.

WORDS TO REMEMBER

2:19 From this day on I will bless you.

²³"'On that day,' declares the Lord Almighty, 'I will take you, my servant Zerubbabel son of Shealtiel,' declares the Lord, 'and I will make you like my signet ring, for I have chosen you,' declares the Lord Almighty."

ᵃ15 Or to the days past

ZECHARIAH

WHO WROTE THIS BOOK?	The prophet Zechariah.
WHY WAS THIS BOOK WRITTEN?	Zechariah encourages the people of Judah to finish building the temple.
WHAT DO WE LEARN ABOUT GOD IN THIS BOOK?	God will cleanse the sin of his people. God will come and rule the earth.
WHAT IS SPECIAL ABOUT THIS BOOK?	Zechariah uses many symbols that are hard to understand, like a flying scroll and a woman in a basket.
WHEN WAS THIS BOOK WRITTEN?	Zechariah was written after many Jews returned to Judah from Babylon, about 520 B.C.
WHAT ARE SOME IMPORTANT CHAPTERS IN THIS BOOK?	God wants his people to love justice and mercy. Zechariah 7–8
	God will come to earth and rule as king. Zechariah 14

A Call to Return to the Lord

1 In the eighth month of the second year of Darius, the word of the Lord came to the prophet Zechariah son of Berekiah, the son of Iddo:

²"The Lord was very angry with your forefathers. ³Therefore tell the people: This is what the Lord Almighty says: 'Return to me,' declares the Lord Almighty, 'and I will return to you,' says the Lord Almighty. ⁴Do not be like your forefathers, to whom the earlier prophets proclaimed: This is what the Lord Almighty says: 'Turn from your evil ways and your evil practices.' But they would not listen or pay attention to me, declares the Lord. ⁵Where are your forefathers now? And the prophets, do they live forever? ⁶But did not my words and my decrees, which I commanded my servants the prophets, overtake your forefathers?

"Then they repented and said, 'The Lord Almighty has done to us what our ways and practices deserve, just as he determined to do.'"

The Man Among the Myrtle Trees

⁷On the twenty-fourth day of the eleventh month, the month of Shebat, in the second year of Darius, the word of the Lord came to the prophet Zechariah son of Berekiah, the son of Iddo.

⁸During the night I had a vision —and there before me was a man riding a red horse! He was standing among the myrtle trees in a ravine. Behind him were red, brown and white horses.

⁹I asked, "What are these, my lord?"

The angel who was talking with me answered, "I will show you what they are."

¹⁰Then the man standing among the myrtle trees explained, "They are the ones the Lord has sent to go throughout the earth."

¹¹And they reported to the angel of the Lord, who was standing among the myrtle trees, "We have gone throughout the earth and found the whole world at rest and in peace."

¹²Then the angel of the Lord said, "Lord Almighty, how long will you withhold mercy from Jerusalem and from the towns of Judah, which you have been angry with these seventy years?" ¹³So the Lord spoke kind and comforting words to the angel who talked with me.

¹⁴Then the angel who was speaking to me said, "Proclaim this word: This is what the Lord Almighty says: 'I am very jealous for Jerusalem and Zion, ¹⁵but I am very angry with the nations that feel secure. I was only a little angry, but they added to the calamity.'

¹⁶"Therefore, this is what the Lord says: 'I will return to Jerusalem with mercy, and there my house will be rebuilt. And the measuring line will be stretched out over Jerusalem,' declares the Lord Almighty.

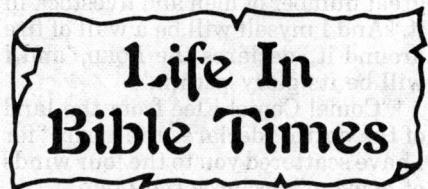

MEASURING LINES

Carpenters did not have measuring tapes in Bible times. They used strings on which they marked distances by tying knots.

---

¹⁷"Proclaim further: This is what the Lord Almighty says: 'My towns will again overflow with prosperity, and the Lord will again comfort Zion and choose Jerusalem.'"

Four Horns and Four Craftsmen

¹⁸Then I looked up—and there before me were four horns! ¹⁹I asked the angel who was speaking to me, "What are these?"

He answered me, "These are the horns that scattered Judah, Israel and Jerusalem."

²⁰Then the LORD showed me four craftsmen. ²¹I asked, "What are these coming to do?"

He answered, "These are the horns that scattered Judah so that no one could raise his head, but the craftsmen have come to terrify them and throw down these horns of the nations who lifted up their horns against the land of Judah to scatter its people."

A Man With a Measuring Line

2 Then I looked up—and there before me was a man with a measuring line in his hand! ²I asked, "Where are you going?"

He answered me, "To measure Jerusalem, to find out how wide and how long it is."

³Then the angel who was speaking to me left, and another angel came to meet him ⁴and said to him: "Run, tell that young man, 'Jerusalem will be a city without walls because of the great number of men and livestock in it. ⁵And I myself will be a wall of fire around it,' declares the LORD, 'and I will be its glory within.'

⁶"Come! Come! Flee from the land of the north," declares the LORD, "for I have scattered you to the four winds of heaven," declares the LORD.

⁷"Come, O Zion! Escape, you who live in the Daughter of Babylon!" ⁸For this is what the LORD Almighty says: "After he has honored me and has sent me against the nations that have plundered you—for whoever touches you touches the apple of his eye— ⁹I will surely raise my hand against them so that their slaves will plunder them.ᵃ Then you will know that the LORD Almighty has sent me.

¹⁰"Shout and be glad, O Daughter of Zion. For I am coming, and I will live among you," declares the LORD. ¹¹"Many nations will be joined with the LORD in that day and will become my people. I will live among you and you will know that the LORD Almighty has sent me to you. ¹²The

LORD will inherit Judah as his portion in the holy land and will again choose Jerusalem. ¹³Be still before the LORD, all mankind, because he has roused himself from his holy dwelling."

Clean Garments for the High Priest

3 Then he showed me Joshuaᵇ the high priest standing before the angel of the LORD, and Satanᶜ standing at his right side to accuse him. ²The LORD said to Satan, "The LORD rebuke you, Satan! The LORD, who has chosen Jerusalem, rebuke you! Is not this man a burning stick snatched from the fire?"

³Now Joshua was dressed in filthy clothes as he stood before the angel. ⁴The angel said to those who were standing before him, "Take off his filthy clothes."

Then he said to Joshua, "See, I have taken away your sin, and I will put rich garments on you."

⁵Then I said, "Put a clean turban on his head." So they put a clean turban on his head and clothed him, while the angel of the LORD stood by.

⁶The angel of the LORD gave this charge to Joshua: ⁷"This is what the LORD Almighty says: 'If you will walk in my ways and keep my requirements, then you will govern my house and have charge of my courts, and I will give you a place among these standing here.

⁸" 'Listen, O high priest Joshua and your associates seated before you, who are men symbolic of things to come: I am going to bring my servant, the Branch. ⁹See, the stone I have set in front of Joshua! There are seven eyesᵈ on that one stone, and I will engrave an inscription on it,' says the LORD Almighty, 'and I will remove the sin of this land in a single day.

¹⁰" 'In that day each of you will invite his neighbor to sit under his vine and fig tree,' declares the LORD Almighty."

ᵃ8,9 Or says after . . . eye: 9"I . . . plunder them." Zechariah   ᶜ1 Satan means accuser.   ᵈ9 Or facets

ᵇ1 A variant of Jeshua; here and elsewhere in

The Gold Lampstand and the Two Olive Trees

4 Then the angel who talked with me returned and wakened me, as a man is wakened from his sleep. ²He asked me, "What do you see?"

I answered, "I see a solid gold lampstand with a bowl at the top and seven lights on it, with seven channels to the lights. ³Also there are two olive trees by it, one on the right of the bowl and the other on its left."

⁴I asked the angel who talked with me, "What are these, my lord?"

⁵He answered, "Do you not know what these are?"

"No, my lord," I replied.

⁶So he said to me, "This is the word of the LORD to Zerubbabel: 'Not by might nor by power, but by my Spirit,' says the LORD Almighty.

⁷"Whatᵃ are you, O mighty mountain? Before Zerubbabel you will become level ground. Then he will bring out the capstone to shouts of 'God bless it! God bless it!' "

⁸Then the word of the LORD came to me: ⁹"The hands of Zerubbabel have laid the foundation of this temple; his hands will also complete it. Then you will know that the LORD Almighty has sent me to you.

¹⁰"Who despises the day of small things? Men will rejoice when they see the plumb line in the hand of Zerubbabel.

"(These seven are the eyes of the LORD, which range throughout the earth.)"

¹¹Then I asked the angel, "What are these two olive trees on the right and the left of the lampstand?"

¹²Again I asked him, "What are these two olive branches beside the two gold pipes that pour out golden oil?"

¹³He replied, "Do you not know what these are?"

"No, my lord," I said.

¹⁴So he said, "These are the two who are anointed toᵇ serve the Lord of all the earth.' "

The Flying Scroll

5 I looked again—and there before me was a flying scroll!

²He asked me, "What do you see?"

I answered, "I see a flying scroll, thirty feet long and fifteen feet wide.ᶜ"

³And he said to me, "This is the curse that is going out over the whole land; for according to what it says on one side, every thief will be banished, and according to what it says on the other, everyone who swears falsely will be banished. ⁴The LORD Almighty declares, 'I will send it out, and it will enter the house of the thief and the house of him who swears falsely by my name. It will remain in his house and destroy it, both its timbers and its stones.' "

The Woman in a Basket

⁵Then the angel who was speaking to me came forward and said to me, "Look up and see what this is that is appearing."

⁶I asked, "What is it?"

He replied, "It is a measuring basket.ᵈ" And he added, "This is the iniquityᵉ of the people throughout the land."

⁷Then the cover of lead was raised, and there in the basket sat a woman! ⁸He said, "This is wickedness," and he pushed her back into the basket and pushed the lead cover down over its mouth.

⁹Then I looked up—and there before me were two women, with the wind in their wings! They had wings like those of a stork, and they lifted up the basket between heaven and earth.

¹⁰"Where are they taking the basket?" I asked the angel who was speaking to me.

¹¹He replied, "To the country of Babyloniaᶠ to build a house for it.

ᵃ7 Or *Who*   ᵇ14 Or *two who bring oil and*
(about 9 meters long and 4.5 meters wide)
appearance   ᶠ11 Hebrew *Shinar*

ᶜ2 Hebrew *twenty cubits long and ten cubits wide*
ᵈ6 Hebrew *an ephah*; also in verses 7-11   ᵉ6 Or

When it is ready, the basket will be set there in its place."

Four Chariots

6 I looked up again—and there before me were four chariots coming out from between two mountains—mountains of bronze! ²The first chariot had red horses, the second black, ³the third white, and the fourth dappled—all of them powerful. ⁴I asked the angel who was speaking to me, "What are these, my lord?"

⁵The angel answered me, "These are the four spiritsᵃ of heaven, going out from standing in the presence of the Lord of the whole world. ⁶The one with the black horses is going toward the north country, the one with the white horses toward the west,ᵇ and the one with the dappled horses toward the south."

⁷When the powerful horses went out, they were straining to go throughout the earth. And he said, "Go throughout the earth!" So they went throughout the earth.

⁸Then he called to me, "Look, those going toward the north country have given my Spiritᶜ rest in the land of the north."

A Crown for Joshua

⁹The word of the Lord came to me: ¹⁰"Take silver and gold from the exiles Heldai, Tobijah and Jedaiah, who have arrived from Babylon. Go the same day to the house of Josiah son of Zephaniah. ¹¹Take the silver and gold and make a crown, and set it on the head of the high priest, Joshua son of Jehozadak. ¹²Tell him this is what the Lord Almighty says: 'Here is the man whose name is the Branch, and he will branch out from his place and build the temple of the Lord. ¹³It is he who will build the temple of the Lord, and he will be clothed with majesty and will sit and rule on his throne. And he will be a priest on his throne. And there will

be harmony between the two.' ¹⁴The crown will be given to Heldai,ᵈ Tobijah, Jedaiah and Henᵉ son of Zephaniah as a memorial in the temple of the Lord. ¹⁵Those who are far away will come and help to build the temple of the Lord, and you will know that the Lord Almighty has sent me to you. This will happen if you diligently obey the Lord your God."

Justice and Mercy, Not Fasting

7 In the fourth year of King Darius, the word of the Lord came to Zechariah on the fourth day of the ninth month, the month of Kislev. ²The people of Bethel had sent Sharezer and Regem-Melech, together with their men, to entreat the Lord ³by asking the priests of the house of the Lord Almighty and the prophets, "Should I mourn and fast in the fifth month, as I have done for so many years?"

⁴Then the word of the Lord Almighty came to me: ⁵"Ask all the people of the land and the priests, 'When you fasted and mourned in the fifth and seventh months for the past seventy years, was it really for me that you fasted? ⁶And when you were eating and drinking, were you not just feasting for yourselves? ⁷Are these not the words the Lord proclaimed through the earlier prophets when Jerusalem and its surrounding towns were at rest and prosperous, and the Negev and the western foothills were settled?' "

⁸And the word of the Lord came again to Zechariah: ⁹"This is what the Lord Almighty says: 'Administer true justice; show mercy and compassion to one another. ¹⁰Do not oppress the widow or the fatherless, the alien or the poor. In your hearts do not think evil of each other.'

¹¹"But they refused to pay attention; stubbornly they turned their backs and stopped up their ears. ¹²They made their hearts as hard as flint and would not listen to the law

---

ᵃ5 Or *winds*   ᵇ6 Or *horses after them*   ᶜ8 Or *spirit*   ᵈ14 Syriac; Hebrew *Helem*
ᵉ14 Or *and the gracious one, the*

or to the words that the Lord Almighty had sent by his Spirit through the earlier prophets. So the Lord Almighty was very angry.

13" 'When I called, they did not listen; so when they called, I would not listen,' says the Lord Almighty. 14'I scattered them with a whirlwind among all the nations, where they were strangers. The land was left so desolate behind them that no one could come or go. This is how they made the pleasant land desolate.' "

The Lord Promises to Bless Jerusalem

8 Again the word of the Lord Almighty came to me. 2This is what the Lord Almighty says: "I am very jealous for Zion; I am burning with jealousy for her."

3This is what the Lord says: "I will return to Zion and dwell in Jerusalem. Then Jerusalem will be called the City of Truth, and the mountain of the Lord Almighty will be called the Holy Mountain."

4This is what the Lord Almighty says: "Once again men and women of ripe old age will sit in the streets of Jerusalem, each with cane in hand because of his age. 5The city streets will be filled with boys and girls playing there."

6This is what the Lord Almighty says: "It may seem marvelous to the remnant of this people at that time, but will it seem marvelous to me?" declares the Lord Almighty.

7This is what the Lord Almighty says: "I will save my people from the countries of the east and the west. 8I will bring them back to live in Jeru-

salem; they will be my people, and I will be faithful and righteous to them as their God."

9This is what the Lord Almighty says: "You who now hear these words spoken by the prophets who were there when the foundation was laid for the house of the Lord Almighty, let your hands be strong so that the temple may be built. 10Before that time there were no wages for man or beast. No one could go about his business safely because of his enemy, for I had turned every man against his neighbor. 11But now I will not deal with the remnant of this people as I did in the past," declares the Lord Almighty.

12"The seed will grow well, the vine will yield its fruit, the ground will produce its crops, and the heavens will drop their dew. I will give all these things as an inheritance to the remnant of this people. 13As you have been an object of cursing among the nations, O Judah and Israel, so will I save you, and you will be a blessing. Do not be afraid, but let your hands be strong."

14This is what the Lord Almighty says: "Just as I had determined to bring disaster upon you and showed no pity when your fathers angered me," says the Lord Almighty, 15"so now I have determined to do good again to Jerusalem and Judah. Do not be afraid. 16These are the things you are to do: Speak the truth to each other, and render true and sound judgment in your courts; 17do not plot evil against your neighbor, and do not love to swear falsely. I hate all this," declares the Lord.

ET'S LIVE IT! Zechariah 7:8–14

WHEN GOD WON'T ANSWER PRAYER ➡ Read Zechariah 7:8–14. Write down in one sentence why God would not listen to the prayers of the people Zechariah writes about (see especially Zechariah 7:13).

Next time you pray, stop first and think. Is there anything you have done wrong that you need to tell God about? When you confess your sins to God and try to do what is right, you can be sure God will listen to your prayers.

¹⁸Again the word of the LORD Almighty came to me. ¹⁹This is what the LORD Almighty says: "The fasts of the fourth, fifth, seventh and tenth months will become joyful and glad occasions and happy festivals for Judah. Therefore love truth and peace."

²⁰This is what the LORD Almighty says: "Many peoples and the inhabitants of many cities will yet come, ²¹and the inhabitants of one city will go to another and say, 'Let us go at once to entreat the LORD and seek the LORD Almighty. I myself am going.' ²²And many peoples and powerful nations will come to Jerusalem to seek the LORD Almighty and to entreat him."

²³This is what the LORD Almighty says: "In those days ten men from all languages and nations will take firm hold of one Jew by the hem of his robe and say, 'Let us go with you, because we have heard that God is with you.'"

Judgment on Israel's Enemies

An Oracle

9 The word of the LORD is
against the land of Hadrach
and will rest upon Damascus—
for the eyes of men and all the
tribes of Israel
are on the LORD—ᵃ
²and upon Hamath too, which
borders on it,
and upon Tyre and Sidon,
though they are very
skillful.
³Tyre has built herself a
stronghold;
she has heaped up silver like
dust,
and gold like the dirt of the
streets.
⁴But the Lord will take away her
possessions
and destroy her power on the
sea,
and she will be consumed by
fire.

⁵Ashkelon will see it and fear;
Gaza will writhe in agony,
and Ekron too, for her hope will
wither.
Gaza will lose her king
and Ashkelon will be deserted.
⁶Foreigners will occupy Ashdod,
and I will cut off the pride of
the Philistines.
⁷I will take the blood from their
mouths,
the forbidden food from between
their teeth.
Those who are left will belong to
our God
and become leaders in Judah,
and Ekron will be like the
Jebusites.
⁸But I will defend my house
against marauding forces.
Never again will an oppressor
overrun my people,
for now I am keeping
watch.

The Coming of Zion's King

⁹Rejoice greatly, O Daughter of
Zion!
Shout, Daughter of Jerusalem!
See, your kingᵇ comes to you,
righteous and having salvation,
gentle and riding on a donkey,
on a colt, the foal of a donkey.
¹⁰I will take away the chariots from
Ephraim
and the war-horses from
Jerusalem,
and the battle bow will be
broken.
He will proclaim peace to the
nations.
His rule will extend from sea to
sea
and from the Riverᶜ to the ends
of the earth.ᵈ
¹¹As for you, because of the blood of
my covenant with you,
I will free your prisoners from
the waterless pit.
¹²Return to your fortress,
O prisoners of hope;
even now I announce that I will

ᵃ1 Or *Damascus. / For the eye of the* LORD *is on all mankind, / as well as on the tribes of Israel,*
ᵇ9 Or *King*   ᶜ10 That is, the Euphrates   ᵈ10 Or *the end of the land*

restore twice as much to
you.

¹³I will bend Judah as I bend my
bow
and fill it with Ephraim.
I will rouse your sons, O Zion,
against your sons, O Greece,
and make you like a warrior's
sword.

The LORD Will Appear

¹⁴Then the LORD will appear over
them;
his arrow will flash like
lightning.
The Sovereign LORD will sound
the trumpet;
he will march in the storms of
the south,

¹⁵ and the LORD Almighty will
shield them.
They will destroy
and overcome with slingstones.
They will drink and roar as with
wine;
they will be full like a bowl
used for sprinkling*a* the corners
of the altar.

¹⁶The LORD their God will save
them on that day
as the flock of his people.
They will sparkle in his land
like jewels in a crown.

¹⁷How attractive and beautiful they
will be!
Grain will make the young men
thrive,
and new wine the young
women.

The LORD Will Care for Judah

10 Ask the LORD for rain in the
springtime;
it is the LORD who makes the
storm clouds.
He gives showers of rain to men,
and plants of the field to
everyone.

²The idols speak deceit,
diviners see visions that lie;
they tell dreams that are false,
they give comfort in vain.

Therefore the people wander like
sheep
oppressed for lack of a
shepherd.

³"My anger burns against the
shepherds,
and I will punish the leaders;
for the LORD Almighty will
care
for his flock, the house of
Judah,
and make them like a proud
horse in battle.

⁴From Judah will come the
cornerstone,
from him the tent peg,
from him the battle bow,
from him every ruler.

⁵Together they*b* will be like
mighty men
trampling the muddy streets in
battle.
Because the LORD is with them,
they will fight and overthrow
the horsemen.

⁶"I will strengthen the house of
Judah
and save the house of Joseph.
I will restore them
because I have compassion on
them.
They will be as though
I had not rejected them,
for I am the LORD their God
and I will answer them.

⁷The Ephraimites will become like
mighty men,
and their hearts will be glad as
with wine.
Their children will see it and be
joyful;
their hearts will rejoice in the
LORD.

⁸I will signal for them
and gather them in.
Surely I will redeem them;
they will be as numerous as
before.

⁹Though I scatter them among the
peoples,
yet in distant lands they will
remember me.

---

a15 Or bowl, / like   *b4,5 Or ruler, all of them together. / 5They*

They and their children will
  survive,
    and they will return.
¹⁰I will bring them back from
  Egypt
    and gather them from Assyria.
I will bring them to Gilead and
  Lebanon,
    and there will not be room
    enough for them.
¹¹They will pass through the sea of
  trouble;
    the surging sea will be subdued
    and all the depths of the Nile
    will dry up.
Assyria's pride will be brought
  down
    and Egypt's scepter will pass
    away.
¹²I will strengthen them in the
  Lord
    and in his name they will
    walk,"
                  declares the Lord.

11 Open your doors,
       O Lebanon,
    so that fire may devour your
    cedars!
²Wail, O pine tree, for the cedar
  has fallen;
    the stately trees are ruined!
Wail, oaks of Bashan;
    the dense forest has been cut
    down!
³Listen to the wail of the
  shepherds;
    their rich pastures are
    destroyed!
Listen to the roar of the lions;
    the lush thicket of the Jordan is
    ruined!

Two Shepherds

⁴This is what the Lord my God
says: "Pasture the flock marked for
slaughter. ⁵Their buyers slaughter
them and go unpunished. Those who
sell them say, 'Praise the Lord, I am
rich!' Their own shepherds do not
spare them. ⁶For I will no longer have
pity on the people of the land," declares the Lord. "I will hand everyone over to his neighbor and his king.
They will oppress the land, and I will

not rescue them from their hands."
⁷So I pastured the flock marked for
slaughter, particularly the oppressed
of the flock. Then I took two staffs
and called one Favor and the other
Union, and I pastured the flock. ⁸In
one month I got rid of the three shepherds.

The flock detested me, and I grew
weary of them ⁹and said, "I will not
be your shepherd. Let the dying die,
and the perishing perish. Let those
who are left eat one another's flesh."
¹⁰Then I took my staff called Favor
and broke it, revoking the covenant I
had made with all the nations. ¹¹It
was revoked on that day, and so the
afflicted of the flock who were watching me knew it was the word of the
Lord.

¹²I told them, "If you think it best,
give me my pay; but if not, keep it."
So they paid me thirty pieces of silver.

¹³And the Lord said to me, "Throw
it to the potter"—the handsome price
at which they priced me! So I took the
thirty pieces of silver and threw them
into the house of the Lord to the potter.

¹⁴Then I broke my second staff
called Union, breaking the brotherhood between Judah and Israel.

¹⁵Then the Lord said to me, "Take
again the equipment of a foolish
shepherd. ¹⁶For I am going to raise up
a shepherd over the land who will not
care for the lost, or seek the young, or
heal the injured, or feed the healthy,
but will eat the meat of the choice
sheep, tearing off their hoofs.

¹⁷"Woe to the worthless shepherd,
  who deserts the flock!
May the sword strike his arm and
  his right eye!
    May his arm be completely
    withered,
    his right eye totally blinded!"

Jerusalem's Enemies to Be Destroyed

An Oracle

12 This is the word of the Lord
       concerning Israel. The Lord,

who stretches out the heavens, who lays the foundation of the earth, and who forms the spirit of man within him, declares: ²"I am going to make Jerusalem a cup that sends all the surrounding peoples reeling. Judah will be besieged as well as Jerusalem. ³On that day, when all the nations of the earth are gathered against her, I will make Jerusalem an immovable rock for all the nations. All who try to move it will injure themselves. ⁴On that day I will strike every horse with panic and its rider with madness," declares the Lord. "I will keep a watchful eye over the house of Judah, but I will blind all the horses of the nations. ⁵Then the leaders of Judah will say in their hearts, 'The people of Jerusalem are strong, because the Lord Almighty is their God.'

⁶"On that day I will make the leaders of Judah like a firepot in a woodpile, like a flaming torch among sheaves. They will consume right and left all the surrounding peoples, but Jerusalem will remain intact in her place.

⁷"The Lord will save the dwellings of Judah first, so that the honor of the house of David and of Jerusalem's inhabitants may not be greater than that of Judah. ⁸On that day the Lord will shield those who live in Jerusalem, so that the feeblest among them will be like David, and the house of David will be like God, like the Angel of the Lord going before them. ⁹On that day I will set out to destroy all the nations that attack Jerusalem.

Mourning for the One They Pierced

¹⁰"And I will pour out on the house of David and the inhabitants of Jerusalem a spirit*a* of grace and supplication. They will look on*b* me, the one they have pierced, and they will mourn for him as one mourns for an only child, and grieve bitterly for him as one grieves for a firstborn son. ¹¹On that day the weeping in Jerusalem will be great, like the weeping of Hadad Rimmon in the plain of Megiddo. ¹²The land will mourn, each clan by itself, with their wives by themselves: the clan of the house of David and their wives, the clan of the house of Nathan and their wives, ¹³the clan of the house of Levi and their wives, the clan of Shimei and their wives, ¹⁴and all the rest of the clans and their wives.

FOUNTAINS

There are many springs of water that bubble out of the earth in the northern part of Israel. When the Bible says "fountain," it usually means a spring, which gives water needed for washing, drinking and watering crops.

*a*10 Or *the Spirit*　　*b*10 Or *to*

LET'S LIVE IT!　　Zechariah 11:15–17

GOOD AND BAD SHEPHERDS ➡ In the Bible, ministers are called "shepherds." Read Zechariah 11:15–17. What does a bad shepherd do? What do you think a good shepherd would do?

If you have younger brothers or sisters, you can be God's shepherd for them! Read this passage to your mom or dad and ask them to help you decide on five ways you can be a good shepherd to your brothers or sisters.

Cleansing From Sin

13 "On that day a fountain will be opened to the house of David and the inhabitants of Jerusalem, to cleanse them from sin and impurity.

2"On that day, I will banish the names of the idols from the land, and they will be remembered no more," declares the LORD Almighty. "I will remove both the prophets and the spirit of impurity from the land. 3And if anyone still prophesies, his father and mother, to whom he was born, will say to him, 'You must die, because you have told lies in the LORD's name.' When he prophesies, his own parents will stab him.

4"On that day every prophet will be ashamed of his prophetic vision. He will not put on a prophet's garment of hair in order to deceive. 5He will say, 'I am not a prophet. I am a farmer; the land has been my livelihood since my youth.ª 6If someone asks him, 'What are these wounds on your body ᵇ?' he will answer, 'The wounds I was given at the house of my friends.'

The Shepherd Struck, the Sheep Scattered

7"Awake, O sword, against my shepherd,
   against the man who is close to me!"
declares the LORD Almighty.
"Strike the shepherd,
   and the sheep will be scattered,
and I will turn my hand against the little ones.
8In the whole land," declares the LORD,
   "two-thirds will be struck down and perish;
   yet one-third will be left in it.
9This third I will bring into the fire;
   I will refine them like silver
   and test them like gold.

They will call on my name
   and I will answer them;
I will say, 'They are my people,'
   and they will say, 'The LORD is our God.'"

The LORD Comes and Reigns

14 A day of the LORD is coming when your plunder will be divided among you.

2I will gather all the nations to Jerusalem to fight against it; the city will be captured, the houses ransacked, and the women raped. Half of the city will go into exile, but the rest of the people will not be taken from the city. 3Then the LORD will go out and fight against those nations, as he fights in the day of battle. 4On that day his feet will stand on the Mount of Olives, east of Jerusalem, and the Mount of Olives will be split in two from east to west, forming a great valley, with half of the mountain moving north and half moving south. 5You will flee by my mountain valley, for it will extend to Azel. You will flee as you fled from the earthquakeᶜ in the days of Uzziah king of Judah. Then the LORD my God will come, and all the holy ones with him.

6On that day there will be no light, no cold or frost. 7It will be a unique day, without daytime or nighttime —a day known to the LORD. When evening comes, there will be light.

8On that day living water will flow out from Jerusalem, half to the eastern seaᵈ and half to the western sea,ᵉ in summer and in winter.

9The LORD will be king over the whole earth. On that day there will be one LORD, and his name the only name.

10The whole land, from Geba to Rimmon, south of Jerusalem, will become like the Arabah. But Jerusalem will be raised up and remain in its place, from the Benjamin Gate to the site of the First Gate, to the Corner

---

ª5 Or *farmer; a man sold me in my youth*   ᵇ6 Or *wounds between your hands*   ᶜ5 Or ⁵My *mountain valley will be blocked and will extend to Azel. It will be blocked as it was blocked because of the earthquake*   ᵈ8 That is, the Dead Sea   ᵉ8 That is, the Mediterranean

Gate, and from the Tower of Hananel to the royal winepresses. ¹¹It will be inhabited; never again will it be destroyed. Jerusalem will be secure.

¹²This is the plague with which the LORD will strike all the nations that fought against Jerusalem: Their flesh will rot while they are still standing on their feet, their eyes will rot in their sockets, and their tongues will rot in their mouths. ¹³On that day men will be stricken by the LORD with great panic. Each man will seize the hand of another, and they will attack each other. ¹⁴Judah too will fight at Jerusalem. The wealth of all the surrounding nations will be collected—great quantities of gold and silver and clothing. ¹⁵A similar plague will strike the horses and mules, the camels and donkeys, and all the animals in those camps.

¹⁶Then the survivors from all the nations that have attacked Jerusalem will go up year after year to worship the King, the LORD Almighty, and to celebrate the Feast of Tabernacles. ¹⁷If any of the peoples of the earth do not go up to Jerusalem to worship the King, the LORD Almighty, they will have no rain. ¹⁸If the Egyptian people do not go up and take part, they will have no rain. The LORD*ᵃ* will bring on them the plague he inflicts on the nations that do not go up to celebrate the Feast of Tabernacles. ¹⁹This will be the punishment of Egypt and the punishment of all the nations that do not go up to celebrate the Feast of Tabernacles.

²⁰On that day HOLY TO THE LORD will be inscribed on the bells of the horses, and the cooking pots in the LORD's house will be like the sacred bowls in front of the altar. ²¹Every pot in Jerusalem and Judah will be holy to the LORD Almighty, and all who come to sacrifice will take some of the pots and cook in them. And on that day there will no longer be a Canaanite*ᵇ* in the house of the LORD Almighty.

ᵃ18 Or part, then the LORD   ᵇ21 Or merchant

MALACHI

WHO WROTE THIS BOOK?

The prophet Malachi.

WHY WAS THIS BOOK WRITTEN?

Malachi shows how the children of the people who returned to Judah from Babylon had strayed from God.

WHAT DO WE LEARN ABOUT GOD IN THIS BOOK?

God deserves our best. God will remember those who love him and talk about him.

WHAT IS SPECIAL ABOUT THIS BOOK?

The prophet answers foolish questions the people ask. His answers teach us how to show love for God.

WHEN WAS THIS BOOK WRITTEN?

Malachi was written between 465 and 430 B.C.

WHAT ARE SOME IMPORTANT PASSAGES IN THIS BOOK?

Honoring God.   Malachi 1:6–11
Robbing God.   Malachi 3:6–12
God's treasured possession.   Malachi 3:16–18

1 An oracle: The word of the LORD to Israel through Malachi. *a*

Jacob Loved, Esau Hated

2"I have loved you," says the LORD.

"But you ask, 'How have you loved us?'

"Was not Esau Jacob's brother?" the LORD says. "Yet I have loved Jacob, 3but Esau I have hated, and I have turned his mountains into a wasteland and left his inheritance to the desert jackals."

4Edom may say, "Though we have been crushed, we will rebuild the ruins."

But this is what the LORD Almighty says: "They may build, but I will demolish. They will be called the Wicked Land, a people always under the wrath of the LORD. 5You will see it with your own eyes and say, 'Great is the LORD—even beyond the borders of Israel!'

Blemished Sacrifices

6"A son honors his father, and a servant his master. If I am a father, where is the honor due me? If I am a master, where is the respect due me?" says the LORD Almighty. "It is you, O priests, who show contempt for my name.

"But you ask, 'How have we shown contempt for your name?'

7"You place defiled food on my altar.

"But you ask, 'How have we defiled you?'

"By saying that the LORD's table is contemptible. 8When you bring blind animals for sacrifice, is that not wrong? When you sacrifice crippled or diseased animals, is that not wrong? Try offering them to your governor! Would he be pleased with you? Would he accept you?" says the LORD Almighty.

9"Now implore God to be gracious to us. With such offerings from your hands, will he accept you?"—says the LORD Almighty.

10"Oh, that one of you would shut the temple doors, so that you would not light useless fires on my altar! I am not pleased with you," says the LORD Almighty, "and I will accept no offering from your hands. 11My name will be great among the nations, from the rising to the setting of the sun. In every place incense and pure offerings will be brought to my name, because my name will be great among the nations," says the LORD Almighty.

12"But you profane it by saying of the Lord's table, 'It is defiled,' and of its food, 'It is contemptible.' 13And you say, 'What a burden!' and you sniff at it contemptuously," says the LORD Almighty.

"When you bring injured, crippled or diseased animals and offer them as sacrifices, should I accept them from your hands?" says the LORD. 14"Cursed is the cheat who has an acceptable male in his flock and vows to give it, but then sacrifices a blemished animal to the Lord. For I am a great king," says the LORD Almighty,

a1 Malachi means my messenger.

▛ET'S LIVE IT!   Malachi 1:1–3

HOW HAS GOD LOVED US? ➡ The people in Malachi's time doubted that God loved them. Malachi reminded them that God had chosen them, the children of Jacob (Israel), as his own people. God said he loved them.

At mealtime, ask your family to help you list answers to the question, "How have you loved us?" (Malachi 1:2). On a 3x5 card write each way God has shown love to your family. Pick a different card at each meal to help you thank God for his special blessing.

"and my name is to be feared among the nations.

Admonition for the Priests

2 "And now this admonition is for you, O priests. ²If you do not listen, and if you do not set your heart to honor my name," says the LORD Almighty, "I will send a curse upon you, and I will curse your blessings. Yes, I have already cursed them, because you have not set your heart to honor me.

³"Because of you I will rebuke*ᵃ* your descendants*ᵇ*; I will spread on your faces the offal from your festival sacrifices, and you will be carried off with it. ⁴And you will know that I have sent you this admonition so that my covenant with Levi may continue," says the LORD Almighty. ⁵"My covenant was with him, a covenant of life and peace, and I gave them to him; this called for reverence and he revered me and stood in awe of my name. ⁶True instruction was in his mouth and nothing false was found on his lips. He walked with me in peace and uprightness, and turned many from sin.

⁷"For the lips of a priest ought to preserve knowledge, and from his mouth men should seek instruction —because he is the messenger of the LORD Almighty. ⁸But you have turned from the way and by your teaching have caused many to stumble; you have violated the covenant with Levi," says the LORD Almighty. ⁹"So I have caused you to be despised and humiliated before all the people, because you have not followed my ways but have shown partiality in matters of the law."

Judah Unfaithful

¹⁰Have we not all one Father*ᶜ*? Did not one God create us? Why do we profane the covenant of our fathers by breaking faith with one another?

¹¹Judah has broken faith. A detestable thing has been committed in Israel and in Jerusalem: Judah has desecrated the sanctuary the LORD loves, by marrying the daughter of a foreign god. ¹²As for the man who does this, whoever he may be, may the LORD cut him off from the tents of Jacob*ᵈ*—even though he brings offerings to the LORD Almighty.

¹³Another thing you do: You flood the LORD's altar with tears. You weep and wail because he no longer pays attention to your offerings or accepts them with pleasure from your hands. ¹⁴You ask, "Why?" It is because the LORD is acting as the witness between you and the wife of your youth, because you have broken faith with her, though she is your partner, the wife of your marriage covenant.

¹⁵Has not ⌊the LORD⌋ made them one? In flesh and spirit they are his. And why one? Because he was seeking godly offspring.*ᵉ* So guard yourself in your spirit, and do not break faith with the wife of your youth.

¹⁶"I hate divorce," says the LORD God of Israel, "and I hate a man's covering himself*ᶠ* with violence as well as with his garment," says the LORD Almighty.

So guard yourself in your spirit, and do not break faith.

The Day of Judgment

¹⁷You have wearied the LORD with your words.

"How have we wearied him?" you ask.

By saying, "All who do evil are good in the eyes of the LORD, and he is pleased with them" or "Where is the God of justice?"

3 "See, I will send my messenger, who will prepare the way before me. Then suddenly the Lord you are seeking will come to his temple; the messenger of the covenant, whom

---

ᵃ3 Or *cut off* (see Septuagint)   *ᵇ3* Or *will blight your grain*   *ᶜ10* Or *father*   *ᵈ12* Or *¹²May the LORD cut off from the tents of Jacob anyone who gives testimony in behalf of the man who does this*   *ᵉ15* Or *¹⁵But the one ⌊who is our father⌋ did not do this, not as long as life remained in him. And what was he seeking? An offspring from God*   *ᶠ16* Or *his wife*

you desire, will come," says the LORD Almighty.

²But who can endure the day of his coming? Who can stand when he appears? For he will be like a refiner's fire or a launderer's soap. ³He will sit as a refiner and purifier of silver; he will purify the Levites and refine them like gold and silver. Then the LORD will have men who will bring offerings in righteousness, ⁴and the offerings of Judah and Jerusalem will be acceptable to the LORD, as in days gone by, as in former years.

⁵"So I will come near to you for judgment. I will be quick to testify against sorcerers, adulterers and perjurers, against those who defraud laborers of their wages, who oppress the widows and the fatherless, and deprive aliens of justice, but do not fear me," says the LORD Almighty.

Robbing God

⁶"I the LORD do not change. So you, O descendants of Jacob, are not destroyed. ⁷Ever since the time of your forefathers you have turned away from my decrees and have not kept them. Return to me, and I will return to you," says the LORD Almighty.

"But you ask, 'How are we to return?'

⁸"Will a man rob God? Yet you rob me.

"But you ask, 'How do we rob you?'

"In tithes and offerings. ⁹You are under a curse—the whole nation of you—because you are robbing me. ¹⁰Bring the whole tithe into the storehouse, that there may be food in my house. Test me in this," says the LORD Almighty, "and see if I will not throw open the floodgates of heaven and pour out so much blessing that you will not have room enough for it. ¹¹I will prevent pests from devouring your crops, and the vines in your fields will not cast their fruit," says the LORD Almighty. ¹²"Then all the nations will call you blessed, for yours will be a delightful land," says the LORD Almighty.

¹³"You have said harsh things against me," says the LORD.

"Yet you ask, 'What have we said against you?'

¹⁴"You have said, 'It is futile to serve God. What did we gain by carrying out his requirements and going about like mourners before the LORD Almighty? ¹⁵But now we call the arrogant blessed. Certainly the evildoers prosper, and even those who challenge God escape.'"

¹⁶Then those who feared the LORD talked with each other, and the LORD listened and heard. A scroll of remembrance was written in his presence concerning those who feared the LORD and honored his name.

¹⁷"They will be mine," says the LORD Almighty, "in the day when I make up my treasured possession.ᵃ I

ᵃ17 Or *Almighty, "my treasured possession, in the day when I act*

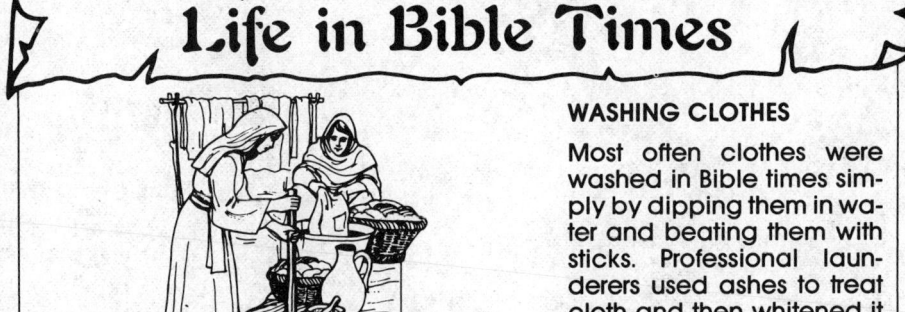

Life in Bible Times

WASHING CLOTHES

Most often clothes were washed in Bible times simply by dipping them in water and beating them with sticks. Professional launderers used ashes to treat cloth and then whitened it in the sun.

will spare them, just as in compassion a man spares his son who serves him. [18]And you will again see the distinction between the righteous and the wicked, between those who serve God and those who do not.

The Day of the LORD

4 "Surely the day is coming; it will burn like a furnace. All the arrogant and every evildoer will be stubble, and that day that is coming will set them on fire," says the LORD Almighty. "Not a root or a branch will be left to them. [2]But for you who revere my name, the sun of righteousness will rise with healing in its wings. And you will go out and leap like calves released from the stall. [3]Then you will trample down the wicked; they will be ashes under the soles of your feet on the day when I do these things," says the LORD Almighty.

[4]"Remember the law of my servant Moses, the decrees and laws I gave him at Horeb for all Israel.

[5]"See, I will send you the prophet Elijah before that great and dreadful day of the LORD comes. [6]He will turn the hearts of the fathers to their children, and the hearts of the children to their fathers; or else I will come and strike the land with a curse."

LET'S LIVE IT!　　　　Malachi 3:16–17

TALKING ABOUT GOD ➠ Read Malachi 3:16–17. God is pleased when you talk with others about him—so pleased that he writes your name in his "scroll of remembrance."

Make your own "book of remembrance." Get a small spiral notebook at the store. At bedtime write what you and others said if you talked about God that day. Try to talk about God with someone each day, so you have something to write in your book. People who love God and talk about him are his "treasured possession."

NEW TESTAMENT

MATTHEW

WHO WROTE THIS BOOK?

Matthew, one of Jesus' twelve disciples, wrote this book.

WHY WAS THIS BOOK WRITTEN?

Matthew shows the Jews that Jesus is the Messiah promised in the Old Testament.

FOR WHOM WAS THIS BOOK WRITTEN?

Matthew was written for the Jewish people.

WHAT HAPPENS IN THIS BOOK?

This book tells about Jesus' birth, his life as an adult, his teaching, death and resurrection.

WHO IS IMPORTANT IN THIS BOOK?

The most important people are Jesus, John the Baptist and Peter.

WHEN DID THIS HAPPEN?

These events took place between 6 B.C. and A.D. 30.

WHERE DID THIS HAPPEN?

Most events took place in towns in Galilee.

WHAT ARE SOME OF THE STORIES IN THIS BOOK?

Wise men visit Jesus.	Matthew 2:1–23
How to be happy.	Matthew 5:1–12
The Lord's prayer.	Matthew 6:9–13
Jesus feeds five thousand people.	Matthew 14:13–21
Jesus walks on water.	Matthew 14:22–33
Lost sheep.	Matthew 18:10–14
Jesus enters Jerusalem.	Matthew 21:1–11
Jesus is crucified.	Matthew 27:32–56
Jesus returns to life.	Matthew 28:1–10
Jesus instructs his followers.	Matthew 28:16–20

The Genealogy of Jesus

1 A record of the genealogy of Jesus Christ the son of David, the son of Abraham:

2Abraham was the father of Isaac,
Isaac the father of Jacob,
Jacob the father of Judah and his brothers,
3Judah the father of Perez and Zerah, whose mother was Tamar,
Perez the father of Hezron,
Hezron the father of Ram,
4Ram the father of Amminadab,
Amminadab the father of Nahshon,
Nahshon the father of Salmon,
5Salmon the father of Boaz, whose mother was Rahab,
Boaz the father of Obed, whose mother was Ruth,
Obed the father of Jesse,
6and Jesse the father of King David.

David was the father of Solomon, whose mother had been Uriah's wife,
7Solomon the father of Rehoboam,
Rehoboam the father of Abijah,
Abijah the father of Asa,
8Asa the father of Jehoshaphat,
Jehoshaphat the father of Jehoram,
Jehoram the father of Uzziah,
9Uzziah the father of Jotham,
Jotham the father of Ahaz,
Ahaz the father of Hezekiah,
10Hezekiah the father of Manasseh,
Manasseh the father of Amon,
Amon the father of Josiah,
11and Josiah the father of Jeconiah*a* and his brothers at the time of the exile to Babylon.

12After the exile to Babylon:
Jeconiah was the father of Shealtiel,
Shealtiel the father of Zerubbabel,
13Zerubbabel the father of Abiud,
Abiud the father of Eliakim,
Eliakim the father of Azor,
14Azor the father of Zadok,
Zadok the father of Akim,
Akim the father of Eliud,
15Eliud the father of Eleazar,
Eleazar the father of Matthan,
Matthan the father of Jacob,
16and Jacob the father of Joseph, the husband of Mary, of whom was born Jesus, who is called Christ.

17Thus there were fourteen generations in all from Abraham to David, fourteen from David to the exile to Babylon, and fourteen from the exile to the Christ.*b*

? DID YOU KNOW?   1:17

Why is this genealogy in Matthew?

A genealogy is a record of a person's ancestors. Matthew wanted us to know that Jesus was a true human being, descended from Adam. Matthew also wanted the Jews to know that Jesus was a descendant of David. Only a descendant of David could be king of the Jews.

The Birth of Jesus Christ

18This is how the birth of Jesus Christ came about: His mother Mary was pledged to be married to Joseph, but before they came together, she was found to be with child through the Holy Spirit. 19Because Joseph her husband was a righteous man and did not want to expose her to public disgrace, he had in mind to divorce her quietly.

20But after he had considered this, an angel of the Lord appeared to him

*a11 That is, Jehoiachin; also in verse 12   b17 Or Messiah. "The Christ" (Greek) and "the Messiah" (Hebrew) both mean "the Anointed One."

in a dream and said, "Joseph son of David, do not be afraid to take Mary home as your wife, because what is conceived in her is from the Holy Spirit. ²¹She will give birth to a son, and you are to give him the name Jesus,^a because he will save his people from their sins."

²²All this took place to fulfill what the Lord had said through the prophet: ²³"The virgin will be with child and will give birth to a son, and they will call him Immanuel"^b—which means, "God with us."

²⁴When Joseph woke up, he did what the angel of the Lord had commanded him and took Mary home as his wife. ²⁵But he had no union with her until she gave birth to a son. And he gave him the name Jesus.

The Visit of the Magi

2 After Jesus was born in Bethlehem in Judea, during the time of King Herod, Magi^c from the east came to Jerusalem ²and asked, "Where is the one who has been born king of the Jews? We saw his star in the east^d and have come to worship him."

³When King Herod heard this he was disturbed, and all Jerusalem with him. ⁴When he had called together all the people's chief priests and teachers of the law, he asked them where the Christ^e was to be born. ⁵"In Bethlehem in Judea," they replied, "for this is what the prophet has written:

⁶" 'But you, Bethlehem, in the land of Judah,
are by no means least among the rulers of Judah;
for out of you will come a ruler who will be the shepherd of my people Israel.'^f"

⁷Then Herod called the Magi secretly and found out from them the exact time the star had appeared. ⁸He sent them to Bethlehem and said, "Go and make a careful search for the child. As soon as you find him, report to me, so that I too may go and worship him."

⁹After they had heard the king, they went on their way, and the star they had seen in the east^g went ahead of them until it stopped over the place where the child was. ¹⁰When they saw the star, they were overjoyed. ¹¹On coming to the house, they saw the child with his mother Mary, and they bowed down and worshiped him. Then they opened their treasures and presented him with gifts of gold and of incense and of myrrh. ¹²And having been warned in a dream not to go back to Herod, they returned to their country by another route.

The Escape to Egypt

¹³When they had gone, an angel of the Lord appeared to Joseph in a dream. "Get up," he said, "take the child and his mother and escape to Egypt. Stay there until I tell you, for

---

^a21 *Jesus* is the Greek form of *Joshua,* which means *the Lord saves.*   ^b23 Isaiah 7:14
^c1 Traditionally *Wise Men*   ^d2 Or *star when it rose*   ^e4 Or *Messiah*   ^f6 Micah 5:2
^g9 Or *seen when it rose*

LET'S LIVE IT!   Matthew 2:1–12

A JESUS BABY BOOK ➠ Parents often keep a baby book for their children. The book has a place for pictures and stories about their child. Ask your mom or dad if you have a baby book and if you can look at it. You can make a baby book for Jesus. Read Matthew 2:1–12, and the first two chapters of Luke to find out about Jesus' birth. In your book draw pictures of the things that happened to Jesus. Pick Bible verses from Matthew and Luke to write under the pictures.

Herod is going to search for the child to kill him."

¹⁴So he got up, took the child and his mother during the night and left for Egypt, ¹⁵where he stayed until the death of Herod. And so was fulfilled what the Lord had said through the prophet: "Out of Egypt I called my son."ᵃ

¹⁶When Herod realized that he had been outwitted by the Magi, he was furious, and he gave orders to kill all the boys in Bethlehem and its vicinity who were two years old and under, in accordance with the time he had learned from the Magi. ¹⁷Then what was said through the prophet Jeremiah was fulfilled:

¹⁸"A voice is heard in Ramah,
    weeping and great mourning,
Rachel weeping for her children
    and refusing to be comforted,
because they are no more."ᵇ

The Return to Nazareth

¹⁹After Herod died, an angel of the Lord appeared in a dream to Joseph in Egypt ²⁰and said, "Get up, take the child and his mother and go to the land of Israel, for those who were trying to take the child's life are dead."

²¹So he got up, took the child and his mother and went to the land of Israel. ²²But when he heard that Archelaus was reigning in Judea in place of his father Herod, he was afraid to go there. Having been warned in a dream, he withdrew to the district of Galilee, ²³and he went and lived in a town called Nazareth. So was fulfilled what was said through the prophets: "He will be called a Nazarene."

John the Baptist Prepares the Way

3 In those days John the Baptist came, preaching in the Desert of Judea ²and saying, "Repent, for the kingdom of heaven is near." ³This is

he who was spoken of through the prophet Isaiah:

"A voice of one calling in the
    desert,
'Prepare the way for the Lord,
    make straight paths for him.' "ᶜ

? DID YOU KNOW?   3:2

What does repent mean?

To repent means to change your heart and mind. John the Baptist told people to repent of their sins. John preached this to help the people of Judea get ready to hear what Jesus would say.

---

⁴John's clothes were made of camel's hair, and he had a leather belt around his waist. His food was locusts and wild honey. ⁵People went out to him from Jerusalem and all Judea and the whole region of the Jordan. ⁶Confessing their sins, they were baptized by him in the Jordan River.

⁷But when he saw many of the Pharisees and Sadducees coming to where he was baptizing, he said to them: "You brood of vipers! Who warned you to flee from the coming wrath? ⁸Produce fruit in keeping with repentance. ⁹And do not think you can say to yourselves, 'We have Abraham as our father.' I tell you that out of these stones God can raise up children for Abraham. ¹⁰The ax is already at the root of the trees, and every tree that does not produce good fruit will be cut down and thrown into the fire.

¹¹"I baptize you withᵈ water for repentance. But after me will come one who is more powerful than I, whose sandals I am not fit to carry. He will baptize you with the Holy Spirit and with fire. ¹²His winnowing fork is in his hand, and he will clear his threshing floor, gathering his wheat into the barn and burning up the chaff with unquenchable fire."

ᵃ15 Hosea 11:1   ᵇ18 Jer. 31:15   ᶜ3 Isaiah 40:3   ᵈ11 Or in

The Baptism of Jesus

¹³Then Jesus came from Galilee to the Jordan to be baptized by John. ¹⁴But John tried to deter him, saying, "I need to be baptized by you, and do you come to me?"

¹⁵Jesus replied, "Let it be so now; it is proper for us to do this to fulfill all righteousness." Then John consented.

¹⁶As soon as Jesus was baptized, he went up out of the water. At that moment heaven was opened, and he saw the Spirit of God descending like a dove and lighting on him. ¹⁷And a voice from heaven said, "This is my Son, whom I love; with him I am well pleased."

The Temptation of Jesus

4 Then Jesus was led by the Spirit into the desert to be tempted by the devil. ²After fasting forty days and forty nights, he was hungry. ³The tempter came to him and said, "If you are the Son of God, tell these stones to become bread."

⁴Jesus answered, "It is written: 'Man does not live on bread alone, but on every word that comes from the mouth of God.'ᵃ"

⁵Then the devil took him to the holy city and had him stand on the highest point of the temple. ⁶"If you are the Son of God," he said, "throw yourself down. For it is written:

" 'He will command his angels
        concerning you,
    and they will lift you up in
        their hands,

so that you will not strike your
        foot against a stone.'ᵇ"

⁷Jesus answered him, "It is also written: 'Do not put the Lord your God to the test.'ᶜ"

⁸Again, the devil took him to a very high mountain and showed him all the kingdoms of the world and their splendor. ⁹"All this I will give you," he said, "if you will bow down and worship me."

¹⁰Jesus said to him, "Away from me, Satan! For it is written: 'Worship the Lord your God, and serve him only.'ᵈ"

¹¹Then the devil left him, and angels came and attended him.

Jesus Begins to Preach

¹²When Jesus heard that John had been put in prison, he returned to Galilee. ¹³Leaving Nazareth, he went and lived in Capernaum, which was by the lake in the area of Zebulun and Naphtali— ¹⁴to fulfill what was said through the prophet Isaiah:

¹⁵"Land of Zebulun and land of
        Naphtali,
    the way to the sea, along the
        Jordan,
    Galilee of the Gentiles—
¹⁶the people living in darkness
        have seen a great light;
on those living in the land of the
        shadow of death
    a light has dawned."ᵉ

¹⁷From that time on Jesus began to preach, "Repent, for the kingdom of heaven is near."

ᵃ4 Deut. 8:3   ᵇ6 Psalm 91:11,12   ᶜ7 Deut. 6:16   ᵈ10 Deut. 6:13   ᵉ16 Isaiah 9:1,2

▨ET'S LIVE IT!   Matthew 4:1–11

FIGHTING TEMPTATION ➡ Read Matthew 4:1–11. Can you find three words that Jesus said each time Satan tempted him?
    The words are, "It is written." Jesus fought each temptation by deciding to obey God and do what God says in the Bible. When you are tempted to do something wrong, you can defeat temptation too. Decide to obey God and do what the Bible says.

The Calling of the First Disciples

18As Jesus was walking beside the Sea of Galilee, he saw two brothers, Simon called Peter and his brother Andrew. They were casting a net into the lake, for they were fishermen. 19"Come, follow me," Jesus said, "and I will make you fishers of men." 20At once they left their nets and followed him.

21Going on from there, he saw two other brothers, James son of Zebedee and his brother John. They were in a boat with their father Zebedee, preparing their nets. Jesus called them, 22and immediately they left the boat and their father and followed him.

Jesus Heals the Sick

23Jesus went throughout Galilee, teaching in their synagogues, preaching the good news of the kingdom, and healing every disease and sickness among the people. 24News about him spread all over Syria, and people brought to him all who were ill with various diseases, those suffering severe pain, the demon-possessed, those having seizures, and the paralyzed, and he healed them. 25Large crowds from Galilee, the Decapolis,*a* Jerusalem, Judea and the region across the Jordan followed him.

The Beatitudes

5 Now when he saw the crowds, he went up on a mountainside and sat down. His disciples came to him, 2and he began to teach them, saying:

3"Blessed are the poor in spirit,
 for theirs is the kingdom of
  heaven.
4Blessed are those who mourn,
 for they will be comforted.
5Blessed are the meek,
 for they will inherit the earth.
6Blessed are those who hunger and
  thirst for righteousness,
 for they will be filled.
7Blessed are the merciful,

a25 That is, the Ten Cities

for they will be shown mercy.
8Blessed are the pure in heart,
 for they will see God.
9Blessed are the peacemakers,
 for they will be called sons of
  God.
10Blessed are those who are
  persecuted because of
  righteousness,
 for theirs is the kingdom of
  heaven.

11"Blessed are you when people insult you, persecute you and falsely say all kinds of evil against you because of me. 12Rejoice and be glad, because great is your reward in heaven, for in the same way they persecuted the prophets who were before you.

❓DID YOU KNOW?   5:3–10

What are the beatitudes?

The beatitudes are special sayings of Jesus. They explain how to be "blessed," or truly happy. Some people look for happiness in money or power. Jesus wants his listeners to know how they can be truly happy.

Salt and Light

13"You are the salt of the earth. But if the salt loses its saltiness, how can it be made salty again? It is no longer good for anything, except to be thrown out and trampled by men.

14"You are the light of the world. A city on a hill cannot be hidden. 15Neither do people light a lamp and put it under a bowl. Instead they put it on its stand, and it gives light to everyone in the house. 16In the same way, let your light shine before men, that they may see your good deeds and praise your Father in heaven.

The Fulfillment of the Law

17"Do not think that I have come to abolish the Law or the Prophets; I have not come to abolish them but to fulfill them. [18]I tell you the truth, until heaven and earth disappear, not the smallest letter, not the least stroke of a pen, will by any means disappear from the Law until everything is accomplished. [19]Anyone who breaks one of the least of these commandments and teaches others to do the same will be called least in the kingdom of heaven, but whoever practices and teaches these commands will be called great in the kingdom of heaven. [20]For I tell you that unless your righteousness surpasses that of the Pharisees and the teachers of the law, you will certainly not enter the kingdom of heaven.

Murder

[21]"You have heard that it was said to the people long ago, 'Do not murder,[a] and anyone who murders will be subject to judgment.' [22]But I tell you that anyone who is angry with his brother[b] will be subject to judgment. Again, anyone who says to his brother, 'Raca,[c]' is answerable to the Sanhedrin. But anyone who says, 'You fool!' will be in danger of the fire of hell.

[23]"Therefore, if you are offering your gift at the altar and there remember that your brother has something against you, [24]leave your gift there in front of the altar. First go and be reconciled to your brother; then come and offer your gift.

[25]"Settle matters quickly with your adversary who is taking you to court. Do it while you are still with him on the way, or he may hand you over to the judge, and the judge may hand you over to the officer, and you may be thrown into prison. [26]I tell you the truth, you will not get out until you have paid the last penny.[d]

Adultery

[27]"You have heard that it was said, 'Do not commit adultery.'[e] [28]But I tell you that anyone who looks at a woman lustfully has already committed adultery with her in his heart. [29]If your right eye causes you to sin, gouge it out and throw it away. It is better for you to lose one part of your body than for your whole body to be thrown into hell. [30]And if your right hand causes you to sin, cut it off and throw it away. It is better for you to lose one part of your body than for your whole body to go into hell.

Divorce

[31]"It has been said, 'Anyone who divorces his wife must give her a certificate of divorce.'[f] [32]But I tell you that anyone who divorces his wife, except for marital unfaithfulness, causes her to become an adulteress, and anyone who marries the divorced woman commits adultery.

Oaths

[33]"Again, you have heard that it was said to the people long ago, 'Do not break your oath, but keep the oaths you have made to the Lord.' [34]But I tell you, Do not swear at all: either by heaven, for it is God's throne; [35]or by the earth, for it is his footstool; or by Jerusalem, for it is the city of the Great King. [36]And do not swear by your head, for you cannot make even one hair white or black. [37]Simply let your 'Yes' be 'Yes,' and your 'No,' 'No'; anything beyond this comes from the evil one.

An Eye for an Eye

[38]"You have heard that it was said, 'Eye for eye, and tooth for tooth.'[g] [39]But I tell you, Do not resist an evil person. If someone strikes you on the right cheek, turn to him the other also. [40]And if someone wants to sue you and take your tunic, let him have your cloak as well. [41]If someone forces you to go one mile, go with him two miles. [42]Give to the one who asks you, and do not turn away from the one who wants to borrow from you.

---

a21 Exodus 20:13   *b22* Some manuscripts *brother without cause*   *c22* An Aramaic term of contempt   *d26* Greek *kodrantes*   *e27* Exodus 20:14   *f31* Deut. 24:1   *g38* Exodus 21:24; Lev. 24:20; Deut. 19:21

Love for Enemies

43"You have heard that it was said, 'Love your neighbor*a* and hate your enemy.' 44But I tell you: Love your enemies*b* and pray for those who persecute you, 45that you may be sons of your Father in heaven. He causes his sun to rise on the evil and the good, and sends rain on the righteous and the unrighteous. 46If you love those who love you, what reward will you get? Are not even the tax collectors doing that? 47And if you greet only your brothers, what are you doing more than others? Do not even pagans do that? 48Be perfect, therefore, as your heavenly Father is perfect.

Life In Bible Times

GIVING TO THE NEEDY

The Jewish people believed that God would bless people who gave money to the poor. But God was not pleased with those who gave only when they were sure others would see them. These people cared more about what people thought of them than about God's blessing.

Giving to the Needy

6 "Be careful not to do your 'acts of righteousness' before men, to be seen by them. If you do, you will have no reward from your Father in heaven.

2"So when you give to the needy, do not announce it with trumpets, as the hypocrites do in the synagogues and on the streets, to be honored by men. I tell you the truth, they have received their reward in full. 3But

when you give to the needy, do not let your left hand know what your right hand is doing, 4so that your giving may be in secret. Then your Father, who sees what is done in secret, will reward you.

Prayer

5"And when you pray, do not be like the hypocrites, for they love to pray standing in the synagogues and on the street corners to be seen by men. I tell you the truth, they have received their reward in full. 6But when you pray, go into your room, close the door and pray to your Father, who is unseen. Then your Father, who sees what is done in secret, will reward you. 7And when you pray, do not keep on babbling like pagans, for they think they will be heard because of their many words. 8Do not be like them, for your Father knows what you need before you ask him.

9"This, then, is how you should pray:

" 'Our Father in heaven,
    hallowed be your name,
10your kingdom come,
    your will be done
        on earth as it is in heaven.
11Give us today our daily bread.
12Forgive us our debts,
    as we also have forgiven our
        debtors.
13And lead us not into temptation,
    but deliver us from the evil one.*c*'

14For if you forgive men when they sin against you, your heavenly Father will also forgive you. 15But if you do not forgive men their sins, your Father will not forgive your sins.

Fasting

16"When you fast, do not look somber as the hypocrites do, for they disfigure their faces to show men they are fasting. I tell you the truth, they have received their reward in full.

---

*a*43 Lev. 19:18   *b*44 Some late manuscripts *enemies, bless those who curse you, do good to those who hate you*   *c*13 Or *from evil*; some late manuscripts *one, / for yours is the kingdom and the power and the glory forever. Amen.*

17But when you fast, put oil on your head and wash your face, 18so that it will not be obvious to men that you are fasting, but only to your Father, who is unseen; and your Father, who sees what is done in secret, will reward you.

Treasures in Heaven

19"Do not store up for yourselves treasures on earth, where moth and rust destroy, and where thieves break in and steal. 20But store up for yourselves treasures in heaven, where moth and rust do not destroy, and where thieves do not break in and steal. 21For where your treasure is, there your heart will be also.

22"The eye is the lamp of the body. If your eyes are good, your whole body will be full of light. 23But if your eyes are bad, your whole body will be full of darkness. If then the light within you is darkness, how great is that darkness!

24"No one can serve two masters. Either he will hate the one and love the other, or he will be devoted to the one and despise the other. You cannot serve both God and Money.

Do Not Worry

25"Therefore I tell you, do not worry about your life, what you will eat or drink; or about your body, what you will wear. Is not life more important than food, and the body more important than clothes? 26Look at the birds of the air; they do not sow or reap or store away in barns, and yet your heavenly Father feeds them. Are you not much more valuable than they? 27Who of you by worrying can add a single hour to his life*a*? 28"And why do you worry about clothes? See how the lilies of the field grow. They do not labor or spin. 29Yet I tell you that not even Solomon in all his splendor was dressed like one of these. 30If that is how God clothes the grass of the field, which is here today and tomorrow is thrown into the fire, will he not much more clothe you, O you of little faith? 31So do not worry, saying, 'What shall we eat?' or 'What shall we drink?' or 'What shall we wear?' 32For the pagans run after all these things, and your heavenly Father knows that you need them. 33But seek first his kingdom and his righteousness, and all these things will be given to you as well. 34Therefore do not worry about tomorrow, for tomorrow will worry about itself. Each day has enough trouble of its own.

Judging Others

7 "Do not judge, or you too will be judged. 2For in the same way you judge others, you will be judged, and with the measure you use, it will be measured to you.

3"Why do you look at the speck of sawdust in your brother's eye and pay no attention to the plank in your own eye? 4How can you say to your brother, 'Let me take the speck out of your eye,' when all the time there is a plank in your own eye? 5You hypocrite, first take the plank out of your own eye, and then you will see clearly to remove the speck from your brother's eye.

6"Do not give dogs what is sacred; do not throw your pearls to pigs. If you do, they may trample them under their feet, and then turn and tear you to pieces.

Ask, Seek, Knock

7"Ask and it will be given to you; seek and you will find; knock and the door will be opened to you. 8For everyone who asks receives; he who seeks finds; and to him who knocks, the door will be opened.

9"Which of you, if his son asks for bread, will give him a stone? 10Or if he asks for a fish, will give him a snake? 11If you, then, though you are evil, know how to give good gifts to your children, how much more will your Father in heaven give good gifts to those who ask him! 12So in everything, do to others what you would

---

a27 Or single cubit to his height

have them do to you, for this sums up the Law and the Prophets.

The Narrow and Wide Gates

13"Enter through the narrow gate. For wide is the gate and broad is the road that leads to destruction, and many enter through it. 14But small is the gate and narrow the road that leads to life, and only a few find it.

A Tree and Its Fruit

15"Watch out for false prophets. They come to you in sheep's clothing, but inwardly they are ferocious wolves. 16By their fruit you will recognize them. Do people pick grapes from thornbushes, or figs from thistles? 17Likewise every good tree bears good fruit, but a bad tree bears bad fruit. 18A good tree cannot bear bad fruit, and a bad tree cannot bear good fruit. 19Every tree that does not bear good fruit is cut down and thrown into the fire. 20Thus, by their fruit you will recognize them.

21"Not everyone who says to me, 'Lord, Lord,' will enter the kingdom of heaven, but only he who does the will of my Father who is in heaven. 22Many will say to me on that day, 'Lord, Lord, did we not prophesy in your name, and in your name drive out demons and perform many miracles?' 23Then I will tell them plainly,

'I never knew you. Away from me, you evildoers!'

The Wise and Foolish Builders

24"Therefore everyone who hears these words of mine and puts them into practice is like a wise man who built his house on the rock. 25The rain came down, the streams rose, and the winds blew and beat against that house; yet it did not fall, because it had its foundation on the rock. 26But everyone who hears these words of mine and does not put them into practice is like a foolish man who built his house on sand. 27The rain came down, the streams rose, and the winds blew and beat against that house, and it fell with a great crash."

28When Jesus had finished saying these things, the crowds were amazed at his teaching, 29because he taught as one who had authority, and not as their teachers of the law.

The Man With Leprosy

8 When he came down from the mountainside, large crowds followed him. 2A man with leprosy[a] came and knelt before him and said, "Lord, if you are willing, you can make me clean."

3Jesus reached out his hand and touched the man. "I am willing," he said. "Be clean!" Immediately he was cured[b] of his leprosy. 4Then Jesus

---

a2 The Greek word was used for various diseases affecting the skin—not necessarily leprosy.
b3 Greek made clean

LET'S LIVE IT!   Matthew 7:1–5

A PRETEND MIRROR ➠ "Judging" means criticizing or condemning someone for something they do. Read Matthew 7: 1–5. What does Jesus say about judging? What are we to do instead of judging?

Often it is easy to be critical, to say bad things about others, without even thinking. Here's a way to help you remember to say good things. On a small card write, "I said something good." Turn the card over and write, "I said something bad." Put the card in your pocket for one whole day. When you say something good about someone, put a check on that side of the card. When you say something bad or not very nice, put a check on the other side of your card. At the end of the day, add up the checks. How did you do?

said to him, "See that you don't tell anyone. But go, show yourself to the priest and offer the gift Moses commanded, as a testimony to them."

The Faith of the Centurion

5When Jesus had entered Capernaum, a centurion came to him, asking for help. 6"Lord," he said, "my servant lies at home paralyzed and in terrible suffering."

7Jesus said to him, "I will go and heal him."

8The centurion replied, "Lord, I do not deserve to have you come under my roof. But just say the word, and my servant will be healed. 9For I myself am a man under authority, with soldiers under me. I tell this one, 'Go,' and he goes; and that one, 'Come,' and he comes. I say to my servant, 'Do this,' and he does it."

10When Jesus heard this, he was astonished and said to those following him, "I tell you the truth, I have not found anyone in Israel with such great faith. 11I say to you that many will come from the east and the west, and will take their places at the feast with Abraham, Isaac and Jacob in the kingdom of heaven. 12But the subjects of the kingdom will be thrown outside, into the darkness, where there will be weeping and gnashing of teeth."

13Then Jesus said to the centurion, "Go! It will be done just as you believed it would." And his servant was healed at that very hour.

Jesus Heals Many

14When Jesus came into Peter's house, he saw Peter's mother-in-law lying in bed with a fever. 15He touched her hand and the fever left her, and she got up and began to wait on him.

16When evening came, many who were demon-possessed were brought to him, and he drove out the spirits with a word and healed all the sick. 17This was to fulfill what was spoken through the prophet Isaiah:

"He took up our infirmities
and carried our diseases."*a*

The Cost of Following Jesus

18When Jesus saw the crowd around him, he gave orders to cross to the other side of the lake. 19Then a teacher of the law came to him and said, "Teacher, I will follow you wherever you go."

20Jesus replied, "Foxes have holes and birds of the air have nests, but the Son of Man has no place to lay his head."

21Another disciple said to him, "Lord, first let me go and bury my father."

22But Jesus told him, "Follow me, and let the dead bury their own dead."

Jesus Calms the Storm

23Then he got into the boat and his disciples followed him. 24Without warning, a furious storm came up on the lake, so that the waves swept over the boat. But Jesus was sleeping. 25The disciples went and woke him, saying, "Lord, save us! We're going to drown!"

26He replied, "You of little faith, why are you so afraid?" Then he got up and rebuked the winds and the waves, and it was completely calm.

27The men were amazed and asked, "What kind of man is this? Even the winds and the waves obey him!"

The Healing of Two Demon-possessed Men

28When he arrived at the other side in the region of the Gadarenes,*b* two demon-possessed men coming from the tombs met him. They were so violent that no one could pass that way. 29"What do you want with us, Son of God?" they shouted. "Have you come here to torture us before the appointed time?"

30Some distance from them a large herd of pigs was feeding. 31The demons begged Jesus, "If you drive us out, send us into the herd of pigs."

a17 Isaiah 53:4   b28 Some manuscripts Gergesenes; others Gerasenes

³²He said to them, "Go!" So they came out and went into the pigs, and the whole herd rushed down the steep bank into the lake and died in the water. ³³Those tending the pigs ran off, went into the town and reported all this, including what had happened to the demon-possessed men. ³⁴Then the whole town went out to meet Jesus. And when they saw him, they pleaded with him to leave their region.

Jesus Heals a Paralytic

9 Jesus stepped into a boat, crossed over and came to his own town. ²Some men brought to him a paralytic, lying on a mat. When Jesus saw their faith, he said to the paralytic, "Take heart, son; your sins are forgiven."

³At this, some of the teachers of the law said to themselves, "This fellow is blaspheming!"

⁴Knowing their thoughts, Jesus said, "Why do you entertain evil thoughts in your hearts? ⁵Which is easier: to say, 'Your sins are forgiven,' or to say, 'Get up and walk'? ⁶But so that you may know that the Son of Man has authority on earth to forgive sins. . . ." Then he said to the paralytic, "Get up, take your mat and go home." ⁷And the man got up and went home. ⁸When the crowd saw this, they were filled with awe; and they praised God, who had given such authority to men.

The Calling of Matthew

⁹As Jesus went on from there, he saw a man named Matthew sitting at the tax collector's booth. "Follow me," he told him, and Matthew got up and followed him.

¹⁰While Jesus was having dinner at Matthew's house, many tax collectors and "sinners" came and ate with him and his disciples. ¹¹When the Pharisees saw this, they asked his disciples, "Why does your teacher eat with tax collectors and 'sinners'?"

¹²On hearing this, Jesus said, "It is not the healthy who need a doctor, but the sick. ¹³But go and learn what this means: 'I desire mercy, not sacrifice.'ᵃ For I have not come to call the righteous, but sinners."

Life In Bible Times

TAX COLLECTORS

In Bible times some tax collectors had outdoor offices by highways. People who traveled had to stop and pay taxes on the goods they carried. The Jews resented the men who collected taxes for the Romans.

Jesus Questioned About Fasting

¹⁴Then John's disciples came and asked him, "How is it that we and the Pharisees fast, but your disciples do not fast?"

¹⁵Jesus answered, "How can the guests of the bridegroom mourn while he is with them? The time will come when the bridegroom will be taken from them; then they will fast.

¹⁶"No one sews a patch of unshrunk cloth on an old garment, for the patch will pull away from the garment, making the tear worse. ¹⁷Neither do men pour new wine into old wineskins. If they do, the skins will burst, the wine will run out and the wineskins will be ruined. No, they pour new wine into new wineskins, and both are preserved."

A Dead Girl and a Sick Woman

¹⁸While he was saying this, a ruler came and knelt before him and said, "My daughter has just died. But come and put your hand on her, and she will live." ¹⁹Jesus got up and went with him, and so did his disciples.

ᵃ13 Hosea 6:6

²⁰Just then a woman who had been subject to bleeding for twelve years came up behind him and touched the edge of his cloak. ²¹She said to herself, "If I only touch his cloak, I will be healed."

²²Jesus turned and saw her. "Take heart, daughter," he said, "your faith has healed you." And the woman was healed from that moment.

²³When Jesus entered the ruler's house and saw the flute players and the noisy crowd, ²⁴he said, "Go away. The girl is not dead but asleep." But they laughed at him. ²⁵After the crowd had been put outside, he went in and took the girl by the hand, and she got up. ²⁶News of this spread through all that region.

Jesus Heals the Blind and Mute

²⁷As Jesus went on from there, two blind men followed him, calling out, "Have mercy on us, Son of David!"

²⁸When he had gone indoors, the blind men came to him, and he asked them, "Do you believe that I am able to do this?"

"Yes, Lord," they replied.

²⁹Then he touched their eyes and said, "According to your faith will it be done to you"; ³⁰and their sight was restored. Jesus warned them sternly, "See that no one knows about this." ³¹But they went out and spread the news about him all over that region.

³²While they were going out, a man who was demon-possessed and could not talk was brought to Jesus. ³³And when the demon was driven out, the man who had been mute spoke. The crowd was amazed and said, "Nothing like this has ever been seen in Israel."

³⁴But the Pharisees said, "It is by the prince of demons that he drives out demons."

The Workers Are Few

³⁵Jesus went through all the towns and villages, teaching in their synagogues, preaching the good news of the kingdom and healing every disease and sickness. ³⁶When he saw the crowds, he had compassion on them, because they were harassed and helpless, like sheep without a shepherd. ³⁷Then he said to his disciples, "The harvest is plentiful but the workers are few. ³⁸Ask the Lord of the harvest, therefore, to send out workers into his harvest field."

Jesus Sends Out the Twelve

10 He called his twelve disciples to him and gave them authority to drive out evil*ᵃ* spirits and to heal every disease and sickness.

²These are the names of the twelve apostles: first, Simon (who is called Peter) and his brother Andrew; James son of Zebedee, and his brother John; ³Philip and Bartholomew; Thomas and Matthew the tax collector; James son of Alphaeus, and Thaddaeus; ⁴Simon the Zealot and Judas Iscariot, who betrayed him.

❓DID YOU KNOW?　　　**10:1**

What did Jesus' disciples do?

Disciple means student or learner. Jesus trained his disciples to preach and teach. The disciples were ordinary men. Many had jobs catching fish, but now they would be "fishers of men."

---

⁵These twelve Jesus sent out with the following instructions: "Do not go among the Gentiles or enter any town of the Samaritans. ⁶Go rather to the lost sheep of Israel. ⁷As you go, preach this message: 'The kingdom of heaven is near.' ⁸Heal the sick, raise the dead, cleanse those who have leprosy,*ᵇ* drive out demons. Freely you have received, freely give. ⁹Do not take along any gold or silver or copper in your belts; ¹⁰take no bag for the journey, or extra tunic, or sandals or

---

ᵃ1 Greek *unclean*　　*ᵇ8* The Greek word was used for various diseases affecting the skin—not necessarily leprosy.

a staff; for the worker is worth his keep.

¹¹"Whatever town or village you enter, search for some worthy person there and stay at his house until you leave. ¹²As you enter the home, give it your greeting. ¹³If the home is deserving, let your peace rest on it; if it is not, let your peace return to you. ¹⁴If anyone will not welcome you or listen to your words, shake the dust off your feet when you leave that home or town. ¹⁵I tell you the truth, it will be more bearable for Sodom and Gomorrah on the day of judgment than for that town. ¹⁶I am sending you out like sheep among wolves. Therefore be as shrewd as snakes and as innocent as doves.

¹⁷"Be on your guard against men; they will hand you over to the local councils and flog you in their synagogues. ¹⁸On my account you will be brought before governors and kings as witnesses to them and to the Gentiles. ¹⁹But when they arrest you, do not worry about what to say or how to say it. At that time you will be given what to say, ²⁰for it will not be you speaking, but the Spirit of your Father speaking through you.

²¹"Brother will betray brother to death, and a father his child; children will rebel against their parents and have them put to death. ²²All men will hate you because of me, but he who stands firm to the end will be saved. ²³When you are persecuted in one place, flee to another. I tell you the truth, you will not finish going through the cities of Israel before the Son of Man comes.

²⁴"A student is not above his teacher, nor a servant above his master. ²⁵It is enough for the student to be like his teacher, and the servant like his master. If the head of the house has been called Beelzebub,ᵃ how much more the members of his household!

²⁶"So do not be afraid of them. There is nothing concealed that will not be disclosed, or hidden that will not be made known. ²⁷What I tell you in the dark, speak in the daylight; what is whispered in your ear, proclaim from the roofs. ²⁸Do not be afraid of those who kill the body but cannot kill the soul. Rather, be afraid of the One who can destroy both soul and body in hell. ²⁹Are not two sparrows sold for a pennyᵇ? Yet not one of them will fall to the ground apart from the will of your Father. ³⁰And even the very hairs of your head are all numbered. ³¹So don't be afraid; you are worth more than many sparrows.

³²"Whoever acknowledges me before men, I will also acknowledge him before my Father in heaven. ³³But whoever disowns me before men, I will disown him before my Father in heaven.

³⁴"Do not suppose that I have come to bring peace to the earth. I did not come to bring peace, but a sword. ³⁵For I have come to turn

" 'a man against his father,
　a daughter against her
　　　mother,
a daughter-in-law against her
　　　mother-in-law—

ᵃ25 Greek *Beezeboul* or *Beelzeboul*　　ᵇ29 Greek *an assarion*

◣ET'S LIVE IT! Matthew 10:24–25a

A FAMILY FUN NIGHT ➡ Plan a family fun night, when everyone dresses up to look the way he or she thinks Jesus looked. Find pictures of Bible times clothing. Wear old bathrobes, make towel headdresses. You might even serve a Bible times meal of fish, fruit, and pita bread.

　　Then read Matthew 10:24–25a together, and talk about ways you can be like Jesus in your daily life.

36 a man's enemies will be the members of his own household.'*a*

37"Anyone who loves his father or mother more than me is not worthy of me; anyone who loves his son or daughter more than me is not worthy of me; 38and anyone who does not take his cross and follow me is not worthy of me. 39Whoever finds his life will lose it, and whoever loses his life for my sake will find it.

40"He who receives you receives me, and he who receives me receives the one who sent me. 41Anyone who receives a prophet because he is a prophet will receive a prophet's reward, and anyone who receives a righteous man because he is a righteous man will receive a righteous man's reward. 42And if anyone gives even a cup of cold water to one of these little ones because he is my disciple, I tell you the truth, he will certainly not lose his reward."

Jesus and John the Baptist

11 After Jesus had finished instructing his twelve disciples, he went on from there to teach and preach in the towns of Galilee.*b*

2When John heard in prison what Christ was doing, he sent his disciples 3to ask him, "Are you the one who was to come, or should we expect someone else?"

4Jesus replied, "Go back and report to John what you hear and see: 5The blind receive sight, the lame walk, those who have leprosy*c* are cured, the deaf hear, the dead are raised, and the good news is preached to the poor. 6Blessed is the man who does not fall away on account of me."

7As John's disciples were leaving, Jesus began to speak to the crowd about John: "What did you go out into the desert to see? A reed swayed by the wind? 8If not, what did you go out to see? A man dressed in fine clothes? No, those who wear fine

clothes are in kings' palaces. 9Then what did you go out to see? A prophet? Yes, I tell you, and more than a prophet. 10This is the one about whom it is written:

" 'I will send my messenger ahead of you,
    who will prepare your way
        before you.'*d*

11I tell you the truth: Among those born of women there has not risen anyone greater than John the Baptist; yet he who is least in the kingdom of heaven is greater than he. 12From the days of John the Baptist until now, the kingdom of heaven has been forcefully advancing, and forceful men lay hold of it. 13For all the Prophets and the Law prophesied until John. 14And if you are willing to accept it, he is the Elijah who was to come. 15He who has ears, let him hear.

16"To what can I compare this generation? They are like children sitting in the marketplaces and calling out to others:

17" 'We played the flute for you,
    and you did not dance;
  we sang a dirge,
    and you did not mourn.'

18For John came neither eating nor drinking, and they say, 'He has a demon.' 19The Son of Man came eating and drinking, and they say, 'Here is a glutton and a drunkard, a friend of tax collectors and "sinners." ' But wisdom is proved right by her actions."

Woe on Unrepentant Cities

20Then Jesus began to denounce the cities in which most of his miracles had been performed, because they did not repent. 21"Woe to you, Korazin! Woe to you, Bethsaida! If the miracles that were performed in you had been performed in Tyre and Sidon, they would have repented long ago in sackcloth and ashes. 22But I tell you, it will be more bearable for

---

a36 Micah 7:6   *b1* Greek *in their towns*   *c5* The Greek word was used for various diseases affecting the skin—not necessarily leprosy.   *d10* Mal. 3:1

Tyre and Sidon on the day of judgment than for you. ²³And you, Capernaum, will you be lifted up to the skies? No, you will go down to the depths.^a If the miracles that were performed in you had been performed in Sodom, it would have remained to this day. ²⁴But I tell you that it will be more bearable for Sodom on the day of judgment than for you."

Rest for the Weary

²⁵At that time Jesus said, "I praise you, Father, Lord of heaven and earth, because you have hidden these things from the wise and learned, and revealed them to little children. ²⁶Yes, Father, for this was your good pleasure.

²⁷"All things have been committed to me by my Father. No one knows the Son except the Father, and no one knows the Father except the Son and those to whom the Son chooses to reveal him.

²⁸"Come to me, all you who are weary and burdened, and I will give you rest. ²⁹Take my yoke upon you and learn from me, for I am gentle and humble in heart, and you will find rest for your souls. ³⁰For my yoke is easy and my burden is light."

Lord of the Sabbath

12 At that time Jesus went through the grainfields on the Sabbath. His disciples were hungry and began to pick some heads of grain and eat them. ²When the Pharisees saw this, they said to him, "Look! Your disciples are doing what is unlawful on the Sabbath."

³He answered, "Haven't you read what David did when he and his companions were hungry? ⁴He entered the house of God, and he and his companions ate the consecrated bread —which was not lawful for them to do, but only for the priests. ⁵Or haven't you read in the Law that on the Sabbath the priests in the temple desecrate the day and yet are innocent? ⁶I tell you that one^b greater than the temple is here. ⁷If you had known what these words mean, 'I desire mercy, not sacrifice,'^c you would not have condemned the innocent. ⁸For the Son of Man is Lord of the Sabbath."

⁹Going on from that place, he went into their synagogue, ¹⁰and a man with a shriveled hand was there. Looking for a reason to accuse Jesus, they asked him, "Is it lawful to heal on the Sabbath?"

¹¹He said to them, "If any of you has a sheep and it falls into a pit on the Sabbath, will you not take hold of it and lift it out? ¹²How much more valuable is a man than a sheep! Therefore it is lawful to do good on the Sabbath."

¹³Then he said to the man, "Stretch out your hand." So he stretched it out and it was completely restored, just as sound as the other. ¹⁴But the Pharisees went out and plotted how they might kill Jesus.

---

^a23 Greek *Hades*   ^b6 Or *something*; also in verses 41 and 42   ^c7 Hosea 6:6

Life in Bible Times

YOKES

Wooden yokes were worn by teams of animals. Oxen yoked together shared the load. Jesus promises to share our load and work beside us.

God's Chosen Servant

¹⁵Aware of this, Jesus withdrew from that place. Many followed him, and he healed all their sick, ¹⁶warning them not to tell who he was. ¹⁷This was to fulfill what was spoken through the prophet Isaiah:

¹⁸"Here is my servant whom I have
    chosen,
  the one I love, in whom I
    delight;
  I will put my Spirit on him,
    and he will proclaim justice to
    the nations.
¹⁹He will not quarrel or cry out;
  no one will hear his voice in the
    streets.
²⁰A bruised reed he will not break,
    and a smoldering wick he will
    not snuff out,
  till he leads justice to victory.
²¹ In his name the nations will
    put their hope."ᵃ

Jesus and Beelzebub

²²Then they brought him a demon-possessed man who was blind and mute, and Jesus healed him, so that he could both talk and see. ²³All the people were astonished and said, "Could this be the Son of David?"

²⁴But when the Pharisees heard this, they said, "It is only by Beelzebub,ᵇ the prince of demons, that this fellow drives out demons."

❓DID YOU KNOW?   12:24

Who was Beelzebub?

Beelzebub was another name for Satan. Jesus' enemies claimed that Jesus cast out demons by using Satan's power. In this passage Jesus showed his enemies that they were foolish and wrong.

---

²⁵Jesus knew their thoughts and said to them, "Every kingdom divided against itself will be ruined, and every city or household divided against itself will not stand. ²⁶If Satan drives out Satan, he is divided against himself. How then can his kingdom stand? ²⁷And if I drive out demons by Beelzebub, by whom do your people drive them out? So then, they will be your judges. ²⁸But if I drive out demons by the Spirit of God, then the kingdom of God has come upon you.

²⁹"Or again, how can anyone enter a strong man's house and carry off his possessions unless he first ties up the strong man? Then he can rob his house.

³⁰"He who is not with me is against me, and he who does not gather with me scatters. ³¹And so I tell you, every sin and blasphemy will be forgiven men, but the blasphemy against the Spirit will not be forgiven. ³²Anyone who speaks a word against the Son of Man will be forgiven, but anyone who speaks against the Holy Spirit will not be forgiven, either in this age or in the age to come.

³³"Make a tree good and its fruit will be good, or make a tree bad and its fruit will be bad, for a tree is recognized by its fruit. ³⁴You brood of vipers, how can you who are evil say anything good? For out of the overflow of the heart the mouth speaks. ³⁵The good man brings good things out of the good stored up in him, and the evil man brings evil things out of the evil stored up in him. ³⁶But I tell you that men will have to give account on the day of judgment for every careless word they have spoken. ³⁷For by your words you will be acquitted, and by your words you will be condemned."

The Sign of Jonah

³⁸Then some of the Pharisees and teachers of the law said to him, "Teacher, we want to see a miraculous sign from you."

³⁹He answered, "A wicked and adulterous generation asks for a miraculous sign! But none will be given it except the sign of the prophet Jo-

---

ᵃ21 Isaiah 42:1-4   ᵇ24 Greek *Beezeboul* or *Beelzeboul*; also in verse 27

nah. ⁴⁰For as Jonah was three days and three nights in the belly of a huge fish, so the Son of Man will be three days and three nights in the heart of the earth. ⁴¹The men of Nineveh will stand up at the judgment with this generation and condemn it; for they repented at the preaching of Jonah, and now one*ᵃ* greater than Jonah is here. ⁴²The Queen of the South will rise at the judgment with this generation and condemn it; for she came from the ends of the earth to listen to Solomon's wisdom, and now one greater than Solomon is here.

⁴³"When an evil*ᵇ* spirit comes out of a man, it goes through arid places seeking rest and does not find it. ⁴⁴Then it says, 'I will return to the house I left.' When it arrives, it finds the house unoccupied, swept clean and put in order. ⁴⁵Then it goes and takes with it seven other spirits more wicked than itself, and they go in and live there. And the final condition of that man is worse than the first. That is how it will be with this wicked generation."

Jesus' Mother and Brothers

⁴⁶While Jesus was still talking to the crowd, his mother and brothers stood outside, wanting to speak to him. ⁴⁷Someone told him, "Your mother and brothers are standing outside, wanting to speak to you."*ᶜ* ⁴⁸He replied to him, "Who is my mother, and who are my brothers?" ⁴⁹Pointing to his disciples, he said, "Here are my mother and my brothers. ⁵⁰For whoever does the will of my Father in heaven is my brother and sister and mother."

The Parable of the Sower

13 That same day Jesus went out of the house and sat by the lake. ²Such large crowds gathered around him that he got into a boat and sat in it, while all the people stood on the shore. ³Then he told them many things in parables, saying: "A farmer went out to sow his seed. ⁴As he was scattering the seed, some fell along the path, and the birds came and ate it up. ⁵Some fell on rocky places, where it did not have much soil. It sprang up quickly, because the soil was shallow. ⁶But when the sun came up, the plants were scorched, and they withered because they had no root. ⁷Other seed fell among thorns, which grew up and choked the plants. ⁸Still other seed fell on good soil, where it produced a crop—a hundred, sixty or thirty times what was sown. ⁹He who has ears, let him hear."

¹⁰The disciples came to him and asked, "Why do you speak to the people in parables?"

¹¹He replied, "The knowledge of the secrets of the kingdom of heaven has been given to you, but not to them. ¹²Whoever has will be given more, and he will have an abundance. Whoever does not have, even what he has will be taken from him. ¹³This is why I speak to them in parables:

"Though seeing, they do not see;
    though hearing, they do not
        hear or understand.

¹⁴In them is fulfilled the prophecy of Isaiah:

" 'You will be ever hearing but
        never understanding;
    you will be ever seeing but
        never perceiving.
¹⁵For this people's heart has
        become calloused;
    they hardly hear with their
        ears,
    and they have closed their eyes.
Otherwise they might see with
        their eyes,
    hear with their ears,
    understand with their hearts
and turn, and I would heal
        them.'*ᵈ*

¹⁶But blessed are your eyes because

ᵃ41 Or something; also in verse 42   *ᵇ43 Greek unclean*   *ᶜ47 Some manuscripts do not have verse 47.*   *ᵈ15 Isaiah 6:9,10*

they see, and your ears because they hear. [17]For I tell you the truth, many prophets and righteous men longed to see what you see but did not see it, and to hear what you hear but did not hear it.

[18]"Listen then to what the parable of the sower means: [19]When anyone hears the message about the kingdom and does not understand it, the evil one comes and snatches away what was sown in his heart. This is the seed sown along the path. [20]The one who received the seed that fell on rocky places is the man who hears the word and at once receives it with joy. [21]But since he has no root, he lasts only a short time. When trouble or persecution comes because of the word, he quickly falls away. [22]The one who received the seed that fell among the thorns is the man who hears the word, but the worries of this life and the deceitfulness of wealth choke it, making it unfruitful. [23]But the one who received the seed that fell on good soil is the man who hears the word and understands it. He produces a crop, yielding a hundred, sixty or thirty times what was sown."

The Parable of the Weeds

[24]Jesus told them another parable: "The kingdom of heaven is like a man who sowed good seed in his field. [25]But while everyone was sleeping, his enemy came and sowed weeds among the wheat, and went away. [26]When the wheat sprouted and formed heads, then the weeds also appeared.

[27]"The owner's servants came to him and said, 'Sir, didn't you sow good seed in your field? Where then did the weeds come from?'

[28] 'An enemy did this,' he replied.

"The servants asked him, 'Do you want us to go and pull them up?'

[29] 'No,' he answered, 'because while you are pulling the weeds, you may root up the wheat with them. [30]Let both grow together until the harvest. At that time I will tell the harvesters: First collect the weeds and tie them in bundles to be burned; then gather the wheat and bring it into my barn.' "

❓DID YOU KNOW?   13:36

What is the parable of the weeds about?

The parable of the weeds is about real Christians and pretend Christians. Jesus said that it is sometimes difficult to tell the difference, so we are to wait, and let God decide who is a real Christian when Jesus returns.

The Parables of the Mustard Seed and the Yeast

[31]He told them another parable: "The kingdom of heaven is like a mustard seed, which a man took and planted in his field. [32]Though it is the smallest of all your seeds, yet when it grows, it is the largest of garden plants and becomes a tree, so that the birds of the air come and perch in its branches."

[33]He told them still another parable: "The kingdom of heaven is like yeast that a woman took and mixed into a large amount[a] of flour until it worked all through the dough."

[34]Jesus spoke all these things to the crowd in parables; he did not say anything to them without using a parable. [35]So was fulfilled what was spoken through the prophet:

"I will open my mouth in
	parables,
I will utter things hidden since
	the creation of the world."[b]

The Parable of the Weeds Explained

[36]Then he left the crowd and went into the house. His disciples came to him and said, "Explain to us the parable of the weeds in the field."

---

[a]33 Greek *three satas* (probably about 1/2 bushel or 22 liters)   [b]35 Psalm 78:2

³⁷He answered, "The one who sowed the good seed is the Son of Man. ³⁸The field is the world, and the good seed stands for the sons of the kingdom. The weeds are the sons of the evil one, ³⁹and the enemy who sows them is the devil. The harvest is the end of the age, and the harvesters are angels.

⁴⁰"As the weeds are pulled up and burned in the fire, so it will be at the end of the age. ⁴¹The Son of Man will send out his angels, and they will weed out of his kingdom everything that causes sin and all who do evil. ⁴²They will throw them into the fiery furnace, where there will be weeping and gnashing of teeth. ⁴³Then the righteous will shine like the sun in the kingdom of their Father. He who has ears, let him hear.

The Parables of the Hidden Treasure and the Pearl

⁴⁴"The kingdom of heaven is like treasure hidden in a field. When a man found it, he hid it again, and then in his joy went and sold all he had and bought that field.

⁴⁵"Again, the kingdom of heaven is like a merchant looking for fine pearls. ⁴⁶When he found one of great value, he went away and sold everything he had and bought it.

The Parable of the Net

⁴⁷"Once again, the kingdom of heaven is like a net that was let down into the lake and caught all kinds of fish. ⁴⁸When it was full, the fishermen pulled it up on the shore. Then they sat down and collected the good fish in baskets, but threw the bad away. ⁴⁹This is how it will be at the end of the age. The angels will come and separate the wicked from the righteous ⁵⁰and throw them into the fiery furnace, where there will be weeping and gnashing of teeth.

⁵¹"Have you understood all these things?" Jesus asked.

"Yes," they replied.

⁵²He said to them, "Therefore every teacher of the law who has been instructed about the kingdom of heaven is like the owner of a house who brings out of his storeroom new treasures as well as old."

A Prophet Without Honor

⁵³When Jesus had finished these parables, he moved on from there. ⁵⁴Coming to his hometown, he began teaching the people in their synagogue, and they were amazed. "Where did this man get this wisdom and these miraculous powers?" they asked. ⁵⁵"Isn't this the carpenter's son? Isn't his mother's name Mary, and aren't his brothers James, Joseph, Simon and Judas? ⁵⁶Aren't all his sisters with us? Where then did this man get all these things?" ⁵⁷And they took offense at him.

But Jesus said to them, "Only in his hometown and in his own house is a prophet without honor."

⁵⁸And he did not do many miracles there because of their lack of faith.

John the Baptist Beheaded

14 At that time Herod the tetrarch heard the reports about Jesus, ²and he said to his atten-

---

▌ET'S LIVE IT!   Matthew 13:53–58

APPRECIATION NIGHT ➠ Read Matthew 13:53–58. People in Jesus' hometown did not appreciate him. Jesus said that people often don't appreciate members of their own family!

Suggest a family appreciation night. Have each person in your family take turns sitting on a chair in the middle of the room. Everyone else says what he or she appreciates about the person in the chair. When each person has had his or her turn, pretend Jesus is sitting in the empty chair. Let everyone tell what he or she appreciates about Jesus.

dants, "This is John the Baptist; he has risen from the dead! That is why miraculous powers are at work in him."

³Now Herod had arrested John and bound him and put him in prison because of Herodias, his brother Philip's wife, ⁴for John had been saying to him: "It is not lawful for you to have her." ⁵Herod wanted to kill John, but he was afraid of the people, because they considered him a prophet.

⁶On Herod's birthday the daughter of Herodias danced for them and pleased Herod so much ⁷that he promised with an oath to give her whatever she asked. ⁸Prompted by her mother, she said, "Give me here on a platter the head of John the Baptist." ⁹The king was distressed, but because of his oaths and his dinner guests, he ordered that her request be granted ¹⁰and had John beheaded in the prison. ¹¹His head was brought in on a platter and given to the girl, who carried it to her mother. ¹²John's disciples came and took his body and buried it. Then they went and told Jesus.

Jesus Feeds the Five Thousand

¹³When Jesus heard what had happened, he withdrew by boat privately to a solitary place. Hearing of this, the crowds followed him on foot from the towns. ¹⁴When Jesus landed and saw a large crowd, he had compassion on them and healed their sick.

¹⁵As evening approached, the disciples came to him and said, "This is a remote place, and it's already getting late. Send the crowds away, so they can go to the villages and buy themselves some food."

¹⁶Jesus replied, "They do not need to go away. You give them something to eat."

¹⁷"We have here only five loaves of bread and two fish," they answered.

¹⁸"Bring them here to me," he said. ¹⁹And he directed the people to sit down on the grass. Taking the five loaves and the two fish and looking up to heaven, he gave thanks and broke the loaves. Then he gave them to the disciples, and the disciples gave them to the people. ²⁰They all ate and were satisfied, and the disciples picked up twelve basketfuls of broken pieces that were left over. ²¹The number of those who ate was about five thousand men, besides women and children.

Jesus Walks on the Water

²²Immediately Jesus made the disciples get into the boat and go on ahead of him to the other side, while he dismissed the crowd. ²³After he had dismissed them, he went up on a mountainside by himself to pray. When evening came, he was there alone, ²⁴but the boat was already a considerable distance[a] from land, buffeted by the waves because the wind was against it.

²⁵During the fourth watch of the night Jesus went out to them, walking on the lake. ²⁶When the disciples saw him walking on the lake, they were terrified. "It's a ghost," they said, and cried out in fear.

²⁷But Jesus immediately said to them: "Take courage! It is I. Don't be afraid."

²⁸"Lord, if it's you," Peter replied, "tell me to come to you on the water."

²⁹"Come," he said.

Then Peter got down out of the boat, walked on the water and came toward Jesus. ³⁰But when he saw the wind, he was afraid and, beginning to sink, cried out, "Lord, save me!"

³¹Immediately Jesus reached out his hand and caught him. "You of little faith," he said, "why did you doubt?"

³²And when they climbed into the boat, the wind died down. ³³Then those who were in the boat worshiped him, saying, "Truly you are the Son of God."

³⁴When they had crossed over, they landed at Gennesaret. ³⁵And when the men of that place recognized

---

a24 Greek *many stadia*

Jesus, they sent word to all the surrounding country. People brought all their sick to him ³⁶and begged him to let the sick just touch the edge of his cloak, and all who touched him were healed.

Clean and Unclean

15 Then some Pharisees and teachers of the law came to Jesus from Jerusalem and asked, ²"Why do your disciples break the tradition of the elders? They don't wash their hands before they eat!"

³Jesus replied, "And why do you break the command of God for the sake of your tradition? ⁴For God said, 'Honor your father and mother'ᵃ and 'Anyone who curses his father or mother must be put to death.'ᵇ ⁵But you say that if a man says to his father or mother, 'Whatever help you might otherwise have received from me is a gift devoted to God,' ⁶he is not to 'honor his fatherᶜ' with it. Thus you nullify the word of God for the sake of your tradition. ⁷You hypocrites! Isaiah was right when he prophesied about you:

⁸" 'These people honor me with
      their lips,
   but their hearts are far from
      me.
⁹They worship me in vain;
   their teachings are but rules
      taught by men.'ᵈ"

¹⁰Jesus called the crowd to him and said, "Listen and understand. ¹¹What goes into a man's mouth does not make him 'unclean,' but what comes out of his mouth, that is what makes him 'unclean.' "

¹²Then the disciples came to him and asked, "Do you know that the Pharisees were offended when they heard this?"

¹³He replied, "Every plant that my heavenly Father has not planted will be pulled up by the roots. ¹⁴Leave them; they are blind guides.ᵉ If a

blind man leads a blind man, both will fall into a pit."

¹⁵Peter said, "Explain the parable to us."

¹⁶"Are you still so dull?" Jesus asked them. ¹⁷"Don't you see that whatever enters the mouth goes into the stomach and then out of the body? ¹⁸But the things that come out of the mouth come from the heart, and these make a man 'unclean.' ¹⁹For out of the heart come evil thoughts, murder, adultery, sexual immorality, theft, false testimony, slander. ²⁰These are what make a man 'unclean'; but eating with unwashed hands does not make him 'unclean.' "

The Faith of the Canaanite Woman

²¹Leaving that place, Jesus withdrew to the region of Tyre and Sidon. ²²A Canaanite woman from that vicinity came to him, crying out, "Lord, Son of David, have mercy on me! My daughter is suffering terribly from demon-possession."

²³Jesus did not answer a word. So his disciples came to him and urged him, "Send her away, for she keeps crying out after us."

²⁴He answered, "I was sent only to the lost sheep of Israel."

²⁵The woman came and knelt before him. "Lord, help me!" she said.

²⁶He replied, "It is not right to take the children's bread and toss it to their dogs."

²⁷"Yes, Lord," she said, "but even the dogs eat the crumbs that fall from their masters' table."

²⁸Then Jesus answered, "Woman, you have great faith! Your request is granted." And her daughter was healed from that very hour.

Jesus Feeds the Four Thousand

²⁹Jesus left there and went along the Sea of Galilee. Then he went up on a mountainside and sat down. ³⁰Great crowds came to him, bringing

---

ᵃ4 Exodus 20:12; Deut. 5:16   ᵇ4 Exodus 21:17; Lev. 20:9   ᶜ6 Some manuscripts *father or his mother*   ᵈ9 Isaiah 29:13   ᵉ14 Some manuscripts *guides of the blind*

the lame, the blind, the crippled, the mute and many others, and laid them at his feet; and he healed them. ³¹The people were amazed when they saw the mute speaking, the crippled made well, the lame walking and the blind seeing. And they praised the God of Israel.

³²Jesus called his disciples to him and said, "I have compassion for these people; they have already been with me three days and have nothing to eat. I do not want to send them away hungry, or they may collapse on the way."

³³His disciples answered, "Where could we get enough bread in this remote place to feed such a crowd?"

³⁴"How many loaves do you have?" Jesus asked.

"Seven," they replied, "and a few small fish."

³⁵He told the crowd to sit down on the ground. ³⁶Then he took the seven loaves and the fish, and when he had given thanks, he broke them and gave them to the disciples, and they in turn to the people. ³⁷They all ate and were satisfied. Afterward the disciples picked up seven basketfuls of broken pieces that were left over. ³⁸The number of those who ate was four thousand, besides women and children. ³⁹After Jesus had sent the crowd away, he got into the boat and went to the vicinity of Magadan.

The Demand for a Sign

16 The Pharisees and Sadducees came to Jesus and tested him by asking him to show them a sign from heaven.

²He replied,ᵃ "When evening comes, you say, 'It will be fair weather, for the sky is red,' ³and in the morning, 'Today it will be stormy, for the sky is red and overcast.' You know how to interpret the appearance of the sky, but you cannot interpret the signs of the times. ⁴A wicked and adulterous generation looks for a miraculous sign, but none will be given it except the sign of Jonah." Jesus then left them and went away.

The Yeast of the Pharisees and Sadducees

⁵When they went across the lake, the disciples forgot to take bread. ⁶"Be careful," Jesus said to them. "Be on your guard against the yeast of the Pharisees and Sadducees."

⁷They discussed this among themselves and said, "It is because we didn't bring any bread."

⁸Aware of their discussion, Jesus asked, "You of little faith, why are you talking among yourselves about having no bread? ⁹Do you still not understand? Don't you remember the five loaves for the five thousand, and how many basketfuls you gathered?

ᵃ2 Some early manuscripts do not have the rest of verse 2 and all of verse 3.

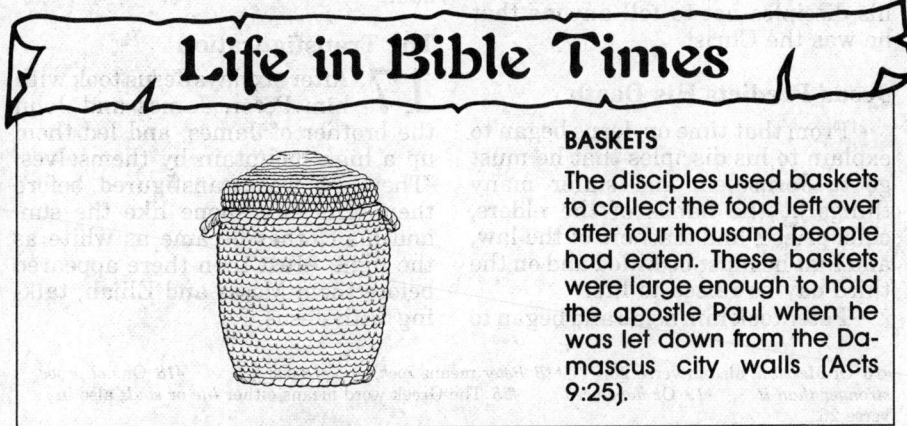

Life in Bible Times

BASKETS

The disciples used baskets to collect the food left over after four thousand people had eaten. These baskets were large enough to hold the apostle Paul when he was let down from the Damascus city walls (Acts 9:25).

¹⁰Or the seven loaves for the four thousand, and how many basketfuls you gathered? ¹¹How is it you don't understand that I was not talking to you about bread? But be on your guard against the yeast of the Pharisees and Sadducees." ¹²Then they understood that he was not telling them to guard against the yeast used in bread, but against the teaching of the Pharisees and Sadducees.

Peter's Confession of Christ

¹³When Jesus came to the region of Caesarea Philippi, he asked his disciples, "Who do people say the Son of Man is?"

¹⁴They replied, "Some say John the Baptist; others say Elijah; and still others, Jeremiah or one of the prophets."

¹⁵"But what about you?" he asked. "Who do you say I am?"

¹⁶Simon Peter answered, "You are the Christ,ᵃ the Son of the living God."

¹⁷Jesus replied, "Blessed are you, Simon son of Jonah, for this was not revealed to you by man, but by my Father in heaven. ¹⁸And I tell you that you are Peter,ᵇ and on this rock I will build my church, and the gates of Hadesᶜ will not overcome it.ᵈ ¹⁹I will give you the keys of the kingdom of heaven; whatever you bind on earth will beᵉ bound in heaven, and whatever you loose on earth will beᵉ loosed in heaven." ²⁰Then he warned his disciples not to tell anyone that he was the Christ.

Jesus Predicts His Death

²¹From that time on Jesus began to explain to his disciples that he must go to Jerusalem and suffer many things at the hands of the elders, chief priests and teachers of the law, and that he must be killed and on the third day be raised to life.

²²Peter took him aside and began to rebuke him. "Never, Lord!" he said. "This shall never happen to you!"

²³Jesus turned and said to Peter, "Get behind me, Satan! You are a stumbling block to me; you do not have in mind the things of God, but the things of men."

❓DID YOU KNOW?   16:18

On what rock will Jesus build his church?

Some people think Jesus meant that Peter is the rock. Other Christians think Jesus meant that the rock is what Peter said, that Jesus is "the Christ, the Son of the living God" (Matthew 16:16).

---

²⁴Then Jesus said to his disciples, "If anyone would come after me, he must deny himself and take up his cross and follow me. ²⁵For whoever wants to save his lifeᶠ will lose it, but whoever loses his life for me will find it. ²⁶What good will it be for a man if he gains the whole world, yet forfeits his soul? Or what can a man give in exchange for his soul? ²⁷For the Son of Man is going to come in his Father's glory with his angels, and then he will reward each person according to what he has done. ²⁸I tell you the truth, some who are standing here will not taste death before they see the Son of Man coming in his kingdom."

The Transfiguration

17 After six days Jesus took with him Peter, James and John the brother of James, and led them up a high mountain by themselves. ²There he was transfigured before them. His face shone like the sun, and his clothes became as white as the light. ³Just then there appeared before them Moses and Elijah, talking with Jesus.

ᵃ16 Or Messiah; also in verse 20   ᵇ18 Peter means rock.   ᶜ18 Or hell   ᵈ18 Or not prove stronger than it   ᵉ19 Or have been   ᶠ25 The Greek word means either life or soul; also in verse 26.

⁴Peter said to Jesus, "Lord, it is good for us to be here. If you wish, I will put up three shelters—one for you, one for Moses and one for Elijah."

⁵While he was still speaking, a bright cloud enveloped them, and a voice from the cloud said, "This is my Son, whom I love; with him I am well pleased. Listen to him!"

⁶When the disciples heard this, they fell facedown to the ground, terrified. ⁷But Jesus came and touched them. "Get up," he said. "Don't be afraid." ⁸When they looked up, they saw no one except Jesus.

⁹As they were coming down the mountain, Jesus instructed them, "Don't tell anyone what you have seen, until the Son of Man has been raised from the dead."

¹⁰The disciples asked him, "Why then do the teachers of the law say that Elijah must come first?"

¹¹Jesus replied, "To be sure, Elijah comes and will restore all things. ¹²But I tell you, Elijah has already come, and they did not recognize him, but have done to him everything they wished. In the same way the Son of Man is going to suffer at their hands." ¹³Then the disciples understood that he was talking to them about John the Baptist.

❓DID YOU KNOW? 17:2

What was the transfiguration?

Transfiguration means to be changed. In the transfiguration Jesus was changed from looking like a normal person to shining brightly. Moses and Elijah came and talked with Jesus during the transfiguration.

The Healing of a Boy With a Demon

¹⁴When they came to the crowd, a man approached Jesus and knelt be-

fore him. ¹⁵"Lord, have mercy on my son," he said. "He has seizures and is suffering greatly. He often falls into the fire or into the water. ¹⁶I brought him to your disciples, but they could not heal him."

¹⁷"O unbelieving and perverse generation," Jesus replied, "how long shall I stay with you? How long shall I put up with you? Bring the boy here to me." ¹⁸Jesus rebuked the demon, and it came out of the boy, and he was healed from that moment.

¹⁹Then the disciples came to Jesus in private and asked, "Why couldn't we drive it out?"

²⁰He replied, "Because you have so little faith. I tell you the truth, if you have faith as small as a mustard seed, you can say to this mountain, 'Move from here to there' and it will move. Nothing will be impossible for you.ᵃ"

²²When they came together in Galilee, he said to them, "The Son of Man is going to be betrayed into the hands of men. ²³They will kill him, and on the third day he will be raised to life." And the disciples were filled with grief.

The Temple Tax

²⁴After Jesus and his disciples arrived in Capernaum, the collectors of the two-drachma tax came to Peter and asked, "Doesn't your teacher pay the temple taxᵇ?"

²⁵"Yes, he does," he replied.

When Peter came into the house, Jesus was the first to speak. "What do you think, Simon?" he asked. "From whom do the kings of the earth collect duty and taxes—from their own sons or from others?"

²⁶"From others," Peter answered.

"Then the sons are exempt," Jesus said to him. ²⁷"But so that we may not offend them, go to the lake and throw out your line. Take the first fish you catch; open its mouth and you will find a four-drachma coin.

ᵃ20 Some manuscripts *you.* ²¹*But this kind does not go out except by prayer and fasting.*
ᵇ24 Greek *the two drachmas*

Take it and give it to them for my tax and yours."

The Greatest in the Kingdom of Heaven

18 At that time the disciples came to Jesus and asked, "Who is the greatest in the kingdom of heaven?"

2He called a little child and had him stand among them. 3And he said: "I tell you the truth, unless you change and become like little children, you will never enter the kingdom of heaven. 4Therefore, whoever humbles himself like this child is the greatest in the kingdom of heaven.

?DID YOU KNOW?   18:3

How are little children great?

When Jesus called a little child, the child came right away to stand beside Jesus. The grown-ups that Jesus had preached to did not obey him as well as the little child did. Great Christians will obey Jesus as this little child did.

5"And whoever welcomes a little child like this in my name welcomes me. 6But if anyone causes one of these little ones who believe in me to sin, it would be better for him to have a large millstone hung around his

neck and to be drowned in the depths of the sea.

7"Woe to the world because of the things that cause people to sin! Such things must come, but woe to the man through whom they come! 8If your hand or your foot causes you to sin, cut it off and throw it away. It is better for you to enter life maimed or crippled than to have two hands or two feet and be thrown into eternal fire. 9And if your eye causes you to sin, gouge it out and throw it away. It is better for you to enter life with one eye than to have two eyes and be thrown into the fire of hell.

The Parable of the Lost Sheep

10"See that you do not look down on one of these little ones. For I tell you that their angels in heaven always see the face of my Father in heaven. [a]

12"What do you think? If a man owns a hundred sheep, and one of them wanders away, will he not leave the ninety-nine on the hills and go to look for the one that wandered off? 13And if he finds it, I tell you the truth, he is happier about that one sheep than about the ninety-nine that did not wander off. 14In the same way your Father in heaven is not willing that any of these little ones should be lost.

A Brother Who Sins Against You

15"If your brother sins against

---

[a]10 Some manuscripts *heaven.* 11*The Son of Man came to save what was lost.*

▌ET'S LIVE IT!   Matthew 18:10–14

GOD'S NOT MAD AT ME! ➡ Read Matthew 18:10–14. In this story the sheep are God's children and God is the shepherd. Wandering off and getting lost is doing something wrong or sinful. After reading this passage, answer these questions: How does God feel about his children? What does God do when we sin? How does God feel when we confess our sin and are "found"?

Cut the figure of a sheep out of cardboard. For wool, glue cotton on one side of the sheep. On the other side write, "He is happy about the one sheep that is found." Put the sheep in your room to remind you that God loves you even when you have done something wrong.

you,[a] go and show him his fault, just between the two of you. If he listens to you, you have won your brother over. [16]But if he will not listen, take one or two others along, so that 'every matter may be established by the testimony of two or three witnesses.'[b] [17]If he refuses to listen to them, tell it to the church; and if he refuses to listen even to the church, treat him as you would a pagan or a tax collector.

[18]"I tell you the truth, whatever you bind on earth will be[c] bound in heaven, and whatever you loose on earth will be[c] loosed in heaven.

[19]"Again, I tell you that if two of you on earth agree about anything you ask for, it will be done for you by my Father in heaven. [20]For where two or three come together in my name, there am I with them."

The Parable of the Unmerciful Servant

[21]Then Peter came to Jesus and asked, "Lord, how many times shall I forgive my brother when he sins against me? Up to seven times?"

[22]Jesus answered, "I tell you, not seven times, but seventy-seven times.[d]

[23]"Therefore, the kingdom of heaven is like a king who wanted to settle accounts with his servants. [24]As he began the settlement, a man who owed him ten thousand talents[e] was brought to him. [25]Since he was not able to pay, the master ordered that he and his wife and his children and all that he had be sold to repay the debt.

[26]"The servant fell on his knees before him. 'Be patient with me,' he begged, 'and I will pay back everything.' [27]The servant's master took pity on him, canceled the debt and let him go.

[28]"But when that servant went out, he found one of his fellow servants who owed him a hundred denarii.[f] He grabbed him and began to choke

him. 'Pay back what you owe me!' he demanded.

[29]"His fellow servant fell to his knees and begged him, 'Be patient with me, and I will pay you back.'

[30]"But he refused. Instead, he went off and had the man thrown into prison until he could pay the debt. [31]When the other servants saw what had happened, they were greatly distressed and went and told their master everything that had happened.

[32]"Then the master called the servant in. 'You wicked servant,' he said, 'I canceled all that debt of yours because you begged me to. [33]Shouldn't you have had mercy on your fellow servant just as I had on you?' [34]In anger his master turned him over to the jailers to be tortured, until he should pay back all he owed.

[35]"This is how my heavenly Father will treat each of you unless you forgive your brother from your heart."

Divorce

19 When Jesus had finished saying these things, he left Galilee and went into the region of Judea to the other side of the Jordan. [2]Large crowds followed him, and he healed them there.

[3]Some Pharisees came to him to test him. They asked, "Is it lawful for a man to divorce his wife for any and every reason?"

[4]"Haven't you read," he replied, "that at the beginning the Creator 'made them male and female,'[g] [5]and said, 'For this reason a man will leave his father and mother and be united to his wife, and the two will become one flesh'[h]? [6]So they are no longer two, but one. Therefore what God has joined together, let man not separate."

[7]"Why then," they asked, "did Moses command that a man give his wife a certificate of divorce and send her away?"

[8]Jesus replied, "Moses permitted

---

a15 Some manuscripts do not have *against you.*   *b16* Deut. 19:15   *c18* Or *have been*
d22 Or *seventy times seven*   *e24* That is, millions of dollars   *f28* That is, a few dollars
g4 Gen. 1:27   *h5* Gen. 2:24

you to divorce your wives because your hearts were hard. But it was not this way from the beginning. ⁹I tell you that anyone who divorces his wife, except for marital unfaithfulness, and marries another woman commits adultery."

¹⁰The disciples said to him, "If this is the situation between a husband and wife, it is better not to marry."

¹¹Jesus replied, "Not everyone can accept this word, but only those to whom it has been given. ¹²For some are eunuchs because they were born that way; others were made that way by men; and others have renounced marriage*a* because of the kingdom of heaven. The one who can accept this should accept it."

The Little Children and Jesus

¹³Then little children were brought to Jesus for him to place his hands on them and pray for them. But the disciples rebuked those who brought them.

¹⁴Jesus said, "Let the little children come to me, and do not hinder them, for the kingdom of heaven belongs to such as these." ¹⁵When he had placed his hands on them, he went on from there.

The Rich Young Man

¹⁶Now a man came up to Jesus and asked, "Teacher, what good thing must I do to get eternal life?"

¹⁷"Why do you ask me about what is good?" Jesus replied. "There is only One who is good. If you want to enter life, obey the commandments."

¹⁸"Which ones?" the man inquired.

Jesus replied, " 'Do not murder, do not commit adultery, do not steal, do not give false testimony, ¹⁹honor your father and mother,'*b* and 'love your neighbor as yourself.'*c* "

²⁰"All these I have kept," the young man said. "What do I still lack?"

²¹Jesus answered, "If you want to be perfect, go, sell your possessions and give to the poor, and you will have treasure in heaven. Then come, follow me."

²²When the young man heard this, he went away sad, because he had great wealth.

²³Then Jesus said to his disciples, "I tell you the truth, it is hard for a rich man to enter the kingdom of heaven. ²⁴Again I tell you, it is easier for a camel to go through the eye of a needle than for a rich man to enter the kingdom of God."

²⁵When the disciples heard this, they were greatly astonished and asked, "Who then can be saved?"

²⁶Jesus looked at them and said, "With man this is impossible, but with God all things are possible."

²⁷Peter answered him, "We have left everything to follow you! What then will there be for us?"

²⁸Jesus said to them, "I tell you the truth, at the renewal of all things, when the Son of Man sits on his glori-

a12 Or *have made themselves eunuchs*   *b19* Exodus 20:12-16; Deut. 5:16-20   *c19* Lev. 19:18

▚ET'S LIVE IT!   Matthew 19:13–15

JESUS LOVES THE CHILDREN ➡ Read Matthew 19:13–15. Just as Jesus loved the little children in this story, he loves you today. He cannot really put his hands on you as he did these children, but he is always there, always watching over you.

To remind yourself and the rest of the people in your family, make special placemats for your family. Take colored construction paper and trace around your hands, the left hand on the left side, the right hand on the right side. Color and decorate the hands with rings and bracelets if you wish. Use the placemats for your next family meal and talk together about how Jesus loves your family.

ous throne, you who have followed me will also sit on twelve thrones, judging the twelve tribes of Israel. ²⁹And everyone who has left houses or brothers or sisters or father or mother*a* or children or fields for my sake will receive a hundred times as much and will inherit eternal life. ³⁰But many who are first will be last, and many who are last will be first.

The Parable of the Workers in the Vineyard

20 "For the kingdom of heaven is like a landowner who went out early in the morning to hire men to work in his vineyard. ²He agreed to pay them a denarius for the day and sent them into his vineyard.

³"About the third hour he went out and saw others standing in the marketplace doing nothing. ⁴He told them, 'You also go and work in my vineyard, and I will pay you whatever is right.' ⁵So they went.

"He went out again about the sixth hour and the ninth hour and did the same thing. ⁶About the eleventh hour he went out and found still others standing around. He asked them, 'Why have you been standing here all day long doing nothing?'

a29 Some manuscripts mother or wife

⁷"'Because no one has hired us,' they answered.

"He said to them, 'You also go and work in my vineyard.'

⁸"When evening came, the owner of the vineyard said to his foreman, 'Call the workers and pay them their wages, beginning with the last ones hired and going on to the first.'

⁹"The workers who were hired about the eleventh hour came and each received a denarius. ¹⁰So when those came who were hired first, they expected to receive more. But each one of them also received a denarius. ¹¹When they received it, they began to grumble against the landowner. ¹²'These men who were hired last worked only one hour,' they said, 'and you have made them equal to us who have borne the burden of the work and the heat of the day.'

¹³"But he answered one of them, 'Friend, I am not being unfair to you. Didn't you agree to work for a denarius? ¹⁴Take your pay and go. I want to give the man who was hired last the same as I gave you. ¹⁵Don't I have the right to do what I want with my own money? Or are you envious because I am generous?'

¹⁶"So the last will be first, and the first will be last."

Life in Bible Times

THE DENARIUS

In the time of the New Testament a day's pay was a single coin, called a denarius. This was enough money to buy food for one day and to rent a small room for the night. The coin was made of silver and was usually stamped with a picture of the Roman emperor. It looked somewhat like our dime.

Jesus Again Predicts His Death

¹⁷Now as Jesus was going up to Jerusalem, he took the twelve disciples aside and said to them, ¹⁸"We are going up to Jerusalem, and the Son of Man will be betrayed to the chief priests and the teachers of the law. They will condemn him to death ¹⁹and will turn him over to the Gentiles to be mocked and flogged and crucified. On the third day he will be raised to life!"

A Mother's Request

²⁰Then the mother of Zebedee's sons came to Jesus with her sons and, kneeling down, asked a favor of him.

²¹"What is it you want?" he asked.

She said, "Grant that one of these two sons of mine may sit at your right and the other at your left in your kingdom."

²²"You don't know what you are asking," Jesus said to them. "Can you drink the cup I am going to drink?"

"We can," they answered.

²³Jesus said to them, "You will indeed drink from my cup, but to sit at my right or left is not for me to grant. These places belong to those for whom they have been prepared by my Father."

²⁴When the ten heard about this, they were indignant with the two brothers. ²⁵Jesus called them together and said, "You know that the rulers of the Gentiles lord it over them, and their high officials exercise authority over them. ²⁶Not so with you. Instead, whoever wants to become great among you must be your servant, ²⁷and whoever wants to be first must be your slave— ²⁸just as the Son of Man did not come to be served, but to serve, and to give his life as a ransom for many."

Two Blind Men Receive Sight

²⁹As Jesus and his disciples were leaving Jericho, a large crowd followed him. ³⁰Two blind men were sitting by the roadside, and when they heard that Jesus was going by, they shouted, "Lord, Son of David, have mercy on us!"

³¹The crowd rebuked them and told them to be quiet, but they shouted all the louder, "Lord, Son of David, have mercy on us!"

³²Jesus stopped and called them. "What do you want me to do for you?" he asked.

³³"Lord," they answered, "we want our sight."

³⁴Jesus had compassion on them and touched their eyes. Immediately they received their sight and followed him.

The Triumphal Entry

21 As they approached Jerusalem and came to Bethphage on the Mount of Olives, Jesus sent two disciples, ²saying to them, "Go to the village ahead of you, and at once you will find a donkey tied there, with her colt by her. Untie them and bring them to me. ³If anyone says anything to you, tell him that the Lord needs them, and he will send them right away."

⁴This took place to fulfill what was spoken through the prophet:

⁵"Say to the Daughter of Zion,
    'See, your king comes to you,
gentle and riding on a donkey,
    on a colt, the foal of a
        donkey.' " *a*

⁶The disciples went and did as Jesus had instructed them. ⁷They brought the donkey and the colt, placed their cloaks on them, and Jesus sat on them. ⁸A very large crowd spread their cloaks on the road, while others cut branches from the trees and spread them on the road. ⁹The crowds that went ahead of him and those that followed shouted,

"Hosanna *b* to the Son of David!"

"Blessed is he who comes in the
    name of the Lord!" *c*

a5 Zech. 9:9   *b9* A Hebrew expression meaning "Save!" which became an exclamation of praise;
also in verse 15   *c9* Psalm 118:26

"Hosanna*a* in the highest!"

¹⁰When Jesus entered Jerusalem, the whole city was stirred and asked, "Who is this?"

¹¹The crowds answered, "This is Jesus, the prophet from Nazareth in Galilee."

Jesus at the Temple

¹²Jesus entered the temple area and drove out all who were buying and selling there. He overturned the tables of the money changers and the benches of those selling doves. ¹³"It is written," he said to them, " 'My house will be called a house of prayer,'*b* but you are making it a 'den of robbers.'*c*"

¹⁴The blind and the lame came to him at the temple, and he healed them. ¹⁵But when the chief priests and the teachers of the law saw the wonderful things he did and the children shouting in the temple area, "Hosanna to the Son of David," they were indignant.

¹⁶"Do you hear what these children are saying?" they asked him.

"Yes," replied Jesus, "have you never read,

" 'From the lips of children and
infants
you have ordained praise'*d*?"

¹⁷And he left them and went out of the city to Bethany, where he spent the night.

The Fig Tree Withers

¹⁸Early in the morning, as he was on his way back to the city, he was hungry. ¹⁹Seeing a fig tree by the road, he went up to it but found nothing on it except leaves. Then he said to it, "May you never bear fruit again!" Immediately the tree withered.

²⁰When the disciples saw this, they were amazed. "How did the fig tree wither so quickly?" they asked.

²¹Jesus replied, "I tell you the truth, if you have faith and do not doubt, not only can you do what was done to the fig tree, but also you can say to this mountain, 'Go, throw yourself into the sea,' and it will be done. ²²If you believe, you will receive whatever you ask for in prayer."

The Authority of Jesus Questioned

²³Jesus entered the temple courts, and, while he was teaching, the chief priests and the elders of the people came to him. "By what authority are you doing these things?" they asked. "And who gave you this authority?"

²⁴Jesus replied, "I will also ask you one question. If you answer me, I will tell you by what authority I am doing these things. ²⁵John's baptism— where did it come from? Was it from heaven, or from men?"

They discussed it among themselves and said, "If we say, 'From heaven,' he will ask, 'Then why didn't you believe him?' ²⁶But if we say, 'From men'—we are afraid of the people, for they all hold that John was a prophet."

²⁷So they answered Jesus, "We don't know."

Then he said, "Neither will I tell you by what authority I am doing these things.

❓**DID YOU KNOW?** 21:27

What is authority?

Authority is the right to do something. Jesus' enemies were upset by Jesus' teachings and by his miracles. They asked him what right he had to say and do these things. This was a foolish question. Jesus could not have done what he did without God's help. So Jesus did not answer this foolish question of his enemies.

---

a9 A Hebrew expression meaning "Save!" which became an exclamation of praise; also in verse 15
b13 Isaiah 56:7   *c13* Jer. 7:11   *d16* Psalm 8:2

The Parable of the Two Sons

28"What do you think? There was a man who had two sons. He went to the first and said, 'Son, go and work today in the vineyard.'

29" 'I will not,' he answered, but later he changed his mind and went.

30"Then the father went to the other son and said the same thing. He answered, 'I will, sir,' but he did not go.

31"Which of the two did what his father wanted?"

"The first," they answered.

Jesus said to them, "I tell you the truth, the tax collectors and the prostitutes are entering the kingdom of God ahead of you. 32For John came to you to show you the way of righteousness, and you did not believe him, but the tax collectors and the prostitutes did. And even after you saw this, you did not repent and believe him.

The Parable of the Tenants

33"Listen to another parable: There was a landowner who planted a vineyard. He put a wall around it, dug a winepress in it and built a watchtower. Then he rented the vineyard to some farmers and went away on a journey. 34When the harvest time approached, he sent his servants to the tenants to collect his fruit.

35"The tenants seized his servants; they beat one, killed another, and stoned a third. 36Then he sent other servants to them, more than the first time, and the tenants treated them the same way. 37Last of all, he sent his son to them. 'They will respect my son,' he said.

38"But when the tenants saw the son, they said to each other, 'This is the heir. Come, let's kill him and take his inheritance.' 39So they took him and threw him out of the vineyard and killed him.

40"Therefore, when the owner of the vineyard comes, what will he do to those tenants?"

41"He will bring those wretches to a wretched end," they replied, "and he will rent the vineyard to other tenants, who will give him his share of the crop at harvest time."

42Jesus said to them, "Have you never read in the Scriptures:

" 'The stone the builders rejected
    has become the capstone[a];
the Lord has done this,
    and it is marvelous in our
        eyes'[b]?

43"Therefore I tell you that the kingdom of God will be taken away from you and given to a people who will produce its fruit. 44He who falls on this stone will be broken to pieces, but he on whom it falls will be crushed."[c]

45When the chief priests and the Pharisees heard Jesus' parables, they knew he was talking about them. 46They looked for a way to arrest him, but they were afraid of the crowd because the people held that he was a prophet.

The Parable of the Wedding Banquet

22 Jesus spoke to them again in parables, saying: 2"The kingdom of heaven is like a king who prepared a wedding banquet for his son. 3He sent his servants to those who had been invited to the banquet to tell them to come, but they refused to come.

4"Then he sent some more servants and said, 'Tell those who have been invited that I have prepared my dinner: My oxen and fattened cattle have been butchered, and everything is ready. Come to the wedding banquet.'

5"But they paid no attention and went off—one to his field, another to his business. 6The rest seized his servants, mistreated them and killed them. 7The king was enraged. He sent his army and destroyed those murderers and burned their city.

8"Then he said to his servants, 'The wedding banquet is ready, but those

---

a42 Or *cornerstone*   b42 Psalm 118:22,23   c44 Some manuscripts do not have verse 44.

I invited did not deserve to come. [9]Go to the street corners and invite to the banquet anyone you find.' [10]So the servants went out into the streets and gathered all the people they could find, both good and bad, and the wedding hall was filled with guests.

[11]"But when the king came in to see the guests, he noticed a man there who was not wearing wedding clothes. [12]'Friend,' he asked, 'how did you get in here without wedding clothes?' The man was speechless.

[13]"Then the king told the attendants, 'Tie him hand and foot, and throw him outside, into the darkness, where there will be weeping and gnashing of teeth.'

[14]"For many are invited, but few are chosen."

Paying Taxes to Caesar

[15]Then the Pharisees went out and laid plans to trap him in his words. [16]They sent their disciples to him along with the Herodians. "Teacher," they said, "we know you are a man of integrity and that you teach the way of God in accordance with the truth. You aren't swayed by men, because you pay no attention to who they are. [17]Tell us then, what is your opinion? Is it right to pay taxes to Caesar or not?"

[18]But Jesus, knowing their evil intent, said, "You hypocrites, why are you trying to trap me? [19]Show me the coin used for paying the tax." They brought him a denarius, [20]and he asked them, "Whose portrait is this? And whose inscription?"

[21]"Caesar's," they replied.

Then he said to them, "Give to Caesar what is Caesar's, and to God what is God's."

[22]When they heard this, they were amazed. So they left him and went away.

Marriage at the Resurrection

[23]That same day the Sadducees, who say there is no resurrection, came to him with a question.

[24]"Teacher," they said, "Moses told us that if a man dies without having children, his brother must marry the widow and have children for him. [25]Now there were seven brothers among us. The first one married and died, and since he had no children, he left his wife to his brother. [26]The same thing happened to the second and third brother, right on down to the seventh. [27]Finally, the woman died. [28]Now then, at the resurrection, whose wife will she be of the seven, since all of them were married to her?"

[29]Jesus replied, "You are in error because you do not know the Scriptures or the power of God. [30]At the resurrection people will neither marry nor be given in marriage; they will be like the angels in heaven. [31]But about the resurrection of the dead —have you not read what God said to you, [32]'I am the God of Abraham, the God of Isaac, and the God of Jacob'[a]? He is not the God of the dead but of the living."

[33]When the crowds heard this, they were astonished at his teaching.

The Greatest Commandment

[34]Hearing that Jesus had silenced the Sadducees, the Pharisees got together. [35]One of them, an expert in the law, tested him with this question: [36]"Teacher, which is the greatest commandment in the Law?"

[37]Jesus replied: " 'Love the Lord your God with all your heart and with all your soul and with all your mind.'[b] [38]This is the first and greatest commandment. [39]And the second is like it: 'Love your neighbor as yourself.'[c] [40]All the Law and the Prophets hang on these two commandments."

Whose Son Is the Christ?

[41]While the Pharisees were gathered together, Jesus asked them, [42]"What do you think about the Christ[d]? Whose son is he?"

"The son of David," they replied.

---

[a]32 Exodus 3:6   [b]37 Deut. 6:5   [c]39 Lev. 19:18   [d]42 Or *Messiah*

43He said to them, "How is it then that David, speaking by the Spirit, calls him 'Lord'? For he says,

44" 'The Lord said to my Lord:
    "Sit at my right hand
    until I put your enemies
        under your feet." ' *a*

45If then David calls him 'Lord,' how can he be his son?" **46**No one could say a word in reply, and from that day on no one dared to ask him any more questions.

Seven Woes

23 Then Jesus said to the crowds and to his disciples: **2**"The teachers of the law and the Pharisees sit in Moses' seat. **3**So you must obey them and do everything they tell you. But do not do what they do, for they do not practice what they preach. **4**They tie up heavy loads and put them on men's shoulders, but they themselves are not willing to lift a finger to move them.

5"Everything they do is done for men to see: They make their phylacteries *b* wide and the tassels on their garments long; **6**they love the place of honor at banquets and the most important seats in the synagogues; **7**they love to be greeted in the mar-

ketplaces and to have men call them 'Rabbi.'

8"But you are not to be called 'Rabbi,' for you have only one Master and you are all brothers. **9**And do not call anyone on earth 'father,' for you have one Father, and he is in heaven. **10**Nor are you to be called 'teacher,' for you have one Teacher, the Christ. *c* **11**The greatest among you will be your servant. **12**For whoever exalts himself will be humbled, and whoever humbles himself will be exalted.

13"Woe to you, teachers of the law and Pharisees, you hypocrites! You shut the kingdom of heaven in men's faces. You yourselves do not enter, nor will you let those enter who are trying to. *d*

15"Woe to you, teachers of the law and Pharisees, you hypocrites! You travel over land and sea to win a single convert, and when he becomes one, you make him twice as much a son of hell as you are.

16"Woe to you, blind guides! You say, 'If anyone swears by the temple, it means nothing; but if anyone swears by the gold of the temple, he is bound by his oath.' **17**You blind fools! Which is greater: the gold, or the temple that makes the gold sacred? **18**You also say, 'If anyone

---

a44 Psalm 110:1   *b5* That is, boxes containing Scripture verses, worn on forehead and arm   *c10* Or *Messiah*   *d13* Some manuscripts *to.* *14Woe to you, teachers of the law and Pharisees, you hypocrites! You devour widows' houses and for a show make lengthy prayers. Therefore you will be punished more severely.*

Life in Bible Times

PHYLACTERIES

When Jewish men prayed, many tied special boxes holding Bible verses to their arm and forehead. These were called phylacteries. Jesus criticized men who did this to make people think they were especially holy.

swears by the altar, it means nothing; but if anyone swears by the gift on it, he is bound by his oath.' ¹⁹You blind men! Which is greater: the gift, or the altar that makes the gift sacred? ²⁰Therefore, he who swears by the altar swears by it and by everything on it. ²¹And he who swears by the temple swears by it and by the one who dwells in it. ²²And he who swears by heaven swears by God's throne and by the one who sits on it.

²³"Woe to you, teachers of the law and Pharisees, you hypocrites! You give a tenth of your spices—mint, dill and cummin. But you have neglected the more important matters of the law—justice, mercy and faithfulness. You should have practiced the latter, without neglecting the former. ²⁴You blind guides! You strain out a gnat but swallow a camel.

²⁵"Woe to you, teachers of the law and Pharisees, you hypocrites! You clean the outside of the cup and dish, but inside they are full of greed and self-indulgence. ²⁶Blind Pharisee! First clean the inside of the cup and dish, and then the outside also will be clean.

❓DID YOU KNOW?　　23:28

What are woes?

Woes are sorrow, grief or trouble. Jesus uses this word to warn the teachers of the law and Pharisees. He tells them seven reasons why they are in trouble with God.

---

²⁷"Woe to you, teachers of the law and Pharisees, you hypocrites! You are like whitewashed tombs, which look beautiful on the outside but on the inside are full of dead men's bones and everything unclean. ²⁸In the same way, on the outside you appear to people as righteous but on the inside you are full of hypocrisy and wickedness.

²⁹"Woe to you, teachers of the law and Pharisees, you hypocrites! You build tombs for the prophets and decorate the graves of the righteous. ³⁰And you say, 'If we had lived in the days of our forefathers, we would not have taken part with them in shedding the blood of the prophets.' ³¹So you testify against yourselves that you are the descendants of those who murdered the prophets. ³²Fill up, then, the measure of the sin of your forefathers!

³³"You snakes! You brood of vipers! How will you escape being condemned to hell? ³⁴Therefore I am sending you prophets and wise men and teachers. Some of them you will kill and crucify; others you will flog in your synagogues and pursue from town to town. ³⁵And so upon you will come all the righteous blood that has been shed on earth, from the blood of righteous Abel to the blood of Zechariah son of Berekiah, whom you murdered between the temple and the altar. ³⁶I tell you the truth, all this will come upon this generation.

³⁷"O Jerusalem, Jerusalem, you who kill the prophets and stone those sent to you, how often I have longed to gather your children together, as a hen gathers her chicks under her wings, but you were not willing. ³⁸Look, your house is left to you desolate. ³⁹For I tell you, you will not see me again until you say, 'Blessed is he who comes in the name of the Lord.'ᵃ"

Signs of the End of the Age

24 Jesus left the temple and was walking away when his disciples came up to him to call his attention to its buildings. ²"Do you see all these things?" he asked. "I tell you the truth, not one stone here will be left on another; every one will be thrown down."

³As Jesus was sitting on the Mount of Olives, the disciples came to him privately. "Tell us," they said, "when will this happen, and what will be the

---

ª39 Psalm 118:26

sign of your coming and of the end of the age?"

⁴Jesus answered: "Watch out that no one deceives you. ⁵For many will come in my name, claiming, 'I am the Christ,ᵃ' and will deceive many. ⁶You will hear of wars and rumors of wars, but see to it that you are not alarmed. Such things must happen, but the end is still to come. ⁷Nation will rise against nation, and kingdom against kingdom. There will be famines and earthquakes in various places. ⁸All these are the beginning of birth pains.

⁹"Then you will be handed over to be persecuted and put to death, and you will be hated by all nations because of me. ¹⁰At that time many will turn away from the faith and will betray and hate each other, ¹¹and many false prophets will appear and deceive many people. ¹²Because of the increase of wickedness, the love of most will grow cold, ¹³but he who stands firm to the end will be saved. ¹⁴And this gospel of the kingdom will be preached in the whole world as a testimony to all nations, and then the end will come.

¹⁵"So when you see standing in the holy place 'the abomination that causes desolation,'ᵇ spoken of through the prophet Daniel—let the reader understand— ¹⁶then let those who are in Judea flee to the mountains. ¹⁷Let no one on the roof of his house go down to take anything out of the house. ¹⁸Let no one in the field go back to get his cloak. ¹⁹How dreadful it will be in those days for pregnant women and nursing mothers! ²⁰Pray that your flight will not take place in winter or on the Sabbath. ²¹For then there will be great distress, unequaled from the beginning of the world until now—and never to be equaled again. ²²If those days had not been cut short, no one would survive, but for the sake of the elect those days will be shortened. ²³At that time if anyone says to you,

'Look, here is the Christ!' or, 'There he is!' do not believe it. ²⁴For false Christs and false prophets will appear and perform great signs and miracles to deceive even the elect—if that were possible. ²⁵See, I have told you ahead of time.

²⁶"So if anyone tells you, 'There he is, out in the desert,' do not go out; or, 'Here he is, in the inner rooms,' do not believe it. ²⁷For as lightning that comes from the east is visible even in the west, so will be the coming of the Son of Man. ²⁸Wherever there is a carcass, there the vultures will gather.

²⁹"Immediately after the distress of those days

" 'the sun will be darkened,
   and the moon will not give its
     light;
the stars will fall from the sky,
   and the heavenly bodies will be
     shaken.'ᶜ

³⁰"At that time the sign of the Son of Man will appear in the sky, and all the nations of the earth will mourn. They will see the Son of Man coming on the clouds of the sky, with power and great glory. ³¹And he will send his angels with a loud trumpet call, and they will gather his elect from the four winds, from one end of the heavens to the other.

³²"Now learn this lesson from the fig tree: As soon as its twigs get tender and its leaves come out, you know that summer is near. ³³Even so, when you see all these things, you know that itᵈ is near, right at the door. ³⁴I tell you the truth, this generationᵉ will certainly not pass away until all these things have happened. ³⁵Heaven and earth will pass away, but my words will never pass away.

The Day and Hour Unknown

³⁶"No one knows about that day or hour, not even the angels in heaven, nor the Son,ᶠ but only the Father. ³⁷As it was in the days of Noah, so it

---

ᵃ5 Or *Messiah*; also in verse 23   ᵇ15 Daniel 9:27; 11:31; 12:11   ᶜ29 Isaiah 13:10; 34:4
ᵈ33 Or *he*   ᵉ34 Or *race*   ᶠ36 Some manuscripts do not have *nor the Son*.

will be at the coming of the Son of Man. ³⁸For in the days before the flood, people were eating and drinking, marrying and giving in marriage, up to the day Noah entered the ark; ³⁹and they knew nothing about what would happen until the flood came and took them all away. That is how it will be at the coming of the Son of Man. ⁴⁰Two men will be in the field; one will be taken and the other left. ⁴¹Two women will be grinding with a hand mill; one will be taken and the other left.

⁴²"Therefore keep watch, because you do not know on what day your Lord will come. ⁴³But understand this: If the owner of the house had known at what time of night the thief was coming, he would have kept watch and would not have let his house be broken into. ⁴⁴So you also must be ready, because the Son of Man will come at an hour when you do not expect him.

⁴⁵"Who then is the faithful and wise servant, whom the master has put in charge of the servants in his household to give them their food at the proper time? ⁴⁶It will be good for that servant whose master finds him doing so when he returns. ⁴⁷I tell you the truth, he will put him in charge of all his possessions. ⁴⁸But suppose that servant is wicked and says to himself, 'My master is staying away a long time,' ⁴⁹and he then begins to beat his fellow servants and to eat and drink with drunkards. ⁵⁰The master of that servant will come on a day when he does not expect him and

at an hour he is not aware of. ⁵¹He will cut him to pieces and assign him a place with the hypocrites, where there will be weeping and gnashing of teeth.

The Parable of the Ten Virgins

25 "At that time the kingdom of heaven will be like ten virgins who took their lamps and went out to meet the bridegroom. ²Five of them were foolish and five were wise. ³The foolish ones took their lamps but did not take any oil with them. ⁴The wise, however, took oil in jars along with their lamps. ⁵The bridegroom was a long time in coming, and they all became drowsy and fell asleep.

⁶"At midnight the cry rang out: 'Here's the bridegroom! Come out to meet him!'

⁷"Then all the virgins woke up and trimmed their lamps. ⁸The foolish ones said to the wise, 'Give us some of your oil; our lamps are going out.'

⁹"'No,' they replied, 'there may not be enough for both us and you. Instead, go to those who sell oil and buy some for yourselves.'

¹⁰"But while they were on their way to buy the oil, the bridegroom arrived. The virgins who were ready went in with him to the wedding banquet. And the door was shut.

¹¹"Later the others also came. 'Sir! Sir!' they said. 'Open the door for us!'

¹²"But he replied, 'I tell you the truth, I don't know you.'

¹³"Therefore keep watch, because you do not know the day or the hour.

▃ET'S LIVE IT!   Matthew 25:1–13

BE READY WHEN JESUS COMES ➡ Jesus told a story about young women with lamps. The young women were waiting for the bridegroom to bring the bride to his home. Some of them ran out of oil. Read Matthew 25:1–13. Jesus told this story to remind us that he is coming back; but since we don't know exactly when, we must always be ready!

You can make a Bible-time lamp with your parents. Pour cooking oil into a shallow glass bowl. Float a bit of linen cloth or a candle wick in the oil, and light the wick. The flickering light will remind you that Jesus may come back to earth at any time.

The Parable of the Talents

14"Again, it will be like a man going on a journey, who called his servants and entrusted his property to them. 15To one he gave five talents*a* of money, to another two talents, and to another one talent, each according to his ability. Then he went on his journey. 16The man who had received the five talents went at once and put his money to work and gained five more. 17So also, the one with the two talents gained two more. 18But the man who had received the one talent went off, dug a hole in the ground and hid his master's money.

19"After a long time the master of those servants returned and settled accounts with them. 20The man who had received the five talents brought the other five. 'Master,' he said, 'you entrusted me with five talents. See, I have gained five more.'

21"His master replied, 'Well done, good and faithful servant! You have been faithful with a few things; I will put you in charge of many things. Come and share your master's happiness!'

22"The man with the two talents also came. 'Master,' he said, 'you entrusted me with two talents; see, I have gained two more.'

23"His master replied, 'Well done, good and faithful servant! You have been faithful with a few things; I will put you in charge of many things. Come and share your master's happiness!'

24"Then the man who had received the one talent came. 'Master,' he said, 'I knew that you are a hard man, harvesting where you have not sown and gathering where you have not scattered seed. 25So I was afraid and went out and hid your talent in the ground. See, here is what belongs to you.'

26"His master replied, 'You wicked, lazy servant! So you knew that I harvest where I have not sown and gather where I have not scattered seed? 27Well then, you should have put my money on deposit with the bankers, so that when I returned I would have received it back with interest.

28" 'Take the talent from him and give it to the one who has the ten talents. 29For everyone who has will be given more, and he will have an abundance. Whoever does not have, even what he has will be taken from him. 30And throw that worthless servant outside, into the darkness, where there will be weeping and gnashing of teeth.'

The Sheep and the Goats

31"When the Son of Man comes in his glory, and all the angels with him, he will sit on his throne in heavenly glory. 32All the nations will be gathered before him, and he will separate the people one from another as a shepherd separates the sheep from the goats. 33He will put the sheep on his right and the goats on his left.

34"Then the King will say to those on his right, 'Come, you who are blessed by my Father; take your inheritance, the kingdom prepared for you since the creation of the world. 35For I was hungry and you gave me something to eat, I was thirsty and you gave me something to drink, I was a stranger and you invited me in, 36I needed clothes and you clothed me, I was sick and you looked after me, I was in prison and you came to visit me.'

37"Then the righteous will answer him, 'Lord, when did we see you hungry and feed you, or thirsty and give you something to drink? 38When did we see you a stranger and invite you in, or needing clothes and clothe you? 39When did we see you sick or in prison and go to visit you?'

40"The King will reply, 'I tell you the truth, whatever you did for one of the least of these brothers of mine, you did for me.'

41"Then he will say to those on his left, 'Depart from me, you who are cursed, into the eternal fire prepared for the devil and his angels. 42For I

---

a15 A talent was worth more than a thousand dollars.

was hungry and you gave me nothing to eat, I was thirsty and you gave me nothing to drink, 43I was a stranger and you did not invite me in, I needed clothes and you did not clothe me, I was sick and in prison and you did not look after me.'

44"They also will answer, 'Lord, when did we see you hungry or thirsty or a stranger or needing clothes or sick or in prison, and did not help you?'

45"He will reply, 'I tell you the truth, whatever you did not do for one of the least of these, you did not do for me.'

46"Then they will go away to eternal punishment, but the righteous to eternal life."

The Plot Against Jesus

26 When Jesus had finished saying all these things, he said to his disciples, 2"As you know, the Passover is two days away—and the Son of Man will be handed over to be crucified."

3Then the chief priests and the elders of the people assembled in the palace of the high priest, whose name was Caiaphas, 4and they plotted to arrest Jesus in some sly way and kill him. 5"But not during the Feast," they said, "or there may be a riot among the people."

Jesus Anointed at Bethany

6While Jesus was in Bethany in the home of a man known as Simon the Leper, 7a woman came to him with an alabaster jar of very expensive perfume, which she poured on his head as he was reclining at the table.

8When the disciples saw this, they were indignant. "Why this waste?" they asked. 9"This perfume could have been sold at a high price and the money given to the poor."

10Aware of this, Jesus said to them, "Why are you bothering this woman? She has done a beautiful thing to me. 11The poor you will always have with you, but you will not always have me. 12When she poured this perfume on my body, she did it to prepare me for

burial. 13I tell you the truth, wherever this gospel is preached throughout the world, what she has done will also be told, in memory of her."

Judas Agrees to Betray Jesus

14Then one of the Twelve—the one called Judas Iscariot—went to the chief priests 15and asked, "What are you willing to give me if I hand him over to you?" So they counted out for him thirty silver coins. 16From then on Judas watched for an opportunity to hand him over.

❓DID YOU KNOW?   26:14

Who was Judas?

Judas was the disciple who betrayed Jesus. Judas took money for showing Jesus' enemies where they could find him at night, when the crowds who believed in him would not see them.

The Lord's Supper

17On the first day of the Feast of Unleavened Bread, the disciples came to Jesus and asked, "Where do you want us to make preparations for you to eat the Passover?"

18He replied, "Go into the city to a certain man and tell him, 'The Teacher says: My appointed time is near. I am going to celebrate the Passover with my disciples at your house.'"

19So the disciples did as Jesus had directed them and prepared the Passover.

20When evening came, Jesus was reclining at the table with the Twelve. 21And while they were eating, he said, "I tell you the truth, one of you will betray me."

22They were very sad and began to say to him one after the other, "Surely not I, Lord?"

23Jesus replied, "The one who has dipped his hand into the bowl with me will betray me. 24The Son of Man will go just as it is written about him. But woe to that man who betrays the

Son of Man! It would be better for him if he had not been born."

²⁵Then Judas, the one who would betray him, said, "Surely not I, Rabbi?"

Jesus answered, "Yes, it is you."ᵃ

²⁶While they were eating, Jesus took bread, gave thanks and broke it, and gave it to his disciples, saying, "Take and eat; this is my body."

²⁷Then he took the cup, gave thanks and offered it to them, saying, "Drink from it, all of you. ²⁸This is my blood of theᵇ covenant, which is poured out for many for the forgiveness of sins. ²⁹I tell you, I will not drink of this fruit of the vine from now on until that day when I drink it anew with you in my Father's kingdom."

³⁰When they had sung a hymn, they went out to the Mount of Olives.

Jesus Predicts Peter's Denial

³¹Then Jesus told them, "This very night you will all fall away on account of me, for it is written:

" 'I will strike the shepherd,
    and the sheep of the flock will
        be scattered.'ᶜ

³²But after I have risen, I will go ahead of you into Galilee."

³³Peter replied, "Even if all fall away on account of you, I never will."

³⁴"I tell you the truth," Jesus answered, "this very night, before the rooster crows, you will disown me three times."

³⁵But Peter declared, "Even if I have to die with you, I will never disown you." And all the other disciples said the same.

Gethsemane

³⁶Then Jesus went with his disciples to a place called Gethsemane, and he said to them, "Sit here while I go over there and pray." ³⁷He took Peter and the two sons of Zebedee along with him, and he began to be

sorrowful and troubled. ³⁸Then he said to them, "My soul is overwhelmed with sorrow to the point of death. Stay here and keep watch with me."

³⁹Going a little farther, he fell with his face to the ground and prayed, "My Father, if it is possible, may this cup be taken from me. Yet not as I will, but as you will."

⁴⁰Then he returned to his disciples and found them sleeping. "Could you men not keep watch with me for one hour?" he asked Peter. ⁴¹"Watch and pray so that you will not fall into temptation. The spirit is willing, but the body is weak."

⁴²He went away a second time and prayed, "My Father, if it is not possible for this cup to be taken away unless I drink it, may your will be done."

⁴³When he came back, he again found them sleeping, because their eyes were heavy. ⁴⁴So he left them and went away once more and prayed the third time, saying the same thing.

⁴⁵Then he returned to the disciples and said to them, "Are you still sleeping and resting? Look, the hour is near, and the Son of Man is betrayed into the hands of sinners. ⁴⁶Rise, let us go! Here comes my betrayer!"

Jesus Arrested

⁴⁷While he was still speaking, Judas, one of the Twelve, arrived. With him was a large crowd armed with swords and clubs, sent from the chief priests and the elders of the people. ⁴⁸Now the betrayer had arranged a signal with them: "The one I kiss is the man; arrest him." ⁴⁹Going at once to Jesus, Judas said, "Greetings, Rabbi!" and kissed him.

⁵⁰Jesus replied, "Friend, do what you came for."ᵈ

Then the men stepped forward, seized Jesus and arrested him. ⁵¹With that, one of Jesus' companions

---

ᵃ25 Or "You yourself have said it"   ᵇ28 Some manuscripts the new   ᶜ31 Zech. 13:7
ᵈ50 Or "Friend, why have you come?"

reached for his sword, drew it out and struck the servant of the high priest, cutting off his ear.

⁵²"Put your sword back in its place," Jesus said to him, "for all who draw the sword will die by the sword. ⁵³Do you think I cannot call on my Father, and he will at once put at my disposal more than twelve legions of angels? ⁵⁴But how then would the Scriptures be fulfilled that say it must happen in this way?"

⁵⁵At that time Jesus said to the crowd, "Am I leading a rebellion, that you have come out with swords and clubs to capture me? Every day I sat in the temple courts teaching, and you did not arrest me. ⁵⁶But this has all taken place that the writings of the prophets might be fulfilled." Then all the disciples deserted him and fled.

Before the Sanhedrin

⁵⁷Those who had arrested Jesus took him to Caiaphas, the high priest, where the teachers of the law and the elders had assembled. ⁵⁸But Peter followed him at a distance, right up to the courtyard of the high priest. He entered and sat down with the guards to see the outcome.

⁵⁹The chief priests and the whole Sanhedrin were looking for false evidence against Jesus so that they could put him to death. ⁶⁰But they did not find any, though many false witnesses came forward.

Finally two came forward ⁶¹and declared, "This fellow said, 'I am able to destroy the temple of God and rebuild it in three days.' "

⁶²Then the high priest stood up and said to Jesus, "Are you not going to answer? What is this testimony that these men are bringing against you?" ⁶³But Jesus remained silent.

The high priest said to him, "I charge you under oath by the living God: Tell us if you are the Christ,ᵃ the Son of God."

⁶⁴"Yes, it is as you say," Jesus re-

plied. "But I say to all of you: In the future you will see the Son of Man sitting at the right hand of the Mighty One and coming on the clouds of heaven."

❓DID YOU KNOW?　26:59

What was the Sanhedrin?

The Sanhedrin was the governing council of the Jews. The Sanhedrin could make laws and put people in prison. The Romans, who ruled much of the world, let most of the nations they conquered govern themselves under a Roman governor.

---

⁶⁵Then the high priest tore his clothes and said, "He has spoken blasphemy! Why do we need any more witnesses? Look, now you have heard the blasphemy. ⁶⁶What do you think?"

"He is worthy of death," they answered.

⁶⁷Then they spit in his face and struck him with their fists. Others slapped him ⁶⁸and said, "Prophesy to us, Christ. Who hit you?"

Peter Disowns Jesus

⁶⁹Now Peter was sitting out in the courtyard, and a servant girl came to him. "You also were with Jesus of Galilee," she said.

⁷⁰But he denied it before them all. "I don't know what you're talking about," he said.

⁷¹Then he went out to the gateway, where another girl saw him and said to the people there, "This fellow was with Jesus of Nazareth."

⁷²He denied it again, with an oath: "I don't know the man!"

⁷³After a little while, those standing there went up to Peter and said, "Surely you are one of them, for your accent gives you away."

⁷⁴Then he began to call down

ᵃ63 Or Messiah; also in verse 68

curses on himself and he swore to them, "I don't know the man!"

Immediately a rooster crowed. 75Then Peter remembered the word Jesus had spoken: "Before the rooster crows, you will disown me three times." And he went outside and wept bitterly.

Judas Hangs Himself

27 Early in the morning, all the chief priests and the elders of the people came to the decision to put Jesus to death. 2They bound him, led him away and handed him over to Pilate, the governor.

3When Judas, who had betrayed him, saw that Jesus was condemned, he was seized with remorse and returned the thirty silver coins to the chief priests and the elders. 4"I have sinned," he said, "for I have betrayed innocent blood."

"What is that to us?" they replied. "That's your responsibility."

5So Judas threw the money into the temple and left. Then he went away and hanged himself.

6The chief priests picked up the coins and said, "It is against the law to put this into the treasury, since it is blood money." 7So they decided to use the money to buy the potter's field as a burial place for foreigners. 8That is why it has been called the Field of Blood to this day. 9Then what was spoken by Jeremiah the prophet was fulfilled: "They took the thirty silver coins, the price set on him by the people of Israel, 10and they used them to buy the potter's field, as the Lord commanded me."a

a10 See Zech. 11:12,13; Jer. 19:1-13; 32:6-9.

Jesus Before Pilate

11Meanwhile Jesus stood before the governor, and the governor asked him, "Are you the king of the Jews?"

"Yes, it is as you say," Jesus replied.

12When he was accused by the chief priests and the elders, he gave no answer. 13Then Pilate asked him, "Don't you hear the testimony they are bringing against you?" 14But Jesus made no reply, not even to a single charge—to the great amazement of the governor.

15Now it was the governor's custom at the Feast to release a prisoner chosen by the crowd. 16At that time they had a notorious prisoner, called Barabbas. 17So when the crowd had gathered, Pilate asked them, "Which one do you want me to release to you: Barabbas, or Jesus who is called Christ?" 18For he knew it was out of envy that they had handed Jesus over to him.

19While Pilate was sitting on the judge's seat, his wife sent him this message: "Don't have anything to do with that innocent man, for I have suffered a great deal today in a dream because of him."

20But the chief priests and the elders persuaded the crowd to ask for Barabbas and to have Jesus executed.

21"Which of the two do you want me to release to you?" asked the governor.

"Barabbas," they answered.

22"What shall I do, then, with Jesus who is called Christ?" Pilate asked.

▌ET'S LIVE IT!   Matthew 26:69–75

SORRY AFTER DOING WRONG ➠ The apostle Peter loved Jesus. But the night before Jesus died, Peter was afraid. Read Matthew 26:69–74 to find out what Peter did. Read Matthew 26:75 to find out how Peter felt after he lied and said he wasn't Jesus' friend.

If we love God, we will feel guilty and miserable after doing wrong. When you feel this way, the best thing to do is pray and tell God you are sorry. He will forgive you, and you will feel better.

They all answered, "Crucify him!" [23]"Why? What crime has he committed?" asked Pilate.

But they shouted all the louder, "Crucify him!"

[24]When Pilate saw that he was getting nowhere, but that instead an uproar was starting, he took water and washed his hands in front of the crowd. "I am innocent of this man's blood," he said. "It is your responsibility!"

[25]All the people answered, "Let his blood be on us and on our children!"

[26]Then he released Barabbas to them. But he had Jesus flogged, and handed him over to be crucified.

❓DID YOU KNOW?   27:24

Who was Pilate?

Pilate was the Roman governor in charge of Judea. The Sanhedrin took Jesus to Pilate because he was the only one who could condemn Jesus to death.

The Soldiers Mock Jesus

[27]Then the governor's soldiers took Jesus into the Praetorium and gathered the whole company of soldiers around him. [28]They stripped him and put a scarlet robe on him, [29]and then twisted together a crown of thorns and set it on his head. They put a staff in his right hand and knelt in front of him and mocked him. "Hail, king of the Jews!" they said. [30]They spit on him, and took the staff and struck him on the head again and again. [31]After they had mocked him, they took off the robe and put his own clothes on him. Then they led him away to crucify him.

The Crucifixion

[32]As they were going out, they met a man from Cyrene, named Simon, and they forced him to carry the cross. [33]They came to a place called Golgotha (which means The Place of the Skull). [34]There they offered Jesus wine to drink, mixed with gall; but after tasting it, he refused to drink it. [35]When they had crucified him, they divided up his clothes by casting lots.[a] [36]And sitting down, they kept watch over him there. [37]Above his head they placed the written charge against him: THIS IS JESUS, THE KING OF THE JEWS. [38]Two robbers were crucified with him, one on his right and one on his left. [39]Those who passed by hurled insults at him, shaking their heads [40]and saying, "You who are going to destroy the temple and build it in three days, save yourself! Come down from the cross, if you are the Son of God!"

[41]In the same way the chief priests, the teachers of the law and the elders mocked him. [42]"He saved others," they said, "but he can't save himself! He's the King of Israel! Let him come down now from the cross, and we will believe in him. [43]He trusts in God. Let God rescue him now if he wants him, for he said, 'I am the Son of God.'" [44]In the same way the robbers who were crucified with him also heaped insults on him.

The Death of Jesus

[45]From the sixth hour until the ninth hour darkness came over all the land. [46]About the ninth hour Jesus cried out in a loud voice, *"Eloi, Eloi,[b] lama sabachthani?"*—which means, "My God, my God, why have you forsaken me?"[c]

[47]When some of those standing there heard this, they said, "He's calling Elijah."

[48]Immediately one of them ran and got a sponge. He filled it with wine vinegar, put it on a stick, and offered it to Jesus to drink. [49]The rest said, "Now leave him alone. Let's see if Elijah comes to save him."

[50]And when Jesus had cried out

---

[a]35 A few late manuscripts *lots that the word spoken by the prophet might be fulfilled: "They divided my garments among themselves and cast lots for my clothing"* (Psalm 22:18)   [b]46 Some manuscripts *Eli, Eli*   [c]46 Psalm 22:1

again in a loud voice, he gave up his spirit.

⁵¹At that moment the curtain of the temple was torn in two from top to bottom. The earth shook and the rocks split. ⁵²The tombs broke open and the bodies of many holy people who had died were raised to life. ⁵³They came out of the tombs, and after Jesus' resurrection they went into the holy city and appeared to many people.

⁵⁴When the centurion and those with him who were guarding Jesus saw the earthquake and all that had happened, they were terrified, and exclaimed, "Surely he was the Son*ᵃ* of God!"

⁵⁵Many women were there, watching from a distance. They had followed Jesus from Galilee to care for his needs. ⁵⁶Among them were Mary Magdalene, Mary the mother of James and Joses, and the mother of Zebedee's sons.

The Burial of Jesus

⁵⁷As evening approached, there came a rich man from Arimathea, named Joseph, who had himself become a disciple of Jesus. ⁵⁸Going to Pilate, he asked for Jesus' body, and Pilate ordered that it be given to him. ⁵⁹Joseph took the body, wrapped it in a clean linen cloth, ⁶⁰and placed it in his own new tomb that he had cut out

ᵃ54 Or *a son*

of the rock. He rolled a big stone in front of the entrance to the tomb and went away. ⁶¹Mary Magdalene and the other Mary were sitting there opposite the tomb.

The Guard at the Tomb

⁶²The next day, the one after Preparation Day, the chief priests and the Pharisees went to Pilate. ⁶³"Sir," they said, "we remember that while he was still alive that deceiver said, 'After three days I will rise again.' ⁶⁴So give the order for the tomb to be made secure until the third day. Otherwise, his disciples may come and steal the body and tell the people that he has been raised from the dead. This last deception will be worse than the first."

⁶⁵"Take a guard," Pilate answered. "Go, make the tomb as secure as you know how." ⁶⁶So they went and made the tomb secure by putting a seal on the stone and posting the guard.

The Resurrection

28 After the Sabbath, at dawn on the first day of the week, Mary Magdalene and the other Mary went to look at the tomb.

²There was a violent earthquake, for an angel of the Lord came down from heaven and, going to the tomb, rolled back the stone and sat on it. ³His appearance was like lightning,

Life in Bible Times

JESUS' TOMB

The tombs of the wealthy were cut into rocky hillsides. A round stone rested in a stone track. The stone was rolled over the opening to seal it. Read Matthew 27:57–61. This is the kind of tomb in which Jesus was buried.

and his clothes were white as snow. [4]The guards were so afraid of him that they shook and became like dead men.

[5]The angel said to the women, "Do not be afraid, for I know that you are looking for Jesus, who was crucified. [6]He is not here; he has risen, just as he said. Come and see the place where he lay. [7]Then go quickly and tell his disciples: 'He has risen from the dead and is going ahead of you into Galilee. There you will see him.' Now I have told you."

[8]So the women hurried away from the tomb, afraid yet filled with joy, and ran to tell his disciples. [9]Suddenly Jesus met them. "Greetings," he said. They came to him, clasped his feet and worshiped him. [10]Then Jesus said to them, "Do not be afraid. Go and tell my brothers to go to Galilee; there they will see me."

The Guards' Report

[11]While the women were on their way, some of the guards went into the city and reported to the chief priests everything that had happened. [12]When the chief priests had met with the elders and devised a plan, they gave the soldiers a large sum of money, [13]telling them, "You are to say, 'His disciples came during the night and stole him away while we were asleep.' [14]If this report gets to the governor, we will satisfy him and keep you out of trouble." [15]So the soldiers took the money and did as they were instructed. And this story has been widely circulated among the Jews to this very day.

WORDS TO REMEMBER

28:19-20 Go and make disciples of all nations .... And surely I am with you always, to the very end of the age.

The Great Commission

[16]Then the eleven disciples went to Galilee, to the mountain where Jesus had told them to go. [17]When they saw him, they worshiped him; but some doubted. [18]Then Jesus came to them and said, "All authority in heaven and on earth has been given to me. [19]Therefore go and make disciples of all nations, baptizing them in[a] the name of the Father and of the Son and of the Holy Spirit, [20]and teaching them to obey everything I have commanded you. And surely I am with you always, to the very end of the age."

---

[a]19 Or into; see Acts 8:16; 19:5; Romans 6:3; 1 Cor. 1:13; 10:2 and Gal. 3:27.

MARK

WHO WROTE THIS BOOK?
A young man named John Mark wrote down stories Peter told about Jesus.

WHY WAS THIS BOOK WRITTEN?
Mark shows people who Jesus was by telling what Jesus did.

FOR WHOM WAS THIS BOOK WRITTEN?
Mark wrote this book for people in the Roman empire who did not understand how the Jews lived.

WHAT HAPPENS IN THIS BOOK?
Jesus shows his power by performing miracles that help people, and he teaches his disciples.

WHO IS IMPORTANT IN THIS BOOK?
Jesus is the important person in this book.

WHEN DID THIS HAPPEN?
Jesus worked miracles and taught from A.D. 26 to 30.

WHERE DID THIS HAPPEN?
Most things in Mark 1–9 happened in Galilee. Most things in Mark 10–16 took place in or near Jerusalem.

WHAT ARE SOME OF THE STORIES IN THIS BOOK?

Jesus heals a paralyzed man.	Mark 2:1–12
Jesus calms a storm.	Mark 4:35–41
Jesus raises a dead girl.	Mark 5:21–43
Jesus walks on water.	Mark 6:45–56
Jesus feeds four thousand people.	Mark 8:1–10
Jesus heals a young boy.	Mark 9:14–32
Jesus holds the Lord's Supper.	Mark 14:12–26
Jesus dies and is buried.	Mark 15:21–47
Jesus is raised again.	Mark 16:1–8

John the Baptist Prepares the Way

1 The beginning of the gospel about Jesus Christ, the Son of God.*a*

²It is written in Isaiah the prophet:

"I will send my messenger ahead
  of you,
    who will prepare your way"*b*—
³"a voice of one calling in the
    desert,
'Prepare the way for the Lord,
    make straight paths for him.'"*c*

⁴And so John came, baptizing in the desert region and preaching a baptism of repentance for the forgiveness of sins. ⁵The whole Judean countryside and all the people of Jerusalem went out to him. Confessing their sins, they were baptized by him in the Jordan River. ⁶John wore clothing made of camel's hair, with a leather belt around his waist, and he ate locusts and wild honey. ⁷And this was his message: "After me will come one more powerful than I, the thongs of whose sandals I am not worthy to stoop down and untie. ⁸I baptize you with*d* water, but he will baptize you with the Holy Spirit."

The Baptism and Temptation of Jesus

⁹At that time Jesus came from Nazareth in Galilee and was baptized by John in the Jordan. ¹⁰As Jesus was coming up out of the water, he saw heaven being torn open and the Spirit descending on him like a dove. ¹¹And a voice came from heaven: "You are my Son, whom I love; with you I am well pleased."

¹²At once the Spirit sent him out into the desert, ¹³and he was in the desert forty days, being tempted by Satan. He was with the wild animals, and angels attended him.

The Calling of the First Disciples

¹⁴After John was put in prison, Jesus went into Galilee, proclaiming the good news of God. ¹⁵"The time has come," he said. "The kingdom of God is near. Repent and believe the good news!"

¹⁶As Jesus walked beside the Sea of Galilee, he saw Simon and his brother Andrew casting a net into the lake, for they were fishermen. ¹⁷"Come, follow me," Jesus said, "and I will make you fishers of men." ¹⁸At once they left their nets and followed him.

¹⁹When he had gone a little farther, he saw James son of Zebedee and his brother John in a boat, preparing their nets. ²⁰Without delay he called them, and they left their father Zebedee in the boat with the hired men and followed him.

Jesus Drives Out an Evil Spirit

²¹They went to Capernaum, and when the Sabbath came, Jesus went into the synagogue and began to teach. ²²The people were amazed at

---

a1 Some manuscripts do not have *the Son of God.*   *b2* Mal. 3:1   *c3* Isaiah 40:3   *d8* Or *in*

Life in Bible Times

FISHING

Fishermen in boats worked on the Sea of Galilee in the first century. The fish they caught in their nets were salted or dried and were sold all through Palestine.

his teaching, because he taught them as one who had authority, not as the teachers of the law. ²³Just then a man in their synagogue who was possessed by an evil*a* spirit cried out, ²⁴"What do you want with us, Jesus of Nazareth? Have you come to destroy us? I know who you are—the Holy One of God!"

²⁵"Be quiet!" said Jesus sternly. "Come out of him!" ²⁶The evil spirit shook the man violently and came out of him with a shriek.

²⁷The people were all so amazed that they asked each other, "What is this? A new teaching—and with authority! He even gives orders to evil spirits and they obey him." ²⁸News about him spread quickly over the whole region of Galilee.

Jesus Heals Many

²⁹As soon as they left the synagogue, they went with James and John to the home of Simon and Andrew. ³⁰Simon's mother-in-law was in bed with a fever, and they told Jesus about her. ³¹So he went to her, took her hand and helped her up. The fever left her and she began to wait on them.

³²That evening after sunset the people brought to Jesus all the sick and demon-possessed. ³³The whole town gathered at the door, ³⁴and Jesus healed many who had various diseases. He also drove out many demons, but he would not let the demons speak because they knew who he was.

Jesus Prays in a Solitary Place

³⁵Very early in the morning, while it was still dark, Jesus got up, left the house and went off to a solitary place, where he prayed. ³⁶Simon and his companions went to look for him, ³⁷and when they found him, they exclaimed: "Everyone is looking for you!"

³⁸Jesus replied, "Let us go somewhere else—to the nearby villages —so I can preach there also. That is why I have come." ³⁹So he traveled throughout Galilee, preaching in their synagogues and driving out demons.

A Man With Leprosy

⁴⁰A man with leprosy*b* came to him and begged him on his knees, "If you are willing, you can make me clean."

⁴¹Filled with compassion, Jesus reached out his hand and touched the man. "I am willing," he said. "Be clean!" ⁴²Immediately the leprosy left him and he was cured.

⁴³Jesus sent him away at once with a strong warning: ⁴⁴"See that you don't tell this to anyone. But go, show yourself to the priest and offer the sacrifices that Moses commanded for your cleansing, as a testimony to them." ⁴⁵Instead he went out and began to talk freely, spreading the news. As a result, Jesus could no longer enter a town openly but stayed outside in lonely places. Yet the people still came to him from everywhere.

Jesus Heals a Paralytic

2 A few days later, when Jesus again entered Capernaum, the people heard that he had come home. ²So many gathered that there was no room left, not even outside the door, and he preached the word to them. ³Some men came, bringing to him a paralytic, carried by four of them. ⁴Since they could not get him to Jesus because of the crowd, they made an opening in the roof above Jesus and, after digging through it, lowered the mat the paralyzed man was lying on. ⁵When Jesus saw their faith, he said to the paralytic, "Son, your sins are forgiven."

⁶Now some teachers of the law were sitting there, thinking to themselves, ⁷"Why does this fellow talk like that? He's blaspheming! Who can forgive sins but God alone?"

⁸Immediately Jesus knew in his

---

a23 Greek *unclean*; also in verses 26 and 27 affecting the skin—not necessarily leprosy.　　*b40* The Greek word was used for various diseases

spirit that this was what they were thinking in their hearts, and he said to them, "Why are you thinking these things? ⁹Which is easier: to say to the paralytic, 'Your sins are forgiven,' or to say, 'Get up, take your mat and walk'? ¹⁰But that you may know that the Son of Man has authority on earth to forgive sins . . . ." He said to the paralytic, ¹¹"I tell you, get up, take your mat and go home." ¹²He got up, took his mat and walked out in full view of them all. This amazed everyone and they praised God, saying, "We have never seen anything like this!"

The Calling of Levi

¹³Once again Jesus went out beside the lake. A large crowd came to him, and he began to teach them. ¹⁴As he walked along, he saw Levi son of Alphaeus sitting at the tax collector's booth. "Follow me," Jesus told him, and Levi got up and followed him.

¹⁵While Jesus was having dinner at Levi's house, many tax collectors and "sinners" were eating with him and his disciples, for there were many who followed him. ¹⁶When the teachers of the law who were Pharisees saw him eating with the "sin-

ners" and tax collectors, they asked his disciples: "Why does he eat with tax collectors and 'sinners'?"

Life In Bible Times

HOUSE ROOFS

House roofs in New Testament times were made by laying branches over roof beams. Mud was packed over the branches. The friends who carried a paralyzed man to Jesus dug through the mud roof of a house and lowered the sick man into the room where Jesus was teaching.

¹⁷On hearing this, Jesus said to them, "It is not the healthy who need a doctor, but the sick. I have not come to call the righteous, but sinners."

Jesus Questioned About Fasting

¹⁸Now John's disciples and the Pharisees were fasting. Some people

---

LET'S LIVE IT!   Mark 1:40–42

REACH OUT TO OTHERS ➡ Leprosy was a terrible disease. The leper's skin had open sores. A person with leprosy was "unclean" and could not worship God with other people or even live in town. Because of the disease, no one came near a leper.

Read Mark 1:40–42. Jesus showed he cared for the leper by touching him and healing him.

Make a list of children you know who might feel as lonely as the leper. Then answer these three questions:

1. Why is he or she left alone? (Because he or she is not nice, is dirty, doesn't wear nice clothes, hits people, looks different?)
2. How do you think he or she feels? (Happy, lonely, afraid, proud, sad, angry, stuck up, other feelings?)
3. How could you show that Jesus cares? (Smile, talk to him, ask her to sit with you at lunch, pick him for your team, tell others to stop being unfriendly?)

What will you do to show that Jesus cares about the lonely today?

came and asked Jesus, "How is it that John's disciples and the disciples of the Pharisees are fasting, but yours are not?"

19Jesus answered, "How can the guests of the bridegroom fast while he is with them? They cannot, so long as they have him with them. 20But the time will come when the bridegroom will be taken from them, and on that day they will fast.

21"No one sews a patch of unshrunk cloth on an old garment. If he does, the new piece will pull away from the old, making the tear worse. 22And no one pours new wine into old wineskins. If he does, the wine will burst the skins, and both the wine and the wineskins will be ruined. No, he pours new wine into new wineskins."

Lord of the Sabbath

23One Sabbath Jesus was going through the grainfields, and as his disciples walked along, they began to pick some heads of grain. 24The Pharisees said to him, "Look, why are they doing what is unlawful on the Sabbath?"

25He answered, "Have you never read what David did when he and his companions were hungry and in need? 26In the days of Abiathar the high priest, he entered the house of God and ate the consecrated bread, which is lawful only for priests to eat. And he also gave some to his companions."

27Then he said to them, "The Sabbath was made for man, not man for the Sabbath. 28So the Son of Man is Lord even of the Sabbath."

3 Another time he went into the synagogue, and a man with a shriveled hand was there. 2Some of them were looking for a reason to accuse Jesus, so they watched him closely to see if he would heal him on the Sabbath. 3Jesus said to the man with the shriveled hand, "Stand up in front of everyone."

4Then Jesus asked them, "Which is lawful on the Sabbath: to do good or to do evil, to save life or to kill?" But they remained silent.

5He looked around at them in anger and, deeply distressed at their stubborn hearts, said to the man, "Stretch out your hand." He stretched it out, and his hand was completely restored. 6Then the Pharisees went out and began to plot with the Herodians how they might kill Jesus.

Crowds Follow Jesus

7Jesus withdrew with his disciples to the lake, and a large crowd from Galilee followed. 8When they heard all he was doing, many people came to him from Judea, Jerusalem, Idumea, and the regions across the Jordan and around Tyre and Sidon. 9Because of the crowd he told his disciples to have a small boat ready for him, to keep the people from crowding him. 10For he had healed many, so that those with diseases were pushing forward to touch him. 11Whenever the evila spirits saw him, they fell down before him and cried out, "You are the Son of God." 12But he gave them strict orders not to tell who he was.

The Appointing of the Twelve Apostles

13Jesus went up on a mountainside and called to him those he wanted, and they came to him. 14He appointed twelve—designatingb them apostles—that they might be with him and that he might send them out to preach 15and to have authority to drive out demons. 16These are the twelve he appointed: Simon (to whom he gave the name Peter); 17James son of Zebedee and his brother John (to them he gave the name Boanerges, which means Sons of Thunder); 18Andrew, Philip, Bartholomew, Mat-

---

a11 Greek unclean; also in verse 30   b14 Some manuscripts do not have designating them apostles.

thew, Thomas, James son of Alphaeus, Thaddaeus, Simon the Zealot [19]and Judas Iscariot, who betrayed him.

Jesus and Beelzebub

[20]Then Jesus entered a house, and again a crowd gathered, so that he and his disciples were not even able to eat. [21]When his family heard about this, they went to take charge of him, for they said, "He is out of his mind."

[22]And the teachers of the law who came down from Jerusalem said, "He is possessed by Beelzebub[a]! By the prince of demons he is driving out demons."

[23]So Jesus called them and spoke to them in parables: "How can Satan drive out Satan? [24]If a kingdom is divided against itself, that kingdom cannot stand. [25]If a house is divided against itself, that house cannot stand. [26]And if Satan opposes himself and is divided, he cannot stand; his end has come. [27]In fact, no one can enter a strong man's house and carry off his possessions unless he first ties up the strong man. Then he can rob his house. [28]I tell you the truth, all the sins and blasphemies of men will be forgiven them. [29]But whoever blasphemes against the Holy Spirit will never be forgiven; he is guilty of an eternal sin."

[30]He said this because they were saying, "He has an evil spirit."

Jesus' Mother and Brothers

[31]Then Jesus' mother and brothers arrived. Standing outside, they sent someone in to call him. [32]A crowd was sitting around him, and they told him, "Your mother and brothers are outside looking for you."

[33]"Who are my mother and my brothers?" he asked.

[34]Then he looked at those seated in a circle around him and said, "Here are my mother and my brothers! [35]Whoever does God's will is my brother and sister and mother."

The Parable of the Sower

4 Again Jesus began to teach by the lake. The crowd that gathered around him was so large that he got into a boat and sat in it out on the lake, while all the people were along the shore at the water's edge. [2]He taught them many things by parables, and in his teaching said: [3]"Listen! A farmer went out to sow his seed. [4]As he was scattering the seed, some fell along the path, and the birds came and ate it up. [5]Some fell on rocky places, where it did not have much soil. It sprang up quickly, because the soil was shallow. [6]But when the sun came up, the plants were scorched, and they withered because they had no root. [7]Other seed fell among thorns, which grew up and choked the plants, so that they did not bear grain. [8]Still other seed fell on good soil. It came up, grew and produced a crop, multiplying thirty, sixty, or even a hundred times."

[9]Then Jesus said, "He who has ears to hear, let him hear."

[10]When he was alone, the Twelve and the others around him asked him about the parables. [11]He told them, "The secret of the kingdom of God has been given to you. But to those on the outside everything is said in parables [12]so that,

" 'they may be ever seeing but
        never perceiving,
    and ever hearing but never
        understanding;
    otherwise they might turn and be
        forgiven!'[b]"

[13]Then Jesus said to them, "Don't you understand this parable? How then will you understand any parable? [14]The farmer sows the word. [15]Some people are like seed along the path, where the word is sown. As soon as they hear it, Satan comes and takes away the word that was sown in them. [16]Others, like seed sown on rocky places, hear the word and at once receive it with joy. [17]But since

---

[a]22 Greek *Beezeboul* or *Beelzeboul*   [b]12 Isaiah 6:9,10

they have no root, they last only a short time. When trouble or persecution comes because of the word, they quickly fall away. ¹⁸Still others, like seed sown among thorns, hear the word; ¹⁹but the worries of this life, the deceitfulness of wealth and the desires for other things come in and choke the word, making it unfruitful. ²⁰Others, like seed sown on good soil, hear the word, accept it, and produce a crop—thirty, sixty or even a hundred times what was sown."

A Lamp on a Stand

²¹He said to them, "Do you bring in a lamp to put it under a bowl or a bed? Instead, don't you put it on its stand? ²²For whatever is hidden is meant to be disclosed, and whatever is concealed is meant to be brought out into the open. ²³If anyone has ears to hear, let him hear."

²⁴"Consider carefully what you hear," he continued. "With the measure you use, it will be measured to you—and even more. ²⁵Whoever has will be given more; whoever does not have, even what he has will be taken from him."

The Parable of the Growing Seed

²⁶He also said, "This is what the kingdom of God is like. A man scatters seed on the ground. ²⁷Night and day, whether he sleeps or gets up, the seed sprouts and grows, though he does not know how. ²⁸All by itself the soil produces grain—first the stalk, then the head, then the full kernel in the head. ²⁹As soon as the grain is ripe, he puts the sickle to it, because the harvest has come."

The Parable of the Mustard Seed

³⁰Again he said, "What shall we say the kingdom of God is like, or what parable shall we use to describe it? ³¹It is like a mustard seed, which is the smallest seed you plant in the ground. ³²Yet when planted, it grows and becomes the largest of all garden plants, with such big branches that the birds of the air can perch in its shade."

³³With many similar parables Jesus spoke the word to them, as much as they could understand. ³⁴He did not say anything to them without using a parable. But when he was alone with his own disciples, he explained everything.

Jesus Calms the Storm

³⁵That day when evening came, he said to his disciples, "Let us go over to the other side." ³⁶Leaving the crowd behind, they took him along, just as he was, in the boat. There were also other boats with him. ³⁷A furious squall came up, and the waves broke over the boat, so that it was nearly swamped. ³⁸Jesus was in the stern, sleeping on a cushion. The

Life in Bible Times

SOWING SEED

Farmers in the first century didn't use machines to sow their fields with seed. They took handfuls of seed and, with a sweeping motion, threw it on the ground they had plowed. A skillful sower could spread grain seeds very evenly.

disciples woke him and said to him, "Teacher, don't you care if we drown?"

³⁹He got up, rebuked the wind and said to the waves, "Quiet! Be still!" Then the wind died down and it was completely calm.

⁴⁰He said to his disciples, "Why are you so afraid? Do you still have no faith?"

⁴¹They were terrified and asked each other, "Who is this? Even the wind and the waves obey him!"

The Healing of a Demon-possessed Man

5 They went across the lake to the region of the Gerasenes.*a* ²When Jesus got out of the boat, a man with an evil*b* spirit came from the tombs to meet him. ³This man lived in the tombs, and no one could bind him any more, not even with a chain. ⁴For he had often been chained hand and foot, but he tore the chains apart and broke the irons on his feet. No one was strong enough to subdue him. ⁵Night and day among the tombs and in the hills he would cry out and cut himself with stones.

⁶When he saw Jesus from a distance, he ran and fell on his knees in front of him. ⁷He shouted at the top of his voice, "What do you want with me, Jesus, Son of the Most High God? Swear to God that you won't torture me!" ⁸For Jesus had said to him, "Come out of this man, you evil spirit!"

⁹Then Jesus asked him, "What is your name?"

"My name is Legion," he replied, "for we are many." ¹⁰And he begged Jesus again and again not to send them out of the area.

¹¹A large herd of pigs was feeding on the nearby hillside. ¹²The demons begged Jesus, "Send us among the pigs; allow us to go into them." ¹³He gave them permission, and the evil spirits came out and went into the pigs. The herd, about two thousand in number, rushed down the steep bank into the lake and were drowned.

¹⁴Those tending the pigs ran off and reported this in the town and countryside, and the people went out to see what had happened. ¹⁵When they came to Jesus, they saw the man who had been possessed by the legion of demons, sitting there, dressed and in his right mind; and they were afraid. ¹⁶Those who had seen it told the people what had happened to the demon-possessed man—and told about the pigs as well. ¹⁷Then the people began to plead with Jesus to leave their region.

¹⁸As Jesus was getting into the boat, the man who had been demon-possessed begged to go with him. ¹⁹Jesus did not let him, but said, "Go home to your family and tell them how much the Lord has done for you, and how he has had mercy on you." ²⁰So the man went away and began to tell in the Decapolis*c* how much Jesus had done for him. And all the people were amazed.

?DID YOU KNOW?   5:18

Can demons really possess people?

Demons are evil spirits that really can make people do evil things. We should have nothing to do with demons, even pretend demons shown in some movies. The movies people make about demons leave out one important thing: Even thousands of demons cannot stand against Jesus. When we invite Jesus Christ into our lives, he protects us.

A Dead Girl and a Sick Woman

²¹When Jesus had again crossed over by boat to the other side of the lake, a large crowd gathered around him while he was by the lake. ²²Then one of the synagogue rulers, named

---

a1 Some manuscripts *Gadarenes*; other manuscripts *Gergesenes*   *b2* Greek *unclean*; also in verses 8 and 13   *c20* That is, the Ten Cities

Jairus, came there. Seeing Jesus, he fell at his feet 23and pleaded earnestly with him, "My little daughter is dying. Please come and put your hands on her so that she will be healed and live." 24So Jesus went with him.

A large crowd followed and pressed around him. 25And a woman was there who had been subject to bleeding for twelve years. 26She had suffered a great deal under the care of many doctors and had spent all she had, yet instead of getting better she grew worse. 27When she heard about Jesus, she came up behind him in the crowd and touched his cloak, 28because she thought, "If I just touch his clothes, I will be healed." 29Immediately her bleeding stopped and she felt in her body that she was freed from her suffering.

30At once Jesus realized that power had gone out from him. He turned around in the crowd and asked, "Who touched my clothes?"

31"You see the people crowding against you," his disciples answered, "and yet you can ask, 'Who touched me?'"

32But Jesus kept looking around to see who had done it. 33Then the woman, knowing what had happened to her, came and fell at his feet and, trembling with fear, told him the whole truth. 34He said to her, "Daughter, your faith has healed you. Go in peace and be freed from your suffering."

35While Jesus was still speaking, some men came from the house of Ja-irus, the synagogue ruler. "Your daughter is dead," they said. "Why bother the teacher any more?"

36Ignoring what they said, Jesus told the synagogue ruler, "Don't be afraid; just believe."

37He did not let anyone follow him except Peter, James and John the brother of James. 38When they came to the home of the synagogue ruler, Jesus saw a commotion, with people crying and wailing loudly. 39He went in and said to them, "Why all this commotion and wailing? The child is not dead but asleep." 40But they laughed at him.

After he put them all out, he took the child's father and mother and the disciples who were with him, and went in where the child was. 41He took her by the hand and said to her, *"Talitha koum!"* (which means, "Little girl, I say to you, get up!"). 42Immediately the girl stood up and walked around (she was twelve years old). At this they were completely astonished. 43He gave strict orders not to let anyone know about this, and told them to give her something to eat.

A Prophet Without Honor

6 Jesus left there and went to his hometown, accompanied by his disciples. 2When the Sabbath came, he began to teach in the synagogue, and many who heard him were amazed.

"Where did this man get these things?" they asked. "What's this wisdom that has been given him, that

---

▌ET'S LIVE IT!　　　　Mark 5:21–23,35–43

PARENTS WHO PRAY ➡ Read Mark 5:21–23,35–43. What did the father do to help his little girl?

　Pretend you are a newspaper reporter. Interview your mother, father, or a grandparent. Ask the questions below. Then write a story about a time someone prayed for you.

　Can you remember a time when you prayed hard for me? Why did you pray then? What did you say when you prayed? Why was an answer to this prayer important? How did God answer the prayer? What things do you ask God for when you pray for me now?

he even does miracles! ³Isn't this the carpenter? Isn't this Mary's son and the brother of James, Joseph,ᵃ Judas and Simon? Aren't his sisters here with us?" And they took offense at him.

⁴Jesus said to them, "Only in his hometown, among his relatives and in his own house is a prophet without honor." ⁵He could not do any miracles there, except lay his hands on a few sick people and heal them. ⁶And he was amazed at their lack of faith.

Jesus Sends Out the Twelve

Then Jesus went around teaching from village to village. ⁷Calling the Twelve to him, he sent them out two by two and gave them authority over evilᵇ spirits.

⁸These were his instructions: "Take nothing for the journey except a staff—no bread, no bag, no money in your belts. ⁹Wear sandals but not an extra tunic. ¹⁰Whenever you enter a house, stay there until you leave that town. ¹¹And if any place will not welcome you or listen to you, shake the dust off your feet when you leave, as a testimony against them."

¹²They went out and preached that people should repent. ¹³They drove out many demons and anointed many sick people with oil and healed them.

John the Baptist Beheaded

¹⁴King Herod heard about this, for Jesus' name had become well known. Some were saying,ᶜ "John the Baptist has been raised from the dead, and that is why miraculous powers are at work in him."

¹⁵Others said, "He is Elijah."

And still others claimed, "He is a prophet, like one of the prophets of long ago."

¹⁶But when Herod heard this, he said, "John, the man I beheaded, has been raised from the dead!"

¹⁷For Herod himself had given orders to have John arrested, and he had him bound and put in prison. He did this because of Herodias, his brother Philip's wife, whom he had married. ¹⁸For John had been saying to Herod, "It is not lawful for you to have your brother's wife." ¹⁹So Herodias nursed a grudge against John and wanted to kill him. But she was not able to, ²⁰because Herod feared John and protected him, knowing him to be a righteous and holy man. When Herod heard John, he was greatly puzzledᵈ; yet he liked to listen to him.

²¹Finally the opportune time came. On his birthday Herod gave a banquet for his high officials and military commanders and the leading men of Galilee. ²²When the daughter of Herodias came in and danced, she pleased Herod and his dinner guests.

The king said to the girl, "Ask me for anything you want, and I'll give it to you." ²³And he promised her with an oath, "Whatever you ask I will give you, up to half my kingdom."

?DID YOU KNOW?　　6:26

Why did Herod kill John the Baptist?

King Herod made a foolish promise to give a dancing girl anything she asked. She asked for the head of John the Baptist. The king knew it was wrong to kill John, but he worried about what his friends would think if he broke his promise. King Herod committed a terrible sin just so he would not be embarrassed.

---

²⁴She went out and said to her mother, "What shall I ask for?"

"The head of John the Baptist," she answered.

²⁵At once the girl hurried in to the king with the request: "I want you to give me right now the head of John the Baptist on a platter."

²⁶The king was greatly distressed,

ᵃ3 Greek *Joses*, a variant of *Joseph*　　ᵇ7 Greek *unclean*　　ᶜ14 Some early manuscripts *He was saying*　　ᵈ20 Some early manuscripts *he did many things*

but because of his oaths and his dinner guests, he did not want to refuse her. ²⁷So he immediately sent an executioner with orders to bring John's head. The man went, beheaded John in the prison, ²⁸and brought back his head on a platter. He presented it to the girl, and she gave it to her mother. ²⁹On hearing of this, John's disciples came and took his body and laid it in a tomb.

Jesus Feeds the Five Thousand

³⁰The apostles gathered around Jesus and reported to him all they had done and taught. ³¹Then, because so many people were coming and going that they did not even have a chance to eat, he said to them, "Come with me by yourselves to a quiet place and get some rest."

³²So they went away by themselves in a boat to a solitary place. ³³But many who saw them leaving recognized them and ran on foot from all the towns and got there ahead of them. ³⁴When Jesus landed and saw a large crowd, he had compassion on them, because they were like sheep without a shepherd. So he began teaching them many things.

³⁵By this time it was late in the day, so his disciples came to him. "This is a remote place," they said, "and it's already very late. ³⁶Send the people away so they can go to the sur-

ᵃ37 Greek take two hundred denarii

rounding countryside and villages and buy themselves something to eat."

³⁷But he answered, "You give them something to eat."

They said to him, "That would take eight months of a man's wagesᵃ! Are we to go and spend that much on bread and give it to them to eat?"

³⁸"How many loaves do you have?" he asked. "Go and see."

When they found out, they said, "Five—and two fish."

³⁹Then Jesus directed them to have all the people sit down in groups on the green grass. ⁴⁰So they sat down in groups of hundreds and fifties. ⁴¹Taking the five loaves and the two fish and looking up to heaven, he gave thanks and broke the loaves. Then he gave them to his disciples to set before the people. He also divided the two fish among them all. ⁴²They all ate and were satisfied, ⁴³and the disciples picked up twelve basketfuls of broken pieces of bread and fish. ⁴⁴The number of the men who had eaten was five thousand.

Jesus Walks on the Water

⁴⁵Immediately Jesus made his disciples get into the boat and go on ahead of him to Bethsaida, while he dismissed the crowd. ⁴⁶After leaving them, he went up on a mountainside to pray.

Life in Bible Times

BAKING BREAD

Women used clay ovens to bake bread. They built a fire inside, and when the oven was hot they put pancake-shaped bread on the outside to cook. Or they scraped the ashes out of the oven and put small loaves of bread inside.

[47]When evening came, the boat was in the middle of the lake, and he was alone on land. [48]He saw the disciples straining at the oars, because the wind was against them. About the fourth watch of the night he went out to them, walking on the lake. He was about to pass by them, [49]but when they saw him walking on the lake, they thought he was a ghost. They cried out, [50]because they all saw him and were terrified.

Immediately he spoke to them and said, "Take courage! It is I. Don't be afraid." [51]Then he climbed into the boat with them, and the wind died down. They were completely amazed, [52]for they had not understood about the loaves; their hearts were hardened.

[53]When they had crossed over, they landed at Gennesaret and anchored there. [54]As soon as they got out of the boat, people recognized Jesus. [55]They ran throughout that whole region and carried the sick on mats to wherever they heard he was. [56]And wherever he went—into villages, towns or countryside—they placed the sick in the marketplaces. They begged him to let them touch even the edge of his cloak, and all who touched him were healed.

Clean and Unclean

7 The Pharisees and some of the teachers of the law who had come from Jerusalem gathered around Jesus and [2]saw some of his disciples eating food with hands that were "unclean," that is, unwashed. [3](The Pharisees and all the Jews do not eat unless they give their hands a ceremonial washing, holding to the tradition of the elders. [4]When they come from the marketplace they do not eat unless they wash. And they observe many other traditions, such as the washing of cups, pitchers and kettles.[a])

[5]So the Pharisees and teachers of the law asked Jesus, "Why don't your disciples live according to the tradition of the elders instead of eating their food with 'unclean' hands?"

?DID YOU KNOW?   7:5

What is the "tradition of the elders"?

The Pharisees thought that all their rules were very important, more important even than God's law and his Word. Jesus said the Pharisees were wrong. Rules made up by people are never as important as God's Word.

---

[6]He replied, "Isaiah was right when he prophesied about you hypocrites; as it is written:

" 'These people honor me with
     their lips,
but their hearts are far from
     me.
[7]They worship me in vain;
     their teachings are but rules
     taught by men.'[b]

[8]You have let go of the commands of God and are holding on to the traditions of men."

[9]And he said to them: "You have a fine way of setting aside the commands of God in order to observe[c] your own traditions! [10]For Moses said, 'Honor your father and your mother,'[d] and, 'Anyone who curses his father or mother must be put to death.'[e] [11]But you say that if a man says to his father or mother: 'Whatever help you might otherwise have received from me is Corban' (that is, a gift devoted to God), [12]then you no longer let him do anything for his father or mother. [13]Thus you nullify the word of God by your tradition that you have handed down. And you do many things like that."

[14]Again Jesus called the crowd to him and said, "Listen to me, everyone, and understand this. [15]Nothing

---

[a]4 Some early manuscripts *pitchers, kettles and dining couches*   [b]6,7 Isaiah 29:13   [c]9 Some manuscripts *set up*   [d]10 Exodus 20:12; Deut. 5:16   [e]10 Exodus 21:17; Lev. 20:9

outside a man can make him 'unclean' by going into him. Rather, it is what comes out of a man that makes him 'unclean.'*a*"

17After he had left the crowd and entered the house, his disciples asked him about this parable. 18"Are you so dull?" he asked. "Don't you see that nothing that enters a man from the outside can make him 'unclean'? 19For it doesn't go into his heart but into his stomach, and then out of his body." (In saying this, Jesus declared all foods "clean.")

20He went on: "What comes out of a man is what makes him 'unclean.' 21For from within, out of men's hearts, come evil thoughts, sexual immorality, theft, murder, adultery, 22greed, malice, deceit, lewdness, envy, slander, arrogance and folly. 23All these evils come from inside and make a man 'unclean.' "

The Faith of a Syrophoenician Woman

24Jesus left that place and went to the vicinity of Tyre.*b* He entered a house and did not want anyone to know it; yet he could not keep his presence secret. 25In fact, as soon as she heard about him, a woman whose little daughter was possessed by an evil*c* spirit came and fell at his feet. 26The woman was a Greek, born in Syrian Phoenicia. She begged Jesus to drive the demon out of her daughter.

27"First let the children eat all they want," he told her, "for it is not right to take the children's bread and toss it to their dogs."

28"Yes, Lord," she replied, "but even the dogs under the table eat the children's crumbs."

29Then he told her, "For such a reply, you may go; the demon has left your daughter."

30She went home and found her child lying on the bed, and the demon gone.

The Healing of a Deaf and Mute Man

31Then Jesus left the vicinity of Tyre and went through Sidon, down to the Sea of Galilee and into the region of the Decapolis.*d* 32There some people brought to him a man who was deaf and could hardly talk, and they begged him to place his hand on the man.

33After he took him aside, away from the crowd, Jesus put his fingers into the man's ears. Then he spit and touched the man's tongue. 34He looked up to heaven and with a deep sigh said to him, *"Ephphatha!"* (which means, "Be opened!"). 35At this, the man's ears were opened, his tongue was loosened and he began to speak plainly.

36Jesus commanded them not to tell anyone. But the more he did so, the more they kept talking about it. 37People were overwhelmed with amazement. "He has done everything well," they said. "He even makes the deaf hear and the mute speak."

Jesus Feeds the Four Thousand

8 During those days another large crowd gathered. Since they had nothing to eat, Jesus called his disciples to him and said, 2"I have compassion for these people; they have already been with me three days and have nothing to eat. 3If I send them home hungry, they will collapse on the way, because some of them have come a long distance."

4His disciples answered, "But where in this remote place can anyone get enough bread to feed them?"

5"How many loaves do you have?" Jesus asked.

"Seven," they replied.

6He told the crowd to sit down on the ground. When he had taken the seven loaves and given thanks, he broke them and gave them to his dis-

---

a15 Some early manuscripts 'unclean.' 16If anyone has ears to hear, let him hear.   *b24 Many early manuscripts Tyre and Sidon*   *c25 Greek unclean*   *d31 That is, the Ten Cities*

ciples to set before the people, and they did so. ⁷They had a few small fish as well; he gave thanks for them also and told the disciples to distribute them. ⁸The people ate and were satisfied. Afterward the disciples picked up seven basketfuls of broken pieces that were left over. ⁹About four thousand men were present. And having sent them away, ¹⁰he got into the boat with his disciples and went to the region of Dalmanutha.

¹¹The Pharisees came and began to question Jesus. To test him, they asked him for a sign from heaven. ¹²He sighed deeply and said, "Why does this generation ask for a miraculous sign? I tell you the truth, no sign will be given to it." ¹³Then he left them, got back into the boat and crossed to the other side.

The Yeast of the Pharisees and Herod

¹⁴The disciples had forgotten to bring bread, except for one loaf they had with them in the boat. ¹⁵"Be careful," Jesus warned them. "Watch out for the yeast of the Pharisees and that of Herod."

¹⁶They discussed this with one another and said, "It is because we have no bread."

¹⁷Aware of their discussion, Jesus asked them: "Why are you talking about having no bread? Do you still not see or understand? Are your hearts hardened? ¹⁸Do you have eyes but fail to see, and ears but fail to hear? And don't you remember? ¹⁹When I broke the five loaves for the five thousand, how many basketfuls of pieces did you pick up?"

"Twelve," they replied.

²⁰"And when I broke the seven loaves for the four thousand, how many basketfuls of pieces did you pick up?"

They answered, "Seven."

²¹He said to them, "Do you still not understand?"

The Healing of a Blind Man at Bethsaida

²²They came to Bethsaida, and some people brought a blind man and begged Jesus to touch him. ²³He took the blind man by the hand and led him outside the village. When he had spit on the man's eyes and put his hands on him, Jesus asked, "Do you see anything?"

²⁴He looked up and said, "I see people; they look like trees walking around."

²⁵Once more Jesus put his hands on the man's eyes. Then his eyes were opened, his sight was restored, and he saw everything clearly. ²⁶Jesus sent him home, saying, "Don't go into the village.ᵃ"

Peter's Confession of Christ

²⁷Jesus and his disciples went on to the villages around Caesarea Philippi. On the way he asked them, "Who do people say I am?"

²⁸They replied, "Some say John the Baptist; others say Elijah; and still others, one of the prophets."

²⁹"But what about you?" he asked. "Who do you say I am?"

Peter answered, "You are the Christ.ᵇ"

³⁰Jesus warned them not to tell anyone about him.

❓DID YOU KNOW?   8:29

Who is Jesus?

People who saw Jesus perform miracles and heard him teach knew he was special. Peter knew just how special! "Christ" means the person chosen by God to be the Savior of his people. The name "Son of Man" tells us Jesus was a real human being (Mark 8:31). The name "Son of God" (Mark 9:7) tells us Jesus is truly God.

ᵃ26 Some manuscripts *Don't go and tell anyone in the village*   ᵇ29 Or *Messiah*. "The Christ" (Greek) and "the Messiah" (Hebrew) both mean "the Anointed One."

Jesus Predicts His Death

31He then began to teach them that the Son of Man must suffer many things and be rejected by the elders, chief priests and teachers of the law, and that he must be killed and after three days rise again. 32He spoke plainly about this, and Peter took him aside and began to rebuke him.

33But when Jesus turned and looked at his disciples, he rebuked Peter. "Get behind me, Satan!" he said. "You do not have in mind the things of God, but the things of men."

34Then he called the crowd to him along with his disciples and said: "If anyone would come after me, he must deny himself and take up his cross and follow me. 35For whoever wants to save his life*a* will lose it, but whoever loses his life for me and for the gospel will save it. 36What good is it for a man to gain the whole world, yet forfeit his soul? 37Or what can a man give in exchange for his soul? 38If anyone is ashamed of me and my words in this adulterous and sinful generation, the Son of Man will be ashamed of him when he comes in his Father's glory with the holy angels."

9 And he said to them, "I tell you the truth, some who are standing here will not taste death before they see the kingdom of God come with power."

The Transfiguration

2After six days Jesus took Peter, James and John with him and led them up a high mountain, where they were all alone. There he was transfigured before them. 3His clothes became dazzling white, whiter than anyone in the world could bleach them. 4And there appeared before them Elijah and Moses, who were talking with Jesus.

5Peter said to Jesus, "Rabbi, it is good for us to be here. Let us put up three shelters—one for you, one for Moses and one for Elijah." 6(He did not know what to say, they were so frightened.)

7Then a cloud appeared and enveloped them, and a voice came from the cloud: "This is my Son, whom I love. Listen to him!"

WORDS TO REMEMBER

9:7 This is my Son, whom I love. Listen to him!

8Suddenly, when they looked around, they no longer saw anyone with them except Jesus.

9As they were coming down the mountain, Jesus gave them orders not to tell anyone what they had seen until the Son of Man had risen from the dead. 10They kept the matter to themselves, discussing what "rising from the dead" meant.

11And they asked him, "Why do the teachers of the law say that Elijah must come first?"

12Jesus replied, "To be sure, Elijah does come first, and restores all things. Why then is it written that the Son of Man must suffer much and be rejected? 13But I tell you, Elijah has come, and they have done to him everything they wished, just as it is written about him."

The Healing of a Boy With an Evil Spirit

14When they came to the other disciples, they saw a large crowd around them and the teachers of the law arguing with them. 15As soon as all the people saw Jesus, they were overwhelmed with wonder and ran to greet him.

16"What are you arguing with them about?" he asked.

17A man in the crowd answered, "Teacher, I brought you my son, who is possessed by a spirit that has robbed him of speech. 18Whenever it seizes him, it throws him to the ground. He foams at the mouth,

---

*a35 The Greek word means either *life* or *soul*; also in verse 36.

gnashes his teeth and becomes rigid. I asked your disciples to drive out the spirit, but they could not."

¹⁹"O unbelieving generation," Jesus replied, "how long shall I stay with you? How long shall I put up with you? Bring the boy to me."

²⁰So they brought him. When the spirit saw Jesus, it immediately threw the boy into a convulsion. He fell to the ground and rolled around, foaming at the mouth.

²¹Jesus asked the boy's father, "How long has he been like this?"

"From childhood," he answered. ²²"It has often thrown him into fire or water to kill him. But if you can do anything, take pity on us and help us."

²³" 'If you can'?" said Jesus. "Everything is possible for him who believes."

²⁴Immediately the boy's father exclaimed, "I do believe; help me overcome my unbelief!"

²⁵When Jesus saw that a crowd was running to the scene, he rebuked the evil^a spirit. "You deaf and mute spirit," he said, "I command you, come out of him and never enter him again."

²⁶The spirit shrieked, convulsed him violently and came out. The boy looked so much like a corpse that many said, "He's dead." ²⁷But Jesus took him by the hand and lifted him to his feet, and he stood up.

²⁸After Jesus had gone indoors, his disciples asked him privately, "Why couldn't we drive it out?"

²⁹He replied, "This kind can come out only by prayer.^b"

³⁰They left that place and passed through Galilee. Jesus did not want anyone to know where they were, ³¹because he was teaching his disciples. He said to them, "The Son of Man is going to be betrayed into the hands of men. They will kill him, and after three days he will rise." ³²But they did not understand what he

meant and were afraid to ask him about it.

Who Is the Greatest?

³³They came to Capernaum. When he was in the house, he asked them, "What were you arguing about on the road?" ³⁴But they kept quiet because on the way they had argued about who was the greatest.

³⁵Sitting down, Jesus called the Twelve and said, "If anyone wants to be first, he must be the very last, and the servant of all."

³⁶He took a little child and had him stand among them. Taking him in his arms, he said to them, ³⁷"Whoever welcomes one of these little children in my name welcomes me; and whoever welcomes me does not welcome me but the one who sent me."

Whoever Is Not Against Us Is for Us

³⁸"Teacher," said John, "we saw a man driving out demons in your name and we told him to stop, because he was not one of us."

³⁹"Do not stop him," Jesus said. "No one who does a miracle in my name can in the next moment say anything bad about me, ⁴⁰for whoever is not against us is for us. ⁴¹I tell you the truth, anyone who gives you a cup of water in my name because you belong to Christ will certainly not lose his reward.

Causing to Sin

⁴²"And if anyone causes one of these little ones who believe in me to sin, it would be better for him to be thrown into the sea with a large millstone tied around his neck. ⁴³If your hand causes you to sin, cut it off. It is better for you to enter life maimed than with two hands to go into hell, where the fire never goes out.^c ⁴⁵And if your foot causes you to sin, cut it off. It is better for you to enter life crippled than to have two feet and be

^a25 Greek *unclean*　　^b29 Some manuscripts *prayer and fasting*　　^c43 Some manuscripts *out,*
⁴⁴*where / " 'their worm does not die, / and the fire is not quenched.'*

thrown into hell.ᵃ ⁴⁷And if your eye causes you to sin, pluck it out. It is better for you to enter the kingdom of God with one eye than to have two eyes and be thrown into hell, ⁴⁸where

" 'their worm does not die,
and the fire is not quenched.'ᵇ

⁴⁹Everyone will be salted with fire.

⁵⁰"Salt is good, but if it loses its saltiness, how can you make it salty again? Have salt in yourselves, and be at peace with each other."

Divorce

10 Jesus then left that place and went into the region of Judea and across the Jordan. Again crowds of people came to him, and as was his custom, he taught them.

²Some Pharisees came and tested him by asking, "Is it lawful for a man to divorce his wife?"

³"What did Moses command you?" he replied.

⁴They said, "Moses permitted a man to write a certificate of divorce and send her away."

⁵"It was because your hearts were hard that Moses wrote you this law," Jesus replied. ⁶"But at the beginning of creation God 'made them male and female.'ᶜ ⁷'For this reason a man will leave his father and mother and be united to his wife,ᵈ ⁸and the two will become one flesh.'ᵉ So they are no longer two, but one. ⁹Therefore what God has joined together, let man not separate."

¹⁰When they were in the house again, the disciples asked Jesus about this. ¹¹He answered, "Anyone who divorces his wife and marries another woman commits adultery against her. ¹²And if she divorces her husband and marries another man, she commits adultery."

The Little Children and Jesus

¹³People were bringing little chil-

dren to Jesus to have him touch them, but the disciples rebuked them. ¹⁴When Jesus saw this, he was indignant. He said to them, "Let the little children come to me, and do not hinder them, for the kingdom of God belongs to such as these. ¹⁵I tell you the truth, anyone who will not receive the kingdom of God like a little child will never enter it." ¹⁶And he took the children in his arms, put his hands on them and blessed them.

The Rich Young Man

¹⁷As Jesus started on his way, a man ran up to him and fell on his knees before him. "Good teacher," he asked, "what must I do to inherit eternal life?"

¹⁸"Why do you call me good?" Jesus answered. "No one is good—except God alone. ¹⁹You know the commandments: 'Do not murder, do not commit adultery, do not steal, do not give false testimony, do not defraud, honor your father and mother.'ᶠ"

²⁰"Teacher," he declared, "all these I have kept since I was a boy."

²¹Jesus looked at him and loved him. "One thing you lack," he said. "Go, sell everything you have and give to the poor, and you will have treasure in heaven. Then come, follow me."

²²At this the man's face fell. He went away sad, because he had great wealth.

²³Jesus looked around and said to his disciples, "How hard it is for the rich to enter the kingdom of God!"

²⁴The disciples were amazed at his words. But Jesus said again, "Children, how hard it isᵍ to enter the kingdom of God! ²⁵It is easier for a camel to go through the eye of a needle than for a rich man to enter the kingdom of God."

²⁶The disciples were even more amazed, and said to each other, "Who then can be saved?"

ᵃ45 Some manuscripts *hell*, ⁴⁶*where / " 'their worm does not die, / and the fire is not quenched.'* ᵇ48 Isaiah 66:24   ᶜ6 Gen. 1:27   ᵈ7 Some early manuscripts do not have *and be united to his wife.*   ᵉ8 Gen. 2:24   ᶠ19 Exodus 20:12-16; Deut. 5:16-20   ᵍ24 Some manuscripts *is for those who trust in riches*

²⁷Jesus looked at them and said, "With man this is impossible, but not with God; all things are possible with God."

²⁸Peter said to him, "We have left everything to follow you!"

²⁹"I tell you the truth," Jesus replied, "no one who has left home or brothers or sisters or mother or father or children or fields for me and the gospel ³⁰will fail to receive a hundred times as much in this present age (homes, brothers, sisters, mothers, children and fields—and with them, persecutions) and in the age to come, eternal life. ³¹But many who are first will be last, and the last first."

Jesus Again Predicts His Death

³²They were on their way up to Jerusalem, with Jesus leading the way, and the disciples were astonished, while those who followed were afraid. Again he took the Twelve aside and told them what was going to happen to him. ³³"We are going up to Jerusalem," he said, "and the Son of Man will be betrayed to the chief priests and teachers of the law. They will condemn him to death and will hand him over to the Gentiles, ³⁴who will mock him and spit on him, flog him and kill him. Three days later he will rise."

The Request of James and John

³⁵Then James and John, the sons of Zebedee, came to him. "Teacher," they said, "we want you to do for us whatever we ask."

³⁶"What do you want me to do for you?" he asked.

³⁷They replied, "Let one of us sit at your right and the other at your left in your glory."

³⁸"You don't know what you are asking," Jesus said. "Can you drink the cup I drink or be baptized with the baptism I am baptized with?"

³⁹"We can," they answered.

Jesus said to them, "You will drink the cup I drink and be baptized with the baptism I am baptized with, ⁴⁰but to sit at my right or left is not for me to grant. These places belong to those for whom they have been prepared."

⁴¹When the ten heard about this, they became indignant with James and John. ⁴²Jesus called them together and said, "You know that those who are regarded as rulers of the

---

LET'S LIVE IT!   Mark 10:35–45

BEING AN IMPORTANT PERSON ➠ Read Mark 10:35–45. Jesus told his disciples that to be really important, they must serve others (Mark 10:43).
    Here are two lists of things children may do. Which list describes a person who is willing to be a servant instead of wanting to be boss? Even boys and girls can be great Christians if they are willing to serve.

List #1
Always wants to be the leader in games.
Brags about high grades.
Wants only the best players on his team.
Always insists "I'm right."
Never listens to others' ideas.

List #2
Takes turns with others being leader.
Helps others out with school work.
Wants friends on team even if they're not best.
Gives in sometimes to others.
Listens to others, and shares own ideas too.

Gentiles lord it over them, and their high officials exercise authority over them. ⁴³Not so with you. Instead, whoever wants to become great among you must be your servant, ⁴⁴and whoever wants to be first must be slave of all. ⁴⁵For even the Son of Man did not come to be served, but to serve, and to give his life as a ransom for many."

Blind Bartimaeus Receives His Sight

⁴⁶Then they came to Jericho. As Jesus and his disciples, together with a large crowd, were leaving the city, a blind man, Bartimaeus (that is, the Son of Timaeus), was sitting by the roadside begging. ⁴⁷When he heard that it was Jesus of Nazareth, he began to shout, "Jesus, Son of David, have mercy on me!"

⁴⁸Many rebuked him and told him to be quiet, but he shouted all the more, "Son of David, have mercy on me!"

⁴⁹Jesus stopped and said, "Call him."

So they called to the blind man, "Cheer up! On your feet! He's calling you." ⁵⁰Throwing his cloak aside, he jumped to his feet and came to Jesus.

⁵¹"What do you want me to do for you?" Jesus asked him.

The blind man said, "Rabbi, I want to see."

⁵²"Go," said Jesus, "your faith has healed you." Immediately he received his sight and followed Jesus along the road.

The Triumphal Entry

11 As they approached Jerusalem and came to Bethphage and Bethany at the Mount of Olives, Jesus sent two of his disciples, ²saying to them, "Go to the village ahead of you, and just as you enter it, you will find a colt tied there, which no one has ever ridden. Untie it and bring it here. ³If anyone asks you, 'Why are you doing this?' tell him,

'The Lord needs it and will send it back here shortly.' "

⁴They went and found a colt outside in the street, tied at a doorway. As they untied it, ⁵some people standing there asked, "What are you doing, untying that colt?" ⁶They answered as Jesus had told them to, and the people let them go. ⁷When they brought the colt to Jesus and threw their cloaks over it, he sat on it. ⁸Many people spread their cloaks on the road, while others spread branches they had cut in the fields. ⁹Those who went ahead and those who followed shouted,

"Hosanna!ᵃ"

"Blessed is he who comes in the name of the Lord!"ᵇ

¹⁰"Blessed is the coming kingdom of our father David!"

"Hosanna in the highest!"

¹¹Jesus entered Jerusalem and went to the temple. He looked around at everything, but since it was already late, he went out to Bethany with the Twelve.

Jesus Clears the Temple

¹²The next day as they were leaving Bethany, Jesus was hungry. ¹³Seeing in the distance a fig tree in leaf, he went to find out if it had any fruit. When he reached it, he found nothing but leaves, because it was not the season for figs. ¹⁴Then he said to the tree, "May no one ever eat fruit from you again." And his disciples heard him say it.

¹⁵On reaching Jerusalem, Jesus entered the temple area and began driving out those who were buying and selling there. He overturned the tables of the money changers and the benches of those selling doves, ¹⁶and would not allow anyone to carry merchandise through the temple courts. ¹⁷And as he taught them, he said, "Is it not written:

ᵃ9 A Hebrew expression meaning "Save!" which became an exclamation of praise; also in verse 10
ᵇ9 Psalm 118:25,26

" 'My house will be called
a house of prayer for all
nations'ᵃ?

But you have made it 'a den of robbers.'ᵇ"

¹⁸The chief priests and the teachers
of the law heard this and began looking for a way to kill him, for they
feared him, because the whole crowd
was amazed at his teaching.

¹⁹When evening came, theyᶜ went
out of the city.

The Withered Fig Tree

²⁰In the morning, as they went
along, they saw the fig tree withered
from the roots. ²¹Peter remembered
and said to Jesus, "Rabbi, look! The
fig tree you cursed has withered!"

²²"Haveᵈ faith in God," Jesus answered. ²³"I tell you the truth, if anyone says to this mountain, 'Go, throw
yourself into the sea,' and does not
doubt in his heart but believes that
what he says will happen, it will be
done for him. ²⁴Therefore I tell you,
whatever you ask for in prayer, believe that you have received it, and it
will be yours. ²⁵And when you stand
praying, if you hold anything against
anyone, forgive him, so that your Fa-

ther in heaven may forgive you your
sins.ᵉ"

The Authority of Jesus Questioned

²⁷They arrived again in Jerusalem,
and while Jesus was walking in the
temple courts, the chief priests, the
teachers of the law and the elders
came to him. ²⁸"By what authority
are you doing these things?" they
asked. "And who gave you authority
to do this?"

²⁹Jesus replied, "I will ask you one
question. Answer me, and I will tell
you by what authority I am doing
these things. ³⁰John's baptism—was
it from heaven, or from men? Tell
me!"

³¹They discussed it among themselves and said, "If we say, 'From
heaven,' he will ask, 'Then why didn't
you believe him?' ³²But if we say,
'From men' ...." (They feared the
people, for everyone held that John
really was a prophet.)

³³So they answered Jesus, "We
don't know."

Jesus said, "Neither will I tell you
by what authority I am doing these
things."

ᵃ17 Isaiah 56:7   ᵇ17 Jer. 7:11   ᶜ19 Some early manuscripts he   ᵈ22 Some early
manuscripts If you have   ᵉ25 Some manuscripts sins. ²⁶But if you do not forgive, neither will your
Father who is in heaven forgive your sins.

Life in Bible Times

CLEARING THE TEMPLE

The great temple in Jeru-
salem had several court-
yards. In the outer court it
had become common for
people to buy and sell animals for the sacrifice.
Jesus was angry about this.
God's temple was for
prayer, not for doing business.

The Parable of the Tenants

12 He then began to speak to them in parables: "A man planted a vineyard. He put a wall around it, dug a pit for the winepress and built a watchtower. Then he rented the vineyard to some farmers and went away on a journey. ²At harvest time he sent a servant to the tenants to collect from them some of the fruit of the vineyard. ³But they seized him, beat him and sent him away empty-handed. ⁴Then he sent another servant to them; they struck this man on the head and treated him shamefully. ⁵He sent still another, and that one they killed. He sent many others; some of them they beat, others they killed.

⁶"He had one left to send, a son, whom he loved. He sent him last of all, saying, 'They will respect my son.'

⁷"But the tenants said to one another, 'This is the heir. Come, let's kill him, and the inheritance will be ours.' ⁸So they took him and killed him, and threw him out of the vineyard.

⁹"What then will the owner of the vineyard do? He will come and kill those tenants and give the vineyard to others. ¹⁰Haven't you read this scripture:

" 'The stone the builders rejected
    has become the capstone*a*;
¹¹the Lord has done this,
    and it is marvelous in our
        eyes'*b*?"

¹²Then they looked for a way to arrest him because they knew he had spoken the parable against them. But they were afraid of the crowd; so they left him and went away.

Paying Taxes to Caesar

¹³Later they sent some of the Pharisees and Herodians to Jesus to catch him in his words. ¹⁴They came to him and said, "Teacher, we know you are a man of integrity. You aren't swayed by men, because you pay no attention to who they are; but you teach the way of God in accordance with the truth. Is it right to pay taxes to Caesar or not? ¹⁵Should we pay or shouldn't we?"

But Jesus knew their hypocrisy. "Why are you trying to trap me?" he asked. "Bring me a denarius and let me look at it." ¹⁶They brought the coin, and he asked them, "Whose portrait is this? And whose inscription?"

"Caesar's," they replied.

¹⁷Then Jesus said to them, "Give to Caesar what is Caesar's and to God what is God's."

And they were amazed at him.

Marriage at the Resurrection

¹⁸Then the Sadducees, who say there is no resurrection, came to him with a question. ¹⁹"Teacher," they said, "Moses wrote for us that if a man's brother dies and leaves a wife but no children, the man must marry the widow and have children for his brother. ²⁰Now there were seven brothers. The first one married and died without leaving any children. ²¹The second one married the widow, but he also died, leaving no child. It was the same with the third. ²²In fact, none of the seven left any children.

---

a10 Or *cornerstone*   *b11* Psalm 118:22,23

Last of all, the woman died too. ²³At the resurrection^a whose wife will she be, since the seven were married to her?"

²⁴Jesus replied, "Are you not in error because you do not know the Scriptures or the power of God? ²⁵When the dead rise, they will neither marry nor be given in marriage; they will be like the angels in heaven. ²⁶Now about the dead rising— have you not read in the book of Moses, in the account of the bush, how God said to him, 'I am the God of Abraham, the God of Isaac, and the God of Jacob'^b? ²⁷He is not the God of the dead, but of the living. You are badly mistaken!"

The Greatest Commandment

²⁸One of the teachers of the law came and heard them debating. Noticing that Jesus had given them a good answer, he asked him, "Of all the commandments, which is the most important?"

²⁹"The most important one," answered Jesus, "is this: 'Hear, O Israel, the Lord our God, the Lord is one.^c ³⁰Love the Lord your God with all your heart and with all your soul and with all your mind and with all your strength.'^d ³¹The second is this: 'Love your neighbor as yourself.'^e There is no commandment greater than these."

WORDS TO REMEMBER

12:30-31 Love the Lord your God with all your heart and with all your soul and with all your mind and with all your strength.... Love your neighbor as yourself. There is no commandment greater than these.

³²"Well said, teacher," the man replied. "You are right in saying that

God is one and there is no other but him. ³³To love him with all your heart, with all your understanding and with all your strength, and to love your neighbor as yourself is more important than all burnt offerings and sacrifices."

³⁴When Jesus saw that he had answered wisely, he said to him, "You are not far from the kingdom of God." And from then on no one dared ask him any more questions.

Whose Son Is the Christ?

³⁵While Jesus was teaching in the temple courts, he asked, "How is it that the teachers of the law say that the Christ^f is the son of David? ³⁶David himself, speaking by the Holy Spirit, declared:

" 'The Lord said to my Lord:
    "Sit at my right hand
until I put your enemies
    under your feet." '^g

³⁷David himself calls him 'Lord.' How then can he be his son?"

The large crowd listened to him with delight.

³⁸As he taught, Jesus said, "Watch out for the teachers of the law. They like to walk around in flowing robes and be greeted in the marketplaces, ³⁹and have the most important seats in the synagogues and the places of honor at banquets. ⁴⁰They devour widows' houses and for a show make lengthy prayers. Such men will be punished most severely."

The Widow's Offering

⁴¹Jesus sat down opposite the place where the offerings were put and watched the crowd putting their money into the temple treasury. Many rich people threw in large amounts. ⁴²But a poor widow came and put in two very small copper coins,^h worth only a fraction of a penny.ⁱ

⁴³Calling his disciples to him,

Jesus said, "I tell you the truth, this poor widow has put more into the treasury than all the others. 44They all gave out of their wealth; but she, out of her poverty, put in everything—all she had to live on."

Signs of the End of the Age

13 As he was leaving the temple, one of his disciples said to him, "Look, Teacher! What massive stones! What magnificent buildings!"

2"Do you see all these great buildings?" replied Jesus. "Not one stone here will be left on another; every one will be thrown down."

3As Jesus was sitting on the Mount of Olives opposite the temple, Peter, James, John and Andrew asked him privately, 4"Tell us, when will these things happen? And what will be the sign that they are all about to be fulfilled?"

5Jesus said to them: "Watch out that no one deceives you. 6Many will come in my name, claiming, 'I am he,' and will deceive many. 7When you hear of wars and rumors of wars, do not be alarmed. Such things must happen, but the end is still to come. 8Nation will rise against nation, and kingdom against kingdom. There will be earthquakes in various places, and famines. These are the beginning of birth pains.

9"You must be on your guard. You will be handed over to the local councils and flogged in the synagogues. On account of me you will stand before governors and kings as witnesses to them. 10And the gospel must first be preached to all nations. 11Whenever you are arrested and brought to trial, do not worry beforehand about what to say. Just say whatever is given you at the time, for it is not you speaking, but the Holy Spirit.

12"Brother will betray brother to death, and a father his child. Children will rebel against their parents and have them put to death. 13All men will hate you because of me, but he who stands firm to the end will be saved.

14"When you see 'the abomination that causes desolation'a standing where itb does not belong—let the reader understand—then let those who are in Judea flee to the mountains. 15Let no one on the roof of his house go down or enter the house to take anything out. 16Let no one in the field go back to get his cloak. 17How dreadful it will be in those days for pregnant women and nursing mothers! 18Pray that this will not take place in winter, 19because those will be days of distress unequaled from the beginning, when God created the world, until now—and never to be equaled again. 20If the Lord had not cut short those days, no one would survive. But for the sake of the elect, whom he has chosen, he has shortened them. 21At that time if anyone says to you, 'Look, here is the Christc!' or, 'Look, there he is!' do not believe it. 22For false Christs and false prophets will appear and perform signs and miracles to deceive the elect—if that were possible. 23So be on your guard; I have told you everything ahead of time.

24"But in those days, following that distress,

" 'the sun will be darkened,
    and the moon will not give its
      light;
25the stars will fall from the sky,
    and the heavenly bodies will be
      shaken.'d

26"At that time men will see the Son of Man coming in clouds with great power and glory. 27And he will send his angels and gather his elect from the four winds, from the ends of the earth to the ends of the heavens.

28"Now learn this lesson from the fig tree: As soon as its twigs get tender and its leaves come out, you know that summer is near. 29Even so, when you see these things happening, you

---

a14 Daniel 9:27; 11:31; 12:11   b14 Or he; also in verse 29   c21 Or Messiah   d25 Isaiah 13:10; 34:4

know that it is near, right at the door. 30I tell you the truth, this generationa will certainly not pass away until all these things have happened. 31Heaven and earth will pass away, but my words will never pass away.

WORDS TO REMEMBER

13:26 Men will see the Son of Man coming in clouds with great power and glory.

The Day and Hour Unknown

32"No one knows about that day or hour, not even the angels in heaven, nor the Son, but only the Father. 33Be on guard! Be alertb! You do not know when that time will come. 34It's like a man going away: He leaves his house and puts his servants in charge, each with his assigned task, and tells the one at the door to keep watch.

35"Therefore keep watch because you do not know when the owner of the house will come back—whether in the evening, or at midnight, or when the rooster crows, or at dawn. 36If he comes suddenly, do not let him find you sleeping. 37What I say to you, I say to everyone: 'Watch!' "

Jesus Anointed at Bethany

14 Now the Passover and the Feast of Unleavened Bread were only two days away, and the chief priests and the teachers of the law were looking for some sly way to arrest Jesus and kill him. 2"But not during the Feast," they said, "or the people may riot."

3While he was in Bethany, reclining at the table in the home of a man known as Simon the Leper, a woman came with an alabaster jar of very expensive perfume, made of pure nard. She broke the jar and poured the perfume on his head.

4Some of those present were saying indignantly to one another, "Why

this waste of perfume? 5It could have been sold for more than a year's wagesc and the money given to the poor." And they rebuked her harshly.

6"Leave her alone," said Jesus. "Why are you bothering her? She has done a beautiful thing to me. 7The poor you will always have with you, and you can help them any time you want. But you will not always have me. 8She did what she could. She poured perfume on my body beforehand to prepare for my burial. 9I tell you the truth, wherever the gospel is preached throughout the world, what she has done will also be told, in memory of her."

10Then Judas Iscariot, one of the Twelve, went to the chief priests to betray Jesus to them. 11They were delighted to hear this and promised to give him money. So he watched for an opportunity to hand him over.

The Lord's Supper

12On the first day of the Feast of Unleavened Bread, when it was customary to sacrifice the Passover lamb, Jesus' disciples asked him, "Where do you want us to go and make preparations for you to eat the Passover?"

13So he sent two of his disciples, telling them, "Go into the city, and a man carrying a jar of water will meet you. Follow him. 14Say to the owner of the house he enters, 'The Teacher asks: Where is my guest room, where I may eat the Passover with my disciples?' 15He will show you a large upper room, furnished and ready. Make preparations for us there."

16The disciples left, went into the city and found things just as Jesus had told them. So they prepared the Passover.

17When evening came, Jesus arrived with the Twelve. 18While they were reclining at the table eating, he said, "I tell you the truth, one of you will betray me—one who is eating with me."

19They were saddened, and one by

---

a30 Or race   b33 Some manuscripts alert and pray   c5 Greek than three hundred denarii one they said to him, "Surely not I?"

²⁰"It is one of the Twelve," he replied, "one who dips bread into the bowl with me. ²¹The Son of Man will go just as it is written about him. But woe to that man who betrays the Son of Man! It would be better for him if he had not been born."

²²While they were eating, Jesus took bread, gave thanks and broke it, and gave it to his disciples, saying, "Take it; this is my body."

²³Then he took the cup, gave thanks and offered it to them, and they all drank from it.

THE LORD'S SUPPER

Jesus told his disciples to celebrate the Lord's Supper, or Communion. The drink reminds us that Jesus shed his blood for us. The bread reminds us that his body was broken on the cross.

²⁴"This is my blood of the ᵃ covenant, which is poured out for many," he said to them. ²⁵"I tell you the truth, I will not drink again of the fruit of the vine until that day when I drink it anew in the kingdom of God."

²⁶When they had sung a hymn, they went out to the Mount of Olives.

Jesus Predicts Peter's Denial

²⁷"You will all fall away," Jesus told them, "for it is written:

"'I will strike the shepherd,
　and the sheep will be
　　scattered.'ᵇ

²⁸But after I have risen, I will go ahead of you into Galilee."

²⁹Peter declared, "Even if all fall away, I will not."

³⁰"I tell you the truth," Jesus answered, "today—yes, tonight—before the rooster crows twiceᶜ you yourself will disown me three times."

³¹But Peter insisted emphatically, "Even if I have to die with you, I will never disown you." And all the others said the same.

Gethsemane

³²They went to a place called Gethsemane, and Jesus said to his disciples, "Sit here while I pray." ³³He took Peter, James and John along with him, and he began to be deeply distressed and troubled. ³⁴"My soul is overwhelmed with sorrow to the point of death," he said to them. "Stay here and keep watch."

³⁵Going a little farther, he fell to the ground and prayed that if possible the hour might pass from him. ³⁶"Abba,ᵈ Father," he said, "everything is possible for you. Take this cup from me. Yet not what I will, but what you will."

³⁷Then he returned to his disciples and found them sleeping. "Simon," he said to Peter, "are you asleep? Could you not keep watch for one hour? ³⁸Watch and pray so that you will not fall into temptation. The spirit is willing, but the body is weak."

³⁹Once more he went away and prayed the same thing. ⁴⁰When he came back, he again found them sleeping, because their eyes were heavy. They did not know what to say to him.

⁴¹Returning the third time, he said to them, "Are you still sleeping and resting? Enough! The hour has come. Look, the Son of Man is betrayed into the hands of sinners. ⁴²Rise! Let us go! Here comes my betrayer!"

Jesus Arrested

⁴³Just as he was speaking, Judas, one of the Twelve, appeared. With

---

ᵃ24 Some manuscripts *the new*　　ᵇ27 Zech. 13:7　　ᶜ30 Some early manuscripts do not have
twice.　　ᵈ36 Aramaic for *Father*

him was a crowd armed with swords and clubs, sent from the chief priests, the teachers of the law, and the elders.

⁴⁴Now the betrayer had arranged a signal with them: "The one I kiss is the man; arrest him and lead him away under guard." ⁴⁵Going at once to Jesus, Judas said, "Rabbi!" and kissed him. ⁴⁶The men seized Jesus and arrested him. ⁴⁷Then one of those standing near drew his sword and struck the servant of the high priest, cutting off his ear.

⁴⁸"Am I leading a rebellion," said Jesus, "that you have come out with swords and clubs to capture me? ⁴⁹Every day I was with you, teaching in the temple courts, and you did not arrest me. But the Scriptures must be fulfilled." ⁵⁰Then everyone deserted him and fled.

⁵¹A young man, wearing nothing but a linen garment, was following Jesus. When they seized him, ⁵²he fled naked, leaving his garment behind.

Before the Sanhedrin

⁵³They took Jesus to the high priest, and all the chief priests, elders and teachers of the law came together. ⁵⁴Peter followed him at a distance, right into the courtyard of the high priest. There he sat with the guards and warmed himself at the fire.

⁵⁵The chief priests and the whole Sanhedrin were looking for evidence against Jesus so that they could put him to death, but they did not find any. ⁵⁶Many testified falsely against him, but their statements did not agree.

⁵⁷Then some stood up and gave this false testimony against him: ⁵⁸"We heard him say, 'I will destroy this man-made temple and in three days will build another, not made by man.'" ⁵⁹Yet even then their testimony did not agree.

⁶⁰Then the high priest stood up before them and asked Jesus, "Are you

not going to answer? What is this testimony that these men are bringing against you?" ⁶¹But Jesus remained silent and gave no answer.

Again the high priest asked him, "Are you the Christ,ᵃ the Son of the Blessed One?"

⁶²"I am," said Jesus. "And you will see the Son of Man sitting at the right hand of the Mighty One and coming on the clouds of heaven."

⁶³The high priest tore his clothes. "Why do we need any more witnesses?" he asked. ⁶⁴"You have heard the blasphemy. What do you think?"

They all condemned him as worthy of death. ⁶⁵Then some began to spit at him; they blindfolded him, struck him with their fists, and said, "Prophesy!" And the guards took him and beat him.

Peter Disowns Jesus

⁶⁶While Peter was below in the courtyard, one of the servant girls of the high priest came by. ⁶⁷When she saw Peter warming himself, she looked closely at him.

"You also were with that Nazarene, Jesus," she said.

⁶⁸But he denied it. "I don't know or understand what you're talking about," he said, and went out into the entryway.ᵇ

⁶⁹When the servant girl saw him there, she said again to those standing around, "This fellow is one of them." ⁷⁰Again he denied it.

After a little while, those standing near said to Peter, "Surely you are one of them, for you are a Galilean."

⁷¹He began to call down curses on himself, and he swore to them, "I don't know this man you're talking about."

⁷²Immediately the rooster crowed the second time.ᶜ Then Peter remembered the word Jesus had spoken to him: "Before the rooster crows twiceᵈ you will disown me three times." And he broke down and wept.

ᵃ61 Or *Messiah*　ᵇ68 Some early manuscripts *entryway and the rooster crowed*　ᶜ72 Some early manuscripts do not have *the second time.*　ᵈ72 Some early manuscripts do not have *twice.*

Jesus Before Pilate

15 Very early in the morning, the chief priests, with the elders, the teachers of the law and the whole Sanhedrin, reached a decision. They bound Jesus, led him away and handed him over to Pilate.

2"Are you the king of the Jews?" asked Pilate.

"Yes, it is as you say," Jesus replied.

3The chief priests accused him of many things. 4So again Pilate asked him, "Aren't you going to answer? See how many things they are accusing you of."

5But Jesus still made no reply, and Pilate was amazed.

6Now it was the custom at the Feast to release a prisoner whom the people requested. 7A man called Barabbas was in prison with the insurrectionists who had committed murder in the uprising. 8The crowd came up and asked Pilate to do for them what he usually did.

9"Do you want me to release to you the king of the Jews?" asked Pilate, 10knowing it was out of envy that the chief priests had handed Jesus over to him. 11But the chief priests stirred up the crowd to have Pilate release Barabbas instead.

12"What shall I do, then, with the one you call the king of the Jews?" Pilate asked them.

13"Crucify him!" they shouted.

14"Why? What crime has he committed?" asked Pilate.

But they shouted all the louder, "Crucify him!"

15Wanting to satisfy the crowd, Pilate released Barabbas to them. He had Jesus flogged, and handed him over to be crucified.

The Soldiers Mock Jesus

16The soldiers led Jesus away into the palace (that is, the Praetorium) and called together the whole company of soldiers. 17They put a purple robe on him, then twisted together a crown of thorns and set it on him. 18And they began to call out to him, "Hail, king of the Jews!" 19Again and again they struck him on the head with a staff and spit on him. Falling on their knees, they paid homage to him. 20And when they had mocked him, they took off the purple robe and put his own clothes on him. Then they led him out to crucify him.

FLOGGING

Before Roman prisoners were crucified, they were beaten with a whip. This whip had sharp pieces of metal or bone in its lashes. Such a whipping drew so much blood that the prisoners died more quickly on the cross.

The Crucifixion

21A certain man from Cyrene, Simon, the father of Alexander and Rufus, was passing by on his way in from the country, and they forced him to carry the cross. 22They brought Jesus to the place called Golgotha (which means The Place of the Skull). 23Then they offered him wine mixed with myrrh, but he did not take it. 24And they crucified him. Dividing up his clothes, they cast lots to see what each would get.

25It was the third hour when they crucified him. 26The written notice of the charge against him read: THE KING OF THE JEWS. 27They crucified two robbers with him, one on his right and one on his left.ᵃ 29Those who passed by hurled insults at him, shaking their heads and saying, "So! You who are going to destroy the

---

ᵃ27 Some manuscripts *left,* 28*and the scripture was fulfilled which says, "He was counted with the lawless ones"* (Isaiah 53:12)

temple and build it in three days, ³⁰come down from the cross and save yourself!"

³¹In the same way the chief priests and the teachers of the law mocked him among themselves. "He saved others," they said, "but he can't save himself! ³²Let this Christ,ᵃ this King of Israel, come down now from the cross, that we may see and believe." Those crucified with him also heaped insults on him.

The Death of Jesus

³³At the sixth hour darkness came over the whole land until the ninth hour. ³⁴And at the ninth hour Jesus cried out in a loud voice, *"Eloi, Eloi, lama sabachthani?"*—which means, "My God, my God, why have you forsaken me?"ᵇ

³⁵When some of those standing near heard this, they said, "Listen, he's calling Elijah."

³⁶One man ran, filled a sponge with wine vinegar, put it on a stick, and offered it to Jesus to drink. "Now leave him alone. Let's see if Elijah comes to take him down," he said.

³⁷With a loud cry, Jesus breathed his last.

³⁸The curtain of the temple was torn in two from top to bottom. ³⁹And when the centurion, who stood there in front of Jesus, heard his cry andᶜ saw how he died, he said, "Surely this man was the Sonᵈ of God!"

⁴⁰Some women were watching from a distance. Among them were Mary Magdalene, Mary the mother of James the younger and of Joses, and Salome. ⁴¹In Galilee these women had followed him and cared for his needs. Many other women who had come up with him to Jerusalem were also there.

The Burial of Jesus

⁴²It was Preparation Day (that is, the day before the Sabbath). So as evening approached, ⁴³Joseph of Arimathea, a prominent member of the Council, who was himself waiting for the kingdom of God, went boldly to Pilate and asked for Jesus' body. ⁴⁴Pilate was surprised to hear that he was already dead. Summoning the centurion, he asked him if Jesus had already died. ⁴⁵When he learned from the centurion that it was so, he gave the body to Joseph. ⁴⁶So Joseph bought some linen cloth, took down the body, wrapped it in the linen, and placed it in a tomb cut out of rock. Then he rolled a stone against the entrance of the tomb. ⁴⁷Mary Magdalene and Mary the mother of Joses saw where he was laid.

The Resurrection

16 When the Sabbath was over, Mary Magdalene, Mary the mother of James, and Salome bought spices so that they might go to anoint Jesus' body. ²Very early on the first day of the week, just after sunrise, they were on their way to the tomb ³and they asked each other, "Who will roll the stone away from the entrance of the tomb?"

⁴But when they looked up, they saw that the stone, which was very large, had been rolled away. ⁵As they entered the tomb, they saw a young man dressed in a white robe sitting on the right side, and they were alarmed.

⁶"Don't be alarmed," he said. "You are looking for Jesus the Nazarene, who was crucified. He has risen! He is not here. See the place where they laid him. ⁷But go, tell his disciples and Peter, 'He is going ahead of you into Galilee. There you will see him, just as he told you.'"

⁸Trembling and bewildered, the women went out and fled from the tomb. They said nothing to anyone, because they were afraid.

[The most reliable early manuscripts and other ancient witnesses do not have Mark 16:9–20.]

ᵃ32 Or *Messiah*　　ᵇ34 Psalm 22:1　　ᶜ39 Some manuscripts do not have *heard his cry and*
ᵈ39 Or *a son*

⁹When Jesus rose early on the first day of the week, he appeared first to Mary Magdalene, out of whom he had driven seven demons. ¹⁰She went and told those who had been with him and who were mourning and weeping. ¹¹When they heard that Jesus was alive and that she had seen him, they did not believe it.

¹²Afterward Jesus appeared in a different form to two of them while they were walking in the country. ¹³These returned and reported it to the rest; but they did not believe them either.

¹⁴Later Jesus appeared to the Eleven as they were eating; he rebuked them for their lack of faith and their stubborn refusal to believe those who had seen him after he had risen.

¹⁵He said to them, "Go into all the world and preach the good news to all creation. ¹⁶Whoever believes and is baptized will be saved, but whoever does not believe will be condemned. ¹⁷And these signs will accompany those who believe: In my name they will drive out demons; they will speak in new tongues; ¹⁸they will pick up snakes with their hands; and when they drink deadly poison, it will not hurt them at all; they will place their hands on sick people, and they will get well."

¹⁹After the Lord Jesus had spoken to them, he was taken up into heaven and he sat at the right hand of God. ²⁰Then the disciples went out and preached everywhere, and the Lord worked with them and confirmed his word by the signs that accompanied it.

LUKE

WHO WROTE THIS BOOK?	Luke, a physician who often traveled with Paul, wrote this book.
WHY WAS THIS BOOK WRITTEN?	Luke tells what many people who knew Jesus remembered of his life and teaching.
FOR WHOM WAS THIS BOOK WRITTEN?	Luke wrote for people who wanted to know the kind of person Jesus was.
WHAT HAPPENS IN THIS BOOK?	Jesus meets, teaches and helps many different kinds of people.
WHO IS IMPORTANT IN THIS BOOK?	Jesus is the important person in this book.
WHEN DID THIS HAPPEN?	Jesus traveled and taught from A.D. 26 to 30.
WHERE DID THIS HAPPEN?	Most of the events in this book happened in Galilee and Judea.

Introduction

1 Many have undertaken to draw up an account of the things that have been fulfilled[a] among us, [2]just as they were handed down to us by those who from the first were eyewitnesses and servants of the word. [3]Therefore, since I myself have carefully investigated everything from the beginning, it seemed good also to me to write an orderly account for you, most excellent Theophilus, [4]so that you may know the certainty of the things you have been taught.

The Birth of John the Baptist Foretold

[5]In the time of Herod king of Judea there was a priest named Zechariah, who belonged to the priestly division of Abijah; his wife Elizabeth was also a descendant of Aaron. [6]Both of them were upright in the sight of God, observing all the Lord's commandments and regulations blamelessly. [7]But they had no children, because Elizabeth was barren; and they were both well along in years.

[8]Once when Zechariah's division was on duty and he was serving as priest before God, [9]he was chosen by lot, according to the custom of the priesthood, to go into the temple of the Lord and burn incense. [10]And when the time for the burning of incense came, all the assembled worshipers were praying outside.

[11]Then an angel of the Lord appeared to him, standing at the right side of the altar of incense. [12]When Zechariah saw him, he was startled and was gripped with fear. [13]But the angel said to him: "Do not be afraid, Zechariah; your prayer has been heard. Your wife Elizabeth will bear you a son, and you are to give him the name John. [14]He will be a joy and delight to you, and many will rejoice because of his birth, [15]for he will be great in the sight of the Lord. He is never to take wine or other fermented drink, and he will be filled with the Holy Spirit even from birth.[b] [16]Many of the people of Israel will he bring back to the Lord their God. [17]And he will go on before the Lord, in the spirit and power of Elijah, to turn the hearts of the fathers to their children and the disobedient to the wisdom of the righteous—to make ready a people prepared for the Lord."

[18]Zechariah asked the angel, "How can I be sure of this? I am an old man and my wife is well along in years."

[19]The angel answered, "I am Gabriel. I stand in the presence of God, and I have been sent to speak to you and to tell you this good news. [20]And now you will be silent and not able to speak until the day this happens, because you did not believe my words, which will come true at their proper time."

[21]Meanwhile, the people were waiting for Zechariah and wondering why he stayed so long in the temple. [22]When he came out, he could not speak to them. They realized he had seen a vision in the temple, for he kept making signs to them but remained unable to speak.

[23]When his time of service was completed, he returned home. [24]After this his wife Elizabeth became pregnant and for five months remained in seclusion. [25]"The Lord has done this for me," she said. "In these days he has shown his favor and taken away my disgrace among the people."

The Birth of Jesus Foretold

[26]In the sixth month, God sent the angel Gabriel to Nazareth, a town in Galilee, [27]to a virgin pledged to be married to a man named Joseph, a descendant of David. The virgin's name was Mary. [28]The angel went to her and said, "Greetings, you who are highly favored! The Lord is with you."

[29]Mary was greatly troubled at his words and wondered what kind of greeting this might be. [30]But the angel said to her, "Do not be afraid,

---

a1 Or been surely believed   *b15 Or from his mother's womb*

Mary, you have found favor with God. ³¹You will be with child and give birth to a son, and you are to give him the name Jesus. ³²He will be great and will be called the Son of the Most High. The Lord God will give him the throne of his father David, ³³and he will reign over the house of Jacob forever; his kingdom will never end."

³⁴"How will this be," Mary asked the angel, "since I am a virgin?"

³⁵The angel answered, "The Holy Spirit will come upon you, and the power of the Most High will overshadow you. So the holy one to be born will be called ᵃ the Son of God. ³⁶Even Elizabeth your relative is going to have a child in her old age, and she who was said to be barren is in her sixth month. ³⁷For nothing is impossible with God."

³⁸"I am the Lord's servant," Mary answered. "May it be to me as you have said." Then the angel left her.

Mary Visits Elizabeth

³⁹At that time Mary got ready and hurried to a town in the hill country of Judea, ⁴⁰where she entered Zechariah's home and greeted Elizabeth. ⁴¹When Elizabeth heard Mary's greeting, the baby leaped in her womb, and Elizabeth was filled with the Holy Spirit. ⁴²In a loud voice she exclaimed: "Blessed are you among women, and blessed is the child you will bear! ⁴³But why am I so favored, that the mother of my Lord should

come to me? ⁴⁴As soon as the sound of your greeting reached my ears, the baby in my womb leaped for joy. ⁴⁵Blessed is she who has believed that what the Lord has said to her will be accomplished!"

Mary's Song

⁴⁶And Mary said:

"My soul glorifies the Lord
⁴⁷ and my spirit rejoices in God
    my Savior,
⁴⁸for he has been mindful
    of the humble state of his
    servant.
From now on all generations will
    call me blessed,
⁴⁹ for the Mighty One has done
    great things for me—
holy is his name.
⁵⁰His mercy extends to those who
    fear him,
from generation to generation.
⁵¹He has performed mighty deeds
    with his arm;
he has scattered those who are
    proud in their inmost
    thoughts.
⁵²He has brought down rulers from
    their thrones
but has lifted up the humble.
⁵³He has filled the hungry with
    good things
but has sent the rich away
    empty.
⁵⁴He has helped his servant Israel,
    remembering to be merciful

ᵃ35 Or *So the child to be born will be called holy,*

⬛ET'S LIVE IT!   Luke 1:26–38

MARY CAN BE OUR EXAMPLE ➡ Many Bible people are good examples for us to follow. Mary is one of the best. Mary was a young woman, engaged to Joseph. When an angel told Mary that God had chosen her to have the Christ child, Mary must have worried. What would Joseph and other people think if she had a baby when she was not married? Read Luke 1:26–38. What did Mary decide?

With one of your parents, talk about times when it is hard to do what God wants because others might laugh at you or be angry with you. When you do what God wants, no matter what others may think, you follow Mary's good example.

55to Abraham and his descendants
forever,
even as he said to our fathers."

56Mary stayed with Elizabeth for
about three months and then returned home.

?DID YOU KNOW?   1:46

What is Mary's song?

This is the song Mary sang when
she visited Elizabeth. Mary praised
God for letting her become the
mother of the Savior. Mary was a
wonderful young woman, with a
wonderful faith in God.

The Birth of John the Baptist

57When it was time for Elizabeth to
have her baby, she gave birth to a
son. 58Her neighbors and relatives
heard that the Lord had shown her
great mercy, and they shared her joy.
59On the eighth day they came to
circumcise the child, and they were
going to name him after his father
Zechariah, 60but his mother spoke up
and said, "No! He is to be called
John."

61They said to her, "There is no one
among your relatives who has that
name."

62Then they made signs to his father, to find out what he would like to
name the child. 63He asked for a writing tablet, and to everyone's astonishment he wrote, "His name is
John." 64Immediately his mouth was
opened and his tongue was loosed,
and he began to speak, praising God.
65The neighbors were all filled with
awe, and throughout the hill country
of Judea people were talking about
all these things. 66Everyone who
heard this wondered about it, asking,
"What then is this child going to be?"
For the Lord's hand was with him.

Zechariah's Song

67His father Zechariah was filled
with the Holy Spirit and prophesied:

68"Praise be to the Lord, the God of
Israel,
because he has come and has
redeemed his people.
69He has raised up a horn*a* of
salvation for us
in the house of his servant
David
70(as he said through his holy
prophets of long ago),
71salvation from our enemies
and from the hand of all who
hate us—
72to show mercy to our fathers
and to remember his holy
covenant,
73   the oath he swore to our father
Abraham:
74to rescue us from the hand of our
enemies,
and to enable us to serve him
without fear
75   in holiness and righteousness
before him all our days.

76And you, my child, will be called
a prophet of the Most High;
for you will go on before the
Lord to prepare the way for
him,
77to give his people the knowledge
of salvation
through the forgiveness of their
sins,
78because of the tender mercy of
our God,
by which the rising sun will
come to us from heaven
79to shine on those living in
darkness
and in the shadow of death,
to guide our feet into the path of
peace."

80And the child grew and became
strong in spirit; and he lived in the
desert until he appeared publicly to
Israel.

The Birth of Jesus

2 In those days Caesar Augustus
issued a decree that a census
should be taken of the entire Roman
world. 2(This was the first census

a69 Horn here symbolizes strength.

that took place while Quirinius was governor of Syria.) ³And everyone went to his own town to register.

⁴So Joseph also went up from the town of Nazareth in Galilee to Judea, to Bethlehem the town of David, because he belonged to the house and line of David. ⁵He went there to register with Mary, who was pledged to be married to him and was expecting a child. ⁶While they were there, the time came for the baby to be born, ⁷and she gave birth to her firstborn, a son. She wrapped him in cloths and placed him in a manger, because there was no room for them in the inn.

The Shepherds and the Angels

⁸And there were shepherds living out in the fields nearby, keeping watch over their flocks at night. ⁹An angel of the Lord appeared to them, and the glory of the Lord shone around them, and they were terrified. ¹⁰But the angel said to them, "Do not be afraid. I bring you good news of great joy that will be for all the people. ¹¹Today in the town of David a Savior has been born to you; he is Christ*a* the Lord. ¹²This will be a sign to you: You will find a baby wrapped in cloths and lying in a manger."

¹³Suddenly a great company of the heavenly host appeared with the angel, praising God and saying,

¹⁴"Glory to God in the highest,
and on earth peace to men on
whom his favor rests."

¹⁵When the angels had left them and gone into heaven, the shepherds said to one another, "Let's go to Bethlehem and see this thing that has happened, which the Lord has told us about."

¹⁶So they hurried off and found Mary and Joseph, and the baby, who was lying in the manger. ¹⁷When they had seen him, they spread the word concerning what had been told them about this child, ¹⁸and all who heard it were amazed at what the shepherds said to them. ¹⁹But Mary treasured up all these things and pondered them in her heart. ²⁰The shepherds returned, glorifying and praising God for all the things they had heard and seen, which were just as they had been told.

Jesus Presented in the Temple

²¹On the eighth day, when it was time to circumcise him, he was named Jesus, the name the angel had given him before he had been conceived.

²²When the time of their purification according to the Law of Moses had been completed, Joseph and Mary took him to Jerusalem to present him to the Lord ²³(as it is

*a*11 Or *Messiah.* "The Christ" (Greek) and "the Messiah" (Hebrew) both mean "the Anointed One"; also in verse 26.

Life in Bible Times

THE STABLE

In Bethlehem cattle were usually kept in a cave rather than a building. The stable where Jesus was born was probably one of these caves.

written in the Law of the Lord, "Every firstborn male is to be consecrated to the Lord"[a]), [24]and to offer a sacrifice in keeping with what is said in the Law of the Lord: "a pair of doves or two young pigeons."[b]

[25]Now there was a man in Jerusalem called Simeon, who was righteous and devout. He was waiting for the consolation of Israel, and the Holy Spirit was upon him. [26]It had been revealed to him by the Holy Spirit that he would not die before he had seen the Lord's Christ. [27]Moved by the Spirit, he went into the temple courts. When the parents brought in the child Jesus to do for him what the custom of the Law required, [28]Simeon took him in his arms and praised God, saying:

[29]"Sovereign Lord, as you have promised,
    you now dismiss[c] your servant in peace.
[30]For my eyes have seen your salvation,
[31]   which you have prepared in the sight of all people,
[32]a light for revelation to the Gentiles
    and for glory to your people Israel."

[33]The child's father and mother marveled at what was said about him. [34]Then Simeon blessed them and said to Mary, his mother: "This child is destined to cause the falling and rising of many in Israel, and to be a sign that will be spoken against, [35]so that the thoughts of many hearts will be revealed. And a sword will pierce your own soul too."

[36]There was also a prophetess, Anna, the daughter of Phanuel, of the tribe of Asher. She was very old; she had lived with her husband seven years after her marriage, [37]and then was a widow until she was eighty-four.[d] She never left the temple but worshiped night and day, fasting and praying. [38]Coming up to them at that very moment, she gave thanks to God and spoke about the child to all who were looking forward to the redemption of Jerusalem.

[39]When Joseph and Mary had done everything required by the Law of the Lord, they returned to Galilee to their own town of Nazareth. [40]And the child grew and became strong; he was filled with wisdom, and the grace of God was upon him.

The Boy Jesus at the Temple

[41]Every year his parents went to Jerusalem for the Feast of the Passover. [42]When he was twelve years old, they went up to the Feast, according to the custom. [43]After the Feast was over, while his parents were returning home, the boy Jesus

---

[a]23 Exodus 13:2,12   [b]24 Lev. 12:8   [c]29 Or promised, / now dismiss   [d]37 Or widow for eighty-four years

stayed behind in Jerusalem, but they were unaware of it. ⁴⁴Thinking he was in their company, they traveled on for a day. Then they began looking for him among their relatives and friends. ⁴⁵When they did not find him, they went back to Jerusalem to look for him. ⁴⁶After three days they found him in the temple courts, sitting among the teachers, listening to them and asking them questions. ⁴⁷Everyone who heard him was amazed at his understanding and his answers. ⁴⁸When his parents saw him, they were astonished. His mother said to him, "Son, why have you treated us like this? Your father and I have been anxiously searching for you."

⁴⁹"Why were you searching for me?" he asked. "Didn't you know I had to be in my Father's house?" ⁵⁰But they did not understand what he was saying to them.

⁵¹Then he went down to Nazareth with them and was obedient to them. But his mother treasured all these things in her heart. ⁵²And Jesus grew in wisdom and stature, and in favor with God and men.

❓DID YOU KNOW?   **2:42**

Why did Jesus go to the temple when he was twelve?

At twelve a Jewish boy was considered old enough to keep God's law as an adult. The Old Testament said Jewish men were supposed to go to the temple to worship on the Passover. Now that Jesus was twelve, he went to Jerusalem to celebrate the Passover in the temple.

John the Baptist Prepares the Way

3 In the fifteenth year of the reign of Tiberius Caesar—when Pontius Pilate was governor of Judea, Herod tetrarch of Galilee, his brother Philip tetrarch of Iturea and Traconitis, and Lysanias tetrarch of Abilene— ²during the high priesthood of Annas and Caiaphas, the word of God came to John son of Zechariah in the desert. ³He went into all the country around the Jordan, preaching a baptism of repentance for the forgiveness of sins. ⁴As is written in the book of the words of Isaiah the prophet:

"A voice of one calling in the
        desert,
'Prepare the way for the Lord,
        make straight paths for him.
⁵Every valley shall be filled in,
        every mountain and hill made
        low.
The crooked roads shall become
        straight,
        the rough ways smooth.
⁶And all mankind will see God's
        salvation.' "ᵃ

⁷John said to the crowds coming out to be baptized by him, "You brood of vipers! Who warned you to flee from the coming wrath? ⁸Produce fruit in keeping with repentance. And do not begin to say to yourselves, 'We have Abraham as our father.' For I tell you that out of these stones God can raise up children for Abraham. ⁹The ax is already at the root of the trees, and every tree that does not produce good fruit will be cut down and thrown into the fire."

¹⁰"What should we do then?" the crowd asked.

¹¹John answered, "The man with two tunics should share with him who has none, and the one who has food should do the same."

¹²Tax collectors also came to be baptized. "Teacher," they asked, "what should we do?"

¹³"Don't collect any more than you are required to," he told them.

¹⁴Then some soldiers asked him, "And what should we do?"

He replied, "Don't extort money and don't accuse people falsely—be content with your pay."

a6 Isaiah 40:3-5

[15]The people were waiting expectantly and were all wondering in their hearts if John might possibly be the Christ.[a] [16]John answered them all, "I baptize you with[b] water. But one more powerful than I will come, the thongs of whose sandals I am not worthy to untie. He will baptize you with the Holy Spirit and with fire. [17]His winnowing fork is in his hand to clear his threshing floor and to gather the wheat into his barn, but he will burn up the chaff with unquenchable fire." [18]And with many other words John exhorted the people and preached the good news to them.

[19]But when John rebuked Herod the tetrarch because of Herodias, his brother's wife, and all the other evil things he had done, [20]Herod added this to them all: He locked John up in prison.

The Baptism and Genealogy of Jesus

[21]When all the people were being baptized, Jesus was baptized too. And as he was praying, heaven was opened [22]and the Holy Spirit descended on him in bodily form like a dove. And a voice came from heaven: "You are my Son, whom I love; with you I am well pleased."

[23]Now Jesus himself was about thirty years old when he began his ministry. He was the son, so it was thought, of Joseph,

the son of Heli, [24]the son of Matthat,
the son of Levi, the son of Melki,
the son of Jannai, the son of Joseph,
[25]the son of Mattathias, the son of Amos,
the son of Nahum, the son of Esli,
the son of Naggai, [26]the son of Maath,
the son of Mattathias, the son of Semein,
the son of Josech, the son of Joda,
[27]the son of Joanan, the son of Rhesa,
the son of Zerubbabel, the son of Shealtiel,
the son of Neri, [28]the son of Melki,
the son of Addi, the son of Cosam,
the son of Elmadam, the son of Er,
[29]the son of Joshua, the son of Eliezer,
the son of Jorim, the son of Matthat,
the son of Levi, [30]the son of Simeon,
the son of Judah, the son of Joseph,
the son of Jonam, the son of Eliakim,
[31]the son of Melea, the son of Menna,
the son of Mattatha, the son of Nathan,
the son of David, [32]the son of Jesse,
the son of Obed, the son of Boaz,
the son of Salmon,[c] the son of Nahshon,
[33]the son of Amminadab, the son of Ram,[d]
the son of Hezron, the son of Perez,
the son of Judah, [34]the son of Jacob,
the son of Isaac, the son of Abraham,
the son of Terah, the son of Nahor,
[35]the son of Serug, the son of Reu,
the son of Peleg, the son of Eber,
the son of Shelah, [36]the son of Cainan,
the son of Arphaxad, the son of Shem,
the son of Noah, the son of Lamech,
[37]the son of Methuselah, the son of Enoch,
the son of Jared, the son of Mahalalel,

---

[a]15 Or *Messiah*   [b]16 Or *in*   [c]32 Some early manuscripts *Sala*   [d]33 Some manuscripts *Amminadab, the son of Admin, the son of Arni*; other manuscripts vary widely.

the son of Kenan, 38the son of Enosh,
the son of Seth, the son of Adam, the son of God.

The Temptation of Jesus

4 Jesus, full of the Holy Spirit, returned from the Jordan and was led by the Spirit in the desert, 2where for forty days he was tempted by the devil. He ate nothing during those days, and at the end of them he was hungry.

3The devil said to him, "If you are the Son of God, tell this stone to become bread."

4Jesus answered, "It is written: 'Man does not live on bread alone.'*a*"

5The devil led him up to a high place and showed him in an instant all the kingdoms of the world. 6And he said to him, "I will give you all their authority and splendor, for it has been given to me, and I can give it to anyone I want to. 7So if you worship me, it will all be yours."

8Jesus answered, "It is written: 'Worship the Lord your God and serve him only.'*b*"

9The devil led him to Jerusalem and had him stand on the highest point of the temple. "If you are the Son of God," he said, "throw yourself down from here. 10For it is written:

" 'He will command his angels
    concerning you
to guard you carefully;
11they will lift you up in their
    hands,
so that you will not strike your
    foot against a stone.'*c*"

12Jesus answered, "It says: 'Do not put the Lord your God to the test.'*d*"

13When the devil had finished all this tempting, he left him until an opportune time.

Jesus Rejected at Nazareth

14Jesus returned to Galilee in the power of the Spirit, and news about him spread through the whole coun-

tryside. 15He taught in their synagogues, and everyone praised him.

? DID YOU KNOW?   4:4

How did Jesus overcome temptation?

Jesus remembered teachings from the Bible and decided to obey God's Word. Studying the Bible is the best way to overcome temptation.

16He went to Nazareth, where he had been brought up, and on the Sabbath day he went into the synagogue, as was his custom. And he stood up to read. 17The scroll of the prophet Isaiah was handed to him. Unrolling it, he found the place where it is written:

18"The Spirit of the Lord is on me,
    because he has anointed me
    to preach good news to the poor.
He has sent me to proclaim
    freedom for the prisoners
and recovery of sight for the
    blind,
to release the oppressed,
19   to proclaim the year of the
        Lord's favor."*e*

20Then he rolled up the scroll, gave it back to the attendant and sat down. The eyes of everyone in the synagogue were fastened on him, 21and he began by saying to them, "Today this scripture is fulfilled in your hearing."

22All spoke well of him and were amazed at the gracious words that came from his lips. "Isn't this Joseph's son?" they asked.

23Jesus said to them, "Surely you will quote this proverb to me: 'Physician, heal yourself! Do here in your hometown what we have heard that you did in Capernaum.' "

24"I tell you the truth," he continued, "no prophet is accepted in his hometown. 25I assure you that there

---

a4 Deut. 8:3   *b8* Deut. 6:13   *c11* Psalm 91:11,12   *d12* Deut. 6:16   *e19* Isaiah 61:1,2

were many widows in Israel in Elijah's time, when the sky was shut for three and a half years and there was a severe famine throughout the land. 26Yet Elijah was not sent to any of them, but to a widow in Zarephath in the region of Sidon. 27And there were many in Israel with leprosy*a* in the time of Elisha the prophet, yet not one of them was cleansed—only Naaman the Syrian."

28All the people in the synagogue were furious when they heard this. 29They got up, drove him out of the town, and took him to the brow of the hill on which the town was built, in order to throw him down the cliff. 30But he walked right through the crowd and went on his way.

Jesus Drives Out an Evil Spirit

31Then he went down to Capernaum, a town in Galilee, and on the Sabbath began to teach the people. 32They were amazed at his teaching, because his message had authority. 33In the synagogue there was a man possessed by a demon, an evil*b* spirit. He cried out at the top of his voice, 34"Ha! What do you want with us, Jesus of Nazareth? Have you come to destroy us? I know who you are—the Holy One of God!"

35"Be quiet!" Jesus said sternly. "Come out of him!" Then the demon threw the man down before them all and came out without injuring him.

36All the people were amazed and said to each other, "What is this teaching? With authority and power he gives orders to evil spirits and they come out!" 37And the news about him spread throughout the surrounding area.

Jesus Heals Many

38Jesus left the synagogue and went to the home of Simon. Now Simon's mother-in-law was suffering from a high fever, and they asked Jesus to help her. 39So he bent over

her and rebuked the fever, and it left her. She got up at once and began to wait on them.

40When the sun was setting, the people brought to Jesus all who had various kinds of sickness, and laying his hands on each one, he healed them. 41Moreover, demons came out of many people, shouting, "You are the Son of God!" But he rebuked them and would not allow them to speak, because they knew he was the Christ.*c*

42At daybreak Jesus went out to a solitary place. The people were looking for him and when they came to where he was, they tried to keep him from leaving them. 43But he said, "I must preach the good news of the kingdom of God to the other towns also, because that is why I was sent." 44And he kept on preaching in the synagogues of Judea.*d*

The Calling of the First Disciples

5 One day as Jesus was standing by the Lake of Gennesaret,*e* with the people crowding around him and listening to the word of God, 2he saw at the water's edge two boats, left there by the fishermen, who were washing their nets. 3He got into one of the boats, the one belonging to Simon, and asked him to put out a little from shore. Then he sat down and taught the people from the boat.

4When he had finished speaking, he said to Simon, "Put out into deep water, and let down*f* the nets for a catch."

5Simon answered, "Master, we've worked hard all night and haven't caught anything. But because you say so, I will let down the nets."

6When they had done so, they caught such a large number of fish that their nets began to break. 7So they signaled their partners in the other boat to come and help them,

---

a27 The Greek word was used for various diseases affecting the skin—not necessarily leprosy. *b33* Greek *unclean*; also in verse 36   *c41* Or *Messiah*   *d44* Or *the land of the Jews*; some manuscripts *Galilee*   *e1* That is, Sea of Galilee   *f4* The Greek verb is plural.

and they came and filled both boats so full that they began to sink.

⁸When Simon Peter saw this, he fell at Jesus' knees and said, "Go away from me, Lord; I am a sinful man!" ⁹For he and all his companions were astonished at the catch of fish they had taken, ¹⁰and so were James and John, the sons of Zebedee, Simon's partners.

Then Jesus said to Simon, "Don't be afraid; from now on you will catch men." ¹¹So they pulled their boats up on shore, left everything and followed him.

The Man With Leprosy

¹²While Jesus was in one of the towns, a man came along who was covered with leprosy.ᵃ When he saw Jesus, he fell with his face to the ground and begged him, "Lord, if you are willing, you can make me clean."

¹³Jesus reached out his hand and touched the man. "I am willing," he said. "Be clean!" And immediately the leprosy left him.

¹⁴Then Jesus ordered him, "Don't tell anyone, but go, show yourself to the priest and offer the sacrifices that Moses commanded for your cleansing, as a testimony to them."

¹⁵Yet the news about him spread all the more, so that crowds of people came to hear him and to be healed of their sicknesses. ¹⁶But Jesus often withdrew to lonely places and prayed.

Jesus Heals a Paralytic

¹⁷One day as he was teaching, Pharisees and teachers of the law, who had come from every village of Galilee and from Judea and Jerusalem, were sitting there. And the power of the Lord was present for him to heal the sick. ¹⁸Some men came carrying a paralytic on a mat and tried to take him into the house to lay him before Jesus. ¹⁹When they could not find a way to do this because of the crowd, they went up on the roof and lowered him on his mat through the tiles into the middle of the crowd, right in front of Jesus.

²⁰When Jesus saw their faith, he said, "Friend, your sins are forgiven."

²¹The Pharisees and the teachers of the law began thinking to themselves, "Who is this fellow who speaks blasphemy? Who can forgive sins but God alone?"

²²Jesus knew what they were thinking and asked, "Why are you thinking these things in your hearts? ²³Which is easier: to say, 'Your sins are forgiven,' or to say, 'Get up and walk'? ²⁴But that you may know that the Son of Man has authority on earth to forgive sins. . . ." He said to the paralyzed man, "I tell you, get up, take your mat and go home." ²⁵Immediately he stood up in front of them, took what he had been lying on and went home praising God. ²⁶Everyone was amazed and gave praise to God. They were filled with awe and said,

---

ᵃ12 The Greek word was used for various diseases affecting the skin—not necessarily leprosy.

▚ET'S LIVE IT!   Luke 5:1–11

PEOPLE JESUS CHOOSES ➠ What kind of person would you want to do a difficult job? Read Luke 5:1–11. We learn at least four things about the men Jesus chose to be his disciples: 1. They worked hard. 2. They were respectful. 3. They followed instructions. 4. They were used to working with other people as a team.

Make a seven-day chart with four columns: Work Hard, Respectful, Obedient, and Get Along with Others. Each day for a week try to live as the disciples did. Each day you work hard, are respectful, obedient, or get along with others, give yourself a check mark in that column.

"We have seen remarkable things today."

The Calling of Levi

27After this, Jesus went out and saw a tax collector by the name of Levi sitting at his tax booth. "Follow me," Jesus said to him, 28and Levi got up, left everything and followed him.

29Then Levi held a great banquet for Jesus at his house, and a large crowd of tax collectors and others were eating with them. 30But the Pharisees and the teachers of the law who belonged to their sect complained to his disciples, "Why do you eat and drink with tax collectors and 'sinners'?"

31Jesus answered them, "It is not the healthy who need a doctor, but the sick. 32I have not come to call the righteous, but sinners to repentance."

Jesus Questioned About Fasting

33They said to him, "John's disciples often fast and pray, and so do the disciples of the Pharisees, but yours go on eating and drinking."

34Jesus answered, "Can you make the guests of the bridegroom fast while he is with them? 35But the time will come when the bridegroom will be taken from them; in those days they will fast."

36He told them this parable: "No one tears a patch from a new garment and sews it on an old one. If he does, he will have torn the new garment, and the patch from the new will not match the old. 37And no one pours new wine into old wineskins. If he does, the new wine will burst the skins, the wine will run out and the wineskins will be ruined. 38No, new wine must be poured into new wineskins. 39And no one after drinking old wine wants the new, for he says, 'The old is better.'"

Lord of the Sabbath

6 One Sabbath Jesus was going through the grainfields, and his disciples began to pick some heads of grain, rub them in their hands and eat the kernels. 2Some of the Pharisees asked, "Why are you doing what is unlawful on the Sabbath?"

3Jesus answered them, "Have you never read what David did when he and his companions were hungry? 4He entered the house of God, and taking the consecrated bread, he ate what is lawful only for priests to eat. And he also gave some to his companions." 5Then Jesus said to them, "The Son of Man is Lord of the Sabbath."

6On another Sabbath he went into the synagogue and was teaching, and a man was there whose right hand was shriveled. 7The Pharisees and the teachers of the law were looking for a reason to accuse Jesus, so they watched him closely to see if he would heal on the Sabbath. 8But Jesus knew what they were thinking and said to the man with the shriveled hand, "Get up and stand in front of everyone." So he got up and stood there.

9Then Jesus said to them, "I ask you, which is lawful on the Sabbath: to do good or to do evil, to save life or to destroy it?"

10He looked around at them all, and then said to the man, "Stretch out your hand." He did so, and his hand was completely restored. 11But they were furious and began to discuss with one another what they might do to Jesus.

The Twelve Apostles

12One of those days Jesus went out to a mountainside to pray, and spent the night praying to God. 13When morning came, he called his disciples to him and chose twelve of them, whom he also designated apostles: 14Simon (whom he named Peter), his brother Andrew, James, John, Philip, Bartholomew, 15Matthew, Thomas, James son of Alphaeus, Simon who was called the Zealot, 16Judas son of James, and Judas Iscariot, who became a traitor.

Blessings and Woes

17He went down with them and stood on a level place. A large crowd of his disciples was there and a great number of people from all over Judea, from Jerusalem, and from the coast of Tyre and Sidon, 18who had come to hear him and to be healed of their diseases. Those troubled by evil*a* spirits were cured, 19and the people all tried to touch him, because power was coming from him and healing them all.

20Looking at his disciples, he said:

"Blessed are you who are poor,
 for yours is the kingdom of God.
21Blessed are you who hunger now,
 for you will be satisfied.
Blessed are you who weep now,
 for you will laugh.
22Blessed are you when men hate you,
 when they exclude you and insult you
 and reject your name as evil,
 because of the Son of Man.

23"Rejoice in that day and leap for joy, because great is your reward in heaven. For that is how their fathers treated the prophets.

24"But woe to you who are rich,
 for you have already received your comfort.
25Woe to you who are well fed now,
 for you will go hungry.
Woe to you who laugh now,
 for you will mourn and weep.
26Woe to you when all men speak well of you,
 for that is how their fathers treated the false prophets.

a18 Greek *unclean*

Love for Enemies

27"But I tell you who hear me: Love your enemies, do good to those who hate you, 28bless those who curse you, pray for those who mistreat you. 29If someone strikes you on one cheek, turn to him the other also. If someone takes your cloak, do not stop him from taking your tunic. 30Give to everyone who asks you, and if anyone takes what belongs to you, do not demand it back. 31Do to others as you would have them do to you.

32"If you love those who love you, what credit is that to you? Even 'sinners' love those who love them. 33And if you do good to those who are good to you, what credit is that to you? Even 'sinners' do that. 34And if you lend to those from whom you expect repayment, what credit is that to you? Even 'sinners' lend to 'sinners,' expecting to be repaid in full. 35But love your enemies, do good to them, and lend to them without expecting to get anything back. Then your reward will be great, and you will be sons of the Most High, because he is kind to the ungrateful and wicked. 36Be merciful, just as your Father is merciful.

Judging Others

37"Do not judge, and you will not be judged. Do not condemn, and you will not be condemned. Forgive, and you will be forgiven. 38Give, and it will be given to you. A good measure, pressed down, shaken together and running over, will be poured into

---

⊾ET'S LIVE IT!   Luke 6:27–36

HOW TO LOVE ENEMIES ➠ Love is not just a feeling. Christian love means caring about people and doing nice things for them.
   Read Luke 6:27–36. Jesus wants us to love all people, even our enemies.
   Do you know anyone who doesn't like you, or is mean to you? Here are some ways to show love to your enemy: Smile. Be friendly. Pray for her. Help him with school work. Say nice things about her. Invite him over to play. Choose her for your team.

your lap. For with the measure you use, it will be measured to you."

39He also told them this parable: "Can a blind man lead a blind man? Will they not both fall into a pit? 40A student is not above his teacher, but everyone who is fully trained will be like his teacher.

41"Why do you look at the speck of sawdust in your brother's eye and pay no attention to the plank in your own eye? 42How can you say to your brother, 'Brother, let me take the speck out of your eye,' when you yourself fail to see the plank in your own eye? You hypocrite, first take the plank out of your eye, and then you will see clearly to remove the speck from your brother's eye.

A Tree and Its Fruit

43"No good tree bears bad fruit, nor does a bad tree bear good fruit. 44Each tree is recognized by its own fruit. People do not pick figs from thornbushes, or grapes from briers. 45The good man brings good things out of the good stored up in his heart, and the evil man brings evil things out of the evil stored up in his heart. For out of the overflow of his heart his mouth speaks.

The Wise and Foolish Builders

46"Why do you call me, 'Lord, Lord,' and do not do what I say? 47I will show you what he is like who comes to me and hears my words and puts them into practice. 48He is like a man building a house, who dug down deep and laid the foundation on rock. When a flood came, the torrent struck that house but could not shake it, because it was well built. 49But the one who hears my words and does not put them into practice is like a man who built a house on the ground without a foundation. The moment the torrent struck that house, it collapsed and its destruction was complete."

The Faith of the Centurion

7 When Jesus had finished saying all this in the hearing of the peo-

ple, he entered Capernaum. 2There a centurion's servant, whom his master valued highly, was sick and about to die. 3The centurion heard of Jesus and sent some elders of the Jews to him, asking him to come and heal his servant. 4When they came to Jesus, they pleaded earnestly with him, "This man deserves to have you do this, 5because he loves our nation and has built our synagogue." 6So Jesus went with them.

He was not far from the house when the centurion sent friends to say to him: "Lord, don't trouble yourself, for I do not deserve to have you come under my roof. 7That is why I did not even consider myself worthy to come to you. But say the word, and my servant will be healed. 8For I myself am a man under authority, with soldiers under me. I tell this one, 'Go,' and he goes; and that one, 'Come,' and he comes. I say to my servant, 'Do this,' and he does it."

CENTURIONS

Centurions were important Roman army officers. Each commanded one hundred soldiers in the Roman army. All of the centurions mentioned in the Bible were friends of the Jewish people and believed in God.

9When Jesus heard this, he was amazed at him, and turning to the crowd following him, he said, "I tell you, I have not found such great faith even in Israel." 10Then the men who had been sent returned to the house and found the servant well.

Jesus Raises a Widow's Son

11Soon afterward, Jesus went to a

town called Nain, and his disciples and a large crowd went along with him. [12]As he approached the town gate, a dead person was being carried out—the only son of his mother, and she was a widow. And a large crowd from the town was with her. [13]When the Lord saw her, his heart went out to her and he said, "Don't cry."

[14]Then he went up and touched the coffin, and those carrying it stood still. He said, "Young man, I say to you, get up!" [15]The dead man sat up and began to talk, and Jesus gave him back to his mother.

[16]They were all filled with awe and praised God. "A great prophet has appeared among us," they said. "God has come to help his people." [17]This news about Jesus spread throughout Judea[a] and the surrounding country.

Jesus and John the Baptist

[18]John's disciples told him about all these things. Calling two of them, [19]he sent them to the Lord to ask, "Are you the one who was to come, or should we expect someone else?"

[20]When the men came to Jesus, they said, "John the Baptist sent us to you to ask, 'Are you the one who was to come, or should we expect someone else?'"

[21]At that very time Jesus cured many who had diseases, sicknesses and evil spirits, and gave sight to many who were blind. [22]So he replied to the messengers, "Go back and report to John what you have seen and heard: The blind receive sight, the lame walk, those who have leprosy[b] are cured, the deaf hear, the dead are raised, and the good news is preached to the poor. [23]Blessed is the man who does not fall away on account of me."

[24]After John's messengers left, Jesus began to speak to the crowd about John: "What did you go out into the desert to see? A reed swayed by the wind? [25]If not, what did you go out to see? A man dressed in fine clothes? No, those who wear expen-

sive clothes and indulge in luxury are in palaces. [26]But what did you go out to see? A prophet? Yes, I tell you, and more than a prophet. [27]This is the one about whom it is written:

" 'I will send my messenger ahead
   of you,
who will prepare your way
   before you.'[c]

[28]I tell you, among those born of women there is no one greater than John; yet the one who is least in the kingdom of God is greater than he."

[29](All the people, even the tax collectors, when they heard Jesus' words, acknowledged that God's way was right, because they had been baptized by John. [30]But the Pharisees and experts in the law rejected God's purpose for themselves, because they had not been baptized by John.)

? DID YOU KNOW? 7:30

Who were the Pharisees and experts in the law?

The Pharisees were religious men who studied the Bible and wanted to please God, but they did not really understand what they read. These men tried to please God by being better than other people. When Jesus showed them they were wrong, they hated him and became his enemies.

---

[31]"To what, then, can I compare the people of this generation? What are they like? [32]They are like children sitting in the marketplace and calling out to each other:

" 'We played the flute for you,
   and you did not dance;
we sang a dirge,
   and you did not cry.'

[33]For John the Baptist came neither eating bread nor drinking wine, and

---

[a]17 Or *the land of the Jews*   [b]22 The Greek word was used for various diseases affecting the skin—not necessarily leprosy.   [c]27 Mal. 3:1

you say, 'He has a demon.' ³⁴The Son
of Man came eating and drinking,
and you say, 'Here is a glutton and a
drunkard, a friend of tax collectors
and "sinners." ' ³⁵But wisdom is
proved right by all her children."

Jesus Anointed by a Sinful Woman

³⁶Now one of the Pharisees invited
Jesus to have dinner with him, so he
went to the Pharisee's house and reclined at the table. ³⁷When a woman
who had lived a sinful life in that
town learned that Jesus was eating
at the Pharisee's house, she brought
an alabaster jar of perfume, ³⁸and as
she stood behind him at his feet
weeping, she began to wet his feet
with her tears. Then she wiped them
with her hair, kissed them and
poured perfume on them.

³⁹When the Pharisee who had invited him saw this, he said to himself,
"If this man were a prophet, he would
know who is touching him and what
kind of woman she is—that she is a
sinner."

⁴⁰Jesus answered him, "Simon, I
have something to tell you."

"Tell me, teacher," he said.

⁴¹"Two men owed money to a certain moneylender. One owed him five
hundred denarii,ᵃ and the other fifty.
⁴²Neither of them had the money to
pay him back, so he canceled the
debts of both. Now which of them will
love him more?"

⁴³Simon replied, "I suppose the one
who had the bigger debt canceled."

"You have judged correctly," Jesus
said.

⁴⁴Then he turned toward the woman and said to Simon, "Do you see
this woman? I came into your house.
You did not give me any water for my
feet, but she wet my feet with her
tears and wiped them with her hair.
⁴⁵You did not give me a kiss, but this
woman, from the time I entered, has
not stopped kissing my feet. ⁴⁶You
did not put oil on my head, but she
has poured perfume on my feet.

⁴⁷Therefore, I tell you, her many sins
have been forgiven—for she loved
much. But he who has been forgiven
little loves little."

⁴⁸Then Jesus said to her, "Your
sins are forgiven."

⁴⁹The other guests began to say
among themselves, "Who is this who
even forgives sins?"

⁵⁰Jesus said to the woman, "Your
faith has saved you; go in peace."

The Parable of the Sower

8 After this, Jesus traveled about
from one town and village to another, proclaiming the good news of
the kingdom of God. The Twelve were
with him, ²and also some women who
had been cured of evil spirits and diseases: Mary (called Magdalene) from
whom seven demons had come out;
³Joanna the wife of Cuza, the manager of Herod's household; Susanna;
and many others. These women were
helping to support them out of their
own means.

⁴While a large crowd was gathering and people were coming to Jesus
from town after town, he told this
parable: ⁵"A farmer went out to sow
his seed. As he was scattering the
seed, some fell along the path; it was
trampled on, and the birds of the air
ate it up. ⁶Some fell on rock, and
when it came up, the plants withered
because they had no moisture. ⁷Other
seed fell among thorns, which grew
up with it and choked the plants.
⁸Still other seed fell on good soil. It
came up and yielded a crop, a hundred times more than was sown."

When he said this, he called out,
"He who has ears to hear, let him
hear."

⁹His disciples asked him what this
parable meant. ¹⁰He said, "The
knowledge of the secrets of the kingdom of God has been given to you, but
to others I speak in parables, so that,

" 'though seeing, they may not
    see;

ᵃ41 A denarius was a coin worth about a day's wages.

though hearing, they may not understand.'ᵃ

11"This is the meaning of the parable: The seed is the word of God. 12Those along the path are the ones who hear, and then the devil comes and takes away the word from their hearts, so that they may not believe and be saved. 13Those on the rock are the ones who receive the word with joy when they hear it, but they have no root. They believe for a while, but in the time of testing they fall away. 14The seed that fell among thorns stands for those who hear, but as they go on their way they are choked by life's worries, riches and pleasures, and they do not mature. 15But the seed on good soil stands for those with a noble and good heart, who hear the word, retain it, and by persevering produce a crop.

A Lamp on a Stand

16"No one lights a lamp and hides it in a jar or puts it under a bed. Instead, he puts it on a stand, so that those who come in can see the light. 17For there is nothing hidden that will not be disclosed, and nothing concealed that will not be known or brought out into the open. 18Therefore consider carefully how you listen. Whoever has will be given more; whoever does not have, even what he thinks he has will be taken from him."

Jesus' Mother and Brothers

19Now Jesus' mother and brothers came to see him, but they were not able to get near him because of the crowd. 20Someone told him, "Your mother and brothers are standing outside, wanting to see you."

21He replied, "My mother and brothers are those who hear God's word and put it into practice."

Jesus Calms the Storm

22One day Jesus said to his disciples, "Let's go over to the other side of the lake." So they got into a boat and set out. 23As they sailed, he fell asleep. A squall came down on the lake, so that the boat was being swamped, and they were in great danger.

24The disciples went and woke him, saying, "Master, Master, we're going to drown!"

He got up and rebuked the wind and the raging waters; the storm subsided, and all was calm. 25"Where is your faith?" he asked his disciples.

In fear and amazement they asked one another, "Who is this? He commands even the winds and the water, and they obey him."

The Healing of a Demon-possessed Man

26They sailed to the region of the Gerasenes,ᵇ which is across the lake from Galilee. 27When Jesus stepped ashore, he was met by a demon-possessed man from the town. For a long time this man had not worn clothes or lived in a house, but had lived in the tombs. 28When he saw Jesus, he cried out and fell at his feet, shouting at the top of his voice, "What do you want with me, Jesus, Son of the Most High God? I beg you, don't torture me!" 29For Jesus had commanded the evilᶜ spirit to come out of the man. Many times it had seized him, and though he was chained hand and foot and kept under guard, he had broken his chains and had been driven by the demon into solitary places.

30Jesus asked him, "What is your name?"

"Legion," he replied, because many demons had gone into him. 31And they begged him repeatedly not to order them to go into the Abyss.

32A large herd of pigs was feeding there on the hillside. The demons begged Jesus to let them go into them, and he gave them permission. 33When the demons came out of the man, they went into the pigs, and the

---

ᵃ10 Isaiah 6:9　　ᵇ26 Some manuscripts *Gadarenes*; other manuscripts *Gergesenes*; also in verse 37
ᶜ29 Greek *unclean*

herd rushed down the steep bank into the lake and was drowned.

³⁴When those tending the pigs saw what had happened, they ran off and reported this in the town and countryside, ³⁵and the people went out to see what had happened. When they came to Jesus, they found the man from whom the demons had gone out, sitting at Jesus' feet, dressed and in his right mind; and they were afraid. ³⁶Those who had seen it told the people how the demon-possessed man had been cured. ³⁷Then all the people of the region of the Gerasenes asked Jesus to leave them, because they were overcome with fear. So he got into the boat and left.

³⁸The man from whom the demons had gone out begged to go with him, but Jesus sent him away, saying, ³⁹"Return home and tell how much God has done for you." So the man went away and told all over town how much Jesus had done for him.

❓DID YOU KNOW?   8:32

How did Jesus show his power over demons?

Jesus made the demons do what he said. Even thousands of demons were not strong enough to oppose Jesus. Jesus is still stronger than any evil spirit.

A Dead Girl and a Sick Woman

⁴⁰Now when Jesus returned, a crowd welcomed him, for they were all expecting him. ⁴¹Then a man named Jairus, a ruler of the synagogue, came and fell at Jesus' feet, pleading with him to come to his house ⁴²because his only daughter, a girl of about twelve, was dying.

As Jesus was on his way, the crowds almost crushed him. ⁴³And a woman was there who had been subject to bleeding for twelve years,ᵃ but

no one could heal her. ⁴⁴She came up behind him and touched the edge of his cloak, and immediately her bleeding stopped.

⁴⁵"Who touched me?" Jesus asked.

When they all denied it, Peter said, "Master, the people are crowding and pressing against you."

⁴⁶But Jesus said, "Someone touched me; I know that power has gone out from me."

⁴⁷Then the woman, seeing that she could not go unnoticed, came trembling and fell at his feet. In the presence of all the people, she told why she had touched him and how she had been instantly healed. ⁴⁸Then he said to her, "Daughter, your faith has healed you. Go in peace."

⁴⁹While Jesus was still speaking, someone came from the house of Jairus, the synagogue ruler. "Your daughter is dead," he said. "Don't bother the teacher any more."

⁵⁰Hearing this, Jesus said to Jairus, "Don't be afraid; just believe, and she will be healed."

✝️ WORDS TO REMEMBER

8:50 Don't be afraid; just believe.

---

⁵¹When he arrived at the house of Jairus, he did not let anyone go in with him except Peter, John and James, and the child's father and mother. ⁵²Meanwhile, all the people were wailing and mourning for her. "Stop wailing," Jesus said. "She is not dead but asleep."

⁵³They laughed at him, knowing that she was dead. ⁵⁴But he took her by the hand and said, "My child, get up!" ⁵⁵Her spirit returned, and at once she stood up. Then Jesus told them to give her something to eat. ⁵⁶Her parents were astonished, but he ordered them not to tell anyone what had happened.

ᵃ43 Many manuscripts *years, and she had spent all she had on doctors*

Jesus Sends Out the Twelve

9 When Jesus had called the Twelve together, he gave them power and authority to drive out all demons and to cure diseases, ²and he sent them out to preach the kingdom of God and to heal the sick. ³He told them: "Take nothing for the journey—no staff, no bag, no bread, no money, no extra tunic. ⁴Whatever house you enter, stay there until you leave that town. ⁵If people do not welcome you, shake the dust off your feet when you leave their town, as a testimony against them." ⁶So they set out and went from village to village, preaching the gospel and healing people everywhere.

⁷Now Herod the tetrarch heard about all that was going on. And he was perplexed, because some were saying that John had been raised from the dead, ⁸others that Elijah had appeared, and still others that one of the prophets of long ago had come back to life. ⁹But Herod said, "I beheaded John. Who, then, is this I hear such things about?" And he tried to see him.

Jesus Feeds the Five Thousand

¹⁰When the apostles returned, they reported to Jesus what they had done. Then he took them with him and they withdrew by themselves to a town called Bethsaida, ¹¹but the crowds learned about it and followed him. He welcomed them and spoke to them about the kingdom of God, and healed those who needed healing.

¹²Late in the afternoon the Twelve came to him and said, "Send the crowd away so they can go to the surrounding villages and countryside and find food and lodging, because we are in a remote place here."

¹³He replied, "You give them something to eat."

They answered, "We have only five loaves of bread and two fish—unless we go and buy food for all this crowd."

¹⁴(About five thousand men were there.)

But he said to his disciples, "Have them sit down in groups of about fifty each." ¹⁵The disciples did so, and everybody sat down. ¹⁶Taking the five loaves and the two fish and looking up to heaven, he gave thanks and broke them. Then he gave them to the disciples to set before the people. ¹⁷They all ate and were satisfied, and the disciples picked up twelve basketfuls of broken pieces that were left over.

❓DID YOU KNOW?   9:13

Why did Jesus feed five thousand people?

The five thousand people who came to hear Jesus were hungry, and Jesus was worried about them. He cares about those who are poor and hungry. It is good for Christians to care about others as Jesus did.

Peter's Confession of Christ

¹⁸Once when Jesus was praying in private and his disciples were with him, he asked them, "Who do the crowds say I am?"

¹⁹They replied, "Some say John the Baptist; others say Elijah; and still others, that one of the prophets of long ago has come back to life."

²⁰"But what about you?" he asked. "Who do you say I am?"

Peter answered, "The Christ*ᵃ* of God."

²¹Jesus strictly warned them not to tell this to anyone. ²²And he said, "The Son of Man must suffer many things and be rejected by the elders, chief priests and teachers of the law, and he must be killed and on the third day be raised to life."

²³Then he said to them all: "If anyone would come after me, he must deny himself and take up his cross

ᵃ20 Or Messiah

daily and follow me. ²⁴For whoever wants to save his life will lose it, but whoever loses his life for me will save it. ²⁵What good is it for a man to gain the whole world, and yet lose or forfeit his very self? ²⁶If anyone is ashamed of me and my words, the Son of Man will be ashamed of him when he comes in his glory and in the glory of the Father and of the holy angels. ²⁷I tell you the truth, some who are standing here will not taste death before they see the kingdom of God."

The Transfiguration

²⁸About eight days after Jesus said this, he took Peter, John and James with him and went up onto a mountain to pray. ²⁹As he was praying, the appearance of his face changed, and his clothes became as bright as a flash of lightning. ³⁰Two men, Moses and Elijah, ³¹appeared in glorious splendor, talking with Jesus. They spoke about his departure, which he was about to bring to fulfillment at Jerusalem. ³²Peter and his companions were very sleepy, but when they became fully awake, they saw his glory and the two men standing with him. ³³As the men were leaving Jesus, Peter said to him, "Master, it is good for us to be here. Let us put up three shelters—one for you, one for Moses and one for Elijah." (He did not know what he was saying.)

³⁴While he was speaking, a cloud appeared and enveloped them, and they were afraid as they entered the cloud. ³⁵A voice came from the cloud, saying, "This is my Son, whom I have chosen; listen to him." ³⁶When the voice had spoken, they found that Jesus was alone. The disciples kept this to themselves, and told no one at that time what they had seen.

The Healing of a Boy With an Evil Spirit

³⁷The next day, when they came down from the mountain, a large crowd met him. ³⁸A man in the crowd called out, "Teacher, I beg you to look at my son, for he is my only child. ³⁹A spirit seizes him and he suddenly screams; it throws him into convulsions so that he foams at the mouth. It scarcely ever leaves him and is destroying him. ⁴⁰I begged your disciples to drive it out, but they could not."

⁴¹"O unbelieving and perverse generation," Jesus replied, "how long shall I stay with you and put up with you? Bring your son here."

⁴²Even while the boy was coming, the demon threw him to the ground in a convulsion. But Jesus rebuked the evil*ᵃ* spirit, healed the boy and gave him back to his father. ⁴³And they were all amazed at the greatness of God.

While everyone was marveling at all that Jesus did, he said to his disciples, ⁴⁴"Listen carefully to what I am about to tell you: The Son of Man is going to be betrayed into the hands of men." ⁴⁵But they did not understand what this meant. It was hidden from them, so that they did not grasp it, and they were afraid to ask him about it.

Who Will Be the Greatest?

⁴⁶An argument started among the disciples as to which of them would be the greatest. ⁴⁷Jesus, knowing their thoughts, took a little child and had him stand beside him. ⁴⁸Then he said to them, "Whoever welcomes this little child in my name welcomes me; and whoever welcomes me welcomes the one who sent me. For he who is least among you all—he is the greatest."

⁴⁹"Master," said John, "we saw a man driving out demons in your name and we tried to stop him, because he is not one of us."

⁵⁰"Do not stop him," Jesus said, "for whoever is not against you is for you."

Samaritan Opposition

⁵¹As the time approached for him to

ᵃ42 Greek unclean

be taken up to heaven, Jesus resolutely set out for Jerusalem. [52]And he sent messengers on ahead, who went into a Samaritan village to get things ready for him; [53]but the people there did not welcome him, because he was heading for Jerusalem. [54]When the disciples James and John saw this, they asked, "Lord, do you want us to call fire down from heaven to destroy them[a]?" [55]But Jesus turned and rebuked them, [56]and[b] they went to another village.

The Cost of Following Jesus

[57]As they were walking along the road, a man said to him, "I will follow you wherever you go."

[58]Jesus replied, "Foxes have holes and birds of the air have nests, but the Son of Man has no place to lay his head."

[59]He said to another man, "Follow me."

But the man replied, "Lord, first let me go and bury my father."

[60]Jesus said to him, "Let the dead bury their own dead, but you go and proclaim the kingdom of God."

[61]Still another said, "I will follow you, Lord; but first let me go back and say good-by to my family."

[62]Jesus replied, "No one who puts his hand to the plow and looks back is fit for service in the kingdom of God."

Jesus Sends Out the Seventy-two

10 After this the Lord appointed seventy-two[c] others and sent them two by two ahead of him to every town and place where he was about to go. [2]He told them, "The harvest is plentiful, but the workers are few. Ask the Lord of the harvest, therefore, to send out workers into his harvest field. [3]Go! I am sending you out like lambs among wolves. [4]Do not take a purse or bag or sandals; and do not greet anyone on the road.

[5]"When you enter a house, first say, 'Peace to this house.' [6]If a man of peace is there, your peace will rest on him; if not, it will return to you. [7]Stay in that house, eating and drinking whatever they give you, for the worker deserves his wages. Do not move around from house to house.

[8]"When you enter a town and are welcomed, eat what is set before you. [9]Heal the sick who are there and tell them, 'The kingdom of God is near you.' [10]But when you enter a town and are not welcomed, go into its streets and say, [11]'Even the dust of your town that sticks to our feet we wipe off against you. Yet be sure of this: The kingdom of God is near.' [12]I tell you, it will be more bearable on that day for Sodom than for that town.

[13]"Woe to you, Korazin! Woe to you, Bethsaida! For if the miracles that were performed in you had been performed in Tyre and Sidon, they would have repented long ago, sitting in sackcloth and ashes. [14]But it will be more bearable for Tyre and Sidon at the judgment than for you. [15]And you, Capernaum, will you be lifted up to the skies? No, you will go down to the depths.[d]

[16]"He who listens to you listens to me; he who rejects you rejects me; but he who rejects me rejects him who sent me."

[17]The seventy-two returned with joy and said, "Lord, even the demons submit to us in your name."

[18]He replied, "I saw Satan fall like lightning from heaven. [19]I have given you authority to trample on snakes and scorpions and to overcome all the power of the enemy; nothing will harm you. [20]However, do not rejoice that the spirits submit to you, but rejoice that your names are written in heaven."

---

[a]54 Some manuscripts *them, even as Elijah did*   [b]55,56 Some manuscripts *them. And he said,* "You do not know what kind of spirit you are of, for the Son of Man did not come to destroy men's lives, but to save them." [56]And   [c]1 Some manuscripts *seventy*; also in verse 17   [d]15 Greek *Hades*

21At that time Jesus, full of joy through the Holy Spirit, said, "I praise you, Father, Lord of heaven and earth, because you have hidden these things from the wise and learned, and revealed them to little children. Yes, Father, for this was your good pleasure.

22"All things have been committed to me by my Father. No one knows who the Son is except the Father, and no one knows who the Father is except the Son and those to whom the Son chooses to reveal him."

23Then he turned to his disciples and said privately, "Blessed are the eyes that see what you see. 24For I tell you that many prophets and kings wanted to see what you see but did not see it, and to hear what you hear but did not hear it."

The Parable of the Good Samaritan

25On one occasion an expert in the law stood up to test Jesus. "Teacher," he asked, "what must I do to inherit eternal life?"

26"What is written in the Law?" he replied. "How do you read it?"

27He answered: " 'Love the Lord your God with all your heart and with all your soul and with all your strength and with all your mind'a; and, 'Love your neighbor as yourself.'b"

28"You have answered correctly," Jesus replied. "Do this and you will live."

29But he wanted to justify himself, so he asked Jesus, "And who is my neighbor?"

30In reply Jesus said: "A man was going down from Jerusalem to Jericho, when he fell into the hands of robbers. They stripped him of his clothes, beat him and went away, leaving him half dead. 31A priest happened to be going down the same road, and when he saw the man, he passed by on the other side. 32So too, a Levite, when he came to the place and saw him, passed by on the other

side. 33But a Samaritan, as he traveled, came where the man was; and when he saw him, he took pity on him. 34He went to him and bandaged his wounds, pouring on oil and wine. Then he put the man on his own donkey, took him to an inn and took care of him. 35The next day he took out two silver coinsc and gave them to the innkeeper. 'Look after him,' he said, 'and when I return, I will reimburse you for any extra expense you may have.'

36"Which of these three do you think was a neighbor to the man who fell into the hands of robbers?"

37The expert in the law replied, "The one who had mercy on him."

Jesus told him, "Go and do likewise."

❓DID YOU KNOW?   10:33

What was a Samaritan?

A Samaritan was a person who lived in Samaria, a district next to Judea and Galilee. The Jews did not like the Samaritans, who were foreigners. Jesus' story shows that anyone can be a good neighbor. We are to help any person in trouble, whatever race or religion or nationality.

At the Home of Martha and Mary

38As Jesus and his disciples were on their way, he came to a village where a woman named Martha opened her home to him. 39She had a sister called Mary, who sat at the Lord's feet listening to what he said. 40But Martha was distracted by all the preparations that had to be made. She came to him and asked, "Lord, don't you care that my sister has left me to do the work by myself? Tell her to help me!"

41"Martha, Martha," the Lord answered, "you are worried and upset

---

a27 Deut. 6:5   b27 Lev. 19:18   c35 Greek two denarii

about many things, [42]but only one thing is needed.[a] Mary has chosen what is better, and it will not be taken away from her."

Jesus' Teaching on Prayer

11 One day Jesus was praying in a certain place. When he finished, one of his disciples said to him, "Lord, teach us to pray, just as John taught his disciples."

[2]He said to them, "When you pray, say:

" 'Father,[b]
hallowed be your name,
your kingdom come.[c]
[3]Give us each day our daily bread.
[4]Forgive us our sins,
    for we also forgive everyone
        who sins against us.[d]
And lead us not into
        temptation.[e]' "

[5]Then he said to them, "Suppose one of you has a friend, and he goes to him at midnight and says, 'Friend, lend me three loaves of bread, [6]because a friend of mine on a journey has come to me, and I have nothing to set before him.'

[7]"Then the one inside answers, 'Don't bother me. The door is already locked, and my children are with me in bed. I can't get up and give you anything.' [8]I tell you, though he will not get up and give him the bread because he is his friend, yet because of the man's boldness[f] he will get up and give him as much as he needs.

[9]"So I say to you: Ask and it will be given to you; seek and you will find; knock and the door will be opened to you. [10]For everyone who asks receives; he who seeks finds; and to him who knocks, the door will be opened.

[11]"Which of you fathers, if your son asks for[g] a fish, will give him a snake instead? [12]Or if he asks for an egg, will give him a scorpion? [13]If you then, though you are evil, know how to give good gifts to your children, how much more will your Father in heaven give the Holy Spirit to those who ask him!"

WORDS TO REMEMBER

11:9 Ask and it will be given to you; seek and you will find; knock and the door will be opened to you.

Jesus and Beelzebub

[14]Jesus was driving out a demon that was mute. When the demon left, the man who had been mute spoke, and the crowd was amazed. [15]But some of them said, "By Beelzebub,[h] the prince of demons, he is driving out demons." [16]Others tested him by asking for a sign from heaven.

[17]Jesus knew their thoughts and said to them: "Any kingdom divided against itself will be ruined, and a house divided against itself will fall. [18]If Satan is divided against himself, how can his kingdom stand? I say this because you claim that I drive out demons by Beelzebub. [19]Now if I drive out demons by Beelzebub, by whom do your followers drive them out? So then, they will be your judges. [20]But if I drive out demons by the finger of God, then the kingdom of God has come to you.

[21]"When a strong man, fully armed, guards his own house, his possessions are safe. [22]But when someone stronger attacks and overpowers him, he takes away the armor in which the man trusted and divides up the spoils.

[23]"He who is not with me is against me, and he who does not gather with me, scatters.

[24]"When an evil[i] spirit comes out of a man, it goes through arid places seeking rest and does not find it.

---

[a]42 Some manuscripts *but few things are needed—or only one*   [b]2 Some manuscripts *Our Father in heaven*   [c]2 Some manuscripts *come. May your will be done on earth as it is in heaven.*
[d]4 Greek *everyone who is indebted to us*   [e]4 Some manuscripts *temptation but deliver us from the evil one*   [f]8 Or *persistence*   [g]11 Some manuscripts *for bread, will give him a stone; or if he asks for*   [h]15 Greek *Beezeboul* or *Beelzeboul*; also in verses 18 and 19   [i]24 Greek *unclean*

Then it says, 'I will return to the house I left.' 25When it arrives, it finds the house swept clean and put in order. 26Then it goes and takes seven other spirits more wicked than itself, and they go in and live there. And the final condition of that man is worse than the first."

27As Jesus was saying these things, a woman in the crowd called out, "Blessed is the mother who gave you birth and nursed you."

28He replied, "Blessed rather are those who hear the word of God and obey it."

The Sign of Jonah

29As the crowds increased, Jesus said, "This is a wicked generation. It asks for a miraculous sign, but none will be given it except the sign of Jonah. 30For as Jonah was a sign to the Ninevites, so also will the Son of Man be to this generation. 31The Queen of the South will rise at the judgment with the men of this generation and condemn them; for she came from the ends of the earth to listen to Solomon's wisdom, and now one*a* greater than Solomon is here. 32The men of Nineveh will stand up at the judgment with this generation and condemn it; for they repented at the preaching of Jonah, and now one greater than Jonah is here.

The Lamp of the Body

33"No one lights a lamp and puts it in a place where it will be hidden, or under a bowl. Instead he puts it on its stand, so that those who come in may see the light. 34Your eye is the lamp of your body. When your eyes are good, your whole body also is full of light. But when they are bad, your body also is full of darkness. 35See to it, then, that the light within you is not darkness. 36Therefore, if your whole body is full of light, and no part of it dark, it will be completely lighted, as when the light of a lamp shines on you."

Six Woes

37When Jesus had finished speaking, a Pharisee invited him to eat with him; so he went in and reclined at the table. 38But the Pharisee, noticing that Jesus did not first wash before the meal, was surprised.

39Then the Lord said to him, "Now then, you Pharisees clean the outside of the cup and dish, but inside you are full of greed and wickedness. 40You foolish people! Did not the one who made the outside make the inside also? 41But give what is inside the dish,*b* to the poor, and everything will be clean for you.

42"Woe to you Pharisees, because you give God a tenth of your mint, rue and all other kinds of garden herbs, but you neglect justice and the love of God. You should have practiced the latter without leaving the former undone.

43"Woe to you Pharisees, because you love the most important seats in the synagogues and greetings in the marketplaces.

44"Woe to you, because you are like unmarked graves, which men walk over without knowing it."

45One of the experts in the law answered him, "Teacher, when you say these things, you insult us also."

46Jesus replied, "And you experts in the law, woe to you, because you load people down with burdens they can hardly carry, and you yourselves will not lift one finger to help them.

47"Woe to you, because you build tombs for the prophets, and it was your forefathers who killed them. 48So you testify that you approve of what your forefathers did; they killed the prophets, and you build their tombs. 49Because of this, God in his wisdom said, 'I will send them prophets and apostles, some of whom they will kill and others they will persecute.' 50Therefore this generation will be held responsible for the blood of all the prophets that has been shed since the beginning of the world,

---

a31 Or something; also in verse 32   *b41 Or what you have*

New Testament Men & Women

MARY   An angel came to tell Mary that she had been chosen by God to be the mother of Jesus.

You can read about Mary in Luke 1:26-38 (page 1242).

JOSEPH   After he was visited by an angel messenger from God, Joseph married Mary, Jesus' mother.

You can read about Joseph in Matthew 1:18-25 (page 1168).

ELIZABETH   When Elizabeth was an old woman, she had a son, John the Baptist, who told the people that Jesus was coming.

You can read about Elizabeth in Luke 1:5-25 (page 1242).

ZECHARIAH   Zechariah could not speak after he was told he was to be the father of John the Baptist.

You can read about Zechariah in Luke 1:5-25 (page 1242).

JOHN THE BAPTIST   John the Baptist was sent by God to tell the people that Jesus the Savior was coming.

You can read about John the Baptist in Luke 3:1-20 (page 1247).

HEROD   King Herod tried to have Jesus killed when Jesus was still a baby.

You can read about Herod in Matthew 2:1-18 (page 1169).

NICODEMUS   Nicodemus came at night to talk to Jesus and was told how he could be born again.

You can read about Nicodemus in John 3:1-21 (page 1291).

THE CENTURION   Jesus said that this centurion, an officer in the Roman army, had more faith than anyone else Jesus had met in Israel.

You can read about the centurion in Matthew 8:5-13 (page 1177).

THE SAMARITAN WOMAN   The Samaritan woman, who had had five husbands, met Jesus at a well, where he offered her living water.

You can read about the Samaritan woman in John 4:4-42 (page 1292).

continued

New Testament Men & Women

MARY AND MARTHA
Mary and Martha opened their home to Jesus whenever he came to Bethany.

You can read about Mary and Martha in Luke 10:38-42 (page 1262).

LAZARUS
Lazarus was the brother of Mary and Martha. When Lazarus got sick and died, Jesus raised him back to life.

You can read about Lazarus in John 11:1-44 (page 1306).

ZACCHAEUS
Zacchaeus was so short that he climbed a tree in order to see Jesus in a crowd; Jesus stopped and spoke directly to Zacchaeus.

You can read about Zacchaeus in Luke 19:1-10 (page 1275).

CAIAPHAS
Caiaphas was high priest when Jesus was arrested and sentenced to die.

You can read about Caiaphas in Matthew 26:57-68 (page 1207).

PILATE
While Pilate was governor of Judea, he allowed Jesus to be crucified.

You can read about Pilate in Matthew 27:11-26 (page 1208).

SIMON
Simon, a man from Cyrene, was forced to carry Jesus' cross to Golgotha, where Jesus was crucified.

You can read about Simon in Matthew 27:32 (page 1209).

JOSEPH OF ARIMATHEA
Joseph of Arimathea asked Pilate for Jesus' body and buried Jesus in a new tomb.

You can read about Joseph of Arimathea in John 19:38-42 (page 1318).

MARY MAGDALENE
Mary Magdalene was the first of Jesus' followers to learn of his resurrection.

You can read about Mary Magdalene in John 20:10-18 (page 1319).

MATTHIAS
Matthias was chosen to replace Judas as one of the twelve apostles after Jesus had gone back to heaven.

You can read about Matthias in Acts 1:15-26 (page 1324).

ANANIAS AND SAPPHIRA
Ananias and Sapphira lied to Peter about some property they had sold.

You can read about Ananias and Sapphira in Acts 5:1-11 (page 1330).

continued

New Testament Men & Women

STEPHEN   Stephen would not deny his belief in Jesus and was the first person to be killed for those beliefs.

You can read about Stephen in Acts 6:8-15; 7:54-60 (page 1332).

SAUL/PAUL   Saul, also called Paul, was a Jew who was persecuting the followers of Jesus until Jesus spoke to him on the road to Damascus.

You can read about Paul in Acts 9—28 (page 1336).

CORNELIUS   Cornelius was the first Gentile to whom Peter brought the message of Jesus' love.

You can read about Cornelius in Acts 10 (page 1338)

BARNABAS   Barnabas, a great missionary in the early church, traveled with Paul on his first missionary journey.

You can read about Barnabas in Acts 13:1-3 (page 1342).

SILAS   Silas traveled with Paul and helped him on some of his missionary journeys.

You can read about Silas in Acts 15:22-35 (page 1347).

PRISCILLA AND AQUILA   Priscilla and Aquila were tentmakers with whom Paul worked and lived while he was in Corinth.

You can read about Priscilla and Aquila in Acts 18 (page 1351).

TIMOTHY   Timothy traveled with Paul on his second missionary journey and from then on helped Paul in his work.

You can read about Timothy in 1 and 2 Timothy (page 1458).

TITUS   Titus was a friend and helper of Paul.

You can read about Titus in the book of Titus (page 1469).

PHILEMON   Paul wrote to ask Philemon to take back a runaway slave, Onesimus.

You can read about Philemon in the book of Philemon (page 1472).

Turn this page over to read about twelve more New Testament men, Jesus' twelve disciples.

THE TWELVE

URING Jesus' life on earth he called twelve
    special men.
When he said, "Come follow me," they did so
    there and then.

NVITED first to join the group, Simon Peter came.
Peter's brother followed too — Andrew
    was his name.

EVERAL more were called by Jesus near the
    Galilean lake.
James and John gave up their nets,
    just for Jesus' sake.

ROWDS that followed Jesus knew Philip
    and Thomas too.
But Thomas had doubts about Jesus
    (more than just a few).

N the group was Matthew, who wrote of Jesus' life.
His book tells many great stories —
    the love, teachings, and strife.

LEASED to be a disciple, James joined
    the throng.
Thaddaeus and Simon also came along.

ATER the one called Judas would betray his
    master's name.
Bartholomew (called Nathanael) was
    another one who came.

ACH of the disciples went out in the world
    to preach,
To tell the message of Jesus to every
    soul they could reach.

INCE we're saved by Jesus, we must follow too;
So listen to Jesus calling —
    calling me and you.

[51]from the blood of Abel to the blood of Zechariah, who was killed between the altar and the sanctuary. Yes, I tell you, this generation will be held responsible for it all.

[52]"Woe to you experts in the law, because you have taken away the key to knowledge. You yourselves have not entered, and you have hindered those who were entering."

[53]When Jesus left there, the Pharisees and the teachers of the law began to oppose him fiercely and to besiege him with questions, [54]waiting to catch him in something he might say.

Warnings and Encouragements

12 Meanwhile, when a crowd of many thousands had gathered, so that they were trampling on one another, Jesus began to speak first to his disciples, saying: "Be on your guard against the yeast of the Pharisees, which is hypocrisy. [2]There is nothing concealed that will not be disclosed, or hidden that will not be made known. [3]What you have said in the dark will be heard in the daylight, and what you have whispered in the ear in the inner rooms will be proclaimed from the roofs.

[4]"I tell you, my friends, do not be afraid of those who kill the body and after that can do no more. [5]But I will show you whom you should fear: Fear him who, after the killing of the body, has power to throw you into hell. Yes, I tell you, fear him. [6]Are not five sparrows sold for two pennies[a]? Yet not one of them is forgotten by God. [7]Indeed, the very hairs of your head are all numbered. Don't be afraid; you are worth more than many sparrows.

[8]"I tell you, whoever acknowledges me before men, the Son of Man will also acknowledge him before the angels of God. [9]But he who disowns me before men will be disowned before the angels of God. [10]And everyone who speaks a word against the Son of Man will be forgiven, but anyone who blasphemes against the Holy Spirit will not be forgiven.

[11]"When you are brought before synagogues, rulers and authorities, do not worry about how you will defend yourselves or what you will say, [12]for the Holy Spirit will teach you at that time what you should say."

The Parable of the Rich Fool

[13]Someone in the crowd said to him, "Teacher, tell my brother to divide the inheritance with me."

[14]Jesus replied, "Man, who appointed me a judge or an arbiter between you?" [15]Then he said to them, "Watch out! Be on your guard against all kinds of greed; a man's life does not consist in the abundance of his possessions."

[16]And he told them this parable: "The ground of a certain rich man produced a good crop. [17]He thought to himself, 'What shall I do? I have no place to store my crops.'

[18]"Then he said, 'This is what I'll do. I will tear down my barns and build bigger ones, and there I will store all my grain and my goods. [19]And I'll say to myself, "You have plenty of good things laid up for many years. Take life easy; eat, drink and be merry." '

[20]"But God said to him, 'You fool! This very night your life will be demanded from you. Then who will get what you have prepared for yourself?'

[21]"This is how it will be with anyone who stores up things for himself but is not rich toward God."

Do Not Worry

[22]Then Jesus said to his disciples: "Therefore I tell you, do not worry about your life, what you will eat; or about your body, what you will wear. [23]Life is more than food, and the body more than clothes. [24]Consider the ravens: They do not sow or reap, they have no storeroom or barn; yet God feeds them. And how much more valuable you are than birds! [25]Who of you by worrying can add a single

[a]6 Greek *two assaria*

hour to his life*a*? 26Since you cannot do this very little thing, why do you worry about the rest?

27"Consider how the lilies grow. They do not labor or spin. Yet I tell you, not even Solomon in all his splendor was dressed like one of these. 28If that is how God clothes the grass of the field, which is here today, and tomorrow is thrown into the fire, how much more will he clothe you, O you of little faith! 29And do not set your heart on what you will eat or drink; do not worry about it. 30For the pagan world runs after all such things, and your Father knows that you need them. 31But seek his kingdom, and these things will be given to you as well.

32"Do not be afraid, little flock, for your Father has been pleased to give you the kingdom. 33Sell your possessions and give to the poor. Provide purses for yourselves that will not wear out, a treasure in heaven that will not be exhausted, where no thief comes near and no moth destroys. 34For where your treasure is, there your heart will be also.

Watchfulness

35"Be dressed ready for service and keep your lamps burning, 36like men waiting for their master to return from a wedding banquet, so that when he comes and knocks they can immediately open the door for him.

a25 Or single cubit to his height

37It will be good for those servants whose master finds them watching when he comes. I tell you the truth, he will dress himself to serve, will have them recline at the table and will come and wait on them. 38It will be good for those servants whose master finds them ready, even if he comes in the second or third watch of the night. 39But understand this: If the owner of the house had known at what hour the thief was coming, he would not have let his house be broken into. 40You also must be ready, because the Son of Man will come at an hour when you do not expect him."

41Peter asked, "Lord, are you telling this parable to us, or to everyone?"

42The Lord answered, "Who then is the faithful and wise manager, whom the master puts in charge of his servants to give them their food allowance at the proper time? 43It will be good for that servant whom the master finds doing so when he returns. 44I tell you the truth, he will put him in charge of all his possessions. 45But suppose the servant says to himself, 'My master is taking a long time in coming,' and he then begins to beat the menservants and maidservants and to eat and drink and get drunk. 46The master of that servant will come on a day when he does not expect him and at an hour he is not aware of. He will cut him to pieces

Life in Bible Times

LILIES OF THE FIELD

Flowers grew wild all over Galilee. No one planted or weeded them. Yet God "dressed" them with beautiful petals. God will care for us too, for we are more important to God than flowers.

and assign him a place with the unbelievers.

47"That servant who knows his master's will and does not get ready or does not do what his master wants will be beaten with many blows. 48But the one who does not know and does things deserving punishment will be beaten with few blows. From everyone who has been given much, much will be demanded; and from the one who has been entrusted with much, much more will be asked.

Not Peace but Division

49"I have come to bring fire on the earth, and how I wish it were already kindled! 50But I have a baptism to undergo, and how distressed I am until it is completed! 51Do you think I came to bring peace on earth? No, I tell you, but division. 52From now on there will be five in one family divided against each other, three against two and two against three. 53They will be divided, father against son and son against father, mother against daughter and daughter against mother, mother-in-law against daughter-in-law and daughter-in-law against mother-in-law."

Interpreting the Times

54He said to the crowd: "When you see a cloud rising in the west, immediately you say, 'It's going to rain,' and it does. 55And when the south wind blows, you say, 'It's going to be hot,' and it is. 56Hypocrites! You know how to interpret the appearance of the earth and the sky. How is it that you don't know how to interpret this present time?

57"Why don't you judge for yourselves what is right? 58As you are going with your adversary to the magistrate, try hard to be reconciled to him on the way, or he may drag you off to the judge, and the judge turn you over to the officer, and the officer throw you into prison. 59I tell you, you will not get out until you have paid the last penny.*"

Repent or Perish

13 Now there were some present at that time who told Jesus about the Galileans whose blood Pilate had mixed with their sacrifices. 2Jesus answered, "Do you think that these Galileans were worse sinners than all the other Galileans because they suffered this way? 3I tell you, no! But unless you repent, you too will all perish. 4Or those eighteen who died when the tower in Siloam fell on them—do you think they were more guilty than all the others living in Jerusalem? 5I tell you, no! But unless you repent, you too will all perish."

6Then he told this parable: "A man had a fig tree, planted in his vineyard, and he went to look for fruit on it, but did not find any. 7So he said to the man who took care of the vineyard, 'For three years now I've been coming to look for fruit on this fig tree and haven't found any. Cut it down! Why should it use up the soil?'

8"'Sir,' the man replied, 'leave it alone for one more year, and I'll dig around it and fertilize it. 9If it bears fruit next year, fine! If not, then cut it down.'"

A Crippled Woman Healed on the Sabbath

10On a Sabbath Jesus was teaching in one of the synagogues, 11and a woman was there who had been crippled by a spirit for eighteen years. She was bent over and could not straighten up at all. 12When Jesus saw her, he called her forward and said to her, "Woman, you are set free from your infirmity." 13Then he put his hands on her, and immediately she straightened up and praised God.

14Indignant because Jesus had healed on the Sabbath, the synagogue ruler said to the people, "There are six days for work. So come and be healed on those days, not on the Sabbath."

15The Lord answered him, "You hypocrites! Doesn't each of you on the

a 59 Greek lepton

Sabbath untie his ox or donkey from the stall and lead it out to give it water? 16Then should not this woman, a daughter of Abraham, whom Satan has kept bound for eighteen long years, be set free on the Sabbath day from what bound her?"

17When he said this, all his opponents were humiliated, but the people were delighted with all the wonderful things he was doing.

The Parables of the Mustard Seed and the Yeast

18Then Jesus asked, "What is the kingdom of God like? What shall I compare it to? 19It is like a mustard seed, which a man took and planted in his garden. It grew and became a tree, and the birds of the air perched in its branches."

20Again he asked, "What shall I compare the kingdom of God to? 21It is like yeast that a woman took and mixed into a large amount*a* of flour until it worked all through the dough."

The Narrow Door

22Then Jesus went through the towns and villages, teaching as he made his way to Jerusalem. 23Someone asked him, "Lord, are only a few people going to be saved?"

He said to them, 24"Make every effort to enter through the narrow door, because many, I tell you, will try to enter and will not be able to. 25Once the owner of the house gets up and closes the door, you will stand outside knocking and pleading, 'Sir, open the door for us.'

"But he will answer, 'I don't know you or where you come from.'

26"Then you will say, 'We ate and drank with you, and you taught in our streets.'

27"But he will reply, 'I don't know you or where you come from. Away from me, all you evildoers!'

28"There will be weeping there, and gnashing of teeth, when you see Abraham, Isaac and Jacob and all the prophets in the kingdom of God, but you yourselves thrown out. 29People will come from east and west and north and south, and will take their places at the feast in the kingdom of God. 30Indeed there are those who are last who will be first, and first who will be last."

Jesus' Sorrow for Jerusalem

31At that time some Pharisees came to Jesus and said to him, "Leave this place and go somewhere else. Herod wants to kill you."

32He replied, "Go tell that fox, 'I will drive out demons and heal people today and tomorrow, and on the third day I will reach my goal.' 33In any case, I must keep going today and tomorrow and the next day—for surely no prophet can die outside Jerusalem!

34"O Jerusalem, Jerusalem, you who kill the prophets and stone those sent to you, how often I have longed to gather your children together, as a hen gathers her chicks under her wings, but you were not willing! 35Look, your house is left to you desolate. I tell you, you will not see me again until you say, 'Blessed is he

a21 Greek three satas (probably about 1/2 bushel or 22 liters)

LET'S LIVE IT!　　Luke 13:18–19

TWO WAYS TO GROW ➡ Read Luke 13:18–19. God's plan for all living things is for them to grow. Ask your mom or dad how many inches long you were when you were born. Mark that many inches on a wall. Then stand by the wall and mark how tall you are now.

People grow spiritually too. Talk with your parents. Ask if they can see ways you have grown spiritually in the past two years.

who comes in the name of the Lord.'*a*"

Jesus at a Pharisee's House

14 One Sabbath, when Jesus went to eat in the house of a prominent Pharisee, he was being carefully watched. ²There in front of him was a man suffering from dropsy. ³Jesus asked the Pharisees and experts in the law, "Is it lawful to heal on the Sabbath or not?" ⁴But they remained silent. So taking hold of the man, he healed him and sent him away.

⁵Then he asked them, "If one of you has a son*b* or an ox that falls into a well on the Sabbath day, will you not immediately pull him out?" ⁶And they had nothing to say.

⁷When he noticed how the guests picked the places of honor at the table, he told them this parable: ⁸"When someone invites you to a wedding feast, do not take the place of honor, for a person more distinguished than you may have been invited. ⁹If so, the host who invited both of you will come and say to you, 'Give this man your seat.' Then, humiliated, you will have to take the least important place. ¹⁰But when you are invited, take the lowest place, so that when your host comes, he will say to you, 'Friend, move up to a better place.' Then you will be honored in the presence of all your fellow guests. ¹¹For everyone who exalts himself will be humbled, and he who humbles himself will be exalted."

¹²Then Jesus said to his host, "When you give a luncheon or dinner, do not invite your friends, your brothers or relatives, or your rich neighbors; if you do, they may invite you back and so you will be repaid. ¹³But when you give a banquet, invite the poor, the crippled, the lame, the blind, ¹⁴and you will be blessed. Although they cannot repay you, you will be repaid at the resurrection of the righteous."

The Parable of the Great Banquet

¹⁵When one of those at the table with him heard this, he said to Jesus, "Blessed is the man who will eat at the feast in the kingdom of God."

¹⁶Jesus replied: "A certain man was preparing a great banquet and invited many guests. ¹⁷At the time of the banquet he sent his servant to tell those who had been invited, 'Come, for everything is now ready.'

¹⁸"But they all alike began to make excuses. The first said, 'I have just bought a field, and I must go and see it. Please excuse me.'

¹⁹"Another said, 'I have just bought five yoke of oxen, and I'm on my way to try them out. Please excuse me.'

²⁰"Still another said, 'I just got married, so I can't come.'

²¹"The servant came back and reported this to his master. Then the owner of the house became angry and ordered his servant, 'Go out quickly into the streets and alleys of the town and bring in the poor, the crippled, the blind and the lame.'

²²"'Sir,' the servant said, 'what you ordered has been done, but there is still room.'

²³"Then the master told his servant, 'Go out to the roads and country lanes and make them come in, so that my house will be full. ²⁴I tell you, not one of those men who were invited will get a taste of my banquet.'"

The Cost of Being a Disciple

²⁵Large crowds were traveling with Jesus, and turning to them he said: ²⁶"If anyone comes to me and does not hate his father and mother, his wife and children, his brothers and sisters—yes, even his own life—he cannot be my disciple. ²⁷And anyone who does not carry his cross and follow me cannot be my disciple. ²⁸"Suppose one of you wants to build a tower. Will he not first sit down and estimate the cost to see if he has enough money to complete it?

a35 Psalm 118:26   *b5* Some manuscripts *donkey*

²⁹For if he lays the foundation and is not able to finish it, everyone who sees it will ridicule him, ³⁰saying, 'This fellow began to build and was not able to finish.'

³¹"Or suppose a king is about to go to war against another king. Will he not first sit down and consider whether he is able with ten thousand men to oppose the one coming against him with twenty thousand? ³²If he is not able, he will send a delegation while the other is still a long way off and will ask for terms of peace. ³³In the same way, any of you who does not give up everything he has cannot be my disciple.

³⁴"Salt is good, but if it loses its saltiness, how can it be made salty again? ³⁵It is fit neither for the soil nor for the manure pile; it is thrown out.

"He who has ears to hear, let him hear."

The Parable of the Lost Sheep

15 Now the tax collectors and "sinners" were all gathering around to hear him. ²But the Pharisees and the teachers of the law muttered, "This man welcomes sinners and eats with them."

³Then Jesus told them this parable: ⁴"Suppose one of you has a hundred sheep and loses one of them. Does he not leave the ninety-nine in the open country and go after the lost sheep until he finds it? ⁵And when he finds it, he joyfully puts it on his shoulders ⁶and goes home. Then he calls his friends and neighbors together and says, 'Rejoice with me; I have found my lost sheep.' ⁷I tell you that in the same way there will be more rejoicing in heaven over one sinner who repents than over ninety-nine righteous persons who do not need to repent.

The Parable of the Lost Coin

⁸"Or suppose a woman has ten silver coins*a* and loses one. Does she not light a lamp, sweep the house and search carefully until she finds it? ⁹And when she finds it, she calls her friends and neighbors together and says, 'Rejoice with me; I have found my lost coin.' ¹⁰In the same way, I tell you, there is rejoicing in the presence of the angels of God over one sinner who repents."

The Parable of the Lost Son

¹¹Jesus continued: "There was a man who had two sons. ¹²The younger one said to his father, 'Father, give me my share of the estate.' So he divided his property between them.

¹³"Not long after that, the younger son got together all he had, set off for a distant country and there squandered his wealth in wild living. ¹⁴After he had spent everything, there was a severe famine in that whole country, and he began to be in need. ¹⁵So he went and hired himself out to

---

*a8 Greek ten drachmas, each worth about a day's wages

Life in Bible Times

THE SHEPHERD'S STAFF

Shepherds in Palestine carried a staff with a hook at one end. The shepherd used it to lift up a sheep that had fallen into a hole or down the side of a cliff.

a citizen of that country, who sent him to his fields to feed pigs. ¹⁶He longed to fill his stomach with the pods that the pigs were eating, but no one gave him anything.

¹⁷"When he came to his senses, he said, 'How many of my father's hired men have food to spare, and here I am starving to death! ¹⁸I will set out and go back to my father and say to him: Father, I have sinned against heaven and against you. ¹⁹I am no longer worthy to be called your son; make me like one of your hired men.' ²⁰So he got up and went to his father.

"But while he was still a long way off, his father saw him and was filled with compassion for him; he ran to his son, threw his arms around him and kissed him.

²¹"The son said to him, 'Father, I have sinned against heaven and against you. I am no longer worthy to be called your son.ᵃ'

²²"But the father said to his servants, 'Quick! Bring the best robe and put it on him. Put a ring on his finger and sandals on his feet. ²³Bring the fattened calf and kill it. Let's have a feast and celebrate. ²⁴For this son of mine was dead and is alive again; he was lost and is found.' So they began to celebrate.

²⁵"Meanwhile, the older son was in the field. When he came near the house, he heard music and dancing. ²⁶So he called one of the servants and asked him what was going on. ²⁷'Your brother has come,' he replied, 'and your father has killed the fattened calf because he has him back safe and sound.'

²⁸"The older brother became angry and refused to go in. So his father went out and pleaded with him. ²⁹But he answered his father, 'Look! All these years I've been slaving for you and never disobeyed your orders. Yet you never gave me even a young goat so I could celebrate with my friends. ³⁰But when this son of yours who has squandered your property with pros-

titutes comes home, you kill the fattened calf for him!'

³¹"'My son,' the father said, 'you are always with me, and everything I have is yours. ³²But we had to celebrate and be glad, because this brother of yours was dead and is alive again; he was lost and is found.'"

The Parable of the Shrewd Manager

16 Jesus told his disciples: "There was a rich man whose manager was accused of wasting his possessions. ²So he called him in and asked him, 'What is this I hear about you? Give an account of your management, because you cannot be manager any longer.'

³"The manager said to himself, 'What shall I do now? My master is taking away my job. I'm not strong enough to dig, and I'm ashamed to beg— ⁴I know what I'll do so that, when I lose my job here, people will welcome me into their houses.'

⁵"So he called in each one of his master's debtors. He asked the first, 'How much do you owe my master?'

⁶"'Eight hundred gallonsᵇ of olive oil,' he replied.

"The manager told him, 'Take your bill, sit down quickly, and make it four hundred.'

⁷"Then he asked the second, 'And how much do you owe?'

"'A thousand bushelsᶜ of wheat,' he replied.

"He told him, 'Take your bill and make it eight hundred.'

⁸"The master commended the dishonest manager because he had acted shrewdly. For the people of this world are more shrewd in dealing with their own kind than are the people of the light. ⁹I tell you, use worldly wealth to gain friends for yourselves, so that when it is gone, you will be welcomed into eternal dwellings.

¹⁰"Whoever can be trusted with very little can also be trusted with

---

ᵃ21 Some early manuscripts son. *Make me like one of your hired men.*   ᵇ6 Greek *one hundred batous* (probably about 3 kiloliters)   ᶜ7 Greek *one hundred korous* (probably about 35 kiloliters)

much, and whoever is dishonest with very little will also be dishonest with much. ¹¹So if you have not been trustworthy in handling worldly wealth, who will trust you with true riches? ¹²And if you have not been trustworthy with someone else's property, who will give you property of your own?

¹³"No servant can serve two masters. Either he will hate the one and love the other, or he will be devoted to the one and despise the other. You cannot serve both God and Money."

¹⁴The Pharisees, who loved money, heard all this and were sneering at Jesus. ¹⁵He said to them, "You are the ones who justify yourselves in the eyes of men, but God knows your hearts. What is highly valued among men is detestable in God's sight.

Additional Teachings

¹⁶"The Law and the Prophets were proclaimed until John. Since that time, the good news of the kingdom of God is being preached, and everyone is forcing his way into it. ¹⁷It is easier for heaven and earth to disappear than for the least stroke of a pen to drop out of the Law.

¹⁸"Anyone who divorces his wife and marries another woman commits adultery, and the man who marries a divorced woman commits adultery.

The Rich Man and Lazarus

¹⁹"There was a rich man who was dressed in purple and fine linen and lived in luxury every day. ²⁰At his gate was laid a beggar named Lazarus, covered with sores ²¹and longing to eat what fell from the rich man's table. Even the dogs came and licked his sores.

²²"The time came when the beggar died and the angels carried him to Abraham's side. The rich man also died and was buried. ²³In hell,ᵃ where he was in torment, he looked up and saw Abraham far away, with Lazarus by his side. ²⁴So he called to him, 'Father Abraham, have pity on

me and send Lazarus to dip the tip of his finger in water and cool my tongue, because I am in agony in this fire.'

²⁵"But Abraham replied, 'Son, remember that in your lifetime you received your good things, while Lazarus received bad things, but now he is comforted here and you are in agony. ²⁶And besides all this, between us and you a great chasm has been fixed, so that those who want to go from here to you cannot, nor can anyone cross over from there to us.'

²⁷"He answered, 'Then I beg you, father, send Lazarus to my father's house, ²⁸for I have five brothers. Let him warn them, so that they will not also come to this place of torment.'

²⁹"Abraham replied, 'They have Moses and the Prophets; let them listen to them.'

³⁰" 'No, father Abraham,' he said, 'but if someone from the dead goes to them, they will repent.'

³¹"He said to him, 'If they do not listen to Moses and the Prophets, they will not be convinced even if someone rises from the dead.' "

❓DID YOU KNOW?   16:22

Is there life after death?

Yes. In Jesus' story about the rich man and the beggar Lazarus, each one died. But after that both were able to talk and think and see and feel! After our bodies are dead, we will still be alive.

Sin, Faith, Duty

17 Jesus said to his disciples: "Things that cause people to sin are bound to come, but woe to that person through whom they come. ²It would be better for him to be thrown into the sea with a millstone tied around his neck than for him to cause one of these little ones to sin. ³So watch yourselves.

ᵃ23 Greek *Hades*

"If your brother sins, rebuke him, and if he repents, forgive him. ⁴If he sins against you seven times in a day, and seven times comes back to you and says, 'I repent,' forgive him."

⁵The apostles said to the Lord, "Increase our faith!"

⁶He replied, "If you have faith as small as a mustard seed, you can say to this mulberry tree, 'Be uprooted and planted in the sea,' and it will obey you.

⁷"Suppose one of you had a servant plowing or looking after the sheep. Would he say to the servant when he comes in from the field, 'Come along now and sit down to eat'? ⁸Would he not rather say, 'Prepare my supper, get yourself ready and wait on me while I eat and drink; after that you may eat and drink'? ⁹Would he thank the servant because he did what he was told to do? ¹⁰So you also, when you have done everything you were told to do, should say, 'We are unworthy servants; we have only done our duty.'"

Ten Healed of Leprosy

¹¹Now on his way to Jerusalem, Jesus traveled along the border between Samaria and Galilee. ¹²As he was going into a village, ten men who had leprosy*ᵃ* met him. They stood at a distance ¹³and called out in a loud voice, "Jesus, Master, have pity on us!"

¹⁴When he saw them, he said, "Go, show yourselves to the priests." And as they went, they were cleansed.

¹⁵One of them, when he saw he was healed, came back, praising God in a loud voice. ¹⁶He threw himself at Jesus' feet and thanked him—and he was a Samaritan.

¹⁷Jesus asked, "Were not all ten cleansed? Where are the other nine? ¹⁸Was no one found to return and give praise to God except this foreigner?" ¹⁹Then he said to him, "Rise and go; your faith has made you well."

The Coming of the Kingdom of God

²⁰Once, having been asked by the Pharisees when the kingdom of God would come, Jesus replied, "The kingdom of God does not come with your careful observation, ²¹nor will people say, 'Here it is,' or 'There it is,' because the kingdom of God is within*ᵇ* you."

²²Then he said to his disciples, "The time is coming when you will long to see one of the days of the Son of Man, but you will not see it. ²³Men will tell you, 'There he is!' or 'Here he is!' Do not go running off after them. ²⁴For the Son of Man in his day*ᶜ* will be like the lightning, which flashes and lights up the sky from one end to the other. ²⁵But first he must suffer many things and be rejected by this generation.

²⁶"Just as it was in the days of Noah, so also will it be in the days of the Son of Man. ²⁷People were eating, drinking, marrying and being given in marriage up to the day Noah en-

---

ᵃ12 The Greek word was used for various diseases affecting the skin—not necessarily leprosy.
ᵇ21 Or *among*　　*ᶜ24* Some manuscripts do not have *in his day*.

▚ET'S LIVE IT! 　　　　Luke 17:11–19

SAYING THANK YOU ➠ Read Luke 17:11–19. Saying thank you to God is one important way we praise him and show love for him.

Take a long sheet of paper and make nine folds in it, as if you were making a large fan. In the folded paper cut the figure of a person without cutting the arms but letting them extend over the folds. Open it, and you have a line of ten figures attached to each other! Color one of the figures your favorite color. Tape the figures to your wall to remind you to be like the man who came back and said thank you to Jesus.

tered the ark. Then the flood came and destroyed them all.

28"It was the same in the days of Lot. People were eating and drinking, buying and selling, planting and building. 29But the day Lot left Sodom, fire and sulfur rained down from heaven and destroyed them all.

30"It will be just like this on the day the Son of Man is revealed. 31On that day no one who is on the roof of his house, with his goods inside, should go down to get them. Likewise, no one in the field should go back for anything. 32Remember Lot's wife! 33Whoever tries to keep his life will lose it, and whoever loses his life will preserve it. 34I tell you, on that night two people will be in one bed; one will be taken and the other left. 35Two women will be grinding grain together; one will be taken and the other left.*a*"

37"Where, Lord?" they asked.

He replied, "Where there is a dead body, there the vultures will gather."

The Parable of the Persistent Widow

18 Then Jesus told his disciples a parable to show them that they should always pray and not give up. 2He said: "In a certain town there was a judge who neither feared God nor cared about men. 3And there was a widow in that town who kept coming to him with the plea, 'Grant me justice against my adversary.'

4"For some time he refused. But finally he said to himself, 'Even though I don't fear God or care about men, 5yet because this widow keeps bothering me, I will see that she gets justice, so that she won't eventually wear me out with her coming!' "

6And the Lord said, "Listen to what the unjust judge says. 7And will not God bring about justice for his chosen ones, who cry out to him day and night? Will he keep putting them off? 8I tell you, he will see that they get justice, and quickly. However, when

the Son of Man comes, will he find faith on the earth?"

The Parable of the Pharisee and the Tax Collector

9To some who were confident of their own righteousness and looked down on everybody else, Jesus told this parable: 10"Two men went up to the temple to pray, one a Pharisee and the other a tax collector. 11The Pharisee stood up and prayed about*b* himself: 'God, I thank you that I am not like other men—robbers, evildoers, adulterers—or even like this tax collector. 12I fast twice a week and give a tenth of all I get.'

13"But the tax collector stood at a distance. He would not even look up to heaven, but beat his breast and said, 'God, have mercy on me, a sinner.'

14"I tell you that this man, rather than the other, went home justified before God. For everyone who exalts himself will be humbled, and he who humbles himself will be exalted."

The Little Children and Jesus

15People were also bringing babies to Jesus to have him touch them. When the disciples saw this, they rebuked them. 16But Jesus called the children to him and said, "Let the little children come to me, and do not hinder them, for the kingdom of God belongs to such as these. 17I tell you the truth, anyone who will not receive the kingdom of God like a little child will never enter it."

The Rich Ruler

18A certain ruler asked him, "Good teacher, what must I do to inherit eternal life?"

19"Why do you call me good?" Jesus answered. "No one is good—except God alone. 20You know the commandments: 'Do not commit adultery, do not murder, do not steal, do not give false testimony, honor your father and mother.'*c*"

---

a35 Some manuscripts *left. 36Two men will be in the field; one will be taken and the other left.*
b11 Or *to*   *c20* Exodus 20:12-16; Deut. 5:16-20

²¹"All these I have kept since I was a boy," he said.

²²When Jesus heard this, he said to him, "You still lack one thing. Sell everything you have and give to the poor, and you will have treasure in heaven. Then come, follow me."

²³When he heard this, he became very sad, because he was a man of great wealth. ²⁴Jesus looked at him and said, "How hard it is for the rich to enter the kingdom of God! ²⁵Indeed, it is easier for a camel to go through the eye of a needle than for a rich man to enter the kingdom of God."

²⁶Those who heard this asked, "Who then can be saved?"

²⁷Jesus replied, "What is impossible with men is possible with God."

²⁸Peter said to him, "We have left all we had to follow you!"

²⁹"I tell you the truth," Jesus said to them, "no one who has left home or wife or brothers or parents or children for the sake of the kingdom of God ³⁰will fail to receive many times as much in this age and, in the age to come, eternal life."

❓ DID YOU KNOW?   18:22

Why did Jesus tell the rich ruler to sell everything he had?

The young man had kept the commandments that tell how to love other people. But Jesus reminded him that the first commandment was to love God with all his heart. Jesus knew that the young ruler's riches were more important to him than God was.

Jesus Again Predicts His Death

³¹Jesus took the Twelve aside and told them, "We are going up to Jerusalem, and everything that is written by the prophets about the Son of Man will be fulfilled. ³²He will be handed over to the Gentiles. They will mock him, insult him, spit on him, flog him

and kill him. ³³On the third day he will rise again."

³⁴The disciples did not understand any of this. Its meaning was hidden from them, and they did not know what he was talking about.

A Blind Beggar Receives His Sight

³⁵As Jesus approached Jericho, a blind man was sitting by the roadside begging. ³⁶When he heard the crowd going by, he asked what was happening. ³⁷They told him, "Jesus of Nazareth is passing by."

³⁸He called out, "Jesus, Son of David, have mercy on me!"

³⁹Those who led the way rebuked him and told him to be quiet, but he shouted all the more, "Son of David, have mercy on me!"

⁴⁰Jesus stopped and ordered the man to be brought to him. When he came near, Jesus asked him, ⁴¹"What do you want me to do for you?"

"Lord, I want to see," he replied.

⁴²Jesus said to him, "Receive your sight; your faith has healed you." ⁴³Immediately he received his sight and followed Jesus, praising God. When all the people saw it, they also praised God.

Zacchaeus the Tax Collector

19 Jesus entered Jericho and was passing through. ²A man was there by the name of Zacchaeus; he was a chief tax collector and was wealthy. ³He wanted to see who Jesus was, but being a short man he could not, because of the crowd. ⁴So he ran ahead and climbed a sycamore-fig tree to see him, since Jesus was coming that way.

⁵When Jesus reached the spot, he looked up and said to him, "Zacchaeus, come down immediately. I must stay at your house today." ⁶So he came down at once and welcomed him gladly.

⁷All the people saw this and began to mutter, "He has gone to be the guest of a 'sinner.'"

⁸But Zacchaeus stood up and said to the Lord, "Look, Lord! Here and

now I give half of my possessions to the poor, and if I have cheated anybody out of anything, I will pay back four times the amount."

9Jesus said to him, "Today salvation has come to this house, because this man, too, is a son of Abraham. 10For the Son of Man came to seek and to save what was lost."

The Parable of the Ten Minas

11While they were listening to this, he went on to tell them a parable, because he was near Jerusalem and the people thought that the kingdom of God was going to appear at once. 12He said: "A man of noble birth went to a distant country to have himself appointed king and then to return. 13So he called ten of his servants and gave them ten minas. a 'Put this money to work,' he said, 'until I come back.'

14"But his subjects hated him and sent a delegation after him to say, 'We don't want this man to be our king.'

15"He was made king, however, and returned home. Then he sent for the servants to whom he had given the money, in order to find out what they had gained with it.

16"The first one came and said, 'Sir, your mina has earned ten more.'

17" 'Well done, my good servant!' his master replied. 'Because you have been trustworthy in a very small matter, take charge of ten cities.'

18"The second came and said, 'Sir, your mina has earned five more.'

19"His master answered, 'You take charge of five cities.'

a13 A mina was about three months' wages.

20"Then another servant came and said, 'Sir, here is your mina; I have kept it laid away in a piece of cloth. 21I was afraid of you, because you are a hard man. You take out what you did not put in and reap what you did not sow.'

22"His master replied, 'I will judge you by your own words, you wicked servant! You knew, did you, that I am a hard man, taking out what I did not put in, and reaping what I did not sow? 23Why then didn't you put my money on deposit, so that when I came back, I could have collected it with interest?'

24"Then he said to those standing by, 'Take his mina away from him and give it to the one who has ten minas.'

25" 'Sir,' they said, 'he already has ten!'

26"He replied, 'I tell you that to everyone who has, more will be given, but as for the one who has nothing, even what he has will be taken away. 27But those enemies of mine who did not want me to be king over them —bring them here and kill them in front of me.' "

The Triumphal Entry

28After Jesus had said this, he went on ahead, going up to Jerusalem. 29As he approached Bethphage and Bethany at the hill called the Mount of Olives, he sent two of his disciples, saying to them, 30"Go to the village ahead of you, and as you enter it, you will find a colt tied there, which no one has ever ridden. Untie it and

---

▌ET'S LIVE IT!   Luke 19:11-24

FIND YOUR GIFTS ➡ Read Luke 19:11-24. Which lessons do you think God wants you to learn from this story? 1. God gives everyone gifts and abilities. 2. God wants me to use my gifts for him. 3. God will praise me when I use my gifts for him.

List some things you do well. Sing? Draw? Write? Play sports? Help others? Ask three adults who know you what gifts they think God has given you. Ask how they think you can use your gifts to serve God.

bring it here. ³¹If anyone asks you, 'Why are you untying it?' tell him, 'The Lord needs it.' "

³²Those who were sent ahead went and found it just as he had told them. ³³As they were untying the colt, its owners asked them, "Why are you untying the colt?"

³⁴They replied, "The Lord needs it."

³⁵They brought it to Jesus, threw their cloaks on the colt and put Jesus on it. ³⁶As he went along, people spread their cloaks on the road.

³⁷When he came near the place where the road goes down the Mount of Olives, the whole crowd of disciples began joyfully to praise God in loud voices for all the miracles they had seen:

³⁸"Blessed is the king who comes in the name of the Lord!"ᵃ

"Peace in heaven and glory in the highest!"

³⁹Some of the Pharisees in the crowd said to Jesus, "Teacher, rebuke your disciples!"

⁴⁰"I tell you," he replied, "if they keep quiet, the stones will cry out."

⁴¹As he approached Jerusalem and saw the city, he wept over it ⁴²and said, "If you, even you, had only known on this day what would bring you peace—but now it is hidden from your eyes. ⁴³The days will come upon you when your enemies will build an embankment against you and encircle you and hem you in on every side. ⁴⁴They will dash you to the ground, you and the children within your walls. They will not leave one stone on another, because you did not recognize the time of God's coming to you."

Jesus at the Temple

⁴⁵Then he entered the temple area and began driving out those who were selling. ⁴⁶"It is written," he said to them, " 'My house will be a house of prayer'ᵇ; but you have made it 'a den of robbers.'ᶜ"

⁴⁷Every day he was teaching at the temple. But the chief priests, the teachers of the law and the leaders among the people were trying to kill him. ⁴⁸Yet they could not find any way to do it, because all the people hung on his words.

WORDS TO REMEMBER

19:46 My house will be a house of prayer.

The Authority of Jesus Questioned

20 One day as he was teaching the people in the temple courts and preaching the gospel, the chief priests and the teachers of the law, together with the elders, came up to him. ²"Tell us by what authority you are doing these things," they said. "Who gave you this authority?"

³He replied, "I will also ask you a question. Tell me, ⁴John's baptism —was it from heaven, or from men?"

⁵They discussed it among themselves and said, "If we say, 'From heaven,' he will ask, 'Why didn't you believe him?' ⁶But if we say, 'From men,' all the people will stone us, because they are persuaded that John was a prophet."

⁷So they answered, "We don't know where it was from."

⁸Jesus said, "Neither will I tell you by what authority I am doing these things."

The Parable of the Tenants

⁹He went on to tell the people this parable: "A man planted a vineyard, rented it to some farmers and went away for a long time. ¹⁰At harvest time he sent a servant to the tenants so they would give him some of the fruit of the vineyard. But the tenants beat him and sent him away empty-handed. ¹¹He sent another servant, but that one also they beat and treated shamefully and sent away

---

ᵃ38 Psalm 118:26   ᵇ46 Isaiah 56:7   ᶜ46 Jer. 7:11

empty-handed. ¹²He sent still a third, and they wounded him and threw him out.

¹³"Then the owner of the vineyard said, 'What shall I do? I will send my son, whom I love; perhaps they will respect him.'

¹⁴"But when the tenants saw him, they talked the matter over. 'This is the heir,' they said. 'Let's kill him, and the inheritance will be ours.' ¹⁵So they threw him out of the vineyard and killed him.

"What then will the owner of the vineyard do to them? ¹⁶He will come and kill those tenants and give the vineyard to others."

When the people heard this, they said, "May this never be!"

¹⁷Jesus looked directly at them and asked, "Then what is the meaning of that which is written:

" 'The stone the builders rejected
    has become the capstone*ᵃ'ᵇ?

¹⁸Everyone who falls on that stone will be broken to pieces, but he on whom it falls will be crushed."

¹⁹The teachers of the law and the chief priests looked for a way to arrest him immediately, because they knew he had spoken this parable against them. But they were afraid of the people.

Paying Taxes to Caesar

²⁰Keeping a close watch on him, they sent spies, who pretended to be honest. They hoped to catch Jesus in something he said so that they might hand him over to the power and authority of the governor. ²¹So the spies questioned him: "Teacher, we know that you speak and teach what is right, and that you do not show partiality but teach the way of God in accordance with the truth. ²²Is it right for us to pay taxes to Caesar or not?"

²³He saw through their duplicity and said to them, ²⁴"Show me a denarius. Whose portrait and inscription are on it?"

²⁵"Caesar's," they replied.

He said to them, "Then give to Caesar what is Caesar's, and to God what is God's."

²⁶They were unable to trap him in what he had said there in public. And astonished by his answer, they became silent.

❓DID YOU KNOW?   20:20

How did spies try to trap Jesus?

The spies asked Jesus about taxes. If Jesus said, "Don't pay taxes," they would report him to the Roman governor. If Jesus said, "Do pay taxes," it would make the people angry, because the people did not think they should pay taxes to Rome. Jesus was too wise to be trapped.

The Resurrection and Marriage

²⁷Some of the Sadducees, who say there is no resurrection, came to Jesus with a question. ²⁸"Teacher," they said, "Moses wrote for us that if a man's brother dies and leaves a wife but no children, the man must marry the widow and have children for his brother. ²⁹Now there were seven brothers. The first one married a woman and died childless. ³⁰The second ³¹and then the third married her, and in the same way the seven died, leaving no children. ³²Finally, the woman died too. ³³Now then, at the resurrection whose wife will she be, since the seven were married to her?"

³⁴Jesus replied, "The people of this age marry and are given in marriage. ³⁵But those who are considered worthy of taking part in that age and in the resurrection from the dead will neither marry nor be given in marriage, ³⁶and they can no longer die; for they are like the angels. They are God's children, since they are children of the resurrection. ³⁷But in the account of the bush, even Moses

---

ᵃ17 Or *cornerstone*   ᵇ17 Psalm 118:22

showed that the dead rise, for he calls the Lord 'the God of Abraham, and the God of Isaac, and the God of Jacob.'[a] 38He is not the God of the dead, but of the living, for to him all are alive."

39Some of the teachers of the law responded, "Well said, teacher!" 40And no one dared to ask him any more questions.

Whose Son Is the Christ?

41Then Jesus said to them, "How is it that they say the Christ[b] is the Son of David? 42David himself declares in the Book of Psalms:

" 'The Lord said to my Lord:
    "Sit at my right hand
43until I make your enemies
    a footstool for your feet." '[c]

44David calls him 'Lord.' How then can he be his son?"

45While all the people were listening, Jesus said to his disciples, 46"Beware of the teachers of the law. They like to walk around in flowing robes and love to be greeted in the marketplaces and have the most important seats in the synagogues and the places of honor at banquets. 47They devour widows' houses and for a show make lengthy prayers. Such men will be punished most severely."

The Widow's Offering

21 As he looked up, Jesus saw the rich putting their gifts into the temple treasury. 2He also saw a poor widow put in two very small copper coins.[d] 3"I tell you the truth," he said, "this poor widow has put in more than all the others. 4All these people gave their gifts out of their wealth; but she out of her poverty put in all she had to live on."

Signs of the End of the Age

5Some of his disciples were remarking about how the temple was adorned with beautiful stones and with gifts dedicated to God. But Jesus said, 6"As for what you see here, the time will come when not one stone will be left on another; every one of them will be thrown down."

7"Teacher," they asked, "when will these things happen? And what will be the sign that they are about to take place?"

8He replied: "Watch out that you are not deceived. For many will come in my name, claiming, 'I am he,' and, 'The time is near.' Do not follow them. 9When you hear of wars and revolutions, do not be frightened. These things must happen first, but the end will not come right away."

10Then he said to them: "Nation will rise against nation, and kingdom against kingdom. 11There will be great earthquakes, famines and pestilences in various places, and fearful events and great signs from heaven.

12"But before all this, they will lay hands on you and persecute you. They will deliver you to synagogues and prisons, and you will be brought before kings and governors, and all on account of my name. 13This will result in your being witnesses to them. 14But make up your mind not to worry beforehand how you will defend yourselves. 15For I will give you words and wisdom that none of your adversaries will be able to resist or contradict. 16You will be betrayed even by parents, brothers, relatives and friends, and they will put some of you to death. 17All men will hate you because of me. 18But not a hair of your head will perish. 19By standing firm you will gain life.

20"When you see Jerusalem being surrounded by armies, you will know that its desolation is near. 21Then let those who are in Judea flee to the mountains, let those in the city get out, and let those in the country not enter the city. 22For this is the time of punishment in fulfillment of all that has been written. 23How dreadful it will be in those days for pregnant women and nursing mothers! There will be great distress in the land and wrath against this people. 24They

---

a37 Exodus 3:6   b41 Or Messiah   c43 Psalm 110:1   d2 Greek two lepta

will fall by the sword and will be taken as prisoners to all the nations. Jerusalem will be trampled on by the Gentiles until the times of the Gentiles are fulfilled.

25"There will be signs in the sun, moon and stars. On the earth, nations will be in anguish and perplexity at the roaring and tossing of the sea. 26Men will faint from terror, apprehensive of what is coming on the world, for the heavenly bodies will be shaken. 27At that time they will see the Son of Man coming in a cloud with power and great glory. 28When these things begin to take place, stand up and lift up your heads, because your redemption is drawing near."

29He told them this parable: "Look at the fig tree and all the trees. 30When they sprout leaves, you can see for yourselves and know that summer is near. 31Even so, when you see these things happening, you know that the kingdom of God is near.

32"I tell you the truth, this generation*a* will certainly not pass away until all these things have happened. 33Heaven and earth will pass away, but my words will never pass away.

34"Be careful, or your hearts will be weighed down with dissipation, drunkenness and the anxieties of life, and that day will close on you unexpectedly like a trap. 35For it will come upon all those who live on the face of the whole earth. 36Be always on the watch, and pray that you may be able to escape all that is about to happen, and that you may be able to stand before the Son of Man."

37Each day Jesus was teaching at the temple, and each evening he went out to spend the night on the hill called the Mount of Olives, 38and all the people came early in the morning to hear him at the temple.

Judas Agrees to Betray Jesus

22 Now the Feast of Unleavened Bread, called the Passover, was approaching, 2and the chief priests and the teachers of the law were looking for some way to get rid of Jesus, for they were afraid of the people. 3Then Satan entered Judas, called Iscariot, one of the Twelve. 4And Judas went to the chief priests and the officers of the temple guard and discussed with them how he might betray Jesus. 5They were delighted and agreed to give him money. 6He consented, and watched for an opportunity to hand Jesus over to them when no crowd was present.

The Last Supper

7Then came the day of Unleavened Bread on which the Passover lamb had to be sacrificed. 8Jesus sent Peter and John, saying, "Go and make preparations for us to eat the Passover."

❓DID YOU KNOW?　　22:8

What was the Last Supper?

The Last Supper was a Passover meal that Jesus ate with his disciples the night before he was crucified. Jesus told his disciples he was about to die. He also told them to keep on celebrating the Lord's Supper until he came again.

9"Where do you want us to prepare for it?" they asked.

10He replied, "As you enter the city, a man carrying a jar of water will meet you. Follow him to the house that he enters, 11and say to the owner of the house, 'The Teacher asks: Where is the guest room, where I may eat the Passover with my disciples?' 12He will show you a large upper room, all furnished. Make preparations there."

13They left and found things just as Jesus had told them. So they prepared the Passover.

14When the hour came, Jesus and

his apostles reclined at the table. 15And he said to them, "I have eagerly desired to eat this Passover with you before I suffer. 16For I tell you, I will not eat it again until it finds fulfillment in the kingdom of God."

17After taking the cup, he gave thanks and said, "Take this and divide it among you. 18For I tell you I will not drink again of the fruit of the vine until the kingdom of God comes."

19And he took bread, gave thanks and broke it, and gave it to them, saying, "This is my body given for you; do this in remembrance of me."

20In the same way, after the supper he took the cup, saying, "This cup is the new covenant in my blood, which is poured out for you. 21But the hand of him who is going to betray me is with mine on the table. 22The Son of Man will go as it has been decreed, but woe to that man who betrays him." 23They began to question among themselves which of them it might be who would do this.

24Also a dispute arose among them as to which of them was considered to be greatest. 25Jesus said to them, "The kings of the Gentiles lord it over them; and those who exercise authority over them call themselves Benefactors. 26But you are not to be like that. Instead, the greatest among you should be like the youngest, and the one who rules like the one who serves. 27For who is greater, the one who is at the table or the one who serves? Is it not the one who is at the table? But I am among you as one who serves. 28You are those who have stood by me in my trials. 29And I confer on you a kingdom, just as my Father conferred one on me, 30so that you may eat and drink at my table in my kingdom and sit on thrones, judging the twelve tribes of Israel.

31"Simon, Simon, Satan has asked to sift you*a* as wheat. 32But I have prayed for you, Simon, that your faith may not fail. And when you have turned back, strengthen your brothers."

33But he replied, "Lord, I am ready to go with you to prison and to death."

34Jesus answered, "I tell you, Peter, before the rooster crows today, you will deny three times that you know me."

35Then Jesus asked them, "When I sent you without purse, bag or sandals, did you lack anything?"

"Nothing," they answered.

36He said to them, "But now if you have a purse, take it, and also a bag; and if you don't have a sword, sell your cloak and buy one. 37It is written: 'And he was numbered with the transgressors'*b*; and I tell you that this must be fulfilled in me. Yes, what is written about me is reaching its fulfillment."

38The disciples said, "See, Lord, here are two swords."

"That is enough," he replied.

Jesus Prays on the Mount of Olives

39Jesus went out as usual to the Mount of Olives, and his disciples followed him. 40On reaching the place, he said to them, "Pray that you will not fall into temptation." 41He withdrew about a stone's throw beyond them, knelt down and prayed, 42"Father, if you are willing, take this cup from me; yet not my will, but yours be done." 43An angel from heaven appeared to him and strengthened him. 44And being in anguish, he prayed more earnestly, and his sweat was like drops of blood falling to the ground.*c*

45When he rose from prayer and went back to the disciples, he found them asleep, exhausted from sorrow. 46"Why are you sleeping?" he asked them. "Get up and pray so that you will not fall into temptation."

Jesus Arrested

47While he was still speaking a crowd came up, and the man who was

---

a31 The Greek is plural.   *b37* Isaiah 53:12   *c44* Some early manuscripts do not have verses 43 and 44.

called Judas, one of the Twelve, was leading them. He approached Jesus to kiss him, ⁴⁸but Jesus asked him, "Judas, are you betraying the Son of Man with a kiss?"

⁴⁹When Jesus' followers saw what was going to happen, they said, "Lord, should we strike with our swords?" ⁵⁰And one of them struck the servant of the high priest, cutting off his right ear.

⁵¹But Jesus answered, "No more of this!" And he touched the man's ear and healed him.

⁵²Then Jesus said to the chief priests, the officers of the temple guard, and the elders, who had come for him, "Am I leading a rebellion, that you have come with swords and clubs? ⁵³Every day I was with you in the temple courts, and you did not lay a hand on me. But this is your hour—when darkness reigns."

Peter Disowns Jesus

⁵⁴Then seizing him, they led him away and took him into the house of the high priest. Peter followed at a distance. ⁵⁵But when they had kindled a fire in the middle of the courtyard and had sat down together, Peter sat down with them. ⁵⁶A servant girl saw him seated there in the firelight. She looked closely at him and said, "This man was with him."

⁵⁷But he denied it. "Woman, I don't know him," he said.

⁵⁸A little later someone else saw him and said, "You also are one of them."

"Man, I am not!" Peter replied.

⁵⁹About an hour later another asserted, "Certainly this fellow was with him, for he is a Galilean."

⁶⁰Peter replied, "Man, I don't know what you're talking about!" Just as he was speaking, the rooster crowed. ⁶¹The Lord turned and looked straight at Peter. Then Peter remembered the word the Lord had spoken to him: "Before the rooster crows today, you will disown me three times." ⁶²And he went outside and wept bitterly.

The Guards Mock Jesus

⁶³The men who were guarding Jesus began mocking and beating him. ⁶⁴They blindfolded him and demanded, "Prophesy! Who hit you?" ⁶⁵And they said many other insulting things to him.

Jesus Before Pilate and Herod

⁶⁶At daybreak the council of the elders of the people, both the chief priests and teachers of the law, met together, and Jesus was led before them. ⁶⁷"If you are the Christ,ᵃ" they said, "tell us."

Jesus answered, "If I tell you, you will not believe me, ⁶⁸and if I asked you, you would not answer. ⁶⁹But from now on, the Son of Man will be seated at the right hand of the mighty God."

⁷⁰They all asked, "Are you then the Son of God?"

He replied, "You are right in saying I am."

⁷¹Then they said, "Why do we need

ᵃ67 Or Messiah

◣ET'S LIVE IT!   Luke 22:39–44

PRAY WHEN HURTING ➠ Read Luke 22:39–44. When he prayed Jesus knew that he would soon be nailed to a cross. Suffering and death were the "cup" Jesus prayed about. What words tell you how Jesus felt when he thought about his suffering? What did God do to help Jesus?

If something terrible ever happens to you or to a friend, the very best thing to do is to pray. When we pray and tell God how we feel, he strengthens us just as he strengthened Jesus.

any more testimony? We have heard it from his own lips.'"

❓DID YOU KNOW?   22:70

Did Jesus ever say he was God?

Yes. He told the Jewish council he was the Son of God (Luke 22:70). Two other times when he said he was God are found in John 5:16–18 and John 8:54–59.

---

23 Then the whole assembly rose and led him off to Pilate. ²And they began to accuse him, saying, "We have found this man subverting our nation. He opposes payment of taxes to Caesar and claims to be Christ,ᵃ a king."

³So Pilate asked Jesus, "Are you the king of the Jews?"

"Yes, it is as you say," Jesus replied.

⁴Then Pilate announced to the chief priests and the crowd, "I find no basis for a charge against this man."

⁵But they insisted, "He stirs up the people all over Judeaᵇ by his teaching. He started in Galilee and has come all the way here."

⁶On hearing this, Pilate asked if the man was a Galilean. ⁷When he learned that Jesus was under Herod's jurisdiction, he sent him to Herod, who was also in Jerusalem at that time.

⁸When Herod saw Jesus, he was greatly pleased, because for a long time he had been wanting to see him. From what he had heard about him, he hoped to see him perform some miracle. ⁹He plied him with many questions, but Jesus gave him no answer. ¹⁰The chief priests and the teachers of the law were standing there, vehemently accusing him. ¹¹Then Herod and his soldiers ridiculed and mocked him. Dressing him in an elegant robe, they sent him back to Pilate. ¹²That day Herod and

Pilate became friends—before this they had been enemies.

¹³Pilate called together the chief priests, the rulers and the people, ¹⁴and said to them, "You brought me this man as one who was inciting the people to rebellion. I have examined him in your presence and have found no basis for your charges against him. ¹⁵Neither has Herod, for he sent him back to us; as you can see, he has done nothing to deserve death. ¹⁶Therefore, I will punish him and then release him.ᶜ"

¹⁸With one voice they cried out, "Away with this man! Release Barabbas to us!" ¹⁹(Barabbas had been thrown into prison for an insurrection in the city, and for murder.)

²⁰Wanting to release Jesus, Pilate appealed to them again. ²¹But they kept shouting, "Crucify him! Crucify him!"

²²For the third time he spoke to them: "Why? What crime has this man committed? I have found in him no grounds for the death penalty. Therefore I will have him punished and then release him."

²³But with loud shouts they insistently demanded that he be crucified, and their shouts prevailed. ²⁴So Pilate decided to grant their demand. ²⁵He released the man who had been thrown into prison for insurrection and murder, the one they asked for, and surrendered Jesus to their will.

The Crucifixion

²⁶As they led him away, they seized Simon from Cyrene, who was on his way in from the country, and put the cross on him and made him carry it behind Jesus. ²⁷A large number of people followed him, including women who mourned and wailed for him. ²⁸Jesus turned and said to them, "Daughters of Jerusalem, do not weep for me; weep for yourselves and for your children. ²⁹For the time will come when you will say, 'Blessed are the barren women, the wombs that

---

ᵃ2 Or *Messiah*; also in verses 35 and 39   ᵇ5 Or *over the land of the Jews*   ᶜ16 Some manuscripts *him.*" ¹⁷*Now he was obliged to release one man to them at the Feast.*

never bore and the breasts that never nursed!' [30]Then

" 'they will say to the mountains,
    "Fall on us!"
and to the hills, "Cover us!" '[a]

[31]For if men do these things when the tree is green, what will happen when it is dry?"

[32]Two other men, both criminals, were also led out with him to be executed. [33]When they came to the place called the Skull, there they crucified him, along with the criminals—one on his right, the other on his left. [34]Jesus said, "Father, forgive them, for they do not know what they are doing."[b] And they divided up his clothes by casting lots.

[35]The people stood watching, and the rulers even sneered at him. They said, "He saved others; let him save himself if he is the Christ of God, the Chosen One."

[36]The soldiers also came up and mocked him. They offered him wine vinegar [37]and said, "If you are the king of the Jews, save yourself."

[38]There was a written notice above him, which read: THIS IS THE KING OF THE JEWS.

[39]One of the criminals who hung there hurled insults at him: "Aren't you the Christ? Save yourself and us!"

[40]But the other criminal rebuked him. "Don't you fear God," he said, "since you are under the same sentence? [41]We are punished justly, for we are getting what our deeds deserve. But this man has done nothing wrong."

[42]Then he said, "Jesus, remember me when you come into your kingdom.[c]"

[43]Jesus answered him, "I tell you the truth, today you will be with me in paradise."

Jesus' Death

[44]It was now about the sixth hour, and darkness came over the whole land until the ninth hour, [45]for the sun stopped shining. And the curtain of the temple was torn in two. [46]Jesus called out with a loud voice, "Father, into your hands I commit my spirit." When he had said this, he breathed his last.

[47]The centurion, seeing what had happened, praised God and said, "Surely this was a righteous man." [48]When all the people who had gath-

[a]30 Hosea 10:8   [b]34 Some early manuscripts do not have this sentence.   [c]42 Some manuscripts come with your kingly power

Life in Bible Times

THE CROSS

The Romans executed only the worst criminals by crucifixion, which was a very painful death. The hands were nailed to the cross bar, and nails were driven through the heels into the post. It usually took a long time to die on the cross.

ered to witness this sight saw what took place, they beat their breasts and went away. ⁴⁹But all those who knew him, including the women who had followed him from Galilee, stood at a distance, watching these things.

Jesus' Burial

⁵⁰Now there was a man named Joseph, a member of the Council, a good and upright man, ⁵¹who had not consented to their decision and action. He came from the Judean town of Arimathea and he was waiting for the kingdom of God. ⁵²Going to Pilate, he asked for Jesus' body. ⁵³Then he took it down, wrapped it in linen cloth and placed it in a tomb cut in the rock, one in which no one had yet been laid. ⁵⁴It was Preparation Day, and the Sabbath was about to begin.

⁵⁵The women who had come with Jesus from Galilee followed Joseph and saw the tomb and how his body was laid in it. ⁵⁶Then they went home and prepared spices and perfumes. But they rested on the Sabbath in obedience to the commandment.

The Resurrection

24 On the first day of the week, very early in the morning, the women took the spices they had prepared and went to the tomb. ²They found the stone rolled away from the tomb, ³but when they entered, they did not find the body of the Lord Jesus. ⁴While they were wondering about this, suddenly two men in clothes that gleamed like lightning stood beside them. ⁵In their fright the women bowed down with their faces to the ground, but the men said to them, "Why do you look for the living among the dead? ⁶He is not here; he has risen! Remember how he told you, while he was still with you in Galilee: ⁷'The Son of Man must be delivered into the hands of sinful men, be crucified and on the third day be raised again.' " ⁸Then they remembered his words.

⁹When they came back from the tomb, they told all these things to the Eleven and to all the others. ¹⁰It was Mary Magdalene, Joanna, Mary the mother of James, and the others with them who told this to the apostles. ¹¹But they did not believe the women, because their words seemed to them like nonsense. ¹²Peter, however, got up and ran to the tomb. Bending over, he saw the strips of linen lying by themselves, and he went away, wondering to himself what had happened.

WORDS TO REMEMBER

24:6 He is not here; he has risen!

On the Road to Emmaus

¹³Now that same day two of them were going to a village called Emmaus, about seven miles ᵃ from Jerusalem. ¹⁴They were talking with each other about everything that had happened. ¹⁵As they talked and discussed these things with each other, Jesus himself came up and walked along with them; ¹⁶but they were kept from recognizing him.

¹⁷He asked them, "What are you discussing together as you walk along?"

They stood still, their faces downcast. ¹⁸One of them, named Cleopas, asked him, "Are you only a visitor to Jerusalem and do not know the things that have happened there in these days?"

¹⁹"What things?" he asked.

"About Jesus of Nazareth," they replied. "He was a prophet, powerful in word and deed before God and all the people. ²⁰The chief priests and our rulers handed him over to be sentenced to death, and they crucified him; ²¹but we had hoped that he was the one who was going to redeem Israel. And what is more, it is the third day since all this took place. ²²In ad-

---

ᵃ13 Greek *sixty stadia* (about 11 kilometers)

dition, some of our women amazed us. They went to the tomb early this morning [23]but didn't find his body. They came and told us that they had seen a vision of angels, who said he was alive. [24]Then some of our companions went to the tomb and found it just as the women had said, but him they did not see."

[25]He said to them, "How foolish you are, and how slow of heart to believe all that the prophets have spoken! [26]Did not the Christ[a] have to suffer these things and then enter his glory?" [27]And beginning with Moses and all the Prophets, he explained to them what was said in all the Scriptures concerning himself.

[28]As they approached the village to which they were going, Jesus acted as if he were going farther. [29]But they urged him strongly, "Stay with us, for it is nearly evening; the day is almost over." So he went in to stay with them.

[30]When he was at the table with them, he took bread, gave thanks, broke it and began to give it to them. [31]Then their eyes were opened and they recognized him, and he disappeared from their sight. [32]They asked each other, "Were not our hearts burning within us while he talked with us on the road and opened the Scriptures to us?"

[33]They got up and returned at once to Jerusalem. There they found the Eleven and those with them, assembled together [34]and saying, "It is true! The Lord has risen and has appeared to Simon." [35]Then the two told what had happened on the way, and how Jesus was recognized by them when he broke the bread.

Jesus Appears to the Disciples

[36]While they were still talking about this, Jesus himself stood among them and said to them, "Peace be with you."

[37]They were startled and frightened, thinking they saw a ghost. [38]He said to them, "Why are you troubled, and why do doubts rise in your minds? [39]Look at my hands and my feet. It is I myself! Touch me and see; a ghost does not have flesh and bones, as you see I have."

[40]When he had said this, he showed them his hands and feet. [41]And while they still did not believe it because of joy and amazement, he asked them, "Do you have anything here to eat?" [42]They gave him a piece of broiled fish, [43]and he took it and ate it in their presence.

[44]He said to them, "This is what I told you while I was still with you: Everything must be fulfilled that is written about me in the Law of Moses, the Prophets and the Psalms."

[45]Then he opened their minds so they could understand the Scriptures. [46]He told them, "This is what is written: The Christ will suffer and rise from the dead on the third day, [47]and repentance and forgiveness of sins will be preached in his name to all nations, beginning at Jerusalem. [48]You are witnesses of these things. [49]I am going to send you what my Father has promised; but stay in the city until you have been clothed with power from on high."

The Ascension

[50]When he had led them out to the vicinity of Bethany, he lifted up his hands and blessed them. [51]While he was blessing them, he left them and was taken up into heaven. [52]Then they worshiped him and returned to Jerusalem with great joy. [53]And they stayed continually at the temple, praising God.

a26 Or *Messiah*; also in verse 46

JOHN

John, the disciple of Jesus, wrote this book.

WHO WROTE THIS BOOK?

WHY WAS THIS BOOK WRITTEN?

FOR WHOM WAS THIS BOOK WRITTEN?

WHAT HAPPENS IN THIS BOOK?

WHO IS IMPORTANT IN THIS BOOK?

WHEN DID THIS HAPPEN?

WHERE DID THIS HAPPEN?

WHAT ARE SOME SPECIAL STORIES IN THIS BOOK?

The book of John shows that Jesus is the Son of God and helps people believe in him.

John was written for everyone who wants to understand who Jesus really is.

John reports miracles and teachings that show Jesus is the Son of God.

Jesus is the important person in this book.

Jesus taught and performed miracles from A.D. 26 to 30.

Most of the things in this book happened in Judea.

The Word Became Flesh

1 In the beginning was the Word, and the Word was with God, and the Word was God. ²He was with God in the beginning.

³Through him all things were made; without him nothing was made that has been made. ⁴In him was life, and that life was the light of men. ⁵The light shines in the darkness, but the darkness has not understood[a] it.

?DID YOU KNOW?   1:1

What is the "Word"?

The "Word" is a special name for Jesus. It means that Jesus is the person who reveals God, or tells us what God is like. The Bible says that Jesus existed forever and that he is God.

---

⁶There came a man who was sent from God; his name was John. ⁷He came as a witness to testify concerning that light, so that through him all men might believe. ⁸He himself was not the light; he came only as a witness to the light. ⁹The true light that gives light to every man was coming into the world.[b]

¹⁰He was in the world, and though the world was made through him, the world did not recognize him. ¹¹He came to that which was his own, but his own did not receive him. ¹²Yet to all who received him, to those who believed in his name, he gave the right to become children of God— ¹³children born not of natural descent,[c] nor of human decision or a husband's will, but born of God.

¹⁴The Word became flesh and made his dwelling among us. We have seen his glory, the glory of the One and Only,[d] who came from the Father, full of grace and truth.

¹⁵John testifies concerning him. He cries out, saying, "This was he of whom I said, 'He who comes after me has surpassed me because he was before me.'" ¹⁶From the fullness of his grace we have all received one blessing after another. ¹⁷For the law was given through Moses; grace and truth came through Jesus Christ. ¹⁸No one has ever seen God, but God the One and Only,[d,e] who is at the Father's side, has made him known.

WORDS TO REMEMBER

1:17 Grace and truth came through Jesus Christ.

John the Baptist Denies Being the Christ

¹⁹Now this was John's testimony when the Jews of Jerusalem sent priests and Levites to ask him who he was. ²⁰He did not fail to confess, but confessed freely, "I am not the Christ.[f]"

²¹They asked him, "Then who are you? Are you Elijah?"

He said, "I am not."

"Are you the Prophet?"

He answered, "No."

²²Finally they said, "Who are you? Give us an answer to take back to those who sent us. What do you say about yourself?"

²³John replied in the words of Isaiah the prophet, "I am the voice of one calling in the desert, 'Make straight the way for the Lord.'"[g]

²⁴Now some Pharisees who had been sent ²⁵questioned him, "Why then do you baptize if you are not the Christ, nor Elijah, nor the Prophet?"

²⁶"I baptize with[h] water," John replied, "but among you stands one you do not know. ²⁷He is the one who

---

a5 Or *darkness, and the darkness has not overcome to every man who comes into the world*   b9 Or *This was the true light that gives light*   c13 Greek *of bloods*   d14,18 Or *the Only Begotten*   e18 Some manuscripts *but the only* (or *only begotten*) *Son*   f20 Or *Messiah.* "The Christ" (Greek) and "the Messiah" (Hebrew) both mean "the Anointed One"; also in verse 25.   g23 Isaiah 40:3   h26 Or *in*; also in verses 31 and 33

comes after me, the thongs of whose sandals I am not worthy to untie."

²⁸This all happened at Bethany on the other side of the Jordan, where John was baptizing.

Jesus the Lamb of God

²⁹The next day John saw Jesus coming toward him and said, "Look, the Lamb of God, who takes away the sin of the world! ³⁰This is the one I meant when I said, 'A man who comes after me has surpassed me because he was before me.' ³¹I myself did not know him, but the reason I came baptizing with water was that he might be revealed to Israel."

❓ DID YOU KNOW? 1:29

What does Lamb of God mean?

In Old Testament times lambs were offered as sacrifices when a person sinned. To call Jesus the Lamb of God meant that he would die as a sacrifice to take away our sins.

---

³²Then John gave this testimony: "I saw the Spirit come down from heaven as a dove and remain on him. ³³I would not have known him, except that the one who sent me to baptize with water told me, 'The man on whom you see the Spirit come down and remain is he who will baptize with the Holy Spirit.' ³⁴I have seen and I testify that this is the Son of God."

Jesus' First Disciples

³⁵The next day John was there again with two of his disciples. ³⁶When he saw Jesus passing by, he said, "Look, the Lamb of God!"

³⁷When the two disciples heard him say this, they followed Jesus. ³⁸Turning around, Jesus saw them following and asked, "What do you want?"

They said, "Rabbi" (which means Teacher), "where are you staying?"

³⁹"Come," he replied, "and you will see."

So they went and saw where he was staying, and spent that day with him. It was about the tenth hour.

⁴⁰Andrew, Simon Peter's brother, was one of the two who heard what John had said and who had followed Jesus. ⁴¹The first thing Andrew did was to find his brother Simon and tell him, "We have found the Messiah" (that is, the Christ). ⁴²And he brought him to Jesus.

Jesus looked at him and said, "You are Simon son of John. You will be called Cephas" (which, when translated, is Peter[a]).

Jesus Calls Philip and Nathanael

⁴³The next day Jesus decided to leave for Galilee. Finding Philip, he said to him, "Follow me."

⁴⁴Philip, like Andrew and Peter, was from the town of Bethsaida. ⁴⁵Philip found Nathanael and told him, "We have found the one Moses wrote about in the Law, and about whom the prophets also wrote—Jesus of Nazareth, the son of Joseph."

⁴⁶"Nazareth! Can anything good come from there?" Nathanael asked.

"Come and see," said Philip.

⁴⁷When Jesus saw Nathanael approaching, he said of him, "Here is a true Israelite, in whom there is nothing false."

⁴⁸"How do you know me?" Nathanael asked.

Jesus answered, "I saw you while you were still under the fig tree before Philip called you."

⁴⁹Then Nathanael declared, "Rabbi, you are the Son of God; you are the King of Israel."

⁵⁰Jesus said, "You believe[b] because I told you I saw you under the fig tree. You shall see greater things than that." ⁵¹He then added, "I tell you[c] the truth, you[c] shall see heav-

---

[a]42 Both *Cephas* (Aramaic) and *Peter* (Greek) mean *rock*.   [b]50 Or *Do you believe . . . ?*
[c]51 The Greek is plural.

en open, and the angels of God ascending and descending on the Son of Man."

Jesus Changes Water to Wine

2 On the third day a wedding took place at Cana in Galilee. Jesus' mother was there, ²and Jesus and his disciples had also been invited to the wedding. ³When the wine was gone, Jesus' mother said to him, "They have no more wine."

⁴"Dear woman, why do you involve me?" Jesus replied. "My time has not yet come."

⁵His mother said to the servants, "Do whatever he tells you."

⁶Nearby stood six stone water jars, the kind used by the Jews for ceremonial washing, each holding from twenty to thirty gallons.ᵃ

Life In Bible Times

WATER JARS

Water was stored in large stone jars and was used for washing and drinking. Jews at the time of Jesus did much ceremonial washing of their hands before eating. These very large jars were the sort that Jesus asked to be filled with water before he changed that water to wine.

---

⁷Jesus said to the servants, "Fill the jars with water"; so they filled them to the brim.

⁸Then he told them, "Now draw some out and take it to the master of the banquet."

They did so, ⁹and the master of the banquet tasted the water that had been turned into wine. He did not realize where it had come from, though

the servants who had drawn the water knew. Then he called the bridegroom aside ¹⁰and said, "Everyone brings out the choice wine first and then the cheaper wine after the guests have had too much to drink; but you have saved the best till now."

¹¹This, the first of his miraculous signs, Jesus performed at Cana in Galilee. He thus revealed his glory, and his disciples put their faith in him.

Jesus Clears the Temple

¹²After this he went down to Capernaum with his mother and brothers and his disciples. There they stayed for a few days.

¹³When it was almost time for the Jewish Passover, Jesus went up to Jerusalem. ¹⁴In the temple courts he found men selling cattle, sheep and doves, and others sitting at tables exchanging money. ¹⁵So he made a whip out of cords, and drove all from the temple area, both sheep and cattle; he scattered the coins of the money changers and overturned their tables. ¹⁶To those who sold doves he said, "Get these out of here! How dare you turn my Father's house into a market!"

¹⁷His disciples remembered that it is written: "Zeal for your house will consume me."ᵇ

¹⁸Then the Jews demanded of him, "What miraculous sign can you show us to prove your authority to do all this?"

¹⁹Jesus answered them, "Destroy this temple, and I will raise it again in three days."

²⁰The Jews replied, "It has taken forty-six years to build this temple, and you are going to raise it in three days?" ²¹But the temple he had spoken of was his body. ²²After he was raised from the dead, his disciples recalled what he had said. Then they believed the Scripture and the words that Jesus had spoken.

²³Now while he was in Jerusalem at the Passover Feast, many people

---

ᵃ6 Greek *two to three metretes* (probably about 75 to 115 liters)   ᵇ17 Psalm 69:9

saw the miraculous signs he was doing and believed in his name. *a* 24But Jesus would not entrust himself to them, for he knew all men. 25He did not need man's testimony about man, for he knew what was in a man.

Jesus Teaches Nicodemus

3 Now there was a man of the Pharisees named Nicodemus, a member of the Jewish ruling council. 2He came to Jesus at night and said, "Rabbi, we know you are a teacher who has come from God. For no one could perform the miraculous signs you are doing if God were not with him."

3In reply Jesus declared, "I tell you the truth, no one can see the kingdom of God unless he is born again. *b* "

4"How can a man be born when he is old?" Nicodemus asked. "Surely he cannot enter a second time into his mother's womb to be born!"

5Jesus answered, "I tell you the truth, no one can enter the kingdom of God unless he is born of water and the Spirit. 6Flesh gives birth to flesh, but the Spirit*c* gives birth to spirit. 7You should not be surprised at my saying, 'You*d* must be born again.' 8The wind blows wherever it pleases. You hear its sound, but you cannot tell where it comes from or where it is going. So it is with everyone born of the Spirit."

9"How can this be?" Nicodemus asked.

10"You are Israel's teacher," said Jesus, "and do you not understand these things? 11I tell you the truth, we speak of what we know, and we testify to what we have seen, but still you people do not accept our testimony. 12I have spoken to you of earthly things and you do not believe; how then will you believe if I speak of heavenly things? 13No one has ever gone into heaven except the one who came from heaven—the Son of Man. *e* 14Just as Moses lifted up the snake in the desert, so the Son of Man must be lifted up, 15that everyone who believes in him may have eternal life.*f*

16"For God so loved the world that he gave his one and only Son,*g* that whoever believes in him shall not perish but have eternal life. 17For God did not send his Son into the world to condemn the world, but to save the world through him. 18Whoever believes in him is not condemned, but whoever does not believe stands condemned already because he has not believed in the name of God's one and only Son. *h* 19This is the verdict: Light has come into the world, but men loved darkness in-

---

Words to Remember

3:16 For God so loved the world that he gave his one and only Son, that whoever believes in him shall not perish but have eternal life.

---

*a*23 Or *and believed in him*   *b*3 Or *born from above; also in verse 7*   *c*6 Or *but spirit*
*d*7 The Greek is plural.   *e*13 Some manuscripts *Man, who is in heaven*   *f*15 Or *believes may have eternal life in him*   *g*16 Or *his only begotten Son*   *h*18 Or *God's only begotten Son*
*i*21 Some interpreters end the quotation after verse 15.

 LET'S LIVE IT!   John 3:1–16

BORN AGAIN ➠ Read John 3:1–16. When you were born, you received physical life. People who are "born again" receive eternal life from God. Physical life ends when people die, but a person with eternal life will live forever with God in heaven.

How can you know that you have been born again? Memorize John 3:16. If you believe in Jesus as your Savior, this verse says that you are born again and have eternal life.

stead of light because their deeds were evil. ²⁰Everyone who does evil hates the light, and will not come into the light for fear that his deeds will be exposed. ²¹But whoever lives by the truth comes into the light, so that it may be seen plainly that what he has done has been done through God." *i*

John the Baptist's Testimony About Jesus

²²After this, Jesus and his disciples went out into the Judean countryside, where he spent some time with them, and baptized. ²³Now John also was baptizing at Aenon near Salim, because there was plenty of water, and people were constantly coming to be baptized. ²⁴(This was before John was put in prison.) ²⁵An argument developed between some of John's disciples and a certain Jew *a* over the matter of ceremonial washing. ²⁶They came to John and said to him, "Rabbi, that man who was with you on the other side of the Jordan—the one you testified about—well, he is baptizing, and everyone is going to him."

²⁷To this John replied, "A man can receive only what is given him from heaven. ²⁸You yourselves can testify that I said, 'I am not the Christ *b* but am sent ahead of him.' ²⁹The bride belongs to the bridegroom. The friend who attends the bridegroom waits and listens for him, and is full of joy when he hears the bridegroom's voice. That joy is mine, and it is now complete. ³⁰He must become greater; I must become less.

³¹"The one who comes from above is above all; the one who is from the earth belongs to the earth, and speaks as one from the earth. The one who comes from heaven is above all. ³²He testifies to what he has seen and heard, but no one accepts his testimony. ³³The man who has accepted it has certified that God is truthful. ³⁴For the one whom God has sent

speaks the words of God, for God *c* gives the Spirit without limit. ³⁵The Father loves the Son and has placed everything in his hands. ³⁶Whoever believes in the Son has eternal life, but whoever rejects the Son will not see life, for God's wrath remains on him." *d*

Jesus Talks With a Samaritan Woman

4 The Pharisees heard that Jesus was gaining and baptizing more disciples than John, ²although in fact it was not Jesus who baptized, but his disciples. ³When the Lord learned of this, he left Judea and went back once more to Galilee.

⁴Now he had to go through Samaria. ⁵So he came to a town in Samaria called Sychar, near the plot of ground Jacob had given to his son Joseph. ⁶Jacob's well was there, and Jesus, tired as he was from the journey, sat down by the well. It was about the sixth hour.

⁷When a Samaritan woman came to draw water, Jesus said to her, "Will you give me a drink?" ⁸(His disciples had gone into the town to buy food.)

⁹The Samaritan woman said to him, "You are a Jew and I am a Samaritan woman. How can you ask me for a drink?" (For Jews do not associate with Samaritans. *e*)

¹⁰Jesus answered her, "If you knew the gift of God and who it is that asks you for a drink, you would have asked him and he would have given you living water."

¹¹"Sir," the woman said, "you have nothing to draw with and the well is deep. Where can you get this living water? ¹²Are you greater than our father Jacob, who gave us the well and drank from it himself, as did also his sons and his flocks and herds?"

¹³Jesus answered, "Everyone who drinks this water will be thirsty again, ¹⁴but whoever drinks the water I give him will never thirst. In-

---

*a25 Some manuscripts *and certain Jews* interpreters end the quotation after verse 30.　*b28 Or *Messiah*　*c34 Greek *he*　*d36 Some　*e9 Or *do not use dishes Samaritans have used*

deed, the water I give him will become in him a spring of water welling up to eternal life."

15The woman said to him, "Sir, give me this water so that I won't get thirsty and have to keep coming here to draw water."

16He told her, "Go, call your husband and come back."

17"I have no husband," she replied.

Jesus said to her, "You are right when you say you have no husband. 18The fact is, you have had five husbands, and the man you now have is not your husband. What you have just said is quite true."

19"Sir," the woman said, "I can see that you are a prophet. 20Our fathers worshiped on this mountain, but you Jews claim that the place where we must worship is in Jerusalem."

21Jesus declared, "Believe me, woman, a time is coming when you will worship the Father neither on this mountain nor in Jerusalem. 22You Samaritans worship what you do not know; we worship what we do know, for salvation is from the Jews. 23Yet a time is coming and has now come when the true worshipers will worship the Father in spirit and truth, for they are the kind of worshipers the Father seeks. 24God is spirit, and his worshipers must worship in spirit and in truth."

25The woman said, "I know that

Messiah" (called Christ) "is coming. When he comes, he will explain everything to us."

26Then Jesus declared, "I who speak to you am he."

The Disciples Rejoin Jesus

27Just then his disciples returned and were surprised to find him talking with a woman. But no one asked, "What do you want?" or "Why are you talking with her?"

28Then, leaving her water jar, the woman went back to the town and said to the people, 29"Come, see a man who told me everything I ever did. Could this be the Christ*a*?" 30They came out of the town and made their way toward him.

31Meanwhile his disciples urged him, "Rabbi, eat something."

32But he said to them, "I have food to eat that you know nothing about."

33Then his disciples said to each other, "Could someone have brought him food?"

34"My food," said Jesus, "is to do the will of him who sent me and to finish his work. 35Do you not say, 'Four months more and then the harvest'? I tell you, open your eyes and look at the fields! They are ripe for harvest. 36Even now the reaper draws his wages, even now he harvests the crop for eternal life, so that the sower and the reaper may be glad together. 37Thus the saying 'One

a29 Or *Messiah*

Life in Bible Times

CARRYING WATER

Getting each day's water supply was the job of women. Each day they came to the town well, filled their jars, and then carried the full water jars home on their heads.

sows and another reaps' is true. [38]I sent you to reap what you have not worked for. Others have done the hard work, and you have reaped the benefits of their labor."

Many Samaritans Believe

[39]Many of the Samaritans from that town believed in him because of the woman's testimony, "He told me everything I ever did." [40]So when the Samaritans came to him, they urged him to stay with them, and he stayed two days. [41]And because of his words many more became believers.

[42]They said to the woman, "We no longer believe just because of what you said; now we have heard for ourselves, and we know that this man really is the Savior of the world."

Jesus Heals the Official's Son

[43]After the two days he left for Galilee. [44](Now Jesus himself had pointed out that a prophet has no honor in his own country.) [45]When he arrived in Galilee, the Galileans welcomed him. They had seen all that he had done in Jerusalem at the Passover Feast, for they also had been there.

[46]Once more he visited Cana in Galilee, where he had turned the water into wine. And there was a certain royal official whose son lay sick at Capernaum. [47]When this man heard that Jesus had arrived in Galilee from Judea, he went to him and begged him to come and heal his son, who was close to death.

[48]"Unless you people see miraculous signs and wonders," Jesus told him, "you will never believe."

[49]The royal official said, "Sir, come down before my child dies."

[50]Jesus replied, "You may go. Your son will live."

The man took Jesus at his word and departed. [51]While he was still on the way, his servants met him with the news that his boy was living.

[52]When he inquired as to the time when his son got better, they said to him, "The fever left him yesterday at the seventh hour."

[53]Then the father realized that this was the exact time at which Jesus had said to him, "Your son will live." So he and all his household believed.

[54]This was the second miraculous sign that Jesus performed, having come from Judea to Galilee.

The Healing at the Pool

5 Some time later, Jesus went up to Jerusalem for a feast of the Jews. [2]Now there is in Jerusalem near the Sheep Gate a pool, which in Aramaic is called Bethesda[a] and which is surrounded by five covered colonnades. [3]Here a great number of disabled people used to lie—the blind, the lame, the paralyzed.[b] [5]One who was there had been an invalid for thirty-eight years. [6]When Jesus saw him lying there and learned that he had been in this condition for a long time, he asked him, "Do you want to get well?"

[7]"Sir," the invalid replied, "I have no one to help me into the pool when the water is stirred. While I am trying to get in, someone else goes down ahead of me."

[8]Then Jesus said to him, "Get up! Pick up your mat and walk." [9]At once the man was cured; he picked up his mat and walked.

The day on which this took place was a Sabbath, [10]and so the Jews said to the man who had been healed, "It is the Sabbath; the law forbids you to carry your mat."

[11]But he replied, "The man who made me well said to me, 'Pick up your mat and walk.' "

[12]So they asked him, "Who is this fellow who told you to pick it up and walk?"

[13]The man who was healed had no idea who it was, for Jesus had slipped

---

[a]2 Some manuscripts *Bethzatha*; other manuscripts *Bethsaida*   [b]3 Some less important manuscripts *paralyzed—and they waited for the moving of the waters. [4]From time to time an angel of the Lord would come down and stir up the waters. The first one into the pool after each such disturbance would be cured of whatever disease he had.*

away into the crowd that was there. ¹⁴Later Jesus found him at the temple and said to him, "See, you are well again. Stop sinning or something worse may happen to you." ¹⁵The man went away and told the Jews that it was Jesus who had made him well.

? DID YOU KNOW? 5:15

Who does John mean when he says "the Jews"?

By "the Jews" John does not mean the Jewish people. This is the way John talks about the religious leaders of the Jews. "The Jews" in John's Gospel are the Pharisees and chief priests and experts in the Old Testament law who did not believe in Jesus.

Life Through the Son

¹⁶So, because Jesus was doing these things on the Sabbath, the Jews persecuted him. ¹⁷Jesus said to them, "My Father is always at his work to this very day, and I, too, am working." ¹⁸For this reason the Jews tried all the harder to kill him; not only was he breaking the Sabbath, but he was even calling God his own Father, making himself equal with God.

¹⁹Jesus gave them this answer: "I tell you the truth, the Son can do nothing by himself; he can do only what he sees his Father doing, because whatever the Father does the Son also does. ²⁰For the Father loves the Son and shows him all he does. Yes, to your amazement he will show him even greater things than these. ²¹For just as the Father raises the dead and gives them life, even so the Son gives life to whom he is pleased to give it. ²²Moreover, the Father judges no one, but has entrusted all judgment to the Son, ²³that all may honor the Son just as they honor the Father. He who does not honor the Son does not honor the Father, who sent him.

²⁴"I tell you the truth, whoever hears my word and believes him who sent me has eternal life and will not be condemned; he has crossed over from death to life. ²⁵I tell you the truth, a time is coming and has now come when the dead will hear the voice of the Son of God and those who hear will live. ²⁶For as the Father has life in himself, so he has granted the Son to have life in himself. ²⁷And he has given him authority to judge because he is the Son of Man.

W ORDS TO REMEMBER

5:24 Whoever hears my word and believes him who sent me has eternal life and will not be condemned.

---

²⁸"Do not be amazed at this, for a time is coming when all who are in their graves will hear his voice ²⁹and come out—those who have done good will rise to live, and those who have done evil will rise to be condemned. ³⁰By myself I can do nothing; I judge only as I hear, and my judgment is just, for I seek not to please myself but him who sent me.

Testimonies About Jesus

³¹"If I testify about myself, my testimony is not valid. ³²There is another who testifies in my favor, and I know that his testimony about me is valid.

³³"You have sent to John and he has testified to the truth. ³⁴Not that I accept human testimony; but I mention it that you may be saved. ³⁵John was a lamp that burned and gave light, and you chose for a time to enjoy his light.

³⁶"I have testimony weightier than that of John. For the very work that the Father has given me to finish, and which I am doing, testifies that the Father has sent me. ³⁷And the Father who sent me has himself testified concerning me. You have never heard his voice nor seen his form, ³⁸nor does his word dwell in you, for

you do not believe the one he sent.
[39]You diligently study[a] the Scriptures because you think that by them you possess eternal life. These are the Scriptures that testify about me, [40]yet you refuse to come to me to have life.

[41]"I do not accept praise from men, [42]but I know you. I know that you do not have the love of God in your hearts. [43]I have come in my Father's name, and you do not accept me; but if someone else comes in his own name, you will accept him. [44]How can you believe if you accept praise from one another, yet make no effort to obtain the praise that comes from the only God[b]?

[45]"But do not think I will accuse you before the Father. Your accuser is Moses, on whom your hopes are set. [46]If you believed Moses, you would believe me, for he wrote about me. [47]But since you do not believe what he wrote, how are you going to believe what I say?"

Jesus Feeds the Five Thousand

6 Some time after this, Jesus crossed to the far shore of the Sea of Galilee (that is, the Sea of Tiberias), [2]and a great crowd of people followed him because they saw the miraculous signs he had performed on the sick. [3]Then Jesus went up on a mountainside and sat down with his disciples. [4]The Jewish Passover Feast was near.

[5]When Jesus looked up and saw a great crowd coming toward him, he said to Philip, "Where shall we buy bread for these people to eat?" [6]He asked this only to test him, for he already had in mind what he was going to do.

[7]Philip answered him, "Eight months' wages[c] would not buy enough bread for each one to have a bite!"

[8]Another of his disciples, Andrew, Simon Peter's brother, spoke up, [9]"Here is a boy with five small barley loaves and two small fish, but how far will they go among so many?"

Life In Bible Times

BARLEY LOAVES

Two kinds of grain, wheat and barley, were used to make bread. Wheat was expensive. Most people were poor, so they ate small round loaves of coarse barley bread.

---

[10]Jesus said, "Have the people sit down." There was plenty of grass in that place, and the men sat down, about five thousand of them. [11]Jesus then took the loaves, gave thanks, and distributed to those who were seated as much as they wanted. He did the same with the fish.

[12]When they had all had enough to eat, he said to his disciples, "Gather the pieces that are left over. Let nothing be wasted." [13]So they gathered them and filled twelve baskets with the pieces of the five barley loaves left over by those who had eaten.

[14]After the people saw the miraculous sign that Jesus did, they began to say, "Surely this is the Prophet who is to come into the world." [15]Jesus, knowing that they intended to come and make him king by force, withdrew again to a mountain by himself.

Jesus Walks on the Water

[16]When evening came, his disciples went down to the lake, [17]where they got into a boat and set off across the lake for Capernaum. By now it was dark, and Jesus had not yet joined them. [18]A strong wind was blowing and the waters grew rough. [19]When

---

[a]39 Or *Study diligently* (the imperative)   [b]44 Some early manuscripts *the Only One*
[c]7 Greek *two hundred denarii*

they had rowed three or three and a half miles,[a] they saw Jesus approaching the boat, walking on the water; and they were terrified. 20But he said to them, "It is I; don't be afraid." 21Then they were willing to take him into the boat, and immediately the boat reached the shore where they were heading.

22The next day the crowd that had stayed on the opposite shore of the lake realized that only one boat had been there, and that Jesus had not entered it with his disciples, but that they had gone away alone. 23Then some boats from Tiberias landed near the place where the people had eaten the bread after the Lord had given thanks. 24Once the crowd realized that neither Jesus nor his disciples were there, they got into the boats and went to Capernaum in search of Jesus.

Jesus the Bread of Life

25When they found him on the other side of the lake, they asked him, "Rabbi, when did you get here?"

26Jesus answered, "I tell you the truth, you are looking for me, not because you saw miraculous signs but because you ate the loaves and had your fill. 27Do not work for food that spoils, but for food that endures to eternal life, which the Son of Man will give you. On him God the Father has placed his seal of approval."

28Then they asked him, "What must we do to do the works God requires?"

29Jesus answered, "The work of God is this: to believe in the one he has sent."

30So they asked him, "What miraculous sign then will you give that we may see it and believe you? What will you do? 31Our forefathers ate the manna in the desert; as it is written: 'He gave them bread from heaven to eat.'[b]"

32Jesus said to them, "I tell you the truth, it is not Moses who has given

you the bread from heaven, but it is my Father who gives you the true bread from heaven. 33For the bread of God is he who comes down from heaven and gives life to the world."

34"Sir," they said, "from now on give us this bread."

35Then Jesus declared, "I am the bread of life. He who comes to me will never go hungry, and he who believes in me will never be thirsty. 36But as I told you, you have seen me and still you do not believe. 37All that the Father gives me will come to me, and whoever comes to me I will never drive away. 38For I have come down from heaven not to do my will but to do the will of him who sent me. 39And this is the will of him who sent me, that I shall lose none of all that he has given me, but raise them up at the last day. 40For my Father's will is that everyone who looks to the Son and believes in him shall have eternal life, and I will raise him up at the last day."

?DID YOU KNOW?   6:35

What does "bread of life" mean?

In this passage bread is a symbol. Jesus is not talking about real bread. Jesus was teaching his listeners that he was the one who could give them spiritual food, and keep them alive.

41At this the Jews began to grumble about him because he said, "I am the bread that came down from heaven." 42They said, "Is this not Jesus, the son of Joseph, whose father and mother we know? How can he now say, 'I came down from heaven'?"

43"Stop grumbling among yourselves," Jesus answered. 44"No one can come to me unless the Father who sent him draws him, and I will raise him up at the last day. 45It is

---

a19 Greek *rowed twenty-five or thirty stadia* (about 5 or 6 kilometers)   b31 Exodus 16:4; Neh. 9:15; Psalm 78:24,25

written in the Prophets: 'They will all be taught by God.'*a* Everyone who listens to the Father and learns from him comes to me. ⁴⁶No one has seen the Father except the one who is from God; only he has seen the Father. ⁴⁷I tell you the truth, he who believes has everlasting life. ⁴⁸I am the bread of life. ⁴⁹Your forefathers ate the manna in the desert, yet they died. ⁵⁰But here is the bread that comes down from heaven, which a man may eat and not die. ⁵¹I am the living bread that came down from heaven. If anyone eats of this bread, he will live forever. This bread is my flesh, which I will give for the life of the world."

⁵²Then the Jews began to argue sharply among themselves, "How can this man give us his flesh to eat?"

⁵³Jesus said to them, "I tell you the truth, unless you eat the flesh of the Son of Man and drink his blood, you have no life in you. ⁵⁴Whoever eats my flesh and drinks my blood has eternal life, and I will raise him up at the last day. ⁵⁵For my flesh is real food and my blood is real drink. ⁵⁶Whoever eats my flesh and drinks my blood remains in me, and I in him. ⁵⁷Just as the living Father sent me and I live because of the Father, so the one who feeds on me will live because of me. ⁵⁸This is the bread that came down from heaven. Your forefathers ate manna and died, but he who feeds on this bread will live forever." ⁵⁹He said this while teaching in the synagogue in Capernaum.

Many Disciples Desert Jesus

⁶⁰On hearing it, many of his disciples said, "This is a hard teaching. Who can accept it?"

⁶¹Aware that his disciples were grumbling about this, Jesus said to them, "Does this offend you? ⁶²What if you see the Son of Man ascend to where he was before! ⁶³The Spirit gives life; the flesh counts for nothing. The words I have spoken to you are spirit*b* and they are life. ⁶⁴Yet there are some of you who do not believe." For Jesus had known from the beginning which of them did not believe and who would betray him. ⁶⁵He went on to say, "This is why I told you that no one can come to me unless the Father has enabled him."

⁶⁶From this time many of his disciples turned back and no longer followed him.

⁶⁷"You do not want to leave too, do you?" Jesus asked the Twelve.

⁶⁸Simon Peter answered him, "Lord, to whom shall we go? You have the words of eternal life. ⁶⁹We believe and know that you are the Holy One of God."

⁷⁰Then Jesus replied, "Have I not chosen you, the Twelve? Yet one of you is a devil!" ⁷¹(He meant Judas, the son of Simon Iscariot, who, though one of the Twelve, was later to betray him.)

Jesus Goes to the Feast of Tabernacles

7 After this, Jesus went around in Galilee, purposely staying away

*a*45 Isaiah 54:13   *b*63 Or *Spirit*

▌ET'S LIVE IT!   John 6:60–69

ONE WAY ➠ Read John 6:60–69. There are many religions in the world. Most teach that people must live good lives in order to go to heaven. What is special about Christianity is that eternal life is a gift, a gift only Jesus can give a person.

Hold up your hand, with one finger pointed up as a "number one" sign. Trace around your hand with the finger pointed up, to show there is only one way to heaven. Color the picture. Add pictures or Bible verses to make your poster tell others Jesus is the only way to eternal life.

from Judea because the Jews there were waiting to take his life. ²But when the Jewish Feast of Tabernacles was near, ³Jesus' brothers said to him, "You ought to leave here and go to Judea, so that your disciples may see the miracles you do. ⁴No one who wants to become a public figure acts in secret. Since you are doing these things, show yourself to the world." ⁵For even his own brothers did not believe in him.

⁶Therefore Jesus told them, "The right time for me has not yet come; for you any time is right. ⁷The world cannot hate you, but it hates me because I testify that what it does is evil. ⁸You go to the Feast. I am not yet*ᵃ* going up to this Feast, because for me the right time has not yet come." ⁹Having said this, he stayed in Galilee.

¹⁰However, after his brothers had left for the Feast, he went also, not publicly, but in secret. ¹¹Now at the Feast the Jews were watching for him and asking, "Where is that man?"

¹²Among the crowds there was widespread whispering about him. Some said, "He is a good man."

Others replied, "No, he deceives the people." ¹³But no one would say anything publicly about him for fear of the Jews.

Jesus Teaches at the Feast

¹⁴Not until halfway through the Feast did Jesus go up to the temple courts and begin to teach. ¹⁵The Jews were amazed and asked, "How did this man get such learning without having studied?"

¹⁶Jesus answered, "My teaching is not my own. It comes from him who sent me. ¹⁷If anyone chooses to do God's will, he will find out whether my teaching comes from God or whether I speak on my own. ¹⁸He who speaks on his own does so to gain honor for himself, but he who works for the honor of the one who sent him is a man of truth; there is nothing false

about him. ¹⁹Has not Moses given you the law? Yet not one of you keeps the law. Why are you trying to kill me?"

²⁰"You are demon-possessed," the crowd answered. "Who is trying to kill you?"

²¹Jesus said to them, "I did one miracle, and you are all astonished. ²²Yet, because Moses gave you circumcision (though actually it did not come from Moses, but from the patriarchs), you circumcise a child on the Sabbath. ²³Now if a child can be circumcised on the Sabbath so that the law of Moses may not be broken, why are you angry with me for healing the whole man on the Sabbath? ²⁴Stop judging by mere appearances, and make a right judgment."

Is Jesus the Christ?

²⁵At that point some of the people of Jerusalem began to ask, "Isn't this the man they are trying to kill? ²⁶Here he is, speaking publicly, and they are not saying a word to him. Have the authorities really concluded that he is the Christ*ᵇ*? ²⁷But we know where this man is from; when the Christ comes, no one will know where he is from."

²⁸Then Jesus, still teaching in the temple courts, cried out, "Yes, you know me, and you know where I am from. I am not here on my own, but he who sent me is true. You do not know him, ²⁹but I know him because I am from him and he sent me."

³⁰At this they tried to seize him, but no one laid a hand on him, because his time had not yet come. ³¹Still, many in the crowd put their faith in him. They said, "When the Christ comes, will he do more miraculous signs than this man?"

³²The Pharisees heard the crowd whispering such things about him. Then the chief priests and the Pharisees sent temple guards to arrest him.

³³Jesus said, "I am with you for only a short time, and then I go to the

---

ᵃ8 Some early manuscripts do not have *yet*.　　*ᵇ26* Or *Messiah*; also in verses 27, 31, 41 and 42 one who sent me. ³⁴You will look for me, but you will not find me; and where I am, you cannot come."

³⁵The Jews said to one another, "Where does this man intend to go that we cannot find him? Will he go where our people live scattered among the Greeks, and teach the Greeks? ³⁶What did he mean when he said, 'You will look for me, but you will not find me,' and 'Where I am, you cannot come'?"

³⁷On the last and greatest day of the Feast, Jesus stood and said in a loud voice, "If anyone is thirsty, let him come to me and drink. ³⁸Whoever believes in me, as*a* the Scripture has said, streams of living water will flow from within him." ³⁹By this he meant the Spirit, whom those who believed in him were later to receive. Up to that time the Spirit had not been given, since Jesus had not yet been glorified.

⁴⁰On hearing his words, some of the people said, "Surely this man is the Prophet."

⁴¹Others said, "He is the Christ."

❓ DID YOU KNOW?   7:42

What does "Christ" mean?

"Christ" is the title given to the one God would send to save his people. When anyone called Jesus the Christ, it meant that person believed Jesus was the one the Old Testament promised would come to save us.

Still others asked, "How can the Christ come from Galilee? ⁴²Does not the Scripture say that the Christ will come from David's family*b* and from Bethlehem, the town where David lived?" ⁴³Thus the people were divided because of Jesus. ⁴⁴Some wanted to seize him, but no one laid a hand on him.

Unbelief of the Jewish Leaders

⁴⁵Finally the temple guards went back to the chief priests and Pharisees, who asked them, "Why didn't you bring him in?"

⁴⁶"No one ever spoke the way this man does," the guards declared.

⁴⁷"You mean he has deceived you also?" the Pharisees retorted. ⁴⁸"Has any of the rulers or of the Pharisees believed in him? ⁴⁹No! But this mob that knows nothing of the law— there is a curse on them."

⁵⁰Nicodemus, who had gone to Jesus earlier and who was one of their own number, asked, ⁵¹"Does our law condemn anyone without first hearing him to find out what he is doing?"

⁵²They replied, "Are you from Galilee, too? Look into it, and you will find that a prophet*c* does not come out of Galilee."

[The earliest and most reliable manuscripts and other ancient witnesses do not have John 7:53–8:11.]

⁵³Then each went to his own home. **8** But Jesus went to the Mount of Olives. ²At dawn he appeared again in the temple courts, where all the people gathered around him, and he sat down to teach them. ³The teachers of the law and the Pharisees brought in a woman caught in adultery. They made her stand before the group ⁴and said to Jesus, "Teacher, this woman was caught in the act of adultery. ⁵In the Law Moses commanded us to stone such women. Now what do you say?" ⁶They were using this question as a trap, in order to have a basis for accusing him.

But Jesus bent down and started to write on the ground with his finger. ⁷When they kept on questioning him, he straightened up and said to them, "If any one of you is without sin, let

---

a37,38 Or / If anyone is thirsty, let him come to me. / And let him drink, 38who believes in me. / As
b42 Greek seed   c52 Two early manuscripts the Prophet

him be the first to throw a stone at her." ⁸Again he stooped down and wrote on the ground.

⁹At this, those who heard began to go away one at a time, the older ones first, until only Jesus was left, with the woman still standing there. ¹⁰Jesus straightened up and asked her, "Woman, where are they? Has no one condemned you?"

¹¹"No one, sir," she said.

"Then neither do I condemn you," Jesus declared. "Go now and leave your life of sin."

The Validity of Jesus' Testimony

¹²When Jesus spoke again to the people, he said, "I am the light of the world. Whoever follows me will never walk in darkness, but will have the light of life."

¹³The Pharisees challenged him, "Here you are, appearing as your own witness; your testimony is not valid."

¹⁴Jesus answered, "Even if I testify on my own behalf, my testimony is valid, for I know where I came from and where I am going. But you have no idea where I come from or where I am going. ¹⁵You judge by human standards; I pass judgment on no one. ¹⁶But if I do judge, my decisions are right, because I am not alone. I stand with the Father, who sent me. ¹⁷In your own Law it is written that the testimony of two men is valid. ¹⁸I am one who testifies for myself; my other witness is the Father, who sent me."

¹⁹Then they asked him, "Where is your father?"

"You do not know me or my Father," Jesus replied. "If you knew me, you would know my Father also." ²⁰He spoke these words while teaching in the temple area near the place where the offerings were put. Yet no one seized him, because his time had not yet come.

²¹Once more Jesus said to them, "I

am going away, and you will look for me, and you will die in your sin. Where I go, you cannot come."

²²This made the Jews ask, "Will he kill himself? Is that why he says, 'Where I go, you cannot come'?"

²³But he continued, "You are from below; I am from above. You are of this world; I am not of this world. ²⁴I told you that you would die in your sins; if you do not believe that I am ͵the one I claim to be͵,ᵃ you will indeed die in your sins."

²⁵"Who are you?" they asked.

"Just what I have been claiming all along," Jesus replied. ²⁶"I have much to say in judgment of you. But he who sent me is reliable, and what I have heard from him I tell the world."

²⁷They did not understand that he was telling them about his Father. ²⁸So Jesus said, "When you have lifted up the Son of Man, then you will know that I am ͵the one I claim to be͵, and that I do nothing on my own but speak just what the Father has taught me. ²⁹The one who sent me is with me; he has not left me alone, for I always do what pleases him." ³⁰Even as he spoke, many put their faith in him.

The Children of Abraham

³¹To the Jews who had believed him, Jesus said, "If you hold to my teaching, you are really my disciples. ³²Then you will know the truth, and the truth will set you free."

³³They answered him, "We are Abraham's descendantsᵇ and have never been slaves of anyone. How can you say that we shall be set free?"

³⁴Jesus replied, "I tell you the truth, everyone who sins is a slave to sin. ³⁵Now a slave has no permanent place in the family, but a son belongs to it forever. ³⁶So if the Son sets you free, you will be free indeed. ³⁷I know you are Abraham's descendants. Yet you are ready to kill me, because you have no room for my word. ³⁸I am telling you what I have seen in the Fa-

---

ᵃ24 Or I am he; also in verse 28   ᵇ33 Greek seed; also in verse 37

ther's presence, and you do what you have heard from your father. *a*"

³⁹"Abraham is our father," they answered.

"If you were Abraham's children," said Jesus, "then you would*b* do the things Abraham did. ⁴⁰As it is, you are determined to kill me, a man who has told you the truth that I heard from God. Abraham did not do such things. ⁴¹You are doing the things your own father does."

"We are not illegitimate children," they protested. "The only Father we have is God himself."

The Children of the Devil

⁴²Jesus said to them, "If God were your Father, you would love me, for I came from God and now am here. I have not come on my own; but he sent me. ⁴³Why is my language not clear to you? Because you are unable to hear what I say. ⁴⁴You belong to your father, the devil, and you want to carry out your father's desire. He was a murderer from the beginning, not holding to the truth, for there is no truth in him. When he lies, he speaks his native language, for he is a liar and the father of lies. ⁴⁵Yet because I tell the truth, you do not believe me! ⁴⁶Can any of you prove me guilty of sin? If I am telling the truth, why don't you believe me? ⁴⁷He who belongs to God hears what God says. The reason you do not hear is that you do not belong to God."

The Claims of Jesus About Himself

⁴⁸The Jews answered him, "Aren't we right in saying that you are a Samaritan and demon-possessed?"

⁴⁹"I am not possessed by a demon," said Jesus, "but I honor my Father and you dishonor me. ⁵⁰I am not seeking glory for myself; but there is one who seeks it, and he is the judge. ⁵¹I tell you the truth, if anyone keeps my word, he will never see death."

⁵²At this the Jews exclaimed, "Now we know that you are demon-possessed! Abraham died and so did the prophets, yet you say that if anyone keeps your word, he will never taste death. ⁵³Are you greater than our father Abraham? He died, and so did the prophets. Who do you think you are?"

⁵⁴Jesus replied, "If I glorify myself, my glory means nothing. My Father, whom you claim as your God, is the one who glorifies me. ⁵⁵Though you do not know him, I know him. If I said I did not, I would be a liar like you, but I do know him and keep his word. ⁵⁶Your father Abraham rejoiced at the thought of seeing my day; he saw it and was glad."

⁵⁷"You are not yet fifty years old," the Jews said to him, "and you have seen Abraham!"

⁵⁸"I tell you the truth," Jesus answered, "before Abraham was born, I am!" ⁵⁹At this, they picked up stones to stone him, but Jesus hid himself, slipping away from the temple grounds.

❓DID YOU KNOW?　　　8:57

How old was Jesus?

Jesus lived about thirty-three years here on earth. But Jesus was also God. As God, Jesus has always existed, even before Abraham was born thousands of years earlier.

Jesus Heals a Man Born Blind

9 As he went along, he saw a man blind from birth. ²His disciples asked him, "Rabbi, who sinned, this man or his parents, that he was born blind?"

³"Neither this man nor his parents sinned," said Jesus, "but this happened so that the work of God might be displayed in his life. ⁴As long as it is day, we must do the work of him who sent me. Night is coming, when

---

*a*38 Or *presence. Therefore do what you have heard from the Father.*　　*b*39 Some early manuscripts *"If you are Abraham's children," said Jesus, "then*

no one can work. ⁵While I am in the world, I am the light of the world."

⁶Having said this, he spit on the ground, made some mud with the saliva, and put it on the man's eyes. ⁷"Go," he told him, "wash in the Pool of Siloam" (this word means Sent). So the man went and washed, and came home seeing.

⁸His neighbors and those who had formerly seen him begging asked, "Isn't this the same man who used to sit and beg?" ⁹Some claimed that he was.

Others said, "No, he only looks like him."

But he himself insisted, "I am the man."

¹⁰"How then were your eyes opened?" they demanded.

¹¹He replied, "The man they call Jesus made some mud and put it on my eyes. He told me to go to Siloam and wash. So I went and washed, and then I could see."

¹²"Where is this man?" they asked him.

"I don't know," he said.

The Pharisees Investigate the Healing

¹³They brought to the Pharisees the man who had been blind. ¹⁴Now the day on which Jesus had made the mud and opened the man's eyes was a Sabbath. ¹⁵Therefore the Pharisees also asked him how he had received his sight. "He put mud on my eyes," the man replied, "and I washed, and now I see."

¹⁶Some of the Pharisees said, "This man is not from God, for he does not keep the Sabbath."

But others asked, "How can a sinner do such miraculous signs?" So they were divided.

¹⁷Finally they turned again to the blind man, "What have you to say about him? It was your eyes he opened."

The man replied, "He is a prophet."

¹⁸The Jews still did not believe that he had been blind and had received his sight until they sent for the man's parents. ¹⁹"Is this your son?" they asked. "Is this the one you say was born blind? How is it that now he can see?"

²⁰"We know he is our son," the parents answered, "and we know he was born blind. ²¹But how he can see now, or who opened his eyes, we don't know. Ask him. He is of age; he will speak for himself." ²²His parents said this because they were afraid of the Jews, for already the Jews had decided that anyone who acknowledged that Jesus was the Christᵃ would be put out of the synagogue. ²³That was why his parents said, "He is of age; ask him."

²⁴A second time they summoned the man who had been blind. "Give glory to God,ᵇ" they said. "We know this man is a sinner."

²⁵He replied, "Whether he is a sinner or not, I don't know. One thing I do know. I was blind but now I see!"

²⁶Then they asked him, "What did

ᵃ22 Or *Messiah*   ᵇ24 A solemn charge to tell the truth (see Joshua 7:19)

▌ET'S LIVE IT!   John 9:1–7

IS SICKNESS PUNISHMENT? ▪➡ Some people think all sickness is punishment for sin. What did Jesus say about this idea? Read John 9:1–5. Jesus healed the man, and called healing "the work of him who sent me [God]" (John 9:4).

Doctors, nurses, and many others work toward the healing of sick people. If there is a doctor in your church, or if your church supports a medical missionary, tell him or her about this Bible story. Ask that person how being a doctor or nurse is doing God's work.

he do to you? How did he open your eyes?"

²⁷He answered, "I have told you already and you did not listen. Why do you want to hear it again? Do you want to become his disciples, too?"

²⁸Then they hurled insults at him and said, "You are this fellow's disciple! We are disciples of Moses! ²⁹We know that God spoke to Moses, but as for this fellow, we don't even know where he comes from."

³⁰The man answered, "Now that is remarkable! You don't know where he comes from, yet he opened my eyes. ³¹We know that God does not listen to sinners. He listens to the godly man who does his will. ³²Nobody has ever heard of opening the eyes of a man born blind. ³³If this man were not from God, he could do nothing."

³⁴To this they replied, "You were steeped in sin at birth; how dare you lecture us!" And they threw him out.

Spiritual Blindness

³⁵Jesus heard that they had thrown him out, and when he found him, he said, "Do you believe in the Son of Man?"

³⁶"Who is he, sir?" the man asked. "Tell me so that I may believe in him."

³⁷Jesus said, "You have now seen him; in fact, he is the one speaking with you."

³⁸Then the man said, "Lord, I believe," and he worshiped him.

³⁹Jesus said, "For judgment I have come into this world, so that the blind will see and those who see will become blind."

⁴⁰Some Pharisees who were with him heard him say this and asked, "What? Are we blind too?"

⁴¹Jesus said, "If you were blind, you would not be guilty of sin; but now that you claim you can see, your guilt remains."

The Shepherd and His Flock

10 "I tell you the truth, the man who does not enter the sheep pen by the gate, but climbs in by some other way, is a thief and a robber. ²The man who enters by the gate is the shepherd of his sheep. ³The watchman opens the gate for him, and the sheep listen to his voice. He calls his own sheep by name and leads them out. ⁴When he has brought out all his own, he goes on ahead of them, and his sheep follow him because they know his voice. ⁵But they will never follow a stranger; in fact, they will run away from him because they do not recognize a stranger's voice." ⁶Jesus used this figure of speech, but they did not understand what he was telling them.

⁷Therefore Jesus said again, "I tell you the truth, I am the gate for the sheep. ⁸All who ever came before me were thieves and robbers, but the sheep did not listen to them. ⁹I am the gate; whoever enters through me will

Life in Bible Times

THE SHEEP PEN

At night flocks of sheep were kept in pens made of stone or branches with thorns. The shepherd slept in the only doorway. If wild animals came near the shepherd was there to protect the sheep.

be saved. *a* He will come in and go out, and find pasture. ¹⁰The thief comes only to steal and kill and destroy; I have come that they may have life, and have it to the full.

¹¹"I am the good shepherd. The good shepherd lays down his life for the sheep. ¹²The hired hand is not the shepherd who owns the sheep. So when he sees the wolf coming, he abandons the sheep and runs away. Then the wolf attacks the flock and scatters it. ¹³The man runs away because he is a hired hand and cares nothing for the sheep.

¹⁴"I am the good shepherd; I know my sheep and my sheep know me— ¹⁵just as the Father knows me and I know the Father—and I lay down my life for the sheep. ¹⁶I have other sheep that are not of this sheep pen. I must bring them also. They too will listen to my voice, and there shall be one flock and one shepherd. ¹⁷The reason my Father loves me is that I lay down my life—only to take it up again. ¹⁸No one takes it from me, but I lay it down of my own accord. I have authority to lay it down and authority to take it up again. This command I received from my Father."

ⓌORDS TO REMEMBER

10:14-15 I am the good shepherd; I know my sheep and my sheep know me ... I lay down my life for the sheep.

---

¹⁹At these words the Jews were again divided. ²⁰Many of them said, "He is demon-possessed and raving mad. Why listen to him?"

²¹But others said, "These are not the sayings of a man possessed by a demon. Can a demon open the eyes of the blind?"

The Unbelief of the Jews

²²Then came the Feast of Dedica-tion *b* at Jerusalem. It was winter, ²³and Jesus was in the temple area walking in Solomon's Colonnade. ²⁴The Jews gathered around him, saying, "How long will you keep us in suspense? If you are the Christ, *c* tell us plainly."

²⁵Jesus answered, "I did tell you, but you do not believe. The miracles I do in my Father's name speak for me, ²⁶but you do not believe because you are not my sheep. ²⁷My sheep listen to my voice; I know them, and they follow me. ²⁸I give them eternal life, and they shall never perish; no one can snatch them out of my hand. ²⁹My Father, who has given them to me, is greater than all *d*; no one can snatch them out of my Father's hand. ³⁰I and the Father are one."

³¹Again the Jews picked up stones to stone him, ³²but Jesus said to them, "I have shown you many great miracles from the Father. For which of these do you stone me?"

³³"We are not stoning you for any of these," replied the Jews, "but for blasphemy, because you, a mere man, claim to be God."

³⁴Jesus answered them, "Is it not written in your Law, 'I have said you are gods' *e*? ³⁵If he called them 'gods,' to whom the word of God came—and the Scripture cannot be broken— ³⁶what about the one whom the Father set apart as his very own and sent into the world? Why then do you accuse me of blasphemy because I said, 'I am God's Son'? ³⁷Do not believe me unless I do what my Father does. ³⁸But if I do it, even though you do not believe me, believe the miracles, that you may know and understand that the Father is in me, and I in the Father." ³⁹Again they tried to seize him, but he escaped their grasp.

⁴⁰Then Jesus went back across the Jordan to the place where John had been baptizing in the early days. Here he stayed ⁴¹and many people came to him. They said, "Though John never performed a miraculous

---

a9 Or *kept safe*   *b22* That is, Hanukkah   *c24* Or *Messiah*   *d29* Many early manuscripts
What my Father has given me is greater than all   *e34* Psalm 82:6

sign, all that John said about this man was true." [42]And in that place many believed in Jesus.

The Death of Lazarus

11 Now a man named Lazarus was sick. He was from Bethany, the village of Mary and her sister Martha. [2]This Mary, whose brother Lazarus now lay sick, was the same one who poured perfume on the Lord and wiped his feet with her hair. [3]So the sisters sent word to Jesus, "Lord, the one you love is sick."

[4]When he heard this, Jesus said, "This sickness will not end in death. No, it is for God's glory so that God's Son may be glorified through it." [5]Jesus loved Martha and her sister and Lazarus. [6]Yet when he heard that Lazarus was sick, he stayed where he was two more days.

[7]Then he said to his disciples, "Let us go back to Judea."

[8]"But Rabbi," they said, "a short while ago the Jews tried to stone you, and yet you are going back there?"

[9]Jesus answered, "Are there not twelve hours of daylight? A man who walks by day will not stumble, for he sees by this world's light. [10]It is when he walks by night that he stumbles, for he has no light."

[11]After he had said this, he went on to tell them, "Our friend Lazarus has fallen asleep; but I am going there to wake him up."

[12]His disciples replied, "Lord, if he sleeps, he will get better." [13]Jesus had been speaking of his death, but his disciples thought he meant natural sleep.

[14]So then he told them plainly, "Lazarus is dead, [15]and for your sake I am glad I was not there, so that you may believe. But let us go to him."

[16]Then Thomas (called Didymus) said to the rest of the disciples, "Let us also go, that we may die with him."

Jesus Comforts the Sisters

[17]On his arrival, Jesus found that Lazarus had already been in the tomb for four days. [18]Bethany was less than two miles[a] from Jerusalem, [19]and many Jews had come to Martha and Mary to comfort them in the loss of their brother. [20]When Martha heard that Jesus was coming, she went out to meet him, but Mary stayed at home.

? DID YOU KNOW?　　　11:15

Why did Jesus let Lazarus die?

Jesus didn't come immediately when Lazarus' sisters sent for him. Jesus let his friend die. But Jesus brought Lazarus back to life again. This miracle showed Jesus' power over death.

[21]"Lord," Martha said to Jesus, "if you had been here, my brother would not have died. [22]But I know that even now God will give you whatever you ask."

[23]Jesus said to her, "Your brother will rise again."

[24]Martha answered, "I know he will rise again in the resurrection at the last day."

[25]Jesus said to her, "I am the resurrection and the life. He who believes in me will live, even though he dies; [26]and whoever lives and believes in me will never die. Do you believe this?"

[27]"Yes, Lord," she told him, "I believe that you are the Christ,[b] the Son of God, who was to come into the world."

[28]And after she had said this, she went back and called her sister Mary aside. "The Teacher is here," she said, "and is asking for you." [29]When Mary heard this, she got up quickly and went to him. [30]Now Jesus had not yet entered the village, but was still at the place where Martha had met him. [31]When the Jews who had been with Mary in the house, comforting her, noticed how quickly she got up

---

[a]18 Greek *fifteen stadia* (about 3 kilometers)　　[b]27 Or *Messiah*

and went out, they followed her, supposing she was going to the tomb to mourn there.

³²When Mary reached the place where Jesus was and saw him, she fell at his feet and said, "Lord, if you had been here, my brother would not have died."

³³When Jesus saw her weeping, and the Jews who had come along with her also weeping, he was deeply moved in spirit and troubled. ³⁴"Where have you laid him?" he asked.

"Come and see, Lord," they replied.

³⁵Jesus wept.

³⁶Then the Jews said, "See how he loved him!"

³⁷But some of them said, "Could not he who opened the eyes of the blind man have kept this man from dying?"

Jesus Raises Lazarus From the Dead

³⁸Jesus, once more deeply moved, came to the tomb. It was a cave with a stone laid across the entrance. ³⁹"Take away the stone," he said.

"But, Lord," said Martha, the sister of the dead man, "by this time there is a bad odor, for he has been there four days."

⁴⁰Then Jesus said, "Did I not tell you that if you believed, you would see the glory of God?"

⁴¹So they took away the stone. Then Jesus looked up and said, "Father, I thank you that you have heard me. ⁴²I knew that you always hear me, but I said this for the benefit of the people standing here, that they may believe that you sent me."

⁴³When he had said this, Jesus called in a loud voice, "Lazarus, come out!" ⁴⁴The dead man came out, his hands and feet wrapped with strips of linen, and a cloth around his face.

Jesus said to them, "Take off the grave clothes and let him go."

The Plot to Kill Jesus

⁴⁵Therefore many of the Jews who had come to visit Mary, and had seen what Jesus did, put their faith in him. ⁴⁶But some of them went to the Pharisees and told them what Jesus had done. ⁴⁷Then the chief priests and the Pharisees called a meeting of the Sanhedrin.

"What are we accomplishing?" they asked. "Here is this man performing many miraculous signs. ⁴⁸If we let him go on like this, everyone will believe in him, and then the Romans will come and take away both our place*a* and our nation."

⁴⁹Then one of them, named Caiaphas, who was high priest that year, spoke up, "You know nothing at all! ⁵⁰You do not realize that it is better for you that one man die for the people than that the whole nation perish."

⁵¹He did not say this on his own, but as high priest that year he prophesied that Jesus would die for the Jewish nation, ⁵²and not only for that nation but also for the scattered children of God, to bring them together and make them one. ⁵³So from that day on they plotted to take his life.

⁵⁴Therefore Jesus no longer moved about publicly among the Jews. Instead he withdrew to a region near the desert, to a village called Ephraim, where he stayed with his disciples.

⁵⁵When it was almost time for the Jewish Passover, many went up from the country to Jerusalem for their ceremonial cleansing before the Passover. ⁵⁶They kept looking for Jesus, and as they stood in the temple area they asked one another, "What do you think? Isn't he coming to the Feast at all?" ⁵⁷But the chief priests and Pharisees had given orders that if anyone found out where Jesus was, he should report it so that they might arrest him.

Jesus Anointed at Bethany

12 Six days before the Passover, Jesus arrived at Bethany, where Lazarus lived, whom Jesus had raised from the dead. ²Here a

---

a48 Or *temple*

dinner was given in Jesus' honor. Martha served, while Lazarus was among those reclining at the table with him. ³Then Mary took about a pint*ᵃ* of pure nard, an expensive perfume; she poured it on Jesus' feet and wiped his feet with her hair. And the house was filled with the fragrance of the perfume.

⁴But one of his disciples, Judas Iscariot, who was later to betray him, objected, ⁵"Why wasn't this perfume sold and the money given to the poor? It was worth a year's wages.*ᵇ*" ⁶He did not say this because he cared about the poor but because he was a thief; as keeper of the money bag, he used to help himself to what was put into it.

⁷"Leave her alone," Jesus replied. "It was intended that she should save this perfume for the day of my burial. ⁸You will always have the poor among you, but you will not always have me."

⁹Meanwhile a large crowd of Jews found out that Jesus was there and came, not only because of him but also to see Lazarus, whom he had raised from the dead. ¹⁰So the chief priests made plans to kill Lazarus as well, ¹¹for on account of him many of the Jews were going over to Jesus and putting their faith in him.

The Triumphal Entry

¹²The next day the great crowd that had come for the Feast heard that Jesus was on his way to Jerusalem. ¹³They took palm branches and went out to meet him, shouting,

"Hosanna!*ᶜ*"

"Blessed is he who comes in the name of the Lord!"*ᵈ*

"Blessed is the King of Israel!"

¹⁴Jesus found a young donkey and sat upon it, as it is written,

¹⁵"Do not be afraid, O Daughter of Zion;
see, your king is coming,
seated on a donkey's colt."*ᵉ*

¹⁶At first his disciples did not understand all this. Only after Jesus was glorified did they realize that these things had been written about him and that they had done these things to him.

¹⁷Now the crowd that was with him when he called Lazarus from the tomb and raised him from the dead continued to spread the word. ¹⁸Many people, because they had heard that he had given this miraculous sign, went out to meet him. ¹⁹So the Pharisees said to one another, "See, this is getting us nowhere. Look how the whole world has gone after him!"

Jesus Predicts His Death

²⁰Now there were some Greeks among those who went up to worship at the Feast. ²¹They came to Philip, who was from Bethsaida in Galilee, with a request. "Sir," they said, "we would like to see Jesus." ²²Philip went to tell Andrew; Andrew and Philip in turn told Jesus.

²³Jesus replied, "The hour has come for the Son of Man to be glorified. ²⁴I tell you the truth, unless a kernel of wheat falls to the ground and dies, it remains only a single seed. But if it dies, it produces many seeds. ²⁵The man who loves his life will lose it, while the man who hates his life in this world will keep it for eternal life. ²⁶Whoever serves me must follow me; and where I am, my servant also will be. My Father will honor the one who serves me.

²⁷"Now my heart is troubled, and what shall I say? 'Father, save me from this hour'? No, it was for this very reason I came to this hour. ²⁸Father, glorify your name!"

Then a voice came from heaven, "I have glorified it, and will glorify it

---

ᵃ3 Greek *a litra* (probably about 0.5 liter)   *ᵇ5* Greek *three hundred denarii*   *ᶜ13* A Hebrew expression meaning "Save!" which became an exclamation of praise   *ᵈ13* Psalm 118:25, 26   *ᵉ15* Zech. 9:9

again." ²⁹The crowd that was there and heard it said it had thundered; others said an angel had spoken to him.

³⁰Jesus said, "This voice was for your benefit, not mine. ³¹Now is the time for judgment on this world; now the prince of this world will be driven out. ³²But I, when I am lifted up from the earth, will draw all men to myself." ³³He said this to show the kind of death he was going to die.

³⁴The crowd spoke up, "We have heard from the Law that the Christ[a] will remain forever, so how can you say, 'The Son of Man must be lifted up'? Who is this 'Son of Man'?"

³⁵Then Jesus told them, "You are going to have the light just a little while longer. Walk while you have the light, before darkness overtakes you. The man who walks in the dark does not know where he is going. ³⁶Put your trust in the light while you have it, so that you may become sons of light." When he had finished speaking, Jesus left and hid himself from them.

The Jews Continue in Their Unbelief

³⁷Even after Jesus had done all these miraculous signs in their presence, they still would not believe in him. ³⁸This was to fulfill the word of Isaiah the prophet:

"Lord, who has believed our
        message
  and to whom has the arm of the
        Lord been revealed?"[b]

³⁹For this reason they could not believe, because, as Isaiah says elsewhere:

⁴⁰"He has blinded their eyes
  and deadened their hearts,
  so they can neither see with their
        eyes,
    nor understand with their
        hearts,
    nor turn—and I would heal
        them."[c]

⁴¹Isaiah said this because he saw Jesus' glory and spoke about him.

⁴²Yet at the same time many even among the leaders believed in him. But because of the Pharisees they would not confess their faith for fear they would be put out of the synagogue; ⁴³for they loved praise from men more than praise from God.

⁴⁴Then Jesus cried out, "When a man believes in me, he does not believe in me only, but in the one who sent me. ⁴⁵When he looks at me, he sees the one who sent me. ⁴⁶I have come into the world as a light, so that no one who believes in me should stay in darkness.

⁴⁷"As for the person who hears my words but does not keep them, I do not judge him. For I did not come to judge the world, but to save it. ⁴⁸There is a judge for the one who rejects me and does not accept my words; that very word which I spoke will condemn him at the last day. ⁴⁹For I did not speak of my own accord, but the Father who sent me commanded me what to say and how to say it. ⁵⁰I know that his command leads to eternal life. So whatever I say is just what the Father has told me to say."

Jesus Washes His Disciples' Feet

13 It was just before the Passover Feast. Jesus knew that the time had come for him to leave this world and go to the Father. Having loved his own who were in the world, he now showed them the full extent of his love.[d]

²The evening meal was being served, and the devil had already prompted Judas Iscariot, son of Simon, to betray Jesus. ³Jesus knew that the Father had put all things under his power, and that he had come from God and was returning to God; ⁴so he got up from the meal, took off his outer clothing, and wrapped a towel around his waist. ⁵After that, he poured water into a basin and be-

---

a34 Or *Messiah*   *b38* Isaiah 53:1   *c40* Isaiah 6:10   *d1* Or *he loved them to the last* gan to wash his disciples' feet, drying them with the towel that was wrapped around him.

⁶He came to Simon Peter, who said to him, "Lord, are you going to wash my feet?"

⁷Jesus replied, "You do not realize now what I am doing, but later you will understand."

⁸"No," said Peter, "you shall never wash my feet."

Jesus answered, "Unless I wash you, you have no part with me."

⁹"Then, Lord," Simon Peter replied, "not just my feet but my hands and my head as well!"

¹⁰Jesus answered, "A person who has had a bath needs only to wash his feet; his whole body is clean. And you are clean, though not every one of you." ¹¹For he knew who was going to betray him, and that was why he said not every one was clean.

¹²When he had finished washing their feet, he put on his clothes and returned to his place. "Do you understand what I have done for you?" he asked them. ¹³"You call me 'Teacher' and 'Lord,' and rightly so, for that is what I am. ¹⁴Now that I, your Lord and Teacher, have washed your feet, you also should wash one another's feet. ¹⁵I have set you an example that you should do as I have done for you.

¹⁶I tell you the truth, no servant is greater than his master, nor is a messenger greater than the one who sent him. ¹⁷Now that you know these things, you will be blessed if you do them.

Jesus Predicts His Betrayal

¹⁸"I am not referring to all of you; I know those I have chosen. But this is to fulfill the scripture: 'He who shares my bread has lifted up his heel against me.'ᵃ

¹⁹"I am telling you now before it happens, so that when it does happen you will believe that I am He. ²⁰I tell you the truth, whoever accepts anyone I send accepts me; and whoever accepts me accepts the one who sent me."

²¹After he had said this, Jesus was troubled in spirit and testified, "I tell you the truth, one of you is going to betray me."

²²His disciples stared at one another, at a loss to know which of them he meant. ²³One of them, the disciple whom Jesus loved, was reclining next to him. ²⁴Simon Peter motioned to this disciple and said, "Ask him which one he means."

²⁵Leaning back against Jesus, he asked him, "Lord, who is it?"

²⁶Jesus answered, "It is the one to

ᵃ18 Psalm 41:9

Life in Bible Times

FOOT WASHING

When visitors came into a house, they took off their sandals. A good host offered them water to wash their dusty feet. Usually the lowest servant in the house was ordered to wash the guests' feet. Jesus was showing us how to be humble when he took the job of washing his disciples' feet.

whom I will give this piece of bread when I have dipped it in the dish." Then, dipping the piece of bread, he gave it to Judas Iscariot, son of Simon. 27As soon as Judas took the bread, Satan entered into him.

"What you are about to do, do quickly," Jesus told him, 28but no one at the meal understood why Jesus said this to him. 29Since Judas had charge of the money, some thought Jesus was telling him to buy what was needed for the Feast, or to give something to the poor. 30As soon as Judas had taken the bread, he went out. And it was night.

Jesus Predicts Peter's Denial

31When he was gone, Jesus said, "Now is the Son of Man glorified and God is glorified in him. 32If God is glorified in him, *a* God will glorify the Son in himself, and will glorify him at once.

33"My children, I will be with you only a little longer. You will look for me, and just as I told the Jews, so I tell you now: Where I am going, you cannot come.

34"A new command I give you: Love one another. As I have loved you, so you must love one another. 35By this all men will know that you are my disciples, if you love one another."

WORDS TO REMEMBER

13:34 Love one another. As I have loved you, so you must love one another.

36Simon Peter asked him, "Lord, where are you going?"

Jesus replied, "Where I am going, you cannot follow now, but you will follow later."

37Peter asked, "Lord, why can't I follow you now? I will lay down my life for you."

38Then Jesus answered, "Will you really lay down your life for me? I tell you the truth, before the rooster crows, you will disown me three times!

Jesus Comforts His Disciples

14 "Do not let your hearts be troubled. Trust in God *b*; trust also in me. 2In my Father's house are many rooms; if it were not so, I would have told you. I am going there to prepare a place for you. 3And if I go and prepare a place for you, I will come back and take you to be with me that you also may be where I am. 4You know the way to the place where I am going."

Jesus the Way to the Father

5Thomas said to him, "Lord, we don't know where you are going, so how can we know the way?"

6Jesus answered, "I am the way and the truth and the life. No one comes to the Father except through me. 7If you really knew me, you would know *c* my Father as well. From now on, you do know him and have seen him."

WORDS TO REMEMBER

14:6 I am the way and the truth and the life. No one comes to the Father except through me.

8Philip said, "Lord, show us the Father and that will be enough for us."

9Jesus answered: "Don't you know me, Philip, even after I have been among you such a long time? Anyone who has seen me has seen the Father. How can you say, 'Show us the Father'? 10Don't you believe that I am in the Father, and that the Father is in me? The words I say to you are not just my own. Rather, it is the Father, living in me, who is doing his work. 11Believe me when I say that I am in the Father and the Father is in me; or

---

a32 Many early manuscripts do not have *If God is glorified in him.*   *b1* Or *You trust in God*
c7 Some early manuscripts *If you really have known me, you will know*

at least believe on the evidence of the miracles themselves. [12]I tell you the truth, anyone who has faith in me will do what I have been doing. He will do even greater things than these, because I am going to the Father. [13]And I will do whatever you ask in my name, so that the Son may bring glory to the Father. [14]You may ask me for anything in my name, and I will do it.

Jesus Promises the Holy Spirit

[15]"If you love me, you will obey what I command. [16]And I will ask the Father, and he will give you another Counselor to be with you forever— [17]the Spirit of truth. The world cannot accept him, because it neither sees him nor knows him. But you know him, for he lives with you and will be[a] in you. [18]I will not leave you as orphans; I will come to you. [19]Before long, the world will not see me anymore, but you will see me. Because I live, you also will live. [20]On that day you will realize that I am in my Father, and you are in me, and I am in you. [21]Whoever has my commands and obeys them, he is the one who loves me. He who loves me will be loved by my Father, and I too will love him and show myself to him."

[22]Then Judas (not Judas Iscariot) said, "But, Lord, why do you intend to show yourself to us and not to the world?"

[23]Jesus replied, "If anyone loves me, he will obey my teaching. My Father will love him, and we will come to him and make our home with him. [24]He who does not love me will not obey my teaching. These words you hear are not my own; they belong to the Father who sent me.

[25]"All this I have spoken while still with you. [26]But the Counselor, the Holy Spirit, whom the Father will send in my name, will teach you all things and will remind you of everything I have said to you. [27]Peace I leave with you; my peace I give you. I do not give to you as the world gives. Do not let your hearts be troubled and do not be afraid.

[28]"You heard me say, 'I am going away and I am coming back to you.' If you loved me, you would be glad that I am going to the Father, for the Father is greater than I. [29]I have told you now before it happens, so that when it does happen you will believe. [30]I will not speak with you much longer, for the prince of this world is coming. He has no hold on me, [31]but the world must learn that I love the Father and that I do exactly what my Father has commanded me.

"Come now; let us leave.

The Vine and the Branches

15 "I am the true vine, and my Father is the gardener. [2]He cuts off every branch in me that bears no fruit, while every branch that does bear fruit he prunes[b] so that it will be even more fruitful. [3]You are already clean because of the word I have spoken to you. [4]Remain in me, and I will remain in you. No branch

---

[a]17 Some early manuscripts *and is*   [b]2 The Greek for *prunes* also means *cleans.*

LET'S LIVE IT!

SUPER HELP WHEN WE NEED IT MOST ➡ Who is the Christian's helper? Read John 14:15–21 to find out.

God the Holy Spirit is our invisible helper. He is in us and stays with us. When we need strength to obey God's commands, the Holy Spirit strengthens us.

Paste a photograph of yourself to a sheet of paper. Then draw and color a giant figure around your photograph. Let the picture remind you that God is with you, to give you strength to do right.

can bear fruit by itself; it must remain in the vine. Neither can you bear fruit unless you remain in me. [5]"I am the vine; you are the branches. If a man remains in me and I in him, he will bear much fruit; apart from me you can do nothing. [6]If anyone does not remain in me, he is like a branch that is thrown away and withers; such branches are picked up, thrown into the fire and burned. [7]If you remain in me and my words remain in you, ask whatever you wish, and it will be given you. [8]This is to my Father's glory, that you bear much fruit, showing yourselves to be my disciples.

[9]"As the Father has loved me, so have I loved you. Now remain in my love. [10]If you obey my commands, you will remain in my love, just as I have obeyed my Father's commands and remain in his love. [11]I have told you this so that my joy may be in you and that your joy may be complete. [12]My command is this: Love each other as I have loved you. [13]Greater love has no one than this, that he lay down his life for his friends. [14]You are my friends if you do what I command. [15]I no longer call you servants, because a servant does not know his master's business. Instead, I have called you friends, for everything that I learned from my Father I have made known to you. [16]You did not choose me, but I chose you and appointed you to go and bear fruit—fruit that will last. Then the Father will give you whatever you ask in my name. [17]This is my command: Love each other.

The World Hates the Disciples

[18]"If the world hates you, keep in mind that it hated me first. [19]If you belonged to the world, it would love you as its own. As it is, you do not belong to the world, but I have chosen you out of the world. That is why the world hates you. [20]Remember the words I spoke to you: 'No servant is greater than his master.'[a] If they persecuted me, they will persecute

you also. If they obeyed my teaching, they will obey yours also. [21]They will treat you this way because of my name, for they do not know the One who sent me. [22]If I had not come and spoken to them, they would not be guilty of sin. Now, however, they have no excuse for their sin. [23]He who hates me hates my Father as well. [24]If I had not done among them what no one else did, they would not be guilty of sin. But now they have seen these miracles, and yet they have hated both me and my Father. [25]But this is to fulfill what is written in their Law: 'They hated me without reason.'[b]

[26]"When the Counselor comes, whom I will send to you from the Father, the Spirit of truth who goes out from the Father, he will testify about me. [27]And you also must testify, for you have been with me from the beginning.

16 "All this I have told you so that you will not go astray. [2]They will put you out of the synagogue; in fact, a time is coming when anyone who kills you will think he is offering a service to God. [3]They will do such things because they have not known the Father or me. [4]I have told you this, so that when the time comes you will remember that I warned you. I did not tell you this at first because I was with you.

The Work of the Holy Spirit

[5]"Now I am going to him who sent me, yet none of you asks me, 'Where are you going?' [6]Because I have said these things, you are filled with grief. [7]But I tell you the truth: It is for your good that I am going away. Unless I go away, the Counselor will not come to you; but if I go, I will send him to you. [8]When he comes, he will convict the world of guilt[c] in regard to sin and righteousness and judgment: [9]in regard to sin, because men do not believe in me; [10]in regard to righteousness, because I am going to the Father, where you can see me no longer;

---

[a]20 John 13:16   [b]25 Psalms 35:19; 69:4   [c]8 Or *will expose the guilt of the world*

¹¹and in regard to judgment, because the prince of this world now stands condemned.

¹²"I have much more to say to you, more than you can now bear. ¹³But when he, the Spirit of truth, comes, he will guide you into all truth. He will not speak on his own; he will speak only what he hears, and he will tell you what is yet to come. ¹⁴He will bring glory to me by taking from what is mine and making it known to you. ¹⁵All that belongs to the Father is mine. That is why I said the Spirit will take from what is mine and make it known to you.

¹⁶"In a little while you will see me no more, and then after a little while you will see me."

The Disciples' Grief Will Turn to Joy

¹⁷Some of his disciples said to one another, "What does he mean by saying, 'In a little while you will see me no more, and then after a little while you will see me,' and 'Because I am going to the Father'?" ¹⁸They kept asking, "What does he mean by 'a little while'? We don't understand what he is saying."

¹⁹Jesus saw that they wanted to ask him about this, so he said to them, "Are you asking one another what I meant when I said, 'In a little while you will see me no more, and then after a little while you will see me'? ²⁰I tell you the truth, you will weep and mourn while the world rejoices. You will grieve, but your grief will turn to joy. ²¹A woman giving birth to a child has pain because her time has come; but when her baby is born she forgets the anguish because of her joy that a child is born into the world. ²²So with you: Now is your time of grief, but I will see you again and you will rejoice, and no one will take away your joy. ²³In that day you will no longer ask me anything. I tell you the truth, my Father will give you whatever you ask in my name. ²⁴Until now you have not asked for anything in my name. Ask and you will receive, and your joy will be complete.

WORDS TO REMEMBER

16:24 Ask and you will receive, and your joy will be complete.

²⁵"Though I have been speaking figuratively, a time is coming when I will no longer use this kind of language but will tell you plainly about my Father. ²⁶In that day you will ask in my name. I am not saying that I will ask the Father on your behalf. ²⁷No, the Father himself loves you because you have loved me and have believed that I came from God. ²⁸I came from the Father and entered the world; now I am leaving the world and going back to the Father."

²⁹Then Jesus' disciples said, "Now you are speaking clearly and without figures of speech. ³⁰Now we can see that you know all things and that you do not even need to have anyone ask you questions. This makes us believe that you came from God."

³¹"You believe at last!"ᵃ Jesus answered. ³²"But a time is coming, and has come, when you will be scattered, each to his own home. You will leave me all alone. Yet I am not alone, for my Father is with me.

³³"I have told you these things, so that in me you may have peace. In this world you will have trouble. But take heart! I have overcome the world."

Jesus Prays for Himself

17 After Jesus said this, he looked toward heaven and prayed:

"Father, the time has come. Glorify your Son, that your Son may glorify you. ²For you granted him authority over all people that he might give eternal life to all those you have given him.

ᵃ31 Or "Do you now believe?"

³Now this is eternal life: that they may know you, the only true God, and Jesus Christ, whom you have sent. ⁴I have brought you glory on earth by completing the work you gave me to do. ⁵And now, Father, glorify me in your presence with the glory I had with you before the world began.

Jesus Prays for His Disciples

⁶"I have revealed you ᵃ to those whom you gave me out of the world. They were yours; you gave them to me and they have obeyed your word. ⁷Now they know that everything you have given me comes from you. ⁸For I gave them the words you gave me and they accepted them. They knew with certainty that I came from you, and they believed that you sent me. ⁹I pray for them. I am not praying for the world, but for those you have given me, for they are yours. ¹⁰All I have is yours, and all you have is mine. And glory has come to me through them. ¹¹I will remain in the world no longer, but they are still in the world, and I am coming to you. Holy Father, protect them by the power of your name—the name you gave me—so that they may be one as we are one. ¹²While I was with them, I protected them and kept them safe by that name you gave me. None has been lost except the one doomed to destruction so that Scripture would be fulfilled.

¹³"I am coming to you now, but I say these things while I am still in the world, so that they may have the full measure of my joy within them. ¹⁴I have given them your word and the world has hated them, for they are not of the world any more than I am of the world. ¹⁵My prayer is not

that you take them out of the world but that you protect them from the evil one. ¹⁶They are not of the world, even as I am not of it. ¹⁷Sanctify ᵇ them by the truth; your word is truth. ¹⁸As you sent me into the world, I have sent them into the world. ¹⁹For them I sanctify myself, that they too may be truly sanctified.

Jesus Prays for All Believers

²⁰"My prayer is not for them alone. I pray also for those who will believe in me through their message, ²¹that all of them may be one, Father, just as you are in me and I am in you. May they also be in us so that the world may believe that you have sent me. ²²I have given them the glory that you gave me, that they may be one as we are one: ²³I in them and you in me. May they be brought to complete unity to let the world know that you sent me and have loved them even as you have loved me.

²⁴"Father, I want those you have given me to be with me where I am, and to see my glory, the glory you have given me because you loved me before the creation of the world.

²⁵"Righteous Father, though the world does not know you, I know you, and they know that you have sent me. ²⁶I have made you known to them, and will continue to make you known in order that the love you have for me may be in them and that I myself may be in them."

Jesus Arrested

18 When he had finished praying, Jesus left with his disciples and crossed the Kidron Valley. On the other side there was an olive grove, and he and his disciples went into it.

²Now Judas, who betrayed him,

ᵃ6 Greek *your name*; also in verse 26   ᵇ17 Greek *hagiazo (set apart for sacred use* or *make holy)*; also in verse 19

knew the place, because Jesus had often met there with his disciples. ³So Judas came to the grove, guiding a detachment of soldiers and some officials from the chief priests and Pharisees. They were carrying torches, lanterns and weapons.

❓DID YOU KNOW?　　17:20

What did Jesus ask God to do for his followers?

Jesus asked God to protect them, to sanctify them, to make them one with God, and to bring them to heaven to see Jesus' glory. If you believe in Jesus, this prayer was for you too.

---

⁴Jesus, knowing all that was going to happen to him, went out and asked them, "Who is it you want?"

⁵"Jesus of Nazareth," they replied.

"I am he," Jesus said. (And Judas the traitor was standing there with them.) ⁶When Jesus said, "I am he," they drew back and fell to the ground.

⁷Again he asked them, "Who is it you want?"

And they said, "Jesus of Nazareth."

⁸"I told you that I am he," Jesus answered. "If you are looking for me, then let these men go." ⁹This happened so that the words he had spoken would be fulfilled: "I have not lost one of those you gave me."[a]

¹⁰Then Simon Peter, who had a sword, drew it and struck the high priest's servant, cutting off his right ear. (The servant's name was Malchus.)

¹¹Jesus commanded Peter, "Put your sword away! Shall I not drink the cup the Father has given me?"

Jesus Taken to Annas

¹²Then the detachment of soldiers with its commander and the Jewish officials arrested Jesus. They bound him ¹³and brought him first to An-

nas, who was the father-in-law of Caiaphas, the high priest that year. ¹⁴Caiaphas was the one who had advised the Jews that it would be good if one man died for the people.

Peter's First Denial

¹⁵Simon Peter and another disciple were following Jesus. Because this disciple was known to the high priest, he went with Jesus into the high priest's courtyard, ¹⁶but Peter had to wait outside at the door. The other disciple, who was known to the high priest, came back, spoke to the girl on duty there and brought Peter in.

¹⁷"You are not one of his disciples, are you?" the girl at the door asked Peter.

He replied, "I am not."

¹⁸It was cold, and the servants and officials stood around a fire they had made to keep warm. Peter also was standing with them, warming himself.

The High Priest Questions Jesus

¹⁹Meanwhile, the high priest questioned Jesus about his disciples and his teaching.

²⁰"I have spoken openly to the world," Jesus replied. "I always taught in synagogues or at the temple, where all the Jews come together. I said nothing in secret. ²¹Why question me? Ask those who heard me. Surely they know what I said."

²²When Jesus said this, one of the officials nearby struck him in the face. "Is this the way you answer the high priest?" he demanded.

²³"If I said something wrong," Jesus replied, "testify as to what is wrong. But if I spoke the truth, why did you strike me?" ²⁴Then Annas sent him, still bound, to Caiaphas the high priest.[b]

Peter's Second and Third Denials

²⁵As Simon Peter stood warming himself, he was asked, "You are not one of his disciples, are you?"

---

a9 John 6:39　　b24 Or (Now Annas had sent him, still bound, to Caiaphas the high priest.)

He denied it, saying, "I am not."

²⁶One of the high priest's servants, a relative of the man whose ear Peter had cut off, challenged him, "Didn't I see you with him in the olive grove?" ²⁷Again Peter denied it, and at that moment a rooster began to crow.

Jesus Before Pilate

²⁸Then the Jews led Jesus from Caiaphas to the palace of the Roman governor. By now it was early morning, and to avoid ceremonial uncleanness the Jews did not enter the palace; they wanted to be able to eat the Passover. ²⁹So Pilate came out to them and asked, "What charges are you bringing against this man?"

³⁰"If he were not a criminal," they replied, "we would not have handed him over to you."

³¹Pilate said, "Take him yourselves and judge him by your own law."

"But we have no right to execute anyone," the Jews objected. ³²This happened so that the words Jesus had spoken indicating the kind of death he was going to die would be fulfilled.

³³Pilate then went back inside the palace, summoned Jesus and asked him, "Are you the king of the Jews?"

³⁴"Is that your own idea," Jesus asked, "or did others talk to you about me?"

³⁵"Am I a Jew?" Pilate replied. "It was your people and your chief priests who handed you over to me. What is it you have done?"

³⁶Jesus said, "My kingdom is not of this world. If it were, my servants would fight to prevent my arrest by the Jews. But now my kingdom is from another place."

³⁷"You are a king, then!" said Pilate.

Jesus answered, "You are right in saying I am a king. In fact, for this reason I was born, and for this I came into the world, to testify to the truth. Everyone on the side of truth listens to me."

³⁸"What is truth?" Pilate asked. With this he went out again to the Jews and said, "I find no basis for a charge against him. ³⁹But it is your custom for me to release to you one prisoner at the time of the Passover. Do you want me to release 'the king of the Jews'?"

⁴⁰They shouted back, "No, not him! Give us Barabbas!" Now Barabbas had taken part in a rebellion.

Jesus Sentenced to be Crucified

19 Then Pilate took Jesus and had him flogged. ²The soldiers twisted together a crown of thorns and put it on his head. They clothed him in a purple robe ³and went up to him again and again, saying, "Hail, king of the Jews!" And they struck him in the face.

⁴Once more Pilate came out and said to the Jews, "Look, I am bringing him out to you to let you know that I find no basis for a charge against him." ⁵When Jesus came out wearing the crown of thorns and the purple robe, Pilate said to them, "Here is the man!"

⁶As soon as the chief priests and their officials saw him, they shouted, "Crucify! Crucify!"

But Pilate answered, "You take him and crucify him. As for me, I find no basis for a charge against him."

⁷The Jews insisted, "We have a law, and according to that law he must die, because he claimed to be the Son of God."

⁸When Pilate heard this, he was even more afraid, ⁹and he went back inside the palace. "Where do you come from?" he asked Jesus, but Jesus gave him no answer. ¹⁰"Do you refuse to speak to me?" Pilate said. "Don't you realize I have power either to free you or to crucify you?"

¹¹Jesus answered, "You would have no power over me if it were not given to you from above. Therefore the one who handed me over to you is guilty of a greater sin."

¹²From then on, Pilate tried to set Jesus free, but the Jews kept shouting, "If you let this man go, you are no friend of Caesar. Anyone who claims to be a king opposes Caesar."

¹³When Pilate heard this, he brought Jesus out and sat down on

the judge's seat at a place known as the Stone Pavement (which in Aramaic is Gabbatha). [14]It was the day of Preparation of Passover Week, about the sixth hour.

"Here is your king," Pilate said to the Jews.

[15]But they shouted, "Take him away! Take him away! Crucify him!"

"Shall I crucify your king?" Pilate asked.

"We have no king but Caesar," the chief priests answered.

[16]Finally Pilate handed him over to them to be crucified.

The Crucifixion

So the soldiers took charge of Jesus. [17]Carrying his own cross, he went out to the place of the Skull (which in Aramaic is called Golgotha). [18]Here they crucified him, and with him two others—one on each side and Jesus in the middle.

[19]Pilate had a notice prepared and fastened to the cross. It read: JESUS OF NAZARETH, THE KING OF THE JEWS. [20]Many of the Jews read this sign, for the place where Jesus was crucified was near the city, and the sign was written in Aramaic, Latin and Greek. [21]The chief priests of the Jews protested to Pilate, "Do not write 'The King of the Jews,' but that this man claimed to be king of the Jews."

[22]Pilate answered, "What I have written, I have written."

[23]When the soldiers crucified Jesus, they took his clothes, dividing them into four shares, one for each of them, with the undergarment remaining. This garment was seamless, woven in one piece from top to bottom.

[24]"Let's not tear it," they said to one another. "Let's decide by lot who will get it."

This happened that the scripture might be fulfilled which said,

"They divided my garments
        among them
    and cast lots for my clothing."[a]

So this is what the soldiers did.

[25]Near the cross of Jesus stood his mother, his mother's sister, Mary the wife of Clopas, and Mary Magdalene. [26]When Jesus saw his mother there, and the disciple whom he loved standing nearby, he said to his mother, "Dear woman, here is your son," [27]and to the disciple, "Here is your mother." From that time on, this disciple took her into his home.

The Death of Jesus

[28]Later, knowing that all was now completed, and so that the Scripture would be fulfilled, Jesus said, "I am thirsty." [29]A jar of wine vinegar was there, so they soaked a sponge in it, put the sponge on a stalk of the hyssop plant, and lifted it to Jesus' lips. [30]When he had received the drink, Jesus said, "It is finished." With that, he bowed his head and gave up his spirit.

[31]Now it was the day of Preparation, and the next day was to be a special Sabbath. Because the Jews did not want the bodies left on the crosses during the Sabbath, they asked Pilate to have the legs broken and the bodies taken down. [32]The soldiers therefore came and broke the legs of the first man who had been crucified with Jesus, and then those of the other. [33]But when they came to Jesus and found that he was already dead, they did not break his legs. [34]Instead, one of the soldiers pierced Jesus' side with a spear, bringing a sudden flow of blood and water. [35]The man who saw it has given testimony, and his testimony is true. He knows that he tells the truth, and he testifies so that you also may believe. [36]These things happened so that the scripture would be fulfilled: "Not one of his bones will be broken,"[b] [37]and, as another scripture says, "They will look on the one they have pierced."[c]

The Burial of Jesus

[38]Later, Joseph of Arimathea asked Pilate for the body of Jesus.

a24 Psalm 22:18   b36 Exodus 12:46; Num. 9:12; Psalm 34:20   c37 Zech. 12:10

Now Joseph was a disciple of Jesus, but secretly because he feared the Jews. With Pilate's permission, he came and took the body away. ³⁹He was accompanied by Nicodemus, the man who earlier had visited Jesus at night. Nicodemus brought a mixture of myrrh and aloes, about seventy-five pounds.ᵃ ⁴⁰Taking Jesus' body, the two of them wrapped it, with the spices, in strips of linen. This was in accordance with Jewish burial customs. ⁴¹At the place where Jesus was crucified, there was a garden, and in the garden a new tomb, in which no one had ever been laid. ⁴²Because it was the Jewish day of Preparation and since the tomb was nearby, they laid Jesus there.

BURIAL

The Jews buried persons the same day they died. The body was wrapped in strips of cloth. For special people, sweet-smelling spices were wrapped with the cloth.

The Empty Tomb

20 Early on the first day of the week, while it was still dark, Mary Magdalene went to the tomb and saw that the stone had been removed from the entrance. ²So she came running to Simon Peter and the other disciple, the one Jesus loved, and said, "They have taken the Lord out of the tomb, and we don't know where they have put him!"

³So Peter and the other disciple started for the tomb. ⁴Both were running, but the other disciple outran Peter and reached the tomb first. ⁵He bent over and looked in at the strips of linen lying there but did not go in. ⁶Then Simon Peter, who was behind him, arrived and went into the tomb. He saw the strips of linen lying there, ⁷as well as the burial cloth that had been around Jesus' head. The cloth was folded up by itself, separate from the linen. ⁸Finally the other disciple, who had reached the tomb first, also went inside. He saw and believed. ⁹(They still did not understand from Scripture that Jesus had to rise from the dead.)

Jesus Appears to Mary Magdalene

¹⁰Then the disciples went back to their homes, ¹¹but Mary stood outside the tomb crying. As she wept, she bent over to look into the tomb ¹²and saw two angels in white, seated where Jesus' body had been, one at the head and the other at the foot.

¹³They asked her, "Woman, why are you crying?"

"They have taken my Lord away," she said, "and I don't know where they have put him." ¹⁴At this, she turned around and saw Jesus standing there, but she did not realize that it was Jesus.

¹⁵"Woman," he said, "why are you crying? Who is it you are looking for?"

Thinking he was the gardener, she said, "Sir, if you have carried him away, tell me where you have put him, and I will get him."

¹⁶Jesus said to her, "Mary."

She turned toward him and cried out in Aramaic, "Rabboni!" (which means Teacher).

¹⁷Jesus said, "Do not hold on to me, for I have not yet returned to the Father. Go instead to my brothers and tell them, 'I am returning to my Father and your Father, to my God and your God.'"

¹⁸Mary Magdalene went to the disciples with the news: "I have seen the Lord!" And she told them that he had said these things to her.

ᵃ39 Greek *a hundred litrai* (about 34 kilograms)

Jesus Appears to His Disciples

19On the evening of that first day of the week, when the disciples were together, with the doors locked for fear of the Jews, Jesus came and stood among them and said, "Peace be with you!" 20After he said this, he showed them his hands and side. The disciples were overjoyed when they saw the Lord.

21Again Jesus said, "Peace be with you! As the Father has sent me, I am sending you." 22And with that he breathed on them and said, "Receive the Holy Spirit. 23If you forgive anyone his sins, they are forgiven; if you do not forgive them, they are not forgiven."

Jesus Appears to Thomas

24Now Thomas (called Didymus), one of the Twelve, was not with the disciples when Jesus came. 25So the other disciples told him, "We have seen the Lord!"

But he said to them, "Unless I see the nail marks in his hands and put my finger where the nails were, and put my hand into his side, I will not believe it."

26A week later his disciples were in the house again, and Thomas was with them. Though the doors were locked, Jesus came and stood among them and said, "Peace be with you!" 27Then he said to Thomas, "Put your finger here; see my hands. Reach out your hand and put it into my side. Stop doubting and believe."

28Thomas said to him, "My Lord and my God!"

29Then Jesus told him, "Because you have seen me, you have believed; blessed are those who have not seen and yet have believed."

30Jesus did many other miraculous signs in the presence of his disciples, which are not recorded in this book. 31But these are written that you maya believe that Jesus is the Christ, the Son of God, and that by believing you may have life in his name.

Jesus and the Miraculous Catch of Fish

21 Afterward Jesus appeared again to his disciples, by the Sea of Tiberias.b It happened this way: 2Simon Peter, Thomas (called Didymus), Nathanael from Cana in Galilee, the sons of Zebedee, and two other disciples were together. 3"I'm going out to fish," Simon Peter told them, and they said, "We'll go with you." So they went out and got into

a31 Some manuscripts *may continue to*   b1 That is, Sea of Galilee

---

Life in Bible Times

FISH SYMBOL

Very early the fish became a symbol of Christianity. During persecution by the Romans, Christians used it as a secret symbol to discover if another person was a Christian or not. The letters of the Greek word for fish (*ichthus*) are the same as the first letters of Jesus Christ, God's Son, Savior.

the boat, but that night they caught nothing.

4Early in the morning, Jesus stood on the shore, but the disciples did not realize that it was Jesus.

5He called out to them, "Friends, haven't you any fish?"

"No," they answered.

6He said, "Throw your net on the right side of the boat and you will find some." When they did, they were unable to haul the net in because of the large number of fish.

7Then the disciple whom Jesus loved said to Peter, "It is the Lord!" As soon as Simon Peter heard him say, "It is the Lord," he wrapped his outer garment around him (for he had taken it off) and jumped into the water. 8The other disciples followed in the boat, towing the net full of fish, for they were not far from shore, about a hundred yards.ᵃ 9When they landed, they saw a fire of burning coals there with fish on it, and some bread.

10Jesus said to them, "Bring some of the fish you have just caught."

11Simon Peter climbed aboard and dragged the net ashore. It was full of large fish, 153, but even with so many the net was not torn. 12Jesus said to them, "Come and have breakfast." None of the disciples dared ask him, "Who are you?" They knew it was the Lord. 13Jesus came, took the bread and gave it to them, and did the same with the fish. 14This was now

the third time Jesus appeared to his disciples after he was raised from the dead.

Jesus Reinstates Peter

15When they had finished eating, Jesus said to Simon Peter, "Simon son of John, do you truly love me more than these?"

"Yes, Lord," he said, "you know that I love you."

Jesus said, "Feed my lambs."

16Again Jesus said, "Simon son of John, do you truly love me?"

He answered, "Yes, Lord, you know that I love you."

Jesus said, "Take care of my sheep."

17The third time he said to him, "Simon son of John, do you love me?"

Peter was hurt because Jesus asked him the third time, "Do you love me?" He said, "Lord, you know all things; you know that I love you."

Jesus said, "Feed my sheep. 18I tell you the truth, when you were younger you dressed yourself and went where you wanted; but when you are old you will stretch out your hands, and someone else will dress you and lead you where you do not want to go." 19Jesus said this to indicate the kind of death by which Peter would glorify God. Then he said to him, "Follow me!"

20Peter turned and saw that the disciple whom Jesus loved was fol-

ᵃ8 Greek *about two hundred cubits* (about 90 meters)

ET'S LIVE IT!   John 21:15–17

DO YOU LOVE ME? ➠ The night before Jesus was crucified Peter said three times that he did not even know Jesus. Peter lied because he was afraid. But later Peter was so sorry that he cried (Mark 14:72). After Jesus was raised from the dead, he went to Peter. Read John 21:15–17. How many times did he ask Peter, "Do you love me"?

Jesus forgave Peter and even told Peter to feed his lambs and sheep. "Feed my lambs" means to care for the people who believe in Jesus.

If you do something wrong and worry that God will be angry, remember this story. Tell Jesus that you love him. He will forgive you and even give you important work to do for him.

lowing them. (This was the one who had leaned back against Jesus at the supper and had said, "Lord, who is going to betray you?") ²¹When Peter saw him, he asked, "Lord, what about him?"

WORDS TO REMEMBER

21:17 Lord, you know all things; you know that I love you.

²²Jesus answered, "If I want him to remain alive until I return, what is

that to you? You must follow me." ²³Because of this, the rumor spread among the brothers that this disciple would not die. But Jesus did not say that he would not die; he only said, "If I want him to remain alive until I return, what is that to you?"

²⁴This is the disciple who testifies to these things and who wrote them down. We know that his testimony is true.

²⁵Jesus did many other things as well. If every one of them were written down, I suppose that even the whole world would not have room for the books that would be written.

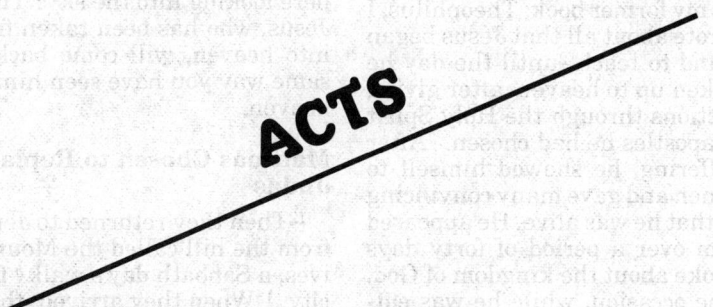

ACTS

Jesus Taken Up Into Heaven

1 In my former book, Theophilus, I wrote about all that Jesus began to do and to teach ²until the day he was taken up to heaven, after giving instructions through the Holy Spirit to the apostles he had chosen. ³After his suffering, he showed himself to these men and gave many convincing proofs that he was alive. He appeared to them over a period of forty days and spoke about the kingdom of God. ⁴On one occasion, while he was eating with them, he gave them this command: "Do not leave Jerusalem, but wait for the gift my Father promised, which you have heard me speak about. ⁵For John baptized with ᵃ water, but in a few days you will be baptized with the Holy Spirit."

⁶So when they met together, they asked him, "Lord, are you at this time going to restore the kingdom to Israel?"

⁷He said to them: "It is not for you to know the times or dates the Father has set by his own authority. ⁸But you will receive power when the Holy Spirit comes on you; and you will be my witnesses in Jerusalem, and in all Judea and Samaria, and to the ends of the earth."

⁹After he said this, he was taken up before their very eyes, and a cloud hid him from their sight.

¹⁰They were looking intently up into the sky as he was going, when suddenly two men dressed in white stood beside them. ¹¹"Men of Galilee," they said, "why do you stand here looking into the sky? This same Jesus, who has been taken from you into heaven, will come back in the same way you have seen him go into heaven."

Matthias Chosen to Replace Judas

¹²Then they returned to Jerusalem from the hill called the Mount of Olives, a Sabbath day's walk ᵇ from the city. ¹³When they arrived, they went upstairs to the room where they were staying. Those present were Peter, John, James and Andrew; Philip and Thomas, Bartholomew and Matthew; James son of Alphaeus and Simon the Zealot, and Judas son of James. ¹⁴They all joined together constantly in prayer, along with the women and Mary the mother of Jesus, and with his brothers.

¹⁵In those days Peter stood up among the believers ᶜ (a group numbering about a hundred and twenty) ¹⁶and said, "Brothers, the Scripture had to be fulfilled which the Holy Spirit spoke long ago through the mouth of David concerning Judas, who served as guide for those who arrested Jesus— ¹⁷he was one of our number and shared in this ministry."

¹⁸(With the reward he got for his wickedness, Judas bought a field; there he fell headlong, his body burst open and all his intestines spilled out. ¹⁹Everyone in Jerusalem heard about this, so they called that field in

---

ᵃ5 Or in   ᵇ12 That is, about 3/4 mile (about 1,100 meters)   ᶜ15 Greek *brothers*

⬛ᴇT'S LIVE IT!   Acts 1:8

POWER TO WITNESS ➡ Read Acts 1:8. Jesus promised to give his followers power to witness. "Witnessing" means telling others what we know about Jesus.

Ask your mom or dad to let you have a size "D" battery to symbolize power. Print John 3:16 on a piece of paper, and tape it to the battery. Carry the battery with you. When people ask you what it is, let them read the verse. Pray when you go out with your battery that the Holy Spirit will give you power to witness, and that your friends will believe in Jesus.

their language Akeldama, that is, Field of Blood.)

²⁰"For," said Peter, "it is written in the book of Psalms,

> " 'May his place be deserted;
>   let there be no one to dwell in
>   it,'ᵃ

and,

> " 'May another take his place of
>   leadership.'ᵇ

²¹Therefore it is necessary to choose one of the men who have been with us the whole time the Lord Jesus went in and out among us, ²²beginning from John's baptism to the time when Jesus was taken up from us. For one of these must become a witness with us of his resurrection."

²³So they proposed two men: Joseph called Barsabbas (also known as Justus) and Matthias. ²⁴Then they prayed, "Lord, you know everyone's heart. Show us which of these two you have chosen ²⁵to take over this apostolic ministry, which Judas left to go where he belongs." ²⁶Then they cast lots, and the lot fell to Matthias; so he was added to the eleven apostles.

The Holy Spirit Comes at Pentecost

2 When the day of Pentecost came, they were all together in one place. ²Suddenly a sound like the blowing of a violent wind came from heaven and filled the whole house where they were sitting. ³They saw what seemed to be tongues of fire that separated and came to rest on each of them. ⁴All of them were filled with the Holy Spirit and began to speak in other tonguesᶜ as the Spirit enabled them.

⁵Now there were staying in Jerusalem God-fearing Jews from every nation under heaven. ⁶When they heard this sound, a crowd came together in bewilderment, because each one heard them speaking in his own language. ⁷Utterly amazed, they asked:

"Are not all these men who are speaking Galileans? ⁸Then how is it that each of us hears them in his own native language? ⁹Parthians, Medes and Elamites; residents of Mesopotamia, Judea and Cappadocia, Pontus and Asia, ¹⁰Phrygia and Pamphylia, Egypt and the parts of Libya near Cyrene; visitors from Rome ¹¹(both Jews and converts to Judaism); Cretans and Arabs—we hear them declaring the wonders of God in our own tongues!" ¹²Amazed and perplexed, they asked one another, "What does this mean?"

¹³Some, however, made fun of them and said, "They have had too much wine.ᵈ"

❓DID YOU KNOW?   2:1

What was Pentecost?

Pentecost was a Jewish holy day. Christians remember Pentecost because God gave Jesus' disciples the Holy Spirit on that day. The disciples spoke in foreign languages, and flames of fire appeared over their heads. These were special signs of the Holy Spirit on that first Christian Pentecost. When many people gathered to see what was happening, Peter preached to them about Jesus.

Peter Addresses the Crowd

¹⁴Then Peter stood up with the Eleven, raised his voice and addressed the crowd: "Fellow Jews and all of you who live in Jerusalem, let me explain this to you; listen carefully to what I say. ¹⁵These men are not drunk, as you suppose. It's only nine in the morning! ¹⁶No, this is what was spoken by the prophet Joel:

¹⁷" 'In the last days, God says,
   I will pour out my Spirit on all
     people.
 Your sons and daughters will
   prophesy,

ᵃ20 Psalm 69:25   ᵇ20 Psalm 109:8   ᶜ4 Or *languages*; also in verse 11   ᵈ13 Or *sweet wine*

your young men will see
visions,
your old men will dream
dreams.
¹⁸Even on my servants, both men
and women,
I will pour out my Spirit in
those days,
and they will prophesy.
¹⁹I will show wonders in the
heaven above
and signs on the earth below,
blood and fire and billows of
smoke.
²⁰The sun will be turned to
darkness
and the moon to blood
before the coming of the great
and glorious day of the
Lord.
²¹And everyone who calls
on the name of the Lord will be
saved.'^a

²²"Men of Israel, listen to this:
Jesus of Nazareth was a man accredited by God to you by miracles, wonders and signs, which God did among you through him, as you yourselves know. ²³This man was handed over to you by God's set purpose and foreknowledge; and you, with the help of wicked men,^b put him to death by nailing him to the cross. ²⁴But God raised him from the dead, freeing him from the agony of death, because it was impossible for death to keep its hold on him. ²⁵David said about him:

" 'I saw the Lord always before
me.
Because he is at my right hand,
I will not be shaken.
²⁶Therefore my heart is glad and
my tongue rejoices;
my body also will live in hope,
²⁷because you will not abandon me
to the grave,
nor will you let your Holy One
see decay.
²⁸You have made known to me the
paths of life;

you will fill me with joy in your
presence.'^c

²⁹"Brothers, I can tell you confidently that the patriarch David died and was buried, and his tomb is here to this day. ³⁰But he was a prophet and knew that God had promised him on oath that he would place one of his descendants on his throne. ³¹Seeing what was ahead, he spoke of the resurrection of the Christ,^d that he was not abandoned to the grave, nor did his body see decay. ³²God has raised this Jesus to life, and we are all witnesses of the fact. ³³Exalted to the right hand of God, he has received from the Father the promised Holy Spirit and has poured out what you now see and hear. ³⁴For David did not ascend to heaven, and yet he said,

" 'The Lord said to my Lord:
"Sit at my right hand
³⁵until I make your enemies
a footstool for your feet." '^e

³⁶"Therefore let all Israel be assured of this: God has made this Jesus, whom you crucified, both Lord and Christ."

³⁷When the people heard this, they were cut to the heart and said to Peter and the other apostles, "Brothers, what shall we do?"

³⁸Peter replied, "Repent and be baptized, every one of you, in the name of Jesus Christ for the forgiveness of your sins. And you will receive the gift of the Holy Spirit. ³⁹The promise is for you and your children and for all who are far off—for all whom the Lord our God will call."

⁴⁰With many other words he warned them; and he pleaded with them, "Save yourselves from this corrupt generation." ⁴¹Those who accepted his message were baptized, and about three thousand were added to their number that day.

---

^a21 Joel 2:28-32   ^b23 Or *of those not having the law* (that is, Gentiles)   ^c28 Psalm 16:8-11
^d31 Or *Messiah.* "The Christ" (Greek) and "the Messiah" (Hebrew) both mean "the Anointed One";
also in verse 36.   ^e35 Psalm 110:1

The Fellowship of the Believers

⁴²They devoted themselves to the apostles' teaching and to the fellowship, to the breaking of bread and to prayer. ⁴³Everyone was filled with awe, and many wonders and miraculous signs were done by the apostles. ⁴⁴All the believers were together and had everything in common. ⁴⁵Selling their possessions and goods, they gave to anyone as he had need. ⁴⁶Every day they continued to meet together in the temple courts. They broke bread in their homes and ate together with glad and sincere hearts, ⁴⁷praising God and enjoying the favor of all the people. And the Lord added to their number daily those who were being saved.

Peter Heals the Crippled Beggar

3 One day Peter and John were going up to the temple at the time of prayer—at three in the afternoon. ²Now a man crippled from birth was being carried to the temple gate called Beautiful, where he was put every day to beg from those going into the temple courts. ³When he saw Peter and John about to enter, he asked them for money. ⁴Peter looked straight at him, as did John. Then Peter said, "Look at us!" ⁵So the man gave them his attention, expecting to get something from them.

⁶Then Peter said, "Silver or gold I do not have, but what I have I give you. In the name of Jesus Christ of Nazareth, walk." ⁷Taking him by the right hand, he helped him up, and instantly the man's feet and ankles became strong. ⁸He jumped to his feet and began to walk. Then he went with them into the temple courts, walking and jumping, and praising God. ⁹When all the people saw him walking and praising God, ¹⁰they recognized him as the same man who used to sit begging at the temple gate called Beautiful, and they were filled with wonder and amazement at what had happened to him.

❓DID YOU KNOW?   3:6

How were Peter and John able to heal?

God gave Peter and John special power. When they healed in Jesus' name, it proved that Jesus really was the Son of God. After healing, Peter preached a sermon and told the people how to be saved.

Peter Speaks to the Onlookers

¹¹While the beggar held on to Peter and John, all the people were astonished and came running to them in the place called Solomon's Colonnade. ¹²When Peter saw this, he said to them: "Men of Israel, why does this surprise you? Why do you stare at us as if by our own power or godliness we had made this man walk? ¹³The God of Abraham, Isaac and Jacob, the God of our fathers, has glorified his servant Jesus. You handed him over to be killed, and you disowned him before Pilate, though he had decided to let him go. ¹⁴You disowned the Holy and Righteous One and asked that a murderer be released to you. ¹⁵You killed the author of life, but

---

▌ET'S LIVE IT!   Acts 2:42–47

POWER TO LOVE ➠ The first Christians loved each other very much. Read Acts 2:42–47. Find in these verses at least five things the early Christians did to show love for each other.

Here are things you can do today to show Christian love: 1. Have a garage sale and give what you earn to needy people. 2. Invite a lonely person to your house for a meal. 3. Have friends in to share family devotions. How is each one like something the early Christians did?

God raised him from the dead. We are witnesses of this. ¹⁶By faith in the name of Jesus, this man whom you see and know was made strong. It is Jesus' name and the faith that comes through him that has given this complete healing to him, as you can all see.

¹⁷"Now, brothers, I know that you acted in ignorance, as did your leaders. ¹⁸But this is how God fulfilled what he had foretold through all the prophets, saying that his Christ*a* would suffer. ¹⁹Repent, then, and turn to God, so that your sins may be wiped out, that times of refreshing may come from the Lord, ²⁰and that he may send the Christ, who has been appointed for you—even Jesus. ²¹He must remain in heaven until the time comes for God to restore everything, as he promised long ago through his holy prophets. ²²For Moses said, 'The Lord your God will raise up for you a prophet like me from among your own people; you must listen to everything he tells you. ²³Anyone who does not listen to him will be completely cut off from among his people.'*b*

²⁴"Indeed, all the prophets from Samuel on, as many as have spoken, have foretold these days. ²⁵And you are heirs of the prophets and of the covenant God made with your fathers. He said to Abraham, 'Through your offspring all peoples on earth will be blessed.'*c* ²⁶When God raised up his servant, he sent him first to you to bless you by turning each of you from your wicked ways."

Peter and John Before the Sanhedrin

4 The priests and the captain of the temple guard and the Sadducees came up to Peter and John while they were speaking to the people. ²They were greatly disturbed because the apostles were teaching the people and proclaiming in Jesus the resurrection of the dead. ³They seized Peter and John, and because it was evening, they put them in jail until the next day. ⁴But many who heard the message believed, and the number of men grew to about five thousand.

⁵The next day the rulers, elders and teachers of the law met in Jerusalem. ⁶Annas the high priest was there, and so were Caiaphas, John, Alexander and the other men of the high priest's family. ⁷They had Peter and John brought before them and began to question them: "By what power or what name did you do this?"

⁸Then Peter, filled with the Holy Spirit, said to them: "Rulers and elders of the people! ⁹If we are being called to account today for an act of kindness shown to a cripple and are asked how he was healed, ¹⁰then know this, you and all the people of Israel: It is by the name of Jesus Christ of Nazareth, whom you crucified but whom God raised from the dead, that this man stands before you healed. ¹¹He is

" 'the stone you builders rejected,
  which has become the
    capstone.*d' e*

¹²Salvation is found in no one else, for there is no other name under heaven given to men by which we must be saved."

¹³When they saw the courage of Peter and John and realized that they were unschooled, ordinary men, they were astonished and they took note that these men had been with Jesus. ¹⁴But since they could see the man who had been healed standing there with them, there was nothing they could say. ¹⁵So they ordered them to withdraw from the Sanhedrin and then conferred together. ¹⁶"What are we going to do with these men?" they asked. "Everybody living in Jerusalem knows they have done an outstanding miracle, and we cannot deny it. ¹⁷But to stop this thing from spreading any further among the people, we must warn these men to

---

a18 Or *Messiah*; also in verse 20   *b23* Deut. 18:15,18,19   *c25* Gen. 22:18; 26:4   *d11* Or *cornerstone*   *e11* Psalm 118:22

speak no longer to anyone in this name."

¹⁸Then they called them in again and commanded them not to speak or teach at all in the name of Jesus. ¹⁹But Peter and John replied, "Judge for yourselves whether it is right in God's sight to obey you rather than God. ²⁰For we cannot help speaking about what we have seen and heard."

²¹After further threats they let them go. They could not decide how to punish them, because all the people were praising God for what had happened. ²²For the man who was miraculously healed was over forty years old.

The Believers' Prayer

²³On their release, Peter and John went back to their own people and reported all that the chief priests and elders had said to them. ²⁴When they heard this, they raised their voices together in prayer to God. "Sovereign Lord," they said, "you made the heaven and the earth and the sea, and everything in them. ²⁵You spoke by the Holy Spirit through the mouth of your servant, our father David:

" 'Why do the nations rage
    and the peoples plot in vain?
²⁶The kings of the earth take their
    stand
    and the rulers gather together
    against the Lord

and against his Anointed
    One.^a'^b

²⁷Indeed Herod and Pontius Pilate met together with the Gentiles and the people^c of Israel in this city to conspire against your holy servant Jesus, whom you anointed. ²⁸They did what your power and will had decided beforehand should happen. ²⁹Now, Lord, consider their threats and enable your servants to speak your word with great boldness. ³⁰Stretch out your hand to heal and perform miraculous signs and wonders through the name of your holy servant Jesus."

³¹After they prayed, the place where they were meeting was shaken. And they were all filled with the Holy Spirit and spoke the word of God boldly.

The Believers Share Their Possessions

³²All the believers were one in heart and mind. No one claimed that any of his possessions was his own, but they shared everything they had. ³³With great power the apostles continued to testify to the resurrection of the Lord Jesus, and much grace was upon them all. ³⁴There were no needy persons among them. For from time to time those who owned lands or houses sold them, brought the money from the sales ³⁵and put it at the

a26 That is, Christ or Messiah   *b26* Psalm 2:1,2   *c27* The Greek is plural.

▉ET'S LIVE IT!   Acts 4:23–31

POWER THROUGH PRAYER ➡ When Peter and John were threatened they asked God for power to do miracles and keep on preaching. Read Acts 4:23–31. Because they knew God had been in control already at creation and at the time of David, they were certain he was still in control and still answering prayer.

Ask your mom or dad what they know about God that makes them sure he can answer prayer. Tell them about what you discovered in this Bible story.

When you pray, it is a good idea to begin as the disciples did, thanking God for his great power and telling him you know he can answer your prayers.

apostles' feet, and it was distributed to anyone as he had need.

³⁶Joseph, a Levite from Cyprus, whom the apostles called Barnabas (which means Son of Encouragement), ³⁷sold a field he owned and brought the money and put it at the apostles' feet.

Ananias and Sapphira

5 Now a man named Ananias, together with his wife Sapphira, also sold a piece of property. ²With his wife's full knowledge he kept back part of the money for himself, but brought the rest and put it at the apostles' feet.

³Then Peter said, "Ananias, how is it that Satan has so filled your heart that you have lied to the Holy Spirit and have kept for yourself some of the money you received for the land? ⁴Didn't it belong to you before it was sold? And after it was sold, wasn't the money at your disposal? What made you think of doing such a thing? You have not lied to men but to God."

⁵When Ananias heard this, he fell down and died. And great fear seized all who heard what had happened. ⁶Then the young men came forward, wrapped up his body, and carried him out and buried him.

⁷About three hours later his wife came in, not knowing what had happened. ⁸Peter asked her, "Tell me, is this the price you and Ananias got for the land?"

"Yes," she said, "that is the price."

⁹Peter said to her, "How could you agree to test the Spirit of the Lord? Look! The feet of the men who buried your husband are at the door, and they will carry you out also."

¹⁰At that moment she fell down at his feet and died. Then the young men came in and, finding her dead, carried her out and buried her beside her husband. ¹¹Great fear seized the whole church and all who heard about these events.

The Apostles Heal Many

¹²The apostles performed many miraculous signs and wonders among the people. And all the believers used to meet together in Solomon's Colonnade. ¹³No one else dared join them, even though they were highly regarded by the people. ¹⁴Nevertheless, more and more men and women believed in the Lord and were added to their number. ¹⁵As a result, people brought the sick into the streets and laid them on beds and mats so that at least Peter's shadow might fall on some of them as he passed by. ¹⁶Crowds gathered also from the towns around Jerusalem, bringing their sick and those tormented by evilᵃ spirits, and all of them were healed.

❓DID YOU KNOW?   5:3

What was the sin of Ananias and Sapphira?

Ananias and Sapphira lied. The money they got from selling some land was theirs to use any way they wanted, but they agreed to lie to the church. Lying to the church is like lying to God, and God punished them.

The Apostles Persecuted

¹⁷Then the high priest and all his associates, who were members of the party of the Sadducees, were filled with jealousy. ¹⁸They arrested the apostles and put them in the public jail. ¹⁹But during the night an angel of the Lord opened the doors of the jail and brought them out. ²⁰"Go, stand in the temple courts," he said, "and tell the people the full message of this new life."

²¹At daybreak they entered the temple courts, as they had been told, and began to teach the people.

When the high priest and his associates arrived, they called together

---

ᵃ16 Greek unclean

the Sanhedrin—the full assembly of the elders of Israel—and sent to the jail for the apostles. 22But on arriving at the jail, the officers did not find them there. So they went back and reported, 23"We found the jail securely locked, with the guards standing at the doors; but when we opened them, we found no one inside." 24On hearing this report, the captain of the temple guard and the chief priests were puzzled, wondering what would come of this.

25Then someone came and said, "Look! The men you put in jail are standing in the temple courts teaching the people." 26At that, the captain went with his officers and brought the apostles. They did not use force, because they feared that the people would stone them.

27Having brought the apostles, they made them appear before the Sanhedrin to be questioned by the high priest. 28"We gave you strict orders not to teach in this name," he said. "Yet you have filled Jerusalem with your teaching and are determined to make us guilty of this man's blood."

29Peter and the other apostles replied: "We must obey God rather than men! 30The God of our fathers raised Jesus from the dead—whom you had killed by hanging him on a tree. 31God exalted him to his own right hand as Prince and Savior that he might give repentance and forgiveness of sins to Israel. 32We are witnesses of these things, and so is the Holy Spirit, whom God has given to those who obey him."

33When they heard this, they were furious and wanted to put them to death. 34But a Pharisee named Gamaliel, a teacher of the law, who was honored by all the people, stood up in the Sanhedrin and ordered that the men be put outside for a little while. 35Then he addressed them: "Men of Israel, consider carefully what you intend to do to these men. 36Some time ago Theudas appeared, claim-

ing to be somebody, and about four hundred men rallied to him. He was killed, all his followers were dispersed, and it all came to nothing. 37After him, Judas the Galilean appeared in the days of the census and led a band of people in revolt. He too was killed, and all his followers were scattered. 38Therefore, in the present case I advise you: Leave these men alone! Let them go! For if their purpose or activity is of human origin, it will fail. 39But if it is from God, you will not be able to stop these men; you will only find yourselves fighting against God."

40His speech persuaded them. They called the apostles in and had them flogged. Then they ordered them not to speak in the name of Jesus, and let them go.

41The apostles left the Sanhedrin, rejoicing because they had been counted worthy of suffering disgrace for the Name. 42Day after day, in the temple courts and from house to house, they never stopped teaching and proclaiming the good news that Jesus is the Christ. *a*

The Choosing of the Seven

6 In those days when the number of disciples was increasing, the Grecian Jews among them complained against the Hebraic Jews because their widows were being overlooked in the daily distribution of food. 2So the Twelve gathered all the disciples together and said, "It would not be right for us to neglect the ministry of the word of God in order to wait on tables. 3Brothers, choose seven men from among you who are known to be full of the Spirit and wisdom. We will turn this responsibility over to them 4and will give our attention to prayer and the ministry of the word."

5This proposal pleased the whole group. They chose Stephen, a man full of faith and of the Holy Spirit; also Philip, Procorus, Nicanor, Timon, Parmenas, and Nicolas from

Antioch, a convert to Judaism. [6]They presented these men to the apostles, who prayed and laid their hands on them.

[7]So the word of God spread. The number of disciples in Jerusalem increased rapidly, and a large number of priests became obedient to the faith.

Stephen Seized

[8]Now Stephen, a man full of God's grace and power, did great wonders and miraculous signs among the people. [9]Opposition arose, however, from members of the Synagogue of the Freedmen (as it was called)—Jews of Cyrene and Alexandria as well as the provinces of Cilicia and Asia. These men began to argue with Stephen, [10]but they could not stand up against his wisdom or the Spirit by whom he spoke.

[11]Then they secretly persuaded some men to say, "We have heard Stephen speak words of blasphemy against Moses and against God."

[12]So they stirred up the people and the elders and the teachers of the law. They seized Stephen and brought him before the Sanhedrin. [13]They produced false witnesses, who testified, "This fellow never stops speaking against this holy place and against the law. [14]For we have heard him say that this Jesus of Nazareth will destroy this place and change the customs Moses handed down to us."

[15]All who were sitting in the Sanhedrin looked intently at Stephen, and they saw that his face was like the face of an angel.

Stephen's Speech to the Sanhedrin

7 Then the high priest asked him, "Are these charges true?"

[2]To this he replied: "Brothers and fathers, listen to me! The God of glory appeared to our father Abraham while he was still in Mesopotamia, before he lived in Haran. [3]'Leave your country and your people,' God said, 'and go to the land I will show you.'[a]

[4]"So he left the land of the Chaldeans and settled in Haran. After the death of his father, God sent him to this land where you are now living. [5]He gave him no inheritance here, not even a foot of ground. But God promised him that he and his descendants after him would possess the land, even though at that time Abraham had no child. [6]God spoke to him in this way: 'Your descendants will be strangers in a country not their own, and they will be enslaved and mistreated four hundred years. [7]But I will punish the nation they serve as slaves,' God said, 'and afterward they will come out of that country and worship me in this place.'[b] [8]Then he gave Abraham the covenant of circumcision. And Abraham became the father of Isaac and circumcised him eight days after his birth. Later Isaac became the father of Jacob, and Jacob became the father of the twelve patriarchs.

[9]"Because the patriarchs were jealous of Joseph, they sold him as a slave into Egypt. But God was with him [10]and rescued him from all his troubles. He gave Joseph wisdom and enabled him to gain the goodwill of Pharaoh king of Egypt; so he made him ruler over Egypt and all his palace.

[11]"Then a famine struck all Egypt and Canaan, bringing great suffering, and our fathers could not find food. [12]When Jacob heard that there was grain in Egypt, he sent our fathers on their first visit. [13]On their second visit, Joseph told his brothers who he was, and Pharaoh learned about Joseph's family. [14]After this, Joseph sent for his father Jacob and his whole family, seventy-five in all. [15]Then Jacob went down to Egypt, where he and our fathers died. [16]Their bodies were brought back to Shechem and placed in the tomb that Abraham had bought from the sons of

Hamor at Shechem for a certain sum of money.

17"As the time drew near for God to fulfill his promise to Abraham, the number of our people in Egypt greatly increased. 18Then another king, who knew nothing about Joseph, became ruler of Egypt. 19He dealt treacherously with our people and oppressed our forefathers by forcing them to throw out their newborn babies so that they would die.

20"At that time Moses was born, and he was no ordinary child.a For three months he was cared for in his father's house. 21When he was placed outside, Pharaoh's daughter took him and brought him up as her own son. 22Moses was educated in all the wisdom of the Egyptians and was powerful in speech and action.

23"When Moses was forty years old, he decided to visit his fellow Israelites. 24He saw one of them being mistreated by an Egyptian, so he went to his defense and avenged him by killing the Egyptian. 25Moses thought that his own people would realize that God was using him to rescue them, but they did not. 26The next day Moses came upon two Israelites who were fighting. He tried to reconcile them by saying, 'Men, you are brothers; why do you want to hurt each other?'

27"But the man who was mistreating the other pushed Moses aside and said, 'Who made you ruler and judge over us? 28Do you want to kill me as you killed the Egyptian yesterday?'b 29When Moses heard this, he fled to Midian, where he settled as a foreigner and had two sons.

30"After forty years had passed, an angel appeared to Moses in the flames of a burning bush in the desert near Mount Sinai. 31When he saw this, he was amazed at the sight. As he went over to look more closely, he heard the Lord's voice: 32'I am the God of your fathers, the God of Abraham, Isaac and Jacob.'c Moses trembled with fear and did not dare to look.

33"Then the Lord said to him, 'Take off your sandals; the place where you are standing is holy ground. 34I have indeed seen the oppression of my people in Egypt. I have heard their groaning and have come down to set them free. Now come, I will send you back to Egypt.'d

35"This is the same Moses whom they had rejected with the words, 'Who made you ruler and judge?' He was sent to be their ruler and deliverer by God himself, through the angel who appeared to him in the bush. 36He led them out of Egypt and did wonders and miraculous signs in Egypt, at the Red Seae and for forty years in the desert.

37"This is that Moses who told the Israelites, 'God will send you a prophet like me from your own people.'f 38He was in the assembly in the desert, with the angel who spoke to him on Mount Sinai, and with our fathers; and he received living words to pass on to us.

39"But our fathers refused to obey him. Instead, they rejected him and in their hearts turned back to Egypt. 40They told Aaron, 'Make us gods who will go before us. As for this fellow Moses who led us out of Egypt —we don't know what has happened to him!'g 41That was the time they made an idol in the form of a calf. They brought sacrifices to it and held a celebration in honor of what their hands had made. 42But God turned away and gave them over to the worship of the heavenly bodies. This agrees with what is written in the book of the prophets:

" 'Did you bring me sacrifices and
    offerings
forty years in the desert,
    O house of Israel?
43You have lifted up the shrine of
    Molech

---

a20 Or was fair in the sight of God   b28 Exodus 2:14   c32 Exodus 3:6   d34 Exodus 3:5,7,8,10   e36 That is, Sea of Reeds   f37 Deut. 18:15   g40 Exodus 32:1

and the star of your god
Rephan,
the idols you made to worship.
Therefore I will send you into
exile'[a] beyond Babylon.

44"Our forefathers had the tabernacle of the Testimony with them in the desert. It had been made as God directed Moses, according to the pattern he had seen. 45Having received the tabernacle, our fathers under Joshua brought it with them when they took the land from the nations God drove out before them. It remained in the land until the time of David, 46who enjoyed God's favor and asked that he might provide a dwelling place for the God of Jacob.[b] 47But it was Solomon who built the house for him.

48"However, the Most High does not live in houses made by men. As the prophet says:

49" 'Heaven is my throne,
　　and the earth is my footstool.
What kind of house will you build
　　for me?
　　　　　　says the Lord.
Or where will my resting place
　　be?
50Has not my hand made all these
　　things?'[c]

51"You stiff-necked people, with uncircumcised hearts and ears! You are just like your fathers: You always resist the Holy Spirit! 52Was there ever a prophet your fathers did not persecute? They even killed those who predicted the coming of the

Righteous One. And now you have betrayed and murdered him— 53you who have received the law that was put into effect through angels but have not obeyed it."

The Stoning of Stephen

54When they heard this, they were furious and gnashed their teeth at him. 55But Stephen, full of the Holy Spirit, looked up to heaven and saw the glory of God, and Jesus standing at the right hand of God. 56"Look," he said, "I see heaven open and the Son of Man standing at the right hand of God."

57At this they covered their ears and, yelling at the top of their voices, they all rushed at him, 58dragged him out of the city and began to stone him. Meanwhile, the witnesses laid their clothes at the feet of a young man named Saul.

59While they were stoning him, Stephen prayed, "Lord Jesus, receive my spirit." 60Then he fell on his knees and cried out, "Lord, do not hold this sin against them." When he had said this, he fell asleep.

8 And Saul was there, giving approval to his death.

The Church Persecuted and Scattered

On that day a great persecution broke out against the church at Jerusalem, and all except the apostles were scattered throughout Judea and Samaria. 2Godly men buried Stephen and mourned deeply for him. 3But Saul began to destroy the church. Go-

---

[a]43 Amos 5:25-27　　[b]46 Some early manuscripts *the house of Jacob*　　[c]50 Isaiah 66:1,2

LET'S LIVE IT!　　　　　　　　　　　Acts 7:54–60

POWER TO DO RIGHT ➠ Stephen was very brave. Stephen became the church's first "martyr," the first person to die for preaching about Jesus.
　　Read Acts 7:54–60. Even when Stephen was being stoned to death, he prayed for the people who were killing him. Picture in your mind a situation where you might have to stand up for what you believe. You may not be stoned like Stephen, but God wants you to stand for what is right. He will make you brave like Stephen.

ing from house to house, he dragged off men and women and put them in prison.

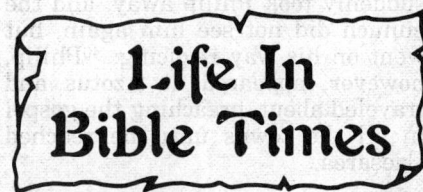

Life In Bible Times

STONING STEPHEN

The Hebrew people executed criminals by throwing heavy stones at them. Stephen was the first Christian martyr. A martyr (MAR-ter) is a person who is put to death because of his or her beliefs. Stephen was stoned because he preached about Jesus.

Philip in Samaria

⁴Those who had been scattered preached the word wherever they went. ⁵Philip went down to a city in Samaria and proclaimed the Christ*a* there. ⁶When the crowds heard Philip and saw the miraculous signs he did, they all paid close attention to what he said. ⁷With shrieks, evil*b* spirits came out of many, and many paralytics and cripples were healed. ⁸So there was great joy in that city.

Simon the Sorcerer

⁹Now for some time a man named Simon had practiced sorcery in the city and amazed all the people of Samaria. He boasted that he was someone great, ¹⁰and all the people, both high and low, gave him their attention and exclaimed, "This man is the divine power known as the Great Power." ¹¹They followed him because he had amazed them for a long time with his magic. ¹²But when they believed Philip as he preached the good news of the kingdom of God and the name of Jesus Christ, they were baptized, both men and women. ¹³Simon

himself believed and was baptized. And he followed Philip everywhere, astonished by the great signs and miracles he saw.

❓ DID YOU KNOW? 8:9

What is sorcery?

Sorcery is a kind of magic. It is supposed to give a person power over others. A sorcerer named Simon saw the power Jesus' apostles had and wanted that power for himself. He offered the apostles money for that power.

¹⁴When the apostles in Jerusalem heard that Samaria had accepted the word of God, they sent Peter and John to them. ¹⁵When they arrived, they prayed for them that they might receive the Holy Spirit, ¹⁶because the Holy Spirit had not yet come upon any of them; they had simply been baptized into*c* the name of the Lord Jesus. ¹⁷Then Peter and John placed their hands on them, and they received the Holy Spirit.

¹⁸When Simon saw that the Spirit was given at the laying on of the apostles' hands, he offered them money ¹⁹and said, "Give me also this ability so that everyone on whom I lay my hands may receive the Holy Spirit."

²⁰Peter answered: "May your money perish with you, because you thought you could buy the gift of God with money! ²¹You have no part or share in this ministry, because your heart is not right before God. ²²Repent of this wickedness and pray to the Lord. Perhaps he will forgive you for having such a thought in your heart. ²³For I see that you are full of bitterness and captive to sin."

²⁴Then Simon answered, "Pray to the Lord for me so that nothing you have said may happen to me."

²⁵When they had testified and proclaimed the word of the Lord, Peter

a5 Or *Messiah*   *b7* Greek *unclean*   *c16* Or *in*

and John returned to Jerusalem, preaching the gospel in many Samaritan villages.

Philip and the Ethiopian

26Now an angel of the Lord said to Philip, "Go south to the road—the desert road—that goes down from Jerusalem to Gaza." 27So he started out, and on his way he met an Ethiopian *a* eunuch, an important official in charge of all the treasury of Candace, queen of the Ethiopians. This man had gone to Jerusalem to worship, 28and on his way home was sitting in his chariot reading the book of Isaiah the prophet. 29The Spirit told Philip, "Go to that chariot and stay near it."

30Then Philip ran up to the chariot and heard the man reading Isaiah the prophet. "Do you understand what you are reading?" Philip asked.

31"How can I," he said, "unless someone explains it to me?" So he invited Philip to come up and sit with him.

32The eunuch was reading this passage of Scripture:

"He was led like a sheep to the
      slaughter,
   and as a lamb before the
         shearer is silent,
      so he did not open his mouth.
33In his humiliation he was
      deprived of justice.
   Who can speak of his
         descendants?
   For his life was taken from the
      earth." *b*

34The eunuch asked Philip, "Tell me, please, who is the prophet talking about, himself or someone else?" 35Then Philip began with that very passage of Scripture and told him the good news about Jesus.

36As they traveled along the road, they came to some water and the eunuch said, "Look, here is water. Why shouldn't I be baptized?" *c* 38And he gave orders to stop the chariot. Then

both Philip and the eunuch went down into the water and Philip baptized him. 39When they came up out of the water, the Spirit of the Lord suddenly took Philip away, and the eunuch did not see him again, but went on his way rejoicing. 40Philip, however, appeared at Azotus and traveled about, preaching the gospel in all the towns until he reached Caesarea.

Saul's Conversion

9 Meanwhile, Saul was still breathing out murderous threats against the Lord's disciples. He went to the high priest 2and asked him for letters to the synagogues in Damascus, so that if he found any there who belonged to the Way, whether men or women, he might take them as prisoners to Jerusalem. 3As he neared Damascus on his journey, suddenly a light from heaven flashed around him. 4He fell to the ground and heard a voice say to him, "Saul, Saul, why do you persecute me?"

? DID YOU KNOW?   9:1

Who was Saul?

The Saul of the New Testament was a Pharisee who hated Christians. After Jesus spoke to Saul, Saul became a Christian. Later, Saul became known by his Greek name, Paul. Paul became the greatest missionary of all time and wrote thirteen books of the New Testament.

5"Who are you, Lord?" Saul asked.

"I am Jesus, whom you are persecuting," he replied. 6"Now get up and go into the city, and you will be told what you must do."

7The men traveling with Saul stood there speechless; they heard the sound but did not see anyone. 8Saul

---

*a*27 That is, from the upper Nile region   *b*33 Isaiah 53:7,8   *c*36 Some late manuscripts
baptized?" *37*Philip said, "If you believe with all your heart, you may." The eunuch answered, "I
believe that Jesus Christ is the Son of God."

got up from the ground, but when he opened his eyes he could see nothing. So they led him by the hand into Damascus. [9]For three days he was blind, and did not eat or drink anything.

[10]In Damascus there was a disciple named Ananias. The Lord called to him in a vision, "Ananias!"

"Yes, Lord," he answered.

[11]The Lord told him, "Go to the house of Judas on Straight Street and ask for a man from Tarsus named Saul, for he is praying. [12]In a vision he has seen a man named Ananias come and place his hands on him to restore his sight."

[13]"Lord," Ananias answered, "I have heard many reports about this man and all the harm he has done to your saints in Jerusalem. [14]And he has come here with authority from the chief priests to arrest all who call on your name."

[15]But the Lord said to Ananias, "Go! This man is my chosen instrument to carry my name before the Gentiles and their kings and before the people of Israel. [16]I will show him how much he must suffer for my name."

[17]Then Ananias went to the house and entered it. Placing his hands on Saul, he said, "Brother Saul, the Lord—Jesus, who appeared to you on the road as you were coming here —has sent me so that you may see again and be filled with the Holy Spirit." [18]Immediately, something like scales fell from Saul's eyes, and he could see again. He got up and was baptized, [19]and after taking some food, he regained his strength.

Saul in Damascus and Jerusalem

Saul spent several days with the disciples in Damascus. [20]At once he began to preach in the synagogues that Jesus is the Son of God. [21]All those who heard him were astonished and asked, "Isn't he the man who raised havoc in Jerusalem among those who call on this name? And

hasn't he come here to take them as prisoners to the chief priests?" [22]Yet Saul grew more and more powerful and baffled the Jews living in Damascus by proving that Jesus is the Christ.[a]

[23]After many days had gone by, the Jews conspired to kill him, [24]but Saul learned of their plan. Day and night they kept close watch on the city gates in order to kill him. [25]But his followers took him by night and lowered him in a basket through an opening in the wall.

Life In Bible Times

PAUL IN A BASKET

Grain and other crops were stored in very large woven baskets. These baskets were so large that Paul's friends were able to use one to let him down over the city wall of Damascus.

---

[26]When he came to Jerusalem, he tried to join the disciples, but they were all afraid of him, not believing that he really was a disciple. [27]But Barnabas took him and brought him to the apostles. He told them how Saul on his journey had seen the Lord and that the Lord had spoken to him, and how in Damascus he had preached fearlessly in the name of Jesus. [28]So Saul stayed with them and moved about freely in Jerusalem, speaking boldly in the name of the Lord. [29]He talked and debated with the Grecian Jews, but they tried to kill him. [30]When the brothers learned of this, they took him down to Caesarea and sent him off to Tarsus.

[31]Then the church throughout Judea, Galilee and Samaria enjoyed a

---

[a]22 Or *Messiah*

time of peace. It was strengthened; and encouraged by the Holy Spirit, it grew in numbers, living in the fear of the Lord.

Aeneas and Dorcas

³²As Peter traveled about the country, he went to visit the saints in Lydda. ³³There he found a man named Aeneas, a paralytic who had been bedridden for eight years. ³⁴"Aeneas," Peter said to him, "Jesus Christ heals you. Get up and take care of your mat." Immediately Aeneas got up. ³⁵All those who lived in Lydda and Sharon saw him and turned to the Lord.

³⁶In Joppa there was a disciple named Tabitha (which, when translated, is Dorcas*ᵃ*), who was always doing good and helping the poor. ³⁷About that time she became sick and died, and her body was washed and placed in an upstairs room. ³⁸Lydda was near Joppa; so when the disciples heard that Peter was in Lydda, they sent two men to him and urged him, "Please come at once!"

³⁹Peter went with them, and when he arrived he was taken upstairs to the room. All the widows stood around him, crying and showing him the robes and other clothing that Dorcas had made while she was still with them.

⁴⁰Peter sent them all out of the room; then he got down on his knees and prayed. Turning toward the dead woman, he said, "Tabitha, get up." She opened her eyes, and seeing Peter she sat up. ⁴¹He took her by the hand and helped her to her feet. Then he called the believers and the widows and presented her to them alive. ⁴²This became known all over Joppa, and many people believed in the Lord. ⁴³Peter stayed in Joppa for some time with a tanner named Simon.

Cornelius Calls for Peter

10 At Caesarea there was a man named Cornelius, a centurion in what was known as the Italian Regiment. ²He and all his family were devout and God-fearing; he gave generously to those in need and prayed to God regularly. ³One day at about three in the afternoon he had a vision. He distinctly saw an angel of God, who came to him and said, "Cornelius!"

⁴Cornelius stared at him in fear. "What is it, Lord?" he asked.

The angel answered, "Your prayers and gifts to the poor have come up as a memorial offering before God. ⁵Now send men to Joppa to bring back a man named Simon who is called Peter. ⁶He is staying with Simon the tanner, whose house is by the sea."

⁷When the angel who spoke to him had gone, Cornelius called two of his servants and a devout soldier who was one of his attendants. ⁸He told

ᵃ36 Both *Tabitha* (Aramaic) and *Dorcas* (Greek) mean *gazelle.*

▟ET'S LIVE IT!   Acts 9:1–31

POWER TO CHANGE ➡ Read Acts 9:1–31. Look carefully at the kind of person Saul was before he was converted (Acts 9:1–2). What kind of person was he after he was converted (Acts 9:20–22,27–28)?

Draw "before" and "after" pictures of Paul's face. How do you think Paul looked when he hated Christians? How do you think Paul looked when he loved Jesus and wanted others to love Jesus too?

Put the "before" and "after" pictures on your wall to remind you that anyone can be converted by trusting Jesus and can become a different person. Let the pictures remind you to pray for people who especially need to change.

them everything that had happened and sent them to Joppa.

Peter's Vision

⁹About noon the following day as they were on their journey and approaching the city, Peter went up on the roof to pray. ¹⁰He became hungry and wanted something to eat, and while the meal was being prepared, he fell into a trance. ¹¹He saw heaven opened and something like a large sheet being let down to earth by its four corners. ¹²It contained all kinds of four-footed animals, as well as reptiles of the earth and birds of the air. ¹³Then a voice told him, "Get up, Peter. Kill and eat."

¹⁴"Surely not, Lord!" Peter replied. "I have never eaten anything impure or unclean."

¹⁵The voice spoke to him a second time, "Do not call anything impure that God has made clean."

¹⁶This happened three times, and immediately the sheet was taken back to heaven.

¹⁷While Peter was wondering about the meaning of the vision, the men sent by Cornelius found out where Simon's house was and stopped at the gate. ¹⁸They called out, asking if Simon who was known as Peter was staying there.

¹⁹While Peter was still thinking about the vision, the Spirit said to him, "Simon, three*ᵃ* men are looking for you. ²⁰So get up and go downstairs. Do not hesitate to go with them, for I have sent them."

²¹Peter went down and said to the men, "I'm the one you're looking for. Why have you come?"

²²The men replied, "We have come from Cornelius the centurion. He is a righteous and God-fearing man, who is respected by all the Jewish people. A holy angel told him to have you come to his house so that he could hear what you have to say." ²³Then Peter invited the men into the house to be his guests.

Peter at Cornelius' House

The next day Peter started out with them, and some of the brothers from Joppa went along. ²⁴The following day he arrived in Caesarea. Cornelius was expecting them and had called together his relatives and close friends. ²⁵As Peter entered the house, Cornelius met him and fell at his feet in reverence. ²⁶But Peter made him get up. "Stand up," he said, "I am only a man myself."

❓DID YOU KNOW?   10:17

Why did God send Peter a vision?

In New Testament times the Jewish people did not associate with non-Jews. God gave Peter a vision of animals to teach him that it was all right to go to a non-Jew's home.

---

²⁷Talking with him, Peter went inside and found a large gathering of people. ²⁸He said to them: "You are well aware that it is against our law for a Jew to associate with a Gentile or visit him. But God has shown me that I should not call any man impure or unclean. ²⁹So when I was sent for, I came without raising any objection. May I ask why you sent for me?"

³⁰Cornelius answered: "Four days ago I was in my house praying at this hour, at three in the afternoon. Suddenly a man in shining clothes stood before me ³¹and said, 'Cornelius, God has heard your prayer and remembered your gifts to the poor. ³²Send to Joppa for Simon who is called Peter. He is a guest in the home of Simon the tanner, who lives by the sea.' ³³So I sent for you immediately, and it was good of you to come. Now we are all here in the presence of God to listen to everything the Lord has commanded you to tell us."

³⁴Then Peter began to speak: "I now realize how true it is that God

---

ᵃ19 One early manuscript *two*; other manuscripts do not have the number.

does not show favoritism ³⁵but accepts men from every nation who fear him and do what is right. ³⁶You know the message God sent to the people of Israel, telling the good news of peace through Jesus Christ, who is Lord of all. ³⁷You know what has happened throughout Judea, beginning in Galilee after the baptism that John preached— ³⁸how God anointed Jesus of Nazareth with the Holy Spirit and power, and how he went around doing good and healing all who were under the power of the devil, because God was with him.

³⁹"We are witnesses of everything he did in the country of the Jews and in Jerusalem. They killed him by hanging him on a tree, ⁴⁰but God raised him from the dead on the third day and caused him to be seen. ⁴¹He was not seen by all the people, but by witnesses whom God had already chosen—by us who ate and drank with him after he rose from the dead. ⁴²He commanded us to preach to the people and to testify that he is the one whom God appointed as judge of the living and the dead. ⁴³All the prophets testify about him that everyone who believes in him receives forgiveness of sins through his name."

⁴⁴While Peter was still speaking these words, the Holy Spirit came on all who heard the message. ⁴⁵The circumcised believers who had come with Peter were astonished that the gift of the Holy Spirit had been poured out even on the Gentiles. ⁴⁶For they heard them speaking in tongues*a* and praising God.

Then Peter said, ⁴⁷"Can anyone keep these people from being baptized with water? They have received the Holy Spirit just as we have." ⁴⁸So he ordered that they be baptized in the name of Jesus Christ. Then they asked Peter to stay with them for a few days.

Peter Explains His Actions

11 The apostles and the brothers throughout Judea heard that the Gentiles also had received the word of God. ²So when Peter went up to Jerusalem, the circumcised believers criticized him ³and said, "You went into the house of uncircumcised men and ate with them."

⁴Peter began and explained everything to them precisely as it had happened: ⁵"I was in the city of Joppa praying, and in a trance I saw a vision. I saw something like a large sheet being let down from heaven by its four corners, and it came down to where I was. ⁶I looked into it and saw four-footed animals of the earth, wild beasts, reptiles, and birds of the air. ⁷Then I heard a voice telling me, 'Get up, Peter. Kill and eat.'

⁸"I replied, 'Surely not, Lord! Nothing impure or unclean has ever entered my mouth.'

⁹"The voice spoke from heaven a second time, 'Do not call anything impure that God has made clean.' ¹⁰This happened three times, and then it was all pulled up to heaven again.

¹¹"Right then three men who had been sent to me from Caesarea stopped at the house where I was staying. ¹²The Spirit told me to have no hesitation about going with them. These six brothers also went with me, and we entered the man's house. ¹³He told us how he had seen an angel appear in his house and say, 'Send to Joppa for Simon who is called Peter. ¹⁴He will bring you a message through which you and all your household will be saved.'

¹⁵"As I began to speak, the Holy Spirit came on them as he had come on us at the beginning. ¹⁶Then I remembered what the Lord had said: 'John baptized with*b* water, but you will be baptized with the Holy Spirit.' ¹⁷So if God gave them the same gift as he gave us, who believed in the Lord Jesus Christ, who was I to think that I could oppose God?"

¹⁸When they heard this, they had no further objections and praised God, saying, "So then, God has grant-

ed even the Gentiles repentance unto life."

The Church in Antioch

19Now those who had been scattered by the persecution in connection with Stephen traveled as far as Phoenicia, Cyprus and Antioch, telling the message only to Jews. 20Some of them, however, men from Cyprus and Cyrene, went to Antioch and began to speak to Greeks also, telling them the good news about the Lord Jesus. 21The Lord's hand was with them, and a great number of people believed and turned to the Lord.

22News of this reached the ears of the church at Jerusalem, and they sent Barnabas to Antioch. 23When he arrived and saw the evidence of the grace of God, he was glad and encouraged them all to remain true to the Lord with all their hearts. 24He was a good man, full of the Holy Spirit and faith, and a great number of people were brought to the Lord.

25Then Barnabas went to Tarsus to look for Saul, 26and when he found him, he brought him to Antioch. So for a whole year Barnabas and Saul met with the church and taught great numbers of people. The disciples were called Christians first at Antioch.

27During this time some prophets came down from Jerusalem to Antioch. 28One of them, named Agabus, stood up and through the Spirit predicted that a severe famine would spread over the entire Roman world. (This happened during the reign of Claudius.) 29The disciples, each according to his ability, decided to provide help for the brothers living in Judea. 30This they did, sending their gift to the elders by Barnabas and Saul.

Peter's Miraculous Escape From Prison

12 It was about this time that King Herod arrested some who belonged to the church, intending to persecute them. 2He had James, the brother of John, put to death with the sword. 3When he saw that this pleased the Jews, he proceeded to seize Peter also. This happened during the Feast of Unleavened Bread. 4After arresting him, he put him in prison, handing him over to be guarded by four squads of four soldiers each. Herod intended to bring him out for public trial after the Passover.

5So Peter was kept in prison, but the church was earnestly praying to God for him.

6The night before Herod was to bring him to trial, Peter was sleeping between two soldiers, bound with two chains, and sentries stood guard at the entrance. 7Suddenly an angel of the Lord appeared and a light shone in the cell. He struck Peter on the side and woke him up. "Quick, get up!" he said, and the chains fell off Peter's wrists.

8Then the angel said to him, "Put on your clothes and sandals." And Peter did so. "Wrap your cloak around you and follow me," the angel told him. 9Peter followed him out of the prison, but he had no idea that what the angel was doing was really happening; he thought he was seeing a vision. 10They passed the first and second guards and came to the iron gate leading to the city. It opened for them by itself, and they went through it. When they had walked the length of one street, suddenly the angel left him.

❓DID YOU KNOW?　　12:7

How did Peter escape from prison?

An angel let Peter out of his chains and led him outside the jail. All Peter's friends were praying for him; but when Peter came to their door, they wouldn't believe it was him!

11Then Peter came to himself and said, "Now I know without a doubt that the Lord sent his angel and rescued me from Herod's clutches and from everything the Jewish people were anticipating."

¹²When this had dawned on him, he went to the house of Mary the mother of John, also called Mark, where many people had gathered and were praying. ¹³Peter knocked at the outer entrance, and a servant girl named Rhoda came to answer the door. ¹⁴When she recognized Peter's voice, she was so overjoyed she ran back without opening it and exclaimed, "Peter is at the door!"

¹⁵"You're out of your mind," they told her. When she kept insisting that it was so, they said, "It must be his angel."

¹⁶But Peter kept on knocking, and when they opened the door and saw him, they were astonished. ¹⁷Peter motioned with his hand for them to be quiet and described how the Lord had brought him out of prison. "Tell James and the brothers about this," he said, and then he left for another place.

¹⁸In the morning, there was no small commotion among the soldiers as to what had become of Peter. ¹⁹After Herod had a thorough search made for him and did not find him, he cross-examined the guards and ordered that they be executed.

Herod's Death

Then Herod went from Judea to Caesarea and stayed there a while. ²⁰He had been quarreling with the people of Tyre and Sidon; they now joined together and sought an audience with him. Having secured the support of Blastus, a trusted personal servant of the king, they asked for peace, because they depended on the king's country for their food supply.

²¹On the appointed day Herod, wearing his royal robes, sat on his throne and delivered a public address to the people. ²²They shouted, "This is the voice of a god, not of a man." ²³Immediately, because Herod did not give praise to God, an angel of the

Lord struck him down, and he was eaten by worms and died.

²⁴But the word of God continued to increase and spread.

²⁵When Barnabas and Saul had finished their mission, they returned from ᵃ Jerusalem, taking with them John, also called Mark.

Barnabas and Saul Sent Off

13 In the church at Antioch there were prophets and teachers: Barnabas, Simeon called Niger, Lucius of Cyrene, Manaen (who had been brought up with Herod the tetrarch) and Saul. ²While they were worshiping the Lord and fasting, the Holy Spirit said, "Set apart for me Barnabas and Saul for the work to which I have called them." ³So after they had fasted and prayed, they placed their hands on them and sent them off.

❓DID YOU KNOW?   13:2

What are missionaries?

Missionaries are people who travel to tell others about Jesus. The first missionaries of the Christian church were Barnabas and Paul (Saul). The rest of the book of Acts tells about the adventures of these missionaries.

On Cyprus

⁴The two of them, sent on their way by the Holy Spirit, went down to Seleucia and sailed from there to Cyprus. ⁵When they arrived at Salamis, they proclaimed the word of God in the Jewish synagogues. John was with them as their helper.

⁶They traveled through the whole island until they came to Paphos. There they met a Jewish sorcerer and false prophet named Bar-Jesus, ⁷who was an attendant of the proconsul, Sergius Paulus. The proconsul, an intelligent man, sent for Barnabas and

Saul because he wanted to hear the word of God. 8But Elymas the sorcerer (for that is what his name means) opposed them and tried to turn the proconsul from the faith. 9Then Saul, who was also called Paul, filled with the Holy Spirit, looked straight at Elymas and said, 10"You are a child of the devil and an enemy of everything that is right! You are full of all kinds of deceit and trickery. Will you never stop perverting the right ways of the Lord? 11Now the hand of the Lord is against you. You are going to be blind, and for a time you will be unable to see the light of the sun."

Immediately mist and darkness came over him, and he groped about, seeking someone to lead him by the hand. 12When the proconsul saw what had happened, he believed, for he was amazed at the teaching about the Lord.

In Pisidian Antioch

13From Paphos, Paul and his companions sailed to Perga in Pamphylia, where John left them to return to Jerusalem. 14From Perga they went on to Pisidian Antioch. On the Sabbath they entered the synagogue and sat down. 15After the reading from the Law and the Prophets, the synagogue rulers sent word to them, saying, "Brothers, if you have a message of encouragement for the people, please speak."

16Standing up, Paul motioned with his hand and said: "Men of Israel and you Gentiles who worship God, listen to me! 17The God of the people of Israel chose our fathers; he made the people prosper during their stay in Egypt, with mighty power he led them out of that country, 18he endured their conduct a for about forty years in the desert, 19he overthrew seven nations in Canaan and gave their land to his people as their inheritance. 20All this took about 450 years.

"After this, God gave them judges until the time of Samuel the prophet.

21Then the people asked for a king, and he gave them Saul son of Kish, of the tribe of Benjamin, who ruled forty years. 22After removing Saul, he made David their king. He testified concerning him: 'I have found David son of Jesse a man after my own heart; he will do everything I want him to do.'

JEWISH SYNAGOGUES

Jews gathered each Sabbath to worship in a synagogue. At the front of the synagogue was a container, called an "ark," where Bible scrolls were kept. Leaders of the synagogue sat on chairs in the front on each side of this ark. Visitors like Paul were often invited to speak to the congregation.

23"From this man's descendants God has brought to Israel the Savior Jesus, as he promised. 24Before the coming of Jesus, John preached repentance and baptism to all the people of Israel. 25As John was completing his work, he said: 'Who do you think I am? I am not that one. No, but he is coming after me, whose sandals I am not worthy to untie.'

26"Brothers, children of Abraham, and you God-fearing Gentiles, it is to us that this message of salvation has been sent. 27The people of Jerusalem and their rulers did not recognize Jesus, yet in condemning him they fulfilled the words of the prophets that are read every Sabbath. 28Though they found no proper ground for a death sentence, they asked Pilate to have him executed. 29When they had carried out all that

a18 Some manuscripts *and cared for them*

was written about him, they took him down from the tree and laid him in a tomb. 30But God raised him from the dead, 31and for many days he was seen by those who had traveled with him from Galilee to Jerusalem. They are now his witnesses to our people.

32"We tell you the good news: What God promised our fathers 33he has fulfilled for us, their children, by raising up Jesus. As it is written in the second Psalm:

" 'You are my Son;
    today I have become your
        Father.'*a' b*

34The fact that God raised him from the dead, never to decay, is stated in these words:

" 'I will give you the holy and
    sure blessings promised to
        David.'*c*

35So it is stated elsewhere:

" 'You will not let your Holy One
    see decay.'*d*

36"For when David had served God's purpose in his own generation, he fell asleep; he was buried with his fathers and his body decayed. 37But the one whom God raised from the dead did not see decay.

38"Therefore, my brothers, I want you to know that through Jesus the forgiveness of sins is proclaimed to you. 39Through him everyone who believes is justified from everything you could not be justified from by the law of Moses. 40Take care that what the prophets have said does not happen to you:

41" 'Look, you scoffers,
    wonder and perish,
for I am going to do something in
    your days
    that you would never believe,
    even if someone told you.'*e*"

42As Paul and Barnabas were leaving the synagogue, the people invited them to speak further about these things on the next Sabbath. 43When the congregation was dismissed, many of the Jews and devout converts to Judaism followed Paul and Barnabas, who talked with them and urged them to continue in the grace of God.

44On the next Sabbath almost the whole city gathered to hear the word of the Lord. 45When the Jews saw the crowds, they were filled with jealousy and talked abusively against what Paul was saying.

46Then Paul and Barnabas answered them boldly: "We had to speak the word of God to you first. Since you reject it and do not consider yourselves worthy of eternal life, we now turn to the Gentiles. 47For this is what the Lord has commanded us:

" 'I have made you*f* a light for
    the Gentiles,
    that you*f* may bring salvation
    to the ends of the earth.'*g*"

48When the Gentiles heard this, they were glad and honored the word of the Lord; and all who were appointed for eternal life believed.

49The word of the Lord spread through the whole region. 50But the Jews incited the God-fearing women of high standing and the leading men of the city. They stirred up persecution against Paul and Barnabas, and expelled them from their region. 51So they shook the dust from their feet in protest against them and went to Iconium. 52And the disciples were filled with joy and with the Holy Spirit.

In Iconium

14 At Iconium Paul and Barnabas went as usual into the Jewish synagogue. There they spoke so effectively that a great number of Jews and Gentiles believed. 2But the Jews who refused to believe stirred up the Gentiles and poisoned their minds against the brothers. 3So Paul and Barnabas spent considerable time there, speaking boldly for the

---

a33 Or *have begotten you*   *b33* Psalm 2:7   *c34* Isaiah 55:3   *d35* Psalm 16:10
e41 Hab. 1:5   *f47* The Greek is singular.   *g47* Isaiah 49:6

Lord, who confirmed the message of his grace by enabling them to do miraculous signs and wonders. ⁴The people of the city were divided; some sided with the Jews, others with the apostles. ⁵There was a plot afoot among the Gentiles and Jews, together with their leaders, to mistreat them and stone them. ⁶But they found out about it and fled to the Lycaonian cities of Lystra and Derbe and to the surrounding country, ⁷where they continued to preach the good news.

In Lystra and Derbe

⁸In Lystra there sat a man crippled in his feet, who was lame from birth and had never walked. ⁹He listened to Paul as he was speaking. Paul looked directly at him, saw that he had faith to be healed ¹⁰and called out, "Stand up on your feet!" At that, the man jumped up and began to walk.

¹¹When the crowd saw what Paul had done, they shouted in the Lycaonian language, "The gods have come down to us in human form!" ¹²Barnabas they called Zeus, and Paul they called Hermes because he was the chief speaker. ¹³The priest of Zeus, whose temple was just outside the city, brought bulls and wreaths to the city gates because he and the crowd wanted to offer sacrifices to them.

¹⁴But when the apostles Barnabas and Paul heard of this, they tore their clothes and rushed out into the crowd, shouting: ¹⁵"Men, why are you doing this? We too are only men, human like you. We are bringing you good news, telling you to turn from these worthless things to the living God, who made heaven and earth and sea and everything in them. ¹⁶In the past, he let all nations go their own way. ¹⁷Yet he has not left himself without testimony: He has shown kindness by giving you rain from heaven and crops in their seasons; he provides you with plenty of food and fills your hearts with joy." ¹⁸Even with these words, they had difficulty keeping the crowd from sacrificing to them.

¹⁹Then some Jews came from Antioch and Iconium and won the crowd over. They stoned Paul and dragged him outside the city, thinking he was dead. ²⁰But after the disciples had gathered around him, he got up and went back into the city. The next day he and Barnabas left for Derbe.

The Return to Antioch in Syria

²¹They preached the good news in that city and won a large number of disciples. Then they returned to Lystra, Iconium and Antioch, ²²strengthening the disciples and encouraging them to remain true to the faith. "We must go through many hardships to enter the kingdom of God," they said. ²³Paul and Barnabas appointed el-

---

▌ET'S LIVE IT!   Acts 14:8–18

POWER IS FROM GOD ➡ Read Acts 14:8–18. What did the people of Lystra do when Paul healed the crippled man? Why were Barnabas and Paul upset?

Tell someone this story and explain what upset the apostles. Ask them these questions:

1. Who did the people think was most important?
2. Who did Paul think was most important?
3. Who do you think is most important?

We can be glad for our leaders, but remember they are not as important as God.

ders[a] for them in each church and, with prayer and fasting, committed them to the Lord, in whom they had put their trust. 24After going through Pisidia, they came into Pamphylia, 25and when they had preached the word in Perga, they went down to Attalia.

26From Attalia they sailed back to Antioch, where they had been committed to the grace of God for the work they had now completed. 27On arriving there, they gathered the church together and reported all that God had done through them and how he had opened the door of faith to the Gentiles. 28And they stayed there a long time with the disciples.

The Council at Jerusalem

15 Some men came down from Judea to Antioch and were teaching the brothers: "Unless you are circumcised, according to the custom taught by Moses, you cannot be saved." 2This brought Paul and Barnabas into sharp dispute and debate with them. So Paul and Barnabas were appointed, along with some other believers, to go up to Jerusalem to see the apostles and elders about this question. 3The church sent them on their way, and as they traveled through Phoenicia and Samaria, they told how the Gentiles had been converted. This news made all the brothers very glad. 4When they came to Jerusalem, they were welcomed by the church and the apostles and elders, to whom they reported everything God had done through them.

5Then some of the believers who belonged to the party of the Pharisees stood up and said, "The Gentiles must be circumcised and required to obey the law of Moses."

6The apostles and elders met to consider this question. 7After much discussion, Peter got up and addressed them: "Brothers, you know that some time ago God made a choice among you that the Gentiles might hear from my lips the message of the gospel and believe. 8God, who knows the heart, showed that he accepted them by giving the Holy Spirit to them, just as he did to us. 9He made no distinction between us and them, for he purified their hearts by faith. 10Now then, why do you try to test God by putting on the necks of the disciples a yoke that neither we nor our fathers have been able to bear? 11No! We believe it is through the grace of our Lord Jesus that we are saved, just as they are."

12The whole assembly became silent as they listened to Barnabas and Paul telling about the miraculous signs and wonders God had done among the Gentiles through them. 13When they finished, James spoke up: "Brothers, listen to me. 14Simon[b] has described to us how God at first showed his concern by taking from the Gentiles a people for himself. 15The words of the prophets are in agreement with this, as it is written:

16" 'After this I will return
    and rebuild David's fallen tent.
  Its ruins I will rebuild,
    and I will restore it,
17that the remnant of men may
      seek the Lord,
  and all the Gentiles who bear
      my name,
  says the Lord, who does these
      things'[c]
18   that have been known for
      ages.[d]

19"It is my judgment, therefore, that we should not make it difficult for the Gentiles who are turning to God. 20Instead we should write to them, telling them to abstain from food polluted by idols, from sexual immorality, from the meat of strangled animals and from blood. 21For Moses has been preached in every city from the earliest times and is

---

[a]23 Or *Barnabas ordained elders*; or *Barnabas had elders elected*   [b]14 Greek *Simeon*, a variant of *Simon*; that is, Peter   [c]17 Amos 9:11,12   [d]17,18 Some manuscripts *things'—* / [18]*known to the Lord for ages is his work*

read in the synagogues on every Sabbath."

The Council's Letter to Gentile Believers

22Then the apostles and elders, with the whole church, decided to choose some of their own men and send them to Antioch with Paul and Barnabas. They chose Judas (called Barsabbas) and Silas, two men who were leaders among the brothers. 23With them they sent the following letter:

The apostles and elders, your brothers,

To the Gentile believers in Antioch, Syria and Cilicia:

Greetings.

24We have heard that some went out from us without our authorization and disturbed you, troubling your minds by what they said. 25So we all agreed to choose some men and send them to you with our dear friends Barnabas and Paul— 26men who have risked their lives for the name of our Lord Jesus Christ. 27Therefore we are sending Judas and Silas to confirm by word of mouth what we are writing. 28It seemed good to the Holy Spirit and to us not to burden you with anything beyond the following requirements: 29You are to abstain from food sacrificed to idols, from blood, from the meat of strangled animals and from sexual immorality. You will do well to avoid these things.

Farewell.

30The men were sent off and went down to Antioch, where they gathered the church together and delivered the letter. 31The people read it and were glad for its encouraging message. 32Judas and Silas, who themselves were prophets, said much to encourage and strengthen the brothers. 33After spending some time there, they were sent off by the brothers with the blessing of peace to return to those who had sent them. *a* 35But Paul and Barnabas remained in Antioch, where they and many others taught and preached the word of the Lord.

Disagreement Between Paul and Barnabas

36Some time later Paul said to Barnabas, "Let us go back and visit the brothers in all the towns where we preached the word of the Lord and see how they are doing." 37Barnabas wanted to take John, also called Mark, with them, 38but Paul did not think it wise to take him, because he had deserted them in Pamphylia and had not continued with them in the work. 39They had such a sharp disagreement that they parted company. Barnabas took Mark and sailed for Cyprus, 40but Paul chose Silas and left, commended by the brothers to the grace of the Lord. 41He went through Syria and Cilicia, strengthening the churches.

Timothy Joins Paul and Silas

16 He came to Derbe and then to Lystra, where a disciple named Timothy lived, whose mother

a33 Some manuscripts *them,* *34but Silas decided to remain there*

was a Jewess and a believer, but whose father was a Greek. [2]The brothers at Lystra and Iconium spoke well of him. [3]Paul wanted to take him along on the journey, so he circumcised him because of the Jews who lived in that area, for they all knew that his father was a Greek. [4]As they traveled from town to town, they delivered the decisions reached by the apostles and elders in Jerusalem for the people to obey. [5]So the churches were strengthened in the faith and grew daily in numbers.

Paul's Vision of the Man of Macedonia

[6]Paul and his companions traveled throughout the region of Phrygia and Galatia, having been kept by the Holy Spirit from preaching the word in the province of Asia. [7]When they came to the border of Mysia, they tried to enter Bithynia, but the Spirit of Jesus would not allow them to. [8]So they passed by Mysia and went down to Troas. [9]During the night Paul had a vision of a man of Macedonia standing and begging him, "Come over to Macedonia and help us." [10]After Paul had seen the vision, we got ready at once to leave for Macedonia, concluding that God had called us to preach the gospel to them.

Lydia's Conversion in Philippi

[11]From Troas we put out to sea and sailed straight for Samothrace, and the next day on to Neapolis. [12]From there we traveled to Philippi, a Roman colony and the leading city of that district of Macedonia. And we stayed there several days.

[13]On the Sabbath we went outside the city gate to the river, where we expected to find a place of prayer. We sat down and began to speak to the women who had gathered there. [14]One of those listening was a woman named Lydia, a dealer in purple cloth from the city of Thyatira, who was a worshiper of God. The Lord opened her heart to respond to Paul's message. [15]When she and the members of her household were baptized, she invited us to her home. "If you consider me a believer in the Lord," she said, "come and stay at my house." And she persuaded us.

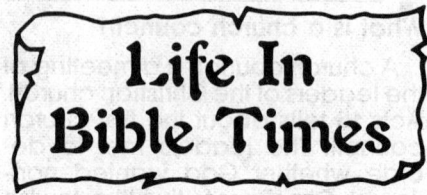

Life In Bible Times

PURPLE CLOTH

Purple dye came from crushing the shells of tiny sea creatures. Hundreds of these shellfish were needed to make enough purple to dye one robe, so purple cloth was very expensive.

Paul and Silas in Prison

[16]Once when we were going to the place of prayer, we were met by a slave girl who had a spirit by which she predicted the future. She earned a great deal of money for her owners by fortune-telling. [17]This girl followed Paul and the rest of us, shouting, "These men are servants of the Most High God, who are telling you the way to be saved." [18]She kept this up for many days. Finally Paul became so troubled that he turned around and said to the spirit, "In the name of Jesus Christ I command you to come out of her!" At that moment the spirit left her.

[19]When the owners of the slave girl realized that their hope of making money was gone, they seized Paul and Silas and dragged them into the marketplace to face the authorities. [20]They brought them before the magistrates and said, "These men are Jews, and are throwing our city into an uproar [21]by advocating customs unlawful for us Romans to accept or practice."

[22]The crowd joined in the attack against Paul and Silas, and the magistrates ordered them to be stripped and beaten. [23]After they had been se-

verely flogged, they were thrown into prison, and the jailer was commanded to guard them carefully. 24Upon receiving such orders, he put them in the inner cell and fastened their feet in the stocks.

25About midnight Paul and Silas were praying and singing hymns to God, and the other prisoners were listening to them. 26Suddenly there was such a violent earthquake that the foundations of the prison were shaken. At once all the prison doors flew open, and everybody's chains came loose. 27The jailer woke up, and when he saw the prison doors open, he drew his sword and was about to kill himself because he thought the prisoners had escaped. 28But Paul shouted, "Don't harm yourself! We are all here!"

29The jailer called for lights, rushed in and fell trembling before Paul and Silas. 30He then brought them out and asked, "Sirs, what must I do to be saved?"

31They replied, "Believe in the Lord Jesus, and you will be saved —you and your household." 32Then they spoke the word of the Lord to him and to all the others in his house. 33At that hour of the night the jailer took them and washed their wounds; then immediately he and all his family were baptized. 34The jailer brought them into his house and set a meal

before them; he was filled with joy because he had come to believe in God—he and his whole family.

35When it was daylight, the magistrates sent their officers to the jailer with the order: "Release those men." 36The jailer told Paul, "The magistrates have ordered that you and Silas be released. Now you can leave. Go in peace."

37But Paul said to the officers: "They beat us publicly without a trial, even though we are Roman citizens, and threw us into prison. And now do they want to get rid of us quietly? No! Let them come themselves and escort us out."

38The officers reported this to the magistrates, and when they heard that Paul and Silas were Roman citizens, they were alarmed. 39They came to appease them and escorted them from the prison, requesting them to leave the city. 40After Paul and Silas came out of the prison, they went to Lydia's house, where they met with the brothers and encouraged them. Then they left.

In Thessalonica

17 When they had passed through Amphipolis and Apollonia, they came to Thessalonica, where there was a Jewish synagogue. 2As his custom was, Paul went into the synagogue, and on three Sabbath

---

LET'S LIVE IT!   Acts 16:16–34

POWER IN PRAISE ➠ Do you ever have a day like Kenny's?

Kenny was miserable. Dad had to work late and couldn't take him to the ball game. Mom made him eat food he hated at supper. And now he had to do homework instead of watching TV.

Have a "Kenny contest." Let each member of your family show how Kenny will probably act by making faces, by the way they walk or sit. Then read Acts 16:16–34. Together list some things Kenny might have praised God for, even though he was disappointed. Then make a list of things your family can praise God for. Post the list where everyone in the family can read it. The list will remind you that praise gives us the power to be happy even when things go wrong.

days he reasoned with them from the Scriptures, ³explaining and proving that the Christ*a* had to suffer and rise from the dead. "This Jesus I am proclaiming to you is the Christ,*a*" he said. ⁴Some of the Jews were persuaded and joined Paul and Silas, as did a large number of God-fearing Greeks and not a few prominent women.

⁵But the Jews were jealous; so they rounded up some bad characters from the marketplace, formed a mob and started a riot in the city. They rushed to Jason's house in search of Paul and Silas in order to bring them out to the crowd.*b* ⁶But when they did not find them, they dragged Jason and some other brothers before the city officials, shouting: "These men who have caused trouble all over the world have now come here, ⁷and Jason has welcomed them into his house. They are all defying Caesar's decrees, saying that there is another king, one called Jesus." ⁸When they heard this, the crowd and the city officials were thrown into turmoil. ⁹Then they made Jason and the others post bond and let them go.

In Berea

¹⁰As soon as it was night, the brothers sent Paul and Silas away to Berea. On arriving there, they went to the Jewish synagogue. ¹¹Now the Bereans were of more noble character than the Thessalonians, for they received the message with great eagerness and examined the Scriptures every day to see if what Paul said was true. ¹²Many of the Jews believed, as did also a number of prominent Greek women and many Greek men.

¹³When the Jews in Thessalonica learned that Paul was preaching the word of God at Berea, they went there too, agitating the crowds and stirring them up. ¹⁴The brothers immediately sent Paul to the coast, but Silas and Timothy stayed at Berea. ¹⁵The men who escorted Paul brought him to Athens and then left

with instructions for Silas and Timothy to join him as soon as possible.

In Athens

¹⁶While Paul was waiting for them in Athens, he was greatly distressed to see that the city was full of idols. ¹⁷So he reasoned in the synagogue with the Jews and the God-fearing Greeks, as well as in the marketplace day by day with those who happened to be there. ¹⁸A group of Epicurean and Stoic philosophers began to dispute with him. Some of them asked, "What is this babbler trying to say?" Others remarked, "He seems to be advocating foreign gods." They said this because Paul was preaching the good news about Jesus and the resurrection. ¹⁹Then they took him and brought him to a meeting of the Areopagus, where they said to him, "May we know what this new teaching is that you are presenting? ²⁰You are bringing some strange ideas to our ears, and we want to know what they mean." ²¹(All the Athenians and the foreigners who lived there spent their time doing nothing but talking about and listening to the latest ideas.)

²²Paul then stood up in the meeting of the Areopagus and said: "Men of Athens! I see that in every way you are very religious. ²³For as I walked around and looked carefully at your objects of worship, I even found an altar with this inscription: TO AN UNKNOWN GOD. Now what you worship as something unknown I am going to proclaim to you.

²⁴"The God who made the world and everything in it is the Lord of heaven and earth and does not live in temples built by hands. ²⁵And he is not served by human hands, as if he needed anything, because he himself gives all men life and breath and everything else. ²⁶From one man he made every nation of men, that they should inhabit the whole earth; and he determined the times set for them and the exact places where they

---

*a*3 Or *Messiah*   *b*5 Or *the assembly of the people*

should live. 27God did this so that men would seek him and perhaps reach out for him and find him, though he is not far from each one of us. 28'For in him we live and move and have our being.' As some of your own poets have said, 'We are his offspring.'

❓DID YOU KNOW?　　17:23

What was Athens like?

Athens was a famous Greek city. The people of Athens loved to talk about religion and important ideas. When Paul came to Athens he talked to people about God, who made the world, and about Jesus, who was raised from the dead. Acts 17 contains Paul's sermon to the people of Athens.

29"Therefore since we are God's offspring, we should not think that the divine being is like gold or silver or stone—an image made by man's design and skill. 30In the past God overlooked such ignorance, but now he commands all people everywhere to repent. 31For he has set a day when he will judge the world with justice by the man he has appointed. He has given proof of this to all men by raising him from the dead."

32When they heard about the resurrection of the dead, some of them sneered, but others said, "We want to hear you again on this subject." 33At that, Paul left the Council. 34A few men became followers of Paul and believed. Among them was Dionysius, a member of the Areopagus, also a woman named Damaris, and a number of others.

In Corinth

18 After this, Paul left Athens and went to Corinth. 2There he met a Jew named Aquila, a native of Pontus, who had recently come from Italy with his wife Priscilla, be-

cause Claudius had ordered all the Jews to leave Rome. Paul went to see them, 3and because he was a tentmaker as they were, he stayed and worked with them. 4Every Sabbath he reasoned in the synagogue, trying to persuade Jews and Greeks.

5When Silas and Timothy came from Macedonia, Paul devoted himself exclusively to preaching, testifying to the Jews that Jesus was the

Life In Bible Times

TENTMAKERS

Tents were made from animal skins or from fabric woven of wool or goats' hair. The tentmaker sewed these materials together using awls and needles and thread. It was expected that every Jewish boy would learn a trade; Paul was trained to be a tentmaker.

Christ.a 6But when the Jews opposed Paul and became abusive, he shook out his clothes in protest and said to them, "Your blood be on your own heads! I am clear of my responsibility. From now on I will go to the Gentiles."

7Then Paul left the synagogue and went next door to the house of Titius Justus, a worshiper of God. 8Crispus, the synagogue ruler, and his entire household believed in the Lord; and many of the Corinthians who heard him believed and were baptized.

9One night the Lord spoke to Paul in a vision: "Do not be afraid; keep on speaking, do not be silent. 10For I am with you, and no one is going to attack and harm you, because I have many people in this city." 11So Paul

a5 Or *Messiah;* also in verse 28

stayed for a year and a half, teaching them the word of God.

¹²While Gallio was proconsul of Achaia, the Jews made a united attack on Paul and brought him into court. ¹³"This man," they charged, "is persuading the people to worship God in ways contrary to the law."

¹⁴Just as Paul was about to speak, Gallio said to the Jews, "If you Jews were making a complaint about some misdemeanor or serious crime, it would be reasonable for me to listen to you. ¹⁵But since it involves questions about words and names and your own law—settle the matter yourselves. I will not be a judge of such things." ¹⁶So he had them ejected from the court. ¹⁷Then they all turned on Sosthenes the synagogue ruler and beat him in front of the court. But Gallio showed no concern whatever.

Priscilla, Aquila and Apollos

¹⁸Paul stayed on in Corinth for some time. Then he left the brothers and sailed for Syria, accompanied by Priscilla and Aquila. Before he sailed, he had his hair cut off at Cenchrea because of a vow he had taken. ¹⁹They arrived at Ephesus, where Paul left Priscilla and Aquila. He himself went into the synagogue and reasoned with the Jews. ²⁰When they asked him to spend more time with them, he declined. ²¹But as he left, he promised, "I will come back if it is God's will." Then he set sail from Ephesus. ²²When he landed at Caesarea, he went up and greeted the church and then went down to Antioch.

²³After spending some time in Antioch, Paul set out from there and traveled from place to place throughout the region of Galatia and Phrygia, strengthening all the disciples.

²⁴Meanwhile a Jew named Apollos, a native of Alexandria, came to Ephesus. He was a learned man, with a thorough knowledge of the Scriptures. ²⁵He had been instructed in the way of the Lord, and he spoke with great fervor^a and taught about Jesus accurately, though he knew only the baptism of John. ²⁶He began to speak boldly in the synagogue. When Priscilla and Aquila heard him, they invited him to their home and explained to him the way of God more adequately.

²⁷When Apollos wanted to go to Achaia, the brothers encouraged him and wrote to the disciples there to welcome him. On arriving, he was a great help to those who by grace had believed. ²⁸For he vigorously refuted the Jews in public debate, proving from the Scriptures that Jesus was the Christ.

Paul in Ephesus

19 While Apollos was at Corinth, Paul took the road through the interior and arrived at Ephesus. There he found some disciples ²and asked them, "Did you receive the Holy Spirit when^b you believed?"

They answered, "No, we have not even heard that there is a Holy Spirit."

³So Paul asked, "Then what baptism did you receive?"

"John's baptism," they replied.

⁴Paul said, "John's baptism was a baptism of repentance. He told the people to believe in the one coming after him, that is, in Jesus." ⁵On hearing this, they were baptized into^c the name of the Lord Jesus. ⁶When Paul placed his hands on them, the Holy Spirit came on them, and they spoke in tongues^d and prophesied. ⁷There were about twelve men in all.

⁸Paul entered the synagogue and spoke boldly there for three months, arguing persuasively about the kingdom of God. ⁹But some of them became obstinate; they refused to believe and publicly maligned the Way. So Paul left them. He took the disciples with him and had discussions daily in the lecture hall of Tyrannus.

---

^{a}25 Or *with fervor in the Spirit* ^{b}2 Or *after* ^{c}5 Or *in* ^{d}6 Or *other languages*

¹⁰This went on for two years, so that all the Jews and Greeks who lived in the province of Asia heard the word of the Lord.

¹¹God did extraordinary miracles through Paul, ¹²so that even hand-kerchiefs and aprons that had touched him were taken to the sick, and their illnesses were cured and the evil spirits left them.

¹³Some Jews who went around driving out evil spirits tried to invoke the name of the Lord Jesus over those who were demon-possessed. They would say, "In the name of Jesus, whom Paul preaches, I command you to come out." ¹⁴Seven sons of Sceva, a Jewish chief priest, were doing this. ¹⁵One day the evil spirit answered them, "Jesus I know, and I know about Paul, but who are you?" ¹⁶Then the man who had the evil spirit jumped on them and overpowered them all. He gave them such a beating that they ran out of the house naked and bleeding.

¹⁷When this became known to the Jews and Greeks living in Ephesus, they were all seized with fear, and the name of the Lord Jesus was held in high honor. ¹⁸Many of those who believed now came and openly confessed their evil deeds. ¹⁹A number who had practiced sorcery brought their scrolls together and burned them publicly. When they calculated the value of the scrolls, the total came to fifty thousand drachmas.ᵃ ²⁰In this way the word of the Lord spread widely and grew in power.

²¹After all this had happened, Paul decided to go to Jerusalem, passing through Macedonia and Achaia. "After I have been there," he said, "I must visit Rome also." ²²He sent two of his helpers, Timothy and Erastus, to Macedonia, while he stayed in the province of Asia a little longer.

The Riot in Ephesus

²³About that time there arose a great disturbance about the Way. ²⁴A silversmith named Demetrius, who made silver shrines of Artemis, brought in no little business for the craftsmen. ²⁵He called them together, along with the workmen in related trades, and said: "Men, you know we receive a good income from this business. ²⁶And you see and hear how this fellow Paul has convinced and led astray large numbers of people here in Ephesus and in practically the whole province of Asia. He says that man-made gods are no gods at all. ²⁷There is danger not only that our trade will lose its good name, but also that the temple of the great goddess Artemis will be discredited, and the goddess herself, who is worshiped throughout the province of Asia and the world, will be robbed of her divine majesty."

❓DID YOU KNOW?   19:17

What was Ephesus like?

Ephesus was one of the largest cities in Asia. It had a great temple, dedicated to a pagan goddess named Artemis. When Paul came to Ephesus he taught about the true God. So many people became Christians that the silversmiths who sold medals of Artemis began to lose business. Acts 19 tells about Paul's adventures in Ephesus.

²⁸When they heard this, they were furious and began shouting: "Great is Artemis of the Ephesians!" ²⁹Soon the whole city was in an uproar. The people seized Gaius and Aristarchus, Paul's traveling companions from Macedonia, and rushed as one man into the theater. ³⁰Paul wanted to appear before the crowd, but the disciples would not let him. ³¹Even some of the officials of the province, friends of Paul, sent him a message begging him not to venture into the theater.

³²The assembly was in confusion:

ᵃ19 A drachma was a silver coin worth about a day's wages.

Some were shouting one thing, some another. Most of the people did not even know why they were there. ³³The Jews pushed Alexander to the front, and some of the crowd shouted instructions to him. He motioned for silence in order to make a defense before the people. ³⁴But when they realized he was a Jew, they all shouted in unison for about two hours: "Great is Artemis of the Ephesians!"

Life In Bible Times

THE TEMPLE OF ARTEMIS

The temple of Artemis at Ephesus was one of the wonders of the world. It was larger than a football field and had 127 columns, each of them as high as a five-story building! People came from all over the world to visit the temple of Artemis.

³⁵The city clerk quieted the crowd and said: "Men of Ephesus, doesn't all the world know that the city of Ephesus is the guardian of the temple of the great Artemis and of her image, which fell from heaven? ³⁶Therefore, since these facts are undeniable, you ought to be quiet and not do anything rash. ³⁷You have brought these men here, though they have neither robbed temples nor blasphemed our goddess. ³⁸If, then, Demetrius and his fellow craftsmen have a grievance against anybody, the courts are open and there are proconsuls. They can press charges. ³⁹If there is anything further you want to bring up, it must be settled in a legal assembly. ⁴⁰As it is, we are in danger of being charged with rioting because of today's events. In that case we would not be able to account for this commotion, since there is no reason for it." ⁴¹After

he had said this, he dismissed the assembly.

Through Macedonia and Greece

20 When the uproar had ended, Paul sent for the disciples and, after encouraging them, said good-by and set out for Macedonia. ²He traveled through that area, speaking many words of encouragement to the people, and finally arrived in Greece, ³where he stayed three months. Because the Jews made a plot against him just as he was about to sail for Syria, he decided to go back through Macedonia. ⁴He was accompanied by Sopater son of Pyrrhus from Berea, Aristarchus and Secundus from Thessalonica, Gaius from Derbe, Timothy also, and Tychicus and Trophimus from the province of Asia. ⁵These men went on ahead and waited for us at Troas. ⁶But we sailed from Philippi after the Feast of Unleavened Bread, and five days later joined the others at Troas, where we stayed seven days.

Eutychus Raised From the Dead at Troas

⁷On the first day of the week we came together to break bread. Paul spoke to the people and, because he intended to leave the next day, kept on talking until midnight. ⁸There were many lamps in the upstairs room where we were meeting. ⁹Seated in a window was a young man named Eutychus, who was sinking into a deep sleep as Paul talked on and on. When he was sound asleep, he fell to the ground from the third story and was picked up dead. ¹⁰Paul went down, threw himself on the young man and put his arms around him. "Don't be alarmed," he said. "He's alive!" ¹¹Then he went upstairs again and broke bread and ate. After talking until daylight, he left. ¹²The people took the young man home alive and were greatly comforted.

Paul's Farewell to the Ephesian Elders

¹³We went on ahead to the ship and

sailed for Assos, where we were going to take Paul aboard. He had made this arrangement because he was going there on foot. [14]When he met us at Assos, we took him aboard and went on to Mitylene. [15]The next day we set sail from there and arrived off Kios. The day after that we crossed over to Samos, and on the following day arrived at Miletus. [16]Paul had decided to sail past Ephesus to avoid spending time in the province of Asia, for he was in a hurry to reach Jerusalem, if possible, by the day of Pentecost.

[17]From Miletus, Paul sent to Ephesus for the elders of the church. [18]When they arrived, he said to them: "You know how I lived the whole time I was with you, from the first day I came into the province of Asia. [19]I served the Lord with great humility and with tears, although I was severely tested by the plots of the Jews. [20]You know that I have not hesitated to preach anything that would be helpful to you but have taught you publicly and from house to house. [21]I have declared to both Jews and Greeks that they must turn to God in repentance and have faith in our Lord Jesus.

[22]"And now, compelled by the Spirit, I am going to Jerusalem, not knowing what will happen to me there. [23]I only know that in every city the Holy Spirit warns me that prison and hardships are facing me. [24]However, I consider my life worth nothing to me, if only I may finish the race and complete the task the Lord Jesus has given me—the task of testifying to the gospel of God's grace.

[25]"Now I know that none of you among whom I have gone about preaching the kingdom will ever see me again. [26]Therefore, I declare to you today that I am innocent of the blood of all men. [27]For I have not hesitated to proclaim to you the whole will of God. [28]Keep watch over yourselves and all the flock of which the Holy Spirit has made you overseers.[a] Be shepherds of the church of God,[b]

which he bought with his own blood. [29]I know that after I leave, savage wolves will come in among you and will not spare the flock. [30]Even from your own number men will arise and distort the truth in order to draw away disciples after them. [31]So be on your guard! Remember that for three years I never stopped warning each of you night and day with tears.

[32]"Now I commit you to God and to the word of his grace, which can build you up and give you an inheritance among all those who are sanctified. [33]I have not coveted anyone's silver or gold or clothing. [34]You yourselves know that these hands of mine have supplied my own needs and the needs of my companions. [35]In everything I did, I showed you that by this kind of hard work we must help the weak, remembering the words the Lord Jesus himself said: 'It is more blessed to give than to receive.' "

[36]When he had said this, he knelt down with all of them and prayed. [37]They all wept as they embraced him and kissed him. [38]What grieved them most was his statement that they would never see his face again. Then they accompanied him to the ship.

On to Jerusalem

21 After we had torn ourselves away from them, we put out to sea and sailed straight to Cos. The next day we went to Rhodes and from there to Patara. [2]We found a ship crossing over to Phoenicia, went on board and set sail. [3]After sighting Cyprus and passing to the south of it, we sailed on to Syria. We landed at Tyre, where our ship was to unload its cargo. [4]Finding the disciples there, we stayed with them seven days. Through the Spirit they urged Paul not to go on to Jerusalem. [5]But when our time was up, we left and continued on our way. All the disciples and their wives and children accompanied us out of the city, and there on the beach we knelt to pray.

---

[a]28 Traditionally *bishops*   [b]28 Many manuscripts *of the Lord*

6After saying good-by to each other, we went aboard the ship, and they returned home.

7We continued our voyage from Tyre and landed at Ptolemais, where we greeted the brothers and stayed with them for a day. 8Leaving the next day, we reached Caesarea and stayed at the house of Philip the evangelist, one of the Seven. 9He had four unmarried daughters who prophesied.

10After we had been there a number of days, a prophet named Agabus came down from Judea. 11Coming over to us, he took Paul's belt, tied his own hands and feet with it and said, "The Holy Spirit says, 'In this way the Jews of Jerusalem will bind the owner of this belt and will hand him over to the Gentiles.'"

12When we heard this, we and the people there pleaded with Paul not to go up to Jerusalem. 13Then Paul answered, "Why are you weeping and breaking my heart? I am ready not only to be bound, but also to die in Jerusalem for the name of the Lord Jesus." 14When he would not be dissuaded, we gave up and said, "The Lord's will be done."

15After this, we got ready and went up to Jerusalem. 16Some of the disciples from Caesarea accompanied us and brought us to the home of Mnason, where we were to stay. He was a man from Cyprus and one of the early disciples.

Paul's Arrival at Jerusalem

17When we arrived at Jerusalem, the brothers received us warmly. 18The next day Paul and the rest of us went to see James, and all the elders were present. 19Paul greeted them and reported in detail what God had done among the Gentiles through his ministry.

20When they heard this, they praised God. Then they said to Paul: "You see, brother, how many thousands of Jews have believed, and all of them are zealous for the law. 21They have been informed that you teach all the Jews who live among the Gentiles to turn away from Moses, telling them not to circumcise their children or live according to our customs. 22What shall we do? They will certainly hear that you have come, 23so do what we tell you. There are four men with us who have made a vow. 24Take these men, join in their purification rites and pay their expenses, so that they can have their heads shaved. Then everybody will know there is no truth in these reports about you, but that you yourself are living in obedience to the law. 25As for the Gentile believers, we have written to them our decision that they should abstain from food sacrificed to idols, from blood, from the meat of strangled animals and from sexual immorality."

26The next day Paul took the men and purified himself along with them. Then he went to the temple to give notice of the date when the days of purification would end and the offering would be made for each of them.

Paul Arrested

27When the seven days were nearly over, some Jews from the province of Asia saw Paul at the temple. They stirred up the whole crowd and seized him, 28shouting, "Men of Israel, help us! This is the man who teaches all men everywhere against our people and our law and this place. And besides, he has brought Greeks into the temple area and defiled this holy place." 29(They had previously seen Trophimus the Ephesian in the city with Paul and assumed that Paul had brought him into the temple area.)

30The whole city was aroused, and the people came running from all directions. Seizing Paul, they dragged him from the temple, and immediately the gates were shut. 31While they were trying to kill him, news reached the commander of the Roman troops that the whole city of Jerusalem was in an uproar. 32He at once took some officers and soldiers and ran down to the crowd. When the rioters saw the commander and his soldiers, they stopped beating Paul.

³³The commander came up and arrested him and ordered him to be bound with two chains. Then he asked who he was and what he had done. ³⁴Some in the crowd shouted one thing and some another, and since the commander could not get at the truth because of the uproar, he ordered that Paul be taken into the barracks. ³⁵When Paul reached the steps, the violence of the mob was so great he had to be carried by the soldiers. ³⁶The crowd that followed kept shouting, "Away with him!"

Paul Speaks to the Crowd

³⁷As the soldiers were about to take Paul into the barracks, he asked the commander, "May I say something to you?"

"Do you speak Greek?" he replied. ³⁸"Aren't you the Egyptian who started a revolt and led four thousand terrorists out into the desert some time ago?"

³⁹Paul answered, "I am a Jew, from Tarsus in Cilicia, a citizen of no ordinary city. Please let me speak to the people."

⁴⁰Having received the commander's permission, Paul stood on the steps and motioned to the crowd.

When they were all silent, he said to them in Aramaic[a]: ¹"Brothers and fathers, listen now to my defense."

22 ²When they heard him speak to them in Aramaic, they became very quiet.

Then Paul said: ³"I am a Jew, born in Tarsus of Cilicia, but brought up in this city. Under Gamaliel I was thoroughly trained in the law of our fathers and was just as zealous for God as any of you are today. ⁴I persecuted the followers of this Way to their death, arresting both men and women and throwing them into prison, ⁵as also the high priest and all the Council can testify. I even obtained letters from them to their brothers in Damascus, and went there to bring these people as prisoners to Jerusalem to be punished.

⁶"About noon as I came near Damascus, suddenly a bright light from heaven flashed around me. ⁷I fell to the ground and heard a voice say to me, 'Saul! Saul! Why do you persecute me?'

⁸" 'Who are you, Lord?' I asked.

" 'I am Jesus of Nazareth, whom you are persecuting,' he replied. ⁹My companions saw the light, but they did not understand the voice of him who was speaking to me.

¹⁰" 'What shall I do, Lord?' I asked.

" 'Get up,' the Lord said, 'and go into Damascus. There you will be told all that you have been assigned to do.' ¹¹My companions led me by the hand into Damascus, because the brilliance of the light had blinded me.

¹²"A man named Ananias came to see me. He was a devout observer of the law and highly respected by all the Jews living there. ¹³He stood beside me and said, 'Brother Saul, receive your sight!' And at that very moment I was able to see him.

¹⁴"Then he said: 'The God of our fathers has chosen you to know his will and to see the Righteous One and to hear words from his mouth. ¹⁵You will be his witness to all men of what

---

a40 Or possibly Hebrew; *also in 22:2*

you have seen and heard. ¹⁶And now what are you waiting for? Get up, be baptized and wash your sins away, calling on his name.'

¹⁷"When I returned to Jerusalem and was praying at the temple, I fell into a trance ¹⁸and saw the Lord speaking. 'Quick!' he said to me. 'Leave Jerusalem immediately, because they will not accept your testimony about me.'

¹⁹"'Lord,' I replied, 'these men know that I went from one synagogue to another to imprison and beat those who believe in you. ²⁰And when the blood of your martyr[a] Stephen was shed, I stood there giving my approval and guarding the clothes of those who were killing him.'

²¹"Then the Lord said to me, 'Go; I will send you far away to the Gentiles.'"

Paul the Roman Citizen

²²The crowd listened to Paul until he said this. Then they raised their voices and shouted, "Rid the earth of him! He's not fit to live!"

²³As they were shouting and throwing off their cloaks and flinging dust into the air, ²⁴the commander ordered Paul to be taken into the barracks. He directed that he be flogged and questioned in order to find out why the people were shouting at him like this. ²⁵As they stretched him out to flog him, Paul said to the centurion standing there, "Is it legal for you to flog a Roman citizen who hasn't even been found guilty?"

²⁶When the centurion heard this, he went to the commander and reported it. "What are you going to do?" he asked. "This man is a Roman citizen."

²⁷The commander went to Paul and asked, "Tell me, are you a Roman citizen?"

"Yes, I am," he answered.

²⁸Then the commander said, "I had to pay a big price for my citizenship."

"But I was born a citizen," Paul replied.

²⁹Those who were about to question him withdrew immediately. The commander himself was alarmed when he realized that he had put Paul, a Roman citizen, in chains.

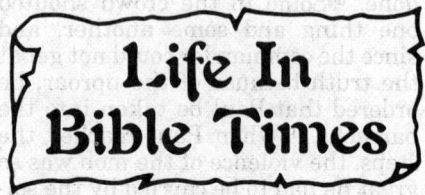

ROMAN CITIZENSHIP

The Romans whipped people they thought might have committed a crime in order to make them confess. But it was against the law to whip a Roman citizen.

Before the Sanhedrin

³⁰The next day, since the commander wanted to find out exactly why Paul was being accused by the Jews, he released him and ordered the chief priests and all the Sanhedrin to assemble. Then he brought Paul and had him stand before them. **23** Paul looked straight at the Sanhedrin and said, "My brothers, I have fulfilled my duty to God in all good conscience to this day." ²At this the high priest Ananias ordered those standing near Paul to strike him on the mouth. ³Then Paul said to him, "God will strike you, you whitewashed wall! You sit there to judge me according to the law, yet you yourself violate the law by commanding that I be struck!"

⁴Those who were standing near Paul said, "You dare to insult God's high priest?"

⁵Paul replied, "Brothers, I did not realize that he was the high priest; for it is written: 'Do not speak evil about the ruler of your people.'[b]"

⁶Then Paul, knowing that some of them were Sadducees and the others Pharisees, called out in the Sanhe-

drin, "My brothers, I am a Pharisee, the son of a Pharisee. I stand on trial because of my hope in the resurrection of the dead." ⁷When he said this, a dispute broke out between the Pharisees and the Sadducees, and the assembly was divided. ⁸(The Sadducees say that there is no resurrection, and that there are neither angels nor spirits, but the Pharisees acknowledge them all.)

⁹There was a great uproar, and some of the teachers of the law who were Pharisees stood up and argued vigorously. "We find nothing wrong with this man," they said. "What if a spirit or an angel has spoken to him?" ¹⁰The dispute became so violent that the commander was afraid Paul would be torn to pieces by them. He ordered the troops to go down and take him away from them by force and bring him into the barracks.

¹¹The following night the Lord stood near Paul and said, "Take courage! As you have testified about me in Jerusalem, so you must also testify in Rome."

The Plot to Kill Paul

¹²The next morning the Jews formed a conspiracy and bound themselves with an oath not to eat or drink until they had killed Paul. ¹³More than forty men were involved in this plot. ¹⁴They went to the chief priests and elders and said, "We have taken a solemn oath not to eat anything until we have killed Paul. ¹⁵Now then, you and the Sanhedrin petition the commander to bring him before you on the pretext of wanting more accurate information about his case. We are ready to kill him before he gets here."

¹⁶But when the son of Paul's sister heard of this plot, he went into the barracks and told Paul.

¹⁷Then Paul called one of the centurions and said, "Take this young man to the commander; he has something to tell him." ¹⁸So he took him to the commander.

The centurion said, "Paul, the prisoner, sent for me and asked me to bring this young man to you because he has something to tell you."

¹⁹The commander took the young man by the hand, drew him aside and asked, "What is it you want to tell me?"

²⁰He said: "The Jews have agreed to ask you to bring Paul before the Sanhedrin tomorrow on the pretext of wanting more accurate information about him. ²¹Don't give in to them, because more than forty of them are waiting in ambush for him. They have taken an oath not to eat or drink until they have killed him. They are ready now, waiting for your consent to their request."

²²The commander dismissed the young man and cautioned him, "Don't tell anyone that you have reported this to me."

Paul Transferred to Caesarea

²³Then he called two of his centurions and ordered them, "Get ready a detachment of two hundred soldiers, seventy horsemen and two hundred spearmen ᵃ to go to Caesarea at nine tonight. ²⁴Provide mounts for Paul so that he may be taken safely to Governor Felix."

²⁵He wrote a letter as follows:

²⁶Claudius Lysias,

To His Excellency, Governor Felix:

Greetings.

²⁷This man was seized by the Jews and they were about to kill him, but I came with my troops and rescued him, for I had learned that he is a Roman citizen. ²⁸I wanted to know why they were accusing him, so I brought him to their Sanhedrin. ²⁹I found that the accusation had to do with questions about their law, but there was no charge against him that deserved death or im-

---

ᵃ23 The meaning of the Greek for this word is uncertain.

prisonment. ³⁰When I was informed of a plot to be carried out against the man, I sent him to you at once. I also ordered his accusers to present to you their case against him.

³¹So the soldiers, carrying out their orders, took Paul with them during the night and brought him as far as Antipatris. ³²The next day they let the cavalry go on with him, while they returned to the barracks. ³³When the cavalry arrived in Caesarea, they delivered the letter to the governor and handed Paul over to him. ³⁴The governor read the letter and asked what province he was from. Learning that he was from Cilicia, ³⁵he said, "I will hear your case when your accusers get here." Then he ordered that Paul be kept under guard in Herod's palace.

The Trial Before Felix

24 Five days later the high priest Ananias went down to Caesarea with some of the elders and a lawyer named Tertullus, and they brought their charges against Paul before the governor. ²When Paul was called in, Tertullus presented his case before Felix: "We have enjoyed a long period of peace under you, and your foresight has brought about reforms in this nation. ³Everywhere and in every way, most excellent Felix, we acknowledge this with profound gratitude. ⁴But in order not to weary you further, I would request that you be kind enough to hear us briefly.

⁵"We have found this man to be a troublemaker, stirring up riots among the Jews all over the world. He is a ringleader of the Nazarene sect ⁶and even tried to desecrate the temple; so we seized him. ⁸By^a examining him yourself you will be able to learn the truth about all these

charges we are bringing against him."

⁹The Jews joined in the accusation, asserting that these things were true.

¹⁰When the governor motioned for him to speak, Paul replied: "I know that for a number of years you have been a judge over this nation; so I gladly make my defense. ¹¹You can easily verify that no more than twelve days ago I went up to Jerusalem to worship. ¹²My accusers did not find me arguing with anyone at the temple, or stirring up a crowd in the synagogues or anywhere else in the city. ¹³And they cannot prove to you the charges they are now making against me. ¹⁴However, I admit that I worship the God of our fathers as a follower of the Way, which they call a sect. I believe everything that agrees with the Law and that is written in the Prophets, ¹⁵and I have the same hope in God as these men, that there will be a resurrection of both the righteous and the wicked. ¹⁶So I strive always to keep my conscience clear before God and man.

¹⁷"After an absence of several years, I came to Jerusalem to bring my people gifts for the poor and to present offerings. ¹⁸I was ceremonially clean when they found me in the temple courts doing this. There was no crowd with me, nor was I involved in any disturbance. ¹⁹But there are some Jews from the province of Asia, who ought to be here before you and bring charges if they have anything against me. ²⁰Or these who are here should state what crime they found in me when I stood before the Sanhedrin— ²¹unless it was this one thing I shouted as I stood in their presence: 'It is concerning the resurrection of the dead that I am on trial before you today.'"

²²Then Felix, who was well acquainted with the Way, adjourned the proceedings. "When Lysias the

<hr>

^a6-8 Some manuscripts *him and wanted to judge him according to our law.* ⁷*But the commander, Lysias, came and with the use of much force snatched him from our hands* ⁸*and ordered his accusers to come before you. By*

commander comes," he said, "I will decide your case." 23He ordered the centurion to keep Paul under guard but to give him some freedom and permit his friends to take care of his needs.

24Several days later Felix came with his wife Drusilla, who was a Jewess. He sent for Paul and listened to him as he spoke about faith in Christ Jesus. 25As Paul discoursed on righteousness, self-control and the judgment to come, Felix was afraid and said, "That's enough for now! You may leave. When I find it convenient, I will send for you." 26At the same time he was hoping that Paul would offer him a bribe, so he sent for him frequently and talked with him.

27When two years had passed, Felix was succeeded by Porcius Festus, but because Felix wanted to grant a favor to the Jews, he left Paul in prison.

The Trial Before Festus

25 Three days after arriving in the province, Festus went up from Caesarea to Jerusalem, 2where the chief priests and Jewish leaders appeared before him and presented the charges against Paul. 3They urgently requested Festus, as a favor to them, to have Paul transferred to Jerusalem, for they were preparing an ambush to kill him along the way. 4Festus answered, "Paul is being held at Caesarea, and I myself am going there soon. 5Let some of your leaders come with me and press charges against the man there, if he has done anything wrong."

6After spending eight or ten days with them, he went down to Caesarea, and the next day he convened the court and ordered that Paul be brought before him. 7When Paul appeared, the Jews who had come down from Jerusalem stood around him, bringing many serious charges against him, which they could not prove.

8Then Paul made his defense: "I have done nothing wrong against the law of the Jews or against the temple or against Caesar."

9Festus, wishing to do the Jews a favor, said to Paul, "Are you willing to go up to Jerusalem and stand trial before me there on these charges?"

10Paul answered: "I am now standing before Caesar's court, where I ought to be tried. I have not done any wrong to the Jews, as you yourself know very well. 11If, however, I am guilty of doing anything deserving death, I do not refuse to die. But if the charges brought against me by these Jews are not true, no one has the right to hand me over to them. I appeal to Caesar!"

12After Festus had conferred with his council, he declared: "You have appealed to Caesar. To Caesar you will go!"

Festus Consults King Agrippa

13A few days later King Agrippa and Bernice arrived at Caesarea to pay their respects to Festus. 14Since they were spending many days there, Festus discussed Paul's case with the king. He said: "There is a man here whom Felix left as a prisoner. 15When I went to Jerusalem, the chief priests and elders of the Jews brought charges against him and asked that he be condemned.

16"I told them that it is not the Roman custom to hand over any man before he has faced his accusers and has had an opportunity to defend himself against their charges. 17When they came here with me, I did not delay the case, but convened the court the next day and ordered the man to be brought in. 18When his accusers got up to speak, they did not charge him with any of the crimes I had expected. 19Instead, they had some points of dispute with him about their own religion and about a dead man named Jesus who Paul claimed was alive. 20I was at a loss how to investigate such matters; so I asked if he would be willing to go to Jerusalem and stand trial there on these charges. 21When Paul made his appeal to be held over for the Emperor's decision, I ordered him held until I could send him to Caesar."

²²Then Agrippa said to Festus, "I would like to hear this man myself."

He replied, "Tomorrow you will hear him."

❓DID YOU KNOW?   25:14

Who were Felix and Festus?

Felix and Festus were Roman governors. Felix kept Paul under arrest for two years. Festus, who replaced Felix, didn't know what to do with Paul. Acts 24–26 tells what happened while Paul was under arrest in Caesarea, and how he happened to be sent to Rome.

Paul Before Agrippa

²³The next day Agrippa and Bernice came with great pomp and entered the audience room with the high ranking officers and the leading men of the city. At the command of Festus, Paul was brought in. ²⁴Festus said: "King Agrippa, and all who are present with us, you see this man! The whole Jewish community has petitioned me about him in Jerusalem and here in Caesarea, shouting that he ought not to live any longer. ²⁵I found he had done nothing deserving of death, but because he made his appeal to the Emperor I decided to send him to Rome. ²⁶But I have nothing definite to write to His Majesty about him. Therefore I have brought him before all of you, and especially before you, King Agrippa, so that as a result of this investigation I may have something to write. ²⁷For I think it is unreasonable to send on a prisoner without specifying the charges against him."

26 Then Agrippa said to Paul, "You have permission to speak for yourself."

So Paul motioned with his hand and began his defense: ²"King Agrippa, I consider myself fortunate to stand before you today as I make my defense against all the accusations of the Jews, ³and especially so because you are well acquainted with all the Jewish customs and controversies. Therefore, I beg you to listen to me patiently.

❓DID YOU KNOW?   25:23

Who was King Agrippa?

Agrippa was a grandson of Herod, who was king when Jesus was born. But Agrippa ruled only the district of Galilee. The Roman governor Festus wanted Agrippa's advice because he did not know what to do with Paul.

---

⁴"The Jews all know the way I have lived ever since I was a child, from the beginning of my life in my own country, and also in Jerusalem. ⁵They have known me for a long time and can testify, if they are willing, that according to the strictest sect of our religion, I lived as a Pharisee. ⁶And now it is because of my hope in what God has promised our fathers that I am on trial today. ⁷This is the promise our twelve tribes are hoping to see fulfilled as they earnestly serve God day and night. O king, it is because of this hope that the Jews are accusing me. ⁸Why should any of you consider it incredible that God raises the dead?

⁹"I too was convinced that I ought to do all that was possible to oppose the name of Jesus of Nazareth. ¹⁰And that is just what I did in Jerusalem. On the authority of the chief priests I put many of the saints in prison, and when they were put to death, I cast my vote against them. ¹¹Many a time I went from one synagogue to another to have them punished, and I tried to force them to blaspheme. In my obsession against them, I even went to foreign cities to persecute them.

¹²"On one of these journeys I was going to Damascus with the authority and commission of the chief

priests. [13]About noon, O king, as I was on the road, I saw a light from heaven, brighter than the sun, blazing around me and my companions. [14]We all fell to the ground, and I heard a voice saying to me in Aramaic,[a] 'Saul, Saul, why do you persecute me? It is hard for you to kick against the goads.'

[15]"Then I asked, 'Who are you, Lord?'

" 'I am Jesus, whom you are persecuting,' the Lord replied. [16]'Now get up and stand on your feet. I have appeared to you to appoint you as a servant and as a witness of what you have seen of me and what I will show you. [17]I will rescue you from your own people and from the Gentiles. I am sending you to them [18]to open their eyes and turn them from darkness to light, and from the power of Satan to God, so that they may receive forgiveness of sins and a place among those who are sanctified by faith in me.'

[19]"So then, King Agrippa, I was not disobedient to the vision from heaven. [20]First to those in Damascus, then to those in Jerusalem and in all Judea, and to the Gentiles also, I preached that they should repent and turn to God and prove their repentance by their deeds. [21]That is why the Jews seized me in the temple courts and tried to kill me. [22]But I have had God's help to this very day, and so I stand here and testify to small and great alike. I am saying nothing beyond what the prophets and Moses said would happen— [23]that the Christ[b] would suffer and, as the first to rise from the dead, would proclaim light to his own people and to the Gentiles."

[24]At this point Festus interrupted Paul's defense. "You are out of your mind, Paul!" he shouted. "Your great learning is driving you insane."

[25]"I am not insane, most excellent Festus," Paul replied. "What I am saying is true and reasonable. [26]The king is familiar with these things,

and I can speak freely to him. I am convinced that none of this has escaped his notice, because it was not done in a corner. [27]King Agrippa, do you believe the prophets? I know you do."

[28]Then Agrippa said to Paul, "Do you think that in such a short time you can persuade me to be a Christian?"

[29]Paul replied, "Short time or long—I pray God that not only you but all who are listening to me today may become what I am, except for these chains."

[30]The king rose, and with him the governor and Bernice and those sitting with them. [31]They left the room, and while talking with one another, they said, "This man is not doing anything that deserves death or imprisonment."

[32]Agrippa said to Festus, "This man could have been set free if he had not appealed to Caesar."

Paul Sails for Rome

27 When it was decided that we would sail for Italy, Paul and some other prisoners were handed over to a centurion named Julius, who belonged to the Imperial Regiment. [2]We boarded a ship from Adramyttium about to sail for ports along the coast of the province of Asia, and we put out to sea. Aristarchus, a Macedonian from Thessalonica, was with us.

[3]The next day we landed at Sidon; and Julius, in kindness to Paul, allowed him to go to his friends so they might provide for his needs. [4]From there we put out to sea again and passed to the lee of Cyprus because the winds were against us. [5]When we had sailed across the open sea off the coast of Cilicia and Pamphylia, we landed at Myra in Lycia. [6]There the centurion found an Alexandrian ship sailing for Italy and put us on board. [7]We made slow headway for many days and had difficulty arriving off Cnidus. When the wind did not allow

---

[a]14 Or *Hebrew*   [b]23 Or *Messiah*

us to hold our course, we sailed to the lee of Crete, opposite Salmone. ⁸We moved along the coast with difficulty and came to a place called Fair Havens, near the town of Lasea.

⁹Much time had been lost, and sailing had already become dangerous because by now it was after the Fast.ᵃ So Paul warned them, ¹⁰"Men, I can see that our voyage is going to be disastrous and bring great loss to ship and cargo, and to our own lives also." ¹¹But the centurion, instead of listening to what Paul said, followed the advice of the pilot and of the owner of the ship. ¹²Since the harbor was unsuitable to winter in, the majority decided that we should sail on, hoping to reach Phoenix and winter there. This was a harbor in Crete, facing both southwest and northwest.

The Storm

¹³When a gentle south wind began to blow, they thought they had obtained what they wanted; so they weighed anchor and sailed along the shore of Crete. ¹⁴Before very long, a wind of hurricane force, called the "northeaster," swept down from the island. ¹⁵The ship was caught by the storm and could not head into the wind; so we gave way to it and were driven along. ¹⁶As we passed to the lee of a small island called Cauda, we were hardly able to make the lifeboat secure. ¹⁷When the men had hoisted

ᵃ9 That is, the Day of Atonement (Yom Kippur)

it aboard, they passed ropes under the ship itself to hold it together. Fearing that they would run aground on the sandbars of Syrtis, they lowered the sea anchor and let the ship be driven along. ¹⁸We took such a violent battering from the storm that the next day they began to throw the cargo overboard. ¹⁹On the third day, they threw the ship's tackle overboard with their own hands. ²⁰When neither sun nor stars appeared for many days and the storm continued raging, we finally gave up all hope of being saved.

²¹After the men had gone a long time without food, Paul stood up before them and said: "Men, you should have taken my advice not to sail from Crete; then you would have spared yourselves this damage and loss. ²²But now I urge you to keep up your courage, because not one of you will be lost; only the ship will be destroyed. ²³Last night an angel of the God whose I am and whom I serve stood beside me ²⁴and said, 'Do not be afraid, Paul. You must stand trial before Caesar; and God has graciously given you the lives of all who sail with you.' ²⁵So keep up your courage, men, for I have faith in God that it will happen just as he told me. ²⁶Nevertheless, we must run aground on some island."

The Shipwreck

²⁷On the fourteenth night we were

Life in Bible Times

CARGO SHIPS

Paul was traveling on one of the large cargo ships that sailed the Mediterranean Sea. These ships were large enough to carry two or three hundred people as well as their cargo.

still being driven across the Adriatic[a] Sea, when about midnight the sailors sensed they were approaching land. 28They took soundings and found that the water was a hundred and twenty feet[b] deep. A short time later they took soundings again and found it was ninety feet[c] deep. 29Fearing that we would be dashed against the rocks, they dropped four anchors from the stern and prayed for daylight. 30In an attempt to escape from the ship, the sailors let the lifeboat down into the sea, pretending they were going to lower some anchors from the bow. 31Then Paul said to the centurion and the soldiers, "Unless these men stay with the ship, you cannot be saved." 32So the soldiers cut the ropes that held the lifeboat and let it fall away.

33Just before dawn Paul urged them all to eat. "For the last fourteen days," he said, "you have been in constant suspense and have gone without food—you haven't eaten anything. 34Now I urge you to take some food. You need it to survive. Not one of you will lose a single hair from his head." 35After he said this, he took some bread and gave thanks to God in front of them all. Then he broke it and began to eat. 36They were all encouraged and ate some food themselves. 37Altogether there were 276 of us on board. 38When they had eaten as much as they wanted, they lightened the ship by throwing the grain into the sea.

39When daylight came, they did not recognize the land, but they saw a bay with a sandy beach, where they decided to run the ship aground if they could. 40Cutting loose the anchors, they left them in the sea and at the same time untied the ropes that held the rudders. Then they hoisted the foresail to the wind and made for the beach. 41But the ship struck a sandbar and ran aground. The bow stuck fast and would not move, and the stern was broken to pieces by the pounding of the surf.

42The soldiers planned to kill the prisoners to prevent any of them from swimming away and escaping. 43But the centurion wanted to spare Paul's life and kept them from carrying out their plan. He ordered those who could swim to jump overboard first and get to land. 44The rest were to get there on planks or on pieces of the ship. In this way everyone reached land in safety.

Ashore on Malta

28 Once safely on shore, we found out that the island was called Malta. 2The islanders showed us unusual kindness. They built a fire and welcomed us all because it was raining and cold. 3Paul gathered a pile of brushwood and, as he put it on the fire, a viper, driven out by the heat, fastened itself on his hand. 4When the islanders saw the snake hanging from his hand, they said to each other, "This man must be a mur-

---

a27 In ancient times the name referred to an area extending well south of Italy.   *b28* Greek *twenty orguias (about 37 meters)*   *c28* Greek *fifteen orguias (about 27 meters)*

 ET'S LIVE IT!   Acts 27:13—44

THE POWER OF TRUST IN GOD ➠ Read this exciting story about the storm and shipwreck that happened to Paul. Paul trusted God and remained calm even when their ship was almost sinking in the storm.

Paul's trust in God helped others on the ship: the sailors (Acts 27:30–32); all 276 on board (Acts 27:33–38); the prisoners (Acts 27:42–44).

Draw a picture of your favorite part of this story. Let it remind you to trust God even when there is danger. If you stay calm in danger because you trust God, you can help others be calm too.

derer; for though he escaped from the sea, Justice has not allowed him to live." [5]But Paul shook the snake off into the fire and suffered no ill effects. [6]The people expected him to swell up or suddenly fall dead, but after waiting a long time and seeing nothing unusual happen to him, they changed their minds and said he was a god.

[7]There was an estate nearby that belonged to Publius, the chief official of the island. He welcomed us to his home and for three days entertained us hospitably. [8]His father was sick in bed, suffering from fever and dysentery. Paul went in to see him and, after prayer, placed his hands on him and healed him. [9]When this had happened, the rest of the sick on the island came and were cured. [10]They honored us in many ways and when we were ready to sail, they furnished us with the supplies we needed.

Arrival at Rome

[11]After three months we put out to sea in a ship that had wintered in the island. It was an Alexandrian ship with the figurehead of the twin gods Castor and Pollux. [12]We put in at Syracuse and stayed there three days. [13]From there we set sail and arrived at Rhegium. The next day the south wind came up, and on the following day we reached Puteoli. [14]There we found some brothers who invited us to spend a week with them. And so we came to Rome. [15]The brothers there had heard that we were coming, and they traveled as far as the Forum of Appius and the Three Taverns to meet us. At the sight of these men Paul thanked God and was encouraged. [16]When we got to Rome, Paul was allowed to live by himself, with a soldier to guard him.

Paul Preaches at Rome Under Guard

[17]Three days later he called together the leaders of the Jews. When they had assembled, Paul said to them:

"My brothers, although I have done nothing against our people or against the customs of our ancestors, I was arrested in Jerusalem and handed over to the Romans. [18]They examined me and wanted to release me, because I was not guilty of any crime deserving death. [19]But when the Jews objected, I was compelled to appeal to Caesar—not that I had any charge to bring against my own people. [20]For this reason I have asked to see you and talk with you. It is because of the hope of Israel that I am bound with this chain."

[21]They replied, "We have not received any letters from Judea concerning you, and none of the brothers who have come from there has reported or said anything bad about you. [22]But we want to hear what your views are, for we know that people everywhere are talking against this sect."

[23]They arranged to meet Paul on a certain day, and came in even larger numbers to the place where he was staying. From morning till evening he explained and declared to them the kingdom of God and tried to convince them about Jesus from the Law of Moses and from the Prophets. [24]Some were convinced by what he said, but others would not believe. [25]They disagreed among themselves and began to leave after Paul had made this final statement: "The Holy Spirit spoke the truth to your forefathers when he said through Isaiah the prophet:

[26]" 'Go to this people and say,
   "You will be ever hearing but
      never understanding;
   you will be ever seeing but
      never perceiving."
[27]For this people's heart has
      become calloused;
   they hardly hear with their
      ears,
   and they have closed their eyes.
Otherwise they might see with
      their eyes,
   hear with their ears,
   understand with their hearts

and turn, and I would heal them.'[a]

28"Therefore I want you to know that God's salvation has been sent to the Gentiles, and they will listen!"[b]

30For two whole years Paul stayed there in his own rented house and welcomed all who came to see him. 31Boldly and without hindrance he preached the kingdom of God and taught about the Lord Jesus Christ.

[a]27 Isaiah 6:9,10   [b]28 Some manuscripts *listen!" 29After he said this, the Jews left, arguing vigorously among themselves.*

ROMANS

WHO WROTE THIS BOOK?

Paul wrote this book to the church in Rome.

WHY WAS THIS BOOK WRITTEN?

Romans shows how Jesus' death makes us right with God and how Jesus will help us live a good life.

FOR WHOM WAS THIS BOOK WRITTEN?

This book is a letter Paul sent to Christians in Rome.

WHEN WAS THIS BOOK WRITTEN?

This book was written about A.D. 57 from the city of Corinth.

WHAT ARE SOME IMPORTANT TEACHINGS IN THIS BOOK?

Everyone sins.	Romans 3:9–20
God saves people who believe.	Romans 4:1–25
Jesus died for us.	Romans 5:1–11
God's Spirit helps us do right.	Romans 8:1–11
God loves us forever.	Romans 8:28–39
God shows us how to love.	Romans 12:9–21

1 Paul, a servant of Christ Jesus, called to be an apostle and set apart for the gospel of God— [2]the gospel he promised beforehand through his prophets in the Holy Scriptures [3]regarding his Son, who as to his human nature was a descendant of David, [4]and who through the Spirit[a] of holiness was declared with power to be the Son of God[b] by his resurrection from the dead: Jesus Christ our Lord. [5]Through him and for his name's sake, we received grace and apostleship to call people from among all the Gentiles to the obedience that comes from faith. [6]And you also are among those who are called to belong to Jesus Christ.

[7]To all in Rome who are loved by God and called to be saints:

Grace and peace to you from God our Father and from the Lord Jesus Christ.

Paul's Longing to Visit Rome

[8]First, I thank my God through Jesus Christ for all of you, because your faith is being reported all over the world. [9]God, whom I serve with my whole heart in preaching the gospel of his Son, is my witness how constantly I remember you [10]in my prayers at all times; and I pray that now at last by God's will the way may be opened for me to come to you.

[11]I long to see you so that I may impart to you some spiritual gift to make you strong— [12]that is, that you and I may be mutually encouraged by each other's faith. [13]I do not want you to be unaware, brothers, that I planned many times to come to you (but have been prevented from doing so until now) in order that I might have a harvest among you, just as I have had among the other Gentiles.

[14]I am obligated both to Greeks and non-Greeks, both to the wise and the foolish. [15]That is why I am so eager to preach the gospel also to you who are at Rome.

[16]I am not ashamed of the gospel, because it is the power of God for the salvation of everyone who believes: first for the Jew, then for the Gentile. [17]For in the gospel a righteousness from God is revealed, a righteousness

ROME

Rome was the largest city in the Roman Empire when Paul wrote this letter. The rich lived very well in beautiful homes with mosaic floors. They ate large meals with many different foods available to them. The poor, however, lived in small rooms in badly built blocks of apartment houses. Their meals were very plain, usually bread or porridge and occasionally a vegetable.

---

[a]4 Or *who as to his spirit*   [b]4 Or *was appointed to be the Son of God with power*

 ET'S LIVE IT!   Romans 1:8–10

PRAYING FOR OTHERS ➡ Paul had never been to Rome or seen the Romans. But he prayed for the Christians there "constantly" and "at all times."

Get the address of a missionary family your church helps to support. Write and ask them to send you letters about their work. When you pray at bedtime, pray for that missionary family as well as for your own family and friends.

that is by faith from first to last,*a* just as it is written: "The righteous will live by faith."*b*

God's Wrath Against Mankind

[18]The wrath of God is being revealed from heaven against all the godlessness and wickedness of men who suppress the truth by their wickedness, [19]since what may be known about God is plain to them, because God has made it plain to them. [20]For since the creation of the world God's invisible qualities—his eternal power and divine nature—have been clearly seen, being understood from what has been made, so that men are without excuse.

[21]For although they knew God, they neither glorified him as God nor gave thanks to him, but their thinking became futile and their foolish hearts were darkened. [22]Although they claimed to be wise, they became fools [23]and exchanged the glory of the immortal God for images made to look like mortal man and birds and animals and reptiles.

[24]Therefore God gave them over in the sinful desires of their hearts to sexual impurity for the degrading of their bodies with one another. [25]They exchanged the truth of God for a lie, and worshiped and served created things rather than the Creator—who is forever praised. Amen.

[26]Because of this, God gave them over to shameful lusts. Even their women exchanged natural relations for unnatural ones. [27]In the same way the men also abandoned natural relations with women and were inflamed with lust for one another. Men committed indecent acts with other men, and received in themselves the due penalty for their perversion.

[28]Furthermore, since they did not think it worthwhile to retain the knowledge of God, he gave them over to a depraved mind, to do what ought not to be done. [29]They have become filled with every kind of wickedness, evil, greed and depravity. They are full of envy, murder, strife, deceit and malice. They are gossips, [30]slanderers, God-haters, insolent, arrogant and boastful; they invent ways of doing evil; they disobey their parents; [31]they are senseless, faithless, heartless, ruthless. [32]Although they know God's righteous decree that those who do such things deserve death, they not only continue to do these very things but also approve of those who practice them.

❓DID YOU KNOW? 1:18

Why is God angry with human beings?

God has shown people his power by creating the universe. But people do not want to know about God and do not thank him. Instead they are wicked and do evil things. Romans 1 tells what people all over the world have done and explains why God is angry with human beings.

God's Righteous Judgment

2 You, therefore, have no excuse, you who pass judgment on someone else, for at whatever point you judge the other, you are condemning yourself, because you who pass judgment do the same things. [2]Now we know that God's judgment against those who do such things is based on truth. [3]So when you, a mere man, pass judgment on them and yet do the same things, do you think you will escape God's judgment? [4]Or do you show contempt for the riches of his kindness, tolerance and patience, not realizing that God's kindness leads you toward repentance?

[5]But because of your stubbornness and your unrepentant heart, you are storing up wrath against yourself for the day of God's wrath, when his righteous judgment will be revealed.

a17 Or is from faith to faith   b17 Hab. 2:4

6God "will give to each person according to what he has done."ᵃ 7To those who by persistence in doing good seek glory, honor and immortality, he will give eternal life. 8But for those who are self-seeking and who reject the truth and follow evil, there will be wrath and anger. 9There will be trouble and distress for every human being who does evil: first for the Jew, then for the Gentile; 10but glory, honor and peace for everyone who does good: first for the Jew, then for the Gentile. 11For God does not show favoritism.

12All who sin apart from the law will also perish apart from the law, and all who sin under the law will be judged by the law. 13For it is not those who hear the law who are righteous in God's sight, but it is those who obey the law who will be declared righteous. 14(Indeed, when Gentiles, who do not have the law, do by nature things required by the law, they are a law for themselves, even though they do not have the law, 15since they show that the requirements of the law are written on their hearts, their consciences also bearing witness, and their thoughts now accusing, now even defending them.) 16This will take place on the day when God will judge men's secrets through Jesus Christ, as my gospel declares.

❓DID YOU KNOW?   2:16

What is God's judgment?

The Bible teaches that someday God will punish people who sin. This is what "God's judgment" means. But God does not punish right away. He is waiting, to give each person a chance to know Jesus and have his or her sins forgiven.

The Jews and the Law

17Now you, if you call yourself a Jew; if you rely on the law and brag about your relationship to God; 18if you know his will and approve of what is superior because you are instructed by the law; 19if you are convinced that you are a guide for the blind, a light for those who are in the dark, 20an instructor of the foolish, a teacher of infants, because you have in the law the embodiment of knowledge and truth— 21you, then, who teach others, do you not teach yourself? You who preach against stealing, do you steal? 22You who say that people should not commit adultery, do you commit adultery? You who abhor idols, do you rob temples? 23You who brag about the law, do you dishonor God by breaking the law? 24As it is written: "God's name is blasphemed among the Gentiles because of you."ᵇ

25Circumcision has value if you observe the law, but if you break the law, you have become as though you had not been circumcised. 26If those who are not circumcised keep the law's requirements, will they not be regarded as though they were circumcised? 27The one who is not circumcised physically and yet obeys the law will condemn you who, even though you have theᶜ written code and circumcision, are a lawbreaker.

28A man is not a Jew if he is only one outwardly, nor is circumcision merely outward and physical. 29No, a man is a Jew if he is one inwardly; and circumcision is circumcision of the heart, by the Spirit, not by the written code. Such a man's praise is not from men, but from God.

God's Faithfulness

3 What advantage, then, is there in being a Jew, or what value is there in circumcision? 2Much in every way! First of all, they have been entrusted with the very words of God.

3What if some did not have faith? Will their lack of faith nullify God's faithfulness? 4Not at all! Let God be

ᵃ6 Psalm 62:12; Prov. 24:12   ᵇ24 Isaiah 52:5; Ezek. 36:22   ᶜ27 Or who, by means of a true, and every man a liar. As it is written:

? DID YOU KNOW?   2:17

What is the law?

The law is every rule in the Old Testament that God gave the Jewish people to live by. Some Jewish people thought God was pleased with them just because they had the law. Paul said that God was only pleased if they kept the law because they loved him.

"So that you may be proved right
    when you speak
and prevail when you judge."[a]

[5]But if our unrighteousness brings out God's righteousness more clearly, what shall we say? That God is unjust in bringing his wrath on us? (I am using a human argument.) [6]Certainly not! If that were so, how could God judge the world? [7]Someone might argue, "If my falsehood enhances God's truthfulness and so increases his glory, why am I still condemned as a sinner?" [8]Why not say —as we are being slanderously reported as saying and as some claim that we say—"Let us do evil that good may result"? Their condemnation is deserved.

No One Is Righteous

[9]What shall we conclude then? Are we any better[b]? Not at all! We have already made the charge that Jews and Gentiles alike are all under sin. [10]As it is written:

"There is no one righteous, not
    even one;
[11] there is no one who
        understands,
    no one who seeks God.
[12]All have turned away,
    they have together become
        worthless;

there is no one who does good,
    not even one."[c]
[13]"Their throats are open graves;
    their tongues practice deceit."[d]
"The poison of vipers is on their
    lips."[e]
[14] "Their mouths are full of
        cursing and bitterness."[f]
[15]"Their feet are swift to shed
        blood;
[16] ruin and misery mark their
        ways,
[17]and the way of peace they do not
        know."[g]
[18] "There is no fear of God before
        their eyes."[h]

[19]Now we know that whatever the law says, it says to those who are under the law, so that every mouth may be silenced and the whole world held accountable to God. [20]Therefore no one will be declared righteous in his sight by observing the law; rather, through the law we become conscious of sin.

? DID YOU KNOW?   3:10

What is righteousness?

In the Bible righteousness means either doing right things, or being right with God. Because everyone has sinned, no one can be right with God by what he or she does. Yet God forgives people who believe in Jesus and says we are right with him. Then God expects Christians to do right things.

Righteousness Through Faith

[21]But now a righteousness from God, apart from law, has been made known, to which the Law and the Prophets testify. [22]This righteousness from God comes through faith in Jesus Christ to all who believe. There is no difference, [23]for all have sinned and fall short of the glory of God, [24]and are justified freely by his grace

---

a4 Psalm 51:4   *b9* Or *worse*   *c12* Psalms 14:1-3; 53:1-3; Eccles. 7:20   *d13* Psalm 5:9
e13 Psalm 140:3   *f14* Psalm 10:7   *g17* Isaiah 59:7,8   *h18* Psalm 36:1

through the redemption that came by Christ Jesus. [25]God presented him as a sacrifice of atonement,[a] through faith in his blood. He did this to demonstrate his justice, because in his forbearance he had left the sins committed beforehand unpunished— [26]he did it to demonstrate his justice at the present time, so as to be just and the one who justifies those who have faith in Jesus.

WORDS TO REMEMBER

3:22 Righteousness from God comes through faith in Jesus Christ to all who believe.

[27]Where, then, is boasting? It is excluded. On what principle? On that of observing the law? No, but on that of faith. [28]For we maintain that a man is justified by faith apart from observing the law. [29]Is God the God of Jews only? Is he not the God of Gentiles too? Yes, of Gentiles too, [30]since there is only one God, who will justify the circumcised by faith and the uncircumcised through that same faith. [31]Do we, then, nullify the law by this faith? Not at all! Rather, we uphold the law.

Abraham Justified by Faith

4 What then shall we say that Abraham, our forefather, discovered in this matter? [2]If, in fact, Abraham was justified by works, he had something to boast about—but not before God. [3]What does the Scripture say? "Abraham believed God, and it was credited to him as righteousness."[b]

[4]Now when a man works, his wages are not credited to him as a gift, but as an obligation. [5]However, to the man who does not work but trusts God who justifies the wicked, his faith is credited as righteousness. [6]David says the same thing when he speaks of the blessedness of the man to whom God credits righteousness apart from works:

[7]"Blessed are they
    whose transgressions are
        forgiven,
    whose sins are covered.
[8]Blessed is the man
    whose sin the Lord will never
        count against him."[c]

[9]Is this blessedness only for the circumcised, or also for the uncircumcised? We have been saying that Abraham's faith was credited to him as righteousness. [10]Under what circumstances was it credited? Was it after he was circumcised, or before? It was not after, but before! [11]And he received the sign of circumcision, a seal of the righteousness that he had by faith while he was still uncircumcised. So then, he is the father of all who believe but have not been circumcised, in order that righteous-

a25 Or *as the one who would turn aside his wrath, taking away sin*   b3 Gen. 15:6; also in verse 22   c8 Psalm 32:1,2

LET'S LIVE IT!   Romans 4:4–8

RECEIVING GOD'S GIFT ➡ We cannot earn forgiveness. God gives us salvation as a gift. When someone brings you a present at Christmas or on your birthday, you take it and say, "Thank you." This is just how you receive God's gift of salvation. All you do is take it and say, "Thank you."

Find an empty box. Write Romans 4:7–8 on a piece of paper and put it in the box. Then wrap the box like a Christmas gift. Keep the gift-wrapped box in your room as a reminder that God has forgiven you. Or use it to show a friend how to become a Christian.

ness might be credited to them. ¹²And he is also the father of the circumcised who not only are circumcised but who also walk in the footsteps of the faith that our father Abraham had before he was circumcised.

¹³It was not through law that Abraham and his offspring received the promise that he would be heir of the world, but through the righteousness that comes by faith. ¹⁴For if those who live by law are heirs, faith has no value and the promise is worthless, ¹⁵because law brings wrath. And where there is no law there is no transgression.

¹⁶Therefore, the promise comes by faith, so that it may be by grace and may be guaranteed to all Abraham's offspring—not only to those who are of the law but also to those who are of the faith of Abraham. He is the father of us all. ¹⁷As it is written: "I have made you a father of many nations."*ᵃ* He is our father in the sight of God, in whom he believed—the God who gives life to the dead and calls things that are not as though they were.

¹⁸Against all hope, Abraham in hope believed and so became the father of many nations, just as it had been said to him, "So shall your offspring be."*ᵇ* ¹⁹Without weakening in his faith, he faced the fact that his body was as good as dead—since he was about a hundred years old—and that Sarah's womb was also dead. ²⁰Yet he did not waver through unbelief regarding the promise of God, but was strengthened in his faith and gave glory to God, ²¹being fully persuaded that God had power to do what he had promised. ²²This is why "it was credited to him as righteousness." ²³The words "it was credited to him" were written not for him alone, ²⁴but also for us, to whom God will credit righteousness—for us who believe in him who raised Jesus our Lord from the dead. ²⁵He was delivered over to death for our sins and was raised to life for our justification.

Peace and Joy

5 Therefore, since we have been justified through faith, we*ᶜ* have peace with God through our Lord Jesus Christ, ²through whom we have gained access by faith into this grace in which we now stand. And we*ᶜ* rejoice in the hope of the glory of God. ³Not only so, but we*ᶜ* also rejoice in our sufferings, because we know that suffering produces perseverance; ⁴perseverance, character; and character, hope. ⁵And hope does not disappoint us, because God has poured out his love into our hearts by the Holy Spirit, whom he has given us.

❓DID YOU KNOW?   4:25

What does justified mean?

Justified is a special word that means we have been declared *not guilty!* When God forgives our sins, he says we are not guilty anymore. Because we are forgiven, we are right with God and can go to heaven.

---

⁶You see, at just the right time, when we were still powerless, Christ died for the ungodly. ⁷Very rarely will anyone die for a righteous man, though for a good man someone might possibly dare to die. ⁸But God demonstrates his own love for us in this: While we were still sinners, Christ died for us.

WORDS TO REMEMBER

5:8 God demonstrates his own love for us in this: While we were still sinners, Christ died for us.

---

⁹Since we have now been justified by his blood, how much more shall we be saved from God's wrath through him! ¹⁰For if, when we were God's en-

---

ᵃ17 Gen. 17:5   *ᵇ18* Gen. 15:5   *ᶜ1,2,3* Or *let us*

emies, we were reconciled to him through the death of his Son, how much more, having been reconciled, shall we be saved through his life! [11]Not only is this so, but we also rejoice in God through our Lord Jesus Christ, through whom we have now received reconciliation.

Death Through Adam, Life Through Christ

[12]Therefore, just as sin entered the world through one man, and death through sin, and in this way death came to all men, because all sinned— [13]for before the law was given, sin was in the world. But sin is not taken into account when there is no law. [14]Nevertheless, death reigned from the time of Adam to the time of Moses, even over those who did not sin by breaking a command, as did Adam, who was a pattern of the one to come.

[15]But the gift is not like the trespass. For if the many died by the trespass of the one man, how much more did God's grace and the gift that came by the grace of the one man, Jesus Christ, overflow to the many! [16]Again, the gift of God is not like the result of the one man's sin: The judgment followed one sin and brought condemnation, but the gift followed many trespasses and brought justification. [17]For if, by the trespass of the one man, death reigned through that one man, how much more will those who receive God's abundant provision of grace and of the gift of righteousness reign in life through the one man, Jesus Christ.

[18]Consequently, just as the result of one trespass was condemnation for all men, so also the result of one act of righteousness was justification that brings life for all men. [19]For just as through the disobedience of the one man the many were made sinners, so also through the obedience of the one man the many will be made righteous.

[20]The law was added so that the trespass might increase. But where sin increased, grace increased all the more, [21]so that, just as sin reigned in death, so also grace might reign through righteousness to bring eternal life through Jesus Christ our Lord.

❓DID YOU KNOW? 5:15

How do we know that God loves us?

Jesus, God's Son, was sent to die for us, even though we were sinners. This shows how much God loves us.

Dead to Sin, Alive in Christ

6 What shall we say, then? Shall we go on sinning so that grace may increase? [2]By no means! We died to sin; how can we live in it any longer? [3]Or don't you know that all of us who were baptized into Christ Jesus were baptized into his death? [4]We were therefore buried with him through baptism into death in order that, just as Christ was raised from the dead through the glory of the Father, we too may live a new life.

[5]If we have been united with him like this in his death, we will certainly also be united with him in his resurrection. [6]For we know that our old self was crucified with him so that the body of sin might be done away with,[a] that we should no longer be slaves to sin— [7]because anyone who has died has been freed from sin.

[8]Now if we died with Christ, we believe that we will also live with him. [9]For we know that since Christ was raised from the dead, he cannot die again; death no longer has mastery over him. [10]The death he died, he died to sin once for all; but the life he lives, he lives to God. [11]In the same way, count yourselves dead to sin but alive to God in Christ Jesus. [12]Therefore do not let

---

a6 Or be rendered powerless

sin reign in your mortal body so that you obey its evil desires. ¹³Do not offer the parts of your body to sin, as instruments of wickedness, but rather offer yourselves to God, as those who have been brought from death to life; and offer the parts of your body to him as instruments of righteousness. ¹⁴For sin shall not be your master, because you are not under law, but under grace.

Slaves to Righteousness

¹⁵What then? Shall we sin because we are not under law but under grace? By no means! ¹⁶Don't you know that when you offer yourselves to someone to obey him as slaves, you are slaves to the one whom you obey—whether you are slaves to sin, which leads to death, or to obedience, which leads to righteousness? ¹⁷But thanks be to God that, though you used to be slaves to sin, you wholeheartedly obeyed the form of teaching to which you were entrusted. ¹⁸You have been set free from sin and have become slaves to righteousness.

SLAVES

There were thousands of slaves in Rome in Paul's day. They worked at many different jobs: potters, household servants, silversmiths, farmers, shepherds, builders, scribes. Most slaves, if they were obedient and did their job well, could plan on eventually being free.

¹⁹I put this in human terms because you are weak in your natural selves. Just as you used to offer the

parts of your body in slavery to impurity and to ever-increasing wickedness, so now offer them in slavery to righteousness leading to holiness. ²⁰When you were slaves to sin, you were free from the control of righteousness. ²¹What benefit did you reap at that time from the things you are now ashamed of? Those things result in death! ²²But now that you have been set free from sin and have become slaves to God, the benefit you reap leads to holiness, and the result is eternal life. ²³For the wages of sin is death, but the gift of God is eternal life in*ᵃ* Christ Jesus our Lord.

An Illustration From Marriage

7 Do you not know, brothers—for I am speaking to men who know the law—that the law has authority over a man only as long as he lives? ²For example, by law a married woman is bound to her husband as long as he is alive, but if her husband dies, she is released from the law of marriage. ³So then, if she marries another man while her husband is still alive, she is called an adulteress. But if her husband dies, she is released from that law and is not an adulteress, even though she marries another man.

⁴So, my brothers, you also died to the law through the body of Christ, that you might belong to another, to him who was raised from the dead, in order that we might bear fruit to God. ⁵For when we were controlled by the sinful nature,*ᵇ* the sinful passions aroused by the law were at work in our bodies, so that we bore fruit for death. ⁶But now, by dying to what once bound us, we have been released from the law so that we serve in the new way of the Spirit, and not in the old way of the written code.

Struggling With Sin

⁷What shall we say, then? Is the law sin? Certainly not! Indeed I would not have known what sin was except through the law. For I would

---

ᵃ23 Or through   ᵇ5 Or the flesh; also in verse 25

not have known what coveting really was if the law had not said, "Do not covet."[a] 8But sin, seizing the opportunity afforded by the commandment, produced in me every kind of covetous desire. For apart from law, sin is dead. 9Once I was alive apart from law; but when the commandment came, sin sprang to life and I died. 10I found that the very commandment that was intended to bring life actually brought death. 11For sin, seizing the opportunity afforded by the commandment, deceived me, and through the commandment put me to death. 12So then, the law is holy, and the commandment is holy, righteous and good.

13Did that which is good, then, become death to me? By no means! But in order that sin might be recognized as sin, it produced death in me through what was good, so that through the commandment sin might become utterly sinful. 14We know that the law is spiritual; but I am unspiritual, sold as a slave to sin. 15I do not understand what I do. For what I want to do I do not do, but what I hate I do. 16And if I do what I do not want to do, I agree that the law is good. 17As it is, it is no longer I myself who do it, but it is sin living in me. 18I know that nothing good lives in me, that is, in my sinful nature.[b] For I have the desire to do what is good, but I cannot carry it out. 19For what I do is not the good I want to do; no, the evil I do not want to do—this I keep on doing. 20Now if I do what I do not want to do, it is no longer I who do it, but it is sin living in me that does it.

21So I find this law at work: When I want to do good, evil is right there with me. 22For in my inner being I delight in God's law; 23but I see another law at work in the members of my body, waging war against the law of my mind and making me a prisoner of the law of sin at work within my members. 24What a wretched man I am! Who will rescue me from this body of death? 25Thanks be to God —through Jesus Christ our Lord!

So then, I myself in my mind am a slave to God's law, but in the sinful nature a slave to the law of sin.

Life Through the Spirit

8 Therefore, there is now no condemnation for those who are in Christ Jesus,[c] 2because through Christ Jesus the law of the Spirit of life set me free from the law of sin and death. 3For what the law was powerless to do in that it was weakened by the sinful nature,[d] God did by sending his own Son in the likeness of sinful man to be a sin offering.[e] And so he condemned sin in sinful man,[f] 4in order that the righteous requirements of the law might be fully met in us, who do not live according to the sinful nature but according to the Spirit.

5Those who live according to the sinful nature have their minds set on what that nature desires; but those who live in accordance with the Spirit have their minds set on what the Spirit desires. 6The mind of sinful man[g] is death, but the mind controlled by the Spirit is life and peace; 7the sinful mind[h] is hostile to God. It does not submit to God's law, nor can it do so. 8Those controlled by the sinful nature cannot please God.

9You, however, are controlled not by the sinful nature but by the Spirit, if the Spirit of God lives in you. And if anyone does not have the Spirit of Christ, he does not belong to Christ. 10But if Christ is in you, your body is dead because of sin, yet your spirit is alive because of righteousness. 11And if the Spirit of him who raised Jesus from the dead is living in you, he who raised Christ from the dead will also

---

a7 Exodus 20:17; Deut. 5:21   b18 Or *my flesh live according to the sinful nature but according to the Spirit,* 8, 9, 12 and 13   c3 Or *man, for sin*   c1 Some later manuscripts *Jesus, who do not* d3 Or *the flesh*; also in verses 4, 5, f3 Or *in the flesh*   g6 Or *mind set on the flesh* h7 Or *the mind set on the flesh*

give life to your mortal bodies through his Spirit, who lives in you.

[12]Therefore, brothers, we have an obligation—but it is not to the sinful nature, to live according to it. [13]For if you live according to the sinful nature, you will die; but if by the Spirit you put to death the misdeeds of the body, you will live, [14]because those who are led by the Spirit of God are sons of God. [15]For you did not receive a spirit that makes you a slave again to fear, but you received the Spirit of sonship.[a] And by him we cry, "Abba,[b] Father." [16]The Spirit himself testifies with our spirit that we are God's children. [17]Now if we are children, then we are heirs—heirs of God and co-heirs with Christ, if indeed we share in his sufferings in order that we may also share in his glory.

Future Glory

[18]I consider that our present sufferings are not worth comparing with the glory that will be revealed in us. [19]The creation waits in eager expectation for the sons of God to be revealed. [20]For the creation was subjected to frustration, not by its own choice, but by the will of the one who subjected it, in hope [21]that[c] the creation itself will be liberated from its bondage to decay and brought into the glorious freedom of the children of God.

[22]We know that the whole creation has been groaning as in the pains of childbirth right up to the present time. [23]Not only so, but we ourselves, who have the firstfruits of the Spirit, groan inwardly as we wait eagerly for our adoption as sons, the redemption of our bodies. [24]For in this hope we were saved. But hope that is seen is no hope at all. Who hopes for what he already has? [25]But if we hope for what we do not yet have, we wait for it patiently.

[26]In the same way, the Spirit helps us in our weakness. We do not know what we ought to pray for, but the Spirit himself intercedes for us with groans that words cannot express. [27]And he who searches our hearts knows the mind of the Spirit, because the Spirit intercedes for the saints in accordance with God's will.

WORDS TO REMEMBER

8:26 We do not know what we ought to pray for, but the Spirit himself intercedes for us.

More Than Conquerors

[28]And we know that in all things God works for the good of those who love him,[d] who[e] have been called according to his purpose. [29]For those God foreknew he also predestined to be conformed to the likeness of his Son, that he might be the firstborn among many brothers. [30]And those he predestined, he also called; those he called, he also justified; those he justified, he also glorified.

WORDS TO REMEMBER

8:28 We know that in all things God works for the good of those who love him.

---

[31]What, then, shall we say in response to this? If God is for us, who can be against us? [32]He who did not spare his own Son, but gave him up for us all—how will he not also, along with him, graciously give us all things? [33]Who will bring any charge against those whom God has chosen? It is God who justifies. [34]Who is he that condemns? Christ Jesus, who died—more than that, who was raised to life—is at the right hand of God and is also interceding for us. [35]Who shall separate us from the love

---

a15 Or *adoption*   *b15* Aramaic for *Father*   *c20,21* Or *subjected it in hope.* [21]*For*
d28 Some manuscripts *And we know that all things work together for good to those who love God*
e28 Or *works together with those who love him to bring about what is good—with those who*

of Christ? Shall trouble or hardship or persecution or famine or nakedness or danger or sword? [36]As it is written:

"For your sake we face death all day long;
we are considered as sheep to be slaughtered."[a]

[37]No, in all these things we are more than conquerors through him who loved us. [38]For I am convinced that neither death nor life, neither angels nor demons,[b] neither the present nor the future, nor any powers, [39]neither height nor depth, nor anything else in all creation, will be able to separate us from the love of God that is in Christ Jesus our Lord.

God's Sovereign Choice

9 I speak the truth in Christ—I am not lying, my conscience confirms it in the Holy Spirit— [2]I have great sorrow and unceasing anguish in my heart. [3]For I could wish that I myself were cursed and cut off from Christ for the sake of my brothers, those of my own race, [4]the people of Israel. Theirs is the adoption as sons; theirs the divine glory, the covenants, the receiving of the law, the temple worship and the promises. [5]Theirs are the patriarchs, and from them is traced the human ancestry of Christ, who is God over all, forever praised![c] Amen.

[6]It is not as though God's word had failed. For not all who are descended from Israel are Israel. [7]Nor because they are his descendants are they all Abraham's children. On the contrary, "It is through Isaac that your offspring will be reckoned."[d] [8]In other words, it is not the natural children who are God's children, but it is the children of the promise who are regarded as Abraham's offspring. [9]For this was how the promise was stated: "At the appointed time I will

return, and Sarah will have a son."[e]
[10]Not only that, but Rebekah's children had one and the same father, our father Isaac. [11]Yet, before the twins were born or had done anything good or bad—in order that God's purpose in election might stand: [12]not by works but by him who calls—she was told, "The older will serve the younger."[f] [13]Just as it is written: "Jacob I loved, but Esau I hated."[g]

[14]What then shall we say? Is God unjust? Not at all! [15]For he says to Moses,

"I will have mercy on whom I have mercy,
and I will have compassion on whom I have compassion."[h]

[16]It does not, therefore, depend on man's desire or effort, but on God's mercy. [17]For the Scripture says to Pharaoh: "I raised you up for this very purpose, that I might display my power in you and that my name might be proclaimed in all the earth."[i] [18]Therefore God has mercy on whom he wants to have mercy, and he hardens whom he wants to harden.

[19]One of you will say to me: "Then why does God still blame us? For who resists his will?" [20]But who are you, O man, to talk back to God? "Shall what is formed say to him who formed it, 'Why did you make me like this?'"[j] [21]Does not the potter have the right to make out of the same lump of clay some pottery for noble purposes and some for common use?

[22]What if God, choosing to show his wrath and make his power known, bore with great patience the objects of his wrath—prepared for destruction? [23]What if he did this to make the riches of his glory known to the objects of his mercy, whom he prepared in advance for glory— [24]even us, whom he also called, not only

---

a36 Psalm 44:22   *b38* Or *nor heavenly rulers*   *c5* Or *Christ, who is over all. God be forever praised!* Or *Christ. God who is over all be forever praised!*   *d7* Gen. 21:12   *e9* Gen. 18:10,14
f12 Gen. 25:23   *g13* Mal. 1:2,3   *h15* Exodus 33:19   *i17* Exodus 9:16   *j20* Isaiah 29:16;
45:9

from the Jews but also from the Gentiles? 25As he says in Hosea:

"I will call them 'my people' who
are not my people;
and I will call her 'my loved
one' who is not my loved
one,"a

26and,

"It will happen that in the very
place where it was said to
them,
'You are not my people,'
they will be called 'sons of the
living God.' "b

27Isaiah cries out concerning Israel:

"Though the number of the
Israelites be like the sand
by the sea,
only the remnant will be saved.
28For the Lord will carry out
his sentence on earth with
speed and finality."c

29It is just as Isaiah said previously:

"Unless the Lord Almighty
had left us descendants,
we would have become like
Sodom,
we would have been like
Gomorrah."d

Israel's Unbelief

30What then shall we say? That the Gentiles, who did not pursue righteousness, have obtained it, a righteousness that is by faith; 31but Israel, who pursued a law of righteousness, has not attained it. 32Why not? Because they pursued it not by faith but as if it were by works. They stumbled over the "stumbling stone." 33As it is written:

"See, I lay in Zion a stone that
causes men to stumble
and a rock that makes them
fall,

and the one who trusts in him
will never be put to
shame."e

10 Brothers, my heart's desire and prayer to God for the Israelites is that they may be saved. 2For I can testify about them that they are zealous for God, but their zeal is not based on knowledge. 3Since they did not know the righteousness that comes from God and sought to establish their own, they did not submit to God's righteousness. 4Christ is the end of the law so that there may be righteousness for everyone who believes.

5Moses describes in this way the righteousness that is by the law: "The man who does these things will live by them."f 6But the righteousness that is by faith says: "Do not say in your heart, 'Who will ascend into heaven?'g" (that is, to bring Christ down) 7"or 'Who will descend into the deep?'h" (that is, to bring Christ up from the dead). 8But what does it say? "The word is near you; it is in your mouth and in your heart,"i that is, the word of faith we are proclaiming: 9That if you confess with your mouth, "Jesus is Lord," and believe in your heart that God raised him from the dead, you will be saved. 10For it is with your heart that you believe and are justified, and it is with your mouth that you confess and are saved. 11As the Scripture says, "Anyone who trusts in him will never be put to shame."j 12For there is no difference between Jew and Gentile—the same Lord is Lord of all and richly blesses all who call on him, 13for, "Everyone who calls on the name of the Lord will be saved."k

14How, then, can they call on the one they have not believed in? And how can they believe in the one of whom they have not heard? And how can they hear without someone preaching to them? 15And how can

a25 Hosea 2:23   b26 Hosea 1:10   c28 Isaiah 10:22,23   d29 Isaiah 1:9   e33 Isaiah 8:14;
28:16   f5 Lev. 18:5   g6 Deut. 30:12   h7 Deut. 30:13   i8 Deut. 30:14
j11 Isaiah 28:16   k13 Joel 2:32

they preach unless they are sent? As it is written, "How beautiful are the feet of those who bring good news!"[a]

[16]But not all the Israelites accepted the good news. For Isaiah says, "Lord, who has believed our message?"[b] [17]Consequently, faith comes from hearing the message, and the message is heard through the word of Christ. [18]But I ask: Did they not hear? Of course they did:

"Their voice has gone out into all the earth,
their words to the ends of the world."[c]

[19]Again I ask: Did Israel not understand? First, Moses says,

"I will make you envious by those who are not a nation;
I will make you angry by a nation that has no understanding."[d]

[20]And Isaiah boldly says,

"I was found by those who did not seek me;
I revealed myself to those who did not ask for me."[e]

[21]But concerning Israel he says,

"All day long I have held out my hands
to a disobedient and obstinate people."[f]

The Remnant of Israel

11 I ask then: Did God reject his people? By no means! I am an Israelite myself, a descendant of Abraham, from the tribe of Benjamin. [2]God did not reject his people, whom he foreknew. Don't you know what the Scripture says in the passage about Elijah—how he appealed to God against Israel: [3]"Lord, they have killed your prophets and torn down your altars; I am the only one left, and they are trying to kill me"[g]? [4]And what was God's answer to him? "I have reserved for myself seven thousand who have not bowed the knee to Baal."[h] [5]So too, at the present time there is a remnant chosen by grace. [6]And if by grace, then it is no longer by works; if it were, grace would no longer be grace.[i]

[7]What then? What Israel sought so earnestly it did not obtain, but the elect did. The others were hardened, [8]as it is written:

"God gave them a spirit of stupor,
eyes so that they could not see
and ears so that they could not hear,
to this very day."[j]

[9]And David says:

"May their table become a snare and a trap,
a stumbling block and a retribution for them.
[10]May their eyes be darkened so they cannot see,
and their backs be bent forever."[k]

a15 Isaiah 52:7　　b16 Isaiah 53:1　　c18 Psalm 19:4　　d19 Deut. 32:21　　e20 Isaiah 65:1
f21 Isaiah 65:2　　g3 1 Kings 19:10,14　　h4 1 Kings 19:18　　i6 Some manuscripts by grace. But if by works, then it is no longer grace; if it were, work would no longer be work. j8 Deut. 29:4; Isaiah 29:10　　k10 Psalm 69:22,23

LET'S LIVE IT! 　　　　　Romans 10:11–15

A BEAUTIFUL CAREER ➠ List five jobs you think it would be fun to have when you grow up. Tell your mom or dad what is on your list, and explain what you like about each job.

Then read Romans 10:11–15. Does anything in this passage make you think a career as a preacher or missionary would be a good one? Talk with your pastor. What does your pastor like about being a preacher?

Ingrafted Branches

[11]Again I ask: Did they stumble so as to fall beyond recovery? Not at all! Rather, because of their transgression, salvation has come to the Gentiles to make Israel envious. [12]But if their transgression means riches for the world, and their loss means riches for the Gentiles, how much greater riches will their fullness bring!

[13]I am talking to you Gentiles. Inasmuch as I am the apostle to the Gentiles, I make much of my ministry [14]in the hope that I may somehow arouse my own people to envy and save some of them. [15]For if their rejection is the reconciliation of the world, what will their acceptance be but life from the dead? [16]If the part of the dough offered as firstfruits is holy, then the whole batch is holy; if the root is holy, so are the branches.

[17]If some of the branches have been broken off, and you, though a wild olive shoot, have been grafted in among the others and now share in the nourishing sap from the olive root, [18]do not boast over those branches. If you do, consider this: You do not support the root, but the root supports you. [19]You will say then, "Branches were broken off so that I could be grafted in." [20]Granted. But they were broken off because of unbelief, and you stand by faith. Do not be arrogant, but be afraid. [21]For if God did not spare the natural branches, he will not spare you either.

[22]Consider therefore the kindness and sternness of God: sternness to those who fell, but kindness to you, provided that you continue in his kindness. Otherwise, you also will be cut off. [23]And if they do not persist in unbelief, they will be grafted in, for God is able to graft them in again. [24]After all, if you were cut out of an olive tree that is wild by nature, and contrary to nature were grafted into a cultivated olive tree, how much more readily will these, the natural branches, be grafted into their own olive tree!

All Israel Will Be Saved

[25]I do not want you to be ignorant of this mystery, brothers, so that you may not be conceited: Israel has experienced a hardening in part until the full number of the Gentiles has come in. [26]And so all Israel will be saved, as it is written:

"The deliverer will come from
    Zion;
he will turn godlessness away
    from Jacob.
[27]And this is[a] my covenant with
    them
when I take away their sins."[b]

[28]As far as the gospel is concerned, they are enemies on your account;

---

[a]27 Or *will be*   [b]27 Isaiah 59:20,21; 27:9; Jer. 31:33,34

Life in Bible Times

GRAFTING

Farmers often tried to improve their crop by grafting new branches on old trees. They cut off an old branch and carefully tied on a new branch in such a way that it could grow there.

but as far as election is concerned, they are loved on account of the patriarchs, [29]for God's gifts and his call are irrevocable. [30]Just as you who were at one time disobedient to God have now received mercy as a result of their disobedience, [31]so they too have now become disobedient in order that they too may now[a] receive mercy as a result of God's mercy to you. [32]For God has bound all men over to disobedience so that he may have mercy on them all.

Doxology

[33]Oh, the depth of the riches of the
    wisdom and[b] knowledge of
    God!
  How unsearchable his
      judgments,
    and his paths beyond tracing
      out!
[34]"Who has known the mind of the
      Lord?
  Or who has been his
      counselor?"[c]
[35]"Who has ever given to God,
    that God should repay him?"[d]
[36]For from him and through him
      and to him are all things.
  To him be the glory forever!
    Amen.

Living Sacrifices

12 Therefore, I urge you, brothers, in view of God's mercy, to offer your bodies as living sacrifices, holy and pleasing to God—this is your spiritual[e] act of worship. [2]Do not conform any longer to the pattern of this world, but be transformed by the renewing of your mind. Then you will be able to test and approve what God's will is—his good, pleasing and perfect will.

[3]For by the grace given me I say to every one of you: Do not think of yourself more highly than you ought, but rather think of yourself with sober judgment, in accordance with the measure of faith God has given you.

[4]Just as each of us has one body with many members, and these members do not all have the same function, [5]so in Christ we who are many form one body, and each member belongs to all the others. [6]We have different gifts, according to the grace given us. If a man's gift is prophesying, let him use it in proportion to his[f] faith. [7]If it is serving, let him serve; if it is teaching, let him teach; [8]if it is encouraging, let him encourage; if it is contributing to the needs of others, let him give generously; if it is leadership, let him govern diligently; if it is showing mercy, let him do it cheerfully.

Love

[9]Love must be sincere. Hate what is evil; cling to what is good. [10]Be devoted to one another in brotherly love. Honor one another above yourselves. [11]Never be lacking in zeal, but keep your spiritual fervor, serving the Lord. [12]Be joyful in hope, patient in affliction, faithful in prayer. [13]Share with God's people who are in need. Practice hospitality.

[14]Bless those who persecute you; bless and do not curse. [15]Rejoice with those who rejoice; mourn with those who mourn. [16]Live in harmony with one another. Do not be proud, but be willing to associate with people of low position.[g] Do not be conceited.

❓DID YOU KNOW?   12:9

How can we show that we love God?

We show we love God by loving and serving others. Romans 12:9–21 lists many ways we can show love to the people around us.

---

[17]Do not repay anyone evil for evil. Be careful to do what is right in the eyes of everybody. [18]If it is possible, as far as it depends on you, live at

---

a31 Some manuscripts do not have *now*.   b33 Or *riches and the wisdom and the*
c34 Isaiah 40:13   d35 Job 41:11   e1 Or *reasonable*   f6 Or *in agreement with the*
g16 Or *willing to do menial work*

peace with everyone. ¹⁹Do not take revenge, my friends, but leave room for God's wrath, for it is written: "It is mine to avenge; I will repay,"ᵃ says the Lord. ²⁰On the contrary:

"If your enemy is hungry, feed
    him;
  if he is thirsty, give him
    something to drink.
In doing this, you will heap
    burning coals on his
    head."ᵇ

²¹Do not be overcome by evil, but overcome evil with good.

Submission to the Authorities

13 Everyone must submit himself to the governing authorities, for there is no authority except that which God has established. The authorities that exist have been established by God. ²Consequently, he who rebels against the authority is rebelling against what God has instituted, and those who do so will bring judgment on themselves. ³For rulers hold no terror for those who do right, but for those who do wrong. Do you want to be free from fear of the one in authority? Then do what is right and he will commend you. ⁴For he is God's servant to do you good. But if you do wrong, be afraid, for he does not bear the sword for nothing. He is God's servant, an agent of wrath to bring punishment on the wrongdoer. ⁵Therefore, it is necessary to submit to the authorities, not only because of

possible punishment but also because of conscience.

⁶This is also why you pay taxes, for the authorities are God's servants, who give their full time to governing. ⁷Give everyone what you owe him: If you owe taxes, pay taxes; if revenue, then revenue; if respect, then respect; if honor, then honor.

Love, for the Day Is Near

⁸Let no debt remain outstanding, except the continuing debt to love one another, for he who loves his fellowman has fulfilled the law. ⁹The commandments, "Do not commit adultery," "Do not murder," "Do not steal," "Do not covet,"ᶜ and whatever other commandment there may be, are summed up in this one rule: "Love your neighbor as yourself."ᵈ ¹⁰Love does no harm to its neighbor. Therefore love is the fulfillment of the law.

¹¹And do this, understanding the present time. The hour has come for you to wake up from your slumber, because our salvation is nearer now than when we first believed. ¹²The night is nearly over; the day is almost here. So let us put aside the deeds of darkness and put on the armor of light. ¹³Let us behave decently, as in the daytime, not in orgies and drunkenness, not in sexual immorality and debauchery, not in dissension and jealousy. ¹⁴Rather, clothe yourselves with the Lord Jesus Christ, and do not think about how to gratify the desires of the sinful nature.ᵉ

ᵃ19 Deut. 32:35   ᵇ20 Prov. 25:21,22   ᶜ9 Exodus 20:13-15,17; Deut. 5:17-19,21   ᵈ9 Lev. 19:18   ᵉ14 Or the flesh

---

▌ET'S LIVE IT!   Romans 13:1–7

DON'T BREAK THE LAW ➥ Read Romans 13:1–7. This passage tells us that God gave governments the right to pass laws and punish people who break the law.

What is the most important reason Christians have for obeying the law? Write a one-page essay on why Christians should obey all laws. See if your church newsletter or the church page in your local newspaper will print your essay.

The Weak and the Strong

14 Accept him whose faith is weak, without passing judgment on disputable matters. ²One man's faith allows him to eat everything, but another man, whose faith is weak, eats only vegetables. ³The man who eats everything must not look down on him who does not, and the man who does not eat everything must not condemn the man who does, for God has accepted him. ⁴Who are you to judge someone else's servant? To his own master he stands or falls. And he will stand, for the Lord is able to make him stand.

⁵One man considers one day more sacred than another; another man considers every day alike. Each one should be fully convinced in his own mind. ⁶He who regards one day as special, does so to the Lord. He who eats meat, eats to the Lord, for he gives thanks to God; and he who abstains, does so to the Lord and gives thanks to God. ⁷For none of us lives to himself alone and none of us dies to himself alone. ⁸If we live, we live to the Lord; and if we die, we die to the Lord. So, whether we live or die, we belong to the Lord.

⁹For this very reason, Christ died and returned to life so that he might be the Lord of both the dead and the living. ¹⁰You, then, why do you judge your brother? Or why do you look down on your brother? For we will all stand before God's judgment seat. ¹¹It is written:

"'As surely as I live,' says the Lord,
'every knee will bow before me;
every tongue will confess to God.'"ᵃ

¹²So then, each of us will give an account of himself to God.

¹³Therefore let us stop passing judgment on one another. Instead, make up your mind not to put any stumbling block or obstacle in your brother's way. ¹⁴As one who is in the Lord Jesus, I am fully convinced that no foodᵇ is unclean in itself. But if anyone regards something as unclean, then for him it is unclean. ¹⁵If your brother is distressed because of what you eat, you are no longer acting in love. Do not by your eating destroy your brother for whom Christ died. ¹⁶Do not allow what you consider good to be spoken of as evil. ¹⁷For the kingdom of God is not a matter of eating and drinking, but of righteousness, peace and joy in the Holy Spirit, ¹⁸because anyone who serves Christ in this way is pleasing to God and approved by men.

¹⁹Let us therefore make every effort to do what leads to peace and to mutual edification. ²⁰Do not destroy the work of God for the sake of food. All food is clean, but it is wrong for a man to eat anything that causes someone else to stumble. ²¹It is better not to eat meat or drink wine or to do anything else that will cause your brother to fall.

²²So whatever you believe about these things keep between yourself and God. Blessed is the man who does not condemn himself by what he approves. ²³But the man who has doubts is condemned if he eats, because his eating is not from faith; and everything that does not come from faith is sin.

15 We who are strong ought to bear with the failings of the weak and not to please ourselves. ²Each of us should please his neighbor for his good, to build him up. ³For even Christ did not please himself but, as it is written: "The insults of those who insult you have fallen on me."ᶜ ⁴For everything that was written in the past was written to teach us, so that through endurance and the encouragement of the Scriptures we might have hope.

⁵May the God who gives endurance and encouragement give you a spirit of unity among yourselves as you follow Christ Jesus, ⁶so that with one heart and mouth you may glorify the

---

ᵃ11 Isaiah 45:23   ᵇ14 Or *that nothing*   ᶜ3 Psalm 69:9

God and Father of our Lord Jesus Christ.

7Accept one another, then, just as Christ accepted you, in order to bring praise to God. 8For I tell you that Christ has become a servant of the Jews*a* on behalf of God's truth, to confirm the promises made to the patriarchs 9so that the Gentiles may glorify God for his mercy, as it is written:

"Therefore I will praise you
    among the Gentiles;
  I will sing hymns to your
    name."*b*

10Again, it says,

"Rejoice, O Gentiles, with his
  people."*c*

11And again,

"Praise the Lord, all you Gentiles,
  and sing praises to him, all you
    peoples."*d*

12And again, Isaiah says,

"The Root of Jesse will spring up,
  one who will arise to rule over
    the nations;
  the Gentiles will hope in him."*e*

13May the God of hope fill you with all joy and peace as you trust in him, so that you may overflow with hope by the power of the Holy Spirit.

Paul the Minister to the Gentiles

14I myself am convinced, my brothers, that you yourselves are full of goodness, complete in knowledge and competent to instruct one another. 15I have written you quite boldly on some points, as if to remind you of them again, because of the grace God gave me 16to be a minister of Christ Jesus to the Gentiles with the priestly duty of proclaiming the gospel of God, so that the Gentiles might become an offering acceptable to God, sanctified by the Holy Spirit.

17Therefore I glory in Christ Jesus in my service to God. 18I will not venture to speak of anything except what Christ has accomplished through me in leading the Gentiles to obey God by what I have said and done— 19by the power of signs and miracles, through the power of the Spirit. So from Jerusalem all the way around to Illyricum, I have fully proclaimed the gospel of Christ. 20It has always been my ambition to preach the gospel where Christ was not known, so that I would not be building on someone else's foundation. 21Rather, as it is written:

"Those who were not told about
  him will see,
  and those who have not heard
    will understand."*f*

22This is why I have often been hindered from coming to you.

Paul's Plan to Visit Rome

23But now that there is no more place for me to work in these regions, and since I have been longing for many years to see you, 24I plan to do so when I go to Spain. I hope to visit you while passing through and to have you assist me on my journey there, after I have enjoyed your company for a while. 25Now, however, I am on my way to Jerusalem in the service of the saints there. 26For Macedonia and Achaia were pleased to make a contribution for the poor among the saints in Jerusalem. 27They were pleased to do it, and indeed they owe it to them. For if the Gentiles have shared in the Jews' spiritual blessings, they owe it to the Jews to share with them their material blessings. 28So after I have completed this task and have made sure that they have received this fruit, I will go to Spain and visit you on the way. 29I know that when I come to you, I will come in the full measure of the blessing of Christ.

30I urge you, brothers, by our Lord Jesus Christ and by the love of the Spirit, to join me in my struggle by

a8 Greek *circumcision*   *b9* 2 Samuel 22:50; Psalm 18:49   *c10* Deut. 32:43
d11 Psalm 117:1   *e12* Isaiah 11:10   *f21* Isaiah 52:15

praying to God for me. [31]Pray that I may be rescued from the unbelievers in Judea and that my service in Jerusalem may be acceptable to the saints there, [32]so that by God's will I may come to you with joy and together with you be refreshed. [33]The God of peace be with you all. Amen.

Personal Greetings

16 I commend to you our sister Phoebe, a servant[a] of the church in Cenchrea. [2]I ask you to receive her in the Lord in a way worthy of the saints and to give her any help she may need from you, for she has been a great help to many people, including me.

[3]Greet Priscilla[b] and Aquila, my fellow workers in Christ Jesus. [4]They risked their lives for me. Not only I but all the churches of the Gentiles are grateful to them.

[5]Greet also the church that meets at their house.

Greet my dear friend Epenetus, who was the first convert to Christ in the province of Asia.

[6]Greet Mary, who worked very hard for you.

[7]Greet Andronicus and Junias, my relatives who have been in prison with me. They are outstanding among the apostles, and they were in Christ before I was.

[8]Greet Ampliatus, whom I love in the Lord.

[9]Greet Urbanus, our fellow worker in Christ, and my dear friend Stachys.

[10]Greet Apelles, tested and approved in Christ.

Greet those who belong to the household of Aristobulus.

[11]Greet Herodion, my relative.

Greet those in the household of Narcissus who are in the Lord.

[12]Greet Tryphena and Tryphosa, those women who work hard in the Lord.

Greet my dear friend Persis, another woman who has worked very hard in the Lord.

[13]Greet Rufus, chosen in the Lord, and his mother, who has been a mother to me, too.

[14]Greet Asyncritus, Phlegon, Hermes, Patrobas, Hermas and the brothers with them.

[15]Greet Philologus, Julia, Nereus and his sister, and Olympas and all the saints with them.

[16]Greet one another with a holy kiss.

All the churches of Christ send greetings.

[17]I urge you, brothers, to watch out for those who cause divisions and put obstacles in your way that are contrary to the teaching you have learned. Keep away from them. [18]For such people are not serving our Lord Christ, but their own appetites. By smooth talk and flattery they deceive the minds of naive people. [19]Everyone has heard about your obedience, so I am full of joy over you; but I want you to be wise about what is good, and innocent about what is evil.

?DID YOU KNOW?   16:1,17

Why does Paul call others in the church his brothers and sisters?

Christians are God's family. From the very beginning of the church, Christians called each other brother and sister to show how close they felt to each other.

[20]The God of peace will soon crush Satan under your feet.

The grace of our Lord Jesus be with you.

[21]Timothy, my fellow worker, sends his greetings to you, as do Lucius, Jason and Sosipater, my relatives.

[22]I, Tertius, who wrote down this letter, greet you in the Lord.

[23]Gaius, whose hospitality I and

---

a1 Or *deaconess*   b3 Greek *Prisca*, a variant of *Priscilla*

the whole church here enjoy, sends you his greetings.

Erastus, who is the city's director of public works, and our brother Quartus send you their greetings.[a]

[25]Now to him who is able to establish you by my gospel and the proclamation of Jesus Christ, according to the revelation of the mystery hidden for long ages past, [26]but now revealed and made known through the prophetic writings by the command of the eternal God, so that all nations might believe and obey him— [27]to the only wise God be glory forever through Jesus Christ! Amen.

---

[a]23 Some manuscripts *their greetings.* [24]*May the grace of our Lord Jesus Christ be with all of you. Amen.*

1 CORINTHIANS

WHO WROTE THIS BOOK?

Paul.

WHY WAS THIS BOOK WRITTEN?

Paul wrote 1 Corinthians to help the Corinthians solve problems in their church.

FOR WHOM WAS THIS BOOK WRITTEN?

This book is a letter that Paul sent to Christians in Corinth.

WHEN WAS THIS BOOK WRITTEN?

This book was written about A.D. 57 from the city of Ephesus.

WHAT ARE SOME IMPORTANT TEACHINGS IN THIS BOOK?

Believers must stop sinning.	1 Corinthians 6:9–11
Each of us is important.	1 Corinthians 12:14–31
What love is really like.	1 Corinthians 13:1–13
Jesus is alive.	1 Corinthians 15:3–8
We will be resurrected too.	1 Corinthians 15:35–58

1 Paul, called to be an apostle of Christ Jesus by the will of God, and our brother Sosthenes,

²To the church of God in Corinth, to those sanctified in Christ Jesus and called to be holy, together with all those everywhere who call on the name of our Lord Jesus Christ—their Lord and ours:

³Grace and peace to you from God our Father and the Lord Jesus Christ.

Thanksgiving

⁴I always thank God for you because of his grace given you in Christ Jesus. ⁵For in him you have been enriched in every way—in all your speaking and in all your knowledge— ⁶because our testimony about Christ was confirmed in you. ⁷Therefore you do not lack any spiritual gift as you eagerly wait for our Lord Jesus Christ to be revealed. ⁸He will keep you strong to the end, so that you will be blameless on the day of our Lord Jesus Christ. ⁹God, who has called you into fellowship with his Son Jesus Christ our Lord, is faithful.

Divisions in the Church

¹⁰I appeal to you, brothers, in the name of our Lord Jesus Christ, that all of you agree with one another so that there may be no divisions among you and that you may be perfectly united in mind and thought. ¹¹My brothers, some from Chloe's household have informed me that there are quarrels among you. ¹²What I mean is this: One of you says, "I follow Paul"; another, "I follow Apollos"; another, "I follow Cephas[a]"; still another, "I follow Christ."

¹³Is Christ divided? Was Paul crucified for you? Were you baptized into[b] the name of Paul? ¹⁴I am thankful that I did not baptize any of you except Crispus and Gaius, ¹⁵so no one can say that you were baptized into my name. ¹⁶(Yes, I also baptized the household of Stephanas; beyond that, I don't remember if I baptized anyone else.) ¹⁷For Christ did not send me to baptize, but to preach the gospel—not with words of human wisdom, lest the cross of Christ be emptied of its power.

Christ the Wisdom and Power of God

¹⁸For the message of the cross is foolishness to those who are perishing, but to us who are being saved it is the power of God. ¹⁹For it is written:

"I will destroy the wisdom of the
     wise;
the intelligence of the
     intelligent I will
     frustrate."[c]

²⁰Where is the wise man? Where is the scholar? Where is the philosopher of this age? Has not God made foolish the wisdom of the world? ²¹For since in the wisdom of God the world

a12 That is, Peter   b13 Or in; also in verse 15   c19 Isaiah 29:14

▌ET'S LIVE IT!   1 Corinthians 1:10–12

WHAT CHURCH DO YOU GO TO? ➠ How many different churches can you name? Here's a start: Baptist, Methodist. Can you name at least three more?

Read 1 Corinthians 1:10–12. When people in the early church formed different groups they quarreled about which group was best. That can happen today too, but you can be proud of your church without thinking you are better than other Christians.

Find out how your denomination or church group started. Find out what is special about your church.

through its wisdom did not know him, God was pleased through the foolishness of what was preached to save those who believe. 22Jews demand miraculous signs and Greeks look for wisdom, 23but we preach Christ crucified: a stumbling block to Jews and foolishness to Gentiles, 24but to those whom God has called, both Jews and Greeks, Christ the power of God and the wisdom of God. 25For the foolishness of God is wiser than man's wisdom, and the weakness of God is stronger than man's strength.

26Brothers, think of what you were when you were called. Not many of you were wise by human standards; not many were influential; not many were of noble birth. 27But God chose the foolish things of the world to shame the wise; God chose the weak things of the world to shame the strong. 28He chose the lowly things of this world and the despised things —and the things that are not—to nullify the things that are, 29so that no one may boast before him. 30It is because of him that you are in Christ Jesus, who has become for us wisdom from God—that is, our righteousness, holiness and redemption. 31Therefore, as it is written: "Let him who boasts boast in the Lord." a

2 When I came to you, brothers, I did not come with eloquence or superior wisdom as I proclaimed to you the testimony about God. b 2For I resolved to know nothing while I was with you except Jesus Christ and him crucified. 3I came to you in weakness and fear, and with much trembling. 4My message and my preaching were not with wise and persuasive words, but with a demonstration of the Spirit's power, 5so that your faith might not rest on men's wisdom, but on God's power.

Wisdom From the Spirit

6We do, however, speak a message of wisdom among the mature, but not the wisdom of this age or of the rulers of this age, who are coming to nothing. 7No, we speak of God's secret wisdom, a wisdom that has been hidden and that God destined for our glory before time began. 8None of the rulers of this age understood it, for if they had, they would not have crucified the Lord of glory. 9However, as it is written:

"No eye has seen,
    no ear has heard,
  no mind has conceived
    what God has prepared for
      those who love him"c—

10but God has revealed it to us by his Spirit.

The Spirit searches all things, even the deep things of God. 11For who among men knows the thoughts of a man except the man's spirit within him? In the same way no one knows the thoughts of God except the Spirit of God. 12We have not received the spirit of the world but the Spirit who is from God, that we may understand what God has freely given us. 13This is what we speak, not in words taught us by human wisdom but in words taught by the Spirit, expressing spiritual truths in spiritual words.d 14The man without the Spirit does not accept the things that come from the Spirit of God, for they are foolishness to him, and he cannot understand them, because they are spiritually discerned. 15The spiritual man makes judgments about all things, but he himself is not subject to any man's judgment:

16"For who has known the mind of
    the Lord
  that he may instruct him?"e

But we have the mind of Christ.

On Divisions in the Church

3 Brothers, I could not address you as spiritual but as worldly— mere infants in Christ. 2I gave you milk, not solid food, for you were not

---

a31 Jer. 9:24   b1 Some manuscripts *as I proclaimed to you God's mystery*   c9 Isaiah 64:4
d13 Or *Spirit, interpreting spiritual truths to spiritual men*   e16 Isaiah 40:13

yet ready for it. Indeed, you are still not ready. ³You are still worldly. For since there is jealousy and quarreling among you, are you not worldly? Are you not acting like mere men? ⁴For when one says, "I follow Paul," and another, "I follow Apollos," are you not mere men?

❓DID YOU KNOW?   2:13

How can we know anything about God?

We cannot see God or hear him. We only know about God through the Bible. Here Paul says that the Holy Spirit gave us the words of the Bible.

---

⁵What, after all, is Apollos? And what is Paul? Only servants, through whom you came to believe—as the Lord has assigned to each his task. ⁶I planted the seed, Apollos watered it, but God made it grow. ⁷So neither he who plants nor he who waters is anything, but only God, who makes things grow. ⁸The man who plants and the man who waters have one purpose, and each will be rewarded according to his own labor. ⁹For we are God's fellow workers; you are God's field, God's building.

¹⁰By the grace God has given me, I laid a foundation as an expert builder, and someone else is building on it. But each one should be careful how he builds. ¹¹For no one can lay any foundation other than the one already laid, which is Jesus Christ. ¹²If any man builds on this foundation using gold, silver, costly stones, wood, hay or straw, ¹³his work will be shown for what it is, because the Day will bring it to light. It will be revealed with fire, and the fire will test the quality of each man's work. ¹⁴If what he has built survives, he will receive his reward. ¹⁵If it is burned up, he will suffer loss; he himself will be saved, but only as one escaping through the flames.

¹⁶Don't you know that you yourselves are God's temple and that God's Spirit lives in you? ¹⁷If anyone destroys God's temple, God will destroy him; for God's temple is sacred, and you are that temple.

¹⁸Do not deceive yourselves. If any one of you thinks he is wise by the standards of this age, he should become a "fool" so that he may become wise. ¹⁹For the wisdom of this world is foolishness in God's sight. As it is written: "He catches the wise in their craftiness"ᵃ; ²⁰and again, "The Lord knows that the thoughts of the wise are futile."ᵇ ²¹So then, no more boasting about men! All things are yours, ²²whether Paul or Apollos or Ce-

ᵃ19 Job 5:13   ᵇ20 Psalm 94:11

Life in Bible Times

LAYING FOUNDATIONS

Buildings in New Testament times were put up on sturdy stone foundations. Expert builders made sure the foundation rested on solid rock. Only buildings with strong foundations could withstand rough weather or earthquakes.

About the New Testament Books

THE GOSPELS

The first four books of the New Testament tell the story of Jesus, how he was born, how he lived, how he died and rose again.

MATTHEW
MARK
LUKE
JOHN

HISTORY

The only book of history in the New Testament tells us how the church began and what happened to some of the people who made up that early church.

ACTS

LETTERS

These books were actual letters, written mostly by Paul. They gave instructions on how to live as a Christian should.

ROMANS
1, 2 CORINTHIANS
GALATIANS
EPHESIANS
PHILIPPIANS
COLOSSIANS
1, 2 THESSALONIANS
1, 2 TIMOTHY
TITUS
PHILEMON
HEBREWS
JAMES
1, 2 PETER
1, 2, 3 JOHN
JUDE

PROPHECY

The only New Testament book of prophecy covers John's vision of what will happen at the end of the world.

REVELATION

Love

PASGE

F O R ♥ K I D S

If I can speak beautifully and can sing like an angel, but don't love others, I sound like a child banging on a piano or a screeching radio.

If I'm very smart, almost a genius, if I can figure out the hardest math problems and understand sentence diagrams, but don't love others, I am nothing.

If I give all my toys away to poor kids and even give up my clothes and my home, but don't love others, what good is it?

Love will stand in line and wait its turn.
Love looks for the good in others.
Love doesn't always want what others have, and it doesn't brag about what it does have.
Love is polite, even when the other person is rude.
Love doesn't always have to be first.
Love doesn't get angry over the small things, and it doesn't remember one reason after another to be hurt.
Love isn't happy when someone else fails but is happy with the truth.
Love will always protect others, especially those who are often picked on or teased.
Love always believes the best about others and is steady and true.

Love never gives up. Preaching will stop someday. So will speeches. Knowledge will come to an end. Today we only know part of what there is to know. We can preach and speak only with a small part of understanding, but when perfection comes then what is imperfect will go away.

I am now young, and so I talk and think and speak like a child. When I become an adult I will put childish ways behind me. Now we see only a poor reflection, like in a mirror; then we will see face to face. Now I only know part of what there is to know; then I will know fully and will be fully known.

Only three things really matter in life:
Faith, Hope and Love.
But the greatest of these is LOVE.

phas[a] or the world or life or death or the present or the future—all are yours, 23and you are of Christ, and Christ is of God.

Apostles of Christ

4 So then, men ought to regard us as servants of Christ and as those entrusted with the secret things of God. 2Now it is required that those who have been given a trust must prove faithful. 3I care very little if I am judged by you or by any human court; indeed, I do not even judge myself. 4My conscience is clear, but that does not make me innocent. It is the Lord who judges me. 5Therefore judge nothing before the appointed time; wait till the Lord comes. He will bring to light what is hidden in darkness and will expose the motives of men's hearts. At that time each will receive his praise from God.

6Now, brothers, I have applied these things to myself and Apollos for your benefit, so that you may learn from us the meaning of the saying, "Do not go beyond what is written." Then you will not take pride in one man over against another. 7For who makes you different from anyone else? What do you have that you did not receive? And if you did receive it, why do you boast as though you did not?

8Already you have all you want! Already you have become rich! You have become kings—and that without us! How I wish that you really had become kings so that we might be kings with you! 9For it seems to me that God has put us apostles on display at the end of the procession, like men condemned to die in the arena. We have been made a spectacle to the whole universe, to angels as well as to men. 10We are fools for Christ, but you are so wise in Christ! We are weak, but you are strong! You are honored, we are dishonored! 11To this very hour we go hungry and thirsty, we are in rags, we are brutally treat-

ed, we are homeless. 12We work hard with our own hands. When we are cursed, we bless; when we are persecuted, we endure it; 13when we are slandered, we answer kindly. Up to this moment we have become the scum of the earth, the refuse of the world.

14I am not writing this to shame you, but to warn you, as my dear children. 15Even though you have ten thousand guardians in Christ, you do not have many fathers, for in Christ Jesus I became your father through the gospel. 16Therefore I urge you to imitate me. 17For this reason I am sending to you Timothy, my son whom I love, who is faithful in the Lord. He will remind you of my way of life in Christ Jesus, which agrees with what I teach everywhere in every church.

18Some of you have become arrogant, as if I were not coming to you. 19But I will come to you very soon, if the Lord is willing, and then I will find out not only how these arrogant people are talking, but what power they have. 20For the kingdom of God is not a matter of talk but of power. 21What do you prefer? Shall I come to you with a whip, or in love and with a gentle spirit?

Expel the Immoral Brother!

5 It is actually reported that there is sexual immorality among you, and of a kind that does not occur even among pagans: A man has his father's wife. 2And you are proud! Shouldn't you rather have been filled with grief and have put out of your fellowship the man who did this? 3Even though I am not physically present, I am with you in spirit. And I have already passed judgment on the one who did this, just as if I were present. 4When you are assembled in the name of our Lord Jesus and I am with you in spirit, and the power of our Lord Jesus is present, 5hand this man over to Satan, so that the sinful nature[b] may be destroyed and his

---

a22 That is, Peter   b5 Or *that his body*; or *that the flesh*

spirit saved on the day of the Lord.

6Your boasting is not good. Don't you know that a little yeast works through the whole batch of dough? 7Get rid of the old yeast that you may be a new batch without yeast—as you really are. For Christ, our Passover lamb, has been sacrificed. 8Therefore let us keep the Festival, not with the old yeast, the yeast of malice and wickedness, but with bread without yeast, the bread of sincerity and truth.

9I have written you in my letter not to associate with sexually immoral people— 10not at all meaning the people of this world who are immoral, or the greedy and swindlers, or idolaters. In that case you would have to leave this world. 11But now I am writing you that you must not associate with anyone who calls himself a brother but is sexually immoral or greedy, an idolater or a slanderer, a drunkard or a swindler. With such a man do not even eat.

12What business is it of mine to judge those outside the church? Are you not to judge those inside? 13God will judge those outside. "Expel the wicked man from among you."*a*

Lawsuits Among Believers

6 If any of you has a dispute with another, dare he take it before the ungodly for judgment instead of before the saints? 2Do you not know that the saints will judge the world? And if you are to judge the world, are you not competent to judge trivial cases? 3Do you not know that we will judge angels? How much more the things of this life! 4Therefore, if you have disputes about such matters, appoint as judges even men of little account in the church!*b* 5I say this to shame you. Is it possible that there is nobody among you wise enough to judge a dispute between believers? 6But instead, one brother goes to law against another—and this in front of unbelievers!

7The very fact that you have lawsuits among you means you have been completely defeated already. Why not rather be wronged? Why not rather be cheated? 8Instead, you yourselves cheat and do wrong, and you do this to your brothers.

9Do you not know that the wicked will not inherit the kingdom of God? Do not be deceived: Neither the sexually immoral nor idolaters nor adulterers nor male prostitutes nor homosexual offenders 10nor thieves nor the greedy nor drunkards nor slanderers nor swindlers will inherit the kingdom of God. 11And that is what some of you were. But you were washed, you were sanctified, you were justified in the name of the Lord Jesus Christ and by the Spirit of our God.

Sexual Immorality

12"Everything is permissible for me"—but not everything is beneficial. "Everything is permissible for me"—but I will not be mastered by anything. 13"Food for the stomach and the stomach for food"—but God will destroy them both. The body is not meant for sexual immorality, but for the Lord, and the Lord for the body. 14By his power God raised the Lord from the dead, and he will raise us also. 15Do you not know that your bodies are members of Christ himself? Shall I then take the members of Christ and unite them with a prostitute? Never! 16Do you not know that he who unites himself with a prostitute is one with her in body? For it is said, "The two will become one flesh."*c* 17But he who unites himself with the Lord is one with him in spirit.

18Flee from sexual immorality. All other sins a man commits are outside his body, but he who sins sexually sins against his own body. 19Do you not know that your body is a temple of the Holy Spirit, who is in you, whom you have received from God?

---

a13 Deut. 17:7; 19:19; 21:21; 22:21,24; 24:7   b4 Or matters, do you appoint as judges men of little account in the church?   c16 Gen. 2:24

You are not your own; ²⁰you were bought at a price. Therefore honor God with your body.

Marriage

7 Now for the matters you wrote about: It is good for a man not to marry.^a ²But since there is so much immorality, each man should have his own wife, and each woman her own husband. ³The husband should fulfill his marital duty to his wife, and likewise the wife to her husband. ⁴The wife's body does not belong to her alone but also to her husband. In the same way, the husband's body does not belong to him alone but also to his wife. ⁵Do not deprive each other except by mutual consent and for a time, so that you may devote yourselves to prayer. Then come together again so that Satan will not tempt you because of your lack of self-control. ⁶I say this as a concession, not as a command. ⁷I wish that all men were as I am. But each man has his own gift from God; one has this gift, another has that.

⁸Now to the unmarried and the widows I say: It is good for them to stay unmarried, as I am. ⁹But if they cannot control themselves, they should marry, for it is better to marry than to burn with passion.

¹⁰To the married I give this command (not I, but the Lord): A wife must not separate from her husband. ¹¹But if she does, she must remain unmarried or else be reconciled to her husband. And a husband must not divorce his wife.

¹²To the rest I say this (I, not the Lord): If any brother has a wife who is not a believer and she is willing to live with him, he must not divorce her. ¹³And if a woman has a husband who is not a believer and he is willing to live with her, she must not divorce him. ¹⁴For the unbelieving husband has been sanctified through his wife, and the unbelieving wife has been sanctified through her believing husband. Otherwise your children would

be unclean, but as it is, they are holy.

¹⁵But if the unbeliever leaves, let him do so. A believing man or woman is not bound in such circumstances; God has called us to live in peace. ¹⁶How do you know, wife, whether you will save your husband? Or, how do you know, husband, whether you will save your wife?

¹⁷Nevertheless, each one should retain the place in life that the Lord assigned to him and to which God has called him. This is the rule I lay down in all the churches. ¹⁸Was a man already circumcised when he was called? He should not become uncircumcised. Was a man uncircumcised when he was called? He should not be circumcised. ¹⁹Circumcision is nothing and uncircumcision is nothing. Keeping God's commands is what counts. ²⁰Each one should remain in the situation which he was in when God called him. ²¹Were you a slave when you were called? Don't let it trouble you—although if you can gain your freedom, do so. ²²For he who was a slave when he was called by the Lord is the Lord's freedman; similarly, he who was a free man when he was called is Christ's slave. ²³You were bought at a price; do not become slaves of men. ²⁴Brothers, each man, as responsible to God, should remain in the situation God called him to.

²⁵Now about virgins: I have no command from the Lord, but I give a judgment as one who by the Lord's mercy is trustworthy. ²⁶Because of the present crisis, I think that it is good for you to remain as you are. ²⁷Are you married? Do not seek a divorce. Are you unmarried? Do not look for a wife. ²⁸But if you do marry, you have not sinned; and if a virgin marries, she has not sinned. But those who marry will face many troubles in this life, and I want to spare you this.

²⁹What I mean, brothers, is that the time is short. From now on those

---

^a1 Or "It is good for a man not to have sexual relations with a woman."

who have wives should live as if they had none; [30]those who mourn, as if they did not; those who are happy, as if they were not; those who buy something, as if it were not theirs to keep; [31]those who use the things of the world, as if not engrossed in them. For this world in its present form is passing away.

[32]I would like you to be free from concern. An unmarried man is concerned about the Lord's affairs—how he can please the Lord. [33]But a married man is concerned about the affairs of this world—how he can please his wife— [34]and his interests are divided. An unmarried woman or virgin is concerned about the Lord's affairs: Her aim is to be devoted to the Lord in both body and spirit. But a married woman is concerned about the affairs of this world—how she can please her husband. [35]I am saying this for your own good, not to restrict you, but that you may live in a right way in undivided devotion to the Lord.

[36]If anyone thinks he is acting improperly toward the virgin he is engaged to, and if she is getting along in years and he feels he ought to marry, he should do as he wants. He is not sinning. They should get married. [37]But the man who has settled the matter in his own mind, who is under no compulsion but has control over his own will, and who has made up his mind not to marry the virgin— this man also does the right thing. [38]So then, he who marries the virgin does right, but he who does not marry her does even better. [a]

[39]A woman is bound to her husband as long as he lives. But if her husband dies, she is free to marry anyone she wishes, but he must belong to the Lord. [40]In my judgment, she is happier if she stays as she is—and I think that I too have the Spirit of God.

Food Sacrificed to Idols

8 Now about food sacrificed to idols: We know that we all possess knowledge. [b] Knowledge puffs up, but love builds up. [2]The man who thinks he knows something does not yet know as he ought to know. [3]But the man who loves God is known by God.

[4]So then, about eating food sacrificed to idols: We know that an idol is nothing at all in the world and that there is no God but one. [5]For even if there are so-called gods, whether in heaven or on earth (as indeed there are many "gods" and many "lords"), [6]yet for us there is but one God, the Father, from whom all things came and for whom we live; and there is but one Lord, Jesus Christ, through whom all things came and through whom we live.

[7]But not everyone knows this. Some people are still so accustomed to idols that when they eat such food they think of it as having been sacrificed to an idol, and since their conscience is weak, it is defiled. [8]But food does not bring us near to God; we are no worse if we do not eat, and no better if we do.

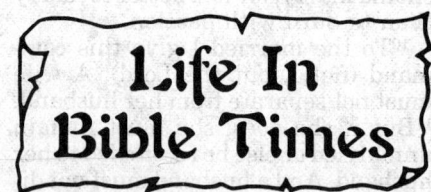

TEMPLE MEAT MARKETS

The meat of animals sacrificed to pagan gods was sold in markets that were part of pagan temples. Most city people in New Testament times bought their meat at these markets.

---

[a]36-38 Or [36]If anyone thinks he is not treating his daughter properly, and if she is getting along in years, and he feels she ought to marry, he should do as he wants. He is not sinning. He should let her get married. [37]But the man who has settled the matter in his own mind, who is under no compulsion but has control over his own will, and who has made up his mind to keep the virgin unmarried—this man also does the right thing. [38]So then, he who gives his virgin in marriage does right, but he who does not give her in marriage does even better.   *[b]1 Or "We all possess knowledge," as you say*

9Be careful, however, that the exercise of your freedom does not become a stumbling block to the weak. 10For if anyone with a weak conscience sees you who have this knowledge eating in an idol's temple, won't he be emboldened to eat what has been sacrificed to idols? 11So this weak brother, for whom Christ died, is destroyed by your knowledge. 12When you sin against your brothers in this way and wound their weak conscience, you sin against Christ. 13Therefore, if what I eat causes my brother to fall into sin, I will never eat meat again, so that I will not cause him to fall.

The Rights of an Apostle

9 Am I not free? Am I not an apostle? Have I not seen Jesus our Lord? Are you not the result of my work in the Lord? 2Even though I may not be an apostle to others, surely I am to you! For you are the seal of my apostleship in the Lord.

3This is my defense to those who sit in judgment on me. 4Don't we have the right to food and drink? 5Don't we have the right to take a believing wife along with us, as do the other apostles and the Lord's brothers and Cephasa? 6Or is it only I and Barnabas who must work for a living?

7Who serves as a soldier at his own expense? Who plants a vineyard and does not eat of its grapes? Who tends a flock and does not drink of the milk? 8Do I say this merely from a human point of view? Doesn't the Law say the same thing? 9For it is written in the Law of Moses: "Do not muzzle an ox while it is treading out the grain."b Is it about oxen that God is concerned? 10Surely he says this for us, doesn't he? Yes, this was written for us, because when the plowman plows and the thresher threshes, they ought to do so in the hope of sharing in the harvest. 11If we have sown spiritual seed among you, is it too much if we reap a material harvest from you? 12If others have this

right of support from you, shouldn't we have it all the more?

But we did not use this right. On the contrary, we put up with anything rather than hinder the gospel of Christ. 13Don't you know that those who work in the temple get their food from the temple, and those who serve at the altar share in what is offered on the altar? 14In the same way, the Lord has commanded that those who preach the gospel should receive their living from the gospel.

15But I have not used any of these rights. And I am not writing this in the hope that you will do such things for me. I would rather die than have anyone deprive me of this boast. 16Yet when I preach the gospel, I cannot boast, for I am compelled to preach. Woe to me if I do not preach the gospel! 17If I preach voluntarily, I have a reward; if not voluntarily, I am simply discharging the trust committed to me. 18What then is my reward? Just this: that in preaching the gospel I may offer it free of charge, and so not make use of my rights in preaching it.

19Though I am free and belong to no man, I make myself a slave to everyone, to win as many as possible. 20To the Jews I became like a Jew, to win the Jews. To those under the law I became like one under the law (though I myself am not under the law), so as to win those under the law. 21To those not having the law I became like one not having the law (though I am not free from God's law but am under Christ's law), so as to win those not having the law. 22To the weak I became weak, to win the weak. I have become all things to all men so that by all possible means I might save some. 23I do all this for the sake of the gospel, that I may share in its blessings.

24Do you not know that in a race all the runners run, but only one gets the prize? Run in such a way as to get the prize. 25Everyone who competes in the games goes into strict training.

a5 That is, Peter   b9 Deut. 25:4

They do it to get a crown that will not last; but we do it to get a crown that will last forever. 26Therefore I do not run like a man running aimlessly; I do not fight like a man beating the air. 27No, I beat my body and make it my slave so that after I have preached to others, I myself will not be disqualified for the prize.

Warnings From Israel's History

10 For I do not want you to be ignorant of the fact, brothers, that our forefathers were all under the cloud and that they all passed through the sea. 2They were all baptized into Moses in the cloud and in the sea. 3They all ate the same spiritual food 4and drank the same spiritual drink; for they drank from the spiritual rock that accompanied them, and that rock was Christ. 5Nevertheless, God was not pleased with most of them; their bodies were scattered over the desert.

6Now these things occurred as examples*a* to keep us from setting our hearts on evil things as they did. 7Do not be idolaters, as some of them were; as it is written: "The people sat down to eat and drink and got up to indulge in pagan revelry."*b* 8We should not commit sexual immorality, as some of them did—and in one day twenty-three thousand of them died. 9We should not test the Lord, as some of them did—and were killed by snakes. 10And do not grumble, as some of them did—and were killed by the destroying angel.

11These things happened to them as examples and were written down as warnings for us, on whom the fulfillment of the ages has come. 12So, if you think you are standing firm, be careful that you don't fall! 13No temptation has seized you except what is common to man. And God is faithful; he will not let you be tempted beyond what you can bear. But when you are tempted, he will also provide a way out so that you can stand up under it.

Idol Feasts and the Lord's Supper

14Therefore, my dear friends, flee from idolatry. 15I speak to sensible people; judge for yourselves what I say. 16Is not the cup of thanksgiving for which we give thanks a participation in the blood of Christ? And is not the bread that we break a participation in the body of Christ? 17Because there is one loaf, we, who are many, are one body, for we all partake of the one loaf.

18Consider the people of Israel: Do not those who eat the sacrifices participate in the altar? 19Do I mean then that a sacrifice offered to an idol is anything, or that an idol is anything? 20No, but the sacrifices of pagans are offered to demons, not to God, and I do not want you to be par-

a6 Or types; also in verse 11   *b7 Exodus 32:6*

▚ET'S LIVE IT!   1 Corinthians 9:24–27

A SPIRITUAL FITNESS TEST ➠ Take this physical fitness test: 1. Do five push-ups. 2. Do ten sit-ups. 3. Touch your toes ten times. 4. Do three pull-ups. 5. Run around your house outside three times without stopping. Do this every day, and you will probably stay physically fit.

Here's a spiritual fitness plan: 1. Read your Bible and think about what God says. 2. Spend time in prayer every day. 3. Pray for others who need special help. 4. Do at least one loving thing for someone each day. 5. Try to please God in everything you do.

In 1 Corinthians 9:24–27 Paul writes about athletes who trained hard. The athletes didn't just want to be fit. They wanted to win! Use the five spiritual fitness steps to train yourself spiritually.

ticipants with demons. ²¹You cannot drink the cup of the Lord and the cup of demons too; you cannot have a part in both the Lord's table and the table of demons. ²²Are we trying to arouse the Lord's jealousy? Are we stronger than he?

The Believer's Freedom

²³"Everything is permissible"— but not everything is beneficial. "Everything is permissible"—but not everything is constructive. ²⁴Nobody should seek his own good, but the good of others.

ᙎORDS TO REMEMBER

10:24 Nobody should seek his own good, but the good of others.

---

²⁵Eat anything sold in the meat market without raising questions of conscience, ²⁶for, "The earth is the Lord's, and everything in it."^a

²⁷If some unbeliever invites you to a meal and you want to go, eat whatever is put before you without raising questions of conscience. ²⁸But if anyone says to you, "This has been offered in sacrifice," then do not eat it, both for the sake of the man who told you and for conscience' sake^b— ²⁹the other man's conscience, I mean, not yours. For why should my freedom be judged by another's conscience? ³⁰If I take part in the meal with thankfulness, why am I denounced because of something I thank God for?

³¹So whether you eat or drink or whatever you do, do it all for the glory of God. ³²Do not cause anyone to stumble, whether Jews, Greeks or the church of God— ³³even as I try to please everybody in every way. For I am not seeking my own good but the good of many, so that they may be

11 saved. ¹Follow my example, as I follow the example of Christ.

Propriety in Worship

²I praise you for remembering me in everything and for holding to the teachings,^c just as I passed them on to you.

³Now I want you to realize that the head of every man is Christ, and the head of the woman is man, and the head of Christ is God. ⁴Every man who prays or prophesies with his head covered dishonors his head. ⁵And every woman who prays or prophesies with her head uncovered dishonors her head—it is just as though her head were shaved. ⁶If a woman does not cover her head, she should have her hair cut off; and if it is a disgrace for a woman to have her hair cut or shaved off, she should cover her head. ⁷A man ought not to cover his head,^d since he is the image and glory of God; but the woman is the glory of man. ⁸For man did not come from woman, but woman from man; ⁹neither was man created for woman, but woman for man. ¹⁰For this reason, and because of the angels, the woman ought to have a sign of authority on her head.

¹¹In the Lord, however, woman is not independent of man, nor is man independent of woman. ¹²For as woman came from man, so also man is born of woman. But everything comes from God. ¹³Judge for yourselves: Is it proper for a woman to pray to God with her head uncovered? ¹⁴Does not the very nature of things teach you that if a man has long hair, it is a disgrace to him, ¹⁵but that if a woman has long hair, it is her glory? For long hair is given to her as a covering. ¹⁶If anyone wants to be contentious about this, we have

---

^a26 Psalm 24:1　　^b28 Some manuscripts *conscience' sake, for "the earth is the Lord's and everything in it"*　　^c2 Or *traditions*　　^d4-7 Or ⁴*Every man who prays or prophesies with long hair dishonors his head.* ⁵*And every woman who prays or prophesies with no covering of hair on her head dishonors her head—she is just like one of the "shorn women."* ⁶*If a woman has no covering, let her be for now with short hair, but since it is a disgrace for a woman to have her hair shorn or shaved, she should grow it again.* ⁷*A man ought not to have long hair*

no other practice—nor do the churches of God.

The Lord's Supper

17In the following directives I have no praise for you, for your meetings do more harm than good. 18In the first place, I hear that when you come together as a church, there are divisions among you, and to some extent I believe it. 19No doubt there have to be differences among you to show which of you have God's approval. 20When you come together, it is not the Lord's Supper you eat, 21for as you eat, each of you goes ahead without waiting for anybody else. One remains hungry, another gets drunk. 22Don't you have homes to eat and drink in? Or do you despise the church of God and humiliate those who have nothing? What shall I say to you? Shall I praise you for this? Certainly not!

23For I received from the Lord what I also passed on to you: The Lord Jesus, on the night he was betrayed, took bread, 24and when he had given thanks, he broke it and said, "This is my body, which is for you; do this in remembrance of me." 25In the same way, after supper he took the cup, saying, "This cup is the new covenant in my blood; do this, whenever you drink it, in remembrance of me."

26For whenever you eat this bread and drink this cup, you proclaim the Lord's death until he comes.

27Therefore, whoever eats the bread or drinks the cup of the Lord in an unworthy manner will be guilty of sinning against the body and blood of the Lord. 28A man ought to examine himself before he eats of the bread and drinks of the cup. 29For anyone who eats and drinks without recognizing the body of the Lord eats and drinks judgment on himself. 30That is why many among you are weak and sick, and a number of you have fallen asleep. 31But if we judged ourselves, we would not come under judgment. 32When we are judged by the Lord, we are being disciplined so that we will not be condemned with the world.

33So then, my brothers, when you come together to eat, wait for each other. 34If anyone is hungry, he should eat at home, so that when you meet together it may not result in judgment.

And when I come I will give further directions.

Spiritual Gifts

12 Now about spiritual gifts, brothers, I do not want you to be ignorant. 2You know that when you were pagans, somehow or other you were influenced and led astray to

---

Life in Bible Times

WOMEN'S VEILS

All respectable Hebrew women wore veils over their faces when they went out in public. Paul here is saying that women should wear such veils when they worshiped. Men then worshiped with their heads uncovered, women with their heads covered. Some churches still follow these rules today.

mute idols. ³Therefore I tell you that no one who is speaking by the Spirit of God says, "Jesus be cursed," and no one can say, "Jesus is Lord," except by the Holy Spirit.

⁴There are different kinds of gifts, but the same Spirit. ⁵There are different kinds of service, but the same Lord. ⁶There are different kinds of working, but the same God works all of them in all men.

⁷Now to each one the manifestation of the Spirit is given for the common good. ⁸To one there is given through the Spirit the message of wisdom, to another the message of knowledge by means of the same Spirit, ⁹to another faith by the same Spirit, to another gifts of healing by that one Spirit, ¹⁰to another miraculous powers, to another prophecy, to another distinguishing between spirits, to another speaking in different kinds of tongues,ᵃ and to still another the interpretation of tongues.ᵃ ¹¹All these are the work of one and the same Spirit, and he gives them to each one, just as he determines.

❓DID YOU KNOW?   **12:1**

What are spiritual gifts?

Spiritual gifts are special abilities the Holy Spirit gives to Christians. Spiritual gifts let us help other people become stronger Christians. There are many different kinds of spiritual gifts.

One Body, Many Parts

¹²The body is a unit, though it is made up of many parts; and though all its parts are many, they form one body. So it is with Christ. ¹³For we were all baptized byᵇ one Spirit into one body—whether Jews or Greeks, slave or free—and we were all given the one Spirit to drink.

¹⁴Now the body is not made up of one part but of many. ¹⁵If the foot should say, "Because I am not a hand, I do not belong to the body," it would not for that reason cease to be part of the body. ¹⁶And if the ear should say, "Because I am not an eye, I do not belong to the body," it would not for that reason cease to be part of the body. ¹⁷If the whole body were an eye, where would the sense of hearing be? If the whole body were an ear, where would the sense of smell be? ¹⁸But in fact God has arranged the parts in the body, every one of them, just as he wanted them to be. ¹⁹If they were all one part, where would the body be? ²⁰As it is, there are many parts, but one body.

²¹The eye cannot say to the hand, "I don't need you!" And the head cannot say to the feet, "I don't need you!" ²²On the contrary, those parts of the body that seem to be weaker are indispensable, ²³and the parts that we think are less honorable we treat with special honor. And the parts that are unpresentable are treated with special modesty, ²⁴while our presentable parts need no special treatment. But God has combined the members of the body and has given greater honor to the parts that lacked it, ²⁵so that there should be no division in the body, but that its parts should have equal concern for each other. ²⁶If one part suffers, every part suffers with it; if one part is honored, every part rejoices with it.

²⁷Now you are the body of Christ, and each one of you is a part of it. ²⁸And in the church God has appointed first of all apostles, second prophets, third teachers, then workers of miracles, also those having gifts of healing, those able to help others, those with gifts of administration, and those speaking in different kinds of tongues. ²⁹Are all apostles? Are all prophets? Are all teachers? Do all work miracles? ³⁰Do all have gifts of healing? Do all speak in tonguesᶜ? Do all interpret? ³¹But eagerly desireᵈ the greater gifts.

ᵃ10 Or *languages*; also in verse 28   ᵇ13 Or *with*; or *in*   ᶜ30 Or *other languages*   ᵈ31 Or *But you are eagerly desiring*

Love

And now I will show you the most excellent way.

13 If I speak in the tongues[a] of men and of angels, but have not love, I am only a resounding gong or a clanging cymbal. [2]If I have the gift of prophecy and can fathom all mysteries and all knowledge, and if I have a faith that can move mountains, but have not love, I am nothing. [3]If I give all I possess to the poor and surrender my body to the flames,[b] but have not love, I gain nothing.

[4]Love is patient, love is kind. It does not envy, it does not boast, it is not proud. [5]It is not rude, it is not self-seeking, it is not easily angered, it keeps no record of wrongs. [6]Love does not delight in evil but rejoices with the truth. [7]It always protects, always trusts, always hopes, always perseveres.

[8]Love never fails. But where there are prophecies, they will cease; where there are tongues, they will be stilled; where there is knowledge, it will pass away. [9]For we know in part and we prophesy in part, [10]but when perfection comes, the imperfect disappears. [11]When I was a child, I talked like a child, I thought like a child, I reasoned like a child. When I became a man, I put childish ways behind me. [12]Now we see but a poor reflection as in a mirror; then we shall see face to face. Now I know in part; then I shall know fully, even as I am fully known.

[13]And now these three remain: faith, hope and love. But the greatest of these is love.

Gifts of Prophecy and Tongues

14 Follow the way of love and eagerly desire spiritual gifts, especially the gift of prophecy. [2]For anyone who speaks in a tongue[c] does not speak to men but to God. Indeed, no one understands him; he utters mysteries with his spirit.[d] [3]But everyone who prophesies speaks to men for their strengthening, encouragement and comfort. [4]He who speaks in a tongue edifies himself, but he who prophesies edifies the church. [5]I would like every one of you to speak in tongues,[e] but I would rather have you prophesy. He who prophesies is greater than one who speaks in tongues,[e] unless he interprets, so that the church may be edified.

[6]Now, brothers, if I come to you and speak in tongues, what good will I be to you, unless I bring you some revelation or knowledge or prophecy or word of instruction? [7]Even in the case of lifeless things that make sounds, such as the flute or harp, how will anyone know what tune is being played unless there is a distinction in the notes? [8]Again, if the trumpet does not sound a clear call, who will get ready for battle? [9]So it is with you. Unless you speak intelligible words with your tongue, how will anyone know what you are saying? You will just be speaking into the air. [10]Un-

---

[a]1 Or *languages*   [b]3 Some early manuscripts *body that I may boast*   [c]2 Or *another language*; also in verses 4, 13, 14, 19, 26 and 27   [d]2 Or *by the Spirit*   [e]5 Or *other languages*; also in verses 6, 18, 22, 23 and 39

▚ET'S LIVE IT!   1 Corinthians 13:4–7

LOVE IS ➡ Love is the main thing God expects of us as Christians. He says we should love him and others. Read 1 Corinthians 13:4–7. This passage explains something of how a loving person will treat others.

Write on a different 3x5 card each thing these verses say Christian love is. At mealtime, when your whole family is together, draw one of the cards. Have each person tell about a time when someone in the family showed this kind of love to him or her.

doubtedly there are all sorts of languages in the world, yet none of them is without meaning. [11]If then I do not grasp the meaning of what someone is saying, I am a foreigner to the speaker, and he is a foreigner to me. [12]So it is with you. Since you are eager to have spiritual gifts, try to excel in gifts that build up the church.

[13]For this reason anyone who speaks in a tongue should pray that he may interpret what he says. [14]For if I pray in a tongue, my spirit prays, but my mind is unfruitful. [15]So what shall I do? I will pray with my spirit, but I will also pray with my mind; I will sing with my spirit, but I will also sing with my mind. [16]If you are praising God with your spirit, how can one who finds himself among those who do not understand[a] say "Amen" to your thanksgiving, since he does not know what you are saying? [17]You may be giving thanks well enough, but the other man is not edified.

[18]I thank God that I speak in tongues more than all of you. [19]But in the church I would rather speak five intelligible words to instruct others than ten thousand words in a tongue.

[20]Brothers, stop thinking like children. In regard to evil be infants, but in your thinking be adults. [21]In the Law it is written:

"Through men of strange tongues
    and through the lips of
        foreigners
I will speak to this people,
    but even then they will not
        listen to me,"[b]
says the Lord.

[22]Tongues, then, are a sign, not for believers but for unbelievers; prophecy, however, is for believers, not for unbelievers. [23]So if the whole church comes together and everyone speaks in tongues, and some who do not understand[c] or some unbelievers come in, will they not say that you are out of your mind? [24]But if an unbeliever or someone who does not understand[d] comes in while everybody is prophesying, he will be convinced by all that he is a sinner and will be judged by all, [25]and the secrets of his heart will be laid bare. So he will fall down and worship God, exclaiming, "God is really among you!"

?DID YOU KNOW?   14:23

What is speaking in tongues?

Speaking in tongues is a spiritual gift that let early Christians speak in unknown languages. Paul had this gift. But Paul said that it is better for people with this spiritual gift to use ordinary talk in church, so everyone can understand what they are saying.

Orderly Worship

[26]What then shall we say, brothers? When you come together, everyone has a hymn, or a word of instruction, a revelation, a tongue or an interpretation. All of these must be done for the strengthening of the church. [27]If anyone speaks in a tongue, two—or at the most three —should speak, one at a time, and someone must interpret. [28]If there is no interpreter, the speaker should keep quiet in the church and speak to himself and God.

[29]Two or three prophets should speak, and the others should weigh carefully what is said. [30]And if a revelation comes to someone who is sitting down, the first speaker should stop. [31]For you can all prophesy in turn so that everyone may be instructed and encouraged. [32]The spirits of prophets are subject to the control of prophets. [33]For God is not a God of disorder but of peace.

As in all the congregations of the saints, [34]women should remain silent

---

[a]16 Or *among the inquirers* inquirer   [b]21 Isaiah 28:11,12   [c]23 Or *some inquirers*   [d]24 Or *or some*

in the churches. They are not allowed to speak, but must be in submission, as the Law says. ³⁵If they want to inquire about something, they should ask their own husbands at home; for it is disgraceful for a woman to speak in the church.

³⁶Did the word of God originate with you? Or are you the only people it has reached? ³⁷If anybody thinks he is a prophet or spiritually gifted, let him acknowledge that what I am writing to you is the Lord's command. ³⁸If he ignores this, he himself will be ignored.^a

³⁹Therefore, my brothers, be eager to prophesy, and do not forbid speaking in tongues. ⁴⁰But everything should be done in a fitting and orderly way.

The Resurrection of Christ

15 Now, brothers, I want to remind you of the gospel I preached to you, which you received and on which you have taken your stand. ²By this gospel you are saved, if you hold firmly to the word I preached to you. Otherwise, you have believed in vain.

³For what I received I passed on to you as of first importance^b: that Christ died for our sins according to the Scriptures, ⁴that he was buried, that he was raised on the third day according to the Scriptures, ⁵and that he appeared to Peter,^c and then to the Twelve. ⁶After that, he appeared to more than five hundred of the brothers at the same time, most of whom are still living, though some have fallen asleep. ⁷Then he appeared to James, then to all the apostles, ⁸and last of all he appeared to me also, as to one abnormally born.

⁹For I am the least of the apostles and do not even deserve to be called an apostle, because I persecuted the church of God. ¹⁰But by the grace of God I am what I am, and his grace to me was not without effect. No, I worked harder than all of them—yet not I, but the grace of God that was with me. ¹¹Whether, then, it was I or they, this is what we preach, and this is what you believed.

The Resurrection of the Dead

¹²But if it is preached that Christ has been raised from the dead, how can some of you say that there is no resurrection of the dead? ¹³If there is no resurrection of the dead, then not even Christ has been raised. ¹⁴And if Christ has not been raised, our preaching is useless and so is your faith. ¹⁵More than that, we are then found to be false witnesses about God, for we have testified about God that he raised Christ from the dead. But he did not raise him if in fact the dead are not raised. ¹⁶For if the dead are not raised, then Christ has not been raised either. ¹⁷And if Christ has not been raised, your faith is futile; you are still in your sins. ¹⁸Then those also who have fallen asleep in Christ are lost. ¹⁹If only for this life we have hope in Christ, we are to be pitied more than all men.

²⁰But Christ has indeed been raised from the dead, the firstfruits of those who have fallen asleep. ²¹For since death came through a man, the resurrection of the dead comes also through a man. ²²For as in Adam all die, so in Christ all will be made alive. ²³But each in his own turn: Christ, the firstfruits; then, when he comes, those who belong to him. ²⁴Then the end will come, when he hands over the kingdom to God the Father after he has destroyed all dominion, authority and power. ²⁵For he must reign until he has put all his enemies under his feet. ²⁶The last enemy to be destroyed is death. ²⁷For he "has put everything under his feet."^d Now when it says that "everything" has been put under him, it is clear that this does not include God himself, who put everything under Christ. ²⁸When he has done this, then the Son himself will be made subject

---

^a38 Some manuscripts *If he is ignorant of this, let him be ignorant*　　^b3 Or *you at the first*
^c5 Greek *Cephas*　　^d27 Psalm 8:6

to him who put everything under him, so that God may be all in all.

²⁹Now if there is no resurrection, what will those do who are baptized for the dead? If the dead are not raised at all, why are people baptized for them? ³⁰And as for us, why do we endanger ourselves every hour? ³¹I die every day—I mean that, brothers—just as surely as I glory over you in Christ Jesus our Lord. ³²If I fought wild beasts in Ephesus for merely human reasons, what have I gained? If the dead are not raised,

"Let us eat and drink,
    for tomorrow we die."ᵃ

³³Do not be misled: "Bad company corrupts good character." ³⁴Come back to your senses as you ought, and stop sinning; for there are some who are ignorant of God—I say this to your shame.

The Resurrection Body

³⁵But someone may ask, "How are the dead raised? With what kind of body will they come?" ³⁶How foolish! What you sow does not come to life unless it dies. ³⁷When you sow, you do not plant the body that will be, but just a seed, perhaps of wheat or of something else. ³⁸But God gives it a body as he has determined, and to each kind of seed he gives its own body. ³⁹All flesh is not the same: Men have one kind of flesh, animals have another, birds another and fish another. ⁴⁰There are also heavenly bodies and there are earthly bodies; but the splendor of the heavenly bodies is one kind, and the splendor of the earthly bodies is another. ⁴¹The sun has one kind of splendor, the moon another and the stars another; and star differs from star in splendor.

⁴²So will it be with the resurrection of the dead. The body that is sown is perishable, it is raised imperishable; ⁴³it is sown in dishonor, it is raised in glory; it is sown in weakness, it is raised in power; ⁴⁴it is sown a natural body, it is raised a spiritual body.

If there is a natural body, there is also a spiritual body. ⁴⁵So it is written: "The first man Adam became a living being"ᵇ; the last Adam, a life-giving spirit. ⁴⁶The spiritual did not come first, but the natural, and after that the spiritual. ⁴⁷The first man was of the dust of the earth, the second man from heaven. ⁴⁸As was the earthly man, so are those who are of the earth; and as is the man from heaven, so also are those who are of heaven. ⁴⁹And just as we have borne the likeness of the earthly man, so shall weᶜ bear the likeness of the man from heaven.

⁵⁰I declare to you, brothers, that flesh and blood cannot inherit the kingdom of God, nor does the perishable inherit the imperishable. ⁵¹Listen, I tell you a mystery: We will not all sleep, but we will all be changed— ⁵²in a flash, in the twinkling of an eye, at the last trumpet. For the trumpet will sound, the dead will be raised imperishable, and we will be changed. ⁵³For the perishable must clothe itself with the imperishable, and the mortal with immortality. ⁵⁴When the perishable has been clothed with the imperishable, and the mortal with immortality, then the saying that is written will come true: "Death has been swallowed up in victory."ᵈ

⁵⁵"Where, O death, is your victory?
    Where, O death, is your
        sting?"ᵉ

⁵⁶The sting of death is sin, and the power of sin is the law. ⁵⁷But thanks be to God! He gives us the victory through our Lord Jesus Christ.

⁵⁸Therefore, my dear brothers, stand firm. Let nothing move you. Always give yourselves fully to the work of the Lord, because you know that your labor in the Lord is not in vain.

ᵃ32 Isaiah 22:13   ᵇ45 Gen. 2:7   ᶜ49 Some early manuscripts *so let us*   ᵈ54 Isaiah 25:8
ᵉ55 Hosea 13:14

The Collection for God's People

16 Now about the collection for God's people: Do what I told the Galatian churches to do. [2]On the first day of every week, each one of you should set aside a sum of money in keeping with his income, saving it up, so that when I come no collections will have to be made. [3]Then, when I arrive, I will give letters of introduction to the men you approve and send them with your gift to Jerusalem. [4]If it seems advisable for me to go also, they will accompany me.

WORDS TO REMEMBER

15:57 Thanks be to God! He gives us the victory through our Lord Jesus Christ.

Personal Requests

[5]After I go through Macedonia, I will come to you—for I will be going through Macedonia. [6]Perhaps I will stay with you awhile, or even spend the winter, so that you can help me on my journey, wherever I go. [7]I do not want to see you now and make only a passing visit; I hope to spend some time with you, if the Lord permits. [8]But I will stay on at Ephesus until Pentecost, [9]because a great door

[a]19 Greek *Prisca*, a variant of *Priscilla*

for effective work has opened to me, and there are many who oppose me.

[10]If Timothy comes, see to it that he has nothing to fear while he is with you, for he is carrying on the work of the Lord, just as I am. [11]No one, then, should refuse to accept him. Send him on his way in peace so that he may return to me. I am expecting him along with the brothers.

[12]Now about our brother Apollos: I strongly urged him to go to you with the brothers. He was quite unwilling to go now, but he will go when he has the opportunity.

[13]Be on your guard; stand firm in the faith; be men of courage; be strong. [14]Do everything in love.

[15]You know that the household of Stephanas were the first converts in Achaia, and they have devoted themselves to the service of the saints. I urge you, brothers, [16]to submit to such as these and to everyone who joins in the work, and labors at it. [17]I was glad when Stephanas, Fortunatus and Achaicus arrived, because they have supplied what was lacking from you. [18]For they refreshed my spirit and yours also. Such men deserve recognition.

Final Greetings

[19]The churches in the province of Asia send you greetings. Aquila and Priscilla[a] greet you warmly in the

---

Life in Bible Times

A HOUSE CHURCH

The homes of wealthy Christians like Aquila and Priscilla (see 1 Corinthians 16:19) were large, with a garden-like area in the middle. Christians went to homes like these to worship instead of to church buildings.

Lord, and so does the church that meets at their house. ²⁰All the brothers here send you greetings. Greet one another with a holy kiss.

²¹I, Paul, write this greeting in my own hand.

²²If anyone does not love the Lord —a curse be on him. Come, O Lord*ᵃ*! ²³The grace of the Lord Jesus be with you.

²⁴My love to all of you in Christ Jesus. Amen.*ᵇ*

ᵃ22 In Aramaic the expression *Come, O Lord* is *Marana tha.*
ᵇ24 Some manuscripts do not have *Amen.*

2 CORINTHIANS

WHO WROTE THIS BOOK?	Paul.
WHY WAS THIS BOOK WRITTEN?	The book of 2 Corinthians lets the Corinthians know that Paul loves them even if their church does have many problems.
FOR WHOM WAS THIS BOOK WRITTEN?	This book is a letter that was sent to Christians in Corinth.
WHEN WAS THIS BOOK WRITTEN?	This book was written about A.D. 58 from Macedonia.

WHAT ARE SOME IMPORTANT TEACHINGS IN THIS BOOK?

Our prayers help leaders.	2 Corinthians 1:8–11
Forgive those who repent.	2 Corinthians 2:5–11
We are God's ministers.	2 Corinthians 5:11–21
Give generously.	2 Corinthians 9:6–15
Help for the weak.	2 Corinthians 12:7–10

1 Paul, an apostle of Christ Jesus by the will of God, and Timothy our brother,

To the church of God in Corinth, together with all the saints throughout Achaia:

²Grace and peace to you from God our Father and the Lord Jesus Christ.

CORINTH

Corinth was an important port city lying on a narrow strip of land between two seas. Cargoes were landed at Corinth and carried overland to the other sea.

The God of All Comfort

³Praise be to the God and Father of our Lord Jesus Christ, the Father of compassion and the God of all comfort, ⁴who comforts us in all our troubles, so that we can comfort those in any trouble with the comfort we ourselves have received from God. ⁵For just as the sufferings of Christ flow over into our lives, so also through Christ our comfort overflows. ⁶If we are distressed, it is for your comfort and salvation; if we are comforted, it is for your comfort, which produces in you patient endurance of the same sufferings we suffer. ⁷And our hope for you is firm, because we know that just as you share in our sufferings, so also you share in our comfort.

⁸We do not want you to be uninformed, brothers, about the hardships we suffered in the province of Asia. We were under great pressure, far beyond our ability to endure, so that we despaired even of life. ⁹Indeed, in our hearts we felt the sentence of death. But this happened that we might not rely on ourselves but on God, who raises the dead. ¹⁰He has delivered us from such a deadly peril, and he will deliver us. On him we have set our hope that he will continue to deliver us, ¹¹as you help us by your prayers. Then many will give thanks on our*a* behalf for the gracious favor granted us in answer to the prayers of many.

Paul's Change of Plans

¹²Now this is our boast: Our conscience testifies that we have conducted ourselves in the world, and especially in our relations with you, in the holiness and sincerity that are from God. We have done so not according to worldly wisdom but according to God's grace. ¹³For we do not write you anything you cannot read or understand. And I hope that, ¹⁴as you have understood us in part, you will come to understand fully that you can boast of us just as we will boast of you in the day of the Lord Jesus.

a11 Many manuscripts *your*

▍ET'S LIVE IT!   2 Corinthians 1:8–11

HE HAS DELIVERED US, TOO ➠ Read 2 Corinthians 1:8–11. To find out about the "deadly peril" Paul was in, read 2 Corinthians 11:23–29.

Most people have hardships and even feel despair at times. Ask your mom or dad or your grandparents if God has delivered them from any really hard times. Ask them to tell you about what happened.

It is good to know that God, who delivered your mom and dad, will deliver you too.

2 CORINTHIANS 1:15   1410

15Because I was confident of this, I planned to visit you first so that you might benefit twice. 16I planned to visit you on my way to Macedonia and to come back to you from Macedonia, and then to have you send me on my way to Judea. 17When I planned this, did I do it lightly? Or do I make my plans in a worldly manner so that in the same breath I say, "Yes, yes" and "No, no"?

18But as surely as God is faithful, our message to you is not "Yes" and "No." 19For the Son of God, Jesus Christ, who was preached among you by me and Silasa and Timothy, was not "Yes" and "No," but in him it has always been "Yes." 20For no matter how many promises God has made, they are "Yes" in Christ. And so through him the "Amen" is spoken by us to the glory of God. 21Now it is God who makes both us and you stand firm in Christ. He anointed us, 22set his seal of ownership on us, and put his Spirit in our hearts as a deposit, guaranteeing what is to come.

23I call God as my witness that it was in order to spare you that I did not return to Corinth. 24Not that we lord it over your faith, but we work with you for your joy, because it is by faith you stand firm. 1So I made up my mind that I would not make another painful visit to you. 2For if I grieve you, who is left to make me glad but you whom I have grieved? 3I wrote as I did so that when I came I should not be distressed by those who ought to make me rejoice. I had confidence in all of you, that you would all share my joy. 4For I wrote you out of great distress and anguish of heart and with many tears, not to grieve you but to let you know the depth of my love for you.

Forgiveness for the Sinner

5If anyone has caused grief, he has not so much grieved me as he has grieved all of you, to some extent—not to put it too severely. 6The pun-ishment inflicted on him by the majority is sufficient for him. 7Now instead, you ought to forgive and comfort him, so that he will not be overwhelmed by excessive sorrow. 8I urge you, therefore, to reaffirm your love for him. 9The reason I wrote you was to see if you would stand the test and be obedient in everything. 10If you forgive anyone, I also forgive him. And what I have forgiven—if there was anything to forgive—I have forgiven in the sight of Christ for your sake, 11in order that Satan might not outwit us. For we are not unaware of his schemes.

Ministers of the New Covenant

12Now when I went to Troas to preach the gospel of Christ and found that the Lord had opened a door for me, 13I still had no peace of mind, because I did not find my brother Titus there. So I said good-by to them and went on to Macedonia.

14But thanks be to God, who always leads us in triumphal procession in Christ and through us spreads everywhere the fragrance of the knowledge of him. 15For we are to God the aroma of Christ among those who are being saved and those who are perishing. 16To the one we are the smell of death; to the other, the fragrance of life. And who is equal to such a task? 17Unlike so many, we do not peddle the word of God for profit. On the contrary, in Christ we speak before God with sincerity, like men sent from God.

3Are we beginning to commend ourselves again? Or do we need, like some people, letters of recommendation to you or from you? 2You yourselves are our letter, written on our hearts, known and read by everybody. 3You show that you are a letter from Christ, the result of our ministry, written not with ink but with the Spirit of the living God, not on tablets of stone but on tablets of human hearts.

4Such confidence as this is ours

a19 Greek *Silvanus*, a variant of Silas

through Christ before God. ⁵Not that we are competent in ourselves to claim anything for ourselves, but our competence comes from God. ⁶He has made us competent as ministers of a new covenant—not of the letter but of the Spirit; for the letter kills, but the Spirit gives life.

The Glory of the New Covenant

⁷Now if the ministry that brought death, which was engraved in letters on stone, came with glory, so that the Israelites could not look steadily at the face of Moses because of its glory, fading though it was, ⁸will not the ministry of the Spirit be even more glorious? ⁹If the ministry that condemns men is glorious, how much more glorious is the ministry that brings righteousness! ¹⁰For what was glorious has no glory now in comparison with the surpassing glory. ¹¹And if what was fading away came with glory, how much greater is the glory of that which lasts!

¹²Therefore, since we have such a hope, we are very bold. ¹³We are not like Moses, who would put a veil over his face to keep the Israelites from gazing at it while the radiance was fading away. ¹⁴But their minds were made dull, for to this day the same veil remains when the old covenant is read. It has not been removed, because only in Christ is it taken away. ¹⁵Even to this day when Moses is read, a veil covers their hearts. ¹⁶But whenever anyone turns to the Lord, the veil is taken away. ¹⁷Now the Lord is the Spirit, and where the Spirit of the Lord is, there is freedom.

¹⁸And we, who with unveiled faces all reflect^a the Lord's glory, are being transformed into his likeness with ever-increasing glory, which comes from the Lord, who is the Spirit.

WORDS TO REMEMBER

3:18 We . . . are being transformed into his likeness.

Treasures in Jars of Clay

4 Therefore, since through God's mercy we have this ministry, we do not lose heart. ²Rather, we have renounced secret and shameful ways; we do not use deception, nor do we distort the word of God. On the contrary, by setting forth the truth plainly we commend ourselves to every man's conscience in the sight of God. ³And even if our gospel is veiled, it is veiled to those who are perishing. ⁴The god of this age has blinded the minds of unbelievers, so that they cannot see the light of the gospel of the glory of Christ, who is the image of God. ⁵For we do not preach ourselves, but Jesus Christ as Lord, and ourselves as your servants for Jesus' sake. ⁶For God, who said, "Let light shine out of darkness,"^b made his light shine in our hearts to give us the light of the knowledge of the glory of God in the face of Christ.

⁷But we have this treasure in jars of clay to show that this all-surpassing power is from God and not from us. ⁸We are hard pressed on every side, but not crushed; perplexed, but

^a18 Or *contemplate*   ^b6 Gen. 1:3

LET'S LIVE IT!   2 Corinthians 3:1–3

READING GOD'S MAIL ➡ How does God send letters to people today? Read 2 Corinthians 3:1–3 to find out. Christians can be a letter from Christ by doing what is right, by loving others, and by telling others about Jesus.

Think about it . . . what kind of letter are you? What do your friends and relatives see and think about Jesus when they look at you?

not in despair; [9]persecuted, but not abandoned; struck down, but not destroyed. [10]We always carry around in our body the death of Jesus, so that the life of Jesus may also be revealed in our body. [11]For we who are alive are always being given over to death for Jesus' sake, so that his life may be revealed in our mortal body. [12]So then, death is at work in us, but life is at work in you.

Life In Bible Times

TREASURE!

Archaeologists have found treasures of silver in cheap clay pots. Clay pots were common, and thousands were made. But they were sometimes used to store the valuable and the precious.

---

[13]It is written: "I believed; therefore I have spoken."[a] With that same spirit of faith we also believe and therefore speak, [14]because we know that the one who raised the Lord Jesus from the dead will also raise us with Jesus and present us with you in his presence. [15]All this is for your benefit, so that the grace that is reaching more and more people may cause thanksgiving to overflow to the glory of God.

[16]Therefore we do not lose heart. Though outwardly we are wasting away, yet inwardly we are being renewed day by day. [17]For our light and momentary troubles are achieving for us an eternal glory that far outweighs them all. [18]So we fix our eyes not on what is seen, but on what is unseen. For what is seen is temporary, but what is unseen is eternal.

Our Heavenly Dwelling

5 Now we know that if the earthly tent we live in is destroyed, we have a building from God, an eternal house in heaven, not built by human hands. [2]Meanwhile we groan, longing to be clothed with our heavenly dwelling, [3]because when we are clothed, we will not be found naked. [4]For while we are in this tent, we groan and are burdened, because we do not wish to be unclothed but to be clothed with our heavenly dwelling, so that what is mortal may be swallowed up by life. [5]Now it is God who has made us for this very purpose and has given us the Spirit as a deposit, guaranteeing what is to come.

[6]Therefore we are always confident and know that as long as we are at home in the body we are away from the Lord. [7]We live by faith, not by sight. [8]We are confident, I say, and would prefer to be away from the body and at home with the Lord. [9]So we make it our goal to please him, whether we are at home in the body or away from it. [10]For we must all appear before the judgment seat of Christ, that each one may receive what is due him for the things done while in the body, whether good or bad.

The Ministry of Reconciliation

[11]Since, then, we know what it is to fear the Lord, we try to persuade men. What we are is plain to God, and I hope it is also plain to your conscience. [12]We are not trying to commend ourselves to you again, but are giving you an opportunity to take pride in us, so that you can answer those who take pride in what is seen rather than in what is in the heart. [13]If we are out of our mind, it is for the sake of God; if we are in our right mind, it is for you. [14]For Christ's love compels us, because we are convinced that one died for all, and therefore all died. [15]And he died for all, that those who live should no longer live for

themselves but for him who died for them and was raised again.

16So from now on we regard no one from a worldly point of view. Though we once regarded Christ in this way, we do so no longer. 17Therefore, if anyone is in Christ, he is a new creation; the old has gone, the new has come! 18All this is from God, who reconciled us to himself through Christ and gave us the ministry of reconciliation: 19that God was reconciling the world to himself in Christ, not counting men's sins against them. And he has committed to us the message of reconciliation. 20We are therefore Christ's ambassadors, as though God were making his appeal through us. We implore you on Christ's behalf: Be reconciled to God. 21God made him who had no sin to be sin*a* for us, so that in him we might become the righteousness of God.

❓DID YOU KNOW?   5:20

What is reconciliation?

To reconcile means to get together again as friends. Jesus died for our sins so we could get together with God and be his friends. God wants us to tell our friends about Jesus, so they can become God's friends too.

6 As God's fellow workers we urge you not to receive God's grace in vain. 2For he says,

"In the time of my favor I heard
    you,
   and in the day of salvation I
    helped you."*b*

I tell you, now is the time of God's favor, now is the day of salvation.

Paul's Hardships

3We put no stumbling block in anyone's path, so that our ministry will not be discredited. 4Rather, as ser-

vants of God we commend ourselves in every way: in great endurance; in troubles, hardships and distresses; 5in beatings, imprisonments and riots; in hard work, sleepless nights and hunger; 6in purity, understanding, patience and kindness; in the Holy Spirit and in sincere love; 7in truthful speech and in the power of God; with weapons of righteousness in the right hand and in the left; 8through glory and dishonor, bad report and good report; genuine, yet regarded as impostors; 9known, yet regarded as unknown; dying, and yet we live on; beaten, and yet not killed; 10sorrowful, yet always rejoicing; poor, yet making many rich; having nothing, and yet possessing everything.

11We have spoken freely to you, Corinthians, and opened wide our hearts to you. 12We are not withholding our affection from you, but you are withholding yours from us. 13As a fair exchange—I speak as to my children—open wide your hearts also.

Do Not Be Yoked With Unbelievers

14Do not be yoked together with unbelievers. For what do righteousness and wickedness have in common? Or what fellowship can light have with darkness? 15What harmony is there between Christ and Belial*c*? What does a believer have in common with an unbeliever? 16What agreement is there between the temple of God and idols? For we are the temple of the living God. As God has said: "I will live with them and walk among them, and I will be their God, and they will be my people."*d*

17"Therefore come out from them
    and be separate,
                  says the Lord.
   Touch no unclean thing,
    and I will receive you."*e*
18"I will be a Father to you,

---

a21 Or *be a sin offering*   *b2* Isaiah 49:8   *c15* Greek *Beliar*, a variant of *Belial*
d16 Lev. 26:12; Jer. 32:38; Ezek. 37:27   *e17* Isaiah 52:11; Ezek. 20:34,41

and you will be my sons and
daughters,
    says the Lord Almighty."ᵃ

7 Since we have these promises,
dear friends, let us purify ourselves from everything that contami-
nates body and spirit, perfecting holiness out of reverence for God.

Paul's Joy

²Make room for us in your hearts.
We have wronged no one, we have
corrupted no one, we have exploited
no one. ³I do not say this to condemn
you; I have said before that you have
such a place in our hearts that we
would live or die with you. ⁴I have
great confidence in you; I take great
pride in you. I am greatly encouraged; in all our troubles my joy
knows no bounds.

⁵For when we came into Macedonia, this body of ours had no rest, but
we were harassed at every turn—
conflicts on the outside, fears within.
⁶But God, who comforts the downcast, comforted us by the coming of
Titus, ⁷and not only by his coming
but also by the comfort you had given
him. He told us about your longing
for me, your deep sorrow, your ardent
concern for me, so that my joy was
greater than ever.

⁸Even if I caused you sorrow by my
letter, I do not regret it. Though I did

regret it—I see that my letter hurt
you, but only for a little while— ⁹yet
now I am happy, not because you
were made sorry, but because your
sorrow led you to repentance. For you
became sorrowful as God intended
and so were not harmed in any way
by us. ¹⁰Godly sorrow brings repentance that leads to salvation and
leaves no regret, but worldly sorrow
brings death. ¹¹See what this godly
sorrow has produced in you: what
earnestness, what eagerness to clear
yourselves, what indignation, what
alarm, what longing, what concern,
what readiness to see justice done. At
every point you have proved yourselves to be innocent in this matter.
¹²So even though I wrote to you, it
was not on account of the one who did
the wrong or of the injured party, but
rather that before God you could see
for yourselves how devoted to us you
are. ¹³By all this we are encouraged.

In addition to our own encouragement, we were especially delighted to
see how happy Titus was, because his
spirit has been refreshed by all of
you. ¹⁴I had boasted to him about you,
and you have not embarrassed me.
But just as everything we said to you
was true, so our boasting about you to
Titus has proved to be true as well.
¹⁵And his affection for you is all the
greater when he remembers that you
were all obedient, receiving him with

ᵃ18 2 Samuel 7:14; 7:8

Life in Bible Times

SENDING A LETTER

Many New Testament
books were letters that
were sent to churches.
There was no post office.
People wrapped up the
letters carefully, tied them,
and asked travelers to take
them to friends.

fear and trembling. [16]I am glad I can have complete confidence in you.

Generosity Encouraged

8 And now, brothers, we want you to know about the grace that God has given the Macedonian churches. [2]Out of the most severe trial, their overflowing joy and their extreme poverty welled up in rich generosity. [3]For I testify that they gave as much as they were able, and even beyond their ability. Entirely on their own, [4]they urgently pleaded with us for the privilege of sharing in this service to the saints. [5]And they did not do as we expected, but they gave themselves first to the Lord and then to us in keeping with God's will. [6]So we urged Titus, since he had earlier made a beginning, to bring also to completion this act of grace on your part. [7]But just as you excel in everything—in faith, in speech, in knowledge, in complete earnestness and in your love for us[a]—see that you also excel in this grace of giving.

[8]I am not commanding you, but I want to test the sincerity of your love by comparing it with the earnestness of others. [9]For you know the grace of our Lord Jesus Christ, that though he was rich, yet for your sakes he became poor, so that you through his poverty might become rich.

[10]And here is my advice about what is best for you in this matter: Last year you were the first not only to give but also to have the desire to do so. [11]Now finish the work, so that your eager willingness to do it may be matched by your completion of it, according to your means. [12]For if the willingness is there, the gift is acceptable according to what one has, not according to what he does not have.

[13]Our desire is not that others might be relieved while you are hard pressed, but that there might be equality. [14]At the present time your plenty will supply what they need, so that in turn their plenty will supply

? DID YOU KNOW?   8:14

Why do Christians give?

Paul urged Christians to give to help other Christians who were hungry. Christians are not *commanded* to give, but they are to share what they have because of their generous hearts.

what you need. Then there will be equality, [15]as it is written: "He who gathered much did not have too much, and he who gathered little did not have too little."[b]

Titus Sent to Corinth

[16]I thank God, who put into the heart of Titus the same concern I have for you. [17]For Titus not only welcomed our appeal, but he is coming to you with much enthusiasm and on his own initiative. [18]And we are sending along with him the brother who is praised by all the churches for his service to the gospel. [19]What is more, he was chosen by the churches to accompany us as we carry the offering, which we administer in order to honor the Lord himself and to show our eagerness to help. [20]We want to avoid any criticism of the way we administer this liberal gift. [21]For we are taking pains to do what is right, not only in the eyes of the Lord but also in the eyes of men.

[22]In addition, we are sending with them our brother who has often proved to us in many ways that he is zealous, and now even more so because of his great confidence in you. [23]As for Titus, he is my partner and fellow worker among you; as for our brothers, they are representatives of the churches and an honor to Christ. [24]Therefore show these men the proof of your love and the reason for our pride in you, so that the churches can see it.

9 There is no need for me to write to you about this service to the

---

[a]7 Some manuscripts *in our love for you*   [b]15 Exodus 16:18

saints. ²For I know your eagerness to help, and I have been boasting about it to the Macedonians, telling them that since last year you in Achaia were ready to give; and your enthusiasm has stirred most of them to action. ³But I am sending the brothers in order that our boasting about you in this matter should not prove hollow, but that you may be ready, as I said you would be. ⁴For if any Macedonians come with me and find you unprepared, we—not to say anything about you—would be ashamed of having been so confident. ⁵So I thought it necessary to urge the brothers to visit you in advance and finish the arrangements for the generous gift you had promised. Then it will be ready as a generous gift, not as one grudgingly given.

Sowing Generously

⁶Remember this: Whoever sows sparingly will also reap sparingly, and whoever sows generously will also reap generously. ⁷Each man should give what he has decided in his heart to give, not reluctantly or under compulsion, for God loves a cheerful giver. ⁸And God is able to make all grace abound to you, so that in all things at all times, having all that you need, you will abound in every good work. ⁹As it is written:

"He has scattered abroad his gifts
    to the poor;
  his righteousness endures
    forever."ᵃ

¹⁰Now he who supplies seed to the sower and bread for food will also

supply and increase your store of seed and will enlarge the harvest of your righteousness. ¹¹You will be made rich in every way so that you can be generous on every occasion, and through us your generosity will result in thanksgiving to God.

¹²This service that you perform is not only supplying the needs of God's people but is also overflowing in many expressions of thanks to God. ¹³Because of the service by which you have proved yourselves, men will praise God for the obedience that accompanies your confession of the gospel of Christ, and for your generosity in sharing with them and with everyone else. ¹⁴And in their prayers for you their hearts will go out to you, because of the surpassing grace God has given you. ¹⁵Thanks be to God for his indescribable gift!

Paul's Defense of His Ministry

10 By the meekness and gentleness of Christ, I appeal to you—I, Paul, who am "timid" when face to face with you, but "bold" when away! ²I beg you that when I come I may not have to be as bold as I expect to be toward some people who think that we live by the standards of this world. ³For though we live in the world, we do not wage war as the world does. ⁴The weapons we fight with are not the weapons of the world. On the contrary, they have divine power to demolish strongholds. ⁵We demolish arguments and every pretension that sets itself up against the knowledge of God, and we take captive every thought to make it obe-

ᵃ9 Psalm 112:9

ET'S LIVE IT!   2 Corinthians 9:6–11

WHY GIVE? ➡ God wants us to give some of our money to help others. And he wants us to do it cheerfully. He promises, then, to make sure we always have enough. Read 2 Corinthians 9:6–11.

   Giving is something everyone can do. Do you have an allowance or a job for which you get paid? After reading these verses, how much of your allowance can you give cheerfully?

dient to Christ. ⁶And we will be ready to punish every act of disobedience, once your obedience is complete.

⁷You are looking only on the surface of things. ᵃ If anyone is confident that he belongs to Christ, he should consider again that we belong to Christ just as much as he. ⁸For even if I boast somewhat freely about the authority the Lord gave us for building you up rather than pulling you down, I will not be ashamed of it. ⁹I do not want to seem to be trying to frighten you with my letters. ¹⁰For some say, "His letters are weighty and forceful, but in person he is unimpressive and his speaking amounts to nothing." ¹¹Such people should realize that what we are in our letters when we are absent, we will be in our actions when we are present.

¹²We do not dare to classify or compare ourselves with some who commend themselves. When they measure themselves by themselves and compare themselves with themselves, they are not wise. ¹³We, however, will not boast beyond proper limits, but will confine our boasting to the field God has assigned to us, a field that reaches even to you. ¹⁴We are not going too far in our boasting, as would be the case if we had not come to you, for we did get as far as you with the gospel of Christ. ¹⁵Neither do we go beyond our limits by boasting of work done by others.ᵇ Our hope is that, as your faith continues to grow, our area of activity among you will greatly expand, ¹⁶so that we can preach the gospel in the regions beyond you. For we do not want to boast about work already done in another man's territory. ¹⁷But, "Let him who boasts boast in the Lord."ᶜ ¹⁸For it is not the one who commends himself who is approved, but the one whom the Lord commends.

Paul and the False Apostles

11 I hope you will put up with a little of my foolishness; but you are already doing that. ²I am jealous for you with a godly jealousy. I promised you to one husband, to Christ, so that I might present you as a pure virgin to him. ³But I am afraid that just as Eve was deceived by the serpent's cunning, your minds may somehow be led astray from your sincere and pure devotion to Christ. ⁴For if someone comes to you and preaches a Jesus other than the Jesus we preached, or if you receive a different spirit from the one you received, or a different gospel from the one you accepted, you put up with it easily enough. ⁵But I do not think I am in the least inferior to those "super-apostles." ⁶I may not be a trained speaker, but I do have knowledge. We have made this perfectly clear to you in every way.

⁷Was it a sin for me to lower myself in order to elevate you by preaching the gospel of God to you free of charge? ⁸I robbed other churches by receiving support from them so as to serve you. ⁹And when I was with you and needed something, I was not a burden to anyone, for the brothers who came from Macedonia supplied what I needed. I have kept myself from being a burden to you in any way, and will continue to do so. ¹⁰As surely as the truth of Christ is in me, nobody in the regions of Achaia will stop this boasting of mine. ¹¹Why? Because I do not love you? God knows I do! ¹²And I will keep on doing what I am doing in order to cut the ground from under those who want an opportunity to be considered equal with us in the things they boast about.

¹³For such men are false apostles, deceitful workmen, masquerading as apostles of Christ. ¹⁴And no wonder, for Satan himself masquerades as an angel of light. ¹⁵It is not surprising,

---

ᵃ7 Or *Look at the obvious facts*   ᵇ13-15 Or ¹³*We, however, will not boast about things that cannot be measured, but we will boast according to the standard of measurement that the God of measure has assigned us—a measurement that relates even to you.* ¹⁴ .... ¹⁵*Neither do we boast about things that cannot be measured in regard to the work done by others.*   ᶜ17 Jer. 9:24

then, if his servants masquerade as servants of righteousness. Their end will be what their actions deserve.

Paul Boasts About His Sufferings

16I repeat: Let no one take me for a fool. But if you do, then receive me just as you would a fool, so that I may do a little boasting. 17In this self-confident boasting I am not talking as the Lord would, but as a fool. 18Since many are boasting in the way the world does, I too will boast. 19You gladly put up with fools since you are so wise! 20In fact, you even put up with anyone who enslaves you or exploits you or takes advantage of you or pushes himself forward or slaps you in the face. 21To my shame I admit that we were too weak for that!

What anyone else dares to boast about—I am speaking as a fool—I also dare to boast about. 22Are they Hebrews? So am I. Are they Israelites? So am I. Are they Abraham's descendants? So am I. 23Are they servants of Christ? (I am out of my mind to talk like this.) I am more. I have worked much harder, been in prison more frequently, been flogged more severely, and been exposed to death again and again. 24Five times I received from the Jews the forty lashes minus one. 25Three times I was beaten with rods, once I was stoned, three times I was shipwrecked, I spent a night and a day in the open sea, 26I have been constantly on the move. I have been in danger from rivers, in danger from bandits, in danger from my own countrymen, in danger from Gentiles; in danger in the city, in danger in the country, in danger at sea; and in danger from false brothers. 27I have labored and toiled and have often gone without sleep; I have known hunger and thirst and have often gone without food; I have been cold and naked. 28Besides everything else, I face daily the pressure of my concern for all the churches. 29Who is weak, and I do not feel weak? Who is led into sin, and I do not inwardly burn?

30If I must boast, I will boast of the things that show my weakness. 31The God and Father of the Lord Jesus, who is to be praised forever, knows that I am not lying. 32In Damascus the governor under King Aretas had the city of the Damascenes guarded in order to arrest me. 33But I was lowered in a basket from a window in the wall and slipped through his hands.

Paul's Vision and His Thorn

12 I must go on boasting. Although there is nothing to be gained, I will go on to visions and revelations from the Lord. 2I know a man in Christ who fourteen years ago was caught up to the third heaven. Whether it was in the body or out of the body I do not know—God knows. 3And I know that this man—whether in the body or apart from the body I do not know, but God knows— 4was caught up to paradise. He heard inexpressible things, things that man is not permitted to tell. 5I will boast about a man like that, but I will not boast about myself, except about my weaknesses. 6Even if I should choose to boast, I would not be a fool, because I would be speaking the truth. But I refrain, so no one will think more of me than is warranted by what I do or say.

7To keep me from becoming conceited because of these surpassingly great revelations, there was given me a thorn in my flesh, a messenger of Satan, to torment me. 8Three times I pleaded with the Lord to take it away from me. 9But he said to me, "My grace is sufficient for you, for my power is made perfect in weakness." Therefore I will boast all the more gladly about my weaknesses, so that Christ's power may rest on me. 10That is why, for Christ's sake, I delight in weaknesses, in insults, in hardships, in persecutions, in difficulties. For when I am weak, then I am strong.

Paul's Concern for the Corinthians

11I have made a fool of myself, but

you drove me to it. I ought to have been commended by you, for I am not in the least inferior to the "super-apostles," even though I am nothing. [12]The things that mark an apostle —signs, wonders and miracles— were done among you with great perseverance. [13]How were you inferior to the other churches, except that I was never a burden to you? Forgive me this wrong!

[14]Now I am ready to visit you for the third time, and I will not be a burden to you, because what I want is not your possessions but you. After all, children should not have to save up for their parents, but parents for their children. [15]So I will very gladly spend for you everything I have and expend myself as well. If I love you more, will you love me less? [16]Be that as it may, I have not been a burden to you. Yet, crafty fellow that I am, I caught you by trickery! [17]Did I exploit you through any of the men I sent you? [18]I urged Titus to go to you and I sent our brother with him. Titus did not exploit you, did he? Did we not act in the same spirit and follow the same course?

[19]Have you been thinking all along that we have been defending ourselves to you? We have been speaking in the sight of God as those in Christ; and everything we do, dear friends, is for your strengthening. [20]For I am afraid that when I come I may not find you as I want you to be, and you may not find me as you want me to be. I fear that there may be quarreling, jealousy, outbursts of anger, factions, slander, gossip, arrogance and disorder. [21]I am afraid that when I come again my God will humble me before you, and I will be grieved over many who have sinned earlier and have not repented of the impurity, sexual sin and debauchery in which they have indulged.

Final Warnings

13 This will be my third visit to you. "Every matter must be established by the testimony of two or three witnesses."[a] [2]I already gave you a warning when I was with you the second time. I now repeat it while absent: On my return I will not spare those who sinned earlier or any of the others, [3]since you are demanding proof that Christ is speaking through me. He is not weak in dealing with you, but is powerful among you. [4]For to be sure, he was crucified in weakness, yet he lives by God's power. Likewise, we are weak in him, yet by God's power we will live with him to serve you.

[5]Examine yourselves to see whether you are in the faith; test yourselves. Do you not realize that Christ Jesus is in you—unless, of course, you fail the test? [6]And I trust that you will discover that we have not failed the test. [7]Now we pray to God that you will not do anything wrong.

[a]1 Deut. 19:15

▌ET'S LIVE IT!   2 Corinthians 12:7–10

HOW TO BE STRONG ➠ "I can't," ten-year-old Jimmy wailed. "I just can't do it." Jimmy could be talking about: Telling the neighbors he broke their window. Taking a hard test at school. Memorizing the multiplication tables. Going back to school after everyone had laughed at him. Standing up in front of everyone at church to recite a poem he memorized.

If you were to say "I can't do it," what would you probably be talking about?

Read 2 Corinthians 12:7–10. When you feel weak you are more likely to ask God for help. What will happen if Jimmy asks God to help him with the situations listed above?

Not that people will see that we have stood the test but that you will do what is right even though we may seem to have failed. ⁸For we cannot do anything against the truth, but only for the truth. ⁹We are glad whenever we are weak but you are strong; and our prayer is for your perfection. ¹⁰This is why I write these things when I am absent, that when I come I may not have to be harsh in my use of authority—the authority the Lord gave me for building you up, not for tearing you down.

Final Greetings

¹¹Finally, brothers, good-by. Aim for perfection, listen to my appeal, be of one mind, live in peace. And the God of love and peace will be with you.

¹²Greet one another with a holy kiss. ¹³All the saints send their greetings.

¹⁴May the grace of the Lord Jesus Christ, and the love of God, and the fellowship of the Holy Spirit be with you all.

GALATIANS

1 Paul, an apostle—sent not from men nor by man, but by Jesus Christ and God the Father, who raised him from the dead— ²and all the brothers with me,

To the churches in Galatia:

³Grace and peace to you from God our Father and the Lord Jesus Christ, ⁴who gave himself for our sins to rescue us from the present evil age, according to the will of our God and Father, ⁵to whom be glory for ever and ever. Amen.

No Other Gospel

⁶I am astonished that you are so quickly deserting the one who called you by the grace of Christ and are turning to a different gospel— ⁷which is really no gospel at all. Evidently some people are throwing you into confusion and are trying to pervert the gospel of Christ. ⁸But even if we or an angel from heaven should preach a gospel other than the one we preached to you, let him be eternally condemned! ⁹As we have already said, so now I say again: If anybody is preaching to you a gospel other than what you accepted, let him be eternally condemned!

¹⁰Am I now trying to win the approval of men, or of God? Or am I trying to please men? If I were still trying to please men, I would not be a servant of Christ.

❓DID YOU KNOW? 1:7

What is the gospel?

The gospel is the Good News that if we believe in Jesus, God will forgive our sins. Any other belief or religion is not God's Good News.

Paul Called by God

¹¹I want you to know, brothers, that the gospel I preached is not something that man made up. ¹²I did not receive it from any man, nor was I taught it; rather, I received it by revelation from Jesus Christ.

¹³For you have heard of my previous way of life in Judaism, how intensely I persecuted the church of God and tried to destroy it. ¹⁴I was advancing in Judaism beyond many Jews of my own age and was extremely zealous for the traditions of my fathers. ¹⁵But when God, who set me apart from birth*a* and called me by his grace, was pleased ¹⁶to reveal his Son in me so that I might preach him among the Gentiles, I did not consult any man, ¹⁷nor did I go up to Jerusalem to see those who were apostles before I was, but I went immediately into Arabia and later returned to Damascus.

❓DID YOU KNOW? 1:17

How was Paul different from the other apostles?

The other apostles were with Jesus when he was here on earth. Paul became a Christian after Jesus died and was raised again. But the other apostles knew that God had called Paul to work as an apostle.

---

¹⁸Then after three years, I went up to Jerusalem to get acquainted with Peter*b* and stayed with him fifteen days. ¹⁹I saw none of the other apostles—only James, the Lord's brother. ²⁰I assure you before God that what I am writing you is no lie. ²¹Later I went to Syria and Cilicia. ²²I was personally unknown to the churches of Judea that are in Christ. ²³They only heard the report: "The man who formerly persecuted us is now preaching the faith he once tried to destroy." ²⁴And they praised God because of me.

---

*a*15 Or *from my mother's womb*   *b*18 Greek *Cephas*

Paul Accepted by the Apostles

2 Fourteen years later I went up again to Jerusalem, this time with Barnabas. I took Titus along also. ²I went in response to a revelation and set before them the gospel that I preach among the Gentiles. But I did this privately to those who seemed to be leaders, for fear that I was running or had run my race in vain. ³Yet not even Titus, who was with me, was compelled to be circumcised, even though he was a Greek. ⁴This matter arose, because some false brothers had infiltrated our ranks to spy on the freedom we have in Christ Jesus and to make us slaves. ⁵We did not give in to them for a moment, so that the truth of the gospel might remain with you.

⁶As for those who seemed to be important—whatever they were makes no difference to me; God does not judge by external appearance—those men added nothing to my message. ⁷On the contrary, they saw that I had been entrusted with the task of preaching the gospel to the Gentiles,ᵃ just as Peter had been to the Jews.ᵇ ⁸For God, who was at work in the ministry of Peter as an apostle to the Jews, was also at work in my ministry as an apostle to the Gentiles. ⁹James, Peterᶜ and John, those reputed to be pillars, gave me and Barnabas the right hand of fellowship when they recognized the grace given to me. They agreed that we should go to the Gentiles, and they to the Jews. ¹⁰All they asked was that we should continue to remember the poor, the very thing I was eager to do.

Paul Opposes Peter

¹¹When Peter came to Antioch, I opposed him to his face, because he was clearly in the wrong. ¹²Before certain men came from James, he used to eat with the Gentiles. But when they arrived, he began to draw back and separate himself from the Gentiles because he was afraid of those who belonged to the circumcision group. ¹³The other Jews joined him in his hypocrisy, so that by their hypocrisy even Barnabas was led astray.

¹⁴When I saw that they were not acting in line with the truth of the gospel, I said to Peter in front of them all, "You are a Jew, yet you live like a Gentile and not like a Jew. How is it, then, that you force Gentiles to follow Jewish customs?

¹⁵"We who are Jews by birth and not 'Gentile sinners' ¹⁶know that a man is not justified by observing the law, but by faith in Jesus Christ. So we, too, have put our faith in Christ Jesus that we may be justified by faith in Christ and not by observing the law, because by observing the law no one will be justified.

¹⁷"If, while we seek to be justified in Christ, it becomes evident that we ourselves are sinners, does that mean that Christ promotes sin? Absolutely not! ¹⁸If I rebuild what I destroyed, I prove that I am a lawbreaker. ¹⁹For through the law I died to the law so

---

ᵃ7 Greek *uncircumcised*   ᵇ7 Greek *circumcised*; also in verses 8 and 9   ᶜ9 Greek *Cephas*; also in verses 11 and 14

⬛ET'S LIVE IT!   Galatians 2:11–16

STAND UP FOR WHAT IS RIGHT ➡ Many times we want to go along with our friends, even if our friends are doing something that is not right. Do you think it's better to just leave when that happens? Or should we tell our friends what they are doing is wrong?

Read Galatians 2:11–16. What did Paul do when Peter and his Christian friends did wrong? If you follow Paul's example, what will you do when your friends do wrong?

that I might live for God. 20I have been crucified with Christ and I no longer live, but Christ lives in me. The life I live in the body, I live by faith in the Son of God, who loved me and gave himself for me. 21I do not set aside the grace of God, for if righteousness could be gained through the law, Christ died for nothing!"*a*

WORDS TO REMEMBER

2:20 Christ lives in me.

Faith or Observance of the Law

3 You foolish Galatians! Who has bewitched you? Before your very eyes Jesus Christ was clearly portrayed as crucified. 2I would like to learn just one thing from you: Did you receive the Spirit by observing the law, or by believing what you heard? 3Are you so foolish? After beginning with the Spirit, are you now trying to attain your goal by human effort? 4Have you suffered so much for nothing—if it really was for nothing? 5Does God give you his Spirit and work miracles among you because you observe the law, or because you believe what you heard?

? DID YOU KNOW?   3:1

How were the Galatians foolish?

The Galatians thought they could become better Christians by trying harder to be good. Paul told them to just trust God to help them. We can do what is right if we trust God to help us, but not if we try to be good by ourselves.

6Consider Abraham: "He believed God, and it was credited to him as righteousness."*b* 7Understand, then, that those who believe are children of Abraham. 8The Scripture foresaw that God would justify the Gentiles by faith, and announced the gospel in advance to Abraham: "All nations will be blessed through you."*c* 9So those who have faith are blessed along with Abraham, the man of faith.

10All who rely on observing the law are under a curse, for it is written: "Cursed is everyone who does not continue to do everything written in the Book of the Law."*d* 11Clearly no one is justified before God by the law, because, "The righteous will live by faith."*e* 12The law is not based on faith; on the contrary, "The man who does these things will live by them."*f* 13Christ redeemed us from the curse of the law by becoming a curse for us, for it is written: "Cursed is everyone who is hung on a tree."*g* 14He redeemed us in order that the blessing given to Abraham might come to the Gentiles through Christ Jesus, so that by faith we might receive the promise of the Spirit.

The Law and the Promise

15Brothers, let me take an example from everyday life. Just as no one can set aside or add to a human covenant that has been duly established, so it is in this case. 16The promises were spoken to Abraham and to his seed. The Scripture does not say "and to seeds," meaning many people, but "and to your seed,"*h* meaning one person, who is Christ. 17What I mean is this: The law, introduced 430 years later, does not set aside the covenant previously established by God and thus do away with the promise. 18For if the inheritance depends on the law, then it no longer depends on a promise; but God in his grace gave it to Abraham through a promise.

19What, then, was the purpose of the law? It was added because of transgressions until the Seed to whom the promise referred had come.

a21 Some interpreters end the quotation after verse 14.   b6 Gen. 15:6   c8 Gen. 12:3; 18:18; 22:18   d10 Deut. 27:26   e11 Hab. 2:4   f12 Lev. 18:5   g13 Deut. 21:23   h16 Gen. 12:7; 13:15; 24:7

The law was put into effect through angels by a mediator. [20]A mediator, however, does not represent just one party; but God is one.

[21]Is the law, therefore, opposed to the promises of God? Absolutely not! For if a law had been given that could impart life, then righteousness would certainly have come by the law. [22]But the Scripture declares that the whole world is a prisoner of sin, so that what was promised, being given through faith in Jesus Christ, might be given to those who believe.

[23]Before this faith came, we were held prisoners by the law, locked up until faith should be revealed. [24]So the law was put in charge to lead us to Christ[a] that we might be justified by faith. [25]Now that faith has come, we are no longer under the supervision of the law.

❓ DID YOU KNOW?   3:24

Why did God give people his law?

God wanted people to know the difference between right and wrong. The law cannot make anyone good. Instead, it helps people see that they have done wrong, and that they need to trust Jesus to forgive their sins.

Sons of God

[26]You are all sons of God through faith in Christ Jesus, [27]for all of you who were baptized into Christ have clothed yourselves with Christ. [28]There is neither Jew nor Greek, slave nor free, male nor female, for you are all one in Christ Jesus. [29]If you belong to Christ, then you are Abraham's seed, and heirs according to the promise.

4 What I am saying is that as long as the heir is a child, he is no different from a slave, although he

owns the whole estate. [2]He is subject to guardians and trustees until the time set by his father. [3]So also, when we were children, we were in slavery under the basic principles of the world. [4]But when the time had fully come, God sent his Son, born of a woman, born under law, [5]to redeem those under law, that we might receive the full rights of sons. [6]Because you are sons, God sent the Spirit of his Son into our hearts, the Spirit who calls out, "Abba,[b] Father." [7]So you are no longer a slave, but a son; and since you are a son, God has made you also an heir.

Life In Bible Times

GUARDIANS

The boy of a well-to-do Greek family had a guardian. This guardian was a slave, who went everywhere with the boy. The child had to obey the slave, who took orders from the child's father. When the boy was old enough, he became a "son," and no longer had a guardian.

Paul's Concern for the Galatians

[8]Formerly, when you did not know God, you were slaves to those who by nature are not gods. [9]But now that you know God—or rather are known by God—how is it that you are turning back to those weak and miserable principles? Do you wish to be enslaved by them all over again? [10]You are observing special days and months and seasons and years! [11]I fear for you, that somehow I have wasted my efforts on you.

[12]I plead with you, brothers, become like me, for I became like you.

---

a24 Or charge until Christ came   *b6 Aramaic for Father*

You have done me no wrong. [13]As you know, it was because of an illness that I first preached the gospel to you. [14]Even though my illness was a trial to you, you did not treat me with contempt or scorn. Instead, you welcomed me as if I were an angel of God, as if I were Christ Jesus himself. [15]What has happened to all your joy? I can testify that, if you could have done so, you would have torn out your eyes and given them to me. [16]Have I now become your enemy by telling you the truth?

[17]Those people are zealous to win you over, but for no good. What they want is to alienate you from us, so that you may be zealous for them. [18]It is fine to be zealous, provided the purpose is good, and to be so always and not just when I am with you. [19]My dear children, for whom I am again in the pains of childbirth until Christ is formed in you, [20]how I wish I could be with you now and change my tone, because I am perplexed about you!

Hagar and Sarah

[21]Tell me, you who want to be under the law, are you not aware of what the law says? [22]For it is written that Abraham had two sons, one by the slave woman and the other by the free woman. [23]His son by the slave woman was born in the ordinary way; but his son by the free woman was born as the result of a promise.

[24]These things may be taken figuratively, for the women represent two covenants. One covenant is from Mount Sinai and bears children who are to be slaves: This is Hagar. [25]Now Hagar stands for Mount Sinai in Arabia and corresponds to the present city of Jerusalem, because she is in slavery with her children. [26]But the Jerusalem that is above is free, and she is our mother. [27]For it is written:

"Be glad, O barren woman,
  who bears no children;
break forth and cry aloud,
  you who have no labor pains;

because more are the children of
    the desolate woman
  than of her who has a
    husband."[a]

[28]Now you, brothers, like Isaac, are children of promise. [29]At that time the son born in the ordinary way persecuted the son born by the power of the Spirit. It is the same now. [30]But what does the Scripture say? "Get rid of the slave woman and her son, for the slave woman's son will never share in the inheritance with the free woman's son."[b] [31]Therefore, brothers, we are not children of the slave woman, but of the free woman.

Freedom in Christ

5 It is for freedom that Christ has set us free. Stand firm, then, and do not let yourselves be burdened again by a yoke of slavery.

[2]Mark my words! I, Paul, tell you that if you let yourselves be circumcised, Christ will be of no value to you at all. [3]Again I declare to every man who lets himself be circumcised that he is obligated to obey the whole law. [4]You who are trying to be justified by law have been alienated from Christ; you have fallen away from grace. [5]But by faith we eagerly await through the Spirit the righteousness for which we hope. [6]For in Christ Jesus neither circumcision nor uncircumcision has any value. The only thing that counts is faith expressing itself through love.

[7]You were running a good race. Who cut in on you and kept you from obeying the truth? [8]That kind of persuasion does not come from the one who calls you. [9]"A little yeast works through the whole batch of dough." [10]I am confident in the Lord that you will take no other view. The one who is throwing you into confusion will pay the penalty, whoever he may be. [11]Brothers, if I am still preaching circumcision, why am I still being persecuted? In that case the offense of the cross has been abolished. [12]As for

those agitators, I wish they would go the whole way and emasculate themselves!

¹³You, my brothers, were called to be free. But do not use your freedom to indulge the sinful nature*ᵃ*; rather, serve one another in love. ¹⁴The entire law is summed up in a single command: "Love your neighbor as yourself."*ᵇ* ¹⁵If you keep on biting and devouring each other, watch out or you will be destroyed by each other.

? DID YOU KNOW?   5:13

What is Christian freedom?

Christians are not free to do whatever they want. Because God helps us, we are free to do what is right.

Life by the Spirit

¹⁶So I say, live by the Spirit, and you will not gratify the desires of the sinful nature. ¹⁷For the sinful nature desires what is contrary to the Spirit, and the Spirit what is contrary to the sinful nature. They are in conflict with each other, so that you do not do what you want. ¹⁸But if you are led by the Spirit, you are not under law.

¹⁹The acts of the sinful nature are obvious: sexual immorality, impurity and debauchery; ²⁰idolatry and witchcraft; hatred, discord, jealousy, fits of rage, selfish ambition, dissen-

sions, factions ²¹and envy; drunkenness, orgies, and the like. I warn you, as I did before, that those who live like this will not inherit the kingdom of God.

²²But the fruit of the Spirit is love, joy, peace, patience, kindness, goodness, faithfulness, ²³gentleness and self-control. Against such things there is no law. ²⁴Those who belong to Christ Jesus have crucified the sinful nature with its passions and desires. ²⁵Since we live by the Spirit, let us keep in step with the Spirit. ²⁶Let us not become conceited, provoking and envying each other.

Doing Good to All

6 Brothers, if someone is caught in a sin, you who are spiritual should restore him gently. But watch yourself, or you also may be tempted. ²Carry each other's burdens, and in this way you will fulfill the law of Christ. ³If anyone thinks he is something when he is nothing, he deceives himself. ⁴Each one should test his own actions. Then he can take pride in himself, without comparing himself to somebody else, ⁵for each one should carry his own load.

⁶Anyone who receives instruction in the word must share all good things with his instructor.

⁷Do not be deceived: God cannot be mocked. A man reaps what he sows. ⁸The one who sows to please his sinful nature, from that nature*ᶜ* will

ᵃ13 Or the flesh; also in verses 16, 17, 19 and 24 flesh   *ᵇ14 Lev. 19:18*   *ᶜ8 Or his flesh, from the*

◣ET'S LIVE IT!   Galatians 5:22–25

FRUIT ON YOUR TREE ➠ Read Galatians 5:22–25. Then cut fruit shapes from different colors of construction paper. Write a different fruit of the Spirit on each. Make five or six of each fruit.

On a very large sheet of paper, draw a large tree with many branches. Each time you do something that shows love or patience or self-control, or another fruit of the Spirit, tape one of that fruit to your tree. Write what you did to earn the fruit on the back before you tape it up. See how much fruit you can have on your tree at the end of one week.

reap destruction; the one who sows to please the Spirit, from the Spirit will reap eternal life. [9]Let us not become weary in doing good, for at the proper time we will reap a harvest if we do not give up. [10]Therefore, as we have opportunity, let us do good to all people, especially to those who belong to the family of believers.

WORDS TO REMEMBER

6:10 Do good to all people, especially to those who belong to the family of believers.

Not Circumcision but a New Creation

[11]See what large letters I use as I write to you with my own hand!

[12]Those who want to make a good impression outwardly are trying to compel you to be circumcised. The only reason they do this is to avoid being persecuted for the cross of Christ. [13]Not even those who are circumcised obey the law, yet they want you to be circumcised that they may boast about your flesh. [14]May I never boast except in the cross of our Lord Jesus Christ, through which[a] the world has been crucified to me, and I to the world. [15]Neither circumcision nor uncircumcision means anything; what counts is a new creation. [16]Peace and mercy to all who follow this rule, even to the Israel of God.

[17]Finally, let no one cause me trouble, for I bear on my body the marks of Jesus.

[18]The grace of our Lord Jesus Christ be with your spirit, brothers. Amen.

[a]14 Or *whom*

EPHESIANS

1 Paul, an apostle of Christ Jesus by the will of God,

To the saints in Ephesus,*a* the faithful*b* in Christ Jesus:

²Grace and peace to you from God our Father and the Lord Jesus Christ.

Spiritual Blessings in Christ

³Praise be to the God and Father of our Lord Jesus Christ, who has blessed us in the heavenly realms with every spiritual blessing in Christ. ⁴For he chose us in him before the creation of the world to be holy and blameless in his sight. In love ⁵he*c* predestined us to be adopted as his sons through Jesus Christ, in accordance with his pleasure and will— ⁶to the praise of his glorious grace, which he has freely given us in the One he loves. ⁷In him we have redemption through his blood, the forgiveness of sins, in accordance with the riches of God's grace ⁸that he lavished on us with all wisdom and understanding. ⁹And he*d* made known to us the mystery of his will according to his good pleasure, which he purposed in Christ, ¹⁰to be put into effect when the times will have reached their fulfillment—to bring all things in heaven and on earth together under one head, even Christ. ¹¹In him we were also chosen,*e* having been predestined according to the plan of him who works out everything in conformity with the purpose of his will, ¹²in order that we, who were the first to hope in Christ, might be for the praise of his glory. ¹³And you also were included in Christ when you heard the word of truth, the gospel of your salvation. Having believed, you were marked in him with a seal, the promised Holy Spirit, ¹⁴who is a deposit guaranteeing our inheritance until the redemption of those who are God's possession—to the praise of his glory.

Thanksgiving and Prayer

¹⁵For this reason, ever since I heard about your faith in the Lord Jesus and your love for all the saints, ¹⁶I have not stopped giving thanks for you, remembering you in my prayers. ¹⁷I keep asking that the God of our Lord Jesus Christ, the glorious Father, may give you the Spirit*f* of wisdom and revelation, so that you may know him better. ¹⁸I pray also that the eyes of your heart may be enlightened in order that you may know the hope to which he has called you, the riches of his glorious inheritance in the saints, ¹⁹and his incomparably great power for us who believe. That power is like the working of his mighty strength, ²⁰which he exerted in Christ when he raised him from the dead and seated him at his right hand in the heavenly realms, ²¹far above all rule and authority, power and dominion, and every title that can be given, not only in the present age but also in the one to come. ²²And God placed all things under his feet and appointed him to be head over everything for the church, ²³which is his body, the fullness of him who fills everything in every way.

❓DID YOU KNOW?   1:11

What has God done to bless you?

Ephesians 1 tells how God the Father chose you, Christ died to forgive you, and the Holy Spirit stays with you to keep you safe. Paul wanted the Ephesian Christians, and us, to remember that we have these "spiritual blessings."

Made Alive in Christ

2 As for you, you were dead in your transgressions and sins, ²in

---

a1 Some early manuscripts do not have *in Ephesus.*   *b1* Or *believers who are*   *c4,5* Or *sight in love.* ⁵*He*   *d8,9* Or *us. With all wisdom and understanding,* ⁹*he*   *e11* Or *were made heirs*   *f17* Or *a spirit*

which you used to live when you followed the ways of this world and of the ruler of the kingdom of the air, the spirit who is now at work in those who are disobedient. [3]All of us also lived among them at one time, gratifying the cravings of our sinful nature[a] and following its desires and thoughts. Like the rest, we were by nature objects of wrath. [4]But because of his great love for us, God, who is rich in mercy, [5]made us alive with Christ even when we were dead in transgressions—it is by grace you have been saved. [6]And God raised us up with Christ and seated us with him in the heavenly realms in Christ Jesus, [7]in order that in the coming ages he might show the incomparable riches of his grace, expressed in his kindness to us in Christ Jesus. [8]For it is by grace you have been saved, through faith—and this not from yourselves, it is the gift of God— [9]not by works, so that no one can boast. [10]For we are God's workmanship, created in Christ Jesus to do good works, which God prepared in advance for us to do.

WORDS TO REMEMBER

2:8 By grace you have been saved, through faith—and this not from yourselves, it is the gift of God.

One in Christ

[11]Therefore, remember that formerly you who are Gentiles by birth and called "uncircumcised" by those who call themselves "the circumcision" (that done in the body by the hands of men)— [12]remember that at that time you were separate from Christ, excluded from citizenship in Israel and foreigners to the covenants of the promise, without hope and without God in the world. [13]But now in Christ Jesus you who once were far away have been brought near through the blood of Christ.

[14]For he himself is our peace, who has made the two one and has destroyed the barrier, the dividing wall of hostility, [15]by abolishing in his flesh the law with its commandments and regulations. His purpose was to create in himself one new man out of the two, thus making peace, [16]and in this one body to reconcile both of them to God through the cross, by which he put to death their hostility. [17]He came and preached peace to you who were far away and peace to those who were near. [18]For through him we both have access to the Father by one Spirit.

[19]Consequently, you are no longer foreigners and aliens, but fellow citizens with God's people and members of God's household, [20]built on the foundation of the apostles and prophets, with Christ Jesus himself as the chief cornerstone. [21]In him the whole building is joined together and rises to become a holy temple in the Lord. [22]And in him you too are being built together to become a dwelling in which God lives by his Spirit.

Paul the Preacher to the Gentiles

3 For this reason I, Paul, the prisoner of Christ Jesus for the sake of you Gentiles—

[2]Surely you have heard about the administration of God's grace that was given to me for you, [3]that is, the mystery made known to me by revelation, as I have already written briefly. [4]In reading this, then, you will be able to understand my insight into the mystery of Christ, [5]which was not made known to men in other generations as it has now been revealed by the Spirit to God's holy apostles and prophets. [6]This mystery is that through the gospel the Gentiles are heirs together with Israel, members together of one body, and sharers together in the promise in Christ Jesus.

[7]I became a servant of this gospel by the gift of God's grace given me

---

a3 Or our flesh

through the working of his power. [8]Although I am less than the least of all God's people, this grace was given me: to preach to the Gentiles the unsearchable riches of Christ, [9]and to make plain to everyone the administration of this mystery, which for ages past was kept hidden in God, who created all things. [10]His intent was that now, through the church, the manifold wisdom of God should be made known to the rulers and authorities in the heavenly realms, [11]according to his eternal purpose which he accomplished in Christ Jesus our Lord. [12]In him and through faith in him we may approach God with freedom and confidence. [13]I ask you, therefore, not to be discouraged because of my sufferings for you, which are your glory.

A Prayer for the Ephesians

[14]For this reason I kneel before the Father, [15]from whom his whole family[a] in heaven and on earth derives its name. [16]I pray that out of his glorious riches he may strengthen you with power through his Spirit in your inner being, [17]so that Christ may dwell in your hearts through faith. And I pray that you, being rooted and established in love, [18]may have power, together with all the saints, to grasp how wide and long and high and deep is the love of Christ, [19]and to know this love that surpasses knowledge —that you may be filled to the measure of all the fullness of God.

[20]Now to him who is able to do immeasurably more than all we ask or imagine, according to his power that is at work within us, [21]to him be glory in the church and in Christ Jesus throughout all generations, for ever and ever! Amen.

Unity in the Body of Christ

4 As a prisoner for the Lord, then, I urge you to live a life worthy of the calling you have received. [2]Be completely humble and gentle; be patient, bearing with one another in

love. [3]Make every effort to keep the unity of the Spirit through the bond of peace. [4]There is one body and one Spirit— just as you were called to one hope when you were called— [5]one Lord, one faith, one baptism; [6]one God and Father of all, who is over all and through all and in all.

WORDS TO REMEMBER

3:20 [God] is able to do immeasurably more than all we ask or imagine.

---

[7]But to each one of us grace has been given as Christ apportioned it. [8]This is why it[b] says:

"When he ascended on high,
  he led captives in his train
  and gave gifts to men."[c]

[9](What does "he ascended" mean except that he also descended to the lower, earthly regions[d]? [10]He who descended is the very one who ascended higher than all the heavens, in order to fill the whole universe.) [11]It was he who gave some to be apostles, some to be prophets, some to be evangelists, and some to be pastors and teachers, [12]to prepare God's people for works of service, so that the body of Christ may be built up [13]until we all reach unity in the faith and in the knowledge of the Son of God and become mature, attaining to the whole measure of the fullness of Christ.

[14]Then we will no longer be infants, tossed back and forth by the waves, and blown here and there by every wind of teaching and by the cunning and craftiness of men in their deceitful scheming. [15]Instead, speaking the truth in love, we will in all things grow up into him who is the Head, that is, Christ. [16]From him the whole body, joined and held together by every supporting ligament, grows and

---

a15 Or *whom all fatherhood*   *b8* Or *God*   *c8* Psalm 68:18   *d9* Or *the depths of the earth*

builds itself up in love, as each part does its work.

Living as Children of Light

[17]So I tell you this, and insist on it in the Lord, that you must no longer live as the Gentiles do, in the futility of their thinking. [18]They are darkened in their understanding and separated from the life of God because of the ignorance that is in them due to the hardening of their hearts. [19]Having lost all sensitivity, they have given themselves over to sensuality so as to indulge in every kind of impurity, with a continual lust for more.

[20]You, however, did not come to know Christ that way. [21]Surely you heard of him and were taught in him in accordance with the truth that is in Jesus. [22]You were taught, with regard to your former way of life, to put off your old self, which is being corrupted by its deceitful desires; [23]to be made new in the attitude of your minds; [24]and to put on the new self, created to be like God in true righteousness and holiness.

[25]Therefore each of you must put off falsehood and speak truthfully to his neighbor, for we are all members of one body. [26]"In your anger do not sin"[a]: Do not let the sun go down while you are still angry, [27]and do not give the devil a foothold. [28]He who has been stealing must steal no longer, but must work, doing something useful with his own hands, that he may have something to share with those in need.

[29]Do not let any unwholesome talk come out of your mouths, but only what is helpful for building others up according to their needs, that it may benefit those who listen. [30]And do not grieve the Holy Spirit of God, with whom you were sealed for the day of redemption. [31]Get rid of all bitterness, rage and anger, brawling and slander, along with every form of malice. [32]Be kind and compassionate to one another, forgiving each other, just as in Christ God forgave you.

5 Be imitators of God, therefore, as dearly loved children [2]and live a life of love, just as Christ loved us and gave himself up for us as a fragrant offering and sacrifice to God.

WORDS TO REMEMBER

5:1 Be imitators of God, therefore, as dearly loved children and live a life of love.

---

[3]But among you there must not be even a hint of sexual immorality, or of any kind of impurity, or of greed, because these are improper for God's holy people. [4]Nor should there be obscenity, foolish talk or coarse joking, which are out of place, but rather thanksgiving. [5]For of this you can be sure: No immoral, impure or greedy person—such a man is an idolater—has any inheritance in the kingdom of Christ and of God.[b] [6]Let no one deceive you with empty words, for because of such things God's wrath comes on those who are disobe-

---

[a]26 Psalm 4:4   [b]5 Or *kingdom of the Christ and God*

ET'S LIVE IT!   Ephesians 4:29–32

LEARNING GOD'S LANGUAGE ➠ Most of the Old Testament was written in Hebrew. The New Testament was written in Greek. But God has a special language for Christians.

Read Ephesians 4:29–32. Discuss these questions with your parents: What are some things a Christian who talks God's language would never say? What are things a Christian who talks God's language might say to others?

dient. [7]Therefore do not be partners with them.

[8]For you were once darkness, but now you are light in the Lord. Live as children of light [9](for the fruit of the light consists in all goodness, righteousness and truth) [10]and find out what pleases the Lord. [11]Have nothing to do with the fruitless deeds of darkness, but rather expose them. [12]For it is shameful even to mention what the disobedient do in secret. [13]But everything exposed by the light becomes visible, [14]for it is light that makes everything visible. This is why it is said:

"Wake up, O sleeper,
    rise from the dead,
and Christ will shine on you."

[15]Be very careful, then, how you live—not as unwise but as wise, [16]making the most of every opportunity, because the days are evil. [17]Therefore do not be foolish, but understand what the Lord's will is. [18]Do not get drunk on wine, which leads to debauchery. Instead, be filled with the Spirit. [19]Speak to one another with psalms, hymns and spiritual songs. Sing and make music in your heart to the Lord, [20]always giving thanks to God the Father for everything, in the name of our Lord Jesus Christ.

[21]Submit to one another out of reverence for Christ.

❓DID YOU KNOW?   5:15

How are Christians to live?

Christians are not to be like other people. We are to be more loving, kind, and forgiving. Ephesians 4 and 5 tell us how to live to please God.

Wives and Husbands

[22]Wives, submit to your husbands as to the Lord. [23]For the husband is the head of the wife as Christ is the head of the church, his body, of which he is the Savior. [24]Now as the church submits to Christ, so also wives should submit to their husbands in everything.

[25]Husbands, love your wives, just as Christ loved the church and gave himself up for her [26]to make her holy, cleansing[a] her by the washing with water through the word, [27]and to present her to himself as a radiant church, without stain or wrinkle or any other blemish, but holy and blameless. [28]In this same way, husbands ought to love their wives as their own bodies. He who loves his wife loves himself. [29]After all, no one ever hated his own body, but he feeds and cares for it, just as Christ does the church— [30]for we are members of his body. [31]"For this reason a man will leave his father and mother and be united to his wife, and the two will become one flesh."[b] [32]This is a profound mystery—but I am talking about Christ and the church. [33]However, each one of you also must love his wife as he loves himself, and the wife must respect her husband.

Children and Parents

6 Children, obey your parents in the Lord, for this is right. [2]"Honor your father and mother"—which is the first commandment with a promise— [3]"that it may go well with you and that you may enjoy long life on the earth."[c]

✦ORDS TO REMEMBER

6:1 Children, obey your parents in the Lord, for this is right.

---

[4]Fathers, do not exasperate your children; instead, bring them up in the training and instruction of the Lord.

---

[a]26 Or *having cleansed*   [b]31 Gen. 2:24   [c]3 Deut. 5:16

Slaves and Masters

⁵Slaves, obey your earthly masters with respect and fear, and with sincerity of heart, just as you would obey Christ. ⁶Obey them not only to win their favor when their eye is on you, but like slaves of Christ, doing the will of God from your heart. ⁷Serve wholeheartedly, as if you were serving the Lord, not men, ⁸because you know that the Lord will reward everyone for whatever good he does, whether he is slave or free.

⁹And masters, treat your slaves in the same way. Do not threaten them, since you know that he who is both their Master and yours is in heaven, and there is no favoritism with him.

The Armor of God

¹⁰Finally, be strong in the Lord and in his mighty power. ¹¹Put on the full armor of God so that you can take your stand against the devil's schemes. ¹²For our struggle is not against flesh and blood, but against the rulers, against the authorities, against the powers of this dark world and against the spiritual forces of evil in the heavenly realms. ¹³Therefore put on the full armor of God, so that when the day of evil comes, you may be able to stand your ground, and after you have done everything, to stand. ¹⁴Stand firm then, with the belt of truth buckled around your waist, with the breastplate of righteousness in place, ¹⁵and with your feet fitted with the readiness that comes from the gospel of peace. ¹⁶In addition to all this, take up the shield of faith, with which you can extinguish all the flaming arrows of the evil one. ¹⁷Take the helmet of salvation and the sword of the Spirit, which is the word of God. ¹⁸And pray in the Spirit on all occasions with all kinds of prayers and requests. With this in mind, be alert and always keep on praying for all the saints.

¹⁹Pray also for me, that whenever I open my mouth, words may be given me so that I will fearlessly make known the mystery of the gospel, ²⁰for which I am an ambassador in chains. Pray that I may declare it fearlessly, as I should.

Final Greetings

²¹Tychicus, the dear brother and faithful servant in the Lord, will tell you everything, so that you also may know how I am and what I am doing. ²²I am sending him to you for this

Life in Bible Times

A SOLDIER'S ARMOR

This description by Paul of a Roman soldier's armor shows how familiar Paul was with Roman soldiers and what they wore. Each part of the soldier's armor was an important part of his defense against the weapons of his enemy. Read Ephesians 6:10–18 to find all the parts of the soldier's armor. Now compare that soldier's armor with the armor you must put on as a Christian.

very purpose, that you may know how we are, and that he may encourage you.

[23]Peace to the brothers, and love with faith from God the Father and the Lord Jesus Christ. [24]Grace to all who love our Lord Jesus Christ with an undying love.

PHILIPPIANS

WHO WROTE THIS BOOK?

Paul.

WHY WAS THIS BOOK WRITTEN?

Philippians thanks the people for their love and gifts and gives them instructions on how to live good Christian lives.

FOR WHOM WAS THIS BOOK WRITTEN?

This book is a letter Paul sent to Christians at Philippi.

WHEN WAS THIS BOOK WRITTEN?

This book was written about A.D. 63 from Rome, where Paul was in prison.

WHAT ARE SOME IMPORTANT TEACHINGS IN THIS BOOK?

Live as good Christians.	Philippians 1:27–30
Live a humble life.	Philippians 2:1–4
How Jesus was humble.	Philippians 2:5–11
The Christian's goal.	Philippians 3:12–16
How to be at peace.	Philippians 4:4–7
Think about good things.	Philippians 4:8–9

1 Paul and Timothy, servants of Christ Jesus,

To all the saints in Christ Jesus at Philippi, together with the overseers[a] and deacons:

[2]Grace and peace to you from God our Father and the Lord Jesus Christ.

Thanksgiving and Prayer

[3]I thank my God every time I remember you. [4]In all my prayers for all of you, I always pray with joy [5]because of your partnership in the gospel from the first day until now, [6]being confident of this, that he who began a good work in you will carry it on to completion until the day of Christ Jesus.

[7]It is right for me to feel this way about all of you, since I have you in my heart; for whether I am in chains or defending and confirming the gospel, all of you share in God's grace with me. [8]God can testify how I long for all of you with the affection of Christ Jesus.

[9]And this is my prayer: that your love may abound more and more in knowledge and depth of insight, [10]so that you may be able to discern what is best and may be pure and blameless until the day of Christ, [11]filled with the fruit of righteousness that comes through Jesus Christ—to the glory and praise of God.

❓DID YOU KNOW?   1:9

How did Paul show love for the Philippians?

Paul showed his love for the Philippians by praying for them. You can pray for people you love too.

Paul's Chains Advance the Gospel

[12]Now I want you to know, brothers, that what has happened to me has really served to advance the gospel. [13]As a result, it has become clear throughout the whole palace guard[b] and to everyone else that I am in chains for Christ. [14]Because of my chains, most of the brothers in the Lord have been encouraged to speak the word of God more courageously and fearlessly.

[15]It is true that some preach Christ out of envy and rivalry, but others out of goodwill. [16]The latter do so in love, knowing that I am put here for the defense of the gospel. [17]The former preach Christ out of selfish ambition, not sincerely, supposing that they can stir up trouble for me while I am in chains.[c] [18]But what does it matter? The important thing is that in every way, whether from false motives or true, Christ is preached. And because of this I rejoice.

Yes, and I will continue to rejoice, [19]for I know that through your prayers and the help given by the Spirit of Jesus Christ, what has happened to me will turn out for my deliverance.[d] [20]I eagerly expect and hope that I will in no way be ashamed, but will have sufficient courage so that now as always Christ will be exalted in my body, whether by life or by death. [21]For to me, to live is Christ and to die is gain. [22]If I am to go on living in the body, this will mean fruitful labor for me. Yet what shall I choose? I do not know! [23]I am torn between the two: I desire to depart and be with Christ, which is better by far; [24]but it is more necessary for you that I remain in the body. [25]Convinced of this, I know that I will remain, and I will continue with all of you for your progress and joy in the faith, [26]so that through my being with you again your joy in Christ Jesus will overflow on account of me.

[27]Whatever happens, conduct yourselves in a manner worthy of the gospel of Christ. Then, whether I come and see you or only hear about you in my absence, I will know that you

---

[a]1 Traditionally *bishops* and 17 in reverse order.   [b]13 Or *whole palace*   [d]19 Or *salvation*   [c]16,17 Some late manuscripts have verses 16

stand firm in one spirit, contending as one man for the faith of the gospel ²⁸without being frightened in any way by those who oppose you. This is a sign to them that they will be destroyed, but that you will be saved —and that by God. ²⁹For it has been granted to you on behalf of Christ not only to believe on him, but also to suffer for him, ³⁰since you are going through the same struggle you saw I had, and now hear that I still have.

Imitating Christ's Humility

2 If you have any encouragement from being united with Christ, if any comfort from his love, if any fellowship with the Spirit, if any tenderness and compassion, ²then make my joy complete by being like-minded, having the same love, being one in spirit and purpose. ³Do nothing out of selfish ambition or vain conceit, but in humility consider others better than yourselves. ⁴Each of you should look not only to your own interests, but also to the interests of others.

⁵Your attitude should be the same as that of Christ Jesus:

⁶Who, being in very nature*ᵃ* God,
did not consider equality with
God something to be
grasped,
⁷but made himself nothing,
taking the very nature*ᵇ* of a
servant,
being made in human likeness.
⁸And being found in appearance as
a man,
he humbled himself

and became obedient to death—
even death on a cross!
⁹Therefore God exalted him to the
highest place
and gave him the name that is
above every name,
¹⁰that at the name of Jesus every
knee should bow,
in heaven and on earth and
under the earth,
¹¹and every tongue confess that
Jesus Christ is Lord,
to the glory of God the Father.

Shining as Stars

¹²Therefore, my dear friends, as you have always obeyed—not only in my presence, but now much more in my absence—continue to work out your salvation with fear and trembling, ¹³for it is God who works in you to will and to act according to his good purpose.

¹⁴Do everything without complaining or arguing, ¹⁵so that you may become blameless and pure, children of God without fault in a crooked and depraved generation, in which you shine like stars in the universe ¹⁶as you hold out*ᶜ* the word of life—in order that I may boast on the day of Christ that I did not run or labor for nothing. ¹⁷But even if I am being poured out like a drink offering on the sacrifice and service coming from your faith, I am glad and rejoice with all of you. ¹⁸So you too should be glad and rejoice with me.

Timothy and Epaphroditus

¹⁹I hope in the Lord Jesus to send

ᵃ6 Or in the form of   *ᵇ7 Or the form*   *ᶜ16 Or hold on to*

▌ET'S LIVE IT!   Philippians 2:1–11

FOLLOW JESUS' EXAMPLE ⟹ A humble Christian is not selfish or conceited. A humble Christian thinks how others feel, and not just about himself or herself. Read Philippians 2:1–11. How was Jesus humble? How could you follow Jesus' example in each of these situations?
   One of the younger children falls down and gets hurt on the bus.
   A friend forgot to bring a bag lunch on a field trip.
   You and your sister want to play with the same friend.

Timothy to you soon, that I also may be cheered when I receive news about you. ²⁰I have no one else like him, who takes a genuine interest in your welfare. ²¹For everyone looks out for his own interests, not those of Jesus Christ. ²²But you know that Timothy has proved himself, because as a son with his father he has served with me in the work of the gospel. ²³I hope, therefore, to send him as soon as I see how things go with me. ²⁴And I am confident in the Lord that I myself will come soon.

WORDS TO REMEMBER

2:14 Do everything without complaining or arguing.

---

²⁵But I think it is necessary to send back to you Epaphroditus, my brother, fellow worker and fellow soldier, who is also your messenger, whom you sent to take care of my needs. ²⁶For he longs for all of you and is distressed because you heard he was ill. ²⁷Indeed he was ill, and almost died. But God had mercy on him, and not on him only but also on me, to spare me sorrow upon sorrow. ²⁸Therefore I am all the more eager to send him, so that when you see him again you may be glad and I may have less anxiety. ²⁹Welcome him in the Lord with great joy, and honor men like him, ³⁰because he almost died for the work of Christ, risking his life to make up for the help you could not give me.

No Confidence in the Flesh

3 Finally, my brothers, rejoice in the Lord! It is no trouble for me to write the same things to you again, and it is a safeguard for you.

²Watch out for those dogs, those men who do evil, those mutilators of the flesh. ³For it is we who are the circumcision, we who worship by the Spirit of God, who glory in Christ Jesus, and who put no confidence in the flesh— ⁴though I myself have reasons for such confidence.

If anyone else thinks he has reasons to put confidence in the flesh, I have more: ⁵circumcised on the eighth day, of the people of Israel, of the tribe of Benjamin, a Hebrew of Hebrews; in regard to the law, a Pharisee; ⁶as for zeal, persecuting the church; as for legalistic righteousness, faultless.

⁷But whatever was to my profit I now consider loss for the sake of Christ. ⁸What is more, I consider everything a loss compared to the surpassing greatness of knowing Christ Jesus my Lord, for whose sake I have lost all things. I consider them rubbish, that I may gain Christ ⁹and be found in him, not having a righteousness of my own that comes from the law, but that which is through faith in Christ—the righteousness that comes from God and is by faith. ¹⁰I want to know Christ and the power of his resurrection and the fellowship of sharing in his sufferings, becoming like him in his death, ¹¹and so, somehow, to attain to the resurrection from the dead.

Pressing on Toward the Goal

¹²Not that I have already obtained all this, or have already been made perfect, but I press on to take hold of that for which Christ Jesus took hold of me. ¹³Brothers, I do not consider myself yet to have taken hold of it. But one thing I do: Forgetting what is behind and straining toward what is ahead, ¹⁴I press on toward the goal to win the prize for which God has called me heavenward in Christ Jesus.

¹⁵All of us who are mature should take such a view of things. And if on some point you think differently, that too God will make clear to you. ¹⁶Only let us live up to what we have already attained.

¹⁷Join with others in following my example, brothers, and take note of those who live according to the pattern we gave you. ¹⁸For, as I have often told you before and now say again

even with tears, many live as enemies of the cross of Christ. ¹⁹Their destiny is destruction, their god is their stomach, and their glory is in their shame. Their mind is on earthly things. ²⁰But our citizenship is in heaven. And we eagerly await a Savior from there, the Lord Jesus Christ, ²¹who, by the power that enables him to bring everything under his control, will transform our lowly bodies so that they will be like his glorious body.

4 Therefore, my brothers, you whom I love and long for, my joy and crown, that is how you should stand firm in the Lord, dear friends!

Exhortations

²I plead with Euodia and I plead with Syntyche to agree with each other in the Lord. ³Yes, and I ask you, loyal yokefellow,ᵃ help these women who have contended at my side in the cause of the gospel, along with Clement and the rest of my fellow workers, whose names are in the book of life.

⁴Rejoice in the Lord always. I will say it again: Rejoice! ⁵Let your gentleness be evident to all. The Lord is near. ⁶Do not be anxious about anything, but in everything, by prayer and petition, with thanksgiving, present your requests to God. ⁷And the peace of God, which transcends all understanding, will guard your hearts and your minds in Christ Jesus.

ᵃ3 Or loyal Syzygus

⁸Finally, brothers, whatever is true, whatever is noble, whatever is right, whatever is pure, whatever is lovely, whatever is admirable—if anything is excellent or praiseworthy—think about such things. ⁹Whatever you have learned or received or heard from me, or seen in me—put it into practice. And the God of peace will be with you.

Thanks for Their Gifts

¹⁰I rejoice greatly in the Lord that at last you have renewed your concern for me. Indeed, you have been concerned, but you had no opportunity to show it. ¹¹I am not saying this because I am in need, for I have learned to be content whatever the circumstances. ¹²I know what it is to be in need, and I know what it is to have plenty. I have learned the secret of being content in any and every situation, whether well fed or hungry, whether living in plenty or in want. ¹³I can do everything through him who gives me strength.

WORDS TO REMEMBER

4:13 I can do everything through him who gives me strength.

---

¹⁴Yet it was good of you to share in my troubles. ¹⁵Moreover, as you Phi-

Life in Bible Times

RUNNING A RACE

In Greek Olympic games and at other games, runners tried to be the first to reach a wooden goal. The wooden goal, instead of a tape, marked the end of the race.

lippians know, in the early days of your acquaintance with the gospel, when I set out from Macedonia, not one church shared with me in the matter of giving and receiving, except you only; [16]for even when I was in Thessalonica, you sent me aid again and again when I was in need. [17]Not that I am looking for a gift, but I am looking for what may be credited to your account. [18]I have received full payment and even more; I am amply supplied, now that I have received from Epaphroditus the gifts you sent. They are a fragrant offer-ing, an acceptable sacrifice, pleasing to God. [19]And my God will meet all your needs according to his glorious riches in Christ Jesus.

[20]To our God and Father be glory for ever and ever. Amen.

Final Greetings

[21]Greet all the saints in Christ Jesus. The brothers who are with me send greetings. [22]All the saints send you greetings, especially those who belong to Caesar's household.

[23]The grace of the Lord Jesus Christ be with your spirit. Amen.[a]

[a]23 Some manuscripts do not have *Amen*.

ET'S LIVE IT!   Philippians 4:8–9

WHAT'S ON YOUR MIND? ➡ Read Philippians 4:8–9. What does God want us to think about?

Often it is easy for people to think bad thoughts. Many times we have bad thoughts because we've put bad things into our minds, perhaps by watching a violent TV program, playing with friends who use rough language, listening to hard rock music.

Now you think of three ways to put good things into your mind. Show the list to your mom or dad. What do they think of it?

COLOSSIANS

WHO WROTE THIS BOOK?

Paul.

WHY WAS THIS BOOK WRITTEN?

Colossians shows that Jesus is supreme and that he saves us completely.

FOR WHOM WAS THIS BOOK WRITTEN?

This book is a letter written to Christians at Colosse.

WHEN WAS THIS BOOK WRITTEN?

Colossians was written about A.D. 62, when Paul was in prison in Rome.

WHAT ARE SOME IMPORTANT TEACHINGS IN THIS BOOK?

Jesus is supreme.   Colossians 1:15–20
Jesus forgives our sins.   Colossians 2:13–15
How to live a holy life.   Colossians 3:12–17

1 Paul, an apostle of Christ Jesus by the will of God, and Timothy our brother,

2To the holy and faithful*a* brothers in Christ at Colosse:

Grace and peace to you from God our Father.*b*

Thanksgiving and Prayer

3We always thank God, the Father of our Lord Jesus Christ, when we pray for you, 4because we have heard of your faith in Christ Jesus and of the love you have for all the saints— 5the faith and love that spring from the hope that is stored up for you in heaven and that you have already heard about in the word of truth, the gospel 6that has come to you. All over the world this gospel is bearing fruit and growing, just as it has been doing among you since the day you heard it and understood God's grace in all its truth. 7You learned it from Epaphras, our dear fellow servant, who is a faithful minister of Christ on our*c* behalf, 8and who also told us of your love in the Spirit.

9For this reason, since the day we heard about you, we have not stopped praying for you and asking God to fill you with the knowledge of his will through all spiritual wisdom and understanding. 10And we pray this in order that you may live a life worthy of the Lord and may please him in every way: bearing fruit in every good work, growing in the knowledge of God, 11being strengthened with all power according to his glorious might so that you may have great endurance and patience, and joyfully 12giving thanks to the Father, who has qualified you*d* to share in the inheritance of the saints in the kingdom of light. 13For he has rescued us from the dominion of darkness and brought us into the kingdom of the Son he loves, 14in whom we have redemption,*e* the forgiveness of sins.

The Supremacy of Christ

15He is the image of the invisible God, the firstborn over all creation. 16For by him all things were created: things in heaven and on earth, visible and invisible, whether thrones or powers or rulers or authorities; all things were created by him and for him. 17He is before all things, and in him all things hold together. 18And he is the head of the body, the church; he is the beginning and the firstborn from among the dead, so that in everything he might have the supremacy. 19For God was pleased to have all his fullness dwell in him, 20and through him to reconcile to himself all things, whether things on earth or things in heaven, by making peace through his blood, shed on the cross. 21Once you were alienated from God and were enemies in your minds because of*f* your evil behavior. 22But now he has reconciled you by Christ's physical body through death to present you holy in his sight, without blemish and free from accusation— 23if you continue in your faith, established and firm, not moved from the hope held out in the gospel. This is the gospel that you heard and that has been proclaimed to every creature under heaven, and of which I, Paul, have become a servant.

❓DID YOU KNOW?   1:15

Is Jesus really God?

Yes, Jesus is God. Colossians 1:15–20 tells us that Jesus created all things and he is more powerful than any other being.

Paul's Labor for the Church

24Now I rejoice in what was suffered for you, and I fill up in my flesh what is still lacking in regard to Christ's afflictions, for the sake of his

---

a2 Or *believing*   *b2* Some manuscripts *Father and the Lord Jesus Christ*   *c7* Some manuscripts *your*   *d12* Some manuscripts *us*   *e14* A few late manuscripts *redemption through his blood*   *f21* Or *minds, as shown by*

body, which is the church. [25]I have become its servant by the commission God gave me to present to you the word of God in its fullness— [26]the mystery that has been kept hidden for ages and generations, but is now disclosed to the saints. [27]To them God has chosen to make known among the Gentiles the glorious riches of this mystery, which is Christ in you, the hope of glory.

[28]We proclaim him, admonishing and teaching everyone with all wisdom, so that we may present everyone perfect in Christ. [29]To this end I labor, struggling with all his energy, which so powerfully works in me.

2 I want you to know how much I am struggling for you and for those at Laodicea, and for all who have not met me personally. [2]My purpose is that they may be encouraged in heart and united in love, so that they may have the full riches of complete understanding, in order that they may know the mystery of God, namely, Christ, [3]in whom are hidden all the treasures of wisdom and knowledge. [4]I tell you this so that no one may deceive you by fine-sounding arguments. [5]For though I am absent from you in body, I am present with you in spirit and delight to see how orderly you are and how firm your faith in Christ is.

Freedom From Human Regulations Through Life With Christ

[6]So then, just as you received Christ Jesus as Lord, continue to live in him, [7]rooted and built up in him, strengthened in the faith as you were taught, and overflowing with thankfulness.

[8]See to it that no one takes you captive through hollow and deceptive philosophy, which depends on human tradition and the basic principles of this world rather than on Christ.

[9]For in Christ all the fullness of the Deity lives in bodily form, [10]and you have been given fullness in Christ,

who is the head over every power and authority. [11]In him you were also circumcised, in the putting off of the sinful nature,[a] not with a circumcision done by the hands of men but with the circumcision done by Christ, [12]having been buried with him in baptism and raised with him through your faith in the power of God, who raised him from the dead.

[13]When you were dead in your sins and in the uncircumcision of your sinful nature,[b] God made you[c] alive with Christ. He forgave us all our sins, [14]having canceled the written code, with its regulations, that was against us and that stood opposed to us; he took it away, nailing it to the cross. [15]And having disarmed the powers and authorities, he made a public spectacle of them, triumphing over them by the cross.[d]

WORDS TO REMEMBER

2:13 He forgave us all our sins.

---

[16]Therefore do not let anyone judge you by what you eat or drink, or with regard to a religious festival, a New Moon celebration or a Sabbath day. [17]These are a shadow of the things that were to come; the reality, however, is found in Christ. [18]Do not let anyone who delights in false humility and the worship of angels disqualify you for the prize. Such a person goes into great detail about what he has seen, and his unspiritual mind puffs him up with idle notions. [19]He has lost connection with the Head, from whom the whole body, supported and held together by its ligaments and sinews, grows as God causes it to grow.

[20]Since you died with Christ to the basic principles of this world, why, as though you still belonged to it, do you submit to its rules: [21]"Do not handle! Do not taste! Do not touch!"? [22]These are all destined to perish with use,

---

a11 Or *the flesh*   *b13* Or *your flesh*   *c13* Some manuscripts *us*   *d15* Or *them in him*

because they are based on human commands and teachings. ²³Such regulations indeed have an appearance of wisdom, with their self-imposed worship, their false humility and their harsh treatment of the body, but they lack any value in restraining sensual indulgence.

Rules for Holy Living

3 Since, then, you have been raised with Christ, set your hearts on things above, where Christ is seated at the right hand of God. ²Set your minds on things above, not on earthly things. ³For you died, and your life is now hidden with Christ in God. ⁴When Christ, who is your*a* life, appears, then you also will appear with him in glory.

⁵Put to death, therefore, whatever belongs to your earthly nature: sexual immorality, impurity, lust, evil desires and greed, which is idolatry. ⁶Because of these, the wrath of God is coming. *b* ⁷You used to walk in these ways, in the life you once lived. ⁸But now you must rid yourselves of all such things as these: anger, rage, malice, slander, and filthy language from your lips. ⁹Do not lie to each other, since you have taken off your old self with its practices ¹⁰and have put on the new self, which is being renewed in knowledge in the image of its Creator. ¹¹Here there is no Greek or Jew, circumcised or uncircumcised, barbarian, Scythian, slave or free, but Christ is all, and is in all.

? DID YOU KNOW?   3:12

What is holiness?

Holiness is doing right and good things because we love Jesus. Colossians 3 gives us some very specific rules for how to live a holy life.

---

¹²Therefore, as God's chosen people, holy and dearly loved, clothe yourselves with compassion, kindness, humility, gentleness and patience. ¹³Bear with each other and forgive whatever grievances you may have against one another. Forgive as the Lord forgave you. ¹⁴And over all these virtues put on love, which binds them all together in perfect unity.

WORDS TO REMEMBER

3:13 Forgive whatever grievances you may have against one another. Forgive as the Lord forgave you.

---

¹⁵Let the peace of Christ rule in your hearts, since as members of one body you were called to peace. And be thankful. ¹⁶Let the word of Christ dwell in you richly as you teach and admonish one another with all wisdom, and as you sing psalms, hymns and spiritual songs with gratitude in your hearts to God. ¹⁷And whatever you do, whether in word or deed, do it all in the name of the Lord Jesus, giving thanks to God the Father through him.

Rules for Christian Households

¹⁸Wives, submit to your husbands, as is fitting in the Lord.

¹⁹Husbands, love your wives and do not be harsh with them.

²⁰Children, obey your parents in everything, for this pleases the Lord. ²¹Fathers, do not embitter your children, or they will become discouraged.

²²Slaves, obey your earthly masters in everything; and do it, not only when their eye is on you and to win their favor, but with sincerity of heart and reverence for the Lord. ²³Whatever you do, work at it with all your heart, as working for the Lord, not for men, ²⁴since you know that you will receive an inheritance from the Lord as a reward. It is the Lord

---

a4 Some manuscripts *our*   *b6* Some early manuscripts *coming on those who are disobedient*

Christ you are serving. ²⁵Anyone who does wrong will be repaid for his wrong, and there is no favoritism.

4 Masters, provide your slaves with what is right and fair, because you know that you also have a Master in heaven.

Further Instructions

²Devote yourselves to prayer, being watchful and thankful. ³And pray for us, too, that God may open a door for our message, so that we may proclaim the mystery of Christ, for which I am in chains. ⁴Pray that I may proclaim it clearly, as I should. ⁵Be wise in the way you act toward outsiders; make the most of every opportunity. ⁶Let your conversation be always full of grace, seasoned with salt, so that you may know how to answer everyone.

Final Greetings

⁷Tychicus will tell you all the news about me. He is a dear brother, a faithful minister and fellow servant in the Lord. ⁸I am sending him to you for the express purpose that you may know about our*a* circumstances and that he may encourage your hearts. ⁹He is coming with Onesimus, our faithful and dear brother, who is one of you. They will tell you everything that is happening here.

¹⁰My fellow prisoner Aristarchus sends you his greetings, as does Mark, the cousin of Barnabas. (You have received instructions about him; if he comes to you, welcome him.) ¹¹Jesus, who is called Justus, also sends greetings. These are the only Jews among my fellow workers for the kingdom of God, and they have proved a comfort to me. ¹²Epaphras, who is one of you and a servant of Christ Jesus, sends greetings. He is always wrestling in prayer for you, that you may stand firm in all the will of God, mature and fully assured. ¹³I vouch for him that he is working hard for you and for those at Laodicea and Hierapolis. ¹⁴Our dear friend Luke, the doctor, and Demas send greetings. ¹⁵Give my greetings to the brothers at Laodicea, and to Nympha and the church in her house.

¹⁶After this letter has been read to you, see that it is also read in the church of the Laodiceans and that you in turn read the letter from Laodicea.

¹⁷Tell Archippus: "See to it that you complete the work you have received in the Lord."

¹⁸I, Paul, write this greeting in my own hand. Remember my chains. Grace be with you.

---

a8 Some manuscripts *that he may know about your*

▌ET'S LIVE IT!   Colossians 3:18–21

YOUR PART IN A HAPPY FAMILY ⟹ Everyone has a part in making a happy family. Read Colossians 3:18–21. What is your dad's part? Your mom's part? What is your part?
How would you obey if your mom or dad said:

1. "It's time for bed."
2. "Be sure to be good on the school bus."
3. "I wish you wouldn't complain about the food I cook."
4. "Don't be mouthy."
5. "Studies come first."

Talk to your mom or dad. Ask them why the whole family is happier when everybody does their part.

1 THESSALONIANS

WHO WROTE THIS BOOK? Paul.

WHY WAS THIS BOOK WRITTEN? The book of 1 Thessalonians teaches the Christians in Thessalonica how to please God.

FOR WHOM WAS THIS BOOK WRITTEN? This book is a letter Paul sent to Christians at Thessalonica.

WHEN WAS THIS BOOK WRITTEN? This book was written about A.D. 51 from Corinth.

WHAT ARE SOME IMPORTANT TEACHINGS IN THIS BOOK?

Being Christian examples.	1 Thessalonians 1:4–10
Living to please God.	1 Thessalonians 4:3–12
Jesus will come again.	1 Thessalonians 4:13–18

1 Paul, Silas[a] and Timothy,

To the church of the Thessalonians in God the Father and the Lord Jesus Christ:

Grace and peace to you.[b]

Thanksgiving for the Thessalonians' Faith

[2]We always thank God for all of you, mentioning you in our prayers. [3]We continually remember before our God and Father your work produced by faith, your labor prompted by love, and your endurance inspired by hope in our Lord Jesus Christ.

[4]For we know, brothers loved by God, that he has chosen you, [5]because our gospel came to you not simply with words, but also with power, with the Holy Spirit and with deep conviction. You know how we lived among you for your sake. [6]You became imitators of us and of the Lord; in spite of severe suffering, you welcomed the message with the joy given by the Holy Spirit. [7]And so you became a model to all the believers in Macedonia and Achaia. [8]The Lord's message rang out from you not only in Macedonia and Achaia—your faith in God has become known everywhere. Therefore we do not need to say anything about it, [9]for they themselves report what kind of reception you gave us. They tell how you turned to God from idols to serve the living and true God, [10]and to wait for his Son from heaven, whom he raised from the dead—Jesus, who rescues us from the coming wrath.

? DID YOU KNOW?   1:6

How did the Thessalonians show they were real Christians?

The Thessalonians started worshiping God and stopped worshiping idols. They also began to tell other people about Jesus.

Paul's Ministry in Thessalonica

2 You know, brothers, that our visit to you was not a failure. [2]We had previously suffered and been insulted in Philippi, as you know, but with the help of our God we dared to tell you his gospel in spite of strong opposition. [3]For the appeal we make does not spring from error or impure motives, nor are we trying to trick you. [4]On the contrary, we speak as men approved by God to be entrusted with the gospel. We are not trying to please men but God, who tests our hearts. [5]You know we never used flattery, nor did we put on a mask to cover up greed—God is our witness. [6]We were not looking for praise from men, not from you or anyone else.

As apostles of Christ we could have been a burden to you, [7]but we were gentle among you, like a mother caring for her little children. [8]We loved you so much that we were delighted to share with you not only the gospel of God but our lives as well, because you had become so dear to us. [9]Surely you remember, brothers, our toil and hardship; we worked night and day in order not to be a burden to anyone while we preached the gospel of God to you.

[10]You are witnesses, and so is God, of how holy, righteous and blameless we were among you who believed. [11]For you know that we dealt with each of you as a father deals with his own children, [12]encouraging, comforting and urging you to live lives worthy of God, who calls you into his kingdom and glory.

[13]And we also thank God continually because, when you received the word of God, which you heard from us, you accepted it not as the word of men, but as it actually is, the word of God, which is at work in you who believe. [14]For you, brothers, became imitators of God's churches in Judea, which are in Christ Jesus: You suf-

---

[a]1 Greek *Silvanus*, a variant of *Silas*   [b]1 Some early manuscripts *you from God our Father and the Lord Jesus Christ*

fered from your own countrymen the same things those churches suffered from the Jews, [15]who killed the Lord Jesus and the prophets and also drove us out. They displease God and are hostile to all men [16]in their effort to keep us from speaking to the Gentiles so that they may be saved. In this way they always heap up their sins to the limit. The wrath of God has come upon them at last. [a]

❓DID YOU KNOW?   2:7

What kind of person was Paul?

Paul was a warm and loving person. In 1 Thessalonians 2:7 we read how Paul treated the new Christians in Thessalonica "like a mother caring for her little children."

Paul's Longing to See the Thessalonians

[17]But, brothers, when we were torn away from you for a short time (in person, not in thought), out of our intense longing we made every effort to see you. [18]For we wanted to come to you—certainly I, Paul, did, again and again—but Satan stopped us. [19]For what is our hope, our joy, or the crown in which we will glory in the presence of our Lord Jesus when he comes? Is it not you? [20]Indeed, you are our glory and joy.

3 So when we could stand it no longer, we thought it best to be left by ourselves in Athens. [2]We sent Timothy, who is our brother and God's fellow worker [b] in spreading the gospel of Christ, to strengthen and encourage you in your faith, [3]so that no one would be unsettled by these trials. You know quite well that we were destined for them. [4]In fact, when we were with you, we kept telling you that we would be persecuted. And it turned out that way, as you well know. [5]For this reason, when I could stand it no longer, I sent to find out about your faith. I was afraid that in some way the tempter might have tempted you and our efforts might have been useless.

Timothy's Encouraging Report

[6]But Timothy has just now come to us from you and has brought good news about your faith and love. He has told us that you always have pleasant memories of us and that you long to see us, just as we also long to see you. [7]Therefore, brothers, in all our distress and persecution we were encouraged about you because of your faith. [8]For now we really live, since you are standing firm in the Lord. [9]How can we thank God enough for you in return for all the joy we have in the presence of our God because of you? [10]Night and day we pray most earnestly that we may see you again and supply what is lacking in your faith.

---

[a]16 Or them fully and God's servant   [b]2 Some manuscripts brother and fellow worker; other manuscripts brother

---

◤ET'S LIVE IT!   1 Thessalonians 3:6–10

KEEP IN TOUCH ⟹ The apostle Paul had friends he cared about. He wrote letters to them. Read 1 Thessalonians 3:6–10.

Do you have a pen pal? Pen pals are friends with whom you exchange letters. If you've moved, children you used to know can be good pen pals. So can cousins who live in a different city or town. If you don't have a pen pal, write a letter to a child in a missionary family to see if he or she would like to write you.

When you write to your pen pals, pray for them just as Paul prayed for his friends when he wrote.

¹¹Now may our God and Father himself and our Lord Jesus clear the way for us to come to you. ¹²May the Lord make your love increase and overflow for each other and for everyone else, just as ours does for you. ¹³May he strengthen your hearts so that you will be blameless and holy in the presence of our God and Father when our Lord Jesus comes with all his holy ones.

Living to Please God

4 Finally, brothers, we instructed you how to live in order to please God, as in fact you are living. Now we ask you and urge you in the Lord Jesus to do this more and more. ²For you know what instructions we gave you by the authority of the Lord Jesus.

³It is God's will that you should be sanctified: that you should avoid sexual immorality; ⁴that each of you should learn to control his own body*a* in a way that is holy and honorable, ⁵not in passionate lust like the heathen, who do not know God; ⁶and that in this matter no one should wrong his brother or take advantage of him. The Lord will punish men for all such sins, as we have already told you and warned you. ⁷For God did not call us to be impure, but to live a holy life. ⁸Therefore, he who rejects this instruction does not reject man but God, who gives you his Holy Spirit.

⁹Now about brotherly love we do not need to write to you, for you yourselves have been taught by God to love each other. ¹⁰And in fact, you do love all the brothers throughout Macedonia. Yet we urge you, brothers, to do so more and more.

¹¹Make it your ambition to lead a quiet life, to mind your own business and to work with your hands, just as we told you, ¹²so that your daily life may win the respect of outsiders and so that you will not be dependent on anybody.

The Coming of the Lord

¹³Brothers, we do not want you to be ignorant about those who fall asleep, or to grieve like the rest of men, who have no hope. ¹⁴We believe that Jesus died and rose again and so we believe that God will bring with Jesus those who have fallen asleep in him. ¹⁵According to the Lord's own word, we tell you that we who are still alive, who are left till the coming of the Lord, will certainly not precede those who have fallen asleep. ¹⁶For the Lord himself will come down from heaven, with a loud command, with the voice of the archangel and with the trumpet call of God, and the dead in Christ will rise first. ¹⁷After that, we who are still alive and are left will be caught up together with them in the clouds to meet the Lord in the air. And so we will be with the Lord forever. ¹⁸Therefore encourage each other with these words.

WORDS TO REMEMBER

4:17 We will be with the Lord forever.

5 Now, brothers, about times and dates we do not need to write to you, ²for you know very well that the day of the Lord will come like a thief in the night. ³While people are saying, "Peace and safety," destruction will come on them suddenly, as labor pains on a pregnant woman, and they will not escape.

⁴But you, brothers, are not in darkness so that this day should surprise you like a thief. ⁵You are all sons of the light and sons of the day. We do not belong to the night or to the darkness. ⁶So then, let us not be like others, who are asleep, but let us be alert and self-controlled. ⁷For those who sleep, sleep at night, and those who get drunk, get drunk at night. ⁸But since we belong to the day, let us be self-controlled, putting on faith and

---

a4 Or *learn to live with his own wife*; or *learn to acquire a wife*

love as a breastplate, and the hope of salvation as a helmet. ⁹For God did not appoint us to suffer wrath but to receive salvation through our Lord Jesus Christ. ¹⁰He died for us so that, whether we are awake or asleep, we may live together with him. ¹¹Therefore encourage one another and build each other up, just as in fact you are doing.

Final Instructions

¹²Now we ask you, brothers, to respect those who work hard among you, who are over you in the Lord and who admonish you. ¹³Hold them in the highest regard in love because of their work. Live in peace with each other. ¹⁴And we urge you, brothers, warn those who are idle, encourage the timid, help the weak, be patient with everyone. ¹⁵Make sure that nobody pays back wrong for wrong, but always try to be kind to each other and to everyone else.

¹⁶Be joyful always; ¹⁷pray continually; ¹⁸give thanks in all circumstances, for this is God's will for you in Christ Jesus.

¹⁹Do not put out the Spirit's fire; ²⁰do not treat prophecies with contempt. ²¹Test everything. Hold on to the good. ²²Avoid every kind of evil.

WORDS TO REMEMBER

5:15 Make sure that nobody pays back wrong for wrong, but always try to be kind to each other and to everyone else.

²³May God himself, the God of peace, sanctify you through and through. May your whole spirit, soul and body be kept blameless at the coming of our Lord Jesus Christ. ²⁴The one who calls you is faithful and he will do it.

²⁵Brothers, pray for us. ²⁶Greet all the brothers with a holy kiss. ²⁷I charge you before the Lord to have this letter read to all the brothers.

²⁸The grace of our Lord Jesus Christ be with you.

2 THESSALONIANS

WHO WROTE THIS BOOK?	Paul.
WHY WAS THIS BOOK WRITTEN?	The book of 2 Thessalonians tells these Christians to work hard until Jesus comes again.
FOR WHOM WAS THIS BOOK WRITTEN?	The book of 2 Thessalonians is a letter Paul sent to Christians at Thessalonica.
WHEN WAS THIS BOOK WRITTEN?	This book was written about A.D. 52 from Corinth.
WHAT ARE SOME IMPORTANT TEACHINGS IN THIS BOOK?	God will punish the wicked. 2 Thessalonians 1:5–10 Everyone should work. 2 Thessalonians 3:6–15

1

Paul, Silas*a* and Timothy,

To the church of the Thessalonians in God our Father and the Lord Jesus Christ:

²Grace and peace to you from God the Father and the Lord Jesus Christ.

Thanksgiving and Prayer

³We ought always to thank God for you, brothers, and rightly so, because your faith is growing more and more, and the love every one of you has for each other is increasing. ⁴Therefore, among God's churches we boast about your perseverance and faith in all the persecutions and trials you are enduring.

⁵All this is evidence that God's judgment is right, and as a result you will be counted worthy of the kingdom of God, for which you are suffering. ⁶God is just: He will pay back trouble to those who trouble you ⁷and give relief to you who are troubled, and to us as well. This will happen when the Lord Jesus is revealed from heaven in blazing fire with his powerful angels. ⁸He will punish those who do not know God and do not obey the gospel of our Lord Jesus. ⁹They will be punished with everlasting destruction and shut out from the presence of the Lord and from the majesty of his power ¹⁰on the day he comes to be glorified in his holy people and to be marveled at among all those who have believed. This includes you, because you believed our testimony to you.

¹¹With this in mind, we constantly pray for you, that our God may count you worthy of his calling, and that by his power he may fulfill every good purpose of yours and every act prompted by your faith. ¹²We pray this so that the name of our Lord Jesus may be glorified in you, and you in him, according to the grace of our God and the Lord Jesus Christ.*b*

The Man of Lawlessness

2

Concerning the coming of our Lord Jesus Christ and our being gathered to him, we ask you, brothers, ²not to become easily unsettled or alarmed by some prophecy, report or letter supposed to have come from us, saying that the day of the Lord has already come. ³Don't let anyone deceive you in any way, for ,that day will not come, until the rebellion occurs and the man of lawlessness*c* is revealed, the man doomed to destruction. ⁴He will oppose and will exalt himself over everything that is called God or is worshiped, so that he sets himself up in God's temple, proclaiming himself to be God.

? DID YOU KNOW?   1:7

When will God punish people for their sins?

God will punish wicked people when Jesus comes back to earth. Until then, people can decide to trust Jesus and have their sins forgiven. When people become Christians, they love Jesus and begin to do good.

---

⁵Don't you remember that when I was with you I used to tell you these things? ⁶And now you know what is holding him back, so that he may be revealed at the proper time. ⁷For the secret power of lawlessness is already at work; but the one who now holds it back will continue to do so till he is taken out of the way. ⁸And then the lawless one will be revealed, whom the Lord Jesus will overthrow with the breath of his mouth and destroy by the splendor of his coming. ⁹The coming of the lawless one will be in accordance with the work of Satan displayed in all kinds of counterfeit miracles, signs and wonders, ¹⁰and in every sort of evil that deceives those

---

*a*1 Greek *Silvanus*, a variant of *Silas*   *b*12 Or *God and Lord, Jesus Christ*   *c*3 Some
manuscripts *sin*

who are perishing. They perish because they refused to love the truth and so be saved. [11]For this reason God sends them a powerful delusion so that they will believe the lie [12]and so that all will be condemned who have not believed the truth but have delighted in wickedness.

Stand Firm

[13]But we ought always to thank God for you, brothers loved by the Lord, because from the beginning God chose you[a] to be saved through the sanctifying work of the Spirit and through belief in the truth. [14]He called you to this through our gospel, that you might share in the glory of our Lord Jesus Christ. [15]So then, brothers, stand firm and hold to the teachings[b] we passed on to you, whether by word of mouth or by letter.

[16]May our Lord Jesus Christ himself and God our Father, who loved us and by his grace gave us eternal encouragement and good hope, [17]encourage your hearts and strengthen you in every good deed and word.

WORDS TO REMEMBER

2:16-17 May our Lord Jesus Christ
. . . encourage your hearts and
strengthen you in every good
deed and word.

Request for Prayer

3 Finally, brothers, pray for us that the message of the Lord may spread rapidly and be honored, just as it was with you. [2]And pray that we may be delivered from wicked and evil men, for not everyone has faith. [3]But the Lord is faithful, and he will strengthen and protect you from the evil one. [4]We have confidence in the Lord that you are doing and will continue to do the things we command. [5]May the Lord direct your hearts into God's love and Christ's perseverance.

Warning Against Idleness

[6]In the name of the Lord Jesus Christ, we command you, brothers, to keep away from every brother who is idle and does not live according to the teaching[c] you received from us. [7]For you yourselves know how you ought to follow our example. We were not idle when we were with you, [8]nor did we eat anyone's food without paying for it. On the contrary, we worked night and day, laboring and toiling so that we would not be a burden to any of you. [9]We did this, not because we do not have the right to such help, but in order to make ourselves a model for you to follow. [10]For even when we were with you, we gave you this rule: "If a man will not work, he shall not eat."

[11]We hear that some among you are idle. They are not busy; they are busybodies. [12]Such people we com-

---

[a]13 Some manuscripts *because God chose you as his firstfruits*   [b]15 Or *traditions*   [c]6 Or *tradition*

▍ET'S LIVE IT!   2 Thessalonians 3:6–10

LEARNING TO WORK ➠ Read 2 Thessalonians 3:6–10. Every adult Christian is supposed to support himself or herself. It's good to learn to work and be responsible when you are still young. Have you thought about earning money so you can buy some of the things you need yourself?

Here are jobs some children do. Collect papers or returnable pop bottles to sell. Do work for your mom or dad around the house. Have a paper route. Wash cars. Rake leaves. Wash windows. Can you think of other work you might do to earn money?

mand and urge in the Lord Jesus Christ to settle down and earn the bread they eat. 13And as for you, brothers, never tire of doing what is right.

14If anyone does not obey our instruction in this letter, take special note of him. Do not associate with him, in order that he may feel ashamed. 15Yet do not regard him as an enemy, but warn him as a brother.

Final Greetings

16Now may the Lord of peace himself give you peace at all times and in every way. The Lord be with all of you.

17I, Paul, write this greeting in my own hand, which is the distinguishing mark in all my letters. This is how I write.

18The grace of our Lord Jesus Christ be with you all.

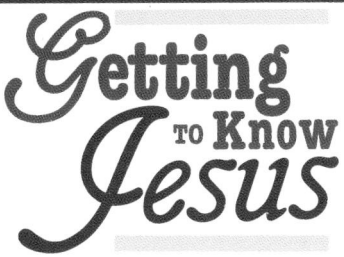

Getting TO Know Jesus

QUESTION: Who is Jesus?
ANSWER: Jesus is God's Son.

Because sin came into the world when Adam and Eve disobeyed
God, God asked Jesus to come to make things right again.
    Jesus was born (just about 2,000 years ago),
    and he lived in a part of the world called Palestine.
When he was about thirty years old, he began to preach and to heal.
    Three or four years later he was nailed to a cross to die.
When the people who loved him went to his grave three days later,
Jesus' body wasn't there.
    He had come back to life, just as he said he would.

QUESTION: Where is Jesus now?
ANSWER: Jesus is in heaven with his Father.

But he has not left us alone here on earth. He sent the Holy Spirit to
live with us —
    to make us strong when we feel like giving up,
      to help us to care about other people
      when we sometimes don't feel like it,
        to tell us that Jesus will always love us.

QUESTION: Why did Jesus have to die?
ANSWER: It was all part of God's great plan to make right
what had become so wrong because of sin.

You see, we all deserve to be punished.
    God loves us so much he sent Jesus to take our punishment.
Because of Jesus we can know for sure that God welcomes us into his
loving arms —
    right now and when we die and go to be with him.

 continued

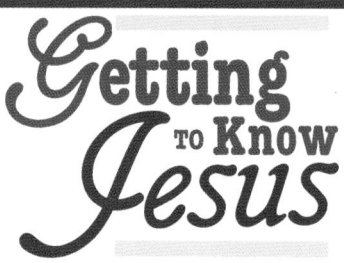

Getting TO Know Jesus

QUESTION: Does Jesus love me?
ANSWER: Jesus loves you more than you can imagine.

He loves you when you cry and when you laugh;
    when you argue with your brother or
        when you've had a bad day.
He loves you so much that he died for you — but he isn't still dead.
He is alive, and he is loving and watching over you every day.

QUESTION: Will Jesus ever stop loving me?
ANSWER: No!

There will be times when you wonder if Jesus is really real.
    There will be times when you wonder if he loves you.
There will be times when you do things that you shouldn't —
    when you act mean to your sister
        or lie to your father.
But when you pray and tell Jesus that you have times when
you doubt;
    when you pray and tell Jesus that you know you've done
wrong and you want to do better —
    you can be sure that he will never let you down.
He will love you your whole life long,
    and you will live with him forever.

QUESTION: How do I know I'm a Christian?
ANSWER: There are many signs.

When you love Jesus with all the love you can give,
    when you know deep down that Jesus loves you,
        when you believe he died to forgive your sins,
            when you want to live for Jesus —
those are good signs that help you know you are a Christian.
    Sure, you're going to fail sometimes,
But, you see, God's love for you is so great that it covers those
times when you fail.
    He sees deep into your heart.
        He knows your desire to live for him,
            and *he loves you.*

1 TIMOTHY

WHO WROTE THIS BOOK?

Paul.

WHY WAS THIS BOOK WRITTEN?

The book of 1 Timothy gives Timothy advice on how to do his important work.

FOR WHOM WAS THIS BOOK WRITTEN?

This book is a letter Paul sent to his young helper Timothy.

WHEN WAS THIS BOOK WRITTEN?

This book was written about A.D. 65 from Macedonia.

WHAT ARE SOME IMPORTANT TEACHINGS IN THIS BOOK?

Beware of false teachers.	1 Timothy 1:3–11
Choosing leaders.	1 Timothy 3:1–16
Be an example.	1 Timothy 4:11–16
The Christian family.	1 Timothy 5:1–2
Don't love money.	1 Timothy 6:3–10
Advice to the rich.	1 Timothy 6:17–21

1 Paul, an apostle of Christ Jesus by the command of God our Savior and of Christ Jesus our hope,

²To Timothy my true son in the faith:

Grace, mercy and peace from God the Father and Christ Jesus our Lord.

❓DID YOU KNOW?   1:2

Who was Timothy?

Timothy was a young companion of Paul. Paul trained Timothy on his missionary journeys. Later Timothy became a leader in the church. Two New Testament books are letters that Paul wrote to Timothy.

Warning Against False Teachers of the Law

³As I urged you when I went into Macedonia, stay there in Ephesus so that you may command certain men not to teach false doctrines any longer ⁴nor to devote themselves to myths and endless genealogies. These promote controversies rather than God's work—which is by faith. ⁵The goal of this command is love, which comes from a pure heart and a good conscience and a sincere faith. ⁶Some have wandered away from these and turned to meaningless talk. ⁷They want to be teachers of the law, but they do not know what they are talking about or what they so confidently affirm.

⁸We know that the law is good if one uses it properly. ⁹We also know that law*a* is made not for the righteous but for lawbreakers and rebels, the ungodly and sinful, the unholy and irreligious; for those who kill their fathers or mothers, for murderers, ¹⁰for adulterers and perverts, for slave traders and liars and perjurers—and for whatever else is contrary to the sound doctrine ¹¹that conforms to the glorious gospel of the blessed God, which he entrusted to me.

The Lord's Grace to Paul

¹²I thank Christ Jesus our Lord, who has given me strength, that he considered me faithful, appointing me to his service. ¹³Even though I was once a blasphemer and a persecutor and a violent man, I was shown mercy because I acted in ignorance and unbelief. ¹⁴The grace of our Lord was poured out on me abundantly, along with the faith and love that are in Christ Jesus.

¹⁵Here is a trustworthy saying that deserves full acceptance: Christ Jesus came into the world to save sinners—of whom I am the worst. ¹⁶But for that very reason I was shown mercy so that in me, the worst of sinners, Christ Jesus might display his unlimited patience as an example for those who would believe on him and receive eternal life. ¹⁷Now to the King eternal, immortal, invisible, the only God, be honor and glory for ever and ever. Amen.

¹⁸Timothy, my son, I give you this instruction in keeping with the prophecies once made about you, so that by following them you may fight the good fight, ¹⁹holding on to faith and a good conscience. Some have rejected these and so have shipwrecked their faith. ²⁰Among them are Hymenaeus and Alexander, whom I have handed over to Satan to be taught not to blaspheme.

Instructions on Worship

2 I urge, then, first of all, that requests, prayers, intercession and thanksgiving be made for everyone— ²for kings and all those in authority, that we may live peaceful and quiet lives in all godliness and holiness. ³This is good, and pleases God our Savior, ⁴who wants all men to be saved and to come to a knowledge of the truth. ⁵For there is one

a9 Or that the law

God and one mediator between God and men, the man Christ Jesus, [6]who gave himself as a ransom for all men—the testimony given in its proper time. [7]And for this purpose I was appointed a herald and an apostle—I am telling the truth, I am not lying—and a teacher of the true faith to the Gentiles.

?DID YOU KNOW?   1:13

Can bad people become good?

Yes. Paul was once a violent man who persecuted Christians. When God saved him, he changed. God can save the worst sinners and make them truly good people.

---

[8]I want men everywhere to lift up holy hands in prayer, without anger or disputing.

[9]I also want women to dress modestly, with decency and propriety, not with braided hair or gold or pearls or expensive clothes, [10]but with good deeds, appropriate for women who profess to worship God.

[11]A woman should learn in quietness and full submission. [12]I do not permit a woman to teach or to have authority over a man; she must be silent. [13]For Adam was formed first, then Eve. [14]And Adam was not the one deceived; it was the woman who was deceived and became a sinner. [15]But women[a] will be saved[b] through childbearing—if they continue in faith, love and holiness with propriety.

Overseers and Deacons

3 Here is a trustworthy saying: If anyone sets his heart on being an overseer,[c] he desires a noble task. [2]Now the overseer must be above reproach, the husband of but one wife,

temperate, self-controlled, respectable, hospitable, able to teach, [3]not given to drunkenness, not violent but gentle, not quarrelsome, not a lover of money. [4]He must manage his own family well and see that his children obey him with proper respect. [5](If anyone does not know how to manage his own family, how can he take care of God's church?) [6]He must not be a recent convert, or he may become conceited and fall under the same judgment as the devil. [7]He must also have a good reputation with outsiders, so that he will not fall into disgrace and into the devil's trap.

[8]Deacons, likewise, are to be men worthy of respect, sincere, not indulging in much wine, and not pursuing dishonest gain. [9]They must keep hold of the deep truths of the faith with a clear conscience. [10]They must first be tested; and then if there is nothing against them, let them serve as deacons.

[11]In the same way, their wives[d] are to be women worthy of respect, not malicious talkers but temperate and trustworthy in everything.

?DID YOU KNOW?   3:2

What kind of people should church leaders be?

Church leaders should be good examples of what Christians are to be like. They should be respectable, hospitable, gentle, not lovers of money. In 1 Timothy 3 Paul lists other important characteristics of church leaders.

---

[12]A deacon must be the husband of but one wife and must manage his children and his household well. [13]Those who have served well gain an excellent standing and great assurance in their faith in Christ Jesus.

[14]Although I hope to come to you

---

[a]15 Greek she   [b]15 Or restored   [c]1 Traditionally bishop; also in verse 2   [d]11 Or way, deaconesses

soon, I am writing you these instructions so that, [15]if I am delayed, you will know how people ought to conduct themselves in God's household, which is the church of the living God, the pillar and foundation of the truth. [16]Beyond all question, the mystery of godliness is great:

> He[a] appeared in a body,[b]
> was vindicated by the Spirit,
> was seen by angels,
> was preached among the
>   nations,
> was believed on in the world,
> was taken up in glory.

Instructions to Timothy

4 The Spirit clearly says that in later times some will abandon the faith and follow deceiving spirits and things taught by demons. [2]Such teachings come through hypocritical liars, whose consciences have been seared as with a hot iron. [3]They forbid people to marry and order them to abstain from certain foods, which God created to be received with thanksgiving by those who believe and who know the truth. [4]For everything God created is good, and nothing is to be rejected if it is received with thanksgiving, [5]because it is consecrated by the word of God and prayer.

[6]If you point these things out to the brothers, you will be a good minister of Christ Jesus, brought up in the truths of the faith and of the good teaching that you have followed. [7]Have nothing to do with godless myths and old wives' tales; rather, train yourself to be godly. [8]For physical training is of some value, but godliness has value for all things, holding promise for both the present life and the life to come.

[9]This is a trustworthy saying that deserves full acceptance [10](and for this we labor and strive), that we have put our hope in the living God, who is the Savior of all men, and especially of those who believe.

[11]Command and teach these things. [12]Don't let anyone look down on you because you are young, but set an example for the believers in speech, in life, in love, in faith and in purity. [13]Until I come, devote yourself to the public reading of Scripture, to preaching and to teaching. [14]Do not neglect your gift, which was given you through a prophetic message when the body of elders laid their hands on you.

[15]Be diligent in these matters; give yourself wholly to them, so that everyone may see your progress. [16]Watch your life and doctrine closely. Persevere in them, because if you do, you will save both yourself and your hearers.

---

[a]16 Some manuscripts *God*   [b]16 Or *in the flesh*

LET'S LIVE IT!

BE AN EXAMPLE ➡ Read 1 Timothy 4:12. What five ways can even young people be good Christians and set an example for others?

Make a Pledge Poster for your wall. Here is what the Pledge Poster might say:

I WILL BE AN EXAMPLE

In speech, I will not gossip or swear.
In life, I will do what pleases God.
In love, I will care about others.
In faith, I will pray and trust God.
In purity, I will choose what is right.

Advice About Widows, Elders and Slaves

5 Do not rebuke an older man harshly, but exhort him as if he were your father. Treat younger men as brothers, ²older women as mothers, and younger women as sisters, with absolute purity.

³Give proper recognition to those widows who are really in need. ⁴But if a widow has children or grandchildren, these should learn first of all to put their religion into practice by caring for their own family and so repaying their parents and grandparents, for this is pleasing to God. ⁵The widow who is really in need and left all alone puts her hope in God and continues night and day to pray and to ask God for help. ⁶But the widow who lives for pleasure is dead even while she lives. ⁷Give the people these instructions, too, so that no one may be open to blame. ⁸If anyone does not provide for his relatives, and especially for his immediate family, he has denied the faith and is worse than an unbeliever.

⁹No widow may be put on the list of widows unless she is over sixty, has been faithful to her husband,ᵃ ¹⁰and is well known for her good deeds, such as bringing up children, showing hospitality, washing the feet of the saints, helping those in trouble and devoting herself to all kinds of good deeds.

¹¹As for younger widows, do not put them on such a list. For when their sensual desires overcome their dedication to Christ, they want to marry. ¹²Thus they bring judgment on themselves, because they have broken their first pledge. ¹³Besides, they get into the habit of being idle and going about from house to house. And not only do they become idlers, but also gossips and busybodies, saying things they ought not to. ¹⁴So I counsel younger widows to marry, to have children, to manage their homes and to give the enemy no opportunity for slander. ¹⁵Some have in fact already turned away to follow Satan.

? DID YOU KNOW? 5:11

What was the list of widows?

The list of widows was a list of Christian women who had no family. The church supported them and gave them special work to do in ministering to other Christians.

---

¹⁶If any woman who is a believer has widows in her family, she should help them and not let the church be burdened with them, so that the church can help those widows who are really in need.

¹⁷The elders who direct the affairs of the church well are worthy of double honor, especially those whose work is preaching and teaching. ¹⁸For the Scripture says, "Do not muzzle the ox while it is treading out the grain,"ᵇ and "The worker deserves his wages."ᶜ ¹⁹Do not entertain an accusation against an elder unless it is brought by two or three witnesses. ²⁰Those who sin are to be rebuked publicly, so that the others may take warning.

²¹I charge you, in the sight of God and Christ Jesus and the elect angels, to keep these instructions without partiality, and to do nothing out of favoritism.

²²Do not be hasty in the laying on of hands, and do not share in the sins of others. Keep yourself pure.

²³Stop drinking only water, and use a little wine because of your stomach and your frequent illnesses.

²⁴The sins of some men are obvious, reaching the place of judgment ahead of them; the sins of others trail behind them. ²⁵In the same way, good deeds are obvious, and even those that are not cannot be hidden.

6 All who are under the yoke of slavery should consider their masters worthy of full respect, so that

---

ᵃ9 Or *has had but one husband*　　ᵇ18 Deut. 25:4　　ᶜ18 Luke 10:7

God's name and our teaching may not be slandered. ²Those who have believing masters are not to show less respect for them because they are brothers. Instead, they are to serve them even better, because those who benefit from their service are believers, and dear to them. These are the things you are to teach and urge on them.

Love of Money

³If anyone teaches false doctrines and does not agree to the sound instruction of our Lord Jesus Christ and to godly teaching, ⁴he is conceited and understands nothing. He has an unhealthy interest in controversies and quarrels about words that result in envy, strife, malicious talk, evil suspicions ⁵and constant friction between men of corrupt mind, who have been robbed of the truth and who think that godliness is a means to financial gain.

⁶But godliness with contentment is great gain. ⁷For we brought nothing into the world, and we can take nothing out of it. ⁸But if we have food and clothing, we will be content with that. ⁹People who want to get rich fall into temptation and a trap and into many foolish and harmful desires that plunge men into ruin and destruction. ¹⁰For the love of money is a root of all kinds of evil. Some people, eager for money, have wandered from the faith and pierced themselves with many griefs.

Paul's Charge to Timothy

¹¹But you, man of God, flee from all this, and pursue righteousness, god-liness, faith, love, endurance and gentleness. ¹²Fight the good fight of the faith. Take hold of the eternal life to which you were called when you made your good confession in the presence of many witnesses. ¹³In the sight of God, who gives life to everything, and of Christ Jesus, who while testifying before Pontius Pilate made the good confession, I charge you ¹⁴to keep this command without spot or blame until the appearing of our Lord Jesus Christ, ¹⁵which God will bring about in his own time—God, the blessed and only Ruler, the King of kings and Lord of lords, ¹⁶who alone is immortal and who lives in unapproachable light, whom no one has seen or can see. To him be honor and might forever. Amen.

¹⁷Command those who are rich in this present world not to be arrogant nor to put their hope in wealth, which is so uncertain, but to put their hope in God, who richly provides us with everything for our enjoyment. ¹⁸Command them to do good, to be rich in good deeds, and to be generous and willing to share. ¹⁹In this way they will lay up treasure for themselves as a firm foundation for the coming age, so that they may take hold of the life that is truly life.

²⁰Timothy, guard what has been entrusted to your care. Turn away from godless chatter and the opposing ideas of what is falsely called knowledge, ²¹which some have professed and in so doing have wandered from the faith.

Grace be with you.

LET'S LIVE IT!
1 Timothy 6:6–10

BEING CONTENT ➡ Make a list of all your favorite toys and possessions. Be sure to include things like your bed, your different clothes, your toys.

Read 1 Timothy 6:6–10. What is really important in life is godliness (being God's person) and having enough to eat and to wear. People who think they have to have more things to be happy are usually unhappy and discontented no matter how much they have.

Look back at the list you made. Draw a line through each thing that you don't need in order to be content.

2 TIMOTHY

WHO WROTE THIS BOOK?
Paul.

WHY WAS THIS BOOK WRITTEN?
This letter encourages Timothy to keep on working hard after Paul dies.

FOR WHOM WAS THIS BOOK WRITTEN?
This book is a letter Paul sent to his young helper Timothy.

WHEN WAS THIS BOOK WRITTEN?
This book was written about A.D. 67, when Paul was in prison a second time.

WHAT ARE SOME IMPORTANT TEACHINGS IN THIS BOOK?
Teach God's truth.   2 Timothy 1:8–15
Teach gently.   2 Timothy 2:22–26
Teach faithfully.   2 Timothy 4:1–5

1 Paul, an apostle of Christ Jesus by the will of God, according to the promise of life that is in Christ Jesus,

²To Timothy, my dear son:

Grace, mercy and peace from God the Father and Christ Jesus our Lord.

Encouragement to Be Faithful

³I thank God, whom I serve, as my forefathers did, with a clear conscience, as night and day I constantly remember you in my prayers. ⁴Recalling your tears, I long to see you, so that I may be filled with joy. ⁵I have been reminded of your sincere faith, which first lived in your grandmother Lois and in your mother Eunice and, I am persuaded, now lives in you also. ⁶For this reason I remind you to fan into flame the gift of God, which is in you through the laying on of my hands. ⁷For God did not give us a spirit of timidity, but a spirit of power, of love and of self-discipline.

WORDS TO REMEMBER

1:8 Do not be ashamed to testify about our Lord.

---

⁸So do not be ashamed to testify about our Lord, or ashamed of me his prisoner. But join with me in suffering for the gospel, by the power of God, ⁹who has saved us and called us to a holy life—not because of anything we have done but because of his own purpose and grace. This grace was given us in Christ Jesus before the beginning of time, ¹⁰but it has now been revealed through the appearing of our Savior, Christ Jesus, who has destroyed death and has brought life and immortality to light through the gospel. ¹¹And of this gospel I was appointed a herald and an apostle and a teacher. ¹²That is why I am suffering as I am. Yet I am not ashamed, because I know whom I have believed, and am convinced that he is able to guard what I have entrusted to him for that day.

¹³What you heard from me, keep as the pattern of sound teaching, with faith and love in Christ Jesus. ¹⁴Guard the good deposit that was entrusted to you—guard it with the help of the Holy Spirit who lives in us.

¹⁵You know that everyone in the province of Asia has deserted me, including Phygelus and Hermogenes.

¹⁶May the Lord show mercy to the household of Onesiphorus, because he often refreshed me and was not ashamed of my chains. ¹⁷On the contrary, when he was in Rome, he searched hard for me until he found me. ¹⁸May the Lord grant that he will find mercy from the Lord on that day! You know very well in how many ways he helped me in Ephesus.

2 You then, my son, be strong in the grace that is in Christ Jesus. ²And the things you have heard me say in the presence of many witnesses entrust to reliable men who will also be qualified to teach others. ³Endure hardship with us like a good soldier of Christ Jesus. ⁴No one serving as a soldier gets involved in civil-

---

LET'S LIVE IT!   2 Timothy 1:13–14

WHAT YOU HEARD ➡ Paul taught Timothy about God and Jesus. Who has taught you about God? Your parents? Teachers? Church school teachers? Minister? Ask each to tell you the most important thing they have taught you—something they want you to remember all your life.

Write down what they tell you. Look at what you've written every few weeks to remind yourself of what you need to learn.

ian affairs—he wants to please his commanding officer. [5]Similarly, if anyone competes as an athlete, he does not receive the victor's crown unless he competes according to the rules. [6]The hardworking farmer should be the first to receive a share of the crops. [7]Reflect on what I am saying, for the Lord will give you insight into all this.

?DID YOU KNOW?   2:3

What are good Christians like?

Good Christians are like soldiers, who obey their commander; like athletes, who train hard to win; like farmers, who work hard and are willing to wait for their rewards.

---

[8]Remember Jesus Christ, raised from the dead, descended from David. This is my gospel, [9]for which I am suffering even to the point of being chained like a criminal. But God's word is not chained. [10]Therefore I endure everything for the sake of the elect, that they too may obtain the salvation that is in Christ Jesus, with eternal glory.

[11]Here is a trustworthy saying:

If we died with him,
  we will also live with him;
[12]if we endure,
  we will also reign with him.
If we disown him,
  he will also disown us;
[13]if we are faithless,
  he will remain faithful,
  for he cannot disown himself.

A Workman Approved by God

[14]Keep reminding them of these things. Warn them before God against quarreling about words; it is of no value, and only ruins those who listen. [15]Do your best to present yourself to God as one approved, a workman who does not need to be ashamed and who correctly handles the word of truth. [16]Avoid godless chatter, because those who indulge in it will become more and more ungodly. [17]Their teaching will spread like gangrene. Among them are Hymenaeus and Philetus, [18]who have wandered away from the truth. They say that the resurrection has already taken place, and they destroy the faith of some. [19]Nevertheless, God's solid foundation stands firm, sealed with this inscription: "The Lord knows those who are his,"[a] and, "Everyone who confesses the name of the Lord must turn away from wickedness."

[20]In a large house there are articles not only of gold and silver, but also of wood and clay; some are for noble purposes and some for ignoble. [21]If a man cleanses himself from the latter, he will be an instrument for noble purposes, made holy, useful to the Master and prepared to do any good work.

WORDS TO REMEMBER

2:22 Pursue righteousness, faith, love and peace, along with those who call on the Lord out of a pure heart.

---

[22]Flee the evil desires of youth, and pursue righteousness, faith, love and peace, along with those who call on the Lord out of a pure heart. [23]Don't have anything to do with foolish and stupid arguments, because you know they produce quarrels. [24]And the Lord's servant must not quarrel; instead, he must be kind to everyone, able to teach, not resentful. [25]Those who oppose him he must gently instruct, in the hope that God will grant them repentance leading them to a knowledge of the truth, [26]and that they will come to their senses and escape from the trap of the devil, who has taken them captive to do his will.

a19 Num. 16:5 (see Septuagint)

Godlessness in the Last Days

3 But mark this: There will be terrible times in the last days. ²People will be lovers of themselves, lovers of money, boastful, proud, abusive, disobedient to their parents, ungrateful, unholy, ³without love, unforgiving, slanderous, without self-control, brutal, not lovers of the good, ⁴treacherous, rash, conceited, lovers of pleasure rather than lovers of God— ⁵having a form of godliness but denying its power. Have nothing to do with them.

⁶They are the kind who worm their way into homes and gain control over weak-willed women, who are loaded down with sins and are swayed by all kinds of evil desires, ⁷always learning but never able to acknowledge the truth. ⁸Just as Jannes and Jambres opposed Moses, so also these men oppose the truth—men of depraved minds, who, as far as the faith is concerned, are rejected. ⁹But they will not get very far because, as in the case of those men, their folly will be clear to everyone.

Paul's Charge to Timothy

¹⁰You, however, know all about my teaching, my way of life, my purpose, faith, patience, love, endurance,

¹¹persecutions, sufferings—what kinds of things happened to me in Antioch, Iconium and Lystra, the persecutions I endured. Yet the Lord rescued me from all of them. ¹²In fact, everyone who wants to live a godly life in Christ Jesus will be persecuted, ¹³while evil men and impostors will go from bad to worse, deceiving and being deceived. ¹⁴But as for you, continue in what you have learned and have become convinced of, because you know those from whom you learned it, ¹⁵and how from infancy you have known the holy Scriptures, which are able to make you wise for salvation through faith in Christ Jesus. ¹⁶All Scripture is God-breathed and is useful for teaching, rebuking, correcting and training in righteousness, ¹⁷so that the man of God may be thoroughly equipped for every good work.

WORDS TO REMEMBER

3:16 All Scripture is God-breathed and is useful for teaching.

4 In the presence of God and of Christ Jesus, who will judge the living and the dead, and in view of his appearing and his kingdom, I give

Life in Bible Times

A LEAFY CROWN

People who won athletic events did not get money or gold. The prize was a wreath made of leaves to wear on their head. In 2 Timothy 4:8 Paul wrote about a crown that would last longer than a crown of leaves. He said he had "finished the race" and would be receiving a "crown of righteousness."

you this charge: [2]Preach the Word; be prepared in season and out of season; correct, rebuke and encourage—with great patience and careful instruction. [3]For the time will come when men will not put up with sound doctrine. Instead, to suit their own desires, they will gather around them a great number of teachers to say what their itching ears want to hear. [4]They will turn their ears away from the truth and turn aside to myths. [5]But you, keep your head in all situations, endure hardship, do the work of an evangelist, discharge all the duties of your ministry.

[6]For I am already being poured out like a drink offering, and the time has come for my departure. [7]I have fought the good fight, I have finished the race, I have kept the faith. [8]Now there is in store for me the crown of righteousness, which the Lord, the righteous Judge, will award to me on that day—and not only to me, but also to all who have longed for his appearing.

Personal Remarks

[9]Do your best to come to me quickly, [10]for Demas, because he loved this world, has deserted me and has gone to Thessalonica. Crescens has gone to Galatia, and Titus to Dalmatia. [11]Only Luke is with me. Get Mark and bring him with you, because he is helpful to me in my ministry. [12]I sent Tychicus to Ephesus. [13]When you come, bring the cloak that I left with Carpus at Troas, and my scrolls, especially the parchments.

[14]Alexander the metalworker did me a great deal of harm. The Lord will repay him for what he has done. [15]You too should be on your guard against him, because he strongly opposed our message.

[16]At my first defense, no one came to my support, but everyone deserted me. May it not be held against them. [17]But the Lord stood at my side and gave me strength, so that through me the message might be fully proclaimed and all the Gentiles might hear it. And I was delivered from the lion's mouth. [18]The Lord will rescue me from every evil attack and will bring me safely to his heavenly kingdom. To him be glory for ever and ever. Amen.

Final Greetings

[19]Greet Priscilla[a] and Aquila and the household of Onesiphorus. [20]Erastus stayed in Corinth, and I left Trophimus sick in Miletus. [21]Do your best to get here before winter. Eubulus greets you, and so do Pudens, Linus, Claudia and all the brothers.

[22]The Lord be with your spirit. Grace be with you.

---

[a]19 Greek *Prisca*, a variant of *Priscilla*

TITUS

WHO WROTE THIS BOOK?

Paul.

WHY WAS THIS BOOK WRITTEN?

The book of Titus shows Titus how to be a good teacher and leader.

FOR WHOM WAS THIS BOOK WRITTEN?

This book is a letter Paul sent to a young helper named Titus.

WHEN WAS THIS BOOK WRITTEN?

Paul wrote this letter to Titus about A.D. 65 from Corinth.

WHAT ARE SOME IMPORTANT TEACHINGS IN THIS BOOK?

How to live a Christian life. Titus 2:1–15
Christians are to do good. Titus 3:3–8

1 Paul, a servant of God and an apostle of Jesus Christ for the faith of God's elect and the knowledge of the truth that leads to godliness— 2a faith and knowledge resting on the hope of eternal life, which God, who does not lie, promised before the beginning of time, 3and at his appointed season he brought his word to light through the preaching entrusted to me by the command of God our Savior,

4To Titus, my true son in our common faith:

Grace and peace from God the Father and Christ Jesus our Savior.

Titus' Task on Crete

5The reason I left you in Crete was that you might straighten out what was left unfinished and appoint*a* elders in every town, as I directed you. 6An elder must be blameless, the husband of but one wife, a man whose children believe and are not open to the charge of being wild and disobedient. 7Since an overseer*b* is entrusted with God's work, he must be blameless—not overbearing, not quick-tempered, not given to drunkenness, not violent, not pursuing dishonest gain. 8Rather he must be hospitable, one who loves what is good, who is self-controlled, upright, holy and disciplined. 9He must hold firmly to the trustworthy message as it has been taught, so that he can encourage others by sound doctrine and refute those who oppose it.

10For there are many rebellious people, mere talkers and deceivers, especially those of the circumcision group. 11They must be silenced, because they are ruining whole households by teaching things they ought not to teach—and that for the sake of dishonest gain. 12Even one of their own prophets has said, "Cretans are always liars, evil brutes, lazy gluttons." 13This testimony is true. Therefore, rebuke them sharply, so that they will be sound in the faith

14and will pay no attention to Jewish myths or to the commands of those who reject the truth. 15To the pure, all things are pure, but to those who are corrupted and do not believe, nothing is pure. In fact, both their minds and consciences are corrupted. 16They claim to know God, but by their actions they deny him. They are detestable, disobedient and unfit for doing anything good.

What Must Be Taught to Various Groups

2 You must teach what is in accord with sound doctrine. 2Teach the older men to be temperate, worthy of respect, self-controlled, and sound in faith, in love and in endurance.

3Likewise, teach the older women to be reverent in the way they live, not to be slanderers or addicted to much wine, but to teach what is good. 4Then they can train the younger women to love their husbands and children, 5to be self-controlled and pure, to be busy at home, to be kind, and to be subject to their husbands, so that no one will malign the word of God.

6Similarly, encourage the young men to be self-controlled. 7In everything set them an example by doing what is good. In your teaching show integrity, seriousness 8and soundness of speech that cannot be condemned, so that those who oppose you may be ashamed because they have nothing bad to say about us.

9Teach slaves to be subject to their masters in everything, to try to please them, not to talk back to them, 10and not to steal from them, but to show that they can be fully trusted, so that in every way they will make the teaching about God our Savior attractive.

11For the grace of God that brings salvation has appeared to all men. 12It teaches us to say "No" to ungodliness and worldly passions, and to live self-controlled, upright and godly lives in this present age, 13while we

---

*a*5 Or *ordain*　　*b*7 Traditionally *bishop*

wait for the blessed hope—the glorious appearing of our great God and Savior, Jesus Christ, [14]who gave himself for us to redeem us from all wickedness and to purify for himself a people that are his very own, eager to do what is good.

[15]These, then, are the things you should teach. Encourage and rebuke with all authority. Do not let anyone despise you.

Doing What Is Good

3 Remind the people to be subject to rulers and authorities, to be obedient, to be ready to do whatever is good, [2]to slander no one, to be peaceable and considerate, and to show true humility toward all men.

WORDS TO REMEMBER

3:1 Be ready to do whatever is good.

---

[3]At one time we too were foolish, disobedient, deceived and enslaved by all kinds of passions and pleasures. We lived in malice and envy, being hated and hating one another. [4]But when the kindness and love of God our Savior appeared, [5]he saved us, not because of righteous things we had done, but because of his mercy. He saved us through the washing of rebirth and renewal by the Holy Spirit, [6]whom he poured out on us generously through Jesus Christ our Savior, [7]so that, having been justified by his grace, we might become heirs having the hope of eternal life. [8]This is a trustworthy saying. And I want you to stress these things, so that those who have trusted in God may be careful to devote themselves to doing what is good. These things are excellent and profitable for everyone.

WORDS TO REMEMBER

3:5 He saved us, not because of righteous things we had done, but because of his mercy.

---

[9]But avoid foolish controversies and genealogies and arguments and quarrels about the law, because these are unprofitable and useless. [10]Warn a divisive person once, and then warn him a second time. After that, have nothing to do with him. [11]You may be sure that such a man is warped and sinful; he is self-condemned.

Final Remarks

[12]As soon as I send Artemas or Tychicus to you, do your best to come to me at Nicopolis, because I have decided to winter there. [13]Do everything you can to help Zenas the lawyer and Apollos on their way and see that they have everything they need. [14]Our people must learn to devote themselves to doing what is good, in order that they may provide for daily necessities and not live unproductive lives.

[15]Everyone with me sends you greetings. Greet those who love us in the faith.

Grace be with you all.

LET'S LIVE IT!   Titus 2:11–14

JUST SAY NO ➡ Read Titus 2:11–14. It tells us that Christians should say no if they are urged to do something wrong. What are some things boys and girls should say no to?

Look in a mirror and practice saying no. Try saying no with a smile. Try to look very serious when you say no. Try an angry look with your no. Which do you think is the best way to say no?

Tell your mom or dad some things you plan to say no to. Ask them which of the looks you've practiced is the best to use when you say no.

PHILEMON

WHO WROTE THIS BOOK?	Paul.
WHY WAS THIS BOOK WRITTEN?	This book asks Philemon to welcome back a runaway slave named Onesimus, who had become a Christian.
TO WHOM WAS THIS BOOK WRITTEN?	This book is a personal letter sent to a Christian named Philemon.
WHEN WAS THIS BOOK WRITTEN?	Philemon was written about A.D. 63 while Paul was in prison in Rome.

[1]Paul, a prisoner of Christ Jesus, and Timothy our brother,

To Philemon our dear friend and fellow worker, [2]to Apphia our sister, to Archippus our fellow soldier and to the church that meets in your home:

[3]Grace to you and peace from God our Father and the Lord Jesus Christ.

Thanksgiving and Prayer

[4]I always thank my God as I remember you in my prayers, [5]because I hear about your faith in the Lord Jesus and your love for all the saints. [6]I pray that you may be active in sharing your faith, so that you will have a full understanding of every good thing we have in Christ. [7]Your love has given me great joy and encouragement, because you, brother, have refreshed the hearts of the saints.

WORDS TO REMEMBER

7 Your love has given me great joy and encouragement.

Paul's Plea for Onesimus

[8]Therefore, although in Christ I could be bold and order you to do what you ought to do, [9]yet I appeal to you on the basis of love. I then, as Paul—an old man and now also a prisoner of Christ Jesus— [10]I appeal to you for my son Onesimus,[a] who became my son while I was in chains. [11]Formerly he was useless to you, but now he has become useful both to you and to me.

[12]I am sending him—who is my very heart—back to you. [13]I would have liked to keep him with me so that he could take your place in helping me while I am in chains for the gospel. [14]But I did not want to do anything without your consent, so that any favor you do will be spontaneous and not forced. [15]Perhaps the reason he was separated from you for a little while was that you might have him back for good— [16]no longer as a slave, but better than a slave, as a dear brother. He is very dear to me but even dearer to you, both as a man and as a brother in the Lord.

[17]So if you consider me a partner, welcome him as you would welcome me. [18]If he has done you any wrong or owes you anything, charge it to me. [19]I, Paul, am writing this with my own hand. I will pay it back—not to mention that you owe me your very self. [20]I do wish, brother, that I may have some benefit from you in the Lord; refresh my heart in Christ. [21]Confident of your obedience, I write to you, knowing that you will do even more than I ask.

[22]And one thing more: Prepare a guest room for me, because I hope to be restored to you in answer to your prayers.

[23]Epaphras, my fellow prisoner in Christ Jesus, sends you greetings. [24]And so do Mark, Aristarchus, Demas and Luke, my fellow workers. [25]The grace of the Lord Jesus Christ be with your spirit.

---

a10 Onesimus means useful.

HEBREWS

The Son Superior to Angels

1 In the past God spoke to our fore-fathers through the prophets at many times and in various ways, ²but in these last days he has spoken to us by his Son, whom he appointed heir of all things, and through whom he made the universe. ³The Son is the radiance of God's glory and the exact representation of his being, sustaining all things by his powerful word. After he had provided purification for sins, he sat down at the right hand of the Majesty in heaven. ⁴So he became as much superior to the angels as the name he has inherited is superior to theirs.

⁵For to which of the angels did God ever say,

"You are my Son;
today I have become your
Father*a*"*b*?

Or again,

"I will be his Father,
and he will be my Son"*c*?

⁶And again, when God brings his firstborn into the world, he says,

"Let all God's angels worship
him."*d*

⁷In speaking of the angels he says,

"He makes his angels winds,
his servants flames of fire."*e*

⁸But about the Son he says,

"Your throne, O God, will last for
ever and ever,
and righteousness will be the
scepter of your kingdom.
⁹You have loved righteousness and
hated wickedness;
therefore God, your God, has set
you above your companions
by anointing you with the oil of
joy."*f*

¹⁰He also says,

"In the beginning, O Lord, you

laid the foundations of the
earth,
and the heavens are the work of
your hands.
¹¹They will perish, but you remain;
they will all wear out like a
garment.
¹²You will roll them up like a robe;
like a garment they will be
changed.
But you remain the same,
and your years will never
end."*g*

¹³To which of the angels did God ever say,

"Sit at my right hand
until I make your enemies
a footstool for your feet"*h*?

¹⁴Are not all angels ministering spirits sent to serve those who will inherit salvation?

? DID YOU KNOW?   1:4

How is Jesus greater than angels?

Jesus is God's Son. Jesus created the angels, and the angels worship him.

Warning to Pay Attention

2 We must pay more careful attention, therefore, to what we have heard, so that we do not drift away. ²For if the message spoken by angels was binding, and every violation and disobedience received its just punishment, ³how shall we escape if we ignore such a great salvation? This salvation, which was first announced by the Lord, was confirmed to us by those who heard him. ⁴God also testified to it by signs, wonders and various miracles, and gifts of the Holy Spirit distributed according to his will.

---

a5 Or *have begotten you*   *b5* Psalm 2:7   *c5* 2 Samuel 7:14; 1 Chron. 17:13   *d6* Deut. 32:43
(see Dead Sea Scrolls and Septuagint)   *e7* Psalm 104:4   *f9* Psalm 45:6,7
g12 Psalm 102:25-27   *h13* Psalm 110:1

Jesus Made Like His Brothers

⁵It is not to angels that he has subjected the world to come, about which we are speaking. ⁶But there is a place where someone has testified:

"What is man that you are
    mindful of him,
  the son of man that you care for
    him?
⁷You made him a little*ᵃ* lower
    than the angels;
  you crowned him with glory and
    honor
⁸ and put everything under his
    feet."*ᵇ*

In putting everything under him, God left nothing that is not subject to him. Yet at present we do not see everything subject to him. ⁹But we see Jesus, who was made a little lower than the angels, now crowned with glory and honor because he suffered death, so that by the grace of God he might taste death for everyone.

¹⁰In bringing many sons to glory, it was fitting that God, for whom and through whom everything exists, should make the author of their salvation perfect through suffering. ¹¹Both the one who makes men holy and those who are made holy are of the same family. So Jesus is not ashamed to call them brothers. ¹²He says,

"I will declare your name to my
    brothers;
  in the presence of the
    congregation I will sing
    your praises."*ᶜ*

¹³And again,

"I will put my trust in him."*ᵈ*

And again he says,

"Here am I, and the children God
    has given me."*ᵉ*

¹⁴Since the children have flesh and blood, he too shared in their humanity so that by his death he might destroy him who holds the power of death—that is, the devil— ¹⁵and free those who all their lives were held in slavery by their fear of death. ¹⁶For surely it is not angels he helps, but Abraham's descendants. ¹⁷For this reason he had to be made like his brothers in every way, in order that he might become a merciful and faithful high priest in service to God, and that he might make atonement for*ᶠ* the sins of the people. ¹⁸Because he himself suffered when he was tempted, he is able to help those who are being tempted.

Jesus Greater Than Moses

3 Therefore, holy brothers, who share in the heavenly calling, fix your thoughts on Jesus, the apostle and high priest whom we confess. ²He was faithful to the one who appointed him, just as Moses was faithful in all God's house. ³Jesus has been found worthy of greater honor than Moses, just as the builder of a house has greater honor than the house itself. ⁴For every house is built by someone, but God is the builder of everything. ⁵Moses was faithful as a servant in all God's house, testifying to what would be said in the future. ⁶But Christ is faithful as a son over God's house. And we are his house, if we hold on to our courage and the hope of which we boast.

Warning Against Unbelief

⁷So, as the Holy Spirit says:

"Today, if you hear his voice,
⁸ do not harden your hearts
  as you did in the rebellion,
    during the time of testing in
    the desert,
⁹where your fathers tested and
    tried me
  and for forty years saw what I
    did.
¹⁰That is why I was angry with
    that generation,

ᵃ7 Or *him for a little while*; also in verse 9   *ᵇ8* Psalm 8:4-6   *ᶜ12* Psalm 22:22
ᵈ13 Isaiah 8:17   *ᵉ13* Isaiah 8:18   *ᶠ17* Or *and that he might turn aside God's wrath, taking away*

and I said, 'Their hearts are
　　always going astray,
and they have not known my
　　ways.'
[11]So I declared on oath in my
　　anger,
'They shall never enter my
　　rest.' "[a]

[12]See to it, brothers, that none of
you has a sinful, unbelieving heart
that turns away from the living God.
[13]But encourage one another daily,
as long as it is called Today, so that
none of you may be hardened by sin's
deceitfulness. [14]We have come to
share in Christ if we hold firmly till
the end the confidence we had at
first. [15]As has just been said:

"Today, if you hear his voice,
　　do not harden your hearts
　　as you did in the rebellion."[b]

[16]Who were they who heard and rebelled? Were they not all those Moses
led out of Egypt? [17]And with whom
was he angry for forty years? Was it
not with those who sinned, whose
bodies fell in the desert? [18]And to
whom did God swear that they would
never enter his rest if not to those
who disobeyed[c]? [19]So we see that
they were not able to enter, because
of their unbelief.

❓DID YOU KNOW?　　3:15

How do people show unbelief?

People who really believe in
God do what God says. People
who do not believe do not obey
God. They rebel and turn away
from him.

A Sabbath-Rest for the People
of God

4 Therefore, since the promise of
entering his rest still stands, let
us be careful that none of you be

found to have fallen short of it. [2]For
we also have had the gospel preached
to us, just as they did; but the message they heard was of no value to
them, because those who heard did
not combine it with faith.[d] [3]Now we
who have believed enter that rest,
just as God has said,

"So I declared on oath in my
　　anger,
'They shall never enter my
　　rest.' "[e]

And yet his work has been finished
since the creation of the world. [4]For
somewhere he has spoken about the
seventh day in these words: "And on
the seventh day God rested from all
his work."[f] [5]And again in the passage above he says, "They shall never
enter my rest."

[6]It still remains that some will enter that rest, and those who formerly
had the gospel preached to them did
not go in, because of their disobedience. [7]Therefore God again set a certain day, calling it Today, when a
long time later he spoke through David, as was said before:

"Today, if you hear his voice,
　　do not harden your hearts."[b]

[8]For if Joshua had given them rest,
God would not have spoken later
about another day. [9]There remains,
then, a Sabbath-rest for the people of
God; [10]for anyone who enters God's
rest also rests from his own work, just
as God did from his. [11]Let us, therefore, make every effort to enter that
rest, so that no one will fall by following their example of disobedience.

[12]For the word of God is living and
active. Sharper than any double-
edged sword, it penetrates even to dividing soul and spirit, joints and marrow; it judges the thoughts and atti-
tudes of the heart. [13]Nothing in all
creation is hidden from God's sight.
Everything is uncovered and laid

---

a11 Psalm 95:7-11　　*b15,7* Psalm 95:7,8　　*c18* Or *disbelieved*　　*d2* Many manuscripts *because*
they did not share in the faith of those who obeyed　　*e3* Psalm 95:11; also in verse 5
f4 Gen. 2:2

bare before the eyes of him to whom we must give account.

Jesus the Great High Priest

¹⁴Therefore, since we have a great high priest who has gone through the heavens,ᵃ Jesus the Son of God, let us hold firmly to the faith we profess. ¹⁵For we do not have a high priest who is unable to sympathize with our weaknesses, but we have one who has been tempted in every way, just as we are—yet was without sin. ¹⁶Let us then approach the throne of grace with confidence, so that we may receive mercy and find grace to help us in our time of need.

5 Every high priest is selected from among men and is appointed to represent them in matters related to God, to offer gifts and sacrifices for sins. ²He is able to deal gently with those who are ignorant and are going astray, since he himself is subject to weakness. ³This is why he has to offer sacrifices for his own sins, as well as for the sins of the people.

⁴No one takes this honor upon himself; he must be called by God, just as Aaron was. ⁵So Christ also did not take upon himself the glory of becoming a high priest. But God said to him,

"You are my Son;
    today I have become your
        Father.ᵇ"ᶜ

⁶And he says in another place,

"You are a priest forever,
    in the order of Melchizedek."ᵈ

⁷During the days of Jesus' life on earth, he offered up prayers and petitions with loud cries and tears to the one who could save him from death, and he was heard because of his reverent submission. ⁸Although he was a son, he learned obedience from what he suffered ⁹and, once made perfect, he became the source of eternal salvation for all who obey him ¹⁰and was designated by God to be high priest in the order of Melchizedek.

? DID YOU KNOW?   5:10

What did a high priest do?

The high priest offered sacrifices to God for people who had sinned, and he prayed to God for them. God appointed the high priests of Israel. Jesus is the high priest God has appointed for us as Christians.

ᵃ14 Or *gone into heaven*   ᵇ5 Or *have begotten you*   ᶜ5 Psalm 2:7   ᵈ6 Psalm 110:4

▌ET'S LIVE IT!   Hebrews 4:14–16

MERCY ➡ Read this story about Eric:

Dad gave Eric money to buy new shoe laces. Instead Eric bought candy. When Eric went home he told his dad he lost the money. Later Eric's dad found out. He took Eric to the store and made him use his allowance to buy the shoe laces. Then he hugged Eric and told him he had done wrong but that he loved him anyway.

Read Hebrews 4:14–16. Do you think Jesus would approve of what Eric's dad did? Why, or why not?

Read this Bible passage to one of your parents. Then act out the story of Eric, with you being Eric. Try different endings. Decide together what Jesus would do if he were your parent.

Warning Against Falling Away

[11]We have much to say about this, but it is hard to explain because you are slow to learn. [12]In fact, though by this time you ought to be teachers, you need someone to teach you the elementary truths of God's word all over again. You need milk, not solid food! [13]Anyone who lives on milk, being still an infant, is not acquainted with the teaching about righteousness. [14]But solid food is for the mature, who by constant use have trained themselves to distinguish good from evil.

6 Therefore let us leave the elementary teachings about Christ and go on to maturity, not laying again the foundation of repentance from acts that lead to death,[a] and of faith in God, [2]instruction about baptisms, the laying on of hands, the resurrection of the dead, and eternal judgment. [3]And God permitting, we will do so.

[4]It is impossible for those who have once been enlightened, who have tasted the heavenly gift, who have shared in the Holy Spirit, [5]who have tasted the goodness of the word of God and the powers of the coming age, [6]if they fall away, to be brought back to repentance, because[b] to their loss they are crucifying the Son of God all over again and subjecting him to public disgrace.

[7]Land that drinks in the rain often falling on it and that produces a crop useful to those for whom it is farmed receives the blessing of God. [8]But land that produces thorns and thistles is worthless and is in danger of being cursed. In the end it will be burned.

[9]Even though we speak like this, dear friends, we are confident of better things in your case—things that accompany salvation. [10]God is not unjust; he will not forget your work and the love you have shown him as you have helped his people and continue to help them. [11]We want each of you to show this same diligence to the very end, in order to make your hope sure. [12]We do not want you to become lazy, but to imitate those who through faith and patience inherit what has been promised.

The Certainty of God's Promise

[13]When God made his promise to Abraham, since there was no one greater for him to swear by, he swore by himself, [14]saying, "I will surely bless you and give you many descendants."[c] [15]And so after waiting patiently, Abraham received what was promised.

[16]Men swear by someone greater than themselves, and the oath confirms what is said and puts an end to all argument. [17]Because God wanted to make the unchanging nature of his purpose very clear to the heirs of what was promised, he confirmed it with an oath. [18]God did this so that, by two unchangeable things in which it is impossible for God to lie, we who have fled to take hold of the hope offered to us may be greatly encouraged. [19]We have this hope as an anchor for the soul, firm and secure. It enters the inner sanctuary behind the curtain, [20]where Jesus, who went before us, has entered on our behalf. He has become a high priest forever, in the order of Melchizedek.

Melchizedek the Priest

7 This Melchizedek was king of Salem and priest of God Most High. He met Abraham returning from the defeat of the kings and blessed him, [2]and Abraham gave him a tenth of everything. First, his name means "king of righteousness"; then also, "king of Salem" means "king of peace." [3]Without father or mother, without genealogy, without beginning of days or end of life, like the Son of God he remains a priest forever.

[4]Just think how great he was: Even the patriarch Abraham gave him a

---

[a]1 Or *from useless rituals*   [b]6 Or *repentance while*   [c]14 Gen. 22:17

tenth of the plunder! ⁵Now the law requires the descendants of Levi who become priests to collect a tenth from the people—that is, their brothers —even though their brothers are descended from Abraham. ⁶This man, however, did not trace his descent from Levi, yet he collected a tenth from Abraham and blessed him who had the promises. ⁷And without doubt the lesser person is blessed by the greater. ⁸In the one case, the tenth is collected by men who die; but in the other case, by him who is declared to be living. ⁹One might even say that Levi, who collects the tenth, paid the tenth through Abraham, ¹⁰because when Melchizedek met Abraham, Levi was still in the body of his ancestor.

❓DID YOU KNOW?   7:11

Who was Melchizedek?

Melchizedek [Mel-KIZ-a-deck] was a priest of God during Abraham's time. Later, only the descendants of Aaron could be priests. Jesus is like Melchizedek. He is a true priest even though he is not a descendant of Aaron.

---

a17 Psalm 110:4

Jesus Like Melchizedek

¹¹If perfection could have been attained through the Levitical priesthood (for on the basis of it the law was given to the people), why was there still need for another priest to come —one in the order of Melchizedek, not in the order of Aaron? ¹²For when there is a change of the priesthood, there must also be a change of the law. ¹³He of whom these things are said belonged to a different tribe, and no one from that tribe has ever served at the altar. ¹⁴For it is clear that our Lord descended from Judah, and in regard to that tribe Moses said nothing about priests. ¹⁵And what we have said is even more clear if another priest like Melchizedek appears, ¹⁶one who has become a priest not on the basis of a regulation as to his ancestry but on the basis of the power of an indestructible life. ¹⁷For it is declared:

"You are a priest forever,
in the order of Melchizedek."ᵃ

¹⁸The former regulation is set aside because it was weak and useless ¹⁹(for the law made nothing perfect), and a better hope is introduced, by which we draw near to God.

²⁰And it was not without an oath!

Life in Bible Times

ANCHORS

In ancient times every ship carried several anchors. They were used not only to anchor a ship in harbor, but to slow it down in a storm. Anchors were made from different materials at different times: stone, iron, lead. Most had two flukes (the part of an anchor that hooks in the ground).

Others became priests without any oath, ²¹but he became a priest with an oath when God said to him:

"The Lord has sworn
  and will not change his mind:
'You are a priest forever.'"ᵃ

²²Because of this oath, Jesus has become the guarantee of a better covenant.

²³Now there have been many of those priests, since death prevented them from continuing in office; ²⁴but because Jesus lives forever, he has a permanent priesthood. ²⁵Therefore he is able to save completelyᵇ those who come to God through him, because he always lives to intercede for them.

²⁶Such a high priest meets our need—one who is holy, blameless, pure, set apart from sinners, exalted above the heavens. ²⁷Unlike the other high priests, he does not need to offer sacrifices day after day, first for his own sins, and then for the sins of the people. He sacrificed for their sins once for all when he offered himself. ²⁸For the law appoints as high priests men who are weak; but the oath, which came after the law, appointed the Son, who has been made perfect forever.

The High Priest of a New Covenant

8 The point of what we are saying is this: We do have such a high priest, who sat down at the right hand of the throne of the Majesty in heaven, ²and who serves in the sanctuary, the true tabernacle set up by the Lord, not by man.

³Every high priest is appointed to offer both gifts and sacrifices, and so it was necessary for this one also to have something to offer. ⁴If he were on earth, he would not be a priest, for there are already men who offer the gifts prescribed by the law. ⁵They serve at a sanctuary that is a copy and shadow of what is in heaven. This is why Moses was warned when he was about to build the tabernacle: "See to it that you make everything according to the pattern shown you on the mountain."ᶜ ⁶But the ministry Jesus has received is as superior to theirs as the covenant of which he is mediator is superior to the old one, and it is founded on better promises.

⁷For if there had been nothing wrong with that first covenant, no place would have been sought for another. ⁸But God found fault with the people and saidᵈ:

"The time is coming, declares the Lord,
    when I will make a new covenant
  with the house of Israel
    and with the house of Judah.
⁹It will not be like the covenant
    I made with their forefathers
  when I took them by the hand
    to lead them out of Egypt,

ᵃ21 Psalm 110:4   ᵇ25 Or forever   ᶜ5 Exodus 25:40   ᵈ8 Some manuscripts may be translated fault and said to the people.

▌ET'S LIVE IT!   Hebrews 7:24–25

JESUS IS ALIVE ➧ Read Hebrews 7:24–25. Jesus is alive and he prays (intercedes) for you! Because Jesus is alive, he will take care of you always.

Here is something to do to remind you that Jesus is alive. At your local Christian bookstore, get small pictures of Jesus praying. Put one on the mirror where you brush your teeth. Put one in your room near your bed. Put one in your school notebook. Think of other places to put the pictures where you will see them during the day and will remember that Jesus is alive.

because they did not remain
　　faithful to my covenant,
and I turned away from them,
　　　　　declares the Lord.
[10]This is the covenant I will make
　　with the house of Israel
after that time, declares the
　　Lord.
I will put my laws in their minds
　　and write them on their hearts.
I will be their God,
　　and they will be my people.
[11]No longer will a man teach his
　　neighbor,
　　or a man his brother, saying,
　　'Know the Lord,'
because they will all know me,
　　from the least of them to the
　　greatest.
[12]For I will forgive their
　　wickedness
　　and will remember their sins no
　　more."[a]

[13]By calling this covenant "new,"
he has made the first one obsolete;
and what is obsolete and aging will
soon disappear.

❓DID YOU KNOW?　　　　8:1

What did Jesus do as our high priest?

Jesus offered himself as the sacrifice for all our sins. Old Testament priests offered animals as sacrifice for sin. More sin required another sacrifice. But Jesus' perfect sacrifice covers our sin once for all.

Worship in the Earthly Tabernacle

9 Now the first covenant had regulations for worship and also an earthly sanctuary. [2]A tabernacle was set up. In its first room were the lampstand, the table and the consecrated bread; this was called the Holy Place. [3]Behind the second curtain was a room called the Most Holy Place, [4]which had the golden altar of incense and the gold-covered ark of the covenant. This ark contained the gold jar of manna, Aaron's staff that had budded, and the stone tablets of the covenant. [5]Above the ark were the cherubim of the Glory, overshadowing the atonement cover.[b] But we cannot discuss these things in detail now.

[6]When everything had been arranged like this, the priests entered regularly into the outer room to carry on their ministry. [7]But only the high priest entered the inner room, and that only once a year, and never without blood, which he offered for himself and for the sins the people had committed in ignorance. [8]The Holy Spirit was showing by this that the way into the Most Holy Place had not yet been disclosed as long as the first tabernacle was still standing. [9]This is an illustration for the present time, indicating that the gifts and sacrifices being offered were not able to clear the conscience of the worshiper. [10]They are only a matter of food and drink and various ceremonial washings—external regulations applying until the time of the new order.

The Blood of Christ

[11]When Christ came as high priest of the good things that are already here,[c] he went through the greater and more perfect tabernacle that is not man-made, that is to say, not a part of this creation. [12]He did not enter by means of the blood of goats and calves; but he entered the Most Holy Place once for all by his own blood, having obtained eternal redemption. [13]The blood of goats and bulls and the ashes of a heifer sprinkled on those who are ceremonially unclean sanctify them so that they are outwardly clean. [14]How much more, then, will the blood of Christ, who through the eternal Spirit offered himself unblemished to God, cleanse our consciences from acts that lead to

---

a12 Jer. 31:31-34　　*b5* Traditionally *the mercy seat*　　*c11* Some early manuscripts *are to come*

death,[a] so that we may serve the living God!

15For this reason Christ is the mediator of a new covenant, that those who are called may receive the promised eternal inheritance—now that he has died as a ransom to set them free from the sins committed under the first covenant.

16In the case of a will,[b] it is necessary to prove the death of the one who made it, 17because a will is in force only when somebody has died; it never takes effect while the one who made it is living. 18This is why even the first covenant was not put into effect without blood. 19When Moses had proclaimed every commandment of the law to all the people, he took the blood of calves, together with water, scarlet wool and branches of hyssop, and sprinkled the scroll and all the people. 20He said, "This is the blood of the covenant, which God has commanded you to keep."[c] 21In the same way, he sprinkled with the blood both the tabernacle and everything used in its ceremonies. 22In fact, the law requires that nearly everything be cleansed with blood, and without the shedding of blood there is no forgiveness.

23It was necessary, then, for the copies of the heavenly things to be purified with these sacrifices, but the heavenly things themselves with better sacrifices than these. 24For Christ did not enter a man-made sanctuary that was only a copy of the true one; he entered heaven itself, now to appear for us in God's presence. 25Nor did he enter heaven to offer himself again and again, the way the high priest enters the Most Holy Place every year with blood that is not his own. 26Then Christ would have had to suffer many times since the creation of the world. But now he has appeared once for all at the end of the ages to do away with sin by the sacrifice of himself. 27Just as man is destined to die once, and after that to face judgment, 28so Christ was sacrificed once to take away the sins of many people; and he will appear a second time, not to bear sin, but to bring salvation to those who are waiting for him.

Christ's Sacrifice Once for All

10 The law is only a shadow of the good things that are coming—not the realities themselves. For this reason it can never, by the same sacrifices repeated endlessly year after year, make perfect those who draw near to worship. 2If it could, would they not have stopped being offered? For the worshipers would have been cleansed once for all, and would no longer have felt guilty for their sins. 3But those sacrifices are an annual reminder of sins, 4because it is impossible for the blood of bulls and goats to take away sins.

5Therefore, when Christ came into the world, he said:

"Sacrifice and offering you did not
    desire,
  but a body you prepared for me;
6with burnt offerings and sin
    offerings
  you were not pleased.
7Then I said, 'Here I am—it is
    written about me in the
    scroll—
  I have come to do your will,
    O God.' "[d]

8First he said, "Sacrifices and offerings, burnt offerings and sin offerings you did not desire, nor were you pleased with them" (although the law required them to be made). 9Then he said, "Here I am, I have come to do your will." He sets aside the first to establish the second. 10And by that will, we have been made holy through the sacrifice of the body of Jesus Christ once for all.

11Day after day every priest stands and performs his religious duties; again and again he offers the same sacrifices, which can never take away sins. [12]But when this priest had offered for all time one sacrifice for sins, he sat down at the right hand of God. [13]Since that time he waits for his enemies to be made his footstool, [14]because by one sacrifice he has made perfect forever those who are being made holy.

ORDS TO REMEMBER

10:10 We have been made holy through the sacrifice of the body of Jesus Christ once for all.

[15]The Holy Spirit also testifies to us about this. First he says:

[16]"This is the covenant I will make with them
after that time, says the Lord.
I will put my laws in their hearts,
and I will write them on their minds."[a]

[17]Then he adds:

"Their sins and lawless acts
I will remember no more."[b]

[18]And where these have been forgiven, there is no longer any sacrifice for sin.

A Call to Persevere

[19]Therefore, brothers, since we have confidence to enter the Most Holy Place by the blood of Jesus, [20]by a new and living way opened for us through the curtain, that is, his body, [21]and since we have a great priest over the house of God, [22]let us draw near to God with a sincere heart in full assurance of faith, having our hearts sprinkled to cleanse us from a guilty conscience and having our bodies washed with pure water. [23]Let us hold unswervingly to the hope we profess, for he who promised is faithful. [24]And let us consider how we may spur one another on toward love and good deeds. [25]Let us not give up meet-

ing together, as some are in the habit of doing, but let us encourage one another—and all the more as you see the Day approaching.

[26]If we deliberately keep on sinning after we have received the knowledge of the truth, no sacrifice for sins is left, [27]but only a fearful expectation of judgment and of raging fire that will consume the enemies of God. [28]Anyone who rejected the law of Moses died without mercy on the testimony of two or three witnesses. [29]How much more severely do you think a man deserves to be punished who has trampled the Son of God under foot, who has treated as an unholy thing the blood of the covenant that sanctified him, and who has insulted the Spirit of grace? [30]For we know him who said, "It is mine to avenge; I will repay,"[c] and again, "The Lord will judge his people."[d] [31]It is a dreadful thing to fall into the hands of the living God.

[32]Remember those earlier days after you had received the light, when you stood your ground in a great contest in the face of suffering. [33]Sometimes you were publicly exposed to insult and persecution; at other times you stood side by side with those who were so treated. [34]You sympathized with those in prison and joyfully accepted the confiscation of your property, because you knew that you yourselves had better and lasting possessions.

[35]So do not throw away your confidence; it will be richly rewarded. [36]You need to persevere so that when you have done the will of God, you will receive what he has promised. [37]For in just a very little while,

"He who is coming will come and
will not delay.
[38]   But my righteous one[e] will live
by faith.
And if he shrinks back,
I will not be pleased with
him."[f]

---

[a]16 Jer. 31:33   [b]17 Jer. 31:34   [c]30 Deut. 32:35   [d]30 Deut. 32:36; Psalm 135:14
[e]38 One early manuscript *But the righteous*   [f]38 Hab. 2:3,4

³⁹But we are not of those who shrink back and are destroyed, but of those who believe and are saved.

By Faith

11 Now faith is being sure of what we hope for and certain of what we do not see. ²This is what the ancients were commended for.

³By faith we understand that the universe was formed at God's command, so that what is seen was not made out of what was visible.

⁴By faith Abel offered God a better sacrifice than Cain did. By faith he was commended as a righteous man, when God spoke well of his offerings. And by faith he still speaks, even though he is dead.

⁵By faith Enoch was taken from this life, so that he did not experience death; he could not be found, because God had taken him away. For before he was taken, he was commended as one who pleased God. ⁶And without faith it is impossible to please God, because anyone who comes to him must believe that he exists and that he rewards those who earnestly seek him.

⁷By faith Noah, when warned about things not yet seen, in holy fear built an ark to save his family. By his faith he condemned the world and became heir of the righteousness that comes by faith.

⁸By faith Abraham, when called to go to a place he would later receive as his inheritance, obeyed and went, even though he did not know where he was going. ⁹By faith he made his home in the promised land like a stranger in a foreign country; he lived in tents, as did Isaac and Jacob, who were heirs with him of the same promise. ¹⁰For he was looking forward to the city with foundations, whose architect and builder is God.

¹¹By faith Abraham, even though he was past age—and Sarah herself was barren—was enabled to become a father because he*a* considered him faithful who had made the promise. ¹²And so from this one man, and he as good as dead, came descendants as numerous as the stars in the sky and as countless as the sand on the seashore.

¹³All these people were still living by faith when they died. They did not receive the things promised; they only saw them and welcomed them from a distance. And they admitted that they were aliens and strangers on earth. ¹⁴People who say such things show that they are looking for a country of their own. ¹⁵If they had been thinking of the country they had left, they would have had opportunity to return. ¹⁶Instead, they were longing for a better country—a heavenly one. Therefore God is not ashamed to be called their God, for he has prepared a city for them.

¹⁷By faith Abraham, when God tested him, offered Isaac as a sacrifice. He who had received the promises was about to sacrifice his one and only son, ¹⁸even though God had said to him, "It is through Isaac that your offspring*b* will be reckoned."*c* ¹⁹Abraham reasoned that God could raise the dead, and figuratively

---

a11 Or *By faith even Sarah, who was past age, was enabled to bear children because she* *b18* Greek *seed*   *c18* Gen. 21:12

▚ET'S LIVE IT!   Hebrews 11:8–12

SHOW YOUR FAITH ➡ How did Abraham show that he had faith in God? Read Hebrews 11:8–12 and find three things Abraham did by faith.

Now write about your faith. Write three sentences. Put your name in the blank. Start each sentence with, "By faith _____," and tell things you have done because you believe in Jesus.

speaking, he did receive Isaac back from death.

²⁰By faith Isaac blessed Jacob and Esau in regard to their future.

²¹By faith Jacob, when he was dying, blessed each of Joseph's sons, and worshiped as he leaned on the top of his staff.

²²By faith Joseph, when his end was near, spoke about the exodus of the Israelites from Egypt and gave instructions about his bones.

²³By faith Moses' parents hid him for three months after he was born, because they saw he was no ordinary child, and they were not afraid of the king's edict.

²⁴By faith Moses, when he had grown up, refused to be known as the son of Pharaoh's daughter. ²⁵He chose to be mistreated along with the people of God rather than to enjoy the pleasures of sin for a short time. ²⁶He regarded disgrace for the sake of Christ as of greater value than the treasures of Egypt, because he was looking ahead to his reward. ²⁷By faith he left Egypt, not fearing the king's anger; he persevered because he saw him who is invisible. ²⁸By faith he kept the Passover and the sprinkling of blood, so that the destroyer of the firstborn would not touch the firstborn of Israel.

²⁹By faith the people passed through the Red Sea*a* as on dry land; but when the Egyptians tried to do so, they were drowned.

³⁰By faith the walls of Jericho fell, after the people had marched around them for seven days.

³¹By faith the prostitute Rahab, because she welcomed the spies, was not killed with those who were disobedient.*b*

³²And what more shall I say? I do not have time to tell about Gideon, Barak, Samson, Jephthah, David, Samuel and the prophets, ³³who through faith conquered kingdoms, administered justice, and gained what was promised; who shut the

mouths of lions, ³⁴quenched the fury of the flames, and escaped the edge of the sword; whose weakness was turned to strength; and who became powerful in battle and routed foreign armies. ³⁵Women received back their dead, raised to life again. Others were tortured and refused to be released, so that they might gain a better resurrection. ³⁶Some faced jeers and flogging, while still others were chained and put in prison. ³⁷They were stoned*c*; they were sawed in two; they were put to death by the sword. They went about in sheepskins and goatskins, destitute, persecuted and mistreated— ³⁸the world was not worthy of them. They wandered in deserts and mountains, and in caves and holes in the ground.

³⁹These were all commended for their faith, yet none of them received what had been promised. ⁴⁰God had planned something better for us so that only together with us would they be made perfect.

❓DID YOU KNOW?   **11:39**

What difference does faith make?

Faith helps believers do great things. Hebrews 11 lists many heroes of faith. It tells what they were able to do because they trusted God.

God Disciplines His Sons

12 Therefore, since we are surrounded by such a great cloud of witnesses, let us throw off everything that hinders and the sin that so easily entangles, and let us run with perseverance the race marked out for us. ²Let us fix our eyes on Jesus, the author and perfecter of our faith, who for the joy set before him endured the cross, scorning its shame, and sat down at the right hand of the throne of God. ³Consider him who endured

---

a29 That is, Sea of Reeds   *b31* Or *unbelieving put to the test;*   *c37* Some early manuscripts *stoned; they were*

such opposition from sinful men, so that you will not grow weary and lose heart.

⁴In your struggle against sin, you have not yet resisted to the point of shedding your blood. ⁵And you have forgotten that word of encouragement that addresses you as sons:

"My son, do not make light of the
    Lord's discipline,
and do not lose heart when he
    rebukes you,
⁶because the Lord disciplines those
    he loves,
and he punishes everyone he
    accepts as a son."ᵃ

⁷Endure hardship as discipline; God is treating you as sons. For what son is not disciplined by his father? ⁸If you are not disciplined (and everyone undergoes discipline), then you are illegitimate children and not true sons. ⁹Moreover, we have all had human fathers who disciplined us and we respected them for it. How much more should we submit to the Father of our spirits and live! ¹⁰Our fathers disciplined us for a little while as they thought best; but God disciplines us for our good, that we may share in his holiness. ¹¹No discipline seems pleasant at the time, but painful. Later on, however, it produces a harvest of righteousness and peace for those who have been trained by it.

¹²Therefore, strengthen your feeble arms and weak knees. ¹³"Make level paths for your feet,"ᵇ so that the lame may not be disabled, but rather healed.

Warning Against Refusing God

¹⁴Make every effort to live in peace with all men and to be holy; without holiness no one will see the Lord. ¹⁵See to it that no one misses the grace of God and that no bitter root grows up to cause trouble and defile many. ¹⁶See that no one is sexually immoral, or is godless like Esau, who for a single meal sold his inheritance rights as the oldest son. ¹⁷Afterward, as you know, when he wanted to inherit this blessing, he was rejected. He could bring about no change of mind, though he sought the blessing with tears.

¹⁸You have not come to a mountain that can be touched and that is burning with fire; to darkness, gloom and storm; ¹⁹to a trumpet blast or to such a voice speaking words that those who heard it begged that no further word be spoken to them, ²⁰because they could not bear what was commanded: "If even an animal touches the mountain, it must be stoned."ᶜ ²¹The sight was so terrifying that Moses said, "I am trembling with fear."ᵈ

²²But you have come to Mount Zion, to the heavenly Jerusalem, the city of the living God. You have come to thousands upon thousands of angels in joyful assembly, ²³to the church of the firstborn, whose names are written in heaven. You have come to God, the judge of all men, to the spirits of righteous men made

---

ᵃ6 Prov. 3:11,12   ᵇ13 Prov. 4:26   ᶜ20 Exodus 19:12,13   ᵈ21 Deut. 9:19

▎ET'S LIVE IT!   Hebrews 12:5–11

PUNISHMENT, RIGHT OR WRONG? ➡ Pretend that you are a parent. Your children tell you they don't think it's right for you to punish them. What can you find in Hebrews 12:5–11 to help you explain why punishment is good instead of bad?

Ask a parent to read this passage too. Talk about these rules for good punishment: Punish me because you love me, not because you are mad at me. Punish me to help me do better, not to get even with me for what I've done.

perfect, 24to Jesus the mediator of a new covenant, and to the sprinkled blood that speaks a better word than the blood of Abel.

25See to it that you do not refuse him who speaks. If they did not escape when they refused him who warned them on earth, how much less will we, if we turn away from him who warns us from heaven? 26At that time his voice shook the earth, but now he has promised, "Once more I will shake not only the earth but also the heavens."a 27The words "once more" indicate the removing of what can be shaken—that is, created things—so that what cannot be shaken may remain.

28Therefore, since we are receiving a kingdom that cannot be shaken, let us be thankful, and so worship God acceptably with reverence and awe, 29for our "God is a consuming fire."b

Concluding Exhortations

13 Keep on loving each other as brothers. 2Do not forget to entertain strangers, for by so doing some people have entertained angels without knowing it. 3Remember those in prison as if you were their fellow prisoners, and those who are mistreated as if you yourselves were suffering.

4Marriage should be honored by all, and the marriage bed kept pure, for God will judge the adulterer and all the sexually immoral. 5Keep your lives free from the love of money and be content with what you have, because God has said,

"Never will I leave you;
   never will I forsake you."c

6So we say with confidence,

"The Lord is my helper; I will not
   be afraid.
What can man do to me?"d

7Remember your leaders, who spoke the word of God to you. Consider the outcome of their way of life and imitate their faith. 8Jesus Christ is the same yesterday and today and forever.

WORDS TO REMEMBER

13:5 Never will I leave you;
      never will I forsake you.

9Do not be carried away by all kinds of strange teachings. It is good for our hearts to be strengthened by grace, not by ceremonial foods, which are of no value to those who eat them. 10We have an altar from which those who minister at the tabernacle have no right to eat.

WORDS TO REMEMBER

13:6 The Lord is my helper; I will not be afraid.

11The high priest carries the blood of animals into the Most Holy Place as a sin offering, but the bodies are burned outside the camp. 12And so Jesus also suffered outside the city gate to make the people holy through his own blood. 13Let us, then, go to him outside the camp, bearing the disgrace he bore. 14For here we do not have an enduring city, but we are looking for the city that is to come.

15Through Jesus, therefore, let us continually offer to God a sacrifice of praise—the fruit of lips that confess his name. 16And do not forget to do good and to share with others, for with such sacrifices God is pleased.

17Obey your leaders and submit to their authority. They keep watch over you as men who must give an account. Obey them so that their work will be a joy, not a burden, for that would be of no advantage to you.

18Pray for us. We are sure that we have a clear conscience and desire to live honorably in every way. 19I par-

---

a26 Haggai 2:6   b29 Deut. 4:24   c5 Deut. 31:6   d6 Psalm 118:6,7

ticularly urge you to pray so that I may be restored to you soon.

20May the God of peace, who through the blood of the eternal covenant brought back from the dead our Lord Jesus, that great Shepherd of the sheep, 21equip you with everything good for doing his will, and may he work in us what is pleasing to him, through Jesus Christ, to whom be glory for ever and ever. Amen.

22Brothers, I urge you to bear with my word of exhortation, for I have written you only a short letter.

23I want you to know that our brother Timothy has been released. If he arrives soon, I will come with him to see you.

24Greet all your leaders and all God's people. Those from Italy send you their greetings.

25Grace be with you all.

JAMES

James, the brother of Jesus, wrote this book.

James shows Christians how to practice their faith in Jesus.

This book was written to Christians everywhere.

James was probably written about A.D. 48.

God does not tempt us.	James 1:12–18
We are to do what God says.	James 1:22–25
Don't show favoritism.	James 2:1–13
Be careful what you say.	James 3:1–12
Don't criticize others.	James 4:11–12
Be patient when you suffer.	James 5:7–11
Pray when you are sick.	James 5:13–16

1 James, a servant of God and of the Lord Jesus Christ,

To the twelve tribes scattered among the nations:

Greetings.

Trials and Temptations

²Consider it pure joy, my brothers, whenever you face trials of many kinds, ³because you know that the testing of your faith develops perseverance. ⁴Perseverance must finish its work so that you may be mature and complete, not lacking anything. ⁵If any of you lacks wisdom, he should ask God, who gives generously to all without finding fault, and it will be given to him. ⁶But when he asks, he must believe and not doubt, because he who doubts is like a wave of the sea, blown and tossed by the wind. ⁷That man should not think he will receive anything from the Lord; ⁸he is a double-minded man, unstable in all he does.

⁹The brother in humble circumstances ought to take pride in his high position. ¹⁰But the one who is rich should take pride in his low position, because he will pass away like a wild flower. ¹¹For the sun rises with scorching heat and withers the plant; its blossom falls and its beauty is destroyed. In the same way, the rich man will fade away even while he goes about his business.

¹²Blessed is the man who perseveres under trial, because when he has stood the test, he will receive the crown of life that God has promised to those who love him.

¹³When tempted, no one should say, "God is tempting me." For God cannot be tempted by evil, nor does he tempt anyone; ¹⁴but each one is tempted when, by his own evil desire, he is dragged away and enticed. ¹⁵Then, after desire has conceived, it gives birth to sin; and sin, when it is full-grown, gives birth to death.

ᗯORDS TO REMEMBER

1:13 God cannot be tempted by evil, nor does he tempt anyone.

¹⁶Don't be deceived, my dear brothers. ¹⁷Every good and perfect gift is from above, coming down from the Father of the heavenly lights, who does not change like shifting shadows. ¹⁸He chose to give us birth through the word of truth, that we might be a kind of firstfruits of all he created.

Listening and Doing

¹⁹My dear brothers, take note of this: Everyone should be quick to listen, slow to speak and slow to become angry, ²⁰for man's anger does not bring about the righteous life that God desires. ²¹Therefore, get rid of all moral filth and the evil that is so prevalent and humbly accept the word planted in you, which can save you.

²²Do not merely listen to the word,

ᐳET'S LIVE IT!   James 1:5–8

WISDOM DIARY ➡ Read James 1:5–8. "Wisdom" in the Bible means knowing the right thing to do. "Believe and not doubt" means that when God shows a person the right thing to do, he must do it.

A wisdom diary is a little notebook in which you write hard decisions you have to make. Pray about them. When you think you know what God wants, do it. Then write down what happens when you do what God wants.

When you look back over your notebook you will find out how wise you were to ask God for wisdom and how good it is to do what is right.

and so deceive yourselves. Do what it says. ²³Anyone who listens to the word but does not do what it says is like a man who looks at his face in a mirror ²⁴and, after looking at himself, goes away and immediately forgets what he looks like. ²⁵But the man who looks intently into the perfect law that gives freedom, and continues to do this, not forgetting what he has heard, but doing it—he will be blessed in what he does.

WORDS TO REMEMBER

1:22 Do not merely listen to the word.... Do what it says.

---

²⁶If anyone considers himself religious and yet does not keep a tight rein on his tongue, he deceives himself and his religion is worthless. ²⁷Religion that God our Father accepts as pure and faultless is this: to look after orphans and widows in their distress and to keep oneself from being polluted by the world.

Favoritism Forbidden

2 My brothers, as believers in our glorious Lord Jesus Christ, don't show favoritism. ²Suppose a man comes into your meeting wearing a gold ring and fine clothes, and a poor man in shabby clothes also comes in. ³If you show special attention to the man wearing fine clothes and say, "Here's a good seat for you," but say to the poor man, "You stand there" or "Sit on the floor by my feet," ⁴have you not discriminated among yourselves and become judges with evil thoughts?

⁵Listen, my dear brothers: Has not God chosen those who are poor in the eyes of the world to be rich in faith and to inherit the kingdom he promised those who love him? ⁶But you have insulted the poor. Is it not the rich who are exploiting you? Are they not the ones who are dragging you into court? ⁷Are they not the ones who are slandering the noble name of him to whom you belong?

Life In Bible Times

RICH PEOPLE

Rich people were well-dressed and wore gold jewelry. Everyone could tell a rich person from a poor one. Christians were told to welcome the poor as well as the rich.

---

⁸If you really keep the royal law found in Scripture, "Love your neighbor as yourself,"ᵃ you are doing right. ⁹But if you show favoritism, you sin and are convicted by the law as lawbreakers. ¹⁰For whoever keeps the whole law and yet stumbles at just one point is guilty of breaking all of it. ¹¹For he who said, "Do not commit adultery,"ᵇ also said, "Do not murder."ᶜ If you do not commit adultery but do commit murder, you have become a lawbreaker.

¹²Speak and act as those who are going to be judged by the law that gives freedom, ¹³because judgment without mercy will be shown to anyone who has not been merciful. Mercy triumphs over judgment!

Faith and Deeds

¹⁴What good is it, my brothers, if a man claims to have faith but has no deeds? Can such faith save him? ¹⁵Suppose a brother or sister is without clothes and daily food. ¹⁶If one of you says to him, "Go, I wish you well; keep warm and well fed," but does nothing about his physical needs, what good is it? ¹⁷In the same way,

---

ᵃ8 Lev. 19:18   ᵇ11 Exodus 20:14; Deut. 5:18   ᶜ11 Exodus 20:13; Deut. 5:17

faith by itself, if it is not accompanied by action, is dead.

¹⁸But someone will say, "You have faith; I have deeds."

Show me your faith without deeds, and I will show you my faith by what I do. ¹⁹You believe that there is one God. Good! Even the demons believe that—and shudder.

---

²⁰You foolish man, do you want evidence that faith without deeds is useless*ᵃ*? ²¹Was not our ancestor Abraham considered righteous for what he did when he offered his son Isaac on the altar? ²²You see that his faith and his actions were working together, and his faith was made complete by what he did. ²³And the scripture was fulfilled that says, "Abraham believed God, and it was credited to him as righteousness,"*ᵇ* and he was called God's friend. ²⁴You see that a person is justified by what he does and not by faith alone.

²⁵In the same way, was not even Rahab the prostitute considered righteous for what she did when she gave lodging to the spies and sent them off in a different direction? ²⁶As the body without the spirit is dead, so faith without deeds is dead.

Taming the Tongue

3 Not many of you should presume to be teachers, my brothers, because you know that we who teach will be judged more strictly. ²We all stumble in many ways. If anyone is never at fault in what he says, he is a perfect man, able to keep his whole body in check.

³When we put bits into the mouths of horses to make them obey us, we can turn the whole animal. ⁴Or take ships as an example. Although they are so large and are driven by strong winds, they are steered by a very small rudder wherever the pilot wants to go. ⁵Likewise the tongue is a small part of the body, but it makes great boasts. Consider what a great forest is set on fire by a small spark. ⁶The tongue also is a fire, a world of evil among the parts of the body. It corrupts the whole person, sets the whole course of his life on fire, and is itself set on fire by hell.

⁷All kinds of animals, birds, reptiles and creatures of the sea are being tamed and have been tamed by man, ⁸but no man can tame the tongue. It is a restless evil, full of deadly poison.

⁹With the tongue we praise our Lord and Father, and with it we curse men, who have been made in God's likeness. ¹⁰Out of the same mouth come praise and cursing. My brothers, this should not be. ¹¹Can both fresh water and salt*ᶜ* water flow from the same spring? ¹²My brothers, can a fig tree bear olives, or a grapevine bear figs? Neither can a salt spring produce fresh water.

Two Kinds of Wisdom

¹³Who is wise and understanding among you? Let him show it by his good life, by deeds done in the humility that comes from wisdom. ¹⁴But if you harbor bitter envy and selfish ambition in your hearts, do not boast about it or deny the truth. ¹⁵Such "wisdom" does not come down from heaven but is earthly, unspiritual, of the devil. ¹⁶For where you have envy and selfish ambition, there you find disorder and every evil practice.

¹⁷But the wisdom that comes from heaven is first of all pure; then peace-loving, considerate, submissive, full of mercy and good fruit, im-

---

ᵃ20 Some early manuscripts dead   ᵇ23 Gen. 15:6   ᶜ11 Greek bitter (see also verse 14)

partial and sincere. [18]Peacemakers who sow in peace raise a harvest of righteousness.

Submit Yourselves to God

4 What causes fights and quarrels among you? Don't they come from your desires that battle within you? [2]You want something but don't get it. You kill and covet, but you cannot have what you want. You quarrel and fight. You do not have, because you do not ask God. [3]When you ask, you do not receive, because you ask with wrong motives, that you may spend what you get on your pleasures.

[4]You adulterous people, don't you know that friendship with the world is hatred toward God? Anyone who chooses to be a friend of the world becomes an enemy of God. [5]Or do you think Scripture says without reason that the spirit he caused to live in us envies intensely?[a] [6]But he gives us more grace. That is why Scripture says:

"God opposes the proud
  but gives grace to the
    humble."[b]

[7]Submit yourselves, then, to God. Resist the devil, and he will flee from you. [8]Come near to God and he will come near to you. Wash your hands, you sinners, and purify your hearts,

you double-minded. [9]Grieve, mourn and wail. Change your laughter to mourning and your joy to gloom. [10]Humble yourselves before the Lord, and he will lift you up.

WORDS TO REMEMBER

4:8 Come near to God and he will come near to you.

---

[11]Brothers, do not slander one another. Anyone who speaks against his brother or judges him speaks against the law and judges it. When you judge the law, you are not keeping it, but sitting in judgment on it. [12]There is only one Lawgiver and Judge, the one who is able to save and destroy. But you—who are you to judge your neighbor?

Boasting About Tomorrow

[13]Now listen, you who say, "Today or tomorrow we will go to this or that city, spend a year there, carry on business and make money." [14]Why, you do not even know what will happen tomorrow. What is your life? You are a mist that appears for a little while and then vanishes. [15]Instead, you ought to say, "If it is the Lord's will, we will live and do this or that." [16]As it is, you boast and brag. All such boasting is evil. [17]Anyone, then,

---

[a]5 Or that God jealously longs for the spirit that he made to live in us; or that the Spirit he caused to live in us longs jealously   [b]6 Prov. 3:34

LET'S LIVE IT!   James 3:1–8

COUNT TO THREE FIRST ➡ Read James 3:1–8. What three things does James say are like the tongue?

Here's a way to control your tongue and keep from saying mean, angry, or wrong things. When you feel mean or angry and are about to say something, count to three first.

Count silently:
  1–bit
  2–rudder
  3–fire

Counting can remind you to control your tongue, so you do not say something you will be sorry about later.

who knows the good he ought to do and doesn't do it, sins.

Warning to Rich Oppressors

5 Now listen, you rich people, weep and wail because of the misery that is coming upon you. [2]Your wealth has rotted, and moths have eaten your clothes. [3]Your gold and silver are corroded. Their corrosion will testify against you and eat your flesh like fire. You have hoarded wealth in the last days. [4]Look! The wages you failed to pay the workmen who mowed your fields are crying out against you. The cries of the harvesters have reached the ears of the Lord Almighty. [5]You have lived on earth in luxury and self-indulgence. You have fattened yourselves in the day of slaughter.[a] [6]You have condemned and murdered innocent men, who were not opposing you.

Patience in Suffering

[7]Be patient, then, brothers, until the Lord's coming. See how the farmer waits for the land to yield its valuable crop and how patient he is for the autumn and spring rains. [8]You too, be patient and stand firm, because the Lord's coming is near. [9]Don't grumble against each other, brothers, or you will be judged. The Judge is standing at the door!

[10]Brothers, as an example of patience in the face of suffering, take the prophets who spoke in the name of the Lord. [11]As you know, we consider blessed those who have persevered. You have heard of Job's perseverance and have seen what the Lord finally brought about. The Lord is full of compassion and mercy.

[12]Above all, my brothers, do not swear—not by heaven or by earth or by anything else. Let your "Yes" be yes, and your "No," no, or you will be condemned.

The Prayer of Faith

[13]Is any one of you in trouble? He should pray. Is anyone happy? Let him sing songs of praise. [14]Is any one of you sick? He should call the elders of the church to pray over him and anoint him with oil in the name of the Lord. [15]And the prayer offered in faith will make the sick person well; the Lord will raise him up. If he has sinned, he will be forgiven. [16]Therefore confess your sins to each other and pray for each other so that you may be healed. The prayer of a righteous man is powerful and effective.

[17]Elijah was a man just like us. He prayed earnestly that it would not rain, and it did not rain on the land for three and a half years. [18]Again he prayed, and the heavens gave rain, and the earth produced its crops.

[19]My brothers, if one of you should wander from the truth and someone should bring him back, [20]remember this: Whoever turns a sinner from the error of his way will save him from death and cover over a multitude of sins.

---

[a]5 Or *yourselves as in a day of feasting*

1 PETER

1 Peter, an apostle of Jesus Christ,

To God's elect, strangers in the world, scattered throughout Pontus, Galatia, Cappadocia, Asia and Bithynia, [2]who have been chosen according to the foreknowledge of God the Father, through the sanctifying work of the Spirit, for obedience to Jesus Christ and sprinkling by his blood:

Grace and peace be yours in abundance.

Praise to God for a Living Hope

[3]Praise be to the God and Father of our Lord Jesus Christ! In his great mercy he has given us new birth into a living hope through the resurrection of Jesus Christ from the dead, [4]and into an inheritance that can never perish, spoil or fade—kept in heaven for you, [5]who through faith are shielded by God's power until the coming of the salvation that is ready to be revealed in the last time. [6]In this you greatly rejoice, though now for a little while you may have had to suffer grief in all kinds of trials. [7]These have come so that your faith—of greater worth than gold, which perishes even though refined by fire—may be proved genuine and may result in praise, glory and honor when Jesus Christ is revealed. [8]Though you have not seen him, you love him; and even though you do not see him now, you believe in him and are filled with an inexpressible and glorious joy, [9]for you are receiving the goal of your faith, the salvation of your souls.

[10]Concerning this salvation, the prophets, who spoke of the grace that was to come to you, searched intently and with the greatest care, [11]trying to find out the time and circumstances to which the Spirit of Christ in them was pointing when he predicted the sufferings of Christ and the glories that would follow. [12]It was revealed to them that they were not serving themselves but you, when they spoke of the things that have now been told you by those who have preached the gospel to you by the Holy Spirit sent from heaven. Even angels long to look into these things.

❓DID YOU KNOW?　　1:3

What is the Christians' hope?

The Christians' hope is that we will someday be with Jesus in heaven. Christians are God's special treasures. And God has treasure for us in heaven. This is why Peter starts his letter with praise for God.

Be Holy

[13]Therefore, prepare your minds for action; be self-controlled; set your hope fully on the grace to be given you when Jesus Christ is revealed. [14]As obedient children, do not conform to the evil desires you had when you lived in ignorance. [15]But just as he who called you is holy, so be holy in all you do; [16]for it is written: "Be holy, because I am holy."[a]

❓DID YOU KNOW?　　1:15

Why should we be holy?

We should be holy because we are God's children, and God is holy. Children are supposed to be like their Father.

---

[17]Since you call on a Father who judges each man's work impartially, live your lives as strangers here in reverent fear. [18]For you know that it was not with perishable things such as silver or gold that you were redeemed from the empty way of life handed down to you from your forefathers, [19]but with the precious blood of Christ, a lamb without blemish or defect. [20]He was chosen before the cre-

[a]16 Lev. 11:44,45; 19:2; 20:7

ation of the world, but was revealed in these last times for your sake. [21]Through him you believe in God, who raised him from the dead and glorified him, and so your faith and hope are in God.

[22]Now that you have purified yourselves by obeying the truth so that you have sincere love for your brothers, love one another deeply, from the heart.[a] [23]For you have been born again, not of perishable seed, but of imperishable, through the living and enduring word of God. [24]For,

"All men are like grass,
    and all their glory is like the
        flowers of the field;
the grass withers and the flowers
        fall,
[25] but the word of the Lord stands
        forever."[b]

And this is the word that was preached to you.

WORDS TO REMEMBER

1:22 Love one another deeply, from the heart.

2 Therefore, rid yourselves of all malice and all deceit, hypocrisy, envy, and slander of every kind. [2]Like newborn babies, crave pure spiritual milk, so that by it you may grow up in your salvation, [3]now that you have tasted that the Lord is good.

The Living Stone and a Chosen People

[4]As you come to him, the living Stone—rejected by men but chosen by God and precious to him— [5]you also, like living stones, are being built into a spiritual house to be a holy priesthood, offering spiritual sacrifices acceptable to God through Jesus Christ. [6]For in Scripture it says:

"See, I lay a stone in Zion,

a chosen and precious
    cornerstone,
and the one who trusts in him
    will never be put to shame."[c]

[7]Now to you who believe, this stone is precious. But to those who do not believe,

"The stone the builders rejected
    has become the capstone,[d] [e]

[8]and,

"A stone that causes men to
        stumble
    and a rock that makes them
        fall."[f]

They stumble because they disobey the message—which is also what they were destined for.

[9]But you are a chosen people, a royal priesthood, a holy nation, a people belonging to God, that you may declare the praises of him who called you out of darkness into his wonderful light. [10]Once you were not a people, but now you are the people of God; once you had not received mercy, but now you have recieved mercy.

[11]Dear friends, I urge you, as aliens and strangers in the world, to abstain from sinful desires, which war against your soul. [12]Live such good lives among the pagans that, though they accuse you of doing wrong, they may see your good deeds and glorify God on the day he visits us.

Submission to Rulers and Masters

[13]Submit yourselves for the Lord's sake to every authority instituted among men: whether to the king, as the supreme authority, [14]or to governors, who are sent by him to punish those who do wrong and to commend those who do right. [15]For it is God's will that by doing good you should silence the ignorant talk of foolish men. [16]Live as free men, but do not

---

a22 Some early manuscripts *from a pure heart*   *b25* Isaiah 40:6-8   *c6* Isaiah 28:16   *d7* Or
cornerstone   *e7* Psalm 118:22   *f8* Isaiah 8:14

use your freedom as a cover-up for evil; live as servants of God. ¹⁷Show proper respect to everyone: Love the brotherhood of believers, fear God, honor the king.

¹⁸Slaves, submit yourselves to your masters with all respect, not only to those who are good and considerate, but also to those who are harsh. ¹⁹For it is commendable if a man bears up under the pain of unjust suffering because he is conscious of God. ²⁰But how is it to your credit if you receive a beating for doing wrong and endure it? But if you suffer for doing good and you endure it, this is commendable before God. ²¹To this you were called, because Christ suffered for you, leaving you an example, that you should follow in his steps.

? DID YOU KNOW?   **2:13**

What does submit mean?

To submit means to do what is right by obeying a person in charge. Christians are supposed to obey their country's laws. Employees are to work hard for the person who hired them. Children are to submit to parents and teachers. 1 Peter 2 and 3 are about submission.

---

²²"He committed no sin,
   and no deceit was found in his
      mouth."ᵃ

ᵃ22 Isaiah 53:9

²³When they hurled their insults at him, he did not retaliate; when he suffered, he made no threats. Instead, he entrusted himself to him who judges justly. ²⁴He himself bore our sins in his body on the tree, so that we might die to sins and live for righteousness; by his wounds you have been healed. ²⁵For you were like sheep going astray, but now you have returned to the Shepherd and Overseer of your souls.

Wives and Husbands

3 Wives, in the same way be submissive to your husbands so that, if any of them do not believe the word, they may be won over without words by the behavior of their wives, ²when they see the purity and reverence of your lives. ³Your beauty should not come from outward adornment, such as braided hair and the wearing of gold jewelry and fine clothes. ⁴Instead, it should be that of your inner self, the unfading beauty of a gentle and quiet spirit, which is of great worth in God's sight. ⁵For this is the way the holy women of the past who put their hope in God used to make themselves beautiful. They were submissive to their own husbands, ⁶like Sarah, who obeyed Abraham and called him her master. You are her daughters if you do what is right and do not give way to fear.

⁷Husbands, in the same way be considerate as you live with your

---

 **LET'S LIVE IT!**   1 Peter 2:9–12

PRAISE PENNANTS ➠ Sometimes people praise God by praying. People can also praise God by singing. Sometimes people raise their hands to praise God. Read 1 Peter 2:9–12. How does living a good life praise God?

Make a family flag display. Hang a string across your dining room or on the wall. Cut triangular pennants from colored construction paper. Each evening have each family member think of one good thing they did that day to please God. Write it on a pennant and tape it to the string. See how soon your string fills up with praise pennants.

wives, and treat them with respect as the weaker partner and as heirs with you of the gracious gift of life, so that nothing will hinder your prayers.

Suffering for Doing Good

⁸Finally, all of you, live in harmony with one another; be sympathetic, love as brothers, be compassionate and humble. ⁹Do not repay evil with evil or insult with insult, but with blessing, because to this you were called so that you may inherit a blessing. ¹⁰For,

"Whoever would love life
  and see good days
must keep his tongue from evil
  and his lips from deceitful
    speech.
¹¹He must turn from evil and do
    good;
  he must seek peace and pursue
    it.
¹²For the eyes of the Lord are on
    the righteous
  and his ears are attentive to
    their prayer,
but the face of the Lord is against
    those who do evil."ᵃ

WORDS TO REMEMBER

3:8 Live in harmony with one another; be sympathetic, love as brothers, be compassionate and humble.

---

¹³Who is going to harm you if you are eager to do good? ¹⁴But even if you should suffer for what is right, you are blessed. "Do not fear what they fearᵇ; do not be frightened."ᶜ ¹⁵But in your hearts set apart Christ as Lord. Always be prepared to give an answer to everyone who asks you to give the reason for the hope that you have. But do this with gentleness and respect, ¹⁶keeping a clear conscience, so that those who speak ma-

liciously against your good behavior in Christ may be ashamed of their slander. ¹⁷It is better, if it is God's will, to suffer for doing good than for doing evil. ¹⁸For Christ died for sins once for all, the righteous for the unrighteous, to bring you to God. He was put to death in the body but made alive by the Spirit, ¹⁹through whomᵈ also he went and preached to the spirits in prison ²⁰who disobeyed long ago when God waited patiently in the days of Noah while the ark was being built. In it only a few people, eight in all, were saved through water, ²¹and this water symbolizes baptism that now saves you also—not the removal of dirt from the body but the pledgeᵉ of a good conscience toward God. It saves you by the resurrection of Jesus Christ, ²²who has gone into heaven and is at God's right hand—with angels, authorities and powers in submission to him.

Living for God

4 Therefore, since Christ suffered in his body, arm yourselves also with the same attitude, because he who has suffered in his body is done with sin. ²As a result, he does not live the rest of his earthly life for evil human desires, but rather for the will of God. ³For you have spent enough time in the past doing what pagans choose to do—living in debauchery, lust, drunkenness, orgies, carousing and detestable idolatry. ⁴They think it strange that you do not plunge with them into the same flood of dissipation, and they heap abuse on you. ⁵But they will have to give account to him who is ready to judge the living and the dead. ⁶For this is the reason the gospel was preached even to those who are now dead, so that they might be judged according to men in regard to the body, but live according to God in regard to the spirit.

⁷The end of all things is near. Therefore be clear minded and self-controlled so that you can pray.

ᵃ12 Psalm 34:12-16   ᵇ14 Or *not fear their threats*   ᶜ14 Isaiah 8:12   ᵈ18,19 Or *alive in the spirit,* ¹⁹*through which*   ᵉ21 Or *response*

8Above all, love each other deeply, because love covers over a multitude of sins. 9Offer hospitality to one another without grumbling. 10Each one should use whatever gift he has received to serve others, faithfully administering God's grace in its various forms. 11If anyone speaks, he should do it as one speaking the very words of God. If anyone serves, he should do it with the strength God provides, so that in all things God may be praised through Jesus Christ. To him be the glory and the power for ever and ever. Amen.

WORDS TO REMEMBER

4:9 Offer hospitality to one another without grumbling.

Suffering for Being a Christian

12Dear friends, do not be surprised at the painful trial you are suffering, as though something strange were happening to you. 13But rejoice that you participate in the sufferings of Christ, so that you may be overjoyed when his glory is revealed. 14If you are insulted because of the name of Christ, you are blessed, for the Spirit of glory and of God rests on you. 15If you suffer, it should not be as a murderer or thief or any other kind of criminal, or even as a meddler. 16However, if you suffer as a Christian, do not be ashamed, but praise God that you bear that name. 17For it is time for judgment to begin with the family of God; and if it begins with us, what will the outcome be for those who do not obey the gospel of God? 18And,

"If it is hard for the righteous to
    be saved,
  what will become of the ungodly
    and the sinner?"[a]

19So then, those who suffer according to God's will should commit themselves to their faithful Creator and continue to do good.

To Elders and Young Men

5 To the elders among you, I appeal as a fellow elder, a witness of Christ's sufferings and one who also will share in the glory to be revealed: 2Be shepherds of God's flock that is under your care, serving as overseers—not because you must, but because you are willing, as God wants you to be; not greedy for money, but eager to serve; 3not lording it over those entrusted to you, but being examples to the flock. 4And when the Chief Shepherd appears, you will receive the crown of glory that will never fade away.

5Young men, in the same way be submissive to those who are older. All of you, clothe yourselves with humility toward one another, because,

"God opposes the proud
  but gives grace to the
    humble."[b]

6Humble yourselves, therefore, under God's mighty hand, that he may lift you up in due time. 7Cast all your anxiety on him because he cares for you.

WORDS TO REMEMBER

5:7 Cast all your anxiety on him because he cares for you.

8Be self-controlled and alert. Your enemy the devil prowls around like a roaring lion looking for someone to devour. 9Resist him, standing firm in the faith, because you know that your brothers throughout the world are undergoing the same kind of sufferings.

10And the God of all grace, who called you to his eternal glory in Christ, after you have suffered a little while, will himself restore you and make you strong, firm and stead-

a18 Prov. 11:31   b5 Prov. 3:34

fast. ¹¹To him be the power for ever and ever. Amen.

Final Greetings

¹²With the help of Silas,ᵃ whom I regard as a faithful brother, I have written to you briefly, encouraging you and testifying that this is the true grace of God. Stand fast in it.

¹³She who is in Babylon, chosen together with you, sends you her greetings, and so does my son Mark. ¹⁴Greet one another with a kiss of love.

Peace to all of you who are in Christ.

ᵃ12 Greek *Silvanus*, a variant of *Silas*

2 PETER

WHO WROTE THIS BOOK?	Peter, the disciple of Jesus, wrote this book.
WHY WAS THIS BOOK WRITTEN?	The book of 2 Peter warns Christians against false teachers.
FOR WHOM WAS THIS BOOK WRITTEN?	This book is a letter Peter sent to Christians everywhere.
WHEN WAS THIS BOOK WRITTEN?	This book was written about A.D 67.
WHAT ARE SOME IMPORTANT TEACHINGS IN THIS BOOK?	What false teachers are like. 2 Peter 2:1–22 How the world will end. 2 Peter 3:1–13

1 Simon Peter, a servant and apostle of Jesus Christ,

To those who through the righteousness of our God and Savior Jesus Christ have received a faith as precious as ours:

²Grace and peace be yours in abundance through the knowledge of God and of Jesus our Lord.

Making One's Calling and Election Sure

³His divine power has given us everything we need for life and godliness through our knowledge of him who called us by his own glory and goodness. ⁴Through these he has given us his very great and precious promises, so that through them you may participate in the divine nature and escape the corruption in the world caused by evil desires.

⁵For this very reason, make every effort to add to your faith goodness; and to goodness, knowledge; ⁶and to knowledge, self-control; and to self-control, perseverance; and to perseverance, godliness; ⁷and to godliness, brotherly kindness; and to brotherly kindness, love. ⁸For if you possess these qualities in increasing measure, they will keep you from being ineffective and unproductive in your knowledge of our Lord Jesus Christ. ⁹But if anyone does not have them, he is nearsighted and blind, and has forgotten that he has been cleansed from his past sins.

¹⁰Therefore, my brothers, be all the more eager to make your calling and election sure. For if you do these things, you will never fall, ¹¹and you will receive a rich welcome into the eternal kingdom of our Lord and Savior Jesus Christ.

Prophecy of Scripture

¹²So I will always remind you of these things, even though you know them and are firmly established in the truth you now have. ¹³I think it is right to refresh your memory as long as I live in the tent of this body, ¹⁴because I know that I will soon put it aside, as our Lord Jesus Christ has made clear to me. ¹⁵And I will make every effort to see that after my departure you will always be able to remember these things.

❓DID YOU KNOW?   1:5

How do Christians grow?

Two ways Christians grow are by being good and by learning more about God. 2 Peter 1:3–11 tells you other secrets about how to grow as a Christian.

---

¹⁶We did not follow cleverly invented stories when we told you about the power and coming of our Lord Jesus Christ, but we were eyewitnesses of his majesty. ¹⁷For he received honor and glory from God the Father when the voice came to him from the Majestic Glory, saying, "This is my Son, whom I love; with him I am well pleased."ᵃ ¹⁸We ourselves heard this voice that came from heaven when we were with him on the sacred mountain.

❓DID YOU KNOW?   1:21

Why do we trust the Bible?

We trust the Bible because we know that God spoke through the people who wrote it. Nothing in the Bible is invented. It is all true.

---

¹⁹And we have the word of the prophets made more certain, and you will do well to pay attention to it, as to a light shining in a dark place, until the day dawns and the morning star rises in your hearts. ²⁰Above all, you must understand that no prophecy of Scripture came about by the prophet's own interpretation. ²¹For prophecy never had its origin in the

---

a17 Matt. 17:5; Mark 9:7; Luke 9:35

will of man, but men spoke from God as they were carried along by the Holy Spirit.

False Teachers and Their Destruction

2 But there were also false prophets among the people, just as there will be false teachers among you. They will secretly introduce destructive heresies, even denying the sovereign Lord who bought them—bringing swift destruction on themselves. ²Many will follow their shameful ways and will bring the way of truth into disrepute. ³In their greed these teachers will exploit you with stories they have made up. Their condemnation has long been hanging over them, and their destruction has not been sleeping.

❓DID YOU KNOW?   2:1

What is a false teacher?

A false teacher is a person who teaches what is not true instead of what the Bible says. Peter uses strong language here to describe what he thinks of false teachers and what will happen to them in the end.

---

⁴For if God did not spare angels when they sinned, but sent them to hell,ᵃ putting them into gloomy dungeonsᵇ to be held for judgment; ⁵if he did not spare the ancient world when he brought the flood on its ungodly people, but protected Noah, a preacher of righteousness, and seven others; ⁶if he condemned the cities of Sodom and Gomorrah by burning them to ashes, and made them an example of what is going to happen to the ungodly; ⁷and if he rescued Lot, a righteous man, who was distressed by the filthy lives of lawless men ⁸(for that righteous man, living among them day after day, was tormented in his righ-

teous soul by the lawless deeds he saw and heard)— ⁹if this is so, then the Lord knows how to rescue godly men from trials and to hold the unrighteous for the day of judgment, while continuing their punishment.ᶜ ¹⁰This is especially true of those who follow the corrupt desire of the sinful natureᵈ and despise authority.

Bold and arrogant, these men are not afraid to slander celestial beings; ¹¹yet even angels, although they are stronger and more powerful, do not bring slanderous accusations against such beings in the presence of the Lord. ¹²But these men blaspheme in matters they do not understand. They are like brute beasts, creatures of instinct, born only to be caught and destroyed, and like beasts they too will perish.

¹³They will be paid back with harm for the harm they have done. Their idea of pleasure is to carouse in broad daylight. They are blots and blemishes, reveling in their pleasures while they feast with you.ᵉ ¹⁴With eyes full of adultery, they never stop sinning; they seduce the unstable; they are experts in greed—an accursed brood! ¹⁵They have left the straight way and wandered off to follow the way of Balaam son of Beor, who loved the wages of wickedness. ¹⁶But he was rebuked for his wrongdoing by a donkey—a beast without speech—who spoke with a man's voice and restrained the prophet's madness.

¹⁷These men are springs without water and mists driven by a storm. Blackest darkness is reserved for them. ¹⁸For they mouth empty, boastful words and, by appealing to the lustful desires of sinful human nature, they entice people who are just escaping from those who live in error. ¹⁹They promise them freedom, while they themselves are slaves of depravity—for a man is a slave to whatever has mastered him. ²⁰If they

---

ᵃ4 Greek *Tartarus*   ᵇ4 Some manuscripts *into chains of darkness*   ᶜ9 Or *unrighteous for punishment until the day of judgment*   ᵈ10 Or *the flesh*   ᵉ13 Some manuscripts *in their love feasts*

have escaped the corruption of the world by knowing our Lord and Savior Jesus Christ and are again entangled in it and overcome, they are worse off at the end than they were at the beginning. [21]It would have been better for them not to have known the way of righteousness, than to have known it and then to turn their backs on the sacred command that was passed on to them. [22]Of them the proverbs are true: "A dog returns to its vomit,"[a] and, "A sow that is washed goes back to her wallowing in the mud."

The Day of the Lord

3 Dear friends, this is now my second letter to you. I have written both of them as reminders to stimulate you to wholesome thinking. [2]I want you to recall the words spoken in the past by the holy prophets and the command given by our Lord and Savior through your apostles.

[3]First of all, you must understand that in the last days scoffers will come, scoffing and following their own evil desires. [4]They will say, "Where is this 'coming' he promised? Ever since our fathers died, everything goes on as it has since the beginning of creation." [5]But they deliberately forget that long ago by God's word the heavens existed and the earth was formed out of water and by water. [6]By these waters also the world of that time was deluged and

destroyed. [7]By the same word the present heavens and earth are reserved for fire, being kept for the day of judgment and destruction of ungodly men.

[8]But do not forget this one thing, dear friends: With the Lord a day is like a thousand years, and a thousand years are like a day. [9]The Lord is not slow in keeping his promise, as some understand slowness. He is patient with you, not wanting anyone to perish, but everyone to come to repentance.

?DID YOU KNOW?　　　3:12

How will the world end?

After Jesus comes back, this universe will be burned up. Then God will create a new heaven and earth to be home for the people who followed and loved Jesus.

---

[10]But the day of the Lord will come like a thief. The heavens will disappear with a roar; the elements will be destroyed by fire, and the earth and everything in it will be laid bare.[b]

[11]Since everything will be destroyed in this way, what kind of people ought you to be? You ought to live holy and godly lives [12]as you look forward to the day of God and speed its coming.[c] That day will bring about the destruction of the heavens by fire,

---

a22 Prov. 26:11　　*b10* Some manuscripts *be burned up*　　*c12* Or *as you wait eagerly for the day of God to come*

▚ET'S LIVE IT!　　　2 Peter 3:10–13

WHAT WILL HAPPEN TO OUR EARTH? ➡ Read 2 Peter 3:10–13. Draw a picture showing what will happen to our earth when Jesus comes again (2 Peter 3:12).

The Bible says that God will then create a new heaven and earth. On the back of the first picture, draw a picture of what you think the new earth might look like (2 Peter 3:13).

God's people, who live holy and godly lives, will enjoy his new heaven and earth. If you are one of God's children, draw yourself on your picture of the new earth.

and the elements will melt in the heat. [13]But in keeping with his promise we are looking forward to a new heaven and a new earth, the home of righteousness.

[14]So then, dear friends, since you are looking forward to this, make every effort to be found spotless, blameless and at peace with him. [15]Bear in mind that our Lord's patience means salvation, just as our dear brother Paul also wrote you with the wisdom that God gave him. [16]He writes the same way in all his letters, speaking in them of these matters. His letters contain some things that are hard to understand, which ignorant and unstable people distort, as they do the other Scriptures, to their own destruction.

[17]Therefore, dear friends, since you already know this, be on your guard so that you may not be carried away by the error of lawless men and fall from your secure position. [18]But grow in the grace and knowledge of our Lord and Savior Jesus Christ. To him be glory both now and forever! Amen.

1 JOHN

1JN
JUD
REV

The Word of Life

1 That which was from the beginning, which we have heard, which we have seen with our eyes, which we have looked at and our hands have touched—this we proclaim concerning the Word of life. ²The life appeared; we have seen it and testify to it, and we proclaim to you the eternal life, which was with the Father and has appeared to us. ³We proclaim to you what we have seen and heard, so that you also may have fellowship with us. And our fellowship is with the Father and with his Son, Jesus Christ. ⁴We write this to make our*ᵃ* joy complete.

Walking in the Light

⁵This is the message we have heard from him and declare to you: God is light; in him there is no darkness at all. ⁶If we claim to have fellowship with him yet walk in the darkness, we lie and do not live by the truth. ⁷But if we walk in the light, as he is in the light, we have fellowship with one another, and the blood of Jesus, his Son, purifies us from all*ᵇ* sin.

⁸If we claim to be without sin, we deceive ourselves and the truth is not in us. ⁹If we confess our sins, he is faithful and just and will forgive us our sins and purify us from all unrighteousness. ¹⁰If we claim we have not sinned, we make him out to be a liar and his word has no place in our lives.

WORDS TO REMEMBER

1:9 If we confess our sins, he is faithful and just and will forgive us our sins and purify us from all unrighteousness.

2 My dear children, I write this to you so that you will not sin. But if anybody does sin, we have one who speaks to the Father in our defense

—Jesus Christ, the Righteous One. ²He is the atoning sacrifice for our sins, and not only for ours but also for*ᶜ* the sins of the whole world.

³We know that we have come to know him if we obey his commands. ⁴The man who says, "I know him," but does not do what he commands is a liar, and the truth is not in him. ⁵But if anyone obeys his word, God's love*ᵈ* is truly made complete in him. This is how we know we are in him: ⁶Whoever claims to live in him must walk as Jesus did.

⁷Dear friends, I am not writing you a new command but an old one, which you have had since the beginning. This old command is the message you have heard. ⁸Yet I am writing you a new command; its truth is seen in him and you, because the darkness is passing and the true light is already shining.

⁹Anyone who claims to be in the light but hates his brother is still in the darkness. ¹⁰Whoever loves his brother lives in the light, and there is nothing in him*ᵉ* to make him stumble. ¹¹But whoever hates his brother is in the darkness and walks around in the darkness; he does not know where he is going, because the darkness has blinded him.

? DID YOU KNOW?   2:9

What is walking in the light?

Walking in the light (1 John 1:7) is being honest with God. If we are walking in the light, we know when we do wrong, and we confess our sin to God. Lying to ourselves or others about doing wrong is what John calls walking in darkness.

¹²I write to you, dear children,
　　because your sins have been
　　　　forgiven on account of his
　　　　name.
¹³I write to you, fathers,

ᵃ4 Some manuscripts your   ᵇ7 Or every   ᶜ2 Or He is the one who turns aside God's wrath,
taking away our sins, and not only ours but also   ᵈ5 Or word, love for God   ᵉ10 Or it

because you have known him
who is from the beginning.
I write to you, young men,
because you have overcome the
evil one.
I write to you, dear children,
because you have known the
Father.
[14]I write to you, fathers,
because you have known him
who is from the beginning.
I write to you, young men,
because you are strong,
and the word of God lives in
you,
and you have overcome the evil
one.

Do Not Love the World

[15]Do not love the world or anything
in the world. If anyone loves the
world, the love of the Father is not in
him. [16]For everything in the world
—the cravings of sinful man, the lust
of his eyes and the boasting of what
he has and does—comes not from the
Father but from the world. [17]The
world and its desires pass away, but
the man who does the will of God
lives forever.

Warning Against Antichrists

[18]Dear children, this is the last
hour; and as you have heard that the
antichrist is coming, even now many
antichrists have come. This is how we
know it is the last hour. [19]They went
out from us, but they did not really
belong to us. For if they had belonged
to us, they would have remained with
us; but their going showed that none
of them belonged to us.
[20]But you have an anointing from
the Holy One, and all of you know the
truth.[a] [21]I do not write to you because you do not know the truth, but
because you do know it and because
no lie comes from the truth. [22]Who is
the liar? It is the man who denies
that Jesus is the Christ. Such a man
is the antichrist—he denies the Father and the Son. [23]No one who denies the Son has the Father; whoever

acknowledges the Son has the Father
also.

?DID YOU KNOW?   2:18

What is an antichrist?

An antichrist is a person who is
against Christ. A person who is
against Christ does not believe
that Jesus really is God. This kind of
person does not know God.

---

[24]See that what you have heard
from the beginning remains in you. If
it does, you also will remain in the
Son and in the Father. [25]And this is
what he promised us—even eternal
life.
[26]I am writing these things to you
about those who are trying to lead
you astray. [27]As for you, the anointing you received from him remains in
you, and you do not need anyone to
teach you. But as his anointing
teaches you about all things and as
that anointing is real, not counterfeit—just as it has taught you, remain in him.

Children of God

[28]And now, dear children, continue
in him, so that when he appears we
may be confident and unashamed before him at his coming.
[29]If you know that he is righteous,
you know that everyone who does
what is right has been born of him.
3 How great is the love the Father
has lavished on us, that we
should be called children of God! And
that is what we are! The reason the
world does not know us is that it did
not know him. [2]Dear friends, now we
are children of God, and what we will
be has not yet been made known. But
we know that when he appears,[b] we
shall be like him, for we shall see him
as he is. [3]Everyone who has this hope
in him purifies himself, just as he is
pure.
[4]Everyone who sins breaks the law;

---

[a]20 Some manuscripts *and you know all things*   [b]2 Or *when it is made known*

in fact, sin is lawlessness. 5But you know that he appeared so that he might take away our sins. And in him is no sin. 6No one who lives in him keeps on sinning. No one who continues to sin has either seen him or known him.

7Dear children, do not let anyone lead you astray. He who does what is right is righteous, just as he is righteous. 8He who does what is sinful is of the devil, because the devil has been sinning from the beginning. The reason the Son of God appeared was to destroy the devil's work. 9No one who is born of God will continue to sin, because God's seed remains in him; he cannot go on sinning, because he has been born of God. 10This is how we know who the children of God are and who the children of the devil are: Anyone who does not do what is right is not a child of God; nor is anyone who does not love his brother.

? DID YOU KNOW?   3:1

How do you know if a person is a child of God?

Children of God believe in Jesus. They show they trust Jesus by obeying God's commands and by loving other Christians.

Love One Another

11This is the message you heard from the beginning: We should love one another. 12Do not be like Cain, who belonged to the evil one and murdered his brother. And why did he murder him? Because his own actions were evil and his brother's were righteous. 13Do not be surprised, my brothers, if the world hates you. 14We know that we have passed from death to life, because we love our brothers. Anyone who does not love remains in death. 15Anyone who hates his brother is a murderer, and you know that no murderer has eternal life in him.

16This is how we know what love is: Jesus Christ laid down his life for us. And we ought to lay down our lives for our brothers. 17If anyone has material possessions and sees his brother in need but has no pity on him, how can the love of God be in him? 18Dear children, let us not love with words or tongue but with actions and in truth. 19This then is how we know that we belong to the truth, and how we set our hearts at rest in his presence 20whenever our hearts condemn us. For God is greater than our hearts, and he knows everything.

21Dear friends, if our hearts do not condemn us, we have confidence before God 22and receive from him anything we ask, because we obey his commands and do what pleases him. 23And this is his command: to believe in the name of his Son, Jesus Christ, and to love one another as he commanded us. 24Those who obey his commands live in him, and he in them. And this is how we know that

◤ET'S LIVE IT!   1 John 3:16–20

LOVE AND ACTIONS ➠ Read 1 John 3:16–20. How do we know God loves us? How do we as Christians show that the love of God is in us?

Play a game at the dinner table. Each person is to say "Love is . . .," and then describe a way to show love by an action. For instance, "Love is helping with the dishes." "Love is praying with me at night." "Love is mowing an invalid's grass." Each person must think of something new in five seconds, or he or she is out.

Count the number of "love is" actions your family can name. Play the game several times, and see how many loving actions you can think of together.

he lives in us: We know it by the Spirit he gave us.

Test the Spirits

4 Dear friends, do not believe every spirit, but test the spirits to see whether they are from God, because many false prophets have gone out into the world. ²This is how you can recognize the Spirit of God: Every spirit that acknowledges that Jesus Christ has come in the flesh is from God, ³but every spirit that does not acknowledge Jesus is not from God. This is the spirit of the antichrist, which you have heard is coming and even now is already in the world.

⁴You, dear children, are from God and have overcome them, because the one who is in you is greater than the one who is in the world. ⁵They are from the world and therefore speak from the viewpoint of the world, and the world listens to them. ⁶We are from God, and whoever knows God listens to us; but whoever is not from God does not listen to us. This is how we recognize the Spirit*ᵃ* of truth and the spirit of falsehood.

God's Love and Ours

⁷Dear friends, let us love one another, for love comes from God. Everyone who loves has been born of God and knows God. ⁸Whoever does not love does not know God, because God is love. ⁹This is how God showed his love among us: He sent his one and only Son*ᵇ* into the world that we might live through him. ¹⁰This is love: not that we loved God, but that he loved us and sent his Son as an atoning sacrifice for*ᶜ* our sins. ¹¹Dear friends, since God so loved us, we also ought to love one another. ¹²No one has ever seen God; but if we love one another, God lives in us and his love is made complete in us.

¹³We know that we live in him and he in us, because he has given us of his Spirit. ¹⁴And we have seen and testify that the Father has sent his Son to be the Savior of the world. ¹⁵If anyone acknowledges that Jesus is the Son of God, God lives in him and he in God. ¹⁶And so we know and rely on the love God has for us.

Words to Remember

4:11 Since God so loved us, we also ought to love one another.

God is love. Whoever lives in love lives in God, and God in him. ¹⁷In this way, love is made complete among us so that we will have confidence on the day of judgment, because in this world we are like him. ¹⁸There is no fear in love. But perfect love drives out fear, because fear has to do with punishment. The one who fears is not made perfect in love.

Did You Know? 4:16

What is love?

God is love. Love is Jesus dying for us. Real love is helping others when they have needs. Because God loves us, we are to love others.

¹⁹We love because he first loved us. ²⁰If anyone says, "I love God," yet hates his brother, he is a liar. For anyone who does not love his brother, whom he has seen, cannot love God, whom he has not seen. ²¹And he has given us this command: Whoever loves God must also love his brother.

Faith in the Son of God

5 Everyone who believes that Jesus is the Christ is born of God, and everyone who loves the father loves his child as well. ²This is how we know that we love the children of God: by loving God and carrying out his commands. ³This is love for God: to obey his commands. And his com-

---

ᵃ6 Or *spirit*　　*ᵇ9* Or *his only begotten Son*　　*ᶜ10* Or *as the one who would turn aside his wrath,*
taking away

mands are not burdensome, 4for everyone born of God overcomes the world. This is the victory that has overcome the world, even our faith. 5Who is it that overcomes the world? Only he who believes that Jesus is the Son of God.

WORDS TO REMEMBER

5:3 This is love for God: to obey his commands.

6This is the one who came by water and blood—Jesus Christ. He did not come by water only, but by water and blood. And it is the Spirit who testifies, because the Spirit is the truth. 7For there are three that testify: 8thea Spirit, the water and the blood; and the three are in agreement. 9We accept man's testimony, but God's testimony is greater because it is the testimony of God, which he has given about his Son. 10Anyone who believes in the Son of God has this testimony in his heart. Anyone who does not believe God has made him out to be a liar, because he has not believed the testimony God has given about his Son. 11And this is the testimony: God has given us eternal life, and this life is in his Son. 12He who has the Son has life; he who does not have the Son of God does not have life.

Concluding Remarks

13I write these things to you who believe in the name of the Son of God so that you may know that you have

eternal life. 14This is the confidence we have in approaching God: that if we ask anything according to his will, he hears us. 15And if we know that he hears us—whatever we ask —we know that we have what we asked of him.

16If anyone sees his brother commit a sin that does not lead to death, he should pray and God will give him life. I refer to those whose sin does not lead to death. There is a sin that leads to death. I am not saying that he should pray about that. 17All wrongdoing is sin, and there is sin that does not lead to death.

WORDS TO REMEMBER

5:13 I write these things to you who believe in the name of the Son of God so that you may know that you have eternal life.

18We know that anyone born of God does not continue to sin; the one who was born of God keeps him safe, and the evil one cannot harm him. 19We know that we are children of God, and that the whole world is under the control of the evil one. 20We know also that the Son of God has come and has given us understanding, so that we may know him who is true. And we are in him who is true—even in his Son Jesus Christ. He is the true God and eternal life.

21Dear children, keep yourselves from idols.

---

a7,8 Late manuscripts of the Vulgate *testify in heaven: the Father, the Word and the Holy Spirit, and these three are one.* 8*And there are three that testify on earth: the* (not found in any Greek manuscript before the sixteenth century)

2 JOHN

¹The elder,

To the chosen lady and her children, whom I love in the truth—and not I only, but also all who know the truth— ²because of the truth, which lives in us and will be with us forever:

³Grace, mercy and peace from God the Father and from Jesus Christ, the Father's Son, will be with us in truth and love.

⁴It has given me great joy to find some of your children walking in the truth, just as the Father commanded us. ⁵And now, dear lady, I am not writing you a new command but one we have had from the beginning. I ask that we love one another. ⁶And this is love: that we walk in obedience to his commands. As you have heard from the beginning, his command is that you walk in love.

⁷Many deceivers, who do not acknowledge Jesus Christ as coming in the flesh, have gone out into the world. Any such person is the deceiver and the antichrist. ⁸Watch out that you do not lose what you have worked for, but that you may be rewarded fully. ⁹Anyone who runs ahead and does not continue in the teaching of

WORDS TO REMEMBER

6 And this is love: that we walk in obedience to his commands.... his command is that you walk in love.

Christ does not have God; whoever continues in the teaching has both the Father and the Son. ¹⁰If anyone comes to you and does not bring this teaching, do not take him into your house or welcome him. ¹¹Anyone who welcomes him shares in his wicked work.

¹²I have much to write to you, but I do not want to use paper and ink. Instead, I hope to visit you and talk with you face to face, so that our joy may be complete.

¹³The children of your chosen sister send their greetings.

3 JOHN

John, the disciple of Jesus, wrote this book.

The book of 3 John shows Christians how to live close to God and other people.

This book is a letter John sent to Christians everywhere.

John probably wrote about A.D 90.

¹The elder,

To my dear friend Gaius, whom I love in the truth.

²Dear friend, I pray that you may enjoy good health and that all may go well with you, even as your soul is getting along well. ³It gave me great joy to have some brothers come and tell about your faithfulness to the truth and how you continue to walk in the truth. ⁴I have no greater joy than to hear that my children are walking in the truth.

⁵Dear friend, you are faithful in what you are doing for the brothers, even though they are strangers to you. ⁶They have told the church about your love. You will do well to send them on their way in a manner worthy of God. ⁷It was for the sake of the Name that they went out, receiving no help from the pagans. ⁸We ought therefore to show hospitality to such men so that we may work together for the truth.

⁹I wrote to the church, but Diotrephes, who loves to be first, will have nothing to do with us. ¹⁰So if I come, I will call attention to what he is doing, gossiping maliciously about us. Not satisfied with that, he refuses to welcome the brothers. He also stops those who want to do so and puts them out of the church.

¹¹Dear friend, do not imitate what is evil but what is good. Anyone who does what is good is from God. Anyone who does what is evil has not seen God. ¹²Demetrius is well spoken of by everyone—and even by the truth itself. We also speak well of him, and you know that our testimony is true.

¹³I have much to write you, but I do not want to do so with pen and ink. ¹⁴I hope to see you soon, and we will talk face to face.

Peace to you. The friends here send their greetings. Greet the friends there by name.

LET'S LIVE IT!

3 John 2–4

GREAT JOY ➡ Read 3 John 2–4. Ask your mother or dad to explain why John says, "I have no greater joy than to hear that my children are walking in the truth" (3 John 4).

It made John glad that his friends were following Jesus and living for him. How do you think you could make your parents glad?

JUDE

WHO WROTE THIS BOOK?	Jude, a brother of Jesus, wrote this book.
WHY WAS THIS BOOK WRITTEN?	Jude warns Christians about false teachers.
FOR WHOM WAS THIS BOOK WRITTEN?	This book is a letter written to Christians everywhere.
WHEN WAS THIS BOOK WRITTEN?	Jude was written about A.D 66.

¹Jude, a servant of Jesus Christ and a brother of James,

To those who have been called, who are loved by God the Father and kept by*a* Jesus Christ:

²Mercy, peace and love be yours in abundance.

The Sin and Doom of Godless Men

³Dear friends, although I was very eager to write to you about the salvation we share, I felt I had to write and urge you to contend for the faith that was once for all entrusted to the saints. ⁴For certain men whose condemnation was written about*b* long ago have secretly slipped in among you. They are godless men, who change the grace of our God into a license for immorality and deny Jesus Christ our only Sovereign and Lord.

⁵Though you already know all this, I want to remind you that the Lord*c* delivered his people out of Egypt, but later destroyed those who did not believe. ⁶And the angels who did not keep their positions of authority but abandoned their own home—these he has kept in darkness, bound with everlasting chains for judgment on the great Day. ⁷In a similar way, Sodom and Gomorrah and the surrounding towns gave themselves up to sexual immorality and perversion. They serve as an example of those who suffer the punishment of eternal fire.

⁸In the very same way, these dreamers pollute their own bodies, reject authority and slander celestial beings. ⁹But even the archangel Michael, when he was disputing with the devil about the body of Moses, did not dare to bring a slanderous accusation against him, but said, "The Lord rebuke you!" ¹⁰Yet these men speak abusively against whatever they do not understand; and what things they do understand by instinct, like unreasoning animals—these are the very things that destroy them.

¹¹Woe to them! They have taken the way of Cain; they have rushed for profit into Balaam's error; they have been destroyed in Korah's rebellion. ¹²These men are blemishes at your love feasts, eating with you without the slightest qualm—shepherds who feed only themselves. They are clouds without rain, blown along by the wind; autumn trees, without fruit and uprooted—twice dead. ¹³They are wild waves of the sea, foaming up their shame; wandering stars, for whom blackest darkness has been reserved forever.

¹⁴Enoch, the seventh from Adam, prophesied about these men: "See, the Lord is coming with thousands upon thousands of his holy ones ¹⁵to judge everyone, and to convict all the ungodly of all the ungodly acts they have done in the ungodly way, and of all the harsh words ungodly sinners have spoken against him." ¹⁶These men are grumblers and faultfinders; they follow their own evil desires; they boast about themselves and flatter others for their own advantage.

A Call to Persevere

¹⁷But, dear friends, remember what the apostles of our Lord Jesus Christ foretold. ¹⁸They said to you, "In the last times there will be scoffers who will follow their own ungodly desires." ¹⁹These are the men who divide you, who follow mere natural instincts and do not have the Spirit.

²⁰But you, dear friends, build yourselves up in your most holy faith and pray in the Holy Spirit. ²¹Keep yourselves in God's love as you wait for the mercy of our Lord Jesus Christ to bring you to eternal life.

WORDS TO REMEMBER

21 Keep yourselves in God's love.

---

a1 Or for; or *in* manuscripts *Jesus*   *b4 Or men who were marked out for condemnation*   *c5 Some early*

²²Be merciful to those who doubt; ²³snatch others from the fire and save them; to others show mercy, mixed with fear—hating even the clothing stained by corrupted flesh.

Doxology

²⁴To him who is able to keep you from falling and to present you before his glorious presence without fault and with great joy— ²⁵to the only God our Savior be glory, majesty, power and authority, through Jesus Christ our Lord, before all ages, now and forevermore! Amen.

REVELATION

WHO WROTE THIS BOOK?

John, the disciple of Jesus, wrote this book.

WHY WAS THIS BOOK WRITTEN?

John wrote this book to tell people about a vision he had of Jesus and about "what must soon take place."

FOR WHOM WAS THIS BOOK WRITTEN?

This book was written for all Christians everywhere.

WHEN WAS THIS BOOK WRITTEN?

John wrote this book about A.D 90.

WHAT ARE SOME IMPORTANT TEACHINGS IN THIS BOOK?

Jesus is God.	Revelation 1:9–18
Letters to seven churches.	Revelation 2–3
God is on his throne.	Revelation 4:1–11
God will judge Satan.	Revelation 20:7–10
God will judge the dead.	Revelation 20:11–15
A new world.	Revelation 21:1–22:6

Prologue

1 The revelation of Jesus Christ, which God gave him to show his servants what must soon take place. He made it known by sending his angel to his servant John, ²who testifies to everything he saw—that is, the word of God and the testimony of Jesus Christ. ³Blessed is the one who reads the words of this prophecy, and blessed are those who hear it and take to heart what is written in it, because the time is near.

Greetings and Doxology

⁴John,

To the seven churches in the province of Asia:

Grace and peace to you from him who is, and who was, and who is to come, and from the seven spirits*ᵃ* before his throne, ⁵and from Jesus Christ, who is the faithful witness, the firstborn from the dead, and the ruler of the kings of the earth.

To him who loves us and has freed us from our sins by his blood, ⁶and has made us to be a kingdom and priests to serve his God and Father —to him be glory and power for ever and ever! Amen.

⁷Look, he is coming with the
clouds,
and every eye will see him,
even those who pierced him;
and all the peoples of the earth
will mourn because of him.
So shall it be! Amen.

WORDS TO REMEMBER

1:5 [Jesus] loves us and has freed us from our sins by his blood.

⁸"I am the Alpha and the Omega," says the Lord God, "who is, and who

was, and who is to come, the Almighty."

One Like a Son of Man

⁹I, John, your brother and companion in the suffering and kingdom and patient endurance that are ours in Jesus, was on the island of Patmos because of the word of God and the testimony of Jesus. ¹⁰On the Lord's Day I was in the Spirit, and I heard behind me a loud voice like a trumpet, ¹¹which said: "Write on a scroll what you see and send it to the seven churches: to Ephesus, Smyrna, Pergamum, Thyatira, Sardis, Philadelphia and Laodicea."

¹²I turned around to see the voice that was speaking to me. And when I turned I saw seven golden lampstands, ¹³and among the lampstands was someone "like a son of man,"*ᵇ* dressed in a robe reaching down to his feet and with a golden sash around his chest. ¹⁴His head and hair were white like wool, as white as snow, and his eyes were like blazing fire. ¹⁵His feet were like bronze glowing in a furnace, and his voice was like the sound of rushing waters. ¹⁶In his right hand he held seven stars, and out of his mouth came a sharp double-edged sword. His face was like the sun shining in all its brilliance.

¹⁷When I saw him, I fell at his feet as though dead. Then he placed his right hand on me and said: "Do not be afraid. I am the First and the Last. ¹⁸I am the Living One; I was dead, and behold I am alive for ever and ever! And I hold the keys of death and Hades.

¹⁹"Write, therefore, what you have seen, what is now and what will take place later. ²⁰The mystery of the seven stars that you saw in my right hand and of the seven golden lampstands is this: The seven stars are the angels*ᶜ* of the seven churches, and the seven lampstands are the seven churches.

ᵃ4 Or the sevenfold Spirit *ᵇ13 Daniel 7:13* *ᶜ20 Or messengers*

To the Church in Ephesus

2 "To the angel*a* of the church in Ephesus write:

These are the words of him who holds the seven stars in his right hand and walks among the seven golden lampstands: ²I know your deeds, your hard work and your perseverance. I know that you cannot tolerate wicked men, that you have tested those who claim to be apostles but are not, and have found them false. ³You have persevered and have endured hardships for my name, and have not grown weary.

⁴Yet I hold this against you: You have forsaken your first love. ⁵Remember the height from which you have fallen! Repent and do the things you did at first. If you do not repent, I will come to you and remove your lampstand from its place. ⁶But you have this in your favor: You hate the practices of the Nicolaitans, which I also hate.

⁷He who has an ear, let him hear what the Spirit says to the churches. To him who overcomes, I will give the right to eat from the tree of life, which is in the paradise of God.

To the Church in Smyrna

⁸"To the angel of the church in Smyrna write:

These are the words of him who is the First and the Last, who died and came to life again. ⁹I know your afflictions and your poverty—yet you are rich! I know the slander of those who say they are Jews and are not, but are a synagogue of Satan. ¹⁰Do not be afraid of what you are about to suffer. I tell you, the devil will put some of you in prison to test you, and you will suffer persecution for ten days. Be faithful, even to the point of death, and I will give you the crown of life.

¹¹He who has an ear, let him hear what the Spirit says to the churches. He who overcomes will not be hurt at all by the second death.

To the Church in Pergamum

¹²"To the angel of the church in Pergamum write:

These are the words of him who has the sharp, double-edged sword. ¹³I know where you live —where Satan has his throne. Yet you remain true to my name. You did not renounce your faith in me, even in the days of Antipas, my faithful witness, who was put to death in your city— where Satan lives.

¹⁴Nevertheless, I have a few things against you: You have people there who hold to the teaching of Balaam, who taught Balak to entice the Israelites to

---

a1 Or *messenger*; also in verses 8, 12 and 18

LET'S LIVE IT!
Revelation 1:9–18

JESUS IS ALMIGHTY GOD ➡ John was a close friend of Jesus. But what happened when he saw Jesus as he truly is in heaven? Read Revelation 1:9–18.
   Find or draw a picture of how Jesus might have looked as a baby. Find or draw a picture of how Jesus might have looked as a grown-up, teaching and healing. Find or draw a picture of Jesus in heaven, as he is in Revelation 1. Put the three pictures together on your wall to remind you that Jesus is God as well as your loving friend.

sin by eating food sacrificed to idols and by committing sexual immorality. ¹⁵Likewise you also have those who hold to the teaching of the Nicolaitans. ¹⁶Repent therefore! Otherwise, I will soon come to you and will fight against them with the sword of my mouth.

¹⁷He who has an ear, let him hear what the Spirit says to the churches. To him who overcomes, I will give some of the hidden manna. I will also give him a white stone with a new name written on it, known only to him who receives it.

To the Church in Thyatira

¹⁸"To the angel of the church in Thyatira write:

These are the words of the Son of God, whose eyes are like blazing fire and whose feet are like burnished bronze. ¹⁹I know your deeds, your love and faith, your service and perseverance, and that you are now doing more than you did at first.

²⁰Nevertheless, I have this against you: You tolerate that woman Jezebel, who calls herself a prophetess. By her teaching she misleads my servants into sexual immorality and the eating of food sacrificed to idols. ²¹I have given her time to repent of her immorality, but she is unwilling. ²²So I will cast her on a bed of suffering, and I will make those who commit adultery with her suffer intensely, unless they repent of her ways. ²³I will strike her children dead. Then all the churches will know that I am he who searches hearts and minds, and I will repay each of you according to your deeds. ²⁴Now I say to the rest of you in Thyatira, to you who do not hold to her teaching and have not learned Satan's so-called deep secrets (I

will not impose any other burden on you): ²⁵Only hold on to what you have until I come.

²⁶To him who overcomes and does my will to the end, I will give authority over the nations—

²⁷'He will rule them with an
　　　iron scepter;
　he will dash them to
　　　pieces like pottery'ᵃ—

just as I have received authority from my Father. ²⁸I will also give him the morning star. ²⁹He who has an ear, let him hear what the Spirit says to the churches.

To the Church in Sardis

3 "To the angelᵇ of the church in Sardis write:

These are the words of him who holds the seven spiritsᶜ of God and the seven stars. I know your deeds; you have a reputation of being alive, but you are dead. ²Wake up! Strengthen what remains and is about to die, for I have not found your deeds complete in the sight of my God. ³Remember, therefore, what you have received and heard; obey it, and repent. But if you do not wake up, I will come like a thief, and you will not know at what time I will come to you.

⁴Yet you have a few people in Sardis who have not soiled their clothes. They will walk with me, dressed in white, for they are worthy. ⁵He who overcomes will, like them, be dressed in white. I will never blot out his name from the book of life, but will acknowledge his name before my Father and his angels. ⁶He who has an ear, let him hear what the Spirit says to the churches.

To the Church in Philadelphia

⁷"To the angel of the church in Philadelphia write:

ᵃ27 Psalm 2:9   ᵇ1 Or *messenger*; also in verses 7 and 14   ᶜ1 Or *the sevenfold Spirit*

These are the words of him who is holy and true, who holds the key of David. What he opens no one can shut, and what he shuts no one can open. ⁸I know your deeds. See, I have placed before you an open door that no one can shut. I know that you have little strength, yet you have kept my word and have not denied my name. ⁹I will make those who are of the synagogue of Satan, who claim to be Jews though they are not, but are liars—I will make them come and fall down at your feet and acknowledge that I have loved you. ¹⁰Since you have kept my command to endure patiently, I will also keep you from the hour of trial that is going to come upon the whole world to test those who live on the earth.

? DID YOU KNOW?   3:1

Who were the angels of the churches mentioned in Revelation 2–3?

Angel means "messenger." John was writing to leaders of these churches. They were God's messengers. Each of the cities mentioned was in Asia Minor, not far from the island where John was a prisoner when he wrote Revelation.

¹¹I am coming soon. Hold on to what you have, so that no one will take your crown. ¹²Him who overcomes I will make a pillar in the temple of my God. Never again will he leave it. I will write on him the name of my God and the name of the city of my God, the new Jerusalem, which is coming down out of heaven from my God; and I will also write on him my new name. ¹³He who has an ear, let him hear what the Spirit says to the churches.

To the Church in Laodicea

¹⁴"To the angel of the church in Laodicea write:

These are the words of the Amen, the faithful and true witness, the ruler of God's creation. ¹⁵I know your deeds, that you are neither cold nor hot. I wish you were either one or the other! ¹⁶So, because you are lukewarm—neither hot nor cold—I am about to spit you out of my mouth. ¹⁷You say, 'I am rich; I have acquired wealth and do not need a thing.' But you do not realize that you are wretched, pitiful, poor, blind and naked. ¹⁸I counsel you to buy from me gold refined in the fire, so you can become rich; and white clothes to wear, so you can cover your shameful nakedness; and salve to put on your eyes, so you can see.

¹⁹Those whom I love I rebuke and discipline. So be earnest, and repent. ²⁰Here I am! I stand at the door and knock. If anyone hears my voice and opens the door, I will come in and eat with him, and he with me.

W ORDS TO REMEMBER

3:20 Here I am! I stand at the door and knock. If anyone hears my voice and opens the door, I will come in and eat with him, and he with me.

²¹To him who overcomes, I will give the right to sit with me on my throne, just as I overcame and sat down with my Father on his throne. ²²He who has an ear, let him hear what the Spirit says to the churches."

The Throne in Heaven

4 After this I looked, and there before me was a door standing open in heaven. And the voice I had first

heard speaking to me like a trumpet said, "Come up here, and I will show you what must take place after this." [2]At once I was in the Spirit, and there before me was a throne in heaven with someone sitting on it. [3]And the one who sat there had the appearance of jasper and carnelian. A rainbow, resembling an emerald, encircled the throne. [4]Surrounding the throne were twenty-four other thrones, and seated on them were twenty-four elders. They were dressed in white and had crowns of gold on their heads. [5]From the throne came flashes of lightning, rumblings and peals of thunder. Before the throne, seven lamps were blazing. These are the seven spirits[a] of God. [6]Also before the throne there was what looked like a sea of glass, clear as crystal.

In the center, around the throne, were four living creatures, and they were covered with eyes, in front and in back. [7]The first living creature was like a lion, the second was like an ox, the third had a face like a man, the fourth was like a flying eagle. [8]Each of the four living creatures had six wings and was covered with eyes all around, even under his wings. Day and night they never stop saying:

> "Holy, holy, holy
> is the Lord God Almighty,
> who was, and is, and is to come."

[9]Whenever the living creatures give glory, honor and thanks to him who sits on the throne and who lives for ever and ever, [10]the twenty-four elders fall down before him who sits on the throne, and worship him who lives for ever and ever. They lay their crowns before the throne and say:

[11]"You are worthy, our Lord and
        God,
    to receive glory and honor and
        power,
for you created all things,

and by your will they were
        created
and have their being."

❓DID YOU KNOW?   4:2

What did John see in heaven?

John saw God on his throne, being worshiped there. Then John saw Jesus, the Lamb of God. In John's vision of the future, Jesus is about to begin punishing the people of earth for their sins.

The Scroll and the Lamb

5 Then I saw in the right hand of him who sat on the throne a scroll with writing on both sides and sealed with seven seals. [2]And I saw a mighty angel proclaiming in a loud voice, "Who is worthy to break the seals and open the scroll?" [3]But no one in heaven or on earth or under the earth could open the scroll or even look inside it. [4]I wept and wept because no one was found who was worthy to open the scroll or look inside. [5]Then one of the elders said to me, "Do not weep! See, the Lion of the tribe of Judah, the Root of David, has triumphed. He is able to open the scroll and its seven seals."

[6]Then I saw a Lamb, looking as if it had been slain, standing in the center of the throne, encircled by the four living creatures and the elders. He had seven horns and seven eyes, which are the seven spirits[a] of God sent out into all the earth. [7]He came and took the scroll from the right hand of him who sat on the throne. [8]And when he had taken it, the four living creatures and the twenty-four elders fell down before the Lamb. Each one had a harp and they were holding golden bowls full of incense, which are the prayers of the saints. [9]And they sang a new song:

> "You are worthy to take the scroll
>   and to open its seals,

a5,6 Or *the sevenfold Spirit*

because you were slain,
   and with your blood you
      purchased men for God
   from every tribe and language
      and people and nation.
¹⁰You have made them to be a
      kingdom and priests to
      serve our God,
   and they will reign on the
      earth."

¹¹Then I looked and heard the voice of many angels, numbering thousands upon thousands, and ten thousand times ten thousand. They encircled the throne and the living creatures and the elders. ¹²In a loud voice they sang:

"Worthy is the Lamb, who was
      slain,
to receive power and wealth and
      wisdom and strength
and honor and glory and praise!"

¹³Then I heard every creature in heaven and on earth and under the earth and on the sea, and all that is in them, singing:

"To him who sits on the throne
      and to the Lamb
be praise and honor and glory and
      power,
   for ever and ever!"

¹⁴The four living creatures said, "Amen," and the elders fell down and worshiped.

The Seals

6 I watched as the Lamb opened the first of the seven seals. Then I heard one of the four living creatures say in a voice like thunder, "Come!" ²I looked, and there before me was a white horse! Its rider held a bow, and he was given a crown, and he rode out as a conqueror bent on conquest.

³When the Lamb opened the second seal, I heard the second living creature say, "Come!" ⁴Then another horse came out, a fiery red one. Its rider was given power to take peace from the earth and to make men slay each other. To him was given a large sword.

⁵When the Lamb opened the third seal, I heard the third living creature say, "Come!" I looked, and there before me was a black horse! Its rider was holding a pair of scales in his hand. ⁶Then I heard what sounded like a voice among the four living creatures, saying, "A quart ᵃ of wheat for a day's wages, ᵇ and three quarts of barley for a day's wages, ᵇ and do not damage the oil and the wine!"

⁷When the Lamb opened the fourth seal, I heard the voice of the fourth living creature say, "Come!" ⁸I looked, and there before me was a pale horse! Its rider was named Death, and Hades was following close behind him. They were given power over a fourth of the earth to kill by

ᵃ6 Greek *a choinix* (probably about a liter)   ᵇ6 Greek *a denarius*

Life in Bible Times

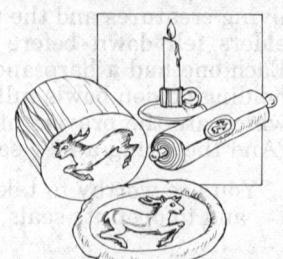

A SEALED SCROLL

Important papers were fastened with seals. Wax or clay held the papers together. A mark was made in the wax or clay when it was soft. No one could open the papers without breaking the seal.

sword, famine and plague, and by the wild beasts of the earth.

⁹When he opened the fifth seal, I saw under the altar the souls of those who had been slain because of the word of God and the testimony they had maintained. ¹⁰They called out in a loud voice, "How long, Sovereign Lord, holy and true, until you judge the inhabitants of the earth and avenge our blood?" ¹¹Then each of them was given a white robe, and they were told to wait a little longer, until the number of their fellow servants and brothers who were to be killed as they had been was completed.

¹²I watched as he opened the sixth seal. There was a great earthquake. The sun turned black like sackcloth made of goat hair, the whole moon turned blood red, ¹³and the stars in the sky fell to earth, as late figs drop from a fig tree when shaken by a strong wind. ¹⁴The sky receded like a scroll, rolling up, and every mountain and island was removed from its place.

¹⁵Then the kings of the earth, the princes, the generals, the rich, the mighty, and every slave and every free man hid in caves and among the rocks of the mountains. ¹⁶They called to the mountains and the rocks, "Fall on us and hide us from the face of him who sits on the throne and from the wrath of the Lamb! ¹⁷For the great day of their wrath has come, and who can stand?"

❓DID YOU KNOW?   6:12

What are the seals in Revelation 6?

The seals are the terrible punishments about to come on millions of people who have sinned.

144,000 Sealed

7 After this I saw four angels standing at the four corners of the earth, holding back the four winds of the earth to prevent any wind from blowing on the land or on the sea or on any tree. ²Then I saw another angel coming up from the east, having the seal of the living God. He called out in a loud voice to the four angels who had been given power to harm the land and the sea: ³"Do not harm the land or the sea or the trees until we put a seal on the foreheads of the servants of our God." ⁴Then I heard the number of those who were sealed: 144,000 from all the tribes of Israel.

⁵From the tribe of Judah 12,000 were sealed,
from the tribe of Reuben 12,000,
from the tribe of Gad 12,000,
⁶from the tribe of Asher 12,000,
from the tribe of Naphtali 12,-000,
from the tribe of Manasseh 12,-000,
⁷from the tribe of Simeon 12,000,
from the tribe of Levi 12,000,
from the tribe of Issachar 12,000,
⁸from the tribe of Zebulun 12,000,
from the tribe of Joseph 12,000,
from the tribe of Benjamin 12,-000.

The Great Multitude in White Robes

⁹After this I looked and there before me was a great multitude that no one could count, from every nation, tribe, people and language, standing before the throne and in front of the Lamb. They were wearing white robes and were holding palm branches in their hands. ¹⁰And they cried out in a loud voice:

"Salvation belongs to our God,
who sits on the throne,
and to the Lamb."

¹¹All the angels were standing around the throne and around the elders and the four living creatures. They fell down on their faces before the throne and worshiped God, ¹²saying:

"Amen!
Praise and glory

and wisdom and thanks and
    honor
and power and strength
be to our God for ever and ever.
Amen!"

¹³Then one of the elders asked me,
"These in white robes—who are they,
and where did they come from?"

¹⁴I answered, "Sir, you know."

And he said, "These are they who
have come out of the great tribula-
tion; they have washed their robes
and made them white in the blood of
the Lamb. ¹⁵Therefore,

"they are before the throne of God
    and serve him day and night in
        his temple;
and he who sits on the throne will
        spread his tent over them.
¹⁶Never again will they hunger;
    never again will they thirst.
The sun will not beat upon them,
    nor any scorching heat.
¹⁷For the Lamb at the center of the
        throne will be their
        shepherd;
    he will lead them to springs of
        living water.
And God will wipe away every
    tear from their eyes."

The Seventh Seal and the Golden Censer

8 When he opened the seventh
seal, there was silence in heaven
for about half an hour.

²And I saw the seven angels who
stand before God, and to them were
given seven trumpets.

³Another angel, who had a golden
censer, came and stood at the altar.
He was given much incense to offer,
with the prayers of all the saints, on
the golden altar before the throne.
⁴The smoke of the incense, together
with the prayers of the saints, went
up before God from the angel's hand.
⁵Then the angel took the censer,
filled it with fire from the altar, and
hurled it on the earth; and there
came peals of thunder, rumblings,

flashes of lightning and an earthquake.

The Trumpets

⁶Then the seven angels who had
the seven trumpets prepared to
sound them.

⁷The first angel sounded his trumpet, and there came hail and fire
mixed with blood, and it was hurled
down upon the earth. A third of the
earth was burned up, a third of the
trees were burned up, and all the
green grass was burned up.

⁸The second angel sounded his
trumpet, and something like a huge
mountain, all ablaze, was thrown
into the sea. A third of the sea turned
into blood, ⁹a third of the living creatures in the sea died, and a third of
the ships were destroyed.

¹⁰The third angel sounded his
trumpet, and a great star, blazing
like a torch, fell from the sky on a
third of the rivers and on the springs
of water— ¹¹the name of the star is
Wormwood.ᵃ A third of the waters
turned bitter, and many people died
from the waters that had become bitter.

¹²The fourth angel sounded his
trumpet, and a third of the sun was
struck, a third of the moon, and a
third of the stars, so that a third of
them turned dark. A third of the day
was without light, and also a third of
the night.

¹³As I watched, I heard an eagle
that was flying in midair call out in
a loud voice: "Woe! Woe! Woe to the
inhabitants of the earth, because of
the trumpet blasts about to be sounded by the other three angels!"

9 The fifth angel sounded his
trumpet, and I saw a star that
had fallen from the sky to the earth.
The star was given the key to the
shaft of the Abyss. ²When he opened
the Abyss, smoke rose from it like the
smoke from a gigantic furnace. The
sun and sky were darkened by the
smoke from the Abyss. ³And out of
the smoke locusts came down upon

ᵃ11 That is, Bitterness

the earth and were given power like that of scorpions of the earth. [4]They were told not to harm the grass of the earth or any plant or tree, but only those people who did not have the seal of God on their foreheads. [5]They were not given power to kill them, but only to torture them for five months. And the agony they suffered was like that of the sting of a scorpion when it strikes a man. [6]During those days men will seek death, but will not find it; they will long to die, but death will elude them.

[7]The locusts looked like horses prepared for battle. On their heads they wore something like crowns of gold, and their faces resembled human faces. [8]Their hair was like women's hair, and their teeth were like lions' teeth. [9]They had breastplates like breastplates of iron, and the sound of their wings was like the thundering of many horses and chariots rushing into battle. [10]They had tails and stings like scorpions, and in their tails they had power to torment people for five months. [11]They had as king over them the angel of the Abyss, whose name in Hebrew is Abaddon, and in Greek, Apollyon.[a]

[12]The first woe is past; two other woes are yet to come.

[13]The sixth angel sounded his trumpet, and I heard a voice coming from the horns[b] of the golden altar that is before God. [14]It said to the sixth angel who had the trumpet, "Release the four angels who are bound at the great river Euphrates." [15]And the four angels who had been kept ready for this very hour and day and month and year were released to kill a third of mankind. [16]The number of the mounted troops was two hundred million. I heard their number.

[17]The horses and riders I saw in my vision looked like this: Their breastplates were fiery red, dark blue, and yellow as sulfur. The heads of the horses resembled the heads of lions, and out of their mouths came fire,

smoke and sulfur. [18]A third of mankind was killed by the three plagues of fire, smoke and sulfur that came out of their mouths. [19]The power of the horses was in their mouths and in their tails; for their tails were like snakes, having heads with which they inflict injury.

[20]The rest of mankind that were not killed by these plagues still did not repent of the work of their hands; they did not stop worshiping demons, and idols of gold, silver, bronze, stone and wood—idols that cannot see or hear or walk. [21]Nor did they repent of their murders, their magic arts, their sexual immorality or their thefts.

❓DID YOU KNOW? 9:20

Will atomic bombs fall on earth?

Some think Revelation 8–9 describe what could happen if there is an atomic war. But the terrible punishments God will bring on our earth are worse than any atomic war could be. These terrible punishments are for those who have rejected God, not for those who have believed in his Son.

The Angel and the Little Scroll

10 Then I saw another mighty angel coming down from heaven. He was robed in a cloud, with a rainbow above his head; his face was like the sun, and his legs were like fiery pillars. [2]He was holding a little scroll, which lay open in his hand. He planted his right foot on the sea and his left foot on the land, [3]and he gave a loud shout like the roar of a lion. When he shouted, the voices of the seven thunders spoke. [4]And when the seven thunders spoke, I was about to write; but I heard a voice from heaven say, "Seal up what the seven thunders have said and do not write it down."

[5]Then the angel I had seen stand-

---

[a]11 *Abaddon* and *Apollyon* mean *Destroyer*.   [b]13 That is, projections

ing on the sea and on the land raised his right hand to heaven. [6]And he swore by him who lives for ever and ever, who created the heavens and all that is in them, the earth and all that is in it, and the sea and all that is in it, and said, "There will be no more delay! [7]But in the days when the seventh angel is about to sound his trumpet, the mystery of God will be accomplished, just as he announced to his servants the prophets."

[8]Then the voice that I had heard from heaven spoke to me once more: "Go, take the scroll that lies open in the hand of the angel who is standing on the sea and on the land."

[9]So I went to the angel and asked him to give me the little scroll. He said to me, "Take it and eat it. It will turn your stomach sour, but in your mouth it will be as sweet as honey." [10]I took the little scroll from the angel's hand and ate it. It tasted as sweet as honey in my mouth, but when I had eaten it, my stomach turned sour. [11]Then I was told, "You must prophesy again about many peoples, nations, languages and kings."

❓ DID YOU KNOW?   10:11

What is an apocalypse?

An apocalypse (uh-POCK-uh-lips) is a description of the end of the world. It uses many words that are symbols. Because many of the symbols are hard to understand, we cannot be sure what everything means. Revelation is an apocalypse. This book pictures the end of the world and God's punishment of sin.

The Two Witnesses

11 I was given a reed like a measuring rod and was told, "Go and measure the temple of God and the altar, and count the worshipers there. [2]But exclude the outer court; do not measure it, because it has been

given to the Gentiles. They will trample on the holy city for 42 months. [3]And I will give power to my two witnesses, and they will prophesy for 1,260 days, clothed in sackcloth." [4]These are the two olive trees and the two lampstands that stand before the Lord of the earth. [5]If anyone tries to harm them, fire comes from their mouths and devours their enemies. This is how anyone who wants to harm them must die. [6]These men have power to shut up the sky so that it will not rain during the time they are prophesying; and they have power to turn the waters into blood and to strike the earth with every kind of plague as often as they want.

[7]Now when they have finished their testimony, the beast that comes up from the Abyss will attack them, and overpower and kill them. [8]Their bodies will lie in the street of the great city, which is figuratively called Sodom and Egypt, where also their Lord was crucified. [9]For three and a half days men from every people, tribe, language and nation will gaze on their bodies and refuse them burial. [10]The inhabitants of the earth will gloat over them and will celebrate by sending each other gifts, because these two prophets had tormented those who live on the earth.

[11]But after the three and a half days a breath of life from God entered them, and they stood on their feet, and terror struck those who saw them. [12]Then they heard a loud voice from heaven saying to them, "Come up here." And they went up to heaven in a cloud, while their enemies looked on.

[13]At that very hour there was a severe earthquake and a tenth of the city collapsed. Seven thousand people were killed in the earthquake, and the survivors were terrified and gave glory to the God of heaven.

[14]The second woe has passed; the third woe is coming soon.

The Seventh Trumpet

[15]The seventh angel sounded his

trumpet, and there were loud voices in heaven, which said:

"The kingdom of the world has
    become the kingdom of our
    Lord and of his Christ,
and he will reign for ever and
    ever."

¹⁶And the twenty-four elders, who were seated on their thrones before God, fell on their faces and worshiped God, ¹⁷saying:

"We give thanks to you, Lord God
    Almighty,
the One who is and who was,
because you have taken your
    great power
and have begun to reign.
¹⁸The nations were angry;
and your wrath has come.
The time has come for judging the
    dead,
and for rewarding your servants
    the prophets
and your saints and those who
    reverence your name,
both small and great—
and for destroying those who
    destroy the earth."

¹⁹Then God's temple in heaven was opened, and within his temple was seen the ark of his covenant. And there came flashes of lightning, rumblings, peals of thunder, an earthquake and a great hailstorm.

The Woman and the Dragon

12 A great and wondrous sign appeared in heaven: a woman clothed with the sun, with the moon under her feet and a crown of twelve stars on her head. ²She was pregnant and cried out in pain as she was about to give birth. ³Then another sign appeared in heaven: an enormous red dragon with seven heads and ten horns and seven crowns on his heads. ⁴His tail swept a third of the stars out of the sky and flung them to the earth. The dragon stood in front of the woman who was about to give birth, so that he might devour her child the moment it was born. ⁵She gave birth to a son, a male child, who will rule all the nations with an iron scepter. And her child was snatched up to God and to his throne. ⁶The woman fled into the desert to a place prepared for her by God, where she might be taken care of for 1,260 days.

⁷And there was war in heaven. Michael and his angels fought against the dragon, and the dragon and his angels fought back. ⁸But he was not strong enough, and they lost their place in heaven. ⁹The great dragon was hurled down—that ancient serpent called the devil, or Satan, who leads the whole world astray. He was hurled to the earth, and his angels with him.

¹⁰Then I heard a loud voice in heaven say:

"Now have come the salvation
    and the power and the
    kingdom of our God,
    and the authority of his Christ.
For the accuser of our brothers,
    who accuses them before our
    God day and night,
    has been hurled down.
¹¹They overcame him
    by the blood of the Lamb
    and by the word of their
      testimony;
they did not love their lives so
    much
    as to shrink from death.
¹²Therefore rejoice, you heavens
    and you who dwell in them!
But woe to the earth and the sea,
    because the devil has gone
      down to you!
He is filled with fury,
    because he knows that his time
      is short."

¹³When the dragon saw that he had been hurled to the earth, he pursued the woman who had given birth to the male child. ¹⁴The woman was given the two wings of a great eagle, so that she might fly to the place prepared for her in the desert, where she would be taken care of for a time, times and half a time, out of the serpent's reach. ¹⁵Then from his mouth the serpent spewed water like a river, to overtake the woman and sweep her

away with the torrent. [16]But the earth helped the woman by opening its mouth and swallowing the river that the dragon had spewed out of his mouth. [17]Then the dragon was enraged at the woman and went off to make war against the rest of her offspring—those who obey God's commandments and hold to the testimony of Jesus.

13 [1]And the dragon[a] stood on the shore of the sea.

The Beast out of the Sea

And I saw a beast coming out of the sea. He had ten horns and seven heads, with ten crowns on his horns, and on each head a blasphemous name. [2]The beast I saw resembled a leopard, but had feet like those of a bear and a mouth like that of a lion. The dragon gave the beast his power and his throne and great authority. [3]One of the heads of the beast seemed to have had a fatal wound, but the fatal wound had been healed. The whole world was astonished and followed the beast. [4]Men worshiped the dragon because he had given authority to the beast, and they also worshiped the beast and asked, "Who is like the beast? Who can make war against him?"

❓ DID YOU KNOW?   13:1

Who is the "beast coming out of the sea"?

Many Bible teachers think the beast will be a world leader who will pretend to be God. Satan will help him try to get people to fight against God.

---

[5]The beast was given a mouth to utter proud words and blasphemies and to exercise his authority for forty-two months. [6]He opened his mouth to blaspheme God, and to slander his name and his dwelling place and those who live in heaven. [7]He was given power to make war against the saints and to conquer them. And he was given authority over every tribe, people, language and nation. [8]All inhabitants of the earth will worship the beast—all whose names have not been written in the book of life belonging to the Lamb that was slain from the creation of the world.[b]

[9]He who has an ear, let him hear.

[10]If anyone is to go into captivity,
   into captivity he will go.
If anyone is to be killed[c] with the
      sword,
   with the sword he will be
      killed.

This calls for patient endurance and faithfulness on the part of the saints.

The Beast out of the Earth

[11]Then I saw another beast, coming out of the earth. He had two horns like a lamb, but he spoke like a dragon. [12]He exercised all the authority of the first beast on his behalf, and made the earth and its inhabitants worship the first beast, whose fatal wound had been healed. [13]And he performed great and miraculous signs, even causing fire to come down from heaven to earth in full view of men. [14]Because of the signs he was given power to do on behalf of the first beast, he deceived the inhabitants of the earth. He ordered them to set up an image in honor of the beast who was wounded by the sword and yet lived. [15]He was given power to give breath to the image of the first beast, so that it could speak and cause all who refused to worship the image to be killed. [16]He also forced everyone, small and great, rich and poor, free and slave, to receive a mark on his right hand or on his forehead, [17]so that no one could buy or sell unless he had the mark, which is the name of the beast or the number of his name.

[18]This calls for wisdom. If anyone has insight, let him calculate the

---

a1 Some late manuscripts And I   *b8 Or written from the creation of the world in the book of life belonging to the Lamb that was slain*   *c10 Some manuscripts anyone kills*

number of the beast, for it is man's number. His number is 666.

The Lamb and the 144,000

14 Then I looked, and there before me was the Lamb, standing on Mount Zion, and with him 144,000 who had his name and his Father's name written on their foreheads. ²And I heard a sound from heaven like the roar of rushing waters and like a loud peal of thunder. The sound I heard was like that of harpists playing their harps. ³And they sang a new song before the throne and before the four living creatures and the elders. No one could learn the song except the 144,000 who had been redeemed from the earth. ⁴These are those who did not defile themselves with women, for they kept themselves pure. They follow the Lamb wherever he goes. They were purchased from among men and offered as firstfruits to God and the Lamb. ⁵No lie was found in their mouths; they are blameless.

The Three Angels

⁶Then I saw another angel flying in midair, and he had the eternal gospel to proclaim to those who live on the earth—to every nation, tribe, language and people. ⁷He said in a loud voice, "Fear God and give him glory, because the hour of his judgment has come. Worship him who made the heavens, the earth, the sea and the springs of water."

⁸A second angel followed and said, "Fallen! Fallen is Babylon the Great, which made all the nations drink the maddening wine of her adulteries."

⁹A third angel followed them and said in a loud voice: "If anyone worships the beast and his image and receives his mark on the forehead or on the hand, ¹⁰he, too, will drink of the wine of God's fury, which has been poured full strength into the cup of his wrath. He will be tormented with burning sulfur in the presence of the holy angels and of the Lamb. ¹¹And the smoke of their torment rises for ever and ever. There is no rest day or night for those who worship the beast and his image, or for anyone who receives the mark of his name." ¹²This calls for patient endurance on the part of the saints who obey God's commandments and remain faithful to Jesus.

¹³Then I heard a voice from heaven say, "Write: Blessed are the dead who die in the Lord from now on."

"Yes," says the Spirit, "they will rest from their labor, for their deeds will follow them."

The Harvest of the Earth

¹⁴I looked, and there before me was a white cloud, and seated on the cloud was one "like a son of man"ᵃ with a crown of gold on his head and a sharp sickle in his hand. ¹⁵Then another angel came out of the temple and called in a loud voice to him who was sitting on the cloud, "Take your sickle and reap, because the time to reap has come, for the harvest of the earth is ripe." ¹⁶So he who was seated on the cloud swung his sickle over the earth, and the earth was harvested.

¹⁷Another angel came out of the temple in heaven, and he too had a sharp sickle. ¹⁸Still another angel, who had charge of the fire, came from the altar and called in a loud voice to him who had the sharp sickle, "Take your sharp sickle and gather the clusters of grapes from the earth's vine, because its grapes are ripe." ¹⁹The angel swung his sickle on the earth, gathered its grapes and threw them into the great winepress of God's wrath. ²⁰They were trampled in the winepress outside the city, and blood flowed out of the press, rising as high as the horses' bridles for a distance of 1,600 stadia.ᵇ

Seven Angels With Seven Plagues

15 I saw in heaven another great and marvelous sign: seven angels with the seven last plagues

ᵃ14 Daniel 7:13   ᵇ20 That is, about 180 miles (about 300 kilometers)

—last, because with them God's wrath is completed. ²And I saw what looked like a sea of glass mixed with fire and, standing beside the sea, those who had been victorious over the beast and his image and over the number of his name. They held harps given them by God ³and sang the song of Moses the servant of God and the song of the Lamb:

"Great and marvelous are your deeds,
    Lord God Almighty.
Just and true are your ways,
    King of the ages.
⁴Who will not fear you, O Lord,
    and bring glory to your name?
For you alone are holy.
All nations will come
    and worship before you,
for your righteous acts have been revealed."

⁵After this I looked and in heaven the temple, that is, the tabernacle of the Testimony, was opened. ⁶Out of the temple came the seven angels with the seven plagues. They were dressed in clean, shining linen and wore golden sashes around their chests. ⁷Then one of the four living creatures gave to the seven angels seven golden bowls filled with the wrath of God, who lives for ever and ever. ⁸And the temple was filled with smoke from the glory of God and from his power, and no one could enter the temple until the seven plagues of the seven angels were completed.

The Seven Bowls of God's Wrath

16 Then I heard a loud voice from the temple saying to the seven angels, "Go, pour out the seven bowls of God's wrath on the earth."

²The first angel went and poured out his bowl on the land, and ugly and painful sores broke out on the people who had the mark of the beast and worshiped his image.

³The second angel poured out his bowl on the sea, and it turned into blood like that of a dead man, and every living thing in the sea died.

⁴The third angel poured out his bowl on the rivers and springs of water, and they became blood. ⁵Then I heard the angel in charge of the waters say:

"You are just in these judgments,
    you who are and who were, the Holy One,
because you have so judged;
⁶for they have shed the blood of
    your saints and prophets,
and you have given them blood
    to drink as they deserve."

⁷And I heard the altar respond:

"Yes, Lord God Almighty,
    true and just are your
        judgments."

⁸The fourth angel poured out his bowl on the sun, and the sun was given power to scorch people with fire. ⁹They were seared by the intense heat and they cursed the name of God, who had control over these plagues, but they refused to repent and glorify him.

¹⁰The fifth angel poured out his bowl on the throne of the beast, and his kingdom was plunged into darkness. Men gnawed their tongues in agony ¹¹and cursed the God of heaven because of their pains and their sores, but they refused to repent of what they had done.

¹²The sixth angel poured out his bowl on the great river Euphrates, and its water was dried up to prepare the way for the kings from the East. ¹³Then I saw three evil[a] spirits that looked like frogs; they came out of the mouth of the dragon, out of the mouth of the beast and out of the mouth of the false prophet. ¹⁴They are spirits of demons performing miraculous signs, and they go out to the kings of the whole world, to gather them for the battle on the great day of God Almighty.

¹⁵"Behold, I come like a thief! Blessed is he who stays awake and

[a]13 Greek *unclean*

keeps his clothes with him, so that he may not go naked and be shamefully exposed."

¹⁶Then they gathered the kings together to the place that in Hebrew is called Armageddon.

¹⁷The seventh angel poured out his bowl into the air, and out of the temple came a loud voice from the throne, saying, "It is done!" ¹⁸Then there came flashes of lightning, rumblings, peals of thunder and a severe earthquake. No earthquake like it has ever occurred since man has been on earth, so tremendous was the quake. ¹⁹The great city split into three parts, and the cities of the nations collapsed. God remembered Babylon the Great and gave her the cup filled with the wine of the fury of his wrath. ²⁰Every island fled away and the mountains could not be found. ²¹From the sky huge hailstones of about a hundred pounds each fell upon men. And they cursed God on account of the plague of hail, because the plague was so terrible.

The Woman on the Beast

17 One of the seven angels who had the seven bowls came and said to me, "Come, I will show you the punishment of the great prostitute, who sits on many waters. ²With her the kings of the earth committed adultery and the inhabitants of the earth were intoxicated with the wine of her adulteries."

❓DID YOU KNOW?   **17:5**

What is Babylon?

Babylon in the book of Revelation does not mean the historical city but is a symbol standing for civilization. Other symbols in these chapters, like the woman on the beast, are hard to understand.

---

³Then the angel carried me away in the Spirit into a desert. There I saw a woman sitting on a scarlet beast that was covered with blasphemous names and had seven heads and ten horns. ⁴The woman was dressed in purple and scarlet, and was glittering with gold, precious stones and pearls. She held a golden cup in her hand, filled with abominable things and the filth of her adulteries. ⁵This title was written on her forehead:

MYSTERY

BABYLON THE GREAT

THE MOTHER OF PROSTITUTES

AND OF THE ABOMINATIONS OF THE

EARTH.

⁶I saw that the woman was drunk with the blood of the saints, the blood of those who bore testimony to Jesus.

When I saw her, I was greatly astonished. ⁷Then the angel said to me: "Why are you astonished? I will explain to you the mystery of the woman and of the beast she rides, which has the seven heads and ten horns. ⁸The beast, which you saw, once was, now is not, and will come up out of the Abyss and go to his destruction. The inhabitants of the earth whose names have not been written in the book of life from the creation of the world will be astonished when they see the beast, because he once was, now is not, and yet will come.

⁹"This calls for a mind with wisdom. The seven heads are seven hills on which the woman sits. ¹⁰They are also seven kings. Five have fallen, one is, the other has not yet come; but when he does come, he must remain for a little while. ¹¹The beast who once was, and now is not, is an eighth king. He belongs to the seven and is going to his destruction.

¹²"The ten horns you saw are ten kings who have not yet received a kingdom, but who for one hour will receive authority as kings along with the beast. ¹³They have one purpose and will give their power and authority to the beast. ¹⁴They will make war against the Lamb, but the Lamb will overcome them because he is Lord of lords and King of kings—and with him will be his called, chosen and faithful followers."

15Then the angel said to me, "The waters you saw, where the prostitute sits, are peoples, multitudes, nations and languages. 16The beast and the ten horns you saw will hate the prostitute. They will bring her to ruin and leave her naked; they will eat her flesh and burn her with fire. 17For God has put it into their hearts to accomplish his purpose by agreeing to give the beast their power to rule, until God's words are fulfilled. 18The woman you saw is the great city that rules over the kings of the earth."

The Fall of Babylon

18 After this I saw another angel coming down from heaven. He had great authority, and the earth was illuminated by his splendor. 2With a mighty voice he shouted:

"Fallen! Fallen is Babylon the
  Great!
She has become a home for
  demons
and a haunt for every evil*a* spirit,
  a haunt for every unclean and
  detestable bird.
3For all the nations have drunk
  the maddening wine of her
  adulteries.
The kings of the earth committed
  adultery with her,
  and the merchants of the earth
  grew rich from her
  excessive luxuries."

4Then I heard another voice from heaven say:

"Come out of her, my people,
  so that you will not share in
  her sins,
  so that you will not receive any
  of her plagues;
5for her sins are piled up to
  heaven,
  and God has remembered her
  crimes.
6Give back to her as she has given;
  pay her back double for what
  she has done.

Mix her a double portion from
  her own cup.
7Give her as much torture and
  grief
  as the glory and luxury she
  gave herself.
In her heart she boasts,
  'I sit as queen; I am not a
  widow,
  and I will never mourn.'
8Therefore in one day her plagues
  will overtake her:
  death, mourning and famine.
She will be consumed by fire,
  for mighty is the Lord God who
  judges her.

9"When the kings of the earth who committed adultery with her and shared her luxury see the smoke of her burning, they will weep and mourn over her. 10Terrified at her torment, they will stand far off and cry:

" 'Woe! Woe, O great city,
  O Babylon, city of power!
In one hour your doom has come!'

11"The merchants of the earth will weep and mourn over her because no one buys their cargoes any more— 12cargoes of gold, silver, precious stones and pearls; fine linen, purple, silk and scarlet cloth; every sort of citron wood, and articles of every kind made of ivory, costly wood, bronze, iron and marble; 13cargoes of cinnamon and spice, of incense, myrrh and frankincense, of wine and olive oil, of fine flour and wheat; cattle and sheep; horses and carriages; and bodies and souls of men.

14"They will say, 'The fruit you longed for is gone from you. All your riches and splendor have vanished, never to be recovered.' 15The merchants who sold these things and gained their wealth from her will stand far off, terrified at her torment. They will weep and mourn 16and cry out:

" 'Woe! Woe, O great city,

*a*2 Greek *unclean*

dressed in fine linen, purple and
scarlet,
and glittering with gold,
precious stones and pearls!
17In one hour such great wealth
has been brought to ruin!'

"Every sea captain, and all who
travel by ship, the sailors, and all
who earn their living from the sea,
will stand far off. 18When they see the
smoke of her burning, they will exclaim, 'Was there ever a city like this
great city?' 19They will throw dust on
their heads, and with weeping and
mourning cry out:

" 'Woe! Woe, O great city,
where all who had ships on the
sea
became rich through her
wealth!
In one hour she has been brought
to ruin!
20Rejoice over her, O heaven!
Rejoice, saints and apostles and
prophets!
God has judged her for the way
she treated you.' "

21Then a mighty angel picked up a
boulder the size of a large millstone
and threw it into the sea, and said:

"With such violence
the great city of Babylon will be
thrown down,
never to be found again.
22The music of harpists and
musicians, flute players and
trumpeters,
will never be heard in you
again.
No workman of any trade
will ever be found in you again.
The sound of a millstone
will never be heard in you
again.
23The light of a lamp
will never shine in you again.
The voice of bridegroom and bride
will never be heard in you
again.
Your merchants were the world's
great men.
By your magic spell all the
nations were led astray.

24In her was found the blood of
prophets and of the saints,
and of all who have been killed
on the earth."

Hallelujah!

19 After this I heard what
sounded like the roar of a
great multitude in heaven shouting:

"Hallelujah!
Salvation and glory and power
belong to our God,
2 for true and just are his
judgments.
He has condemned the great
prostitute
who corrupted the earth by her
adulteries.
He has avenged on her the blood
of his servants."

3And again they shouted:

"Hallelujah!
The smoke from her goes up for
ever and ever."

4The twenty-four elders and the
four living creatures fell down and
worshiped God, who was seated on
the throne. And they cried:

"Amen, Hallelujah!"

5Then a voice came from the
throne, saying:

"Praise our God,
all you his servants,
you who fear him,
both small and great!"

6Then I heard what sounded like a
great multitude, like the roar of rushing waters and like loud peals of
thunder, shouting:

"Hallelujah!
For our Lord God Almighty
reigns.
7Let us rejoice and be glad
and give him glory!
For the wedding of the Lamb has
come,
and his bride has made herself
ready.
8Fine linen, bright and clean,
was given her to wear."

(Fine linen stands for the righteous acts of the saints.)

⁹Then the angel said to me, "Write: 'Blessed are those who are invited to the wedding supper of the Lamb!'" And he added, "These are the true words of God."

¹⁰At this I fell at his feet to worship him. But he said to me, "Do not do it! I am a fellow servant with you and with your brothers who hold to the testimony of Jesus. Worship God! For the testimony of Jesus is the spirit of prophecy."

The Rider on the White Horse

¹¹I saw heaven standing open and there before me was a white horse, whose rider is called Faithful and True. With justice he judges and makes war. ¹²His eyes are like blazing fire, and on his head are many crowns. He has a name written on him that no one knows but he himself. ¹³He is dressed in a robe dipped in blood, and his name is the Word of God. ¹⁴The armies of heaven were following him, riding on white horses and dressed in fine linen, white and clean. ¹⁵Out of his mouth comes a sharp sword with which to strike down the nations. "He will rule them with an iron scepter."ᵃ He treads the winepress of the fury of the wrath of God Almighty. ¹⁶On his robe and on

ᵃ15 Psalm 2:9

his thigh he has this name written:

KING OF KINGS AND LORD OF LORDS.

¹⁷And I saw an angel standing in the sun, who cried in a loud voice to all the birds flying in midair, "Come, gather together for the great supper of God, ¹⁸so that you may eat the flesh of kings, generals, and mighty men, of horses and their riders, and the flesh of all people, free and slave, small and great."

¹⁹Then I saw the beast and the kings of the earth and their armies gathered together to make war against the rider on the horse and his army. ²⁰But the beast was captured, and with him the false prophet who had performed the miraculous signs on his behalf. With these signs he had deluded those who had received the mark of the beast and worshiped his image. The two of them were thrown alive into the fiery lake of burning sulfur. ²¹The rest of them were killed with the sword that came out of the mouth of the rider on the horse, and all the birds gorged themselves on their flesh.

The Thousand Years

20 And I saw an angel coming down out of heaven, having the key to the Abyss and holding in his hand a great chain. ²He seized the dragon, that ancient serpent, who is

Life in Bible Times

HORSES

When rulers rode on horses it meant they were going to war. When rulers came in peace they rode donkeys. Jesus is pictured here in Revelation as a warrior coming on a horse to conquer Satan finally and forever.

the devil, or Satan, and bound him for a thousand years. ³He threw him into the Abyss, and locked and sealed it over him, to keep him from deceiving the nations anymore until the thousand years were ended. After that, he must be set free for a short time.

?DID YOU KNOW? 19:11

How will Jesus come?

When it is time to judge the world, Jesus will come back as a warrior, with all the armies of heaven. He will punish God's enemies then and defeat Satan.

⁴I saw thrones on which were seated those who had been given authority to judge. And I saw the souls of those who had been beheaded because of their testimony for Jesus and because of the word of God. They had not worshiped the beast or his image and had not received his mark on their foreheads or their hands. They came to life and reigned with Christ a thousand years. ⁵(The rest of the dead did not come to life until the thousand years were ended.) This is the first resurrection. ⁶Blessed and holy are those who have part in the first resurrection. The second death has no power over them, but they will be priests of God and of Christ and will reign with him for a thousand years.

Satan's Doom

⁷When the thousand years are over, Satan will be released from his prison ⁸and will go out to deceive the nations in the four corners of the earth—Gog and Magog—to gather them for battle. In number they are like the sand on the seashore. ⁹They marched across the breadth of the earth and surrounded the camp of God's people, the city he loves. But fire came down from heaven and devoured them. ¹⁰And the devil, who deceived them, was thrown into the lake of burning sulfur, where the beast and the false prophet had been thrown. They will be tormented day and night for ever and ever.

?DID YOU KNOW? 20:10

What will happen to Satan?

Satan will be thrown into a lake of fire, to be punished there forever. People who do not believe in Jesus will be in the lake of fire also.

The Dead Are Judged

¹¹Then I saw a great white throne and him who was seated on it. Earth and sky fled from his presence, and there was no place for them. ¹²And I saw the dead, great and small, standing before the throne, and books were opened. Another book was opened, which is the book of life. The dead were judged according to what they had done as recorded in the books. ¹³The sea gave up the dead that were in it, and death and Hades gave up the dead that were in them, and each person was judged according to what he had done. ¹⁴Then death and Hades were thrown into the lake of fire. The lake of fire is the second death. ¹⁵If anyone's name was not found written in the book of life, he was thrown into the lake of fire.

The New Jerusalem

21 Then I saw a new heaven and a new earth, for the first heaven and the first earth had passed away, and there was no longer any sea. ²I saw the Holy City, the new Jerusalem, coming down out of heaven from God, prepared as a bride beautifully dressed for her husband. ³And I heard a loud voice from the throne saying, "Now the dwelling of God is with men, and he will live with them. They will be his people, and God himself will be with them and be their God. ⁴He will wipe every tear from their eyes. There will be no more death or mourning or crying or pain, for the old order of things has passed away."

❓ DID YOU KNOW?   21:4

What will heaven be like?

Revelation 21–22 are about heaven. Heaven will be a beautiful place. There will be no sorrow or tears there. Everything will be new. Best of all, we will be with God forever.

---

⁵He who was seated on the throne said, "I am making everything new!" Then he said, "Write this down, for these words are trustworthy and true."

⁶He said to me: "It is done. I am the Alpha and the Omega, the Beginning and the End. To him who is thirsty I will give to drink without cost from the spring of the water of life. ⁷He who overcomes will inherit all this, and I will be his God and he will be my son. ⁸But the cowardly, the unbelieving, the vile, the murderers, the sexually immoral, those who practice magic arts, the idolaters and all liars—their place will be in the fiery lake of burning sulfur. This is the second death."

⁹One of the seven angels who had the seven bowls full of the seven last plagues came and said to me, "Come, I will show you the bride, the wife of the Lamb." ¹⁰And he carried me away in the Spirit to a mountain great and high, and showed me the Holy City, Jerusalem, coming down out of heaven from God. ¹¹It shone with the glory of God, and its brilliance was like that of a very precious jewel, like a jasper, clear as crystal. ¹²It had a great, high wall with twelve gates, and with twelve angels at the gates. On the gates were written the names of the twelve tribes of Israel. ¹³There were three gates on the east, three on the north, three on the south and three on the west. ¹⁴The wall of the city had twelve foundations, and on them were the names of the twelve apostles of the Lamb.

¹⁵The angel who talked with me had a measuring rod of gold to measure the city, its gates and its walls. ¹⁶The city was laid out like a square, as long as it was wide. He measured the city with the rod and found it to be 12,000 stadia^a in length, and as wide and high as it is long. ¹⁷He measured its wall and it was 144 cubits^b thick,^{c} by man's measurement, which the angel was using. ¹⁸The wall was made of jasper, and the city of pure gold, as pure as glass. ¹⁹The foundations of the city walls were decorated with every kind of precious stone. The first foundation was jasper, the second sapphire, the third chalcedony, the fourth emerald, ²⁰the fifth sardonyx, the sixth carnelian, the seventh chrysolite, the eighth beryl, the ninth topaz, the tenth chrysoprase, the eleventh jacinth, and the twelfth amethyst.^{d} ²¹The twelve gates were twelve pearls, each gate made of a single pearl. The great street of the city was of pure gold, like transparent glass.

²²I did not see a temple in the city, because the Lord God Almighty and the Lamb are its temple. ²³The city does not need the sun or the moon to shine on it, for the glory of God gives it light, and the Lamb is its lamp. ²⁴The nations will walk by its light, and the kings of the earth will bring their splendor into it. ²⁵On no day will its gates ever be shut, for there will be no night there. ²⁶The glory and honor of the nations will be brought into it. ²⁷Nothing impure will ever enter it, nor will anyone who does what is shameful or deceitful, but only those whose names are written in the Lamb's book of life.

---

^{a}16 That is, about 1,400 miles (about 2,200 kilometers) ^{b}17 That is, about 200 feet (about 65 meters) ^{c}17 Or *high* ^{d}20 The precise identification of some of these precious stones is uncertain.

The River of Life

22 Then the angel showed me the river of the water of life, as clear as crystal, flowing from the throne of God and of the Lamb ²down the middle of the great street of the city. On each side of the river stood the tree of life, bearing twelve crops of fruit, yielding its fruit every month. And the leaves of the tree are for the healing of the nations. ³No longer will there be any curse. The throne of God and of the Lamb will be in the city, and his servants will serve him. ⁴They will see his face, and his name will be on their foreheads. ⁵There will be no more night. They will not need the light of a lamp or the light of the sun, for the Lord God will give them light. And they will reign for ever and ever.

⁶The angel said to me, "These words are trustworthy and true. The Lord, the God of the spirits of the prophets, sent his angel to show his servants the things that must soon take place."

Jesus Is Coming

⁷"Behold, I am coming soon! Blessed is he who keeps the words of the prophecy in this book."

⁸I, John, am the one who heard and saw these things. And when I had heard and seen them, I fell down to worship at the feet of the angel who had been showing them to me. ⁹But he said to me, "Do not do it! I am a fellow servant with you and with

a16 The Greek is plural.

your brothers the prophets and of all who keep the words of this book. Worship God!"

¹⁰Then he told me, "Do not seal up the words of the prophecy of this book, because the time is near. ¹¹Let him who does wrong continue to do wrong; let him who is vile continue to be vile; let him who does right continue to do right; and let him who is holy continue to be holy."

¹²"Behold, I am coming soon! My reward is with me, and I will give to everyone according to what he has done. ¹³I am the Alpha and the Omega, the First and the Last, the Beginning and the End.

WORDS TO REMEMBER

22:12 Behold! I am coming soon!

---

¹⁴"Blessed are those who wash their robes, that they may have the right to the tree of life and may go through the gates into the city. ¹⁵Outside are the dogs, those who practice magic arts, the sexually immoral, the murderers, the idolaters and everyone who loves and practices falsehood.

¹⁶"I, Jesus, have sent my angel to give you*a* this testimony for the churches. I am the Root and the Offspring of David, and the bright Morning Star."

¹⁷The Spirit and the bride say,

LET'S LIVE IT!   Revelation 21:1—22:6

WHAT IS HEAVEN LIKE? ➡ Read Revelation 21:1—22:6. These verses tell us a lot about what heaven will look like. Name three jewels that will be found in heaven. What will the streets be made of? Will there be a sun or moon?

Revelation 21:4 tells us four things that will *not* be in heaven. Can you find them?

Today tell at least one friend why you are glad Jesus died so you can go to heaven someday.

"Come!" And let him who hears say, "Come!" Whoever is thirsty, let him come; and whoever wishes, let him take the free gift of the water of life.

[18]I warn everyone who hears the words of the prophecy of this book: If anyone adds anything to them, God will add to him the plagues described in this book. [19]And if anyone takes words away from this book of prophecy, God will take away from him his share in the tree of life and in the holy city, which are described in this book.

[20]He who testifies to these things says, "Yes, I am coming soon."

Amen. Come, Lord Jesus.

[21]The grace of the Lord Jesus be with God's people. Amen.

WEIGHTS AND MEASURES

	BIBLICAL UNIT		APPROXIMATE AMERICAN EQUIVALENT		APPROXIMATE METRIC EQUIVALENT	
WEIGHTS	talent	*(60 minas)*	75	pounds	34	kilograms
	mina	*(50 shekels)*	1 1/4	pounds	0.6	kilogram
	shekel	*(2 bekas)*	2/5	ounce	11.5	grams
	pim	*(2/3 shekel)*	1/3	ounce	7.6	grams
	beka	*(10 gerahs)*	1/5	ounce	5.5	grams
	gerah		1/50	ounce	0.6	gram
LENGTH	cubit		18	inches	0.5	meter
	span		9	inches	23	centimeters
	handbreadth		3	inches	8	centimeters

CAPACITY

DRY MEASURE

	BIBLICAL UNIT		AMERICAN		METRIC	
cor [homer]	*(10 ephahs)*		6	bushels	220	liters
lethek	*(5 ephahs)*		3	bushels	110	liters
ephah	*(10 omers)*		3/5	bushel	22	liters
seah	*(1/3 ephah)*		7	quarts	7.3	liters
omer	*(1/10 ephah)*		2	quarts	2	liters
cab	*(1/18 ephah)*		1	quart	1	liter

LIQUID MEASURE

bath	*(1 ephah)*		6	gallons	22	liters
hin	*(1/6 bath)*		4	quarts	4	liters
log	*(1/72 bath)*		1/3	quart	0.3	liter

The figures of the table are calculated on the basis of a shekel equaling 11.5 grams, a cubit equaling 18 inches and an ephah equaling 22 liters. The quart referred to is either a dry quart (slightly larger than a liter) or a liquid quart (slightly smaller than a liter), whichever is applicable. The ton referred to in the footnotes is the American ton of 2,000 pounds.

This table is based upon the best available information, but it is not intended to be mathematically precise; like the measurement equivalents in the footnotes, it merely gives approximate amounts and distances. Weights and measures differed somewhat at various times and places in the ancient world. There is uncertainty particularly about the ephah and the bath; further discoveries may give more light on these units of capacity.

INDEX

This index will help you find where certain subjects or people are written about in the special features of your Adventure Bible. For example, if you want to know more about Solomon and his wisdom, you could look under *Solomon* or *wisdom* in this index. The page numbers listed will guide you to a feature that covers those topics. If you're looking for the meaning of a word, or if you want to know where a Bible verse on a particular topic or person is found, turn to page 1561 to look it up in the dictionary-concordance.

ACTIVITIES

If you want to not only *read* your Adventure Bible but also *do* something with what you've learned, these next pages are just for you. Some of these activities can be done alone; some can be done with your friends or family. The three main headings give you three types of activities. Take your pick . . . then turn to one of the pages listed for some great ideas for things to discuss, things to do, or things to make.

ABBREVIATIONS FOR THE BOOKS OF THE BIBLE

Genesis	Ge	Nahum	Na
Exodus	Ex	Habakkuk	Hab
Leviticus	Lev	Zephaniah	Zep
Numbers	Nu	Haggai	Hag
Deuteronomy	Dt	Zechariah	Zec
Joshua	Jos	Malachi	Mal
Judges	Jdg	Matthew	Mt
Ruth	Ru	Mark	Mk
1 Samuel	1Sa	Luke	Lk
2 Samuel	2Sa	John	Jn
1 Kings	1Ki	Acts	Ac
2 Kings	2Ki	Romans	Ro
1 Chronicles	1Ch	1 Corinthians	1Co
2 Chronicles	2Ch	2 Corinthians	2Co
Ezra	Ezr	Galatians	Gal
Nehemiah	Ne	Ephesians	Eph
Esther	Est	Philippians	Php
Job	Job	Colossians	Col
Psalms	Ps	1 Thessalonians	1Th
Proverbs	Pr	2 Thessalonians	2Th
Ecclesiastes	Ecc	1 Timothy	1Ti
Song of Songs	SS	2 Timothy	2Ti
Isaiah	Isa	Titus	Tit
Jeremiah	Jer	Philemon	Phm
Lamentations	La	Hebrews	Heb
Ezekiel	Eze	James	Jas
Daniel	Da	1 Peter	1Pe
Hosea	Hos	2 Peter	2Pe
Joel	Joel	1 John	1Jn
Amos	Am	2 John	2Jn
Obadiah	Ob	3 John	3Jn
Jonah	Jnh	Jude	Jude
Micah	Mic	Revelation	Rev

DICTIONARY-CONCORDANCE

This dictionary-concordance will help you understand the meanings of difficult words that you may read while you are using your Adventure Bible. It will also help you find Bible verses on certain subjects or people for which you may be looking. Just look up the word in this dictionary-concordance and use the information you find there. If you are looking for the place where certain subjects or people are covered in the special features of this Adventure Bible, you will want to turn to the index that begins on page 1545.

A

Aaron—the brother of Moses; he served as Moses' spokesman before Pharaoh (Ex 4:14-16,27-31; 7:1-2); Israel's first high priest (Ex 28:1; Nu 17; Heb 5:1-4).

Abba—the word for *father* in Aramaic, one of the three languages Jesus spoke.
Ro 8:15 And by him we cry "*A*, Father."
Gal 4:6 the Spirit who calls out, "*A*, Father"

Abel—the second son of Adam (Ge 4:2); he offered the proper sacrifice to God (Ge 4:4; Heb 11:4), but was murdered by his brother Cain (Ge 4:8; Mt 23:35; 1Jn 3:12).

abhor—to hate or to turn away from.

Abigail—the wife of Nabal; she helped save David's life (1Sa 25:14-35) and later became his wife (1Sa 25:36-42).

abolish—to destroy completely; to put an end to.

abomination—a thing to be hated.

abound—to be more than enough; to overflow.

Abraham—the father of the Jewish nation. God established a covenant with him in which God promised that he would make a mighty nation of Abraham's children and would give them the land of Canaan (Ge 15; 17; 22; Ro 4; Heb 6:13-15). A son, Isaac, was born to Sarah and Abraham in their old age (Ge 17:16; 18:9-15; 21:1-7; Heb 11:11-12). Later, as a test, God told him to offer Isaac as a sacrifice (Ge 22; Heb 11:17-19) but withdrew this command when Abraham showed that he would trust the Lord even in this matter.

Absalom—a son of David (2Sa 3:3); he fled from Israel after murdering his half-brother Amnon (2Sa 13). Upon his return, he plotted to take David's throne. He met death when his long hair became entangled in an oak tree and Joab, David's commander, thrust javelins into his heart (2Sa 14-18).

abstain—to keep yourself from doing something.

accordance—agreement.

accredited—officially approved.

accursed—to be condemned or doomed by a curse.

Achan—an Israelite who kept spoil from the conquest of Jericho for himself; as a result of Achan's stealing what belonged to God, the Israelites were defeated at Ai and he and his family were stoned to death (Jos 7; 22:20).

acknowledge—to know and to say that something is true.

acquit—to free from punishment or blame.

acts—deeds.
Ps 150:2 Praise him for his *a* of power
Isa 64:6 all our righteous *a* are like filthy

Adam—the first man God created (Ge 1:26-2:25); he sinned by disobeying God (Ge 3) thereby bringing all people under the curse of sin (Ro 5:12-21).

admonish—to give warning or advice in a caring way.

adorn—to make more beautiful.

adultery—having sexual relations with someone other than one's husband or wife.
Ex 20:14 You shall not commit *a*
Mt 5:28 lustfully has already committed *a*

adversary—enemy; opponent.

advocate—1. (*v.*) to speak in favor of. 2. (*n.*) someone who speaks in another person's defense. Jesus is our advocate.

affliction—trouble or pain that lasts a long time.
Ro 12:12 patient in *a*, faithful in prayer.

aforethought—thought about or planned ahead of time.

Ahab—a wicked king of Israel; the husband of Jezebel (1Ki 16:31). He caused Israel to worship Baal rather than God (1Ki 16:31-33) and was opposed by God's prophet Elijah (1Ki 17:1; 18; 21).

alabaster—a hard marblelike material that can be made into jars, vases or sculptures.

alien—a foreigner or stranger.
Ex 22:21 "Do not mistreat an *a*
Eph 2:19 no longer foreigners and *a*, but fellow citizens
1Pe 2:11 as *a* and strangers in the world

alienate—to make unfriendly; to turn a person's interest or affection away from another person or thing.

allot—to divide and give away in parts. In Old Testament times the land of Canaan was allotted to the twelve tribes of Israel.

Almighty—a name used to show how strong and powerful God is.
Ge 17:1 "I am God *A;* walk before me
Isa 6:3 "Holy, holy, holy is the LORD *A*

altar—a raised platform, made of stones, metal, dirt or wood, on which sacrifices were made.

Amen—So be it; Let it become true.

Ananias—1. the husband of Sapphira; he was struck dead for lying to God (Ac 5:1-11); 2. the disciple who baptized Saul (Ac 9:10-19); 3. the high priest before whom Paul was tried in Jerusalem (Ac 22:30-24:1).

Ancient of Days—a name for God that was often used to tell of his wisdom and dignity.

Andrew—one of the twelve apostles; the brother of Peter (Mt 4:18; 10:2; Ac 1:13).

angel—a heavenly being.
Ps 34:7 The *a* of the LORD encamps
Heb 1:14 Are not all *a* ministering spirits
Heb 2:7 made him a little lower than the *a*
1Pe 1:12 Even *a* long to look

annals—historical writings.

annihilate—to destroy completely.

anoint—to pour oil on a person's head.

antichrist—a person who is against Christ.
1Jn 2:18 have heard that the *a* is coming
1Jn 2:22 a man is the *a*—he denies

anxiety—worry.
1Pe 5:7 Cast all your *a* on him

Apollos—a Christian from Alexandria who knew the Scriptures well (Ac 18:24-28) and helped Paul to minister in Corinth (Ac 19:1; 1Co 1:12).

apostle—1. the twelve men Jesus chose to work with him during his earthly ministry; after being equipped by the Holy Spirit, they were sent out to preach about Jesus; The twelve are: Andrew, James the son of Alphaeus, James the son of Zebedee, John, Judas Iscariot, Matthew, Nathanael (Bartholomew), Peter, Philip, Simon, Thaddaeus (Judas), and Thomas. 2. later, someone who had been with Jesus, had seen his miracles and then taught others about him.

Mk 3:14 twelve—designating them *a*—
1Co 12:28 God has appointed first of all *a*
1Co 15:9 For I am the least of the *a*

aqueduct—a channel for bringing water from one place to another.

Aquila—the husband of Priscilla; Aquila and Priscilla were co-workers with Paul in Corinth (Ac 18; Ro 16:3).

Aramaic—the main language used in the countries east of the Mediterranean Sea during Jesus' earthly ministry.

archangel—an angel of high rank; a leader of other angels.

archives—the official records of a government.

ark of the Testimony—a large gold-covered box housed in the Tabernacle, with two gold cherubim on its lid. It contained the Ten Commandments (Tablets of Testimony), a jar of manna and Aaron's staff, and was kept inside the Most Holy Place in the Tent of Meeting. It was a sign to the Israelites of God's presence with them, and was also the place where God revealed to his people, through the priests, what was his will for them.

Armageddon—the site of the final battle between God and Satan.
Rev 16:16 that in Hebrew is called *A*.

armor—protective clothing worn in battle, usually made of metal
Eph 6:11 Put on the full *a* of God.

arrogant—proud; conceited.

ascend—to go up. Jesus ascended to heaven to return to God the Father.

ascribe—to think of as caused by, coming from or belonging to.
1Ch 16:28 *a* to the LORD glory and strength

assert—to say positively.

astray—mistaken; not on the right path; lost.

atone—to make right, by paying the penalty, the relationship between God and humans that we broke through sin. In the Old Testament people atoned symbolically for their sins by offering sacrifices to God. In the New Testament Jesus corrected the relationship between God and people once and for all by dying for our sins.

atonement—the payment that corrects the relationship between God and humans that we broke through sin.
Lev 17:11 it is the blood that makes *a*
Lev 23:27 this seventh month is the Day of *A*.
Ro 3:25 presented him as a sacrifice of *a,*
Heb 2:17 that he might make *a* for the sins

authority—the right and power to give orders.
Mt 9:6 the Son of Man has *a* on earth
Mt 28:18 "All *a* in heaven and on earth has
Ro 13:1 for there is no *a* except that which
Heb 13:17 your leaders and submit to their *a*.

avenge—to get back at or punish someone who has done wrong.
Dt 32:35 It is mine to *a;* I will repay.

awe—respect and wonder; a holy fear of God because of his great power.
Ecc 5:7 Therefore stand in *a* of God.

Ac 2:43 Everyone was filled with *a*
Heb 12:28 acceptably with reverence and *a*

B

Baal—the name of many false gods in Canaan. Each section of Canaan had its own Baal, for example, Baal of Peor, Baal of Hermon, Baal-Berith.
1Ki 18:25 Elijah said to the prophets of *B*

Babylon—the beautiful capital of Babylonia; it was a powerful and influential city in the Near East from the eighteenth to the sixth centuries B.C. The Babylonians destroyed Jerusalem in 602 B.C. and took many Israelites, such as Daniel and his friends, to Babylon. These captives lived there for about seventy years. In the New Testament, Babylon represents the godless city.
Ps 137:1 By the rivers of *B* we sat and wept

Balaam—a seer who tried to curse Israel during their journey to the promised land, but God would not allow it (Nu 22-24).

balm—a skin cream used to heal sores and relieve pain.

banish—to force a person away from a place.

baptize—a religious ceremony in which water is used as a symbol of cleansing from sin. Some churches today baptize by sprinkling or pouring water over a person. Baptism is a sign that our sins are washed away and that Jesus has taken us to be his own.
Mk 1:9 and was *b* by John in the Jordan.
Mk 16:16 believes and is *b* will be saved,
Ac 1:5 but in a few days you will be *b*
Ac 2:38 Repent and be *b*, every one of you,
Ac 16:33 he and all his family were *b*.
Ac 18:8 heard him believed and were *b*.

Barabbas—the Jews chose this criminal, rather than Jesus, to be released by Pilate (Mt 27:26).

Barnabas—an apostle; he was a co-worker with Paul on his first missionary journey (Ac 9:27; chs 13-15).

barren—1. unable to have children. 2. unable to produce crops.

Bartholomew—one of the twelve apostles (Mt 10:3; Ac 1:13). He was also probably known as Nathanael (Jn 1:45-49; 21:2).

Bathsheba—the wife of Uriah; she committed adultery with David and later became his wife (2Sa 11); the mother of Solomon (2Sa 12:24).

Beelzebub—the prince of demons; Satan.
Lk 11:15, "By *B*, the prince of demons,

believe—to accept as true; to trust; to have faith.
Mk 1:15 Repent and *b* the good news!"
Mk 9:24 "I do *b;* help me overcome my
Jn 1:7 that through him all men might *b*.
Jn 3:18 does not *b* stands condemned
Jn 20:27 Stop doubting and *b*."
Ac 16:31 They replied,"*B* in the Lord Jesus,
Ro 3:22 faith in Jesus Christ to all who *b*.
1Th 4:14 We *b* that Jesus died and rose again

Benjamin—the twelfth son of Jacob. Rachel was his mother and he was the younger brother of Joseph (Ge 35:16-24; chs. 42-45).

bereaved—left alone, especially because of the death of a close friend or relative.

besiege—to surround a city or town completely with an army, so that nothing can go in or out.

bestow—to give.

Bethlehem—the city in Judea where Jesus was born (Mt 2:1).

betray—to turn a friend over to his or her enemies; to be unfaithful to.

betroth—to promise to marry.

bewildered—confused; puzzled.

bier—a platform on which a coffin or dead body is carried.

birthright—the special rights of the firstborn son. In the Old Testament, after the father died the oldest son received the father's power and right to make decisions for the entire family. He also got twice as much money and property as each of his brothers.
Ge 25:34 So Esau despised his *b*.

blameless—without fault.
Ge 17:1 walk before me and be *b*.
1Co 1:8 so that you will be *b* on the day
Php 2:15 so that you may become *b* and pure

blaspheme—to speak carelessly, falsely or insultingly about God or holy things.
Mk 3:29 whoever *b* against the Holy Spirit

blemish—a spot or mark that makes something imperfect.

bless—1. to make holy; 2. to show favor to; 3. to ask God to show favor to.
Ge 2:3 And God *b* the seventh day
Ge 12:3 I will *b* those who *b* you,
Mt 5:3 saying "*B* are the poor in spirit
Ro 12:14 *b* those who persecute you; *b*

blight—a disease in plants that makes them shrivel up and die.

blood—
Ex 12:13 and when I see the *b*, I will pass
Mt 26:28 This is my *b* of the covenant
Ro 5:9 have now been justified by his *b*
Eph 1:7 we have redemption through his *b*
Heb 9:12 once for all by his own *b*
Rev 5:9 with your *b* you purchased men
Rev 7:14 white in the *b* of the Lamb.

boast—to brag.
Ps 34:2 My soul will *b* in the LORD
Gal 6:14 May I never *b* except in the cross

Boaz—a wealthy man who lived in Bethlehem in the days of the judges; he married Ruth (Ru 2; 4).

body—
Ro 6:13 Do not offer the parts of your *b*
Ro 12:1 to offer your *b* as living sacrifices,
1Co 6:19 not know that your *b* is a temple
1Co 12:12 The *b* is a unit, though it is made up
Eph 5:30 for we are members of his *b*.

bondage—slavery.
Ezr 9:9 God has not deserted us in our *b*.

booty—valuables taken from a conquered people.

branch—
Isa 4:2 In that day the *B* of the Lord will
Jer 33:15 I will make a righteous *B* sprout
Jn 15:5 "I am the vine; you are the *b*.

bread—
Dt 8:3 that man does not live on *b* alone
Pr 30:8 but give me only my daily *b*.
Isa 55:2 Why spend money on what is not *b*
Mt 6:11 Give us today our daily *b*.
Jn 6:35 Jesus declared, "I am the *b* of life.

breastpiece—a decorated square of linen cloth worn by the high priest when he entered the Holy Place. The breastpiece was worn chest-high and over a robe. On it were twelve gems, one for each of the twelve tribes of Israel.
Ex 28:15 "Fashion a *b* for making decisions

breastplate—a chest-covering made of metal or leather, worn by soldiers for protection.

brother—
Ge 4:9 "Am I my *b* keeper?"
Ps 133:1 is when *b* live together in unity!
Mt 18:15 'If your *b* sins against you

burden—a heavy load.
Mt 11:30 my yoke is easy and my *b* is light.
Gal 6:2 Carry each other's *b*

C

Caesar—the title of many Roman emperors.
Lk 2:1 In those days *C* Augustus
Mt 22:21 "Give to *C* what is Caesar's

Cain—Adam and Eve's firstborn son; he murdered his brother Abel (Ge 4:1-16).

calamity—a disaster, usually causing great loss and suffering.

caldron—a large clay or metal pot.

Caleb—one of the twelve men who spied out Canaan. He came back with a positive report and encouraged the Israelites to take possession of Canaan. His faith allowed him to enter Canaan (Nu 13:6-14:38; Dt 1:36) whereas those Israelites who believed the report of the other ten spies died during Israel's forty years of wandering in the wilderness.

call (*v.*)—
2Ch 7:14 if my people, who are *c*
Ps 145:18 near to all who *c* on him
Isa 65:24 Before they *c* I will answer
Mt 9:13 come to *c* the righteous
Jn 10:3 He *c* his own sheep by name
Ro 8:30 And those he predestined, he also *c*
Ro 10:12 and richly blesses all who *c* on him
1Pe 2:9 of him who *c* you out of darkness

call, calling (*n.*)—
Ro 11:29 gifts and his *c* are irrevocable
Eph 4:1 worthy of the *c* you have received
2Pe 1:10 all the more eager to make your *c*

Canaan—1. the land God promised to the nation of Israel; 2. the promised land.
1Ch 16:18 "To you I will give the land of *C*

capstone—the stone that holds two walls together; the stone that finishes a wall.
1Pe 2:7 has become the *c*,

censer—a bowl or dish used for carrying hot coals or for burning incense.

centurion—a Roman army officer in charge of one hundred soldiers.

chaff—the seed covering of a grain such as wheat. In Bible times the grain and chaff were separated by tossing the grain into the air so the wind could blow the chaff away.
Ps 1:4 they are like *c*
Mt 3:12 up the *c* with unquenchable fire

chariot—a two-wheeled vehicle pulled by horses.
2Ki 6:17 and *c* of fire all around Elisha

chasten—to correct or improve by punishment or suffering.

cheerful—
Pr 15:13 A happy heart makes the face *c*
2Co 9:7 for God loves a *c* giver.

cherub—an angel, with an appearance something like a human being. The word for more than one cherub is *cherubim*.

children—
Ps 8:2 from the lips of *c* and infants
Pr 17:6 Children's *c* are a crown
Mt 19:14 "Let the little *c* come to me
Ro 8:16 with our spirit that we are God's *c*.
Eph 6:1 *C*, obey your parents in the Lord,
Eph 6:4 do not exasperate your *c;* instead
1Jn 3:1 that we should be called *c* of God

choose—
Jos 24:15 then *c* for yourselves this day
Jn 15:16 You did not *c* me,
Jn 15:16 But I *c* you to go and bear fruit
Eph 1:4 He *c* us in him before the creation
2Th 2:13 from the beginning God *c* you

chosen—
Mt 22:14 For many are invited, but few are *c*
Jn 15:19 but I have *c* you out of the world
1Pe 2:9 But you are a *c* people, a royal

Christ—the official title of Jesus, meaning "the Anointed One." It is a Greek word, and it means the same as the Hebrew word *Messiah*.
Mt 1:16 was born Jesus, who is called *C*.
Mt 16:16 Peter answered, "You are the *C*
Jn 1:41 found the Messiah" (that is, the *C*).
Jn 20:31 you may believe that Jesus is the *C*
Ro 5:8 While we were still sinners, *C* died
1Co 1:23 but we preached *C* crucified
1Co 12:27 Now you are the body of *C*
Eph 5:2 as *C* loved us and gave himself up
Eph 5:23 as *C* is the head of the church
Php 1:21 to live is *C* and to die is gain.
2Th 2:1 the coming of our Lord Jesus *C*

Christian—a believer in or follower of Christ.
Ac 11:26 The disciples were first called *C*
1Pe 4:16 as a *C*, do not be ashamed,

chronicles—a history of events in the order in which they took place.

church—
Mt 16:18 and on this rock I will build my *c*
Eph 5:23 as Christ is the head of the *c*
Col 1:24 the sake of his body, which is the *c*.

circumcise—to cut off the loose fold of skin at the end of the penis.

Ge 17:10 Every male among you shall be c.

cistern—a pit dug into the ground for storing rainwater.

citadel—a tower or building equipped for war, especially one in a city.

city of refuge—one of six cities set aside by Moses and Joshua for those who had accidentally killed someone. Such people would be safe there until a fair trial could be held.

clean animals—animals God allowed the Israelites to sacrifice and eat.

cleanse—to make clean; to wash.

cloak—a loose-fitting coat without sleeves.

co-heir—one of two persons who receive an inheritance. Because of Christ's death and resurrection, we are co-heirs with him of our inheritance in God.

Ro 8:17 heirs of God and c with Christ

comfort—

Ps 23:4 rod and your staff, they c me.

Zec 1:17 and the LORD will again c Zion

2Co 1:4 so that we can c those

commandment—an order given by God. God gave the Ten Commandments to the Israelites while they were encamped in the area of Mount Sinai.

Ex 20:6 who love me and keep my c.

Mt 22:38 This is the first and greatest c.

Jn 13:34 "A new c I give you: Love one

commemorate—to remember an event with a special celebration or ceremony.

commend—1. to praise; 2. to hand over to someone for safekeeping.

compassion—sympathy; pity.

Ps 103:4 and crowns me with love and c.

Mt 9:36 When he saw the crowds, he had c

Ro 9:15 and I will have c on whom I have c.

Col 3:12 clothe yourselves with c, kindness,

compassionate—

Ne 9:17 gracious and c, slow to anger

complacent—contented; unconcerned.

conceive—1. to become pregnant; 2. to think up or imagine.

Mt 1:20 what is c in her is from the Holy

1Co 2:9 no mind has c

concubine—in Bible times, a woman who belonged to a man but did not have the rights of a wife. She was often one of the spoils of war, and her primary purpose was to bear children for the man.

condemn—to give out punishment to; to pronounce guilty.

Jn 3:17 Son into the world to c the world,

Ro 8:34 Who is he that c? Christ Jesus

condemnation—

Ro 8:1 there is now no c for those who are

confess—1. to say what you believe; 2. to tell your sins to someone.

Lev 26:40 "But if they will c their sins

Ro 10:9 That if you c with your mouth

Php 2:11 every tongue c that Jesus Christ is

1Jn 1:9 If we c our sins, he is faithful

conform—to agree with and try to be like someone; to do what others say to do.

Ro 8:29 predestined to be c to the likeness

1Pe 1:14 do not c to the evil desires you had

conscience—the sense of knowing if something is good or bad; a sense of right and wrong.

Ro 2:15 their c also bearing witness

Tit 1:15 their minds and c are corrupted.

Heb 9:14 cleanse our c from acts that lead

conscript—1. to take for government use; 2. to force to serve in an army.

consecrate—to set aside or dedicate for God's use.

Ex 13:2 "C to me every firstborn male

Lev 20:7 "C yourselves and be holy

console—to comfort.

conspire—to plan together to do evil.

consume—1. to use up or eat up; 2. to destroy completely.

Jn 2:17 "Zeal for your house will c me."

Heb 12:29 for our God is a c fire.

contempt—lack of respect; looking down on someone or something as being worthless.

Pr 14:31 He who oppresses the poor shows c

1Th 5:20 do not treat prophecies with c.

content—

Php 4:11 to be c whatever the circumstances,

Heb 13:5 and be c with what you have

contrite—to feel sorry for one's sins; to feel repentant.

Ps 51:17 a broken and c heart

Isa 66:2 he who is humble and c in spirit

convert—a person who has changed from one belief to another.

1Ti 3:6 He must not be a recent c

convict—1. to prove one wrong; 2. to make a person feel sorrow.

Jn 16:8 he will c the world of guilt in regard

convulsion—a wild shaking of the body; violent contraction and expansion of one's muscles.

Cornelius—a Roman to whom Peter preached the gospel; he became the first Gentile Christian (Ac 10).

cornerstone—the first or most important stone laid when constructing a building.

Eph 2:20 with Christ Jesus himself as the chief c.

corrupt—1. (v.) to change from good to bad; 2. (adj.) wicked.

Ge 6:11 Now the earth was c in God's sight

1Co 15:33 "Bad company c good character."

counsel—to give advice to.

Counselor—another name for the Holy Spirit.

Jn 14:26 But the C, the Holy Spirit,

Jn 15:26 "When the C comes, whom I will

covenant—1. an agreement between two people or two groups of people, in which usually both make specific promises. 2. the promises of God for salvation.

Ge 9:9 "I now establish my c with you

Ge 17:2 I will confirm my c between me

Ex 19:5 if you obey me fully and keep my c

Jer 31:31 "when I will make a new c

Eze 37:26 I will make a *c* of peace with them
1Co 11:25 "This cup is the new *c* in my blood
Heb 9:15 Christ is the mediator of a new *c*

covet—to want for yourself something that belongs to another person.
Ex 20:17 You shall not *c* your neighbor's

create—to make; to bring into being. God created the world; the world is God's creation; God is the Creator.
Ge 1:1 In the beginning God *c* the heavens
Ps 51:10 *C* in me a pure heart, O God
Col 1:16 For by him all things were *c*
Rev 10:6 who *c* the heavens and all that is

cross—
Mt 10:38 and anyone who does not take his *c*
Gal 6:14 in the *c* of our Lord Jesus Christ
Php 2:8 even death on a *c*!
Col 2:14 he took it away, nailing it to the *c*
Heb 12:2 set before him endured the *c*

crown—
Pr 4:9 present you with a *c* of splendor."
Isa 61:3 to bestow on them a *c* of beauty
1Co 9:25 it to get a *c* that will last forever.
2Ti 4:8 store for me the *c* of righteousness
Rev 2:10 and I will give you the *c* of life.

crucify—to put to death by nailing or tying a person's body to a cross.
Mt 27:22 They all answered,"*C* him!"
Jn 19:18 Here they *c* him, and with him two
1Co 1:23 but we preach Christ *c*: a stumbling
Gal 2:20 I have been *c* with Christ

curse—(*v.*) to ask God to bring evil or injury to; (*n.*) a prayer or desire that evil or injury come upon someone.
Lev 20:9 "If anyone *c* his father or mother
Dt 21:23 hung on a tree is under God's *c*.
Lk 6:28 bless those who *c* you, pray
Gal 3:13 *C* is everyone who is hung on a tree
Jas 3:9 with it we *c* men, who have been

D

Daniel—a young Jewish exile; he lived in Babylon during the reign of several kings, including Nebuchadnezzar. He was found praying to God, contrary to an edict prohibiting for thirty days subjects from praying to anyone except the king. For this he was thrown into a lion's den (Da 1-6).

David—the son of Jesse; in early life: anointed by Samuel to become king of Israel (1Sa 16:1-13); killed the giant Goliath (1Sa 17); and was pursued by Saul. After Saul's death (2Sa 1) he was made king (2Sa 5:1-4), and it was during his reign that Israel's place in the land of Canaan was made secure.

day—
Ge 1:5 God called the light "*d* "
Ps 118:24 This is the *d* the Lord has made;
Ecc 12:1 Creator in the *d* of your youth,
Joel 2:31 and dreadful *d* of the Lord.
Mic 4:1 in the last *d*
Lk 11:3 Give us each *d* our daily bread.
Heb 1:2 in these last *d* he has spoken to us

2Pe 3:8 With the Lord a *d* is like

deacon—a church leader chosen to take care of money matters and to give money to the widows and the poor.
1Ti 3:8 *D*, likewise, are to be men worthy

death—
Ps 23:4 the valley of the shadow of *d*,
Ecc 7:2 for *d* is the destiny of every man;
Isa 25:8 he will swallow up *d* forever.
Ro 6:23 For the wages of sin is *d*,
1Co 15:21 For since *d* came through a man,
1Co 15:55 Where, O *d*, is your sting?"
Rev 1:18 And I hold the keys of *d* and Hades
Rev 21:4 There will be no more *d*

debauchery—living an immoral life or a life without religion; living to please only yourself.

Deborah—a prophetess who led Israel to victory over the Canaanites (Jdg 4-5).

debt—something that one person owes another. (Also, debtor.)
Mt 6:12 Forgive us our *d*,

deceive—(*v.*) to fool or trick; to lie (*n.* deceit, deception; *adj.* deceitful).
Ge 3:13 "The serpent *d* me, and I ate."
1Co 3:18 Do not *d* yourselves.
Gal 6:7 Do not be *d*: God cannot be
1Jn 1:8 we *d* ourselves and the truth is not

decree—an order or law given by someone with power and authority.

dedicate—to set apart for a special purpose, often for God's use.

defect—imperfection; fault.

defile—to make something that is good and pure impure or unclean.

defraud—to cheat someone by trickery.

Deity—God.
Col 2:9 of the *D* lives in bodily form,

deliver—to rescue; to set free.

demon—evil spirit. A demon-possessed person is one who is controlled by evil spirits.
Mk 5:15 possessed by the legion of *d*
Ro 8:38 neither angels not *d*, neither
1Co 10:20 of pagans are offered to *d*,
1Ti 4:1 spirits and things taught by *d*.
Jas 2:19 Good! Even the *d* believe that
Rev 16:14 of *d* performing miraculous signs

denarius—a small Roman coin made of silver. During Jesus' earthly ministry, one denarius was the payment for about one day's work.

denounce—to say a person or thing is evil.

depraved—evil or sinful.
Php 2:15 fault in a crooked and *d* generation

depravity—
Ro 1:29 of wickedness, evil, greed and *d*.
2Pe 2:19 they themselves are slaves of *d*

desecrate—to treat without respect or reverence.

desolate—not lived in; lonely; deserted.

destine—(*v.*) to decide ahead of time (*n.* destiny).

destitute—not having necessary things such as money and food.

detest—to hate.

devil—
Lk 4:2 forty days he was tempted by the *d.*
Eph 4:27 and do not give the *d* a foothold.
Eph 6:11 stand against the *d* schemes.
2Ti 2:26 and escape from the trap of the *d,*
Jas 4:7 Resist the *d,* and he will flee
1Pe 5:8 Your enemy the *d* prowls
1Jn 3:8 was to destroy the *d* work.
Rev 12:9 that ancient serpent called the *d*

devote—to set apart for a special person or for a special reason; to set apart for God's use.

devout—religious; giving much time to prayer and worship.

die—
Ge 2:17 when you eat of it you will surely *d*
2Ki 14:6 each is to *d* for his own sins."
Ecc 3:2 a time to be born and a time to *d*
Eze 3:18 that wicked man will *d* for his sin
Eze 18:4 soul who sins is the one who will *d.*
Jn 11:26 and believes in me will never *d.*
Ro 14:8 and if we *d,* we *d* to the Lord.
1Co 15:22 in Adam all *d,* so in Christ all will
Php 1:21 to live is Christ and to *d* is gain.
Rev 14:13 Blessed are the dead who *d*

dirge—a song of deep sadness, usually sung at funerals.

discern—to understand; to come to know the difference between two or more things.
Php 1:10 you may be able to *d* what is best

disciple—a follower or student, especially one who believes what the leader teaches. Anyone who believes in Jesus is his disciple.
Lk 14:27 and follow me cannot be my *d.*
Jn 13:35 men will know that you are my *d*

discipline—(*v.*) to correct; to teach what is right; (*n.*) training that corrects, molds or perfects moral character.
Ps 39:11 You rebuke and *d* men for their sin
Pr 15:5 A fool spurns his father's *d*
Pr 29:17 *D* your son, and he will give you
Heb 12:6 the Lord *d* those he loves
Rev 3:19 Those whom I love I rebuke and *d.*

disclose—to show or reveal.

discourse—1. (*v.*) to talk together; 2. (*n.*) a conversation or speech.

discriminate—to make a difference where no such difference should or does exist; to treat two persons or things differently because one seems better than the other.
Jas 2:4 have you not *d* among yourselves

disgrace—to bring shame to.

disown—to reject someone or something so completely that it no longer belongs to you.
Mt 26:35 to die with you, I will never *d* you."
2Ti 2:12 if we *d* him,

disperse—to scatter; to spread around.

dissension—disagreement; quarreling.

dissipation—living only for your own pleasure; wasting your life on foolish or evil pleasures.

divination—seeing into the future by magic.
Lev 19:26 " 'Do not practice *d* or sorcery.

divine—given by God; belonging to God.
Ro 1:20 his eternal power and *d* nature

2Co 10:4 they have *d* power

divorce—
Mal 2:16 "I hate *d,*" says the Lord God
Mt 19:3 for a man to *d* his wife for any
1Co 7:11 And a husband must not *d* his wife.

doctrine—teachings or beliefs about God.
1Ti 4:16 Watch your life and *d* closely.
Tit 2:1 is in accord with sound *d.*

dominion—power; rule.
Ps 22:28 for *d* belongs to the Lord
Eph 1:21 far above all rule and authority, power and *d*

doom—1. (*v.*) to make certain something will fail or be destroyed; 2. (*n.*) fate; condemnation; ruin.

door—
Mt 7:7 and the *d* will be opened to you.
Rev 3:20 I stand at the *d* and knock.

doubt—
Mt 21:21 if you have faith and do not *d*
Mk 11:23 and does not *d* in his heart
Jas 1:6 he must believe and not *d*

dropsy—puffiness or swelling of the body caused by a disease of the kidneys, liver or heart.

E

earth—
Ge 1:1 God created the heavens and the *e.*
Ps 24:1 *e* is the Lord's and everything
Mt 6:10 done on *e* as it is in heaven.
Mt 24:35 Heaven and *e* will pass away
Lk 2:14 on *e* peace to men
Php 2:10 in heaven and on *e* and under the *e*
2Pe 3:13 to a new heaven and a new *e*

edict—an order or law made by a person who has the power to enforce it.

edify—to teach someone to live a godly life, or to help someone to live in such a way.
1Co 14:4 but he who prophesies *e* the church

elders—1. the older men of a town or nation. They were the leaders of their community and made all the important decisions. Each town had its own groups of elders. After the Jews returned from exile in Babylon, the elders made up the Sanhedrin, the ruling council of the Jews. 2. the leaders of the church.
1Ti 5:17 The *e* who direct the affairs
Tit 1:5 and appoint *e* in every town

election—
Ro 9:11 God's purpose in *e* might stand
2Pe 1:10 to make your calling and *e* sure.

Eli—the high priest with whom Samuel spent the early years of his life (1Sa 2:11-26).

Elijah—a prophet of the Lord during the reign of Ahab. He predicted a famine in Israel (1Ki 17:1), and defeated the prophets of Baal at Carmel in the test of whose God would set fire to the altar (1Ki 18:16-46). He was taken to heaven in a whirlwind (2Ki 2:11-12) and later appeared with Moses at the transfiguration of Jesus (Mk 9:1-8).

Elisha—the prophet who succeeded Elijah. He was present when God took Elijah to heaven, and he took his place as prophet to Israel (2Ki 2:1-18).

Elizabeth—the mother of John the Baptist. She became pregnant when she was very old; Mary went to visit her when she found out she, too, was pregnant (Lk 1:5-58).

enchanter—a magician or snake charmer.

endure—to continue; to keep on going; to bear something that is difficult or painful.
 Ps 136:1 His love *e* forever.
 Mal 3:2 who can *e* the day of his coming
 2Ti 2:3 *E* hardship with us like a good

enmity—hatred or bad feelings that make two people or two groups enemies.
 Ge 3:15 And I will put *e*

Enoch—a man who "walked with God." Later in life, God "took him away" (Ge 5:18-24).

envy—to want for yourself something that belongs to another person.
 1Co 13:4 It does not *e*, it does not boast

ephod—a linen apron worn by a priest over his robe. It was decorated with gold, blue, purple and scarlet yarns.

Ephraim—1. one of Joseph's sons; 2. one of the tribes of Israel. Its members were descendants of Ephraim. 3. a name for the northern kingdom of Israel after the ten tribes of Israel and the two tribes of Judah separated from each other.
 Ge 41:52 The second son he named *E*
 Isa 7:17 unlike any since *E* broke away from Judah

epileptic—a person afflicted with a disorder of the brain that makes one lose control of his or her muscles and sometimes causes unconsciousness. In Bible times epilepsy was a dreaded disease; but today it can be controlled by medicine.

equity—fairness.

Esau—the firstborn son of Isaac and twin of Jacob (Ge 25:21-26). He sold his birthright to Jacob for a pot of stew (Ge 25:29-34) and was tricked out of his blessing by this same brother (Ge 27). Later in his life he and Jacob met and were reconciled (Ge 33).

esteem—1. (*v.*) to value; to consider important; 2. (*n.*) high regard or respect.

Esther—a Jewish woman who lived in Persia (Est 2:7). Xerxes chose her to be queen (Est 2:8-18). Upon being told of a plot by Haman to kill the Jews, she went to the king and pleaded for the Jewish people and thus saved them (Est 3-4; 7-9).

eternal—without beginning or end; forever; timeless. God is eternal.
 Dt 33:27 The *e* God is your refuge,
 Jn 3:16 him shall not perish but have *e* life.
 Ro 6:23 but the gift of God is *e* life
 1Jn 5:13 you may know that you have *e* life.

eunuch—1. the most important official after the king or queen; 2. a man whose sex organs have been removed so that he cannot produce children.

evangelist—a person who preaches the good news about Jesus.
 Ac 21:8 stayed at the house of Philip the *e*
 Eph 4:11 some to be prophets, some to be *e*

Eve—the first woman God created (Ge 2:20-24). Her name means, Mother of all the living (Ge 3:20).

everlasting—forever; without end.
 Ps 90:2 from *e* to *e* you are God.
 Isa 9:6 *E* Father, Prince of Peace
 Isa 55:3 I will make an *e* covenant with you
 Jn 6:47 the truth, he who believes has *e* life.
 2Th 1:9 punished with *e* destruction

evil—wicked; doing things against God's will.
 Ge 2:9 of the knowledge of good and *e*
 Ps 23:4 I will fear no *e*
 Isa 13:11 I will punish the world for its *e*
 Isa 55:7 and the *e* man his thoughts.
 Mt 6:13 but deliver us from the *e* one."
 Ro 12:9 Hate what is *e;* cling
 Ro 12:17 Do not repay anyone *e* for *e*.
 Eph 6:16 all the flaming arrows of the *e* one.
 Jas 1:13 For God cannot be tempted by *e*

exalt—to praise; to raise to an important position.
 Ps 118:28 you are my God, and I will *e* you.
 Ps 148:13 for his name alone is *e*
 Pr 14:34 Righteousness *e* a nation
 Mt 23:12 For whoever *e* himself will be

exile—(*v.*) to force someone to leave his or her country or home; (*n.*) forced removal from one's country or home.
 2Ch 36:20 He carried into *e* to Babylon

exodus—the departure of a large group of people from one place to go to another. The book of Exodus is the story of the Israelites' journey from Egypt to Canaan.

exploit—to take unfair advantage of.

extol—to praise.
 Ps 34:1 I will *e* the LORD at all times
 Ps 95:2 and *e* him with music and song.

extortion—something gotten from a person by force or by using other illegal means.

Ezekiel—a priest who was called to be a prophet to the Jewish people when they were in exile in Babylon (Eze 1-3). He had many visions from the Lord (Eze 37; 40).

Ezra—a priest and teacher of the Law; he led a group of Jewish exiles back to Israel and helped them reestablish the temple of God and restore proper worship (Ezr 7-8).

F

faction—a group of people trying to get its own way or promote its own interests.

faith—belief and trust in God; knowing that God is real, even though we can't see him.
 Hab 2:4 but the righteous will live by his *f*
 Mt 17:20 if you have *f* as small as a mustard
 Lk 7:9 I have not found such great *f*
 Ro 1:17 "The righteous will live by *f.*"
 Ro 3:22 comes through *f* in Jesus Christ

1Co 13:2 and if I have a *f* that can move
2Co 5:7 We live by *f*, not by sight.
Eph 6:16 to all this, take up the shield of *f*,
1Ti 6:12 Fight the good fight of the *f*.
Heb 11:1 *f* is being sure of what we hope for
Heb 11:8 By *f* Abraham, when called to go
Heb 12:2 the author and perfecter of our *f*
Jas 2:26 so *f* without deeds is dead.

faithful—trustworthy; loyal. God is faithful.
Ps 145:13 the LORD is *f* to all his promises
Mt 25:21 "Well done, good and *f* servant!
Ro 12:12 patient in affliction, *f* in prayer.
1Co 10:13 And God is *f*; he will not let you be
1Jn 1:9 he is *f* and just and will forgive us
Rev 1:5 who is the *f* witness, the firstborn

faithfulness—
Ps 86:15 to anger, abounding in love and *f*.
La 3:23 great is your *f*.
Gal 5:22 patience, kindness, goodness, *f*

falsehood—a lie.

family—
Ps 68:6 God sets the lonely in *f*
Lk 9:61 go back and say good-by to my *f*."
Lk 12:52 in one *f* divided against each other
1Ti 3:4 He must manage his own *f* well
1Ti 5:4 practice by caring for their own *f*

father—
Ge 2:24 this reason a man will leave his *f*
Ge 17:4 You will be the *f* of many nations.
Ex 20:12 "Honor your *f* and your mother
Pr 23:22 Listen to your *f*, who gave you life
Mt 6:9 "Our *F* in heaven
Lk 11:11 "Which of you *f*, if your son asks
Lk 23:34 Jesus said, "*F*, forgive them
Jn 10:30 I and the *F* are one."
Jn 14:2 In my *F* house are many rooms
Jn 14:6 No one comes to the *F*

fear—(*v.*) 1. to respect highly; to feel reverence and awe for; 2. to be afraid of. (n.) profound reverence toward God; anticipation or awareness of danger.
Dt 6:13 *F* the LORD your God, serve him
Job 1:8 a man who *f* God and shuns evil."
Ps 91:5 You will not *f* the terror of night
Ps 111:10 *f* of the LORD is the beginning
Isa 41:10 So do not *f*, for I am with you
Php 2:12 to work out your salvation with *f*

fellowship—companionship or friendship.
1Jn 1:6 claim to have *f* with him yet walk
1Jn 1:7 we have *f* with one another,

fig—1. a brownish pear-shaped fruit that grows in countries near the Mediterranean Sea; 2. the tree that grows this fruit.

firstborn—a family's first male child. The firstborn son became the head of the family when his father died. He also received twice as much money and property as each of his brothers.
Ex 11:5 Every *f* son in Eygpt will die

firstfruits—the first vegetables, fruits and grains harvested from the field.
Ex 23:19 "Bring the best of the *f* of your soil

flawless—without fault or defect; perfect.

flog—to beat with a stick or a whip.

forbearance—patience; tolerance.

forefather—a male ancestor.

foreknow—to know ahead of time.
Ro 8:29 For those God *f* he
Ro 11:2 not reject his people, whom he *f*

forgive—to pardon or excuse; no longer to blame or be angry with someone who had done you wrong.
Mt 6:14 For if you *f* men when they sin
Lk 23:34 Jesus said, "Father, *f* them
Col 3:13 *F* as the Lord forgave you.
1Jn 1:9 and just and will *f* us our sins

forsake—to leave another completely alone, with no hope that you will ever return.
Jos 1:5 I will never leave you or *f* you.
Isa 55:7 Let the wicked *f* his way
Mt 27:46 my God, why have you *f* me?

frankincense—an incense burned for its sweet smell.

free—
Jn 8:32 and the truth will set you *f*."
Ro 6:18 You have been set *f* from sin

freedom—
2Co 3:17 the Spirit of the Lord is, there is *f*.
Gal 5:13 But do not use your *f* to indulge

friend—
Pr 18:24 there is a *f* who sticks closer
Jn 15:13 that one lay down his life for his *f*.
Jas 4:4 Anyone who chooses to be a *f*

fruitful—productive; yielding much fruit.
Ge 1:22 "Be *f* and increase in number
Jn 15:2 clean so that it will be even more *f*.

fulfill—to complete a promise or project.
Ps 116:14 I will *f* my vows to the LORD
Mk 14:49 But the Scriptures must be *f*."
Lk 24:44 Everything must be *f* that is

fulfillment—
Ro 13:10 Therefore love is the *f* of the law.

G

Gabriel—the angel who announced the births of John the Baptist and Jesus (Lk 1:11-20, 26-38).

Galilee—the northern part of Palestine. Palestine had three main parts: Galilee, Samaria and Judea. Jesus grew up, preached and did most of his miracles in Galilee. Today this area is in northern Israel.

gall—1. a plant with an extremely bitter-tasting fruit; 2. the liquid made by the liver.
Mt 27:34 mixed with *g*; but after tasting it

genealogy—a list of a person's ancestors or descendants; a family tree.

generation—the entire number of people born and living at about the same time. Grandparents, parents and children are three different generations.
Ps 102:12 your renown endures through all *g*.
Lk 1:48 now on all *g* will call me blessed

Gentile—anyone who is not a Jew.

Ro 3:9 and *G* alike are all under sin.
Ro 11:13 as I am the apostle to the *G*
Eph 3:6 the gospel the *G* are heirs together

Gideon—a judge who freed Israel from the rule and terror of the Midianites (Jdg 6-8). He asked for a sign from God, and God showed him his will by means of dew and a fleece (Jdg 6:36-40).

gift—
Ro 6:23 but the *g* of God is eternal life
1Co 12:4 There are different kinds of *g*,
2Co 9:15 be to God for his indescribable *g*!

gleanings—the grain or fruit left behind after harvesting. Poor people were allowed to pick up and use these leftovers.

glory—1. honor; praise; 2. a source of pride or worthiness.
Ps 8:5 and crowned him with *g* and honor.
Ps 19:1 The heavens declare the *g* of God
Lk 2:14 saying, "*G* to God in the highest
Jn 1:14 We have seen his *g*, the *g* of the one
1Co 10:31 whatever you do, do it all for the *g*
Rev 4:11 to receive *g* and honor and power

glutton—a person who eats too much.

gnash—to grind (one's teeth) together.

God—
Ge 1:1 In the beginning *G* created
Ge 17:1 "I am *G* Almighty; walk before me
Ge 50:20 but *G* intended it for good
Ex 8:10 is no one like the LORD our *G*.
Ex 20:5 the LORD your *G*, am a jealous *G*
Nu 23:19 *G* is not a man, that he should lie
Dt 4:31 the LORD your *G* is a merciful *G*
Dt 6:4 LORD our *G*, the LORD is one.
Dt 6:5 Love the LORD your *G*
Dt 32:4 A faithful *G* who does no wrong
Ne 9:17 But you are a forgiving *G*
Ps 46:1 *G* is our refuge and strength
Ps 71:22 harp for your faithfulness, O my *G*
Jn 1:18 ever seen *G*, but *G* the only Son
Jn 3:16 "For *G* so loved the world that he
Jn 4:24 *G* is spirit, and his worshipers must
1Co 10:13 *G* is faithful; he will not let you be
1Co 14:33 For *G* is not a *G* of disorder
Heb 12:10 but *G* disciplines us for our good
Jas 1:13 For *G* cannot be tempted by evil
1Jn 4:16 *G* is love.
Rev 4:8 holy is the Lord *G* Almighty

Golgotha—the hill outside Jerusalem where Jesus was hung on a cross.
Jn 19:17 (which in Aramaic is called *G*).

Goliath—the Philistine giant who was killed by David (1Sa 17; 21:9).

gospel—1. the good news that Jesus died for our sins and rose again; 2. Gospel, any of the first four books of the New Testament.
Ro 1:16 I am not ashamed of the *g*
Ro 15:16 duty of proclaiming the *g* of God
1Co 9:16 Woe to me if I do not preach the *g*!
1Co 15:2 By this *g* you are saved
2Co 9:13 your confession of the *g*
1Th 2:4 by God to be entrusted with the *g*

grace—an undeserved favor or gift; the undeserved forgiveness, kindness and mercy that God gives us.

Ro 3:24 and are justified freely by his *g*
Ro 5:20 where sin increased, *g* increased all
2Co 12:9 "My *g* is sufficient for you
Eph 2:5 it is by *g* you have been saved.
Tit 3:7 having been justified by his *g*

guilty—having broken a law or commandment; deserving punishment.
Ex 34:7 does not leave the *g* unpunished
1Co 11:27 in an unworthy manner will be *g*
Heb 10:22 to cleanse us from a *g* conscience
Jas 2:10 at just one point is *g* of breaking all

H

Hades—hell; the place where the spirits of the dead live.
Mt 16:18 the gates of *H* will not overcome it.

Hagar—a servant of Sarah and one of Abraham's wives; the mother of Ishmael (Ge 16:1-6; 25:12). After giving birth to Isaac, Sarah drove Hagar away (Ge 21:9-21).

Haggai—a prophet who encouraged the Israelites who returned from exile in Babylon to rebuild the temple (Ezr 5:1; Hag 1-2).

hallelujah—praise the Lord; a song of praise.
Rev 19:1 "*H*! Salvation and glory and power

hallow—to make holy; to set apart as special.

Hannah—the wife of Elkanah; she prayed for a son and God gave her Samuel. She dedicated him to God and he lived in the temple as a boy and became a prophet and judge (1Sa 1-2).

harlot—a woman who lets a man use her body for sex in exchange for money.

haughty—proud.
Pr 16:18 a *h* spirit before a fall.

heart—
Dt 6:5 LORD your God with all your *h*
1Sa 16:7 but the LORD looks at the *h*."
1Ch 28:9 for the LORD searches every *h*
Ps 51:10 Create in me a pure *h*, O God
Ps 119:11 I have hidden your word in my *h*
Ps 139:23 Search me, O God, and know my *h*
Jer 29:13 when you seek me with all your *h*.
Eze 36:26 I will give you a new *h*
Mt 5:8 Blessed are the pure in *h*
Mt 22:37 the Lord your God with all your *h*
Ro 10:10 is with your *h* that you believe

heaven—
Ge 14:19 Creator of *h* and earth.
Mt 19:23 man to enter the kingdom of *h*.
Mk 16:19 he was taken up into *h*
Php 3:20 But our citizenship is in *h*.
Rev 21:1 Then I saw a new *h* and a new earth

Hebrew—1. another name for an Israelite; a descendant of Abraham; 2. the language spoken by the Jews. The Old Testament was written in Hebrew.

heir—someone who receives the property or blessings of a person who has died. In Bible times an heir was usually male.
Ro 8:17 then we are *h*—*h* of God
Eph 3:6 gospel the Gentiles are *h* together

heresy—false teaching about God.

Herod—the family name of five kings who ruled Palestine under the Roman emperor: Herod the Great (Mt 2:16); Herod Antipas (Mk 6:14-29); Herod Philip (Mt 14:3; Mk 6:17); Herod Agrippa I (Ac 12:1-4,19-23); Herod Agrippa II (Ac 23:35; 25:13-26:32).

Herodias—the wife of Herod Antipas; she persuaded her daughter to ask Antipas for the head of John the Baptist (Mk 6:17).

Hezekiah—a king of Judah; he restored the temple, reinstituted proper worship and sought the Lord's help against the Assyrians. He showed his faith when, suffering from a serious illness, he prayed to God and was healed; yet he also showed the Babylonians his treasures and God punished him and the Israelites for this (2Ch 29-31; 2Ki 18-20).

high priest—the chief religious official in the Jewish religion. In the Old Testament he offered the most important sacrifices to God in behalf of the people. In Jesus' time he was also the head of the Sanhedrin (the highest Jewish court), and a powerful political leader—even having a small army.

hinder—to hold back; to prevent; to delay.

holy—(v.) set apart for God; (adj.) belonging to God; pure; godly.
    Ex 20:8 the Sabbath day by keeping it h.
    Lev 11:44 and be h, because I am h.
    Isa 6:3 "H, h, h is the Lord Almighty
    Ro 12:1 as living sacrifices, h and pleasing
    Rev 4:8 "H, h, h is the LORD Almighty

Holy Spirit—the third person of the Trinity; the Spirit lives and works in our hearts and minds. Jesus promised his disciples that he would send his Spirit (Jn 14:16-26), and it came at Pentecost in a powerful way (Ac 2). Other names are: the Spirit, Counselor and Comforter.

homage—honor; respect.

homosexual—someone who has sexual relations with a person of the same sex.
    1Co 6:9 male prostitutes nor h offenders

hope (v.; n.)—
    Ps 42:5 Put your h in God
    Isa 40:31 but those who h in the LORD
    Ro 8:24 But h that is seen is no h at all.
    1Co 15:19 for this life we have h in Christ
    Heb 11:1 faith is being sure of what we h for

hosanna—a Hebrew word of praise meaning "save."
    Mt 21:9 "H in the highest!"

hospitality—welcoming people into one's home; sharing one's home and food with others.
    Ro 12:13 Practice h.
    1Pe 4:9 Offer h to one another

humble—(v.) to make humble in spirit or manner; (adj.) not proud; not pretending to be important.
    Ps 147:6 The LORD sustains the h
    Mt 23:12 whoever exalts himself will be h
    Jas 4:10 H yourselves before the Lord

humiliate—to make humble; to reduce to a lower position; to make ashamed.
    1Co 11:22 and h those who have nothing?

hymn—a song of praise to God.

hypocrite—a person who pretends to love God.
    Mt 6:5 when you pray, do not be like the h
    Mt 7:5 you h, first take the plank out

hyssop—a plant used to sprinkle water or blood for religious cleansing.
    Ps 51:7 with h, and I will be clean

I

idol—a statue made by people and worshiped as if it had the power of a god; anything that takes the place of God in a person's life. Worshiping idols is called idolatry.
    1Co 8:4 We know that an i is nothing at all
    Col 3:5 evil desires and greed, which is i.

Immanuel—a name for Jesus meaning "God with us."
    Isa 7:14 birth to a son, and will call him I.
    Mt 1:23 and they will call him I"

immortal—free from death; not able to die.
    1Ti 1:17 Now to the King eternal, i

immortality—
    1Co 15:53 and the mortal with i.

imperishable—not able to die or to be destroyed.
    1Pe 1:23 not of perishable seed, but of i

impure—not pure; not clean.
    1Th 4:7 For God did not call us to be i

incense—1. spices burned to make a sweet-smelling smoke, as a way of worshiping God; 2. the sweet smell or the smoke of burning spices.
    Ps 141:2 my prayer be set before you like i
    Mt 2:11 him with gifts of gold and of i

incensed—very angry; filled with rage.

indignation—anger.

infirmity—physical weakness; disease.
    Isa 53:4 Surely he took up our i

inherit—to receive money, property or keepsakes from a person after his or her death.
    Mt 5:5 for they will i the earth.
    Mk 10:17 "what must I do to i eternal life?"

inheritance—money, property or keepsakes received from a person after his or her death.
    Dt 4:20 to be the people of his i
    1Pe 1:4 and into an i that can never perish

iniquity—sin; wickedness.
    Ps 51:2 Wash away all my i
    Ps 103:10 or repay us according to our i.
    Isa 53:6 the i of us all.
    Mic 7:19 and hurl all our i into the depths.

injustice—unfairness.

inscription—1. the writing on a coin; 2. a written title or message.

insolent—proud, in an insulting way.

institute—to establish; to begin.

insurrection—revolt or rebellion against a government.

integrity—complete honesty.

intercede—to beg or plead for another person.
Ro 8:26 but the Spirit himself *i* for us

intercession—
Isa 53:12 and made *i* for the transgressors.

intermarry—to marry someone from a different race or religion.
Dt 7:3 Do not *i* with them.

irrevocable—not able to be taken back or changed.

Isaac—the promised son of Abraham and Sarah (Ge 17:19; 21:1-7); offered as a sacrifice by Abraham (Ge 22); married Rebekah (Ge 24) and was the father of Esau and Jacob (Ge 25). Rebekah and Jacob plotted together to trick Isaac into blessing Jacob instead of Esau (Ge 27).

Isaiah—prophet called by God (Isa 6) to prophesy to Judah (Isa 1:1). Some of his prophesies are about the coming Messiah (Isa 53).

Ishmael—the son of Abraham and Hagar (Ge 16); he was not to be the son of the covenant (Ge 17:18-21). Sarah and Abraham sent both Hagar and Ishmael away from them (Ge 21:8-21).

Israel—1. the nation made up of descendants of the twelve sons of Jacob. Israel became a nation when God took his people out of Egypt (Ex 1-14); 2. the new name God gave to Jacob (Ge 32:28); 3. the northern ten tribes after they separated from Judah and Benjamin.
Dt 6:4 Hear, O *I;* The LORD our God
Eze 39:23 of *I* went into exile for their sin
Lk 22:30 judging the twelve tribes of *I.*
Eph 3:6 Gentiles are heirs together with *I*

Israelites—the people of Israel.
Ex 14:22 and the *I* went through the sea
Ro 9:27 the number of the *I* be like the sand

J

Jacob—the second son of Isaac and Rebekah; he was the twin brother of Esau (Ge 25:21-26). He bought Esau's birthright for a pot of stew (Ge 25:29-34) and later tricked Isaac into giving him the blessing that belonged to Esau (Ge 27:1-37). After running away from Esau, he wrestled with God, and his name was changed to Israel (Ge 32:22-32). He had twelve sons and all of them eventually went to Egypt during a famine (Ge 42-43). He settled in Egypt, but was buried by his son Joseph in Canaan, the promised land (Ge 46; 50).

James—1. one of the twelve apostles; the brother of John (Mt 4:21-22). He was present at the transfiguration (Mt 17:1-13); he was later killed by Herod (Ac 12:2); 2. one of the twelve apostles; the son of Alphaeus (Mt 10:3); 3. the brother of Jesus (Mk 6:30); he waited with the believers for the promised Holy Spirit after Christ's ascension (Ac 2:1-3); became a leader in the church in Jerusalem (Ac 12:17; 15; 21:18; Gal 2:9); author of the epistle of James (Jas 1:1).

Japheth—one of the sons of Noah (Ge 5:32);

he was blessed because he covered his father's nakedness (Ge 9:18-28).

jealous—1. afraid of losing someone's love or affection; 2. angry or unhappy because of what someone else has; 3. careful to guard or keep what one has.
Joel 2:18 the LORD will be *j* for his land
2Co 11:2 I am *j* for you with a godly jealousy

jealousy—
Gal 5:20 hatred, discord, *j,* fits of rage

Jeremiah—a prophet called by God (Jer 1) to prophesy to Judah (Jer 1:1-3). His life was in danger because of what he prophesied (Jer 11:18-23:26), and he was subsequently put in stocks (Jer 20:1-2), imprisoned (Jer 37), and thrown in a cistern (Jer 38). He was forced to flee to Egypt from the Babylonians (Jer 43). He is often referred to as the prophet of gloom, because he prophesied about the destruction of Judah.

Jeroboam—an official in Solomon's court; he rebelled and became the first king of Israel (the northern ten tribes) (1Ki 11:26-40; 12:1-20).

Jerusalem—the political and religious center of Judah.
2Ki 23:27 and I will reject *J,* the city I chose
Ne 2:17 Come, let us rebuild the wall of *J*
Ps 137:5 If I forget you, O *J*
Jn 4:20 where we must worship is in *J.*"
Rev 21:2 I saw the Holy City, the new *J*

Jeshua—see Joshua (2).

Jew—an Israelite; one of the chosen people of God; a descendant of Abraham through Jacob.
Mt 2:2 who has been born king of the *J* ?
Ro 3:29 Is God the God of *J* only?
Gal 3:28 There is neither *J* nor Greek

Jezebel—the Sidonian wife of King Ahab (1Ki 16:31). She promoted Baal worship in Israel (1Ki 16:32-33); had many prophets of God killed (1Ki 18:4,13); and opposed the prophet Elijah (1Ki 18:1-2). Elijah prophesied her death (1Ki 21:17-24).

Joash—the boy-king of Judah; he repaired the temple (2Ki 12).

Job—a wealthy man from the land of Uz who feared God (Job 1:1-5). His righteousness was tested by disaster (Job 1:6-22) and personal affliction (Job 2), but, in the end, God restored wealth and honor to him (Job 42).

John—1. John the Baptist (Mk 1:2-8); the son of Zechariah and Elizabeth (Lk 1). He preached in the desert, preparing the people for Jesus (Mt 3:11-12); baptized Jesus in the Jordan River (Mt 3:13-17); was arrested (Mk 1:14) and executed by Herod (Mk 6:14-29); 2. one of the twelve apostles; brother of the apostle James (Lk 5:1-10). He was present at Jesus' transfiguration (Lk 9:28-36); became one of the leaders of the church at Jerusalem (Ac 4:1-3); wrote the Gospel of John, the letters of John (2Jn 1; 3Jn 1) and the book of Revelation (Rev 1:1; 22:8).

John, Mark (see Mark, John).

Jonah—a prophet in the days of Jeroboam II of Israel (2Ki 14:25). He was called to preach

to Nineveh but instead fled to Tarshish (Jnh
1:1-3). While at sea a great storm arose because
of his disobedience; he was thrown into the sea
and was swallowed by a large fish (Jnh 1:4-17).
He then repented and went to Nineveh and
preached, telling the people to repent (Jnh 3).

Jonathan—a son of King Saul (1Sa 13:16). He
had a special friendship with David (1Sa 18:1-
4); 19-20; 23:16-18). When he was killed (1Sa
31) David mourned greatly for him (2Sa 1).

Jordan—a river in Palestine that flows between the Sea of Galilee and the Dead Sea.
> Jos 4:22 Israel crossed the *J* on dry ground."
> Mt 3:6 baptized by him in the *J* River.

Joseph—1. the son of Jacob and Rachel (Ge
30:24). He was favored by his father, but hated
by his brothers (Ge 37:3-4). He was sold into
slavery by his brothers (Ge 37:12-36), taken to
Egypt and there served Potiphar until put in
prison on a false charge (Ge 39). While in prison
he interpreted the dreams of Pharaoh's servants (Ge 40), and then interpreted Pharaoh's
dreams (Ge 41:4-40). For this, he was given a
high position under Pharaoh (Ge 41:41-57).
During a famine his brothers came to Egypt to
buy grain, and so Joseph was reunited with his
aged father and with his brothers (Ge 42-47);
2. the husband of Mary and childhood father
of Jesus (Mt 1:16-24; 2:13-19); 3. a disciple of
Jesus from Arimathea; he gave his tomb for
Jesus' burial (Mt 27:57-61); 4. the original
name of Barnabas (Ac 4:36).

Joshua—1. the son of Nun (Nu 13:8); Moses'
aide on Mount Sinai, when God revealed how
Israel was to live as his chosen people (Ex
24:13); spied out the land of Canaan (Nu 13);
and he and Caleb, though members of the generation of Israelites who had showed a lack of
faith forty years earlier, were allowed to enter
the promised land (Nu 14:6,30). As the successor of Moses (Dt 31:1-18), he led the Israelites
across the Jordan River into Canaan (Jos 3-4);
was the commander in the conquest of Jericho
(Jos 6), Ai (Jos 7-8), and a large part of Canaan
(Jos 10-12); oversaw the dividing up of the
promised land among the twelve tribes of Israel
(Jos 13-22); 2. the high priest in Israel during
the rebuilding of both the temple (Hag 1-2) and
the altar (Ezr 3:2,8); also called Jeshua.

Judah—1. Jacob's fourth son; 2. the tribe of
Israel whose members were descendants of Judah; 3. a name for the southern kingdom after
Judah and Benjamin separated from the northern ten tribes.
> Ge 29:35 So she named him *J.*
> Jer 13:19 All *J* will be carried into exile,
> Zec 10:4 From *J* will come the cornerstone

Judaism—the teachings of the Jewish religion.

Judas—1. one of the twelve apostles (Lk 6:16;
Ac 1:13); was probably also called Thaddaeus
(Mt 10:3); 2. one of the brothers of Jesus (Mt
13:55); author of the last letter in the New Testament (Jude 1); 3. one of the twelve apostles,
also called Iscariot; he betrayed Jesus (Mk 3:19;
14:10-50) and then hung himself (Mt 27:3-5).

judge—to decide if something is good or bad;
to condemn.
> Ps 9:8 He will *j* the world in righteousness
> Mt 7:1 Do not *j*, or you too will be judged.
> 2Ti 4:1 who will *j* the living and the dead.

judgment—1. a decision or opinion; 2. a decision of guilt or innocence made by a judge in
a court of law; punishment decided on by a
court; 3. a decision from God, especially the final judgment when God will reward those who
believe in him and condemn all others to hell.
> Dt 1:17 of any man, for *j* belongs to God.
> Ps 119:66 Teach me knowledge and good *j*
> Isa 66:16 the Lord will execute *j*
> Mt 5:21 who murders will be subject to *j.*
> Mt 12:36 have to give account on the day of *j*
> Jn 5:22 but has entrusted all *j* to the Son
> Ro 14:10 stand before God's *j* seat.
> 2Co 5:10 appear before the *j* seat of Christ

jurisdiction—one's power and right to rule.

justice—fairness.
> Isa 30:18 For the LORD is a God of *j.*
> Isa 61:8 "For I, the LORD, love *j*
> Zec 7:9 'Administer true *j;* show mercy
> Lk 11:42 you neglect *j* and the love of God.

justification—God's action in treating us as if
we had never sinned.
> Ro 4:25 and was raised to life for our *j.*
> Ro 5:18 of righteousness was *j* that brings

justify—to erase someone's sins; to declare
righteous.
> Ac 13:39 him everyone who believes is *j*
> Ro 3:24 and are *j* freely by his grace
> Ro 5:1 since we have been *j* through faith
> Gal 3:24 to Christ that we might be *j* by faith

KL

kingdom—
> Ex 19:6 you will be for me a *k* of priests
> Mt 6:33 But seek first his *k* and his
> Mt 16:19 the keys of the *k* of heaven
> Jn 18:36 "My *k* is not of this world.
> 1Co 15:24 hand over the *k* to God the Father
> Rev 11:15 of the world has become the *k*

kingdom of heaven (also called, kingdom of
God)—God's rule in the lives of his chosen people and in his creation. Anyone who is born
again by believing in Jesus enters this kingdom.
> Mt 3:2 "Repent, for the *k* of heaven is near,"
> Mt 5:3 for theirs is the *k* of heaven.

kinsman-redeemer—a close male relative
who had the right to marry a widow and buy
("redeem") her husband's property.
> Ruth 3:9 over me, since you are a *k.*"

Laban—the brother of Rebekah (Ge 24:29-51)
and father of Rachel and Leah (Ge 29-31).

lamb—
> Isa 53:7 he was led like a *l* to the slaughter
> 1Co 5:7 our Passover *l*, has been sacrificed.
> Rev 5:6 Then I saw a *L*, looking

Lamb of God—a name for Jesus that reminds

us that he is like the lambs offered for sacrifice in the Old Testament.

Jn 1:29 *L* of God, who takes away the sin

lament—a cry of grief. (Also, lamentation)

law—1. God's rules, which help his people know what is right and wrong. The Ten Commandments are part of God's law; 2. Law, the first five books of the Bible, written by Moses.

Ne 8:8 from the Book of the *L* of God
Ps 1:2 and on his *l* he meditates day
Ps 19:7 the *l* of the Lord is perfect
Ps 119:97 Oh, how I love your *l* !
Mt 22:40 All the *L* and the Prophets hang
Ro 8:3 For what the *l* was powerless to do
Ro 13:10 love is the fulfillment of the *l*
Gal 3:24 So the *l* was put in charge to lead us

Lazarus—1. the poor man in one of Jesus' parables (Lk 16:19-31); 2. the brother of Mary and Martha; Jesus raised him from the dead (Jn 11:1-12:19).

Leah—the wife of Jacob; she had six sons and one daughter (Ge 29:16-30:21).

legion—1. a group of 6,000 soldiers in the Roman army; 2. any very large group of people or things.

leprosy—a word used in the Bible for many different skin diseases and infections.

Levite—a member of the tribe of Levi. The Levites took care of the temple. Only Levites could become priests, but not all Levites were priests.

Nu 1:53 The *L* are to be responsible

lewd—indecent; wicked.

life—
physical life
Ge 2:7 into his nostrils the breath of *l*
Ps 23:6 all the days of my *l*
Jer 10:23 that a man's *l* is not his own
Mk 10:45 to give his *l* as a ransom for many."
Jn 15:13 lay down his *l* for his friends.
Eph 4:1 I urge you to live a *l* worthy
Col 1:10 order that you may live a *l* worthy
spiritual life
Mt 6:25 Is not *l* more important than food
Mt 10:39 Whoever finds his *l* will lose it
Jn 1:4 In him was *l*, and that *l* was
Jn 3:15 believes in him may have eternal *l*.
Jn 3:36 believes in the Son has eternal *l*
Jn 11:25 "I am the resurrection and the *l*.
Jn 14:6 am the way and the truth and the *l*.
Jn 20:31 that by believing you may have *l*
Ro 6:13 have been brought from death to *l*
Ro 6:23 but the gift of God is eternal *l*
1Jn 3:14 we have passed from death to *l*

light—
Ge 1:3 "Let there be *l*," and there was *l*
2Sa 22:29 Lord turns my darkness into *l*.
Ps 27:1 Lord is my *l* and my salvation
Ps 119:105 and a *l* for my path.
Isa 9:2 have seen a great *l*
Mt 5:16 let your *l* shine before men
Jn 8:12 he said, "I am the *l* of the world.
2Co 4:6 made his *l* shine in our hearts
1Jn 1:5 God is *l;* in him there is no

live—

Ex 20:12 so that you may *l* long
Ro 1:17 "The righteous will *l* by faith."
2Co 5:7 We *l* by faith, not by sight.
Php 1:21 to *l* is Christ and to die is gain.

locusts—a type of grasshopper. When they would settle in a grain field, orchard or other cultivated area in Bible times, they could devastate the crop.

Lord—
Mt 3:3 'Prepare the way for the *L*
Mt 22:37 " 'Love the *L* your God
Lk 2:9 glory of the *L* shone around them
Ac 16:31 replied, "Believe in the *L* Jesus
Ro 10:13 on the name of the *L* will be saved
Php 2:11 confess that Jesus Christ is *L*
Heb 13:6 *L* is my helper
2Pe 1:16 and coming of our *L* Jesus Christ
Rev 17:14 he is *L* of lords and King of kings
Rev 22:20 Come, *L* Jesus

Lord (Yahweh)—
Ge 2:4 When the *L* God made the earth
Ex 20:2 "I am the *L* your God, who
Ps 23:1 The *L* is my shepherd, I shall lack
Ps 103:1 Praise the *L*, O my soul
Pr 1:7 The fear of the *L* is the beginning
Isa 6:3 Holy, holy, holy is the *L* Almighty
Isa 55:6 Seek the *L* while he may be found

Lot—the nephew of Abraham (Ge 12:5). He chose to live in Sodom (Ge 13). At one point Abraham rescued him from four kings (Ge 14), and later he pleaded with God for Lot's life when God was about to destroy Sodom (Ge 19:1-29).

lot—one of the ways used in Bible times to find out God's will about a matter. It is something like drawing straws.

Mt 27:35 divided up his clothes by casting *l*.
Ac 1:26 Then they drew *l*, and the *l* fell

love (*v.*; *n.*)—
Ex 20:6 showing *l* to thousands who *l* me
Ps 23:6 Surely goodness and *l* will follow
Ps 136:1-26 His *l* endures forever.
Isa 61:8 "For I, the Lord, *l* justice
Mt 3:17 "This is my Son, whom I *l*
Mt 5:44 *L* your enemies and pray
Mt 19:19 and '*l* your neighbor as yourself.' "
Jn 13:34 I give you: *L* one another.
Jn 15:13 Greater *l* has no one than this
Ro 13:10 Therefore *l* is the fulfillment
Gal 5:22 But the fruit of the Spirit is *l*, joy
Eph 1:4 in *l* he predestined us
1Jn 3:10 anyone who does not *l* his brother
1Jn 3:16 This is how we know what *l* is
1Jn 4:7 for *l* comes from God.
1Jn 4:10 This is *l;* not that we loved God
1Jn 4:16 God is *l*.

Luke—a co-worker with Paul; he wrote the books of Luke and Acts (Col 4:14).

lust—a strong desire for something wrong.
Pr 6:25 Do not *l* in your heart
Ro 1:26 God gave them over to shameful *l*.

lute—a stringed musical instrument, with a pear-shaped body and neck. It is played in the same way as a guitar.

lyre—a small lap harp with three to twelve strings.

m

Magi—men of Arabia and Persia who studied the stars. People thought they had the power to tell the meaning of dreams.

Mt 2:1 *M* from the east came to Jerusalem

maimed—crippled; having lost a part of one's body, such as an arm or leg.

majestic—great and powerful.

Ex 15:6 was *m* in power.
Ps 8:1 how *m* is your name in all the earth!
Ps 111:3 Glorious and *m* are his deeds

malice—hatred; wishing harm on someone else.

manger—a feedbox for cows or other animals.

Lk 2:7 in strips of cloth and lying in a *m*."

manna—the special food God gave daily to the Israelites until they reached the promised land.

Ex 16:31 people of Israel called the bread *m*.
Jn 6:49 Your forefathers ate the *m*

Mark, John—the cousin of Barnabas (Col 4:10); a helper to Paul and Barnabas (Ac 13:5); later a co-worker with Barnabas (Ac 15:39) and then Paul (Phm 24); author of the second Gospel, according to early church tradition.

marriage—

Mt 22:30 neither marry nor be given in *m*
Ro 7:2 she is released from the law of *m*.
Heb 13:4 by all, and the *m* bed kept pure

Martha—the sister of Mary and Lazarus, the man whom Jesus raised from the dead (Jn 11; 12:2).

martyr—a person who suffers greatly or dies for what he or she believes in.

marvel—to be surprised; to be filled with wonder.

Mary—1. the mother of Jesus (Mt 1:16-25; Mk 3:31; Jn 19:25-27; Ac 1:14); 2. Mary Magdalene—a woman whom Jesus freed from demons (Lk 8:2); became a supporter of Jesus' ministry (Lk 8:1-3); was present at the cross (Mk 15:40); and was one of the women who came on Easter morning to the tomb (Mt 27:61), where she saw the angel (Lk 24:1-12) and the resurrected Jesus (Jn 20:1-18); 3. the sister of Martha and Lazarus, the man whom Jesus raised from the dead (Jn 11); she washed Jesus' feet with expensive perfume (Jn 12:1-8).

Matthew—a tax collector who became one of the twelve apostles (Mt 9:9-13); also called Levi (Mk 2:14-17).

mediator—one who makes peace between two people or two groups who are displeased and/or angry with each other. Jesus is the mediator between us and God.

1Ti 2:5 and one *m* between God and men
Heb 9:15 For this reason Christ is the *m*

meditate—to think seriously and carefully.

Ps 1:2 and on his law he *m* day and night.
Ps 119:15 I *m* on your precepts

medium—a person who can supposedly talk with the spirits of people who have died.

meek—patient; mild; gentle.

Mt 5:5 Blessed are the *m*

mercy—kindness and forgiveness, especially when given to a person who doesn't deserve it.

Mic 6:8 To act justly and to love *m*
Ro 9:15 "I will have *m* on whom I have *m*
1Pe 1:3 In his great *m* he has given us new

Messiah—the "Anointed One"; Christ; the one the Jews expected to come and be their king.

Jn 1:41 "We have found the *M*" (that is

Methuselah—a man in early Bible times who lived 969 years (Ge 5:27).

midwife—a woman who helped with the birth of a baby.

millstone—one of a pair of stones used to crush grain for flour.

Lk 17:2 sea with a *m* tied around his neck

minister—(*v.*) to serve; to give care or attention to; (*n.*) one who serves; one who gives care or attention to.

1Sa 3:1 The boy Samuel *m*
2Co 3:6 as *m* of a new covenant
1Ti 4:6 you will be a good *m*

miracle—an unusual happening, one that goes against the normal laws of nature. Miracles are done by the power of God.

Ps 77:14 You are the God who performs *m*
Jn 14:11 the evidence of the *m* themselves.
Ac 2:22 accredited by God to you by *m*
Heb 2:4 it by signs, wonders and various *m*

Miriam—the sister of Moses and Aaron (Nu 26:59); led the Israelites in praising God in dance and song after he had parted the waters of the Red Sea (Ex 15:20-21); later temporarily struck with leprosy because she criticized Moses (Nu 12).

money—

Ecc 5:10 Whoever loves *m* never has *m*
Mt 6:24 You cannot serve both God and *M*.
1Co 16:2 set aside a sum of *m* in keeping
1Ti 6:10 For the love of *m* is a root

mortal—human; able to die.

1Co 15:53 and the *m* with immortality.

Moses—the leader of Israel from the flight out of Egypt to their arrival outside the promised land. As a baby, his mother and sister placed him in a basket in the Nile River to save his life; he was discovered by Pharaoh's daughter (Ex 2:1-10), who raised him at the royal court. After killing an Egyptian he fled to Midian (Ex 2:11-15), where he was called by the Lord to deliver Israel (Ex 3-4). Pharaoh refused to listen to God's warnings (Ex 5), and God punished him and his people with ten plagues (Ex 7-11). Moses instructed the people in their initial observance of the Passover and led them in the exodus out of Egypt, culminating in their passing through the Red Sea (Ex 12-14). He received the law of God at Sinai (Ex 19-23) and gave it to the people of Israel. He supervised the building of the tabernacle (Ex 36-40), set apart Aaron and priests to lead the Israelites in worshiping God (Ex 8-9), and, under his supervision, twelve spies were sent into Canaan (Nu 13). When ten of the spies returned with a pessimistic report, the Israelites believed this account, thereby showing a lack of faith in God. God in turn punished them with forty years of wandering outside the promised land (Nu 14). Moses was allowed to view the land of Canaan from the top of Mount Nebo, but died without entering it (Nu 20:1-13; Dt 34:5-12).

muster—to gather together, especially to gather soldiers for war.

mute—unable to speak.

myrrh—the sweet-smelling sap of the myrrh bush. It was used to make the sacred anointing oil.

Mt 2:11 of gold and of incense and of *m*.

n

Naomi—the mother-in-law of Ruth (Ru 1); she advised Ruth to seek marriage with Boaz (Ru 2-4).

nard—a pleasant-smelling oil from the spikenard, a plant that grew in India. Since this oil had to be brought from India to Israel, it was very expensive.

Nathanael—one of the twelve apostles (Jn 1:45-49); was probably also called Bartholomew (Mt 10:3).

Nazarene—1. a person who lived in or came from the town of Nazareth in Galilee. 2. a member of an early sect of Jewish converts to Christianity who retained the Mosaic ritual.

Mk 16:6 looking for Jesus the *N*

Nazirite—a person who separated himself or herself by taking a vow to do special work for God. This included a promise not to cut one's hair and not to drink wine.

Jdg 13:5 because the boy is to be a *N*

Nehemiah—the Jewish "cupbearer" of King Artaxerxes of Persia (Ne 2:1); a trusted and highly placed official in the court of Artaxerxes; temporarily appointed governor of Judah; while in Jerusalem rebuilt the walls of the city (Ne 2-6) and with Ezra reestablished the worship of God there after the Babylonian exile (Ne 8).

Nicodemus—a Pharisee who visited Jesus at night (Jn 3) and learned about being born again. With Joseph of Arimathea, he prepared Jesus' body for burial (Jn 19:38-42).

Noah—"a righteous man" in early Bible times; he built an ark, as God commanded him (Ge 6-8). God made a covenant with him never again to cover the entire earth with a flood (Ge 9).

nullify—to make of no value; to make unimportant.

o

oath—a promise in which one asks God to witness that something is true.

obey—to do as asked; to yield to some- one's commands or wishes.

Dt 6:3 careful to *o* so that it may go well

Dt 13:4 Keep his commands and *o* him
1Sa 15:22 To *o* is better than sacrifice
Jn 14:23 loves me, he will *o* my teaching.
Ac 5:29 "We must *o* God rather than men!
Eph 6:1 *o* your parents in the Lord

offend—to make someone angry by what you do.

offering—1. something given to God as an act of worship; 2. the killing of an animal to make the relationship between God and man right again. In the Old Testament, animals and grains were regularly used as offerings, in an attempt to bring the people closer to God.

Ge 22:8 provide the lamb for the burnt *o*
Isa 53:10 the LORD makes his life a guilt *o*
Mk 12:33 is more important than all burnt *o*
Eph 5:2 as a fragrant *o* and sacrifice to God.

offshoot—a branch off the main stem of a tree or plant.

offspring—children.

Ge 3:15 and between your *o* and hers
Ge 12:7 "To your *o* I will give this land."

omen—an event or sign believed to foretell the future.

oppress—to control people unfairly and cruelly by the use of one's power.

Isa 53:7 He was *o* and afflicted
Zec 7:10 Do not *o* the widow

oracle—1. a saying or answer; 2. the word of the Lord.

ordain—1. to set apart for a specific office or duty; 2. to order or command.

ordinance—1. an official law; 2. a law made or commanded by God.

overseer—a person who watches over and takes care of others. *Overseer* was one of the terms used for leaders in the early church.

Ac 20:28 the Holy Spirit has made you *o*.
1Ti 3:2 Now the *o* must be above reproach

p

pagan—a person who does not worship God, especially someone who worships idols.

1Pe 2:12 such good lives among the *p* that

papyrus—1. a large water plant, similar to the reed, that grows in marshes and lakes. Moses' mother put him in a basket made from papyrus (Ex 2:3); 2. a paper made from this plant.

parable—a story that tells a special lesson or truth. Jesus told many parables.

paradise—a perfect place; heaven.

Lk 23:43 today you will be with me in *p*."

paralytic—a person who is unable to move certain parts of his or her body.

Mk 2:3 bringing to him a *p*, carried by four

parents—

Pr 17:6 and *p* are the pride of their children.
Eph 6:1 Children, obey your *p* in the Lord
Col 3:20 obey your *p* in everything

Passover—an annual Jewish holiday that yet today reminds the Jewish people of how God freed them from slavery in Egypt. At the Passover feast, the Jews eat bread made without yeast (unleavened bread), bitter herbs and lamb. With the unleavened bread they remember that they left Egypt hastily. There was no time to wait for yeast bread to rise. Bitter herbs remind them of their suffering in Egypt. The lamb reminds them of the lamb they killed at the first Passover and how they put its blood on their doorframes. The Lord "passed over" the homes so marked, but he killed all the other firstborn in Egypt.

Ex 12:11 Eat it in haste; it is the LORD's *P*.

Passover Lamb—the lamb killed on the Passover as a sacrifice. Jesus is our Passover Lamb. He was sacrificed for our deliverance from sin, in the same way a lamb was sacrificed to show deliverance from Egypt.

1Co 5:7 our *P* lamb, has been sacrificed.

patience—
Gal 5:22 joy, peace, *p*, kindness, goodness

patient—able to put up with problems or pain without complaining or becoming angry.
Ro 12:12 Be joyful in hope, *p* in affliction
1Co 13:4 Love is *p*, love is kind.

patriarch—the father and ruler of a family; the head of a tribe.

Paul—a Pharisee from Tarsus (Ac 9:11); named Saul at birth (Ac 13:9). Jesus appeared to him on the road to Damascus, and in this way God turned one of the fiercest persecutors of the Christian church into one of its mightiest servants (Ac 9:4-9; 26:12-18). Paul became an apostle (Gal 1), and preached the Good News to the Gentiles. His first missionary journey was to Cyprus and Galatia (Ac 13-14); his second journey, with Silas, took him to Macedonia (Ac 16:6-10). After his return to Jerusalem, he was arrested (Ac 21), but continued to preach (Ac 23:1-11). He was then transferred to Caesarea (Ac 23:12-35), where he was tried before Felix (Ac 24). After being imprisoned for two years Paul was tried further, first before Festus and then before King Agrippa (Ac 25; 26). Despite shipwreck on the voyage to Rome (Ac 27), he arrived safely and was put under house arrest (Ac 28). It seems evident from Paul's writings that he was released from this first Roman imprisonment and that he ministered further to the growing Christian church. He died, perhaps beheaded, in Rome. Paul's writings make up a significant portion of the New Testament, and range from intricate theology to passionate letters to struggling churches.

peace—freedom from disturbance; calm.
Isa 9:6 Everlasting Father, Prince of *P*
Lk 2:14 on earth *p* to men on whom his
Jn 14:27 *P* I leave with you; my *p*
Ro 5:1 we have *p* with God
Gal 5:22 joy, *p*, patience, kindness
1Pe 3:11 he must seek *p* and pursue it.

Pentecost—a Jewish feast celebrated fifty days after the Passover. Today the Christian church celebrates Pentecost because it was the day the Holy Spirit came to dwell with Christ's followers.
Ac 2:1-4

people—
Jer 24:7 They will be my *p*
Ac 15:14 from the Gentiles a *p*
2Co 6:16 and they will be my *p*."
1Pe 2:9 you are a chosen *p*

perishable—able to spoil; able to be destroyed.
1Co 15:42 the body that is sown is *p*

perjurer—a person who lies under oath.

persecute—to continually treat someone cruelly and unfairly, even though that person has done nothing wrong. The early Christians were persecuted for believing in Jesus as the Son of God.
Jn 15:20 they *p* me, they will *p* you
Ro 12:14 Bless those who *p* you; bless

persecution—
Ro 8:35 or hardship or *p* or famine

perseverance—
Ro 5:3 we know that suffering produces *p*
Ro 5:4 *p*, character; and character, hope.
Heb 12:1 run with *p* the race marked out

persevere—to refuse to give up; to keep on trying; to continue in one's actions or beliefs in spite of problems.
Heb 10:36 You need to *p* so that

pervert—to use wrongly; to turn from what is right.

pestilence—a plague; a disease that spreads quickly and kills many people.

Peter—one of the twelve apostles; the brother of Andrew, also called Simon (Lk 6:14) and Cephas (Jn 1:42). Although Jesus predicted that Peter would deny him (Mk 14:27-31), and though he did deny Jesus three times (Mk 14:66-72), after his resurrection Jesus commissioned Peter to shepherd his flock (Jn 21:15-23). At Pentecost he becomes bold and preaches a sermon (Ac 2), and he continues to heal (Ac 3:1-10) and preach (Ac 3:11-26), even though challenged by the Sanhedrin (Ac 4:1-22). Later God speaks to him in a vision and Peter goes to the Gentile Cornelius to tell him about Jesus (Ac 10).

Pharisees—a group of Jews who obeyed very strictly both God's laws and all their own rules about God's laws.
Mt 5:20 surpasses that of the *P*

Philip—1. one of the twelve apostles (Mt 10:3); 2. a deacon (Ac 6:1-7) and evangelist in Samaria; he witnessed to an Ethiopian (Ac 8:4-40).

phylactery—a small leather box containing verses from the Old Testament; male Jews wore these boxes on their foreheads and left arms when they prayed.
Mt 23:5 They make their *p* wide

piety—love and reverence for God; devotion to God.

Pilate—the governor of Judea who questioned Jesus (Lk 22:66-23:25) and then sent him to Herod (Lk 23:6-12). Pilate finally consented to Jesus' crucifixion when the crowds chose Barabbas rather than Jesus to be released (Lk 23:13-25).

plague—1. a disease that kills many people, such as the plague of boils; 2. an event that causes much suffering or loss, especially a trouble in which there is a great number of offending agents, such as the plague of locusts.

plowshare—the pointed part of the plow; it cuts into the soil to make rows.

Isa 2:4 They will beat their swords into p

plunder—1. (v.) to loot or rob during a war; 2. (n.) property taken by plundering.

pomegranate—a reddish fruit about the size of an orange. It has many seeds and a juicy pulp.

poor—
Dt 15:4 there should be no p among you
Ps 82:3 maintain the rights of the p
Pr 14:31 oppresses the p shows contempt
Isa 61:1 me to preach good news to the p.
Mt 5:3 "Blessed are the p in spirit
Mt 26:11 the p you will always have
1Co 13:3 If I give all I possess to the p
2Co 8:9 yet for your sakes he became p

praise—(v.) to glorify; to say good things about someone or something; (n.) approval; worship.
Ex 15:2 He is my God, and I will p him
Ps 119:175 Let me live that I may p you
Eph 1:12 might be for the p of his glory

pray—
2Ch 7:14 will humble themselves and p
Mt 6:5 "But when you p, do not be like
Ro 8:26 do not know what we ought to p.
1Th 5:16,17 Be joyful always; p continually

precept—command; law; rule.
Ps 19:8 the p of the LORD are right
Ps 119:69 I keep your p with all my heart.

predestine—to decide or decree ahead of time.
Ro 8:30 And those he p, he also called
Eph 1:5 In love he p us to be adopted

prevail—to triumph or succeed.

pride—
Pr 8:13 I hate p and arrogance
Pr 16:18 P goes before destruction
Gal 6:4 Then he can take p in himself

priest—a Levite who offered sacrifices and prayers to God for the people.
Heb 4:14 have a great high p who has gone
Heb 7:26 Such a high p meets our need

proclaim—to announce or declare.
1Ch 16:23 p his salvation day after day
Ps 19:1 the skies p the work of his hands.
1Co 11:26 you p the Lord's death

profane—to make a holy thing impure by treating it with disrespect or irreverence.
Lev 22:32 Do no p my holy name.

prone—naturally inclined; having a tendency toward or liking for.

prophecy—a message from God that a prophet brings to the people.
1Co 13:8 where there are p, they will cease
2Pe 1:20 you must understand that no p

prophesy—to give the message of God to the people.
Joel 2:28 Your sons and daughters will p
1Co 14:39 my brothers, be eager to p

prophet—a person who receives messages from God to tell to his people. A prophet is called by God to speak for him.
Dt 18:18 up for them a p like you
Lk 24:25 believe all that the p have spoken!
Ac 10:43 All the p testify about him that
2Pe 1:19 word of the p made more certain

prostitute—a person who lets someone use his or her body for sexual relations, in exchange for money.
Lk 15:30 property with p comes home
1Co 6:9 male p nor homosexual offenders

prostrate—lying facedown on the ground.

provoke—to make angry; to cause trouble.

psalm—poetry written to praise God.
Eph 5:19 Speak to one another with p

purify—to make pure or clean.
1Jn 1:7 of Jesus, his Son, p us from all sin.
1Jn 1:9 and p us from all unrighteousness

Purim—an annual Jewish holiday for celebrating Queen Esther's rescue of the Jews when Haman plotted to destroy them.

R

Rachel—the daughter of Laban (Ge 29:16); she became Jacob's wife (Ge 29:28) and bore him two sons, Joseph and Benjamin (Ge 30:22-24; 35:16-24).

ransom—the price paid to get back a person who is held as a slave. Because we were slaves of sin, a ransom had to be paid for us. That ransom was the death of a sinless person. Jesus, the perfect one, paid our ransom when he died on the cross for us.
Mt 20:28 and to give his life as a r for many."
Heb 9:15 as a r to set them free

reap—1. to cut down grain at harvest time; to gather a crop together; 2. to get as a result or reward.
Gal 6:7 A man r what he sows.

Rebekah—the sister of Laban and Isaac's wife (Ge 24); the mother of Esau and Jacob (Ge 25:19-26). With her encouragement Jacob tricked his father into giving him the blessing that belonged to Esau (Ge 27:1-17).

rebel—1. (v.) to disobey and turn against those in authority; 2. (n.) a person who disobeys and flaunts authority.

rebuke—to scold sharply.
2Ti 4:2 correct, r and encourage
Rev 3:19 Those whom I love I r

recompense—to pay or repay; to make up for.

reconcile—to return to friendship after a quarrel.
Mt 5:24 First go and be r to your brother
Ro 5:10 we were r to him through death

reconciliation—
Ro 5:11 whom we have now received r.
2Co 5:18 and gave us the ministry of r
2Co 5:19 committed to us the message of r

redeem—1. to free from evil by paying a price (Gal 3:13); 2. to buy back.
> Ex 6:6 slaves to them and will *r* you
> Gal 3:13 Christ *r* us from the curse

redemption—the act of being bought back.
> Eph 1:7 In him we have *r* through his blood
> Col 1:14 in whom we have *r*, the forgiveness

Rehoboam—the son of Solomon; he became king after his father's death (1Ki 11:43). Because of his harsh treatment of the people, Israel was divided into two kingdoms (1Ki 12:1-24; 14:21-31).

rejoice—to express joy or gladness.
> Ps 118:24 let us *r* and be glad in it.
> Lk 1:47 and my spirit *r* in God my Savior
> Php 4:4 *R* in the Lord always.

repent—to turn away from sin; to be sorry for what you have done and to promise not to do it again.
> Mt 4:17 "*R*, for the kingdom of heaven is
> Lk 13:3 unless you *r*, you too will all perish.
> Ac 2:38 Peter replied, "*R* and be baptized,

repentance—
> Lk 3:8 Produce fruit in keeping with *r*.
> 2Co 7:10 Godly sorrow brings *r* that leads

reproach—1. (*v*.) to blame or accuse; 2. (*n*.) something for which one can be blamed or criticized; blame, criticism.

restore—to bring back; to return something to its former condition.
> Ps 23:3 he *r* my soul.
> Ps 51:12 *R* to me the joy of your salvation

resurrection—the act of coming back to life after being dead.
> Jn 11:25 Jesus said to her, "I am the *r*
> Ro 1:4 Son of God by his *r* from the dead
> 1Co 15:12 some of you say that there is no *r*

retribution—punishment for doing wrong.
> Jer 51:56 For the LORD is a God of *r*

revelation—the act of making known or telling about.
> Gal 1:12 I received it by *r* from Jesus Christ.
> Rev 1:1 *r* of Jesus Christ, which God gave

revenge—to hurt or punish a person who has wronged you; to get back at someone who has hurt you.
> Lev 19:18 "Do not seek *r* or bear a grudge
> Ro 12:19 Do not take *r*, my friends

revere—to feel respect for.

reverence—a feeling of respect and honor.
> Ps 5:7 in *r* will I bow down
> Col 3:22 of heart and *r* for the Lord.

revile—to call someone a bad name; to scold in an insulting way.

reward (*v*.; *n*.)—
> Ps 127:3 children a *r* from him.
> Jer 17:10 to *r* a man according to his conduct
> Mt 5:12 because great is your *r* in heaven
> Mt 6:5 they have received their *r* in full.
> Rev 22:12 I am coming soon! My *r* is with me

righteous—without sin; doing what is right.
> Isa 64:6 and all our *r* acts are like filthy rags
> Mt 13:49 and separate the wicked from the *r*
> Ro 1:17 as it is written: "The *r* will live
> Ro 3:10 "There is no one *r*, not even one

> 1Jn 3:7 does what is right is *r*, just as he is *r*.

righteousness—
> Ge 15:6 and he credited it to him as *r*.
> Ps 23:3 He guides me in paths of *r*
> Mt 5:6 those who hunger and thirst for *r*
> Mt 6:33 But seek first his kingdom and his *r*
> Ro 4:3 and it was credited to him as *r*."
> 2Ti 3:16 correcting and training in *r*

Ruth—a Moabite widow who went with her mother-in-law Naomi to Bethlehem (Ru 1). There she gathered the gleanings from the field of Boaz (Ru 2), whom she later married (Ru 3-4:12). She was an ancestor of David (Ru 4:13-22) and of Jesus (Mt 1:5).

S

Sabbath—the seventh day of the week; the Jewish day of rest and worship. It extended from Friday sunset until Saturday sunset.
> Ex 20:8 "remember the *S* day

sackcloth—a rough cloth, usually woven from goats' hair. Clothing made of sackcloth was worn as a sign of mourning for the dead or as a sign that a person was sorry for his or her sins.

sacred—holy; set apart for God in a special way.

sacrifice—(*v*.) to offer as a sacrifice, (*n*.) an offering given to God for the sins of the people. In the Old Testament God commanded the people to pay for their sins by sacrificing cattle, lambs, goats, doves or pigeons. The animals were killed, their blood splattered against the altar and their bodies burned on the altar. People who were very poor could bring flour to be burned on the altar. These sacrifices were pictures of Jesus' coming as a once-for-all sacrifice for sinners.
> Ge 22:2 *S* him there as a burnt offering
> Ex 12:27 "It is the Passover *s* to the LORD
> 1Sa 15:22 To obey is better than *s*
> Ro 12:1 to offer your bodies as living *s*
> Heb 9:28 so Christ was *s* once
> 1Jn 2:2 He is the atoning *s* for our sins

Sadducees—a group of Jewish leaders, many of them priests, who accepted only the written law of God. They opposed the Pharisees, who had many additional laws that had been passed down to them by their religious teachers. Unlike the Pharisees, the Sadducees did not believe in a resurrection of the dead, but they agreed with the Pharisees in their hatred of Jesus.
> Mk 12:18 *S*, who say there is no resurrection

saints—Christians; people whom God has made holy. A saint can be either a Christian who is alive on earth or one who is already in heaven.
> Ro 8:27 intercedes for the *s* in accordance
> Eph 1:1 To the *s* in Ephesus,

salvation—deliverance from the guilt and power of sin. By his death and resurrection,

Jesus brings salvation to people who believe in him.

Ps 27:1 The LORD is my light and my *s*
Lk 2:30 For my eyes have seen your *s*
Ac 4:12 *S* is found in no one else,
2Co 7:10 brings repentance that leads to *s*
Php 2:12 to work out your *s* with fear
Heb 2:3 escape if we ignore such a great *s*?

Samaritan—a person of late Old Testament or New Testament times who lived in or came from Samaria. The Samaritans were only partly Jewish, and they worshiped God differently than Jews in Israel. Jews from Judea and Galilee hated the Samaritans. They would go out of their way to travel around Samaria (Lk 10:30-37).

Samson—an Israelite judge whose birth was foretold by an angel (Jdg 13). He married a Philistine woman (Jdg 14) and later took vengeance on the Philistines for forcing his wife to tell the answer to the riddle with which he had challenged them (Jdg 15). He was again betrayed by a woman, Delilah, but in the end became obedient to God and was used by God to punish the Philistines (Jdg 16).

Samuel—often called the last of Israel's judges and the first of her prophets (see also Heb 11:32). His birth was earnestly prayed for by his mother Hannah (1Sa 1:10-18), and when he was old enough she brought him to the temple and he was dedicated to the Lord (1Sa 1:21-28). There he was raised by Eli (1Sa 2:11; 18-26) and was called to be a prophet (1Sa 3). He anointed Saul as king (1Sa 9-10), but later announced God's rejection of Saul (1Sa 15). He anointed David as king (1Sa 16) and protected him from Saul (1Sa 19:18-24).

sanctify—to make holy. Our sanctification begins when we become Christians. It is continued by the ongoing work of the Holy Spirit in our hearts.

Ro 15:16 to God, *s* by the Holy Spirit.
1Th 5:23 *s* you through and through.
2Th 2:13 through the *s* work of the Spirit

sanctuary—a place where God is worshiped; a holy place.

Sanhedrin—the ruling council of the Jews in Jesus' time. It was made up of seventy men, and the leader was the high priest. Even though the Romans had conquered Palestine and a Roman governor ruled the country, the Jews were allowed to judge many of their own matters. The Sanhedrin could decide whether someone was innocent or guilty of breaking a Jewish law, but it could not put anyone to death without the permission of the Roman governor.

Mk 14:55 and the whole *S* were looking for evidence

Sarah—the wife of Abraham and mother of Isaac; first called Sarai (Ge 11:29-31). God promised her that, though she had been barren throughout her life, she would give birth to a son in her old age (Ge 17:15-21; 18:10-15).

Satan—the devil; the leader of the fallen spirits; the most powerful enemy of God and humans.

Mk 4:15 *S* comes and takes away the word

2Co 11:14 for *S* himself masquerades
Rev 12:9 serpent called the devil or *S*

Saul—1. the first king of Israel (1Sa 9-10). He was anointed by Samuel but was later rejected by God because he failed to destroy all of the Amalekites (1Sa 15). When David killed Goliath (1Sa 17), Saul attempted to kill him (1Sa 18; 19). Although pursued by Saul, David spared the king's life twice (1Sa 24; 26). Saul was wounded by the Philistines in battle and took his own life (1Sa 31). 2. See Paul.

Savior—a name for Jesus that means he saves his people from sin.

Isa 43:11 and apart from me there is no *s*.
Lk 1:47 and my spirit rejoices in God my *S*
1Ti 4:10 who is the *S* of all men
1Jn 4:14 Son to be the *S* of the world

scabbard—the case that a knife, dagger or sword is carried in.

scepter—a rod or stick held by a king or queen as a sign of royal power and authority.

scorpion—a spider-like animal with a poisonous stinger at the end of its tail.

scribe—a person with the important task of copying letters, books and legal papers.

Scripture—all or part of the Bible. When the Bible uses this word it means the Old Testament, since the New Testament had not yet been written. Today we call the Old and New Testaments the Bible or Scripture.

Jn 10:35 and the *S* cannot be broken
2Ti 3:16 All *S* is God-breathed
2Pe 1:20 that no prophecy of *S* came about

scroll—a book made of a long piece of leather or paper that was rolled around a stick at both ends.

Eze 3:1 eat what is before you, eat this *s*

seal—1. a tool with a design raised on it or cut into it; 2. the mark made by pressing this tool onto wax, paper or other soft material. A seal was used to close a letter or legal paper or to prove the authority of the paper.

2Co 1:22 set his *s* of ownership on us
Rev 5:2 "Who is worthy to break the *s*

sect—a group of people who hold one or more beliefs in common; especially, a small religious group that has separated from a larger group.

seer—a prophet; a person who, with God's help, can see what will happen in the future.

1Sa 9:9 of today used to be called a *s*.

self-control—the ability to control your own actions and feelings.

Gal 5:23 faithfulness, gentleness and *s*.
2Pe 1:6 and to knowledge, *s;* and to *s*

self-indulgence—doing whatever you feel like doing. Self-indulgence is the opposite of self-control.

sensual—appealing to the body's senses; caring too much for physical pleasures.

sexual immorality—using sex in ways God says are wrong.

1Co 6:13 body is not meant for *s* immorality
1Th 4:3 that you should avoid *s* immorality

shekel—a specific weight of silver, used as money.

Shem—one of the three sons of Noah (Ge 5:32). He, along with his brother Japheth, covered his father when he was naked (Ge 9:21-31). Abraham was one of his descendants (Ge 11:10-32).

shepherd—
Ps 23:1 LORD is my *s*, I shall lack nothing.
Jer 31:10 will watch over his flock like a *s*.'
Jn 10:11 The good *s* lays down his life
Ac 20:28 Be *s* of the church of God

sickle—a tool with a long, curved blade and a short handle, used for cutting grain.

signet—a ring with a design on it. The design was stamped in wax to seal a letter or legal paper. Signet rings were usually worn by people in authority.

Simon—1. see Peter; 2. one of the twelve apostles; also called the Zealot (Mt 10:4; Ac 1:13); 3. a sorcerer in Samaria who had great influence on the Samaritan people during the early days of the church; he was severely rebuked by Peter (Ac 8:9-24) for attempting to buy the power of the Holy Spirit.

sin—(*v.*) to break the law of God; (*n.*) the act of not doing what God wants.
Nu 32:23 be sure that your *s* will find you
1Ki 8:46 for there is no one who does not *s*
Ps 51:2 and cleanse me from my *s*.
Ps 119:11 that I might not *s* against you.
Jn 1:29 who takes away the *s* of the world!
Ro 3:23 for all have *s* and fall short
Ro 6:23 For the wages of *s* is death
2Co 5:21 God made him who had no *s* to be *s*
1Jn 3:6 No one who lives in him keeps on *s*

sinner—
Ps 1:1 or stand in the way of *s*
Ps 51:5 Surely I have been a *s* from birth
Mt 9:13 come to call the righteous, but *s*."
Lk 15:7 in heaven over one *s* who repents
Lk 18:13 'God, have mercy on me, a *s*.'
Ro 5:8 While we were still *s*, Christ died

sins—
Isa 1:18 "Though your *s* are like scarlet
Mt 1:21 he will save his people from their *s*."
Mt 18:15 "If your brother *s* against you
Lk 11:4 Forgive us our *s*
Ac 22:16 be baptized and wash your *s* away
Eph 2:1 dead in your transgressions and *s*
Heb 7:27 He sacrificed for their *s* once for all
1Pe 2:24 He himself bore our *s* in his body
1Jn 1:9 If we confess our *s*, he is faithful
Rev 1:5 has freed us from our *s* by his blood

slander—(*v.*) saying untrue things about another person in order to hurt him or her; (*n.*) false charges or misrepresentations about another person.
Lev 19:16 " 'Do not go about spreading *s*
Tit 3:2 to *s* no one, to be peaceable

Sodom and Gomorrah—the two cities destroyed by God because the people were so wicked.
Ge 19:24 rained down burning sulfur on S

Solomon—the son of David and Bathsheba (2Sa 12:24). He became king of Israel after David died (1Ki 1). He asked God for wisdom and was given it (1Ki 3), and he built the temple (1Ki 5-7) and dedicated it to God with prayer

(1Ki 8). His many foreign wives turned his heart away from God (1Ki 11:1-13). Jeroboam, one of his officials, rebelled against him (1Ki 11:26-40).

son—
Pr 10:1 A wise *s* brings joy to his father
Joel 2:28 Your *s* and daughters will prophesy
Jn 12:36 so that you may become *s* of light."
Ro 8:14 by the Spirit of God are *s* of God
1Jn 4:9 only S into the world that we might

Son of Man—a name for Jesus. Jesus used this name to show he was the Messiah prophesied about in Daniel 7:13.
Mt 20:18 and the S of Man will be betrayed
Mk 14:62 you will see the S of Man sitting
Lk 19:10 For the S of Man came to seek
Jn 3:14 so the S of Man must be lifted up

soothsayer—a person who could foretell the future.

sorcerer—a magician.

soul—the spiritual part of a person; the part of a person that does not die.
Dt 6:5 with all your *s* and with all your
Ps 23:3 he restores my *s*.
Mt 10:28 kill the body but cannot kill the *s*.
Mt 11:29 and you will find rest for your *s*.
Mt 16:26 yet forfeits his *s*? Or what can
Mt 22:37 with all your *s* and with all your

sovereign—having authority over everything.

sow—to plant seeds. In Jesus' time seeds were sown by scattering them by hand over the ground.
Job 4:8 and those who *s* trouble reap it
Gal 6:7 A man reaps what he *s*.

spirit—1. the part of a person that is not the body; the soul; 2. beings who do not have bodies; 3. another name for Holy Spirit.
1. spirit
Ps 31:5 Into your hands I commit my *s*
Eze 36:26 you a new heart and put a new *s*
Mt 5:3 saying: "Blessed are the poor in *s*
Mt 26:41 *s* is willing, but the body is weak."
2. spirit
1Jn 4:1 Dear friends, do not believe every *s*
3. Spirit
Ge 1:2 and the S of God was hovering
Ps 51:11 or take your Holy S from me.
Mt 1:18 to be with child through the Holy S.
Mt 3:11 will baptize you with the Holy S
Mt 3:16 he saw the S of God descending
Mt 28:19 and of the Son and of the Holy S
Jn 14:26 But the Counselor, the Holy S.
Jn 20:22 and said, "Receive the Holy S.
Ac 1:5 will be baptized with the Holy S."
Ac 2:4 of them were filled with the Holy S
Ac 2:38 will receive the gift of the Holy S.
Ro 8:26 the S helps us in our weakness.
1Co 2:10 God has revealed it to us by his S.
1Co 6:19 body is a temple of the Holy S,
Gal 5:22 But the fruit of the S is love, joy,
Eph 5:18 Instead, be filled with the S.

squall—a sudden, strong wind often accompanied by rain or snow.

staff—a stick used to lean on; a rod used by a shepherd.
Ps 23:4 your rod and your *s*

stature—height; normal growth or development.
Lk 2:52 And Jesus grew in wisdom and *s*

stiff-necked—stubborn.

stone—to kill or to try to kill someone by throwing rocks or stones at him or her.

strength—
Ex 15:2 The LORD is my *s* and my song
Dt 6:5 all your soul and with all your *s*.
Ps 46:1 God is our refuge and *s*
Isa 40:31 will renew their *s*.
Php 4:13 through him who gives me *s*

subdue—to bring under control; to conquer.

submission—humbleness; obedience.
1Co 14:34 but must be in *s*, as the Law says.
1Ti 2:11 learn in quietness and full *s*.

submit—
Ro 13:1 Everyone must *s* himself
Eph 5:21 *S* to one another out of reverence
Col 3:18 Wives, *s* to your husbands
Jas 4:7 *S* yourselves, then, to God.

suffer—
Mk 8:31 the Son of Man must *s* many things
Lk 24:26 the Christ have to *s* these things
1Co 12:26 If one part *s*, every part *s* with it

suffering—
Isa 53:3 of sorrows, and familiar with *s*.
Ac 5:41 worthy of *s* disgrace for the Name.
Ro 8:17 share in his *s* in order that we may
2Ti 1:8 But join with me in *s* for the gospel

supplication—a humble prayer to God; pleading or begging.

sustain—to give support; to help; to comfort.
Ps 18:35 and your right hand *s* me;
Ps 146:9 and *s* the fatherless and the widow,

symbol—an object or action that stands for or suggests something else. The cross is a symbol of Jesus' death.

synagogue—the Jewish place of worship and religious teaching.
Lk 4:16 the Sabbath day he went into the *s*
Ac 17:2 custom was, Paul went into the *s*

T

tabernacle—the tent used by the Israelites for meeting with God; the place where God chose to show his presence. The tabernacle was made by God's command and according to his plans. It is described in detail in Exodus 26.
Ex 40:34 the glory of the LORD filled the *t*.

talent—a large amount of silver or gold, worth very much money.
Mt 25:15 to another one *t*, each according

teach—
Ex 33:13 *t* me your ways so I may know you
Ps 90:12 *T* us to number our days aright
Lk 11:1 said to him, "Lord, *t* us to pray
Jn 14:26 will *t* you all things and will remind

temperate—moderate; having self-control.

tempest—a violent storm.

temple—1. the place where the Jewish people worshiped and sacrificed in Jerusalem. The first temple was built by King Solomon as a house for God. 2. the human body.
1Ki 8:27 How much less this *t* I have built!
Ac 17:24 does not live in *t* built by hands.
1Co 6:19 you not know that your body is a *t*
2Co 6:16 For we are the *t* of the living God.

tempt—to try to get someone to do wrong.
Mt 4:1 into the desert to be *t* by the devil.
1Co 7:5 again so that Satan will not *t* you.

temptation—
Mt 6:13 And lead us not into *t*
1Co 10:13 No *t* has seized you except what

testimony—a statement made by a witness to prove that something is true.
Lk 18:20 not give false *t*, honor your father

tetrarch—a ruler over one-fourth of a kingdom.

Thaddaeus—one of the twelve apostles (Mk 3:18); son of James and probably also known as Judas (Lk 6:16; Ac 1:13).

thanks—
1Ch 16:8 give *t* to the LORD, call
Ps 100:4 give *t* to him and praise his name.
1Co 15:57 *t* be to God! He gives us the victory
2Co 9:15 *T* be to God for his indescribable
1Th 5:18 give *t* in all circumstances

thanksgiving—
Ps 100:4 Enter his gates with *t*
Php 4:6 by prayer and petition, with *t*

Thomas—one of the twelve apostles (Lk 6:15; Ac 1:13); he doubted Jesus' resurrection but upon seeing Jesus believed (Jn 20:24-28).

threshing floor—the place where grain was trampled by oxen or beaten with a stick to separate it from the stalk.

Timothy—fellow-traveler and official representative of the apostle Paul. He and his mother and grandmother were led by Paul to see Christ as the fulfillment of the Old Testament law (2Ti 1:5). He joined Paul on his second missionary journey (Ac 16-20), and at one point in this journey Paul sent him to minister to the church at Corinth (1Co 4:17; 16:10). He was the leader of the church at Ephesus (1Ti 1:3) and a co-writer with Paul (1Th 1:1; 2Th 1:1; Phm 1).

tithe—the giving to God of one-tenth of what you earn.
Lev 27:30 " 'A *t* of everything from the land
Mal 3:8 the whole *t* into the storehouse

Titus—a Gentile co-worker with Paul (Gal 2:1-3; 2Ti 4:10). Paul sent him to Corinth to aid in solving some of the problems there (2Co 2:13; 7-8; 12:18).

tomb—a burial place. In Bible times, tombs often were either caves or were dug into stone cliffs.
Mt 27:65 make the *t* as secure as you know
Lk 24:2 the stone rolled away from the *t*

tongue—
Ps 39:1 and keep my *t* from sin
Ac 2:4 and began to speak in other *t*
Php 2:11 every *t* confess that Jesus Christ
Jas 1:26 does not keep a tight rein on his *t*

tradition of the elders—the rules that the Jewish religious leaders gave to the people and which they in turn passed on to their children; laws added to the Old Testament by the Jewish leaders.

Mt 15:2 break the *t* of the elders?

trance—a condition of being partly awake and partly in a dream-like state.

transfigure—to change the appearance of; to make bright and glorious.

Mt 17:2 There he was *t* before them.

transgression—sin; disobeying the law of God.

Ps 32:1 whose *t* are forgiven,
Isa 53:5 But he was pierced for our *t*
Eph 2:1 you were dead in your *t* and sins

treaty—an agreement between two people or groups or nations.

trespass—sin; wrongdoing.

Ro 5:17 For if, by the *t* of the one man

true—

Ps 119:160 All your words are *t*
Jn 17:3 the only *t* God, and Jesus Christ
Ro 3:4 Let God be *t*, and every man a liar.
Php 4:8 whatever is *t*, whatever is noble

trust (*v.*); (*n.*)—

Ps 37:3 *T* in the LORD and do good
Pr 3:5 *T* in the LORD with all your heart
Isa 30:15 in quietness and *t* is your strength
Jn 14:1 *T* in God; *t* also in me.
1Co 4:2 been given a *t* must prove faithful.

truth—

Ps 51:6 Surely you desire *t*
Zec 8:16 are to do: Speak the *t* to each other
Jn 8:32 Then you will know the *t*
Jn 8:32 and the *t* will set you free."
Jn 14:6 I am the way and the *t* and the life.
Ro 1:25 They exchanged the *t* of God.
1Co 13:6 in evil but rejoices with the *t*.
Eph 4:15 Instead, speaking the *t* in love
Heb 10:26 received the knowledge of the *t*
1Jn 1:6 we lie and do not live by the *t*.
1Jn 1:8 deceive ourselves and the *t* is not

tunic—a long shirt worn by men in Bible times.

Lk 6:29 do not stop him from taking your *t*.

turban—a head-covering made by winding a cloth around the head.

uv

unbelief—doubt.

Mk 9:24 help me overcome my *u*!

unbeliever—one who does not believe in Jesus.

2Co 6:14 Do not be yoked together with *u*.

unclean animals—animals the Israelites were not allowed to sacrifice or to eat.

unity—being one.

Ps 133:1 when brothers live together in *u*!
Col 3:14 them all together in perfect *u*.

unleavened bread—bread made without

yeast. It is usually flat, like a pancake or cracker.

Ex 12:17 "Celebrate the Feast of *U* Bread

unrepentant—sorry for one's sins.

upright—honest; doing what is right and good.

usury—very high and unfair interest charged on a loan.

Ne 5:10 But let the exacting of *u* stop!

vain—worthless; unsuccessful; foolish. "In vain" means without success or result.

vassal—1. a servant or slave; 2. someone who is under another person's protection. The vassal received land and protection from a lord. In return, he owed the lord his loyalty and obedience, part of his crops, and, in case of war, help in fighting.

vengeance—hurt or punishment done to another person who has done something wrong to you.

Isa 34:8 For the LORD has a day of *v*,

vile—disgusting, evil.

vindicate—to defend; to provide justice for; to set free.

violate—1. to rape; 2. to make something unholy; 3. to fail to obey.

virgin—a woman or girl who has never had sexual intercourse.

Isa 7:14 The *v* will be with child
Mt 1:23 "The *v* will be with child

vision—a dream from God.

Nu 12:6 I reveal myself to him in *v*
Joel 2:28 your young men will see *v*.
Ac 26:19 disobedient to the *v* from heaven.

vow—a solemn promise made before God or to God.

Jdg 11:30 Jephthah made a *v* to the LORD
Ps 116:14 I will fulfill my *v* to the LORD

w

wail—to cry loudly.

walk—

Ps 1:1 who does not *w* in the counsel
Isa 2:5 let us *w* in the light of the LORD.
Mic 6:8 and to *w* humbly with your God.
2Jn 6 his command is that you *w* in love.

wash—

Ps 51:7 *w* me and I will be whiter
Ac 22:16 be baptized and *w* your sins away

watch—

Jer 31:10 will *w* over his flock like a shepherd.'
Mt 26:41 "*W* and pray so that you will not fall

way—

2Sa 22:31 "As for God, his *w* is perfect
Ps 1:1 or stand in the *w* of sinners
Ps 37:5 Commit your *w* to the LORD
Isa 53:6 each of us has turned to his own *w*
Jn 14:6 "I am the *w* and the truth

2Co 12:31 will show you the most excellent w.

wicked—sinful.
Ps 1:1 walk in the counsel of the w
Isa 55:7 Let the w forsake his way

will (v.; n.)—
Ps 143:10 Teach me to do your w
Isa 53:10 Yet it was the Lord's w
Mt 6:10 your w be done
Mt 26:39 Yet not as I w, but as you w."
Ro 12:2 and approve what God's w is
Eph 5:17 understand what the Lord's w is.
1Jn 5:14 we ask anything according to his w
Rev 4:11 and by your w they were created

work—(v.; n.)—
Ex 23:12 "Six days do your w
Jn 9:4 we must do the w of him who sent
Php 2:12 continue to w out your salvation
2Ti 3:17 equipped for every good w.

world—
Mt 5:14 "You are the light of the w.
Mk 16:15 into all the w and preach the good
Jn 1:29 who takes away the sin of the w!
Jn 3:16 so loved the w that he gave his one
Jn 8:12 he said, "I am the light of the w.
1Jn 2:15 not love the w or anything in the w.

worldly—loving the things of the world more than the things of God.
Tit 2:12 to ungodliness and w passions

worship—(v.) to give praise, honor and respect to God; (n.) reverence given to God.
Ps 95:6 Come, let us bow down in w
Jn 4:24 and his worshipers must w in spirit

worthy—having value; honorable; deserving.
1Ch 16:25 For great is the Lord and most w
Eph 4:1 to live a life w of the calling you
Rev 5:2 "Who is w to break the seals

wrath—great anger; the strong anger of God.
Pr 15:1 A gentle answer turns away w

Ro 5:9 saved from God's w through him!

wretch—1. a very unhappy person; someone who has had many bad or difficult things happen to him or her; 2. an evil person.

yz

yearn—to long for; to want very much.

yoke—1. (v.) to join together; 2. (n.) a wooden bar that goes over the necks of two animals, usually oxen. The yoke holds the animals together as they pull an object, such as a plow or a cart.
Mt 11:29 Take my y upon you and learn
2Co 6:14 Do not be y together

zeal—eagerness; strong desire.
Ro 12:11 Never be lacking in z

Zealot—a member of the Jewish group that wanted to fight against and overthrow the Roman government.

Zechariah—a prophet and priest who returned to Jerusalem from the Babylonian captivity; he encouraged the Jews to rebuild the temple (Ezr 5:1; 6:14; Zec 1:1).

Zerubbabel—a descendant of David (1Ch 3:19) and heir to the throne of Judah (1Ch 3:17-19); he led the return from the Babylonian captivity and was appointed governor of Judah by Cyrus, king of Persia (Ezr 1-3; Ne 7:7; Hag 1-2; Zec 4).

Zion—1. the hill on which the city of Jerusalem first stood; David's royal palace and the temple were both built on Mount Zion; 2. the entire city of Jerusalem.
Jer 50:5 They will ask the way to Z
Ro 11:26 "The deliverer will come from Z